WASHINGTON

COURT RULES

VOLUME III – LOCAL

2016

SUPERIOR, DISTRICT, AND MUNICIPAL COURTS

THOMSON REUTERS

Mat #41608746

© 2015 Thomson Reuters

This publication was created to provide you with accurate and authoritative information concerning the subject matter covered; however, this publication was not necessarily prepared by persons licensed to practice law in a particular jurisdiction. The publisher is not engaged in rendering legal or other professional advice, and this publication is not a substitute for the advice of an attorney. If you require legal or other expert advice, you should seek the services of a competent attorney or other professional.

ISBN: 978–0–314–67506–4

West's and Westlaw are registered in the U.S. Patent and Trademark Office.

PREFACE

Designed for use in the office or courtroom, this pamphlet contains the Washington local rules.

WHAT'S NEW

Washington Court Rules, Volume III – Local, 2016, includes rules and associated material governing practice before the Washington Superior, District, and Municipal courts. It replaces the 2015 edition. It is current with amendments received through August 15, 2015.

Washington Rule GR 7(a) provides:

"(a) Generally. Fifty copies of rules of court authorized by law to be adopted or amended by courts other than the Supreme Court must be filed with the state Administrator for the Courts. New proposed rules and amendments must be filed on or before July 1, to be effective September 1 of the same year. Promulgation or amendment of rules that describe only the structure, internal management and organization of the court but do not affect courtroom procedures are not governed by the time limitations above."

CONTACT US

For additional information or research assistance, call the West reference attorneys at 1-800-REF-ATTY (1-800-733-2889). Contact West's editorial department directly with your questions and suggestions by e-mail at west.editor@thomson.com.

Thank you for subscribing to this product. Should you have any questions regarding this product please contact Customer Service at 1-800-328-4880 or by fax at 1-800-340-9378. If you would like to inquire about related publications, or to place an order, please contact us at 1-800-344-5009 or visit us online.

THE PUBLISHER

September 2015

TABLE OF CONTENTS

ADAMS COUNTY

Table of Courts

Superior Court

Adams County Superior Court Rules.

District Courts

Othello District Court—[No Local Rules].
Ritzville District Court Rules.

SUPERIOR COURT
ADAMS COUNTY SUPERIOR COURT RULES

Including Amendments Received Through
August 15, 2015

Table of Rules

LOCAL RULES

RULE 1. SCHEDULING

A. Sessions and Hours. There shall be one continuous session of Court from 9:00 a.m. to 4:30 p.m. each day from January 1st through December 31st excepting non-judicial days designated by law as legal holidays, or specifically designated as non-judicial days by the State Supreme Court.

B. General Motion Docket. The general motion docket shall be each Monday except when the Monday is a legal holiday, or when canceled by prior order of the Court. All hearings in civil, probate, family law, adoption, guardianship and other matters (except juvenile court matters) not requiring testimony, shall be scheduled to the motion docket for 9:00 a.m. Criminal matters shall be scheduled for 10:00 a.m. The form at **Appendix LR–1B** shall be used to note motions. Argument shall be limited to ten minutes per side and the moving party may reserve some portion of said ten minutes for rebuttal argument. Hearings requiring more than 30 minutes shall be scheduled in the same manner as trials.

C. Juvenile Matters (Offender). Juvenile offender matters, other than fact-findings/arraignments and/preliminary appearances shall be heard on the first Thursday of each month at 9:00 a.m., unless said Thursday is a non-judicial day in which case they shall be heard on the following Thursday which is not a non-judicial day. Fact-finding hearings shall be scheduled for 1:30 p.m. on said Thursdays. In every case not resolved within fourteen calendar days prior to the fact-finding there shall be a status hearing at 10:00 a.m. on the general motion docket occurring on the Monday of the week preceding the date of fact-finding. The juvenile's appearance at the status hearing is mandatory.

D. Juvenile Matters (Dependency). Juvenile court matters, other than offender matters, shall be scheduled for the first Tuesday of each month at 9:00 a.m., unless said Tuesday is a non-judicial day in which case, they shall be heard on the following Tuesday which is not a non-judicial day. All parties and their witnesses shall be present and available at 9:00 a.m. Counsel shall first confer as to which matters can be resolved by agreed orders or without testimony, those matters shall then be put on the record or argued. Matters requiring testimony shall then be heard. Shelter Care hearings shall be special set with the Superior Court Administrator. Social studies and predisposition reports are to be presented to the Court no later than three days prior to disposition, or as otherwise directed by the Court.

E. Ex Parte Matters. Noncriminal ex parte matters shall be heard on all judicial days at 11:00 a.m. Personal appearance is required if the party requests an ex parte order seeking to restrain another party from the family home or contact with the other party or children. Unless notice is specifically excluded by statute, no ex parte order shall be presented without notice to opposing counsel or opposing party without counsel. If counsel for any party, or a party, has appeared either formally or informally, notice is required. If necessary, notice may be by telephone or facsimile. This rule applies regardless of whether service is required on the attorney or a party pursuant to CR 5(b)(4). The movant shall be responsible for making arrangements to have the clerk deliver the court file for the hearing. Parties are advised to telephone the Superior Court Administrator in advance to ensure that there will be a judicial officer available to hear the ex parte calendar.

F. Civil Trials. Civil cases may be noted to the motion docket for trial setting at any time after the pleadings are closed. Cases noted for trial setting will be assigned for trial by the Court Administrator. The form at **Appendix LR–1F** shall be used to note cases for trial. Counsel is not required to appear at the trial setting unless they are objecting to the trial setting.

G. Criminal Cases and Pre–trials. Criminal trials shall be scheduled to begin at 9:00 a.m. on the fourth Tuesday of each calendar month. The jury, if necessary, will be scheduled to arrive at 1:30 p.m. of that day. In every criminal case, whether it is specifically ordered or not, there shall be a pretrial hearing on Monday at 1:30 p.m. in the calendar week preceding the calendar week of trial unless it is a non-judicial day in which case it shall be held on the Monday immediately preceding which is not a non-judicial day. Attendance by the defendant at the pretrial hearing is mandatory. If the defendant does not attend the pretrial hearing a warrant may be issued for his or her arrest and the trial date reset. All motions in limine shall be filed and served five days in advance of the pretrial hearing for hearing on that day and shall be deemed waived if not so presented. Responsive pleadings shall be filed and served one day before the pretrial hearing.

Jury instructions shall be filed, served and bench-copied on or before the pretrial hearing. Sanctions may be imposed for failure to do so.

H. Support Enforcement Calendar. The support enforcement calendar shall be heard on the first

Wednesday of January, March, May, July, September, and November commencing at 9:00 a.m.

[Adopted on an emergency basis effective June 9, 2015; adopted on a permanent basis effective September 1, 2015.]

RULE 2. FILING

Except in consolidated cases, no documents shall be filed with more than one case number, unless sufficient copies are simultaneously provided for each cause. Where there are multiple cases numbers and no copies provided, the Clerk shall place the documents only in the first case number designated.

For all causes wherein an Order for Consolidation has been entered for the purpose of trial, the caption shall include the separate titles of the consolidated actions, along with the specific cause numbers, an indication to the clerk of which cause number the pleadings shall be filed under. The party filing the pleadings shall provide copies for each cause listed. If no indication is made and a copy is not provided for each cause the clerk shall place the pleadings into the lowest or earliest filed cause.

In all causes wherein an Order for Consolidation has been entered said order shall designate in what action all future pleadings shall be filed, and a copy of said order shall be filed in each case. Said order would be the last document filed in the undesignated case number.

Facsimile and Electronic filing shall not be allowed absent court order. All pleadings, and other papers presented for filing with the Clerk shall be on 8 ½ by 11 paper and shall be printed on one side only. The Clerk may refuse to file any papers not in conformance with this rule.

[Adopted on an emergency basis effective June 9, 2015; adopted on a permanent basis effective September 1, 2015.]

RULE 3. JUVENILE OFFENDER MATTERS

A. Costs. Attorney's fees may be assessed against the juvenile, parent, or other person legally obligated to support the juvenile, when public funded counsel is used for defense (RCW 13.40.145). Partial detention costs for adjudicated offenders may be assessed pursuant to RCW 13.40.220. Detention costs shall be based on the parties ability to pay but not to exceed $150.00 per day of detention. The State of Washington Determination of Indigency Report form, pursuant to RCW 10.101.020, shall be used in determining parental financial obligations.

A hearing, judgment and order determining parental financial obligations shall take place following disposition, or as otherwise directed by the Court.

B. Sealing. On the first Thursday of each month at 9:00 a.m., there will be a "hearing to seal juvenile court records" which will be sealed administratively unless the court receives an objection or compelling reason (e.g., legal financial obligation still owing) not

to seal. If said date falls on a non-judicial day, these hearings shall be scheduled for the first Thursday of the month following which is not a non-judicial day. These hearings shall be scheduled for the first hearing following the date the juvenile turns 18 years of age or, if the juvenile is determined to be on supervision, or on a JRA commitment, or parole beyond his/her 18th birthday or the first hearing following scheduled termination of supervision/parole (assuming the juvenile serves maximum number of months in his/her commitment range.) The hearing date will be set by the disposition order which shall note same as a clerk's action if the juvenile qualifies for an administrative sealing. The juvenile is not required to be present at the hearing.

Psychological and other treatment evaluation reports as well as predisposition reports shall be considered and shall be filed under seal in the "confidential side" of the official juvenile court file which shall be open to the parties and the judge, but not open to the public unless ordered by the court. Said exhibits may be returned or destroyed pursuant to the rules governing other exhibits.

[Adopted on an emergency basis effective June 9, 2015; adopted on a permanent basis effective September 1, 2015.]

RULE 4. JUVENILE NON–OFFENDER MATTERS [RESERVED]

RULE 5. DOMESTIC RELATIONS MATTERS

A. Show Cause Hearings. In all show cause orders where a party is directed to "personally" appear and show cause, said party shall appear in person and subject himself to examination by counsel. Any such party must be given at least five days' notice of the time and place of the show cause hearing.

B. Testimony Required. The sworn testimony of at least one of the parties shall be required to support the entry of a decree of dissolution or a final parenting plan or modification thereof.

C. Affidavits. Affidavits or Declarations in all contested motion hearings, shall not exceed five (5) double spaced pages (exclusive of exhibits). Responsive affidavits shall be served and filed no later than 12:00 p.m. (noon) the day before the hearing. Reply affidavits shall be provided to opposing counsel/party no later than 5:00 p.m. the day before the hearing. Reply affidavits shall be limited to a maximum of three (3) double spaced pages and shall be in strict reply to the responsive affidavit.

[Adopted on an emergency basis effective June 9, 2015; adopted on a permanent basis effective September 1, 2015.]

RULE 6. CRIMINAL MATTERS

PROCEEDURE[1] FOLLOWING ARREST WITHOUT WARRANT

A. [See CrR 3.1 (d)] Appointment of counsel for indigent defendants shall be made by the Court as soon as is feasible following arrest. Upon such an appointment, the Court shall promptly provide defense counsel with notice of his/her appointment.

B. Indigent criminal defendants appealing from District Court Judgments shall, within five days after giving Notice of Appeal, request the Superior Court for appointed counsel. If appropriate, the Court shall appoint counsel by written order. Ordinarily, counsel appearing in District Court will be appointed.

C. [See CrR 3.1 (2)] No defense counsel, whether retained or appointed, shall be permitted to withdraw as such without prior Court approval; provided, however, that after a verdict has been entered, counsel may withdraw without prior approval by the Court.

D. Discovery. [See CrR 4.7] The Prosecuting Attorney shall provide to the defendant, either directly or through the defendant's counsel, a copy of all criminal history record information in a Prosecutor's possession at the Omnibus Order compliance date.

E. [See CrR 3(b), (c), (d)] All persons arrested on felony charges and held in custody shall, as soon as feasible during the first day upon which the Court is open, be brought before the Superior Court at 11:00 a.m. to be advised of their rights.

F. A person arrested without a warrant shall have a determination of probable cause no later than forty-eight (48) hours following the person's arrest. Non judicial days shall not be excluded in the calculation of said forty eight (48) hours. The Court shall determine probable cause on the sworn testimony of a peace officer or prosecuting attorney. The sworn testimony may be by written affidavit or electronically recorded, and in either case the testimony shall be preserved.

[Adopted on an emergency basis effective June 9, 2015; adopted on a permanent basis effective September 1, 2015.]

[1] So in original copy.

RULE 7. CIVIL MATTERS [RESERVED]

RULE 8. SPECIAL PROCEEDINGS MATTERS [RESERVED]

RULE 9. PLEADINGS/MOTIONS

A. Time for Filing. Parties desiring to submit an application to the Court, legal brief, memorandum of authorities, and any supporting affidavits or other documents on a motion, hearing or trial to be heard shall, unless otherwise particularized under a specific State or local rule, serve and file the same with the Clerk of the Court no later than five (5) court days before the date the party wishes the motion to be considered. Any responsive materials shall be served and filed with the Clerk of the Court by 12:00 noon

two days prior to the time set for the hearing or trial. Any documents in strict reply shall be similarly filed and served no later than 12:00 noon on the court day before the hearing. No documents shall be submitted to the Court unless opposing counsel or the self-represented litigants have been timely provided with copies. Reapplication for order. When an order has been applied for and refused in whole or in part (unless without prejudice), or has been granted conditionally and the condition has not been performed, the same application for an order shall not be made except upon an alleged different statement of facts or law. It shall be shown by affidavit what application was made, when, and to what judge; what order or decision was made thereon; and what new facts or law are claimed to be shown.

B. Motions in Limine. Motions to limit the introduction of evidence should be presented for resolution not later than the regular motion day immediately preceding the assigned trial date or such other date as may be set by the Court.

C. Form. Necessary provisions in orders requiring personal attendance; in all civil proceedings wherein an Order is to be issued requiring the personal attendance of a person to be examined in open Court, the Order shall include the following works [1] in capital letters:

YOUR FAILURE TO APPEAR AS ABOVE SET FORTH AT THE TIME, DATE, AND PLACE STATED MAY CAUSE THE COURT TO ISSUE A BENCH WARRANT FOR YOUR APPREHENSION AND CONFINEMENT IN JAIL UNTIL SUCH TIME AS THE MATTER CAN BE HEARD OR UNTIL BAIL IS POSTED.

No bench warrant shall be issued in such cases for the apprehension of the cited person if such language has been omitted

D. Delivery. Working copies of papers requiring thorough consideration by the Court shall be delivered to the Judge's chambers in an appropriate period prior to trial or the hearing therein, but not less than two (2) working days prior to the commencement thereof. Working copies need not be delivered until a hearing has been set in the cause of action involved.

E. Documents. Such papers shall include briefs, memorandums of authority, lengthy affidavits, pleadings, and admitted exhibits. Said briefs or memorandums of authority shall contain statements of the legal issues involved and the authority supporting the same. Nothing herein shall be construed to restrict the right of any parties to submit further briefs or memorandums of authority at any other time during the trial of the case.

F. Three Hole Punched. All working copies shall be punched for a three-ring binder and shall not be stapled.

G. **All pleadings** shall be typed and double-spaced on pleading paper (numbered lines). The practice of incorporating hand written statements by witnesses or parties by addending same to declarations or affidavits will not be allowed.

[Adopted on an emergency basis effective June 9, 2015; adopted on a permanent basis effective September 1, 2015.]

  1 So in original.

RULE 10. PROPOSED JURY INSTRUCTIONS

A. Proposed jury instruction/s shall be typewritten. Each instruction shall be typed on a separate sheet of paper which bears no marking identifying either the party or the attorney presenting the instruction. No citation or other extraneous matter shall appear on a proposed instruction, except as hereinafter provided.

B. On or before the pretrial hearing, the proposed instructions shall be distributed as follows:

1. One assembled and numbered copy containing citations of authority, including the number of any applicable Washington Pattern Instruction, shall be filed with the Clerk;

2. The original, unassembled, unnumbered and without citations shall be delivered to the Court;

3. One copy numbered, assembled, and containing the citations of supporting authorities, including the number of any applicable Washington Pattern Instruction, shall be delivered as follows: one to the Court and one to opposing counsel.

C. Copies of Washington Pattern Instructions are not provided by the Court. If such instructions are proposed, they must be submitted in typed form with the suitable number of copies as outlined above.

[Adopted on an emergency basis effective June 9, 2015; adopted on a permanent basis effective September 1, 2015.]

RULE 11. EXHIBITS

A. **Pre–Marking.** Counsel shall arrange with the Clerk for the marking of all exhibits prior to the trial.

B. **Copies.** Unless the making of copies is impractical, legible copies of exhibits shall be furnished to opposing counsel and the court, and numbered the same as marked by the Clerk. This rule shall not apply to rebuttal or impeachment exhibits not required to be offered in the party's case in chief.

C. A descriptive list of the proposed exhibits shall be e-mailed to the clerk no later than two working days prior to the trial date.

D. **Offers for Admission.** Counsel shall offer exhibits for admission. A motion for admission is not required.

[Adopted on an emergency basis effective June 9, 2015; adopted on a permanent basis effective September 1, 2015.]

RULE 12. COURT REPORTING

A. Pre-trial and post-trial civil motions and other proceedings will not be recorded by a reporter unless requested by a party to the action, or as directed by the Court.

B. Civil trials will be reported only on a request of a party to the action, which party shall arrange for a court reporter to be in attendance. The cost of such reporter shall be an expense of the requesting party or parties.

C. In criminal matters, all pre-trial motions and appearances will be recorded electronically, and the Court will arrange for a court reporter to be in attendance for criminal trials at the expense of Adams County.

D. If partial transcripts are made of the record during proceedings in Superior Court, a copy of such transcription shall be furnished to the Judge.

[Adopted on an emergency basis effective June 9, 2015; adopted on a permanent basis effective September 1, 2015.]

RULE 13. JURORS

a. **Examination of Jurors.**

1. At the commencement of trial the Clerk will assign numbers randomly, beginning with the number one, to all jurors called for trial. If a criminal defendant objects to this procedure the numbers will be drawn by the Clerk in open court at the beginning of the trial.

  a. Prior to the questioning of prospective jurors by counsel, the Court will allow time for counsel to review juror profiles and questionnaires.

  b. These jurors will be given placards with their assigned numbers on them. These will be large enough to be easily read by the Court, counsel, and the court reporter. The jurors will arrange themselves in order as directed by the Court.

  c. If alternate jurors are to be selected, the parties are encouraged to stipulate that all preemptory challenges will be exercised against the entire panel. Otherwise, each side will only be allowed the number of peremptory challenges(s) against the alternate juror or jurors as allowed by CR 47(b).

2. The Court will then ask general questions of the prospective jurors.

  A. "General questions" mean those questions that are designed to discover those jurors who should be excused for cause (e.g., those prospective jurors who are related to a party or who cannot be available for the full time the trial is estimated to take).

  B. Counsel may request general questions to be asked by the Court as long as they meet the definition in section (2)(A) above.

3. After prospective jurors have been excused for cause, the Court may excuse those jurors who are in excess of the number needed for the trial. The number needed for the trial will be equal to 12 plus the number of alternates, plus the total number of peremptory challenges to which all parties are entitled, plus two to five additional as a cushion for possible additional challenges for cause.

4. Counsel will then question the remaining prospective jurors.

A. Each side will have ninety (90) minutes for questioning. Each side may reserve that amount of the allotted time as allowed by the Court for additional questions following the questioning by the other side. Any time expended in arguing a challenge for cause will not be charged to either side.

B. The times set forth in section (4)(A) above may be expanded by the Court for good cause shown, such as an extremely complicated case or multiple parties.

C. Counsel may use their allotted time in any manner and may question prospective jurors in any order. Counsel may ask group questions or ask jurors to respond to remarks made by other members of the jury panel (e.g., the first question may be addressed to juror #3 in the box, then a question addressed to the entire panel, or just to jurors #3 and #9 etc.)

D. Challenges for cause must be made when they are discovered.

E. Objections to questions are made in the usual manner.

F. If counsel is pursuing an important issue that relates to the qualifications of the prospective jurors to serve, and time has run out, counsel may request that the Court grant additional time.

G. The entire panel of prospective jurors is passed for cause when counsel so announces or when the time allotted has been consumed.

H. The procedure set forth in this rule shall not apply to cases involving charges of aggravated first degree murder as defined by RCW 10.95.020 if a notice of special sentencing proceeding has been filed.

5. The parties then exercise their peremptory challenges.

A. All peremptory challenges shall be exercised in open court.

B. Challenges may be made to jurors who are not seated in the box.

C. When a peremptory challenge is exercised, the next juror on the bench with the lowest number shall replace the juror who was excused from the jury box.

D. The parties are encouraged to stipulate regarding peremptory challenges per Rule 47(a)(2)(A).

E. Upon request of counsel, time will be allowed between voir dire and the exercise of peremptory challenges.

6. Additional Provisions.

A. Counsel may submit, and Court may allow, special questionnaires focused to the specific case (or type of case) to be submitted to the jurors to answer on the morning of trial before the voir dire process begins. Copies will be made and available to counsel during the questioning of the jurors. Counsel must submit proposed questionnaires to the Court and serve copies on opposing counsel at least five days prior to trial. If this is not done, the Court, in its discretion may not allow special questionnaires. (If a standard questionnaire has been adopted by the Court for particular types of cases counsel may refer to the standard questionnaire rather than serving copies.)

b. **Jury—Jurors.** Jurors shall be called on a one trial/one day basis. Those persons selected to serve on a jury will be obligated for the duration of that one trial.

[Adopted on an emergency basis effective June 9, 2015; adopted on a permanent basis effective September 1, 2015.]

RULE 14. GUARDIAN AD LITEM TRAINING AND QUALIFICATION

A. Registry. The Court Administrator shall maintain a registry of persons who are willing and qualified to act as Guardians Ad Litem in guardianship matters. The Court will select as guardians ad litem only persons appearing in the registry, except in extraordinary circumstances.

B. Eligibility. In order to be eligible for the registry, a person must file with the court administrator a written Statement of Qualifications as prescribed by RCW 11.88.090 (3)(b)(i) and Certificate of Completion of Training evidencing the completion of the training program approved by the Superior Court.

C. Appointment. The Court shall appoint as guardian ad litem only a person free from influence of anyone interested in the result of the proceeding. A copy of the guardian ad litem Certificate of Completion of Training shall be filed in each proceeding in which the person is appointed guardian ad litem.

D. Guardian Ad Litem Training Program. Training shall be pursuant to RCW 11.88.090. This training program will be given in conjunction and cooperation with other Washington counties and is scheduled throughout the year by the Administrative Office of the Courts.

[Adopted on an emergency basis effective June 9, 2015; adopted on a permanent basis effective September 1, 2015.]

RULE 15. RESCISSION, MODIFICATION OR RENEWAL OF NO–CONTACT ORDERS

A protected party or parent/guardian of a protected party who is a minor desiring to rescind, modify or renew a statutory no contact order may contact the Clerk of the Court for pre-printed forms necessary.

Such motions shall be noted to the motion docket and be served personally upon the respondent at least five days in advance thereof. In the case of no contact orders issued in a criminal case, the office of the Adams County Prosecuting Attorney shall also be served. Proof of service shall be filed before the matter is heard.

The factors the Court will consider in determining whether to rescind, modify or review no-contact orders include but are not limited to whether the victim has had a chance to make alternate plans for safety, the status and nature of any criminal proceedings against the respondent/defendant. The respondent's/defendant's compliance with the terms of his/her Judgment and Sentence, whether the respondent/defendant has completed any course of education or counseling addressing perpetrators of violence, and other risk factors.

Petitioners are strongly recommended to consult with a domestic violence advocate prior to the hearing.

The clerk of the court shall maintain a list/directory of domestic violence victim advocacy programs available in Adams County and abutting counties.

If a no-contact order is rescinded, modified or renewed the order rescinding, modifying or renewing the original order shall be forwarded to applicable law enforcement agencies by the Clerk of the court.

[Adopted on an emergency basis effective June 9, 2015; adopted on a permanent basis effective September 1, 2015.]

RULE 16. SUSPENSION OR MODIFICATION OF RULES

The Court may suspend or modify any of the foregoing rules, in any given case, upon good cause being shown therefore or upon the Court's own motion.

[Adopted on an emergency basis effective June 9, 2015; adopted on a permanent basis effective September 1, 2015.]

RULE 17. EFFECTIVE DATE

The rules replace and supercede all existing Adams County Superior Court rules and become effective June 9, 2015. They shall be cited as ACLR (Adams County Local Rules)

[Adopted on an emergency basis effective June 9, 2015; adopted on a permanent basis effective September 1, 2015.]

APPENDIX LR–1B.   MOTION NOTE–UP SLIP

Superior Court of Washington
County of

Petitioner,	No.
and	**Note for Calendar**
	(NTC)
	Clerk's Action Required
Respondent.	

To the Clerk of Court and to:

1. Please note that this case will be placed on the calendar for hearing on _____, on the date set out below.
2. A hearing has been set for the following date, time and place.

Date: _____   Time: _____a.m./p.m.
Place: _____   Room/Department: _____
Dated: _____

Signature of Requesting Party or Lawyer/WSBA No.

_____

Print or Type Name
Notice to party: (you may list an address that is not your residential address where you agree to accept legal documents. Any time this address changes while this action is pending, you must notify the opposing parties in writing and file an updated Confidential Information Form (WPF DRPSCU 09.0200) with the court clerk.)

_____

Address

_____

[Adopted on an emergency basis effective June 9, 2015; adopted on a permanent basis effective September 1, 2015.]

APPENDIX LR–1F. TRIAL NOTE–UP SLIP

SUPERIOR COURT OF WASHINGTON FOR ADAMS COUNTY

Plaintiff,	) NO.)) NOTE FOR TRIAL)
vs.	))
Defendant.	))

TO THE CLERK OF THE COURT AND
TO: _____

_____

_____

PLEASE TAKE NOTE that this case will be brought on the trial setting docket for assignment for a trial date on the ___ day of _____, 20 ___, A list of your available trial dates must be filed with the court before the setting date.

FAILURE TO PROVIDE THE COURT WITH A LIST OF AVAILABLE DATES COULD RESULT IN THE DENIAL OF ANY MOTION FOR CONTINUANCE BECAUSE OF CONFLICTS IN SCHEDULE.

1. Nature of this case: _____
2. Is a jury demand?: _____

         6 member ( )   12 member ( )

3. Estimated trial time: _____

THE COURT TRIAL CALENDAR IS PRE–SET. CASES WILL NOT BE PERMITTED TO CONTINUE BEYOND THE TIME ESTIMATED FOR TRIAL. IF THE NON–SETTING PARTIES DO NOT AGREE WITH THE ESTIMATE IN THIS NOTICE THEY MUST FILE THEIR OWN ESTIMATE BEFORE THE TRIAL SETTING DATE.

DATED this _____ day of _____ 20 ____.

                        SIGNED: _____

                        ATTORNEY FOR: _____

SERVE ON ALL PARTIES AND FILE WITH THE CLERK

[Adopted on an emergency basis effective June 9, 2015; adopted on a permanent basis effective September 1, 2015.]

LOCAL RULES FOR MANDATORY ARBITRATION (LRMA) [DELETED]

APPENDICES

DISTRICT COURTS

OTHELLO DISTRICT COURT—
[No Local Rules]

PUBLISHER'S NOTE

This district court follows the Ritzville District Court Rules.

RITZVILLE DISTRICT COURT RULES

Including Amendments Received Through
August 15, 2015

Table of Rules

LOCAL RULES

[INTRODUCTION]

These Local Rules have been adopted under the provisions of General Rule 7 promulgated by the Washington State Supreme Court. The numbering used in these Local Rules conforms to the numbering system and format of the Superior Court Criminal Rules (CrR), Civil Rules for Courts of Limited Jurisdiction (CRLJ), and Infraction Rules for Courts of Limited Jurisdiction (IRLJ), which are in effect as of the adoption of these Local Rules.

[Adopted effective September 1, 2015.]

I. LOCAL ADMINISTRATIVE RULES

LARLJ 1. SCOPE OF RULES

(a) Operating and administrative policies and procedures of the Ritzville District Court shall be in accordance with Local Court Rules adopted pursuant to GR 7, et seq.

(b) In the absence of a rule governing a particular procedure, or policy, the Presiding Judge shall resolve the issue pending the establishment of a new rule.

(c) Prior Rules Repealed. All prior rules of the Ritzville District Court are repealed upon adoption of these Rules.

[Adopted effective September 1, 2015.]

LARLJ 2. ADVISORY RULES COMMITTEE

(a) To facilitate regular review of established Local Court Rules, policies and procedures, and to insure maximum participation by all jurisdictions, an Advisory Committee shall be established composed of the following representative participants:

(1) City Attorney for Ritzville

(2) Adams County Prosecutor

(3) Adams County Public Defender

(4) Court Administrator

(5) Adams County Bar Association

(6) Presiding Judge, who will serve as Chairman

(7) Chief of Police of City of Ritzville

(8) Adams County Sheriff

(9) Sergeant of Ritzville Detachment of Washington State Patrol

(b) The Advisory Committee shall meet annually at the Adams County Courthouse, Ritzville District Court. Meeting arrangements, including the date, shall be facilitated by the Court Administrator, for the convenience of the Committee. Additional meetings may be called as needed by the Presiding Judge.

(c) The Committee shall evaluate written recommendations for the revision or establishment of Local Court Rules. The committee shall review all written suggestions and/or recommendations on Local Court Rules received by the Court during the preceding quarter.

(d) The Committee shall also consider proposed changes in Court policies and procedures which are not governed by Court Rules.

[Adopted effective September 1, 2015.]

LARLJ 3. MISCELLANEOUS PROVISIONS

(a) All requests for Local Court Rules or rule changes must be submitted in writing to be considered by the Advisory Committee.

(b) Immediately following each Advisory Committee meeting, the Presiding Judge shall present the Committee recommendations to the elected Judge and Court Administrator for appropriate action.

(c) In evaluating any proposed Local Court Rules, the Judge shall take into consideration the fiscal impact of additional services in view of budget restraints.

[Adopted effective September 1, 2015.]

LARLJ 9. CONFIDENTIAL RECORDS AND INFORMATION

(a) Public Records. Unless the trial judge rules otherwise in a particular case, the following are considered public records and may be viewed and copied by the public:

(1) Court pleadings;

(2) Dockets, both civil and criminal, regardless of the current status of the proceeding;

(3) Indexes to civil and criminal cases;

(4) Tape recordings of court proceedings;

(5) Search warrants, affidavits, and inventories, after execution and return of the warrant.

(b) Private Records. The following are considered exempt from disclosure unless they have been admitted into evidence, incorporated into a court pleading, or are the subject of a stipulation on the record which places them into public record:

(1) Witness statements and police reports;

(2) Pre–sentence reports and reports related to compliance with conditions of sentence;

(3) Copies of driving records or criminal history records subject to RCW 10.97;

(4) Correspondence received by the court regarding sentencing and compliance with the terms of probation.

(c) Quasi–Public Documents. The following are not subject to public review, but are subject to review by the defendant and his/her attorney:

(1) Witness statements;

(2) Pre–sentence reports and reports related to compliance with conditions of sentence;

(3) Copies of driving records or criminal history records subject to RCW 10.97;

(4) Correspondence received by the court regarding sentencing and compliance with the terms of probation, except when the information is provided on the condition it remain confidential or when a finding of good cause is made for its confidentiality.

(d) Court Assistance.

(1) Court facilities are available to the public to assist in disclosure, subject to local court rule.

(2) For security purposes, the court may require identification from the reviewing party.

(e) Judicial Review. To assure that only public records are reviewed by the public, judicial review of disclosure may be requested by the prosecuting authority, defendant, court clerks, or other interested parties. The court may withhold dissemination until a hearing may reasonably be held. Following the hearing, the court may make such restrictive orders as are necessary.

(f) Statutes Not Superseded. Nothing in this rule shall be construed to supersede existing statutes or subsequent amendments thereto.

[Adopted effective September 1, 2015.]

II. LOCAL GENERAL RULES

LGR 1. DESIGNATION

The District Courts in Adams County shall be designated:

Othello District Court

Ritzville District Court

These Rules apply only to the Ritzville District Court.

[Adopted effective September 1, 2015.]

LGR 2. HOURS OF OPERATION

The District Court Shall be open for business Monday through Friday, except holidays, from 8:30 a.m. to 4:30 p.m. District Court will be closed daily from 12:00 p.m. to 1:00 p.m. for lunch. Special hearings and motions may be set by appointment with the Court. The "next judicial day" as referred to in RCW 46.61.50571 means the next day upon which Court is held in the Ritzville District Court, Adams County, Washington.

[Adopted effective September 1, 2015.]

LGR 3. FORM OF PLEADING

Every paper presented to the Judge for signature or delivered to the Court Clerk for filing shall be a clearly readable original and shall include:

(a) number and title of case;

(b) designation of what the paper purports to be;

(c) name, original signature, office address, telephone number and Washington State Bar Association Number of counsel.

[Adopted effective September 1, 2015.]

LGR 4. INSTRUCTIONS TO JURY

(a) Proposed. Unless otherwise requested by the trial judge on timely notice to counsel, proposed instructions shall be submitted when the case is called for trial. Proposed instructions upon questions of law developed by the evidence, which could not reasonably be anticipated, may be submitted at any time before the court has instructed the jury.

(b) Submission. Submission of proposed instructions shall be by delivering the original and three or more copies as required by the trial judge, by filing one copy with the clerk, identified as the party's proposed instructions, and by serving one copy upon each opposing counsel.

(c) Form. Each proposed instruction shall be typewritten or printed on a separate sheet of letter-size (8–½ by 11 inches) paper. Except for one copy of each, the instructions delivered to the trial court shall not be numbered or identified as to the proposing party. One copy delivered to the trial court, and the copy filed with the clerk, and copies served on each opposing counsel shall be numbered and identified as to proposing party, and may contain supporting annotations.

[Adopted effective September 1, 2015.]

LGR 5. COST OF JURY

When a cause assigned a date for trial as a jury case is settled, or will not be tried by a jury for any reason whatsoever, notice of that fact shall be given immediately to the Court. Terms may be sought against the responsible party should this case be settled after the jury has been called. Any such terms imposed by the Court for payment shall be paid as directed by the Court.

[Adopted effective September 1, 2015.]

LGR 6. JUDGE'S COPY

Whenever a trial brief or memorandum of authority is filed with the Court, a copy shall be served upon opposing counsel, with an extra copy provided for the Judge.

[Adopted effective September 1, 2015.]

LGR 7. SCHEDULE OF FEES

The following cost of documents/official services provided by the Ritzville District Court Clerk can be found on the Ritzville District Court website at *www. co.adams.wa.us*.

Anti Harassment

Appeal to Superior Court

Appeal Preparation Fee

Certified Copy

Civil

Civil Supplemental Proceedings

Copy of Proceedings on disc

Deferred Finding Assessments

Domestic Violence

Duplication of Electronic Records

Fax Transmission Fees

Impound

Name Change

NSF check-handling fee

Photo Copy Expenses (per page)

Postage

Small Claims

Transcript of Judgment

Writ of Garnishment

[Adopted effective September 1, 2015.]

LGR 8. COURT'S MOTION

Any of these Rules may be suspended or modified by the Court upon its own motion.

[Adopted effective September 1, 2015.]

LGR 9. ENUMERATED POWERS

Court Clerks and Court Commissioners shall have only powers enumerated by the Judge appointing them and as restricted by State Statute or Court Rule.

[Adopted effective September 1, 2015.]

LGR 10. CELL PHONES, PAGERS, AND OTHER DEVICES

No person shall be in the Ritzville District Court while in possession of a cell phone, pager, smart phone, hand held device, or other electronic device capable of producing a ring tone, beep, or other noise or signal unless such device is turned off or is in a "silent" or "vibrate" mode.

Any person found having any of the articles or devices heretofore mentioned which are not turned off or in a "silent" or "vibrate" mode while in the Ritzville District Court is subject to having such devices seized

by law enforcement officers, bailiffs on court order, or as otherwise directed by the Court.

In addition, any person violating this rule shall be subject to punishment for contempt of court.

[Adopted effective September 1, 2015.]

LGR 11. COURTROOM SAFETY

No person shall be in the Ritzville District Court while armed with ANY firearm or taser or explosive device or any knife having a blade length of more than three inches or any billy club, blackjack, truncheon or bat, nor shall any such person be in the afore-mentioned area while possessing any gas gun or other device used for the spraying of tear gas, mace or other noxious chemical substance, nor any incendiary device.

Any person found having any of the articles or devices heretofore mentioned which are banned from the Ritzville District Court (when being used for court purposes) is subject to having such articles or devices seized by law enforcement officers, bailiffs on court order, or as otherwise directed by the Court.

Any person violating this rule shall be subject to punishment for contempt of court and prosecuted under RCW 9.41.300.

[Adopted effective September 1, 2015.]

LGR 12. USE OF A COLLECTION AGENCY AND ASSESSMENT AS COURT COST OF AMOUNTS PAID FOR COLLECTION SERVICES

(a) The Court shall use the services of a collection agency for the purposes of collecting unpaid and delinquent penalties on infraction, criminal fines, costs, assessments, and forfeitures, on the terms and conditions of the contract for collection services between Ritzville District Court for Adams County and said collection agency, and may be subsequently amended.

(b) The collection agency's fee or charge, as set forth in said contract, shall be added by the collection agency as a cost to the total judgment of the Court against each defendant whose account is referred by the Court to the collection agency.

(c) Nothing in this section shall prevent the Court from notifying the Department of Licensing of the defendant's failure to pay a fine or cost as ordered by the Court.

[Adopted effective September 1, 2015.]

III. LOCAL CIVIL RULES

LCRLJ 3. COMMENCEMENT OF ACTION

Actions filed deliberately in the wrong venue on motion for change of venue, shall carry an award of reasonable attorney fees to the moving party. Any

action filed in the wrong venue shall be presumed to have been done with deliberation, and the burden to show otherwise is hereby placed upon the filing party. A motion for voluntary non-suit shall not be granted while there is a motion pending for correction of venue.

[Adopted effective September 1, 2015.]

LCRLJ 16. CIVIL JURY PRE–TRIAL PROCEDURE

All cases set for jury trial shall be set for pretrial conference which shall be held at least two weeks prior to trial. No order shall be required for this mandatory pre-trial conference. The attorneys who are to conduct the trial and all parties shall be present to consider such matters as will promote a fair and expeditious trial. All discovery should be completed three days prior to said conference. Opposing counsel or party must be given seven days notice on pre-trial motions to be heard at the pre-trial conference. Any pre-trial motions requiring testimony of witnesses for argument may, in the discretion of the Court, be continued to the day of trial. All amendments, pleas, and motions should be made or be completed at this conference. Upon failure to appear, the Judge may proceed with the conference ex-parte, if necessary, and enter any appropriate order including striking the jury demand and may impose terms.

[Adopted effective September 1, 2015.]

LCRLJ 26. DISCOVERY

Prior permission of the Court is required before taking depositions pursuant to Rules 30 through 32 of the Superior Court Civil Rules. The request for Admissions, Written Interrogatories and all other discovery procedures authorized by Rules 26 through 37 of the Superior Court Civil Rules shall be available to all parties in a cause of action without prior permission of the Court.

[Adopted effective September 1, 2015.]

LCRLJ 39. ADMISSIBILITY OF CERTAIN DOCUMENTS AT TRIAL

The documents listed below, if relevant, are presumed admissible at the trial, but only if: (1) the party offering the document serves on all parties at least 14 days prior to the trial date a notice, accompanied by a copy of the document and the name, address, and telephone number of its author or maker; and (2) the party offering the document similarly furnishes all other parties with copies of all other related documents from the same author or maker. This Rule does not restrict argument or proof related to the weight of evidence admitted, nor does it restrict the Court's authority to determine the weight of the evidence after hearing all of the evidence and the arguments of opposing parties.

Any other party may subpoena the author or maker of a document admissible under this Rule, at the party's expense, and examine the author or maker as if under cross-examination. The documents presumed admissible under this Rule are:

(a) A bill, report, chart or record of a hospital, doctor, dentist, registered nurse, licensed practical nurse, physical therapist, psychologist or other health care provider, on a letterhead or billhead;

(b) A bill for drugs, medical appliances or other related expenses on a letterhead or billhead;

(c) A bill, or an estimate of property damage on a letterhead or billhead. In the case of an estimate, the party intending to offer the estimate shall forward with the notice to the adverse party a statement indicating whether or not the property was repaired, and if it was, whether the estimated repairs were made in full or in part, attaching a copy to the receipted bill showing the items or repair and the amount paid;

(d) A police, weather, wage lost, or traffic signal report, or standard United States government life expectancy table to the extent it is admissible under the Rules of Evidence, but without the need for formal proof of authentication or identification;

(e) A photograph, x-ray, drawing, map, blueprint, or similar documentary evidence, to the extent it is admissible under the Rules of Evidence, but without the need for formal proof of authentication or identification;

(f) A document not specifically covered by any of the foregoing provisions by having equivalent circumstantial guarantees of trustworthiness, the admission of which would serve the interest of justice.

[Adopted effective September 1, 2015.]

LCRLJ 40. CONTINUANCE

(a) **Bench Trials.** Once a trial date has been set, a continuance will be granted only upon written stipulation of the parties filed, or order of the Court upon showing of good cause.

(b) **Jury Trials.**

(1) Prior to or at the pre-trial conference, request for continuance shall be granted upon written stipulation of the parties filed, or upon order of the Court upon showing good cause.

(2) After pre-trial conference, all requests for a continuance must be made in the form of a written motion and affidavit with reasonable notice provided to the opposing counsel and the Court. A continuance will be granted by the Court only upon showing of good cause.

(c) In any case, continuances shall be granted for only so long as is necessary taking into account not only the request or consent of the parties, but also the public interest in prompt disposition of cases.

[Adopted effective September 1, 2015.]

LCRLJ 41. DISMISSAL

(a) **Voluntary Dismissal.** Voluntary non-suits requested on the trial date are subject, at the discretion of the Court, to the allowance of costs and witness fees and reasonable attorney fees to those appearing on such trial date.

(b) Dismissal on Clerk's Motion. In all civil cases in which no action of record has occurred during the previous 12 months, the Clerk of the Court shall notify the attorneys of record by mail that the court will dismiss the case unless, within 30 days following the mailing of such, a party takes action of record or files a status report with the court indicating the reason for inactivity and projecting future activity and a case completion date. If the court does not receive such a status report, it shall, on motion of the clerk, dismiss the case without prejudice and without cost to any party.

The clerk shall mail notice of impending dismissal not later than 30 days after the case becomes eligible for dismissal because of inactivity. A party who does not receive the clerk's notice shall be entitled to reinstatement of the case, without cost, upon motion brought within a reasonable time after learning of the dismissal.

[Adopted effective September 1, 2015.]

LCRLJ 54. JUDGMENT AND COSTS

(a) Attorney fees. When any party claims the right to recover attorney fees by contract, statute, or court rule, that fact shall be brought to the attention of the Court immediately following its decision on the merits of the case, or the delivery of the jury verdict. If the Court then determines that an award of attorney fees may be appropriate, the Court may require the party requesting attorney fees to provide the Court with an affidavit detailing the fees incurred. The Court may either make an award of attorney fees and include it in the judgment, or schedule the matter for further argument.

[Adopted effective September 1, 2015.]

LCRLJ 55. DEFAULT AND JUDGMENT

(a) Entry of Default. In the event the Defendant does not appear within one half hour of the time set for trial, the Plaintiff may move for entry of default and a default judgment pursuant to CRLJ 55. A motion and affidavit for default judgment for failure to appear, plead, or otherwise defend as provided by this Rule shall be in substantially the same format hereinafter set forth.

(b) Entry of Default Judgment.

(1) *Assigned Claims.* A default judgment will not be entered on an assigned claim unless the original written assignment is filed with the Court.

(2) *Interest.* No judgment for interest shall be allowed unless proof of the factors necessary for computation of interest including applicable dates, rate of interest, and amount subject to interest, in addition to the final amount of interest claimed, is submitted in writing.

(3) *Notice.* The prevailing party shall notify the Defendant of the entry of default judgment by mailing a copy of the judgment to the defendant at his last known address within 5 days after entry of judgment.

(4) *Attorney Fees.* Where authorized by written instrument or statute, excluding those cases governed by the provisions of RCW 12.20.060, the Court may award reasonable attorney fees in cases where default judgment is entered in the amount of $200.00, unless at the time of judgment is entered, the prevailing party presents competent evidence to the Court that a larger sum should be awarded.

[Adopted effective September 1, 2015.]

LCRLJ 87. NAME CHANGES

(a) Requirements. An applicant who applies to the court for a change of name pursuant to RCW 4.24.130 must meet the following requirements:

(1) *Birth Certificate.* A certified copy of any minor applicant's birth certificate or suitable identification must be presented to the clerk for verification and copying.

(2) *Minors: Parental Consent.* All applicants under eighteen (18) years of age must be represented by a parent or legal guardian, and both biological or legal parents or guardian must approve the change of name either by personal appearance or by verified affidavit.

(3) *Separate Application.* Each applicant requesting a change of name must present a separate Change of Name Order and pay a separate filing fee and recording fee.

[Adopted effective September 1, 2015.]

IV. LOCAL CRIMINAL RULES

LCrRLJ 3.2. RELEASE OF ACCUSED

Any defendant charged with a criminal offense shall at his first court appearance be ordered released on his personal recognizance pending trial unless the Court determines that such recognizance will not reasonably assure his appearance, when required, or the Court finds that release on personal recognizance should be denied based on other criteria in pre-trial release rules applicable to Courts of Limited Jurisdiction.

If the Court finds that release should be denied, the Court shall proceed to determine whether probable cause exists to believe that the accused committed the offense charged, unless this determination has previously been made by a Court. Before making this determination, the Court may only consider affidavits or certificates under oath filed, or sworn testimony and further may examine under oath the affiant and any other witnesses he may produce. If probable cause is not established, the defendant shall be released.

Any person arrested for a crime classified as Domestic Violence under RCW 10.99 shall be held in jail without bail pending his first appearance.

No bail pending first appearance shall apply to all such offenses listed under Section 10.99 irrespective of their classification as felony, gross misdemeanor or misdemeanor.

[Adopted effective September 1, 2015.]

LCrRLJ 3.5–3.6. EVIDENCE SUPPRESSION PROCEDURE/CONFESSION SUPPRESSION PROCEDURE

All demands for hearings on admissibility of confessions, statements, or evidence must be made no later than the pre-trial hearing. The plaintiff shall be responsible for the subpoena of all witnesses necessary to meet its burden of proof at the CrRLJ 3.5–3.6 hearing. All CrRLJ 3.5–3.6 hearings shall be specially set.

(i) Deferred Prosecution Petition. Deferred Prosecution petitions shall be in substantially the same format as the petition attached to this Rule. Each petition shall include a case history and an evaluation attached as exhibits.

[Adopted effective September 1, 2015.]

PETITION FOR DEFERRED PROSECUTION

**DISTRICT COURT, STATE OF
WASHINGTON, ADAMS COUNTY**

_____,	No: _____
Plaintiff	**Petition for Deferred Prosecution**
vs.	**(DPPF)**
_____,	**Charges:** _____
Defendant	**Violation Date:** _____

Comes Now the defendant and petitions the court for deferred prosecution pursuant to RCW Chapter 10.05, and states as follows:

1. I allege the wrongful conduct charged is the result of or caused by [ ] *Alcoholism* [ ] *Drug Addiction* [ ] *Mental Problems*, for which I need treatment.

2. Unless I receive treatment for my problem, the probability of future reoccurrence is great.

3. I agree to pay for the cost of diagnosis and treatment, if financially able to do so, subject to RCW 10.05.130.

4. I understand that the court will not accept a petition for deferred prosecution from a person who sincerely believes that he or she is innocent of the crime(s) charged or does not suffer from alcoholism, drug addiction, or mental problems.

5. If this charge is a violation of Title 46 or similar municipal ordinance, I have not previously been placed on a deferred prosecution for a Title 46 or similar municipal ordinance violation.

6. A case history and assessment have been filed with this petition pursuant to RCW 10.05.020.

7. I understand and acknowledge I have the following rights: (a) to have a lawyer represent me at all hearings; (b) to have a lawyer appointed at public expense if I cannot afford one; (c) to a speedy, public jury trial; (d) to appeal any conviction; (e) to remain silent and not testify; (f) to question witnesses who testify against me; (g) to call witnesses to testify for me, at no cost; (h) to be presumed innocent unless the charge(s) against me is proven beyond a reasonable doubt; and (i) to present evidence and a defense. By deferring prosecution on these charges, I understand I give up my right to: (a) a speedy trial; (b) a jury; (c) testify; (d) question witnesses; (e) call witnesses; and (f) present evidence or a defense.

8. I stipulate to the admissibility and sufficiency of the facts in the attached police reports. I acknowledge that the above items will be entered and used to support a finding of guilty if the deferred prosecution is revoked.

9. If my deferred prosecution is revoked and I am found guilty, I understand that I may be sentenced up to the maximum penalty allowed by law.

10. I understand that if I proceed to trial and I am found guilty, I may be allowed to seek suspension of some or all fines and incarceration if I seek treatment. I understand that I may seek treatment from a public or private agency at any time, whether or not I have been found guilty or placed on deferred prosecution.

11. I understand that for some crimes, a deferred prosecution will enhance mandatory penalties for subsequent offenses committed within a seven-year period. I understand that a deferred prosecution will be a prior offense under RCW 46.61.5055 (driving under the influence, physical control of a vehicle under the influence, negligent driving if originally charged as driving under the influence or physical control of a vehicle under the influence, vehicular homicide, or vehicular assault).

12. I understand that if the court grants this Petition, I may not operate a motor vehicle on the public highways without a valid operator's license and proof of liability insurance pursuant to RCW 46.29.490. I understand that if my wrongful conduct is

the result of or caused by alcohol dependency, I shall also be required to install an ignition interlock under RCW 46.20.720. The required periods of use of the interlock shall be not less than the periods provided for in RCW 46.20.720(2)(a), (b) and (c). I may also be required to pay restitution to victims, pay court costs, and pay probation costs authorized by law. To help ensure continued sobriety and reduce the likelihood of re-offense, the court may order reasonable conditions during the period of the deferred prosecution including, but not limited to, attendance at self-help recovery support groups for alcoholism or drugs, complete abstinence from alcohol and all non-prescribed mind-altering drugs, periodic urinalysis or breath analysis, and maintaining law-abiding behavior. Alcoholism programs shall require a minimum of two self-help recovery groups per week for the duration of the treatment program. The court may terminate the deferred prosecution program if I violate this paragraph.

13. I understand that if the court grants this Petition, during the period of deferred prosecution I will be required to contact my probation officer, the probation director or designee, or the court if there is no probation department, to request permission to travel or transfer to another state if my wrongful conduct involves: (i) an offense in which a person has incurred direct or threatened physical or psychological harm; (ii) an offense that involves the use or possession of a firearm; (iii) a second or subsequent misdemeanor offense of driving while impaired by drugs or alcohol; (iv) a sexual offense that requires me to register as a sex offender in Washington state. I understand that I will be required to pay an application fee with my travel or transfer request.

14. I understand that if I fail or neglect to comply with any part of my treatment plan or with any ignition interlock requirements, then the court will hold a hearing to determine whether I should be removed from the deferred prosecution program. After the hearing the court will either order that I continue with treatment or be removed from deferred prosecution and enter judgment. If I am convicted of a similar offense during the deferred prosecution, the court will revoke the deferred prosecution and enter judgment.

15. I understand that the charge(s) against me in this case will be dismissed three years from the end of the two-year treatment program, and following proof to the court that I have complied with the conditions imposed by the court following successful completion of the two-year treatment program, but no less than five years from the date the deferred prosecution is granted, if the court grants my petition for deferred prosecution and if I fully comply with all the terms of the court order placing me on deferred prosecution.

I certify under penalty of perjury under the laws of the state of Washington that I have read the foregoing and agree with all of its provisions and that all statements made are true and correct.

Dated at _____, Washington this ___ day of _____, _____.

_____   _____
Petitioner–Defendant   Defense Attorney   WSBA No.

[Adopted effective September 1, 2015.]

DEFERRED PROSECUTION FINDINGS OF FACT, CONCLUSIONS OF LAW, AND ORDER

DISTRICT COURT, STATE OF WASHINGTON, ADAMS COUNTY

STATE OF WASHINGTON, CITY OF RITZVILLE,	)	
	)	No.
Plaintiff,	)	
	)	
vs.	)	DEFERRED PROSECUTION
_____,	)	FINDINGS OF FACT,
	)	CONCLUSIONS OF LAW, AND
Defendant.	)	ORDER
_____	)	

This matter coming before the court on the defendant's Petition for Deferred Prosecution, and the court having considered the Petition, evaluation and treatment plan filed by the defendant, and the arguments of counsel, now makes the following findings of fact:

I. Findings of Fact

1. The defendant was evaluated by an approved alcoholism treatment facility or an approved drug treatment center; said agency's evaluation meets the requirements of RCW 10.05.040 and is attached to this Order. A certified alcoholism treatment facility or drug treatment center has prepared a treatment plan meeting the requirements of RCW 10.05.150 and has committed to provide treatment. Said treatment plan and commitment to treatment is attached to this Order, and incorporated by reference herein.

2. The defendant has agreed to pay, or arranged for the payment of, the costs of treatment.

3. The defendant has agreed to complete the two-year treatment program set forth in the treatment plan attached to this Order and to follow the other conditions of the court's Order.

4. The defendant has been advised of the following rights and has knowingly and voluntarily waived each of them:

(a) The right to a jury trial;

(b) The right to a speedy trial;

(c) The right to present evidence in his or her defense;

(d) The right to hear and question all witnesses who testify against the defendant;

(e) The right to compel witnesses to appear and testify on behalf of the defendant at no cost to the defendant;

(f) The right to testify.

5. The defendant has stipulated to the admissibility and sufficiency of the facts contained in the written police reports and understands these facts will be considered by the court in any criminal hearing on the underlying offense or offenses held subsequent to revocation of the order granting deferred prosecution. The defendant has agreed that the facts contained in the stipulated police reports are sufficient to allow the court to find the petitioner guilty, beyond a reasonable doubt, of the charged offenses.

6. The defendant has agreed, and the court finds, that any statements made by the defendant contained in the stipulated police reports were made knowingly and voluntarily.

7. the charge is a violation of RCW Title 46 or similar municipal ordinance, the defendant has affirmed, and the court finds, that the defendant has not previously participated in a prior deferred prosecution program for a violation of RCW Title 46 or any similar municipal ordinance.

From the foregoing Findings of Fact, the court makes the following Conclusions of Law:

II. Conclusions of Law

1. The court has jurisdiction over the subject matter and petitioner in this case.

2. The petition meets the requirements of RCW 10.05.020

3. The diagnostic evaluation and treatment plan met the requirements of RCW 10.05.040, RCW 10.05.050 and RCW 10.05.150.

4. The Petition was made freely, voluntarily and knowingly.

III. Order

Based on the foregoing Findings of Fact and Conclusions of Law, the court hereby grants the Petition for Deferred Prosecution and allows the defendant to enter into a deferred prosecution program. The defendant shall remain under the jurisdiction of the court during the two year treatment plan, and for three years after the court receives proof of successful completion of the two-year treatment program, but not less than five years from the <u>date of this Order</u>. The defendant shall, while under the court's jurisdiction, comply with the following conditions:

1. The defendant shall fully comply with and complete the two-year treatment program attached to this Order and incorporated by reference in Paragraph 2 of the court's Findings. In the event there are any inconsistencies between this order and the attached treatment plan, the terms and conditions set forth in this order shall be controlling.

2. The defendant shall pay, or arrange for payment of, the costs of the treatment program.

3. The defendant shall maintain total abstinence from alcohol and all other non-prescribed mind altering drugs.

4. The defendant shall not commit any crimes. The definition of "commit" includes, but is not limited to, any criminal charge resolved by a stay of proceedings, a stipulated order of continuance, or any other agreement which consists of a continuance with conditions, even if the ultimate disposition of the criminal charge is a dismissal, amendment of charge, or a finding of not guilty.

5. The defendant shall not refuse to submit to a breath or blood test if a police officer has reasonable grounds to believe that the defendant is driving or is in physical control of a motor vehicle while under the influence of intoxicating liquor or drugs.

6. The defendant shall not operate a motor vehicle upon the public highways without a valid operator's license and proof of liability insurance in an amount not less than that established by RCW 46.29.490.

7. The defendant shall not change treatment agencies without written permission of the court.

8. The treatment facility shall file with Ritzville District Court **monthly** treatment status/compliance reports. Those reports shall be sent to:

Ritzville District Court
210 W. Broadway
Ritzville, WA 99169
Phone # 509–659–1002
Fax # 509–659–3245

9.   The defendant shall provide **in writing** to the court any change in mailing address.

10.   The defendant [ ] shall [ ] shall not be required to pay a $600.00 administrative fee.

11.   The defendant [ ] shall [ ] shall not be required to pay a $125 breath test fee.

12.   [ ] The defendant [ ] shall [ ] shall not be required to reimburse Adams County for the cost of his/her court appointed attorney in the amount of $ ___.

13.   [ ] The defendant shall pay restitution in the amount of $ ___.   [ ] A restitution hearing shall be held on ___ / 20 to determine what amount of restitution should be paid by the defendant

14.   This matter shall be set for review at any time as may be deemed appropriate by the court. In the event the defendant fails or neglects to undertake, complete or comply with any term or condition of this Order, the court, upon receiving notice of such failure, neglect, or violation, shall hold a hearing to determine whether the sufficient cause exists to remove the defendant from the deferred prosecution program. In the event the defendant is convicted of a similar offense, the court shall remove the defendant from the deferred prosecution program.

15.   In the event the court finds cause to revoke the deferred prosecution, the court (sitting without a jury) will consider the stipulated police reports, including any statements made by the defendant, and determine whether the stipulated evidence supports the charge(s) beyond a reasonable doubt

16.   In the event the defendant complies with the conditions of this Order the court shall, three years after receiving proof of successful completion of the two-year treatment program, but not before five years following entry of this Order, dismiss the charges pending against the defendant

17.   Other: _____

_____

Dated _____ / _____ 20 _____

_____
DISTRICT COURT JUDGE

Presented by:

Copy received; approved as to form:

_____   _____
Attorney for Defendant   WSBA   #Prosecuting Attorney   WSBA #

Copy received; terms and conditions of Order accepted by:

_____

Defendant

Attached to this Order are:

A.   Alcohol/drug evaluation, treatment plan and commitment to provide treatment.

B.   Police reports.

[Adopted effective September 1, 2015.]

23

LCrRLJ 3.7. PRESENCE OF THE PROSECUTOR

In all criminal cases, a representative of the Prosecuting Attorney's Office or the Office of City Attorney responsible for the case shall be present to conduct the case for the plaintiff. This rule applies to arraignments, pretrial hearings, motions, trials and other dispositions.

[Adopted effective September 1, 2015.]

LCrRLJ 4.5. JURY PRE–TRIAL PROCEDURE

(a) Pre–Trial Hearings. All cases scheduled for jury trial shall be set for pre-trial hearing. Pre–trial hearings shall be held prior to the jury trial. The State or City Prosecutor, defense counsel and defendant shall attend the pre-trial hearings. If the defendant does not appear for the pre-trial hearing, a warrant for the arrest of the defendant shall issue and the jury trial date will be stricken unless a written waiver of pretrial hearing has been filed with the Court. If the Prosecutor fails to appear at pre-trial hearing, the Court may impose terms and other sanctions created by Court Rule and State law. Pre–trial hearing may be waived by filing a written stipulation signed by both parties which states there are no pretrial motions and the case will proceed to jury trial on the specified date.

A defendant may also waive the first pre-trial hearing by filing a written waiver and request to set the case over to the next regularly scheduled pre-trial or motion calendar. A written motion must be filed on any issues to be argued at the second or third pretrial or motion calendar.

(b) Motions. Pre–Trial motions shall be made at the time of the pre-trial hearing. Motions shall not be considered at the time of trial unless they could not have been raised at the time of pre-trial hearing or the Judge at the time of the pre-trial hearing expressly continues such motions to the time of trial. Absent good cause, motions for dismissal or suppression of evidence in criminal cases shall be in writing and shall be provided to the Prosecutor or City Attorney at least 48 hours before the pre-trial hearing. Dispositions and bench trials will not be heard on the date set for jury trial. Lengthy motions or motions requiring witnesses to be subpoenaed will be specially set by the court.

[Adopted effective September 1, 2015.]

LCrRLJ 7.2. SENTENCING

Conditions and Payment. Any deferred or suspended sentence in which the defendant is ordered to pay a fine, restitution, court cost, or attorney fees, shall, unless other specific provision is made by the Court, include by reference the following provision:

(1) *Time Payments.* Regular monthly payments may be required if the fine is not paid in full at sentencing until all fines, penalties, fees and costs are paid. Unless otherwise specified by the Court, all fine payments, costs, fees, and restitution paid through the Court shall be scheduled to be paid on a set date each month. Each payment agreement shall include a statement that the account will be referred to a collection agency if payment is not received by due date and the defendant will be liable for any and all costs. Upon finding that such payment is delinquent, the Clerk shall mail the Defendant a delinquent payment notice. If payment is not received within 30 days, then the matter is turned over to collection and Department of Licensing is notified of Defendant's failure to respond.

(2) *Collection Process/Costs.* If a Defendant fails to make all payments as directed or otherwise fails to respond to the Court within 30 days after the date of a delinquency notice, the delinquent account will be referred to a collection agency pursuant to RCW 3.02.045. The amount agreed to between the Court and the collection agency as remuneration for services will be assessed as cost and added to the judgment.

(3) *Attorney Fee/Reimbursement.* Upon motion of the Plaintiff, the Court will evaluate the financial status of Defendants represented by appointed counsel. Those Defendants found by the Court to be financially able at the time of sentencing to reimburse the City or County for all or a portion of attorney fees will be ordered by the Court to make reimbursement. Unless otherwise ordered by the Court, such reimbursement shall be made within 90 days of sentencing.

(4) *Probation Fees.* Pursuant to RCW 10.64.120, a defendant may be required to pay a fee for probation services.

(5) *Revocation of Probation/Hearing.* Revocation of a deferred or suspended sentence for nonpayment of fines, costs, attorney fees or probation fees or a finding of contempt pursuant to RCW 10.01.180 shall occur only after a hearing and upon such a finding by the Court that the defendant has willfully failed to make such payments while having the financial ability to do so or has willfully failed to make a good faith reasonable effort to acquire a means to make such payments. Further, the Court should consider whether alternative means of payment through time payments or performance of community service has been available to the Defendant, prior to imposition of a jail sentence.

(6) *Petition to Modify.* The Defendant may, at any time, petition to the Court to adjust the amount of any payment established in accordance with this Rule, due to his or her changed financial position or to relieve undue hardship to the Defendant and his or her family.

[Adopted effective September 1, 2015.]

LCrRLJ 8.2. MOTIONS

Notation for Hearing. Motions may be noted on the Court's docket by delivery of a written Note for Motion Docket. Counsel shall indicate on the docu-ment whether the motion will require live testimony and the estimated time for disposition. Motions requiring ten minutes or less will be given preference on the motion docket.

[Adopted effective September 1, 2015.]

V. LOCAL INFRACTION RULES

LIRLJ 2.4. RESPONSE TO NOTICE

Any person who has been served with a notice of infraction and who desires to use option (1) as provided in IRLJ 2.4(b)(1), may arrange time payments on the monetary penalty according to the policy then in force when the infraction is filed. A fee shall be assessed at the time of establishing a time payment agreement, as a nonrefundable cost for usage of the service. A minimum payment of $25.00 is required each month.

[Adopted effective September 1, 2015.]

LIRLJ 2.6. INFRACTION PRE–HEARING CONFERENCE

(a) Pre–hearing Conference Required—Waiver. A defendant charged with an infraction who requests a hearing to contest the infraction shall first appear at a pre-hearing conference, in which motions, not witnesses will be heard. The pre-hearing conference shall be scheduled in accordance with the provisions of IRLJ 2.6(a)(1)(i). If the defendant does not intend to bring any pre-hearing motion, the requirement that the defendant appear at the pre-hearing conference may be waived by the defendant in writing; provided the waiver is received by the court before the time set for the pre-hearing conference. If the defendant does not appear for the pre-hearing he is deemed to have waived his right to bring any pre-hearing motions, and the infraction will be set on the next contested hearing date. In waiving the pre-hearing conference, the defendant shall complete a waiver form approved by the court. In the event that the defendant submits a waiver in a form other than that approved by the court, said waiver shall be ineffective unless it is in substantial compliance with the same format hereinafter set forth.

(ii) *Setting Contested Hearing.* If the infractions are not resolved following the pre-hearing conference, a contested hearing shall be scheduled for not more than ninety (90) days from the date of the prehearing conference. If the pre-hearing conference is waived, a contested hearing shall be scheduled for not more than ninety (90) days from the date the waiver of the pre-hearing conference is received by the court.

(iii) *Pre–hearing Motions for Contested Infrac-tions—Written Notice Required—Time Limits for Oral Argument.* All motions, including the cited authority(s), to exclude evidence or dismiss an infraction shall be filed no later than the conclusion of the pre-hearing conference. If a defendant elects to waive his or her appearance at the pre-hearing conference, any motion, including the cited authority, must be noted on the waiver form filed with the court pursuant to IRLJ 2.6(a). Any motion(s) not timely filed shall be waived and shall not be considered by the court.

All motions timely noted shall be addressed by the court at the time of the contested hearing. Unless otherwise ordered by the court, parties shall have a total of ten (10) minutes each to argue and/or respond to motions before the court. Any argument in support of, or in response to, motions before the court that will require more than ten (10) minutes to present shall be submitted in brief form.

[Adopted effective September 1, 2015.]

WAIVER OF PRE–HEARING

DISTRICT COURT, STATE OF WASHINGTON, ADAMS COUNTY

STATE OF WASHINGTON, CITY OF RITZVILLE, Plaintiff, vs. _____, Defendant.	)))))))))))

No. _____

WAIVER OF PRE–HEARING

The undersigned defendant, having been advised of his/her right to a pre-hearing conference for the contested citation number # _____, hereby freely, knowingly and voluntarily, waives said right.

_____   _____
Date   Defendant's Signature

_____   _____
Date   Defendant's Attorney   WSBA No.

_____   _____
Date   DISTRICT COURT JUDGE

[Adopted effective September 1, 2015.]

LIRLJ 3.1. CONTESTED HEARINGS— PRELIMINARY PROCEEDINGS

(a) Subpoena. The defendant and the plaintiff may subpoena witnesses necessary for the presentation of their respective cases. Subpoena requests must be filed with the court at least fourteen (14) days prior to the contested hearing and witnesses should be served at least 7 days before the hearing. The subpoena may be issued by a judge, court commissioner, or clerk of the court or by a party's lawyer. If a party's lawyer issues a subpoena, a copy shall be filed with the court and with the office of the prosecuting authority assigned to the court in which the infraction is filed on the same day it is sent out for service. A request that an officer appear at a contested hearing pursuant to rule 3.3(c) shall be filed on a separate pleading. A subpoena may be directed for service within their jurisdiction to the sheriff of any county or any peace officer of any municipality in the state in which the witness may be or it may be served as provided in CR45(c), or it may be served by first-class mail, postage prepaid, sent to the witnesses' last known address. Service by mail shall be deemed complete upon the third day following the day upon which the subpoena was placed in the mail. If the subpoena is for a witness outside the county, a judge must approve of the subpoena.

(b) If the defendant who requests a hearing to contest the determination that an infraction was committed has a criminal charge pending, and said criminal charge arises out of the same occurrence as the infraction, the hearing on the infraction may be heard at the same time as the trial on the criminal charge at the request of the defendant, the City Attorney, County Attorney, or the court as authorized by the Infraction Rules for Courts of Limited Jurisdiction.

[Adopted effective September 1, 2015.]

LIRLJ 3.3. PROCEDURE AT CONTESTED HEARING

(b) Plaintiff Witness–Representation by Lawyer. In contested traffic infraction hearings the Plaintiff shall be represented by a lawyer representative of the Prosecuting Attorney or City Attorney in all contested hearings where witnesses have been subpoenaed, or discovery requested, and where the Defendant is represented by a lawyer.

[Adopted effective September 1, 2015.]

LIRLJ 3.5. HEARINGS VIA MAIL/E-MAIL

(a) Contested or Mitigation Hearings. Upon receipt of a request for contested or mitigation hearing (including e-mail submissions), the Court shall set the matter for hearing and send the Defendant a letter and the appropriate forms. The Defendant shall return the completed declaration to the Court in writing (including e-mail submissions). Upon receipt of the completed declaration the hearing will be cancelled. The Declaration contesting or mitigating an infraction must certify or declare under penalty of perjury under the laws of the State of Washington that the statement is true and correct. The Declaration must also contain a statement that if it is determined that the respondent committed the infraction, the respondent promises to pay the monetary penalty authorized by law and assessed by the court. Any witness statement submitted by the Defendant contesting the infraction must also be sworn. The Court shall review the officer's sworn statement and declarations submitted by the defendant. The examination may be held in Chambers and shall not be governed by the rules of evidence. The Court will then determine whether the plaintiff has proved by a preponderance of evidence whether it is more likely than not that the defendant has committed the infraction and render its decision and/or what penalty, if any, was imposed, by mail.

If the defendant chooses to contest or mitigate by mail, he or she waives the right to appeal the court's decision to the Superior Court under IRLJ 3.5. **The Court must receive declarations no later than seven (7) days prior to the scheduled hearing time or they will not be considered.**

STATE OF WASHINGTON,	)
CITY OF RITZVILLE,	)
	)
	) DECLARATION OF:
Plaintiff,	)
	) Infraction No.
vs.	)
	)

Defendant.   )
_____)

MY SWORN STATEMENT IS AS FOLLOWS: (Use reverse side if necessary)

_____
_____
_____
_____
_____
_____
_____
_____
_____

I certify (or declare) under penalty of perjury under the laws of the State of Washington that the foregoing is true and correct.

I promise that if it is determined that I committed the infraction for which I was cited, I will pay the monetary penalty authorized by law and assessed by the Court.

Dated this ___ day of _____, 20 ___, at _____ (City), _____ (County), _____ (State).

_____

Defendant

(c) Deferred Findings. The court may defer findings regarding traffic infractions for up to one year pursuant to RCW 46.63.070(5)(a).

(1) *Limit.* A person may not receive more than one deferral within a seven-year period for moving violations and one deferral within a seven-year period for non-moving violations.

(2) *Conditions.* For both moving and non-moving violations a person who is the holder of an active commercial driver's license may not receive a deferral under this section. The conditions shall include payment of an administrative fee.

(3) Administrative Fees can be found on the Ritzville District Court website *www. co.adams.wa.us* under Filing and Miscellaneous Fees.

(4) *Dismissal.* After the end of the deferral period, the court will dismiss the infraction if the person has met all the conditions of the deferral and has not committed another respective traffic infraction during the period.

(5) A petition for a deferred finding which is denied by the Court will be treated as a request for a mitigation hearing.

(6) Failure to comply with any conditions, will result in the infraction being found committed and reported to the Department of Licensing.

[Adopted effective September 1, 2015.]

LIRLJ 4.2. FAILURE TO PAY FOR TRAFFIC INFRACTION

Defendants who owe penalties on traffic infractions must report to the cashier/clerk immediately after leaving the courtroom to make payment arrangements. Failure to do so may be considered a failure to pay. The Court may assess the appropriate penalty for failure to pay or appear, and may rescind any reduction in the penalty imposed. The court reserves the right to assign the account to a third party agency for the collection of the penalties, fines, and costs owed.

[Adopted effective September 1, 2015.]

LIRLJ 6.2. MONETARY PENALTY SCHEDULE FOR INFRACTIONS

(b) Unscheduled Infractions.

(1) *Mandatory Liability Insurance Violations—Proof of Insurance.* If a defendant who is charged with driving a motor vehicle without having proof of valid insurance pursuant to RCW 46.30.020 and that defendant presents satisfactory evidence that they have obtained valid insurance to the Clerk of the Court within 15 days of the date of the citation, for the vehicle the defendant was operating on the day he/she was cited, then the bail for the offense shall be reduced. If the defendant presents satisfactory evidence of valid insurance being in effect at the time the citation was issued, for the vehicle the defendant was operating, within 15 days of the date of the citation, then the offense shall be dismissed upon payment of the $25 administrative fee.

(2) *No Valid Operators License—Show License.* If a defendant is charged with the infraction of driving a motor vehicle without having a valid driver's license issued to Washington residents pursuant to RCW 46.20.015, and that defendant presents a valid license or satisfactory evidence that the defendant has obtained a valid driver's license to the court clerk, then the bail for the offense shall be reduced and the defendant will be entitled to post and forfeit that penalty without the need to appear in court on that charge.

(3) *Expired Vehicle License.* If a person charged with the violation of RCW 46.16A.030.5.L (Expired Vehicle Registration Less than Two Months) or RCW 46.16A.030.5.O (Expired Vehicle Registration Over Two Months) is able to provide proof prior to any scheduled hearing the person has subsequently obtained a valid registration then the penalty shall be reduced and a finding of committed entered.

[Adopted effective September 1, 2015.]

LIRLJ 6.6. SPEED MEASURING DEVICE: DESIGN AND CONSTRUCTION CERTIFICATION

(b) Speed Measuring Device Certifications. Any certificate, affidavit, or foundation evidentiary document allowed or required by IRLJ 6.6 can be filed with the Clerk of the Court and maintained by the court as a public record. The records will be available for inspection by the public. Copies will be provided on request, subject to a charge for any allowable copying fees.Speed measuring device certification documents can be obtained from the court clerk during normal business hours prior to a contested hearing. Speed measuring device certifications are not subject to discovery.

(c) Request for Speed Measuring Device (SMD) Expert. Defense request to produce an electronic or laser SMD expert pursuant to IRLJ 6.6(e) for a contested hearing shall be contained in a separate document clearly designated as a request for a SMD expert, served on the prosecuting authority with a conformed copy filed with the Clerk of the Court. If the charging law enforcement agency's SMD expert maintains a schedule for monthly appearances in the Ritzville District Court for Adams County, a request for a SMD expert shall be deemed by the court to be a request to set (or re-set) the hearing to a day scheduled for the agency's SMD expert.

(1) The Party filing the above demand shall specifically call it to the Court Clerk's attention so the case will be set on the appropriate SMD expert's trial date so as to avoid a continuance under IRLJ 6.6(c).

In the absence of proof of a request to produce an electronic speed measuring device (SMD) expert, a certificate in substantially the form provided under CrRLJ 6.13, IRLJ 6.6 is admissible in lieu of an expert witness in any court proceeding in which the design and construction of an electronic speed measuring device (SMD) is an issue.

[Adopted effective September 1, 2015.]

VI. LOCAL RULES FOR APPEAL OF DECISIONS

VI. LOCAL RULES FOR APPEAL OF DECISIONS

Refer to Washington Court Rules (State).

[Adopted effective September 1, 2015.]

VII. LOCAL COURTROOM PRACTICE AND DECORUM

VII. LOCAL COURTROOM PRACTICE AND DECORUM

(a) Examination of Witnesses and Argument of Counsel.

(1) During opening statement, examination of witnesses, and arguments, counsel should remain at counsel table unless otherwise authorized by the Court.

(2) Do not approach a witness without asking permission of the Court. When permission is granted for the purpose of working with an exhibit, resume the examination from counsel table when finished with the exhibit.

(3) Rise when addressing the Court and when making objections as this calls the Court's attention to you.

(b) Objections to Questions and Evidence.

(1) When objecting, state only that you are objecting and specify the ground or grounds of objection. Do not use objections for the purpose of making a speech, recapitulating testimony, or attempting to guide the witness.

(2) Argument upon the objection will not be heard until permission is given or argument is requested by the Court.

(c) Decorum.

(1) Address all remarks to the Court. Colloquy or argument between attorneys is not permitted.

(2) In a jury case, if there is an offer of stipulation, first confer with opposing counsel and obtain the Court's permission before submitting it to the jury.

(3) Counsel during trial shall not exhibit familiarity with witnesses, jurors, or opposing counsel. The use of first names or nicknames is to be avoided. During jury argument, no juror shall be addressed individually or by name.

(4) During the argument of opposing counsel, remain seated at the counsel table and be respectful. Never divert the attention of the Court or the jury.

(d) Witnesses and Ruling of the Court.

(1) Witnesses shall at all times be treated with fairness, consideration and respect.

(2) No person shall ever by facial expression or other conduct exhibit any opinion concerning any testimony, which is being given by a witness, or as to a ruling by the Court. Counsel will admonish their clients and witnesses about this very common occurrence.

(e) Court Hours and Promptness.

(1) The Court will make every effort to commence proceedings at the time set. Promptness is expected from counsel and witnesses.

(2) Counsel should make every effort to schedule witnesses in order to use full utilization of the trial day.

(f) Exhibits.

(1) All exhibits should be pre-marked for identification prior to trial. The Bailiff assigned to each Judge will cooperate with counsel in facilitating the marking and management of the exhibits.

(2) Documents and other exhibits should be shown to opposing counsel before their use in Court.

(3) Ordinarily, exhibits should be offered in evidence when they become admissible rather than at the end of counsel's case.

(4) Marking on exhibits should only be made after receiving the Court's permission to do so.

(g) Opening Statement. Confine your opening statement to what you expect the evidence to show. It is not proper to use the opening statement to argue the case or instruct as to the law.

[Adopted effective July 1, 1997. Amended effective September 1, 2008; September 1, 2015.]

ASOTIN COUNTY

Table of Courts

Superior Court

Hells Canyon Circuit Local Rules.

District Court

Asotin County District Court.

SUPERIOR COURT

HELLS CANYON CIRCUIT LOCAL RULES
[PREVIOUSLY KNOWN AS THE LOCAL RULES OF THE SUPERIOR COURT OF THE STATE OF WASHINGTON FOR THE JUDICIAL DISTRICT OF ASOTIN, COLUMBIA, AND GARFIELD COUNTIES]

PUBLISHER'S NOTE

The Hells Canyon Circuit Local Rules (Previously Known as the Local Rules for the Superior Courts of Asotin, Columbia, and Garfield Counties) are set forth under Hells Canyon Circuit.

DISTRICT COURT
ASOTIN COUNTY DISTRICT COURT

Including Amendments Received Through
August 15, 2015

Table of Rules

RULE 1. [SCOPE OF RULES]

Asotin County District Court Sits for:

Asotin County District Court matters
Clarkston Municipal matters, and
Asotin Municipal matters

These rules apply to all.

[Adopted effective September 1, 2009. Amended effective September 2, 2014.]

RULE 2. OPERATION

Weekdays—8:30 by teleconference with Asotin County jail.

The District Court does bond hearings for all jurisdictions, (including Superior Court when the Superior Court Judge isn't available.)

Monday—10:00—12:00 Omnibus Motions docket

1:30 Traffic mitigations and contested cases; Restraining Order Hearings; Collections, and Small Claims

Tuesday—Clarkston Municipal Docket

10:00—12:00 Entry and Trial Set

1:30—Arraignment

3:00—Review

Wednesday—Asotin County District Court and City of Asotin Municipal Court

Asotin Co. District

10:00—12:00 Entry and Trial Set

1:30—Arraignment

3:00—Review

Asotin Municipal

1:30—Arraignment

3:00—Review

4:00 Entry and Trial Set

Thursdays and Fridays

Trials

[Adopted effective September 1, 2009. Amended effective September 2, 2014.]

RULE 3. FEES

The Court may charge a monthly probation fee for domestic violence, DUI, and other cases determined by the court.

The Court may charge a fee, not inconsistent with statute, for a payment schedule rather than a single payment.

The Court may charge a fee for making copies of CD's

The fees for documents and official services can be found in the schedule of fees listed in RCW 3.62.060

[Adopted effective September 1, 2009. Amended effective September 2, 2014.]

RULE 4. [RECORDS]

The Court is a Court of Record which is kept on CD.

Records kept by the Court are:

Public Records.

1. Court Pleadings initiating a case and the disposition unless otherwise sealed, expunged or violative of a person's right to privacy.

Quasi–Public Documents. These are not subject to public review, but, unless otherwise ordered by the Court are subject to review by the parties and their attorneys (plaintiff and defendant and their attorneys.[1]

a.   Witness statements

b.   Pre–Sentence Reports and Probation Reports

c.   Copies of driving records or criminal history

d.   Correspondence received by the Court regarding sentencing or reports on terms of probation.

[Adopted effective September 1, 2009. Amended effective September 2, 2014.]

[1] So in original.

RULE 5.   PRETRIAL RELEASE

Defendants in Criminal cases are not entitled to release until a bond hearing but maybe released according to bail schedules set out in CrLJ or promulgated by the Sheriff's department.

[Adopted effective September 1, 2009. Amended effective September 2, 2014.]

RULE 6.   JURY FEES

When a cause is assigned a date for jury trial and is settled or otherwise not heard for any reason whatsoever, notice of that fact shall be given immediately to the Court. Terms may be sought against the responsible party should this case be settled after the jury has been called. Any such terms imposed by the Court for payment shall be paid as directed by the Court.

[Adopted effective September 1, 2009. Amended effective September 2, 2014.]

RULE 7.   [TELECONFERENCING]

"Pleas of Guilty" and "Judgments and Sentences" may be heard by the Court using the teleconferencing system with the defendant at jail, represented by his or her counsel present or at the Jail, if all parties agree and the court has the signed plea and can follow the proposed Judgment and Sentence.

[Adopted effective September 1, 2009. Amended effective September 2, 2014.]

BENTON COUNTY

Table of Courts

Superior Court

Local Rules of the Superior Court of Washington in and for Benton and Franklin Counties.

District Court

Benton County District Court.

SUPERIOR COURT

LOCAL RULES OF THE SUPERIOR COURT OF WASHINGTON IN AND FOR BENTON AND FRANKLIN COUNTIES

Including Amendments Received Through
August 15, 2015

Table of Rules

LOCAL GENERAL RULES (LGR)

LGR 2. ADMINISTRATIVE PRESIDING JUDGE AND ASSISTANT ADMINISTRATIVE PRESIDING JUDGE

(a) Election, Term, Vacancies, and Removal.

(1) *Election.* The administrative presiding judge and assistant administrative presiding judge shall be elected by a majority vote of the judges. Said elections shall occur at the December judge's meeting in odd numbered years.

(2) *Term.* The administrative presiding judge and assistant administrative presiding judge shall each serve for a term of two years. The terms of the presiding judge and assistant presiding judge first elected pursuant to this rule shall expire on December 31, 2003.

(3) *Vacancies.*

(A) Administrative Presiding Judge. In the event of a vacancy in the office of the administrative presiding judge prior to the completion of the two-year term of the administrative presiding judge, the assistant administrative presiding judge shall serve as administrative presiding judge for the remainder of the un-expired term.

(B) Assistant Administrative Presiding Judge. In the event of a vacancy in the office of the assistant administrative presiding judge prior to the completion of the two year term of the assistant administrative presiding judge, a new assistant administrative presiding judge shall be elected pursuant to subsection (1) above at the next regularly scheduled judge's meeting. The newly elected assistant administrative presiding judge shall serve for the remainder of the un-expired term.

(4) *Removal.* The administrative presiding judge and assistant administrative presiding judge may be removed by a majority vote of the judges after noting the issue on the agenda for the next regularly scheduled judge's meeting.

(5) *Executive Committee.* The Judges of the Superior Court, sitting as a whole as an executive committee, shall advise and assist the administrative presiding judge in the administration of the court.

(6) *Liaison Judges.* Individual judges may be assigned responsibility for certain management areas and court functions. The responsibility of the assigned judge is to act as a liaison between the court and others concerned about matters that fall within the management area or court function. The assigned judge shall keep the administrative presiding judge and executive committee informed about the management area or court function and shall make such reports as are necessary to the executive committee at the regularly scheduled judges meetings. The court administrator shall maintain the list of the liaison assignments that shall be available, upon request, to the public.

(7) *Court Administrator.* The court administrator shall, under the direction of the executive committee, supervise the administration of the court.

[Adopted effective April 9, 2002. Amended effective September 1, 2010.]

LOCAL CIVIL RULES (LCR)

LCR 4. CIVIL CASE SCHEDULE

(a) **Case Schedule.** Except as otherwise provided in these rules or ordered by the Court, when an initial pleading is filed and a new case file is opened, the Court Administrator or Superior Court Clerk will prepare and file a scheduling order (referred to in these rules as a "Case Schedule") and will provide one copy to the party filing the initial pleading.

(b) **Effective Date.** This rule shall apply to all cases filed on or after January 1, 2001 except as provided below.

(c) **Cases Not Governed by a Civil Case Schedule.** Unless otherwise ordered by the Court, the following cases will not be issued a Case Schedule on filing:

(1) Change of name;

(2) Proceedings under RCW title 26.

(3) Paternity

(4) Harassment (RCW chapter 10.14);

(5) Proceedings under RCW title 13;

(6) Unlawful detainer;

(7) Foreign judgment;

(8) Abstract or transcript of judgment;

(9) Petition for Writ of Habeas Corpus, Mandamus, Restitution, or Review, or any other Writ;

(10) Civil commitment;

(11) Proceedings under RCW chapter 10.77;

(12) Proceedings under RCW chapter 70.96A;

(13) Proceedings for isolation and quarantine;

(14) Injunction;

(15) Guardianship/Petitions under TEDRA;

(16) Probate;

(17) Proceedings under RCW chapter 36.70C;

(18) Tax Warrants;

(19) Lower Court Appeals;

(20) Administrative Law Reviews (Appeals of Administrative Agency Decisions);

(21) Emancipation of Minor;

(22) Defacto Parenting;

(23) Minor Settlements;

(24) Condemnations;

(25) Petitions for Transfers of Structured Settlements under RCW 19.205;

(26) Tax Foreclosures; and

(27) Actions brought under the Public Records Act, RCW Chapter 42.56.

(d) Service of Case Schedule on Other Parties.

(1) The party filing the initial pleading shall promptly provide a copy of the Case Schedule to all other parties by (a) serving a copy of the Case Schedule on the other parties along with the initial pleading, or (b) serving the Case Schedule on the other parties within 10 days after the later filing of the initial pleading or service of any response to the initial pleading, whether that response is a notice of appearance, an answer, or a CR 12 motion.

(2) A party who joins an additional party in an action shall serve the additional party with the current Case Schedule together with the first pleading served on the additional party.

(e) Amendment of Case Schedule. The Court, either on motion of a party or on its own initiative, or at a Status Conference requested by the parties, may modify the Case Schedule for good cause. The Court shall freely grant a motion to amend the case schedule when justice so requires. The motion shall include a proposed Amended Case Schedule. If a Case Schedule is modified on the Court's own motion, the Court Administrator will prepare and file the Amended Case Schedule and promptly mail it to all parties. Parties may not amend a Case Schedule by stipulation without approval of the Court. If a trial is continued after the Pretrial Management Conference, Court Administration will, as soon as practicable, schedule a mandatory Status Conference for the purpose of scheduling a new trial and the development of a new Case Schedule Order.

(f) Form of Case Schedule.

(1) *Case Schedule.* A Case Schedule for each type of case, which will set the time period between filing and trial and the scheduled events and deadlines for that type of case, will be established by the Court by General Order, based upon relevant factors, including statutory priorities, resources available to the Court, case filings, and the interests of justice.

(2) *Form.* A Case Schedule will be in generally the following form:

SUPERIOR COURT OF THE STATE OF WASHINGTON
IN AND FOR BENTON AND FRANKLIN COUNTIES

Plaintiff(s))	Case No.
)	
)	**CIVIL CASE**
)	**SCHEDULE ORDER**
V.)	**(ORSCS)**
)	
)	
Defendant(s))	

I. SCHEDULE

	DUE DATE
1. Cancellation / Confirmation of Status Conference	3 Months
2. Status Conference	4 Months
3. Plaintiff's Disclosure of Lay and Expert Witnesses...........	4 Months
4. Defendant's Disclosure of Lay and Expert Witnesses	6 Months
5. Last Date for Filing Statement of Arbitrability	6 ½Months
6. Disclosure of Plaintiff's Rebuttal Witnesses	6 ½ Months
7. Disclosure of Defendant's Rebuttal Witnesses	7 Months
8. Discovery Completed..........	9 ½ Months
9. Last Date for Filing Jury Demand	10 Months
10. Settlement Position Statements filed by all parties	10 Months
11. Last Date for Hearing Dispositive Pretrial Motions	10 ½ Months
12. Settlement Conference	11 Months
13. Last Date for Filing and Serving Trial Management Report	11 ½ Months
15.¹ Pretrial Management Conference	11 ½ Months
16. Trial Memoranda and Motions in Limine to be filed	2 Weeks to Trial
17. Trial Date and Motions in Limine	12 Months

II. ORDER

IT IS ORDERED that all parties comply with the foregoing schedule.

DATED this _____ day of _____, _____

_____

Judge

NOTICE TO PLAINTIFF:

The plaintiff may serve a copy of the Case Schedule Order on the defendant(s) along with the summons and complaint. Otherwise, the plaintiff shall serve the Case Schedule Order on the defendant(s) within ten (10) days after the latter of: (1) the filing of the summons and complaint or (2) service of the defendant's first response to the complaint, whether that response is a Notice of Appearance, an Answer, or a CR 12 Motion.

(g) Monitoring. At such times as the Presiding Judge may direct, the Court Administrator will monitor cases to determine compliance with these rules.

(h) Witness Disclosure; Enforcement; Sanctions.

(1) *Disclosure of Possible Lay and Expert Witnesses.*

(A) Disclosure of Primary Witnesses. Each party shall, no later than the date for disclosure designated in the Case Schedule, disclose all persons with relevant factual or expert knowledge whom the party believes are reasonably likely to be called at trial.

(B) Disclosure of Rebuttal Witnesses. Each party shall, no later than the date for disclosure designated in the Case Schedule, disclose all persons whose knowledge did not appear relevant until the primary witnesses were disclosed and whom the party reserves the option to call as witnesses at trial.

(C) Scope of Disclosure. Disclosure of witnesses under this rule shall include the following information:

i. All Witnesses. Name, address, and phone number.

ii. Lay Witnesses. A brief description of the anticipated subject matter of the witness' testimony.

iii. Experts. A summary of the expert's opinions and the basis therefor and a brief description of the expert's qualifications.

(D) Exclusion of Testimony. Any person not disclosed in compliance with this rule may not be called to testify at trial, unless the Court orders otherwise for good cause and subject to such conditions as justice requires, including the payment of terms.

(E) Discovery Not Limited. This rule does not modify a party's responsibility under court rules to respond to or seasonably supplement responses to discovery or otherwise to comply with discovery before the deadlines set by this rule.

(2) If the Court finds that an attorney or party has failed to comply with the Case Schedule, failed to provide all of the information required in witness disclosures or disclosed witnesses that are not reasonably likely to be called at trial and has no reasonable excuse, the Court may order the attorney or party to pay monetary sanctions to the Court, or terms to any other party who has incurred expense as a result of the failure to comply, or both; in addition, the Court may impose such other sanctions as justice requires.

(3) As used with respect to the Case Schedule, "terms" means costs, attorney fees, and other expenses incurred or to be incurred as a result of the failure to comply; the term "monetary sanctions" means a financial penalty payable to the Court; the term "other sanctions" includes but is not limited to the exclusion of evidence.

(4) Except for good cause shown, trials in all civil cases subject to Rule 4 shall trail for one day. That is, trials of cases in Benton County will be called on Mondays, but the parties must be prepared to begin trial on the next day (Tuesday). Similarly, trials of case in Franklin County will be called on Wednesdays, but the parties must be prepared to begin trial on the next day (Thursday).

[Adopted effective September 1, 2000. Amended effective September 1, 2001; September 1, 2003; September 1, 2004; September 1, 2005; September 1, 2006; September 1, 2007; September 1, 2009; September 1, 2010; September 1, 2011; September 2, 2013; September 2, 2014; September 1, 2015.]

1 Numbering as provided in original.

LCR 4.1. CANCELLATION OR CONFIRMATION OF STATUS CONFERENCE

(a) Scope. This rule shall apply to all cases governed by a Case Schedule pursuant to LR 4.

(b) Cancellation or Confirmation of Status Conference; Form. If all parties do not sign the Cancellation or Confirmation of Status Conference form or give telephonic authority for signature on the form, a status conference shall be held. The plaintiff shall, after conferring with all other parties, file, serve, and provide to the Court Administrator's Office, a form entitled "Cancellation or Confirmation;" which will be in substantially the following form:

SUPERIOR COURT OF THE STATE OF WASHINGTON IN AND FOR BENTON AND FRANKLIN COUNTIES

Plaintiff(s)	)	Case No.
	)	
V.	)	**CANCELLATION/CONFIRMATION**
	)	**OF STATUS CONFERENCE**

)
Defendant(s)   )

_____

I. CANCELLATION

☐ The parties make the following joint representations and hereby cancel the scheduled
Status Conference:
1. No additional parties will be joined.
2. All parties have been served or have waived service.
3. All mandatory pleadings have been filed.
4. No additional claims or defenses will be raised.
5. None of the parties desire revision to the case schedule
6. All parties have cooperated in completing this report.

II. CONFIRMATION

☐ The parties are unable to make the foregoing joint representation and require a status conference, as explained below:

IF THE ABOVE BOX IS CHECKED, THERE _WILL_ BE A TELEPHONIC STATUS CONFERENCE, AS NOTED IN THE CASE SCHEDULE, AT WHICH ALL PARTIES OR THEIR ATTORNEYS MUST APPEAR.

☐ An additional party will be joined.

☐ A party remains to be served.

☐ An additional claim or defense will be raised.

☐ One or more parties desire revision to the Case Schedule.

☐ A party has refused to cooperate in drafting this report.

☐ Other explanation: _____

In order to obtain the Court's direction in the matters described above, the parties will appear at an initial telephonic conference, the date of which, as stated in the Case Schedule, is: _____

PLAINTIFF or PLAINTIFF'S ATTORNEY

   DATED: _____   SIGNED: _____

Typed Name: _____   WSBA #: _____
Address: _____
Phone: _____
Attorney(s) for: _____

. DEFENDANT or DEFENDANT'S ATTORNEY

   DATED: _____   SIGNED: _____

Typed Name: _____   WSBA #: _____
Address: _____
Phone: _____
Attorney(s) for: _____

(c) Parties to Confer in Completing Form. The plaintiff shall confer with all other parties in completing the form. If any party fails to cooperate in completing the form, any other party may file and serve the form and note the refusal to cooperate.

(d) Status Conference. All parties must, on the date designated by the Court in the Case Schedule, participate in a telephonic status conference with a Judge, Commissioner or Special Master designated by the Court Administrator. See LR 4.2.

(e) Additional Parties, Claims, and Defenses. No additional parties may be joined, and no additional claims or defenses may be raised, after the date designated in the Case Schedule for Status Conference, unless the Court orders otherwise for good cause and subject to such conditions as justice requires.

(f) Party-initiated Status Conference. Parties are encouraged at any time to contact the Court Administrator to schedule a telephonic status conference to assist the parties in resolving case scheduling problems, including requests to change the trial date.

(g) Cases Subject to Mandatory Arbitration. If a statement of arbitrability pursuant to LMAR 2.1 is filed, the case will then be governed by LMARs unless and until there is a request for a trial de novo or the case is otherwise removed from the Mandatory Arbitration Calendar pursuant to LMAR 7.1

[Former LCR 4.1 adopted effective September 1, 2000. Amended effective September 1, 2001; September 1, 2009; amended and renumbered as LCR 4.1 effective September 1, 2011.]

LCR 4.2. STATUS CONFERENCE; NONCOMPLIANCE HEARING

(a) Scope. This rule shall apply to all cases governed by a Case Schedule pursuant to LR 4.

(b) Non–Compliance Hearing. If a party fails to appear for a required Status Conference as set by the Case Schedule, the Court shall issue an order to show cause addressing a non-compliance hearing to be held before the Judge, Commissioner or Special Master. At that hearing the Court may enter an order of default against the party that failed to appear, may order the Case Schedule to be met by specific dates, continue the hearing, dismiss the case, impose terms or sanctions, or take other action to enforce the court rules regarding the Case Schedule. Attendance at the compliance hearing is mandatory for every party that failed to appear at the Status Conference. Attendance at the compliance hearing is mandatory for every party that failed to appear at the Status Conference.

[Former LCR 4.3 adopted effective September 1, 2000; amended effective September 1, 2009; amended and renumbered as LCR 4.2 effective September 1, 2011; amended effective September 1, 2012; September 2, 2013.]

LCR 5. BRIEFS AND ELECTRONIC SERVICE

(a) Electronic Service. The Court and Clerk may transmit to all attorneys orders, notices and other documents electronically, via e-mail or other process. Unless an attorney provides a different e-mail address, the Court and Clerk will send documents to the electronic mailbox address shown on the Washington State Bar Association online Attorney Directory. The Court or Clerk may electronically transmit notices, orders, or other documents to a party who has filed electronically or has agreed to accept electronic documents from the Court, and has provided the Clerk the address of the party's electronic mailbox. It is the responsibility of all attorneys and the filing or agreeing party to maintain an electronic mailbox sufficient to receive electronic transmissions of notices, orders, and other documents. Parties are reminded that, pursuant to CR5(b)(7), a party may serve pleadings electronically on another party only with the consent of the other party. An optional form Agreement to Accept Electronic Notification is available on the Court's website.

(b) Briefs. All motions, brief, declarations, affidavits, and other supporting written documentation pertaining to trials, summary judgements[1] motions, lower court appeals and appeals from decisions of administrative agencies (except the record transferred by the agency) and any other motions, and other documents submitted for hearings, such as trial management reports, proposed findings of fact and conclusions of law and judgements,[2] motions and sentencing position statements in criminal matters, and guardian ad litem reports (including criminal and domestic relations), shall be served and filed in the cause.

(c) Bench Copies. Unless a party does not have access to a computer or the internet, bench copies of all such documents, as well as settlement positions statement in civil and domestic cases, shall be submitted electronically via the internet at http://www.benton-franklinsuperiorcourt.com/submit-bench-copies/ or http://motion.co.franklin.wa.us/. Parties without access to a computer and the internet shall deliver bench copies to the Court Administrator at the Benton County Justice Center. All bench copies must be submitted not later than noon one court day prior to the scheduled hearing, proceeding or trial. No bench copies, except settlement position statements, shall be submitted to the Court unless a copy has been served upon or mailed to opposing counsel or party if unrepresented if they are entitled to notice by law.

Bench copies submitted electronically are deleted from the system forty-five days after the associated hearing. Bench copies submitted on paper are destroyed five (5) court days after the associated hearing unless counsel requests copies be returned, with return postage arranged, or unless Court Administration is advised of the new hearing date. When hearings are continued, the parties shall amend the hearing date associated with all bench copies submitted electronically.

If a party fails to submit bench copies as set forth above the Court may continue the hearing, impose terms and enter other orders as may be appropriate.

Bench copies of the following documents should not be electronically submitted: Notices of hearings, notes for dockets, transmittal letters, proposed statements of defendant on plea of guilty, proposed judgments and sentences and proofs of service (unless service is at issue), and briefs and supporting materials in uncontested summary judgment motions in state paternity cases need not be submitted.

[Adopted effective April 1, 1986; amended effective September 1, 2000; September 1, 2001; September 1, 2002; September 1, 2003; September 1, 2004; September 1, 2005; September 1, 2007; September 1, 2009; September 1, 2011; September 1, 2012; September 2, 2014; September 1, 2015.]

¹ So in original.

² So in original.

LCR 7. PLEADINGS ALLOWED; FORM OF MOTIONS

(b) Motions and Other Papers.

(1) *Memorandum of Authorities and Affidavits Required.*

(A) The moving party shall serve and file with his or her Motion a brief written statement of the Motion and a brief containing reasons and citations of the authorities on which he or she relies. If the Motion requires the consideration of the facts not appearing of record, he or she shall also serve and file copies of all affidavits and photographic or other documentary evidence he intends to present in support of the motion. Bench copies shall be submitted as provided in LCR 5.

(B) Each party opposing the Motion shall at least by noon, one (1) day prior to the argument, serve upon counsel for the moving party and file with the Clerk a brief containing reasons and citations of the authorities upon which he relies, together with all affidavits and photographic or other documenta-

ry evidence any supporting material. Bench copies shall be submitted as provided in LCR 5.

(2) *Necessary Provision in Pleadings Relating to Supplemental Proceedings and Show Cause Hearings for Contempt.* In all supplemental proceedings wherein an order is to be issued requiring the personal attendance of a party to be examined in open court, and in orders to show cause for contempt, the order must include the following words in capital letters:

YOUR FAILURE TO APPEAR AS ABOVE SET FORTH AT THE TIME, DATE, AND PLACE THEREOF WILL CAUSE THE COURT TO ISSUE A BENCH WARRANT FOR YOUR APPREHENSION AND CONFINEMENT IN JAIL UNTIL SUCH TIME AS THE MATTER CAN BE HEARD OR UNTIL BAIL IS POSTED.

No bench warrant will be issued in such cases for the apprehension of the cited person if such language has been omitted.

(3) *Counsel Fees.* Appointed counsel submitting motions for fixing or payment of fees and counsel requesting that the Court fix fees in any other case (except for temporary fees in domestic relation cases) should itemize their time, services rendered, or other detailed basis for the fees requested and attach a copy thereof to the motion.

(4) *Action Required by Clerk.* All documents filed with the Clerk, other than a note for the motion or trial dockets (see LCR 40) which require any action (other than filing) by the Clerk shall contain a motion in the caption specifying the nature of the document the words: "CLERK'S ACTION REQUIRED."

(5) *Motion to Shorten Time.* All motions to shorten time must be in writing and supported by declaration or affidavit that (a) states exigent circumstances or other compelling reasons why the matter must be heard on shortened time and (b) demonstrates due diligence in the manner and method by which notice, or attempted notice, was provided to all other parties regarding the presentation of the motion to shorten time. If the moving party, after showing due diligence, has been unable to notify all parties of the motion to shorten time, it is within the judicial officer's discretion to proceed with the motion to shorten time. The judicial officer shall indicate on the order shortening time the minimum amount of notice to be provided the responding party, which, barring extraordinary circumstances as set forth in the declaration or affidavit supporting the motion, shall not be less than 48 hours. The court file must be presented along with the motion to shorten time, declaration or affidavit, and the proposed order to the judicial officer considering the request.

(6) *Document Format.* Documents prepared for a judge's signature must contain at least two (2) lines of text on the signature page.

(7) *Hearing of Motion Calendar.*

(A) Note for Motion Docket. Any attorney desiring to bring any issue of law on for Hearing shall file with the Clerk and serve on all opposing counsel, not later than six (6) court days prior to the day on which the attorney desires it to be heard, a note for the motion docket which shall contain the title of the court, the cause number, a brief title of the cause, the date when the same shall be heard, the words "Note for Motion Docket," the name or names of each attorney involved in the matter, the nature of the motion, and by whom made. It shall be subscribed by the attorney filing the same and shall bear the designation of whom the attorney represents. The foregoing provisions shall not prohibit the hearing of emergency motions at the discretion of the Court.

(B) Over 10 Minutes for Hearing. If the moving party expects the motion to take more than ten (10) minutes to argue by all sides collectively, the movant shall designate on the note for motion docket that the matter is "over 10 minutes."

(C) Confirmation of Summary Judgment and Over–Ten–Minute Hearings. The moving party shall confirm with the clerk that summary judgment and over-ten-minute hearings will be heard on the date set during the following time periods:

    i. Summary judgment and over-ten-minute hearings shall be confirmed in Benton County no sooner than Monday at 8:00 a.m. and no later than Tuesday noon of the week in which the motion is noted for hearing.

    ii. Summary judgment and over-ten-minute hearings shall be confirmed in Franklin County no sooner than Tuesday at 8:30 a.m. and no later than Thursday noon of the week preceding the week in which the motion is noted for hearing.

    Confirmations may be by telephone, or by e-mail to the addresses stated below in LCR 7 (b)(7)(F).

    iii. The clerk shall not allow more than a total of three (3) summary judgment and three (3) over-ten-minute hearings to be confirmed for any one date. The maximum for such motions may be changed by resolution of the judges.

(D) Removal of Motion. If the motion is not so served, mailed, and filed the Court may strike the same from the calendar.

(E) Service of Notice. The motion will not be heard unless there is on file proof of service of notice upon the attorney for the opposing party or there is an admission of service by opposing counsel.

(F) Continuance or Striking of Noted Motions by Parties. A matter noted on the motion docket may be continued pursuant to the following:

    i. The moving party may strike or continue a motion at any time without cause with adequate notice to the opposing parties. Sanctions may be imposed if the opposing party's appearance at the hearing could have been avoided through due diligence of the moving party.

    ii. Upon a showing of cause, the Court, in its discretion, may grant the nonmoving party's request for a continuance.

    iii. The party striking any matter may give notice to the non-moving parties by any means reasonably likely to provide actual notice. The clerk may be notified either by written notice or by e-mail notification. Notice to the Franklin County Clerk may be emailed to the following address: civilclerk@co.franklin.wa.us for civil cases; and domesticclerk@co.franklin.wa.us for domestic cases. Notice to the Benton County Clerk may be emailed to the following address: clerk@co.benton.wa.us.

    iv. If the matter is stricken and the moving party desires a hearing, a new note for motion docket must be filed with the Clerk in accordance with section (A), above. Except for matters continued in open court, a new note for docket is required for motions that are continued.

(G) Calling Docket—Priority for Pro Bono Counsel. The causes on the civil docket for each motion day will be called in order, and the moving party, if no one appears in opposition, may take the order moved for upon proper proof of notice, unless the Court shall deem it unauthorized. In order to encourage participation in pro bono legal representation, all motions, where one or both parties are represented by pro bono counsel, shall, at the request of the pro bono attorney be given priority on the docket. Such priority shall be given without any reference as to the reason why. All parties are to appear in person.

(H) Continuances by Court. Any motion or hearing may be continued by the Court to a subsequent motion day or set down by the Court for hearing at another specified time, and the Court may alter the order of hearing as may be necessary to expedite the business of court.

(I) Frivolous Motions. Upon hearing any motion, if the Court is of the opinion that such motion is frivolous, or upon granting a continuance of any matter, terms may be imposed by the Court against the party filing such motion, or against the party at whose instance such continuance is granted.

(J) Ex Parte—Notice to Opposing Counsel. Lawyers should not ask the Court for ex parte orders without proper notice to opposing counsel, if counsel has appeared either formally or informally. This rule applies to temporary restraining orders and orders to show cause in domestic relations cases, as well as all other types of matters. (*See Rule 65.*)

(K) Decisions Without Oral Argument. Upon agreement of the parties, or upon request of the Court, a motion may be determined without oral argument. Matters may be noted for decision without oral argument only on the dates and times established for regular calendars. The moving party shall certify in the note for docket that every party has consented to determination without oral argument.

(L) Discovery Motions. The Court will not entertain any Motion or objection with respect to Rules 26, 27, 30, 31, 33, 34, 35 or 36, Civil Rules for Superior Court unless it affirmatively appears that counsel have met and conferred with respect thereto. Counsel for the moving or objecting party shall arrange such a conference. If the Court finds that counsel for any party, upon whom a Motion for an objection with respect to matters covered by such rules is served, willfully refused to meet and confer, or having met, willfully refused or fails to confer in good faith, the Court may take appropriate action to encourage future good faith compliance. In the event of an emergency, the Court will entertain Motion objections which would otherwise be governed by the above rule.

(M) Argument Limitations. Argument on the civil docket shall be limited to (thirty) 30 minutes per case.

[Adopted April 1, 1986. Amended effective August 1, 1990; September 1, 2002; September 1, 2009; September 1, 2011; September 2, 2013; September 2, 2014; September 1, 2015.]

LCR 16. PRE–TRIAL PROCEDURE

(a) **Settlement Conferences.** In all cases governed by a Case Schedule pursuant to LR 4, the Court shall schedule a settlement conference.

(1) *Preparation for Conference.*

(A) No later than the date set forth on the civil case schedule order, all parties shall prepare a position statement which shall be submitted to the Court as set forth in LCR 5(c). No fax copies will be accepted by the court. Position statements shall not be filed in the court file. No party shall be required to provide a copy of the position statement to any other party. The position statement shall include the following:

(i) A brief non-argumentative summary of the case.

(ii) A statement of whether liability is admitted, and if not, the plaintiff's theory or theories of liability and the defendant's theory or theories on non-liability.

(iii) A list of all items of special damages claimed by the plaintiff and a statement of whether any or all of those are admitted by the defendant.

(iv) An explanation of the general damages, including a summary of the nature and extent of any claimed disability or impairment.

(v) A statement of what settlement offers have been made thus far, if any.

(vi) The position statement is to be a summary only. It is not to include a copy of any exhibits, medical reports, expert witness reports, etc. Generally the length of the summary will be 1—5 pages. The summary should take the form of a letter that begins with a reference to the name of the case and the cause number. It should not be in the form of a pleading.

(2) *Parties to Be Available.*

(A) The parties and counsel shall attend the settlement conference except on prior order of the Court upon good cause shown.

(B) Representative of Insurer and Guardians ad Litem. Parties whose defense is provided by a liability insurance company need not personally attend the settlement conference, but a representative of the insurer of said parties shall be available by telephone or in person with sufficient authority to bind the insurer to a settlement. Guardians ad Litem shall be available by telephone or appear in person.

(3) *Private Mediation.* Regardless of whether mediation is court-ordered, parties may seek an order allowing them to opt out of the settlement conference by filing a stipulation and order with Court Administration. The request must include a letter from a mediator and signed on behalf of all parties that the case has been mediated or that mediation has been scheduled to occur on or before the date of the settlement conference.

(4) *Failure to Attend.*

(A) Sanctions. Failure to comply with the provisions of paragraphs 1 and 2 above may result in the imposition of terms and sanctions as the Court may deem appropriate.

(B) Default. Failure to appear at the settlement conference, without prior approval of the court, may constitute an act of default. Any party appearing at the settlement conference may move for default pursuant to CR 55. Costs and terms may be assessed at the discretion of the court.

(5) *Proceedings Privileged.* Proceedings of said settlement conference shall in all respects be privileged and not reported or recorded. No party shall be bound unless a settlement is reached. When a settlement has been reached, the Judge may in his/her discretion order the settlement agreement in whole, or, in case of a partial agreement, then the terms thereof, to be reported or recorded.

(6) *Continuances.* Continuances of settlement conferences may be authorized only by the Court on timely application.

(7) *Pretrial Power of Court.* If the case is not settled at a settlement conference, the Judge may nevertheless make such orders as are appropriate in a pretrial conference under CR 16.

(8) *Judge Disqualified for Trial.* A Judge presiding over a settlement conference shall be disqualified from acting as the trial Judge in that matter, as well as any subsequent summary judgment motions, unless all parties agree otherwise in writing.

(a)[1] Pretrial Conference/Trial Exhibits. In cases that are governed by a Case Schedule pursuant to LR 4, the Court shall schedule a Pretrial Conference, which shall be attended by the lead trial attorney of each party who is represented by an attorney and by each party who is not represented by an attorney. The parties must jointly prepare a Trial Management Report.

Trial counsel shall submit to the court clerk at the Pre–Trial Conference all proposed trial exhibits which shall be marked for identification by the clerk as set forth in the Trial Management Report. Unless ordered otherwise, exhibit numbers 1 through 100 shall be allocated to the plaintiff(s) and exhibit numbers 101 and above are allocated to the defendant(s).

(b) Trial Management Report. In cases governed by a Civil Case Schedule Order pursuant to LR 4, the parties must jointly prepare a Trial Management Report. The plaintiff shall prepare an initial report and serve it upon all opposing parties no later than two weeks prior to the date it is due under the Civil Case Schedule Order. The Report shall be filed with the Court, with a copy served on the court administrator. The Report shall contain:

(1) Nature and brief, non-argumentative summary of the case;

(2) List of issues that are not in dispute;

(3) List of issues that are disputed;

(4) Index of exhibits (excluding rebuttal or impeachment exhibits);

(5) List of plaintiff's requests for Washington Pattern Jury Instructions;

(6) List of defendant's requests for Washington Pattern Jury Instructions;

(7) List of names of all lay and expert witnesses, excluding rebuttal witnesses;

(8) Suggestions by either party for shortening the trial.

(c) Parties to Confer in Completing Report. The attorneys for all parties in the case shall confer in completing the Trial Management Report. If any party fails to cooperate in completing the report, any

other party may file and serve the report and note the refusal to cooperate.

(d) Sanctions. On motion or on its own, the court may issue any just orders, including those set forth herein, if a party or its attorney: (i) fails to appear at a scheduling or other pretrial conference; (ii) is substantially unprepared to participate—or does not participate in good faith—in the conference; or (iii) fails to obey a scheduling or other pretrial order. Sanctions may include the following:

(1) Prohibiting the disobedient party from supporting or opposing designated claims or defenses, or from introducing designated matters in evidence;

(2) Striking pleadings in whole or in part;

(3) Staying further proceedings until the order is obeyed;

(4) Dismissing the action or proceeding in whole or in part;

(5) Rendering a default judgment against the disobedient party; or

(6) Treating as contempt of court the failure to obey any order except an order to submit to a physical or mental examination.

Instead of or in addition to any other sanction, the court must order the party, its attorney, or both to pay the reasonable expenses—including attorney's fees—incurred because of any noncompliance with this rule, unless the noncompliance was substantially justified or other circumstances make an award of expenses unjust.

(f)[2] Form of Trial Management Report. A trial management report will be in generally the following form:

SUPERIOR COURT OF THE STATE OF WASHINGTON IN AND FOR BENTON AND FRANKLIN COUNTIES

Plaintiff(s)	Case No.
V.	**TRIAL MANAGEMENT REPORT**
Defendant(s)	

Pursuant to Lr 16, this Trial Management Report must be filed and served in all cases governed by a Civil Case Schedule. Failure to file and serve this report or to appear at the Pretrial Conference may result in the imposition of monetary sanctions, dismissal of the case, or entry of a default judgment. Failure to fully disclose all items required on this report may result in exclusion or restriction on use of evidence at trial. This is a joint report, requiring counsel to meet, confer and attempt to resolve differences in the matters addressed in this report. A copy of this report must be provided to the assigned judge

A. **MEETING:** The parties, by their attorneys, _____

(address)

met at on _____ and could not settle the case and are prepared to proceed to trial.

B. **NATURE OF CASE** (Provide a joint, brief, non-argumentative description of the case suitable for reading to the jury panel):

C. **TOTAL NUMBER OF TRIAL DAYS** (total of plaintiff's and defendant's case): _____

D. **LIST OF ISSUES WHICH ARE NOT IN DISPUTE:**

E. **LIST OF EACH ISSUE THAT IS DISPUTED** (Issues not identified here may not be raised at trial without leave of the Court):

F. **EXHIBITS** (Trial counsel shall meet with the trial court clerk at the Pre–Trial Conference, to submit all proposed trial exhibits, which admissibility has been stipulated to by the parties, and to index said exhibits numerically. Unless ordered otherwise, exhibit numbers 1 through 99 are allocated to the plaintiff(s) and exhibit numbers 100 and above are allocated to the defendant(s)):

Counsel met on _____, _____, conferred and reviewed a list of all exhibits that will be offered at trial. Any exhibit which is not on said list of exhibits will not be considered except by leave of the court.

G. **INDEX OF EXHIBITS** (The index shall indicate: (1) the exhibit number, (2) by whom offered, (3) a brief description, (4) whether the parties have stipulated to admissibility, and if not, (5) the legal grounds for the objection(s). Rebuttal or impeachable exhibits need not be listed): List first those exhibits for which admissibility has been stipulated to by the parties.

EXHIBIT NUMBER	DESCRIP- TION	STIPULA- TION AS TO ADMISSI- BILITY	OBJECTION / GROUNDS (CITE ER)

H. **LIST OF PLAINTIFF'S REQUESTS FOR WASH- INGTON PATTERN JURY INSTRUCTIONS** (If special and not WPI/WPIC or pattern instructions including bracketed material, attach a copy):

I. **LIST OF DEFENDANT'S REQUESTS FOR WASH- INGTON PATTERN JURY INSTRUCTIONS** (If special and not WPI/WPIC or pattern instructions including bracketed material, attach a copy):

J. **LIST OF NAMES AND SCHEDULE OF ALL LAY AND EXPERT WITNESSES** (Describe type of witness (lay, treating, expert) and party calling witness. Please estimate all necessary time for presentation of all direct and cross examination. Rebuttal witnesses need not be listed):

NAME	PARTY	ESTIMATED DATE AND TIME FOR WITNESS TESTIMONY

I certify under penalty of perjury under the laws of the State of Washington that the foregoing is true and correct.

Signed: _____   Signed: _____
Dated: _____   Dated: _____
WSBA #: _____   WSBA #: _____
Phone Number: _____   Phone Number: _____
Attorney For: _____   Attorney For: _____

[Adopted April 1, 1986. Amended effective September 1, 2000; September 1, 2002; September 1, 2003; September 1, 2007; September 1, 2009; September 1, 2011; September 1, 2012; September 2, 2013; September 2, 2014; September 1, 2015.]

1 So in original.
2 So in original.

LCR 40. ASSIGNMENT OF CASES

(a) Notice of Trial—Note of Issue.

(1) *Of Fact—Note for Trial Docket—Cases Not Subject to Civil Case Schedule Order.*

(A) Any party desiring to bring any issue of fact to trial, except for cases governed by LCR 4 and LCR 04.04W, shall file with the Clerk and Court Administrator's Office and serve upon the other parties or their attorneys a "Notice of Trial Setting and Certificate of Readiness," in the form maintained by the Court Administrator's Office, which shall contain the title for the court, a brief title of the case, the case number, the nature of the case, whether jury or non-jury, whether there has been a 12–person jury demand, whether a 6–person jury would be acceptable, estimated trial time, the name and address and telephone number of each attorney assigned to the case, whether there should be a pre-trial conference, preferential trial dates or times, and anything further that would assist the Court in setting a trial date, and shall be subscribed by the attorney filing the same.

(B) An attorney noting a case for trial thereby certifies that the case is at issue, that there has been a reasonable opportunity for discovery, that discovery will be complete by the trial date, that necessary witnesses will be available, and that to his/her knowledge, no other parties will be served with a summons and no further pleadings will be filed prior to trial.

(C) The attorney noting the case for trial shall confer with all other counsel prior to noting the case for trial setting to determine if there is any objection to setting. If there is no objection, the attorney shall so certify on the notice of setting. If there is objection and the setting attorney believes the objections to readiness are not justified, the attorney shall so indicate on the setting notice and the matter shall be heard by the Presiding Judge on the motion calendar.

(D) In the event all parties agree the case is ready for trial or will be ready for trial by a specific date, but have objections to particular dates, they shall notify the Court Administrator's Office of un-available dates within five (5) days after receiving the notice of trial setting.

(b) Methods.

(1) *Court Administrator to Assign Dates.* The Court Administrator shall assign trial dates under the supervision of the Presiding Judge who shall be in direct charge of the trial calendar. To the extent practical, cases shall be set chronologically according to noting date, except for cases having statutory pref-erence.

(2) *Jury and Non-jury Trials.* Upon the serving and filing of a "Notice of Trial Setting and Certificate of Readiness," the Court Administrator shall forthwith assign a specific trial date and notify the Clerk and counsel of the date assigned.

(3) *Advancing Trial Dates.* Any case assigned a specific date may, at the discretion of the Presiding Judge, be advanced to an earlier date or may be reset if the court calendar permits. Notice shall be given at least five (5) days prior to the new trial date assigned.

(4) *One Day Trailing.* Except for good cause shown, all non-domestic civil cases shall trail for one day. That is, trials of cases in Benton County will be called on Mondays, but the parties must be prepared to begin trial on the next day (Tuesday). Similarly, trials of cases in Franklin County will be called on Wednesdays, but the parties must be prepared to begin trial on the next day (Thursday).

(5) *Notice of Settlement.* Notice of the settlement of a case set for trial shall be immediately given to the Court Administrator or, if unable to contact the Court Administrator, to the Clerk. Any circumstance pre-venting any case from going to trial as scheduled, immediately upon becoming known to counsel, shall be communicated to the Court Administrator. Failure to comply with this rule may result in the assessment of terms including the expense of a jury panel.

(c) Stipulated Continuances. No trial setting shall be continued by stipulation of counsel without good cause and without approval of the Civil Presiding Judge or Court Administrator within twenty (20) days of the date set for trial. More than twenty (20) days before trial, stipulations for continuance will normally be honored unless the Court concludes a continuance is unwarranted. All stipulations to continue must be supported by an affidavit setting forth the reasons for the continuance and submitted to the Court Adminis-trator's office for review by the Civil Presiding Judge.

(d) Change of Judge.

(1) *Affidavit—Judge.*

(A) Under RCW 4.12.050, the motion and the affidavit must be filed with the clerk, and a copy delivered to Court Administration and to all other parties. If the party has not filed another motion and affidavit, and the motion and affidavit meet the requirements of RCW 4.12.050, the designated judge shall recuse himself or herself, without fur-ther order.

(B) Requests for Recusal. A party requesting the recusal of a judge may do so by motion and affidavit filed with the Clerk and a copy delivered to Court Administration and to all other parties. The matter shall be heard on the record by the judge against whom the request is made.

(2) *Affidavit—Court Commissioner.* Affidavits of prejudice or for change of Court Commissioner will not be recognized. The remedy of a party is for a motion for revision under RCW 2.24.050.

(e) Pre–Assignment of Judge. Judges will be pre-assigned to cases only by court order, for good cause, and will be assigned in order from the list maintained by Court Administration.

(f) Writ of Habeas Corpus Relating to Custody of Minor Children. Applications for Writs of Habeas Corpus relating to custody of minor children shall be presented to and returnable to the presiding judge of the Superior Court for Benton and Franklin Counties on court days between the hours of 8:30 a.m. to noon and 1:00 to 4:00 p.m.

[Adopted April 1, 1986; amended effective September 1, 1998; September 1, 2000; September 1, 2002; September 1, 2003; September 1, 2004; September 1, 2008; September 1, 2010; September 1, 2011; September 1, 2012; September 2, 2014.]

LCR 42. CONSOLIDATION; SEPARATE TRIALS

(a) Consolidated Cases for Trial. When two or more cases are consolidated for trial only, all docu-ments shall be submitted with an original for each file so consolidated. Consolidated cases shall be pre-sumed to be consolidated for trial only, unless other-wise indicated.

[Adopted effective August 1, 1990; amended effective Sep-tember 1, 2007.]

LCR 47. JURORS

(a) Voir Dire. The trial judge may examine the prospective juror touching their qualification to act as fair and impartial jurors in the case before him or her; provided that thereafter the trial judge shall give leave to respective counsel to ask the jurors such supplementary questions as may be deemed by the trial judge proper and necessary. The voir dire exam-ination of prospective jurors shall, as nearly as possi-ble, be limited to those matters having a reasonably direct bearing on prejudice or qualifications and shall not be used by opposing counsel as a means of argu-ing or trying their case on voir dire. The "struck method" of voir dire examination is allowed. That is, the parties may direct questions to individual jurors or to the panel or to portions thereof, in the discretion of the examiner.

(e) Challenge.

(9) *Peremptory Challenges.* All peremptory challenges allowed by law shall be exercised in the following manner:

The bailiff will deliver to counsel for the plaintiff and counsel for the defendant, in turn, a prepared form upon which each counsel shall endorse the name of the challenged juror in the space designated, or his acceptance of the jury as constituted. The bailiff will then exhibit this form after each challenge to the opposing counsel, and the Court. After all challenges have been exhausted, the Court will excuse those jurors who have been challenged and will seat the jury as finally selected.

A waiver by a party indicates an acceptance by that party of all jurors seated up to that point.

The purpose of this rule is to preserve the secrecy of peremptory challenges and all parties and their counsel shall conduct themselves to that end. This procedure may be modified if appropriate.

(k) Selection of Jurors. The Benton County Superior Court and the Franklin County Superior Court shall employ a properly programmed electronic data processing system or device to make random selection of jurors as required by RCW 2.36.060.093. It is determined that fair and random selection may be achieved without division of the county into three (3) or more jury districts. During the month of July of each year, a master jury list shall be selected by an unrestricted random sample in accordance with RCW 2.36.055.

[Adopted effective April 1, 1986; amended effective September 1, 2011.]

LCR 48. JURIES OF LESS THAN TWELVE

(a) Stipulation: Procedure. The parties may stipulate that the jury shall consist of any number of persons less than twelve (12) but not less than three (3). Counsel shall call the stipulation to the attention of the Presiding Judge when the case is called for trial. The stipulation, if in writing, shall be filed in the cause; if oral, it shall be noted by the clerk in the minutes of the trial.

(b) Challenges Not Affected. The stipulation shall not affect the number of challenges, nor the manner of making them, unless the parties expressly agree otherwise. (See RCW 4.44.120, et seq.)

[Adopted effective April 1, 1986.]

LCR 51. INSTRUCTIONS TO JURY AND DELIBERATION

(a) Proposed.

(1) *Instructions Required of Plaintiff.* Plaintiff's counsel shall prepare and present to the Court a cover instruction containing the title and file number of

proceedings, the name of the attorney for each party properly designated, and appropriate blank space where the name of the judge hearing the case can be inserted, and entitled "Instructions of the Court."

(2) *Instructions in the Alternative.* Instructions, the form of which are dependent upon rulings of the Court, may be submitted in the alternative and counsel shall have the right to withdraw those instructions made unnecessary or inappropriate by reason of said rulings at any time prior to the submission of the Court's instructions to the jury.

(b) Submission.

(1) *Distribution.* Sets of proposed instructions shall be prepared and distributed as follows:

(A) Original, which shall be assembled and numbered and contain citations, shall be filed with the clerk;

(B) One copy, which shall be assembled, numbered and contain citations, shall be provided to counsel for each other party;

(C) One copy, which shall be assembled and numbered, shall be retained by the counsel preparing them;

(D) One copy, which shall be assembled, numbered and contain citations, shall be provided to the trial judge;

(E) One copy, without numbers or citations, shall be provided to the trial judge.

(F) Citations, as required by the rule, shall include applicable WPI or WPIC numbers and shall appear on the bottom of the proposed instructions.

(2) *Time for Serving Instructions.* Unless requested earlier by the trial judge, all instructions, shall be submitted at the beginning of the first day of trial. Upon request of the trial judge to all counsel and made not more than seven (7) days before the date of trial, counsel shall prepare and deliver to the trial judge and to other counsel, not less than three (3) days before the day on which the case is set for trial, the required number of copies of proposed instructions insofar as counsel may then be able to determine them.

(c) Verdict Forms. Each verdict form shall be headed with title and cause number of the proceeding. This shall also apply to special interrogatories. A date line shall be typed above the line for the foreman.

(d) Published Instructions.

(1) *Request.* The Court has not adopted a local rule to allow instructions appearing in the Washington Pattern Instructions (WPI or WPIC) to be requested by reference to the published number.

(2) *Modified Instructions.* Whenever a Washington Pattern Instruction (WPI or WPIC) is modified by the addition of, the deletion of, or the modification of certain language, the party proposing the instruction

must cite the instruction as follows: "WPI or WPIC No. Modified."

(e) Disregarding Requests. The trial court may disregard any proposed instruction not proposed or submitted in accordance with this rule.

(f) Civil and Criminal. This rule applies to instructions for civil and criminal cases.

(g) Duties Relating to Return of Verdict. Attorneys awaiting a verdict shall keep the clerk advised of where they may be reached by phone. Attorneys desiring to be present for the verdict shall be at the courthouse within fifteen (15) minutes of the time they are called. In a criminal case, at least one attorney for each party and the prosecuting attorney or deputy prosecuting attorney shall be present for the receipt of the verdict, unless excused by the Court. The defense attorney is responsible for advising the defendant to be present for the verdict unless defendant is in custody.

[Adopted effective April 1, 1986; amended effective September 1, 2003; September 1, 2005; September 1, 2009; September 1, 2011.]

LCR 52. FINDINGS OF FACT AND CONCLUSIONS OF LAW

Unless the presiding judicial officer directs that entry of Findings of Fact and Conclusions of Law are to be handled differently, the Findings, Conclusions and Judgment shall be entered in the following manner:

(a) Submission. Within fifteen (15) days after the decisions rendered, the prevailing party shall submit Findings of Fact and Conclusions of Law and shall deliver the same together with the Proposed Judgment to the opposing counsel. If the prevailing party fails to submit proposed findings in a timely manner, the other party may do so, and shall thereupon note the matter for presentment, giving the prevailing party at least seven (7) business days notice of the hearing.

(b) Objections. A non-prevailing party objecting to the Findings, Conclusions or Judgment shall, within fifteen (15) days after receipt of the same, deliver to proposing counsel two (2) copies of the objections thereto in writing, and the proposed substitutions. Upon receipt of the objections, the proposing attorney shall mail the proposed Findings, Conclusions and proposed Judgment together with one (1) copy of the objections and the proposed substitutions received from opposing counsel to the trial judge.

(1) If there are no objections received within the fifteen (15) day period aforesaid, counsel may forward the submittal to the judge who shall, within ten (10) days thereafter, either (a) sign the proposed Findings of Fact, Conclusions of Law and Judgment and forward to the Clerk for filing with conformed copies to all counsel, or (b) return the Findings of Fact, Conclu-

sions of Law and Judgment, if deficient, to all counsel noting the Court's requested changes or additions thereto.

(2) If objections are made, the Court shall arrange for a chamber conference to settle the issues as soon as practicable.

(c) Intent. It is the intent of this rule that Findings of Fact, Conclusions of Law and Judgment will be settled and filed as soon as possible, and that such matters shall not be noted on the Motion Docket; provided however, that if the Findings of Fact, Conclusions of Law and Judgment are not settled within sixty (60) days after the Court's oral or written decision, either party may note entry of the Findings of Fact, Conclusions of Law and Judgment on the Motion Docket.

(d) Application. This rule only applies to the entry of Findings of Fact and Conclusions of Law when the same are required under CR 52, and does not apply to entry of orders or judgments unless Findings of Fact and Conclusions of Law are required.

[Adopted effective April 1, 1986; amended effective September 1, 2011; September 2, 2014.]

LCR 53.2. COURT COMMISSIONERS

(e) Revision by the Court.

(1) *Motion Content and Service Deadlines.* A party seeking revision off a Court Commissioner's ruling shall within ten (10) days of entry of the written order, file and serve a Motion for Revision. The motion must set forth specific grounds for each claimed error and argument and legal authorities in support thereof. The motion shall be accompanied by a copy of the order for which revision is sought, along with copies of all papers which were before the Commissioner in support, or in opposition in the original proceedings. A copy of the motion and all supporting documents shall be provided to all other parties to the proceedings and to the Court Administrator who shall refer the motion to the appropriate Judge for consideration. The responding party shall have five (5) working days from the receipt of the motion to file a written response with the Clerk and provide copies to all other parties and to the Court Administrator.

(2) *Transcript Required.* When seeking revision of a ruling of the Court Commissioner which was based on testimony, such testimony must be transcribed and attached to the motion. If the transcript is not timely available, the moving party must set forth arrangements which have been made to secure the transcript.

(3) *Review is De Novo.* Review of the Commissioner's order shall be de novo based on the pleadings and transcript submitted and without oral argument unless requested by the reviewing Judge.

(4) *Scope of Motion.* The Judge may deny the motion, revise any order or judgment which is related to the issue raised by the motion for revision or

remand to the Commissioner for further proceedings. The Judge may not consider evidence or issues which were not before the Commissioner or not raised by the motion for revision. The Judge may consider a request for attorney fees by either party for the revision proceedings.

(5) *Effect of Commissioner's Order.* The Court Commissioner's written order shall remain effective unless and until revised by the Judge or unless stayed by the Judge pending proceedings related to the motion for revision.

[Adopted effective September 1, 2003.]

LCR 56. SUMMARY JUDGMENT

(c) Motion and Proceedings.

(1) *Briefs.* Briefs, or statements of points and authorities, shall be mandatory with respect to all motions for summary judgment. The original is to be filed with the Superior Court Clerk. Bench copies shall be submitted in accordance with LCR 5.

If a party fails to submit electronic bench copies as directed in LCR 5, the Court shall issue an order to show cause addressing a non-compliance hearing to be held before the Judge, Commissioner or Special Master. At that hearing the Court may continue the hearing, impose terms or sanctions, or take other action to enforce the court rules regarding submission of electronic bench copies prior to hearings. Attendance at the non-compliance hearing is mandatory for every party that failed to comply with the requirements under LCR 5.

(2) *Continuance and Confirmation.* In the event a motion for summary judgment or partial summary judgment is noted, and the non-moving party believes that a continuance is warranted, the non-moving party shall file a motion for a continuance, supporting the same with sworn pleadings. Said motion shall be heard at least one week before the scheduled date of the summary judgment hearing.

(A) In the event the moving party unreasonably refuses to continue the case or the opposing party unreasonably is not prepared for the hearing, terms may be assessed.

(B) The moving party shall confirm with the clerk that the motion will be heard on the date set during the time periods set forth in LCR 7(b). However, the clerk shall not allow more than three (3) summary judgment hearings and three (3) over-ten-minute hearings to be confirmed for any one date. The maximum for such motions may be changed by resolution of the judges. A moving party contacting the clerk to confirm a summary judgment for a date for which the maximum number of summary judgments and over-ten-minute hearings have previously been confirmed may continue the hearing to the next reasonably available setting and provide notice of the continuance to the other parties in the action and shall re-confirm the

continued setting in accordance with the above rules. Twenty-eight (28) days notice is not required for setting a new hearing hereunder. The new hearing date may be after the last date specified for filing dispositive motions in the Civil Case Schedule Order, but in no event less than fourteen (14) days before trial.

(3) *Motion—Contents of.* The moving party shall specify with particularity the documentary evidence, including depositions, on which the motion is based.

(4) *Continuance After Confirmation.* Once confirmed, no summary judgment hearing shall be continued without permission of the presiding Judge, and the moving party must appear at the docket.

[Adopted effective April 1, 1986. Amended effective September 1, 1998; September 1, 2003; September 1, 2006; September 1, 2009; September 1, 2011; September 2, 2013; September 2, 2014.]

LCR 58. ENTRY OF JUDGMENT

(a) When.

(1) *Judgments and Orders to Be Filed Forthwith.* Any order, judgment or decree which has been signed by the Court shall not be taken from the courthouse, but must be filed forthwith by the attorney obtaining it with the Clerk's Office or with the clerk in the courtroom. If signed outside the courthouse, the attorney procuring the order shall mail it to the appropriate clerk the same day, or file it by the next judicial day.

(2) *Settlement.* Upon settlement of any action a judgment of dismissal shall be entered forthwith.

(b) Effective Time.

(1) *Effective on Filing in Clerk's Office.* Judgments, orders and decrees shall be effective from the time of filing in the Clerk's Office, unless filed in accordance with CR 5(e).

(2) *Not to Be Entered Until Signed.* The clerk will enter no judgment or decree until the same has been signed by the judge.

[Adopted effective April 1, 1986. Amended effective September 1, 2015.]

LCR 59. NEW TRIAL, RECONSIDERATION, AND AMENDMENT OF JUDGMENTS

(e) Hearing on Motion.

(1) *Motions for New Trial, Reconsideration, or Judgment NOV.* Motions for New Trial, reconsideration, or for judgment NOV shall be submitted without oral argument unless the Court orders otherwise as hereinafter provided. The motion shall be served and filed as provided in CR 59(b). At the time of filing the motion, the moving party shall serve and file a statement of points and authorities and deliver a copy of the motion, supporting documents and memorandum

to the trial judge. The trial judge may (1) grant, deny or modify the motion, (2) call for a written response from the opposing party, or (3) call for oral argument.

[Adopted effective April 1, 1986. Amended effective September 1, 2015.]

LCR 64. SEIZURE OF PERSON OR PROPERTY

All bench warrants issued in a civil proceeding shall be valid for one year from the date of issuance, unless quashed earlier. All such warrants issued in a civil proceeding shall contain substantially the following language: This warrant shall expire at the end of one year from the date of issuance.

[Adopted effective August 1, 1990; September 1, 2003.]

LCR 65. INJUNCTIONS

(b) Temporary Restraining Order; Hearing: Duration. The party applying for an emergency order which would require or forbid the doing of some act, if a public body is involved, or if the opponent's counsel is known, shall notify the opponent or opposing counsel and shall request opponent's presence at the presentation of the order, unless good cause to the contrary is shown. If the opponent does not appear, the judge shall require a full showing with respect to the notice given.

(c) All applications for temporary restraining orders (except in domestic relation cases) shall be presented to the Presiding Judge, if available, or to such other judge as he may designate to handle such matters if available.

[Adopted effective April 1, 1986.]

LCR 77. SUPERIOR COURTS AND JUDICIAL OFFICERS

(a) Reapplication for Order. When an order has been applied for and refused in whole or in part or has been granted conditionally and the condition has not been performed, the same application for an order must not be presented to another judge without advising the second judge of the fact that the order was previously refused or conditioned.

(d) Court Hours. Court will be in session, unless otherwise ordered, on all judicial days except Saturdays. Court hours will be from 8:30 a.m. to 12:00 noon and from 1:00 p.m. to 4:00 p.m. Counsel shall be present in court at 8:30 a.m. on the first day of a jury trial. In criminal cases, defense counsel shall have the defendant in court at 8:30 a.m. the first day of trial unless the defendant is in custody.

[Adopted effective April 1, 1986. Amended effective September 1, 1998; September 1, 2003; September 1, 2004; September 1, 2005; September 1, 2009; September 1, 2011.]

LCR 79. BOOKS AND RECORDS KEPT BY THE CLERK

(d) Other Books and Records of Clerk.

(1) *Withdrawal of Files from Clerk's Office.* Files generally shall remain in the Clerk's offices. The Clerk or employees thereof may take files to courtrooms or to judicial officers. Judicial officers, court reporters and court administration staff may check files out. Attorneys may also review court files, with convenient and appropriate areas for such review designated by the Clerk.

The statement of facts, after having been settled and signed, shall not be withdrawn from the Clerk's office except by order of the Court.

(2) *Exhibits.*

(A) Temporary Withdrawal. Exhibits may be withdrawn temporarily from the clerk's office only by:

(i) The judge having the cause under consideration;

(ii) Official court reporters for use in connection with their duties, without court order; and,

(iii) An attorney of record, upon court order.

(B) Videotaped Depositions. Videotaped depositions published in open court shall be treated as court exhibits, with the same retention standards. A party who wishes to make a published videotaped deposition part of the court file must submit a certified transcript of the deposition.

(3) *Return of Contraband Exhibits.* When contraband, alcoholic beverages, tobacco products or controlled substances are being held by the clerk of the court as part of the records and files in any criminal case, and all proceedings in the case have been completed, the court may order the clerk to deliver such contraband or substances to an authorized representative of the law enforcement agency initiating the prosecution for disposition according to law.

(4) *Return of Exhibits and Unopened Depositions.* When a civil case is finally concluded, and upon stipulation of the parties or court order, the clerk of the court may return all exhibits and unopened depositions, or destroy the same.

(5) *Disposition of Exhibits.* After final disposition of a civil cause, the Court after hearing, may order the clerk to destroy or otherwise dispose of physical evidence which cannot, because of bulk or weight, be retained in the case file provided that all parties of record are given thirty (30) days written notice of any such hearing.

(6) *Return of Administrative Records.* When a case for review of an administrative record is finally completed, the clerk shall return the administrative record to the officer or agency certifying the same to the court.

(7) *Verbatim Record of Proceedings.* A verbatim report of proceedings shall not be withdrawn from the clerk's office except by court order.

(8) *Transcripts.* A request for a copy of a transcript prepared by a court reporter in the possession of the clerk of the court, shall be referred to the court reporter that prepared said transcript.

(9) *Electronic Recording of Proceedings.* The court clerks shall maintain custody of electronic recordings created in any civil or criminal proceedings.

(10) *Video Recording of Proceedings.* The court clerks shall maintain custody of video recordings offered and/or admitted as evidence in any civil or criminal proceedings.

[Adopted effective April 1, 1986. Amended effective September 1, 2002; September 1, 2007; September 2, 2014.]

LCR 81. APPLICABILITY IN GENERAL

(a) To What Proceedings Applicable.

(1) *Generally.* In general, procedure in this Court shall be in accordance with pertinent Washington Court Rules as heretofore or hereafter adopted by the Supreme Court of Washington. These local rules are intended only to supplement those rules and are numbered, insofar as possible, to conform to the CR numbering system. The Rules shall also apply to criminal cases insofar as they are applicable.

(2) *Suspension of Rules.* The Court may modify or suspend any of these Rules in any given case, upon good cause being shown therefore, or upon the Court's own motion.

[Adopted effective April 1, 1986; Amended effective September 1, 2003.]

DOMESTIC RELATIONS

LCR 94.04W. DOMESTIC RELATIONS

(a) Family Court.

(1) *Jurisdiction.* All cases filed under Title 26 RCW shall be transferred to the Family Court for adjudication.

(2) *Judicial Officers.* Each of the judges and court commissioners of the Benton and Franklin Counties Judicial District are designated as Judges of the Family Court and Commissioners of the Family Court.

(3) *Effective Dates.* Sections (b) and (c), below, are effective and apply to all cases pending on January 1, 1999 or filed on or after January 1, 1999.

(b) Automatic Mutual Temporary Order.

(1) *Contents.* Upon the filing of a summons and petition in any action subject to this rule, the court, on its own motion, shall automatically issue a mutual temporary order that includes the following provisions unless specifically otherwise ordered by the court:

(A) The parties are restrained from transferring, removing, encumbering, concealing, or in any way disposing of any property except in the usual course of business or for the immediate necessities of life or as agreed upon in writing by the parties. Each party shall notify the other party of any extraordinary expenditure made after the order is issued.

(B) The parties are restrained from assigning, transferring, borrowing, lapsing, surrendering or changing entitlements of any insurance policies of either or both parties, whether medical, health, life or auto insurance, except as agreed in writing by the parties.

(C) Each party is immediately responsible for any debts he or she incurs after the order is issued, whether by open account, credit card, loan, security interest or mortgage, except as agreed in writing by the parties.

(D) Each party shall have access to all tax, financial, legal and household records and reasonable access to such records shall not be denied.

(E) In every action in which children are involved:

(i) Each parent is restrained from changing the residence of the child(ren) until further order of the court, except as agreed in writing by the parties.

(ii) Each parent shall insure that the child(ren) not be exposed to negative comments about the other parent.

(2) *Effective Date.* The petitioner is subject to the order from the time of its entry upon filing of the summons and petition. The petitioner shall serve a copy of the order on the respondent. The respondent is subject to the order from the time that it is served. The order shall remain in effect until further order of the court.

(c) Domestic Case Scheduling Order.

Except as otherwise provided in these rules or ordered by the Court, when an initial pleading is filed and a new case file is opened, the Court Administrator will prepare a domestic case schedule and the Superior Court Clerk will file the Domestic Case Scheduling Order (referred to in these rules as a "Case Schedule") and will provide one copy to the party filing the initial pleading.

(1) *Waiver of Domestic Case Scheduling Order.* The Court may order that the Case Scheduling Order be waived in Petitions to Modify Child Support, upon motion by either party.

(d) Effective Date.

This rule shall apply to all cases filed on or after September 1, 2010.

(e) Service of Domestic Case Schedule on Other Parties.

The party filing the initial pleading shall promptly provide a copy of the Domestic Case Schedule to all other parties by (a) serving a copy of the

Domestic Case Schedule on the other parties along with the initial pleading, or (b) serving the Domestic Case Schedule on the other parties within 10 days after the later filing of the initial pleading or service of any response to the initial pleading, whether that response is a notice of appearance or an answer.

(f) Amendment of Domestic Case Schedule. The Court, either on motion of a party or on its own initiative, may modify the Domestic Case Schedule for good cause. The Court shall freely grant a motion to amend the Domestic case schedule when justice so requires. The motion shall include a proposed Amended Domestic Case Schedule. If a Domestic Case Schedule is modified on the Court's own motion, the Court Administrator will prepare and file the Amended Domestic Case Schedule and promptly mail it to all parties. Parties may not amend a Domestic Case Schedule by stipulation without approval of the Court.

(g) Form of Domestic Case Schedule.

(1) *Domestic Case Schedule.* A Domestic Case Schedule for each type of case, which will set the time period between filing and trial and the scheduled events and deadlines for that type of case, will be established by the Court by General Order, based upon relevant factors, including statutory priorities, resources available to the Court, case filings, and the interests of justice.

(2) *Form.* A Domestic Case Schedule will be in generally the following form:

IN THE SUPERIOR COURT FOR THE
STATE OF WASHINGTON
IN AND FOR BENTON AND FRANKLIN COUNTIES

Petitioner,	)	Case No.
	)	
and	)	DOMESTIC CASE
	)	SCHEDULE ORDER
	)	(ORSCS)
	)	
Respondent.	)	
	)	
	)	
_____	)	

I. SCHEDULE
(Week of _____)

1. Mandatory Status Conference/Parenting Seminars/Adequate Cause	2 months
2. Assign GAL	4 months
3. Final Parenting Plan	4 months
4. Appraisal Report Due	4 months
5. Additional Discovery Pursuant to LCR 94.04W(j)(4)(A–H)	4 months
6. Additional Status Conference	4 months
7. Mediation (with or without children) ..	7 months
8. GAL Report Due	6 months
9. Additional Discovery Completed	6–½ months
10. Written Settlement Proposal (Petitioner)	1 week (Prior to STLCON)
11. Written Settlement Proposal (Respondent)	2 days (Prior to STLCON)
12. Settlement/Pretrial Conference	7–½ months
13. Trial Date	9 months

II. ORDER

IT IS ORDERED that all parties comply with the foregoing schedule.

Dated this _____ day of _____, _____.

SUPERIOR COURT JUDGE/COMMISSIONER

(h) Mandatory Status Conference.

(1) *Scheduling.* All dissolution actions shall be scheduled for a status conference to occur within 60 days of filing. The petitioner or joint petitioners shall note the dissolution action for status conference by serving notice of the conference with the original service of process or by timely service in the manner required for service and filing of pleadings and other papers pursuant to Civil Rule 5. The Notice of Status Conference will advise the respondent and the clerk of the date, time, and place of the status conference. Attendance by all counsel and parties to the action is mandatory absent any compelling reasons determined by the judicial officer. *See* Cancellation/Confirmation of Status Conference form LCR 94.04W(j).

(2) *Preparation.* At the status conference, both parties shall be present and shall be prepared to advise the court of the nature of all disputed issues, of the need for temporary orders, of the need for investigation by professionals, of allegations of domestic violence and/or child abuse and of any other issues affecting the timely disposition of the dissolution action.

(3) *Financial Declarations.* At the status conference all parties shall file and serve a financial declaration in the form prescribed by the Office of the Administrator for the Courts together with the following documents:

(A) Support Worksheets. If child support is an issue, Washington State Child Support Worksheets (ALL PAGES), signed by the submitting party;

(B) Tax Returns. Complete tax returns for the past two calendar years together with all schedules and W–2 forms;

(C) Partnership and Corporate Tax Returns. Complete partnership and/or corporate tax returns for the past two years together with all schedules and attachments for all partnerships and corporations in which a party has had an interest of five percent or greater.

(D) Pay Stubs. All pay stubs showing income for the past six months or since January 1 of the Calendar year, whichever period is greater.

(4) *Domestic Case Scheduling Order.* At the initial status conference the Court shall review with the parties the nature of the issues in dispute.

(5) *Guardian ad Litem.* The guardian ad litem intake packet shall be completed and submitted to the court no later than the second status conference.

(6) *Mediation Required for All Disputed Issues.* All disputed issues shall be submitted to mandatory mediation. All disputed child custody and visitation issues shall be submitted to mandatory mediation pursuant to LCR 94.06W. Mediation shall be completed pursuant to the Domestic Case Scheduling Order.

(7) *Evaluations.* The court may for good cause order a custody or parenting evaluation, mental health evaluation, alcohol or drug evaluation, mediation, treatment, counseling, and/or physical examination. The Court will determine the need for appointment of professionals and direct either or both parties to pay for services deemed necessary.

The issue of costs shall be addressed in the order requiring said services and shall contain an hourly rate and maximum payment if costs are to be at public expense.

(8) *Business Valuations.* If the value of the community interest in a business or professional practice is in dispute, the court shall appoint an appraiser to report to the court and the parties on the value of the business or professional practice. The parties may agree upon an appraiser to be appointed by the court. If the parties are unable to agree, each party shall, at the status conference, designate a valuation expert, and the experts so designated shall, within ten days following the status conference, recommend to the court a valuation expert to be appointed as an appraiser by the court.

(i) Mandatory Settlement and Pretrial Conferences.

(1) *Combined Settlement and Pretrial Conferences.* A combined settlement and pretrial conference shall be held in all contested domestic relations cases. The purpose of the conference is to explore settlement of all issues and to identify disputed issues. Parties are not bound by the settlement recommendations of the Court, but are required to attend and participate. Attendance by all counsel and parties is mandatory. Failure to appear at the settlement conference, without prior permission of the court, shall constitute an act of default. The present party may move for default pursuant to CR 55.

(2) *Discovery; Filing Position Statements.* All discovery shall be completed thirty (30) days prior to the settlement conference. Petitioner shall prepare his or her position statement and mail or deliver the same to respondent and the court administrator seven (7) days prior to the settlement conference. No fax copies will be accepted by the court. Respondent shall file with the court administrator and serve his or her position statement, in the same format as the petitioner, incorporating the petitioner's data, and mail or deliver the same to the petitioner and the court administrator two (2) days prior to the settlement conference. Position statements shall not be filed in the court file.

(3) *Court Imposed Sanctions.* Failure to appear at the settlement conference (without prior permission of the court) or failure to timely submit a Position Statement, shall subject the non-complying party and/or their attorney to a sanction of $200, paid to the Clerk of the Court. Payment shall be due within 20 days of the order. A party or attorney may petition the Court for relief from sanctions, which shall be filed within the same 20 day period and shall be noted for hearing.

(4) *Position Statements.*

(A) Form. Position statements for the purpose of the settlement conference shall be substantially in the form maintained by the Court Administrator's Office. The position statement will indicate the proposed disposition of assets and liabilities, proposed spousal maintenance, and residential placement of children, as applicable. The position statement shall not be used for any purpose at trial, unless otherwise agreed by the parties.

(B) Asset/Liability List. If distribution of assets or liabilities is an issue, each party shall file and serve a list of assets and liabilities known to the party, together with the position statement, and shall indicate the party's good faith opinion as to the fair market value of any asset as of the date of separation. The parties may also indicate the current fair market value if there is a significant difference. The list shall be signed by the party under penalty of perjury. This list may be used at trial, subject to the rules of evidence.

(C) Needs/Abilities Statement. If spousal maintenance or attorney's fees is at issue, each party shall file and serve a statement containing a list of all income and assets, including any retirement benefits, together with a list of current monthly living expenses and liabilities together with the position statement. The information regarding liabilities shall indicate the total amount owed as of the date of separation, the amount the party has paid on the debt(s) since the date of separation, and the monthly payment on the debt(s). The statement shall also include information concerning the needs and abilities of the party, including age, education, work experience, and mental and physical health. This statement shall be signed by the party under penalty of perjury. This statement may be used at trial, subject to the rules of evidence.

(D) Pretrial Statement. At the conclusion of the settlement conference, if the case is not then settled, the parties shall complete a Joint Pretrial

Statement, in the form maintained by the Court Administrator's Office. Both parties and attorneys shall sign the Joint Pretrial Statement.

(5) *Discovery Required.* In addition to discovery required under 94.04 W(i)(3)(A–D), the parties are required to file and exchange, as appropriate, the following documents no later than the discovery cutoff date:

(A) A copy of the most recent statement of balances due on mortgages, real estate purchase contracts, deeds of trust, installment purchase contracts, and time payment accounts owed by or to the parties;

(B) The most recent employers' ERISA statement, and a statement of contribution since that statement, of any pension plan of either party;

(C) A written appraisal of any real estate, antiques, jewelry, or other items of special, unusual, or extraordinary value or a summary of the evidence which will be relied upon;

(D) A verified extract or copy of the most recent N.A.D.A. Official Used Car Guide or Appraisal Guide showing both average loan and wholesale and retail values for any automobiles.

(E) A summary of the source and tracing of any property asserted to be the separate property or obligation of either party.

(F) A statement from each life insurance company issuing a policy of insurance on the life of either party as to its cash value and any loans on the cash value.

(G) A written appraisal of any proprietorship, partnership, or closely held corporation of the parties, or a summary of the evidence which will be relied upon.

(H) Expert witnesses shall be disclosed at or before the pretrial conference.

(j) Entry of Decree.

(1) *Time of Presenting Documents for Signature.* At the time of hearing of a non-contested dissolution case, the necessary documents to be signed must be presented to the Court for signature. If signed, they shall be filed with the clerk forthwith. For good cause shown, the Court may extend the time for presentation.

(2) *Disposition of Issues.* No decree of dissolution shall be entered unless the decree disposes of all issues over which the Court has jurisdiction.

(k) Orders Pendente Lite. Ex parte orders in domestic relations matters which restrain one party from the family home or from contact with the other party or children shall not be entered unless the Court finds (and the order provides) that irreparable injury could result if the order is not entered. No ex parte orders shall be issued changing the custody of minor children without a clear showing of present

danger to a child (children) and/or that the custodial person will, unless custody change is immediate, remove the said child (children) from the State of Washington. The attorney presenting the order shall specifically advise the Court that the order presented contains such a provision.

(*l*) Modification of Divorce Decree—Re: Support. If a petition to modify any order, judgment or decree is with regard only to support of minor children, then it shall be heard upon affidavit only, which shall concern change of circumstances and other appropriate matters, unless the petitioner therein has obtained leave of Court to hear said matter upon oral testimony, in which event the notice of hearing shall so provide. The respondent, prior to the return date, may obtain leave of Court to present oral testimony.

(m) Actions for Modification of Custody. A motion for modification of the custody provisions of a decree of dissolution or other custody decree shall be brought on by noting the adequate cause hearing required by RCW 26.09.270 on the motion calendar. The notice shall inform the other party of the time and place of hearing, the right of the other party to file opposing affidavits, and that the Court will take the following action:

(A) If adequate cause for hearing is not established by the affidavits, the motion for modification of the custody decree will be denied.

(B) If adequate cause for hearing is established by the affidavits, an order will be issued fixing a trial date and requiring the other party to show cause why the motion for modification should not be granted.

(C) If venue or jurisdiction is an issue, either party may apply to the Presiding Judge for an expedited hearing on this issue, which shall be heard promptly prior to a hearing on the merits.

(2) [1] *Motions for Temporary Custody.* Except with respect to pending actions for dissolution, legal separation, or a decree of invalidity, motions for temporary custody will not be heard until adequate cause has been established. Once adequate cause is established, the Court may proceed immediately to the hearing of the motion for temporary custody or continue the same, as justice requires.

(3) *Actions for Modification of Visitation.* Actions to clarify or change established visitation rights shall not require an adequate cause hearing.

(n) One Day Trailing of Trial Dates. Except for good cause shown, all domestic cases shall trail for one day. For example, if a domestic trial is set to be begin on Wednesday, the parties must be prepared to begin trial on Thursday as well.

(*o*) Cancellation/Confirmation of Status Conference. The following form is to be used for Cancellation/Confirmation of Status Conference.

SUPERIOR COURT OF THE STATE OF WASHINGTON
IN AND FOR BENTON AND FRANKLIN COUNTIES
IN RE THE MARRIAGE OF:

	)	
Petitioner	)	Case No.
	)	
V.	)	CANCELLATION
	)	OF STATUS CONFERENCE
	)	
Respondent	)	

I. CANCELLATION

The parties make the following joint representations and hereby cancel the Status Conference(s) scheduled on _____ and _____ (dates):

1. All parties have been served or have signed an acceptance of service.
2. All mandatory pleadings and financial information have been filed.
3. All parenting seminars have been completed (certificates attached) or are not required.
4. No unresolved issues remain for the court's intervention.
5. This matter has been placed on the uncontested domestic docket for entry of final documents on _____ (Notice for Docket attached)
6. A copy of this document will be provided to Court Administration.

PETITIONER OR PETITIONER'S ATTORNEY

DATED: _____ SIGNED: _____

Typed Name: _____ WSBA #: _____
Address: _____
Phone: _____
Attorney for: _____

RESPONDENT OR RESPONDENT'S ATTORNEY

DATED: _____ SIGNED: _____

Typed Name: _____ WSBA #: _____
Address: _____
Phone: _____
Attorney for: _____

[Adopted effective April 1, 1986. Amended effective September 1, 1998; September 1, 1999; September 1, 2001; September 1, 2003; September 1, 2005; September 1, 2007; September 1, 2009; September 1, 2010; September 1, 2011; September 1, 2012; September 2, 2013; September 2, 2014.]

1 Numbering as provided in original.

LCR 94.05W. MANDATORY PARENTING SEMINARS

(a) **Applicable Cases.** This rule shall apply to all cases filed after January 1, 1997 under Chapter 26.09, Chapter 26.10, or Chapter 26.26 RCW which require a parenting plan or residential plan for minor children; including dissolutions, legal separations, major modifications, paternity actions in which paternity has been established, and non-parental custody actions.

(b) **Mandatory Attendance.** In all cases governed by this rule, all parties shall complete a parenting seminar approved by the court. Standards for par-

enting seminars shall be established by the court and providers approved by the court.

(c) **Timing.** Parties required by this rule to participate in a parenting seminar shall complete an approved parenting seminar within 60 days of service of a petition or motion initiating the action which is subject to this rule. In the case of paternity actions initiated by the prosecuting attorney's office, the parenting seminar shall be required only when paternity is established or acknowledged and a parenting plan is requested. The class will be completed prior to entry of a permanent parenting or residential plan.

(d) **Fees.** Each party attending a seminar shall pay a fee charged by the approved provider and sanctioned by the court. The court may waive the fee for indigent parties.

(e) **Special Consideration/Waiver.**

(1) In no case shall opposing parties be required to attend a seminar together.

(2) If the court determines that attendance at a seminar is not in the children's best interest, pursuant to Chapter 26.12 RCW, the court shall either:

(A) waive the requirement of completion of the seminar; or

(B) allow participation in an alternative parenting seminar if available.

(3) The court may waive a party's attendance or extend the time required for attendance at a seminar for good cause shown.

(f) **Failure to Comply.** Willful refusal to participate in a parenting seminar or willful delay in completion of a court ordered parenting seminar by any party will constitute contempt of court and may result in sanctions, including, but not limited to, imposition of monetary terms, striking of pleadings, or denial of affirmative relief to a party not in compliance with this rule.

[Adopted effective January 1, 1997; amended effective September 1, 1999.]

LCR 94.06W. MANDATORY MEDIATION OF CHILD PLACEMENT AND VISITATION ISSUES

(a) **Effective Date.** This rule applies to all cases filed on or after January 1, 1999.

(b) **Child Placement Proceeding Defined.** For purposes of this rule, a child placement proceeding shall be defined as any proceeding before the court in which placement or visitation is at issue, except juvenile court dependency proceedings.

(c) **Mediation Required.** All placement or visitation issues shall be referred to mandatory mediation pursuant to the Domestic Case Scheduling Order. The mediation requirement may be waived by the court for good cause. A written motion for waiver of mediation shall be noted before the court. An Order Waiving Mediation shall be filed with the court prior to the case being set for settlement conference.

(d) Superior Court Jurisdiction and Other Rules—Show Cause Hearings. The requirement of mediation shall not prevent the court or court commissioner from entering temporary orders.

(e) Authority of Mediator. The mediator has the authority to determine the time, place, and duration of mediation. In appropriate cases, the mediator shall have the authority to terminate the mediation prior to completion.

(f) Attendance. Mediation session shall normally include the parties only, but may, by agreement of the parties and mediator, include other persons. Attendance at mediation sessions is mandatory.

(g) Declaration of Completion. Within seven (7) days of completion, a declaration of completion shall be filed by the mediator. The counsel and parties shall be advised by the mediator, on a separate document attached to the declaration of completion, the results and recommendations of the mediator. The mediator shall advise the court only whether an agreement has been reached.

(h) Mediation Unsuccessful. If the parties fail to reach an agreement in mediation of the issues of placement and visitation, a Guardian Ad Litem or a family court investigation may be ordered. The family court investigator shall not be the same person who mediated the case. Upon completion of the investigation, written recommendation shall be filed with the court.

(i) Confidentiality. The work product of the mediator and all communications during mediation shall be privileged and not subject to compulsory disclosure. The mediator shall not appear or testify in any court proceedings.

(j) Guardian ad Litem (GAL)/Family Court Investigator (FCI).

(1) *Appointment.* Upon motion of the parties or on the Court's own motion, the court may appoint a Guardian Ad Litem or a Family Court Investigator. The order shall be the court's mandated "Order Appointing Guardian ad Litem or Family Court Investigator" form.

(2) *Notice for Hearing.* Pursuant to the civil rules, from the date of the appointment, the GAL/FCI shall receive copies of all documents that are to be served on parties, copies of all discovery, and notice of all hearings and presentations related to the child custody or visitation five (5) Court days prior to the hearing or presentation.

(3) *Notice for Trial.* Any party who requires the GAL/FCI at a trial related to child custody or visitation issues, shall prepare and serve a subpoena on the GAL/FCI for mandatory appearance by GAL/FCI.

(4) *Discharge.* Unless otherwise set forth in these rules, the GAL/FCI shall be discharged only by order of the Court upon motion or upon completion of the case when the final orders are filed with the approval of the appointed GAL/FCI.

(5) *Declaration.* In any case where a GAL/FCI has been appointed, prior to entry of the final parenting plan or residential schedule, the GAL/FCI must either sign the final parenting plan or residential schedule or sign a Declaration indicating the GAL/FCI has reviewed the final order and approves, does not approve, or approves in part. If the GAL/FCI does not approve of all provisions in the final plan, the GAL/FCI must state in the Declaration what provisions are objected to and why.

[Adopted effective September 1, 1998. Amended effective September 1, 2008; September 1, 2011; September 2, 2013; September 2, 2014; September 1, 2015.]

LCR 94.07W. DOMESTIC RELATIONS MOTIONS

(a) Family Court Motions. Family court motions shall be scheduled on the family court dockets in Benton and Franklin counties in accordance with the docket schedule approved by the Superior Court judges. Docket days and times are available through the Superior Court Administrator's Office or the Superior Court Clerk's office.

(1) *Benton County Family Court Motions.*

(A) Benton County family court motions requiring more than ten minutes for argument shall be noted on the over-ten domestic docket which starts at 8:30 a.m. Should more than fifty (50) cases be noted for argument on the morning docket, those in excess of fifty (50) shall automatically be scheduled to be heard on the afternoon domestic docket of the same day and the parties shall be notified of such by the Superior Court Clerk's office. Any case scheduled but not heard on the morning docket shall be heard on the afternoon domestic docket of the same day which starts at 1:30 p.m.

(B) All Benton County family court motions requiring less than ten (10) minutes for argument and all pro se domestic motions, except for motions regarding relocation, shall be heard on the afternoon domestic relations docket which starts at 1:30 p.m.

(C) Benton County relocation motions shall be heard on the Prosser domestic docket.

(D) Franklin County relocation motions shall be noted as a special setting with the Court Administrator and filed with the Clerk.

(2) *Declarations (Benton and Franklin Counties).*

(A) Generally. Absent prior authorization from the court, the entirety of all declarations and affidavits, including attachments, from the moving party, including any expert or non-expert witnesses, in support of a motions hearing (or a continuation of a motions hearing), including any reply by the moving party, shall be limited to a sum total of twenty-five (25) pages, excluding cover page and fax transmittal affidavit, which shall be filed in the Clerk's office and served on the other party by noon on the day prior to the hearing. The entirety of all declarations and affidavits, including attachments, submitted in response by the non-moving party, to a motions hearing (or a continuation of a motions hearing) shall be limited to a sum total of 20 pages. If the declarations and affidavits, including attachments, are in excess of the page limitations, the entirety of the submission will not be reviewed or considered by the court. All declarations and affidavits must comply with GR14 (format for pleadings and other papers), be legibly hand-printed or typed in at least twelve (12) point type.

(i) Authorization to exceed the declaration page limitation shall be in writing and filed under the respective cause number in the Superior Court Clerk's office.

(ii) Any motion to exceed the page limit shall be in writing with notice to the opposing party, and shall be brought before the judicial officer that will be deciding the original motion.

(iii) In no event shall the page limit exceed 35 pages.

(B) Exhibits. Exhibits to any declaration shall count towards the above page limit.

(C) Financial declarations. Financial declarations, child support worksheets, and financial documents do not count toward the page limit.

(D) Expert reports and evaluations. Declarations, affidavits, and reports from Family Court Investigator, and Guardians ad Litem do not count toward the page limit.

(E) Miscellaneous exceptions. Copies of declarations or affidavits clearly marked as previously filed for a motion already ruled upon and supplied only as a convenience to the court in lieu of the court file do not count toward the page limit.

(3) *Time for Argument.*

(A) Each side on the over-ten family Court motion docket is allowed seven (7) minutes for oral argument including rebuttal unless otherwise authorized by the court. Authorization to exceed the oral argument time limit by up to four minutes may be granted if the court determines that exceptional circumstances warrant authorization. Such authorization must be obtained prior to commencement of the docket.

Each side on the regular domestic docket is allowed five (5) minutes for oral argument including rebuttal.

(B) Bench Copies. All motions, briefs, declarations, affidavits, and other supporting written documentation pertaining to trials, summary judgment motions, appeals from decisions of administrative agencies (except the record transferred by the agency) and any other motions, and other documents submitted for hearings, such as pre-trial position statements in domestic cases, trial management reports, proposed findings of fact and conclusions of law and judgments, and guardian ad litem reports (including criminal and domestic relations), shall be served and filed in the cause. Unless a party does not have access to a computer or the internet, bench copies of all such documents, as well as settlement position statements, shall be submitted electronically via the internet at http://motion. co.franklin.wa.us/. Parties without access to a computer and the internet shall deliver bench copies to the Court Administrator at the Benton County Justice Center. All bench copies must be submitted not later than noon one court day prior to the scheduled hearing, proceeding or trial. No bench copies, except settlement position statements, shall be submitted to the Court unless a copy has been served upon or mailed to opposing counsel or party if unrepresented. Bench copies submitted electronically are deleted from the system forty-five (45) days after the associated hearing. Bench copies submitted on paper are destroyed five (5) court days after the associated hearing unless counsel requests copies be returned, with return postage arranged, or unless Court Administration is advised of the new hearing date. When hearings are continued, the parties shall amend the hearing date associated with all bench copies submitted electronically.

If a party fails to submit bench copies as set forth above the Court may continue the hearing, impose terms and enter other orders as may be appropriate.

[Adopted effective September 1, 2007. Amended effective September 1, 2009; September 2, 2013; September 2, 2014; September 1, 2015.]

LCR 95.00W. DOMESTIC RELATIONS WAIVER OF AGE TO MARRY

Applications for waiver of minimum age to marry shall be made through the Juvenile Department of the Superior Court. Application shall contain such information and supporting documentation as may be prescribed by the Director of Juvenile Court. Before Court hearing, applicants must give evidence of completion of a program of premarital counseling by a licensed counselor, a counseling agency, or their rabbi, priest or minister, together with such counselor's recommendation, and shall be interviewed by a probation counselor of the Juvenile Department who may offer recommendations to the Court.

[Adopted effective April 1, 1986.]

LCR 96.00W. CHANGE OF NAME OF STEPCHILD

When a change of name to that of the stepfather is sought for a child under eighteen (18) years of age, notice must be given to the natural father in the manner of giving notice to a non-consenting parent in an adoption, and in addition, written consent will be required of any child over fourteen (14) years of age.

[Adopted effective April 1, 1986.]

LOCAL SPECIAL PROCEEDINGS RULES (LSPR)

LSPR 98.18. COURT-CREATED TRUSTS

(a) Special Needs Trusts and Trust governed by SPR 98.16W shall be approved in accord with the following requirements:

(1) A copy of the proposed trust document, note for hearing and trustee's fee schedule shall be submitted to the Guardianship Monitoring Program one week in advance of the hearing. The entire matter may be presented Ex Parte with the Clerk's office, unless notice has been requested by another party.

(2) An independent Guardian Ad Litem, specifically qualified in the area of court-created trusts, must be appointed to evaluate the proposed trust unless:

(a) The Court has ordered that the trust be drafted by independent trust counsel; or

(b) The basis for eligibility for a special needs trust in a physical disability only and the adult beneficiary is competent. However, the Court may, in its discretion, appoint a Guardian ad Litem for an otherwise competent beneficiary if it determines that he or she may not fully appreciate all the issues involved in creating the trust.

(3) The proponent of a trust must identify any other roles expected for trustees or members of a trust advisory committee in the life of the beneficiary. This would include caregivers, professional advisors, family or others who might receive direct or indirect economic benefit from trust expenditures.

(4) The order approving the trust may only be entered in a file with a probate/guardianship type "4" case assignment number to facilitate tracking. The order must have space designated on the face page to highlight due dates for accountings and other required filings. The trust document must be filed in the Superior Court file.

(5) The trustee is required to furnish annual accountings to the Court for approval on notice to any interested parties.

(6) The trust may not provide for removal to another venue or jurisdiction without order of this Court.

(7) A parent of a minor beneficiary is not the sole trustee or, if co-trustee, is not able to authorize a trust disbursement without Court approval.

(8) The appointment of any successor trustee is subject to approval of the Court.

(9) A trustee, other than a bank or trust company, is required to post a bond in the full amount of trust funds not placed in blocked accounts.

(10) Amendment of the trust shall only be by order of this Court.

(11) The trustee must file an inventory with the Court within 30 days of the funding of the trust. An amended inventory must be filed within 30 days if additional funding, in excess of $3,000, takes place after the filing of the initial inventory.

(12) The trustee must file with the Court an outline of the beneficiary's projected needs and significant trust expenditures within 30 days of their appointment and annually at the time of each accounting to the Court.

[Adopted effective September 1, 2009.]

LSPR 98.20. ESTATES—GUARDIANSHIPS

(a) **Hearings.** All proceedings in guardianship will normally be presented Ex Parte at the Court Administrator's office—with the Guardianship Monitoring Program. Matters that require a hearing shall be placed on the Probate Calendar.

(b) **Pleadings.** Parties are required to use those guardianship forms approved by the Benton and Franklin Counties Superior Court for guardianship proceedings.

(c) **Presentation of Reports and Care Plans.**

(1) The original of any report, accounting or care plan shall be filed in the Clerk's Office.

(2) A copy of the report, accounting or care plan shall be clearly marked "BENCH COPY" provided to the Superior Court Guardianship Monitoring Program together with an original and one copy of a proposed order approving the report, accounting and/or care plan and a stamped, self-addressed envelope.

(3) Copies of any supporting documentation for accountings shall be provided to the Superior Court Guardianship Monitoring Program. This shall include monthly bank statements, canceled checks or substitute images thereof provided by the financial institution, and receipts as appropriate. If the guardian of the estate is a bank or trust/agency company, it may file a computer printed statement of account in lieu of receipts or canceled checks. However, it must still complete the Report and Accounting form. Guardians shall retain copies of the supporting documentation for

four (4) years. Upon request of the Court, supporting documentation shall be re-submitted to the Guardianship Monitoring Program.

(d) Final Accounting. When a guardianship of the estate terminates and a guardian files a final account, an order shall be presented to the court setting a hearing on notice pursuant to RCW 11.92.053. The order shall be on a form approved by the court. The Guardianship Monitoring Program shall audit the final accounting. However, if the sole basis for the guardianship is the minority of the incapacitated person, the guardian may settle the account by filing a declaration of completion and serving notice thereof, on forms approved by the court, in accord with RCW 11.88.140. If the guardian of the estate resigns or is removed, but the guardianship continues, the court may in its discretion, settle the account as an ex parte intermediate account or require a hearing on notice.

(e) Attorney of Record. The attorney representing the Guardianship shall be considered the attorney of record until his or her withdrawal. Should the attorney representing the estate choose to withdraw, the attorney must advise the court of the name and address of the party to be notified, should that be necessary, of a delinquent report, accounting or Periodic Personal Care Plan. The notice to the court shall be filed prior to the effective date of the withdrawal of the attorney.

(f) Noncompliance Calendar.

(1) The Guardianship Monitoring Program office shall record all due dates for guardian's reports, and filings as set by the court. This shall include, but not be limited to an inventory, care plan, designation of standby-guardian, report and accounting or receipt for blocked account. The Court Administrator shall set a periodic Noncompliance Calendar for those cases in which guardians have not met the required due dates.

(2) *Order to Appear.* If reports and filings are not presented timely, an order to appear on the guardianship noncompliance calendar shall be sent to the attorney of record and/or the guardian citing the parties into court. Appearance on the calendar is mandatory. The attorney and/or the guardian shall have at least five days' notice, in accordance with CR 6, to appear.

(3) *Attendance at Noncompliance Calendar Excused.* If the guardian files the required document(s) referenced in the noncompliance notice at least five days in advance of the calendar date, they shall be excused from attendance at the calendar.

(4) *Sanctions on the Noncompliance Calendar.* The judicial officer assigned to hear the guardianship noncompliance calendar may impose monetary sanctions, increase the bond, suspend the duties of the guardian, appoint a guardian ad litem, and/or remove the guardian.

(g) Review Hearing/Conference. If after initial review of a guardian's report or other filing, it is found unacceptable by the Court, the guardian shall be notified of the additional information or corrective action required. Additionally, the Court may cite the guardian in to appear at an informal review conference or in-court review hearing. The Court may then take appropriate action to resolve any concerns regarding the guardian's performance of their fiduciary duties.

[Adopted effective September 1, 2009. Amended effective September 2, 2013; September 1, 2015.]

LOCAL GUARDIAN AD LITEM RULES (LGAL)

LGAL 1. SCOPE

(a) This rule covers the maintenance and administration of the Guardian ad Litem Registries maintained by the Superior Court Administrator's office pursuant to RCW 4.08.060 as amended, RCW 8.25.270 as amended, RCW 11.88.090 as amended, Superior Court Guardian ad Litem Rules GALR as amended, and RCW 26.12 as amended. (The Guardian ad Litem Registry for dependency cases pursuant to RCW 13.34 is maintained and administered by the Juvenile Court Administrator's office).

(b) These rules shall be supplemented by administrative rules and policies adopted by the Court.

[Adopted effective September 1, 2003. Amended effective September 2, 2013.]

LGAL 2. REGISTRY ADMINISTRATION

(a) The Court shall maintain and administer Guardian ad Litem registries for Adoption, Guardianship, and Family Law. These registries shall not include Juvenile Court Guardians ad Litem, or Court Appointed Special Advocates, which shall continue to be administered independently by their respective programs. These requirements and procedures also apply to persons not listed on a registry who are appointed to serve as a Guardian ad Litem in a field for which there is a registry.

(b) The Court shall maintain a completed application form, and background information records pertaining to each person on a registry. Persons listed on a registry or registries shall reapply and update background information annually on a date specified for each registry. Background Information Records, as required by RCW 26.12.175(3), shall be available for public inspection.

(c) Persons shall be selected to serve on each registry at the discretion of the Court giving due consideration to: (a) having a sufficient number of Guardians ad Litem available to fulfill the requests for appointment; (b) achieving and maintaining a high level of knowledge, skill and competence within each given field. In some cases there may be more qualified applicants than will be needed or would benefit the program, so that not all persons applying will be selected.

(d) The Court may sponsor or approve training which registry applicants shall be required to attend to maintain and improve their level of proficiency. Title 11 Guardian ad Litem registry applicants must complete any training required by RCW 11.88.090 prior to placement of the applicant's name on the guardianship registry.

(e) Each registry may be reconstituted periodically. The Court may remove persons listed on a registry and allow additional applicants to be added to a registry at the discretion of the Court.

(f) The Court may impose an application fee and/or charge a fee for the training programs.

[Adopted effective September 1, 2003. Amended effective September 1, 2004; September 1, 2015.]

LGAL 5. APPOINTMENT OF GUARDIAN AD LITEM

(a) Equitable Distribution of Workload/Appointment of Guardian Ad Litem From Registry.

(1) *Adoption Registry.*

(A) Any person listed on the Adoption registry may be appointed upon stipulation of the parties and agreement of the Guardian ad Litem to accept the case.

(B) Absent a stipulation to a particular person listed on the registry, the Court Administrator/or designee shall, upon order of the Court, appoint a Guardian ad Litem from the registry on a rotational basis subject to the Guardian ad Litem's agreement to accept the case.

(2) *Guardianship Registry.*

(A) A party needing an appointment from the Guardianship registry shall provide by e-mail, fax or letter a written request to the Superior Court Administrator's Office, which office shall, except in extraordinary circumstances, appoint as Guardian ad Litem that person whose name next appears on the registry on a rotational basis and meets the requirements of RCW 11.88.090 (3) (a) subject to that person's acceptance of the appointment.

(B) The person appointed by the Court Administrator's Office shall serve upon the parties a notice of acceptance and qualifications in conformance with RCW 11.88.090.

(C) Guardian ad Litems appointed pursuant to RCW Title 11 shall be compensated in accordance with the provisions of RCW 11.88.090 and RCW 11.88.097 provided, however, that in the event it is

shown by motion supported by affidavit that the county shall be responsible for such costs, the fees shall not exceed $1,000.00 per case. The affidavit in support of a motion for Court paid fees shall set forth the financial position of the alleged incapacitated person, including assets, potential causes of action, monthly income and monthly expenses. If additional fees beyond the $1,000.00 per case are requested such request shall be by a separate motion supported by appropriate affidavits. The order authorizing disbursal of County funds shall provide that those fees shall be reimbursed to the County in the event the estate obtains, within a reasonable period of time, sufficient assets.

(D) Should any person appointed herein fail to accept such appointment more than twice in a calendar year, or fail to accept a County pay appointment if the Guardian ad Litem is selected on the rotational registry, such persons name will be deleted from the registry at the Court's discretion.

(3) *Family Law (Title 26) Registry.* Guardians ad Litem appointed pursuant to RCW Title 26 shall be appointed in the following manner:

(A) A Guardian ad Litem shall be appointed within (120) days of filing of the action. Upon either the motion of the Court or a party to an action and subsequent decision of the Court to appoint a Guardian ad Litem, each party to the action shall be provided with a list of three names from the registry along with background information as specified in RCW 26.12.175(3), including their hourly rate for services. Each party may, within seven (7) judicial days, strike one name from the list. If more than one name remains on the list, the Court shall select the first named Guardian ad Litem not stricken by a party. In the event all three names are stricken, the Court shall select the alternate named Guardian ad Litem on the list as placed on the list pursuant to section (C) below. Parties shall file an Order Appointing Guardian ad Litem within thirty (30) days of the selection by the Court. Guardian ad Litem retainer fee and intake packets must be received by the Guardian ad Litem prior to the filing of the Order Appointing Guardian ad Litem. The Guardian ad Litem shall immediately begin their work upon filing of the Order Appointing Guardian ad Litem.

(B) The Superior Court Administrator or his or her designee shall, at such time as is ordered by the Superior Court, shall prepare a strike list packet.

(C) Said strike list packets shall be prepared by randomly selecting three names from the registry.

Additionally, for each strike list packet, one additional name shall be randomly selected as the alternate Guardian ad Litem.

(D) The Court may, for good cause and upon written finding, appoint a specific Guardian ad Litem to a case upon recommendation of the parties.

Good cause may include expertise in a particular area, previous appointment of a Guardian ad Litem to the specific case, or such other reason as determined by the Court. The hourly rate for services charged by a Guardian ad Litem does not constitute good cause for the appointment of a specific Guardian ad Litem upon recommendation of the parties.

(E) Title 26 Guardian ad Litems are required to accept up to two (2) county-paid abuse and neglect cases in a calendar year. Appointments shall be made in alphabetical rotation in the event that the Court's Family Court Investigator (FCI) is unable to accept the case. Failure to accept county-paid appointments may result in removal from the Registry at the Court's discretion.

(b) Procedure to Address Complaints by Guardians ad Litem. Complaints by Guardians ad Litem regarding registry or appointment matters shall be made in writing and be addressed to the Court Administrator. The Administrative Presiding Judge, Assistant Administrative Presiding Judge or Court Administrator shall provide written response to the complainant within 45 business days of receipt of the complaint.

[Adopted effective September 1, 2002; Amended effective September 1, 2003; September 1, 2004; September 1, 2009; September 1, 2010; September 1, 2011; September 2, 2014; September 1, 2015.]

LGAL 7. GRIEVANCE PROCEDURE

(a) Purpose Statement. The procedure for handling grievances and/or imposing discipline against a Guardian ad Litem provided hereunder are intended to facilitate a process which is fair, expedited, and protective of all participants as well as respectful of judicial time and resources.

(b) Procedures for Filing a Grievance.

(1) Only a party to a case may file a grievance against a Guardian ad Litem. Grievances against Guardians ad Litem shall be made in writing, be signed under the penalty of perjury, and be addressed to the Court Administrator. Neither the grievance nor any documentation related to the grievance, including a decision on the grievance, shall be filed in the court file.

(2) The grievance must include the following information:

A. The name, mailing address, telephone number, and e-mail address (if any) of the party filing the grievance;

B. The case number and case name;

C. The name of the judge or court commissioner hearing the case;

D. The trial date;

E. Whether the party filing the grievance has discussed the grievance with the Guardian ad Litem

F. What action the Guardian ad Litem has taken to address the grievance;

G. Which provision of the Order Appointing Guardian ad Litem or of these rules the party filing the grievance is claiming the Guardian ad Litem has violated;

H. A complete statement of the specific facts underlying each alleged violation, as set forth in subsection (3) below;

I. What the party filing the grievance is requesting be done to correct the problem complained of and why.

(3) The grievance must state with specificity the act or failure to act of concern to the complaining party as it relates to the grounds outlined below which are also grounds for denial of listing on, removal from or temporarily suspending the Guardian ad Litem from the registry:

A. There has been a violation of the Guardian ad Litem Code of Conduct,

B. There has been a misrepresentation of his or her qualification to be a Guardian ad Litem, or

C. Has not met the annual update requirements set forth in LGAL rule 2(b); or

D. Any reason that would place the suitability of the person to act as Guardian ad Litem in question, including, but not limited to the following:

i.   Breach of confidentiality.

ii. Falsifying information on the application.

iii. Falsifying information in a Court report.

iv. Failure to report abuse of a child.

v.   Ex-parte communication.

vi. Representing the court in a public forum, without prior approval of the Court.

vii. Violation of state, or local laws, rules of the policy, while a Guardian ad Litem.

viii. Dissemination of Bi–Pen (Bi–County Police Information) records.

(c) Initial Screening of Grievance. The Court Administrator shall forthwith forward the grievance to the Administrative Presiding Judge for initial screening. If it is clear on the face of the grievance that the grievance is without merit, the Administrative Presiding Judge shall dismiss the grievance, providing a copy of such dismissal to the complaining party and the affected Guardian ad Litem. The Administrative Presiding Judge shall endeavor to complete the initial screening within fourteen (14) days of filing of the grievance. The matter will be closed and the grievance shall be held as a confidential, sealed record in the files of the Court Administrator for six (6) years following dismissal of the grievance unless specifically directed otherwise by the Administrative Presiding Judge.

(d) Grievances Filed During the Pendency of a Case.

(1) If a grievance is not dismissed under section (c) and the grievance pertains to a pending case or if trial in the pending case is underway, the Court Administrator shall, within three (3) business days of receipt, forward the grievance to the Administrative Presiding Judge or if trial is underway, to the judicial officer assigned to hear the trial, to handle the grievance, with a copy being sent to the affected Guardian ad Litem.

If the grievance is forwarded to the Administrative Presiding Judge, he/she shall assign responsibility for the investigation and decision on the grievance to the Administrative Presiding Judge, the Assistant Administrative Presiding Judge, another judicial officer, or a committee composed of three (3) judicial officers of the Administrative Presiding Judge's choosing. Whomever the grievance is forwarded to shall be known as the "judicial officer for the grievance".

(2) The Guardian ad Litem shall be allowed to file a response to the grievance within fourteen (14) days of receiving notice from the court by forwarding a copy of the response to the complaining party with the original response being sent to the Court Administrator who will deliver same to the judicial officer for the grievance. In addition, an appropriate investigation may be made by the judicial officer, including, but not limited to, interviews with the complainant, the Guardian ad Litem, and other persons with relevant knowledge.

(3) Upon receipt of the response from the Guardian ad Litem or upon passage of the fourteen (14) day response period, whichever is sooner, the judicial officer assigned to grievance shall review the response, complete the investigation and thereafter issue a final written or oral disposition of the matter. The judicial officer for the grievance will endeavor to issue a final decision within no later than forty-five (45) days after the filing of the grievance.

The original of a written disposition or a transcript of an oral disposition shall be placed in the grievance file with copies of the written disposition being forwarded to the complaining party and to the Guardian ad Litem.

(4) If the final disposition is that the grievance should be dismissed, the procedure with regard to retention of the grievance set forth in section (c) above shall be followed. If, as part of the final disposition, there has been a finding that the grievance was not brought in good faith or was otherwise frivolous or designed to impact the pending proceedings through increased costs to the other party or Guardian ad Litem, terms in the form of costs or other sanctions may be imposed against the grieving party.

(5) If, upon a finding by a preponderance of the evidence that one or more of the grounds in section (b)(2) have been established, and the final disposition is that the grievance was brought in good faith and has been determined to be well-founded, there shall be a method of discipline to be imposed upon the Guardian ad Litem set forth in the disposition which shall take effect immediately. Accepted forms of discipline shall consist of one or more of the following: (1) a verbal or written reprimand, (2) removal from the pending case; (3) suspension of the Guardian ad Litem from the registry for a period not to exceed one (1) year; (4) suspension of the Guardian ad Litem from the registry until such time as the Guardian ad Litem has provided satisfactory proof of completing additional training in a specific area described in the disposition; (5) imposition of terms in the form of costs or other monetary sanctions; and/or (6) permanent removal of the Guardian ad Litem from the registry for Title 11, Title 13, and/or Title 26 cases.

If the discipline imposed is permanent removal from any Guardian ad Litem registry, notification of same shall be forwarded to the Office of the Administrator for the Courts for circulation to other counties. The confidential file of the grievance shall include the original grievance, the Guard ad Litem's response, and the written initial and final dispositions of the matter and shall be maintained by the Court Administrator for a period for no less than six (6) years.

(6) A Guardian ad Litem who ceases to be on the registry and who still has active or incomplete cases shall immediately report this circumstance to the Court Administrator who will forthwith reassign such cases.

(7) Timelines stated herein may be modified by the Administrative Presiding Judge or judicial officer for the grievance for good cause. In calculating times, items mailed shall be deemed received by the addressee three (3) days after the date of mailing.

(e) Grievances Filed After the Conclusion of a Case or After Discharge of the Guardian ad Litem. If the grievance pertains to a case in which final orders have been entered or an order discharging the Guardian ad Litem has been entered, the Court Administrator shall, within three (3) business days, forward the grievance to the judicial officer who presided over the trial in the case or who signed the final orders/order of discharge which a copy to the affected Guardian ad Litem, as the judicial officer for the grievance.

Thereafter, the procedures set forth in section (d) shall be followed.

(f) Interim Suspension for Grievances Handled Under Sections (d) and (e). For all grievances received and processed under sections (d) and (e) above, at the discretion of the Administrative Presiding Judge or the judicial officer for the grievance as set forth in this rule, the Guardian ad Litem's participation in the registry may be suspended pending resolution of the grievance.

A Guardian ad Litem whose participation is suspended pending resolution and who still has active or incomplete cases shall immediately report this circumstance to the Superior Court Administrator who may reassign such cases upon instruction from the judicial officer assigned to the grievance.

(g) Reconsideration of Decision Under Sections (d) and (e). A Guardian ad Litem seeking reconsideration of the decision shall do so in writing to the Superior Court Administrator, who shall forward the request and supporting documents to the judicial officer for the grievance for final decision. The Guardian ad Litem shall be notified in writing of the final decision.

[Adopted effective September 1, 2002. Amended effective September 1, 2003; September 1, 2010; September 2, 2014; September 1, 2015.]

LOCAL MANDATORY ARBITRATION RULES (LMAR)

LMAR 1.1. APPLICATION OF RULES

The purpose of mandatory arbitration of civil actions under RCW 7.06 as implemented by the Mandatory Arbitration Rules is to provide a simplified and economical procedure for obtaining the prompt and equitable resolution of disputes involving claims not exceeding fifty thousand dollars ($50,000). The Mandatory Arbitration Rules as supplemented by these local rules are not designed to address every question which may arise during the arbitration process and the rules give considerable discretion to the arbitrator. The arbitrator should not hesitate to be informal and expeditious, consistent with the purpose of the statute and rules.

[Adopted September 1, 1996; Amended March 1, 1997; September 1, 2003; amended on an emergency basis effective January 1, 2006; amended on a permanent basis effective September 1, 2006.]

LMAR 1.2. MATTERS SUBJECT TO ARBITRATION

By implementation of these rules the Superior Court of Washington for Benton and Franklin Counties authorizes mandatory arbitration under RCW 7.06. 010, and approves such arbitration in civil actions in which no party asserts, on the party's own behalf, a claim in excess of fifty thousand dollars ($50,000) exclusive of interest, attorney's fees, and costs under RCW 7.06.020 as amended.

[Adopted September 1, 1996; Amended March 1, 1997; amended on an emergency basis effective January 1, 2006; amended on a permanent basis effective September 1, 2006.]

LMAR 2.1. TRANSFER TO ARBITRATION

(a) Statement of Arbitrability. In every civil case, following the commencement of the action, but no later than the date set forth in the case schedule order pursuant to LCR 4 or for cases filed on or before December 31, 2000 where no case schedule order has been issued, no later than sixty (60) days prior to a properly noted and set trial, any party may, upon the form prescribed by the court and maintained in the Court Administrator's Office, complete a statement of arbitrability. The statement of arbitrability shall be filed in the superior court clerk's office and a duplicate copy delivered to the court administrator's office and the opposing party or parties. A party failing to file and serve a statement of arbitrability within the time prescribed shall be deemed to have waived arbitration, and may subject the matter to mandatory arbitration thereafter only upon leave of the court for good cause shown.

(b) Response to Statement of Arbitrability. Any party disagreeing with the statement of arbitrability shall serve and file a response on the form prescribed by the Court and maintained in the Court Administrator's Office. A duplicate copy of the response shall be delivered to the court administrator. In the absence of such a response, the statement of arbitrability shall be deemed correct. Any response opposing the statement of arbitrability shall be filed within 10 court days after receipt of the statement of arbitrability. A notice of issue shall be filed with any response objecting to the statement of arbitrability, noting the matter for hearing on the issue of arbitrability within 10 court days of filing the response.

(c) Failure to File—Amendments. A person failing to serve and file an original response within the times prescribed may later do so only upon leave of the court. A party may amend a statement of arbitrability or response at any time before assignment of an arbitrator or assignment of a trial date, and thereafter only upon leave of the court for good cause shown.

(d) When Transfer to Arbitration Occurs for Purposes of Application of Local Rules. The case is transferred to arbitration upon the filing of a statement of arbitrability indicating that the case is subject to arbitration unless an objection to arbitration of the case is received within the time limits found in LMAR 2.1(b). This transfer shall also trigger the restriction on discovery contained in MAR 4.2 and LMAR 4.2.

(e) Civil Case Schedule Order Stricken. Any civil case schedule order entered in an action pursuant to LCR 4 shall be stricken upon the filing of a statement of arbitrability unless an objection to arbitration of the case is received within the time limits found in LMAR 2.1(b) in which event the civil case schedule order shall be stricken upon issuance of an order directing the case to mandatory arbitration following a hearing on the objection.

[Adopted Effective September 1, 1996. Amended effective September 1, 1998; September 1, 1999; September 1, 2002; September 1, 2003; September 1, 2011; September 1, 2015.]

LMAR 2.3. ASSIGNMENT TO ARBITRATOR

(a) Generally; Stipulations. When a case is transferred to arbitration, but not less than ninety (90) days following filing and service on all parties subject to arbitration, a list of five proposed arbitrators will be furnished to all parties. A master list of arbitrators will be made available upon request. The parties are encouraged to stipulate to an arbitrator. In the absence of a stipulation, the arbitrator will be chosen from among the five proposed arbitrators in the manner defined by this rule. If the parties stipulate to an arbitrator who is not one of the five proposed arbitrators, they must obtain the arbitrator's consent to appointment prior to submitting the stipulation to the Court.

(b) Response by Parties. Each party may, within 10 court days of the date mailed by the court, after a list of proposed arbitrators is furnished to the parties, nominate one or two arbitrators and strike one or two arbitrators from the list. If both parties respond, an arbitrator nominated by both parties will be appointed. If no arbitrator is nominated by both parties, the court administrator will randomly appoint an arbitrator from among those not stricken by either party.

(c) Response by Only One Party. If only one party responds within 10 court days of the date mailed by the court, the court administrator will appoint an arbitrator nominated by that party.

(d) No Response. If neither party responds within 10 court days of the date mailed by the court, the court administrator will randomly select and appoint one of the five proposed arbitrators.

(e) Additional Arbitrators for Additional Parties. If there are more than two adverse parties, at least two additional proposed arbitrators shall be added to the list with the above principles of selection to be applied. The number of adverse parties shall be determined by the court administrator, subject to review by a superior court judge.

(f) List of Proposed Arbitrators. Parties do not have to serve choices upon each other and the court administrator must keep selections confidential. The court administrator must retain returned lists of proposed arbitrators until the time for appeal has expired or a request for trial de novo is received, whichever is sooner.

[Adopted September 1, 1996; Amended September 1, 1998; September 1, 2006.]

LMAR 3.1. QUALIFICATIONS OF ARBITRATORS

(a) Arbitration Panel. There shall be a panel of arbitrators in such numbers as the administrative committee may from time to time determine. A person desiring to serve as an arbitrator shall complete an information sheet on the form prescribed by the Court. A list showing the names of arbitrators available to hear cases and the information sheets will be available for public inspection in the court administrator's office. The oath of office on the form prescribed by the Court must be completed and filed prior to an applicant being placed on the panel.

(b) Qualification. Unless otherwise stipulated, an arbitrator must be a member of the Washington State Bar for 5 years or a retired judge.

(c) Refusal; Disqualification. The appointment of an arbitrator is subject to the right of that person to refuse to serve. An arbitrator must notify the court administrator within three court days of receipt of the notice of appointment if refusing to serve or if any cause exists for the arbitrator's disqualification from the case upon any of the grounds of interest, relationship, bias or prejudice set forth in CJC Canon 3(c) governing the disqualification of Judges. If disqualified, the arbitrator must immediately return all materials in a case to the court administrator. A party may challenge the qualifications of an arbitrator by motion to the Court if the motion is made within 10 court days of the appointment of the arbitrator.

[Adopted effective September 1, 1996; amended effective September 1, 2003; September 1, 2011.]

LMAR 3.2. AUTHORITY OF ARBITRATORS

(a) Authority. An arbitrator has the authority to:

(1) Determine the time, place, and procedure to present a motion before the arbitrator.

(2) Require a party and/or attorney to pay the reasonable expenses, including attorney fees, caused by the failure of such party and/or attorney to obey an order of the arbitrator unless the arbitrator finds that the failure was substantially justified or that other circumstances make an award of expenses unjust. The arbitrator shall make a special award for such expenses and shall file such award with the clerk of the superior court, with proof of service on each party. The aggrieved party shall have 10 days thereafter to appeal the award of such expense in accordance with the procedure described in RCW 2.24.050. If, within 10 days after the award is filed no party appeals, a judgment shall be entered in the manner described generally under MAR 6.3.

(3) Award attorney fees, as authorized by these rules, by contract, or by law.

(2)[1] Determine the time and place for the arbitration hearing.

(3)[2] Award, by judgment or offset, the fee paid by a party to initiate arbitration where the arbitrability is clear and the party responsible for filing the statement of arbitrability unreasonably delayed in the filing of a statement or arbitrability, regardless of which party substantially prevails.

(b) Motions. All motions shall be presented to the arbitrator, unless a) arbitrability is at issue, b) assignment of arbitrator is disputed, c) motion is for involuntary dismissal, d) motion is for summary judgment, e) motion is for failure to state a cause of action, or f) motion is to add or change parties.

(c) Immunity. Arbitrators shall have immunity to the same extent as provided for superior court judges in Washington State.

[Adopted effective September 1, 1996; amended effective September 1, 2011.]

> 1 So in original, probably should be (4).
> 2 So in original, probably should be (5).

LMAR 4.2. DISCOVERY

(a) Additional Discovery. In determining when additional discovery beyond that directly authorized by MAR 4.2 is reasonably necessary, the arbitrator shall balance the benefits of discovery against the burdens and expenses. The arbitrator shall consider the nature and complexity of the case, the amount in controversy, values at stake, the discovery that has already occurred, the burdens on the party from whom discovery is sought, and the possibility of unfair surprise which may result if discovery is restricted. Authorized discovery shall be conducted in accordance with the Superior Court Civil Rules, except motions concerning discovery shall be determined by the arbitrator. Except as provided in MAR 4.2, discovery pending when a case is transferred to arbitration is stayed except on stipulation of the parties. All discovery admissible under the Superior Court Civil Rules and Washington Rules of Evidence is admissible at arbitration, whether produced before or after the appointment of the arbitrator.

(b) Notwithstanding the Foregoing. The following interrogatories may be submitted to any party:

(1) State the amount of general damages being claimed;

(2) State each item of special damages being claimed and the amount thereof;

(3) List the name, address, and telephone number of each person having knowledge of any facts regarding liability;

(4) List the name, address, and telephone number of each person having knowledge of any facts regarding the damage claimed;

(5) List the name, address, and telephone number of each expert witness you intend to call at the arbitration hearing. For each expert, state the subject matter on which the expert is expected to testify; state the substance of the facts and opinions to which the expert is expected to testify, and a summary of the grounds for each opinion.

(6) If you are claiming bodily injury damages, please describe your present physical condition as the same relates to the incident giving rise to your complaint and being specific as to the area(s) of your body you claim was injured.

(7) If you are claiming bodily injury damages, please list the name, address, and telephone number of each and every health care provider with whom you treated, consulted with, or were examined by: (a) in the ten (10) years preceding the incident giving rise to your complaint; and (b) from the date of said incident to the present date.

(8) Identify the existence of and the contents of any insurance agreement under which any person carrying on an insurance business may be liable to satisfy part of all of a judgment which may be entered in the action or to indemnify or reimburse for payments made to satisfy the judgment; and any documents affecting coverage (such as denying coverage, extending coverage, or reserving rights) from or on behalf of such person to the covered person or the covered person's representative. For purposes of this section, an application for insurance shall not be treated as part of an insurance agreement. Discovery produced pursuant to this subsection shall not be disclosed to the arbitrator.

(9) Identify all parties who you contend have not been properly served with the summons and complaint.

Upon request, all records reflecting the treatments, consultations, and examinations must be produced unless the requester is provided a medical authorization sufficient to allow the requester to obtain independent access to said records at his or her own expense. Alternatively, the requesting party may also request records through depositions upon written questions as allowed by CR 31.

Only these interrogatories, with the exact language as set out above, are permitted.

[Adopted effective September 1, 1996; amended effective September 1, 1998; September 1, 2003; September 1, 2010; September 1, 2011.]

LMAR 4.4. NOTICE OF SETTLEMENT

(a) Notice of Settlement. After any settlement that fully resolves all claims against all parties, the plaintiff shall, within 5 days or before the arbitration hearing, whichever is sooner, file and serve a written notice of settlement on the form prescribed by the Court. The notice shall be filed with both the arbitrator and the Court. Where notice cannot be filed with the arbitrator before the arbitration hearing, the plaintiff shall notify the arbitrator of the settlement by telephone prior to the hearing, and the written notice shall be filed and served within five days after the settlement.

(b) Dismissal by the Court. If an order dismissing all claims against all parties is not entered within 60 days after written notice of settlement is filed, or within 60 days after the scheduled arbitration hearing date, whichever is earlier, the court administrator will mail notice to the attorneys of record that the case will be dismissed by the Court for want of prosecution unless, within 10 court days after the mailing, a party makes a written application to the Court, showing good cause why the case should not be dismissed. If good cause is shown, the case may be reinstated to the original arbitrator for an additional 90 days or for such period of time as the Court may designate. If an order dismissing all claims against all parties is not entered during that additional period of time, the court administrator shall issue another notice as described above.

[Adopted September 1, 1996; Amended September 1, 1998.]

LMAR 5.1.   NOTICE OF HEARING

(a) Time For Hearing. The arbitrator shall set the time, date, and place of the hearing and shall give reasonable notice of the hearing date to the parties. Except by stipulation or for good cause shown, the hearing shall be scheduled to take place not sooner than 21 days, nor later than 63 days, from the date of the assignment of the case to the arbitrator, however, in no instance shall the original hearing date be set later than 120 days from the appointment of the arbitrator. The arbitrator may grant a continuance of the hearing date not to exceed 60 days beyond the original hearing date. In the absence of agreement of the parties and arbitrator on the date for any hearing, the arbitrator shall have the authority to set a hearing date over the objection of the parties which is consistent with this rule. Any setting of the original hearing date later than 120 days from the appointment of the arbitrator or any continuance of a hearing date more than 60 days from the original hearing date must be noted on the civil motion docket before the Presiding Judge and will be granted only for good cause shown.

(b) Confirmation of Hearing. Parties must confirm the hearing date with the arbitrator one week prior to hearing. Failure to confirm the hearing with the arbitrator may result in the cancellation of hearing at the arbitrator's discretion. Parties must notify arbitrator of a settlement reached prior to the scheduled hearing date in accordance with LMAR 4.4.

[Adopted effective September 1, 1996; Amended effective September 1, 1998; September 1, 2003.]

LMAR 5.2.   PRE–HEARING STATEMENT OF PROOF—DOCUMENT FILED WITH COURT

In addition to the requirements of MAR 5.2, each party shall also furnish the arbitrator with copies of pleadings and other documents contained in the court file which that party deems relevant. The court file shall remain with the county clerk.

[Adopted effective September 1, 1996.]

LMAR 6.1.   FORM AND CONTENT OF AWARD

(a) Exhibits. All exhibits offered during the hearing shall be returned to the offering parties.

(b) Attorney Fees/Statutory Costs. Any motion for actual attorney fees/statutory costs, whether pursuant to contract, statute, or recognized ground in equity, must be presented to the arbitrator as follows:

(1) Any motion for an award of attorney fees/statutory costs must be submitted to the arbitrator and served on opposing counsel within five court days of receipt of the award. There shall be no extension of this time, unless the moving party makes a request for an extension before the five day period has expired, in writing, and served on both the arbitrator and opposing counsel;

(2) Any response to the motion for attorney fees/statutory costs must be submitted to the arbitrator and served on opposing counsel within five court days after receipt of the motion;

(3) The arbitrator shall render a decision on the motion, in writing, within ten court days after receipt of the motion;

(4) If the arbitrator awards attorney fees/statutory costs, the arbitrator shall file an amended award. If attorney fees are denied, the decision shall be filed and served on the parties;

(5) It is within the arbitrator's discretion to hold a hearing on the issue of attorney fees;

(6) The time for appeal of the arbitrator's decision in any case where attorney fees/statutory costs have been timely requested, as set forth above, shall not run until the service and filing of the amended award, or the denial thereof.

[Adopted effective September 1, 1996; amended effective September 1, 2003; September 1, 2008.]

LMAR 6.2.   FILING OF AWARD

The Clerk shall file all arbitration awards under seal.

A request by an arbitrator for an extension of the time for the filing of an award under MAR 6.2 may be presented to a superior court judge ex parte. The arbitrator shall give the parties notice of an extension granted.

[Adopted effective September 1, 1996. Amended effective September 1, 2015.]

LMAR 7.1.   REQUEST FOR TRIAL DE NOVO—CALENDAR— JURY DEMAND

(a) Assignment of Trial Date. If there is a request for a trial de novo, or the case is otherwise removed from the Mandatory Arbitration calendar, the Court will assign a trial date.

(b) Appeal Period—Attorney Fees. In any case in which a party makes a motion for attorney fees pursuant to LMAR 6.1 (b), the 20–day period for appeal shall not commence until the arbitrator has filed and served either the amended award or the written denial thereof.

(c) Case Schedule. Cases originally governed by a Case Schedule pursuant to LCR 4, 4.1, or 4.1A will again become subject to a Case Schedule if a trial de novo is requested. Promptly after the request for trial de novo is filed, the Court will mail to all parties a Notice of Trial Date together with an Amended Case Schedule, which will govern the case until the trial de novo. The Amended Case Schedule will include the following deadlines:

SCHEDULE	DUE DATE
1. Plaintiff's Disclosure of Lay and Expert Witnesses	1 months
2. Defendant's Disclosure of Lay and Expert Witnesses	3 months
3. Disclosure of Plaintiff's Rebuttal Witnesses	4 months
4. Disclosure of Defendant's Rebuttal Witnesses	5 months
5. Discovery Cutoff	5 ½ months
6. Settlement Position Statement filed by all parties	6 months
7. Last Date for Hearing Dispositive Pretrial Motions	6 months
8. Settlement Conference	6 ½ months
9. Last Date for Filing and Serving Trial Management Report	7 months
10. Pretrial conference	7 months
11. Trial Memoranda, Motions in Limine, Jury Instructions	2 wks. to trial
12. Trial Date	8 months

(d) Jury Demand. The appealing party may file and serve on the other party or parties a jury demand at the same time as the request for a trial de novo. The non-appealing party shall have 14 calendar days after the request for the trial de novo is served on that party to file a jury demand.

[Adopted effective September 1, 1996. Amended effective September 1, 1998; September 1, 2000; September 1, 2003; September 1, 2015.]

LMAR 8.3. EFFECTIVE DATE

Contingent upon funding by the county legislative authority, these rules, as amended, become effective on the first day of January 1997, subject to amendment thereafter. With respect to civil cases pending on that date, if the case has not at that time received a trial date, or if the trial date has been set for later than the first day of April, 1997, any party may serve and file a statement of arbitrability indicating that the case is subject to mandatory arbitration in accordance with the provisions of LMAR 2.1 (a). If, within 10 court days, no party files a response indicating that the case is not subject to arbitration in accordance with the provisions of LMAR 2.1 (b), the case will be transferred to the arbitration calendar. A case set for trial earlier than the first day of April, 1997, will be transferred to arbitration only by stipulation of all parties.

[Adopted effective September 1, 1996; Amended effective September 1, 2003.]

LMAR 8.4. TITLE AND CITATION

These rules are known and cited as the Benton and Franklin Counties Superior Court Local Mandatory Arbitration Rules. LMAR is the official abbreviation.

[Adopted effective September 1, 1996.]

LMAR 8.6. COMPENSATION OF ARBITRATOR

(a) Generally. Arbitrators shall be compensated in the same amount and manner as judges pro tempore of the superior court; provided, however, that said compensation shall not exceed $1,000.00 for any case unless approved by the judge assigned to the arbitration administrative committee. Compensation may be requested for hearing time and reasonable preparation time. Arbitrators may be reimbursed a sum not to exceed $25.00 for costs incurred.

(b) Form. When the award is filed, the arbitrator shall submit to the court administrator a request for payment on a form prescribed by the court.

[Adopted effective September 1, 1996; amended effective September 1, 2009; September 2, 2014.]

LMAR 8.7. ADMINISTRATION

(a) Court Administrator. The court administrator, under the supervision of the Administrative Presiding Judge, shall implement the procedures mandated by these rules and perform any additional duties which may be designated by the Administrative Presiding Judge.

(b) Duties of Administrative Presiding Judge. In the administration of the mandatory arbitration program for Benton and Franklin Counties Superior Court, the Administrative Presiding Judge shall have the power and duty to:

(1) Supervise the Court Administrator in the implementation of mandatory arbitration;

(2) Select and appoint attorneys to the panel of arbitrators;

(3) Remove a person from the panel of arbitrators;

(4) Establish procedures for selecting an arbitrator not inconsistent with the Mandatory Arbitration Rules or these rules, and;

(5) Review the administration and operation of the arbitration program periodically and make changes as he/she deems appropriate to improve the program.

[Adopted effective September 1, 1996. Amended effective September 2, 2014.]

LOCAL CRIMINAL RULES (LCrR)

LCrR 2.3. REVIEW OF SEALED AFFIDAVITS AND SEARCH WARRANTS

(a) Review. The court may review orders sealing search warrants and/or affidavits in support thereof at any time upon the request of the prosecuting attorney or upon motion of the court.

(b) Notice to and Response from Prosecuting Attorney. In each case in which the court reviews a previously entered order sealing a search warrant and/or affidavit in support thereof, the prosecuting attorney will be provided at least 14 days prior written notice of such review. Prior to such review the prosecuting attorney may submit to the court a memorandum generally setting forth the state's position with regard to unsealing all portions of or none of the sealed affidavit and/or search warrant.

(c) Filing of Responsive Memoranda. The original of any memorandum submitted pursuant to subsection (b) will be filed, unsealed, with the order sealing the affidavit and/or search warrant, and the prosecuting attorney will provide a bench copy to the court. The court will consider any requests by the state to seal all or portions of any affidavits or declarations filed in support of the state's memorandum, and, if granted, enter an appropriate order.

(d) Order on Review. After considering the state's position and reviewing in camera the order and the affidavit and/or search warrant sealed pursuant thereto, the court will enter an order that (a) the affidavit and/or search warrant continue to be sealed as previously ordered, (b) designated portions of the affidavit and/or search warrant continue to be sealed and that the remainder thereof be unsealed, or (c) the affidavit and/or search warrant be unsealed.

[Adopted effective September 1, 2004.]

LCrR 3.1. RIGHT TO AND ASSIGNMENT OF COUNSEL

(a) Appointment of Counsel. Defendants who request appointment of counsel may be required to promptly execute a financial disclosure under oath, which shall be filed.

All appointments of counsel by reason of indigence are expressly contingent upon indigence and full disclosure of assets. Where assets are discovered or acquired subsequent to appointment which would indicate that defendant can afford counsel, or if the defendant can afford part payment, fees may be ordered paid, pursuant to the appointment agreement, by the Court.

Upon appointment of counsel for indigent criminal defendants or other litigants, the clerk shall promptly provide counsel with notice of the appointment.

Attorneys representing defendants in criminal cases, except for appointed attorneys, must serve prompt written notice of their appearance upon the prosecuting attorney and file the same with the Clerk of the Court.

Whenever an attorney appears for a defendant in a criminal case at arraignment, the appearance shall be unconditional. No appearance shall be conditioned on payment of fees or for any other reason.

(b) Services Other than Counsel. Pursuant to the authority under CrR 3.1(f), all requests and approval for expert services expenditures are hereby delegated to the Benton and Franklin Counties Office of Public Defense. Upon finding that investigative, expert or other services are necessary to an adequate defense and that defendant is financially unable to obtain them, the Benton and Franklin Counties Office of Public Defense (OPD) shall authorize the services. Where services are denied in whole or in part, the defendant may move for *de novo* review to the Presiding Judge. Should the defendant seek an order sealing the moving papers, defendant shall present, along with the moving papers, a motion and proposed order sealing the documents to the OPD. The OPD shall submit the motion to seal and proposed order with the moving papers regarding request for expert services and the OPD's order on the motion for expert services to the Presiding Judge.

(c) Upon Appeal. In cases involving appeals from another court to the Superior Court in which the defendant wishes counsel to be appointed in the Superior court on the basis of indigence, the following will apply:

(1) The trial attorney shall be responsible for:

(A) Perfecting the appeal to the Superior Court.

(B) Noting the issue of appointment of counsel upon the next criminal motion docket following the perfection of the appeal.

(C) Preparing an affidavit of indigence.

(D) Representing the defendant at such hearing.

(2) The defendant shall be present at the hearing upon the motion to establish indigence.

[Adopted effective April 1, 1986; Amended effective September 1, 2003; September 1, 2009.]

LCrR 3.2. RELEASE OF ACCUSED

(a) Bail and Recognizance. Defendants on bail or recognizance are expected to be available for non-scheduled appearances upon seventy-two (72) hours notice to defendant or defendant's attorney. They are expected to be present and on time at all scheduled appearances concerning which they have received either oral or written notice. Failure to appear in accordance with this rule may result in forfeiture of bail, revocation of recognizance, issuance of a bench warrant for arrest or additional criminal charges.

(b) New Conditions of Release. In the event that bail is forfeited for any reason, new conditions of release must be entered and a new bond posted. No order reinstating a previously forfeited bond shall be issued by the court; however, the court may, for good cause shown, vacate the judgment of forfeiture.

(c) Separate Bond Required. All case filings wherein conditions of release requiring bail are set shall require a separate and distinct bond posted by the surety in the specific amount specified for each case. A bond in the aggregate amount for multiple cases will not be allowed nor shall any order be presented to the court that fails to specify the exact amount of bail for each matter addressed in the order.

(d) Post–Conviction Release. No plea of guilty shall be conditioned upon any agreement concerning the conditions of release provided for in CrR 3.2(f).

[Adopted effective April 1, 1986; Amended effective September 1, 2004; September 1, 2009.]

LCrR 3.4. COURT APPEARANCE OF DEFENDANTS

All preliminary and timely arrangements for the court appearance of any defendant held in custody shall be the responsibility of the Prosecutor in charge of the case.

[Adopted effective April 1, 1986.]

LCrR 4.2. PLEAS AND CONTINUANCES

(a) When Heard. If a criminal case is set for trial, but is to be disposed of by a change of plea, the plea shall be heard on or before the pre-trial hearing unless the court authorizes a continuance until a later date.

(b) Court Commissioners. Superior Court Commissioners appointed under Article 4, Section 23 of the Washington State Constitution are authorized to accept and enter a plea of guilty.

[Adopted effective April 1, 1986; Amended effective September 1, 2000; September 1, 2003.]

LCrR 4.5. OMNIBUS HEARINGS

In every criminal case (except appeals) an omnibus hearing date will be set at the time of arraignment. Normally, it will be set for four (4) weeks from the date of arraignment. At the time of the hearing, it will be expected that defense counsel and Prosecuting Attorney will have already met and disposed of all matters on the omnibus application that can be disposed of and that plea bargaining will have been considered.

If there are any unresolved matters, they will be determined by the Court at the hearing. If it is necessary to hold a suppression hearing, a date certain will be set for such hearing at the time of the omnibus hearing. The defendant shall be present at the omnibus hearing.

If there will be no pre-trial motions or hearings in a case, and all parties agree that an omnibus hearing would not be beneficial, waiver of the hearing may be requested by written stipulation which shall be signed by counsel and defendant. Such a request constitutes an assurance that the case is ready for trial on the date set and that all pre-trial matters have been disposed of.

All rulings of the Court at omnibus hearings or otherwise made in the Criminal Motion Department shall be binding on the parties and shall not be re-litigated at trial.

All briefs, declarations, affidavits, trial briefs, proposed jury instructions, motions, proposed findings of fact and conclusions of law, sentencing position statements, and pre-sentence investigation reports shall be served and filed in the cause. Unless a party does not have access to a computer or the internet, bench copies of all such documents shall be submitted electronically via the internet at http://motion.co.franklin.wa.us/. Parties without access to a computer and the internet shall deliver bench copies to the Court administrator. All bench copies must be submitted not later than nine (9:00) o'clock a.m., one (1) court day prior to the scheduled hearing, proceeding or trial. No bench copies shall be submitted to the Court unless prior thereto or simultaneously therewith a copy thereof has been served upon or mailed to opposing counsel. All paper bench copies will be destroyed one (1) week after the original date noted for hearing unless counsel requests copies be returned with return postage arranged, or unless Court Administration is advised of the new hearing date. When hearings are continued, the parties shall amend the hearing date associated with all bench copies submitted electronically.

[Adopted effective April 1, 1986; amended effective September 1, 2011.]

LCrR 4.9. PRE–TRIAL HEARINGS

(a) General Provisions. In every criminal case, a hearing shall be held for the purpose of determining whether the parties have fully considered the possibility of disposition of the case without trial; for the purpose of entering a plea should a plea be tendered; for considering the matter of requests for continuance; and for any other appropriate matters.

Such hearing shall be mandatory and the defendant's presence at such hearing shall be mandatory.

The hearing shall be set on the criminal law and motion docket (2) dockets prior to the trial date. It shall be the responsibility of each defense attorney, upon receipt of the notice of the trial date, to notify the defendant of this hearing. The failure of the defendant to be present at such hearing (unless the case has been previously disposed of) will result in the revocation of bail or personal recognizance and the issuance of a bench warrant for the defendant's arrest. It may also result in the imposition of the sanctions.

(b) Pleadings. All briefs, memorandums, declarations, affidavits, and motions to be argued or used in connection with a CrR 3.5, CrR 3.6, or other Pre–Trial evidentiary hearing shall be served and filed in the cause. Bench copies shall be submitted in accordance with LCR 5.

(c) Sanctions, Enforcement, and Non–Compliance Hearing. If a party fails to submit electronic bench copies the Court may continue the hearing, impose terms and enter other orders as may be appropriate.

[Adopted effective April 1, 1986; amended effective September 1, 2009; September 2, 2014.]

LCrR 4.11. TRIAL CONFIRMATION

Prosecuting attorneys and defense counsel shall confirm with the Court Administrator's office all criminal jury trials in Benton County no later than 4:00 p.m. on the Thursday prior to the trial date and in Franklin County no later than 12:00 p.m. on the Friday prior to the trial date.

[Adopted effective September 1, 2005; amended effective September 1, 2011.]

LCrR 7.1. PROCEDURE BEFORE SENTENCING

A defendant convicted of a crime shall be sentenced as soon thereafter as possible, consistent with the necessity for securing a pre-sentence report and related diagnostic evaluations, where appropriate. In no case will any order be entered which has the effect of delaying sentencing pending the initiation or completion of a rehabilitative treatment program (as distinguished from a diagnostic evaluation).

[Adopted effective April 1, 1986; Amended effective September 1, 2003.]

LCrR 7.2. SENTENCING

(e) Pre–Sentence Reports. Pre-sentence reports may be ordered by the Court from one or more of the following sources:

(1) The Washington State Office of Adult Probation and Parole.

(2) The Prosecuting Attorney and defense counsel.

All pre-sentence reports should present alternatives to incarceration in those cases in which it may appear that the public security can be accomplished and the defendant's behavior altered by such an alternative.

All pre-sentence reports should indicate the loss or injury to the victim by description and in dollar amounts where applicable.

Immediately upon the Court's ordering of a pre-sentence investigation, the clerk shall notify the Washington State Office of Adult Probation and Parole.

[Adopted effective April 1, 1986.]

LCrR 8.1. JUSTIFICATION OF SURETIES [REPEALED]

[Adopted effective September 1, 2004. Amended effective September 1, 2006. Repealed effective September 1, 2009.]

LOCAL JUVENILE COURT RULES (LJuCr)

TITLE I. GENERAL PROVISIONS, SCOPE AND APPLICATION OF RULES

LJuCr 1.1. SCOPE OF RULES, PURPOSE OF RULES, EFFECTIVE DATE, AMENDMENTS

(A) Scope. These local rules relate to the procedure in the Juvenile Court of Benton and Franklin Counties and shall supplement the State Superior Juvenile Court Rules. These rules shall also govern the policy and administration of the Juvenile Court.

(B) Purpose. The express purpose of the local rules is to develop standardized policy and procedures to ensure the fair and efficient operation of the Benton–Franklin Juvenile Division of the Superior Court of the State of Washington in Benton and Franklin County.

(C) Effective Date. These rules shall take effect on the 1st day of April 1988. All previous existing local Juvenile Court rules are hereby superseded and declared void by the adoption of these rules.

(D) Amendments. The Judges of the Benton–Franklin County Superior Court may from time to time amend these rules.

[Adopted effective April 1, 1988; amended effective September 1, 2003.]

LJuCr 1.6. JUVENILE COURT ADMINISTRATOR DUTIES AND AUTHORITY

(A) Juvenile Court Administrator.

1. In accordance with RCW 13.04.035, the Juvenile Court will be directed by an Administrator who is appointed by the Judges of the Superior Court and shall serve at their pleasure.

2. The Administrator shall direct the Juvenile Court in accordance with the policies and rules of the Judges and shall be directly responsible to the presiding Juvenile Court Judge for all departmental operations and for the carrying out of court rules and policies.

3. The Administrator shall establish written departmental rules and procedures to carry out the statutory duties of the court and to comply with court rules and policy. Such written rules and procedures shall be approved by the Superior Court Judges.

4. In accordance with RCW 13.04.040, the Administrator shall appoint probation counselors who shall serve at the pleasure of the Administrator. The Administrator may also designate a Deputy Administrator subject to concurrence of the Judges.

5. The Administrator shall have the authority to organize the personnel of the department as the Administrator may deem appropriate for the carrying out of the statutory duties of the court and to comply with court rules and policy.

6. The Administrator shall have the authority to administer the approved budget of the department, to contract for expenditures, and authorize payment in accordance with state law and county policy. All contracts are subject to review as to form by the respective County Prosecuting Attorney.

7. The Administrator shall have the authority to establish written working agreements with other agencies in regard to the carrying out of the statutory work of the court. Such written working agreements are subject to review as to form by the respective County Prosecuting Attorney.

8. The Administrator shall, in accordance with RCW 13.04.037, adopt written standards for the regulation and government of the juvenile detention facility and services and shall appoint a detention counselor who shall have charge of the detention facility and shall be responsible to the Administrator for compliance with the adopted detention standards. Such standards shall be reviewed and the detention facilities shall be inspected annually by the Administrator.

9. The Administrator shall establish written departmental rules concerning the assignment and use of all equipment, including all motor vehicles registered or assigned to the Juvenile Court to ensure the equipment is being used for the business of the court and in accordance with state law and county policy.

10. The Administrator shall establish written rules regarding employee working hours and conditions. The Administrator may authorize or prescribe deviations from the normal workday as the business of the court or department may require. The Administrator shall represent the court in any negotiations with employees regarding working conditions, hours and rules.

11. The Administrator shall establish written rules for employee discipline, which may include, but are not limited to, verbal and/or written reprimand, suspension without pay or termination, in accordance with state law and county policy.

12. The Administrator in conjunction with an ad hoc committee comprise of one (1) panel attorney, the prosecuting attorneys or one (1) deputy prosecuting attorney from each county, one (1) attorney from the local Washington State Attorney General Office, a representative from the court's legal process unit and the juvenile court commissioner shall annually review the Juvenile Court policy and rules, the departmental rules and procedures, and the detention standards and facilities and shall prepare and present a written annual report to the Superior Court Judges.

13. The Administrator shall establish and maintain a central record keeping system. Written rules and procedures shall be established governing the record keeping system. Such rules and procedures shall be subject to review by the Judges. Such record keeping system may be computerized.

14. The Administrator shall prepare annually a plan for the Juvenile court, which shall include a proposed budget for the next calendar year.

15. The Administrator shall perform such other duties as required by the Judges.

[Adopted effective April 1, 1988; amended effective September 1, 2005.]

LJuCr 1.7. COURT FORMS

(A) Generally. It shall be the policy of the court to use standardized court forms whenever possible. Pursuant to RCW 13.34.035 standardized forms are required in all dependency matters.

(B) Review. All court forms shall be subject to review by the Judges and Court Commissioners.

[Adopted effective April 1, 1988. Amended effective September 1, 2015.]

LJuCr 1.8. PUBLICATION

(A) Generally. Any party may file with the Clerk of the Court a Motion and Affidavit requesting an Order for the publication of Notice and/or Summons.

(B) Procedure. Upon the issuing of an Order to publish with the Clerk of Court, the Clerk shall forward the notice and summons and order for publication to the newspaper that is named in said order.

1. Upon receipt of an Affidavit of Publication, the Clerk shall file the original affidavit and provide copies to appropriate parties.

(C) Costs. The costs of publication shall be borne by the county.

1. Nothing in this Rule shall prevent the court from ordering a party to reimburse the county for the costs of publication.

[Adopted effective April 1, 1988. Amended effective September 2, 2013.]

LJuCr 1.9. CONTINUANCES

(A) Generally. Continuances or other delays may be granted only as follows:

1. Upon written agreement of the parties, which must be personally signed by counsel representing all the parties and must be approved by the Court.

2. On the motion of a party, the court may continue a juvenile offender matter when required in the due administration of justice and none of the parties to the action will be substantially prejudiced in the presentation of their case.

3. On the motion of a party, the court may continue an action pursuant to RCW 13.32A, RCW 13.34, or RCW 13.50 when good cause is established and none of the parties to the action will be substantially prejudiced in the presentation of their case.

4. The court must state its reasons on the record for granting a motion for a continuance.

5. All continuances shall be to a date certain and confirmed by written order.

(B) Trial Dates/Fact–Finding Hearings. All motions for a continuance of a trial date in offender matters or fact-finding hearings pursuant to RCW 13.32A, RCW 13.34 or RCW 13.50 shall be presented in open court by the moving party.

[Adopted effective April 1, 1988; amended effective September 1, 2005.]

LJuCr 1.10. ISSUANCE AND SERVICE

(A) Generally.

1. Juvenile offenders and their parent(s), guardian(s), or custodian(s) may be served by mail, postage prepaid. The respective Clerk of the Court shall be responsible for the mailing of the necessary documents and for the filing of an Affidavit of Mailing. The respective Prosecuting Attorney's office shall be responsible for the preparation of such documents.

  a. Exceptions. The above procedure shall apply to all offender matters except diversion terminations and community supervision violations. In those matters, juvenile court/diversion unit staff shall be responsible for the preparation of the appropriate documents, including the Notice/Summons.

2. Parties to juvenile dependency, guardianship and termination of parental rights proceedings and matters may be served by certified mail, return receipt requested. The respective Clerk of the Court shall be responsible for the filing of an Affidavit of Mailing and the returned receipt. The Attorney General's Office shall be responsible for preparing the appropriate documents for dependency, guardianship, and termination of parental rights matters.

(B) Failure to Appear on Summons—Offender Matters.

1. If a person fails to appear in response to a Notice/Summons, or if service is not effected within a reasonable time, a warrant for arrest shall be issued. A reasonable time to effect service shall be defined as service within ten (10) days of the filing of the information.

[Adopted effective April 1, 1988. Amended effective September 2, 2013; September 1, 2015.]

LJuCr 1.11. MEDICAL CONSENT AUTHORIZATION

(A) Generally. A request on behalf of a juvenile for medical authorization shall be submitted in writing. The request shall be in petition form, verified, and shall set forth the following, if known:

1. Full name of the child;

2. Date of birth of the child;

3. Child's place of residence;

4. Name of the child's father;

5. Name of the child's mother;

6. The parent's place of birth;

7. Parent's age;

8. Cultural heritage of the child;

9. Whereabouts of the parents, guardian or custodian;

10. The treatment required;

11. The reason for treatment;

12. The necessity of the authorization by the court;

13. Full names and relationship to the child of the petitioner, and;

14. Any other matter which might be relevant.

(B) Emergency Requests. Emergency requests for medical consent authorization may be made by telephone and telephonically approved by the court. A record of such telephonic authorizations shall be made and a written authorization submitted for signature of the court the next judicial day.

(C) Form. An appropriate form may be used to initiate such authorization.

[Adopted effective April 1, 1988; amended effective September 1, 2005.]

LJuCr 1.12. BRIEFS AND OTHER DOCUMENTS

All pleadings [including, motions, briefs, proposed findings of fact and conclusions of law and proposed judgments] pertaining to dependency, termination, guardianship and juvenile criminal proceedings shall be served and filed with the respective Superior Court Clerk. The originals of all ISSP's and GAL Reports shall be submitted to the Court via the Juvenile Legal Process Staff.

Unless a party does not have access to a computer or the Internet, bench copies of all such documents (except as stated herein) shall be submitted electronically via the internet at http://jmotion.co.franklin.wa.us/ for dependency matters, and http://motion.co.franklin.wa.us/ for juvenile criminal matters. When hearings are continued, the parties shall amend the hearing date associated with all bench copies submitted electronically.

Parties without access to a computer and the Internet shall deliver bench copies to the Benton Franklin Counties Juvenile Court Legal Process Staff, 5606 W. Canal Place, Suite 106, Kennewick, WA 99336. All bench copies must be submitted not later than nine (9:00) o'clock a.m. one court day prior to the scheduled hearing, proceeding or trial. No bench copies shall be submitted to the Court unless prior thereto or simultaneously therewith a copy thereof has been served upon or mailed to opposing counsel. All paper bench copies will be destroyed one (1) week after the original date noted for hearing unless counsel requests copies be returned, with return postage arranged, or unless the Legal Process Staff is advised of the new hearing date.

Bench copies of the following documents need not be provided: Notices of hearings, notes for dockets, proposed statements of defendant on plea of guilty, proposed judgments and sentences, probation violation reports, preliminary disposition reports, detention reports, review hearing reports, decline reports, juvenile offender diagnostic/predisposition reports, and proposed orders establishing conditions of release. Bench copies of trial exhibits to be offered in termination trials may, but need not be submitted, and if submitted, may but need not be submitted electronically.

As used in this rule, juvenile probation counselors and staff of the Juvenile Court are not parties. This rule shall not apply to BECCA matters including Children in Need of Services, At–Risk Youth, and Truancy.

Pursuant to GR 30(b)(4) participants in dependency, termination and guardianship are deemed to electronically accept service of all documents as of the time and date the documents are uploaded to jMotion. This does not preclude parties from serving documents as authorized in CR 5. This shall not apply to service of original process.

[Adopted effective September 1, 2012. Amended effective September 2, 2013; September 1, 2015.]

TITLE II. SHELTER CARE PROCEEDINGS

LJuCr 2.3. SHELTER CARE HEARINGS

(A) Generally. A shelter care hearing shall be held in all cases where a child has been taken into custody pursuant to RCW 13.34.060 and/or RCW 26.44.050 and a petition has been filed. The hearing shall be held within 72 hours, excluding weekends and holidays.

1. In all cases initiated by a lay person filing a dependency petition and the taking of a child into custody pursuant to the above-referenced statute, a caseworker shall be assigned to the matter in order to provide a recommendation to the court as to the need for shelter care. Juvenile court staff shall immediately notify the Attorney General's office of any dependency cases initiated by an individual or agency other than the Department of Social and Health Services.

(B) Notice. Notice shall be given to all parties as required by RCW 13.34.060 and JuCr 2.3.

(C) Procedure. At the hearing the court shall:

1. Advise the parties of their rights pursuant to statute and court rules;

2. Enter an order of shelter care and continuing the matter for a contested proceeding.

3. At the contested hearing, the court shall take testimony and/or admit documentary evidence concerning the circumstances for taking the child into custody and the need for shelter care;

4. Consider the recommendation made to the court by the Department of Social and Health Services;

5. Enter an appropriate Order.

[Adopted effective April 1, 1988. Amended effective September 1, 2006.]

LJuCr 2.4. CASE SCHEDULE

At the initial shelter care hearing, case hearing dates and related dates through the disposition hearing will be approved by the Court and entered on the Dependency Order Setting Case Schedule. All parties will be provided a copy of the case schedule at the shelter care hearing.

[Adopted effective September 1, 2003. Amended effective September 1, 2006.]

TITLE III. DEPENDENCY PROCEEDINGS

LJuCr 3.2. DEPENDENCY PETITIONS

(A) Generally. Any person may file a petition alleging a dependency. Each petition shall be verified by the individual filing the petition as including allegations, which are supported by documents and/or statements by third parties. Each petition must contain a statement of facts constituting a dependency, and the names and residence, if known to the petitioner, of the parents, guardian or custodian of the alleged dependent child. A layperson requesting to file a petition shall be initially referred to the Department of Social and Health Services to file a CPS referral for appropriate investigation.

(B) Verification. All petitions shall be verified and contain a statement of facts constituting such dependency.

(C) Upon filing of a dependency petition, the Court will appoint counsel for the parent, guardians or custodians and will appoint counsel or a guardian ad litem for the child. The parent, guardian or custodian must complete the financial statement documents as requested by the court for further court approval of appointment of counsel.

[Adopted effective April 1, 1988. Amended effective September 1, 2006.]

LJuCr 3.3. CASE CONFERENCE

(A) Generally. All parties shall participate in a case conference to address the following issues:

1. Placement of the child;

2. Visitation;

3. Services being recommended for the children and parents;

4. Whether other case issues can be agreed and stipulated to;

5. Whether entry of a dependency fact-finding order is agreed to;

6. Whether disposition order provisions are agreed to; and

7. Any other outstanding issue.

(B) Conference Date. The case conference shall be held within four weeks after the filing of the petition on the date established by the case schedule order.

[Adopted effective September 1, 2003. Amended effective September 1, 2006.]

LJuCr 3.4. TELEPHONE STATUS CONFERENCE

(A) Generally. The court shall conduct a telephonic conference with the attorneys and guardian ad litem, who shall participate to ascertain the status of the case. Issues to be determined will be the accomplishment of service, whether the case conference issues discussed by the parties are agreed or contested, whether any motions are anticipated, and any other outstanding issues.

(B) Agreed Orders. If the parties are in agreement, the process for entering an agreed order will be established.

(C) Contested Issues. If there are contested issues, the parties shall address:

1. Continuances;

2. Trial date, length of trial, and time to be allotted to each party;

3. Discovery matters;

4. Motions;

5. Briefing schedule; and

6. Witnesses and exhibits.

(D) Telephone Status Conference Date. The Court shall schedule the telephone status conference on the date established in the case schedule order. The status conference may be rescheduled for good cause shown.

[Adopted effective September 1, 2003. Amended effective September 1, 2006.]

LJuCr 3.5. UNCONTESTED FACT–FINDING DATE

(A) Generally. Any remaining issues not resolved at the status conferences, including service issues, shall be addressed at the uncontested docket date. Default and agreed orders shall be entered.

(B) Uncontested Docket Date. The uncontested fact-finding hearing shall be held pursuant to the Order Setting Case Schedule.

(C) Witness and Exhibit Lists. On the Friday immediately following the uncontested, fact-finding date, the parties shall exchange witness and exhibit lists. Witness lists shall include the names, addresses, and telephone numbers of the witnesses.

[Adopted effective September 1, 2003. Amended effective September 1, 2006.]

LJuCr 3.6. CONTESTED FACT FINDING HEARINGS

(A) Generally. Unless an agreed order or default order has been entered, the Court shall hold a fact-finding trial as to whether the child is dependent pursuant to statutory definitions.

(B) Hearing Date. Contested fact finding trials shall commence within 75 days of the filing of the petition, unless continued by the Court due to exceptional circumstances. The Court shall initially set the hearing for a three-day trial to be held approximately six weeks after the telephonic status conference.

[Adopted effective September 1, 2003. Amended effective September 1, 2006.]

LJuCr 3.7. DISPOSITION HEARING

(A) Generally. After a child is agreed to be dependent or found by the court to be dependent, a hearing shall be held to address disposition issues, including but not limited to, placement of the child, visitation, and services to be provided to the family during the course of the dependency. A social study, (Individual Service and Safety Plan), consisting of a written evaluation of matters relevant to the disposition of the case shall be made. The study shall include all social records and shall be made available to the court.

(B) Contents. All social study (ISSP) and predisposition reports will address the factors listed in RCW 13.34.120.

(C) Times. All dispositional hearings will be held immediately following the fact-finding hearing unless there is good cause to continue the matter for up to fourteen days. The Court may continue the dispositional hearing longer than fourteen days if there is good cause shown.

1. Reports including the agency's social study and proposed service plan (ISSP) shall be provided and/or mailed to the court, the parties, and counsel no later than ten (10) working days prior to the dispositional hearing.

1.[1] Parties and other respondents shall provide written responses, accompanied by supporting documentation to all matters contained in the ISSP, GAL reports and filed motions of which they have substantial disagreement no later than nine (9:00) o'clock a.m. one court day prior to the review or disposition hearing. Failure to file a written response will not be considered good cause for a continuance.

(D) Initial Review Hearing. The initial review hearing shall be held no later than six (6) months from the initial out of home placement or no more than ninety days from the entry of the disposition order, whichever comes first. The court shall schedule the initial review hearing at the time of the dispositional hearing.

(D)[2] Review Hearing. The court shall schedule a review hearing at the time of the dispositional hearing.

[Formerly LJuCr 3.8, adopted effective April 1, 1988; amended effective September 1, 2003; September 1, 2006; renumbered LJuCr 3.7 and amended effective September 1, 2012.]

1 Numbering as provided in original.

2 Lettering as provided in original.

LJuCr 3.8. DEPENDENCY REVIEW HEARING

(A) Generally. The status of all children found to be dependent shall be reviewed by the court at least every six (6) months at a hearing where it shall be determined whether court supervision should continue. The court shall receive a written evaluation of matters relevant and material to the need for further court supervision and placement of the child.

(B) Sources. A written evaluation may be ordered by the court from the following sources:

1. Department of Social and health Services or related agency; or

2. Any other source that can provide relevant and material information on the issue of the need for further Court supervision and placement of the child.

3. Written responses to the evaluation from the parties will include supporting documentation, if applicable, and will be provided to the court not later than nine (9:00) o'clock a.m. one court day prior a review hearing.

(C) Contents. All written evaluations will address the factors listed in RCW 13.34.130.

(D) Times. All dependency review hearings shall be set as to date and time in open court at the time of the previous hearing.

1. All ISSP's will be provided to the court and counsel no later than ten (10) working days prior to the review hearing.

2. Addenda to ISSP's or GAL reports may be provided to the court and the parties not later than nine (9:00) o'clock a.m. one court day prior to the hearing. Otherwise, the information must be provided to the court verbally at the hearing.

3. Parties and other respondents shall provide written responses, accompanied by supporting documentation, to all matters contained in the ISSP, GAL reports and filed motions of which they have substantial disagreement not later than nine (9:00) o'clock a.m. one court day prior to the review or disposition hearing. Failure to file a written response will not be considered good cause for a continuance.

[Formerly LJuCr 3.9, adopted effective April 1, 1988; amended effective September 1, 2006; renumbered LJuCr 3.8 and amended effective September 1, 2012.]

LJuCr 3.9. GUARDIANSHIP IN JUVENILE COURT

(A) Generally. Any party to a dependency proceeding may file a petition requesting that guardianship be created as to a dependent child pursuant to RCW 13.36.030.

(B) Procedure. Once a petition has been filed with the Clerk of the Court, the petitioner shall:

1. Notify the Department of Social and Health Services;

2. Schedule a date and time for a hearing on the petition and file a Notice and Summons stating such information;

(C) Order. If the court establishes a guardianship pursuant to RCW 13.36.030, et. seq., the court shall enter an Order to that effect that addresses the matters required by statute, including RCW 13.36.050.

[Formerly LJuCr 3.11, adopted effective April 1, 1988. Amended effective September 1, 2006. Renumbered LJuCr

3.9 and amended effective September 1, 2012; September 1, 2015.]

LJuCr 3.10.   FINAL PARENTING PLANS

(A) Generally. Upon the Court granting concurrent jurisdiction from the dependency court, a party to a dependency action may file the necessary pleadings for entry of a final parenting plan in the dependency court, pursuant to RCW 13.34.155 and RCW 26.

(B) Procedure. The procedure to follow shall be posted at the Benton County website at www.co.benton.wa.us.

[Adopted effective September 2, 2013.]

TITLE IV.   PROCEEDINGS TO TERMINATE PARENT–CHILD RELATIONSHIP

LJuCr 4.1.   INVOKING JURISDICTION OF JUVENILE COURT

(A) Generally. Juvenile Court jurisdiction is invoked over a proceeding to terminate a parent-child relationship and to establish a Chapter 13.36 guardianship by filing a petition.

(B) New and Separate Cause Number. All petitions to terminate a parent-child relationship and to establish a Chapter 13.36 guardianship filed with the Court shall be assigned a new and separate cause number, and the respective Superior Court Clerk shall open a file separate from any original dependency file.

[Adopted effective April 1, 1988. Amended effective September 1, 2006; September 2, 2013; September 1, 2015.]

LJuCr 4.2.   PLEADINGS

(A) Petition. All petitions to terminate a parent-child relationship shall contain the elements required in JuCr 3.3, be verified, and shall state the facts and circumstances which underlie each of the allegations required by RCW 13.34.180 and 13.34.190. Petitions involving voluntary relinquishment of parental rights shall attach the relinquishment rights and consent form signed by the parent(s).

(B) Answer. All petitions to terminate a parent-child relationship and to establish a Chapter 13.36 guardianship shall be answered by the parties. All answers shall be in written form and shall conform to the Superior Court Civil Rules. Failure to answer the petition may constitute grounds for entry of termination or guardianship by default in the Juvenile Court's discretion.

[Adopted effective April 1, 1988. Amended effective September 1, 2015.]

LJuCr 4.3.   NOTICE OF TERMINATION HEARING

(A) Generally. Notice of the termination hearing and a copy of the petition shall be served on all parties

in the manner defined by RCW 13.34.070(7) and (8) or published in the manner defined by RCW 13.34.080. Notice of the date and time of the termination hearing and any pre-trial hearings shall be sent to all parties in the manner defined by RCW 13.34.070(7) and (8) if their addresses or location can be ascertained.

(B) Indian Children. If the petitioner knows or has reason to know that the child involved is a member of an Indian tribe, the petitioner shall notify the child's tribe in the manner required by RCW 13.34.070(10), 25 U.S.C. 1912 and 13.38.070.

[Adopted effective April 1, 1988. Amended effective September 1, 2015.]

LJuCr 4.4.   DISCOVERY IN PROCEEDINGS TO TERMINATE PARENT–CHILD RELATIONSHIP

(A) Generally. Discovery shall be conducted according to the Superior Court Civil Rules. Witness lists and exhibit lists shall be provided per the Order Setting Case Schedule. Failure to provide a witness list may result in sanctions in the discretion of the Juvenile Court.

[Adopted effective April 1, 1988. Amended effective September 1, 2015.]

LJuCr 4.5.   SCHEDULING THE TERMINATION HEARING OF PARENTAL RIGHTS HEARING/PRE–TRIAL HEARING

(A) At the initial hearing, case hearing dates and related dates through the trial date will be approved by the Court and entered on the Termination Order Setting Case Schedule. All parties will be provided a copy of the case schedule at the initial hearing

[Adopted effective April 1, 1988. Amended effective September 1, 2006.]

TITLE V.   PROCEEDINGS FOR ALTERNATIVE RESIDENTIAL PLACEMENT [RESCINDED]

LJuCr 5.2.   ALTERNATE RESIDENTIAL PLACEMENT PETITIONS [RESCINDED]

[Rescinded effective September 1, 2015.]

LJuCr 5.6.   DISPOSITION HEARING [RESCINDED]

[Rescinded effective September 1, 2015.]

LJuCr 5.7.   REVIEW HEARINGS; ALTERNATIVE RESIDENTIAL PLACEMENTS [RESCINDED]

[Rescinded effective September 1, 2015.]

TITLE VI.   JUVENILE OFFENSE PROCEEDINGS DIVERSION AGREEMENTS

LJuCr 6.6.   TERMINATION/MODIFICATION OF DIVERSION AGREEMENTS

(A) Generally. Diversion unit(s) shall have the authority to file with the Clerk of the Court a petition and affidavit alleging a substantial violation of a juvenile's diversion agreement and seek termination or modification of the agreement.

(B) Procedure. Once the petition and affidavit alleging violation of a juvenile's diversion agreement has been filed, the diversion unit shall immediately inform the respective Prosecuting Attorney's Office and the appropriate Juvenile Court unit to ensure the matter is scheduled and all appropriate parties are notified of the hearing date, time and place.

1. The diversion unit will prepare a written report on the alleged violations. Copies will be provided to all appropriate parties.

2. A representative of the diversion unit familiar with the particular case will be present at such hearing.

(C) Issuance of Notice/Summons. The Clerk of the Court shall be delegated the authority to issue Notice/Summons pursuant to a petition to terminate/modify a diversion agreement without the need for a formal order from the court.

[Adopted effective April 1, 1988.]

TITLE VII.   JUVENILE OFFENSE PROCEEDINGS IN JUVENILE COURT

LJuCr 7.3.   DETENTION AND RELEASE

(A) Generally. No juvenile offender or alleged juvenile offender will be released from court-ordered detention unless a written Order to that effect has been approved by the parties and signed by a Court Commissioner or Superior Court Judge.

(B) Procedure. The Juvenile Court detention staff, probation counselors and Prosecuting Attorneys will establish written procedures to be followed. Such procedures will be subject to review by the judges.

[Adopted effective April 1, 1988.]

LJuCr 7.6.   ARRAIGNMENT AND PLEAS

(A) Generally. Unless waived pursuant to these rules, an arraignment hearing shall be held no later than twenty-one (21) days after the information is filed. Attendance by the alleged juvenile offender is mandatory. At arraignment, the juvenile shall be arraigned on the charges set forth in the information. If a juvenile is detained, his/her arraignment hearing shall be held no later than fourteen (14) days after the information is filed.

(B) Procedure.

1. The juvenile and his/her counsel shall review, prepare and complete the following forms and present them to the court at the hearing:

   a. Juvenile's Acknowledgement of Advisement of Rights; and

   b. Juvenile's Notice/Advisement of Records.

2. At arraignment, the court shall:

   a. Appoint or confirm assignment of counsel;

   b. Confirm the juvenile is aware of his/her rights; and the record provisions of RCW 13.50;

   c. Take a plea from the juvenile of either guilty, not guilty or not guilty by reason of insanity;

   d. Determine if discovery has been given; and

   e. Set the next appropriate court date.

3. *Group Arraignments.* The court may advise juvenile respondents of their rights and explain the record provisions of RCW 13.50 in a group proceeding. All other portions of the arraignment shall be accomplished individually.

(C) Name and Date of Birth. The juvenile respondent shall be asked his/her true name and date of birth. If the juvenile alleges that his/her true name and/or date of birth is other than indicated on the information, it shall be entered in the Minutes of the court and subsequent proceedings shall be had against the respondent by the indicated name and date of birth.

(D) Reading. The information shall be read to the juvenile respondent, unless the reading is waived, and a copy shall be provided to the respondent and his/her counsel.

[Adopted effective April 1, 1988; amended effective September 1, 2005.]

LJuCr 7.7. PLEAS OF GUILTY

(A) Generally. When a case has been set for trial, the attorney for the juvenile respondent should give the prosecutor notice of confirmation of trial or change of plea not less than three (3) court days before the trial date. Similar notice shall be given to the Juvenile Court staff.

(B) Procedure. The juvenile respondent and his/her counsel shall prepare and complete a Statement of Juvenile on Plea of Guilty before appearing in court. The juvenile respondent and his/her counsel shall present the completed statement to the court. After receiving the completed statement, the court shall conduct a detailed inquiry addressing:

1. The meaning and effect of a plea of guilty;

2. The elements of the offense alleged;

3. The juvenile's acknowledgement of his/her guilty on each and every element of the offense alleged;

4. The standard sentencing range and the maximum punishment for the offense alleged;

5. The juvenile's understanding of and the meaning of the prosecutor's recommendation; and

6. Any other appropriate matters.

Upon acceptance of the plea, the court shall have the juvenile respondent sign the statement in open court. The statement shall be filed with the Clerk of the Court.

(C) Withdrawal of Plea of Guilty. A motion to withdraw a plea of guilty may be made only before sentence is imposed and upon a showing of good cause. The court may set aside an Order of Disposition and permit a juvenile respondent to withdraw his/her plea of guilty to correct an injustice.

(D) Form. The Statement of Juvenile on Plea of Guilty will conform substantially with JuCr 7.7.

[Adopted effective April 1, 1988.]

LJuCr 7.12. DISPOSITIONAL HEARING— OFFENDER PROCEEDINGS

(A) Time. If the respondent pleads guilty or is found guilty of the allegations in the information, the court shall enter its findings upon the record and proceed immediately to the disposition unless:

1. The court believes additional information is necessary, or

2. The court believes additional time is needed to determine an appropriate custody or living situation, or

3. Commitment is to be considered and additional time is necessary to seek alternatives, or

4. The court deems a continuance is otherwise necessary.

(B) Sources. Predispositional reports may be ordered by the court from one or more of the following sources:

1. The Benton–Franklin County Juvenile court staff;

2. The Prosecuting Attorney;

3. The defense counsel; and

4. Any other source that can provide relevant and material information on the issue off an appropriate disposition.

(C) Form. All predispositional reports will address the various factors required by RCW 13.40.150. All predispositional reports should present alternatives to commitment in those cases, which it may appear that public security can be accomplished, and the offender's behavior altered by such an alternative. All reports shall be provided to the court and counsel no later than one (1) day prior to the dispositional hearing.

(D) Community Diagnostic Evaluation. A diagnostic evaluation may be ordered by the court after a showing that such an evaluation is necessary and will aid the court in reaching an appropriate disposition.

(E) Restitution. All predispositional reports shall indicate the loss or injury to the victim by description and dollar amount. It will be the duty of the predispositional report writer to ascertain the necessary information and make a recommendation to the court as to a juvenile's ability to make full or partial restitution. The court shall fix the amount of restitution at the dispositional hearing.

(F) Court Costs, Attorney's Fees and Victim's Assessment. The predispositional report writer shall make a recommendation to the court as to a juvenile's ability to reimburse the county for any court costs, fees for court-appointed counsel and the victim assessment fee.

(G) Manifest Injustice Findings. If the court imposes a sentence based upon a finding of manifest injustice, the court shall set forth those portions of the record material to the disposition.

[Adopted effective April 1, 1988; amended effective September 1, 2005.]

LJuCr 7.15. MOTIONS—JUVENILE OFFENSE PROCEEDINGS

(A) Generally. All motions, including motions to suppress evidence, motion regarding admissions, and other motions requiring testimony, shall be heard at the time of trial unless otherwise set by the Court, together with a brief which shall include a summary of the facts upon which the motions are based, not later than five (5) days before the adjudicatory hearing. Reply briefs shall be served and filed with the Court no later than noon of the Court day before the hearing.

(B) To Dismiss for Delay in Referral of Offense. The Court may dismiss information if it is established that there has been an unreasonable delay in referral of the offense to the Court. For purposes of this rule, a delay of more than thirty (30) days from the date of completion of the police investigation of the offense to the time of filing of the charge shall be deemed prima facie evidence of an unreasonable delay. Upon a prima facie showing of unreasonable delay, the Court shall then determine whether or not dismissal or other appropriate sanction will be imposed. Among those factors otherwise considered, the Court shall consider the following:

1. The length of the delay;

2. The reason for the delay;

3. The impact of the delay on ability to defend against the charge; and

4. The seriousness of the alleged offense.

Unreasonable delay shall constitute an affirmative defense which must be raised by motion not less than one (1) week before trial. Such motion may be considered by affidavit.

[Adopted effective April 1, 1988; amended effective September 1, 2005.]

LJuCr 7.16. BAIL

(A) Generally. All juveniles held in detention on probable cause shall have the right to have bail addressed in their first court appearance. If bail is granted, it may be posted by either cash or bond. The juvenile will be released from detention to an approved party only on the referral or cause number for which bail is posted. The court may impose additional conditions of release pursuant to RCW 13.40.040(4).

(B) Procedure. The following steps shall be followed:

1. The issue of bail shall be first addressed at the first appearance hearing.

2. If bail is authorized by the Court, it shall be posted with the respective County Clerk during normal business hours or with the Benton–Franklin Counties Detention Center when the respective County Clerk's Office is closed. Prior to release, the juvenile shall be advised of the next hearing date, any other conditions of release and that failure to appear may result in bail forfeiture and prosecution for bail jumping. When a bond is filed with the Clerk of the Court in Benton or Franklin County, the Clerk in the respective County shall issue a certified copy of the original bond to juvenile detention.

3. A juvenile detainee will not be released from detention unless detention staff has physical possession of the certified copy of the original bond from the Clerk of the Court, a verified receipt for posted bail from the Clerk of the Court or an original authorized bond or cash bail is posted with detention during hours that the County Clerk's Office is closed.

4. Pursuant to the provisions of RCW 13.40.056, when bail is posted, by bond or by cash, ten dollars of the amount posted as bail shall be collected in cash as a nonrefundable bail fee.

(C) Forms. Forms for this procedure shall be subject to review by the judges.

[Adopted effective April 1, 1988. Amended effective September 1, 2006; September 2, 2013.]

LJuCr 7.17. BENCH WARRANTS

(A) Generally. Upon proper application to the court, a bench warrant may be issued for a juvenile:

1. Who, without justification, fails to appear at a scheduled court hearing after receiving proper notice;

2. Who is alleged to have violated the terms of his/her community supervision;

3. Who is alleged to have violated the terms of his/her release of detention; and

4. Any other appropriate situation.

(B) Procedure. Once an Order to issue a bench warrant has been approved by the court, the Clerk of the respective Court shall issue the warrant for the arrest of the named juvenile:

1. The warrant may be served by law enforcement officers or by probation counselors pursuant to RCW 13.04.040(5).

[Adopted effective April 1, 1988. Amended effective September 2, 2013.]

LJuCr 7.18. VIOLATIONS OF COMMUNITY SUPERVISION

(A) Generally. Probation counselors shall have the authority to file with the respective Clerk of the Court a motion and affidavit alleging a violation of community supervision.

(B) Procedure. Once the motion and affidavit alleging a violation of community supervision has been filed, the probation counselor shall contact the appropriate juvenile court unit to ensure the matter is scheduled and all appropriate parties are notified of the hearing date, time and place.

1. The probation counselor shall prepare a written report of the alleged violations. Copies will be provided to all appropriate parties no later than one (1) day prior to the hearing.

2. The probation counselor shall be present at such hearing to respond to questions concerning the matter.

(C) Absconding From Placement. All juvenile respondents placed on community supervision shall strictly follow the terms and conditions of his/her probation contract as well as any instructions of his/her probation counselor, including placement. If a juvenile respondent voluntarily and without authority absents himself/herself from a placement pursuant to the terms of his/her community supervision, this will be deemed a violation of the juvenile's community supervision and is sufficient grounds for a warrant of arrest to be issued.

1. A juvenile respondent placed in confinement as a result of a warrant of arrest issued pursuant to this rule shall not be released unless ordered by the court.

(D) Warrants. The court may order a warrant for the arrest of a juvenile respondent. A warrant may be served by law enforcement or a probation counselor.

(E) Guidelines. The following guidelines are established for probation counselors with respect to alleged violations of community supervision:

1. A minor or technical violation and the respondent's whereabouts are known: file the appropriate motion and have the respective Clerk of the Court issue a Summons.

2. A serious violation of the criminal law or condition of community supervision and the respondent's whereabouts are known: immediate arrest by law enforcement or probation counselor followed by filing the appropriate motion and schedule of detention hearing.

3. A violation of the criminal code or condition of community supervision and the respondent's whereabouts are unknown: file the appropriate motion and request the issuance of a warrant.

(F) Issuance of Notice/Summons. The respective Clerk of the Court shall be delegated the authority to issue Notice/Summons pursuant to a motion alleging violations of community supervision without the need for a formal order from the court.

[Adopted effective April 1, 1988. Amended effective September 2, 2013.]

TITLE VIII. DECLINING JUVENILE COURT JURISDICTION OVER AN ALLEGED JUVENILE OFFENDER

LJuCr 8.3. DECLINING JUVENILE COURT JURISDICTION OVER AN ALLEGED JUVENILE OFFENDER

(A) Generally. In accordance with RCW 13.40.110 and Juvenile Court Rule 8.1, any party may file an appropriate motion and supporting affidavit to decline jurisdiction with the respective Clerk of the Court.

(B) Report. A declination investigation report shall be prepared by the juvenile court staff.

The report shall:

1. Address the following factors:

a. The seriousness of the alleged offense to the community and whether the protection of the community requires waiver of juvenile court jurisdiction;

b. Whether the alleged offense was committed in an aggressive, violent, premeditated or willful manner;

c. Whether the alleged offense was against persons or against property;

d. The prosecutive merit of the complaint;

e. The desirability of trial and disposition of the entire offense in one court;

f. The sophistication and maturity of the juvenile as determined by consideration of his home, environmental situation, emotional attitude and pattern of living;

g. The record and previous history of the juvenile, including previous contacts with law enforcement agencies, juvenile courts and other jurisdictions, prior periods of probation/community supervision, or prior commitments to juvenile institutions;

h. The prospects for adequate protection of the public and the likelihood of reasonable rehabilitation of the juvenile (if he is found to have committed the alleged offense) by the use of procedures, services and facilities currently available to the juvenile court.

2. Address any other factors relevant to the motion; and

3. Make a recommendation to the court as to the motion.

(C) Hearing. The writer of the declination investigation report will be present at the declination hearing to testify, if so requested.

[Adopted effective April 1, 1988. Amended effective September 2, 2013.]

TITLE IX. RIGHT TO LAWYER AND EXPERTS IN ALL JUVENILE COURT PROCEEDINGS

LJuCr 9.2. RIGHT TO COUNSEL

(A) Appointments. Legal counsel shall be provided at the expense of the county in the following circumstances:

1. *For a Juvenile Respondent:*

   a. Alleged to be a juvenile offender;

   b. Alleged to have violated the terms of his/her community supervision;

   c. Who may be a party to a diversion agreement who has not waived his right to counsel, and who requests counsel be appointed for the purpose of advising him as to whether he desires to participate in the diversion process or to decline to participate;

   d. When the Prosecuting Attorney or diversion unit has filed a petition to terminate or modify a diversion agreement;

   e. When a dependency petition has been filed alleging the child to be dependent pursuant to RCW 13.34.040, and the child is eight (8) years of age or older and a guardian ad litem has not been appointed to represent the best interests of the child;

   f. When a review hearing is to be held pursuant to RCW 13.32A or RCW 13.34, and the child is eight (8) years of age or older and a guardian ad litem has not been appointed to represent the best interests of the child;

   g. When a petition to terminate the rights of the parent or parents of the juvenile has been filed and the child is eight (8) years of age or older and a guardian ad litem has not been appointed to represent the vest[1] interests of the child;

   h. When a petition asking for the creation of a guardianship over the child has been filed pursuant to RCW 13.36, and the child is eight (8) years of age or older and a guardian ad litem has not been appointed to represent the best interests of the child.

2. *For a Parent, Guardian or Custodian:*

   a. Who is a party to a:

   (1) Dependency proceeding;

   (2) Proceeding for the termination of the parent-child relationship;

   (3) Proceeding pursuant to RCW 13.40 and a juvenile under the age of twelve for whom a parent, guardian or custodian is responsible is requesting to waive a right or object to a proceeding;

   (4) Proceeding pursuant to RCW 13.36 requesting a guardianship be created;

   (6)[2] Proceeding and who requests that the court appoint counsel because of an inability to obtain counsel due to financial hardship and the court finds the party indigent.

3. Whenever ordered by the court.

(B) Retained Counsel. Any party may be represented by retained counsel in any proceeding before the Juvenile Court.

(C) Procedure for Appointment of Counsel. At or prior to the initial appearance of the parties, the court or a representative of the court may inquire as to the financial status of any party who requests counsel to be appointed. Upon the filing of a motion and affidavit for assignment of a lawyer by a party, the court may schedule a hearing on the subject of the parents, guardian, or custodian and/or the child's ability to pay all or part of the expense of counsel. Upon a finding that the party requesting appointment of counsel is indigent, the court shall appoint counsel. If it appears that the party can partially afford counsel, the court shall appoint counsel but may direct that the party pay an amount certain to the Clerk of the Court.

1. An appropriate form may be used to determine the financial status of a party.

(D) Notice of Appearance. Attorneys, representing parties in juvenile matters, except for appointed attorneys, must serve prompt written notice of their appearance upon all other parties or their counsel of record, the legal process unit of the court and file the same with the Clerk of the Court.

(E) Recovery of County Expense for Appointed Counsel. Nothing in this rule shall prevent the court from ordering, as a condition of community supervision, that juvenile offenders pay court costs and fees for court-appointed counsel.

[Adopted effective April 1, 1988. Amended effective September 1, 2005; September 1, 2015.]

1 So in original.

2 So in original.

LJuCr 9.4. APPOINTMENT OF NON-LAWYER GUARDIAN AD LITEM

(A) Generally. It shall be the policy of the court to appoint a non-lawyer guardian ad litem for a juvenile in lieu of an attorney in all proceedings other than offender matters involving juveniles under the age of eight (8) years. The court may appoint a non-lawyer guardian ad litem in lieu of or in addition to an attorney in all proceedings other than offender matters involving juveniles who are eight (8) years of age or older. A guardian ad litem is deemed a party to the proceeding upon appointment.

(B) Procedure.

1. *Dependency/Guardianship/Termination Proceedings.* The court may appoint a guardian ad litem for a child after the court has entered a finding of dependency pursuant to RCW 13.34 or at any other appropriate stage of a proceeding. In cases involving more than one child from the same family unit, the court may appoint one guardian ad litem to represent the interests of all the children.

2. *Other Proceedings.* The court may appoint a guardian ad litem when it deems such an appointment necessary.

(C) Role. The guardian ad litem shall be an advocate on behalf of and in the best interests of the child. The guardian ad litem shall serve as a participant in court proceedings. A guardian ad litem shall be entitled to full access to all parties and relevant records and to receive notice as a party.

(D) Certification. No guardian ad litem shall be appointed to represent a child until he/she has successfully completed an approved training course supervised by the court and administered an oath of office by the court. A guardian ad litem shall be free of influence from anyone interested in the result of the proceeding.

(E) Reports. In all proceedings, the guardian ad litem shall submit a written report to the court addressing all relevant factors and making a recommendation to the court as to an appropriate disposition in the best interests of the child. All reports submitted by a guardian ad litem will be provided to the court and parties no later than ten (10) days prior to the scheduled hearing. A report received within five (5) days of a hearing may constitute good cause of a continuance if a party requests a continuance.

(F) Representation by Attorney. A guardian ad litem may be represented by an attorney.

[Adopted effective April 1, 1988. Amended effective September 1, 2008; September 1, 2015.]

TITLE X.   JUVENILE COURT RECORDS

LJuCr 10.2. RECORDING JUVENILE COURT PROCEEDINGS

(A) Generally. All proceedings in the Benton-Franklin County Superior Court Juvenile Division shall be recorded unless waived pursuant to statute.

1. The electronic recording devise installed at the court is approved for all hearings and for all purposes.

(B) Request for Transcript. Upon written motion by any party to a proceeding, the court may order a written verbatim transcript to be prepared. The individual preparing the transcript shall certify that it accurately reflects the electronic record of the proceeding.

1. *Dependency, Guardianship, or Termination of Parental Rights, Proceedings.* All written verbatim transcripts prepared for proceedings involving dependent children, or termination of parental rights proceedings shall be sealed. An individual make[1] inspect such a transcript only after obtaining written court order.

[Adopted effective April 1, 1988. Amended effective September 1, 2015.]

[1] So in original.

LJuCr 10.3. INSPECTION/RELEASE OF INFORMATION

(A) Generally. All records, other than the official court record, are confidential and may be released only as provided in state statute and court rule. All requests for information shall be made in writing. Such requests shall state the reason for the inspection or release of information and all parties to the underlying cause shall be provided written notice of the request by the requesting party.

(B) Procedure.

1. *Juvenile Offender Matters.* The agency receiving the written request shall refer the written request to the originating agency of the records. The agency will review the request and decide if the request is proper pursuant to statute and court rule. The requesting party shall be notified in writing as to the appropriateness of his/her request by the originating agency.

2. *Juvenile Dependency/Termination of Parental Rights Matters.* The agency receiving the written request shall refer the written request to the originating agency. The agency will review the request and decide if the request is proper pursuant to statute and court rule. The requesting party shall be notified in writing as to the appropriateness of his/her request by the originating agency.

(C) Release. Only complete information will be released.

(D) Research Requests. Requests for information concerning legitimate research for educational, scientific or public purposes may be approved by the court if:

1. The individual or agency is engaged in legitimate research for educational, scientific or public purposes; and

2. The anonymity of all person mentioned in the records/information will be preserved.

3. The juvenile court administrator shall establish written policy and procedure addressing research requests.

[Adopted effective April 1, 1988. Amended effective September 1, 2015.]

LJuCr 10.10. NOTICE AND ADVISEMENT JUVENILE OFFENDER RECORDS

(A) **Generally.** Any juvenile to whom the record provisions of RCW 13.50.050 may apply shall be given written notice of his or her rights under the referenced statute.

(B) **Procedure.** The following procedure shall be followed:

1. In the case of a juvenile offender, a written form signed by the juvenile in which a juvenile is advised of rights pursuant to RCW 13.50.050 and acknowledges being so advised shall be filed with the Clerk of the Court at the time of his or her arraignment.

2. In the case of a juvenile referred to a diversion unit, a similar written form as in the above paragraph shall be signed by the juvenile and filed as part of the diversion agreement.

[Adopted effective April 1, 1988.]

TITLE XI. SUPPLEMENTAL PROVISIONS [RESERVED]

DISTRICT COURT
BENTON COUNTY DISTRICT COURT LOCAL COURT RULES

**Including Amendments Received Through
August 15, 2015**

Table of Rules

BCDCR 3.1. SERVICES OTHER THAN LAWYER

Pursuant to the authority under CrRLJ 3.1(f), all requests and approval for expert services expenditures are hereby delegated to the Benton County Office of Public Defense (OPD). Upon finding that investigative, expert or other services are necessary to an adequate defense and that the defendant is financially unable to obtain them, the OPD shall authorize the services. Where services are denied in whole or in part, the defendant may move for de novo review to the Presiding Judge. Should the defendant seek an order sealing the moving papers, defendant shall present, along with the moving papers, a motion and proposed order sealing the documents to the OPD. The OPD shall submit the motion to seal and proposed order with the moving papers regarding request for expert services and the OPD's order on the motion for expert services to the Presiding Judge. The motion may be made ex-parte. All compensation for investigative, expert or other services shall be paid by the OPD.

[Adopted effective September 1, 2015.]

BCDIR 3.5. DECISION ON WRITTEN STATEMENTS

A person who has received a traffic or civil infraction may request by mail or e-mail to mitigate their traffic infraction. Mitigation hearings based on written statements may be heard in chambers.

This court does not accept written statements for contested infractions.

[Adopted effective September 1, 2011.]

CHELAN COUNTY

Table of Courts

Superior Court

Local Rules for the Superior Court of the State of Washington for Chelan County.

District Court

Local Rules for the District Court of the State of Washington for Chelan County.

Municipal Courts

Chelan Municipal Court Local Rules.

SUPERIOR COURT

LOCAL RULES FOR THE SUPERIOR COURT OF THE STATE OF WASHINGTON FOR CHELAN COUNTY

Including Amendments Received Through
August 15, 2015

Table of Rules

PREFACE

1. Promulgation. These rules shall be known as the Local Rules for the Superior Court of the State of Washington for Chelan County. Copies of these rules will be filed with the Clerk of Court for Chelan County and will be distributed to all law offices in Chelan and Douglas Counties. Additional copies will be available at the office for the Clerk for Chelan County. These rules shall be effective September 1, 2011 and supersede all prior rules of this court.

2. Numbering. Consistent with CR 83(a), Washington Court Rules, these rules conform in numbering system and in format to those rules and facilitate the use of both. The number of each rule is preceded by the abbreviation such as "LR," designating the rule as local to this court and supplemental to the corresponding Washington Court Rule.

[Adopted effective September 1, 1999; amended effective September 1, 2000; September 1, 2001; September 1, 2002.; September 1, 2011; September 1, 2015.]

LOCAL RULES

LR .01. COURTROOM SAFETY

No person (except for duly and regularly commissioned law enforcement officers of the State of Washington and other states of the United States of America not appearing on their own family law matter) shall be on the Fifth Floor of the Chelan County Regional Law and Justice Center, Juvenile Justice Center or Auditorium (when being used for court purposes) while armed with ANY firearm or taser or explosive device or any knife having a blade length of more than three inches or any billyclub, blackjack, truncheon or bat, nor shall any such person be in any of the fore-mentioned areas while possessing any gas gun or other device used for the spraying of tear gas, mace or other noxious chemical substance, nor any incendiary device.

Any person found having any of the articles or devices heretofore mentioned which are banned from the fifth floor of the Chelan County Regional Law and Justice Center, Juvenile Justice Center and Auditorium (when being used for court purposes) is subject to having such articles or devices seized by law enforcement officers, bailiffs on court order, or as otherwise directed by the Court.

Any person violating this rule shall be subject to punishment for contempt of court and prosecuted under RCW 9.41.300.

[Former LR 1 Adopted effective September 1, 1999; renumbered effective September 1, 2002; amended effective September 1, 2004.]

LR. 02.   PRESIDING JUDGE

(a) Election.   The judges of the superior court shall elect a presiding judge and assistant presiding judge as required by GR 29. The first election shall occur on or before July 1, 2002. Each succeeding election shall occur on or before January 1 of even-numbered years, beginning with 2004. The election shall be conducted at a meeting of all judges of the district by open vote.

(b) Term.   The term of the presiding judge and assistant presiding judge shall be for two years commencing on January 1 of the year in which the term begins. The term of the initial presiding judge pursuant to this rule shall be from date of election until December 31, 2003.

(c) Vacancies.   Interim vacancies of the office of presiding judge or assistant presiding judge shall be filled as provided in LGR 29(a).

(d) Executive Committee.   The two judges not serving as presiding judge and the court administrator shall constitute an executive committee to advise the presiding judge. The responsibilities of the presiding judge, as set forth in GR 29, may be shared with members of the executive committee.

[Adopted effective September 1, 2002; amended effective September 1, 2015.]

LR 5.   SERVICE AND FILING OF PLEADINGS AND OTHER PAPERS

(d) Filing.

(5) *Documents Not to be Filed.*   Photocopies of reported cases, statutes or texts shall not be filed as an appendix to a brief or otherwise but shall be furnished directly to the judge hearing the matter.

Documents or copies thereof produced during discovery and other items, which should properly be received as exhibits rather than as a part of the court file shall not be included in the court file.

(6) *Case Information Cover Sheet.*   Each new civil and domestic case filing shall be accompanied by a Case Information Cover Sheet prepared and submitted by the party filing said new civil or domestic case. Attached as Exhibit A to this rule is the form of the Case Information Cover Sheet.

(7) *Electronic Filing of Documents.*   Electronic filing of documents shall be permitted provided that the electronic transmission of documents is done in a manner approved by the Superior Court Clerk.

(A) Signatures: Use of electronic filing by a party or attorney shall constitute compliance CR11's signature requirement. A printed copy of the electronically filed document with original signatures shall be maintained by the filing party and made available for inspection by other parties or the Court upon request. Documents containing signatures of third-parties (i.e., unopposed motions, affidavits, stipulations, etc.) may also be filed electronically by indicating in the original signatures are maintained by the filing party in paper-format.

(B) Time for Filing and Effect of Use of Efiling: Any pleading filed electronically shall be considered as filed with the Court when transmission is completed ("authorized date and time"). Any document Efiled with the Court by 5:00 PT shall be deemed filed with the Court on that date.

(C) Form of Documents Electronically Filed: All electronically filed pleadings shall be formatted in accordance with the applicable rules governing formatting of paper pleadings.

(D) Payment Of Statutory Filing Fees: All statutory filing fees shall be collected and paid for electronically filed documents according to the then current methods approved by the Clerk of the Chelan County Superior Court.

[Adopted effective September 1, 1999; amended effective September 1, 2001.]

LR 5 EXHIBIT A.   CASE INFORMATION COVER SHEET

Case Information Cover Sheet

Case Number _____   Case Title _____

Attorney Name _____   Bar Membership Number _____

Please check the <u>one</u> category that best describes this case for indexing purposes. Accurate case indexing not only saves time in docketing new cases, but also helps in forecasting needed judicial resources. Cause of action definitions are listed on the back of this form. Thank you for your cooperation.

APPEAL/REVIEW
- _____ Administrative Law Review (ALR 2)
- _____ Civil, Non-Traffic (LCA 2)
- _____ Civil, Traffic (LCI 2)

CONTRACT/COMMERCIAL
- _____ Breach of Contract (COM 2)
- _____ Commercial Contract (COM 2)
- _____ Commercial Non-Contract (COL 2)
- _____ Third Party Collection (COL 2)

DOMESTIC RELATIONS
- _____ Annulment/Invalidity (INV 3)
- _____ Child Custody (CUS 3)
- _____ Dissolution with Children (DIC 3)
- _____ Dissolution with no Children (DIN 3)
- _____ Legal Separation (SEP 3)
- _____ Mandatory Wage Assignment (MWA 3)
- _____ Modification (MOD 3)
- _____ Out-of-State Custody (OSC 3)
- _____ Reciprocal, Respondent in County (RIC 3)
- _____ Reciprocal, Respondent Out of County (ROC 3)

JDGMENT 1
- _____ Abstract Only (ABJ 2)
- _____ Foreign Judgment (FJU 2)
- _____ Judgment, Another County (ABJ 2)
- _____ Judgment, Another State (FJU 2)
- _____ Tax Warrant (TAX 2)
- _____ Transcript of Judgment (TRJ 2)

MENTAL ILLNESS
- _____ Alcoholic Treatment (ALT 6)
- _____ Mental Illness—Adult (MI 6)
- _____ Mental Illness—Juvenile (MIJ 6)

OTHER COMPLAINT/PETITION
- _____ Action to Compel/Confirm Private Binding Arbitration (MSC 2)
- _____ Change of Name (CHN 2)
- _____ Civil Harassment (HAR 2)
- _____ Deposit of Surplus Funds (MSC 2)
- _____ Domestic Violence (DVP 2)
- _____ Injunction (INJ 2)
- _____ Interpleader (MSC 2)
- _____ Minor Settlement (No guardianship) (MST 2)
- _____ Subpoenas (MSC 2)

PATERNITY/ADOPTION
- _____ Adoption (ADP 5)
- _____ Paternity (PAT 5)
- _____ Relinquishment (REL 5)
- _____ Termination of Parent-Child Relationship (TER 5)

PROBATE/GUARDIANSHIP
- _____ Absentee (ABS 4)
- _____ Disclaimer (DSC 4)
- _____ Estate (EST 4)
- _____ Foreign Will (FNW 4)
- _____ Guardianship (GDN 4)
- _____ Guardianship/Estate (G/E 4)
- _____ Limited Guardianship (LGD 4)
- _____ Minor Settlement (With guardianship) (MST 4)
- _____ Will Only (WLL 4)

PROPERTY
- _____ Condemnation (CON 2)
- _____ Foreclosure (FOR 2)
- _____ Quiet Title (QTI 2)
- _____ Unlawful Detainer (UND 2)

TORT, MEDICAL MALPRACTICE
- _____ Hospital (MED 2)
- _____ Medical Doctor (MED 2)
- _____ Other Health Care Professional (MED 2)

TORT, MOTOR VEHICLE
- _____ Death (TMV 2)
- _____ Non-Death Injuries (TMV 2)
- _____ Property Damage Only (TMV 2)

TORT, NON-MOTOR VEHICLE
- _____ Asbestos (PIN 2)
- _____ Other Malpractice (MAL 2)
- _____ Personal Injury (PIN 2)
- _____ Products Liability (TTO 2)
- _____ Property Damage (TTO 2)
- _____ Wrongful Death (WDE 2)

WRIT
- _____ Habeas Corpus (WHC 2)
- _____ Mandamus (WRM 2)
- _____ Restitution (WRR 2)
- _____ Review (WRV 2)

IF YOU CANNOT DETERMINE THE APPROPRIATE CATEGORY, PLEASE DESCRIBE THE CAUSE OF ACTION BELOW.

_____

_____

_____

[Adopted effective September 1, 1999.]

1 So in original.

LR 7. PLEADINGS ALLOWED; FORM OF MOTIONS

(b) Motions and Other Papers.

(1) *How Made.*

(A) Reapplication on Same Facts. When a motion has been denied in whole or in part (unless without prejudice) or when a motion has been granted conditionally and the condition has not been performed, the same motion may not be presented to another judge. Reapplication shall be made in the same manner as a motion to reconsider. NOTE: SEE LR 56 FOR SUMMARY JUDGMENT MOTIONS.

(B) Subsequent Motion; Different Facts. If a subsequent motion is made upon alleged different facts, the moving party must show by affidavit what motion was previously made, when and to which judge, what order or decision was made on it, and what new facts are claimed to be shown.

(C) Notes for Motion Calendar; Time for Filing. Any party desiring to bring any motion prior to trial, other than a motion for summary judgment, must file with the Clerk and serve all parties and the Judge assigned to hear the motion or the Presiding Judge at least five (5) court days before the date fixed for such hearing. A BENCH COPY OF THE MOTION AND ALL SUPPORTING DOCUMENTS SHALL BE DELIVERED TO THE CHELAN COUNTY COURTHOUSE OR MAILED OT THE JUDGE. THE MAILING ADDRESS FOR ALL JUDGES IS P.O. BOX 880, WENATCHEE, WA 98807-0880. The documents should include a Note for Motion, the motion and supporting documents.

(i) Note for Motion—Dissolution Actions. See Washington Pattern Form.

(ii) Other Actions. The note must contain the title of the court; the date, the time when the same shall be heard; the words "Note for Motion", the names of the attorneys for all parties or parties pro se; the nature of the motion; and by whom the motion is made. Attached as Exhibit B to this Rule is an example form of a Note for Motion that may be used for Chelan County causes. Any sections of Exhibit B that do not apply to the particular motion may be deleted from the form prior to filing. This note for motion must be signed by the attorney or party pro se filing the same, with the designation of the party represented.

(iii) The note or other document shall provide a certificate of mailing of all documents relating to the motion. If a party noting the matter for hearing: (a) has a limited ability to speak or understand the English Language, or (b) knows or, after reasonable inquiry has reason to believe, that any other party to the action has limited ability to speak or understand the English Language, the party noting the matter for hearing shall indicate on the Note for Motion form that an interpreter is needed. The party filing the Note for Motion shall simultaneously with such filing provide a copy of the Note for Motion to Judges Chambers. This paragraph shall not apply to State-initiated child support enforcement or modification actions or to State-initiated paternity actions so long as the State provides an interpreter for such proceedings.

Responding documents and briefs must be filed with the Clerk and copies served on all parties and the Judge scheduled to hear the motion, no later than noon two (2) court days prior to the hearing. Copies of any additional responding or reply documents must be filed with the Clerk and served on all parties no later than noon of the court day prior to the hearing.

(D) Late Filing; Terms. Any material offered at a time later than required by this rule, over objection of counsel, may be rejected by the Court, or the matter may be continued and the court may impose appropriate terms or sanctions.

(E) Telephonic Hearing. Any party may request to argue any motion by telephone conference call. The requesting party shall contact the judge or commissioner scheduled to hear the motion at least three (3) days before the hearing for permission under such conditions as ordered by the court. All parties retain the right to argue motions in person, even if the other party appears by telephone.

(F) Special Settings. To special set any matter before the assigned judge you may:

(i) contact the person responsible for scheduling that judge's calendar; or

(ii) contact Judges Chambers at 509–667–6210 or via e-mail at SuperiorCourt.Judge@co.chelan. wa.us.

[Adopted effective September 1, 1999. Amended effective September 1, 2000; September 1, 2001; September 1, 2002; September 1, 2003; September 1, 2006; amended on an emergency basis effective January 1, 2009; amended on a permanent basis effective September 1, 2009; September 1, 2011; September 2, 2013; September 2, 2014; September 1, 2015.]

LR 7 EXHIBIT B. NOTE FOR MOTION

LR 7   EXHIBIT B

IN THE SUPERIOR COURT OF THE STATE OF WASHINGTON
IN AND FOR THE COUNTY OF CHELAN

Plaintiff,	No.
vs.	NOTE FOR MOTION
	[ ] **Interpreter needed**[1]
	[ ] **Spanish**
	[ ] **Other language:** _____
	(specify)
Defendant.	[ ] **ASL**

TO: CLERK OF THE COURT

AND TO:

NOTE FOR LAW AND MOTION CALENDAR

_____ Please note that this matter will be heard on the regularly scheduled Law and Motion
Calendar on the _____ day of _____, 20__, at 9:30 a.m. (adoption – 9:00 a.m.).

Nature of Hearing: _____

NOTE FOR SHOW CAUSE CALENDAR

_____ Please note that this matter will be heard on the regularly scheduled Show Cause
Calendar on the _____ day of _____, 20__, before Court Commissioner Vandegrift
at 1:30 p.m.

NOTE FOR DISSOLUTION CALENDAR

_____ Please note that this matter will be heard on the regularly scheduled Dissolution Calendar
on the _____ day of _____, 20__, before the Court Commissioner Vandegrift at
1:30 p.m.

NOTE FOR DOMESTIC VIOLENCE CALENDAR

_____ Please note that this matter will be heard on the regularly scheduled Domestic Violence
Calendar on the ____ day of _____, 20____ before the Motion Judge at 9:00 a.m.

Nature of Hearing: _____

---

[1] If an interpreter is needed, a copy of the Note for Motion must be provided to the Judicial Assistant
simultaneously with the filing of this document. LR 7(b)(1)(c)(iii)

NOTE FOR PRO SE SUPPORT MODIFICATION HEARING

_____ Please note that this matter will be heard on Thursday, the ____ day of _____, 20____, before the Motion Judge at 3:00 p.m.

All summary judgment motions must be special set for the judge assigned to preside over the case.

NOTE FOR SPECIAL SETTING

All dates and times for special settings must be obtained from the person responsible for scheduling for the Judge or Commissioner before which the motion is to be set.

_____ Please note that this Summary Judgment has been specially set before the Honorable _____, on the ____ day of _____, 20___, at _____ a.m./p.m.

Note: <u>CONFIRMATION</u>: ON ANY MOTION FOR SUMMARY JUDGMENT, COUNSEL FOR THE MOVING PARTY SHALL CONTACT THE PERSON RESPONSIBLE FOR SCHEDULING FOR THE JUDGE OR COMMISSIONER (LR7(F)) THREE COURT DAYS PRECEDING THE DATE SET FOR HEARING AND ADVISE WHETHER THE MOTION WILL BE HEARD. IF NOTIFICATION IS NOT MADE, THE MOTION WILL BE STRICKEN FOR RESETTING PURSUANT TO LR 56(k).

_____ Please note that this matter has been specially set before Court Commissioner _____ on the ____ day of _____, 20___, at _____ a.m./p.m.

Nature of Hearing: _____

USE THIS SECTION <u>ONLY</u> IF NONE OF THE ABOVE APPLY

_____ Please note that this matter has been specially set before the Honorable _____, on the ____ day of _____, 20___, at _____ a.m./p.m.

Nature of Hearing: _____

Dated this ____ day of _____, 20___.

By: _____

Attorney for _____

[Amended September 1, 2015]

[Adopted effective September 1, 1999. Amended effective September 1, 2000; September 1, 2007; amended on an emergency basis effective January 1, 2009; amended on a permanent basis effective September 1, 2009; amended effective September 1, 2010; amended on an emergency basis effective October 1, 2011; amended on a permanent basis effective September 1, 2012; September 2, 2013; September 1, 2015.]

LR 8. SHOW CAUSE ORDERS

(g) Certified copies of show cause orders shall not be issued by the Clerk of the Court without payment in advance.

[Adopted effective September 1, 1999.]

LR 10. FORM OF PLEADINGS

(f) Any document or correspondence presented to the Court for filing which does not have the correct cause number on the face of such document or correspondence may not be filed and may be returned to the presenter.

[Adopted effective September 1, 1999.]

LR 16. PRETRIAL PROCEDURE AND FORMULATING ISSUES

(c) **Pre–Trial Conference.** Any order for a pre-trial conference shall be in the form of and include the provisions as set forth in the Exhibit "C" attached to this rule. The pre-trial conference shall be held not less than two weeks prior to the trial date.

(d) **Pre–Trial Order.** A pre-trial order in the form of Exhibit "D" attached to this rule shall be prepared by counsel within ten (10) days after the conclusion of the pre-trial conference.

(e) **Exhibits.** Parties shall notify the trial judge and the opposing party by letter if that party anticipates offering 25 exhibits or more at the time of trial. Said notice shall be given no less than two (2) weeks prior to the trial date.

(f) **Settlement Conferences.**

(1) *On Motion by Party.* Any party in any pending case may serve and file a motion for a settlement conference directed to the department to which the settlement is assigned in accordance with paragraph (5) below.

(2) *On Court's Motion.* The court to which a case is assigned for trial may, upon its own motion after a trial date has been set, order a settlement conference in any pending case, and a settlement conference shall be held unless all parties file objections thereto.

(3) *Subsequent Motion by Party.* Where a motion for a settlement conference is defeated by the filing of an objection or objections, any party in said cause may file another motion for a settlement conference after thirty days following the filing of the last previous motion for a settlement conference.

(4) *Order for Settlement Conference.* Upon the entry of an order for a settlement conference, the judge shall fix a specific date and hour for the conference. If the party presenting such order has limited ability to speak or understand the English Language, or if such party knows or, after reasonable inquiry has reason to believe, that any other party to the action has limited ability to speak or understand the English Language, the party presenting such Order for entry shall indicate on such order that an interpreter is needed and the language for which the interpretation is needed. The party presenting such order for entry shall, substantially simultaneously with the entry of such order, provide a copy thereof to Judges Chambers.

(5) *Assignment of Judge.* A judge not assigned to preside over the trial shall conduct the settlement conference.

(6) *Preparation and Attendance.* The attorney personally in charge of each party's case shall personally attend all settlement conferences and shall, not less than three (3) days prior to the date set for the settlement conference, serve on the assigned judge and the attorney for the opposing party a letter succinctly addressing the following:

    a. A brief factual summary;

    b. Issues regarding liability;

    c. Issues regarding damages, both special and general

    d. History of any settlement negotiations; and

    e. Current position on settlement.

In family law cases, counsel shall also serve on the assigned judge and attorney for the opposing party the completed matrix included herein as Exhibit B to LR 94.04.

Each attorney shall be prepared to discuss the foregoing in detail at the settlement conference.

(7) *Attendance of Parties.* The parties shall in all cases attend the settlement conference.

Parties whose defense is provided by a liability insurance company need not personally attend said settlement conference, but a representative of the insurer of such party, if such a representative is available in Chelan–Douglas counties, shall attend with sufficient authority to bind the insurer to a settlement. In the event such a representative is not available, counsel representing the party whose defense is provided by the insurer shall make a good faith effort to obtain settlement authority to bind the insurer to a settlement prior to the settlement conference.

Attendance of any party may be excused by the court where by reason of health, or other good and sufficient reason, compelling his personal attendance would be unduly burdensome. Whether or not the attendance of any party is required shall rest in the discretion of the judge presiding at the settlement conference. Request for excuse shall be made at least three (3) days prior to the hearing.

(8) *Proceedings Privileged.* Proceedings of said settlement conference shall, in all respects, be privileged and shall not be reported or recorded. No party shall be bound unless a settlement is reached. When a settlement has been reached, the judge may,

at the request of any party, in his or her discretion, order the settlement to be reported or recorded.

(9) *Sanctions.* Where a party has failed to comply with any of the provisions of this rule the court shall make such orders as are just, which shall include the award of reasonable expenses, including attorney's fees, caused by the failure, unless the court finds that the failure was substantially justified or that other circumstances make an award of expenses unjust. [Adopted effective September 1, 1999; amended effective September 1, 2000; September 1, 2006; September 1, 2015.]

LR 16 EXHIBIT C. ORDER FOR PRETRIAL CONFERENCE

IN THE SUPERIOR COURT OF THE STATE OF WASHINGTON
IN AND FOR THE COUNTY OF CHELAN

	)	
	)	
	)	
	)	
Plaintiff(s),	)	
	)	
vs.	)	No.
	)	
	)	
	)	ORDER FOR PRETRIAL
	)	CONFERENCE
	)	
Defendant(s).	)	

THIS CAUSE appearing to be at issue and ready for trial, it is

1. ORDERED AND ADJUDGED THAT a pretrial conference will be held in Chambers at ____.m. at the Chelan County Courthouse on the ___ day of _____, 20___. Total time allocated for the conference will be _____. The attorneys who will conduct the trial must attend this conference.

All discovery procedures shall be completed by the time of this conference.

2. ORDERED AND ADJUDGED THAT at least five working days prior to this conference, the attorneys shall submit to the trial judge and to opposing counsel a Pretrial Statement containing the following:

(a) A list designating those pleadings upon which the case goes to trial;

(b) A succinct statement of the cause of action in regard to each claim or defense;

(c) A clear statement of the issues to be tried;

(d) An itemized list of the claimed special damages;

(e) A statement of the principles of law involved in the case, supported by citations of authority;

(f) A statement of facts, which his client will admit;

(g) A list of the names and addresses of all persons who have knowledge of relevant facts and the general nature of their testimony;

(h) A list of all exhibits and documentary evidence, which may be used at the trial;

(i) A complete set of written jury instructions, standard and special, which will be proposed for use at the trial, including verdict forms;

(j) Any request for preliminary rulings on questions of law with citations in regard thereto;

(k) Any trial brief that either party wishes the court to consider.

3. ORDERED AND ADJUDGED THAT at the time of the conference, the first thirty minutes of the conference will be set aside for a meeting between counsel to:

(a) Inspect all documentary evidence and transportable exhibits listed in their Pretrial Statements. Exhibits not easily transportable will be made available for inspection at a time and place fixed at the conference.

(b) Mark each document and exhibit using consecutive numerals for the plaintiff and the defendant.

(c) Object to the admissibility of the evidence, reserving the appropriate objections.

(d) Object to the jury instructions filed with the Pretrial Statements, reserving the appropriate objections.

(e) Stipulate on all matters of fact and law upon which the parties are in agreement.

DONE AND ORDERED in Chambers in Chelan County, Washington, this day of _____ 20___.

_____

JUDGE

[Adopted effective September 1, 1999; amended effective September 1, 2000.]

LR 16 EXHIBIT D.   PRETRIAL ORDER

IN THE SUPERIOR COURT OF THE STATE OF WASHINGTON
IN AND FOR THE COUNTY OF CHELAN

	)	
	)	
	)	
	)	
Plaintiff(s),	)	
	)	
vs.	)	No.
	)	
	)	
	)	PRETRIAL ORDER
	)	
	)	
Defendant(s).	)	

I.   BASIS

1.1   The above matter has been noted for trial setting.

1.2   A pretrial conference was held and the following persons were present:

For Plaintiff(s):   For Defendant(s):

II.   ORDER

2.1   Names and addresses of attendant lawyers who will try the case and are authorized to enter into binding stipulations:

For Plaintiff(s):   For Defendant(s):

2.2   Summary of plaintiff's case:

2.3   Summary of defense and counterclaim:

2.4   The following amendments are allowed to the pleadings:

2.5   Names and addresses of plaintiff's witnesses and summary of testimony expected from each:

2.6   Names and addresses of defendant's witnesses and summary of testimony expected from each:

Additional Witnesses: If additional witnesses are discovered, who by the use of reasonable diligence could not have been discovered before the Pretrial Conference, the party intending to use such witness shall immediately report the names, addresses and summary of the testimony of such witness to opposing counsel and the court.

2.7 Facts admitted by stipulation and agreement:

2.8 Exhibits produced for admission:

a. The following exhibits were marked, identified and admitted without objection, no further identification or offers of admission shall be required at trial:

b. The following exhibits were produced and offered but were objected to for competency, relevancy and materiality; they may be introduced at the trial without formal identification, their authenticity being agreed to:

c. The admission of the following exhibits will be contested:

d. The following exhibits will be sent to opposing counsel within _____ days and within five days of receipt forwarded to the court with any objections thereto; in the event no objections are raised the exhibits will be admitted in accordance with the provisions of (a) above.

Additional Exhibits: If additional exhibits or documents are discovered which could not have been discovered by reasonable diligence before the Pretrial Conference, the party intending to use them shall immediately exhibit them to opposing counsel and submit them to the court to be marked for identification. Opposing counsel shall immediately indicate to the court his or her position with respect to such exhibit, i.e., whether his or her position falls under (a), (b) or (c) above.

2.9 Unresolved issues:

2.10 Points of law passed upon by the court:

2.11 Estimated length of trial: Jury:

2.12 Other matters that may aid the trial:

Set for trial:

Approved, stipulated and agreed:

_____   _____
Attorney for Plaintiff   Attorney for Defendant

IT IS ORDERED that the stipulations be carried out as outlined above.

DATED: _____   _____
                                   JUDGE

[Adopted effective September 1, 1999; amended effective September 1, 2000.]

LR 32. USE OF DEPOSITIONS IN COURT PROCEEDINGS

(a) Use of Depositions.

(6) *Video Depositions.* When presenting video depositions, a written deposition must also be filed. The videotape may be returned after the appeal period, regardless if it is published or not.

[Adopted effective September 1, 1999.]

LR 37. FAILURE TO MAKE DISCOVERY; SANCTIONS

(f) Completion of Discovery. Unless otherwise stipulated to by the parties, or ordered by the Court upon good cause shown and such terms and conditions as are just, all discovery allowed under CR 26 through 37, including responses and supplementations thereto, must be completed no later than 35 calendar days prior to the date assigned for trial. Nothing herein stated shall modify a party's responsibility to seasonably supplement responses to discovery requests or otherwise comply with discovery prior to the 35–day cutoff.

[Adopted effective September 1, 1999.]

LR 47. JURORS

(k) Counsel or the parties shall not contact or interview jurors or cause jurors to be contacted or interviewed after trial without first having been granted leave to do so by the Court.

[Adopted effective September 1, 1999.]

LR 49. VERDICTS

(1) Receiving Verdict During Absence of Counsel. A party or attorney desiring to be present at the return of the verdict must remain in attendance at the courthouse or be available by telephone call. If a party or attorney fails to appear within 20 minutes of telephone notice to the attorney's office, home or other number, the court may proceed to take the verdict in the absence of such party or attorney. In such case, the jury shall be individually polled and the identity of any dissenting jurors recorded.

[Adopted effective September 1, 1999.]

LR 52. DECISIONS, FINDINGS AND CONCLUSIONS

(f) In all actions tried to the court, counsel for each party shall, two (2) days prior to trial, provide the Court and opposing counsel with proposed findings of fact and conclusions of law. Provided, that proposed findings and conclusions are not required in domestic cases of any kind, except that the court may, at its discretion, require proposed findings and conclusions, in a particular case or the parties may voluntarily submit such findings and conclusions.

(g) Time Limit for Presentation. In cases tried to the court, findings of fact, conclusions of law and a proposed judgment shall be presented within twenty (20) days of the court's oral or memorandum decision; provided however, that in the event post-trial motions are filed, the twenty (20) days shall run from the date of ruling on such motions.

In the event that said findings of fact, conclusions of law and the proposed judgment are presented to the court in excess of twenty (20) days of the court's oral decision, the party presenting such findings of fact, conclusions of law and proposed judgment shall, if requested by the court, prepare and file a transcript of the court's oral decision.

[Adopted effective September 1, 1999.]

LR 56. SUMMARY JUDGMENT

(i) Special Setting. Summary judgments shall be heard by the judge who is assigned to preside over the trial.

ALL MOTIONS FOR SUMMARY JUDGMENT MUST BE SPECIAL SET. SPECIAL SETTINGS SHALL BE OBTAINED BY CONTACTING THE PERSON RESPONSIBLE FOR SCHEDULING AS SET FORTH IN LR 7(b)(1)(F).

(j) Service and Filing.

FOR ALL JUDICIAL DEPARTMENTS

A working copy for the judge of the motion, all supporting documents and all responding documents shall be delivered to the courthouse or mailed to the judge at the time of filing the originals.

FOR DEPARTMENT 2 (HONORABLE T.W. SMALL)

In addition to paper working copies, it is preferred that working copies be submitted via e-mail in PDF format with hyperlinks to all cited cases and statutes. E–mailed documents should be sent to Karen. Komoto@co.chelan.wa.us and SuperiorCourt.Judge@ co.chelan.wa.us.

The mailing address for all judges is P.O. Box 880, Wenatchee, WA 98807–0880. If working copies are not received, the judge may strike the hearing.

Where depositions or interrogatories are a part of the evidence relied upon, counsel's affidavits, briefs and arguments must cite the depositions or interrogatories by page and line.

ANY MATERIAL OFFERED AT A TIME LATER THAN REQUIRED BY THIS RULE OVER OBJECTION OF COUNSEL SHALL NOT BE ACCEPTED AND CONSIDERED BY THE COURT EXCEPT UPON THE IMPOSITION OF APPROPRIATE TERMS OR SANCTIONS, INCLUDING THE RIGHT TO A CONTINUANCE IF REQUESTED.

Any motion for summary judgment or responsive pleadings to a motion for summary judgment shall list and identify all evidence the Court should consider.

(k) Confirmation. On any motion for summary judgment, counsel for the moving party shall contact the person responsible for scheduling for the judge or commissioner (LR7(F)) three court days preceding the date set for hearing and advise whether the motion will be heard. If notification is not made, the motion will be stricken for resetting.

[Adopted effective September 1, 1999. Amended effective September 1, 2000; September 1, 2010; September 1, 2011; September 2, 2013; September 1, 2015.]

LR 58. ENTRY OF JUDGMENT

(m) Judgment on a Promissory Note. No judgment on a promissory note will be signed until the original note has been filed with the Clerk, absent proof of loss or destruction.

[Adopted effective September 1, 1999.]

LR 59. MOTION FOR RECONSIDERATION

(3) Nature of Hearing.

(A) A motion for reconsideration or for a new trial shall be submitted on briefs and declarations or affidavits only, without oral argument, unless the trial judge, on application from counsel or on the judge's own motion, allows oral argument. The judge will notify counsel if oral argument is to be allowed. Copies of such motions for reconsideration, copy of note for motion calendar and responses thereto shall be delivered to the judge at the time of filing.

(B) The scheduled hearing date will not ordinarily involve oral argument. However, it will be the earliest date that the court will consider the merits of the motion.

[Adopted effective September 1, 1999. Amended effective September 1, 2000; September 2, 2013.]

LR 65. INJUNCTIONS

(b) Temporary Restraining Order; Notice; Hearing; Duration.

(1) *Notice to Opponent.* Failure to give notice as required by CR 65 may result in the imposition of terms and/or sanctions on the moving party.

[Adopted effective September 1, 1999.]

LR 77. SUPERIOR COURTS AND JUDICIAL OFFICERS

(*o*) Court Calendar.

(1) The Motion Judge will hold Probate and Law and Motion Calendars each Friday at 9:30 a.m. Adoption hearings will be heard at 9:00 a.m. on the Law and Motion Calendar.

(2) The Judges rotate as Motion Judge according to the schedule published periodically by the Judges.

The Motion Judge's schedule is as follows:

Monday:	Criminal Calendar
Tuesday:	9:00 Domestic Violence Calendar
Wednesday:	Criminal Calendar
Thursday:	9:30 Special Set Criminal Matters (week prior to criminal trials)
Friday:	9:30 Law & Motion Calendar/Adoptions at 9:00 AM (Second and Fourth Friday. First and Third Friday the Law & Motion Calendar is presided over by the court commissioner.)

To obtain a special set please call (509) 667–6210 or e-mail SuperiorCourt.Judge@co.chelan.wa.us.

A COURT REPORTER WILL NOT BE PROVIDED FOR ANY CIVIL MATTER SCHEDULED, EXCEPT PATERNITY ACTIONS, UNLESS REQUESTED AT LEAST TWO COURT DAYS BEFORE THE HEARING OR TRIAL.

(3) Except as otherwise provided in LR 77(*o*)(3)(a) hereof, Domestic Relations and Domestic Show Cause hearings where an attorney has appeared will be held each Monday at 1:30 p.m. Court Commissioner Vandegrift will preside. Domestic Relations and Domestic Show Cause hearings where the parties are pro se will be specially set before the assigned judge.

(a) Domestic Relations and Domestic Show Cause hearings requiring more than 30 minutes will be scheduled by special setting before the judge assigned to hear the trial. See LR 7(b)(1)(F).

A COURT REPORTER WILL NOT BE PROVIDED FOR ANY DOMESTIC RELATIONS SHOW CAUSE HEARING UNLESS REQUESTED AT LEAST TWO COURT DAYS BEFORE THE DATE OF THE HEARING.

(4) *Default Dissolution Hearings* will be held on Tuesdays at 1:30 p.m. Court Commissioner Vandegrift will preside.

(5) *Juvenile Calendars* will be held on Tuesdays, Thursdays 8:30 a.m. or such other time as matters are set. Court Commissioner Vandegrift will preside over juvenile calendars.

(6) *Dependency Hearings* will be held on Wednesdays or such other time as matters are set. Court Commissioner Vandegrift will preside.

(7) *Holiday Scheduling*—any court calendar falling on an official court holiday will be cancelled.

(A) The Judges may, by order, further alter these court schedules as needed and as available courtroom space requires.

(p) Ex parte Matters.

(1) *Non–Emergency.* Non-emergency ex parte orders shall be left in the Judges Chambers box in the County Clerk's Office or in the mailbox outside the door to Judges Chambers for consideration. Orders left prior to 10:30 a.m. will be considered by the Court and available for pick-up in the County Clerk's office not later than 4:30 p.m. that same day. Orders left after 10:30 a.m. will be available for pick up not later than 4:30 p.m. on the following day.

(2) *Emergency Orders.* Emergency orders may be presented directly to Judges Chambers and will be considered by any available judge, or as soon as a judge becomes available.

(q) Special Settings. Any civil matter which will require more than twenty minutes of argument shall be specially set at a time arranged with the Court. See LR 7(b)(1)(F).

(r) The Judges will preside over all matters scheduled on a calendar even though the matter is assigned to another department, except for sentencings, motions for summary judgment or matters where there is a conflict.

[Adopted effective September 1, 1999. Amended effective September 1, 2000; September 1, 2001; September 1, 2002; September 1, 2003; September 1, 2006; September 1, 2007; September 1, 2009; September 1, 2011; amended on an emergency basis effective October 1, 2011; amended on a permanent basis effective September 1, 2012; September 2, 2013; September 1, 2015.]

LR 78. CLERKS

(g) Pleadings or other papers requiring action on the part of the Clerk of the Court (other than filing, stamping, docketing and placing in the court file) shall constitute action documents. Action documents shall include a special caption directly below the case number on the first page such as "Clerk's Action Required". The specific action required of the Clerk shall be stated with particularity in the body of the pleading or other paper requiring action on the part of the Clerk.

[Adopted effective September 1, 1999.]

LSPR 94.04. FAMILY LAW PROCEEDINGS

A. Applicability of the Rule. Unless otherwise specified, this rule applies to all family law proceedings, including paternity actions and non-parental custody and/or visitation actions, defined as follows: Any proceeding in which the court is requested to adjudicate or enforce the rights of the parties or their children regarding the determination or modification of child custody, visitation, parenting plan, child support or spousal maintenance, or the temporary distribution of property or obligations.

B. Non–Contested Dissolution Hearings.

(1) *Hearing.* Non-contested dissolution cases will be heard on a calendar set by the Superior Court Judges and Clerk. The days and times are set forth in LR 77. The Clerk shall not place any case on the non-contested calendar unless the file shows one of the following:

a. The applicant's opponent has joined in the petition for dissolution of marriage; or

b. The applicant's opponent has waived notice or has signed a consent to hearing on the date noted; or

c. An order for default has been applied for or entered.

The Clerk shall not place any case on the non-contested calendar unless proof is filed that summons was served more than ninety (90) days before the date selected for hearing or that the case has been on file more than ninety days and both parties have submitted to the jurisdiction of the court.

(2) *Note for Non-contested Calendar–Attorney.* A notice of hearing on the non-contested calendar must be filed by counsel with the Clerk at least three court days before the date of the hearing.

(3) *Note for Non–Contested Calendar—Without Attorney (Self–Represented).* A notice of hearing on the non-contested calendar by a self-represented party shall be accompanied by pre-approved pleadings which the party proposes to submit to the court as final orders. Such proposed pleadings shall include Findings of Fact and Conclusions of Law or Waiver of same signed by all parties, Decree, Parenting Plan and/or Residential Schedule, Child Support Worksheets, Order of Child Support, and a Residential Time Summary, where applicable.

The Clerk shall not place any case on the non-contested calendar upon application by any self-represented party unless it is accompanied by the party's pre-approved, proposed pleadings.

(4) *Self–Represented Note for Show Cause Calendar—Without Attorney.* All self-represented parties, at the time of scheduling a show cause hearing, must provide the Clerk copies of all pre-approved pleadings which the self-represented party proposes to submit to the court as orders. Such proposed pleadings shall include Temporary Orders, Temporary Parenting Plans/Residential Schedules, Temporary Order of Child Support, etc, where applicable.

(5) *Self–Represented Emergency Ex Parte Orders.* Parties shall not be required to obtain pre-approval of pleadings submitted for emergency ex parte orders.

(6) Self-represented parties shall obtain pre-approval of all final documents only from the Chelan County or Douglas County Superior Courthouse Facilitator, or a private attorney. Pre-approval shall be designated in a manner clearly ascertainable and approved by the Chelan County Clerk.

The Clerk shall not file said proposed pleadings, but shall instead place all proposed pleadings on the fly leaf of the court file.

(7) *Order on Non–Contested Calendar.* The order of the calendars shall be as follows:

    a. Matters where attorneys appear;

    b. Self–represented matters in which pleadings are complete for the court's review;

    c. All other matters.

(8) *Mandatory JIS Search for All Cases Involving Children.* At least three (3) days prior to scheduled hearing for entry of final orders, self-represented parties and attorneys must complete and submit the form in Exhibit 1. If orders are to be presented ex parte, this completed form must accompany the final documents when presented to the court for signature.

(9) *Withdrawal of Consent.* Before a decree is entered, a party may move to withdraw any consent or waiver previously given. Such motion must be supported by affidavit showing good cause and shall be noted for hearing on the show cause calendar.

(10) *Disposition of Issues in Decree.* No decree of dissolution shall be entered unless the decree disposes of all issues over which the court has jurisdiction relating to disposition of property and liabilities of the parties and support or maintenance of either spouse. For good cause shown, the court may in its discretion enter a decree of dissolution stating that it retains jurisdiction to dispose of issues relating to parenting and child support.

C. Contested Dissolutions.

(1) *Pretrial Forms.* In all final hearings or trials in domestic relations matters, each party shall provide to the judge or commissioner, and serve on the opposing party, a written statement as to the issues in controversy at least three (3) days prior to trial. The written statement may be in any form chosen by the attorney to convey the following:

    (a) A brief factual summary;

    (b) Issues in dispute [whether property, debts or custody];

    (a)[1] Case law, if it will be argued, supporting your position;

    (b) Proposed distribution of assets and debts, proposed parenting plan and child support amount, if in dispute;

    (c) Areas of agreement.

If one of the parties is seeking maintenance or child support, both parties shall complete the financial declaration contained in Exhibit A to LR 94.04.

If the parties are in dispute as to the distribution of assets and debts, both parties shall complete Exhibit B to LR 94.04. The pretrial forms shall not be filed with the Clerk.

Unless explained otherwise by the parties, the values shown on the pretrial form should include proposed pension, retirement, profit sharing or other deferred benefit or financial security plan; the cash surrender value of all life insurance policies; the amounts of accounts receivable, inheritance due, and trust accounts; the fair market value of all other property including collections, antiques; and in the case of automobiles, the average between wholesale and retail blue book values.

(2) *Enforcement.* If either party fails to comply with paragraph B(1) set forth above, the trial judge may order such party or his attorney to pay an appropriate attorney's fee to the opponent for any additional work or delay caused by the failure to comply. If either party fails to comply, the trial date may be stricken.

(3) *Continuances.* Stipulations or motions to continue a case already on the trial calendar must be in writing, supported by a declaration showing sufficient grounds for the requested continuance. The moving party shall present a written order for entry.

D. Child Custody or Parenting Plan Proceedings.

(1) *Parenting Plans.*

    (a) Proposed, Temporary and Permanent Parenting plans shall be in the form required by State law. Proposed temporary parenting plans need not have the dispute resolution and decision making sections completed.

E. Dating and Mailing of Decrees and Orders.

(1) When any decree or order is filed in a dissolution matter, the attorney for the party presenting the order, or the party if the matter is presented pro se, shall immediately deliver or mail to the opposing party, or to the opposing party's last known address, or to opposing counsel, a true copy of the decree or order with the date of entry indicated on each copy. A declaration of mailing of such true copy shall be filed.

F. Hearings—Show Cause—Preliminary and Temporary Orders.

(1) *Hearings.* See Local Rule 77.

(2) *Hearings by Documentary Evidence.* All show cause hearings pertaining to requests for temporary support money and/or attorney's fees shall be heard and determined by documentary evidence only, unless the parties request that oral testimony be given and the court, in its discretion, agrees.

(3) *Supporting Worksheet.* A motion for order to show cause for temporary support shall be supported by a child support worksheet in the form prescribed by state law and may also include a financial declaration in the form designated in Exhibit A attached to this rule. No order shall be signed setting a show

cause hearing for temporary support unless the signed worksheet accompanies the motion.

(4) *Information Considered Notwithstanding Non-Appearance.* An affidavit or child support worksheet filed by a non-appearing respondent shall be considered by the court at the time of hearing on show cause hearings and upon hearing default dissolutions.

(5) *Limitations on Declarations.*

(a) Application. This section (5) of this rule does not apply to domestic violence petitions or domestic violence motions.

(b) Children's Statements. Declarations by minors are disfavored.

(c) Format. All filed documents and copies provided as "Working Papers" and served on other parties and attorneys shall be legible. If typed or computer printed, documents shall be in 12 point or larger type, double-spaced between the lines.

(d) Page Limits.

(i.) Generally. Absent prior authorization from the court, the entirety of all declarations and affidavits from the parties and any non-expert witnesses in support of motions (except financial declarations), including any reply, shall be limited to a sum total of twenty-five (25) pages. The entirety of all declarations and affidavits submitted in response to motions shall be limited to a sum total of twenty (20) pages.

(ii.) Exhibits. Exhibits that consist of declarations or affidavits of parties or witnesses shall count towards the above page limit. All other exhibits attached to a declaration or affidavit shall not be counted toward the page limit.

(iii.) Financial Declarations. Financial Declarations and financial documents do not count toward the page limit.

(iv.) Expert Reports and Evaluations. Declarations, affidavits, and reports from Court Appointed Special Advocates (CASA), Guardians Ad Litem (GAL) and expert witnesses do not count toward the page limit.

(v.) Miscellaneous Exceptions. Copies of declarations or affidavits previously filed for a motion already ruled upon and supplied only as a convenience to the court in lieu of the court file do not count toward the page limit. Deposition excerpts shall not count toward the page limit.

G. Disposal of Proposed Parenting Plan. The Clerk is authorized to remove from the file and dispose of all proposed parenting plans after the Permanent Parenting Plan has been entered and the time for appeal has elapsed.

H. Mandatory Information Education Workshop. The Chelan County Superior Court finds that it is in the best interest of any child whose parents or custodians are involved in specific court proceedings to provide such parents with an educational workshop concerning the impact of family restructuring has on their child. The workshop offers parents tools to help ensure that their child's emotional needs will not be overlooked during the legal process, to encourage parents to agree on child-related matters, and to aid in maximizing the use of court time.

(1) *Types of Proceedings Required.* Each person named as a party in the following types of proceedings filed after January 1, 1997, must comply with LSPR 94.04I:

1. Dissolution of Marriage with child(ren) under 18 years old;

2. Legal Separation or Declaration of Invalidity with child(ren) under 18 years old;

3. Petition to establish custody or visitation including paternity; and/or

4. Post-judgment petition involving custody or visitation.

(2) *Service on Parties.* The Clerk of the court shall provide a copy of this rule (LR94.04 I) to the initiating party for service upon all parties against whom relief is sought, together with a statement describing the program including contact telephone numbers, addresses, statement of costs, and an explanation of how to request a waiver or deferral of the program registration fee.

(3) *Mandatory.* Each party who files an appearance in a proceeding of the types described above in Section (1) shall complete the program unless exempted by the court. **No final order approving any residential or parenting plan shall be entered without proof of completion of such education program by the parents or legal guardians unless otherwise ordered by the court.**

(4) *Ninety (90) Day Deadline.* Each party shall attend and complete an approved parenting workshop within ninety (90) days of filing a proceeding specified in Section (1) above.

I. Mandatory JIS Search for All Cases Involving Children. At least three (3) days prior to scheduled hearing for entry of final orders, self-represented parties and attorneys must complete and submit the form in Exhibit C to LSPR 94.04. If orders are to be presented ex parte, this completed form must accompany the final documents when presented to the court for signature.

[LR 94.04 adopted effective September 1, 1999. Amended effective September 1, 2000; September 1, 2001; September 1, 2006; amended on an emergency basis effective January 1, 2009; amended on a permanent basis effective September 1, 2009; September 1, 2011; September 2, 2013. Renumbered LSPR 94.04 and amended effective September 1, 2015.]

1 Lettering as provided in original.

LSPR 94.04 EXHIBIT A.   FINANCIAL DECLARATION (FNDCLR)

EXHIBIT A TO LSPR 94.04

SUPERIOR COURT OF WASHINGTON
COUNTY OF CHELAN

In re:	
	NO.
Petitioner,	FINANCIAL DECLARATION
and	[ ] PETITIONER
	[ ] RESPONDENT
	(FNDCLR)
Respondent.	

Name: _____   Date of Birth: _____
Social Security Number: _____

I. SUMMARY OF BASIC INFORMATION

Declarant's Total Monthly Net Income (from § 3.3 below) $ _____

Declarant's Total Monthly Household Expenses (from § 5.9 below) $ _____

Declarant's Total Monthly Debt Expenses (from § 5.11 below) $ _____

Declarant's Total Monthly Expenses (from § 5.12 below) $ _____
Estimate of the other party's gross monthly income (from § 3.1f below) [ ] $ _____
                                                                                                       [ ]   unknown

II. PERSONAL INFORMATION

2.1   Occupation:

2.2   The highest year of education completed:

2.3   Are you presently employed? [ ] Yes [ ] No

    a. If yes: (1)   Where do you work (name and address)?

                            (2)   When did you start work there (month/year)?   _____

    b. If no: (1)   When did you last work (month/year)?   _____

(2)   What were your gross monthly earnings? $ _____
(3)   Why are you presently unemployed?

III. INCOME INFORMATION

If child support is at issue, complete the Washington State Child Support Worksheet(s), skip Paragraphs 3.1 and 3.2.
If maintenance, fees, costs or debts are at issue and child support is NOT an issue this entire section should be
completed. (Estimate of other party's income information is optional.)

3.1   GROSS MONTHLY INCOME.
       If you are paid on a weekly basis, multiply your weekly gross pay by 4.3 to determine your monthly wages
       and salaries. If you are paid every two weeks, multiply your gross pay by 2.15. If you are paid twice
       monthly, multiply your gross pay by 2. If you are paid once a month, list that amount below.

		Petitioner	Respondent
a.	Wages and Salaries	$ _____	$ _____
b.	Interest and Dividend Income	$ _____	$ _____
c.	Business Income	$ _____	$ _____
d.	Spousal Maintenance From Other Relationships	$ _____	$ _____
e.	Other Income	$ _____	$ _____
f.	Total Gross Monthly Income (add lines 3.1a through 3.1e)	$ _____	$ _____
g.	Actual Gross Income (Year to date)	$ _____	$ _____

3.2   MONTHLY DEDUCTIONS FROM GROSS INCOME.

a.	Income Taxes	$ _____	$ _____
b.	FICA/Self-employment Taxes	$ _____	$ _____
c.	State Industrial Insurance Deductions	$ _____	$ _____
d.	MANDATORY Union/Professional Dues	$ _____	$ _____
e.	Pension Plan Payments	$ _____	$ _____
f.	Spousal Maintenance Paid	$ _____	$ _____
g.	Normal Business Expenses	$ _____	$ _____
h.	Total Deductions from Gross Income (add lines 3.2a through 3.2g)	$ _____	$ _____

3.3   MONTHLY NET INCOME. (Line 3.1f minus line 3.2h or $ _____ $ _____
       line 3 from the Child Support Worksheet(s).)

3.4   MISCELLANEOUS INCOME.

a.	Child support received from other relationships	$ _____	$ _____
b.	Other miscellaneous income (list source and amounts):	$ _____	$ _____
	_____	$ _____	$ _____

	$ _____	$ _____
	$ _____	$ _____
	$ _____	$ _____

c.   Total Miscellaneous Income (add lines 3.4a through 3.4c) $ _____ $ _____

3.5   Income of Other Adults in Household $ _____ $ _____

3.6   If the income of either party is disputed, state monthly income you believe is correct and explain below:

IV. AVAILABLE ASSETS

4.1   Cash on hand $ _____

4.2   On deposit in banks $ _____

4.3   Stocks and Bonds, cash value of life insurance $ _____

4.4   Other liquid assets: $ _____

V. MONTHLY EXPENSE INFORMATION

Monthly expenses for myself and _____ dependents are: (Expenses should be calculated for the future, after separation, based on the anticipated residential schedule for the children.)

5.1   HOUSING.
   Rent, 1st mortgage or contract payments $ _____

   Installment payments for other mortgages or encumbrances $ _____

   Taxes & insurance (if not in monthly payment) $ _____

   Total Housing $ _____

5.2   UTILITIES.
   Heat (gas & oil) $ _____

   Electricity $ _____

   Water, sewer, garbage $ _____

   Telephone $ _____

   Cable $ _____

   Other $ _____

   Total Utilities $ _____

5.3   FOOD AND SUPPLIES.
   Food for _____ persons $ _____

Supplies (paper, tobacco, pets)	$ _____
Meals eaten out	$ _____
Other	$ _____
Total Food Supplies	$ _____

5.4 CHILDREN.

Day Care/Babysitting	$ _____
Clothing	$ _____
Tuition (if any)	$ _____
Other child related expenses	$ _____
Total Expenses Children	$ _____

5.5 TRANSPORTATION.

Vehicle payments or leases	$ _____
Vehicle insurance & license	$ _____
Vehicle gas, oil, ordinary maintenance	$ _____
Parking	$ _____
Other transportation expenses	$ _____
Total Transportation	$ _____

5.6 HEALTH CARE. (Omit if fully covered)

Insurance	$ _____
Uninsured dental, orthodontic, medical, eye care expenses	$ _____
Other uninsured health expenses	$ _____
Total Health Care	$ _____

5.7 PERSONAL EXPENSES (Not including children).

Clothing	$ _____
Hair care/personal care expenses	$ _____
Clubs and recreation	$ _____
Education	$ _____
Books, newspapers, magazines, photos	$ _____
Gifts	$ _____
Other	$ _____
Total Personal Expenses	$ _____

5.8 MISCELLANEOUS EXPENSES.

Life insurance (if _not_ deducted from income)	$ _____
Other _____	$ _____

Other _____ $ _____

Total Miscellaneous Expenses $ _____

5.9   TOTAL HOUSEHOLD EXPENSES (The total of Paragraphs 5.1 through 5.8) $ _____

5.10   INSTALLMENT DEBTS INCLUDED IN PARAGRAPHS 5.1 THROUGH 5.8.

Creditor	Description of Debt	Balance	Month of Last Payment
_____	_____	_____	_____
_____	_____	_____	_____
_____	_____	_____	_____
_____	_____	_____	_____

5.11   OTHER DEBTS AND MONTHLY EXPENSES NOT INCLUDED IN PARAGRAPHS 5.1 THROUGH 5.8.

Creditor	Description of Debt	Balance	Month of Last Payment	Monthly Payment
_____	_____	_____	_____	$ _____
_____	_____	_____	_____	$ _____
_____	_____	_____	_____	$ _____
_____	_____	_____	_____	$ _____
_____	_____	_____	_____	$ _____
_____	_____	_____	_____	$ _____
_____	_____	_____	_____	$ _____

Total Monthly Payments for Other Debts and Monthly Expenses $ _____

5.12   TOTAL EXPENSES (Add Paragraphs 5.9 and 5.11) $ _____

VI. ATTORNEY FEES

6.1   Amount paid for attorney fees and costs to date: $ _____

6.2   The source of this money was:

6.3   Fees and costs incurred to date: $ _____

6.4   Arrangements for attorney fees and costs are:

6.5   Other:

I declare under penalty of perjury under the laws of the State of Washington that the foregoing is true and correct.

Signed at _____ on _____.
            [Place]   [Date]

_____
Signature

_____
Print or Type Name

THE OTHER PARTY MUST BE SERVED COPIES OF YOUR TAX RETURNS FROM THE LAST TWO YEARS AND COPIES OF YOUR PAY STUBS FOR THE LAST SIX MONTHS TO VERIFY YOUR INCOME. YOU SHOULD ALSO BRING COPIES OF YOUR TAX RETURNS FROM THE LAST TWO YEARS AND COPIES OF YOUR PAY STUBS FOR THE LAST SIX MONTHS TO YOUR COURT HEARINGS.

[LR 94.04 Exhibit A adopted effective September 1, 1999; amended effective September 1, 2000. Renumbered LSPR 94.04 Exhibit A and amended effective September 1, 2015.]

LSPR 94.04 EXHIBIT B.   STATEMENT OF ASSETS AND LIABILITIES

ITEM NO.	IN RE THE MARRIAGE OF: AND ASSETS AND LIABILITIES (ALL REAL AND PERSONAL PROPERTY; YEAR OF ACQUISITION; ALL DEBTS AND ADJUSTMENTS)	COMMUNITY OR SEPARATE PROPERTY	ACQUISITION COST	HUSBAND'S VALUATION & PROPOSED DISTRIBUTION	WIFE'S VALUATION & PROPOSED DISTRIBUTION	COURT'S DISTRIBUTION
1						
2						
3						
4						
5						
6						
7						
8						
9						
10						
11						
12						
13						
14						
15						
16						

EXHIBIT B TO LSPR 94.04

[LR 94.04 Exhibit B adopted effective September 1, 1999.   Renumbered LSPR 94.04 Exhibit B and amended effective September 1, 2015.]

LSPR 94.04 EXHIBIT C.   JIS SEARCH FOR ALL CASES INVOLVING CHILDREN

EXHIBIT C TO LSPR 94.04

Case Number: _____

Hearing Date: _____

CHELAN COUNTY SUPERIOR COURT

JIS SEARCH FOR ALL CASES INVOLVING CHILDREN

Under the parenting plan or residential schedule proposed to the court, the child(ren) will spend the majority of their time living with the (**check one**):

☐ Petitioner   or   ☐ Respondent

	Name / Alias used	Birthdate	Court Use Only
Petitioner(s)	1 2	1 2	JIS/JABS checked ☐ ☐ SCOMIS checked ☐ ☐ Information attached ☐ ☐ No information found ☐ ☐
Other Adult(s) living in Petitioner's home or spending a significant amount of time in Petitioner's home	1 2 3	1 2 3	JIS/JABS checked ☐ ☐ ☐ SCOMIS checked ☐ ☐ ☐ Information attached ☐ ☐ ☐ No information found ☐ ☐ ☐
Respondent(s)	1 2	1 2	JIS/JABS checked ☐ ☐ SCOMIS checked ☐ ☐ Information attached ☐ ☐ No information found ☐ ☐
Other Adult(s) living in Respondent's home or spending a significant amount of time in Respondent's home	1 2 3	1 2 3	JIS/JABS checked ☐ ☐ ☐ SCOMIS checked ☐ ☐ ☐ Information attached ☐ ☐ ☐ No information found ☐ ☐ ☐

Date: _____

Presented By: _____

☐ Self Represented   or   ☐ Attorney for Petitioner   or   ☐ Attorney for Respondent

This form must be filed by both parties at the Court Facilitator's Office at least three days prior to scheduled hearing for entry of final orders. If orders are to be presented ex parte, this cover sheet must accompany the final documents when presented to the court for signature.

[LR 94.04 Exhibit C adopted on an emergency basis effective January 1, 2009; adopted on a permanent basis effective September 1, 2009. Renumbered LSPR 94.04 Exhibit C and amended effective September 1, 2015.]

LSPR 96.04. CHANGE OF NAME OF STEPCHILD

When changing the name of a child under the age of 18 to the name of the child's stepfather, the petitioner shall give notice of such proceeding except as provided by statute to:

a. The father, if the child has been born during marriage, or

b. The father, if paternity is established, or

c. Any other person with a paternal interest by virtue of an adoption.

In addition, written consent shall be required of any child over 14 years of age.

[LR 96.04 adopted effective September 1, 1999. Renumbered LSPR 96.04 and amended effective September 1, 2015.]

LSPR 98.04. ESTATES—PROBATE

(a) Ex Parte. All probate matters that are not contested and in which notice is not required by statute, rule, or duly filed request for notice under R.C.W. 11.28.240 or where such notice has been waived, may be done ex parte.

(b) Contents of File for Ex Parte Presentation. The following documents will be presented before ex parte presentation:

(1) Original will;

(2) Affidavits of subscribing witnesses;

(3) Certified copy of Death Certificate—SSN redacted;

(4) Order admitting will to probate or order appointing administrator if petition is by surviving spouse;

(5) Petition for order of solvency if solvency is requested;

(6) An inventory or partial inventory of assets and debts sufficient to prove solvency;

(7) An order of solvency.

(c) Presentation by Mail. An original probate application may be presented by mail under the following conditions.

(1) All documents required by 98.04(b) shall be presented in the mailing;

(2) All documents shall bear the personal original signature of counsel or party pro se presenting same;

(3) *Covering Letter.* All documents shall be accompanied by a covering letter of explanation personally signed by the presenter and shall request the Clerk to deliver the documents to a Judge or a Court Commissioner for signing;

(4) *Return Envelope.* A self-addressed return envelope bearing sufficient postage paid shall be included for the return of any request conformed copies.

[LR 98.04 adopted effective September 1, 1999; amended effective September 1, 2006. Renumbered LSPR 98.04 and amended effective September 1, 2015.]

LSPR 98.09. GUARDIANSHIP FUNDS

In all guardianships in which the funds are held by the guardian as trustee for the ward, the funds shall be placed in a designated bank account and the passbook for such account shall be deposited with the Clerk of the Court and withdrawals made from such account only upon order of the Court.

The tax identification number or social security number of the ward should be included in any order where the Clerk of the Court is required to invest funds.

[LR 98.09A adopted effective September 1, 1999. Renumbered LR 98.09 effective September 1, 2000. Renumbered LSPR 98.09 and amended effective September 1, 2015.]

LGALR 98.10. CHELAN COUNTY SUPERIOR COURT GUARDIAN AD LITEM ROTATIONAL REGISTRY (TITLES 11 AND 26)

SCOPE/PURPOSE

This local rule covers the maintenance and administration of the Guardian ad Litem Registry maintained by the Registry Administrator.

DEFINITIONS

None.

POLICY

A. Registry Administration.

1.1 The court shall maintain and administer the GAL registries. These registries are limited to Titles 11.88 and 26 GAL's. These requirements and procedures also apply to persons not listed on a registry who are appointed to serve as a Guardian ad Litem in a field for which there is a registry.

1.2 The Court shall maintain an application form and background information records pertaining to each person on a registry. Persons listed on the registry shall reapply and update background information annually on a date specified for the registry. All application and background information, with the exception of personal identifying information in family law cases and pending complaints, shall be available for public inspection.

1.3 Persons shall be selected to serve on the registry at the discretion of the Court giving due consideration to: (1) having a sufficient number of GAL's available to fulfill the requests for appointment; (2) achieving and maintaining diversity; and (3) retaining panels of persons with substantial experience and special knowledge within given fields. In some cases there may be more qualified applicants that will be needed or would benefit the program, so that not all persons applying will be selected.

1.4 The court shall periodically sponsor or approve training programs which registry applicants shall be required to attend to maintain and improve their level of proficiency. Training programs may be co-sponsored or offered by the state or local bar association under the oversight of the court.

1.5 The registry may be reconstituted periodically after and [1] open application period has been announced. The court may allow additional applicants to be added to the registry periodically.

1.6 The court may impose an application processing fee and/or charge a fee for the training programs.

B. Education and Experience Requirements.

2.1 *Attorneys.*

a. Member of the Washington State Bar Association in good standing; and

b. For initial placement on registry, completion of any training as required by statute. For retention on registry, completion of any continuing training, as may be required by statute or the court from time to time.

2.2 *Non–Attorneys.*

a. For initial placement on registry, completion of any training as required by statute. For retention on registry, completion of any continuing training, as may be required by statute or the court from time to time.

b. Eligibility to be determined by the court.

C. Application. Each person requesting to be listed on the Guardian Ad Litem Registry (or registries) shall submit an application on the current form provided by the court.

D. Appointment of a Guardian ad Litem From Registry.

4.1 If the parties agree on the appointment of a GAL, they may choose any GAL from the court registry in private pay cases. If the parties cannot agree, or if the GAL is to be paid by county funds, the Registry Administrator shall appoint the next available GAL on the rotational list.

4.2 The party or parties needing the Registry Administrator to appoint a GAL from the rotational list shall request the same of the Registry Administrator, who shall appoint as GAL that person whose name next appears on the registry on a rotational basis, subject to that person's acceptance of the appointment.

4.3 The person appointed by the Registry Administrator shall serve upon the parties a notice of appointment.

E. Retention on Registry.

5.1 Persons on the registry shall promptly inform the court of any temporary unavailability to serve, or of their intent to resign from the registry.

5.2 A person who files an annual update when the same is requested by the Registry Administrator shall remain on the registry unless the person is removed or suspended as set forth in Section F.

5.3 A person may be denied listing on, or may be temporarily suspended from, the registry for any reason that places the suitability of the person to act as GAL in question.

5.4 A GAL who ceases to be on the registry and who still has active or incomplete cases shall immediately report this circumstance to the Registry Administrator, who shall reassign such cases.

5.5 A person's retention on the registry shall be reviewed upon the court's receipt of a complaint regarding performance in office or the court's receipt of adverse information regarding the suitability of a person to serve as a GAL. Complaints shall be reviewed in accordance with Section F.

F. Complaint Procedure.

6.1 There shall be a complaint review committee consisting of the Superior Court Presiding Judge, the Juvenile Court Administrator and a representative of the Chelan/Douglas Counties Bar Association.

6.2 All complaints must be in writing and must be submitted to the Superior Court Presiding Judge.

6.3 Upon receipt of a written complaint, the Presiding Judge shall convene the Complaint Review Committee within 10 business days to review the complaint. Upon review of the complaint, the complaint Review Committee shall either:

a. Make a finding that the complaint has no merit on it's face, and decline to review the complaint and so inform the complainant; or

b. Make a finding that the complaint does appear to have merit and request a written response from the GAL within 10 business days, detailing the specific issues in the complaint to which the Committee desires a response. The Committee shall provide the GAL with a copy of the original complaint. A GAL's failure to respond within the required 10 business days will result in the immediate suspension of the GAL from all registries.

c. In considering whether the complaint has merit, the Complaint Review Committee shall consider whether the complaint alleges the GAL has:

1. Violated the code of conduct;

2. Misrepresented his or her qualifications to serve as GAL;

3. Not met the annual update requirements set forth in Paragraph 1.2 of this policy;

4. Breached the confidentiality of the parties;

5. Falsified information in a report to the court or in testimony before the court;

6. Failed to report abuse of a child;

7. Communicated with a judicial officer ex-parte;

8. Represented the court in a public forum without prior approval of the court;

9. Violated state or local laws, rules, or this policy in the person's capacity as a GAL; or,

10. Taken or failed to take any other action which would reasonable [2] place the suitability of the person to serve as GAL in question.

6.4 Upon receipt of a written response to a complaint from the GAL, the Complaint Review Committee shall, within 10 business days, make a finding as to each of the issues delineated in the Committee's letter to the GAL that either there is no merit to the issues based upon the GAL's response or that there is merit to the issue. The Review Committee may, at their discretion, extended [3] the time for entering findings to conduct additional investigation if necessary, however, in no case shall that extension be for more than 20 business days and the GAL shall be notified.

6.5 The Complaint Review Committee shall have the authority to issue a written admonishment, a written reprimand, refer the GAL to additional training, recommend to the court, upon it's [4] own motion to remove the GAL from the instant case, or suspend or remove the GAL from the registry. In considering a response, the Committee shall take into consideration any prior complaints which resulted in an admonishment, reprimand, referral to training, removal of the GAL from a particular case, or suspension or removal from a registry. If a GAL is listed on more than one registry, the suspension or removal may apply to each registry the GAL is listed on at the discretion of the Committee.

6.6 The complainant and the GAL shall be notified in writing of the Committee's decision within 10 business days of receipt of the GAL response.

6.7 A GAL may, within 5 business days of receipt of notification that they have been suspended or [5] review the Committee's decision. The court shall designate a hearing officer. The sole purpose of the hearing shall be to review the appropriateness of the suspension or removal from the registry. The hearing officer shall review the written record of the instant case and any prior complaints upon which the Committee relied and hear oral arguments from the GAL and a representative of the Committee. Said hearing shall be conducted within 20 days of the receipt of the request for the hearing.

G. Payment of Guardian ad Litem.

7.1 There shall be no payment of a GAL by anyone, except as authorized by order of the court.

7.2 Each order appointing GAL shall set forth the hourly rate of compensation for the investigative/legal work; source of payment, if determined; and unless waived, shall require the GAL to seek court authorization to provide services in excess of fifty hours per case, not including court appearances.

7.3 The order appointing a GAL may include a provision for a retainer fee, as evidenced by itemized accounting, shall be returned to the parties according to their proportionate responsibility for payment of the GAL.

7.4 All fee requests by the GAL submitted to the court shall contain time records, which distinguished investigative/legal, administrative/clerical, and travel time and shall also be served upon the parties.

7.5 GAL fees shall be the responsibility of a party or parties unless the court has entered and order [6] authorizing payment at public expense.

[LR 98.10 adopted effective September 1, 1999. Amended effective September 1, 2000; September 1, 2012; September 2, 2013. Renumbered LGALR 98.10 and amended effective September 1, 2015.]

[1] So in original.

[2] So in original.

[3] So in original.

[4] So in original.

[5] So in original. Probably should be followed by "removed".

[6] So in original.

LGALR 98.11. COMPLAINT PROCEDURE FOR TITLE 13 GUARDIANS AD LITEM

Any complaint filed against a Title 13 guardian ad litem, whether the guardian ad litem is a member of the Chelan–Douglas CASA/GAL Program or an attorney guardian ad litem appointed by the court, will follow the complaint procedure outlined in LGALR 98.10(F).

[LR 98.11 adopted effective September 1, 2002. Renumbered LGALR 98.11 and amended effective September 1, 2015.]

LOCAL CRIMINAL RULES FOR SUPERIOR COURT

LCrR 1.6. DUTIES

The full time Chelan County Court Commissioner shall have the authority to accept pleas in criminal matters.

[Adopted effective September 1, 2000.]

LCrR 2.2. WARRANT OF ARREST AND SUMMONS

(g) Warrants by Fax Machine or E–Mail. Law enforcement officials in outlaying areas of Chelan County may send by Fax machine or e-mail a motion, affidavit and order for a search warrant or an arrest warrant to the Court at fax number (509) 667–6588 or e-mail superiorcourt.warrant@co.chelan.wa.us, or other e-mail as directed by the Court. Upon authorization and entry by the Court, a signed copy of the order shall be sent back by Fax machine or e-mail to the law enforcement official for execution. Each faxed or e-mailed document shall indicate the date and time sent. The original of the order shall be presented and signed at the earliest possible time for filing with the Court.

[Adopted effective September 1, 1999; amended effective September 1, 2001; September 2, 2014; September 1, 2015.]

LCrR 3.1. RIGHT TO AND ASSIGNMENT OF LAWYER

(d)(4) Defendants who request appointment of counsel may be required to promptly execute and file a financial disclosure under oath, which shall substantially comply with the form set forth in Exhibit A attached hereto, or the defendant may be required to provide the information orally to the court.

(5) All appointments of counsel by reason of indigency are expressly contingent upon indigency and full disclosure of assets. Where income or assets are discovered or change subsequent to appointment which enable the defendant to afford counsel, or if the defendant can afford partial payment, fees may be ordered to be reimbursed to the court.

(6) Upon appointment of counsel for indigent criminal defendants or other litigants, the Clerk shall promptly provide counsel with notice of the appointment.

(e)(1) Attorneys representing defendants in criminal cases, except when appointed by the court, must serve prompt written notice of their employment upon the prosecuting attorney and file the same with the Clerk of the Court, and note the same for a hearing. No withdrawal will be granted by the Court, except for cause deemed sufficient by the Court. Approval of withdrawal may, if necessary to prevent a continuance of a trial or hearing, be denied, and such attorney be required to proceed with the trial.

[Adopted effective September 1, 1999; amended effective September 1, 2000.]

DECLARATION OF INDIGENCY

IN THE SUPERIOR COURT OF THE STATE OF WASHINGTON
IN AND FOR THE COUNTY OF CHELAN

State of Washington,   )
) DECLARATION OF INDIGENCY
            Plaintiff,   )
) NO.: _____
v.   )
)
_____,   )
)
          Defendant.   )
_____)

STATE OF WASHINGTON   )
) ss
COUNTY OF CHELAN   )

I, _____ , the above named defendant, do want a lawyer to represent me in the case. I am without income or assets with which to retain an attorney.

1. GENERAL INFORMATION

   (a) Name: _____
   (b) Address: _____
   (c) Telephone number: _____
   (d) Marital status: [ ] Single [ ] Married [ ] Separated
       Spouses Name: _____
       Spouses Address: _____
   (e) Number of dependents: _____
       Age of dependents: _____
       Are you presently employed: [ ] Yes [ ] No
       Length of employment: _____ Occupation: _____
   (f) Name and address of employer: _____
       Prior employer: _____
   (g) Is spouse employed? [ ] Yes [ ] No
       Length of employment: _____ Occupation: _____
       Name of spouse's employer: _____

2. INCOME
   (a) Gross monthly income (mine) $_____
   (b) Gross monthly income (spouse) $_____
   (c) Other income $_____

3. ASSETS
   (a) Cash on hand $_____
   (b) Savings account $_____
   (c) Checking account $_____
   (d) Home (cash value less amount owing) $_____
   (e) Vehicles (cash value less amount owing) $_____
       Make and year: _____
   (f) Other assets and property $_____

4. MONTHLY LIVING EXPENSES
   (a) Rent or mortgage $_____
   (b) Food $_____

  (c) Utilities $_____

  (d) Transportation $_____

  (e) Medical, dental, and insurance $_____

  (f) Other $_____

5. DEBTS

  Name of Creditors: **AMOUNT OWED:**

  _____ $_____

  _____ $_____

  _____ $_____

  _____ $_____

Should there be any change in my income or assets, I will advise the court immediately.

I have been advised that I may be required to repay all or part of the costs of court appointed counsel.

I declare under penalty of perjury, under the laws of the State of Washington, that the above information is true and correct.

              _____

              Signature

              _____

              Date signed

              _____

              Place signed

[Adopted effective September 1, 1999.]

LCrR 3.4. PRESENCE OF THE DEFENDANT

(d) All preliminary and timely arrangements for the court appearance of any defendant held in custody shall be the responsibility of the deputy prosecutor in charge of the case, who shall advise the jail staff of the defendant's required appearance.

[Adopted effective September 1, 1999.]

LCrR 3.6. SUPPRESSION HEARINGS– DUTY OF COURT

Threshold hearings may be stricken upon stipulation by the prosecuting attorney that the defendant has made a preliminary showing for the 3.6 hearing.

[Adopted effective September 1, 1999.]

LCrR 4.2. PLEAS

(i) If a criminal case is set for trial but will be disposed of by a change of plea, the guilty plea shall be heard on or before the trial date. The court may authorize a continuance and hear the change of plea at a later date.

[Adopted effective September 1, 1999.]

LCrR 4.5. OMNIBUS HEARINGS

(d)(1) *Motions.* All rulings of the Court at omnibus hearings or on motions shall be binding on the parties and shall not be relitigated at trial.

(i) If there is no dispute regarding omnibus requests, the motion shall be signed by both parties and presented to the Court ex parte for signature before the date of omnibus hearing.

(ii) A defendant need not appear at the omnibus hearing if there are no disputed omnibus requests.

[Adopted effective September 1, 1999; amended effective September 1, 2005.]

LCrR 7.1. PROCEDURES BEFORE SENTENCING

(b)(1) *When Required; Time of Service.* Unless otherwise directed by the Court, the prosecuting attorney and the defendant's attorney shall, not less than ten (10) days before the sentencing date, serve a copy of any presentence report upon the opposing party and send the original to the sentencing judge. The Department of Corrections shall serve a copy of its report upon the prosecuting attorney and the defense attorney and the original to the sentencing judge not less than ten days before the sentencing date.

(2) *Contents of Defendant's Report.* The defendant's presentence report which requests a sentence outside of the standard range shall outline any proposed programs, specifically state, among the other details, what community resources are available for implementation of the program.

If the defendant is not requesting a sentence outside of the standard range, the defense presentence report shall indicate the recommended sentence, the type of program that should be afforded the defendant, and reasons therefore.

(3) *Penalties for Violation.* A violation of this rule may result in the refusal of the Court to proceed with the sentencing until after reports have been served and filed as directed herein, and in the imposition of terms, or the Court may proceed to impose sentence without regard to the violation.

(4) *Preliminary Confidential Filing of Report.* The Clerk of the Court shall file under seal and not permit examination of the pre-sentence report, any psychological, sociological, and mental health examinations, sex offender treatment evaluations, and polygraph examinations until further order of the court. Upon request for the inspection of such documents, the court shall reasonably promptly inspect the file and provide for inspection of all non-confidential and disclosable information to the requesting individual.

[Adopted effective September 1, 1999.]

LCrR 7.8. PAYMENT OF COSTS

(a) In all criminal cases, except where the Court Order is to the contrary, the Judgment and Sentence shall provide that the Clerk shall disperse monies received from the criminal defendant in the following order:

(1) Restitution;

(2) Crime Victims Compensation;

(3) Court Costs;

(4) Attorneys Fees;

(5) Drug Fund;

(6) Fines.

[Adopted effective September 1, 1999. Formerly LCrR 7.3, renumbered effective September 1, 2000.]

CHELAN COUNTY LOCAL RULES FOR MANDATORY ARBITRATION

LMAR 1.1. APPLICATION OF RULES— PURPOSE AND DEFINITIONS

(a) Purpose. The purpose of mandatory arbitration of civil actions under RCW 7.06 as implemented by the Mandatory Arbitration Rules is to provide a simplified and economical procedure for obtaining the prompt and equitable resolution of disputes involving claims of $50,000 or less. The Mandatory Arbitration Rules as supplemented by these local rules are not designed to address every question, which may arise during the arbitration process, and the rules give considerable discretion to the Arbitrator. The Arbitrator should not hesitate to exercise that discretion. Arbitration hearings should be informal and expeditious, consistent with the purpose of the statutes and rules.

[Adopted effective September 1, 1999; amended effective September 1, 2006; September 1, 2011.]

LMAR 1.3. RELATIONSHIP TO THE SUPERIOR COURT JURISDICTION AND OTHER RULES—MOTION

All motions before the Court relating to mandatory arbitration shall be noted on the civil motions calendar in accordance with LR 77, except as otherwise provided in these rules of arbitration.

[Adopted effective September 1, 1999; amended effective September 1, 2011.]

LMAR 2.1. TRANSFER TO ARBITRATION

(a) **Statement of Arbitrability.** In every civil case the party filing the Note for Trial Docket provided by Civil Rule 30 shall, upon the form prescribed by the court, complete a Statement of Arbitrability.* Within 14 days after the Note for Trial and Statement of Arbitrability have been served and filed, any party disagreeing with the Statement of Arbitrability or willing to stipulate to arbitration shall serve and file a response to the Statement of Arbitrability on the form prescribed by the Court.** In the absence of such response, the Statement of Arbitrability shall be deemed correct, and the case shall be deemed set for arbitration. If a party asserts that its claim exceeds $50,000 or seeks relief other than a money judgment, the case is not subject to arbitration except by stipulation.

(b) **Failure to File—Amendments.** A party failing to serve and file an original response within the time prescribed may later do so only upon leave of court. A party may amend the Statement of Arbitrability or response at any time before assignment of an Arbitrator or assignment of trial date and thereafter only upon leave of court for good cause shown.***

If a party noting the matter for trial setting: (a) has a limited ability to speak or understand the English Language, or (b) knows, or after reasonable inquiry has reason to believe, that any other party to the action has limited ability to speak or understand the English Language, the party noting the matter for trial shall indicate on the Note for Trial Setting and Initial Statement of Arbitrability that an interpreter is needed. The party filing such Notice of Trial Setting and Initial Statement of Arbitrability shall, simultaneously with such filing, provide a copy of the Notice of Trial Setting and Initial Statement of Arbitrability to the Judicial Assistant.

(c) **By Stipulation.** A case in which all parties file a stipulation to arbitrate under MAR 8.1 will be placed on the arbitration calendar regardless of the nature of the case or amount in controversy.****

[Adopted effective September 1, 1999; amended effective September 1, 2000; September 1, 2006; September 1, 2011.]

* Form LMAR 2.1(a)1

** Form LMAR 2.1(a)2

*** Form LMAR 2.1(b)

**** Form LMAR 2.1(c)

LMAR 2.1(a)1 (FORM).   NOTE FOR TRIAL SETTING
AND INITIAL STATEMENT OF ARBITRABILITY

IN THE SUPERIOR COURT OF THE STATE OF WASHINGTON
IN AND FOR THE COUNTY OF CHELAN

,
 	
 Plaintiff,
 	
 vs.
 	
 ,
 	
 Defendant.
	No.
	
	 NOTE FOR TRIAL SETTING AND INITIAL STATEMENT OF ARBITRABILITY
	
	 [ ] **Interpreter needed**[2]
	    [ ] **Spanish**
	    [ ] **Other language:** _____
	                  (specify)
	
	 [ ] **ASL**

TO THE CLERK OF THE COURT AND TO:

_____

_____

_____

CERTIFICATION OF READINESS FOR TRIAL OR ARBITRATION

THE UNDERSIGNED HEREBY CERTIFIES THAT THIS CASE IS AT ISSUE AS OF _____ (date answer/response filed) AND THAT THER HAS BEEN A REASONABLE TIME FOR DISCOVERY, THAT DISCVOERY WILL BE COMPLETE IN ACCORDANCE WITH LR 37(F), THAT ALL NECESSARY WITNESSES WILL BE AVAILABLE, AND THAT THE CASE IS IN EVERY WAY READY FOR TRIAL OR ARBITRATION.

Please take note that this case will be brought on the trial setting docket for assignment

for trial date on the _____, 20___.

    1.   Nature of case: _____

    2.   Is Jury demanded? _____6 member ( ) 12 member ( )

    3.   Estimated trial time: _____ hours _____ days

_____

[2]If an interpreter is needed, a copy of the Note for Motion must be provided to the Judicial Assistant simultaneously with the filing of this document. LR 7(b)(1)(c)(iii). LMAR 2.1(b)

SERVE ON ALL PARTIES AND FILE WITH THE COUNTY CLERK.
Form LMAR 2.1(a)1
[Amended September 1, 2015]

4.   Dates unavailable for trial:

_____

INITIAL STATEMENT FO ARBITRABILITY (LMAR 2.1)

_____ This case is subject to arbitration because the sole relief sought is a money judgment and involves no claim in excess of $50,000, exclusive of attorney fees, interest and costs. (MAR 1.2)

_____ This case is not subject to mandatory arbitration because:

     _____ Plaintiff's claim exceeds $50,000.

     _____ Plaintiff seeks relief other than a money judgment.

     _____ Defendant's counter or cross-claim exceeds $50,000.

     _____ Defendant's counter or cross-claim seeks relief other than a monetary judgment.

_____ The undersigned contends that its claim exceeds $50,000 but hereby waives any claim in excess of $50,000 for purposes of arbitration (MAR 1.2).

DATED: _____   Signed: _____

                                  Attorney for: _____

Names, Addresses and Phone Numbers of all Counsel of Record:

Plaintiff Attorney: _____   Bar ID: _____

Address: _____   Phone: _____

Defense Attorney: _____   Bar ID: _____

Address: _____   Phone: _____

Other: _____   Bar ID: _____

Address: _____   Phone: _____

SERVE ON ALL PARTIES AND FILE WITH THE COUNTY CLERK.
Form LMAR 2.1(a)1
[Amended September 1, 2015]

[Adopted effective September 1, 1999; amended effective September 1, 2000; September 1, 2006; September 1, 2007; September 1, 2011; September 1, 2015.]

LMAR 2.1(a)(2) (Form). RESPONSE TO NOTE FOR TRIAL SETTING AND INITIAL STATEMENT OF ARBITRABILITY

SUPERIOR COURT OF WASHINGTON FOR CHELAN COUNTY

_____,) Plaintiff,)) vs.)) _____,) Defendant.) _____)	No. _____ RESPONSE TO NOTE FOR TRIAL SETTING AND INITIAL STATEMENT OF ARBITRABILITY

The undersigned attorney disagrees with the Initial Statement of Arbitrability filed in this case and contends that:

_____   This case is subject to arbitration because the sole relief sought is a money judgment and involves no claim in excess of $50,000, exclusive of attorney fees, interest and costs. (MAR 1.2)

_____   This case is not is not subject to mandatory arbitration because:

_____   Plaintiff's claim exceeds $50,000.
_____   Plaintiff seeks relief other than a money judgment.
_____   Defendant's counter or cross-claim exceeds $50,000.
_____   Defendant's counter or cross-claim seeks relief other than a money judgment.

_____   The undersigned contends that its claim exceeds $50,000 but herby waives any claim in excess of $50,000 for purposes of arbitration (MAR 1.2).

DATED: _____   SIGNED: _____

Attorney for : _____

Type Name: _____

Address: _____

_____

SERVE ON ALL PARTIES AND FILE WITH THE COUNTY CLERK.
Form LMAR 2.1(a)2

[Adopted effective September 1, 1999; September 1, 2006; amended effective September 1, 2011.]

LMAR 2.1(b) (Form). AMENDED STATEMENT OF ARBITRABILITY

SUPERIOR COURT OF WASHINGTON FOR CHELAN COUNTY

_____,	)	No. _____
Plaintiff,	)	
	)	
vs.	)	AMENDED STATEMENT
	)	OF ARBITRABILITY
_____,	)	
Defendant.	)	
_____)		

_____ This form amends an Original Statement of Arbitrability.
_____ This form amends Response to the Statement of Arbitrability.

_____ This case is subject to arbitration because the sole relief sought is a money judgment and involves no claim in excess of $50,000, exclusive of attorney fees, interest and costs. (MAR 1.2)

_____ This case is not subject to mandatory arbitration because:

_____ Plaintiff's claim exceeds $50,000.
_____ Plaintiff seeks relief other than a money judgment.
_____ Defendant's counter or cross-claim exceeds $50,000.
_____ Defendant's counter or cross-claim seeks relief other than a money judgment.

_____ The undersigned contends that its claim exceeds $50,000 but herby waives any claim in excess of $50,000 for purposes of arbitration (MAR 1.2).

DATED: _____   SIGNED: _____

Attorney for: _____

An amendment to a Statement of Arbitrability for a case already assigned to an arbitrator or already assigned a trial date must be presented as a motion before a Judge. (LMAR 1.3)

SERVE ON ALL PARTIES, THE ARBITRATION ADMINISTRATOR AND FILE WITH THE COUNTY CLERK.
Form LMAR 2.1(b)

[Adopted effective September 1, 1999; amended effective September 1, 2006; September 1, 2011.]

LMAR 2.1(c) (Form). STIPULATION TO ARBITRATION

SUPERIOR COURT OF WASHINGTON FOR CHELAN COUNTY

_____,)
             Plaintiff,)   No. _____
)
      vs.   )   STIPULATION TO
)   ARBITRATION
_____,)
             Defendant.)
_____)

Although this case is not subject to mandatory arbitration, the undersigned attorneys are willing to stipulate that the case be assigned to arbitration without limit on the award. (MAR 8.1 – LMAR 8.1)

Signed:_____   Signed:_____
    Attorney for Plaintiff   Attorney for Defendant

Typed Name:_____   Typed Name:_____

Address:_____   Address:_____

_____   _____

Signed:_____   Signed:_____
    Attorney for Plaintiff   Attorney for Defendant

Typed Name:_____   Typed Name:_____

Address:_____   Address:_____

_____   _____

FILE WITH THE COUNTY CLERK AND THE ARBITRATION ADMINISTRATOR
Form LMAR 2.1(c)

[Adopted effective September 1, 1999; amended effective September 1, 2000; September 1, 2011.]

LMAR 2.3. ASSIGNMENT TO ARBITRATOR

(a) **Generally; Stipulations.** When a case is set for arbitration, a list of five proposed arbitrators will be furnished to the parties.* A master list of arbitrators will be made available upon request. The parties are encouraged to stipulate to an arbitrator.** In the absence of a stipulation, the arbitrator will be chosen from among the five proposed arbitrators in the manner defined by this rule.

(b) **Response by Parties.** Each party may, within 14 days after the list of proposed arbitrators is furnished to the parties, nominate one or two arbitrators and strike two arbitrators from the list. If both parties respond, an arbitrator nominated by both parties will be appointed. If no arbitrator has been nominated by both parties, the Arbitration Administrator will randomly appoint an arbitrator from among those not stricken by either party.

(c) **Response by Only One Party.** If only one party responds within 14 days, the Arbitration Administrator will appoint an arbitrator nominated by that party.

(d) **No Response.** If neither party responds within 14 days, the Arbitration Administrator will randomly appoint one of the five proposed arbitrators.

(e) **Additional Arbitrators for Additional Parties.** If there are more than two adverse parties, all represented by different counsel, two additional proposed arbitrators shall be added to the list for each additional party so represented with the above principles of selection to be applied. The number of adverse parties shall be determined by the Arbitration Administrator, subject to review by the Presiding Judge.

[Adopted effective September 1, 1999; amended effective September 1, 2011.]

* Form LMAR 2.3(a)
** Form LMAR 2.3(a)2

LMAR 2.3(a) (Form).   NOTICE OF PROPOSED ARBITRATORS

SUPERIOR COURT OF WASHINGTON FOR CHELAN COUNTY

_____ ,)
          Plaintiff,   )
)
          vs.   )
)
)
_____ ,)
          Defendant.   )
_____)
	No. _____
	
	NOTICE OF PROPOSED
	ARBITRATORS

TO: The parties and their attorneys
FROM: Arbitration Administrator

This case has been transferred to arbitration. You are encouraged to stipulate to an arbitrator. A list of Chelan County attorneys who have volunteered to serve as arbitrators is available in the Arbitration Administrator's Office at the Chelan County Courthouse. If you stipulate, please contact the Arbitrator jointly to determine whether he or she is willing and able to serve. Complete the separate "Stipulation to Arbitrator" form and return it to the Arbitration Administrator.

In the absence of a stipulation, pursuant to LMAR 2.3, the arbitrator will be chosen from the following list:

    1.   4.
    2.   5.
    3.

Each party may recommend two (please circle) and reject two (please strike through) arbitrators from the list.
The form or a completed "Stipulation to Arbitrator" form must be returned to the Arbitration Administrator within 14 days of receipt.

At the expiration of the above date, an Arbitrator will be selected in this action according to the procedure established in Local Rule 2.3.

Dated:_____   Signed:_____
A copy of this form to be
Returned within 14 days of   Typed Name:_____
receipt to:
                                 Address:_____
Arbitration Administrator
P.O. Box 880   Attorney for:_____
Wenatchee, WA 98807
Form LMAR 2.3(a)

[Adopted effective September 1, 1999; amended effective September 1, 2011.]

LMAR 2.3(a)2 (Form).　STIPULATION TO ARBITRATOR

SUPERIOR COURT OF WASHINGTON FOR CHELAN COUNTY

_____,	)	No. _____
Plaintiff,	)	
	)	
vs.	)	STIPULATION TO
	)	ARBITRATOR
_____,	)	
Defendant.	)	
_____	)	

The parties stipulate to the following person as Arbitrator:

Arbitrator's name:_____

Address:_____

ARBITRATOR HAS BEEN CONTACTED JOINTLY AND AGREES TO SERVE.

Signed:_____　　　　Signed:_____
　　Attorney for Plaintiff　　　　　　　Attorney for Defendant

Typed Name:_____　　　　Typed Name:_____

Address:_____　　　　Address:_____

_____　　　　_____

Signed:_____　　　　Signed:_____
　　Attorney for Plaintiff　　　　　　　Attorney for Defendant

Typed Name:_____　　　　Typed Name:_____

Address:_____　　　　Address:_____

_____　　　　_____

A completed copy of this form must be returned within 14 days of receipt to:

Arbitration Administrator
P.O. Box 880
Wenatchee, WA 98801-0880

Form LMAR 2.3(a)2

[Adopted effective September 1, 1999; amended effective September 1, 2000; September 1, 2011.]

LMAR 3.1. QUALIFICATIONS

(a) Arbitration Panel. There shall be a panel of arbitrators in such numbers as the Superior Court Judges may from time to time determine. A person desiring to serve as an arbitrator shall complete an information sheet on the form prescribed by the Court. A list showing the names of arbitrators available to hear cases and the information sheets will be available for public inspection in the Arbitration Administrator's Office. The oath of office on the form prescribed by the Court must be completed and filed prior to an applicant being placed on the panel.

(b) Refusal; Disqualification. The appointment of an arbitrator is subject to the right of that person to refuse to serve. An arbitrator must notify the Arbitration Administrator immediately if refusing to serve or if any cause exists for the arbitrator's disqualification from the case upon any of the grounds of interest, relationship, bias or prejudice set forth in CJC Cannon 3(c) governing the disqualification of judges. If disqualified, the Arbitrator must immediately return all materials in a case to the Arbitration Administrator.

[Adopted effective September 1, 1999; amended effective September 1, 2011.]

LMAR 3.2. AUTHORITY OF ARBITRATORS

An arbitrator has the authority to:

(a) Determine the time, place and procedure to present a motion before the arbitrator.

(b) Require a party or attorney advising such party or both to pay the reasonable expenses, including attorney's fees, caused by the failure of such party or attorney or both to obey an order of the arbitrator unless the arbitrator finds that the failure was substantially justified or that other circumstances make an award of expenses unjust. The arbitrator shall make a special award for such expenses and shall file such award with the clerk of the court, with proof of service on each party. The aggrieved party shall have 10 days thereafter to appeal the award of such expense in accordance with the procedures described in RCW 2.24.050. If within 10 days after the award is filed no party appeals, a judgment shall be entered in a manner described generally under MAR 6.3.

(c) Award attorney's fees as authorized by these rules, by contract or law.

[Adopted effective September 1, 1999; amended effective September 1, 2011.]

LMAR 4.2. DISCOVERY

In determining when additional discovery beyond that directly authorized by MAR 4.2 is reasonably necessary, the Arbitrator shall balance the benefits of discovery against the burdens and expenses. The Arbitrator shall consider the nature and complexity of the case, the amount of controversy, values at stake, the discovery that has already occurred, the burdens on the party from whom discovery is sought, and the possibility of unfair surprise which may result if discovery is restricted. Authorized discovery shall be conducted in accordance with the civil rules except that motions concerning discovery shall be determined by the Arbitrator.

[Adopted effective September 1, 1999; amended effective September 1, 2011.]

LMAR 5.1. NOTICE OF HEARING—TIME AND PLACE—CONTINUANCE

An arbitration hearing may be scheduled at any reasonable time and place chosen by the Arbitrator.* The Arbitrator may grant a continuance without court order. The parties may stipulate to a continuance only with the permission of the Arbitrator. The Arbitrator shall give reasonable notice of the hearing date and any continuance to the Arbitration Administrator.**

[Adopted effective September 1, 1999; amended effective September 1, 2011.]

* Form LMAR 5.1(a)

** Form LMAR 5.1(b)

LMAR 5.1(a) (Form). NOTICE OF ARBITRATION HEARING DATE

SUPERIOR COURT OF WASHINGTON FOR CHELAN COUNTY

_____,	)	No. _____
Plaintiff,	)	
	)	
vs.	)	NOTICE OF ARBITRATION
	)	HEARING DATE
_____,	)	
Defendant.	)	
	)	

The hearing in this case has been scheduled for:

Date:_____

Time:_____

Place:_____

_____

The prehearing statement of proof under MAR 5.2 and LMAR 5.2 must be furnished to the Arbitrator and served on all parties at least 14 days before the hearing.

DATED:_____   Arbitrator:_____

Address:_____

_____

Telephone No._____

Copies must be sent to the parties and to:

Arbitration Administrator
P.O. Box 880
Wenatchee, WA 98807-0880

Form LMAR 5.1(a)

[Adopted effective September 1, 1999; amended effective September 1, 2000; September 1, 2011.]

LMAR 5.1(b) (Form).   ORDER OF CONTINUANCE OF ARBITRATION HEARING DATE

SUPERIOR COURT OF WASHINGTON FOR CHELAN COUNTY

_____,)
              Plaintiff,   )   No. _____
)
      vs.   )   ORDER OF CONTINUANCE OF
)   ARBITRATION HEARING DATE
_____,)
             Defendant.   )
_____)

The attorney for the _____ has moved for a continuance
of the arbitration hearing date in this case.
The reasons given are:_____

_____

_____

The opposing attorney has not objected or has been overruled; therefore,

IT IS ORDERED that the date of the arbitration hearing in this case is now set for
_____, _____, 20 ___, at _____ a.m./p.m.

DATED:_____   _____
                                          ARBITRATOR

Copies must be sent to the parties and to:

Arbitration Administrator
P.O. Box 880
Wenatchee, WA 98807-0880

Form LMAR 5.1(b)

[Adopted effective September 1, 1999; amended effective September 1, 2000; September 1, 2011.]

LMAR 5.2. PREHEARING STATEMENT OF PROOF—DOCUMENTS FILED WITH THE COURT

In addition to the requirements of MAR 5.2, each party shall also furnish the Arbitrator with copies of pleadings and other documents contained in the court file which that party deems relevant. The court file shall remain with the County Clerk. The Arbitrator shall strictly enforce the provisions of MAR 5.2 and is encouraged to withhold permission to present evidence at time of hearing if the parties have failed to comply with this rule.

[Adopted effective September 1, 1999; amended effective September 1, 2011.]

LMAR 5.3. CONDUCT OF HEARING— WITNESSES—RULES OF EVIDENCE

(a) **Oath or Affirmation.** The Arbitrator shall place a witness under oath or affirmation before the witness presents testimony.

(b) **Recording.** The hearing may be recorded electronically or otherwise by any party at his or her expense.

(c) **Certain Documents Presumed Admissible.** The documents listed below, if relevant, are presumed admissible at an arbitration hearing, but only if (1) the party offering the document serves on all parties a notice, accompanied by a copy of the document and the name, address, and telephone number of its author or maker, at least 14 days prior to the hearing in accordance with MAR 5.2; and (2) the party offering the document similarly furnishes all other parties with copies of all other related documents from the same author or maker. This rule does not restrict argument or proof relating to the weight of the evidence after hearing all of the evidence and the arguments of opposing parties. The documents presumed admissible under this rule are:

1. A bill, report, chart or record of a hospital, doctor, dentist, registered nurse, licensed practical nurse, physical therapist, psychologist or other health care provider, on a letterhead or billhead;

2. A bill for drugs, medical appliances or other related expenses on a letterhead or billhead;

3. A bill for or an estimate of property damage on a letterhead or billhead. In the case of an estimate, the party intending to offer the estimate shall forward with the notice to the adverse party, a statement indicating whether or not the property was repaired, and if it was, whether the estimated repairs were made in full or in part, attaching a copy to the receipted bill showing the items of repair and the amount paid.

4. A police, weather, wage loss, or traffic signal report, or standard United States government life expectancy table to the extent it is admissible under the Rules of Evidence, but without the need for formal proof of authentication or identification;

5. A photograph, x-ray, drawing, map, blueprint or similar documentary evidence, to the extent it is admissible under the Rules of Evidence, but without the need for formal proof of authentication or identification;

6. The written statement of any other witness, including the written report of an expert witness, and including a statement of opinion which the witness would be allowed to express if testifying in person, if it is made by affidavit or by declaration under penalty of perjury;

7. A document not specifically covered by any of the foregoing provisions but having equivalent circumstantial guarantees of trustworthiness, the admission of which would serve the interest of justice.

(e) **Opposing Party May Subpoena Author or Maker as Witness.** Any other party may subpoena the author or maker of a document admissible under this rule, at that party's expense, and examine the author or maker as if under cross-examination.*

[Adopted effective September 1, 1999; amended effective September 1, 2011.]

* Form 5.3(e)1 or Form 5.3(e)2

LMAR 5.3(e)1 (Form). SUBPOENA
SUPERIOR COURT OF WASHINGTON FOR CHELAN COUNTY

_____,)
        Plaintiff,)   No. _____
)
     vs.   )   SUBPOENA
)
_____,)
       Defendant.)
_____)

TO: _____
ADDRESS:_____

YOU ARE COMMANDED TO APPEAR AT AN ARBITRATION HEARING ON:

_____ at _____
     Date   Time

AT:_____
    Room Number

Address:

_____
    Street   City

To testify in this case on behalf of the _____ and to remain in
attendance until you have been dismissed or excused by the Arbitrator.

FAILURE TO COMPLY MAY BE CONTEMPT OF COURT.

DATED:_____   Signature:_____

Address:_____

_____   _____ Arbitrator

Phone:_____   _____ Attorney for Plaintiff

                                  _____ Attorney for Defendant

                                  _____ Attorney for _____

                              (Check applicable box)

Form LMAR 5.3(e)1

[Adopted effective September 1, 1999; amended effective September 1, 2011.]

LMAR 5.3(e)2 (Form). SUBPOENA DUCES TECUM
SUPERIOR COURT OF WASHINGTON FOR CHELAN COUNTY

```
_____,        )
                Plaintiff,    )      No. _____
                              )
          vs.                 )      SUBPOENA  DUCES TECUM
                              )
_____,        )
                Defendant.    )
_____         )
```

TO: _____

ADDRESS:_____

YOU ARE COMMANDED TO APPEAR AT AN ARBITRATION HEARING ON:

_____ at _____
          Date   Time

AT:_____

          Room Number

Address: _____

          _____
          Street   City

To testify in this case on behalf of the _____ and to remain in
attendance until you have been dismissed or excused by the Arbitrator.

FAILURE TO COMPLY MAY BE CONTEMPT OF COURT.

DATED:_____   Signature:_____

Address:_____

_____   _____ Arbitrator

Phone:_____   _____ Attorney for Plaintiff

                                     _____ Attorney for Defendant

                                     _____ Attorney for_____

                                     (Check applicable box)

Form LMAR 5.3(e)2

[Adopted effective September 1, 1999. Amended effective September 1, 2011.]

LMAR 6.1. FORM AND CONTENT OF AWARD

(a) Form. The award shall be prepared on the form prescribed by the Court.*

(b) Exhibits. All exhibits offered during the hearing shall accompany the award and be filed with the Clerk.

[Adopted effective September 1, 1999; amended effective September 1, 2011.]

* Form LMAR 6.1(a)

LMAR 6.1(a) (Form). ARBITRATION AWARD

SUPERIOR COURT OF WASHINGTON FOR CHELAN COUNTY

_____,	)		
Plaintiff,	)	No. _____	
	)		
vs.	)	ARBITRATION AWARD	
	)		
_____,	)		
Defendant.	)		
_____	)		

The issues in arbitration having been heard on _____, 20 ___, I make the following award:

Twenty days after the award has been filed with the Clerk, if no party has sought a trial de novo under MAR 7.1, any party on notice to all parties may present to the Presiding Judge a judgment on the arbitration award for entry as final judgment in this case.

Was any part of this award based on the failure of a party to participate?

_____ Yes   _____ No

If yes, please identify the party and explain:

DATED:_____   _____

ARBITRATOR

Originals to be filed with the Clerk of the Superior Court, Chelan County Courthouse, together with proof of service on the parties. A copy must also be sent to:

Arbitration Administrator
P.O. Box 880
Wenatchee, WA 98807-0880

Form LMAR 6.1(a)

[Adopted effective September 1, 1999. Amended effective September 1, 2011.]

LMAR 6.2. FILING OF AWARD

A request by an Arbitrator for an extension of time for the filing of an award under MAR 6.2 may be presented to the Presiding Judge, ex parte. The Arbitrator shall give the parties notice of any extension granted.

[Adopted effective September 1, 1999; amended effective September 1, 2011.]

LMAR 6.3. JUDGMENT ON AWARD

(a) Presentation. A judgment on an award shall be presented to the Presiding Judge, by any party, on notice in accordance with MAR 6.3.

[Adopted effective September 1, 1999; amended effective September 1, 2011.]

LMAR 7.1. REQUEST FOR TRIAL DE NOVO—CALENDAR

Trial Date: Jury Demand. Every case transferred to the arbitration calendar shall maintain its position on the trial calendar as if the case had not been transferred to arbitration. A case that has been given a trial date will not lose that date by reason of being transferred to arbitration. The case shall be stricken from the trial calendar after the twenty (20)–day period within which a party may request a trial de novo has elapsed. Any jury demand shall be served and filed by the appealing party along with the request for a trial de novo, and by a non-appealing party within 14 calendar days after the request for trial de novo is served on that party. If no jury demand is timely filed, it is deemed waived.

*Form LMAR 7.1

[Adopted effective September 1, 1999; amended effective September 1, 2000; September 1, 2002; September 1, 2011.]

LMAR 7.1 (Form). REQUEST FOR TRIAL DE NOVO
AND FOR CLERK TO SEAL THE AWARD
SUPERIOR COURT OF WASHINGTON FOR CHELAN COUNTY

_____,	)	No. _____
Plaintiff,	)	
	)	
vs.	)	REQUEST FOR TRIAL DE
	)	NOVO AND FOR CLERK TO
_____,	)	SEAL THE AWARD
Defendant.	)	
_____	)	

Please take notice that the aggrieved party _____, requests a Trial De Novo from the award filed _____, 20____.

1. A trial De Novo is requested in this case pursuant to MAR 7.1 and LMAR7.1.
2. The Arbitration Award shall be sealed pursuant to LMAR 7.1 and LMAR 7.2.
3. Pursuant to LMAR 7.1, a jury demand:

[ ]   IS being filed and served upon all parties at the same time as the filing of this Request for Trial De Novo by the undersigned as the aggrieved party.

[ ]   IS NOT being filed by the aggrieved party. The non-aggrieved party has fourteen (14) calendar days from the date of service of Request for Trial De Novo to file a jury demand.

DATED:_____   _____

Signed

Typed Name:_____

Address:_____

_____

Attorney for _____

File with the Clerk of the Court, Chelan County Courthouse. Copies to be served on the parties and a copy sent to:

Arbitration Administrator
P.O. Box 880
Wenatchee, WA 98807-0880

Form LMAR 7.1

[Adopted effective September 1, 1999. Amended effective September 1, 2002; September 1, 2011.]

LMAR 7.2. PROCEDURE AT TRIAL

The Clerk shall seal arbitration awards at the time they are filed.

[Adopted effective September 1, 1999; amended effective September 1, 2011.]

LMAR 8.4. TITLE AND CITATION

These rules are known and cited as the Chelan County Mandatory Arbitration Rules. LMAR is the official abbreviation.

[Adopted effective September 1; 1999; amended effective September 1, 2011.]

LMAR 8.5. COMPENSATION OF ARBITRATOR

(a) Generally. Arbitrators shall be compensated in the same amount and manner as Judges Pro Tempore of the Superior Court; provided, however, that said compensation shall not exceed $1000.00 for any case unless prior approval is granted by a judge. Hearing time and reasonable preparation time are compensable.

(b) Form. When the award is filed, the Arbitrator shall submit to the Court a request for payment on a form prescribed by the Court. The Presiding Judge shall determine the amount of compensation and costs to be paid.

[Adopted effective September 1, 1999. Amended effective September 1, 2011; September 2, 2013. Rescinded effective September 2, 2014. Reinstated effective September 1, 2015.]

LMAR 8.6. ADMINISTRATION

The Arbitration Administrator, under the supervision of the Superior Court Judges, shall supervise arbitration under these rules and perform any additional duties, which may be delegated by the judges.

[Adopted effective September 1, 1999; amended effective September 1, 2011.]

DISTRICT COURT

LOCAL RULES FOR THE DISTRICT COURT OF THE STATE OF WASHINGTON FOR CHELAN COUNTY

Including Amendments Received Through
August 15, 2015

Table of Rules

CIVIL RULES

LCRLJ 38. CIVIL JURY TRIAL

(A) Demand. The request for jury trial in civil cases shall be by filing a demand with the clerk and paying the jury fee not later than seven days from the date of the trial setting notice issued from the court. Failure to comply with this rule is a waiver of the right to a jury trial.

(B) Imposition of Costs. Whenever any cause assigned for jury trial is settled or will not be tried by the jury for any reason, notice of that fact shall be given immediately to the court. If notification is not given forty-eight hours prior to the time of the trial, and in any event after the jury has been summoned orally or in writing, the court in its discretion may order payment of the actual costs of the jury panel by the offending party.

(NOTE: THERE IS NO PROVISION FOR REFUND OF THE JURY FEES.)

(C) Pre-trial Procedure. All cases set for jury trial shall be set for pre-trial conference, which shall be held at least two weeks prior to trial. The attorneys who are to conduct the trial and all parties shall be present to consider such matters as will promote a fair and expeditious trial. All discovery should be completed five days prior to said conference. Opposing counsel or party must be given five days notice of pre-trial motions to be heard at the pre-trial conference. Any pre-trial motions requiring the testimony of witnesses for argument may, in the discretion of the court, be continued to the day of trial. All amendments, pleadings, and motions should be made or be completed at this conference. Upon failure to appear, the judge may proceed with the conference ex-parte, and enter any appropriate order including striking the jury demand and may impose terms. Insofar as practical, the conference shall deal with any matter cognizable by Superior or District Court Rule and failure to raise the matter may result in the waiver of the same.

[Adopted effective September 1, 1998.]

LCRLJ 54. ATTORNEY FEES

In civil default cases where attorney fees are authorized by statute or by written agreement, the following fee schedule shall be deemed reasonable in all default cases unless the parties present evidence of circumstances that convinces the court that a larger or smaller fee should be awarded, provided, however, the court shall have authority to vary from this schedule on its own motion:

SCHEDULE FOR REASONABLE ATTORNEY FEES IN DEFAULT CASES

(Unless limited by statute)

$0 to $1,000	$300
$1,000.01 to $1,500	$325
$1,500.01 to $2,000	$350
$2,000.01 to $2,500	$375
$2,500.01 to $3,000	$400
$3,000.01 to $4,000	$425
$4,000.01 to $5,000	$450

For judgment amounts exceeding $5,000, reasonable attorney fees may be allowed of 10% of any balance over $5,000, without formal justification or documentation.

NSF Checks: When RCW 62A.3–515 has been followed, reasonable attorney fees will be awarded in an amount to be determined by reference to RCW 12.20.060 unless the attorney convinces the court that a larger fee should be awarded and provides an itemized affidavit as to actual time spent and hourly rate expended by the attorney in the case, in which case the court shall determine a reasonable fee. A reasonable handling fee awarded pursuant to 62A.3–515 shall not exceed $40 per check.

Where only statutory attorney fees are authorized, the default judgment shall include, and the court will approve, only attorney fees in the statutory amount as applicable at the time of entry of the judgment.

[Adopted effective September 1, 1998; amended effective September 1, 2001; September 1, 2005; September 1, 2011.]

CRIMINAL RULES

LCrRLJ 3.1(d). RIGHT TO AND ASSIGNMENT OF LAWYER

Indigent defendants shall have counsel appointed to represent them in all criminal cases unless the right to counsel is waived. Indigency shall mean an inability to pay an attorney a reasonable fee for the services which appear to be required by reason of the crime charged without substantial hardship to the defendant or the defendant's family. Defendants who request appointment of counsel may be required to promptly execute a financial disclosure under oath, which shall be filed in substantially the form set forth in Exhibit LCrRLJ 3.1(d)(1) and (2).

All appointments of counsel by reason of indigency are expressly contingent upon indigency and full disclosure of assets. Where assets are discovered or acquired subsequent to appointment which would indicate that the defendant can afford to retain counsel, or if the defendant can afford partial payment, fees may be ordered paid, pursuant to the appointment agreement, by the court.

Upon appointment of counsel for indigent criminal defendants or other litigants, the Clerk shall promptly provide counsel with notice of the appointment.

An attorney representing a defendant in a criminal case must promptly serve a written notice of appearance upon the prosecuting attorney and file the same with the clerk of the court. The attorney must certify to the court that he or she complies with the applicable Standards for Indigent Defense approved by the Supreme Court.

[Adopted effective September 1, 1998. Amended effective September 2, 2013.]

EXHIBIT LCrRLJ 3.1(d)(1). AFFIDAVIT OF INDIGENCY

Exhibit LCrRLJ 3.1(d)(1)

CHELAN COUNTY DISTRICT COURT
AFFIDAVIT OF INDIGENCY

The undersigned on oath states that I am financially unable to obtain the service of a lawyer without causing substantial hardship to myself or my family; and **I DECLARE UNDER PENALTY OF PERJURY THAT THE FOLLOWING PERSONAL AND FINANCIAL INFORMATION IS TRUE AND INTENDED TO BE RELIED UPON BY THE COURT IN DETERMINING MY ELIGIBILITY FOR LEGAL SERVICES TO BE FURNISHED ME AT PUBLIC EXPENSE.** Should there be any change in the following circumstances, I will advise the court immediately.

To qualify for a public defender the following must be filled out **completely**.

GENERAL INFORMATION: Name: _____

Address: _____ City: _____ State: _____ Zip: _____

Social Security Number: _____ Telephone ( ) _____ Date of Birth: _____

Martial Status: [ ] Single   [ ] Married   [ ] Divorced   [ ] Separated   Spouse's Name _____

My Employer: _____ Hours worked per week _____ Hourly/Monthly wage: _____

Spouse's Employer: _____ Hours worked per week _____ Hourly/Monthly wage: _____

Total Monthly Income:_____ No. of Dependents: _____ Ages: ____, ____, ____, ____, ____

EXPENSES		ASSETS	
Rent/Mortgage	$ _____	Cash, Checking, Savings	$_____
Food	$ _____	Home (Equity)	$_____
Utilities	$ _____	Vehicles (Cash or equity value)	$_____
Medical & Dental Expenses	$ _____	Investments	$_____
Installment Payments (credit cards)	$ _____	Property	$_____
Auto Expenses (payments, gas, repairs, ins.)	$ _____	Other: (furniture, jewelry, boats, etc)	$_____
Miscellaneous	$ _____	Miscellaneous	$_____
TOTAL EXPENSES	$ _____	TOTAL ASSETS	$_____

_____ I ACKNOWLEDGE THAT IF MY FINANCIAL SITUATION CHANGES, I MAY BE REQUIRED TO REIMBURSE THE COURT FOR THE EXPENSE OF MY PUBLIC DEFENDER, AND THAT I AM REQUIRED TO REPORT TO THE COURT ANY SUCH CHANGE IN FINANCIAL CONDITION.

_____ I UNDERSTAND AND AGREE TO KEEP ALL APPOINTMENTS AS SCHEDULED BY THE PUBLIC DEFENDER OR I MAY LOSE THE RIGHT TO REPRESENTATION BY THE PUBLIC DEFENDER.

Date: _____   _____

                                         Signature

Sworn and subscribed on:

Date: _____   _____

                                         Judge/Pro Tem

(PLEASE SEE OTHER SIDE FOR ACKNOWLEDGEMENT OF LIABILITY FOR ATTORNEY FEES)

Revised April 2006

[Adopted effective September 1, 1998. Amended effective September 1, 2006; September 2, 2013.]

EXHIBIT LCrRLJ 3.1(d)(2). ACKNOWLEDGMENT OF NOTICE OF POTENTIAL LIABILITY FOR ATTORNEY FEES

CHELAN COUNTY DISTRICT COURT
CHELAN COUNTY, STATE OF WASHINGTON

STATE OF WASHINGTON	)	
CITY OF WENATCHEE	)	
Plaintiff,	)	CASE NO. _____
Vs.	)	
	)	ACKNOWLEDGMENT OF NOTICE OF
	)	POTENTIAL LIABILITY FOR
	)	ATTORNEY FEES
_____	)	
Defendant.	)	

The undersigned defendant, having requested the appointment of an attorney due to indigency, hereby acknowledges that in connection with such request he/she has been advised that the court may impose the obligation of repaying the fees and costs of the attorney appointed on the following conditions:

1. That the imposition of the obligation to repay such costs and attorney fees would be based upon a foreseeable ability of the undersigned to pay.

2. That the undersigned would be entitled to the same exemption as civil judgment debtors at execution.

3. The order imposing the obligation to pay would not be enforceable by contempt or by revocation of suspended sentence unless non-payment is intentional or in bad faith.

Fully understanding the above advice, the undersigned hereby requests that an attorney be appointed to represent him/her in the above matters.

DATED this ___ day of _____, 20 ___.

_____
Defendant

_____
Address

City, State, Zip

[Adopted effective September 1, 1998. Amended effective September 1, 2001; September 1, 2006; September 2, 2013.]

LCrRLJ 3.1(e). WITHDRAWAL OF LAWYER

Whenever a case has been set for trial, no lawyer shall be allowed to withdraw except upon the consent of the court for good cause shown and upon the substitution of another lawyer or upon the defendant's knowing and voluntary decision to proceed without a lawyer. Consent may be denied if necessary to prevent a continuance.

All counsel shall be automatically terminated as counsel of record upon the following:

(1) entry of a sentence following a plea of guilty;

(2) at the conclusion of the 30–day appeal period following sentencing as a result of conviction after trial; or

(3) entry of an order deferring sentencing, a dispositional order of continuance, an order deferring prosecution, or any final disposition which is appealable;

provided that; in cases involving a subsequent hearing as a direct consequence of the sentence, such as a restitution hearing, representation will terminate upon completion of such hearing.

[Adopted effective September 1, 1998. Amended effective September 2, 2013.]

LCrRLJ 4.1(d). CRIMES REQUIRING DEFENDANT'S APPEARANCE AT ARRAIGNMENT

A lawyer may not enter a written plea of not guilty on behalf of a client, if the charging document states that one or more of the charges involves domestic violence, harassment, violation of an anti-harassment or protection order, stalking, or driving while under the influence of intoxicants, driving while under the age of 21 after having consumed alcohol, or physical control of a vehicle while under the influence of intoxicants. For such charges, the defendant must appear in person for arraignment; and the court shall determine the necessity of imposing conditions of pre-trial release.

[Adopted effective September 1, 1998.]

LCrRLJ 4.2(i). DEFERRED PROSECUTION

A petition for deferred prosecution pursuant to RCW 10.05 must be filed with the court no later than seven (7) days prior to trial unless good cause exists for delay. Sample forms for such a petition are attached hereto as Exhibits LCrRLJ 4.2(i) A, B, C, and D. The court shall have the discretion to impose court costs at the time of the approval of a deferred prosecution.

[Effective September 1, 2000.]

EXHIBIT LCrRLJ 4.2(i)(A).   PETITION FOR DEFERRED PROSECUTION

DISTRICT COURT OF WASHINGTON,
FOR CHELAN COUNTY

NO: _____

_____,
                    Plaintiff

VS.

_____,
                    Defendant

PETITION FOR DEFERRED
PROSECUTION (DPPF)
CHARGES: _____

VIOLATION DATE: _____

COMES NOW the defendant and petitions the court for deferred prosecution pursuant to RCW Chapter 10.05, and states as follows:

1. I allege the wrongful conduct charged is the result of or caused by
    [ ] ALCOHOLISM   [ ] DRUG ADDICTION   [ ] MENTAL PROBLEMS,
    for which I need treatment.
2. Unless I receive treatment for my problem, the probability of future reoccurrence is great.
3. I agree I must pay, or arrange payment for, all diagnostic and treatment costs associated with the Deferred Prosecution.
4. I understand that the court will not accept a petition for deferred prosecution from a person who sincerely believes that he or she is innocent of the crime(s) charged or does not suffer from alcoholism, drug addiction, or mental problems.
5. If this charge is a violation of Title 46 or similar municipal ordinance, I have not previously been placed on a deferred prosecution for a Title 46 or similar municipal ordinance violation.
6. A case history and assessment have been filed with this petition pursuant to RCW 10.05.020.
7. I understand and acknowledge I have the following rights: (a) to have a lawyer represent me at all hearings; (b) to have a lawyer appointed at public expense if I cannot afford one; (c) to a speedy, public jury trial; (d) to appeal any conviction; (e) to remain silent and not testify; (f) to question witnesses who testify against me; (g) to call witnesses to testify for me, at no cost; (h) to be presumed innocent unless the charge(s) against me is proven beyond a reasonable doubt; and (i) to present evidence and a defense. By deferring prosecution on these charges, I understand I give up my right to: (a) a speedy trial; (b) a jury; (c) testify; (d) question witnesses; (e) call witnesses; and (f) present evidence or a defense.
8. I stipulate to the admissibility and sufficiency of the facts in the attached police reports. I acknowledge that the above items will be entered and used to support a finding of guilty if the deferred prosecution is revoked.
9. If my deferred prosecution is revoked and I am found guilty, I understand that I may be sentenced up to the maximum penalty allowed by law.
10. I understand that if I proceed to trial and I am found guilty, I may be allowed to seek suspension of some or all fines and incarceration if I seek treatment. I understand that I may seek treatment from a public or private agency at any time, whether or not I have been found guilty or placed on deferred prosecution.
11. I understand that for some crimes, a deferred prosecution will enhance mandatory penalties for subsequent offenses committed within a seven-year period. I understand that a deferred prosecution will be a prior offense under RCW 46.61.5055 (driving under the influence, physical control of a vehicle under the influence, negligent driving if originally charged as driving under the influence or physical control of a vehicle under the influence, vehicular homicide, or vehicular assault).
12. I understand that if the court grants this Petition, I may not operate a motor vehicle on the public highways without a valid operator's license and proof of liability insurance pursuant to RCW 46.29.490. I understand I shall also be required to install an ignition interlock or other device on any motor vehicle I operate as set forth in RCW 46.20.720. I may also be required to pay restitution to victims, pay court costs, and pay probation costs authorized by law. The court may terminate the deferred prosecution program if I violate this paragraph.

13. I understand that if I fail or neglect to comply with any part of my treatment plan or with any ignition interlock requirements, then the court will hold a hearing to determine whether I should be removed from the deferred prosecution program. After the hearing the court will either order that I continue with treatment or be removed from deferred prosecution and enter judgment. If I am convicted of a similar offense during the deferred prosecution, the court will revoke the deferred prosecution and enter judgment.

14. I understand that the charge(s) against me in this case will be dismissed three years from the end of the two-year treatment plan, but no less than five years from the date the deferred prosecution is granted, if the court grants my petition for deferred prosecution and if I fully comply with all the terms of the court order placing me on deferred prosecution.

I certify under penalty of perjury under the laws of the state of Washington that I have read the foregoing and agree with all of its provisions and that all statements made are true and correct.

Dated at _____, Washington this ___ day of _____, 20 ___.

_____

Petitioner–Defendant

_____

Defense Attorney

[Effective September 1, 2000; amended effective September 1, 2001.]

EXHIBIT LCrRLJ 4.2(i)(B). ORDER OF REFERRAL FOR EVALUATION

IN THE DISTRICT COURT OF THE STATE OF WASHINGTON
IN AND FOR THE COUNTY OF CHELAN

STATE OF WASHINGTON   )
) NO. _____
          Plaintiff,   )
) ORDER OF REFERRAL
vs.   ) FOR EVALUATION
)
)
_____,   )
          Defendant.   )
_____   )

THIS matter coming on before the above-entitled court on defendant's Petition for Deferred Prosecution, and the court having examined the petition filed by the defendant and the affidavit attached thereto, finds that the defendant is charged with a gross misdemeanor crime of Driving While Intoxicated which may be the result of or caused by an alcohol problem for which the defendant is in need of treatment; that, unless the problem is treated, the probability of future reoccurrence of the alleged crime is great, and the defendant has agreed to pay the costs of diagnosis and evaluation.

NOW, THEREFORE, said defendant is hereby referred to _____ located at _____ in _____, WASHINGTON, an approved treatment agency, for an evaluation and diagnosis of defendant's alcohol problem to determine, after a thorough investigation and examination, if:

1. The defendant suffers from the problem mentioned herein;

2. If the problem is not treated whether there is a probability that similar misconduct will occur in the future;

3. Whether extensive and long-term treatment is required and would be effective if instituted; and

4. Whether effective treatment is available and what that treatment would include.

The approved treatment agency shall report, in writing, to the court its findings and recommendations; and if treatment is recommended it shall set out a treatment plan showing:

(a) The type of treatment;

(b) The nature of the treatment;

(c) The length of said treatment;

(d) A treatment time schedule; and

(e) The approximate cost of said treatment plan.

Said report shall be filed with this court for its consideration on or before the ___ day of _____, 20 ___, A copy of said report shall be furnished to the defendant's attorney and to the prosecuting attorney.

DATED this ___ day of _____, 20 ___.

_____
DISTRICT COURT JUDGE

Presented by:

_____

_____

WSBA _____

Attorney for Defendant

[Effective September 1, 2000; amended effective September 1, 2001.]

EXHIBIT LCrRLJ 4.2(i)(C). STATEMENT OF DEFENDANT ON PETITION FOR DEFERRED PROSECUTION/STIPULATION TO FACTS

IN THE DISTRICT COURT OF THE STATE OF WASHINGTON
IN AND FOR THE COUNTY OF CHELAN

STATE OF WASHINGTON,	)	
	)	NO. _____
Plaintiff,	)	
	)	STATEMENT OF DEFENDANT ON
vs.	)	PETITION FOR DEFERRED
	)	PROSECUTION/STIPULATION TO
_____,	)	FACTS
	)	
Defendant.	)	
_____	)	

1. My true name is above set forth. My date of birth is _____, and I have completed the _____ grade of school.

2. I understand that I am charged with the offense(s) of _____ which occurred in Washington State, with a violation date of _____. I am petitioning for deferred prosecution on the above charge(s).

3. The court has advised me of the following constitutional rights:

(a) I have the right to representation by a lawyer, and if I cannot afford to pay for a lawyer, one will be provided for me at public expense.

(b) I have the right to a speedy and public trial by an impartial jury in the place where the crime is alleged to have been committed.

(c) I have the right to remain silent, before and during trial, and I need not testify against myself.

(d) I have the right at trial to confront witnesses who testify against me, and I have the right at trial to have witnesses testify for me, and they can be made to appear at no expense to me.

(e) I am presumed innocent until a charge is proved beyond a reasonable doubt, or I enter a plea of guilty.

(f) I have the right to appeal a finding, after trial, of guilt.

4. If I proceed to trial and am found guilty, I may be allowed to seek suspension of some or all of the fines or incarceration (jail sentence) that may be ordered, upon the condition that I seek treatment.

5. I may seek treatment from public and private agencies at any time without regard to whether or not I am guilty of the offense(s) charged.

6. I understand that the court will not accept a petition for deferred prosecution from a person who sincerely believes he or she is innocent of the offense(s) charged or does not, in fact, suffer from the problems alleged in the petition. I sincerely believe I suffer from the problems alleged in my petition for deferred prosecution. I further do not sincerely believe that I am innocent of the charge(s) indicated above.

7. I understand that as a condition of granting the deferred prosecution petition, the court may order me to pay restitution for any damages incurred by individuals as a result of the offense for which I am charged, and the court may order payment of court costs. I further understand that the court may terminate/revoke my deferred prosecution program for failure to pay restitution or court costs.

8. I understand that as a condition of granting a deferred prosecution petition, the court will enter an order that I may not operate a motor vehicle upon a public highway without a valid operator's license and proof of liability insurance. The court may also order the installation of an ignition interlock or other device pursuant to

RCW 46.20.720, and may enter an order requiring that I attend a DUI Victim Impact Panel. I further understand that the court will terminate/revoke my deferred prosecution program if I am convicted of a similar offense, and that the court may terminate/revoke my deferred prosecution program for failure to comply with any of the conditions established by the court as part of my deferred prosecution program.

9. I am submitting my case on the record pursuant to RCW 10.05.020. I understand that by doing so I am stipulating to the admissibility, sufficiency, and accuracy of the evidence contained in the reports and relevant materials (including but not limited to the written police report, DUI ARREST REPORT, and any attachment thereto). I understand that if I am revoked from the deferred prosecution program, my case will be set for trial and the reports and relevant materials will be entered and used to support a finding of guilt. I agreed that there is sufficient evidence contained in the reports and relevant materials to convict me of the charge(s) above. I understand that my trial will consist of a judge reading the reports and relevant materials and deciding on that evidence alone if I am guilty of the charge.

10. I understand that by submitting my case on the record, I am giving up the Constitutional right to a jury trial, the right to a speedy trial, the right to hear and question witnesses, the right to call witnesses in my own behalf, and the right to testify or not to testify. I understand that I am waiving the right to raise any defenses I may have to the above charge.

11. No one has made any threats or promises to persuade me to submit my case on the record. I agree that I have knowingly and voluntarily submitted my case on the record, and that I understand the contents of this document. I understand that this document will be entered and used to support a finding of guilt if the court finds cause to revoke my deferred prosecution. I have read, or have had read to me this document, understand its contents, and have no further questions to ask of the court.

I hereby certify under penalty of perjury under the laws of the State of Washington that the forgoing is true and correct.

Dated in Wenatchee, Washington this ___ day of _____, 20 ___.

_____

Defendant

This matter coming before the court for entry of an Order Deferring Prosecution, the court makes the following findings with regard to the defendant/petitioner's execution of the foregoing statement. The above statement as well as these findings shall be incorporated into the Order Deferring Prosecution by this reference thereto.

(a) That the petitioner has stipulated to the admissibility and sufficiency of the facts as contained in the written police report and other relevant materials referenced above.

(b) That the petitioner has acknowledged the admissibility of the stipulated facts in any criminal hearing on the underlying offense or offenses held subsequent to revocation of the order granting deferred prosecution.

(c) That the petitioner has acknowledged and waived the right to testify, the right to a speedy trial, the right to call witnesses to testify, the right to present evidence in his or her defense, and the right to a jury trial.

(d) That the petitioner's statements were made knowingly and voluntarily.

Presented by: Approved for entry:

_____   _____
Deputy Prosecuting Attorney   Defense Counsel

Approved this ___ day of _____ 20 ___.

_____

Judge

[Effective September 1, 2000; amended effective September 1, 2001.]

EXHIBIT LCrRLJ 4.2(i)(D).   ORDER DEFERRING PROSECUTION

IN THE DISTRICT COURT OF THE STATE OF WASHINGTON
IN AND FOR THE COUNTY OF CHELAN

STATE OF WASHINGTON, CITY OF WENATCHEE,	)	No.
Plaintiff,	)	ORDER DEFERRING PROSECUTION
vs.	)	
	)	
_____,	)	
Defendant.	)	

FINDINGS OF FACT

1.1   The Petitioner suffers from alcoholism, drug addiction, or mental problems and has agreed to comply with the terms and conditions of the treatment plan prepared pursuant to RCW 10.05, and to pay the costs of diagnosis and treatment;

1.2   The Petitioner has stipulated to the admissibility and sufficiency of the facts as contained in the written police report(s);

1.3   The Petitioner has agreed and acknowledged that the written police reports and any other documents, reports or evidence filed in this case are admissible against the Petitioner in any criminal hearing on the underlying offense or offenses held subsequent to revocation of the order granting deferred prosecution;

1.4   The Petitioner has acknowledged and waived the right to a speedy trial, the right to a jury trial, the right to testify and to call witnesses to testify, the right to confront and question witnesses; and the right to present evidence in his or her defense;

1.5   The Petitioner's stipulations, admissions, and statements were made knowingly and voluntarily.

ORDER

IT IS HEREBY ORDERED that the Defendant is accepted for deferred prosecution and shall comply with the following conditions:

2.1   The Defendant shall comply with all of the terms and conditions of the two-year treatment program, a copy of which is attached and incorporated herein by reference. The Defendant shall pay for the costs of treatment and shall not change treatment agencies without prior approval of the Court.

2.2   The Defendant shall authorize the treatment agency to communicate freely with the Court and the Probation Office regarding the Defendant's treatment progress. The treatment agency shall submit monthly reports to the Probation Office for the entire treatment period. In the event that the Defendant fails or neglects to comply with any term or condition of the treatment program, the treatment agency shall immediately submit a written report of such breach to the Probation Office.

2.3   The Petitioner will be under the deferred prosecution supervision of the Chelan County District Court Probation Office for five (5) years and will comply with all terms and conditions established by that office to monitor and enforce compliance with this Order and shall pay all costs of supervision through the Probation Department.

2.4   The Defendant shall pay court costs of $250, an Alcohol Violators fee of $200 pursuant to RCW 46.61.5054, and a public defender recoupment of ___, for a total of ___, not including probation fees or restitution.

2.5   The Defendant shall immediately notify the Court Clerk as well as the Probation Department, in writing, of all changes in address.

2.6   The Defendant shall not operate a motor vehicle upon the public highways without a valid operator's license and proof of liability insurance as established by RCW 46.29.490.

2.7   The Defendant will not refuse to submit to a breath, blood, or urine test for alcohol or drug content upon request by law enforcement, the probation department, treatment provider, or the court.

2.8   The Defendant will not possess, consume or otherwise acquire any alcohol, non-prescribed controlled substances, or drug paraphernalia and will not enter any bar, tavern, or alcohol establishment for the entire length of the deferred prosecution period (five years).   Such prohibition includes medical marijuana unless otherwise specifically ordered by the court.

2.9   The Defendant shall attend a DUI victim impact panel within 60 days of entry of this order.

2.10   For a period of ___ year(s) or as directed by the Department of Licensing, the Defendant shall have a functioning ignition interlock installed in any motor vehicle that he or she operates.   The Defendant shall provide written verification of the installation to the Probation Department within 30 days of entry of this order deferring prosecution.   The Defendant shall comply with all rules and regulations of the Department of Licensing regarding the ignition interlock device and ignition interlock license.

2.11   The Defendant shall not commit any criminal law violations, including but not limited to any alcohol or drug-related offenses, during the five-year period of the deferred prosecution.

2.12   Restitution shall be paid to the following victims:

Name: _____ Amount: _____

Address: _____

Name: _____ Amount: _____

Address: _____

2.13   Other: _____

_____

_____.

DONE IN OPEN COURT this ___ day of _____, ___.

_____

JUDGE/JUDGE PRO TEM

Presented by: Copy Received:

_____   _____

Attorney for Defendant, WSBA#   Defendant

Copy received and approved as to form:

_____

Deputy Prosecuting Attorney, WSBA#

[Effective September 1, 2000.   Amended effective September 1, 2001; September 1, 2006; September 1, 2011; September 2, 2013.]

LCrRLJ 4.8. WITNESSES—PROCESS— SUBPOENAS [WITHDRAWN]

[Adopted effective September 1, 1998. Withdrawn effective September 2, 2013.]

LCrRLJ 6.1. PRE–JURY TRIAL CONFERENCE/READINESS HEARING

6.1(a) Pre–Jury Trial Conference. In every criminal case in which the right to trial by jury has not been waived, there will be a pre-jury trial conference for the purpose of presenting and scheduling motions and for setting a readiness conference and jury trial date.

The defendant and counsel are required to attend pre-trial hearings unless excused by the court. Failure of the defendant to attend any pre-trial hearing may result in the issuance of a bench warrant and forfeiture of any bail or bond.

6.1(b) Readiness Hearing. A readiness hearing shall be set in all cases set for jury trial. The prosecuting attorney, defense counsel and the defendant are required to attend the readiness hearing, unless otherwise excused by the court. Failure of the defendant to appear at the readiness hearing may result in the issuance of a bench warrant, forfeiture of bail and/or bond, and striking of the trial.

At the readiness hearing, the parties shall indicate their readiness for trial and advise the court of any factors affecting readiness for trial; such as, exchange of witness lists, availability of witnesses, and unresolved motions. Upon conclusion of the readiness hearing, the court will accept amendments of charges only upon good cause shown.

Any case confirmed for jury trial at the readiness hearing that does not proceed to trial, absent good cause, may be subject to sanctions as deemed appropriate by the judge, including but not limited to actual jury costs, witness fees, and terms.

Prior to readiness hearing, the parties may file a Notice of Settlement and a Waiver of Right to Speedy Trial, signed by the defendant. Upon receipt of such notice and waiver, the readiness hearing may be stricken and the cause set for entry of plea and sentencing.

[Adopted effective September 1, 1998. Amended effective September 2, 2013.]

LCrRLJ 6.13(b). EVIDENCE—BLOOD DRAW CERTIFICATION

(1) Certification of Qualification to Draw Blood and of Blood Draw Procedure.

(A) *Admission of Blood Draw Certificate.* In the absence of a request to produce the person who drew blood from the defendant made at least 7 days prior to trial, certificates substantially in the following form are admissible in lieu of a witness in any court proceeding held pursuant to RCW 46.61.502 through RCW 46.61.506 for the purposes of determining whether a person was operating or in actual physical control of a vehicle while under the influence of intoxicating liquors and/or drugs:

BLOOD DRAW CERTIFICATION:

I, _____, do certify under penalty of perjury of the laws of the State of Washington the following: I am a (physician) (registered nurse) (qualified technician) and I am qualified by medical training and experience to draw blood from the human body.

On _____ (date) at ___ (time) I drew ___ (number of samples) blood samples from _____ (name of person) at the direction and in the presence of _____ (name of officer).

I further certify that with each sample the blood draw site was sterilized with a non-alcoholic preparation (betadine) (other _____), and that each blood sample was drawn into a chemically clean dry container (hereinafter referred to as blood draw containers) consistent with the size of the sample and sealed with an inert leak-proof stopper. The blood draw containers are known by me to contain a suitable anti-coagulant and enzyme poison sufficient in amount to prevent clotting and stabilize the alcohol concentration. The anti-coagulant and enzyme poison utilized in this blood draw were (sodium fluoride and potassium oxalate) (other: _____). To the best of my knowledge, no foreign substances or chemicals, including alcohol, were involved in the blood draw process other than those listed above.

_____   _____
Date and Place   **Signature of person making certification**

[Adopted effective September 1, 1998.]

LCrRLJ 8.2. MOTIONS

At the pre-jury trial conference, the parties must state with specificity all motions. If the motion has not been submitted in writing with a supporting memorandum of authorities before or during the pre-jury trial conference, the court will establish a briefing schedule. The court will determine if an evidentiary hearing is required and will set a time for a hearing on the motion(s).

Except on good cause or as to routine matters, e.g., a motion to exclude witnesses, motions in limine and supporting memoranda, shall be filed at least one business day prior to trial.

[Adopted effective September 1, 1998. Amended effective September 2, 2013.]

INFRACTION RULES

LIRLJ 2.6(c). MITIGATION HEARING ON WRITTEN STATEMENT

Written Request for Penalty Reduction. A defendant requesting a reduction of an infraction penalty may have such a determination based upon his or her written statement explaining the mitigating circumstances. The statement shall contain the person's promise to pay the monetary penalty imposed by the court after reviewing the statement. The statement shall be executed in compliance with RCW 9A.72.085, in substantially the following form:

> I certify [or declare] under the penalty of perjury under the laws of the State of Washington that the foregoing is true:
>
> I promise that if it is determined that I committed the infraction for which I was cited, I will pay the monetary penalty authorized by law and assessed by the Court.

_____   _____
[Date and Place]   [Signature]

Further, the examination of the statement may be held in chambers.

[Adopted effective September 1, 1998.]

LIRLJ 3.1. CONTESTED HEARINGS— PRELIMINARY PROCEEDINGS

(a)(1) *Subpoenas.* In contested cases, the defendant and the plaintiff may subpoena witnesses necessary for the presentation of their respective cases. The request for a subpoena may be made in person or by mail. In order to request a subpoena, the request must be made in writing informing the clerk of the court of the name and address of the witness and of the date of the contested hearing. The subpoena may be issued by a judge, court commissioner, clerk of the court, or by a party's attorney. The responsibility for serving subpoenas on witnesses, including law enforcement witnesses and the Speed Measuring Device Expert (SMD Expert) is upon the party requesting the subpoena. Such subpoenas may be served as stated in IRLJ 3.1(a).

(2) *Timeliness.* In cases where the request for a subpoena is made 14 days or less prior to the scheduled hearing, the Court may deny the request for the subpoena or condition the issuance of the subpoena upon a continuance of the hearing date. (See following rule for time frame for Speed Measuring Device Expert.)

(3) *Speeding Measuring Device Expert.* Defense requests for a Speed Measuring Device Expert must be made to the Office of the Prosecuting Attorney no less than 30 days prior to the date set for the contested hearing. A request for a SMD expert may be treated by the Court as a request for a continuance to the next date on which the prosecuting attorney has scheduled the appearance of the SMD Expert. In cases where either party requests a Speed Measuring Device Expert (SMD Expert), those cases shall be consolidated to the extent possible on one calendar. (See Exhibit LIRLJ 3.1(a)(3).)

(4) *Costs and Witness Fees.* Each party is responsible for costs incurred by that party, including witness fees, as set forth in RCW 46.63.151. In cases where a party requests a witness to be subpoenaed, the party requesting the witness shall pay the witness fees and mileage expenses due that witness.

[Adopted effective September 1, 1998.]

LIRLJ 3.3(b). REPRESENTATION BY LAWYER

At a contested hearing, the plaintiff shall be represented by a lawyer representative of the prosecuting authority when the defendant is represented by a lawyer; or when the defendant has served upon the prosecution a demand for discovery, requested a speed measuring device expert to appear, or filed motions requesting relief based upon an alleged failure by the plaintiff/prosecution to perform duties required by law.

A notice of appearance must be filed by a lawyer representing a defendant at a contested hearing within 7 days from the date the defendant files a request for a contested hearing. Upon receipt of the lawyer's notice of appearance, the clerk shall reset the contested hearing to the appropriate jurisdiction's next available contested hearing infraction calendar with a lawyer representative of the prosecuting authority or if appropriate to the next contested hearing calendar for the designated law enforcement agency's speed measuring device expert. The failure to timely file a notice of appearance may result in the contested hearing being held beyond the 120 days from the date of notice of infraction or the date the default judgment was set aside, as required by IRLJ 2.6(a).

[Adopted effective September 1, 2010.]

LIRLJ 3.3(b)(1). WAIVER OF PERSONAL APPEARANCE

At a contested hearing and in lieu of a personal appearance, a defendant charged with a traffic infraction may appear by and through counsel.

[Adopted effective september 1, 1998.]

LIRLJ 3.3(b)(2). NOTICE OF APPEARANCE BY COUNSEL

A defendant charged with a traffic infraction and represented by counsel must provide written notice to the prosecuting authority and the clerk of the court of such representation at least 7 days from the date the original request for a contested hearing is mailed by the defendant. Upon receipt of counsel's notice of appearance, the clerk shall reset the contested hearing to the appropriate jurisdiction's next available speed measuring device expert/infraction calendar for the designated law enforcement agency. Failure to timely submit a notice of appearance may result in the contested hearing being held beyond the 120 days from the date of notice of infraction or the date a default judgment is set aside, as required by IRLJ 2.6(a).

[Adopted effective September 1, 1998.]

LIRLJ 3.5. DECISION ON WRITTEN STATEMENTS

(a) Contested Hearings. Contested hearings based on written statements, as provided for in IRLJ 2.4(b)(4) and IRLJ 2.6(c), are authorized.

(1) *Timeliness.* Written statements must be received by the court at least three (3) business days before the scheduled hearing.

(2) *Procedure.* The court shall examine the citing officer's report and any statement submitted by the defendant. The examination shall take place within 120 days after the defendant filed the response to the notice of infraction. The examination may be held in chambers and shall not be governed by the Rules of Evidence.

(3) *Factual Determination.* The court shall determine whether the plaintiff has proved by a preponderance of all evidence submitted that the defendant committed the infraction.

(4) *Disposition.* If the court determines that the infraction was committed, it may assess a penalty in accordance with IRLJ 3.3.

(5) *Notice to Parties.* The court shall notify the parties in writing whether an infraction was found to have been committed and what penalty, if any, was imposed.

(6) *No Appeal Permitted.* The judge's decision based on written statements is final and may not be appealed.

(b) Mitigation Hearings. Mitigation hearings based on written statements may be held in chambers.

[Adopted effective September 1, 2015.]

MUNICIPAL COURTS
CHELAN MUNICIPAL COURT LOCAL RULES
Including Amendments Received Through
August 15, 2015

Table of Rules

---

1. SCOPE, PURPOSE, AND CONSTRUCTION

CMCLR 1.1. SCOPE

These rules govern the procedure in the Chelan Municipal Court of the City of Chelan in all criminal proceedings and supplement CrRLJ, ARLJ and IRLJ. They shall be interpreted and supplemented in light of the common law and the decisional law of this city. These rules shall not be construed to affect or derogate from the constitutional rights of any defendant.

[Adopted effective September 1, 1998.]

CMCLR 1.2. PURPOSE AND CONSTRUCTION

These rules are intended to provide for the just determination of every criminal proceeding. They shall be construed to secure simplicity in procedure, fairness in administration, effective justice, and the elimination of unjustifiable expense and delay.

[Adopted effective September 1, 1998.]

CMCLR 1.3. EFFECT

Except as otherwise provided elsewhere in these rules, on their effective date:

a) Any acts done before the effective date in any proceedings then pending or any action taken in any proceeding pending under rules of procedure in effect prior to the effective date of these rules are not impaired by these rules.

b) These rules also apply to any proceedings in court then pending or thereafter commenced regardless of when the proceedings were commenced, except to the extent that in the opinion of the court, the former procedure should continue to be made applicable in a particular case in the interest of justice or because of in feasibility of application of the procedures of these rules.

[Adopted effective September 1, 1998.]

CMCLR 1.4. DEFINITIONS

As used in these rules, unless the context clearly requires otherwise:

a) "Next Judicial day" means the next regularly scheduled court calendar day.

b) "Next business day" means the next day the court is open for business.

[Adopted effective September 1, 1999; Amended effective September 1, 2003.]

CMCLR 1.6. CONDUCT OF COURT

All judicial proceedings and trials shall be conducted in accordance with these rules. If no procedure is specifically prescribed by rule, the court may proceed in any lawful manner not inconsistent with these rules, or with any applicable statute. The trial judge shall determine questions pertaining to the conduct of the court not covered by these rules or appropriate statutes.

a) The Clerk's Office shall be open during regular business days and hours.

b) Regular judicial days shall be scheduled on a regular basis, taking into account the schedules of regularly appearing counsel and the part-time staff of the court. In the event of holidays or other preemptions, Court may be held on a specially scheduled day.

In custody hearings will be held the next court business day.

c) Judges pro tempore shall have the full powers of the regular judge during regular Court sessions for which he/she is appointed. The Court Administrator shall keep a record of judges pro tempore which have been sworn into service.

[Adopted effective September 1, 1998; Amended effective September 1, 2003.]

CMCLR 1.7. LOCAL COURT RULES—ADOPTION

These rules are adopted pursuant to CrRLJ 1.7. These local rules for Criminal matters, Infractions and Appeals are assembled and numbered to conform with the numbering system and format adopted by the Supreme Court of the State of Washington as required under GR 7.

These rules supplement CrRLJ, ARLJ and IRLJ. Because of jurisdiction, no specific Chelan Municipal Rules of Civil Procedure are adopted.

[Adopted effective September 1, 1998.]

CMCLR 1.8. TITLE OF RULES

These rules may be known and cited as Chelan Municipal Court Local Rules, and shall be referred to as CMCLR.

[Adopted effective September 1, 1998.]

2. PROCEDURES PRIOR TO ARREST AND OTHER SPECIAL PROCEEDINGS

CMCLR 2.5. PROCEDURE ON FAILURE TO OBEY CITATION AND NOTICE

The court may order the issuance of a bench warrant for the arrest of any defendant who has failed to appear before the court, either in person or by a lawyer, in answer to a citation and notice, or an order of the court, upon which the defendant has promised in writing to appear, or of which the defendant has otherwise received notice to appear, if the sentence for the offense charged may include confinement in jail.

If the charge does not include confinement as a punishment, the court may find the defendant in Contempt of Court. A new notice informing the defendant of the additional charge will be issued for the defendant to appear in court. Warrant may be issued if defendant continues to disregard notices and fail to appear.

[Adopted effective September 1, 1998.]

3. RIGHTS OF DEFENDANTS

CMCLR 3.2. RELEASE OF ACCUSED

a) Bail Schedule. The court shall establish bail schedules from time to time for use by the Chelan Police Department. The schedule shall designate those types of criminal cases, if any, wherein the defendant will be allowed to forfeit bail in lieu of arraignment. Unless prior arrangements have been made, the bail must be paid in full prior to the assigned arraignment date.

b) Proceedings Before the Judge. For persons who have been arrested, appearance before a judge of this court at the jail shall include a 48–hour probable cause telephonic hearing, if there has been no probable cause determination prior to such arrest. A judicial authorization has been issued to the Chelan Police

Department duty supervisor to issue Personal Recognizance Bond/Bail or Bond Collection and Setting Conditions of Release Before Arraignment on all Chelan Municipal Court custodial arrests.

[Adopted effective September 1, 1998.]

CMCLR 3.3. TIME FOR TRIAL

h) Continuances. Continuances and other delays may be granted as follows:

1) On request of the prosecuting authority or the defense with approval from the prosecuting authority.

2) Jury trial continuance may be granted if notice is given 7 days in advance of trial and a signed speedy trial waiver has been filed. Waiver of Jury trial must be signed and filed with the court at least 7 days in advance of trial.

[Adopted effective September 1, 1998.]

CMCLR 3.6. SUPPRESSION PROCEDURE

Written motions to suppress physical, oral or identification evidence shall be presented in writing at least 7 days in advance of an evidentiary hearing.

[Adopted effective September 1, 1998.]

6. PROCEDURES AT TRIAL

CMCLR 6.1.1. TRIAL BY JURY

Any case confirmed for jury trial at the readiness hearing shall remain set for a jury trial. On the last regular court day preceding the trial date, the prosecutor, defense attorney or the defendant, if appearing pro se, shall confirm the jury trial via telephone to the clerk of the court before 3:00 pm, or advise that some other disposition has been reached.

Failure of the defense attorney to confirm the jury trial as required shall cause the case to be stricken as a jury trial, and reset as a bench trial, at which the defendant and counsel must be present.

Any case confirmed as a jury trial and not proceeding to a jury, whether by entry of a plea or otherwise, shall be subject to terms, including costs for an unused jury, witness fees, and other terms deemed appropriate by the court.

[Adopted effective September 1, 1998.]

7. PROCEDURES FOLLOWING CONVICTION

CMCLR 7.9. PAYMENT ARRANGEMENTS

Time payments may be arranged with the approval of the court at the time of sentencing. Payments should be arranged to be paid in full by the end of the probation period. If undue hardship can be proven, the court may reduce payments. If payments cannot be made as agreed, the defendant shall call the court or write the court to request review. Failure to notify the court of missed payments, may result in the issuance of FTA to the Department of Licensing, the assignment of the case to a collection agency and/or issuance of a bench warrant for failure to pay. Failure to keep the court current with mailing address may also result in the above penalties. Willful failure to pay fines, costs or other assessments may be cause for violation of conditions of sentence.

[Adopted effective September 1, 1998; Amended effective September 1, 2003.]

CMCLR 7.10. COMMUNITY SERVICE

The court may impose community service or jail time in lieu of monetary payments in appropriate cases. Community service may be performed at a non-profit organization with prior approval from the court. The court shall keep a list of participating community service organizations within the City of Chelan.

[Adopted effective September 1, 1998.]

8. MISCELLANEOUS

CMCLR 8.13. USE OF COLLECTION AGENCY, ACCEPTANCE OF CREDIT CARD

The court shall use the services of a collection agency for the purposes of collecting unpaid and delinquent penalties on infractions, criminal fines, costs, assessments and forfeitures, on the terms and conditions of the contract for collection services between the City of Chelan and said collection agency, and as may be subsequently amended.

The collection agency's fee, as set forth in said contract, shall be added by the collection agency as a court cost to the total judgment of the court against each defendant whose account is referred by the court to said collection agency. The court shall also collect a portion of interest that has been assessed by the collection agency.

Credit cards, VISA and MasterCard, shall be accepted by the court and the Chelan Police Department for payment of fines and/or bail. A fee set by the court shall be assessed at the time of credit card use to be charged as a non-refundable cost for usage of the service.

[Adopted effective September 1, 1998.]

CMCLR 8.14. JUDGE AUTHORIZATIONS

The Chelan Police Department has been given authorization for the Duty Supervisor to sign the "Personal Recognizance Bond/Bail or Bond Collection and Setting Condition of Release", see Form 1.

The Court Administrator has been given authorization to sign all court correspondence and forms, with the exception of bench warrants and subpoenas.

[Adopted effective September 1, 1998.]

CMCLR 8.15. NO CONTACT ORDER CONDITIONS OF RELEASE FROM JAIL IN DOMESTIC VIOLENCE CASES

In cases where an individual is arrested on a domestic violence or domestic violence related charge, and where that individual is released prior to appearing before a judge, for arraignment, bail hearing or any other hearing where conditions of release could be set, including instances where the individual posts bail or bond to secure his or her release, there shall be imposed a No Contact Order as a condition of release, prohibiting the arrested individual from having any contact with the alleged victim involved in the incident involved in his/her arrest, and from having any contact with the alleged victim's place of residence or employment or any other place where the victim is, or is believed to be. This No Contact Order shall be effective until the next business day or when the arrested individual is next before the court and further orders of the court are issued in connection with the matters involved in the individual's arrest.

[Adopted effective September 1, 1998.]

CMCLR 8.16. RECALL OF WARRANTS

If the defendant fails to appear for a hearing before the court and the Judge orders a warrant issued, the warrant can be recalled and case rescheduled if defendant calls before 5:00 pm on the date the warrant was ordered, unless specifically ordered otherwise. Thereafter, the warrant cannot be recalled unless authorized by the court. The defendant will then be required to appear in court on a regularly scheduled court date. The defendant may call to schedule a court date for appearance, but the warrant will not be recalled.

[Adopted effective September 1, 1998.]

CMCLR 8.17. SCHEDULE OF FEES

The following shall be the schedule of fees charged for certain services provided by the Municipal Court. These amounts are consistent with RCW 3.62. 060.

Duplication of Electronic Records	$10.00/tape
Paper Copy/Fax Expenses	$1.00/1st Page .50 ea add page
Certified Copy	$5.00/document
Postage	Actual cost
Criminal History Checks	$15.00

JIS Data Dissemination charges will be set in accordance with the Office of the Administration of the Courts.

[Adopted effective September 1, 1998.]

CMCLR 8.18. WAIVER OF ACCOUNT BALANCES

Delinquent account balances under $15.00 on adjudicated cases where all other conditions of sentencing have been satisfied may be waived administratively and closed on a case-by-case basis.

[Adopted effective September 1, 1998.]

9. DE NOVO APPEALS

The Chelan Municipal Court is governed by De Novo Appeals. Appeals can be filed as per CrRLJ 9.

[Adopted effective September 1, 1998.]

10. INFRACTION PROCEDURES

CMCLR 10.1. MANDATORY LIABILITY INSURANCE VIOLATIONS—PROOF OF INSURANCE

If a person who has been cited with a violation of RCW 46.30.020 presents to the court clerk evidence that the person had in effect at the time of the citation liability insurance as required by RCW 46.30.020, then, upon payment of twenty-five dollars ($25.00), the case shall be dismissed and the court clerk shall be authorized to make appropriate notation of the dismissal in the court file.

[Adopted effective September 1, 1998.]

CMCLR 10.2. MITIGATION HEARINGS

Mitigation hearings may be submitted to the Court on a written statement. Upon receipt of a request for a written hearing, the Court shall set the matter for hearing and send the defendant a letter and the appropriate forms. The defendant shall return the completed declaration to the court. Upon receipt of the completed declaration the hearing date will be cancelled. The court will then decide the issue from the evidence presented and render its decision by mail.

[Adopted effective September 1, 1998.]

CMCLR 10.3. PROCEDURE AT CONTESTED HEARINGS

Each party at a contested hearing is responsible for subpoenaing his/her own witnesses including the Speed Measuring Device Expert (SMD Expert) or as pursuant to IRLJ 6.6(b). Any party issuing said subpoena must also file with the court proof of its timely issuance and service prior to the court hearing. Each party shall bear the cost of their own subpoenaed witness including the SMD Expert as set forth in RCW 46.63.151.

The officer's presence is not required. The parties must request the officer to be present at least 10 days in advance of the set contested hearing. If the officer has been requested to be present, the hearing will not be rescheduled unless 7 days notice is given to the court.

Written statements may be taken for contested hearings. However, the plaintiff must acknowledge in writing that they understand there will be no appeal from a decision based on their written statements, pursuant to IRLJ 3. 5(e).

This rule is not intended to supersede or conflict with any statutes covering procedures for infractions or the IRLJ, specifically IRLJ 3.1(a), 6. 6 or CrRLJ 6.13(d).

[Adopted effective September 1, 1998; Amended effective September 1, 2003.]

CMCLR 10.4. PAYMENT OF INFRACTION FINES AND PENALTIES

Infractions shall be paid in full within 15 days from date of issue or at the conclusion of any requested hearing. Time payment agreement may be signed if extenuating circumstances can be shown that payment cannot be made in full. If time payments are allowed, they must be paid within three months or an agreed upon time by the court.

If the defendant fails to respond to a notice of infraction, the court shall proceed as required by IRLJ 2.5. An FTR penalty shall also be added to boating and non-traffic infractions. The court shall notify the defendant in writing of penalties added. Within this notice, the court shall also inform the defendant that if full payment, to include penalty, is not paid within 30 days, the account will be turned over to a collection agency.

The court may impose community service or jail time in lieu of monetary payments in appropriate cases.

[Adopted effective September 1, 1998; Amended effective September 1, 2003.]

FORM 1

City of Chelan Municipal Court
State of Washington

_____

CITY OF CHELAN

                Plaintiff,   Citation Number # _____
   vs

  ☐ **PERSONAL RECOGNIZANCE BOND**

_____ ☐ **BAIL OR BOND COLLECTION**

            Defendant   **AND SETTING CONDITIONS OF RELEASE**

Mailing Address: _____ **RELEASE BEFORE ARRAIGNMENT**

_____

KNOW ALL MEN BY THESE PRESENTS:

    That I, _____, as principal, am held and firmly bound unto the City of Chelan in the amount of $ __ for my appearance before the Judge of the above entitled Court, Chelan, Washington on the __ day of _____, 20__ at __ a.m. in the court room located at the 143 E Johnson Avenue, Chelan, Washington to answer to the charge(s) of _____.

    Failure to appear for this arraignment shall result in the issuance of a warrant for my arrest, forfeiture of posted bond/bail and may cause the suspension of my driving privileges. Further I am hereby given notice of the following additional conditions of release. Failure to comply with these conditions will be considered Contempt of Court and will result in my re-arrest to be held without bail until my first appearance before a judge.

    THE CONDITION of the above obligation is such, that

    Whereas, the defendant herein has been charged by complaint duly filed and sworn to with the above named crime; and

    Whereas, said defendant has been released on his personal recognizance or posted bail/bond and the following conditions of release:

    _____ No Contact with _____,

    _____ Keep away from the area of _____,

    _____ No further consumption of intoxicating liquor before arraignment,

    _____ No frequenting of establishments where liquor is sold by the drink,

    _____ No driving of a motor vehicle for __ hours,

    _____ No driving of a motor vehicle until properly licensed and insured;

    I fully understand the above conditions of my release and promise to appear for the above court date.

Dated this _____ day of _____, ___.   _____
                                          Defendant's Signature

_____ _____
Issuing Officer's Signature   Authorized by Judge/Judge Protem

[Adopted effective September 1, 1998; Amended effective September 1, 2003.]

CLALLAM COUNTY

Table of Courts

Superior Court

Clallam County Superior Court Rules.

District Courts

District I Court of Clallam County Local Rules.
Local Rules for Clallam County District Court II.

Municipal Courts

Port Angeles Municipal Court—[No Local Rules].
Sequim Municipal Court—[No Local Rules].

SUPERIOR COURT

CLALLAM COUNTY SUPERIOR COURT RULES

Including Amendments Received Through
August 15, 2015

Table of Rules

LOCAL ADMINISTRATIVE RULES (LAR)

RULE 0.1. [PRESIDING JUDGE; ASSISTANT PRESIDING JUDGE]

The Presiding Judge and Assistant Presiding Judge shall be elected to serve for a two (2) year term commencing on January 1, 2002. The Presiding Judge shall manage administrative and policy matters of the court. The Assistant Presiding Judge shall serve as the Acting Presiding Judge during the absence of, or upon the request of, the Presiding Judge.

[Adopted effective September 1, 2002.]

RULE 0.2. SEALED REPORTS; ADULT CRIMINAL AND JUVENILE DELINQUENCY PROCEEDINGS; PSYCHOLOGICAL, CHEMICAL DEPENDENCY, AND MENTAL EVALUATIONS AND REPORTS [RESCINDED]

[Rescinded effective September 1, 2015.]

RULE 0.3. SEALED REPORTS; ADULT CRIMINAL PROCEEDINGS AND JUVENILE DELINQUENCY PROCEEDINGS; PRESENTENCE INVESTIGATION REPORTS, BILLING STATEMENTS [RESCINDED]

[Rescinded effective September 1, 2015.]

RULE 0.4. [SEALED REPORTS; DEFENDANT'S CASE HISTORY INFORMATION]

The clerk of the court shall seal defendant's case history information obtained from the Judicial Information System whether filed separately or attached to a document as a schedule or exhibit.

[Adopted effective September 1, 2002.]

RULE 0.5. ADMINISTRATIVE RECORDS, DISCOVERY DOCUMENTS OR COPIES

The clerk shall treat the administrative record as an exhibit. Exhibits in all cases shall be kept by the Clerk separate from the files or the case and returned or destroyed at the end of the case, once the appeal time has run.

Documents or copies produced during discovery or other items that should properly be received as exhibits shall not be included in the court file.

[Adopted effective September 1, 2009.]

RULE 0.6. CLERK'S ACTION REQUIRED

Any order or document that is filed in the Clerk's Office requiring action by the Clerk must contain language on the first page of the document in the upper right hand side as follows: "Clerk's Action Required" and be properly marked/identified that action is required.

When the Clerk is to forward a copy of an order to law enforcement, the order must clearly state that the Clerk is to forward a copy of the order to law enforcement and include the name of the law enforcement agency where the order is to be sent.

[Adopted effective September 1, 2009.]

RULE 0.7. FORMAT FOR PLEADINGS AND OTHER PAPERS

All Pleadings, motions, and other papers filed with the court shall comply with General Rule 14 and documents shall be in 12 point or larger type, double-spaced between the lines.

[Adopted effective September 1, 2009.]

LOCAL CIVIL RULES FOR SUPERIOR COURT (LCR)

RULE 0.6. REAPPLICATION FOR ORDER

(a) When an order has been applied for and refused in whole or in part or has been granted conditionally and the condition has not been performed, the same application for an order must not be presented to another Judge, without disclosure of the prior refusal.

(b) If a subsequent application is made upon an alleged different state of facts, it must be shown by affidavit what application was made, when and to what Judge, what order or decision was made thereon, and what new facts are claimed to be shown.

(c) Any order entered in violation of this rule may be set aside upon motion.

[Adopted effective June 30, 1993.]

RULE 0.7. COUNSEL FEES

Appointed counsel moving for the fixing or payment of fees, and counsel moving the court to fix fees in any other case, shall itemize time, services rendered, and other detailed basis for the fees requested in affidavit form. The affidavit submitted by appointed counsel shall be in the form of Exhibit A–1. The affidavit

submitted by counsel who are not appointed by the court shall be substantially in the form of Exhibit A–2.

[Adopted effective June 30, 1993.]

RULE 1. PRIORITY TRIAL SETTING

To obtain a priority civil setting (including cases with statutory priority), the requesting party shall note the trial setting for hearing on the regular civil calendar and shall by motion and affidavit set forth the basis for the priority settings. The Court Administrator shall not set cases as "Priority" without written order of the court.

[Adopted effective June 30, 1993.]

RULE 2. REVISION OF COMMISSIONER'S RULING

(a) A party or counsel moving for revision of a ruling by a Court Commissioner shall comply with RCW 2.24.050.

(b) A motion for revision shall be submitted on the record, together with supporting memoranda, if any, without oral argument, unless otherwise ordered by the court.

(c) Copies of the motion for revision and any memoranda in support thereof shall be served upon all other parties and copies thereof shall also be delivered to the Judge assigned to decide the motion at the time the originals thereof are filed with the Clerk. The Judge assigned shall review the motion and shall request the non-moving party to respond unless the motion is summarily denied. The Judge's decision may be in the form of a final order, in which case it shall be expressly entitled as such.

[Adopted effective June 30, 1993.]

RULE 7(b). NECESSARY PROVISION IN PLEADINGS RELATING TO SUPPLE- MENTAL PROCEEDINGS AND SHOW CAUSE HEARINGS FOR CONTEMPT

(1) In all supplemental proceedings wherein an order is to be issued requiring the personal attendance of a party to be examined in open court, and in orders to show cause for contempt, the order must include substantially the following words in capital letters:

YOUR FAILURE TO APPEAR AS ABOVE SET FORTH AT THE TIME, DATE AND PLACE THEREOF WILL CAUSE THE COURT TO ISSUE A BENCH WARRANT FOR YOUR APPREHEN- SION AND CONFINEMENT IN JAIL UNTIL SUCH TIME AS THE MATTER CAN BE HEARD OR UNTIL BAIL IS POSTED.

No bench warrant will be issued in such cases for the apprehension of the cited person if such language has been omitted.

(2) Orders to show cause for contempt shall be served on the alleged contemnor in the manner of service of a summons and complaint.

[Adopted effective June 30, 1993.]

RULE 31. [PERSONAL IDENTIFIERS— CHILDREN]

(1) **Complete names of children, sealed case types:** The complete names of children shall be used in cases that are deemed confidential pursuant to state or federal statutes, including cases filed pursuant to Chapter 13.32A RCW (family reconciliation), Chapter 13.34 RCW (dependency and termination), Chapter 4.24 RCW (special rights of action), Chapter 26.33 (adoption), Chapter 26.26 (parentage) and Chapter 71.34 (mental health services for minors).

(2) **Confidential Information Form:** The complete names of children and other identifiers shall be included in the Confidential Information Form or similar document for cases filed under Title 26.

(3) **Domestic Relations Filings and Orders:** Court orders concerning the financial support or the custody or residential schedule of a child (including temporary and permanent parenting plans and similar documents) and orders establishing or disestablishing paternity shall include the full name of the child. The date of birth of a child shall be included in court records only as authorized by GR 22.

(4) **Child who is alleged to be a victim of a crime:** The complete name of a child who is alleged to be a victim of a crime may be included on subpoenas and in jury instructions. Nothing in this rule requires that subpoenas be routinely filed in the court file.

(5) **Child who is charged with a crime:** The complete name of a child charged with a crime shall be included in any indictment or information filed with the court pursuant to CrR 2.1 or JuCR 7.2, as part of an affidavit or declaration of probable cause or for any other purpose deemed necessary for the prosecution or defense of the criminal or juvenile offender matter.

(6) **Orders issued for the protection of a child:** If a child is a person protected by a criminal no contact order issued pursuant to 10.99 RCW, an anti-harassment order issued pursuant to 10.14 RCW, an order of protection under issued pursuant to 26.50 RCW or a restraining order or order of protection issued pursuant to 26.09 RCW, 26.10 RCW, 26.26 RCW, RCW 26.52.020, or any other court order entered for the protection of the child, the child's full name and other identifiers shall be included on petitions and orders as necessary for entry of the order into the judicial Information System (JIS) and/or the Washington Crime Information Center (WACIC).

(7) **Conditions of release:** If access to a child is restricted pursuant to CrR 3.2(d)(1), the court may include the full name of the child on the order if deemed necessary for effective enforcement of the order.

(8) **Orders restraining child from contacting or harassing others:** Whenever a child is named as a respondent in an order listed in (3) or (6) above, the child's full name and other personal identifiers shall be included on the petition and order as necessary for entry of the order in the Judicial Information System (JIS) and/or the Washington Crime Information Center (WACIC).

(9) **Petitions and notices filed pursuant to Chapter 11.28, RCW (children as heirs to estate):** The full names and ages of children and other information required by RCW 11.28.110 and RCW 11.28.330 shall be included, however the date of birth may be included only as authorized by GR 22.

(10) **General authority:** Nothing in this rule shall prohibit a court from authorizing the use of a child's full name or date of birth when necessary for the orderly administration of justice, consistent with the requirements of GR 22.

[Adopted effective September 1, 2005.]

RULE 40(b). TRIAL SETTINGS AND CONTINUANCES

(1) Counsel shall note cases for trial on forms substantially like that found in Exhibit B annexed hereto.

(2) All contested motions for continuance shall be in writing to the court, giving detailed reasons for the request. The court may grant or deny the continuance, and if granted, may impose terms.

[Adopted effective June 30, 1993.]

RULE 40(f). AFFIDAVITS OF PREJUDICE

(1) A party or counsel filing a motion and affidavit of prejudice shall comply with RCW 4.12.050.

(2) A party or counsel filing a motion and affidavit of prejudice shall provide a copy to the Court Administrator.

[Adopted effective June 30, 1993.]

RULE 40.1. NOTICE TO COURT OF CALENDAR AND JURY TRIAL CHANGES

Whenever a case has been set for trial and thereafter is settled or will not be tried for any reason, or if a jury is thereafter waived, notice shall be immediately given to the Court Administrator. Upon violation of this rule, the court may assess actual costs. Actual costs shall include venireperson mileage and per diem, bailiff wages, and witness fees paid by the court.

[Adopted effective June 30, 1993.]

RULE 51(c). JURY INSTRUCTIONS

(a) Assembling and Distribution. Proposed jury instructions shall be assembled and distributed as follows:

(1) Original to trial Judge to be unnumbered without citations.

(2) One copy numbered and with supporting citations to each of the following:

Clerk, for court file
Judge, for work copy
Counsel for each opposing party

(b) Citations. Washington Pattern Jury Instructions are to be cited. On the copy of Proposed Jury Instructions delivered to the trial court, the Clerk, and opposing counsel, those Washington Pattern Jury Instructions proposed shall be so identified by WPI number. If the WPI is changed or modified in any way (except for the selection of alternate WPI wording), the citation shall include the word "modified".

[Adopted effective June 30, 1993.]

RULE 54. JUDGMENTS AND COSTS

(f) Presentation

(3) *Presentation by Mail.* Counsel may present agreed orders and ex parte orders, based upon the record in the file, by use of the United States mail addressed either to the Court or to the Clerk. When signed, the Judge/Commissioner will file such order with the Clerk. When rejected, the Judge/Commis-

sioner may return the papers by United States mail to the counsel sending them, without prejudice to presentation by counsel in person. An addressed stamped envelope shall be provided for return of any conformed materials and/or rejected orders. The clerk may charge an ex parte fee.

(4) *Presentation by Legal Assistant.* Legal Assistants who are duly registered with the Clallam County Bar Association or any local bar association of this state may personally present agreed, ex parte and uncontested orders based solely upon the documents presented and the record in the file.

[Adopted effective September 1, 2002.]

RULE 59(e). MOTION FOR RECONSIDERATION OR NEW TRIAL

(1) A motion for reconsideration and any supporting documents shall be filed and served (with a copy delivered to the trial Judge at the time of filing) within ten (10) days of the entry of the order, judgment, oral opinion, memorandum opinion, or other action of the court that is sought to be reconsidered.

(2) A motion for reconsideration or for new trial shall be submitted on briefs and affidavits only, without oral argument, unless the trial Judge orders otherwise.

(3) The court shall review the motion and either deny the motion or request counsel for the non-moving party to respond to the motion within ten (10) days of the notice to respond. Thereafter, the court may request further information or oral argument, or may decide the motion following the ten (10) day period for response. The court's decision may be in the form of a final order, in which case it shall be expressly entitled as such.

[Adopted effective June 30, 1993.]

RULE 77(k). HEARING OF MOTION CALENDAR

(1) Motion calendar shall be held on Friday.

(2) Department I motions for non-domestic civil matters shall be noted for 1:30 p.m. All Department I trial settings shall be noted for 8:45 a.m., unless otherwise arranged with the Court Administrator.

(3) Department II motions for non-domestic civil matters shall be noted for 9:00 a.m. All Department II trial settings shall be noted for 8:45 a.m., unless otherwise arranged with the Court Administrator.

(4) Department III motions for domestic matters concerning dissolutions, modifications of dissolutions and custody cases shall be noted for 9:00 a.m. before the Court Commissioner. All paternity matters shall be noted for 1:30 p.m. before the Court Commissioner. Adoption hearings shall be noted for 8:45 a.m. before the Court Commissioner. All Domestic Violence and

Anti–Harassment Protection Order hearings shall be noted for 10:30 a.m.

(5) All motions shall be noted for the civil motion calendar as provided in CR 40(a)(2). When any matter which has been noted as provided in CR 40(a)(2) is resolved by settlement or continuance, the Court Administrator shall be immediately notified so the court may be relieved from responsibility of reviewing the file. All matters noted for the calendar shall be confirmed with the Superior Court Clerk by noon of the second day before the motion is to be heard. If the matter is not confirmed, it shall be at the discretion of the court whether or not the motion is heard on the date noted.

(6) All briefs, memoranda, or affidavits on a motion (other than a motion for summary judgment) including all responsive pleadings, shall be served and filed with the clerk no later than 4:30 p.m. on the second court day preceding the date set for the hearing, i.e., for a Friday hearing, no later than 4:30 p.m., Wednesday.

(7) With regard to rebuttal affidavits, the court shall consider such affidavits, provided they are filed not later than 1:00 p.m. on the day preceding the hearing (usually 1:00 p.m. on Thursday), and further provided bench copies of such rebuttal affidavits are delivered to the Court Administrator at the time the originals thereof are filed.

[Adopted effective June 30, 1993; revised January 1, 1996; amended effective September 1, 2009.]

RULE 78. PROCEDURE FOR EMANCIPATION PETITIONS

Emancipation petitions filed on or after January 3, 1994 shall not be considered by the court until such time as a supplement (Exhibit G attached to these rules) is filed for the court's consideration.

After an emancipation petition is filed, the petitioner shall cause to be served upon his or her parent(s)/guardian(s) a copy of the petition and a blank copy of the response to the petition for emancipation (Exhibit H attached to these rules). Thereafter the petitioner shall file a declaration or affidavit of service with the court.

Emancipation petitions shall be heard contemporaneous with the juvenile dependency calendar by the Judge or Commissioner presiding on the date the hearing is scheduled.

[Adopted effective March 16, 1994.]

RULE 81. APPLICABILITY IN GENERAL

(a) Procedure in this court shall be in accordance with pertinent Washington Court Rules as heretofore or hereafter adopted by the Supreme Court of Washington. These Local Rules are only to supplement those rules and are numbered, insofar as possible, to conform in numbering with them.

(b) The court may modify or suspend any of these Rules, in any given case, upon good cause.

[Adopted effective June 30, 1993.]

RULE 94(a). FAMILY COURT HEARINGS AND MOTIONS

(1) When a hearing is set in a matter involving RCW Chapter 26, either by an Order to Show Cause or Notice of Issue, the moving party's motions, orders and accompanying documents shall be served by noon on the ninth day before the hearing (normally Wednesday), unless a shorter time is ordered or agreed to by opposing counsel. Responses shall be served by noon on the second day before the hearing (normally Wednesday). Reply affidavits or declarations strictly limited to matters in the response shall be served by noon on the day prior to the hearing. When a motion is supported by affidavit or other documents, the affidavit or other documents shall be served with the motion.

(2) **Limitations on Declarations.**

(a) *Application.* This section (2) does not apply to domestic violence petitions or domestic violence motions.

(b) *Children's statements.* Declarations by minors are disfavored.

(c) *Page limits.*

[i] Generally. Absent prior authorization from the court, the entirety of all declarations and affidavits from the parties and any non-expert witnesses in support of motions (except financial declarations), including any reply, shall be limited to a sum total of twenty-five (25) pages. The entirety of all declarations and affidavits submitted in response to motions shall be limited to a sum total of twenty (20) pages. If a counter-motion is included in the response, then the limit is (25) pages total.

[ii] Exhibits. Exhibits that consist of declarations or affidavits of parties or witnesses shall count towards the above page limit. All other exhibits attached to a declaration or affidavit shall not be counted toward the page limit.

[iii] Financial Declarations. Financial Declarations and financial documents do not count toward the page limit.

[iv] Expert Reports and Evaluations. Declarations, affidavits, and reports from Court Appointed Special Advocates (CASA), Guardians-ad-litem (GAL) and court appointed expert witnesses do not count toward the page limit.

[v] Miscellaneous Exceptions. Copies of declarations or affidavits previously filed for a motion already ruled upon and supplied only as a convenience to the court do not count toward the page

limit. Deposition excerpts shall not count toward the page limit.

(3) When temporary support, maintenance, attorney fees or costs are at issue, each party shall file and serve with their pleadings a Financial Declaration. (Washington Pattern Form DR01.0550).

(4) Each party shall submit a bench copy of their motion or response and accompanying documents at the time the originals are filed.

(5) Temporary family law issues will normally be determined by affidavits or declaration alone. Oral testimony may be permitted in limited circumstances at the Court's discretion.

[Adopted effective June 30, 1993; amended effective September 1, 2002; September 1, 2005; September 1, 2009.]

RULE 94(b). DOMESTIC RELATIONS FINAL HEARING ON CONTESTED MATTERS

In all final hearings or trials in domestic relations matters, each party filing a written pretrial affidavit and personal property form shall file and serve the same by 1:30 p.m. of the judicial day prior to trial. The pretrial Affidavit shall be substantially in the form set forth in Exhibit C attached to these rules.

[Adopted effective June 30, 1993.]

RULE 94(c). DOMESTIC RELATIONS WAIVER OF AGE TO MARRY

Applications for waiver of minimum age to marry shall be made to the Superior Court. Before court hearing, applicants must give evidence of completion of a program of pre-marital counseling, together with such counselor's recommendation.

[Adopted effective June 30, 1993.]

RULE 94(d). DOMESTIC RELATIONS NOTICE TO SUPERIOR COURT OF JUVENILE PROCEEDINGS

All parties and their attorneys to a proceeding involving custody or adoption in the Superior Court are obligated to disclose to the Superior Court the pendency of any Juvenile Court proceedings of which they are aware regarding those minor children.

[Adopted effective June 30, 1993.]

RULE 94(e). ENTRY OF DISSOLUTION DECREE BY DECLARATION OF JURISDICTIONAL FACTS

The Court will enter an agreed or default decree of dissolution of marriage without a final hearing or oral testimony when at least one of the parties is represented by an attorney, the petitioner completes a Request for Entry of Decree and Declaration of Jurisdictional Facts in the form set forth in Exhibit F and:

(1) the respondent or respondent's attorney approves all of the final papers including the Request for Entry of Decree and Declaration of Jurisdictional Facts, or

(2) the respondent is in default, and the decree provides for only that relief requested in the petition,

(3) the respondent or co-petitioner joined in the petition and is unavailable to sign the final papers, and the decree provides for only that relief requested in the petition.

[Adopted effective September 1, 2002.]

RULE 94(f). DOMESTIC RELATIONS SETTLEMENT CONFERENCES

(1) A settlement conference shall be held in all contested domestic relations cases, including dissolution, legal separation, paternity, 3rd party custody, domestic partnership, marriage-like relationships, or modification of any custody order. The settlement conference shall be held with a Court Commissioner or Judge.

(2) Domestic relations cases shall not be set for trial under LCR 40(b) without a settlement conference, except in the following circumstances;

a. The requirement is waived, upon good cause shown, by a Judge or Court Commissioner; or

b. A settlement is not reached in an initial settlement conference because of a party's violation of one or more provisions of LCR 94(f). In such instances, a trial date may be set, but a second settlement conference will be scheduled to occur prior to the established trial date.

(3) Once a response to the petition has been filed, a settlement conference is scheduled by noting the matter before the Court Administrator on the Friday 8:45 a.m. trial setting calendar.

(4) The personal appearance of the parties and their attorneys is mandatory at the settlement conference. In cases where domestic violence is at issue, or where a party no longer resides within the State of Washington, appearance may be by phone. In all other instances, or unless otherwise agreed by the parties, appearing by phone is not considered a personal appearance. If the parties do not agree, the requesting party may seek an exception to this rule by filing a motion, prior to the scheduled settlement conference, to waive the appearance requirement. Such motions will be filed pursuant to the terms of LCR 94(a). The Court shall impose a sanction in the amount of $250 against a party who violates this provision.

(5) If parties agree to reset a settlement conference, they will inform the Court Administrator of that agreement as soon as possible, but in no case later than the business day prior to the scheduled conference.

(6) Parties will prepare for and participate in good faith in scheduled settlement conferences. One week prior to the scheduled settlement conference, each party shall file a Settlement Statement in form substantially similar to the pattern form set forth in Exhibit A. The Settlement Statement is intended to provide the narrative and documentary information necessary to inform the court and the opposing party of the submitting party's position on the major issues to be resolved. The Settlement Statement will not be filed in the Court file, but the original will be provided to the judicial officer conducting the settlement conference, with a copy provided to the opposing party or his/her attorney.

(7) If both parties fail to provide the Settlement Statement one week prior to the scheduled settlement conference, the Court shall issue an order which:

a. Strikes the settlement conference; and

b. Directs the parties to appear before the Court Administrator to select a new settlement conference date.

(8) If only one party fails to file the Settlement Statement one week prior to the scheduled settlement conference, the Court shall issue an order which imposes a sanction on the offending party in the amount of $500, to be reduced to $250 if the Settlement Statement is filed before the scheduled settlement conference. If, at the beginning of the settlement conference, the party that complied with the original deadline requests a continuance of the settlement conference, the conference will be reset to a new date.

(9) If the Court finds that a Settlement Statement is materially deficient, or that a party's lack of preparation prohibits a meaningful settlement conference, the Court may impose additional sanctions or other remedies as the Court deems appropriate.

(10) If the provisions of LCR 94(f) have been followed and a case fails to settle at the settlement conference, the parties will immediately appear before the Court Administrator following the settlement conference to select a trial date. Unless otherwise agreed, the trial will not be scheduled to occur sooner than forty-five days, nor later than 120 days, following the unsuccessful settlement conference. Trials for the types of cases identified in LCR 94(f)(1) may be set to commence on either Monday or Tuesday.

[Adopted effective June 30, 1993; amended effective September 1, 2009.]

RULE 95. MANDATORY PARENTING SEMINARS

(A) **Definition of Applicable Cases.** This rule applies to all cases filed under Ch. 26.09 or Ch. 26.26 of the RCW filed after January 1, 1996, including dissolutions, legal separations, major modifications and paternity actions (in which paternity has been established) where the parties are parents of children under the age of 18, and where a parenting plan or residential plan is required which involves more than purely financial issues.

(B) **Parenting Seminars; Mandatory Attendance.** In all cases referred to in Section (A) above, and in those additional cases arising under Title 26 RCW where a court makes a discretionary finding that a parenting seminar would be in the best interest of the children, both parents, and such nonparent parties as the court may direct, shall participate in, and successfully complete, an approved parenting seminar. Standards for an approved parenting seminar shall be established by Administrative Order of this court. Successful completion shall be evidenced by a certificate of attendance filed by the provider agency with the court.

(C) **Special Considerations/Waiver.**

(1) In no case shall opposing parties be required to attend a seminar together.

(2) Upon a showing of domestic violence or abuse which would not require mutual decision making pursuant to RCW 26.09.191, or that a parent's attendance at a seminar is not in the children's best interest, the court shall either:

(a) waive the requirement of completion of the seminar; or

(b) provide an alternative voluntary parenting seminar for battered spouses.

(3) The Court may waive the seminar requirement for one or both parents in any case for good cause shown.

(D) **Failure to Comply.** Nonparticipation, or default, by one parent does not excuse participation by the other parent. Respondent's refusal, delay or default will not delay the progress of the case to a final decree; however, Respondent will not be allowed to seek affirmative relief in this or subsequent proceedings, except certain Temporary Orders, on parenting issues until the seminar has been successfully completed. Petitioner's refusal or delay will prevent the case from being tried or any final order affecting the parenting/residential plan being entered in Petitioner's favor. Willful refusal or delay by either parent may constitute contempt of court and result in sanctions imposed by the court or may result in the imposition of monetary terms, default and/or striking of pleadings.

(E) Petitioners in all applicable cases as defined in subsection (A) above shall serve a notice as provided by the Clerk's Office upon Respondents notifying them of the requirements of this court rule. The notice shall be served with the initial pleadings.

[Adopted effective January 1, 1996.]

ADMINISTRATIVE ORDER OF JANUARY 1, 1996 ESTABLISHING STANDARDS FOR PARENTING SEMINARS AS REQUIRED BY LCR 95

The Clallam County Superior Court hereby adopts the following standards for parenting seminars:

(a) Mandatory Requirement. Where required by local court rule or by court order, parties shall participate in, and successfully complete, an approved parenting seminar within 60 days after service of a petition or initiating motion on the respondent.

(b) Approved Parenting Seminar. An approved parenting seminar is one that complies with the seminar content and instructor qualifications standards set forth in paragraphs (d) and (e) of this Order and has received Court approval.

(c) Fees. Each parent attending a seminar shall pay a fee charged by the approved provider agency. A sliding fee scale shall be available. The seminars shall be conducted at no cost to the County.

(d) Seminar Content. The seminar content will be approved by the Court, and shall include, at a minimum:

(1) the developmental stages of childhood;

(2) stress indicators in children;

(3) age appropriate expectations of children;

(4) the impact of divorce on children;

(5) the grief process;

(6) reducing stress for children through an amicable divorce;

(7) the long term impact of parental conflict on children;

(8) visitation recommendations to enhance the child's relationship with both parents;

(9) financial obligations of child rearing;

(10) conflict management and dispute resolution;

(11) communication skills for divorced parents;

(12) practical skills for working together; and

(13) the impact on children when stepparents and blended families enter their lives.

(e) Qualifications of Instructors. Parenting seminars will be conducted by a team of two instructors, including one male and one female. In certain circumstances, where two instructors are unavailable, then one instructor may conduct the seminar. Instructors shall have the following minimum credentials and experience

(1) a bachelor's degree in social work, psychology or other related behavioral science;

(2) supervised experience in treatment of emotionally disturbed children, adolescents and their families;

(3) experience in providing a wide range of mental health services to children and families, with specific experience in the areas of separation/divorce, loss and grief, and blended families;

(4) extensive knowledge of child development, age appropriate expectations for children, and positive parenting;

(5) experience in group treatment and/or facilitating classes and seminars;

(6) an ability to work with other agencies as part of a collaborative program; and

(7) strong oral communication skills.

When parties choose to use agencies or religious organizations which are not already approved by the Court, the Court may modify or waive the foregoing qualifications for the instructors upon a showing of other indicia of competence and experience.

(f) Length. The seminars shall, at a minimum, be three hours in length.

(g) Referrals for Other Services. During the seminar, referral resources will be made available to the parents, and their children, including individual and family counseling drug/alcohol counseling, anger management counseling, parenting classes, mediation, etc. These services are optional, and the parties must seek their own funding resources.

Dated this 29th day of December, 1995

LOCAL CRIMINAL RULES FOR SUPERIOR COURT (LCrR)

RULE 0.6. REAPPLICATION FOR ORDER

(a) When an order has been applied for and refused in whole or in part or has been granted conditionally and the condition has not been performed, the same application for an order must not be presented to another Judge, without disclosure of the prior refusal.

(b) If a subsequent application is made upon an alleged different state of facts, it must be shown by affidavit what application was made, when and to what Judge, what order or decision was made thereon, and what new facts are claimed to be shown.

(c) Any order entered in violation of this rule may be set aside upon motion.

[Adopted effective June 30, 1993.]

RULE 0.7. COUNSEL FEES

Appointed counsel moving for the fixing or payment of fees, and counsel moving the court to fix fees in any other case, shall itemize time, services rendered, and other detailed basis for the fees requested in affidavit form. The affidavit submitted by appointed counsel shall be in the form of Exhibit A–1. The affidavit submitted by counsel who are not appointed by the court shall be substantially in the form of Exhibit A–2.

[Adopted effective June 30, 1993.]

RULE 1. JUSTIFICATION OF SURETIES

(1) Any person or corporation desiring to post bail bonds in Clallam County Superior Court shall first obtain an Order of Justification.

(2) All Petitions for an Order of Justification shall be in writing to the Court and shall provide the following information:

(A) *All Sureties.*

1. Types of bonds—an outline of the types of bonds posted by the surety.

2. Current suretyship obligations—a current list of all suretyship obligations to all courts within the geographical limits of Washington State, including the following:

   a. The name of the court.

   b. The name of the defendant.

   c. The amount of the bond.

   d. The date issued.

3. Current bond foreclosures—a list of the current obligations to the courts in the way of bond forfeitures or other obligations incurred by the surety which have not been paid, or a statement that there are none.

4. Presentation—identity of the names and addresses of all persons who will be delivering or presenting bonds on behalf of the bonding surety.

5. Jurisdictions where surety has previously been authorized to post bail bonds and jurisdictions denying such authorization.

(B) *Corporations.*

1. Power of Attorney.

   a. Names of the agents authorized to execute bonds on behalf of the surety.

   b. The maximum dollar amount of any single bond which each agent is authorized to execute.

2. A copy of the current Certificate of Authority issued by the Insurance Commissioner for the state of Washington.

3. Resident corporate agent.

   a. The name of the resident agent(s) for the corporate surety in the state of Washington authorized to appear and accept service on behalf of the corporate surety.

   b. A copy of the power of attorney appointing said person(s) as resident agent(s).

(C) *Individuals.*

1. Individual name(s) of applicant(s).

2. All fictitious names used by the applicant(s).

3. Resident address of individual applicant(s).

4. Business address of all individual applicant(s).

5. Marital status of applicant(s) and, if applicable, name(s) of spouse(s).

6. Verified Financial Statement:

   A. Assets.

   i. Real property:

   a. Legal description of property.

   b. Current appraisal of the property by a qualified real estate appraiser who is a member of the American Institute of Appraisers, or a statement of the appraiser that there has been no change in the value of the property since the last appraisal of the property.

   c. If the real estate is being purchased on contract or subject to mortgage, deed of trust, or other encumbrance, disclose:

   1. How the property is being obtained.

   2. Amount of purchase price.

   3. Amount of unpaid balance.

   4. Notarized confirmation, etc.

   d. Property tax statements and verification that real property taxes have been paid in full.

   e. Verification that real property and structures thereon are insured against loss or damage.

   ii. Personal property.

   a. Statement that the personalty is properly insured against loss, including a statement indicating the insurance coverage limits.

   iii. Savings (bank deposits).

   iv. Stocks and Bonds.

   a. Lists of individual stocks and bonds.

   b. Statement of current value of stocks and bonds.

   v. Cash (including checking accounts).

   vi. Other investments.

   B. Liabilities, including unsatisfied judgments. If unsatisfied judgment(s) is included, list court, title of cause, cause number, judgment creditor, and amount of unsatisfied judgment.

   C. Net worth.

7. Current Property Bond Obligations in the State of Washington.

   a. Name of court.

   b. Name of defendant.

   c. Amount of the bond.

   d. Date of issuance of bond.

8. Driver's License.

    a. Driver's license number.

    b. State of issuance.

9. Criminal History—provide any criminal history conviction information for all persons identified in paragraph (C) 1. and (C) 5.

    a. Name of criminal offense convicted of committing.

    b. Type of criminal offense. (misdemeanor, gross misdemeanor, felony; exclude traffic infractions);

    c. Name of sentencing court.

    d. Date of offense.

    e. Date of sentencing.

(3) All petitions for an Order of Justification shall be verified under oath or certified under penalty of perjury as authorized by RCW 9A.72.085.

(4) All initial Orders of Justification shall be effective until the 30th day of April, next following the entry of the Order of Justification.

(5) All Orders of Justification, other than the initial Order for that surety, shall be effective from May 1 of one year until April 30 of the following year.

(6) All Petitions for an Order of Justification shall be accompanied by a proposed Order of Justification in substantially the form set out in Exhibit D of these rules.

[Adopted effective June 30, 1993.]

RULE 1.1. APPLICABILITY IN GENERAL

(a) Procedure in this court shall be in accordance with pertinent Washington Court Rules as heretofore or hereafter adopted by the Supreme Court of Washington. These Local Rules are only to supplement those rules and are numbered, insofar as possible, to conform in numbering with them.

(b) The court may modify or suspend any of these Rules, in any given case, upon good cause.

[Adopted effective June 30, 1993.]

RULE 1.2. COURT COMMISSIONER AUTHORITY

In adult criminal cases, any Court Commissioner appointed to serve in the Clallam County Superior Court and qualified under Article 4, Section 23 of the Constitution of the State of Washington shall have the power, authority and jurisdiction, concurrent with the Superior Court Judges, to preside over arraignments, preliminary appearances, initial extradition hearings, and noncompliance proceedings pursuant to RCW 9.94A.200; to accept pleas; to appoint counsel; to make determinations of probable cause; to set, amend, and review conditions of pretrial release; to set bail; to set

trial and hearing dates; to authorize continuances and to accept waivers of the right to speedy trial.

[Adopted effective June 8, 2000.]

RULE 4.5(c). STATUS HEARINGS

(1) A hearing shall be set at arraignment in every criminal case for approximately one month before trial at which time the status of the trial preparation will be disclosed to the court.

(2) The defendant must personally appear at the status hearing, unless otherwise ordered.

(3) A Status Report and Order will be filed at the conclusion of the status hearing and shall be in the form of Exhibit E.

[Adopted effective June 30, 1993.]

RULE 6.11(c). AFFIDAVITS OF PREJUDICE

(1) A party or counsel filing a motion and affidavit of prejudice shall comply with RCW 4.12.050.

(2) A party or counsel filing a motion and affidavit of prejudice shall provide a copy to the Court Administrator.

[Adopted effective June 30, 1993.]

RULE 6.1. NOTICE TO COURT OF CALENDAR AND JURY TRIAL CHANGES

Whenever a case has been set for trial and thereafter is settled or will not be tried for any reason, or if a jury is thereafter waived, notice shall be immediately given to the Court Administrator. Upon violation of this rule, the court may assess actual costs. Actual costs shall include venireperson mileage and per diem, bailiff wages, and witness fees paid by the court.

[Adopted effective June 30, 1993.]

RULE 6.15. JURY INSTRUCTIONS

(a) Assembling and Distribution. Proposed jury instructions shall be assembled and distributed as follows:

(1) Original to trial Judge to be unnumbered without citations.

(2) One copy numbered and with supporting citations to each of the following:

Clerk, for court file

Judge, for worked copy

Counsel for each opposing party

(b) Citations. Washington Pattern Jury Instructions are to be cited. On the copy of Proposed Jury Instructions delivered to the trial court, the Clerk, and opposing counsel, those Washington Pattern Jury Instructions proposed shall be so identified by WPI number. If the WPI is changed or modified in any way (except for the selection of alternate WPI wording), the citation shall include the word "modified".

[Adopted effective June 30, 1993.]

EXHIBITS TO LOCAL CIVIL RULES AND LOCAL CRIMINAL RULES
EXHIBIT A.   EXHIBIT A TO LCR 94(F) SETTLEMENT CONFERENCE STATEMENT

SUPERIOR COURT OF Washington
COUNTY OF Clallam

In re

)
)   NO.
)   SETTLEMENT CONFERENCE
)   STATEMENT
)

A.   Introductory Information

1.   Name of submitting party:

2.   Date of settlement conference:

3.   Type of case:

4.   Names and ages of children:

B.   Stipulations

1.   The parties have reached a stipulated to the following:

C.   Parenting Plan

1.   I assert that the following factors set forth in RCW 26.09.191 apply:

2.   I assert that based upon the RCW 26.09.191 factors, the following restrictions need to be included in the parenting plan:

3.   Attached as Exhibit A is my proposed final parenting plan.

D.   Child Support/Maintenance

1.   My monthly gross income is $ _____ and my monthly net income is $ _____.

2.   I assert that the opposing party's gross income is $ _____ and net income is $ _____.

3.   I propose that child support be set at $ _____ per month.

4.   I assert that the following constitutes a basis for deviation from the standard child support amount:

5.   I propose that spousal maintenance be set as follows (include duration and amount):

6.   Attached as Exhibit B is my most recent year-to-date pay stub (no later than 60 days old):

7.   Attached as Exhibit C is my current financial declaration (or I incorporate the financial declaration filed with the court on _____ by this reference:

E.   Division of Assets/Liabilities

1.   I claim that the following is separate property or liability:

2.   This claim of separate property or liability is based upon the following facts:

3.   The following is my position regarding each parcel of real property:

a.   Street address of each parcel:

b.   Who should be awarded each parcel:

c.   Fair market value of each parcel:

d.   Amount of encumbrances secured by each parcel:

4. Attached as Exhibit D is the document I would submit to the court, at trial, as evidence of the value of the real property in this matter.

5. The following information relates to the liabilities to be allocated in this proceeding:

    a.   Name of each creditor:

    b.   Truncated account number for each creditor:

    c.   Amount owing at time of separation:

    d.   Amount currently owing:

    e.   Attached as Exhibit E are the monthly statements from each creditor for the month of separation and for the most recent month (attach that portion of the statement which shows the account number and balance).

6. The following information relates to each banking or investment account:

    a.   The name of each account:

    b.   Truncated account number for each account:

    c.   Account balance at time of separation:

    d.   Account balance currently:

    e.   Attached as Exhibit F are the statements for each account for the month of separation and the most recent month (attach that portion of the statement which shows the account number and balance).

7. The following information relates to each retirement account:

    a.   The name of each account:

    b.   Truncated account number for each account:

    c.   Nature of each account (IRA / 401K / Deferred Compensation / Defined Benefit plan, etc.)

    c.   Account balance at time of marriage:

    d.   Account balance at time of separation:

    e.   Account balance in most recent statement:

    f.   Attached as Exhibit G are the statements for each account for the month marriage, the month of separation and the most recent month (attach that portion of the statement which shows the account number and balance).

8. Attached as Exhibit H is my proposed division of personal property, showing who should receive each item, and what I believe to be the value of each item. Attached as Exhibit I are the documents to support those values (i.e. Blue Book statements, appraisals, etc.) (Note: It is not necessary to list all items of property, but rather only those items over which there is a dispute. Further it is not necessary to document all values under this provision unless a party believes that there is significant dispute as to the value).

F. Legal Citations

1. I ask the court to review the following legal citations (cases or statutes) prior to the scheduled conference:

[Adopted effective September 1, 2009.]

EXHIBIT A–1. AFFIDAVIT REGARDING ATTORNEY FEES

IN THE SUPERIOR COURT OF THE STATE OF WASHINGTON
IN AND FOR THE COUNTY OF CLALLAM

Plaintiff,	))) NO. _____)
vs	) AFFIDAVIT REGARDING) ATTORNEY FEES)
Defendant.	)))))

1.   The undersigned being first duly sworn on oath states: The following is a true and accurate summary of dates, times the services rendered on behalf of _____, who is the _____ in the above case.

Date   Service   Time

(calendar date)   (must be in sufficient detail to fully advise court of   (to nearest
                    service rendered)   ⅒oth hour)

(computer printout containing this information may be
incorporated by reference)

TOTAL TIME _____.

2.   The above services have been segregated between the following accounts:

SUPERIOR COURT _____

JUVENILE COURT DELINQUENCY _____

JUVENILE COURT DEPENDENCY _____

COSTS _____

_____

Attorney for _____

(NOTARY STATEMENT)

EXHIBIT A–1 TO LOCAL RULES FOR SUPERIOR COURT

[Adopted effective June 30, 1993.]

EXHIBIT A-2. AFFIDAVIT REGARDING ATTORNEY FEES

IN THE SUPERIOR COURT OF THE STATE OF WASHINGTON
IN AND FOR THE COUNTY OF CLALLAM

Plaintiff,	) NO. _____)) AFFIDAVIT REGARDING) ATTORNEY FEES
vs.	
Defendant.	

1.   The undersigned being first duly sworn on oath states: The following is a true and accurate summary of dates, times and services rendered on behalf of _____, who is the _____ in the above case.

Date   Service   Time

(calendar date)   (must be in sufficient detail to fully advise court of   (to nearest
                   service rendered)   ⅒th hour)

(computer printout containing this information
may be incorporated by reference)

TOTAL TIME_____

2.   The usual and customary hourly fee charged by the undersigned to the great majority of hourly clients is $_____ and that has been the undersigned's rate since _____. (provide rates for all periods covered by paragraph 1. above.

_____

Attorney for _____

(NOTARY STATEMENT)

EXHIBIT A-2 TO LOCAL RULES FOR SUPERIOR COURT

[Adopted effective June 30, 1993.]

EXHIBIT B. NOTICE FOR TRIAL SETTING

SUPERIOR COURT OF WASHINGTON
COUNTY OF CLALLAM

NO. _____

NOTICE FOR TRIAL SETTING
[LCR 40(b)]

TO DEFENDANT(S): _____

AND TO OPPOSING COUNSEL: _____

AND TO THE CLERK OF THE ABOVE–ENTITLED COURT:

PLEASE TAKE NOTICE that the issue of law in this cause will be calendared as follows:

Friday, the ____ day of _____, 19___, at _____;
and the Clerk is requested to note this cause on the docket for that day.
Counsel filing this notice certifies as follows:

1. The case is at issue.

2. Nature of the case: _____

3. [   ] Non–Jury [ ] Jury [ ] 12 Person [ ] 6 Person

4. [   ] Jury fee paid

5. Length of trial: _____ days.

6. [   ] The attorneys for the parties stipulate that the following dates are available for trial setting: _____

7. [   ] The parties shall appear before the Clerk to select a trial date, and if such date cannot be agreed upon, before the Judge assigned to hear the case on his Motion Calendar.

DATED this ____ day of _____, 19___.

Stipulated Dates Agreed To: Notice Filed By:

Printed/Typed Name: _____   Printed/Typed Name: _____
WSBA #: _____   WSBA #: _____
OF: _____   OF: _____
Attorney(s) For: _____   Attorney(s) For: _____

[Adopted effective June 30, 1993.]

Exhibit C   CLALLAM COUNTY

EXHIBIT C.   PRETRIAL AFFIDAVIT

IN THE SUPERIOR COURT OF THE STATE OF WASHINGTON
IN AND FOR THE COUNTY OF CLALLAM

IN RE THE MARRIAGE OF

_____   ) NO. _____

Petitioner,   ) PRETRIAL AFFIDAVIT OF

and

_____

Respondent.

STATE OF WASHINGTON   )
) ss.
County of Clallam   )

_____, being first duly sworn on oath, deposes and says:

I—GENERAL INFORMATION

1.1   Name of Wife: _____ Age: _____ Date of Birth: _____
1.2   Name of Husband: _____ Age: _____ Date of Birth: _____
1.3   Dependent Children:

a.   Of this marriage:

Name	Date of Birth	Age	With Whom Residing

b.   Of Former Marriages:

	Name	Age	With Whom Residing

1.4   Support, maintenance and attorney fees I (request) (am willing to pay):

a.   Monthly support for each dependent child $_____
b.   Monthly maintenance for _____ months $_____
c.   Attorney Fees $_____

II—INCOME AND EMPLOYMENT

2.1   Husband:

a.   Employer: _____
b.   Position: _____
c.   Average gross monthly wage: _____ $_____
d.   Deductions:
         Withholding tax: $_____
         Social Security (FICA) $_____
         Other: $_____
Net Employment Income: $_____
Other Income (per month): $_____

TOTAL DISPOSABLE INCOME: $_____

2.2   Wife:

    a.   Employer: _____

    b.   Position: _____

    c.   Average gross monthly wage: $_____

    d.   Deductions:

             Withholding Tax: $_____

             Social Security (FICA) $_____

             Other: $_____

    Net Employment Income: $_____

    Other Income (per month): $_____

          TOTAL DISPOSABLE INCOME: $_____

III—RETIREMENT BENEFITS

3.1   Retirement benefits—future

	Employee Monthly Contrib.	Employee Accrued Contrib.	Percent Accrued During Marriage	Age– Earliest Eligibility	Estim. Present Value
Husband:	$_____	$_____	_____%	_____	$_____
Wife:	$_____	$_____	_____%	_____	$_____

IV—MONTHLY LIVING EXPENSES

4.1   Affiant's current monthly living expenses, excluding the debts set forth in paragraph VII, are as follows:

V—COMMUNITY ASSETS

Description of Item	Fair Market Value	Encumbrance	Net Value	Awarded Husband/Wife
Totals:	$_____	$_____	$_____	

VI—SEPARATE ASSETS

Description of Item	Fair Market Value	Encumbrance	Net Value	Awarded Husband/Wife
Totals:	$_____	$_____	$_____	

VII—LIABILITIES

Creditor	Monthly Payment	Unpaid Balance	Assumed by Husband/Wife
Totals:	$_____	$_____	

VIII—SUMMARY

Assets to Husband: $ _____

(Debts) to Husband: $ ( ) _____

(Less)/plus judgment/lien: $ _____

TOTAL: $ _____

Assets to Wife: $ _____

(Debts) to Wife: $ ( ) _____

(Less)/plus judgment/lien: $ _____

TOTAL: $ _____

IX—OTHER FACTORS

IF ANY BEARING ON FINANCIAL ISSUES (e.g. physical disabilities, dependent children of prior marriages, etc.)

_____

Signature

SUBSCRIBED and SWORN to before me this ___ day of _____, 19___.

_____

Notary Public in and for the State of Washington.

Commission Expires: _____.

IN RE THE MARRIAGE OF_____ CLALLAM COUNTY CAUSE NO. _____

PROPERTY VALUATION AND DISTRIBUTION, Page No. _____

NO.	ITEM (OF PROPERTY)	WIFE'S PROPOSED AWARDS		HUSBAND'S PROPOSED AWARDS		COURT'S AWARDS		COURT REMARKS
		TO WIFE AT THIS VALUE	TO HUSBAND AT THIS VALUE	TO WIFE AT THIS VALUE	TO HUSBAND AT THIS VALUE	TO WIFE AT THIS VALUE	TO HUSBAND AT THIS VALUE	

[Adopted effective June 30, 1993.]

EXHIBIT D. ORDER OF JUSTIFICATION

IN THE SUPERIOR COURT OF THE STATE OF WASHINGTON
IN AND FOR THE COUNTY OF CLALLAM

IN RE THE JUSTIFICATION OF:)

) ORDER OF JUSTIFICATION

)

      Surety.   )

_____)

This matter having come on before the Court on the Petition for Justification filed herein by _____ to justify qualifications to post bail bonds in criminal matters pending in Superior Court in and for the County of Clallam; and the Court having considered the contents of the aforementioned petition and being of the opinion that the same should be granted; now, therefore, it is hereby,

ORDERED that _____ be, and the same is hereby granted authorization to post bail bonds in connection with criminal matters pending in the Superior Court in and for the County of Clallam under the following terms and conditions:

(1) That _____ may post bail bonds secured by the assets of the same _____ in amounts up to and including $_____;

(2) Each bond shall be approved by an officer authorized by law; and it is further

ORDERED that this order shall be effective until _____ and not thereafter.

DONE this ___ day of _____, 19___.

JUDGE

Presented by:

_____

[Adopted effective June 30, 1993.]

EXHIBIT E. STATUS REPORT AND ORDER

IN THE SUPERIOR COURT OF THE STATE OF WASHINGTON
IN AND FOR THE COUNTY OF CLALLAM

STATE OF WASHINGTON,	)	NO.
	)	
Plaintiff,	)	STATUS REPORT AND ORDER
	)	
vs.	)	
	)	
	)	
	)	
Defendant.	)	
	)	

THIS REPORT is submitted to the Court for the purpose of disclosing the present status of this case as it relates to trial preparation and Court scheduling.

1. The Defendant received discovery materials from the Prosecuting Attorney on _____, 19___.

2. The Defendant has reviewed the discovery materials with Defendant's Attorney.

3. Defendant received a plea offer from the Prosecuting Attorney on _____, 19___.

4. The Defendant has discussed/reviewed the Plea Offer with Defendant's Attorney.

5. The Plea Offer is:
    (a) (__) Accepted (Acceptance does not waive time limits of CrR 3.3)
    (b) (__) Not Accepted.
        1. (__) Additional omnibus hearing is required.
            Specific issues are: _____
            _____

            Hearing is set _____ o'clock __.m. on
            _____, 19___.
        (__) Additional omnibus hearing is waived.
        2. (__) Defendant requests 3.5/3.6 hearing.
            Hearing is set for _____ o'clock __.m. on
            _____, 19___.

_____   _____
Attorney for Defendant   (Deputy) Prosecuting Attorney

_____
Defendant

_____

ORDER

The Court has reviewed the status of his case and orders the hearings set forth above.

DATED this ___ day of _____, 19___.

_____
JUDGE

[Adopted effective June 30, 1993.]

EXHIBIT F.   EXHIBIT F TO LCR 94(E) ENTRY OF DISSOLUTION DECREE BY DECLARATION OF JURISDICTIONAL FACTS

SUPERIOR COURT OF WASHINGTON
COUNTY OF CLALLAM

In re the Marriage of:)
)   NO.
          Petitioner,)   REQUEST FOR ENTRY OF
              and)   DECREE AND DECLARATION
        Respondent.)   OF JURISDICTIONAL FACTS
_____)

REQUEST	The petitioner requests immediate entry of Findings of Fact, Conclusions of Law and Decree of Dissolution of Marriage without a final hearing, and states:
RESIDENCE	I was a resident of the state of Washington when the petition was filed.
TIME LIMITS	More than 90 days have elapsed since the later of _____, the date on which the Petition was filed, and _____, the date:

[ ]   the respondent signed an acceptance of service.

[ ]   the summons and petition were personally served upon the respondent.

[ ]   the summons and petition were mailed pursuant to an order for service by mail.

[ ]   the summons was first published pursuant to an order for service by publication.

MARRIAGE	The parties were married on _____.
PREGNANCY	The wife is not now pregnant.
DEPENDENT CHILDREN	All dependent children of the marriage are identified in the proposed decree. The proposed Parenting Plan is in the children's best interest; the Child Support Worksheets are accurate.
PROPERTY & DEBTS IF DEFAULT	All property and all debts of the parties are fairly and completely divided in the Decree. If entry of the decree is sought after default of the Respondent, The decree provides for only that relief requested in the petition.
PERJURY DECLARATION	I DECLARE UNDER PENALTY OF PERJURY UNDER THE LAWS OF THE STATE OF WASHINGTON THAT THE FOREGOING IS TRUE AND CORRECT.

DATED: _____, 20___   _____
At _____, Washington.   Petitioner
Presented by:

_____   _____
    Attorney for Petitioner   Respondent

[Adopted effective September 1, 2002.]

EXHIBIT G. SUPPLEMENT TO EMANCIPATION PETITION

SUPPLEMENT TO EMANCIPATION PETITION

Please answer each of the questions fully and attach, as exhibits to the petition, such additional information as is requested, or that you feel would be helpful to the court's determination of this petition. All answers should be typed or legibly printed or written in ink. Please use additional pages if the spaces provided are insufficient for the answer.

PERSONAL DATA

1. Provide your name, date of birth and social security number.

_____

_____

_____

2. Provide a list of the names, addresses and telephone numbers of your parents or guardians and your siblings.

_____

_____

_____

_____

3. Provide the names, birth dates and present addresses of your children, if any.

_____

_____

4. Explain how long you have lived in Washington State.

_____

_____

5. Describe your general health including any major illnesses, accidents or disabilities you have incurred up to this point in your life.

_____

_____

_____

_____

6. List the names, addresses and telephone numbers of the persons with whom you have resided for the past three years.

_____

_____

_____

EDUCATIONAL INFORMATION

1. Explain how much education you have received and what is the last grade you completed in school.

_____

_____

_____

_____

_____

2. Attach a copy of school transcript for the past two years.

3. Describe what future education plans you presently have, if any.

_____
_____
_____
_____
_____
_____

4. Describe the clubs and activities you may have been involved in during the past two years, whether these were school related or not.

_____
_____
_____
_____
_____
_____
_____

FINANCIAL INFORMATION

1. List the name, address and telephone number of your present employer, if any, and describe your responsibilities at work.

_____
_____
_____
_____
_____
_____
_____
_____

2. List the names, addresses and telephone numbers of your previous employers and include the dates during which you were employed by each of these persons or businesses.

_____
_____
_____
_____
_____
_____

3. Attach a copy of a completed financial certificate to the petition.

4. Describe how you intend to meet your financial needs if emancipated.

_____
_____
_____
_____
_____
_____

5. If an attorney is helping you with this process, explain how that attorney is being paid.

_____

_____
_____
_____

CRIMINAL HISTORY

1. List all of the crimes or traffic offenses for which you have received convictions or diversions.

_____
_____
_____

2. Attach a copy of your criminal history, or a certificate from the juvenile court which states that you do not have any criminal history.

3. Describe what criminal charges, if any, may be pending against you at this time, including pending court hearings or financial obligations.

_____
_____
_____

REFERENCES

1. Provide the names, addresses and telephone numbers of three adult references who support your petition. These references should not include your parents or guardians.

_____
_____
_____
_____
_____
_____
_____
_____
_____

STATEMENT OF GOALS

1. Provide a brief statement of your personal goals for the future and how you plan to achieve them.

_____
_____
_____
_____
_____
_____

2. Describe how you intend to pay for medical and dental care if you are emancipated.

_____
_____
_____
_____

NOTE: There should be 3 attachments to this supplement.

I declare under penalty of perjury of the laws of the State of Washington that the foregoing is true and correct.

Signed at   _____ on _____.
          (City and State)   (Date)

_____
          (Signature)

[Adopted effective March 16, 1994.]

EXHIBIT H. RESPONSE TO PETITION FOR EMANCIPATION

IN THE SUPERIOR COURT OF THE STATE OF WASHINGTON
IN AND FOR THE COUNTY OF CLALLAM

In re the Emancipation of:) NO.
)
) RESPONSE TO PETITION
) FOR EMANCIPATION

The undersigned parent(s)/guardian(s) acknowledge(s) receipt of a copy of the Petition For Emancipation.

(please designate by placing your initials next to your response to the petition)

_____ 1. I agree with the Petition For Emancipation and will attend the hearing as scheduled.

_____ 2. I agree with the Petition For Emancipation and will not attend the hearing as scheduled.

_____ 3. I do not agree with the Petition For Emancipation and will attend the hearing as scheduled.

_____ 4. I do not agree with the Petition For Emancipation, but will not attend the hearing as scheduled.

(Please print your name, address and telephone number)

_____
Name

_____
Address

_____
Telephone Number

Dated this ___ day of _____, 19___.

_____   _____
Parent/Guardian   Parent/Guardian

RESPONSE TO PETITION
FOR EMANCIPATION
EXHIBIT H
[Adopted effective March 16, 1994.]

LOCAL MANDATORY ARBITRATION RULES (LMAR)
I. SCOPE AND PURPOSE OF RULES

LMAR 1.1. APPLICATION OF RULES

The purpose of mandatory arbitration of civil actions under RCW 7.06 as implemented by the Mandatory Arbitration Rules is to provide a simplified and economical procedure for obtaining the prompt and equitable resolution of disputes involving claims of $50,000.00 or less. The Mandatory Arbitration Rules as supplemented by these local rules are not designed to address every question which may arise during the arbitration process and the rules give considerable discretion to the arbitrator. The arbitrator should not hesitate to be informal and expeditious, consistent with the purpose of the statute and rules.

[Adopted effective January 1, 1994.]

LMAR 1.2. MATTERS SUBJECT TO ARBITRATION

By implementation of these rules the Superior Court of Washington for Clallam County authorizes mandatory arbitration under RCW 7.06.010, and approves such arbitration in civil actions in which no party asserts, on the party's own behalf, a claim in excess of $50,000.00 exclusive of interest, attorney's fees and costs under RCW 7.06.020 as amended.

[Adopted effective January 1, 1994.]

LMAR 1.3. CLAIM LIMIT

The limit for claims subject to mandatory arbitration is $50,000.00, exclusive of interest, attorney's fees and costs. For the purpose of this rule, a "claim" is defined to be the net value of the claim, after all reductions for comparative negligence or setoffs; e.g. if the plaintiff's damages are $100,000.00 and the plaintiff is 50% comparatively negligent, the plaintiff's claim is for $50,000.00.

[Adopted effective January 1, 1994.]

II. TRANSFER OF ARBITRATION AND ASSIGNMENT OF ARBITRATOR

LMAR 2.1. TRANSFER TO ARBITRATION

(a) Statement of Arbitrability. In every civil case, the party filing the note for trial setting (Exhibit A) provided by CR 40(a)(1) and LCR 40(B)(1), or any party prior to the time for trial setting, may upon the form prescribed by the court, complete a statement of arbitrability, which will be filed In the Superior Court Clerk's office and a duplicate copy delivered to the Court Administrator's office and the opposing party or parties. A party failing to file and serve a statement of arbitrability within the times prescribed shall be deemed to have waived arbitration, and may subject the matter to mandatory arbitration thereafter only upon leave of the court for good cause shown.

(b) Response to Statement of Arbitrability. Any party disagreeing with the statement of arbitrability shall serve and file a response on the form prescribed by the court (Exhibit B). A duplicate copy of the response shall be delivered to the Court Administrator. In the absence of such a response, the statement of arbitrability shall be deemed correct. Any response opposing the statement of arbitrability shall be filed within seven days after the receipt of the statement of arbitrability. A notice of issue shall be filed with any response objecting to the statement of arbitrability, noting the matter for hearing on the issue of arbitrability within 14 days of filing the response.

(c) Failure to File — Amendments. A person failing to serve and file an original response within the times prescribed may later do so only upon leave of the court. A party may amend a statement of arbitrability or response at any time before assignment of an arbitrator or assignment of a trial date, and thereafter only upon leave of the court for good cause shown.

(d) By Stipulation. A case in which all parties file a stipulation to arbitrate under MAR 8.1(b) will be placed on the arbitration calendar regardless of the nature of the case or amount in controversy.

(e) When Transfer to Arbitration Occurs for Purposes of Application of Local Rules. The case is transferred to arbitration upon the filing of a statement of arbitrability indicating that the case is subject to arbitration, and the filing of a motion for appointment of arbitrator, unless an objection to arbitration of the case is received within the time limits found in LMAR 2.1(b). This transfer shall also trigger the restriction on discovery contained in MAR 4.2 and LMAR 4.2.

[Adopted effective January 1, 1994.]

LMAR 2.2. ASSIGNMENT TO ARBITRATOR

(a) Generally; Stipulations. When a case is set for arbitration, a list of five proposed arbitrators will be furnished to the parties. A master list of arbitrators will be made available on request. The parties are encouraged to stipulate to an arbitrator. In the absence of a stipulation, the arbitrator will be chosen from among the five proposed arbitrators in the manner defined by this rule.

(b) Response by Parties. Each party may, within 14 days after a list of proposed arbitrators is furnished to the parties, nominate one or two arbitrators and strike two arbitrators from the list. If both parties respond, an arbitrator nominated by both parties will be appointed. If no arbitrator has been nominated by both parties, a superior court judge or commissioner will randomly appoint an arbitrator from among those not stricken by either party.

(c) Response by Only One Party. If only one party responds within 14 days, a superior court judge or commissioner will appoint an arbitrator nominated by that party.

(d) No Response. If neither party responds within 14 days, a superior court judge or commissioner will appoint one of the five proposed arbitrators.

[Adopted effective January 1, 1994.]

III. ARBITRATORS

LMAR 3.2. AUTHORITY OF ARBITRATORS

(a) An arbitrator has the authority to:

(1) Determine the time, place and procedure to present a motion before the arbitrator.

(2) Require a party or attorney, advising such party, or both, to pay the reasonable expenses, including attorney fees, caused by the failure of such party or attorney, or both, to obey an order of the arbitrator unless the arbitrator finds that the failure was substantially justified or that other circumstances make an award of expenses unjust. The arbitrator shall make a special award for such expenses and shall file such award with the clerk of the superior court, with proof of service on each party. The aggrieved party shall have 10 days thereafter to appeal the award of such expense in accordance with the procedure described in RCW 2.24.050. If, within 10 days after the award is filed no party appeals, a judgment shall be entered in manner described generally under MAR 6.3.

(3) Award attorney fees, as authorized by these rules, by a contract or by law.

(4) Decide the location for the arbitration hearing.

(b) Arbitrators shall have immunity to the same extent as provided for superior court judges in Washington State.

[Adopted effective January 1, 1994.]

IV. PROCEDURES AFTER ASSIGNMENT

LMAR 4.2. DISCOVERY

(a) Additional Discovery. In determining when additional discovery beyond that directly authorized by MAR 4.2 is reasonably necessary, the arbitrator shall balance the benefits of discovery against the burdens and expenses. The arbitrator shall consider the nature and complexity of the case, the amount in controversy, values at stake, the discovery that has already occurred, the burdens on the party from whom discovery is sought, and the possibility of unfair surprise which may result if discovery is restricted. Authorized discovery shall be conducted in accordance with the civil rules, except that motions concerning discovery shall be determined by the arbitrator.

(b) Notwithstanding the Foregoing. The following interrogatories may be submitted to any party:

(1) State the amount of general damages being claimed;

(2) State each item of special damages being claimed and the amount thereof;

(3) List the name, address and phone number of each person having knowledge of any facts regarding liability;

(4) List the name, address and phone number of each person having knowledge of any facts regarding the damages claimed;

(5) List the name, address and phone number of each expert witness you intend to call at the arbitration. For each such expert, state the subject matter on which the expert is expected to testify; state the substance of the facts and opinions to which the expert is expected to testify, and a summary of the grounds for each opinion.

Only these interrogatories, with the exact language as set out above, are permitted.

[Adopted effective January 1, 1994.]

V. HEARING

LMAR 5.2. PREHEARING STATEMENT OF PROOF—DOCUMENT FILED WITH COURT

In addition to the requirements of MAR 5.2, each party shall also furnish the arbitrator with copies of pleadings and other documents contained in the court file which that party deems relevant. The court file shall remain with the county clerk.

[Adopted effective January 1, 1994.]

VI. AWARD

LMAR 6.1. FORM AND CONTENT OF AWARD

(a) Exhibits. All exhibits offered during the hearing shall be returned to the offering parties.

(b) Attorney Fees. Any motion for actual attorney fees, whether pursuant to contract, statute, or recognized ground in equity, must be presented to the arbitrator, as follows:

(1) Any motion for an award of attorney fees must be submitted to the arbitrator and served on opposing counsel within seven calendar days of receipt of the award. There shall be no extension of this time — unless the moving party makes a request for an extension before the seven day period has expired, in writing, served on both the arbitrator and opposing counsel;

(2) Any response to the motion for fees, must be submitted to the arbitrator and served on opposing counsel within seven calendar days after receipt of the motion;

(3) The arbitrator shall render a decision on the motion, in writing, within 14 days after the motion is made;

(4) If the arbitrator awards fees, the arbitrator shall file an amended award. If fees are denied, the decision shall be filed and served on the parties;

(5) It is within the arbitrator's discretion to hold a hearing on the issue of fees;

(6) The time for appeal of the arbitrator's decision in any case where attorney fees have been timely requested, as set forth above, shall not run until the service and filing of the amended award, or the denial thereof.

[Adopted effective January 1, 1994.]

LMAR 6.2. FILING OF AWARD

A request by an arbitrator for an extension of the time for the filing of an award under MAR 6.2 may be presented to a superior court judge or commissioner ex parte. The arbitrator shall give the parties notice of an extension granted.

[Adopted effective January 1, 1994.]

VII. TRIAL DE NOVO

LMAR 7.1. REQUEST FOR TRIAL DE NOVO—CALENDAR

(a) A written request for a trial de novo shall be accompanied by a note of issue noting the matter for trial setting. Failure to submit the note of issue is not grounds for dismissal; however, the court may impose terms in its discretion.

(b) In any case in which a party makes a motion for attorney fees pursuant to LMAR 6.1c, the 20 day period for appeal shall not commence until the arbitra-

tor has either filed and served the amended award, or the written denial thereof.

(c) The appealing party may file and serve on the other party or parties a jury demand at the same time as the request for a trial de novo and note of issue are filed. The non-appealing party shall have until the time the case is set for trial to file a jury demand. If no jury demand is timely filed, it is waived:

(d) When a case is transferred to the arbitration calendar it will lose its trial date.

[Adopted effective January 1, 1994.]

VIII. GENERAL PROVISIONS

LMAR 8.3. EFFECTIVE DATE

These rules, as amended, become effective on the 1st day of January, 1994, subject to amendment thereafter. With respect to civil cases pending on that date, if the case has not at that time received a trial date, or if the trial date has been set for later than the 1st day of April, 1994, any party may serve and file a statement of arbitrability indicating that the case is subject to mandatory arbitration. If, within 14 days, no party files a response indicating that the case is not subject to arbitration, the case will be transferred to the arbitration calendar. A case set for trial earlier than the 1st day of April, 1994, will be transferred to arbitration only by stipulation of all parties.

[Adopted effective January 1, 1994.]

LMAR 8.6. COMPENSATION OF ARBITRATOR

(a) **Generally.** Arbitrators shall be compensated in the same amount and manner as judges pro tempore of the superior court; provided, however, that said compensation shall not exceed $500.00 for any case unless prior approval is granted by the presiding judge. Hearing time and reasonable preparation time are compensable. Arbitrators may be reimbursed a sum not to exceed $25.00 for costs incurred.

(b) **Form.** When the award is filed, the arbitrator shall submit to the presiding court ex parte a request on a form prescribed by the court. The presiding judge shall determine the amount of compensation and costs, if any are to be paid.

[Adopted effective January 1, 1994.]

LMAR 8.7. ADMINISTRATION

(a) **Court Administrator.** The court administrator and superior court clerk, under the supervision of the Superior Court Judges shall implement the procedures mandated by these rules and perform any additional duties which may be delegated by the judges.

(b) **Administrative Committee.** There shall be an administrative committee composed of both Superior Court judges, a Court commissioner, and three members of the Washington State Bar Association, chosen by the Clallam County Bar Association. The bar members of the committee shall serve for staggered three year terms and may be reappointed. Terms of the initial committee shall be determined by lot.

(c) **Administrative Committee — Duties.** The administrative committee shall have the power and duty to:

(1) Select its chairperson and provide for its procedures;

(2) Select and appoint the panel of arbitrators;

(3) Remove a person from the panel of arbitrators;

(4) Establish procedures for selecting an arbitrator not inconsistent with the Mandatory Arbitration Rules or these rules;

(5) Review the administration and operation of the arbitration program periodically and make recommendations as it deems appropriate to improve the program.

[Adopted effective January 1, 1994.]

LMAR 8.8. WANT OF PROSECUTION

The Superior Court Clerk shall file a clerk's motion to dismiss for want of prosecution in any case assigned for arbitration where there is no activity for a period of one year.

[Adopted effective January 1, 1994.]

[EXHIBITS]
NOTE FOR ARBITRATION

SUPERIOR COURT OF WASHINGTON
COUNTY OF CLALLAM

```
                              )
               Plaintiff,     )
                              )  NO:
vs                            )
                              )  NOTE FOR ARBITRATION
               Defendant.     )
                              )
_____
```

CASE CATEGORY:

Commercial/Contract (COL)	_____	Personal Injury (PIN)	_____
Construction (CONS)	_____	Real Estate (COM)	_____
Family Law (DIS)	_____	Other (Specify)	_____

PLAINTIFF'S ATTORNEY:
   Name:
   Address:
   Telephone:
   WSBA#

DEFENDANT'S ATTORNEY
   Name:
   Address:
   Telephone:
   WSBA#

(Please note additional attorneys on the other side)

STATEMENT OF ARBITRABILITY

[ ] This case is subject to arbitration because the sole relief sought is a money judgment and involves no claim in excess of $50,000, exclusive of attorneys fees, interest and costs.

[ ] The undersigned contends that its claim exceeds $50,000 but hereby waives any claim in excess of $35,000 for the purposes of arbitration.

RESPONSE TO STATEMENT OF ARBITRABILITY

[ ] This case is not subject to mandatory arbitration because:
   [ ] Plaintiff's claim exceeds $50,000;
   [ ] Plaintiff seeks relief other than a money judgment;
   [ ] Defendant's counter or cross claim exceeds $50,000;
   [ ] Defendant's counter or cross claim seeks relief other than a money judgment.

DATED: _____ SIGNED: _____ WSBA# _____

[Adopted effective January 1, 1994.]

NOTICE FOR TRIAL SETTING

SUPERIOR COURT OF WASHINGTON
COUNTY OF CLALLAM

Plaintiff,	)
	) NO:
vs	)
	) NOTICE FOR TRIAL SETTING
Defendant.	)
	)

TO DEFENDANTS: _____

AND TO OPPOSING COUNSEL: _____

AND TO THE CLERK OF THE ABOVE ENTITLED COURT:

PLEASE TAKE NOTICE that the issue of law in this cause will be calendared as follows:

Friday, the ___ day of _____, 200 ___, at _____; and the Clerk is requested to note this cause on the docket for that day.

Counsel filing this notice certifies as follows:
1. The case is at issue.
2. Nature of the case: _____
3. [ ] Non–jury   [ ] Jury   [ ] 12 Person   [ ] 6 Person
4. [ ] Jury fee paid
5. Length of trial: _____ days.
6. [ ] The attorneys for the parties stipulate that the following dates are available for trial setting: _____
7. [ ] The parties shall appear before the Clerk to select a trial date, and if such date cannot be agreed upon, before the Judge assigned to hear the case on his Motion Calendar.

DATED this _____ day of _____ 200 _____.

Notice filed by:

_____

WSBA #
Attorney for _____

[Adopted effective January 1, 1994.]

APPEALS FROM COURTS OF LIMITED JURISDICTION

Pursuant to the provisions of RALJ 4, the Superior Court in and for Clallam County adopts the following mandatory procedures for appeals from Courts of Limited Jurisdiction:

I. LRALJ 4.1. AUTHORITY OF COURTS PENDING APPEAL

A. Superior Court. Jurisdiction is invoked upon the filing of a Notice of Appeal with the Superior Court Clerk.

B. Court of Limited Jurisdiction. After a Notice of Appeal has been filed, and while the case is on appeal, authority to act in a case is limited to RALJ except as expanded by these rules.

C. Questions Relating to Indigency. The Court of Limited Jurisdiction shall decide questions relating to indigency concerning the appointment of counsel at public expense. The Superior Court shall decide questions relating to indigency concerning all other expenses the party wants waived or provided at public expense.

1. *Motion for Order of Indigency and Appointment of Counsel at Public Expense.*

a. Criminal Cases. A party seeking review partially or wholly at public expense from a decision of a Court of Limited Jurisdiction must move in the lower court for an Order of Indigency and Appointment of Counsel at Public Expense. The motion must be supported by an affidavit setting forth the moving party's total assets; monthly income, expenses and liabilities of the party; and a statement of the amount, if any, the party can contribute toward the expense of counsel.,

b. Civil Cases. A party seeking review of a civil case partially or wholly at public expense must move in the lower court for an Order of Indigency and Appointment of counsel at Public Expense. The Motion must be supported by an affidavit meeting substantially the same requirements as set forth in subsection (a) above. In addition, the party must also demonstrate in the motion or the supporting affidavit that the party has a constitutional right to review partially or wholly at public expense.

2. *Motion for Order of Payment of Costs at Public Expense.* A party seeking review partially or wholly at public expense from a decision of a Court of Limited Jurisdiction must move in the Superior Court for an Order of Payment of Costs at Public Expense. The motion must be supported by a statement of the costs the party wants waived or provided at public expense.

3. *Action by the District/Municipal Court.* The lower court shall decide the motion for an Order of Indigency and Appointment of Counsel at Public Ex-

pense, after a hearing if the circumstances warrant, as follows:

a. Denial Generally. The lower court shall deny the motion if a party has adequate means to pay all of the cost of a lawyer for appellant review. The order denying the motion for an Order of Indigency and Appointment of Counsel at Public Expense shall contain findings designating the funds or source of funds available to the party to pay the cost for a lawyer.

b. Approval Generally (Criminal). The lower court shall grant the motion and enter an Order of Indigency and Appointment of Counsel at Public Expense if the party seeking public funds is unable by reason of poverty to pay all or some of the costs of a lawyer for review.

c. Approval Generally (Civil). If the case is civil case, and the party is unable by reason of poverty to pay all or some of the costs of lawyer for review, and if the party has a constitutional right to review partially or wholly at public expense, the lower court shall enter findings of indigency.

d. The Motion, Affidavit and Order Re: Indigency and Appointment of Counsel at Public expense shall be transmitted to the Superior Court by the Lower Court Clerk as a part of the record on review.

4. *Action by the Superior Court.* The Superior Court shall decide the motion for Order of Payment of Costs at Public Expense, after a hearing if the circumstances warrant.

5. *Order of Indigency and Order of Payment of Costs at Public Expense.* The Order(s) shall designate the items of expense which are to be paid with public funds and, where appropriate, the items of expense to be paid by a party or the amount which the party must contribute toward the expense of review. The Order shall designate the extent to which public funds are to be used for payment of the expense of the record on review, limited to those parts of the record reasonably necessary to review issues argued in good faith. Verbatim transcripts of Voir Dire and/or opening statements shall not be paid at public expense without specific court approval. The transcript, to be paid at public expense, shall contain only those portions of the electronic recording necessary to present the issues on appeal.

6. A party and counsel for the party who have been granted an Order pursuant to this rule must promptly bring to the attention of the Superior Court

any significant improvement, during review, in the financial condition of the parties. The Superior court will give a party the benefit of an Order granted pursuant to this rule throughout the review unless the Superior Court finds that the party's financial condition has improved to the extent that the party is no longer indigent.

7. *Appointment and Withdrawal of Counsel in Trial Court.* The lower court shall determine questions relating to the appointment and withdrawal of counsel for an indigent party on review.

8. *Conditions for Payment.* The expenses for an indigent party which are necessarily incident to review by the Superior Court will be paid from public funds, by the Superior Court, only if an Order of Payment meets the requirements of paragraph 5 above and is included in the record on review.

[Adopted effective June 8, 2000.]

II. SMALL CLAIMS APPEAL

Small Claims Court's judgments appealed to the Superior Court shall be subject to the mandatory arbitration requirements of Superior Court and shall follow the procedural rules relating to arbitration. A Trial De Novo on an appeal from Small Claims Court shall not be allowed unless the parties have participated in mandatory arbitration pursuant to the local rules.

[Adopted effective June 8, 2000.]

SELECTED LOCAL ADMINISTRATIVE ORDERS

AO 98–2–5–1. [ADMINISTRATIVE ORDER OF JUNE 1, 1998, ESTABLISHING CLERK'S PROCEDURE FOR PRESENTENCE INVESTIGATION REPORT]

The presentence investigation report containing such information as defendant's criminal history, information about the defendant's characteristics, financial condition, the circumstances affecting the defendant's behavior as may be relevant in imposing sentence or in the correctional treatment of the defendant, and information about the victim; NOW, THEREFORE,

IT IS HEREBY ORDERED that presentence investigation reports shall be sealed upon filing with the Clallam County Superior Court Clerk. Presentence investigation reports may be opened by petitioning the Court with a proper motion and notice to each party and the victim if applicable.

DATED this 1st day of June, 1998

[Adopted June 1, 1998.]

DISTRICT COURTS

DISTRICT I COURT OF CLALLAM COUNTY LOCAL RULES

Including Amendments Received Through
August 15, 2015

Table of Rules

I. CIVIL PROCEEDINGS

LRCRLJ 6.40(g). MEDIATION FOR SMALL CLAIMS COURT

Mediation is strongly encouraged before a trial is allowed in Small Claims Court. The court will set the date for mediation at the time of filing. Both parties must attend the mediation or formally opt-out. If the plaintiff fails to appear, a dismissal may be entered. If the defendant fails to appear or formally opt-out, their answer, if one was filed, may be stricken and default judgment entered. Parties must bring their evidence to the mediation, however, no witnesses are allowed. The purpose of mediation is to settle the case if possible; if no settlement is made at mediation, the case will be set for trial. Attorneys and paralegals may not represent parties at mediation.

[Adopted effective July 1, 1997. Amended effective September 1, 2003; July 1, 2004; September 1, 2015.]

II. CRIMINAL MATTERS

LRCrRLJ 2.1(a)(1)(i). PROSECUTION RESPONSIBLE[1] FOR DIVERSION OF DWLS3

The Prosecutor from each jurisdiction may implement a pre file diversion program for DWLS3, as authorized by law. All complaints and citations for DWLS3 shall be reviewed prior to being filed with the court for eligibility into the Prosecutor's program.

[Adopted effective September 1, 2009. Amended effective September 1, 2015.]

[1] So in original.

LRCrRLJ 2.2(b)(5). WARRANTS ISSUED FOR FAILING TO APPEAR

Defendants that fail to appear, or to provide documentation to the court that they have completed their conditions of Judgment and Sentence prior to the scheduled review hearing, will have warrants issued for their arrest.

[Adopted effective September 1, 2003. Amended effective July 1, 2004; July 5, 2005; September 1, 2015.]

LRCrRLJ 3.1(3)(e). COURT APPOINTED ATTORNEY WITHDRAWLS[1]

Court appointed attorneys may withdraw 180 days after a Warrant of Arrest has been issued, or disposition is entered by way of a Judgment and Sentence, Order of Dismissal or Order Modifying but does not include Stipulated Order of Continuances, Deferred Sentences, Deferred Findings or a Deferred Prosecution.

[Adopted effective September 1, 2009. Amended effective September 1, 2011; September 2, 2013; September 1, 2015.]

[1] So in original.

LRCrRLJ 3.2.1(e)(3). PROCEDURE AT PRELIMINARY APPEARANCE

(1) Any accused detained in jail must be brought before the court before the close of business on the next court day as specified by CrRLJ 3.2.1(d)(1).

(2) Any defendant given a preliminary appearance date by citation, criminal complaint, or summons shall appear as scheduled.

(3) At the preliminary appearance, the defendant shall sign a Rights Form and Conditions of Release. Preliminary appearance of the defendant shall only be excused under unusual circumstances by order of the court. When preliminary appearance is excused the Promise to Return and Conditions of Release shall be entered, setting arraignment date and conditions of release, by telephonic record in open court. The clerk shall forward a copy of this Order to counsel for the plaintiff and defendant, or defendant if pro-se, thereby providing notice for arraignment.

[Adopted effective July 1, 1997. Amended effective September 1, 2003; July 1, 2004; July 1, 2005; September 1, 2015.]

LRCrRLJ 3.3(c)(3). TIME FOR ARRAIGNMENT AND TRIAL [REPEALED]

[Adopted effective July 1, 1997; Amended effective July 1, 2004; repealed effective September 1, 2009.]

LRCrRLJ 4.1(d)(1). APPEARANCE BY DEFENDANT'S LAWYER

The defendant must appear in person for arraignment with their lawyer unless the defendant knowingly and voluntarily waives his/her right to counsel in writing. Appearance at arraignment is not waived by the defendant's lawyer filing an appearance and plea of not guilty on behalf of a client. At arraignment appearance of either the defendant or lawyer shall only be excused under unusual circumstances by order of the court. When the defendant and the defendant's lawyer are present at the regular scheduled preliminary appearance calendar arraignment may be conducted. The entry of plea, conditions of release on the Promise to Return and Order Pending Trial, and Order Setting Schedule and Directing Pretrial Procedure may all be entered; thereby, eliminating the need for a separate arraignment appearance.

[Adopted effective July 1, 1997. Amended effective July 1, 2004; September 1, 2008; September 1, 2009; September 1, 2015.]

LRCrRLJ 4.5(a). PRETRIAL HEARINGS

(1) **Pretrial Motions.** Written 3.6 and *Knapstad* motions shall be filed within 28 days of the arraignment. Failure to file a written motion by that date shall constitute a waiver unless the date is extended by the court for good cause.

(2) **Jury Readiness Hearing.** On Tuesday two weeks prior to trial setting, a Jury Readiness Hearing will be held. All parties and counsel shall be present and all pretrial matters shall be concluded. The presence of the defendant may not be waived except under extraordinary circumstances by order of the court. Failure of the defendant to be present at the Jury Readiness Hearing will result in the issuance of a bench warrant and the striking of the jury trial date.

(3) **Trial Confirmation.** On Tuesday the day before trial, a Trial Confirmation Hearing will be held. After the Trial Confirmation Hearing is held, notice not later than 4:30 p.m. must be given to the Court Clerk to cancel the jury or costs may be assessed to the appropriate party.

[Adopted effective July 1, 1997. Amended effective September 1, 2001; September 1, 2002; September 1, 2003; July 1, 2004; September 1, 2008; September 1, 2009; September 1, 2011; September 2, 2013; September 1, 2015.]

LRCrRLJ 4.8(b)(1)(a). DRIVING WHILE SUSPENDED SUBPOENA DUCES TECUM

A defendant accused of a charge of Driving While Suspended may, through his/her attorney, issue a subpoena Duces Tecum upon the Department of Licensing in Olympia for records reasonably relating to the existence and service of the drivers license suspension alleged. Said subpoena shall permit the Department of Licensing no less than 14 days from the completion of service to comply with the subpoena. The subpoena shall also permit the Department of Licensing to comply by fax or first class mail, postage prepaid to the attorney's business address.

[Adopted effective July 1, 2004. Amended effective July 1, 2005; September 1, 2015.]

LRCrRLJ 8.1(c)(1). MOTIONS

When setting a hearing on a jurisdictional calendar a notice of issue along with an agreed order shortening time shall be filed with the court by 12:00 on the day prior to the jurisdictional calendar.

When setting a hearing on a non-jurisdictional calendar a motion shall be filed in accordance with

CrRLJ 8.1(c). In extraordinary circumstances the court may allow a motion and order shorting time.

[Adopted effective September 2, 2013. Amended effective September 1, 2015.]

III. INFRACTIONS

LRIRLJ 2.4(4). WRITTEN STATEMENT FOR MITIGATING CIRCUMSTANCES

Submitting a written statement explaining mitigating circumstances, is authorized. Prior to submitting the statement a person must promise to pay the monetary penalty authorized by law if the infraction is found to be committed. Written statements may be submitted to the court by email at: https://websrv7.clallam.net/mitigations/mitiform.php?CourtID=1.

[Adopted effective September 1, 2015.]

LRIRLJ 3.1(b)(1). CONTESTED HEARINGS DISCOVERY

Speed measuring device certifications are not subject to discovery. Local speed measuring devices certification documents can be obtained from the court clerk during normal business hours prior to a contested hearing. Washington State Patrol's speed measuring device certifications are located at: www.wsp.wa.gov/traveler/smdhome.htm.

[Adopted effective July 1, 2004. Amended effective July 1, 2005; September 1, 2011; September 1, 2015.]

LOCAL RULES FOR CLALLAM COUNTY DISTRICT COURT II

Including Amendments Received Through
August 15, 2015

Table of Rules

I. INTRODUCTION

LARLJ 2. SCOPE OF RULES AND ADOPTION

(a) **Effect of Local Rules.** These rules shall be known as the Local Rules for Clallam County District Court II. These rules are supplemental to the Rules for Courts of Limited Jurisdiction, as adopted or amended by the Supreme Court of the State of Washington, and shall not be construed in conflict with them.

(b) **Adoption and Amendment.** These rules are adopted pursuant to GR 7, CRLJ 83 and CrRLJ 1.7 and may be amended in the discretion of the District Court II Judge.

(c) **Prior Rules Repealed.** All prior rules of Clallam County District Court II are repealed upon adoption of these rules.

[Adopted effective September 1, 2002.]

II. CIVIL PROCEEDINGS

LCRLJ 5. SERVICE AND FILING OF PLEADINGS AND OTHER PAPER

(i) **Filing by Facsimile or Email.** The court accepts documents filed by facsimile or email (PDF format preferred), subject to the provisions of GR 17. A document properly filed by facsimile or email shall constitute an original for all purposes.

[Adopted effective September 1, 2011.]

LCRLJ 38. CIVIL JURY TRIAL

(a) **Demand.** The request for jury trial in civil cases shall be made by filing a demand with the clerk and paying the jury fee not later than seven days from the date of the trial setting notice issued from the court. Failure to comply with this rule is a waiver of the right to a jury trial.

(b) **Imposition of Costs.** The court shall be notified immediately if a case scheduled for jury trial is settled or will not be tried by the jury for any reason. An assessment for jury costs may be imposed if the parties fail to notify the court at least 24 hours before the trial is scheduled to begin.

[Adopted effective September 1, 2002.]

LCRLJ 40(1). SMALL CLAIMS MANDATORY MEDIATION

(a) **Mediation Conference.** A Mediation Conference is mandatory before trial. The court will set a

Mediation Conference date at the time of filing an answer to the Complaint. Both parties must attend the Mediation Conference. If the plaintiff fails to appear, a dismissal may be entered. If the defendant fails to appear, their answer, if one was filed, may be stricken and a default judgment entered. Parties must bring their evidence to the mediation, however, no witnesses are allowed. The purpose of mediation is to settle the case if possible; if no settlement is made at mediation, the case will proceed to trial. Lawyers and paralegals may not represent the parties at mediation or in Small Claims Court.

(b) Exemption from Mediation. The parties may request exemption from mandatory Mediation Conference by filing an affidavit within 14 days of receipt of the notice of the mandatory mediation conference, wherein the parties state they have attempted to settle all issues in dispute by participating in formal mediation or arbitration prior to filing the case.

If the parties have already submitted the case to another type of mediation or arbitration service, the case may proceed directly to trial at the discretion of the court. The parties shall file with the court notice from the prior mediation/arbitration agency showing such prior attempt to settle.

(c) Completing Mediation. Any case assigned to mediation must be completed within 90 days of assignment, unless otherwise ordered by the court.

(1) In all cases assigned to mediation in which a settlement is reached, the parties shall report such settlement to the mediator and the mediator shall file written notice of such settlement with the court.

(2) The results of mediation shall be reported to the court as either "settled" or "not settled".

(3) If a case is reported as "settled", the terms of the agreement, including a date of final compliance, shall be signed in writing by the parties and filed by the mediator with the clerk of the court within 10 judicial days.

(i) The mediator shall provide the creditor with a form to report compliance or non-compliance with the terms of the settlement agreement.

(ii) Should the creditor fail to file a report of compliance or non-compliance within 30 days after the final date for compliance, or reports the terms of the settlement have been met, the court may dismiss the case.

(iii) Upon notice by a creditor of non-compliance with the terms of the settlement agreement, the clerk of the court shall refer the case to a judge for disposition.

(4) If the parties are not able to settle a mediated case, the case will be set for trial.

[Adopted on an emergency basis effective March 10, 2014; June 2, 2014; adopted on a permanent basis effective September 2, 2014.]

LCRLJ 40(2). CONTINUANCE OF MEDIATION OR SMALL CLAIM TRIAL

The party requesting a continuance must contact the other party who must also agree to the continuance in writing.

If one party will not agree to the continuance, the party seeking the continuance must make a written motion for continuance and set a hearing date prior to the scheduled mediation or trial date. The motion and notice of hearing must be served on the opposing party not less than five days prior to the date set for the motion to continue. At the hearing, the Judge will make a ruling whether the matter will be continued.

If there are less than five days prior to the mediation or trial date to serve the opposing party, the party requesting the continuance may contact the Court to explain the circumstances which require the mediation or trial to be continued. The matter may be continued by the Court upon showing of good cause.

[Adopted on an emergency basis effective March 10, 2014; June 2, 2014; adopted on a permanent basis effective September 2, 2014.]

LCRLJ 51. JURY INSTRUCTIONS

(a) Assembling and Distribution. Proposed jury instructions shall be assembled and distributed as follows:

(1) One copy (including cover page) to judge to be unnumbered, paper clipped (not stapled) and without citations;

(2) One copy with supporting citations, numbered and stapled, to each of the following:

Clerk, for court file

Judge, for work copy

Counsel for each opposing party

(b) Citations. Washington Pattern Jury Instructions are to be cited. On the copies of proposed jury instructions delivered to the judge, clerk and opposing counsel, pattern instructions shall be identified by WPI number. If a pattern instruction is changed or modified in any way, the citation shall include the word "modified."

[Adopted effective September 1, 2002.]

III.　CRIMINAL PROCEEDINGS

LCrRLJ 3.3.　CONTINUANCES

(a) Continuances may be granted:

(1) Upon written agreement of all parties which must be authorized by the defendant(s). Agreements lacking evidence of approval of all parties will not be considered by the court. The agreement must set forth the basis for the continuance and include a proposed order of continuance. The agreement is not effective unless approved by the court.

(2) By motion, if such motion complies with relevant rules for motions, including CrRLJ 3.3(h)(2).

(3) Only if the continuance is to a date within the speedy trial requirements of CrRLJ 3.3 or the defendant executes a waiver of speedy trial.

[Adopted effective September 1, 2002.]

LCrRLJ 3.4.　AGREEMENT TO VIDEO CONFERENCING [RESCINDED]

[Adopted effective September 1, 2002; rescinded effective September 1, 2011.]

LCrRLJ 8.4.　SERVICE, FILING, AND SIGNING OF PAPERS

(e) Filing by Facsimile or Email. The court accepts documents filed by facsimile or email (PDF format preferred), subject to the provisions of GR 17. A document properly filed by facsimile or email shall constitute an original for all purposes.

[Adopted effective September 1, 2011.]

LCrRLJ 38.　CRIMINAL JURY TRIAL

(a) Imposition of Costs. The court shall be notified immediately if a case scheduled for jury trial is settled or will not be tried by the jury for any reason. An assessment for jury costs may be imposed if the parties fail to notify the court at least 24 hours before the trial is scheduled to begin.

[Adopted effective September 1, 2002.]

LCrRLJ 51.　JURY INSTRUCTIONS

(a) Assembling and Distribution. Proposed jury instructions shall be assembled and distributed as follows:

(1) One copy (including cover page) to judge to be unnumbered, paper clipped (not stapled) and without citations;

(2) One copy with supporting citations, numbered and stapled, to each of the following:

　Clerk, for court file

　Judge, for work copy

　Counsel for each opposing party

(b) Citations. Washington Pattern Jury Instructions are to be cited. On the copies of proposed jury instructions delivered to the judge, clerk and opposing counsel, pattern instructions shall be identified by WPI number. If a pattern instruction is changed or modified in any way, the citation shall include the word "modified."

[Adopted effective September 1, 2002.]

IV.　INFRACTION RULES

LIRLJ 2.4.　RESPONSE TO NOTICE

(c) Method of Response. A person may respond to a notice of infraction in person or by mail. A response by mail must be postmarked no later than midnight of the day the response is due. Written instructions about infraction hearing procedures will be provided to anyone timely responding to an infraction. The written instructions explain the procedures for mitigating or contesting infractions in person; by mail; or online, using the court's website.

[Adopted effective September 1, 2011.]

LIRLJ 3.1.　CONTESTED HEARINGS— PRELIMINARY PROCEEDINGS

(a) Timeliness of Requests for Subpoenas. If a request for a subpoena pursuant to IRLJ 3.1 is made 14 days or less before a scheduled hearing, the court may deny the request or condition the issuance of the subpoena on a continuance of the hearing date.

(b) Speed Measuring Device Expert. Defense requests for a Speed Measuring Device Expert must be made to the appropriate prosecuting attorney's office no less than 30 days before a contested hearing.

(c) Costs and Witness Fees. Each party is responsible for costs incurred by that party, including witness fees. In cases where a party requests a witness to be subpoenaed, the party requesting the witness shall pay the witness fees and mileage expenses due that witness.

[Adopted effective September 1, 2002.]

LIRLJ 3.5.　DECISION ON WRITTEN STATEMENTS

The procedure authorized in IRLJ 3.5 is adopted by this court.

[Adopted effective September 1, 2002.]

LIRLJ 6.6.　SPEED MEASURING DEVICE; DESIGN AND CONSTRUCTION

(d) Maintaining Certificates as Public Records. IRLJ 6.6 certificates are maintained as public records by the Washington State Patrol and are available on the WSP website: http://www.wsp.wa.gov. The court is entitled to take judicial notice of certificates available online at the WSP website. The court will not maintain separate records of such certificates. Evidence will not be suppressed merely because a certificate is available online, as opposed to being provided by the prosecuting authority. Evidence shall be suppressed if the certificate is insufficient.

[Adopted effective September 1, 2011.]

MUNICIPAL COURTS
PORT ANGELES MUNICIPAL COURT—
[No Local Rules]

PUBLISHER'S NOTE

This municipal court follows District Court I of Clallam County Local Rules

SEQUIM MUNICIPAL COURT—
[No Local Rules]

PUBLISHER'S NOTE

This municipal court follows the District Court I of Clallam County Local Rules

CLARK COUNTY

Table of Courts

Superior Court

Local Rules of the Superior Court for Clark County.

District Court

Local Rules of the District Court of Clark County, State of Washington.

Municipal Courts

Municipal Courts of Battle Ground, Ridgefield, and La Center.
Camas–Washougal Municipal Court—[No Local Rules].
Vancouver Municipal Court—[No Local Rules].
Yacolt Municipal Court—[No Local Rules].

SUPERIOR COURT

LOCAL RULES OF THE SUPERIOR COURT FOR CLARK COUNTY

Originally Effective January 1, 1987

Including Amendments Received Through August 15, 2015

Table of Rules

ORIGINALLY EFFECTIVE
JANUARY 1, 1987

Pursuant to Rule 83 of the Civil Rules for Superior Court, the following rules are hereby adopted by the Superior Court of Clark County, Washington, to be in effect after January 1, 1987, superseding all former rules and special rules.

SCOPE OF RULES

These rules are assembled to conform with the requirements of CR 83. Each rule is given the CR number, section or subsection which most clearly deals with the same subsection. These rules are supplemental to the State rules and are not to be construed in derogation thereof. Numerical omissions indicate that there are no local rules on this subject.

I. ADMINISTRATIVE RULES

RULE 0.1. DEPARTMENTS, SENIORITY AND MANAGEMENT

(a) Departments. The Superior Court for Clark County shall be divided into as many individual numbered departments as there are judges authorized by law. Each judge in the order of seniority shall select an unassigned courtroom.

(b) Seniority. Seniority shall be established by the length of continuous service as a judge of the Superior Court. In the event two or more judges have equal length of service, their seniority shall be determined by lot.

(c) Assignments. The assignment of courtrooms, whenever necessary, shall be incorporated into an order signed by the Presiding Judge and filed with the Clerk of the Court.

[Amended effective September 1, 2002.]

RULE 0.2. COURT MANAGEMENT AND ORGANIZATION

(a) Authorities. The authority to manage and conduct the court shall be vested in:

(1) The Superior Court Judges through regular monthly or special meetings of a majority of the Judges;

(2) The Presiding Judge and the Assistant Presiding Judge in the interim between meetings of the Judges.

(b) Duties and Responsibilities.

(1) The Judges, en banc, have final authority over any matters pertaining to court organization and operation and over any individual or committee of the court.

(2) Decisions made between meetings of the judges and particularly matters of policy affecting the court and its operation, shall be presented to the judges at the next meeting by the Presiding Judge for approval, ratification, modification or rejection.

(3) The Presiding Judge and Assistant Presiding Judge shall be elected by a majority vote of the Court's Judges for a term not to exceed two years and shall perform all duties of the position required by General Rule 29 (f).

(4) There shall be a Chief Family Law Division Judge, appointed by the Presiding Judge for a term of two years. The duties of the Chief Family Law Judge shall include assignment of work, creation of special calendars, supervision of the implementation of case management tools, development of policy for alternative dispute resolution, supervision of Family Treatment Court and Family Law Guardianship services and such other duties as may be delegated by the Court or Presiding or Assistant presiding Judge.

(c) Judicial Assistants and Reporters. Judicial Assistants are subject to the direct supervision and authority of the department to which they are assigned.

(1) Judicial Assistants shall attend to the affairs of the court from 8:00 a.m. to 5:00 p.m. daily unless otherwise ordered by the court or required by court duties.

(d) Court Commissioners. Full-time Court Commissioners appointed pursuant to RCW 2.24.010 are authorized to perform all of the duties authorized by RCW 2.24.040.

[Amended effective September 1, 1996; September 1, 2000; September 1, 2002; September 1, 2004; September 1, 2008; September 2, 2014.]

RULE 0.2.5.   COURT ADMINISTRATOR

(a) Selection. The court administrator shall be appointed by a majority of all of the judges and shall serve at the pleasure of the appointing authority under the direction and supervision of the Presiding and Assistant Presiding Judge.

(b) Powers and Duties. The powers and duties of the court administrator include but are not limited to the following:

(1) *Administrative.* Administrative control of all non-judicial activities of the court.

(2) *Policies.* Implement all policies regarding judicial functions of the court.

(3) *Supervisory.* Supervision of all court employees, except commissioners, juvenile court employees and departmental employees.

(4) *Budgetary.* Preparation and administration of the budget.

(5) *Representative.* Representation of the court in dealings with the State Court Administrator.

(6) *Assist.* Assist the Presiding Judge in meeting with representatives of governmental bodies, and other public and private groups regarding court management matters.

(7) *Agenda Preparation.* Prepare the agenda for judges' meetings and act as recording secretary at those meetings and at committee meetings where the administrator's presence would be reasonable and productive.

(8) *Record Preparation and Maintenance.* Prepare reports and compile statistics as required by the judges or state court administration and maintain records of informal activities of the court.

(9) *Recommendations.* Make recommendations to the judges for the improvement of the administration of the court.

[Amended effective September 1, 1996; September 1, 2002; September 2, 2014.]

RULE 0.3.   CASE ASSIGNMENT AND DOCKETS

(a) Case Assignment. All criminal and civil cases shall be specifically assigned by department in a random manner to assure even distribution between the departments. Each department shall be responsible for all cases assigned to it and shall hear all matters pertaining thereto except as set forth below in paragraph (B). This rule shall not preclude the transfer of cases, trials, or preliminary matters between departments when in the interest of administration of justice it may be necessary or when necessitated by disqualification of a judge as provided for by law or court rule.

(b) Criminal Judge. A criminal judge shall be designated on a rotating basis to hear criminal proceedings for all departments except trials and trial related matters, suppression motion and CrR 3.5 hearings. The criminal judge shall be designated on a rotating basis in accordance with a published rotation schedule.

(1) A criminal first appearance hearing shall be conducted daily by the criminal judge or designated commissioner at a regularly designated time. All persons arrested prior to midnight shall be brought before the criminal judge for consideration of right to counsel if one has not previously been made available under CrR 3.1, pre-trial release under CrR 3.2, advice

as to charges filed or to be filed, and for scheduling of arraignment and further proceedings.

(c) Schedule. Judges will schedule events and trials in accordance with the published judicial calendar and judge rotation schedule.

(1) Contempt matters shall be cited on the civil calendar of the judge issuing the order.

(d) Calendars. Calendars shall be prepared under the direction of the Court Administrator to reflect the departments in which the various matters are to be heard, the subject involved, and the times.

(e) Jury Sessions. There shall be jury sessions each month of the year for each department. The method to be employed in obtaining the required number of jurors shall be in accordance with RCW 2.36.054 utilizing the electronic data processing random selection provided for in RCW 2.36.063 et seq.

[Amended effective September 1, 2000; September 2, 2014.]

RULE 0.4. GENERAL

(a) Attire of Counsel and Litigants. All attorneys appearing before the court or in chambers shall be attired in a manner that is consistent with the current generally prevailing and accepted business attire for professional men and women in the local community. Any attire that is distracting or detrimental to the seriousness of the proceedings or disruptive of decorum should be avoided. The parties should wear clean and neat appearing clothing, and to avoid such items as sandals, clogs, sport togs, sweatshirts, tee-shirts, body-exposing garments or anything that contains emblazoned figures or words.

(b) Local Rule Re: E-mail Communication.

Purpose: The purpose of this rule is to provide guidelines for the use of e-mail in communicating with court staff. This rule does not apply to the other forms of communication, and does not establish a preference for e-mail communication over any other form of communication.

Use of judge's individual address prohibited: The only address to be used by attorneys, pro se self-represented litigants or others who need to communicate with court staff about a case is the individual department's judicial assistant's e-mail address. Absent express invitation by the judge, the judge's individual e-mail address is not to be used.

Guidelines for use of e-mail: E-mail communication with the department is appropriate in the following typical situations:

To obtain a date for an in-court hearing;

To submit proposed orders;

To determine the judge's availability for a settlement conference;

To determine the availability of equipment needed for trial (such as a video player or speaker phone);

To determine the judge's preference as to number of copies of jury instructions required for trial;

To advise the court of a settlement (to be immediately followed by formal written notice pursuant to CR 41(e);

To determine whether the judge will accept pleadings, jury instructions, legal memoranda, and the like, in the form of an e-mail submission;

Other matters of a similar nature that would be appropriate to handle by way of a phone call to court staff.

Ex parte communication prohibited: The prohibitions regarding ex parte contact with the court are fully applicable to e-mail communication. If an attorney/party is communicating substantive information to court staff, the e-mail must also be sent to opposing counsel/party and so indicate on its face. Substantive information includes information regarding the likelihood of settlement, the timing of witnesses, anticipated problems with scheduling, concerns regarding security and other case-specific issues.

Service of working copies and pleadings: Absent prior permission of the court, e-mail may not be used to provide working copies of legal pleadings, including jury instructions. Absent agreement of counsel/opposing party or express permission of the court, e-mail may not be used for service of pleadings on opposing parties, even in those situations where the court has agreed to accept working copies by e-mail.

Retention of e-mail: The court is not obligated to retain any electronic communications. Original documentation shall be filed with the County Clerk's Office.

[Amended effective September 1, 2008; September 2, 2014.]

RULE 0.5. JUVENILE DEPARTMENT

(d) Reports to Be Confidential: Unless otherwise ordered by the court, all predisposition reports, including SSODA evaluations and CDDA evaluations, shall be confidential. These reports shall be filed in a confidential envelope and are not considered part of the official juvenile court file.

[Amended effective September 1, 2015.]

RULE 0.6. FAMILY COURT

(a) Authority. Each Superior Court judge is designated as a judge of the Family Court. Matters affecting the welfare of minor children may also be heard by the Court Commissioner.

(b) Petition. When a controversy exists between parties that may affect the welfare of minor children, either party may petition the court (using Form No. DR–001) for the purpose of investigating the welfare of the minor children and the relevant factors for determining custody, visitation rights or modifications of either.

(c) Preliminary Determinations. The court shall make a preliminary determination of the necessity for Family Court Services based upon the petition and supporting documents on the family law motion calendar before any matter is referred. Only cases where material facts are alleged that circumstances affecting the welfare of the minor children exist will be referred for Family Court services.

(d) Additional Documents Required. When a matter is referred to Family Court Services, each party shall fully complete and submit prior to the interview the following:

(1) Family Information Statement (Form No. DR–002)

(2) Financial Statement (Form No. DR–003)

Appropriate consent(s) to release of information shall be executed upon request of the Family Court Coordinator.

(e) Order to Appear. Upon referral of a matter for Family Court Services, an order to appear shall be issued and served on the non-petitioning party requiring him/her to contact Family Court Services within five (5) days of service for a personal interview to be scheduled within fifteen (15) days of service.

(1) Failure to comply with the order to appear and complete the interview process will allow the court to determine custody, visitation, or modification of either on the basis of available information.

(2) If there has been no service of the order to appear obtained within thirty (30) days of its issuance, the court, being satisfied that good faith efforts to obtain service have been made, may enter such further orders as may be proper in the circumstances.

(3) The petitioning party shall within five (5) days of the issuance of the order to appear, contact Family Court Services for an interview to be scheduled within fifteen (15) days of the order of referral.

(f) Preliminary Report. After completion of the Family Court Services interviews, a preliminary report shall be prepared and submitted to the court and counsel (parties). The court may then proceed to enter such orders for custody, visitation, or modification as it deems proper and/or may refer the parties for such professional services as may be indicated appropriate.

(g) Professional Services/Report. When the parties are referred for family professional services, a final report shall be submitted to the court and counsel (parties) by Family Court Services, attaching reports and other information obtained concerning the welfare of the children, custody, visitation, and related issues.

(h) Costs. The court may assess each party a fee for the cost of professional services if initially provided at public expense due to economic hardship.

(i) Suggested Visitation Schedule. In order to facilitate reasonable resolution of visitation disputes, the parties should consider the following guide which the court would be inclined to accept as reasonable in most cases:

The children should reside with the primary residential parent, except the children should reside with the non-residential parent pursuant to the following schedule:

(1) *Weekends.* Alternating weekends from 6:00 p.m. Friday until 6:00 p.m. Sunday.

(2) *Summers.* Alternate weeks during the summer, commencing the first Friday after school is out. The primary residential parent shall have even years and the other parent shall have odd years.

(3) *Winter holidays.* In odd-numbered years (whether or not the children are in school, as calculated by the local school year calendar), winter holiday time beginning at 6:00 p.m. on the day school recesses and continuing until December 24th at 8:00 p.m.; in even-numbered years, December 24th from 8:00 p.m. and continuing until noon the day before school commences.

(4) *Spring holiday.* Alternating spring vacations (whether or not the children are in school, as calculated by the local school year calendar). The non-residential parent should have the children in even-numbered years, not to interrupt the weekend schedule set forth above.

(5) *Other holidays.* The children should spend Thanksgiving with the residential parent in even-numbered years. The children should spend Thanksgiving with the non-residential parent in odd-numbered years. Thanksgiving should be defined as commencing at 6:00 p.m. the day school is out before Thanksgiving Day, and continuing until 6:00 p.m. the Sunday immediately following the holiday. Monday holidays shall be spent with the parent having residential time over the preceding weekend. The Memorial Day holiday shall be with the non-residential parent every year and the Labor Day weekend shall be with the residential parent every year.

[Amended effective May 12, 1993; September 1, 2010; September 2, 2014.]

RULE 0.7. DOMESTIC VIOLENCE PETITIONS

(a) Filing. The clerk may refer a petitioner to either the District Court or Superior Court for issuance of an ex parte temporary order for protection pursuant to RCW 26.50.070. All hearings for an order for protection issued pursuant to RCW 26.50.060 shall be scheduled before the Superior Court Commissioner in accordance with the court's published schedule.

(b) Pending domestic violence criminal cases are outside the scope of domestic relations settlement conferences. Parties will not be permitted to attempt to negotiate criminal cases or make settlement offers contingent upon the alleged victim's position in a pending criminal case, and parties will not be allowed to include pending criminal charges as part of the settlement conference agreement. Any party who makes a settlement offer contingent upon the alleged victim's input, position, etc., in a pending criminal case, or otherwise attempts to negotiate a criminal case in the context of a domestic relations settlement conference, will be considered to be acting in bad faith, and terms will be assessed.

[Amended effective June 27, 1995.]

RULE 0.8. CIVIL BENCH WARRANT

(a) Identification of Arrestee. Any person requesting a civil warrant of arrest shall provide the following information, if known, on the face of the warrant: full name, date of birth, social security number, height, weight, race, gender, eye color, hair color, and last known address.

(b) Affidavits in Support of Warrant. An affidavit, stating the reason(s) for the issuance of a warrant, shall be provided to the issuing Judicial Officer at the time the warrant is requested.

[Adopted effective September 1, 1991; Amended effective September 1, 2002.]

RULE 0.9. WRITS OF HABEAS CORPUS IN CHILD CUSTODY MATTERS

(a) Rule to Control in Conjunction with RCW 7.36. This Local Rule shall, in conjunction with Chapter 7.36, control the procedure and legal right to retain custody of a child in Clark County, Washington through a writ of habeas corpus.

(b) Who May Petition. Only a person or entity with a previously established right to custody of a child will be granted a writ of habeas corpus. The applicant must be able to document the pre-existing legal right to custody of the child paramount to the right of any other person or entity. The pre-existing custody order must be issued by a court of competent jurisdiction and have been obtained through a court action where the other party had notice of the action and the opportunity to be heard.

(c) Presentment. A Petition for Writ of Habeas Corpus should be presented to either the Presiding or the Family Law Judge of the Superior Court of Clark County.

(d) Forms. Applicants for Writs of Habeas Corpus in Child Custody matters shall use exclusively those forms approved by the Clark County Superior Court available at the Clark County Superior Court Clerk's Office including the Sealed Source Mission Child Information Declaration.

[Adopted effective September 1, 2005.]

II. CIVIL RULES

RULE 4.1. DISSOLUTION OF MARRIAGE, MODIFICATIONS, ETC.

(a) Cases in which Declaration Accepted. When a party is represented by an attorney, a declaration will be accepted in lieu of testimony in cases in which parties have stipulated to entry or in default cases in which the relief requested is the same as the relief requested in the Petition for dissolution. In those cases in which the relief requested is different or more specific than the original petition, and the respondent has defaulted, the party requesting relief which varies from the petition must appear on the Dissolution Docket and present testimony in support of the request, with a decision to be made by the judge or commissioner.

The declaration in lieu of testimony must be made after the expiration of the ninety (90) day period.

The declaration must be in substantially the same form as the Declaration in Support of Entry of Decree of Dissolution. The declaration must include the certification of attorney.

(b) Show Cause Orders; Temporary Restraining Orders. When the court, in its discretion, decides to order the personal appearance of a party, a show cause order shall be issued and made returnable not less than 5 days, excluding weekends and holidays, prior to the hearing, unless a shorter time is ordered by the court. Immediate restraining orders will not be granted unless it is clearly shown by affidavit setting forth facts that irreparable injury could result prior to the hearing.

(c) Standards and Worksheets. Prior to hearing an application for any support or maintenance, the parties shall prepare, serve and file applicable worksheets in accordance with RCW 26.19 taking into consideration the standards for determination of child support as published by the Washington State Child Support Commission.

(d) Scope of Hearings. A show cause order or citation may include notice of hearing all relief sought by the applicant. All temporary hearings shall be heard only on affidavit unless otherwise ordered by the court. Supporting affidavits shall be limited to 4 per party excluding affidavits from expert witnesses. Affidavits from parties shall not exceed 6 pages and supplemental affidavits shall not exceed 2 pages. All affidavits and declarations shall be typewritten and double spaced and no smaller than eleven point type.

(e) Modification Proceedings.

(1) *Procedure.*

(A) Requests for modification under RCW Chapter 26, initiated by summons and petition, shall be served on the other party by personal service, or as otherwise provided in CR 4, or as to actions pursuant to RCW 26.09.175, as provided in RCW 26.09.175(2). Service shall be required twenty (20) days prior to hearing or sixty (60) days if served out of state.

(2) *Custody Matters.* Preliminary ex-parte requests for order to show cause or for immediate temporary custody will be denied except in extraordinary circumstances. See RCW 26.09.270.

(3) *Default.* The Notice/Petition shall contain a statement that if the party served fails to respond by the hearing date, the relief requested will be granted by default.

[Amended effective September 12, 1989; October 6, 1989; May 19, 1993; August 19, 1995; September 1, 1996; September 2, 2014.]

RULE 6. POLICY RE: FILING TIMES/DATES

(d) For matters set on any regular Court Dockets, not including Domestic relations motions defined below in subparagraph (e), all responsive documents must be served on the parties and filed with the Clerk no later than two days before the scheduled hearing. Courtesy copies must be provided to the judicial officer hearing the matter at the same time.

(e) Domestic relations motions (Show Cause docket matters, Modification/Contempt docket matters and Family Law Motion docket matters) shall be filed and served upon all parties no later than ten (10) court days before the time specified for the hearing. Responses shall be filed and served on all parties not later than 4:30 p.m. five (5) court days before the time specified for the hearing. Replies shall be filed and served on all parties not later than 4:30 p.m. three (3) court days before the hearing. Courtesy copies must be provided to the judicial officer hearing the matter at the same time.

Practical examples of CCLR 6 as to Domestic Relations Motions:

Show Cause Dockets:
Hearing Date set for Wednesday April 30
Moving Party serves and files motion—Wednesday April 16
Responding Party serves and files response—Wednesday April 23
Moving Party Serves and files reply—Friday April 25

Modification/Contempt Dockets:
Hearing Date set for Thursday May 15
Moving Party served and files motion—Thursday May 1
Responding Party serves and files response—Thursday May 8
Moving Party serves and files reply—Monday May 12

Motion Dockets:
Hearing Date set for Friday May 16
Moving Party serves and files motion—Friday May 2
Responding Party serves and files response—Friday May 9
Moving Party serves and files reply—Tuesday May 13

[Amended effective September 1, 1996; September 1, 2012; September 2, 2014.]

RULE 7. PLEADINGS

(b) **Motions and Other Papers.**

(1) *How made.*

(A) **Reapplication on Same Facts.** When an order has been refused in whole or part (unless without prejudice), or has been granted conditionally and the condition has not been performed, the same application may not be presented to another judge.

(B) **Subsequent Application, Different Facts.** If a subsequent application is made upon an alleged different state of facts, the same must be shown by affidavit what application was made, when and to what judge, what order or decision was made on it and what new facts are claimed to be shown; for failure to comply with this requirement, any order made upon subsequent application may be set aside and sanctions imposed.

RULE 10. FORM OF PLEADINGS

(e) **Format Recommendations.**

(3) *Bottom Notation.*

(A) Signatures Required. Every order presented for a Judge's signature shall include a portion of the text on the signature page and shall be signed by the individual attorney presenting it on the lower left-hand corner of the page to be signed.

(B) Pleadings to be Dated and Names Typed. All pleadings, motions and other papers to be filed with the clerk shall be dated by the person preparing the same. The names of all persons signing a pleading or other paper should be typed under the signature. If signed by an attorney, the attorney's Washington State Bar Association number must be set forth.

(C) Self-represented litigant pleadings shall be typewritten or neatly printed, shall conform to the format recommendations of CR 10(e), and shall contain the party's telephone number(s), mailing address and street address where service of process and other papers may be made upon him/her or the same may be rejected for filing by the clerk.

[Amended effective September 25, 1989; September 1, 2010; September 2, 2014.]

RULE 11. SIGNING OF PLEADINGS

(a) Pro Se Parties. Any party appearing on his or her own behalf shall certify in writing that all documents and pleadings were prepared personally or with the advice of an attorney authorized to practice before the court and that he or she understands that the court by entering a decree or other order does not relieve the party of the responsibility for any omissions, defects, or inaccuracies in the file or matters presented or any consequences resulting therefrom.

RULE 26. GENERAL PROVISIONS [RESCINDED]

[Rescinded effective March 30, 1989.]

RULE 38. DEMAND FOR JURY

(b)(1) *Non-arbitration cases.* Except for cases submitted for arbitration, failure to demand a jury (and pay the required fee) within 30 days of the filing of the Notice to Set for Trial or the Response will be deemed a waiver of the right to a jury trial. The time period may be extended by court order.

(b)(2) *Arbitration cases.* In the event a trial de novo is requested under MAR 7.1, the parties must file a Notice to Set for Trial with the request for trial de novo and demand jury pursuant to (b)(1) above.

[Amended effective September 1, 1996.]

RULE 40. ASSIGNMENT OF CASES

(b) Methods—Civil Cases.

(1) *Notice to Set for Trial.* An attorney or party desiring to place a case on the trial readiness calendar shall file a "Notice to Set for Trial" on a form prescribed by the court.

(2) *Certification.* The attorney by filing a Notice to Set for Trial certifies that the case is fully at issue with all necessary parties joined, all anticipated discovery has been or will be completed before trial and that all other counsel have been served with copy of the Notice.

(3) *Response to Notice to Set for Trial.* An attorney who objects to a case being set for trial, or who otherwise disagrees with the information on the "Notice," shall file and serve a "Response to Notice to Set for Trial" on a form prescribed by the court within 10 days of the date of service of the "Notice." The Response shall be noted for hearing the objection not more than 25 days after the date of service of the "Notice to Set for Trial." No Response is necessary if counsel agrees with the "Notice to Set for Trial." See Rule 38 re: Demand for Jury.

(4) *Call for Trial.* Any case placed on the readiness calendar will be subject to call for trial or to be assigned a specific date for trial. The court will give reasonable notice of the trial date assigned.

(5) *Continuances.* When a case has been called from the readiness calendar and set, it shall proceed to trial or be dismissed, unless good cause is shown for continuance, or the court may impose such terms as are reasonable and in addition may impose costs upon counsel who has filed a Notice to Set for Trial, or who has failed to object thereto and is not prepared to proceed to trial. No request for continuance will be considered without the written acknowledgement of the client on the pleadings and an affidavit giving the particulars necessitating a continuance in accordance with CR 40(d) and (e). Continued cases may be removed from the trial calendar at the discretion of the court and, if removed, will be re-calendared only upon filing a new Notice to Set for Trial.

(6) *Mandatory Settlement Conferences.* All cases involving dissolution of marriage or modification of prior decrees, except those meeting the requirements for accelerated setting (see Notice form) will be scheduled for a mandatory settlement conference following the filing of a Notice to Set for Trial. No case subject to this section will be set for trial without a pre-trial settlement conference first being held unless a judicial waiver is obtained.

(A) Settlement Conference Affidavit. Each party must complete the Pre–Trial Domestic Relations Settlement Conference Affidavit on the form available from the Superior Court Administrator. The original must be filed with the Superior Court Clerk and a copy served on the opposing attorney or party if not represented by an attorney, no later than 4:00 p.m. one week prior to the scheduled conference. At the same time, a copy of the Affidavit, to be used by the judge or commissioner conducting the conference, must be filed with the Superior Court Administrator. Failure to file and serve the Affidavit one week prior to the conference shall subject the person failing to do so to an assessment of not less than $150.00 and up to $500.00. Failure to file an affidavit and/or appear at the conference may subject a party or attorney to additional sanctions.

(c) Preferences.

(1) Criminal cases shall be accorded priority and shall be assigned trial dates in accordance with CrR 3.3(f).

[Amended effective September 1, 1996; September 1, 2000; September 1, 2004; September 1, 2010; September 2, 2014.]

RULE 45. SUBPOENA [RESCINDED]

[Amended effective September 1, 1997. Rescinded effective September 2, 2014.]

RULE 47. JURORS

(a) Examination of Jurors.

(1) *Voir Dire.* The trial judge may examine the prospective jurors touching their qualifications to act as fair and impartial jurors in the case before him, and counsel shall advise the court in advance of the names of witnesses then intended to be called for this pur-

pose. Thereafter, the trial judge shall allow the respective parties to ask the jurors such supplementary questions as may be deemed proper and necessary by the trial judge. The voir dire examination of prospective jurors shall, as nearly as possible, be limited to those matters having a reasonably direct bearing on prejudice, and shall not be used by counsel:

(A) as a means of arguing or trying their cases, or

(B) as an effort to indoctrinate, visit with or establish rapport with jurors, or

(C) for the purpose of questioning concerning anticipated instructions of the court or theories of law, or

(D) for the purpose of asking the jurors what kind of verdict they might return under any circumstance. Personal questions should be asked collectively of the entire panel whenever possible.

(2) Juror questionnaires may not be removed from or viewed outside the office of the Superior Court Administrator or the courtrooms of the Superior or District Courts without the express approval of the trial judge.

(k) **Random Selection.** Jurors shall be selected at random by a properly programmed electronic data processing system as provided by RCW 2.36.63.

[Amended effective September 1, 1996.]

RULE 52. DECISIONS, FINDINGS, CONCLUSIONS

(c) **Presentation.**

(1) *Time Limit.* All findings of fact, conclusions of law and verdicts shall be presented to the judge having heard the matter not later than 15 days after the decision or verdict was rendered.

RULE 53.2. MOTIONS FOR REVISION OF A COMMISSIONER'S ORDER

(a) A motion for revision of a Commissioner's order shall be served and filed within 10 days of entry of the written order, as provided in RCW 2.24.050, along with a written notice of hearing that gives the other parties at least 5 days notice, excluding weekends and legal holidays, of the time, date and place of the hearing on the motion for revision. The motion shall specify the error claimed

(b) The party seeking revision of a Commissioner's order shall schedule the motion for hearing on the assigned Family Law Judge's Motion Docket. The motion shall be scheduled and heard by the assigned Judge within 21 days of entry of the Commissioner's order. If the assigned Judge does not have a Motion Docket within 21 days of entry of the Commissioner's order, the motion shall be heard on the first available Motion Docket thereafter, unless otherwise ordered by the Judge or Commissioner. Failure to hear the motion within 21 days or the first available Motion

Docket thereafter shall result in dismissal of the motion.

(1) Motions for revision of a Commissioner's order shall be based on the written materials submitted or available to the Commissioner, including papers and pleadings in the court file, as provided in RCW 2.24.050. The standard of review shall be *de novo* if the record does not include live testimony. Oral arguments on motions to revise shall be limited to 5 minutes per side. No additional affidavits or other non-brief materials shall be filed. If a brief or memorandum of law was filed by a party before the Commissioner, no new brief or memorandum shall be submitted by that party on the motion for revision.

(2) With the exception of juvenile criminal cases, the filing of a motion for revision does not automatically stay the Commissioner's order, and the order shall remain in force unless a separate motion is made and an order staying the Commissioner's order is granted by the assigned Judge or the Commissioner who signed the order.

(3) The party seeking revision shall, at least 5 days before the hearing, deliver to the assigned Judge the motion, notice of hearing and copies of all papers submitted by all parties to the Commissioner; or with the assigned Judge's consent, an alternative to copies of all papers submitted, a listing of those papers in a form similar to a designation of clerk's papers.

(4) For cases in which a timely motion for reconsideration of the Commissioner's order has been filed, the time for filing a motion for revision of the Commissioner's order shall commence on the date of the filing of the Commissioner's written order of judgment on reconsideration.

[Adopted effective September 1, 2000; amended effective September 1, 2007; September 1, 2008.]

RULE 56. SUMMARY JUDGMENT

(c) **Motion and Proceedings**

(1) *Confirmation Process.* In the event a motion for summary judgement is to be argued, counsel must notify the assigned department, in person or by telephone, by 4:30 p.m. two court days prior to the hearing; otherwise, the matter will be stricken. If no opposition is anticipated, the assigned Judge should be so informed.

[Amended effective September 1, 1996.]

RULE 59. NEW TRIAL, RECONSIDERATION, AND AMENDMENT OF JUDGMENTS

(b) **Time for Motions; Contents of Motions.** A motion for new trial or reconsideration shall be served and filed not later than 10 days after the entry of the judgment or order in question. The opposing party shall have 10 days after service of such motion to file and serve a response, if necessary. No reply will be permitted. The moving party shall provide copies of the motion (and response, if any) to the Judge. No oral argument shall be permitted without express approval of the court. The court shall issue a written ruling on the motion.

[Adopted effective September 1, 2001.]

RULE 71.   WITHDRAWAL BY ATTORNEY

(c)(1) Notice of Intent to Withdraw. The Notice of Intent to Withdraw filed pursuant to CR 71 shall include the names, last known addresses and telephone number(s) of the person(s) represented by the withdrawing attorney, unless disclosure would violate the Rules of Professional Conduct.

(e) Notice to Court. An attorney filing any notice of intent to withdraw, order authorizing withdrawal, notice of withdrawal and substitution or notice of appearance by any subsequent attorney, shall provide a conformed copy of the notice or order to the Judge to whom the case is assigned if the case has been set for trial.

[Adopted effective September 1, 2009. Amended effective September 1, 2010.]

RULE 77.   SUPERIOR COURT AND JUDICIAL OFFICERS

(5) *Powers of Judges of Superior Courts.*

(A) Presiding Judge. There shall be a Presiding Judge of the court who shall be designated to serve pursuant to GR29.

(i) The Presiding Judge shall preside when the judges meet en banc, and shall receive and dispose of all communications intended for the Superior Court but not personally addressed to any department or relating to the business which has been assigned to any department or designated as the responsibility of the Presiding Judge.

(ii) Any judge may sign orders in all cases, if approved by opposing counsel, except continuances, findings, conclusions and judgments and orders on motions for judgment N.O.V. or for new trial in contested cases.

(iii) Applications for emergency or temporary orders or writs shall be made to the assigned judge when available. If unavailable, they may be signed by any other judge.

(9) *Judges Pro Tempore.* Consent to trial before a judge pro tempore (RCW 2.08.180) may be indicated by a party or attorney on the Notice to Set for Trial and the Response to Notice to Set for Trial.

(10) *Change of Judge.*

(A) Change of Commissioner. Affidavits of Prejudice with reference to court commissioners will not be recognized. The proper remedy of a party is a motion for revision under RCW 2.24.050.

(f) Sessions.

(1) *Court Hours.* The courts will be in session on all judicial days, except Saturday and Sunday. Trials will be conducted from 9:00 a.m. until 12:00 noon and from 1:30 p.m. to 4:30 p.m. unless otherwise ordered.

(h) Summer Recess.[1]

(i) Motion Day.

(1) *Law and Motion Day.* Civil motions, show cause orders, contempt proceedings, other docket items will be heard by the various departments of the court according to the published schedule available through the Court Administrator's Office. If no one appears in opposition, the moving party may take the order unless the court deems it unauthorized. If no one appears for the motion or show cause, it shall be stricken from the docket. Any item so stricken must be re-noted in order to be heard.

(2) *Continuances.* Motions and show cause matters may be continued by the court to a subsequent motion day or set down for hearing at a specific time.

(3) *Order of Hearing and Argument Under the Rule.* The judge shall determine the order in which the various matters docketed shall be heard. Temporary support orders shall be presented upon affidavit; however, the court may call for testimony to clarify discrepancies. Matters requiring argument may be placed at the bottom of the docket by the judge. In no event will testimony be taken on the motion docket unless notice of intent to do so is given the opposing party and the concurrence of the court is obtained. See also Rule 94.04.

[Amended effective September 2, 2014.]

1 So in original. Heading enacted without accompanying text.

RULE 79.   BOOKS AND RECORDS KEPT BY CLERK

(d) Other Books and Records of Clerk.

(1) *Exhibits.*

(A) Filing and Substitution. All exhibits and other papers received in evidence on the trial of any cause must be filed at that time, but the court may, either then or by leave granted thereafter, upon notice, permit a copy of any such exhibit or other paper to be filed or substituted in the files, in lieu of the original.

(B) Storage. The exhibits in all cases shall be kept by the clerk separate from the files of the case.

(C) Inspection. No exhibits shall be inspected in the Clerk's Office except in the presence of the clerk or one of his or her deputies.

(D) Exhibits Not Evidence Unless Ordered. Exhibits filed pursuant to subsection (A) hereof shall not be evidence in the cause unless by order of the trial judge entered on notice and hearing.

(E) Temporary Withdrawal. Exhibits may be withdrawn temporarily from the custody of the clerk only by:

(i) The judge having the cause under consideration;

(ii) Official court reporter, without court order for use in connection with their duties.

(iii) Attorneys of record, upon court order, after notice to or with the consent of opposing counsel.

(iv) The clerk shall take an itemized receipt for all exhibits withdrawn, and upon return of the exhibit or exhibits they shall be checked by the clerk against original receipts. The clerk shall keep all receipts for such exhibits for the period of three years from date of receipt.

(F) Withdrawal and Disposition. Within ninety (90) days after the final disposition of any cause, including all appellate processes, each party shall withdraw all exhibits offered by such party and give the clerk a receipt therefore. In the event a party shall fail to withdraw the exhibits within such time, the clerk is authorized to destroy the same after 30 days from the mailing to a party of notice of intent to destroy exhibits.

(i) Drugs or Dangerous Items. When any controlled substances or dangerous items have been admitted in evidence or have been identified, and are being held by the clerk as a part of the records and files in any criminal cause, and all proceedings in the cause have been completed, the prosecuting attorney may apply to the court for an order directing the clerk to deliver such drugs and/or dangerous items, to an authorized representative of the law enforcement agency initiating the prosecution for disposition according to law. If the court finds these facts, and is of the opinion that there will be no further need for such drugs, it shall enter an order accordingly. The clerk shall then deliver the drugs and/or dangerous items and take from the law enforcement agency a receipt which he or she shall file in the cause. The Clerk shall also file any certificate issued by an authorized federal or state agency and received by him or her showing the nature of such drugs.

(2) *Withdrawal of Files and Documents from Clerk's Office.*

(A) Files. The clerk shall permit no file to be taken from the office, except to the courtroom or to a judge, court commissioner, referee or official court reporter, unless authority has first been obtained from the Clerk. All of the clerk's files which are in the hands of an attorney for the purposes of any trial or hearing must be returned to the clerk at the close thereof. The clerk, or a designated deputy, may in his or her discretion and on application in writing, grant authority to the applicant to withdraw one or more files from the clerk's custody for a period not to exceed three days. The court may, upon written application showing cause therefore, authorize the withdrawal of specified clerk's files for a period in excess of three days. Only attorneys with a WSBA number or an employee of that firm's office may make a written request to withdraw a file from the Clerk's office. An attorney's employee must provide the attorney's business card giving permission from the attorney to withdraw any confidential file. Adoption files may only be withdrawn by an attorney with a Notice of Appearance filed in that case. Any request to withdraw a file from the Clerk's office within one calendar week of its being scheduled for a court hearing or trial shall not be granted.

(B) Statement of Facts. Statements of facts, after having been settled and signed, shall not be withdrawn from the Clerk's Office.

(3) *Return of Files, Documents or Exhibits.*

(A) Failure to Return Files or Exhibits; Sanctions. In the event that an attorney or other person fails to return files or exhibits which were temporarily withdrawn by him or her within the time required, and fails to comply with the clerk's request for their return, the clerk may, without notice to the attorney or other person concerned, apply to the presiding judge for an order for immediate return of such files or exhibits. A certified copy of such order, if entered, shall then be served upon the attorney or other person involved.

(B) Return of Exhibits and Unopened Depositions. In any civil cause on a stipulation of the parties that when judgment in the cause shall become final, or shall become final after an appeal, or upon judgment of dismissal or upon filing a satisfaction of judgment, the Clerk may return all exhibits and unopened depositions, or may destroy them. The court may enter an order accordingly.

(C) Return of Administrative Record. Upon completion of a case under review of administrative record, the Clerk shall either return the administrative record to the officer or agency certifying the same to the court or destroy the record if the offering officer or agency has given authorization.

(4) *Access to Sealed Documents and Files.*

(A) Examination of Documents and Files. The clerk shall not permit the examination of any sealed document or sealed file except by order of the presiding or assigned judge or in accordance with GR 15 or GR 22.

(B) Documents filed after the sealing of an entire court file. Any document filed with the Clerk after the entire court file has been sealed shall include a special caption directly below the case number on the first page such as "Sealed File".

[Adopted effective September 1, 2008.]

III. MANDATORY ARBITRATION RULES (LMAR)

I. SCOPE AND PURPOSE OF RULES

RULE 1.1. APPLICATION OF RULE—DEFINITION

(a) Purpose. The Mandatory Arbitration Rules as supplemented by these local rules are not designed to address every question which may arise during the arbitration process, and the rules give considerable discretion to the arbitrator. The arbitrator should not hesitate to exercise that discretion.

(b) "Director" Defined. In these rules, "Director" means the Court Administrator for the Clark County Superior Court.

RULE 1.2. MATTERS SUBJECT TO ARBITRATION

(a) Amount. The amount of claims subject to arbitration shall not exceed $50,000.

[Amended effective June 19, 1990; September 1, 2005.]

II. TRANSFER TO ARBITRATION AND ASSIGNMENT OF ARBITRATOR

RULE 2.1. TRANSFER TO ARBITRATION

(a) Statement of Arbitrability. In every civil case the party filing the Notice to Set for Trial provided by Local Rule 40, shall, upon the form prescribed by the Court, complete a Statement of Arbitrability.

(b) Response to Statement of Arbitrability. Any party who disagrees with the Statement of Arbitrability shall serve and file a Response to the Statement of Arbitrability on the form prescribed by the Court pursuant to L.R.40. In the absence of such response, the Statement of Arbitrability shall be deemed correct and the case shall be deemed arbitrable. If a party asserts that its claim exceeds $50,000 or seeks relief other than a money judgment, the case is not subject to arbitration except by stipulation.

(c) Failure to File—Amendments. A party failing to serve and file an original response within the time prescribed may later do so only upon leave of court. A party may amend the Statement of Arbitrability or Response at any time before assignment of an arbitrator or assignment of a trial date and thereafter only upon leave of Court for good cause shown.

[Amended effective September 1, 2004; September 1, 2005.]

RULE 2.3. ASSIGNMENT TO ARBITRATOR

(a) Generally; Stipulations. When a case is set for arbitration, a list of seven proposed arbitrators will be furnished to the parties. A master list of arbitrators will be made available on request. The parties are encouraged to stipulate to an arbitrator. In the absence of a stipulation, the arbitrator will be chosen from among the seven proposed arbitrators in the manner defined by this rule.

(b) Response by Parties. Each party may, within 14 days after a list of proposed arbitrators is furnished to the parties, nominate up to three arbitrators and strike up to three arbitrators from the list. If both parties respond, an arbitrator nominated by both parties will be appointed. If no arbitrator has been nominated by both parties, the Director will randomly appoint an arbitrator from among those not stricken by either party.

(c) Response by Only One Party. If only one party responds within 14 days, the Director will appoint an arbitrator nominated by that party.

(d) No response. If neither party responds within 14 days, the Director will randomly appoint one of the seven proposed arbitrators.

(e) Additional Arbitrators for Additional Parties. If there are more than two adverse parties, all represented by different counsel, three additional proposed arbitrators shall be added to the list for each additional party so represented with the above principles of selection to be applied. The number of adverse parties shall be determined by the Director, subject to review by the Presiding Judge.

[Amended effective July, 1995; November, 1997.]

III. ARBITRATORS

RULE 3.1. QUALIFICATIONS

(a) Arbitration Panel. There shall be a panel of arbitrators in such numbers as the Superior Court judges may from time to time determine. A person desiring to serve as an arbitrator shall complete an information sheet on the form prescribed by the court. A list showing the names of arbitrators available to hear cases and the information sheets will be available for public inspection in the Director's office. The oath of office on the form prescribed by the court must be completed and filed prior to an applicant being placed on the panel.

(b) Refusal; Disqualification. The appointment of an arbitrator is subject to the right of that person to refuse to serve. An arbitrator must notify the Director immediately if refusing to serve or if any cause exists for the arbitrator's disqualification from the case upon any of the grounds of interest, relationship, bias or prejudice set forth in CJC Canon 3(c) governing the disqualification of judges. If disqualified, the arbitrator must immediately return all materials in a case to the Director.

RULE 3.2. AUTHORITY OF ARBITRATORS

An arbitrator has the authority to:

(1) Determine the time, place and procedure to present a motion before the arbitrator.

(2) Require a party or attorney advising such party or both to pay the reasonable expenses, including attorney's fees, caused by the failure of such party or attorney or both to obey an order of the arbitrator unless the arbitrator finds that the failure was substantially justified or that other circumstances make an award of expenses unjust. The arbitrator shall make a special award for such expenses and shall file such award with the Clerk of the Superior Court, with proof of service of a party on each party. The aggrieved party shall have 10 days thereafter to appeal the award of such expense in accordance with the procedures described in RCW 2.24.050. If within 10 days after the award is filed no party appeals, a judgment shall be entered in a manner described generally under MAR 6.3.

(3) Award attorney's fees as authorized by these rules, by contract or by law.

[Amended effective November, 1997.]

V. HEARING

RULE 5.1. LOCATION OF HEARING

The arbitrator shall set the time, date and place of the hearing which shall be conducted at a location within Clark County.

[Adopted effective September 1, 2002.]

RULE 5.2. PRE–HEARING STATEMENT OF PROOF—DOCUMENTS FILED WITH COURT

In addition to the requirements of MAR 5.2, each party shall also furnish the arbitrator with copies of pleadings and other documents contained in the court file which that party deems relevant. The court file shall remain with the County Clerk.

RULE 5.3. CONDUCT OF HEARING— WITNESSES—RULES OF EVIDENCE

(a) **Witnesses.** The arbitrator shall place a witness under oath or affirmation before the witness presents testimony.

(b) **Recording.** The hearing may be recorded electronically or otherwise by any party at his or her expense.

(c) **Rules of Evidence, Generally.** The Rules of Evidence, to the extent determined by the arbitrator to be applicable, should be liberally construed to promote justice. The parties should stipulate to the admission of evidence when there is no genuine issue as to its relevance or authenticity.

(d) **Certain Documents Presumed Admissible.** The documents listed below, if relevant, are presumed admissible at an arbitration hearing, but only if (1) the party offering the document serves on all parties a notice, accompanied by a copy of the document and the name, address and telephone number of its author or maker, at least 14 days prior to the hearing in accordance with MAR 5.2; and (2) the party offering the document similarly furnishes all other parties with copies of all other related documents from the same author or maker. This rule does not restrict argument or proof relating to the weight of the evidence admitted, nor does it restrict the arbitrator's authority to determine the weight of the evidence after hearing all of the evidence and the arguments of opposing parties. The documents presumed admissible under this rule are:

(1) A bill, report, chart, or record of a hospital, doctor, dentist, registered nurse, licensed practical nurse, physical therapist, psychologist or other health care provider, on a letterhead or billhead;

(2) A bill for drugs, medical appliances or other related expenses on a letterhead or billhead;

(3) A bill for, or an estimate of, property damage on a letterhead or a billhead. In the case of an estimate, the party intending to offer the estimate shall forward with the notice to the adverse party a statement indicating whether or not the property was repaired, and if it was, whether the estimated repairs were made in full or in part, attaching a copy to the receipted bill showing the items of repair and the amount paid.

(4) A police, weather, wage loss, or traffic signal report, or standard United States government life expectancy table to the extent it is admissible under the Rules of Evidence, but without the need for formal proof of authentication or identification;

(5) A photograph, x-ray, drawing, map, blueprint or similar documentary evidence, to the extent it is admissible under the Rules of Evidence, but without the need for formal proof of authentication or identification;

(6) The written statement of any other witness, including the written report of an expert witness, and including a statement of opinion which the witness would be allowed to express if testifying in person, if it is made by affidavit or by declaration under penalty of perjury;

(7) A document not specifically covered by any of the foregoing provisions but having equivalent circum-

stantial guarantees of trustworthiness, the admission of which would serve the interests of justice.

(e) Opposing Party May Subpoena Author or Maker as Witness. Any other party may subpoena the author or maker of a document admissible under this rule, at that party's expense, and examine the author or maker as if under cross examination.

VI. AWARD

RULE 6.1. FORM AND CONTENT OF AWARD

(a) Form. The award shall be prepared on the form prescribed by the court.

(b) Return of Exhibits. When an award is filed, the arbitrator shall return all exhibits to the parties who offered them during the hearing.

RULE 6.3. JUDGMENT ON AWARD

A judgment on award shall be presented to the "assigned" judge, by any party, on notice in accordance with MAR 6.3.

VII. TRIAL DE NOVO

RULE 7.1. REQUEST FOR TRIAL DE NOVO

The appealing party shall file and serve on the other party or parties a Notice to Set for Trial pursuant to Local Rule 40.

[Amended effective September 1, 1996.]

RULE 7.2. PROCEDURE AT TRIAL

The clerk shall seal any award if a trial de novo is requested.

VIII. GENERAL PROVISIONS

RULE 8.1. STIPULATION—EFFECT ON RELIEF GRANTED

If a case not otherwise subject to mandatory arbitration is transferred to arbitration by stipulation, the arbitrator may grant any relief which could have been granted if the case were determined by a judge.

RULE 8.3. EFFECTIVE DATE

These rules shall take effect on July 1, 1986. With respect to civil cases pending trial on that date, if the case has not at that time received a trial date, or if the trial has been set later than October 1, 1986, any party may serve and file a statement of arbitrability indicating that the case is subject to mandatory arbitration. If within 14 days no party files a response indicating the case is not subject to arbitration, the case will be transferred to the arbitration calendar. A case set for trial earlier than October 1, 1986, will be transferred to arbitration only upon order of the court.

RULE 8.4. TITLE AND CITATION

These rules are known and cited as the Clark County Superior Court Mandatory Arbitration Rules. LMAR is the official abbreviation.

RULE 8.6. COMPENSATION OF ARBITRATOR

(a) Generally. Arbitrators shall be compensated in the same amount and manner as judges pro tempore of the Superior Court. Hearing time and reasonable preparation time are compensable.

(b) Form. When the award is filed, the arbitrator shall submit to the Director a request for payment on a form prescribed by the Court. The Director shall determine the amount of compensation to be paid. The decision of the Director will be reviewed by the Chief Administrative Judge at the request of the arbitrator.

RULE 8.7. ADMINISTRATION

The Director, under the supervision of the Superior Court judges, shall supervise arbitration under these rules and perform any additional duties which may be delegated by the judges.

[Adopted effective July 15, 1986.]

IV. SPECIAL PROCEEDINGS RULES

RULE 92.04. SHOW CAUSE ORDER

In supplemental hearings and contempt proceedings wherein a show cause order is issued requiring the personal attendance of a party to be examined in open court, the order to show cause must include the following words in capital letters:

> YOUR FAILURE TO APPEAR AS ABOVE SET FORTH AT THE TIME, DATE AND PLACE THEREOF MAY CAUSE THE COURT TO ISSUE A BENCH WARRANT FOR YOUR APPREHENSION AND CONFINEMENT IN JAIL UNTIL SUCH TIME AS THE MATTER CAN BE HEARD, UNLESS BAIL IS FURNISHED AS PROVIDED IN SAID BENCH WARRANT.

If such wording is not included as above required, the moving party shall not be entitled to a bench warrant for the apprehension of such person.

RULE 98.08. ESTATES–PROBATE–ETC.

(1) Method of Presenting Proof. Proof of all matters in probate may be by verified petition, or by other evidence, such as personal testimony, affidavit or deposition.

(2) Proof of Wills. In uncontested will proceedings, testimony in support of a will may be given in person or by deposition or by affidavit to which is attached the original or a facsimile of the will. RCW 11.20.020 (2). For other methods see RCW 11.20.140. It is necessary to present a certificate of testimony for the court's signature.

RULE 98.16W. REGARDING SETTLEMENT OF CLAIMS OF MINOR AND INCAPACITATED PERSONS

(a) Rule to Control in Conjunction With SPR 98.16W. In every settlement of a claim, whether or not filed in court, involving the beneficial interest of an unemancipated minor or person determined to be disabled or incapacitated under RCW 11.88, this Local Rule shall, in **conjunction with the terms of SPR.98.16W, control the disposition of the settlement funds or the** value of other property remaining after deduction for all approved fees, bills and expenses ("net settlement").

(b) More than $25,000. For net settlements greater than $25,000, SPR 98.16W (2) will apply.

(c) $25,000 or Less. For net settlements of $25,000 or less, every order approving settlements of minors or incapacitated persons shall contain the following:

(1) "Clerk's Action Required, See Addendum Paragraph 5" [or renumbered paragraph, as appropriate] immediately below the title of the pleading in the case caption; *and*

All orders approving settlement of minors or incapacitated persons shall include exclusively the following addendum language approved by the Clark County Superior Court.

The addendum is below.

ADDENDUM REGARDING BLOCKED ACCOUNT, ANNUITY, OR TRUST DEPOSIT

1. The net proceeds of the settlement to the minor or incapacitated person shall be in the form of a check made payable to: ☐ Settlement Guardian ad Litem, ☐ Plaintiff's counsel, ☐ Defense counsel, or ☐ the Clerk of the Court.

2. The check shall then be endorsed by the person designated in paragraph 1 and held pending disposition according to the terms of this order by the ☐ Settlement Guardian ad Litem, ☐ Plaintiff's counsel, or ☐ Defense counsel. If none appear in the action the Clerk of the Court shall request that the presiding judge appoint a Settlement Guardian ad Litem.

3. The ☐ Settlement Guardian ad Litem; ☐ Plaintiff's counsel; ☐ Defense counsel shall be responsible for:

☐ Opening of a blocked account with a state or federally regulated and insured financial institution located in the state of Washington, using the minor or incapacitated person's Social Security number, with provision that withdrawals cannot be made except as provided in the trust instrument, as ordered by the court, or paid to the minor at his or her age of majority, to wit, _____ [insert date of 18th birthday] following compliance with RCW 11.88.140 if applicable. The ☐ Settlement Guardian ad Litem, ☐ Plaintiff's counsel, or ☐ Defense counsel shall be responsible for the deposit of the check into the blocked account and for the completion and filing of the "Receipt of Funds Into Blocked Account" with the Superior Court and shall provide a conformed copy of the Receipt to the ☐ Settlement Guardian ad Litem, ☐ Plaintiff's counsel, or ☐ Defense counsel;

☐ Causing the purchase of an annuity contract consistent with the terms of the foregoing order; or

☐ Delivering the funds to a court-approved guardian or trustee and, if the guardian or trustee is constituted in another proceeding, filing proof of letters of guardianship or copy of trust in these proceedings.

4. The Settlement Guardian ad Litem shall not be discharged and Plaintiff's counsel and Defense counsel will not withdraw from the case until the actions specified above are completed and the receipt, copy of annuity contract, or letters of guardianship or copy of trust has been filed with the court, dismissal of the injury action or civil proceeding notwithstanding.

5. This matter shall be set on for review by the undersigned judge on _____, 20 ___ [**Not later than 30 days after entry of order**] to confirm that ☐ receipt, ☐ annuity, ☐ letters of guardianship, ☐ trust has been filed.

6. In the event that the ☐ receipt, ☐ annuity, ☐ letters of guardianship, ☐ trust is not filed within 30 days of entry of this Order (unless this period is extended by the court, for good cause shown), the persons designated in Paragraphs 2 and 3 are required to appear on the Probate Docket on _____. 20 ___, and show cause why the blocked account has not been opened, why the funds have not been deposited, why the receipt has not been filed, why letters of guardianship have not been filed, why the trust has not been filed, and/or why an annuity has not been purchased.

7. In the event of any inconsistencies between the terms of the Addendum and the order to which it is attached, the terms of the Addendum shall supersede those of the order.

Dated and signed in open court this ___ day of _____, 20 ___.

_____
Judge

[Adopted effective September 1, 2005. Amended effective September 1, 2015.]

RULE 98.20. GUARDIANSHIPS AND TRUSTS [RESCINDED]

[Adopted effective September 1, 2008. Rescinded effective September 1, 2012.]

RULE 98.30. REASONABLENESS HEARINGS

(a) **Reasonableness Hearings.** Reasonableness hearings pursuant to RCW 4.22.060 shall be heard by the judge assigned to the particular matter by affidavit only unless the court shall deem necessary an evidentiary hearing. Affidavits of the parties shall be submitted setting forth all facts justifying the settlement as proposed by the parties or in opposition thereto. A summary affidavit of the attorneys for the parties setting forth each of the factors governing reasonableness hearings shall also be submitted.

(b) **Scheduling.** A reasonableness hearing shall be scheduled in the assigned department at a time mutually convenient to the parties and the court with at least 10 days notice to all parties named in the lawsuit. The hearings shall not be scheduled on a regular motion docket without prior written order of the judge hearing the matter.

(c) **Additional Defendants.** If a party seeks to preserve rights against or cut off contribution rights of a person or other entity who is not named as a party in the suit, that party shall secure the addition of the unnamed party to the suit as a "reasonableness hearing defendant." This may be done by motion to the court. The "reasonableness hearing defendant" shall then be served with the following items in the same manner as summons may be served in a civil action:

(1) Notice of the reasonableness hearing;

(2) The summons and complaint and responses thereto together with any amendments thereto;

(3) All affidavits to be submitted to the court for the reasonableness hearing.

(d) **Discovery.** The "reasonableness defendant" shall be allowed to request production of documents, depositions, or other relevant materials from any party subject to CR 26 and CR 34.

(e) **Affidavits; Defenses.** The "reasonableness hearing defendant" shall be entitled to submit affidavits or other material for the reasonableness hearing as any other party, and shall be allowed to raise any manner of defense germane to the court's consideration at a reasonableness hearing including but not limited to jurisdiction and sufficiency of process.

(f) **Notice.** No less than thirty (30) days notice of the reasonableness hearing shall be given to the "reasonableness hearing defendant." If the "reasonableness hearing defendant" is served out-of-state or by publication, no less than sixty (60) days notice of the reasonableness hearing shall be given. If the "reasonableness hearing defendant" does not appear in person or through counsel at the reasonableness hearing, the "reasonableness hearing defendant" shall be deemed to be in default, and the court shall proceed to determine the issue of reasonableness.

V. CRIMINAL RULES

RULE 2.2. WAIVERS OF PROBABLE CAUSE [RESCINDED]

[Amended September 1, 1996. Rescinded effective September 2, 2014.]

RULE 2.4. CRIMINAL APPEALS

(1) If the appellant is represented in District Court by court-appointed counsel or retained counsel, that attorney has the duty to file an appeal, and if appointed counsel on appeal is sought, to obtain an order of indigency from District Court. Trial counsel shall docket the matter as soon as possible before the assigned Superior Court Judge for appointment of

counsel on appeal, if necessary, and, for entry of a scheduling order. District Court counsel should appear with the client on the superior Court Docket, and may withdraw upon appointment of appellate counsel. Appellate counsel, or appellant, if there is no counsel retained or appointed in Superior Court, shall be responsible for perfecting the record and obtaining the necessary media and/or verbatim report of proceedings.

(2) If the defendant appears Pro se in District Court, the Superior Court Clerk, upon receiving notice of appeal, shall docket the matter before the assigned Superior court Judge, and shall notify the appellant and the appropriate respondent of the court date, and of the obligation to appear at the hearing before the assigned Superior Court Judge for appointment of counsel and entry of a scheduling order. The notice to the appellant shall further advise that failure to appear at the hearing may result in dismissal of the appeal. If the District Court has not made a finding of indigency relating to the appeal, at such hearing before the Superior Court, the Court shall proceed to consider whether such a finding is appropriate.

(3) The Superior Court department to whom the appeal is assigned will have the duty to contact appellate counsel, and confirm that counsel has received the notice of appointment and scheduling order.

[Adopted effective September 1, 2008.]

RULE 2.5. CIVIL APPEALS

(1) The procedure in civil cases, except small claims, will be the same as in criminal cases, except that neither an order of indigency or appointment of counsel will be required.

[Adopted effective September 1, 2008.]

RULE 3.1. RIGHT TO AND ASSIGNMENT OF COUNSEL

(d) Assignment of Counsel.

(3) Although counsel may have communicated with a defendant under the provisions of CrR 3.1 prior to the first appearance, the court shall determine the question of indigence and the actual assignment of a particular attorney to represent a defendant at public expense.

(f) Services Other Than Counsel. Pursuant to the authority under CrR 3.1(f), all requests for expenditure for investigative and expert services are hereby delegated to the Clark County Indigent Defense Coordinator. If a request is denied in whole or in part, defendant may move for review before the assigned judge.

[Amended effective September 1, 2007.]

RULE 3.2. PROPERTY BONDS IN LIEU OF BAIL

(a) Requirements for Acceptable Property Bonds in Lieu of Bail Bond or Cash.

(1) Current title report on Clark County property.

(2) Documentation of current assessed value of the property.

(3) Documentation of the current status of any encumbrances on the property.

(4) A signed form of promissory note in the amount of the bond, plus 10% administrative fees, payable on demand upon forfeiture of the property bond. Any amount of the administrative fee not expended will be refunded.

(5) A signed form of deed of trust to Clark County to secure the promissory note to be recorded by County Auditor after the order approving bond is entered, filed with the County Clerk.

(6) Tender of cash or certified check to pay the cost to record the note and deed of trust made payable to "Clark County Auditor."

(7) A covenant that, in the event of foreclosure, all costs of foreclosure, sale, improvements needed to make the property marketable, and the county's attorney

(8) The bond must be in first priority on the property, or accompanied by a subordination of any superior encumbrances, OR the property must be free and clear

(9) The bond, plus 10% must not exceed 70% of the owner's equity based on the Clark County Assessor's assessed value.

(b) Motions for acceptance of property bonds shall be considered by the court on a case by case basis, including colloquy with the property owner, at the discretion of the court.

(c) Any event that causes a reduction in the value of the property posted in lieu of bail bond or cash may result in a review of the sufficiency of the security for the bond either upon motion of the Prosecutor or the Court's own motion.

[Added effective September 1, 2008.]

RULE 3.2.1. BAIL SETTING AND BAIL REVIEW

At a defendant's first appearance on a criminal charge, in those cases where the court determines that bail should be required, the Court shall proceed to set a reasonable bail, taking into account the factors set forth in CrR 3.2 (c).

At the time set for arraignment, the Court hearing the matter may review the bail previously set, in the event that new information is made known to the court, or in the event that material circumstances have changed since the original bail setting. Thereafter, bail may be reconsidered only by proper written motion before the assigned judge, with timely notice to the Prosecuting Attorney, and only upon granting of permission by the assigned judge to hear such matter.

RULE 3.4. PRESENCE OF THE DEFENDANT

(a) When Necessary.

(1) Defendant shall be present at all proceedings except omnibus when it is presented by stipulation or expressly waived.

[Amended on an emergency basis effective January 23, 2006; amended on a permanent basis effective September 1, 2006; amended effective September 1, 2007; September 2, 2014.]

RULE 4.5. OMNIBUS HEARING

(d) Motions. Motions for a CrR 3.5 Hearing and/or Suppression Hearing shall be set forth and filed separately from the omnibus application and stipulation and shall inform the court of the specific ground therefor. Briefs and authorities shall be supplied to the court and opposing counsel 2 days before the hearing.

(g) Stipulations.

(1) At or prior to the time set for omnibus hearing, the parties may file a written stipulation to the effect that all discovery requested by the other party has been supplied or will be provided not later than 10 days prior to trial and indicate thereon whether or not there are statements of the defendant which require a pre-trial hearing under CrR 3.5 and/or evidence which may require a pre-trial suppression hearing. The written stipulation will be accepted by the court provided it is signed by the prosecuting attorney, defense counsel and the defendant. The court may then set a time prior to trial or if deemed more expedient at the trial for hearing such matters as are requested hereunder.

RULE 7.12. PRESENTENCE INVESTIGATION

(b) Report.

(1) *Additional Reports.* The court may consider, in addition to the formal pre-sentence report, any reports prepared by the defendant, his counsel, law enforcement agencies, the prosecuting attorney and all victim impact statements.

[Amended effective September 1, 1997; September 2, 2014.]

VI. MENTAL RULES

RULE 2.4. PROBABLE CAUSE HEARING

(c) Hearing. Upon filing of all necessary papers with the court by the mental health professional and notice to the court and prosecuting attorney that a probable cause hearing is to be held, the clerk will notify the court who will through the Clerk of Court schedule the hearing within 72 hours of the date and time of initial detention. The probable cause hearing will be at the facility where the person is detained.

VII. GUARDIAN AD LITEM RULES

RULE 5.0. APPOINTMENT OF GUARDIAN AD LITEM

When the appointment of a guardian ad litem is required, the appointee shall be from the appropriate Court-approved Guardian ad Litem registry maintained for Titles 11, 13 or 26, respectively.

[Adopted effective September 1, 2002.]

RULE 5.1. FEES

Fees paid guardians ad litem shall be at the rate set by Superior Court administrative policy. If additional fees are requested, a written motion for same, accompanied by supporting affidavit(s) must be filed.

[Adopted effective September 1, 2002.]

RULE 7.0. GUARDIAN AD LITEM GRIEVANCE PROCEDURES

These rules apply to guardians ad litem and Court Appointed Special Advocates appointed on any case heard by the Court under Titles 11, 13 and 26 of the Revised Code of Washington.

[Adopted effective September 1, 2002.]

RULE 7.1. GUARDIAN AD LITEM ADVISORY COMMITTEE

The Court's Guardian ad Litem Advisory Committee, hereinafter referred to as the "Committee," will administer complaints about guardians ad litem.

[Adopted effective September 1, 2002.]

RULE 7.2. SUBMISSION OF COMPLAINTS

All complaints must be in writing and must be submitted to the Superior Court Administrator. All complaints must bear the signature, name and address of the person filing the complaint.

[Adopted effective September 1, 2002.]

RULE 7.3. REVIEW OF COMPLAINT

(1) Upon receipt of a written complaint, the Court Administrator shall convene the Committee to review the complaint. Upon review of the complaint, the Committee shall either:

(A) Make a finding that the complaint is with regard to a case then pending in the court and decline to review the complaint and so inform the complainant. In such instances the Committee shall advise the complainant that the complaint may only be addressed in the context of the case at bar, either by seeking the removal of the guardian ad litem or by contesting the information or recommendation contained in the guardian ad litem's report or testimony. In such cases the Committee and its members shall perform its role in such a manner as to assure that the trial judge remains uninformed as to the complaint; or

(B) Make a finding that the complaint has no merit on its face, and decline to review the complaint and so inform the complainant; or

(C) Make a finding that the complaint appears to have merit and request a written response from the Guardian ad Litem within 10 business days, detailing the specific issues in the complaint to which the Committee desires a response. The Committee shall provide the Guardian ad Litem with a copy of the original complaint. In considering whether the complaint has merit, the Committee shall consider whether the complaint alleges the Guardian ad Litem has:

(1) Violated a code of conduct;

(2) Misrepresented his or her qualifications to serve as a Guardian ad Litem;

(3) Breached the confidentiality of the parties;

(4) Falsified information in a report to the court or in testimony before the court;

(5) Failed, when required, to report abuse of a child;

(6) Communicated with a judicial officer ex-parte concerning a case for which he or she is serving as a guardian ad litem;

(7) Violated state or local laws or court rules; or,

(8) Taken or failed to take any other action which would reasonably place the suitability of the person to serve as a Guardian ad Litem in question.

[Adopted effective September 1, 2002.]

RULE 7.4. RESPONSE AND FINDINGS

(1) Upon receipt of a written response to a complaint from the Guardian ad Litem, the Committee shall make a finding as to each of the specific issues in the complaint to which the Committee desires a response, as delineated in the Committee's letter to the Guardian ad Litem. Such findings shall state that either there is no merit to the issue based upon the Guardian ad Litem's response or that there is merit to the issue.

(2) The Committee shall have the authority to issue a written admonishment, a written reprimand, refer the Guardian ad Litem to additional training, or recommend to the Presiding Judge that the Court suspend or remove the Guardian ad Litem from the registry. In considering a response, the Committee shall take into consideration any prior complaints that resulted in an admonishment, reprimand, referral to training, or suspension or removal from a registry. If a Guardian ad Litem is listed on more than one registry, the suspension or removal may apply to each registry on which the Guardian ad Litem is listed, at the discretion of the Committee.

(3) The complainant and the Guardian ad Litem shall be notified in writing of the Committee's decision following receipt of the Guardian ad Litem's response.

[Adopted effective September 1, 2002.]

RULE 7.5. CONFIDENTIALITY

(1) A complaint shall be deemed confidential for all purposes unless the Committee has determined that it has merit under 7.4, above.

(2) Any record of complaints filed which are not deemed by the Committee to have merit shall be confidential and shall not be disclosed except by court order.

[Adopted effective September 1, 2002.]

RULE 7.6. COMPLAINT PROCESSING TIME STANDARDS

(1) Complaints shall be resolved within twenty-five (25) days of the date of receipt of the written complaint if a case is pending.

(2) Complaints shall be resolved within sixty (60) days of the date of the receipt of the written complaint if the complaint is filed subsequent to the conclusion of a case.

[Adopted effective September 1, 2002.]

RULE 7.7. REMOVAL FROM REGISTRY

(1) When a guardian ad litem is removed from the Court's registry pursuant to the disposition of a grievance hereunder, the Court Administrator shall send a notice of such removal to the Administrative Office of the Courts.

(2) When the Court Administrator receives notice from the Administrative Office of the Courts that a guardian ad litem on the Court's registry has been removed from the registry of any other Washington Superior Court, the Administrator shall advise the Presiding Judge of such removal.

[Adopted effective September 1, 2002.]

VIII.   RULES FOR APPEALS OF DECISIONS OF LOWER[1] OF LIMITED JURISDICTIONS

[1] So in original.

RULE 2.0.   SMALL CLAIMS APPEALS

(1) This rule applies only to an appeal of the decision of a Small Claims Court operating under RCW 12.40. Small claims appeals shall be heard de novo, based solely upon the record certified from the District Court pursuant to RCW 12.36.

(2) After a small claims appeal has been perfected, the District Court Clerk will notify the parties in writing of the Superior Court cause number, and the name and department number of the assigned Superior Court Judge. The Superior Court Clerk will notify the assigned department when the record has been received, and the appeal is ready to be reviewed.

(3) The assigned Judge will schedule a hearing to consider the oral argument of the parties. Oral argument shall not exceed 15 minutes per side without prior approval by the Court. No witness testimony, or presentation of additional evidence, will be permitted. The parties may request additional time for argument, or to submit written authorities, by motion directed to the assigned Judge.

(4) The decision of the Court shall be entered by written judgment. When the Court's ruling is against the appellant, judgment shall be entered against the appellant and the sureties of the posted appeal bond, as required by RCW 12.36.090.

[Adopted effective September 1, 2007.]

DISTRICT COURT

LOCAL RULES OF THE DISTRICT COURT OF CLARK COUNTY, STATE OF WASHINGTON

Including Amendments Received Through
August 15, 2015

Table of Rules

GENERAL RULES

LGR 14. FORMAT FOR PLEADING AND OTHER PAPERS

(a) Format Requirements. All pleadings, motions, and other papers filed with the court shall be legibly written or printed. The use of letter-size paper (8–1/2 by 11 inches) is mandatory. The writing or printing shall appear on only one side of the page. The top margin of the first page shall be a minimum of three inches, the bottom margin shall be a minimum of one inch and the side margins shall be a minimum of one inch. All subsequent pages shall have a minimum of one inch margins. Papers filed shall not include any colored pages, highlighting or other colored markings.

(1) *Format Recommendations.* (3) Bottom Notation. (A) Signatures Required. Every order present-ed for a Judge's signature shall include a portion of the text on the signature page and shall be signed by the individual attorney presenting it on the lower left-hand corner of the page to be signed. Every page shall include the case number.

(2) *Pleading to be Dated and Names Typed.* All pleadings, motions, and other papers to be filed with the clerk shall be dated by the person preparing the same. The names of all persons signing a pleading or other paper should be typed under the signature. If signed by an attorney, the attorney's Washington Bar Association number must be set forth.

(3) Pro se pleadings shall be typewritten or neatly printed, shall conform to the format recommendations of CRLJ 10(e), and shall contain the party's mailing

address and street address where service of process and other papers may be made upon him/her or the same may be rejected for filing by the clerk.

(4) *Audio/Visual Exhibits.* When testimony or evidence is to be given via video tape or motion pictures, it is the responsibility of the party introducing the testimony or evidence to provide the proper equipment for viewing such testimony or evidence, or to provide the court the testimony or evidence in CD or DVD format.

(5) *Small Claims and Name Change Format Requirements.* All Small Claims and Name Change pleadings must conform to Clark County District Court forms. Prescribed forms are available on the court's website. Any pleadings not meeting such requirements may be rejected for filing and returned, then resubmitted after compliance with this rule.

(d) In addition to the format requirements of GR14 and CR10, all pleadings motions and other papers filed with the District Court shall be legibly written or printed with numbered lines, double-spaced type except for generally recognized exceptions such as lengthy quotes or exhibits, twelve (12) point type , and using bonded or at least 20 lb. grade of paper. Any submission not meeting such requirements may be returned for resubmission in compliance with the rule.

[Adopted March 5, 2002; amended on an emergency basis effective April 26, 2007; amended on a permanent basis effective September 1, 2007; September 1, 2008; September 1, 2009; September 1, 2012.]

LGR 30. MANDATORY ELECTRONIC FILING

(B) Electronic Filing.

(5) Effective September 1, 2013, unless this rule provides otherwise, attorneys shall electronically file (e–file) documents with the District Court Clerk's office using the Clark County Court E–Filing System. Non–attorneys are not required to e-file documents.

(A.) Documents That Shall Not Be E–Filed. Documents required by law to be filed in non-electronic media must be filed in paper-form. Exceptions to e-filing include the following documents:

(i) Certified records of proceedings for purposes of appeal;

(ii) Documents presented for filing during a court hearing or trial;

(iii) Foreign (out of state) Judgments under official seal;

(iv) New cases or fee based documents filed with an Order in Forma Pauperis;

(vi)[1] Bail bonds;

(v) Trial Exhibits.

Comment: Negotiable instruments, exhibits, and trial notebooks are examples of items that are not to be filed in the court file either in paper form or by e-filing.

(B.) Documents That May Be E–Filed. The following documents may be e-filed:

(i) Voluminous Documents—Voluminous documents of 500 pages or more may be e-filed or filed in paper form.

(ii) Answers to Writs of Garnishment

(iii) Documents from governments or other courts under official seal. If filed electronically, the filing party must retain the original document during the pendency of any appeal and until at least sixty (60) days after completion of the instant case, and shall present the original document to the court if requested to do so. This does not include documents that are or will be submitted as an exhibit in a hearing or trial.

(E.) Filing Fees, Electronic Filing Fees.

(1) Documents being e-filed that require a fee must include a copy of the payment confirmation. Court payment may be made through the court's authorized payment processing agency.

[Adopted effective September 2, 2013.]

1 Numbering as provided in original.

I. ADMINISTRATIVE RULES

LARLJ 0.1. COURT ORGANIZATION AND MANAGEMENT

The general management of the court shall be vested in the Presiding Judge and his/her duties and powers are as set forth below, pursuant to and in conjunction with ARLJ 5 and GR 29.

[Effective June 30, 1997.]

LARLJ 0.2. ATTIRE OF COUNSEL AND LITIGANTS

All attorneys appearing before the court shall be attired in a manner that is consistent with the current generally prevailing and accepted business attire for professional men and women in the local community. Male attorneys shall wear coats and ties. Female attorneys shall wear dresses, skirts, pants suits or jacket and slacks. Any attire that is distracting or detrimental to the seriousness of the proceedings or disruptive of decorum should be avoided. Counsel are responsible for informing litigants that they should wear clean and neat-appearing clothing.

[Adopted on an emergency basis effective April 26, 2007; adopted on a permanent basis effective September 1, 2007.]

LARLJ 5. PRESIDING JUDGE

(a) **Appointment and Term.** The term of Presiding Judge is to be two (2) years in duration, unless terminated earlier by a vote of the majority of all the sitting Judges. The Presiding Judge shall be elected by a majority of the sitting Judges on or before October 31st of each year so that notice of election may be given pursuant to GR 29. The Presiding Judge may be re-elected for additional terms.

(b) Duties.

(1) The Presiding Judge will act as Chief Administrative Judge and will see that policy of the Court, as determined by a majority of the Judges, is implemented by the Court Administrator.

(2) The Presiding Judge will call meetings of the Court and preside over said meetings.

(3) The Presiding Judge will adopt and implement a Court schedule with the consent of the majority of the Judges.

(4) The Presiding Judge will be the spokesperson for the Court in response to media inquiries.

(5) The Presiding Judge will be responsible for long range planning.

(6) The Presiding Judge will be responsible for relations with other elected officials, and other duties consistent with GR 29.

(7) All major policy decisions will require the approval of a majority of the Judges, however, the Presiding Judge will be responsible for overseeing the budget, implementation of new technologies and the administrative function of the Court. The Presiding Judge may delegate any of his/her responsibilities to other Judges and create departments or committees to handle complex problems or functions as he or she sees fit.

[Effective June 30, 1997; amended effective September 1, 2002; September 1, 2006.]

LARLJ 5.1. ACTING PRESIDING JUDGE

(a) Election. The Court may by vote of a majority of the sitting Judges appoint an Acting Presiding Judge to conform to the Administrative Rules for Courts of Limited Jurisdiction.

(b) Duties. The Acting Presiding Judge will assume the duties of the Presiding Judge in the case of a prolonged absence, death or incapacity of the Presiding Judge.

(c) Status. The Acting Presiding Judge shall have the same status as all other sitting Judges with regard to duties and assignments by the Presiding Judge and eligibility to be elected Presiding Judge.

[Effective June 30, 1997.]

II. CIVIL RULES

LCRLJ 5. SERVICE AND FILING OF PLEADINGS AND OTHER PAPERS

(d) Filing.

(5) *Motions.* No motion for any order shall be heard unless the pleadings and citation have been filed with the Clerk not less than five court days before the hearing unless a motion for order shortening time has been filed and granted by the court.

(6) *Documents Not to Be Filed:*

(i) Interrogatories and depositions without written permission of Court, unless necessary for the disposition of a motion or objection;

(ii) Unanswered request for admissions unless necessary for the disposition of a motion or objection;

(iii) Photocopies of reported cases, statutes or texts appended to a brief or otherwise, shall not be filed, but may be furnished directly to the Judge hearing the matter.

(iv) Documents or copies thereof which should be received as exhibit rather than part of the court file.

(v) Requests for discovery and/or answer shall not be filed unless necessary for the disposition of a motion or objection.

(7) *Offers of Settlement.* An offer of settlement made pursuant to Chapter 4.84 of the Revised Code of Washington shall not be filed or communicated to the trier of the fact in violation of Section 4.84.280 of the Revised Code of Washington prior to completion of trial. A violation of this order shall result in the denial of the reasonable attorney fee. (See LCRLJ 68A)

[Adopted effective June 30, 1997; amended effective September 1, 2011.]

LCRLJ 33. INTERROGATORIES TO PARTIES

(e) Limited Interrogatories Without Prior Approval of the Court: Parties Represented by Attorneys. In those civil actions in which all parties are represented by counsel, any party may serve upon any other party no more than two sets of written interrogatories containing not more than 20 questions per set without prior permission of the Court. Any subsections shall be treated as a question for purposes of the 20 questions limitation. Interrogatories authorized under this local rule shall conform to the provisions of Civil Rule 33.

[Effective June 30, 1997.]

LCRLJ 40. ASSIGNMENT OF CASES

(c) Methods.

(1) *Notice to Set for Trial.* A party desiring to place a case on the trial readiness calendar shall file a "Notice to Set for Trial" on a form prescribed by the Court, a copy of which is attached at the end of this section.

(2) *Certification.* By filing a Notice to Set for Trial, a party certifies that the case is fully at issue with all necessary parties joined, all anticipated discovery has been or will be completed before trial and all other counsel have been served with a copy of the Notice.

(3) *Response to Notice to Set for Trial.* A party who objects to a case being set for trial, or who otherwise disagrees with the information on the "Notice," shall file and serve a "Response to Notice to Set for Trial" on a form prescribed by the Court within 10 days of the date of mailing or personal service of the "Notice." (See attached.) The Response shall be noted for hearing the objection not more than 25 days after the date of mailing or personal service of the "Notice to Set for Trial." No response is necessary if the party agrees with the "Notice to Set for Trial."

(4) *Call for Trial.* Any case placed on the readiness calendar will be subject to call for trial to be assigned a specific date for trial. The Court will give reasonable notice of the trial date assigned.

(5) *Continuances.* When a case has been called from the readiness calendar and set, it shall proceed to trial or be dismissed, unless good cause is shown for continuance, or the Court may impose such terms as are reasonable and in addition may impose costs upon counsel who has filed a Notice to Set for Trial, or who has failed to object thereto and is not prepared to proceed to trial. No request for continuance, including stipulated motions, will be considered without an affidavit giving the particulars necessitating a continuance in accordance with CRLJ 40(d) and (e). Continued cases may be removed from the trial calendar at the discretion of the court and, if removed, will be recalendared upon filing a new Notice to Set for Trial.

[Effective June 30, 1997.]

LCRLJ 43. TAKING OF TESTIMONY

(e) Evidence on Motions.

(1) Motions shall be heard on the pleadings, affidavits, published depositions and other papers filed unless otherwise directed by the Court. Any counter-affidavit shall be served upon the opposing party not later than (3) three days prior to the date of the hearing, or movant shall have the option of a postponement of the hearing. Affidavits strictly in reply to a counter-affidavit may be served and considered at the hearing.

[Effective June 30, 1997.]

LCRLJ 54. JUDGMENTS AND COSTS

(c) Demand for Default Judgment—Method—Ex–Parte Judgments and Orders. Counsel present-

ing a judgment or seeking entry of an order shall be responsible for seeing that all applicable papers are filed and that the Court file is provided to the Judge. Counsel may present routine ex-parte or stipulated matters based on the record in the file by mail addressed to the assigned Judge. Self addressed, stamped envelopes shall be provided for return of any conformed materials and/or rejected orders. All judgments shall contain a Judgment Summary in conformity with RCW 4.64.030.

(d) Costs—Attorney Fees.

(1) Reasonable attorney fees when allowed by statute or contract will be determined on a case by case basis and awarded in the sound discretion of the Court upon satisfactory justification, which may include documentation of time and charges.

In appropriate cases, when a Default Judgment is entered, there will be a minimum of $250. Additional reasonable attorney fees may be allowed on the basis of a maximum of 50% of the first $500.00 of the principal amount of the judgment, plus 10% of any balance over $500.00, without formal justification or documentation.

(2) If reasonable attorney fees are requested based on a contract provision, the contract provision must be conspicuously highlighted or *underlined* to be readily ascertainable.

(3) Specific citation of authority must accompany requests for reasonable attorney fees on any basis other than contract provision.

(4) Statutory attorney fees may be granted when reasonable attorney fees are not authorized. (See RCW 12.20.060)

(5) *Offers of Settlement.* Improper communication of an offer of settlement shall result in the denial of reasonable attorney fees (see LCRLJ 5(d)(7) and LCRLJ 68).

[Effective June 30, 1997.]

LCRLJ 58. ENTRY OF JUDGMENTS

(d) Judgment on a Promissory Note. No judg-
ment on a promissory note will be signed until the original note has been filed with the Court, absent proof of loss or destruction.

[Effective June 30, 1997.]

LCRLJ 68A. OFFER OF SETTLEMENT

(a) Form. An Offer of Settlement shall clearly
state it is an Offer of Settlement and specifically refer to Chapter 4.84 of the Revised Code of Washington.

(1) *Method of Service.* Service shall be made as permitted in CRLJ 5.

(2) *Time of Service.* Service shall be made in accordance with RCW 4.84.280 and/or CRLJ 68.

(3) *Pro-Se Parties.* Offers of Settlement served on pro-se parties shall include a statement that failure or

refusal to accept this offer may result in a reasonable attorney fee being assessed at the time of judgment. Failure to include such wording will be grounds for the Court to deny reasonable attorney fees.

[Effective June 30, 1997.]

LCRLJ 69. EXECUTION, SUPPLEMENTAL PROCEEDINGS AND GARNISHMENTS

(a) **Scope.** Execution, supplemental proceedings and garnishments are governed by Statute (See Titles 6 and 7 of the Revised Code of Washington).

(1) *Supplemental Proceedings.* In all supplemental proceedings wherein an order is issued pursuant thereto requiring the personal attendance of a party to be examined in open court and in orders to show cause the order must include the following words in capital letters.

YOUR FAILURE TO APPEAR AS SET FORTH AT THE TIME, DATE, AND PLACE THEREOF MAY CAUSE THE COURT TO ISSUE A BENCH WARRANT FOR YOUR APPREHENSION AND CONFINEMENT IN JAIL UNTIL SUCH TIME AS THE MATTER CAN BE HEARD, UNLESS BAIL IS FURNISHED AS PROVIDED IN SUCH BENCH WARRANT.

The failure to include such wording will be grounds for the Court to refuse to issue a bench warrant.

(2) *Bench Warrant.* In the event the judgment debtor fails to appear for examination in a supplemental proceeding, the Court may issue a Bench Warrant for the defendant's arrest upon plaintiff's motion, provided that proof of personal service on the judgment debtor of the order to appear for examination has been filed. Such Bench Warrant shall provide for bail in the presumptive amount of $500.00, unless the size

of the judgment warrants setting a greater or lesser amount. Upon arrest on a Civil Bench Warrant, the defendant shall be released by the jail upon posting the bail amount or surety bond. In the event that the defendant is unable to post bail, the defendant shall be brought before the Court at the next regularly scheduled "in custody" time. Verbal or oral notice of the bench warrant hearing will be given to the opposing party or counsel one (1) hour or more prior to the scheduled hearing. In the event the opposing party is unavailable for said hearing, the defendant may be released by order of the District Court conditioned upon the party's appearance at a rescheduled hearing.

Upon completion of the examination of the judgment debtor, the bail posted shall be exonerated unless the Court orders otherwise.

(3) *Judgment Against Garnishee; Order to Disburse.*

(i) No judgment against a garnishee defendant, or order to pay into Court, or order to the clerk to pay out any sum received pursuant to a Writ of Garnishment, will be signed except after judgment is entered against the defendant and until the party who caused the writ to issue shall have filed proof of service and sufficient time shall have elapsed as provided by statute. (RCW 6.27).

(ii) The pattern form of "Judgment and Order to Disburse on Answer of Garnishee Defendant", as proposed by the Office of the Administrator for the Courts of the State of Washington, is hereby adopted for use in Clark County District Court as modified to include a provision for disbursement. Failure to follow such form may be grounds for denial of the order.

[Effective June 30, 1997. Amended effective September 1, 2006.]

III. SMALL CLAIMS RULES

LSC 1. COUNTERCLAIM

The defendant may counterclaim against the plaintiff for an amount up to the jurisdictional limit provided in RCW 12.40.010. The defendant must notify the plaintiff of such counterclaim at least 21 days prior to the trial date unless waived by the Court.

[Effective June 30, 1997; Amended May 5, 2002; September 1, 2015.]

LSC 2. MOTION TO SET ASIDE DEFAULT JUDGMENT

(a) **Filing.** A party may file a motion to set aside a default judgment or dismissal entered at time of trial for failure of such party to have appeared for trial. The motion shall set forth "good cause" reasons for having failed to appear for trial.

(b) **Time for Motion.** The written motion must be filed within 30 days of entry of such default.

(c) **Reset Fee.** Before the Court will set a hearing on a motion to set aside a default judgment, the moving party must pay a reset fee of $50.00 to the Court. The reset fee will be paid over to the opposing party regardless of the outcome of the case.

[Effective June 30, 1997; Amended May 5, 2002.]

LSC 3. CLERK'S DISMISSAL

In all small claims cases wherein there has been no action of record during the preceding 12 months, the clerk of the Court shall mail notice to the parties that the case will be dismissed by the Court for want of prosecution unless within 30 days following the mailing, action of record is made or an application in writing is made to the Court and good cause shown why it should be continued as a pending case. If such application is not made or good cause is not shown, the Court shall dismiss each such case without prejudice. The cost of filing such order of dismissal with the clerk shall not be assessed against either party.

[Effective June 30, 1997.]

LSC 4. SMALL CLAIMS MEDIATION

(a) Mediation Conference. Mediation Conference is mandatory before trial. The court will set Mediation Conference date at the time of filing of answer to the complaint. Both parties must attend the Mediation Conference. If the plaintiff fails to appear, a dismissal will be entered. If the defendant fails to appear, their answer, if one was filed, will be stricken and a default judgment entered. Parties must bring their evidence to the mediation, however, no witnesses are allowed. The purpose of mediation is to settle the case if possible; if no settlement is made at mediation, the case will go to trial. Attorneys and paralegals may not represent the parties at mediation.

(b) Exemption from Mediation. The parties may request exemption from mandatory mediation conference by filing an affidavit within 14 days of receipt of the notice of mandatory mediation conference, wherein the parties state they have attempted to settle all issues in dispute by participating in mediation prior to filing the case.

If the parties have already submitted the case to another type of mediation or arbitration service, the case may proceed directly to trial.

(c) Completing Mediation. Any case assigned to mediation must complete mediation within 90 days of assignment, unless otherwise ordered by the court.

(1) In all cases assigned to mediation in which a settlement is reached, the parties shall report such settlement to the mediator and the mediator shall file a notice of such settlement with the court.

(2) The results of mediation hearings shall be reported to the court as either "settled" or "not settled".

(3) If a case is reported as "settled", the terms of the agreement, including a date of final compliance, shall be signed by the parties and filed by the mediator with the clerk of the court within 10 judicial days.

(i) The mediator shall provide the creditor with a form to report compliance or non-compliance with the terms of the settlement agreement.

(ii) Should the creditor fail to file a report of compliance or non-compliance within 30 days after the final date for compliance, or reports the terms of the settlement have been met, the clerk of the court shall dismiss the case.

(iii) Upon notice by a creditor of non-compliance with the terms of the settlement agreement, the clerk of the court shall refer the case to a judge for disposition.

(4) If the parties are not able to settle a mediated case, the case will be set for trial and not be required to arbitrate.

[Adopted April 14, 2004.]

IV. CRIMINAL RULES

LCrRLJ 2.1. COMPLAINT–CITATION AND NOTICE

(b) Citation and Notice to Appear.

(7) *Mandatory Appearance for Alcohol Violators.* A defendant who is charged with an offense involving alcohol as defined in RCW 46.61.502, 46.61. 503, and 46.61.504 shall be required to appear in person before a judicial officer within seven days from the time of arrest or issuance of a citation pursuant to RCW 46.61.50571. Appearances required are mandatory and may not be waived.

[Adopted effective September 1, 2003; amended effective September 1, 2011.]

LCrRLJ 2.2. WARRANT OF ARREST

(a) Issuance of Warrant.

(2) *Probable Cause*

(i) Waivers of Probable Cause are Presumed to be Valid Until Challenged. A challenge to the

waiver will trigger a new 48 hour period for the prosecuting agency to establish probable cause.

[Adopted effective September 1, 2006.]

LCrRLJ 3.1. RIGHT TO AND ASSIGNMENT OF LAWYER

(d) Assignment of Lawyer.

(1) Unless waived, counsel shall be provided to any person who is financially unable to obtain an attorney without causing substantial hardship to the defendant or the defendant's family.

(2) *Financial Screening.*

(i) The initial interview and financial screening to determine eligibility for counsel at public expense shall be conducted by the County Corrections Department. Said department shall make an immediate determination of eligibility. If a person is found to be partially eligible, a recommendation indicating this shall be completed and sent to the judge.

(ii) The County Corrections Department may perform the initial screening at any time without a referral from the Court as long as the person has not appeared in court. Once a person has appeared, screening may be done only after receipt of a signed referral or as noted in LCrRLJ 3.1(d)(iv) below.

(iii) The County Corrections Department shall not rescreen a defendant to determine eligibility unless it has received a referral signed by a District Court Judge.

(iv) The County Corrections Department shall rescreen, without referral, any defendant who wishes to appeal a conviction in District Court. This rescreening shall be done using Superior Court guidelines.

(v) If at any time it appears that a person has retained private counsel, has funds sufficient to do so, or is otherwise not eligible for defense services, the appointed attorney may notify the Court and ask its guidance. Conversely, if it appears that counsel previously retained by a person has withdrawn, or that a person thought to have funds sufficient to obtain private counsel is not in fact able to do so, the defendant may be referred for a redetermination of eligibility.

(3) *Reimbursement of Attorney Fees.*

(i) Partial ability to pay. A person found to be partially eligible for defense services shall be required to make reimbursement to Clark County as agreed at the time of appointment.

(ii) Reimbursement not required by appointed counsel. In no case shall appointed counsel set or attempt to obtain reimbursement for the costs of defense services.

(e) Withdrawal of Lawyer.

(1) *Duties of Attorney Before Withdrawal.*

(a) Before asking permission to withdraw from the court, or filing a notice of withdrawal, counsel of record should attempt to determine whether or not a client who has been sentenced, or who is facing sentencing, intends to pursue an appeal of his or her conviction.

(b) Upon being notified that a client who has been sentenced or is facing sentencing wishes to file an appeal, the attorney of record shall do the following before withdrawing from the representation:

(i) Prepare and file the notice of appeal in the form prescribed by the court rule.

(ii) In the case of an indigent client, prepare a motion and order in forma pauperis (IFP), providing for the preparation of the record, and transmittal of clerk's papers at public expense, waiving the filing fee for the appeal, and providing for appointment of new counsel on appeal. This order should be presented to the sentencing court, and filed with the clerk by the withdrawing attorney. The order shall require the clerk of the

court to promptly notify new counsel of the appointment for the appeal.

(iii) Present and file an order setting conditions of release on appeal.

(f) Services Other Than a Lawyer.

(2) Pursuant to the authority under CcRLJ[1] 3.1(f) all requests for expenditure for investigative and expert services for State cases and City of Vancouver cases are hereby delegated to the Clark County Indigent Defense Coordinator and the City of Vancouver Indigent Defense Coordinator respectively.

[Effective June 30, 1997. Amended on an emergency basis, effective April 26, 2007; amended on a permanent basis, effective September 1, 2007; September 2, 2013.]

1 So in original. Probably should be "CrRLJ".

LCrRLJ 3.2. PRETRIAL RELEASE

(a) Personal Recognizance.

(1) Designated members of the staff of the Clark County Corrections Department Monitoring Unit are authorized to release persons who are charged with misdemeanor offenses on their own recognizance. When released, the defendant shall be given a date to appear in court as specified in the District Court bail schedule.

(2) The arresting officer shall indicate "to be set" in the space for court date on the citation for any defendant detained at the jail for a misdemeanor or gross misdemeanor. The exception to this occurs when the arresting officer releases the defendant on personal recognizance. In such cases, the officer shall specify a return date for appearance in court as specified in the District Court bail schedule.

(3) When no one from the County Corrections Department Monitoring Unit is on duty, Jail supervisory personnel may grant recognizance to certain defendants charged only with misdemeanor or gross misdemeanor offenses. The defendant shall be given an appearance date as specified in the District Court bail schedule. This authority is to be used for defendants who have been residents of Clark County for more than one year.

(b) Bail.

(1) Misdemeanor bail shall not be combined with felony bail. If cash is received, it shall be kept separate. If a bail bond agent posts bail, he or she shall post separate bonds. A separate bond shall be posted for each new complaint.

(2) If someone other than the defendant posts cash bail, the person receiving the bail shall obtain the correct name and address of the payer.

(3) A defendant who is released on bail shall be given an appearance date as specified in the District Court bail schedule.

(c) Bail Schedule. The Court shall periodically publish a bail schedule which will include any bail schedule and penalty promulgated by the Supreme Court of the State of Washington. The schedule will also include appearance days and times.

Said schedule shall be provided to all law enforcement officers within the county.

Said schedule shall have the force and effect of local court rule for all the courts under the authority of the District Court of Clark County.

(d) Forfeiture. A copy of the Notice of Trial Setting shall be furnished to the bail bond agent for a defendant.

If the defendant fails to appear as directed by the Court, a bail forfeiture shall be immediately issued. The bail bond agent shall have 60 days to locate the defendant. At the end of the 60 days, the full amount of the bond shall be due.

If the bail bond agent presents the defendant to the Court before the 60 days has elapsed, costs may be imposed against the defendant. The costs shall be $50.00 for failure to appear at arraignment, pretrial or sentencing; $100.00 for failure to appear for trial; or $300.00 for failure to appear at a jury trial.

If the defendant fails to appear for sentencing or pretrial or arraignment, but does appear within (5) five days of the original appearance date, the court costs shall be waived. There shall be no such waiver for a defendant who fails to appear for trial.

[Effective June 30, 1997.]

LCrRLJ 3.3. TIME FOR TRIAL

(h) Continuances. All motions for continuance shall be heard by notice and citation on the appropriate motion docket. Only in extreme emergencies shall the presiding judge or the trial judge consider a motion for continuance without the proper notice and citation.

[Effective June 30, 1997.]

LCrRLJ 3.4(d). VIDEO CONFERENCE PROCEEDINGS

Trial Court proceedings including entry of Statement of Defendant of Guilty and sentencing and post sentencing hearings may be conducted by video conference upon agreement of the parties either in writing or on the record, and upon approval of the trial court judge.

[Effective October 1, 2004.]

LCrRLJ 4.1. ARRAIGNMENT

(d) Appearance by Defendant's Lawyer. Attorneys at law, admitted to practice in the State of Washington, may enter a plea of not guilty in writing on all cases filed in the District Court. Defendants are required to appear in person for driving under the influence and domestic violence arraignments.

(e) Deferred Prosecution. A petition for deferred prosecution under RCW 10.05 shall be on the form prescribed by the Court, which is attached as an appendix to these rules and available in the District Court clerk's office. [Adopted effective March 12, 1997.]

[Adopted effective March 12, 1997. Amended effective September 1, 2006.]

LCrRLJ 4.5. PRETRIAL PROCEDURES

(a) Pretrial Conference. The court shall set pretrial conferences for all cases where a not guilty plea has been entered. Pro se defendants who enter a plea of not guilty at arraignment shall appear on the date scheduled by the court for a pretrial conference with the prosecuting attorney/city attorney to discuss their cases. Failure to appear for the pretrial conference may result in the issuance of a bench warrant and/or forfeiture of any bail or bond. Defense attorneys shall make arrangements with the prosecuting attorney/city attorney to exchange information and discuss the case.

(b) Pretrial Hearing.

(1) In all cases in which a defendant has entered a plea of not guilty, a pretrial hearing shall be set approximately 45 days after arraignment. Said hearing shall provide an opportunity for plea negotiations, omnibus, resolution of discovery issues, and trial setting. Following the hearing, if a plea is not negotiated, an order shall be entered setting forth the following: (i) discovery schedule, (ii) date and nature of pretrial motions, (iii) date of readiness hearing, (iv) date of trial and (v) time for filing witness lists.

(2) The prosecuting attorney/city attorney, defense attorney, and defendant shall be required to attend the pretrial hearing, with the exception that a defendant represented by counsel may waive his/her appearance on the form prescribed by the court, a copy of which will be made available in the District Court clerk's office. The waiver shall not be executed more than 7 days prior to the pretrial hearing. Absent a waiver, failure to attend may result in the issuance of a bench warrant and/or forfeiture of any bail or bond.

(c) Readiness Hearing. The prosecuting attorney/city attorney, defense attorney and defendant shall appear in court on the date scheduled for readiness hearing to confirm their readiness to proceed with the scheduled trial. In the event the defendant fails to appear, the jury shall be canceled, a bench warrant may be issued, bail or bond may be forfeited, and costs may be imposed at the discretion of the court. In the event the defendant waives the jury trial subsequent to the readiness hearing, costs may be imposed at the discretion of the court.

[Adopted effective March 12, 1997.]

LCrRLJ 4.8. SUBPOENAS

(a) Issuance for Witnesses. If a witness in a criminal matter is to be subpoenaed, the person making the request should prepare the subpoena and present it to the Court for signature on the subpoena. All subpoenas must be prepared in triplicate prior to the presentation for signature.

Any request for more than three subpoenas must be approved by the Court.

[Effective June 30, 1997.]

LCrRLJ 4.11. [REPEALED]

LCrRLJ 4.12. [REPEALED]

V. INFRACTION RULES

LIRLJ 2.4. RESPONSE TO NOTICE OF INFRACTION

(a) Generally. A person who has been served with a notice of infraction must respond to the notice within 15 days of the date the notice is personally served or, if the notice is served by mail, within 18 days of the date the notice is mailed.

(b) Alternatives. A person may respond to a notice of infraction by:

(1) Paying the amount of the monetary penalty in accordance with applicable law, in which case the court shall enter a judgment that the defendant has committed the infraction;

(2) Contesting the determination that an infraction occurred by requesting a hearing in accordance with applicable law;

(3) Requesting a hearing to explain mitigating circumstances surrounding the commission of the infraction in accordance with applicable law; or

(4) Submitting a written statement either contesting the infraction or explaining mitigating circumstances. The statement shall contain the person's promise to pay the monetary penalty authorized by law if the infraction is found to be committed. For contested hearing the statement shall be executed in substantially the following form:

I hereby state as follows:

I promise that if it is determined that I committed the infraction for which I was cited, I will pay the monetary penalty authorized by law and assessed by the court. I certify (or declare) under penalty of perjury under the laws of the State of Washington that the foregoing is true and correct.

_____   _____
(Date and Place)   (Signature)

I understand that if this form is submitted by e-mail, my typed name on the signature line will qualify as my signature for purposes of the above certification.)

For mitigation hearings, the statement shall be executed in substantially the following form:

I hereby state as follows:

I promise to pay the monetary penalty authorized by law or, at the discretion of the court, any reduced penalty that may be set.

I certify (or declare) under penalty of perjury under the laws of the State of Washington that the foregoing is true and correct.

_____   _____
(Date and Place)   (Signature)

I understand that if this form is submitted by e-mail, my typed name on the signature line will qualify as my signature for purposes of the above certification.

(c) Method of Response. A person may respond to a notice of infraction either personally, or by mail or by e-mail. If the response is mailed or e-mailed, it must be postmarked or e-mailed not later than midnight of the day the response is due.

[Adopted effective September 1, 2001; amended effective September 1, 2010.]

LIRLJ 2.6. INFRACTION HEARINGS

(c) Decisions on Written Statements. Mitigation hearings shall generally be held in open court. The procedure set forth in IRLJ 3.5, allowing decisions on written statements is authorized

[Adopted March 4, 1998; amended May 5, 2002].

LIRLJ 3.5. DECISION ON WRITTEN STATEMENTS

(a) Contested Hearings. The court shall examine the citing officer's report and any statement submitted by the defendant. The examination shall take place within 120 days after the defendant filed the response to the notice of infraction. The examination may be held in chambers and shall not be governed by the Rules of Evidence.

(1) *Factual Determination.* The court shall determine whether the plaintiff has proved by a preponderance of all evidence submitted that the defendant has committed the infraction.

(2) *Disposition.* If the court determines that the infraction has been committed, it may assess a penalty in accordance with rule 3.3.

(3) *Notice to Parties.* The court shall notify the parties in writing whether an infraction was found to

have been committed and what penalty, if any, was imposed.

(4) *No Appeal Permitted.* There shall be no appeal from a decision on written statements.

(b) Mitigation Hearings. Mitigation hearings based upon written statements may be held in chambers.

[Adopted effective September 1, 2001; amended effective September 1, 2010.]

MUNICIPAL COURTS

MUNICIPAL COURTS OF BATTLE GROUND, RIDGEFIELD, AND LA CENTER

Including Amendments Received Through
August 15, 2015

Table of Rules

* Heading supplied by Publisher based on corresponding heading in the Criminal Rules or Infraction Rules for Courts of Limited Jurisdiction.

CRIMINAL RULES

L CrRLJ 1.7. [LOCAL COURT RULES—AVAILABILITY]

(a) Pursuant to CrRLJ 1.7 and GR 7, the Local Rules of the combined Municipal Courts for the City of Battle Ground, Washington, and the towns of Ridgefield and La Center, Washington, should be the Criminal Rules for Courts of Limited Jurisdiction, together with any amendments or changes thereto approved by the Supreme Court of the State of Washington, and the Local Rules set forth below.

(b) Where a conflict exists between the CrRLJ and these Local Rules, the Local Rules shall be read so as to conform to the CrRLJ as closely as possible, with the intent of protecting the Constitutional rights of each individual Defendant and the just and speedy adjudications of the matter before the Court.

[Adopted effective September 1, 2000.]

L CrRLJ 3.2.1. [PROCEEDINGS BEFORE THE JUDGE—PROCEDURE FOLLOWING EXECUTION OF A WARRANT, OR ARREST WITHOUT A WARRANT—PROBABLE CAUSE FOR DETERMINATION—BAIL—PRELIMINARY HEARING]

(a) The Court hereby designates the judges of the Clark County Superior and District Courts to make the initial probable cause determination for any Defendant held in custody on a case filed in the Municipal Courts effected by these rules, given the limited meeting times of this Court.

(d)(1) The "next business day" of the Court is defined for the purposes of this rule as the Thursday next following the arrest and detention of the Defendant. The preliminary appearance shall be combined with the arraignment of the Defendant, given the limited number of court days per month of these Courts.

[Adopted effective September 1, 2000.]

L CrRLJ 3.3. [TIME FOR TRIAL]

(h) Continuances.

(3) Any requests for continuance, made orally in open court or in writing by Defendant's counsel or the Defendant, shall require the Court to reinform the Defendant of his or her speedy trial rights before the motion is granted or denied. The Court shall not grant a motion for continuance beyond the Defendant's originally calculated speedy trial time, unless the Defendant (or Defendant's counsel, upon counsel's representation that the Defendant has been informed of his or her speedy trial rights and has authorized counsel to waive them) signs a Waiver of Speedy Trial upon a form supplied by the Court. The Defendant or counsel must understand, before signing the waiver, that the Court will be waiving the Defendant's speedy trial rights to a date certain, upon which date the applicable 60 day or 90 day period will begin to run anew.

[Adopted effective September 1, 2000.]

L CrRLJ 3.4. [PRESENCE OF THE DEFENDANT]

(a)(1) (present text)

(a)(2) An attorney licensed to practice law in the State of Washington may file a Notice of Appearance on behalf of a Defendant and waive the Defendant's presence at any hearing subsequent to arraignment; however, all Defendants charged with either Driving Under the Influence of Alcohol or Drugs, Physical Control, or any crime designated as a "domestic violence crime" are required to personally appear at their arraignment.

[Adopted effective September 1, 2000.]

L CrRLJ 4.1. [ARRAIGNMENT]

(e) Arraignments will normally be held on the next court day after the Defendant has been cited and released or, if in custody, on the next court day after their arrest. At arraignment, the Defendant will be provided with a "Statement of Rights/Plea Form" and,

if they are requesting a court-appointed attorney, a "Financial Declaration" form to fill out and present to the Judge before entering a plea. The Court shall assure itself that the Defendant understands his/her rights and the charge(s) before taking a plea. If an interpreter is necessary for the Defendant to understand their rights, the Court may set over the arraignment until such interpretation services can be secured. At the arraignment, the Court shall set a pretrial hearing date approximately one month later and a trial date within the speedy trial time as determined by the Court.

[Adopted effective September 1, 2000.]

L CrRLJ 4.5. [PRETRIAL HEARING]

(a) (original text)

(b) At the first pretrial hearing, either party may make pretrial motions, engage in settlement discussions, request modifications to any previous orders, or address any other issues between the parties.

(c) At the first or subsequent pretrial hearings, the Court shall set a mandatory pretrial hearing at least two weeks prior to the scheduled trial date. The Defendant's presence at the mandatory pretrial hearing shall be required. At the mandatory pretrial hearing, the Court shall determine whether both parties are ready to proceed on the appointed trial date, make appropriate orders in aid of an expeditious resolution of the matter, and set a cut-off date for discovery and subpoenaing witnesses, unless those dates have already been set.

[Adopted effective September 1, 2000.]

L CrRLJ 6.3. SELECTING THE JURY]

Normally, the clerk will take the first eighteen names from the Elections Division list that personally appear for jury duty on the date set for trial. Should at least 18 qualified jurors fail to appear, the Court may either delay the trial date, after assuring itself that no prejudice will result to either party, or may go ahead with less than six jurors upon the Defendant's consent.

[Adopted effective September 1, 2000.]

INFRACTION RULES

LIRLJ 1.1. SCOPE AND PURPOSE OF RULES

(a) Scope of Rules. These rules are adopted pursuant to GR 7 and IRLJ 1.3 of the Washington State Court Rules, governing the procedure in Courts of Limited Jurisdiction for all cases involving "infractions". Infractions are civil non-criminal violations of law defined by statute.

(b) The Court may modify or suspend any of these Local Court Rules in any given case upon good cause being shown or upon the Court's own motion.

[Adopted effective September 2, 2014.]

LIRLJ 1.2. DEFINITIONS

For the purposes of these rules:

(a) Infraction Case. "Infraction case" means a civil proceeding initiated in a court of limited jurisdiction pursuant to a statute that authorizes offenses to be punished as infractions.

(b) Notice of Infraction. "Notice of infraction" means a document initiating an infraction case when issued and filed pursuant to statute and these rules.

(c) Defendant. "Defendant" means a person cited for an infraction, a registered owner of a vehicle cited for a parking infraction, or the person who responds to the parking infraction or the requests of a hearing.

(d) Court. "Court" means a court of limited jurisdiction organized pursuant to RCW Title 3, RCW Title 35, or RCW Title 35A.

(e) Judgment. "Judgment" means any final decision in an infraction case, including, but not limited to, a finding entered after a hearing governed by these rules or after payment of a monetary penalty in lieu of a hearing.

(f) Plaintiff. "Plaintiff" means the governmental unit issuing the notice of infraction, including, but not limited to, the state, a county, or a municipality.

(g) Department. "Department" means the Washington State Department of Licensing.

(h) Lawyer. "Lawyer" means any person authorized by Supreme Court rule to practice law.

(i) Statute. "Statute" means any state statute, local or county ordinance, resolution, or regulation, or agency regulation.

(j) Citing Officer. "Citing officer" means a law enforcement officer or other official authorized by law to issue a notice of infraction.

(k) Prosecuting Authority. "Prosecuting authority" includes prosecuting attorneys, city attorneys, corporation counsel, and their deputies and assistants, or such other persons as may be designated by statute.

(*l*) Judge. "Judge" means any judge of any court of limited jurisdiction and shall include every judicial officer authorized to preside over infraction cases.

(m) Community Restitution. "Community restitution" means compulsory service, without compensation, performed for the benefit of the community by the defendant.

[Adopted effective September 2, 2014.]

LIRLJ 1.3.   LOCAL COURT RULES

(a) Adoption. Each court may adopt special infraction rules not inconsistent with these general rules.

(b) Formulated. These local rules are formulated pursuant to IRLJ 1.3

(c) Filing. Local rules become effective only after they are filed with the Administrator for the Courts in accordance with GR 7.

[Adopted effective September 1, 2000. Amended effective September 2, 2014.]

LIRLJ 1.4.   CONTINUANCES

A. Mitigation Hearing: A Court Clerk may grant one telephone request for a continuance. The continuance must be requested by 5:00 p.m. the day before the scheduled hearing.

B. Contested Hearing: A Court Clerk may grant one telephone request for a continuance. The continuance must be requested not less than three (2)[1] days before the scheduled Contested hearing.

[Adopted effective September 2, 2014.]

1 So in original.

LIRLJ 1.5.   ELECTRONIC FILING NOTICE OF INFRACTIONS & OFFICERS REPORTS

Pursuant to GR 30, Battle Ground Municipal Court will accept electronic filings initiated by a law enforcement officer when that officer is presumed to have signed the document, when the officer uses his or her USER ID and password to electronically submit the document to the court or prosecutor through the Washington State approved application, and the court will also accept the officers report electronically. Unless otherwise specified, the signature shall be presumed to have been made under Penalty of perjury under the laws of the State of Washington and on the date and at the place set forth in the citation.

This rule shall be effective immediately upon filing with the Administrator of the Courts and shall apply retroactively to any pending cases.

[Adopted effective September 2, 2014.]

LIRLJ 2.4.   RESPONSE TO NOTICE

(a) Generally. A person who has been served with a notice of infraction must respond to the notice within 15 days of the date the notice is personally served or, if the notice is served by mail, within 18 days of the date the notice is mailed.

(b) Alternatives. A person may respond to a notice of infraction by:

(1) Paying the amount of the monetary penalty in accordance with applicable law, in which case the court shall enter a judgment that the defendant has committed the infraction;

(2) Contesting the determination that an infraction occurred by requesting a hearing in accordance with applicable law; Or submitting a written statement;

(3) Requesting a hearing to explain mitigating circumstances surrounding the commission of the infraction in accordance with applicable law; Or submitting a written statement;

(4) *In addition to the requirements of IRLJ 2.4(b)* 4. When a person is submitting a written statement either contesting the infraction or explaining mitigating circumstances, using this method the person gives up their right to an in-person hearing, and its concom-

itant right to hear and question the plaintiff's witnesses, as well as giving up the right to have their own witnesses, as well as giving up their right to have their own witnesses come to court and testify on their behalf, if this alternative is authorized by local court rule. The statement shall contain the person's promise to pay the monetary penalty authorized by law if the infraction is found to be committed. For a written contested hearing the statement shall be executed in substantially the following form:

I hereby state as follows:

I promise that if it is determined that I committed the infraction for which I was cited, I will pay the monetary penalty authorized by law and assessed by the court. I certify (or declare) under penalty of perjury under the laws of the State of Washington that the foregoing is true and correct.

_____ _____
   (Date and Place)   (Signature)

I understand that if this form is submitted by e-mail, my typed name on the signature line will qualify as my signature for purposes of the above certification.)

For a written mitigation hearing, the statement shall be executed in substantially the following form:

I hereby state as follows:

I promise to pay the monetary penalty authorized by law or, at the discretion of the court, any reduced penalty that may be set.

I certify (or declare) under penalty of perjury under the laws of the State of Washington that the foregoing is true and correct.

_____ _____
   (Date and Place)   (Signature)

I understand that if this form is submitted by e-mail, my typed name on the signature line will qualify as my signature for purposes of the above certification.

(c) Method of Response. A person may respond to a notice of infraction either in person, by mail, by phone, or by e-mail, or by completing and submitting the court form electronically. If the response is mailed or e-mailed, it must be postmarked or e-mailed no later than midnight of the day the response is due.

[Adopted effective September 1, 2000. Amended effective September 2, 2014.]

LIRLJ 2.6. [SCHEDULING OF HEARINGS] [RESCINDED]

[Adopted effective September 1, 2000. Rescinded effective September 2, 2014.]

LIRLJ 3.1. REQUEST FOR SUBPOENA

Any request for a subpoena to be issued by the court must be filed in writing at least 14 days before the hearing, or such lesser time as the court deems proper. The request cannot be combined with a notice of appearance or any other pleading.

If a defendant does not have a lawyer and wants witnesses to testify on their behalf, the defendant must provide a list of the witnesses with the following information:

(i) the witnesses' true name;

(ii) the witnesses' mailing or street address.

The defendant should also be informed that the prosecuting authority may waive the officer's presence, unless the defendant requests it.

[Adopted effective September 1, 2000. Amended effective September 2, 2014.]

LIRLJ 3.3. PROCEDURE AT CONTESTED HEARING

The prosecuting authority, if no witnesses have been subpoenaed, may waive the presence of a lawyer on its behalf and elect to proceed solely on the sworn statement of the citing officer. If the Defendant wants the citing officer available for cross-examination at the hearing, the defendant shall be required to request the officer's presence at the hearing in writing pursuant to Rule IRLJ 3.1(a), supra.

[Adopted effective September 1, 2000. Amended effective September 2, 2014.]

LIRLJ 3.5. DECISION ON WRITTEN STATEMENTS

In lieu of a defendant's personal appearance for a mitigation or contested hearing, the person who has been issued a notice of civil infraction may respond to the Battle Ground Municipal Court either in person, by phone, or in writing by mail or by e-mail in a written statement form, in lieu of making a personal appearance at a mitigation or contested hearing.

(a) Contested Hearings. The court shall examine the citing officer's report and any statement submitted by the defendant. The examination shall take place within 120 days after the defendant filed the response to the notice of infraction. The examination may be held in chambers and shall not be governed by the Rules of Evidence.

(1) *Factual Determination.* The court shall determine whether the plaintiff has proved by a preponder-

ance of all evidence submitted that the defendant has committed the infraction.

(2) *Disposition.* If the court determines that the infraction has been committed, it may assess a penalty in accordance with rule 3.3.

(3) *Notice to Parties.* The court shall notify the parties in writing whether an infraction was found to have been committed and what penalty, if any, was imposed.

(b) Mitigation Hearings. Mitigation hearings based upon written statements may be held in chambers.

In accordance with the provisions of IRLJ 3.5, such hearings are not governed by the Rules of Evidence, and there shall be no appeal from a decision on written or e-mail statement(s).

This rule shall be effective immediately upon filing with the Administrator of the Courts and shall apply retroactively to any pending cases.

[Adopted effective September 2, 2014.]

LIRLJ 3.6.   INFRACTION WITNESS FEES

Each party is responsible for costs incurred by that party as set forth in RCW 46.63.151. The party requesting the witness shall pay the witness fees and mileage expenses due that witness. Any person who requests production of an electronic speed measuring device expert, and who is thereafter found by the Court to have committed the infraction, shall be required to pay the fee charged by the expert as a cost incurred by the party.

[Adopted effective September 2, 2014.]

LIRLJ 3.7.   SPEED MEASURING DEVICE EXPERT

When any Speed Measuring Device Expert is required to testify in a contested infraction hearing, the expert may testify from a location other than the courtroom such as: via speakerphone or other electronic means acceptable to the court.

[Adopted effective September 2, 2014.]

CAMAS—WASHOUGAL MUNICIPAL COURT—
[No Local Rules]

PUBLISHER'S NOTE

This municipal court follows the Local Rules of the District Court of Clark County.

VANCOUVER MUNICIPAL COURT—
[No Local Rules]

PUBLISHER'S NOTE

This municipal court follows the Local Rules of the District Court of Clark County.

YACOLT MUNICIPAL COURT—
[No Local Rules]

PUBLISHER'S NOTE

This municipal court follows the Local Rules of the District Court of Clark County.

COLUMBIA COUNTY

Table of Courts

Superior Court

Hells Canyon Circuit Local Rules.

District Court

Columbia County District Court Local Rules.

Municipal Court

Dayton Municipal Court.

SUPERIOR COURT

HELLS CANYON CIRCUIT LOCAL RULES
[PREVIOUSLY KNOWN AS THE LOCAL RULES OF THE SUPERIOR COURT OF THE STATE OF WASHINGTON FOR THE JUDICIAL DISTRICT OF ASOTIN, COLUMBIA, AND GARFIELD COUNTIES]

PUBLISHER'S NOTE

The Hells Canyon Circuit Local Rules (Previously Known as the Local Rules for the Superior Courts of Asotin, Columbia, and Garfield Counties) are set forth under Hells Canyon Circuit.

DISTRICT COURT

COLUMBIA COUNTY DISTRICT COURT LOCAL RULES

**Including Amendments Received Through
August 15, 2015**

Table of Rules

INTRODUCTION

These local rules have been adopted under the provisions of General Rule 7 promulgated by the Washington State Supreme Court and conform in numbering and format to GR 7. These rules supplement ARLJ, CRLJ, RALJ, CrRLJ, IRLJ and RALJ in accordance with RCW 3.30.080 and GR 7. Insofar as practicable the Washington Court Rules are not repeated and the user of these Local Rules should refer to the pertinent rule as adopted by the Supreme Court.

[Amended effective September 1, 2011.]

I. ADMINISTRATIVE RULES (LARLJ)

LARLJ 1. JURY ADMINISTRATIVE REIMBURSEMENT FEE

A party demanding a jury trial shall, before 1:30 p.m. three business days prior to the scheduled trial date, contact the Columbia County District Court Clerk and confirm that the jury is still required. When a cause assigned a date for trial as a jury case is settled, or will not be tried by a jury for any reason, notice of that fact shall be given immediately to the Court Clerk. In the event the notice is given to the Court Clerk less than three days prior to the scheduled trial date, the party electing not to have their case heard by a jury (Criminal Cases: Defendant who waives jury; or State if jury waiver follows Jury Demand by State; Civil Cases: jury waiver by party after demand) shall pay a jury administrative reimbursement fee equal to the actual costs incurred by the Court for jury fee payments and mileage reimbursements, unless the Judge determines that those costs and fees shall not be paid.

[Adopted effective September 1, 2006; amended effective September 1, 2011.]

LARLJ 2. NEXT JUDICIAL DAY

The state law requires that defendants arrested for driving while under the influence, driving under age twenty-one after consuming alcohol, or being in physical control of a vehicle while under the influence appear in court within one judicial day. Such judicial day is defined as the first date following arrest when court is in session.

[Adopted effective September 1, 2006; amended effective September 1, 2011.]

LARLJ 3. MISCELLANEOUS FEES

The following shall be the schedule of fees charged for certain official services provided by the Columbia County District Court Clerk. These amounts are consistent with **RCW 3.62.060.**

Duplication of Electronic Records	$10.00
Photocopy Expenses	$ .50/page
Certified Copy	$ 6.00
Appeals (Preparation of Tapes–ONLY . . .	$40.00
Return of Check Fee (NSF or Account closed checks)	$35.00

The Court Administrator shall provide procedures and staff for requests made for research in the files of the Court. In the event a request is made to research the contents of files, which have been archived, an Archive Research Fee of $25 per hour shall be charged to the requesting party with a minimum of one hour paid prior to the research commencing. Also see LARJ 3, relating to other applicable fees.

These fees may be changed by general court order without amending these rules.

[Adopted effective September 1, 2006; amended effective September 1, 2011.]

LARLJ 4. DISCLOSURE OF PUBLIC RECORDS

A. The following records and files of this Court are declared confidential:

(a) Affidavits for probable cause for arrest warrants before the warrant has been served and returned.

(b) Mental health, psychiatric, and medical reports.

(c) Alcohol and drug evaluations and follow up reports.

(d) Deferred Prosecution petitions and orders.

(e) Unless admitted into evidence, certified copies of driving records, abstracts of driving records, and compiled reports of arrests and convictions;

(f) Judges notes and work sheets.

B. Access to confidential records is limited to persons authorized by statute or who obtain a Court order.

[Adopted effective September 1, 2006; amended effective September 1, 2011.]

II. CIVIL RULES (LCRLJ)

LCRLJ 1. FILING OF PLEADINGS AND OTHER PAPERS

A. Documents to Be Filed. [Reserved]

B. Documents Not to Be Filed

(a) Interrogatories and depositions without written permission of Columbia County District Court unless necessary for the disposition of a motion or objection.

(b) Unanswered request for admissions unless necessary for the disposition of the motion or objection.

(c) Total copies of reported cases, statutes or texts appended to a brief, or otherwise, may only be filed with a copy marked "bench copy" furnished directly to the judge hearing the matter; and

C. An offer of settlement made pursuant to RCW chapter 4.84 shall not be filed or communicated to the trier of fact in violation of RCW 4.84.280 of the Revised Code of Washington prior to the completion of trial. A violation of this order may result in denial of the reasonable attorney fee.

[Adopted effective September 1, 2006; amended effective September 1, 2011.]

LCRLJ 2. PRE–TRIAL HEARING

When matters of fact are put in issue by responsive pleadings served and filed with the court and if one of the parties has noted the case for pre-trial hearing, a

pre-trial will be set. If both parties stipulate and the Court agrees, the pre-trial hearing may be specially set on the docket for a telephone conference hearing. **Wherever possible, 5 days notice must be given to the Clerk for approval by the Judge and scheduling.** At the pre-trial hearing all parties must appear (in person or telephonically) or through counsel. If a party does not appear at the pre-trial hearing, the non-appearing party's pleadings shall be stricken, unless good cause is shown, and the court may grant a judgment of default or dismissal against the non-appearing party. If no parties appear, the court may dismiss all pending claims without prejudice. At the pre-trial hearing, the court will also perform the following functions:

1. Determine any pre-trial motions.

2. Assign trial and/or further motion dates.

3. Acknowledge and approve settlement agreements.

4. Enter default or judgments on pleadings.

5. Pre admit exhibits for trial.

6. Enter discovery order and completion dates.

Counsel shall appear at the pre-trial hearing with a schedule of dates of availability for trial or any other necessary proceeding.

The pre-trial hearing procedure shall not preclude the entry of default judgments, judgments on pleadings, or any other orders not inconsistent with these rules or the Civil Rules for Courts of Limited Jurisdiction (CRLJ) prior to the date of the pre-trial hearing.

[Adopted effective September 1, 2006; amended effective September 1, 2011.]

LCRLJ 3. INSTRUCTIONS TO JURY

It is the responsibility of the parties to submit proposed jury instructions to the Columbia County District Court and to opposing parties no later than the time the case is called for trial or at a time ordered by the court. If the party demanding a jury trial fails to comply with this requirement, the right to jury trial shall be deemed waived and jury panel dismissed unless all opposing parties move to retain the jury and the court finds good cause therefore.

[Adopted effective September 1, 2006; amended effective September 1, 2011.]

LCRLJ 4. DISMISSAL ON CLERK'S MOTION

In all cases where there has been no action of record during the 12 months just past, the Columbia County District Court Clerk shall mail notice to the parties or the attorneys of record that such case will be dismissed by the court for want of prosecution unless within thirty (30) days following said mailing, written application of action of record is made to the court and good cause shown why the case should be continued as a pending case. If such application is not made or good cause is not shown, the court shall dismiss each such case without prejudice. The cost of filing such order of dismissal with a clerk shall not be assessed against either party.

[Adopted effective September 1, 2006; amended effective September 1, 2011.]

LCRLJ 5. DEFAULT JUDGMENTS

ATTORNEY FEES. When a party is entitled to an award of reasonable attorney fees (in lieu of those statutory fees provided for by **RCW 12.20.060**), the fees provided in the following attorney fees schedule are deemed reasonable in all default cases unless the party presents evidence of circumstances which convince the court a larger or smaller fee should be awarded; provided, however, the court shall have authority to vary from the schedule on its own motion:

Schedule for attorney fees in default cases

$0.00 to $2,500	$250.00
$2,501 to $5,000	$350.00
$5,001 to $10,000	$450.00
$10,001 to $15,000	$600.00

Attorney's fee requests in excess of $450 must be itemized.

[Adopted effective September 1, 2006; amended effective September 1, 2011.]

LCRLJ 6. PAYMENT OF MONIES ON JUDGMENTS

After payments of monies on judgments are paid to the receiving party, or the receiving party's attorney, a satisfaction of judgment shall be filed within the following thirty (30) days of receipt of the funds and a satisfaction of judgment shall be filed within said thirty days in the amount received.

[Adopted effective September 1, 2006; amended effective September 1, 2011.]

LCRLJ 7. CIVIL JURY

Pre-trial Procedure. All cases, set for jury trial shall be set for a pre-trial conference which shall be held at least two weeks prior to trial. The attorneys who are to conduct the trial and all parties shall be present (parties may be excused by the court for good cause) to consider such matters as will promote a fair and expeditious trial. All discovery shall be completed within ten (10) days following the pre-trial conference. Opposing counsel or party, and the Court must be given ten (10) days notice prior to the pre-trial conference. Opposing counsel or party must be given ten (10) days prior written notice of any pre-trial motions to be heard at the pre-trial conference. Any motions not made at the pre-trial conference shall be deemed waived.

[Adopted effective September 1, 2006; amended effective September 1, 2011.]

LCRLJ 8. NAME CHANGES

A. Minors—Parental Consent. All applications for change of name of a person less than 18 years of age must be represented by a parent or legal guardian. The petitioner must file proof of service of petition and notice of hearing to either biological or legal parents or guardians if the applicant has not filed a written approval of change of name by both biological or legal parents and guardians. Said notices shall be served on other parties at least ten (10) days prior to the hearing.

B. Each petition requesting a change of name must present a separate change of name order and pay a separate filing fee and a recording fee for each person whose name is being changed.

[Adopted effective September 1, 2006; amended effective September 1, 2011.]

III. INFRACTION RULES (LIRLJ)

LIRLJ 1. DECISIONS ON WRITTEN OR EMAIL STATEMENTS

A. In place of the defendant's personal appearance at a mitigation infraction hearing, defendants may submit their statement in writing (including email submissions).

B. The court shall examine the citing officer's report and any statement(s) submitted by the defendant. The examination shall take place within 120 days after the defendant filed a response to the notice of infraction. The examination may be held in Chambers and shall not be governed by the rules of evidence.

[Adopted effective September 1, 2006; amended effective September 1, 2011.]

LIRLJ 2. MANDATORY LIABILITY INSURANCE VIOLATIONS— PROOF OF INSURANCE

A. If a person who has been cited with a violation of **RCW 46.30.020** presents to the Court Clerk evidence that the person had in effect at the time of the citation liability insurance as required by **RCW**

46.30.020, then, upon payment of twenty-five ($25.00), the case shall be dismissed and the court clerk shall be authorized to make appropriate notation of the dismissal in the court file.

B. If a person charged with violation of **RCW 46.30.00**, for failure to have liability insurance is able to show evidence that the person has subsequently obtained liability insurance in conformity with the requirements of **RCW 46.30.020**, then the penalty shall be reduced to seventy five ($75.00). Upon payment, the case shall be dismissed and the court clerk shall be authorized to make appropriate notation of the dismissal in the court file.

[Adopted effective September 1, 2006; amended effective September 1, 2011.]

LIRLJ 3. DEFERRED INFRACTIONS

If a defendant is granted a deferral on an infraction pursuant to the provisions of RCW 46.63.070, meeting the statutory qualifications, the Court shall charge an administrative fee of $150.00, payable within 30 days of the entry of deferral.

[Adopted effective September 1, 2007; amended effective September 1, 2011.]

IV. CRIMINAL RULES (LCrRLJ)

LCrRLJ 1. EXHIBITS

In a criminal case every exhibit in the court's custody, which is not contraband and for which ownership is not in dispute, shall be returned to the party who produced that exhibit upon motion of the party, or upon the court's motion and expiration of the appeal period. Exhibits not withdrawn shall be delivered by the court to the applicable law enforcement agency for disposition as abandoned property; or if contraband, for destruction. No exhibit shall be released by the court without its being receipted for by the receiving person.

[Adopted effective September 1, 2006; amended effective September 1, 2011.]

LCrRLJ 2. OBLIGATION OF DEFENDANTS TO APPEAR IN COURT, AND CONSEQUENCES OF FAILURES TO APPEAR IN CASES WHERE A PUBLIC DEFENDER HAS BEEN APPOINTED

A. The appointment of a public defender attorney, for any defendant deemed to be indigent shall be conditioned upon the defendant appearing in court for all hearings where his/her appearance has been required by the court.

B. If any defendant for which a public defender has been appointed fails to appear in court when so

required on two occasions without being excused in advance by the court, the order/appointment whereby the public defender was appointed for said defendant may be vacated immediately upon such second failure to appear.

C. Upon such appointment being vacated the public defender shall be relieved from any requirements to appear in court with such defendant.

D. The provisions of this rule, however, do not preclude the defendant from reapplying to the court for the appointment of a public defender to represent him/her.

[Adopted effective September 1, 2006; amended effective September 1, 2011.]

LCrRLJ 3.2. RELEASE OF ACCUSED

A. DUI/Physical Control Cases. In cases where an individual is arrested for Driving a Motor Vehicle While Under the Influence of Intoxicants and/or Drugs or for Physical Control of a Motor Vehicle While Under the Influence of Intoxicants and/or Drugs or Minor Operating a Motor Vehicle After Consuming Alcohol, the individual so arrested shall be held in custody without bail pending a first appearance before a Judge, UNLESS, in the discretion of jail supervisory staff, incarceration may create health or safety issues, jail space/transport is not available, or any other good cause which calls for conditional release.

B. Domestic Violence Cases. Any individual arrested for a crime classified, as Domestic Violence under Section **10.99** of the Revised Code of Washington shall be held in custody without bail pending a first appearance before a Judge, UNLESS, in the discretion of jail supervisory staff, incarceration may create health or safety issues, jail space/transport is not available, or any other good cause which calls for conditional release.

C. Conditions of Release in Felony Preliminary Appearance Hearings

The Court shall set conditions of release for individuals alleged to have committed a felony by affidavit of probable cause pursuant to CrRLJ 3.2.1(d) & (e) or by criminal complaint pursuant to CrRLJ 3.2.1(g) at a preliminary appearance hearing. If a surety bond is required the surety bond may be approved if it is recites that it is issued jointly in favor of the District Court and in favor of the Superior Court in the event of a filing of information in Superior Court. If cash bail is required and paid the Columbia County Sheriff shall deposit all felony cash bail with the District Court Clerk. Upon notice that information has been filed in Superior Court the District Court Clerk shall forward surety bonds or cash bail to the Superior Court Clerk. In the event a criminal complaint is filed charging a misdemeanor or gross misdemeanor following a preliminary appearance hearing on an alleged felony, the Clerk shall retain surety bonds or cash bail received. In the event neither a criminal complaint nor information is filed within 72 hours of the accused detention in jail, exclusive of weekends and holidays, the surety or cash bail will be returned to the accused.

[Adopted effective September 1, 2006; amended effective September 1, 2011.]

LCrRLJ 4. READINESS HEARING

In order to efficiently schedule the calling of jurors, to avoid unnecessary disruptions of jurors lives, and to avoid the waste of public funds the following readiness hearing procedures have been adopted:

Not less than 7 days prior to an assigned jury trial date, there shall be held a readiness hearing. At the readiness hearing it shall be mandatory that the prosecuting attorney, the defense counsel, and the defendant be present. The requirements of this rule can be waived only by the Judge appointed to the case. In the event the defendant fails to appear, the jury trial setting shall be canceled, a bench warrant may be issued, bail or bond may be forfeited, and costs may be imposed at the discretion of the court. In the event the defendant waives the jury trial subsequent to the readiness hearing, costs may be imposed pursuant to LARLJ 1. At the readiness hearing, the following matters will be concluded:

1. All plea negotiations

2. Exchange of witness lists

3. Providing of any discovery not previously completed by the pretrial hearing held prior to the readiness hearing.

4. Motions on legal issues arising subsequent to the pretrial hearing or on issues arising due to new evidence.

5. Filing with the court proposed non-WPI (Washington Pattern Instructions) jury instructions and voire dire questions for the prospective jurors which either party requests to be asked by the court. Note ALL jury instructions will need to be filed 5 working days prior to a jury trial including WPI by the prosecution and 3 days prior to trial by the defendant.

At the conclusion of the readiness hearing, the court will no longer grant any further motions to amend or motions to dismiss the charge(s) unless good cause is shown (involving unique and unexpected events/factors). Therefore, the case will be tried by jury, unless waived by the defendant, or concluded by a guilty plea to the original charge (s), See LARLJ 1 regarding administrative reimbursement of jury fees for those who do not give at least 3 days notice of settlement to the clerk of the court.

[Adopted effective September 1, 2006; amended effective September 1, 2011.]

V. RULES FOR APPEAL (LRALJ)

LRALJ 1. FAILURE TO DESIGNATE THE RECORD

The Court will advise Superior Court in writing if a party fails to designate the portions of the record necessary for review as provided in RALJ 6.2(a). Failure to designate the record may be considered a failure to diligently pursue the appeal and cause the Court to revoke any stay of enforcement of the judgment under RALJ 4.2 and RALJ 4.3. At the time notice of failure to designate the record is transmitted

to Superior Court, the Clerk shall also send notice to the parties of a hearing at which the Court shall consider revocation of the stay due to the failure to diligently pursue the appeal.

[Adopted effective September 1, 2006; amended effective September 1, 2011.]

LRALJ 3. COPY OF RECORDING FOR PARTIES

Requests for duplicates of recorded tapes shall be in writing on a form prescribed by the Court. Duplicates of tapes and of the log for the record shall be delivered only after payment of the actual costs, un-

less the party is otherwise excused by statute or by the Constitution.

[Adopted effective September 1, 2006; amended effective September 1, 2011.]

MUNICIPAL COURT

DAYTON MUNICIPAL COURT LOCAL RULES

Including Amendments Received Through
August 15, 2015

Table of Rules

INTRODUCTION

These local rules have been adopted under the provisions of General Rule 7 promulgated by the Washington State Supreme Court and conform in numbering and format to GR 7. These rules supplement ARLJ, CRLJ, RALJ, CrRLJ, IRLJ and RALJ in accordance with RCW 3.30.080 and GR 7. Insofar as practicable the Washington Court Rules are not repeated and the user of these Local Rules should refer to the pertinent rule as adopted by the Supreme Court.

[Adopted effective September 1, 2011.]

I. ADMINISTRATIVE RULES (LARLJ)

LARLJ 1. JURY ADMINISTRATIVE REIMBURSEMENT FEE

A party demanding a jury trial shall, before 1:30 p.m. three business days prior to the scheduled trial date, contact the Columbia County District Court Clerk and confirm that the jury is still required. When a cause assigned a date for trial as a jury case is settled, or will not be tried by a jury for any reason, notice of that fact shall be given immediately to the Court Clerk. In the event the notice is given to the Court Clerk less than three days prior to the scheduled trial date, the party electing not to have their case heard by a jury (Criminal Cases: Defendant who waives jury; or State if jury waiver follows Jury Demand by State; Civil Cases: jury waiver by party after demand) shall pay a jury administrative reimbursement fee equal to the actual costs incurred by the Court for jury fee payments and mileage reimbursements, unless the Judge determines that those costs and fees shall not be paid.

[Adopted effective September 1, 2011.]

LARLJ 2. NEXT JUDICIAL DAY

The state law requires that defendants arrested for driving while under the influence, driving under age twenty-one after consuming alcohol, or being in physical control of a vehicle while under the influence appear in court within one judicial day. Such judicial day is defined as the first date following arrest when court is in session.

[Adopted effective September 1, 2011.]

LARLJ 3. MISCELLANEOUS FEES

The following shall be the schedule of fees charged for certain official services provided by the Columbia County District Court Clerk. These amounts are consistent with **RCW 3.62.060.**

Duplication of Electronic Records	$10.00
Photocopy Expenses	$ .50/page
Certified Copy	$ 6.00
Appeals (Preparation of Tapes–ONLY	$40.00
Return of Check Fee (NSF or Account closed checks)	$35.00

The Court Administrator shall provide procedures and staff for requests made for research in the files of the Court. In the event a request is made to research the contents of files, which have been archived, an Archive Research Fee of $25 per hour shall be charged to the requesting party with a minimum of one hour paid prior to the research commencing. Also see LARJ 3, relating to other applicable fees.

These fees may be changed by general court order without amending these rules.

[Adopted effective September 1, 2011.]

LARLJ 4. DISCLOSURE OF PUBLIC RECORDS

A. The following records and files of this Court are declared confidential:

(a) Affidavits for probable cause for arrest warrants before the warrant has been served and returned.

(b) Mental health, psychiatric, and medical reports.

(c) Alcohol and drug evaluations and follow up reports.

(d) Deferred Prosecution petitions and orders.

(e) Unless admitted into evidence, certified copies of driving records, abstracts of driving records, and compiled reports of arrests and convictions;

(f) Judges notes and work sheets.

B. Access to confidential records is limited to persons authorized by statute or who obtain a Court order.

[Adopted effective September 1, 2011.]

II. CIVIL RULES (LCRLJ)

LCRLJ 1. FILING OF PLEADINGS AND OTHER PAPERS

A. Documents to Be Filed. [Reserved]

B. Documents Not to Be Filed

(a) Interrogatories and depositions without written permission of Columbia County District Court unless necessary for the disposition of a motion or objection.

(b) Unanswered request for admissions unless necessary for the disposition of the motion or objection.

(c) Total copies of reported cases, statutes or texts appended to a brief, or otherwise, may only be filed with a copy marked "bench copy" furnished directly to the judge hearing the matter; and

C. An offer of settlement made pursuant to RCW chapter 4.84 shall not be filed or communicated to the trier of fact in violation of RCW 4.84.280 of the Revised Code of Washington prior to the completion of trial. A violation of this order may result in denial of the reasonable attorney fee.

[Adopted effective September 1, 2011.]

LCRLJ 2. PRE–TRIAL HEARING

When matters of fact are put in issue by responsive pleadings served and filed with the court and if one of the parties has noted the case for pre-trial hearing, a pre-trial will be set. If both parties stipulate and the Court agrees, the pre-trial hearing may be specially set on the docket for a telephone conference hearing.

Wherever possible, 5 days notice must be given to the Clerk for approval by the Judge and scheduling. At the pre-trial hearing all parties must appear (in person or telephonically) or through counsel. If a party does not appear at the pre-trial hearing, the non-appearing party's pleadings shall be stricken, unless good cause is shown, and the court may grant a judgment of default or dismissal against the non-appearing party. If no parties appear, the court may dismiss all pending claims without prejudice. At the pre-trial hearing, the court will also perform the following functions:

1. Determine any pre-trial motions.

2. Assign trial and/or further motion dates.

3. Acknowledge and approve settlement agreements.

4. Enter default or judgments on pleadings.

5. Pre admit exhibits for trial.

6. Enter discovery order and completion dates.

Counsel shall appear at the pre-trial hearing with a schedule of dates of availability for trial or any other necessary proceeding.

The pre-trial hearing procedure shall not preclude the entry of default judgments, judgments on pleadings, or any other orders not inconsistent with these rules or the Civil Rules for Courts of Limited Jurisdiction (CRLJ) prior to the date of the pre-trial hearing.

[Adopted effective September 1, 2011.]

LCRLJ 3.   INSTRUCTIONS TO JURY

It is the responsibility of the parties to submit proposed jury instructions to the Columbia County District Court and to opposing parties no later than the time the case is called for trial or at a time ordered by the court. If the party demanding a jury trial fails to comply with this requirement, the right to jury trial shall be deemed waived and jury panel dismissed unless all opposing parties move to retain the jury and the court finds good cause therefore.

[Adopted effective September 1, 2011.]

LCRLJ 4.   DISMISSAL ON CLERK'S MOTION

In all cases where there has been no action of record during the 12 months just past, the Columbia County District Court Clerk shall mail notice to the parties or the attorneys of record that such case will be dismissed by the court for want of prosecution unless within thirty (30) days following said mailing, written application of action of record is made to the court and good cause shown why the case should be continued as a pending case. If such application is not made or good cause is not shown, the court shall dismiss each such case without prejudice. The cost of filing such order of dismissal with a clerk shall not be assessed against either party.

[Adopted effective September 1, 2011.]

LCRLJ 5.   DEFAULT JUDGMENTS

ATTORNEY FEES. When a party is entitled to an award of reasonable attorney fees (in lieu of those statutory fees provided for by **RCW 12.20.060**), the fees provided in the following attorney fees schedule are deemed reasonable in all default cases unless the party presents evidence of circumstances which convince the court a larger or smaller fee should be awarded; provided, however, the court shall have authority to vary from the schedule on its own motion:

Schedule for attorney fees in default cases

$0.00	to $2,500	$250.00
$2,501	to $5,000	$350.00
$5,001	to $10,000	$450.00
$10,001	to $15,000	$600.00

Attorney's fee requests in excess of $450 must be itemized.

[Adopted effective September 1, 2011.]

LCRLJ 6.   PAYMENT OF MONIES ON JUDGMENTS

After payments of monies on judgments are paid to the receiving party, or the receiving party's attorney, a satisfaction of judgment shall be filed within the following thirty (30) days of receipt of the funds and a satisfaction of judgment shall be filed within said thirty days in the amount received.

[Adopted effective September 1, 2011.]

LCRLJ 7.   CIVIL JURY

Pre-trial Procedure. All cases, set for jury trial shall be set for a pre-trial conference which shall be held at least two weeks prior to trial. The attorneys who are to conduct the trial and all parties shall be present (parties may be excused by the court for good cause) to consider such matters as will promote a fair and expeditious trial. All discovery shall be completed within ten (10) days following the pre-trial conference. Opposing counsel or party, and the Court must be given ten (10) days notice prior to the pre-trial conference. Opposing counsel or party must be given ten (10) days prior written notice of any pre-trial motions to be heard at the pre-trial conference. Any motions not made at the pre-trial conference shall be deemed waived.

[Adopted effective September 1, 2011.]

LCRLJ 8.   NAME CHANGES

A.   Minors—Parental Consent. All applications for change of name of a person less than 18 years of age must be represented by a parent or legal guardian. The petitioner must file proof of service of petition and notice of hearing to either biological or legal parents or guardians if the applicant has not filed a written approval of change of name by both biological or legal parents and guardians. Said notices shall be served on other parties at least ten (10) days prior to the hearing.

B.   Each petition requesting a change of name must present a separate change of name order and pay a separate filing fee and a recording fee for each person whose name is being changed.

[Adopted effective September 1, 2011.]

III. INFRACTION RULES (LIRLJ)

LIRLJ 1.   DECISIONS ON WRITTEN OR EMAIL STATEMENTS

A.   In place of the defendant's personal appearance at a mitigation infraction hearing, defendants may submit their statement in writing (including email submissions).

B.   The court shall examine the citing officer's report and any statement(s) submitted by the defendant. The examination shall take place within 120 days after the defendant filed a response to the notice of infraction. The examination may be held in Chambers and shall not be governed by the rules of evidence.

[Adopted effective September 1, 2011.]

LIRLJ 2. MANDATORY LIABILITY INSURANCE VIOLATIONS— PROOF OF INSURANCE

A. If a person who has been cited with a violation of RCW46.30.020 presents to the Court Clerk evidence that the person had in effect at the time of the citation liability insurance as required by RCW 46.30.020, then, upon payment of twenty-five ($25.00), the case shall be dismissed and the court clerk shall be authorized to make appropriate notation of the dismissal in the court file.

B. If a person charged with violation of RCW 46.30.00, for failure to have liability insurance is able to show evidence that the person has subsequently obtained liability insurance in conformity with the requirements of RCW46.30.020, then the penalty shall be reduced to seventy five ($75.00) Upon payment, the case shall be dismissed and the court clerk shall be authorized to make appropriate notation of the dismissal in the court file.

[Adopted effective September 1, 2011.]

LIRLJ 3. DEFERRED INFRACTIONS

If a defendant is granted a deferral on an infraction pursuant to the provisions of RCW 46.63.070, meeting the statutory qualifications, the Court shall charge an administrative fee of $150.00, payable within 30 days of the entry of deferral.

[Adopted effective September 1, 2011.]

IV. CRIMINAL RULES (LCrRLJ)

LCrRLJ 1. EXHIBITS

In a criminal case every exhibit in the court's custody, which is not contraband and for which ownership is not in dispute, shall be returned to the party who produced that exhibit upon motion of the party, or upon the court's motion and expiration of the appeal period. Exhibits not withdrawn shall be delivered by the court to the applicable law enforcement agency for disposition as abandoned property; or if contraband, for destruction. No exhibit shall be released by the court without its being receipted for by the receiving person.

[Adopted effective September 1, 2011.]

LCrRLJ 2. OBLIGATION OF DEFENDANTS TO APPEAR IN COURT, AND CONSEQUENCES OF FAILURES TO APPEAR IN CASES WHERE A PUBLIC DEFENDER HAS BEEN APPOINTED

A. The appointment of a public defender attorney, for any defendant deemed to be indigent shall be conditioned upon the defendant appearing in court for all hearings where his/her appearance has been required by the court.

B. If any defendant for which a public defender has been appointed fails to appear in court when so required on two occasions without being excused in advance by the court, the order/appointment whereby the public defender was appointed for said defendant may be vacated immediately upon such second failure to appear.

C. Upon such appointment being vacated the public defender shall be relieved from any requirements to appear in court with such defendant.

D. The provisions of this rule, however, do not preclude the defendant from reapplying to the court for the appointment of a public defender to represent him/her.

[Adopted effective September 1, 2011.]

LCrRLJ 3.2. RELEASE OF ACCUSED

A. DUI/Physical Control Cases. In cases where an individual is arrested for Driving a Motor Vehicle While Under the Influence of Intoxicants and/or Drugs or for Physical Control of a Motor Vehicle While Under the Influence of Intoxicants and/or Drugs or Minor Operating a Motor Vehicle After Consuming Alcohol, the individual so arrested shall be held in custody without bail pending a first appearance before a Judge, UNLESS, in the discretion of jail supervisory staff, incarceration may create health or safety issues, jail space/transport is not available, or any other good cause which calls for conditional release.

B. Domestic Violence Cases. Any individual arrested for a crime classified, as Domestic Violence under Section 10.99 of the Revised Code of Washington shall be held in custody without bail pending a first appearance before a Judge, UNLESS, in the discretion of jail supervisory staff, incarceration may create health or safety issues, jail space/transport is not available, or any other good cause which calls for conditional release.

C. Conditions of Release in Felony Preliminary Appearance Hearings. The Court shall set conditions of release for individuals alleged to have committed a felony by affidavit of probable cause pursuant to CrRLJ 3.2.1(d)&(e) or by criminal complaint pursuant to CrRLJ 3.2.1(g) at a preliminary appearance hearing. If a surety bond is required the surety bond may be approved if it is recites that it is issued jointly in favor of the District Court and in favor of the Superior Court in the event of a filing of information in Superior Court. If cash bail is required and paid the

Columbia County Sheriff shall deposit all felony cash bail with the District Court Clerk. Upon notice that information has been filed in Superior Court the District Court Clerk shall forward surety bonds or cash bail to the Superior Court Clerk. In the event a criminal complaint is filed charging a misdemeanor or gross misdemeanor following a preliminary appearance hearing on an alleged felony, the Clerk shall retain surety bonds or cash bail received. In the event neither a criminal complaint nor information is filed within 72 hours of the accused detention in jail, exclusive of weekends and holidays, the surety or cash bail will be returned to the accused.

[Adopted effective September 1, 2011.]

LCrRLJ 4. READINESS HEARING

In order to efficiently schedule the calling of jurors, to avoid unnecessary disruptions of jurors lives, and to avoid the waste of public funds the following readiness hearing procedures have been adopted:

Not less than 7 days prior to an assigned jury trial date, there shall be held a readiness hearing. At the readiness hearing it shall be mandatory that the prosecuting attorney, the defense counsel, and the defendant be present. The requirements of this rule can be waived only by the Judge appointed to the case. In the event the defendant fails to appear, the jury trial setting shall be canceled, a bench warrant may be issued, bail or bond may be forfeited, and costs may be imposed at the discretion of the court. In the event the defendant waives the jury trial subsequent

to the readiness hearing, costs may be imposed pursuant to LARLJ 1. At the readiness hearing, the following matters will be concluded:

1. All plea negotiations

2. Exchange of witness lists

3. Providing of any discovery not previously completed by the pretrial hearing held prior to the readiness hearing.

4. Motions on legal issues arising subsequent to the pretrial hearing or on issues arising due to new evidence.

5. Filing with the court proposed non-WPI (Washington Pattern Instructions) jury instructions and voire dire questions for the prospective jurors which either party requests to be asked by the court. Note ALL jury instructions will need to be filed 5 working days prior to a jury trial including WPI by the prosecution and 3 days prior to trial by the defendant.

At the conclusion of the readiness hearing, the court will no longer grant any further motions to amend or motions to dismiss the charge(s) unless good cause is shown (involving unique and unexpected events/factors). Therefore, the case will be tried by jury, unless waived by the defendant, or concluded by a guilty plea to the original charge (s), See LARLJ 1 regarding administrative reimbursement of jury fees for those who do not give at least 3 days notice of settlement to the clerk of the court.

[Adopted effective September 1, 2011.]

V. RULES FOR APPEAL (LRALJ)

LRALJ 1. FAILURE TO DESIGNATE THE RECORD

The Court will advise Superior Court in writing if a party fails to designate the portions of the record necessary for review as provided in RALJ 6.2(a). Failure to designate the record may be considered a failure to diligently pursue the appeal and cause the Court to revoke any stay of enforcement of the judgment under RALJ 4.2 and RALJ 4.3. At the time notice of failure to designate the record is transmitted to Superior Court, the Clerk shall also send notice to the parties of a hearing at which the Court shall

consider revocation of the stay due to the failure to diligently pursue the appeal.

[Adopted effective September 1, 2011.]

LRALJ 3. COPY OF RECORDING FOR PARTIES

Requests for duplicates of recorded tapes shall be in writing on a form prescribed by the Court. Duplicates of tapes and of the log for the record shall be delivered only after payment of the actual costs, unless the party is otherwise excused by statute or by the Constitution.

[Adopted effective September 1, 2011.]

COWLITZ COUNTY

Table of Courts

Superior Court

Local Rules of the Superior Court for Cowlitz County.

District Court

Cowlitz County District Court Local Rules.

Municipal Courts

Castle Rock Municipal Court—[No Local Rules].
Kalama Municipal Court—[No Local Rules].
Kelso Municipal Court—[No Local Rules].
Longview Municipal Court—[No Local Rules].
Woodland Municipal Court—[No Local Rules].

SUPERIOR COURT

LOCAL RULES OF THE SUPERIOR COURT FOR COWLITZ COUNTY

Originally Effective February 1, 1981

**Including Amendments Received Through
August 15, 2015**

Table of Rules

PART I. RULES OF GENERAL APPLICATION

GENERAL RULES (CCLGR)

RULE 22. ACCESS TO FAMILY LAW COURT RECORDS

(d) Restricted Personal Identifiers Not Required—Except.

(4) Should any party file an acknowledgement of paternity, declination of paternity or birth certificate, that document shall be placed in the sealed portion of the court file.

[Amended effective September 1, 2015.]

PART IV. RULES FOR SUPERIOR COURT

ADMINISTRATIVE RULES (CCLAR)

RULE 1. DEPARTMENTS OF SUPERIOR COURT

(a) Departments. The Superior Court of Cowlitz County shall be divided into as many departments as there are judges authorized by law. Said departments are presided over and by the following judges, and each said judge shall be designated and known as judge of said department until otherwise changed by amendment of this local rule.

Department No. 1: Judge Gary B. Bashor

Department No. 2: Judge Stephen M. Warning

Department No. 3: Judge Michael H. Evans

Department No. 4: Judge Marilyn K. Haan

Department No. 5: Vacant

[Effective September 1, 1997; amended effective September 1, 2000; September 1, 2002; September 1, 2006; September 1, 2011; September 1, 2012.]

RULE 8. COURT ORGANIZATION AND MANAGEMENT

(a) Management. The judges of the Superior Court shall elect, by majority vote, a Presiding Judge who shall serve for a period of two years. The election will take place in December of even-numbered years. The presiding judge's term shall commence January 1. That judge shall have all powers enumerated in GR 29.

At the same time, the judges shall elect an Acting Presiding Judge. The Acting Presiding Judge shall serve in the absence of the Presiding Judge or upon the request of the Presiding Judge in accordance with GR29.

[Original CCLAR 2 was amended effective September 1, 1993; September 1, 1995; September 1, 1997; September 1, 2000; September 1, 2002; renumbered as CCLAR 8 and amended effective September 1, 2005; amended effective September 1, 2006; September 1, 2012; September 1, 2015.]

RULE 10. EMAIL COMMUNICATION

a. Purpose: The purpose of this rule is to provide guidelines for the use of e-mail in communicating with the judges and/or court staff. This rule does not apply to other forms of communication and does not establish a preference for e-mail communication over any other form of communication. E–mail is another tool to provide information as may have been through a telephone call or delivery of documents but it is not intended to substitute as oral argument on any issue.

b. Guidelines for Use of Email: The Court will accept electronic bench copies of pleadings prior to a hearing provided the following guidelines are followed. All parties or their counsel must be provided contemporaneous copies of the email. Attached documents to an e-mail must be in a PDF format. A party must advise the court and parties of any later updated or changed versions of a document previously sent via email. No argument of the issues will be allowed within the e-mail. The purpose of the rule is solely to permit electronic transmission of copies of pleadings.

c. Appropriateness: Email communication with court staff is appropriate in the following typical situations:

i. To obtain a date for an in-court hearing;

ii. To submit proposed orders and/or bench copies of pleadings or trial aides;

iii. To determine the judge's availability;

iv. To determine the availability of equipment needed for trial (such as a projector, video / compact disc player or speaker phone);

v. To advise the court of a settlement (to be immediately followed by formal written notice pursuant to CR 41(e));

viii[1]. Other matters of a similar nature that would be appropriate to handle by way of a phone call to court staff.

d. Ex Parte Communication Prohibited: The prohibitions regarding ex parte contact with the court are fully applicable to e-mail communication. To avoid ex parte contact, all parties must be included in the email and that they appear as additional recipients in the email. If all parties are not included, the judge will not review the email or its content. If an attorney or party is communicating substantive information to court staff, the email must also be sent to the all opposing attorneys /parties and so indicate on its face. Substantive information includes information regarding the likelihood of settlement, the timing of witnesses, anticipated problems with scheduling, concerns regarding security and other case-specific issues.

e. Electronic Service of Working Copies and Pleadings:

1. Absent agreement of the opposing party or express permission of the court, e-mail may not be used for service of pleadings on opposing parties.

2. Bench or work copies of pleadings may be transmitted to the assigned judge in advance of any hearing, provided that all parties to the case are copied on the e-mail including any attachments. Any e-mail which fails to copy all parties will be deleted without review.

3. There shall be no editorial, comment or argument included in the emails; however, information as to the time, date and docket of the matter shall be permitted.

4. Submission by e-mail is an accommodation and in no case shall it be a requirement for any party to submit any document via e-mail, absent a specific order of the Court. Parties are still encouraged to provide a hard copy of any working papers for judges to Court Administration.

f. Retention of Email: The Court is not obligated to retain any electronic communications.

[Adopted effective September 1, 2012. Amended effective September 2, 2013; September 1, 2015.]

[1]So in original.

RULE 11. INTERPRETERS

(a) A written request must be made to the Interpreter Coordinator at least two weeks in advance if an interpreter is needed for a Superior Court hearing or trial. Requests can be emailed to the Interpreter Coordinator at Court Administration. (See Local Administrative Court Rule 10 for ex-parte emailing rules and/or Superior Court's website at www.cowlitzsuperiorcourt.us for additional information.) More advanced notice should be given for specialized and/or high demand languages, longer hearings, or if multiple interpreters are needed. If these timelines are not followed, an interpreter may not be available for a hearing and may require the matter be continued to allow for the presence of an interpreter.

(b) The request for an interpreter should include the following information:

i. Date, time, estimated length and type of hearing.

ii. Language or other type of interpreter needed (for specialized/indigenous languages please indicate the city and/or region where the Limited English Proficiency person is from).

(c) Immediately notify the Interpreter Coordinator if a hearing is continued or set over. Failure to do so at least two days before the hearing may result in the party being charged for the cost of the interpreter if the interpreter cannot be cancelled without a fee.

(d) A confirmation of the request for the interpreter will be sent to the requesting party by the Interpreter Coordinator within five days of receiving the request. If the requesting party has not received confirmation of the request for an interpreter, then the requesting party should immediately contact the

Interpreter Coordinator to verify the request has been received and the necessary interpreter is available for the scheduled hearing.

[Adopted effective September 1, 2012. Amended on an emergency basis, effective January 1, 2013; April 1, 2013; June 6, 2013; amended on a permanent basis, effective September 2, 2013; September 1, 2015.]

CIVIL RULES (CCLCR)
3. PLEADINGS AND MOTIONS (Rules 7–16)

RULE 7. PLEADINGS ALLOWED; FORM OF MOTIONS

(b) Motions and Other Papers.

(1) *How Made.*

(A) Application on Same Facts. When an order has been refused in whole or in part (unless without prejudice) or has been granted conditionally and the condition has not been performed, the same application for an order may not be presented to another judge.

(B) Subsequent Application, Different Facts. If a subsequent application is made upon an alleged different state of facts, it must be shown by affidavit that previous application was made, when and to what judge, what order or decision was made on it, and what new facts are claimed to be shown; and for a failure to comply with this requirement, any order made upon such subsequent application may be set aside, and appropriate sanctions applied.

(C) Request for Bench Warrant. In all supplemental proceedings wherein an order is to be issued requiring the personal attendance of a party to be examined in open court, and in orders to show cause for contempt, the order shall be certified and personally served on that party and must include the following words, in capital letters:

YOUR FAILURE TO APPEAR AS ABOVE SET FORTH AT THE TIME, DATE AND PLACE THEREOF WILL CAUSE THE COURT TO ISSUE A BENCH WARRANT FOR YOUR APPREHENSION AND CONFINEMENT IN JAIL UNTIL SUCH TIME AS THE MATTER CAN BE HEARD OR UNTIL BAIL IS POSTED.

No bench warrant will be issued in such cases for the apprehension of the cited person if said language has been omitted.

[Effective September 1, 1997; amended effective September 1, 2012; September 1, 2015.]

RULE 10. FORM OF PLEADINGS AND OTHER PAPERS

(a) Caption.

(4) *Bench Copies of Pleadings.*

(i) All courtesy copies of a pleading provided to the court shall have the date and time of the pending hearing on the upper right-hand corner of the first page of the pleading.

(ii) A courtesy PDF copy of a pleading may be emailed to a judge in accordance with CCLAR 10, but a hard copy should also be provided for the judge.

(e) Bottom Notation.

(3) All attorney and/or pro se party's signature lines shall also include their email addresses, if available.

(f) Date of Documents. All documents presented to a judge for signature shall provide for a date on which the document is signed, immediately above the judge's signature.

(g) Pleadings to be Dated. All pleadings, motions and other papers to be filed with the clerk shall be dated by the lawyer, party, or individual preparing the same.

(h) The court may refuse to sign, and the clerk may refuse to file, any pleading not complying with this Rule and GR 14(a).

(i) *Sealed Pleadings.* In all cases subject to GR 31, any request to seal a pleading or document shall be accompanied by the appropriate fee. The fee schedule is available from the County Clerk or online at www.co.cowlitz.wa.us/clerk. If payment is in the form of a check, it should be made to "Cowlitz County Clerk."

(ii) [1]

[Amended effective September 1, 1995; September 1, 2002; September 1, 2005; September 1, 2009; September 1, 2010; September 1, 2012; September 2, 2014; September 1, 2015.]

[1] No text in original.

RULE 11. SIGNING AND DRAFTING OF PLEADINGS, MOTIONS, AND LEGAL MEMORANDA; SANCTIONS

(a) Address of Party Appearing Pro Se. A party appearing pro se shall state on all pleadings filed, a mailing address for that party, a street address where service of process and other papers may be made on that party, and a telephone number where that party can be contacted during the day unless that information is made confidential by statute. When a party appears pro se without filing a pleading or other paper, the clerk shall cause the party to insert in the file a paper, or other special indication, that the party has appeared without a lawyer and the party's mailing address, a street address where service of process or other papers may be made, a telephone number where the party can be contacted during the day and an email address (if available).

[Effective September 1, 1997; amended effective September 1, 2012.]

RULE 16. PRETRIAL PROCEDURE AND FORMULATING ISSUES

(c) Whenever requested by a party, or at the discretion of the Court in the absence of such request and prior to obtaining a trial date, there shall be entered a "Case Scheduling Order," substantially in the form set forth below. If the parties cannot agree on compliance dates, then they shall place the matter before the Court on the appropriate Motion Calendar / Docket for entry of those dates.

(d) Except where otherwise specifically stated by court rule or court order, copies of all legal memorandums, final witness lists, exhibit index, family financial status, and all other pleadings for trial shall be submitted to Court Administration no later than three (3) court days prior to the scheduled date of trial readiness hearing.

16 Appendix A
Civil Case Scheduling Order

SUPERIOR COURT OF WASHINGTON FOR COUNTY OF COWLITZ

_____,

Plaintiff,

vs.

_____,

Defendant.

No. _____

CASE SCHEDULING ORDER
CIVIL

Based on the motion filed by [ ] Plaintiff [ ] Defendant on _____, 20_____, or in the alternative based on the Court's discretion, and the records and files herein, the Court orders the following:

Check the box if the item is applicable to the case and then indicate the required information for that item.

[ ]   BIFURCATION OR CONSOLIDATION: All motions for bifurcation or consolidation (CR 42) shall be made by _____, 20_____

[ ]   MASTERS IN DISCOVERY: All requests for appointment of masters in discovery matters (CR 53.3) shall be submitted by: _____, 20_____

[ ]   INTERPRETERS: All requests for an interpreter shall be submitted in accordance with CCLCR 11 by: _____, 20_____

[ ]   LOCAL MANDATORY ARBITRATION (LMAR):
The parties have determined that MAR [ ] does [ ] does not apply.

[ ] JOINDER OF ADDITIONAL PARTIES: Additional parties to this action, if any, shall be joined by:_____, 20_____

[ ] AMENDMENT OF PLEADINGS:
Amendments of the pleadings, if any, shall be made by:_____, 20_____

[ ] EXPERT WITNESSES:
All expert witness information shall be provided by plaintiff by:_____, 20_____
All expert witness information shall be provided by defendant by: _____, 20_____
Information provided shall be as required under CR 26(b)(5).
All expert witness depositions shall be completed by: _____, 20_____

[ ] WRITTEN DISCOVERY (CR 33, 34, 36):
All written discovery (including interrogatories, requests for production, and requests for admissions) shall be submitted by: _____, 20_____

[ ] REQUESTS FOR ENTRY UPON LAND (CR 34):
All parties shall make any requests for entry upon land for inspection and other purposes no later than:_____, 20_____

[ ] PHYSICAL AND MENTAL EXAMINATIONS OF PERSONS:
All parties shall make any request for physical or mental examination of persons no later than:_____, 20_____

[ ] DISPOSITIVE MOTIONS:
All dispositive motions shall be heard by: _____, 20_____

[ ] NON-DISPOSITIVE MOTIONS AND MOTIONS IN LIMINE:
All non-dispositive motions and motions in limine shall be heard by: _____,20_____

[ ] ALTERNATE DISPUTE RESOLUTION:
Alternate dispute resolution shall be completed by: _____, 20_____

[ ] PRETRIAL ORDER:
A proposed pretrial order shall be prepared by the parties and shall be filed by plaintiff by _____, 20_____

[ ] ALTERNATE DISPUTE RESOLUTION:
[ ] Trial Before Referee (RCW 4.48)
[ ] The parties have filed their consent to trial by referee with the Clerk.
[ ] Plaintiff [ ] Defendant states that an issue of fact, namely,

_____

[ ] Mediation:
[ ] The parties do not want or cannot agree on mediation.
[ ] The parties shall complete mediation no later than_____, 20_____

[ ] Arbitration:

[ ] The parties do not want or cannot agree on arbitration.
[ ] The parties shall consider entering arbitration not later than
_____, 20_____ (not mandatory).

[ ]   OTHER:

_____

_____

_____

_____

_____

_____

Any party wishing to enforce any requirements of this order or any other matter shall note the matter for hearing on the appropriate docket. Pursuant to LCR 40(b) no trial date will be set until all the above has been complied with and the parties have filed a "Trial Setting Notice and Certification of Readiness."

Dated: _____, 20_____.

_____
                          JUDGE

Presented by:

_____

Approved as to form, notice of presentation waived:

_____

16 Appendix B
Domestic Relations Case Scheduling Order

SUPERIOR COURT OF WASHINGTON FOR COUNTY OF COWLITZ

_____,	No. _____
Petitioner,	**CASE SCHEDULING ORDER**
vs.	**DOMESTIC RELATIONS**
_____,	(Use when at least one party has an attorney)
Respondent.	

　　　Based on the motion filed by [ ] Petitioner [ ] Respondent on _____, 20____, or in the alternative based on the Court's discretion, and issues remain that need to be resolved, the Court orders the following:

　　　Check the box if the item is applicable to the case, and then indicate the required information for that item.

[ ]　　　WRITTEN DISCOVERY (CR 33, 34, 36):
　　　All supplemental written discovery (including interrogatories, requests for production, and requests for admissions) shall be submitted by: _____, 20_____

[ ]　　　DISCOVERY RESPONSES (CR 33, 34, 36):
　　　All discovery (including interrogatories, requests for production, and requests for admissions) responses shall be submitted by: _____, 20_____

[ ]　　　WITNESSES:
　　　All primary and expert witness information shall be provided to opposing party by:
　　　_____, 20_____
　　　All possible additional witness information shall be provided to opposing party by:
　　　_____, 20_____

[ ]　　　DEPOSITIONS:
　　　All depositions shall be taken by:_____, 20_____

[ ]   GUARDIAN AD LITEM (GAL) REPORT: The Guardian ad Litem (GAL) Report shall be
       submitted by: _____, 20____. [90 days after appointment
       and at least 60 days before trial provided an extension is not granted by the Court.]

[ ]   STATEMENT OF FAMILY FINANCIAL STATUS:
       The Statement of Family Financial Status, legal memorandums, final witness lists, exhibits and
       index shall be submitted by: _____, 20_____

[ ]   OBJECTIONS: Objections to any exhibits based upon authenticity or admissibility shall be
       submitted by: _____, 20_____

[ ]   JOINT STATEMENT OF PENDING ISSUES:
       The attorneys' joint statement of pending issues shall be submitted by:
       _____, 20_____

[ ]   OTHER:

       _____

       _____

       _____

       _____

       _____

Any party wishing to enforce any requirements of this order or any other matter shall note the matter for
hearing on the appropriate docket. Pursuant to LCR 40(b) no Settlement Conference date will be set until
all the above has been complied with and the parties have filed a "Certificate of Readiness and Trial
Setting Notice."

Dated: _____, 20_____

                                                    _____
                                                    JUDGE / COMMISSIONER
Presented by:

_____

Approved as to form, notice of presentation waived:

_____

16 Appendix C
Domestic Relations Case Scheduling Order
For Cases Without Attorneys

SUPERIOR COURT OF WASHINGTON FOR COWLITZ COUNTY

In re:

_____,

          Petitioner,

   and

_____,

          Respondent.

No.

CASE SCHEDULING ORDER
PRO SE DOMESTIC RELATIONS
(Use when neither party has an attorney)

NOTICE TO ALL PARTIES:

All parties should make themselves familiar with the Cowlitz County Local Rules (CCLCR) as well as the Washington State Court Rules. These can be found at www.courts.wa.gov/court_rules and www.co.cowlitz.wa.us/superiorcourt. Failure to follow Court Rules may result in your case being delayed or your request not being considered.

*If you or the other parent receives public assistance (TANF and/or Medicaid) for the child(ren), you must serve or give a copy of **all** documents you file to the Prosecuting Attorney (Support Enforcement) at 1338 Commerce Avenue, Suite 305, Longview, WA 98632.*

All requirements are based on the date this order was signed by the Court, plus the noted number of days afterwards.

For example: If this order was signed on August 1st and the requirement for the GAL investigation order is to be completed "+ 60 days," then you must complete the order for the Guardian ad Litem (GAL) investigation by October 1 (which is 60 days from August 1ˢᵗ).

CASE SCHEDULE

CASE #:_____

This order was signed by the Court on _____ **20**____.

**All deadlines listed below are based on this date plus (+) the additional days listed below. **

TASK COMPLETE no later than the above date of order plus the number of days below.

File a Response if you are the Respondent	+60 days / _____
Enter order for Guardian ad Litem (GAL) investigation *This is only required if you cannot agree who the children will live with the majority of the time, you are requesting a substantially equal residential time, or if there are serious issues (drugs, violence, etc.). Forms at: www.cowlitzsuperiorcourt.us	+60 days / _____
Provide the following asset and income information to the other party and Support Enforcement (if the parties receive public assistance): 1) Last 2 years of tax returns and W-2 forms 2) Last 6 months of bank statements 3) Last 6 months of wage stubs from all jobs 4) Last 6 months of investment information (401k, retirement, pension, stocks, money market accounts, etc.) 5) Copies of all statements of contested assets/debts you want the Court to award to you or the other party (i.e., house value, vehicle values, etc.).	+90 days / _____
Provide the following debt information to the other party and Support Enforcement (if the parties receive public assistance): 1) Copies of debts (mortgage, credit cards, car payment, etc.) 2) Copies of any child support orders for any of your children.	+90 days / _____
Propose and file a Parenting Plan and Child Support Worksheet See: https://fortress.wa.gov/dshs/csips/ssgen for help with a child support worksheet	+90 days / _____
Send a settlement letter to the other party with your proposed Parenting Plan and Child Support Worksheet. **Make a good faith effort with the other party to settle your issues at this time.**	+120 days / _____
Fill out the Statement of Family Financial Status form. www.cowlitzsuperiorcourt.us	+160 days/ _____
If there are children involved, meet with courthouse facilitator or an attorney to review your final pleadings. (This can be done as soon as there is an agreement in your case.)	**ANY TIME** you have agreed final orders

If you completed the above tasks AND have not settled your case, you may now schedule your case for a Settlement Conference by filling out and filing with the Clerk's Office a Trial Setting and Certificate of Readiness order located at www.cowlitzsuperiorcourt.us. You should mail a conformed copy of that document to the other party and the Prosecuting Attorney - Support Enforcement, if a child receives public assistance, at least two (2) weeks prior to the docket date you requested and then appear on that docket to set your matter for conference/trial. Settlement conferences are required in divorce (dissolution) cases but you may request one in any family law case.

IT IS ORDERED. FAILURE TO COMPLY WITH THE PROVISIONS OF THIS ORDER MAY RESULT IN DISMISSAL OR OTHER SANCTIONS.

Dated: _____

_____
JUDGE / COMMISSIONER

_____	_____
Petitioner's Printed Name	Respondent's Printed Name
_____	_____
Email address if available	Email address if available
_____	_____
Mailing Address	Mailing Address
_____	_____
City, State, Zip	City, State, Zip
_____	_____
Phone Number (if available)	Phone Number (if available)

ADDITIONAL NOTICES:

1) You may file for additional requests (Temporary Orders, Contempt, etc.) at any time.

2) Forms and information are available online at www.court.wa.gov/forms and www.washingtonlawhelp.org and www.co.cowlitz.wa.us/clerk/resources and http://www.cowlitzsuperiorcourt.us

3) If you reach an agreement with the other party and the Prosecuting Attorney, Child Support Office, if it is a public assistance case, regarding all issues, you may settle your case at any time. If you reach an agreement, fill out the documents necessary to finalize your case, have all parties sign and then schedule your case for a final hearing.

4) If you are low-income and want assistance in this case, call CLEAR at 1-888-201-1014 (Monday through Friday, from 9:10 a.m. to 12:25 p.m.) to see if you qualify and whether legal services are available. Information about your legal rights and self-help legal packets can be found at www.washingtonlawhelp.org.

[Effective September 1, 1997; amended effective September 1, 2002; September 1, 2012; amended on an emergency basis effective January 1, 2015; April 1, 2015; amended on a permanent basis effective September 1, 2015.]

6. TRIALS (Rules 38–53.4)

RULE 40. ASSIGNMENT OF CASES

(b) Methods.

(i) *Trial Assignment.* Court Administration shall schedule all trial dates which will be typically be set the "week of". The moving party shall serve and file a request for a Trial Setting/Certificate of Readiness substantially in the form set forth at the end of these civil rules. The parties shall appear on the appropriate trial assignment docket and Court Administration will schedule the trial. Proof of service of the trial setting notice shall be filed with the clerk by the moving party prior to the time of trial setting. If any issue arises which prevents Court Administration from issuing a trial date and/or a Trial Scheduling Order, the parties shall note the matter onto the appropriate Civil or Domestic Relations Motion Docket for resolution by the presiding judge.

(ii) No cause appearing on the assignment docket will be set for trial unless there is a response filed, there has been a Certificate of Readiness filed which is not contested, and at least one of the parties or their attorney either personally appears or contacts the court on or before the commencement of the docket.

(iii) Should any party believe the case is not yet ready for trial, or that the Case Scheduling Order has not been completed, they shall file and serve an objection to the Certificate of Readiness and note the matter for hearing on the appropriate motion calendar. This will remove the matter from the Court Administration's trial assignment docket.

(iv) In the event one or more attorneys to the cause fail to appear for trial setting, after being given proper notice of the application by the movant, and without advising the court, in writing, of non-available trial dates, the trial date shall be assigned, absent good cause shown, and subject to whatever reasonable terms may be applied by the court. If no attorney or party appears for the trial assignment, the assignment request will be stricken. An attorney may have a trial set without personal appearance provided they furnish a letter to the file indicating their intention not to personally appear and suggesting time preferences, restrictions, estimated length or other relevant information.

(v) The initial request for trial setting shall be accompanied by a list of the names and addresses of all persons entitled to notice. All parties have the obligation to inform the Court Administration promptly of any errors or changes in this list.

(vi) *Trial Setting / Certificate of Readiness and Trial Scheduling Order Format.* The approved Certificate of Readiness and Trial Setting Notice is as follows: (See 40 Appendix A–1 and 40 Appendix B–1)

40 APPENDIX A-1
Civil Trial Setting Notice and Certificate of Readiness

SUPERIOR COURT OF WASHINGTON FOR COUNTY OF COWLITZ

_____,

                     Plaintiff,

vs.

_____,

                     Defendant.

NO.

CIVIL CERTIFICATE OF READINESS
AND
TRIAL SETTING NOTICE

** CLERK'S ACTION REQUIRED **

I. HEARING DATE

WEDNESDAY, _____TRIAL SETTING DOCKET at 12:45 p.m. (Courtroom 7).

II. TRIAL SETTING

2.1   Type of Trial: _____ Jury (6) _____ Jury (12) or _____ Non-Jury

                                 Jury fee has been paid in full: ( ) Yes ( ) No

            Duration of Trial: _____ Hours or _____ Days

            Prioritization Factors: [ ] Bumped Previously [ ] Involving Children (Family Law Cases)

                               [ ]Other_____

            Interpreter Services: [ ] Plaintiff [ ] Defendant request in accordance to CCLCR11

                               Language: _____

2.2   Nature of the case:_____

III. CERTIFICATE OF READINESS

3.1   The undersigned certify that:

     a.   This case is at issue.

     b.   No affirmative pleading remains unanswered and no additional claims or defenses will be raised.

     c.   All parties necessary for a full and complete disposition of this case have been joined and have either appeared or an Order of Default was entered against them.

     d.   All discovery, including answers to interrogatories, response to requests for production, requests for admission, subpoenas to third parties (except trial subpoenas), CR 35 medical examinations, all lay and expert depositions have been completed and all motions to compel discovery have been heard and ruled upon.

e. No further dispositive motions, including 12(b) motions, motions to dismiss, motions for more definite statement, and motions for summary judgment shall be made.

f. This case is ready for trial.

g. This case ____does ___ does not involve claims for attorney fees and costs (other than statutory.)

Plaintiff claims attorney fees and costs on the basis of: _____

_____

Defendant claims attorney fees and costs on the basis of: _____

_____

h. Other considerations: _____

_____

The undersigned attest the foregoing is true and correct.

DATED this _____ day of _____, 20_____.

_____
Party or Attorney for
Address:

Phone:
Email:

_____
Party or Attorney for
Address:

Phone:
Email:

_____
Party or Attorney for
Address:

Phone:
Email:

_____
Party or Attorney for
Address:

Phone:
Email:

40 APPENDIX B-1
Domestic Relations Trial Setting Notice and Certificate of Readiness

SUPERIOR COURT OF WASHINGTON FOR COUNTY OF COWLITZ

_____,	NO:
Petitioner,	DOMESTIC RELATIONS **CERTIFICATE OF READINESS** and **TRIAL SETTING NOTICE**
vs.	
_____,	****CLERK'S ACTION REQUIRED****
Respondent.	

I. HEARING DATE

MONDAY, _____ 20____ TRIAL SETTING DOCKET at 8:30 a.m. (Courtroom 7).

II. TRIAL SETTING

2.1   Type of Trial: _____ Mandatory Settlement Conference (MSC)
                                _____ Non-Jury Trial (MSC heard by:_____)
                                _____ Support Modification
                                _____ Other (Describe:_____)

         Duration of Trial: _____ Hours or _____ Days

         Prioritization Factors: [ ] Bumped Previously   [ ] Involving Children
                                  [ ] Other_____

         Interpreter Services: [ ] Petitioner   [ ] Respondent   Request in Accordance to CCLCR11
                                 Language: _____

☐   **CERTIFICATE OF READINESS FOR MANDATORY SETTLEMENT CONFERENCE**
      (Please check if setting for MSC)

3.1   The undersigned certify that the case is ready for Mandatory Settlement Conference (MSC) as follows:

      a.   This case is at issue.

      b.   No affirmative pleading remains unanswered and no additional claims or defenses will be raised.

c. All parties necessary for a full and complete disposition of this case have been joined and have either appeared or an Order of Default was entered against them.

d. ~~All discovery, including answers to interrogatories, response to requests for production, requests for admission, subpoenas to third parties (except trial subpoenas), CR 35 medical examinations, all lay and expert depositions have been completed and all motions to compel discovery have been heard and ruled upon.~~

e. No further dispositive motions, including 12(b) motions, motions to dismiss, motions for more definite statement, and motions for summary judgment shall be made.

f. The parties have exchanged settlement proposals and engaged in settlement negotiations.

g. This case is ready for mandatory settlement conference.

h. The GAL report (if ordered) was filed on _____

i. Other considerations: _____

_____

☐   CERTIFICATE OF READINESS FOR TRIAL   (Please check if setting for trial)

3.2   The undersigned certify that the case is ready for trial as follows:

a. This case is at issue.

b. No affirmative pleading remains unanswered and no additional claims or defenses will be raised.

c. All parties necessary for a full and complete disposition of this case have been joined and have either appeared or an Order of Default was entered against them.

d. All discovery, including answers to interrogatories, response to requests for production, requests for admission, subpoenas to third parties (except trial subpoenas), CR 35 medical examinations, and all lay and expert depositions have been completed, and all motions to compel discovery have been heard and ruled upon.

e. No further dispositive motions, including 12(b) motions, motions to dismiss, motions for more definite statement, and motions for summary judgment shall be made.

f. The GAL report (if ordered) was filed on _____
**

g. The parties have exchanged settlement proposals and engaged in settlement negotiations.

h. This case is ready for trial.

i. This case ___does ___does not involve claims for attorney fees and costs (other than statutory.)

j.   Other considerations: _____

Plaintiff claims attorney fees and costs on the basis of: _____
_____

Defendant claims attorney fees and costs on the basis of: _____
_____

The undersigned attest the foregoing is true and correct.

DATED this _____ day of _____, 20____.

_____   _____
Party (or Attorney for)   Party (or Attorney for)
Address: Address:

Phone: Phone:
Email: Email:

_____   _____
Party (or Attorney for)   Party (or Attorney for)
Address: Address:

Phone: Phone:
Email: Email:

   (vi) *Trial Scheduling Orders.* The Court shall file and send to the parties a Trial Scheduling Order for the case after Court Administration assigns a trial / MSC date. The Trial Scheduling Order shall be substantially in the form approved by the Court, as shown in this rule. (See 40 Appendix "A–2" for Civil forms, 40 Appendix "B–2" for Domestic Relations forms). These Trial Scheduling Orders may be amended only by leave of the Court upon motion. Motions for continuance, even if agreed, shall only be granted upon showing of good cause.

   (vii) The requirements of this rule can be waived or modified upon a written motion.

40 APPENDIX A-2
CIVIL TRIAL SCHEDULING ORDER

SUPERIOR COURT OF WASHINGTON FOR COUNTY OF COWLITZ

_____,

Plaintiff,

vs.

_____,

Defendant.

NO.

TRIAL SCHEDULING ORDER (CIVIL)

CLERK'S ACTION REQUIRED

Based on the records and files herein it is hereby ordered that trial and other matters in this case are scheduled as follows:

Trial Readiness Review: Thursday, _____ 20 _____ at 8:30 a.m.
   (*Your Appearance Is Required. The trial's actual start date will be determined at this time.*)

TRIAL TYPE: [ ] Jury, [ ] Non-Jury

TRIAL DATE: [ ] Week of_____, 20_____.

[ ] Date _____, 20 _____.

Start Time: _____ [ ] a.m. [ ] p.m.   **Length**: _____ (hours / days / weeks)

Location: [ ] Hall of Justice   [ ] Youth Services Center [ ] Other:_____

Interpreter Services Request in accordance to CCLCR 11:   [ ] Plaintiff [ ] Defendant

   Language:_____

CASE PRE-ASSIGNMENT:
This case is pre-assigned to Judge _____ by an order dated _____

PROPOSED STATEMENT OF CASE (for jury trials):   The parties shall prepare a proposed statement of the case which shall be filed with the court by the plaintiff no later than _____ days before trial.

JOINT STATEMENT OF EVIDENCE: A joint statement of evidence shall be prepared by the parties and shall be filed by plaintiff by Wednesday prior to trial.

PERPETUATION DEPOSITIONS:
Perpetuation Depositions shall be completed no later than 14 days prior to trial.

JURY INSTRUCTIONS (pursuant to CR 51):   Plaintiff's and Defendant's proposed jury instructions shall be served and filed no later than 10 days before trial.

PROPOSED FINDINGS OF FACT AND CONCLUSIONS OF LAW: When requested by the judge, all parties shall file and serve proposed findings of fact and proposed conclusions of law 7 days prior to trial date.

TRIAL BRIEFS:
Plaintiff's trial brief shall be filed and served on defense counsel 14 days prior to trial.
Defendant's trial brief shall be filed and served on plaintiff counsel 10 days prior to trial.
Court's courtesy copies shall be provided to Court Administration 10 days prior to trial.

EXCHANGE OF OFFERS:
Each party shall exchange written offers no later than 30 days prior to trial.

Per Cowlitz County Superior Court Local Rule 40(i), all counsel (or the parties if unrepresented by an attorney) shall appear at the at the trial calendar review on the Thursday a week prior to the assigned trial date at 8:30 am. Failure to do so will result in sanctions, which may include striking of the trial date at the discretion of the court. CourtCall may be used to attend this hearing.

It is your responsibility to confirm your trial / hearing start date by calling Court Administration at (360) 577-3085.

In all jury trials, witnesses shall be prohibited from the Second Floor Lobby of the Hall of Justice until after the jury has been selected and seated. Parties and their counsel shall avoid the second floor lobby until a jury has been selected and seated.

The following-named attorneys and/or parties have been sent a copy of this notice:

_____   _____
_____   _____
_____   _____
_____   _____

_____   _____
_____   _____
_____   _____
_____   _____

Dated: _____, 20____   _____

                                         _____
                                         JUDGE / COMMISSIONER

40 APPENDIX B-2
Domestic Relations Trial Scheduling Order

SUPERIOR COURT OF WASHINGTON FOR COUNTY OF COWLITZ

_____, Petitioner, vs. _____, Respondent.	NO. TRIAL SCHEDULING ORDER (DOMESTIC RELATIONS) ** CLERK'S ACTION REQUIRED **

Trial Readiness Review: Thursday, _____ 20_____ at 8:30 a.m.
    (_Your Appearance Is Required. The trial's actual start date will be determined at this time._)

TRIAL TYPE: [ ] Jury,   [ ] Non-Jury

TRIAL DATE: [ ] Week of_____, 20_____.

                [ ] Date _____, 20_____.

Start Time: _____ [ ] a.m. [ ] p.m.   **Length**: _____ (hours / days / weeks)

Location: [ ] Hall of Justice   [ ] Youth Services Center   [ ] Other: _____

Interpreter Services Request in accordance to CCLCR 11:   [ ] Plaintiff   [ ] Defendant

      Language: _____

Type of case: [ ] **Mandatory Settlement Conference (MSC)**
                 [ ] **Non-Jury Trial**
                 [ ] Involving Parenting Plan/Custody issues   [ ] Not involving Parenting Plan/Custody issues
                 [ ] **Support Modifications on Declarations**

CASE PRE-ASSIGNMENT:
This case is pre-assigned to Judge _____ by an order dated _____

PERPETUATION DEPOSITIONS:
Perpetuation Depositions shall be completed no later than 14 days prior to trial.

TRIAL BRIEFS:

Petitioner's trial brief shall be filed and served on respondent's counsel 14 days prior to trial.
Respondent's trial brief shall be filed and served on petitioner's counsel 10 days prior to trial.
Court's courtesy copies shall be provided to Court Administration 10 days prior to trial.

EXCHANGE OF OFFERS:
Each party shall exchange written offers to each opposing side no later than 30 days prior to trial.

Per Cowlitz County Superior Court Local Rule 40(i), all counsel (or the parties if unrepresented by an attorney) shall appear at the at the trial calendar review on the Thursday a week prior to the assigned trial date at 8:30 am. (This requirement does not apply to participants in Mandatory Settlement Conferences and Support Modifications on Declarations.) Failure to do so will result in sanctions, which may include striking of the trial date at the discretion of the court. CourtCall may be used to attend this hearing.

It is your responsibility to confirm your trial / hearing start date by calling Court Administration at (360) 577-3085.

The following-named attorneys and/or parties have been sent a copy of this order:

_____   _____
_____   _____
_____   _____
_____   _____

_____   _____
_____   _____
_____   _____

Dated: _____, 20_____.

_____
JUDGE / COMMISSIONER

(g) Pre–Assignment of Cases.

(i) *By the Court.* The Judges may select those cases deemed appropriate for pre-assignment due to length of trial or complexity of issues.

(ii) *By Motion.* The parties by stipulation may request that a case be preassigned, or any party may place a motion for pre-assignment upon the appropriate motion calendar.

(iii) *Discretionary Act.* Pre-assignment of cases is a discretionary act. Affidavits of prejudice against the assigned judge which are not based on actual cause will be deemed waived unless filed before pre-assignment.

(iv) *All Matters to be Heard by Pre-assigned Judge.* After selection of the trial judge in the pre-assigned case, the trial, all motions, conferences and other matters and proceedings, except settlement conferences, should be heard before that Judge, if available.

(h) Notice to Court of Calendar and Trial Changes. Whenever a cause which has been set for trial is settled or will not be tried for any reason, or if a jury is subsequently waived the parties shall file a notice with the Clerk's Office. The parties shall also give either telephonic notice to Court Administration and all other parties no later than the next business day, with written confirmation, OR electronic notice to Court Administration and all other parties no later than the next business day.

(i) If it becomes apparent that the time allocated for a trial will not be adequate to complete the trial, the parties shall promptly notify the Court Administration of that fact and of the time necessary to complete the trial.

(ii) The Court may assess actual costs or other sanctions for a violation of this rule.

(i) Trial Readiness Review. In all cases set for trial, all parties, or their attorneys shall appear on the readiness review docket at 8:30 on the Thursday morning the week prior to trial. (This requirement does not apply for Mandatory Settlement Conferences or Child Support Modifications on Declarations.) Parties and/or counsel may appear via CourtCall (www.courtcall.com). Final instructions from the Court, including the specific start date and time of the trial will be given by the Court at the combined readiness review. Failure to appear may result in the striking of the assigned trial date and/or other sanctions as deemed appropriate by the Court.

(j) Call Calendar.

(i) The causes appearing on a motion docket shall be called and the movant, if no one appears in opposition, may take the order moved for if approved by the court. If no one appears for a motion or petition, it shall be deemed waived and stricken.

(ii) A party or his/her attorney may appear on any civil or domestic relations motion docket via CourtCall® (go to www.courtcall.com), except a party who has been properly served with an order to show cause or other order requiring his/her personal appearance. The responding party in that circumstance must appear in person unless otherwise ordered by the court.

[Effective September 1, 1997; amended effective September 1, 2002; September 1, 2005; September 1, 2006; September 1, 2012; amended on an emergency basis effective January 1, 2015; April 1, 2015; amended on a permanent basis effective September 1, 2015.]

RULE 45. SUBPOENA

(a) For Attendance of Witnesses. Subpoenas issued by pro se litigants must be approved by a superior court judge. The judge may choose to require an ex parte hearing to determine if the witness has legally relevant information. This Rule shall be liberally construed. The purpose of this Rule is to prevent the abuse of the subpoena process.

(g) When Excused. A witness subpoenaed to attend in any case, criminal or civil, is dismissed and excused from further attendance as soon as he has given his testimony in chief for the party in whose instance he was called and has been cross-examined thereon, unless either party makes request in open court that the witness remain in attendance. Witness fees will not be allowed any witness after the day on which his testimony is given except when the witness has in open court been required to remain in further attendance; and, when so required, the clerk shall make a minute entry to that effect, and the party making the request that the witness remain in attendance shall be solely responsible for any additional witness fees incurred by that witness as a result of that further attendance.

[Effective September 1, 1997; amended effective September 1, 2003.]

RULE 47. JURORS

(e) Challenge.

(9) *Peremptory Challenges.* All peremptory challenges allowed by law shall be exercised in the following manner:

The Clerk shall keep a list of jurors passed for cause and when it is complete will provide the list to the attorneys for the parties who will, in turn, exercise challenges by striking the name of each challenged juror without oral comment. After all challenges have been exhausted or waived, the judge will excuse those jurors who have been challenged and will seat the jury as finally selected.

[Amended effective September 1, 1995; September 1, 1997; September 1, 2012; September 1, 2015.]

7. JUDGMENT (Rules 54–63)

RULE 56. SUMMARY JUDGMENT

(c) Motion and Proceedings.

(3) Summary judgments shall be heard during the Court's regularly scheduled motion calendar/docket; PROVIDED, if the parties or their attorneys antici-

pate that the matter may exceed 30 minutes, the matter must be noted on the appropriate trial assignment docket for a special set hearing time.

(4) Cross-motions for summary judgment will be treated as a new motion for summary judgment. Unless otherwise agreed to by the parties, the timeline for the cross motion shall be in accordance with CR 56 and the first filed motion for summary judgment will proceed as scheduled except as otherwise ordered by the Court.

(5) The attorney for the moving party (whether original motion or cross–motion) shall notify the Clerk of the Court and Court Administration no later than three (3) court days preceding the date set for hearing and advise whether the motion will in fact be argued. If such notification is not timely made, the motion will be stricken for resetting.

[Amended effective September 1, 1995; September 1, 2002; September 1, 2012; September 1, 2015.]

RULE 59. NEW TRIAL, RECONSIDERATION, AND AMENDMENT OF JUDGMENTS

(e) Hearing on Motion.

(3) *Nature of Hearing.*

(A) In Cowlitz County a motion for reconsideration or for a new trial shall be submitted on briefs and affidavits only, without oral argument, unless the trial judge, on written application from the attorney or on his/her own motion, allows oral argument. Copies of such motion, which must be made within the time limits set forth in CR 59, shall be delivered to the court administration and delivered to the opposing party and/or their attorney at the time of filing. Any response thereto shall be filed with the clerk and thereafter a copy delivered to opposing party and/or their attorney and the court administration within ten (10) days after the filing of the motion for reconsideration. The trial judge shall either rule and advise the attorneys of the ruling or advise the attorneys of desired further proceedings pursuant to CR 59.

[Effective September 1, 1997; amended effective September 1, 2003; September 1, 2012.]

10. SUPERIOR COURTS AND CLERKS (Rules 77–80)

RULE 77. SUPERIOR COURT AND JUDICIAL OFFICERS

(d) Superior Court Always Open.

(1) *Trial Hours.* Sessions of trial departments, except as otherwise provided for in these Rules, shall be from 8:45 a.m. until 12 noon and from 1:00 p.m. until 4:30 p.m., Monday through Friday, unless otherwise ordered by the trial judge. Special sessions of any court may be held on Saturday, or at earlier or later times, at the discretion of the trial judge, to hear any and all matters that such judge sets for hearing before him/her and at such hours upon said day as the judge shall fix.

(f) Sessions.

(1) *Superior Court Sessions.* There shall be one continuous session of court from January 1 until December 31 of each year.

(2) *Jury Terms.* Jury trials, both civil and criminal, shall be set throughout the year.

(k) Motion Day—Local Rules.

(1) *Schedules.* A copy of court dockets and hearing days is posted in the clerk's office, and a copy may be requested from superior court administration. Provided, however, in the event a legal holiday prevents the conduct of a docket or hearing day, the same may, on the order of the presiding judge, be rescheduled and notice thereof posted prominently in the clerk's office.

(2) *Hearing Assignment.* With the court's approval, any matter set on a motion docket may be assigned a specific date and time for hearing.

(3) *Time Limitations.* Attorneys will be allowed not more than five (5) minutes each for argument on a motion, unless further time is granted by special order of the court.

(4) *Presentation of Papers.* At the commencement of hearing on each probate final report, the lawyer for the personal representative shall present a proposed order approving final report and decree of distribution. For good cause, the court may extend the time for presentation of such findings, conclusions, orders and decrees.

(5) *Noted Cases.* All materials to be considered on a motion docket, except domestic relations, must be filed in the clerk's office not later than 10:00 a.m. at least two (2) court days preceding the docket in question. A copy of any pleading filed less than five (5) working days prior to a scheduled hearing must be provided to the assigned judge, or if no judge is yet assigned, to the Court Administration with a note in the upper right hand corner of the first page indicating the date, time and type of hearing/calendar docket. If no copy is provided, those pleadings may not be considered, at the discretion of the judge.

[Amended effective September 1, 1993; September 1, 1995; September 1, 1996; September 1, 2000; September 1, 2002; September 1, 2003; September 1, 2005; September 1, 2012; September 1, 2015.]

11. GENERAL PROVISIONS (Rules 81–86)

RULE 83. LOCAL RULES OF SUPERIOR COURT

(c) Suspension. The court may modify or suspend any of these Rules, in any given case, upon good cause being shown therefore or upon the court's own motion.

[Effective September 1, 1997.]

12. FAMILY LAW (Rules 87–95)

RULE 88. CONTESTED HEARINGS

The following rules shall apply to all contested hearings in these domestic relations matters: motions for temporary orders, hearings to determine adequate cause, motions for contempt, and hearings on declarations for modification of child support.

(a) Discretion of the Court. The above matters will be heard on affidavits submitted in accordance with this Rule and arguments only, unless:

(1) In the judgment and discretion of the Court, the facts reveal unusual circumstances which, in the furtherance of justice, require oral testimony; or, consideration of non-complying pleadings.

(b) Filing and Service of Motions, Responses, Replies, and Affidavits. Such matters shall not be heard unless affidavits are served and filed as required by this Rule and CR 6(a).

(1) The moving party shall serve and file supporting affidavit(s) together with the petition, motion, or order to show cause.

(2) Domestic relations motions shall be filed and served upon all parties not later than nine (9) court days before the time specified for the hearing. Responses shall be filed and served on all parties not later than 3:00 p.m., four (4) court days before the time specified for the hearing. Replies shall be filed and served on all parties not later than 3:00 p.m., two (2) court days before the hearing.

(3) Pleadings filed later than 3:00 p.m. two (2) court days before the hearing may be considered if good cause for the delay appears within those pleadings. A copy of any pleading filed after 3:00 p.m. three (3) court days prior to the hearing must be given to the assigned judge. The clerk's office will not be responsible for getting late pleadings in the court file prior to hearing. The Court will not consider pleadings that are filed after 3:00 p.m. two (2) court days prior to hearing deadline if no copy is provided to the assigned judge. All bench copies must have in the upper right hand on the first page a notation of date, time and type of hearing/calendar docket.

Practical Example of LCR 88 (b)

Below is an example of the practical application of CCLCR 88 (b):

Monday, May 1—Moving party serves and files motion.

Monday, May 8—Responding party serves and files response.

Wednesday, May 10—Moving party serves and files reply.

Monday, May 15—Hearing date.

(c) Length and Format of Affidavits. The following limits shall apply, unless waived by the court upon written motion, which may be heard on the ex parte docket with reasonable prior notice to the opposing party or their attorney.

(1) Affidavits must be typed, double-spaced and on pleading paper. Affidavits not in this format may not be considered.

(2) Initial affidavits will be limited to six (6) pages (exclusive of exhibits) from the parties and four (4) pages from other witnesses. Each party is limited to a total of four (4) affidavits in support of or in response to a motion. The moving party may also file and serve affidavits of no more than four (4) pages in total in rebuttal.

(d) Preparation and Presentation of Orders. All orders will be prepared by the moving party. The Court will set a presentation date at the time of the hearing on the motion. The proposed order shall be filed with the Court and provided to the other party or his/her attorney not less than five (5) court days prior to the presentation date. Objections, shall be filed with the Court by the objecting party along with proposed orders not less than two (2) court days prior to the presentation date.

[Adopted effective September 1, 2005. Amended on an emergency basis, effective March 1, 2006; amended on a permanent basis, effective September 1, 2006; September 1, 2007; September 1, 2012; amended on an emergency basis, effective June 6, 2013; amended on a permanent basis, effective September 2, 2013; September 2, 2014; September 1, 2015.]

RULE 91. MANDATORY SETTLEMENT CONFERENCES IN DOMESTIC RELATIONS ACTIONS

(a) Policy Statement. It is the finding of the court that settlement conferences are a valuable tool to promote the amicable resolution of disputes and promote the efficient use of court resources. Settlement conference time is also a valuable resource. It is expected that all parties who participate in settlement conferences as mandated by the court be prepared to participate when scheduled and not squander this valuable resource.

(b) Settlement Conferences Required. A settlement conference is mandatory in all contested actions in which a dissolution/declaration of invalidity/legal separation of marriage or domestic partnership is sought. A settlement conference may be requested in any family law matter with the agreement of all parties. No trial date will be set unless the required settlement conference has occurred or has been waived by a judge for good cause.

Parties may comply with this rule by participating in a mediation or settlement conference using a court approved mediation service, and filing a certificate from that service with the court. Should parties choose to go through private mediation to comply with this rule, they shall be responsible for all costs of said mediation. Approved mediators shall be listed on the Court's website, and are available from the Court Administration, the Clerk and the court facilitator's office.

(c) Request for Settlement Conference. A request to schedule a settlement conference may not be made until after an answer has been filed. The request for settlement conference shall be signed and filed with the clerk.

(1) *Form.* The request shall be substantially in the form approved by the court and available on the court's website, from the county clerk or court facilitator, or from superior court administration.

(d) Readiness Statement. Each party shall complete the Certificate of Readiness Statement and Mandatory Settlement Conference / Trial Setting Notice which shall be signed and filed with the clerk. This document will include a statement, verified by each party or his/her attorney, that negotiations have been attempted between the parties.

(1) *Form.* The request shall be substantially in the form approved by the court and available on the court's website, from the county clerk or court facilitator, or from superior court administration.

(e) Settlement Conference Affidavit. Each party must complete a statement of family financial status. If the parenting plan or child support is at issue, each party will provide a proposed parenting plan and child support worksheets. Appraisals, bluebook printouts, or other documents supporting contested issues should be included with the affidavit. It is helpful if the parties can agree on a format for any proposed balance sheets. The affidavit and supporting documents shall not be filed with the superior court clerk. The affidavit and supporting documents shall be served on the opposing attorney or party if not represented by an attorney, and an additional copy will be provided to the Superior Court Administration for the use of the presiding judicial officer conducting the settlement conference, no later than 4:00 p.m. five (5) court days prior to the scheduled conference.

(1) If the state has filed a Notice of Appearance in a domestic relations case in which child support is involved and the only states interest is medical assistance provided for the children of the parties and preservation of state's collections of child support arrears owed to it, the state may not appear at the mandatory settlement conference if the following language is included in the Mandatory Settlement Conference Affidavit:

Petitioner/Respondent agree to include in the Order of Child Support preservation of the state's right to collect arrears owed to it and the statutorily mandated language regarding medical insurance coverage contained in Paragraph 3.18 and uninsured medical expenses in Paragraph 3.19 as requested by the state in this matter and (check the applicable box):

___ 1. There is insufficient evidence at this time regarding the availability / accessibility of medical insurance coverage and cost of medical insurance coverage for the children at this time and medical insurance coverage may be enforced through the Division of Child Support as provided in RCW 26.18.170.

___ 2. Petitioner/Respondent has available and accessible health insurance coverage for the child/ren at a premium cost of $ ___ (the portion of the premium cost for the children's coverage only). He/she shall provide such insurance coverage on behalf of the children as required by law and stated in Paragraph 3.18.1(B) Findings and (C) Parents Obligations. The insurance premium and the other party's contribution shall be included in the child support calculation.

The state shall be served with the final proposed Order of Child Support and Child Support Worksheets for review and approval within the statutory time limits required by RCW 26.23.130 for the state's review prior to entry of final orders. If the medical or other provisions do not comply with the state's requests for medical insurance coverage language and arrears preservation, these issues shall remain contested and shall be set for hearing.

(2) *Form.* The request shall be substantially in the form approved by the court and available on the court's website, from the County Clerk or court facilitator, or from Superior Court Administration.

(f) Sanctions. Failure to file the documents pursuant to sections (d) and (e) above may result in sanctions.

Failure to appear at the conference shall subject a party and/or attorney to additional sanctions upon motion of the opposing party. A party in compliance with this rule may seek fees and costs against a noncompliant party by way of motion to the court and such terms shall be at the discretion of the court.

(g) Conference Procedure. Participation in the settlement conference shall be mandatory. All parties, and their attorneys if represented, shall appear at the settlement conference.

(h) Completion of Conference. If the settlement conference results in a partial or full settlement of the case, a record of the settlement shall be made, either by a written CR 2A settlement agreement, signed by both parties and their attorneys, or by placing the agreement on the record in open court. If the settlement conference is not successful, the supervising presiding judicial officer shall file a notice of completion of the conference with the clerk. A private mediator may also file the notice of completion of conference if private mediation is used to comply with this rule.

Form. The completion notice and/or the CR2A agreement cover page shall be substantially in the form approved by the court and available on the court's website, from the county clerk or court facilitator, or from superior court administration.

(i) Notice of Settlement or Change. Whenever a cause has been set for mandatory settlement conference and thereafter is settled or will not proceed for any reason, notice (available from the superior court administration) shall immediately be given to the court and the clerk by the close of the next business day. In the event of a violation of this Rule, the court may, in its discretion, assess actual costs incurred, as a result of the violation, plus such other sanction as appears appropriate against the offending attorney and/or party.

[Adopted effective September 1, 2005; amended effective September 1, 2007; repealed on an emergency basis effective May 1, 2009; repealed on a permanent basis effective September 1, 2009; adopted on an emergency basis, effective January 19, 2010; amended on a permanent basis effective September 1, 2010; September 1, 2012; September 1, 2015.]

RULE 92.   FINALIZING FAMILY LAW CASES

(a) Review of Final Pleadings. All final decrees, final orders and accompanying findings of fact, conclusions of law, parenting plans, orders of child support, and child support worksheets for family law cases involving children shall be reviewed for form and completeness prior to presentation to a judicial officer by an attorney of record in the case, an attorney who approved the pleadings as to form and completeness, or the courthouse facilitator.

(Note: If the parties are proposing a Substantially Equal Residential Time plan, there must be a Guardian ad Litem (GAL) report filed per LCR 98.)

(b) Pro Se Parties.

(1) In a dissolution or non-parental custody action where the moving party is proceeding without representation by an attorney, the party's proposed final pleadings shall be delivered to the Clerk of the Court at least five (5) days prior to the scheduled hearing date. The courthouse facilitator shall review all those pleadings and, if they appear appropriate, shall sign and file a "Certificate of Courthouse Facilitator" to that effect. The Clerk of the Court shall not accept for filing any such proposed final document which appears to be incomplete; with specific reference to the child support computation worksheet, all sections and parts thereof must be fully completed or marked "not applicable" where such is the case. The Court will not conduct a final hearing in the matter unless the "Certificate of Courthouse Facilitator" is filed.

(c) Presentation of Papers. At the commencement of a hearing upon a default or uncontested dissolution, invalidity, legal separation, paternity, or non-parental custody matter, the petitioner or petitioner's attorney shall present to the court proposed findings of fact, conclusions of law, and decree.

(d) Filing Agreements and Contracts. All property settlement agreements or separation contracts reduced to writing and signed shall be filed as a part of the record of said cause.

(e) Finalization of Dissolutions by Affidavit. Parties who come to a final agreement in their dissolution case may present final statutory testimony by declaration without further court appearance, unless a judge otherwise orders in-person testimony. The declaration must be in a form approved by the Court. The declaration shall accompany the final papers and shall be filed with the Clerk to be handled by the ex parte judge. If neither party is represented by an attorney, then a Certificate of Courthouse Facilitator, as set forth in 92(b)(1) above, must also accompany the final papers before consideration can be made by the ex parte judge. There shall be an ex parte fee for finalization of dissolution matters by way of declaration. The fee schedule is available from the County Clerk or online at www. co.cowlitz.wa.us/clerk.

(f) Form. The declaration and certification of Final Testimony by Affidavit shall be substantially in the form approved by the Court and available on the Court's website, from the County Clerk or court facilitator, or from Superior Court Administration.

SUPERIOR COURT OF WASHINGTON FOR COWLITZ COUNTY

In re Marriage of: No. *
&, Petitioner,
and   **FINAL TESTIMONY BY**
&, Respondent. **AFFIDAVIT PER CCLR 92(e)**

I, _____, am the [ ] Petitioner [ ] Respondent in this matter and make this declaration in support of the entry of final orders in this case.

1. At least one of us was a legal resident of the State of Washington at the time the petition was filed.

2. More than ninety (90) days have passed since the petition was filed, And the responding party received his / her copy of the petition.

3. We were married on _____ in _____.

4. We separated from each other on _____.

5. Our Marriage is irretrievably broken, and we are requesting the Court to enter a Decree of Dissolution.

6. We have agreed to a division of our property and our debts that is both fair and equitable.

[ ] The Separation Contract dated _____ is approved as being fair at the time of execution.

7. We have [ ] no children OR [ ] the following children born as issue of the marriage who are dependent upon us for support.

Name _____ Age _____

Name _____ Age _____

Name _____ Age _____

Name _____ Age _____

The wife is not currently pregnant.

8. We have agreed to the entry of the attached Findings and Conclusions of Law, the Decree of Dissolution, and (if applicable) a Parenting Plan, Child Support Order and Child Support Worksheet.

9. Pick One:

[ ] The proposed agreed child support order does not deviate from the standard table amount under the support guidelines

–OR–

[ ] The proposed agreed child support order deviates from the standard table amount under the support guidelines for the following reasons (agreement of the parties is not sufficient):

_____

_____

10. The child(ren) [ ] do [ ] do not receive public assistance benefits in the form of a TANF cash grant and/or medical assistance (Medicaid).

[ ] The child(ren) receive public assistance as checked above and the State of Washington, through the Cowlitz County Prosecuting Attorney, Child Support Division located at 1338 Commerce Ave. Suite 305, Longview WA 98632, has been timely served as required by RCW 26.23.130 (20 days prior to entry of the final orders) with the proposed Order of Child Support and Child Support Worksheets and has reviewed and signed the Order of Child Support and Worksheets.

11. We are requesting the Court to enter the following name changes, which are not made to defraud creditors:

Petitioner's New Name:

Respondent's New Name:

I declare under penalty of perjury under the laws of the State of Washington that the foregoing is true and correct to the best of my knowledge.

Signed at _____, Washington.

DATED:

[ ] Petitioner [ ]Respondent

[Original CCLCR 94.08 was adopted effective September 1, 2003. Renumbered as CCLCR 92 and amended effective September 1, 2005; amended on an emergency basis effective May 1, 2009; amended on a permanent basis effective September 1, 2009; September 1, 2010; September 1, 2012; September 2, 2014; amended on an emergency basis effective November 10, 2014; November 24, 2014; February 24, 2015.]

RULE 95. WAIVER OF AGE TO MARRY

Applications for waiver of minimum age to marry, pursuant to RCW 26.04.010, shall be made through the superior court clerk's office. Upon application, the Court shall appoint a Guardian ad Litem to investigate and make a recommendation to the Court on the application. Applicants shall provide such information and supporting documentation as may be prescribed by the Guardian ad Litem. Before court hearing, applicants must give evidence of completion of a program of premarital counseling by a counselor, a counseling agency, or rabbi, priest or minister, together with such counselor's recommendation, and shall be interviewed by the Guardian ad Litem.

[Adopted effective September 1, 2005. Amended effective September 2, 2014.]

RULE 97. FINANCIAL PROVISIONS

(a) When Financial Information is Required.

(1) Absent exigent circumstances, each party shall complete, sign, file, and serve on all parties a financial declaration for any motion, trial, or settlement conference that concerns the following issues:

(A) Payment of a child's expenses, such as tuition, costs of extracurricular activities, medical expenses, or college;

(B) Child support or spousal maintenance; or

(C) Any other financial matter, including payment of debt, attorney and expert fees, or the costs of an investigation or evaluation.

(2) A party may use a previously-prepared financial declaration if all information in that declaration remains accurate.

(3) Financial declarations need not be provided when presenting an order by agreement or default.

(b) Supporting Documents to be filed with the Financial Declaration. Parties who file a financial declaration shall also file the following supporting documents, to be filed under seal as required by GR 22;

(1) Pay stubs for the past six months (or the most recent pay stub if it includes year-to-date information for the prior six months). If a party does not receive pay stubs, other documents shall be provided that show all income received from whatever source, and the deductions from earned income for these periods;

(2) Complete personal tax returns for the prior two years, including all Schedules and all W–2s;

(3) If either party owns an interest of 5% or more in a corporation, partnership or other entity that generates its own tax return, the complete tax return

for each such corporation, partnership or other entity for the prior two years;

(4) Any other document containing Personal Financial Information and/or Personal Identifiers (such as social security number or bank account numbers) shall be filed under seal.

(c) If a party asks the Court to order or change child support or order payment of other expenses for a child, each party shall also file completed Washington State Child Support Worksheets.

[Adopted effective September 1, 2012; amended effective September 1, 2015.]

RULE 98. GUARDIAN AD LITEMS

(a) **Appointment of Guardian ad Litem.** When the appointment of a Guardian ad Litem is required, the appointee shall be from the appropriate Court-approved Guardian ad Litem registry maintained for Titles 11 or 26, respectively.

(1) *Substantially Equal Residential Time:* When a Parenting Plan sets a residential schedule of substantially equal time, then a Guardian ad Litem (GAL) shall be appointed to make a recommendation to the Court regarding the adoption of the schedule. The recommendation of the Guardian ad Litem shall be filed with the Court, and a copy to each party, prior to the Court's finalization of the schedule. This rule applies whether or not the parties agree to the residential schedule.

(b) **Fees.** Fees paid Guardians ad Litem shall be at the rate set by Superior Court administrative policy. If additional fees are requested, a written motion for same, accompanied by supporting affidavit(s) must be filed.

(c) **Guardian ad Litem grievance procedures.** These rules apply to Guardians ad Litem and Court Appointed Special Advocates appointed on any case heard by the Court under Titles 11 or 26 of the Revised Code of Washington.

(d) **Guardian ad Litem advisory committee.** The Court's Guardian ad Litem Advisory Committee, hereinafter referred to as the "Committee," will administer complaints about Guardians ad Litem in accordance with Local Court Rule GAL 8.

(e) **Policies and procedures.** Such policies and procedures will be implemented as necessary to carry out this rule.

[Adopted effective September 2, 2014; amended on an emergency basis effective November 10, 2014; February 10, 2015; amended on a permanent basis effective September 1, 2015.]

CRIMINAL RULES (CCLCrR)

3. RIGHTS OF DEFENDANTS

RULE 3.1. RIGHT TO AND ASSIGNMENT OF ATTORNEY

(g) **Appearance of Attorney.** Attorneys representing defendants in criminal cases as a retained attorney must serve prompt written notice of their appearance upon the prosecuting attorney and file the same with the clerk of the court.

[Effective September 1, 1997; amended effective September 1, 2005; September 1, 2012; September 1, 2015.]

4. PROCEDURES PRIOR TO TRIAL

RULE 4.2. PLEAS

(i) **Plea by Court Commissioner.** Pursuant to RCW 2.24.040(15) a duly appointed Superior Court Commissioner may accept a guilty plea in felony matters. After the guilty plea is accepted, the matter shall be referred to a judge for disposition.

[Adopted on an emergency basis effective April 1, 2008; adopted on a permanent basis effective September 1, 2008.]

RULE 4.11. MISCELLANEOUS

(a) **Criminal Trial Calendar Review.** A review shall be held at 8:30 a.m. the Thursday before the week of trial to determine if the case is ready to proceed to trial. Counsel for all parties shall appear and advise the Court of readiness for trial, the expected length of trial, and any restrictions as to particular days of the week or affidavits under RCW 4.12.050.

[Adopted effective September 1, 2012; amended effective September 1, 2015.]

LOCAL MANDATORY ARBITRATION RULES (LMAR)

LMAR 1.1. APPLICATION OF RULES— PURPOSE AND DEFINITIONS

The purpose of mandatory arbitration of civil actions under RCW 7.06 as implemented by the Superior Court Mandatory Arbitration Rules (MAR) is to provide a simplified and economical procedure for obtaining the prompt and equitable resolution of disputes involving claims of $50,000 or less. Claims in which the sole relief sought is the establishment, modification, or termination of maintenance or child support payments shall not be subject to mandatory arbitration. The Mandatory Arbitration Rules as supplemented by these local rules are not designed to address every question which may arise during the arbitration process, and the rules give considerable discretion to the arbitrator. The arbitrator should not hesitate to be informal and expeditious, consistent with the purpose of the statue [1] and rules.

[Adopted effective September 1, 2011.]

[1] So in original, probably should be "statute".

LMAR 1.2. MATTERS SUBJECT TO ARBITRATION

By implementation of these rules the Superior Court of Washington for Cowlitz County authorizes mandatory arbitration under RCW 7.06.010, and approves such arbitrations in civil actions in which no party asserts a claim in excess of $50,000, exclusive of interest and costs under RCW 7.06.020 as amended, effective September 1, 2011.

[Adopted effective September 1, 2011.]

LMAR 2.1. TRANSFER TO ARBITRATION

(a) **Statement of Arbitrability.** In every civil case after a response has been filed and at any time thereafter that a case meets Mandatory Arbitration guidelines, the parties shall, upon the form approved by the court, (forms available on the court's website or from the County Clerk) request the case be transferred to arbitration. The party requesting arbitration shall serve a statement of arbitrability, substantially in the form attached to these local rules on the opposing party. The Court may transfer a case to arbitration on its own motion if it determines a case meets the MAR requirements.

The request for transfer to MAR/Statement of Arbitrability shall be promptly provided to the Superior Court Administration. The approved Request to Transfer to MAR and Statement of Arbitrability is listed below in Appendix A.

(b) **Response to Statement of Arbitrability.** Any party disagreeing with the statement of arbitrability shall file and serve a response stating his or her objections within ten (10) days of the service of the statement of arbitrability.

A copy of the statement and response shall be furnished or served upon the Court Administration by the responding party at the time of filing. In the absence of such a response, the statement of arbitrability shall be deemed correct and a non-responding party shall be deemed to have stipulated to arbitration if the statement of arbitrability provides that the case is subject to arbitration. Otherwise, the case will not be subject to arbitration except by stipulation of the parties, or court order.

A $220 fee will be charged for all cases assigned to arbitration. Business checks or money orders should be made payable to the Clerk's Office. No arbitrator will be assigned until the fee is paid in full.

(c) **Failure to File Amendments.** A party failing to serve and file an original response to a statement of arbitrability within the time prescribed may do so later only upon leave of court. A party may amend the statement of arbitrability or response thereto at any time prior to assignment of an arbitrator and thereafter only by leave of court for good cause shown.

[Adopted effective September 1, 2011. Amended effective September 1, 2012; amended on an emergency basis, effective January 1, 2013; April 1, 2013; June 6, 2013; amended on a permanent basis, effective September 2, 2013.]

LMAR 2.3. ASSIGNMENT TO ARBITRATOR

(a) **Generally, Stipulations.** When a case is set for arbitration, a list of five proposed arbitrators will be furnished to the parties. A master list of arbitrators will be made available on request. The parties are encouraged to stipulate to an arbitrator using a form prescribed by the court. In the absence of a stipulation, the arbitrator will be chosen from among the five proposed arbitrators in the manner defined by this rule.

(b) **Response by Parties.** Each party may, within fourteen (14) days after a list of proposed arbitrators has been furnished to the parties, nominate one (1) or two (2) arbitrators and strike two (2) arbitrators from the list. If both parties respond, an arbitrator nominated by both parties will be appointed. If no arbitrator has been nominated by both parties, a judge will appoint an arbitrator from among those not stricken by either party.

(c) **Response by Only One Party.** If only one party responds within fourteen (14) days, a judge will appoint an arbitrator nominated by that party.

(d) **No Response.** If neither party responds within fourteen (14) days, a judge will appoint one of the five proposed arbitrators.

(e) **Additional Arbitrators for Additional Parties.** If there are more than two (2) adverse parties, all represented by different attorneys, two (2) additional proposed arbitrators shall be added to the list for each additional party so represented with the above principles of selection to be applied.

[Adopted effective September 1, 2011; amended effective September 1, 2012.]

LMAR 3.1. QUALIFICATIONS

(a) Minimum Qualifications. An arbitrator must be a member of the Washington State Bar Association who has been admitted to the Bar for a minimum of five (5) years, or who is a retired Washington State Judge or Commissioner and will conform to the Superior Court Policy and Procedures for MARs. By stipulation the parties to a case may agree to an arbitrator not on the Cowlitz County arbitration panel if the arbitrator so chosen is a duly qualified member of an arbitration panel established under Local Mandatory Arbitration Rules of another county in the state of Washington. The parties may stipulate to a non-lawyer arbitrator upon approval of a judge.

(b) Application. A person desiring to serve as an arbitrator shall complete an application on a form prescribed by the court. The form shall contain a list of areas of law subject to arbitration whereby the applicant marks the area he/she is willing to be considered as an arbitrator. A copy of said application will be available upon request by any party considering the person as an arbitrator and will be mailed to a requesting party at the party's own expense. The oath of office on the form prescribed by the court must be completed and filed prior to an appointed applicant being placed on the arbitration panel.

(c) Refusal, Disqualification. The appointment of an arbitrator is subject to the right of that person to refuse to serve. An arbitrator must notify the court administration immediately if refusing to serve or if any cause exists for the arbitrator's disqualification from the case upon any of the grounds of interest, relationship, bias or prejudice set forth in CJC Cannon (3) governing the disqualification of judges.

[Adopted effective September 1, 2011; amended effective September 1, 2012; September 1, 2015.]

LMAR 3.2. AUTHORITY OF ARBITRATORS

An arbitrator has the authority to:

(a) Motions. Determine a reasonable time, place, and procedure to present a motion before the arbitrator, excluding motions for summary award and involuntary dismissal.

(b) Expenses. Require a party or attorney advising such party or both to pay the reasonable expenses, including attorney's fees, caused by the failure of such party or attorney or both to obey an order of the arbitrator unless the arbitrator finds that the failure was substantially justified or that other circumstances make an award of expenses unjust. The arbitrator shall make a special award for such expenses and shall file such award with the clerk of the superior court, with proof of service on each party. The aggrieved party shall have ten (10) days thereafter to appeal the award of such expenses in accordance with the procedures described in RCW 2.24.050. If within ten (10) days after the award is filed no party appeals, a judgment shall be entered in a manner described generally under MAR 6.3.

(c) Attorney's Fees. Award attorney's fees as authorized by these LMARs, by contract or by law.

[Adopted effective September 1, 2011.]

LMAR 4.2. DISCOVERY

(a) Additional Discovery. In determining when additional discovery beyond that directly authorized by MAR 4.2 is reasonably necessary, the arbitrator shall balance the benefits of discovery against the burdens and expenses. The arbitrator shall consider the nature and complexity of the case, the amount in controversy, values at stake, the discovery that has already occurred, the burdens on the party from whom discovery is sought, and the possibility of unfair surprise which may result if discovery is restricted. Authorized discovery shall be conducted in accordance with the superior court civil rules except that motions concerning discovery shall be determined by the arbitrator.

(b) Discovery Pending. Discovery pending at the time the case is assigned to an arbitrator is stayed pending order from the arbitrator or except as the parties may stipulate or except as authorized by MAR 4.2.

[Adopted effective September 1, 2011.]

LMAR 5.1. NOTICE OF HEARING—TIME AND PLACE—CONTINUANCE

An arbitration hearing may be scheduled at any reasonable time and place chosen by the arbitrator; except by stipulation with permission of the arbitrator, the hearing shall be scheduled to take place not later than ninety (90) days from the date of assignment to the arbitrator. The arbitrator may grant a continuance without court approval. The arbitrator shall give reasonable notice of the hearing date on a Notice of Arbitration Hearing Date form approved by the court, and any continuance on an Order of Continuance of Arbitration Hearing Date form approved by the court to the court administration.

[Adopted effective September 1, 2011; amended effective September 1, 2012.]

LMAR 5.2. PREHEARING STATEMENT OF PROOF—DOCUMENTS FILED WITH THE COURT

Generally. In addition to the requirements of MAR 5.2, each party shall also furnish the arbitrator with copies of pleadings and other documents contained in the court file which that party deems relevant. The court file shall remain with the County Clerk. The arbitrator shall strictly enforce the provisions of MAR 5.2 and is encouraged to withhold permission to present evidence at the time of hearing if the parties have failed to comply with this rule.

[Adopted effective September 1, 2011; amended effective September 1, 2012.]

LMAR 6.1. FORM AND CONTENT OF AWARD

(a) Form. The award shall be prepared on an Arbitration Award approved by the court and filed with the county clerk along with proof of service on the parties.

(b) Return of Exhibits. When an award is filed, the arbitrator shall return all exhibits to the parties who offered them during the hearing.

[Adopted effective September 1, 2011.]

LMAR 6.2. FILING OF AWARD

A request by an arbitrator for an extension of time for the filing of an award shall be presented to the court administration, and may be extended up to an additional fourteen (14) days by a judge. The arbitrator shall give the parties notice of any extension granted. Recurring delays in the filing of awards will result in the removal of the arbitrator from the panel.

[Adopted effective September 1, 2011; amended effective September 1, 2012.]

LMAR 6.3. JUDGMENT ON AWARD

Presentation. A judgment on an award shall be presented at the ex parte docket, by any party, on notice in accordance with MAR 6.3 no sooner than twenty (20) days after the award is entered if no party has sought trial *de novo*.

[Adopted effective September 1, 2011; amended effective September 1, 2012.]

LMAR 7.1. REQUEST FOR TRIAL DE NOVO

Request. The Request for Trial de Novo and Sealing of Award shall be filed with the county clerk on such form as approved by the court. A copy shall be provided to the court administration.

[Adopted effective September 1, 2011; amended effective September 1, 2012.]

LMAR 8.1. STIPULATIONS—EFFECT ON RELIEF GRANTED

If a case not otherwise subject to mandatory arbitration is transferred to arbitration by stipulation, the arbitrator may grant any relief which could have been granted if the case were determined by a judge. Stipulated arbitrations are not governed by these rules unless expressly agreed to by the parties. Compensation of arbitrators performing stipulated arbitrations is the responsibility of the parties.

[Adopted effective September 1, 2011.]

LMAR 8.4. TITLE AND CITATION

These rules are known and cited as the Cowlitz County Superior Court Mandatory Arbitration Rules. LMAR is the official abbreviation.

[Adopted effective September 1, 2011.]

LMAR 8.5. COMPENSATION OF ARBITRATOR

(a) Generally. Arbitrators shall be compensated in the same amount and manner as judges pro tempore of the superior court. The maximum compensation is capped at the six hours times the applicable hourly rate as provided by the Administrative Office of the Courts, unless approved by a superior court judge.

(b) Form. When the award is filed, the arbitrator shall submit to the court administrator two original requests for payment on a form prescribed by the court within sixty (60) days of the filing of the award. The court administration shall determine the amount of compensation and costs to be paid, subject to approval by a judge. Compensation to the arbitrator and cost reimbursement shall be pursuant to standards set and periodically revised by the court.

[Adopted effective September 1, 2011; amended effective September 1, 2012.]

LMAR 8.6. ADMINISTRATION

(a) Generally. The court administrator, under the superior court judges, shall supervise arbitration under these rules and perform any additional duties which may be delegated by the judges.

(b) Administrative Committee. There shall be an administrative committee composed of two (2) judges chosen by the presiding judge and three members of the Washington State Bar Association chosen by the Cowlitz–Wahkiakum County Bar Association. The members of the committee shall serve for staggered three-year terms and may be re-appointed.

(c) Powers and Duties. The administrative committee shall have the power and duty to:

(1) Select its chairperson and provide for its procedures;

(2) Make recommendations to the presiding judge for removal of a person from a panel of arbitrators. Such recommendation for removal must be in writing and state the basis for the request;

(3) Review the administration and operation of the arbitration program periodically and make recommendations as it deems appropriate to improve the program.

[Adopted effective September 1, 2011.]

MANDATORY GUARDIAN AD LITEM RULES (CCLGALR)
Formerly Mandatory Juvenile Court Rules (CCLJuCR)
TITLE III. DEPENDENCY PROCEEDINGS

RULE 3. ESTABLISHMENT OF CASA LOCAL RULES

(a) Title. These Rules shall be known as the CASA Local Rules for Cowlitz County, Washington.

(b) Scope. These Rules shall be applicable to all dependency cases in the Cowlitz County Juvenile Court. These cases include children who are alleged to be dependent, neglected, or abandoned; in all cases in which termination of parental rights is involved; or in any other appropriate dependency proceeding pending in Cowlitz County Juvenile Court. Once CASA has been appointed for a child(ren), that appointment will continue until further order of the court irrespective of the increasing age of the child(ren).

(c) Application. These Rules shall supplement the existing local rules and the Washington Juvenile Court Rules (JuCR) which shall apply in addition to these Rules. These Rules may be modified or waived by the sitting juvenile court judge, by special order, when, in the opinion of said Judge, such waiver or modification is necessary in order to do justice, or to arrive at the equities of the case between, or among, the parties involved. Each person appearing in this court is charged with the knowledge of all applicable rules.

(d) Definitions.

(1) *Juvenile Rules Definitions.* The definitions of JuCR 1.3 shall apply in these cases.

(A) "CASA" means The Cowlitz County CASA, which is the non-profit corporation that provides specially trained and sworn adults to the court as CASA volunteers. It is the designated CASA organization for all Cowlitz County CASA cases. CASA also stands for "Court Appointed Special Advocates," which refers to the organization's volunteers.

(B) A "CASA Volunteer" means a responsible adult who has been specially trained as a court appointed special advocate and who has taken a special oath from a superior court judge. The person is charged with making recommendations in the form of reports and testimony to the judge regarding the best interests of the child(ren). The volunteer serves only upon the order of and at the discretion of the judge.

i. "CASA" Volunteer Affiliate" means a CASA volunteer who has met the state training requirements to perform the duties of a guardian ad litem in juvenile court dependency matters but who is required to perform these duties under direct supervision of a CASA volunteer mentor for a minimum of six (6) months.

ii. A "CASA Volunteer Certified" means a CASA volunteer who has met the state training requirements to perform the duties of a guardian ad litem in juvenile court dependency matters and who has successfully completed a minimum of six (6) months of direct supervision by a CASA volunteer mentor as a CASA volunteer affiliate.

iii. A qualified "CASA Volunteer Mentor" means a CASA volunteer who has performed the duties of a guardian ad litem as a CASA volunteer certified for a minimum of one (1) year and has been identified by the Cowlitz County CASA as a mentor.

(C) "CASA Report" means any report prepared by the CASA volunteer addressed to the judge giving a thorough background investigation of the child(ren), including, but not limited to, information about the parents, relatives, and others who have knowledge about or concerning the child(ren). The report contains advisory recommendations as to the best interest of the child(ren).

(D) "CASA Order" means the order signed by a judge, or a court commissioner, which appoints CASA as guardian ad litem. The order remains effective until CASA is ordered released from the child(ren)'s case.

(E) "CASA Director" means the executive director of the Cowlitz County CASA, as hired by its board of directors, or as designated by its board of directors.

The CASA director is the person charged with the supervision of all CASA volunteers, CASA reports, and CASA cases.

(e) Establishment of CASA Cases and Orders.

(1) *Requests for CASA.* The court may appoint a CASA volunteer upon its own initiative, or a request for appointment of a CASA volunteer to a case or for a child(ren) may be made by any person or agency having knowledge of facts which indicate that a CASA volunteer is appropriate. A request for a CASA volunteer may be made by motion filed by any person or agency. The court clerk shall accept the filing of the motion and note upon it the date and time of filing.

(2) *Preliminary Inquiry.* Except in situations where the court orders a CASA volunteer appointed upon its own initiative, the clerk shall forward a copy of any request or motion filed to the CASA director within ten (10) days of its filing. The CASA director will make a preliminary investigation of the case. If

the case appears appropriate, the director will recommend to the court the signing of a CASA order and provide the name of an available CASA volunteer. If the case does not appear appropriate, the CASA director will recommend that CASA not be appointed to the case. The preliminary inquiry shall be completed within ten (10) days of receiving the request or motion from the court clerk.

(3) *Hearing.* Within ten (10) days after a request or motion for a CASA volunteer is filed, the CASA director will file with the court a response to the motion based upon the preliminary inquiry conducted. Thereafter, the court may, if necessary, hold a hearing, at which time any person or agency may present proof for or against appointment of a CASA volunteer. Following the hearing, or, in the event a hearing is not necessary and the court has received a response, the court shall enter an order either granting or denying the request or motion. Notwithstanding the above, the court may enter an order appointing a CASA volunteer at any time for a child(ren) in a proceeding, upon its own initiative, during or following the preliminary inquiry and with or without conducting any hearing, by signing a CASA order.

(4) *CASA Order.* The CASA order may be signed by the judge or a court commissioner in any case. The order shall be effective when signed and shall continue in full force and effect until a subsequent order is signed which orders the CASA volunteer released from the case. The CASA volunteer shall continue to serve on a pending case so long as the child(ren) continues under the jurisdiction of the court. The clerk of the court shall furnish the CASA director with a copy of each CASA order within five (5) days of entry of the order. The CASA order will also be served upon all parties or their attorney of record. Each CASA order shall have a copy of the relevant petition attached and a notice of the next scheduled hearing date, time, and location.

(5) *Scope of the CASA Order.* Upon entry of a CASA order appointing a CASA volunteer to a case, all persons and agencies are under an obligation to cooperate with the CASA volunteer to assist in determining the best interest of the child(ren). The CASA volunteer shall have access to the child(ren) (including any child(ren) in detention), the parents, any caretaker, or any other agency or party having information related to the child(ren). The CASA volunteer has the right to inspect and/or copy any documents deemed relevant by the volunteer to the child(ren)'s situation. The CASA volunteer shall consult and work with any attorney guardian ad litem appointed for the child(ren), as is necessary. The CASA volunteer shall maintain any information received during an investigation in a confidential manner. The CASA volunteer shall not disclose any such information except in reports to the court and to parties to the proceeding, unless disclosure of any information has been limited by the court pursuant to CASA Rule 5(c).

Nothing contained in these Rules shall be construed as permitting any non-attorney CASA volunteer to practice law before the court.

(f) Guardian Ad Litem Appointments.

(1) *Appointment.* In cases involving CASA volunteers, the court may have appointed an attorney guardian ad litem who may represent the child(ren) in all legal proceedings, and who shall then serve with the CASA volunteer to so represent the child(ren) in all legal proceedings.

(2) *Legal Services.* The CASA volunteer shall not act as the legal representative of any child(ren) in any legal proceeding, unless the CASA volunteer is a licensed attorney. The CASA volunteer may fully participate in any proceedings involving the child(ren) for whom the CASA volunteer has been appointed. If called as a witness by the court or any party, the CASA volunteer shall testify as a witness in any proceeding.

(3) *Compensation.* The CASA volunteer shall not receive any compensation from the court or from any party to the proceedings. The CASA volunteer serves the court and as such shall receive no compensation or remuneration.

(4) *Release.* A CASA volunteer who wishes to be released from a case shall so petition the court, having first obtained the approval therefor from the CASA director.

(g) CASA Court Attendance and Reports.

(1) *Attending Hearings.* The CASA volunteer is charged with the notice of all hearings which involve the child(ren) assigned, and will attend all such hearings. In the event of a conflict, the CASA volunteer may request a continuance for good cause shown or may be excused by the court from appearing. Any party may call the CASA volunteer as a witness in the proceeding. CASA may be compelled to attend by any party with the service of a subpoena for the CASA volunteer, made by service upon the volunteer or by serving the CASA director, giving at least five (5) days' notice prior to the hearing, excluding Saturdays, Sundays, and legal holidays.

(2) *Filing Reports.* The CASA representative shall, absent special circumstances or unless excused by the judge, submit a written report at least five (5) working days prior to each dispositional or review hearing involving the child(ren). The report shall be addressed to the judge and shall contain such attachments and documents as are relevant to the proceedings. The report when filed shall become a permanent part of the applicable juvenile court legal file. The volunteer shall sign the report, but not under oath. The court is in no way bound by or obligated to adopt any CASA recommendations, the report being advisory in nature.

(3) *Inspection of Reports; Confidentiality.* Generally, the child(ren), the attorney, the parent, guardian

or legal guardian, the attorney guardian ad litem, and any state or other agency involved in the proceedings, shall be entitled to inspect the CASA report, and all documents attached thereto except that information protected from disclosure by law. However, the court, in its discretion, may decline to permit inspection of CASA reports, or portions thereof, to anyone other than a party or an attorney of record in the proceeding, if it determines that such inspection would be detrimental to the child(ren). The court shall issue such orders as are necessary to maintain the confidential nature of information so classified.

(h) Special Compliance Reviews. The CASA volunteer is responsible for monitoring compliance with all court orders issued in any case or proceeding involving the child(ren) for whom the CASA volunteer was appointed. To that end, in the event that the CASA volunteer believes that any court orders are not being complied with by any party, and the volunteer's efforts to obtain compliance have been unsuccessful, the volunteer may request the clerk of the court to place the case on the court's docket for early review, and the clerk shall give notice thereof. The judge may then examine the CASA volunteer, and any other witness, at a hearing to determine compliance or noncompliance with its orders. The court may issue such remedial order(s) as may be necessary or may issue a show cause order to any party to determine why compliance with its orders has failed. Special reviews may also be conducted by the court to determine compliance with the CASA order by any person or agency as described in CASA Rules 3(d) and 3(e).

[Adopted effective May 1, 1994; amended effective September 1, 2000; September 1, 2002; September 1, 2005; September 1, 2006; September 1, 2012.]

RULE 7. GUARDIAN AD LITEM DISCIPLINARY PROCEDURES FOR CASA VOLUNTEERS

(a) There shall be a complaint review committee, hereinafter referred to as the "committee," consisting of three (3) individuals designated by the superior court judges of Cowlitz County. The committee is empowered by the court to review all complaints made regarding the guardian ad litem services provided by CASA volunteers.

7.[1] One member of the committee shall be a superior court judge.

(b) All complaints must be in writing and must be submitted to the complaint review committee. Complaints shall remain confidential until resolved.

(c) Upon receipt of a written complaint concerning a CASA volunteer, the superior court judge shall advise the director of the Cowlitz County CASA of the complaint. If the judge finds the complaint sufficiently serious, the matter will be referred directly to the committee. Otherwise, the complaint will be forwarded to the director who will meet with all parties

involved in the dispute in an attempt to resolve the problem at the director's level.

(1) A copy of the complaint and the resolution or lack of resolution shall be forwarded to the juvenile court administrator.

(2) If the complaint is not resolved to the satisfaction of the complainant, the matter will move to (d) of this policy.

(d) Upon receipt of the written complaint (unresolved) and findings from the director of the Cowlitz County CASA, or upon a direct referral from a judge, the juvenile court administrator shall convene the committee within ten (10) business days to review the complaint. Upon review of the complaint, the committee shall either:

Make a finding that the complaint has no merit on its face, and decline to review the complaint and so inform the complainant; or

Make a finding that the complaint does appear to have merit and request a written response from the CASA volunteer within ten (10) business days, detailing the specific issues in the complaint to which the committee desires a response. The committee shall provide the CASA volunteer with a copy of the original complaint. The failure of a CASA volunteer, subject to the complaint, to respond within the required ten (10) business days, in the absence of good cause shown, will result in the immediate suspension of the CASA volunteer.

In considering whether the complaint has merit, the committee shall consider, but not be limited to, whether the complaint alleges the CASA volunteer has:

(1) Violated the code of conduct;

(2) Misrepresented his or her qualifications to serve;

(3) Not met the annual training update requirements set forth in the statute;

(4) Breached the confidentiality of the parties;

(5) Falsified information in a report to the court or in testimony before the court;

(6) Failed to report abuse of a child;

(7) Communicated with a judicial officer ex-parte;

(8) Represented the court in a public forum without prior approval of the court;

(9) Violated state or local laws, rules, or this policy in the person's capacity as a CASA volunteer; or,

(10) Taken, or failed to take, any other action which would reasonably place the suitability of the person to serve as a CASA volunteer in question.

(e) Upon receipt of a written response to a complaint from the CASA volunteer, the committee shall, within ten (10) business days, make a finding as to each of the issues delineated in the committee's letter to the CASA volunteer that either there is no merit to the issue based upon the response of the CASA volunteer or that there is merit to the issue. The committee may, at its discretion, extend the time for entering findings to conduct additional investigation if necessary; however, in no case shall that extension be for more than twenty (20) business days and the CASA volunteer shall be notified.

(f) The committee shall have the authority to issue a written admonishment, written reprimand, refer the CASA volunteer to additional training, recommend to the presiding judge that the court, upon its own motion, remove the CASA volunteer from the current case or suspend or remove the CASA volunteer from the registry. In considering a response, the committee shall take into consideration any prior complaints which resulted in an admonishment, reprimand, referral to training, removal of the CASA volunteer from a particular case, or suspension or removal from a registry. If a CASA volunteer is listed on more than one registry, the suspension or removal may apply to each registry the CASA volunteer is listed on at the discretion of the committee.

(g) The complainant, the CASA volunteer, and the director of Cowlitz County CASA, shall be notified in writing of the committee's decision within ten (10) business days of receipt of the response of the CASA volunteer or longer if additional time for investigation is necessary pursuant to paragraph (e) above.

(h) A CASA volunteer may, within five (5) business days of receipt of notification that he/she has been suspended or removed from a registry, request a hearing on the committee's decision. The presiding judge shall designate a hearing officer. The sole purpose of the hearing shall be to review the appropriateness of the suspension or removal from the registry. The hearing officer shall review the written record of the instant complaint and any prior complaints the committee considered, and hear oral arguments from the CASA volunteer or his or her representative and a representative of the committee. Said hearing shall be conducted within twenty (20) days of the receipt of the request for the hearing. The decision of the hearing officer shall be final and binding upon the parties.

[Adopted effective September 1, 2002; amended effective September 1, 2012.]

1 Numbering as provided in original.

TITLE IV. GUARDIAN AD LITEM RULES

RULE 8. GUARDIAN AD LITEM DISCIPLINARY PROCEDURES

(1) Guardian Ad Litem Advisory Committee. The Court's Guardian ad Litem Advisory Committee hereinafter referred to as the "Committee," will administer complaints about guardians ad litem.

(2) Submission of Complaints. All complaints must be in writing and must be submitted to the Superior Court Administrator. All complaints must bear the signature, name and address of the person filing the complaint.

(3) Review of Complaint. Upon receipt of a written complaint, the Court Administrator shall convene the Committee to review the complaint. Upon review of the complaint, the Committee shall either:

(a) Make a finding that the complaint is with regard to a case then pending in the court and decline to review the complaint and so inform the complainant. In such instances the Committee shall advise the complainant that the complaint may only be addressed in the context of the case at bar, either by seeking the removal of the guardian ad litem or by contesting the information or recommendation contained in the guardian ad litem's report or testimony. In such cases the Committee and its members shall perform its role in such a manner as to assure that the trial judge remains uninformed as to the complaint; or

(b) Make a finding that the complaint has no merit on its face, and decline to review the complaint and so inform the complainant; or

(c) Make a finding that the complaint appears to have merit and request a written response from the Guardian ad Litem within 10 business days, detailing the specific issues in the complaint to which the Committee desires a response. The Committee shall provide the Guardian ad Litem with a copy of the original complaint. In considering whether the complaint has merit, the Committee shall consider whether the complaint alleges the Guardian ad Litem has:

(1) Violated a code of conduct;

(2) Misrepresented his or her qualifications to serve as a Guardian ad Litem;

(3) Breached the confidentiality of the parties;

(4) Falsified information in a report to the court or in testimony before the court;

(5) Failed, when required, to report abuse of a child;

(6) Communicated with a judicial officer ex-parte concerning a case for which he or she is serving as a guardian ad litem;

(7) Violated state or local laws or court rules; or,

(8) Taken or failed to take any other action which would reasonably place the suitability of the person to serve as a Guardian ad Litem in question.

(4) Response and Findings.

(a) Upon receipt of a written response to a complaint from the Guardian ad Litem, the Committee shall make a finding as to each of the specific issues in the complaint to which the Committee desires a response, as delineated in the Committee's letter to the Guardian ad Litem. Such findings shall state that either there is no merit to the issue based upon the Guardian ad Litem's response or that there is merit to the issue.

(b) The Committee shall have the authority to issue a written admonishment, a written reprimand, refer the Guardian ad Litem to additional training, or recommend to the Presiding Judge that the Court suspend or remove the Guardian ad Litem from the registry. In considering a response, the Committee shall take into consideration any prior complaints that resulted in an admonishment, reprimand, referral to training, or suspension or removal from a registry. If a Guardian ad Litem is listed on more than one registry, the suspension or removal may apply to each registry the Guardian ad Litem is listed on, at the discretion of the Committee.

(c) The complainant and the Guardian ad Litem shall be notified in writing of the Committee's decision following receipt of the Guardian ad Litem's response.

(5) Confidentiality.

(a) A complaint shall be deemed confidential for all purposes unless the committee has determined that it has merit under LGAL 8(4) above.

(b) Any record of complaints filed which are not deemed by the committee to have merit shall be confidential and shall not be disclosed except by court order.

(6) Complaint Processing Time Standards.

(a) Complaints shall be resolved within twenty-five (25) days of the date of receipt of the written complaint if a case is pending.

(b) Complaints shall be resolved within sixty (60) days of the date of receipt of the written complaint if the complaint is filed subsequent to the conclusion of a case.

(7) Removal from Registry.

(a) When a guardian ad litem is removed from the court's registry pursuant to the disposition of a grievance hereunder, the Court Administrator shall send a notice of such removal to the Office of the Administrator for the Courts.

(b) When the Court Administrator receives notice from the Office of the Administrator for the Courts that a guardian ad litem on the court's registry has been removed from the registry of any other Washington Superior Court the Administrator shall advise the Presiding Judge of such removal.

[Adopted effective September 1, 2012.]

PART V. RULES OF APPEAL OF DECISIONS OF COURTS OF LIMITED JURISDICTION (CCLRALJ)
TITLE 2. INITIATING AN APPEAL

RULE 2.4. HOW TO INITIATE AN APPEAL

(b) Filing Fee.

(1) If the party seeking to appeal has had judgment rendered against him or her in an infraction or other civil matter and has not been declared indigent in a court of limited jurisdiction, any application for a waiver of filing fee in superior court must be approved by a judge of the superior court. The office of the county clerk will furnish application forms for such fee waiver.

[Effective September 1, 1997; amended effective September 1, 2005.]

RULE 2.6. CONTENT OF NOTICE OF APPEAL

(c) Designation of Claimed Errors.

(1) *Identification.* The appealing party shall identify in writing, as to each claimed error, by reference to the numerical (digital) count on the electronic record as disclosed by the log, the beginning and the end of each portion of the recorded proceedings relevant to the claimed error.

[Effective September 1, 1997.]

APPENDICES

APPENDIX A.   REQUEST FOR TRANSFER TO ARBITRATION AND STATEMENT OF ARBITRABILITY

SUPERIOR COURT OF WASHINGTON FOR COWLITZ COUNTY

In re:	No.
Plaintiff	**REQUEST FOR TRANSFER TO ARBITRATION AND STATEMENT OF ARBITRABILITY**
vs.	
Defendant.	***CLERK'S ACTION REQUIRED***

TO: Clerk of the above-entitled Court; and

TO: All Parties and/or Attorneys listed under Part II.

REQUEST FOR TRANSFER TO ARBITRATION

SPECIAL NOTE: _____

_____

PROOF OF SERVICE: The undersigned certifies that all counsel have been served with a copy of this Notice either personally or by mail.

I. STATEMENT OF ARBITRABILITY

1.1   _____   This case is subject arbitration because the sole relief sought is a money judgment and it involves no claim in excess of $50,000, exclusive of Attorney fees, interest, and costs.

1.2   _____   The undersigned contends that its claim exceeds $50,000, but for purposes of arbitration waives any claim in excess of $50,000.

Because this case is subject to Mandatory Arbitration, the undersigned certifies further that a copy of this document has been provided to Court Administration.

II. PARTIES

2.1   The names & addresses of the parties and/or their attorneys are as follows:

2.1.1

2.1.2

2.1.3

Date: _____   _____
                         Name of Attorney, WSB #
                         Attorney for Plaintiff / Defendant

[Adopted on an emergency basis effective January 1, 2013; April 1, 2013; June 6, 2013; amended on a permanent basis, effective September 2, 2013.]

DISTRICT COURT

COWLITZ COUNTY DISTRICT COURT LOCAL RULES

Including Amendments Received Through
August 15, 2015

Table of Rules

LOCAL GENERAL RULES

RULE 29. PRESIDING JUDGE

Before January 1 of each odd numbered year, the judges shall by majority vote elect a presiding judge and an assistant presiding judge, to serve a two-year term starting January 1 of the year after the election. In the event of an interim vacancy, the judges shall by majority vote elect a replacement within 30 days after the vacancy occurs.

[Effective September 1, 2010.]

LOCAL INFRACTION RULES

RULE 2.4. HEARINGS ON WRITTEN STATEMENTS

(a) The court authorizes mitigation hearings and contested hearings on written statements in lieu of a defendant's personal appearance. A written statement that does not clearly request to contest a notice of infraction will be treated as a request to explain mitigating circumstances.

(b) A defendant may submit a written statement as a response to a notice of infraction within 15 days of the date the notice is personally served or, if the notice is served by mail, within 18 days of the date the notice is mailed. Additionally, a defendant who has requested a mitigation hearing or a contested hearing may submit a written statement later in lieu of personally appearing at the hearing. The written statement must be received by the time of the hearing.

(c) A written statement may be delivered to the court in person, by United States mail or any other delivery service, by facsimile, or by email. The court's contact information is as follows:

Address:	Cowlitz County District Court 312 SW 1st Avenue Kelso WA 98626
Facsimile:	(360) 577–3132
Email:	dctcourt@co.cowlitz.wa.us

or through the court's web site:

www.co.cowlitz.wa.us/districtcourt

(d) A written statement shall contain the person's promise to pay the monetary penalty authorized by law if the infraction is found to be committed. The statement shall be executed in compliance with RCW 9A.72.085, in substantially the following form:

I certify (or declare) under penalty of perjury under the laws of the State of Washington that the foregoing is true. I promise that if it is determined that I committed the infraction for which I was cited, I will pay the monetary penalty authorized by law and assessed by the court.

_____ _____
(Date and Place)   (Signature)

[Effective September 1, 2004.]

RULE 3.1. REQUEST FOR SUBPOENA

Any request for a subpoena to be issued by the court must be filed in writing at least 14 days before the hearing, or such lesser time as the court deems proper. The request cannot be combined with a notice of appearance or any other pleading.

[Effective September 1, 2004.]

RULE 6.6. REQUEST FOR SPEED MEASURING DEVICE EXPERT; REMOTE TESTIMONY

Any request to produce a speed measuring device expert must be filed in accordance with IRLJ 6.6(b). The request cannot be combined with a notice of appearance or any other pleading. The court may allow the speed measuring device expert to testify from a location other than the courtroom, via speaker-phone or other electronic means acceptable to the court.

[Effective September 1, 2004; Amended effective September 1, 2005.]

LOCAL CRIMINAL RULES

RULE 3.2(o). DEFENDANTS WHO MUST BE SEEN BEFORE RELEASE

(1) A person subjected to custodial arrest for a domestic violence assault charge is to be held until the next judicial day if—

(a) The person has been convicted of or placed on deferred prosecution for any domestic violence assault charge in any jurisdiction occurring within the last seven years, and/or

(b) The person has a pending domestic violence assault charge in any jurisdiction. A pending charge means a charge with no final disposition, and includes but is not limited to a charge on deferred prosecution, stipulated continuance, or similar arrangement.

(2) A person subjected to custodial arrest for driving under the influence of alcohol and/or any drug ("DUI") or physical control under the influence of alcohol and/or any drug ("physical control") is to be held until the next judicial day if—

(a) The person has been convicted of or placed on deferred prosecution for any charge of DUI, physical control, vehicular homicide, or vehicular assault in any jurisdiction occurring within the last seven years, and/or

(b) The person has a pending DUI or physical control charge in any jurisdiction. A pending charge

means a charge with no final disposition, and includes but is not limited to a charge on deferred prosecution, stipulated continuance, or similar arrangement; and/or

(c) The current case involved an accident that resulted in injury to a person other than the defendant.

[Adopted effective September 1, 2007.]

RULE 3.4. PRESENCE OF THE DEFENDANT

Other trial court proceedings including the entry of a Statement of Defendant on Plea of Guilty may be conducted by video conference, in accordance with CrRLJ 3.4(d).

[Adopted effective September 1, 2005.]

RULE 4.1. ARRAIGNMENT

Appointment of counsel eliminates the need for a further arraignment. Upon the appointment of counsel, the court shall enter a plea of "not guilty" and set the appropriate hearing(s). Appointment of counsel shall commence the running of the time periods established in CrRLJ 3.3, unless the time periods have previously been commenced by an appearance in open court.

[Adopted effective September 1, 2007.]

MUNICIPAL COURTS

CASTLE ROCK MUNICIPAL COURT—
[No Local Rules]

PUBLISHER'S NOTE

This municipal court follows the Cowlitz County District Court Local Rules.

KALAMA MUNICIPAL COURT—
[No Local Rules]

PUBLISHER'S NOTE

This municipal court follows the Cowlitz County District Court Local Rules.

KELSO MUNICIPAL COURT—
[No Local Rules]

PUBLISHER'S NOTE

This municipal court follows the Cowlitz County District Court Local Rules.

LONGVIEW MUNICIPAL COURT—
[No Local Rules]

PUBLISHER'S NOTE

This municipal court follows the Cowlitz County District Court Local Rules.

WOODLAND MUNICIPAL COURT—
[No Local Rules]

PUBLISHER'S NOTE

This municipal court follows the Cowlitz County District Court Local Rules.

DOUGLAS COUNTY

Table of Courts

Superior Court

Local Rules for the Superior Court of the State of Washington for Douglas County.

District Court

Local Court Rules of Douglas County District Court.

Municipal Courts

Bridgeport Municipal Court—[No Local Rules].
East Wenatchee Municipal Court—[No Local Rules].
Rock Island Municipal Court—[No Local Rules].
Waterville Municipal Court—[No Local Rules].

SUPERIOR COURT

LOCAL RULES FOR THE SUPERIOR COURT OF THE STATE OF WASHINGTON FOR DOUGLAS COUNTY

Including Amendments Received Through
August 15, 2015

Table of Rules

PREFACE

1. Promulgation. These rules shall be known as the Local Rules for the Superior Court of the State of Washington for Douglas County. Copies of these rules will be filed with the Clerk of the Court for Douglas County and will be distributed to all law offices in Chelan and Douglas Counties. Additional copies will be available at the office of the Clerks for Douglas County. These rules will be effective September 1, 1999, and supersede all prior rules of these courts.

2. Numbering. Consistent with CR 83(a), Washington Court Rules, these rules conform in numbering system and in format to those rules and facilitate the use of both. The number of each rule is preceded by the abbreviation "LR" designating the rule as local to these courts and supplemental to the corresponding Washington Court Rule.

3. Revisions and Additions. These rules have been prepared in loose-leaf form to facilitate revision, additions or deletions in the future by page without the necessity of republication.

[Adopted effective September 1, 1999.]

LOCAL RULES

LR 5. SERVICE AND FILING OF PLEADINGS AND OTHER PAPERS

(d) Filing.

(5) *Documents Not to be Filed.* Photocopies of reported cases, statutes or texts shall not be filed as an appendix to a brief or otherwise but may be furnished directly to the judge hearing the matter. Documents or copies thereof produced during discovery and other items which should properly be received as exhibits rather than as a part of the court file shall not be included in the court file.

(6) *Case Information Cover Sheet.* Each new civil and domestic case filing shall be accompanied by a Case Information Cover Sheet prepared and submitted by the party filing said new civil or domestic case. Attached as *Exhibit A* to this rule is the form of the Case Information Cover Sheet.

[Adopted effective September 1, 1999.]

LR 5 EXHIBIT A.   CASE INFORMATION SHEET

_____ COUNTY SUPERIOR COURT
CASE INFORMATION COVER SHEET

Case Number _____ Case Title _____
Attorney Name _____ Bar Membership Number _____
Please check one category that best describes this case for indexing purposes.
Accurate case indexing not only saves time in docketing new cases, but helps in
forecasting needed judicial resources. Cause of action definitions are listed on
the back of this form. Thank you for your cooperation.

APPEAL/REVIEW
____ Administrative Law Review (ALR 2)
____ Appeal of a Department of Licensing
      Revocation (DOL 2)
____ Civil, Non–Traffic (LCA 2)
____ Civil, Traffic (LCI 2)
CONTRACT/COMMERCIAL
____ Breach of Contract (COM 2)
____ Commercial Contract (COM 2)
____ Commercial Non–Contract (COL 2)
____ Third Party Collection (COL 2)
DOMESTIC RELATIONS
____ Annulment/Invalidity (INV 3)
____ Child Custody (CUS 3)
____ Dissolution with Children (DIC 3)
____ Dissolution with no Children (DIN 3)
____ Foreign Judgment (FJU 3)
____ Legal Separation (SEP 3)
____ Mandatory Wage Assignment (MWA 3)
____ Meretricious Relationship (MER 2)
____ Modification (MOD 3)
____ Out-of-State Custody (OSC 3)
____ Reciprocal, Respondent in County (RIC 3)
____ Reciprocal, Respondent Out of County
      (ROC 3)
DOMESTIC VIOLENCE/ANTIHARASSMENT
____ Civil Harassment (HAR 2)
____ Confidential Name Change (CHN 5)
____ Domestic Violence (DVP 2)
JUDGMENT
____ Abstract Only (ABJ 2)
____ Foreign Judgment (FJU 2)
____ Judgment, Another County (ABJ 2)
____ Judgment, Another State (FJU 2)
____ Tax Warrant (TAX 2)
____ Transcript of Judgment (TRJ 2)
MENTAL ILLNESS
____ Alcoholic Treatment (ALT 6)
____ Mental Illness—Adult (MI 6)
____ Mental Illness—Juvenile (MIJ 6)
PROBATE/GUARDIANSHIP
____ Absentee (ABS 4)
____ Disclaimer (DSC 4)
____ Estate (EST 4)
____ Foreign Will (FNW 4)
____ Guardianship (GDN 4)
____ Guardianship/Estate (G/E 4)
____ Limited Guardianship (LGD 4)
____ Minor Settlement (With guardianship)
____ (MST 4)
____ Non–Probate Notice to Creditors (NNC 4)
____ Will Only (WLL 4)

ADOPTION/PATERNITY
____ Adoption (ADP 5)
____ Confidential Intermediary (MSC 5)
____ Initial Pre–Placement Report (PPR 5)
____ Modification (MOD 5)
____ Paternity (PAT 5)
____ Paternity/URESA/UIFSA (PUR 5)
____ Relinquishment (REL 5)
____ (Title 26) Termination of Parent–Child
      Relationship (TER 5)
OTHER COMPLAINT/PETITION
____ Action to Compel/Confirm Private Binding
____ Arbitration (MSC 2)
____ Change of Name (CHN 2)
____ Deposit of Surplus Funds (MSC 2)
____ Emancipation of Minor (EOM 2)
____ Injunction (INJ 2)
____ Interpleader (MSC 2)
____ Malicious Harassment (MHA 2)
____ Minor Settlement (No guardianship)
      (MST 2)
____ Petition for Civil Commitment (Sexual
      Predator) (PCC 2)
____ Seizure of Property from the Commission of
      a Crime (SPC 2)
____ Seizure of Property Resulting from a Crime
      (SPR 2)
____ Subpoenas (MSC 2)
PROPERTY RIGHTS
____ Condemnation (CON 2)
____ Foreclosure (FOR 2)
____ Land Use Petition (LUP 2)
____ Property Fairness (PFA 2)
____ Quiet Title (QTI 2)
____ Unlawful Detainer (UND 2)
TORT, MEDICAL MALPRACTICE
____ Hospital (MED 2)
____ Medical Doctor (MED 2)
____ Other Health Care Professional (MED 2)
TORT, MOTOR VEHICLE
____ Death (TMV 2)
____ Non–Death Injuries (TMV 2)
____ Property Damage Only (TMV 2)
TORT, NON–MOTOR VEHICLE
____ Asbestos (PIN 2)
____ Other Malpractice (MAL 2)
____ Personal Injury (PIN 2)
____ Products Liability (TTO 2)
____ Property Damage (PRP 2)
____ Wrongful Death (WDE 2)
WRIT
____ Habeas Corpus (WHC 2)
____ Mandamus (WRM 2)
____ Restitution (WRR 2)
____ Review (WRV 2)

IF YOU CANNOT DETERMINE THE APPROPRIATE CATEGORY, PLEASE DESCRIBE THE CAUSE OF ACTION BELOW.

_____

_____

[Adopted effective September 1, 1999.]

LR 7. PLEADINGS ALLOWED; FORM OF MOTIONS

(b) Motions and Other Papers.

(1) *How Made.*

(A) Notes for Motion Calendar; Time for Filing. Any party desiring to bring any motion prior to trial, other than a motion for summary judgment, must file with the Clerk and serve all parties and the Judge at least five (5) court days before the date fixed for such hearing. **A COPY OF THE MOTION AND ALL SUPPORTING DOCUMENTS SHALL BE DELIVERED TO THE DOUGLAS COUNTY COURTHOUSE OR MAILED TO THE JUDGE. THE MAILING ADDRESS FOR THE DOUGLAS COUNTY SUPERIOR COURT JUDGE IS P. O. BOX 488, WATERVILLE, WASHINGTON 98858.** The documents should include a Note for Motion, the motion and supporting documents.

(i) Note for Motion—Dissolution Actions. See Washington Pattern Form.

(ii) Other Actions. The note must contain the title of the court; the date, the time when the same shall be heard; the words "Note for Motion", the names of the attorneys for all parties or parties pro se; the nature of the motion; and by whom the motion is made. Attached as *Exhibit A* to this Rule is an example form of a Note for Motion that may be used for Douglas County cases. Any sections of Exhibit A that do not apply to the particular motion may be deleted from the form prior to filing. This note for motion must be signed by the attorney or party pro se filing the same, with the designation of the party represented.

The note or other document shall provide a certificate of mailing of all documents relating to the motion.

Responding documents and briefs must be filed with the Clerk and copies served on all parties and the Judge of Douglas County, no later than noon (2) court days prior to the hearing. Copies of any additional responding or reply documents must be filed with the Clerk and served on all parties no later than noon of the court day prior to the hearing.

(D) Late Filing; Terms. Any material offered at a time later than required by this rule, upon objection of counsel, may be rejected by the Court, or the matter may be continued and the court may impose appropriate terms or sanctions.

[Adopted effective September 1, 1999.]

LR 7 EXHIBIT A. NOTE FOR MOTION

IN THE SUPERIOR COURT OF THE STATE OF WASHINGTON
IN AND FOR THE COUNTY OF DOUGLAS

```
                              )
                              )
                              )
                              )  No.
                              )
                              )  NOTE FOR MOTION
                              )
                              )
_____ )
```

TO:

NOTE FOR LAW AND MOTION CALENDAR

Nature of Hearing:

__ Please note that this matter will be heard on the **regularly scheduled Law and Motion Calendar** on the _____ day of _____ 19 ____ , 1:30 p.m.

__ Please note that this matter has been **specially set on the Law and Motion Calendar** before the **Honorable** _____ , on the _____ day of _____ , 19 ____ at ____ a.m./p.m.

USE THIS SECTION ONLY IF THE ABOVE DOES NOT APPLY

NOTE FOR SPECIAL SETTING

All summary judgments in Douglas County must be special set. All dates and times for special settings must be obtained from the Douglas County Court Administrator.

__ Please note that this matter has been **specially set** before the **Honorable** _____ ,on the _____ day of _____ , 19 ____ , at ____ a.m./p.m.

__ Please note that this matter has been **specially set** before **Court Commissioner** _____ on the _____ day of _____ , 19 ____ at ____ , a.m./p.m.

Dated this _____ day of _____ , 19 ____ .

By:_____

[Adopted effective September 1, 1999.]

LR 7(E). [FILING BY FACSIMILE]

(E) Filing by facsimile with the Court, and serving parties by facsimile, shall be pursuant to General Rule 17.

[Adopted effective September 1, 2002; amended effective September 1, 2005.]

LR 8. SHOW CAUSE ORDERS

(g) Certified copies of show cause orders shall not be issued by the Clerk of the Court without payment in advance.

[Adopted effective September 1, 1999.]

LR 10. FORM OF PLEADINGS

Any document or correspondence presented to the Court for filing which does not have the correct cause number on the face of such document or correspondence may not be filed and may be returned to the presenter.

[Adopted effective September 1, 1999.]

LR 16. PRETRIAL PROCEDURE AND FORMULATING ISSUES

(c) **Pre-Trial Conference.** Any order for a pre-trial conference shall be in the form of and include the provisions as set forth in the *Exhibit "A"* attached to this rule. The pre-trial conference shall be held not less than two weeks prior to the trial date.

(d) **Pre-Trial Order.** A pre-trial order in the form of *Exhibit "B"* attached to this rule shall be prepared by counsel within ten (10) days after the conclusion of the pre-trial conference.

(e) **Exhibits.** Parties shall notify the trial judge and the opposing party by letter if that party anticipates offering 25 exhibits or more at time of trial. Said notice shall be given no less than 2 weeks prior to the trial date.

(f) **Settlement Conference.**

(1) *On Court's Motion.* The court to which a case is assigned for trial may, upon its own motion after a trial date has been set, order a settlement conference in any pending case, and a settlement conference shall be held.

(2) *Order for Settlement Conference.* Upon the entry of an order for a settlement conference, the judge shall fix a specific date and hour for the conference.

(3) *Preparation and Attendance.* The attorney personally in charge of each party's case shall personally attend all settlement conferences and shall, not less than three (3) days prior to the date set for the settlement conference, serve on the assigned judge and the attorney for the opposing party a letter succinctly addressing the following:

a. A brief factual summary;

b. Issues regarding liability;

c. Issues regarding damages, both special and general;

d. History of any settlement negotiations; and

e. Current position on settlement.

Each attorney shall be prepared to discuss the foregoing in detail at the settlement conference.

(4) *Attendance of Parties.* The parties shall in all cases attend the settlement conference.

Parties whose defense is provided by a liability insurance company need not personally attend said settlement conference, but a representative of the insurer of such party, if such a representative is available in Chelan–Douglas counties, shall attend with sufficient authority to bind the insurer to a settlement. In the event such a representative is not available, counsel representing the party whose defense is provided by the insurer shall make a good faith effort to obtain settlement authority to bind the insurer to a settlement prior to the settlement conference.

Attendance of any party may be excused by the court where by reason of health, or other good and sufficient reason, compelling his personal attendance would be unduly burdensome. Whether or not the attendance of any party is required shall rest in the discretion of the Judge. Request for excuse shall be made at least three (3) days prior to the hearing.

(5) *Proceedings Privileged.* Proceedings of said settlement conference shall, in all respects, be privileged and shall not be reported or recorded. No party shall be bound unless a settlement is reached. When a settlement has been reached, the judge may, at the request of any party, in his discretion, order the settlement to be reported or recorded.

(6) *Sanctions.* Where a party has failed to comply with any of the provisions of this rule the court shall make such orders as are just which shall include the award of reasonable expenses, including attorney's fees, caused by the failure, unless the court finds that the failure was substantially justified or that other circumstances make an award of expenses unjust.

[Adopted effective September 1, 1999.]

LR 16 EXHIBIT A. ORDER FOR PRETRIAL CONFERENCE

IN THE SUPERIOR COURT OF THE STATE OF WASHINGTON
IN AND FOR THE COUNTY OF DOUGLAS

	)
	)
	)
	)
Plaintiff(s),	)
	)
vs.	) No.
	)
	)
	) ORDER FOR PRETRIAL
	) CONFERENCE
	)
Defendant(s).	)

THIS CAUSE appearing to be at issue and ready for trial, it is

1. ORDERED AND ADJUDGED THAT a pretrial conference will be held in Chambers at _____ .m. at the _____ County Courthouse on the _____ day of _____ , 19 ____ . Total time allocated for the conference will be _____ . The attorneys who will conduct the trial must attend this conference.

All discovery procedures shall be completed by the time of this conference.

2. ORDERED AND ADJUDGED THAT at least five working days prior to this conference, the attorneys shall submit to the trial judge and to opposing counsel a Pretrial Statement containing the following:

(a) A list designating those pleadings upon which the case goes to trial;

(b) A succinct statement of the cause of action in regard to each claim or defense;

(c) A clear statement of the issues to be tried;

(d) An itemized list of the claimed special damages;

(e) A statement of the principles of law involved in the case, supported by citations of authority;

(f) A statement of facts which his client will admit;

(g) A list of the names and addresses of all persons who have knowledge of relevant facts and the general nature of their testimony;

(h) A list of all exhibits and documentary evidence which may be used at the trial;

(i) A complete set of written jury instructions, standard and special, which will be proposed for use at the trial, including verdict forms;

(j) Any request for preliminary rulings on questions of law with citations in regard thereto;

(k) Any trial brief that either party wishes the court to consider.

3. ORDERED AND ADJUDGED THAT at the time of the conference, the first thirty minutes of the conference will be set aside for a meeting between counsel to:

(a) Inspect all documentary evidence and transportable exhibits listed in their Pretrial Statements. Exhibits not easily transportable will be made available for inspection at a time and place fixed at the conference.

(b) Mark each document and exhibit using consecutive numerals for the plaintiff and the defendant.

(c) Object to the admissibility of the evidence, reserving the appropriate objections.

(d) Object to the jury instructions filed with the Pretrial Statements, reserving the appropriate objections.

(e) Stipulate on all matters of fact and law upon which the parties are in agreement.

DONE AND ORDERED in Chambers in Douglas County, Washington, this _____ day of _____ 19 ____ .

_____

JUDGE

[Adopted effective September 1, 1999.]

LR 16 EXHIBIT B.   PRETRIAL ORDER FORM

IN THE SUPERIOR COURT OF THE STATE OF WASHINGTON
IN AND FOR THE COUNTY OF DOUGLAS

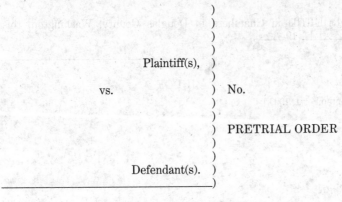

```
                                  )
                                  )
                                  )
                                  )
              Plaintiff(s),       )
                                  )
        vs.                       )   No.
                                  )
                                  )
                                  )   PRETRIAL ORDER
                                  )
                                  )
              Defendant(s).       )
_____)
```

I.   BASIS

1.1   The above matter has been noted for trial setting.

1.2   A pretrial conference was held and the following persons were present:

      For Plaintiff(s):   For Defendant(s):

II.   ORDER

2.1   Names and addresses of attendant lawyers who will try the case and are authorized to enter into binding stipulations:

      For Plaintiff(s):   For Defendant(s):

2.2   Summary of plaintiff's case:

2.3   Summary of defense and counterclaim:

2.4   The following amendments are allowed to the pleadings:

2.5   Names and addresses of plaintiff's witnesses and summary of testimony expected from each:

2.6   Names and addresses of defendant's witnesses and summary of testimony expected from each:

Additional Witnesses: If additional witnesses are discovered, who by the use of reasonable diligence could not have been discovered before the Pretrial Conference, the party intending to use such witness shall immediately report the names, addresses and summary of the testimony of such witness to opposing counsel and the court.

2.7   Facts admitted by stipulation and agreement:

2.8   Exhibits produced for admission:

  a.   The following exhibits were marked, identified and admitted without objection, no further identification or offers of admission shall be required at trial:

b.. The following exhibits were produced and offered but were objected to for competency, relevancy and materiality; they may be introduced at the trial without formal identification, their authenticity being agreed to:

c. The admission of the following exhibits will be contested:

d. The following exhibits will be sent to opposing counsel within _____ days and within five days of receipt forwarded to the court with any objections thereto; in the event no objections are raised the exhibits will be admitted in accordance with the provisions of (a) above.

Additional Exhibits: If additional exhibits or documents are discovered which could not have been discovered by reasonable diligence before the Pretrial Conference, the party intending to use them shall immediately exhibit them to opposing counsel and submit them to the court to be marked for identification. Opposing counsel shall immediately indicate to the court his or her position with respect to such exhibit, i.e., whether his or her position falls under (a), (b) or (c) above.

2.9   Unresolved issues:

2.10 Points of law passed upon by the court:

2.11 Estimated length of trial: Jury:

2.12 Other matters that may aid the trial:

Set for trial:

Approved, stipulated and agreed:

_____   _____
Attorney for Plaintiff   Attorney for Defendant

   IT IS ORDERED that the stipulations be carried out as outlined above.

DATED: _____   _____
                                       JUDGE

[Adopted effective September 1, 1999.]

LR 32. USE OF DEPOSITIONS IN COURT PROCEEDINGS

(a) Use of Depositions.

(6) Video Depositions. When presenting video depositions, a written deposition must also be filed. The videotape may be returned after the appeal period, regardless if it is published or not.

[Adopted effective September 1, 1999.]

LR 37. FAILURE TO MAKE DISCOVERY; SANCTIONS

(f) Completion of Discovery. Unless otherwise stipulated to by the parties, or ordered by the Court upon good cause shown and such terms and conditions as are just, all discovery allowed under CR 26 through 37, including responses and supplementations thereto, must be completed no later than 35 calendar days prior to the date assigned for trial. Nothing herein stated shall modify a party's responsibility to seasonably supplement responses to discovery requests or otherwise comply with discovery prior to the 35–day cutoff.

[Adopted effective September 1, 1999.]

LR 47. JURORS

(k) Counsel or the parties shall not contact or interview jurors or cause jurors to be contacted or interviewed after trial without first having been granted leave to do so by the Court.

[Adopted effective September 1, 1999.]

LR 49. VERDICTS

(*l*) Receiving Verdict During Absence of Counsel. A party or attorney desiring to be present at the return of the verdict must remain in attendance at the courthouse or be available by telephone call. If a party or attorney fails to appear within 20 minutes of telephone notice to the attorney's office, home or other number, the court may proceed to take the verdict in the absence of such party or attorney. In such case, the jury shall be individually polled and the identity of any dissenting jurors recorded.

[Adopted effective September 1, 1999.]

LR 52. DECISIONS, FINDINGS AND CONCLUSIONS

(a) through (e), Washington Court Rules

(f) In all actions tried to the court, counsel for each party shall, two days prior to trial, provide the Court and opposing counsel with proposed findings of fact and conclusions of law. Provided, that proposed findings and conclusions are not required in domestic cases of any kind, except that the court may, at its discretion, require proposed findings and conclusions, in a particular case or the parties may voluntarily submit such findings and conclusions.

(g) Time Limit for Presentation. In cases tried to the court, findings of fact, conclusions of law and a proposed judgment shall be presented within twenty (20) days of the court's oral or memorandum decision; provided however, that in the event post-trial motions are filed, the twenty (20) days shall run from the date of ruling on such motions.

In the event that said findings of fact, conclusions of law and the proposed judgment are presented to the court in excess of twenty (20) days of the court's oral decision, the party presenting such findings of fact, conclusions of law and proposed judgment shall, if requested by the court, prepare and file a transcript of the court's oral decision.

[Adopted effective September 1, 1999.]

LR 56. SUMMARY JUDGMENT

(a) through (h), Washington Court Rules

(i) Special setting. Douglas County summary judgments shall be heard by the Judge of Douglas County.

ALL MOTIONS FOR SUMMARY JUDGMENTS IN DOUGLAS COUNTY *MUST* BE SPECIAL SET. SPECIAL SETTINGS SHALL BE OBTAINED BY CALLING JUDGES' CHAMBERS IN DOUGLAS COUNTY (745–9063 or 884–9430) AND REQUESTING TO SET A MATTER ON THE JUDGE'S CALENDAR.

(j) Service and Filing.

A WORKING COPY FOR THE JUDGE OF THE MOTION, ALL SUPPORTING DOCUMENTS AND ALL RESPONDING DOCUMENTS SHALL BE DELIVERED TO THE COURTHOUSE OR MAILED TO THE JUDGE AT THE TIME OF FILING THE ORIGINALS. THE MAILING ADDRESS FOR THE JUDGE IS P. O. BOX 488, WATERVILLE, WASHINGTON 98858–0488. IF WORKING COPIES ARE NOT RECEIVED, THE JUDGE MAY STRIKE THE HEARING.

Where depositions or interrogatories are a part of the evidence relied upon, counsel's affidavits, briefs and arguments must cite the depositions or interrogatories by page and line.

ANY MATERIAL OFFERED AT A TIME LATER THAN REQUIRED BY THIS RULE OVER OBJECTION OF COUNSEL SHALL NOT BE ACCEPTED AND CONSIDERED BY THE COURT EXCEPT UPON THE IMPOSITION OF APPROPRIATE TERMS OR SANCTIONS, INCLUDING THE RIGHT TO A CONTINUANCE IF REQUESTED.

Any motion for summary judgment or responsive pleadings to a motion for summary judgment shall list and identify all evidence the Court should consider.

(k) Confirmation. On any motion for summary judgment in Douglas County, counsel for the moving party shall contact the Court Administrator three court days preceding the date set for hearing and advise whether the motion will be heard. If notification is not made, the motion may be stricken for resetting.

[Adopted effective September 1, 1999.]

LR 58. ENTRY OF JUDGMENT

(m) Judgment on a Promissory Note. No judgment on a promissory note will be signed until the original note has been filed with the Clerk, absent proof of loss or destruction.

[Adopted effective September 1, 1999.]

LR 59. MOTION FOR RECONSIDERATION

(e) Hearing on Motion.

(3) *Nature of Hearing.*

(A) A motion for reconsideration or for a new trial shall be submitted on briefs and declarations or affidavits only, without oral argument, unless the trial judge, on application from counsel or on the judge's own motion, allows oral argument. The judge will notify counsel if oral argument is to be allowed. Copies of such motions for reconsideration, copy of note for motion calendar and responses thereto shall be delivered to the judge at the time of filing.

(B) The scheduled hearing date will not ordinarily involve oral argument. However, it will be the earliest date that the court will consider the merits of the motion. In the event that oral argument has been allowed, counsel for the moving party shall notify the Clerk of the Court by noon, three days preceding the date set for hearing and advise whether the motion will be argued.

[Adopted effective September 1, 1999.]

LR 65. INJUNCTIONS

(b) Temporary Restraining Order; Notice; Hearing; Duration.

(1) *Notice to Opponent.* Failure to give notice as required by CR 65 may result in the imposition of terms and/or sanctions on the moving party.

[Adopted effective September 1, 1999.]

LR 77. SUPERIOR COURTS AND JUDICIAL OFFICERS

(o) Court Calendar for Douglas County. The Judge will hold Probate and Law and Motion Calendars the second and fourth Tuesday at 1:30 p.m.

Adoption hearings will be held at 1:30 p.m., in Chambers, on the Law & Motion Calendar,

Douglas County's Court schedule is as follows:

Monday:	Criminal Calendar at 10:00 a.m. via video and 1:30 p.m. for in-person appearances

Tuesday:	
Domestic violence hearings:	1:00 p.m.
2nd and 4th Tuesdays:	Civil Calendar at 1:30 p.m.
1st and 3rd Tuesdays:	Truancies at 3:00 p.m. at District Court in East Wenatchee
3rd Tuesday	DV and Civil Calendar at 1:00 p.m. at District Court in East Wenatchee

Wednesday:	
1st, 2nd and 3rd:	Juvenile Calendar at 9:00 a.m. and 1:00 p.m.
4th Wednesday:	Dependency Calendar at 9:00 a.m.

Thursday:	
2nd and 4th Thursdays:	Criminal trials at 9:00 a.m.

To obtain a special setting, contact the Court Administrator at 509–745–9063.

A COURT REPORTER WILL NOT BE PROVIDED FOR ANY MATTER SCHEDULED ON ANY CALENDAR. ALL MATTERS WILL BE DIGITALLY AUDIO RECORDED.

(a) Domestic Relations Show Cause hearings requiring more than 30 minutes will be scheduled by special setting.

A COURT REPORTER WILL NOT BE PROVIDED FOR ANY MATTER SCHEDULED ON ANY CALENDAR. ALL MATTERS WILL BE DIGITALLY AUDIO RECORDED.

(2) Holiday Scheduling—These Court schedules will be altered when affected by Holidays as set out in Exhibit A to this rule.

(A) The Judge may by order further alter these court schedules as needed and as available courtroom space requires.

(p) Ex parte matters and emergency orders and writs will be considered at the opening of court each day prior to the commencement of trial or the regular court calendar or at such other time as the judges and/or court commissioners are available. Non–emergency matters shall be left with the Clerk and the judges/commissioner will consider the same when available.

(q) Special Settings. Any matter which will require more than ten minutes of argument per party shall be specially set at a time arranged with the Court.

[Adopted effective September 1, 1999. Amended effective September 1, 2000; September 1, 2005; September 1, 2015.]

LR 77 EXHIBIT A. HOW HOLIDAYS WILL AFFECT THIS SCHEDULE

Holiday on a Monday

Judge's Calendar:

Monday's Criminal Calendar will be cancelled at the Judge's discretion.

[Adopted effective September 1, 1999; amended effective September 1, 2000.]

LR 78. "ACTION" DOCUMENTS

Pleadings or other papers requiring action on the part of the Clerk of the Court (other than filing, stamping, docketing and placing in the court file) shall constitute action documents. Action documents shall include a special caption directly below the case number on the first page such as "Clerk's Action Required". The specific action required of the Clerk shall be stated with particularity in the body of the pleading or other paper requiring action on the part of the Clerk.

[Adopted effective September 1, 1999.]

LR 80. COURT REPORTERS

A COURT REPORTER WILL NOT BE PROVIDED FOR ANY MATTER HEARD IN DOUGLAS COUNTY SUPERIOR COURT. ALL MATTERS WILL BE DIGITALLY AUDIO RECORDED. IF ANY PARTY WISHES ANY MATTER TO BE REPORTED BY A COURT REPORTER, THAT PARTY IS RESPONSIBLE TO PROVIDE A COURT REPORTER.

[Adopted effective September 1, 2000; amended effective September 1, 2005.]

LR 94.04. MARRIAGE DISSOLUTION ACTIONS

A. Non-Contested Dissolution Hearings.

(1) *Hearing.* Non-contested dissolution cases may be heard on a calendar set by the Superior Court Judge and Clerk. The days and times are set forth in LR 77. Non contested dissolution cases may also be presented to the Superior Court Judge in Chambers without the appearance of either party. For the Superior Court Judge to sign a non contested Decree of Dissolution, Legal Separation or other document, the parties must have executed all documents and have their signatures notarized, *including any Joinder executed by the adverse party.* The jurisdictional testimony and other testimony in support of the dissolution must be done in affidavit form and verified.

(2) *Note for Non-Contested Calendar.* A notice of hearing on the non-contested calendar must be filed with the Clerk at least three court days before the date of hearing. The Clerk shall not place any case on the non-contested calendar unless the file shows one of the following:

(a) The opposing party has joined in the petition for dissolution of marriage and his or her signature is notarized on the joinder; or

(b) The opposing party has waived notice or has signed a consent to hearing on the date noted; or

(c) An order for default has been applied for or entered.

The Clerk shall not place any case on the non-contested calendar unless proof is filed that summons was served more than ninety (90) days before the date selected for hearing or that the case has been on file more than ninety (90) days and both parties have submitted to the jurisdiction of the court.

(3) *Withdrawal of Consent.* Before a decree is entered, a party may move to withdraw any consent or waiver previously given. Such motion must be supported by affidavit showing good cause and shall be noted for hearing on the show cause calendar.

(4) *Order of Non-Contested Calendar.* The order of the non-contested calendar will be as follows:

(a) Matters where attorneys appear;

(b) Pro se matters.

(5) *Entry of Decree.* At the time of hearing of a non-contested dissolution case, the necessary documents to be signed must be presented to the court for signature. If signed they shall be filed with the Clerk forthwith. For good cause shown, the court may extend the time for presentation.

(6) *Disposition of Issues in Decree.* No decree of dissolution shall be entered unless the decree disposes of all issues over which the court has jurisdiction relating to disposition of property and liabilities of the parties and support or maintenance of either spouse. For good cause shown, the court may in its discretion enter a decree of dissolution stating that it retains jurisdiction to dispose of issues relating to parenting and child support.

B. Contested Dissolutions.

(1) *Pretrial Forms.* In all final hearings or trials in domestic relations matters, each party shall provide to the judge or commissioner and serve on the opposing party a written statement as to the issues in controversy at least three days prior to trial. The written statement may be in any form chosen by the attorney to convey the following:

(a) A brief factual summary;

(b) Issues in dispute [whether property, debts or custody];

(c) Case law, if it will be argued, supporting your position;

(d) Proposed distribution of assets, debts and proposed parenting plan and child support amount, if in dispute;

(e) Areas of agreement.

If one of the parties is seeking maintenance or child support, *both* parties shall complete the financial declaration contained in Form A.

If the parties are in dispute as to the distribution of assets and debts, *both* parties shall complete Form LC

94.04 Exhibit B. The pretrial forms shall not be filed with the Clerk.

Unless explained otherwise by the parties, the values shown on the pretrial form for proposed distribution of assets shall be present cash value of any pension, retirement, profit sharing or other deferred benefit or financial security plan; the cash surrender value of all life insurance policies; the amounts of accounts receivable, inheritance due, and trust accounts; the fair market value of all other property including collections, antiques; and in the case of automobiles, the average between wholesale and retail blue book values.

(2) *Enforcement.* If either party fails to comply with paragraph B(1) set forth above, the trial judge may order such party or his attorney to pay an appropriate attorney's fee to the opponent for any additional work or delay caused by the failure to comply. If either party fails to comply, the trial date may be stricken.

(3) *Continuances.* Stipulations or motions to continue a case already on the trial calendar must be in writing, supported by a declaration showing sufficient grounds for the requested continuance. The moving party shall present a written order for entry.

C. Child Custody or Parenting Plan Proceedings.

(1) *Parenting Plans.*

(a) Proposed, Temporary and Permanent Parenting plans shall be in the form required by State law. Proposed temporary parenting plans need not have the dispute resolution and decision making sections completed.

D. Dating and Mailing of Decrees and Orders.

(1) When any decree or order is filed in a dissolution matter, the attorney for the party presenting the order, or the party if the matter is presented pro se, shall immediately deliver or mail to the opposing party to the opposing party's last known address, or to opposing counsel, a true copy of the decree or order with the date of entry indicated on each copy. A declaration of mailing of such true copy shall be filed.

E. Hearings—Show Cause—Preliminary and Temporary Orders.

(1) *Hearings.* See Local Rule 77.

(2) *Hearing by Documentary Evidence.* All show cause hearings pertaining to request for temporary support money and/or attorney's fees shall be heard and determined by documentary evidence only, unless the parties request that oral testimony be given and the court in its discretion agrees.

(3) *Supporting Worksheet.* A motion for order to show cause for temporary support shall be supported by a child support worksheet in the form prescribed by state law and may also include a financial declaration in the form designated in *Exhibit A* attached to this rule. No order shall be signed setting a show cause hearing for temporary support unless the signed worksheet accompanies the motion.

(4) *Information Considered Notwithstanding Non-Appearance.* An affidavit or child support worksheet filed by a non-appearing respondent shall be considered by the court at the time of hearing on show cause hearings and upon hearing default dissolutions.

F. Disposal of Proposed Parenting Plan. The Clerk is authorized to remove from the file and dispose of all proposed parenting plans after the Permanent Parenting Plan has been entered and the time for appeal has elapsed.

In request to have law enforcement assist in procuring a child or individual that petitioner alleges is being held in violation of a court order, custody decree or other lawful proceeding shall be done by writ of habeas corpus.

G. Appointment of Optional Guardian Ad Litem.

(1) *Optional Guardian Ad Litem.* In any domestic relations matter the court may, upon its own motion, or motion of either party, appoint a guardian ad litem to represent the interests of any child, or children, of the parties. If any decree illegitimizes a child or may result in a child becoming illegitimate, the court may require that a guardian ad litem be appointed for the child.

(2) *Appointment.* The guardian ad litem shall be appointed from the court-approved registry for Title 26 RCW. Said person shall have such powers, as granted by the court, to ascertain what is in the best interests of the child or children, and to take whatever steps the court deems appropriate to effectuate a result consistent with the best interest of the child or children.

(3) *Duties of Guardian Ad Litem.* The court may direct the guardian ad litem to report to the court, either orally or in writing. The guardian ad litem has the right to attend and participate at trial or any other proceeding, and shall be given all other rights accorded a party, including notice. The guardian ad litem may be called as a witness at trial by either party, or the court.

H. Mandatory Information Program for Parents. The Douglas County Superior Court finds that it is in the best interest of any child whose parents or custodians are involved in specific court proceedings to provide such parents with an educational workshop concerning the impact family restructuring has on their child. The workshop offers parents tools to help ensure that their child's emotional needs will not be overlooked during the legal processes, to encourage parents to agree on child-related matters, and to aid in maximizing the use of court time.

(1) *Types of Proceedings Required.* Each person named as a party in the following types of proceedings filed after January 1, 1999 must comply with Local Rule 94.04H:

   1. Dissolution of Marriage with child(ren) under 18 years old;

   2. Legal Separation or Declaration of Invalidity with child(ren) under 18 years old.

   3. Petition to establish custody or visitation including paternity, and/or

   4. Post-judgment petition involving custody or visitation.

(2) *Service on Parties.* The Clerk of the court shall provide a copy of this rule (LR 94.04H) to the initiating party for service upon all parties against whom relief is sought, together with a statement describing the program including contact telephone numbers, addresses, statement of costs, and an explanation of how to request a waiver or deferral of the program registration fee.

(3) *Mandatory.* Each party who files an appearance in a proceeding of the types described above in Section (1) shall complete the program unless exempted by the court. **No final order approving any residential or parenting plan shall be entered without proof of completion of such education program by the parents or legal guardians unless otherwise ordered by the court.**

(4) *Ninety (90) Day Deadline.* Each party shall attend and complete an approved parenting workshop within ninety (90) days of filing a proceeding specified in Section (1) above.

(5) *Exemption.* The Court may exempt one or both parties from completion of the program if, after reviewing the requesting party's motion and supporting affidavit, the Court determines that participation is unnecessary.

(6) *Approved Program.* The parent education program sponsored by the Washington State University (WSU) Extension Service is an approved program. Other programs may be approved by application to the Court.

(7) *Proof of Completion.* Upon completion of the program, the workshop provider shall issue a certificate of completion to each program participant. The certificate of completion shall be filed with the Clerk of the Court.

(8) *Non–Complying Parties–Attorney's Fees Sanctions.* A party who has completed the program shall have the right to request entry of an order from the court compelling the non-complying party's completion of the program. Should the non-complying party fail to complete the program in a timely manner without good reason, the court shall enter an award of reasonable attorney fees incurred for obtaining an order for compliance in favor of the complying party who uses this option to force the non-complying party into compliance or other sanctions as set forth below.

(9) *Other Sanctions.* If upon order of the court a non-complying party continues to refuse participation, the refusal may be considered by the Court in making its ruling on issues that are in dispute and/or may be grounds for contempt.

(10) *Fees.* Each party shall pay the fee charged by the approved provider. The Court shall reduce the fee to fifteen dollars ($15.00) whenever the filing fee has been waived. The court may waive the entire fee upon special application to the Court.

WRIT OF HABEAS CORPUS–POLICIES AND PROCEDURES

1. The following forms are adopted by this Local Rule of the Douglas County Superior Court:

- Order to Issue Writ of Habeas Corpus and Warrant in Aid of Writ
- Writ of Habeas Corpus
- Warrant in Aid of Writ of Habeas Corpus

The text of the above forms may not be altered. Obsolete or altered forms will not be accepted by law enforcement.

2. A Habeas Corpus must be commenced by the filing of a signed and verified Petition. The Petition must set forth the information required by RCW 7.36.030. A mandatory Petition form has not been adopted.

3. The Order to Issue Writ must be signed by a Judge/Court Commissioner and filed with the clerk of the Superior Court. Obtain a certified copy of the Order to Issue Writ at the time of filing, as the certified copy will be necessary for the Sheriff's office. Filing fees, writ fees and certified copy fees will be payable to the Clerk of the Court at that time.

4. On filing the Order to Issue Writ, the Clerk of the Douglas County Superior Court will issue the Writ of Habeas Corpus and the Warrant in Aid of Writ of Habeas Corpus. The originals will be given to the petitioner's attorney.

5. The following **must** be provided to the Sheriff's office:

- A **certified** copy of the Order to Issue Writ
- The **original** Writ of Habeas Corpus
- The **original** Warrant in Aid of Writ of Habeas Corpus
- Information Sheet, which contains information regarding the parties and child(ren)
- A copy of the Petition for Writ of Habeas Corpus
- A copy of the most recent Order or Decree which grants petitioner custody

- A recent photograph of the child(ren), if available

- A recent photograph of respondent, if available

- Payment of the base fee for service of the Writ. Mileage and additional services fees will be subsequently billed.

6. A law enforcement interview of the petitioner or petitioner's attorney is strongly encouraged in order to obtain information helpful towards locating the child(ren) and assuring officer safety.

7. The petitioner, petitioner's attorney, family members and private investigators may not accompany law enforcement during attempts to execute the Writ.

8. When a child is recovered, both petitioner and respondent will be immediately notified by law enforcement. The child is then brought immediately before the Superior Court. A child will never be directed returned to the petitioner. If the Superior Court is not in session, then the child will be placed in temporary care through DSHS. Temporary care is avoided if at all possible and, unless specifically ordered by the Court, Writs are not served on weekends, holidays, or after Court hours.

[Adopted effective September 1, 1999; amended effective September 1, 2000.]

IN THE SUPERIOR COURT OF THE STATE OF WASHINGTON
IN AND FOR THE COUNTY OF DOUGLAS

In re Custody of,	)	
	)	
	)	
─────────────────────────────────,	)	No.
Minor Child/Children	)	
	)	
	)	
─────────────────────────────────,	)	WARRANT IN AID OF
Petitioner,	)	WRIT OF HABEAS CORPUS
	)	
and	)	
	)	
	)	
─────────────────────────────────,	)	
Respondent.	)	

The State of Washington To: The Sheriff of Douglas County
And To: Any peace officer in the State of Washington

YOU ARE HEREBY AUTHORIZED to break and enter any outer or inner door or other opening of any building, structure, vehicle, or other enclosure in which you have reason to believe the child/children _____ is/are located or where information pertaining to the location of the child/children may be found, and as necessary to secure the body/bodies of the child/children and bring him/her/them before the Douglas County Superior Court; and

YOU ARE FURTHER ORDERED to arrest any persons who obstruct or otherwise prevent your efforts to carry out the Order of this Court the execution of the Writ of Habeas Corpus and to bring such persons before the Douglas County Superior Court for questioning; and

YOU ARE FURTHER ORDERED, in the event the Superior Court is not in session at the time of arrest, to hold any person obstructing or otherwise preventing your efforts to carry out the Order of the Court and the Writ of Habeas Corpus in the Chelan County Regional Jail until the next day on which the Superior Court is in session.

Witness_____

Judge/Court Commissioner of the Superior Court In and for Douglas County this ____ day of _____, 1999.

Attest: My hand and seal of the Superior Court this ____ day of _____, 1999.

Clerk_____

By _____, Deputy

IN THE SUPERIOR COURT OF THE STATE OF WASHINGTON
IN AND FOR THE COUNTY OF DOUGLAS

In re Custody of,

_____,) No.
            Minor Child/Children

_____,) ORDER TO ISSUE WRIT OF
            Petitioner,   ) HABEAS CORPUS AND
) WARRANT IN AID OF WRIT
and

_____,)
            Respondent.   )

THIS MATTER having come on before the undersigned this day on the Petitioner's motion for the issue of a Writ of Habeas Corpus, Petitioner appearing by and through his/her attorney, _____, the Court having reviewed the file and the supporting affidavit(s), and having heard the statements of counsel, it is now

ORDERED, ADJUDGED AND DECREED that a Writ of Habeas Corpus issue directing the Sheriff of Douglas County and any other peace officer in the State of Washington to locate and take _____ into immediate custody and bring such child/children before the Douglas County Superior Court; it is further

ORDERED, ADJUDGED AND DECREED that in the event the Superior Court is not in session at the time such child/children is/are taken into custody, the child/children shall be placed in the care, custody and control of the Department of Social and health Services until the next day on which the Superior Court is in session; it is further

ORDERED, ADJUDGED AND DECREED that the Department of Social and Health services shall place the child/children into protective custody and shall only release the child/children to the Sheriff or any other peace officer of the State of Washington acting pursuant to this Order, or upon a further Order of this Court to a person specifically authorized to receive the care, custody and control of the child/children; it is further

ORDERED, ADJUDGED AND DECREED that the Sheriff and any other peace officer may break and enter any outer or inner door or other opening of any building, structure, vehicle, or other enclosure in which they have reason to believe the child/children is/are located or where information pertaining to the location of the child/children may be found; it is further

ORDERED, ADJUDGED AND DECREED that the Sheriff and any other peace officer may arrest any person who stands in the way, obstructs or otherwise prevents their lawful efforts to obtain immediately custody of the child/children and to bring such person(s) before the Douglas County Superior Court for questioning; it is further

ORDERED, ADJUDGED AND DECREED that, in the event the Superior Court is not in session at the time of arrest, the Sheriff and any other peace officer shall hold any person who stands in the way, obstructs or otherwise prevents lawful efforts to obtain immediate custody of the child/children in the Chelan County Regional Jail until the next day on which the Superior Court is in session.

DATE: _____   _____
                                          JUDGE/COURT COMMISSIONER

Presented by:

_____
        , WSBA #_____
Attorney for Petitioner

IN THE SUPERIOR COURT OF THE STATE OF WASHINGTON
IN AND FOR THE COUNTY OF DOUGLAS

In re Custody of,   )
)
)
_____,) No.
            Minor Child/Children   )
)
)
_____,)
                Petitioner,   ) WRIT OF HABEAS CORPUS
)
and   )
)
)
_____,)
                Respondent.   )

The State of Washington To: The Sheriff of Douglas County
And To: Any peace officer in the State of Washington
And To: The Department of Social and Health Services

THE SHERIFF AND ANY PEACE OFFICER ARE HEREBY COMMANDED to secure custody of the body/bodies of _____, wherever he/she/they may be detained and bring him/her/them before the Douglas County Superior Court. In the event the Superior Court is not in session at the time such child/children is/are taken into custody, you shall place the child/children in the care, custody and control of the Department of Social and Health Services until such time as this matter may be heard on the next day on which the Superior Court is in session.

THE DEPARTMENT OF SOCIAL SERVICES IS HEREBY COMMANDED to take custody of the child/children from law enforcement and place the child/children into protective custody until such time as this matter may be heard by the Superior Court. The Department of Social and Health Services shall only release the child/children to the Douglas County Sheriff or any other peace officer of the State of Washington acting pursuant to this Writ or, upon a further Order of this Court, to a person specifically authorized to receive the care, custody and control of the child/children.

THE SHERIFF AND ANY PEACE OFFICER ARE FURTHER ORDERED to break and enter any outer or inner door or other opening of any building, structure, vehicle, or other enclosure in which you have reason to believe the child/children is/are located or where information pertaining to the location of the child/children may be found, and as necessary to secure the body of the child/children and bring him/her/them before the Superior Court.

Witness_____

Judge/Court Commissioner of the Superior Court in and for Douglas County this ____ day of _____, 1999.

Attest: My hand and seal of the Superior Court

This _____ day of _____, 1999.

Clerk_____

By _____, Deputy

LR 94.04 EXHIBIT A. DECLARATION RE FINANCIAL ABILITY

SUPERIOR COURT OF WASHINGTON
COUNTY OF DOUGLAS

In re:	)
	)
	) NO.
	) FINANCIAL DECLARATION
Petitioner	) ( ) Petitioner
and	) ( ) Respondent
	)
	)
Respondent	)
	)
_____)	(FNDCLR)

Name: Date of Birth:
Social Security Number:

I. SUMMARY OF BASIC INFORMATION

Declarant's Total Monthly Net Income
(from § 3.3 below) $_____

Declarant's Total Monthly Household Expenses
(from § 5.9 below) $_____

Declarant's Total Monthly Debt Expenses
(from § 5.11 below) $_____

Declarant's Total Monthly Expenses
(from § 5.12 below) $_____

Estimate of the other party's gross monthly income
(from § 3.1f below) $_____

II. PERSONAL INFORMATION

2.1 Occupation:_____

2.2 The highest year of education completed: _____

2.3 Are you presently employed? [ ] Yes [ ] No

    a. If yes:

        (1) Where do you work? _____

            _____

            (Name and Address)

        (2) When did you start work there (month/year)? _____

    b. If no: (1) When did you last work (month/year)? _____

           (2) What were your gross monthly earnings? _____

           (3) Why are you presently unemployed? _____

                 _____

                 _____

III. INCOME INFORMATION

If child support is at issue, complete the Washington State Child Support Worksheet(s), skip Paragraphs 3.1 and 3.2. If maintenance, fees, costs or debts are at issue and child support is NOT an issue this entire section should be completed. (Estimate of other party's income information is optional.)

3.1   GROSS MONTHLY INCOME.

If you are paid on a weekly basis, multiply your weekly gross pay by 4.3 to determine your monthly wages and salaries. If you are paid every two weeks, multiply your gross pay by 2.15. If you are paid twice monthly, multiply your gross pay by 2. If you are paid once a month, list that amount below.

		Petitioner	Respondent
a.	Wages and Salaries	$_____	$_____
b.	Interest and Dividend Income	$_____	$_____
c.	Business Income	$_____	$_____
d.	Spousal Maintenance From Other Relationships	$_____	$_____
e.	Other Income	$_____	$_____
f.	Total Gross Monthly Income (add lines 3.1a through 3.1e)	$_____	$_____
g.	Actual Gross Income (Year to date)	$_____	$_____

3.2   MONTHLY DEDUCTIONS FROM GROSS INCOME.

		Petitioner	Respondent
a.	Income Taxes	$_____	$_____
b.	FICA/Self-employment Taxes	$_____	$_____
c.	State Industrial Insurance Deductions	$_____	$_____
d.	MANDATORY Union/Professional Dues	$_____	$_____
e.	Pension Plan Payments	$_____	$_____
f.	Spousal Maintenance Paid	$_____	$_____
g.	Normal Business Expenses	$_____	$_____
h.	Total Deductions from Gross Income (add lines 3.2a through 3.2g)	$_____	$_____

3.3   MONTHLY NET INCOME.

(Line 3.1f minus line 3.2h or line 3 from the Child Support Worksheet(s).) $_____ $_____

3.4   MISCELLANEOUS INCOME.

		Petitioner	Respondent
a.	Child support received from other relationships	$_____	$_____
b.	Other miscellaneous income (list source and amounts):	$_____	$_____
	Other:	$_____	$_____
		$_____	$_____
		$_____	$_____
		$_____	$_____
c.	Total Miscellaneous Income (add lines 3.4a through 3.4c)	$_____	$_____

3.5   Income of Other Adults in Household $_____ $_____

3.6 If the income of either party is disputed, state monthly income you believe is correct and explain below:

IV. AVAILABLE ASSETS

4.1 Cash on hand $_____ $_____

4.2 On deposit in banks $_____ $_____

4.3 Stocks and Bonds, cash value of life insurance $_____ $_____

4.4 Other liquid assets: $_____ $_____

V. MONTHLY EXPENSE INFORMATION

Monthly expenses for myself and _____ dependents are: (Expenses should be calculated for the future, after separation, based on the anticipated residential schedule for the children.)

5.1 HOUSING.

Rent, 1st mortgage or contract payments $_____
Installment payments for other mortgages or encumbrances $_____
Taxes & Insurance (if not in monthly payment) $_____
Total Housing $_____

5.2 UTILITIES.

Heat (gas & oil) $_____
Electricity $_____
Water, sewer, garbage $_____
Telephone $_____
Cable $_____
Other $_____
Total Utilities $_____

5.3 FOOD AND SUPPLIES.

Food for _____ persons $_____
Supplies (paper, tobacco, pets) $_____
Meals eaten out $_____
Other: $_____
Total Food Supplies $_____

5.4 CHILDREN.

Day Care/Babysitting $_____
Clothing $_____
Tuition (if any) $_____
Other child related expenses $_____
Total Expenses Children $_____

5.5 TRANSPORTATION.

Vehicle payments or leases $_____
Vehicle insurance & license $_____
Vehicle gas, oil, ordinary maintenance $_____
Parking $_____
Other transportation expenses $_____
Total Transportation $_____

5.6   HEALTH CARE. (Omit if fully covered)

Insurance $_____
Uninsured dental, orthodontic, medical, eye
care expenses $_____
Other uninsured health expenses $_____
Total Health Care $_____

5.7   PERSONAL EXPENSES (Not including children).

Clothing $_____
Hair care/personal care expenses $_____
Clubs and recreation $_____
Education $_____
Books, newspapers, magazines, photos $_____
Gifts $_____
Other $_____
Total Personal Expenses $_____

5.8   MISCELLANEOUS EXPENSES.

Life insurance (if <u>not</u> deducted from income) $_____
Other: $_____
Other: $_____
Total Miscellaneous Expenses $_____

5.9   TOTAL HOUSEHOLD EXPENSES

(The total of Paragraphs 5.1 through 5.8) $_____

5.10   INSTALLMENT DEBTS INCLUDED IN PARAGRAPHS 5.1 THROUGH 5.8.

Creditor/Debt	Description	Balance	Month of Last Payment

5.11   OTHER DEBTS AND MONTHLY EXPENSES NOT INCLUDED IN PARAGRAPHS 5.1 THROUGH 5.8.

Creditor/Debt	Description	Balance	Month of Last Payment	Amount of Monthly Payment	Payment

Total Monthly Payments for Other Debts and
Monthly Expenses $_____

5.12   TOTAL EXPENSES (Add Paragraphs 5.9 and 5.11) $_____

VI. ATTORNEY FEES

6.1   Amount paid for attorney fees and costs to date: $_____

6.2   The source of this money was:

_____
_____
_____

6.3   Fees and costs incurred to date: $_____

6.4   Arrangements for attorney fees and costs are:

_____
_____
_____

6.5   Other: _____
_____
_____

I DECLARE under penalty of perjury under the laws of the State of Washington that the foregoing is true and correct.

Signed at _____, on _____.

_____
Declarant

THE OTHER PARTY MUST BE SERVED COPIES OF YOUR TAX RETURNS FROM THE LAST TWO YEARS AND COPIES OF YOUR PAYSTUBS FOR THE LAST SIX MONTHS TO VERIFY YOUR INCOME. *ATTACH COPIES TO THIS DOCUMENT. YOU SHOULD ALSO BRING COPIES OF YOUR TAX RETURNS FROM THE LAST TWO YEARS AND COPIES OF YOUR PAY-STUBS FOR THE LAST SIX MONTHS TO YOUR COURT HEARINGS.

[Adopted effective September 1, 1999.]

LR 94.04 EXHIBIT B.   STATEMENT OF ASSETS AND LIABILITIES

ITEM NO.	IN RE THE MARRIAGE OF: and ASSETS AND LIABILITIES (ALL REAL AND PERSONAL PROPERTY; YEAR OF ACQUISITION; ALL DEBTS AND ADJUSTMENTS)	COMMUNITY OR SEPARATE PROPERTY	ACQUISITION COST	HUSBAND'S VALUATION AND PROPOSED DISTRIBUTION		WIFE'S VALUATION AND PROPOSED DISTRIBUTION		COURTS DISTRIBUTION	
				TO HUSBAND	TO WIFE	TO HUSBAND	TO WIFE	TO HUSBAND	TO WIFE
1									
2									
3									
4									
5									
6									
7									
8									
9									
10									
11									
12									
13									
14									
15									
16									
17									
18									
19									

ITEM NO.	ASSETS AND LIABILITIES (ALL REAL AND PERSONAL PROPERTY; YEAR OF ACQUISITION, ALL DEBTS AND ADJUSTMENTS)	COMMUNITY OR SEPARATE PROPERTY	ACQUISITION COST	HUSBAND'S VALUATION AND PROPOSED DISTRIBUTION		WIFE'S VALUATION AND PROPOSED DISTRIBUTION		COURTS DISTRIBUTION	
				TO HUSBAND	TO WIFE	TO HUSBAND	TO WIFE	TO HUSBAND	TO WIFE
20									
21									
22									
23									
24									
25									
26									
27									
28									
29									
30									
TOTAL									

[Adopted effective September 1, 1999.]

LR 94.04H. MANDATORY PARENT EDUCATION WORKSHOP

H. MANDATORY INFORMATION PROGRAM FOR PARENTS. The Douglas County Superior Court finds that it is in the best interest of any child whose parents or custodians are involved in specific court proceedings to provide such parents with an educational workshop concerning the impact family restructuring has on their child. The workshop offers parents tools to help ensure that their child's emotional needs will not be overlooked during the legal processes, to encourage parents to agree on child-related matters, and to aid in maximizing the use of court time.

(1)*I Types of Proceedings Required.* Each person named as a party in the following types of proceedings filed after January 1, 1999 must comply with Local Rule 94.04H:

    1. Dissolution of Marriage with child(ren) under 18 years old;

    2. Legal Separation or Declaration of Invalidity with child(ren) under 18 years old.

    3. Petition to establish custody or visitation including paternity, and/or

    4. Post–judgment petition involving custody or visitation.

(2) *Service on Parties.* The Clerk of the court shall provide a copy of this rule (LR 94.04H) to the initiating party for service upon all parties against whom relief is sought, together with a statement describing the program including contact telephone numbers, addresses, statement of costs, and an explanation of how to request a waiver or deferral of the program registration fee.

(3) *Mandatory.* Each party who files an appearance in a proceeding of the types described above in Section (1) shall complete the program unless exempted by the court. **No final order approving any residential or parenting plan shall be entered without proof of completion of such education program by the parents or legal guardians unless otherwise ordered by the court.**

(4) *Ninety (90) Day Deadline.* Each party shall attend and complete an approved parenting workshop within ninety (90) days of filing a proceeding specified in Section (1) above.

(5) *Exemption.* The Court may exempt one or both parties from completion of the program if, after reviewing the requesting party's motion and supporting affidavit, the Court determines that participation is unnecessary.

(6) *Approved Program.* The parent education program sponsored by the Washington State University (WSU) Extension Service is an approved program.

Other programs may be approved by application to the Court.

(7) *Proof of Completion.* Upon completion of the program, the workshop provider shall issue a certificate of completion to each program participant. The certificate of completion shall be filed with the Clerk of the Court.

(8) *Non–Complying Parties—Attorney's Fees Sanctions.* A party who has completed the program shall have the right to request entry of an order from the court compelling the non-complying party's completion of the program. Should the non-complying party fail to complete the program in a timely manner without good reason, the court shall enter an award of reasonable attorney fees incurred for obtaining an order for compliance in favor of the complying party who uses this option to force the non-complying party into compliance or other sanctions as set forth below.

(9) *Other Sanctions.* If upon order of the court a non-complying party continues to refuse participation, the refusal may be considered by the Court in making its ruling on issues that are in dispute and/or may be grounds for contempt.

(10) *Fees.* Each party shall pay the fee charged by the approved provider. The Court shall reduce the fee to fifteen dollars ($15.00) whenever the filing fee has been waived. The court may waive the entire fee upon special application to the Court.

[Adopted effective September 1, 2002.]

LR 96.04. CHANGE OF NAME OF STEPCHILD

When changing the name of a child under the age of 18 to the name of the child's stepfather, the petitioner shall give notice of such proceeding except as provided by statute to:

    a. The father, if the child has been born during marriage, or

    b. The father, if paternity is established, or

    c. Any other person with a paternal interest by virtue of an adoption.

In addition, written consent shall be required of any child over 14 years of age.

[Adopted effective September 1, 1999.]

LR 98.04. ESTATES—PROBATE

A. Ex Parte. All probate matters that are not contested and in which notice is not required by statute, rule, or duly filed request for notice under R.C.W. 11.28.240 or where such notice has been waived, may be done ex parte.

B. Contents of File for Ex Parte Presentation. The following documents will be presented before ex parte presentation.

    (1) Original will.

(2) Affidavits of subscribing witnesses.

(3) Certified copy of Death Certificate.

(4) Order admitting will to probate or order appointing administrator if petition is by surviving spouse.

(5) Petition for order of solvency if solvency is requested.

(6) An inventory or partial inventory of assets and debts sufficient to prove solvency.

(7) An order of solvency.

C. Presentation by Mail. An original probate application may be presented by mail under the following conditions.

(1) All documents required by 98.04(B) shall be presented in the mailing.

(2) All documents shall bear the personal original signature of counsel or party pro se presenting same.

(3) *Covering Letter.* All documents shall be accompanied by a covering letter of explanation personally signed by the presenter and shall request the Clerk to deliver the documents to a Judge or a Court Commissioner for signing.

(4) *Return Envelope.* A self-addressed return envelope bearing sufficient postage paid shall be included for the return of any requested conformed copies.

[Adopted effective September 1, 1999.]

LR 98.09A. GUARDIANSHIP FUNDS

In all guardianships in which the funds are held by the guardian as trustee for the ward, the funds shall be placed in a designated bank account and the passbook for such account shall be deposited with the Clerk of the Court and withdrawals made from such account only upon order of the Court.

The tax identification number or social security number of the ward should be included in any order where the Clerk of the Court is required to invest funds.

[Adopted effective September 1, 1999.]

LR 98.10. DOUGLAS COUNTY SUPERIOR COURT GUARDIAN AD LITEM ROTATIONAL REGISTRY (TITLES 11 AND 26)

SCOPE/PURPOSE

This local rule covers the maintenance and administration of the Guardian ad Litem Registry maintained by the Registry Administrator.

DEFINITIONS

None.

POLICY

A. Registry Administration

1.1 The court shall maintain and administer the GAL registries. These registries are limited to Titles 11.88 and 26 GAL's. These requirements and procedures also apply to persons not listed on a registry who are appointed to serve as a Guardian ad Litem in a field for which there is a registry.

1.2 The Court shall maintain an application form and background information records pertaining to each person on a registry. Persons listed on the registry shall reapply and update background information annually on a date specified for the registry. All application and background information, with the exception of personal identifying information in family law cases and pending complaints, shall be available for public inspection.

1.3 Persons shall be selected to serve on the registry at the discretion of the Court giving due consideration to:

(1) having a sufficient number of GAL's available to fulfill the requests for appointment;

(2) achieving and maintaining diversity; and

(3) retaining panels of persons with substantial experience and special knowledge within given fields. In some cases there may be more qualified applicants that will be needed or would benefit the program, so that not all persons applying will be selected.

1.4 The court shall periodically sponsor or approve training programs which registry applicants shall be required to attend to maintain and improve their level of proficiency. Training programs may be co-sponsored or offered by the state or local bar association under the oversight of the court.

1.5 The registry may be reconstituted periodically after and open application period has been announced. The court may allow additional applicants to be added to the registry periodically.

1.6 The court may impose an application processing fee and/or charge a fee for the training programs.

B. Education and Experience Requirements

2.1 Attorneys

a. Member of the Washington State Bar Association in good standing; and

b. For initial placement on registry, completion of any training as required by statute. For retention on registry, completion of any continuing training, as may be required by statute or the court from time to time.

2.2 Non-attorneys

a. For initial placement on registry, completion of any training as required by statute. For retention on registry, completion of any continuing training, as may be required by statute or the court from time to time.

b. Eligibility to be determined by the court.

C. Application

Each person requesting to be listed on the Guardian Ad Litem Registry (or registries) shall annually submit an application on the current form provided by the court, which shall include the following:

3.1 The name, business address, and telephone number of the applicant.

3.2 The level of formal education of the applicant and, if the applicant is an attorney, the year admitted to practice in Washington State and any other States in which the attorney is licensed to practice.

3.3 A listing of training relating the GAL's duties.

3.4 The number of years experience as a GAL.

3.5 The number of appointments as a GAL and the County or Counties of appointment.

3.6 The applicant's criminal history as defined by RCW 9.94A.030.

3.7 Evidence of the person's knowledge, training, and experience.

3.8 A statement describing the nature, status, and outcome of any complaints, investigations, disciplinary actions, lawsuits, or liability claims lodged against the GAL related to the persons duties as a GAL and any orders for removal of the GAL entered prior to the completion of the GAL's duties for any reason other than a conflict of interest where the GAL had no prior knowledge that the conflict existed.

3.9 A description of the fees charged by the applicant (hourly rate and any required retainer) and a statement of the applicant's willingness to accept cases on a reduced fee basis.

3.10 Agreement to advise the court immediately in the event of any complaint, investigation, or action being commenced related to the applicants duties as a GAL in the instant or any other case which could lead to:

1. Discipline of the applicant;

2. The suspension or revocation of the applicant's professional license(s).

3.11 Agreement to advise the court immediately upon the filing of criminal charges for a felony or a crime involving allegations of theft, dishonesty, or moral turpitude.

D. Appointment of a Guardian Ad Litem from Registry

4.1 A party needing an appointment from a GAL registry shall serve a written request upon the Registry Administrator, who shall appoint as GAL that person whose name next appears on the registry on a rotational basis, subject to that person's acceptance of the appointment.

4.2 The person appointed by the Registry Administrator shall serve upon the parties a notice of appointment.

E. Retention on Registry

5.1 Persons on the registry shall promptly inform the court of any temporary unavailability to serve, or of their intent to resign from the registry.

5.2 A person shall remain on the registry unless the person fails to maintain a current application with attachments or the person is removed or suspended as set forth in Section F.

5.3 A person may be denied listing on, or may be temporarily suspended from, the registry for any reason that places the suitability of the person to act as GAL in question.

5.4 A GAL who ceases to be on the registry and who still has active or incomplete cases shall immediately report this circumstance to the Registry Administrator, who shall reassign such cases.

5.5 A person's retention on the registry shall be reviewed upon the court's receipt of a complaint regarding performance in office or the court's receipt of adverse information regarding the suitability of a person to serve as a GAL. Complaints shall be reviewed in accordance with Section F.

F. Complaint Procedure

6.1 There shall be a complaint review committee consisting of the Superior Court Presiding Judge, the Juvenile Court Administrator and a representative of the Chelan/Douglas Counties Bar Association.

6.2 All complaints must be in writing and must be submitted to the Superior Court Presiding Judge.

6.3 Upon receipt of a written complaint, the Presiding Judge shall convene the Complaint Review Committee within 10 business days to review the complaint. Upon review of the complaint, the complaint Review Committee shall either:

a. Make a finding that the complaint has no merit on it's face, and decline to review the complaint and so inform the complainant; or

b. Make a finding that the complaint does appear to have merit and request a written response from the GAL within 10 business days, detailing the specific issues in the complaint to which the Committee desires a response. The Committee shall provide the GAL with a copy of the original complaint. A GAL's failure to respond within the required 10 business days will result in the immediate suspension of the GAL from all registries.

c. In considering whether the complaint has merit, the Complaint Review Committee shall consider whether the complaint alleges the GAL has:

1. Violated the code of conduct;

2. Misrepresented his or her qualifications to serve as GAL;

3. Not met the annual update requirements set forth in Paragraph 1.2 of this policy;

4. Breached the confidentiality of the parties;

5. Falsified information in a report to the court or in testimony before the court;

6. Failed to report abuse of a child;

7. Communicated with a judicial officer ex-parte;

8. Represented the court in a public forum without prior approval of the court;

9. Violated state or local laws, rules, or this policy in the person's capacity as a GAL; or,

10. Taken or failed to take any other action which would reasonably place the suitability of the person to serve as GAL in question.

6.4 Upon receipt of a written response to a complaint from the GAL, the Complaint Review Committee shall, within 10 business days, make a finding as to each of the issues delineated in the Committee's letter to the GAL that either there is no merit to the issues based upon the GAL's response or that there is merit to the issue. The Review Committee may, at their discretion, extended the time for entering findings to conduct additional investigation if necessary, however, in no case shall that extension be for more than 20 business days and the GAL shall be notified.

6.5 The Complaint Review Committee shall have the authority to issue a written admonishment, a written reprimand, refer the GAL to additional training, recommend to the court, upon it's own motion to remove the GAL from the instant case, or suspend or remove the GAL from the registry. In considering a response, the Committee shall take into consideration any prior complaints which resulted in an admonishment, reprimand, referral to training, removal of the GAL from a particular case, or suspension or removal from a registry. If a GAL is listed on more than one registry, the suspension or removal may apply to each registry the GAL is listed on at the discretion of the Committee.

6.6 The complainant and the GAL shall be notified in writing of the Committee's decision within 10 business days of receipt of the GAL response.

6.7 A GAL may, within 5 business days of receipt of notification that they have been suspended or review the Committee's decision. The court shall designate a hearing officer. The sole purpose of the hearing shall be to review the appropriateness of the suspension or removal from the registry. The hearing officer shall review the written record of the instant case and any prior complaints upon which the Committee relied and hear oral arguments from the GAL and a representative of the Committee. Said hearing shall be conducted within 20 days of the receipt of the request for the hearing.

G. Payment of Guardian Ad Litem

7.1 There shall be no payment of a GAL by anyone, except as authorized by order of the court.

7.2 Each order appointing GAL shall set forth the hourly rate of compensation for the investigative/legal work; source of payment, if determined; and unless waived, shall require the GAL to seek court authorization to provide services in excess of fifty hours per case, not including court appearances.

7.3 The order appointing a GAL may include a provision for a retainer fee, as evidenced by itemized accounting, shall be returned to the parties according to their proportionate responsibility for payment of the GAL.

7.4 All fee requests by the GAL submitted to the court shall contain time records, which distinguished investigative/legal, administrative/clerical, and travel time and shall also be served upon the parties.

7.5 GAL fees shall be the responsibility of a party or parties unless the court has entered and order authorizing payment at public expense.

H. Appointment Procedures

8.1 Requesting Attorney — Send a letter to the registry administrator requesting the appointment of a GAL. The letter should state the name of the case the GAL is for, the case number, and a brief outlining of the case. The outline should provide sufficient information for the prospective GAL to make a determination as to whether or not he or she will accept the case.

8.2 Registry Administrator — The registry administrator will select the next available GAL appearing on the registry and fax or mail a Notice of Appointment to the GAL along with the letter received from the requesting attorney.

a. Check the GAL Rotational Assignments list and determine who is to receive the next appointment.

b. Check the GAL Appointment Summaries to determine the last appointment number assigned.

c. Write in the next Appointment Number to the GAL to receive the assignment on the Rotational Assignment List.

d. Complete a Notice of Appointment form and fax it to the GAL.

e. Prepare and Assignment Summary Sheet.

8.3 Guardian Ad Litem — The GAL may contact the requesting attorney for more information. The GAL will return the Notice of Appointment to the Registry Administrator. If the GAL rejects the appointment or a conflict exists, the process goes back to step two. If the GAL accepts the appointment, the GAL shall comply with all the provisions of the appropriate RCW.

8.4 Registry Administrator — Upon return receipt of a Notice of Appointment, which has been accepted, the Registry Administrator shall forward a copy of the acceptance to the requesting attorney.

8.5 Requesting Attorney — Upon receipt of a Notice of Appointment that has been accepted, the requesting attorney shall see that an Order of Appointment is filed with the Court. A copy of the Order of Appointment shall be provided to the Registry Administrator.

[Adopted effective September 1, 2002.]

LOCAL CRIMINAL RULES FOR SUPERIOR COURT

LCrR 1.2. COURT COMMISSIONER AUTHORITY

In adult criminal cases, any Court Commissioner appointed to serve in the Douglas County Superior Court and qualified under Article 4, Section 23 of the Constitution of the State of Washington shall have the power, authority and jurisdiction, concurrent with the Superior Court Judges, to preside over arraignments, preliminary appearances, initial extradition hearings, and noncompliance proceedings pursuant to RCW 9.94A.200; to accept pleas; to appoint counsel; to make determinations of probable cause; to set, amend, and review conditions of pretrial release; to set bail; to set trial and hearing dates; to authorize continuances and to accept waivers of the right to speedy trial.

[Adopted effective September 1, 2002.]

LCrR 2.2. WARRANT OF ARREST AND SUMMONS

(c) **Warrants and Fax Machine.** Law enforcement officials in Douglas County may send by Fax machine a motion, affidavit and order for a search warrant or an arrest warrant to the Superior Court in Waterville. Upon authorization and entry by the Court, a signed copy of the order shall be sent back by Fax machine to the law enforcement official for execution. Each faxed document shall indicate the date and time sent. The original of the order shall be presented and signed at the earliest possible time for filing with the Court.

Warrants sent by Fax machine to the Superior Court Judge for Douglas County shall be sent to Fax number (509)745–8027.

[Adopted effective September 1, 1999.]

LCrR 3.1. RIGHT TO AND ASSIGNMENT OF COUNSEL

Indigent defendants shall have counsel appointed to represent them in all criminal cases unless the right to counsel is waived. Indigency shall mean an inability to pay an attorney a reasonable fee for the services which appear to be required by reasons of the crime charged without substantial hardship to himself or his family. Defendants who request appointment of counsel may be required to promptly execute and file a financial disclosure under oath, which shall substantially comply with the form set forth in Exhibit A, or the defendant may be required to provide the information orally to the court.

All appointments of counsel by reason of indigency are expressly contingent upon indigency and full disclosure of assets. Where income or assets are discovered or change subsequent to appointment which enable the defendant to afford counsel, or if the defendant can afford partial payment, fees may be ordered to be reimbursed to the court.

Upon appointment of counsel for indigent criminal defendants or other litigants, the Clerk shall promptly provide counsel with notice of the appointment.

Attorneys representing defendants in criminal cases, except when appointed by the Court, must serve prompt written notice of their employment upon the prosecuting attorney and file the same with the Clerk of the Court. To withdraw, an attorney must serve a motion to withdraw upon the prosecuting attorney, file the same with the Clerk of the Court, and note the same for a hearing. No withdrawal will be granted by the Court, except for cause deemed sufficient by the Court. Approval of withdrawal may, if necessary to prevent a continuance of a trial or hearing, be denied, and such attorney be required to proceed with the trial.

SUPERIOR COURT OF THE STATE OF WASHINGTON
IN AND FOR THE COUNTY OF DOUGLAS

State of Washington,   )
)   *DECLARATION OF INDIGENCY*
                    Plaintiff,   )
)   No.: _____
v.   )
)
_____,   )
)
                    Defendant.   )

_____

STATE OF WASHINGTON   )
) ss
COUNTY OF DOUGLAS   )

   I, _____, the above named defendant, do want a lawyer to represent me
in this case. I am without income or assets with which to retain an attorney.

1. GENERAL INFORMATION

      (a) Name: _____
      (b) Address: _____
      (c) Telephone number: _____
      (d) Marital status: [   ] Single [   ] Married [   ] Separated
           Spouse's Name: _____
           Spouses Address: _____
      (e) Number of dependents: _____
           Age of dependents: _____
           Are you presently employed: [   ] Yes [   ] No
           Length of employment: _____ Occupation: _____
      (f) Name and address of employer: _____
           Prior employer: _____
      (g) Is spouse employed? [   ] Yes [   ] No
           Length of employment: _____ Occupation: _____
           Name of spouse's employer: _____

2. INCOME
      (a) Gross monthly income (mine) $_____
      (b) Gross monthly income (spouse) $_____
      (c) Other income $_____

3. ASSETS
      (a) Cash on hand $_____
      (b) Savings account $_____
      (c) Checking account $_____
      (d) Home (cash value less amount owing) $_____
      (e) Vehicles (cash value less amount owing) $_____
           Make and year: _____
      (f) Other assets and property $_____

4. MONTHLY LIVING EXPENSES
      (a) Rent or mortgage $_____
      (b) Food $_____

    (c) Utilities $_____

    (d) Transportation $_____

    (e) Medical, dental, and insurance $_____

    (f) Other $_____

5.   DEBTS

    Name of Creditors: AMOUNT
OWED:

_____ $_____

_____ $_____

_____ $_____

_____ $_____

Should there be any change in my income or assets, I will advise the court immediately.

I have been advised that I may be required to repay all or part of the costs of court appointed counsel.

I declare under penalty of perjury, under the laws of the State of Washington, that the above information is true and correct.

_____

Signature

_____

Date signed

_____

Place signed

[Adopted effective September 1, 1999.]

LCrR 3.4. COURT APPEARANCE OF CRIMINAL DEFENDANTS

All preliminary and timely arrangements for the court appearance of any defendant held in custody shall be the responsibility of the deputy prosecutor in charge of the case, who shall advise the jail staff of the defendant's required appearance.

[Adopted effective September 1, 1999.]

LCrR 3.4(d)(2). [VIDEO CONFERENCES]

In criminal matters, in addition to those proceedings allowed by CrR 3.4(d)(1), all trial court proceedings, including, but not limited to, entry of a statement of Defendant on plea of guilty and sentencing, may be conducted by video conference by agreement of all parties in writing or on the record.

[Adopted effective September 1, 2002.]

LCrR 4.1. PROCEDURES PRIOR TO TRIAL

Court commissioners shall have authority in all matters allowed by the Constitution of the State of Washington, case law, and statutes; including, but not limited to, the authority noted in RCW 2.24.040 to accept guilty pleas.

[Adopted effective June 8, 2000.]

LCrR 4.2. PLEAS AND CONTINUANCES

If a criminal case is set for trial but will be disposed of by a change of plea, the guilty plea shall be heard on or before the trial date. The court may authorize a continuance and hear the change of plea at a later date.

[Adopted effective September 1, 1999.]

LCrR 4.5. OMNIBUS HEARINGS

(d) **Motions.** All rulings of the Court at omnibus hearings or on motions shall be binding on the parties and shall not be relitigated at trial.

(i) If there is no dispute regarding omnibus requests, the motion shall be signed by both parties and presented to the Court ex parte for signature before date of omnibus hearing.

[Adopted effective September 1, 1999.]

LCrR 7.2. PRESENTENCE INVESTIGATION

(a) **When Required; Time of Service.** Unless otherwise directed by the Court, in all cases where a person is to be sentenced for commission of a felony, the prosecuting attorney and the defendant's attorney shall, not less than ten days before the sentencing date, serve a copy of any presentence report upon the opposing party, a copy to the sentencing Judge, and send the original to the Clerk of the Court. The Community Corrections Office shall serve a copy of its report upon the prosecuting attorney and the defense attorney and the original to the sentencing judge not less than ten days before the sentencing date.

(b) **Contents of Defendant's Report.** The defendant's presentence report which requests a sentence outside of the standard range shall outline any proposed programs, specifically state, among the other details, what community resources are available for implementation of the program.

If the defendant is not requesting a sentence outside of the standard range, the defense presentence report shall indicate the recommended sentence, the type of program that should be afforded the defendant, and reasons therefore.

(c) **Penalties for Violation.** A violation of this rule may result in the refusal of the Court to proceed with the sentencing until after reports have been served and filed as directed herein, and in the imposition of terms, or the Court may proceed to impose sentence without regard to the violation.

[Adopted effective September 1, 1999.]

LCrR 7.3. PAYMENT OF COSTS

In all criminal cases, except where the Court Order is to the contrary, the Judgment and Sentence shall provide that the Clerk shall disperse monies received from the criminal defendant in the following order:

(a) Restitution

(b) Crime Victims Compensation

(c) Court Costs

(d) Attorneys Fees

(e) Drug Fund

(f) Fines

[Adopted effective September 1, 1999.]

DOUGLAS COUNTY LOCAL RULES FOR MANDATORY ARBITRATION [RESCINDED EFFECTIVE SEPTEMBER 1, 2015]

DISTRICT COURT

LOCAL COURT RULES OF DOUGLAS COUNTY DISTRICT COURT

Including Amendments Received Through
August 15, 2015

Table of Rules

INTRODUCTORY

1. Promulgation. These rules shall be known as the Local Rules for the District Court of the State of Washington for Douglas County. These rules will be effective September 1, 2008 and supersede all prior rules of this court. The provisions of these local rules are supplemental to the rules adopted by the Supreme Court of the State of Washington for courts of limited jurisdiction, and shall not be construed in conflict with them.

[Adopted effective June 15, 1987; amended effective September 1, 2000; September 1, 2008.]

ADMINISTRATIVE RULES

LARLJ 9(g). DISCLOSURE OF PUBLIC RECORDS

Access to confidential records is strictly limited to persons or entities authorized by statute or court order to obtain such records. Request for access to court records shall be made in writing on the form provided by the Court and shall be granted or denied only by a judge, or designee, who shall state the reasons for denial in writing. Any person objecting to a denial of access may file a Motion for Reconsideration with supporting affidavit. Costs of researching, copying and transcribing shall be paid in advance by the person or entity asking for such copies. No documents or electronic data may be removed from the court offices without the written order of the court.

[Adopted effective September 1, 2000.]

CIVIL RULES

LCRLJ 38. CIVIL JURY TRIAL

(A) Demand. The request for jury trial in civil cases shall be made by filing a demand with the clerk and paying the jury fee not later than seven days from the date of the trial setting notice issued from the court. Failure to comply with this rule is a waiver of the right to a jury trial.

(B) Imposition of costs. Whenever any cause assigned for jury trial is settled or will not be tried by the jury for any reason, notice of that fact shall be given immediately to the court. If notification is not given forty-eight hours prior to the time of the trial, and in any event after the jury has been summoned orally or in writing, the court in its discretion may order payment of the actual costs of the jury panel by the offending party.

(NOTE: THERE IS NO PROVISION FOR RE-FUND OF THE JURY FEES.)

(C) Pre-trial Procedure. All cases set for jury trial shall be set for pre-trial conference, which shall be held at least two weeks prior to trial. The attorneys who are to conduct the trial and all parties shall be present to consider such matters as will promote a fair and expeditious trial. All discovery should be completed five days prior to said conference. Opposing counsel or party must be given five days notice of pre-trial motions to be heard at the pre-trial conference. Any pre-trial motions requiring the testimony of witnesses for argument may, in the discretion of the court, be continued to the day of trial. All amendments, pleadings and motions should be made or be completed at this conference. Upon failure to appear, the judge may proceed with the conference ex parte, and enter any appropriate order including striking the jury demand and may impose terms. Insofar as practicable the conference shall deal with any matter cognizable by Superior Court Rule CR 4.5, and failure

to raise that matter may result in the waiver of the same.

[Adopted effective June 15, 1987; amended effective September 1, 2000; renamed from LJCR 38 effective September 1, 2008.]

LCRLJ 54. ATTORNEY FEES

In civil default cases where attorney fees are authorized by statute or by written agreement, the following schedule shall be deemed reasonable in all default cases unless the parties present evidence of circumstances that convinces the court that a larger or smaller fee should be awarded, provided, however, the court shall have authority to vary from this schedule on its own motion:

$1.00– to $ 999	$300
$1,000.00 to $1,500	$325
$1,500.01 to $2,000	$350
$2,000.01 to $2,500	$375
$2,500.01 to $3,000	$400
$3,000.01 to $4,000	$425
$4,000.01 to $5,000	$450

For judgments exceeding $5,000, reasonable attorney fees may be allowed of 10% of any balance over $5,000 without formal justification or documentation.

NSF checks. When RCW 62A.3–515 has been followed, reasonable attorney fees will be awarded in an amount to be determined by reference to RCW 12.20.060 unless the attorney convinces the court that a larger fee should be awarded and provides an itemized affidavit as to actual time spent and hourly rate expended by the attorney in the case, in which case the court shall determine a reasonable fee.

Where only statutory attorney fees are authorized, the default judgment shall include, and the court will approve, only attorney fees in the statutory amount as applicable at the time of entry of judgment.

[Adopted effective June 15, 1987; amended effective September 1, 2000; renamed and amended effective September 1, 2008.]

CRIMINAL RULES

LCrRLJ 3.1(d). RIGHT TO AND ASSIGNMENT OF COUNSEL

Indigent defendants shall have counsel appointed to represent them in all criminal cases unless the right to counsel is waived. Indigency shall mean an inability to pay an attorney a reasonable fee for the services, which appear to be required by reasons of the crime charged without substantial hardship to himself or his family. Defendants who request appointment of counsel shall be required to promptly execute a financial disclosure under oath on a form supplied by the court.

Upon appointment of counsel for indigent criminal defendants, the Clerk shall promptly provide counsel with notice of the appointment.

Attorneys representing defendants in criminal cases must serve prompt written notice of their employment upon the prosecuting attorney and file the same with the clerk of the court. To withdraw, the attorney must serve notice of such intention upon the prosecuting attorney and file the same with the clerk of the court. No withdrawal will be recognized by the court, except for cause deemed sufficient by the court. Approval of withdrawal may, if necessary to prevent a continuance, be denied, and such attorney be required to proceed with the trial.

Appointed counsel by reason of indigency shall be automatically relieved of their appointment upon: (1) entry of a sentence on a guilty plea (2) at the conclusion of the appeal time following sentencing as a result of a conviction in a contested trial, (3) upon entry of an order deferring prosecution (4) upon issuance of a warrant for failure to appear.

[Adopted effective June 15, 1987; amended effective September 1. 2000; renamed from LCrRLJ 3.1(d) and amended effective September 1, 2008.]

LCrRLJ 3.3. CONTINUANCES

After the first appearance all requests to continue a pre-trial hearing, motion or trial dates will require a written order of continuance signed by both parties and submitted to the judge for approval. No continuance will be accepted after noon on the day before the law and motion calendar. The court will not continue the trial or hearing date beyond the CrRLJ 3.3 dates without a speedy trial waiver.

After conviction, requests for continuance of review or revocation dates may be submitted by letter or motion to the court and may be submitted off the record to the judge for approval.

[Adopted effective September 1, 2008.]

LCrRLJ 4.1(d). CRIMES REQUIRING DEFENDANT'S APPEARANCE AT ARRAIGNMENT

A lawyer may not enter a written plea of not guilty on behalf of a client, if the charging document states that one or more of the charges involves domestic violence, harassment, violation of an anti-harassment or protection order, stalking, or driving while under the influence of intoxicants, driving while under the age of 21 after having consumed alcohol, or physical control of a vehicle while under the influence of intoxicants. For such charges, the defendant must appear in person for arraignment; and the court shall determine the necessity of imposing conditions of pre-trial release.

[Adopted effective June 15, 1987; amended effective September 1, 2000; renamed from LJCrR 4.1(d) and amended September 1, 2008.]

LCrRLJ 4.2. DEFERRED PROSECUTION

A petition for deferred prosecution pursuant to RCW 10.05 must be filed with the court no later than seven (7) days prior to readiness hearing unless good cause exists for delay. The petition and the accompanying declarations shall be in a form set forth in CrRLJ 4.2. A complete copy of the police report of the defendant's conduct giving rise to the charge shall be attached to the petition. The Order for Deferred Prosecution shall provide for supervision for 60–months, completion of a treatment plan, payment of costs, abstinence from consumption of alcohol and non-prescription drugs, no traffic offenses, a requirement that all vehicles driven by the defendant be equipped with an ignition interlock device as required by statute and no driving without proper license and insurance.

[Adopted effective September 1, 2008.]

LCrRLJ 4.8. WITNESSES—PROCESS— SUBPOENAS

When application is made for a subpoena for a witness residing outside of Douglas County and the Greater Wenatchee area, such application shall be accompanied by an affidavit showing to the satisfaction of the court the materiality of the testimony which is expected to be obtained from such witness. The court in its discretion may waive this requirement.

Preparation of subpoenas shall be the responsibility of the applicant and shall be submitted with the application requesting issuance of the subpoena. Service of the subpoenas shall be the responsibility of the applicant.

[Adopted effective June 15, 1987; amended effective September 1, 2000; renumbered from LJCrR 4.8 effective September 1, 2008.]

LCrRLJ 6.1. TRIAL BY JURY OR BY THE COURT

6.1(a)(1) In every criminal or traffic case in which the defendant is entitled to a jury trial, the Clerk shall set a date for a pre-trial conference to be held within five weeks of the date a plea of not guilty is entered. The purpose of said conference is to determine if discovery is completed and if pretrial motions are necessary and to set a readiness hearing and trial date. Discovery shall be in the hands of the party requesting same at least two (2) working days prior to the pre-trial conference. See Local Rule LCrRLJ 8.02 concerning notice to opposing parties of the nature of pretrial motions and the necessity of witnesses at the hearing.

If the defendant fails to appear at any scheduled hearing without good cause, bail will be ordered forfeited and the court will order a Bench Warrant issued for the arrest of the defendant.

In the event it comes to the attention of the court that there is a likelihood that the defendant will not be available for his jury trial, as evidenced, for example by defendant's failure to remain in contact with his lawyer, the court will schedule an additional pre-trial conference to inquire as to the availability of the defendant. If the defendant does not appear, the jury trial date will be stricken, bail forfeited, and the court will order a bench warrant for the arrest of the defendant.

6.1(a)(2) Readiness conference. A readiness hearing shall be set in all cases set for jury trial. The prosecuting attorney, defense counsel and defendant are required to appear at the hearing. The court will inquire as to whether the case is expected to go to trial; the number of witnesses to be called by each side; the anticipated length of trial, and all motions, discovery and plea negotiations shall be concluded. Any case confirmed for jury trial at the readiness hearing not proceeding to jury trial shall be subject to such sanctions as deemed appropriate by the judge including but not limited to jury costs, witness fees and terms.

[Adopted effective June 15, 1987; amended effective September 1, 2000; renamed from LJCrR 6.1 effective September 1, 2008.]

LCrRLJ 8.2. MOTIONS AND APPLICATIONS— NOTICE—SERVICE

All amendments to the charges, pleas, or pre-trial motions shall be made at the time of the readiness hearing. Motions shall be supported by an affidavit or declaration under penalty of perjury of a person with testimonial knowledge, setting forth the facts to be elicited at an evidentiary hearing. Motions shall not be considered at the time of trial unless they could not have been raised at the time of the readiness hearing or the judge at the time of readiness hearing expressly continues such motions to the time of trial. Absent good cause, motions for dismissal or suppression of evidence in criminal cases shall be in writing and shall be provided to the Court and the opposing party at least 10 days before the readiness hearing. Response briefs are due two days before the hearing. Any witnesses necessary to establish issues on motions shall be subpoenaed by the moving party. If a proper motion is not received by the court 10 days prior to the scheduled hearing, the motion hearing shall be stricken.

[Adopted effective June 15, 1987; amended effective September 1, 2000; renamed from LJCrR 8.2 and amended effective September 1, 2008.]

LJCrR 10.05. DEFERRED PROSECUTION [DELETED]

[Adopted effective June 15, 1987; amended effective September 1, 2000; deleted effective September 1, 2008.]

TRAFFIC INFRACTION RULES

LIRLJ 2.4. RESPONSE TO NOTICE

The procedure authorized in IRLJ 2.4(b)(4) is adopted by this court

[Adopted effective June 15, 1987.]

LIRLJ 3.1. CONTESTED HEARINGS– PRELIMINARY PROCEEDINGS

Speed Measuring Device Expert. Defense requests for a Speed Measuring Device Expert must be made to the Office of the Prosecuting Attorney no less than 30–days prior to the date set for the contested hearing. The request shall be contained in a separate document clearly designated as a request for an SMD expert. A request for a SMD expert may be treated by the Court as a request for a continuance to the next date on which the prosecuting attorney has scheduled the appearance of the SMD Expert. An SMD expert called as a witness by either party may testify by telephone; however, any party intending to elicit telephonic testimony from an SMD expert shall notify the court and opposing party at least five days prior to the date set for the contested hearing.

[Adopted effective June 15, 1987; amended effective September 1, 2000; September 1, 2008.]

LIRLJ 3.2. FAILURE TO APPEAR

Setting Aside Judgment Upon Failure to Appear—Good Cause Petition

A defendant may file a written motion on forms provided by the court to set aside a default judgment for Failure to Appear at a requested hearing. The court will examine the written motion and make a decision without the defendant being required to appear. Only one motion shall be allowed on any case. A mitigation hearing may be granted upon setting aside the judgment. A contested hearing shall not be allowed unless by special written order.

[Adopted effective June 15, 1987; amended effective September 1, 2008.]

LIRLJ 3.3(b)(1). REPRESENTATION BY LAWYER

At a contested hearing where an attorney has appeared for the defendant or witnesses have been subpoenaed, a lawyer representative of the Prosecutor's office shall appear. A defendant charged with a traffic infraction and represented by counsel must provide written notice to the prosecuting authority and clerk of the court of such representation at least seven days from the date the original request for a contested hearing is mailed by the defendant. Upon receipt of counsel's notice of appearance, the clerk shall reset the contested hearing to the appropriate calendar.

[Adopted effective June 15, 1987; amended effective September 1, 2008.]

LIRLJ 3.5. DECISION ON WRITTEN STATEMENTS

The procedure authorized by IRLJ 3.5 is adopted by this court.

[Adopted effective June 15, 1987.]

LIRLJ 4.2. FAILURE TO PAY OR COMPLETE COMMUNITY SERVICE FOR TRAFFIC INFRACTION

(d) Failure to make payment. Defendants who owe penalties on traffic infractions must report to the court clerk immediately after leaving the courtroom. Failure to do so will be considered a failure to pay or complete community service. The Court will assess the appropriate penalty for failure to pay or appear, and will rescind any reduction in the penalty imposed. Failure to comply with the time payment agreement on an infraction will cause the court to rescind any penalty reduction previously granted by the court.

[Adopted effective June 15, 1987; amended effective September 1, 2000.]

MUNICIPAL COURTS

BRIDGEPORT MUNICIPAL COURT—
[No Local Rules]

PUBLISHER'S NOTE

This municipal court follows the Local Court Rules of Douglas County District Court.

EAST WENATCHEE MUNICIPAL COURT—
[No Local Rules]

ROCK ISLAND MUNICIPAL COURT—
[No Local Rules]

PUBLISHER'S NOTE

This municipal court follows the Local Court Rules of Douglas County District Court.

WATERVILLE MUNICIPAL COURT—
[No Local Rules]

PUBLISHER'S NOTE

This municipal court follows the Local Court Rules of Douglas County District Court.

FERRY COUNTY

Table of Courts

Superior Court

Local Rules for the Superior Courts of Ferry, Pend Oreille and Stevens Counties.

District Court

Ferry District Court Local Rules.

SUPERIOR COURT

LOCAL RULES FOR THE SUPERIOR COURTS OF FERRY, PEND OREILLE AND STEVENS COUNTIES

Including Amendments Received Through
August 15, 2015

Table of Rules

LOCAL ADMINISTRATIVE RULES (Cite as LAR)

LAR 1.   DEPARTMENTS OF COURT

The Superior Courts of Stevens, Ferry and Pend Oreille Counties shall be divided into as many departments as there are judges authorized by law. The departments shall be numbered consecutively in the order of the creation, as follows:

DEPARTMENT	CREATED
No. 1	June 13, 1860
No. 2	April 13, 1982

[Adopted September 1, 1991; amended effective September 1, 2004.]

LAR 2.   COURT SCHEDULE—MOTIONS

Motions and other pre-trial proceedings will be scheduled for hearing on a Law and Motion Docket, unless by prior arrangement through the court administrator.

The calendar shall be prepared and published by the court administrator and the presiding judge or his/her designee-judge on a monthly basis for the ensuing six months, and shall be distributed to the attorneys in each county and made available to the public from the Clerks' offices for each of the three counties. The Law and Motion Days and times may be changed by the court administrator as needed to accommodate the judges' schedules, jury terms in each county, and caseload demands. Attorneys and parties are advised to consult the calendar, the County Clerk, or the court administrator to confirm Law and Motion Docket dates and times prior to noting a motion.

[Adopted September 1, 1991; amended effective September 1, 2004.]

LAR 3.   COURT MANAGEMENT

(a) General Management. The general management of the court shall be vested in the presiding judge under policy established by the judges at regular and special meetings.

(b) Presiding Court Rotation. The presiding judge shall be selected, serve, and, if necessary, be removed in accordance with GR 29. In the event of the lack of a majority vote of the judges, the Supreme Court shall be requested to appoint a superior court judge from another jurisdiction to participate in the decision.

(c) Duties of the Presiding Judge. The presiding judge's responsibilities, duties and authority shall be as provided in GR 29 as now or hereafter amended.

(d) Duties of the Court Administrator. The court administrator shall assist the presiding judge in his or her administrative responsibilities. Subject to the general supervision of the presiding judge, the court administrator's duties shall include:

(1) Administrative control of all non-judicial activities of the court;

(2) Case setting and trial calendar management;

(3) Preparation and administration of the budget;

(4) Coordination with state Administrative Office of the Courts;

(5) Assisting the presiding judge in dealing with county governments, bar associations, news media and other public and private groups having a reasonable interest in the administration of the court;

(6) Preparation of such reports and compilation of such statistics as may be required by the judges or state Administrative Office of the Courts;

(7) Making recommendations to the judges for the improvement of the administration of the court.

[Adopted September 1, 1991; amended effective September 1, 2004.]

LAR 4.   JUVENILE COURT AND FAMILY LAW DEPARTMENT

Juvenile Department. There shall be a juvenile department of the court, in which shall be heard all matters arising under the juvenile court laws. Both judges are designated as judges of the juvenile and family courts. Each court commissioner of each of the three counties is authorized to hear juvenile cases and family law cases in his or her respective county in these departments as assigned by the presiding judge. See also LJuCRs below.

[Adopted September 1, 1991; amended effective September 1, 2004.]

LOCAL CIVIL RULES (Cite as LCR)

1. COMMENCEMENT OF ACTIONS

LCR 5. SERVICE AND FILING OF PLEADINGS AND OTHER PAPERS

(b)(2) *Service by Mail, Facsimile or Email.*

(A) By Mail. See CR 5(b)(2)(A) and (B).

(B) By Facsimile. Service by facsimile shall be allowed only under the following conditions consistent with GR17:

(i) The party or attorney of record to whom service is delivered has a publicly available fax number or has given written consent to receive fax service to the sending party or attorney;

(ii) The attorney or party sending the document via fax shall retain the original signed document until 60 days after completion of the case. Documents to be transmitted by fax shall bear the notation: "SENT on (DATE) VIA FAX FOR FILING IN COURT."

(iii) Documents transmitted by fax shall be letter size (8–½ by 11 inches). Documents over 10 pages in length may not be served by fax without prior approval of the receiving party.

(iv) Any document transmitted by fax must be accompanied by a fax transmittal sheet in a form that includes the case number (if any), case caption, number of pages, the sender's name, and the senders voice and facsimile telephone numbers. Transmittal sheets are not considered legal filings.

(v) A document transmitted directly to the receiving party shall be deemed received at the time the receiving party's fax machine electronically registers the transmission of the first page, regardless of when final printing of the document occurs, except that a document received after the close of normal business hours shall be considered received the next judicial day. If a document is not completely transmitted, it will not be considered received. A document transmitted to another for filing with the clerk of the court will be deemed filed when presented to the clerk in the same manner as an original document.

(vi) [Rescinded effective September 2, 2014]

(vii) Facsimile Machine Not Required. Nothing in this rule shall require a party, an attorney or a Clerk of a court to have a facsimile machine.

(C) By Email. Parties (or attorneys of record) may serve opposing parties by email only if they have written consent from the receiving party. Working copies may be emailed to the court as follows:

(i) Any document (except original actions and personal restraint petitions) may be emailed as an attachment to an email message if:

(a) The body of the email message to which the document is attached is no more than 100 words and includes: case name, case number, name, phone number, bar number and email address of the person sending the document; and does not include prohibited ex parte communications.

(b) Any appendices attached to a brief, motion or pleading do not exceed a total of 25 pages.

(c) The attached document complies with the Civil Rules, except where these protocols provide otherwise.

(d) The attached document is subscribed with the name and bar number of the sender and the original signed document is retained in the sender's file.

(e) The Email must be properly addressed to the email address provided by the court administrator for each of the counties in the judicial district.

(f) The subject line must include "Working Copy for [Cause No.][Case Name] for Hearing on [Date of Hearing] before [Name of Judge].

(g) The date and time the email was sent must be evident on the received email and show on any printout of that email.

(h) The email must also be sent as a courtesy copy to any other party that has an email address and has so requested by filing a Request for Email Copies in substantially the following form: "[Party Name] requests that all working copies emailed to the court under LCR5(b)(2) also be emailed to the above at the following email address: [Email Address]."

(ii) No signature is required on an attached document, if all protocols are followed.

(iii) The date and time the attachment to email is deemed received will be no sooner than the date and time of actual filing of the document's original with the Clerk.

(iv) The use of PDF format or Microsoft WORD is encouraged, but not required. If the conversion software used by the court is unable to convert a document, the party submitting the document will be notified to submit the document in written form.

(i) Documents Not to Be Filed. In addition to the discovery material specified in CR 5(i), photocopies of reported cases, statutes or texts shall not be filed as an appendix to a brief or otherwise, but may be furnished directly to the judge hearing the matter; provided, any items submitted to the judge shall be provided to opposing parties or counsel at the same time.

[Adopted September 1, 1991; amended effective September 1, 2004; September 2, 2014.]

LCR 6. TIME

(d) Motions and Other Papers.

(1) *Scope of Rules.* Except when specifically provided in another rule, this rule governs all motions in civil cases. See, for example, LCR 56 and LCR 94.04.

(2) *Dates of Filing, Hearing and Consideration.*

(A) Filing and Scheduling of Motion. The moving party shall serve and file all motion papers no later than six (6) court days before the date the party wishes the motion to be considered. A motion must be scheduled by a party for hearing on an appropriate motion docket for the type of matter to be heard.

(B) Working Copies. The working copies of all papers shall be marked on the upper right corner of the first page with the date, time and county of hearing and the name of the judge.

(i) HARD COPIES: Working copies of the motion and all papers in support or opposition, if provided, shall be delivered to the judge who is to hear the motion no later than the day they are to be served on all other parties, at 215 South Oak Street, #209, Colville, WA 99114, regardless of which county in which the motion is filed.

(ii) ELECTRONIC COPIES: Email transmission is authorized for judge's working copies, provided that the email transmission of documents is done in a manner approved by the Stevens County Superior Court Clerk. The Clerk may assess a fee for the email submission of working copies.

(C) Opposing Papers. Any party opposing a motion shall file the original responsive papers in opposition to a motion, serve copies on parties and deliver any working copies to the judge as in (B) above no later than 12:00 noon two court days before the date the motion is to be heard.

(D) Reply. Any papers in strict reply shall be filed, copies served on parties, and any working copies delivered to the hearing judge as in (B) above no later than 12:00 noon on the court day before the date of the hearing.

(E) Sanctions. Any material offered at a time later than required by this rule, and any reply material which is not in strict reply, will not be considered by the Court over objection of counsel except upon the imposition of appropriate sanctions, unless the Court orders otherwise.

[Adopted effective September 1, 2004. Amended effective September 2, 2014.]

4. PLEADINGS AND MOTIONS

LCR 16. PRETRIAL PROCEDURES AND FORMULATING ISSUES

(a) Hearing Matters Considered. Upon the motion of a party or the court's own initiative, the presiding judge or, in the case of a preassigned case, the judge so designated will decide whether any civil case would benefit from a pretrial scheduling conference.

(b) Pretrial Order. The conference procedures and form of the pretrial order shall be determined by the judge to whom the matter is assigned.

(c) Settlement Conference. Upon the motion of a party or the court's own initiative, the presiding judge or designated judge may order private mediation or a mandatory settlement conference with respect to any civil case.

Any settlement conference ordered will be held before a designated settlement judge at least thirty (30) days before the scheduled trial date. At least five (5) court days before the settlement conference each party shall supply a confidential position statement to the settlement judge. The statement shall include:

(1) A general factual summary of the case;

(2) Disputed and admitted facts;

(3) A statement of legal issues, together with authorities; and

(4) A general position statement.

(5) In domestic relations cases, the party's position, in precise terms, concerning issues of:

(a) property,

(b) debts,

(c) maintenance,

(d) child support,

(e) parenting plan, and

(f) any other matters requiring resolution.

The attorneys who will be in charge of each party's case shall attend the settlement conference personally and shall come prepared to discuss in detail and in good faith the issues of fact and law remaining, the evidence pertaining to liability and damages, or, in a domestic relations case, the various categories of issues subject to the court's jurisdiction, and the respective positions of the various parties on settlement. The attorneys shall be accompanied by their clients or representatives possessing authority to settle unless such clients or representatives are available by telephone or are otherwise excused by the judge, or unless the attorney himself or herself has full authority with respect to settlement.

The proceedings of the settlement conference shall be privileged and not recorded. If a settlement is not reached the settlement judge shall not make any order or preside at the trial on the merits without consent of all parties.

(d) Pre-assignment to a Particular Judge. Upon written application of any party with notice to the other parties, or on the court's own motion, the presiding judge may preassign cases involving complex issues and/or extensive pretrial procedures to a particular judge for pretrial procedures and trial. The burden of establishing the need for pre-assignment shall be on the party or parties requesting the same. Pretrial conferences and hearings and trial scheduling shall be arranged directly with the preassigned judge and the court administrator.

(e) Methods.

(1) *Summary Judgment.* See LCR 56.

(2) *Filing of Motions, Memoranda and Affidavits—General.* See LCR 6(d) for times for filing motions, responses and replies. The moving party shall file with the Note for Hearing—Issue of Law form the following: The motion being noted, all supporting affidavits and documentary evidence, and a brief or memorandum of authorities, unless the legal position is fully and adequately stated in the motion or issue of law form.

(3) *Copies of Briefs or Memoranda.* A copy of the brief or memorandum and supporting affidavits shall be furnished to the assigned judge at the time of filing. The judge's working copies, with a notation thereon as to the date and time of hearing on the

motion, shall be delivered or mailed to the judge at 215 South Oak Street, #209, Colville, WA 99114, regardless of in which county the motion is being filed. Working copies of responsive materials should likewise note the date of hearing and be delivered or mailed to judge hearing the matter at the above address. Failure to comply with these requirements may result in a continuance and/or imposition of terms.

(4) *Affidavits or Declarations.* All affidavits or declarations shall be sworn or affirmed under penalty of perjury, made on personal knowledge, set forth such facts as would be admissible in evidence, and show affirmatively that the affiant or declarant is competent to testify to the matters stated therein.

(5) *Motion Calendar Hearing Procedures.* The Law and Motion calendar will commence at times designated in the respective county's court calendar as distributed by the court administrator and County Clerk's offices. Matters shall be noted for the particular time designated in the court calendar. Agreed orders and defaults will be heard at the beginning of the docket. Motions other than summary judgment shall be limited to ten (10) minutes each side. Motions which will exceed the time limit of this rule, if allowed by the motion judge, will ordinarily be placed at the end of the motion docket.

(f) Change of Judge. In the event that a motion is scheduled for hearing before a judge on a specified day and an affidavit of prejudice is filed against that judge, the scheduled motion will be transferred for hearing by the court administrator to another judge or court commissioner; provided, however, motions for summary judgment and any other motion which would be dispositive of a claim of any party shall be heard only by a judge, except as otherwise authorized under Rule 0.6.

[Adopted September 1, 1991; amended effective September 1, 2004.]

6. TRIALS

LCR 40. ASSIGNMENT OF CASES

Notice of Trial and Certificate of Readiness. Any party desiring to bring an issue of fact to trial shall serve and file a properly completed Notice for Trial Setting and/or Settlement Conference and Certificate of Readiness on a form available from the court administrator. The party filing the Notice and Certificate shall, after conferring with opposing counsel, specify (a) whether a settlement conference is requested and (b) whether a short notice setting will be acceptable. An attorney noting a case for trial and any party or counsel of record who does not file a timely objection to trial setting thereby certifies that the case is at issue, that there has been reasonable opportunity for discovery, that discovery will be com-

plete by the trial date, that necessary witnesses will be available, and that the time estimated for trial is accurate. Any party contending the case is not ready for trial or that the estimated length of trial is not correct shall serve and file a counter notice of trial or objection to trial setting and notice of argument thereon within five (5) days of the date of service of the notice for trial setting which objection shall be noted for hearing on the next Law and Motion day.

[Adopted September 1, 1991; amended effective September 1, 2004.]

LCR 43. TAKING OF TESTIMONY

(a) Testimony.

(3) *Excusing Witnesses.* A witness under subpoena is excused from further attendance as soon as testimony has been given, unless either party makes request in open court that the witness remain in attendance or be subject to recall. Witness fees will not be allowed on subsequent days unless the court has required the witness to remain in attendance, which fact shall be noted by the clerk in the court.

(4) *Telephonic Testimony.* Witnesses may not testify telephonically except upon prior court approval.

(e) Evidence on Motions.

(1) *Generally.* Motions for temporary support, attorney's fees and costs, restraining orders, injunctions, to dissolve injunctions and to quash or dissolve attachments shall be heard only on the pleadings, affidavits or declarations, published depositions and other papers filed unless the court otherwise directs.

[Adopted September 1, 1991; amended effective September 1, 2004.]

LCR 47. JURORS

(e) Challenge.

(9) *Peremptory Challenges.* The exercise or waiver of peremptory challenges shall be noted silently.

(k) Statement of Case. Each party in a civil case shall submit a brief statement of the case suitable to be read to the jury before the voir dire examination.

[Adopted September 1, 1991; amended effective September 1, 2004.]

LCR 49. VERDICTS

(k) Receiving Verdict During Absence of Counsel. A party or attorney desiring to be present at the return of the verdict must remain in attendance at the courthouse or be available by telephone call. If a party or attorney fails to appear within 20 minutes of telephone notice to the attorney's office, home or other number, the court may proceed to take the verdict in the absence of such party or attorney. In such case the jury shall be individually polled and the identity of any dissenting jurors recorded.

[Adopted effective September 1, 1991.]

LCR 51. INSTRUCTIONS TO JURY AND DELIBERATION

(b) Submission. Each party shall file with the Clerk the original proposed instructions, numbered and with citations, and shall provide the judge with one copy numbered and with citations and one copy unnumbered and without citations. One copy, numbered and with citations, shall be served on each other party.

[Adopted September 1, 1991; amended effective September 1, 2004.]

LCR 52. DECISIONS, FINDINGS AND CONCLUSIONS

(a) Requirements.

(6) *Time.* Unless the judge has included formal findings of fact and conclusions of law in a written opinion or memorandum of decision pursuant to CR 52(a)(4) or they are otherwise unnecessary by reason of CR 52(a)(5), the attorney of record for the prevailing party shall prepare proposed findings of fact and conclusions of law, along with the proposed form of decree, order or judgment as required by CR 54(e). At the time of the decision the court shall enter an order fixing a date by which the proposed findings, conclusions and decree, order or judgment shall be prepared and served and establishing a date of presentation.

[Adopted September 1, 1991; amended effective September 1, 2004.]

7. JUDGMENT

LCR 54. JUDGMENTS AND COSTS

(f) Presentation.

(3) *Method—Ex Parte Judgments and Orders.* Counsel presenting a judgment or seeking entry of an order shall be responsible to see that all papers pertaining thereto are filed and that the court file is provided to the judge by the Clerk. Counsel may present routine *ex parte* or stipulated matters based on the record in the file by mail addressed to the Clerk. Self-addressed, stamped envelopes shall be provided for return of any conformed materials and/or rejected orders, and the appropriate *ex parte* fee shall be submitted prior to presentation.

[Adopted September 1, 1991; amended effective September 1, 2004.]

LCR 56. SUMMARY JUDGMENT

(c) Motion and Proceedings. In the event a motion for summary judgment, partial summary judgment or dismissal is to be argued, counsel for the moving party is required to confirm the motion with the court administrator by telephone by 4:30 p.m. at least four (4) court days before the hearing. Working copies of the motions, all accompanying documents, and all responsive and reply papers, shall be provided by the respective parties to the judge at the time of filing at 215 South Oak, #209, Colville, WA 99114, regardless of the county in which the motion is filed.

[Adopted September 1, 1991; amended effective September 1, 2004.]

9. PROVISIONAL AND FINAL REMEDIES

LCR 69. EXECUTION

(a) Procedure—Delinquent Support. No writ of execution or attachment shall be issued for the collection of delinquent child support or spousal maintenance until a judgment determining the amount due has been entered.

(b) Supplemental Proceedings. In all supplemental proceedings wherein a show cause order is issued requiring the personal attendance of the party to be examined in open court and in orders to show cause in re contempt, the order to show cause must include the following words in capital letters:

YOUR FAILURE TO APPEAR AS SET FORTH AT THE TIME, DATE AND PLACE SET FORTH IN THIS ORDER MAY CAUSE THE COURT TO ISSUE A BENCH WARRANT FOR YOUR APPREHENSION AND CONFINEMENT IN JAIL UNTIL SUCH TIME AS THE MATTER CAN BE HEARD, UNLESS BAIL IS FURNISHED AS PROVIDED IN SUCH WARRANT.

The failure to include such wording will be grounds for the court to refuse to issue a bench warrant for the apprehension of such person.

[Adopted effective September 1, 1991.]

10. SUPERIOR COURTS AND CLERKS

LCR 77. SUPERIOR COURTS AND JUDICIAL OFFICERS

(o) Conference Calls. Motions or other matters may not, without the advance approval of the court, be heard by conference call. The specific time shall be arranged with the court administrator. Conference calls are discouraged for Law and Motion Docket days. Conference calls will be recorded only at the request of either party made to the court administrator at the time of scheduling the call.

(p) Trial Status. Not less than ten (10) days prior to any scheduled trial, each counsel or self-represented party shall contact the court administrator to advise the status of the case and of settlement negotiations, if any, and whether it is anticipated trial will take place as scheduled.

[Adopted September 1, 1991; amended effective September 1, 2004.]

LCR 79. BOOKS AND RECORDS KEPT BY THE CLERK

(g) Other Books and Records of Clerk.

(1) *Exhibits.* Exhibits shall be kept separately from the court file. Any inspection of an exhibit must be in the presence of the clerk or a deputy clerk unless authorized by a court order.

(2) *Rejection of Unsuitable Materials.* The Clerk shall not accept for filing in the court file material which should be filed as an exhibit or other materials not to be included by reason of CR 5(i) and LCR 5(i). When the Clerk is uncertain as to whether material is suitable for filing, he or she shall seek the advice of the presiding judge before filing the same.

(3) *Return of Contraband Exhibits.* When contraband, alcoholic beverages, tobacco products, controlled substances or fish or wildlife parts are being held by the Clerk as part of the records and files in any criminal case, and all proceedings in the case have been completed, the court may order the Clerk to deliver such contraband or substances to an authorized representative of the law enforcement agency initiating the prosecution for disposition according to law. The Clerk shall then deliver the contraband and take from the law enforcement agency a receipt which shall be filed in the case. The Clerk shall also file any certificate issued by an authorized federal or state agency and received by the Clerk showing the nature of such contraband or substances.

(4) *Return of Administrative Record on Appeal.* When a case for review of an administrative record is finally completed, the Clerk shall treat the administrative record as an exhibit. The Clerk shall return the administrative record to the officer or agency certifying the same to the Court.

(h) At the discretion of the Clerk, a file may be removed from the courthouse by a resident attorney, a representative of a title company with proper authorization, or a judicial officer. Authorization for an attorney to remove a file from the courthouse may be given in writing by the Clerk or Clerk's deputy and shall not exceed two (2) court days. Files may be withdrawn to be taken to a courtroom by the following persons: judicial officers, deputy clerks, bailiffs, the court administrator or his/her staff, and resident attorneys.

In instances of mail or telephonic requests by nonresident attorneys, the file will be mailed by certified mail to the Clerk of the county where such applicant attorney is a resident. All costs of mailing shall be borne by the applicant attorney. All files so withdrawn must be returned to the Clerk's office within the period specified by the Clerk, but in no event will this period exceed two (2) court days. The court may, upon written application showing cause therefor, authorize the withdrawal of specified Clerk's files for a period in excess of tow (2) court days.

Any person found in violation of the provisions of this rule shall be subject to sanctions as ordered by the court.

[Adopted September 1, 1991; amended effective September 1, 2004.]

LCR 80. REPORTING OF COURT PROCEEDINGS

(c) General Reporting Requirements.

(1) *Electronic Recording.* All proceedings required to be on the record shall be recorded by electronic recording pursuant to CR 80. The original tapes or compact disks shall be kept by the clerk of the court.

(2) *Oral Decision.* Oral decisions or rulings by a judge which are transcribed shall first be submitted to the judge for review prior to delivery and a final copy shall be furnished to the judge for his/her file.

(3) *Transcripts.* With the exception of transcripts provided under RALJ 6.3A, the official transcript or verbatim report of proceedings of any matters shall be prepared by or under the direction of the court administrator. Anyone wishing to order an official transcript or verbatim report of proceedings shall make such request to the court administrator and shall at the same time make arrangements for payment thereof. With the exception of RALJ appeal matters, transcripts or verbatim reports of proceedings not obtained through the court administrator are subject to being stricken from the record upon the request of any party or on the court's own motion.

[Adopted September 1, 1991; amended effective September 1, 2004.]

12. SPECIAL MATTERS

LCR 94.04. DOMESTIC RELATIONS ACTIONS

(a) Preliminary and Temporary Orders.

(1) *Affidavit or Declaration of Financial Affairs.* A party applying for temporary support, maintenance, debt or income-producing property allocation, attorney's fees or other financial relief pending trial must serve and file with his or her motion an affidavit or declaration under penalty of perjury respecting financial affairs. The responding party, if contesting the motion, shall likewise submit such an affidavit or declaration which shall be served and filed. The notice of hearing or show cause order shall notify the responding party of this requirement.

(b) Ex Parte Hearing. Non-contested actions for marriage dissolution, separation or invalidity decrees, and paternity decrees, which have been approved for entry by all parties or their counsel may be presented for final hearing before the judge assigned to hear *ex parte* matters on any regular court day. Except as required by the judge or judicial officer reviewing the proposed decree, oral testimony will not be required at such hearings. The attorney or party shall request that the clerk present the original court file to the *ex parte* judge at the time of presentment, together with the proposed findings of fact, conclusions of law and decree. Presentation of such agreed decrees may be by mail to the Clerk of the Court. The appropriate *ex parte* fee and return, postage paid and pre-addressed envelopes for any conformed copies shall be submitted prior to presentation. The person submitting the *ex parte* request shall assure proof of compliance with LCR 95.04, if applicable.

[Adopted September 1, 1991; amended effective September 1, 2004.]

LCR 95.04. MANDATORY PARENT EDUCATION WORKSHOP

The Ferry, Stevens and Pend Oreille Counties Superior Courts find that it is in the best interest of any child whose parents or custodians are involved in specific court proceedings to provide such parents with an educational workshop concerning the impact family restructuring has on their child. The workshop offers parents tools to help ensure that their child's emotional needs will not be overlooked during the legal processes, to encourage parents to agree on child-related matters, and to aid in maximizing the use of court time.

(1) **Types of Proceedings Required.** Each person named as a party in the following types of proceedings filed after October 1, 1999, must comply with Local Rule 95.04:

1. Dissolution of marriage with child(ren) under 18 years old;

2. Legal separation or declaration of invalidity of marriage with child(ren) under 18 years old;

3. Petition to establish custody or visitation including paternity; and/or

4. Post–judgment petition involving custody or visitation.

(2) **Service on Parties.** The Clerk of the Court shall provide a copy of this rule (LR 95.04) in a conspicuous place together with information from court approved parenting education providers.

(3) **Mandatory.** Each party who files an appearance in a proceeding of the types described above in Section (1) shall complete the program unless exempted by the court. No final order approving any residential or parenting plan shall be entered without proof of completion of such education program by the

parents or legal guardians unless otherwise ordered by the court.

(4) Ninety (90) Day Deadline. Each party shall attend and complete an approved parenting workshop within ninety (90) days of filing a proceeding specified in Section (1) above.

(5) Exemption. The Court may exempt one or both parties from completion of the program if, after reviewing the requesting party's motion and supporting affidavit, the Court determines that participation is unnecessary.

(6) [Rescinded September 2, 2014.]

(7) Proof of Completion. Upon completion of the parenting education program, each program participant shall file the certificate of completion with the Clerk of the Court.

(8) Non–Complying Parties—Attorney's Fees Sanctions. A party who has completed the program shall have the right to request entry of an order from the court compelling the non-complying party's completion of the program. Should the non-complying party fail to complete the program in a timely manner without good reason, the court shall enter an award of reasonable attorney's fees and costs incurred for ob-

taining an order for compliance in favor of the complying party who uses this option to force the non-complying party into compliance. Other sanctions as set forth in Section (9) below may also be ordered.

(9) Other Sanctions. If upon order of the court a non-complying party continues to refuse participation, the refusal may be considered by the court in making its rulings on issues which are in dispute and may be grounds for contempt, striking of pleadings, and/or default.

(10) [Rescinded September 2, 2014.]

[Adopted effective September 1, 1999. Amended effective September 2, 2014.]

LCR 99. LOCAL RULES OF SUPERIOR COURT

Local Rules Committee. There shall be a standing rules committee composed of the presiding judge (or his/her designee), at least two members of the bar from the tri-county judicial district, and one of the three County Clerks. The rules committee will meet as determined by the presiding judge.

[Adopted September 1, 1991; amended effective September 1, 2004; September 2, 2014.]

LOCAL CRIMINAL RULES (Cite as LCrR)

LCrR 3.1. ARRAIGNMENT, TRIAL AND OTHER HEARINGS

(a) Arraignment Order. Criminal trials shall be set at the time of arraignment. At the same time, the court shall schedule an omnibus hearing and a trial status conference. The order on arraignment shall specify whether defendant shall be required to appear at omnibus hearing.

(b) Omnibus Hearing. Unless an agreed omnibus order has been submitted by both sides prior to or at the time of the omnibus hearing, defendant's attorney of record shall appear personally at the omnibus hearing. If the order on arraignment has required defendant's personal attendance at omnibus, defendant shall personally appear, or a bench warrant may issue.

(c) Status Hearing. Both defendant and defendant's attorney of record shall appear personally at the status hearing. Failure to appear at status hear-

ing is grounds for sanctions and/or issuance of a bench warrant for defendant's arrest.

[Adopted effective September 1, 2004.]

LCrR 6.1. TRIAL BY JURY

Notice to Court of Calendar and Jury Trial Changes; Sanctions for Late Notice. Whenever a case has been set for trial and thereafter is settled or will not be tried for any reason, or if a jury is thereafter waived, notice shall be given by the defendant's attorney of record to the court administrator, no later than two working days prior to the scheduled trial date. Failure to give notice as required in this rule may be grounds for assessment of actual costs. Actual costs shall include jury venire mileage and fees, bailiff wages, clerk overtime costs incurred in contacting jury venire persons, and witness fees paid by the court.

[Adopted effective September 1, 2004.]

LOCAL JUVENILE COURT RULES (Cite as LJuCR)

LJuCR 2.5. AMENDMENT OF SHELTER CARE ORDER

Hearings to review an existing shelter care order shall be set for hearing no later than thirty (30) days after the prior shelter care hearing. When the De-

partment of Social and Health Services is the petitioner, the Department shall submit for entry a continuing shelter care order, maintaining the existing orders, no more than three (3) judicial days prior to the date of the shelter care review hearing unless: (1) a party files and serves an objection to continued shelter care on or before three (3) judicial days prior to the hearing date for the shelter care review hearing; (2) any party formally notes a shelter care hearing; or (3) the entry of a court order (such as an order of dependency) has made continued shelter care unnecessary.

[Adopted effective September 1, 2004.]

LJuCR 3.8. DISPOSITION HEARINGS

(c) **Evidence.** At disposition, review and permanency planning hearings, the court shall consider the social file, social study (Individual Service and Safety Plan), and other appropriate predisposition studies, including diagnostic, treatment and progress reports and recommendations from service providers who have provided services to parties under prior court order. Any predisposition study shall be made available to the other parties a reasonable time prior to the hearing.

[Adopted effective September 1, 2004.]

LJuCR 3.9. REVIEW HEARINGS

(a) **Testimony.** All contested review hearings, including permanency planning reviews, shall be held without oral testimony, unless a motion is properly and timely made by a party with due notice to all other parties, and the motion is granted by the court to allow oral testimony. The parties may present further evidence in written affidavit or declaration form, and the social file and other appropriate diagnostic, treatment and progress reports and recommendations from service providers shall also be considered at the request of any party. Any written materials shall be made available to the other parties at a reasonable time prior to the hearing.

(b) **Parties to Be Heard.** Unless the court orders further testimony pursuant to subsection (a) above, the only persons who may be heard at review hearings shall be the current caseworker, the parent(s) or guardian/custodian of the child, the guardian ad litem, and any foster or relative caregiver entitled to an opportunity to be heard under state or federal law.

[Adopted effective September 1, 2004.]

LOCAL GUARDIAN AD LITEM GRIEVANCE RULES (Cite as LRGAL)

LRGAL 1. GUARDIAN AD LITEM COMPLAINT REVIEW COMMITTEE

There shall be a complaint review committee (hereinafter referred to as the "committee"), consisting of a judge, as designated by the presiding judge, the court administrator or Clerk, and a representative of the county bar association designated by its president, to administer complaints about guardians ad litem involved in Titles 11, 13 and 26 RCW.

[Adopted effective September 1, 2004.]

LRGAL 2. SUBMISSION OF COMPLAINTS

All complaints shall be in writing, signed by at least one individual with his/her address and phone number, and submitted to the court administrator.

[Adopted effective September 1, 2004.]

LRGAL 3. REVIEW OF COMPLAINT

Upon receipt of a written complaint, the court administrator shall convene the complaint review committee within ten (10) business days to review the complaint. Upon review of the complaint, the committee shall either:

(a) Make a finding that the complaint concerns a case then pending in the court and decline to review the complaint and so inform the complainant. In such instances, the committee shall advise the complainant that the complaint may only be addressed in the context of the case at bar, either by motion seeking

the removal of the guardian ad litem or by contesting the information or recommendation contained in the guardian ad litem's report or testimony. In such cases, the committee and its members shall perform their roles in such a manner as to assure that the trial judge or court commissioner remains uninformed as to the complaint; or

(b) Make a finding that the complaint has no merit on its face, and decline to review it and so inform the complaining party; or

(c) Make a finding that the complaint appears to have merit and request a written response from the guardian ad litem within ten (10) business days detailing the specific issues in the complaint to which the committee desires a response. The committee shall provide the guardian ad litem with a copy of the original complaint. A guardian ad litem's failure to respond within the required ten (10) business days shall result in the immediate suspension of the guardian ad litem from all registries. In considering whether the complaint has merit, the committee shall consider whether the complaint alleges the guardian ad litem has:

(1) Violated the Rules of Professional Conduct;

(2) Misrepresented his or her qualifications to serve as a guardian ad litem;

(3) Not met the annual training requirements set forth in the registry requirements;

(4) Breached the confidentiality of the parties;

(5) Falsified information in a report to the court or in testimony before the court;

(6) Failed to report abuse of a child;

(7) Communicated with a judge/commissioner *ex parte*, except as allowed by law (such as in obtaining an emergency restraining order);

(8) Purported to represent the court in a public forum without prior approval of the presiding judge;

(9) Violated state or local laws, or court rules in the person's capacity as guardian ad litem;

(10) Taken or failed to take any other action which would reasonably call the suitability of the person to serve as guardian ad litem into question;

(11) Failed to keep information confidential from non-parties or disclosed protected information to a party;

(12) Intentionally lied or presented information in a false light to the court, another party or a third party; or

(13) Talked about a case for which the guardian ad litem was appointed to the media or public without the permission of all parties and/or the court.

[Adopted effective September 1, 2004.]

LRGAL 4. RESPONSE AND FINDINGS

Upon receipt of a written response to a complaint from the guardian ad litem, the complaint review committee shall, within ten (10) business days, make a finding as to each of the issues delineated in the committee's written request to the guardian ad litem that based on the response, there is either no merit to the issue, or there is merit to the issue. In any case where the committee finds that there is merit to an issue, the committee may conduct further investigation, including the examination of witnesses, documents, and such other evidence as the committee may, in the exercise of its discretion, choose to examine. The committee may extend the time for entering findings of fact during such examination, provided, however, that no such extension shall exceed thirty (30) days beyond the date the committee determined that there is merit to any issue.

[Adopted effective September 1, 2004.]

LRGAL 5. CONFIDENTIALITY

(a) A complaint shall be deemed confidential for all purposes unless the committee has determined that it has merit under LRGAL 1.3(c).

(b) Any record of complaints filed which are found by the committee not to have merit shall be and remain confidential and shall not be disclosed except by court order.

[Adopted effective September 1, 2004.]

LRGAL 6. COMPLAINT PROCESSING TIME STANDARDS

(a) Complaints shall be resolved within twenty-five (25) days of the date of receipt of the written complaint if a case is pending.

(b) Complaints shall be resolved within sixty (60) days of the date or receipt of the written complaint if the complaint is filed subsequent to the conclusion of the case.

(c) The complainant and the guardian ad litem shall be notified in writing of the committee's decision within ten (10) business days of the entry of the committee's findings and decision.

(d) Complaints filed under this rule must be filed within three (3) years from the date of the occurrence of the matters complained of. The committee shall find complaints filed after this time not to have cause to proceed. This limitation applies to all complaints, whether filed during the pendency or after the conclusion of a case.

[Adopted effective September 1, 2004.]

LRGAL 7. SANCTIONS

The committee shall have the authority to issue a written admonishment, issue a written reprimand, refer the guardian ad litem to additional testing, recommend to the presiding judge either that the court, on its own motion, remove the guardian ad litem from the instant case, or that the presiding judge suspend or remove the guardian ad litem from the registry. In considering a sanction, the committee shall take into consideration any prior complaints which resulted in an admonishment, reprimand, referral to training, removal of the guardian ad litem from a particular case, or suspension or removal from a registry. If a guardian ad litem is listed on more than one registry, at the discretion of the committee, the suspension or removal may apply to each registry on which the guardian ad litem is listed. When a guardian ad litem is removed from a registry pursuant to the disposition of a grievance, the court shall send notice of such removal to the state Administrative Office of the Courts (AOC).

[Adopted effective September 1, 2004.]

LRGAL 8. REQUEST FOR RECONSIDERATION BY GUARDIAN AD LITEM

A guardian ad litem may, within five (5) business days of receipt of notification that he or she has been suspended or removed from a registry, request a hearing for reconsideration of the committee's decision. The presiding judge shall designate a hearing officer to preside over and conduct such review. The sole purpose of the review shall be to review the appropriateness of the suspension or removal from the registry. The hearing officer shall review the written record of the instant case and any prior complaints upon which the committee relied and hear oral argument from the guardian ad litem and a representative of the committee. Said hearing shall be conducted within twenty (20) days of receipt of a request for the hearing.

[Adopted effective September 1, 2004.]

LRGAL 9. MAINTAINING RECORDS OF GRIEVANCES

The superior court administrator shall maintain a record of grievances filed and of any sanctions issued pursuant to the grievance procedure.

[Adopted effective September 1, 2004.]

LRGAL 10. UNAVAILABILITY OF PRESIDING JUDGE

In the event the presiding judge is not able to sit on the committee, issue an order or make an assignment as required by these rules, on account of being the judge who is assigned to a particular case, or is recused or may otherwise be disqualified, the other sitting judge shall act in the place and stead of the presiding judge. In the event both judges are unable to so act, the court administrator shall arrange for a court commissioner or visiting judge, so to act.

[Adopted effective September 1, 2004.]

LOCAL RULES FOR APPEAL OF DECISIONS OF COURTS OF LIMITED JURISDICTION (Cite as LRALJ)

LRALJ 3.1. PROCEDURE

(a) **Scheduling.** When a notice of appeal has been filed, the Clerk shall provide the presiding judge with a suggested schedule of dates for filing the transcript, for submission of briefs as provided by RALJ 6.3A and 7.2, and for oral argument. The presiding judge shall then enter an order which requires the parties to comply with a schedule for such filings and to appear for a hearing for oral argument. The Clerk shall give notice of the appeal scheduling order to all parties, which notice shall include a notice sent directly to any criminal defendant, even if represented by counsel. The scheduling order shall bear the following legend above the judge's signature:

ATTENTION APPELLANT: **You are ultimately responsible for ensuring that your appeal is prosecuted in a timely manner, even if you have an attorney assisting you in prepar-**

ing your appeal. **You must maintain contact with your attorney and the court to ensure that this scheduling order is being followed. If you or your attorney fail to meet the deadlines set out in this scheduling order, or fail to timely seek an extension of time pursuant to RALJ 10.3, sanctions may be assessed against you, or your appeal may be involuntarily dismissed pursuant to RALJ 10.2(a).**

(b) **Transcripts.** In the event the transcript or briefs are not timely filed, a party or the Clerk may note the matter on the motion docket either for dismissal for want of prosecution or for order of reversal.

(c) **Argument.** Arguments on appeal will be limited to 20 minutes per side, except on prior order of the court.

[Adopted September 1, 1991; amended effective September 1, 2004.]

APPENDICES

APPENDIX A.   FINANCIAL STATEMENT (RCW 26.09.090)

_____   (Clerk's Date Stamp)

SUPERIOR COURT OF
WASHINGTON
COUNTY OF _____

In re the marriage of:

Petitioner:

and:

         CASE NO. _____

Respondent: FINANCIAL STATEMENT

I.   GENERAL INFORMATION

1.1   Name of wife: Age: Date of birth:
1.2   Name of husband: Age: Date of birth:
1.3   Dependent children:
     a.   Of this marriage:

	Date of		
Name	Birth	Age	With Whom Residing

     b.   Of former marriages:

Parent (Husband or Wife)	Name	Age	With Whom Residing

1.4   Support and attorney fees I (request) (am willing to pay):
     a.   Monthly support for each dependent child $_____
     b.   Attorney fees $_____

II.   INCOME AND EMPLOYMENT

2.1   Husband:
     a.   Occupation:
     b.   Net take-home pay per month:
        (Calculate on basis of 4⅓ weeks per month. Do <u>not</u> deduct such things as
        savings bonds, credit union payments, etc.)
          Employer   Address
                                         $ _____
                                           $ _____

     c.   Other income (per month):
          Source
                                           $ _____
                                           $ _____
                                           $ _____

TOTAL MONTHLY INCOME $ _____

d. If not employed, work for which trained and the approximate net amount capable of earning:

2.2 Wife
     a. Occupation:
     b. Net take-home pay per month:
        (Calculate on basis of 4⅓ weeks per month. Do <u>not</u> deduct such things as savings bonds, credit union payments, etc.)
             <u>Employer</u>   <u>Address</u>

                                                $ _____
                                                $ _____

     c. Other income (per month):
             <u>Source</u>

                                                $ _____
                                                $ _____
                                                $ _____

TOTAL MONTHLY INCOME $ _____

d. If not employed, work for which trained and the approximate net amount capable of earning:

III. RETIREMENT BENEFITS

(Including defined-benefit pension plans, defined-contribution retirement plans, sick leave plans, permanent insurance, stock programs and deferred compensation agreements.)

3.1 Present benefits

     a. Estimated monthly retirement benefits: $_____
        Date on which they (did) commence:
        Period of time benefits will be payable:

3.2 Future benefits

     a. I am or will be entitled to retirement benefits from:

     b. The last statement from the retirement plan is attached.
        If no statement is available I provide the following:

(1) Amount of contributions monthly $_____
(2) Total contributions to date $_____
(3) Age at which I can first draw benefits:
(4) Effect of remarriage on receipt or loss of benefits:

IV. MONTHLY EXPENSES AND DEBTS

4.1 Current monthly living expenses paid by me (including expenses for dependent children living with me).

Food	_____	Life insurance	_____
House payment or rent	_____	Medical expense (insur-	
Utilities (heat, electricity,		ance, medicine, drugs,	
water, garbage)	_____	doctor, dentist	_____
Telephone	_____	Clothing & laundry	_____
Auto (gas, repairs,		School expense	_____
license, insurance)	_____	Babysitter	_____
Homeowner's insurance	_____	Support & alimony	_____
Recreation	_____	Miscellaneous	_____

TOTAL $ _____

4.2 Monthly debt payments for which I am solely responsible

Payee (Creditor)	Amount Due/Month	Amount

TOTAL $ _____

TOTAL OF 4.1 AND 4.2 $ _____

4.3 Monthly debt payments for which the community is responsible:

Payee (Creditor)	Amount Due/Month	Monthly Payment By Me

TOTAL PAID BY ME $ _____

TOTAL OF MONTHLY EXPENSES AND DEBTS (4.1 + 4.2 + 4.3) $ _____

Under penalty of perjury I certify that the within Financial Statement is full, true and correct to the best of my knowledge.

DATED this _____ day of _____, 19____.

_____
Petitioner/Respondent

APPENDIX B. STATEMENT OF ASSETS AND LIABILITIES AND PROPOSED DISTRIBUTION

IN THE SUPERIOR COURT OF THE STATE OF WASHINGTON
IN AND FOR THE COUNTY OF _____

In re the Marriage of:

)
)
) No. _____
)
) STATEMENT OF ASSETS AND
) LIABILITIES AND PROPOSED
) DISTRIBUTION
)
)
)
)
)

The attached Statement of Assets and Liabilities and Proposed Distribution is submitted to the Court pursuant to Local Rule 94.04(c).

Date: _____   _____
                                                    Petitioner

Date: _____   _____
                                                    Respondent

SCHEDULE I.   COMMUNITY ASSETS

No.	Item	Proposed Value			Proposed Disposition*			Decision	
		Hus.	Wife	Agreed	By Hus.	By Wife	Agreed	Hus.	Wife
1.									
2.									
3.									
4.									
5.									
6.									
7.									
8.									
9.									
10.									
11.									
12.									
13.									
14.									

15. _____

16. _____

17. _____

18. _____

19. _____

20. _____

* Insert "H" or "W" to indicate to whom disposition is proposed

SCHEDULE II. COMMUNITY DEBTS

No.	Item	Proposed Value			Proposed Disposition*			Decision	
		Hus.	Wife	Agreed	By Hus.	By Wife	Agreed	Hus.	Wife
1.									
2.									
3.									
4.									
5.									
6.									
7.									
8.									
9.									
10.									
11.									
12.									
13.									
14.									
15.									
16.									
17.									
18.									
19.									
20.									

* Insert "H" or "W" to indicate to whom disposition is proposed

SCHEDULE III. HUSBAND'S SEPARATE PROPERTY

No.	Item	Proposed Value			Proposed Disposition*			Decision	
		Hus.	Wife	Agreed	By Hus.	By Wife	Agreed	Hus.	Wife

1. _____
2. _____
3. _____
4. _____
5. _____
6. _____
7. _____
8. _____
9. _____
10. _____
11. _____
12. _____
13. _____
14. _____
15. _____
16. _____
17. _____
18. _____
19. _____
20. _____

* Insert "H" or "W" to indicate to whom disposition is proposed

SCHEDULE IV. WIFE'S SEPARATE PROPERTY

No.	Item	Proposed Value			Proposed Disposition*			Decision	
		Hus.	Wife	Agreed	By Hus.	By Wife	Agreed	Hus.	Wife
1.									
2.									
3.									
4.									
5.									
6.									
7.									
8.									
9.									

10. _____

11. _____

12. _____

13. _____

14. _____

15. _____

16. _____

17. _____

18. _____

19. _____

20. _____

* Insert "H" or "W" to indicate to whom disposition is proposed

SCHEDULE V. PROPERTY THE CHARACTER
OF WHICH IS CONTESTED

No.	Item	Proposed Value			Proposed Disposition*			Decision	
		Hus.	Wife	Agreed	By Hus.	By Wife	Agreed	Hus.	Wife
1.									
2.									
3.									
4.									
5.									
6.									
7.									
8.									
9.									
10.									
11.									
12.									
13.									
14.									
15.									
16.									
17.									
18.									

19. _____

20. _____

* Insert "H" or "W" to indicate to whom disposition is proposed

SCHEDULE VI. SUMMARY

	Community Property		Separate Property	
	Husband	Wife	Husband	Wife
Assets				
Liabilities				
TOTALS				

DISTRICT COURT
FERRY DISTRICT COURT LOCAL RULES

Including Amendments Received Through
August 15, 2015

Table of Rules

I. LOCAL ADMINISTRATIVE RULES

LARLJ 2. SCOPE OF RULES AND ADOPTION

(a) Effect of Local Rules. These rules shall be known as the Local Rules for the District Court of the State of Washington for Ferry County. These rules will be effective September 1, 2011. These rules conform with, to the extent possible, the numbering system and in format to the rules adopted by the Supreme Court of the State of Washington for courts of limited jurisdiction.

The provisions of these local rules are supplemental to the rules adopted by the Supreme Court of the State of Washington for courts of limited jurisdiction, and shall not be construed in conflict with them.

(b) Adoption and Amendments. These rules are adopted and may be amended from time to time in accordance with GR 7, CRLJ 83, CrRLJ 1.7 and IRLJ 1.3 of the Washington Court Rules. The court may modify or suspend any of these local rules in any given case upon good cause shown or upon the court's own motion.

[Adopted effective September 1, 2011.]

LARLJ 2.1. DECORUM

Courtroom Decorum. All attorneys and other individuals in the courtroom shall abide by the following rules of conduct:

(a) Always be prompt. Be in the courtroom ready to proceed at the appointed time.

(b) Stand when the judge or the jury enters or leaves the courtroom.

(c) Do not make personal attacks on opposing counsel or parties.

(d) Do not interrupt. Wait your turn. Address all remarks to the Judge. Argument between litigants or their attorneys is not permitted.

(e) After the judge has ruled, ask the Judge's permission before arguing further.

(f) Rise when addressing the Judge and when making objections as this calls the Judge's attention to you.

(g) Dress Appropriately to the Serious Nature of the Matters Before the Court. Shorts and other kinds of beach apparel are not appropriate. Clothing advertising alcoholic beverages or illegal drugs are not appropriate. Hats are not to be worn in the courtroom.

(h) No food or beverage of any kind are not to be brought into the courtroom, except for empanelled jurors.

(i) Do not approach a witness, the jury or the Judge without asking permission of the Judge.

(j) No person shall be in Ferry County District Court while in possession of a cell phone, pager, smart phone or other such device unless it is turned off or is in a silent or vibrate mode. Any person having any of these items not turned off or in silent or vibrate mode is subject to having such device seized upon direction of the Court. In addition, any person violating this rule shall be subject to punishment for contempt of court.

[Adopted effective September 1, 2011.]

LARLJ 5. COURT ADMINISTRATOR

(d) Selection. The court administrator shall be appointed by the judge and shall serve at the pleasure of the appointing authority under the direction and supervision of the judge.

(e) Powers and duties. The powers and duties of the court administrator include but are not limited to the following:

(1) Administrative control of all non-judicial activities of the court.

(2) Implement all policies regarding judicial functions of the court.

(3) Supervision of all court employees.

(4) Preparation and administration of the court budget.

(5) Representation of the court in dealings with the State Court Administrator.

(6) Assist the judge in meeting with representatives of governmental bodies, and other public and private groups regarding court management matters.

(7) Prepare reports and compile statistics as required by the judge or state court administrator and maintain records or informal activities of the court.

(8) Make recommendations to the judge for the improvement of the administration of the court.

The Court administrator may delegate such duties to court employees as deemed appropriate.

[Adopted effective September 1, 2011.]

LARLJ 6. APPEARANCE BY TELEPHONE

Hearings of any type will not be conducted by telephone without prior approval of the judge on a showing of good cause.

[Adopted effective September 1, 2011.]

LARLJ 7. SECURITY OF COURTROOMS AND RELATED AREAS

Weapons: No weapons designed for offensive or defensive purposes shall be allowed in any space assigned to the District Court and a violation of this order shall constitute contempt of court.

Exceptions: This rule shall not apply to Judges, commissioned police officers, corrections officers, or federal law enforcement officers.

[Adopted effective September 1, 2011.]

II. LOCAL CIVIL RULES

LCRLJ 55. DEFAULT

(a) Entry of Default Judgment.

(5) All necessary papers required for entry of a default judgment shall be filed at the same time as the motion for default judgment, unless extended by court order to correct a clerical error or omission or for furnishing of any proof required by the court. Default judgments shall be subject to the following:

(6) No default judgment shall be granted except upon motion by plaintiff's attorney of record, or if none, by motion by plaintiff.

(7) No default judgment shall be granted except upon proof satisfactory to the court. The court shall require at least the following to be on file with the motion for default judgment, unless otherwise excused by the court for good cause:

(i) on assigned causes of action, the assignment instrument;

(ii) on causes of action based on negotiable instrument, the original negotiable instrument;

(iii) on causes of action based on retail sales contract, chattel mortgage, or conditional sales contract, the original contract (or a copy if the original has been filed with a governmental agency). Where applicable, an automobile title or bill of sale must be filed;

(iv) on causes of action based on open account where the complaint is not specific, a written statement of account setting forth all charges and credits and the dates thereof, the nature of merchandise or services furnished, and a statement of any interest or surcharges which are included;

(v) on causes of action for rent based on oral lease, a statement of account setting forth the dates of accrued rent, dates of delinquency, late charges and any other costs. If any claim is made for damages or repairs to premises, such claim must be itemized separately;

(vi) on causes of action for rent based on a written lease, a copy of the lease and a statement of account setting forth the dates of accrued rent, dates of delinquency, late charges and any other costs. If any claim is made for damages or repairs to premises, such claim must be itemized separately;

(vii) on causes of action based on all other contracts, oral testimony to prove performance may be required, together with filing of a copy of the contract, if written; and filing or proving the items of account and any credits;

(viii) on causes of action for tort, the proof required shall be the same as required above for proving contract balances except that the following additional proof of the amount of damage shall be required:

(a) Property damage may be proved by repair bills or estimates;

(b) Loss of use claims, loss of wages, and pain and suffering shall be proved by oral testimony.

(c) Hospital and doctor bills may be proved by written bills, whether paid or not.

(8) No judgment for interest shall be allowed unless citation to applicable authority is presented and there is on file proof of the factors necessary for computation of interest including applicable dates, rate of interest, amounts subject to interest, and a computation of the total interest claimed due. For prejudgment interest the document that contains the rate of interest shall be included, with the rate of interest underlined and highlighted in yellow for the court.

(9) Default judgments must be accompanied by:

(i) Affidavit of Service if not previously filed.

(ii) Affidavit of Soldiers' and Sailors' Relief Act.

(g) Collection and handling charges and attorney fees on actions brought to collect dishonored checks shall not be allowed unless proof of the following is provided:

(1) The statutory form of notice of dishonor has been sent as required by RCW chapter 62.A–3 and a copy is filed with the court.

(2) An accounting statement, or some reasonable alternate means of determining plaintiff's collection costs, is filed with the court.

[Adopted effective September 1, 2011.]

III. LOCAL CRIMINAL RULES

LCrRLJ 2.5. PROCEDURE ON FAILURE TO OBEY CITATION AND NOTICES TO APPEAR

(a) **Recall of Failure to Appear Arrest Warrants.** The Court Administrator, or delegate, shall have authority to recall Failure to Appear Arrest Warrants issued because the defendant failed to appear or respond to the citation or summons under the following provisions:

(1) The Failure to Appear Arrest Warrant has not yet been sent to the Sheriff for entry into the NCIC.

(2) The defendant personally appears at the counter to sign for a court date or appears through counsel, and/or posts bail.

(3) In cases of clerical error.

(b) In all other cases, the defendant shall present himself/herself to the Ferry County Jail unless otherwise directed by the Court Administrator.

[Adopted effective September 1, 2011.]

LCrRLJ 4.5. PRE–TRIAL CONFERENCE

(a) **Date set at arraignment.** When a plea of not guilty is entered, the court shall set a time for a pre-trial conference, approximately 30 days after the arraignment.

(b) **Mandatory Appearance.** All parties and their attorneys shall be present at the pre-trial hearing. Failure of a defendant to attend the pre-trial conference may result in the issuance of a bench warrant, the forfeiture of any bond, bail or other security posted by or on behalf of the defendant, and the striking of the trial date from the trial calendar.

(c) **Discovery Complete.** By the time of the pre-trial hearing, the parties should have completed discovery and concluded plea negotiations.

(d) **Pre-trial Motions.** All pre-trial motions (including Petitions for Deferred Prosecution) other than motions in limine, must be noted at the pre-trial hearing. The court will set a time for a hearing on the motions and set a briefing schedule. The motions must be made in writing accordance with the briefing schedule, with a memorandum of authorities, and, where appropriate, an affidavit setting forth the specific facts the party expects to elicit at the hearing.

(e) **Jury Trial.** The Trial Readiness Hearing and the Jury Trial will be confirmed at this time.

[Adopted effective September 1, 2011.]

LCrRLJ 6.1. JURY TRIAL READINESS HEARING

A Jury Trial Readiness Hearing will be scheduled during the week prior to the jury term week. The Defendant must be present with his or her attorney.

The failure of the Defendant to appear at this hearing, unless excused by the Court, may result in the issuance of a bench warrant and the jury trial being stricken, and shall be deemed a waiver of the Defendant's Right to Speedy Trial. At the hearing the following matters will be concluded:

1. All plea negotiations;

2. Exchange of witness lists;

3. Providing any discovery not previously completed by the Pre–Trial Conference; and,

4. Motions on legal issues arising subsequent to the Jury Pre–Trial Conference or on issues arising due to new evidence.

[Adopted effective September 1, 2011.]

LCrRLJ 6.15. JURY INSTRUCTIONS

(a) Unless otherwise noted by the court, proposed jury instructions shall be filed with the court and served upon opposing counsel by 3 PM on Monday of Jury Trial Week. Each party shall file two original sets of instructions: one with citations and one without citations, and shall serve a copy with citations on each party. Additional instructions, which could not be reasonably anticipated, shall be served and filed at any time before the court has instructed the jury. Each proposed instruction shall be on a separate sheet of paper. The original without citations shall neither be numbered nor include citations of authority.

[Adopted effective September 1, 2011.]

LCrRLJ 7.6. PROBATION MONITORING FEES

Defendants placed on probation shall be required to pay a monthly monitoring fee, unless otherwise stated in the judgment and sentence.

[Adopted effective September 1, 2011.]

LCrRLJ 8.2(f). NO CONTACT ORDERS

A request to extinguish or modify a No Contact Order in a Domestic Violence case may only be made by a party to the case and must be made in writing. A verified safety plan must in place for any victim of Domestic Violence. All parties and the alleged victim must be served with written notice at least five court days before any hearing to consider such a request.

[Adopted effective September 1, 2011.]

LCrRLJ 38. CRIMINAL JURY TRIAL

(a) Imposition of Costs. The Court shall be notified immediately if a case scheduled for jury trial is settled or will not be tried by the jury for any reason. An assessment for jury costs may be imposed if the parties fail to notify the court at least 24 hours before the trial is scheduled to begin. The responsible party will be required to pay a jury administrative reimbursement fee equal to the actual costs incurred by the Court for the jury trial, unless the Judge determines that those costs and fees shall not be paid. Costs include jury fee payments, mileage reimbursements and all postage costs to summon the jury. Any such terms imposed by the Court shall be paid as directed by the Court.

[Adopted effective September 1, 2011.]

IV. LOCAL INFRACTION RULES

LIRLJ 2.6. SCHEDULING OF HEARINGS

(A)(1)(i) A Respondent who requests a contested hearing may first be scheduled for a prehearing conference, which shall be scheduled in accordance with the provisions of IRLJ 2.6(a)(1)(i).

(ii) The prehearing conference may be waived in accordance with the provisions of IRLJ 2.6(a)(1)(ii). However, a respondent who waives the prehearing conference may not be entitled to seek deferral of the infraction(s) alleged. If the respondent fails to timely waive or appear at the prehearing conference, then a default judgment shall be entered.

[Adopted effective September 1, 2011.]

LIRLJ 3.2. MOTION FOR VACATION OF DEFAULT JUDGMENT FOR FTA

(b) A defendant against whom a judgment for a traffic infraction has been entered by default for failure to appear, may file a motion in writing, on forms provided by the court, requesting that the judgment be set aside. The motion will then be presented to the court ex parte for determination.

The motion will be evaluated in conformity with CRLJ 60(b). If the Court grants said motion, the matter will be set for a hearing of the kind requested by the defendant on an upcoming calendar date.

[Adopted effective September 1, 2011.]

LIRLJ 3.5. DECISION ON WRITTEN OR EMAIL STATEMENTS

Mitigation and Contested hearings regarding infractions are authorized. The procedure set out in IRLJ 3.5 is adopted. In place of the defendant's personal appearance at a contested or mitigated infraction hearing, defendants may submit their statement in writing (including email submissions). The sworn, written statements must be received by the Court no later than seven (7) calendar days before the scheduled hearing or it will not be considered. The Court shall examine the citing officer's report and any statements from the defendant. The examination shall take place within 120 days after the defendant filed a response to the notice of infraction. The examination may be held in Chambers and shall not be governed by the rules of evidence. Any Defendant electing to request that the Court hold a contested hearing under this rule waives the right to appeal the Court's decision to Superior Court under IRLJ 3.5. Upon reaching a decision, the court will notify the person of the Judge's determination. The person must remit any amount set by the Judge. If the amount set by the Judge is not paid by the specified date the failure to respond fee will be added and the matter turned over to a collection agency. If the citation is a traffic infraction, the Department of Licensing will be notified if the person fails to respond or to pay.

[Adopted effective September 1, 2011.]

LIRLJ 3.6.　DEFERRED FINDINGS

(a) Deferred Findings. The court may defer findings regarding traffic infractions prior to a contested hearing, or defer entry of an order following a mitigation for up to one year and impose conditions on that person.

(b) Limit. A person may not receive more than one deferral within a seven-year period for moving violations and one deferral within a seven year period for nonmoving violations.

(c) Conditions. For moving violations the conditions may include attendance at traffic safety school (if available), payment of some or all of the presumptive fine and an administrative fee. For nonmoving violations the conditions may include payment of some or all of the presumptive fine and an administrative fee.

(d) Administrative Fee. An administrative fee shall be charged.

(e) Dismissal. After the end of the deferral period, the court will dismiss the infraction if the person has met all the conditions of the deferral and has not committed another traffic infraction during the period.

(f) Subsequent Violation During the Deferral Period. The court will notify a person during the pending deferment of a violation by first class mail to the address provided by the deferred person. The Court will note the deferred violation as committed and transmit the Notice of Infraction to the Department of Licensing. The Court shall of no other obligation to the deferred person in this regard.

[Adopted effective September 1, 2011.]

LIRLJ 6.6.　SPEED MEASURING DEVICE CERTIFICATION; REQUEST FOR SPEED MEASURING DEVICE EXPERT; REMOTE TESTIMONY

Any certificate admissible under LIRLJ 6.6(b), and any other document related to a Speed Measuring Device, can be filed with the clerk of the court and maintained by the court as a public record, and shall be available for inspection by the public. Copies shall be provided by the clerk's office on request. There shall be no charge for the copy if it relates to an infraction filed against the person making the request. These records shall be available without a formal request for discovery. The court shall be entitled to take judicial notice of the fact that any document filed pursuant to this rule has been filed with the court.

Requests to produce the electronic measuring device expert shall be contained in a separate document and filed in accordance with IRLJ 6.6(b), and served on the prosecuting attorney with a conformed copy filed with the Clerk of the Court. The request cannot be combined with a notice of appearance or any other pleading.

The Court may allow the speed measuring device expert to testify from a location other than the courtroom, via speakerphone.

[Adopted effective September 1, 2011.]

FRANKLIN COUNTY

Table of Courts

Superior Court

Local Rules of the Superior Court of Washington in and for Benton and Franklin Counties.

District Court

Franklin County District Court

Municipal Courts

Connell Municipal Court—[No Local Rules].
Kahlotus Municipal Court—[No Local Rules].
Pasco Municipal Court Rules.

SUPERIOR COURT

LOCAL RULES OF THE SUPERIOR COURT OF WASHINGTON IN AND FOR BENTON AND FRANKLIN COUNTIES

PUBLISHER'S NOTE

The Local Rules for the Superior Courts of Benton and Franklin Counties are set forth in Benton County.

DISTRICT COURT
FRANKLIN COUNTY DISTRICT COURT

Including Amendments Received Through
August 15, 2015

Table of Rules

Rule
IRLJ 3.5.   Decision on Written Statements.

IRLJ 3.5.   DECISION ON WRITTEN STATEMENTS

(a) Contested Hearings. The court shall examine the citing officer's report and any statement submitted by the defendant. The examination shall take place within 120 days after the defendant filed the response to the notice of infraction. The examination may be held in chambers and shall not be governed by the Rules of Evidence.

(1) Factual Determination. The court shall determine whether the plaintiff has proved by a preponderance of all evidence submitted that the defendant has committed the infraction.

(2) Disposition. If the court determines that the infraction has been committed, it may assess a penalty in accordance with rule 3.3.

(3) Notice to Parties. The court shall notify the parties in writing whether an infraction was found to have been committed and what penalty, if any, was imposed.

(4) No appeal Permitted. There shall be no appeal from a decision on written statements.

(b) Mitigation Hearings. Mitigation hearings based upon written statements may be held in chambers.

[Adopted effective September 1, 2009.]

MUNICIPAL COURTS

CONNELL MUNICIPAL COURT—
[No Local Rules]

KAHLOTUS MUNICIPAL COURT—
[No Local Rules]

PASCO MUNICIPAL COURT RULES

Including Amendments Received Through
August 15, 2015

Table of Rules

LOCAL RULES

PMCLR 1.7. ADOPTION OF LOCAL RULES

These rules are adopted pursuant to CrRLJ 1.7.

[Adopted effective September 1, 1996.]

PMCLR 1.8. TITLE OF RULES

These rules may be known and cited as Pasco Municipal Court Local Rules, and shall be referred to as PMCLR.

[Adopted effective September 1, 1996.]

PMCLR 2.0. EFFECT OF LOCAL RULES

The provisions of the Local Rules are supplemental to the Rules for Courts of Limited Jurisdiction, as adopted or hereafter amended by the Supreme Court of the State of Washington, and shall not be construed in conflict with them.

[Adopted effective September 1, 1996.]

PMCLR 3.1. WITHDRAWAL OF COUNSEL

Pursuant to CrRLJ 3.1(e), no attorney may withdraw except upon consent of the court for good cause shown when a case has not been concluded. Except in cases where withdrawal is mandated by the Rules of Professional Conduct, the court should not permit withdrawal unless there is simultaneous substitution of a lawyer who is prepared to proceed on the scheduled trial date. A motion to substitute counsel not mandated by the Rules of Professional Conduct which is accompanied by a motion to continue the trial date should only be granted upon actual payment of terms and/or costs.

[Adopted effective September 1, 1996.]

PMCLR 3.2(m). BAIL

When required to reasonably assure appearance in court for those persons arrested and detained in jail for new offenses, bail shall be set in accordance with a schedule, approved by the presiding judge, and available from the court clerk. Bail shall not be set for accused persons arrested for new offenses involving domestic violence except at the preliminary appearance or arraignment.

[Adopted effective September 1, 1996.]

PMCLR 3.3. TIME FOR TRIAL— OBJECTIONS TO TRIAL DATE

(a) A defendant who objects to the trial date set by the court pursuant to CrRLJ 3.3(f) shall file and serve upon the plaintiff a written motion and shall, within three court days (excluding Saturdays, Sundays or legal holidays) of the filing of the motion, appear in court at the time court is scheduled to commence, and advise the judge that the motion has been made. Failure to comply with this rule shall be a waiver of the objection.

(h) Continuances. Continuances or other delays of criminal trials shall be granted only upon written motion, and for reasons provided in CrRLJ 3.3. Orders granting continuances or other delays of criminal trials must be in writing.

(k) Deferred Prosecution. A petition for Deferred Prosecution under section 10.05 of the Revised Code of Washington shall be filed fourteen (14) days before the date set for trial on forms approved by the Court.

The written assessment prepared by an approved treatment facility shall be accompanied by a recommendation from the Probation Office, or such other Court Appointee authorized under Chapter 10.05 of the Revised Code of Washington.

When the Court denies the Petition for a Deferred Prosecution, timely filed under this rule, the case shall proceed to trial as previously set.

In the event the Petition for Deferred Prosecution is approved by the Court, the Defendant may be under the supervision of the Probation Department, or Court Appointee pursuant to Section 10.05.170 of the Revised Code of Washington. A defendant who refuses, fails or neglects to comply with an order, or request of the Probation Office or Court Appointee, or the terms of supervision, or conditions of supervision, or conditions of deferred prosecution may have the deferred prosecution revoked.

[Adopted effective September 1, 1996.]

PMCLR 3.4. PRESENCE OF THE DEFENDANT

(1) Defendant shall be present at all proceedings except when expressly waived.

[Adopted effective September 1, 1996.]

PMCLR 4.1. PROCEEDINGS BEFORE THE JUDGE—APPEARANCE

(d) Appearance by Defendant's Lawyer.

(7) Attorneys retained by defendants must promptly serve written notice of their appearance upon the prosecuting attorney, and file the same with the Clerk. The notice of appearance shall be contained in a separate document. If an appearance has already been filed on behalf of a defendant, a new attorney retained by defendant must promptly serve written notice of substitution of counsel, which includes the signature of the defendant and signed withdrawal of defendant's previous counsel, upon the prosecuting attorney, and file the same with the Clerk.

[Adopted effective September 1, 1996.]

PMCLR 4.2. PROCEDURE UPON A PLEA OF GUILTY

Guilty Plea Statement. It shall be the duty of the defense attorney to have a properly completed written statement of the defendant on a guilty plea. Proper forms may be obtained from the Clerk's Office without charge.

[Adopted effective September 1, 1996.]

PMCLR 4.5. TRIAL READINESS HEARING

(a) The Court shall schedule a trial readiness hearing in each criminal case which is set for trial.

(b) Appearance by the attorneys and the defendant is REQUIRED. Appearance by the attorneys who will be trying the case is preferred. For good cause, substitute counsel may attend on behalf of trial counsel so long as counsel is prepared to answer the inquiries of the court. If the Defendant fails to appear without good cause and the court finds no reasonable assurance from counsel that the case will proceed on schedule to jury trial, a jury will not be called in to hear the case as scheduled. The case will be listed a "call case" on the trial date.

(c) At the trial readiness hearing, the Judge may inquire as to whether the case is expected to go to trial, whether the defendant expects to waive the jury, the number of witnesses expected to be called, the anticipated length of the trial and any other matter necessary to administer the trial calendar efficiently. Any other anticipated problems should be brought to the court's attention.

(d) Any continuance of the trial date must include a continuance of the trial readiness hearing unless expressly agreed by the Judge.

(e) Trial Notification Requirements. All parties shall contact the Clerk's office two (2) days prior to the date set for trial and notify the Clerk whether (a) the case will proceed to trial; (b) the anticipated length of the trial; (c) existence of a jury trial waiver, if any; (d) requirements for interpreters, if any, and (e) if pretrial matters remain for hearing.

[Adopted effective September 1, 1996.]

PMCLR 4.7. DISCOVERY

(e) Discretionary Disclosure.

(3) Any motion for items and information not covered by Section (a) and (d) of CrRLJ 4.7 shall be accompanied by an affidavit and memoranda setting forth in detail the reasons the requested items and information are material and significant enough to amount to a denial of the right to a fair trial, if not ordered discoverable, so that the Court may have a basis for its ruling.

[Adopted effective September 1, 1996.]

PMCLR 6.1.1. TRIAL BY JURY OR BY THE COURT

(a) Trial by Jury—Waiver. A defendant charged with a criminal offense punishable by a loss of freedom shall be scheduled for a jury trial, unless specifically waived by the filing of a Jury Trial Waiver at any time prior to trial. Failure of the defendant to file written Notice of Jury Waiver with the Court at least two (2) court days prior to trial shall result in imposition of terms in the amount of $180.00, absent exigent circumstances.

[Adopted effective September 1, 1996.]

PMCLR 7.2. POST–SENTENCING REVIEWS

Except pursuant to a signed, agreed order, judges pro tempore shall not enter orders suspending the balance of sentences previously imposed, nor shall they grant temporary releases from the jail. This rule does not apply to cases in which the judge pro tempore to whom the motion is addressed originally imposed sentence in the case.

[Adopted effective September 1, 1996.]

PMCLR 8.2.1. MOTIONS

Pre-trial motions other than motions in limine shall be set forth in writing and served prior to the pre-trial hearing and a memorandum of points and authorities and an affidavit setting forth specifically the facts which counsel expects to elicit at a hearing. These pleadings are to be served on opposing counsel and upon the judge presumed to sit in the court in which the pre-trial hearing was last heard. Based upon the pleadings, the court will decide whether and when a hearing will be set, and will notify counsel.

(a) Length of Memoranda. Memoranda relating to motions shall not exceed ten (10) pages. Waiver of page limitations may be granted only upon motion demonstrating good cause which may be heard ex parte.

(b) Motion Hearing Procedures. Oral argument on motions shall be limited to ten (10) minutes for each side, exclusive of testimony, unless the assigned Judge determines otherwise, in which case the motion may be placed at the end of the docket.

[Adopted effective September 1, 1996.]

PMCLR 8.2.2. CONTINUANCES

Requests for continuances to the clerk shall be in writing, and must be served on the prosecutor and filed with a time for trial waiver which shall be for at least the same number of days as the continuance request. Time for trial waivers shall be on the approved speedy trial waiver form. These forms are available from the court clerk at no charge.

[Adopted effective September 1, 1996.]

PMCLR 8.9. SANCTIONS

Any violation of these rules, in addition to the court's inherent right to enter or deny such orders as it deems proper, shall subject the offending attorney to such terms as the court may order.

[Adopted effective September 1, 1996.]

LOCAL INFRACTION RULES

LIRLJ 9.1. SCHEDULING OF CONTESTED HEARINGS FOR TRAFFIC INFRACTIONS

A defendant charged with a traffic infraction who requests a hearing to contest the determination that a traffic infraction occurred may first be scheduled to appear at a prehearing conference. If the defendant fails to appear at the prehearing conference, a default judgment shall be entered. A summary of this rule shall be given or mailed to each defendant scheduled for a prehearing conference.

[Adopted effective September 1, 1996; renumbered from LIRLJ 2.6 and amended effective September 1, 2008.]

LIRLJ 9.2. PROCEDURE FOR CONTESTED AND MITIGATION HEARINGS FOR TRAFFIC INFRACTIONS

A. HEARINGS ON WRITTEN STATEMENTS

1. **Generally.** Mitigation and contested infraction hearings, decided upon written statements which are certified under penalty of perjury, as provided for in IRLJ 2.4(b)(4) and IRLJ 2.6(c), are authorized and adopted by this Court as well as the procedures authorized by IRLJ 3.5. For a statement to be considered the written statement(s) must be received by the Court timely pursuant to written instructions provided to the parties by the Court.

2. **Mitigation Hearings By Statements.** Upon a request by the defendant to have a mitigation hearing by statement instead of appearing in person at a scheduled court hearing, the Court will review in chambers the defendant's statement addressing any mitigation factors that the defendant believes might affect the amount of the penalty imposed. Within the statement there will be a promise by the defendant to pay the monetary penalty authorized by law, or at the discretion of the Court, any reduced penalty assessed by the court. The defendant will be advised in writing by the court of the amount of the penalty and the date the penalty is to be paid to the Court. There is no appeal of the decision by the Court as to the monetary amount to be paid by the defendant for a mitigation infraction.

3. Prehearing Conference for Contested Infractions. Prior to a contested hearing, whether held in person, on the record, or decided by statements alone, the parties will be scheduled for a "pre-hearing conference" authorized by former local court rule IRLJ 2.6, now cited as PMCLR 9.1. At the time of the scheduled pre-hearing conference the parties may exchange certified statements intended to be submitted to the Court for its review in chambers.

4. Decision on Written Statement for Contested Infractions. The certified statements submitted by both the City and defendant are examined by the Court. The examination will be held in chambers, and it is not governed by the Rules of Evidence. The Court however, shall determine whether or not the plaintiff (City) has proven by a preponderance of all the evidence submitted that the defendant committed the infraction(s).

   a. Disposition. If the Court determines that the infraction has been committed, then it may assess the penalty authorized by law in accordance with IRLJ 3.3.

   b. Notice to Parties of Contested Decision. The Court shall notify the parties in writing whether an infraction was found to have been committed or not and what penalty, if any, was imposed.

   c. No Appeal Permitted. There shall be no appeal from a decision on written statements.

B. COURT HEARING FORM CONTESTED TRAFFIC OFFENSES

1. Procedure for Contested Traffic Offenses. Court Rule IRLJ 3.3 provides for the procedure when a defendant requests a contested hearing on the record. This procedure is requested by a defendant when he wants to appear in person, in court, or on a scheduled day and time, to present evidence on his behalf. The plaintiff's witnesses as well as the defendant and defendant's witnesses would be placed under oath on the record, and would testify as to the events.

2. Rules of Evidence. The Rules of Evidence and statutes that relate to evidence in infraction cases shall apply to contested court hearings.

3. Officer's Testimony. With the adoption of the Decision on Written Statement option for contested hearings by local court rule the certificate of the officer may be used by the Plaintiff instead of the officer appearing in person at the contested court hearing. Should the defendant wish to officer to be present at the hearing then he may subpoena the officer as his witness pursuant to IRLJ 3.1. Each party is responsible for his or her own witness costs which includes the costs for the officer to be appear.

4. Factual Determination at Contested Court Hearing. The Court shall determine whether the Plaintiff has proven by a preponderance of the evidence that the defendant committed the infraction. If the Court finds the infraction was committed, it shall enter an appropriate order on its records. If the Court fines the infraction not committed, it shall enter an order of dismissal.

5. Disposition. If the infraction is found committed the Judge may assess a monetary penalty against the defendant which may not exceed that provided by law.

6. Appeal. After a finding of committed at a contested court hearing the defendant may appeal the decision to Superior Court within the rules as provided in IRLJ 5, Appeals, and CRLJ 6. The appellant must comply with any costs for appeal that Superior Court may assess.

[Adopted effective September 1, 2008.]

LIRLJ 9.3. SPEED MEASURING DEVICE, DESIGN, AND CONSTRUCTION CERTIFICATE

The Court cites and adopts herein the procedure to permit the Speed Measuring Device Certificate in the form as provided in IRLJ 636 in lieu of live testimony by the speed measuring device expert in traffic infraction cases. However, pursuant to IRLJ 636 a defendant may request that the SMD expert be present at his contested court hearing instead of the certificate being admitted into evidence. In that case the defendant must follow the procedures set forth in IRLJ 6.6

[Adopted effective September 1, 2008.]

GARFIELD COUNTY

Table of Courts

Superior Court

Hells Canyon Circuit Local Rules.

District Court

Garfield County District Court Local Rules.

SUPERIOR COURT

HELLS CANYON CIRCUIT LOCAL RULES
[PREVIOUSLY KNOWN AS THE LOCAL RULES OF THE SUPERIOR COURT OF THE STATE OF WASHINGTON FOR THE JUDICIAL DISTRICT OF ASOTIN, COLUMBIA, AND GARFIELD COUNTIES]

PUBLISHER'S NOTE

The Hells Canyon Circuit Local Rules (Previously Known as the Local Rules for the Superior Courts of Asotin, Columbia, and Garfield Counties) are set forth under Hells Canyon Circuit.

DISTRICT COURT
GARFIELD COUNTY DISTRICT COURT LOCAL RULES

Including Amendments Received Through
August 15, 2015

Table of Rules

LOCAL RULES (GCDCLR)

RULE 3.5. MITIGATION HEARING ON WRITTEN STATEMENT

Mitigation Hearings may be submitted to the Court in writing, and the Court will consider and rule on mitigation if all of the following conditions are met:

(1) The submission must contain a brief explanation of the need for a hearing by mail rather than an in-court, personal hearing.

(2) The submission must contain a written explanation of the mitigating circumstances to be considered.

(3) The submission must contain the following:

I declare under penalty of perjury under the laws of the state of Washington that the information I have supplied is true and correct.

Executed this ___ day of _____, 20 ___, at _____ (city) _____ (state).

_____

signature

(4) The submission must be signed on the "signature" line.

(5) The submission must be accompanied by a cashier's check or money order (no personal or business checks) in the full, exact amount specified on the notice of infraction.

If all of the above conditions are met, the Court will (within 60 days) examine (in chambers) the officer's report (if any) and the explanation from the defendant. The process is not governed by the rules of evidence.

If the Court considers mitigation appropriate, it will reduce the original penalty and will return to the defendant any amount submitted that is in excess of the adjusted penalty.

No appeal may be taken from a decision rendered on a mitigation hearing on a written statement.

[Effective September 1, 2004.]

GRANT COUNTY

Table of Courts

Superior Court

The Local Rules of the Superior Court of Washington in and for the County of Grant.

District Court

Local Rules for the District Court of the State of Washington for Grant County.

Municipal Courts

Coulee City Municipal Court—[No Local Rules].
Electric City Municipal Court—[No Local Rules].
Ephrata Municipal Court—[No Local Rules].
George Municipal Court—[No Local Rules].
Grand Coulee Municipal Court—[No Local Rules].
Mattawa Municipal Court—[No Local Rules].
Moses Lake Municipal Court—[No Local Rules].
Quincy Municipal Court—[No Local Rules].
Royal City Municipal Court—[No Local Rules].
Soap Lake Municipal Court—[No Local Rules].
Warden Municipal Court—[No Local Rules].

SUPERIOR COURT

THE LOCAL RULES OF THE SUPERIOR COURT OF WASHINGTON IN AND FOR THE COUNTY OF GRANT

Including Amendments Received Through August 15, 2015

Table of Rules

389

SECTION 1.   ADMINISTRATIVE RULES

LAR 1.   TITLE AND SCOPE

(a) Title. These rules shall be known as "The Local Rules of the Superior Court of Washington in and for the County of Grant." The brief title of these rules is "Grant County Local Rules." These rules may be cited in the following format: "LAR 1" (for Administrative Rules); "LCR 7" (for Civil Rules); "LCrR 1.1" (for Criminal Rules); "LRMA 1.1" (for Mandatory Arbitration Rules); "LRMM 1" (for Mandatory Mediation Rules).

(b) Scope. Unless otherwise provided herein, these rules apply to all criminal and civil proceedings, family and domestic matters, mental health proceedings, juvenile court offender and dependency proceedings, appeals from lower courts, tribunals and agencies, and other matters brought before the Grant County Superior Court. To the extent these rules supplement rules of statewide application adopted by the Supreme Court of Washington, both local and statewide rules apply. To the extent these rules conflict with statewide rules, the statewide rules apply.

(c) Arbitration. By order dated April 20, 1988, Grant County Superior Court adopted local rules for mandatory arbitration ("LRMA") which apply to original civil actions with limited money claims, and to other actions upon stipulation of the parties.

(d) Mediation. By order dated May 28, 2012 Grant County Superior Court adopted local rules for mandatory mediation ("LRMM") which apply to disputed issues in family law cases, as defined in said rules.

(e) Waiver. Any provision of these rules may be waived or modified by order of the court for good cause shown, or as required in the interests of justice.

(f) Numbering. In compliance with CR 83, the local civil rules in Section 2 and the local criminal rules in Section 3 are numbered consistent with the numbers of the most closely associated Civil Rules for Superior Court and Criminal Rules for Superior Court.

[Formerly LR 1, adopted effective April 1, 1997; renumbered LAR 1 and amended effective September 1, 2012.]

LAR 2. JUDICIAL OFFICERS

(a) Departments. There shall be four departments of this court, identified as Civil Department, Criminal Department, Juvenile Court, and Court Commissioner's Department. The judicial officers of this court will be assigned, on a rotating basis, for such periods as the Presiding Judge may from time to time determine, among the departments of this court.

(b) Presiding Judge. (1) *Election.* During the month of December of each even-numbered year, the judges of the court shall elect, by such manner as they may then agree or, in the absence of such agreement, by secret written ballot, one of their number to serve as Presiding Judge. In the same fashion, the judges shall elect an Acting Presiding Judge. Vacancies in either position will be filled in the same manner as soon as practicable after vacancy occurs.

(2) *Removal.* The Presiding Judge or Acting Presiding Judge may be removed by the unanimous vote of the other judges of the court.

(3) *Term.* The Presiding Judge shall be elected to a term of two years, commencing on January 1 of each odd-numbered year.

(4) *Special Inquiry Judge.* By virtue of office, the Presiding Judge shall be the Special Inquiry Judge designated by the judges of the court as required by RCW 10.27.050. In the event the Presiding Judge is disqualified from any special inquiry proceeding, the Acting Presiding Judge will be deemed to be the special inquiry judge so designated.

(5) *Library Board.* By virtue of office, the Presiding Judge, or his or her designee, shall be a member of the Grant County Law Library Board.

(c) Juvenile Judge. The judge assigned to the Juvenile Court pursuant to section (a) of this rule shall be designated as the Juvenile Court Judge, as provided in chapter 13.40 RCW.

(d) Court Commissioners. The judges will employ at least one court commissioner, assigned to the Court Commissioner's Department, unless otherwise assigned by the Presiding Judge. The Court Commissioner will ordinarily preside over weekly dependency dockets, and dockets and trials of brief duration in domestic and paternity cases.

The judge of the Grant County District Court assigned to the Moses Lake district will ordinarily be appointed as a commissioner of the superior court. In such capacity, the court commissioner may sign ex parte orders. Ex parte orders signed at a location other than the Grant County Courthouse shall be transmitted by the commissioner to the Clerk of this court; original orders shall not be returned to the party or attorney requesting the same.

The Presiding Judge may appoint pro tempore court commissioners from time to time as may be required for due administration of the business of the court.

[Formerly LR 2, adopted effective April 1, 1997; amended effective September 1, 2005; renumbered LAR 2 and amended, effective September 1, 2012.]

LAR 3. STAFF POSITIONS

(a) Court Reporter. There shall be at least one official reporter, selected by a majority of the judges, appointed and serving in the manner, and performing the functions, prescribed by law.

(b) Court Administrator. The administrative operation of the court will be coordinated by a Court Administrator, appointed by the judges and serving at their pleasure. The Court Administrator will schedule all court calendars, and perform such other duties as the Presiding Judge may from time to time direct.

(c) Interpreter Coordinator and Arbitration Administrator. The court shall employ an Interpreter Coordinator, who shall be certified by the Administrative Office for the Courts as an interpreter in the Spanish language. The Interpreter Coordinator will attend court proceedings when directed by a judge, and will arrange for the retention and assignment of other interpreters as the business of the court may require. The Interpreter Coordinator may be permitted, by written policies of the court, to perform interpretation services for private party litigants.

The Interpreter Coordinator may, when directed by the judges of the court, also serve as Arbitration Administrator, as provided in the Local Rules for Mandatory Arbitration.

(d) Jury Administrator. The court shall employ a Jury Administrator to perform all administrative functions necessary for calling, selecting, and compensating petit jurors.

(e) Other Staff. The judges may appoint such other staff, including assistants, bailiffs, deputies and others, as may from time to time be necessary to the efficient operation of the court.

[Formerly LR 3, adopted effective April 1, 1997; renumbered LAR 3 and amended effective September 1, 2012.]

LAR 4. MOTION CALENDARS

(a) Law and Motion Calendars. Except as otherwise ordered from time to time as necessary in the administration of the court, regular law and motion calendars will be heard as follows:

Civil Department:

Civil motions: Friday, 9:00

Adoption motions and hearings: Friday, 11:00

Sentence compliance: 1st, 3rd and 5th Fridays, 1:30

Criminal Department:

Criminal motions: Monday and Tuesday, 9:00

CrR 3.5, CrR 3.6 hearings: Wednesday and Thursday, 10:00

Commissioner Department:

Dependency docket: Tuesday, 1:30

Paternity, support enforcement: Thursday, 9:00

Domestic and family law:

Motions, decrees with counsel: Friday, 9:00

Pro se decrees: Friday, 1:30

Pro se motions: Friday, 2:00

Juvenile Court:

Offender motions: Monday, 9:00

Truancy, at-risk youth: Tuesday, 9:00

Protection orders: Tuesday, 1:30

(b) Holiday Schedule. When Monday is a court holiday, the criminal docket will be called on the following Tuesday and Wednesday, and the Monday Juvenile offender docket will be called on the following Wednesday, unless otherwise ordered by the court. When Friday is a court holiday, all regularly-scheduled dockets will be called on the preceding Thursday, unless otherwise ordered by the court. When a Tuesday, Wednesday or Thursday court holiday affects a docket, the docket will be specially scheduled by the court.

[Renumbered from LR 4(a)–(b) and amended effective September 1, 2012.]

LAR 5. GRIEVANCES AS TO GUARDIANS AD LITEM

(a) Scope. This rule applies to grievances from litigants, witnesses, attorneys, or other persons regarding guardians ad litem (GAL) and court-appointed special advocates (CASA) appointed pursuant to Titles 11, 13, and 26 RCW.

(b) Form. All grievances regarding the qualifications, conduct or performance of a GAL or CASA must be in writing, submitted to the Presiding Judge of the Superior Court.

(c) Assignment for investigation. The Presiding Judge shall promptly designate a judicial officer to investigate a grievance. The judicial officer assigned may be any judge or court commissioner, whether or not said officer is otherwise involved in a pending case from which the grievance arises. When it is necessary, in the judgment of the Presiding Judge, to appoint an investigator who is not a judicial officer, or who is not otherwise associated with the court, the Presiding Judge may appoint any qualified person to investigate the grievance.

(d) Initial Determination of Merit. The investigating judicial officer shall initially determine whether or not the grievance raises issues of arguable merit. In making this determination, the officer shall consider whether the grievance alleges, and whether there is

evidence to support, that the GAL or CASA has (1) violated an applicable code of conduct; (2) misrepresented his or her qualifications to serve in the appointed capacity; (3) breached a duty of confidentiality; (3)[1] falsified or mischaracterized information in testimony or a report to the court; (4) failed to report abuse or neglect of a child; (5) communicated with a judicial officer *ex parte* in contravention of law; (6) purported to represent the court in a public forum without prior approval of the court; (7) violated state or local laws, rules, or policies in the capacity as GAL or CASA; (8) failed to complete assigned duties with reasonable diligence; or (9) taken or failed to take any other action which would reasonably place in question the GAL or CASA's fitness to serve.

(e) Meritless Claims. Upon determining that the grievance raises no issues of arguable merit, the investigating judicial officer shall decline to further investigate and shall so inform the grievant and the Presiding Judge in writing.

(f) Claims of Arguable Merit. Upon determining that the grievance raises issues of arguable merit, the investigating judicial officer shall request a written response from any GAL or CASA involved therein. The GAL or CASA shall submit a written response within 14 days of the request, unless additional time is allowed upon request to the investigating judicial officer. The investigating judicial officer may make any other contacts, inquiries, or reviews he or she deems necessary to resolution of any issue of arguable merit. He or she shall submit a written report of findings of fact and conclusions of the investigation to all other judicial officers of the court. Upon the majority vote of said judicial officers, a final written report will be provided to the grievant and to every GAL and CASA involved.

(g) Assignments During Investigation. Unless expressly ordered otherwise upon the recommendation of the investigating judicial officer, the court shall make no additional assignments of a GAL or CASA named in a grievance until completion of the investigation. The investigating judicial officer may recommend to the Presiding Judge that a GAL or CASA be ordered to perform no additional services pursuant to any existing appointment until completion of the investigation.

(h) Time to Complete Investigation. Unless otherwise directed by the Presiding Judge for good cause, investigations under this rule shall be completed within 60 days of receipt of a grievance.

(i) Action After Investigation. A final written report by a majority of the judicial officers of the court may order (1) that a GAL or CASA remain on the court's registry with no further action taken; (2) that a GAL or CASA be suspended from the registry pending completion of designated remedial measures; (3) that a GAL or CASA be removed from the court's registry; or (4) any other measures necessary to resolution of issues raised in the grievance. If removal from the registry is ordered, the court shall send notice thereof to the Administrative Office of the Courts.

(j) Confidentiality. A record of all written complaints or grievances regarding any GAL or CASA shall be maintained by the court. Grievances shall be confidential until completion of any investigation conducted pursuant to this rule. A record of any action ordered by the court in response to a grievance shall be placed in the GAL or CASA's file.

[Adopted effective September 2, 2014.]

1 So in original.

SECTION 2. CIVIL RULES

LCR 7. MOTIONS

(a) Time Limits. (1) *Length of hearing.* Civil and domestic/family law and motion dockets are limited to matters requiring no more than ten minutes per side. Matters expected to exceed that limitation must be specially set by the court administrator.

(2) *Responsive declarations.* In matters on the domestic and family docket, and the paternity docket, responsive declarations must be served and filed by noon on the calendar day immediately prior to the docket, or 24 hours before the scheduled docket, whichever is later, unless the court expressly permits later service and/or filing.

(b) Noting Matters on Motion Dockets. Except as otherwise provided in this section, or with leave of the judicial officer presiding on the docket, matters to be heard on a motion docket must be noted with the clerk five days prior to the docket. If the judicial officer assigned to hear a docket is unavailable, another judge may consider and grant an ex parte motion for order shortening time to note a matter on a docket.

(c) Required Special Settings. The following matters may not be noted on the court's regular dockets, but must be specially set with the court administrator: motions for summary judgment; arguments on the merits in appeals from lower courts or tribunals; child hearsay (Ryan) hearings.

Once a time and date for a special setting are obtained from the court administrator, the moving party must file and serve a notice of the setting in the same manner in which motions are noted for regular dockets.

(d) Telephonic argument. (1) *Unreported.* Arguments on motions are to be conducted in person, except that, by specific arrangement with the court administrator at least two days before a hearing, argument may be made by telephone, Provided, (1) that all parties agree to telephonic argument; (2) that the judicial officer before whom the hearing will be conducted approves of telephonic argument; and (3) that no verbatim record is requested (or the record is made by a party). A party may withhold agreement to telephonic argument only for reasonable, articulable cause.

For good cause shown, on motion of a party, the court may order telephonic argument of a motion in the absence of such agreement. A motion to require telephonic argument shall itself be argued by telephone unless all affected parties are before the court when the motion is made.

(2) *Verbatim record.* The requirement that there be no verbatim record may be waived by the court only if: (1) no participant other than the court uses a speaker phone; (2) no speaking participant is on a cellular telephone; and (3) the reported call will begin with each party's stipulation to the following:

"This conference call argument is being reported by the official court reporter. Each party stipulates that any portion of the proceedings which is inaudible to the reporter will be noted as such in the record without jeopardy to the reporter or to any transcript being deemed accurate and complete."

[Renumbered from LR 4(c)–(e), LR 11, and amended effective September 1, 2012; amended effective September 1, 2015.]

LCR 16. PRETRIAL CONFERENCE AND TRIAL CONFERENCE

(a) Pretrial conference. A pretrial conference may be conducted in civil cases in the manner, and for the purposes, set forth in CR 16.

(b) Trial conference. Civil jury trials will be preceded by a conference, on the record unless a record of the trial has been waived, beginning at 9:00 a.m. on the first trial day unless otherwise ordered by the court. If the conference is expected to exceed 60 minutes, the parties shall obtain a specially-set time from the court administrator. Counsel for the parties shall attend. The conference will address administrative matters relating to the trial, and resolve motions *in limine* and other motions entertained by the court.

Civil bench trials may be preceded by a conference on request of a party or on the court's motion.

[Renumbered from LR 5(a), LR 6(a), and amended effective September 1, 2012.]

LCR 16A. PARENTING SEMINARS

(a) Cases Affected. Pursuant to RCW 26.12.170, this rule applies to all actions in which the court is petitioned to adopt a parenting plan or residential schedule involving minor children, and, if ordered by the court, to an action in which modification of such a plan or schedule is sought.

(b) Seminar Required. The judges of this court shall, by administrative order maintained in the records of the clerk, from time to time designate one or more providers of parenting seminars. Each party who is a parent shall, within thirty days after initiating or being served with initial documents in a case covered by this rule, contact a designated provider to schedule attendance at a parenting seminar. Prior to trial in such a case, or prior to entry of a final parenting plan or residential schedule if no trial is held, each such party shall attend and complete a parenting seminar, and file proof thereof with the court.

(c) Exemption and Enforcement. A party may seek exemption from the requirements of this rule on the basis of substantial hardship, established by motion of the party supported by written declaration or oral testimony. A party who has completed a parenting seminar, pursuant to this rule or otherwise, within twenty-four months before institution of the present action is, upon filing proof thereof, also exempt from part (b) of this rule, unless otherwise ordered by the court. Unless exempted, a party who fails to comply may be sanctioned by civil contempt remedies, by an order striking pleadings, or in such other manner as the court deems appropriate.

[Formerly LR 13, adopted effective April 1, 1997; renumbered as LCR 16A and amended effective September 1, 2012.]

LCR 16B. ASSETS AND DEBTS IN MARRIAGE DISSOLUTION AND SIMILAR CASES

(a) Statement Required. Not later than noon on the court day before the day on which an action for dissolution of marriage, dissolution of a registered domestic partnership, division of assets of a committed intimate relationship, or similar case, is called for trial, when there exists a dispute between the parties regarding the characterization, valuation or distribution of any asset or debt, each party shall file with the trial judge and serve on the other party a statement in spreadsheet format of all assets and debts of the parties within the court's jurisdiction.

(b) Contents of Statement. (1) *Assets.* The statement shall sequentially number and identify each asset with sufficient particularity to distinguish it from other assets of the same type. As to each asset, the statement shall set forth, unless unknown to the party, the following information: date, manner and cost of acquisition; the party's characterization of the asset as community (or "shared") or separate property, and if separate, the basis for that claim; present fair market value; and proposed distribution by the court. The statement shall separately identify any asset in the possession of either party claimed to be the property of a third person, in whole or in part.

(2) *Debts.* The statement shall sequentially number and specifically identify (including creditor and account number) each debt claimed to be owed by either party or both. As to each debt, the statement shall set forth, unless unknown to the party, the following information: the date(s) on which the debt was incurred, the purpose for which it was incurred, any security given for the debt; the balance owed at the time of trial and at the time of separation; payments made by either party after separation; whether, and to what extent, the debt is claimed to be the separate or individual debt of either party; and the proposed distribution by the court.

(3) *Other relief.* Each party's statement shall also set forth any other financial relief requested, other than child support, including a monetary judgment to balance the division of assets and debts, spousal maintenance, and award of costs and attorney fees.

[Formerly LR 15, adopted effective September 1, 2005; renumbered as LCR 16B and amended effective September 1, 2012.]

LCR 16C. SETTLEMENT CONFERENCE

(a) When Held. Subject to available time on the court's calendar, a settlement conference may be held in any civil or domestic case by agreement of the parties, or, in the absence of agreement, upon order of the court

(b) Time and Judicial Officer. A settlement conference will be held at a time set by the court administrator, and shall be conducted by a judicial officer other than the officer to whom the case is, or likely will be, assigned for trial.

(c) Persons Attending. The attorney in charge of each party's case shall attend the settlement conference. The parties to a domestic case shall attend the conference; in other civil cases, the parties, or persons with settlement authority for a party, shall be available, and the judicial officer conducting the conference shall decide whether the parties shall be present in the conference room. When the defense of a party is provided by an insurer, a representative of the insurer with authority to bind the insurer to a settlement, must be in attendance or immediately available by telephone to the attorney for that party. Attendance of any party or representative may be excused for good cause shown.

(d) Preconference Submittal. At least two days before the date set for the settlement conference, the attorney, or pro se party, personally in charge of each party's case shall present to the judicial officer conducting the conference a letter succinctly addressing those issues required to be addressed.

(e) Privilege. Settlement conferences shall, in all respects, be privileged proceedings and not reported or recorded. No party is bound by any position taken during a settlement conference unless a settlement is reached. When a settlement has been reached, the judicial officer may, and at the request of any party shall, cause the settlement to be made a matter of record. The judicial officer presiding over the settlement conference shall be disqualified from acting as the trial judge in that matter, unless all parties otherwise agree in writing.

[Formerly LR 17, adopted effective September 1, 2005; renumbered as LCR 16C and amended effective September 1, 2012.]

LCR 26F. SCHEDULING ORDER

(a) **Status Conference.** In civil cases in which the complaint has been served on any defendant, the court administrator will schedule a status conference, to be conducted by telephone not sooner than 90 days, nor later than 120 days after the complaint is filed, and will give notice thereof to counsel and unrepresented parties who have appeared. The purpose of the status conference is to schedule deadlines for completion of all measures necessary to prepare the case for trial. Notice of the status conference shall be in the form appended hereto as Form LR 8–A, and will be accompanied by a blank status conference statement (Form LR 8–B) and blank note-up slip for trial setting (Form LR 8–C).

After a request for trial de novo following mandatory arbitration, the court administrator will schedule a status conference in the manner set forth above, to be conducted by telephone within 60 days of the filing of the request.

(b) **Scheduling Order.** Following the status conference, or upon receipt of a status conference statement agreed to by all parties, the court will issue a Scheduling Order in the form appended hereto as Form LR 8–D. Deadlines established in the Scheduling Order may be extended by stipulation of the parties only upon leave of the court. The court may, upon motion of a party made before expiration of a deadline, extend any deadline in the Scheduling Order for good cause shown.

(c) **Cases Excluded.** Unless otherwise ordered by a judge, the scheduling procedure provided in LR 8(a) will not be employed in domestic relations, paternity; adoption; change of name; domestic violence (chapter 26.50 RCW); harassment (chapter 10.14 RCW); interstate support enforcement; juvenile dependency; minor settlement; probate; guardianship; petition for writ of habeas corpus, mandamus, review or other writ; unlawful detainer; civil commitment; proceedings under chapter 10.77 RCW; proceedings under chapter 70.96A RCW; and cases in which pretrial time limits are expressed in statute.

(d) **Trial Setting.** See LR 40(a).

[Renumbered from LR 8(a)–(b) and amended effective September 1, 2012; September 2, 2014.]

LCR 40. TRIAL

(a) **Trial Setting.** Each party completing or stipulating to a status conference statement (Form LR 8–B) shall, to the extent practicable, indicate therein the approximate number of court days anticipated to be needed for trial, including jury orientation, selection, and deliberation if a jury demand has been, or is expected to be, made.

(b) **Civil Trials.** Civil trials shall be scheduled by the court administrator at such times as are conducive to the efficient operation of the court and the expeditious resolution of cases. Generally, civil jury trials will begin on Mondays or Tuesdays at 9:00 a.m.

(c) **Domestic Trials.** Trials in domestic relations and family law cases shall be set for trial by the court administrator in the same manner as civil trials. Trials not expected to exceed one-half day may be set in the Commissioner's Department.

(d) **Paternity Trials.** Trials expected to exceed one-half day will generally be set by the court administrator as civil trials. Otherwise, paternity trials will be scheduled in the Commissioner's Department on Thursday afternoons, unless a special setting is obtained from the court administrator.

[Renumbered from LR 4(f), (h)–(i), LR 8(a)(3), and amended effective September 1, 2012; September 2, 2014.]

LCR 47. JURY SELECTION

(a) **Panel.** The jury administrator will randomly assign sequential numbers, beginning with "1," to all prospective jurors who have timely appeared for trial, and will cause them to be seated in the courtroom in that order when directed by the trial judge to do so. The judge and counsel will be provided with a roster of the panel as seated.

(b) **Examination.** Unless otherwise ordered by the judge presiding at trial, juries will be selected after panel examination. The judge will conduct orientation and general questioning of the panel. Thereafter, counsel will, in turn, be permitted to question the panel, or individual members thereof, for a stated period of time set by the judge. The judge may allow a second period of questioning by each side. For good cause shown, the judge may extend the period of questioning, or allow additional rounds, on motion of a party.

(c) **Challenges.** Challenges for cause shall be made openly or at sidebar, as the judge may direct. After examination of the panel, counsel will, in turn, exercise peremptory challenges by striking names from a roster of those panel members not previously dismissed. After peremptory challenges, the remaining unchallenged jurors with the twelve (or, in appropriate cases, six) lowest roster numbers shall be seated as the jury. The remaining juror(s) with the next lowest roster number(s) will be seated as the alternate juror(s).

[Renumbered from LR 10(a) and amended effective September 1, 2012.]

LCR 51. JURY INSTRUCTIONS

Each party wishing to propose jury instructions shall file with the clerk, deliver to the judge, and serve on other parties one cited copy and one clean copy of each instruction proposed. Cited copies shall include marginal citation of the authority relied upon in proposing the instruction, and will be sequentially lettered or numbered. Clean copies shall not include citations, letters or numbers.

[Renumbered from LR 10(b) and amended effective September 1, 2012.]

LCR 59. RECONSIDERATION AND RE-APPLICATION

(a) Motion for Reconsideration. (1) *Noting for hearing.* As provided in CR 59(b), a party filing a motion for reconsideration will also file a note-up slip noting the motion for hearing on an appropriate law and motion docket, designating the judicial officer whose decision the motion seeks to reconsider. The date for hearing shall be at least ten days after filing of the motion.

(2) *Hearing.* Upon receiving for filing a motion for reconsideration and note-up slip, the clerk shall cause the same to be delivered to the judicial officer whose decision the motion seeks to reconsider. The judicial officer will promptly determine, as provided in CR 59(e), whether the motion should be denied on its face, or, if not, whether the motion is to be heard on oral argument or submitted on briefs. The judicial officer will enter an order expressing such determinations, including a briefing schedule and a date for argument, when appropriate. The court administrator will cause copies of the order to be delivered to all counsel and unrepresented parties.

(b) Re-application. When an order has been applied for and denied in whole or in part, or has been granted conditionally and the condition has not been performed, the same application for an order may not be presented to a different judicial officer unless that officer is clearly advised of the fact of the previous denial or unfulfilled condition.

[Formerly LR 14, adopted effective September 1, 2005; renumbered LCR 59 and amended effective September 1, 2012.]

LCR 70. CIVIL CONTEMPT PROCEEDINGS

This rule shall apply to all civil contempt proceedings whether brought under chapter 7.21 RCW or other statutes, but shall not apply to summary contempt proceedings under RCW 7.21.050.

(a) Warning. The order to show cause shall advise the responding party, in prominent language, that failure to appear could result in issuance of a warrant for the arrest of that party.

(b) Service. Unless otherwise authorized by order of the court, or by the express terms of a statute under which the contempt motion is brought, or by written stipulation of the parties, the order to show cause, together with the motion and supporting declarations or other materials, must be personally served on the responding party.

(c) Failure to Appear. At the hearing, if the responding party fails to appear and upon proof of service of the pleadings required by this rule, the court may order arrest of the responding party. Other requested remedies may also be ordered upon default, even if a warrant is not ordered.

[Formerly LR 16, adopted effective September 1, 2005; renumbered LCR 70 and amended effective September 1, 2012.]

LCR 79. LIMITED ACCESS TO PATERNITY FILES

(a) Persons. Only the following persons shall have access to paternity files of this court: the mother, the presumed father, any alleged father who has not been dismissed from the case, an attorney representing any of the foregoing or the child (after filing a notice of appearance), any guardian *ad litem* appointed in the cause and not discharged, the State of Washington as represented by the Attorney General's office or Grant County Prosecutor's Office (or other contracted counsel), and any other person upon permission from a judge or commissioner of the court.

(b) Limited Access. Access to a paternity file by the mother, or presumed or alleged father is limited to review of the file at the office of the clerk of the court when no final Judgment and Order Determining Paternity has been entered. After entry of such Judgment and Order, any party referred to in the order may, upon paying the applicable fee, receive a copy of the order and any visitation order, parenting plan, residential schedule or child support order in the file.

(c) Access by Court Officers. Any attorney, guardian *ad litem*, or employee or contractor of the Attorney General or Prosecutor authorized by part (a) of this rule to have access to a paternity file may examine or otherwise handle the file in the clerk's office pursuant to policies of the clerk.

(d) Segregation of File. The Clerk of this Court may segregate Paternity files into two or more volumes, ending the first (or subsequent) volume upon entry of an Order Establishing Paternity. Said Order, together with pleadings filed thereafter may be filed in a separate volume or volumes. When such segregation is made by the Clerk, the limitations on access expressed in this rule will be deemed only to apply to the volume(s) closed with filing of the Order Establishing Paternity

[Formerly LR 12, adopted effective April 1, 1997; renumbered LCR 79 and amended effective September 1, 2012.]

FORMS

FORM LR 8–A. NOTICE OF STATUS CONFERENCE (NTSC)

Superior Court of Washington
County of Grant

		No.
	Plaintiff(s),	**Notice of Status Conference** (NTSC)
vs.		
	Defendant(s).	Date:
		Time:
		Department:

A telephonic status conference will be held in this cause on the date and time shown above. *The plaintiff(s) shall arrange for and place the conference telephone call.*

The following rules apply to this status conference procedure:

DISTRIBUTION OF THIS NOTICE. The court has provided this notice to all parties who have appeared herein. Plaintiff(s) shall immediately forward a copy of this notice to any party who has not yet appeared, but whom plaintiff(s) or counsel expect to appear before the date set above.

PARTIES TO CONFER. At least <u>15 days before the status conference</u>, all parties must confer regarding the following subject: (a) service of process; (b) jurisdiction and venue; (c) anticipated motions; (d) anticipated discovery; (e) appropriate time limits for disclosure of experts, amendment of pleadings, addition of parties, discovery and dispositive motions; (f) likelihood of jury demand; (g) anticipated length of trial.

STATUS CONFERENCE STATEMENT. Accompanying this notice is a blank Status Conference Statement (Form LR8–B), which must be completed by each party and filed with the court <u>at least seven court days before the status conference</u>. **Please provide a copy to the Court Administrator.** If an agreed Status Conference Statement is filed, the conference will be stricken. If no statements are on file seven days before the status conference, the court will strike the hearing for non-compliance and you will not receive a scheduling order nor trial date.

CONFERENCE CALL. When placing the conference call to the court (509–754–2011), advise the courthouse switchboard operator that this is a conference call for the department indicated above, or you may give the extension number as listed above.

PARTIES SHALL PROVIDE UNAVAILABLE DATES, AS WELL AS, ANTICI-PATED TRIAL LENGTH AT LEAST 7 DAYS PRIOR TO THE STATUS CONFERENCE. THE TRIAL DATE WILL BE SET BY THE COURT AD-MINISTRATOR BASED ON THE INFORMATION PROVIDED BY THE PAR-TIES. IF NO STATEMENTS ARE ON FILE SEVEN DAYS PRIOR TO THE STATUS CONFERENCE, YOU WILL NOT BE GIVEN A SCHEDULING ORDER NOR TRIAL DATE.

DATED: By Order Of: _____

                              JUDGE OF THE SUPERIOR COURT

CERTIFICATE OF MAILING: The undersigned certifies, under penalty of perjury of the laws of the State of Washington, that on the date stated above, (s)he deposited a copy of this Notice of Status Conference in the U.S. Mail, with sufficient postage prepaid, addressed to the persons and addresses named below or on the attached sheet.

NAME   NAME
TITLE   TITLE
ADDRESS   ADDRESS

Grant County Superior Court

P.O. Box 37

Ephrata, WA 98823

(509) 754–2011, ext.

(509) 754–6036 fax

[Effective April 1, 1997. Amended effective September 1, 2012; September 1, 2015.]

FORM LR 8–B. STATUS CONFERENCE STATEMENT (ST)

Superior Court of Washington
County of Grant

No.

Plaintiff(s),   **Status Conference Statement**
vs.   (ST)

_____
Defendant(s).

THIS FORM MUST BE FILED AT LEAST 3 DAYS
BEFORE STATUS CONFERENCE

Is this case subject to mandatory arbitration? ☐NO ☐Yes

(Case is subject to mandatory arbitration if sole relief sought is money judgment not over $50,000 exclusive of costs & interest).

If case is subject to mandatory arbitration, do not complete the remainder of this form; sign the form and return it to the court along with the arbitration filing fee.

Anticipated form of trial: ☐ Non-jury   ☐ Jury of 6   ☐ Jury of 12

Anticipated number of trial days needed: ___ days (including jury voir dire, closing argument, deliberations)

The parties who have not settled or been released (i.e., who will participate in trial) are:

Complete the following request for deadlines to be included in the Scheduling Order. Pretrial steps are listed in most common order. If no request, "Default Schedule" will be used.

	REQUESTED SCHEDULE	DEFAULT SCHEDULE
1. DISCLOSE EXPERTS		
Plaintiff	_____	60 days after status conference
Defendant	_____	90 days after status conference
Responsive	_____	120 days after status conference
2. JOIN ADDITIONAL PARTIES	_____	120 days after status conference
3. AMEND PLEADINGS	_____	180 days after status conference
4. COMPLETE ALL DISCOVERY & DEPOSITIONS	_____	90 days before trial
5. ARGUE DISPOSITIVE MOTIONS	_____	45 days before trial

A pretrial conference (see LCR 16):

[ ] can most likely be completed in 30 minutes and thus may be held at 9:00 am on first trial day.

[ ] will likely exceed 30 minutes and should therefore be specially set by the court administrator. _Please notify the court administrator if your response to this item changes before the trial._

A settlement conference before a judge other than the trial judge ☐ is ☐ is not requested.

Beginning six months after the status conference date, I (or "we" if this is a joint statement) am unavailable for trial—due to now-existing scheduled trials, hearings, or travel—on the following dates:

Each undersigned certifies that (s)he has conferred with all other counsel and pro se parties regarding the matters set forth herein, and that all parties:

☐ Do agree to the requested schedule.

☐ Do not agree to the requested schedule.

_____   _____

Attorney for: Attorney for:

_____   _____

Attorney for: Attorney for:

[Effective April 1, 1997. Amended effective September 1, 2012; September 1, 2015.]

FORM LR 8–C. NOTE–UP SLIP FOR TRIAL SETTING

Superior Court of Washington
County of Grant

                                              No.

               PLAINTIFF(S),   **Note–Up Slip For Trial Setting**
                                  (NTTRS)

and

                                   Hearing Date:
                                   Time:

               DEFENDANT(S).

THIS FORM MUST BE FILED WITHIN 30 DAYS AFTER DISCOVERY DEADLINE.

EACH PARTY BY OR AGAINST WHOM CLAIMS REMAIN UNRESOLVED COMPLETE THE FOLLOWING:

This case remains unresolved after completion of discovery, and requires a trial of ___ days.

[ ] Bench trial [ ] Jury of: ☐6 ☐12 (Jury demand filed by _____)

A pretrial conference:

[ ] Can be completed in 30 minutes and so may be held at 9:00 a.m. on the first day of trial.

[ ] Will likely exceed 30 minutes and should be specially set by the Court Administrator.

The parties who have not settled or otherwise released (i.e., who will participate in the trial) are:

I am unavailable for trial on the following dates:

A settlement conference before a judge other than the trial judge ☐ is ☐ is not requested.

DATE: _____   _____

                                 Attorney for: _____

                                 _____

                                 Address

                                 _____

                                 _____

                                 _____

                                 Phone Number

[Effective April 1, 1997. Amended effective September 1, 2012.]

FORM LR 8–D. SCHEDULING ORDER (ORSCS)

SUPERIOR COURT OF WASHINGTON
COUNTY OF GRANT

	)	NO.
Plaintiff(s)	)	
vs.	)	
	)	SCHEDULING ORDER
	)	(ORSCS)
Defendant(s)	)	

PLEASE TAKE NOTICE OF THE FOLLOWING:

A ☐ Non–Jury, ☐ Jury 6, ☐ Jury 12 TRIAL in this case is set for **days**, beginning:

Date: Time: Setting:
Date: Time: Setting:
Date: Time: Setting:

NOTICE: Trial is limited to number of days stated above. If trial is expected to exceed that limit, please notify the Court Administrator immediately.

☐   HEARING(S) in this cause are set as follows:

Nature of Hearing   Time Allotted   Date, Time, & Judge

The parties hereto will complete trial preparation according to the following schedule:

DISCLOSE EXPERT
WITNESSES: Join Additional Parties:

    Plaintiff(s):   Amend Pleadings:

    Defendant(s):   Complete Discovery &
                                  Depositions: (90 days before trial)

    Responsive: Argue Dispositive Motions: (45 days before trial)

MODIFICATION OF SCHEDULE: The court may, on motion of a party, after notice and hearing, modify any of the foregoing dates for good cause shown. Schedule deadlines may be amended by stipulation of the parties only upon leave of the court.

ORDERED BY THE COURT this date: _____

_____
Judge

CERTIFICATE OF MAILING: The undersigned certifies, under penalty of perjury of the laws of the State of Washington, that on the date stated above, (s)he deposited a copy of this Notice of Status Conference in the U.S. Mail, with sufficient postage prepaid, addressed to the persons and addresses named below or on the attached sheet.

NAME   NAME
TITLE   TITLE
ADDRESS   ADDRESS

_____

Grant County Superior Court
P.O. Box 37
Ephrata, WA 98823
(509) 754–2011, ext.

(509) 754–6036 fax

[Effective April 1, 1997. Amended effective September 1, 2012; September 1, 2015.]

FORM LR 8–E. NOTICE OF TRIAL/HEARING DATES

Superior Court of Washington
County of Grant

                                 No.

,

                       Plaintiff,   **NOTICE OF:**

vs.

                                   ☐ **Trial Date(s) (NTTD)**

,

                 Respondent.   ☐ **Hearing Date(s) (NTHG)**

PLEASE TAKE NOTICE OF THE FOLLOWING:

A ☐ **Non–Jury,** ☐ **Jury 6,** ☐ **Jury 12 TRIAL** in this case is set for **1 day**, beginning:

Date: _____   Time: _____   Setting: _____
Date: _____   Time: _____   Setting: _____
Date: _____   Time: _____   Setting: _____

NOTICE: Trial is limited to number of days stated above. If trial is expected to exceed that limit, please notify the Court Administrator immediately.

☐   HEARING(S) in this cause are set as follows:

Nature of Hearing	Time Allotted	Date, Time, & Judge
_____	_____	_____
_____	_____	_____
_____	_____	_____

I certify under penalty of perjury of the laws of the State of Washington, that on the date stated below I deposited a copy of the foregoing in the U.S. Mail addressed to each party and address identified below.

DATE: _____   _____

                                 Grant County Superior Court
                                 P.O. Box 37
                                 Ephrata, WA 98823
                                 (509) 754–2011, ext.

cc:

[Effective September 1, 2012.]

FORM LR 8–F. CRIMINAL CASE SCHEDULING ORDER

SUPERIOR COURT OF WASHINGTON IN AND FOR GRANT COUNTY

STATE OF WASHINGTON, Plaintiff,	)	
	)	NO. _____
vs.	)	
	)	**CRIMINAL CASE SCHEDULING**
	)	
_____,	)	
Defendant.	)	

PROS'R: _____ DEF'R: _____ LANG. _____

CrR 3.3 COMMENC'MT DATE: _____ TRIAL DEADLINE: _____

OMNIBUS HRG. _____ READINESS _____ TRIAL _____

** *Defendant must attend Omnibus Hearing, Readiness Hearing, and Trial, each set at 9:00 a.m.* **

IT IS ORDERED AS FOLLOWS:

1. On or before the Omnibus Hearing date, **counsel for the State** shall disclose to counsel for Defendant all materials and information identified in CrR 4.7(a). On or before said date, **counsel for Defendant** shall disclose to counsel for the State all materials and information identified in CrR 4.7(b).

2. Motions requiring hearings in excess of ten minutes per side, or involving live testimony, including hearings under CrR 3.5 and CrR 3.6, shall be filed or made orally at the Omnibus Hearing. Hearings upon such matters will be docketed only when requested at the time the motion is filed or made orally.

3. At the Omnibus Hearing, the court may, upon its own motion or at the request of counsel, schedule additional status hearings or a Pretrial Conference pursuant to CrR 4.5(c)(v).

4. At the Omnibus Hearing, counsel shall certify to the court: (a) the status of discovery and compliance with disclosure obligations; (b) that counsel have conferred in good faith to consider resolution of the case without trial; and (c) that a plea agreement has or will be proposed, or will not be considered, and the withdrawal date of any outstanding settlement offer.

5. At the Readiness Hearing, each side will either confirm its readiness to proceed to Trial or move for Trial continuance. If Trial is continued, the court shall also schedule an additional readiness hearing accordingly.

6. *Notice to Defendant:* If Trial does not commence on the date scheduled, and a new trial date is not expressly ordered by the court, Readiness Hearing and Trial will be deemed continued to the following week. Defendant shall appear the following Monday (Tuesday if Monday is a holiday) for Readiness Hearing, and the following Wednesday (Thursday if Monday is a holiday) for Trial.

DONE IN OPEN COURT _____   _____
                                              JUDGE

Receipt of copy acknowledged by Defendant: _____

[Effective September 1, 2012.]

SECTION 3.   CRIMINAL RULES

LCrR 1.1.   APPLICABILITY OF CIVIL RULES

Unless otherwise expressly provided herein, the following Local Rules apply in criminal cases as well as in civil cases: LR 7(b), except that initial appearances, motions to revoke conditions of release, and emergency furlough motions may be noted on any criminal docket without advance notice; LR 7(c) and (d); LR 47; LR 51; LR 59.

[Adopted effective September 1, 2012.]

LCrR 3.3.   TRIAL SCHEDULING

(a) Criminal trials will ordinarily be scheduled to begin on Wednesday at 9:00 a.m. (delayed by one day when Monday is a court holiday). The court will maintain a calendar of cases set for trial; cases will be called for trial in the order of their speedy trial deadline, and for cases having the same deadline, in order of their cause numbers, unless otherwise ordered by the court. The court may, by administrative order, specify further particulars regarding calling criminal cases for trial, the obligation of counsel and parties in trailing cases, and so on.

(b) A case on the trial calendar which is not resolved or expressly continued to a new trial date will be deemed continued for trial to the following week without change to its trial deadline.

[Renumbered from LR 4(g) and amended effective September 1, 2012.]

LCrR 3.5.   CONFESSION HEARING

At or before the omnibus hearing, the prosecution shall serve on the defendant and file with the court a brief description of the defendant's statements the prosecution intends to offer in evidence at trial. Not later than twenty four hours before a hearing pursuant to CrR 3.5, the parties may file memoranda of legal authorities relating to admission or exclusion of the defendant's statements.

[Renumbered from LR 9(a) and amended effective September 1, 2012.]

LCrR 3.6.   SUPPRESSION HEARING

At least one week prior to a hearing under CrR 3.6, the defendant shall serve on the prosecutor and file with the court a written motion for suppression, identifying the item(s) to be suppressed and briefly stating the grounds. The defendant shall serve and file with the motion a memorandum of authorities upon which defendant relies for suppression.

The prosecution shall file a memorandum of authorities upon which it relies for admissibility of the challenged evidence not later than twenty-four hours before the hearing.

[Renumbered from LR 9(b) and amended effective September 1, 2012.]

LCrR 4.1.   SCHEDULING ORDER

In criminal cases, at the time of arraignment, the court will adopt a schedule for the case by completing a Scheduling Order in the form appended hereto as Form LR 8–F. The court will cause the original Scheduling Order to be filed with the clerk, and will cause copies to be delivered to the court administrator, prosecuting attorney, defense attorney and defendant.

[Renumbered from LR 8(c) and amended effective September 1, 2012.]

LCrR 4.5.   OMNIBUS AND READINESS HEARINGS

The scheduling order required by LR 8 shall establish dates for omnibus hearing, readiness hearing, and trial, each of which the defendant shall attend unless excused in advance by the court. The omnibus hearing shall be conducted in the manner anticipated in CrR 4.5. At the readiness hearing, the court will confirm that all parties are ready to proceed to trial, or will continue trial to a date certain.

[Renumbered from LR 5(b) and amended effective September 1, 2012.]

LCrR 6.1.   TRIAL CONFERENCE

Unless otherwise ordered, criminal trials will begin with a conference, on the record, to resolve pretrial and trial issues. The conference will begin at such time as the court directs during the readiness hearing If the conference is expected to require more than 60 minutes, counsel shall so advise the court at the readiness hearing. Counsel and the defendant shall attend the trial conference. The conference will address administrative matters relating to the trial, admissibility of evidence of prior convictions or other contested evidentiary matters, motions *in limine*, and other motions entertained by the court.

[Renumbered from LR 6(b) and amended effective September 1, 2012.]

LOCAL RULES FOR MANDATORY ARBITRATION

[INTRODUCTION TO MANDATORY ARBITRATION RULES]

As authorized by MAR 8.2, the Superior Court of Grant County, by Order dated April 20, 1988, adopted these Local Rules for Mandatory Arbitration (LRMA).

I. SCOPE AND PURPOSE OF RULES

LRMA 1.1. PURPOSE OF RULES—OTHER RULES—DEFINITIONS

(a) Purpose and Scope. The purpose of these Local Rules for Mandatory Arbitration is to supplement the Mandatory Arbitration Rules (MAR) adopted by the Supreme Court in order to provide a simplified, economical procedure for the prompt and equitable resolution of disputes involving claims of $50,000 or less. THESE RULES MUST BE READ AND APPLIED IN CONJUNCTION WITH THE MANDATORY ARBITRATION RULES.

These rules are not intended to address every question which may arise during arbitration, and thus leave considerable discretion to the arbitrator. Arbitrators should liberally employ such discretion in order to assure that hearings are informal and expeditious, consistent with the purposes of the statutes and rules.

(b) Administrator. As used in these rules, "Administrator" means the employee of the Grant County Superior Court who may, from time to time, be assigned by the judges thereof the position and responsibilities of Arbitration Administrator.

[Amended effective May 1, 1990; September 1, 2012.]

LRMA 1.2. AMOUNT IN CONTROVERSY

Pursuant to RCW 7.06.020, civil matters shall be subject to mandatory arbitration if the amount claimed by any party does not exceed $50,000 exclusive of attorney fees, interest and costs, or if the parties waive claims in excess thereof for the purposes of arbitration.

[Amended effective May 1, 1990; September 1, 2012.]

LRMA 1.3. MOTIONS

All motions before the court relating to mandatory arbitration shall be noted on the civil motions calendar in accordance with LR 7, except as otherwise provided in these arbitration rules.

[Amended effective September 1, 2012.]

II. TRANSFER TO ARBITRATION AND ASSIGNMENT OF ARBITRATOR

LRMA 2.1. TRANSFER TO ARBITRATION

(a) Statement of Arbitrability. In every civil case to which the scheduling procedure set forth in LR 26F applies, each party filing and serving a status conference statement (Form LR 8–B) shall indicate thereon whether or not the case is subject to mandatory arbitration. Alternatively, any party who asserts that a case is subject to mandatory arbitration may at any time file and serve on all other parties a statement of arbitrability.

(b) Response. A party who disputes another party's assertion that the case is or is not subject to mandatory arbitration shall so advise the court in any one of these ways: (1) by so indicating in the status conference statement (Form LR 8–B); (2) by so indicating at the commencement of the status conference required by LR 26F(a); or (3) by serving and filing a written response to another party's statement of arbirtrability [1] within 14 days of service thereof.

(c) Amendment. A party may amend a statement of arbitrability, response, or other assertion regarding arbitrability of the case at any time before assignment of an arbitrator, and thereafter only upon leave of the court for good cause shown.

(d) Failure to File. If no response or other dispute regarding arbitrability is filed or brought to the attention of the court as provided in this rule, then a statement that the case is subject to mandatory arbitration will be deemed correct.

(e) By Stipulation. A case in which all parties file a stipulation to arbitrate under MAR 8.1 will be transferred to arbitration regardless of the nature of the case or the amount in controversy.

[Amended effective May 1, 1990; September 1, 2012.]

1 So in original.

LRMA 2.3. ASSIGNMENT TO ARBITRATOR

(a) Generally—Stipulations. When a case is set for arbitration, a list of five proposed arbitrators will be furnished to the parties. A master list of arbitrators will be made available on request. The parties are encouraged to stipulate to an arbitrator. In the absence of a stipulation, the arbitrator will be chosen from among the five proposed arbitrators in the manner set forth in this rule.

(b) Response by Parties. Each party may, within 14 days after a list of proposed arbitrators is furnished to the parties, nominate one or two arbitrators and strike two arbitrators from the list. If both parties respond, an arbitrator nominated by both parties will be appointed. If no arbitrator has been nominated by both parties, the Administrator will randomly appoint an arbitrator from among those not stricken by either party.

(c) Response by Only One Party. If only one party responds within 14 days, the Administrator will appoint an arbitrator nominated by that party.

(d) No Response. If no party responds within 14 days, the Administrator will randomly appoint one of the five proposed arbitrators.

(e) Additional Parties. If there are more than two adverse parties, all represented by different counsel, two additional proposed arbitrators shall be added to the list for each additional party so represented with the procedures for selection set forth in this rule to be applied. The number of adverse parties shall be determined by the Administrator, subject to review by the Presiding Judge.

[Amended effective September 1, 2012.]

III. ARBITRATORS

LRMA 3.1. QUALIFICATIONS

(a) Arbitration Panel. There shall be a panel of arbitrators in such numbers as the Superior Court Judges may from time to time determine. A person desiring to serve as an arbitrator shall complete an information sheet on the form prescribed by the court. A list of the names of arbitrators available to hear cases, and the information sheets filed by them, will be available for public inspection at the Administrator's office. The oath of office, in a form prescribed by the court, must be completed and filed prior to an applicant being placed on the arbitration panel.

(b) Refusal—Disqualification. The appointment of an arbitrator is subject to the right of that person to decline to serve. An arbitrator must notify the Administrator immediately if declining to serve or if any cause exists for the arbitrator's disqualification from the case upon any of the grounds of interest, relationship, bias, or prejudice set forth in the Code of Judicial Conduct, Rule 2.11 governing the disqualification of judges. If disqualified, the arbitrator will immediately return all materials in a case to the Administrator.

[Amended effective September 1, 2012.]

IV. PROCEDURES AFTER ASSIGNMENT

LRMA 4.2. DISCOVERY

In determining when additional discovery beyond that directly authorized by MAR 4.2 is reasonably necessary, the arbitrator shall balance the benefits of discovery against the burdens and expenses. The arbitrator shall consider the nature and complexity of the case, the amount in controversy, values at stake, the discovery that has already occurred, the burdens on the party from whom discovery is sought, and the possibility of unfair surprise which may result if discovery is restricted. Authorized discovery shall be conducted in accordance with the civil rules except that motions concerning discovery shall be resolved by the arbitrator. Nothing in this rule shall prohibit the arbitrator from considering, in ruling on the merits of the case, any other discovery devices which may have been completed prior to assignment of the case to the arbitrator.

[Amended effective September 1, 2012.]

V. HEARING

LRMA 5.1. NOTICE OF HEARING—TIME AND PLACE—CONTINUANCE

An arbitration hearing may be scheduled at any reasonable time and place chosen by the arbitrator. The arbitrator may grant a continuance without court order. The parties may stipulate to a continuance only with leave of the arbitrator. The arbitrator shall give reasonable notice of the hearing date and any continuance to the Administrator.

[Amended effective September 1, 2012.]

LRMA 5.2. PREHEARING STATEMENT OF PROOF—DOCUMENTS FILED WITH THE COURT

The statements of witnesses and exhibits required by MAR 5.2 shall be simultaneously exchanged by all parties. In addition to the requirements of MAR 5.2, each party shall also furnish the arbitrator with copies of pleadings and other documents contained in the court file which that party deems relevant. The court file shall remain in the custody of the County Clerk.

[Amended effective September 1, 2012.]

LRMA 5.3. CONDUCT OF HEARING— WITNESSES—RULES OF EVIDENCE

(a) Oath or Affirmation. The arbitrator shall place a witness under oath or affirmation, substantially in the following form, before the witness presents testimony: *"Do you solemnly swear or affirm, under penalty of perjury under the laws of the State of Washington, that the testimony you give in this matter will be the truth?"*

(b) Recording. The hearing may be recorded electronically or otherwise by any party at his or her expense, providing that the means of recording do not interfere with conduct of the hearing.

(c) Rules of Evidence Generally. The Rules of Evidence, to the extent determined by the arbitrator to be applicable, should be liberally construed to promote justice and economical dispute resolution.

[Amended effective September 1, 2012.]

VI. AWARD

LRMA 6.1. FORM AND CONTENT OF AWARD

(a) Form. The arbitrator's award shall be prepared on a form prescribed by the court.

(b) Exhibits. All exhibits offered during the arbitration hearing shall be filed with the Clerk at the time of filing the award.

[Amended effective September 1, 2012.]

LRMA 6.2. FILING OF AWARD— EXTENSION

A request by the arbitrator for extension of the time for filing an award under MAR 6.2 may be presented *ex parte* to the Presiding Judge. The arbitrator shall give all parties notice of any extension granted.

[Amended effective September 1, 2012.]

LRMA 6.3. PRESENTATION OF JUDGMENT

A judgment on an award shall be presented to the Presiding Judge, by any party, on notice in accordance with MAR 6.3.

VII. TRIAL DE NOVO

LRMA 7.1. REQUEST FOR TRIAL DE NOVO—TRIAL SETTING

Any party desiring trial de novo after an arbitration award must give notice thereof as provided in MAR 7.1(a) notwithstanding that the case is not ripe for trial setting under LR 40. If a trial date has been assigned prior to the filing of an arbitration award, it shall remain in place if a request for trial de novo is filed pursuant to MAR 7.1(a), and shall be stricken if no such request is filed within the time permitted by MAR 7.1(a).

[Amended effective September 1, 2012.]

LRMA 7.2. SEALING ARBITRATION AWARD [WITHDRAWN]

[Withdrawn effective September 1, 2012.]

VIII. GENERAL PROVISIONS

LRMA 8.1. STIPULATIONS—EFFECT ON RELIEF GRANTED

If a case not otherwise subject to mandatory arbitration is transferred to the arbitration calendar by stipulation, the arbitrator may grant award any relief which could have been granted if the case were determined by a judge.

[Amended effective September 1, 2012.]

LRMA 8.3. EFFECTIVE DATE [WITHDRAWN]

[Withdrawn effective September 1, 2012.]

LRMA 8.4. TITLE AND CITATION

These rules are known and cited as the Grant County Superior Court Local Rules for Mandatory Arbitration. "LRMA" is the official abbreviation.

[Amended effective September 1, 2012.]

LRMA 8.6. COMPENSATION OF ARBITRATORS

(a) Generally. Arbitrators shall be compensated for time spent in preparation, hearings, and preparation of an award, at an hourly rate established by the Office of Administrator of the Courts. Hourly compensation shall not include travel time. Arbitrators shall also be compensated for their reasonable costs, including mileage.

(b) Determination and Payment. The Administrator shall determine the amount of compensation and costs to be paid, and shall cause the costs and one-half of the compensation to be promptly paid from funds of Grant County, without deductions. The Administrator will promptly submit a request for payment of the remaining one-half of compensation, less deductions required by law, from funds of the State of Washington.

(c) Form. When the arbitrator's award is filed, the arbitrator shall submit to the court a request for payment on a form prescribed by the court.
[Renumbered from LRMA 8.5 and amended effective September 1, 2012.]

LRMA 8.7. ADMINISTRATION

The Administrator, under the supervision of the Court Administrator and the Superior Court Judges, shall supervise arbitration under these rules and perform such additional duties relating thereto as the judges or court administrator may direct.
[Renumbered from LRMA 8.6 and amended effective September 1, 2012.]

LOCAL RULES FOR MANDATORY MEDIATION

LRMM 1. GENERAL PROVISIONS

(a) Mediation Required. Contested issues in family law cases are subject to mandatory mediation in accordance with this rule. No trial or hearing shall be conducted to resolve any such issue until either (1) the parties have engaged in mediation; or (2) the court has, for good cause, waived the mediation requirement of this rule. Attorneys for the parties may attend mediation proceedings. Mediation proceedings will be completed at least 30 days before trial.

(b) Family Law Cases.

(1) Family law cases subject to mandatory mediation under this rule are as follows:

   a. Dissolution or declaration of invalidity of marriage or domestic partnership.

   b. Legal separation.

   c. Child custody proceedings involving parents, presumed or putative parents, *de facto* parents, or non-parents (after a finding adequate cause when required).

   d. Paternity cases after entry of a judgment determining parentage.

   e. Proceedings to establish child support or maintenance obligations.

   f. Proceedings relating to the termination of marriage-like relationships.

(2) Unless otherwise ordered by the court, mediation under this rule is not required for the following cases or issues:

   a. Dependency and termination cases.

   b. Contempt proceedings regarding compliance with court orders.

   c. Petitions for Domestic Violence Protection Orders.

   d. Adoption proceedings.

   e. Petitions for emancipation of a minor or for change of name.

   f. Motions to waive the requirements of this rule for good cause.

(c) Contested Issues.

(1) Contested issues subject to mandatory mediation under this rule include the following:

   a. Characterization, valuation and/or division of assets and debts.

   b. Establishment of final parenting plan or residential schedule.

   c. Modification of a final parenting plan or residential schedule after a finding of adequate cause.

   d. Modification of a temporary parenting plan or residential schedule.

   e. Establishment of child support or maintenance (other than initial temporary order).

   f. Modification of temporary or permanent child support or maintenance order.

(2) Unless otherwise ordered by the court, contested issues subject to mandatory mediation under this rule do not include the following:

   a. Entry of initial temporary support order.

   b. Entry of initial temporary parenting plan or residential schedule.

   c. Entry of other initial temporary orders, including restraining orders; orders for the use, possession, disposition or preservation of assets; orders allocating responsibility for debt service; and similar temporary orders.

(d) Waiver. On its own motion, or on motion of a party, the court may waive the mediation requirements or time limits of this rule for good cause. Good cause will be presumed in cases where mediation would require a party subjected to domestic violence to meet in close proximity with a perpetrator of that violence.

[Adopted effective September 1, 2012.]

LRMM 2. MEDIATOR

(a) **Appointment of Mediator.** The parties may stipulate to appointment of a person to perform the mediation required by this rule by filing with the court a written stipulation including the name, address and date of appointment of the mediator. In the absence of stipulation, the court will, on its own motion or the motion of a party, appoint a mediator. The person or organization appointed by the parties or the court shall immediately be notified of the appointment. Any person so appointed may decline the appointment and promptly notify the parties and the court thereof.

(b) **Compensation.** The mediator shall set a reasonable fee for mediation. The parties shall promptly pay the mediator's fee in the proportions agreed by the parties or, in the absence of agreement, as ordered by the court.

(c) **Authority and Duties.** The mediator shall set the time, place, manner, and duration of mediation, which may be adjourned from time to time to facilitate resolution of issues. Within seven (7) days after completion of mediation, the mediator shall file with the court, and provide copies to the parties and attorneys who participated in the mediation, a declaration setting forth (1) the date(s) of mediation; (2) the contested issues mediated; and (3) the manner in which any party failed, in the judgment of the mediator, to participate in good faith.

(d) **Mediator as Witness.** The mediator may not be subpoenaed to testify, nor shall the mediator agree or volunteer to testify, in any discovery procedure or court hearing regarding the statements, communications, or proposals, written or oral, made by any party, attorney or other participant in the mediation process.

[Adopted effective September 1, 2012.]

LRMM 3. MEDIATION PROCESS

(a) **Required Materials.** At least two days before mediation proceedings, each party will submit to the mediator proposed orders sought to be entered by the court or equivalent written statements of the resolution of all contested issues subject to mediation. When support issues are being mediated, each party will include a financial declaration and completed child support worksheets. When characterization, valuation, and/or division of assets or debts is being mediated, each party shall submit a statement in the form required by LR 15. The parties shall timely submit any additional materials requested by the mediator. Materials submitted to the mediator shall not be filed with the Clerk of court.

(b) **Good Faith Obligation.** The parties shall mediate in good faith. Failure to fully participate in mediation, including failure to submit required materials, refusal to discuss a contested issue, or refusal to consider a proposed resolution, shall be evidence of

lack of good faith. A party may be sanctioned for failing to mediate in good faith; sanctions may include assessment of all costs of mediation, an award of attorney fees and costs to a party participating in good faith, or other sanctions ordered by the court.

(c) **Appearance.** For good cause shown, the mediator may permit any participant in mediation to appear by telephone. At the mediator's discretion, persons other than the parties and their attorneys may be permitted to attend the mediation, *Provided,* that a party seeking permission for a non-party to attend shall give reasonable advance written notice of the request to every opposing party.

(d) **Agreement.** Any agreement between the parties reached during the mediation process shall be reduced to writing before conclusion of the mediation and shall be endorsed by all parties, participating attorneys, and the mediator. The mediator may, upon notice to a person participating by telephone, endorse the agreement on behalf of that person. The mediator will cause a copy of the endorsed agreement to be provided to each party before conclusion of the mediation.

[Adopted effective September 1, 2012.]

LRMM 4. CONFIDENTIALITY

(a) **Disclosure of Communications.** The work product of the mediator, and all statements by, and communications between, the mediator and any participant in the mediation proceedings, or by or between any participant and another participant or counsel for a participant, shall be confidential, and shall not be disclosed to any person, except as follows: (1) the mediator shall report to appropriate law enforcement and/or child welfare authorities information relating to the abuse of any child when such information comes to the mediator at any time in the mediation proceedings and the information appears to be evidence of a crime against a child; and (2) any written agreement endorsed by the parties as set forth in this rule may be filed with or disclosed to the court.

(b) **Admonition to Participants.** The mediator shall provide in writing to all participants in the mediation process a copy of the foregoing provision prior to commencement of mediation.

[Adopted effective September 1, 2012.]

LRMM 5. OTHER PROVISIONS

(a) **Discovery.** The mediation process does not stay, prohibit, supersede or otherwise affect the rights and obligations of the parties to conduct or provide discovery as set forth in applicable rules of court, or modify in any way the provisions of law for compelling the same.

(b) **Title and Citation.** These rules are known and cited as the Grant County Superior Court Local Rules for Mandatory Mediation. "LRMM" is the official abbreviation.

(c) Effective Date. This rule shall apply to all causes of action pending before the court on or after the 1st day of September, 2012, except those cases in which trial has commenced.

[Adopted effective September 1, 2012.]

DISTRICT COURT

LOCAL RULES FOR THE DISTRICT COURT OF THE STATE OF WASHINGTON FOR GRANT COUNTY

Including Amendments Received Through
August 15, 2015

Table of Rules

PREFACE

1. Promulgation. These rules shall be known as the Local Rules for the District Court of the state of Washington for Grant County. Copies of these rules will be filed with District Court for Grant County and will be distributed to all law offices in Grant County. Additional copies will be available at the office of the Grant County District Court Administrator. These rules will be effective September 1, 2004.

2. Numbering. Consistent with CRLJ 83(a) and CrRLJ 1.7, Washington Court rules, these rules, to the extent possible, conform in numbering system and in format to those rules and facilitate the use of both. The number of each rule is preceded by the abbreviation "L" designating the rule as local to this court and supplemental to the corresponding Washington Court Rule.

3. Revisions and Additions. These rules have been prepared in loose-leaf form to facilitate revision, additions or deletions in the future by page without the necessity of republication.

[Adopted effective July 1, 1994; amended effective September 1, 1999; September 1, 2003; September 1, 2004.]

ADMINISTRATIVE RULES

L–ARLJ .01.   FOREWORD

Administrative Rules

These Local Rules for Civil, Criminal, Infraction, and Appeals are assembled to conform in numbering system and in format to the rules adopted by the Supreme Court as required by GR 7.

These rules supplement ARLJ, CRLJ, CrRLJ, RALJ, and IRLJ in accordance with RCW 3.30.080 and GR 7. Local Rules are cited as L- ARLJ, L- CRLJ, L–CrRLJ, L–RALJ, and L–IRLJ. Insofar as practicable the Washington Court Rules are not repeated and the user of these Local rules should refer to the pertinent rule as adopted by the Supreme Court.

[Adopted effective September 1, 2003; amended effective September 1, 2004.]

L–ARLJ .02.   PRESIDING JUDGE

Presiding Judge and Court Governance

(a) Election, Term, Vacancies, Removal and Selection Criteria

(1) *Election.* The Presiding Judge shall be elected by majority vote of the Grant County District Court judges for a term of not less than two years. In the same manner, the judges shall elect an Assistant Presiding Judge of the court who shall serve as Acting Presiding Judge during the absence or upon the request of the Presiding Judge and who shall perform such further duties as the Presiding Judge shall direct. If the judges fail or refuse to elect a Presiding Judge or Assistant Presiding Judge, the Presiding Judge then in office shall notify the Supreme Court of said failure or refusal and the Supreme Court shall appoint a Presiding Judge or Assistant Presiding Judge pursuant to GR 29(a)(1).

(2) *Term.* The Presiding Judge shall be elected for a term of not fewer than two years, subject to reelection. The term of the Presiding Judge shall commence on January 1 of the year in which the Presiding Judge's term begins.

(3) *Vacancies.* Interim vacancies of the office of Presiding Judge or Acting Presiding Judge shall be filled as provided in (a)(1).

(4) *Removal.* The Presiding Judge may be removed by a majority vote of the judges of the court.

(5) *Selection Criteria.* A Presiding Judge must have at least four years of experience as a judge, unless this requirement is waived by a majority vote of the judges of the court. Selection of a Presiding Judge should be based on the judge's

a) Management and administrative ability

b) Interest in serving in the position.

c) Experience and familiarity with a variety of trial court assignments, and

d) Ability to motivate and educate other judicial officers and court personnel.

(6) *Notification of Chief Justice.* The Presiding Judge so elected shall send notice of the election of the Presiding Judge and Assistant Presiding Judge to the Chief Justice of the Supreme Court within 30 days of election.

(7) *Caseload Adjustment.* To the extent possible, the judicial caseload should be adjusted to provide the Presiding Judge with sufficient time and resources to devote to the management and administrative duties of the office.

(8) *General Responsibilities.* The Presiding Judge is responsible for leading the management and administration of the court's business, recommending policies and procedures that improve the court's effectiveness, and allocating resources in a way that maximizes the court's ability to resolve disputes fairly and expeditiously.

(9) *Duties and Authority.* The judicial and administrative duties set forth in this rule cannot be delegated to persons in either the legislative or executive branches of government. A Presiding Judge may delegate the performance of ministerial duties to court employees; however, it is still the Presiding Judge's responsibility to ensure they are performed in accordance with this rule. In addition to exercising general administrative supervision over the court, the Presiding Judge shall:

a) Supervise the business of the court and judicial officers in such manner as to ensure the expeditious and efficient processing of all cases and equitable distribution of the workload among judicial officers;

b) Assign judicial officers to hear cases pursuant to statute or rule. The court may establish general policies governing the assignment of judges;

c) Coordinate judicial officers' vacations, attendance at education programs, and similar matters;

d) Develop and coordinate statistical and management information;

e) Supervise the daily operation of the court including:

1) All personnel assigned to perform court functions; and

2) All personnel employed under the judicial branch of government including but not limited to working conditions, hiring, discipline, and termination decisions except wages, or benefits directly related to wages; and

3) The Court Administrator, who shall report directly to the Presiding Judge. (see.03)

f) Supervise the court's accounts and audit the procurement and disbursement of appropriations and preparation of the court's annual budget request;

g) Appoint standing and special committees of judicial officers necessary for the proper performance of the duties of the court;

h) Promulgate local rules as a majority of the judges may approve or as the Supreme Court shall direct;

i) Supervise the preparation and filing of reports required by statute and court rule;

j) Act as the official spokesperson for the court in all matters with the executive or legislative branches of state and local government and the community unless the Presiding Judge shall designate another judge or employee to serve in this capacity;

k) Preside at meetings of the judicial officers of the court;

l) Determine the qualifications of and establish a training program for pro tem judges and pro tem court commissioners; and

m) Perform other duties as may be assigned by statute or court rule.

10) *Enabling Authority.* The Presiding Judge shall have the general responsibilities, duties and authority set forth in GR 29.

[Adopted effective September 1, 2003; amended effective September 1, 2004.]

L–ARLJ .03.   COURT ADMINISTRATOR

Court Governance and Responsibility

(a) **Selection.** The Court Administrator shall be appointed by the judges, and shall serve at the pleasure of the judges under the direction and supervision of the Presiding Judge.

(b) **Qualifications.** Refer to Grant District Court job description for Court Administrator.

(1) *General responsibilities.* The Court Administrator is responsible for assisting the Presiding Judge in the management and administration of the court's business, recommending policies and procedures that improve the court's effectiveness and recommending the allocation of resources to maximize the court's efficiency.

(c) **Powers and Duties.** The powers and duties of the Court Administrator include but are not limited to the following:

(1) Administrative control of all non-judicial activities of the court.

(2) Implementation of all policies regarding judicial functions of the court.

(3) Supervision of all court employees including the Probation Department; including but not limited to working conditions, hiring, discipline and termination decisions.

(4) Preparation and administration of the court budget.

(5) Representation of the court in dealings with the State Court Administrator.

(6) Representation of the court in meeting with representatives of governmental bodies, and other public and private groups regarding court management matters at the direction of the Presiding Judge.

(7) Preparation of reports and compilation of statistics as required by the Presiding Judge or State Court Administrator and maintain records or informal activities of the court.

(8) Recommendations to the Presiding Judge for the improvement of the administration of the court.

(9) Administration of the coordination of judicial services to municipalities as identified in the Districting Plan; Provision of legislative updates to all affected parties.

(10) Coordination efforts with Administrative Office of the Courts (AOC) and local Law Enforcement Agencies (LEA's).

(11) Assistance to the Presiding Judge in promulgating local rules.

(12) Coordination, dissemination and implementation of local rules to all affected parties.

(13) Supervision of the process and ministrations of procuring Pro Tempore Judges.

(14) Attendance to judges' meetings and preparation of the agenda for and minutes of those meetings.

(15) Supervision of the Court's accounts and audit of the procurement and disbursement of appropriations.

(d) **Enabling Authority.** The Court Administrator shall have the general responsibilities, duties, and authority set forth in GR 29; Reports directly to the Presiding Judge. The Court Administrator may delegate such duties to court employees as deemed appropriate.

[Adopted effective September 1, 2003; amended effective September 1, 2004.]

CIVIL RULES

LCRLJ 38.   CIVIL JURY PRE–TRIAL PROCEDURE

All cases set for jury trial shall be set for pre-trial conference which shall be held at least two weeks prior to trial. No order shall be required for this mandatory pre-trial conference. The attorneys who are to conduct the trial and all parties shall be present to consider such matters as will promote a fair and expeditious trial. All discovery should be completed three days prior to said conference. Opposing counsel or party must be given seven days notice on pre-trial motions to be heard at the pre-trial conference. Any pre-trial motions requiring the testimony of witnesses for argument may, in the discretion of the Court, be rescheduled or continued to the day of trial. All amendments, pleas, and motions should be made or be completed at this conference. Upon failure to appear, the Judge may proceed with the conference ex-parte, if necessary, and enter any appropriate order including striking the jury demand and may impose terms.

[Adopted effective September 1, 1999. Amended effective September 1, 2003.]

LCRLJ 64.   GARNISHMENT AND DENIAL OF NON–RESPONSIVE EXEMPTION CLAIM

A blank Exemption Claim or one that does not claim an exemption shall be denied without a court hearing if the garnishing party files and serves a Notice of Non–Responsive Exemption Claim, within seven days of receipt of the Exemption Claim. If filing and/or service is had by mail, compliance with this rule shall be deemed complete if the described Notice is posted in the US Mail on or before the seventh day after the garnishing party received the Exemption Claim.

[Adopted effective September 1, 1999; amended effective September 1, 2003.]

LCRLJ 65. CIVIL–NAME CHANGES

(a) **Separate Petitions Required.** A separate petition shall be filed for each name a party wishes changed.

(b) **Hearing.** All hearings on petitions for name changes shall be in open court and on the record.

(c) **Minors.**

(1) Birth Certificate. A certified copy of any minor applicant's birth certificate or suitable identification must be presented to the clerk for verification and copying.

(2) Parental Notification.

(a) A person petitioning to change the name of a minor child or ward must establish that both parents consent to the change in writing, or that the nonpetitioning parent has been served at least ten days before the hearing with a notice that includes the hearing date, the minor's current name, the name the petitioner desires the minor to assume, and the reasons for requesting the change of name.

(b) A person petitioning to change the name of a minor child may move the court for an order authorizing notice to a parent by publication. The requesting parent must certify under penalty of perjury that the whereabouts of the other parent are unknown. If authorized by the court, notice by publication one time in a newspaper of general circulation in the county of the nonpetitioning parent's last known address shall be deemed sufficient if it satisfied the requirements of LCRLJ 65(c)(2)(a).

(d) **Contents of Petition.** A petition for change of name must be sworn under oath and state the following:

(1) The Petitioner's full present name and the full name the petitioner wishes to assume;

(2) The Petitioner's date of birth;

(3) That the Petitioner resides in Grant County;

(4) The reason for the request;

(5) The application is not made for any illegal or fraudulent purpose;

(6) The name change will not be detrimental to the interests of any other person;

(7) The name of the Petitioner's father and mother, or, if brought on behalf of a minor, the name of the minor's father and mother;

(8) Whether the Petitioner is subject to the jurisdiction of the Washington State Department of Corrections and, if so, that Petitioner has provided a copy of the Petition to the Department at least five days before any hearing on the name change request;

(9) Whether the Petitioner is subject to the sex offender registration laws of the State of Washington and, if so, that Petitioner has provided copies of the Petition to the county sheriff and the Washington State Patrol at least five days before any hearing on the name change request.

(e) **Contents of Proposed Order.** A Petitioner for change of name must file a proposed Order Changing Name that includes the following:

(1) The Petitioner's full name;

(2) The full name Petitioner seeks to assume;

(3) If the Petition is brought on behalf of a minor, a finding that both parents or guardians consent to the change, or that a non consenting parent was served with notice of the proposed change as required by these rules, or that a non consenting parent's legal rights were previously terminated by court order;

(4) A finding whether the Petitioner is subject to the jurisdiction of the Washington State Department of Corrections and, if so, whether Petitioner provided a copy of the Petition to the Department at least five days before the Order is to be entered;

(5) A finding whether the Petitioner is subject to the sex offender registration laws of the State of Washington and, if so, whether Petitioner provided copies of the Petition to the county sheriff and Washington State Patrol at least five days before the Order is to be entered;

(6) A finding that the Petition is not made for illegal or fraudulent purposes;

(7) A finding that the change of name will not be detrimental to the interests of any other person;

(8) If the Petition is brought on behalf of a minor, a finding that the name change is in the best interests of the minor.

[Adopted effective September 1, 2009.]

CRIMINAL RULES

LCrRLJ 3.3.   CONTINUANCES

(a) Continuances may be granted:

(1) Upon written agreement of all parties which must be authorized by the defendant(s). Agreements lacking evidence of approval of all parties will not be considered by the court. The agreement must set forth the basis for the continuance and include a proposed order of continuance. The agreement is not effective unless approved by the court.

(2) By motion, if such motion complies with relevant rules for motions, including CrRLJ 3.3(h)(2).

(3) Only if the continuance is to a date within the speedy trial requirements of CrRLJ 3.3 or the defendant executes a waiver of speedy trial.

[Adopted effective September 1, 2009.]

LCrRLJ 3.4(d)(2).   VIDEO ARRAIGNMENT AGREEMENT

(2) *Agreement.* Other trial court proceedings including the entry of a Statement of Defendant on Plea of Guilty as provided for by CrRLJ 4.2 may be conducted by video conference only by agreement of the parties, either in writing or on the record, and upon the approval of the trial court judge. For purposes of video conference proceedings, the electronic or facsimile signatures of the defendant, counsel, interested parties and the Court shall be treated as if they were an original signature. This includes all orders on Judgment and Sentence, No Contact Orders, Statements of Defendant on Pleas of Guilty, and other documents or pleadings as the Court shall determine are appropriate or necessary.

[Adopted on an emergency basis, effective April 6, 2012.]

LCrRLJ 4.5.   PRE TRIAL CONFERENCE/READINESS HEARING

a) In every criminal or traffic case in which the defendant is entitled to a jury trial, the Clerk shall set a date for a pre-trial conference. The purpose of said conference is for presentation and setting of motions, completion of plea bargaining, and to set a trial date. Discovery shall be in the hands of the party requesting same at least two (2) working days PRIOR TO said conference. The Clerk will then proceed to notify the prospective jurors as provided by law. See Local Rule LJCrR 8.2 concerning notice to opposing parties of the nature of the pre-trial motions and the necessity of witnesses at the hearing.

If the party or his attorney fails to appear at said conference without adequate cause then known to the court, bail will be ordered forfeited and the Court will order a Bench Warrant issued for the arrest of the defendant.

In the event it comes to the attention of the court that there is a likelihood that the defendant will not be available for jury trial, as evidenced, for example, by defendant's failure to remain in contact with his lawyer, the court will schedule an additional hearing to inquire as to the availability of the defendant. If the defendant does not appear, the jury trial date will be stricken, bail forfeited, and the court will order a bench warrant for the arrest of the defendant.

b) Within ten (10) days, excluding weekends and holidays, prior to an assigned jury trial date, there shall be held a readiness hearing. At such a hearing, it shall be mandatory that the prosecuting authority, the defense counsel, and the defendant be present. At such a hearing, the following matters will be concluded:

1. All plea bargaining

2. Exchange of witness lists

3. Providing of any discovery not previously exchanged at the pre-jury conference

4. Motions on the legal issues arising subsequent to the pre-jury conference or on issues arising due to new evidence

At the conclusion of the readiness hearing, the court will no longer accept any plea bargaining arrangements. Thereafter, the case will be tried by jury, unless waived by the defendant, or concluded by a guilty plea to the original charge, or a dismissal of the charge(s). A failure of the defendant to be present at the readiness hearing will result in the issuance of a bench warrant for failure to appear and the vacating of the jury trial date. The requirements of this rule can be waived only by the judge assigned to the case or the Presiding Judge of the Grant County District Court.

[Adopted effective September 1, 1999.]

LCrRLJ 8.2.   MOTIONS AND APPLICATIONS— NOTICE—SERVICE

All amendments to the charges, pleas, or pre-trial motions shall be made at the time of the pre-trial hearing. Motions shall not be considered at the time of trial unless they could not have been raised at the time of the pre-trial hearing or the judge at the time of the pre-trial hearing expressly continues such motions to the time of trial. Absent good cause, motions for dismissal or suppression of evidence in criminal cases shall be in writing and shall be provided to the prosecutor at least 48 hours before the pre-trial hearing. Witnesses necessary to establish issues of fact or law on motions shall be subpoenaed by moving party.

In the event lengthy motions or motions requiring witnesses to be subpoenaed or scheduled cannot be heard at the pre-trial conference due to time limitations or scheduling conflict, the moving party shall notify the clerk's office so that the matter may be given a special setting.

[Adopted effective July 1, 1994; amended effective September 1, 1999.]

INFRACTION RULES

LIRLJ 2.6(c). DECISION ON WRITTEN STATEMENTS

Decision on written statements, given under penalty of perjury, are allowed.

[Adopted effective September 1, 1999.]

LIRLJ 3.1. CONTESTED HEARINGS— PRELIMINARY PROCEEDINGS

(a)(1) *Subpoenas.* In contested cases, the defendant and the plaintiff may subpoena witnesses necessary for the presentation of their respective cases. The request for a subpoena may be made in person or by mail. In order to request a subpoena, the request must be made in writing informing the clerk of the court of the name and address of the witness and of the date of the contested hearing. The subpoena may be issued by a judge, court commissioner, clerk of the court, or by a party's attorney. The responsibility for serving subpoenas on witnesses, including law enforcement witnesses and the Speed Measuring Device Expert (SMD Expert) is upon the party requesting the subpoena. Such subpoenas may be served as stated in IRLJ 3.1(a).

(2) *Timeliness.* In cases where the request for a subpoena is made 14 days or less prior to the scheduled hearing, the Court may deny the request for the subpoena or condition the issuance of the subpoena upon a continuance of the hearing date. (See following rule for time frame for Speed Measuring Device Expert.)

(3) *Speed Measuring Device Expert.* Defense requests for a Speed Measuring Device Expert must be made to the Office of the Prosecuting Attorney no less than 30 days prior to the date set for the contested hearing. A request for a SMD expert may be treated by the Court as a request for a continuance to the next date on which the prosecuting attorney has scheduled the appearance of the SMD Expert. In cases where either party requests a Speed Measuring Device Expert (SMD Expert), those cases shall be consolidated to the extent possible on one calendar. (See Exhibit LIRLJ 3.1(a)(3).)

(4) *Costs and Witness Fees.* Each party is responsible for costs incurred by that party, including witness fees, as set forth in RCW 46.63.151. In cases where a party requests a witness to be subpoenaed, the party requesting the witness shall pay the witness fees and mileage expenses due that witness. Any person who requests production of an electronic speed measuring device expert, and who is thereafter found by the court to have committed the infraction, shall be required to pay the fee charged by the expert as a cost incurred by that party.

[Adopted effective September 1, 1999; amended effective September 1, 2002.]

LIRLJ 3.1(b). PLAINTIFF'S LAWYER

Plaintiff's lawyer for discovery purposes would be the Grant County Prosecuting Attorney. Notice sent to the court clerk is ineffective. A request for discovery may require that the court date be reset to a date when the prosecutor is in court.

[Adopted effective September 1, 2002.]

LIRLJ 6.2(a). NO VALID OPERATORS LICENSE—SHOW LICENSE

If a defendant is charged with the infraction of driving a motor vehicle without having a valid driver's license issued to Washington residents pursuant to RCW 46.20, and that defendant presents a valid license or satisfactory evidence that the defendant has obtained a valid driver's license to the court clerk, then the bail for the offense shall be reduced to $150.00 and the defendant will be entitled to post and forfeit that penalty without the need to appear in court on that charge.

[Adopted effective September 1, 1999; amended effective September 1, 2002; September 1, 2003; September 1, 2004.]

LIRLJ 6.2(b). INSURANCE— SHOW PROOF

If a defendant is charged with driving a motor vehicle without having proof of valid insurance pursuant to RCW 46.20, and that defendant presents satisfactory evidence that they have obtained valid insurance to the court clerk, then the bail for the offense shall be as set forth below and the defendant will be entitled to post and forfeit that penalty without the need to appear in court on that charge.

  i) insurance in effect at the time of the citation: $25.00

  ii) 1st offense: $ 150.00

  iii) 2nd offense: $ 200.00

  iv) 3rd offense: $ 250.00

  v) subsequent offense(s)—court appearance mandatory

[Adopted effective September 1, 1999; amended effective September 1, 2002; September 1, 2003; September 1, 2004.]

MUNICIPAL COURTS

COULEE CITY MUNICIPAL COURT—
[No Local Rules]

PUBLISHER'S NOTE

All municipal courts in Grant County follow the Grant County District Court Local Rules.

ELECTRIC CITY MUNICIPAL COURT—
[No Local Rules]

PUBLISHER'S NOTE

All municipal courts in Grant County follow the Grant County District Court Local Rules.

EPHRATA MUNICIPAL COURT—
[No Local Rules]

PUBLISHER'S NOTE

All municipal courts in Grant County follow the Grant County District Court Local Rules.

GEORGE MUNICIPAL COURT—
[No Local Rules]

PUBLISHER'S NOTE

All municipal courts in Grant County follow the Grant County District Court Local Rules.

GRAND COULEE MUNICIPAL COURT—
[No Local Rules]

PUBLISHER'S NOTE

All municipal courts in Grant County follow the Grant County District Court Local Rules.

MATTAWA MUNICIPAL COURT—
[No Local Rules]

PUBLISHER'S NOTE

All municipal courts in Grant County follow the Grant County District Court Local Rules.

MOSES LAKE MUNICIPAL COURT—
[No Local Rules]

PUBLISHER'S NOTE

All municipal courts in Grant County follow the Grant County District Court Local Rules.

QUINCY MUNICIPAL COURT—
[No Local Rules]

PUBLISHER'S NOTE

All municipal courts in Grant County follow the Grant County District Court Local Rules.

ROYAL CITY MUNICIPAL COURT—
[No Local Rules]

PUBLISHER'S NOTE

All municipal courts in Grant County follow the Grant County District Court Local Rules.

SOAP LAKE MUNICIPAL COURT—
[No Local Rules]

PUBLISHER'S NOTE

All municipal courts in Grant County follow the Grant County District Court Local Rules.

WARDEN MUNICIPAL COURT—
[No Local Rules]

PUBLISHER'S NOTE

All municipal courts in Grant County follow the Grant County District Court Local Rules.

GRAYS HARBOR COUNTY

Table of Courts

Superior Court

Local Rules of the Superior Court for Grays Harbor County.

District Court

Local Rules of Grays Harbor County District Court.

Municipal Courts

Aberdeen Municipal Court Rules.
Cosmopolis Municipal Court—[No Local Rules].
Elma Municipal Court Local Court Rules.
Hoquiam Municipal Court Local Court Rules.
McCleary Municipal Court Local Court Rules.
Montesano Municipal Court Local Court Rules.
Oakville Municipal Court Local Court Rules.
Ocean Shores Municipal Court Local Rules.
Westport Municipal Court Local Court Rules.

SUPERIOR COURT

LOCAL RULES OF THE SUPERIOR COURT FOR GRAYS HARBOR COUNTY

**Including Amendments Received Through
August 15, 2015**

Table of Rules

LOCAL GENERAL RULES (LGR)

RULE 29. PRESIDING JUDGE IN SUPERIOR COURT DISTRICT

(a) Election, Term, Vacancies, Removal and Selection Criteria—Multiple Judge Courts.

(1) *Election.* The Grays Harbor Superior Court Judges shall elect a Presiding Judge by majority vote at a meeting held in October or November of even numbered years.

(2) *Term.* The Presiding Judge shall be elected for a term of two years, subject to reelection.

(3) *Vacancies.* Interim vacancies in the office of Presiding Judge shall be filled by a majority vote of the Superior Court Judges at the first Judges meeting held after the vacancy is known to exist.

[Adopted effective September 1, 2015.]

LOCAL CIVIL RULES (LCR)

II. COMMENCEMENT OF ACTION; SERVICE OF PROCESS, PLEADINGS, MOTIONS AND ORDERS

RULE 5. SERVICE AND FILING OF PLEADINGS AND OTHER PAPERS

(a) Service—When Required.

(1) *Bench Copies.* All pleadings and other papers that a party wants the Court to consider at a scheduled trial or hearing must be filed and served on all parties with a bench copy to be provided to the Court. Bench copies must clearly indicate on the top of the first page of the document the current date and time set for the proceeding, the name of the assigned judicial officer, if known, and the cause number. Bench copies that do not include the required information on the first page may be disregarded by the judicial officer and the party submitting the defective bench copies may be subject to other sanctions as provided in CR 5(d)(2).

(b) Service—How Made.

(8) *Bench Copies.* Bench copies shall be submitted to the Court on the day of filing, **but in no case later than the day prior to the hearing,** by delivering a paper copy of the documents to the office of the Court Administrator or electronically with permission of Court Administration. Bench copies provided electronically must comply with the rules regarding time and format.

[Adopted effective September 2, 2014. Amended effective September 1, 2015.]

RULE 6. TIME

(d) For Motions—Affidavits. The moving party shall file and serve all motions and supporting documents by noon five days before the scheduled proceeding. All material in response to a motion shall be filed and served by noon the court day before the scheduled proceeding.

(E) *Ex Parte Matters.* No allotted time for ex parte matters exists. Ex parte matters may be presented to the Judge in chambers or presented through the Clerk's office for a fee. Counsel is responsible for obtaining the Court file when presenting ex parte matters in chambers.

[Adopted effective September 2, 2014.]

III. PLEADINGS AND MOTIONS

RULE 7. PLEADINGS ALLOWED; FORM OF MOTIONS

(b) Motions and Other Papers.

(1) *How Made.*

(A) Reapplication on Same Facts. When an order has been applied for and refused in whole or in part or has been granted conditionally and the condition has not been performed, the same application for an order shall not be presented to another Judge without advising the second Judge of the fact that the order was previously refused or conditioned.

(B) Subsequent Motion, Different Facts. If a subsequent application is made upon an alleged different set of facts, it shall be shown by affidavit what application was made, when and to what Judge, what order or decision was made thereon, and what different facts are claimed to be shown. Any order obtained in violation of this section may be set aside.

(5) *Telephonic Argument.* Telephonic appearances are not allowed on motion docket calendars. All other requests for appearing at hearings by telephone for purposes of oral argument shall be approved by the Court and specially set by the Court Administrator.

[Amended effective September 1, 2010; amended on an emergency basis, effective January 1, 2012; amended on a permanent basis effective September 1, 2012; September 2, 2014.]

RULE 11. SIGNING AND DRAFTING OF PLEADINGS, MOTIONS, AND LEGAL MEMORANDA; SANCTIONS

(a) (1) *Frivolous Motions.* Terms and sanctions may be imposed if the Court finds that any motion or its opposition is frivolous.

[Adopted effective September 2, 2014.]

RULE 16. PRETRIAL PROCEDURE AND FORMULATING ISSUES

(b) Pretrial Order.

(1) *Settlement Conference.* The Court may order a settlement conference in any civil case. The parties or the attorneys who will be in charge of each party's case shall attend personally and shall be prepared to discuss in detail and in good faith the issues of fact and law remaining, the evidence pertaining to liability and damages and the respective positions of the par-

ties on settlement. The attorneys shall be accompanied by their clients or representatives possessing authority to settle unless excused by the Judge. The proceedings of the settlement conference shall be privileged and not recorded. If a settlement is not reached, the settlement Judge shall not make any order or preside at that trial on the merits without consent of all parties.

(2) *Pretrial Conference.* In all civil cases the Court may order a pretrial conference on its own motion or that of any party. The order for a pretrial conference should specify the duties of the parties prior to the conference, whether attendance by the parties is mandatory, the information to be submitted prior to the conference, and items to be discussed at the conference.

(3) *Scheduling Orders.* If no agreed scheduling order is filed within sixty days after the trial date is assigned, the Court Administrator, under the supervision of the Court, may set a scheduling order for the case. The scheduling order should include dates for the disclosure of primary witnesses and rebuttal witnesses. Other provisions may be required on a case by case basis. This pretrial schedule may be amended in writing by the mutual agreement of the parties only upon approval of the Court.

(i) Disclosure of Primary Witnesses. The date by which each party shall have disclosed all persons

with relevant factual or expert knowledge whom the party intends to call at trial.

(ii) Disclosure of Rebuttal Witnesses. The date by which each party shall have disclosed all persons whose knowledge did not appear relevant until the primary witnesses were disclosed and whom the party reserves the option to call as witnesses at trial.

(iii) Scope of Disclosure. Disclosure of witnesses under this rule shall include the witnesses name, address, and phone number, along with a brief description of the witnesses relevant knowledge. Disclosure of expert witnesses shall also include a summary of the expert's opinions and the basis therefore and a brief description of the expert's qualifications.

(iv) Exclusion of Testimony. Any person not disclosed in compliance with this rule and a scheduling order may not be called to testify at trial, unless the Court orders otherwise for good cause and subject to such conditions as justice requires.

(v) Discovery not Limited. This rule does not modify a party's responsibility to seasonably supplement responses to discovery requests or otherwise to comply with discovery by the deadlines set by a scheduling order.

[Amended effective September 2, 2014.]

VI. TRIALS

RULE 40. ASSIGNMENT OF CASES

(b) Methods. All parties shall file a request for trial setting utilizing the format set forth in Form 1 located in the Appendix to these Rules and shall include a list of persons entitled to notice with their addresses. All parties have the obligation to inform the Court Administrator promptly of any errors or changes in this list. A copy of the request shall be provided to the opposing party or his or her attorney and to the Court Administrator. Ten days after receipt of the first request, the Court Administrator shall schedule the trial. All trial settings will be mailed by the Court Administrator to the parties at the addresses provided in the Note for Trial and Statement of Arbitrability unless a party has submitted a completed authorization to receive notification by email to the Court Administrator. Forms for authorizing notification by email are available from the Court Administrator.

(d) Trials.

(1) *Trial Briefs.* Trial briefs shall be submitted in all cases. The submitting party shall file the original with the Clerk and provide a bench copy to the Judge and one copy to each opposing party. Plaintiff's brief shall be served and filed not less than four days before

the trial and Defendant's brief by noon of the court day before the trial.

(2) *Jury Trials.* Counsel shall report to the Judge at least one-half hour before the scheduled beginning of a jury trial and provide the Judge with a written list of the names and city of residence of witnesses and general voir dire questions to be asked of the jury. Counsel shall be prepared to present any final pretrial matters to the Court. Pretrial matters requiring argument shall be noted for hearing prior to the morning of the trial. Jury trials should be conducted with minimal interruptions of the jury's time. To this end, matters which need to be heard outside the presence of the jury should be anticipated so that they can be considered during jury breaks or before or after the jury's day. Unless otherwise ordered or agreed, plaintiffs shall occupy the counsel table closest to the jury.

(e) Continuances. Motions for trial continuances shall be in writing. Continuances of trials may be granted only by a Judge in writing for good cause shown. Continuances shall be to a date certain which shall be obtained through the Court Administrator.

(g) Pre-assignment of Cases.

(1) *By the Court.* The Judges may select those cases deemed appropriate for pre-assignment due to length of trial or complexity of issues. The Court shall notify the parties of any pre-assignment.

(2) *By Motion.* The parties by stipulation may request that a case be pre-assigned, or any party may place a motion for pre-assignment upon the appropriate motion calendar.

(3) Affidavits of prejudice against the assigned Judge which are not based on actual cause will be deemed waived unless filed by a party before receiving notice of pre-assignment.

(4) *All Matters to be Heard by Pre-assigned Judge.* Once a case has been pre-assigned, all subsequent matters and proceedings except settlement conferences shall be heard before the assigned judicial officer, if available.

(h) Notice of Calendar and Trial Changes. Whenever a cause which has been set for trial is settled or will not be tried for any reason, or if a jury is subsequently waived, the parties shall immediately notify the Court Administrator. If it becomes apparent that the time allocated for a trial will not be adequate to complete the trial, the parties shall promptly notify the Court Administrator of that fact and of the time necessary to complete the trial. The Court may assess actual costs or other sanctions for a violation of this rule.

[Amended effective September 2, 2014.]

RULE 47. JURORS

(k) Appeals on Written Record. Cases set for jury trial which are appeals based on a written record which is read to the jury may be heard without the presence of a Judge or court reporter during the reading of the record. The rulings of the hearing official will stand unless objections are renewed before trial. Counsel will meet and confer before trial and agree as much as possible on the order of the record and what portions will be read. Counsel shall notify the trial Judge before the jury is empaneled of those portions of the record upon which the trial Judge will be asked to rule and of any other matters relating to the reading of the record that need to be resolved prior to trial.

[Amended effective September 2, 2014.]

RULE 49. VERDICTS

(e) **(1)** *Proceedings When Jurors Have Agreed.* A party or attorney desiring to be present at the return of the verdict must remain in attendance at the courthouse or be available by telephone call. If a party or attorney fails to appear within twenty minutes of telephone notice to the attorney's office, home or other number, the Court may proceed to take the verdict in the absence of such party or attorney.

[Amended effective September 2, 2014.]

RULE 51. INSTRUCTIONS TO JURY AND DELIBERATION

(b) Submission. Proposed instructions utilizing Washington Pattern Jury Instructions shall be submitted by each party no later than the day before trial. The proposed instructions shall be formatted to be consecutive and contiguous rather than one per page. One printed copy each of annotated proposed instructions shall be provided to the clerk, the trial Judge, and each opposing party. Any modification to the Washington Pattern Jury Instructions shall be clearly noted on the annotated copies. A digital copy of the proposed instructions without citation shall also be provided to the trial Judge. The digital copy may be emailed to Court administration or delivered on electronic writable media storage.

[Amended effective September 2, 2014; September 1, 2015.]

RULE 52. DECISIONS, FINDINGS AND CONCLUSIONS

(a) Presentation. When the entry of Findings of Fact and Conclusions of Law are required either by rule or statute, the prevailing party, within fifteen (15) days of the decision being rendered, shall file along with proposed Findings of Fact and Conclusions of Law and a Proposed Judgment/Order and deliver a copy of same to the Court and to all other parties with a timely notice of presentment setting the matter for a date certain. On the prevailing party's failure to do so, any other party to the matter may timely note the matter for presentment subject to filing and delivery of the same required documents identified herein.

(1) *Objections.* Any party objecting to the proposed final orders submitted by another party shall file written objections with proposed substitutions and deliver a copy of same to the prevailing party and the Court by noon the day before the scheduled presentment hearing. The objecting party shall notify all parties and the Court Administrator that a special setting is required for entry of orders and that the original presentment date should be stricken.

(2) *Transcript of Ruling.* Any party obtaining a transcript of the ruling for which final orders are required shall provide a copy of same to all other parties and the Court. At the time of the hearing on entry of orders, the Court shall determine who shall ultimately be responsible for the costs of the transcript.

(3) *Intent.* The Court's intent is to finalize all matters as early as possible after oral decisions are rendered.

[Adopted effective September 2, 2014.]

VII. JUDGMENT

RULE 59. NEW TRIAL, RECON-SIDERATION, AND AMEND-MENT OF JUDGMENTS

(e) Hearing on Motion.

(4) *Reconsideration.* A motion for reconsideration shall be submitted on briefs and affidavits only, without oral argument, unless the trial Judge requests oral argument. The moving party shall file the motion and all supporting affidavits, documents and briefs at the same time, and on the date of filing, serve on or mail a copy thereof to opposing counsel, and deliver a copy thereof to the trial Judge which copy shall show the date of filing. The trial Judge shall either deny the motion and advise counsel of the ruling or request responding briefs and direct the movant to note the motion for hearing.

[Adopted effective September 2, 2014.]

X. SUPERIOR COURTS AND CLERKS

RULE 77. SUPERIOR COURTS AND JUDICIAL OFFICERS

(f) Sessions. The Court shall be in session on all judicial days from 8:30 a.m. to 12:00 noon, and from 1:15 p.m. to 4:30 p.m. Cases may be set for other dates and times. Normally jury trials begin at 8:30 a.m. and non-jury trials begin at 9:30 a.m. In case of conflict, the cases will be heard according to priority assigned because of the nature of the case. In event of a conflict which prevents a trial from beginning as scheduled, parties will be expected to be available to commence the trial at a later time in the day or week. The Court Administrator's office will be open from 8:30 a.m. to noon and from 1:15 p.m. until 4:30 p.m. on every court day; however, no documents will be accepted for filing in this office nor will documents be accepted for delivery to the Court as bench copies beyond the deadlines set forth in these rules.

(1) *Motion Dockets.* The civil, family law and criminal motion dockets shall be conducted on Monday, as more specifically set forth below. If Monday is a holiday, the motion dockets will be heard on the next regular court day. Motion dockets will not occur during judicial conference weeks. A list of those dates will be posted each year on the Grays Harbor County Superior Court Website.

(A) Civil Motion Docket. The civil motion docket will begin at 8:30 a.m. at the courthouse in Montesano. Summary judgment motions and motions requiring argument longer than five minutes per side will be heard on Monday afternoon beginning at 1:30 p.m. All motions requiring an afternoon setting shall be scheduled through the Court Administrator or specially set by a Judge.

(B) Family Law Motion Docket. The family law motion docket will begin at 9:00 a.m. at the courthouse in Montesano.

(C) Time Allowed for Oral Argument. On the morning civil and family law motion dockets, the parties shall be limited to five minutes of oral argument. At the conclusion of the time limit, argument shall cease and the matter shall be deemed submitted provided that if the Court desires to hear further argument, it may place the matter at the end of the motion docket, set the matter for further argument on the afternoon docket, or continue the matter to a specified date.

(D) Other Motion Dockets. The Court shall conduct a motion docket for paternity cases and default domestic cases on Mondays at 1:30 p.m. at the Juvenile Court Facility located in Aberdeen, Washington. The domestic violence protection order petitions will be heard on Monday at 3:00 p.m. at the courthouse in Montesano.

(E) Scheduling Motions. All matters for the morning dockets shall be noted through the Clerk's office. All matters for the afternoon or special setting dockets shall be set by the Court Administrator.

(i) Confirmation Process. Any motion noted on an afternoon docket will be stricken from the calendar unless the hearing is confirmed with the Court Administrator in person, by email, or by telephone at 360–249–5311. Such confirmation shall be given by noon on the Thursday prior to the hearing.

(ii) Continuances. Motions may be continued one time by stipulation of the parties. Additional continuances require approval of the Court. If a moving party is not ready to argue his or her motion at the time it is called by the Court for reasons other than lack of service duly attempted, the matter shall be stricken subject to being renoted by the moving party at a later date.

(F) Petitions for Adoption. Uncontested petitions for adoption shall be specially set for Mondays at 8:15 a.m. after first obtaining approval of the Court Administrator.

[Amended effective September 2, 2014.]

RULE 79. BOOKS AND RECORDS KEPT BY THE CLERK

(d) Other Books and Records of Clerk.

(1) *Exhibits.* When an exhibit is marked for identification it becomes part of the Court record and, except when used in the courtroom or on appeal, shall not be removed from the Clerk's custody without a Court order. After 30 days' written notice to all parties of record following final disposition of a civil or family law case, the Court may order the Clerk to destroy or dispose of physical evidence unless good cause is shown why it should be preserved.

[Amended effective September 2, 2014.]

LOCAL FAMILY LAW CIVIL RULES (LFLCR)

RULE 1. SCOPE OF RULES

The Superior Court Civil Rules (CR) and the Grays Harbor County Local Superior Court Civil Rules (LCR) govern procedure for all civil matters including family law matters except where superseded by a local family law court rule (LFLCR). In family law matters, if a conflict exists between a LCR and a LFLCR, the LFLCR shall be [1] take precedence and govern.

[Adopted effective September 2, 2014.]

[1] So in original.

RULE 16. PRETRIAL PROCEDURE AND FORMULATING ISSUES

(b) Pretrial Order.

(1) *Settlement Conference.* The Court may order a settlement conference in any family law case on its own motion or on the motion of a party. The motion of a party for a settlement conference shall be noted on the family law motion calendar. If a settlement conference is ordered, all parties and their attorneys, if any, shall attend personally unless excused by the settlement Judge and all persons in attendance shall be prepared to discuss in detail and in good faith the issues of fact and law remaining, the evidence pertaining to the issues, and the respective positions of the parties on settlement. Settlement conference proceedings shall be privileged and not recorded. If a settlement is not reached, the settlement Judge shall not make any subsequent rulings or preside at that trial on the merits without consent of all parties.

(2) *Pretrial Conference.* In all family law cases, the Court Administrator will schedule a pretrial conference on the family law motion calendar the week before the week the case is scheduled for trial. Prior to the pretrial conference, if the parties have not agreed on the division of the parties' assets and liabilities, each party shall, utilizing a format consistent with that set forth in Form 2 located in the Appendix to these Rules, file and exchange a document setting forth that party's proposed allocation and the estimated values of the items before the Court for division. The attorneys and/or parties shall attend the pretrial conference to discuss the status of the case and readiness for trial.

(A) Pretrial Statement. In any contested family law action in which property division, the parenting plan, spousal maintenance, or child support is at issue, each party shall serve on the other party and file with the Court a written summary setting forth a brief statement of the issues in dispute and a brief statement of the party's proposed resolution of the issues.

Unless otherwise excused by the Court, each party's pretrial statement must be served and filed no later than the day of pretrial conference or settlement conference, whichever occurs first, unless otherwise ordered by the Court. Failure to timely serve and file the pretrial statement as required may result in sanctions.

[Adopted effective September 2, 2014.]

LOCAL MANDATORY ARBITRATION RULES (LMAR)

I. SCOPE AND PURPOSE OF RULES

RULE 1.1. APPLICATION OF RULES

The Mandatory Arbitration Rules as supplemented by these local rules are not designed to address every question which may arise during the arbitration process and the rules give considerable discretion to the arbitrator. The arbitrator should not hesitate to be informal and expeditious, consistent with the purpose of the statute and rules.

[Amended effective September 2, 2014.]

RULE 1.2. MATTERS SUBJECT TO ARBITRATION

The Superior Court of Washington for Grays Harbor County authorizes mandatory arbitration on all matters where no party asserts a claim for damages in excess of fifty thousand dollars pursuant to MAR 1.2. and subject to the payment of any filing fees required by local ordinance for such matters.

[Amended on an emergency basis effective January 27, 2006. Amended effective September 2, 2014; amended on an emergency basis effective December 8, 2014; amended on a permanent basis effective September 1, 2015.]

RULE 1.3. RELATIONSHIP TO SUPE-RIOR COURT JURISDICTION AND OTHER RULES

(c) Motions. All motions in which a party is requesting the matter be submitted to arbitration shall be noted on the civil motions calendar in accordance with Grays Harbor County Local Rules, except as otherwise provided in these arbitration rules.

[Amended effective September 2, 2014.]

II. TRANSFER TO ARBITRATION AND ASSIGNMENT OF ARBITRATOR

RULE 2.1. TRANSFER TO ARBITRATION

(a) Statement of Arbitrability. In every civil or family law case to be arbitrated, the party filing the note for trial shall complete a statement of arbitrability substantially in the form set forth in Form 1 in the Appendix of Forms for the LCRs.

(b) Response to Statement of Arbitrability. Any party disagreeing with the statement of arbitrability shall serve and file a response to the statement of arbitrability with a copy of the statement of arbitrability and note for trial setting objected to within ten days of the service of the statement of arbitrability and note for trial setting. A copy of both the statement and response shall be furnished to the Court Administrator by the responding party at the time of filing so that an objection calendar may be prepared. In the absence of such a response, the statement of arbitrability shall be deemed correct, and a nonresponding party shall be deemed to have stipulated to arbitration if the statement of arbitrability provides that the case is arbitrable. Otherwise, the case will not be subject to arbitration except by stipulation of the parties or Court order and will be set for trial on the trial calendar.

(d) By Stipulation. If all parties file a stipulation to arbitration under MAR 8.1, the case will be placed on the arbitration calendar regardless of the nature of the case or amount in controversy.

[Amended effective September 2, 2014.]

III. ARBITRATORS

RULE 3.1. QUALIFICATIONS

(a) Arbitration Panel. There shall be a panel of arbitrators in such numbers as the Presiding Judge or his/her designee may from time to time determine. A person desiring to serve as an arbitrator shall complete an application on a form prescribed by the Court and submit the application to the Court Administrator. A copy of said application of a person appointed as an arbitrator will be available upon request by any party and will be mailed to a requesting party at the party's own expense. The oath of office on the form prescribed by the Court must be completed and filed with the Court Administrator prior to an appointed applicant being placed on the panel.

(b) Declining An Appointment. Any arbitrator to whom a case has been assigned may decline to serve based on unavailability, conflict of interest, or other reason premised on good cause by immediately notifying the presiding Judge or his/her designee of such declination and the grounds for same. Upon declining to serve, the arbitrator must return all case materials to the presiding Judge or his/her designee.

[Amended effective September 2, 2014.]

IV. PROCEDURES AFTER ASSIGNMENT

RULE 4.2. DISCOVERY

(b) Discovery Pending at the Time Arbitrator is Assigned. Discovery pending at the time the case is assigned to an arbitrator is stayed pending order from the arbitrator or as the parties may stipulate or as authorized by MAR 4.2.

[Amended effective September 2, 2014.]

V. HEARING

RULE 5.1. NOTICE OF HEARING

An arbitration hearing may be scheduled at any reasonable time and place chosen by the arbitrator considering available dates indicated by the parties. The arbitrator may grant a continuance without Court order. The parties may stipulate to a continuance only with the permission of the arbitrator. The arbitrator shall give reasonable notice of the hearing date and any continuance to the presiding Judge or designee.

[Amended effective September 2, 2014.]

RULE 5.2. PREHEARING STATEMENT OF PROOF

(a) Generally. In addition to the requirements of MAR 5.2, each party shall also furnish the arbitrator

with copies of pleadings and other documents contained in the court file which that party deems relevant.

[Amended effective September 2, 2014.]

VI. AWARD

RULE 6.2. FILING OF AWARD

(a) Extensions of Time. A request by an arbitrator for an extension of time for the filing of an award shall be presented to the Presiding Judge or his/her designee. The arbitrator shall give the parties notice of any extension granted. Recurring delays in the filing of awards will result in the removal of the arbitrator from the panel at the discretion of the Court.

(b) Return of Exhibits. When an award is filed, the arbitrator shall return all exhibits to the parties who offered them during the hearing.

[Amended effective September 2, 2014.]

RULE 6.4. COSTS AND ATTORNEY FEES

(a) Request.

(1) *Compensation of Arbitrator.* Arbitrators shall be compensated at a rate to be set by the state. This compensation shall not exceed $1,000.00 without re-

ceiving prior approval from the Presiding Judge or his/her designee. Requests to exceed the $1,000.00 limit shall be submitted in advance if possible to the Presiding Judge or his/her designee. In situations where the arbitrator goes over the limit without gaining prior approval, a written explanation shall be attached to the arbitrator's request for compensation. Hearing time and reasonable preparation time by the arbitrator are compensable. Arbitrators may be reimbursed a sum not to exceed $25.00 for costs incurred unless otherwise authorized in advance by the Presiding Judge or his/her designee.

(2) *Form.* When the award is filed, the arbitrator shall submit to the Court Administrator a request for payment on a form prescribed by the Court. The Court Administrator shall screen these requests, consult with the Presiding Judge or his/her designee in unusual circumstances, and process the compensation requests for payment.

[Adopted effective September 2, 2014.]

VII. TRIAL DE NOVO

RULE 7.1. REQUEST FOR TRIAL DE NOVO

(a) Service and Filing. The request for trial de novo shall be accompanied by a request for trial

setting using Form 1 in the Appendix of Forms to these local rules.

(d) Calendar. When a trial de novo is requested, trial shall be set by the Court Administrator.

[Amended effective September 2, 2014.]

VIII. GENERAL PROVISIONS

RULE 8.1. STIPULATIONS

(c) To Arbitrate Other Cases. If a case not otherwise subject to mandatory arbitration is transferred to arbitration by stipulation, the arbitrator may grant any relief which could have been granted if the case were determined by a Judge.

[Amended effective September 2, 2014.]

RULE 8.4. TITLE AND CITATION

These rules are known and cited as the Local Mandatory Arbitration Rules for the Superior Court of Grays Harbor County. LMAR is the official abbreviation.

[Amended effective September 2, 2014.]

RULE 8.7. ADMINISTRATION

(a) Court Administrator. The Court Administrator, under the supervision of the Superior Court Judges, shall supervise arbitration under these rules and perform any additional duties which may be delegated by the Judges.

(b) Duties. The Court Administrator, under the supervision of the Superior Court Judges, shall have the power and duty to:

(1) Develop and maintain local arbitration procedural rules;

(2) Select and appoint the panel of arbitrators provided in Rule 3.1(a);

(3) Remove a person from a panel of arbitrators;

(4) Establish procedures for selecting an arbitrator not inconsistent with the Mandatory Arbitration Rules or these rules;

(5) Review the administration and operation of the arbitration program periodically and make recommen-dations to the Superior Court Judges as he/she deems appropriate to improve the program.

[Amended effective September 2, 2014.]

LOCAL GUARDIAN AD LITEM RULES (LGALR)

RULE 1.   SCOPE AND DEFINITIONS

(b) Definitions. As used in this rule, the following additional term means:

(5) *Client.* "Client" for purposes of these rules shall mean the person(s) for whom the guardian ad litem has been appointed.

(c) Appointment of Guardian Ad Litem. Unless the parties to the case agree on the appointment of a specific guardian ad litem, the Judge shall select a guardian ad litem from the applicable registry as required. For Title 13 cases, the Court shall appoint the individual or individuals to whom the Grays Harbor County contract for service as a guardian ad litem in dependency actions is currently awarded or to a Court Appointed Special Advocate ("CASA") volunteer program unless a conflict exists. Where a conflict exists in such actions, the Court shall then appoint a guardian ad litem who has met all other qualifications for inclusion on a Title 13 RCW Guardian Ad Litem registry. For Title 26 RCW paternity cases requiring appointment of a guardian ad litem who has entered into a contract with the State of Washington to provide such services, the Court shall only appoint individuals who are currently under contract with the state to provide such services unless no such individual is available.

[Adopted effective September 1, 2012. Amended effective September 2, 2014; September 1, 2015.]

RULE 2.   GENERAL RESPONSIBILITIES OF THE GUARDIAN AD LITEM

The general responsibilities of guardians ad litem operating in this county shall be consistent with the state rules with the following clarifications and additions:

(a) Represent best interests. A guardian ad litem who is also an attorney may, however, answer simple procedural questions of another party who is unrepresented by counsel to facilitate clarity in the proceedings.

(m) Ex parte communications. During the pendency of a case, a guardian ad litem shall communicate privately with the Judge only for purposes of obtaining special instructions from the Judge as to the scope of the guardian ad litem's investigation, to communicate an agreement of the parties, to present agreed orders, to obtain an ex parte restraining order or ex parte contempt show cause order for the protection of the guardian ad litem's client, to obtain access to sealed or confidential court files, or in an emergency situation to protect the life of the guardian ad litem's client. In all such cases, the guardian ad litem should notify the parties or their counsel of such communications and the content of same within a reasonable period of time.

(q) Records of time and expenses.

(1) For Title 11 RCW and Title 26 RCW cases where the county guarantees payment of the guardian ad litem fees and costs, the guardian ad litem shall file with the Court a notice and motion in the form prescribed by the Court with an itemized statement for payment of the guardian ad litem fees and costs and provide a copy of same to each party.

(2) For Title 13 RCW cases where the county guarantees payment of the guardian ad litem fees and costs, the guardian ad litem, if not serving under an annual contract for services with the county, shall file with the Court a petition and proposed order with an itemized statement for payment of said fees and costs.

(3) For paternity cases where the state guarantees payment of the guardian ad litem fees and costs, the guardian ad litem shall complete the form provided by the state and attach an itemized statement and submit same to the Grays Harbor County Deputy Prosecuting Attorney for the Office of Support Enforcement within sixty days of entry of final orders.

(4) For private pay cases, the guardian ad litem shall either submit an invoice and itemized statement to the parties for payment or submit a notice, motion and itemized statement to the Court for entry of a judgment and order for payment of fees.

At any time during the course of an active case, any party may request an itemized statement from the guardian ad litem of the fees and costs incurred to date which the guardian ad litem shall provide within ten working days. For cases where the county guarantees payment of the guardian ad litem fees and costs, to avoid additional charges for court appearances and related costs to prepare such documents, the notice and motion or petition for payment may be made at the end of the case rather than as progressive motions at the discretion of the guardian ad litem.

[Adopted effective September 1, 2012. Amended effective September 2, 2014.]

RULE 3. ROLES AND RESPONSIBILITIES OF GUARDIAN AD LITEM IN TITLE 13 RCW JUVENILE COURT PROCEEDINGS

(b) Concurrent planning. In Title 13 RCW juvenile court proceedings, a guardian ad litem shall explore concurrent planning and make a timely recommendation to the Court for a permanent plan for the child. In order to accommodate the guardian ad litem's duties in Title 13 RCW juvenile court proceedings, the guardian ad litem shall be timely notified of and invited to all Department staffings, meetings, and other proceedings involving the dependency to which counsel for the parents are provided notice and shall be provided access to and/or copies of all documentation in the possession of the Department involving the parties to the dependency within thirty days of the appointment of the guardian ad litem and at no cost to the guardian ad litem subject to the Department's responsibility to redact certain identifying information and to provide updated information as it becomes available to the Department as set forth in Title 13 RCW.

[Adopted effective September 1, 2012. Amended effective September 2, 2014; September 1, 2015.]

RULE 5. APPOINTMENTS OF GUARDIAN AD LITEM

(c) Guardian Ad Litem Registries. Meeting the minimum qualifications necessary to be eligible for inclusion on any Grays Harbor County guardian ad litem registry does not guarantee that an individual will be approved for such inclusion. The Grays Harbor Superior Court judiciary reserves the right establish an application process and to reject any applicant.

[Adopted effective September 1, 2012. Amended effective September 2, 2014.]

RULE 7. GRIEVANCE PROCEDURES

(k) Purpose statement. The procedure for handling grievances and/or imposing discipline against a guardian ad litem provided hereunder are intended to facilitate a process which is fair, expedited, and protective of all participants.

(*l*) Procedure for Filing a Grievance.

(1) *Filing the Grievance.* Only a party to a case may file a grievance against a guardian ad litem. The grievance must be in writing and filed with the Court Administrator. The complaint must state with specificity the act or failure to act of concern to the complaining party and shall include the following information:

(A) The name, mailing address, telephone number, and e-mail address (if any) of the person filing the grievance;

(B) The case number and case name;

(C) The name of the Judge or Court Commissioner hearing the case;

(D) The trial date;

(E) Whether the party filing the grievance has discussed the complaint with the guardian ad litem;

(F) What action the guardian ad litem has taken to address the complaint;

(G) Which provision of the Order Appointing Guardian Ad Litem or of these rules the party filing the grievance is claiming the guardian ad litem has violated;

(H) A brief, concise statement of the specific facts underlying each alleged violation; and

(I) What the party filing the grievance is requesting be done to correct the problem complained of and why.

(2) *Grievances Filed During the pendency of a Case.*

(A) If the grievance pertains to a pending case or if trial in the pending case is underway, the Court Administrator shall, within three business days of receipt, forward the grievance to the presiding or assigned judicial officer to handle the grievance with a copy being sent to the affected guardian ad litem.

(B) Within three business days of receiving the grievance, the judicial officer shall make an initial determination of whether or not there is adequate cause to proceed with the grievance.

(C) If the initial determination is that the grievance is without adequate cause, the matter will be closed and all parties will be so notified. The grievance shall be held as a confidential, sealed record in the files of the Court Administrator for six years following dismissal of the grievance unless specifically directed otherwise by the judicial officer making the initial determination.

(D) If the initial determination is that there is adequate cause to proceed with the grievance, the guardian ad litem shall be allowed to file a response to the grievance within fourteen days of receiving notice from the Court by forwarding a copy of the response to the complaining party with the original response being sent to the Court Administrator who will deliver same to the judicial officer making the initial determination.

(E) Upon receipt of the response from the guardian ad litem or upon passage of the fourteen day response period, whichever is sooner, the judicial officer shall review the response and thereafter issue a final written or oral disposition of the matter no later than twenty-five days following the filing of the grievance. The original copy of a written disposition or a transcript of an oral disposition shall be placed in the grievance file with copies of the written disposition being forwarded to the complaining party and to the guardian ad litem.

(F) If the final written disposition is that the grievance should be dismissed, the procedure with regard to retention of the grievance set forth in paragraph 7(*l*)(2)(C) above shall be followed. If, as part of the final disposition, there has been a finding that the grievance was not brought in good faith or was otherwise frivolous or designed to impact the pending proceedings through increased costs to the other party or guardian ad litem, terms in the form of costs or other sanctions may be imposed against the grieving party.

(G) If the final written disposition is that the grievance was brought in good faith and has been determined to be well-founded, there shall be a method of discipline to be imposed upon the guardian ad litem set forth in the disposition which shall take effect immediately. Accepted forms of discipline shall consist of one or more of the following: (1) a verbal or written reprimand, (2) removal from the pending case; (3) suspension of the guardian ad litem from the registry for a period not to exceed ninety days, (4) suspension of the guardian ad litem from the registry until such time as the guardian ad litem has provided satisfactory proof of completing additional training in a specific area described in the disposition, (5) imposition of terms in the form of costs or other monetary sanctions, and/or (6) permanent removal of the guardian ad litem from the registry for Title 11 RCW, Title 13 RCW, and/or

Title 26 RCW cases. If the discipline imposed is permanent removal from any guardian ad litem registry, notification of same shall be forwarded to the Office of the Administrator for the Courts for circulation to other counties. The confidential file of the grievance shall include the original grievance, the guardian ad litem's response, and the written initial and final dispositions of the matter and shall be maintained by the Court Administrator for a period for no less than six years.

(H) Timelines stated herein may be modified by the judicial officer for good cause. In calculating times, items mailed shall be deemed received by the addressee three days after the date of mailing.

(3) *Grievances Filed After the Conclusion of a Case or After Discharge of the Guardian Ad Litem.* If the grievance pertains to a case in which final orders have been entered or an order discharging the guardian ad litem has been entered, the Court Administrator shall, within five business days, forward the grievance to the judicial officer who presided over the trial in the case or who signed the final orders/order of discharge with a copy to the affected guardian ad litem. Thereafter, the procedures set forth in section 7(*l*)(2) shall be followed except that five additional business days shall be added to each subsequent deadline indicated in that section.

[Adopted effective September 1, 2012. Amended effective September 2, 2014.]

LOCAL CRIMINAL RULES (LCrR)

3. RIGHTS OF DEFENDANTS

RULE 3.1. RIGHT TO AND ASSIGNMENT OF LAWYER

(d) **Assignment of Lawyer.** Unless the defendant has indicated an intent to hire private counsel, appointment of counsel for indigent defendants shall be made by the Court at the preliminary appearance. The clerk shall notify the appointed attorney and the attorney shall file a written notice of appearance. The Prosecuting Attorney shall email copies of the Information, Motion and Declaration for Arrest Warrant, Defendant's Criminal History and Adult Risk Assessment to the defense attorney on the same day as the first appearance or when counsel is appointed. In addition, the Prosecutor shall file as confidential the Adult Risk Assessment if one was created.

(4)(a) *Compliance With Standards for Indigent Defense and County Contracts.* Attorneys appointed to provide indigent defense services under this Rule shall submit the required compliance certification to the Court Administrator each quarter and a caseload update and proof of insurance to the County Commissioners as required under the attorney contract for

services. Failure of an attorney to submit the required compliance certifications will result in requests for payment being denied until compliance has been achieved.

[Amended effective September 1, 2010; September 2, 2014; September 1, 2015.]

RULE 3.2. RELEASE OF ACCUSED

(b) **Relevant Factors.** In applying for pretrial release, a defendant should be prepared to provide the Court with information under CrR 3.2(b) and other relevant information subject to the right of the defendant not to give evidence of an incriminating nature against himself. An application form will be available in the courtrooms.

[Amended effective September 1, 2010; September 2, 2014.]

RULE 3.3. TIME FOR TRIAL

(f) **Setting of Trial Date.** The State and the defendant or defense counsel shall set trial, selecting from a list the Court Administrator provides, at the arraignment hearing.

[Amended effective September 1, 2010; September 2, 2014; September 1, 2015.]

4.   PROCEDURES PRIOR TO TRIAL

RULE 4.2.   PLEAS

When a case is set for trial, the Court Administrator shall assign a date for a pretrial conference which shall be at least two weeks prior to the trial date. Pleas of guilty should be entered by the pretrial conference. The Court may refuse to grant a discretionary reduction or dismissal of charges or counts if a plea is entered after the time for the pretrial conference. If the defendant fails to appear at the pretrial conference, the Court may strike the trial date and issue a warrant for the defendant's arrest.

[Adopted effective September 2, 2014.]

RULE 4.5.   OMNIBUS HEARING

(d) Motions.

(1) *How Made.* The moving party shall note motions in a timely manner so that all hearings and motions (other than final pretrial motions which can be completed before the time the trial is set to begin) will be heard at least seven days prior to the date of trial. Failure to timely note motions for hearing in accordance with this rule shall be deemed a waiver of the pretrial hearing on such motions. The civil rules relating to motions and hearings (LCR 7) apply to criminal cases.

(2) *Legal Authority in Support of Motions.* Counsel shall submit briefs that specify legal authority in support of, or in opposition to, a pending motion. The brief of the moving party shall be submitted at least four days before the scheduled hearing, and the brief of the responding party shall be filed at least by noon one day prior to the day of the hearing. Copies of all motion briefs shall be submitted to the Judge who has been assigned to hear the motion.

(3) *Reapplication on Same Facts.* When a motion seeking relief has been refused in whole or in part or has been granted conditionally and the condition has not been performed, the same application for relief shall not be presented to another Judge without advising the second Judge of the fact that the prior motion was previously refused or conditioned.

(4) *Subsequent Motion, Different Facts.* If a subsequent motion for relief is made upon an alleged different state of facts, it shall be shown by affidavit what application was made, when and to what Judge, what order or decision was made thereon, and what new facts are claimed to be shown. Any order obtained in violation of this section may be set aside.

(h) Memorandum. The parties may submit an agreed order on omnibus. If an agreed order will not be submitted, each party shall prepare and submit an omnibus application substantially in the form set forth in Criminal Rules for Superior Court on or before the time set for the omnibus hearing. It is not necessary to make separate written motions where such motions have been checked on the party's omnibus application. The moving party shall note such motions for hearing in accordance with these rules. Briefs and supporting documents shall be submitted as required by these local rules.

[Amended effective September 1, 2010; September 2, 2014.]

6.   PROCEDURES AT TRIAL

RULE 6.1.   TRIAL BY JURY
OR BY THE COURT

If a party fails to comply with these local rules regarding trial procedures, the Court may impose monetary sanctions, or enter such other orders, as the Court deems appropriate to address and remedy the failure to comply.

(a) Trial by Jury.

(1) *Pretrial matters on or before Trial Day.* Counsel shall report to the assigned Trial Judge at least one-half hour before the scheduled beginning of a jury trial and provide the Judge with a written list of the names and city of residence of witnesses and general voir dire questions to be asked of the jury. Counsel shall be prepared to present any final pretrial matters to the Court. Pretrial matters requiring argument shall be noted for hearing prior to the morning of the trial. Jury trials should be conducted with minimal interruptions of the jury's time. To this end, matters which need to be heard outside the presence of the jury should be anticipated so that they can be considered during jury breaks or before or after the jury's day. Unless otherwise ordered or agreed, plaintiffs shall occupy the counsel table closest to the jury.

(e) Trial Briefs. Trial briefs shall be required in all cases. The original shall be filed with the Clerk, with one copy provided to the Judge and one copy provided to each opposing party. The prosecuting attorney's brief shall be served and filed not less than four court days before the trial and the defendant's brief shall be served and filed by noon of the court day before the trial.

[Adopted effective September 1, 2010. Amended effective September 2, 2014.]

RULE 6.15. INSTRUCTIONS AND ARGUMENTS

(a) Proposed Instructions. Proposed instructions utilizing Washington Pattern Jury Instructions shall be submitted by each party no later than three days before trial. The proposed instructions shall be for-matted to be consecutive and contiguous rather than one per page. One printed copy each of annotated proposed instructions shall be provided to the clerk, the trial Judge, and each opposing party. Any modification to the Washington Pattern Jury Instructions shall be clearly noted on the annotated copies. A digital copy of the proposed instructions without citation shall also be provided to the trial Judge. The digital copy may be emailed to Court administration or delivered on electronic writable media storage.

[Adopted effective September 2, 2014. Amended effective September 1, 2015.]

7. PROCEDURES FOLLOWING CONVICTION

RULE 7.1. PROCEDURES BEFORE SENTENCING

(d) Other Reports.

(1) *Counsel's Presentence Reports.* All counsel shall submit written presentence reports to the Court no later than noon on the court day preceding sentencing.

[Adopted effective September 2, 2014.]

RULE 7.2. SENTENCING

(a) Generally. A sentencing hearing shall be set on Fridays at 8:30 a.m. for defendants whose standard range sentence exceeds 365 days and requires imprisonment with the Department of Corrections. The sentencing hearing shall be set with the Court Administrator unless ordered by the Court.

(e) Work Release. Defendants requesting work release shall submit an application, a form for which will be available in the courtrooms. Work release applications shall be submitted to the corrections facility staff for comment before being submitted to the Court for approval.

(f) Release of Information. Whenever a person is allowed to receive credit against a jail sentence for time spent in a place other than the Grays Harbor County Jail, the County Corrections Department may require the person to complete an appropriate release of information form so that the corrections staff can fully monitor the time served.

[Amended effective September 2, 2014; September 1, 2015.]

LOCAL JUVENILE COURT RULES (LJuCR)

TITLE I. SCOPE AND APPLICATION OF RULES

RULE 1.0. COURT SCHEDULE

Juvenile Court proceedings are generally held at the Grays Harbor County Juvenile Facility located at 103 Hagara Street, Aberdeen, Washington, with calendars scheduled as follows:

The times and dates for Dependency, Truancy, CHINS & At–Risk–Youth calendar schedules will be posted on the Superior Court Website as well as the Superior Court Clerk's Office and the Juvenile Court facility bulletin board.

The time and place for Juvenile Criminal trials, Dependency and Termination of Parental Rights testimonial proceedings will be as set by the Court Administrator.

[Amended effective September 1, 2010; September 2, 2014; amended on an emergency basis effective December 8, 2014; amended on a permanent basis effective September 1, 2015.]

RULE 1.6. COUNSEL

Insofar as applicable, the rules relating to appointment of counsel, withdrawal, and fees in criminal cases shall likewise apply to juvenile cases. No attorney for parent or child, whether privately retained or appointed, shall be permitted to withdraw without Court approval.

[Amended effective September 2, 2014.]

RULE 9.2. ADDITIONAL RIGHT TO REPRESENTATION BY LAWYER

(d)(1)(a) *Compliance With Standards for Indigent Defense and County Contracts.* Attorneys appointed to provide indigent defense services under this Rule shall submit the required compliance certification to the Court Administrator each quarter and a caseload update and proof of insurance to the County Commissioners as required under the attorney contract for services. Failure of an attorney to submit the required compliance certifications will result in requests for payment being denied until compliance has been achieved.

[Adopted effective September 2, 2014.]

LOCAL RULES FOR APPEAL OF DECISIONS OF COURTS OF LIMITED JURISDICTION (LRALJ)

TITLE 7.   BRIEFS

RULE 7.1.   GENERALLY

At the time of the filing of appellant's brief, the appellant shall also note the matter for hearing on the motion docket for a hearing date not less than 30 days from the date of filing of appellant's brief. The hearing should be set for no later than five months after the date the appeal is taken.

[Adopted effective September 2, 2014.]

FORMS

FORM 1. NOTE FOR TRIAL AND INITIAL STATEMENT OF ARBITRABILITY

SUPERIOR COURT OF WASHINGTON IN AND FOR GRAYS HARBOR COUNTY	No.
vs. Plaintiff,	**NOTE FOR TRIAL AND INITIAL STATEMENT OF ARBITRATION LCR 40(b); LMAR 2.1(A)**
Defendant.	**(CLERK'S ACTION REQUIRED)**

TO: Opposing counsel or party and Court Administrator, the undersigned requests a trial date and certifies that the case is at issue and further certifies:

1. Nature of the case:_____
2. Jury of twelve_____   Jury of six___   Non-Jury___
3. Estimated trial time: My case____ days (hours).   Total:____ days (hours).
4. Number of witnesses I will call: Expert:____   Non-expert:____
5. Dates unavailable to me:_____
_____
_____

6. An accurate list of the names and addresses of all persons entitled to notice is attached hereto or has previously been provided.

INITIAL STATEMENT OF ARBITRABILITY

☐ This case is subject to arbitration because the sole relief being sought is a money judgment and involves no claim in excess of fifty thousand dollars ($50,000), exclusive of attorney fees, interest and costs.

☐ This case is not subject to mandatory arbitration because:
    ___ This is a domestic matter and the parties do not stipulate to arbitration.
    ___ Plaintiff's claim exceeds $50,000.
    ___ Plaintiff seeks relief other than a money judgment.
    ___ Defendant's counter or cross claim exceeds $50,000.
    ___ Defendant's counter or cross claim seeks relief other than a money judgment.

NOTE FOR TRIAL AND INITIAL STATEMENT OF ARBITRABILITY - Page 1 of 2

☐ This case is not subject to mandatory arbitration but the undersigned stipulates that the case may
be submitted to arbitration.

Date:_____

Signed:_____

Typed name:_____

WSBA No._____

Attorney for:_____

Address:_____

_____

Phone:_____

E-mail:_____

<u>List of the names and addresses or all persons that received notice:</u>

Name:_____   Name:_____

Attorney for:_____   Attorney for:_____

Address:_____   Address:_____

_____   _____

Phone:_____   Phone:_____

E-mail:_____   E-mail:_____

Name:_____   Name:_____

Attorney for:_____   Attorney for:_____

Address:_____   Address:_____

_____   _____

Phone:_____   Phone:_____

E-mail:_____   E-mail:_____

NOTE FOR TRIAL AND INITIAL STATEMENT OF ARBITRABILITY - Page 2 of 2

[Adopted on an emergency basis effective December 8, 2014; adopted on a permanent basis
effective September 1, 2015.]

FORM 2. PROPOSED DIVISION OF ASSETS AND LIABILITIES IN FAMILY LAW CASES

In re Marriage of

	ASSETS & DEBTS	Date of Value	Gross Value	Liens/ Debts	NET VALUE	TO HUSBAND		TO WIFE	
						COMM	SEP	COMM	SEP
1	Sample property - house	#####	550,000	320,000	230,000		20,000	210,000	
2	Sample property - 401k	#####	621,418		621,418	621,418			
3	Sample inheritance - Schwab ***1234	#####	161,000		161,000		161,000		
4	Sample debt - VISA	#####		12,250	-12,250			-12,250	
5					0				
6					0				
7					0				
8					0				
9					0				
10					0				
11					0				
12					0				
13					0				
14					0				
15					0				
16					0				
17					0				
18					0				
19					0				
20					0				
21					0				
22					0				
23					0				
24					0				
25					0				
26					0				
27					0				
28					0				
29					0				
30					0				
31					0				
32					0				
33					0				
34					0				
35					0				
36					0				
37					0				
38					0				
39					0				
40					0				
41					0				
42					0				
43					0				
44					0				
45					0				
46					0				
47					0				
48					0				
49					0				
50					0				
	TOTALS		1,332,418	332,250	1,000,168	621,418	181,000	197,750	0

	MARITAL LIEN >	-252,792	252,792
Wife's percentage (entered by user) 55.0%	Each party's total dollars	368,626	450,542
Husband's percentage (automatic) 45.0%	Each party's percentage	45%	55%

Reimbursements owed party-to-party *outside the division of community property*:

Husband owed for daycare overpayment:	150	
Husband owed for separate property interest in residence:	20,000	
Husband owed:		
Wife owed for support arrearages:		2,300
Wife owed:		
Wife owed:		
FINAL TRANSFER PAYMENT = MARITAL LIEN + SUM OF REIMBURSEMENTS >	-234,942	234,942

[Adopted on an emergency basis effective October 17, 2014; adopted on a permanent basis effective September 1, 2015.]

DISTRICT COURT

LOCAL RULES OF GRAYS HARBOR COUNTY DISTRICT COURT

Including Amendments Received Through
August 15, 2015

Table of Rules

I. LOCAL ADMINISTRATIVE RULES

LAR 5. COURT ORGANIZATION; PRESIDING JUDGE

(a) Court Organization; Departments. The Grays Harbor County District Court district includes all of Grays Harbor County. Grays Harbor County District Court has two departments: Department No. 1, located in Montesano, Washington, and Department No. 2, located in Aberdeen, Washington. The district judges are authorized to hear cases in either department.

(b) Assignment and Filing of Cases by Departments.

(1) All cases filed with the Grays Harbor County District Court shall be filed, maintained and heard in the department designated by the Presiding Judge.

(2) Pursuant to a reorganization of the court in 2003, Dept. 1 will be designated as the department where all criminal cases will be filed and heard, and Dept. 2 will be designated as the department where all civil cases will be filed and heard.

(3) The Presiding Judge may order the transfer of any case to another judge or department to assure the expeditions and efficient handling of all cases and equal distribution of the case load among the district

judges. In the event of recusal or other disqualification of a department's judge, the court administrator shall cause the case to be heard by another judge, visiting judge or judge pro tempore. The case file shall not be transferred to another department unless ordered by the Presiding Judge.

[Adopted effective September 1, 1999. Amended effective September 1, 2003.]

LAR 11. OFFICE HOURS

At least one of the two Grays Harbor County District Court departments and offices with a clerk in attendance shall be open to the public each judicial day, except Saturday, from 8:00 a.m. to 12:00 p.m. and 1:00 p.m. to 5:00 p.m.

[Adopted effective September 1, 1999; amended effective September 1, 2003.]

II. LOCAL CIVIL RULES

LCR 7. PLEADINGS ALLOWED; FORM [DELETED]

[Adopted effective September 1, 1999; deleted effective September 1, 2009.]

LCR 26. DISCOVERY

(a) **Limited Discovery Permitted.** Except as provided in LCRLJ 30, 33, and 34, the procedures authorized by Rules 26—37 of the Superior Court Civil Rules (CR) applicable for use in the Superior Court may be available only upon prior permission of the court. Appropriate sanctions as permitted by CR 37 will be applicable for a party's failure to comply with LCR 30, 33, and 34.

[Adopted effective September 1, 1999.]

LCR 30. DEPOSITIONS UPON ORAL EXAMINATION

(a) **Deposition of a Party.** A party will be entitled to take one deposition of another party without prior permission of the court, and in accordance with CR 30.

[Adopted effective September 1, 1999.]

LCR 33. INTERROGATORIES TO PARTIES

(a) **Limited Interrogatories without Prior Approval of the Court.** Any party may serve upon any other party not more than one set of written interrogatories containing not more than thirty questions, including those authorized by CRLJ 26(b), without prior permission of the court. Separate sections, paragraphs or categories contained in one interrogatory shall be considered separate questions for the purpose of this rule.

[Adopted effective September 1, 1999.]

LCR 34. REQUESTS FOR PRODUCTION OF DOCUMENTS AND THINGS

(b) **Limited Request for Production.** A party will be entitled to request the production of five separate sets or groups of documents or things, including those authorized by CRLJ 26(b), without prior permission of the court.

[Adopted effective September 1, 1999.]

LCR 38. CIVIL JURY TRIAL

(a) **Demand.** The request for jury trial in civil cases shall be by filing a demand with the clerk and paying the jury fee not later than the date of serving and filing a request for a trial setting. Failure to comply with this rule is a waiver of the right to a jury trial.

[Adopted effective September 1, 1999.]

LCR 40. ASSIGNMENT OF CIVIL CASES FOR TRIAL

(a) **Civil Motions/Trial Setting Calendar.** Civil motions and requests for trial settings shall be scheduled as follows:

Dept. 2: Days and times as determined by the Presiding Judge. Contact the court office for more information.

(b) **Method.** A party desiring have a trial date set for a case shall file with the court and serve upon all parties a request for trial setting at least 5 days prior to the time provided by this rule for setting causes for trial. All other parties shall serve and file a similar request or appear at the date and time the cause is to be set. The initial request for trial setting shall be accompanied by a list of the names and addresses of all persons entitled to notice. All parties have the obligation to inform the court promptly of any errors or changes in this list. Each party and their attorney should include in their request for trial setting a schedule of unavailable dates.

(c) **Notice to Court of Calendar and Trial Changes.** Whenever a cause which has been set for trial is settled or will not be tried for any reason, or if a jury is subsequently waived, the attorneys shall immediately give notice to the court. The court may assess actual costs or other sanctions for a violation of this rule.

[Adopted effective September 1, 1999; amended effective September 1, 2003; September 1, 2009.]

LCR 41. DISMISSAL OF ACTIONS

(b) **Dismissal on Clerk's Motion.** In all civil cases where there has been no action of record due in the twelve months just past, the clerk shall mail notice to the parties or their attorneys of record that such case will be dismissed for want of prosecution unless within thirty days following said mailing, action of record is made or an application in writing is made to the court and good cause shown why it should be continued as a pending case. If such application is not made or good cause is not shown, the court shall dismiss each such case without prejudice. The costs of filing such order of dismissal with the clerk shall not be assessed against either party.

[Adopted effective September 1, 1999.]

LCR 54. ATTORNEY FEES AND COSTS

(a) **Reasonable Attorney Fees; Proof Required.** Reasonable attorney fees when allowed by statute or contract will be determined on a case by case basis and awarded in the sound discretion of the court upon satisfactory proof, which may include documentation of time and charges.

(b) **Default Judgment; Fees Allowed Without Justification.** In appropriate cases, when a Default Judgment is entered, reasonable attorney fees may be allowed on the basis of a maximum of 50% of the first $500 of the principal amount of the judgment, plus 10% of any balance over $500, without formal justification or documentation.

(c) **Original Note or Check Required; Offer of Settlement After Appearance or Answer.** The original note and any checks sued upon shall be filed as a condition for the award of reasonable attorney fees and collections costs. In all other cases where reasonable attorney fees are claimed either by virtue of a written instrument or a bona fide offer of settlement in a claim for damages, a copy of the offer of settlement together with proof of service or copy of the written instrument shall be filed. An attorney fee as provided for in RCW 4.84.250–.310 shall not be awarded upon a default judgment except when either a Notice of Appearance or responsive pleading (other than a consent to judgment) has been filed and an offer of settlement is served thereafter pursuant to statute or court rule.

[Adopted effective September 1, 1999.]

LCR 65. SMALL CLAIMS

(a) **Filing.** Small Claims cases shall be filed on a form approved by the Court.

(b) **Mediation Mandatory.** Mediation is mandatory before a trial is allowed. A date for mediation will be set on or after the return calendar. All parties must attend the mediation. If the plaintiff fails to appear, a dismissal will be entered. If the defendant fails to appear, defendant's answer will be stricken and a default judgement entered. Parties must bring their evidence to the mediation, however, no witnesses are allowed. The purpose of mediation is to provide the parties an opportunity to settle the case if possible without a trial; if no settlement is made after media-

tion, the court will set a trial date. Attorneys and paralegals may not represent parties at mediation. If the parties have already submitted the case to another type of mediation or arbitration service, or if the court finds good cause to waive mediation, the case may proceed directly to trial.

(c) **Continuance of Mediation and Trial of Small Claim Cases.** Any party requesting a continuance of a scheduled mediation session or small claim case must contact the court in writing and explain the circumstances which may require the mediation session or trial to be continued to another date and time. If all parties agree to a continuance, the court will grant the request. If all parties do not agree, the case may be continued by the Court upon a showing of good cause for a continuance. If the request is not granted by the court, the mediation and trial will proceed as currently scheduled. The Court, upon its own motion, may continue a trial for any reason.

[Adopted effective September 1, 1999; amended on an emergency basis effective July 1, 2007; amended on a permanent basis effective September 1, 2007.]

LCR 66. NAME CHANGES

(a) **Separate Petitions Required.** A separate petition shall be filed for each name a party wishes changed.

(b) **Minors.**

(1) *Birth Certificate.* A certified copy of any minor applicant's birth certificate or suitable identification must be presented to the clerk for verification and copying.

(2) *Parental Notification.* A parent or guardian who has not consented in writing to a minor's change of name and whose parental rights have not been previously terminated must be given actual notice or notice by publication as provided in CRLJ 4.

(3) *Notice by Publication.* Publication of a single notice in a newspaper of general circulation in the county of the parent or guardian's last known residence shall be sufficient so long as the notice contains a hearing date, the name of the minor, the name the petitioner desires the child to assume, and sets for the reasons for requesting the change of name.

(c) **Form of Order.** An Order for Name Change should conform to the format required by Chapter 65.04 RCW to facilitate recording with the County Auditor.

[Adopted effective September 1, 1999.]

LCR 69. PAYMENT OF MONIES ON JUDGMENTS [DELETED]

[Adopted effective September 1, 1999; deleted effective September 1, 2009.]

III. LOCAL CRIMINAL RULES

2. PROCEDURES PRIOR TO ARREST AND OTHER SPECIAL PROCEEDINGS

LCrR 2.1(d). FILING OF CITATION AND NOTICE TO APPEAR [DELETED]

[Adopted effective September 1, 1999; deleted effective September 1, 2009.]

LCrR 2.5. PROCEDURE ON FAILURE TO OBEY CITATION AND NOTICE [DELETED]

[Adopted effective September 1, 1999; deleted effective September 1, 2009.]

3. RIGHTS OF DEFENDANTS

LCrR 3.1(e). AUTOMATIC WITHDRAWAL OF ATTORNEY APPOINTED AT PUBLIC EXPENSE

Unless a Notice of Appeal has been filed, an attorney appointed at public expense shall be deemed automatically withdrawn from representation thirty days following a final decision of the court as defined in RALJ without need to file any document with the court.

[Adopted effective September 1, 1999.]

LCrR 3.2. BAIL SCHEDULE

The court shall periodically publish a bail schedule, which will include any bail schedule and penalty schedule promulgated by the Supreme Court of the State of Washington. The schedule will also include appearance days and times. The schedule shall be provided to all law enforcement agencies within the county. The bail schedule shall be intended as a guideline, but shall not be construed as limiting the authority of the court in individual cases to set bail in a different amount.

(m) **Bail in Criminal Cases.** When required to reasonable assure appearance in court, bail for a person arrested for the offenses listed in CrRLJ 3.2(m)—(s) shall be the amount listed therein. The court for good cause recited in a written order may set a different amount. Forfeiture of bail shall not constitute a final disposition for offenses listed in CrRLJ 3.2(m) without a written order of the court showing the reasons.

(n) **Domestic Violence Cases.** [Repealed effective July 1, 2007].

[Adopted effective September 1, 1999; amended on an emergency basis effective July 1, 2007; amended on a permanent basis effective September 1, 2007; amended effective September 1, 2009.]

LCrR 3.3(h). CONTINUANCES

A motion for continuance of trial must be filed on or before the date set for pre-trial hearing, unless circumstances beyond the control of the moving party prevent such motion from being timely filed.

[Adopted effective September 1, 1999.]

4. PROCEDURES PRIOR TO TRIAL

LCrR 4.5. PRE–TRIAL HEARING

(a) All cases scheduled for jury trial shall be set for pre-trial hearing. The court should set all pre-trial hearings no later than 45 days after arraignment. The prosecutor, defense counsel and the defendant shall attend the pre-trial hearing. If the defendant fails to appear for the pre-trial hearing, a warrant for the arrest of the defendant may issue. If the prosecutor or defense counsel fails to appear at the pre-trial hearing, the court may impose terms and any other sanctions authorized by law, and the court may continue or strike any scheduled hearing or trial date.

(c) All demands for a CrRLJ 3.5 hearing on admissibility of confessions or statements must be in writing and made no later than the pre-trial hearing. The plaintiff shall be responsible for the subpoena of all witnesses necessary at the CrRLJ 3.5 hearing. The court will schedule the date and time for all CrRLJ 3.5 hearings.

[Adopted effective December 1, 1987; amended effective September 1, 1999; September 1, 2001; September 1, 2009.]

LCrR 4.8. NOTIFICATION OF COURT AND WITNESSES

When a case docketed for trial or other hearing is settled or will not otherwise proceed to hearing, the parties shall immediately give notice of that fact to the court. It shall be the duty of each party to notify its own witnesses, not only of the date and time of trial, but also of continuances, pre-trial hearings, motions and other proceedings. The court will not pay witness fees to witnesses who appear for a case that has been continued or settled without trial or hearing. Such costs shall be borne by the party, or attorney, who called, subpoenaed or requested a subpoena for the witness.

[Adopted effective December 1, 1987; amended effective September 1, 1999.]

LCrR 5.1.1. JURY TRIAL—CONFIRMA-TION—NOTIFICATION OF COURT

(a) All cases set for a jury trial will also be set for a Confirmation Hearing prior to the jury trial date. The prosecutor, defense counsel and the defendant shall attend the confirmation hearing. If the defendant fails to appear for the confirmation hearing, a warrant for the arrest of the defendant may issue, and the court may continue or strike any scheduled hearing or trial date. If the prosecutor or defense counsel fails to appear at the pre-trial hearing, the court may impose terms and any other sanctions authorized by law, and the court may continue or strike any scheduled hearing or trial date. At the Confirmation Hearing, all parties are expected to verify readiness to proceed to trial, or to propose an alternate disposition. When a case assigned for jury trial is settled or will not be tried by the jury for any reason, notice of that fact shall be given immediately to the court. The court may impose terms including requiring payment of the actual costs of the jury in the event a case settles after the Confirmation Hearing.

[Adopted effective September 1, 1999; amended effective October 1, 2000; September 1, 2001; September 1, 2009.]

LCrR 5.1.2. BENCH TRIAL—CONFIRMA-TION—NOTIFICATION OF COURT

(a) All cases set for trial to the court without a jury may be set for a Confirmation Hearing prior to the trial date. The prosecutor, defense counsel and the defendant shall attend the confirmation hearing. If the defendant fails to appear for the confirmation hearing, a warrant for the arrest of the defendant may issue, and the court may continue or strike any scheduled hearing or trial date. If the prosecutor or defense counsel fails to appear at the pre-trial hearing, the court may impose terms and any other sanctions authorized by law, and the court may continue or strike any scheduled hearing or trial date. At the Confirmation Hearing, all parties are expected to verify readiness to proceed to trial, or to propose an alternate disposition. When a case assigned for trial to the court is settled or will not be tried for any reason, notice of that fact shall be given immediately to the court. The court may impose terms in the event a case settles after the Confirmation Hearing.

[Adopted effective September 1, 2003; amended on an emergency basis effective July 1, 2007; amended on a permanent basis effective September 1, 2007; amended effective September 1, 2009.]

LCrR 6.1.1. JURY TRIAL—WAIVER

A defendant that is charged with a criminal offense punishable by a loss of freedom should be scheduled for a jury trial, unless specifically waived by the filing of a Jury Trial Waiver prior to trial.

[Adopted effective September 1, 1999.]

8. MISCELLANEOUS

LCrR 8.2. MOTIONS

CrRLJ 8.1(c) and CrRLJ 8.2 shall govern motions in criminal cases.

[Adopted effective December 1, 1987; amended effective September 1, 1999.]

LCrR 8.2(f). NO CONTACT ORDERS

A request to extinguish or modify a No Contact Order in a Domestic Violence case may only be made by a party to the case and must be in writing. All parties and the alleged victim must be served with written notice at least five court days before any hearing to consider such a request.

[Adopted effective September 1, 1999.]

LCrR 8.5. RETURN OF EXHIBITS

Every exhibit in a criminal case will be returned to the party/or attorney who produced that exhibit for identification. The return shall be made upon written application, two weeks following termination of the time for appeal. Exhibits not requested to be returned during that period by the producing attorney or party may be delivered by the court clerk to the local police authority for disposition as abandoned property; or if contraband, for destruction. No exhibit shall be withdrawn or delivered without being receipted for by the receiving party.

[Adopted effective December 1, 1987; amended effective September 1, 1999.]

IV. LOCAL INFRACTION RULES

LIR 2.4. TIME PAYMENTS ON INFRACTIONS

Any person who has been served with a notice of infraction and who desires to use option (1) as provided in IRLJ 2.4(b)(1), may arrange time payments on the monetary penalty by signing a court approved time payment agreement.

[Adopted effective September 1, 1999.]

LIR 3.1. MOTIONS

All motions in infraction cases shall be governed by CRLJ 7(b). Motions shall be filed and served no later than 3 days prior to the scheduled hearing date unless the court orders otherwise.

[Adopted on an emergency basis effective July 1, 2007; adopted on a permanent basis effective September 1, 2007.]

LIR 3.3(b). REPRESENTATION BY LAWYER [REPEALED]

[Adopted effective December 1, 1987; amended effective September 1, 1999; repealed on an emergency basis effective November 4, 2009; repealed on a permanent basis effective September 1, 2010.]

LIR 3.5. DECISIONS ON WRITTEN STATEMENTS

Upon the request of the defendant made in writing at least 1 day prior to the date and time set for a contested hearing, the court may consider and decide the case on the basis of written statements, according to the procedure set forth in IRLJ 3.5, as now or hereafter amended. The court may also decide cases set for mitigation hearing on the basis of written statements upon request of the defendant.

[Adopted effective September 1, 1999.]

MUNICIPAL COURTS
ABERDEEN MUNICIPAL COURT RULES

Including Amendments Received Through
August 15, 2015

Table of Rules

LOCAL RULES

AMCLR 1.7. ADOPTION OF LOCAL RULES

These rules are adopted pursuant to GR7, CrRLJ 1.7 and IRLJ 1.3 of the Washington Court Rules. These rules govern the procedure in Aberdeen Municipal Court and are supplemental to the rules enacted by the Washington State Supreme Court for the Courts of Limited Jurisdiction. The court may modify or suspend any of these local Court rules in any given case upon good cause being shown or upon the Court's own motion in the interest of justice and/or the efficient operation of the Court.

[Adopted effective September 2, 2014.]

AMCLR 1.8. TITLE OF RULES

These rules shall be known as the Aberdeen Municipal Court Local Rules and shall be cited as AMCLR, and the Aberdeen Municipal Court Local Infraction Rules and shall be cited as AMCLIR.

[Adopted effective September 2, 2014.]

AMCLR 3.2. RELEASE OF ACCUSED

(a) Bail Schedule. Pursuant to CrRLJ 3.2 (b) (7), the court shall periodically publish a bail schedule, which will include any bail schedule and penalty schedule promulgated by the Supreme Court of the State of Washington. The bail schedule shall be intended as a guideline and shall not be construed as limiting the authority of the court in individual cases to set bail in a different amount.

(b) New Domestic Violence Offenses. Defendants arrested on domestic violence offenses shall be detained without bail until appearance on the next judicial day.

[Adopted effective September 2, 2014.]

AMCLR 3.4. PRESENCE OF THE DEFENDANT

Defendants must attend every scheduled court proceeding. The only exception to this rule is if an attorney, in compliance with CrRLJ 4.1(g), has entered an appearance or a plea of not guilty on behalf of a defendant not charged with a domestic violence crime or a violation of RCW 46.61.502 (Driving under the influence), RCW 46.61.503 (Driving under twenty-one consuming alcohol), or RCW 46.61.504 (Physical control of vehicle under the influence), and then the defendant's presence at arraignment is not required. If a defendant fails to appear as required, a warrant shall issue for the defendant's arrest. Any scheduled hearing or trial date shall be stricken, and costs may be imposed.

[Adopted effective September 2, 2014.]

AMCLR 3.5. CONFESSION PROCEDURE

All demands for CrRLJ 3.5 hearings shall be in writing and filed not less than 14 days prior to the pretrial hearing. Copies of the demand must be served contemporaneously on the prosecuting attorney. All CrRLJ 3.5 hearings shall be scheduled by the Court.

[Adopted effective September 2, 2014.]

AMCLR 4.1.   ARRAIGNMENT

Defendants charged with Driving under the influence (RCW 46.61.502), Driving under twenty-one consuming alcohol (RCW 46.61.503), and Physical control of vehicle under the influence (RCW 46.61.504) shall be arraigned on the next judicial day after arrest.

[Adopted effective September 2, 2014.]

AMCLR 6.13.   EVIDENCE

(a) BAC Verifier/Maintenance Operator Demand. Any demand for the appearance of a BAC verifier/maintenance operator shall be by separate document and shall be filed with the Court and served contemporaneously on the prosecuting attorney not less than 14 days prior to the pretrial hearing.

(b) Return of Exhibits. Every exhibit in a criminal case which is not contraband will be returned to the party or attorney who produced the exhibit for identification upon written application, following ter-

mination of the time for appeal. Exhibits not requested to be returned during the appeal period by the producing party or attorney may be delivered by the Court Administrator to the local police authority for disposition as abandoned property. No exhibit shall be released or delivered without it first being receipted for by the receiving party.

[Adopted effective September 2, 2014.]

AMCLR 8.1.   PRETRIAL MOTIONS

All pretrial motions, including motions to dismiss, motions to suppress and motions in limine, shall be in writing and filed with the court and served on the opposing party not less than 14 days prior to the pretrial hearing. All motions shall state the grounds for the motion and shall be supported by a brief and memorandum of authorities. All responses and opposing memorandums shall be filed not less than 5 days prior to the pretrial hearing. All pretrial motions shall be heard at the pretrial hearing unless otherwise scheduled by the Court.

[Adopted effective September 2, 2014.]

INFRACTION RULES

AMCLIR 2.4.   RESPONSE TO NOTICE—TIME PAYMENTS

Any person who has been served with a notice of infraction and desires to pay the infraction pursuant to IRLJ 2.4(b)(1) may arrange for time payments on the monetary penalty by signing the court-approved time payment agreement. An administrative fee for the establishing, monitoring and processing of the time pay agreement shall be added as costs.

[Adopted effective September 2, 2014.]

AMCLIR 2.6.   SCHEDULE OF HEARINGS—CONTINUANCES

A court clerk may grant one telephone request for a continuance. For a mitigation hearing, the continuance must be requested by 5:00 p.m. the day before the scheduled hearing. For a contested hearing, the continuance must be requested not less than three

weeks before the scheduled hearing. Thereafter, all requests must be in writing and approved by the court.

[Adopted effective September 2, 2014.]

AMCLIR 6.6.   SPEED MEASURING DEVICE—EXPERT WITNESS FEE

Each party is responsible for costs incurred by that party as set forth in RCW 46.63.151. The party requesting a witness shall pay the witness fees and mileage expenses due that witness. Any person who requests production of an electronic speed measuring device expert, and who is thereafter found by the court to have committed the infraction, shall be required to pay the fee charged by the expert as a cost incurred by the party.

[Adopted effective September 2, 2014.]

COSMOPOLIS MUNICIPAL COURT—
[No Local Rules]

ELMA MUNICIPAL COURT LOCAL COURT RULES

Including Amendments Received Through
August 15, 2015

Table of Rules

RULE 1. ADOPTION

These rules are adopted pursuant to CrRLJ 1.7.

[Adopted effective September 1, 1999.]

RULE 2. RESERVATION OF DISCRETION

The Court reserves the authority to interpret and/or suspend or modify these rules in individual cases on motion of a party for good cause shown or its own motion in the interest of justice and/or the efficient operation of the Court.

[Adopted effective September 1, 1999, CrRLJ 1.2.]

RULE 3. COURT SESSIONS

Regular Court sessions shall be on the second and fourth Friday of each month commencing at 12:30 p.m. in the Elma City Hall and at such other times and places as the Court may deem necessary for its proper administration.

[Effective September 1, 1999, CrRLJ 1.6.]

RULE 4. BAIL SCHEDULE

The Court shall, by written order filed with the Clerk, establish bail schedules for use by the police. The schedule shall designate those types of criminal cases, if any, wherein the defendant shall be allowed to forfeit bail in lieu of arraignment.

[Effective September 1, 1999, CrRLJ 3.2(m).]

RULE 5. ARRAIGNMENT DATE AND DETENTION

A. The arresting officer shall set the defendant's arraignment date and time when issuing a citation in all cases charging a criminal offense. The date set shall be the next Friday Court date at 12:30 p.m. until the Sunday five days prior to such Court session. Thereafter, the arraignment is to be set for the Court date following. All citations shall be filed upon issuance.

B. In the event that any person is arrested on probable cause (i.e. citation as opposed to warrant) and placed in the Grays Harbor County jail, then the County jail is hereby authorized to release said person from its facility no later than 48 hours after that persons detention at the Grays Harbor County jail, unless a judge has held a probable cause hearing.

The police department shall file a photocopy of the police reports or a Certificate of Probable Cause with the Grays Harbor County jail staff for the judge's review as to probable cause upon booking of any defendant into the Grays Harbor County jail.

[Effective September 1, 1999, CrRLJ 3.2.1.]

RULE 6. COMBINING DOCUMENTS

A Notice of Appearance and Plea of Not Guilty may be in one document. A Waiver of a, jury trial or speedy trial may be separate and signed by the defendant or the defendant's attorney if the attorney certifies that the Waiver has been expressly approved by the defendant. A Demand for the appearance of a breathalyzer/datamaster-verifier maintenance operator shall be by a separate document. Discovery demands shall be by a separate document.

[Effective September 1, 1999, CrRLJ 4.1(b);(d).]

RULE 7. DISCOVERY

"Blanket" discovery forms may be used, in addition to specific request, in which case each item requested shall contain a box or square in the left margin and shall be checked by the demanding party if that item is to be applicable to the particular case. Demands not applicable shall not be checked. Sanctions may be imposed for violation of this rule including, but not limited to, the quashing of the entire demand. Failure to provide discovery materials, including bills of particulars, shall be deemed waived unless the Court is notified in writing not less than two weeks prior to trial.

[Effective September 1, 1999, CrRLJ 4.7.]

RULE 8. PRE-TRIAL HEARINGS

A. Hearings. All cases scheduled for a jury trial shall be set for a pre-trial hearing not less than two weeks prior to the trial. The City Attorney, the defendant and the defense attorney, if any, shall attend the hearing. If a defendant not represented by counsel fails to appear for the hearing, a warrant for his or her arrest shall issue, and the jury trial setting stricken, If a defendant represented by counsel fails to appear, a warrant for the defendant's arrest may issue, and the jury trial setting may be stricken. In any case where a defendant fails to appear for the hearing, the period of time from that hearing to the defendant's next personal appearance in Court shall not be included in any speedy trial time limitation requirements.

B. Motions. All amendments to the charges, pleas or other motions shall be heard at the pre-trial hearing. The Court in its notification of trial date shall set the date upon which all motions shall be scheduled, generally the pre-trial hearing immediately prior to the scheduled trial date. Motions may not be considered at the time of trial unless they have been raised at the pre-trial hearing, or the Court, on its own motion, continues a matter to the time of trial. The party requiring the attendance of a witness at the pre-trial hearing shall be responsible for subpoenas of such witness except that the City Attorney shall subpoena necessary witnesses for a CrRLJ 3.5 hearing if the defendant or his attorney has requested in writing such attendance.

[Effective September 1, 1999, CrRLJ 3.3 and 3.4.]

RULE 9. CONTINUANCES

A. Bench Trials—Stipulations. The Court will grant a continuance after a bench trial date has been set upon a stipulation of counsel not less than three days prior to the date set.

B. Bench Trials—Written Motion. All requests for a continuance made five working days or less prior to a non-jury trial not stipulated to by the opposing party shall be presented by written motion and affidavit after notice to the opposing party. Twenty-four hours prior notice to the opposing party shall meet the requirement of this sub-section. The Court may grant a continuance on a showing of good cause.

C. Jury Trials. All requests for a continuance of a jury trial shall be presented by a written motion and affidavit with notice provided to the opposing party. Such motions may be heard at the pre-trial hearing or the date set by the clerk in the trial notification letter for motions. A continuance will be granted only upon a showing of good cause.

D. Good Cause. The following shall be deemed to be good cause:

1. Illness;

2. Unavoidable and/or unforeseen conflicts;

3. Unforeseen unavailability of witnesses; or,

4. Lack of discovery or new evidence requiring investigation.

E. Imposition of Costs. Payment of costs of the Court and the opposing party may be a condition for granting a continuance.

F. Speedy Trial Waiver. A Waiver of the speedy trial rule shall be required as a condition for granting a continuance.

G. Infraction Hearings. One telephone request for a continuance may be granted by the Court Clerk.

Thereafter, the request must be in writing and approved by the Court.

[Effective September 1, 1999, CrRLJ 3.3(h).]

RULE 10. JURY INSTRUCTIONS

A. When Submitted. Jury instructions are required to be filed with the Court and provided to the opposing party by the date set forth in the trial notification letter issued by the Clerk of the Court, said date generally being the Friday prior to the scheduled trial date.

B. How Submitted. Three sets of instructions shall be submitted on plain 8 1/2 by 11 inch paper. Citations of authority shall not appear on the unnumbered set. One additional set shall be served upon the opposing party.

C. Pattern Instructions. All instructions must be prepared by the offering party. The court has no pattern jury instructions.

[Effective September 1, 1999, CrRLJ 6.15.]

RULE 11. PLEAS IN CRIMINAL CASES—JURY TRIAL SET

The Court shall be notified of a plea agreement not less than ten days prior to a jury trial. Failure to comply with this Rule will result in imposition of jury costs, in addition to any other sentence imposed. If a case is resolved by a plea agreement or dismissed between the time a jury is called (ten days prior to trial) and 24 hours prior to trial, the Court shall assess costs of at least $40.00 against the defendant, or counsel, as part of the plea agreement, or against the City or its counsel in the event of a dismissal. For cases that are resolved by plea agreement or dismissal, within 24 hours of trial, the Court shall assess costs in the amount of at least $120.00, against defendant or counsel as part of any plea agreement, or against the City or its counsel in the event of a dismissal.

[Effective September 1, 1999, CrRLJ 4.2.]

RULE 12. TELEPHONIC COMMUNICATION

All proceedings except infraction hearings and criminal changes of pleas or trials may be heard by telephone conference call at the request of either party at the Courts discretion.

[Effective September 1, 1999.]

RULE 13. RETURN OF EXHIBITS

Every exhibit shall be returned to the party who produced it in a case that was not appealed upon written application not earlier than twenty-one (21) days after the trial. Exhibits not so withdrawn shall be destroyed after thirty (30) days or, if contraband, delivered to the police for destruction.

[Effective September 1, 1999.]

RULE 14. PAYMENT OF FINES AND PENALTIES

A. Infractions. Infraction penalties imposed shall be paid at the conclusion of any requested hearing.

B. Attorney and Jury Fees—Reimbursement. In the event of a conviction, the Court may require partial or full reimbursement to the City for the cost of Court appointed counsel and/or jury fees from those defendants the Court finds able to pay the same.

C. Jail Costs—Reimbursement. In the event of a conviction, the Court may require partial or full reimbursement to the City for the cost of jail time, as set by the Grays Harbor County Sheriff's Department, from those defendants the Court finds are able to pay the same.

D. Conditions of Time Payment. All legal financial obligations shall be paid at the rate of $50.00 per month or the total amount due divided by the number of probation months, not to exceed twelve months, whichever amount is greater, unless a different payment schedule is expressly approved by the Court.

E. Credit for Jail Time. The Court may give credit to a defendant of $25.00 per day for sitting out a fine. However, said credit shall not relieve the defendant of any requirement of reimbursement for jail costs.

F. Community Service. The Court may impose community service in lieu of monetary payments in appropriate cases.

G. Petition to Modify. The defendant may petition the Court to modify monetary payments at any time due to his or her changed financial condition.

H. Revocation of Probation or Imposition of Suspended Jail Time and/or Fines. Probation shall be revoked and previously suspended jail time and/or fines may be imposed for willful failure to pay fines.

[Effective September 1, 1999.]

HOQUIAM MUNICIPAL COURT LOCAL COURT RULES

Including Amendments Received Through
August 15, 2015

Table of Rules

RULE 1. ADOPTION

These rules are adopted pursuant to CrRLJ 1.7.

[Adopted May 30, 2002.]

RULE 2. RESERVATION OF DISCRETION

The court reserves the authority to interpret, suspend or modify these rules in individual cases on motion of a party for good cause shown, or its own motion in the interests of justice or the efficient operation of the court.

[Adopted May 30, 2002.]

RULE 3. COURT SESSIONS

Court sessions shall be at such times and places as the court may deem necessary for its proper administration.

[Adopted May 30, 2002.]

RULE 4. JUDGE ASSIGNMENT

All cases filed in the court are assigned to the appointed judge of the court.

[Adopted May 30, 2002.]

RULE 5. BAIL SCHEDULE

The court may establish a bail schedule for use by the police department. The schedule may designate those criminal charges wherein the defendant will be allowed to forfeit bail in lieu of appearing at arraignment. If a criminal charge is not included on a bail schedule, the defendant's appearance at arraignment shall be mandatory. Bail or bond for release from jail shall be in the amount of $500.00 or as otherwise determined by the court in all cases, except those alleging domestic violence for which no bail or bond shall be set.

[Adopted May 30, 2002.]

RULE 6. ARRAIGNMENT DATE

The arresting officer shall set a defendant's arraignment date and time when issuing a citation charging a criminal charge. The date set shall be consistent with a schedule to be provided by the court clerk. If the charge is driving under the influence or being in physical control while under the influence, the arraignment date shall be set on the next day in which court is in session. If the charge is driving under the influence or being in physical control while under the influence, or any charge involving alleged domestic violence, the defendant shall appear personally at the arraignment. In all other cases, the defendant may appear at the arraignment through an attorney. All citations shall be filed upon issuance.

[Adopted May 30, 2002.]

RULE 7. DOCUMENTS

A notice of appearance and plea of not guilty may be included in one document. A waiver of jury trial or speedy trial may be separate or combined in one document, and signed by the defendant, or by the defendant's attorney if the attorney certifies that the waiver has been expressly approved by the defendant. A demand for the appearance of a BAC technician or a Speed Measuring Device expert pursuant to CrRLJ 6.13 shall be made in a separate document filed with the court and served upon the city attorney. Pleadings or documents may be filed with the court by facsimile, provided that hard copies of the pleadings or documents are subsequently filed with the court and copies are served upon the opposing party.

[Adopted May 30, 2002.]

RULE 8. DISCOVERY

Discovery demands shall be by a separate document. Discovery shall be completed by the date set for the pretrial hearing. Failure to provide discovery materials, including bill of particulars if ordered, shall be deemed waived unless the court is notified at the time of the pretrial hearing.

[Adopted May 30, 2002.]

RULE 9. MOTIONS AND HEARINGS

(A) Pretrial Hearings. A pretrial hearing shall be set in all cases which have not been resolved at the arraignment. The city attorney, the defendant, and the defense attorney, if any, shall attend the pretrial hearing. At the pretrial hearing, the parties shall inform the court whether discovery has been completed, whether a plea bargain agreement has been reached, and if not, whether the case shall be continued, set for a bench trial, or set for a jury trial if a waiver of jury trial has not been previously made. If the case is set for a jury trial, an additional pretrial hearing shall be scheduled at least one week prior to the date set for the jury trial.

(B) Motions. All motions, including but not limited to amendments to the charges, for continuance and CrRLJ 3.5 hearings shall be heard at the pretrial hearing. Motions will not be considered at the time of trial unless they could not have been raised at the pretrial hearing, or the court on its own motion continued a matter to the time of trial.

(C) Subpoenas. A party wishing the attendance of a witness at a hearing shall be responsible for securing a subpoena for the witness except that the city attorney shall subpoena necessary witnesses for a CrRLJ 3.5 hearing if the defendant or defense attorney has requested in writing such attendance and has given notice for such motion as set forth herein. A party requesting the court to subpoena a witness shall provide the name and address of such witness, and, unless found to be indigent, payment of $50.00 per requested subpoena to pay for the witness and mileage fees, at least ten (10) days prior to the date set for trial.

(D) Testimonial Hearing Notice. A party bringing a motion which will require testimony, including CrRLJ 3.5 hearings, shall give separate notice of such to the clerk and the opposing party not less than five (5) court days prior to the hearing. Failure to comply with this rule may result in the striking of the motion, its denial, or in the imposition of terms.

(E) Attendance Required. The Defendant must attend every scheduled court proceeding. If a defendant fails to attend a scheduled court proceeding, a warrant may issue for his/her arrest and all scheduled court dates, including trial dates, may be stricken at the discretion of the court. The time period from the date of the hearing missed by a defendant until his/her next appearance in court shall not be included in any time limitation requirements.

[Adopted May 30, 2002.]

RULE 10. CONTINUANCES

(A) Bench Trials—Stipulations. The court will grant a continuance of a bench trial date upon the stipulation of the parties, if filed with the court at least one day prior to the date set for trial.

(B) Bench Trials—Written Motion. All requests for a continuance of a bench trial date not stipulated to by the opposing party shall be made by written motion and affidavit at least five (5) working days prior to the date set for trial, after notice to the opposing party.

(C) Jury Trials. All requests for a continuance of a jury trial shall be presented by a written motion and affidavit with notice provided to the opposing party. Such motions shall be made at the pretrial hearing.

(D) Good Cause. A motion for continuance of a bench trial or a jury trial will be granted only upon a showing of good cause. The following shall be deemed good cause:

(1) Illness with such verification as may be required by the court; or,

(2) Unavoidable and/or unforseen conflicts; or

(3) Lack of discovery or discovery of new evidence requiring investigation; or

(4) Other causes, in the discretion of the court.

(E) Imposition of Costs. Payment of costs of the court and the opposing party may be a condition for granting a motion for continuance.

(F) Speedy Trial Waiver. A waiver of the right to a speedy trial may be required as a condition for granting a motion for continuance. A motion for continuance made by the defendant or defense attorney shall be deemed a waiver of speedy trial, effective at least until the next date scheduled for the trial.

(G) Infraction Hearings. One telephonic request for a continuance may be granted by the court clerk. Thereafter, a request must be in writing and approved by the court.

[Adopted May 30, 2002.]

RULE 11. JURY INSTRUCTIONS

(A) When Submitted. Proposed jury instructions shall be submitted when the case is called for trial.

(B) How Submitted. Three sets of instructions shall be submitted to the court on plain 8½ by 11 paper. These sets shall not be numbered. Another set shall be submitted to the opposing party. Citations of authority shall not appear on the unnumbered sets, but can be included on additional sets to be submitted to the trial judge and the opposing party.

[Adopted May 30, 2002.]

RULE 12. PLEAS IN CRIMINAL CASES— JURY TRIAL SETTINGS

The court shall be notified of a plea bargain agreement not less than two weeks prior to a jury trial. Failure to comply with this rule may result in the imposition of costs in addition to any other sentence imposed.

[Adopted May 30, 2002.]

RULE 13. TELEPHONIC AND ELECTRONIC COMMUNICATION

All proceedings except infraction hearings, criminal changes of plea or criminal trials may be heard by telephone conference call at the request of either party with written notice to the court and at the discretion of the judge.

[Adopted May 30, 2002.]

RULE 14. RETURN OF EXHIBITS

Every exhibit shall be returned to the party who produced it in a case that is not appealed upon application not earlier than thirty (30) days following the trial or entry of judgment and sentence, whichever was later. Exhibits not so returned may be destroyed after sixty (60) days following the trial or entry of judgment, unless an appeal is filed, or, if contraband, delivered to the police department for destruction.

[Adopted May 30, 2002.]

RULE 15. PAYMENT OF FINES AND PENALTIES

(A) Infractions. Infraction penalties shall be paid no later than at the conclusion of any requested hearing. A defendant who does not request a contested hearing or a mitigation hearing, but who would like to make payments towards the applicable infraction penalty without appearing in court, may make payment arrangements with the court clerk within fifteen (15) days of the issuance of the notice of infraction.

(B) Attorney and Jury Fees—Reimbursement. The court may require partial or full reimbursement to the city for the cost of court appointed counsel and/or jury fees from those defendants the court finds able to pay.

(C) Conditions of Time Payment. All time payments in criminal payments shall be paid at the rate of $50.00 per month or the total amount due divided by eleven, whichever is greater, unless a different payment schedule is approved by the court.

(D) Community Service. The court may impose community service in lieu of monetary payments in appropriate cases.

(E) Petition to Modify. The defendant may petition the court to modify monetary payments at any time due to his/her changed financial condition.

(F) Revocation of Probation. Probation shall be revoked for willful failure to pay fines, costs or other assessments.

[Adopted May 30, 2002.]

RULE 16. AUTHORITY OF COURT CLERK

The court clerk shall have authority to execute and issue the following temporary orders: No Contact Orders, Pretrial Release Orders, Orders Continuing Custody, Commitment Orders, Orders setting court dates, Warrants for Arrest and Electronic Home Monitoring Orders, provided that these temporary orders shall expire on the date set for the defendant's next appearance in court.

[Adopted May 30, 2002.]

RULE 17. ELECTRONIC HOME MONITORING

In appropriate cases, the court may order that a defendant be incarcerated in the Hoquiam Jail and released subject to electronic home monitoring. In such cases, the defendant shall be deemed to be in custody. Any wilful violation of the terms of the order imposing electronic home monitoring shall constitute contempt of court, violation of probation and/or escape from custody. In the event that the agency administering the electronic home monitoring believes that the defendant has removed the monitoring device or otherwise wilfully violated the terms of the order imposing electronic home monitoring, the agency shall:

(1) If possible, deliver the defendant to the Hoquiam Police Department for immediate incarceration pursuant to the defendant's original sentence or order of commitment, in which case the court shall be notified of the alleged violation and a hearing date shall be set; or

(2) Report the violation to the Hoquiam Police Department or to the court, at which time the court shall issue a warrant for the arrest of the defendant.

[Adopted May 30, 2002.]

RULE 18. PUBLIC ACCESS

Persons who wish to utilize the public access features of the court's computerized records system must schedule an appointment to do so through the court clerk in advance. Each appointment shall be limited to thirty (30) minutes. There shall be a charge of $1.00 per page for any records printed by the court.

[Adopted May 30, 2002.]

McCLEARY MUNICIPAL COURT LOCAL COURT RULES

Including Amendments Received Through
August 15, 2015

Table of Rules

RULE 1. ADOPTION

These rules are adopted pursuant to GR7, CrRLJ 1.7 and IRLJ 1.3.

[Adopted effective September 3, 1991; amended effective September 1, 2001.]

RULE 2. RESERVATION OF DISCRETION

The Court reserves the authority to interpret, suspend or modify these rules in individual cases on motion of a party for good cause shown or on its own motion in the interest of justice or the efficient operation of the court.

[Adopted effective September 1, 1991.]

RULE 3. COURT SESSIONS

Court sessions shall begin at 9:00 a.m. on the second and fourth Friday of each month in the McCleary City Hall, and at such other times and places as the court may deem necessary for its proper administration.

[Adopted effective September 3, 1991; amended effective September 1, 2001.]

RULE 4. JUDGE ASSIGNMENT

All cases filed in the court are assigned to the appointed judge of the court.

[Adopted effective September 3, 1991.]

RULE 5. BAIL SCHEDULE

The court may establish a bail schedule for use by the police. The schedule may designate those criminal charges wherein the defendant will be allowed to forfeit bail in lieu of arraignment. In the absence of a schedule, the defendant's appearance at arraignment shall be mandatory. Bond for release from jail shall be $500.00 in all cases, except those alleging domestic violence for which no bond shall be set.

[Formerly Rule 4. Adopted September 3, 1991.]

RULE 6. ARRAIGNMENT DATE

The arresting officer shall set a defendant's arraignment date and time when issuing a citation charging a criminal offense. The date set shall be consistent with a schedule to be provided by the court clerk. All citations shall be filed upon issuance.

[Formerly Rule 5. Adopted September 3, 1991.]

RULE 7. NOTICE OF APPEARANCE, COMBINING DOCUMENTS, DEMAND FOR BAC VERIFIER MAINTENANCE OPERATOR AND MOTIONS

(A) Notice of Appearance to City Attorney. Attorneys appearing for a defendant shall provide a copy of the Notice of Appearance to the City Attorney contemporaneously with filing the same with the court.

(B) Combining Documents. A Notice of Appearance and plea of not guilty may be combined in one document.

(C) BAC Verifier Maintenance Operator Demand. Any demand for the appearance of a BAC Verifier maintenance operator shall be by separate document to be filed with the court and served on the

City Attorney contemporaneously with filing the same with the court.

(D) Motions. Any motion filed on behalf of any party shall be provided to the attorney representing the opposing party or, if not represented, to the opposing party contemporaneously with filing the same with the court.

[Adopted September 3, 1991; amended effective September 1, 2001.]

RULE 8. DISCOVERY

Discovery demands shall be by a separate document. "Blanket" discovery forms may be used, provided that each item requested shall contain a box or square in the left margin and shall be checked by the demanding party if that item is to be applicable to the particular case. Demands not applicable shall not be checked. Sanctions may be imposed for violation of this rule, including but not limited to the quashing of the entire demand. Failure to provide discovery materials, including bills of particulars if ordered, shall be deemed waived unless the court is notified in writing not less than two weeks prior to the trial.

[Formerly Rule 7. Adopted September 3, 1991.]

RULE 9. MOTIONS AND HEARINGS

(A) Pre-trial Hearings. All cases set for a jury or non-jury trial shall be set for a pre-trial hearing prior to the trial date. The City Attorney, the defendant and the defense attorney, if any, shall attend the hearing.

(B) Motions. All motions, including but not limited to amendment to the charges, for continuance and CrRLJ 3.5 hearings shall be heard at the pre-trial hearing. Motions will not be considered at the time of trial unless they could not have been raised at the pre-trial hearing, or the court on its own motion continued a matter to the time of trial.

(C) Subpoenas. A party wishing the attendance of a witness at a hearing shall be responsible for subpoenas of such witnesses, except that the City Attorney shall subpoena necessary witnesses for a CrRLJ 3.5 hearing if the defendant or his attorney has requested in writing such attendance and has given notice for such motion as set forth herein. A party requesting the court to subpoena a witness shall provide the name and address of the witness, a statement of the relevance of the testimony, and payment of $50.00 per requested subpoena to pay for the witness fee and mileage, and costs of service.

(D) Testimonial Hearing Notice. A party bringing a motion which will require testimony, including CrRLJ 3.5 hearings, shall give separate notice of such to the clerk and the opposing party not less than two weeks prior to the hearing. Failure to comply with this rule may result in the striking of the motion, its denial or terms.

(E) Attendance Required. The defendant must attend every scheduled court proceeding. If a defendant fails to attend, a bench warrant may issue for his/her arrest by the judge or court personnel upon direction of the judge and all scheduled court dates may be stricken at the discretion of the court. The court may impose an additional fee for the issuance of any bench warrant for failure to appear. The time period from the hearing missed by a defendant to his/her next appearance in court shall not be included in any time limitation requirements but rather time limits shall begin anew from such next appearance.

[Adopted September 3, 1991; amended effective September 1, 2001.]

RULE 10. CONTINUANCES

(A) Bench Trials—Stipulations. The court will grant a continuance after a bench trial date has been set upon a stipulation of the parties not less than one day prior to the date set.

(B) Bench Trials—Written Motion. All requests for a continuance made five working days or less prior to a bench trial not stipulated to by the opposing party shall be presented by written motion and affidavit after notice to the opposing party. Twenty–four hours prior notice to the opposing party shall meet the requirement of this subsection. The court may grant a continuance on a showing of good cause.

(C) Jury Trials. All requests for a continuance of a jury trial shall be presented by a written motion and affidavit with notice provided to the opposing party. Such motions may be heard at the pre-trial hearing. A continuance will be granted only upon a showing of good cause.

(D) Good Cause. The following shall be deemed good cause:

(1) Illness with such verification as may be required by the court; or,

(2) Unavoidable and/or unforeseen conflicts; or,

(3) Lack of discovery or new evidence requiring investigation.

(E) Imposition of Costs. Payment of costs of the court and the opposing party may be a condition for granting a continuance.

(F) Speedy Trial Waiver. A waiver of the right to a speedy trial may be required as a condition for granting a continuance.

(G) Infraction Hearings. One telephonic request for a continuance may be granted by the clerk. Thereafter such a request must be in writing and approved by the court.

[Formerly Rule 9. Adopted September 3, 1991; amended effective September 1, 2001.]

RULE 11.   JURY INSTRUCTIONS

(A) When Submitted. Proposed jury instructions shall be submitted when the case is called for trial.

(B) How Submitted. Three sets of instructions shall be submitted on plain 8–1/2 × 11 inch paper. Citations of authority shall not appear on the unnumbered set. One additional set shall be served upon the opposing party.

(C) Pattern Instructions. The court does not maintain pattern instructions. All instructions must be prepared by the offering party.

[Formerly Rule 10. Adopted September 3, 1991; amended effective September 1, 2001.]

RULE 12.   PLEAS IN CRIMINAL CASES— JURY TRIAL SETTINGS

The court shall be notified of a plea agreement not less than two weeks prior to a jury trial. Failure to comply with this rule may result in the imposition of costs, including but not limited to witness, jury, and service of process fees in addition to any other sentence imposed.

[Formerly Rule 11. Adopted September 3, 1991; amended effective September 1, 2001.]

RULE 13.   TELEPHONIC COMMUNICATION

All proceedings, except infraction hearings, and criminal changes of plea or trials, may be heard by telephone conference call at the request of either party or the court.

[Formerly Rule 12. Adopted September 3, 1991.]

RULE 14.   RETURN OF EXHIBITS

Every exhibit shall be returned to the party who produced it in a case that was not appealed upon written application not earlier than twenty one days after the trial or sentencing, whichever was later. Exhibits not so withdrawn may be destroyed after thirty days or, if contraband, delivered to the police for destruction.

[Formerly Rule 13. Adopted September 3, 1991.]

RULE 15.   PAYMENT OF FINES AND PENALTIES

(A) Infractions. Infraction penalties shall be paid at the conclusion of any requested hearing, or upon such schedule as may be set by a court approved time payment agreement.

(B) Attorney and Jury Fees—Reimbursement. The court may require partial or full reimbursement to the city for the cost of court appointed counsel and/or jury fees from those defendants the court finds able to pay such.

(C) Conditions of Time Payment. All criminal time payments shall be paid at the rate of $50.00 per month or the total amount due divided by eleven, whichever amount is greater, unless the court approves a different payment schedule.

(D) Community Service. The court may impose community service in lieu of monetary payments in appropriate cases.

(E) Petition to Modify. The defendant may petition the court to modify monetary payments at any time due to his/her changed financial condition.

(F) Revocation of Probation. Probation shall be revoked for willful failure to pay fines, costs or other assessments.

[Formerly Rule 14. Adopted September 3, 1991; amended effective September 1, 2001.]

RULE 16.   NOTICE OF APPEARANCE IN CONTESTED INFRACTION CASE AND SCHEDULING OF PRE–HEARING CONFERENCE

(A) Notice of Appearance to City Attorney. Attorneys appearing for a defendant in a contested infraction case shall provide a copy of a Notice of Appearance to the City Attorney contemporaneously with filing the same with the court.

(B) Pre-Hearing Conference Required. All contested infractions wherein an attorney represents the defendant shall be set for a pre-hearing conference prior to the setting of a contested hearing.

[Adopted effective September 1, 2001.]

RULE 17.   USE OF A COLLECTION AGENCY AND ASSESSMENT AS COURT COST OF AMOUNTS PAID FOR COLLECTION SERVICES

(A) Contract for Collection. The court may use the services of a collection agency for the purposes of collecting unpaid and delinquent penalties on infractions, criminal fines, costs, assessments and forfeitures, on the terms and conditions of the contract for collection services between the City of McCleary and said collection agency, and as may be subsequently amended.

(B) Collection Agency Fee as Cost. The collection agency's fee or charge, as set forth in said contract, shall be added by the collection agency as a court cost to the total judgment of the court against each defendant whose account is referred to the collection agency.

[Adopted effective September 1, 2001.]

MONTESANO MUNICIPAL COURT LOCAL COURT RULES

Including Amendments Received Through
August 15, 2015

Table of Rules

RULE 1. ADOPTION

These rules are adopted pursuant to GR7, CrRLJ 1.7 and IRLJ 1.3.

[Adopted September 3, 1991; amended effective September 1, 2001; September 1, 2010.]

RULE 2. RESERVATION OF DISCRETION

The court reserves the authority to interpret, suspend or modify these rules in individual cases on motion of a party for good cause shown or on its own motion in the interest of justice or the efficient operation of the court.

[Adopted September 3, 1991; amended effective September 1, 2010.]

RULE 3. COURT SESSIONS

Court sessions shall be held in the Montesano City Hall, and at such other times and places as the court may deem necessary for its proper administration on the following schedule:

(A) 2:45 p.m. on the second Tuesday of each month for arraignments, mitigation and contested hearings, sentencing, show cause and review hearings and such other matters as the court may schedule;

(B) 9:00 a.m. on the third Wednesday of each month for Jury Trials, Special hearings and such other matters as the court may schedule;

(C) 12:45 p.m. on the fourth Tuesday of each month for pre-trial conferences, arraignments, mitigation and contested hearings, sentencing, show cause and review hearings and such other matters as the court may schedule.

(D) 10:30 a.m. on the fourth Tuesday of each month for non-jury trials;

[Adopted September 3, 1991; amended effective September 1, 2001; September 1, 2003; September 1, 2004; September 1, 2010; September 1, 2011; September 2, 2014.]

RULE 4. JUDGE ASSIGNMENT

All cases filed in the court are assigned to the appointed judge of the court.

[Adopted September 3, 1991; amended effective September 1, 2010.]

RULE 5. RELEASE OF THE ACCUSED

A. Bail: Montesano Municipal Court will follow the bail schedule set forth in Washington Court Rule CrRLJ 3.2(*o*) except where the charges involve domestic violence offenses or charges of DUI (RCW 46.61.502) or Physical Control (RCW 46.61.504).

B. Domestic Violence Offenses: Bail shall not be set for a person arrested for a new domestic violence offense unless set by a judge telephonically at the time of arrest, or at a preliminary appearance, arraignment or subsequent court appearance. "Domestic violence" includes, but is not limited to any of the misdemeanor or gross misdemeanor offenses listed in RCW 10.99.020(5), or similar municipal ordinance, when committed by one family or household member against another. "Family or household members" are those persons listed in RCW 10.99.020(3) or similar municipal ordinance.

C. DUI or Physical Control: Bail shall not be set for a person arrested for a new DUI or Physical Control offense unless set by a judge telephonically at the time of arrest, or at a preliminary appearance, arraignment or subsequent court appearance or by written court order.

[Adopted September 3, 1991; amended effective September 1, 2010; September 2, 2014.]

RULE 6. ARRAIGNMENT DATE

The arresting officer shall set a defendant's arraignment date and time when issuing a citation charging a criminal offense. The date set shall be consistent with a schedule to be provided by the court clerk. All citations shall be filed upon issuance.

[Adopted September 3, 1991; amended effective September 1, 2010.]

RULE 7. NOTICE OF APPEARANCE, COMBINING DOCUMENTS, DEMAND FOR BAC VERIFIER MAINTENANCE OPERATOR AND MOTIONS

(A) Notice of Appearance to City Attorney. Attorneys appearing for a defendant shall provide a copy of the Notice of Appearance to the City Attorney contemporaneously with filing the same with the court.

(B) Combining Documents. A Notice of Appearance and plea of not guilty may be combined in one document.

(C) BAC Verifier Maintenance Operator Demand. Any demand for the appearance of a BAC Verifier maintenance operator shall be by separate document to be filed with the court and served on the City Attorney contemporaneously with filing the same with the court.

(D) Motions. Any motion filed on behalf of any party shall be provided to the attorney representing the opposing party or, if not represented, to the opposing party contemporaneously with filing the same with the court.

[Adopted September 3, 1991; amended effective September 1, 2001; September 1, 2010.]

RULE 8. DISCOVERY

Discovery demands shall be by a separate document. "Blanket" discovery forms may be used, provided that each item requested shall contain a box or square in the left margin and shall be checked by the demanding party if that item is to be applicable to the particular case. Demands not applicable shall not be checked. Sanctions may be imposed for violation of this rule, including but not limited to the quashing of the entire demand. Failure to provide discovery materials, including bills of particulars if ordered, shall

be deemed waived unless the court is notified in writing not less than two weeks prior to the trial.

[Adopted September 3, 1991; amended effective September 1, 2010.]

RULE 9. MOTIONS AND HEARINGS

(A) Pre-trial Hearings. All cases set for a jury or non-jury trial shall be set for a pre-trial hearing prior to the trial date. The City Attorney, the defendant and the defense attorney, if any, shall attend the hearing.

(B) Motions. All motions, including but not limited to amendment to the charges, for continuance and CrRLJ 3.5 hearings, shall be heard at the pre-trial hearing. Motions will not be considered at the time of trial unless they could not have been raised at the pre-trial hearing, or the court on its own motion continued a matter to the time of trial.

(C) Subpoenas. A party wishing the attendance of a witness at a hearing shall be responsible for subpoenas of such witnesses, except that the City Attorney shall subpoena necessary witnesses for a CrRLJ 3.5 hearing if the defendant or his attorney has requested in writing such attendance and has given notice for such motion as set forth herein. A party requesting the court to subpoena a witness shall provide the name and address of the witness, a statement of the relevance of the testimony, and payment of $50.00 per requested subpoena to pay for the witness fee and mileage, and costs of service.

(D) Testimonial Hearing Notice. A party bringing a motion which will require testimony, including CrRLJ 3.5 hearings, shall give separate notice of such to the clerk and the opposing party not less than two weeks prior to the hearing. Failure to comply with this rule may result in the striking of the motion, its denial or terms.

(E) Attendance Required. The defendant must attend every scheduled court proceeding. If a defendant fails to attend, a bench warrant may issue for his/her arrest by the judge or court personnel upon direction of the judge and all scheduled court dates may be stricken at the discretion of the court. The court may impose an additional fee for the issuance of any bench warrant for failure to appear. The time period from the hearing missed by a defendant to his/her next appearance in court shall not be included in any time limitation requirements but rather time limits shall begin anew from such next appearance.

[Adopted September 3, 1991; amended effective September 1, 2001; September 1, 2010.]

RULE 10. CONTINUANCES

(A) Bench Trials—Stipulations. The court will grant a continuance after a bench trial date has been set upon a stipulation of the parties not less than one day prior to the date set.

(B) Bench Trials—Written Motion. All requests for a continuance made five working days or less prior to a bench trial not stipulated to by the opposing party shall be presented by written motion and affidavit after notice to the opposing party. Twenty-four hours prior notice to the opposing party shall meet the requirement of this subsection. The court may grant a continuance on a showing of good cause.

(C) Jury Trials. All requests for a continuance of a jury trial shall be presented by a written motion and affidavit with notice provided to the opposing party. Such motions may be heard at the pre-trial hearing. A continuance will be granted only upon a showing of good cause.

(D) Good Cause. The following shall be deemed good cause:

(1) Illness with such verification as may be required by the court; or

(2) Unavoidable and/or unforeseen conflicts; or

(3) Lack of discovery or new evidence requiring investigation.

(E) Imposition of Costs. Payment of costs of the court and the opposing party may be a condition for granting a continuance.

(F) Waiver of Time for Trial Right. A waiver of time for trial right may be required as a condition for granting a continuance.

(G) Infraction Hearings. One telephonic request for a continuance may be granted by the clerk. Thereafter such a request must be in writing and approved by the court.

[Adopted September 3, 1991; amended effective September 1, 2001; September 1, 2010.]

RULE 11. JURY INSTRUCTIONS

(A) When Submitted. Proposed jury instructions shall be submitted when the case is called for trial.

(B) How Submitted. Three sets of instructions shall be submitted on plain 8–1/2 × 11 inch paper. Citations of authority shall not appear on the unnumbered set. One additional set shall be served upon the opposing party.

(C) Pattern Instructions. The court does not maintain pattern instructions. All instructions must be prepared by the offering party.

[Adopted September 3, 1991; amended effective September 1, 2001; September 1, 2010.]

RULE 12. PLEAS IN CRIMINAL CASES— JURY TRIAL SETTINGS

The court shall be notified of a plea agreement not less than two weeks prior to a jury trial. Failure to comply with this rule may result in the imposition of costs, including but not limited to witness, jury, and service of process fees in addition to any other sentence imposed.

[Adopted September 3, 1991; amended effective September 1, 2001; September 1, 2010.]

RULE 13. TELEPHONIC COMMUNICATION

All proceedings, except infraction hearings and criminal changes of plea or trials, may be heard by telephone conference call at the request of either party or the court.

[Adopted September 3, 1991; amended effective September 1, 2010.]

RULE 14. RETURN OF EXHIBITS

Every exhibit shall be returned to the party who produced it in a case that was not appealed upon written application not earlier than twenty one days after the trial or sentencing, whichever was later. Exhibits not so withdrawn may be destroyed after thirty days or, if contraband, delivered to the police for destruction.

[Adopted September 3, 1991; amended effective September 1, 2010.]

RULE 15. PAYMENT OF FINES AND PENALTIES

(A) Infractions. Infraction penalties shall be paid at the conclusion of any requested hearing, or upon such schedule as may be set by a court approved time payment agreement. A $10 fee shall be assessed per payment plan, traffic infraction only. 46.43.110 [6][c]

(B) Attorney and Jury Fees—Reimbursement. The court may require partial or full reimbursement to the City for the cost of court-appointed counsel and/or jury fees from those defendants the court finds able to pay such.

(C) Conditions of Time Payment. All criminal time payments shall be paid at the rate of $50.00 per month or the total amount due divided by eleven, whichever amount is greater, unless the court approves a different payment schedule.

(D) Community Restitution. The court may impose community restitution in lieu of monetary payments in appropriate cases.

(E) Petition to Modify. The defendant may petition the court to modify monetary payments at any time due to his/her changed financial condition.

(F) Revocation of Probation. Probation shall be revoked for willful failure to pay fines, costs or other assessments.

[Adopted September 3, 1991; amended effective September 1, 2001; September 1, 2010.]

RULE 16. NOTICE OF APPEARANCE IN CONTESTED INFRACTION

(A) Notice of Appearance to City Attorney. Attorneys appearing for a defendant in a contested infraction case shall provide a copy of a Notice of Appearance to the City Attorney contemporaneously with filing the same with the court.

[Adopted September 1, 2001; amended effective September 1, 2010.]

RULE 17. AUTOMATIC WITHDRAWAL OF ATTORNEY AT PUBLIC EXPENSE

Unless a Notice of Appeal has been filed, an attorney appointed at public expense shall be deemed automatically withdrawn from representation thirty days following a final decision of the court as defined in RALJ without need to file any document with the court.

[Adopted September 1, 2001; amended effective September 1, 2010.]

RULE 18. DECISIONS ON WRITTEN STATEMENTS [RESCINDED]

[Adopted effective September 1, 2010. Rescinded effective September 2, 2014.]

RULE 19. USE OF A COLLECTION AGENCY AND ASSESSMENT AS COURT COST OF AMOUNTS PAID FOR COLLECTION SERVICES

(A) Contract for Collection. The court may use the services of a collection agency for the purposes of collecting unpaid and delinquent penalties on infractions, criminal fines, costs, assessments and forfeitures, on the terms and conditions of the contract for collection services between the City of Montesano and said collection agency, and as may be subsequently amended.

(B) Collection Agency Fee as Cost. The collection agency's fee or charge, as set forth in said contract, shall be added by the collection agency as a court cost to the total judgment of the court against each defendant whose account is referred to the collection agency.

[Adopted effective September 1, 2010.]

OAKVILLE MUNICIPAL COURT LOCAL COURT RULES

Including Amendments Received Through August 15, 2015.

Table of Rules

RULE 1. ADOPTION

These rules are adopted pursuant to GR7, CrRLJ 1.7 and IRLJ 1.3.

[Adopted effective September 1, 2011.]

RULE 2. RESERVATION OF DISCRETION

The court reserves the authority to interpret, suspend or modify these rules in individual cases on motion of a party for good cause shown or on its own motion in the interest of justice or the efficient operation of the court.

[Adopted effective September 1, 2011.]

RULE 3. COURT SESSIONS

Court sessions shall be held in the Oakville City Hall, and at such other times and places as the court may deem necessary for its proper administration on the following schedule:

(A) 5:30 p.m. on the second and fourth Monday of each month for arraignments, mitigation and contested hearings, sentencings, show cause and review hearings and such other matters as the court may schedule;

(B) 1:00 p.m. on the fourth Friday of each month for Special hearings and such other matters as the court may schedule;

(C) 6:00 p.m. on the second Monday of each month for non-jury trials;

(D) 5:35 p.m. on the second Monday of each month for pre-trial conferences, arraignments, mitigation and contested hearings, sentencings, show cause and review hearings and such other matters as the court may schedule

[Adopted effective September 1, 2011.]

RULE 4. JUDGE ASSIGNMENT

All cases filed in the court are assigned to the appointed judge of the court.

[Adopted effective September 1, 2011.]

RULE 5. BAIL SCHEDULE

The court may establish a bail schedule for use by the police. The schedule may designate those criminal charges wherein the defendant will be allowed to forfeit bail in lieu of arraignment. In the absence of a schedule, the defendant's appearance at arraignment shall be mandatory.

[Adopted effective September 1, 2011.]

RULE 6. ARRAIGNMENT DATE

The arresting officer shall set a defendant's arraignment date and time when issuing a citation charging a criminal offense. The date set shall be consistent with a schedule to be provided by the court clerk. All citations shall be filed upon issuance.

[Adopted effective September 1, 2011.]

RULE 7. NOTICE OF APPEARANCE, COMBINING DOCUMENTS, DEMAND FOR BAC VERIFIER MAINTENANCE OPERATOR AND MOTIONS

(A) Notice of Appearance to City Attorney. Attorneys appearing for a defendant shall provide a copy of the Notice of Appearance to the City Attorney contemporaneously with filing the same with the court.

(B) Combining Documents. A Notice of Appearance and plea of not guilty may be combined in one document.

(C) BAC Verifier Maintenance Operator Demand. Any demand for the appearance of a BAC Verifier maintenance operator shall be by separate document to be filed with the court and served on the City Attorney contemporaneously with filing the same with the court.

(D) Motions. Any motion filed on behalf of any party shall be provided to the attorney representing the opposing party or, if not represented, to the opposing party contemporaneously with filing the same with the court.

[Adopted effective September 1, 2011.]

RULE 8. DISCOVERY

Discovery demands shall be by a separate document. "Blanket" discovery forms may be used, provided that each item requested shall contain a box or square in the left margin and shall be checked by the demanding party if that item is to be applicable to the particular case. Demands not applicable shall not be checked. Sanctions may be imposed for violation of this rule, including but not limited to the quashing of the entire demand. Failure to provide discovery materials, including bills of particulars if ordered, shall be deemed waived unless the court is notified in writing not less than two weeks prior to the trial.

[Adopted effective September 1, 2011.]

RULE 9. MOTIONS AND HEARINGS

(A) Pre-trial Hearings. All cases set for a jury or non-jury trial shall be set for a pre-trial hearing prior to the trial date. The City Attorney, the defendant and the defense attorney, if any, shall attend the hearing.

(B) Motions. All motions, including but not limited to amendment to the charges, for continuance and CrRLJ 3.5 hearings, shall be heard at the pre-trial hearing. Motions will not be considered at the time of trial unless they could not have been raised at the pre-trial hearing, or the court on its own motion continued a matter to the time of trial.

(C) Subpoenas. A party wishing the attendance of a witness at a hearing shall be responsible for subpoenas of such witnesses, except that the City Attorney shall subpoena necessary witnesses for a CrRLJ 3.5 hearing if the defendant or his attorney has requested in writing such attendance and has given notice for such motion as set forth herein. A party requesting the court to subpoena a witness shall provide the name and address of the witness, a statement of the relevance of the testimony, and payment of $50.00 per

requested subpoena to pay for the witness fee and mileage, and costs of service.

(D) Testimonial Hearing Notice. A party bringing a motion which will require testimony, including CrRLJ 3.5 hearings, shall give separate notice of such to the clerk and the opposing party not less than two weeks prior to the hearing. Failure to comply with this rule may result in the striking of the motion, its denial or terms.

(E) Attendance Required. The defendant must attend every scheduled court proceeding. If a defendant fails to attend, a bench warrant may issue for his/her arrest by the judge or court personnel upon direction of the judge and all scheduled court dates may be stricken at the discretion of the court. The court may impose an additional fee for the issuance of any bench warrant for failure to appear. The time period from the hearing missed by a defendant to his/her next appearance in court shall not be included in any time limitation requirements but rather time limits shall begin anew from such next appearance.

[Adopted effective September 1, 2011.]

RULE 10. CONTINUANCES

(A) Bench Trials—Stipulations. The court will grant a continuance after a bench trial date has been set upon a stipulation of the parties not less than one day prior to the date set.

(B) Bench Trials—Written Motion. All requests for a continuance made five working days or less prior to a bench trial not stipulated to by the opposing party shall be presented by written motion and affidavit after notice to the opposing party. Twenty-four hours prior notice to the opposing party shall meet the requirement of this subsection. The court may grant a continuance on a showing of good cause.

(C) Jury Trials. All requests for a continuance of a jury trial shall be presented by a written motion and affidavit with notice provided to the opposing party. Such motions may be heard at the pre-trial hearing. A continuance will be granted only upon a showing of good cause.

(D) Good Cause. The following shall be deemed good cause:

(1) Illness with such verification as may be required by the court; or

(2) Unavoidable and/or unforeseen conflicts; or

(3) Lack of discovery or new evidence requiring investigation.

(E) Imposition of Costs. Payment of costs of the court and the opposing party may be a condition for granting a continuance.

(F) Waiver of Time for Trial Right. A waiver of time for trial right may be required as a condition for granting a continuance.

(G) Infraction Hearings. One telephonic request for a continuance may be granted by the clerk. Thereafter such a request must be in writing and approved by the court.

[Adopted effective September 1, 2011.]

RULE 11. JURY INSTRUCTIONS

(A) When Submitted. Proposed jury instructions shall be submitted when the case is called for trial.

(B) How Submitted. Three sets of instructions shall be submitted on plain 8–1/2 × 11 inch paper. Citations of authority shall not appear on the unnumbered set. One additional set shall be served upon the opposing party.

(C) Pattern Instructions. The court does not maintain pattern instructions. All instructions must be prepared by the offering party.

[Adopted effective September 1, 2011.]

RULE 12. PLEAS IN CRIMINAL CASES— JURY TRIAL SETTINGS

The court shall be notified of a plea agreement not less than two weeks prior to a jury trial. Failure to comply with this rule may result in the imposition of costs, including but not limited to witness, jury, and service of process fees in addition to any other sentence imposed.

[Adopted effective September 1, 2011.]

RULE 13. TELEPHONIC COMMUNICATION

All proceedings, except infraction hearings and criminal changes of plea or trials, may be heard by telephone conference call at the request of either party or the court.

[Adopted effective September 1, 2011.]

RULE 14. RETURN OF EXHIBITS

Every exhibit shall be returned to the party who produced it in a case that was not appealed upon written application not earlier than twenty one days after the trial or sentencing, whichever was later. Exhibits not so withdrawn may be destroyed after thirty days or, if contraband, delivered to the police for destruction.

[Adopted effective September 1, 2011.]

RULE 15. PAYMENT OF FINES AND PENALTIES

(A) Infractions. Infraction penalties shall be paid at the conclusion of any requested hearing, or upon such schedule as may be set by a court approved time payment agreement. A $10 fee shall be assessed per payment plan, traffic infraction only. 46.43.110 [6][c]

(B) Attorney and Jury Fees—Reimbursement. The court may require partial or full reimbursement to the City for the cost of court-appointed counsel and/or jury fees from those defendants the court finds able to pay such.

(C) Conditions of Time Payment. All criminal time payments shall be paid at the rate of $50.00 per month or the total amount due divided by eleven, whichever amount is greater, unless the court approves a different payment schedule.

(D) Community Restitution. The court may impose community restitution in lieu of monetary payments in appropriate cases.

(E) Petition to Modify. The defendant may petition the court to modify monetary payments at any time due to his/her changed financial condition.

(F) Revocation of Probation. Probation shall be revoked for willful failure to pay fines, costs or other assessments.

[Adopted effective September 1, 2011.]

RULE 16. NOTICE OF APPEARANCE IN CONTESTED INFRACTION

(A) Notice of Appearance to City Attorney. Attorneys appearing for a defendant in a contested infraction case shall provide a copy of a Notice of Appearance to the City Attorney contemporaneously with filing the same with the court.

[Adopted effective September 1, 2011.]

RULE 17. AUTOMATIC WITHDRAWAL OF ATTORNEY AT PUBLIC EXPENSE

Unless a Notice of Appeal has been filed, an attorney appointed at public expense shall be deemed automatically withdrawn from representation thirty days following a final decision of the court as defined in RALJ without need to file any document with the court.

[Adopted effective September 1, 2011.]

RULE 18. DECISIONS ON WRITTEN STATEMENTS

(A) Upon the request of the defendant made in writing at least 1 day prior to the date and time set for a contested hearing, the court may consider and decide the case on the basis of written statements, according to the procedure set forth in IRLJ 3.5, as now or hereafter amended. The court may also decide cases set for mitigation hearing on the basis of written statements upon request of the defendant.

(B) The court shall allow written statements through e-mail procedures as established by the presiding judge through administrative order. E-mail procedures shall meet the requirements of IRLJ 3.5.

[Adopted effective September 1, 2011.]

RULE 19. USE OF A COLLECTION AGENCY AND ASSESSMENT AS COURT COST OF AMOUNTS PAID FOR COLLECTION SERVICES

(A) **Contract for Collection.** The court may use the services of a collection agency for the purposes of collecting unpaid and delinquent penalties on infractions, criminal fines, costs, assessments and forfeitures, on the terms and conditions of the contract for collection services between the City of Montesano and said collection agency, and as may be subsequently amended.

(B) **Collection Agency Fee as Cost.** The collection agency's fee or charge, as set forth in said contract, shall be added by the collection agency as a court cost to the total judgment of the court against each defendant whose account is referred to the collection agency.

[Adopted effective September 1, 2011.]

OCEAN SHORES MUNICIPAL COURT LOCAL RULES

Including Amendments Received Through
August 15, 2015

Table of Rules

RULE 1. ADOPTION

These rules are adopted pursuant to GR7 CrRLJ 1.7. and IRLJ 1.3

[Adopted effective July 1, 2005; amended effective September 1, 2011.]

RULE 2. RESERVATION OF DISCRETION

The court reserves the authority to interpret, suspend or modify these rules in individual cases on motion of a party for good cause shown, or its own motion in the interests of justice or the efficient operation of the court.

[Adopted effective July 1, 2005.]

RULE 3. REGULAR COURT SESSIONS

A. Criminal Matters. Regular sessions for criminal matters pending in Ocean Shores Municipal Court shall be held on the third Wednesday of each month, commencing at 1:30 p.m., at the Ocean Shores Convention Center, and/or at such other times and places as the court may deem necessary for its proper administration.

B. Infractions. Regular sessions for traffic infractions and/or other civil infractions pending in Ocean Shores Municipal Court may be held on the third Wednesday of each month, and/or the third Thursday of each month, commencing at 1:30 p.m., at the Ocean Shores Convention Center, and/or, at such other times and places as the court may deem necessary for its proper administration.

[Adopted effective July 1, 2005.]

RULE 4. JUDGE ASSIGNMENT

All cases filed in the court are assigned to the appointed judge of the court.

[Adopted effective July 1, 2005.]

RULE 5. BAIL SCHEDULE

The court shall by written order filed with the court administrator establish bail schedules for use by the Ocean Shores Police Department. The schedule shall designate those types of criminal cases, if any, wherein the defendant may forfeit bail in lieu of arraignment.

[Adopted effective July 1, 2005.]

RULE 6. ARRAIGNMENT DATE

Arraignments shall be in conformance with CrRLJ 3.4 and 4.1. The arresting officer shall set a defendant's arraignment date and time when issuing a citation charging a criminal charge. The dates set shall be consistent with the schedule to be provided by the court administrator. If the charging document states that one or more of the charges against a defendant involves domestic violence, harassment, violation of a no contact order, protection order or anti-harassment order, stalking, driving under the influence of intoxicants and/or drugs, physical control or minor under 21 operating a motor vehicle after consuming alcohol the defendant's arraignment shall be set on the next day in which the court is in session and the defendant's presence shall be mandatory. In all other cases the defendants may appear at the arraignment through an attorney. All citations shall be filed upon issuance.

[Adopted effective July 1, 2005.]

RULE 7. COMBINING DOCUMENTS

A notice of appearance and plea of not guilty may be included in one document. A waiver of jury trial or speedy trial may be separate or combined in one document, and signed by the defendant, or by the defendant's attorney if the attorney certifies that the waiver has been expressly approved by the defendant. A demand for the appearance of a BAC technician, Washington State Toxicologist or a Speed Measuring Device expert pursuant to CrRLJ 6.13 shall be made in a separate document filed with the court and served upon the city attorney. Pleadings or documents may be filed with the court by facsimile, provided that hard copies of the pleadings or documents are subsequently filed with the court and copies are served upon the opposing party.

[Adopted effective July 1, 2005.]

RULE 8. DISCOVERY

Discovery demands shall be by a separate document. Discovery shall be completed by the date set for the pretrial hearing. Failure to provide discovery materials, including bill of particulars if ordered, shall be deemed waived unless the court is notified at the time of the pretrial hearing.

[Adopted effective July 1, 2005.]

RULE 9. MOTIONS AND HEARINGS

A. Pretrial Hearings. A pretrial hearing shall be set in all cases which have not been resolved at the arraignment. The city attorney, the defendant, and the defense attorney, if any, shall attend the pretrial hearing. At the pretrial hearing, the parties shall inform the court whether discovery has been completed, whether a plea bargain agreement has been reached, and if not, whether the case shall be continued, set for a bench trial, or set for a jury trial if a waiver of jury trial has not been previously made. If the case is set for a jury trial, an additional pretrial hearing shall be scheduled at least one (1) week prior to the date set for the jury trial.

B. Motions—All motions including, but not limited to amendments to the charges, for continuance and CrRLJ 3.5 hearing shall be heard at the pretrial hearing. Motions shall not be considered at the time of trial unless they could not have been raised at the pretrial hearing or the court on its own motion continued a matter to the time of trial.

(1) *Filing and Service of Motions*—All motions including supporting briefs, memoranda, documents and affidavits shall be filed and served at least twenty (20) days prior to the scheduled hearing date. The responding party shall file and serve any responding motions, briefs, memoranda, documents and affidavits

at least five (5) days prior to hearing date. The court retains the authority to waive this requirement for good cause shown or if justice otherwise requires. The moving party shall notify the court administrator at the time of the setting of any motion herein if oral testimony is required and shall also provide to the court administrator the estimated time required, for the motion hearing. This rule does not authorize oral testimony when the facts are undisputed or can adequately be presented by affidavit and/or other documentary evidence.

(2) *Judge Working Copy*—A copy of all motions, briefs, memoranda, documents and affidavits and responding motions, briefs, memoranda, documents and affidavits shall be provided to the judge after being filed with the court.

(3) *Motion Hearing Procedure*—Oral argument on motions not requiring testimony shall be limited to fifteen (15) minutes for each side unless the Judge allows additional time, in which case the motion may be placed at the end of the court docket. Hearings requiring testimony shall be heard at the end of the docket or on a date and time to be scheduled by the court administrator. Failure to comply with these rules may result in the striking of the motion, denial of motion or imposition of terms.

C. Subpoenas. A party wishing the attendance of a witness at a hearing shall be responsible for securing a subpoena for the witness except that the city attorney shall subpoena necessary witnesses for a CrRLJ 3.5 hearing if the defendant or defense attorney has requested in writing such an attendance and has given notice for such motion as set forth herein. A party requesting the court to subpoena a witness shall provide the name and address of such witness, and, unless found to be indigent, payment of $50.00 per requested subpoena to pay for the witness and mileage fees, at least ten (10) days prior to the date set for trial.

D. Attendance Required. The Defendant must attend every scheduled court proceeding. If a defendant fails to attend a scheduled court proceeding, a warrant may issue for his/her arrest and all the scheduled court dates, including trial dates, may be stricken at the discretion of the court. The time period from the date of the hearing missed by a defendant until his/her next appearance in court, shall not be included in any time limitation requirements.

[Adopted effective July 1, 2005.]

RULE 10. CONTINUANCES

A. Arraignments. The court administrator may, for good cause, continue an arraignment at the request of the defendant or counsel to the next available court session except in those cases when the charging document states that one or more of the charges involves domestic violence, harassment, violation of a no contact order, protection order or anti-harassment order, stalking, driving under the influence of intoxicants and/or drugs, physical control or minor under 21 operating a motor vehicle after consuming alcohol.

B. Bench Trials—Stipulations. The court will grant a continuance of a bench trial date upon the stipulation of the parties, if filed with the court at least three (3) business days prior to the date set for trial.

C. Bench Trials—Written Motion. All requests for a continuance of a bench trial date not stipulated to by the opposing party shall be made by written motion and affidavit at least five (5) business days prior to the date set for trial, after notice to the opposing party.

D. Jury Trials. All requests for a continuance of a jury trial shall be presented by a written motion and affidavit with notice provided to the opposing party. Such motions shall be made at the pretrial hearing.

E. Good Cause. A motion for continuance of an arraignment, bench trial or a jury trial will be granted only upon a showing of good cause. The following shall be deemed good cause:

1. Illness with such verification as may be required by the court; or,

2. Unavoidable and/or unforeseen conflicts; or,

3. For trials, lack of discovery or discovery of new evidence requiring investigation; or,

4. Other causes, in the discretion of the court.

F. Imposition of Costs. Payment of costs of the court and the opposing party may be a condition for granting a motion for continuance.

G. Speedy Trial Waiver. A waiver of the right to a speedy trial may be required as a condition for granting a motion for continuance. A motion for continuance made by the defendant or defense attorney shall be deemed a waiver of speedy trial, effective until the next date scheduled for the trial.

H. Infraction Hearings. One telephonic request for a continuance may be granted by the court administrator. Thereafter, a request must be in writing and approved by the court.

[Adopted effective July 1, 2005.]

RULE 11. JURY INSTRUCTIONS

A. When Submitted. Proposed jury instructions shall be submitted when the case is called for trial.

B. How Submitted. Three sets of instructions shall be submitted to the court on plain 8 ½ by 11 paper. These sets shall not be numbered. Another set shall be submitted to the opposing party. Citations of authority shall not appear on the unnumbered sets, but can be included on additional sets to be submitted to the trial judge and the opposing party.

C. Pattern Instructions. The court does not maintain pattern instructions. All instructions must be prepared by the offering party.

[Adopted effective July 1, 2005.]

RULE 12. PLEAS IN CRIMINAL CASES— JURY TRIAL SETTINGS

The court shall be notified of a plea bargain agreement not less than two (2) weeks prior to a jury trial. Failure to comply with this rule may result in the imposition of costs in addition to any other sentence imposed.

[Adopted effective July 1, 2005.]

RULE 13. TELEPHONIC AND ELECTRONIC COMMUNICATION

All proceedings except infraction hearings, criminal changes of plea or criminal trials may be heard by telephone conference call at the request of either party with written notice to the court and at the discretion of the judge.

[Adopted effective July 1, 2005.]

RULE 14. RETURN OF EXHIBITS

Every exhibit shall be returned to the party who produced it in a case that is not appealed upon application not earlier than thirty (30) days following the trial or entry of judgment and sentence, whichever was later. Exhibits not so returned may be destroyed after sixty (60) days following the trial or entry of judgment, unless an appeal is filed, or, if contraband, delivered to the police department for destruction.

[Adopted effective July 1, 2005.]

RULE 15. PAYMENT OF FINES AND PENALTIES

A. Infractions. Infraction penalties shall be paid no later than at the conclusion of any requested hearing. A defendant who does not request a contested hearing or a mitigation hearing, but who would like to make payments towards the applicable infraction penalty without appearing in court, may make payment arrangements with the court administrator within fifteen (15) days of the issuance of the notice of infraction.

B. Attorney and Jury Fees—Reimbursement. The court may require partial or full reimbursement to the city for the cost of court appointed counsel and/or jury fees from those defendants the court finds able to pay.

C. Other Costs and Fees. The court may require reimbursement to the city of other costs and fees as provided by statute including but not limited to: costs of incarceration, interpreter fees, emergency response fees, blood/breath testing, and expenses incurred for service of warrants. Assessments of costs and fees shall be subject to limitations provided by statute.

D. Conditions of Time Payment. All time payments in criminal payments shall be paid at the rate of fifty dollars ($50.00) per month or the total amount due divided by eleven, whichever is greater, unless a different payment schedule is approved by the court.

E. Petition to Modify. The defendant may petition the court to modify monetary payments at any time due to his/her changed financial condition.

F. Revocation of Probation. Probation shall be revoked for willful failure to pay fines, costs or other assessments.

[Adopted effective July 1, 2005.]

RULE 16. ELECTRONIC HOME MONITORING

In appropriate cases the court will allow electronic home monitoring in lieu of incarceration for pretrial monitoring and sentencing subject to conditions set forth by the court.

[Adopted effective July 1, 2005.]

RULE 17. RELEASE OF THE ACCUSED

A. Bail. When required to reasonably assure appearance in court for those persons arrested and detained in jail for new offenses, bail shall be set by the court. Bail shall not be set for accused persons arrested for new offenses involving domestic violence, violation of an anti-harassment order, violation of a protection order, or stalking, except at the preliminary appearance or arraignment.

B. Conditions of Release. The court may impose conditions of release pending trial, including, but not limited to: a no-contact order, ignition interlock device, electronic home monitoring, or any other conditions which are appropriate as set forth in CrRLJ 3.2 (a), (b), and (c).

[Adopted effective July 1, 2005.]

RULE 18. AUTOMATIC WITHDRAWAL OF ATTORNEY AT PUBLIC EXPENSE

Unless a Notice of Appeal has been filed, an attorney appointed at public expense shall be deemed automatically withdrawn from representation thirty days following a final decision of the court as defined in RALJ without need to file any document with the court.

[Adopted effective September 1, 2011.]

RULE 19. DECISIONS ON WRITTEN STATEMENTS

A) Upon the request of the defendant made in writing at least 1 day prior to the date and time set for a contested infraction hearing, the court may consider and decide the case on the basis of written statements, according to the procedure set forth in IRLJ 3.5, as now or hereafter amended. The court may also decide cases set for a mitigation hearing on the basis of written statements upon request of the defendant.

B) The court shall allow written statements through e-mail procedures as established by the presiding judge through administrative order. E-mail procedures shall meet the requirements of IRLJ 3.5

[Adopted effective September 1, 2011.]

RULE 20. INFRACTION WITNESS FEES

Each party is responsible for costs incurred by that party as set forth in RCW 46.63.151. The party requesting the witness shall pay the witness fees and mileage expense due that witness. Any person who requests production of an electronic speed measuring devise[1] expert and who is thereafter found by the court to have committed the infraction shall be required to pay the fee charged by the expert as a cost incurred by the party.

[Adopted effective September 2, 2013.]

[1] So in original.

WESTPORT MUNICIPAL COURT LOCAL COURT RULES

Including Amendments Received Through
August 15, 2015

Table of Rules

RULE 1. ADOPTION

These rules are adopted pursuant to GR 7.

[Adopted February 2, 1992.]

RULE 2. RESERVATION OF DISCRETION

The Court reserves the authority to interpret and/or suspend or modify these rules in individual cases on motion of a party for good cause shown or its own motion in the interest of justice and/or the efficient operation of the court.

[Adopted February 2, 1992.]

RULE 3. COURT SESSIONS

Regular court sessions shall be on the first and third Fridays of each month commencing at 9:00 A.M. in the Westport City Hall Council Chambers and at such other times and places as the court may deem necessary for its proper administration.

[Adopted February 2, 1992.]

RULE 4. BAIL SCHEDULE

The court shall by written order filed with the clerk establish bail schedules for use by the police. The schedule shall designate those types of criminal cases, if any, wherein the defendant will be allowed to forfeit bail in lieu of arraignment.

[Adopted February 2, 1992.]

RULE 5. ARRAIGNMENT DATE

The arresting officer will set the defendant's arraignment date and time when issuing a citation in all cases charging a criminal offense. The date set shall be the next Friday court date at 9:00 A.M. until the Sunday immediately preceding a court session. Thereafter, the arraignment is to be set for the court date following. All citations shall be filed upon issuance.

A defendant cited for a violation of RCW 46.61.502, 503 and 504 is required to appear pursuant to RCW 46.61.5051 one (1) judicial day after that arrest. A judicial day may be defined as the first friday of the next month of the third Friday of the month the citation was written in, if the citation was served between the first and third Friday of that month. Appearances at this hearing are mandatory and may not be waived by an appearance of an attorney.

[Adopted February 2, 1992. Amended January 15, 1999.]

RULE 6. COMBINING DOCUMENTS

The notice of appearance and plea of not guilty may be in one document. Waivers of a jury trial or speedy trial shall be separate and signed by the defendant or by the defendant's attorney if the attorney certifies that the defendant has expressly approved the waiver. A demand for the appearance of a breathalyzer/verifier maintenance operator shall be by a separate document. Discovery demands shall be by a separate document.

[Adopted February 2, 1992.]

RULE 7. DISCOVERY

"Blanket" discovery forms may be used provided that each item requested shall contain a box or square in the left margin and shall be checked by the demanding party if that item is to be applicable to the particular case. Demands not applicable shall not be checked. Sanctions may be imposed for violation of this rule including, but not limited to, the quashing of the entire demand. Failure to provide discovery materials, including bills of particulars, shall be deemed waived unless the court is notified in writing not less than two weeks prior to trial.

[Adopted February 2, 1992.]

RULE 8.　PRE–TRIAL HEARINGS

(A) **Hearings.** All cases scheduled for a jury trial shall be set for a pre-trial hearing not less than one month prior to the trial. The city attorney, the defendant and the defense attorney, if any, shall attend the hearing. If a defendant not represented by counsel fails to appear for the hearing, a warrant for his or her arrest shall issue, and the jury trial setting stricken. If a defendant represented by counsel fails to appear, a warrant for defendant's arrest may issue, and the jury trial setting may be stricken. In any case where a defendant fails to appear for the hearing, the period of time from that hearing to the defendant's next personal appearance in court shall not be included in any time limitation requirements.

(B) **Motions.** All amendments to the charges, pleas or other motions shall be heard at the pre-trial hearing. Motions may not be considered at the time of trial unless they could not have been raised at the pre-trial hearing, or the court, on its motion, continues a matter to the time of trial. The party wishing the attendance of a witness at the pre-trial hearing shall be responsible for subpoenas of such witness except that the city attorney shall subpoena necessary witnesses for a CrRLJ 3.5 hearing if the defendant or his attorney has requested in writing such attendance.

[Adopted February 2, 1992.]

RULE 9.　CITIZEN COMPLAINTS

Citizen complaints will be accepted only after approval of the city attorney.

[Adopted February 2, 1992.]

RULE 10.　CONTINUANCES

(A) **Bench Trials—Stipulations.** The court will grant a continuance after a bench trial date has been set upon a stipulation of counsel not less than one day prior to the date set. The defendant must sign all orders of continuance.

(B) **Written Motion: Bench Trials.** All requests for a continuance made five working days or less prior to a non-jury trial not stipulated to by the opposing party shall be presented by written motion and affidavit after notice to the opposing party. Twenty four hours prior notice to the opposing party shall meet the requirement of this sub-section. The court may grant a continuance on a showing of good cause.

(C) **Jury Trials.** A written motion and affidavit shall present all requests for a continuance of a jury trial with notice provided to the opposing party. Such motions may be heard at the pre-trial hearing. A continuance will be granted only upon a showing of good cause.

(D) **Good Cause.** The following shall be deemed to be good cause:

(1) Illness;

(2) Unavoidable and/or unforeseen conflicts;

(3) Unforeseen unavailability of witnesses; or,

(4) Lack of discovery or new evidence requiring investigation.

(E) **Imposition of Costs.** Payment of costs of the court and the opposing party may be a condition for granting a continuance.

(F) **Speedy Trial Waiver.** A waiver of the speedy trial rule may be required as a condition for granting a continuance. Waivers must be to a date certain.

(G) **Infraction Hearing.** The court clerk may grant one telephone request for a continuance. Thereafter, the request must be in writing and approved by the court.

[Adopted February 2, 1992.]

RULE 11.　JURY INSTRUCTIONS

(A) **When Submitted.** Proposed jury instructions shall be submitted when the case is called for trial.

(B) **How Submitted.** Three sets of instructions shall be submitted on plain 8½ × 11 inch paper. Citations of authority shall not appear on the unnumbered set. One additional set shall be served upon the opposing party.

(C) **Pattern Instructions.** Only instructions approved by the court and availability to it in photocopy form may be requested by reference. The offering party must prepare all other instructions.

[Adopted February 2, 1992.]

RULE 12.　PLEAS IN CRIMINAL CASES—JURY TRIAL SET

The court shall be notified of a plea agreement not less than one week prior to a jury trial. Failure to comply with this rule may result in the imposition of costs in addition to any other sentence imposed.

[Adopted February 2, 1992.]

RULE 13.　TELEPHONIC COMMUNICATION

All proceedings except criminal changes of pleas or trials may be heard by telephone conference call at the request of either party or the court.

[Adopted February 2, 1992.]

RULE 14.　RETURN OF EXHIBITS

Every exhibit shall be returned to the party who produced it in a case that was not appealed upon written application not earlier than twenty one days after the trial. Exhibits not so withdrawn shall be destroyed after thirty days, or, if contraband, delivered to the police for destruction.

[Adopted February 2, 1992.]

RULE 15. PAYMENT OF FINES AND PENALTIES

(A) Infractions. Infraction penalties imposed shall be paid at the conclusion of any requested hearing unless the court specifically orders otherwise.

(B) Attorney and Jury Fees—Reimbursement. The court may require partial or full reimbursement to the city for the cost of court appointed counsel and/or jury fees from those defendants the court finds able to pay such.

(C) Conditions of Time Payment. All criminal time payments shall be paid at the rate of $50.00 per month or the total amount due divided by the number of probation months, not to exceed twelve months, which ever amount is greater, unless a different payment schedule is expressly approved by the court.

(D) Community Service. The court may impose community service in lieu of monetary payments in appropriate cases.

(E) Petition to Modify. The defendant may petition the court to modify monetary payments at any time due to his or her changed financial condition.

(F) Revocation of Probation. Probation shall be revoked for willful failure to pay fines, costs or other assessments.

[Adopted February 2, 1992.]

RULE 16. WEAPONS IN AREA OF COURT

No person except on duty police officers shall possess any weapon in the Westport City Hall during court sessions.

At all times no person shall possess any weapon in the court office or hallway in front of the court office.

The clerk shall post a copy of this rule on the entrance door in the court office and the courtroom when the court is in session.

The Chief of police or his designee is designated as the custodian of weapons and shall provide a procedure for the receipt, storage and return of all weapons pursuant to Chapter 396, Laws of 1993.

[Adopted 1993.]

HELLS CANYON CIRCUIT

Table of Courts

Superior Court

Hells Canyon Circuit Local Rules.

SUPERIOR COURT

HELLS CANYON CIRCUIT LOCAL RULES
[PREVIOUSLY KNOWN AS THE LOCAL RULES OF THE SUPERIOR COURT OF THE STATE OF WASHINGTON FOR THE JUDICIAL DISTRICT OF ASOTIN, COLUMBIA, AND GARFIELD COUNTIES]

Including Amendments Received Through
August 15, 2015

Table of Rules

HCCLR 1 TO HCCLR 24.   [RESCINDED]

[Rescinded effective September 2, 2014.]

LCR 5. SERVICE AND FILING OF PLEADINGS AND OTHER PAPERS

(e) Filing with the Court.

(1) *Bench Copies.* Bench copies of documents may, but need not be, submitted electronically via email to the court administrator at Superior.Court@co.asotin.

wa.us. Parties without access to a computer and the internet shall deliver bench copies to the Court Administrator. All bench copies must be submitted not later than nine (9:00) o'clock a.m. one court day prior to the scheduled hearing, proceeding or trial. No bench copies shall be submitted to the Court unless prior thereto or simultaneously therewith a copy thereof has been served upon or mailed to opposing counsel.

(2) *Documents Not to be Filed.* Photocopies of reported cases, statutes or texts shall not be filed as an appendix to a brief or otherwise but may be

furnished directly to the judge hearing the matter. Documents or copies thereof produced during discovery and other items which should properly be received as exhibits rather than as a part of the court file shall not be included in the court file.

[Adopted effective September 2, 2014.]

LCR 6. TIME

(d) For Motions—Affidavits.

(1) *Notes for Civil Motions Calendar.* Responding documents and briefs must be filed with the clerk and copies served on all parties and the court no later than 12:00 noon two (2) court days prior to the hearing. Copies of any documents replying to the response must be filed with the clerk and served on all parties and the court not later than 12 noon of the court day prior to the hearing. This section does not apply to CR 56 summary judgment motions. Absent prior approval of the court, responsive or reply materials will not include either audio or video tape recordings.

(2) *Notes for Family Law Motion Calendar.* Any party desiring to bring any family law motion, other than a motion to reconsider (governed by LCR 59), on the family law motion calendar must file such motion documents with the Clerk and serve all parties and the court at least twelve (12) days before the date fixed for such hearing. Responding documents and briefs must be filed with the clerk and copies served on all parties and the court no later than 12:00 noon, five (5) court days before the hearing. Copies of any additional responding or reply documents must be filed with the clerk and served on all parties and the Court not later than 12:00 noon three (3) court days before the hearing. Absent prior approval of the court, responsive or reply materials will not include either audio or video tape recordings.

(3) *Late Filing.* Any material submitted later than required by this rule, upon objection of counsel, may be rejected by the Court, or the matter may be continued and/or the court may impose appropriate terms or sanctions.

[Adopted effective September 2, 2014.]

LCR 7. MOTIONS AND HEARINGS

(5) **Telephonic argument.** Arguments on motions are to be conducted in person, except that, by specific arrangement with the court administrator at least two days before a hearing, argument may be made by telephone PROVIDED, (1) that all parties agree to telephonic argument; and (2) that the judicial officer before whom the hearing will be conducted approves of telephonic argument. A party may withhold agreement to telephonic argument only for reasonable, articulable cause. For good cause shown, on motion of a party, the court may order telephonic argument of a motion in the absence of such agreement. A motion to allow or disallow telephonic argument shall itself be argued by telephone unless all affected parties are before the court when the motion is made.

(6) **Verbatim record.** By utilizing and/or consenting to the option to appear and argue telephonically, each party stipulates that any portion of the proceedings which is inaudible to any the reporter transcribing the record will be noted as such in the record without jeopardy to the reporter or to any transcript being deemed accurate and complete.

(7) **Time Limits for Hearings.** Civil and domestic/family law and motion dockets are limited to matters typically requiring no more than ten (10) minutes to present. Matters expected to exceed that limitation must be specially set by the Court or its administrator.

(8) **Required Special Settings.** The following matters may not be noted on the court's regular dockets, but must be specially set with the court administrator: motions for summary judgment; arguments on the merits in appeals from lower courts or tribunals; child hearsay (Ryan) hearings.

(9) **Hearings on Requests for Temporary Orders.** Hearings with respect to all temporary orders, including adequate cause, in dissolution, parentage and family law matters shall be held and determined upon affidavits, declarations, and argument only. Said affidavits or declarations shall be filed and served in the same manner as other pleadings and orders in civil cases and as prescribed by this rule. When any order has been applied for and refused in whole or in part or has been granted conditionally and the condition has not been performed, the same application for an order must not be presented to another judge without advising the second judge of the fact that the order was previously refused or conditioned and that application is again being made.

(10) **Non–contested Dissolution.** These cases may be heard on the Court Docket days set forth in LCR77. Non contested dissolution cases may also be presented to the Superior Court Judge in Chambers without the appearance of either party. The jurisdictional testimony and other testimony in support of the dissolution must be done in affidavit form or a declaration pursuant to GR 13.

(11) **Proposed Orders.** A proposed form of order, which the Court may adopt, modify, or reject consistent with the decision of the Court, shall be served with the motion or response to motion. Proposed orders should not be filed with the clerk.

(12) **Originals of Proposed Orders.** Originals of proposed orders shall be retained by counsel for presentation at the hearing on the motion.

[Adopted effective September 2, 2014.]

LCR 16. PRETRIAL PROCEDURE AND FORMULATING ISSUES/MEDIATION

(c) Pre–Trial Conference in Non Domestic Civil Cases. Any pre-trial conference should be held not less than two weeks prior to the trial date unless otherwise scheduled by the Court.

(d) Exhibits. Parties shall notify the trial judge and the opposing party by letter, fax copy, or electronic mail if that party anticipates offering 25 exhibits or more at time of trial. Said notice shall be given no less than 2 weeks prior to the trial date unless the proffering party could not reasonably known of their existence prior to that time.

(e) Settlement Conference in Non Family Law Cases on Court's Motion. The court to which a case is assigned for trial may, upon its own motion, either before or after a trial date has been set, order a settlement conference in any pending case, and a settlement conference shall be held.

(1) *Preparation and Attendance.* The attorney personally in charge of each party's case shall personally attend all settlement conferences unless telephonic participation has been approved by the Court. Not less than three (3) days prior to the date set for the settlement conference, serve on the assigned judge or commissioner and the attorney for the opposing party a letter succinctly addressing the following:

    a. A brief factual summary;

    b. Issues regarding liability;

    c. Issues regarding damages, both special and general;

    d. History of any settlement negotiations; and

    e. Current position on settlement.

(2) *Attendance of Parties.* The parties shall in all cases attend the settlement conference. Parties whose defense is provided by a liability insurance company need not personally attend said settlement conference, but a representative of the insurer of such party, if such a representative is available in the county in which the matter is pending, shall attend with sufficient authority to bind the insurer to a settlement. In the event such a representative is not available, counsel representing the party whose defense is provided by the insurer shall make a good faith effort to obtain settlement authority to bind the insurer to a settlement prior to the settlement conference. Attendance of any party may be excused by the court where by reason of health, or other good and sufficient reason, compelling his personal attendance would be unduly burdensome. Whether or not the attendance of any party is required shall rest in the discretion of the Judge or Commissioner scheduled to conduct the conference.

(3) *Proceedings Privileged.* Proceedings of said settlement conference shall, in all respects, be privileged and shall not be reported or recorded. No party shall be bound unless a settlement is reached. When a settlement has been reached, the judge may, at the request of any party, in his discretion, order the settlement to be reported or recorded.

(4) *Sanctions.* Where a party has wilfully failed to comply with any of the provisions of this rule the court may make such orders as are just which may also include the award of reasonable expenses, including attorney's fees, caused by the failure, unless the court finds that the failure was substantially justified or that other circumstances make an award of expenses unjust.

(f) Pre–Trial Procedure in Domestic Relation Cases.

(1) *Mandatory Mediation in Domestic Relations Cases.* All contested issues in every domestic relations case, except matters limited to child support, establishment of paternity, or the existence of adequate cause, shall be submitted to mandatory mediation before proceeding to trial. Mediation shall be completed 30 days prior to trial. The mediation requirement or time limits may be waived or modified by the Court upon motion for good cause shown or upon the Court's motion. Sanctions in accordance subsection (e)(4) above may be imposed by the Court against a party found not to have participated in mediation in good faith.

(2) *Mediation No Stay.* Mediation does not stay or otherwise affect the rights and duties of the parties established by statute, court rule, or court order.

(3) *Selection of Mediator.* The parties may choose their own mediator approved by the Court. Absent an agreement, upon motion of either party, the Court will select a mediator. The parties are responsible for the cost of mediation equally unless otherwise ordered by the Court.

(4) *Authority of Mediator.* The mediator has the authority to set the time, place, manner, duration of mediation, and retainer required to be paid by both parties before mediation will commence. The mediator also has the right to terminate mediation.

(5) *Participation.* Only the parties and their counsel shall attend mediation sessions, unless leave is granted by the mediator for other persons to attend and/or participate. The mediator is empowered to exclude non-parties from the premises where the mediation is taking place in order to minimize disruption to the process.

(6) *Report.* Within seven (7) days of completion of mediation, a declaration of completion shall be filed with the Court by the mediator. The parties shall be advised by the mediator of the results of mediation in writing. The mediator shall advise the Court whether or not an agreement has been reached on some or all of the issues.

(7) *Payment.* Mediators shall be paid by the parties in accordance with their agreement, and if none,

as determined in mediation or ordered thereafter by the Court.

(8) *Proceedings Privileged.* The work product of the mediator and all communications to the mediator during the mediation process are confidential and may not be disclosed. The mediator shall not appear to testify in any court action except as may be necessary to secure payment of the mediator's fees.

(g) Pretrial Statement–Contested Dissolutions. In any action for dissolution of a marriage in which property division, the parenting plan, spousal maintenance or child support is an issue, each party shall serve on the other party and file with the court a written summary setting forth:

(1) Statement of the issues.

(2) A statement of the party's proposed resolution of the issues.

(3) A description and valuation of the assets and liabilities of the parties, together with a proposed division thereof.

(4) The party's proposed parenting plan.

(5) Child Support calculations.

Each party's written summary must be served and filed no later than four days before the pretrial conference or settlement conference, whichever occurs first. Failure to timely serve and file the summary as required may result in sanctions.

[Adopted effective September 2, 2014.]

LCR 32. USE OF DEPOSITIONS IN COURT PROCEEDINGS

(a) Use of Depositions.

(6) *Video Depositions.* When presenting video depositions, a written deposition must also be filed. The videotape may be returned after the appeal period, regardless of whether it is published or not.

[Adopted effective September 2, 2014.]

LCR 37. FAILURE TO MAKE DISCOVERY; SANCTIONS

(f) Completion of Discovery. Unless otherwise stipulated to by the parties, or ordered by the Court upon good cause shown and such terms and conditions as are just, all discovery allowed under CR 26 through 37, including responses and supplementation thereto, must be completed no later than 35 calendar days prior to the date assigned for trial. Nothing herein stated shall modify a party's responsibility to seasonably supplement responses to discovery requests or otherwise comply with discovery prior to the 35–day cutoff.

[Adopted effective September 2, 2014.]

LCR 47. JURY SELECTION

(d) Procedure. The Court will use a struck jury method of jury selection as follows:

(1) *Jury Pool.* A list constituting the jury pool and copies of juror profiles for a particular trial will be available prior to or on the morning of trial.

(2) *Assigning seat numbers for jurors.* The jury administrator shall assign seat numbers to jurors in consecutive order based on their order of appearance in a randomly generated list. Counsel and parties do not need to be present during this process.

(3) *Seating jurors.* The Jury Administrator and/or bailiff will provide each prospective juror with a badge identifying the jurors seating number. With the assistance of the Jury Administrator and/or the bailiff, the jurors will be seated in the courtroom on the spectator benches in numerical order with their seating number badges prominently displayed. In the event a juror is absent after the seating numbers have been assigned, that juror's seat will remain vacant. Counsel may be seated facing the prospective jurors.

(4) *Questions by the court.* The judge will begin the voir dire process with introductory information and general questions. The court may excuse a juror for cause at anytime grounds for dismissal are established. Counsel may challenge for cause at anytime after the judge has completed his or her examination. Any party may request the Court to ask prospective jurors appropriate additional general questions proposed in advance in writing and submitted with jury instructions.

(5) *Questions by counsel.* The attorneys or parties will then question the jurors.

(6) *Peremptory challenges.* When questioning by the court and counsel is completed, the Court will allow the private exercise of peremptory challenges by striking name of the first exercised challenge from the panel of the first 12 jurors remaining after the entire panel has been passed for cause. Subsequent strikes will be made from the panel of the first twelve remaining after each successive peremptory strike.

(7) *Alternate jurors.* If the Court elects to seat an alternate juror, the alternate is the next juror remaining in numerical order after the jury of twelve has been selected. Additional peremptory challenges will be added for the alternate and may be exercised in the same fashion as with respect to the regular jurors.

[Adopted effective September 2, 2014.]

LCR 51. JURY INSTRUCTIONS

(b) Submission. Ten (10) days prior to trial, Plaintiff/Petitioner shall prepare, file, and serve a two sets of proposed instructions. The first set shall numbered and shall contain citations either to the WPI number or the appropriate authority for the instruction. The second set shall be "clean" and will be unnumbered and contain no citations to authorities. Plaintiff/Petitioner shall also submit a cover sheet, verdict form(s), and witness list along with its proposed jury instructions. The Defendant/Respondent shall prepare, file, and serve any new or additional instructions without duplication of the instructions submitted by Plaintiff/Petitioner, and a witness list. In civil cases, a statement of the case to the prospective jurors shall be submitted at the same time.

(c) Numbering and Arrangement. Citations shall be in the lower left-hand corner. All instructions shall be arranged in a logical order. All instructions with citations of authority shall be numbered by the submitting party at the top center of the first page.

[Adopted effective September 2, 2014.]

LCR 53.2. COURT COMMISSIONERS

(e) Revision by the Court.

(1) *Motion Content and Service Deadlines.* A party seeking revision off a Court Commissioner's ruling shall within ten (10) days of entry of the written order, file and serve a Motion for Revision. The motion must set forth specific grounds for each claimed error and argument and legal authorities in support thereof. The motion shall be accompanied by a copy of the order for which revision is sought, along with copies of all papers which were before the Commissioner in support, or in opposition in the original proceedings. A copy of the motion and all supporting documents shall be provided to all other parties to the proceedings and to the Court Administrator who shall refer the motion to the appropriate Judge for consideration. The responding party shall have five (5) working days from the receipt of the motion to file a written response with the Clerk and provide copies to all other parties and to the Court Administrator.

(2) *Transcript Required.* When seeking revision of a ruling of the Court Commissioner which was based on testimony, such testimony must be transcribed and attached to the motion. If the transcript is not timely available, the moving party must set forth arrangements which have been made to secure the transcript.

(3) *Review is De Novo.* Review of the Commissioner's order shall be de novo based on the pleadings and transcript submitted and without oral argument unless requested by the reviewing Judge.

(4) *Scope of Motion.* The Judge may deny the motion, revise any order or judgment which is related to the issue raised by the motion for revision or remand to the Commissioner for further proceedings. The Judge may not consider evidence or issues which were not before the Commissioner or not raised by the motion for revision. The Judge may consider a request for attorney fees by either party for the revision proceedings.

(5) *Effect on Commissioner's Order.* The Court Commissioner's written order shall remain effective unless and until revised by the Judge or unless stayed by the Judge pending proceedings related to the motion for revision.

[Adopted effective September 2, 2014.]

LCR 59. MOTION FOR RECONSIDERATION

(e) Hearing on Motion.

(3) *Nature of Hearing.* A motion for reconsideration or for a new trial shall be submitted on briefs and declarations or affidavits only, without oral argument, unless the trial judge, on application from counsel or on the judge's own motion, allows oral argument. The judge will notify counsel if oral argument is to be allowed. Copies of such motions for reconsideration, copy of note for motion calendar and responses thereto shall be delivered to the judge at the time of filing.

[Adopted effective September 2, 2014.]

LCR 77. SUPERIOR COURTS AND JUDICIAL OFFICERS

(f) Sessions. The Court shall be in session on all judicial days from 8:45 a.m. to 12:00 noon, and from 1:15 p.m. to 4:30 p.m. Cases may be set for other dates and times. Normally jury trials begin at 9:00 a.m. and non-jury trials begin at 9:30 a.m. In case of conflict, the cases will be heard according to priority assigned on the basis of the nature and age of the case. In event of a conflict which prevents a trial from beginning as scheduled, parties will be expected to be available to commence the trial at the next available date.

(1) At this time, the regular docket days for each county are:

Asotin County's Superior Court schedule is as follows: 1st, 3rd and 4th Mondays of the month; and 1st and 3rd Tuesdays of the month:

Columbia County's Superior Court schedule is as follows: 1st and 3rd Wednesdays of the month:

Garfield County's Superior Court schedule is as follows: 1st and 3rd Thursdays of the month:

For updated information regarding the Court's calendar or to to obtain a special setting for matters requiring more than ten (10) minutes to present, contact the Court Administrator at 509–243–2082. Additional information for each county can be found online.

A COURT REPORTER WILL NOT BE PROVIDED FOR ANY MATTER SCHEDULED ON ANY CALENDAR. ALL MATTERS WILL BE DIGITALLY AUDIO RECORDED.

(2) *Holiday Scheduling*—These Court schedules will be altered when affected by Holidays. Please check with the Court Administrator for the next docket date—(509) 243–2082.

(3) The Judge may by order further alter these court schedules as needed and as available courtroom space requires.

(4) Ex parte matters and emergency orders and writs will be considered at the opening of court each day prior to the commencement of trial or the regular court calendar or at such other time as the judges and/or court commissioners are available.

Non-emergency matters shall be left with the Clerk and the judge/commissioner will consider the same when available.

[Adopted effective September 2, 2014.]

LCR 81.　APPLICABILITY IN GENERAL

(a) To What Proceedings Applicable.

(1) *Generally.* In general, procedure in this Court shall be in accordance with pertinent Washington Court Rules as heretofore or hereafter adopted by the Supreme Court of Washington. These local rules are intended only to supplement those rules and are numbered, insofar as possible, to conform to the existing numbering system. The Rules shall also apply to criminal cases insofar as they are applicable.

(2) *Suspension of Rules.* The Court may modify or suspend any of these Rules in any given case, upon good cause being shown therefore, or upon the Court's own motion.

[Adopted effective September 2, 2014.]

LGALR 2.　GENERAL RESPONSIBILITIES OF GUARDIAN AD LITEM

(d) Any person successfully completing the CASA GAL training program offered by the Second Judicial District for the State of Idaho in Nez Perce County with Washington supplementation or similar training in this State shall qualify for the Court's R.C.W. 13.34.102 registry for any county in the District upon request and submission of credentials.

[Adopted effective September 2, 2014.]

LGALR 7.　GRIEVANCE PROCEDURES

(1) **Complaint.** Any grievance or dispute regarding any Guardian ad Litem shall be presented in writing to the Court for submission to a committee of not less than three persons selected by the Court, two of whom must be elected for the respective county, and the third, the Juvenile Court Administrator of the respective county. The committee shall have the authority to obtain a written response, hold a hearing, and make recommendations to the Court ranging from dismissal of the grievance to removal and replacement of the Guardian ad Litem.

(2) **CASA.** If the complaint involves a Guardian ad Litem from the Court Appointed Special Advocates Association, the grievance resolution procedure set forth by the association may be substituted by order of the Court provided that the resolution can occur within the time frame set forth in subsection (3) below.

(3) **Time.** The complaint must be resolved within 25 days for any complaint filed while a case is pending or 60 days for any complaint filed subsequent to the conclusion of a case.

[Adopted effective September 2, 2014.]

LSPR 98.16W.　APPROVAL OF FEES IN CERTAIN CASES

(f) When the Court is called upon to fix the compensation for acting on behalf of a minor or a disabled person, the following guidelines shall be considered:

(1) *Settlement less than $500,000.* If the case is settled and the amount of settlement is $500,000 or less, the attorney's fees should not exceed 1/3 of the amount recovered, exclusive of costs of suit.

(2) *Settlement over $500,000.* If the amount of a settlement is over $500,000, the attorney's fees should not exceed 1/3 of the first $500,000 recovered, exclusive of costs of suit, and 25% of the excess over $500,000 recovered, exclusive of costs of suit.

(3) *Costs of Suit Defined.* For these purposes, "costs of suit" shall mean the expenses of litigation.

(4) If there is an appeal, an additional reasonable fee will be considered.

[Adopted effective September 2, 2014.]

LCrR 4.9.　FINAL PRETRIAL CONFERENCE

(a) Counsel shall report to the Judge at least one day before the scheduled beginning of a jury trial and provide the Judge with a written list of the names and city of residence of witnesses and general voir dire questions to be asked of the jury. Counsel shall advise the Court of any final pretrial matters to be decided by the court. Pretrial matters requiring argument shall be noted for hearing prior to the morning of the trial. Jury trials should be conducted with minimal interruptions of the jury's time. To this end, matters which need to be heard outside the presence of the jury should be anticipated so that they can be considered during jury breaks or before or after the jury's day.

[Adopted effective September 2, 2014.]

LCrR 6.3.　SELECTING THE JURY

(a) The procedure used for jury selection in a criminal case shall be as set forth in LCR 47.

[Adopted effective September 2, 2014.]

ISLAND COUNTY

Table of Courts

Superior Court

Local Rules of the Superior Court for Island County.

District Court and Municipal Courts

Local Rules of the District Court of Island County and the Municipal Courts of the City of Oak Harbor and the Town of Coupeville.
Langley Municipal Court Local Rules.

SUPERIOR COURT

LOCAL COURT RULES OF THE SUPERIOR COURT FOR ISLAND COUNTY

Including Amendments Received Through
August 15, 2015

Table of Rules

PART I. LOCAL CIVIL RULES (LCR)

1. INTRODUCTORY
(Rules 1–2A)

LCR 1. SCOPE OF RULES

Unless specifically designated otherwise, these rules shall govern the local procedure in the Island County Superior Court. These rules are subject to amendment at the direction of the judges. Counsel and litigants should check with the court administrator or county clerk to assure that the rules applicable to their matters are currently in effect. These local rules are supplemental to the Washington State Supreme Court Civil Rules (CR). In all cases where the word "counsel" is used, the provisions shall apply equally to a party appearing without counsel, which party is also known as a "party *pro se.*"

[Adopted effective September 1, 1999; amended effective September 1, 2000; September 1, 2008; September 1, 2011; September 1, 2012.]

2. COMMENCEMENT OF ACTION; SERVICE OF PROCESS, PLEADINGS, MOTIONS AND ORDERS
(Rules 3–6)

LCR 3–4.2. *[NO LOCAL RULES]*

LCR 5. SERVICE AND FILING OF PLEADINGS AND OTHER PAPERS

(a) Service—When Required.

(1) *Emergency Orders.* A party applying for an emergency order which will require or forbid the doing of some act shall notify the opponent or his or her counsel, if known, and shall request his or her presence at presentation of the order, unless good cause to the contrary is shown. If the opponent or opponent's counsel does not appear, the judge shall require a full showing with respect to the notice given.

(b)—(c) (No Local Rules)

(d) Filing.

(1) *Time.* All notices for the law and motion calendar shall be filed with the clerk of the court no later than 4:30 p.m. seven (7) days preceding the date of the hearing.

(2)—(3) *(No Local Rules)*

(e) Filing With the Court Defined.

(1) *Filing with the Clerk.* The filing of pleadings and other papers with the court as required by these rules shall be made by filing them with the clerk of the court, and not the court administrator's office or the judge.

(2) *Facsimile Filing of Pleadings with Clerk.* Documents, including pleadings, may be filed with the clerk by facsimile transmission, in accordance with GR 17, with the following change: In addition to the requirements of a fax transmittal sheet contained in GR 17(b)(2), the fax transmittal sheet shall also contain the title and number of pages for each document sent in the transmission.

(3) *Courtesy Copies for Judges.* Courtesy copies of pleadings and other papers shall be provided to the court administrator's office for the judge assigned to the case at the same time as such pleadings and other papers are required to be served on the opposing party. Such courtesy copies shall have the words "Judge's Courtesy Copy" in the upper right hand corner of the first page, the judge's name, and the date and time of the hearing. Courtesy copies are discarded after ten (10) days from the assigned hearing date. It is the responsibility of the parties or counsel to provide new courtesy copies to the judge thereafter as provided herein.

(f)—(j) (No Local Rules)

(k) Special Set Hearings. In the event argument on the motion is expected to be longer than 15 minutes, the moving party shall confer with the opposing counsel or party, and then contact the court administrator's office to obtain a special set hearing date and time that takes into account the opposing party's reasonable conflicts.

[Effective September 1, 2002; amended effective September 1, 2008; September 1, 2011; September 1, 2012.]

LCR 6. TIME

(a)—(c) (No Local Rules)

(d) For Motions—Affidavits.

(1) *Time.* Notwithstanding CR 6(d), a written motion, other than one which may be heard *ex parte*, and notice of the hearing thereof shall be served not later than twelve (12) days before the time specified for the hearing, unless a different period is fixed by these rules or by order of the court. Such an order may for cause shown be made on *ex parte* application as set

forth in LCR 6(f). When a motion is supported by affidavit, the affidavit shall be served with the motion, and, except as otherwise provided in CR 59(c), opposing affidavits may be served no later than 4 p.m. six (6) calendar days prior to the hearing. Reply affidavits in strict reply to the opposing affidavits may be served no later than 4 p.m. four (4) calendar days prior to the hearing. No additional responses or replies shall be permitted from either party without permission of the court. All motions, affidavits and other documents served on opposing party shall be fully conformed as to signatures, dates signed, date filed, and all other information as it appears on the filed original.

(2) *Conformed Copies.* Court documents served on opposing parties shall be fully conformed as to signatures, dates signed, date filed, and all other information as it appears on the original once it is filed.

(3) *Signatures.* Declarations or affidavits shall be signed by the declarant or affiant.

(e) (No Local Rules).

(f) **Motion to Shorten Time.** A motion to shorten time for LCR 6(d) shall be granted only upon good cause shown. The party requesting an order to shorten time shall give verbal and written notice as soon as possible to opposing party or his or her counsel, if known, regardless of when the motion is prepared and provided. Copies of the motion, declaration, proposed order, and other applicable pleadings and papers shall be provided to the opposing party or his or her counsel, if possible. The motion shall contain a written certification that *pro se* parties or counsel were notified of the time and place when the motion to shorten time is to be heard, or the reasons why such notice was not given. Failure to provide notice may result in terms.

[Effective September 1, 2002; Amended effective September 1, 2006; September 1, 2008; September 1, 2011; September 1, 2012; September 1, 2015.]

3. PLEADINGS AND MOTIONS
(Rules 7–16)

LCR 7. PLEADINGS ALLOWED; FORM OF MOTIONS

(a) (No Local Rules).

(b) **Motions and Other Papers.**

(1)—(3) *(No Local Rules)*

(4) *Identification of Evidence.* The evidence on which the motion or reply is based shall be identified with particularity. Deposition testimony, discovery pleadings, and documentary evidence must be quoted verbatim, or a photocopy of relevant pages must be attached. Deposition testimony in connection with a motion shall not require publication unless a challenge is made and opposing party shows good cause for such publication. Depositions used in this fashion shall remain unopened and not a part of the court file unless otherwise ordered by the court.

(5) *Telephonic Argument.* Oral argument on civil motions, including family law motions, may be heard by conference telephone call through the CourtCall Telephonic Appearance Program ("CourtCall"). The court shall hear CourtCall appearances in the order in which they are noted on the calendar, unless the court exercises its discretion to call cases in a different manner.

(A) Hearings Unsuitable for CourtCall. The following matters are currently deemed unsuitable for CourtCall appearances: Judgment debtor examinations; settlement conferences; hearings or trial at which oral testimony may be presented; hearings in which oral argument is anticipated to exceed 15 minutes. (no criminal cases may be heard by courtcall)

(B) Scheduling CourtCall. CourtCall appearances are scheduled by the party desiring to use CourtCall not less than seven (7) court days prior to the hearing date by calling CourtCall (1–888–882–6878), filling out any required forms, paying the stated fee, and following all procedures set by CourtCall. The court may shorten the time for requesting CourtCall for good cause shown. No calls with a cellular or cordless telephone device or through a personal computer shall be permitted. The party making a CourtCall appearance shall eliminate to the greatest extent possible all ambient noise from the calling location and speak directly into a telephone headset. No private recordings may be made of telephonic appearances.

(C) CourtCall Appearances at Hearing. Parties utilizing CourtCall shall call the court's designated toll free teleconference line approximately five (5) minutes prior to the scheduled time and check-in with the clerk. All persons calling after the check-in period shall be considered to be late for the hearing and shall be treated by the court in the same manner as if the party had personally appeared late for the hearing. Any party appearing by CourtCall shall not utilize the "hold" button, as it is not within the policy of the court to wait for any person to rejoin the line.

(D) Court May Reject or Halt CourtCall Appearances. The court reserves the right, at any time, to reject any request for CourtCall appearances. When the court rejects a request, it shall order a refund of deposited telephonic appearance fees and notify CourtCall, LLC. The court reserves the right to halt the telephonic hearing on any matter and order the attorneys to personally appear at a later date and time, in which case no refund is permitted

(c)—(d) (No Local Rules)

(e) Motions and Orders to Be Separate. Motions and orders shall not be combined into one document. An order shall always be set forth in a separate document.

[Effective September 1, 2002; amended effective September 1, 2004; September 1, 2005; September 1, 2008; September 1, 2011; September 1, 2012; September 2, 2014.]

LCR 8. GENERAL RULES OF PLEADING [NO LOCAL RULE]

[Repealed effective September 1, 2011.]

LCR 9. PLEADING SPECIAL MATTERS [NO LOCAL RULE]

[Repealed effective September 1, 2011.]

LCR 10. FORM OF PLEADINGS AND OTHER PAPERS

(a)—(c) (No Local Rules)

(d) Format Requirements. [See GR 14.]

(1) *Tabs or Separators in Documents.* Any tabs or separators used within documents shall be placed at the bottom of the page only.

(2) *Typing or Legible Printing.* All court documents submitted for filing must be typed or printed legibly using black or dark blue ink. Cursive writing is not allowed. All typing or printing shall be double-spaced.

(3) *Photocopies.* Photocopies of documents shall be legible.

(e) Format Recommendations.

(1)—(6) *(No Local Rules)*

(7) *Black and White Photographs.* Color photographs do not produce usable scanned or microfilmed images. Black and white reproductions are preferred.

(f)—(g) (No Local Rules)

[Effective September 1, 2002; amended effective September 1, 2008; September 1, 2011; September 1, 2012.]

LCR 11. SIGNING AND DRAFING OF PLEADINGS, MOTIONS, AND LEGAL MEMORANDA; SANCTIONS[1]

(a) Violations of Local Court Rules. Violation of these local court rules may result in sanctions as set forth in CR 11.

(b) (No Local Rules)

[Effective September 1, 2002; amended effective September 1, 2008; September 1, 2011; September 1, 2012.]

[1] So in original

LCR 12–15. *[NO LOCAL RULES]*

LCR 16. PRETRIAL PROCEDURE AND FORMULATING ISSUES

(a)—(b) (No Local Rules)

(c) Pretrial Readiness Hearings.

(1) *Time.* The court administrator shall set pretrial readiness hearings in all civil and domestic cases approximately a month prior to the assigned trial date.

(2) *Matters Considered.* Matters to be considered at the readiness hearing may include, but are not limited to, the following: Completion of mandatory mediation, completion of mandatory parenting seminar, witness availability, confirmation of length of trial, continuance of trial date pursuant to LCR 40(e), and pretrial motions.

(3) *Completion of Discovery.* Unless otherwise stipulated by the parties, or ordered by the court upon good cause shown and on such terms and conditions as are just, all discovery allowed under CR 26–37, including responses and supplementation thereto, must be completed no later than the scheduled date of the pretrial readiness hearing. Nothing herein stated shall modify a party's responsibility to promptly supplement responses to discovery or otherwise comply with discovery.

(4) *Statement of Readiness for Trial.* If there are no matters to be resolved by the court, a party's personal appearance at the readiness hearing may be waived, provided the party has certified his or her readiness for trial with a written statement of readiness for trial filed with the court. *See,* Forms Appendix G.

(d) Settlement Conference. Any party in a civil action may schedule a pretrial settlement conference through the court administrator for hearing no later than 21 days prior to trial. The settlement conference shall be before a judge who has not been assigned to preside at any subsequent trial. Attendance at the settlement conference by all parties and counsel shall be mandatory, unless the court determines that circumstances exist precluding another party's attendance. Attendance by non-parties is permissible upon agreement by the parties. The parties shall provide documentation clearly stating the issues involved to the settlement conference judge at least two (2) days prior to the settlement conference.

[Effective September 1, 2002; amended effective September 1, 2005; September 1, 2008; September 1, 2011; September 1, 2012; September 1, 2015.]

4. PARTIES
(Rules 17–25) *[No Local Rules]*

5. DEPOSITIONS AND DISCOVERY
(Rules 26–37)

LCR 26–32. *[NO LOCAL RULES]*

LCR 33. INTERROGATORIES TO PARTIES

(a) Availability; Procedures for Use. Interrogatories and answers thereto shall not be filed with the court, unless they are submitted as evidence in support of the motion or petition. A copy of the face page containing proof of service may be filed with the court.

[Effective September 1, 2002; amended effective September 1, 2004; September 1, 2008; September 1, 2011.]

LCR 34–37. *[NO LOCAL RULES]*

6. TRIALS
(Rules 38–53.4)

LCR 38. JURY TRIAL OF RIGHT [NO LOCAL RULE]

[Repealed effective September 1, 2011.]

LCR 39. TRIAL BY JURY OR BY THE COURT [NO LOCAL RULE]

[Repealed effective September 1, 2011.]

LCR 40. ASSIGNMENT OF CASES

(a) Notice of Trial—Note of Issue.

(1)—(5) *(No Local Rules).*

(6) *Trial Brief in Civil Trials.* In all civil trials, each party shall prepare a trial brief or memorandum of authorities containing the issues involved and the authorities supporting the same. The trial briefs shall be filed with the clerk, copies served on opposing counsel and a copy provided to the assigned judge by noon on the Friday before the date set for commencement of trial.

(b) Methods.

(1) *Note for Trial Setting.* Counsel shall file with the court administrator and serve on all parties, including the guardian ad litem, a Note for Trial Setting and a Notice of Conflict Dates in the form set forth in the Forms Appendix E & F. Conflict dates shall be limited to previously scheduled vacations and trial dates. Counsel or parties appearing *pro se* should request sufficient time for the trial; overestimation of the length of trial is preferred to underestimation of time needed.

On the date requested for trial assignment, the court administrator, without the parties appearing, shall assign cases a specific trial date and notify the parties, including the guardian ad litem, if any, by mail.

(2) *Confirmation of Trials.* Counsel shall confirm with the court administrator no earlier than seven (7) court days or no later than two (2) court days prior to the trial date that their trial will proceed on the scheduled trial date.

(c)—(d) (No Local Rules).

(e) Continuances. Continuances may be granted upon mutual agreement of the parties and upon presentation of an order of continuance if the continuance is sought more than thirty (30) days of the assigned trial date. A continuance sought within thirty (30) days of the assigned trial date shall be made by written motion. Within ten (10) days after a continuance is granted, either by stipulation or by motion, the parties shall file a new Note for Trial Setting and a Notice of Conflict Dates as set forth above, and a new trial date shall be assigned by the court administrator.

(f) (No Local Rules).

(g) Related Cases. Cases are randomly assigned by the Clerk of Court to the judges of the Superior Court on an equal basis at the time of filing, with the following exception: For (1) family law petitions seeking dissolution of marriage, declaration of invalidity, legal separation, parentage and nonparental actions for child custody, (2) actions brought by parties to non-marital relationships involving parenting or distribution of assets and liabilities, and (3) dependency cases, the same judge shall be assigned to all such cases involving the same parents and children pursuant to unified family court principles. Whenever such a case is assigned to the same judge pursuant to this rule, the other judge shall then be assigned an additional case to equalize the case assignments between the judges.

[Effective September 1, 2002. Amended effective September 1, 2004; September 1, 2008; September 1, 2011; September 1, 2012; September 2, 2014.]

LCR 41. DISMISSAL OF ACTIONS

(a)—(d) (No Local Rules)

(e) Notice of Settlements. If the parties fail to comply with CR 41(e) and the court incurs unnecessary expenses, such as jury expenses, the court may in its discretion assess such costs to the parties.

[Adopted effective September 1, 2011.]

LCR 42. CONSOLIDATION; SEPARATE TRIALS [NO LOCAL RULE]

LCR 43. TAKING OF TESTIMONY

(a)—(b) (No Local Rules)

(c) Mode and Order of Interrogation and Presentation. [See ER 611]

(1) *Trial Exhibits.* [*See also,* GR 15(i)]. Counsel shall provide all exhibits, except exhibits intended for impeachment purposes, to the clerk at least one day in advance of trial to be marked for identification. Copies of all exhibits, except large maps or large drawings, shall be given to opposing counsel and to the trial judge at the same time as such exhibits are offered into evidence. Counsel shall also provide the clerk with an 8×11–inch version of any large trial exhibit.

(2) *Records in Administrative Appeals.* Records of proceedings and exhibits filed as the record in an appeal of any administrative hearing shall be presumed to be exhibits to the file in the superior court. Any video conference tapes or audio tapes shall have a transcript filed in addition to the video or audio tape.

[Effective September 1, 2002; amended effective September 1, 2008; September 1, 2011; September 1, 2012.]

LCR 44–50. *[NO LOCAL RULES]*

LCR 51. INSTRUCTIONS TO JURY AND DELIBERATION

(a) Proposed. Proposed jury instructions shall be submitted prior to commencement of trial but in no event later than 9 a.m. the day on which the case is called for trial.

(b)—(i) (No Local Rules)

[Adopted effective September 1, 2012.]

LCR 52–53.4   [NO LOCAL RULES]

7. JUDGMENT
(Rules 54–63)

LCR 54. JUDGMENT AND COSTS

(a)—(e) (No Local Rules)

(f) Presentation.

(1)—(2) *(No Local Rules)*

(3) *Ex Parte Presentation and Fees.* Agreed orders, orders when notice of presentation is waived, and *ex parte* orders based upon the record in the file may be presented by mail. The original order, supporting materials, and the required fee as set forth in the clerk's fee schedule (LCR 79(d)(1)) must be included in the mail or delivery. If accepted by the clerk, the proposed order will be presented to the *ex parte* judge for consideration. If rejected by the clerk, the proposed order will be returned to the sender for resubmission or in-person presentation. Self-addressed, stamped envelopes, along with copies of the proposed order, must be provided if return of any conformed materials or rejected order is sought.

[Adopted effective September 1, 2012.]

LCR 55. DEFAULT AND JUDGMENT

(a) (No Local Rules)

(b) Entry of Default Judgment.

(1)—(4) *(No Local Rules)*

(5) *Default Orders, Decrees or Judgments.* If an order, decree or judgment has been entered by default, counsel representing the prevailing party, or the prevailing party if not represented by counsel, shall immediately mail a conformed copy of the order, decree or judgment signed by the judge, including the date the order was filed with the clerk, to the opponent or opponent's counsel at his or her last known address. An affidavit or declaration showing proof of service by mailing shall be filed with the clerk.

(c)—(f) (No Local Rules)

[Adopted effective September 1, 2011. Amended effective September 1, 2012.]

LCR 56. SUMMARY JUDGMENT

(a)—(b) (No Local Rules)

(c) Motion and Proceedings.

(1) *Confirmation of Summary Judgment Motions.* The moving party shall confirm his or her summary judgment motion with the court administrator no earlier than seven (7) court days or no later than two (2) court days prior to the hearing.

(d)—(h) (No Local Rules)

[Adopted effective September 1, 2004; amended effective September 1, 2008; September 1, 2011; September 1, 2012.]

LCR 57–63. [NO LOCAL RULES]

8. PROVISIONAL AND FINAL REMEDIES
(Rules 64–71) *[No Local Rules]*

9. APPEALS
(Rules 72–76) *[No Local Rules]*

10. SUPERIOR COURTS AND CLERKS (Rules 77–80)

LCR 77. SUPERIOR COURTS AND JUDICIAL OFFICERS

(a) (No Local Rules).

(b) Powers of Superior Courts.

(1) *Powers of Court in Conduct of Judicial Proceedings.* [See RCW 2.28.010.]

(A) Conduct and Dress Code. All participants and spectators shall follow the Conduct and Dress Code adopted by the judges and posted outside the courtrooms. A copy of the local conduct and dress code may be found in the Forms Appendix K.

(B) Professional Conduct. Counsel shall adhere to the Guidelines for Professional courtesy, as well as the "Courtroom Decorum and Practice Guidelines," a copy of which may be found in the Forms Appendix L.

(2)—(3) No Local Rules

(c) (No Local Rules).

(d) Superior Courts Always Open. Unless otherwise ordered, the Island County Superior Court shall be open as set forth in CR 77(d) from 8:30 a.m. to noon, and from 1:00 p.m. to 4:30 p.m. Non-judicial days are designated as Saturday and Sunday and those days designated by law as legal holidays.

(e) No Court on Legal Holidays—Exceptions. [See RCW 2.28.100]. The court shall observe all legal holidays.

(f) Sessions.

(1) *Involuntary Commitment Hearings.* Involuntary commitment hearings shall be held as occasion demands to expedite the hearing, availability of medical testimony, and the convenience of the court. The prosecuting attorney shall notify the office of the court administrator immediately upon the filing of an application, and the time and place of the hearing shall be set by the court administrator at the earliest date compatible with the foregoing factors.

(g)—(j) (No Local Rules).

(k) Motion Day—Local Rules. The Island County docket shall be as follows:

(1) *Law and Motion Calendars.* The civil, adult criminal, and juvenile offender law and motion calendar for Island County shall be on Monday of each week in the assigned departments. If Monday falls on a legal holiday, then the motion calendar shall be heard on the following Tuesday. If any matter on the law and motion calendars is expected to last longer than 15 minutes total, the parties must obtain a specially set hearing date from the court administrator pursuant to LCR 5(k).

(A) Civil Motion Calendar. Closed civil hearings, including adoptions, shall be heard at 9 a.m. Open civil hearings shall be heard from 9:30 a.m. to noon in the following order: Ex parte matters; supplemental proceedings; readiness hearings; parentage motions where paternity has previously been determined; uncontested matters in probates and guardianships; uncontested dissolutions; all orders to show cause and motions in domestic actions; other orders to show cause and motions in civil case; motions and orders subsequent to judgment and motions for summary judgment.

(B) Criminal and Juvenile Offender Calendars. The criminal and juvenile offender calendars shall be heard from 1:30 p.m. to 4:15 p.m. Criminal and juvenile offender preliminary hearings and hearings on bench warrants shall be heard Monday during the criminal and juvenile offender calendar and at 1:15 p.m. on Tuesday through Friday.

(2) *Court Commissioner Calendars.* The court commissioner, or judge when necessary, shall hear the following matters every *Tuesday*:

(A) **At-risk youth, CHINS, and emancipation** proceedings shall be heard at 9:00am

(B) **Domestic Violence, antiharassment, and sexual assault protection order cases** shall be heard at 1:00pm.

(C) **Truancy proceedings** cahll[1] be heard at 3:00pm.

The court commissioner, or judge when necessary, shall hear the following matters every *Wednesday*:

(A) **Shelter Care** hearings shall be held at 8:30a.m. (If such hearings must be held on a day other than Wednesday, such hearings shall be held at 8:30am on Friday.)

(B) **Parentage Actions** shall be heard at 9:00 a.m.

(C) **Dependency** motions and hearings shall be held at 9:30am.

(3) *Pro Se Dissolution Calendar.* Pro Se dissolutions will be heard at 8:30 a.m. on Wednesday.

(3) *Pro Se Dissolution Calendar.* [2] Pro Se dissolutions will be heard at 8:30 a.m. on Wednesday.

(4) *Ex Parte Calendar.* The ex parte calendar shall be heard on the Monday civil motion calendar and at 1 p.m. on Tuesday through Friday.

(5) *Drug Court Calendars.* The Family Treatment Court shall be heard at 10:30 a.m. on Tuesday. Adult Drug Court shall be heard at 10:30 a.m. on Thursday. Juvenile Drug Court shall be heard at 3 p.m. on Thursday.

(6) *Jury Trials.* Jury trials in Island County Superior Court shall be on the date assigned by the court administrator and shall be held from 9:30 a.m. until 4:15 p.m., with a break from noon until 1:30 p.m., or at such other times and for such duration as designated in advance by the court as the docket of cases warrants.

[Effective September 1, 2002; amended effective September 1, 2008; September 1, 2011; September 1, 2012; September 2, 2014; September 1, 2015.]

[1] So in original.

[2] So in original.

LCR 78. CLERKS

(a)—(f) (No Local Rules)

(g) Payment and Disbursal of Trust Funds.

(1) *Payment of Trust Funds.* Trust funds shall be paid to the Clerk with one of the following methods of payment: cash, cashier's check, money order, certified check, government check, attorney's check, or company's check.

(2) *Disbursal of Trust Funds.* Trust funds that are paid by attorney's check or company's check will be available to be disbursed eight court days after receipt by the Clerk. Trust funds that are paid by any other method listed in subsection (1) above will normally be available to be disbursed the first or second court day following receipt by the Clerk.

[Adopted effective September 1, 2012.]

LCR 79. BOOKS AND RECORDS KEPT BY THE CLERK

(a)—(c) (No Local Rules)

(d) Other Books and Records of Clerk.

(1) *Clerk's Fee Schedule.* The clerk of the court will maintain a schedule of charges authorized by law for clerk's services. The schedule shall be available for public inspection and will be maintained in the clerk's office and on the clerk's website.

(2) *Filing Family Court Documents.* The clerk shall file the petition for Family Court and other documents in a special file maintained for such matters, if no dissolution action has been filed previously. Such Family Court documents may be kept in one file and numbered serially. If the petition states that a dissolution action has been filed, the clerk shall file all Family Court documents in the dissolution file as a part of that cause of action, bearing the same cause number.

(3) *Court Files.* The clerk shall permit no file to be taken from the Clerk's office or the Clerk's custody, except to the courtroom, or to a judge, commissioner, referee, bailiff, official court reporter, or the Court Administrator or deputy unless written authority has first been obtained from the Clerk. The Clerk may with discretion and on application in writing, grant written authority to the applicant to withdraw one or more files from the Clerk's custody for a period not exceeding 3 days. Only attorneys with a WSBA number or an employee of that firm's office may make a written request to withdraw a file from the Clerk's office. Such applicant shall return the file, and all of its papers, in good order, and shall not remove, even temporarily, any papers from the file. Any request to withdraw a file from the Clerk's office within one calendar week of its being scheduled for a court hearing or trial shall not be granted. For case files maintained electronically, no person may remove the electronic media on which the record is kept from the custody of the Clerk unless an account is established. Copies of a file or of the documents therein may be obtained from the Clerk as provided by law and rule.

(e) Destruction of Records. After final judgment, if the time of the appeal has elapsed and no appeal has been taken, the court, upon application of any party or other person entitled to the possession of one or more exhibits, may in its discretion order the withdrawal of such exhibit or exhibits and delivery thereof to such party or other person.

(f) List of Pending Decisions. (No Local Rules).

[Amended effective September 1, 2011; September 1, 2012; September 2, 2014.]

LCR 80. COURT REPORTERS

(a) Matters Not Reported. Unless requested by a party and expressly directed by the judge, the following matters will not be reported: Opening statements and closing arguments in non-jury civil trials; *ex parte* matters on the law and motion calendar; verbal statements in a tape recording; video tape recording used at trial or in a hearing.

(b)—(c) (No Local Rules)

[Effective September 1, 2002; September 1, 2004; September 1, 2008; September 1, 2011.]

11. GENERAL PROVISIONS
(Rules 81–86)

LCR 81–84. [NO LOCAL RULES]

LCR 85. TITLE OF RULES

These rules shall be known and cited as the Local Civil Rules for Island County Superior Court. LCR is the official abbreviation.

[Adopted effective September 1, 2011. Amended effective September 1, 2012.]

LCR 86. [NO LOCAL RULE]

PART II. LOCAL/SPECIAL PROCEEDINGS RULES (SPR)

SPR 94.04. FAMILY LAW RULES

(a) Scope of Rules. These special proceeding rules are supplemental to the Washington State Supreme Court Civil Rules (CR) and to the Island County Local Court Rules (ICLCR). Unless otherwise specifically directed otherwise, these rules shall apply to all cases filed after September 1, 2007, in all (1) family law petitions seeking dissolution of marriage, declaration of invalidity, legal separation, parentage and nonparental actions for child custody; and (2) actions brought by parties to non-marital relationships involving parenting or distribution of assets and liabilities. This rule shall also apply to all modification actions filed in the specified cases.

(b) Court's Automatic Temporary Restraining Order. Upon filing a summons and petition in any of the actions specified in SPR 94.04(a), the court on its own motion shall automatically issue the temporary order set forth in the Forms Appendix A, entitled "Court's Temporary Order, Re: SPR 94.04."

(c) Blank Affidavits and Notices Required for *Pro Se* Parties. When either of the parties are *pro se*, a blank affidavit or declaration shall be attached to the motion for a temporary order and show cause order and served on the other party. In addition, the motion for a temporary order and show cause order shall contain the following language:

"At the hearing, the court will consider written sworn affidavits or declarations made under penalty of perjury, which must be signed and must include the date and place of signing. You are not allowed to argue any facts that are not included in affidavits or declarations. Prior to the hearing you must (1) file your affidavits and declarations and any supporting attachments with the clerk of the court, (2) provide a copy of those documents to the court administrator as a courtesy copy for the judge, (3) serve the other party or the other party's attorney with copies of your documents, and (4) complete your filing of the documents within the time period required by Island County Superior Court Local Court Rule 6(d). If you need more information, you are advised to consult an attorney or a court facilitator.

"FAILURE TO APPEAR AS SET FORTH ABOVE MAY RESULT IN A TEMPORARY ORDER BEING ENTERED BY THE COURT THAT GRANTS THE RELIEF REQUESTED IN THE MOTION WITHOUT FURTHER NOTICE TO YOU."

(d) Financial Declarations and Verified Statement of Assets and Liabilities. Within 30 days after the filing of an answer or other responsive pleading in any of the actions specified in SPR 94.04(a), each party shall serve the opposing party with (1) a Financial Declaration (WPF DRPSCU 01.1550) and all attachments in all cases involving a request for child support, maintenance or attorney fees, and (2) a Verified Statement of Assets and Liabilities in the form set out in the Forms Appendix B. The Financial Declaration shall be filed with the court. All parties have a duty to supplement the documents when additional information becomes available. Each party shall file with the court a Declaration of Mailing, in the form set out in the Appendix, attesting that Financial Declaration and all attachments and the Verified Statements of Assets and Liabilities has been provided to the other party within the 30–day time limit.

(e) Parenting Seminars. This rule shall apply to all cases in which the court is being asked to enter a parenting plan for minor children.

(1) *Mandatory Attendance.* Unless waived as provided herein, within 30 days of filing an appearance, answer or other responsive pleading in an action involving a parenting plan for minor children, both parties shall register for a court-approved parent education seminar on the effects of family transitions on children, unless the parties have previously attended such a course within the last three years. Each party shall attend the seminar within 60 days of registering.

(2) *Certificate of Completion.* Upon completion of the seminar, each party shall file with the court the seminar completion certificate provided by the sponsoring agency or provider. Additionally, a copy of the

certificate of completion shall be provided to the judge at presentation of final documents.

(3) *Fees.* Each party attending a seminar shall pay a fee charged by the approved provider and authorized by the court.

(4) *Seminar Providers.* The court shall establish standards for parenting seminars and shall approve seminar providers. A list of approved parenting seminars shall be available from the court administrator, juvenile court administrator, or county clerk. If a parenting seminar is not included on the list, then the court, upon proper motion, may allow other seminar providers to fulfill this requirement on a case-by-case basis.

(5) *Waiver and Special Consideration*

(A) Opposing Parties. In no case shall opposing parties be required to attend a seminar together.

(B) Domestic Violence or Abuse. Upon a showing of domestic violence or abuse which would not require mutual decision-making pursuant to RCW 26.09.191, or if the court determines that attendance at a seminar is not in the children's best interest pursuant to Ch. 26.12 RCW, the court shall either waive the requirement of completion of the seminar or allow participation in an alternative parenting seminar if available.

(C) Proposed Parenting Plan Required. Within 14 days of completing the parenting seminar as described above, each parent shall provide the other parent with a Proposed Parenting Plan, if they have not already done so.

(D) Willful Refusal. Willful refusal to participate in a parenting seminar or willful delay in completing a court-ordered parenting seminar may result in a finding of contempt and imposition of sanctions. (*See* Order to Show Cause Re: Parenting Class in the Forms Appendix H.)

(f) Mandatory Mediation.

(1) *Requirement for Mandatory Mediation.* In all cases specified in SPR 94.04(a) with unresolved issues, both parties shall in good faith engage in mediation with a court-approved mediator in an effort to resolve the case, unless waived as set forth herein. Mediation shall be completed at least 60 days prior to the scheduled trial date.

(2) *Waiver of Mandatory Mediation.* Mediation shall not be required in the following cases:

(A) Good Cause. For good cause shown upon motion and approval by the court; or

(B) Restraining or Protection Order. Where a domestic violence retraining order or protection order (excluding *ex parte* orders) involving the parties has been entered by a court at any time within the previous 12 months;

(C) No Contact Order. Where a domestic violence no contact order exists pursuant to RCW 10.99;

(D) Domestic Abuse. Where the court upon motion finds that domestic abuse has occurred between the parties and that such abuse would interfere with arm's-length mediation.

(E) Order to Require Mediation. Notwithstanding the foregoing, either party may by motion seek a court order requiring mandatory mediation in a case where it would not be required if the moving party believes that the parties would be able to mediate their dispute at arm's length under the particular circumstances of the case.

(3) *Settlement Conference After Mandatory Mediation.* If, after mediation in good faith or where mediation is not required, there remain unresolved issues in any case specified by in SPR 94.04(a), the parties may participate in a settlement conference, pursuant to LCR 16(d).

(4) *Effect on Court Proceedings.* Mediation does not stay or otherwise affect the rights and duties of the parties established by statute, court rule, or court order. The court may enter temporary orders and the parties may conduct discovery prior to or during the mediation process.

(5) *Cost of Mediation.* Mediators shall be paid by the parties in accordance with the agreement of the parties, or in the absence of agreement, as determined in mediation.

(6) *Responsibility for Compliance.* The parties shall be responsible for arranging for and completing all mediation requirements established under this rule.

(7) *Failure to Comply with Mandatory Mediation.* Willful refusal to participate in mediation or willful delay in completing mediation may result in a finding of contempt and imposition of sanctions.

(8) *Approval of Mediators.* Mediators performing mediation services pursuant to this rule must fulfill certain minimum qualifications established by the court. The court administrator shall maintain a list of such minimum qualifications for distribution to the public. In order to fulfill the mediation requirements of this rule, the parties must use the services of a court-approved mediator. The court administrator shall maintain a list of approved mediators, either persons or agencies, for distribution to the public. The list shall contain the following information: each mediator's name, organization, if any, address and telephone number, and fee schedule.

(9) *Selection of Mediator; Right of Mediator to Decline.* The parties may either agree to a mediator from the court-approved list or the mediator will be determined by use of a strike list. A mediator has the right to decline to serve in a particular case. If a mediator declines to serve, the parties shall select a

different mediator, using the same selection process by which the preceding mediator was selected.

(10) *Authority of Mediator.* The mediator has the authority to determine the time, place, manner, and duration of mediation. In appropriate cases, the mediator shall have the authority to terminate the mediation prior to completion.

(11) *Attendance at Mediation.* The parties shall personally attend all mediation sessions, unless the mediator permits telephonic or other attendance. The mediator shall have the authority to require other persons to attend.

(12) *Declaration of Completion of Mediation.* Within seven (7) days of completion of mediation, a declaration that mediation has been completed shall be filed with the court by the mediator. The mediator shall advise counsel and the parties of the results of mediation in writing. The mediator shall advise the court only whether an agreement has been reached on some or all of the issues.

(13) *Confidentiality.* [*See* RCW 5.60.070]. The work product of the mediator and all communications during the mediation shall be privileged and confidential and not subject to compulsory disclosure. The mediator shall not appear to testify in any court proceedings.

(14) *Effective Date.* This rule shall apply to all cases described herein filed after January 1, 1997.

(g) Jurisdictional Declaration in Non–Contested Dissolution Cases. If a decree is entered under RCW 26.09 by joinder, agreement, or default, an attorney representing the petitioner or the respondent may present jurisdictional testimony pursuant to a "Request for Entry of Decree and Declaration of Jurisdictional Facts," found in the Forms Appendix I. If both parties are not represented by counsel, at least one party's presence in court is required.

(h) Required Documents in Dissolution Trials. In addition to the trial briefs required under LCR 40(a), in all contested trial in domestic relations matters, each party shall provide the court with (1) a current Financial Declaration (WPF DRPSCU 01.1550) and all attachments; (2) a written Pretrial Affidavit indicating a proposed division of assets and liability, which form can be found in the Forms Appendix J; and (3) if children are involved, a proposed parenting plan and child support worksheets. All required documents shall be filed with the clerk, copies served on opposing counsel and a copy provided to the assigned judge by noon on the Friday before the date set for commencement of trial.

(i) Parenting Plans and Child Support Orders Submitted by *Pro Se* Parties—Review. In any action in which the residential care or child support of a minor child or children is at issue and in which none of the parties are represented by counsel, the parenting plan and child support documents shall first be reviewed, approved and initialed by the court facilitator in the county in which the action is pending, or if there is no court facilitator, by the juvenile court administrator. A proposed parenting plan does not need to be initialed and approved before filing, but any parenting plan submitted for court approval must be so initialed and approved before the court will consider it.

(j) Family Court—Reconciliation. A party requesting a hearing for reconciliation before Family Court under RCW 26.09.030 shall file a petition with the superior court clerk and obtain a specially set hearing date and time from the court administrator.

[Adopted effective September 1, 2011. Amended effective September 1, 2012; September 1, 2015.]

SPR 98.04. ESTATES—PROBATE— GUARDIANSHIPS

(a) Guardianship Hearing Dates. In all reports required by RCW 11.92 *et seq.*, the title shall contain, in addition to the name of the report, a notice to the clerk to set the next report date, i.e., **"Clerk's Action Required: Next Hearing Date and Time: (date) at 9:30 a.m."**

[Adopted effective September 1, 2011.]

PART III. LOCAL GUARDIAN AD LITEM RULES (GALR)

GALR 1–4. [NO LOCAL RULES]

GALR 5. APPOINTMENTS OF GUARDIANS AD LITEM

(a) Equitable Distribution of Workload. The parties may either agree to a guardian ad litem from the court-approved list or the guardian ad litem will be determined by use of a strike list. A guardian ad litem has the right to decline to serve in a particular case. If a guardian ad litem declines to serve, the parties shall select a different guardian ad litem, using the same selection process by which the preceding guardian ad litem was selected.

(b) Procedure to Address Complaints. Any complaints made by a guardian ad litem regarding registry or appointment matters shall be written and given to the court administrator.

(c) Form of Order Appointing Guardian ad Litem. In any case in which a guardian ad litem is appointed for a minor, any party may request an "Order Appointing Guardian ad Litem (Supplemental)" found in the Forms Appendix C in addition to the mandatory "Order Appointment Guardian ad Litem" found at http://www.courts.wa.gov/forms.

[Adopted effective September 1, 2011. Amended effective September 1, 2012.]

GALR 6.   LIMITED APPOINTMENTS [NO LOCAL RULE]

GALR 7.   GRIEVANCE PROCEDURES

(a) Clear and Concise. (No Local Rules)

(b) Separate Procedures. All complaints or grievances made by or against a guardian ad litem shall be in writing and shall be submitted to the court administrator. All complaints or grievances must bear the signature, name and address of the person filing the complaint, and the case number of the action.

(1) *Pending Cases.* Upon receipt of the written complaint or grievance, the court administrator shall check to see if the complaint or grievance involves a pending case. If the complaint or grievance involves a pending case, the court administrator shall send out a form letter no later than 14 days after receiving the complaint or grievance advising the complainant that the matter must be handled in context of the pending case, either by seeking the removal of the guardian ad litem or by contesting the information or recommendations contained in the guardian ad litem's report or testimony.

(2) *Grievances Filed Subsequent to Conclusion of Case.* If the complaint or grievance does not involve a pending case and the time for appeal has expired or any appeal has been concluded, the court administrator shall assign the complaint or grievance to the judge who was not assigned to the case. The reviewing judge shall then investigate the complaint or grievance and respond in writing to the complainant or grievance within 30 days of receiving such complaint or grievance, informing the complainant of the action that will be taken. The reviewing judge shall either determine that the complaint or grievance has no merit on its face and decline to review the complaint or grievance and so inform the complainant, or determine that the complaint pr [1] grievance has potential merit and inform the complainant that the guardian ad litem has been requested to respond to the complaint or grievance. The reviewing judge shall provide the complainant with a copy of these grievance procedures.

(3) *Considerations as to Merit.* In considering whether any complaint or grievance has merit or potential merit, the reviewing judge shall consider whether the complaint or grievance alleges the guardian ad litem has (i) violated a code of conduct, (ii) misrepresented his or her qualifications to serve as a guardian ad litem, (iii) breached the confidentiality of the parties, (iv) falsified information in a report to the court or in testimony before the court, (v) failed, when required, to report abuse of a child, (vi) communicated

with a judicial officer *ex parte* concerning a case for which he or she is serving as guardian ad litem, (vii) violated state or local laws or court rules, or (viii) taken or failed to take any other action which would reasonably place the suitability of the person to serve as a guardian ad litem in question.

(c) Fair Treatment of Grievances. (No Local Rules)

(d) CASA Grievance Procedures. Grievances against any Court Appointed Special Advocate shall be handled as set forth in the Island County CASA Volunteer Policies and Procedures, a copy of which is available from the CASA director upon request.

(e) Confidentiality. A complaint or grievance shall be deemed confidential for all purposes unless the reviewing judge has made a final determination that the complaint or grievance has merit. Any record of complaints or grievances filed which involve a pending case or which are not deemed by the reviewing judge to have merit shall be confidential and shall not be disclosed except by court order, upon good cause shown, after the person against whom the complaint or grievance was brought has been given notice and an opportunity to be heard.

(f) Response to Complaint. If the reviewing judge determines that the complaint or grievance has potential merit, the reviewing judge shall inform the guardian ad litem in writing within 30 days of receiving the complaint or grievance that a complaint or grievance has been brought against him or her which has potential merit and request the guardian ad litem to make a written response to the complaint or grievance within 20 days. The reviewing judge shall provide the guardian ad litem with a copy of these grievance procedures and a copy of the original complaint or grievance.

(g) Complaint Resolution Time Standards; Procedures.

(1) *Time.* Complaints or grievance filed subsequent to the conclusion of a case shall be resolved within 60 days of the date of receipt of the written complaint or grievance. A copy of the reviewing judge's written final determination shall be mailed to the guardian ad litem and to the complaining party.

(2) *Final Determination.* Upon receipt of a written response to a complaint or grievance, the reviewing judge shall make a final determination either (i) that the complaint or grievance has no merit and dismiss the complaint or grievance, or (ii) that the complaint or grievance has merit and impose sanctions or discipline, if appropriate.

(3) *Sanctions/Discipline.* The reviewing judge shall have the authority to issue a written admonition or a written reprimand, refer the guardian ad litem to additional training, suspend, remove the guardian ad litem from the registry, or impose other appropriate sanctions. In considering an appropriate form of

discipline, the reviewing judge shall take into consideration any prior complaints or grievances that resulted in an admonition, reprimand, referral to training, suspension, removal from the registry, or any other mitigating or aggravating factors.

(4) *Finality of Disposition.* All resolutions of complaints or grievances shall be final and not subject to further appeal, except removal of a guardian ad litem from the registry. The complainant and the guardian ad litem shall be notified in writing of the reviewing judge's final determination and in the case of an appeal, the final disposition and any sanctions imposed.

(5) *Appeal Process.* A guardian ad litem who has been removed from the registry may appeal to the Superior Court bench by written notice to the Presiding Judge within ten (10) days of receipt of a written notice of removal from a registry. The notice of appeal shall clearly state the basis for the appeal. The Superior Court bench shall consider the written material considered by the reviewing judge and any written communication from the guardian ad litem. Neither the guardian ad litem nor any complainant may personally appear to argue issues to be consid-

ered by the Superior Court bench on such appeal. The Superior Court bench shall inform the parties of the final disposition of the appeal in writing within 20 days of receipt of the appeal.

(h) Records of grievances. (No Local Rules)

(i) Removal from Registry.

(1) *Removal from Other Local Registries.* If the guardian ad litem against whom the discipline is directed is listed on more than one registry within the court in which the guardian ad litem is practicing, the suspension or removal may apply to each local registry the guardian ad litem is listed on, at the reviewing judge's discretion.

(2) *Notice to Office of Administrator of the Courts.* Notice of removal of the guardian ad litem from a county's registry shall be sent to the Office of Administrator of the Courts after the guardian ad litem's appeal process has concluded or expired.

(j) Implementation. (No Local Rules)

[Adopted effective September 1, 2011. Amended effective September 1, 2012.]

1 So in original. Probably should be "or".

PART IV. LOCAL CRIMINAL RULES (LCrR)

1. SCOPE, PURPOSE AND CONSTRUCTION
(RULES 1.1–1.5) *[No Local Rules]*

2. PROCEDURES PRIOR TO ARREST AND OTHER SPECIAL PROCEEDINGS
(RULES 2.1–2.3) *[No Local Rules]*

3. RIGHTS OF DEFENDANTS
(RULES 3.1–3.6) *[No Local Rules]*

4. PROCEDURES PRIOR TO TRIAL
(RULES 4.1–4.10)

LCrR 4.1. (NO LOCAL RULE)

LCrR 4.2. PLEAS

(a)—(h) (No Local Rules)

(i) Authority of Court Commissioners. Court Commissioners qualified under Article 4, section 23 of the Washington Constitution are authorized to preside over arraignments, preliminary appearances, initial extradition hearings, and noncompliance proceedings pursuant to RCW 9.94A.200; accept guilty pleas as authorized in this local rule pursuant to RCW 2.24.040(15); appoint counsel; make determinations of probable cause; set, amend, and review conditions of

pretrial release; set bail; set trial and hearing dates; authorize continuances and accept waivers of the right to speedy trial.

[Effective September 1, 2002; amended effective September 1, 2008; September 1, 2011; September 1, 2012.]

LCrR 4.3–4.4. (NO LOCAL RULES)

LCrR 4.5. OMNIBUS HEARING

(a)—(c) (No Local Rules)

(d) Motions. Unless otherwise scheduled, motions in limine and other preliminary matters in criminal cases shall be heard at 8:30 a.m. on the first scheduled day of trial. All other pretrial motions in criminal matters shall be specially set with the court administrator at least ten (10) days prior to trial.

(e)—(h) (No Local Rules)

[Formerly LCrR 5, adopted effective September 1, 2012. Renumbered LCrR 4.5, effective September 2, 2014.]

5. VENUE
(RULES 5.1–5.2) *[No Local Rules]*

6. PROCEDURES AT TRIAL
(RULES 6.1–6.16)

LCrR 6.1. TRIAL BY JURY OR BY THE COURT

(a) Trial Brief or Memorandum. In criminal trials with contested legal or evidentiary issues, each party shall prepare a trial brief or memorandum of authorities containing the issues involved and the authorities supporting same and provide the same to the clerk, opposing counsel and assigned judge by noon

LCrR 4.6–4.10. (NO LOCAL RULES)

two (2) days prior to the date set for commencement of trial.

(b) Exhibits. LCR 43(b) shall apply in criminal trials.

(c) Jury Instructions. LCR 5 shall apply in criminal trials.

[Effective September 1, 2002; amended effective September 1, 2008; September 1, 2011.]

7. PROCEDURES FOLLOWING CONVICTION
(RULES 7.1–7.8) *[No Local Rules]*

8. MISCELLANEOUS
(RULES 8.1–8.9)

LCrR 8.1. TIME

Time shall be computed and enlarged in accordance with CR 6, and not by the civil local court rules.

[Adopted effective September 1, 2006; amended effective September 1, 2008; September 1, 2011.]

LCrR 8.2. MOTIONS

(a) Motion Calendar. Criminal motion calendar shall be set at 1:30 p. m. on Monday in Island County.

(b) CourtCall Does Not Apply. Unless changed by the Local Criminal Court Rules, Criminal Rules 3.5 and 3.6, Civil Rule 7(b), and LCR 7 shall govern

motions in criminal cases. CourtCall does not apply to criminal cases.

(c) Presentation of Final Documents. If a movant's motion is granted in whole or in part, the moving party shall be responsible to prepare and present any written findings, conclusions, and orders necessary as a result of the decision, unless the court orders otherwise.

[Effective September 1, 2002; amended effective September 1, 2004; September 1, 2006; September 1, 2008; September 1, 2011; September 1, 2012.]

LCrR 8.3–8.9 [NO LOCAL RULES]

PART V. LOCAL JUVENILE COURT RULES (LJuCR)

TITLE I. SCOPE AND APPLICATION OF RULES

LJuCR 1.1—1.3. [NO LOCAL RULES]

LJuCR 1.4. APPLICABILITY OF OTHER RULES

(a) Criminal Rules. The Superior Court Criminal Rules and Local Criminal Rules shall apply in juvenile

offense proceedings when not inconsistent with these rules and applicable statutes.

[Effective September 1, 2002; amended effective September 1, 2008; September 1, 2011.]

LJuCR 1.5. [NO LOCAL RULE]

LJuCR 1.6. COURT APPOINTED SPECIAL ADVOCATE PROGRAM

This judicial district has a Court Appointed Special Advocate program. Rules and details may be obtained from Juvenile Court Services.

[Adopted effective September 1, 2005; amended effective September 1, 2008; September 1, 2011.]

TITLE II. SHELTER CARE PROCEEDINGS

LJuCR 2.1–2.4. [NO LOCAL RULES]

LJuCR 2.5. AMENDMENT OF SHELTER CARE ORDER

(a) 30–Day Shelter Care Review. If a parent, guardian ad litem, or court-appointed special advocate wishes to contest placement of a child or any service ordered at the shelter care hearing, he or she must file and serve on all parties and counsel a notice of contested issues no later than three (3) court days before the 30–day shelter care review hearing. The notice of contested hearing shall be accompanied by written evidence in support of the issue. Unless good cause is shown, failure to provide timely notice of contested issues shall constitute a waiver of the right to raise such issues at the 30–day shelter care review hearing.

[Adopted effective September 1, 2004; amended effective September 1, 2008; September 1, 2011.]

TITLE III. DEPENDENCY PROCEEDINGS

LJuCR 3.1—3.8. [NO LOCAL RULES]

LJuCR 3.9. REVIEW HEARING

(a) Department's Written Review Report. A written review report shall be prepared by the department and shall be filed and served on all counsel and parties not less than ten (10) days prior to the review hearing.

(b) Notice of Contested Issues. After receipt of the department's report, if a parent, guardian ad litem, or court-appointed special advocate wishes to contest any issue, he or she must file and serve a notice of contested issues no later than three (3) court days before the hearing. The notice of contested hearing shall be accompanied by written evidence in support of the issue. Unless good cause is shown, failure to provide timely notice of contested issues shall constitute a waiver of the right to contest any issue, except the department's permanency plan.

[Adopted effective September 1, 2004; amended effective September 1, 2008; September 1, 2011.]

LJuCR 3.10–3.11. [NO LOCAL RULES]

TITLE IV.   PROCEEDINGS TO TERMINATE PARENT–CHILD RELATION-SHIP
(RULES 4.1–4.3) *[No Local Rules]*

TITLE V.   PROCEEDINGS FOR CHILDREN IN NEED OF SERVICES
(RULES 5.1–5.7) *[No Local Rules]*

TITLE 5A.   PROCEEDINGS FOR AT–RISK YOUTH
(RULES 5A.1–5A.6) *[No Local Rules]*

TITLE VI.   JUVENILE OFFENSE PROCEEDINGS—DIVERSION AGREE-MENTS
(RULES 6.1–6.6) *[No Local Rules]*

TITLE VII.   JUVENILE OFFENSE PROCEEDINGS IN JUVENILE COURT

LJuCR 7.1—7.2.   [NO LOCAL RULES]

LJuCR 7.3.   DETENTION AND RELEASE
(a)—(f) (No Local Rules)
(g) **Detention Facilities in Island County.** The Island County juvenile court shall designate appropriate juvenile detention facilities for use; provided, that the detention area within the Island County jail may be used for detention of juveniles prior to an initial court appearance if no adult prisoners are housed in the same detention area. Names of designated facilities may be obtained from Island County Juvenile Court Services.

[Effective September 1, 2002; amended effective September 1, 2008; September 1, 2011; September 1, 2012.]

LJuCR 7.5–7.15.   [NO LOCAL RULES]

TITLE VIII. DECLINING JUVENILE COURT JURISDICTION OVER AN ALLEGED JUVENILE OFFENDER
(RULES 8.1–8.2) *[No Local Rules]*

TITLE IX. RIGHT TO LAWYER AND EXPERTS IN ALL JUVENILE COURT PROCEEDINGS
(RULES 9.1–9.3) *[No Local Rules]*

TITLE X. JUVENILE COURT RECORDS
(RULES 10.1–10.9) *[No Local Rules]*

TITLE XI. SUPPLEMENTAL PROVISIONS

LJuCR 11.1–11.3. [NO LOCAL RULES]

LJuCR 11.4. COURT SHEDULES FOR JUVENILE MATTERS[1]

See LCR 77(k)

[Amended effective September 1, 2011; renumbered from LJuCR 11.3 and amended effective September 1, 2012.]

[1] So in original.

LJuCR 11.5. FINANCIAL RESPONSIBILITY

(a) Financial Obligation. Pursuant to the intent and standards set forth in RCW 13.16.085 and RCW 13.40.145, in any juvenile court proceeding regarding the detention, disposition or modification regarding a juvenile offender, or in any at risk youth, CHINS, truancy or dependency proceeding, the court may order the parent or parents, guardian, or other person legally obligated to support the juvenile, to pay a reasonable sum for the cost of detention and/or legal services provided by publicly funded counsel.

(b) Assessment of Costs. The assessment for the cost of detention and publicly funded counsel should not exceed actual costs to the county. The costs shall be assessed and ordered paid in a reasonable time unless a sworn financial statement is presented to the court at said proceeding justifying reduction or elimination of any such assessment, or there are other circumstances recognized by the court for reducing or not imposing the assessment.

(c) Notice. It shall be the duty of the Juvenile Court Services and/or the prosecuting attorney, to notify the parent or parents, guardian, or other person legally obligated to support the juvenile of this rule prior to said proceeding and to provide all necessary documents in order for such person to adequately prepare for said proceeding. Notice shall be provided to the parties five days in advance of any proceeding to assess costs.

(d) Time. Proceedings to assess costs shall not be held prior to sentencing or contempt hearing.

(e) Payments Forwarded. Juvenile Court Services, the public defense department, or the county clerk's office shall receive payments in a manner appropriate to local and state auditing regulations and shall forward such payments to the county treasurer.

(f) Sanctions. A show cause hearing with timely notice by Juvenile Court Services or the prosecuting attorney to the delinquent person or agency may be held to inquire into the delinquency of the assessment and the sanctions available under RCW 13.16.085 and RCW 13.40.145.

[Adopted effective September 1, 2004; amended effective September 1, 2008; September 1, 2011; September 1, 2012.]

LJuCR 11.6—11.22. [NO LOCAL RULES]

[APPENDICES]

[Appendices were adopted effective September 1, 1998; amended and renumbered effective September 1, 2000; September 1, 2002; September 1, 2004; September 1, 2005; September 1, 2008; September 1, 2011; September 1, 2012; September 2, 2014.]

APPENDIX A. TEMPORARY RESTRAINING ORDER

SUPERIOR COURT OF WASHINGTON
COUNTY OF ISLAND

In Re _____ of:

           Petitioner,

and

           Respondent.

NO.

COURT'S TEMPORARY RESTRAINING ORDER
RE: SPR 94.04(b)

I. NOTICE TO PARTIES

1.1 An action has been started in this court that affects your rights. Both parties are now required to obey the following order unless the court changes it. Either of you may ask the court to change or clarify this order. The court has the authority to punish violations of this order and to require the violator to pay attorney fees to the other party for having to bring the violation before the court.

1.2 The financial restraints in section 2.1 below and the requirement to fill out the attached "Verified Statement of Assets and Liabilities" only apply in actions for (1) dissolution of marriage, legal separation, or marriages declared to be invalid, or (2) non-marital relationships involving distribution of assets and liabilities.

II. ORDER

IT IS ORDERED:

2.1 TEMPORARY ORDERS FOR ALL PARTIES

(a) Both parties are restrained from transferring, removing, encumbering, concealing, damaging or in any way disposing of any property except in the usual course of business or for the necessities of life or as agreed in writing by the parties. Each party shall notify the other of any extraordinary expenditure made after this order is issued.

(b) Both parties are restrained from assigning, transferring, borrowing, lapsing, surrendering or changing entitlement of any insurance policies of either or both parties or of any dependent children, whether medical, health, life or auto insurance, except as agreed in writing by the parties.

(c) Unless the court orders otherwise, both parties are responsible for their own future debts whether incurred by credit card, loan, security interest or mortgage, except as agreed in writing by the parties.

(d) Both parties shall have access to all tax, financial, legal, and household records. Reasonable access to records shall not be denied without order of the court.

(e) Within 30 days after the filing of any general appearance, answer or other responsive pleading, each party shall provide the other party with **a completed Financial Declaration (WPF DRPSCU 01.1550) and a Verified Statement of Assets and Liabilities** (form available at www.islandcounty.net/superiorcourt/forms or see Forms Appendix B herein). Each party shall

COURT'S TEMPORARY ORDER – SPR 94.04
Page 1 of 2

FORMS APPENDIX A

then file a Declaration of Mailing showing that these documents have been provided to the other party within the time limit. In all cases involving a request for child support, maintenance or attorney fees, the completed Financial Declaration shall also be filed with the court. All parties have a duty to supplement the financial information when additional information becomes available.

2.2 TEMPORARY ORDERS FOR PARTIES WITH MINOR CHILD(REN).

(a) Both parents are restrained from changing the residence of the child(ren) until further court order, except as agreed in writing by the parties.
(b) Each parent shall have full access to the child(ren)'s educational and medical records, unless otherwise ordered by the court.
(c) Each parent shall insure that the child(ren) are not exposed to negative comments about the other parent. Neither parent shall make negative comments about the other parent in the presence of the child(ren).
(d) Within 30 days of filing an appearance, answer or other responsive pleading in this action, both parties shall register for a court-approved parent education seminar. Each party shall attend the seminar within 60 days of registering. Upon completion of the seminar, each party shall file with the court the seminar completion certificate provided by the sponsoring agency or provider. In no case shall opposing parties be required to attend a seminar together.
(e) Within 14 days of completing the above-ordered parent education seminar, each parent shall provide the other parent with a Proposed Parenting Plan, if they have not already done so.

2.2 MEDIATION AND SETTLEMENT CONFERENCE

If the parties are not able to agree on the final terms of their Decree, they shall be required to participate in mediation of unresolved disputes. Mediation is not required in cases involving domestic violence. For purposes of this order, domestic violence has occurred in the relationship if (1) a domestic violence restraining order or protection order (excluding *ex parte* orders) involving the parties has been entered by a court at any time within the previous 12 months; (2) a domestic violence no contact order exists pursuant to RCW 10.99; or (3) the court upon motion makes a finding that domestic violence has occurred between the parties and that such abuse would interfere with arm's-length mediation. If, after mediation, there remain unresolved issues, the parties may participate in a settlement conference, pursuant to LCR 16(d).

2.3 EFFECTIVE DATE OF ORDER

The Petitioner is subject to this order from the time of filing the Petition. **The Petitioner shall serve a copy of this on the Respondent and file a declaration of service in the court file.** The Respondent is subject to this order from the time that the order is served. This order shall remain in effect until further court order.

Dated:_____

_____
JUDGE/Commissioner

[Amended effective September 1, 2011; September 1, 2012.]

APPENDIX B. VERIFIED STATEMENT OF ASSETS/LIABILITIES SPR 94.04(d)

DO NOT FILE THIS DOCUMENT WITH THE COURT

VERIFIED STATEMENT OF ASSETS AND LIABILITIES
SPR 94.04(d)
(Attach additional sheets in the same form if necessary.)
Strike-Order of Dismissal entered on 03/31/15
DO NOT FILE THIS DOCUMENT WITH THE COURT
Within 30 days after the filing of any general appearance, answer or other responsive pleading, each party shall provide the other party with **a completed Financial Declaration (WPF DRPSCU 01-1550) and a Verified Statement of Assets and Liabilities.**

Petitioner:_____ Respondent:_____ Case #:_____

Date of separation from Spouse:_____ Date Petition for Dissolution filed:_____

1. I am the [ ] Petitioner [ ] Respondent in this action.

2. To my knowledge, as of the date of separation, the following community and separate assets and liabilities existed. *(Note: Generally "**Community assets**" means those assets that were acquired during marriage, except by inheritance or gift. "**Community liabilities**" means all debts incurred during the marriage, regardless of whose name the debt is in. "**Separate assets**" means those assets owned before marriage, or acquired after separation, or acquired during the marriage by inheritance or gift. "**Separate liabilities**" means those debts incurred before the marriage or after separation.*

COMMUNITY ASSETS   **SEPARATE ASSETS**

Real Property:

1. _____   1. _____
2. _____   2. _____

Vehicles (autos, trailers, boats, etc.):

1. _____   1. _____
2. _____   2. _____
3. _____   3. _____
4. _____   4. _____

VERIFIED STATEMENT OF ASSETS/LIABILITIES
SPR 94.04(d)
Page | 1   FORMS APPENDIX B

Bank Accounts:

Bank Name/Branch	Account No.		Bank Name/Branch	Account No.
1.			1.	
2.			2.	
3.			3.	
4.			4.	

Pensions/Retirement Accounts:

1. _____   1. _____
2. _____   2. _____

Business Interests:

1. _____   1. _____
2. _____   2. _____

Stocks/Bonds/Investments:

1. _____   1. _____
2. _____   2. _____
3. _____   3. _____

Life Insurance:

1. _____   1. _____
2. _____   2. _____

Household Goods/Furnishings/Appliances valued over $250:

1. _____   1. _____
2. _____   2. _____
3. _____   3. _____
4. _____   4. _____
5. _____   5. _____

VERIFIED STATEMENT OF ASSETS/LIABILITIES
SPR 94.04(d)   FORMS APPENDIX B
Page | 2

Sporting Goods/Tools & Equipment valued over $250:

1. _____   1. _____
2. _____   2. _____
3. _____   3. _____
4. _____   4. _____

Jewelry/Artwork valued over $250:

1. _____   1. _____
2. _____   2. _____
3. _____   3. _____
4. _____   4. _____

Electronics and Accessories valued over $250:

1. _____   1. _____
2. _____   2. _____
3. _____   3. _____
4. _____   4. _____

Other:

1. _____   1. _____
2. _____   2. _____
3. _____   3. _____

COMMUNITY LIABILTIES

Mortgage:	Balance at Separation	Current Balance
1. _____	$ _____	$ _____
2. _____	$ _____	$ _____

VERIFIED STATEMENT OF ASSETS/LIABILITIES
SPR 94.04(d)   FORMS APPENDIX B
Page | 3

Loans (vehicles/student/personal):

1. _____ $ _____ $ _____
2. _____ $ _____ $ _____
3. _____ $ _____ $ _____
4. _____ $ _____ $ _____

Credit Cards:

1. _____ $ _____ $ _____
2. _____ $ _____ $ _____
3. _____ $ _____ $ _____
4. _____ $ _____ $ _____
5. _____ $ _____ $ _____
6. _____ $ _____ $ _____

Other (overdue utility/phone bills, IRS, hospital/doctor bills, collection):

1. _____ $ _____ $ _____
2. _____ $ _____ $ _____
3. _____ $ _____ $ _____
4. _____ $ _____ $ _____
5. _____ $ _____ $ _____
6. _____ $ _____ $ _____

Business Debts:

1. _____ $ _____ $ _____
2. _____ $ _____ $ _____
3. _____ $ _____ $ _____
4. _____ $ _____ $ _____

VERIFIED STATEMENT OF ASSETS/LIABILITIES
SPR 94.04(d)   FORMS APPENDIX B
Page | 4

SEPARATE LIABILITIES

Describe type:

1. _____ $ _____ $ _____
2. _____ $ _____ $ _____
3. _____ $ _____ $ _____
4. _____ $ _____ $ _____
5. _____ $ _____ $ _____

Since the time of separation, there has been the following substantial change in the assets listed above: *(NOTE: Describe how, when and why any of the above assets were sold, traded, consumed or otherwise disposed.)*

_____

_____

_____

_____

_____

I anticipate receiving the following in the future:

a) **Inheritance** [ ] Yes [ ] No

b) **Settlement proceeds from a lawsuit** [ ] Yes [ ] No

c) **Settlement proceeds from a work-related injury** [ ] Yes [ ] No

d) **Money owed to me by another** [ ] Yes [ ] No

I declare under penalty of perjury of the laws of the State of Washington that the above is true and correct to the best of my knowledge.

DATED this _____ **day of** _____, 20_____.

at _____, **Washington.**

_____
Declarant

VERIFIED STATEMENT OF ASSETS/LIABILITIES
SPR 94.04(d)   FORMS APPENDIX B
Page | 5

[Amended effective September 1, 2011; September 1, 2012; September 1, 2015.]

APPENDIX C.   ORDER APPOINTING GUARDIAN
AD LITEM (SUPPLEMENTAL–GALR 5(c))

SUPERIOR COURT FOR WASHINGTON
COUNTY OF ISLAND

In re:	Case No.
_____	
Plaintiff/Petitioner,	**ORDER APPOINTING GUARDIAN**
vs.	**AD LITEM (SUPPLEMENTAL)**
_____	**GALR 5(c)**
Respondent/Defendant.	

Supplementing the Order Appointing Guardian ad Litem, entered on _____, the
Guardian ad Litem appointed in this cause shall:

☐ 1. Investigate and make recommendations regarding:

    ☐ Paternity
        ☐ Establishment   ☐ Dis-establishment

    ☐ Residential Schedule
        ☐ Initial Parenting Plan (RCW 26.09.187, 26.09.191)
        ☐ Modification of Parenting Plan (RCW 26.09.240)
        ☐ Non-Parental Custody (RCW 26.10.030)
        ☐ Non-Parental Visitation (RCW 26.09.230)

☐ 2. Investigate the following:

☐ Abuse of the Child	☐ Mental health issues, including
☐ Performance of parenting functions	substance abuse
☐ Child's relationship to parents	☐ Family conflict, including
☐ Child's relationship to significant others	Domestic Violence
☐ School placement/Adjustment of child	☐ Special needs of child
☐ Criminal behavior	☐ Cultural factors
☐ Other _____	

Dated: _____   _____
                                JUDGE/COURT COMMISSIONER

Attorney for Petitioner:
(Sign) _____
(Print Name) _____
WSBA #: _____
Address: _____

_____
Phone: _____

Petitioner:
(Sign) _____
(Print Name) _____
Address: _____

_____
Home Phone: _____
Cell Phone: _____
Employer: _____
Work Phone: _____

Attorney for Respondent:
(Sign) _____
(Print Name) _____
WSBA#: _____
Address: _____

_____
Phone: _____

Respondent:
(Sign) _____
(Print Name) _____
Address: _____

_____
Home Phone: _____
Cell Phone: _____
Employer: _____
Work Phone: _____

ORDER APPOINTING GUARDIAN
AD LITEM (SUPPLEMENTAL-GALR 5(c)
Page | 2   FORMS APPENDIX C

[Amended effective September 1, 2011; September 1, 2012; September 1, 2015.]

APPENDIX D. NOTE FOR MOTION CALENDAR LCR 77(k)(1)

SUPERIOR COURT FOR WASHINGTON
COUNTY OF ISLAND

In re:

_____
          Plaintiff/Petitioner,

vs.

_____
          Respondent/Defendant.

Case No.

NOTE FOR MOTION CALENDAR
LCR 77(k)(1)

CLERK'S ACTION REQUIRED

TO THE CLERK OF THE COURT AND TO:

PLEASE TAKE NOTICE that a hearing on the motion listed below will be held at the date and time given in the Law & Justice Center, 1st Floor, 101 North East 6th Street, Coupeville, Washington.

Date: _____

Time: _____

Room: _____

Nature of Motion: _____

Dated: _____

_____
Signature of Attorney or Party

_____
Print or Type Name

_____
Address

_____

> **If you require an interpreter and/or ADA accommodations, please provide a minimum of 10 days' advance notice to us.**
> **TTY/TTD users, please call the Washington Relay Service at 1-800-833-6388**

NOTE FOR MOTION CALENDAR
LCR 77(k)(1)

FORMS APPENDIX D

[Amended effective September 1, 2011; September 1, 2012; September 1, 2015.]

APPENDIX E. NOTE FOR TRIAL SETTING

SUPERIOR COURT OF WASHINGTON
COUNTY OF ISLAND

_____

Plaintiff/Petitioner,

vs/and

_____

Defendant/Respondent.

NO._____

NOTE FOR TRIAL SETTING
LCR 40(b)(1)

(Clerk's Action Required)

TO: The Clerk of the Court
AND TO: _____

ADDRESS: _____

AND TO: _____

ADDRESS: _____

Please take notice that the above captioned action is now fully at issue. The clerk is requested to note this case on the regular Trial Assignment Calendar.

Date requested for trial assignment: _____

(Monday – No Appearance) (See LCR 40(b)(1)

Nature of the case: _____

Issues in Dispute: _____

Estimated Length of Trial: _____

A jury ☐ of 6 ☐ of 12 ☐ has ☐ has not been demanded.

Mandatory mediation under Local Rule 16 ☐ does ☐ does not apply to this case.

The parties have completed mandatory mediation: ☐ yes ☐ no ☐ N/A

Dated: _____

(Sign) _____
(Print Name) _____
Attorney for _____
WSBA# _____
Address: _____

NOTE FOR TRIAL SETTING   FORMS APPENDIX E

[Amended effective September 1, 2011; September 1, 2012.]

APPENDIX F. NOTICE OF CONFLICT DATES

SUPERIOR COURT OF WASHINGTON
COUNTY OF ISLAND

_____ Plaintiff/Petitioner, vs/and _____ Defendant/Respondent.	NO._____ NOTICE OF CONFLICT DATES LCR 40(b)(1)

TO: The Clerk of the Court
AND TO: _____
ADDRESS: _____
                   _____

AND TO: _____
ADDRESS: _____

Please take notice that the above captioned case has been noted for trial assignment on the following date: _____

The following are the undersigned's conflict dates, which are limited to previously scheduled vacations and trial dates:

Dates of Counsel's Unavailability	Reason for Unavailability	Reference (Court and Cause No.)
_____	_____	_____
_____	_____	_____
_____	_____	_____
_____	_____	_____

Dated: _____

                    (Sign) _____

                    (Print Name) _____

                    Attorney for _____
                    WSBA# _____
                    Address: _____

[Amended effective September 1, 2011; September 1, 2012.]

APPENDIX G.   STATEMENT OF READINESS FOR TRIAL

SUPERIOR COURT OF WASHINGTON
COUNTY OF ISLAND

_____	NO._____
Plaintiff/Petitioner,	STATEMENT OF READINESS FOR TRIAL
vs/and	LCR 16(c)(4)
_____	
Defendant/Respondent.	

TO: The Clerk of the Court
AND TO:
ADDRESS: _____
AND TO: _____
ADDRESS: _____

COMES NOW _____ by and through his/her
attorney of record and pursuant to LCR 40(b)(1) certifies as follows:

1. This case is subject to mandatory mediation: ☐yes ☐no
   If so, mandatory mediation has been completed: ☐yes ☐no   ☐N/A
2. This case is subject to mandatory parenting seminar: ☐yes ☐no
   If so, the parenting seminar has been completed: ☐yes ☐no   ☐N/A
3. Declarant's witnesses are available for trial: ☐yes ☐no   ☐N/A
4. All discovery has been completed: ☐yes ☐no
5. All necessary pleadings have been filed: ☐yes ☐no
6. The parties are ready for trial: ☐yes ☐no
7. The estimated length of trial is _____ days.

Declarant hereby requests that his/her personal presence at the court scheduled Readiness Hearing be
waived.

Dated: _____

(Sign) _____

(Print Name)_____
Attorney for _____
WSBA# _____
Address: _____

[Amended effective September 1, 2011; September 1, 2012; September 2, 2014.]

APPENDIX H. ORDER TO SHOW CAUSE RE: PARENTING SEMINAR

SUPERIOR COURT OF WASHINGTON
COUNTY OF ISLAND

In Re the Marriage of:

_____

_____ Petitioner,

and

_____

_____ Respondent.

NO._____

ORDER TO SHOW CAUSE
RE: PARENTING SEMINAR
SPR 94.04(e)(5)(D)

IT IS HEREBY ORDERED, ADJUDGED, AND DECREED:

By sua sponte order of the court:

The petitioner/respondent herein, _____ , shall complete the mandatory parenting seminar, "Helping Children Through Divorce," no later than _____. Proof of completion shall be filed with the court no later than _____. In the event petitioner/respondent has failed to complete this course, he/she shall be subject to contempt and sanctions, including forfeiture of visitation, by the court.

IT IS FURTHER ORDERED:

_____ shall appear in person before this court at the place and time below and show cause why sanctions should not be entered cause for failure to comply with this order.

Date: _____
Time: _____
Place: _____
Room/Department: _____

IF YOU FAIL TO APPEAR IN PERSON AND DEFEND AT THESE PROCEEDINGS THE COURT MAY ORDER SANCTIONS, INCLUDING CONTEMPT OR FORFEITURE OF VISITATION, AND/OR ISSUE A BENCH WARRANT FOR YOUR ARREST WITHOUT FURTHER NOTICE TO YOU.

Other:

In the event proof of compliance with the seminar is filed with the court on or before _____, the hearing shall be stricken.

This order may be served by mail.

Dated: _____ _____
JUDGE/Commissioner

[Amended effective September 1, 2011; September 1, 2012; September 2, 2014.]

APPENDIX I. REQUEST FOR ENTRY OF DECREE AND DECLARATION OF JURISDICTIONAL FACTS SPR 94.04(g)

SUPERIOR COURT FOR WASHINGTON
COUNTY OF ISLAND

In re:	Case No.
_____ Plaintiff/Petitioner, vs. _____ Respondent/Defendant.	**REQUEST FOR ENTRY OF DECREE AND DECLARATION OF JURISDICTIONAL FACTS** SPR94.04(g) *(For use by Attorney Only)*

REQUEST: The petitioner requests immediate entry of Findings of Fact, Conclusions of Law and ☐ Decree of Dissolution of Marriage, ☐ Decree of Legal Separation, or ☐ Declaration of Invalidity without a final hearing, and states:

RESIDENCE: I was a resident of the state of Washington when the petition was filed.

TIME LIMITS: More than 90 days have elapsed since the date of _____, 20__, the date on which the Petition was filed, and _____, 20__, the date on which:

☐ the respondent signed an acceptance of service and the respondent has either
☐ signed the final documents or
☐ waived notice *and* the final documents provide for only that relief requested in the petition.

Or
☐ the summons and petition were personally served upon the respondent, *or*
☐ the summons was first published pursuant to an order for service by publication, *or*
☐ the summons and petition were mailed pursuant to an order for service by mail.

REQUEST FOR ENTRY OF DECREE AND
DECLARATION OF JURISDICTIONAL FACTS
SPR94.04(g) Page | 1   FORMS APPENDIX I

MARRIAGE &
SEPARATION: The parties were married on _____, _____, *(date)* at
              _____, *(city and state)* and separated on
              _____, 20___.

    ☐ The marriage is irretrievably broken, *or*
    ☐ The parties wish to be legally separated, *or*
    ☐ The marriage of the parties is invalid.

PREGNANCY: ☐ The wife is not pregnant, *or*
    ☐ The wife is pregnant. The father of the unborn child is ☐ the husband,
        ☐ not the husband,   ☐ undetermined.

DEPENDENT
CHILDREN: ☐ All dependent children of the marriage are identified and the Child Support
              Worksheets are accurate.

PARENTING
CLASS: ☐ Both parties have completed the mandatory court-approved parent
              education seminar and the certificates of completion <u>are attached.</u>
              ☐ The parent education seminar has been waived by the court.

PROPERTY &
DEBTS: ☐ All property and all debts of the parties are fairly and completely divided in
              the Decree.

MEDIATION: ☐ The parties have complied with mandatory mediation and a certification of
              completion by the mediator <u>is attached</u>.
              ☐ Mediation has been waived by the court.

IF DEFAULT: ☐ If entry of the Decree is sought after default of the Respondent, the final
              documents provide for only that relief requested in the petition.

PERJURY
DECLARATION: ☐ I declare under penalty of perjury under the laws of the State of
              Washington that the foregoing is true and correct.

REQUEST FOR ENTRY OF DECREE AND
DECLARATION OF JURISDICTIONAL FACTS
SPR94.04(g) Page | 2   FORMS APPENDIX I

Dated this date _____

at _____, Washington

Signature of Petitioner

Presented by:

Approved, notice of presentation waived:

_____
Signature of Petitioner's Attorney

_____
Signature of Respondent's Attorney

_____
Signature of Respondent

REQUEST FOR ENTRY OF DECREE AND
DECLARATION OF JURISDICTIONAL FACTS
SPR94.04(g)   Page | 3

FORMS APPENDIX I

[Amended effective September 1, 2011; September 1, 2012; September 1, 2015.]

APPENDIX J. PRE–TRIAL AFFIDAVIT

SUPERIOR COURT FOR WASHINGTON
COUNTY OF ISLAND

In re:

_____
         Plaintiff/Petitioner,

vs.

_____
         Respondent/Defendant.

Case No.

PRE-TRIAL AFFIDAVIT OF:
☐ Petitioner
☐ Respondent
        SPR 94.04(h)

NOTE: This form shall be filed and served by noon two judicial days before trial.

I. PERSONAL DATA

Name: _____, Age: _____   Occupation: _____

Marriage/Relationship date: _____   Employer: _____

Separation date: _____   Gross monthly income: _____

Child's name: _____, Age: _____   Net monthly income: _____

Child's name: _____, Age: _____   Other income: _____

II. SUGGESTED RESIDENTIAL TIME FOR CHILDREN

With Petitioner _____
_____
_____
_____

With
Respondent _____
_____
_____
_____

III. SUGGESTED CHILD SUPPORT

If child support is at issue, complete and file an updated set of Washington State Child Support Worksheets and your most current pay stubs for the last four months. Based on current Worksheets, the presumptive amount of child support for ____ children is $ _____ per month. Child support should be set at $ _____ per month, because _____

_____

_____

_____

_____

_____

_____

IV. SUGGESTED MAINTENANCE

If maintenance is at issue, complete and attach the updated Washington State Financial Declaration and page 1 – 2 of the Washington State Child Support Worksheets (showing income and deductions).

Maintenance of $ _____ per month should be paid to the ☐ petitioner ☐ respondent, until _____, because _____

_____

_____

V. ASSETS AND DEBTS

If the other party *has not* **yet filed a Pretrial Affidavit:** fill in and attach four separate schedules, listing each community asset, separate asset, community debt, and separate debt. For each item, insert your figures in the appropriate columns for "Petitioner" or "Respondent."

If the other party *has* **filed a Pretrial Affidavit:** on their four schedules, add your own figures for each item in the appropriate columns. If the other party omitted any assets or debts, add them to the appropriate schedule. Attach copies of your completed schedules.

Transfer your totals from the Community Assets and Community Debts schedules to this chart, showing your proposed division of community property and debt:

	Petitioner	Respondent
Community Assets:		
Community Debts:		
Subtract Debts from Assets:		
Proposed judgment transfer (+/-):		
FINAL TOTALS:		

VI. OTHER FACTORS

List any other factors which you believe should be considered by the court, such as special income situations, physical disabilities, dependent children of other relationships, etc.

_____

_____

_____

_____

_____

I certify under penalty of perjury under the laws of the State of Washington that the foregoing is true and correct:

Signed this _____ day of _____, at _____, Washington.

_____
Petitioner/Respondent

DATED _____ By: _____

Attorney for _____ WSBA No. _____

PRE-TRIAL AFFIDAVIT OF: • Petitioner   • Respondent
SPR94.04(h) Page | 3   FORMS APPENDIX J

Article I.   COMMUNITY ASSETS

Asset #	Description of Community Asset	Related Debt #	Petitioner's Position			Respondent's Position		
			Fair Mkt Value	To Petitioner	To Respondent	Fair Mkt Value	To Petitioner	To Respondent
CA-1								
CA-2								
CA-3								
CA-4								
CA-5								
CA-6								
CA-7								
CA-8								
CA-9								
CA-10								
CA-11								
CA-12								
CA-13								
CA-14								
CA-15								
CA-16								
CA-17								
CA-18								
CA-19								
CA-20								
CA-21								
CA-22								
CA-23								
CA-24								
COMMUNITY ASSET TOTALS:								

PRE-TRIAL AFFIDAVIT OF: • Petitioner   • Respondent   FORMS APPENDIX J
SPR 94.04(h) Page | 4

Article II.   SEPARATE ASSETS

Asset #	Description of Separate Asset	Related Debt #	Petitioner's Position			Respondent's Position		
			Fair Mkt Value	To Petitioner	To Respondent	Fair Mkt Value	To Petitioner	To Respondent
SA-1								
SA-2								
SA-3								
SA-4								
SA-5								
SA-6								
SA-7								
SA-8								
SA-9								
SA-10								
SA-11								
SA-12								
SA-13								
SA-14								
SA-15								
SA-16								
SA-17								
SA-18								
SA-19								
SA-20								
SA-21								
SA-22								
SA-23								
SA-24								
SEPARATE ASSET TOTALS:								

PRE-TRIAL AFFIDAVIT OF: • Petitioner   • Respondent   FORMS APPENDIX J
SPR94.04(h) Page | 5

Article III. COMMUNITY DEBTS

Asset #	Description of Community Debt	Related Asset #	Petitioner's Position			Respondent's Position		
			Balance at Separation	To Petitioner	To Respondent	Balance at Separation	To Petitioner	To Respondent
CD-1								
CD-2								
CD-3								
CD-4								
CD-5								
CD-6								
CD-7								
CD-8								
CD-9								
CD-10								
CD-11								
CD-12								
CD-13								
CD-14								
CD-15								
CD-16								
CD-17								
CD-18								
CD-19								
CD-20								
CD-21								
CD-22								
CD-23								
CD-24								

COMMUNITY DEBT TOTALS:

PRE-TRIAL AFFIDAVIT OF: • Petitioner   • Respondent   FORMS APPENDIX J

SPR94.04(h) Page 6

Article IV. SEPARATE DEBTS

Asset #	Description of Separate Debt	Related Asset #	Petitioner's Position			Respondent's Position		
			Balance at Separation	To Petitioner	To Respondent	Balance at Separation	To Petitioner	To Respondent
SD-1								
SD-2								
SD-3								
SD-4								
SD-5								
SD-6								
SD-7								
SD-8								
SD-9								
SD-10								
SD-11								
SD-12								
SD-13								
SD-14								
SD-15								
SD-16								
SD-17								
SD-18								
SD-19								
SD-20								
SD-21								
SD-22								
SD-23								
SD-24								
SEPARATE DEBT TOTALS:								

PRE-TRIAL AFFIDAVIT OF: • Petitioner • Respondent   FORMS APPENDIX J

SPR94.04(h) Page | 7

[Amended effective September 1, 2011; September 1, 2012; September 1, 2015.]

APPENDIX K.   ISLAND COUNTY SUPERIOR COURT CONDUCT AND DRESS CODE

ISLAND COUNTY SUPERIOR COURT CONDUCT AND DRESS CODE LCR 77(b)(1)(A)

THE FOLLOWING CONDUCT AND DRESS CODE SHALL APPLY WHEN COURT IS IN SESSION:

1.   No firearms or other weapons, including knives, shall be allowed in the courtroom.

2.   No food or drinks, except water, shall be allowed in the courtroom.

3.   No cell phones or pages, with audible signals activated, shall be allowed in the courtroom.

4.   All persons in the courtroom shall be attired in a manner appropriate to the dignity and decorum of the courtroom setting. As minimum standards, the following rules shall apply:

- Men shall wear shirts, trousers and shoes.
- Women shall wear shoes and either dresses, skirts and tops, or pants and tops.
- Shorts, halter-tops, tank tops, hats, caps, torn clothing, shirts or other clothing with obscene or profane pictures or messages, and "flip-flop" footwear, shall not be worn.
- Male attorneys shall wear coats, slacks and ties.
- Women attorneys shall wear professionally appropriate attire.

5.   All persons in the courtroom shall in their speech and actions conduct themselves in a manner appropriate to the dignity and decorum of the courtroom setting. As minimum standards, the following rules shall apply:

- Spectators and persons not then actively engaged in court proceedings shall be quiet; any speech which does occur shall be as unobtrusive as possible.
- All persons shall refrain from any gestures and from conduct or behavior, which manifest disrespect for the court, counsel, litigants, witnesses, court staff, law enforcement personnel, or other persons.
- Children shall be closely controlled by adults inside and outside the courtrooms.

[Amended effective September 1, 2011; September 1, 2012.]

APPENDIX L. COURTROOM DECORUM AND PRACTICE GUIDELINES

COURTROOM DECORUM AND PRACTICE GUIDELINES LCR 77(b)(1)(B)

PREFACE

The pursuit of justice is a serious undertaking and conduct during the litigation process, both within and outside the courtroom, must at all times satisfy the appearance as well as the reality of fairness and equal treatment. Dignity, order and decorum are indispensable to the proper administration of justice.

A trial is an adversary proceeding, and lawyers must advocate for their clients' positions. However, conduct that may be characterized as discriminatory, abusive, or obstructive impedes the fundamental goal of resolving disputes rationally, peacefully and efficiently. Such conduct tends to delay and often to deny justice.

Attorneys are privileged to participate in the administration of justice in a unique way, and are responsible to their own consciences, to their clients, to one another, and to the public to conduct themselves in a manner which will facilitate, and never detract from, the administration of justice.

A trial is a truth-seeking process designed to resolve human and societal problems in a rational and efficient manner. A lawyer's conduct should be characterized at all times by personal courtesy and professional integrity in the fullest sense of those terms. A judge's conduct should be characterized at all times by courtesy, patience, and fairness toward all participants. The courts belong to the people of this state. The guidelines are intended to facilitate access to the courts for the fair resolution of disputes and should never be applied to deny access.

Application

The purpose of these guidelines is to provide lawyers, judges, and parties with a reasonable standard of conduct in judicial proceedings. However, these guidelines are not intended to homogenize conduct or remove individuality from the courtroom. To facilitate professional growth and foster voluntary compliance with these guidelines, the WSBA Court Congestion and Improvement Committee periodically review these guidelines. Comments are considered by the committee and changes are incorporated as needed.

All participants in judicial proceedings should voluntarily adhere to these guidelines. These guidelines shall not be used as a basis for litigation or for sanctions or penalties. Nothing in these guidelines supersedes or detracts from existing codes or rules of conduct or discipline or alters existing standards by which lawyer negligence may be determined.

COURTROOM DECORUM

I. General Courtroom Decorum

A. Always be prompt.

B. Stand when the judge enters or leaves the courtroom.

C. Do not make personal attacks on opposing counsel.

D. Do not interrupt. Wait your turn.

E. Enhancing courtroom decorum is a cooperative venture among bench and bar. It is appropriate to call to the attention of opposing counsel any perceived violations of these guidelines out of the presence of the jury. After the court has ruled, ask the court's permission before arguing further.

F. Advise clients and witnesses of the formalities of the court, the appropriate guidelines, and any rulings on motions in limine. Encourage their cooperation. This applies both to attorneys and to *pro se* parties.

G. If there is a live microphone at counsel table, remember not to confer with others or rustle papers near the microphone.

H.   Courtrooms equipped for videotaped reporting may require special precautions, such as remaining near a microphone.

I.   Treat everyone in the courtroom with fairness, consideration, and respect. Refrain from conduct that discriminates on the basis of race, color, national origin, religion, creed, sex, age, disability, sexual orientation, or marital status.

II.   General Trial Conduct

A.   Offers of and requests for stipulations are appropriate to facilitate the presentation of a case, but should not be employed to communicate to the jury a party's willingness or unwillingness to stipulate.

B.   During trial, maintain appropriate respect for witnesses, jurors, and opposing counsel, avoiding informality.   Address adults by their titles or surnames unless permission has been given to use first names.   Avoid referring to adults by biased and demeaning expressions or labels such as "girl," "gal," or "boy."   Address jurors individually or by name only during *voir dire.*

C.   Treat jurors with respect and dignity, avoiding fawning, flattery, or pretended solicitude.   Suggestions regarding the comfort or convenience of jurors should generally be made to the court out of the jury's hearing.

D.   During the opening statement and argument of opposing counsel, never inappropriately divert the attention of the court or the jury.

E.   Avoid expressing an opinion to the jury about the testimony of a witness, a ruling of the court, or argument of counsel through exaggerated facial expressions or other contrived conduct.

F.   When practical, give the court advance notice of any legal issue that is likely to be complex, difficult, and which you expect to require argument.

G.   Do not argue the case in the opening statement.

H.   Counsel should not express to the jury personal knowledge or personal opinions about the evidence.

I.   Address your remarks to the court, not to opposing counsel except when extending necessary courtesies, e.g., thank you.

J.   Only attorney, parties, court personnel, and witnesses, when called to the stand, are permitted within the bar of the courtroom, unless otherwise allowed by the court.

III.   Examination of Witnesses

A.   When examining a witness, avoid undue repetition of the witness' answer.

B.   Make objections for evidentiary reasons without delivering a speech or guiding a witness.   Recapitulate testimony only as needed to put an objection in context.

C.   If a witness was on the stand at a recess or adjournment, have the witness ready to proceed when the court is resumed.

D.   Attempt to anticipate witness scheduling problems and discuss them with opposing counsel and the court.   Try to schedule witnesses in advance of trial.

IV.   Exhibits and Documents

A.   Premark exhibits with the clerk for identification prior to trial where appropriate.   Hand all unmarked exhibits to the clerk for marking before using them in trial.

B.   If practical, have photocopies of an exhibit for the court, opposing counsel, and the witness.   Avoid illegible copies if possible.

C.   Return all exhibits to the clerk at each adjournment.

D.   Whenever referring to an exhibit, mention the exhibit number.

E.   Give to the clerk all papers intended for the court.

F. Show the proposed exhibit to opposing counsel prior to offering the exhibit in evidence.

V. *Scheduling*

A. When practical, consult opposing counsel before scheduling hearings and discovery appearances in an effort to avoid scheduling conflicts. Assert a scheduling conflict only if the requested time is not available, not to obtain any unfair advantage.

B. If opposing counsel fails promptly to accept or reject a time offered for hearing or discovery appearance, raises an unreasonable number of conflicts, or consistently fails to comply with this standard, agreement is not required.

C. Where time associated with scheduling agreements could cause damage or harm to a client's case, then a lawyer is justified in setting a hearing or discovery appearance without first consulting with opposing counsel.

D. Give notice of cancellation of appearances and hearings to all involved at the earliest possible time.

VI. *Preferences of Individual Judges*

Counsel are advised to determine the preferences of individual judges with respect to movement within the courtroom. Following are some examples of individual preferences.

A. Stand when addressing the court and when making objections.

B. Stand during opening statement and closing argument.

C. Approach the bench only with permission.

D. Maintain an appropriate distance from the witness and the jury.

E. In the presence of the jury, address the judge as "Your Honor."

VII. *Discovery*

A. Make reasonable efforts to conduct all discovery by agreement. Consider agreeing to an early voluntary exchange of information.

B. Comply with all reasonable discovery requests in a timely manner.

C. Stipulate to facts unless there is a genuine dispute.

D. Conduct yourself in a professional manner and treat other lawyers, the opposing party, and all involved with courtesy and civility at all times. Clients should be counseled that civility and courtesy are required.

E. Be punctual in fulfilling all professional commitments and in communicating with the court and other lawyers.

F. Concentrate discovery responses on matters of substances and content, avoiding quarrels over form or style.

G. Clearly identify for other counsel or parties all changes made in documents submitted for review.

H. Fully respond to discovery, unless making a specific and clear objection warranted by existing law or a reasonable extension thereof. Do not produce documents in a manner designed to hide or obscure the existence of particular documents.

VIII. *Depositions*

A. Advise clients regarding appropriate behavior, attire and other matters involved with depositions and other proceedings.

B. Take depositions only when actually needed to ascertain facts or information or to perpetuate testimony.

C. Make only good-faith objections to discovery, and avoid objections solely for the purpose of withholding or delaying the disclosure of relevant information.

[Adopted effective September 1, 2011. Amended effective September 1, 2012.]

DISTRICT AND MUNICIPAL COURT

LOCAL RULES OF THE DISTRICT COURT OF ISLAND COUNTY AND THE MUNICIPAL COURTS OF THE CITY OF OAK HARBOR, THE TOWN OF COUPEVILLE AND THE CITY OF LANGLEY

Including Amendments Received Through
August 15, 2015

Table of Rules

CRIMINAL RULES

LCrRLJ 1.1. SCOPE

These rules apply to all criminal hearings in Island County District Court, Oak Harbor Municipal Court, Coupeville Municipal Court and Langley Municipal Court.

[Adopted effective September 1, 2000; amended effective September 1, 2001; September 1, 2008.]

LCrRLJ 3.1. APPEARANCE OF COUNSEL

(e) A notice of appearance by counsel is considered effective through the first disposition of the case. Once a dismissal is entered, the defendant is sentenced without appeal being taken, or the defendant enters into a deferred prosecution or sentence program counsel may withdraw without further formality. A new notice of appearance must be filed prior to appearing at any subsequent hearing such as a probation violation or show cause hearing.

[Adopted effective September 1, 2000; amended effective September 1, 2001.]

LCrRLJ 3.2. BAIL

1. Bail is to be set at the first appearance for all domestic violence offenses when a defendant has been arrested and confined pursuant to RCW 10.31.100 (2) (c).

2. Law enforcement and the Court Clerk may receive bail in the form of cash, cashier's check, certified check, money order, traveler's check, credit card charge, checks drawn on a trust account or bail bond. Recognizance bonds must be approved by the prosecuting attorney or by the Court.

[Adopted effective September 1, 2000; amended effective September 1, 2001; September 2, 2014.]

LCrRLJ 3.3. TRIAL SCHEDULING

(f) When the defendant pleads not guilty either personally or through a notice of appearance by counsel, the Clerk will schedule a pretrial hearing. All parties shall be expected to have exchanged discovery. Parties shall discuss the need for hearing any motions, including but not limited to 3.5, 3.6, Hamrick and Knapstad motions. At the pre trial hearing, parties must resolve the case or advise that the case is ready for trial, at which time, a readiness hearing and trial date will be set. The defendant's presence at a readiness hearing is required unless excused by the Court. If an attorney has had no contact with his/her client by the date of the readiness hearing, a warrant shall issue. At the readiness conference, cases declared ready for trial will be assigned for trial. Juries will be called based on trial assignments at the Readiness Calendar. If a case settles after readiness, and a jury is called but not used, statutory costs may be assessed to the responsible party. Juries may be called off by notifying the Court Administrator by 4:30 PM on the afternoon immediately preceding the assigned trial date.

(g) Continuances:

(1) *By stipulation.* Prior to the pretrial hearing the parties may agree in writing to reset the next hearing or hearings. The defendant shall consent in writing to the change in dates. Any agreements to change dates shall be submitted at least 24 hours before the next scheduled hearing. Notice of the new dates will be provided to the parties. All continuances on or after the pre-trial hearing must be approved by the trial judge.

(2) *By motion.* On motion of any party or the court, the court may continue the case when required in the interest of justice if the defendant will not be substantially prejudiced in the presentation of defenses. The motion must be filed on or before the date of the next scheduled hearing. The court must state on the record the reasons for the continuance if it is granted and may also assess terms as it deems appropriate.

(3) The court will not continue a trial date or other disposition beyond the applicable final day for speedy trial under CrRLJ 3.3 without a speedy trial waiver signed by the defendant.

(4) Requests for additional hearings such as bail reviews; requests to change previously scheduled hearings to new dates or to change the nature of the hearing must be requested in writing. Notice shall be given to the opposing party or counsel not less than twenty four hours prior to the new hearing. The clerk will then set the hearing at the requested time or notify the parties if the date set by the court is different than the requested date.

(h) Motions Calendar:

(1) Motions which will require more than five minutes for disposition will be heard on the criminal motion calendars. The Municipal Courts motions will be set at 9:00 AM Monday mornings; the State motions will be set at 2:00 PM Monday afternoon, unless otherwise scheduled by the Court. Motions to modify a No Contact Order shall be set at 10:30 AM on Monday mornings.

(2) Motions which will require less than five minutes for disposition may be heard during the arraignment calendar, the pretrial hearing, or during any regularly scheduled hearing with the court's approval and by agreement of the parties.

(*l*) Disposition Calendar:

(1) Guilty pleas may be entered at arraignment and pretrial hearings or may be noted for the 1:30 PM disposition calendar each Tuesday afternoon and may be noted for hearing at 8:30 AM any court day.

[Adopted effective September 1, 2000; amended effective September 1, 2001; September 1, 2008; September 1, 2009; September 2, 2014.]

LCrRLJ 3.4. PERSONAL APPEARANCE REQUIRED

A defendant who has signed a promise to appear for a hearing or trial must personally appear or submit a signed acknowledgment for the next agreed date. Failure to personally appear or submit such a signed acknowledgment is grounds to issue a warrant for the defendant's arrest and to strike all further hearings until the defendant next appears in person before the court. Represented defendants may file a waiver of attendance permitting their attorney to appear on their behalf. The form attached to these rules may be used for waiver of appearance. The defendant must personally appear at readiness, at trial, for any evidentiary hearings, at arraignments for all domestic violence offenses, and for preliminary appearances following an arrest and release for driving under the influence or physical control charges.

[Adopted effective September 1, 2000; amended effective September 1, 2001; September 2, 2014.]

LCrRLJ 3.7. PRESENCE OF THE PROSECUTOR AND PUBLIC DEFENDER

(1) In all criminal cases, a representative of the Prosecuting Attorney's Office or the Office of City Attorney responsible for the case shall be present to conduct the case for the plaintiff. This rule applies to preliminary hearings, bail reviews, arraignments, pretrial hearings, motions, trials and other dispositions.

(2) **Presence of the Public Defender.** A representative of the Public Defender's Office must be present for all hearings unless excused by the Court.

[Adopted effective September 1, 2000. Amended effective September 2, 2014.]

LCrRLJ 4.1.

(a) The filing of any notice of appearance shall eliminate the need for further arraignment, pursuant to CrRLJ 4.1. Upon the filing of any notice of appearance, the Court shall enter a Not Guilty plea on behalf of the defendant and will set the case for a pretrial hearing. Notwithstanding this provision, the defendant shall appear on the originally scheduled arraignment date for all hearings at which the review of conditions of release or protection orders is mandatory.

[Adopted effective September 1, 2008; amended effective September 1, 2009.]

LCrRLJ 6.1.1.   JURY TERM

(e) Criminal cases will be tried before a jury if jail is a possible sentence unless the defendant waives a jury in writing and the court consents to the waiver. A defendant who files a waiver of jury must file a request to withdraw the waiver within 10 days provided by the rules or before the pretrial hearing whichever first occurs.

(f) Trial terms are set on the first Thursday/Friday of each month for the Municipal Courts; the second, third and fourth Thursday and Friday for District Court and the fifth Thursday/Friday for civil trials. Cases will be assigned for trial at the readiness hearing. When two or more cases are ready they will go to trial in the order assigned by the Court at the Readiness Hearing or thereafter.

[Adopted effective September 1, 2000; amended effective September 1, 2001; September 1, 2003; September 1, 2008; September 2, 2014.]

LCrRLJ 7.6.   PROBATION FEES

(c) Defendants placed on probation shall pay a monthly probation fee in an amount set by the Court.

[Adopted effective September 1, 2000. Amended effective September 1, 2003; September 1, 2008; September 2, 2014.]

LCrRLJ 8.2.   DEFERRED PROSECUTIONS

(a) No order deferring prosecution will be approved and signed unless the defendant is actually in a treatment program or is to begin treatment on a date certain within 15 days of the date the order is signed.

(b) No final order deferring prosecution shall be approved and signed unless the defendant has either obtained an ignition interlock driver's license or a waiver of that requirement.

(c) Motions and orders for deferred prosecutions must be submitted in conformity with the model forms available in probation and at the front counter of the clerk's office. The qualifying evaluation, treatment plan and recommendation from probation must accompany the order. The statutory fees for the administration of the deferred prosecution must be paid before the order will be signed by the Judge unless otherwise ordered by the Court.

(d) Deferred prosecutions requests should be submitted on or before the pretrial conference. If submitted on the day of trial, jury costs may be assessed.

[Adopted effective September 1, 2000; amended effective September 1, 2008; September 1, 2009; September 2, 2014.]

LCrRLJ 10.   VIDEO CONFERENCE PROCEDURES

(a) Criminal. Preliminary appearances, arraignments, bail hearings, and readiness conferences may be conducted by video conference in which all participants can simultaneously see, hear and speak with each other. All video conferences are public, and the public must be able to see all participants and be able to speak as

(b) Permitted by the trial judge. Any party may request an in person hearing, which may be granted in the trial judge's discretion.

(c) Other trial court proceedings including the entry of a guilty plea may be conducted by video conference only by agreement of the parties, either in writing or on the record.

(d) Standards. The judge, counsel, all parties, and the public must be able to see and hear each other during proceedings and be able to speak when permitted by the Judge. Video conference facilities must provide for confidential communication between attorney and client. Normally public access will be provided in the courtroom. Confidential communications will be provided to counsel and interpreters, if any being present with the defendant in the conference room at the secure facility.

[Adopted effective September 1, 2000; amended effective September 1, 2001; September 1, 2008; September 1, 2009.]

INFRACTION RULES

LIRLJ 3.1.   PROCEDURE AT CONTESTED HEARING

(b) Representation by Lawyer. At a contested hearing the plaintiff *may* be represented by a lawyer for the prosecuting authority. The defendant may be represented by a lawyer.

(c) When both parties are represented by lawyers the matter will be heard as if it were a bench trial. If the defendant is not represented the hearing will be assigned to the normal contested hearing calendar for the appropriate court.

(e) If a lawyer appears for the defendant at a regular scheduled contested hearing without previously filing a notice of appearance, the matter may be rescheduled to the Tuesday, 3PM calendar to permit appearance by a lawyer representing the plaintiff.

(f) Witness fees: Each party is responsible for costs incurred by that party as set forth in RCW 46.63.151. Subpoenas may be issued by the Court or a party's lawyer with a copy filed at the Court. Out of county witnesses must be approved by the Judge.

(g) Speed measuring device experts may appear by telephone, video conference call, or in person.

[Adopted effective September 1, 2000; amended effective September 1, 2001; September 1, 2003; September 1, 2009; September 2, 2014.]

LIRLJ 3.5. DECISION ON WRITTEN STATEMENTS

(a) The court will consider requests for contested or mitigation traffic hearings by mail.

(b) To contest a hearing by mail the individual requesting the hearing must:

1) submit full payment with their request;

2) include a statement that they understand that there is no appeal for a decision based on written statements;

3) include a sworn statement of the circumstances of the incident and any other evidence they wish the judge to consider;

4) include a brief justification for the need for a hearing by mail rather than a personal hearing.

Once these items are submitted, the court will examine the officer's report and matters submitted by the individual requesting the hearing. This examination may be done in chambers and will take place within 120 days after the individual submits the required information and tenders payment. The hearing is not governed by the rules of evidence. The court will determine whether the plaintiff has proved by a preponderance of all evidence submitted that the infraction was committed. If the court determines that it was committed it may assess a penalty in accordance with IRLJ 3.3. The court will notify the parties in writing whether an infraction was found to have been committed and what penalty, if any, was imposed.

(c) To request a mitigation hearing by mail, the individual requesting the hearing must:

1) submit full payment with their request;

2) include a statement of the circumstances of the incident and any other evidence they wish the judge to consider;

3) include a brief justification of the need for a hearing by mail rather than a personal hearing.

Once these items are submitted, the court will review the submission and the individual's driving record. This review will be done in chambers and will take place within 120 days after the individual submits the required information. If the court believes that mitigation is proper it will mitigate the penalty and return the amount tendered in excess of the penalty.

(d) No Appeal Permitted. No appeal may be taken from a decision on written statements on either contested or mitigated traffic infractions.

[Adopted effective September 1, 2000; amended effective September 1, 2001; September 1, 2008; September 2, 2014.]

LIRLJ 3.6. DEFERRED FINDINGS

(a) Deferred Findings: The court may defer findings regarding traffic infractions following a contested hearing or defer entry of an order following a mitigation hearing for up to one year pursuant to RCW 46.63.070.

(b) Limit. A person may not receive more than one deferral within a seven-year period for moving violations and one deferral within a seven-year period for nonmoving violations.

(c) Conditions. For moving violations the conditions *shall* include attendance at traffic safety school, payment of the presumptive fine and an administrative fee. For nonmoving violations the conditions *shall* include payment of the presumptive fine and an administrative fee.

(d) Administrative Fee. The administrative fee shall be $25.

(e) Dismissal: After the end of the deferral period, the court will dismiss the infraction if the person has met all the conditions of deferral and has not committed another traffic infraction during the period.

[Adopted effective September 1, 2000; amended effective September 1, 2001.]

FORMS

INTRODUCTION

The following new forms are approved for use in Island County District Court:

(1) Waiver of Jury Trial

(2) Waiver of Speedy Trial

(3) Waiver of Attendance of Represented Defendant

(4) Waiver of Right to Lawyer (Trial)

(5) Waiver of Right to Lawyer (Arraignment)

[Adopted effective September 1, 2000; amended effective September 1, 2009.]

FORM 1. WAIVER OF JURY TRIAL

ISLAND COUNTY DISTRICT COURT
OAK HARBOR MUNICIPAL COURT
COUPEVILLE MUNICIPAL COURT
LANGLEY MUNICIPAL COURT

_____ , Plaintiff, vs. _____ , Defendant	)) Case No. _____) WAIVER OF JURY TRIAL)) (Clerk's Action Required))

WAIVER OF JURY TRIAL

1. I understand that I have a right to a trial by jury.
2. I do not want a jury trial. I want my case tried by a judge without a jury.
3. I understand that if I change my mind, I may request a jury trial within 10 days from today.

Date: _____   _____
                                             Defendant

[Adopted effective September 1, 2000; amended effective September 1, 2008; renumbered from Form 2 and amended effective September 1, 2009.]

FORM 2. WAIVER OF SPEEDY TRIAL

ISLAND COUNTY DISTRICT COURT
OAK HARBOR MUNICIPAL COURT
COUPEVILLE MUNICIPAL COURT
LANGLEY MUNICIPAL COURT

,	))	CASE NO._____
Plaintiff,	)	WAIVER OF SPEEDY TRIAL
vs.	))	(Clerk's Action Required)
	)	
Defendant	'	

_____

1. I understand that I have a right to have a trial in this matter within:

    (a) [ ] 90 days following the date of my arraignment
    (b) [ ] 60 days following the date of my arraignment because I am in
        custody on this charge.

2. I wish to give up this right and agree that this matter may be tried no later
    than

    _____.
          Month   Day   Year

Date: _____
                                                Defendant

3. [ ] I am the lawyer for the above defendant. I waive application on behalf of
    my client and represent that I have express authority from my client to execute
    this waiver. On behalf of my client I agree that this matter may be tried no
    later than

    _____.
          Month   Day   Year

Date: _____
                        Attorney for Defendant

_____
                        Bar Number

[Adopted effective September 1, 2000; amended effective September 1, 2008; renumbered from
Form 1 and amended effective September 1, 2009.]

FORM 3. WAIVER OF ATTENDANCE OF REPRESENTED DEFENDANT

ISLAND COUNTY DISTRICT COURT
OAK HARBOR MUNICIPAL COURT
COUPEVILLE MUNICIPAL COURT
LANGLEY MUNICIPAL COURT

, Plaintiff, vs. , Defendant	)) CASE NO._____) WAIVER OF ATTENDANCE OF) REPRESENTED DEFENDANT))

COMES NOW the above named Defendant, by and through counsel of record, _____, and does hereby submit the Waiver of Attendance.

Dated this _____ day of _____, 20 _____.

_____
                    Attorney for Defendant

DECLARATION OF DEFENDANT

1. I am the defendant in the above-entitled matter.

2. I understand that I have a right to be present at all court proceedings involving my case.

3. I understand that I have a right to have hearings set to a date certain by the court and be notified of those dates by the court.

4. I am represented by the above named attorney who is presenting this Waiver to the court.

5. I do hereby waive my right to be present at any pretrial hearings, readiness hearings, trial assignment hearings or other hearings on various motions which may be brought before the court.

6. I do further waive the right to have hearings set to a date certain by the court and be notified by the court of those future dates. By waiving this right, I fully understand that it will be the responsibility of my attorney to keep me informed of any court dates which my attendance is required, such as any trial dates. I understand that a failure of my attorney to keep me informed of any hearing dates where my presence is required, could result in a warrant being issued for my arrest.

7. I also understand that I have a continuing obligation to my attorney to keep my attorney at all times informed of my mailing address and telephone numbers where I may be reached.

I declare under penalties of perjury under the Laws of the State of Washington that I have read the forgoing Declaration and that the contents thereof are true and correct to the best of my knowledge and information.

Dated this ___ day of _____, 20 ___. _____ Defendant

[Adopted effective September 1, 2000; amended effective September 1, 2008; renumbered from Form 7 and amended effective September 1, 2009.]

FORM 4. WAIVER OF RIGHT TO LAWYER (TRIAL)

DISTRICT COURT FOR THE STATE OF WASHINGTON
FOR ISLAND COUNTY AND THE CITIES OF OAK HARBOR, COUPE-
VILLE, AND LANGLEY

STATE OF WASHINGTON
COUNTY OF ISLAND
CITY OF _____)
              Plaintiff   ) No._____
)
vs   ) Waiver of Right to Lawyer (Trial)
_____)
             Defendant   )

I understand that I have the right to be defended by a lawyer at trial and that such a lawyer will be appointed for me by the court at no expense to me if I can not afford to hire a lawyer. Despite that right I wish to defend myself and do not wish to have a lawyer appointed for me and I have chosen not to hire one. The judge has explained to me that I am charged with the crime(s) of

_____

_____

_____

and that I face the possibility of being sentenced to a maxim of _____.

The judge has explained to me, and I understand, the risks I run by defending myself including the technical problems that I will face under the rules of evidence and procedure. I understand that I will have to comply with the rules just like a lawyer and I understand the prosecutor is a lawyer and is probably more familiar with these rules than I am. I understand that there is much more to a criminal defense than simply being given the chance to tell my story. I understand that jury selection, arguments, examination of witnesses, presentation of evidence and motions all have technical rules which will apply to me, and that I may be unable to present important evidence to the court if I do not comply with these rules. The judge has also advised me that in his opinion I would be better off with a lawyer assisting me. Despite this advice, I wish to defend myself and do not want a lawyer appointed for me. No promises or inducements of any kind have been made to me to get me to give up my right to a lawyer.

Signed _____

Date _____

I find the defendant knowingly and intelligently waived counsel. _____

[Adopted effective September 1, 2000; amended effective September 1, 2008; September 1, 2009.]

FORM 5. WAIVER OF RIGHT TO LAWYER (ARRAIGNMENT)

DISTRICT COURT FOR THE STATE OF WASHINGTON
FOR ISLAND COUNTY AND THE CITIES OF OAK
HARBOR, COUPEVILLE AND LANGLEY

STATE OF WASHINGTON
COUNTY OF ISLAND
CITY OF _____)
           Plaintiff)   )   No._____
)
vs   )   Waiver of Right to Lawyer
)   (Arraignment)
)
_____)
          Defendant   )

I am the defendant in this case. I understand that:

1.1 I am charged with the crime of:

[a]

[b]

[c]

1.2 This crime has the following maximum penalty:

[a]

[b]

[c]

1.3 I understand that I have the right to be represented by a lawyer including a public defender appointed at no expense to me if I am indigent, and that I have the right to have such a lawyer present at all hearings to defend me.

1.4 I understand that this Court will not continue further with this arraignment until a lawyer is here to help me if I request that a lawyer be here.

1.5 I further understand that waiving or giving up my right to a lawyer at this hearing does not prevent me from claiming a right to a lawyer in future proceedings in this case and have been so informed by this Court.

WAIVER

I voluntarily and with knowledge of the above rights give up my right to an attorney at arraignment. No promises or other inducements have been given or made to me to get me to give up this right.

Dated and signed this ___ day of _____, 20 ___.

_____
     Defendant

[Adopted effective September 1, 2000; amended effective September 1, 2008; renumbered from Form 3 and amended effective September 1, 2009. Previous Form 5 was renumbered as Form 7 effective September 1, 2009.]

FORM 6. MOTION FOR ORDER OF CONTINUANCE AND ORDER FOR DIAGNOSTIC EVALUATION (MENTAL NON-DRIVING RELATED)

[ ] ISLAND COUNTY DISTRICT COURT

[ ] OAK HARBOR MUNICIPAL COURT

[ ] State of Washington	)
[ ] City of Oak Harbor	) Cause Number: _____
	)
Plaintiff,	) MOTION FOR ORDER OF
	) CONTINUANCE AND ORDER
vs.	) FOR DIAGNOSTIC EVALUATION
	) {Mental Non–Driving Related}
_____	) [MDP:MFC & DE]
	) RCW 10.05
Defendant.	)
	)

COMES NOW the above-named Defendant, [ ] without counsel, [ ] by and through counsel of record, _____ , and moves the court for a continuance of the case and for an Order Referring the Defendant for a Diagnostic Evaluation for the following reasons:

1. The wrongful conduct charged may be the result of mental problems for which the defendant may be in need of treatment and unless treatment is received, the probability of future recurrence is great.

2. The defendant agrees to pay or arrange for the payment of the costs of a diagnosis of the problem and treatment.

3. The defendant waives the right to a speedy trial for an additional 90 day period commencing on the date the Order of Continuance is entered.

This motion is based upon the records and files herein and upon the following Declaration of the Defendant.

DATED this _____ day of _____, 19__

_____

Printed Name:

[ ] Attorney for Defendant

[ ] Defendant

DECLARATION OF DEFENDANT

I declare under penalties of perjury under the Laws of the State of Washington that I have read the forgoing Motion for Continuance, that the contents thereof are true and correct to the best of my knowledge and information.

Dated this _____ day of _____, _____
             (day)   (month),   (year)

_____

Defendant

Order Granting Deferred Prosecution (Mental Non-Driving Related)

[ ] ISLAND COUNTY DISTRICT COURT

[ ] OAK HARBOR MUNICIPAL COURT

[ ] State of Washington [ ] City of Oak Harbor	)) Cause Number: _____)
Plaintiff,	) ORDER GRANTING DEFERRED) PROSECUTION
vs.	) {Mental Non–Driving Related}) [MDP:ODP] RCW 10.05)
_____	)) CLERK ACTION REQUIRED
Defendant.	))

THIS MATTER having come on regularly before the above-entitled Court upon the defendant's Petition for Deferred Prosecution; the above named defendant appearing, [ ] without counsel, [ ] by and through counsel of record,_____; the Court having considered the records and files herein, including but not limited to the reports attached hereto, Now Therefore, the Court enters the following:

FINDINGS OF FACT

1. The Defendant is charged with a crime for which the Defendant seeks to be granted a Deferred Prosecution under RCW 10.05.

2. The Defendant is amenable to treatment as set forth in the treatment plan filed with the Petition for Deferred Prosecution.

3. The defendant has been advised and fully understands that the defendant has the following rights:

(a) the right to have a lawyer represent the defendant and that if the defendant cannot afford to pay for a lawyer one will be provided at no expense to the defendant. The court may, however, order the defendant to reimburse the plaintiff for the cost of the court appointed attorney.

(b) the right to a speedy trial by jury within 90 days of arraignment.

(c) the right now and at trial to testify or remain silent. If the right to remain silent is exercised, there cannot be any inference of guilt drawn from the defendant's silence, and the Judge or Jury must decide the case on the evidence presented at trial.

(d) the right to compel witnesses to testify on behalf of the defendant at no cost. The court, however, may require reimbursement for the costs of securing the attendance of witnesses.

(e) the defendant is presumed innocent until a charge is proved by the plaintiff by the standard of beyond a reasonable doubt or until the defendant enters a plea of guilty.

(f) the right to appeal a conviction and sentence after trial.

4. The defendant has, as a condition of receiving treatment, and waived the right to testify, the right to a speedy trial, the right to call witnesses to testify, the right to present evidence in defense to the charge, and the right to a jury trial. The defendant further understands if the defendant proceeds to trial and is found guilty, the defendant may be allowed to seek suspension of some or all of the fines; that incarceration may be ordered upon the condition that the defendant seeks treatment; that the defendant may seek treatment from public and private agencies at any time without regard to whether or not the defendant is found guilty of the offense(s) charged. Having a complete understanding of rights as an accused the defendant stipulated to the admissibility and sufficiency of the facts contained in the written police report, including but not limited to the BAC test result (if any), witness statements and driving record. A copy of the police report is attached to the Petition and incorporated herein by this reference. The defendant understands and agrees that the police report will be entered and used to support a finding of guilty if the court finds cause to revoke the order granting deferred prosecution.[1]

CONCLUSIONS OF LAW

1. The Defendant meets the qualification requirements for a Deferred Prosecution.

2. The treatment plan filed with the Petition for Deferred Prosecution satisfy the statutory minimum criteria.[2]

ORDER GRANTING DEFERRED PROSECUTION

IT IS HEREBY ORDERED, ADJUDGED AND DECREED that the defendant's Petition for Deferred Prosecution pursuant to RCW 10.05 is granted upon the following terms and conditions:

1. Defendant shall complete the treatment plan as set forth in the report(s) attached and/or filed with the Petition for Deferred Prosecution and by this reference made part of this order.

2. Defendant shall pay for or arrange for the payment of the cost of treatment.

3. Defendant shall keep the Probation Department at all times fully informed of both the defendant's mailing address, and domicile address and employer's address.

4. Defendant shall comply with all reasonable terms and conditions imposed by the Probation Department.

5. Defendant shall report in person to the Probation Department within five (5) court days of the entry of this order.

6. Defendant is authorized to perform community service in order to work off the $150.00 filing fee and the $35.00 Probation Setup fee at a rate determined by the Probation Department.

7. Defendant is placed on supervised probation during the deferral period, and shall pay, on a monthly basis, the costs of probation of $50.00 per month for the entire treatment period.

IT IS FURTHER ORDERED, ADJUDGED AND DECREED AS FOLLOWS:

1. **The Treatment Facility** shall file with the Probation Department status reports every three (3) months for the first year and every six (6) months for the second year describing the Defendant's cooperation and progress in treatment.

2. **The Clerk of the Court** shall remove this file from the regular court docket files and place this file in the court's special Deferred Prosecution file.

IT IS FURTHER ORDERED, ADJUDGED AND DECREED AS FOLLOWS:

1. If the defendant fails or neglects to carry out and fulfill any term or condition of the treatment plan, or any term or condition imposed in connection with the installation of an ignition interlock device, entity administering the treatment or the ignition interlock device shall immediately report such breach to the court, the prosecutor, and the defendant or the defendant's attorney of record, together with its recommendation. The court upon receiving such a report shall hold a hearing to determine whether the defendant should be removed from the deferred prosecution program. If the court removes the defendant from the program the court shall enter judgment pursuant to RCW 10.05.020 and if the charge is a Title 46 RCW crime, the court shall notify the department of licensing of the removal and entry of judgment.[3]

2. If the defendant is subsequently convicted of a similar offense that was committed while the defendant is in this deferred prosecution program, upon notice the court shall remove the defendant from the deferred prosecution program and enter judgment.[4]

IT IS FURTHER ORDERED, ADJUDGED AND DECREED that the Defendant shall comply with the following additional conditions:

[ ] The defendant shall not operate a motor vehicle unless it is equipped with a functioning ignition interlock device and with an ignition interlock endorsement on the defendant's Washington State driver's license for the duration of the treatment program period.

[ ] Defendant shall remain totally abstinent from the use of alcoholic beverages and non-prescribed mind altering drugs during the period of deferred prosecution.

[ ] Defendant shall commit no alcohol related offenses during the deferral period.

[ ] Defendant shall not operate a motor vehicle without possession of a valid driver's license and proof of liability insurance in a minimum amount as set forth by Washington State law or higher if deemed appropriate by the Probation Department.

[ ] Other: _____

NOTICE TO DEFENDANT

Violation of any of the terms and conditions of this order may be punishable as Contempt of Court and subject the Defendant to imprisonment

Dated this _____ Day of _____ , _____

_____

Judge

Presented by: Approved for entry; copy received:

_____   _____
Defendant or Defendant's Attorney   Prosecuting Attorney

[Adopted effective September 1, 2000.]

1 RCW 10.05.020(2)

2 RCW 10.05.150

3 RCW 10.05.090

4 RCW 10.05.100

FORM 7. MOTION FOR ORDER OF CONTINUANCE AND ORDER FOR DIAGNOSTIC EVALUATION (ALCOHOL/DRUG DRIVING RELATED)

[ ]ISLAND COUNTY DISTRICT COURT
[ ]OAK HARBOR MUNICIPAL COURT

[ ] City of Oak Harbor	) Cause Number:_____
	)
Plaintiff,	) **MOTION FOR ORDER OF**
	) **CONTINUANCE AND ORDER**
vs.	) **FOR DIAGNOSTIC EVALUATION**
	) **{Alcohol/Drug Driving Related}**
_____	) **[ADP:MFC & DE]**
	) **RCW 10.05**
Defendant.	)
	)

COMES NOW the above-named Defendant, [ ] without counsel, [ ] by and through counsel of record, _____ , and moves the court for a continuance of the case and for an Order Referring the Defendant for a Diagnostic Evaluation for the following reasons:

1.   The wrongful conduct charged may be the result of [ ] Alcoholism [ ] drug addiction for which the defendant may be in need of treatment and unless treatment is received, the probability of future recurrence is great.

2.   The defendant agrees to pay or arrange for the payment of the costs of a diagnosis of the problem and treatment.

3.   The defendant waives the right to a speedy trial for an additional 90 day period commencing on the date the Order of Continuance is entered.

The defendant understands that the treatment facility will forward the results of the evaluation to the Department of Licensing, and that the Department of Licensing may suspend the defendant's driver's license or privilege to drive until such time as the defendant has enrolled or successfully completed an extensive treatment program, whether or not the defendant elects to petition the court for a Deferred Prosecution.

This motion is based upon the records and files herein and upon the following Declaration of the Defendant.

DATED this _____ day of _____ , 19__

_____

Printed Name:

[ ] Attorney for Defendant

[ ] Defendant

DECLARATION OF DEFENDANT

I declare under penalties of perjury under the Laws of the State of Washington that I have read the forgoing Motion for Continuance, that the contents thereof are true and correct to the best of my knowledge and information.

Dated this _____ day of _____, _____
           (day)   (month)   (year)

_____

Defendant

Order of Continuance for Diagnostic Evaluation
(Alcohol/Drug Driving Related)

[ ]ISLAND COUNTY DISTRICT COURT

[ ]OAK HARBOR MUNICIPAL COURT

<table>
<tr><td>[ ] State of Washington
[ ] City of Oak Harbor</td><td>)
)
)</td><td>Cause Number:_____</td></tr>
<tr><td align="center">Plaintiff,</td><td>)
)
)</td><td>ORDER OF CONTINUANCE
FOR DIAGNOSTIC EVALUATION</td></tr>
<tr><td align="center">vs.</td><td>)
)</td><td>{Alcohol/Drug Driving Related}
[ADP:OCDP] RCW 10.05</td></tr>
<tr><td>_____</td><td>)
)</td><td>CLERK ACTION REQUIRED</td></tr>
<tr><td align="center">Defendant.</td><td>)
)
)</td><td></td></tr>
</table>

THIS MATTER having come before the above-entitled Court upon the defendant's Motion for Order of Continuance for Diagnostic Evaluation; the above-named defendant appearing, [ ] without counsel, [ ] by and through counsel of record, _____ ; the Court having considered the records and files herein and determining that good cause exists to continue this matter; the Court having found that the defendant has waived the right to a speedy trial for an additional 90 days from the date of this Order, **NOW THEREFORE,**

IT IS ORDERED that the defendant shall obtain a diagnostic investigation and evaluation from:

[ ] **[Alcoholism]** an approved alcoholism treatment program as designated in chapter 70.96A RCW

[ ] **[Drug addiction]** an approved drug program as designated by chapter 71.24 RCW

IT IS FURTHER ORDERED that the facility shall conduct an investigation and examination to determine:

1. Whether the defendant suffers from the problem described;

2. Whether the problem is such that if not treated there is a probability that similar misconduct will occur in the future;

3. Whether extensive and long term treatment is required;

4. Whether effective treatment for the defendant's problem is available; and

5. Whether the person is amenable to treatment.

IT IS FURTHER ORDERED that the facility shall make a written report to the court stating its findings and recommendations after the examination required by RCW 10.05.040.

IT IS FURTHER ORDERED that if the facility's findings and recommendations support treatment, the facility shall comply with RCW 10.05.050.[1]

IT IS FURTHER ORDERED that the report shall be filed with this Court within 30 days from the date of this order and a copy furnished to the defendant, the prosecuting attorney, if requested, and the defendant's attorney, if any.

IT IS FURTHER ORDERED that the defendant shall contact the Probation Department (360) 675–0777 and schedule an appointment with said department at least two weeks before the next scheduled court date. The defendant shall pay the sum of $35.00 at that time for the cost of the probation set up fee.

IT IS FURTHER ORDERED that this matter is continued to the date and time set forth below for further hearing on this matter. The defendant shall appear personally and with counsel, if any. If the defendant elects to file a Petition for

Deferred Prosecution, said petition shall be filed no later than 5 working days before the date of said hearing.

NEXT HEARING

DATE: _____

TIME: _____

DONE IN OPEN COURT this _____ day of _____ , _____ .

_____

JUDGE

Presented by: Approved for entry; copy received:

_____   _____
Defendant or Defendant's Attorney   Prosecuting Attorney

Petition for Deferred Prosecution (Alcohol/Drug Driving Related)

[ ]ISLAND COUNTY DISTRICT COURT

[ ]OAK HARBOR MUNICIPAL COURT

[ ] State of Washington [ ] City of Oak Harbor	) Cause Number:_____
	)
Plaintiff,	) **PETITION FOR**
	) **DEFERRED PROSECUTION**
vs.	) **{Alcohol/Drug Driving Related}**
	) **[ADP:PFDP]**
_____	) **RCW 10.05**
	)
Defendant.	)
	)

COMES NOW the above-named Defendant, [ ] without counsel, [ ] by and through counsel of record, _____ , and makes this Petition for Deferred Prosecution pursuant to RCW 10.05 *et seq.* stating as follows:

1. **GROUNDS.** The wrongful conduct charged is the result of or caused by [ ] alcoholism, [ ] drug addiction, for which the defendant is in need of treatment and unless treated the probability of future reoccurrence is great.

The defendant has never previously been granted a Deferred Prosecution.

2. **COSTS.** The defendant agrees to pay or arrange for the payment of the costs of a diagnosis and treatment of the problem or problems.

3. **FILING FEE.** [ ] The filing fee of $150.00 accompanies this Petition.
    [ ] The defendant is indigent and unable to pay the $150.00 filing fee and therefore requests that the court authorized community service at minimum wage as a method of paying the filing fee.

4. **BAC FEE.** The BAC fee of $125.00 accompanies this Petition or will be paid on the date set for the hearing of this Petition.

5. **CASE HISTORY.** The case history and written assessment prepared by one of the following is attached hereto and incorporated herein by this reference as though fully set forth herein:

[ ] Alcoholism treatment program as designated in chapter 70.96A

[ ] Drug treatment program as designated in chapter 71.24 RCW

6. **ACKNOWLEDGMENT OF RIGHTS.** The defendant has been advised and fully understands that the defendant has the following rights:

(a) the right to have a lawyer represent the defendant and that if the defendant cannot afford to pay for a lawyer one will be provided at no expense to the defendant. The court may, however, order the defendant to reimburse the plaintiff for the cost of the court appointed attorney.

(b) the right to a speedy trial by jury within 90 days of arraignment.

(e) the right now and at trial to testify or remain silent. If the right to remain silent is exercised, there cannot be any inference of guilt drawn from the defendant's silence, and the Judge or Jury must decide the case on the evidence presented at trial.

(f) the right to compel witnesses to testify on behalf of the defendant at no cost. The court, however, may require reimbursement for the costs of securing the attendance of witnesses.

(g) the defendant is presumed innocent until a charge is proved by the plaintiff by the standard of beyond a reasonable doubt or until the defendant enters a plea of guilty.

(h) the right to appeal a conviction and sentence after trial.

7. **WAIVER OF RIGHTS AND STIPULATION TO POLICE REPORTS** [10.05.020(2).] As a condition of receiving treatment the defendant acknowledges and waives the right to testify, the right to a speedy trial, the right to call witnesses to testify, the right to present evidence in defense to the charge, and the right to a jury trial. The defendant further understands if the defendant proceeds to trial and is found guilty, the defendant may be allowed to seek suspension of some or all of the fines; that incarceration may be ordered upon the condition that the defendant seeks treatment; that the defendant may seek treatment from public and private agencies at any time without regard to whether or not the defendant is found guilty of the offense(s) charged. Having a complete understanding of rights as an accused the defendant stipulates to the admissibility and sufficiency of the facts contained in the written police report, including but not limited to the BAC test result (if any), witness statements and driving record. A copy of the police report is attached to this Petition. The defendant understands and agrees that the attached police report will be entered and used to support a finding of guilty if the court finds cause to revoke the order granting deferred prosecution.

The defendant is aware that the Court will not accept a petition for deferred prosecution from a person who sincerely believes that he or she is innocent of the charges or sincerely believes that he or she does not, in fact, suffer from alcoholism or drug addiction.

8. **ACKNOWLEDGMENT OF CONDITIONS OF DEFERRED PROSECUTION**

a. The defendant understands that an approved Deferred Prosecution treatment plan must contain minimum requirements which are set forth RCW 10.05.150 [2]. The defendant accepts and agrees to comply with these requirements as well as those which are contained in the written evaluation which was prepared by an approved treatment facility and filed herewith. The defendant has signed the evaluation acknowledging the defendant's commitment to treatment which is also filed herewith.

b. The defendant understands that as a condition of the Deferred Prosecution, the Court will require that the defendant not operate a motor vehicle without possession of a valid driver's license and liability insurance in an amount which may be set by the court. The defendant further understands that the defendant will be required to show proof of a valid license and liability insurance with acceptable limits before the defendant can drive and that failure to do so will constitute grounds for revocation of the Deferred Prosecution.

c. The defendant understands that the Court may place the defendant on supervised probation during the deferral period to monitor the defendant's progress in treatment and compliance with the other conditions imposed by the Court. Probation will include, but not be limited to monthly contacts between the Probation Department and treatment facility and a semiannual review of the defendant's driving record as maintained by the Department of Licensing. The defendant further understands that a probation supervision fee for the deferred prosecution will be imposed at a rate of $50.00 per month for the entire two year treatment period and $10.00 per month for the remainder of the probationary period of an additional three years which is a total of $1,560.00.

d. The defendant further understands that the court will order the defendant not operate a motor vehicle unless it is equipped with functioning ignition interlock device for the duration of the treatment program if: (a) the defendant was previously convicted of a violation of RCW 46.61.502 (DUI) or RCW 46.61.504 (Physical Control) or an equivalent local ordinance, or (b) if in this case the defendant had an alcohol concentration of at least .15, or (c) by reason of the defendant's refusal to take a test offered pursuant to RCW 46.20.308.

e. The defendant understands that the court may order the defendant to not operate a motor vehicle unless it is equipped with a functioning ignition interlock device for a period of time as the court in the exercise of its discretion deems appropriate regardless of the defendant's alcohol concentration in this case.

f. The defendant understands that if the defendant is convicted of a subsequent similar offense within seven years from the date the defendant is granted a Deferred Prosecution, the defendant understands that the Deferred Prosecution may be considered as a prior DUI conviction for the purpose of enhancement of punishment when imposing mandatory penalties and suspensions under RCW 46.61.515.

OTHER _____

_____

_____

This Petition is based upon the records and files herein and upon the following Declaration of the Defendant.

DATED this _____ day of _____ , 19_____

_____

[ ] Attorney for Defendant

[ ] Defendant

DECLARATION OF DEFENDANT

I declare under penalties of perjury under the Laws of the State of Washington that I have read the forgoing Petition for Deferred Prosecution, that the contents thereof are true and correct to the best of my knowledge and information.

Dated this _____ day of _____, _____
        (day)   (month)   (year)

_____

Defendant

Order Granting Deferred Prosecution (Alcohol/Drug Driving Related)

[ ]ISLAND COUNTY DISTRICT COURT

[ ]OAK HARBOR MUNICIPAL COURT

[ ] State of Washington	)
[ ] City of Oak Harbor	) Cause Number:_____
	)
Plaintiff,	) ORDER GRANTING DEFERRED
	) PROSECUTION
vs.	) {Alcohol/Drug Driving Related}
	) [ADP:ODP] RCW 10.05
_____	)
	) CLERK ACTION REQUIRED
Defendant.	)
_____	)

THIS MATTER having come on regularly before the above-entitled Court upon the defendant's Petition for Deferred Prosecution; the above named defendant appearing, [ ] without counsel, [ ] by and through counsel of record,_____; the Court having considered the records and files herein including but not limited to the reports attached hereto, Now Therefore, the Court enters the following:

FINDINGS OF FACT

1. The Defendant is charged with a crime for which the Defendant seeks to be granted a Deferred Prosecution under RCW 10.05.

2. The Defendant is amenable to treatment as set forth in the treatment plan filed with the Petition for Deferred Prosecution.

3. The defendant has been advised and fully understands that the defendant has the following rights:

(a) the right to have a lawyer represent the defendant and that if the defendant cannot afford to pay for a lawyer one will be provided at no expense to the defendant. The court may, however, order the defendant to reimburse the plaintiff for the cost of the court appointed attorney.

(b) the right to a speedy trial by jury within 90 days of arraignment.

(c) the right now and at trial to testify or remain silent. If the right to remain silent is exercised, there cannot be any inference of guilt drawn from the defendant's silence, and the Judge or Jury must decide the case on the evidence presented at trial.

(d) the right to compel witnesses to testify on behalf of the defendant at no cost. The court, however, may require reimbursement for the costs of securing the attendance of witnesses.

(e) the defendant is presumed innocent until a charge is proved by the plaintiff by the standard of beyond a reasonable doubt or until the defendant enters a plea of guilty.

(f) the right to appeal a conviction and sentence after trial.

4. The defendant has, as a condition of receiving treatment, and waived the right to testify, the right to a speedy trial, the right to call witnesses to testify, the right to present evidence in defense to the charge, and the right to a jury trial. The defendant further understands if the defendant proceeds to trial and is found guilty, the defendant may be allowed to seek suspension of some or all of the fines; that incarceration may be ordered upon the condition that the defendant seeks treatment; that the defendant may seek treatment from public and private agencies at any time without regard to whether or not the defendant is found guilty of the offense(s) charged. Having a complete understanding of rights as an accused the defendant stipulated to the admissibility and sufficiency of the facts contained in the written

police report, including but not limited to the BAC test result (if any), witness statements and driving record. A copy of the police report is attached to the Petition and incorporated herein by this reference. The defendant understands and agrees that the police report will be entered and used to support a finding of guilty if the court finds cause to revoke the order granting deferred prosecution.[3]

CONCLUSIONS OF LAW

1. The Defendant meets the qualification requirements for a Deferred Prosecution.

2. The treatment plan filed with the Petition for Deferred Prosecution satisfy the statutory minimum criteria.[4]

ORDER GRANTING DEFERRED PROSECUTION

IT IS HEREBY ORDERED, ADJUDGED AND DECREED that the defendant's Petition For Deferred Prosecution pursuant to RCW 10.05 is granted upon the following terms and conditions:

1. Defendant shall complete the treatment plan as set forth in the report(s) attached and/or filed with the Petition for Deferred Prosecution and by this reference made part of this order.

2. Defendant shall pay for or arrange for the payment of the cost of treatment.

3. Defendant shall remain totally abstinent from the use of alcoholic beverages and non-prescribed mind altering drugs during the period of deferred prosecution.

4. Defendant shall commit no alcohol related offenses during the deferral period.

5. Defendant shall not operate a motor vehicle without possession of a valid driver's license and proof of liability insurance in a minimum amount as set forth by Washington State law or higher if deemed appropriate by the Probation Department.

6. Defendant shall keep the Probation Department at all times fully informed of both the defendant's mailing address, and domicile address and employer's address.

7. Defendant shall comply with all reasonable terms and conditions imposed by the Probation Department, including but not limited to the following:

A. Submitting to random urinalysis testing and/or providing breath samples on a Portable Breath Testing device or a BAC verifier.

B. Providing proof of attendance at all alcoholism self-help recovery support groups.

C. Providing proof of liability insurance as requested by the Probation Department from time to time.

8. Defendant shall report in person to the Probation Department within five (5) court days of the entry of this order.

9. Defendant shall pay the $125.00 BAC Verifier fee at a rate of no less than $10.00 per month if payment has not already been made.

10. Defendant is authorized to perform community service in order to work off the $150.00 filing fee and the $35.00 Probation Setup fee at a rate determined by the Probation Department.

11. Defendant is placed on supervised probation during the deferral period, and shall pay, on a monthly basis, the costs of probation of $50.00 per month for the entire treatment period, and $10.00 per month for the remainder of the probationary period of three (3) years.

12. [ ] The defendant shall not operate a motor vehicle unless it is equipped with a functioning ignition interlock device and with an ignition interlock endorsement on the defendant's Washington State driver's license shall for the duration of the treatment program period for the following reasons:

[ ] The defendant was previously convicted of DUI or Physical Control

[ ] The defendant had an alcohol concentration of at least .15

[ ] The defendant had refused to take a test offered pursuant to RCW 46.20.308

[ ] The court, in it's exercise of discretion, deems that it is appropriate after considering the file and records of this case.

   [ ] The ignition interlock device is not required at this time, however, the court reserves the authority to subsequently order its installation.

IT IS FURTHER ORDERED, ADJUDGED AND DECREED AS FOLLOWS:

   1. **The Treatment Facility** shall file with the Probation Department status reports every three (3) months for the first year and every six (6) months for the second year describing the Defendant's cooperation and progress in treatment.

   2. **The Clerk of the Court** shall remove this file from the regular court docket files and place this file in the court's special Deferred Prosecution file.

   3. **The Clerk of the Court** shall send an abstract of the defendant's acceptance for Deferred Prosecution to the Department of Licensing.

IT IS FURTHER ORDERED, ADJUDGED AND DECREED AS FOLLOWS:

   1. If the defendant fails or neglects to carry out and fulfill any term or condition of the treatment plan, or any term or condition imposed in connection with the installation of an ignition interlock device, entity administering the treatment or the ignition interlock device shall immediately report such breach to the court, the prosecutor, and the defendant or the defendant's attorney of record, together with its recommendation. The court upon receiving such a report shall hold a hearing to determine whether the defendant should be removed from the deferred prosecution program. If the court removes the defendant from the program the court shall enter judgment pursuant to RCW 10.05.020 and if the charge is a Title 46 RCW crime, the court shall notify the department of licensing of the removal and entry of judgment.[5]

   2. If the defendant is subsequently convicted of a similar offense that was committed while the defendant is in this deferred prosecution program, upon notice the court shall remove the defendant from the deferred prosecution program and enter judgment.[6]

   3. Three years after receiving proof of successful completion of the two-year treatment program, but not before five years following entry of this order, the court shall dismiss the charges pending against the Defendant.

   IT IS FURTHER ORDERED, ADJUDGED AND DECREED that the Defendant shall comply with the following additional conditions:

   [ ] None

   [ ] _____

_____

_____

_____

NOTICE TO DEFENDANT

Violation of any of the terms and conditions of this order may be punishable as Contempt of Court and subject the Defendant to imprisonment

_____

Dated this _____ Day of _____ , _____

_____

Judge

Presented by: Approved for entry; copy received:

<u>Defendant or Defendant's Attorney</u>   <u>Prosecuting Attorney</u>

/   [Adopted effective September 1, 2000; renumbered from Form 5 effective September 1, 2009.]

1 The facility shall make a written report to the court stating its findings and recommendations after the examination required by RCW 10.05.040. If its findings and recommendations support treatment, it shall also recommend a treatment plan setting out: (1) the type; (2) nature; (3) length; (4) a treatment time schedule; and (5) approximate cost of the treatment.

The report with the treatment plan shall be filed with the court and a copy given to the petitioner and the petitioner's counsel. A copy of the treatment plan shall be given to the prosecutor by petitioner's counsel at the request of the prosecutor. The evaluation facility making the written report shall append to the report a commitment by the treatment facility that it will provide the treatment in accordance with this chapter. The facility shall agree to provide the court with a statement every three months for the first year and every six months for the second year regarding (a) the petitioner's cooperation with the treatment plan proposed and (b) the petitioner's progress or failure in treatment. Those statements shall be made as a declaration by the person who is personally responsible for providing the treatment.

2 RCW 10.05.150 A deferred prosecution program for alcoholism shall be for a two-year period and shall include, but not be limited to, the following requirements:

(1) Total abstinence from alcohol and all other nonprescribed mind-altering drugs;

(2) Participation in an intensive inpatient or intensive outpatient program in a state-approved alcoholism treatment facility;

(3) Participation in a minimum of two meetings per week of an alcoholism self-help recovery support group, as determined by the assessing agency, for the duration of the treatment program;

(4) Participation in an alcoholism self-help recovery support group, as determined by the assessing agency, from the date of court approval of the plan to entry into intensive treatment;

(5) Not less than weekly approved outpatient counseling, group or individual, for a minimum of six months following the intensive phase of the treatment;

(6) Not less than monthly outpatient contact, group or individual for the remainder of the two-year deferred prosecution period;

(7) The decision to include the use of prescribed drugs, including disulfiram, as a condition of treatment shall be reserved to the treating facility and the petitioner's physician;

(8) All treatment within the purview of this section shall occur within or be approved by a state-approved alcoholism treatment facility as described in chapter 70.96A RCW;

(9) Signature of the petitioner agreeing to the terms and conditions of the treatment program.

3 RCW 10.05.020(2)

4 RCW 10.05.150

5 RCW 10.05.090

6 RCW 10.05.100

MUNICIPAL COURTS
LANGLEY MUNICIPAL COURT LOCAL RULES

Including Amendments Received Through
August 15, 2015

Table of Rules

LOCAL RULE REQUIRING ATTENDANCE AT DWI VICTIMS PANEL

This local rule of the City of Langley Municipal Court is promulgated for the purpose of establishing a workable procedure for the City's requirement that persons convicted of driving while intoxicated or of physical control in the Langley Municipal Court attend and complete the educational program of the DWI Task Force Victims Panel at 2722 Colby Avenue, Everett, Washington.

1. Every person who is convicted of driving while under the influence of intoxicating liquor or drugs, or of being in actual physical control of a motor vehicle while under the influence of intoxicating liquor or drugs, may be sentenced to attend and complete the educational program of the DWI Task Force Victims Panel on the first such conviction within a 5–year period. After the expiration of 5 years from the date of first such conviction (that is, upon the beginning of a subsequent 5–year period), the defendant would again be sentenced to attend the DWI Victims Panel.

2. Defendants shall attend the DWI Victims Panel designated by this rule, unless another DWI victims educational program shall be specifically allowed by the court in a particular case.

3. Defendants shall attend and complete the DWI victims educational program within 60 days of sentencing, or such other time as may be specifically allowed in individual cases by the court. Extensions beyond 60 days may be allowed by the court for good and sufficient cause.

4. Before leaving the courthouse, the defendant shall complete a standard form maintained in the court, or such other place within the courthouse as the court may in the future designate. The standard form will gather the information necessary for the City's requirement to attend the educational program, and this form may be amended administratively by the court as necessary.

5. Before leaving the courthouse, the defendant shall pick up a standard form of instructions on how to contact the DWI Task Force and advising him/her of the penalty for failure to attend.

6. The DWI Task Force sponsoring the DWI Victims Panel will inform the court of those defendants assigned to attend their program who have failed to attend or complete the program. The DWI Task Force will fill out a standard form order to show cause and forward this to the court.

7. Upon a showing that a defendant has failed to attend or complete the DWI Victims Panel, the court will enter the standard form order requiring the defendant to appear and show cause why his probation should not be revoked, or why he should not be held in contempt. The hearing shall be scheduled approximately 45 days after entry of the order, at such a date and time as the court will set.

8. The order to show cause shall be served on the defendant and upon any defense attorney of record, if any, by mail, or other recognized form of service.

9. Procedures at enforcement hearing: The custodian of the attendance records of the DWI Task Force may appear at the enforcement hearing with the attendance records and give such testimony as may be required by the court concerning attendance or completion of the educational program of the DWI Victims Panel. The defendant shall be allowed to testify. Any other witnesses, by whomever produced, having material evidence shall also be allowed to testify. For a willful violation of the court's order to attend the DWI Victims Panel, the defendant shall be punished, as deemed appropriate by the court and as allowed by law. The punishment shall not excuse the defendant from attendance and completion of the DWI Victims

Panel, and such further enforcement order to compel attendance and completion as the court deems appropriate may be entered.

10. Procedure for enforcement for defendants not attending the DWI Victims Panel serving the Langley Municipal Court: Defendants not required to attend the aforementioned designated DWI Victims Panel shall provide the court with written proof of attendance at such other DWI victims educational program as they attended. Upon failure of such defendant to provide proof of attendance and completion, the court will prepare an order to show cause. The procedure at the enforcement hearing will be the same as in other cases.

11. Defendants ordered to show cause may attend and complete the educational program of the DWI Victims Panel during the interval between being summoned and the date of the show cause hearing. If written proof of attendance and completion is furnished, the court may, but need not, excuse the defendant from attendance at the enforcement hearing.

12. This local rule is effective the 1st day of August, 1992.

13. The court will cause standard forms necessary or useful for the operation of this rule to be devised, and may amend such standard forms as the court deems necessary.

[Adopted September 10, 1992.]

JEFFERSON COUNTY

Table of Courts

Superior Court

Local Rules of the Superior Court of Jefferson County.

District Court

Local Rules for the District Court of the State of Washington for Jefferson County.

SUPERIOR COURT

LOCAL RULES OF THE SUPERIOR COURT OF JEFFERSON COUNTY

Including Amendments Received Through
August 15, 2015

Table of Rules

Rule

LCrR 8.11. Criminal No Contact Orders.

LCrR 8.12. Criminal Hearing Continuances.

LOCAL RULES CONFORMING TO GENERAL RULES

LGR 31. Personal Identifiers—Children.

APPENDICES

App.

1. Request for Entry of Decree and Declaration of Jurisdictional Facts (Dissolution of Marriage).
2. Request for Entry of Decree and Declaration of Jurisdictional Facts (Legal Separation).

App.

3. Note for Motion Docket (NTMTDK).
4. Domestic Relations Information Form.
5. Pretrial Schedule for Complex Civil Litigation.
6. Note for Trial Setting (NTTRS) (Clerk's Action Required).
7. Request for Entry of Decree and Declaration of Jurisdictional Facts (Registered Domestic Partnership).
8. Fax Transmittal Sheet for Filing in the Jefferson County Superior Court of the State of Washington (per GR17).
9. Facsimile Affidavit/Declaration.

I. ADMINISTRATIVE RULES

LCR 1. SCOPE OF RULES

(a) Authority. These local rules are promulgated pursuant to CR 83.

(b) Application of Local Rules. Unless specifically designated otherwise, all local rules apply to all parties be they pro se or represented by an attorney.

(c) Suspension of Local Rules. The court may modify, remove or suspend the application of any of these local rules, in any given case, upon good cause being shown therefore or upon the court's own motion.

[Adopted effective September 1, 2003; amended effective September 1, 2011.]

II. CIVIL RULES

LCR 5. SERVICE AND FILING OF PLEADINGS AND OTHER PAPERS

5.1 Trial or Hearing Briefs—Timing. Trial or hearing briefs shall be filed and served three court days prior to the trial or hearing date. Nothing in this rule shall be construed to restrict the right of any party to submit further briefs or memoranda of authority at any other time during the trial of the case.

5.2 Documents Not To Be Filed. Photocopies of reported cases, statutes or texts shall not be filed as an appendix to a brief or otherwise, but may be furnished directly to the judge hearing the matter, and to all other parties. Also, photocopies of pleadings already filed in the case record shall not be attached to new pleadings, nor shall you attach copies of pleadings served to the proof of service filed. The clerk is authorized to remove all said attachments. Documents or copies produced during discovery, including interrogatories, and other items that should properly be received as exhibits shall not be included in the court file. Documents in a digital or video format are not acceptable for filing.

5.3 By Mail. Counsel may present agreed orders and ex parte orders based upon the record in the file by use of the United States mail addressed to the court, and submission of the ex-parte fee set by the clerk. When signed, the order shall be filed with the clerk. When rejected, the papers shall be returned by mail to the counsel sending them, without prejudice to presentation by counsel in person to the same judge. Self-addressed, stamped envelopes, along with copies of the order to be signed, shall be provided for return of any conformed materials and/or rejected orders.

5.4 Facilitator Review. The courthouse facilitator prior to submission to the court shall review all final pro se ex-parte or non-contested domestic relations documents.

5.5 Filing and Scheduling of Motions and Responses.

(a) *Filing and Scheduling of Motions.* Not withstanding any provision of CR 6(d) to the contrary, a party filing any motion shall serve and file such motion no later than seven (7) days prior to the date noted for argument on the motion. Motions requiring a longer period of notice pursuant to court rule or statute shall be filed as required by the applicable court rule or statute.

All documents supporting the motion shall be filed and served with the motion.

Unless other arrangements are made with the Court Administrator, all motions shall be scheduled for the appropriate Motion Docket. Unless other arrangements are made with the Court Administrator, hearings on any motion shall not include live testimony and argument may be limited in time.

A notice of issue or note for motion docket identifying the nature of the motion, names of the parties, the names of the attorneys if any, and the date and time for argument on the motion shall be filed and served with the motion.

(b) *Response Documents.* Any party opposing a motion or any part thereof shall file all original responsive documents and serve copies upon all parties not later than 12:00 noon two court days prior to the scheduled date for argument on the motion.

(c) *Reply to Response Documents.* All reply documents to the response documents as provided for in (b) of this rule shall be filed and served on all parties no later than 12:00 noon one court day prior to the date set for argument on the motion. No additional documents shall be filed, served or considered by the court after that date and time.

(d) *Affidavits and Declarations.* Affidavits and declarations in support of or in the opposition to any motion or part thereof shall be made only on personal knowledge, shall set forth only such facts as would be admissible in evidence, and shall show affirmatively that the affiant or declarant is competent to testify to the specific matters set forth therein. Argument, comment, and non-expert opinion shall be excluded from affidavits and declarations.

(e) *Hearing on Short Notice.* All motions and orders shortening time shall detail why the seven (7) day window should be reduced and indicate how service was made on the other parties.

(f) *Terms.* Terms and sanctions may be imposed for failure to comply with this rule, including the striking of any documents filed in violation of this rule.

[Adopted effective September 1, 2003; amended effective September 1, 2007; September 1, 2008; amended on an emergency basis effective September 24, 2008; amended on a permanent basis effective September 1, 2009; amended effective September 1, 2010; September 1, 2011; September 1, 2012; September 2, 2014.]

LCR 7. PLEADINGS ALLOWED; FORM OF MOTIONS

7.1 Motion Days. Motions shall be noted at the time and place stated in Local Rule 77(k)(1).

7.2 Ex–Parte Fee. Any ex-parte or agreed application presented without a note for motion docket will be subject to the mandatory ex-parte fee of $20.00.

7.3 Note For Motion Calendar. The notice of issue must be on a form approved by the court such as that in Appendix 3.

7.4 Bench Copy. At the time of filing any moving or responsive papers, a bench copy for the court, labeled "bench copy" and with the date of hearing contained thereon, shall be provided. All bench copies shall be legible. Any reproductions of photographs must be sufficiently clear to be meaningful. Bench copies shall be served on the court administrator. If the matter is to be heard before a visiting judge, it shall be the responsibility of counsel or the party to deliver any bench copies to that visiting judge. If

counsel requests the court administrator to forward the documents via email the fee will be .25¢ per page.

7.5 Hearing Continuances. If the moving party wishes to continue their matter, they must appear in person on the date and time noted and request such continuance, or they may wish to strike the motion and renote it for another date and time. The non-moving party may obtain a one week extension of time for the hearing of the motion by filing with the court and serving the opposing party a certification stating that additional time is needed to properly prepare a response to the motion, and that they believe in good faith that the moving party will not be prejudiced by a one week continuance. The certificate must be filed and served on or before the date that a responsive pleading would have been due.

If the moving party seeks a continuance of more than one week, that party must file a motion with the court seeking such relief.

7.6 Reapplication On Same Facts. When an order has been refused in whole or in part (unless without prejudice) or when an order has been granted conditionally and the condition has not been performed, the same motion may not be presented to another judge.

7.7 Reapplication on Different Facts. If a subsequent motion is made upon an alleged different statement of facts, the moving party must show by affidavit what motion was previously made, when and to what judge, what order or decision was made on it, and what new facts are claimed to be shown. For a failure to comply with this requirement, any order made upon such subsequent motion may be set aside.

7.8 Sanctions. The court may impose sanctions or terms for any frivolous motion, non-appearance, or in granting a continuance of any matter.

7.9 Attorneys Fees and Costs.

7.9.1 A party requesting that the court award attorneys fees or order payment of fees in any case shall itemize in affidavit form the time expended, services rendered, or other basis for the fees requested. All claims of a party for attorney fees and expenses must be submitted in the form of a motion and order. All claims for services must be submitted within 30 days of completion of the case, or they may be denied.

7.9.2 Appointed counsel submitting claims for services shall also itemize expenses incurred, i.e., long distance telephone and photocopy expenses. Extraordinary expenses by counsel will not be allowed without prior approval of the court. No expenses for third party services or experts shall be allowed without prior approval of the court.

7.10 Contested Pretrial Motions. Contested pretrial motions, however designated, the purpose of which is to expand or restrict the issues or limit the introduction of evidence (motions in limine) and motions for judgment on the pleadings, should be presented for resolution on a regular motion calendar before the day assigned for trial. The failure to comply with this rule may result in the court's refusal to hear such motion on the day of trial, or in the imposition of terms for the expense caused to adverse parties and the county by resulting delays.

7.11 Change of Judge. In the event that a motion is scheduled for hearing before a superior court judge on a specified court day and an affidavit of prejudice is filed against that judge, or a recusal is made by the sitting judge, the scheduled motion will be referred for hearing to the court administrator for a superior court commissioner or visiting judge for a time to be determined.

7.12 Length of Argument.

7.12.1 *Time for Argument.* No more than ten minutes to each side for argument shall be allowed unless greater time is specially authorized by the court.

7.12.2 *Arguments Longer Than Ten Minutes.* If the moving party expects the motion to take more than ten minutes to argue by all sides collectively, movant shall designate on the note for motion docket that the matter is over ten minutes and contact the court administrator for a specific time to hear said extended motion.

7.12.3 *CourtCall Telephonic Appearance Rule.*

7.12.3.1 **Program Overview.**

(a) The CourtCall Telephonic Appearance Program ("CourtCall"), 1–888–882–6878, organizes a procedure for telephonic appearance by attorneys or pro se parties as a reasonable alternative to personal appearances in appropriate cases and situations. CourtCall is fully voluntary and no person is required to utilize CourtCall, however, any telephonic appearance must be scheduled using CourtCall.

(b) Hearings will be held on a specific calendar in the usual manner, unless the court exercises its discretion to call cases in a different order.

(c) Hearings are conducted in open court. All attorneys or pro se parties making CourtCall Appearances call a designated toll free teleconference number a few minutes before the calendar is scheduled, to check in with the clerk. Attorneys or pro se parties remain on the court's speakerphone-telephone line and hear the same business that those present in the court may be hearing. Attorneys or pro se parties not participating telephonically appear in person. The court calls cases for hearing. All attorneys or pro se parties on a case participate in the hearing. All present in the courtroom hear the discourse of those making CourtCall Appearances.

(d) CourtCall Appearances should be scheduled by contacting CourtCall at 1–888–882–6878 at least three (3) days prior to the hearing and by paying the stated fee for each CourtCall Appearance.

7.12.3.2. **Participation in CourtCall Appearances.**

(a) **Court.**

(i) The court shall hear CourtCall Appearances in the order in which they are noted on the calendar, unless the court exercises its discretion to call cases in a different manner.

(ii) Subject to the court's right to amend this list, the following matters are currently deemed unsuitable for CourtCall Appearances.

1. Judgment Debtor Examinations;

2. Mandatory Settlement Conferences;

3. Hearings and trials at which oral testimony may be presented;

4. Hearings in which oral argument is anticipated to exceed 10 minutes, unless the matter has been specifically set by the court administrator and appropriately scheduled through CourtCall

(iii) The court reserves the right, at any time, to reject any Request for CourtCall Appearance. When the court rejects a request it shall order a refund of deposited telephonic appearance fees and notify CourtCall, LLC.

(iv) The court reserves the right to halt the telephonic hearing on any matter and order attorneys to personally appear at a later date and time, in which case no refund is permitted.

(v) If a matter is continued prior to the actual hearing date, the prior filing of a Request for CourtCall Appearance form shall remain valid for the continued date of the hearing.

(vi) Existing rules and procedures regarding making of the record by a court reporter or electronic device or obtaining a transcript after the hearing shall apply to hearings at which CourtCall Appearances are made.

(vii) Upon proper motion, the court in its discretion may waive the CourtCall fee for a party who is found by the court to be indigent or for his or her counsel.

(b) **Attorneys and Pro Se Parties.**

(i) Attorneys and pro se parties electing to make a CourtCall Appearance shall serve, on all other parties in the case, the Request for CourtCall Appearance form, fax or otherwise deliver a copy of the form to CourtCall, LLC, and pay the CourtCall Appearance Fee in the method prescribed, before the hearing date.

(c) **Proposed Orders and Bench Copies.**

(i) Parties appearing telephonically may send an original order with a bench copy directly to the court administrator for presentation during the hearing.

7.12.3.3   Appearance Procedure.

(a) An attorney or pro se party making a CourtCall Appearance shall:

(i) Eliminate to the greatest extent all possible ambient noise from the calling locations;

(ii) Be required, during the speaker's appearance, to speak directly into a telephone handset;

(iii) Not call in with cellular or cordless telephone devices or through a personal computer;

(b) An attorney or pro se party making a CourtCall Appearance shall call the court's designated toll free teleconference line approximately five (5) minutes prior to the scheduled hearing time and check-in with the clerk. All persons calling after the check-in period shall be considered to be late for the hearing and shall be treated by the court in the same manner as if the person had personally appeared late for the hearing.

(c) An attorney or pro se party appearing telephonically shall state his or her name for the record each time the person speaks and shall participate in the appearance with the same degree of courtesy and courtroom etiquette as is required for a personal appearance. An attorney or pro se party shall not utilize the "hold" button, as it is not within the policy of the court to wait for any person to rejoin the line.

7.12.4 *Temporary Family Law Issues.* Temporary family law issues will normally be determined by affidavits or declarations alone. Oral testimony may be permitted in limited circumstances at the court's discretion.

[Adopted effective September 1, 2003. Amended effective September 1, 2006; September 1, 2007; September 1, 2008; September 1, 2009; September 1, 2011; September 2, 2014.]

LCR 10.   FORM OF PLEADINGS AND OTHER PAPERS

10.1   Format Requirements. All documents filed shall be clear, legible and permanent, and hand printed or typewritten on non-translucent paper suitable for microfilming and laserfiche. Tissue or onionskin paper shall not be used. Two sided documents are not permitted. The type size shall be no smaller than size 10 font. All pleadings shall be first impressions with original signatures. Documents presented for filing shall contain no staples.

10.2   Signature Requirements. Any order or other paper presented to a judge for signature shall contain an original signature, except for those documents filed by facsimile, on the left hand side of the page by the individual presenting the document. A

place for the judge's signature shall be below the last line of the order or other paper on the right hand side of the page. Attorneys signing shall include their Washington State Bar Association Membership numbers.

10.3   Address of Party Appearing Pro Se. A party appearing pro se shall state on all pleadings filed, (a) the party's mailing address, (b) a street address where service of process and other papers may be made on that party, and (c) a telephone number where the party can be contacted during the business day.

10.4   Clerk's Action Required. Pleadings or other papers requiring action on the part of the clerk (other than file stamping, docketing and placing in the court file) shall be considered action documents. Action documents shall include a special caption directly below the case number of the first page, stating:

CLERK'S ACTION REQUIRED: (state the action requested)

For Example: "PLACE ON MOTION DOCKET" "ENTER PROPERTY JUDGMENT" "ISSUE LETTERS TESTAMENTARY"

Action documents which do not, on their face, comply with LCR 10.4 may not be processed. Responsibility to pursue a remedy rests with the parties, who may contact the clerk for direction.

10.5   Civil Bench Warrant. Any person requesting a civil warrant of arrest shall provide as much of the following information as possible on the person to be served the warrant to the clerk of the court: full name, date of birth, height, weight, race, gender, eye color, hair color and last known address.

10.6   Information Required in Caption. Below the case number and description of the document, every motion and supporting document shall contain the following information in substantially the following format:

Date of Hearing   _____
Judge/Department   _____
Nature of Motion   _____

10.7   Deleted

10.8   Proposed Orders. Proposed orders received by the clerk's office prior to a hearing will be filed in the court file. Parties will need to present an original final order at the time of the hearing or send in an original for presentation with an ex parte fee.

[Adopted effective September 1, 2003. Amended effective September 1, 2006; September 1, 2007; September 1, 2008; September 1, 2009; September 1, 2010; September 1, 2011; September 1, 2012.]

LCR 12.   DEFENSES

12.1   Bankruptcy. Any party that wishes to assert the protection of the Federal Bankruptcy laws shall, by the next judicial business day after the bankruptcy filing, file a copy of the Bankruptcy Court Notice of Commencement of Case Under Bankruptcy Code, or by a certificate reflecting that the copies are true and accurate, filed under the Superior Court caption for each case to which the matter pertains. A copy shall be served on all other parties, and a copy provided to assigned judge, if any. A claim of bankruptcy protection asserted in an answer or other pleading is not sufficient to advise the clerk or court of the pendency of bankruptcy. The parties will seasonably update the court as to the status of a bankruptcy case.

[Adopted effective September 1, 2003; amended effective September 1, 2011.]

LCR 16.   PROCEDURES

16.1 Status/Scheduling Conferences. A status/scheduling conference is a conference at an early state of the litigation held for the purpose of addressing issues such as adequacy of service, discovery, pleadings, need for additional parties, timing of pre-trial motions, and other matters. Status/scheduling conferences shall be scheduled only upon motion by one of the parties to the litigation, or by agreement of counsel.

16.2   Settlement Conferences.

16.2.1 *Domestic Relations Settlement Conferences.* In all domestic relations matters, involving children, settlement conferences are mandatory. The presence of the parties and counsel is mandatory unless excused by the court. If a party fails to attend the mandatory settlement conference the settlement commissioner may strike the trial date and the attending party would then be able to move for an order of default and for terms. Each party shall provide his/her proposed parenting plan and pre-trial affidavits are required. If child support or payment for day care is an issue, both parties shall provide their set of Washington State Child Support Schedule Worksheets. Additionally each parent shall provide:

(a) Federal income tax returns for the past three tax years;

(b) Wage & hour (payroll) statements for the previous three months;

(c) Documents establishing medical and/or dental insurance on the child(ren);

(d) Documentation for day care expenses for the previous three months.

All documents identified above are to be furnished to the court and opposing party two working days before the scheduled settlement conference.

Guardian Ad Litems shall not attend mandatory settlement conferences unless ordered by the court.

16.2.2 *Other Settlement Conferences.* Except in domestic relations cases, settlement conferences shall be held only by agreement of the parties, and shall be heard by a court commissioner. Parties wanting to set up a settlement conference shall contact the court administrator for available dates and times.

16.2.3 *Dependency Case Conferences.* In dependency matters a case conference shall be held one month after the shelter care hearing, for the purpose of attempting to develop a written service plan that is acceptable to all parties and consistent with any prior orders of the court. All parties shall attend the case conference, which shall be facilitated by the Division of Children and Family Services. First set fact finding shall be set two weeks after the case conference.

16.3 Pre–Trial Conferences. Upon motion of either party to the litigation, or upon the court's own motion, a pre-trial conference may be conducted by the trial judge, and shall not be reported unless ordered by the trial judge. Pre-trial conferences shall be held prior to trial, and shall be conducted without interference in the scheduling of any jury. Issues, which should be discussed in the pre-trial conference, include, but are not limited to:

(a) Hearing of non-dispositive motions;

(b) Simplification of the issues;

(c) Necessity or desirability of amendment to pleadings;

(d) Addressing admissions of fact and admission of documents;

(e) Limitation of number of expert witnesses;

(f) Court's estimate of length of trial;

(g) Proposed jury instructions;

(h) Possibility of compromise settlement;

(i) Scheduling difficulties.

16.4 Procedures Immediately Before Trial. The parties shall exchange, not later than 5 court days before the scheduled trial date:

(a) Lists of the witnesses whom each party expects to call at trial;

(b) Lists of the exhibits that each party expects to offer at trial, except for exhibits to be used only for impeachment;

(c) Copies of all documentary exhibits, except for those to be used for illustrative purposes only;

(d) Non–documentary exhibits shall be made available for inspection by the other party.

The proposed witness and exhibit lists, with bench copy, shall be delivered to the trial court and filed with the clerk at least three days prior to trial. Original exhibits shall also be delivered to the clerk at least three days prior to trial for pre-marking along with a descriptive exhibit list.

Any witness or exhibit not listed may not be used at trial, unless the court orders otherwise for good cause and subject to conditions, as justice requires.

16.5 Minor Settlements. The attorney personally in charge of the case of the minor, if any, the minor child, and at least one parent or legal custodian shall personally appear at any hearing at which application is made for approval of a settlement. Personal attendance for any guardian is required. A receipt for funds deposited in a blocked account shall be filed with the court no later than thirty days from the date the bank receives the funds.

16.6 Procedures in Complex Litigation in Non–Criminal Matters. Prior to the scheduling of a trial, any party may move for the adoption of the Detailed Pretrial Schedule (Appendix 5). Grounds for requesting the adoption of the Detailed Pretrial Schedule include, but are not limited to:

(a) Large number of lay witnesses.

(b) A significant number of expert witnesses.

(c) Disputed fact issues of a technical or scientific nature.

(d) A history of procedural difficulties between the parties.

(e) A case involving more than two parties.

[Adopted effective September 1, 2003; amended effective September 1, 2007; September 1, 2011; September 2, 2014.]

LCR 31. PERSONAL IDENTIFIERS— CHILDREN

31.1–31.11 Renumbered as LGR 31.1–31.11

[Adopted effective September 1, 2005; redesignated as LGR 31 effective September 1, 2008.]

LCR 32. USE OF DEPOSITIONS IN COURT PROCEEDINGS

32.1 Video/Audio Depositions. When presenting portions of a video or audio deposition, a printed transcript thereof must be filed within 10 days of its presentation. The video or audiotape will be treated as though it were an exhibit and will be returned after the appeal period.

32.2 Equipment for Viewing. A party offering testimony or evidence by videotape or audiotape shall arrange for or obtain the proper equipment for viewing or listening.

[Adopted effective September 1, 2003; amended effective September 1, 2011.]

LCR 38. JURY TRIAL

38.1 Impaneling the Jury. On the day of trial, the jurors shall sign in on the computer print out provided by the jury manager. After all of the jurors have signed in, the bailiff shall deliver the sign-in sheet to the jury administrator. The jury administrator will randomly assign a number to each name. The list of assigned numbers shall be given to the bailiff who will distribute the numbers to the jurors. Any jurors wishing to be excused from serving on the trial shall be brought before the judge and examined in the presence of the parties. Those not excused shall be returned to the bailiff, who will then seat the panel in the courtroom in numerical order.

38.2 Examination of Jurors. The voir dire examination of the jurors shall be conducted under the direction and control of the court with the following guidelines:

(a) The court shall ask all general questions and thereafter give leave to the respective parties to ask such supplementary questions as may be deemed proper and necessary by the court. The plaintiff shall begin the questioning and may not re-examine the panel after the conclusion of the defendant's examination. The questions shall be designed to determine a prospective juror's bias and prejudice, and shall not be used to try a party's case. The parties shall submit all proposed general questions to the court in writing at the pre-trial conference.

(b) The court may intervene without objection in instances of inappropriate questioning and may limit the amount of time each party has to examine a juror or jury panel. It is expected that each party shall conduct its voir dire in one hour or less.

(c) At the conclusion of each party's questioning, the party shall either challenge a particular juror for cause or pass the panel for cause. After both parties have passed the panel for cause, the first twelve (12) jurors, or if appropriate, six (6) jurors, plus alternates, shall be seated in the jury box. Preemptory challenges shall be open unless on motion for good cause shown.

(d) Counsel may submit, and the court may allow, special questionnaires focused to the specific case to be submitted to the jurors to answer on the morning of trial before the voir dire process begins. Copies will be made available to counsel during the questioning of the jurors. Counsel must submit proposed questionnaires to the court and serve copies on opposing counsel at least three days prior to trial.

(e) At the conclusions of voir dire, any juror questionnaires or forms shall be immediately returned to the Court. No questionnaires or information forms shall be copied or removed from the courtroom without express permission of the trial judge. All jury questionnaires will be destroyed after the jury is impaneled.

38.3 Alternate Juror. The alternate juror shall be designated by random drawing to be announced after closing argument.

38.4 Jury Administrative Reimbursement Fee. In the event that a trial is cancelled subsequent to the jury call having been processed, counsel or parties to the action shall be subject to a jury administrative reimbursement fee equal to the actual costs incurred by the court for jury fee payments or administrative costs in calling the jury panel. Upon a showing of good cause, said fee may be waived by the court.

38.5 PreTrial Matters. Counsel shall report to the judge at 8:45 a.m. the morning the jury trial is to commence, and provide the judge with a written list of the names and residences of witnesses, and general voir dire questions to be asked of the jury. Counsel shall be prepared to present any final pretrial matters to the court. Pretrial matters requiring argument shall be noted for hearing prior to the morning of the trial to avoid inconvenience of the jury pool. Jury trials should be conducted with minimal interruptions of the jury's time. To this end, matters that need to be heard outside the presence of the jury should be anticipated so that they can be considered during jury breaks or before or after the jury's day. Unless otherwise ordered or agreed, plaintiffs shall occupy the counsel table closest to the jury in criminal cases.

38.6 Witnesses. Counsel are directed to subpoena their witnesses no earlier than 11:00 a.m. on the first morning of trial to prevent possible jury contamination.

38.7 Jury Questionnaires. Proposed jury questionnaires shall be delivered to the trial court, filed with the clerk and served on all other parties at least three days prior to trial.

[Adopted effective September 1, 2003; amended effective September 1, 2005; September 1, 2007; September 1, 2011.]

LCR 40. ASSIGNMENT OF CASES

40.1 When Cases May Be Set For Trial.

40.1.1 *Cases Not At Issue.* A note for trial setting must not be filed until all of the issues have been fully joined.

40.1.2 *Administrative Review Cases.* A trial setting involving solely the review of the record of a decision of an administrative agency shall not be set for trial until the record and transcript has been certified and filed with the clerk. The record prepared by the agency shall be numbered and reflect the total number of pages. The administrative record shall be treated as an exhibit and returned following trial upon completion of the appeal period. An Exhibit List itemizing the documents by exhibit document number, document name and page number(s) shall be required at the time that the record is submitted to the clerk. If documents in the record have already been scanned a digital copy of the record shall be provided to the court in addition to the paper record. Contact the clerk to arrange transmission of digital record.

40.2 Responsibility of Parties.

40.2.1 Any party desiring to bring an issue of fact to trial shall file with the clerk, and serve upon all of the other parties, a Note for Trial Setting (Appendix 6), substantially in the form approved by the court. The attorney or pro se litigant noting the case for trial will provide notice to any guardian ad litem appointed in the case.

40.2.2 A Note for Trial Docket must contain the following information:

(a) Nature of the case;

(b) Estimated length of the trial;

(c) Addresses and phone numbers of all attorneys for the parties and pro se parties;

(d) Whether it is a jury or non-jury trial;

(e) Whether the case may be heard by a judge pro tem or commissioner;

(f) Counsel's available trial dates and proposed dates for trial;

(g) If domestic relations, whether a mandatory settlement conference is required;

(h) If there is agreement, the Note for Trial Docket shall reflect in its body that there is agreement of counsel or parties to the dates stated therein;

(i) Motion calendar date and time the assignment of trial is to be heard.

40.2.3 *Response to Note for Trial Docket.* Any attorney or party who objects to a case being set for trial or excepting to the requested trial dates, shall do so by serving on opposing party(s) and filing with the court a response to note for trial setting. The court administrator, prior to the hearing date noted, shall attempt to resolve any scheduling objections. If the administrator is unable to resolve the objections, counsel will be required to appear at the noted hearing date and time, and the judge shall hear the contested trial setting.

40.3 Setting of Trial Date.

40.3.1 *Court Administrator to Assign Dates.* The court administrator shall assign trial dates under the supervision of the judge who shall be in direct charge of the trial calendar. Cases shall be set chronologically according to noting dates, except for cases given statutory preference, or court ordered preference.

40.3.2 *Motion For Early Trial Date.* Any party who believes the case warrants priority may request an early trial date by serving a motion, together with supporting documents, and note it for hearing before the court.

40.4 Pre–Assignment of Cases. No preassignment of cases will occur without the filing of a motion for preassignment, argument and determination by the court that said case should be preassigned.

40.5 Trials.

40.5.1 *Trial Briefs and Jury Instructions.* Three days prior to trial, counsel must file with the court and serve copies on opposing counsel, any trial briefs or memorandum of authorities, and in the event of a jury trial, a copy of the proposed jury instructions.

40.5.2 *Reporting for Trial.* All parties shall report to the court at 8:45 a.m. on the date set for trial, unless otherwise notified by the court administrator. If no trial department is available for immediate trial, the judge shall hold the parties for such time as circumstances dictate, thereby placing the case on "standby" status, or release the parties from the trial date.

40.5.3 *Calendar Management—Conflict Notification.* The administrator shall not release the attorneys from responsibility for appearing at a trial on the date it is set any earlier than noon the court day before it is set. As to those cases unable to proceed on the date set by reason of court congestion, the parties shall remain available for trial for a reasonable period of time, unless the case is continued or reset.

40.5.4 *Trial Days.* Normally trials will be held on each court day except Thursday and Friday.

40.5.5 *Notice of Settlement.* It shall be the obligation of counsel in all cases to immediately notify the court administrator when a case is settled or otherwise will not come on for trial as scheduled. The court may assess actual costs or other sanctions for a violation of this rule.

40.5.6 *Consolidation of Cases for Trial.* When two or more cases are consolidated for trial only, all documents shall be submitted with an extra copy for each file so consolidated.

40.5.7 *Resetting.* When a case is not tried on the date set, the parties are responsible for renoting the matter for trial setting.

40.5.8 *Dissolution Trials.* In all final hearings or trials in domestic relations matters, each party shall provide to the judge and serve on the opposing party a written statement as to the issues in controversy at least three days prior to trial, which contains the following:

    (a) A brief factual summary;

    (b) Issues in dispute, whether property, debts or custody;

    (c) Case law, if it will be argued, supporting the party's position;

    (d) Proposed distribution of assets, debts, liabilities and proposed parenting plan and child support amount, if in dispute;

    (e) Areas of agreement;

    (f) If seeking maintenance or child support, both parties shall complete a financial declaration;

    (g) Domestic Relations Information (Appendix 4).

40.6 Trial Continuances. When a case has been set for trial, it shall proceed to trial, unless good cause is shown for a continuance. The motion for continuance shall be made in writing, and supported by affidavit or declaration of counsel, and signed by the party requesting the continuance. Such motions shall be heard at least ten days prior to trial.

[Adopted effective September 1, 2003; amended effective September 1, 2008; September 1, 2011.]

LCR 49. VERDICTS

49.1 Presence of Party or Attorney at Return of Verdict. Attorneys awaiting a verdict shall keep the clerk advised of where they may be reached by telephone. Attorneys desiring to be present for the verdict shall be present within 10 minutes of telephone notice to the attorney's office, home or other number. The court may proceed to take the verdict in the absence of such party or attorney. In such case the jury shall be individually polled and the identity of the dissenting jurors recorded. In a criminal case, at least one attorney for each party and the prosecuting attorney (or deputy prosecutor) shall be present for the receipt of the verdict, unless excused by the court. The defense attorney is responsible for advising the defendant to be present for the verdict unless the defendant is in custody.

49.2 Jury Polled. The court shall order that the jury be polled, unless the parties waive the poll.

[Adopted effective September 1, 2003; amended effective September 1, 2011.]

LCR 51. INSTRUCTIONS TO JURY AND DELIBERATIONS

51.1 Proposed Instructions. All parties shall read and follow CR 51. The copy which is filed with the clerk shall be numbered and annotated, and shall include a title page identifying the party who is submitting the proposed instructions. The trial judge shall be given a working copy of the annotated set. A copy of the annotated set shall also be furnished to each party. One unannotated set shall be submitted to the court administrator.

51.2 Time for Filing and Service. Proposed jury instructions shall be delivered to the trial court, filed with the clerk and served on all other parties at least three days prior to trial.

51.3 Additional Proposed Instructions. Supplemental instructions shall have a title page and be numbered.

[Adopted effective September 1, 2003; amended effective September 1, 2011.]

LCR 52. DECISIONS, FINDINGS AND CONCLUSIONS

52.1 Presentation. In civil cases tried to the court, unless the judge has included formal findings of fact and conclusions of law in a written opinion, or counsel have stipulated that no appeal shall be taken on the case, the prevailing party shall prepare a bench copy of proposed findings of fact, conclusions of law, and a proposed form of order or judgment.

52.2 Time for Presentation. Presentation of the findings of fact, conclusions of law and judgment shall be noted within thirty (30) days after the decision or verdict was rendered. Hearing on contested findings, conclusions and judgment may be heard telephonically or in person on a regularly scheduled motions calendar or at a time arranged with the court administrator. Proposed findings & conclusions shall be submitted to the court at the time of filing the notice of presentation.

52.3 Entry of Dissolution Decree by Declaration of Jurisdictional Facts. The court may enter an agreed or default decree of dissolution of marriage without a final hearing or oral testimony when the petitioner completes a Request for Entry of Decree and Declaration of Jurisdictional Facts in the form set forth in Appendix 1, and:

(a) The respondent or respondent's attorney approves all of the final papers including the Request for entry of Decree and Declaration of Jurisdictional Facts; or

(b) If the respondent is in default, the decree provides for only that relief requested in the petition; or

(c) If the respondent or co-petitioner joined in the petition and is unavailable to sign the final papers, and the decree provides for only that relief requested in the petition.

[Adopted effective September 1, 2003; amended effective September 1, 2011.]

LCR 53.2. REVISION OF COMMISSIONER RULINGS

53.2.1 Validity of Commissioner's Orders. The filing of a motion for revision does not stay the commissioner's ruling. All orders granted by a court commissioner shall remain valid and in effect pending outcome of the motion for revision, unless stayed upon motion and order properly noted before the commissioner granting the order or before the presiding judge.

53.2.2 Contents of Motion. All motions shall state with specificity any portion of the commissioner's order or judgment sought to be revised. The moving party shall identify those findings of fact or conclusions of law sought to be revised, and cite those portions to the record. Any portion not so specified shall not be revised.

53.2.3 Disposition of Motion. See LCR 59.

[Adopted effective September 1, 2003; amended effective September 1, 2011.]

LCR 55. DEFAULT AND JUDGMENT

55.1 Delivery of Decree to Other Party. In default dissolution cases, at the time of entry of the decree of dissolution, the moving party or counsel shall immediately deliver to or mail to the other party at their last known address, a conformed copy of the decree. Failure to do so may result in vacating the order of default and decree.

[Adopted effective September 1, 2003; amended effective September 1, 2009; September 1, 2011.]

LCR 56. SUMMARY JUDGMENT

56.1 Filing and Hearing Date. All motions for summary judgment shall be noted for hearing on a regularly scheduled motions calendar. However, the court administrator shall not allow more than three summary judgment hearings to be scheduled for any one date.

56.2 Judge's Bench Copies. Bench copies for the judge, labeled "bench copy", shall be forwarded by counsel to the court administrator, and shall contain the name of the judge hearing the motion, the date of the hearing, and by whom these papers are being delivered.

56.3 Deleted

56.4 Scheduling. Summary judgments shall be heard during the court's regularly scheduled civil motion calendar; provided, if arguments of counsel are anticipated to exceed more than 10 minutes per side or a total of thirty minutes in total, then a special setting shall be arranged with the court administrator.

[Adopted effective September 1, 2003; amended effective September 1, 2008; September 1, 2011.]

LCR 59. MOTIONS FOR RECONSIDERATION

(e) Hearing on Motion. A motion for reconsideration shall be submitted on briefs and affidavits only, without oral argument, unless the trial judge on application from counsel or on his own motion allows oral argument. The moving party shall file the motion and all supporting affidavits, documents and briefs at the same time, and on the date of filing serve or mail a copy thereof to opposing counsel, and deliver a copy thereof to the trial judge, which copy shall show the date of filing. The trial judge will consider the motion and will advise counsel of the ruling or of the desired further proceedings pursuant to CR 59 and this rule.

[Adopted effective September 1, 2003; amended effective September 1, 2008; September 1, 2011.]

LCR 77. SUPERIOR COURTS

77(k)(1) *Motion Days Schedules.* Motion calendars or dockets are subject to change without notice. If a particular judge or commissioner is required for a hearing, counsel must call the court administrator to confirm the attendance of that judge or commissioner on that particular docket. Failure to confirm availability can result in the matter not being heard. Normally, matters shall be heard pursuant to the following schedule:

Each Tuesday @ 9:00 & 10:30 a.m.   –   Mandatory Settlement Conferences

Each Wednesday @ 9:00 & 10:30 a.m.	–	Mandatory Settlement Conferences
Each Wednesday @ 9:00 a.m.	–	Juvenile Offenders
Each Wednesday @ 10:00 a.m.	–	Juvenile Offenders–Kitsap Youth Center
Each Wednesday @ 1:00 p.m.	–	Adoption Calendar
Each Thursday @ 7:45 a.m.	–	Drug Court Staffing
Each Thursday @ 8:30 a.m.	–	Drug Court Calendar
Each Thursday @ 10:00 a.m.	–	Family Therapeutic Staffing
Each Thursday @ 10:30 a.m.	–	Family Therapeutic Court
Each Thursday @ 1:00 p.m.	–	Juvenile Dependency Calendar
Each Thursday @ 1:00 p.m.	–	YAR & CHINS Calendar
1st & 3rd Thursday @ 2:30 p.m.	–	Topside Staffing
1st & 3rd Thursday @ 3:00 p.m.	–	Topside Calendar
2nd & 4th Thursdays @ 3:00 p.m.	–	Truancy Calendar
Each Friday @ 8:30 a.m.	–	Adult Criminal Calendar
2nd Friday @ 8:30 a.m.	–	Pay or Appear Calendar
Each Friday @ 1:00 p.m.	–	Civil/Guardianship/Probate
Each Friday @ 2:00 p.m.	–	DV/Anti Harassment/Domestic
Daily @ 11:30 a.m.	–	Fresh Arrest Adult Video Calendar

77.1 Special Christmas Eve Hours. The superior court, court administrator and clerk's offices shall be open each year on Christmas Eve day from 8:30 a.m. to 12:00 p.m. only or as otherwise resolved by the board of county commissioners.

[Adopted effective September 1, 2003; amended effective September 1, 2007; September 1, 2008; amended on an emergency basis effective September 24, 2008; amended on a permanent basis effective September 1, 2009; amended on an emergency basis effective January 1, 2010; March 9, 2010; amended on a permanent basis effective September 1, 2010; September 1, 2011; September 1, 2012; September 2, 2014.]

LCR 78. DUTIES OF THE CLERK/COURT ADMINISTRATOR

78.1 In addition to the other powers and duties prescribed by RCW 2.32.050, 36.18.020, and CR 78, the Clerk/Court Administrator's Office shall have the following powers and duties:

78.1.1 *Time of Filing.* All original pleadings or other papers with proper caption and cause number will be file stamped, docketed, and secured in the legal file by the clerk in the order received. The clerk shall have all filed papers available for inspection in the legal file within three court days of filing.

78.1.2 *Correcting Obvious Errors.* The clerk is authorized to correct obvious errors in cause numbers and captions when the error is of a clerical nature, or in instances where the mathematical addition in criminal judgment and sentences is incorrect.

78.1.3 *Registry of the Court.* Bail is to be returned after the sentencing or dismissal of a criminal case. In all other instances the clerk shall not disburse any funds paid into the registry of the court without a specific written court order, except with bail.

78.1.4 *Unsuitable Materials.* Whenever any paper or other material is presented to the clerk for filing but is deemed by the clerk that the format is improper or inappropriate for filing, the clerk shall affix the file mark thereto and may forthwith orally apply to the court for a determination of the propriety of the filing format of the material presented. If the court determines that the paper or material should not be made a part of the file, the court may order that the unsuitable material be returned to the submitting party.

78.1.5 *Inspection or Withdrawal of Files.* The clerk shall permit no file to be taken from the clerk's office by anyone other than a judge, visiting judge, court commissioner or judge pro tem.

78.1.6 All pleadings, motions and other papers presented for filing with the clerk shall be on 8-1/2 × 11 paper and shall be printed on one side only. The clerk may refuse to file any papers not in conformance with this rule.

78.1.7 *Facsimile Filing of Pleadings With Clerk.* Documents, including pleadings, may be filed with the clerk by facsimile transmission, in accordance with GR 17, with the following change: In addition to the requirements of a fax transmittal sheet contained in GR 17(b)(2) (Appendix 9), the fax transmittal sheet shall also contain the title and number of pages for each document sent in the transmission (Appendix 8). Payment must be made in advance as per instructions listed on fax transmittal sheet.

78.1.8 Only the following persons shall have access to paternity files of the court when no final judgment and order determining paternity has been entered: the mother, the presumed father, any alleged father who has not been dismissed from the case, an attorney representing any of the foregoing or the child (after filing a notice of appearance), any guardian ad litem appointed in the cause and not discharged, the State of Washington as represented by the attorney general's office or Jefferson County Prosecuting Attorney's office, and any other person granted permission in writing by a Jefferson County Superior Court judge. After entry of the judgment and order determining paternity has been entered, the clerk of the court shall seal all pleadings prior to the judgment and order, but shall allow all subsequent pleadings to be open to the public, and shall open a new type 3 case per administrative order.

78.1.9 The clerk shall not accept personal checks in criminal or juvenile offender cases.

78.1.10 The standard fee for faxing to or from the clerk shall be $5.00 for the first page and $1.00 for each page thereafter.

78.1.11 The clerk's fee schedule periodically updated by the clerk is hereby adopted.

78.1.12 The clerk shall promptly notify appointed counsel of any such court appointment by placing a copy of the court order in their receptacle or telephoning them if their client is in custody. In the alternative counsel can be notified by email if they request the same with the clerk's office.

78.1.13 The clerk shall maintain a confidential and sealed file of all search warrants and affidavits in support thereof. After the filing of the inventory and a return of service, said records shall be available for public inspection.

78.1.14 The clerk shall maintain as confidential those mental health, psychiatric and medical records received directly by the court; except, however, those reports attached to and incorporated therein by counsel or parties are not subject to said confidentiality without a court order.

78.1.15 The court administrator shall maintain the judges' notes and worksheets as confidential.

78.1.16 *Exhibits.*

(a) All exhibits should be premarked for identification by the courtroom clerk at least 3 days prior to trial. The courtroom clerk will cooperate with counsel in facilitating the marking and management of the exhibits. The exhibits will be premarked numerically on a first come basis and sequentially from there on. Counsel will produce exhibits allowing sufficient time for this process to occur in an orderly and accurate manner.

(b) Documents and other exhibits should be shown to opposing counsel before their use in court.

(c) Ordinarily, exhibits should be offered in evidence when they become admissible rather than at the end of counsel's case.

(d) Marking on exhibits should only be made after receiving the court's permission to do so.

(e) For cause shown, the court may permit a copy of any document admitted in evidence to be substituted for the original.

(f) Exhibits containing blood borne pathogens, drugs, firearms or dangerous weapons shall be properly packaged and labeled before acceptance by the court or clerk. To meet packaging and labeling requirements, exhibits shall conform to the following criteria when presented:

(i) Blood borne pathogens shall be packaged in sturdy plastic containers. If contained in a vial or hypodermic, each shall be placed in an individual sturdy plastic container. All items shall be labeled to identify the contents as potentially biologically hazardous materials.

(ii) Drugs shall be placed in sealed containers to prevent or reduce emissions for the container. They shall be labeled identifying the contents.

(iii) Firearms shall be unloaded, any breech mechanism or cylinder shall be open, and a secured trigger lock shall be in place.

(iv) Dangerous weapons shall have any sharp or pointed portions sheathed in a manner to prevent injury or contact with the sharp or pointed portions.

(v) Paper bags alone shall not constitute proper packaging.

(g) GR 20, governing security in handling exhibits shall apply, with proviso the Court may also order withdrawal and substitution on its own merit.

(h) All exhibits, some exceptions apply, will be held by the clerk following trial for safekeeping pending appeal or further court order. Those exhibits that fall under the exception will be returned forthwith to the investigating law enforcement agency pending appeal or further court order.

(i) An 8.5 × 11 reproduction or color copy of each large-scale exhibit must be provided and shall be substituted for marking and filing with permission of the court.

(j) After final disposition of a civil matter, the court, after hearing, may order the clerk to destroy or otherwise dispose of physical evidence, which cannot, because of bulk or weight, be retained in the case file, provided that all parties of record are given thirty days written notice of any such hearing.

[Adopted effective September 1, 2003; amended effective September 1, 2007; September 1, 2008; September 1, 2009; September 1, 2010; September 1, 2011; September 2, 2014.]

LCR 79(b)(10). ABSTRACT OF JUDGMENT

(a) The abstract of a judgment shall contain (1) the name of the party, or parties, in whose favor the judgment was rendered; (2) the name of the party, or parties, against whom the judgment was rendered; (3) the date of the rendition of the judgment; and (4) the amount for which the judgment was rendered.

(b) A transcript of a judgment is an abstract, plus an exact copy of the judgment itself. A transcript is required when filing a judgment from a district court or other court of limited jurisdiction in the superior court.

[Adopted effective September 1, 2012.]

LCR 80. COURT REPORTERS

80.1 Transcripts. The official transcript of any electronically recorded proceeding in the Superior Court shall be prepared by or under the direction of the court administrator. Anyone wishing to order an official transcript shall make such request to the court administrator and shall at the same time make arrangements for payment thereof. The electronic court reporter will not begin work on the transcript until the estimate is paid in full to the registry of the court.

[Adopted effective September 1, 2003; amended effective September 1, 2011.]

LCR 81.1. COURTROOM PRACTICE AND DECORUM

81.1.1 Deleted

81.1.2 Deleted

81.1.3 Deleted

81.1.4 Renumbered as 78.1.16

[Adopted effective September 1, 2003. Amended effective September 1, 2006; September 1, 2008; September 1, 2011.]

III. RULES FOR APPEAL OF DECISIONS OF COURTS OF LIMITED JURISDICTION

LRALJ 2.6(a)(1). CONTENT OF NOTICE OF APPEAL

A Notice of Appeal from the District Court shall be (1) titled "Notice of Appeal", (2) identify the party or parties appealing, (3) designate each decision which the party wants reviewed, (4) name the court to which the appeal is taken, (5) provide the name and address of the lawyer for each of the parties represented by a lawyer and the address of the parties who are not represented by counsel, and if a criminal case, it shall include the address of the defendant, (6) state whether the case appealed is criminal (if so, provide RCW for charge), civil or an infraction, and (7) name the court and cause number from which the appeal is taken, and (8) state the name of the judge or commissioner making the original ruling.

[Adopted effective September 1, 2003; amended effective September 1, 2008; September 1, 2011.]

LRALJ 6.3.1. TRANSCRIPT OF ELECTRONIC RECORD

(a) Unless the Superior Court orders otherwise, the appellant shall, in District Court, designate and identify the specific portion of the electronic recording of proceedings as provided in section (c) of this rule. The disk of the designated electronic record will be transmitted to the Superior Court by the District Court. The appellant shall not request or provide a transcript at county expense unless specifically ordered by the Superior Court.

(b) If the respondent wishes to add to or challenge the electronic record as designated by the appellant of the proceedings, then the respondent shall designate and identify the specific portion of the electronic record as provided in section (c) of this rule. The disk of the designated electronic record will be transmitted to the Superior Court by the District Court. The respondent shall not request or provide a transcript at county expense unless specifically ordered by the Superior Court.

(c) Content of electronic record. The designated record shall contain only those portions of the electronic record necessary to present the issues raised on appeal. The designation filed in District Court shall specify the exact time of the alleged error for the Superior Court to consider. If the appellant intends to urge that a verdict or finding of fact is not supported by the evidence, the appellant shall include in the designated record all testimony relevant to the disputed verdict or finding. If the appellant intends to urge that the court erred in giving or failing to give an instruction, the appellant shall include all objections to the instructions given and refused and the court's rulings.

[Adopted effective September 1, 2012.]

LRALJ 8.4. BRIEFING SCHEDULE

Appeals from Courts of Limited Jurisdiction under RALJ, upon filing with the Superior Court, shall be issued a case schedule setting forth the briefing schedule of the parties and the time designated for oral argument. Parties shall comply with all RALJ rules covering traffic infractions, criminal and civil proceedings.

[Adopted effective September 1, 2003; amended effective September 1, 2011.]

IV. JUVENILE COURT RULES

LJUCR 11. FINANCIAL RESPONSIBILITY— JUVENILE COSTS

11.1 Assessment of Costs. The assessment for the cost of detention and publicly funded counsel should not exceed actual costs to the county. The costs shall be assessed and ordered paid in a reasonable time unless a sworn financial statement is presented to the court at a proceeding to justify reduction or elimination of any such assessment, or there are other circumstances recognized by the court for reducing or not imposing the assessment.

11.2 Notice. It shall be the duty of the juvenile court services to notify the parent or parents, guardian or other person legally obligated to support the juvenile of this rule prior to said proceeding and to provide all necessary documents in order for such person to adequately prepare for said proceeding.

11.3 Sanctions. A show cause hearing with timely notice by the clerk's office to the delinquent person may be held to inquire into the delinquency of the assessment and the sanctions available under RCW 13.16.085 and RCW 13.40.145.

[Adopted effective September 1, 2003; amended effective September 1, 2011.]

V. SPECIAL PROCEEDING RULES

LSPR 94. NOTICE TO SUPERIOR COURT OF JUVENILE PROCEEDINGS

All parties to a proceeding involving custody or adoption in the Superior Court are obligated to disclose to said court the pendency of any juvenile proceedings regarding minor children.

[Original LSPR 94(j) was adopted effective September 1, 2003. Renumbered as LSPR 94 effective September 1, 2005; amended effective September 1, 2011.]

LSPR 95. MANDATORY PARENTING SEMINARS

(a) Definition of Applicable Cases. This rule applies to all cases filed under Ch. 26.09 or Ch. 26.26 of the RCWs after September 1, 1997, including dissolutions, legal separations, major modifications and paternity actions (in which paternity has been established) where the parties are parents of a child under the age of 18, and where a parenting plan or residential plan is required which involves the care of any child.

(b) Parenting Seminars Mandatory Attendance. Both parents, and such nonparent parties as the court may direct, shall participate in and successfully complete an approved parenting seminar. The seminar shall be completed within 60 days of service of the motion or petition. Successful completion shall be evidenced by a certificate of attendance filed by the provider agency with the court.

(c) Fees. Each party attending the parenting seminar shall pay a fee charged by the approved provider and authorized by the court.

(d) Special Consideration Waiver.

(1) In no case shall opposing parties be required to attend a seminar together.

(2) The court may, for good cause shown:

(a) waive the seminar requirement for one or both parents, or

(b) allow an alternative parenting seminar.

(e) Failure to Comply. Nonparticipation or default by one parent does not excuse participation by the other parent. Respondent's refusal, delay or default will not delay the progress of the case to a final decree; however, respondent will not be allowed to seek affirmative relief in this or subsequent proceedings, except certain temporary orders, on parenting issues until the seminar has been successfully completed. Petitioner's refusal or delay will prevent the case from being tried or any final order affecting the parenting/residential plan being entered in petitioner's favor. Willful refusal or delay by either parent may constitute contempt of court and result in sanctions imposed by the court or may result in the imposition of monetary terms, default, and/or striking of pleadings.

(f) Service. Petitioner, in all applicable cases as defined in Subsection (a) above, shall serve a copy of this Local Court Rule on Respondent. The notice shall be served with the initial pleadings.

[Adopted effective September 1, 2003; amended effective September 1, 2009; September 1, 2011.]

LSPR 96. LOCAL GUARDIANSHIP PROCEEDINGS

(1) Duties of Judge or Court Commissioner. The judicial officer presented with an order appointing guardian or approving order of accounting shall set the date of the hearing for presentation of the next accounting and annual personal care plan.

(2) Duties of Attorney. Should the attorney representing the estate choose to withdraw, the attorney must advise the court of the name and address of the party to be notified, should that be necessary, of a delinquent accounting and annual Personal Care Plan. The notice to the court shall be filed prior to the effective date of the withdrawal of the attorney.

(3) Deleted

[Adopted effective September 1, 2003; amended effective September 1, 2009; September 1, 2011.]

VI. GUARDIAN AD LITEM RULES (TITLES 11 AND 26)

LGALR. LOCAL GUARDIAN AD LITEM PROCEDURES

1.1 Registry. The Jefferson County Superior Court Administrator or designee shall be responsible for maintaining a registry of those qualified to serve as a Guardian ad Litem in guardianship proceedings as provided in RCW 11 and RCW 26.

1.2 Qualifications. All registry applicants must meet the certification and qualifications set forth in the statutes to be considered for placement on the registry. The registry shall be open for new applica-

tions one time a year, between January 1st and March 1st. All required information must be received by the Jefferson County Superior Court Administrator no later than March 1st of each year. The registry shall be defined by April 1st of each year. All persons on the registry must update their background and qualifications information annually no later than March 1st of each year.

1.3 Notification. Persons applying will be notified of their placement on the registry and shall then be eligible for appointment as a Guardian ad Litem.

1.4 File. The Court Administrator or designee shall maintain a file on each Guardian ad Litem. Each file shall include the Certificate of Completion of training, Background and Qualification Statement, together with all formal complaints or grievances related to the person's service as a Guardian ad Litem. Each file for members of the registry shall be open for public review during normal business hours.

1.5 Code of Conduct. All applicants shall abide by the Guardian ad Litem Code of Conduct, these procedures and the laws of the State of Washington.

1.6 Appointment of Guardian Ad Litem From Registry. Application to the Court for appointment of a Guardian ad Litem shall be made by submitting an Order Appointing Guardian ad Litem to the Office of the Superior Court Administrator. Parties may agree to the appointment of a qualified guardian ad litem whose name appears on the rotational list. If the parties are not in agreement, the Superior Court Administrator shall write in the name which is next on the rotational list and initial the same. The Order shall then be submitted to a Judge or Commissioner for signature or such other action as may be appropriate. Any Judge or Commissioner who does not appoint the person next on the rotational list shall make an appropriate record of the reasons for said deviation. The Order, once signed, shall be presented to the Superior Court Administrator. In the event a Judge or Commissioner approves a person who is not next on the rotation list, the appointed person's name shall go to the bottom of the rotation list. In the event the person nominated as Guardian ad Litem chooses not to serve, regardless of the reason, his/her name shall go to the bottom of the rotational list just as if he/she had served.

1.7 Retention on Guardian Ad Litem Registry. A person shall remain on the registry so long as he/she meets the statutory certification requirements for the registry, and has not been removed.

1.8 Grievance Procedure.

1.8.1 Any person may file a complaint against a guardian ad litem. The complaint must be in writing and filed with the Court Administrator. The complaint must state the specific act or failure to act of concern to the complaining person and shall include: (a) the name, mailing address, and telephone number of the person filing the complaint; (b) the status of the underlying case including the case number and case name; (c) whether the complaining person told the guardian ad litem about the complaint; (d) what action the guardian ad litem has taken to address the complaint; (e) which section of the Code of Conduct or Order of Appointment or statute was violated, and the specific facts involved for each violation; and (f) what the complaining person would like done to fix the problem which is the subject of the complaint.

1.8.2 Complaints filed under this rule must be filed within one year from the date of occurrence of the matters complained of.

1.8.3 If it is determined that the grievance concerns a completed case and the person making the grievance is a party to the case, or is their attorney, a copy of the grievance shall be sent to the Guardian ad Litem and a written response shall be requested from the Guardian ad Litem. A grievance concerning pending or not completed case shall be directed to the judicial officer presiding over the case.

1.8.4 At the discretion of the Superior Court Judge, the Guardian ad Litem's further participation on the registry may be suspended or denied pending resolution of the grievance.

1.8.5 The Judge or Court Administrator shall decide any grievance, including the decision to suspend or remove any Guardian ad Litem from the registry, and shall provide written notice of any decision to the complaining person, the guardian ad litem, and any counsel of record. A copy of the decision shall be placed in the file of the guardian ad litem.

1.8.6 A person may have additional, reasonable requirements imposed upon them which permit them to continue to serve as a Guardian ad Litem, they may be denied listing on the registry; or they may be removed from the registry for any other reason that places the suitability of the person to act as a Guardian ad Litem in question.

1.9 Code of Conduct—Title 11 Guardian Ad Litem.

1.9.1 The Guardian ad Litem shall represent the best interests of the persons for whom he or she is appointed.

1.9.2 The Guardian ad Litem shall make a reasonable inquiry as to the facts and issues in dispute and shall decline the appointment if the Guardian ad Litem is not qualified, competent, or able to complete the matter in a timely manner.

1.9.3 The Guardian ad Litem shall maintain the ethical principles of the Guardian ad Litem's own profession.

1.9.4 The Guardian ad Litem shall remain qualified for the registry to which the Guardian ad Litem is appointed and shall promptly advise the court of any grounds for disqualification or unavailability to service.

1.9.5 The Guardian ad Litem shall maintain independence and objectivity in the Guardian ad Litem investigation.

1.9.6 The Guardian ad Litem shall avoid any actual or apparent conflict of interest or impropriety in the conduct of the Guardian ad Litem's duties. The Guardian ad Litem shall avoid self-dealing or association from which the Guardian ad Litem might directly or indirectly benefit, other than for compensation as

Guardian ad Litem. The Guardian ad Litem shall take action immediately to resolve any potential conflict or impropriety. The Guardian ad Litem shall advise the court and the parties of action taken or resign from the matter as may be necessary to resolve the conflict or impropriety.

1.9.7 The Guardian ad Litem shall treat the parties with respect, courtesy, fairness, and good faith regardless of race, color, creed, religion, national origin, cultural heritage, gender, age, education, economic status, marital status, sexual orientation or disability.

1.9.8 The Guardian ad Litem shall make reasonable efforts to become informed about the facts of the case, and locate professional resources, as necessary, to assist in the Guardian ad Litem's evaluation and recommendations.

1.9.9 The Guardian ad Litem shall inform the court concerning all relevant information disclosed or made available to the Guardian ad Litem.

1.9.10 The Guardian ad Litem shall not guarantee or create the impressions that any portion of the investigations will remain confidential.

1.9.11 The Guardian ad Litem shall maintain the privacy of the parties, and shall make no disclosures about the case or investigation except in reports to the court or as necessary to perform the duties of the Guardian ad Litem.

1.9.12 Any Guardian ad Litem report submitted to the Court **shall** comply with RCW 11.88.090(f)(i) thorough (viii).

1.9.13 The Guardian ad Litem shall perform his or her duties in a prompt and timely manner. The Guardian ad Litem shall maintain adequate documentation to substantiate recommendations and conclusions. The Guardian ad Litem shall keep complete and contemporaneous records of actions taken and the time and expense incurred.

1.9.14 The Guardian ad Litem shall report to D.S.H.S. and the court, any adult abuse as defined in RCW 74.34.020(2).

1.10 Code of Conduct—Title 26 Guardian Ad Litem.

1.10.1 The Guardian ad Litem shall investigate and report to the court, the factors relevant to the parenting and best interests of the person for whom he or she is appointed.

1.10.2 The appointed Guardian ad Litem shall make a reasonable inquiry as to the facts and issues in dispute and shall decline the appointment if they are not qualified, competent, have a conflict of interest or unable to complete the matter in a timely manner.

1.10.3 The Guardian ad Litem shall maintain the ethical principles of their own profession.

1.10.4 The Guardian ad Litem shall remain qualified for the registry to which they are appointed and shall promptly advise the court of any ground for disqualification or unavailability to serve.

1.10.5 The Guardian ad Litem shall maintain independence and objectivity in their investigation.

1.10.6 The Guardian ad Litem shall avoid any actual or apparent conflict of interest or impropriety in the conduct of their duties. The Guardian ad Litem shall avoid self-dealing or association from which the Guardian ad Litem might directly or indirectly benefit, other than from compensation as Guardian ad Litem. The Guardian ad Litem shall take action immediately to resolve any potential conflict or impropriety. The Guardian ad Litem shall advise the court and the parties of action taken, or resign from the matter, as may be necessary to resolve the conflict or impropriety.

1.10.7 The Guardian ad Litem shall treat the parties with respect, courtesy, fairness and good faith regardless of race, color, religion, national origin, cultural heritage, gender, age, education, economic status, sexual orientation or disability.

1.10.8 The Guardian ad Litem shall inform the court concerning all pertinent information disclosed or made available to them during the course of their appointment.

1.10.9 The Guardian ad Litem shall not guarantee or create the impression that any portion of the investigation will remain confidential, and shall inform all witnesses that information gathered by the Guardian ad Litem must be reported to the court.

1.10.10 The Guardian ad Litem shall maintain the privacy of the parties, and shall make no disclosures about the case or investigation except in reports to the court, to the parties and their attorneys, or as necessary to perform the duties of the Guardian ad Litem.

1.10.11 The Guardian ad Litem shall perform his or her duties in a prompt and timely manner, and shall file any report as required by court order or statute.

1.10.12 The Guardian ad Litem shall maintain adequate documentation of the investigation conducted, to substantiate the reported facts, as well as any recommendations or conclusions.

1.10.13 The Guardian ad Litem shall keep complete and contemporaneous records of actions taken, time spent, and expense incurred during the investigation.

1.10.14 All records, including time and expense records, of the Guardian ad Litem shall promptly be made available to the parties and their attorneys for review upon request, without formal discovery request(s) being made. Copies of the records may be made by the parties and their attorneys under circumstances, which assure that the file remains complete, organized and intact.

1.10.15 The Guardian ad Litem shall not have ex parte contact with any judicial officer involving in a matter in which they are appointed or serving.

1.10.16 The Guardian ad Litem shall be available to testify.

1.11 Compensation. The rate of compensation shall be established by the Court and reviewed on an annual basis. The court administrator shall keep a record of the established rates to be allowed. The Guardian Ad Litem shall not charge for travel time, however, may bill for mileage at the applicable Washington State reimbursement rate.

1.12 Notice. If a guardian ad litem is appointed, the guardian ad litem is entitled to notice of all proceedings, including trial.

[Adopted effective September 1, 2003; amended effective September 1, 2011.]

VII. GUARDIAN AD LITEM RULES (TITLE 13)

LGALR. ESTABLISHMENT OF LOCAL RULES FOR COURT APPOINTED SPECIAL ADVOCATES

1.1 Roster. The Director of Juvenile and Family Court Services, through the GAL Coordinator, shall maintain a roster of volunteer Guardians ad Litem who are currently qualified under the GAL Program.

1.2 Qualifications. All volunteer Guardians ad Litem must meet the minimum requirements set out by the GAL Program, and must complete training as prescribed by state law and by GAL Program policy.

1.3 Swearing In/Eligibility to Serve. Upon successful completion of the Initial Training and acceptance into the GAL Program by the Director of Juvenile and Family Court Services, the volunteer Guardian ad Litem will be sworn in by the Superior Court Judge or designee, and then will be eligible to serve.

1.4 Appointment. Upon receipt of an order appointing the GAL Program as Guardian ad Litem for a child, the GAL Coordinator will assign a volunteer Guardian ad Litem to the case, if one is available, and will notify the court and parties of the assignment, and the assignment will take effect immediately. The court shall appoint the person recommended by the program. If a volunteer Guardian ad Litem is not available, the GAL Coordinator shall serve as Guardian ad Litem until a volunteer becomes available.

1.5 File. The GAL Program shall maintain a file on each volunteer Guardian ad Litem. Each file shall contain the volunteer's Application, Authorization for Background Inquiry, results of Criminal History Check, Background Information Record, and documentation of any instances of removal of a case for cause. At the beginning of each case the GAL Program will provide to the court and parties, through their attorneys, copies of the volunteer GAL's Background Information Record. The BIR will include: Level of Education; Training Related to GAL duties; Number of Years' Experience as a GAL; Number of Assignments as a GAL; Criminal History; Dismissals for Cause. The information in the BIR shall be updated annually.

1.6 Code of Conduct. The volunteer GAL shall abide by the Code of Conduct as set out in these Rules, and by GAL Program Policies, as well as the Court Rules of the Courts of the State of Washington, which are incorporated herein.

1.6.1 The volunteer Guardian Ad Litem shall represent the best interests of the child for whom he or she is appointed. If the Guardian ad Litem learns that a conflict exists between the best interests of the child and the child's desires, the GAL will bring this conflict to the court's attention and request an attorney be appointed for the child.

1.6.2 The volunteer Guardian Ad Litem shall complete an independent, thorough investigation of the child's situation.

1.6.3 A volunteer Guardian Ad Litem shall identify himself or herself to parties or other individuals involved in the case as a Guardian ad Litem and shall explain the role of the Guardian ad Litem.

1.6.4 The volunteer Guardian Ad Litem shall complete and submit to the court in a timely manner a written report that addresses the historical and current facts of the child's situations, the GAL's conclusions based on these facts, and the GAL's recommendations in the best interests of the child.

1.6.5 The volunteer Guardian ad Litem shall not guarantee or create the impression that any portion of the investigation will remain confidential, and shall inform all persons interviewed that all pertinent information gathered by the Guardian Ad Litem must be reported to the court.

1.6.6 The volunteer Guardian Ad Litem shall maintain the privacy of parties in a manner consistent with GAL Program Policies.

1.6.7 The volunteer Guardian Ad Litem shall appear in court for all hearings involving the child, unless prior arrangements have been made with the GAL Coordinator to stand in for the GAL.

1.6.8 The volunteer Guardian Ad Litem shall maintain independence, objectivity, and the appearance of fairness in dealing with parties and professionals, both in and out of the courtroom, and shall act in a professional manner.

1.6.9   The volunteer Guardian Ad Litem shall timely report to the court any changes in the situation of the child for whom the GAL is appointed.

1.6.10   The volunteer Guardian Ad Litem shall remain qualified for the GAL Program Roster by passing periodic background checks, meeting continuing education requirements, and by abiding by the policies of the GAL Program.

1.6.11   The volunteer Guardian ad Litem shall avoid actual conflicts of interest or the appearance thereof.

1.6.12   The volunteer Guardian ad Litem shall treat the parties with respect, courtesy, fairness, and good faith regardless of race, color, creed, religion, national origin, cultural heritage, gender, age, education, economic status, sexual orientation or disability.

1.6.13   The volunteer Guardian ad Litem shall maintain adequate documentation of his/her investigation.

1.6.14   The volunteer Guardian Ad Litem shall not have ex parte contact with any judicial officer involving a matter in which they are appointed or serving.

1.6.15   The volunteer Guardian Ad Litem will perform only those duties that are within the scope of the role of the Guardian Ad Litem and included in the GAL job description.

1.7   Grievance Procedure.   Any party can file a complaint against a volunteer Guardian ad Litem. The complaint should be made in writing, and should be addressed to the Director of Juvenile and Family Court Services, P. O. Box 1220, Port Townsend, WA 98368.   The complaint must state the specific act or failure to act of concern to the complaining person and shall include:

(a) The name, mailing address, and telephone number of the person filing the complaint;

(b) The status of the underlying case including the case number, if known, and the case name;

(c) Whether the complaining person told the Guardian ad Litem and/or the Guardian Ad Litem Coordinator about the complaint;

(d) What action the Guardian ad Litem or the Guardian ad Litem Coordinator has taken to address the complaint;

(e) Which section of the Code of Conduct or statute was violated, and the specific facts of each violation;

(f) What the complaining person would like done to fix the problem which is the subject of the complaint.

The Director of Juvenile and Family Court Services will determine whether the complaint is substantive in nature and meets the criteria above.   The Director will contact the complaining party for clarification of the complaint as needed.   If the person making the complaint is a party to a pending case, or the attorney of a party to the case, a copy of the complaint will be sent to the judicial officer and parties.   A copy of the complaint will also be sent to the volunteer Guardian ad Litem, and to the Guardian ad Litem Coordinator, and a written response shall be requested of the volunteer Guardian ad Litem, and the Guardian ad Litem Coordinator if appropriate.

The Director of Juvenile and Family Court Services will investigate the complaint and either the Judge or Director shall decide any grievance that concerns:

(a) A case that is closed,

(b) A complaint made by a person not a party to a pending case, or

(c) A case that is open, and the complaint is brought by a party or his/her attorney, but the complaining party has not moved the court to decide the matter.

The decision of the Judge or Director may include whether to remove the volunteer Guardian ad Litem from the case or the GAL Program Roster.

Decisions made by the Director of Juvenile and Family Court Services regarding a grievance pertaining to an open case may be brought before the presiding judicial officer for review and resolution of the matter.

Any party to an open case who is filing a grievance may bring the complaint, through proper procedure, to the court's attention and move the court to resolve the complaint and/or dismiss the volunteer Guardian ad Litem from the case.

Removal of a volunteer Guardian ad Litem from the Guardian ad Litem Program Roster pursuant to a grievance shall be decided by the Judge or Director of Juvenile and Family Court Services, in consultation with the GAL Coordinator and the GAL Program Attorney.

A copy of the decision shall be placed in the file of the volunteer Guardian Ad Litem.   Dismissals from a case pursuant to a grievance are included in the volunteer Guardian ad Litem's Background Information Record.

Complaints under this rule may be filed at any time during the pendency of a case and up to six months following the dismissal of the case.

[Adopted effective September 1, 2005; amended effective September 1, 2011.]

VIII. CRIMINAL RULES

LCrR 1. SCOPE, PURPOSE AND CONSTRUCTION

1.1 Scope. The Local Civil Rules shall apply in all criminal proceedings when not inconsistent with these rules, the Superior Court Criminal Rules or applicable statutes.

[Adopted effective September 1, 2003; amended effective September 1, 2011.]

LCrR 3.2. RELEASE OF ACCUSED

3.2.1. Drug Court Participants. No drug court participant booked into the Jefferson County Jail on new criminal charges or drug court violations shall be released on bail prior to appearing in drug court by video the following business day at 11:30 am. It will be the Court Administrator's responsibility to keep the participant list current at the Jefferson County Jail.

[Adopted effective September 1, 2006; amended effective September 1, 2011.]

LCrR 3.4. PRESENCE OF THE DEFENDANT

3.4(d)(2) *Video Conference Proceedings—Agreement.* In criminal matters, in addition to those proceedings specifically mentioned in CrR 3.4(d)(1), all trial court proceedings may be conducted by video conference by agreement of the parties on the record. If neither party objects on the record to the proceeding being held by video conference, the participation in the proceeding will constitute "agreement on the record" to the use of video conference for that proceeding.

[Adopted effective September 1, 2010; amended effective September 1, 2011.]

LCrR 3.6. SUPPRESSION HEARINGS

(a) Pleadings. Motions to suppress physical, oral or identification evidence, other than a motion pursuant to rule 3.5, shall be in writing and a bench copy of said motion must be provided for the court at time of filing. Opposing counsel may be ordered to serve and file a memorandum of authorities in opposition to the motion. The court shall determine whether an evidentiary hearing is required based upon the moving papers.

[Adopted effective September 1, 2003; amended effective September 1, 2005; September 1, 2010; September 1, 2011.]

LCrR 4.9. CRIMINAL PRETRIAL HEARINGS

4.9.1 Pretrial hearings shall be set on all felony charges.

4.9.2 Pretrial hearings shall be set on the 8:30 a.m. Friday motion calendar at least ten (10) days prior to the trial date.

4.9.3 The defendant shall be present at the pretrial hearing. Should defendant fail to appear, unless good cause is shown, the trial date shall be stricken and a warrant for arrest of the defendant shall issue.

4.9.4 At the pretrial hearing the court shall determine: (i) whether discovery has been completed, (ii) whether discovery has been reviewed by defendant and counsel, (iii) whether a plea offer from the prosecuting attorney has been received by defendant and counsel, (iv) whether defendant is going to change his plea, (v) whether the defendant is going to petition for Drug Court or Diversion, and (vi) such other matters as may be appropriate.

4.9.5 If defendant advises the court that he intends to enter a guilty plea or petition for Drug Court or Diversion, the trial date will be stricken and a date scheduled for entry of plea or Drug Court or Diversion contract. If defendant does not indicate an intent to enter a guilty plea or petition for Drug Court or Diversion, the case will proceed to trial on the charge(s) as filed.

4.9.6 In the event that a trial is cancelled after pretrial subsequent to the jury call having been processed, counsel or parties to the action shall be subject to a jury administrative reimbursement fee equal to the actual costs incurred by the court for jury fee payments or administrative costs in calling the jury panel. Upon a showing of good cause, said fee may be waived by the court.

[Adopted effective September 1, 2003; amended effective September 1, 2011.]

LCrR 8.10. COURT COMMISSIONERS IN CRIMINAL CASES

In adult criminal cases, any court commissioner appointed to serve in the Jefferson County Superior Court, and qualified under Article 4, Section 23 of the Washington State Constitution, shall have the power, authority and jurisdiction, concurrent with superior court judges, to preside over arraignments, preliminary appearances, initial extradition hearings, and noncompliance proceedings pursuant to RCW 9.94A.634; to accept pleas; appoint counsel; make determinations of probable cause; set, amend and review conditions of pretrial release; set bail; set trial and hearing dates; authorize continuances; and accept waivers of the right to speedy trial.

[Adopted effective September 1, 2003; amended effective September 1, 2011.]

LCrR 8.11. CRIMINAL NO CONTACT ORDERS

At the time of the entry of any criminal Judgment and Sentence, Judgment of Acquittal, Order of Dismissal or other order disposing of a criminal cause of action, the Office of the Prosecuting Attorney shall enter a new Domestic Violence No Contact Order which reflects the extension of any initial order, or in the alternative, an order that reflects the vacation of any initial order.

[Adopted effective September 1, 2003; amended effective September 1, 2011.]

LCrR 8.12. CRIMINAL HEARING CONTINUANCES

Criminal motions will only be continued with the consent of the judge and in open court. Continuances shall not be granted by telephone.

[Adopted effective September 1, 2003; amended effective September 1, 2011.]

LOCAL RULES CONFORMING TO GENERAL RULES

LGR 31. PERSONAL IDENTIFIERS— CHILDREN

31.1 Complete names of children, sealed case types. The complete names of children shall be used in cases that are deemed confidential pursuant to state or federal statutes; including cases filed pursuant to RCW 13 (excluding offender cases); RCW 4.24; RCW 26.33 (Adoption); and, RCW 71.34 (Mental Health Services for Minors).

31.2 Confidential Information Form. The complete names of children and other identifiers shall be included in the Confidential Information Form or similar document for cases filed under Title 26.

31.3 Domestic Relations Orders. Court orders concerning the financial support or the custody or residential schedule of a child (including temporary or permanent parenting plans and similar documents) and orders establishing or disestablishing paternity shall include the full name of the child. The date of the birth of a child shall be included in court records only as authorized by General Rule 22.

31.4 Child who is alleged to be a victim in a crime. The complete name of a child who is alleged to be a victim of a crime may be included in subpoenas and in jury instructions. Nothing in this rule requires that subpoenas be routinely filed in the court file.

31.5 Child who is charged with a crime. The complete name of a child charged with a crime shall be included in any indictment or information filed with the court pursuant to CrR 2.1 or JuCR 7.2, as part of an affidavit or declaration of probable cause or for any other purpose deemed necessary for the prosecution or defense of the criminal or juvenile offender matter.

31.6 Child who is the subject of minor settlement. The complete name and date of birth of a child who is the subject of a minor settlement shall be included in the petition and any dispositive orders, pursuant to Rule 98.16W of the Superior Court Rules on Special Proceedings.

31.7 Orders issued for the protection of a child. If a child is a person protected by a criminal no contact order issued pursuant to RCW 10.99, an antiharassment order issued pursuant to RCW 10.14, an order of protection issued pursuant to RCW 26.50 or a restraining order or order of protection issued pursuant to RCW 26.09, RCW 26.10, RCW 26.26, RCW 26.52.020, or any other court order entered for the protection of the child, the child's full name and other identifiers shall be included on petitions and orders as necessary for entry of the order in the Judicial Information System (JIS) and/or the Washington Crime Information Center (WACIC).

31.8 Orders on release of criminal defendant. If access to a child is restricted pursuant to CrR 3.2(d)(1), the court may include the full name of the child on the order if deemed necessary for effective enforcement of order.

31.9 Orders restraining child from contacting or harassing others. Whenever a child is named as a respondent in an order listed in (3) above, the child's full name and other personal identifiers shall be included on the petition and order as necessary for entry of the order in the Judicial Information System (JIS) and/or the Washington Crime Information Center (WACIC)

31.10 Petitions and Notices filed pursuant to RCW 11.28 (children as heirs to estate). The full names and ages of children and other information required by RCW 11.28.110 and RCW 11.28.330 shall be included. However, the date of birth may be included only as authorized by General Rule 22.

31.11 General Authority. Nothing in this rule shall prohibit a court from authorizing the use of a child's full name or date of birth when necessary for the orderly administration of justice, consistent with the requirements of General Rule 22.

[Adopted effective September 1, 2005; redesignated from LCR 31 effective September 1, 2008; amended effective September 1, 2011.]

APPENDICES

APPENDIX 1. REQUEST FOR ENTRY OF DECREE AND DECLARATION OF JURISDICTIONAL FACTS (DISSOLUTION OF MARRIAGE)

APPENDIX 1

SUPERIOR COURT OF WASHINGTON
COUNTY OF JEFFERSON

In Re the Marriage of:)	
)	NO.
_____,)	
Petitioner,)	REQUEST FOR ENTRY OF DECREE AND
)	DECLARATION OF JURISDICTIONAL FACTS
and)	(DISSOLUTION OF MARRIAGE)
)	
_____,)	
Respondent.)	
_____)	

REQUEST   The petitioner requests immediate entry of Findings of Fact, Conclusions of Law and Decree of Dissolution of Marriage without a final hearing, and states:

RESIDENCE   I was a resident of the state of Washington when the petition was filed.

TIME LIMITS   More than 90 days have elapsed since the later of _____, ____, the date on which the Petition was filed, and _____, ____, the date:

[ ] the respondent signed a joinder.

[ ] the respondent signed an acceptance of service.

[ ] the summons and petition were personally served upon the respondent.

[ ] the summons and petition were mailed pursuant to an order for service by mail.

[ ] the summons was first published pursuant to an order for service by publication.

[ ] default has been taken.

[ ] default has not been taken.

MARRIAGE &   The parties were married on _____ ____, at [city, state]

SEPARATION   _____ and separated on _____, ____.

The marriage is now irretrievably broken.

PREGNANCY   The wife is not now pregnant.

DEPENDENT   All dependent children of the marriage are identified in the proposed Decree.

CHILDREN   The proposed Parenting Plan is in the children's best interest; the Child Support Worksheets are accurate.

PROPERTY   All property and all debts of the parties are fairly and completely divided in the

& DEBTS   Decree.

IF DEFAULT   If entry of the Decree is sought after default of the Respondent, the Decree provides for only that relief requested in the petition.

PERJURY   I declare under penalty of perjury under the laws of the State of Washington that

DECLARATION   the foregoing is true and correct.

Dated:_____, 20____.   [Signed]_____

at _____, Washington   Petitioner

Presented by: Approved, notice of presentation waived:

[Signed]_____   [Signed]_____

           Petitioner   Respondent

[Adopted effective September 1, 2003; amended on an emergency basis effective April 2, 2009; amended on a permanent basis effective September 1, 2009; September 1, 2011; September 2, 2014.]

APPENDIX 2. REQUEST FOR ENTRY OF DECREE AND DECLARATION OF JURISDICTIONAL FACTS (LEGAL SEPARATION)

APPENDIX 2

SUPERIOR COURT OF WASHINGTON
COUNTY OF JEFFERSON

In Re the Marriage of:)
)   NO.
_____ ,   )
                        Petitioner,   )   REQUEST FOR ENTRY OF DECREE AND
)   DECLARATION OF JURISDICTIONAL FACTS
and   )   (LEGAL SEPARATION)
)
_____ ,   )
                        Respondent.   )
_____   )

REQUEST	The petitioner requests immediate entry of Findings of Fact, Conclusions of Law and Decree of Legal Separation without a final hearing, and states:
RESIDENCE	I was a resident of the state of Washington when the petition was filed.
STATUS	[ ] the respondent signed a joinder.
	[ ] the respondent signed an acceptance of service.
	[ ] the summons and petition were personally served upon the respondent.
	[ ] the summons and petition were mailed pursuant to an order for service by mail.
	[ ] the summons was first published pursuant to an order for service by publication.
	[ ] default has been taken.
	[ ] default has not been taken.
MARRIAGE &	The parties were married on _____ ____, at [city, state]
SEPARATION	_____ and separated on _____ , ____.
	The petitioner wishes to be legally separated.
PREGNANCY	The wife is not now pregnant.
DEPENDENT	All dependent children of the marriage are identified in the proposed Decree.
CHILDREN	The proposed Parenting Plan is in the children's best interest; the Child Support Worksheets are accurate.
PROPERTY	All property and all debts of the parties are fairly and completely divided in the
& DEBTS	Decree.
IF DEFAULT	If entry of the Decree is sought after default of the Respondent, the Decree provides for only that relief requested in the petition.
PERJURY	I declare under penalty of perjury under the laws of the State of Washington that
DECLARATION	the foregoing is true and correct.

Dated:_____, 20____.   [Signed]_____
at_____, Washington   Petitioner

Presented by: Approved, notice of presentation waived:

[Signed]_____   [Signed]_____
            Petitioner   Respondent

[Adopted effective September 1, 2003. Former Appendix 2 was deleted and new Appendix 2 was adopted effective September 1, 2009; amended effective September 1, 2011; September 2, 2014.]

APPENDIX 3. NOTE FOR MOTION DOCKET (NTMTDK)

APPENDIX 3

**Superior Court of Washington
County of Jefferson**

_____,	No. _____
Plaintiff/Petitioner	**NOTE FOR MOTION DOCKET**
vs.	**(NTMTDK)**
_____,	
Defendant/Respondent	

TO THE CLERK OF THE COURT AND

TO:

AND:

Please take notice that the undersigned will bring on for hearing:

NATURE OF MOTION:

The hearing is to be held:

   DATE:_____ TIME:_____

AT: Superior Court of Jefferson County
   1820 Jefferson Street
   Port Townsend, WA 98368

DATED:_____   Signed:_____

               Lawyer for_____

               Address:_____

                     _____

                     _____

               Telephone:_____

[Adopted effective September 1, 2003; amended effective September 1, 2011.]

APPENDIX 4.   DOMESTIC RELATIONS INFORMATION FORM

APPENDIX 4

DOMESTIC RELATIONS INFORMATION FORM

Date: _____   ☐ Husband   ☐ Petitioner

Cause No.: _____   ☐ Wife   ☐ Respondent

PARTIES:

HUSBAND/FATHER		WIFE/MOTHER	
Name:	Age:	Name:	Age:
Address:		Address:	

Date of Marriage:	Date of Separation:

DEPENDENT CHILDREN:

Name	Age	This Marriage	Prior Marriage	Percent Residential Time		Since
				Father %	Mother %	

CHILD SUPPORT:

1.

	NET INCOME	SUPPORT
Husband/Father:	$	
Wife/Mother:	$	

2.   Tax Exemptions allocated as follows: _____

3.   Exceptional support considerations: _____

_____

4.   Child Support presently being paid $_____ per month; since _____

5.   Summary of proposed residential arrangements for the children: _____

_____

_____

_____

> YOU MUST ATTACH:
> 1. Proposed Child Support Order, Support Worksheets and current pay stubs. Form WPF DR 01-050.
> 2. Completed Financial Declaration. Form WPF DR 01-055
> 3. Proposed Parenting Plan, if disputed.

MAINTENANCE:

1.   Requested: $_____ per month, duration: _____

2.   Presently being paid: $_____ per month, for _____ months.

HUSBAND/FATHER INCOME:

Employer/Other Source	Length	Gross Income	Net Income
		Total Income	

WIFE/MOTHER INCOME:

Employer/Other Source	Length	Gross Income	Net Income
		Total Income	

FACTORS RELATING TO AWARD OF MAINTENANCE: _____

_____

_____

_____

_____

IF ATTORNEY FEES ARE AT ISSUE:

1.	Incurred to Date	$	Paid To Date	$
2.	Ordered to Date	$	Paid to Date	$
3.	Requested to Date	$	Estimate to Trial	$

PROPERTY DIVISION:

ASSETS:	Fair Market Value	Debt Owed	Net to Husband	Net to Wife
Real Estate:				
Home	$	$	$	$
Other Real Property	$	$	$	$
	$	$	$	$
Vehicles (Year/Make):				
	$	$	$	$
	$	$	$	$
Household Goods	$	$	$	$
Tools/Equipment	$	$	$	$
Recreational/Hobby Equipment	$	$	$	$
Business/Profession:				
Husband	$	$	$	$
Wife	$	$	$	$
Investments	$	$	$	$
Life Insurance Cash Value	$	$	$	$
Retirement:				
Husband	$	$	$	$
Wife	$	$	$	$
IRA's, TSP's, 401-K's, etc.:				
Husband	$	$	$	$
Wife	$	$	$	$
Receivables	$	$	$	$
Other Assets:				
	$	$	$	$
	$	$	$	$
	$	$	$	$
	$	$	$	$
Debts:	($)	($)	($)	($)
TOTALS	$	$	$	$
Equalization:	$	- $	divided by two (2)	= $

Proposed Percentage Division: _____ % to Husband   _____ % to Wife

Effects of Proposed Division: $_____ to Husband $_____ to Wife

[Adopted effective September 1, 2003; amended effective September 1, 2011.]

APPENDIX 5.   PRETRIAL SCHEDULE FOR COMPLEX CIVIL LITIGATION

APPENDIX 5

Superior Court of Washington
County of Jefferson

_____ , Plaintiff/Petitioner vs. _____ , Defendant/Respondent	No. _____ PRETRIAL SCHEDULE FOR COMPLEX CIVIL LITIGATION

TRIAL DATE:_____

NON-EXPERT WITNESS LIST TO BE EXCHANGED AND FILED BY_____

MOTIONS TO AMEND AND/OR TO ADD ADDITIONAL PARTIES MUST BE FILED BY_____

EXPERT WITNESS LIST EXCHANGED AND FILED BY_____

SECOND EXPERT WITNESS LIST EXCHANGED AND FILED BY_____ (A party may only list witnesses in the same category and same number as those listed by the opposing party in its original witness list).

DISCOVERY CLOSES_____ (Interrogatories and Production Requests must be propounded so that the answers are due by this date).

DISPOSITIVE MOTIONS MUST BE FILED AND HEARD BY_____

IN LIMINE MOTIONS MUST BE FILED AND HEARD BY_____

TRIAL BRIEFS AND JURY INSTRUCTIONS FILED BY_____

PROPOSED DEPOSITIONS TESTIMONY TO BE USED (PAGE AND LINE NUMBER) MUST BE FILED BY_____(This rule does not apply to the use of deposition testimony to cross examine witnesses.)
Dated:_____   _____
                                            JUDGE/COURT COMMISSIONER

Presented by:

_____   _____
Attorney   WSBA #   Attorney   WSBA #
_____   _____
Address:_____   Address:_____
_____   _____
Phone:_____   Phone:_____

[Adopted effective September 1, 2005; amended effective September 1, 2009; September 1, 2011.]

APPENDIX 6. NOTE FOR TRIAL SETTING (NTTRS) (CLERK'S ACTION REQUIRED)

APPENDIX 6

Superior Court of Washington
County of Jefferson

_____, Plaintiff/Petitioner vs. _____, Defendant/Respondent	No. _____ **NOTE FOR TRIAL SETTING** **(NTTRS)** **(Clerk's Action Required)**

TO THE CLERK OF THE COURT AND TO:

Please take notice that this case will be placed on the trial setting docket for assignment of trial on Friday, the _____ day of _____, 20____ at ⊔ 1:00 civil or ⊔ 2:00 domestic.

1. Nature of Case: _____
2. A Jury   ⊐has been demanded   ⊐12 person   ⊐6 person   ⊐has not been demanded
3. Estimated length of trial: ⊔ _____ hours   ⊐_____ days
   Plaintiff(s)/Petitioner(s) case:_____ hours/days   Defendant(s)/Respondent(s) case: _____ hours/days
4. Preferred trial dates: _____
5. Dates unavailable for trial: _____
6. Case may be heard by a judge pro tem   ⊐ Yes   ⊐ No
7. Visiting Judge Required: ⊏ Yes   ⊏ No
8. Mandatory Settlement Conference Required: ⊏ Yes   ⊏ No

CHECK APPROPRIATE SQUARES:
☐ I have contacted all counsel and they agree the trial may be set anytime after _____ (date).
⊔ I have contacted all counsel and am unable to obtain agreement on trial dates. The Court will set the trial date.
⊓ No contact has been made with other counsel/party, but all have been served with a copy of this notice in time to allow a response within 10 days.

I hereby represent to the Court that this case is at issue and should be set for trial.

⊔ Plaintiff's claim exceeds $50,000.00
☐ Plaintiff seeks relief other than a money judgment.
⊓ Defendant's counter or cross claim exceeds $50,000.00.
☐ Defendant's counter or cross claim seeks relief other than a money judgment.

Any party not in agreement with the information or estimates given in Note for Trial Setting shall file and serve at least (3) days prior to the trial setting date a counter notice or written objection to setting. If an objection to setting is filed, counsel shall appear on the setting day before the motions judge, to argue the objection.

Date:_____   SIGNED _____
                                          Lawyer for:_____
                                          Address:_____
                                          Telephone Number:_____

[Adopted effective September 1, 2006. Amended effective September 1, 2010; September 1, 2011.]

APPENDIX 7.   REQUEST FOR ENTRY OF DECREE AND DECLARATION OF JURISDICTIONAL FACTS (REGISTERED DOMESTIC PARTNERSHIP)

APPENDIX 7

SUPERIOR COURT OF WASHINGTON
COUNTY OF JEFFERSON

In Re the Domestic Partnership of:)
)
_____   )   NO.
                              ,   )
                      Petitioner,   )   REQUEST FOR ENTRY OF DECREE AND
)   DECLARATION OF JURISDICTIONAL FACTS
and   )   (REGISTERED DOMESTIC PARTNERSHIP)
)
_____   )
                              ,   )
                      Respondent.   )
_____   )

REQUEST	The petitioner requests immediate entry of Findings of Fact, Conclusions of Law and Decree of Dissolution of Registered Domestic Partnership without a final hearing, and states:
RESIDENCE TIME LIMITS	I was a resident of the state of Washington when the petition was filed. More than 90 days have elapsed since the later of _____, ____, the date on which the Petition was filed, and _____, ____, the date: [] the respondent signed a joinder. [] the respondent signed an acceptance of service. [] the summons and petition were personally served upon the respondent. [] the summons and petition were mailed pursuant to an order for service by mail. [] the summons was first published pursuant to an order for service by publication. [] default has been taken. [] default has not been taken.
REGISTRATION & SEPARATION	The parties' domestic partnership was registered with the Secretary of State (Washington) on _____, ____. The parties separated on _____, ____. The domestic partnership is now irretrievably broken.
PREGNANCY	Neither party is currently pregnant.
DEPENDENT CHILDREN	All dependent children of the partnership are identified in the proposed Decree. The proposed Parenting Plan is in the children's best interest; the Child Support Worksheets are accurate.
PROPERTY & DEBTS	All property and all debts of the parties are fairly and completely divided in the Decree.
IF DEFAULT	If entry of the Decree is sought after default of the Respondent, the Decree provides for only that relief requested in the petition.
PERJURY DECLARATION	I declare under penalty of perjury under the laws of the State of Washington that the foregoing is true and correct.

Dated:_____, 20____ .   [Signed]_____
at _____, Washington   Petitioner

Presented by: Approved, notice of presentation waived:

[Signed]_____   [Signed]_____
            Petitioner   Respondent

[Adopted effective September 1, 2012.   Amended effective September 2, 2014.]

APPENDIX 8. FAX TRANSMITTAL SHEET FOR FILING IN THE JEFFERSON COUNTY SUPERIOR COURT OF THE STATE OF WASHINGTON (PER GR 17)

APPENDIX 8

FAX TRANSMITTAL SHEET
FOR FILING IN THE JEFFERSON COUNTY SUPERIOR COURT
OF THE STATE OF WASHINGTON (per GR 17)

ONLY FOR DOCUMENTS TO BE FILED IN THE COURT FILE - FEE REQUIRED

RUTH GORDON, JEFFERSON COUNTY CLERK   360-385-9125

FAX Number: (360) 385-5672

FAX Fee = $5.00 1st page + $1.00 per page thereafter.

Cause Number:	Case Caption: VS
Person Filing:	Date:
Firm Name:	FAX Contact:
Address:	City/State/Zip:
Phone Number:( )	FAX Number:( )
# Pages (not counting this Sheet):	Payment Verification #

PAGE LIMIT: To send single transmissions exceeding twenty (20) pages during regular business hours (8:30 a.m. to 4:30 p.m. Monday through Friday), you must have permission from the Clerk's Office. (Please call in advance) The transmission may need to be scheduled for low use hours. We do not count the FAX COVER SHEET toward this limit. There is no page limit for transmissions after regular business hours. FAX filing is available 24 hours per day, 7 days per week. **Do Not Send the Original. (Attach GR 17(b)(2) Affidavit/Declaration – LCR Appendix 9)**

FAX FEE: The Clerk's FAX fee is $5.00 for the first page and $1.00 for each page thereafter. You must also prepay any fees normally required upon filing pleadings in our court. You may pay by credit or debit card or via the "Court Payments" link on our web page, http://www.co.jefferson.wa.us/Clerk/default.asp. **You must enter the last four digits of your Payment Verification Number in appropriate field above.** Read and sign the "FAX FEE REMITTANCE CERTIFICATION", below. Our payment agent will charge you a convenience fee for using their service in addition to your filing fees and FAX fees.

FILING FEE: Documents requiring filing fees may be FAXed. These include, but are not limited to, original petitions or complaints, jury demands, writs, notices of appeal, and petitions to modify child support. Payment must be made prior to FAX filing. Verification number must be indicated above.

> FAX FEE PAYMENT NOTICE: I have prepaid all necessary fees and have included my verification number above for $_____, which includes the FAX fee for _____ pages of the accompanying document. Signature_____

USE ONLY THIS COVER SHEET TO FILE BY FAX

[Adopted effective September 1, 2006. Amended effective September 1, 2007; September 1, 2009; amended on an emergency basis, effective November 12, 2009; March 9, 2010; amended on a permanent basis, effective September 1, 2010; September 1, 2011; September 2, 2013; September 2, 2014.]

APPENDIX 9.   FACSIMILE AFFIDAVIT/DECLARATION

Superior Court of Washington
County of Jefferson

_____,
                    Plaintiff/Petitioner

vs.

_____,
                    Defendant/Respondent

No. _____

FACSIMILE
AFFIDAVIT/DECLARATION

(AF)

I, _____ (name), _____ (title), with
_____ (firm/organization), declare and state the following:

The attached is a facsimile transmission of _____
_____ (titles   of   documents)
submitted by_____ (name), _____ (title),
in the above-entitled matter.

The attached document(s), prepared for filing on the _____ day of _____, 20_____
and consisting of _____ pages, including this affidavit page, has been examined and
determined by me to be complete and legible.

DATED: _____   SIGNED: _____

                                  Address: _____

                                           _____

                                  Phone: _____

[Adopted effective September 1, 2007.   Amended effective September 1, 2008; September 1,
2011; September 2, 2013.]

DISTRICT COURT

LOCAL RULES FOR THE DISTRICT COURT OF THE STATE OF WASHINGTON FOR JEFFERSON COUNTY

Including Amendments Received Through
August 15, 2015

Table of Rules

I. ADMINISTRATIVE RULES

LARLJ 2. SCOPE OF RULES AND ADOPTION

(a) **Effect of Local Rules.** These rules shall be known as the Local Rules for the District Court of the State of Washington for Jefferson County. These rules will be effective on September 1, 1999 and will supersede all prior rules of this court. These rules conform, to the extent possible, with the numbering system and in format to the rules adopted by the Supreme Court of the State of Washington for courts of limited jurisdiction.

The provisions of these local rules are supplemental to the rules adopted by the Supreme Court of the State of Washington for courts of limited jurisdiction, and shall not be construed in conflict with them.

(b) **Adoption and Amendments.** These Rules are adopted and may be amended from time to time in accordance with GR 7, CRLJ 83, CrRLJ 1.7 and IRLJ 1.3. The court may modify or suspend any of these local rules in any given case upon good cause shown or upon the court's own motion.

(c) Prior Rules Repealed. All prior rules of the Jefferson County District Court are repealed upon adoption of these rules.

[Adopted effective September 1, 1999.]

LARLJ 5.   COURT ADMINISTRATOR AND PROBATION OFFICERS

(d) Selection. The court administrator shall be appointed by the judge and shall serve at the pleasure of the appointing authority under the direction and supervision of the judge.

(e) Powers and Duties. The powers and duties of the court administrator include but are not limited to the following:

(1) Administrative control of all non-judicial activities of the court.

(2) Implement all policies regarding judicial functions of the court.

(3) Supervision of all court and probation employees.

(4) Preparation and administration of the court budget.

(5) Representation of the court in dealings with the State Court Administrator.

(6) Assist the judge in meeting with representatives of governmental bodies, and other public and private groups regarding court management matters.

(7) Prepare reports and compile statistics as required by the judge or state court administrator and maintain records or informal activities of the court.

(8) Make recommendations to the judge for the improvement of the administration of the court.

The court administrator may delegate such duties to court employees as deemed appropriate.

(f) Probation Officers. The probation officer(s) shall perform such duties as are assigned by the Court, including pre-sentence evaluations and reports, determining eligibility for waiver of probation fees and probation supervision.

[Adopted effective September 1, 1999. Amended effective September 1, 2002; September 1, 2015.]

LARLJ 9.   DISCLOSURE OF RECORDS

All requests for release of records/information shall be governed by the Judicial Information System Committee's Data Dissemination Policy GR 31(g), JISCR 15 and ARLJ 9.

(d) Court Assistance.

(3) Court facilities are available to the public to assist disclosure. A copy fee of $.15 per page or $25.00 per CD shall be charged. Certified copies shall be $6.00 per document. Research fees shall be $30.00 per hour for all requests taking longer than one hour. Research fee shall be assessed beginning the second hour.

[Adopted effective September 1, 1999. Amended effective June 28, 2005; September 1, 2015.]

II.   CIVIL PROCEEDINGS

LCRLJ 5.   SERVICE AND FILING OF PLEADINGS AND OTHER PAPERS

(d) Filing.

(5) *Motions.* No motion for any order shall be heard unless the papers pertaining to it have been properly filed with the Clerk.

(6) Documents not to be filed:

(i) Interrogatories and depositions without written permission of Court, unless necessary for the disposition of a motion or objection;

(ii) Unanswered requests for admissions unless necessary for the disposition of a motion or objection;

(iii) Photocopies of reported cases, statutes, or texts, whether appended to a brief or other pleading, shall not be filed but may be furnished directly to the Judge hearing the matter;

(iv) Documents or copies thereof which should be received and/or admitted as an exhibit rather than included in the court file.

(v) Requests for discovery and/or answers unless necessary for the disposition of a motion or objection.

(7) *Offers of Settlement.* An offer of settlement made pursuant to Chapter 4.84 of the Revised Code of Washington shall not be filed or communicated to the trier of fact in violation of Section 4.84.280 of the Revised Code of Washington prior to the completion of trial. A violation of this order shall result in the denial of attorney's fees. (See LCRLJ 68)

(j) Service by Facsimile; see GR 17. Service by facsimile shall be allowed only under the following conditions:

(1) The party or attorney of record to whom service is delivered has a publicly available fax number or has given written consent to receive fax service to the sending party or attorney.

(2) The attorney or party sending the document via fax shall retain the original signed document until 60 days after completion of the case. Document to be transmitted by fax shall bear the notation: "SENT on (DATE) VIA FAX FOR FILING IN COURT".

(3) Documents transmitted by fax shall be letter size (8–½ by 11 inches). Documents over 10 pages in length may not be served by fax without prior approval of the receiving party.

(4) Any document transmitted by fax must be accompanied by a fax transmittal sheet in a form that includes the case number (if any), case caption, number of pages, the sender's name, and senders voice and facsimile telephone numbers. Transmittal sheets are not considered legal findings.

(5) A document transmitted directly to the receiving party shall be deemed received at the time the receiving party's fax machine electronically registers the transmission of the first page, regardless of when the final printing of the document occurs, except that a document received after the close of normal business hours shall be considered received the next judicial day. If a document is not completely transmitted, it will not be considered received. A document transmitted to another for filing with the clerk of the court will be deemed filed when presented to the clerk in the same manner as on original document.

(k) Fees for Facsimile Filing. The standard fee for faxing to or from the clerk shall be $3.00 for the first page and $1.00 for each page thereafter. Faxes will not be filed until payment is received by the court.

(*l*) Service by Email. See GR30.2(d)

[Adopted effective September 1, 1999. Amended effective June 28, 2005; September 1, 2015.]

LCRLJ 10.　FORM OF PLEADINGS

(f) Change of Address. Upon a change of office address, the attorney shall within 10 days after the change, furnish his/her Washington State Bar Association Membership Number, the previous address and telephone number, clearly identified as such, the new address and telephone number, clearly identified as such, and the effective date of the change.

(g) Change of Name. Upon a change of the attorney's name, the attorney shall furnish his or her Washington State Bar Association Membership Number, the previous name, clearly identified as such, the full new name, clearly identified as such, and the effective date of the change.

[Adopted effective September 1, 1999.]

LCRLJ 38.　JURY TRIAL

(d) Impaneling the Jury.

(7) *Random Selection.* On the day of trial, the jurors shall sign in on the computer print-out provided by the Jury Manager. After all of the jurors have signed in, the Bailiff shall deliver the sign-in sheet to the jury administrator. The jury administrator will randomly assign a number to each name. The list of assigned numbers shall be given to the Bailiff who will distribute juror numbers. Any jurors wishing to be excused from serving on the trial shall be brought before the judge and examined in the presence of the parties. Those not excused shall be returned to the bailiff, who will then seat the panel in the courtroom in numerical order.

(8) *Juror Questionnaires.* At the conclusion of voir dire, Juror Questionnaires and/or any juror information forms shall be immediately returned to the Court. Juror Questionnaires and/or any juror information forms shall not be copied or removed from the courtroom without the express permission of the trial judge. The jury questionnaires will be destroyed after the jury is impaneled.

(9) *Examination Of Jurors.* The voir dire examination of jurors shall be conducted under the direction and control of the Court with the following guidelines:

a. It is expected that voir dire, in most cases, will consume one hour time or less.

b. The Court shall ask all general questions and thereafter shall give leave to the respective parties to ask such supplementary questions as may be deemed proper and necessary by the Court. The parties shall submit all proposed general questions in writing prior to voir dire.

c. The Court may intervene without objection in instances of inappropriate questioning and may limit the amount of time each party has to examine a juror or jury panel.

d. The jury shall consist of the first six (6) unchallenged jurors on the panel following exercise of peremptory challenges and/or acceptance of the panel.

(10) *Trial Confirmation.* In civil cases set for jury trial, it is mandatory that the attorneys, or parties in a pro se case, notify the court by 3:00 p.m. the day prior to trial whether or not they will proceed to jury trial. The purpose of this requirement is to permit the cancellation of unneeded jury panels and the savings of the costs thereof. If this required communication is not received, the jury panel may be canceled by the court. It will be deemed a waiver of the jury for the next day and terms may be assessed against the attorneys and/or parties.

[Adopted effective September 1, 1999. Amended effective September 1, 2006.]

LCRLJ 40.　ASSIGNMENT OF CASES

(b) Methods.

(1) *Note for Trial Setting.* Any party desiring to bring any issue to trial may note the matter on the civil motion calendar. The Court Administrator shall schedule all trial dates. The party desiring to set a civil case for trial shall file with the Court and serve upon the opposing party a Note for Trial Setting which will include not less than three (3) proposed dates during which the matter can be tried. If any of these proposed dates are satisfactory to the opposing party, he or she will notify the Court Administrator

within five (5) days of receiving the Note for Trial Setting and trial shall be set for that date.

(2) *Attendance at Trial Setting—Contested Setting.* If setting of trial date is contested, the trial setting shall be presented to the court for assignment of trial date.

(3) *Stipulation for Trial Date.* At any time that all counsel can agree on an available trial date from the calendar, they can indicate their agreement to the clerk of the court on the Note of Trial Setting form.

(4) *Priority Setting.* To obtain a priority civil setting, the requesting party shall note the matter for trial setting, as set out above, indicating that a priority setting is requested. Any priority setting shall be supported by an affidavit which sets out the basis for the request. No case shall be set as a priority without court order.

(5) When a case is not tried on the date set, the parties are responsible for renoting the matter for trial setting.

(e) Continuances.

(1) *Trials—Written Motion.* All requests for a continuance shall be presented by written motion and affidavit after notice to the opposing party or by stipulation and agreed order. If there is no agreement by the parties, the court will grant a continuance only upon a showing of good cause. Twenty-four (24) hours prior notice to the opposing party will meet the requirements of this subsection. Except where the case has been preempted or where the order of continuance recites the new trial date, no case will be reset until the order of continuance has been filed.

(2) *Good Cause.* The following shall be examples of good cause:

    (i) Illness.

    (ii) Unavoidable, unforeseen conflicts.

    (iii) Unforeseen unavailability of witnesses.

    (iv) Lack of discovery when caused by the opposing party's conduct or newly discovered evidence requiring investigation.

(3) *Payment of Terms and Costs.* If a continuance is granted it shall be upon the condition that the moving party shall pay all appropriate costs and terms reflecting inconvenience to others occasioned by the continuance.

(4) *Emergency Suspension.* The court may, in cases of emergency, suspend the requirements set forth in this rule and require such verification as is reasonable.

(g) Motion Setting—Civil.

(1) *Filing Note for Hearing.* The Note for Hearing—Issue of Law must be served and filed no later than ten (10) days prior to the hearing (CRLJ 6 and CRLJ 40). Any responding documents must be served and filed at least seven (7) days before the hearing.

Reply documents must be served and filed at least two (2) days before the hearing. In the event a motion, or one continued from a prior date, is to be argued, counsel for the moving party shall notify the District Court Civil Clerk by 12:00 Noon, two (2) days before the hearing. Failure to comply with the provisions of this rule shall result in the motion being stricken from the motion calendar.

(2) *Motion Setting–Summary Judgment.* Motion for summary judgment and dismissal must be served and filed at least twelve (12) days prior to the hearing (CRLJ 56) and heard at least two (2) weeks prior to the date the case is set for trial. The motion shall be set in accordance with the provisions of paragraph (b) above; and a continuance may be granted only in accordance with the provisions of paragraph (e) above.

(3) *Filings of Motions. Memoranda and Affidavits–General.* The moving party shall file with the Note for Hearing–Issue of Law form, the following: The motion being noted, all supporting affidavits and documentary evidence, and a brief memorandum of authorities, unless the legal position is fully and adequately covered by the "authorities" section of the issue of Law form. If the responding party files a response to the issue of law, or any counter-affidavits, briefs, or memoranda of authorities, such document must be served and filed no later than five (5) days before the hearing. The responding party must also file any pleading to which the motion is directed. Failure to timely comply with these filing requirements may result in a continuance or the motion being stricken from the calendar and imposition of terms.

(4) *Length of Memoranda.* Memoranda relating to motions shall not exceed fifteen (15) pages. Attached copies of foreign and federal decisions are not included in the fifteen (15) page limitation. Waiver of page limitations may be granted only upon motion demonstrating good cause which may be heard ex parte.

(5) *Copies of Motions, Memoranda and Affidavits.* A copy of the motion, brief, memorandum, documents and affidavit shall be furnished to the Clerk at the time of filing for delivery to the assigned Judge for preparation. Responding briefs, memoranda and other documents shall be filed with copies provided for the preparation of the assigned Judge. Failure to comply with this requirement may result in a continuance and imposition of terms.

(6) *Motion Hearing Procedures.* Oral argument on motions shall be limited to ten (10) minutes for each side unless the Judge determines otherwise, in which case the motion may be placed at the end of the calendar.

[Adopted effective September 1, 1999.]

LCRLJ 43. TAKING OF TESTIMONY

(e) Evidence on Motions. Motions shall be heard only on the pleadings, affidavits, published deposition, and other papers filed unless otherwise directed by the Court. Any counter-affidavit shall be served on the opposing party within five (5) days before the hearing or the moving party shall have the option of a postponement of the hearing. Affidavits strictly in reply to a counter-affidavit may be served and considered at the hearing.

[Adopted effective September 1, 1999.]

LCRLJ 49. VERDICTS

(f) Manner of Giving Verdict.

(1) *Receiving Verdict During Absence of Counsel.* A party or attorney desiring to be present at the return of the verdict must remain in attendance at the courthouse or be available by telephone call. If a party or attorney fails to appear within ten (10) minutes of telephone notice to the attorney's office, home, or other number, the Court may proceed to take the verdict in the absence of such party or attorney. In such case, the Jury shall be individually polled and the identity of any dissenting jurors recorded.

[Adopted effective September 1, 1999.]

LCRLJ 54. JUDGMENTS AND COSTS

(c) Demand for judgment.

(1) *Method—Ex Parte Judgments and Orders.* Counsel, legal interns and registered legal assistants presenting a judgment or seeking entry of an order shall be responsible to see that all papers pertaining thereto are filed and that the court file is provided to the judge. Counsel may present routine ex parte or stipulated matters based on the record in the file by mail addressed to the Court Administrator. Self-addressed, stamped envelopes shall be provided for return of any conformed materials and/or rejected orders.

(d) Costs—Attorney Fees.

(1) Reasonable attorney fees when allowed by statute or contract will be determined on a case by case basis and awarded in the sound discretion of the Court upon satisfactory justification, which shall include documentation of time and charges. In appropriate cases, when a default judgment is entered, where authorized and instead of those statutory fees set by RCW 12.20.060, reasonable attorney's fees may be allowed on the basis of a maximum of 50% of the first $500.00 of the principal amount of the judgment, plus 10% of any balance over $500.00, without formal justification or documentation.

(2) If reasonable attorney fees are requested based on a contract provision, the contract provision must be conspicuously highlighted or underlined to be readily ascertainable.

(3) Specific citation of authority must accompany requests for reasonable attorney's fees on any basis other than contract provision.

(4) Statutory attorney's fees may be granted when reasonable attorney's fees are not authorized. (See RCW 12.20.060).

(5) *Assigned Claims.* Before costs and attorney's fees will be allowed by the Court on assigned claims, proof shall be furnished the Court that Notice and Demand for Payment of disputed amount has been sent to the defendant by the assignee, and he/she has had reasonable opportunity of not less than thirty (30) days to pay the disputed amount prior to the suit. Reasonable attorney's fees, when allowed, shall not exceed either ten percent (10%) of the disputed amount, or the statutory attorney's fee, whichever is greater unless there is documentation of time and charges. A statutory attorney's fee shall be allowed when the amount in dispute is paid any time prior to trial on assigned claims. A reasonable attorney's fee shall not be allowed absent satisfactory justification including documentation of time and charges.

(6) 'Offer of Settlement' under RCW chapter 4.84 means a written offer served in the manner provided by CRLJ 5 for service of pleadings, and in an amount as set by the pleadings. A cross-claim will be treated (between cross-claimant and cross-claim defendant) as if it were a separate action.

(7) An offer of settlement must be served after the time the answer or the response to any counter-claim has been served and no later than fourteen (14) days before the trial date. The acceptance of any offer of settlement must be served no later than five (5) judicial days prior to the trial date. An acceptance must be in writing and must be served in the same manner as is required for an offer of settlement.

(8) The offer of settlement shall be substantially in the following form:

Jefferson County District Court
State of Washington

```
_____  )
Plaintiff                 )  No. _____
            v.            )  OFFER OF JUDGMENT
_____  )
Defendant                 )
```

The party named below, in total settlement of this damage action, offers to allow judgment to be entered in this lawsuit against the defendant in the sum of $_____, plus court costs. This offer is made pursuant to RCW 4.84.250 through RCW 4.84.300.

If you wish to accept this offer, you must do so, by written notice, to the undersigned attorney and file a copy of your response with the court named above. The response must be served within ten (10) days, and not later than five (5) days before trial.

If you do not accept this offer within that time period, and the offeror subsequently obtains a judgment which is at least as favorable to the offeror, the amount of the judgment may be increased by an award of additional costs and/or reasonable attorney's fees as authorized by RCW 4.84.250 through RCW 4.84.300, CRLJ 68, and LCRLJ 54.

Name of Offeror: _____
Date: _____
Attorney for Offeror: _____
Address: _____

[Adopted effective September 1, 1999.]

LCRLJ 55.　DEFAULT

(a) **Entry of Default Judgment.**

(5) All necessary papers required for entry of a default judgment shall be filed at the same time as the motion for default judgment, unless extended by court order to correct a clerical error or omission or for furnishing of any proof required by the court. Default judgments shall be subject to the following:

(6) No default judgment shall be granted except upon motion by plaintiff's counsel of record, or if none, by motion of plaintiff.

(7) No default judgment shall be granted except upon proof satisfactory to the court. The court shall require at least the following to be on file with the motion for default judgment, unless otherwise excused by the court for good cause:

(i) on assigned causes of action, the assignment instrument;

(ii) on causes of action based on a negotiable instrument, the original negotiable instrument;

(iii) on causes of action based on a retail sales contract, chattel mortgage, or conditional sales contract, the original contract (or a copy if the original has been filed with a government agency). Where applicable, an automobile title or bill of sale must be filed;

(iv) on causes of action based on open account where the complaint is not specific, a written statement of account setting forth all charges and credits and the dates thereof, the nature of merchandise or services furnished, and a statement of any interest or surcharges which are included;

(v) on causes of action for rent based on an oral lease, a statement of account setting forth the dates of accrued rent, dates of delinquency, late charges and any other costs. If any claim is made for damages or repairs to premises, such claim must be itemized separately;

(vi) on causes of action for rent based on a written lease, a copy of the lease and a statement of account setting forth the dates of accrued rent, dates of delinquency, late charges and any other costs allowed by the lease;

(vii) on causes of action based on all other contracts, oral testimony to prove performance may be required, together with filing of a copy of the con-

tract, if written; and filing or proving the items of account and any credits;

(viii) on causes of action for tort, the proof required shall be the same as required above for proving contract balances except that the following additional proof of the amount of damage shall be required:

Property damage may be proved by repair bills or estimates;

Loss of use claims, loss of wages, and pain and suffering shall be proved by oral testimony;

Hospital and doctor bills may be proved by written bills, whether paid or not.

(8) No judgment for interest shall be allowed unless citation to applicable authority is presented and there is on file proof of the factors necessary for computation of interest including applicable dates, rate of interest, amounts subject to interest, and a computation of the total interest claimed due.

(9) Default Judgments must be accompanied by:

(i) Affidavit of Service if not previously filed.

(ii) Affidavit of Soldiers' and Sailors' Relief Act.

(g) **Collection and handling charges and attorneys fees** on actions brought to collect dishonored checks shall not be allowed unless proof of the following is provided:

(1) The statutory form of notice of dishonor has been sent as required by RCW chapter 62.A–3 and a copy is filed with the court.

(2) An accounting statement, or some reasonable alternate means of determining the plaintiff's collection costs is filed with the court.

[Adopted effective September 1, 1999.]

LCRLJ 58.　ENTRY OF JUDGMENTS

(k) **Judgment on a Promissory Note.** No judgment on a promissory note will be signed until the original note has been filed with the Court, absent proof of loss or destruction.

[Adopted effective September 1, 1999.]

LCRLJ 59.　NEW TRIAL, RECONSIDERATION, AND AMENDMENT OF JUDGMENTS

(k) A motion for reconsideration shall be submitted on brief and affidavits only, without oral argument, unless the trial judge on application from counsel or on his own motion allows oral argument. The moving party shall file the motion and all supporting affidavits, documents and briefs at the same time, and on the date of filing serve or mail a copy thereof to opposing counsel, deliver a copy thereof to the trial judge which copy shall show the date of filing. The trial judge shall either deny the motion and advise counsel of the ruling or advise counsel of desired further proceedings pursuant to CR 59 and this rule.

[Adopted effective September 1, 1999.]

LCRLJ 69. EXECUTION AND SUPPLEMENTAL PROCEEDINGS AND GARNISHMENTS

(b) Supplemental Proceedings.

(1) In all supplemental proceedings wherein a show cause order is issued pursuant thereto requiring the personal attendance of a party to be examined in open Court, and in orders to show cause in re contempt, the order to show cause must include the following words in capital letters:

> YOUR FAILURE TO APPEAR AS SET FORTH AT THE TIME, DATE, AND PLACE THEREOF MAY CAUSE THE COURT TO ISSUE A BENCH WARRANT FOR YOUR APPREHENSION AND CONFINEMENT IN JAIL UNTIL SUCH TIME AS THE MATTER CAN BE HEARD, UNLESS BAIL IS FURNISHED AS PROVIDED IN SUCH BENCH WARRANT.

The failure to include such wording will be grounds for the Court to refuse to issue a bench warrant.

(2) *Bench Warrant.* In the event the judgment debtor fails to appear for examination in supplemental proceedings, the Court may issue a Bench Warrant for the defendant's arrest upon plaintiff's motion, provided that proof of service on the judgment debtor of the order to appear for examination has been filed. Such Bench Warrant shall provide for bail in the amount of $250.00 unless the total judgment, including costs and fees, is less than $250.00, in which case bail shall be set at such lesser amount. Upon arrest on a Civil Bench Warrant, the defendant shall be released by the jail upon posting the bail amount in cash or surety bond. The jail shall require the defendant to sign a jail release form to appear at 1:15 p.m. the next judicial day before the Court Administrator. The Court Administrator shall set a new date and time for the Supplemental Proceeding and notify both parties. If the judgment debtor is not released on bail or bond, he/she shall be brought before a judge, not later than the next judicial day, who shall set a new date and time for the examination of Supplemental Proceedings, and notify both parties. Upon completion of the examination of the judgment debtor, the bail shall be exonerated unless the Court orders otherwise.

(c) Judgment Against Garnishee. No judgment against a garnishee defendant, or order to pay into Court, or order to the Clerk to pay out any sum pursuant to a Writ of Garnishment, will be signed except after judgment is entered against the defendant and until the party who caused the writ to issue shall have proof of service in the manner provided by statute and twenty (20) days shall have elapsed from the filing of the answer of the garnishee defendant. There shall be attached proof of mailing of Notice of Intent to present Default Judgment against garnishee defendant by certified mail of not less than seven (7) days. No funds shall be paid into the Registry of the Court without a court order.

(d) Payment of Judgment. All payment of monies on judgments (including awards of costs) shall be made to the party and/or attorney, unless otherwise ordered. The receiving party, or party's attorney, shall within thirty (30) days of receipt file a satisfaction of the judgment in the amount received.

(e) Order to Pay. The pattern form of "Judgment and Order to Pay", set out in RCW 6.27.265 (as amended), is hereby adopted for use in Jefferson County District Court. Failure to follow such form may be grounds for denial of the order.

(f) Federal Government as Garnishee Defendant.

(i) Whenever the federal government is named as a garnishee defendant the clerk of the court shall, upon submittal of a notice in the appropriate form by the requesting party, issue a notice which directs the garnishee defendant to disburse any non-exempt earnings to the court.

(ii) Funds received by the clerk from a garnishee defendant may be deposited into the registry of the court or, in the case of negotiable instruments, may be retained in the court file. Upon presentation of an order directing the clerk to disburse the funds received, the clerk shall pay or endorse the funds over to the party entitled to same. Except for good cause shown, the funds shall not be paid or endorsed to the judgment creditor prior to the expiration of any minimum statutory period allowed to the judgment debtor for filing an exemption claim.

(iii) The party requesting the writ of garnishment shall supply a copy of the notice to the garnishee defendant with a preaddressed envelope to the Court which has the cause number displayed thereon and to the garnished party in the same manner as is permitted for service of the writ of garnishment.

(iv) The notice to the federal government employer shall be in substantially the following form:

JEFFERSON COUNTY DISTRICT COURT
STATE OF WASHINGTON

	)	No.
	)	
Plaintiff,	)	NOTICE OF FEDERAL
	)	GOVERNMENT GARNISHEE
vs.	)	DEFENDANT
	)	
Defendant.	)	
	)	
Garnishee Defendant	)	
	)	

TO: THE GOVERNMENT OF THE UNITED STATES AND ANY DEPARTMENT, AGENCY OR DIVISION THEREOF

You have been named as the garnishee defendant in the above-entitled cause. A writ of Garnishment accompanies this Notice. The Writ of Garnishment directs you hold the non-exempt earnings of the above-named defendant, but does not instruct you to disburse the funds you hold.

BY THIS NOTICE THE COURT DIRECTS YOU TO WITHHOLD ALL NON–EXEMPT EARNINGS AND DISBURSE THEM, IN ACCORDANCE WITH YOUR NORMAL PAY AND DISBURSEMENT CYCLE, TO THE FOLLOWING:

( ) Jefferson County District Court
PO Box 1220
Port Townsend WA 98368

Cause #_____

PLEASE REFERENCE THE DEFENDANT EMPLOYEE'S NAME AND THE ABOVE CASE NUMBER ON ALL DISBURSEMENTS.

The following Writ also directs you to respond to the Writ within twenty (20) days, but you are allowed thirty (30) days to respond under federal law.

DATED this _____ day of _____ 19 _____.

_____
Clerk of the Court

[Adopted effective September 1, 1999; amended effective September 1, 2002.]

LCRLJ 79. BOOKS AND RECORDS KEPT BY THE CLERK

(a) Other Books and Records Kept by Clerk.

(1) *Exhibits.* Exhibits shall be kept separate from the Court file. Any inspection of an exhibit must be in the presence of a clerk unless authorized by an order of the Court.

(2) *Rejection of Unsuitable Material.* The Clerk shall not accept for filing in the court file, matters which should be filed as an exhibit or other material not to be included by reason of LCRLJ 5 (d) (6). When the Clerk is uncertain as to whether a matter is suitable for filing, he/she shall seek the advice of the Judge before filing the same.

(3) *Removal of Files.* No file may removed from the Clerk's Office without an order of the Court, except as herein provided; an attorney, legal intern, legal assistant, District Court Probation Officer, may check out a file without a specific order of the court. A person taking a file and failing to return same file by the close of business of the same day the file was checked out, shall lose the privilege of checking out files until the previously taken file is returned. Failure to return the file after notice from the Clerk's' Office of a violation of this rule may result in the imposition of terms or other appropriate sanctions. Any person checking out a file and leaving it with a judge or clerk shall have the duty to correct the check-out record in the Clerk's Office, showing with whom the file was left.

(4) Items Required to be Sealed by the Clerk's Office are as follows:

(i) Alcohol evaluations and reports;

(ii) Mental health evaluations and reports;

(iii) Drug evaluations and reports;

(iv) Pre-trial release evaluations and recommendations; and

(v) Any other item ordered to be sealed by a judge or classified as confidential by statute, rule or regulation (See LARLJ 9).

(vi) Determinations of Indigency.

[Adopted effective September 1, 1999.]

III. CRIMINAL MATTERS
LCrRLJ 1.5. STYLE AND FORM

The format requirements for papers being filed with a court are as specified in GR 14, except exhibits, the citation and notice, and forms approved by the Office of the Administrator for the Courts need not be on letter size paper (81/2 by 11 inches). The citation and notice shall be on a form prescribed or approved by the office of the Administrator for the Courts.

(a) Filing with Court. (See: CrRLJ 8.4(c) and CRLJ 5)

(1) *Action Documents.* Pleadings or other papers requiring action on the part of the Clerk/Court (other than file stamping, docketing and placing in the court file) shall be considered action documents. Action documents shall include a special caption directly below the case number on the first page, stating:

"Clerks Action Required: (here state the action requested)."

(2) *Format Recommendations.* It is recommended that all pleadings and other papers include or provide for the following:

(i) Service and Filing. Space should be provided at top of the first page of a document allowing on the right half for the clerk's filing stamp, and in the left half for proof of, or acknowledgment of, service. The papers should when feasible, such as common pleading or service forms, be pre-drilled or punched at the page top for fastening in court files.

(ii) Numbered Paper. All pleadings, motions, affidavits, briefs, and other supporting documents prepared by attorneys/parties should be on paper with line numbering in the left hand margin.

(3) *Handling by Clerk.* All pleadings or other papers with proper caption and cause number will be date receipted, docketed and secured/placed in the court file by the Clerk of the District Court in the order received.

Example LCrRLJ 1.5

IN THE JEFFERSON COUNTY DISTRICT COURT
IN AND FOR THE STATE OF WASHINGTON

_____)	
PLAINTIFF)	CAUSE NO. XXXXXXX
v.)	CLERK'S ACTION REQUIRED:
)	SET THIS MOTION FOR HEARING
_____)	
DEFENDANT)	MOTION CHALLENGING COMPLAINT SUFFICIENCY

The clerks will *not* search out action items. They will not search through letters, notices of appearance, requests for discovery, or other materials, to locate possible requests for action, such as: preservation of jury trial, or non-waiver of 60/90 day rule (this needs a request to set within the correct time, see CrRLJ 3.3), or concern with witnesses. Amongst CrRLJs impacted by this rule are:

CrRLJ 1.5 Style and Form

CrRLJ 3.3(e) Objection to Arraignment Date

CrRLJ 3.3(f) Setting of Trial Date—Waiver of Objection

CrRLJ 4.3 Joinder of Offenses and Defendants

CrRLJ 4.3.1 Consolidation for Trial

CrRLJ 4.4 Severance of Offenses and Defendants

CrRLJ 4.7 Discovery (regulation of, not requests for)

CrRLJ 4.8 Subpoenas

[Adopted effective September 1, 2012.]

LCrRLJ 2.3. SEARCH AND SEIZURE

(h) Search Warrants. The magistrate authorizing a search warrant shall retain custody and control of the original affidavit for search warrant until such warrant is executed and/or returned unexecuted.

(1) After execution, the search warrant shall be filed by number and description of the person or property to be searched. An index will be maintained and available to the public by the Clerk's Office.

(2) The affidavit and accompanying papers including the return of service shall be filed in accordance with the provisions of CrRLJ 8.10 and ARLJ 9.

[Adopted effective September 1, 1999.]

LCrRLJ 2.5. PROCEDURE ON FAILURE TO OBEY CITATION AND NOTICES TO APPEAR

(a) Recall of Failure to Respond Arrest Warrants. The Court Administrator, or delegate, shall have authority to recall Failure to Respond Arrest Warrants issued because the defendant failed to respond to the citation or a summons under the following provisions:

(1) The Failure to Respond Arrest Warrant has not yet been sent to the Sheriff for entry into the NCIC.

(2) The defendant personally appears at the counter to sign for a court date or appears through counsel, and/or posts bail.

(3) In case of clerical error.

(b) In all other cases, the defendant shall present himself/herself to the Jefferson County Correctional Facility unless directed otherwise by the Court Administrator.

[Adopted effective September 1, 1999.]

LCrRLJ 3.2.   RELEASE OF ACCUSED

(a) Forfeiture. Criminal offenses disposable by bond forfeiture shall be approved by the Judge. Nothing in this rule restricts a case by case disposition of a criminal matter.

(b) Uniform Bail Schedule. The District Court shall follow the bail schedule set forth in CrRLJ 3.2 (o) (u).

(4) Bail for unscheduled misdemeanor shall be $250 unless otherwise set by statute or ordinance.

(5) Bail as set forth in this rule, CrRLJ 3.2 or in any similar rule, shall only be available to defendants who have provided sufficient information to establish a positive and verifiable identity and home address. Absent such information, no bail may be established by court hearing.

(c) Release of Intoxicated Persons. No person issued a citation and/or arrested for the crime of Driving While Intoxicated or Being in Physical Control of a Motor Vehicle While Intoxicated shall be released on bail prior to appearance in court unless:

i.   The person has no known prior alcohol related driving offenses;

ii.   The person has a valid driver's license;

iii.   The person has been under the observation of the jail staff for a minimum of six (6) hours; and

iv.   The release will be during the daylight hours.

If the defendant cannot meet the criteria, he/she shall be held until the next arraignment calendar when the Court will set bail.

(d) Release of Intoxicated Minors. No person issued a citation and/or arrested for the crime of Driver Under Twenty–One Consuming Alcohol shall be released on bail prior to appearance in court unless:

i.   The person has no known prior alcohol related driving offenses;

ii.   The person has been under the observation of the jail staff for a minimum of six (6) hours; and

iii.   The release will be during the daylight hours.

iv.   Person under the age of eighteen shall only released to a parent, legal guardian, or the department of social and health services.

If the defendant cannot meet the criteria, he/she shall be held until the next arraignment calendar when the Court will set bail.

(e) Domestic Violence Offenses.

(1) No person issued a citation and/or arrested for a domestic violence offense shall be released on bail prior to appearance in court. At the time a person is book into jail for a domestic violence offense, a Pre–Arraignment Domestic Violence No Contact Order prohibiting any contact with the protected person, including contact through third parties, shall issue. This order shall terminate at initial appearance or within 72 hours of issuance, whichever is sooner.

"Domestic Violence" includes but is not limited to any of the misdemeanor or gross misdemeanor offenses listed in RCW 10.99.020 (5), or similar municipal ordinance, when committed by one family or household member against another. "Family or household members are those person listed in RCW 10.99.020 (1) or similar municipal ordinance."

(2) No order issued under RCW 10.99.020 and/or RCW 10.99.040 shall be quashed until and unless the victim has successfully completed a Domestic Violence Protection Hearing.

[Adopted effective September 1, 1999. Amended effective September 1, 2002; June 28, 2005; September 1, 2006; September 1, 2015.]

LCrRLJ 3.3.   TIME FOR TRIAL

(e) Pre–Trial Hearings. At arraignment the Judge will schedule a pre-trial hearing. The parties shall confer in good faith prior to the pre-trial hearing in an attempt to reach an agreed disposition. The defendant shall be required to attend the pre-trial hearing unless excused by the Court. Failure to attend may result in issuance of a bench warrant and/or forfeiture of any bond. If the case is not resolved at the pre-trial hearing, a trial date will be set. A readiness hearing shall also be set one week before the trial date. The defendant shall be required to attend the readiness hearing unless excused by the court.

(k) Deferred Prosecution.

(1) Petition for Deferred Prosecution under Section 10.05 of the Revised Code of Washington, shall be filed fourteen (14) days before the date set for trial on forms approved by the Court.

(2) The written assessment prepared by an approved treatment facility shall be accompanied by a recommendation from the Probation Office, or such other Court Appointee authorized under Chapter 10.05 of the Revised Code of Washington.

(3) When the Court denies the Petition for a Deferred Prosecution timely filed under this rule, the case shall proceed to trial as previously set.

(4) In the event the Petition for Deferred Prosecution is approved by the Court, the defendant may be under the supervision of the Probation Department, or Court Appointee pursuant to Section 10.05.170 of the Revised Code of Washington. A defendant who refuses, fails, or neglects to comply with an order, or

request of the Probation Office or Court Appointee, or the terms of supervision, or conditions of supervision, or conditions of deferred prosecution may have the deferred prosecution revoked.

[Adopted effective September 1, 1999. Amended effective September 1, 2015.]

LCrRLJ 4.1. PROCEEDINGS BEFORE THE JUDGE APPEARANCE—BAIL

(e) Appearance by Defendant's Lawyer.

(7) Retained attorneys or public defenders who have assumed representation of defendants must promptly serve written notice of their appearance upon the Prosecuting Attorney, and file the same with the Clerk. The notice of appearance shall be contained in a separate document.

(8) A lawyer may enter an appearance on behalf of a client, except in cases in which the docket or charging document states that one or more of the charges involves DUI, Physical Control, Minor DUI, Reckless Driving, Reckless Endangerment, Assault 4th degree with Sexual Motivation, any Domestic Violence Charge, including, but not limited to, Assault 4th DV, Malicious Mischief DV, Harassment, Violation of an Antiharassment/No Contact Order, Stalking, or Harassment, whereupon the defendant's presence is mandatory and cannot be waived.

(f) Counter–Appearance. A defendant, in response to a Summons and Complaint, Citation and Notice to Appear, or a Jail Release Appearance form may first appear at the District Court clerk's window to obtain an arraignment or Pre–Trial Hearing date if one has not been set and to obtain a Determination of Indigency form for appointment of a public defender.

[Adopted effective September 1, 1999. Amended effective September 1, 2006; September 1, 2015.]

LCrRLJ 4.2. PROCEDURE UPON A PLEA OF GUILTY

(i) Guilty Plea Statement. It shall be the duty of the Defense Attorney to have a properly completed written statement of the defendant on a guilty plea. Forms shall be furnished by the Court Administrator without charge.

[Adopted effective September 1, 1999.]

LCrRLJ 4.5. PRETRIAL HEARING

(a) At arraignment a defendant shall be given a pre-trial date only.

(b) All parties shall be expected to have exchanged discovery. Parties shall discuss the need for hearing any motions, including but not limited to 3.5, 3.6, *Hamrick* and *Knapstad* motions.

(c) At pretrial the parties must resolve the case or advise that the case is ready for trial, at which time, a readiness hearing and trial date will be set.

(d) If an attorney has had no contact with his/her client by the date of the readiness hearing, a warrant shall issue.

[Adopted effective September 1, 1999.]

LCrRLJ 6.3. SELECTING THE JURY

See LCRLJ 38.

(a) In criminal cases set for jury trial, it is mandatory that the attorneys, or defendant in a pro se case, notify the court at readiness hearing whether or not they will proceed to jury trial. If the trial is cancelled at a party's request following readiness hearing but before the time for notification set forth in subsection (b), terms may be assessed against the attorneys in an amount equal to the cost of summoning a jury panel.

(b) In criminal cases set for jury trial, it is mandatory that the attorneys, or parties in a pro se case, notify the court by 3:00 p.m. the day prior to trial whether or not they will proceed to jury trial. The purpose of this requirement is to permit the cancellation of unneeded jury panels and the savings of the costs thereof. If this required communication is not received, terms may be assessed against the attorneys and/or parties.

[Adopted effective September 1, 1999.]

LCrRLJ 6.13. EVIDENCE—COURT'S CUSTODY OF EXHIBITS

(f) In a criminal case every exhibit in the courts custody, which is not contraband and for which ownership is not in dispute, shall be returned to the party who produced that exhibit upon motion of that party and expiration of the appeal period. In the event of a finding of guilty, for purpose of this rule, the appeal period shall begin on the day of sentencing or deferral of sentence by the court. Exhibits not returned shall be delivered by the court to the applicable law enforcement agency for disposition as abandoned property; or if contraband, for destruction.

[Adopted effective September 1, 2002.]

LCrRLJ 7.6. PROBATION FEES

(c) Defendants placed on probation shall pay a fee of up to $1500 unless specified differently by the court in the judgment and sentence or by separate order of the court. If placed on bench probation the fee will be up to $300.

[Adopted effective June 28, 2005. Amended effective September 1, 2015.]

LCrRLJ 8.2. MOTIONS

(a) Motion Day. Motions shall be noted for and will be set the 2nd and 4th Friday of each month unless otherwise authorized by the court.

(b) Filing of Motions, Memoranda, and Affidavits. The content and length of the Note for Hearing,

Brief, Memoranda, and Affidavits are governed by LCRLJ 40 (b).

(c) Copies of Motions, Memoranda and Affidavits. A copy of the motion, brief, memoranda, documents and affidavits shall be furnished to the Judge after the originals have been filed. Responding briefs, memoranda, and other documents shall also be filed with the Clerk, and copies furnished to the assigned Judge. Failure to comply with this requirement may result in a continuance and imposition of terms.

[Adopted effective September 1, 1999. Amended effective June 28, 2005; September 1, 2015.]

IV. INFRACTIONS

LIRLJ 3.3. PROCEDURE AT CONTESTED HEARING

(b) Representation by Lawyer. At a contested hearing, the plaintiff shall be represented by a lawyer, representative of the Prosecuting Attorney, or the City Attorney when the defendant is represented by an attorney.

[Adopted effective September 1, 1999.]

LIRLJ 3.5. DECISION OF WRITTEN STATEMENTS

The procedure authorized by IRLJ 3.5 is adopted by this court.

(f) Scheduling. Upon a request for a hearing, the court shall send the defendant a letter and the appropriate form. Defendant shall return the completed form to the Court. The officer will be sent notice from the Court of the defendant's request and shall submit his/her sworn declaration. The Court will decide the issue from the evidence presented and render its decision in writing by mail.

[Adopted effective September 1, 1999.]

LIRLJ 6.2. MONETARY PENALTY SCHEDULE

(e) Penalty for Unscheduled Infractions and Infractions Not Covered by IRLJ 6.2. A penalty schedule for persons charged with miscellaneous infractions not covered by Supreme Court Rule shall be established by local county or city ordinances.

[Adopted effective September 1, 1999.]

LIRLJ 6.6. SPEED MEASURING DEVICE; DESIGN AND CONSTRUCTION CERTIFICATION

(d) Requests to produce the electronic measuring device expert shall be contained in a separate document and served on the Prosecuting Attorney with a conformed copy filed with the Clerk of the Court.

(e) Maintaining Certificates as Public Records. Any certificate, affidavit or foundational evidentiary document allowed or required by this rule can be filed with the court and maintained by the court as a public record. The records will be available for inspection by the public. Copies will be provided on request. The court may charge any allowable copy fees. The records are available without a formal request for discovery. The court is entitled to take judicial notice of the fact that the document has been filed with the court. Evidence will not be suppressed merely because there is not a representative of the prosecuting authority present who actually offers the document. Evidence shall be suppressed pursuant to IRLJ 6.6(c) if the evidence in the certificate, affidavit or document is insufficient, or if it has not been filed as required.

[Adopted effective September 1, 1999; amended effective September 1, 2000.]

V. SMALL CLAIMS PROCEDURES

LRSC 1. FIRST APPEARANCE

(a) The term "appear" means personal appearance of the parties involved. At the first appearance, an employee or agent (not an attorney) may appear if that employee/agent has the sufficient facts in order to present the case, and is authorized to bind the party represented.

(b) If the plaintiff and defendant both appear on the assigned first appearance date the case will be assigned a mediator and will mediate that same day. Mediation is mandatory before a trial is allowed. Parties must bring their evidence to the mediation, however, no witnesses are allowed. The purpose of mediation is to settle the case if possible; if no settlement is made at mediation, the case will be set for trial. Attorneys and paralegals may not represent parties at mediation. If the parties have already submitted the case to another type of mediation or arbitration service, the case may proceed directly to trial. If agreement is reached the parties will sign an agreement which will be entered into the record. Parties will receive a copy of the agreement. No judgment will be entered. If the agreement is breached, the non-breaching party may return to the court for judgment after serving and filing a motion and affidavit setting forth the failure to comply with the terms of the agreement.

(c) If the plaintiff fails to appear, a dismissal will be entered. In cases where the defendant has filed a written counterclaim against the plaintiff and proof of service is presented, the defendant may be allowed judgment against the Plaintiff on the counterclaim. Oral counterclaims are allowed only if both parties appear at the first hearing, and then only if the counterclaim arises out of the same transaction or event upon which the Plaintiff's claim is based.

(d) If the defendant fails to appear and proof of service is presented, and if the plaintiff's testimony supports the claim, the plaintiff will be granted a default judgment against defendant up to the amount claimed and for costs.

(e) If neither party appears the case will be dismissed without prejudice.

[Adopted effective September 1, 1999.]

LRSC 2. TRIAL

If a trial is necessary, both plaintiff and defendant will appear, testify, call witnesses, and present exhibits for the court to consider. If it is inconvenient or overly expensive to call a witness to appear personally, affidavits of witnesses can be presented. Any affidavit expected to be considered by the court shall be served on the other party at least five (5) days (excluding Saturday, Sunday and Holidays) before the trial. A responsive affidavit may be presented at the trial. Copies of such affidavits must be made available to the other party before the trial commences. A simple "signed statement" will not be considered an affidavit and will not be accepted as evidence. The

same rules apply at this hearing as applied at the first appearance if the parties fail to appear.

[Adopted effective September 1, 1999.]

LRSC 3. CONTINUANCE OF MEDIATION OR SMALL CLAIM TRIAL

The party requesting the continuance must contact the other party who must also agree to the continuance. Both parties must contact the court in person or by telephone. If one party will not agree to the continuance, the party seeking the continuance may make a written motion for continuance and set a hearing date prior to the scheduled mediation or trial date. The motion and notice of hearing must be served on the opposing party not less than five days prior to the date set for the motion to continue. At the hearing, the judge will determine whether the matter will be continued. If there are less than five days prior to the mediation or trial date to serve the opposing party, the party requesting the continuance may contact the court to explain the circumstances which require the mediation or trial to be continued. The matter may be continued by the court upon showing of good cause.

[Adopted effective September 1, 1999.]

LRSC 4. DISCOVERY

Discovery, if any, shall proceed in an informal manner. No formal discovery such as interrogatories, requests for production, and/or depositions shall be permitted without prior written approval of the court.

[Adopted effective September 1, 1999.]

VI. SPECIAL PROCEEDINGS

LRSP 1. NAME CHANGES

(a) Requirements. An applicant who applies to the court for a change of name pursuant to RCW 4.24.130 must meet the following requirements:

(1) *Birth Certificate.* A certified copy of any minor applicant's birth certificate or suitable identification must be presented to the clerk for verification and copying.

(2) *Minors: Parental Consent.* All applicants under eighteen (18) years of age must be represented by a parent or legal guardian, and both biological or legal parents or guardian must approve the change of name either by personal appearance or by verified affidavit.

(3) *Separate Applications.* Each applicant requesting a change of name must present a separate Change of Name Order and pay a separate filing fee and recording fee.

[Adopted effective September 1, 1999.]

LRSP 2. UNLAWFUL HARASSMENT PROCEEDINGS

(a) Jurisdiction. If the circumstances alleged in the petition for unlawful harassment meet the statutory criteria, the court shall hear the case unless the parties are already involved in a pending dissolution, dependency or paternity proceeding in which case the matter shall be transferred to Superior Court. The court may require a petitioner to appear and provide testimony prior to issuance of an ex parte temporary order.

(b) Indigent Filing. Upon request of the applicant, the Court shall assess the applicant's financial resources to determine if that individual may proceed in forma pauperis. For the purpose of determining whether grounds for waiver of the filing fee exist, the applicant must complete under oath and submit an Application For Waiver of Fees. No order authorizing waiver of the filing fee shall issue unless the mandatory financial information is submitted to the Court.

(c) Hearing. In unlawful harassment actions only the parties may testify without cross examination, or make statements as allowed by the court. The court may take testimony if it appears to the court necessary for an adequate determination of the matter. [Adopted effective September 1, 1999.]

KING COUNTY

Table of Courts

Superior Court

Local Rules of the Superior Court for King County.

District Court

Local Rules of the District Court for King County.

Municipal Courts

Auburn Municipal Court Local Rules.
Bellevue Municipal Court—[No Local Rules].
Black Diamond Municipal Court Local Rules.
Bothell Municipal Court Local Rules.
Burien Municipal Court—[No Local Rules].
Carnation Municipal Court—[No Local Rules].
Covington Municipal Court—[No Local Rules].
Des Moines Municipal Court Local Rules.
Duvall Municipal Court—[No Local Rules].
Enumclaw Municipal Court Local Rules.
Federal Way Municipal Court Local Rules.
Issaquah Municipal Court Local Rules.
Kenmore Municipal Court—[No Local Rules].
Kent Municipal Court Local Rules.
Kirkland Municipal Court Local Rules.
Lake Forest Park Municipal Court Local Rules.
Maple Valley Municipal Court Local Rules.
Mercer Island Municipal Court Local Rules.
Normandy Park Municipal Court Local Rules.
North Bend Municipal Court—[No Local Rules].
Pacific/Algona Municipal Court Local Rules.
Redmond Municipal Court—[No Local Rules].
Renton Municipal Court Local Rules.
Sammamish Municipal Court—[No Local Rules].
Seatac Municipal Court Local Rules.
Seattle Municipal Court Local Rules.
Shoreline Municipal Court—[No Local Rules].
Skykomish Municipal Court—[No Local Rules].
Snoqualmie Municipal Court—[No Local Rules].
Tukwila Municipal Court Local Rules.
Woodinville Municipal Court—[No Local Rules].

SUPERIOR COURT
LOCAL RULES OF THE SUPERIOR COURT FOR KING COUNTY

Originally Effective September 1, 1974

**Including Amendments Received Through
August 15, 2015**

Table of Rules

ZERO LOCAL RULES

Zero Local Rules Credit

[Effective September 1, 1986; amended effective July 20, 1990; September 2, 1990; September 3, 1990; September 1, 1993; September 1, 1994; September 1, 1996; November 21, 1996; November 19, 1998; September 1, 2000; April 1, 2003; September 1, 2004; September 1, 2008; September 1, 2010.]

FOREWORD

The Zero Local Rules have been adopted for the internal management and operation of the King County Superior Court in conformance with GR 29.
[Effective September 1, 1986.]

LCR 0.1. DEPARTMENT NUMBER AND SENIORITY

(a) Departments. The Superior Court for King County shall be divided into as many individual numbered departments as there are judges authorized by law. When a judge leaves office, the department number shall be assigned to his or her successor. Each judge in order of seniority may select an unassigned courtroom at such time as the Presiding Judge establishes for assignment of unassigned courtrooms.

(b) Seniority. For matters decided by seniority, such as courtroom assignments, seniority will be determined by length of service on the King County

Superior Court. If a judge has a break in service, the prior period of service on this bench will count for seniority purposes. If more than one judge is sworn in on the same day, seniority will be decided by a means agreed upon by the new judges, or, if they cannot agree, by lot.

(c) **Assignments.** The assignment of department numbers and courtrooms whenever necessary, shall be incorporated into an order signed by the Presiding Judge and filed with the Clerk.

(d) **Report to County Election Department.** Before the time for filing a declaration of candidacy for superior court judge, the Presiding Judge will report to the County Election Department the departmental numbers of the positions to be filled. The position numbers on the ballot shall be the assigned departmental numbers.

[Amended effective September 1, 2008.]

LCR 0.2.   COURT MANAGEMENT

(a) **Authority.** The authority to manage and conduct the court is vested in the superior court judges and shall be exercised through regular monthly or special meetings of the judges. Judges have the final authority over any matters pertaining to court organization and operation and over any individual or committee of the court, except as indicated below.

(b) **Judges' Meetings.** Regular meetings shall be held once a month. Special meetings may be called by the Presiding Judge as needed. A quorum shall consist of one-third of the judges of the bench. Meetings of the judges and of the Executive Committee shall be conducted under Robert's Rules of Order, where not inconsistent with these rules. The Presiding Judge shall chair the meetings. The Presiding Judge shall preside from the Maleng Regional Justice Center for the February, April, June, August, October and December meetings, unless one of the extended judges' meetings is scheduled for a month in which the meeting would otherwise be held at the Maleng Regional Justice Center. At least three times a year, the judges meeting shall be scheduled for an entire afternoon, with the expectation that all judges will attend in person.

(c) **Majority of Judges.** Except where these rules specify otherwise, decisions shall be made by a majority of judges who are in attendance at a meeting.

(d) **Executive Session.** The Judges or the Executive Committee may, by majority vote, enter executive session to discuss matters involving personnel and pending, impending and potential litigation, or other matters deemed confidential for purposes of the attorney-client privilege. A motion to enter executive session shall set forth the purpose of the executive session, which shall be included in the general minutes. The motion shall state specifically the purpose for the closed session. Reference to the motion and the stated purpose for the closed session shall be included

in the general session minutes. The presiding judge shall restrict the consideration of matters during the closed portions of meetings only to those purposes specifically exempted and stated in the motion. The presiding judge shall designate the Chief Administrative Officer or a member present to take minutes, which shall be kept separately from the minutes of the regular meeting.

[Amended effective September 1, 2008. Amended effective September 1, 2010.]

LCR 0.3.   DIVISION OF MANAGEMENT AUTHORITY

(a) **Powers and Duties of the Judges.**

(1) Elect and remove at-large members of the Executive Committee.

(2) Elect and remove a Presiding Judge.

(3) Elect and remove an Assistant Presiding Judge.

(4) Appoint and remove commissioners.

(5) Attend judges' meetings.

(6) Attend committee meetings.

(7) Create and dissolve standing committees.

(8) Create and abolish departments. See LCR 0.7

(9) *Enact Local Rules.* Local rules shall be enacted only by a majority of all judges of the court. See CR 83.

(10) Adopt policies that govern or provide guidelines for management of the court.

(11) Adopt general policies for the assignment of cases and judges, as recommended by the Presiding Judge and Executive Committee.

(12) Approve the budget of the court.

(13) Review of decisions made by the Executive Committee when such decisions are not otherwise reserved to the judges as a whole: If four members of the Executive Committee vote to refer the matter for decision by the judges as a whole, the decision shall be referred to the judges for final decision at the next regular judges' meeting. Attend and participate in a meeting of the Executive Committee, if a judge chooses to do so. Only judges who are members of the Executive Committee, except a committee chair under LCR 0.5(e), may vote.

(14) Participate in administration of the court consistent with CJC 3(B)(1).

(b) **Powers and Duties of Presiding Judge.**

(1) Lead the management and administration of the court's business, recommend policies and procedures that improve the court's effectiveness, and allocate financial resources in a way that maximizes the court's ability to resolve disputes fairly and expeditiously.

(2) Serve as the spokesperson for the court in all dealings with the executive and legislative branches

and with the media. If the matter is of such a nature that the Presiding Judge requires advice and counsel, he/she shall contact the members of the Executive Committee, if possible under the circumstances.

(3) Call such special meetings of the judges and Executive Committee as may be required.

(4) Assign judicial officers to calendars, departments and special calendars to hear cases and other matters pursuant to general policies established by the judges of the court.

(5) Assign judicial officers to the various special and standing committees of the court and appoint the chairperson of such committees.

(6) Assign Judges to the King County Superior Court Facilities. In making these assignments, the Presiding Judge shall consider all relevant factors including the willingness of a judge to serve, the need for diversity, and what assignments will be in the best interest of the court as a whole.

(7) Select, in consultation with the Executive Committee, the chief judges of the juvenile, civil, criminal and unified family court departments and of the Maleng Regional Justice Center.

(8) Coordinate the vacations and educational leaves of judicial officers.

(9) Approve exceptions to the duty-time policy.

(10) Serve as the direct supervisor of the court commissioners, subject to delegation to other judges as appropriate.

(11) Supervise all personnel under the judicial branch, including the Chief Administrative Officer and the Director of the Department of Judicial Administration.

(12) With the assistance of the Chief Administrative Office and Director of the Department of Judicial Administration, develop and coordinate statistical and management information.

(13) Ensure that the annual training on record keeping is held, as required by LCR 0.09(g).

(14) Supervise the preparation and filing of reports required by statute and court rules.

(15) Perform such other duties as are provided in these rules, or as are assigned by a majority of the judges.

(c) Powers and Duties of the Assistant Presiding Judge.

(1) Serve as Acting Presiding Judge during the absence or upon the request of the Presiding Judge.

(2) Perform such further duties as these rules, the Presiding Judge, Executive Committee or a majority of the judges shall direct.

(d) Powers and Duties of the Executive Committee.

(1) Decide matters of policy affecting the court, not reserved to the judges as a whole. Decisions shall be final unless referred to the judges as a whole pursuant to sec. (a)(13) of this rule. Provided, however, that decisions involving urgent matters may be implemented after notice to the judges.

(2) Make recommendations on policy matters to the judges at any meeting of the judges.

(3) Recommend the designation and duties of the committees of the court and receive reports and recommendations from committees. Whenever matters to be considered by the Executive Committee concern the work of another committee, the chair of that committee shall be notified of the meeting and shall be considered a member of the Executive Committee for the limited purpose of voting on such matter.

(4) Act in an advisory capacity to the Presiding Judge.

(5) Review and advise the Presiding Judge concerning his or her decision, in the capacity of Presiding Judge, to report a judge or commissioner to the Judicial Conduct Commission.

(6) Determine whether disciplinary action of a commissioner, short of termination, is appropriate.

(7) Approve an expenditure budget and review and approve actual unfunded items.

(8) Determine the general qualifications of and establish a training program for pro tem judges and pro tem court commissioners. Training may be delegated to the relevant standing committee.

(9) Conduct the annual performance review of the Chief Administrative Officer and the Director of Judicial Administration.

(10) Meet at least once a month and provide written agenda and timely notice of the regular Executive Committee meetings to all judges and commissioners. If attachments are available in electronic form, they shall be distributed with the agenda.

(11) Promptly distribute to the judges written minutes of action taken by the Executive Committee.

(12) In the absence of the Presiding and Assistant Presiding Judge, the senior member of the Executive Committee shall serve as Acting Presiding Judge.

[Amended effective September 1, 2008; September 1, 2010; September 1, 2015.]

LCR 0.4. QUALIFICATIONS FOR PRESIDING OR ASSISTANT PRESIDING JUDGE

Only those judges who have served for at least four years as a member of the King County Superior Court bench are eligible to be elected Presiding Judge or Assistant Presiding Judge.

[Amended effective September 1, 2008.]

LCR 0.5. MEMBERSHIP OF THE EXECUTIVE COMMITTEE

(a) The Presiding Judge and Assistant Presiding Judge shall serve as members of the Executive Committee.

(b) The immediate past Presiding Judge shall serve as a member of the Executive Committee for the year following the judge's service as Presiding Judge.

(c) The chief judges of the juvenile, civil, criminal and unified family court departments and of the Maleng Regional Justice Center shall serve as members of the Executive Committee.

(d) There shall be six additional members of the Executive Committee (seven if there is no immediate past Presiding Judge) elected at large. The member elected to fill the seventh position, in the absence of an immediate past Presiding Judge, shall be elected for a one year term, as determined by lot drawn from all newly elected members.

(e) When the Executive Committee is considering a report or recommendation made by a committee, the chair of that committee shall be invited to attend the meeting and may vote on issues pertaining to that committee.

[Amended effective September 1, 2008. Amended effective September 1, 2010.]

LCR 0.6. ELECTIONS

(a) General Provisions. Each elected position (Presiding Judge, Assistant Presiding, and Executive Committee) shall be handled by a separate election. The procedures set forth below shall be undertaken separately for each position in the following order: Presiding Judge, Assistant Presiding Judge and members of the Executive Committee.

(b) Terms of Office.

(1) The Presiding Judge shall serve a three-year term. The term shall commence on January 1 of the year in which the Presiding Judge's term begins.

(2) The Assistant Presiding Judge shall serve a one-year term, commencing on January 1. A candidate for Assistant Presiding Judge who wishes to serve in year three of the term of the Presiding Judge shall indicate an intention to seek the position of Presiding Judge for the following term.

(3) The elected members of the Executive Committee shall serve a two-year term. The terms are to be staggered such that approximately half the elected members are chosen in odd-numbered years and half in even-numbered years. Terms shall commence on January 1.

(c) Solicitation of Candidate. Prior to each election, a questionnaire shall be circulated to every judge to determine whether that judge wishes to be a candidate for the position at issue. The solicitation for the position of Presiding Judge shall occur no later than October 1 of the year in which a Presiding Judge is to be elected. Immediately after a Presiding Judge has been elected, candidates for the position of Assistant Presiding Judge shall be solicited and an election for that position shall be held. Immediately after the election of an Assistant Presiding Judge, candidates for the Executive Committee shall be solicited. The questionnaire for each position shall include a description of the election process and the deadline by which the questionnaire must be returned.

(d) Candidate Information. A list of all judges who have responded affirmatively to the questionnaire shall be available from the Chief Administrative Officer throughout the nomination process. One week prior to the deadline for returning the questionnaires, the Chief Administrative Officer shall provide each judge with a list of all persons who have answered affirmatively regarding the race in question.

(e) Reconsideration of Previously Submitted Questionnaire. Up until the deadline for returning questionnaires, a judge may withdraw a previously submitted questionnaire and re-submit a new questionnaire indicating whether that judges wishes to be a candidate for the position in question.

(f) Distribution of Ballots. Except where there is only one candidate for a position, ballots will be immediately circulated to all judges after the deadline for returning the questionnaire for that position has passed. Each judge shall return the ballot in the time allotted. Voting may be by absentee ballot when necessary.

(g) Counting. Ballots shall be counted by the three most junior judges present at the King County Courthouse on the first judicial day following the return date specified in the ballot.

(h) Run-off Elections. A candidate who receives a majority of votes cast shall be elected. If one candidate does not receive a majority of votes cast, there shall be a run-off election.

(i) Single Candidate. When only one candidate has submitted his or her name for consideration, that candidate shall be deemed elected without the need for the distribution and counting of ballots.

(j) Vacancies. If a judge who has been elected to any office resigns from office or is otherwise unable to complete a term, the Presiding Judge shall promptly establish an election process consistent with the method provided in these rules.

[Amended effective September 1, 2008. Amended effective September 1, 2010.]

LCR 0.7. SPECIAL DEPARTMENTS

(a) Special Departments. Special departments of the court shall be established and assigned such business as is provided by law, by rules adopted by the Supreme Court or Washington State Superior Court Judges' Association (RCW 2.08.230), by these rules, or by the Presiding Judge. The following special departments are established:

(1) Presiding Judge's Department

(2) Unified Family Court Department

(3) Juvenile Court Department

(4) Ex Parte and Probate Department

(5) Criminal Department

(6) Civil Department

(b) Assignment of Judicial Officers. The Presiding Judge shall assign each judicial officer to one of the special departments to facilitate the efficient assignment of cases and motions. However, all judges shall have full authority to hear any case properly filed in King County Superior Court, regardless of that judge's regular departmental assignment. No judge may reject a case assignment on the basis of departmental assignment.

(c) Departmental Manuals. Departments may maintain and develop departmental policy manuals. The manuals shall be updated as needed by the Chief Judge of the department, with any major policy changes to be approved by the Executive Committee.

[Amended effective September 1, 2008; September 1, 2010.]

LCR 0.8. CHIEF JUDGES

(a) Selection. The Presiding Judge, in consultation with the Executive Committee, shall select a chief judge of the following special departments: Civil, Criminal, Juvenile and Unified Family Court and the Chief Judge of the Maleng Regional Justice Center. A presiding judge shall select chief judges only for the year in which the Presiding Judge holds office.

(b) Term. Each chief judge shall serve a term of twelve months, beginning January 1. The judge may be reappointed for successive one-year terms, in accordance with LR 0.8(a).

[Amended effective September 1, 2008; September 1, 2010.]

LCR 0.9. STANDING AND SPECIAL COMMITTEES

(a) Standing Committees. There shall be the following standing committees of judges and commissioners:

(1) *ADR:* Oversee and make recommendations concerning the mandatory arbitration program and other court-annexed alternate dispute resolution programs

(2) *Security, Construction and Facilities:* Develop policies to ensure the safety and security of all courthouse users. Assist in planning for court facilities; make recommendations about maintenance and upgrading of facilities; monitor construction of facilities.

(3) *Courts and Community:* Promote public understanding of the justice system through public presentations, teaching, and community events; strive to eliminate barriers to justice that may result from

differences in culture, economic status, language, and physical or mental disabilities; ensure that the court's commitment to a diverse workforce is reflected in its policies.

(4) *Ex Parte/Probate:* Work with Ex Parte Commissioners to oversee the ex parte calendars and the handling of probate matters. The Ex Parte committee shall be chaired by the Chief Civil Judge.

(5) *Family Law:* Oversee and make recommendations concerning the handling of family law matters. The Family Law committee shall be chaired by the Chief Judge of the Unified Family Court.

(6) *Interpreter:* Oversee and make recommendations concerning the work of the court's interpreter staff.

(7) *Local Rules:* Review existing rules and suggest new rules as appropriate based on changes in the law or court procedures.

(8) *Jury:* Make recommendations as to policies concerning jurors.

(9) *Mental Health Committee:* Oversee and make recommendations for the handling of the civil commitment calendar.

(10) *Sealed Files/Adoption:* Oversee and make recommendations concerning the court's handling of sealed files and adoptions and review requests made by persons who wish to review a sealed adoption file or who need copies of documents in a file or an original from the department of vital statistics.

(11) *Technology:* Plan for use of technology in the court including computer and video, and make recommendations about hardware, software and staffing.

(12) *Self-Represented Parties (Pro Se):* Identify procedural and substantive barriers faced by self-represented civil litigants and mitigate those barriers through education, programs and procedures.

(b) Administrative Committees. The Presiding Judge shall appoint the following committees:

(1) *Audit:* Develop procedures for and approve expenditures of county funds for indigent litigants subject to the provisions of King County Local Rule 98.50–Sexually Violent Predator–Office of Public Defense and King County Local Criminal Rule 3.1(f)–Right to and Assignment of Counsel–Services Other than Counsel.

(2) *Budget:* Draft and recommend to the Court a budget for adoption by the judges.

(3) *Personnel:* Develop personnel policies for adoption by the court.

(c) Special Committees. The Presiding Judge may appoint such special committees as he/she may deem advisable and for a term to be set by the Presiding Judge. Special committees have a duty to study and make recommendations to the Presiding Judge in connection with any subject matters assigned to them. As needed, the Presiding Judge shall convene a long-range planning committee as a special committee.

(d) Departmental, Maleng Regional Justice Center, Special Calendar Committees. The Criminal, Civil, Mental Illness, Unified Family Court, and Juvenile Departments, and the Maleng Regional Justice Center shall each have a committee that shall include all of the judges assigned to that department, special calendar or facility.

(e) Appointment of Committee Chairs and Members. The Presiding Judge in December of each year shall solicit from each judge and commissioner committee preferences and thereafter appoint the chair and members of each committee, effective January 1. Any judge or commissioner may join any standing or departmental/special calendar committee.

(f) Duties. Standing, administrative, and departmental/special calendar committees shall have the responsibilities outlined above and shall carry out specific assignments from the Presiding Judge or the Executive Committee. By March 1 each committee chair shall submit to the Executive Committee the goals that the committee will seek to accomplish that year. At the end of each year each committee shall report to the Executive Committee concerning the work of the committee during the year, and shall make recommendations concerning additional matters the committee should address in the future. Committees shall keep minutes of meetings, and the chair shall include an agenda with the written notice of meetings.

(g) Training on Record Keeping: Each year, the court, by February 15, shall conduct a training concerning the taking of minutes and other record-keeping duties of committees which shall be attended by the chairpersons of all committees and assigned staff.

[Amended effective September 1, 2008; September 1, 2010; September 1, 2012.]

LCR 0.10. COMMISSIONERS

(a) Appointment. Court commissioners shall be appointed by the judges and serve at the pleasure of the judges.

(b) Recruitment. The judges may select a commissioner for a vacant position by transferring another commissioner to the vacant position, by appointing from the eligibility list or by conducting an open selection process. In the event that an open selection process is to be utilized, the Chief Administrative Officer shall advertise the vacancy in state and local bar publications and accept applications from attorneys.

(c) Selection Committee. There shall be a special committee appointed by the Presiding Judge vested with the responsibility for conducting investigations and interviews as it deems appropriate. Any judge or commissioner may attend and participate, and any judge may attend, participate and vote as a member of the Selection Committee in this selection process, so long as this judge has attended all meetings and interviews. The Selection Committee may submit a list of names of applicants to the screening committees of the various bar associations for evaluations to be completed within 45 days. The Selection Committee shall make a report and recommendation to the Executive Committee, which shall make a recommendation to the judges.

(d) Final Selection. The selection of a commissioner shall be made by a majority vote of the judges meeting in executive session. Upon receiving a recommendation from the Selection Committee and the Executive Committee, the judges by a majority vote may transfer a commissioner to a vacant court commissioner's position without considering other candidates.

(e) Eligibility List. After the selection of a commissioner pursuant to the procedure established above, there shall be an "eligibility list" maintained for three years by the Chief Administrative Officer. The list shall contain the names and all related information of applicants considered in accordance with the above-described procedure. If the court needs to appoint another commissioner during the three-year period that the list is maintained, the judges, upon receiving a recommendation from the Selection Committee and Executive Committee, may appoint someone from that list. The court may also supplement this eligibility list, at any time, through an open recruitment process, in the absence of a specific Commissioner position vacancy.

(f) Performance Review. Performance reviews shall be conducted by the Personnel Committee in consultation with the relevant standing committee. The conclusions of the review shall be provided to the members of the Executive Committee and to the commissioner.

(g) Retirement. Commissioners shall retire at the same age at which state law requires judges to retire.

(h) Disciplinary Process. The Presiding Judge and the Executive Committee shall determine whether disciplinary action, short of termination, is appropriate. A commissioner may not be terminated without the consent of the judges as a whole.

(i) Annual Report. Commissioners shall file an annual report with the Presiding Judge by April 15 of each year in a format specified by the Executive Committee. The reports may be reviewed by the Commissioner Performance Review Committee as necessary.

[Amended effective September 1, 2007; September 1, 2008; September 1, 2012; September 1, 2015.]

LCR 0.11. PRO TEMPORE JUDGES AND PRO TEMPORE COMMISSIONERS

(a) Pro Tempore Judges and Pro Tempore Commissioners. The Presiding Judge, with the advice of the relevant standing committees, shall be responsible for the selection of pro tem judges and pro tem commissioners and shall ensure that such pro tem judges and pro tem commissioners are properly trained.

Pro tem judges and pro tem commissioners:

(1) Serve at the pleasure of the Presiding Judge and Executive Committee. A pro tem judge or pro tem commissioner shall work fewer than nine hundred ten (910) hours in a calendar year, except for Term Limited appointments. The pro tem judge, or pro tem commissioner, or the Court may terminate an appointment as pro tem judge or pro tem commissioner at any time without cause or prior notice.

(2) Are not subject to the Court's personnel rules or any other employee handbook except for policies that *explicitly apply* to pro tem judges and pro tem commissioners.

(3) Are not eligible for leave, overtime pay, medical or retirement benefits or any other employment-related benefits.

(4) May be required to attend training pertaining to the particular services being provided. Attendance at a Court-required training is mandatory and a condition of continued placement as a pro tem judge or pro tem commissioner.

(b) Assignments. The Court has the discretion to make calendar assignments and to change assignments.

[Adopted effective September 1, 2007; amended effective September 1, 2008; September 1, 2010.]

LCR 0.12. CHIEF ADMINISTRATIVE OFFICER

(a) Appointment. The Chief Administrative Officer shall be appointed by a majority of all of the judges and serve at the pleasure of the judges. Under the direction and supervision of the Presiding Judge, the specific powers and duties of the Chief Administrative Officer include, but are not limited to, the following:

(1) Administer all non-judicial activities of the court, including case setting and the utilization of jurors.

(2) Employ, assign, supervise and direct the work of the employees of the court except the commissioners, special masters, referees, and each judge's bailiff.

(3) Prepare and administer the budget of the court.

(4) Stay abreast of current best practices in court administration and advise the Presiding Judge of potential changes to current court policies.

(5) In consultation with the Presiding Judge, implement the court's strategic plan and provide leadership and continuity in court initiatives.

(6) Represent the court in dealings with the state Administrative Office of the Courts.

(7) Assist the Presiding Judge in representing the court on all management matters in dealing with governmental bodies, and other public and private groups having a reasonable interest in the administration of the court.

(8) Prepare the agenda, arrange, attend and act as recording secretary for judges' meetings, and for those committee meetings where the Chief Administrative Officer's presence would be reasonable and productive.

(9) Prepare an annual report to the court.

(b) Vacancy. Upon a vacancy in the office of Chief Administrative Officer, the Executive Committee shall recruit qualified applicants for the position. This may include appointment of a special committee. The Executive and Special Committee will interview and screen candidates for the position, and shall present no more than three final candidates to the judges for their review and consideration. The candidate receiving a majority vote of all of the judges shall be named to the vacancy.

[Renumbered from LR 0.11 effective September 1, 2007; amended effective September 1, 2008; September 1, 2010.]

LCR 0.13. DIRECTOR OF JUDICIAL ADMINISTRATION

(a) Appointment. The Director of Judicial Administration shall be appointed by a majority of all of the judges and serve at the pleasure of the judges. Under the direction and supervision of the Presiding Judge, the specific powers and duties of the Director of Judicial Administration include, but are not limited to, the following:

(1) Administer the Department of Judicial Administration, including the maintaining of the official court files, (including those maintained in electronic form), records and indexes necessary for the efficient administration of justice and the court system, and supervising the performance of such other duties assigned to the department by the Presiding Judge or a majority of the judges.

(2) Employ, assign, supervise and direct the work of the employees of the Department of Judicial Administration.

(3) Assist the Presiding Judge in representing the court in dealing with governmental bodies, and other public and private groups having a reasonable interest in the record keeping of the court.

(4) Prepare a report for and attend judges' meetings and attend those committee meetings where the

presence of the Director of Judicial Administration would be reasonable and productive.

(5) Prepare an annual report to the court concerning the activities of the department.

(b) Vacancy. Upon a vacancy in the office of Director of Judicial Administration, the Executive Committee shall recruit qualified applicants for the position. This may include appointment of a special committee. The Executive and Special Committees will interview and screen candidates for the position, and shall present no more than three final candidates to the judges for their review and consideration. The candidate receiving a majority vote of all of the judges shall be named to the vacancy.

[Renumbered from LR 0.12 effective September 1, 2007; amended effective September 1, 2008.]

LCR 0.14. BAILIFFS

Each judge shall be limited to one bailiff and shall appoint and supervise his or her own bailiff. The bailiff shall serve at the pleasure of the judge.

In the absence of the judge, and unless assigned to other duties by the judge, the bailiff shall be supervised by the Chief Administrative Officer. The Chief Administrative Officer shall appoint and supervise as many additional general bailiffs as are needed.

[Renumbered from LR 0.13 effective September 1, 2007; amended effective September 1, 2008; September 1, 2010.]

LCR 0.15. SELECTION OF MEMBERS TO THE BOARD OF TRUSTEES OF THE SUPERIOR COURT JUDGES ASSOCIATION

(a) Membership. Each judge is a member of the Superior Court Judges Association established by RCW 2.16.010.

(b) Board of Trustees. Two judges shall serve as members of the Board of Trustees of the Superior Court Judges Association as representatives of Association District No. 1. The two representatives shall serve staggered terms of three years, commencing at the close of the Annual Spring Meeting of the Association at which the member is elected.

(c) Method of Selection. In the year preceding the election of a District No. 1 Board member and after the election of the Executive Committee, a questionnaire shall be circulated soliciting candidates for the position of nominee for District No. 1 Board member. Voting and election of such nominee shall proceed as set forth in Rule 0.6. In case of a vacancy, and on the request of the Board of Trustees, the same election procedure shall be followed.

(d) Notification to Association. Upon conclusion of the balloting procedure set forth in (c) above, the Presiding Judge shall notify the President–Judge of the Association of the name of the judge elected and request that such name be transmitted to the nominating committee of the association with the recommendation that such name be submitted to the membership at the next Annual Spring Meeting of the association as the nominee for the Association District No. 1 position on the Board of Trustees.

[Renumbered from LR 0.14 effective September 1, 2007; amended effective September 1, 2008.]

LCR 0.16. PILOT PROJECTS

Pilot projects in King County Superior Court shall operate through published procedures approved by the Presiding Judge and the Executive Committee.

[Renumbered from LR 0.15 effective September 1, 2007; amended effective September 1, 2008.]

LCR 0.17. INVESTIGATIONS BY THE JUDICIAL CONDUCT COMMISSION: ACCESS TO SEALED FILES AND DOCUMENTS

(a) Confidential Use: Upon request, the clerk of the court shall provide copies of or otherwise describe the contents of sealed files to a representative of the State Commission on Judicial Conduct, who is conducting a confidential investigation pursuant to WA Const. Art. IV sec. 31.

(b) Public Use: No materials in a sealed file may be made public, unless the Commission has first obtained an order pursuant to GR 15 and LR 79(d)(5). Motions to obtain such an order shall be made to the Presiding Judge.

[Renumbered from LR 0.16 effective September 1, 2007.]

LOCAL RULES CONFORMING TO CR RULES AS REQUIRED BY CR 83

I. INTRODUCTORY (Rules 1-2A)

LCR 1. INTRODUCTION

[Reserved]

[Adopted effective September 1, 2001; amended effective September 1, 2004; removed effective September 1, 2008.]

II. COMMENCEMENT OF ACTION: SERVICE OF PROCESS, PLEADINGS, MOTIONS AND ORDERS

LCR 3. COMMENCEMENT OF ACTION

(No Local Rule)

[Deleted effective September 1, 1993.]

LCR 4. CIVIL CASE SCHEDULE

(a) **Case Schedule.** Except as otherwise provided in these rules or ordered by the Court, when an initial pleading is filed and a new civil case file is opened, the Clerk will prepare and file a scheduling order (referred to in these rules as a "Case Schedule"). When an initial pleading is filed electronically the Clerk will provide an electronic copy to the party filing the initial pleading. When an initial pleading is filed in paper form the Clerk will provide two copies to the party filing the initial pleading.

(b) **Cases not Governed by a Case Schedule.** Unless otherwise ordered by the Court, the following cases will not be issued a Case Schedule on filing:

(1) Change of name;

(2) Domestic violence protection (RCW chapter 26.50);

(3) Anti-harassment protection (RCW chapter 10.14);

(4) Uniform Reciprocal Enforcement of Support Act (URESA) and Uniform Interstate Family Support Act (UIFSA). See LFLR 5;

(5) Unlawful detainer;

(6) Foreign judgment;

(7) Abstract or transcript of judgment;

(8) Petition for Writ of Habeas Corpus, Mandamus, Restitution, or Review, or any other Writ;

(9) Civil commitment;

(10) Proceedings under RCW chapter 10.77;

(11) Proceedings under RCW chapter 70.96A;

(12) Proceedings for isolation and quarantine;

(13) Vulnerable adult protection (RCW 74.34);

(14) Proceedings referred to referee under RCW 4.48. See LCR 53.1;

(15) Adoptions;

(16) Sexual Assault protection (RCW 7.90)

(17) Emancipation of a Minor. See LFLR 18;

(18) Will Contests, Probate and TEDRA Matters;

(19) Marriage Age Waiver Petitions. See LFLR 19;

(20) Receivership Proceedings (filed as an independent action and not under an existing proceeding);

(21) Work Permits;

(22) Small Claims Appeals;

(23) Petition to Approve Minor/Incapacitated Adult Settlement (when filed as an independent action and not under an existing proceeding).

(c) **Service of Case Schedule on Other Parties.**

(1) The party filing the initial pleading shall promptly provide a copy of the Case Schedule to all other parties by (a) serving a copy of the Case Schedule on the other parties along with the initial pleading, or (b) serving the Case Schedule on the other parties within 10 days after the later of the filing of the initial pleading or service of any response to the initial pleading, whether that response is a notice of appearance, an answer, or a CR 12 motion. The Case Schedule may be served by regular mail, or electronically when the party being served has agreed to accept electronic service pursuant to GR 30(b)(4), with proof of service to be filed promptly in the form required by CR 5.

(2) A party who joins an additional party in an action shall serve the additional party with the current Case Schedule together with the first pleading served on the additional party.

(d) **Amendment of Case Schedule.** The Court, either on motion of a party or on its own initiative, may modify any date in the Case Schedule for good cause, except that the trial date may be changed only as provided in LCR 40(e). If a party by motion requests an amendment of the Case Schedule, that party shall prepare and present to the Court for signature an Amended Case Schedule, which upon approval of the Court shall be promptly filed and served on all other parties. The motion shall include a proposed Amended Case Schedule. If a Case Schedule is modified on the Court's own motion, the Court will prepare and file the Amended Case Schedule and promptly issue it to all parties. Parties may not amend a Case Schedule by stipulation without approval of the assigned Judge, except as provided below:

(1) The Deadline for Disclosure of Possible Primary Witnesses and/or the deadline for Disclosure of Additional Witnesses (LCR 26 (b)) may be extended by written stipulation of all parties without the necessity of a court order for an additional period not to exceed 14 days without first applying for approval of the assigned judge, provided that the stipulation contains the following provision: "No party may assert this delay in the Disclosure of Witnesses as a basis for a continuance of the established trial date".

(2) The Discovery Cutoff (LCR 37(g)) may be extended by written stipulation of all parties without the

necessity of a court order for an additional period not
to exceed 14 days without first applying for approval
of the assigned judge, provided that the stipulation
contains the following provision: "No party may assert this extension of the Discovery Cutoff as a basis
for a continuance of the established trial date".

(e) Form of Case Schedule.

(1) *Case Schedule.* A Case Schedule for each type
of case, which will set the time period between filing
and trial and the scheduled events and deadlines for
that type of case, will be established by the Court by
General Order, based upon relevant factors including
statutory priorities, resources available to the Court,
case filings, and the interests of justice.

(2) A Case Schedule, which will be customized for
each type of case, will be in generally the following
form:

Filing:	0
Confirmation of Issues (LFLR 4(c) for disso-	F+16
lution and modification cases):	
Status Conference, if needed (Domestic Re-	F+20
lations cases only-see LFLR 4(e)):	
Confirmation of Joinder (LCR 4.2(a) for civil	F+23
cases):	
Last Day for Filing Statement of Arbitrabili-	F+23
ty without a Showing of Good Cause for	
Late Filing (LMAR 2.1):	
Confirmation of Completion of Genetic Test-	F+34
ing (LFLR 4(d) for paternity cases):	
Disclosure of Possible Primary Witnesses	T-22
(LCR 26(b)):	
Disclosure of Possible Additional Witnesses	T-16
(LCR 26(b)):	
Final Date to Change Trial and to File Jury	T-14
Demand (non-family law civil cases)(LCR	
38(b)(2)):	
Discovery Cutoff (LCR 37(g)):	T-7
Deadline for Engaging in Alternative Dis-	T-4
pute Resolution:	
Deadline for filing "Joint Confirmation Re-	T-3
garding Trial Readiness" (LCR 16):	
Exchange of Witness and Exhibit Lists and	T-3
Documentary Exhibits(LCR 4(j)):	
Deadline for Hearing Dispositive Pretrial	T-2
Motions (LCR 56, CR 56):	
Deadline for filing Trial Briefs, Proposed	T-1
Findings of Fact and Conclusions of Law	
and Jury Instructions:	
Joint Statement of Evidence (LCR 4(k)):	T-1
Trial:	T

IT IS ORDERED that all parties shall comply with
the foregoing schedule and that sanctions, including
but not limited to those set forth in CR 37, may be
imposed for noncompliance. IT IS FURTHER OR-
DERED that the party filing this action must serve
this Order Setting Case Schedule on all other parties.

Dated: _____ _____

Judge

I understand that a copy of this document must be
given to all parties: _____ (Signature)

Note: a number in the right column preceded by an
"F" refers to the number of weeks after filing; a
number in the right column preceded by a "T" refers
to the number of weeks before trial.

(f) Monitoring. At such times as the Presiding
Judge may direct, the Clerk will monitor cases to
determine compliance with these rules.

(g) Enforcement; Sanctions; Dismissal; Terms.

(1) Failure to comply with the Case Schedule may
be grounds for imposition of sanctions, including dismissal, or terms.

(2) The Court, on its own initiative or on motion of
a party, may order an attorney or party to show cause
why sanctions or terms should not be imposed for
failure to comply with the Case Schedule established
by these rules.

(3) If the Court finds that an attorney or party has
failed to comply with the Case Schedule and has no
reasonable excuse, the Court may order the attorney
or party to pay monetary sanctions to the Court, or
terms to any other party who has incurred expense as
a result of the failure to comply, or both; in addition,
the Court may impose such other sanctions as justice
requires.

(4) As used with respect to the Case Schedule,
"terms" means costs, attorney fees, and other expenses incurred or to be incurred as a result of the
failure to comply; the term "monetary sanctions"
means a financial penalty payable to the Court; the
term "other sanctions" includes but is not limited to
the exclusion of evidence.

(h) Failure to Follow Schedule. The court may
enter an order of dismissal without prejudice and
without further notice for failure to attend a status
conference required by these rules as designated on
the Case Schedule or to appear in response to the
order to show cause issued for failure to appear for a
status conference. In family law cases where the
parties have agreed upon a final disposition, the dismissal may be set aside by an Ex Parte Commissioner.

(i) Failure to Appear on Scheduled Trial Date.

(1) The failure of a party seeking affirmative relief
or asserting an affirmative defense to appear for trial
on the scheduled trial date will result in dismissal of
the claims or affirmative defenses without further
notice.

(2) If the party against whom claims are asserted
fails to appear, the party seeking relief must proceed
with the trial on the record. Unless final orders are
entered at the time of trial, the party shall file their
proposed final documents within thirty days of the
trial decision.

(j) Exchange of Witness and Exhibit Lists. In
cases governed by a Case Schedule pursuant to LCR
4, the parties shall exchange, no later than 21 days

before the scheduled trial date: (A) lists of the witnesses whom each party expects to call at trial; (B) lists of the exhibits that each party expects to offer at trial, except for exhibits to be used only for impeachment; and (C) copies of all documentary exhibits, except for those to be used only for illustrative purposes. In addition, non-documentary exhibits, except for those to be used only for illustrative purposes, shall be made available for inspection by all other parties no later than 14 days before trial. Any witness or exhibit not listed may not be used at trial, unless the Court orders otherwise for good cause and subject to such conditions as justice requires. See LCR 26 (witness disclosure requirements.)

(k) Joint Statement of Evidence. In cases governed by a Case Schedule pursuant to LCR 4 the parties shall file, no later than 5 court days before the scheduled trial date, a Joint Statement of Evidence, so entitled, containing (A) a list of the witnesses whom each party expects to call at trial and (B) a list of the exhibits that each party expects to offer at trial. The Joint Statement of Evidence shall contain a notation for each exhibit as to whether all parties agree as to the exhibit's authenticity or admissibility.

(*l*) Non-dispositive Pretrial Motions. All non-dispositive pretrial motions and supporting materials, including but not limited to motions to exclude evidence, shall be served and filed pursuant to the requirements of LCR 7(b). Responsive documents shall also be served and filed pursuant to the requirements of LCR 7(b). In addition, working copies of all motion documents shall be provided pursuant to the requirements of LCR 7(b).

(m) Trial Briefs, Proposed Findings of Fact and Conclusions of Law, and Jury Instructions. Except as otherwise ordered by the Court, parties shall serve copies of the trial brief or memorandum of authorities, proposed findings of fact and conclusions of law in non-jury cases, and proposed jury instructions for jury cases, upon opposing parties, with a working copy submitted to the assigned Judge, no later than five court days before the scheduled trial date.

[Adopted effective January 1, 1990; amended effective September 1, 1992; September 1, 1993; September 1, 1996; September 1, 2001; September 1, 2002; September 1, 2003; September 1, 2004; September 1, 2008; June 1, 2009; September 1, 2010; amended on an emergency basis, effective December 1, 2010; March 1, 2011; June 1, 2011; amended on a permanent basis, effective September 1, 2011; September 1, 2012; September 2, 2013.]

Official Comment

1. Time Standards. The Court has adopted the following time standards for the timely disposition of cases. In view of the backlog of cases and the scarcity of judicial resources, it may take some time before these standards can be met.

(a) General Civil. Ninety percent of all civil cases should be settled, tried, or otherwise concluded within 12 months of the date of case filing; 98 percent within 18 months of filing; and the remainder within 24 months of filing, except for individual cases in which the Court determines that exceptional circumstances exist and for which a continuing review should occur.

(b) Summary Civil. Proceedings using summary hearing procedures, such as those landlord-tenant and replevin actions not requiring full trials, should be concluded within 30 days of filing.

(c) Family Law. Ninety percent of all family law matters should be settled, tried, or otherwise concluded within nine months of the date of case filing, with custody cases given priority; 98 percent within 12 months and 100 percent within 15 months, except for individual cases in which the Court determines that exceptional circumstances exist and for which a continuing review should occur.

(d) Criminal and Juvenile. Criminal and juvenile cases should be heard within the times prescribed by CrR 3.3 or JuCR 7.8.

2. Case Schedule. The term "plaintiff" throughout these rules is intended to include a "petitioner" if that is the correct term for the party initiating the action.

If there is more than one plaintiff, it is the responsibility of each plaintiff to see that the Case Schedule is properly served upon each defendant. This does not mean that multiple copies of the Case Schedule must be served upon each defendant, only that every plaintiff will be held accountable for a failure to serve a copy of the Case Schedule upon a defendant. Multiple plaintiffs should decide among themselves who will serve the Case Schedule upon each defendant.

3. Attorneys and parties are expected to exercise good faith in complying with this rule—for example, by not listing a witness or exhibit that the attorney or party does not actually expect to use at trial.

4. A party wishing to present the testimony of a witness who has been listed by another party may not rely on the listing party to obtain the witness's attendance at trial. Instead, a subpoena should be served on the witness, unless the party is willing to risk the witness's failure to appear.

5. All witnesses must be listed, including those whom a party plans to call as a rebuttal witness. The only exception is for witnesses the need for whose testimony cannot reasonably be anticipated before trial; such witnesses obviously cannot be listed ahead of time.

6. The deadlines in the Case Schedule do not supplant the duty of parties to timely answer interrogatories requesting the names of individuals with knowledge of the facts or with expert opinions. Disclosure of such witnesses known to a party should not be delayed to the deadlines established by this rule.

LCR 4.1. CONFIRMATION OF SERVICE

[Reserved]

[Adopted effective January 1, 1990; amended effective September 1, 1992; September 1, 1996; September 1, 2004; deleted effective September 1, 2008.]

LCR 4.2. CONFIRMATION OF JOINDER OF PARTIES AND ISSUES IN CIVIL AND FAMILY LAW CASES; COMPLETION OF TESTING IN PATERNITY CASES

(a) Civil Non–Family Law Cases; Confirmation of Joinder of Parties, Claims and Defenses; Form. This rule applies to all civil cases with a Case Schedule that are not governed by LFLR 1.

(1) *Confirmation of Joinder; Form.* No later than the designated deadline for joining additional parties and raising additional claims and defenses, as stated in LCR 4(e)(2), the plaintiff(s)/petitioner(s) shall, file and serve a report entitled "Confirmation of Joinder of Parties, Claims, and Defenses," which will be in substantially the following form:

CONFIRMATION OF JOINDER OF PARTIES, CLAIMS, AND DEFENSES

I.   [ ] Plaintiff(s)/petitioner(s) makes the following representations:

1. This case is not subject to mandatory arbitration.

[If it is, this report should not be filed; instead, no later than the deadline for filing this report, a statement of arbitrability should be filed, pursuant to LMAR 2.1(a).]

2. All parties have been served or have waived service.

3. All mandatory pleadings have been filed.

II. [ ] Plaintiff(s)/petitioner(s) do not make the foregoing representations because (if appropriate, check both the box at left and every applicable box below). The Court may set a hearing.

[ ] This case is subject to mandatory arbitration, but not yet ready for the Statement of Arbitrability to be filed.

[ ] A party remains to be served.

[ ] A mandatory pleading remains to be filed.

[ ] Other explanation:

_____

_____

_____

DATED: _____ SIGNED: _____

Plaintiff/Petitioner/Attorney (If attorney, WSBA #: ___)

Typed Name: _____

Address: _____

_____

Phone: _____

Attorney(s) For: _____

(2) *Cases Subject to Mandatory Arbitration.* If a statement of arbitrability pursuant to LMAR 2.1(a) is filed on or before the deadline for filing the Confirmation of Joinder of Parties, Claims, and Defenses, the Confirmation of Joinder need not be filed and no show cause hearing will be held. See LFLR 4(c).

(b) Family Law Dissolution and Modification Cases; Confirmation of Issues; Referral to Mediation; Form. See LFLR 4(c).

(c) Paternity Cases; Confirmation of Completion of Genetic Testing; Form. See LFLR 4(d).

[Adopted effective September 1, 1996; amended effective April 14, 1997; September 1, 1997; September 1, 1999; September 1, 2001; September 1, 2002; September 1, 2003; September 1, 2004; September 1, 2008; September 1, 2015.]

LCR 4.3. STATUS CONFERENCE; NON–COMPLIANCE HEARING

(a) Withdrawn. See LFLR 4.

[Adopted effective September 1, 1996; amended effective April 14, 1997; September 1, 1997; September 1, 2002; September 1, 2004; September 1, 2008.]

LCR 5. SERVICE AND FILING OF PLEADINGS AND OTHER PAPERS

(a)–(c) [Reserved].

(d) Filing. No motion for any order shall be heard unless the original documents pertaining to it have been filed with the Clerk.

(k) Copies of Cases Not to be Filed. Working copies of cases shall be provided to a judge pursuant to LCR 7(b), but shall not be filed with the clerk. The copies provided to the judge and all parties should be in the same form, including but not limited to markings, highlights, and color copies.

[Amended effective September 1, 1994; September 1, 1999; September 1, 2002; September 1, 2008; September 1, 2009; September 2, 2013.]

III. PLEADINGS AND MOTIONS (Rules 7–16)

LCR 7. CIVIL MOTIONS

(b) Motions and Other Documents.

(1) *Scope of Rules.* Except when specifically provided in another rule, this rule governs all motions in

civil cases. See, for example, LCR 12, LCR 26, LCR 40, LCR 56, and the LFLR's.

(2) *Hearing Times and Places.* Hearing times and places will also be available from the Clerk's Office/Department of Judicial Administration (E609 King County Courthouse, Seattle, WA 98104 or 401 Fourth Avenue North, Room 2C, Maleng Regional Justice Center, Kent WA 98032; or for Juvenile Court at 1211 East Alder, Room 307, Seattle, WA 98122) by telephone at (206) 296–9300 or by accessing http://www.kingcounty.gov/courts/clerk. Schedules for all regular calendars (family law motions, ex parte, chief civil, etc.) will be available at the information desk in the King County Courthouse and the Court Administration Office in Room 2D of the Regional Justice Center.

(3) *Argument.* All nondispositive motions and motions for orders of default and default judgment shall be ruled on without oral argument, except for the following:

(A) Motions for revision of Commissioners' rulings, other than rulings regarding involuntary commitment and Title 13 proceedings;

(B) Motions for temporary restraining orders and preliminary injunctions;

(C) Family Law motions under LFLR 5;

(D) Motions to be presented in person to the Ex Parte and Probate Department pursuant to the Ex Parte and Probate Department Presentation of Motions and Hearings Manual ("Motions and Hearings Manual") issued by the Clerk;

(E) Motions for which the Court allows oral argument.

(4) *Dates of Filing, Hearing and Consideration.*

(A) Filing and Scheduling of Motion. The moving party shall serve and file all motion documents no later than six court days before the date the party wishes the motion to be considered. A motion must be scheduled by a party for hearing on a judicial day. For cases assigned to a judge, if the motion is set for oral argument on a non-judicial day, the moving party must reschedule it with the judge's staff; for motions without oral argument, the assigned judge will consider the motion on the next judicial day.

(B) Scheduling Oral Argument on Dispositive Motions. The time and date for hearing shall be scheduled in advance by contacting the staff of the hearing judge.

(C) Oral Argument Requested on All Other Motions. Any party may request oral argument by placing "ORAL ARGUMENT REQUESTED" prominently on the first page of the motion or opposition.

(D) Opposing Documents. Any party opposing a motion shall file and serve the original responsive papers in opposition to a motion, serve copies on parties, and deliver working copies to the hearing judge no later than 12:00 noon two court days before the date the motion is to be considered. Working copies shall be submitted pursuant to the requirements in this rule.

(E) Reply. Any documents in strict reply shall be similarly filed and served no later than 12:00 noon on the court day before the hearing.

(F) Working Copies. Working copies of the motion and all documents in support or opposition shall be delivered to the hearing judge, commissioner, or appropriate judicial department no later than on the day they are to be served on all parties. The copies provided to the judge and all parties should be in the same form, including but not limited to markings, highlights, and color copies. Working copies shall be submitted as follows:

(i) Electronic Submission of Working Copies. Judges' working copies of an e-filed motion and all documents in support or opposition may be electronically submitted using the Clerk's eFiling application. The Clerk may assess a fee for the electronic submission of working copies.

(ii) E–Filed Documents For Which Working Copies Shall Not Be Electronically Submitted. Judges' working copies shall not be electronically submitted for any document of 500 pages or more in length or for any documents filed in paper form. These working copies must be submitted in paper form pursuant to the requirements in this rule.

(iii) Delivery of Working Copies in Paper Form. The upper right corner of all judges' working copies submitted in paper form shall be marked "working copies" and note the date of consideration or hearing, the name of the hearing judge or commissioner or the name of the calendar on which the motion is to be heard, by whom the documents are being presented ("moving party," "opposing party," or other descriptive or identifying term), and shall be delivered to the judges' mailroom or appropriate department in the courthouse in which the judge or commissioner is located.

(G) Terms. Any material offered at a time later than required by this rule, and any reply material which is not in strict reply, will not be considered by the court over objection of counsel except upon the imposition of appropriate terms, unless the court orders otherwise.

(H) Confirmation and Cancellation. Confirmation is not necessary, but if the motion is stricken, the parties shall immediately notify the opposing parties and notify the staff of the hearing judge.

(5) *Form of Motion and Responsive Pleadings.*

(A) Note for Motion. A Note for Motion shall be filed with the motion. The Note shall identify the moving party, the title of the motion, the name of the hearing judge, the trial date, the date for hearing, and the time of the hearing if it is a motion for which oral argument will be held. A Note for Motion form is available from the Clerk's Office.

(B) Form of Motion and of Responsive Pleadings. The motion shall be combined with the memorandum of authorities into a single document, and shall conform to the following format:

(i) Relief Requested. The specific relief the court is requested to grant or deny.

(ii) Statement of Facts. A succinct statement of the facts contended to be material.

(iii) Statement of Issues. A concise statement of the issue or issues of law upon which the Court is requested to rule.

(iv) Evidence Relied Upon. The evidence on which the motion or opposition is based must be specified with particularity. Deposition testimony, discovery pleadings, and documentary evidence relied upon must be quoted verbatim or a photocopy of relevant pages must be attached to an affidavit identifying the documents. Parties should highlight those parts upon which they place substantial reliance. Copies of cases shall not be attached to original pleadings. Responsive pleadings shall conform to this format.

(v) Authority. Any legal authority relied upon must be cited. Copies of all cited non–Washington authorities upon which parties place substantial reliance shall be provided to the hearing Judge and to counsel or parties, but shall not be filed with the Clerk. See LCR 5(k).

(vi) Page Limits. The initial motion and opposing memorandum shall not exceed 12 pages without authorization of the court; reply memoranda shall not exceed five pages without the authority of the court.

(C) Form of Proposed Orders; Mailing Envelopes; E-mail Address. The moving party and any party opposing the motion shall include with their submissions a proposed order. The original of each proposed order shall be submitted to the hearing judge along with any working copies. If the motion is to be considered without oral argument, the moving party shall at the time of filing the motion provide to the court either pre-addressed stamped envelopes addressed to each party/counsel, or e-mail addresses, for the court's use in providing courtesy copies of entered orders. Where working copies are provided via the Clerk's eWorking Copies Application, the parties shall request courtesy copies of entered order(s) through the Clerk's application.

(6) *Motions to Reconsider.* See LCR 59.

(7) *Reopening Motions.* No party shall remake the same motion to a different judge without showing by affidavit what motion was previously made, when and to which judge, what the order or decision was, and any new facts or other circumstances that would justify seeking a different ruling from another judge.

(8) *Motions for Revision of a Commissioner's Order.* For all cases except juvenile and involuntary treatment proceedings:

(A) A motion for revision of a commissioner's order shall be served and filed within 10 days of entry of the written order, as provided in RCW 2.24.050, along with a written notice of hearing that gives the other parties at least six days notice of the time, date and place of the hearing on the motion for revision. The motion shall identify the error claimed.

(B) A hearing on a motion for revision of a commissioner's order shall be scheduled within 21 days of entry of the commissioner's order, unless the assigned Judge or, for unassigned cases, the Chief Civil Judge, orders otherwise.

(i) For cases assigned to an individual Judge, the time and date for the hearing shall be scheduled in advance with the staff of the assigned Judge.

(ii) For cases not assigned to an individual Judge, the hearing shall be scheduled by the Chief Civil Department for Seattle case assignment area cases. For Kent case assignment area cases, the hearing shall be scheduled by the Maleng Regional Justice Center Chief Judge. For family law cases involving children the hearing shall be scheduled by the Chief Unified Family Court Judge.

(iii) All motions for revision of a commissioner's order shall be based on the written materials and evidence submitted to the commissioner, including documents and pleadings in the court file. The moving party shall provide the assigned judge a working copy of all materials submitted to the commissioner in support of and in opposition to the motion, as well as a copy of the electronic recording, if the motion before the commissioner was recorded. Oral arguments on motions to revise shall be limited to 10 minutes per side. Working copies shall be submitted pursuant to the requirements of LCR 7(b).

(iv) The commissioner's written order shall remain in effect pending the hearing on revision unless ordered otherwise by the assigned Judge, or, for unassigned cases, the Chief Judge.

(v) The party seeking revision shall, at least 5 days before the hearing, deliver to the assigned judge or Chief Judge working copies of the motion, notice of hearing, and copies of all documents submitted by all parties to the commissioner, pursuant to LCR 7(b).

(vi) For cases in which a timely motion for reconsideration of the commissioner's order has been filed, the time for filing a motion for revision of the commissioner's order shall commence on the date of the filing of the commissioner's written order of judgment on reconsideration.

(9) *Motion for Order to Show Cause.* Motions for Order to Show Cause shall be presented without oral argument to the Ex Parte and Probate Department through the Clerk's office. For cases where the return on the order to show cause is before the hearing judge, the moving party shall obtain a date for such hearing from the staff of the assigned judge before presenting the motion to the Ex Parte and Probate Department.

(10) *Motion Shortening Time.*

(A) The time for notice and hearing of a motion may be shortened only for good cause upon written application to the court in conformance with this rule.

(B) A motion for order shortening time may not be incorporated into any other pleading.

(C) As soon as the moving party is aware that he or she will be seeking an order shortening time, that party must contact the opposing party to give notice in the form most likely to result in actual notice of the pending motion to shorten time. The declaration in support of the motion must indicate what efforts have been made to notify the other side.

(D) Except for emergency situations, the court will not rule on a motion to shorten time until the close of the next business day following filing of the motion (and service of the motion on the opposing party) to permit the opposing party to file a response. If the moving party asserts that exigent circumstances make it impossible to comply with this requirement, the moving party shall contact the bailiff of the judge assigned the case for trial to arrange for a conference call, so that the opposing party may respond orally and the court can make an immediate decision.

(E) Proposed agreed orders to shorten time: if the parties agree to a briefing schedule on motion to be heard on shortened time, the order may be presented by way of a proposed stipulated order, which may be granted, denied or modified at the discretion of the court.

(F) The court may deny or grant the motion and impose such conditions as the court deems reasonable. All other rules pertaining to confirmation, notice and working papers for the hearing on the motion for which time was shortened remain in effect, except to the extent that they are specifically dispensed with by the court.

(11) *Motion for Stay of Proceedings.*

(A) Motions for stay of proceedings shall be heard by the individual judge assigned or if not assigned by the Chief Civil Judge, Chief Judge of the Maleng Regional Justice Center or Chief Unified Family Court Judge. The order staying proceedings shall indicate a future date by which the case status will be reviewed.

[Amended effective September 1, 1984; May 1, 1988; September 1, 1992; September 1, 1993; September 1, 1994; March 1, 1996; September 1, 1996; April 14, 1997; September 1, 1997; September 1, 1999; September 1, 2001; September 1, 2002; September 1, 2004; September 1, 2006; September 1, 2007; September 1, 2008; amended on an emergency basis, effective January 1, 2009; amended on a permanent basis, effective September 1, 2009; September 1, 2011; September 1, 2012; September 2, 2013; September 2, 2014.]

LCR 10. FORM OF PLEADINGS AND OTHER PAPERS [RESERVED]

[Amended effective September 1, 1994; September 1, 2001; September 1, 2004; deleted effective September 1, 2008.]

LCR 11. SIGNING OF PLEADINGS

(a) Self–Represented Parties (Pro Se).

(1) *Address of Party Appearing Pro Se.* A party appearing pro se shall state on each document filed by him/her, a mailing address for that party, a street address where service can be made on that party and a telephone number where that party can be contacted during the day unless that information is made confidential by statute.

(2) *Clerk's File to Indicate Pro Se Appearance.* When a party appears pro se, without filing a pleading or other document, the clerk shall cause the party to insert in the file a document indicating that the party has appeared without attorney.

(3) *Notice of Rule Requirements.* When a party appears in court without an attorney and without filing a written pleading or other document, pursuant to process served upon him/her, the clerk shall deliver to him/her a printed form containing the substance of subsection (a) of this rule, together with appropriate blanks for the name, address and telephone number the party, and shall request the party to file his/her name, a mailing address, a street address where service of process or other papers may be made, and a telephone number where the party can be contacted during the day. The clerk shall make a minute entry that such printed form has been delivered.

[Amended effective September 1, 2001; September 1, 2004; September 1, 2008; September 2, 2014.]

LCR 12. PRELIMINARY HEARINGS

(d) Motions under CR 12(b) shall be subject to the page limitations and scheduling requirements of CR 56 and LCR 56.

[Adopted effective September 1, 2012.]

LCR 15. AMENDED AND SUPPLEMENTAL PLEADINGS [RESERVED]

[Amended effective September 1, 2001; September 1, 2004; deleted effective September 1, 2008]

LCR 16. PRETRIAL DEADLINES AND PROCEDURES

(a) Pretrial Procedures—Civil Cases and Family Law Cases Not Involving Children.

(1) *Mandatory Joint Confirmation of Trial Readiness.* Parties shall complete a Joint Confirmation of Trial Readiness form, file it with the clerk, and provide a working copy to the assigned judge by the deadline on the case schedule. Failure to complete and file the form by the deadline may result in sanctions, including possible dismissal of this case. The Joint Confirmation of Trial Readiness Report shall include, at minimum:

(A) Type of trial and estimated trial length;

(B) Trial week attorney conflicts;

(C) Interpreter needs;

(D) To what extent alternative dispute resolution has been used in the case;

(E) Any other factors to assist the court to bring about a just, speedy, and economical resolution of the matter.

(b) Alternative Dispute Resolution (ADR) All Cases. See also LCR 4.

(1) Unless excused by (1) an order signed by the judge to whom a case is assigned or (2) a family law commissioner in the case of a family law matter, or (3) the Order Setting Case Schedule issued does not, itself, provide for a deadline for participating in ADR, the parties in every case governed by an order setting case schedule as set forth by LCR 4(b) shall participate in a settlement conference or other alternative dispute resolution process conducted by a neutral third party.

(2) *Preparation for Conference.*

(A) Attendance and Preparation Required. The attorney in charge of each party's case shall personally attend all alternative resolution proceedings and shall come prepared to discuss in detail and in good faith the following:

(i) All liability issues.

(ii) All items of special damages or property damage.

(iii) The degree, nature and duration of any claimed disability.

(iv) General damages.

(v) Explanation of position on settlement.

(B) Family Law Cases—Requirements. See LFLR 16.

(3) *Parties to Be Available.*

(A) Presence in Person. The parties shall personally attend all alternative resolution processes, unless excused, in advance, by the person conducting the proceeding.

(B) Representative of Insurer. Parties whose defense is provided by a liability insurance company need not personally attend the settlement conference or other dispute resolution process, but a representative of the insurer of said parties, if such a representative is available in King County, shall attend in person with sufficient authority to bind the insurer to a settlement. If the representative is not available in King County, the representative shall be available by telephone at the parties' expense.

(4) *Failure to Attend.* Failure to attend the dispute resolution procedure in accordance with paragraphs (A) and (B) above may result in the imposition of terms and sanctions that the judge may deem appropriate.

(5) *Judge Disqualified for Trial.* A judge presiding over a settlement conference shall be disqualified from acting as the trial judge in the matter, unless all parties agree in writing that he/she should so act.

[Amended effective September 1, 1977; September 1, 1981; January 1, 1990; September 1, 1992; September 1, 1993; September 1, 1994; September 1, 2001; January 2, 2004; September 1, 2004; September 1, 2007; September 1, 2008; September 1, 2009; September 1, 2012; September 2, 2013; September 2, 2014; September 1, 2015.]

IV. PARTIES (Rules 17–25)

LCR 23. CLASS ACTIONS [RESERVED]

[Amended effective September 1, 1994; September 1, 1996; deleted effective September 1, 2008.]

V. DEPOSITIONS AND DISCOVERY (Rules 26–37)

LCR 26. DISCOVERY, INCLUDING DISCLOSURE OF POSSIBLE WITNESSES AND PROTECTIVE ORDERS

(b) Discovery Limits.

(1) *Scope.* This rule shall apply to all cases governed by a Case Schedule pursuant to LCR 4.

(2) *Interrogatories.*

(A) Cases With Court–Approved Pattern Interrogatories. In cases where a party has propounded pattern interrogatories pursuant to LCR 33, a party may serve no more than 15 interrogatories, including all discrete subparts, in addition to the pattern interrogatories.

(B) Cases Without Court–Approved Pattern Interrogatories. In cases where a party has not propounded pattern interrogatories pursuant to LCR 33, a party may serve no more than 40 interrogatories, including all discrete subparts.

(3) *Depositions.* A party may take no more than 10 depositions, with each deposition limited to one day of seven hours; provided, that each party may conduct one deposition that shall be limited to two days and seven hours per day.

(4) *Requests for Admission.* A party may serve no more than 25 requests for admission upon any other party in addition to requests for admission propounded to authenticate documents.

(5) *Modification.*

(A) Stipulation of the Parties. These limitations may be increased or decreased by written stipulation of the parties based on the scope of the legal and factual issues presented. Nothing in this rule precludes the parties from engaging in the informal exchange of information in lieu of formal discovery. The parties may establish a written timetable for discovery and develop a discovery plan that will facilitate the economical and efficient resolution of the case. Such plan need not be submitted to the court for approval.

(B) Court Order. If the parties do not agree that discovery in excess of that provided by these rules is necessary, a party may file a motion to submit additional discovery pursuant to LCR 7(b). The proposed order shall include details of what additional discovery is required. A certificate of compliance as required by LCR 37(f) shall be filed with the motion.

(6) *Discovery Requests in Violation of Rule.*

(A) Unless authorized by order of court or written stipulation, a party may not serve requests for admission or interrogatories or note depositions except as authorized by this rule.

(B) Absent a court order or stipulation altering the scope of discovery, the party served with interrogatories or requests for admission in violation of this rule shall be required to respond only to those requests, in numerical order, that comply with LCR 26(b). No motion for protective order is required. The party shall indicate in the answer section of the Interrogatories or Requests for Admission that the party is refusing to respond to the remaining questions because they exceed the discovery limits.

(C) Absent a court order or stipulation altering the scope of discovery, a party served with a notice of deposition in violation of this rule shall inform all parties to the case that he or she will not be attending the deposition. This notification shall occur as soon as possible and, absent extraordinary circumstances, shall not be later than 24 hours before the scheduled deposition. Notice shall be in writing and shall be provided in the manner that is most likely to provide actual notice of the objection. Fax or e-mail notification is permitted, provided (1) the parties have previously agreed to receive pleadings in this manner or (2) the objecting party also provides telephonic notification.

(7) *Applicability.* These discovery limitations do not apply to family law proceedings as defined by LFLR 1, supplemental proceedings undertaken pursuant to LCR 69(b) or other post-judgment proceedings.

(c) Motions to Seal/ Protective Orders. A motion to seal must be made separately pursuant to LGR 15 and cannot be submitted as part of a protective order. Motions for protective order, even if agreed, shall be presented to the assigned judge and not to the ex parte department. If the case is not assigned to a judge, the motion shall be made to the Chief Civil judge for cases with an SEA designation and to the Chief Judge of the MRJC for cases with a KNT designation.

(e) Discovery Not Limited. This rule does not modify a party's responsibility to seasonably supplement responses to discovery requests or otherwise to comply with discovery before the deadlines set by this rule.

(k) Disclosure of Primary Witnesses. Required Disclosures.

(1) *Disclosure of Primary Witnesses.* Each party shall, no later than the date for disclosure designated in the Case Schedule, disclose all persons with relevant factual or expert knowledge whom the party reserves the option to call as witnesses at trial.

(2) *Disclosure of Additional Witnesses.* Each party shall, no later than the date for disclosure designated in the Case Schedule, disclose all persons whose knowledge did not appear relevant until the primary

witnesses were disclosed and whom the party reserves the option to call as witnesses at trial.

(3) *Scope of Disclosure.* Disclosure of witnesses under this rule shall include the following information:

(A) All Witnesses. Name, address, and phone number.

(B) Lay Witnesses. A brief description of the witness' relevant knowledge.

(C) Experts. A summary of the expert's opinions and the basis therefore and a brief description of the expert's qualifications.

(4) *Sanctions.* Failure to comply with this rule or the court's Order Setting Case Schedule may result in sanctions, including the exclusion of witnesses.

[Adopted effective January 1, 1990; amended effective September 1, 1992; September 1, 2001; September 1, 2003; September 1, 2005, September 1, 2007; September 1, 2008; September 1, 2010; September 1, 2011; September 2, 2014; September 1, 2015.]

Comment:

See LGR 15 and LFLR 11 for procedures relevant to motions to seal.

Official Comment

This rule does not require a party to disclose which persons the party intends to call as witnesses at trial, only those whom the party might call as witnesses. Cf. LCR 4(j) (requiring the parties, not later than 21 days before trial, to exchange lists of witnesses whom each party "expects to call" at trial) and Official Comment to LCR 4 All Witnesses must be listed, including those whom a party plans to call as a rebuttal witness. The only exception is when the party calling a witness could not reasonably anticipate needing that witness before trial.

This rule sets a minimum level of disclosure that will be required in all cases, even if one or more parties have not formally requested such disclosure in written discovery. The rule is not intended to serve as a substitute for the discovery procedures that are available under the civil rules to preclude or inhibit the use of those procedures. Indeed, in section (e) the rule specifically provides to the contrary.

The prior version of Section 4 of this rule was, in essence, struck down by the Supreme Court in *Jones v. Seattle,* 179 Wn2d. 322, 314 P.3d 380 (2013). The *Jones* court emphasized that trial courts must follow the three-part test of *Burnet v. Spokane Ambulance,* 131 Wn2d. 484, 933 P.2d 1036 (1997) prior to entering an order excluding a witness.

Official Comment

Publisher's Note:

According to a Clerk's Office Alert dated September 27, 2005, "The King County Superior Court adopted local rules imposing discovery limits in civil proceedings (LR 26 and LR 33) went into effect September 1, 2005. Pursuant to General Administrative Order signed September 21, 2005, these new discovery rule provisions apply only to those cases filed on or after September 1, 2005. The discovery limits do not apply to family law proceedings or post-judgment civil proceedings."

LCR 33. INTERROGATORIES

(a) Pattern Interrogatories for Specific Areas of Practice: (Reserved)

Comment: The King County Superior Court will adopt a process for approving Pattern Interrogatories for use in discrete practice areas. The process and the pattern interrogatories will be available from the KSCS website: http://www.kingcounty.gov/kcsc/, as well as through the office of the King County Clerk.

(b) Appropriate Use of Pattern Interrogatories. It is not required nor recommended that all interrogatories contained in a pattern set be used in every case. It shall be the obligation of counsel or a party to determine which interrogatories are appropriate to the facts of the case.

(c) Format. All Pattern Interrogatories should be contained in a separate document. Although minor variations may be made to these interrogatories to fit the circumstances of a particular case, identifying the document as Pattern Interrogatories is a warranty by the attorney or party signing the interrogatories that such interrogatories are identical in substance to the Pattern Interrogatories approved by the court.

[Adopted effective September 1, 2005; amended effective September 1, 2008.]

Publisher's Note:

According to a Clerk's Office Alert dated September 27, 2005, "The King County Superior Court adopted local rules imposing discovery limits in civil proceedings (LR 26 and LR 33) went into effect on September 1, 2005. Pursuant to General Administrative Order signed September 21, 2005, these new discovery rule provisions apply only to those cases filed on or after September 1, 2005. The discovery limits do not apply to family law proceedings or post-judgment civil proceedings."

LCR 37. FAILURE TO MAKE DISCOVERY; SANCTIONS

(d) (Withdrawn).

(e) Conference of Counsel. See CR 26(i).

(f) Certificate of Compliance. See CR 26(i).

(g) Completion of Discovery. Unless otherwise ordered by the Court for good cause and subject to such terms and conditions as are just, all discovery allowed under CR 26–37, including responses and supplementations thereto, must be completed no later than 49 calendar days before the assigned trial date (provided that deadlines shall be 28 days in all parentage cases and 35 days in all other family law proceedings as defined in LFLR 1). Discovery requests must be served early enough that responses will be due and depositions will have been taken by the cutoff date. Discovery requests that do not comply with this rule will not be enforced. Nothing in this rule shall modify a party's responsibility to seasonably supplement responses to discovery requests or otherwise to comply with discovery prior to the cutoff.

[Adopted effective January 1, 1983. Amended effective September 1, 1986; January 1, 1990; September 1, 1992; Sep-

tember 1, 1999; September 1, 2001; September 1, 2007; September 1, 2008; September 1, 2010; September 1, 2015.]

VI.   TRIALS (Rules 38–52)

LCR 38.   JURY TRIAL OF RIGHT

(b) Demand for Jury

(1) *Separate Document.* The demand for jury trial shall be contained in a separate document.

(2) *Deadline for Filing Demand.* In cases governed by a Case Schedule pursuant to LCR 4 (excluding domestic and paternity cases), a jury demand shall be filed and served no later than the final date to change trial designated in the Case Schedule, which shall be deemed the date on which the case is called to be set for trial within the meaning of CR 38(b).

[Amended effective January 1, 1990; September 1, 1992; September 1, 2001; September 1, 2008.]

LCR 40.   ASSIGNMENT OF CASES AND WHERE MOTIONS ARE TO BE HEARD

(a) Notice of Trial—Note of Issue.

(1) *Assignment of Case to Judge.* The Clerk at filing will issue for all civil cases, except those noted in LCR 4(b), a trial date and a case schedule, and will assign the case to a judge. A Notice of Trial, as provided in CR 40(a), shall not be filed in any civil case.

(b) Where Motions and Proceedings to Be Noted.
See LCR 7(b)(2) with respect to calendar locations and times. All motions and other proceedings in a civil case, shall be brought before the assigned judge, in accordance with LCR 7, or if no assigned judge to the Ex Parte and Probate Department in accordance with LCR 40.1, except as follows:

(1) Motions for default orders and default judgments shall be presented to the Ex Parte and Probate Department, unless any defendant has appeared in the matter, in which case it shall be noted before the assigned judge, or if no judge has been assigned, to the Chief Civil Judge for SEA case designations and the Chief Judge at the Maleng Regional Justice Center for KNT case designations.

(2) *Family Law Proceedings.* See LFLR 5.

(3) *Adoption Proceedings.* Adoption proceedings, except Confidential Intermediary Petitions which are assigned to the Judges Sealed File Committee, shall be heard in the Ex Parte and Probate Department or a judge by special setting. Contested proceedings may be referred by the commissioner to the Clerk who will issue a trial date and a case schedule and will assign the case to a judge. All hearings to finalize an

Adoption Petition shall be noted for a hearing on the appropriate calendar. All other matters shall be presented via the Clerk.

(4) *Small Claims Appeals.* The clerk at filing will issue a Notice of Decision Date and Assignment of Judge for review of the record without oral argument. The decision shall be issued to the parties.

(5) *Antiharassment, Sexual Assault, Domestic Violence and Vulnerable Adult Petitions.* See LCR 40.1

(6) *Order Vacating Conviction.* These motions shall be noted before the judges to whom post sentencing motions have been assigned. The motion is to be noted pursuant LCR 7. See official comment.

(7) *Frivolous Liens.* If the motion to discharge a purportedly frivolous lien is a new action and not part of an underlying proceeding, the motion shall be set before the Chief Civil Judge for Seattle case assignment area cases. Kent case assignment area cases shall be set before the Chief Judge of the Maleng Regional Justice Center. If the motion is part of an underlying proceeding, the matter should be noted before the assigned judge.

(8) *Marriage Age Waiver Petitions.* See LFLR 19.

(9) *Involuntary Treatment Proceedings.* The hearings in involuntary treatment proceedings shall be heard on the involuntary treatment act calendar.

(10) *Receivership Proceedings.* See LCR 40.1(b)(2).

(11) *Supplemental Proceedings.* Hearings on supplemental proceedings shall be set before the Seattle Chief Civil Judge for Seattle case assignment area cases. Kent case assignment area cases shall be set before the Chief Judge of the Maleng Regional Justice Center. The supplemental proceedings fee must be received before hearings will be set by the clerk.

(12) *Work Permits/Variances for Minors.* Applications for work permits for minors, sought pursuant to RCW 26.28.060, shall be presented to the e[1] Chief Civil Judge in Seattle for cases with a SEA designation and to the Chief Judge of the Maleng Regional Justice Center for cases with a KNT designation.

(13) *Writs.*

(a) Extraordinary writs (writs of review, coram nobis mandamus, prohibition and certiorari): See LCR 98.40.

(b) For other writs (pre-judgment garnishment, attachment, replevin, restitution, assistance) the initial application shall be presented without oral argument to the Ex Parte and Probate Department through the Clerk's office. See also LCR 40.1(b)(2)(Q).

(14) *Adult Structured Settlements.* Approvals of structured settlements pursuant to Chapter 19.205 RCW shall be given a case schedule and set before the Chief Civil judge for cases with a SEA designation and to the Chief Judge of the Maleng Regional Justice Center for cases with a KNT assignment.

(15) *Quash of Subpoena.* Motions to quash subpoena from outside the jurisdiction shall be brought before the Chief Civil Judge or the Chief Maleng Regional Justice Center Judge.

(16) *Restoration of Right to Possess Firearm.* A petition to restore the right to possess a firearm shall be noted before the King County Superior Court judge to whom post-sentencing motions have been assigned if the conviction resulting in loss of the right occurred in King County Superior Court. If the conviction resulting in loss of the right occurred in a court of limited jurisdiction or the Superior Court of another county, the petitioner must file an original cause of action in King County Superior Court and the motion shall be noted without oral argument before the Chief Criminal Judge or the Chief Maleng Regional Justice Center Judge pursuant to LCR 7. For cases in which the loss of the right resulted from an involuntary commitment, the petitioner must file an original petition in a separate cause of action and the motion shall be noted without oral argument before the Chief Civil Judge or the Chief Maleng Regional Justice Center Judge pursuant to LCR 7. [For cases in which loss of firearms resulted in a juvenile matter refer to the Juvenile rules.] See official comment.

(c) **Trial Dates.** In guardianship, TEDRA, probate, receiverships and unlawful detainer matters, the motion shall be made before the Ex Parte Department. In all other cases not assigned to a judge, the motions shall be made to the Chief Civil Judge in Seattle for cases with a SEA designation and to the Chief Judge at the Maleng Regional Justice Center for cases with a KNT designation. The motion, which shall be decided without oral argument, shall briefly describe the case, including whether a jury demand has been filed, the expected length of the trial, and any other information relevant to the setting of a trial date. If the assigned trial date has passed and the case has not been dismissed, any party may apply by motion to the assigned judge, or if no assigned judge, to the Seattle Chief Civil Department for cases with a Seattle designation and to the Chief Regional Justice Center Judge in Kent for cases with a Kent assignment, for assignment of a trial date and a case schedule.

(e) **Continuances/Change of Trial Date.**

(1) *Limited Adjustment of Trial Date to Resolve Schedule Conflict.* In cases that are governed by a Case Schedule; the trial date may be adjusted, prior to the Final Date to Change Trial, by motion, to a Monday no more than 28 days before or 28 days after the trial date listed in the Case Schedule.

(2) *Change of Trial Date.* A motion to strike a trial date, or change a trial date more than 28 days before or after the original date, shall be made in writing to the assigned Judge, or if there is no assigned Judge, to the Chief Civil Department, and shall be decided without oral argument. If a motion to change the trial date is made after the Final Date to Change Trial Date, as established by the Case Schedule, the motion will not be granted except under extraordinary circumstances where there is no alternative means of preventing a substantial injustice. A motion to strike or change a trial date may be granted subject to such conditions as justice requires.

(3) *Amended Case Schedule.* When a trial date is changed, the judge changing the trial date may amend the case schedule or may direct that the parties confer and propose a new schedule. Unless some other deadline for submitting the proposed case schedule is set by the court, the parties must submit a proposed case schedule for signature by the assigned judge no later than twenty days after the order changing the trial date is signed.

(4) *Change of Trial Date on Court's Motion.* The Court on its own initiative may, if necessary, change the trial date.

(f) **Change of Judge.** For affidavits of prejudice see RCW 4.12.050.

[Amended September 1, 1977; September 1, 1978; September 1, 1980; amended effective January 1, 1983; September 1, 1984; December 1, 1988; January 1, 1990; September 1, 1992; September 1, 1993; September 1, 1996; April 14, 1997; September 1, 1997; September 1, 1999; September 1, 2001; September 1, 2002; September 1, 2004; September 1, 2005; September 1, 2006; September 1, 2008; January 1, 2009; September 1, 2009; September 1, 2010; September 1, 2011; September 1, 2012; September 2, 2014; September 1, 2015.]

¹ So in original.

Official Comment

Petitions for certificates of rehabilitation is a term sometimes used to describe the Order Vacating Conviction (LCR 40(b)(6)) and Restoration of Rights (LCR 40(b)(16)) process, though this is no longer part of Washington state law.

LCR 40.1. EX PARTE AND PROBATE DEPARTMENT

(a) Ex Parte and Probate Department.

(1) *Ex Parte and Probate Department Presentation of Motions and Hearings Manual.* The Ex Parte and Probate Department and probate Presentation of Motions and Hearings Manual ("Motions and Hearings Manual") is issued by the Clerk and shall contain a list of all matters that shall be presented to the Ex Parte and Probate Department and specifically indicate

which matters shall be heard in person and which shall be submitted in writing, without oral argument, through the Clerk's office. The Motions and Hearings Manual shall contain specific procedural information on how to present matters through the Clerk's office. The Motions and Hearings Manual shall be made available online at www.kingcounty.gov/courts/clerk and in paper form through the Clerk's office and the Ex Parte and Probate Department.

(b) Motions and Other Procedures.

(1) *Scope of Rules.* This rule governs all matters presented to the Ex Parte and Probate Department.

(2) *Cases Not Assigned.* Except as provided otherwise in these rules, all motions and proceedings pertaining to cases not assigned a case schedule or judge on filing shall be presented to the Ex Parte and Probate Department. The following cases or motions are heard by the Ex Parte and Probate Department:

(A) Adoption Proceedings. Adoption proceedings, except Confidential Intermediary Petitions which are assigned to the Judges Sealed File Committee, shall be heard in the Ex Parte and Probate Department or a judge by special setting. Contested proceedings may be referred by the commissioner to the Clerk who will issue a trial date and a case schedule and will assign the case to a judge. All hearings to finalize an Adoption Petition shall be noted for a hearing on the appropriate calendar. All other matters shall be presented via the Clerk.

(B) Agreed and Default Family Law Decrees and Modifications. See LFLR 5.

(C) Antiharassment, Domestic Violence, Sexual Assault and Vulnerable Adult Protection Orders:

(i) Antiharassment Petitions. Applications for temporary antiharassment protection orders shall be presented to the Ex Parte and Probate Department. Hearings on final antiharassment protection orders shall be set by the Clerk or Judicial Officer on the Antiharassment/Sexual Assault Protection Order calendar.

(ii) Domestic Violence Protection Orders. See LFLR 12.

(iii) Sexual Assault Protection Orders. Applications for temporary sexual assault protection orders shall be presented in the Ex Parte and Probate Department. Hearings on final sexual assault protection orders shall be set by the Clerk or Judicial Officer on the Antiharassment/Sexual Assault Protection Order calendar.

(iv) Vulnerable Adult Protection Orders. Applications for temporary vulnerable adult protection orders shall be presented to the Ex Parte and Probate Department. Hearings on final vulnerable adult protection orders shall be set by the Clerk or Judicial Officer before the Ex Parte and Probate Department.

(D) Guardianships, Probates and Other Settlements of Claim involving Incapacitated Adults or Minors. All proceedings brought under Title 11 which include but are not limited to Guardianships, Probates, and trust matters, as well as motions to approve settlement of a claim on behalf of a minor or incapacitated adult pursuant to SPR 98.16, shall be set on the Guardianship/Probate calendar in the Ex Parte and Probate Department either through the Clerk's office or in person, pursuant to the policy guidelines in the Motions and Hearings Manual issued by the Clerk's office. If the matter is contested, it may be referred by the judicial officer to the Clerk who will issue a trial date and will assign the case to a judge.

(E) Judgments on Arbitration Awards. Judgments on Arbitration Awards shall be presented to the Ex Parte and Probate Department with notice to the other parties.

(F) Orders to Show Cause. All Motions for Show Cause shall be presented to the Ex Parte and Probate Department. For cases where the return on the order to show cause is before the assigned trial court, the moving party shall obtain a date for such hearing from the staff of the assigned trial court before presenting to the Ex Parte and Probate Department. See also LCR 7(b)(9). For all cases where the return on the order to show cause is to a calendar, rather than before the assigned judge, the moving party shall select the return date and state the calendar in the proposed order. See also LCR 7(b)(3); LFLR 5.

(G) Orders Waiving Filing Fees. In Forma Pauperis Motions where the party is attempting to seek a waiver of the initial filing fee shall be presented to the Ex Parte and Probate Department. See GR 34. Forms and instructions for these waivers are available at the Clerk's Office or on the Clerk's website: www.kingcounty.gov/courts/clerk.

(H) Requests to Waive Ex Parte via the Clerk and ECR On–Line Fees. Requests to waive fees for Ex Parte via the Clerk shall be presented to the Clerk. Forms and instructions for these waivers are available at the Clerk's Office or on the Clerk's website: www.kingcounty.gov/courts/clerk. See LCR 78 regarding the waiver of ECR On-line fees.

(I) Orders Waiving Other Fees. Waiver of fees other than initial filing fees shall be presented to the assigned judge, or if no assigned judge to the Chief Civil Judge. See RAP 15 for waiver of appellate fees and costs. See GR 34. Forms and instructions for these waivers are available at the Clerk's Office or on the Clerk's website: www.kingcounty.gov/courts/clerk.

(J) Orders to Remove non-ECR Files. Orders to remove non-ECR files from clerk's office shall be presented to the Ex Parte and Probate Department.

(K) Orders Vacating a Dismissal. Orders vacating a dismissal of any civil case combined with a final dispositive order shall be presented to the Ex Parte and Probate Department.

(L) Receivership Proceedings. If the petition is a new action and not part of an underlying proceeding, the initial hearings shall be set in the Ex Parte and Probate Department, and be presented in person; contested proceedings may be referred by the commissioner to the Clerk who will issue a trial date and a case schedule and will assign the case to a judge.

(M) Sealed Files. See LGR 15, LCR 26(b), LCR 77(i)(11) and LFLR 11.

(N) Temporary Restraining Orders. Temporary restraining orders seeking relief pending a hearing on show cause shall be presented to the Ex Parte and Probate Department, and may be presented along with the Motion for Show Cause.

(O) Unlawful Detainer Actions. The orders to show cause, and any agreed orders or orders that do not require notice, shall be obtained by presenting the orders, through the Clerk's office, to the Ex Parte and Probate Department, without oral argument. The initial hearing on order to show cause shall be heard in person in the Ex Parte and Probate Department, provided that contested proceedings may be referred by the judicial officer to the Clerk who will issue a trial date and a case schedule and will assign the case to a judge.

(P) Unopposed Matters. Unopposed matters are to include any agreed order or any order that does not require notice to any other party, interested person or entity and does not require the approval of the assigned judge and is not reserved to any other calendar by any statute, court rule or court order. Motions for default orders and default judgments shall be presented to the Ex Parte and Probate Department, unless any defendant has appeared in the matter, in which case it shall be noted before the assigned judge, or if no judge has been assigned to the Chief Civil Judge for SEA case designations and the Chief Judge at the Maleng Regional Justice Center for KNT case designations in accordance with LCR 7.

(Q) Writs. For pre-judgment garnishment, attachment, replevin, restitution and assistance writs the initial application shall be presented without oral argument to the Ex Parte and Probate Department through the Clerk's office. For other writs, see LCR 40 (b)(13).

(3) *Assigned Cases.* Although assigned to a judge (IC judge), the following civil matters shall be presented to the Ex Parte and Probate Department except as provided otherwise in these rules or by the Court:

(A) In civil proceedings, including family law proceedings, all agreed orders, judgments and decrees, and any orders that do not require notice to any other party, interested person, or entity, including motions for orders to show cause, provided that the order does not affect the case schedule, direct the Clerk to seal a document or file, provide for a protective order pursuant to LCR 26(c) or purport to direct the manner in which another Department or Judge handles a hearing (i.e. a motion to exceed page limits or shorten time), and is not reserved to any other calendar by any statute, court rule, or court order. See LCR 40 and LFLR 5.

(B) Motions to approve or disapprove the settlement of a claim on behalf of an incapacitated person or minor. See SPR 98.16.

(C) Judgments on arbitration awards. See LMAR 6.3.

(D) Civil and family law emergency restraining orders, including domestic violence, sexual assault, and anti-harassment protection orders where either no notice or shortened notice has been given to the opposing parties.

(E) Any other matters as directed by these rules or the Court.

(4) *Matters Not Presented to the Ex Parte and Probate Department.* Regardless of the type of motion, the following types of cases are not heard in the Ex Parte and Probate Department except as otherwise directed by the Court: juvenile court proceedings; civil commitment and sexual predator proceedings; criminal matters; and family law matters given a UFS or UFK designation and assigned to an individual judicial officer for intensive case management. See LFLR 5 and the Motions and Hearings Manual with respect to what types of family law motions shall be presented to the Ex Parte and Probate Department.

(5) *Argument.* Matters presented to the Ex Parte and Probate Department are heard either with or without oral argument as determined by this rule.

(A) Matters With Oral Argument. Generally, emergency orders of protection, other specific emergent matters, matters requiring notice, matters requiring testimony, and matters directed specifically by the Court will be heard in person, with oral argument, on the assigned Ex Parte and Probate Calendar. The parties shall comply with the Motions and Hearings Manual to determine if a specific matter shall be permitted oral argument.

(B) Matters Without Oral Argument. All other matters not presented in person shall be submitted to the Ex Parte and Probate Department in writing, without oral argument, through the Clerk's office. Parties must deliver or mail their paperwork to the Clerk's office directly. The Clerk's office will assess a processing fee. The processing fee must be paid or waived at the time of submission. Parties shall comply with the specific process set forth in the Motions and Hearings Manual for submitting their paperwork.

(C) Matters Required to be Noted. Matters required to be noted for hearing in the Ex Parte and Probate Department must be presented by the parties in person at the time of the noted hearing. Matters may not be noted in the Ex Parte and Probate Department for hearing without oral argument.

[Adopted on an emergency basis effective January 1, 2009; adopted on a permanent basis and amended effective September 1, 2009. Amended effective September 1, 2010; September 1, 2012; September 1, 2015.]

LCR 41.   DISMISSAL OF ACTIONS

(b) Involuntary Dismissal.

(2) *Dismissal on Clerk's Motion.*

(A) Failure to Appear for Trial. If the court has not been previously notified that the trial is no longer necessary, an order of dismissal will be entered on the date the trial is to be commenced. If the court has been notified that the trial is no longer necessary and the case has not been disposed of within 45 days after the scheduled trial date, the case will be dismissed without prejudice on the clerk's motion without prior notice to the parties, unless the parties have filed a certificate of settlement as provided in LCR 41(e)(3). The clerk will mail all parties or their attorneys of record a copy of the order of dismissal.

(B) Failure to File Final Order on Settlement. If an order disposing of all claims against all parties is not entered within 45 days after a written notice of settlement is filed, and if a certificate of settlement without dismissal is not filed as provided in section (e)(3) below, the clerk shall notify the parties that the case will be dismissed by the court. If a party makes a written application to the court within 14 days of the issuance of the notice showing good cause why the case should not be dismissed, the court may order that the case may be continued for an additional period of time. If an order disposing of all claims against all parties is not entered during that additional period of time, the clerk shall enter an order of dismissal without prejudice.

(C) Failure to File Final Orders after a Certificate of Settlement Without Dismissal is Filed. If an order disposing of all claims against all parties is not entered by the date the parties agreed to in the certificate of settlement without dismissal, the clerk shall notify the parties that the case will be dismissed without prejudice. If a party makes a written application to the court within 21 days of the issuance of the notice showing good cause why the case should not be dismissed, the court may order that the case be continued for an additional period of time. If an order disposing all claims against all parties is not entered during that additional period

of time, the clerk shall enter an order of dismissal without prejudice.

(D) Failure to File Judgment or Appeal Following an Arbitration Award. At least 45 days after an arbitration award, the Court may, upon notice to parties, enter an order of dismissal without prejudice for failure to file a judgment or appeal following an arbitration award.

(E) Lack of Action of Record. The Court may enter an order of dismissal without prejudice for failure to take action of record during the past 12 months. The clerk shall issue notice to the attorneys of record that such case will be dismissed by the court unless within 45 days following such issuance a status report is filed with the court indicating the reason for inactivity and projecting future actions and a case completion date. If such status report is not received or if the status is disapproved by the court, the case shall be dismissed without prejudice.

(F) Failure to Return from Stay. If after 90 days beyond the review date no renewing stay order has been filed and there are no future hearing dates, the case shall be dismissed without prejudice by the court for want of prosecution upon further notice to the parties.

(G) Failure to complete an Unlawful Detainer. If no action of record is taken for 45 days, and no future hearing date is scheduled, then the case may be administratively closed by the clerk.

(c) Dismissal of Counterclaim, Cross–Claim, or Third Party Claim.   No local rule.

(d) Costs of Previously Dismissed Action.   No local rule.

(e) Notice of Settlements.

(1) *Advising the Court of Settlement.* After any settlement that fully resolves all claims against all parties, the parties shall, within five days or before the next scheduled court hearing, whichever is sooner, file and serve a written notice of settlement. If the case is assigned to an individual judge and such written notice cannot be filed with the clerk before the trial date, the assigned judge shall be notified of the settlement by telephone, or orally in open court, to be confirmed by filing and serving the written notice or certificate of settlement within five days.

(2) *Notice of Settlement with Prompt Dismissal.* If the action is to be dismissed within 45 days, the notice of settlement shall be in substantially the following form:

NOTICE OF SETTLEMENT OF ALL CLAIMS AGAINST ALL PARTIES

Notice is hereby given that all claims against all parties in this action have been resolved. Any trials or other hearings in this matter may be stricken from the court calendar. This notice is being filed with the consent of all parties.

If an order dismissing all claims against all parties is not entered within 45 days after the written notice of settlement is filed, or within 45 days after the scheduled trial date, whichever is earlier, and if a certificate of settlement without dismissal is not filed as provided in LCR 41(e)(3), the case may be dismissed on the clerk's motion pursuant to LCR 41(b)(2)(B).

Date	Attorney for Defendant
	WSBA No.
Date	Attorney for Plaintiff
	WSBA No.

(Signatures by attorneys on behalf of all parties.)

(3) *Settlement With Delayed Dismissal.* If the parties have reached a settlement fully resolving all claims against all parties, but wish to delay dismissal beyond the period set forth in section (e)(2) above, the parties may file a certificate of settlement without dismissal in substantially the following form (or as amended by the court):

CERTIFICATE OF SETTLEMENT WITHOUT DISMISSAL

I. BASIS

1.1 Within 30 days of filing of the Notice of Settlement of All Claims required by King County Local Rule 41(e), the parties to the action may file a Certificate of Settlement Without Dismissal with the Clerk of the Superior Court.

II. CERTIFICATE

2.1 The undersigned counsel for all parties certify that all claims have been resolved by the parties. The resolution has been reduced to writing and signed by every party and every attorney. Solely for the purpose of enforcing the settlement agreement, the court is asked not to dismiss this action.

2.2 The original of the settlement agreement is in the custody

of: _____

at: _____.

2.3 No further court action shall be permitted except for enforcement of the settlement agreement. The parties contemplate that the final dismissal of this action will be appropriate as

of: _____.

Date: _____

III. SIGNATURES

Attorney for Plaintiff(s)/ Petitioner WSBA No. _____	Attorney for Defendant(s)/ Respondent WSBA No. _____
Attorney of Plaintiff(s)/ Petitioner WSBA No. _____	Attorney for Defendant(s)/ Respondent WSBA No. _____

IV. NOTICE

The filing of this Certificate of Settlement Without Dismissal with the clerk automatically cancels any pending due dates of the Case Schedule for this action, including the scheduled trial date.

On or after the date indicated by the parties as appropriate for final dismissal, if the parties do not dismiss their case, the clerk will notify the parties that the case will be dismissed by the court for want of prosecution unless within 14 days after the issuance a party makes a written application to the court, showing good cause why the case should not be dismissed.

[Adopted effective September 1, 1993; amended effective September 1, 1994; September 1, 1996; September 1, 2001; September 1, 2002; September 1, 2004; September 1, 2006; September 1, 2008; September 1, 2011; September 2, 2014.]

Official Comment

1. Notice of Settlement. Subsections (b)(2) and (e)(1) are intended to prevent a case from entering a state of suspended animation after the parties reach a settlement. The rule creates a mechanism for a settled case to be formally closed by judgment or dismissal. A case will not be removed from the trial calendar on the basis of a settlement unless the settlement resolves all claims against all parties.

LCR 42. CONSOLIDATION; SEPARATE TRIALS

(a) **Motions to Consolidate.** Motions to consolidate cases for trial or other purposes, or to reassign a case to a different judge for reasons of the efficient administration of justice, shall be made in writing to the Chief Civil Judge for SEA case designations and the Chief Judge at the Maleng Regional Justice Center for KNT case designations. Cases without a case schedule or an assigned judge may be consolidated into another case by any judicial officer on the Court's own motion.

[Adopted effective September 1, 2012.]

LCR 43. TAKING OF TESTIMONY

[Reserved]

[Adopted effective September 1, 1996; September 1, 2004; deleted effective September 1, 2008.]

LCR 53.1. REFEREES

(a) Orders of Reference. Before the Court can order a matter referred to a referee under RCW 4.48, a complaint or petition shall be filed with the Clerk. If an order of reference by consent is sought under RCW 4.48.010, the motion requesting the reference, including a summary showing the referee is qualified under RCW 4.48.040, and the written consent shall be filed with the Clerk, and the action shall be exempt from Local Civil Rule 4. If assignment without consent is sought by a party under RCW 4.48.020 a motion requesting that a case be referred to a referee shall be brought for hearing before the department to which the case has been assigned, or, if not assigned to a particular department, to the Chief Civil Judge in Seattle for cases with an SEA designation or to the Chief Judge of the Maleng Regional Justice Center for cases with a KNT designation.

(b) Public Proceedings. All proceedings before a referee pursuant to RCW 4.48 shall be open to the public unless the Court orders otherwise.

(c) Posting of Notice of Trial. At least five days before the date the case is scheduled for trial before a referee, counsel shall provide the Clerk with two copies of a notice, suitable for posting, that sets forth the caption, cause number, name of referee, and the date and place of trial. If the court has ordered that the proceedings shall be closed to the public, the notice shall so state. One copy of the notice shall be posted by the Clerk; the other copy shall be filed in the court file.

(d) Termination of Case. If a case referred to a referee is terminated without the filing of a final judgment, the parties shall have an order of dismissal entered or file with the Clerk a notice or certificate of settlement as provided in LCR 41(e).

[Adopted effective September 1, 1993; amended effective September 1, 2003; September 1, 2008.]

LCR 53.2. COURT COMMISSIONERS

(a)–(e) Reserved.

(f) Affidavits—Court Commissioners. Affidavits of prejudice or for change of Court Commissioner will not be recognized. The remedy of a party is for a motion for revision under RCW 2.24.050.

[Adopted effective September 1, 2012.]

VII. JUDGMENT (Rules 54–63)

LCR 54. JUDGMENTS AND COSTS

(f) *Presentation*.

(3) Presentation by Legal Assistant. Legal assistants who are duly registered with the King County Bar Association or any local bar association of this state may personally present ex parte orders based solely upon the documents presented and the record in the file.

(g) *Interlineations*.

(1) Orders and Judgments. Any interlineations, corrections, and deletions in orders and judgments signed by the judge/commissioner must be initialed by the judge/commissioner.

[Amended effective September 1, 1984; amended effective September 1, 1993; September 1, 2008; amended on an emergency basis effective January 1, 2009; amended on a permanent basis effective September 1, 2009.]

LCR 55. DEFAULT AND JUDGMENT

(a) Entry of Default.

(1) *Order of Default*. When there has not been an appearance by any non-moving party, the moving party shall seek entry of an Order of Default from the Ex Parte and Probate Department through the Clerk's office. When there has been an appearance by any non-moving party, the motion for default shall be noted without oral argument before the assigned Judge, or if none, in the courtroom of the Chief Civil Department for Seattle case assignment area cases and the Chief Judge of the Maleng Regional Justice Center for Kent case assignment area cases. The Motion in support of the Order for Default shall affirmatively state whether or not there has been an appearance by any non-moving party. Failure to so state shall result in the denial of the motion for default without prejudice.

(2) *Late Appearance or Answer*. When a non-moving party has appeared or answered before consideration of the Motion for Order of Default, the moving party shall notify the hearing judge or commissioner.

(b) Entry of Default Judgment. Upon entry of an Order of Default, a party shall move for entry of judgment against the party in default from the Ex Parte and Probate Department through the Clerk's office. If the Court determines that testimony is required, the moving party shall schedule the matter to be heard in person in the Ex Parte and Probate Department.

(c) Setting Aside Default Judgments. Orders to show cause to vacate default judgments shall be presented to the Ex Parte and Probate Department either through the Clerk's office or in person, pursuant to the policy guidelines in the Motions and Hearings Manual issued by the Clerk. Orders to show cause are returnable to the assigned judge. If no judge is assigned, orders to show cause are returnable to the Chief Civil Judge for Seattle cases and the Chief Judge of the Maleng Regional Justice Center for Kent cases. See LCR 7(b)(8). Also see LCR 60(e)(1).

(d) Failure to Appear at Trial. The failure of a party to appear at trial is not governed by this rule. (See LCR 43.)

(e) Family Law Cases. See LFLR 5.

[Adopted effective September 1, 1996. Amended effective September 1, 2003; September 1, 2004; September 1, 2008; amended on an emergency basis effective January 1, 2009; amended on a permanent basis effective September 1, 2009; September 1, 2015.]

LCR 56. SUMMARY JUDGMENT

(c) Motions and Proceedings

(1) *Argument.* The court shall decide all summary judgment motions after oral argument, unless the parties waive argument. The assigned judge shall determine the length of oral argument.

(2) *Dates of Filing and Hearing.* The deadlines for moving, opposing, and reply documents shall be as set forth in CR 56 and the Order Setting Case Schedule. In all other regards, parties shall file and deliver documents and the court shall set all hearings in conformance with LCR 7.

(3) *Form of Motion and Opposition Documents.* The parties shall conform all moving, opposing, and reply documents to the requirements of LCR 7(b)(4), except that moving and opposing memoranda shall not exceed 24 pages. Reply memoranda shall not exceed five pages without authority of the court.

(4) *Motions to Reconsider.* The parties shall conform all motions to reconsider to the requirements of CR 59 and LCR 7(b)(5).

(5) *Reopening.* Reopenings are subject to the requirements of LCR 7(b)(6).

(e) Form of Affidavits; Nonconforming Evidence. A party objecting to the admissibility of evidence submitted by an opposing party must state the objection in writing in a responsive pleading, a separate submission shall only be filed if the objection is to materials filed in the reply.

[Note: Judgment upon multiple claims or involving multiple parties, see CR 54(b).]

[Amended effective September 1, 1983; September 1, 1984; May 1, 1988; January 1, 1990; September 1, 1992; September 1, 1993; September 1, 1994; September 1, 1996; September 1, 2001; September 1, 2004; September 1, 2005; September 1, 2008; September 1, 2011.]

Official Comment

Amended effective September 1, 2011, Subsection (e) is added to obviate the filing of motions to strike objectionable evidence, to relieve parties of the need to file such motions six days in advance and thus, under LCR 7, to file an accompanying motion to shorten tile for a timely consideration of the objection. This rule is intended to clarify local practice

and to conform to *Cameron v. Murray*, 151 Wash. App 646,658, 214 P.3d 150 (Div. I, 2009).

LCR 58. ENTRY OF JUDGMENT

(a) When.

(1) *Judgments and Orders to Be Filed Forthwith.* Any order, judgment or decree which has been signed by the Court shall not be taken from the Courthouse, but must be filed forthwith by the attorney obtaining it with the Clerk's office or with the Clerk in the courtroom.

(b) Effective Time.

(1) *Effective on Filing in Clerk's Office.* Judgments, orders and decrees shall be effective from the time of filing in the Clerk's central office.

(2) *Evaluation and Treatment Orders.* Orders issued pursuant to RCW 71.05.150(2) to detain a person to a designated evaluation and treatment facility for not more than seventy-two-hour evaluation and treatment period, shall be effective immediately from the time of issuance.

(h) Reporting to Department of Licensing.

(1) The Clerk is required to report data about certain civil judgments involving motor vehicle cases (Title 46 RCW) to the Washington State Department of Licensing. To ensure the necessary data is available to the Clerk for reporting purposes, parties to such judgments shall provide to the Clerk a completed "DOL Reporting Data Sheet", which is available at the Clerk's Office or on the Clerk's website: www. kingcounty.gov/courts/clerk, within thirty days after entry of judgment.

[Amended effective September 1, 2004; September 1, 2008; September 1, 2011; September 1, 2015.]

Official Comment

"The court deleted LCR 58(c) as unnecessary. This issue is addressed by the best evidence rule."

LCR 59. NEW TRIAL, RECONSIDERATION, AND AMENDMENT OF JUDGMENTS

(a) *Motion and Notice of Hearing.* The form of motion and notice of hearing shall conform to LCR 7(b)(4). The motion will be considered without oral argument unless called for by the court.

(b) *Response and Reply.* No response to a motion for reconsideration shall be filed unless requested by the court. No motion for reconsideration will be granted without such a request. If a response is called for, a reply may be filed within two days of service of the response.

(c) *Form of Proposed Order; Mailing Envelopes.* The moving party and any party given leave to file a memorandum in opposition shall attach an original proposed order to the working copies submitted to the hearing judge. If the working copies are submitted in paper form, pre-addressed stamped envelopes for each party/counsel shall also be submitted to the hearing judge. Working copies shall be submitted pursuant to the requirements of LCR 7(b) to the extent not inconsistent with this rule.

[Adopted effective September 1, 2008; amended effective September 1, 2009.]

LCR 60.   RELIEF FROM JUDGMENT OR ORDER

(e) Procedure on Vacation of Judgment.

(1) *Default Judgment*: The return on the order to show cause to set aside a default judgment shall be as follows:

(A) Case originally assigned to a judge who has not been assigned (transferred) to a new case designation area or to juvenile court: The order to show cause shall be returned to the judge to whom the case had been originally assigned, regardless of which judicial officer signed the judgment of default.

(B) Case originally assigned to a judge who has left the court or who has transferred to a court facility other than that reflected in the case designa-

tion: The order to show cause shall be returned to the Chief Civil Judge in Seattle or the Maleng Regional Justice Center Chief Judge, according to the designation of the case or in family law cases involving children before the Chief Unified Family Court Judge.

(C) Case not assigned to a judge: The order to show cause shall be returned to the department that entered the default judgment

(2) *Judgment following trial:* The return on the order to show cause to set aside a judgment following trial shall be before the judge who presided over the trial. If that judge has left the court, the return on the order to show cause shall be before the Chief Civil Judge in Seattle or the Maleng Regional Justice Center Chief Judge, depending upon the designation of the case or in family law cases involving children before the Chief Unified Family Court Judge.

(3) *Resetting the trial date:* Where the relief sought includes the right to a trial, a motion to re-set trial date shall be filed contemporaneously with the motion for relief from judgment.

[Adopted effective September 1, 2004; amended effective September 1, 2007; September 1, 2008.]

VIII.   PROVISIONAL AND FINAL REMEDIES (Rules 64–71)

LCR 65.   INJUNCTIONS

(b) *Temporary Restraining Order*

(1) **Where heard:** Except for family law cases, a party seeking a temporary restraining order shall present the motion for temporary restraining order to the Ex Parte and Probate Department through the Clerk's Office. For family law cases, see the LFLR's (Local Family Law Rules).

(2) **Calendaring requirement:** Prior to appearing in the Ex Parte and Probate Department on a motion for a temporary restraining order, the moving party shall obtain a date for hearing on the motion for preliminary injunction from the trial department to which the case is assigned. The hearing shall be set in conformance with the timing requirements of CR 65(b).

[Adopted effective September 1, 2004; amended effective September 1, 2008; amended on an emergency basis effective January 1, 2009; amended on a permanent basis effective September 1, 2009.]

LCR 66.   RECEIVERSHIP PROCEEDINGS

(a) *Generally.*

(1) **Petition and Notice.** A petition for appointment of a receiver may be filed in an underlying proceeding, as provided in RCW 7.60 or as a new action as otherwise provided by statute. Reasonable notice of the time and place of the hearing to determine the appointment of a receiver and the name of

any proposed receiver recommended by the petitioner shall be served upon all parties. If the petition is filed as a new action, the initial hearing shall be noted in the Ex Parte and Probate Department, be presented directly by the parties, and an order to show cause shall be served on all parties. Contested proceedings may be referred by the commissioner to the assigned Judge. Petitions filed in a pending action shall be heard by the assigned Judge, and do not require an Order to Show Cause if all parties have been served and appeared in the action. Upon the appointment of a receiver, the receiver shall notify all parties of the appointment.

(2) **Procedure.** Court rules for motion practice will apply to applications for appointment of a receiver.

(3) **Status Conference.** After the appointment of a receiver, any party may note a status conference before the assigned Judge for the purpose of determining the course of proceedings in the receivership, including amending the case schedule and such other matters as may be appropriate for the receivership.

(4) **Ancillary Proceedings.** Any actions filed by or against a receiver shall be assigned to the Judge overseeing the receivership, unless otherwise ordered by that Judge.

[Amended effective September 1, 1997; September 1, 2008; amended on an emergency basis effective January 1, 2009; amended on a permanent basis effective September 1, 2009.]

LCR 69. EXECUTION

(b) Supplemental Proceedings.

(1) *Time.* Supplemental proceedings shall be conducted commencing at such time as assigned by the Court in the Courtroom of the Chief Civil Department for Seattle case assignment area cases and by the Chief Maleng Regional Justice Center Judge for Kent case assignment area cases.

(2) *Failure to Appear.* Failure of the person to be examined to appear shall result in issuance of a bench warrant by the Court. Failure of the examining attorney to appear without prior notification to the Court shall result in release of the person to be examined and may result in imposition of terms against that attorney if subsequent supplemental proceedings are scheduled for the same debtor.

[Adopted effective September 1, 1984; amended effective September 1, 1996; September 1, 2003; September 1, 2008.]

X. SUPERIOR COURTS AND CLERKS (Rules 77–80)

LCR 77. SUPERIOR COURTS AND JUDICIAL OFFICERS

(f) Sessions.

(1) *Continuous Session.* There shall be one continuous session of court from January 1 to December 31 of each year, excepting those days designated as legal holidays and such days in connection therewith as shall be specifically designated from time to time by the court.

(2) *Court Hours.*

(A) Presiding Department. The court shall be open from 8:30 AM to 12:00 noon and 1:30 PM to 4:30 PM, Monday through Friday and Saturday from 10:00–12:00. No judge need attend personally on Saturdays except upon call. When not personally present, the Presiding Judge shall keep posted in a conspicuous place on the courtroom door and also on the door of the County Clerk's office a notice giving the names and telephone numbers where the Presiding Judge or acting Presiding Judge and clerk may be reached during court hours.

(B) Trial Departments. Sessions of trial departments other than the Juvenile and Special Calendars Departments shall be from 9:00 AM until 12 noon and from 1:30 PM until 4 PM, Monday through Friday, unless otherwise ordered by the judge. Special sessions of any court may be held on Saturday at the discretion of the judge presiding in the particular department, to hear any and all matters that such judge sets for hearing before him/her and at such hours upon said day as the departmental judge shall fix.

(C) Ex Parte Department. The Ex Parte Department shall be open from 9 AM until 12 noon and from 1:30 PM until 4:15 PM, Monday through Friday. See LCR 40.1

(i) Sessions Where More Than One Judge Sits— Effect on Decrees, Orders, Etc.

(1) *Presiding Judge; Duties.* The Presiding Judge shall preside when the court sits *en banc*, shall preside over the Department of the Presiding Judge and shall receive and dispose of all communications intended for the Superior Court not personally addressed to any judge nor relating to business which has been assigned to any particular department.

(2) —*Same; Jurors.* The Presiding Judge shall have general charge of all jurors and shall determine requests for excuse from jury service. The Presiding Judge may delegate the determination for requests for excuse from jury service to senior jury staff.

(3) —*Same; Liaison With Departments.* If, for any reason, a departmental judge cannot hear a matter, he/she shall return it to the Chief Civil Department for Seattle case assignment area cases and the Chief Maleng Regional Justice Center Judge for Kent case assignment area cases, for hearing or reassignment.

(4) —*Same; Criminal Arraignments, Emergency Orders and Writs.* The Chief Criminal Judge shall hear or assign for hearing the criminal arraignment calendar. Applications for Writs of Habeas Corpus relating to custody of minor children shall be presented to the most senior UFC Judge at the Maleng Regional Justice Center. Applications for emergency and miscellaneous applications on criminal or infraction matters shall be presented to the Chief Criminal Judge or Chief Judge of the Maleng Regional Justice Center. No other judge shall sign emergency orders or grant writs while the Presiding Judge or Chief Civil Judge is on duty unless the matter is specifically assigned to that judge by or under the direction of the Presiding Judge or Chief Civil Judge or Chief Judge of the Maleng Regional Justice Center, or except as provided in LCR 98.40. Any order procured in violation of this paragraph may be set aside by the Presiding Judge or Chief Civil Judge or Chief Judge of the Maleng Regional Justice Center upon the application of the party against whom the order has been issued made within 24 hours after service of the order. (See also CR 65(a)(1), Notice.)

(5) —*Same; Ex Parte Orders.* The Chief Civil Department or Chief Judge of the Maleng Regional Justice Center may hear any matters assigned to or arising out of the Ex Parte Department.

(6) —*Same; Judges Pro Tempore.* All judges pro tempore shall be appointed by the Presiding Judge.

(7) —*Same; Absence.* The Presiding Judge in case of disability or necessary absence, may designate another judge to act as Presiding Judge temporarily when the Assistant Presiding Judge is not available.

(8) —*Same; Delegation of Duties.* The Presiding Judge may delegate all duties not required by law to be performed by a Superior Court judge in person.

(9) *Orders to Show Cause.* The court shall make orders to show cause returnable in not less than five days except for good cause shown.

[Amended effective September 1, 1986; September 1, 1993; September 1, 1996; September 1, 1999; September 1, 2001; September 1, 2003; September 1, 2007; September 1, 2008; amended on an emergency basis effective January 1, 2009; amended on a permanent basis effective September 1, 2009; September 1, 2012; September 1, 2015.]

Comment:

See also LFLR 5(c) (*Where to Schedule Specific Motions in Family Law Proceedings*).

LCR 78. CLERKS

(a) *Powers and Duties of Clerk.*

(1) **Certification.** The Clerk, upon application and payment of the fee provided by law, shall certify any one or more of the rules of this Court, or subsections thereof.

(c) *Orders by Clerk.*

(1) **Commission to Take Testimony in Probate and Adoption Proceedings.** Upon the filing of a request the Clerk shall issue a commission to take testimony in any probate or adoption proceeding, unless otherwise ordered by the Court.

(f) *Bonds.*

(1) **Cash Bonds; Minimum Amount.** Cash bonds ordered to be posted with the Clerk in probate and other matters will be in the amount of at least $25 and shall be paid in cash.

(2) —**Same; Withdrawal.** The party posting a cash bond, promptly at the conclusion of the matter to which it relates, shall present to the Court an order authorizing withdrawal, and forthwith upon its entry, withdraw the bond.

(g) *Payment and Disbursal of Trust Funds.*

(1) **Payment of Trust Funds.** Trust funds shall be paid to the Clerk with one of the following methods of payment: cash, cashier's check, money order, certified check, government check, attorney's check, or company's check.

(2) **Disbursal of Trust Funds.** Trust funds that are paid by attorney's check or company's check will be available to be disbursed eight court days after receipt by the Clerk. Trust funds that are paid by any other method listed in subsection (1) above will normally be available to be disbursed the first or second court day following receipt by the Clerk.

(h) *Interest Bearing Accounts.*

(1) Requests and orders directing the Clerk to place trust funds in amounts exceeding $2,000.00 into an interest bearing account, must be delivered to the Cashier Section of the King County Superior Court Clerk's Office. If the request or order was filed prior to payment of the trust funds, a copy of the request or order must be delivered to the Cashier Section at the time the trust funds are paid.

(i) **Waiver of ECR On–Line fees.** Requests to waive fees for ECR On-line shall be presented to the Clerk. Forms and instructions for these waivers are available at the Clerk's Office or on the Clerk's website: www.kingcounty.gov/courts/clerk

[Amended effective September 1, 1996; September 1, 2008; September 1, 2009.]

LCR 79. BOOKS AND RECORDS KEPT BY CLERK

(d) **Other Books and Records of Clerk.**

(1) *Exhibits; Filing and Substitution.* All exhibits and other documents received in evidence on the trial of any cause must be filed at that time, but the court may, either then or by leave granted thereafter, upon notice, permit a copy of any such exhibit or other document to be filed or substituted in the files, in lieu of the original.

(A) Exhibit Files. The exhibits in all cases shall be kept by the clerk separate from the files of the case.

(B) Exhibits–Inspection. No exhibits shall be inspected in the clerk's office except in the presence of the clerk or one of his/her deputies.

(C) Original Court Record–Copies. No original court record shall be admitted as an exhibit, but a copy thereof may be so admitted.

(D) Cardboard Exhibits. Pictures and diagrams shall not be permanently affixed to large cardboards used for display. The clerk is permitted to remove pictures and diagrams from the cardboard for storage purposes.

(2) *Unsuitable Materials as Exhibits.* Whenever there is presented to the clerk for filing in a cause any document or other material that is deemed by the clerk to be improper or inappropriate for filing, the clerk shall affix his/her file mark thereto and may forthwith orally apply to the court for a determination of the propriety of filing the material presented. If the court determines that the document or material should not be made a part of the file, an order shall be entered to that effect and the material shall be retained by the clerk as an exhibit in the cause. The court may order that the unsuitable material be sealed, in which event it shall be available for inspection only by order of the court except to the parties or their attorneys of record.

(3) —*Same; Not Evidence Unless Ordered.* Exhibits filed pursuant to subsection (2) hereof shall not be evidence in the cause unless by order of the trial judge entered on notice and hearing.

(4) *Withdrawal of Files and Exhibits.*

(A) Files. The clerk shall permit no original paper documents to be taken from his/her office or from his/her custody, by anyone other than court personnel, unless written authority has first been obtained. All of the clerk's files which are in the hands of an attorney for the purposes of any trial or hearing must be returned by the attorney to the clerk at the close thereof. The clerk, or a designated deputy, may in his/her discretion and on application in writing, grant written authority to the applicant to withdraw one or more original paper files from the clerk's custody for a period not exceeding ten days. The court may, upon written application showing cause therefore, authorize the withdrawal of specified clerk's files for a period in excess of ten days. For case files maintained electronically, no person may remove the electronic media on which the record is kept from the custody of the Clerk, but copies of a file or of the documents therein may be obtained from the Clerk as provided by law and rule.

(B) —Same; Statement of Facts. Statements of facts in cases where the original record remains in paper form, after having been settled and signed, shall not be withdrawn from the Clerk's office.

(C) Exhibits; Temporary Withdrawal. Exhibits may be withdrawn temporarily from the custody of the Clerk only by:

(i) The Judge having the cause under consideration;

(ii) Official court reporters, without court order, for use in connection with their duties;

(iii) Attorneys of record, upon court order, after notice to or with the consent of opposing counsel. The Clerk shall take an itemized receipt for all exhibits withdrawn, and upon return of the exhibit or exhibits they shall be checked by the Clerk against the original receipts. The Clerk shall keep all receipts for such exhibits for the period of three years from date.

(D) Failure to Return Files or Exhibits; Sanctions. In the event that an attorney or other person fails to return files or exhibits which were temporarily withdrawn by him/her within the time required, and fails to comply with the Clerk's request for their return, the Clerk may, without notice to the attorney or other person concerned, apply to the Presiding Judge for an order for the immediate return of such files or exhibits. A certified copy of such order, if entered, shall then be served upon the attorney or other person involved.

(E) Exhibits; Permanent Withdrawal. After final judgment, the time for appeal having elapsed, and no appeal having been taken, the Court, on application of any party or other person entitled to the possession of one or more exhibits, and for good cause shown, may in its discretion order the withdrawal of such exhibit or exhibits and delivery thereof to such party or other person.

(i) —Exhibits; Narcotics. See LGR 20.

(F) Return of Exhibits and Unopened Depositions. In any civil cause on a stipulation of the parties that when judgment in the cause shall become final, or shall become final after an appeal, or upon judgment of dismissal or upon filing a satisfaction of judgment, the Clerk may return all exhibits and unopened depositions, or may destroy them. The Court may enter an order accordingly.

(5) *Document or File Sealed by Court Order.* The Clerk shall not permit the examination of any sealed document or file except by order of the Court entered pursuant to LCR 77(i)(10).

(6) *Documents Sealed By Court Order.* Once the court order has been signed, the filing party shall place the words "Sealed document per (date) court order" in the caption of any document to be sealed. The filing party must then place the sealed document in a manila envelope marked "Sealed document" on the outside before delivering it to the clerk for filing.

(7) *Documents Redacted by Court Order.* Once the court order has been signed allowing redaction, parties shall file redacted copies of the entire document with the words "Redacted copy pursuant to (date) Order" in the caption.

[Amended effective September 1, 2001, September 1, 2003; September 1, 2004; September 1, 2007; September 1, 2008; September 2, 2014.]

LCR 80. COURT REPORTERS AND TRANSCRIPTS

(a) **Scope of Rule.** The provisions of this rule apply to official court reporters, visiting judge court reporters and, court reporters *pro tempore* and to anyone who produces an official transcript, for example a transcript used for appellate purposes.

(b) **Reserved.**

(c) **Reserved.**

(d) **General Reporting Requirements.**

(1) *Separate Civil and Criminal Notes.* Court reporters shall keep separate notes for civil and criminal cases.

(2) *Arguments; Voir Dire; Information Discussion.* Unless expressly requested by a party or directed by the trial Judge, the following matters will not be reported or recorded:

(A) Opening statements and closing arguments in civil cases, both jury and nonjury.

(B) Voir dire in civil jury cases.

(C) Informal discussions relating to proposed instructions.

(D) Administrative Law Reviews

(3) *Oral Rulings and Decisions.* If the Judge orders in a minute entry that the judge requests to review a transcript of the oral decision before the transcript is filed, the transcriptionist shall electronically transmit a copy of the oral decision to the Judge. The Judge's corrections, if any, shall be returned to the transcriptionist within 14 days of transmittal. If the Judge does not return corrections within 14 days, the transcript shall be filed as presented to the Judge, without further notice.

(4) *Verbatim Report of Proceedings.* Preparation of an official transcript of electronically recorded proceedings conducted in Superior Court (including videotape, audiotape, and digital recordings) shall be completed by a court-approved transcriber in accordance with procedures developed by the Office of the Administrator for the Courts and the King County Superior Court Clerk.

(A) To be included on the King County Superior Court Approved Transcriber List, reporters must complete the Affidavit Requesting Transcriber Status provided by the Superior Court Clerk.

(e) Transcripts and Statements of Fact.

(1) *Transcripts; Notice to Opposing Counsel.* Subject to making satisfactory arrangements for payment of cost, reporters shall furnish promptly all transcripts ordered by counsel. Upon request by one counsel for a transcript of any portion of the record, the reporter shall give prompt notice of the request to opposing counsel.

(2) *Statements of Fact; Ordered in Writing.* Counsel ordering statements of fact shall make a timely request, in writing. Subject to making satisfactory arrangements for payment of the cost, reporters shall furnish promptly all statements of fact on written order from counsel.

(3) *Substitution of Reporters.* In the event there is a substitution of reporters, counsel may order the transcript or statement of facts from the reporter first assigned, who shall notify the substitute reporter of the order.

(f) Filing of Notes.

(1) *Separate Civil and Criminal Notes.* Reporters shall file their notes for civil and criminal cases separately with the Clerk's office within thirty days after the conclusion of the trial or proceeding unless governed by SPRC 3.

(2) *Index.* Reporters shall attach and file an index, with the numbers and titles of all trials reported, for each set of notes.

(3) *Withdrawal of Notes; Return.* After filing the notes, reporters may withdraw them for such time as is necessary to prepare transcripts, by giving a receipt therefore to the Clerk. Reporters shall return notes to the Clerk's office as the transcripts are completed, or on demand of the Clerk.

[Amended effective September 1, 1989; September 1, 2008; September 1, 2011; amended on an emergency basis, effective October 3, 2011; January 3, 2012; April 2, 2012; July 2, 2012; amended on a permanent basis, effective September 1, 2012.]

XI. GENERAL PROVISIONS (Rules 81–86)

LCR 82. CASE ASSIGNMENT AREA

(e) Location for Court Proceedings for Civil Cases Filed in King County; Filing of Documents and Pleadings and Designation of Case Assignment Area.

(1) *Designation of Case Assignment Area.* Each case filed in the Superior Court shall be accompanied by a Case Assignment Designation Form [in the form set forth at LCR 82(e)(8)] on which the party filing the initial pleading has designated whether the case fits within the Seattle Case Assignment Area or the Kent Case Assignment Area, under the standards set forth in Sections (2) through (7), below. Juvenile Offender cases and Involuntary Treatment Act cases are all designated to the Seattle Case Assignment Area. Civil cases filed prior to September 1, 1995 and criminal cases filed prior to June 1, 1996 are defaulted to the Seattle Case Assignment Area unless otherwise ordered by the Court.

(2) *Where Proceedings Held.* All proceedings of any nature shall be conducted at the Court facility in the case assignment area designated on the Case Assignment Designation Form unless the Court has otherwise ordered on its own motion or upon motion of any party to the action.

(3) *Boundaries of Case Assignment Areas.* For purposes of this rule King County shall be divided into case assignment areas as follows:

(A) Seattle Case Assignment Area. All of King County north of Interstate 90 and including all of the Interstate 90 right-of-way; all of the cities of Seattle, Mercer Island, Bellevue, Issaquah and North Bend; and all of Vashon and Maury Islands.

(B) Kent Case Assignment Area. All of King County south of Interstate 90 except those areas included in the Seattle Case Assignment Area.

(C) Change of Area Boundaries. The Presiding Judge may adjust the boundaries between areas when required for the efficient and fair administration of justice in King County.

(4) *Standards for Case Assignment Area Designation, and Revisions Thereof.*

(A) Location Designated by Party Filing Action. Initial designations shall be made upon filing as follows:

(i) Family Law, Paternity and Adoption Cases. For adoption cases, the area where the petitioner(s) resides; for paternity cases, the area where the child resides; and for all other family law cases, the area where either the petitioner or respondent resides or if neither party resides in King County, in the Seattle case assignment area.

(ii) Probate, Guardianship and Trust Cases. For probate cases, the area where the decedent principally resided or if the decedent did not reside in King County, the area in which any part of the estate may be; for guardianship cases, the area where the ward resides; and for trust cases, the area where the principal place of administration of the trust is located. If no principal residence or estate is located in King County, the action may be filed in either case assignment area.

(iii) Orders for Protection and Orders for Antiharassment. For orders for protection or for antiharassment, the area where the petitioner resides unless the petitioner has left the residence or household to avoid abuse; in that case, in either the case assignment area of the previous or the new household or residence.

(iv) Other Civil Cases. For civil cases involving personal injury or property damage, the area where the injury or damage occurred; for cases involving condemnation, quiet title, foreclosure, unlawful detainer or title to real property, the area where the property is located; for all other civil cases, including administrative law reviews, the area where a defendant or respondent resides, or if there is no defendant or respondent, or if defendant or respondent does not reside in King County, the area where the plaintiff or petitioner resides.

(v) Appeals from Courts of Limited Jurisdiction. For cases subject to RALJ, the case assignment area in which the court of original jurisdiction is located.

(vi) Transcripts of Judgment. For transcripts of judgment, the case assignment area where the court of original jurisdiction is located.

(vii) Small Claims Appeals. For small claims appeals, the case assignment area where the court of original jurisdiction is located.

(viii) Appeals from Department of Licensing Orders of Suspension. For appeals from Department of Licensing Orders of Suspension, the Seattle case assignment area.

(ix) Actions filed pursuant to RCW 36.01.050. For actions filed pursuant to RCW 36.01.050 (adjoining counties), either case assignment area.

(x) Domestic Modifications and Support Adjustments. Any Modification Petition or Motion for Support Adjustment in either domestic or paternity cases shall be accompanied by a new Case Assignment Designation form.

(xi) Cases filed pursuant to Trust and Dispute Resolution Act, ch. 11.96A, RCW. Seattle if the primary residence or estate of decedent was in the Seattle case assignment area; all other such cases shall be designated to Kent. If no principal residence or estate is located in King County, the action may be filed in either assignment area.

(B) Improper Designation/Lack of Designation. The designation of the improper case assignment area shall not be a basis for dismissal of any action, but may be a basis for imposition of terms. The lack of designation of case assignment area at initial case filing may be a basis for imposition of terms and will result in assignment to a case assignment area at the Court's discretion.

(C) Assignment or Transfer on Court's Motion. The Court on its own motion may assign or transfer cases to another case assignment area in the county whenever required for the just and efficient administration of justice in King County.

(D) Motions By Party to Transfer. Motions to transfer court proceedings from one case assignment area to another shall be presented to the Chief Civil Judge or the Chief Judge of the Maleng Regional Justice Center. Such motions shall be made in writing as required by LCR 7; shall be ruled on by the Court without oral argument; and shall be noted for consideration no later than 14 days after the date for filing the Confirmation of Joinder of Parties, Claims, and Defenses in civil cases, as required in LCR 4.2(a), or the date for filing of the Confirmation of Issues in domestic cases, as required by LFLR 4(c). All cases shall proceed in the original case assignment area until an order of transfer is entered. Proceedings in the assigned area shall not preclude the timely filing of a motion to transfer.

(E) Venue not Affected. This rule shall not affect whether venue is proper in any Superior Court facility in King County.

(5) *Where Pleadings and Documents Filed.* Pursuant to LGR 30, all pleadings and documents for any civil action in King County must be electronically filed with the Clerk using the Clerk's e-filing application. Documents identified as exceptions to mandatory e-filing must be filed in paper form with the Clerk of the Superior Court at any court facility in any case assignment area in the county. Working copies of docu-

ments for the judge or commissioner must be submitted pursuant to the requirements of LCR 7(b).

(6) *Ex Parte Proceedings.* Proceedings in the Ex Parte Department shall be heard in the case assignment area of the case, except that ex parte matters which do not require court case file review may be heard in any court facility of King County Superior Court.

(7) *Inclusion of Case Assignment Area Code.* All pleadings and documents shall contain after the cause number the case assignment area code assigned by the Clerk (or the default case assignment area code pursuant to LCR 82(e)(1)) for the case assignment area in which court proceedings are to be held. The Clerk may reject pleadings or documents that do not contain this case assignment area code.

(8) *Case Assignment Designation Form.* The Case Assignment Designation Form shall be in substantially the following form:

Attachment to Case Indexing Cover Sheet
CASE ASSIGNMENT DESIGNATION

I certify that this case meets the case assignment criteria, described in King County LCR 82(e), for the:

___ Seattle Area, defined as

All of King County north of Interstate 90 and including all of the Interstate 90 right-of-way; all of the cities of Seattle, Mercer Island, Bellevue, Issaquah and North Bend; and all of Vashon and Maury Islands.

___ Kent Area, defined as

All of King County south of Interstate 90 except those areas included in the Seattle Case Assignment Area.

_____ _____
Signature of Petitioner/Plaintiff   Date

or

_____ _____
Signature of Attorney for   Date
Petitioner/Plaintiff

_____
WSBA Number

(9) *Jury Assignment Area.* See LGR 18. The rule provides for Seattle and Kent jury assignment areas, consisting of registered voters and licensed drivers and identicard holders residing in each jury assignment area.

[Effective September 1, 1995; amended effective September 1, 1996; April 14, 1997; September 1, 1997; September 1, 1999; September 1, 2001; September 1, 2004, September 1, 2006, September 1, 2007; September 1, 2008; June 1, 2009; September 8, 2009; September 1, 2010; September 1, 2012; September 2, 2013.]

LCR 83. LOCAL RULES OF SUPERIOR COURT

Except in case of emergency or other circumstances justifying immediate change, and except for rules that describe only the structure, internal management and organization of the court as provided in GR 7(a), the court shall submit to the Bar proposals for amendment of local rules so that members of the bar may submit comments or objections prior to the adoption of proposed amendments.

[Amended effective September 1, 1977; September 1, 1981; September 1, 1993; September 1, 2001; September 1, 2008.]

LCR 84. "FORMS"

(a) Requirements.

(1) All original pleadings or other documents with proper caption and cause number will be file stamped, docketed and secured in the legal file by the Clerk of the Superior Court in the order received.

(2) *Action documents.* Pleadings or other documents requiring action on the part of the Clerk/Court (other than file stamping, docketing and entry in the court file) shall be considered action documents. Action documents must contain a special caption of "Clerk's Action Required" directly below the document title and specify the action required on the first page.

[Adopted effective September 1, 1984; amended effective September 1, 2004; September 1, 2007; September 1, 2008.]

XII. SPECIAL PROCEEDINGS RULES

LCR 93.04. ADOPTION PROCEEDINGS

(a) *Where Hearings are to be Held.* All adoption hearings shall be heard in the Ex Parte and Probate Department of the case assignment area designated for that case unless specially set before a Judge. All hearings shall be noted in conformity with paragraph (b) of this rule.

(b) *Notice of Hearing.* All adoption hearings requiring notice shall be noted for hearing, on the approved Notice for Hearing form, at least 14 days in advance of the hearing date unless otherwise required for the hearing by law. The moving party shall serve and file all motions documents no later than 14 days before the hearing date.

(c) *Notice to Adoption Service.* Upon the filing of any initial pleadings for adoption of a minor child, the petitioner shall immediately notify the King County Family Court Adoption Service, on a form approved by the Court, of the filing of such proceeding and the names and addresses of all parties and attorneys. Copies of all Notices for Hearing for temporary custody, termination or relinquishment of parental rights or for the entry of a Decree of Adoption of a minor child shall be served upon the Adoption Service in conformity with paragraph (b) of this rule.

(d) *Court's Working Copies.* Working copies of pleadings and Notice for Hearing shall be submitted to the hearing judge or commissioner, pursuant to the requirements of LCR 7(b), no later than 14 days prior to the date set for hearing.

(e) *Post Placement Reports and Services.* No person shall provide post-placement services in a private or independent adoption until authorized by the Court. Unless otherwise specifically ordered by the Court, the adoption agency having legal custody of the child may be appointed to prepare the post-placement report required by statute. In independent adoptions, the motion to appoint a qualified person to provide post-placement services shall be supported by a written curriculum vita or resume.

(f) *Case Schedule. [Reserved]*

(g) *Confirmation of Consent.* Except where legal custody of the adoptee is held by a licensed child placing agency, King County Family Court Services shall investigate and provide to the Court a report confirming the voluntariness of any consent to relinquish parental rights. No consent to relinquish parental rights shall be approved until the Court has received a report complying with this rule. The petitioner or Adoption Facilitator shall immediately notify the Adoption Service that a Consent to Relinquish Parental Rights of Consent to Adoption is anticipated and that a Confirmation of Consent report will be required.

(h) *File Review.* The Adoption Service shall review and forward to the Court the original court file, approved adoption checklist, court docket and working copies not less than two court days prior to any properly noted hearing. The Adoption Service shall notify the Court and parties of any deficiencies noted in the court file.

(i) *Disclosure of Fees and Costs.* A completed financial disclosure form shall be filed by the petitioner and considered by the Court at any hearing which may result in the termination of parental rights, award of temporary custody or entry of an adoption decree.

[Amended effective September 20, 1990; September 1, 1996; September 1, 1999; September 1, 2004; September 1, 2008; September 1, 2009.]

LCR 94.04. FAMILY LAW PROCEEDINGS

[Deleted effective September 1, 2004, See the LFLR's (local family law rules)]

[Amended September 1, 1978; September 1, 1981; July 17, 1985; September 1, 1985; September 1, 1986; May 1, 1988; December 1, 1988; January 1, 1990; September 1, 1990; September 1, 1992; September 1, 1993; September 1, 1994;

September 1, 1996; April 14, 1997; September 1, 1997; September 1, 2001; September 1, 2002; September 1, 2004.]

LCR 98.04. ESTATES—PROBATE— NOTICES

(a) *Probate Hearings.* Probate matters shall be presented to the Ex Parte and Probate Department in accordance with the policy guidelines in the probate manual issued by the Court and the Motions and Hearings Manual issued by the Clerk. The judicial officer may refer contested proceedings to the Clerk who shall issue a case schedule and assign a judge.

(b) *Clerk's File and Noticed Hearings Required.* The following matters shall be noted for hearing at least 14 days in advance:

(1) All guardianship and decedent's estate matters involving the approval of periodic reports, final accounts or the expenditure of funds;

(2) Petitions for Nonintervention Powers, unless notice has been waived by the parties or is not required by law;

(3) Interim accounts in estate matters;

(4) Motion for confirmation of sale of real estate; or

(5) Any other matter in which the court is requested to find that certain procedural steps have been taken.

(6) Working copies of all documents in contested matters and those matters requiring notice must be submitted to the Ex Parte and Probate Department, hearing judge, or commissioner, not later than seven days preceding the hearing. Response documents including briefs, if any, must be filed with the clerk, copies shall be served on all parties, and working copies shall be submitted to Ex Parte, the hearing judge, or commissioner, no later than noon four court days prior to the hearing time. Documents in strict reply thereto shall be similarly filed and served no later than noon two court days prior to the hearing. Working copies shall be submitted pursuant to the requirements of LCR 7(b) to the extent not inconsistent with this rule.

(c) *Bonds to be Signed by Principal.* All bonds required of personal representatives shall be signed by the principal and shall contain the address of the surety.

(d) *Order for Production of Wills.* Upon filing any petition showing jurisdictional facts as to the estate of a deceased person and alleging that it is believed that a will exists and is in a safety deposit box to which the deceased had access, any person having control of such safety deposit box may be directed by court order to open such box in the presence of the petitioner, and if a document purporting to be a will of the deceased is found, the custodian of such safety deposit box shall deliver the same to counsel for the petitioner for immediate filing or to the clerk of the court.

(e) *Appointments; Eligibility of County Employees.* No county employee shall be appointed guardian or administrator in any matter in which compensation is allowed, unless he/she has an interest or blood kinship, or as an heir, or of a financial nature.

(f) *Probate Homesteads; Prior Claims.* In all cases where a petition for allowance in lieu of homestead or in addition thereto is filed by the surviving spouse, vouchers showing the payment of funeral expenses, expenses of last sickness and of administration including fees of appraisers, or a signed written statement by the creditor that such payment has been provided for, must be filed at or before the time of the hearing of said petition.

(g) *Oaths.* The Personal Representative(s) name must be typed or printed on the oath as it appears in the order. When a Personal Representative in an estate changes his or her name, he or she must obtain an order for new letters and file an oath under the new name in order to receive new letters. The expiration date of the letters shall remain the same unless changed by the new order.

(h) *Order Appointing Personal Representative.* The order shall contain the name(s) of the Personal Representative as it appears in the oath.

(i) *Notification of Change of Address.* Any person appointed as Personal Representative or Administrator of an estate must file a notice of change of address with the court within 30 days of the change.

[Amended effective September 1, 1984; September 1, 1999; September 1, 2001; September 1, 2004; September 1, 2005; September 1, 2006; September 1, 2008; amended on an emergency basis effective January 1, 2009; amended on a permanent basis effective September 1, 2009.]

LCR 98.14. TRUST AND ESTATE DISPUTE RESOLUTION ACT AND POWER OF ATTORNEY

(a) *Applicability.* This rule shall apply to all judicial proceedings under RCW 11.96A.090 or 11.96A.300. All documents filed under this rule shall be captioned as *In re the Estate of.* Documents may be further sub-captioned to identify specific parties as circumstances warrant.

(b) *Hearings.* Judicial proceedings shall be assigned to the Ex Parte and Probate department. Hearings shall be noted at least 14 days in advance and at least 20 days after service and filing of the TEDRA petition. See also LR 98.04(b)(6). If a need for an extended hearing arises, the matter will be certified for trial. The Clerk's Office will issue a judicial assignment and a trial date.

(c) *Performance Requirements.* All issues initiated under TEDRA that pertain to an estate must be resolved before the estate can be closed. If the TEDRA proceeding was filed as an incidental action under a separate cause number, when all issues are resolved and the case is ready to be closed, a document shall be filed in the matter indicating that a complete resolution has been achieved.

[Adopted effective September 1, 2006; amended effective September 1, 2008.]

LCR 98.16. SETTLEMENT OF CLAIMS OF MINORS AND INCAPACITATED PERSONS

(a) *Representation.*

(1) Working Copies. Working copies of reports of the settlement guardian ad litem, independent counsel, and of the general guardian in regard to the proposed settlement shall be provided to the Ex Parte and Probate Department not later than seven days preceding the hearing. Working copies shall be submitted pursuant to the requirements of LCR 7(b) to the extent not inconsistent with this rule.

(2) Ex Parte and Probate Department to Hear. All matters requiring the attention of the Court shall be presented to the Ex Parte and Probate Department.

(3) Independent Counsel. A plaintiff attorney representing the incapacitated person may be found to be an independent attorney upon application to the Court and entry of findings per SPR 98.16W. An attorney may not be specially retained by the parties for the purpose of serving as independent counsel, but may be appointed by the Court.

(4) Performance of Requirements; Review. If there is no general guardian at the time a settlement is authorized, the Court shall thereupon follow procedures for review and checking on the case until all requirements of the Court incident to the settlement have been complied with and appropriate receipts have been placed on file.

(5) File Number Case Type. All settlements other than those occurring in cases that already have a King County case number shall be filed with a guardianship case number.

(6) Report Date. Upon signing of the order appointing a settlement guardian ad litem or independent counsel, the Court will note on the order when the report is due.

(7) Reports and Accounting. Periodic reports and accountings required of guardians ad litem who are custodians of an incapacitated person's estate shall be filed and noted for hearing at least 14 days before the scheduled date.

(8) Appointment. The appointment of settlement or litigation guardians ad litem, trust drafters, and independent counsel are subject, as appropriate, to the provisions of LGALR 1-7.

(b) *Control and Orders for Remaining Funds.* For all settlements in which the funds will be retained in a blocked account, a receipt must be submitted on a form approved by the court. The Order approving Minor Settlement shall note a date by which an order to disburse funds will be presented to the court.

[Amended effective September 1, 1984; September 1, 1993; September 1, 1996; September 1, 1999; September 1, 2006; September 1, 2008; September 1, 2009.]

LCR 98.20. GUARDIANSHIPS AND TRUSTS

(a) Hearing Date (Initial Appointment). Upon application, the clerk shall set a date and time for hearing on petitions for the appointment or removal of a guardian, limited guardian or trustee. Unless otherwise directed by court order, the date for an appointment hearing shall be not less than 45 days nor more than 60 days from the date of filing of the petition.

(b) Service and Filing of Reports (Initial Appointment). The report of the guardian ad litem, medical or psychological report, proof of service and other documents offered in support of the petition or in anticipation of the hearing shall be served and filed not less than 15 days in advance of the hearing date. Working copies of the guardian ad litem report, medical or psychological report, and any additional affidavits shall be submitted to the Ex Parte and Probate Department, or the appropriate hearing judge or commissioner, not later than 15 days preceding the hearing. Response documents including briefs, if any, must be filed with the clerk, copies must be served on all parties, and working copies must be submitted to the Ex Parte and Probate Department, or the appropriate hearing judge or commissioner, no later than noon four court days prior to the hearing time. Documents in strict reply thereto shall be similarly filed and served no later than noon two court days prior to the hearing. Working copies shall be submitted pursuant to the requirements of LCR 7(b) to the extent not inconsistent with this rule.

(c) Report Date.

(1) Upon signing of the order appointing guardian or declaring a trust and appointing a trustee, the next report shall be within 90 days of the anniversary of the appointment. The order shall include a Clerk's Action Summary on the first page in a format approved by the Court and posted on the King County Superior Court Clerk's website.

(2) Guardianships in which venue is changed to King County shall retain the reporting period established by the previous jurisdiction until the next accounting is reviewed by the court.

(3) Guardianships with multiple guardians and/or trustees shall have all reports due on the anniversary of the appointment of the first guardian/trustee. The court may designate a different term (i.e. annual, biennial or triennial) for the guardian or trustee report.

(4) If a successor guardian or trustee is appointed, reports shall be due on the anniversary of that appointment.

(5) Any changes to the reporting cycle of a guardian or trustee shall be approved by the court on a form provided by the Clerk's Office.

(d) Reports and Accountings and Contested or Noted Matters. Periodic reports and accountings required of guardians and trustees and other contested or noted matters shall be filed and noted for hearing at least 14 days before the scheduled date. Working copies of all reports, accountings, and contested matters otherwise noted or requiring notice must be submitted to the Ex Parte and Probate Department, or the appropriate hearing judge or commissioner, not later than 14 days preceding the hearing. Response documents, including briefs, if any, must be filed with the clerk and copies served on all parties and submitted to the Ex Parte and Probate Department, or the appropriate hearing judge or commissioner, no later than noon four court days prior to the hearing time; documents in strict reply thereto shall be similarly filed and served no later than noon two court days prior to the hearing. Working copies shall be submitted pursuant to the requirements of LCR 7(b) to the extent not inconsistent with this rule.

(e) Delinquency Calendar. The clerk of the court will track and notify the court of cases in which accountings are delinquent. The court will direct the guardian, trustee, and counsel to appear at a hearing in which sanctions may be imposed or the personal representative removed.

(f) Mailed Reports. Guardianship and trust reports and accountings may be presented for approval by mail without the necessity of noting the case on the appropriate motion calendar, provided that if any person has requested special notice of proceedings or is entitled to notice pursuant to any court order or notice of appearance, the party submitting an order by mail must obtain the approval and signature of the party entitled to notice on any proposed order of approval.

(g) Oaths. The guardian name(s) must be typed or printed on the oath as it appears in the order. When a guardian changes his or her name he or she must obtain an order for new letters and file an oath under the new name in order to receive new letters of guardianship. The expiration date of the letters shall remain the same unless changed by the new order.

(h) Order Approving Guardian's Report and Accounting. The order shall include a Clerk's Action Summary on the first page in a format approved by the Court and posted on the King County Superior Court Clerk's website. The order shall also contain the name(s) of the guardian and address as it appears in the oath and clearly identify whether acting full or limited guardian over the person and/or estate. The order shall be obtained within sixty (60) days of filing the report and accounting.

(i) Vulnerable Adult Protection (VAP) Petitions. Any petition protecting a vulnerable adult shall be filed as a civil matter separate from any guardianship matter. If there is an existing guardianship case when the VAP is filed, a copy of the Protection order may be placed in that file.

(j) Loss of Voting Rights

(1) In accordance with RCW 11.88.010(5), if an incapacitated person loses the right to vote, the Order Appointing Guardian or Approving Report shall include a specific finding on the loss of the right to vote.

(2) The Guardian Ad Litem shall also submit a Notice of Loss of Voting Rights to the court that shall include the name, address, and date of birth of the incapacitated person and that shall direct the Clerk to forward the Notice of Loss of Voting Rights to the County Auditor.

(3) If the guardianship is terminated by a determination of competency of the individual, the court shall direct the Clerk to send to the County Auditor a certified copy of the Order Restoring Voting Rights including the same personal identifiers as the Notice of Loss of Voting Rights.

[Adopted effective September 20, 1990. Amended effective September 1, 1996; September 1, 1999; September 1, 2001; September 1, 2003; September 1, 2004; September 1, 2005. Amended on an emergency basis effective January 1, 2006; amended on a permanent basis effective September 1, 2006; amended effective September 1, 2008; September 1, 2009; September 1, 2015.]

LCR 98.30. MENTAL ILLNESS PROCEEDINGS [RESCINDED]

[Effective September 1, 1995; amended effective September 1, 2001; September 1, 2008. Rescinded effective September 2, 2014.]

LCR 98.40. WRITS OF REVIEW, MANDAMUS, PROHIBITION

(a) Applicability. This rule shall apply to a writ filed pursuant to ch. 7.16, RCW.

(b) Notice to Adverse Party. Except in extraordinary circumstances, no writ shall issue unless the adverse party has been given timely notice pursuant to CR 6, LR 7, of the application for writ. If the notice was not given in a timely manner, the hearing on the application for writ shall be continued. No stay of proceedings shall issue without notice to all parties to the underlying cause from which the writ is sought. No stay of proceedings shall be issued by a judge *pro tempore* absent express written authority of the presiding judge or, in her or his absence, the assistant presiding judge.

(c) Contents of Application for Writ. The following documents must be filed with the application for the writ:

(1) Statement of relief requested;

(2) Legal memorandum explaining why there is no adequate remedy at law;

(3) Declaration or affidavit in support of the factual assertions in the writ;

(4) Declaration of notice to adverse party or statement as to why notice should be excused.

(d) Scheduling of Hearing on Application for Writ: The hearing on a writ from a criminal or infraction case shall be noted before the Chief Criminal Judge for Seattle case assignment area cases. The hearing on a writ in any other case shall be noted before the Chief Civil Judge for Seattle case assignment are cases. All hearings for Kent case assignment area cases shall be noted before the Chief RJC Judge. Where a stay of proceedings has been entered, the dispositive hearing on the writ shall be heard within thirty days of the issuance of the writ.

(e) Motion to File Writ in Forma Pauperis. The Chief Criminal Judge, in criminal and infraction cases, or the Chief Civil Judge in other cases shall review a motion to file *in forma pauperis* before a hearing on the application for a writ shall be scheduled. If the motion is granted, the clerk shall accept the application for filing without requiring a filing fee and shall assign a case number.

(f) Issuance of Case Schedule. When the court has found adequate cause for issuance of a writ, the filing party shall obtain a trial date and a case schedule from the clerk who will also assign the case to a Judge.

[Adopted effective September 1, 2001; amended September 1, 2002; September 1, 2003; September 1, 2005; September 1, 2008.]

LCR 98.50. SEXUALLY VIOLENT PREDATOR—OFFICE OF PUBLIC DEFENSE

Pursuant to RCW 71.09.055, requests for expert services are funded by the Washington State Office of Public Defense (WSOPD). A request for funds in excess of those authorized by WSOPD or for a second evaluator shall be addressed to the assigned trial judge. If the assigned trial judge disqualifies him or herself on the motion for expert services, the judge will refer the motion to the Chief Civil Judge.

The motion may be made *ex parte*, and, upon a showing of good cause, the moving papers may be ordered sealed by the court, and shall remain sealed until further order of the court. Respondent shall provide a copy of the motion to seal and proposed order to the petitioner.

Nothing in this rule limits requirements for the timely disclosure of experts intended to be called by the respondent at trial.

[Adopted effective September 1, 2008. Amended effective September 1, 2015.]

XIII.   GENERAL RULES (LGR)

LGR 15.   DESTRUCTION, SEALING, AND REDACTION OF COURT RECORDS

(c) Sealing or Redacting Court Record.

(1) *Motions to Destroy, Redact or Seal Previously Filed Documents.*

(A) Civil. Motions to destroy, redact or seal all or part of a previously filed civil or domestic relations court record shall be filed with the clerk and presented, in accordance with GR 15 and GR 22, to the assigned judge or if there is no assigned judge, to the Seattle Chief Civil Judge for civil cases with a Seattle designation and to the Chief Judge of the Maleng Regional Justice Center for civil cases with a Kent designation, the Chief Unified Family Court Judge for family law cases with children, with the following exceptions.

(B) Criminal. Motions for cases that are not pending trial shall be presented to the assigned judge or his or her successor or, if there is no trial assigned judge or successor, to the Seattle Chief Criminal Judge or the Chief Judge of the Maleng Regional Justice Center.

(C) Guardianship, Trusts and Probate. (Title 11) Motions may be presented to any regularly sitting Ex Parte Commissioner. Pro tem commissioners are not authorized to seal documents.

(D) Vulnerable Adult Protection Order. (RCW 74.04) Motions may be presented to any regularly sitting (but not a pro tem) Ex Parte Commissioner.

(E) Minor/Incapacitated Settlement. The motion shall be presented to the judicial officer who approved the minor settlement unless the judicial officer who approved the minor settlement is a pro tem commissioner, in which case the motion shall be brought before the assigned judge or any regularly sitting Ex Parte Commissioner.

(F) Name Changes Based on Domestic Violence. If no assigned judge, motion may be presented by the requesting party to any regularly sitting (but not a pro tem) Ex Parte Commissioner.

(G) Financial Source Documents, Personal Health Care Records and Confidential Reports in Title 26 Cases. In a proceeding brought pursuant to RCW 26, "financial source document", "personal health care record" and "confidential report" as defined under and submitted in accordance with GR 22 will be automatically sealed by the clerk without

court order, if accompanied by the proper cover sheet. See, also, LFLR 5(c) and LFLR 11 with respect to family law court records in general. Motions to seal documents pursuant to GR 22 where the filing party did not attach the appropriate coversheet may be presented to a regular sitting Ex Parte commissioner. Pro tem commissioners are not authorized to seal documents.

(2) *Motions to Seal/Redact When Submitted Contemporaneously With Confidential Document—Not to Be Filed.*

(A) Motions to Seal Documents Regarding Expert Witnesses and Other Services in Criminal Cases Pending Trial. Submit to the Chief Criminal Judge, pursuant to the protocol in the Criminal Department Manual: www.kingcounty.gov/courts/SuperiorCourt/criminal.

(B) Motions to Seal Documents Regarding Expert Witnesses and Other Services in Sexually Violent Predator Cases Pending Trial. Submit to assigned judge, pursuant to (E) below.

(C) Motions to Seal Documents Regarding Expert Witnesses and Other Services in Dependency and Termination Cases Pending Fact Finding. Submit to the Chief Juvenile Judge, pursuant to the published protocol available on the Court's Website www.kingcounty.gov/courts/JuvenileCourt/dependency.

(D) Motions to Seal Documents Regarding Expert Witnesses and Other Services in Juvenile Offender Cases Pending Trial. Submit to the Chief Juvenile Judge, pursuant to the protocol in the Juvenile Department Offender Manual: www.kingcounty.gov/courts/JuvenileCourt/offenders.

(E) All Other Motions.

(i) The moving party shall provide the following directly to the hearing judge and not file:

a) The original unredacted copy of the document(s) the party seeks to file under seal to the hearing judge in an envelope for in camera review. The words "SEALED PER COURT ORDER DATED [insert date]" shall be written on the unredacted document(s). The following information shall be written on the envelope: The case caption and cause number; a list of the document(s) under review; and the words "SEALED PER COURT ORDER DATED [insert date]."

b) A proposed redacted copy of the subject document(s).

c) A proposed order granting the motion to seal, with specific proposed findings setting forth the basis for sealing the document(s).

d) A self-addressed envelope with appropriate postage for the return of the document, should the party request said return.

(ii) If the hearing judge denies, in whole or in part, the motion to seal, the judge will return the original unredacted document(s) and the proposed redacted document(s) to the submitting party upon request to return if envelope with postage was provided and will file the order denying the motion to seal.

(iii) If the hearing judge grants the motion to seal the judge will file the sealed document(s) contemporaneously with a separate order granting the motion. If the judge grants the motion by allowing redaction, the judge shall write the words "SEALED PER COURT ORDER DATED [insert date]" in the caption of the unredacted document before filing.

(e) Motions to Unseal or Examine.

Sealed Files. Applications to examine sealed files shall be made as follows: civil, domestic, paternity and dependency cases to the assigned judge, or respective Chief Judge, and petitions to review or remove a will from the will repository to the Ex Parte and Probate Department, with oral argument, presented in person; adoption cases to the Sealed Adoption File Committee judges; dependency cases to the Juvenile Department; mental illness cases to the mental illness calendar. No order permitting the examination of any sealed file shall be entered without a written motion establishing justification under applicable court rules and case law. The court may, in its discretion, require notice to be given to any party in interest before permitting such examination.

(f) Orders to Destroy, Redact or Seal. Any order containing a directive to destroy, redact or seal all or part of a court record must be clearly captioned as such and may not be combined with any other order other than a protective order in criminal cases. The clerk may call to the attention of the judicial officer any deviation from the requirements of the rule.

[Adopted effective September 1, 2008. Amended on an emergency basis, effective January 1, 2009; amended on a permanent basis, effective September 1, 2009; September 1, 2010; September 2, 2013; September 1, 2015.]

LGR 18.   JURY ASSIGNMENT AREA

(e) Location for Jury Assignment Areas for Civil and Criminal Cases Filed in King County.

(1) *Designation of Jury Assignment Areas.* The jury source list shall be divided into a Seattle jury assignment area and a Kent jury assignment area that consist of registered voters and licensed drivers and identicard holders residing in each jury assignment area. The area within each jury assignment area shall be identified by zip code and documented on a list maintained by the chief administrative officer for the court.

(2) *Where Jurors Report.* Individuals receiving a jury summons shall report for service to the Court facility in the jury assignment area identified on the face of the summons.

(3) *Adjustment of Jury Assignment Area Boundaries.* The jury assignment areas contained in this rule may be adjusted by the administrative office of the courts based on the most current United States census data at the request of the majority of the judges of the superior court when required for the efficient and fair administration of justice.

[Adopted effective September 1, 2007; suspended effective September 1, 2008; amended effective September 1, 2009.]

Comment

This rule implements RCW 2.36.055, which allows the jury source list in King County to be divided into jury assignment areas that consist of registered voters and licensed drivers and identicard holders residing in each jury assignment area. The purpose of the statute and this rule is to lessen the burdens borne by jurors in traveling long distances to attend court proceedings by narrowing the geographic area from which jurors are drawn while maintaining a random and proportionate jury pool.

LGR 20.   SECURITY IN HANDLING COURT EXHIBITS

(i) **—Exhibits—Narcotics.** When narcotic or dangerous drugs have been admitted in evidence or have been identified, and are being held by the Clerk as a part of the records and files in any criminal cause, and all proceedings in the cause have been completed, the prosecuting attorney may apply to the Court for an order directing the Clerk to deliver such drugs to an authorized representative of the law enforcement agency initiating the prosecution for disposition according to law. If the Court finds these facts, and is of the opinion that there will be no further need for such drugs, it shall enter an order accordingly. The Clerk shall then deliver the drugs and take from the law enforcement agency a receipt which he/she shall file in the cause. He/she shall also file any certificate issued by an authorized federal or state agency and received by him/her showing the nature of such drugs. See also LCR 79(d).

[Adopted effective September 1, 2008.]

LGR 30.   MANDATORY ELECTRONIC FILING AND SERVICE

(b) Electronic Filing Authorization, Exception, Service, and Technology Equipment.

(4) *Electronic Filing and Service.*

(A) Mandatory Electronic Filing. Attorneys shall electronically file (e-file) all documents using the Clerk's online eFiling application unless this rule provides otherwise. Non–attorneys are not required to e-file but may do so.

(i) Documents That Shall Not Be E–Filed. The following documents must be filed in paper form rather than e–filed:

- Original wills and codicils, including new probate cases that include original wills or codicils;

- Certified records of proceedings for purposes of appeal;

- Documents presented for filing during a court hearing or trial;

- Documents for filing in an Aggravated Murder case;

- Administrative Law Review (ALR) Petitions;

- Interpleader or Surplus Funds Petitions;

- Documents submitted for *in camera* review, including documents submitted pursuant to LGR 15;

- Affidavits for Writs of Garnishment and Writs of Execution;

- New cases or fee based documents filed with an Order in Forma Pauperis.

Comment: Negotiable instruments, exhibits, and trial notebooks are examples of items that are not to be filed in the court file either in paper form or by e-filing.

(ii) Documents That May Be E–Filed. The following documents may be e-filed:

- Voluminous Documents—Voluminous documents of 500 pages or more may be e-filed or filed in paper form.

- Answers to Writs of Garnishment.

- Appeals of lower court decisions.

- Documents from governments or other courts under official seal including adoption documents. If filed electronically, the filing party must retain the original document during the pendency of any appeal and until at least sixty (60) days after completion of the instant case, and shall present the original document to the court if requested to do so. This does not include documents that are or will be submitted as an exhibit in a hearing or trial.

(iii) Working Copies for E–Filed Documents. Judges' working copies for e-filed documents may be electronically submitted to the Clerk using the Clerk's eFiling application and pursuant to LCR 7 unless this rule provides otherwise. The Clerk may assess a fee for the electronic delivery of working copies. Working copies of documents of 500 pages or more in length shall not be submit-

ted electronically. Working copies shall be delivered pursuant to LCR 7, LFLR 6 or the applicable rule for that case type.

(iv) Waiver of the Requirement to E–File. If an attorney is unable to e-file documents, the attorney may request a waiver. The attorney must make a showing of good cause and explain why he or she needs to file paper documents in that particular case. The Clerk will make waiver request forms available. The Clerk will consider each application and provide a written approval or denial to the attorney. Attorneys who receive a waiver shall file a copy of the waiver in each case in which they file documents. Attorneys who have received a waiver shall place the words "Exempt from e-filing per waiver filed on (date)" in the caption of all paper documents they file for the duration of the waiver.

(v) Non–Compliance With This Rule. If an attorney files a document in paper form and does not have an approved waiver from e-filing, the Clerk will assess a fee against the attorney pursuant to King County Code 4A.630.060 for each paper document filed.

(B) Mandatory Electronic Service.

(i) Effecting E–Service. When a party e-files a document, the party must electronically serve (e-serve) the document via the e-service feature within the Clerk's online eFiling application. A related document that is not filed but which must be served—e.g., a proposed order or a document served to comply with LCR 7(b)(4)(F)—shall also be e-served via the eFiling application using the "Upload Additional Documents to E–Serve" feature. E–service under this subsection (b)(4)(B)(i) constitutes service under CR 5 and is complete as stated in CR 5(b)(7). *Exceptions:* This subsection (b)(4)(B)(i) does not apply when a statute or rule requires that a document be personally served on the receiving party, the receiving party is not represented by an attorney and has not registered to accept e-service, or the receiving attorney has a waiver under subsection (b)(4)(A)(iv) above.

(ii) Accepting E–Service. Attorneys must promptly register (opt in) to accept e-service via the Clerk's eFiling application in each case in which the attorney appears (unless the attorney has a waiver under subsection (b)(4)(A)(iv) above). Likewise, a party that is not represented by an attorney must promptly register (opt in) to accept e-service via the Clerk's eFiling application in each case in which the party e-files a document.

(d) Authentication of Electronic Documents.

(2) *Signatures.*

(D) Law enforcement officer signatures on documents signed under penalty of perjury.

(ii) The King County Electronic Log of Detective Investigations is designated as a local and secure system for law enforcement to submit electronically signed documents to the King County Prosecuting Attorney for filing in Superior Court.

[Adopted effective June 1, 2009; amended effective September 1, 2010; September 1, 2011; September 1, 2012; amended on an emergency basis, effective January 1, 2014; April 1, 2014; June 27, 2014; amended on a permanent basis, effective September 2, 2014; September 1, 2015.]

LGR 31. ACCESS TO COURT RECORDS

(d) Access.

(2) On-line access to the Clerk's electronic records system outside of the clerk's office and outside of King County's wide area network shall be restricted to cases filed November 1, 2004 and forward and shall be limited to the following case types:

(i) all criminal cases, defined as those categorized with a number 1 as the third digit of the case number;

(ii) all civil cases, defined as those categorized with a number 2 as the third digit of the case number, with the exceptions of petitions for domestic violence protection orders and petitions for anti-harassment protection orders;

(iii) all probate cases, defined as those cases categorized with a number 4 as the third digit of the case number, except for guardianship cases.

(iv) final parenting plans, decrees, and child support orders in cases filed under RCW 26.09, 26.10, and 26.26.130(7)(b).

[Adopted effective November 5, 2004. Amended effective September 1, 2005; amended on an emergency basis effective February 28, 2006; amended on a permanent basis effective September 1, 2006; September 1, 2015.]

Official Comment

1. Procedures, terms and conditions for on-line access are available in the Clerk's office and online at www.kingcounty.gov/courts/clerk.

XIV. FAMILY LAW RULES (KCLFLR)

LFLR 1. APPLICABILITY

These rules, along with applicable State and Local rules, shall apply to all family law proceedings, except for adoptions. Family law proceedings for the purpose of this rule include actions to divide the property or debts of a domestic partnership or quasi-marital relationship. Failure to follow the rules may result in the court imposing sanctions, which can include requiring one party to pay the other party's attorney fees, refusing to hear a party's motion, not considering documents filed by a party, or any other sanction deemed appropriate.

Official Comment

RCW 26.12.010 confers authority upon Family Courts to hear any proceedings under Title 26 as well as any proceedings in which the court is asked to adjudicate or enforce the rights of the parties or their children regarding the determination or modification of parenting plans, child custody, visitation, or support, or the distribution of property or obligations. Family Law Commissioners are empowered to exercise all the powers and duties of court commissioners under the Washington State Constitution, Article IV, Sec. 23, when operating under the authority of RCW 26.12. See, RCW 26.12.060.

[Adopted effective September 1, 2004]

LFLR 2. DAYS AND TIMES FOR SCHEDULING HEARINGS; COURT HOLIDAYS

Family law motions shall not be scheduled on legal holidays and non-judicial days. Hearing dates and times for the Ex Parte Department, Family Law Motions, and Support Modification/Trial by Affidavit Calendars, as well as a list of legal holidays and non-judicial days, may be obtained from the Clerk's Office/Department of Judicial Administration (E609 King County Courthouse, Seattle WA 98104 or the Maleng Regional Justice Center, 401 4th Ave. N. Room 2C, Kent, WA 98032), by telephone at 206–296–9300 or by accessing http://www.kingcounty.gov/kcscc. Schedules for the Family Law Motions and Ex Parte Department calendars are also available online on the Clerk's website, at the information desk in the King County Courthouse and the Court Administration Office in Room 2D of the Maleng Regional Justice Center. See Local Civil Rule (LCR) 7 with respect to scheduling a motion before a judge.

[Adopted effective September 1, 2004; amended effective September 1, 2008.]

LFLR 3. MANDATORY FORMS TO BE USED

The Washington State mandatory family law forms shall be used except where a mandatory form is designated "optional", local forms have been promulgated by the Court or no mandatory form exists for the particular matter. State and local forms, including Note for Motion forms, may be obtained from the King County Superior Court Clerk, the King County Facilitator's Office, the King County Superior Court Law Library, or by accessing http://www.kingcounty.gov/kcscc.

[Adopted effective September 1, 2004; amended effective September 1, 2008.]

LFLR 4.   CASE SCHEDULE

(a) **Case Schedule.** At the time of the filing of the petition in any domestic relations case, the clerk may issue a case schedule. The parties must strictly comply with all deadlines in the case schedule. The only notice that the parties will receive of certain deadlines (including the date for the status conference) is the case schedule, and failure to comply with the case schedule may result in sanctions or dismissal. See also LR 16.

(b) **Requirement of Service of Case Schedule.** The petitioner must serve a copy of the case schedule on the other party, along with the summons and petition and other documents required by this rule.

(c) **Confirmation of Issues/Status Conference.**

(1) **Confirmation of Issues; Referral to Mediation.**

(A) Deadline for Raising Additional Issues. No additional issues may be raised after the date designated in the Case Schedule for Confirmation of Issues, unless the Court orders otherwise for good cause and subject to such conditions as justice requires.

(B) Confirmation of Issues; Form. If all parties do not sign the Confirmation of Issues form or give telephonic authority for signature of the form, a status conference shall be held. No later than the designated deadline for raising additional issues, as described in subsection (c)(1)(A) above, the petitioner shall, after conferring with the respondent, file and serve a report entitled "Confirmation of Issues," which shall be in substantially the form provided by the court and available from the Clerk's Office or by accessing http://www.kingcounty.gov/kcscc.

(d) **Paternity Cases; Confirmation of Completion of Genetic Testing; Form.**

(1) The form Confirmation of Completion of Genetic Testing shall be filed by the petitioner no later than the date specified in the Case Schedule and shall be in substantially the following form:

[ ]   The petitioning party represents that:
(IF THIS BOX IS CHECKED, THERE WILL NOT BE A STATUS CONFERENCE AS NOTED IN THE CASE SCHEDULING ORDER.)
1.   Paternity genetic testing of all named parties has been completed, the results of the tests are available to all parties, and no party has requested additional testing, OR
2.   Genetic testing is not necessary in this case because paternity has been admitted.

[ ]   The petitioning party represents that:
(IF THIS BOX IS CHECKED, THERE WILL BE A STATUS CONFERENCE, AS NOTED IN THE CASE SCHEDULING ORDER, AT WHICH ALL PARTIES OR THEIR ATTORNEYS MUST APPEAR.)
1.   Paternity genetic testing of all named parties has not been completed, or the results are not yet available to all parties, or a party has requested additional testing, AND
2.   Genetic testing is necessary in this case because paternity is not admitted.

In order to obtain the Court's direction in the matters described above, the parties will appear at a Status Conference, the date of which (as stated in notices on the Case Schedule) is: _____.

NOTICE: You may list an address that is not your residential address where you agree to accept legal documents.

DATED: _____ SIGNED: _____

Petitioner/Attorney (If Attorney, WSBA #)

Typed Name: _____

Address: _____

_____

Phone: _____

Attorney(s) For: _____

(e) **Status Conference; When Required**. A status conference will be held in family law cases when:

(1) no confirmation of issues form or completion of blood testing form has been filed; or

(2) when the filed form indicates that requirements regarding joinder of parties and issues and/or testing remain outstanding.

(f) **Amendment of Case Schedule.** The court, either on its own initiative or on motion of a party, may issue an amended case schedule. A motion to change trial date, even by agreement, must comply with LR 40(e). Motions to amend the case schedule or change trial date must be brought before the judge who is assigned to the case and will not be heard by the family law commissioners or in the Ex Parte Department.

(g) **Completion of Discovery.** All discovery must be completed no later than 28 days before the trial date in parentage cases and no later than 35 days in all other family law proceedings in accordance with the provisions of LR 37(g).

[Adopted effective September 1, 2004; amended effective September 1, 2007; September 1, 2008.]

LFLR 5. WHERE TO SCHEDULE MOTIONS IN FAMILY LAW PROCEEDINGS

(a) **Location of Courthouse (Case Assignment) and Courtrooms.** Except as otherwise ordered or directed, all proceedings filed under a case with a "UFK" or "KNT" designation shall be heard at the Maleng Regional Justice Center, 401 4th Ave. N. in Kent, and all proceedings filed under a "UFS" or "SEA" designation shall be heard at the King County Courthouse, 516 Third Avenue in Seattle. See LCR 82 as to the designation of case assignment areas.

(b) **Where to Schedule Motions; General Rule.** Except as otherwise provided in these rules, contested pre-trial and post-trial motions in family law proceedings, including non-marital relationships involving parenting and/or the distribution of assets/liabilities, shall be heard on the Family Law Motions Calendar. See LFLR 6 for Family Law Motions Calendar Procedures. Agreed orders and orders to show cause shall be presented without oral argument to the Ex Parte and Probate Department through the Clerk's office.

(c) **Where to Schedule Specific Types of Motions; Exceptions to General Rule [LFLR 5(b)].** The following specific types of Family Law Motions are to be scheduled as follows:

(1) *Entry of Agreed and Default Final Decrees Parenting Plans and Custody Orders:* Uncontested final Decrees of Marriage Dissolution and Legal Separation as well as all Final Parenting Plans or Residential Schedules and Final Dissolution of Domestic Partnership Orders shall be presented to the Ex Parte and Probate Department by noting the motion on the uncontested dissolution calendar on at least fourteen (14) days notice, provided that, the matter need not be noted for hearing when presented by an attorney of record, who as an officer of the court, has signed and filed a certificate of compliance in the form prescribed by the court. At least one party shall appear to provide oral testimony or formal proof with respect to entry of a final decree of dissolution or legal separation unless a final parenting plan with respect to all dependent children of the relationship has already been entered or there are no dependent children of the relationship and the final proposed orders are presented by an attorney, in which case the final orders may presented through the Clerk's Office pursuant to LCR 40.1 and shall be accompanied by the certificate of compliance as well as a declaration under penalty of perjury signed by one of the parties within the last 30 days stating that the wife is not pregnant and there are no dependent children of the relationship. The declaration shall be in substantially the same form as set forth in Appendix 1 and shall be available online at www.kingcounty.gov/courts/clerk. All final non-parental custody orders entered by agreement or default shall be presented on the uncontested dissolution calendar on at least 14 days notice, whether or not the parties are represented by counsel, provided that they may also be presented at the time of the Mandatory Case Review hearing (as set forth in the Case Schedule).

APPENDIX I—Model Form Declaration in lieu of Formal Proof for Decree of Dissolution, Invalidity or Legal Separation

SUPERIOR COURT OF WASHINGTON
COUNTY OF KING

In Re the Marriage of:

_____,   NO.

Petitioner,

And   DECLARATION IN LIEU OF FORMAL PROOF

_____,

Respondent.

REQUEST: The [ ] petitioner [ ] respondent requests immediate entry of Findings of Fact, Conclusions of Law and Decree without the necessity of a personal appearance, and states:

650

RESIDENCE: Either the petitioner or respondent was a resident of the State of Washington or was a member of the Armed Forces and was stationed in the State of Washington when the petition was filed.

90 DAY WAITING PERIOD: If this is a dissolution of marriage, the marriage is now irretrievably broken and more than 90 days have elapsed since the later of

_____,

20 _____, the date on which the Petition was filed, and _____,

20 _____, the date:

    [ ] the respondent signed an acceptance of service.

    [ ] the summons and petition were personally served upon the respondent.

    [ ] the summons and petition were mailed pursuant to an order for service by mail.

    [ ] the summons was first published pursuant to an order for service by publication.

DEFAULT: The respondent is _____ is not _____ in default.

MARRIAGE: The parties were married on _____ 20

_____, at [city, state]

_____ and separated on _____, 20

_____.

PREGNANCY: The wife is not now pregnant.

CHILDREN: The following children have been born to or adopted by either party:

Name   Date of Birth   Father of child   Mother of child

DEPENDENT CHILDREN: [SELECT ONE]:

[ ] A final parenting plan has been entered for all dependent children of the marriage.

[ ] There are no children under the age of 18 years of age born to or adopted by the wife or who are otherwise dependent upon the wife, or, all such children were born before the marriage and have not been adjudicated or acknowledged to be the husband's child.

PROPERTY: All property and all debts of the parties are fairly and completely divided in the Decree.

DEFAULT: If entry of the Decree is sought after default of the Respondent, the Decree provides for only that relief requested in the petition.

PERJURY: I declare under penalty of perjury under the laws of the State of Washington that this foregoing is true and correct.

Dated: _____, 20_____.

[Signed] _____ at _____,
Washington

Presented by: [Signed] _____

Bar Number: _____

Approved, notice of presentation waived:

    [Signed] _____

(2) *Support Modification Calendar:* Pre-trial Motions related to the support modification calendar shall be brought as set forth in LFLR 14.

(3) *Motions to be Scheduled Before Judges:* Motions scheduled before judges shall be brought using the timelines required by the applicable civil and local rules, including but not limited to CR 12, CR 56, and LCR 7. Unless otherwise required, motions scheduled before judges shall be heard on at least six (6) court days notice and without oral argument unless otherwise directed by the court. The following motions shall be scheduled before the assigned judge, or if there is no assigned judge, by the Chief Civil Judge or in family law cases involving children before the Chief Unified Family Court Judge:

    (A) Motions to seal a file or a document within a file, even if agreed;

(B) Motions to change the trial date, or a deadline in the case schedule;

(C) Motions for summary judgment, except for summary judgment motions in paternity actions which shall be heard on the family law motions calendar;

(D) Motions to resolve which court shall exercise jurisdiction under the Uniform Child Custody Jurisdiction and Enforcement Act (Chapter 26.27 RCW);

(E) Motions related to discovery. Motions to obtain discovery, such as to appoint an expert or to require an evaluation of a party, valuation of a business or property, or inspection of property, shall be scheduled on the family law motions calendar. Motions for a protective order, to compel a party to comply with a discovery request, or for sanctions related to discovery shall be scheduled before the assigned judge. See LFLR 14 for child support and spousal maintenance modifications and adjustments.

(F) Motions to Enforce a CR2A Agreement.

(G) Motions for Revision of a Commissioner's Order. See LCR 7(b)(8).

(H) Motions to reinstate a case that has been dismissed. If the trial date has passed, the case no longer has an assigned judge; therefore, motions to reinstate the case or vacate the order of dismissal must be brought before the Chief Civil Judge or in family law cases involving children before the Chief Unified Family Court Judge.

(I) Uncontested final decrees of invalidity. Hearings shall be noted with oral argument before the assigned judge or before the judge or commissioner presently assigned to the status/noncompliance calendar. At least one party shall appear to provide oral testimony with respect to entry of a final decree of invalidity.

(J) Motions for Temporary Orders to Restrain or Authorize Relocation of a Child (Objection to Relocation RCW 26.09.510): Hearings shall be noted with oral argument.

(4) *Motions related to Trials and Appeals:* Presentation of final orders related to a trial, motions to reconsider or vacate a judgment or decree entered after trial, and motions relating to the appeal of a final order entered after a motion or a trial (including motions to waive fees for the appeal, to stay the underlying order), shall be noted before the trial judge. If a commissioner entered the final order that is appealed, such motions shall be noted before the Chief Civil Judge/RJC Judge or in family law cases involving children before the Chief Unified Family Court Judge. Motions in limine and trial motions shall be brought before the trial judge.

(5) *Motions to Vacate Orders.*

(A) An agreed order to vacate an order shall be presented without oral argument to the Ex Parte and Probate Department through the Clerk's office, unless the effect of the order would be to reinstate a case that has been dismissed or where the trial date has passed, in which case the agreed order shall be presented pursuant to LCR 60.

(i) Default Order. The return on the order to show cause to set aside a default order shall be as follows:

(a) Case originally assigned to a judge who has not been assigned (transferred) to a new case designation area or to juvenile court. The order to show cause shall be returned to the judge to whom the case had been originally assigned, regardless of which judicial officer signed the order of default.

(b) Case originally assigned to a judge who has left the court or who has transferred to a court facility other than that reflected in the case designation. The order to show cause shall be returned to the Chief Civil Judge in Seattle or the Regional Justice Center Chief Judge, according to the designation of the case or in family law cases involving children before the Chief Unified Family Court Judge.

(c) Case not assigned to a judge. The order to show cause shall be returned to the department that entered the default order provided the relief requested does not impact the case schedule, in which case the order to show cause shall be returned to the Chief Civil Judge in Seattle or the Regional Justice Center Chief Judge, according to the designation of the case or in family law cases involving children before the Chief Unified Family Court Judge.

(ii) Order or decree following trial. The return on the order to show cause to set aside an order or decree following trial shall be before the judge who presided over the trial. If that judge has left the court, the return on the order to show cause shall be before the Chief Civil Judge in Seattle or the Regional Justice Center Chief Judge, depending upon the designation of the case or in family law cases involving children before the Chief Unified Family Court Judge.

(iii) Where the relief sought includes the setting of a new trial date, a motion to re-set trial date shall be filed contemporaneously with the motion for relief from the order or decree.

(B) An agreed order to vacate a Clerk's dismissal so that parties may enter final orders shall be presented without oral argument to the Ex Parte and Probate Department through the Clerk's office.

(C) A motion to vacate an order signed by a judge shall be noted before that judge, unless the original order was entered by agreement or after a default, in which case the motion to vacate shall be noted before the Chief Civil/RJC Judge or in family law cases involving children before the Chief Unified Family Court Judge.

(D) A motion to vacate an order signed by a commissioner shall be noted on the family law motions calendar unless the effect of that motion would be to reinstate a case that has been dismissed. *See* section (3)(H) above.

(6) *Change of Case Assignment Area or Consolidation of Cases:* A motion to change the case assignment area or consolidate two or more actions under one case schedule shall be brought before the Chief Civil Judge/RJC Judge or in family law cases involving children before the Chief Unified Family Court Judge provided that family law commissioners may consolidate a domestic violence protection order proceeding under a family law proceeding.

(7) *Motions for Reconsideration.* See LCR 59.

(8) *Motions for Default Orders and Default Judgments.*

(A) When notice is not required, motions for default orders and judgments shall be presented without oral argument to the Ex Parte and Probate Department through the Clerk's office. If notice to an opposing party is required (for example, when an appearance but no answer has been filed), motions for default orders and judgments shall be noted on the family law motions calendar in accordance with LFLR 6.

(B) Appearance by Responding Parties without Filing a Response. If a party has appeared in the proceeding, but not filed a Response to the Petition, any other party may move for an Order of Default on the Family Law Motion Calendar, to be presented without oral argument through the Clerk's office. Upon entry of the Order of Default, the evidence may be reviewed and a default judgment (including an order setting support) may be entered in the Ex Parte and Probate Department.

(9) *Orders Shortening Time.* Motions for Orders Shortening Time shall be heard in accordance with LCR 7 except that the motion shall be heard by the same judicial officer or calendar that is assigned under these rules to hear the substantive motion.

(10) *Writs of Habeas Corpus.* Application for Writs of Habeas Corpus Relating to Minor Children shall be presented to and returnable to the judge of the Unified Family Court Department currently assigned to the Status/Noncompliance calendar at the Maleng Regional Justice Center (MRJC) in Kent or, in the event of his or her absence, to the most senior judge assigned to the Unified Family Court Department at the MRJC. Contact the office of Court Operations at the MRJC (206–477–2600)

to find out which judge is handling Habeas Corpus matters relating to miner[1] children.

[Adopted effective September 1, 2004. Amended effective September 1, 2006; September 1, 2007; September 1, 2008; amended on an emergency basis, effective January 1, 2009; amended on a permanent basis, effective September 1, 2009; September 1, 2010; September 2, 2013; September 2, 2014.]

[1] So in original.

LFLR 6. FAMILY LAW MOTIONS CALENDAR PROCEDURES

(a) **Applicability.** This rule applies to the family law motions calendar only and does not apply to motions before judges.

(b) **Notice and Hearing.**

(1) Note for Motion Calendar forms are required and may be obtained from the Clerk's Office or by accessing www.kingcounty.gov/courts/clerk. Times and days for scheduling specific types of motions may also be obtained by calling 206–296–9300. See also LFLR 2.

(2) The original of the motion together with all supporting documents (including briefs, affidavits and/or declarations pursuant to RCW 9A.72.085) must be filed with the Clerk and copies served on all parties at least fourteen (14) calendar days before the date of the hearing. Response documents including briefs, if any, must be filed with the Clerk and copies served on all parties no later than noon four (4) court days prior to the hearing time; and documents in strict reply thereto shall be similarly filed and served no later than noon two (2) court days prior to the hearing.

(3) An additional working copy of all documents shall be submitted to the Family Law Motions Coordinator no later than noon three (3) court days prior to the hearing, except that documents in strict reply may be submitted by noon two (2) court days prior to the hearing. For any motion which requests the modification, adjustment, clarification, enforcement (including contempt), reconsideration or vacation of an earlier order, the working copies shall include a copy of the earlier order. Working copies shall be submitted to the Family Law Department pursuant to the requirements of LCR 7(b) to the extent not inconsistent with this rule.

(c) **Confirmations.**

(1) The moving party shall confirm the motion (including motions for presentation of orders), with the Family Law Confirmations Coordinator in person, by telephone or on the King County Superior Court website for Family Law Motions Confirmation Online. Confirmations by phone or in person must be done by either A) three (3) court days prior to the hearing between 2:30 and 4:15 PM or B) two (2) court days before the hearing between 8:30 AM and 12:00 noon. Confirmations via the King County Superior Court website can be done anytime between 12:01 PM three

(3) court days prior to the hearing until 12:00 noon two (2) court days before the hearing. The phone number to confirm Seattle case assignment area cases is 206–477–1523. The phone number to confirm Kent case assignment area cases is 206–477–2750. If not timely confirmed, the motion will be stricken and all working papers destroyed.

(2) Motions cannot be confirmed in person, by telephone or via the website unless the moving party's working copies have been received by the Family Law Department.

(d) **Agreed Continuances.** The parties may agree to continue a hearing only once on the family law motions calendar, and only prior to the end of the confirmation period, as follows:

(1) The parties may continue the motion to any court day that is at least five (5) court days after the scheduled hearing date. The moving party must notify the Family Law Motions Coordinator of the new agreed hearing date by telephone within the confirmation period set forth in LFLR 6(c) above. If agreement to continue the hearing is reached during the confirmation period, the motion must first be confirmed. Continuances cannot be requested through the King County Superior Court website.

(2) The moving party must re-confirm the motion for the new hearing date in accordance with LFLR 6(c) above. Confirmation may be done through the King County Superior Court website.

(3) A request for a continuance after the expiration of the confirmation period set forth in LFLR 6(c) above must be brought before the commissioner at the original confirmed hearing date and time and will ordinarily not be granted.

(e) **Limitations on Declarations.**

(1) *Application.* This section (e) of this rule does not apply to domestic violence petitions or domestic violence motions.

(2) *Children's Statements.* Declarations by minors are disfavored.

(3) *Formats.*

(A) All motions shall follow LCR 7 and LCR 10 to the extent they are not inconsistent with this rule, and use the forms required by LFLR 3.

(B) All filed documents and copies provided as working copies and served on other parties and attorneys shall be legible. If typed or computer printed, documents shall be in 12 point or larger type, double-spaced between the lines.

(4) *Basis.* Evidence, including written evidence in affidavits and declarations by the parties and lay witnesses, must comply with the rules of evidence. The rules of evidence provide that they need not be applied in domestic violence and anti-harassment protection order proceedings. See Rules of Evidence (ER) 1101(c) (4).

(5) *Page Limits.*

(A) Generally. Absent prior authorization from the court, the entirety of all declarations and affidavits from the parties and any non-expert witnesses in support of motions (except financial declarations), including any reply, shall be limited to a sum total of twenty-five (25) pages. The entirety of all declarations and affidavits submitted in response to motions shall be limited to a sum total of twenty (20) pages.

(B) Exhibits. Exhibits that consist of declarations or affidavits of parties or witnesses shall count towards the above page limit. All other exhibits attached to a declaration or affidavit shall not be counted toward the page limit.

(C) Financial Declarations. Financial Declarations and financial documents, as specified in LFLR 10, do not count toward the page limit.

(D) Expert Reports and Evaluations. Declarations, affidavits, and reports from Court Appointed Special Advocates (CASA), Family Court Services (FCS) and expert witnesses do not count toward the page limit.

(E) Miscellaneous Exceptions. Copies of declarations or affidavits previously filed for a motion already ruled upon and supplied only as a convenience to the court in lieu of the court file do not count toward the page limit. Deposition excerpts shall not count toward the page limit.

(6) See LCR 7 for format and page limits on motions, opposition papers, briefs and memorandum of authorities.

(f) Time for Argument.

(1) Each side is allowed five (5) minutes for oral argument, including rebuttal, unless otherwise authorized by the court.

(2) By written stipulation of all parties, any motion except a motion for contempt may be set without oral argument.

(A) Motions heard without oral argument shall be set for a specific date and are subject to the same requirements (including confirmation) as other motions.

(B) Each party shall provide working copies including a proposed order(s) and shall timely serve the opposing party. Working copies shall be submitted pursuant to the requirements of LCR 7(b) to the extent not inconsistent with this rule. Parties submitting working copies in paper form shall also conspicuously include the words "Without Oral Argument" in the upper right corner of each document and the moving party shall provide stamped envelopes addressed to each party/counsel.

(C) The commissioner may order the parties to appear for argument.

(g) Special Settings.

(1) *Additional Time for Argument.* A request for a special setting for oral argument that will require more than five minutes per side, or for other special settings shall be made in writing addressed to the Family Law Motions Coordinator.

(A) The request should state the extraordinary features of the case and explain why additional time for oral argument is needed. The request should state the length of time requested, and whether the other parties agree with the request. The written request shall include working copies of the motion and supporting documents, and all responses received.

(B) The written request shall be filed with the Clerk and working copies shall be submitted to the Family Law Coordinator, and served on all other parties at least six (6) court days prior to the scheduled hearing date. Any response to the request shall be similarly filed and delivered to the Coordinator and other parties by noon at least two (2) court days prior to the scheduled hearing date. Replies are not permitted. Working copies shall be submitted to the Family Law Department pursuant to the requirements of LCR 7(b) to the extent not inconsistent with this rule.

(C) An order granting the request cannot be entered by stipulation or agreement.

(D) No other motion may be joined with a request for additional time.

(E) If granted, the Court will set the date and time for additional time for argument on the Family Law Motions Calendar.

(2) *Motions to Permit Live Testimony at a Hearing.* Except for domestic violence protection order proceedings, a party seeking to present live testimony at a hearing must file a request in writing in the same manner as a request for additional time for argument (in LFLR 6(g)(1) above).

(A) An order Permitting Testimony cannot be entered by stipulation.

(B) If granted, the court will notify the parties of the hearing date and time.

(h) Order on Hearing. Unless otherwise ordered by the Court, immediately following each hearing, an order reflecting the ruling of the Court shall be presented for signature.

[Adopted effective September 1, 2004. Amended effective September 1, 2008; September 1, 2009; September 2, 2014; September 1, 2015.]

LFLR 7. UNIFIED FAMILY COURT

(a) Purpose of Unified Family Court. The purpose of the Unified Family Court (UFC) is to promote effective judicial management of cases involving the health and welfare of children, and to facilitate the prompt resolution of these cases.

(b) UFC Case Management is Suspended.

[Adopted effective September 1, 2004. Amended effective September 2, 2014.]

LFLR 8. MOTIONS FOR EX PARTE RESTRAINING ORDERS

(a) Applicability. This rule applies to motions for temporary restraining orders (also known as Ex Parte Restraining Orders) entered on an emergency basis to prevent immediate injury, loss or damage. See also CR 65. This local rule does not apply to domestic violence protection orders entered under Chapter 26.50 RCW.

(b) Notice of Motion. The party asking for an Ex Parte Restraining Order (the moving party) shall give prior written or oral notice to the attorney for the opposing party or, if unrepresented, to the opposing party. The moving party or attorney shall certify to the court in writing the efforts which have been made to give notice to the opposing party. Such notice is required in all cases unless the moving party clearly shows by sworn declaration that immediate injury, loss or damage will result if notice is given.

(c) Where Presented. The moving party shall present the Motion for Ex Parte Restraining Order and Order to Show Cause in the Ex Parte Department.

(d) Return Hearing. The Order to Show Cause shall schedule a return hearing to review the Ex Parte Restraining Order on the Family Law Motions Calendar. All requirements of LFLR 6 shall apply.

(e) Duration and Extension of Ex Parte Restraining Order. The return hearing shall be held no more than fourteen (14) days from entry of the Ex Parte Restraining Order, unless the Court extends this deadline for good cause, such as to allow time to comply with the notice requirements of LFLR 6.

(f) Motion to Quash Ex Parte Restraining Orders Entered Without Notice. Unless otherwise directed by the court, a party seeking to quash an Ex Parte Restraining Order entered without notice shall present the motion to the Ex Parte Department, giving the notice required by CR 65(b).

[Adopted effective September 1, 2004.]

LFLR 9. COMMENCEMENT OF NONPARENTAL CUSTODY PROCEEDINGS

An action for custody of a child brought by a non-parent is commenced by a summons and petition under a new cause number and may not be commenced under an existing dissolution, paternity or other case. Upon filing, the Clerk's Office will issue a case schedule. The petitioners must obtain a Washington State Patrol and Child Protective Services (CPS) background check on themselves and all adult household members. The King County local form order for obtaining a CPS background check, available from the Clerk's office or at www.kingcounty.gov/kcscc, shall be used. Petitioners must also obtain an Order finding Adequate Cause before the date specified in the Case Schedule and attend a mandatory case review hearing. See Chapter 26.10 RCW, these rules and the Order Issuing Case Schedule for other requirements.

[Adopted effective September 1, 2004; amended effective September 1, 2008.]

LFLR 10. FINANCIAL PROVISIONS

(a) When Financial Information is Required.

(1) Each party shall complete, sign, file, and serve on all parties a financial declaration for any motion, trial, or settlement conference that concerns the following issues:

(A) Payment of a child's expenses, such as tuition, costs of extracurricular activities, medical expenses, or college;

(B) Child support or spousal maintenance; or

(C) Any other financial matter, including payment of debt, attorney and expert fees, or the costs of an investigation or evaluation.

(2) A party may use a previously-prepared financial declaration if all information in that declaration remains accurate.

(3) Financial declarations need not be provided when presenting an order by agreement or default.

(b) Supporting Documents to be filed with the Financial Declaration. Parties who file a financial declaration shall also file the following supporting documents:

(1) Pay stubs for the past six months. If a party does not receive pay stubs, other documents shall be provided that show all income received from whatever source, and the deductions from earned income for these periods;

(2) Complete personal tax returns for the prior two years, including all Schedules and all W–2s;

(3) If either party owns an interest of 5% or more in a corporation, partnership or other entity that generates its own tax return, the complete tax return

for each such corporation, partnership or other entity for the prior two years;

(4) All statements related to accounts in financial institutions in which the parties have or had an interest during the last six (6) months. "Financial institutions" includes banks, credit unions, mutual fund companies, and brokerages.

(5) If a party receives or has received non-taxable income or benefits (for example, from a trust, barter, gift, etc.), documents shall be provided that show receipts, the source, and any deductions for the last two (2) years.

(6) Check registers shall be supplied within fourteen (14) days if requested by the other party.

(7) If a party asks the court to order or change child support or order payment of other expenses for a child, each party shall also file completed Washington State Child Support Worksheets.

(8) For additional requirements for a Settlement Conference, see LFLR 16.

(c) Documents to be filed under Seal. Tax returns, pay stubs, bank statements, and the statements of other financial institutions should not be attached to the Financial Declaration but should be submitted to the clerk under a cover sheet with the caption "Sealed Financial Source Documents". If so designated, the Clerk will file these documents under seal so that only a party to the case or their attorney can access these documents from the court file without a separate court order.

[Adopted effective September 1, 2004.]

LFLR 11.   SEALED COURT RECORDS

(a) Court Records Are Generally Public. Documents filed with the court will in most cases be available for public inspection and copying and for all cases filed beginning 1/1/2000 are maintained in electronic format. Only a document or court file type that is specifically sealed by law, court rule, or court order will be unavailable for public inspection and copying.

(b) Some Documents Subject to Restricted Access. The following documents, if properly identified by the person filing the documents, will be sealed by the Clerk without a court order: income tax returns and schedules, W–2 forms, wage stubs, credit card statements, financial institution statements, and check registers. See also GR 22. These records should only be filed by first attaching the "Sealed Financial Source Documents" cover sheet (Mandatory Form No. WPF DRPSCU–09.0220) and writing the word "SEALED" on the first page of each attachment. Only those documents allowed by GR 22 may be filed under the "Sealed Financial Source Documents" cover sheet without first obtaining a court order to seal the document.

(c) Identifying Information to be Removed. Except for documents that are automatically sealed or where the following information is essential to a determination, parties shall black out social security numbers, driver's license numbers, telephone numbers, children's dates of birth, and all but the last four digits in account numbers, in documents filed with the court.

(d) Requirements for Orders Sealing Records.

(1) *Motion and Declaration required.* The proposed order, even if agreed, must be accompanied by a motion and declaration or affidavit demonstrating a basis for the order consistent with GR 15(c) and Article I, Sec. 10, Washington State Constitution. See also GR 22. See LFLR 5(c) with respect to where to present a motion to seal a file.

(2) *Form of Order to be used.* An order to redact or seal a court record must be made separately and may not be combined with any other order. The order shall either state that the Clerk's Office is directed to seal the entire court record or shall designate the specific documents to be sealed.

Comment: See LR 79(d) for procedures relevant to redacting and sealing.

[Adopted effective September 1, 2004; amended effective September 1, 2007.]

LFLR 12.   DOMESTIC VIOLENCE PROTECTION ORDERS

(a) Applicability. This rule applies to all petitions for domestic violence protection orders brought pursuant to the Domestic Violence Prevention Act, whether filed separately or under another cause of action.

(b) Mandatory Forms. The parties shall utilize any applicable local and state mandatory forms, including form Orders. Forms are available from the King County Clerk's Office, the Protection Order Advocate's Office, and www.metrokc.gov/kcscc.

(c) Return Hearing. Every Temporary Order of Protection or Order of Modification entered without notice shall set a return hearing on the family law calendar on such notice as prescribed in Chapter 26.50 RCW. At the hearing, both parties may testify and the court may consider other relevant evidence. Copies of any writings or other documentary evidence provided to the court must be provided to the other party's attorney. If the other party is not represented, the copies should be handed to either courtroom staff or a domestic violence advocate in the courtroom with a request that they provide the copies to the other party.

[Adopted effective September 1, 2004.]

LFLR 13.   PARENTING PLAN AND CHILD CUSTODY PROCEDURES

(a) Information Required. In child custody, visitation, or parenting plan disputes, each party shall submit the following information:

(1) A proposed custodial or visitation plan or parenting plan, except in actions brought under Chapter 26.10 RCW.

(2) If not in the verified petition, a Uniform Child Custody Jurisdiction Enforcement Act Declaration and Declaration Regarding Other Proceedings, which must be timely supplemented throughout the pendency of the proceedings.

(b) Referral for Mediation, Evaluation, and Investigation.

(1) *Mandatory Mediation.* All parties to parenting plan, custody or visitation disputes shall participate in some form of alternative dispute resolution, such as mediation, unless waived by court order for good cause. See also LFLR 16.

(2) *Investigation by Professionals.* In all parenting plans, custody and visitation cases not resolved by mediation or other dispute resolution process, the matter may be referred to Family Court Services or other suitable person or agency for investigation upon motion or by stipulation. When so referred, a report shall be provided in writing to the Court and the parties in advance of trial.

(3) *Evaluations.* The Court may, upon motion, order a mental health evaluation or physical examination when appropriate. The issues of costs shall be addressed in the order.

(4) *Child Advocate.*

(A) Appointment. Upon motion of the parties or on the Court's own motion, the Court may appoint a child advocate who may be a Guardian ad Litem, A Court Appointed Special Advocate, or an attorney for the child. See also KCLGALR 1–7. The order shall designate the appointee, the duties, and make provision for the payment of fees.

(B) Notice. From the date of the appointment, the child advocate shall receive copies of all documents that are to be served on parties, copies of all discovery, and notice of all hearings, presentations and trials.

(C) Discharge. Unless otherwise set forth in these rules, the child advocate shall be discharged only by order of the Court upon motion or upon completion of the case when final orders are filed with approval of the appointed child advocate.

(5) *Costs of Mediation, Evaluation or Investigation.* Unless waived pursuant to an in forma pauperis petition, the parties shall pay the costs of a Family Court Services mediation or investigation based upon their incomes on a sliding scale basis. The costs of a private mediator, investigator, evaluator or child advocate shall be apportioned between the parties based on their income and resources or as otherwise ordered. Except as otherwise agreed, the fees of a child advocate or evaluator shall be set by the Court.

(c) Seminar for Parenting Plans.

(1) *Applicability.* This rule applies to all cases filed under Chapters 26.09 RCW, and 26.26 RCW related to custody, visitation, or parenting of minor children, including dissolutions of marriage, legal separations, major modifications, and parentage actions in which parentage has been established. This rule does not apply to modification cases based solely upon relocation. In the case of parentage actions initiated by the Prosecuting Attorney's Office, the Seminar for Parenting Plans shall be required only after an order establishing parentage has been entered and a parenting plan is requested.

(2) *Parenting Seminars; Mandatory Attendance.* In all cases referred to in Section (1) above, both parents and such other parties as the court may direct shall participate in and successfully complete an approved parenting seminar within sixty (60) days after service of a petition on the responding party. Successful completion shall be evidenced by a certificate of attendance filed with the court by the provider agency.

(3) *Special Considerations/Waiver.*

(A) In no case shall opposing parties be required to attend a seminar together.

(B) Upon showing of domestic violence, abuse, safety concerns, or 26.09.191 allegations, or that a parent's attendance at a seminar is not in the children's best interest, the court shall either:

waive the requirement of completion of the seminar; or

provide an alternative Seminar For Parenting Plans.

(C) The court may waive the seminar requirement for one or both parents in any case for good cause shown.

(4) *Failure to Comply.* Delay, refusal or default by one parent does not excuse timely compliance by the other parent. Unless attendance at the seminar is waived, a parent who delays beyond the 60 day deadline, or who otherwise fails or refuses to complete the parenting seminar, shall be precluded from presenting any final order affecting the parenting/residential plan or finalizing the parenting plan in this action, until the seminar has been successfully completed. The court may also refuse to allow the non-complying party to seek affirmative relief in this or subsequent proceedings until the seminar is successfully completed. Willful refusal or delay by either parent may constitute contempt of court and result in sanctions imposed by the court, or may result in the imposition of monetary terms, default, and/or striking of pleadings.

(5) *Finalizing Parenting Plans.* All parties are required to attach to their proposed Final Parenting Plan a true and accurate signed and dated copy of the certificate of completion of the Seminar For Parenting Plans. No final parenting plan shall be entered with-

out said certificate or a court order waiving attendance.

(6) *Fee.* Each party attending a seminar shall pay a fee charged by the provider and sanctioned by the court. The court may waive the fee for indigent parties.

(d) Permanent Parenting Plan, Custody or Visitation Modifications.

(1) *Starting an Action to Modify a Permanent Parenting Plan.*

(A) This rule applies to actions to modify final parenting plans, and final custody or visitation orders, except for adjustments related to the relocation of a child. See LFLR 15 for proceedings involving relocation of a child.

(B) The moving party shall attach to the petition a copy of the current parenting plan and all other effective orders affecting parenting, custody, and visitation. Copies of any orders which were entered outside King County shall be certified.

(2) *Adequate Cause Hearing.*

(A) Adequate Cause Requirement. A threshold determination of adequate cause is required for any modification or adjustment of a final parenting plan, whether major, minor, residential or non-residential in nature. An order of adequate cause may be entered by agreement of the parties, by default, or after an adequate cause hearing. This rule does not limit the Court's authority under Chapter 26.50 RCW.

(B) Timing of Adequate Cause Hearing: The adequate cause hearing may not be heard before the deadline for filing the response to the petition has passed. All requirements of LFLR 6 shall apply to the adequate cause hearing.

(C) Finding of Adequate Cause: If adequate cause is found, the matter shall remain scheduled for trial. A copy of the Adequate Cause Order shall be attached to the Confirmation of Issues.

(3) *Entry of Temporary Orders.*

(A) Types of Temporary Orders. Once a finding of adequate cause has been found, the court may enter temporary orders, including but not limited to: a temporary parenting plan, a referral for mediation, investigation, or evaluation; appointment of an evaluator, attorney for the child or Guardian ad Litem; or a referral to Unified Family Court.

(B) Combined with Adequate Cause Hearing. A party may, but is not required to, schedule motions for temporary orders for the same time as the adequate cause hearing. Any party seeking the entry of temporary orders at the adequate cause hearing must make that request by motion pursuant to the format and notice requirements of LFLR 6.

(C) Emergency Temporary Orders. For good cause shown, any party may move for emergency temporary orders at any time, including prior to the finding of adequate cause.

[Adopted effective September 1, 2004. Amended effective September 2, 2014.]

LFLR 14. CHILD SUPPORT AND SPOUSAL MAINTENANCE MODIFICATIONS AND ADJUSTMENTS

(a) *Scope of This Rule.*

(1) This rule applies child support and spousal maintenance adjustments that are brought independently from a petition to modify a parenting plan, or child custody or visitation order. This rule does not apply to support modifications that are based on a substantial change of circumstances if there is a pending proceeding to modify a parenting plan, or child custody or visitation order.

(2) In cases where a modification of a parenting plan, child custody, or visitation has been resolved, the court may transfer the support issues to the Trial by Affidavit Calendar, and this rule will then apply.

(3) A child support adjustment, which merely implements a periodic adjustment clause in an Order of Child Support or is limited to the relief authorized by RCW 26.09.170(9) and (10), shall be brought on the Family Law Motions Calendar under LFLR 6. Each party must also follow LFLR 10.

(4) In a Child Support modification proceeding, the court may grant relief limited to the scope of a child support adjustment, if the case does not meet the requirements for a modification but does meet the requirements for an adjustment.

(b) *Support Modification Proceedings.*

(1) Documents Required to Be Served and Filed

(A) Documents Required from Petitioner. A party petitioning for modification of child support or spousal maintenance shall file and serve upon all other parties the Summons and Petition, a completed Financial Declaration, child support worksheets (if applicable), and the financial documents specified in LFLR 10. The petitioning party shall serve the other party a copy of the Order Setting Case Schedule (issued by the Clerk) with the Summons. If the existing support order was not issued by King County Superior Court, a certified copy of the order must be filed with the Petition.

(B) Documents Required from Responding Parties. Each responding party shall file and serve a Response to Petition, a completed Financial Declaration, child support worksheets (if applicable), and the financial documents specified in LFLR 10, by the deadline established by service of the Summons.

(c) *Motions.*

(1) Pre-trial Motions re Support-only Modifications. All pre-trial motions relating to support-only modifications, including motions to change the trial date, to permit testimony, or relating to discovery, shall be decided on the Trial by Affidavit Calendar without oral argument. Motions shall be noted for hearing fourteen (14) or more days in advance. The procedure for such motions shall conform to LCR 7 and LFLR 6 to the extent not inconsistent with this rule. There is no requirement to confirm such motions. Motion documents shall be filed with the Clerk and working copies shall be provided to the court. Working copies shall be submitted pursuant to the requirements of LCR 7(b) to the extent not inconsistent with this rule. Working copies submitted in paper form must be delivered to the Trial by Affidavit mailbox in the judges' mailroom of the courthouse where the matter will be heard.

(2) Motions to Permit Live Testimony.

(A) Testimony is ordinarily in the form of declarations and affidavits. Oral argument is allowed at all trials by affidavit. A party seeking permission to present live testimony at the time of the trial by affidavit (in addition to oral argument) must file a motion with a supporting declaration setting forth the reasons why live testimony is necessary. The motion and supporting documents shall be noted, filed and served not later than the deadline set forth in the case schedule.

(B) The supporting documents must demonstrate the extraordinary features of the case warranting live testimony. Factors which may be considered include: substantial questions of credibility on a major issue, insufficiency or inconsistency in discovery materials not correctable by further discovery, or particularly complex circumstances requiring expert testimony.

(C) A Motion to Permit Testimony may not be entered by stipulation. If the motion is granted, a hearing will be set.

(3) Motions for Temporary Orders. Motions for Temporary Support Orders will not ordinarily be considered in support-only modification proceedings. Exceptions may apply in exigent circumstances, such as when there has been a change in residential care, a party has requested a continuance of the trial date, or when the lack of a temporary order would substantially prejudice a party. A motion for temporary support shall be noted on the Family Law Motions Calendar; the court in its discretion may also consider an oral motion for temporary support at the time of the support modification trial where the matter is being continued for reasons unrelated to the conduct of the party requesting the temporary support order.

(d) *Method of Disposition of Support Modification Proceedings.*

(1) Trial by Affidavit. The trial of support-only modification petitions shall be heard on affidavits,

declarations, pleadings, and discovery materials obtained pursuant to CR 26–37, unless the court authorizes live testimony pursuant to a motion brought under LFLR 14(c)(2) above.

(2) Proposed Orders. The petitioning party is obliged to provide proposed findings of fact and conclusions of law, child support worksheets, and orders to the other parties and the court not later than the time of trial. The proposed orders shall not be filed with the clerk. Working copies of the proposed orders for the judge shall be submitted pursuant to the requirements of LCR 7(b) to the extent not inconsistent with this rule. If the petitioner is not present and has not presented proposed orders, the matter may be dismissed.

(3) Judicial Officer Presiding. Unless otherwise assigned by the court, support-only modification trials shall be heard on the Trial by Affidavit Calendar by a Family Law Commissioner.

(4) Affidavits of Prejudice Not Recognized. See LCR 40(g).

(5) Independent Proceedings. Except as otherwise stated, Petitions for Modification of Support shall proceed as original determinations, with no threshold or adequate cause hearing required.

(6) Arbitration. The parties may stipulate to arbitrate the issues in the petition pursuant to the state and local Mandatory Arbitration Rules. The stipulation must be in writing, in a form as prescribed by the Court. The stipulation must state whether the issues will be handled by private arbitration or will be submitted to the King County Arbitration Department for assignment of an arbitrator.

(A) Motions for Temporary Relief. Once an arbitrator has been appointed, all motions shall be decided by the arbitrator.

(B) Appeals from Arbitration. Requests for a trial de novo from the decision of an arbitrator shall be heard on the Trial by Affidavit Calendar.

(7) Trial by Affidavit Procedure. Parties shall file the originals of all documents to be considered with the Clerk. Settings on the Trial by Affidavit Calendar must be confirmed by the submission of a copy of these materials either in paper form to the Trial by Affidavit mailbox at the courthouse where the matter will be heard or electronically through the Clerk's e-filing system by the deadline in the case schedule. Each party to the proceeding will have a maximum of ten (10) minutes, including rebuttal, to present oral argument to the court. No new evidence may be offered at the time of trial unless stipulated by the parties or authorized by the court for good cause shown. Parties may attend the trial by telephone, provided that prior arrangements have been made with the court. A party is not obligated to attend the hearing.

(8) Procedure on Default.

(A) Default Procedures. See LFLR 5(c)(9).

(B) Failure of a responding party to be present in person or by counsel at the time of trial shall not constitute a default, as the presentation of oral argument is optional. If counsel or a pro se party is not present, the court will decide the matter based upon the working papers and the oral argument of those present.

[Adopted effective September 1, 2004; amended effective September 1, 2008; September 1, 2009.]

LFLR 15. RELOCATION OF CHILDREN

(a) **Notice Required.** Where a parenting plan or custody order has been entered, a parent seeking to relocate a child outside of his or her school district shall provide notice in accordance with RCW 26.09.430–440. A parent objecting to relocation shall file and serve the form Objection to Relocation/Petition for Modification (DRPSCU 07.0700). If the objecting party is seeking to restrain an immediate move, that party shall file and serve a motion in accordance with LFLR 5(c)(3)(J) within fifteen (15) days of the filing of the Objection to Relocation/Petition for Modification.

(b) **Presentation of Proposed Parenting Plan.** In the absence of an objection, but no earlier than thirty (30) days after the relocating party has served a proposed parenting plan on the person entitled to residential time with the children, any party to the relocation action may present the relocating party's proposed parenting plan to the Ex Parte and Probate Department through the Clerk's office for entry.

(c) **Motion for Default.** If a response to an objection to relocation is not filed within the deadline for filing, a motion for default may be presented to the Family Law Department motions calendar upon fourteen (14) days notice.

(d) **Motions for Temporary Orders.** Motions for temporary orders shall not be heard until the deadline for filing an objection to relocation has passed, unless exigent circumstances require immediate relief. *See* LFLR 5(c)(3)(J).

(e) **Concurrent Actions.** If a petition for dissolution or modification is already pending at the time a notice of intent to relocate is served and if the objecting party serves an Objection to Relocation/Petition for Modification, that action shall be assigned to the same judge assigned to hear the initial action and no new case schedule shall issue. If, after the filing of an Objection to Relocation/Petition for Modification, a party seeks to modify the parenting plan pursuant to RCW 26.09.260, the modification action shall be assigned to the same judge who is assigned the relocation action and a modification case schedule shall be issued which shall govern both actions. A party who seeks to amend the case schedule based on the filing of the second action shall note a motion pursuant to LCR 7(b) with the assigned trial judge.

(f) **Mediation/Alternative Dispute Resolution.** The parties shall participate in mediation or some other form of alternative dispute resolution before trial unless waived by court order.

[Adopted effective September 1, 2004; amended effective September 1, 2008; amended on an emergency basis effective January 1, 2009; amended on a permanent basis effective September 1, 2009; September 2, 2014.]

LFLR 16. ALTERNATIVE DISPUTE RESOLUTION (ADR)

(a) **Alternative Dispute Resolution Required.** Except in cases involving domestic violence, child support only modifications (RCW 26.09.175), or where waived by a court order, the parties in every case shall participate in a settlement conference, mediation or other alternative dispute resolution process conducted by a neutral third person no later than thirty (30) days before trial.

(b) **Attendance at the Alternative Dispute Resolution Proceeding.** All parties and their attorneys, if any, shall personally attend and participate in all alternative resolution proceedings and shall come prepared to discuss all unresolved issues.

(c) **Required Materials.** Proposed final orders, a financial declaration and, if parenting is at issue, a proposed parenting plan, as well as any other materials requested by the neutral third person must be provided to the neutral third person and all parties no later than two (2) working days before the day scheduled for the conference. The materials are not to be filed with the Clerk. When the division of property or debt is at issue, the parties shall provide a table listing all their property and debt substantially the following format:

Description of Property	Community or Separate?	Gross and Net value	Amount owed/ Cost of Sale	Award to husband or wife?

Description of Debt	Community or Separate?	Amount owing	Post–Separation?	Award to husband or wife?

Totals: Property to Wife $ _____

Property to Husband $ _____

Debt to Wife $ _____

Debt to Husband $ _____

Other Requests: _____

The above property and debt distribution is proposed by: _____

Signature: _____ Date: _____

(d) **Duty of Good Faith.** Each party is under an obligation to act in good faith in an attempt to resolve the issues without the need for trial. Failure to act in good faith or failure to abide by the provisions of this rule may result in the imposition of sanctions by the assigned judge.

(e) Pretrial Procedures in Family Law Cases Involving Children.

(1) *Pretrial Conference.* In dissolution cases involving families with children, non-parental custody cases, paternity cases not filed by the prosecutor, domestic relocation cases, cases to establish or disestablish paternity and set residential schedules, and in actions to establish or modify a parenting plan, the Court will schedule a pretrial conference, which shall be attended by the lead trial attorney of each party who is represented by an attorney and by each party who is unrepresented. The conference may include:

(A) Hearing of non dispositive pretrial motions;

(B) Filing of trial briefs;

(C) The Court's estimate of length of trial;

(D) Any other matters that might simplify the issues and bring about a just, speedy and economical resolution of the matter.

[Adopted effective September 1, 2004. Amended effective September 1, 2008; September 2, 2013.]

LFLR 17. CONTEMPT AND OTHER ENFORCEMENT ACTIONS

(a) Civil Contempt Proceedings. See also Chapter 7.21 RCW (regarding general contempt of court), RCW 26.18.050 (regarding failure to pay support or maintenance), and RCW 26.09.160 (parenting plan contempt).

(1) Contempt proceedings shall be started by presenting and obtaining an Order to Show Cause re Contempt from the Ex Parte and Probate Department through the clerk's office, accompanied by a Motion and Declaration for Order to Show Cause Re Contempt and a copy of the order that is alleged to have been violated. The hearing on the contempt proceeding shall be scheduled on the Family Law Motions Calendar in accordance with LFLR 6.

(2) Unless otherwise ordered, a copy of the Order to Show Cause and all supporting documents shall be personally served upon the person alleged to be in contempt. A copy of these documents must also be delivered to that person's attorney, if any, the Family Law Motions coordinator, and all other parties to the action, including any Guardian Ad Litem. All provisions of LFLR 6 shall apply.

(3) If the person alleged to be in contempt is properly served and fails to appear for the Show Cause hearing, the court may grant an order to issue a warrant. The party requesting contempt must deliver the original order and proposed warrant to the Clerk's Office. Upon the Clerk's issuance of the warrant, the party requesting contempt must then deliver the warrant to the King County Sheriff's office at the Courthouse.

(4) If a warrant is issued and the person alleged to be in contempt is arrested, a "Return on Warrant"

hearing will be held the next court day following the arrest on the Family Law Motions Calendar at 1:30 p.m. Except in cases where the warrant was requested by the State, the court will arrange for the arrested party to be transported to the hearing from the jail. If the arrested party has posted bail and has been released from jail, that party shall appear in court at 1:30 p.m. on the next court day.

(b) Other Enforcement Actions. See Chapter 26.23 RCW regarding enforcement of child support orders by the Washington State Support Registry and the Division of Child Support; Chapter 6.27 RCW regarding garnishments; and RCW 26.09.120, RCW 26.23.050 and RCW 26.18.070 regarding wage assignments. See CR 69 and LCR 69 regarding Supplemental Proceedings.

[Adopted effective September 1, 2004. Amended effective September 1, 2008; September 1, 2015.]

LFLR 18. EMANCIPATION OF MINORS

Petitions for Emancipation of a Minor shall be noted before the Chief Unified Family Court Judge, who may refer the matter to Family Court Services for investigation.

[Adopted effective September 1, 2009.]

LFLR 19. MARRIAGE AGE WAIVER PETITIONS

Petitions for Waiver of Marriage Age shall be noted before the Chief Unified Family Court Judge, who may refer the matter to Family Court Services for investigation.

[Adopted effective September 1, 2009.]

LFLR 20. ORIENTATION PROGRAM IN FAMILY LAW MATTERS

(a) Description and Applicability. To assist self-represented parties involved in family law matters and improve the efficiency of the court, King County Superior Court Family Court shall conduct an Orientation Program for parties in all cases filed under Chapter 26.09 RCW, including dissolutions of marriage, legal separations and major parenting plan modifications. Parties modifying only Child Support shall not be required to attend.

(b) Mandatory Attendance. In all cases referred to in Section (a) above, all self-represented parties shall successfully complete the Orientation Program within thirty (30) days of filing or service of the summons and petition. Successful completion shall be evidenced by a certificate of attendance filed with the court by Family Court Operations staff. Any party attending the Orientation Program prior to obtaining a King County Superior Court cause number shall be responsible for filing his or her certificate of attendance in the court file when the cause number is obtained.

(1) *Out of County Resident.* A party residing outside of King County shall be excused from attending the Orientation Program if attendance would be a hardship. Such parties are required to review the Orientation Program materials and file a sworn declaration that they have done so.

(2) *Represented Parties.* Attendance at the Orientation Program shall be excused for a party represented by counsel, provided that if the party becomes self-represented before entry of final orders, such party shall attend the orientation seminar, unless waived for good cause.

(3) *Good Cause.* The court may excuse a party from attending the Orientation Program or permit a party to review the materials and file a sworn declaration that he or she has done so as an alternative to in-person attendance, for good cause shown.

(4) *Service.* The petitioner shall serve the Notice of Mandatory Orientation Program on all respondents at the time the Summons and Petition is served. If a joinder to the petition is filed, the petitioner shall provide the Notice of Mandatory Orientation Program to any joining party within seven (7) days of filing of the joinder.

(5) *Special Considerations.* Opposing parties shall not be required to attend the Orientation Program together.

(6) *Renewal.* The court may reinstitute the requirement to attend the Orientation Program at any time in cases where attendance was previously excused.

(c) Failure to Comply. Delay, refusal or default by one party does not excuse timely compliance by any other party. The Orientation Registration Form shall be submitted to Family Court Services. *See section (a) above.* Unless attendance at the seminar is excused, any party requesting a hearing, including those parties seeking to enter final orders in the action, and any party responding to a request for hearing, shall attend the Orientation Program prior to obtaining affirmative relief. Attendance at the Orientation Program shall not be required prior to emergency hearings or the issuance of restraining orders. Willful refusal or delay by any party may constitute contempt of court and result in sanctions imposed by the court, including the imposition of monetary terms, default or striking of pleadings.

(d) Fee. Each party attending the Orientation Program, or who has been approved to review the materials in lieu of attendance, shall pay a fee charged by Family Court Operations and approved by the court. The court shall provide the service at no expense for indigent parties.

[Adopted on an emergency basis, effective January 1, 2011; amended on an emergency basis, effective April 1, 2011;

adopted on a permanent basis, effective September 1, 2011; September 2, 2014.]

LFLR 21. SIMPLE DISSOLUTION (DIVORCE) PROGRAM

(a) Purpose. To facilitate early resolution of family law cases where the parties:

(1) Are not represented by an attorney in the case; and

(2) Are in agreement on all issues in the case *or* where the respondent is in default; and

(3) Do not have minor children; and

(4) Do not have substantial property or debt to divide between the parties; and

(5) At least one party resides in King County.

(b) Application. The Family Law Courthouse Facilitators and staff who provide basic services under GR 27(c)(3), authorized by RCW 26.12.24, shall determine whether or not pro-se litigants are eligible for the Simple Dissolution (Divorce) Program according to established program guidelines. They shall require each party, or the petitioner in cases where a default order is obtained, to complete and sign an application disclaiming any attorney-client relationship and attorney-client confidentiality as well as disclosing the character and agreed distribution of assets and liabilities.

(c) Finalization. For cases eligible for the Simple Dissolution (Divorce) Program, Courthouse Family Law Facilitators and staff shall transfer the information provided on the application onto the appropriate final orders. A Facilitator Program attorney may present final orders with a completed and signed Declaration In Lieu of Formal Proof to the judicial officer conducting the Status Non–Compliance Calendar or the Chief UFC Judge. Presentation of final orders shall occur pursuant to the time frame established by statute. The Declaration In Lieu of Formal Proof shall be in substantially the same format as set forth in Appendix 1 of LFLR 5 except that these Declarations may be signed any time after filing and prior to entry of the final orders.

(d) Case Schedule. Participating in the Simple Dissolution (Divorce) Program does not waive the parties' obligation to comply with the deadlines set forth in the Order Setting Domestic Case Schedule.

(e) Fee. The Simple Dissolution (Divorce) Program may administer a fee for the service in compliance with King County local rules, Washington State rules and Washington law. The fee shall be waived for indigent parties.

[Adopted on an emergency basis, effective October 28, 2014; January 27, 2015; adopted on a permanent basis effective September 1, 2015.]

XV. LOCAL CRIMINAL RULES (Cite as LCrR)

LCrR 0.1. GRAND JURY

A grand jury shall be under the direct charge and supervision of the Judge, or Judges, to whom the Court may assign that duty by a majority vote of the Judges.

LCrR 0.2. COMMISSIONERS

When so assigned by the Presiding Judge or the Chief Criminal Judge for Seattle case assignment area cases and the Chief RJC Judge for Kent case assignment area cases, commissioners may preside over arraignments, preliminary appearances, initial extradition hearings, noncompliance hearings pursuant to RCW 9.94A.200, accept guilty pleas, appoint counsel, make determinations of probable cause, set and review conditions of pretrial release, set bail, set trial and hearing dates, and hear continuance motions.

[Adopted effective September 1, 2001; amended effective September 1, 2003.]

LCrR 1.1. LOCAL PROCEDURES

The current procedures for handling and processing criminal cases in King County Superior Court are contained in the Criminal Department Manual. Copies of the Manual are available from the courtrooms of the Chief Criminal Judge in Seattle and Chief RJC Judge in Kent. A link to the Manual can be found on the Court's web site at: http://www.metrokc.gov/kcsc/.

[Amended effective September 1, 2001; September 1, 2003; September 1, 2007.]

LCrR 2.2. WARRANT UPON INDICTMENT OR INFORMATION

(b) Issuance of Summons in Lieu of Warrant.

(1) *When Summons Must Issue.* Absent a showing of cause for issuance of a warrant, a summons shall issue for a person who has been released on personal recognizance by a magistrate by the exercise of discretion on the preliminary appearance calendar. The person shall be directed to appear on the arraignment calendar.

(g) Information to Be Supplied to the Court. When a charge is filed in Superior Court and a warrant is requested, the court shall be provided with the following information about the person charged:

(1) The pretrial release interview form, if any, completed by either a bail interviewer or by the defense counsel.

(2) By the prosecuting attorney, insofar as possible.

(A) A brief summary of the alleged facts of the charge;

(B) Information concerning other known pending or potential charges;

(C) A summary of any known criminal record;

(D) Any other facts deemed material to the issue of pretrial release;

(E) Any ruling of a magistrate at a preliminary appearance.

[Amended effective September 1, 2001.]

LCrR 3.1. RIGHT TO AND ASSIGNMENT OF COUNSEL

(d) Assignment of Lawyer.

(4) Appointed and assigned counsel shall file quarterly, with the Clerk, on the form recommended by the Supreme Court, a certificate declaring that counsel is in compliance with the applicable Standards for Indigent Defense promulgated by the Supreme Court of Washington. An appointed or assigned attorney who is not in compliance with the applicable standards, or who has not filed a certificate prior to appearing or filing a notice of appearance, shall so advise the court at every hearing.

(f) Services Other Than Counsel. Pursuant to the authority under CrR 3.1(f), all requests and approval for expert services expenditures are hereby delegated to the King County Office of the Public Defender. Upon finding that investigative, expert or other services are necessary to an adequate defense and that defendant is financially unable to obtain them, the King County Office of the Public Defender (OPD) shall authorize the services. Where services are denied in whole or in part, the defendant may move for *de novo* review to the Chief Criminal Judge or the Chief Judge of the Maleng Regional Justice Center. Should defendant seek an order sealing the moving papers, defendant shall present, along with the moving papers, a motion and proposed order sealing the documents to the OPD. OPD shall submit the motion to seal and proposed order with the moving papers regarding request for expert services and OPD's order on the motion for expert services to the Chief Criminal Judge or the Chief Judge of the Maleng Regional Justice Center.

[Effective January 1, 1996; amended effective September 1, 2008; September 1, 2011; amended on an emergency basis, effective November 29, 2011; March 2, 2012; amended on a permanent basis, effective September 1, 2012; amended on an emergency basis, effective September 27, 2012; December 21, 2012; May 17, 2013; July 1, 2013; amended on a permanent basis, effective September 2, 2013.]

LCrR 3.2. PRETRIAL RELEASE

(a) Personal Bond; Ten Percent Deposit.

(1) Whenever bond has been set, either by use of a bail schedule, or by order in an individual case, unless the court order setting bond specifically provides to the contrary, the bond requirement may be met by deposit in the registry of the court in cash of a sum equal to ten percent of the amount of the bond and by

the filing of a personal appearance bond in a form provided by the court.

(2) The appearance bond shall obligate the defendant to appear for all required court hearings and for trial and to keep a correct address and phone number on file with the court.

(3) Failure to comply with the obligations of the appearance bond without just cause will result in:

(A) Liability for the entire amount of the bond; and

(B) Forfeiture of the cash posted.

(4) Failure to comply with those obligations without just cause will also constitute grounds for imprisonment pending trial.

(5) The cash deposit will be returned to the person who posted the bond upon a showing that the defendant has fulfilled the conditions of the bond and upon presentation of an order showing the defendant has fulfilled the conditions and exonerating bond.

[Amended effective September 1, 1992; September 1, 2001.]

LCrR 4.5. OMNIBUS HEARINGS

(d) **Motions.** All rulings of the Court at omnibus hearings or otherwise made in the criminal motion department shall be binding on the parties and shall not be relitigated at trial.

(i) **Waiver.** If there will be no pretrial motions or hearings in a case, and all parties agree that an omnibus hearing would not be beneficial, waiver of the hearing may be requested by written stipulation on a form provided by the Court. Such a request constitutes an assurance that the parties will be ready to begin jury selection immediately on the morning of trial.

(j) **Preparation.** Discovery shall be completed to the extent possible during the plea bargaining period following initial arraignment. The parties shall have completed and furnished to the criminal motion Judge and to counsel copies of their respective omnibus applications before the hearing.

LCrR 4.11. VIDEO CONFERENCE PROCEEDINGS

(a) **Criminal.** Preliminary appearances as defined by CrR 3.2(b) and CrRLJ 3.2.1(d), arraignments as defined by CrR 3.4 and 4.1 and CrRLJ 3.4 and 4.1, bail hearings as defined by CrR 3.2 and CrRLJ 3.2, and trial settings, as defined by CrR 3.3 and CrRLJ 3.3(f), conducted via video conference in which all participants can simultaneously see, hear, and speak as authorized by the Court, shall be deemed held in open court and in the defendant's presence for the purposes of any statute, court rule, or policy. All video conference hearings conducted pursuant to this rule shall be public, and the public shall be able to simultaneously see and hear all participants and speak as permitted by the trial court Judge. Any party may

request an in-person hearing which may, in the Judge's discretion, be granted.

(b) **Agreement.** Other trial court proceedings may be conducted by video conference only by agreement of the parties either in writing or on the record and upon the approval of the Judge.

(c) **Standards for Video Conference Proceedings.** The Judge, counsel, all parties, and the public attending the hearing must be able to see, hear, and speak as authorized by the Court during proceedings. Video conference facilities must provide for confidential communications between attorney and client and security sufficient to protect the safety of all participants and observers. In interpreted proceedings, the interpreter should be located next to the defendant, and the proceeding must be conducted to assure that the interpreter can hear all participants.

[Effective September 1, 1996]

LCrR 5.1. COMMENCEMENT OF ACTIONS; CASE ASSIGNMENT AREA

(d) **Location for Court Proceedings for Criminal Cases Filed in King County; Filing of Documents and Pleadings and Designation of Case Assignment Area.**

(1) *Designation of Case Assignment Area.* Each criminal case filed in the Superior Court shall be accompanied by a designation of the Case Assignment Area.

(2) *Boundaries of Case Assignment Areas.* For purposes of this rule King County shall be divided into case assignment areas as follows:

(A) Seattle Case Assignment Area. All of King County north of Interstate 90 and including all of the Interstate 90 right-of-way; all of the cities of Seattle, Mercer Island, Bellevue, Issaquah and North Bend; the unincorporated areas of King County Sheriff's Precinct 4; and including all of Vashon and Maury Islands.

(B) Kent Case Assignment Area. All of King County south of Interstate 90 except those areas included in the Seattle Case Assignment Area.

(C) Change of Area Boundaries. The Presiding Judge may adjust the boundaries between areas when required for the efficient and fair administration of justice in King County.

(3) *Standards for Case Assignment Area Designation, and Revisions Thereof.*

(A) Case Assignment Area Designated by Prosecuting Attorney. The indictment or information filed with the Clerk shall contain the Case Assignment Area designation of the case.

(B) Standard for Designation. Except as provided in Section (C) below, the Prosecuting Attorney shall assign the case to the Case Assignment Area where the offense is alleged to have been committed.

(C) Exceptions to Standard Designation.

(i) The Prosecuting Attorney may designate a case assignment area different than provided in (B) above:

a) Where the location of the offense within the county cannot be easily ascertained or the offense was committed in more than one area of the county;

b) Where multiple offenses charged were committed in more than one area of the county;

(ii) The following case categories shall be designated to the Seattle Case Assignment Area:

a) Fugitives from justice.

b) Appeals in criminal cases from District Courts.

c) Cases accepted into Drug Court.

(iii) When a defendant has an action pending, any new action filed against that defendant shall be assigned to the same case assignment area as the pending case.

(D) Improper Designation/Lack of Designation. The designation of the improper case assignment area shall not be a basis for dismissal of any action.

(E) Assignment or Transfer on Court's Motion. The Court on its own motion or on the motion of a party may assign or transfer cases to another case assignment area in the county whenever required for the just and efficient administration of justice in King County.

(F) Motions by Party to Transfer. Motions to transfer court proceedings from one case assignment area to another shall be made in writing, with proper notice to all parties. Motions to transfer shall generally be heard prior to trial setting only. All cases shall proceed in the original case assignment area until an order of transfer is entered.

(G) Venue Not Affected. This rule shall not affect whether venue is proper in any Superior Court facility in King County.

(H) Pre–Filing Requests for Exceptions. The Prosecutor in advance of filing a particular case, for good cause shown, may apply ex parte to the Chief Criminal Judge for an exception to the normal case assignment area.

(4) *Where Pleadings and Documents Filed.* Pursuant to LGR 30, all pleadings and documents for any criminal action in King County must be electronically filed with the Clerk using the Clerk's e-filing system. Documents identified as exceptions to mandatory e-filing must be filed in paper form with the Clerk of the Superior Court at the court facility in the case assignment area of the case. Service of documents on the Prosecuting Attorney and the defendant's attorney shall be made at the office of the Prosecutor and defense attorney located in the case assignment area of the case at the time of service.

(5) *Inclusion of Case Assignment Area Code.* All pleadings and documents shall contain after the cause number the case assignment area code. The Clerk may reject pleadings or documents that do not contain this case assignment area code.

(6) *Jury Assignment Area.* See LGR 18. The rule provides for Seattle and Kent jury assignment areas, consisting of registered voters and licensed drivers and identicard holders residing in each jury assignment area.

[Adopted effective June 1, 1996; amended effective September 1, 2001; December 1, 2001; September 1, 2004; September 1, 2007; June 1, 2009; September 8, 2009; September 1, 2010.]

LCrR 7.1.   PRESENTENCE INVESTIGATION

(a) *When Required; Time of Service.* Unless otherwise directed by the court, in all cases where a person is to be sentenced for commission of a felony, the prosecuting attorney and the defendant's attorney shall, not less than three days before the sentencing date, serve a copy of his/her presentence report upon the opposing party and the original to the sentencing judge. The Department of Corrections shall serve a copy of its report when ordered upon the prosecuting attorney and the defense attorney and the original to the sentencing judge not less than three days before the sentencing date.

(b) *Penalties for Violation.* A violation of this rule may result in the refusal of the court to proceed with the sentencing until after reports have been filed as directed herein, and in the imposition of terms; or the court may proceed to impose sentence without regard to the violation.

(c) *Working Copies.* Any party requesting that the court impose an exceptional sentence shall serve a working copy of the proposed findings in support of the request for an exceptional sentence to the court and opposing counsel no later than seven days before the date scheduled for sentencing. Working copies shall be submitted pursuant to LCR 7(b) to the extent not inconsistent with this rule.

[Amended effective September 1, 2002; September 1, 2009. Former LCrR 7.2 renumbered and amended effective September 1, 2001.]

LCrR 9.1.   IN FORMA PAUPERIS– APPEAL–COURT REPORTER LOG

The Motion for Order of Indigency shall contain the names and dates of appearance for all court reporters who recorded sessions for which authorization for transcription is requested.

[Adopted effective September 1, 1999.]

XVI.   LOCAL JUVENILE COURT RULES
(Cite as LJuCR)

LJuCR 1.1.   SCOPE OF RULES [RESERVED]

[Reserved effective September 2, 2013.]

LJuCR 1.2.   JURISDICTION OF JUVENILE COURT

(a) **Generally.** Reserved

(b) **Indian Children.** In the case of an Indian child, as defined by the federal Indian Child Welfare Act of 1978 and RCW 13.38, jurisdiction and proceedings under these rules shall be in accordance with those acts. Court validation of a voluntary consent to foster care placement of Indian Children shall be in accordance with RCW 13.34.245 and RCW 13.38.150.

[Adopted effective September 2, 2013.]

LJuCR 1.3.   DEFINITIONS [RESERVED]

[Reserved effective September 2, 2013.]

LJuCR 1.4.   APPLICABILITY OF OTHER RULES

(a) **Reserved**

(b) **Reserved**

(c) **Reserved**

(d) **Reserved**

(e) **Discovery.**

(1) *Generally.* Discovery procedures in cases involving alleged dependent or dependent children (including termination and guardianship proceedings) shall generally be governed by CR 26–37.

(2) *Completion of Discovery.* Unless otherwise ordered by the Court for good cause and subject to such terms and conditions as are just, all discovery allowed under CR 26–37, including responses and supplementations thereto, must be completed as provided in the case schedule. Discovery requests must be served early enough that responses will be due and depositions will have been completed by the applicable cutoff date. Discovery requests that do not comply with this rule will not be enforced, absent a written agreement of all parties, and the parties shall not enter into such an agreement if it is likely to affect the trial date. Nothing in this rule shall modify a party's responsibility to reasonably supplement responses to discovery requests or otherwise to comply with discovery prior to the cutoff.

(f) **Summary Judgment.**

(1) *Motion.* A motion for summary judgment may be filed by any party in accordance with LCR 56.

[Adopted effective September 2, 2013.]

LJuCR 1.5.   CONTINUATION OF ACTIONS [RESERVED]

[Reserved effective September 2, 2013.]

TITLE II.   SHELTER CARE PROCEEDINGS

LJuCR 2.0.   RIGHT TO APPOINTED COUNSEL

(a) **Appointment.** A child's parent, legal guardian, or legal custodian has the right to be appointed an attorney, if qualified on the basis of indigency, as provided in RCW 13.34.090. The Court shall not appoint an attorney for any parent, legal guardian, or legal custodian not present at a hearing unless the Court makes a specific finding that a compelling reason for such appointment exists. Representation by a Court appointed attorney for a parent, legal guardian, or legal custodian in a dependency proceeding is limited by the provisions of these rules and the notice set forth in LJuCR 3.4(b).

(b) **Motion for Appointment.** At any point in an RCW Chapter 13.34 proceeding including proceedings for termination of parental rights or to establish dependency guardianships, a party who is not represented by an attorney may move the Court for appointment of an attorney, or referral therefor, pursuant to this rule.

(c) **Demonstration of Eligibility.** At any point in an RCW Chapter 13.34 proceeding, the Court may require on the motion of a party or the Court's own motion, a child's parent, legal guardian, or legal custodian to demonstrate current financial eligibility for a Court appointed attorney.

[Adopted effective March 20, 1997.]

LJuCR 2.1.   PLACEMENT OF JUVENILE IN SHELTER CARE GENERALLY [RESERVED]

[Effective January 2, 1994. Amended effective September 1, 2005. Reserved effective September 2, 2013.]

LJuCR 2.2.   RELEASE OF JUVENILE FROM SHELTER CARE WITHOUT HEARING [RESERVED]

[Effective January 2, 1994. Reserved effective September 2, 2013.]

LJuCR 2.3. RIGHT TO AND NOTICE OF SHELTER CARE HEARING

(a) Notice of Right to Shelter Care Hearing. The notice of the 72–hour and 30–day shelter care hearings shall be given to the child's parents, guardians, or legal custodians, and child's Tribe as soon as reasonably possible after the child is taken into custody. Notice may be made by any means reasonably certain of notifying the parents, guardians or custodians of the child, and child's Tribe, including but not limited to written, telephone or in person communication and shall specify the time and place of the hearing, the right to an attorney and the general allegations of the petition or motion to take child into custody. Proof of notice or of attempts to provide notice of the hearings shall be made by testimony, written declaration or affidavit and submitted for the legal file at the 72–hour hearing. Notice shall also be given to children age 12 and over and they shall be advised of their right to attend the hearings and their right to be represented by an attorney. If a child age 12 and over wishes to attend the 72–hour or 30–day shelter care hearing, the agency having custody of the child shall be responsible for arranging transportation for the child.

(b) Shelter Care Hearing Required. The party filing a dependency petition and setting a 72–hour shelter care hearing shall at the time of filing the petition also set a second shelter care hearing to be held on the Juvenile Court "Contested Calendar" within 30 days of the 72–hour shelter care hearing and a fact-finding hearing to be held at King County Superior Court within 75 days of the filing of the petition. The Clerk shall issue a case schedule and a notice and summons pursuant to RCW 13.34.070 for a pretrial conference and a fact-finding hearing, setting the fact finding hearing within 75 days of the petition being filed. In all dependency cases filed, the petitioner shall be responsible for ensuring service of the summons and notice on all necessary parties.

(c) Notice of Shelter Care Hearing. The petition and/or motion to take child into custody, the notice of custody and rights required by RCW 13.34.062 and the notice and summons for the fact-finding hearing shall be served on the parents, guardians or legal custodians, child's Tribe and to any child age 12 and older as soon as reasonably possible and a receipt signed by the receiving party or a declaration or affidavit of service shall be filed in the legal file. If the notice and summons for the fact-finding hearing cannot be served on a required party prior to or at the 72–hour hearing, it must be served as soon as possible pursuant to the requirements of RCW 13.34.070, 13.34.080, and 13.38.070.

(d) Indian Children. Reserved

(e) Notice to Attorneys of Record. Where there is already a previously assigned or retained attorney of record for any party, including an attorney or CASA for the child, in a dependency proceeding presently pending in Juvenile Court, they shall be provided notice of the shelter care and fact-finding hearings no later than 24 hours prior to the 72–hour shelter care hearing whenever reasonably possible.

(f) Courtesy Notice to Public Defender Agencies and CASA. The petitioning party in a dependency and/or the moving party for an order to take a child into custody shall make available an electronic copy of the petition and any resultant order to OPD, the CASA program, and contracted defense agencies responsible for providing attorney-of-the-day services on the day the petition is filed. The public defender office and CASA program shall be responsible for obtaining said copies.

(g) Continuances of the 72–Hour Hearing. Any person or agency entitled to such notice as set forth above may move for a continuance of the 72–hour hearing if it appears they did not receive timely notice of the hearing. A continuance may be granted by the Court under such conditions as shall ensure the safety and well-being of any child subject to the proceeding. If a child remains in the home of a parent, guardian or legal custodian, the Court may allow the parties to continue the initial shelter care hearing to a new date to be set no later than 14 days from the filing of the petition under such conditions as shall ensure the safety and well-being of any child subject to the proceedings.

(h) Subsequent Shelter Care Hearing for Unavailable Party. Whenever it appears that a parent, guardian, or legal custodian was unable to attend the initial shelter care hearing, such person may request a hearing by written application to the Court showing good cause for their inability to attend the initial hearing. Such subsequent hearing, if granted, shall be conducted within 72 hours of the request (excluding Saturdays, Sundays and holidays).

[Effective January 2, 1994. Amended effective September 1, 2005; September 2, 2013.]

LJuCR 2.4. PROCEDURE AT INITIAL SHELTER CARE HEARING

(a) Inform Parties of Rights. The court shall inform parties of their rights as set forth in RCW 13.34.090. Any parent, guardian and/or legal custodian of the child, or child age 12 or older, who appears at the 72–hour hearing may be represented, at this hearing, by Court-appointed counsel regardless of financial status unless the party expressly waives this right or has retained counsel.

(b) Hearing and Decision. At the 72–hour hearing the Court shall:

(1) Determine whether those persons entitled to notice under RCW 13.34 and RCW 13.38 and these rules have received notice of custody and rights pursuant to RCW 13.34.060 and ensure that all parties are informed of their legal rights.

(2) Receive evidence from the petitioner regarding efforts made to notify the parties to this action, and the child's Tribe and determine whether additional service of process or publication of notice is necessary. Any party to this action who was personally served notice and summons of the fact-finding hearing pursuant to RCW 13.34.070 or who is present at the 72–hour hearing shall be deemed to have received timely and proper notice of the fact-finding hearing.

(3) Determine whether a CASA shall be appointed for the child.

(4) Determine whether an attorney shall be appointed or a referral to the Office of Public Defense for screening be made for any party, including the child, in accordance with the provisions of LJuCR 2.0 and RCW 13.38.110.

(5) Consider and approve agreements pertaining to custody and services pending the 30–day shelter care hearing. The parties may enter into and submit for Court approval an agreed shelter care order. Any such order, if signed by the parent and their attorney, shall constitute sufficient record that the waiver of the 72–hour hearing is knowing and voluntary if the order contains written notice of the rights of the parties to a court hearing and waiver thereof. Agreed orders which are presented without the signature of an attorney for any party must be approved by the Court with the parties present, at which time the Court will inquire into whether the order has been signed knowingly and voluntarily.

(6) Release a child alleged to be dependent to the care, custody, and control of the child's parent, guardian, or legal custodian, unless the Court makes specific findings that the requirements of RCW 13.34.065(2) have been satisfied. The Court may order return of the child subject to specific conditions and/or provision of services.

(7) Hear such evidence as may be presented by the parties as to the issues set forth in LJuCR 2.4(c)(6) and otherwise as to the need for shelter care, consistent with the requirements of RCW 13.34.065. All parties have the right to present evidence in the form of offers of proof, affidavits, statements, testimony, and arguments in the context of the reasonable cause standard.

(8) Enter appropriate findings of fact as to whether the child and all persons with parental or custodial rights have received notice of the hearing and which of the material facts are undisputed. Notice must be given by any party moving to establish dependency at subsequent shelter care hearings upon a showing of undisputed facts sufficient to establish dependency pursuant to RCW 13.34.030(5).

(9) Enter orders of protection or temporary restraining orders or preliminary injunctions pursuant to RCW 26.44 and 26.50 as may be necessary to protect the child or the person having custody of the child, or to allow a child to remain in the family home.

(10) Order the necessary placement, conditions of visitation or contact with the child, services and other relief as necessary to protect the child's right to conditions of basic nurture, physical and mental health and safety. Specific conditions may be set by the Court to facilitate a return of the child or increased contact between parent and child, including assessments as provided by RCW 26.44.053. Upon request the Court may provide for an additional protective order regarding confidentiality of the assessment that does not violate the mandatory reporter provisions of RCW 26.44.

(11) Termination of publication (T.O.P.) hearings shall be set by the petitioner and the Clerk of the Court at least 70 days in the future. It shall be the responsibility of the petitioner to show by the petition or other verified statement or certification that the identity or the whereabouts of a necessary party is unknown or that no other method of service is likely to be successful.

(12) *Alternate Dispute Resolution (ADR):* The Court may order the case set for mediation, settlement conference, or other ADR process and may adjust the case schedule as necessary to accommodate the ADR schedule.

(c) **Release of Juvenile on Conditions.** The court may release the juvenile on those conditions it deems appropriate.

[Adopted effective September 1, 1983. Amended effective January 2, 1994; March 20, 1997; September 1, 2001; September 1, 2005; September 2, 2013.]

LJuCR 2.5. AMENDMENT OF SHELTER CARE ORDER

(a) **Time.** The second hearing shall be set within 30 days of the first hearing, unless by the agreement on the record or in writing of all parties or the order of the Court.

(b) **Procedure.** Unless a party has filed and served written notice of new issues as outlined below, a hearing in open court will not occur; parties presence will be excused; and an order continuing the terms of the 72 hour shelter care hearing will be entered by the court.

(c) **New Issues:** Reasonable advance written notice shall be given to the court and other parties of the new issues any party seeks to raise at the 30 day hearing. The party seeking to modify terms or enforce compliance with the terms of a 72 hour shelter care order shall give written notice to the Court and other parties not later than noon three days prior to the hearing. Responses will be provided by noon the day before the hearing. All other issues require six days written notice to the parties and the court according to LCR 7.

(d) Procedure for Additional Shelter Care Hearing. An additional shelter care hearing can be set on the contested-hearing calendar upon the filing of a note for calendar and a written "Motion and Affidavit of Change of Circumstances" with six court days' notice to all parties. The motion shall specify the change in circumstances, relief requested, statement of facts and the evidence relied upon, and shall be properly served on all parties. All responsive pleadings shall be submitted to the Court and parties

pursuant to LCR 7. The hearing date shall be obtained from the Court.

[Effective January 2, 1994. Amended effective July 1, 1994; March 20, 1997; September 1, 2005; September 1, 2008; September 2, 2013.]

LJuCR 2.6. SUMMARY JUDGMENT [RESCINDED]

[Adopted effective September 1, 2005. Rescinded effective September 2, 2013.]

TITLE III. DEPENDENCY PROCEEDINGS

LJuCR 3.1. INVOKING JURISDICTION OF JUVENILE COURT [RESERVED]

[Effective January 2, 1994. Reserved effective September 2, 2013.]

LJuCR 3.2. WHO MAY FILE PETITION—VENUE

(a) Reserved

(b) Reserved

(c) Location for Court Proceedings for Dependency Actions Filed in King County; Filing of Documents and Pleadings and Designation of Case Assignment Area.

(1) All proceedings of any nature shall be conducted in the case assignment area designated on the dependency petition unless the Court has otherwise ordered on its own motion or upon motion of any party to the action.

(2) Standards for case assignment area designation, and revisions thereof.

(A) Location Designated by Party Filing Action. Initial designations shall be made upon the filing of the petition alleging dependency. Case Assignment Area designations shall not be changed between the time of filing of a dependency petition and the entry of a disposition order except as necessary to correct a mistaken designation, to prevent undue hardship to a party or by the Court on its own motion as required for the just and efficient administration of justice.

(1) For petitions for dependency the case area designation shall be based on the DCFS office filing the petition.

(a) Seattle Case Assignment Area. All petitions from the Martin Luther King Office and for children known to be protected by the Indian Child Welfare Act.

(b) Kent Assignment Area. All petitions from the King South, King East, and White Center DCFS office.

(c) Boundaries of Case Assignment Areas. For purposes of this rule King County shall be

divided into case assignment areas for petitions filed from the King West and Adoptions and Permanency office and any non-DCFS filed petition as follows:

(i) Seattle Case Assignment Area. All of King County except for the areas included in the Kent Case Assignment Area.

(ii) Kent Case Assignment Area. All of the areas of King County using the following postal zip codes: 98001; 98002; 98003; 98010; 98022; 98023; 98025; 98031; 98032; 98038; 98042; 98047; 98048; 98051; 98054; 98055; 98056; 98057; 98058; 98059; 98092; 98146; 98148; 98158; 98166; 98168; 98178; 98188; 98198.

(iii) Change of Area Boundaries. The Presiding Judge may adjust the boundaries between areas when required for the efficient and fair administration of justice in King County.

(2) For cases regarding Children in Need of Services and At Risk Youth, the case area designation shall be based on where the custodial parent resides.

(B) Change of Case Assignment Area Designation. The Court may order that a juvenile's case assignment area designation change upon the establishment of dependency and the entry of a disposition order based on one of the following reasons: hardship to one of parties; transfer of the case within the supervising agency or to a new agency; a need for judicial continuity of control over the case; transfer is in the best interest of the child; correction of a mistaken designation or for such other reason deemed just and proper by the Court or when required for the just and efficient administration of justice. A case should not be transferred solely to accommodate an attorney.

(1) Method. A motion for change of case assignment area designation may be made by any party to the dependency or by the Court on its own motion. Such a motion shall only be made in writing as required by LJuCR 3.12 and shall be titled Motion to Change Case Assignment Area and shall specify the factors for change of case assignment area. A proposed Order to Change

Case Assignment Area shall be included with the working papers submitted for the Court. If the motion is agreed to by the parties, the motion shall so state and the proposed order shall include the signatures of the parties. The Order to Change Case Assignment Area shall be filed by the prevailing party. All cases shall proceed in the original case assignment area until the order is entered and filed. Proceedings in the assigned area shall not preclude the timely filing of a motion to transfer.

(C) Improper Designation/Lack of Designation. The designation of the improper case assignment area shall not be a basis for dismissal of any action, but may be a basis for imposition of terms. The lack of designation of case assignment area at initial case filing may be a basis for imposition of terms and will result in assignment to a case assignment area at the Court's discretion.

(D) Assignment or Transfer on Court's Motion. The Court on its own motion may assign or transfer cases to another case assignment area in the county whenever required for the just and efficient administration of justice in King County.

(E) Venue not Affected. This rule shall not affect whether venue is proper in any Superior Court facility in King County.

(3) *Where Pleadings and Documents Filed.* Pursuant to LGR 30, all pleadings and documents for any dependency proceeding in King County must be electronically filed with the Clerk of the Superior Court using the Clerk's e-filing system. Documents identified as exceptions to mandatory e-filing must be filed in paper form at the court facility in the case assignment area of the case. Working copies must be provided for the judge pursuant to the requirements of LCR 7(b) to the extent not inconsistent with this rule.

(4) *Inclusion of Case Assignment Area Code.* All pleadings and documents shall contain after the cause number the case assignment designation code assigned by the Clerk for the case assignment area in which court proceedings are to be held. The Clerk may reject pleadings or documents that do not contain this case assignment area code.

[Adopted effective January 2, 1994. Amended effective October 1, 1996; September 1, 2004; September 1, 2005; September 1, 2009; April 1, 2011; amended on a permanent basis, effective September 1, 2011; September 2, 2013.]

LJuCR 3.3. CONTENT OF DEPENDENCY PETITION

A dependency petition shall contain:

(a), (b), (d)—(g) reserved

(c) Indian Children. If the petitioner knows or has reason to know that the juvenile is or may be an Indian child as defined in RCW 13.38, the petition shall so state and shall state the name of the Indian Tribe, or if not known, the basis of the child's Indian heritage.

(h) Verification. If the petition is prepared by a Juvenile Court Liaison worker on behalf of the petitioning DSHS social worker, or the private agency coordinator on behalf of an individual or private agency, it shall contain a verified statement by the Liaison worker or private agency coordinator that the information contained therein was provided by the petitioning social worker and that the finalized petition accurately reflects said information.

[Effective January 2, 1994. Amended effective September 1, 2005; September 2, 2013.]

LJuCR 3.4. NOTICE AND SUMMONS— SCHEDULING OF FACTFINDING HEARING

(a) Notice and Summons. At the time of filing the petition, a Notice and Summons and case schedule shall be issued by the Clerk of the Court and served by the petitioner pursuant to RCW 13.34.070. Service by publication shall conform to the requirement of RCW 13.34.080. A 72–hour shelter care hearing date, a pre-trial conference date and a fact finding date shall be obtained at the time of filing and set out in the notice. The notice shall state that a petition begins a process, which if the juvenile is found dependent, may result in permanent termination of the parent-child relationship.

(b) Advice to Be Contained in Notice and Summons.

(1) A notice directed to the juvenile and/or to the juvenile's parent, legal custodian, or guardian shall contain an advisement of rights conforming to requirements of RCW 13.34.062, RCW 13.34.070 and RCW 13.34.090 clearly setting forth the right of a party to a hearing before a Judge and to representation by a lawyer, including appointment of a lawyer to a child, parent, guardian, or legal custodian who cannot afford one.

(2) The Notice and Summons shall also advise the parties that attendance at the pre-trial conference is mandatory, unless excused in advance by the Court.

(3) The Notice and Summons shall also advise the parties that failure of a party to appear or otherwise plead or respond to the petition shall be the basis for the Court to enter an Order of Default and Findings of Dependency and Disposition against that party at the pre-trial conference.

(c) Scheduling Fact Finding Hearing. The Court shall schedule a pre-trial conference and a fact finding hearing. The fact-finding hearing shall be set to be held within 75 days of the filing of the petition alleging dependency. The parties may waive their right to a hearing within 75 days and stipulate to continue the hearing to a later time based on exceptional circumstances subject to Court approval.

(d) Indian Children. If the petitioner knows or has reason to know that the child involved is or may be an Indian child as defined in RCW 13.38, the petitioner shall notify the child's tribe or band of the fact-finding hearing in the manner required by RCW 13.34.070(10), **13.38.070** and 25 U.S.C. 1912.

[Effective January 2, 1994. Amended effective July 1, 1994; March 20, 1997; August 20, 1998; September 1, 2005; September 2, 2013.]

LJuCR 3.5. AMENDMENT OF PETITION [RESERVED]

[Effective January 2, 1994. Reserved effective September 2, 2013.]

LJuCR 3.6. ANSWER TO PETITION

(a) When to File. The parents or other respondents shall file an answer to the petition not later than the date provided in the case schedule. If the petition is amended subsequent to filing, the parents and other respondents shall file an answer to the amended portions of the petition within fourteen (14) days of the amendment or at the date provided in the case schedule, whichever occurs later.

(b) Age of Child Who May Answer. A child aged twelve or older may file an answer to the petition, but shall not be required to do so.

(c) Content of Answer. The answer shall specifically address and admit or deny each allegation in the petition. Denials shall fairly meet the substance of allegations denied. When a parent or other respondent intends in good faith to deny only a part of or to qualify an allegation, he or she shall specify so much of it as is true and material and shall deny only the remainder. If a parent or other respondent is without knowledge or information sufficient to form a belief as to the truth of an allegation, he or she shall so state and this shall have the same effect as a denial. The answer may be signed by the parent or other respondent, the attorney representing the parent or other respondent, or both. If the answer is signed only by the attorney representing the parent or other respondent, the answer shall include a certification by the attorney that the specific admissions and denials contained in the answer have been discussed with that attorney and approved by the parent or respondent that the attorney represents.

[Effective January 2, 1994; amended effective March 20, 1997.]

LJuCR 3.7. FACT–FINDING HEARING

(a) Procedure at Hearing. The court shall hold a factfinding hearing on the petition in accordance with RCW 13.34.110. All fact-finding hearings shall be assigned per the direction of the Court at the pre-trial conference.

(b) Reserved

(c) Burden of Proof. In a fact-finding hearing on a petition alleging dependency pursuant to RCW 13.34.030(6), the facts alleged in the petition must be proven by a preponderance of the evidence.

(d) Reserved

(e) Procedure at Pre-trial Conference.

(1) The Court shall hold a pre-trial conference on the date set in the case schedule which shall be at least 6 days prior to the scheduled date of the fact-finding hearing, at the location specified in the case schedule, unless modified by Court order. All parties must be present at the pre-trial conference unless specifically excused by the Court. Failure of a party to appear or to otherwise plead or respond to the petition, shall be the basis for the Court to enter an Order of Default and Findings of Dependency and Disposition against that party at the pre-trial conference. All parties shall attempt to reach agreement, in advance of the pre-trial conference, on issues regarding discovery, witnesses, evidentiary and other pre-trial questions including a continuance of a trial date. Parties must comply with the requirement of LJuCR 1.4(e) prior to seeking sanctions for failure to provide discovery.

(2) At the pre-trial conference, the Court will inquire into the readiness of the case for trial and compliance with the case schedule. Failure to comply with the case schedule may be the basis for Court ordered sanctions.

(3) For those cases in which a parent or other respondent appears at the pre-trial conference and states their wish to proceed to trial, but has not filed an answer to the petition in a timely fashion pursuant to LJuCR 3.6, and if the Court decides to allow the case to proceed to trial, a continuance of the pre-trial conference may be granted at the request of any other party sufficient to allow the other parties at least five days following the filing of the answer, which shall be filed no later than at the time of the pre-trial conference unless otherwise authorized by the Court due to circumstances beyond the control of the attorney for the answering party, to gather information necessary for completion of the Statement of Evidence based upon the allegations at issue.

(4) For those cases for which an answer has been filed in compliance with LJuCR 3.6, or following a continuance to allow time for preparation of the Statement of Evidence, as provided above, the Court will consider matters of law, may certify the case for an alternative dispute resolution process, and otherwise define the specific procedural course of the fact finding hearing, such as determine the number of witnesses, the length and scope of the fact-finding hearing defined by the allegations actually at issue as determined by the pleadings, stipulations, and other

agreement based upon a "Statement of Evidence" prepared prior to the pre-trial conference.

(5) All motions filed after the pre-trial conference order has been entered shall be brought pursuant to LCR 7 before the designated dependency Judge, unless otherwise assigned.

(f) Agreed Orders of Dependency or Disposition. The parent, guardian or legal custodian of a child may waive his or her right to a fact finding hearing by stipulating or agreeing to the entry of an order of dependency or disposition pursuant to RCW 13.34.110.

(1) Prior to entry of any stipulated or agreed order of dependency, the parent, guardian or legal custodian must appear before the court or waive his or her right to appear by executing, in writing, a waiver of the right to appear. The Court must establish on the record that the parent, guardian, or legal custodian possesses the knowledge and understanding of the legal effect of the stipulated order as required by RCW 13.34.110(2)(c).

(2) If the parent, guardian, or legal custodian fails to appear before the court after stipulating to entry of an agreed order of dependency, the Court may approve entry of the order upon a finding that the parent, guardian, or legal custodian had actual notice of the right to appear and chose not to do so.

[Amended effective September 1, 1983; January 2, 1994; March 20, 1997; August 20, 1998; September 1, 2005; September 2, 2013.]

LJuCR 3.8. DISPOSITION HEARING

(a) Time. If a juvenile has been found to be dependent, the Court shall immediately hold a disposition hearing unless there is good cause for continuing the matter. Pending disposition, the terms and conditions of any current shelter care order will continue in effect unless otherwise ordered by the Court.

(b) Reserved

(c) Evidence.

(1) *Agency Reports.* The petitioner or supervising agency and CASA shall submit a report regarding a long range plan in accordance with RCW 13.34.120 and .130 clearly stating goals for the next six months. The parent, guardian, or legal custodian may also file a report to aid the court in disposition. In those disposition hearings set before a particular judge, working copies of all reports shall be provided to the judge two court days prior to the hearing. Judicial working copies shall be submitted pursuant to LCR 7(b) to the extent not inconsistent with this rule. Copies shall be served on counsel and parties six court days prior to the disposition hearing. Unless otherwise ordered by the Court, no written response is required. However, if provided, it shall be served two court days prior to the hearing.

(2) No report shall be submitted to the Court prior to the fact-finding hearing, but shall be served on the parties and counsel as required by this section.

(3) The Court shall consider the social study and other appropriate pre-dispositional studies and evaluations in addition to information produced at the fact-finding and disposition hearings. Pursuant to ER 1101, the Rules of Evidence need not apply in disposition hearings.

(d) Reserved

(e) Transferring Legal Custody. A disposition which orders removal of the juvenile from his or her home shall have the effect of transferring legal custody to the agency or legal custodian charged with the juvenile's care. The transfer of legal custody shall give the legal custodian the following rights and duties:

(1) To maintain the physical custody of the juvenile;

(2) To protect, educate and discipline the juvenile;

(3) To provide food, clothing, shelter, education as required by law, and routine medical care for a juvenile; and

(4) To consent to emergency medical care, surgical care, including anesthetics, administration of medications as prescribed by the child's treating physician, and to sign releases of medical information to appropriate authorities, pursuant to law. Reasonable efforts shall be made by the custodial agency to contact and secure the consent of the child's parents, if they are available, to any emergency medical and surgical care needed by the child. If the parents disagree with the proposed emergency medical or surgical care, either they or the custodial agency may set an emergency hearing with notice to all parties. The Court may, in its disposition order, modify the rights and duties granted to the legal custodian as a result of the transfer of legal custody.

(f) Transfer to New Agency. In the event of transfer of legal custody to an agency other than the original agency, the newly appointed custodian shall have the same rights and duties as outlined in (f) above, unless modified by the Court.

(g) Agreed Disposition. If the parties agree to a disposition plan and order, the proposed order will be submitted to the Court with all reports. The Court may set the case for a hearing on its own motion with notice to the parties accompanied by a statement of reasons for such setting.

(h) Contested Dispositional Hearing. In the event parties enter agreed dependency orders and seek to set a contested dispositional hearing, the contested dispositional hearing shall be set on the Contested Motions Calendar in accordance with LJuCR 3.12 provided the matter is not expected to exceed 30 minutes. If the matter is expected to take longer than 30 minutes, a pretrial conference order shall be entered identifying the contested issues and setting the matter for judicial assignment.

(i) Retention of Case. A Judge hearing a dependency proceeding may elect to retain authority over that case for future dependency hearings on the motion of a party or the Court's own motion. All orders entered in the proceeding shall specify that the case has been retained until such time as it is released by the Court. All time periods and procedures set forth in these rules and the applicable statutes shall be complied with by the parties and Court. Hearings and motions shall be set with the retaining Judge's bailiff. In the event an emergency hearing or motion is necessary and the moving party certifies that the retaining Judge is not available, the moving party shall set the hearing or motion on the designated contested dependency motions calendar in accordance with these rules.

[Amended effective September 1, 1983; January 2, 1994; July 1, 1994; September 1, 2005; September 1, 2009; September 2, 2013.]

LJuCR 3.9. REVIEW HEARING

(a) Dependency Review Hearings. The status of all dependent children must be reviewed by the Court at least every six months from the beginning date of placement episode or the date dependency is established, whichever is first and shall make findings as required by RCW 13.34.138. Initial review hearings will be per the procedure set out in LJuCR 3.9(b). Contested dependency motions will be per the motion procedure set out in LJuCR 3.12 and permanency planning hearings will be per the procedure set out in LJuCR 3.9(c)

(b) Initial Review. The first dependency review hearing held after dependency is initially established shall be an in-court review and shall be set within six months from the beginning date of the placement episode and no more than ninety ("90") days from entry of the dispositional order, whichever comes first. The initial review may be a permanency planning hearing when necessary to meet the time frames set forth in RCW 13.34.145(3) or 13.34.134, or when otherwise appropriate.

(c) Permanency Planning Review Hearing. The Court shall hold permanency planning review hearings for every child in out-of-home care pursuant to RCW 13.34.130. The first permanency planning review hearing shall be held as specified in RCW 13.34.145 and there shall be a subsequent permanency planning review hearing every 12 months thereafter until a permanency planning goal is achieved or the dependency is dismissed, whichever occurs first. The agency supervising the placement of the child shall submit a permanency plan for care of the child to the parties and the Court. Any such plan submitted shall not affect efforts to provide services for the reunification of the family pending approval or implementation of the permanency planning goal unless the Court specif-

ically orders otherwise. All permanency planning review hearings shall be held in court unless all parties to the dependency, including the child, agree in writing to the entry of a permanency planning order.

(d) Scheduling and Noting Contested Issues.

(1) *Scheduling an Initial Review, Dependency Review, or Permanency Planning Hearing.* Cases set for an initial review, dependency review, or permanency planning hearing shall be heard as follows: The petitioner shall set the case for hearing by obtaining an open date from the Court Coordinator via email at calendar.dependencyseattle@kingcounty.gov or calendar.dependencykent@kingcounty.gov; any party may move to set a case for a review or permanency planning review hearing to ensure that such a review is held within the time periods specified by law; or the Court on its own motion and order may set a case for a review or permanency planning hearing at any time during the dependency by providing the parties with 14 days notice of the hearing, an identification of the issues to be addressed, and a briefing schedule if appropriate.

(2) *Reports and Contested Issues.*

(A) The person or agency supervising the dependency will file and serve a written report and proposed order to all parties not less than 14 days prior to the scheduled hearing. Responsive reports of parties not in agreement with the supervising agency's proposed court order must be filed and served on the supervising person or agency, and all other parties at least seven days prior to the hearing. Documents in strict reply, if any, shall be filed and served no later than noon of the second court day prior to the hearing. All pleadings filed shall contain the name of the judicial officer expected to hear the matter or the courtroom assigned, and the date and time of the hearing in the upper right hand corner of the pleading.

(B) Any party wishing to request clarification, modification, or enforcement of the dispositional order, prior review or permanency planning order, or are requesting additional relief from the Court shall utilize the procedures set out for motions in LJuCR 3.12, and shall attach to their pleadings a copy of the order sought to be modified. Failure to do so will prevent that party from being heard on the contested issue at the hearing. If during the course of a hearing, a contested issue arises that could not have been reasonably anticipated by the affected party or their counsel, the Court may consider the contested issue or continue the hearing.

(C) Working Copies. Working copies of all pleadings be time stamped and submitted to the Court Coordinator by noon three court days prior to the hearing, and all replies shall be submitted to the Court Coordinator by the close of business two days prior to the hearing.

(3) *Hearings.* All review and permanency planning hearings shall be in-court hearings and the court will make findings as required by RCW 13.34.138, RCW 13.34.145, and/or other applicable statute.

(4) *Agreed Continuances.* By agreement a hearing may be continued for reasons approved by the court, provided that the hearing may not be continued past the date at which a review or permanency planning order for the child must be entered. If a hearing is continued past the date at which a review or permanency planning order must be entered for any reason, the Court may enter an order maintaining the status quo pending the hearing. If the supervising agency fails to submit a timely report, and any party makes a request to the supervising agency, at least seven days prior to the hearing, to continue the hearing due to the agency's untimely report, the supervising agency shall take responsibility for obtaining a new date from the Court Coordinator via email at calendar.dependencyseattle@kingcounty.gov or calendar.dependencykent@kingcounty.gov, and for seeking an agreed order by all parties to continue the hearing. If an agreed order continuing the hearing is entered in advance of the hearing, the parties need not appear.

[Effective January 2, 1994. Amended effective July 1, 1994; September 1, 1996; September 1, 2004; September 1, 2005; September 1, 2009; September 2, 2013.]

LJuCR 3.10. MODIFICATION OF ORDER

Any party may move to change, modify, or set aside an order only upon a showing of a change of circumstances. The motion must be in writing pursuant to LJuCR 3.12 and must clearly state the basis for the motion and the relief requested.

[Formerly LJuCR 3.13, amended effective September 1, 1983; January 2, 1994; September 1, 2005. Renumbered LJuCR 3.10 and amended, effective September 2, 2013.]

LJuCR 3.11. GUARDIANSHIP IN JUVENILE COURT

(a) Petition for Guardianship for Dependent Child. A petition requesting the establishment of a guardianship may be filed in the Juvenile Court. The petition shall conform to the requirements of RCW 13.36.030.

(b) Scheduling and Notice. The scheduling and notice of hearings on the guardianship petition shall be in accordance with that required for termination proceedings in Title IV. of these rules.

(c) Procedure; Evidence; Burden of Proof. The court shall hold a hearing on the petition in accordance with RCW 13.36.040.

(d) Motions to Modify or Terminate a RCW 13.34 Dependency Guardianship. Any party to dependency guardianship established under RCW 13.34.232 except a parent whose rights have been terminated may move to modify or terminate a dependency guardianship, or substitute or remove a guard-

ian. The motion shall be set on the Contested Dependency Motions Calendar as per LJuCR 3.12 and all parties including the dependency guardian shall be notified as provided in these rules. If the youth is age twelve (12) or older and not represented by counsel, notice shall additionally be given to the Office of Public Defense for appointment of counsel for the youth. The dependency guardianship may be modified or terminated if the Court finds by a preponderance of the evidence that there has been a substantial change in circumstances subsequent to the establishment of the dependency guardianship and that modification or termination of the dependency guardianship is in the best interest of the child. If a dependency guardianship order is terminated, the case shall return to the underlying dependency status and be set for review as required in LJuCR 3.9.

(e) Petition to Convert a RCW 13.34 Dependency Guardianship to RCW 13.36 Guardianship. A dependency guardian or the Department or Supervising agency may request that juvenile court convert a dependency guardianship established under RCW 13.34.232 to a guardianship under RCW 13.36 by filing a petition in conformity with RCW 13.36.030. The petitioner shall give reasonable notice of the petition to all parties in the dependency.

(1) Upon filing a petition to convert to a ch. 13.36 RCW guardianship, the clerk's office shall issue a case schedule setting a preliminary hearing, pre-trial conference and fact-finding trial as outlined in Title IV of these rules.

(2) If the dependency guardian, youth age twelve (12) or older, and the Department or Supervising agency agree that the dependency guardianship should be converted to a guardianship under RCW 13.36, the petitioner may present an agreed order to that effect, and the court shall strike all remaining hearings listed in the case schedule, and shall dismiss the underlying dependency.

(f) Motions to Modify a RCW 13.36 Guardianship. A guardian, youth age twelve (12) or older, or parent of the child may petition the court to modify the visitation provisions of a guardianship order by filing with the court a motion for modification and an affidavit setting forth facts supporting the modification. The motion shall be heard as a contested motion pursuant to LJuCR 3.10, and if the court finds the motion was brought in bad faith, it may assess attorneys' fees and costs against the moving party in accordance with RCW 13.36.060.

[Formerly LJuCR 3.14, amended effective September 1, 1983; January 2, 1994; July 1, 1994; August 20, 1998; September 1, 2005; September 1, 2009. Renumbered LJuCR 3.11 and amended, effective September 2, 2013.]

LJuCR 3.12. CONTESTED DEPENDENCY MOTIONS

(a) Contested Motions Calendar—Procedure. Contested dependency motions may be set by a party or by the Court on its own motion. Motion hearings may include full dependency reviews but shall be limited to particular noted issues and will not include 72–hour shelter care, 30–day shelter care, or permanency planning hearings.

(b) Scheduling a Contested Hearing.

(1) *By a Party.* A party may set a contested dependency motion hearing by following the procedure outlined in this rule. If the contested hearing will include a full dependency review and the date for the hearing is more than six months from the beginning date of the placement episode or the entry of the previous dependency review order or order of dependency (whichever is first), a status quo order will be entered as provided in LJuCR 3.9(d)(4). Once a contested motion hearing is scheduled, any party to the dependency may raise additional issues or designate it as a full dependency review by filing a motion to expand issues and noting the matter for hearing with the Court Coordinator via email at calendar.dependencyseattle@kingcounty.gov or calendar.dependencykent@kingcounty.gov to a date which provides all the parties with at least 14 days' notice of the new issues, and notifying the Juvenile Court Coordinator's Office. Motions to expand issues are not permitted if the party initially noting the motion for contested hearing designates the motion as an emergency.

(2) *By the Court.* When the Court has set a matter on for a full dependency review, the parties will be notified by the Court of the issue(s) to be addressed, in writing at least 14 days prior to the Court-scheduled contested motion hearing, and the parties must respond with written material which support their respective positions on the issue(s) set for hearing by the Court in the same manner as a party responding to a motion as set out in LJuCR 3.12.

(3) *Court–Approved Date.* The Court Coordinator shall administer the scheduling of all contested dependency review motion hearings via email at calendar.dependencyseattle@kingcounty.gov or calendar.dependencykent@kingcounty.gov. All proposed dates for such matters must be approved by the Coordinator via email at calendar.dependencyseattle@kingcounty.gov or calendar.dependencykent@kingcounty.gov. The approval will be based on the availability of time to hear the matter on the proposed date, unless ordered by the Court as an overset.

(c) Motions Format and Procedures.

(1) *Motions to Be in Writing.* Motions must be in writing dated and signed by the attorney or party, and shall conform to LJuCR 3.12(d).

(2) *Motions Documents and Notes—Time and Place for Filing and Scheduling.*

(i) Any party desiring to bring a motion for a contested hearing shall file with the Clerk and serve upon all parties at least 14 days before the date fixed for such hearing, the motion together with all supporting documents including affidavits and a note for the motion calendar. The note must contain the title of the Court; the case number and a title of the cause; the designation "Juvenile Dependency Motions"; the date and time when the same shall be heard; the words "Note For Motion Calendar"; the names, addresses and telephone numbers of attorneys for all parties; the nature of the motion; and by whom made. This note shall be signed by the attorney or party filing the same, with the designation of party represented.

(ii) Working copies of the note and motion together with all supporting documents including affidavits shall be submitted to the Dependency Court Coordinator's Office by noon three court days prior to the hearing.

(iii) Responsive documents and briefs shall be filed with the Clerk and served upon all parties no later than noon seven days prior to the hearing; and documents in strict reply thereto shall be similarly filed and served no later than noon of the second court day prior to the hearing. All responsive documents shall have the name of the judicial officer expected to hear the matter or the assigned courtroom, and the hearing date and time noted on the upper right corner. Working copies of the response shall be submitted to the Court Coordinator's Office by the noon three days prior to the hearing, and the reply shall be submitted to the Court Coordinator by the close of business two days prior to the hearing.

(d) Motion—Contents of. A motion for a contested hearing must conform to the following format:

(1) *Relief Requested.* The specific relief the Court is requested to grant.

(2) *Statement of Facts.* A succinct statement of the facts contended to be material.

(3) *Statement of Issues.* A concise statement of the issue(s) on which the Court is requested to rule.

(4) *Evidence Relied Upon.* The evidence on which the motion or reply is based must be attached to the motion or reply documents and specified with particularity. Such evidence may include written statements or reports relating to the provision of services and the response of the parties thereto or otherwise relating to compliance with court orders and disposition plans. Hearsay evidence must be provided by sworn statements or declarations unless a reasonable basis exists why such statements could not be procured, in which case the proponent of the evidence must identify the source of the hearsay and its basis of knowledge for the facts or opinions asserted. Any party wishing to request clarification, modification, or enforcement of a prior order shall attach to their pleadings a copy of the order sought to be modified.

(5) *Authority.* Any legal authority relied upon must be cited.

(6) *Proposed Order.* A copy of a proposed order shall be served with the motion and shall be included with the working copies provided for the Court. The original of the proposed order shall not be filed with the Clerk, nor included with the working copies for the Court, but brought to the hearing by the moving party.

(e) Striking Hearing or Changing Hearing Date. A contested dependency motion hearing may be stricken, or the hearing date changed, in the following manner:

(1) *Striking Hearing.* A hearing on a contested dependency motion may be stricken at any time by the moving party, unless another party has previously filed and served a motion to expand issues under LJuCR 3.12(b). Notice that the motion hearing is being stricken shall be given to all parties not later than noon on the day before the scheduled hearing by the means most likely to give actual notice to the party or person in question. Such notice shall be confirmed by filing with the Clerk a Note for Calendar indicating that the hearing has been stricken and serving the notice on all parties. The Note for Calendar should be filed by noon on the business day before the date of the hearing and should be served on the Court Coordinator for distribution to the Judge or Court Commissioner scheduled to hear the matter.

(2) *Changing Hearing Date.* The hearing date on a contested dependency motion may be changed once by agreement of all parties. A new date must be obtained from the Court Coordinator via email at calendar.dependencyseattle@kingcounty.gov or calendar.dependencykent@kingcounty.gov. A Note for Calendar reflecting the new date should be filed with the Clerk at the time that the hearing is changed and should reflect that the original hearing date is stricken.

(3) *Hearings Where There is a Motion to Expand Issues.* Where another party has filed a motion to expand issues under LJuCR 3.12(b), the hearing originally noted may not be stricken unless the party who filed the original motion agrees, or the court orders that the hearing be continued to accommodate resolution of the expanded issues. The hearing date may be changed by agreement of all parties in the manner described under subsection 3.12(e)(2) supra.

(f) Time of Hearing. The hearing of the motion will commence at such time as is designated by the Court.

(1) *Unopposed Matters.* The Court will, on request, enter the order moved for if no one appears in opposition 30 minutes after the time set for hearing unless the Court deems it inappropriate. The opposing party may move to strike a matter if the moving party fails to appear 30 minutes after the time set for hearing unless the Court deems it inappropriate.

(2) *Hearing Order.* Motions will be heard in the order designated by the Court.

(3) *Time for Argument.* No more than five minutes per party or less as directed by the judicial officer hearing the matter, will be allowed for argument unless specially authorized by the Court upon prior application to the judicial officer who will be hearing the matter.

(g) Motions Without Oral Argument. Non-dispositive motions, which a party reasonably believes can be resolved on pleadings alone, may be noted without oral argument in the same manner as other motions except that:

(1) The moving party must clearly designate in their note for calendar that the motion is to be heard without oral argument, and must attach a proposed order to their working copies, and

(2) A party may object to the motion being heard without oral argument by clearly noting their objection in their responsive pleadings and timely filing and serving their response.

(3) If the court determines that oral argument is necessary it will issue an order resetting the hearing to occur with oral argument.

(h) Motion for Oral Testimony. Any party seeking authority to present oral testimony must file a motion requesting oral testimony together with affidavits setting forth the reasons testimony is necessary to a just adjudication of the issues, and an identification of the witnesses sought to be called.

(1) The motion for oral testimony shall be filed before or at the time the motion or response of that party is being filed and shall be decided without oral argument. Working copies of these materials must also be submitted to the Judge assigned to the calendar on which the motion is set and that Judge will determine whether oral testimony will be allowed and/or set out any limitations without oral argument. Working copies shall be submitted to the Judge pursuant to the requirements of LCR 7(b) to the extent not inconsistent with this rule.

(2) The affidavits and exhibits must demonstrate the extraordinary features of the case. Factors which may be considered include substantial questions of credibility on a major issue, insufficiency or inconsistency in discovery materials not correctable by further discovery, or particularly complex circumstances requiring expert testimony.

(3) A motion for oral testimony may be joined by the other party, but an order providing for oral testimony cannot be entered by stipulation. The assigned Judge's decision will be communicated by writing or by telephone no later than 48 hours before the hearing. If granted such a motion may require the setting

of a special hearing time as determined by the assigned Judge.

(i) Imposition of Sanctions or Terms. The Court may impose sanctions or terms for any frivolous motion or in granting a continuance of any matter. Nonappearance on a motion by the moving party may result in the imposition of sanctions or terms by the Court on counsel or on one or more of the parties as appropriate.

[Formerly LJuCR 3.10, adopted effective September 1, 2005; amended effective September 1, 2009. Renumbered LJuCR 3.12 and amended, effective September 2, 2013.]

LJuCR 3.13. EMERGENCY HEARINGS AND HEARINGS SET ON SHORTENED TIME

(a) Emergency Hearings. Any party or their attorney may set a contested hearing based upon their certification that an emergency exists that cannot be addressed on shortened time. In this event the matter shall be heard upon reasonable notice following the same procedure as for a 72–hour hearing pursuant to LJuCR 2.3. The Court may impose sanctions against a person or party who wrongly designates a matter to be an emergency hearing.

(b) Removal Hearings For Currently Adjudicated Dependent Children. If a dependent child is removed from a parent, guardian, or custodian pursuant to RCW 13.34.138(3)(b), an agreed order authorizing the removal shall be entered, or the supervising agency removing the child shall note an emergency hearing to be heard within 72–hours of removal (excluding Saturdays, Sundays, and Holidays) and the hearing shall have the same priority as a 72–hour hearing pursuant to LJuCR 2.4(b). Such hearing may be continued by agreement or order of the court if necessary to allow full briefing of the issue.

(c) Motion Shortening Time.

(1) The time for notice and hearing of a motion may otherwise be shortened only for good cause upon written application to the court in conformance with this rule. For purposes of this rule, good cause requires the moving party to demonstrate that the matter is sufficiently time sensitive and of a nature that it needs to be addressed by the court in less time than would otherwise be required by the rules, and the party bringing the motion could not have reasonably anticipated the matter so as to bring with the normally required notice.

(2) A motion for order shortening time may not be incorporated into any other pleading.

(3) As soon as the moving party is aware that he or she will be seeking an order shortening time, that party must contact the opposing party to give notice in the form most likely to result in actual notice of the pending motion to shorten time, as well as the time and place that the motion to shorten time will be presented. The declaration in support of the motion to shorten time must indicate what efforts have been made to notify the other side of the motion to shorten time, whether efforts to notify were successful, and whether the other side opposes the order shortening time.

(4) Proposed agreed orders to shorten time: if the parties agree to a briefing schedule on motion to be heard on shortened time, the order may be presented by way of a proposed stipulated order, which may be granted, denied or modified at the discretion of the court.

(5) The court may deny or grant the motion and impose such conditions as the court deems reasonable. If the court grants the motion shortening time, the order shall specify deadlines for responsive pleadings or otherwise direct the manner in which the hearing will proceed.

[Formerly LJuCR 3.11, adopted effective September 1, 2005; amended effective September 1, 2009. Renumbered LJuCR 3.13 and amended, effective September 2, 2013.]

LJuCR 3.14. RECONSIDERATION AND REVISION

(a) Reconsideration: Presentation of Orders.

(1) *Motion and notice of Hearing.* The form of motion and notice of hearing shall conform to LCR 7(b)(4) and be filed within the time limits of CR 59. The motion will be considered without oral argument unless called for by the court.

(2) *Response and Reply.* No response to a motion for reconsideration shall be filed unless requested by the court. No motion for reconsideration will be granted without such a request. If a response is called for, the court shall direct a date for the response, which shall be no less than six court days from the court's directive. A reply may be filed within two days of service of the response.

(3) The moving party and any party given leave to file a memorandum in opposition shall attach an original proposed order to the working copies submitted to the hearing judge/commissioner.

(b) Revision of Commissioner's Ruling.

(1) *Service and Filing of Motion.* A motion for revision of a Commissioner's order shall be served and filed within ten (10) days of entry of the written order, as provided in RCW 2.24.050, and noted for consideration within twenty seven (27) days of entry of the Commissioner's order. A written note for motion must be provided to all other parties with at least fourteen (14) days notice of the date and place that the motion for revision will be considered. The motion must set forth specific grounds for revision and the arguments and authorities therefore, and must attach all paperwork originally submitted by all parties to the Commissioner. It shall be noted without oral argument.

(2) *Providing Copies to the Judge.* The party seeking revision must provide the designated dependency Judge with working copies of the motion, the note for motion, and all paperwork originally submitted by all parties to the Commissioner within two business days of filing. The moving party must also provide a copy of the Commissioner's order, a proposed Order on Revision and pre-addressed stamped envelopes for each counsel/party. The designated dependency Judge shall rule on the motion for revision or assign the motion to another judge according to court administration policy. If assigned to another judge, all parties will be provided notice of the reassignment by the bailiff or clerk of the Judge to which the motion has been reassigned.

(3) *Providing Copies to the Bailiff or Judge's Clerk.* When a hearing has been recorded, the bailiff or clerk of the hearing Judge will coordinate with the Clerk's Office to obtain access to the recording within two days of the clerk's receipt of the request. Unless objection is filed to that recording within one week following the demand for revision, the recording shall be deemed certified as the record for revision, together with the legal files in the case.

(4) *Responsive Document.* Responsive documents must be served, and filed, no later than 12:00 noon, seven (7) days before the motion is to be decided. Any documents in strict reply are due no later than 12:00 noon, two (2) days before the motion is to be decided. Working copies of responsive documents must be submitted to the hearing Judge no later than two business days after filing, and working copies of any documents in strict reply must be submitted to the hearing Judge by the close of business the day of filing.

(5) *Oral Argument.* Oral argument on the motion for revision will be scheduled only upon request of the hearing Judge.

(6) *Effect of Commissioner's Order.* The Commissioner's written order shall remain in effect pending the hearing on revision unless ordered otherwise by the reviewing judge.

(7) *Time of Filing.* For cases in which a timely motion for reconsideration of the Commissioner's order has been filed, the time for filing a motion for revision of the Commissioner's order shall commence on the date of the filing of the Commissioner's written order of judgment on reconsideration.

[Formerly LJuCR 3.12, adopted effective September 1, 2005. Amended effective September 1, 2009. Renumbered LJuCR 3.14 and amended effective September 2, 2013. Amended effective September 1, 2015.]

LJuCR 3.15. JUVENILE AUTHORITY OVER FAMILY LAW MATTERS

(a) **Granting of Concurrent Jurisdiction.**[1]

(b) **Scope of Concurrent Jurisdiction.** Any Juvenile Court order granting concurrent jurisdiction shall be cross-filed under the RCW Title 26 action cause number and may, after notice, hearing, and entry of an appropriate protective order in Juvenile Court, authorize access to the Juvenile Court legal file and to any files and records maintained by the petitioning or supervising agency or the CASA of the child or children. A grant of concurrent jurisdiction shall not confer party status in the RCW Title 26 action on the petitioning or supervising agency in the dependency proceeding.

(c) **Authority of Juvenile Court to Hear and Determine Family Law Issues.**

(1) Juvenile Court may hear and determine RCW Title 26 issues in a dependency proceeding as necessary to facilitate a permanency plan for the child or children in the following circumstances:

(A) Agreed Issues: As part of a dependency disposition order or a dependency review order or as otherwise necessary to implement a permanency plan of care for a child and dismiss the dependency, the parents, guardians, or legal custodians of the child may agree subject to Juvenile Court approval to establish a parenting plan, a non-parental custody order, or modify a previously entered parenting plan in order to resolve issues of residential placement and/or visitation between them. Such agreed parenting plan, non-parental custody order, or modification thereof, must have the concurrence of the other parties to the dependency including the supervising agency, the CASA of the child, and the child if age 12 or older, and the court must find such action to be in the best interest of the child.

(i) For purposes of orders entered pursuant to this section ("agreed orders") a parent who was defaulted or has failed to respond in the ongoing dependency action may also be defaulted in the title 26 action if that parent does not appear or respond.

(B) Contested Issues: Following a fact-finding hearing on the dependency petition and a finding by Juvenile Court that a child has been abused or neglected or otherwise subject to such treatment or condition that it is in the best interest of the child, the Juvenile Court may enter a parenting plan, a non-parental custody order, or modify an existing parenting plan, in order to resolve issues of residential placement and/or visitation between the parents, guardians or legal custodians of the child and to implement a permanency plan of care for said child when doing so will result in dismissal of the dependency.

(i) Juvenile Court may enter an amended case schedule in the parenting or non-parental custody action as needed to resolve the issues presented.

(ii) Any party may move the court to transfer the parental or non-parental custody action to the family law department of superior court for further resolution. The court may only grant the motion upon entry of a written finding that it is in the best interest of the child.

(C) In any parenting plan entered or modified in Juvenile Court pursuant to this rule, all issues pertaining to division of marital property shall be referred to or retained by the Family Law Department of King County Superior Court or the appropriate court in other counties. Issues of child support should be referred to or retained by the Family Law Department of King County Superior Court or the appropriate court in other counties but may be resolved by the Juvenile Court.

(D) Any Juvenile Court order determining RCW Title 26 issues is subject to modification upon the same showing and same standards as a Family Law Court order determining Title 26 issues.

(2) Any pleadings filed in Juvenile Court establishing or modifying a parenting plan, or establishing a non-parental custody order shall be cross-filed in the RCW Title 26 action in the Family Law Department of King County Superior Court or in the appropriate court in other counties by the prevailing party, and if the petitioning or moving party has been found indigent and appointed counsel at public expense in the

dependency proceeding, no filing fee shall be imposed by the clerk. Once filed in the RCW Title 26 action, any order establishing or modifying a parenting plan, or establishing a non-parental custody order shall survive the dismissal of the dependency proceeding. Juvenile Court may retain jurisdiction as long as is necessary to protect the child.

(3) Whenever the court is asked to establish or modify a parenting plan or non-parental custody order under this section, and in accordance with RCW 26.12.175 and 26.12.177, the court may appoint a guardian ad litem to represent the interests of the child when the court believes the appointment is necessary to protect the best interests of the child. In accordance with RCW 26.09.110, the court may appoint an attorney to represent the interests of the child with respect to provisions for the parenting or non-parental custody plan.

[Formerly LJuCR 3.16, adopted effective September 1, 1995. Amended effective September 1, 2005; September 1, 2009. Renumbered LJuCR 3.15 and amended, effective September 2, 2013.]

1 So in original.

TITLE IV.   PROCEEDINGS TO TERMINATE PARENT–CHILD RELATIONSHIP

LJuCR 4.1.   INVOKING JURISDICTION OF JUVENILE COURT [RESERVED]

[Effective January 2, 1994. Reserved effective September 2, 2013.]

LJuCR 4.2.   PLEADINGS

(a) **Petition.** A Petition requesting the termination of a parent-child relationship may be filed in Juvenile Court. The petition shall conform to the requirements of LJuCR 3.2 and 3.3, shall be verified, and shall state the facts which underlie each of the allegations required by RCW 13.34.180.

(b) **Amendment of Petition.** A termination petition may be amended as provided in LJuCR 3.5.

(c) **Answer.** A parent shall file an answer to the petition as provided in LJuCR 3.6. A CASA for a child or a child aged twelve or older may file an answer to the petition, but shall not be required to do so. Answers shall be due not later than 65 days after the filing of the petition, or at such other time as may be set by the Court. In no event shall an answer be required less than 20 days after service of the Notice and Summons and Petition.

[Adopted effective January 2, 1994. Amended effective August 20, 1998; September 1, 2005; September 2, 2013.]

LJuCR 4.3.   NOTICE OF TERMINATION HEARINGS

(a) **Generally. Notice and Summons & Notice to Counsel.**

(1) *Notice and Summons.* A notice and summons of the preliminary hearing, pre-trial conference and termination fact-finding trial shall be issued by the Clerk of the Court or petitioner and served by the petitioner along with a copy of the termination petition and order setting case schedule on all parties, including a child who at the time of the scheduled termination fact-finding trial will be age 12 or over, in the manner defined by RCW 13.34.070 or published in the manner defined by RCW 13.34.080.

(2) *Notice to Counsel.* In all cases where a party is represented by counsel in the underlying dependency action, the petitioner shall also provide counsel with a copy of the petition, notice and summons, and order setting case schedule. If the youth is age twelve (12) or older and not represented by counsel, a copy shall be given to the Office of Public Defense for appointment of counsel for the youth.

(3) *Advice to be contained in the Notice and Summons.*

(A) The notice shall clearly state the date, time and place for the hearings and shall contain an advisement of rights substantially conforming to the requirements of RCW 13.34.180 for termination petitions, the requirements of RCW 13.36.030 for guardianship petitions, and RCW 13.34.062 and RCW 13.34.090 so as to inform the party of the right to a hearing before a Judge and to representation by a lawyer, including appointment of a lawyer to a party who cannot afford one.

(B) The notice and summons shall also advise the parties that failure to appear or otherwise plead or respond to the Petition shall be the basis for the Court to enter an Order of Default against that party.

(b) Indian Children. If the petitioner knows or has reason to know that the child involved is or may be an Indian child as defined in RCW 13.38, the petitioner shall notify the Tribe(s) in the manner required by RCW 13.34.070(10), 13.38.070 and 25 U.S.C. 1912.

(c) Case Schedule. Upon the filing of a termination petition, the Clerk of the Court will prepare and file an order setting case schedule and provide one copy to the petitioner. The petitioner shall serve a copy of the case schedule on all parties as provided in these rules. The case schedule shall be in a format set by the Court and shall set the termination fact-finding trial no more than 150 days after the filing of the termination petition. The case schedule will also identify the designated dependency judge to whom the termination fact-finding proceeding is assigned.

(d) Preliminary Hearing. The case schedule will set a preliminary hearing on the termination petition no more than 90 days after the filing of the petition. The preliminary hearing shall be set on the juvenile court dependency calendar and the Court shall determine whether any party shall be found in default and an order of termination of the parent-child relationship entered as to that party.

Nothing in this rule shall preclude any party from noting any additional motions prior to the pretrial conference pursuant to local or civil rule, and shall be set on the juvenile court dependency calendar.

(e) Pre-trial Conference. The Court shall hold a pre-trial conference on the termination petition no more than 120 days after the filing of the petition at a location and time specified at the preliminary hearing, unless modified by Court order. The pre-trial conference shall be set on the juvenile court pre-trial calendar. All parties must be present at the pre-trial conference unless specifically excused by the Court. The pre-trial conference shall be conducted as provided in LJuCR 3.7(a)(2)(5), All motions filed after the pre-trial conference order has been entered shall be brought pursuant to LCR 7 before the designated dependency Judge, unless otherwise assigned.

[Effective January 2, 1994. Amended effective July 1, 1994; August 20, 1998; September 1, 2005; amended on an emergency basis, effective January 1, 2006; amended on a permanent basis, effective September 1, 2006; September 2, 2013.]

LJuCR 4.4. AMENDMENT OF CASE SCHEDULE

(a) Generally. The Court, either on motion of a party or on its own initiative, may modify any date in the case schedule for good cause, except that the fact-finding trial date may be changed only as provided below. If a case schedule is modified on motion of a party, that party shall prepare and present to the Court for signature an amended case schedule, which the party shall promptly file and serve on all other parties. If a case schedule is amended on the Court's own motion, the Court will prepare and file the amended case schedule and promptly mail it to all parties.

(b) Change of Fact–Finding Date.

(1) *Limited Adjustment of Fact–Finding Date to Resolve Schedule Conflict.* Any party to a termination proceeding may move for an adjustment of the fact-finding trial date to resolve schedule conflicts by making a written motion in accordance with LCR 7. The motion must be brought within 30 days of the filing of the termination petition, notice and summons and order setting case schedule, but only to a day no more than 28 days before or 28 days after the fact-finding trial date listed in the case schedule.

(2) *Continuance of Fact–Finding.* Any motion to continue the fact-finding trial date made more than 30 days after filing of the termination petition, or to continue the fact-finding more than 28 days after the original fact-finding date, will not be granted unless the motion is supported by a showing of good cause. The motion must be made in writing in accordance with LCR 7. If a motion to change the trial date is made after the pre-trial conference, the motion will not be granted except under extraordinary circumstances where there is no alternative means of preventing a substantial injustice. A continuance motion may be granted subject to such conditions as justice requires.

(3) *Approval of Party.* A motion for continuance made under subsection (2) above will not be considered unless it is signed by both the party making the motion and the party's attorney, if any, or contains an explanation of why it was impracticable for the party to sign the motion and a certification that a copy of the motion has been mailed or otherwise delivered to the party.

(4) *Order Striking Fact Finding Date.* An Order striking Fact Finding Date shall be filed upon any resolution of the case short of the trial date.

[Adopted effective January 2, 1994. Amended effective August 20, 1998; September 2, 2013.]

LJuCR 4.5. REINSTATEMENT OF PREVIOUSLY TERMINATED PARENTAL RIGHTS

(a) Who May File and Appointment of Counsel for Youth/Child. A child or his/her counsel may file a petition for reinstatement of previously terminated parental rights without paying a filing fee.

(b) Pro Se Youth. If a child seeks to file such a petition without counsel, the clerk shall refer the child to his or her attorney or to the dependency court, which will enter an order directing the King County Office of Public Defense to assign counsel who was previously assigned to the youth under the dependency case number or to assign new counsel if the youth does not have a dependency attorney. The petition shall indicate the case designation of the dependency case and the clerk shall assign the same designation to the reinstatement case. Appointed counsel shall serve as counsel for the reinstatement case and the dependency case.

(c) Case Schedule. Upon filing of the petition, the clerk shall assign a new case number and generate a case schedule and provide a copy to the attorney for the child. A threshold hearing shall be scheduled before the juvenile court dependency calendar.

(d) Notice.

(1) In addition to service of process, counsel for the child shall deliver a copy of the petition and supporting documents and the case schedule to the Department of Social and Health Services social worker assigned to the dependency case and shall provide a copy to the CASA or GAL, if any, for the dependency case. Delivery to the CASA can be to the CASA program office. Counsel shall deliver a copy of the petition to the Office of the Attorney General by mail, facsimile or e-mail.

(2) The Department of Social and Health Services shall deliver a copy of the petition and case schedule to the child's former parent whose parental rights are the subject of the petition, any parent whose rights have not been terminated, the child's current foster parent, relative caregiver, guardian or custodian, and the child's tribe, if applicable.

(e) Concurrent Dependency Reviews. Any dependency review or permanency planning hearing scheduled for the dependency matter shall be heard by the dependency judge or the judge to whom the dependency judge assigns the reinstatement action. An order relative to the dependency review or permanency plan will be entered at both the hearing on the merits and the six month review hearing, in addition to the orders on the reinstatement of parental rights. The clerk shall cross-file orders from these hearings in both the dependency case and the reinstatement case.

(f) Threshold Hearing.

(1) At the threshold hearing, the court will determine, prima facie, the parent or parents' apparent fitness and interest in reinstatement of parental rights.

(2) The court shall also determine whether the best interests of the child may be served by reinstatement of parental rights.

(3) If the court concludes that the case should go forward, then it shall immediately hold a pretrial conference, and set a discovery schedule. If the judicial officer concludes that the matter should not go

forward, then the hearing on the merits already set before the designated dependency judge shall be stricken, and the petition shall be dismissed.

(g) Hearing on the Merits. At the hearing on the merits, if the court conditionally grants the petition, the court shall continue the case for six months during which time the child shall be placed in the custody of the parent or parents.

(h) Hearing on Final Review. At the six month hearing, if the court finds that the child's placement with the parent or parents has been successful, the court shall enter an order reinstating parental rights and shall dismiss the dependency.

[Adopted effective January 2, 1994. Amended effective August 20, 1998; September 1, 2005; September 1, 2008; September 2, 2013.]

LJuCR 4.6. REINSTATEMENT OF PREVIOUSLY TERMINATED PARENTAL RIGHTS

(1) A child or his/her counsel may file a petition for reinstatement of previously terminated parental rights without paying a filing fee. If a child seeks to file such a petition without counsel, the clerk shall refer the child to his or her attorney or to the dependency court, which will enter an order directing the King County Office of the Public Defender to assign counsel who was previously assigned to the youth under the dependency case number or to assign new counsel if the youth does not have a dependency lawyer. The petition shall indicate the case designation of the dependency case and the clerk shall assign the same designation to the reinstatement case. Appointed counsel shall serve as counsel for the reinstatement case and the dependency case.

(2) Upon filing of the petition, the clerk shall assign a new case number and generate a case schedule and provide a copy to the attorney for the child. A threshold hearing shall be scheduled before the dependency commissioner or other judicial officer.

(3) In addition to service of process, counsel for the child shall deliver a copy of the petition and supporting documents and the case schedule to the Department of Social and Health Services social worker assigned to the dependency case and shall provide a copy to the CASA or GAL, if any, for the dependency case. Delivery onto the CASA can be to the CASA program office. Counsel shall deliver a copy of the petition to the office of the attorney general by mail, facsimile or e-mail.

(4) The Department of Social and Health Services shall deliver a copy of the petition and case schedule to the child's former parent whose parental rights are the subject of the petition, any parent whose rights have not been terminated, the child's current foster parent, relative caregiver, guardian or custodian, and the child's tribe, if applicable.

(5) At the threshold hearing, the judicial officer will determine, prima facie, the parent or parents' apparent fitness and interest in reinstatement of parental rights, and determine whether the best interests of the child may be served by reinstatement of parental rights. If the judicial officer so determines, then the matter will be set for a hearing on the merits of the petition before the dependency judge. The judicial officer shall immediately hold a pretrial conference, setting a discovery schedule. If the judicial officer concludes that the matter should not go forward, it shall be dismissed.

(6) At the hearing on the merits, if the court conditionally grants the petition, the court shall continue the case for six months during which time the child shall be placed in the custody of the parent or parents. At the six month hearing, if the court finds that the child's placement with the parent or parents has been successful, the court shall enter an order reinstating parental rights and shall dismiss the dependency.

(7) Any dependency review and permanency planning hearings scheduled for the dependency matter shall be set at the same time as the hearing on the merits of the reinstatement petition or the final six month hearing, to be heard by the dependency judge or the judge to whom the dependency judge assigns the matter. An order relative to the dependency review or permanency plan will be entered at both the hearing on the merits and the six month review hearing, in addition to the orders on the reinstatement of parental rights. The clerk shall cross-file orders from these hearings in both the dependency case and the reinstatement case.

[Adopted effective September 1, 2008.]

LJuCR 6.6. TERMINATION OF DIVERSION AGREEMENT

NOTE: This is now covered in RCW 13.40.080.

[Amended effective September 1, 1983; September 1, 2012.]

LJuCR 7.1. LOCAL PROCEDURES

The current procedures for handling and processing criminal cases in King County Superior Court Juvenile Division are contained in the Juvenile Division Offender Manual. Copies of the Manual are available from the courtroom of the Chief Juvenile Judge in Seattle a link to the Manual can be found on the Court's web site http://www.kingcounty.gov/sites/courts/Juvenilecourt.

[Adopted effective September 1, 2012.]

LJuCR 7.3. DETENTION AND RELEASE WITHOUT HEARING [RESCINDED]

[Former LJuCR 7.4 renumbered and amended effective September 1, 1983; amended effective January 1, 2002; rescinded effective September 1, 2012.]

LJuCR 7.4. DETENTION HEARING [RESCINDED]

[Adopted effective September 1, 1983; rescinded effective September 1, 2012.]

LJuCR 7.6. ARRAIGNMENT—JUVENILE OFFENSE PROCEEDINGS

(a) Time and Procedure for Arraignment.

(1) A case shall be set for the Arraignment Calendar on the court day after it is filed if the juvenile is in detention on that case, and within two weeks of filing in other cases.

(2) Parties shall be present at Court for the arraignment at a time designated in the summons. Absent permission of the court, upon a finding of good cause, a respondent may not waive arraignment, if he or she has not appeared in court on the scheduled date. A waiver of arraignment shall be signed by the juvenile, or the juvenile's counsel, with the permission of the juvenile, and the prosecuting attorney and shall substitute for an in-court arraignment. The waiver shall be on the form adopted by the court. In lieu of accepting a waiver of arraignment, the court may continue arraignment for the presence of the respondent. Examples of good cause for failure to appear at arraignment include:

(A) the juvenile is in custody in a state or out-of-county detention facility;

(B) the juvenile is in a residential treatment program and it is against treatment recommendations to attend court;

(C) the juvenile resides out of state or more than one hundred miles from Court.

(3) An in-court appearance by the juvenile and counsel is required, unless waived by the Court pursuant to (2)(A)(B)(C) for all cases in which the crime charged is a felony or for a gross misdemeanor or misdemeanor alleged to involve domestic violence (including violation of a domestic violence protection or no contact order), a sex offense, including any offense filed with an allegation of sexual motivation, a prostitution-related offense or any offense involving allegations of animal cruelty. Even if a case would otherwise qualify for an arraignment waiver, a juvenile who is seeking to waive speedy trial must appear in court for formal arraignment.

(4) Absent court direction to the contrary, the respondent may waive formal arraignment for all cases not specified in (3) of this rule, unless the prosecuting attorney, juvenile probation counselor, parent or other responsible adult requests that the arraignment occur in court.

[Amended September 1, 1981; amended effective September 1, 1983; February 24, 2000; September 1, 2011; September 2, 2014.]

LJuCR 7.8. TIME FOR ADJUDICATORY HEARING—JUVENILE OFFENSE PROCEEDINGS [RESCINDED]

[Amended effective September 1, 1983; rescinded effective September 1, 2011.]

LJuCR 7.11. ADJUDICATORY HEARING INADMISSIBILITY OF STATEMENTS MADE TO JUVENILE PROBATION COUNSELOR

(b) Evidence. When a case is set for fact finding, any written report by the juvenile probation counselor prepared for the purpose of disposition on that case shall not be inspected by the Court prior to entry of a finding. The juvenile probation counselor shall not testify at a fact finding hearing as to any facts disclosed or discovered in the course of the social investigation without the juvenile's permission.

[Amended effective September 1, 1983; September 1, 2012.]

LJuCR 7.12. PLEA AND DISPOSITION HEARING

(a) A plea and disposition hearing shall be set not more than two weeks after the date of the case setting hearing if the juvenile is out of custody or one weeks after the case setting hearing if the juvenile is detained, except that: if the disposition would result in a commitment to the Juvenile Rehabilitation Administration or if the disposition is for a youth who sexually offended, disposition shall be set three weeks after case setting if the juvenile is out of custody, or two weeks, if the juvenile is detained. When required by good cause, the Court may extend or contract these time limits.

(b) Probation counselors shall provide the court, the prosecutor and defense counsel with a copy of their written disposition no later than noon the day before the scheduled disposition hearing.

(c) If either party or the juvenile probation counselor is seeking a manifest injustice disposition, the materials in support of such disposition shall be provided to the court, the non-moving party(ies) and the juvenile probation counselor, no later than three working days prior to the scheduled disposition hearing.

[Amended September 1, 1981; amended effective September 1, 1983; September 1, 2009; September 1, 2012.]

LJuCR 7.14. MOTIONS—JUVENILE OFFENSE PROCEEDINGS

(a) Generally. All motions, including motions to suppress evidence, motions regarding admissions, and other motions requiring testimony, shall be heard at the time of trial unless otherwise set by the Court. Motions to suppress pursuant to CrR 3.6 and to dismiss (other than for failure of a witness to appear for fact finding) shall be served on all parties and filed with the Court, together with a brief which shall include a summary of the facts upon which the motions are based, not later than five days before the adjudicatory hearing. Response briefs shall be served and filed with the Court not later than noon of the court day before the date set for hearing.

(b) To Dismiss for Delay in Referral of Offense. The Court may dismiss an information if it is established that there has been an unreasonable delay in referral of the offense by the police to the prosecutor and respondent has been prejudiced. For purposes of this rule, a delay of more than two weeks from the date of completion of the police investigation of the offense to the time of receipt of the referral by the prosecutor shall be deemed prima facie evidence of an unreasonable delay. Upon a prima facie showing of unreasonable delay the Court shall then determine whether or not dismissal or other appropriate sanction will be imposed. Among those factors otherwise considered the Court shall consider the following: (1) the length of the delay; (2) the reason for the delay; (3) the impact of the delay on the ability to defend against the charge; and (4) the seriousness of the alleged offense. Unreasonable delay shall constitute an affirmative defense which must be raised by motion not less than one week before trial. Such motion may be considered by affidavit.

[Amended effective September 1, 1983; September 1, 2001; September 1, 2012.]

LJuCR 7.15. INFRACTIONS

(a) Scope of Rule. This rule governs the procedure in juvenile court for all cases involving "infractions". Infractions are noncriminal violations of law defined by statute or ordinance.

(b) Notice of Infraction. An infraction case is initiated by the issuance, service, and filing of a notice of infraction in accordance with this rule. The notice shall identify the infraction which the respondent is alleged to have committed, the accompanying statutory citation or ordinance number, the date the infraction occurred, and the date of the prehearing conference.

(c) Service of Notice. Upon the prosecuting authority filing the notice of infraction with the court, the clerk of the court shall have the notice served by mail, postage prepaid, on the person named in the notice of infraction at his or her address.

(d) Prehearing Conference. The prehearing conference shall be set no sooner than 14 days and no later than 60 days after the filing of the notice of infraction. At the conference, the juvenile may (1) pay the amount of the monetary penalty in accordance with applicable law, in which case the court shall enter a judgment that the respondent has committed the infraction; (2) explain any mitigating circumstances surrounding the commission of the infraction; or (3) contest the determination that an infraction occurred by requesting a contested hearing;

(e) Mitigation Hearing. If the respondent indicates that there are mitigating circumstances, the court shall hold an informal hearing which shall not be governed by the Rules of Evidence. The court shall determine whether the respondent's explanation of the events justifies reduction of the monetary penalty. The court shall enter an order finding the respondent committed the infraction and may assess a monetary penalty. The court may not impose a penalty in excess of the monetary penalty provided for the infraction by law. The court may waive or suspend a portion of the monetary penalty, or provide for time payments, or in lieu of monetary payment provide for the performance of community service as provided by law. The court has continuing jurisdiction and authority to supervise disposition for not more than 1 year.

(f) Contested Hearing. The contested hearing shall be scheduled for not more than 60 days from the date of the prehearing conference. The court shall determine whether the plaintiff has proved by a preponderance of the evidence that the respondent committed the infraction. If the court finds the infraction was committed, it shall enter an appropriate order on its records and it may assess a monetary penalty against the respondent. The monetary penalty assessed may not exceed the monetary penalty provided for the infraction by law. The court may waive or suspend a portion of the monetary penalty, or provide for time payments, or in lieu of monetary payment provide for the performance of community service as provided by law. The court has continuing jurisdiction and authority to supervise disposition for not more than 1 year. If the court finds the infraction was not committed, it shall enter an order dismissing the case.

(g) Failure to Appear. If the respondent fails to respond to a notice of infraction or fails to appear for a court hearing, the court shall enter an order finding that the respondent has committed the infraction and shall assess any monetary penalties provided for by law.

[Adopted effective May 1, 2002.]

LJuCR 7.16. MOTIONS TO SEAL CONVICTION, FOR RESTORATION OF FIREARM RIGHTS AND FOR RELIEF FROM SEX REGISTRATION REQUIREMENTS

Motions to seal juvenile convictions, for restoration of the right to possess a firearm flowing from a juvenile conviction and for relief from the duty to register as a sex offender following conviction of a juvenile offense shall be filed in the Juvenile Division of King County Superior Court. The court will maintain, on its website, appropriate forms and procedures

at www.kingcounty.gov/sites/courts/Juvenilecourt. For restoration of the right to possess a firearm stemming from an adult conviction, See Local Rule 40(b)(17).

[Adopted effective September 1, 2012.]

LJuCR 9.2. ADDITIONAL RIGHT TO REPRESENTATION BY COUNSEL

(d) Juvenile Offense Proceedings.

(1) Appointed and assigned counsel shall file quarterly, with the Clerk, on the form recommended by the Supreme Court, a certificate declaring that counsel is in compliance with the applicable Standards for Indigent Defense promulgated by the Supreme Court of Washington. An appointed or assigned attorney who is not in compliance with the applicable standards, or who has not filed a certificate prior to appearing or filing a notice of appearance, shall so advise the court at every hearing.

[Adopted on an emergency basis, effective September 27, 2012; December 21, 2012; May 17, 2013; July 1, 2013; adopted on a permanent basis, effective September 2, 2013.]

LJuCR 9.3. RIGHT TO APPOINTMENT OF EXPERTS IN JUVENILE OFFENSE PROCEEDINGS

(c) Services Other Than Counsel. Pursuant to the authority under CrR 3.1(f) and JuCR 9.3, all requests and approval for expert services expenditures are hereby delegated to the King County Office of the Public Defense (OPD). Upon finding that investigative, expert or other services are necessary to an adequate defense and that respondent is financially unable to obtain them, the OPD shall authorize the services. Where services are denied in whole or in part, the respondent may move for de novo review to the Chief Juvenile Court Judge. Should respondent seek an order sealing the moving paper or a protective order, respondent shall present, along with the moving papers, a motion and proposed order sealing and/or a proposed protective order to OPD. OPD shall submit the motion to seal and proposed order with the moving papers regarding request for expert services and OPD's order on the motion for expert services to the Chief Juvenile Court Judge.

[Adopted effective September 1, 2012.]

LJuCR 11.23. REVISION OF COURT COMMISSIONER'S RULING [RESERVED]

[Amended effective September 1, 2001; September 1, 2004; reserved effective September 1, 2009.]

TITLE XII. TRUANCY PROCEEDINGS

LJuCR 12.1. TRUANCY CASE ASSIGNMENT AREA

(e) Location for Court Proceedings for Truancy Cases Filed in King County; Filing of Documents and Pleadings and Designation of Case Assignment Area.

(1) *Designation of Case Assignment Area.* In order to facilitate the division of cases between the King County Courthouse and the Maleng Regional Justice Center facilities, it is required that from and after the first day of August 1997, each truancy petition filed in the Superior Court shall be accompanied by a Case Assignment Designation Form [in the form set forth in Section (8) below] on which the party filing the initial pleading has designated whether the case fits within the Seattle Case Assignment Area or the Kent Case Assignment Area, under the standards set forth in Sections (2) through (4) below.

(2) *Where Proceedings Held.* Commencing with the 1997–1998 school year, all proceedings of any nature shall be conducted in the case assignment area designated on the Case Assignment Designation Form unless the Court has otherwise ordered on its own motion or upon motion of any party to the action.

(3) *Boundaries of Case Assignment Areas.* For purposes of this rule King County shall be divided into case assignment areas as follows:

(A) Seattle Case Assignment Area. The school districts in the Seattle Case Assignment area are: Seattle (1); Mercer Island (400); Vashon (402); Skykomish (404); Bellevue (405); Riverview (407); Snoqualmie (410); Issaquah (411); horeline (412); Lake Washington (414); and Northshore (417).

(B) Kent Case Assignment Area. The districts in the Kent Case Assignment area are: Federal Way (210); Enumclaw (216); Renton (403); South Central (406); Auburn (408); Tahoma (409); Kent (415); and Highline (401).

(C) Change of Area Boundaries. The Presiding Judge may adjust the boundaries between areas when required for the efficient and fair administration of justice in King County.

(4) *Standards for Case Assignment Area Designation, and Revisions Thereof.*

(A) Location Designated by Party Filing Action. Initial designations shall be made upon filing of the petition alleging truancy and shall be based on the school district that originates the petition.

(B) Improper Designation/Lack of Designation. The designation of the improper case assignment area shall not be a basis for dismissal of any action, but may be a basis for imposition of terms. The lack of designation of case assignment area at initial case filing may be a basis for imposition of terms

and will result in assignment to a case assignment area at the Court's discretion.

(C) Assignment or Transfer on Court's Motion. The Court on its own motion may assign or transfer cases to another case assignment area in the county whenever required for the just and efficient administration of justice in King County.

(D) Motions by Party to Transfer. Motions to transfer court proceedings from one case assignment area to another shall be made in writing and shall be ruled on by the Court without oral argument. All cases shall proceed in the original case assignment area until an order of transfer is entered. Proceedings in the assigned area shall not preclude the timely filing of a motion to transfer. A change of case assignment area designation may be authorized by the Chief Judge of Juvenile Court or by the commissioner regularly assigned to the Truancy Calendars.

(E) Venue not Affected. This rule shall not affect whether venue is proper in any Superior Court facility in King County.

(5) *Where Pleadings and Documents Filed.* Pursuant to LGR 30, all pleadings and documents for any truancy action in King County must be electronically filed with the Clerk of the Superior Court using the Clerk's e-filing system. Documents identified as exceptions to mandatory e-filing must be filed in paper form at the court facility in the case assignment area of the case.

(6) *Inclusion of Case Assignment Area Code.* All pleadings and document shall contain after the cause number the case assignment area code assigned by the Clerk for the case assignment area in which court proceedings are to be held. The Clerk may reject pleadings or documents that do not contain this case assignment area code.

(7) *Case Assignment Designation Form.* The Case Assignment Designation Form shall be in substantially the following form:

CASE ASSIGNMENT DESIGNATION

I certify that this case meets the case assignment criteria, described in King County for the:

____ Seattle Area, defined as

Seattle (1); Mercer Island (400); Vashon (402); Skykomish (404); Bellevue (405); Riverview (407); Snoqualmie (410); Issaquah (411); Shoreline (412); Lake Washington (414); and Northshore (417).

____ Kent Area, defined as

Federal Way (210); Enumclaw (216); Renton (403); South Central (406); Auburn (408); Tahoma (409); Kent (415); and Highline (401).

_____   _____
Signature of Petitioner   Date

[Adopted effective April 14, 1997. Amended effective September 1, 1999; September 1, 2004; September 1, 2008; September 1, 2009; September 1, 2015.]

TITLE XIII. AT–RISK YOUTH & CHILD IN NEED OF SERVICES PROCEEDINGS

LJuCR 13.1. AT–RISK YOUTH & CHILD IN NEED OF SERVICES CASE ASSIGNMENT AREA

(a) Location for Court Proceeding for At–Risk Youth and Child in Need of Services Actions Filed in King County; Filing of Documents and Pleadings and Designation of Case Assignment Area.

(1) *Designation of Case Assignment Area and Revisions Thereof.* Cases filed under RCW 13.32A shall be filed in the case assignment area in which the primary custodial parent resides, as defined by JuCR 3.2. A motion to change the case assignment area designation may be authorized by the Chief Judge of Juvenile Court or by the commissioner regularly assigned to the Becca Calendars.

[Adopted effective September 1, 2015.]

KING COUNTY LOCAL RULES FOR MANDATORY ARBITRATION

I. SCOPE AND PURPOSE OF RULES

LMAR 1.1. APPLICATION OF RULES— PURPOSE AND DEFINITIONS

(a) Purpose. The purpose of mandatory arbitration of civil actions under RCW 7.06 as implemented by the Mandatory Arbitration Rules is to provide a simplified and economical procedure for obtaining the prompt and equitable resolution of disputes involving claims subject to arbitration by state law. The Mandatory Arbitration Rules as supplemented by these local rules are not designed to address every question that may arise during the arbitration process, and the rules give considerable discretion to the arbitrator. The arbitrator should not hesitate to exercise that discretion. Arbitration hearings should be informal and expeditious, consistent with the purpose of the statutes and rules.

(b) "Supervisor" Defined. In these rules, "Supervisor" means the Supervisor of Arbitration for the King County Superior Court or the Supervisor's designee.

[Amended effective June 10, 1982; September 1, 2008; September 1, 2009.]

LMAR 1.3. RELATIONSHIP TO SUPERIOR COURT JURISDICTION AND OTHER RULES—MOTIONS [RESERVED]

[Amended effective September 1, 2003; September 1, 2008; reserved effective September 1, 2009.]

II. TRANSFER TO ARBITRATION AND ASSIGNMENT OF ARBITRATOR

LMAR 2.1. TRANSFER TO ARBITRATION

(a) Statement of Arbitrability. A party believing a case to be suitable for mandatory arbitration pursuant to MAR 1.2 shall file a statement of arbitrability upon a form prescribed by the Court before the case schedule deadline. After the date indicated on the case schedule has passed, the party wishing to transfer a case to arbitration must obtain an order from the Court upon a showing of good cause.

(b) Response to a Statement of Arbitrability.

(1) Within 14 days after the statement of arbitrability is served and filed, a party who objects to the statement of arbitrability, on the ground that the objecting party's own claim or counterclaim is not arbitrable, shall serve and file a response on a form prescribed by the Court. If such a response is timely served and filed, the matter shall be administratively removed from arbitration. In the absence of such timely response, the statement of arbitrability shall be deemed correct. A party who fails to serve and file a response within the time prescribed may later do so only upon leave of the Court for good cause shown.

(2) A party who objects to a statement of arbitrability on the ground that a claim of the party who filed the statement is not subject to arbitration shall note a motion before the assigned judge.

(c) Filing Amendments. A party may amend or withdraw a statement of arbitrability or response at any time before assignment of an arbitrator and thereafter only upon leave of the court for good cause shown.

(d) By Stipulation: A case in which all parties file a stipulation to arbitrate under MAR 8.1(b) will be placed on the arbitration calendar regardless of the nature of the case or amount in controversy, by leave of the Court.

[Amended effective September 1, 1981; June 10, 1982; January 1, 1990; September 1, 1992; September 1, 2003; September 1, 2009.]

LMAR 2.3. ASSIGNMENT TO ARBITRATOR

(a) Generally. When a case is set for arbitration, a list of proposed arbitrators will be furnished to the parties. The number of proposed arbitrators is based upon the number of adverse parties in the case. The number of adverse parties shall be determined by the Supervisor, subject to review by the Presiding Judge.

(b) Stipulations. The parties are encouraged to stipulate to an arbitrator. In the absence of a stipula-tion, the arbitrator will be chosen from among the proposed arbitrators in the manner defined by this rule.

(c) Response by Parties. Each party may, within 14 days after the list of proposed arbitrators is furnished to the parties, nominate one or two arbitrators and strike two arbitrators from the list. If both parties respond, an arbitrator nominated by both parties will be appointed. If no arbitrator has been nominated by both parties, the Supervisor will appoint an arbitrator from among those not stricken by either party.

(d) Response by Only One Party. If only one party responds within 14 days, the Supervisor will appoint an arbitrator nominated by that party.

(e) No Response. If neither party responds within 14 days, the Supervisor will appoint one of the proposed arbitrators.

[Amended September 1, 1981; September 1, 2008; September 1, 2009.]

III. ARBITRATORS

LMAR 3.1. QUALIFICATIONS

(a) Arbitration Panel. A person desiring to serve as an arbitrator shall complete an oath of office and information sheet on the form prescribed by the Court. The Arbitration Department will maintain and make available a list of arbitrators available to hear cases.

(b) Refusal; Disqualification. The appointment of an arbitrator is subject to the right of that person to refuse to serve. An arbitrator must notify the Supervisor immediately if refusing to serve or if any cause exists for the arbitrator's disqualification from the case upon any of the grounds of interest, relationship, bias or prejudice set forth in CJC Canon 3(c) governing the disqualification of Judges. If disqualified, the arbitrator must immediately return all materials in a case to the Supervisor.

[Amended on an emergency basis effective November 27, 2007; amended on a permanent basis effective September 1, 2008; amended effective September 1, 2009.]

LMAR 3.2. AUTHORITY OF ARBITRATORS

See MAR 3.2(a)(1)–(9). In addition to the authority granted to arbitrators by MAR 3.2 (a), an arbitrator has the authority to:

(a) Determine the time, place and procedure to present a motion before the arbitrator.

(b) Require a party or attorney or both to pay the reasonable expenses, including attorney fees, caused by the failure of such party or attorney or both to obey an order of the arbitrator unless the arbitrator finds that the failure was substantially justified or that other circumstances make an award of expenses unjust. The arbitrator shall make a special award for such expenses and shall file such award with the Clerk of the Superior Court, with proof of service of a party on each party. The aggrieved party shall have ten days thereafter to appeal the award of such expense in accordance with the procedures described in RCW 2.24.050. If within ten days after the award is filed no party appeals, a judgment shall be entered in a manner described generally under MAR 6.3.

(c) See MAR 3.2 for the relationship between the arbitrator's and judge's authority over a case in arbitration.

[Amended effective January 1, 1990; September 1, 1992; September 1, 2009; September 1, 2012.]

IV. PROCEDURES AFTER ASSIGNMENT

LMAR 4.2. DISCOVERY

(a) In determining when additional discovery beyond that directly authorized by MAR 4.2 is reasonably necessary, the arbitrator shall balance the bene-fits of discovery against the burdens and expenses. The arbitrator shall consider the nature and complexity of the case, the amount in controversy, values at stake, the discovery that has already occurred, the burdens on the party from whom discovery is sought, and the possibility of unfair surprise which may result if discovery is restricted. Authorized discovery shall be conducted in accordance with the civil rules except that motions concerning discovery shall be determined by the arbitrator.

(b) Discovery Pending at the Time Arbitrator is Assigned. Discovery pending at the time the case is assigned to an arbitrator is stayed pending order from the arbitrator or except as the parties may stipulate or except as authorized by MAR 4.2.

[Amended September 1, 1981.]

LMAR 4.4. NOTICE OF SETTLEMENT

(a) Notice of Settlement. After any settlement that fully resolves all claims against all parties, the plaintiff shall, within five court days or before the arbitration hearing, whichever is sooner, file and serve a written notice of settlement. The notice shall be filed with both the arbitrator and the Court. Where the notice cannot be filed with the arbitrator before the arbitration hearing, the plaintiff shall notify the arbitrator of the settlement by telephone prior to the hearing, and the written notice shall be filed and served within five court days after the settlement.

(b) Form of Notice. The notice of settlement shall be in substantially the following form:

NOTICE OF SETTLEMENT OF ALL CLAIMS AGAINST ALL PARTIES

Notice is hereby given that all claims against all parties in this action have been resolved. Any trials or other hearings in this matter may be stricken from the court calendar. This notice is being filed with the consent of all parties.

If an order dismissing all claims against all parties is not entered within 45 days after the written notice of settlement is filed, or within 45 days after the scheduled trial date, whichever is earlier, and if a certificate of settlement without dismissal is not filed as provided in LMAR 4.4(d), the case may be dismissed on the Clerk's motion pursuant to LMAR 4.4(c).

Date	Attorney for Plaintiff

WSBA No. _____

(c) Dismissal on Clerk's Motion. See LCR 41(b)(2).

(d) Settlement Without Dismissal. If the parties have reached a settlement fully resolving all claims against all parties, but wish to postpone dismissal beyond the period set forth in section (c) above, the parties may, within 30 days after filing the Notice of Settlement of All Claims, file a Certificate of Settle-ment Without Dismissal in substantially the following form (or as amended by the Court):

CERTIFICATE OF SETTLEMENT WITHOUT DISMISSAL

I. BASIS

1.1 Within 30 days of filing of the Notice of Settlement of All Claims required by King County Local Rules for Mandatory Arbitration 4.4(a), the parties to the action may file a Certificate of Settlement Without Dismissal with the Clerk of the Superior Court.

II. CERTIFICATE

2.1 The undersigned counsel for all parties certify that all claims have been resolved by the parties. The resolution has been reduced to writing and signed by every party and every attorney. Solely for the purpose of enforcing the settlement agreement, the Court is asked not to dismiss this action.

2.2 The original of the settlement agreement is in the custody

of: _____

at: _____.

2.3 No further Court action shall be permitted except for enforcement of the settlement agreement. The parties contemplate that the final dismissal of this action will be appropriate as

of: _____.

Date: _____

III. SIGNATURES

_____	_____
Attorney for Plaintiff/Petitioner WSBA No. _____	Attorney for Defendant/Respondent WSBA No._____
_____	_____
Attorney for Plaintiff/Petitioner WSBA No. _____	Attorney for Defendant/Respondent WSBA No._____

IV. NOTICE

The filing of this Certificate of Settlement Without Dismissal with the Clerk automatically cancels any pending due dates of the Case Schedule for this action, including the scheduled hearing date.

On or after the date indicated by the parties as appropriate for final dismissal, the Clerk will notify the parties that the case will be dismissed by the Court for want of prosecution, unless within 14 days after the issuance a party makes a written application to the Court, showing good cause why the case should not be dismissed.

[Adopted effective January 1, 1990; amended effective September 1, 1992; September 1, 1993; September 1, 2004; September 1, 2009.]

V. HEARING

LMAR 5.1. NOTICE OF HEARING—TIME AND PLACE—CONTINUANCE

An arbitration hearing may be scheduled at any reasonable time and place chosen by the arbitrator. The arbitrator may grant a continuance without court order. The parties may stipulate to a continuance only with the permission of the arbitrator. The arbitrator shall give reasonable notice of the hearing date and any continuance to the Supervisor.

[Amended effective September 1, 2008.]

LMAR 5.2. PREHEARING STATEMENT OF PROOF—DOCUMENTS FILED WITH COURT

In addition to the requirements of MAR 5.2, each party shall also furnish the arbitrator with copies of pleadings and other documents contained in the court file that the party deems relevant.

[Amended effective September 1, 2009.]

LMAR 5.3. CONDUCT OF HEARING—WITNESSES—RULES OF EVIDENCE [RESERVED]

[Reserved effective September 1, 2009.]

VI. AWARD

LMAR 6.1. FORM AND CONTENT OF AWARD

(a) Form. The award shall be prepared on the form prescribed by the Court.

(b) Return of Exhibits. After an award is filed, the arbitrator shall make available to, and parties shall collect, any exhibits offered during the hearing.

[Amended effective September 1, 2009.]

LMAR 6.2. FILING OF AWARD

(a) Extension of Time. A request by an arbitrator for an extension of time for the filing of an award under MAR 6.2 shall be presented in writing to the Supervisor, ex parte. The Supervisor may grant or deny the request, subject to review by the Presiding Judge. The arbitrator shall give the parties notice of any extension granted.

[Amended effective September 1, 1999; September 1, 2008; September 1, 2009; September 1, 2012.]

LMAR 6.3. JUDGMENT ON AWARD

(a) Presentation. A judgment on an award shall be presented to the Ex Parte Department, by any party, on notice in accordance with MAR 6.3.

VII. TRIAL DE NOVO

LMAR 7.1. REQUEST FOR TRIAL DE NOVO—CALENDAR—JURY DEMAND

(a) Assignment of Trial Date. If there is a request for a trial de novo, the Court will assign an accelerated trial date. A request for trial de novo may include a request for assignment of a particular trial date or dates, provided that the date or dates requested have been agreed upon by all parties and are between 60 and 120 days from the date the request for trial de novo is filed.

(b) Jury Demand. Any jury demand shall be served and filed by the appealing party along with the request for trial de novo, and by a non-appealing party within 14 calendar days after the request for trial de novo is served on that party. If no jury demand is timely filed, it is deemed waived.

(c) Case Schedule. Promptly after the request for trial de novo is filed, the Court will issue to all parties a Notice of Trial Date together with the Trial De Novo Case Schedule, which will govern the case until the trial de novo. The Amended Case Schedule will include the following deadlines:

	Weeks Before Trial
Disclosure of Possible Witnesses (LCR 26):	12
Discovery Cutoff (LR 37(g)):	7

(d) Motion to Change Trial Date. No later than 21 days after the date of the filing of the Notice of Trial Date, any party may move to change the trial date, but no such motion will be granted unless it is supported by a showing of good cause. If a motion to change the trial date is made later than 21 days after the filing of the Notice of Trial Date, the motion will not be granted except under extraordinary circumstances where there is no alternative means of preventing a substantial injustice.

[Amended September 1, 1981; March 21, 1985; amended effective January 1, 1990; September 1, 1992; September 1, 2004; September 1, 2008; September 1, 2009.]

LMAR 7.2. PROCEDURE AT TRIAL [RESERVED]

[Reserved effective September 1, 2009.]

LMAR 7.3. COSTS AND ATTORNEY FEES [RESERVED]

[Reserved effective September 1, 2009.]

VIII. GENERAL PROVISIONS

LMAR 8.1. STIPULATIONS—EFFECT ON RELIEF GRANTED

If a case not otherwise subject to mandatory arbitration is transferred to arbitration by stipulation, the arbitrator may grant any relief which could have been granted if the case were determined by a Judge.

LMAR 8.3. EFFECTIVE DATE [RESERVED]

[Reserved effective September 1, 2009.]

LMAR 8.4. TITLE AND CITATION

These rules are known and cited as the King County Superior Court Mandatory Arbitration Rules. LMAR is the official abbreviation.

LMAR 8.5. COMPENSATION OF ARBITRATOR

(a) Generally. Arbitrators shall be compensated in the same amount and manner as Judges pro tempore of the Superior Court. Hearing time and reasonable preparation time are compensable.

(b) Form. When the award is filed, the arbitrator shall submit to the Supervisor a request for payment on a form prescribed by the Court. The Supervisor shall determine the amount of compensation to be paid. The decision of the Supervisor will be reviewed by the Presiding Judge at the request of the arbitrator.

[Amended effective September 1, 2008.]

LMAR 8.6. ADMINISTRATION [SUSPENDED]

[Suspended on an emergency basis effective November 27, 2007; suspended on a permanent basis effective September 1, 2008.]

LOCAL RULES FOR APPEAL OF DECISIONS OF COURTS OF LIMITED JURISDICTION (KCLRALJ)

TITLE 2.   INITIATING AN APPEAL

KCLRALJ 2.6.   CONTENT OF NOTICE OF APPEAL

See RALJ 2.6

[Amended effective September 1, 1987; September 1, 1996; September 8, 2009; September 1, 2010.]

KCLRALJ 2.7.   [NOTICE OF APPEAL]

(a) **Case Schedule.** The clerk shall issue a Case Scheduling Order and judge assignment upon the filing of a Notice of Appeal.

[Adopted effective September 8, 2009. Amended effective September 1, 2010.]

TITLE 3.   ASSIGNMENT OF CASES IN SUPERIOR COURT

KCLRALJ 3.1.   MOTIONS

(a) **Motions.** Motions to continue, for stay, sanctions, dismissal, or for other relief shall be noted before the assigned judge in compliance with the requirements of LCR 7(b). If a party is seeking oral argument on a motion, the party shall direct a specific request to the assigned judge. Motions to consolidate two or more cases shall be noted before the Chief Criminal Judge, the Chief Civil Judge or the Chief Judge of the Maleng Regional Justice Center, in accordance with the case assignment area and case type of the appeal.

[Amended effective September 1, 1987; September 1, 1989; September 1, 1993, September 1, 1996; September 1, 2001; September 1, 2004; September 8, 2009; September 1, 2010.]

KCLRALJ 3.2.   CHANGE OF SUPERIOR COURT JUDGE

(e) **Affidavit of Prejudice.** CrR 8.9 shall apply to an affidavit of prejudice filed with the assigned judge.

[Amended effective September 1, 1987; September 1, 2001; September 8, 2009; September 1, 2010.]

TITLE 7.   BRIEFS

KCLRALJ 7.1.   BRIEFS [REPEALED]
[Repealed effective September 1, 2011]

KCLRALJ 7.3.   FORMAT OF BRIEFS
(b) **Motion for overlength brief.** Any party seeking to file an overlength brief shall submit the request by motion to the assigned judge.

[The effect of these amendments is to enforce the limits on briefs set forth in RALJ 7.3(b)]

[Adopted effective September 1, 2011.]

TITLE 8.   ORAL ARGUMENT

KCLRALJ 8.3.   TIME ALLOWED AND ORDER OF ARGUMENT

(a) **Waiver of argument.** See RALJ 8.4.

(b) **Conduct of hearing.** At the appeal hearing, the court will permit oral argument of ten minutes per side. The first party to file a notice of appeal is entitled to open and conclude oral argument, unless otherwise ordered by the Court. A respondent who has not served and filed a brief seven days in advance of the scheduled hearing date will not be permitted to make oral argument.

(c) **Courtesy copy of brief.** Each of the parties shall deliver a courtesy copy of its brief to the assigned Judge no later than five days before the argument. The courtesy copy of the brief shall be marked on the upper right corner of the first page with the date of the argument and the name of the judge.

[Amended effective September 1, 1987; June 1, 2009; September 8, 2009; September 1, 2010.]

TITLE 9.   SUPERIOR COURT DECISION

KCLRALJ 9.1.   BASIS OF DECISION ON APPEAL

(f) Form of Decision. Unless the court prepares its own decision, the decision of the Superior Court shall be prepared by the prevailing party, and shall be filed with the clerk's office within 15 days, see CR 54(e) and CR 58(a) and (b).

[Amended effective September 1, 1987; September 1, 2001.]

KCLRALJ 9.2.   ENTRY OF DECISION

(c) Court of Limited Jurisdiction. The clerk of the Superior Court shall transmit a copy of the decision of the Superior Court on appeal to the court of limited jurisdiction rendering the decision that was the subject of the appeal and a copy to each party in the case within 30 days following the filing of the Superior Court decision.

(d) Motion for Reconsideration. All motions for reconsideration must comply with the procedure set forth in LCR 59.

[Amended effective September 1, 1987; September 1, 2001; September 8, 2009; September 1, 2010.]

TITLE 10.   VIOLATION OF RULES—SANCTIONS AND DISMISSAL

KCLRALJ 10.1.   VIOLATION OF RULES GENERALLY

See RALJ 10.1.

[Amended effective September 1, 1987; September 8, 2009; September 1, 2010.]

KCLRALJ 10.2.   DISMISSAL OF APPEAL

See RALJ 10.2.

[Amended effective September 1, 1987; September 1, 1989; September 1, 2004; September 8, 2009; September 1, 2010.]

TITLE 12.   SUPERIOR COURT DECISION AND PROCEDURE AFTER DECISION

KCLRALJ 12.1.   MANDATE

(a) Mandate Defined. A "mandate" is the written notification by the Clerk of the Superior Court to the court of limited jurisdiction and to the parties of a Superior Court decision terminating review.

(b) When Mandate Issued by Superior Court. The Clerk of the Superior Court issues the mandate for a Superior Court decision terminating review upon written stipulation of the parties that no party will file a notice of appeal or notice of discretionary review to the Court of Appeals. In the absence of that stipulation, the Clerk issues the mandate:

(1) 30 days after the clerk files the Superior Court decision, unless any party has filed a notice of appeal or notice of request for discretionary review to the Court of Appeals or Supreme Court; or

(2) If a party has filed a notice of appeal or notice of request for discretionary review and the Court of Appeals or Supreme Court has denied jurisdiction on the appeal or denied the request for discretionary review, upon receipt of the denial of the petition for review.

[Amended effective September 1, 1987; September 8, 2009; September 1, 2010.]

KING COUNTY LOCAL GUARDIAN AD LITEM RULES

LGALR 1.   APPLICABILITY

These rules for guardians ad litem shall be referred to as KCLGALR. These rules apply to guardians ad litem appointed by the court pursuant to Title 11, Title 13 or Title 26 RCW, and to guardians ad litem appointed pursuant to Special Proceeding Rule (SPR) 98.16W, RCW 4.08.050 and RCW 4.08.060.

These rules do not apply to guardians ad litem or Special Representatives appointed pursuant Chapter 11.96A RCW; Court Appointed Special Advocates (CASA) with respect to whom other grievance procedures apply; persons appointed to serve as Custodians for Minors pursuant to Chapter 11.114 RCW, or guardians ad litem to hold funds for incapacitated persons under Title 11 RCW.

Complaints by guardians ad litem or by other persons against guardians ad litem (also referred to as "grievances") shall be administered by this process.

[Adopted effective September 1, 2003.]

LGALR 2.   REGISTRIES

The court shall establish rotational registries for the appointment of guardians ad litem to whom this Rule applies. Absent a finding of good cause the court shall appoint from the registry in rotational sequence.

The qualifications and processes for application, selection, education, compensation, and retention for guardians ad litem on each of the registries shall be as set forth in Administrative Procedures adopted by the court. These administrative procedures may be obtained from the King County Superior Court Clerk's website or by contacting the Court's Guardian Ad Litem Registry Manager.

[Adopted effective September 1, 2003.]

LGALR 3. DUTIES OF THE GUARDIAN AD LITEM

A guardian ad litem (GAL) shall comply with the court's instructions as set out in the order appointing a guardian ad litem, and shall not provide or require services beyond the scope of the court's instructions unless by motion and on adequate notice to the parties, a guardian ad litem obtains additional instruction, clarification or expansion of the scope of such appointment.

[Adopted effective September 1, 2003.]

LGALR 4. COMPENSATION

Each order appointing a Guardian ad Litem shall specify a limit on the hourly rate and total compensation for the GAL. These amounts may be increased or modified only upon application to the court in advance of the GAL providing further services. All fee requests are subject to review and approval by the court. An application to increase the fee limits shall be presented upon notice to all parties. An order authorizing an increase in the fee limits shall set forth a specific new limit or amount of increase, and shall indicate generally the duties to be provided during such additional time.

[Adopted effective September 1, 2003.]

LGALR 5. GRIEVANCES MADE BY OR AGAINST GUARDIANS AD LITEM

(a) **Filing a Grievance.** A guardian ad litem having a complaint or a person having a grievance against a guardian ad litem shall complete a complaint in a form approved by the court and file it with the Registry Manager.

(1) The Registry Manager shall immediately deliver the complaint to the presiding judge or to such person designated by the presiding judge to resolve such complaints. Such designee shall be a judge of the King County Superior Court.

(2) Upon receipt of the complaint, the Presiding Judge may retain the matter for decision or assign it to a designee for decision.

(b) **Procedure for Processing Complaint.** The presiding judge or designee will make an initial determination as to whether the complaint has potential merit. If potential merit is found, a response to the complaint will be requested, and the complaining par-

ty will be given an opportunity to reply to the response. The Presiding Judge or designee may schedule a hearing, request additional materials, or enter a decision based upon a review of the record alone. The decision of the presiding judge or designee shall be the final resolution of the complaint. If the complaint relates to a pending case the complaint shall be resolved within 25 days of the receipt of the complaint. If the complaint is made subsequent to the conclusion of a case, the complaint shall be resolved within 60 days of receipt.

(c) **Remedies.** If the complaint is sustained, in whole or in part, the court may suspend or remove of the guardian ad litem from the Registry; or impose other appropriate sanctions. During the pendency of this process the Guardian ad Litem may continue to receive appointments and shall continue to serve in appointed cases, unless otherwise provided by order of the Presiding Judge or designee.

(d) **Fair Treatment of Grievances.** All notices, proceedings and other activities taken pursuant to the grievance process shall observe provisions for fair treatment, due process, notice, the right to be heard and the appearance of fairness.

(e) **Confidentiality.** The complaint, investigation, report and all aspects of the grievance process shall remain confidential until merit is found.

(f) **Records of Grievances.** The court shall maintain a record of grievances filed and of any sanctions issued pursuant to the court's grievance procedure.

(g) **Notice to the Administrative Office of the Courts (AOC).** When a Guardian ad Litem is removed from a Registry pursuant to the disposition of a grievance, the Registry Manager shall promptly send notice of the removal to AOC.

[Adopted effective September 1, 2003.]

LGALR 6. ACTUAL OR APPARENT CONFLICTS OF INTEREST

(a) **Representation of More Than One Person in the Same Proceeding.** A Guardian ad Litem may represent the interests of two or more persons in the same family or class when expressly permitted by court order. Such multiple representation may be reviewed by the court upon request of the Guardian ad Litem or any other party who requests a review of the propriety of the multiple representation or further instruction, such as when a conflict, actual or apparent, arises as among those whose best interests are represented by the Guardian ad Litem.

(b) **Disclosures in Statement of Qualifications.** A Guardian ad litem shall include in the Statement of Qualifications filed pursuant to RCW 11.88.090 a statement as to whether the guardian ad litem currently represents any professional guardians, and if so, the name(s) of such guardian(s).

(c) Multiple Roles in Same Proceeding; Self–Dealing. Absent written order, a Guardian ad Litem shall not solicit or accept employment in any other capacity in the same cause or which pertains to the party on whose behalf the Guardian ad Litem was appointed during or after the Guardian ad Litem's service. Other capacities include, without limitation, attorney for another party, estate planner, guardian, trustee, fiduciary appointee, mediator, arbitrator, adjudicator, or care provider. A GAL may, upon court order, be re-appointed subsequently in the proceeding. With court order, Guardians ad Litem who are attorneys may draft pleadings to initiate related proceedings, in fulfillment of the duties in the proceeding for which they were first appointed.

(d) Recommendations Made in the Self–Interest of the Guardian ad Litem. A Guardian ad Litem shall not recommend the appointment or employment of a person or entity in which the Guardian ad Litem, a member of the Guardian ad Litem's family, or a business associate of the Guardian ad Litem has any interest. A Guardian ad Litem may recommend a person or entity who is or has been a client of the Guardian ad Litem only upon full written disclosure of the material facts to all parties, interested persons and the court; and provided that such disclosure does not violate any privilege or confidence of the client.

[Adopted effective September 1, 2003.]

LGALR 7. EFFECTIVE DATE

This rule shall apply to all appointments or reappointments of guardians ad litem made after the effective date of this rule.

[Adopted effective September 1, 2003.]

KING COUNTY LOCAL MENTAL PROCEEDING RULES

LMPR 1.5. TRIAL SETTINGS OR OTHER ADMINISTRATIVE HEARINGS

(a) Video Conferencing of Administrative Hearings. The Court may conduct hearings to set trial dates on petitions for 90– or 180–day involuntary treatment or other administrative hearings by video conference.

[Adopted effective September 2, 2014.]

LMPR 1.6. PRESENCE WAIVERS

(a) Presence Waivers. The respondent may waive his or her presence at any hearing through a written presence waiver or, for good cause, through an oral presence waiver presented by respondent's counsel.

[Adopted effective September 2, 2014.]

LMPR 1.7. GUARDIANS AD LITEM

(a) Appointment of a Guardian ad Litem. Upon representation by the respondent's counsel on the record that a Guardian ad Litem is needed in a case, the Court may appoint a Guardian ad Litem on behalf of the respondent without requiring the respondent to appear in court. The request for the appointment of a GAL shall be on the record with petitioner's counsel present. In the event the petitioner objects to the appointment of a Guardian ad Litem in the respondent's absence or if respondent's counsel requests, the Court may require the respondent to appear to allow the Court to conduct an inquiry with the respondent to determine that a Guardian ad Litem should be appointed.

(b) Discharge of a Guardian ad Litem. Upon representation by the respondent's counsel on the record that the Guardian ad Litem has concluded that his or her services are no longer necessary and that respondent's counsel has been able to communicate with the respondent, the Court may discharge the Guardian ad Litem.

[Adopted effective September 2, 2014.]

LMPR 1.8. TAKING TESTIMONY VIA VIDEO OR TELEPHONE

(a) General. The Court may take testimony from any witness, including the respondent, via video, telephone, or other electronic means consistent with CR 43(a). The testimony shall be taken in open court with the respondent present, unless the respondent waives his or her presence.

(b) Standards for Video Proceedings. For any hearing conducted via video, the technology used must permit the presiding judicial officer, counsel, all parties, and the witness to be able to see, hear, and speak when authorized, during the proceedings and allow attorneys to use exhibits or other materials during trial. To the extent there are any statutes, case law, or constitutional standards relating to conducting video proceedings, such standards are incorporated herein by reference.

(c) Video Pilot Projects. The court may implement video pilot projects consistent with KCLCR 0.16.

[Adopted effective September 2, 2014.]

LMPR 1.9. PRE–HEARING MOTIONS AND PROCEDURE

(a) Notice and Hearing. The original of any motion together with all supporting documents (including exhibits and briefs) must be filed and copies served on all parties and the Court not later than 10:00 AM on the date the case is first scheduled for a hearing, unless otherwise allowed for good cause shown.

(b) Response. The response may be filed and served in writing or may be made by oral presentation on the record, at the election of the responding party. The responding party shall notify the Court and all other parties of the request to submit a written response not later than the expiration of the case, if applicable, or 12:00 PM on the date the case is first scheduled for hearing, whichever is earlier. The Court may continue the hearing to permit the responding party to submit written response if the request for a continuance is made prior to expiration and the Court determines that such a continuance is in the interest of the administration of justice, or if such continuance is made by agreement of the parties.

[Adopted effective September 2, 2014.]

LMPR 1.10. REVISION OF A COMMISSIONER'S ORDER

(a) **Service and Filing of Motion.** A motion for revision of a Commissioner's order in a proceeding for involuntary treatment or to revoke a less restrictive treatment order shall be served and filed within 10 calendar days of entry of the written order, as provided in RCW 2.24.050. Revision motions shall be filed with the Clerk and will be assigned to a Judge in Seattle or at the MRJC by Court Operations Civil Section staff in Seattle to be heard in chambers by the assigned Judge. Court Operations shall notify counsel of record of the assigned judge as promptly as possible.

(b) **Record of Hearing.** The Assigned Judge will review the FTR recording of the hearing.

(c) **Responsive Document.**

(1) *Motion Relating to Order for 14-Day Commitment.* A written response shall be served and filed within two (2) judicial days of receipt of the motion for revision.

(2) *Motion Relating to Any Other Order.* When the motion involves any other order, such as an order for involuntary treatment for 90 days or for 180 days or the revocation of a less restrictive order, a written response shall be filed not later than three (3) judicial days after receipt of the motion for revision.

(3) *Unopposed Motions.* If the responding party fails to submit a written opposition to the motion, the

Assigned Judge may proceed on the assumption that the motion is unopposed.

(d) **Decision on the Motion for Revision of Commissioner's Order.**

(1) *Hearing and Record.* The hearing on the motion for revision of the Commissioner's order shall be without oral argument and will be based on the record before the Commissioner.

(2) *Ruling on Motion Relating to Order for 14-Day Commitment.* To the extent practicable, the Assigned Judge shall issue an order on the motion for revision within two (2) judicial days of the deadline for receiving a written response to the motion.

(3) *Ruling on Motion Relating to Any Other Order.* To the extent practicable, the Assigned Judge shall issue an order on the motion for revision within five (5) judicial days of the deadline for receiving a written response to the motion.

(e) **Effect of Commissioner's Order.** The Commissioner's written order shall remain in effect pending the Assigned Judge's decision on the motion for revision.

[Adopted effective September 2, 2014.]

LMPR 1.11. FINDINGS OF FACT AND CONCLUSIONS OF LAW

(a) **Hearing.** In any case tried to the Court without a jury, the Court shall state its findings of fact and enter its decision on the record. Written findings at this stage of the proceedings may be in abbreviated form.

(b) **Supplemental Written Findings and Conclusions on Appeal.** The Court shall enter supplemental written findings and conclusions in a case that is appealed to the courts of appeal. The findings and conclusions may be entered after the notice of appeal is filed. The prosecution must submit such proposed findings and conclusions, together with a copy of the taped report of proceedings, to the appropriate Judge or Commissioner, and opposing counsel of record within 21 days after receiving the respondent's notice of appeal.

[Adopted effective September 2, 2014.]

DISTRICT COURT

LOCAL RULES OF THE DISTRICT COURT FOR KING COUNTY

Including Amendments Received Through
August 15, 2015

Table of Rules

LOCAL ADMINISTRATIVE RULES

INTRODUCTION

The Local Administrative Rules have been adopted for the internal management and operation of the King County District Court pursuant to General Rule (GR) 29.

[Adopted effective January 1, 1991; amended effective October 18, 2002.]

LARLJ 0.1. ADMINISTRATION

(a) GENERAL. The responsibility to set policy and to oversee the administration of the Court resides in the elected and appointed judges of the Court. The judges, as outlined in these rules, delegate authority to an Executive Committee, a Chief Presiding Judge, an Assistant Presiding Judge, and a Chief Administrative Officer. The judges retain final authority to set modify or terminate policy or the execution of policy by the Executive Committee or any of the parties listed above through the appeal process set forth in LARLJ 0.2 APPEALS.

(b) EXECUTIVE COMMITTEE. The Executive Committee shall consist of five (5) judges: The Chief Presiding Judge and the Assistant Presiding Judge, and three (3) Division Presiding judges, one from each of the three Administrative Divisions. The Chief Presiding Judge, Assistant Presiding Judge and each member of the Executive Committee shall serve a term of two (2) years, from January 1st through December 31st, or until a successor shall be elected. The Executive Committee is responsible for the establishment of policies regarding the administrative operations of the Court.

(c) CHIEF PRESIDING JUDGE. The Chief Presiding Judge is given the duties set forth in GR 29; is responsible for the supervision of the business of the Court and for ensuring that the business of the Court is conducted in accordance with these rules; shall propose policy to the Executive Committee; shall carry out the policies set by the Executive Committee; shall supervise the Chief Administrative Officer; shall be responsible for general supervision of the current budget; shall be responsible for the preparation of the yearly proposed budget for the court; and after approval of the Executive Committee, shall present the yearly proposed budget to the County Executive and County Council. Should the County Council modify the proposed budget, the Budget Committee and the Chief Presiding Judge shall thereafter formulate and recommend a final budget to the Executive Committee for approval.

(d) ASSISTANT PRESIDING JUDGE. The Assistant Presiding Judge shall assist the Chief Presiding Judge and shall serve as Acting Chief Presiding Judge during the temporary absence or disability of the Chief Presiding Judge. Unless otherwise directed by the Presiding Judge, the Assistant Presiding Judge shall be the chair of the Budget Committee.

(e) DIVISION PRESIDING JUDGE. Each of the Court's three Administrative Divisions shall have a Division Presiding Judge who shall have the responsibilities and the authority delegated by Presiding Judge under GR29.

(f) CHIEF ADMINISTRATIVE OFFICER. The Chief Administrative Officer, under the supervision of the Chief Presiding Judge, shall have responsibility and authority, subject to delegation to the Deputy Chief Administrative Officer and Directors, where the Chief Administrative Officer deems appropriate, over the hiring, supervision, discipline and termination of all non-judicial personnel. The Chief Administrative Officer shall develop and implement uniform court, administrative and personnel procedures and, where appropriate, centralization of court administration to achieve cost savings. The Executive Committee is responsible for the hiring of the Chief Administrative Office. The Chief Administrative Office serves at the pleasure of the Executive Committee.

(g) DEPUTY CHIEF ADMINISTRATIVE OFFICER. The Deputy Chief Administrative Officer, under the supervision of the Chief Administrative Officer, shall have the responsibility and authority delegated by the Chief Administrative Officer. The Deputy Chief Administrative Officer shall be hired by the Chief Administrative Officer only with the concurrence of the Executive Committee. The Deputy Chief Administrative Officer serves at the pleasure of the Executive Committee.

(h) DIRECTOR OF PROBATION SERVICES. The Director of Probation Services, under the supervision of the Chief Presiding Judge, shall have responsibility and authority for operations of the Court's Probation Services, including the hiring, training, placement, discipline and termination of personnel. Responsibility for establishment of policies regarding the operations of Probation Services is placed with the Executive Committee. The Executive Committee is responsible for the hiring of the Director of Probation Services. The Director of the Probation Services serves at the pleasure of the Executive Committee.

(i) DIRECTORS. Division Directors shall have such responsibility and authority, as the Chief Administrative Officer deems appropriate, over the hiring, supervision, discipline, and termination of all non-judicial personnel located in the King County District Court Division to which they are assigned. Division Directors shall be hired by the Chief Administrative Officer only with the concurrence of the majority of the judges in the affected Administrative Division. The Chief Administrative Officer or a judge involved in the concurrence process may appeal a decision not to hire a Division Director to the Executive Committee. Division Directors serve at the pleasure of the Executive Committee.

Directors assigned to the Office of the Presiding Judges shall be selected by the Chief Administrative Officer and hired only with the concurrence of the Executive Committee. These Directors shall have such responsibility and authority as the Chief Administrative Officer deems appropriate over the hiring, supervision, discipline, and termination of non-judicial personnel under their supervision. Directors assigned to the Office of Presiding Judge serve at the pleasure of the Executive Committee.

[Adopted effective January 1, 1991. Amended effective January 1, 2000; October 18, 2002; September 1, 2007; September 2, 2013.]

LARLJ 0.2. APPEALS

(a) A decision of the Chief Presiding Judge may be appealed to the Executive Committee by any judge.

(b) A decision of the Chief Presiding Judge or Executive Committee may be appealed directly to the judges by obtaining the consent of at least five (5) other judges and filing such appeal with the Office of the Presiding Judge for inclusion on the next general judges' meeting agenda. An affirmative vote of at least two-thirds of those judges voting is required to reverse the Chief Presiding Judge's or Executive Committee's decision.

[Adopted effective January 1, 1991; amended effective January 1, 2000; October 18, 2002.]

LARLJ 0.3. REGULAR MEETINGS

Regular meetings of the Executive Committee shall be held every month on the first and third Tuesday. Regular meetings of the judges shall be held on the fourth Friday of January, April, June and October, or on such other day as may be designated by the Chief Presiding Judge. Provided, the Chief Presiding Judge may cancel an Executive Committee meeting or a regular meeting of the judges when there are no scheduled topics of discussion or when reasonably required by scheduling conflicts.

[Adopted effective January 1, 1991; amended effective January 1, 2000; October 18, 2002.]

LARLJ 0.4. SPECIAL MEETINGS

Special meetings of the Executive Committee may be called by the Chief Presiding Judge at any time. Notice of any such meeting shall be provided to each member at least 24 hours in advance by personal contact, email or in writing left at the judge's assigned chambers. Special meetings of the judges may be called at any time by the Chief Presiding Judge or by any six (6) judges acting jointly. Notice of any such meeting shall be provided each judge at least 24 hours in advance by personal contact or in writing left at the judge's assigned chambers.

[Adopted effective January 1, 1991; amended effective January 1, 2000; October 18, 2002.]

LARLJ 0.5. VOTING

Executive Committee members unable to attend a meeting of the Executive Committee shall be allowed to give a written proxy to another judge from that Division who may then participate and vote at the Executive Committee meeting in the same manner as the absent member could have. At a regular judges' meeting, each judge shall have the right to cast one vote on any issue before the judges. Voting by proxy at a regular judges' meeting shall be allowed only if a written proxy has been executed and filed with the Office of the Presiding Judge. Such proxy authorizes another judge to cast his or her vote as directed.

[Adopted effective January 1, 1991; amended effective January 1, 1992; September 1, 1993; January 1, 2000; October 18, 2002.]

LARLJ 0.6. QUORUMS

A quorum for the conduct of business by the entire judges shall be ten (10) judges and for the conduct of business by the Executive Committee four (4) judges.

[Adopted effective January 1, 1991; amended effective January 1, 2000; October 18, 2002.]

LARLJ 0.7. RECORDING SECRETARY

The recording secretary for all regular and special meetings of the Executive Committee and the judges shall be such person as the Chief Administrative Officer may designate. The recording secretary shall record and send to all judges the minutes of the proceedings of the Executive Committee and the judges meetings within five (5) working days following the meeting. The records of all proceedings of the judges and the prior association shall be maintained at the office of the Presiding Judge.

[Adopted effective January 1, 1991; amended effective January 1, 2000.]

LARLJ 0.8. COMMITTEES

The Chief Presiding Judge may from time to time, with or without a motion for such, set up ad-hoc or special committees for specific purposes, and appoint judges to serve on such committees. Permanent committees which shall be appointed annually by the Chief Presiding Judge shall be:

RULES. The rules committee shall be charged with the regular review and revision of all of the local and administrative rules that govern the operation of the judges of the King County District Court. Except in emergencies, all rules revisions and new rules shall be first referred to this committee for drafting.

PROBATION. The probation committee shall be charged with assisting the Probation Director and the Chief Presiding Judge in the development of policy under which the probation department shall operate.

BUDGET. The budget committee shall be charged with the development of the proposed budget for the coming year for the King County District Court. This committee shall coordinate and consider the requests from each Division and develop a recommended budget for consideration of the Executive Committee.

PERSONNEL. The personnel committee shall be charged with the development of all recommended policies that affect the people working in the Divisions, including union contract provisions, recommended salaries and working condition rules and regulations. These recommendations shall be then referred to the Executive Committee for action.

CASELOAD. The Executive Committee will serve as the caseload committee.

[Adopted effective January 1, 1991; amended effective January 1, 2000; October 18, 2002.]

LARLJ 0.9. COMMITTEE REPORTS

All committees having held meetings since the last regular or special meeting of either the Executive Committee or the judges shall report orally or in writing the business conducted by that committee at such meeting. Such report shall be made at the next regular or special meeting of either the Executive Committee or the judges.

[Adopted effective January 1, 1991. Amended effective September 1, 2006.]

LARLJ 0.10. ELECTIONS

Elections for the Chief Presiding Judge and Assistant Presiding Judge shall be held at the regular judges' meeting in October. Elections for Chief Presiding Judge and Assistant Presiding Judge shall be decided by a majority vote of all the judges at the October election meeting. Elections for the Administrative Division representatives to the Executive Committee (Division Presiding Judge) shall be held no later than the Friday following the October judges' meeting. If no judge from an Administrative Division receives a majority of the votes to be elected Division Presiding Judge, then the Chief Presiding Judge shall draw names by lot from the top two finalists to fill the position. The Chief Presiding Judge shall be notified of the Division election results no later than November 5th.

[Adopted effective January 1, 1991; amended effective January 1, 1992; January 1, 2000; October 18, 2002; September 1, 2007.]

LARLJ 0.11. VACANCIES

Vacancies occurring in the Executive Committee shall be filled by a vote of the judges of the administrative division in the same manner as provided in LARLJ 0.10 above.

[Adopted effective January 1, 1991; amended effective September 1, 2007.]

LARLJ 0.12. MEETING AGENDAS

The Chief Presiding Judge shall prepare agendas for both the Executive Committee and judges' meetings and shall deliver the agenda to all appropriate members for each meeting by hand delivery, email or mail, five (5) calendar days before the meeting.

[Adopted effective January 1, 1991; amended effective January 1, 2000; October 18, 2002.]

LARLJ 0.13. RECALL OF ELECTED MEMBERS

The Chief Presiding Judge, Assistant Presiding Judge or any member of the Executive Committee may be recalled from office upon motion made and seconded and approved by two-thirds of those entitled to vote on the issue as provided in paragraph LARLJ 0.10 above. A motion to recall the Chief Presiding Judge, Assistant Presiding Judge, or any member of the Executive Committee may only be voted upon at a meeting of the judges called for that purpose

[Adopted effective January 1, 1991; amended effective October 18, 2002.]

LARLJ 0.14. RULE ON RULES

(a) Notice. Copies of proposed rules or amendments to rule(s), including proposed changes to these administrative rules, should be sent by mail or email to all judges at least three (3) weeks before consideration by the Executive Committee.

(b) Executive Committee Action.

(1) The Executive Committee, if it determines circumstances justify, may adopt the proposed rule(s), except changes to these Administrative Rules, as submitted or as modified at the Executive Committee meeting for immediate effect subject to an automatic review by the judges at the first regular meeting of the judges following such Executive Committee action.

(2) If the Executive Committee determines there is not a need for immediate enactment of the proposed rule(s), it shall nevertheless pass on the advisability of such rule(s), and any amendments considered at such meeting, and forward the proposed rule(s) to a meeting of the judges which is at least twenty-eight (28) days ahead. The Recording Secretary shall send to all judges copies of the proposed rule(s) and the Executive Committee's recommendation(s) regarding adoption or rejection at least five (5) days prior to the regular judges' meeting.

(3) Any Division or judge may request a specific local rule (as opposed to a uniform local rule) for a Division in supplementation of the uniform local rules by obtaining the approval of the Executive Committee and adoption according to GR 7.

(c) Judges. "Judges" are defined to mean all the then current validly appointed or elected King County District Court Judges, and a meeting of such judges includes those present personally and those present by means of proxy voting as authorized by these Local Administrative Rules.

(d) Printing of Rules. Copies of all adopted rules shall be filed as directed by GR 7 and available at all courthouses. Adopted as a goal is the desire to have the Local Court Rules reviewed on an annual basis in time to be accepted for publication by book companies. The Chief Presiding Judge may at any time make typographical error corrections of printed rules.

(e) Emergency Bail Schedule Changes. The Chief Presiding Judge may without prior notice add to, delete, or amend the King County District Court's Uniform Bail Schedule to conform with legislative change or Supreme Court rule change.

(f) Suspension of rules. No local rule of this Court shall be adopted, rescinded or changed without a majority vote of all the judges at a regular or special judges' meeting and only after seven days notice of a motion thereof; *provided,* a rule may be temporarily suspended for a special purpose by a vote requested thereon. The Chief Presiding Judge shall announce the rule suspended and the judges may proceed accordingly.

[Adopted effective January 1, 1991; amended effective September 1, 1993; January 1, 2000; October 18, 2002.]

LARLJ 0.15.   RULES OF ORDER

The latest edition of Roberts Rules of Order shall govern parliamentary procedures at all meetings of the judges and committees

[Adopted effective January 1, 1991.]

LARLJ 0.16.   COURT BUSINESS HOURS AND WEDDINGS

(a) The King County District Court shall be open to the public for business from at least 8:30 AM to 4:30 PM Monday through Friday of each week except for holidays scheduled by the State of Washington Supreme Court and closures ordered by the Presiding Judge when necessitated by inclement weather or other emergency.

(b) Any judge performing a wedding ceremony during the hours the Court is open to the public for business must comply with the requirements of Canon 5(C)(8) of the Code of Judicial Conduct and any applicable statutes.

[Adopted effective January 1, 1991; amended effective January 1, 2000; October 18, 2002.]

LARLJ 0.17.   NAME OF COURT

Beginning January 1, 2007, the King County District Court will be comprised of five electoral districts operating in courthouses throughout King County. Reference to a particular courthouse location shall include the Administrative Division of the King County District Court. Beginning January 1, 2007, the Administrative Divisions are the East, South and West. The courthouse facilities located within the Administrative Divisions are as follows:

South Division

(a) Kent, 1210 South Central Kent, WA 98031

(b) Burien, 601 SW 149th Street, Burien, WA 98166

(c) Regional Justice Center, 401 Fourth Avenue North, Kent, WA 98032

(d) Vashon Facility (c/o Burien Courthouse, 601 SW 149th Street, Burien, WA 98166)

East Division

(a) Bellevue, 585—112th Avenue SE, Bellevue, WA 98004

(b) Issaquah, 5415—220th Avenue SE, Issaquah, WA 98029

(c) Redmond, 8601—160th Avenue NE, Redmond, WA 98052

West Division

(a) Seattle, E–327 King County Courthouse, 516 3rd Avenue, Seattle, WA 98104

(b) Shoreline, 18050 Meridian Avenue N, Shoreline, WA 98133

(c) King County Correctional Facility (c/o Seattle Courthouse, 516 Third Avenue, Room E–327, Seattle, WA 98104

[Formerly LARLJ 0.18, adopted effective January 1, 1991; amended effective January 1, 1992; September 1, 1997; January 1, 2000. Renumbered as LARLJ 0.17 and amended effective October 18, 2002. Amended effective June 26, 2004; September 1, 2007.]

LARLJ 0.18.   ALTERNATE FILING

(a) Chief Presiding Judge. In order to assure the expeditious and efficient handling of all cases and an equitable distribution of workload among the Administrative Divisions, the Chief Presiding Judge, with the approval of the Executive Committee, may by written order, direct that certain types of cases be filed in different Administrative Divisions than otherwise provided in these rules for a designated period of time, or until further ordered. It is recommended, but not required, that the Chief Presiding Judge consult with the Executive Committee, affected Administrative Divisions, affected law enforcement agencies, and other affected parties prior to making such a recommendation to the Executive Committee.

(b) All Judges. Any judge may direct the transfer of a pending case to another Administrative Division for good cause, upon the court's own motion or upon the motion of any party.

(c) Courtesy Hearing. Without transferring the case to another Administrative Division, a hearing may be held in a Division other than the one in which the case is filed for the purpose of setting bail, first appearance after being booked on a warrant, or other purpose agreed to by the court where the case is filed.

[Formerly LARLJ 0.19, adopted effective January 1, 1991; amended effective January 1, 1992; September 1, 1997; January 1, 2000. Renumbered as LARLJ 0.18 and amended effective October 18, 2002; amended effective September 1, 2007.]

LARLJ 0.19. REMOTE PUBLIC ACCESS TO ON-LINE COURT RECORDS

Access to on-line district court records shall be made available to the public subject to the following fees.

(a) **Per Page.** The fee assessed for remote access to on-line district court records shall be twenty-five cents per page. No fee shall be charged to view district court records using terminals that are made available to the public at district court facilities.

(b) **Collection.** Subject to the approval of the Chief Presiding Judge, the district court chief administrative officer shall establish a procedure for the collection of this fee.

[Adopted on an emergency basis effective January 1, 2009; adopted on a permanent basis effective September 1, 2009. Former LARLJ 0.19 adopted effective January 1, 1991; amended effective November 1, 1993; January 1, 2000; amended and renumbered as LARLJ 0.18 effective October 18, 2002.]

LOCAL CIVIL RULES

LCRLJ 3.1. FILING OF CIVIL, IMPOUND, AND SMALL CLAIMS CASES

(a) "Venue" for all civil, impound, and small claims shall be that as prescribed in RCW 3.66.040. For purposes of this rule the term "district" in RCW 3.66.040 shall refer to King County. Cases shall be heard in the division designated by the applicable General Administrative Rule found at LCRLJ.

[Adopted effective January 1, 1991; amended effective September 1, 1993; September 1, 1999; July 1, 2000; September 1, 2009; September 2, 2014.]

LCRLJ 3.2. CASE INFORMATION COVER SHEET

Each new civil case filing, except small claims, petitions for domestic violence protection orders, anti-harassment orders and name changes, shall be accompanied by a Case Information Cover sheet prepared and submitted by the plaintiff or plaintiff's attorney. The minimum requirements of the Case **Information** Cover Sheet shall be established by the court and made available at www.kingcounty.gov/courts/District Court.

[Formerly LCRLJ 11, adopted effective September 15, 2000. Renumbered LCRLJ 3.2 and amended, effective September 2, 2014.]

LCRLJ 4(d)(2). SERVICE OF SUMMONS AND COMPLAINT

Personal service of process shall be as provided by CRLJ 4(d)(2) and RCW 12.04.050. No officer or employee of any party or the assignor of any party shall serve the summons and complaint.

[Adopted effective January 1, 1991; amended effective July 1, 2000; September 2, 2014.]

LCRLJ 26. DISCOVERY

(g) **Time for Discovery.** The parties may agree, with the permission of the court, to discovery cut-off dates which modify the time for discovery within CRLJ 26(d). A notice, signed by all parties, of an agreed schedule shall be filed with the court, and shall become binding upon the parties upon approval by the court. Any party may propose a discovery schedule which modifies the time for discovery within CRLJ 26(d).

(1) Any party intending to propose a discovery schedule under this rule must serve the proposed discovery schedule on all parties, within 90 days of service of the summons and complaint, or counter-claim, or cross complaint, whichever is longer.

(2) Such discovery schedule shall be deemed approved by the court if no objection or counter proposal is served and filed within 14 days of the date of filing.

(3) If an objection or other proposed schedule is filed within 14 days of the filing of a proposed discovery schedule, the court shall note the case for a discovery conference and set discovery deadlines.

(4) No ex-parte fee will be charged.

[Adopted effective January 1, 1991; amended effective September 1, 1994; July 1, 2000; September 2, 2014.]

LCRLJ 35. PHYSICAL AND MENTAL EXAMINATION OF PERSONS

Superior Court Rule (CR) 35 is adopted in its entirety.

[Adopted effective September 2, 2014.]

LCRLJ 38. CIVIL JURY

Demand. Either the Plaintiff or the Defendant may request a jury trial in a civil case which shall be made by filing a demand with the clerk, supplying a copy to the opposing party or counsel and paying the jury fee. If a party only notes the matter for trial and does not either request a jury trial or does not pay the jury fee, the other party may request a jury trial and pay the fee within 10 days of receiving the note for trial. Failure to comply with this rule shall waive the right to a jury trial.

[Adopted effective January 1, 1991; amended effective July 1, 2000; September 2, 2014.]

LCRLJ 39. ADMISSIBILITY OF DOCUMENTS

(a) **Certain Documents Deemed Admissible.** ER 904 shall apply and documents listed there under will be deemed admissible unless objection is made pursuant to this rule under section (c). In addition, the following documents will also be deemed admissible: a police or fire report or other investigative body's report, a wage loss statement, the written statement of any other witness including the written report of an expert witness, and including a statement of opinion which the witness would be allowed to express if testifying in person, if the written statement is made by affidavit or by declaration under penalty of perjury; and, any other document not specifically covered by the foregoing provisions of ER 904 and this rule but having the equivalent circumstantial guarantees of trustworthiness, the admission of which would serve the policies and purposes expressed in King County Superior Court Local Rule LMAR 1.1 and the interests of justice.

Any other party may subpoena the author or maker of the document admissible under this rule, at that party's expense, and examine the author or maker as if under cross-examination.

(b) Notice. The party offering the document must serve on all parties at least fourteen (14) days prior to the trial date and in accordance with CRLJ 5, a notice, accompanied by a copy of the document(s) and the name, address and telephone number or its author or maker if it is not apparent on the face of the document.

(c) Objection. No later than three days prior to the scheduled hearing the other party may serve on all parties a written objection to any document offered under this rule. The objection must contain a brief statement as to why it is objectionable. If there is a failure to object and provide an explanation, then the documents will be presumed admissible subject to (d) below.

(d) Effect of Rule. This rule does not restrict argument or proof relating to the weight to be accorded the evidence submitted, nor does it restrict the trier of fact's authority to determine the weight of the evidence after hearing all of the evidence and the arguments of opposing parties.

[Adopted effective September 2, 2014.]

LCRLJ 54. ATTORNEY FEES

The following attorneys fee schedule, where authorized and instead of those statutory fees set by RCW 12.20.060, shall be deemed reasonable in all default cases unless the parties present evidence of circumstances that convince the court that a larger or smaller fee should be awarded, provided however, the court shall have authority to vary from this schedule on its own motion:

SCHEDULE FOR REASONABLE ATTORNEY FEES IN DEFAULT CASES

(Other than Statutory Attorney Fees)

From	To	Amount
$.01	$1,000	$250
$1,000.01	$1,500	$300
$1,500.01	$2,000	$350
$2,000.01	$2,500	$400
$2,500.01	$3,000	$450
$3,000.01	$4,000	$500
$4,000.01	$5,000	$550

$5,000.01 Set at court's discretion.

[Adopted effective January 1, 1991; amended effective January 1, 1991; May 5, 1992; September 1, 1993; July 1, 2000; September 2, 2014.]

LCRLJ 55. DEFAULT JUDGMENTS

(g) Form of Submission. Any party seeking a default judgment shall submit at least the following to the court contemporaneously with the motion for default judgment, unless otherwise excused by the court for good cause, regardless of whether any of these required documents have been filed with the court prior to the motion.

(1) A copy of the original proof of service shall be attached to the motion for every default judgment.

(2) In assigned causes of action: every assignment instrument relating back to each original debt.

(3) In causes of action based upon all contracts: sworn testimony to prove performances may be required, together with filing of a copy of the contract, if written; filing or proving the items of account and any credits; and the final amount of the principal should be underlined and highlighted in yellow as should the interest amount; in addition:

(a) In causes of action based on a negotiable instrument: the original negotiable instrument or a certified copy of the original negotiable instrument with an attestation that the original has been destroyed or a facsimile of the original negotiable instrument or other proof as provided by a bank defined in RCW 62-A.4-105;

(b) In causes of action based on a retail sales contract chattel mortgage, or conditional sales contract: the contract. Where applicable, an automobile title or bill of sale must be filed;

(c) In causes of action based on open account: a written statement of account setting forth all charges and credits and the dates thereof on the principal and separately listing any statement of any interest or surcharges, and a statement of the nature of merchandise or services furnished;

(d) In causes of action based upon credit card debt: billing statements in the debtors name showing cumulative charges to the extent available, interest, interest rate, payments, credits and, if available, a statement of the nature of merchandise or services furnished;

(e) In causes of action for rent based on an oral lease: a statement of account similar to that required in actions on open account. If any claim is made for damages or repairs to premises, such claim must be itemized separately;

(f) In causes of action for rent based on a written lease: a copy of the lease and a statement of the account.

(4) In causes of action based in tort:

(a) Proof of liability shall be made by sworn statement of a witness with competent knowledge of the event (for automobile accident cases, see RCW 46.52.080 (police accident report not admissible);

(b) Otherwise, the proof required showing the amount of damages shall be the same as required above for proving contract balances except that the following additional proof of the amount of damage shall be required:

(i) Property damage may be proven by repair bills of estimates;

(ii) Loss of use claims, and pain and suffering shall be proved by sworn testimony;

(iii) Loss of wages may be proven by sworn declaration from the Employer or employer's agent; and

(iv) Hospital, doctor, and other medical expenses may be proved by written bills or statements, whether paid or not.

(h) **Conformed Copies.** If the default motion is by mail, the Plaintiff shall file a self-addressed, stamped envelope for the clerk to return a conformed copy of the default judgment to the plaintiff.

(i) **Prejudgment Interest.** In order for a judgment for prejudgment interest to be allowed, the following must be presented to the court:

(1) The date interest commenced, and the document that contains that date. The document with the date should have the date underlined and highlighted in yellow for the court;

(2) The date to which the interest is calculated.

(3) The amount of interest and the rate at which the interest is calculated, and the document that contains the rate of interest. The document with the rate of interest should have the rate of interest underlined and highlighted in yellow for the court; and

(4) The computation of the interest claimed due.

[Adopted effective January 1, 1991; amended effective July 1, 2000; September 1, 2006; September 1, 2007; September 2, 2014.]

LCRLJ 56. SUMMARY JUDGMENTS

(j) **Providing a Copy of the Rule.** A party moving for summary judgment shall, along with its motion for summary judgment, serve a copy of CRLJ 56 on all opposing parties who are not represented by counsel in the action.

[Adopted effective July 1, 2000. Amended effective September 2, 2014.]

LOCAL CRIMINAL RULES

LCrRLJ 1.5. STYLE AND FORM FACILITATING PROOF OF SERVICE AND FILING OF PAPERS

(a) **Style and Form.** (See: CRLJ 5 and 10 and CrRLJs. 1.5 and 8.4)

(b) **Filing with Court.** (See: CrRLJ 8.4(c) and CRLJ 5)

(1) *Action Documents.* Pleadings or other papers requiring action on the part of the Clerk/Court (other than file stamping, docketing and placing in the court electronic file) shall be considered action documents. Action documents shall include a special caption directly below the case number on the first page, stating:

"Clerks Action Required: (here state the action requested)."

(2) *Format Recommendations.* It is recommended that all pleadings and other papers include or provide for the following:

(i) *Service and Filing.* Space should be provided at top of the first page of a document allowing on the right half for the clerk's filing stamp, and in the left half for proof of, or acknowledgment of, service.

(ii) *Numbered Paper.* All pleadings, motions, affidavits, briefs, and other supporting documents prepared by attorneys/parties should be on paper with line numbering in the left hand margin.

(3) *Handling by Clerk.* All pleadings or other papers with proper caption and cause number will be date receipted, docketed and placed within the court electronic file by the Clerk of the District Court in the order received.

[Adopted effective January 1, 1991; amended effective September 1, 2007.]

EXAMPLE LCrRLJ 1.5

Example LCrRLJ 1.5
SPACE FOR SERVICE PROOF/SPACE FOR COURT/FILING STAMP

IN THE KING COUNTY DISTRICT COURT
IN AND FOR THE STATE OF WASHINGTON
_____ Division
_____ Facility

	)	
PLAINTIFF	)	CAUSE NO.
	)	XXXXXXX
v.	)	CLERK'S ACTION
	)	REQUIRED:
	)	SET THIS MOTION
	)	FOR HEARING
	)	
DEFENDANT	)	MOTION
	)	CHALLENGING

COMPLAINT SUFFICIENCY

The clerks will *not* search out action items. They will not search through letters, notices of appearance, requests for discovery, or other materials, to locate possible requests for action, such as: preservation of jury trial, or non-waiver of [60/90] day rule (this needs a request to set within the correct time, see CrRLJ 3.3), or concern with witnesses. Amongst CrRLJs impacted by this rule are:

CrRLJ 1.5	Style and Form
CrRLJ 3.3(e)	Objection to Arraignment Date
CrRLJ 3.3(f)	Setting of Trial Date ... Waiver of Objection
CrRLJ 4.3	Joinder of Offenses and Defendants
CrRLJ 4.3.1	Consolidation for Trial
CrRLJ 4.4	Severance of Offenses and Defendants
CrRLJ 4.7	Discovery (regulation of, not requests for)
CrRLJ 4.8	Subpoenas

[Adopted effective January 1, 1991; amended effective September 1, 2007.]

LCrRLJ 2.2(a). WARRANT OF ARREST AND BENCH WARRANT OF ARREST

(1) **Warrants Expiration Date.** All warrants of arrest issued by King County District Court shall carry on their face a three (3) year expiration date. If not served during that time the warrant expires and the case file shall be closed subject to motion to re-open.

(2) **Bench Warrants for Unpaid Fines.** Bench warrants of arrest for failure to pay fines or make arrangements to perform alternate service, in lieu of payment of a fine, should issue only in the amount of the unpaid fine, or dollar equivalent of unperformed alternative service.

[Adopted effective January 1, 1991.]

LCrRLJ 2.6. eSUPERFORM

Prosecuting Attorneys may file electronic Super-forms ("eSuperforms") into the District Court Online Records System by following the procedure established by GR 30. The probable cause statement in the eSuperform must be authenticated by a law enforcement officer using a digital signature that complies with the requirements of RCW 19.34 or GR 30, or by the arresting or citing officer explicitly signing the statement and transmitting the eSuperform within the King County Booking and Referral System, as permitted by GR 30.

[Adopted on an emergency basis effective March 6, 2008; adopted on a permanent basis effective September 1, 2009.]

LCrRLJ 3.1. SERVICES OTHER THAN COUNSEL

All initial requests and approval for expert services for county and state case expenditures are hereby delegated to the King County Office of Public Defense.

[Adopted on an emergency basis effective June 24, 2005; adopted permanently effective September 1, 2005.]

LCrRLJ 3.2(*o*). BAIL

(1) **Bail Forfeiture.** No forfeiture of bail shall be allowed except in those matters designated by the King County District Court Uniform Bail Schedule as forfeitable offenses. *Provided,* that in extraordinary cases the court shall have discretion to permit forfeiture for offenses designated as nonforfeitable. In any such case the state or city involved shall be permitted an opportunity to resist such forfeiture if desired. The court may at any time for good cause shown order a mandatory hearing for violations designated in the King County District Court Uniform Bail Schedule as forfeitable offenses.

(a) IF A PERSON WHO IS ARRESTED AND HELD FOR A NEW OFFENSE OF DRIVING WHILE UNDER THE INFLUENCE, RCW 46.61.502, DRIVING UNDER THE AGE OF 21 AFTER CONSUMING ALCOHOL OR MARIJUANA, RCW 46.61.503, OR BEING IN PHYSICAL CONTROL OF A VEHICLE WHILE UNDER THE INFLUENCE, RCW 46.61.504 OR AN EQUIVALENT LOCAL ORDINANCE OF ANY OF THESE OFFENSES, AND SUCH PERSON ARRESTED DOES NOT HAVE A PRIOR OFFENSE AS DEFINED IN RCW 46.61.5055 WITH TEN YEARS, THEN THIS PERSON ARRESTED MAY POST BAIL IN THE AMOUNT SCHEDULED BY COURT RULE UNLESS RELEASED WITHOUT POSTING BAIL, OR A DIFFERENT BAIL AMOUNT HAS BEEN SET BY A JUDGE AT THE TIME OF THE ARREST OR BOOKING.

(b) IF A PERSON WHO IS ARRESTED FOR A NEW OFFENSE OF DRIVING WHILE UNDER THE INFLUENCE, RCW 46.61.502, DRIVING UNDER THE AGE OF 21 AFTER CONSUMING ALCOHOL OR MARIJUANA, RCW 46.61.503, OR BEING IN PHYSICAL CONTROL OF A VEHICLE WHILE UNDER THE INFLUENCE, RCW 46.61.504, OR AN EQUIVALENT LOCAL ORDINANCE OF ANY OF THESE OFFENSES, AND SUCH PERSON ARRESTED HAS A PRIOR OFFENSE AS DEFINED IN RCW 46.61.5055 WITHIN TEN YEARS, THEN THIS PERSON ARRESTED SHALL BE HELD WITHOUT RELEASE UNTIL HE OR SHE HAS APPEARED BEFORE A

JUDGE, UNLESS RELEASE OR BAIL HAS BEEN SET BY A JUDGE.

(c) IF A PERSON IS ARRESTED FOR A NEW DOMESTIC VIOLENCE OFFENSE AS IS NOW OR HEREAFTER DEFINED BY THE REVISED CODE OF WASHINGTON THIS PERSON SHALL NOT BE RELEASED UNLESS BAIL IS SET BY A JUDGE AT THE TIME OF THE ARREST OR AT A SUBSEQUENT COURT APPEARANCE.

(2) **Verification of Identity and Address.** Bail, as set forth in, CrRLJ 3.2, or in any similar rule, shall only be available to defendants who have provided sufficient information to establish a positive and verifiable identity and home address. Absent such information, no bail may be accepted until established by court hearing.

[Formerly LCrRLJ 3.2(m), adopted effective January 1, 1991; amended effective January 1, 1991; September 1, 1993; July 1, 1996; September 1, 1999; July 1, 2000; September 1, 2001; renumbered as LCrRLJ 3.2(o) and amended on an emergency basis, effective October 24, 2014.]

LCrRLJ 3.3.   CONTINUANCES

Unless otherwise duly noted for Motion (see CrRLJ 8.2 and CRLJ 6 and 7), all requests to continue pre-trial hearings, motions, trial dates and/or other final dispositions will require the agreement of both parties before such request will be submitted to a judge for approval. The court will not continue a trial date or other final disposition beyond the applicable time for trial under CrRLJ 3.3 without a signed speedy trial waiver.

Requests for continuance of dates set for review/revocation may be made by letter or written motion filed with the court and will be submitted to the judge off the record for approval without the advance agreement of the opposing party.

[Adopted effective September 1, 1996.]

LCrRLJ 4.1.   APPEARANCE BY COUNSEL

Whenever a lawyer will be formally appearing and waiving an arraignment pursuant to CrRLJ 4.1(d), the lawyer may contact the court by telephone and obtain the pre-trial hearing date. The lawyer shall thereafter immediately cause to be filed the written appearance, waiver of arraignment and confirmation of the assigned pre-trial hearing date. No arraignment will be waived until receipt by the court of the written appearance and waiver.

[Adopted effective September 1, 1996.]

LCrRLJ 4.5.   PRE–TRIAL HEARING

(a) Unless otherwise ordered by the judge in a specific case for good cause, all cases in which a defendant enters a plea of not guilty shall be set for a pre-trial hearing.

(b)(1) The pre-trial hearing shall provide an opportunity for negotiation between the parties. The parties shall confer in good faith regarding any agreed disposition prior to trial. The defendant shall be required to attend the pre-trial hearing unless excused by the court. Failure to attend may result in the issuance of a bench warrant and/or forfeiture of any bond. In the event of a disposition, the parties shall execute the appropriate documents for the judge to consider the matter on the record.

(b)(2) In cases which will proceed to trial, the parties shall fully complete the pre-trial order form provided by the court unless the judge in a specific case waives the requirement of filing the written order. Any division may adopt a rule waiving the requirement of a written order in any case to be tried to the bench when the parties stipulate on the record that the matter is ready for trial and all pre-trial motions are waived. All pre-trial orders will be presented to and signed by the judge in open court on the record, unless otherwise ordered by the judge in a specific case.

(b)(3) In the written pre-trial order form, the parties shall identify with specificity all motions and counsel may be required to articulate on the record the basis for any motion. All rulings made at the pre-trial hearing or subsequent motions hearing(s) shall be binding on the parties and shall not be relitigated at trial. Any motions not filed at pre-trial may be deemed waived unless otherwise allowed by the court. Counsel shall file only those motions for which there is a good faith belief that the motion is well grounded in fact and is warranted by existing law or a good faith argument for the extension, modification or reversal of existing law.

(c) The court shall assign dates and give written notice to the parties for Motion hearings and Trial at the time of the Pre-trial Conference and shall, insofar as is reasonably possible, schedule those hearings in consultation with defense counsel. Other factors, such as witness availability, shall also be considered.

(d)(1) A Jury Call/Readiness hearing will be scheduled in all cases proceeding to jury unless specifically waived by the judge in a particular case for good cause shown. This calendar will be held during the week prior to the first day of the jury term. The defendant shall be required to attend this hearing unless excused by the court. Failure to attend may result in the issuance of a bench warrant and/or forfeiture of bond.

(d)(2) A request for a jury trial date constitutes an assurance that the parties will be ready to begin jury selection immediately on the morning of trial.

[Adopted effective September 1, 1996.]

LCrRLJ 4.11.   VIDEO CONFERENCE PROCEEDINGS

(a) **Criminal.** Preliminary appearances as defined by CrR 3.2(b) and CrRLJ 3.2.1(d), arraignments as defined by CrR 3.4 and 4.1 and CrRLJ 3.4 and 4.1, bail hearings as defined by CrR 3.2 and CrRLJ 3.2, and trial settings, as defined by CrR 3.3 and CrRLJ 3.3(f), conducted via video conference in which all participants can simultaneously see, hear, and speak as authorized by the Court, shall be deemed held in open court and in the defendant's presence for the purposes of any statute, court rule, or policy. All video conference hearings conducted pursuant to this rule shall be public, and the public shall be able to simultaneously see and hear all participants and speak as permitted by the trial court Judge. Any party may request an in-person hearing which may, in the Judge's discretion, be granted.

(b) Agreement. Other trial court proceedings may be conducted by video conference only by agreement of the parties either in writing or on the record and upon the approval of the Judge.

(c) Standards for Video Conference Proceedings. The Judge, counsel, all parties, and the public attending the hearing must be able to see, hear, and speak as authorized by the Court during proceedings. Video conference facilities must provide for confidential communications between attorney and client and security sufficient to protect the safety of all participants and observers. In interpreted proceedings, the interpreter should be located next to the defendant, and the proceeding must be conducted to assure that the interpreter can hear all participants.

[Adopted effective December 1, 1997.]

LCrRLJ 5.1. FILING OF CRIMINAL AND CRIMINAL TRAFFIC CASES

All criminal and criminal traffic actions shall be filed in the division where the violation is alleged to have occurred, except as may otherwise by ordered pursuant to LARLJ 0.19 Alternate Filing.

[Adopted effective January 1, 1991; amended effective September 1, 1993.]

LCrRLJ 6.1. JURY WEEK

The following courthouses: Bellevue, Issaquah, Redmond and Shoreline will each select a different week during each month for jury trials, except in jury weeks containing a court holiday jury weeks may overlap.

[Adopted effective September 1, 1996; amended effective June 26, 2004.]

LCrRLJ 6.13. EVIDENCE—COURT'S CUSTODY OF EXHIBITS

In a criminal case every exhibit in the courts custody, which is not contraband and for which ownership is not in dispute, shall be returned to the party who produced that exhibit upon motion of that party and expiration of the appeal period. In the event of a finding of guilty, for purpose of this rule, the appeal period shall begin on the day of sentencing or deferral of sentence by the court. Exhibits not withdrawn

shall be delivered by the court to the applicable law enforcement agency for disposition as abandoned property; or if contraband, for destruction. No exhibit shall be released by the court without its being receipted for by the receiving person.

[Adopted effective January 1, 1991.]

LCrRLJ 7.2(a). SENTENCING— GENERALLY

(1) Statement of Fine. Unless otherwise stated at the time of sentencing, all assessable court costs including witness fees, filing fees and service of process shall be in addition to the stated sentence. Any statutory penalty assessment shall be in addition to the stated fine.

(2) Deferred Prosecution. If it comes to the attention of a sentencing judge on any mandatory-court-appearance offense that the defendant being sentenced is on a deferred prosecution program, the sentencing judge shall cause notice of the offense and sentence to be sent to the judge supervising the deferred prosecution.

[Adopted effective January 1, 1991; amended effective September 1, 1993.]

LCrRLJ 8.1(b). TIME—ENLARGEMENT

Upon the non-appearance of a defendant at the time and place scheduled by the court and a warrant of arrest issued, the defendant's bail or bond may be ordered forfeited with or without further proceedings upon motion of the prosecuting attorney or upon the court's own motion. If the necessary witnesses does not appear at the time scheduled by the court, the court may dismiss such action unless a good cause for such non-appearance is shown. No such action shall be taken until sixty (60) minutes after the scheduled appearance time.

[Adopted effective January 1, 1991.]

LCrRLJ 8.2. MOTIONS

(1) Motion for Deferred Prosecution. Defendants requesting a Title 46 deferred Prosecution for an alcohol or drug related offense, shall submit a (1) Petition For Deferred Prosecution, (2) a Statement of Defendant's Rights at Deferred Prosecution Hearing, and (3) Findings of Fact, Conclusion of Law and Order Granting Deferred Prosecution in the form approved by the Court. A copy of the documents required by this rule will be made available upon request. Such documents may be submitted in the original form provided by the Court or may be reprinted and submitted in substantially the same form. All substantive revisions to these forms must be made known to the Court at each hearing where a request for Deferred Prosecution is made.

(2) Motion of Countywide Significance. Upon the filing of a motion in a criminal case, any party may request that such motion be designated as an "issue of countywide significance". A judge in any division of the Court may, on his/her own motion or upon receiving such a request from a party, request of the Presiding Judge that such motion be designated as an "issue of countywide significance". Upon receiving such request from a judge, the Presiding Judge may designate such motion as an "issue of county-wide significance".

Upon designation of a motion as an "issue of countywide significance", the Presiding Judge shall assign three judges to act as a panel to hear the motion. The panel of judges shall hear testimony and argument and enter Findings of Fact and Conclusions of Law and Decision ("Ruling") on the motion. Judges of the Court shall then have the following options: (1) accept such Ruling in its entirety; (2) not accept such Ruling and schedule a hearing before such judge for the presentation of testimony and argument; or (3) accept the Findings of Fact and Conclusions of Law, in whole or in part, and make a separate Decision thereon. The record made before such panel shall be taken before a court reporter and a transcript shall be made available to any judge of the Court upon his or her request. Copies of the transcript shall be made available through the court reporter to any person upon payment of the costs of transcription.

[Adopted effective January 1, 2000; amended effective September 1, 2001.]

LCrRLJ 8.3. STIPULATED ORDERS OF CONTINUANCE

a) At any time prior to trial, the parties may move for entry of a Stipulated Order of Continuance (hereinafter "SOC").

b) Unless waived by the Court upon motion of the parties, each and every SOC shall be signed by the defendant, his or her attorney of record, and the prosecuting attorney.

c) At a minimum each SOC form shall include the following:

(1) A clear statement that the defendant, by entering into a SOC, agrees to the facts in the police report and/or other documents in the event that the conditions of the SOC are not met.

(2) A clear statement that the police report currently contained in the court file or attached to the SOC as an exhibit, or other specified documents, shall be deemed admissible at trial.

(3) A clear statement that the police report and/or other documents shall be submitted to the court and may be marked as exhibits, but will not be admitted into evidence unless the case proceeds to trial.

(4) A clear statement that the parties agree that in the event that the conditions of the SOC are not met, the evidence at trial shall be limited to the police report currently contained in the court file or attached to the SOC as an exhibit and/or other specified documents submitted to the court at the time that the SOC is approved.

(5) A clear statement that all parties, by entering into a SOC, waive their constitutional right to a jury trial, their right to hear and question witness, their right to call witnesses, and the defendant's right to testify or not to testify.

(6) A clear statement of the period of continuance, which shall be no more than 2 years.

(7) A clear statement that the defendant, by entering into a SOC, is waiving his right to a speedy trial for the duration of the SOC, and that the new commencement date for speedy trial purposes is the last day of the period of continuance.

(8) A clear statement of each and every condition of the SOC, each condition being set forth in a separate paragraph.

(9) A clear statement of the outcome of the case if all conditions of the SOC are met.

(10) A clear statement acknowledging the requirement that the defendant will report to and be supervised by [ ] KCDC probation services or [ ] Bellevue probation services or [ ] probation monitoring, and will pay probation fees accordingly, provided that if this condition is specifically waived there must be a clear statement of that fact and the reasons therefore.

(11) A clear statement that the defendant fully understands that in case of non-compliance, a warrant for his or her arrest may issue, and that the likely result of non-compliance will be a conviction for the crime charged and imposition of up to the maximum penalties allowed by law.

(12) A clear statement of the elements of the offense(s) that must be proven in order to convict the defendant.

(13) A clear statement of the maximum penalties allowed by law, any mandatory minimum penalties and/or any other applicable restrictions/requirements under the law.

(14) A clear statement that advising the defendant that if he or she is not a citizen of the United States, any finding of guilt to any offense punishable as a crime under state law is grounds for deportation, exclusion from admission to the United States, or denial of naturalization pursuant to the laws of the United States.

(15) A clear statement that the defendant agrees that his or her decision to enter the SOC is made freely, knowingly, intelligently and voluntarily; that no one has threatened harm of any kind to the defendant or to any other person to case the defendant to enter into the SOC, and that no one has made any promises of any kind, except those contained in the SOC agreement, to cause the defendant to enter into the SOC.

(16) A clear statement that the defendant has done one or more of the following: (a) read the SOC in its entirety and/or (b) has had the SOC read to him or her in its entirety by someone else (if that person is an interpreter the interpreter shall submit the appropriate declaration with the SOC).

(17) No SOC shall be effective until approved by the Court.

[Adopted effective January 1, 2000; amended effective September 1, 2001; September 1, 2008.]

LOCAL INFRACTION RULES

LIRLJ 2.3. FILING

Infraction citations shall be filed in the division where the violation is alleged to have occurred, except as may otherwise be ordered pursuant to LARLJ 0.18 Alternate Filing.

[Adopted effective January 1, 1991; amended effective September 1, 1993; amended on an emergency basis effective July 22, 2011; June 29, 2012; amended on a permanent basis effective September 1, 2012.]

LIRLJ 2.4. TIME PAYMENTS ON INFRACTIONS

Any person who has been served with a notice of infraction and who desires to use option (1) as provided in IRLJ 2.4(b)(1), may arrange time payments on the monetary penalty according to the policy then in force in the division in which the infraction is filed.

[Adopted effective January 1, 1991; amended effective September 1, 1993.]

LIRLJ 2.6. SCHEDULING OF CONTESTED HEARINGS

Upon receipt of a request for the subpoena of a citing officer, or upon receipt of a subpoena for a citing officer, the court may reschedule the associated contested hearing to the next appropriate date scheduled for the appearance of citing officers.

[Original LIRLJ 2.6 was repealed effective June 26, 2004. Current LIRLJ 2.6 was adopted on an emergency basis effective June 24, 2005, and adopted permanently effective September 1, 2005.]

LIRLJ 2.6(a)(i), (ii) and (iii). PRE-HEARING CONFERENCE

(i) A defendant who requests a contested hearing may first be scheduled for a prehearing conference, which shall be scheduled for not less than 14 days from the date the written notice of the hearing is sent by the court nor more than 45 days from the date of the notice of infraction or the date a default judgment is set aside, unless otherwise agreed by the defendant in writing.

(ii) The prehearing conference may be waived by the defendant in writing if the waiver is received by the court before the time set for the prehearing conference. If the prehearing conference is waived, the case will be set for contested hearing. The contested hearing shall be scheduled for not more than 90 days from the date of the prehearing conference or, if the prehearing conference is waived, from the date of the waiver of the prehearing conference is received by the court.

(iii) **Pre-hearing and Witnesses.** The Court may schedule a prehearing for infractions if it deems it necessary for the convenience of parties and witnesses. If a party requests a witness the Court may reschedule the contested hearing to another date.

[Adopted on an emergency basis effective June 24, 2005; adopted on a permanent basis effective September 1, 2005. Amended on an emergency basis effective July 28, 2014; October 24, 2014.]

LIRLJ 3.5. DECISION ON WRITTEN STATEMENTS

(E) Mitigation and contested hearings based on sworn written statements, as provided in IRLJ 2.4(b)(4) and IRLJ 2.6 are authorized. The Court may accept electronically submitted statements or requests for deferred findings through a link provided at its website. The written statement(s) or electronically transmitted statement(s) or requests must be received by the Court no later than seven (7) calendar days before the scheduled hearing or it will not be considered. The hearing shall be held in accordance with IRLJ 3.5. A form for the defendant's statement(s) and the link for electronically transmitted statement(s) or requests can be found at www.kingcounty.gov/court/DistrictCourt.

[Adopted effective September 1, 2001. Amended on an emergency basis effective July 28, 2014; October 24, 2014.]

LIRLJ 3.6. PLEADINGS—STYLE AND FORM FACILITATING PROOF OF SERVICE AND FILING OF PAPERS

(a) **Style and Form.** (See GR 14)

(b) **Filing with Court.**

(1) *Action Documents.* Pleadings or other papers requiring action on the part of the clerk/court (other than file stamping, docketing and placing in the court file) shall be considered action documents. Action documents shall include a special caption directly below the case number on the first page, stating:

"**Clerk's Action Required:** (herein state the specific action requested)."

Clerks will not search through letters, notices of appearance, requests for discovery or other materials to locate possible requests for action.

[Adopted effective June 26, 2004.]

LIRLJ 6.7(a). RELIEF FROM JUDGMENT OR ORDER

(a) **Clerical Mistakes.** Clerical mistakes in judgments, orders or other parts of the record and errors therein arising from oversight or omission may be corrected by the court at any time of its own initiative or on the motion of any party and after such notice, if any, as the court orders. Such mistakes may be so corrected before review is accepted by the superior court and thereafter may be corrected by order of the superior court.

(b) **Mistakes; Inadvertence; Excusable Neglect; Newly Discovered Evidence; Fraud; etc.** On motion and upon such terms as are just, the court may relieve a party from a final judgment, order, or proceeding for the following reasons:

(1) Mistakes, inadvertence, surprise, excusable neglect or irregularity in obtaining a judgment or order;

(2) Newly discovered evidence which by due diligence could not have been discovered in time to move for a new trial under the provisions of CrRLJ 7.5;

(3) Fraud (whether heretofore denominated intrinsic or extrinsic), misrepresentation, or other misconduct of an adverse party;

(4) The judgment is void; or

(5) Any other reason justifying relief from the operation of the judgment.

(c) The motion shall be made within a reasonable time and for reasons (1) and (2) not more than 1 year after the judgment, order, or proceeding was entered or taken. A motion under this section does not affect the finality of the judgment or suspend its operation.

(d) **Procedure on Vacation of Judgment.**

(1) *Motion.* Application shall be made by motion stating the grounds upon which relief is asked, and supported by affidavit or declaration of the applicant or applicant's attorney, setting forth a concise statement of the facts or errors upon which the motion is based.

(2) *Consideration of Motion.*

(i) The court may decide the motion without hearing based on section (b) (1) if the motion, affidavit or declaration, and court's records establish the moving party is entitled to the requested relief.

(ii) If a contested hearing on the merits was previously held, and the moving party is seeking to modify the finding, a show cause hearing with notice to the adverse party shall be scheduled.

(iii) The court may deny the motion without a hearing if the facts alleged in the affidavit or declaration do not establish grounds for relief.

(iv) The court may enter an order fixing a time and place for hearing and directing the adverse party to appear and show cause why the relief asked for should not be granted.

(3) *Interim Relief.* The court may enter an order recalling any notice to the Department of Licensing regarding the party's failure to appear or failure to respond to an infraction or referral to collections pending the outcome on the motion.

(4) *Service.* No later than 14 days before the scheduled show cause hearing, the moving party shall serve a copy of the motion, affidavit or declaration, and order to show cause upon the other party or the party's attorney, as provided in CrRLJ 8.4(b), and file proof of service with the court.

[Adopted effective Jan. 22, 2010.]

MUNICIPAL COURTS

AUBURN MUNICIPAL COURT LOCAL RULES

Including Amendments Received Through
August 15, 2015

Table of Rules

[INTRODUCTION]

Any of these rules maybe suspended or modified, upon good cause shown, by Stipulation of the parties, or by the court upon its own motion.

LOCAL COURT GENERAL RULES

RULE 1A. LOCAL COURT GENERAL RULE #1A

Parties or witnesses who fail to appear within thirty minutes of the time scheduled for a hearing or trial shall be deemed as having failed to appear unless excused by the court.

[Adopted effective September 1, 2002.]

RULE 1B. LOCAL COURT GENERAL RULE #1B

Sixty days after sentencing and / or final disposition the clerk of the court shall remove from the record the names of any attorneys of record unless a notice of appeal has been filed or the court has received a written indication from the attorney indicating a desire to continue representation of a defendant.

[Adopted effective September 1, 2002.]

LOCAL COURT CRIMINAL RULES

RULE 1. LOCAL COURT CRIMINAL RULE NUMBER ONE: VIDEO CONFERENCE PROCEEDINGS

(A) Preliminary appearances as defined by CrR 3.2(B) and CrRLJ 3.2(d), arraignments as defined by CrR 3.4 and 4.1 and CrRLJ 3.4 and 4.1, bail hearings as defined by CrR 3.2 and CrRLJ 3.2, and trial settings as defined by CrR 3.3 and CrRLJ 3.3(f), conducted via video conference in which all participants can simultaneously see, hear, and speak with each other shall be deemed held in open court and in the defendant's presence for the purposes of any statute, court rule or policy. All video conference hearings conducted pursuant to this rule shall be public, and the public shall be able to simultaneously see and hear all participants and speak as permitted by the trial court judge. Any party may request an in person hearing, which may in the trial court judge's discretion be granted.

(B) All other trial court proceedings including the entry of a Statement of Defendant on Plea of Guilty as defined by CrR 4.2 and CrRLJ 4.2 may be conducted by video conference only by agreement of the parties, either in writing or on the record, and upon the approval of the court.

[Adopted effective September 1, 1999.]

RULE 2. LOCAL COURT CRIMINAL RULE NUMBER TWO

The appointment by this court of a public defender attorney for any defendant deemed to be indigent and deserving of the appointment of a public defender shall be conditioned on the defendant appearing in court for all hearings where his/her appearance has been required by the court.

If any defendant for whom a public defender has been appointed fails to appear in court when so required without being excused in advance by the court, the order/appointment whereby the public defender was appointed for said defendant shall be vacated immediately upon such failure to appear.

Upon such appointment being vacated, the public defender shall be relieved from any requirements to appear in court with such defendant.

The provisions of this Rule, however, do not preclude the defendant from reapplying to the court for the appointment of the public defender to represent him/her.

[Adopted effective September 1, 1999; renumbered from Rule 2A effective September 1, 2008.]

RULE 2A. LOCAL CRIMINAL RULE NO. 2A [RENUMBERED]

[Renumbered as Local Criminal Rule Two effective September 1, 2008.]

RULE 3. LOCAL CRIMINAL RULE NO. 3

Proponents of motions to suppress at a CrRLJ 3.6 hearing shall submit in writing supported by an affidavit or document as provided in RCW 9A.72.085 a statement setting forth the facts the moving party anticipates will be elicited at the hearing no later than fourteen days before the hearing. Failure to timely file shall result in the striking of the motion. If the facts are disputed the respondent shall submit an affidavit or similar document within seven days of the hearing and an evidentiary hearing shall take place at the hearing to address the disputed facts. Failure to timely respond shall result in the court ruling on the motion on the evidence asserted by the proponent. Parties wishing to brief CrRLJ 3.6 motions to suppress shall submit briefs no later that fourteen days before the hearing if they are the proponent and responses, if any, no later seven days before the hearing. Failure to comply with this schedule may result in the court refusing to accept and/or read the briefs, at the court's discretion. Filing of the statements and briefs may be accomplished be facsimile machine transmission no later than midnight of the date in question.

[Adopted effective September 1, 2003; deleted and renumbered from Rule 5 effective September 1, 2008.]

RULE 4. LOCAL CRIMINAL RULE NO. 4

All Pleadings and other papers may be filed with this court by facsimile transmission Monday through Friday, except holidays, between the hours of eight a.m. and five p.m.

[Adopted effective September 1, 2003; deleted and renumbered from Rule 6 effective September 1, 2008.]

RULE 5. LOCAL CRIMINAL RULE NO. 5 [RENUMBERED]

[Adopted effective September 1, 2003; renumbered as Rule 3 effective September 1, 2008.]

RULE 6. LOCAL CRIMINAL RULE NO. 6 [RENUMBERED]

[Adopted effective September 1, 2003; renumbered as Rule 4 effective September 1, 2008.]

LOCAL COURT INFRACTION RULES

RULE 1. LOCAL COURT INFRACTION RULE NUMBER ONE

1. If a person who has been cited with a violation of RCW 46.30.020 presents to the court clerk evidence that the person had in effect at the time of the citation liability insurance as required by RCW 46.30.020, then upon payment of twenty-five dollars ($25.00) administrative costs, the case shall be dismissed and the court clerk shall be authorized to make appropriate notation of the dismissal in the court file.

2. If a person charged with violation of RCW 46.30.020, for failure to have liability insurance is able to show evidence that the person has subsequently obtained liability insurance in conformity with the requirement of RCW 46.30.020, then the penalty shall be reduced to three hundred and fifty dollars ($350.00) and upon payment of the three hundred and fifty dollar ($350.00) penalty, the clerk shall be authorized to enter a finding that the infraction was committed, and make appropriate notations in the court record, and the person will be relieved of any further need to appear in court in connection with the infraction.

[Adopted effective September 1, 1999; renumbered from Rule Three and amended effective September 1, 2008.]

RULE 2. LOCAL COURT INFRACTION RULE NUMBER TWO

A defendant who objects to the hearing date set by the court pursuant to IRLJ 2.6, shall file with the court and serve upon the plaintiff a written motion for a speedy hearing date; said motion shall be filed and served no later than ten days from the date of written notice of the hearing date. Failure to comply with this rule shall be a waiver of the objection.

[Adopted effective September 1, 1999; renumbered from Rule Four effective September 1, 2008.]

RULE 3. LOCAL COURT INFRACTION RULE NUMBER THREE

Discovery requests other than copy of the infraction, the officer's report and the speed measuring device certification must be set for hearing to determine the relevance of such requests.

[Adopted effective September 1, 1999; renumbered from Rule 5 effective September 1, 2008.]

RULE 4. LOCAL COURT INFRACTION RULE NUMBER FOUR

If a person charged with a violation of city ordinance 10.36.268 for parking in disabled space without proper parking placard, license plate or picture identification, presents to the court clerk evidence that the person had in effect at the time of citation the required parking placard, and an identification card bearing picture, name and date of birth of the permit holder, as well as the placard's serial number, then upon payment of twenty five dollars ($25.00) administrative costs, the infraction shall be dismissed and the court clerk shall be authorized to make appropriate notation of the dismissal in court record.

[Adopted effective September 1, 1999; renumbered from Rule 6 effective September 1, 2008.]

RULE 5. LOCAL COURT INFRACTION RULE NUMBER FIVE

(a) A defendant charged with an infraction who requests a hearing to explain mitigating circumstances, pursuant to Rule 2.4 of the Infraction Rules for Courts of Limited Jurisdiction (IRLJ), and pursuant to Section 46.63.070 of the Revised Code of Washington (RCW), shall appear before the Municipal Court at the time of date for which such hearing is scheduled. The judge's determination of the disposition shall be final, and is not subject to review before any court.

(b) A defendant charged with an infraction who requests a hearing to contest the determination that an infraction occurred shall first appear before the Municipal Court for a prehearing/settlement conference, at the time and date for which such hearing is scheduled (normally on a mitigation calendar) in accordance with IRLJ 2.3(a). The judge may waive the prehearing/settlement conference on his/her own motion. If the prehearing conference is waived the case will be set for a contested hearing. If the defendant fails to waive or appear at the prehearing conference, a default judgment shall be entered.

(c) If the defendant who requests a hearing to contest the determination that an infraction was committed has a criminal charge pending in Auburn Municipal Court, and said criminal charge arises out of the same occurrence as the infraction, the hearing on the infraction may be heard at the same time as the trial on the criminal charge at the request of the defendant, the City Attorney or the court and as authorized by the Infraction Rules for Courts of Limited Jurisdiction.

(d) A defendant who requests a hearing to contest the determination that an infraction was committed may file upon the court a written demand that the court subpoena the officer who caused the notice to be issued or whose written statement was the basis for the issuance of the notice if the demand is filed with the court at least fifteen (15) days prior to the contested hearing. Upon receipt of such a demand to assure the officer's presence, upon written notice to the defendant. A defendant is responsible for obtaining and serving subpoenas in accordance with IRLJ 3.1 in all other circumstances.

(e) The plaintiff need not be represented by a lawyer at a contested hearing unless witnesses have been subpoenaed to appear for the hearing.

(f) A motion to set aside a judgment entered upon a failure to appear, per IRLJ 3.2(b), shall be presented into the Municipal Court at a walk-in calendar.

(g) If a defendant fails to respond to a notice of infraction within fifteen days, fails to satisfy a judgment, or fails to appear for a contested or mitigation hearing, the delinquent judgment may be referred to a collection agency pursuant to RCW 3.02.045. Remuneration for collection services will be assessed as costs, at the rate agreed to between the Court and the collection agency, and added to the judgment.

[Adopted effective September 1, 1999; renumbered from Rule 8 effective September 1, 2008.]

RULE 6. LOCAL COURT INFRACTION RULE NUMBER SIX

The party requesting the court to subpoena any witnesses whose testimony relies on expertise or on information obtained through their employment as to any speed measuring device shall be responsible for any cost, including reasonable fees normally charged by such a witness for this service and shall be responsible for all cost related to that witnesses, appearance in court, whether the witness testifies or not, as a cost assessed.

A witness so subpoenaed may be allowed to appear and testify telephonically as the court determines is appropriate.

[Adopted effective September 1, 1999; renumbered from Rule 9 and amended effective September 1, 2008.]

RULE 7. LOCAL COURT INFRACTION RULE NUMBER 7

Pursuant to IRLJ 2.6 (c) upon receipt of written statement on infraction cases involving contested hearings and mitigation hearings, the court is authorized to enter decision based upon such written statements consistent with IRLJ 3.5.

[Adopted effective September 1, 1999; amended effective September 1, 2002; renumbered from Rule 10 effective September 1, 2008.]

RULE 8. LOCAL INFRACTION RULE NUMBER 8

The clerks of the court are authorized to resolve an infraction through a deferred finding as authorized by RCW 46.63.070(5). The conditions of a deferred finding are that the defendant waives their contested/mitigation hearing, have no deferred findings within the prior seven years, pay an administrative fee of $150.00 within 120 days, and within one year complete defensive driving school and have no other traffic infrac-

tions. Successful compliance with the conditions shall result in a dismissal of the of the infraction. Failure of a defendant to comply with any of the terms of deferred finding shall result in a finding of committed and an assessment of the original infraction penalty as well as an assessment of $48.00. Any monies previously paid shall not be credited toward the penalty imposed or the assessment.

[Adopted effective September 1, 2002; renumbered from Rule 11 effective September 1, 2008.]

RULE 9. LOCAL INFRACTION RULE NUMBER 9

Defendants in all infraction cases as an alternate procedure may elect to have the court address a motion to set aside a finding of committed, due to either the defendant's failure to appear for a hearing or failure to timely request a hearing by submitting a written motion to the court supported by an affidavit, setting forth the grounds for the motion and, if a contested hearing is requested, the facts constituting a defense to the infraction.

Upon receipt of the motion the court shall forward a copy of the motion and affidavit to the plaintiff. Should the plaintiff choose to respond, the plaintiff shall cause such response to be filed with the court within five days (exclusive of weekends and holidays) of the receipt of the motion and affidavit and the plaintiff shall cause a copy of the response to be mailed to the defendant.

Upon the expiration of five days from the plaintiff's receipt of the defendant's motion or receipt of the plaintiff's response, the court shall promptly issue its ruling on the basis of the documents submitted without oral hearing unless the court otherwise indicates. All pleadings filed with the court may be filed directly or by facsimile machine.

[Adopted effective September 1, 2002; renumbered from Rule 12 effective September 1, 2008.]

RULE 10. LOCAL INFRACTION RULE NUMBER 10 [RENUMBERED]

[Adopted effective September 1, 2002; renumbered as Rule 7 effective September 1, 2008.]

RULE 11. LOCAL COURT INFRACTION RULE NUMBER 11 [RENUMBERED]

[Adopted effective September 1, 2003; renumbered as Rule 8 effective September 1, 2008.]

RULE 12. LOCAL COURT INFRACTION RULE NUMBER 12 [RENUMBERED]

[Adopted effective July 11, 2005; renumbered as Rule 9 effective September 1, 2008.]

BELLEVUE MUNICIPAL COURT—
[No Local Rules]

PUBLISHER'S NOTE

This municipal court follows the Local Rules of the District Court for King County.

BLACK DIAMOND MUNICIPAL COURT LOCAL RULES

Including Amendments Received Through
August 15, 2015

Table of Rules

PURPOSE, SCOPE AND CONSTRUCTION

1.1.   ADOPTION OF LOCAL RULES

These rules are adopted pursuant to GR 7, CrRlJ 1.7 and IRLJ 1.3.   The effective date of these rules shall be July 1, 2004, except as to those rules governed by GR 7, in which case the effective date will be September 1, 2004.

[Adopted effective September 1, 2004.]

1.2.   TITLE OF RULES

These rules may be known and cited as Black Diamond Municipal Court Local Rules, and shall be referred to as BDMCLR.

[Adopted effective September 1, 2004.]

1.3.   EFFECT OF LOCAL RULES

The provisions of the Local Rules are supplemental to the Rules for the Courts of Limited Jurisdiction, as adopted or hereafter amended by the Supreme Court of the State of Washington, and shall not be construed in conflict with them.

[Adopted effective September 1, 2004.]

1.4.   RESERVATION OF DISCRETION

The Black Diamond Municipal Court reserves the authority to interpret and/or suspend or modify these rules in individual cases on motion of a party for good cause or on a motion of the Court in the interest of justice and/or the efficient operation of the Court.

[Adopted effective September 1, 2004.]

1.5.   JUDICIAL DAY [STRICKEN]

[Adopted effective September 1, 2004; stricken on an emergency basis effective May 7, 2008; stricken on a permanent basis effective September 1, 2008.]

1.6.   NEXT JUDICIAL DAY

The requirement of RCW 46.61.50571 that defendants arrested for driving while under the influence, driving under age twenty-one after consuming alcohol, or being in physical control of a vehicle while under the influence appear in court within one judicial day is waived.   All such defendants shall be required to appear at the earliest practicable day following arrest, such date being defined as the first date following arrest when court is in session.   The following definition shall apply to this rule:

A.   "Earliest practicable day" means the next regularly scheduled day that Court is in session, which may be determined by calling the Black Diamond Municipal Court offices.

[Adopted effective September 1, 2004; amended on an emergency basis effective May 7, 2008; amended on a permanent basis effective September 1, 2008.]

1.7. CONTINUANCES [STRICKEN]

[Adopted effective September 1, 2004; stricken on an emergency basis effective May 7, 2008; stricken on a permanent basis effective September 1, 2008.]

LOCAL CRIMINAL RULES

2.1. QUASHING WARRANTS

(a) The defendant or defendant's attorney may file a motion and order to quash a warrant or pay an administrative fee to quash a warrant subject to subsection (b). The filing of a motion to quash a warrant will not stay the warrant and the defendant remains subject to arrest on the warrant. The motion to quash the warrant will be reviewed by the Judge and the court will either grant or deny the motion, or set a show case [1] hearing for the parties to appear. If a show cause hearing is set by the Judge the warrant will remain outstanding until the proper bond is posted, the defendant is arrested, or the defendant appears in open court and the Judge quashes the warrant and the defendant signs for a new court date.

(b) Warrants issued in an amount of $5,000 dollars or less are subject to an administrative warrant quash procedure whereby the defendant shall pay a nonrefundable administrative fee of $50.00 to the Court for the Court to quash the warrant and the defendant must sign for their next court date to appear. The warrant will not be quashed unless the defendant appears in person to sign for their next court date. Warrants issued in an amount over $5,000 are not subject to be quashed administratively by posting the administrative fee.

[Formerly Rule 2.2, adopted effective September 1, 2004. Renumbered Rule 2. 1 and amended, effective September 2, 2013.]

[1] So in original. Probably should be "cause".

2.3. LOCAL BAIL SCHEDULE

Black Diamond Municipal Court adopts the uniform bail schedule as set forth in CrRLJ 3.2(o) with the following exceptions:

(1) Any case designated as a domestic violence offense as defined in RCW 10.99. In these cases bail shall be set at $100,000 subject to judicial review under CrRLJ 3.2.1.

(2) Any driving under the influence or physical control cases cited under RCW 46.61.502 or 504. In these cases, when required to reasonably assure appearance in court or when the defendant is subject to custodial arrest, bail shall be set at $7,500 subject to judicial review under CrRLJ 3.2.1.

[Adopted effective September 2, 2013.]

2.4. MANDATORY APPEARANCE AT ARRAIGNMENT

A defendant charged with a domestic violence offense (as defined in RCW 10.99), driving under the influence (RCW 46.61.502), physical control (RCW 46.61.504), minor driving after consuming alcohol (RCW 46.61.503), or any sex crime including communication with a minor for immoral purpose, prostitution, or public indecency crime must appear personally for arraignment on the next arraignment calendar following arrest.

[Adopted effective September 2, 2013.]

2.5. WAIVER OF ARRAIGNMENT

An attorney may enter an appearance and/or plea of not guilty on behalf of a client in any criminal or criminal traffic offense. Said appearance or plea shall be made in writing. In all cases not listed in BDMCLR 2.4, an attorney may waive arraignment. A written appearance and waiver of arraignment shall commence the running of the time periods established in CrRLJ 3.3 from the date of receipt by the Court. A written appearance and waiver of arraignment without a plea shall be considered a plea of not guilty and waives any defect in the complaint other than failure to state a crime. The Court does not accept telephonic notices or requests.

[Adopted effective September 2, 2013.]

2.6. DEFERRED PROSECUTION PETITION AND ORDER

A Petition for Deferred Prosecution pursuant to RCW 10.05 must be filed with the Court and the prosecuting authority no later than seven (7) days prior to proposed entry unless good cause exists for delay.

An Order deferring prosecution will not be granted unless proof of compliance with the following is shown:

1. Petition for Deferred Prosecution is submitted on the form identified in CrRLJ 4.2.

2. Order for Deferred Prosecution is submitted on a form approved for use by the Court.

3. Petitioner has written verification that he or she has begun treatment in the program contained in the petition and order for deferred prosecution.

[Adopted effective September 1, 2015.]

2.7. CRIMINAL MOTIONS

All dates for testimonial or over length motion hearings shall be scheduled in court at the pre-trial hearing. These include, but are not limited to CrRLJ 3.5 and CrRLJ 3.6 motions. At the pre-trial hearing where the motion date is requested, the moving party shall file or have already filed a copy of the brief and all supporting documentation on the opposing party and the court. The court shall then set a motion hearing date and may set a briefing schedule for the nonmoving party's response and moving party's reply.

Any motion not identified at the pre-trial hearing or subsequent motion hearings may be deemed waived unless otherwise allowed by the court.

[Adopted effective September 1, 2015.]

2.8. READINESS HEARING

Within ten (10) days prior to an assigned jury trial date, or as set by the court, there shall be held a readiness hearing. All parties must be present and the following matters will be concluded: plea bargaining, exchange of witness lists, exchange of discovery, and motions on any newly discovered evidence creating legal issues. Any motions in liminae that are anticipated to take longer than 30 minutes to litigate must be served on the court and opposing party no later than 2 days prior to trial.

Following conclusion of the readiness hearing the court will set conditions for the confirmation of the jury trial pursuant to BDMCLC 2.9–CrRLJ 4.5(b). Conditions may include the defendant calling and/or meeting with their attorney prior to the scheduled trial date. Failure to comply with the conditions may result in the jury trial being stricken and sanctions imposed pursuant to BDMCLC 2.9–CrRLJ 4.5(b).

[Adopted effective September 1, 2015.]

2.9. JURY CONFIRMATION

(i) Confirmation Required. No later than 3:00 p.m., two (2) days prior to the date of the assigned jury trial, the defendant, if appearing pro se, or the defendant's attorney, if represented by legal counsel, and the City Prosecutor shall contact the Court Clerk and confirm that the case will proceed to jury trial.

(ii) Failure to Confirm. Failure of a party to confirm the jury trial or to advise the Court Clerk that another disposition has been reached may cause the case to be stricken from the jury trial calendar. Failure of the defendant, if appearing pro se, or the defendant's attorney, if represented by legal counsel, to confirm the jury trial or to advise the Court Clerk that another disposition has been reached shall constitute an excluded period of the defendant's speedy trial right pursuant to CrRLJ 3.3(e)(3). Likewise, failure

to comply with any conditions set at the readiness hearing pursuant to BDMCLC 2.8–CrRLJ 4.5(a) may result in the jury trial being stricken and the finding of an excluded period pursuant to CrRLJ 3.3(e)(3).

(iii) Failure to Appear. Failure of the defendant to appear on the jury trial date may result in the issuance of a bench warrant and the forfeiture of any posted bail unless a disposition has been confirmed by all parties. Any disposition will be heard on the next regularly scheduled court day unless an alternative date is set by the parties and is approved by the judge, judge pro tem or court commissioner.

(iv) Sanctions. Failure to comply with this rule or BDMCLC 2.8–CrRLJ 4.5(a) or any case confirmed under this section and not proceeding to trial may result in the imposition of sanctions, including but not limited to jury costs, witness fees and terms, as deemed appropriate by the trial court. If a failure of a party to comply with this rule results in a jury pool actually appearing at the court unnecessarily, sanctions of not less than $250 plus jury costs will be assessed against the offending party.

[Adopted effective September 1, 2015.]

3.0. VIDEO COURT PROCEEDINGS

(1) Authorization. Preliminary appearances held pursuant to CrRLJ 3.2.1(d), arraignments held pursuant to CrRLJ 3.4 and 4.1, bail hearings held pursuant to CrRLJ 3.2, and trial settings held pursuant to CrRLJ 3.3(f), may be conducted by video conference in which all participants can simultaneously see, hear and speak with each other. Such proceedings shall be deemed held in open court and in the defendant's presence for the purpose of any statute, court rule or policy.

All video conference hearings conducted pursuant to this rule shall be public, and the public shall be able to simultaneously see and hear all participants and speak as permitted by the judge, judge pro tem or court commissioner. Any party may request an in-person hearing which may be granted at the discretion of the judge, judge pro tem or court commissioner.

(2) Agreement. Other trial court proceedings, including entry of a Statement of Defendant on Plea of Guilty as provided for by CrRLJ 4.2, may be conducted by video conference only by agreement of the parties, either in writing or on the record, and upon the approval of the judge, judge pro tem or court commissioner.

(3) Standards. The standards for video conference proceedings shall be as specified in CrRLJ 3.4(d)(3).

[Adopted effective September 1, 2015.]

LOCAL INFRACTION RULES

4.1. CONTESTED HEARINGS PRELIMINARY MOTIONS

Motions challenging the authority of the Court, the constitutionality of the Court, the constitutionality of any statute, ordinance or court rule pertaining to an infraction, the authority of the prosecuting attorney prosecuting an infraction, and/or the authority of the law enforcement agency or officer filing an infraction must be made in writing. Such motions, together with citations to authority and argument, must be filed with the Court and served upon the opposing party no later than fourteen days prior to a contested infraction hearing. Such motions may be decided by the Court with or without oral argument, as the Court may determine.

[Adopted effective September 1, 2015.]

4.2. SERVICE & FILING OF SUBPOENAS

The respondent, the plaintiff and respondent's attorney will subpoena witnesses in accordance with IRLJ 3.1(a). Service of subpoenas will be in accordance with IRLJ 3.1(a). Black Diamond Municipal Court will not serve a subpoena on an officer or witness for the respondent, plaintiff or respondent's attorney. Each party must serve their own subpoenas.

Any request for the Speed Measuring Device Expert shall be in accordance with IRLJ 6.6. The Speed Measuring Device Expert may appear telephonically for the hearing.

[Adopted effective September 1, 2015.]

BOTHELL MUNICIPAL COURT LOCAL RULES

Effective September 1, 2000

Including Amendments Received Through August 15, 2015

Table of Rules

LOCAL CRIMINAL RULES

BTM–CrRLJ 3.4(d).   VIDEO CONFERENCE PROCEEDINGS

(1) Authorization. Preliminary appearances held pursuant to CrRLJ 3.2.1(d), arraignments held pursuant to CrRLJ 3.4 and 4.1, bail hearings held pursuant to CrRLJ 3.2, and trial settings held pursuant to CrRLJ 3.3(f), may be conducted by video conference in which all participants can simultaneously see, hear and speak with each other. Such proceedings shall be deemed held in open court and in the defendant's presence for the purpose of any statute, court rule or policy. All video conference hearings conducted pursuant to this rule shall be public, and the public shall be able to simultaneously see and hear all participants and speak as permitted by the judge or judge pro tem. Any party may request an in-person hearing which may be granted at the discretion of the judge or judge pro tem.

(2) Agreement. Other trial court proceedings, including entry of a Statement of Defendant on Plea of Guilty as provided for by CrRLJ 4.2, may be conducted by video conference only by agreement of the parties, either in writing or on the record, and upon the approval of the judge or judge pro tem.

(3) Standards. The standards for video conference proceedings shall be as specified in CrRLJ 3.4(d)(3).
[Adopted effective September 2, 2013.]

BTM–CrRLJ 3.4(e).   QUASHING WARRANTS—POSTING FEES

The Court may permit a defendant who has an outstanding warrant in the Bothell Municipal Court to appear in person and post a $100.00 non-refundable warrant fee. Upon so doing, the warrant will be quashed and a new hearing will be set. A defendant may utilize this program one time only.

[Formerly Rule 4, adopted effective September 1, 2001. Amended effective September 1, 2011; renumbered CrRLJ 3.4(e) and amended, effective September 1, 2012; amended effective September 2, 2013.]

BTM–CrRLJ 4.1(a).   D.U.I. APPEARANCE—LOCAL WAIVER [RESCINDED]

[Formerly Rule 1, adopted effective September 1, 2000. Renumbered CrRLJ 4.1(a) and amended, effective September 1, 2012. Rescinded effective September 2, 2013.]

BTM–CrRLJ 4.5(a).   JURY CONFIRMATION

(i) Confirmation Required. No later than two (2) days prior to the date of the assigned jury trial, the defendant, if appearing pro se, or the defendant's attorney, if represented by legal counsel, and the City Prosecutor shall contact the Court Clerk between 9:00 a.m. and 3:00 p.m. and confirm the case is going to proceed to jury trial or that another disposition has been reached.

(ii) Failure to Confirm. Failure of a party to confirm the jury trial or to advise the Court Clerk that another disposition has been reached may cause the case to be stricken from the jury trial calendar. Failure of the defendant, if appearing pro se, or the defendant's attorney, if represented by legal counsel, to confirm the jury trial or to advise the Court Clerk that another disposition has been reached shall constitute an excluded period of the defendant's speedy trial rights pursuant to CrRLJ 3.3(e)(3).

(iii) Failure to Appear. Failure of the defendant to appear on the jury trial date may result in the issuance of a bench warrant for the defendant's arrest and forfeiture of any posted bail, unless a disposition has been confirmed by all parties. Any disposition will be heard on the next regularly scheduled court day unless an alternative date is set by the parties and

is approved by the judge, judge pro tem or court commissioner.

(iv) Sanctions. Any case confirmed for jury under this subsection and not proceeding to jury trial shall be subject to such sanctions, including but not limited to jury costs, witness fees and terms, as deemed appropriate by the trial judge.

[Formerly Rule 6, adopted effective September 1, 2010. Renumbered CrRLJ 4.5(a) and amended, effective September 1, 2012; amended effective September 2, 2013.]

LOCAL INFRACTION RULES

BTM–IRLJ 3.1(f). MOTIONS—CONTESTED INFRACTION HEARINGS

Motions challenging the authority of the Court, the constitutionality of the Court, the constitutionality of any statute, ordinance or court rule pertaining to an infraction, the authority of the prosecuting attorney prosecuting an infraction, and/or the authority of the law enforcement agency or officer filing an infraction must be made in writing. Such motions, together with citations to authority and argument, must be filed with the Court and served upon the opposing party no later than ten days prior to a contested infraction hearing. Such motions may be decided by the Court with or without oral argument, as the Court may determine.

[Formerly Rule 3, adopted effective September 1, 2000. Renumbered IRLJ 3.1(f) and amended, effective September 1, 2012; amended effective September 2, 2013.]

BTM–IRLJ 3.3(b). NOTICE OF APPEARANCE—CONTESTED INFRACTIONS [RESCINDED]

[Formerly Rule 2, adopted effective September 1, 2000. Renumbered IRLJ 3.3(b) and amended, effective September 1, 2012. Rescinded effective September 2, 2013.]

BTM–IRLJ 3.5. DECISION ON WRITTEN STATEMENTS

At the request of the respondent, the Court will conduct a mitigation hearing authorized by RCW 46.63.100 or consider a petition to defer a finding under RCW 46.63.070(5), or conduct a contested hearing authorized by RCW 46.63.090, upon the written statements of the City's witness(es) and the respondent, pursuant to IRLJ 3.5. A petition for a deferred finding which is denied by the Court will be treated as a request for a mitigation hearing on written statements.

[Formerly Rule 7, adopted effective September 1, 2010; renumbered IRLJ 3.5 and amended, effective September 1, 2012.]

BURIEN MUNICIPAL COURT—
[No Local Rules]

PUBLISHER'S NOTE

This municipal court follows the Local Rules of the District Court for King County.

CARNATION MUNICIPAL COURT—
[No Local Rules]

PUBLISHER'S NOTE

This municipal court follows the Local Rules of the District Court for King County.

COVINGTON MUNICIPAL COURT—
[No Local Rules]

PUBLISHER'S NOTE

This municipal court follows the Local Rules of the District Court for King County.

DES MOINES MUNICIPAL COURT LOCAL RULES

Including Amendments Received Through
August 15, 2015

Table of Rules

LOCAL CRIMINAL RULES

DMMCLR 1.0. ADOPTION OF LOCAL RULES

These rules are adopted pursuant to CrRLJ 1.7.

[Adopted effective July 1, 1998; Amended effective August 26, 2003.]

DMMCLR 2.0. TITLE OF RULES

These rules may be known and cited as the Des Moines Municipal Court Local Rules and shall be referred to as DMMCLR.

[Adopted effective July 1, 1998; amended effective August 26, 2003.]

DMMCLR 3.0. FILING OF PAPERS AND FORM OF PLEADINGS

(a) **Action Documents.** Pleadings or other papers requiring action on the part of the court or court clerk (other than file stamping, docketing and placing in the court file) shall be considered action documents. Action documents shall include a special caption directly below the case number on the first page, stating: "Clerk's Action Required". The action to be taken must be stated next to or directly beneath the special caption. The clerk will not search through letters, notices of appearance, requests for discovery, or other materials to locate possible requests for action items.

(b) **Format.** All pleadings and other papers shall include the following, unless otherwise authorized by the court:

(1) Service and Filing. Space should be provided at the top of the first page of a document allowing on the right half for the clerk's filing stamp, and in the left half for proof of, or acknowledgement of, service.

(2) Numbered Paper. All pleadings, motions, affidavits, briefs, and other supporting documents prepared by parties should be on paper with line numbering in the left hand margin.

(c) **Handling by Clerk.** All pleadings or other papers with proper caption and cause number will be date receipted, docketed and placed in the court file by the Clerk of the Municipal Court in the order received.

(d) Form of Pleadings. Pleadings in compliance with this rule shall be in substantially the following form:

SPACE FOR SERVICE   /   SPACE FOR COURT FILING
PROOF   /   STAMP
                                    /

<u>IN THE MUNICIPAL COURT FOR THE CITY OF DES MOINES,
KING COUNTY, STATE OF WASHINGTON</u>

City of Des Moines,)	CAUSE NO. XXXXXXXX
Plaintiff,)	
)	CLERK'S ACTION REQUIRED
)	(note action required here
)	or in first paragraph)
)	
vs.)	MOTION TO SET REVIEW
_____,)	
Defendant.)	

CLERK'S ACTION REQUIRED: (note action required here or in caption).

[Adopted effective September 1, 2004.]

DMMCLR 4.0. VIDEO CONFERENCE PROCEEDINGS

(a) Criminal. Preliminary appearances as defined by CrR 3.2(b) and CrRLJ 3.2.1(d), arraignments as defined by CrR 3.4 and 4.1 and CrRLJ 3.4 and 4.1, bail hearings as defined by CrR 3.2 and CrRLJ 3.2, and trial settings, as defined by CrR 3.3 and CrRLJ 3.3(f), conducted via video conference in which all participants can simultaneously see, hear, and speak as authorized by the Court, shall be deemed held in open court and in the defendant's presence for the purposes of any statute, court rule, or policy. All video conference hearings conducted pursuant to this rule shall be public, and the public shall be able to simultaneously see and hear all participants and speak as permitted by the trial court Judge. Any party may request an in-person hearing which may, in the Judge's discretion be granted.

(b) Agreement. Other trial court proceedings may be conducted by video conference only by agreement of the parties either in writing or on the record and upon the approval of the Judge.

(c) Standards for Video Conference Proceedings. The Judge, counsel, all parties, and the public attending the hearing must be able to see, hear, and speak as authorized by the Court during proceedings. Video conference facilities must provide for confidential communications between attorney and client and security sufficient to protect the safety of all participants and observers. In interpreted proceedings, the interpreter should be located next to the defendant, and the proceeding must be conducted to assure that the interpreter can hear all participants.

[Adopted effective September 1, 2004.]

DMMCLR 5.0. DECISION ON WRITTEN STATEMENTS

Mitigation and contested hearings based on sworn written statements, as provided in IRLJ 2.4(b)(4) and IRLJ 2.6 are authorized. The written statement(s) must be received by the Court no later than seven (7) calendar days before the scheduled hearing or it will not be considered.

[Adopted effective September 1, 2004.]

DMMCLR 6.0. PRESIDING JUDGE

(a) The Judge duly appointed as Judge of the Des Moines Municipal Court will be known as the Presiding Judge.

(b) The Presiding Judge shall be responsible for the efficient administration of the court. The Presiding Judge shall supervise the preparation and filing of all reports required by statute or rule and shall perform such other duties as may be prescribed by statute, ordinance or rule.

(c) The Presiding Judge shall direct the work of the Court Administrator who will have direct supervision over all administrative, non-judicial functions and all other court personnel except that the Presiding Judge shall directly supervise the Judge Pro–Tempore(s) and magistrate(s).

[Adopted effective September 1, 2004.]

DMMCLR 7.0. MAGISTRATES

The Court may employ judicial officers as magistrates, who shall serve at the pleasure of the Judge. Each must be appointed in accordance with RCW 35.20.200, 35.20.205, and the Des Moines Municipal Code as judge pro tempore. Magistrates shall hear infraction cases as provided by the infraction rules for courts of limited jurisdiction and RCW 46.63, or any law amendatory thereof. Magistrates shall also, perform such other duties as may be assigned to them by the judge.

[Adopted effective September 1, 2004.]

DMMCLR 8.0. REQUIREMENT FOR PAYMENT ON COURTESY WARRANT CALENDAR

A defendant who has been charged with a criminal violation and has an outstanding warrant in the Des Moines Municipal Court may requests to attend the courtesy warrant calendar Court costs shall be collected by the Des Moines Municipal court when the defendant appears in court and requests to appear on the courtesy warrant calendar.

[Adopted effective July 1, 1998; amended effective August 26, 2003.]

DMMCLR 9.0. TIME—ENLARGEMENT

Upon the non-appearance of a defendant at the time and place scheduled by the court and warrant of arrest issued, the defendant's bail or bond may be ordered forfeited with or without further proceedings upon motion of the City Attorney or upon the court's own motion. If the necessary witnesses do not appear at the time scheduled by the court, the court may dismiss such action unless a good cause for such non-appearance is shown. No such action shall be taken until fifteen (15) minutes after the scheduled appearance time.

[Adopted effective July 1, 1998.]

DMMCLR 10.0. EVIDENCE—COURTS CUSTODY OF EXHIBITS

In a criminal case every exhibit in the court's custody, which is not contraband and for which ownership is not in dispute, shall be returned to the party who produced that exhibit upon motion of that party and expiration of the appeal period. In the event of finding of guilty, for purpose of this rule, the appeal period shall begin on the day of sentencing or deferral of sentencing by the court. Exhibits not withdrawn shall be delivered by the court to the Des Moines Police Department for disposition as abandoned property; or if contraband, for destruction. No exhibit shall be released by the court without its being receipted for by the receiving person.

[Adopted effective July 1, 1998.]

DMMCLR 11.0. USE OF A COLLECTION AGENCY AND ASSESSMENT AS COURT COST OF AMOUNTS PAID FOR COLLECTION SERVICES

(a) The court shall use the services of a collection agency for the purposes of collecting unpaid and delinquent penalties on infractions, criminal fines, costs, assessments and forfeitures, on the terms and conditions of the contract for collection services between the City of Des Moines and said collection agency, and may be subsequently amended.

(b) The collection agency's fee or charge, as set forth in said contract, shall be added by the collection agency as a court cost to the total judgment of the court against each defendant whose account is referred by the court to the collection agency.

[Adopted effective July 1, 1998.]

DMMCLR 12.0. BAIL SCHEDULE

A Defendant who is detained in jail after the initial arrest for a misdemeanor or gross misdemeanor shall be released upon posting bail in the amount of $500 for a misdemeanor and $1,000 for a gross misdemeanor, except for the following offenses:

1. **Domestic Violence Offenses:** Defendants shall be held in non-bailable status pending hearing the next court day following booking for any crime alleging domestic violence under RCW 10.99.020(5) or applicable local ordinance.

2. **Driving Under the Influence/Physical Control:** Defendants shall be held in non-bailable status pending hearing the next court day following booking for Driving Under The Influence (RCW 46.61.502) or Physical Control of a Motor Vehicle While Under The Influence (RCW 46.61.504).]

3. **Prostitution Related Offenses:** Defendants shall be released upon posting bail in the amount of $1,000 for any prostitution related offense under RCW 9A.88.030, RCW 9A.88.090, or RCW 9A.88.110 or DMMC 9.76.040, DMMC 9.76.050 or DMMC 9.76.060

4. **Other Non–Bailable Offenses Pending First Court Appearance by Defendant:** Defendants shall be held in non-bailable status pending hearing the next court day following booking for these crimes:

(a) Assault in the fourth degree (RCW 9A.36.041)

(b) Harassment (RCW 9A.46.020)

(c) Violation of an anti-harassment order (RCW 9A.46.040)

(d) Stalking (RCW 9A.46.110)

(e) Communicating with a minor for immoral purposes (RCW 9.68A.090)]

[Adopted effective September 1, 2005; amended effective September 1, 2011.]

LOCAL INFRACTION RULES

DMMCLIR 1.0. SPEED MEASURING DEVICE: DESIGN AND CONSTRUCTION CERTIFICATION

Any person who requests production of an electronic speed measuring device expert, and who is thereafter found by the court to have committed by the infraction, shall be required to pay the fee charged by the expert as a cost incurred by that party, as provided in RCW 46.63.151.

[Adopted effective July 1, 1998.]

DMMCLIR 2.0. REQUIREMENTS FOR PAYMENT FOLLOWING INFRACTION HEARINGS

(a) If a defendant who has been charged with a traffic or other infraction filed with the Des Moines Municipal Court is found to have committed that infraction, the defendant shall make payment in full of the amount of the penalty at the time of the hearing in which the defendant was found to have committed the infraction. The court may reduce a fine penalty amount only upon a showing of exceptional circumstances.

(b) Time payments on infractions will be permitted upon court order, at the time of the hearing on the contested infraction. The court's decision to authorize time payments in infraction cases shall be subject to the conditions set at the time of the order authorizing time payments.

(c) Failure to make payment on the penalties on the committed infractions shall be enforceable pursuant to otherwise applicable court rules, state law or administrative code regulations.

[Adopted effective September 1, 2004.]

DMMCLIR 3.0. INFRACTION— PREHEARING CONFERENCE

(a) Prehearing Conference Required—Waiver. A person cited with an infraction who requests a hearing to contest the infraction shall first appear at a prehearing conference. The prehearing conference shall be scheduled in accordance with the provisions of IRLJ 2.6(a)(1). The requirement that the person appear at the prehearing conference may be waived, in writing, provided the waiver is received by the court before the time set for the prehearing conference. If the defendant fails to timely waive or appear at the prehearing conference, a default judgment shall be entered.

(b) Setting Contested Hearing. If the infractions are not resolved following the prehearing conference, a contested hearing shall be scheduled for not more than ninety (90) days from the date of the prehearing conference. If the prehearing conference is waived, a contested hearing shall be scheduled for not more than ninety (90) days from the date the waiver of the prehearing conference is received by the court.

(c) Prehearing Motions For Contested Infractions—Written Notice Required. All motions to exclude evidence or dismiss an infraction shall be filed no later than the conclusion of the prehearing conference. If a defendant elects to waive his or her appearance at the prehearing conference, any motion must be noted on the waiver form filed with the court pursuant to DMMCLIR 3.0(a). A motion(s) not timely filed shall be waived and shall not be considered by the court. Motions timely noted shall be addressed by the court at the time of the contested hearing.

[Adopted on an emergency basis effective January 12, 2006; re-adopted on an emergency basis effective July 12, 2006; October 12, 2006; January 12, 2007; April 12, 2007; re-adopted on a permanent basis effective September 1, 2007.]

DUVALL MUNICIPAL COURT—
[No Local Rules]

PUBLISHER'S NOTE

This municipal court follows the Local Rules of the District Court for King County.

ENUMCLAW MUNICIPAL COURT LOCAL RULES

Including Amendments Received Through
August 15, 2015

Table of Rules

INTRODUCTION/ADOPTION

These Local Rules have been adopted under the provisions of General Rule 7, (GR 7), promulgated by the Washington State Supreme Court. The numbering used in these Local Rules conforms to the numbering system and format of the Administrative Rules for Courts of Limited Jurisdiction (ARLJ), Criminal Rules for Courts of Limited Jurisdiction (CrRLJ), and Infraction Rules for Courts of Limited Jurisdiction (IRLJ), which are in effect as of the adoption of these Local Rules.

[Adopted effective September 1, 2012.]

COURTROOM PRACTICE AND PROFESSIONALISM

As a proud member of the legal profession, the Court endorses the following principles of civil-professional-conduct:

1. In dealing with attorneys, parties, witnesses, members of the bench, and court staff; all parties shall be civil, courteous, and guided by the fundamental tenets of integrity and fairness.

2. Your word is your bond in dealing with the Court, fellow counsel, and others.

3. Endeavor to resolve differences through cooperation and negotiation, giving due consideration to alternative dispute resolution.

4. Honor appointments, commitments, and case schedules. Be timely in all communications.

5. Design the timing, manner of service, and scheduling of hearings only for proper purposes. The objective should never be to oppress or inconvenience the opponent.

6. Conduct yourself professionally during negotiations, depositions, and any other interaction with opposing counsel or a witness as if you were in the presence of a judge.

7. Be forthright and honest in dealing with the Court, opposing counsel, and others.

8. Be respectful of the Court, the legal profession, and the litigation process in attire and demeanor.

9. As an officer of the Court, as an advocate, and as an attorney; uphold the honor and dignity of the Court and of the legal profession. Strive always to instill and encourage a respectful attitude toward the Court, the litigation process, and the legal profession.

[Adopted effective September 1, 2012.]

GENERAL RULES

EMCLGR 1. APPLICATION

These Rules apply only to the Enumclaw Municipal Court.

[Adopted effective September 1, 2012.]

EMCLGR 2. COURT BUSINESS HOURS/JUDICIAL DAYS

The Enumclaw Municipal Court shall be open to the public for business Monday through Friday from 9:00 a.m. to 5:00 p.m. excluding holidays scheduled by the Washington State Supreme Court and closures ordered by the Presiding Judge when necessitated by union contract, inclement weather, or the oversight of the Court.

Judicial days shall be defined as Tuesday each week. Jury Trials shall be held the third Friday of each month. The Presiding Judge has the discretion to use Monday of any week as a "judicial day" when necessary in the oversight of the Court.

[Formerly EMCLR 1.4 adopted effective September 1, 1999; renumbered EMCLGR 2 and amended, effective September 1, 2012.]

EMCLGR 3. PLEADINGS

Every paper presented to the Judge for signature or delivered to the Court for filing shall be a clearly readable original and shall include:

(a) number and title of case,

(b) designation of what the paper purports to be, and

(c) name, original signature, office address, office telephone number, and WSBA number of counsel.

(d) Pleadings or any other document requesting action by the Court or its clerk, (other than confirming receipt and placing in the court file) shall be considered action documents. Action documents shall include a separate caption directly below the cause number on the first page, in the following form:

CLERK'S ACTION REQUIRED:

(Specify the action(s) requested)

Except to take the action(s) specifically captioned, the court clerk will not otherwise inspect any pleading or document for any request for action.

[Adopted effective September 1, 2012.]

EMCLGR 4. JURY INSTRUCTIONS

Where a jury is to be instructed in writing, proposed "non-WPIC" instructions shall be submitted on plain paper with no identifying mark. The original, without citations of authority and one copy with citations of authority shall be submitted to the Court at the Readiness Hearing.

[Adopted effective September 1, 2012.]

EMCLGR 5. FAX TRANSMISSIONS

(A)(1) Except as set forth in subsection (a)(5) of GR 17, the clerks of the Court may accept for filing documents sent directly to the clerk or to another by electronic facsimile (fax) transmission. The original shall replace a fax copy within five (5) working days. Documents to be transmitted by fax shall bear the notation: "SENT ON (date) VIA FAX FOR FILING IN ENUMCLAW MUNICIPAL COURT".

[Adopted effective September 1, 2012.]

ADMINISTRATIVE RULES

EMCAR 1. COMMISSIONERS

(A) The Court may employ judicial officers as commissioners, who shall serve at the pleasure of the Presiding Judge.

(B) Each must be appointed in accordance with RCW 35.20.205 and the Enumclaw Municipal Code as judge pro tempore.

(C) Commissioners may hear infraction cases as provided by the infraction rules for courts of limited jurisdiction and RCW 46.63, or any amendatory law thereof. Commissioners may also perform such other duties as may be assigned by the Presiding Judge.

[Adopted effective September 1, 2012.]

EMCAR 2. SCOPE OF RULES

(A) Operating and administrative policies and procedures of the Enumclaw Municipal court shall be in accordance with these Local Rules adopted pursuant to GR 7, CrRLJ 1.7, and IRLJ 1.3.

(B) In the absence of a rule governing a particular policy or procedure, the Presiding Judge shall resolve the issue pending the establishment of a local rule.

[Adopted effective September 1, 2012.]

CRIMINAL RULES

EMCCrR 3.1. RELEASE OF ACCUSED

(A) Delay of Release. (1) Bail shall not be set for a person arrested and booked into jail for violation of RCW 46.61.502, 503, 504, or RCW 46.25.110 unless set by a judge telephonically at the time of arrest or at a preliminary appearance, arraignment, or subsequent court appearance. A person arrested and released for a violation of RCW 46.61.502, 503, 504, or RCW 46.25.110 shall be required to appear before a judge pursuant to RCW 46.61.5051 the next judicial day following the arrest. Appearances are mandatory and may not be waived by the appearance of an attorney. (2) Bail shall not be set for a person arrested and booked into jail for a domestic violence offense unless set by a judge telephonically at the time of arrest or at a preliminary appearance, arraignment, or subsequent court appearance. In matters where a person is arrested and released for a domestic violence offense prior to appearing before a judge for arraignment, bail hearing, or any other hearing where conditions of release may be set; there shall be a No Contact Order imposed as a condition of release from custody prohibiting the arrested person from having any contact with the alleged victim involved in the incident and from having any contact with the alleged victim's residence, place of employment, or any other place where the alleged victim may be found or believed to be. Said No Contact Order shall remain effective until the next judicial day when the arrested, cited, and released person shall be required to appear before a judge OR fourteen (14) days if the arrested person is released, but not cited. Appearances are mandatory and may not be waived by the appearance of an attorney. "Domestic Violence" includes, but is not limited to, any misdemeanor or gross misdemeanor offenses listed in RCW 10.99.020(3) or similar municipal ordinance when committed by one family or household member against another. "Family or household members" are those persons listed in RCW 10.99.020(1) or similar municipal ordinance. (3) Bail as set forth in this Rule or any similar rule or order shall be available to those accused that have provided sufficient information to establish a positive and verifiable identity and home address. Absent such information, no bail may be accepted until established by the Court.

(B) Bail. When required to reasonably assure appearance in court, the Court shall follow the bail schedule set forth in the Enumclaw Municipal Court Uniform Bail Schedule, as may be amended, modified, and filed periodically by the Court for use by the Enumclaw Police Department.

[Adopted effective September 1, 2012.]

EMCCrR 3.2. PLEAS

Deferred Prosecution. A written petition shall be filed at the time the defendant moves the Court to grant a deferred prosecution under RCW 10.05 and an order approving the deferred prosecution. A copy of the documents required by this rule will be made available upon request. Said documents may be submitted in the original form provided by the Court or may be reprinted and submitted in substantially the same form. All substantive revisions to these forms must be made known to the Court at the hearing when presented.

[Adopted effective September 1, 2012.]

EMCCrR 3.3. PRETRIAL HEARINGS

(A) Pretrial. When a plea of "not guilty" is entered, the Court shall schedule a pretrial hearing. The prosecuting authority, the defendant, and the defendant's attorney (if any) shall attend the pretrial hearing. Failure of the defendant to appear may result in the issuance of a bench warrant.

(B) Readiness Hearing. A readiness hearing shall be set prior to the trial date. All parties mentioned above shall appear unless waived in the pretrial order. Failure of the defendant to appear when required shall cause the trial date to be stricken and the issuance of a bench warrant.

(C) Telephonic Communications. Pretrial hearings may be conducted by telephonic conference call at the request of either party once approved by the Court.

[Adopted effective September 1, 2012.]

EMCCrR 3.4. TRIAL BY JURY

(A) Any case confirmed for jury trial at the readiness hearing shall remain set for a jury trial. On the last regular court day preceding the trial date, the prosecuting authority and defense attorney or defendant, if appearing pro se, shall confirm the jury trial telephonically to the clerk of the court before 3 p.m., or advise that some other disposition has been reached. Failure to confirm the jury trial as required shall be deemed a waiver of the right to a jury trial, cause the jury to be stricken, and the matter set before the bench. If the failure to confirm the jury trial is on behalf of the defendant and the defendant requests that the case be reset before a jury, then the defendant is deemed to have extended the time for trial to the date next scheduled for jury trial.

(B) Any case confirmed as a jury trial and not proceeding to a jury trial, whether by entry of a plea or otherwise, shall be subject to terms, including costs for the unused jury, witness fees, and other terms deemed appropriate by the Court.

[Adopted effective September 1, 2012.]

INFRACTION RULES

EMCIR 1. PROCEDURE AT CONTESTED HEARING

At a contested hearing, the City may elect to be present at the hearing or the City may waive its presence. The respondent may be represented by an attorney.

No attorney shall appear for a respondent without first filing a Notice of Appearance no less than two (2) days prior to any scheduled hearing. Upon the filing of a Notice of Appearance, the Court shall schedule the contested hearing on a date available to both parties.

[Formerly EMLIR 3.3, adopted on an emergency basis, effective March 1, 2011; renumbered EMCIR 1 and amended on a permanent basis, effective September 1, 2012.]

EMCIR 2. DECISION ON WRITTEN STATEMENT

(A) Generally. The Court shall examine the citing officer's report and any statement submitted by the respondent. The examination shall take place within 120 days after the respondent has filed a response to the notice of infraction. The examination may be held in chambers and shall not be governed by the Rules of Evidence.

(B) Factual Determination. The Court shall determine whether the plaintiff has proved by a preponderance of all evidence submitted that the respondent has committed the infraction if contested.

(C) Disposition. If the Court determines that the infraction has been committed, it may assess a penalty in accordance with IRLJ 3.3. If the Court defers a finding for a specified period of time on certain conditions, it may assess an administrative fee to process the infraction notice.

(D) Notice to Parties. The Court shall notify the parties in writing whether the infraction was found to be committed, deferred, or dismissed and what penalty or administrative fee, if any, was imposed.

(E) The court administrator and/or court clerks shall have the authority to resolve "Failure to Provide Proof of Insurance" infractions at the court office window as follows: a) If respondent had insurance in force on the day the citation was issued, and the respondent provides such proof to the court staff member, the court staff member shall copy the proof of insurance verification which shall be attached to the infraction, and the case will be dismissed upon payment of a $25.00 fee to cover administrative costs. (b) If respondent did not have insurance of the date of the citation, but has now obtained insurance, the citation will be entered as "committed" but the court staff member shall reduce the fine from $550.00 to $250.00. The court staff member shall copy the proof of insurance verification, shall enter the appropriate decision on each ticket, enter the monetary amount due by respondent, and sign and date the ticket.

(F) No Appeal Permitted. There shall be no appeal from a decision made upon written statements.

[Formerly EMLIR 3.5, adopted on an emergency basis, effective March 1, 2011; renumbered EMCIR 2 and amended on a permanent basis, effective September 1, 2012.]

FEDERAL WAY MUNICIPAL COURT LOCAL RULES

Including Amendments Received Through
August 15, 2015

Table of Rules

LOCAL ADMINISTRATIVE RULES

FWMCLAR 2. SCOPE OF RULES PHOTO ENFORCEMENT

Unless otherwise provided, all Infraction Rules for Courts of Limited Jurisdiction (IRLJ) and all local infraction rules (FWMCLIR) apply to photo enforcement proceedings. Subject to supervision and control of the court, the court may delegate administrative functions, filing of Notices of Infraction, docketing of cases, and collection of fines generated by Notices of Infraction issued under RCW 46.63.170 to a third party vendor.

[Adopted effective September 1, 2011.]

FWMCLAR 11. MISDEMEANANT PROBATION

The court provides probation services pursuant to ARLJ 11 through a contract with a third-party vendor.

[Adopted effective September 1, 2010; amended effective September 1, 2011.]

FWMCLAR 12. REGISTRATION BY COURTS OF LIMITED JURISDICTION COURT BUSINESS HOURS

The Federal Way Municipal Court shall be open to the public for business from 8:30 a.m. to 4:30 p.m. Monday through Friday of each week except for Holidays scheduled by Order of the State of Washington Supreme Court or the Federal Way Municipal Court Presiding Judge.

[Adopted effective September 1, 2010. Amended effective September 2, 2013.]

LOCAL GENERAL RULES

FWMCLGR 30. ELECTRONIC FILING AND ELECTRONIC SIGNATURES

(b)(1) While JIS remains the official depository of case information, the court uses Justice Web in conjunction with Just Ware as a means to facilitate electronic filing of documents and data. Attorneys, defendants, and other involved parties are allowed to set up password protected accounts in Justice Web that will allow for the transmission of data and documents to the court and to the parties as provided in (b)(3). Permissions are given based upon the profile of the user and such permission is restricted to cases in which the user is involved. The court may choose to update data in Just Ware/Justice Web from other sources to maintain consistency with JIS data, but it is the primary responsibility of the account holder to keep all personal contact data in the account updated and accurate.

(b)(3) Attorneys with Justice Web accounts will receive all documents from the court in electronic format in Justice Web. Defendants or other involved parties with a JusticeWeb account may elect to receive documents electronically by setting up an account in JusticeWeb and choosing the option to receive documents in electronic format. The court may simply notify recipients to log into their JusticeWeb account to access the document(s). The court, as a convenience, may send reminder notifications of court dates, but failure to receive such a notification shall not relieve the recipient of the obligation to appear or respond as required. It is the responsibility of all parties to maintain current electronic mailbox addresses and memory sufficient to receive electronic transmissions or notifications from the court.

(b)(4) The court will not deny paper filings, but strongly encourages the creation of JusticeWeb accounts pursuant to (b)(1) and (b)(3) once such accounts become available.

> **Comment:** It is anticipated that JusticeWeb accounts will be available as of October 15, 2015. The court anticipates making efiling mandatory effective September 1, 2016.

(d)(1)(A) See (b)(1)

(d)(2)(A) *Judicial Electronic Signatures*: Judicial officers may also sign orders and search warrants with a digital signature as defined in GR 30 in one of the following formats:

i. The judicial officer affixes the electronic signature, saves the signed document in .pdf format, and emails the document to the intended recipients using the judge's secure email account; or,

ii. The judicial officer affixes the electronic signature in the body of an email using the judge's secure email account; or,

iii. The judicial officer instructs the officer via secured email to affix the judge's signature to the search warrant; or,

iv. The judicial officer uses any other reliable means approved by the court by general order.

Documents may be signed by judicial officers using a facsimile of the judicial officer's signature so long as the original facsimile of the signature used in the document is only accessible by the judicial officer.

The document or email may also be signed in the following format if the document or email is sent from the judge's secure email account:

Judge X

Federal Way Municipal Court

33325 8th Avenue South

Federal Way, WA 98003

Telephone: (253) 835–3000

Fax: (253) 835–3020

E–mail: First.Last@cityoffederalway.com

The printed version of the document signed by the judge pursuant to this rule shall constitute an original document that shall be made part of the court file or search warrant return file.

Nothing herein alters the ability of the judge to sign documents in person or delegate the affixing of signatures by others if allowed by law or court rule.

(d)(2)(D)(i) Speed Measuring Device Certifications will be deemed filed with the court pursuant to IRLJ 6.6(b) at the time the document is added by the prosecutor's office to a secure website that allows the documents to be viewed by the public through a hyperlink on the court's website.

(d)(2)(D)(ii) The electronic signature of the officer applied to a Notice of Infraction pursuant to FWMCLIR 2.2 is presumed to be under penalty of perjury.

[Adopted effective September 1, 2012. Amended effective September 2, 2013; September 2, 2014; September 1, 2015.]

LOCAL CRIMINAL RULES

FWMCLR 1.　ADOPTION OF LOCAL RULES

These rules are adopted pursuant to GR 7, CrRLJ 1.7 and IRLJ 1.3.

[Adopted effective April 3, 2000; renumbered from FMCLR 1.7 effective September 1, 2007.]

FWMCLR 1.8.　TITLE OF RULES

These rules may be known and cited as the Federal Way Municipal Court Local Criminal Rules and shall be referred to as FWMCLR.

[Adopted effective September 1, 2010.]

FWMCLR 2.　TITLE OF RULES

These rules may be known and cited as the *Federal Way Municipal Court Local Rules* and *Federal Way Municipal Court Local Infraction Rules* and shall be referred to as FMCLR and FMCLIR.

[Adopted effective April 3, 2000; renumbered from FMCLR 1.8 effective September 1, 2007.]

FWMCLR 2.3.　APPLICATIONS FOR SEARCH WARRANTS IN ELECTRONIC FORMAT

(c) Sworn testimony provided by a police officer for a search warrant may be provided to the judge by electronic means by email or other reliable means if the sworn statement is signed under penalty of perjury pursuant to GR 30(2)(D)(ii).

[Adopted effective September 2, 2014.]

FWMCLR 3.　COURT BUSINESS HOURS

The Federal Way Municipal Court shall be open to the public for business from 8:30 AM to 12:00 PM and 1:00 PM to 4:30 PM Monday through Friday of each week except for holidays scheduled by Order of the State of Washington Supreme Court or the Federal Way Municipal Court Presiding Judge.

[Adopted effective April 3, 2000; renumbered from FMCLR 1.9 and amended effective September 1, 2007.]

FWMCLR 3.2.　RELEASE OF ACCUSED BAIL SCHEDULE

The court adopts the following bail schedule pursuant to CrRLJ 3.2(b)(7) and CrRLJ 3.2(o):

A Defendant who is booked and detained in jail after the initial arrest for a misdemeanor or gross misdemeanor shall be released upon promising to appear in court and posting bail in the amount of $500 for a misdemeanor and $1,000 for a gross misdemeanor, except for the following offenses:

1. Domestic Violence Offenses: Defendants booked and detained in jail after the initial arrest shall be held in non-bailable status pending hearing the next court day following booking for any crime alleging domestic violence under RCW 10.99.020(5) or domestic violence violations alleged under FWRC 6.35.070 and/or FWRC 6.35.090.

2. Driving Under the Influence/Physical Control: Defendants booked and detained in jail after the initial arrest shall be held in non-bailable status pending hearing the next court day following booking for Driving Under The Influence pursuant to RCW 46.61.502 or Physical Control of a Motor Vehicle While Under The Influence pursuant to RCW 46.61.504.

3. Other Crimes: Defendants booked and detained in jail after the initial arrest shall be held in non-bailable status pending hearing the next court day for the following crimes:

(a) Assault in the fourth degree—RCW 9A.36.041

(b) Harassment—RCW 9A.46.020

(c) Violation of an anti-harassment order—RCW 9A.46.040 and FWRC 6.35.060

(d) Stalking—RCW 9A.46.110

(e) Communicating with a minor for immoral purposes—RCW 9.68A.090

(f) Indecent Exposure—RCW 9A.88.010

(g) Aiming or Discharge of a Firearm—RCW 9.41.230

(h) Loaded Firearm in a Vehicle—RCW 9.41.050(2)

(i) Unloaded Firearm in a Vehicle—RCW 9.41.050.1A

(j) Altering a Firearm—RCW 9.41.140

(k) Carrying Concealed Pistol w/o a license in Vehicle—RCW 9.41.050(2)(a)

(*l*) Carrying Concealed Pistol w/o a license on Person—RCW 9.41.050(1)(a)

(m) Leaving Unloaded Pistol in Vehicle—RCW 9.41.050(3)(a)

(n) Unlawful Carrying or Display of Weapons—RCW 9.41.270

(o) Weapons in a Prohibited Area—RCW 9.41.300

(p) Weapons in a Prohibited Area—Court—RCW 9.41.300

(q) Possession of Dangerous Weapon—RCW 9.41.250

(r) Possession of Dangerous Weapon—School—RCW 9.41.280

(s) Malicious Mischief in the third degree—RCW 9A.48.090

(t) Menacing—FWRC 6.35.020

(u) Firearm on Liquor Sale Premises—FWRC 6.25.030

(v) Firearm in Restricted Area—FWRC 6.25.040

(w) Discharge of firearms prohibited—FWRC 6.25.050

(x) Firearm in Park—FWRC 4.05.220, 4.05.040

[Adopted effective September 1, 2011.]

FWMCLR 3.4. PRESENCE OF THE DEFENDANT—VIDEO CONFERENCE HEARINGS

All in-custody arraignments, bail hearings, and trial settings will be conducted via video conference pursuant to CrRLJ 3.4. Consent to proceed via video conference will be implied for all other hearings, excluding trial, unless an objection is made before or during the hearing to proceeding in this manner. However, this consent will not be implied if the defendant is not accompanied or represented by counsel at the hearing. A defendant who is not accompanied or represented by counsel must affirmatively give consent on the record to proceed via video conference.

[Adopted effective September 1, 2010; amended effective September 1, 2012.]

FWMCLR 4. COMMISSIONERS

The Court may employ judicial officers as commissioners, who shall serve at the pleasure of the Presiding Judge. A commissioner shall be appointed in accordance with RCW 3.50.075 and Federal Way Municipal Ordinance 99–339, section 2–311. Commissioners shall perform such other duties and hear matters as may be assigned to them by the Presiding Judge of the Court.

[Adopted effective April 3, 2000; renumbered from FMCLR 2.4 and amended effective September 1, 2007.]

FWMCLR 4.1. ARRAIGNMENT— MANDATORY APPEARANCES AND CONTINUANCES

a. Continuances: If a defendant requests a continuance of his or her arraignment date in person for crimes not specified in subsection (e) of this local rule, the Clerk is authorized to continue and reset the arraignment to a date not later than seven (7) days after the date on which the arraignment was initially set. This continuance may be granted by the Clerk if the defendant signs a notice and promise to appear for the new arraignment date and waives any objection to the later arraignment date in writing.

g. Mandatory Appearance: Defendant's appearance is mandatory and may not be waived or continued in cases involving alleged Driving Under the Influence, Physical Control, any crime alleging domestic violence, or any of the following crimes:

(1) Assault in the fourth degree—RCW 9A.36.041

(2) Harassment—RCW 9A.46.020

(3) Violation of an anti-harassment order—RCW 9A.46.040 and FWRC 6.35.060

(4) Stalking—RCW 9A.46.110

(5) Communicating with a minor for immoral purposes—RCW 9.68A.090

(6) Indecent Exposure—RCW 9A.88.010

(7) Aiming or Discharge of a Firearm—RCW 9.41.230

(8) Loaded Firearm in a Vehicle—RCW 9.41.050(2)

(9) Unloaded Firearm in a Vehicle—RCW 9.41.050.1A

(10) Altering a Firearm—RCW 9.41.140

(11) Carrying Concealed Pistol w/o a license in Vehicle—RCW 9.41.050(2)(a)

(12) Carrying Concealed Pistol w/o a license on Person—RCW 9.41.050(1)(a)

(13) Leaving Unloaded Pistol in Vehicle—RCW 9.41.050(3)(a)

(14) Unlawful Carrying or Display of Weapons—RCW 9.41.270

(15) Weapons in a Prohibited Area—RCW 9.41.300

(16) Weapons in a Prohibited Area—Court—RCW 9.41.300

(17) Possession of Dangerous Weapon—RCW 9.41.250

(18) Possession of Dangerous Weapon—School—RCW 9.41.280

(19) Malicious Mischief in the third degree—RCW 9A.48.090

(20) Menacing—FWRC 6.35.020

(21) Firearm on Liquor Sale Premises—FWRC 6.25.030

(22) Firearm in Restricted Area—FWRC 6.25.040

(23) Discharge of firearms prohibited—FWRC 6.25.050

(24) Firearm in Park—FWRC 4.05.220, 4.05.040

[Adopted effective September 1, 2010. Amended effective September 1, 2011; September 2, 2013.]

FWMCLR 5. FILING OF PAPERS AND FORM OF PLEADINGS

(a) **Action Documents.** Pleadings or other papers requiring action on the part of the court or court clerk (other than file stamping, docketing and placing in the court file) shall be considered action documents. Action documents shall include a special caption directly below the case number on the first page, stating: "Clerk's Action Required". The action to be taken must be stated next to or directly beneath the special caption. The clerk will not search through letters, notices of appearance, requests for discovery, or other materials to locate possible requests for action items.

(b) **Format.** All pleadings and other papers shall include the following, unless otherwise authorized by the court:

(1) *Service and Filing.* Space should be provided at the top of the first page of a document allowing on the right half for the clerk's filing stamp, and in the left half for proof of, or acknowledgement of, service.

(2) *Numbered Paper.* All pleadings, motions, affidavits, briefs, and other supporting documents prepared by parties should be on paper with line numbering in the left hand margin.

(c) **Handling by Clerk.** All pleadings or other papers with proper caption and cause number will be date receipted, docketed and placed in the court file by the Clerk of the Municipal Court in the order received. Provided, however, parties may file pleadings in the lockbox at the clerk's window, but must date stamp the original of any such documents using the stamp provided by the court and place the pleadings in the box by no later than 4:30 p.m. to be counted as filed on that day. The clerk shall correct any mis-stamped documents.

(d) **Form of Pleadings.** Pleadings in compliance with this rule shall be in substantially the following form:

SPACE FOR SERVICE/SPACE FOR COURT PROOF/FILING STAMP

IN THE MUNICIPAL COURT FOR
THE CITY OF FEDERAL WAY
KING COUNTY, STATE OF WASHINGTON

City of Federal Way,	)	
	)	CAUSE NO. XXXXX
Plaintiff,	)	
	)	CLERK'S ACTION REQUIRED
	)	(note action required here or
	)	in first paragraph)
	)	
vs.	)	
	)	MOTION TO SET FOR REVIEW

_____,)
Defendant   )

CLERK'S ACTION REQUIRED: (note action required here or in caption).

[Adopted effective September 1, 2007; amended effective September 1, 2008.]

FWMCLR 6.   PRE–TRIAL HEARINGS

A. Unless otherwise ordered by the Court in a specific case for good cause, all cases in which a defendant enters a plea of not guilty should be set for a pre-trial hearing. The defendant shall be required to attend all hearings unless excused by the Court.

B. The first pre-trial hearing set on a case will be continued upon an agreed motion of the parties. The clerk is authorized to approve such orders, enter the agreed upon date in the record, and add such matters to the docket as requested in the agreed order. The clerk can decline the proposed date if they determine that there is sufficient court congestion to warrant selection of another date.

[Adopted effective April 3, 2000; amended effective September 1, 2005; renumbered from FMCLR 3.1 and amended effective September 1, 2007; amended effective September 1, 2008.]

FWMCLR 6.15.   JURY INSTRUCTIONS

(a) Jury instructions shall be provided as follows:

(1) The parties shall exchange a full set of cited and numbered proposed instructions on the day of trial and file a copy of the cited and numbered proposed instructions with the court. In addition, each party shall provide the judge with one set of unnumbered and uncited instructions in the same sequential order as the cited and numbered proposed instructions filed with the court. The unnumbered and uncited instructions may be provided to the judge in Word electronic format in lieu of a hard copy.

(2) *Numbering and Arrangement of Cited and Numbered Instructions.* On the cited and numbered copy of instructions filed with the court the citations shall be in the lower left-hand corner. The instructions shall be arranged in a logical order and numbered sequentially by the submitting party at the top center of each page (Example: "Instruction No. 1" would be at the top center of the first proposed instruction, "Instruction No. 2" would be at the top center of the second proposed instruction, and so forth).

[Adopted effective September 2, 2013.]

FWMCLR 7.   BAIL

Federal Way Municipal Court will follow the bail schedule set forth in Washington Court Rule CrRLJ 3.2 and the Federal Way City Code (FWCC).

[Adopted effective September 1, 2005; renumbered from FMCLR 3.20 effective September 1, 2007.]

FWMCLR 7.3.   JUDGMENT— COSTS/ASSESSMENTS/COLLECTION

The Court may require partial or full reimbursement for the cost of court appointed counsel, interpreters, booking fees, warrant fees, jury fees, conviction fees, and all other costs and assessments allowed by law.

The Court may use the services of a collection agency for the purposes of collecting unpaid and delinquent criminal fines, costs, assessments and forfeitures. The terms and conditions of the contract for collection services shall be between the Federal Way Municipal Court, the City, and said collection agency, and may be amended as necessary.

The collection agency's fee or charge, as set forth in said contract, shall be added by the collection agency as a Court cost to the total judgment of the Court against each Defendant whose account is referred by the Court to the collection agency.

Nothing in this section shall prevent the Court from notifying the Department of Licensing of the defendant's failure to pay a fine and/or costs as ordered by the Court.

[Adopted effective September 1, 2010.]

FWMCLR 8.   RECALL NO CONTACT ORDERS

When a case is dismissed, any No Contact Order shall be recalled.

[Adopted effective September 1, 2002; renumbered from FMCLR 3.23 effective September 1, 2007.]

FWMCLR 8.2.   MOTIONS

a. Time for Hearing. Motions shall be filed and served as follows:

1. *Motion Requested at Time of Trial Setting:* If a motion date is set at the same time the case is set for trial then the moving party's brief and all supporting documents shall be served on the opposing party and filed with the court at least 14 days before the date scheduled for the hearing.

2. *Motion Requested at Time Other than at Trial Setting:* If a motion is filed at any other time by either party, the moving party must file a note for motion, the moving party's brief, and all supporting documents at the time the motion is filed. The note for motion and supporting documents shall be served and filed with the court at least 21 days before the date requested for the hearing by the moving party.

b. Responsive Documents. The non-moving party's brief and all supporting documents shall be served and filed at least 7 days before the date scheduled for the hearing. The moving party's reply and all supporting documents shall be served and filed at least 2 days before the date scheduled for the hearing.

c. Proof of Service. The parties must file suitable proof showing that the opposing party was served with the documents filed by the party.

[Adopted effective September 1, 2010.]

FWMCLR 8.4. SIGNING OF AGREED ORDERS

(a) Counsel seeking the approval of an agreed order by the court shall obtain the signature of opposing counsel before filing the order with the court. The court may deny the motion if the document is filed without the signature of opposing counsel. "Signature" includes electronic signatures in compliance with GR 30.

[Adopted effective September 2, 2014.]

FWMCLR 9. EVIDENCE—COURTS CUSTODY OF EXHIBITS

In a criminal case every exhibit in the court's custody, which is not contraband and for which ownership is not in dispute, shall be returned to the party who produced that exhibit upon motion of that party and expiration of the appeal period. In the event of finding of guilty, for purpose of this rule, the appeal period shall begin on the day of sentencing or deferral of sentencing by the court. Exhibits not withdrawn shall be delivered by the court to the Federal Way Police Department for disposition as abandoned property; or if contraband, for destruction. No exhibit shall be released by the court without its being receipted for by the receiving person.

[Adopted effective September 1, 2007.]

FWMCLR 10. AUTHORIZATION FOR CONTINUANCE OF ARRAIGNMENTS

If a defendant requests a continuance of his or her arraignment date in person, the Clerk of the Court is authorized to continue and reset the arraignment to a date not later than seven (7) days after the date on which the arraignment was initially set, without the matter needing to come before the Court in open session to consider the request for a continuance of the arraignment, on the condition that the defendant shall sign a notice of the new arraignment date.

This authorization for continuance of arraignment shall not apply to cases involving alleged DUI, Physical Control, or any crime of Domestic Violence.

[Adopted effective April 3, 2000; renumbered from FMCLR 3.3 and amended effective September 1, 2007.]

FWMCLR 11. CONTINUANCE OF ARRAIGNMENT

Pursuant to RCW 46.61.50571, the arraignment and the appearance of a defendant charged under RCW 46.61.502, 503 and 504 may be moved by the clerk from the judicial day following service of the citation to the next regularly scheduled arraignment calendar if such a change is requested in writing by the defendant.

[Adopted effective April 3, 2000; renumbered from FMCLR 3.4 and amended effective September 1, 2007; rescinded and renamed effective September 1, 2008.]

FWMCLR 12. ARRAIGNMENT

Arraignment: A lawyer may, pursuant to CrRLJ 4.1, enter an appearance on behalf of a client and waive arraignment except charges involving DUI, Physical Control, or any Domestic Violence offense, whereupon the defendant's presence is mandatory and cannot be waived.

[Adopted effective April 3, 2000; renumbered from FMCLR 4.1 and amended effective September 1, 2007; renumbered from FWMCLR 13 and amended effective September 1, 2008.]

FWMCLR 13. CONFIRMATION OF MOTIONS

For any motion set pursuant to CrRLJ 3.5 and 3.6, the moving party shall notify the non-moving party by 4:30 PM, two business days before the day the Motion is set for, that the moving party intends to proceed with their motion. If the non-moving party does not receive confirmation that the motion will be heard on the day it is set for, the non-moving party may advise its witnesses that they do not need to appear for that hearing.

[Adopted effective September 1, 2005; renumbered from FMCLR 3.7 and amended effective September 1, 2007; renumbered from FWMCLR 12 effective September 1, 2008.]

FWMCLR 14. USE OF A COLLECTION AGENCY AND ASSESSMENT AS COURT COST OF AMOUNTS PAID FOR COLLECTION SERVICES

A. The Court may use the services of a collection agency for the purposes of collecting unpaid and delinquent penalties on infractions, criminal fines, costs, assessments and forfeitures. The terms and conditions of the contract for collection services shall be between the Federal Way Municipal Court and said collection agency, and may be amended as necessary.

B. The collection agency's fee or charge, as set forth in said contract, shall be added by the collection agency as a Court cost to the total judgment of the

Court against each defendant whose account is referred by the Court to the collection agency.

C. Nothing in this section shall prevent the Court from notifying the Department of Licensing of the defendant's failure to pay a fine and/or costs as ordered by the Court.

[Adopted effective April 3, 2000; renumbered from FMCLR 8.2 effective September 1, 2007.]

FWMCLR 15. PRESIDING JUDGE

A. The Presiding Judge shall be responsible for the efficient management and administration of the Court, recommending policies and procedures that improve the court's effectiveness, and allocating resources in a way that maximizes the court's ability to resolve disputes fairly and expeditiously. The Presiding Judge shall supervise the preparation and filing of all reports required by statute or rule and shall perform such other duties as may be prescribed by statute, ordinance or rule.

B. The Presiding Judge shall direct the work of the Court Administrator who will have direct supervision over all administrative, nonjudicial functions and all other court personnel except that the Presiding Judge shall directly supervise the Commissioner(s) and Judge Pro–Tempore(s).

[Adopted effective April 3, 2000; renumbered from FMCLR 10.2 and amended effective September 1, 2007.]

FWMCLR 16. VIDEO CONFERENCE PROCEEDINGS

A. *Criminal:* Pursuant to GR 19, preliminary appearances as defined by CrRLJ 3.2.1(d), arraignments as defined by CrRLJ 3.4 and 4.1, bail hearings as defined by CrRLJ 3.2, and trial settings as defined by CrRLJ 3.3(d), may be conducted via video conference in which all participants can simultaneously see, hear, and speak with each other shall be deemed held in open court and in the defendant's presence for the purposes of any statute, court rule or policy. All videoconference hearings conducted pursuant to this rule shall be public, and the public shall be able to simultaneously see and hear all participants and speak as permitted by the Court. Any party may request an in-person hearing which may, in the Court's discretion, be granted.

B. *Agreement:* Other trial court proceedings including but not limited to pre-trial hearings and the entry of a Statement of Defendant on Plea of Guilty as defined by CrRLJ 4.2 may be conducted by video conference only by agreement of the parties.

For purposes of videoconference proceedings, the facsimile signature(s) of the defendant, counsel, interested parties and the Court will be treated as if it were an original. This includes all other documents as the Court determines are appropriate or necessary.

[Adopted effective April 3, 2000; renumbered from FMCLR 13.1 and amended effective September 1, 2007; amended effective September 1, 2008.]

LOCAL INFRACTION RULES

FWMCLIR 1. DISCOVERY REQUESTS

Upon written request of a defendant the clerk shall provide copies of the Notice of Infraction, the officer's reports, witness statements, and the speed measuring device certification that are contained in the court's file. Any other requests for discovery shall be set for hearing to determine the relevance of such requests.

[Adopted effective April 3, 2000; renumbered from FMCLIR 1.1 effective September 1, 2007; amended effective September 1, 2008.]

FWMCLIR 1.2. DEFINITIONS DEFENDANT IN PHOTO ENFORCEMENT CASES

(c) In a photo enforcement case, the court is authorized to amend the identity of the named defendant if that new named defendant indicates that they were driving the vehicle at the time alleged in the Notice of Infraction.

[Adopted effective September 1, 2011.]

FWMCLIR 2. SUBPOENAS AND WITNESSES

A request by a defendant for the court to authorize a subpoena of a witness must be received 14 days before the date of the contested hearing. This includes the police officer whose presence is not required unless subpoenaed. In cases where the request for a subpoena is made 14 days or less prior to the scheduled hearing, the Court may deny the request for the subpoena or condition the issuance of the subpoena upon a continuance of the hearing date.

It is the responsibility of the party requesting the subpoena to arrange for proper service of the subpoena on the witness.

[Adopted effective September 1, 2001; renumbered from FMCLIR 3.1 and amended effective September 1, 2007; renumbered from FWMCLIR 3 and amended effective September 1, 2008.]

FWMCLIR 2.2. INITIATION OF INFRACTION CASES PHOTO ENFORCEMENT

(b)(1) For a photo enforcement Notice of Infraction, the officer signs the Notice of Infraction when the officer approves the Notice of Infraction and his or her name is affixed to the Notice of Infraction in the computer system provided for that purpose.

(d) A photo enforcement Notice of Infraction signed by an officer pursuant to FWMCLIR 2.2(b)(1) is filed with the court when it is made part of the computer system of the third party vendor authorized in FWMCLAR 2. There is a rebuttable presumption that the date the Notice of Infraction is made part of the computer system of the third party vendor is the same as the date of issuance of the first Notice of Infraction against the defendant.

[Adopted effective September 1, 2011.]

FWMCLIR 2.6. SCHEDULING OF HEAR-INGS—PHOTO ENFORCEMENT [RE-SCINDED]

[Rescinded effective September 1, 2011.]

FWMCLIR 3. HANDLING OF REQUESTS FOR HEARINGS AFTER FAILURE TO RESPOND

A. If a defendant who has failed to appear or respond to a notice of infraction, on not more than one occasion, as required by RCW 46.63.070 and Rule 2.4 of the Infraction Rules for Courts of Limited Jurisdiction (IRLJ), requests that the Court set his/her case for a hearing, the Clerk of the Court shall be authorized to set a date for the originally requested hearing, and recall any Failure to Appear Fees, pleadings or correspondence from the Department of Licensing reflects the failure to respond or appear, if any was sent, on the following conditions:

(1) The defendant, within 30 days of the date by which a request for a hearing should have been received by the Court, delivers to the Court an envelope containing his/her request for a hearing, with a postmark clearly indicating that the envelope was addressed and mailed to the Federal Way Municipal Court within the time frame for requesting a hearing pursuant to statute and Court rule, and with the envelope indicating that it was returned to the defendant, or;

(2) The Court, within 30 days of the date by which a request for a hearing should have been received by the Court, receives in the mail an envelope containing the defendant's request for a hearing, with the envelope showing a postmark clearly indicating that the envelope was mailed to the Court within the time frame for requesting a hearing pursuant to statute and Court rule.

[Adopted effective April 3, 2000; amended effective September 1, 2005; renumbered from FMCLIR 2.5 effective September 1, 2007; renumbered from FWMCLIR 2 effective September 1, 2008.]

FWMCLIR 3.1. CONTESTED HEARINGS—SUBPOENAS AND WITNESSES

A request by a defendant for the court to authorize a subpoena of a witness must be received by the court at least 14 days before the date of the contested hearing. This includes the police officer whose presence is not required unless subpoenaed. The Court will deny the request for the subpoena or condition the issuance of the subpoena upon a continuance of the hearing date if the request for a subpoena is made less than 14 days prior to the scheduled hearing.

All officer subpoena cases shall be heard on a special calendar and a request to subpoena the officer will result in the case being rescheduled to the date and time of that special calendar.

It is the responsibility of the party requesting the subpoena to arrange for proper service of the subpoena on the witness.

Adopted effective September 1, 2010.

FWMCLIR 3.3. PROCEDURE AT CONTESTED HEARING—ATTORNEYS AT CONTESTED CODE COMPLIANCE HEARINGS

The court may require that the city have an attorney appear at contested code compliance infraction hearings.

[Adopted effective September 1, 2010.]

FWMCLIR 3.5. DECISION ON WRITTEN STATEMENTS DISPOSITION BY WRITTEN STATEMENT, E–MAIL STATEMENT, AND BY VIOLATIONS BUREAU

a. Hearings by Mail or E–Mail. Traffic infractions may be heard by the Court based on written or e-mail submissions from the City and the defendant. Written or e-mail submissions must be provided to the Court five (5) business days in advance of the date set for contested hearing or mitigation hearing in compliance with Infraction Rules of Limited Jurisdiction (IRLJ). A finding of committed may be entered and the full fine assessed if written or e-mail submissions are not timely provided and defendant fails to appear for the in-person hearing.

b. Dispositions by Violations Bureau. The defendant may request an in-person contested or mitigation hearing for any offense, but a defendant may agree in writing to waive an in-person hearing and permit the clerk to enter the following dispositions for the following offenses:

1. *Proof of Insurance.* If a defendant who is charged with driving a motor vehicle without having proof of valid insurance presents to the clerk satisfactory evidence of valid insurance in effect for the defendant or the vehicle the defendant was operating at the time the citation was issued, then the charge will be dismissed and $25.00 in court costs shall be assessed.

2. *Disabled Parking.* If a person charged with violation of parking in a disabled space without proper parking placard, license plate or picture identification, presents to the court clerk evidence that the person had in effect at the time of citation the required parking placard, and an identification card bearing picture, name and date of birth of the permit holder as well as the placard's serial number, the infraction shall be dismissed and the court clerk shall be authorized to make appropriate notation of the dismissal in court records.

3. *Expired Vehicle License Tabs.* The clerk is authorized to enter a committed finding and judgment in the amounts set forth below if defendant shows proof that the vehicle license tabs for the vehicle in question have been renewed and are current:

Expired tabs under two months—$85

Expired tabs over two months—$140

[Adopted effective September 1, 2010; amended effective September 1, 2011.]

FWMCLIR 4. VACATING DEFAULT ON FTA

A defendant against whom a judgment for a traffic infraction has been entered by default for failure to appear within the past 180 days, may file a motion in writing, requesting that said judgment be set aside with payment of the Fail to Appear Fee as set by State Law. The motion will then be set for hearing with the Defendant present. The motion will be evaluated in conformity with CLRJ 60(b). If the Court grants the motion, the matter will be set for a hearing of the kind requested by the defendant. Hearings may be heard at the time of the motion at the discretion of the Judge.

[Adopted effective April 3, 2000; renumbered from FMCLIR 3.2 and amended effective September 1, 2007.]

FWMCLIR 4.2. FAILURE TO PAY OR COMPLETE COMMUNITY RESTITUTION FOR TRAFFIC INFRACTION— USE OF COLLECTION AGENCIES

The Court may use the services of a collection agency for the purposes of collecting unpaid and delinquent penalties on infractions, assessments and forfeitures. The terms and conditions of the contract for collection services shall be between the Federal Way Municipal Court, the City, and said collection agency, and may be amended as necessary.

The collection agency's fee or charge, as set forth in said contract, shall be added by the collection agency as a Court cost to the total judgment of the Court against each Defendant whose account is referred by the Court to the collection agency.

Nothing in this section shall prevent the Court from notifying the Department of Licensing of the defendant's failure to pay a fine and/or costs as ordered by the Court.

[Adopted effective September 1, 2010.]

FWMCLIR 5. DECISION ON WRITTEN OR E–MAIL STATEMENTS

Traffic infractions may be heard by the Court on the basis of written or e-mail submissions from the City and the defendant. Written or e-mail submissions must be provided to the Court in advance of the date set for contested hearing or mitigation in compliance with Infraction Rules of Limited Jurisdiction (IRLJ).

[Adopted effective April 3, 2000; amended effective September 1, 2001; September 1, 2005; renumbered from FMCLIR 3.5 and amended effective September 1, 2007.]

FWMCLIR 6. PROOF OF INSURANCE

If a defendant who is charged with driving a motor vehicle without having proof of valid insurance pursuant to RCW 46.20, presents satisfactory evidence of valid insurance being in effect at the time the citation was issued, for the defendant or the vehicle the defendant was operating, then $25.00 in court costs shall be assessed and the charge dismissed.

[Adopted effective April 3, 2000; amended effective September 1, 2005. renumbered from FMCLIR 4.0 and amended effective September 1, 2007.]

FWMCLIR 6.2. MONETARY PENALTY SCHEDULE FOR INFRACTIONS— PHOTO ENFORCEMENT MONETARY PENALTIES

Unless a different penalty is provided for by state law or local ordinance, the monetary penalty for an infraction issued through means of a photo enforcement system shall not exceed the following amounts:

Red Light Enforcement—$124

School Zone Speeding 1–5 MPH over speed limit—$189

School Zone Speeding 6–10 MPH over speed limit—$210

School Zone Speeding 11+ MPH over speed limit—$250

[Adopted effective September 1, 2010.]

FWMCLIR 6.3. TITLE AND CITATION OF RULES

These rules may be known and cited as the Federal Way Municipal Court Local Infraction Rules and shall be referred to as FWMCLIR.

[Adopted effective September 1, 2010.]

FWMCLIR 6.6. SPEED MEASURING DEVICE: FILING OF DESIGN AND CONSTRUCTION CERTIFICATION

(d) Speed Measuring Device Certifications required to be filed by the prosecutor pursuant to IRLJ 6.6(b) may be filed with the court by adding the documents to the collection of documents available for online public viewing and inspection pursuant to FWMCGR 30(b)(5). The prosecutor is permitted to provide the address to the court's website as the response to requests for such certifications.

[Adopted effective September 2, 2013.]

FWMCLIR 7. DISABLED PARKING

If a person charged with violation of parking in a disabled space without proper parking placard, license plate or picture identification, presents to the court clerk evidence that the person had in effect at the time of citation the required parking placard, and an identification card bearing picture, name and date of birth of the permit holder as well as the placard's serial number, the infraction shall be dismissed and the court clerk shall be authorized to make appropriate notation of the dismissal in court records.

[Adopted effective April 3, 2000; renumbered from FMCLIR 4.1 effective September 1, 2007.]

FWMCLIR 8. PHOTO ENFORCEMENT

A. The clerk may delegate administrative functions, docketing of cases, and collection of fines generated by Notices of Infraction issued under RCW 46.63.170 pursuant to the terms of an agreement between the court and a third party.

B. Hearings for disposition of such offenses may be heard in open court or as provided for in FWMCLIR 5.

[Adopted effective September 1, 2008.]

FWMCLIR 9. ATTORNEYS AT CONTESTED CODE COMPLIANCE HEARINGS

The court may require that the city have an attorney appear at contested code compliance infraction hearings.

[Adopted effective September 1, 2008.]

FWMCLIR 10. PHOTO ENFORCEMENT MONETARY PENALTY

Unless a different penalty is provided for by state law or local ordinance, the monetary penalty for an infraction issued through means of a photo enforcement system shall not exceed the following amounts:

Red Light Enforcement—$124

School Zone Speeding 1–5 MPH over speed limit—$189

School Zone Speeding 6–10 MPH over speed limit—$210

School Zone Speeding 11+ MPH over speed limit—$250

[Adopted on an emergency basis effective April 23, 2009; adopted on a permanent basis effective September 1, 2009; amended on an emergency basis December 1, 2009; adopted on a permanent basis effective September 1, 2010.]

ISSAQUAH MUNICIPAL COURT LOCAL RULES

Including Amendments Received Through
August 15, 2015

Table of Rules

LOCAL COURT RULES ("IMC")

IMC 1.   NOTICE OF APPEARANCE—INFRACTIONS

Attorneys appearing on behalf of clients shall file a Notice of Appearance with the court and prosecutor no later than fourteen (14) court days prior to the hearing. Failure to provide such notice shall be grounds for continuing the case to the next available calendar when the prosecutor will be present.

[Adopted effective September 1, 2008. Amended effective September 1, 2011; September 2, 2013.]

IMC 2.   TIME FOR HEARING—OBJECTIONS TO DATE

A defendant who objects to the hearing date set by the court pursuant to IRLJ 2.6 shall file with the court and serve upon the city attorney a written motion for a new speedy hearing date. Such motion shall be filed and served no later than ten (10) days from the date of written notice of the hearing date. Failure to comply with this rule shall become a waiver of the objection.

[Adopted effective September 1, 2008.]

IMC 3.   REQUEST FOR SPEED MEASURING DEVICE EXPERT—TESTIMONY BY PHONE

Any request to produce a speed measuring device expert must be filed in accordance with IRLJ 6.6(b).

The request cannot be combined with a notice of appearance or any other pleading. The court may allow the speed measuring device expert to testify from a location other than the courtroom via speakerphone or other electronic means acceptable to the court.

[Adopted effective September 1, 2008.]

IMC 4.   SPEED MEASURING DEVICE EXPERT—COST TO BE PAID

Any person who requests production of an electronic speed measuring device expert, and who is thereafter found by the court to have committed the infraction, shall be required to pay the fee charged by the expert as a cost incurred by that party, as provided in RCW 46.63.151.

[Adopted effective September 1, 2008.]

IMC 5.   RELEASE OF ACCUSED—BAIL SCHEDULE

The court adopts the following bail schedule pursuant to CrRLJ 3.2(b)(7) and CrRLJ 3.2(o):

A Defendant who is booked and detained in jail after the initial arrest for a misdemeanor or gross misdemeanor shall be released upon promising to appear in court and posting bail in the amount of $500 for a misdemeanor and $1,000 for a gross misdemeanor, except for the following offenses:

1. Domestic Violence Offenses: Defendants booked and detained in jail after the initial arrest shall be held in non-bailable status pending hearing the next court day following booking for any crime alleging domestic violence under RCW 10.99.020(5) or domestic violence violations alleged under IMC 9.30.030.

2. Driving Under the Influence/Physical Control: Defendants booked and detained in jail after the initial arrest shall be held in non-bailable status pending hearing the next court day following booking for Driving Under The Influence pursuant to RCW 46.61.502 or Physical Control of a Motor Vehicle While Under The Influence pursuant to RCW 46.61.504.

3. Other Crimes: Defendants booked and detained in jail after the initial arrest shall be held in non-bailable status pending hearing the next court day for the following crimes:

(a) Assault in the fourth degree—RCW 9A.36.041

(b) Harassment—RCW 9A.46.020

(c) Placing a Person in Fear or Apprehension—IMC 9.30.020

(d) Coercion—9A.36.070

(e) Violation of an anti-harassment order—RCW 9A.46.040

(f) Stalking—RCW 9A.46.110

(g) Communicating with a minor for immoral purposes—RCW 9.68A.090

(i)[1] Indecent Exposure and/or Public Indecency—RCW 9A.88.010

(j) Aiming or Discharge of a Firearm—RCW 9.41.230

(k) Inhaling Toxic Fumes—RCW 9.07.030

[Adopted effective September 2, 2013.]

1 Lettering as provided in original.

IMC 6. MOTIONS

a. Time for Hearing. Motions shall be filed and served as follows:

1. *Motion Requested at Time of Trial Setting*: If a motion date is set at the same time the case is set for trial then the moving party's brief and all supporting documents shall be served on the opposing party and filed with the court at least 14 days before the date scheduled for the hearing.

2. *Motion Requested at Time Other than at Trial Setting*: If a motion is filed at any other time by either party, the moving party must file a note for motion, the moving party's brief, and all supporting documents at the time the motion is filed. The note

for motion and supporting documents shall be served and filed with the court at least 21 days before the date requested for the hearing by the moving party.

b. Responsive Documents. The non-moving party's brief and all supporting documents shall be served and filed at least 7 days before the date scheduled for the hearing. The moving party's reply and all supporting documents shall be served and filed at least 2 days before the date scheduled for the hearing.

c. Motions to Shorten Time. No party shall seek a motion for order shortening time for hearing a motion unless said party has first notified opposing counsel or the opposing party(s) that such a motion will be sought. The moving party's motion shall be supported by an affidavit or declaration under penalty of perjury detailing the nature of the emergency necessitating the shortening of time and further stating that opposing counsel/party has been provided with a copy of the motion together and the time and place of the hearing wherein the moving party is seeking an order shortening time. Such affidavit or declaration shall state when and where opposing counsel was served with the motion and notice of hearing. The Court shall not grant an order shortening time unless it is satisfied that an emergency justifying the shortening of time truly exists and that the moving party has exercised due diligence in timely advising the opposing counsel/party of the hearing on said motion.

d. Agreed Orders. Where appropriate, agreed orders will be considered by the court at the earliest possible date.

d.[1] Proof of Service. The parties must file suitable proof showing that the opposing party was served with the documents filed by the party.

[Adopted effective September 2, 2013.]

1 Lettering as provided in original.

IMC 7. PRESENCE OF THE DEFENDANT—VIDEO CONFERENCE HEARINGS

All in-custody arraignments, bail hearings, and trial settings will be conducted via video conference pursuant to CrRLJ 3.4. Consent to proceed via video conference will be implied for all other hearings, excluding trial, unless an objection is made before or during the hearing to proceeding in this manner. However, this consent will not be implied if the defendant is not accompanied or represented by counsel at the hearing.

[Adopted effective September 2, 2013.]

LOCAL CIVIL RULES ("IMC–CRLJ")

IMC–CRLJ 10. FORM OF PLEADINGS—STYLE AND FORM—FACILITATING PROOF OF SERVICE AND FILING OF PAPERS

(a) **Action Documents.** Pleadings or other papers requiring action on the part of the Clerk/Court (other than file stamping, docketing and placing in the court file) shall be considered action documents. Action documents shall include a special caption directly below the case number on the first page, stating: "Clerk's Action Required". The action to be taken must be stated either next to the special caption or in the first paragraph on the first page. The clerk will not search through letters, notices of appearance, requests for discovery, or other materials to locate possible requests for action items.

(b) **Format.** All pleadings and other papers shall include or provide for the following, unless otherwise authorized by the court:

(1) *Service and Filing.* Space should be provided at the top of the first page of a document allowing on the right half for the clerk's filing stamp, and in the left half for proof of, or acknowledgement of, service. The papers should when feasible, such as common pleading or service forms, be pre-drilled or punched at the page top for fastening in court files.

(2) *Numbered Paper.* All pleadings, motions, affidavits, briefs, and other supporting documents prepared by attorneys/parties should be on paper with line numbering in the left hand margin.

(c) **Handling by Clerk.** All pleadings or other papers with proper caption and cause number will be date receipted, docketed and secured/placed in the court file by the Clerk of the Municipal Court in the order received.

(d) **Form of Pleadings.** Pleadings in compliance with this rule shall be in substantially the following form:

SPACE FOR SERVICE PROOF	/	SPACE FOR COURT FILING STAMP
	/	
	/	

IN THE MUNICIPAL COURT FOR THE CITY OF ISSAQUAH,
KING COUNTY, STATE OF WASHINGTON

_____,)
)   CAUSE NO. XXXXXXXX
       Plaintiff,   )
)   CLERK'S ACTION REQUIRED:
)   (note action required here or in
)   first paragraph)
       vs.   )
)   MOTION TO SET REVIEW
_____,)
)
       Defendant   )

CLERK'S ACTION REQUIRED: (note action required here or in caption).

[Adopted effective January 1, 2005; Readopted April 1, 2005.]

LOCAL CRIMINAL RULES ("IMC–CrRLJ")

IMC–CrRLJ 1.5.   STYLE AND FORM

The format requirements for papers being filed with the court shall be as specified in CrRLJ 1.5 and IMC–CRLJ 10.

[Adopted effective January 1, 2005; Readopted April 1, 2005.]

IMC–CrRLJ 3.4(d).   VIDEO CONFERENCE PROCEEDINGS [RESCINDED]

[Adopted effective January 1, 2005; Readopted April 1, 2005. Rescinded effective September 2, 2013.]

LOCAL INFRACTION RULES ("IMC–IRLJ")

IMC–IRLJ 3.5.   DECISIONS ON WRITTEN STATEMENTS

(a) Request for Decision on Written Statement. If the defendant submits a timely request for a hearing to contest or mitigate an infraction, the defendant may elect to seek a decision on written statement pursuant to the provisions of IRLJ 3.5 and IMC–IRLJ 3.5. A defendant who elects to contest or mitigate an infraction by decision on written statement shall be deemed to have waived an in-court hearing to contest or mitigate the infraction in person.

(b) Time for Submitting Request for Decision on Written Statement. The request for a decision by written statement shall be submitted no later than fourteen (14) days prior to the date set for the in-court mitigation or contested hearing.

(c) Declaration for Written Statement Required. A defendant wishing to proceed by decision on written statement shall provide a written statement which sets forth the facts and/or defense(s) that the defendant would like the court to consider. A written statement submitted pursuant to this rule shall be submitted by declaration as follows: "I declare under penalty of perjury under the laws of the state of Washington that the foregoing is true and correct," and shall be in substantially the following form:

Name of Defendant:
Address:
Infraction Number (upper right corner of citation):
Violation Date:

I wish to mitigate the infraction
I wish to contest the infraction

Statement:

_____

_____

_____

_____

_____

I declare under penalty of perjury under the laws of the state of Washington that the above information is true and correct.

Executed this ___ day of _____, 20 ___ at
_____ (city/state).

_____
Signature

_____

The written statement shall be submitted at the same time as the request for decision on written statement.

(d) Time for Examination, Factual Determination, Disposition and Notice to Parties. The time for examination, factual determination, disposition and notice to parties shall be pursuant to IRLJ 3.5(a)–(d).

(e) No Appeal Permitted. There shall be no appeal from a decision on written statements.

[Adopted effective January 1, 2005; readopted April 1, 2005.]

KENMORE MUNICIPAL COURT—
[No Local Rules]

PUBLISHER'S NOTE

This municipal court follows the Local Rules of the District Court for King County.

KENT MUNICIPAL COURT LOCAL RULES

Including Amendments Received Through
August 15, 2015

Table of Rules

LOCAL CIVIL RULES ("KMC–CRLJ")

KMC–CRLJ 10.   FORM OF PLEADINGS—STYLE AND FORM—FACILITATING PROOF OF SERVICE AND FILING OF PAPERS

(a) Action Documents. Pleadings or other papers requiring action on the part of the Clerk/Court (other than file stamping, docketing and placing in the court file) shall be considered action documents. Action documents shall include a special caption directly below the case number on the first page, stating: "Clerk's Action Required". The action to be taken must be stated either next to the special caption or in the first paragraph on the first page. The clerk will not search through letters, notices of appearance, requests for discovery, or other materials to locate possible requests for action items.

(b) Format. All pleadings and other papers shall include or provide for the following, unless otherwise authorized by the court:

(1) *Service and Filing.* Space should be provided at the top of the first page of a document allowing on the right half for the clerk's filing stamp, and in the left half for proof of, or acknowledgement of, service. The papers should when feasible, such as common pleading or service forms, be pre-drilled or punched at the page top for fastening in court files.

(2) *Numbered Paper.* All pleadings, motions, affidavits, briefs, and other supporting documents prepared by attorneys/parties should be on paper with line numbering in the left hand margin.

(c) Handling by Clerk. All pleadings or other papers with proper caption and cause number will be date receipted, docketed and secured/placed in the court file by the Clerk of the Municipal Court in the order received.

(d) Form of Pleadings. Pleadings in compliance with this rule shall be in substantially the following form:

SPACE FOR SERVICE   /   SPACE FOR COURT FILING

PROOF   /   STAMP

                /

IN THE MUNICIPAL COURT FOR THE CITY OF KENT, KING COUNTY, STATE OF WASHINGTON

_____,	)	CAUSE NO. XXXXXXXX
Plaintiff,	)))	CLERK'S ACTION REQUIRED: (note action required here or in first paragraph)
vs.	))))	MOTION TO SET REVIEW
_____,	))	
Defendant	)	

CLERK'S ACTION REQUIRED: (note action required here or in caption).

[Adopted effective September 1, 2003.]

LOCAL CRIMINAL RULES ("KMC–CrRLJ")

KMC–CrRLJ 1.5. STYLE AND FORM

The format requirements for papers being filed with the court shall be as specified in CrRLJ 1.5 and KMC–CRLJ 10.

[Adopted effective September 1, 2003.]

KMC–CrRLJ 3.1. ASSIGNMENT OF A LAWYER—PROVISIONAL APPOINTMENT

(a) At the preliminary hearing or arraignment, all persons whether in-custody or out-of-custody shall automatically be appointed a lawyer on a provisional basis to assist them solely with that proceeding unless otherwise ordered by the court. Any person requesting further assignment of counsel must meet with the court's public defense screener who will then make the determination of indigence pursuant to the provisions of chapter 10. 101 RCW. Notwithstanding any screening procedures, the judge may at any time appoint a lawyer in the administration of justice.

(b) This rule does not preclude any person from representing themselves at the preliminary hearing or arraignment. If the defendant chooses to proceed without a lawyer, the court shall determine on the record that the waiver is made voluntarily, competently and with knowledge of the consequences. The defendant must be advised that waiver of a lawyer at arraignment does not preclude the defendant from asserting the right to a lawyer later in the proceedings.

[Adopted effective September 1, 2008.]

KMC–CrRLJ 3.2. RELEASE OF ACCUSED

(b) **Bail Schedule:** A bail schedule may be set by administrative order of the court.

(o)(2) **Hold Pending Appearance Before A Judge:**

(i) _Domestic Violence Offenses:_ Except as may be permitted by a bail schedule adopted pursuant to KMC–CrRLJ 3.2(b)(7), a Defendant arrested and charged with a Domestic Violence Related Offense shall be held in non-bailable status pending hearing the next court day following booking.

(ii) _DUI/Physical Control Offenses:_ Except as may be permitted by a bail schedule adopted pursuant to KMC–CrRLJ 3.2(b)(7), a Defendant arrested and charged with Driving Under The Influence (DUI) or Physical Control Of A Motor Vehicle While Under The Influence (Physical Control) shall be held in non-bailable status pending hearing the next court day following booking.

[Adopted effective September 1, 2002; amended effective September 1, 2005; repealed and adopted as a new rule effective September 1, 2008.]

KMC–CrRLJ 3.4(d). VIDEO CONFERENCE PROCEEDINGS

(1) **Authorization.** Preliminary appearances held pursuant to CrRLJ 3.2.1(d), arraignments held pursuant to CrRLJ 3.4 and 4.1, bail hearings held pursuant to CrRLJ 3.2, and trial settings held pursuant to CrRLJ 3.3(f), may be conducted by video conference in which all participants can simultaneously see, hear and speak with each other. Such proceedings shall be

deemed held in open court and in the defendant's presence for the purpose of any statute, court rule or policy. All video conference hearings conducted pursuant to this rule shall be public, and the public shall be able to simultaneously see and hear all participants and speak as permitted by the Kent Municipal Court judge, judge pro-tem or court commissioner. Any party may request an in-person hearing which may be granted at the discretion of the Municipal Court judge, judge pro-tem or court commissioner.

(2) Agreement. Other trial court proceedings, including the entry of a Statement of Defendant on Plea of Guilty as provided for by CrRLJ 4.2, may be conducted by video conference only by agreement of the parties, either in writing or on the record, and upon the approval of the Kent Municipal Court judge, judge-pro tem or court commissioner.

(3) Standards for Video Conference Proceedings. The standards for video conference proceedings shall be as specified in CrRLJ 3.4(d)(3).

[Adopted effective September 1, 2003.]

KMC–CrRLJ 4.8(a). SUBPOENAS

The copy of any subpoena filed with the court pursuant to CrRLJ 4.8(a) shall be file stamped and placed in a subpoena file corresponding with the month the witness is commanded to appear. Upon an issue or request for enforcement arising under CrRLJ 4.8(b) or (e), or CrRLJ 4.10, the copy of the subpoena at issue shall be removed from the subpoena file, docketed and placed in the case file. Otherwise, copies of subpoenas filed shall be destroyed after 90 days has passed from the date the witness is commanded to appear.

[Adopted effective September 1, 2005.]

KMC–CrRLJ 7.3(j). JUDGMENT

Any fine, assessment or cost that is not in an even dollar amount shall be amended to a higher amount which produces the next greatest even dollar total. Provided however, this provision shall not apply if the total monetary penalty resulting from any increase shall exceed the maximum possible fines, costs and assessments allowed by law.

[Adopted effective September 1, 2005.]

LOCAL INFRACTION RULES ("KMC–IRLJ")

KMC–IRLJ 2.6. INFRACTION— PREHEARING CONFERENCE

(a) Prehearing Conference Required—Waiver. Unless otherwise ordered by the court, a defendant charged with an infraction who requests a hearing to contest the infraction shall first appear at a prehearing conference. The prehearing conference shall be scheduled in accordance with the provisions of IRLJ 2.6(a)(1)(i). The requirement that the defendant appear at the prehearing conference may be waived by the defendant, in writing, provided the waiver is received by the court before the time set for the prehearing conference. If the defendant fails to timely waive or appear at the prehearing conference, a default judgment shall be entered. In waiving the prehearing conference, the defendant shall complete a waiver form approved by the court. In the event that the defendant submits a waiver in a form other than that approved by the court, said waiver shall be ineffective unless it is in substantial compliance with the court approved form.

(b) Waiver of Prehearing Conference Constitutes a Waiver of Opportunity to Seek Deferral of Infraction. A defendant who waives his or her presence at the prehearing conference shall not be entitled to seek deferral of the infraction(s) charged.

(c) Setting Contested Hearing. If the infractions are not resolved following the prehearing conference, a contested hearing shall be scheduled for not more than ninety (90) days from the date of the prehearing conference. If the prehearing conference is waived, a contested hearing shall be scheduled for not more than ninety (90) days from the date the waiver of the prehearing conference is received by the court.

(d) Prehearing Motions for Contested Infractions—Written Notice Required—Time Limits for Oral Argument. All motions to exclude evidence or dismiss an infraction shall be filed no later than the conclusion of the prehearing conference. If a defendant elects to waive his or her appearance at the prehearing conference, any motion must be noted on the waiver form filed with the court pursuant to KMC–IRLJ 2.6(a). Any motion(s) not timely filed shall be waived and shall not be considered by the court. All motions timely noted shall be addressed by the court at the time of the contested hearing. Unless otherwise ordered by the court, parties shall have a total of ten (10) minutes each to argue and/or respond to motions before the court. Any argument in support of, or in response to, motions before the court that will require more than ten (10) minutes to present shall be submitted in brief form.

[Adopted effective September 1, 2002. Amended effective September 2, 2014.]

KMC–IRLJ 3.5. DECISIONS ON WRITTEN STATEMENTS

(a) Request for Decision on Written Statement. If the defendant submits a timely request for a hearing to contest or mitigate an infraction, the defendant may elect to seek a decision on written statement pursuant to the provisions of IRLJ 3.5 and KMC–IRLJ 3.5. A defendant who elects to contest or mitigate an infraction by decision on written statement shall be deemed to have waived an in-court hearing to contest or mitigate the infraction in person.

(b) Time for Submitting Request for Decision on Written Statement. The request for a decision by written statements shall be submitted no later than fourteen (14) days prior to the date set for the in-court mitigation or contested hearing.

(c) Declaration for Written Statement Required. A defendant wishing to proceed by decision on written statement shall provide a written statement which sets forth the facts and/or defense(s) that the defendant would like the court to consider. A written statement submitted pursuant to this rule shall be submitted by declaration as follows: "I declare under penalty of perjury under the laws of the state of Washington that the foregoing is true and correct," and shall be in substantially the following form:

Name of Defendant:
Address:
Infraction Number (upper right corner of citation):
Violation Date:

I wish to mitigate the infraction   ☐
I wish to contest the infraction   ☐

Statement:

_____

_____

_____

_____

_____

_____

I declare under penalty of perjury under the laws of the state of Washington that the above information is true and correct.

Executed this _____ day of _____, 20 ____
at _____ (city/state).

_____
Signature

The written statement shall be submitted at the same time as the request for decision on written statement.

(d) Time for Examination, Factual Determination, Disposition and Notice to Parties. The time for examination, factual determination, disposition and notice to parties shall be pursuant to IRLJ 3.5(a)–(d).

(e) Court May Require In–Person Appearance. In its discretion, the court may deny a defendant's request to proceed by Decision on Written Statement and may require the defendant to appear for an in-person hearing before the court.

(f) No Appeal Permitted. There shall be no appeal from a decision on written statement.

[Adopted effective September 1, 2002. Amended effective September 2, 2014.]

LOCAL GENERAL RULES ("KMC–GR")

KMC–GR 13. USE OF UNSWORN STATEMENT IN LIEU OF AFFIDAVIT—DIGITAL OR WRITTEN SIGNATURE

Law enforcement officers may use a digital signature that complies with the requirements of RCW 19.34 or GR 30 or by the officer explicitly signing the certification or declaration.

[Adopted effective September 1, 2008.]

KMC–GR 16. COURTROOM DECORUM

A. Photography, Recording, Televising, Broadcasting. The taking of photographs or the electronic recording of proceedings in the courtroom or its environs in connection with any judicial proceeding and the broadcasting of judicial proceedings by radio, television or other means is prohibited, except as provided in this rule.

As used herein, "judicial proceeding" means: (1) any hearing required to be held "on the record" by Supreme Court rule including but not limited to preliminary hearings, arraignments, pre-trial proceedings, motions, criminal and civil trials, sentencing, post-conviction relief hearings, mitigation and contested hearings; (2) any proceeding before a judicial officer, including a judge, court commissioner, traffic magistrate judge or judge pro-tem; (3) all sessions of any jury trial including jury orientation or selection, and (4) it shall include any person participating in a judicial proceeding, including witnesses, jurors, judicial officers and court employees.

"Courtroom" of the Kent Municipal Court means the courtroom itself, witness or jury rooms, and any location where civil infraction proceedings are conducted.

"Environs" means any area located within the interior confines of the Kent Municipal Courthouse, including but not limited to the entrances, hallways, corridors, foyers, conference rooms, restrooms and lobbies therein including probation or other offices.

B. Cell Phones, Electronic Devices and Text Messaging. Lawyers, defendants and members of the public may carry cell phones or other portable electronic devices into the court facility. When in any courtroom, all phones or other portable electronic devices shall either be turned off or silenced. No phone calls or text messages shall be sent or received within any courtroom. If silenced, the possessor of the device shall make certain that any transmissions do not interfere with court proceedings.

Failure to comply with this section may result in the confiscation of the cell phone or other portable electronic device and may include a fine or incarceration for Contempt.

C. Exceptions

1. The following exception applies to sections A and B above:

a. Court, probation or law enforcement personnel conducting official business.

2. With the consent of the courtroom's judicial officer, or the presiding judge of the court, the following exceptions may be granted to sections A and B above:

a. News media conditions and limitations as addressed in GR 16;

b. Ceremonial proceedings, including, but not limited to weddings or a judge or judicial officer's investiture;

c. For the limited purpose of presenting evidence, perpetuation of the record of proceedings, and security;

d. For the purposes of judicial administration;

e. As otherwise authorized by the court.

[Adopted effective September 1, 2011.]

KIRKLAND MUNICIPAL COURT LOCAL RULES

Including Amendments Received Through
August 15, 2015

Table of Rules

LOCAL GENERAL RULES

KMCLGR 1.   COURTROOM DECORUM

A.   Photography, Recording, Televising, Broadcasting. The taking of photographs or the electronic recording of proceedings in the courtroom or its environs in connection with any judicial proceeding and the broadcasting of judicial proceedings by radio, television or other means is prohibited, except as provided in this rule.

As used herein, "judicial proceeding" means: (1) any hearing required to be held "on the record" by Supreme Court rule including but not limited to preliminary hearings, arraignments, pre-trial proceedings, motions, criminal and civil trials, sentencing hearings, post-conviction relief hearings, mitigation and contested hearings; (2) any proceeding before a judicial officer, including a judge, court commissioner, traffic magistrate judge or judge pro-tem; (3) all sessions of any jury trial including jury orientation or selection, and (4) it shall include witnesses, jurors, judicial officers and court employees.

"Courtroom" of the Kirkland Municipal Court means the courtroom itself, witness or jury rooms, and any location where civil infraction proceedings are conducted.

"Environs" means any area located within the interior confines of the Kirkland Municipal Courthouse, including but not limited to the entrances, hallways, corridors, foyers, conference rooms, restrooms and lobbies therein including probation or other offices.

B.   Cell Phones, Electronic Devices and Text Messaging. Lawyers, defendants and members of the public may carry cell phones or other portable electronic devices into the court facility. When in any courtroom, all phones or other portable electronic devices shall either be turned off or silenced. No phone calls or text messages shall be sent or received within any courtroom. If silenced, the possessor of the device shall make certain that any transmissions do not interfere with court proceedings.

Failure to comply with this section may result in the confiscation of the cell phone or other portable electronic device and may include a fine or incarceration for Contempt.

C. Exceptions.

1. The following exception applies to sections A and B above:

a) Court, probation or law enforcement personnel conducting official business.

2. With the consent of the courtroom's judicial officer, or the presiding judge of the court, the following exceptions may be granted to sections A and B above:

a) News media conditions and limitations as addressed in GR 1

b) Ceremonial proceedings, including, but not limited to weddings or a judge or judicial officer's investiture;

c) For the limited purpose of presenting evidence, perpetuation of the record of proceedings, and security;

d) For the purposes of judicial administration;

e) As otherwise authorized by the court.

[Adopted effective September 1, 2011.]

KMCLGR 2. JUDICIAL SIGNATURES

Judicial Signatures: Judicial officers may sign orders with a digital signature, as defined in GR 30. In addition, documents may be signed by judicial officers using an electronic form that contains an electronic copy of the judicial officer's signature so long as the form is saved only on a directory that is accessible only by the judicial officers and so long as the electronic signature is protected so that it cannot be electronically copied.

The printed version of these documents shall constitute an original order and shall be placed in the court file. This rule may be amended or supplemented during the year by general order.

[Adopted effective September 2, 2013.]

LOCAL CRIMINAL RULES

KMCLR 1. ADOPTION OF LOCAL RULES

These rules are adopted pursuant to CrRLJ 1.7.

[Adopted effective September 1, 2001]

KMCLR 2. TITLE OF RULES

These rules may be known and cited as the Kirkland Municipal Court Local Criminal Rules. The criminal rules shall be referred to as KMCLR.

[Adopted effective September 1, 2001. Amended effective September 1, 2006.]

KMCLR 3. PRESIDING JUDGE

The Presiding Judge shall conduct duties of the office pursuant to GR 29.

[Adopted effective September 1, 2001. Amended effective September 1, 2006.]

KMCLR 4. FORM OF PLEADINGS— STYLE AND FORM—FACILITATING PROOF OF SERVICE AND FILING OF PAPERS

(a) Action Documents. Pleadings or other papers requiring action on the part of the Clerk/Court (other than file stamping, docketing and placing in the court file) shall be considered action documents. Action documents shall include a special caption directly below the case number on the first page, stating: "Clerk's Action Required". The action to be taken must be stated either next to the special caption or in

the first paragraph on the first page. The clerk will not search through letters, notices of appearance, requests for discovery, or other materials to locate possible requests for action items.

(b) Format. All pleadings and other papers shall include or provide for the following, unless otherwise authorized by the court:

(1) *Service and Filing.* Space should be provided at the top of the first page of a document allowing on the right half for the clerk's filing stamp, and in the left half for proof of, or acknowledgement of, service. The papers should when feasible, such as common pleading or service forms, be pre-drilled or punched at the page top for fastening in court files.

(2) *Numbered Paper.* All pleadings, motions, affidavits, briefs, and other supporting documents prepared by attorneys/parties should be on paper with line numbering in the left hand margin.

(c) Handling by Clerk. All pleadings or other papers with proper caption and cause number will be date receipted, docketed and secured/placed in the court file by the Clerk of the Municipal Court in the order received.

(d) Form of Pleadings. Pleadings in compliance with this rule shall be in substantially the following form:

SPACE FOR SERVICE / SPACE FOR COURT
PROOF   / FILING STAMP
                                      /

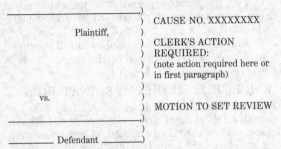

IN THE MUNICIPAL COURT FOR THE CITY OF
KING COUNTY, STATE OF WASHINGTON

_____,)	
Plaintiff,)	CAUSE NO. XXXXXXXX
)	CLERK'S ACTION
)	REQUIRED:
)	(note action required here or
)	in first paragraph)
)	
vs.)	
)	MOTION TO SET REVIEW
_____,)	
)	
_____ Defendant _____)	

CLERK'S ACTION REQUIRED: (note action required here or in caption).

[Adopted effective September 1, 2006.]

KMCLR 5. BAIL FORFEITURES FOR SPECIFIC CRIMES [RESCINDED]

[Adopted effective September 1, 2001. Amended effective
September 1, 2006; rescinded effective September 1, 2012.]

KMCLR 6. BAIL/DOMESTIC VIOLENCE NEW OFFENSES

When required to reasonably assure appearance in
Court for those persons arrested and detained in jail
for new offenses, bail shall not be set for accused
persons arrested for new offenses involving domestic
violence, violation of a court ordered no contact order
or protection order, or violation an anti-harassment
order, except at the preliminary appearance or arraignment.

[Adopted effective September 1, 2001. Amended effective
September 1, 2006.]

KMCLR 7. PRE–TRIAL AND READINESS HEARINGS.

(a) Unless otherwise ordered by the Court in a
specific case for good cause, all cases in which a
defendant enters a plea of not guilty shall be set for a
pre-trial hearing.

(b) (1) The pre-trial hearing shall provide an opportunity for negotiation between the parties. The parties shall confer in good faith regarding any agreed
disposition prior to trial. The defendant shall be
required to attend the pretrial hearing unless excused
by the Court. Failure to attend may result in the
issuance of a bench warrant and/or forfeiture of any
bail/bond. In the event of a disposition, the parties
shall execute the appropriate documents for the Judge
to consider the matter on the record.

(2) In cases that proceed to trial, the parties shall
identify with specificity all motions and counsel may
be required to articulate on the record the basis for
any motion. All rulings made at the pre-trial hearing
or subsequent motion hearing(s) shall be binding on
the parties and shall not be re-litigated at trial. Any

motion not identified at pre-trial may be deemed
waived unless otherwise allowed by the Court. Counsel shall identify only those motions for which there is
a good faith belief that the motion is well grounded in
fact and is warranted by existing law or a good faith
argument for the extension, modification or reversal of
existing law.

(c) The Court shall assign dates and give written
notice to the parties for motion hearings and trial at
the time of the pre-trial conference and shall, in so far
as is reasonably possible, schedule those hearings
after consultation with all counsel. Other factors,
such as witness availability, shall also be considered.

(d) (1) A jury call/readiness hearing will be scheduled in all cases proceeding to jury unless specifically
waived by the Court in a particular case for good
cause shown. This calendar will be held during the
week prior to the scheduled jury trial. The defendant
shall be required to attend this hearing unless excused
by the Court. Failure to attend the readiness hearing
may result in the issuance of a bench warrant, the
case being stricken from the month's jury calendar,
and/or forfeiture of bail/bond.

(2) A request for a jury trial date constitutes an
assurance that the parties will be ready to begin jury
selection immediately on the morning of trial.

(e) A Jury trial must be confirmed by the defendant, or defense council, or prosecuting attorney by
notifying the court at or before 1:30 p.m. the court day
prior to trial. Failure to do so may result in witness
or jury costs being imposed.

[Adopted effective September 1, 2001. Amended effective
September 1, 2006.]

KMCLR 8. DEFENSE CONTINUANCES

A request for continuance must be made either by
the defendant or defendant's attorney 48 hours before
the scheduled hearing. Only the following hearings
are eligible for a one-time continuance by the clerk:

1) Non–Prosecutor Contested Hearings

2) Non–DV and Non–DUI Arraignments

3) For a first time continuance of a Pre trial hearing, the Court will require an agreed motion to continue, filed with a speedy waiver if applicable at least 48
hours before the scheduled hearing. Upon receiving
the agreed order and/or waiver, the clerk will reschedule the hearing.

If a motion for continuance is received and it is not
agreed, the clerk will file the motion in the court file.
The motion to continue will be determined by the
Judge at the scheduled hearing.

[Adopted effective September 1, 2001. Amended effective
September 1, 2006.]

KMCLR 9. PETITIONS FOR DEFERRED PROSECUTION

Petitions for deferred prosecution submitted pursuant to RCW 10.05 shall include a waiver of jury trial signed by the defendant and counsel, if any. Such petitions shall be presented to the Prosecutor and the Court no later than seven days prior to the time the Court is requested to grant the order. The petition shall include the petition, appropriate assessment, treatment plan, and proposed order.

[Adopted effective September 1, 2001]

KMCLR 10. REQUIREMENTS FOR PAYMENT OF JURY FEES

(a) If a defendant requests a jury trial, and does not waive his or her right to a jury trial within 24 hours prior to the scheduled trial or otherwise notifies the Court that the jury trial will not proceed, and the Court incurs the expense of summing the jurors, the defendant may be responsible for payment to the Court in the amount of costs incurred.

(b) If a jury trial is scheduled and the prosecutor does not notify the court within 24 hours the jury trial will not proceed due to known evidentiary problems, and the Court incurs the expense of summing the jurors, the Prosecutor may be responsible for payment to the Court in the amount of costs incurred.

[Adopted effective September 1, 2001. Amended effective September 1, 2006.]

KMCLR 11. CONFIRMATION OF JURY TRIAL

Both parties shall confirm with the Court Clerk whether or not a case set for jury trial is going to be tried to a jury no later than 1:30 p.m. on the court day preceding the date that the case is set for jury trial. Failure to confirm may result in the imposition of sanctions against either or both parties, pursuant to KMCLR 10.

[Adopted effective September 1, 2001. Amended effective September 1, 2006.]

KMCLR 12. REQUIREMENT FOR PAYMENT OF ADMINISTRATIVE PROBATION FEES

The Court may impose an administrative probation fee up to the maximum fee permitted under the current state statute.

[Adopted effective September 1, 2001]

KMCLR 13. REQUIREMENT FOR PAYMENT ON COURTESY WARRANT CALENDAR

A defendant, who has been charged with a criminal violation and has an outstanding warrant in the Kirkland Municipal Court, may request to have the matter

head on the weekly walk-in warrant calendar. The following terms and conditions shall apply:

Bench warrant amount is $1–1,000:

Option 1:

Pay $100 bench warrant fee. Bench warrant will be quashed and hearing will be set by the clerk of court.

Option 2:

Turn him/herself into the Kirkland Jail

Bench warrant amount is $1,001—$5,000:

Option 1:

Post cash bail in the amount of 10% of bench warrant amount ($100 of this amount will be put towards bench warrant cost.) Bench warrant will be quashed and hearing on next available walk-in calendar will be scheduled.

Option 2:

Pay $100 bench warrant fee. Bench warrant will remain active and hearing on next available walk-in calendar will be scheduled

Option 3:

Turn him/herself into the Kirkland Jail

Bench warrant amount is greater than $5,000

Option 1:

Post cash bail in the amount of 100% of bench warrant amount ($100 of this amount will be put towards bench warrant cost.) Bench warrant will be quashed and hearing on next available walk-in calendar will be scheduled.

Option 2:

Pay $100 bench warrant fee. Bench warrant will remain active and hearing on next available walk-in calendar will be scheduled

Option 3:

Turn him/herself into the Kirkland Jail

[Adopted effective September 1, 2001. Amended effective September 1, 2006; September 1, 2009.]

KMCLR 14. VIDEO CONFERENCE PROCEEDINGS

(1) Authorization. Preliminary appearances held pursuant to CrRLJ 3.2.1(d), arraignments held pursuant to CrRLJ 3.4 and 4.1, bail hearings held pursuant to CrRLJ 3.2, and trial settings held pursuant to CrRLJ 3.3(f), may be conducted by video conference in which all participants can simultaneously see, hear and speak with each other. Such proceedings shall be deemed held in open court and in the defendant's presence for the purpose of any statute, court rule or policy. All video conference hearings conducted pursuant to this rule shall be public, and the public shall be able to simultaneously see and hear all participants and speak as permitted by the Kirkland Municipal

Court judge, judge pro-tem or court commissioner. Any party may request an in-person hearing which may be granted at the discretion of the Municipal Court judge, judge pro-tem or court commissioner.

(2) **Agreement.** Other trial court proceedings, including the entry of a Statement of Defendant on Plea of Guilty as provided for by CrRLJ 4.2, may be conducted by video conference only by agreement of the parties, either in writing or on the record, and upon the approval of the Kirkland Municipal Court judge, judge-pro tem or court commissioner.

(3) **Standards for Video Conference Proceedings.** The standards for video conference proceedings shall be as specified in CrRLJ 3.4(d)(3).

[Adopted effective September 1, 2006.]

KMCLR 15. SENTENCING [RESCINDED]

[Rescinded effective September 1, 2006.]

KMCLR 16. WITHDRAWAL OF COUNSEL

Counsel for the defendant may not withdraw from a pending criminal matter without authorization by the Court. Counsel's failure to appear for any hearing without prior authorization from the Court may result in sanctions being imposed against counsel at a show cause hearing.

[Adopted effective September 1, 2001.]

KMCLR 17. RESTITUTION

Where the Court orders that a defendant pay restitution, but does not set an amount at the time of disposition, the prosecuting attorney shall, within 60 days, file with the Court a proposed amount, with documentation in support thereof. The Prosecutor shall mail to the defendant's last known address the proposed amount, with copies of the supporting documents. If the defendant wishes to contest the proposed amount, the defendant shall file with the Court an objection within 30 days of the date of the proposed amount was mailed to the defendant's last known address. Upon receipt of an objection by the Court, the Court shall schedule a restitution hearing, and shall send notice to the Prosecutor and the defendant.

If the defendant does not object, the proposed amount shall be entered as a judgment.

[Adopted effective September 1, 2001. Amended effective September 1, 2006.]

KMCLR 18. REQUIREMENTS FOR PAYMENT FOLLOWING IMPOSITION OF FINES, COSTS, ASSESSMENTS AND FORFEITURES

(a) Upon imposition of a fine, cost, assessment or forfeiture for a criminal charge filed with the Kirkland Municipal Court, absent extenuating circumstances, the defendant shall make payment in full at the time of imposition.

(b) Payment agreement may be authorized upon permission from the Court. The authorization of a payment agreement shall be subject to the conditions set at the time of the order.

(c) Failure to make payment pursuant to the agreement shall be enforceable pursuant to otherwise applicable Court rules, state law or administrative code regulations.

[Adopted effective September 1, 2001.]

KMCLR 19. USE OF A COLLECTION AGENCY AND ASSESSMENT AS COURT COSTS OF AMOUNTS PAID FOR COLLECTION SERVICES

(a) The Court shall use the services of a collection agency for the purposes of collecting unpaid and delinquent penalties on infractions, criminal fines, costs, assessments and forfeitures, on the terms and conditions of the contract for collection services between the City of Kirkland and said collection agency, and may be subsequently amended.

(b) The collection agency's fee or charge, as set forth in said contract, shall be added by the collection agency as a Court cost to the total judgment of the Court against each defendant whose account is referred by the Court to the collection agency.

[Adopted effective September 1, 2001.]

LOCAL INFRACTION RULES

KMCLIR 1. ADOPTION OF LOCAL RULES

These rules are adopted pursuant to IRLJ 1.3.

[Adopted effective September 1, 2001.]

KMCLIR 2. TITLE OF RULES

These rules may be known and cited as the Kirkland Municipal Court Infraction Local Rules. The infraction rules shall be referred to as KMCLIR.

[Adopted effective September 1, 2001. Amended effective September 1, 2006.]

KMCLIR 3. SPEED MEASURING DEVICE: DESIGN AND CONSTRUCTION CERTIFICATION

Any person who requests production of an electronic speed measuring device expert, and who is thereafter found by the Court to have committed the infraction, shall be required to pay the fee charged by the expert as a cost incurred by that party, as provided in RCW 46.63.151.

[Adopted effective September 1, 2001.]

KMCLIR 4. DECISIONS ON WRITTEN STATEMENTS

(a) Request for Decision on Written Statement or E-mail. If the defendant submits a timely request for a hearing to contest or mitigate an infraction, the defendant may elect to seek a decision or request for Deferred Finding on written statement, or email, pursuant to the provisions of IRLJ 3.5 and KMCLIR 4. A defendant who elects to contest or mitigate an infraction by decision on written statement or email shall be deemed to have waived an in-court hearing to contest or mitigate the infraction in person.

In the case where a defendant requests or petitions for a Deferred Finding which is denied by the court, will be treated as a request for a mitigation hearing on written statement or email.

(b) Time for Submitting Request for Decision on Written Statement or E-mail. The request for a decision or request for a Deferred Finding by written statements or email shall be submitted no later than the scheduled hearing time or they will not be considered.

(c) Declaration for Written Statement or E-mail Required. A defendant wishing to proceed by decision or request for Deferred Finding on written statement or email shall provide a written statement or email which sets forth the facts and/or defense(s) that the defendant would like the court to consider. A written statement or email submitted pursuant to this rule shall be submitted by declaration as follows:

"I declare under penalty of perjury under the laws of the state of Washington that the foregoing is true and correct," and shall be in substantially the following form:

Name of Defendant:

Address:

Infraction Number (upper right corner of citation):

Violation Date:

I wish to request a Deferred Finding [ ]

I wish to mitigate the infraction [ ]

I wish to contest the infraction [ ]

Statement:

_____

_____

_____

_____

_____

_____

_____

_____

I declare under penalty of perjury under the laws of the state of Washington that the above information is true and correct.

Executed this ___ day of _____, 20 ___ at _____ (city/state).

_____

Signature

The written statement or email shall be submitted at the same time as the request for decision on written statement or email.

(d) Time for Examination, Factual Determination, Disposition and Notice to Parties. The time for examination, factual determination, disposition and notice to parties shall be pursuant to IRLJ 3.5(a)–(b).

(e) No Appeal Permitted. There shall be no appeal from a decision on written statements or email.

[Adopted effective September 1, 2001; amended effective September 1, 2011.]

KMCLIR 5. NOTICE OF APPEARANCE REQUIRED FOR CONTESTED HEARINGS

Attorneys appearing on behalf of clients shall file a Notice of Appearance with the Court and Prosecutor no later than 3 court days prior to the hearing. Failure to provide such notice shall be grounds for continuing the case to the next available calendar when the Prosecutor will be present.

[Adopted effective September 1, 2001; amended effective September 1, 2002; September 1, 2007.]

KMCLIR 6. PROOF OF INSURANCE

If a defendant who is charged with driving a motor vehicle without having proof of valid insurance pursuant to RCW 46.20, and that defendant presents satisfactory evidence that they have obtained valid insurance to the Clerk of the Court within 15 days of the date of the citation, for the vehicle the defendant was operating on the day he/she was cited, then the bail for the offense shall be reduced to $250.00.

If, within fifteen (15) days of the date of the citation, the defendant presents satisfactory evidence of valid insurance being in effect at the time the citation was issued, then the offense shall be dismissed upon payment of the $25.00 administrative fee.

"Satisfactory evidence" shall mean 1) written identification card from the insurance company, and 2) proof that the defendant was insured to drive the vehicle s/he was operating at the time of the violation. If the defendant is not named on the insurance card, the defendant must provide:

(a) a copy of the policy verifying the defendant is noted as a named insured on the policy; (b) a copy of the policy showing who is covered (i.e. that it covers all other drivers who operate the vehicle with the permission of the owners); or (c) a letter from the insurance agent clearly stating that the defendant would have been covered under the policy provisions on the date charged.

[Adopted effective September 1, 2001. Amended effective September 1, 2006; September 1, 2011.]

KMCLIR 7. REQUIREMENTS FOR PAYMENT FOLLOWING INFRACTION HEARING

(d) If a defendant who has been charged with a traffic or other infraction filed with the Kirkland Municipal Court is found to have committed that infraction, absent extenuating circumstances, the defendant shall make payment in full of the amount of the penalty at the time of the hearing in which the defendant was found to have committed the infraction.

(e) Payment agreements on infractions may be authorized upon permission from the Court upon timely request. The authorization of time payments in infraction cases shall be subject to the conditions set at the time of the order authorizing time payments.

(f) Failure to make payment on the penalties on the committed infractions shall be enforceable pursuant to otherwise applicable Court rules, state law or administrative code regulations.

[Adopted effective September 1, 2001.]

KMCLIR 8. TIME FOR HEARING— OBJECTIONS TO DATE

The Court shall follow the provisions of IRLJ 2.6.

[Adopted effective September 1, 2001. Amended effective September 1, 2006.]

KMCLIR 9. DRIVING WITHOUT A LICENSE

If a defendant who is charged with driving a motor vehicle without having a valid driver's license issued to Washington residents pursuant to RCW 46.20, and that defendant presents valid license proof to the court clerk, then the fine for the offense shall be reduced to $250.

[Adopted effective September 1, 2006.]

KMCLIR 10. INFRACTION PREHEARING CONFERENCE [RESCINDED]

[Rescinded effective September 1, 2011.]

LAKE FOREST PARK MUNICIPAL COURT LOCAL RULES

Including Amendments Received Through
August 15, 2015

Table of Rules

LOCAL RULES

LFPMCLR 1.7. ADOPTION OF LOCAL RULES

These rules are adopted pursuant to CrRLJ 1.7 and IRLJ 1.3 and replace any previous local rules adopted by the court.

[Adopted effective September 1, 1998.]

LFPMCLR 1.8. TITLE OF RULES

These rules may be known and cited as the Lake Forest Park Municipal Court Local Rules, and shall be referred to as LFPMCLR.

[Adopted effective September 1, 1998.]

LFPMCLR 3.2. RELEASE OF ACCUSED

A. Bail: Lake Forest Park Municipal Court will follow the bail schedule set forth in Washington Court Rule CrRLJ 3.2(*o*) except where the charges involve domestic violence offenses or charges of DUI (RCW 46.61.502) or Physical Control (RCW 46.61.504).

B. Domestic Violence Offenses: Bail shall not be set for a person arrested for a new domestic violence offense unless set by a judge telephonically at the time of arrest, or at a preliminary appearance, arraignment or subsequent court appearance. "Domestic violence" includes, but is not limited to any of the misdemeanor or gross misdemeanor offenses listed in RCW 10.99.020(5), or similar municipal ordinance, when committed by one family or household member against another. "Family or household members" are those persons listed in RCW 10.99.020(3) or similar municipal ordinance.

C. DUI or Physical Control: Bail shall not be set for a person arrested for a new charge of DUI (RCW 46.61.502) or Physical Control (RCW 46.61.504) unless set by a judge telephonically at the time of arrest or at a preliminary appearance, arraignment or subsequent court appearance or by written court order.

[Adopted effective September 1, 2012. Amended on an emergency basis effective May 14, 2014; amended on a permanent basis effective September 2, 2014.]

LFPMCLR 4.2. PLEAS [REPEALED]

[Repealed effective September 1, 2011.]

LFPMCLR 4.7. DISCOVERY [REPEALED]

[Repealed effective September 1, 2002.]

LFPMCLR 5.4. PRE–TRIAL HEARINGS

(a) Unless the defendant pleads guilty or submits on the record at an arraignment, a pre-trial hearing (PTH) shall be held. If the defendant or defendant's counsel appears at arraignment and enters a plea of

"Not Guilty", then notice shall be provided by the court at the arraignment to the defendant or defendant's counsel of the date and time of the PTH. If an attorney, pursuant to CrRLJ 4.1(d), submits a written notice of appearance, waiving arraignment and entering a plea of "Not Guilty" on behalf of a defendant, then the court clerk shall issue notice of the date and time of the PTH to defendant's counsel.

(b) The defendant and all counsel must be present at the PTH. Failure of the defendant to appear at a PTH may result in the issuance of a bench warrant.

(c) The PTH shall be held no later than thirty (30) days after the date of arraignment, unless a later date for the PTH is approved by the court.

[Adopted effective September 1, 1998.]

LFPMCLR 6.13. EVIDENCE

The court shall follow the provisions of CrRLJ 6.13 on Evidence subject to the following provisions:

(a) Return of Exhibits. Every exhibit in a criminal/traffic case in the court's custody, which is not contraband and for which ownership is not in dispute, shall be returned to the party who produced that exhibit upon motion of that party and expiration of the appeal period. In the event of a finding of guilty, for purpose of this rule, the appeal period shall begin on the day of sentencing or deferral of sentence by the court. Exhibits not withdrawn shall be delivered by the court clerk to the appropriate law enforcement agency for disposition as abandoned property; or if contraband, for destruction. No exhibit shall be released by the court without its being receipted for by the receiving person.

(b) Request for Speed Measuring Device Expert. The court shall follow the provisions of CrRLJ 6.13(d) concerning the request for a speed measuring device (SMD) expert, except that a request for such a SMD expert shall be in writing and must be received by the court clerk at least seven working days prior to trial.

[Adopted effective September 1, 1998.]

LFPMCLR 7.2. SENTENCING

(a) The court shall follow the provisions of CrRLJ 7.2 on Sentencing, with the addition of the provisions of LFPMCLR 7.2(b) as set out below.

(b) Assessment of Court Costs Upon Dismissal of Insurance Charge. If a defendant is charged with the violation of RCW 46.30.020, "No Valid Insurance" and subsequently appears in person before the court and provides written evidence that at the time the person was cited, he or she was in compliance with the financial responsibility requirements of RCW 46.30.020, then pursuant to the provisions of RCW 46.30.020(2), the charge shall be dismissed and court administrative costs of $25 shall be assessed, unless the costs are specifically waived by the Court.

[Adopted effective September 1, 1998.]

LFPMCLR 7.6.1. RESTITUTION

Where the court orders that a defendant pay restitution, but does not set an amount at the time of disposition, the City Prosecutor shall, within ninety (90) days, file with the court a proposed amount, with documentation in support thereof. The court shall mail to defendant's last known address the proposed amount, with copies of the supporting documents. If the defendant wishes to contest the proposed amount, the defendant shall file with the court an objection within thirty (30) days of the date the proposed amount was mailed to defendant's last known address. Upon receipt of an objection by the court, the court shall schedule a restitution hearing, and shall send notice to the City Prosecutor and the defendant. If defendant does not object, the proposed amount shall be entered as a judgment.

[Adopted effective September 1, 1998.]

LFPMCLR 8.2.1. MOTIONS

Pre-trial motions, other than motions in limine, shall be noted in writing at the pre-trial hearing (PTH). These pleadings are to be served on opposing counsel and on the court. Based upon the pleadings, the court will decide whether and when a hearing will be set and will notify counsel.

[Adopted effective September 1, 1998.]

LFPMCLR 8.2.2. CONTINUANCES

(a) Motions for continuances of hearings and trials shall be presented in writing to the court.

(b) No case shall be continued for hearing or trial unless good cause has been shown. The motion shall set forth specific facts showing good cause that a continuance is necessary and justification for the specific length of the continuance.

(c) In ruling on a motion to continue, the following factors will be considered by the court:

(1) The diligence of the counsel in noting the motion and notifying opposing counsel at the earliest possible date and in attempting to avoid the continuance;

(2) The proximity of the motion to the trial date, the age of the case, the established time limits for processing cases and the nature of any previous continuance orders entered;

(3) Whether the continuance may be avoided by stipulation regarding testimony; and

(4) The earliest possible date all parties will be ready to proceed to trial.

(d) The following factors do not necessarily establish good cause for continuance:

(1) Convenience to or stipulation between the parties;

(2) Failure to expeditiously prepare for trial;

(3) Failure of client to adhere to financial agreement with attorney;

(4) Settlement negotiations not yet completed, including the need to communicate an offer to a client appearing through counsel; and

(5) Recent substitution of trial counsel, except where required by the Rules of Professional Conduct.

[Adopted effective September 1, 1998.]

LFPMCLR 8.2.3.   JURY TRIAL SETTINGS

(a) The jury term will be the first week of the month unless otherwise set by the Court.

(b) At the defendant's Pre-trial Hearing, the case will be set for the start of the jury term that falls within the defendant's speedy trial period. The case will also be set for a Readiness Hearing to be held the week before the start of the jury term, unless the court sets another date.

(c) At the Readiness Hearing, each side will advise the Court whether or not the case will proceed to jury trial on the set jury date.

(d)   At the Readiness Hearing, the Judge will set a date and time for both parties to confirm to the Clerk of Court whether or not the case is going to be tried to a jury. This date and time will be set in open court and provided to the parties in writing. The date will be no later than 48 hours before the start of the jury term.

(e) A party who fails to follow procedures set forth in sub-section (d) may be subject to court sanctions. A party who confirms a jury date and disposes of the case without a jury after the jury has reported may be subject to court sanctions.

[Adopted effective September 1, 2000.]

LFPMCLR 8.11.   DISCLOSURE OF RECORDS

The court clerk shall make available the public records of the court in accordance with the provisions of ARLJ 9, subject to the following provisions:

(a) The disclosure provisions of LFPMCLR 4.7 shall govern all material discoverable under that rule. The disclosure of all other public records of the court shall be governed by the provisions of this rule.

(b) Requests for copies of the public records of the court must be in writing and must be received by the court clerk during the City's normal business hours prior to the commencement of court and a scheduled hearing on any matter for which copies are sought. The name, address and phone number of the person requesting copies of the public records of the court shall be in the written request for such records.

(c) Duplication Fees. Duplication fees shall be in accordance with the fee schedule adopted by the City by ordinance.

[Adopted effective September 1, 1998.]

LOCAL INFRACTION RULES

LFPMCLIR 2.2.   FILING OF NOTICE: PHOTO ENFORCEMENT

For purposes of IRLJ 2.2(d), a Notice of Infraction issued pursuant to RCW 46.63.170 and LFPMC 10.06.020 for an infraction detected through the use of an automated traffic safety camera is filed upon the date issued by the officer if the Notice is electronically transmitted or assigned to a third party, delegated administrative functions for traffic safety camera tickets.

[Adopted effective September 1, 2011.]

LFPMCLIR 2.6.   SCHEDULE OF HEARINGS: PHOTO ENFORCEMENT

The court may delegate administrative functions, docketing of cases, and collection of fines generated by Notices of Infraction issued under RCW 46.63.170 and LFPMC 10.06 pursuant to the terms of an agreement between the court and a third party.

Hearings for disposition of such offenses may be heard in open court under IRLJ 2.6 or as provided for in LFPMCLIR 3.5.

[Adopted effective September 1, 2011.]

LFPMCLIR 3.1(a).   SERVICE AND FILING OF SUBPOENAS

The defendant, the plaintiff, and defendant's attorney will subpoena witnesses in accordance with IRLJ 3.1(a).   Service of subpoenas will be in accordance with IRLJ 3.1(a).   Lake Forest Park Municipal Court will not serve a subpoena on an officer or witness for either the defendant, the plaintiff or defendant's attorney.   Each party must serve their own subpoenas in accordance with Lake Forest Park Municipal Court written procedures determined by the presiding judge.   These procedures are available from the clerk of court or on the court website.

[Adopted effective September 1, 2004.]

LFPMCLIR 3.1(b).   CONTESTED HEARINGS—PRELIMINARY PROCEEDINGS—DISCOVERY

(1) Repealed.

(2) No motion to dismiss or to suppress evidence will be granted for failure to provide discovery not required by IRLJ 3.1(b) unless the moving party has previously obtained an order from the Court compelling production of the additional discovery.

(3) A request for discovery must be served, in accordance with IRLJ 3.1(b), on the city of Lake Forest Park prosecuting authority. Service must be made at Lake Forest Park City Hall, where the prosecutor receives mail for Lake Forest Park Municipal Court criminal and infraction cases. The defendant must provide proof of such timely service at the time of a motion to dismiss or suppress evidence for failure to provide discovery.

(4) A request for discovery is considered properly served when it is served on the prosecutor at Lake Forest Park City Hall at 17425 Ballinger Way NE, Lake Forest Park, WA, 98155. The request must be addressed to the current city prosecutor by name, followed by the words, "City Prosecutor" or addressed to "City of Lake Forest Park Prosecutor". Service of a request for discovery on the court will not be considered service upon the prosecutor's office. Addressing the request either to "the court" or "city attorney" will not be deemed proper service.

[Adopted effective September 1, 2002; amended effective September 1, 2004; amended on an emergency basis effective August 22, 2014.]

LFPMCLIR 3.3(1). CONTINUANCE

A motion for a continuance in a scheduled contested or mitigation traffic hearing must be made in writing and filed 7 days prior to the date of the hearing. The motion shall show good cause for continuance and the defendant shall post $52 as a reschedule fee. This money is held in trust by the court until the next scheduled court date. Upon failure to appear, the $52 is forfeited. Upon a finding of committed, the money is applied toward any fine imposed. Upon a finding of not committed, the $52 is refunded.

[Adopted effective September 1, 2005.]

LFPMCLIR 3.5. DECISION ON WRITTEN STATEMENTS

(1) The court shall follow the provisions of IRLJ 3.5, Decision on Written Statements.

(2) The court shall allow written statements through e-mail procedures as established by the presiding judge through administrative order. E-mail procedures shall meet the requirements of IRLJ 3.5.

[Adopted effective September 1, 1998; amended effective September 1, 2004.]

LFPMCLIR 6.6. SPEED MEASURING DEVICE

The court shall follow the provisions of IRLJ 6.6 concerning the request for a speed measuring device (SMD) expert. The request for such a SMD expert must be served on the prosecuting authority and filed with the clerk of the court at least thirty (30) days prior to trial.

[Adopted effective September 1, 1998.]

LFPMCLIR 6.7. CHANGE OF JUDGE

A party to an infraction hearing in Lake Forest Municipal Court may file an affidavit of prejudice, but only in accordance with CRLJ 40(f). An affidavit of prejudice not filed in accordance with the time restrictions of CRLJ 40(f) will be denied.

[Adopted effective September 1, 2004.]

LFPMCLIR 6.8. DEFERRED FINDINGS

Lake Forest Park Municipal Court will grant deferred findings in a traffic infraction case in accordance with RCW 46.63.070. The presiding judge will create local requirements for the terms of the deferred finding by administrative order. Except for a deferred finding granted pursuant to this rule, no other types of deferred findings or orders will be allowed in any traffic infraction case. No person who has had a deferred finding in another court or participated in the Shorecrest Youth Traffic Court, within 7 years of the pending infraction, is entitled to another deferred finding or deferral of any kind.

[Adopted effective September 1, 2004.]

MAPLE VALLEY MUNICIPAL COURT LOCAL RULES

Including Amendments Received Through
August 15, 2015

Table of Rules

MVMCLR 1.4. JUDICIAL DAY

In 2014, a judicial day will be January 6 and 27, February 3 and 24, March 3 and 24, April 7 and 21, May 5 and 19, June 2 and 16, July 7 and 21, August 4 and 18, September 8 and 22, October 6 and 20, November 3 and 24, and December 8 and 22, when the Court is regularly in session.

In 2014, a judicial day will also be January 15, February 12, March 12, April 16, May 14, June 11, July 16, August 13, September 17, October 15, November 19, and December 17, if and when a jury trial is conducted on that date.

[Adopted effective September 1, 1999. Amended effective September 1, 2011; January 1, 2013; September 2, 2013.]

MVMCLR 1.5. FORM OF PLEADINGS— ACTION DOCUMENTS

Pleadings or any other document requesting action by the Court or its clerk, (other than confirming receipt and placing in the court file) shall be considered action documents. Action documents shall include a separate caption directly below the cause number on the first page, in the following form:

CLERK'S ACTION REQUIRED:

(Specify the action(s) requested)

Except to take the action(s) specifically captioned, the court clerk will not otherwise inspect any pleading or document for any request for action(s).

[Adopted effective September 1, 2001; amended effective September 1, 2011.]

MVMCCLCRRLJ 3.2. FINAL DISPOSITIONS; FORFEITURE OF BAIL [RESCINDED]

MVMCLCrRLJ 4.11. READINESS HEARING

When the defendant has not waived, or the plaintiff has made demand for, the right to a jury trial, all cases shall be set for a readiness hearing.

At this hearing:

a) Each party will announce its intention to proceed to jury trial;

b) All remaining pretrial issues will be raised and resolved, including, but not limited to, requests for subpoena and subpoena duces tecum, motions for joinder or severance, and motions to compel compliance with any court rules or order. Issues not raised at the conclusion of this hearing will be deemed waived, except when court efficiency or due process of law requires further hearing for presentation of evidence, submission of pertinent legal authority, and/or argument;

c) The case will be set for jury trial, if not waived by defendant or demanded by the plaintiff pursuant to CrRLJ 6.1.1(b); and

d) Each party will acknowledge in writing that it is subject to and bound to comply with MVMCLCrRLJ 4.12 in all respects.

The presence of the parties at this hearing is mandatory, unless waived by order of the court.

[Adopted effective September 1, 2011.]

MVMCLCrRLJ 4.12. CONFIRMATION OF JURY TRIAL

Whenever a case is set for jury trial, each party is required to confirm that the case will proceed to trial by jury pursuant to this rule:

a) Deadline for written confirmation. The confirmation must be in writing, and filed with the court by 4:00 pm on the Tuesday immediately preceding the regular jury setting, or by 4:00 pm two days prior to a special jury setting (excluding weekends and City holidays).

b) Contents. The written confirmations must be a certified or sworn statement to the court attesting to the truth of the following facts:

1) The party intends in good faith to proceed to trial by jury;

2) Each of the party's essential witnesses have been either:

A. Personally served a subpoena for the jury trial; or

B. Summoned by other lawful subpoena process for, and have personal knowledge of the date and time of, the jury trial; and

3) The party understands that it is directly responsible for full compliance with this rule, and it is likewise bound by the action or inaction of its legal representative to comply with this rule.

c) Courts action upon noncompliance. In the event either party fails to timely comply with the mandates of this rule, the Court will as soon as practicable:

1) Notify the opposing party, or its legal representative, by the most recent telephone number given to the court by the party or its attorney, of the failure to comply; and

2) Notify all citizens summoned for the jury trial that the trial will not be held and the requirement of their presence has been waived. This notification will be recorded on the court's telephone by 5:00 pm the day preceding the jury trial setting, excluding weekends and City holidays.

Nothing in this provision shall be construed as waiving or excusing the presence of the parties, or its legal representatives, at the date and time which was set for the jury trial.

d) Sanction for plaintiff's noncompliance. If the plaintiff fails to comply with this rule, then, upon motion of the defendant, the court will dismiss the case without prejudice.

Upon good and sufficient cause shown, the court may deny the defendant's motion to dismiss, or grant the motion with prejudice.

e) Sanctions for defendant's non compliance. If the defendant fails to comply with this rule, then the jury trial will be stricken, and in its stead, the court will conduct a hearing on the failure to comply.

Furthermore, in the event the defendant fails to comply with this rule, the Court will continue trial pursuant to CrRLJ 3.3 (f).

[Adopted effective September 1, 2011.]

MVMCIRLJ 2.4(b)(5).   FINANCIAL RESPONSIBILITY INFRACTIONS

If a defendant responds to a notice of infraction for violation of RCW 46.30.020 (driving w/o proof of financial responsibility) pursuant to IRLJ 2.4(a), admits the infraction, and, prior to the initial hearing, provides to the clerk of the court satisfactory evidence that the defendant complied with the financial responsibility requirements of RCW 46.30.020 at the time of the infraction, then the notice of infraction will be dismissed administratively upon payment of $25.00 court costs.

[Adopted effective September 1, 2011. Amended effective September 1, 2012; September 2, 2013.]

MVMCIRLJ 2.4(b)(6).   NO VALID DRIVER LICENSE WITH IDENTIFICATION INFRACTIONS [RESCINDED]

[Adopted effective September 1, 2011. Amended effective September 1, 2012. Rescinded effective September 2, 2013.]

MVMCIRLJ 2.4(b)(7).   DECISION ON WRITTEN STATEMENTS

Upon timely request for a hearing to contest or mitigate a traffic infraction, the Court shall send the defendant written notice of the hearing date and time. The defendant will also be sent a letter describing the hearing by mail option and a declaration form that must be completed by the defendant and any witnesses. If a defendant elects to proceed by mail, the Court shall review the police officer's statement and declarations submitted by the defendant and issue a written decision by mail. Declarations must be received by the Court no later than two working days before any scheduled hearing time or they will not be considered.

[Adopted effective September 1, 2011.]

MVMCIRLJ 3.5.   INFRACTION HEARINGS BY MAIL

(a) The court adopts by reference Infraction Rule for the Courts of Limited Jurisdiction (IRLJ) 3.5 (a) through (e), and amendments thereof.

(b) Any statement submitted by the defendant must be received by the court at least two working days before the scheduled hearing.

[Adopted effective September 1, 2011.]

MERCER ISLAND MUNICIPAL COURT LOCAL RULES

Including Amendments Received Through
August 15, 2015

Table of Rules

LOCAL CRIMINAL RULES

MIMCLR 1. ADOPTION OF LOCAL RULES

These rules are adopted pursuant to CrRLJ 1.7.

[Adopted effective September 1, 2006.]

MIMCLR 2. TITLE OF RULES

These rules may be known and cited as the Mercer Island Municipal Court Local Criminal Rules. The criminal rules shall be referred to as MIMCLR.

[Adopted effective September 1, 2006.]

MIMCLR 3. PRE–TRIAL AND READINESS HEARINGS

(a) Unless otherwise ordered by the Court in a specific case for good cause, all cases in which a defendant enters a plea of not guilty shall be set for a pre-trial hearing.

(b) (1) The pre-trial hearing shall provide an opportunity for negotiation between the parties. The parties shall confer in good faith regarding any agreed disposition prior to trial. The defendant shall be required to attend the pretrial hearing unless excused by the Court. Failure to attend may result in the issuance of a bench warrant and/or forfeiture of any bail/bond. In the event of a disposition, the parties shall execute the appropriate documents for the Judge to consider the matter on the record.

(2) In cases that proceed to trial, the parties shall identify with specificity all motions and counsel may be required to articulate on the record the basis for any motion. All rulings made at the pre-trial hearing or subsequent motion hearing(s) shall be binding on the parties and shall not be re-litigated at trial. Any motion not identified at pre-trial may be deemed waived unless otherwise allowed by the Court. Counsel shall identify only those motions for which there is a good faith belief that the motion is well grounded in fact and is warranted by existing law or a good faith argument for the extension, modification or reversal of existing law.

(c) The Court shall assign dates and give written notice to the parties for motion hearings and trial at the time of the pre-trial conference and shall, in so far as is reasonably possible, schedule those hearings after consultation with all counsel. Other factors, such as witness availability, shall also be considered.

(d) (1) A jury call/readiness hearing will be scheduled in all cases proceeding to jury unless specifically waived by the Court in a particular case for good cause shown. This calendar will be held during the week prior to the scheduled jury trial. The defendant shall be required to attend this hearing unless excused by the Court. Failure to attend the readiness hearing may result in the issuance of a bench warrant, the case being stricken from the month's jury calendar, and/or forfeiture of bail/bond.

(2) A request for a jury trial date constitutes an assurance that the parties will be ready to begin jury selection immediately on the morning of trial.

(e) A Jury trial must be confirmed by the defendant, or defense council, or prosecuting attorney by notifying the court at or before 1:30 p.m. the court day prior to trial. Failure to do so may result in witness or jury costs being imposed.

[Adopted effective September 1, 2006.]

MIMCLR 4. DEFENSE CONTINUANCES

A request for continuance must be made either by the defendant or defendant's attorney 48 hours before the scheduled hearing. Only the following hearings are eligible for a one-time continuance by the clerk:

1) Non-Prosecutor Contested Hearings

2) Non-DV and Non-DUI Arraignments

3) For a first time continuance of a Pre trial hearing, the Court will require an agreed motion to continue, filed with a speedy waiver if applicable at least 48 hours before the scheduled hearing. Upon receiving the agreed order and/or waiver, the clerk will reschedule the hearing.

If a motion for continuance is received and it is not agreed, the clerk will file the motion in the court file. The motion to continue will be determined by the Judge at the scheduled hearing.

[Adopted effective September 1, 2006.]

MIMCLR 5. REQUIREMENTS FOR PAYMENT OF JURY FEES

(a) If a defendant requests a jury trial, and does not waive his or her right to a jury trial within 24 hours prior to the scheduled trial or otherwise notifies the Court that the jury trial will not proceed, and the Court incurs the expense of summing the jurors, the defendant may be responsible for payment to the Court in the amount of costs incurred.

(b) If a jury trial is scheduled and the prosecutor does not notify the court within 24 hours the jury trial will not proceed due to known evidentiary problems, and the Court incurs the expense of summing the jurors, the Prosecutor may be responsible for payment to the Court in the amount of costs incurred.

[Adopted effective September 1, 2006.]

MIMCLR 6. CONFIRMATION OF JURY TRIAL

Both parties shall confirm with the Court Clerk whether or not a case set for jury trial is going to be tried to a jury no later than 1:30 p.m. on the court day preceding the date that the case is set for jury trial. Failure to confirm may result in the imposition of sanctions against either or both parties, pursuant to MIMCLR 5.

[Adopted effective September 1, 2006.]

MIMCLR 7. VIDEO CONFERENCE PROCEEDINGS

(1) Authorization. Preliminary appearances held pursuant to CrRLJ 3.2.1(d), arraignments held pursuant to CrRLJ 3.4 and 4.1, bail hearings held pursuant to CrRLJ 3.2, and trial settings held pursuant to CrRLJ 3.3(f), may be conducted by video conference in which all participants can simultaneously see, hear and speak with each other. Such proceedings shall be deemed held in open court and in the defendant's presence for the purpose of any statute, court rule or policy. All video conference hearings conducted pursuant to this rule shall be public, and the public shall be able to simultaneously see and hear all participants and speak as permitted by the Mercer Island Court judge, judge pro-tem or court commissioner. Any party may request an in-person hearing which may be granted at the discretion of the Municipal Court judge, judge pro-tem or court commissioner.

(2) Agreement. Other trial court proceedings, including the entry of a Statement of Defendant on Plea of Guilty as provided for by CrRLJ 4.2, may be conducted by video conference only by agreement of the parties, either in writing or on the record, and upon the approval of the Mercer Island Court judge, judge-pro tem or court commissioner.

(3) Standards for Video Conference Proceedings. The standards for video conference proceedings shall be as specified in CrRLJ 3.4(d)(3).

[Adopted effective September 1, 2006.]

LOCAL INFRACTION RULES

MIMCLIR 1. ADOPTION OF LOCAL RULES

These rules are adopted pursuant to IRLJ 1.3.

[Adopted effective September 1, 2006.]

MIMCLIR 2. TITLE OF RULES

These rules may be known and cited as the Mercer Island Municipal Court Infraction Local Rules. The infraction rules shall be referred to as MIMCLIR.

[Adopted effective September 1, 2006.]

MIMCLIR 3. SPEED MEASURING DEVICE: DESIGN AND CONSTRUCTION CERTIFICATION

Any person who requests production of an electronic speed measuring device expert, and who is thereafter found by the Court to have committed the infraction, shall be required to pay the fee charged by the expert as a cost incurred by that party, as provided in RCW 46.63.151.

[Adopted effective September 1, 2006.]

MIMCLIR 4. DECISION ON WRITTEN STATEMENTS

Upon timely request for a hearing to contest or mitigate a traffic infraction, the Court shall send the defendant written notice of the hearing date and time. The defendant will also be sent a letter describing the hearing by mail option and a declaration form that must be completed by the defendant and any witnesses. If a defendant elects to proceed by mail, the Court shall review the police officer's statement and declarations submitted by the defendant and issue a written decision by mail. Declarations must be received by the Court no later than the scheduled hearing time or they will not be considered.

[Adopted effective September 1, 2006.]

MIMCLIR 5. NOTICE OF APPEARANCE REQUIRED FOR CONTESTED HEARINGS

Attorneys appearing on behalf of clients shall file a Notice of Appearance with the Court and Prosecutor no later than 3 court days prior to the hearing. Failure to provide such notice shall be grounds for continuing the case to the next available calendar when the Prosecutor will be present, even if the date is beyond speedy trial requirements.

[Adopted effective September 1, 2006.]

MIMCLIR 6. PROOF OF INSURANCE

If a defendant who is charged with driving a motor vehicle without having proof of valid insurance pursuant to RCW 46.20, and that defendant presents satisfactory evidence that they have obtained valid insurance to the Clerk of the Court within 15 days of the date of the citation, for the vehicle the defendant was operating on the day he/she was cited, then the bail for the offense shall be reduced to $250.00.

If the defendant presents satisfactory evidence of valid insurance being in effect at the time the citation was issued, for the vehicle the defendant was operating, within 15 days of the date of the citation, then the offense shall be dismissed upon payment of the $25 administrative fee.

[Adopted effective September 1, 2006.]

MIMCLIR 7. DRIVING WITHOUT A LICENSE

If a defendant who is charged with driving a motor vehicle without having a valid driver's license issued to Washington residents pursuant to RCW 46.20, and that defendant presents valid license proof to the court clerk, then the fine for the offense shall be reduced to $250.

[Adopted effective September 1, 2006.]

NORMANDY PARK MUNICIPAL COURT LOCAL RULES

Including Amendments Received Through
August 15, 2015

Table of Rules

LOCAL CRIMINAL RULES

NPMCLR 1.0. ADOPTION OF LOCAL RULES

These rules are adopted pursuant to CrRLJ 1.7.

[Adopted effective September 1, 2005.]

NPMCLR 2.0. TITLE OF RULES

These rules may be known and cited as the Normandy Park Municipal Court Local Rules and shall be referred to as NPMCLR.

[Adopted effective September 1, 2005.]

NPMCLR 3.0. FILING OF PAPERS AND FORM OF PLEADINGS

(a) **Action Documents.** Pleadings or other papers requiring action on the part of the court or court clerk (other than file stamping, docketing and placing in the court file) shall be considered action documents. Action documents shall include a special caption directly below the case number on the first page, stating: "Clerk's Action Required". The action to be taken must be stated next to or directly beneath the special caption. The clerk will not search through letters, notices of appearance, requests for discovery, or other materials to locate possible requests for action items.

(b) **Format.** All pleadings and other papers shall include the following, unless otherwise authorized by the court:

(1) *Service and Filing.* Space should be provided at the top of the first page of a document allowing on the right half for the clerk's filing stamp, and in the left half for proof of, or acknowledgement of, service.

(2) *Numbered Paper.* All pleadings, motions, affidavits, briefs, and other supporting documents prepared by parties should be on paper with line numbering in the left hand margin.

(c) **Handling by Clerk.** All pleadings or other papers with proper caption and cause number will be date receipted, docketed and placed in the court file by the Clerk of the Municipal Court in the order received.

(d) Form of Pleadings. Pleadings in compliance with this rule shall be in substantially the following form:

SPACE FOR SERVICE / SPACE FOR COURT FILING
PROOF / STAMP
/

IN THE MUNICIPAL COURT FOR THE CITY OF NORMANDY PARK,
KING COUNTY, STATE OF WASHINGTON

City of Normandy Park,	)	
Plaintiff,	)	CAUSE NO. XXXXXXX
	)	
	)	CLERK'S ACTION REQUIRED
	)	(Note action required here or in
	)	first paragraph)
	)	
	)	MOTION TO SET REVIEW
vs.	)	
	)	
_____,	)	
Defendant	)	

CLERK'S ACTION REQUIRED: (note action required here or in caption).

[Adopted effective September 1, 2005.]

NPMCLR 4.0. VIDEO CONFERENCE PROCEEDINGS

(a) Criminal. Preliminary appearances as defined by CrR 3.2(b) and CrRLJ 3.2.1(d), arraignments as defined by CrR 3.4 and 4.1 and CrRLJ 3.4 and 4.1, bail hearings as defined by CrR 3.2 and CrRLJ 3.2, and trial settings, as defined by CrR 3.3 and CrRLJ 3.3(f), conducted via video conference in which all participants can simultaneously see, hear, and speak as authorized by the Court, shall be deemed held in open court and in the defendant's presence for the purposes of any statute, court rule, or policy. All video conference hearings conducted pursuant to this rule shall be public, and the public shall be able to simultaneously see and hear all participants and speak as permitted by the trial court Judge. Any party may request an in-person hearing which may, in the Judge's discretion be granted.

(b) Agreement. Other trial court proceedings may be conducted by video conference only by agreement of the parties either in writing or on the record and upon the approval of the Judge.

(c) Standards for Video Conference Proceedings. The Judge, counsel, all parties, and the public attending the hearing must be able to see, hear, and speak as authorized by the Court during proceedings.

Video conference facilities must provide for confidential communications between attorney and client and security sufficient to protect the safety of all participants and observers. In interpreted proceedings, the interpreter should be located next to the defendant, and the proceeding must be conducted to assure that the interpreter can hear all participants.

[Adopted effective September 1, 2005.]

NPMCLR 5.0. PRESIDING JUDGE

(a) The Judge duly appointed as Judge of the Normandy Park Municipal Court will be known as the Presiding Judge.

(b) The Presiding Judge shall be responsible for the efficient administration of the court. The Presiding Judge shall supervise the preparation and filing of all reports required by statute or rule and shall perform such other duties as may be prescribed by statute, ordinance or rule.

(c) The Presiding Judge shall direct the work of the Court Administrator who will have direct supervision over all administrative, non-judicial functions and all other court personnel except that the Presiding Judge shall directly supervise the Judge Pro–Tempore(s) and magistrate(s).

[Adopted effective September 1, 2005.]

NPMCLR 6.0. MAGISTRATES

The Court may employ judicial officers as magistrates, who shall serve at the pleasure of the Judge. Each must be appointed in accordance with RCW

35.20.200, 35.20.205, and the Normandy Park Municipal Code as judge pro tempore. Magistrates shall hear infraction cases as provided by the infraction rules for courts of limited jurisdiction and RCW 46.63, or any law amendatory thereof. Magistrates shall also, perform such other duties as may be assigned to them by the judge.

[Adopted effective September 1, 2005.]

NPMCLR 7.0. REQUIREMENT FOR PAYMENT ON COURTESY WARRANT CALENDAR

A defendant who has been charged with a criminal violation and has an outstanding warrant in the Normandy Park Municipal Court may requests to attend the courtesy warrant calendar Court costs shall be collected by the Normandy Park Municipal court when the defendant appears in court and requests to appear on the courtesy warrant calendar.

[Adopted effective September 1, 2005.]

NPMCLR 8.0. TIME—ENLARGEMENT

Upon the non-appearance of a defendant at the time and place scheduled by the court and warrant of arrest issued, the defendant's bail or bond may be ordered forfeited with or without further proceedings upon motion of the City Attorney or upon the court's own motion. If the necessary witnesses do not appear at the time scheduled by the court, the court may dismiss such action unless a good cause for such non-appearance is shown. No such action shall be taken until fifteen (15) minutes after the scheduled appearance time.

[Adopted effective September 1, 2005.]

NPMCLR 9.0. EVIDENCE—COURTS CUSTODY OF EXHIBITS

In a criminal case every exhibit in the court's custody, which is not contraband and for which ownership is not in dispute, shall be returned to the party who produced that exhibit upon motion of that party and expiration of the appeal period. In the event of finding of guilty, for purpose of this rule, the appeal period shall begin on the day of sentencing or deferral of sentencing by the court. Exhibits not withdrawn shall be delivered by the court to the Normandy Park Police Department for disposition as abandoned property; or if contraband, for destruction. No exhibit shall be released by the court without its being receipted for by the receiving person.

[Adopted effective September 1, 2005.]

NPMCLR 10.0. USE OF A COLLECTION AGENCY AND ASSESSMENT AS COURT COST OF AMOUNTS PAID FOR COLLECTION SERVICES

(a) The court shall use the services of a collection agency for the purposes of collecting unpaid and delinquent penalties on infractions, criminal fines, costs, assessments and forfeitures, on the terms and conditions of the contract for collection services between the City of Normandy Park and said collection agency, and may be subsequently amended.

(b) The collection agency's fee or charge, as set forth in said contract, shall be added by the collection agency as a court cost to the total judgment of the court against each defendant whose account is referred by the court to the collection agency.

[Adopted effective September 1, 2005.]

NPMCLR 11.0. BAIL SCHEDULE

A Defendant who is detained in jail after the initial arrest for a misdemeanor or gross misdemeanor shall be released upon posting bail in the amount of $500 for a misdemeanor and $1,000 for a gross misdemeanor, except for the following offenses:

1. **Domestic Violence Offenses:** Defendants shall be held in non-bailable status pending hearing the next court day following booking for any crime alleging domestic violence under RCW 10.99.020(5) or applicable local ordinance.

2. **Driving Under the Influence/Physical Control:** Defendants shall be held in non-bailable status pending hearing the next court day following booking for Driving Under The Influence (RCW 46.61.502) or Physical Control of a Motor Vehicle While Under The Influence (RCW 46.61.504).]

3. **Prostitution Related Offenses:** Defendants shall be released upon posting bail in the amount of $1,000 for any prostitution related offense under RCW 9A.88.030, RCW 9A.88.090, or RCW 9A.88.110 or DMMC 9.76.040 DMMC 9. 76.050 or DMMC 9.76.060

4. **Other Non–Bailable Offenses Pending First Court Appearance by Defendant:** Defendants shall be held in non-bailable status pending hearing the next court day following booking for these crimes:

(a) Assault in the fourth degree (RCW 9A.36.041)

(b) Harassment (RCW 9A.46.020)

(c) Violation of an anti-harassment order (RCW 9A.46.040)

(d) Stalking (RCW 9A.46.110)

(e) Communicating with a minor for immoral purposes (RCW 9.68A.090)]

[Adopted effective September 1, 2005; amended effective September 1, 2011.]

LOCAL INFRACTION RULES

NPMCLIR 1.0. SPEED MEASURING DEVICE: DESIGN AND CONSTRUCTION CERTIFICATION

Any person who requests production of an electronic speed measuring device expert, and who is thereafter found by the court to have committed the infraction, shall be required to pay the fee charged by the expert as a cost incurred by that party, as provided in RCW 46.63.151.

[Adopted effective September 1, 2005.]

NPMCLIR 2.0. REQUIREMENTS FOR PAYMENT FOLLOWING INFRACTION HEARINGS

a) If a defendant who has been charged with a traffic or other infraction filed with the Normandy Park Municipal Court is found to have committed that infraction, the defendant shall make payment in full of the amount of the penalty at the time of the hearing in which the defendant was found to have committed the infraction. The court may reduce a fine penalty amount only upon a showing of exceptional circumstances.

b) Time payments on infractions will be permitted upon court order, at the time of the hearing on the contested infraction. The court's decision to authorize time payments in infraction cases shall be subject to the conditions set at the time of the order authorizing time payments.

c) Failure to make payment on the penalties on the committed infractions shall be enforceable pursuant to otherwise applicable court rules, state law or administrative code regulations.

[Adopted effective September 1, 2005.]

NPMCLIR 3.0. DECISION ON WRITTEN STATEMENTS

Mitigation and contested hearings based on sworn written statements, as provided in IRLJ 2.4(b)(4) and IRLJ 2.6 are authorized. The written statement(s) must be received by the Court no later than seven (7) calendar days before the scheduled hearing or it will not be considered.

[Adopted effective September 1, 2005.]

NPMCLIR 4.0. INFRACTION—PREHEARING CONFERENCE

(a) Prehearing Conference Required—Waiver. A person cited with an infraction who requests a hearing to contest the infraction shall first appear at a prehearing conference. The prehearing conference shall be scheduled in accordance with the provisions of IRLJ 2.6(a)(1). The requirement that the person appear at the prehearing conference may be waived, in writing, provided the waiver is received by the court before the time set for the prehearing conference. If the defendant fails to timely waive or appear at the prehearing conference, a default judgment shall be entered.

(b) Setting Contested Hearing. If the infractions are not resolved following the prehearing conference, a contested hearing shall be scheduled for not more than ninety (90) days from the date of the prehearing conference. If the prehearing conference is waived, a contested hearing shall be scheduled for not more than ninety (90) days from the date the waiver of the prehearing conference is received by the court.

(c) Prehearing Motions For Contested Infractions—Written Notice Required. All motions to exclude evidence or dismiss an infraction shall be filed no later than the conclusion of the prehearing conference. If a defendant elects to waive his or her appearance at the prehearing conference, any motion must be noted on the waiver form filed with the court pursuant to NPMCLIR 4.0(a). A motion(s) not timely filed shall be waived and shall not be considered by the court. Motions timely noted shall be addressed by the court at the time of the contested hearing.

[Adopted on an emergency basis effective January 12, 2006; re-adopted on an emergency basis effective July 12, 2006; October 12, 2006; January 12, 2007; April 12, 2007; re-adopted on a permanent basis effective September 1, 2007.]

NORTH BEND MUNICIPAL COURT—
[No Local Rules]

PUBLISHER'S NOTE

This municipal court follows the Local Rules of the District Court for King County.

PACIFIC/ALGONA MUNICIPAL COURTS

Including Amendments Received Through
August 15, 2015

Table of Rules

ALGONA MUNICIPAL COURT LOCAL RULES

ALGMCLR 1.4.   JUDICIAL DAY

The Algona Municipal Court will operate according to the **Pacific Municipal Court Local Rules,** with the exception of PACMCLR 1.4:

The provisions of PACMCLR 1.4 will apply to Algona Municipal Court cases only when an appearance is mandated by RCW 10.99.045 and RCW 46.61.50571.

Otherwise, "judicial day" is defined as the third Monday of the month, unless that calendar is a special set as a result of a holiday.

[Adopted effective September 1, 2009.]

PACIFIC MUNICIPAL COURT LOCAL RULES

PAMCLR 1.0.   COURT CLOSURE DAYS

In addition to the legal holidays recognized in RCW 1.16.050, the Pacific and Algona Municipal Courts will be closed on Columbus Day and Christmas Eve (city recognized holidays), and on Saturdays.

When a court closure day falls on Saturday, the Court will be closed the preceding Friday.

When a court closure day falls on Sunday, the Court will be closed the following Monday.

[Adopted on an emergency basis effective November 11, 2011; adopted on a permanent basis effective September 1, 2012.]

PAMCLR 1.4.   JUDICIAL DAY

"Judicial day" means:

For Pacific Municipal Court: The first and third Wednesday, and the second Thursday morning of the month;

For Algona Municipal Court: In 2013, the third Monday, and the second Thursday afternoon (subject to prosecutor availability), of the month; In January 2014, the first Thursday, and the second Thursday afternoon (subject to prosecutor availability), of the month;

For any jury trials: The last Monday of the month (unless special set upon agreement of the Court and the parties);

upon which the regular sessions of the court are set.

[Adopted effective September 1, 1999. Amended effective September 1, 2005; September 1, 2007; September 1, 2008; September 1, 2009; September 1, 2011; September 2, 2013.]

PAMCLR 1.5.   FORM OF PLEADINGS—
ACTION DOCUMENTS

Pleadings or any other document requesting action by the Court or its clerk (other than confirming receipt and placing in the court file) shall be considered action documents. Action documents shall include a separate caption directly below the cause number on the first page, in the following form:

<u>CLERK'S ACTION REQUIRED:</u>

(Specify the action(s) requested)

Except to take the action(s) specifically captioned, the court clerk will not otherwise inspect any pleading or document for any request for action(s).

[Adopted effective September 1, 2001; amended effective September 1, 2011.]

PAMCLR 2.6. NO CONTACT ORDER HEARING

In any case where a no contact order has been issued and is in effect, a hearing shall be held, upon the written request of the protected person in the order or a party, to consider vacation or modification of the no contact order. This hearing should be held the next judicial day following the request, when practicable, with notice to all parties.

[Adopted effective September 1, 2015.]

PAMCLCrRLJ 3.2. FINAL DISPOSITIONS; FORFEITURE OF BAIL [RESCINDED]

[Adopted effective September 1, 2002; amended effective September 1, 2003; September 1, 2007; September 1, 2011; rescinded effective September 1, 2012.]

PAMCLCrRLJ 4.11. READINESS HEARING

When the defendant has not waived, or the plaintiff has made demand for, the right to a jury trial, all cases shall be set for a readiness hearing.

At this hearing:

(a) Each party will announce its intention to proceed to jury trial;

(b) All remaining pretrial issues will be raised and resolved, including, but not limited to, requests for subpoena and subpoena duces tecum, motions for joinder or severance, and motions to compel compliance with any court rules or order. Issues not raised at the conclusion of this hearing will be deemed waived, except when court efficiency or due process of law requires further hearing for presentation of evidence, submission of pertinent legal authority, and/or argument;

(c) The case will be set for jury trial, if not waived by defendant or demanded by the plaintiff pursuant to CrRLJ 6.1.1(b); and

(d) Each party will acknowledge in writing that it is subject to and bound to comply with PAMCLCrRLJ 4.12 in all respects.

The presence of the parties at this hearing is mandatory, unless waived by order of the court.

[Adopted effective September 1, 2005; amended effective September 1, 2011.]

PAMCLCrRLJ 4.12. CONFIRMATION OF JURY TRIAL

Whenever a case is set for jury trial, each party is required to confirm that the case will proceed to trial by jury pursuant to this rule:

a) Deadline for written confirmation. The confirmation must be in writing, and filed with the court by 4:00 pm on the Thursday immediately preceding the regular jury setting, or by 4:00 pm two days prior to a special jury setting (excluding weekends and City holidays).

b) Contents. The written confirmations must be a certified or sworn statement to the court attesting to the truth of the following facts:

1) The party intends in good faith to proceed to trial by jury;

2) Each of the party's essential witnesses have been either:

A. Personally served a subpoena for the jury trial; or

B. Summoned by other lawful subpoena process for, and have personal knowledge of the date and time of, the jury trial; and

3) The party understands that it is directly responsible for full compliance with this rule, and it is likewise bound by the action or inaction of its legal representative to comply with this rule.

c) Courts action upon noncompliance. In the event either party fails to timely comply with the mandates of this rule, the Court will as soon as practicable:

1) Notify the opposing party, or its legal representative, by the most recent telephone number given to the court by the party or its attorney, of the failure to comply; and

2) Notify all citizens summoned for the jury trial that the trial will not be held and the requirement of their presence has been waived. This notification will be recorded on the court's telephone by 5:00 pm the day preceding the jury trial setting, excluding weekends and City holidays.

Nothing in this provision shall be construed as waiving or excusing the presence of the parties, or its legal representatives, at the date and time which was set for the jury trial.

d) Sanction for plaintiff's noncompliance. If the plaintiff fails to comply with this rule, then, upon motion of the defendant, the court will dismiss the case without prejudice.

Upon good and sufficient cause shown, the court may deny the defendant's motion to dismiss, or grant the motion with prejudice.

e) Sanctions for defendant's non compliance. If the defendant fails to comply with this rule, then the jury trial will be stricken, and in its stead, the court will conduct a hearing on the failure to comply.

Furthermore, in the event the defendant fails to comply with this rule, the court will continue trial pursuant to CrRLJ 3.3(f).

[Adopted effective September 1, 2005; amended effective September 1, 2009; September 1, 2011.]

PAMCIRLJ 2.4(b)(5). FINANCIAL RESPONSIBILITY INFRACTIONS

A. If a defendant responds to a notice of infraction for violation of RCW 46.30.020 (driving w/o proof of financial responsibility) pursuant to IRLJ 2.4(a), admits the infraction, and, prior to the initial hearing, provides to the clerk of the court satisfactory evidence that the defendant complied with the financial responsibility requirements of RCW 46.30.020 at the time of the infraction, then the notice of infraction will be dismissed administratively upon payment of $25.00 court costs.

B. If a defendant responds to a notice of infraction for violation of RCW 46.30.020 pursuant to IRLJ 2.4(a), admits the infraction, and, prior to the initial hearing, provides to the clerk of the court satisfactory evidence that defendant has obtained the financial responsibility required by RCW 46.30.020, then the penalty may be assessed administratively without further hearing as follows:

I.   First offense in 5 years (pursuant to D.O.L. Abstract of Driving Record and the JIS Case history): $100.00

II.   Second offense in 5 years (pursuant to D.O.L. Abstract of Driving Record and the JIS Case history): $200.00

III.   Third offense in 5 years (pursuant to D.O.L. Abstract of Driving Record and the JIS Case history): $300.00

[Adopted effective September 1, 2002; renumbered from PACMLIR 2.4(b)(5) effective September 1, 2011.]

PAMCIRLJ 2.4(b)(6). NO VALID DRIVER LICENSE WITH IDENTIFICATION INFRACTIONS

A. If a defendant responds to a notice of infraction for violation of RCW 46.20.015 (no valid driver license with identification) pursuant to IRLJ 2.4(a), admits the infraction, and, prior to the initial hearing, provides satisfactory proof to the clerk of the court that the defendant has obtained a valid driver's license, then the penalty may be reduced to $50.00 plus statu-

tory costs and assessments (Total $102.50), without further hearing.

B. If a defendant responds to a notice of infraction for violation of RCW 46.20.015 pursuant to IRLJ 2.4(a), admits the infraction, and upon the defendant's request, then the penalty may be assessed administratively as follows:

I.   First offense in 5 years (pursuant to D.O.L. Abstract of Driving Record and the JIS Case history): $150.00

II.   Second offense in 5 years (pursuant to D.O.L. Abstract of Driving Record and the JIS Case history): $250.00

III.   Third offense in 5 years (pursuant to D.O.L. Abstract of Driving Record and the JIS Case history): $350.00

[Adopted effective September 1, 2002; amended effective September 1, 2011.]

PAMCIRLJ 2.4(b)(7). DECISION ON WRITTEN STATEMENTS

Upon timely request for a hearing to contest or mitigate a traffic infraction, the Court shall send the defendant written notice of the hearing date and time. The defendant will also be sent a letter describing the hearing by mail option and a declaration form that must be completed by the defendant and any witnesses.

If a defendant elects to proceed by mail, the Court shall review the police officer's statement and declarations submitted by the defendant and issue a written decision by mail. Declarations must be received by the Court no later than the day before any scheduled hearing time or they will not be considered.

[Adopted effective September 1, 2011.]

PAMCIRLJ 3.5. INFRACTION HEARINGS BY MAIL

(a) The court adopts by reference Infraction Rule for the Courts of Limited Jurisdiction (IRLJ) 3.5 (a) through (e), and amendments thereof.

(b) Any statement submitted by the defendant must be received by the Court no later than the day before any scheduled hearing time or they will not be considered.

[Adopted effective September 1, 2005; amended effective September 1, 2009; September 1, 2011.]

PAMCIRLJ 6.2(e). REQUIREMENT FOR PAYMENT FOLLOWING INFRACTION HEARINGS

I. If a person admits committing, or is found to have committed, any infraction, absent extenuating circumstances, he or she shall pay in full the amount of the penalty imposed by the court at the time of the hearing.

II. Time payments on infractions will be permitted upon a showing of extenuating circumstances, at the time of the hearing on the infraction. Time payments will be at a minimum of $40.00 each month, unless specifically authorized by the judge. The court's decision to authorize time payments in infraction cases shall be subject to the conditions set at the time of the order authorizing time payments. The court may impose an additional administrative fee for the costs of establishing, monitoring and processing a time payment agreement.

[Adopted effective September 1, 2002; amended effective September 1, 2011.]

REDMOND MUNICIPAL COURT—
[No Local Rules]

PUBLISHER'S NOTE

This municipal court follows the Local Rules of the District Court for King County.

RENTON MUNICIPAL COURT LOCAL RULES

Including Amendments Received Through
August 15, 2015

Table of Rules

RMCLR 1.7. ADOPTION OF LOCAL RULES

These rules are adopted pursuant to CrRLJ 1.7.

[Adopted effective September 1, 2001.]

RMCLR 1.8. TITLE OF RULES

These rules shall be known as Renton Municipal Court Local Rules and shall be referred to as RMCLR.

[Adopted effective September 1, 2001.]

RMCLR 1.9. COURTROOM AND OFFICE HOURS

(a) Court Hours. The Renton Municipal Court shall be in session on all judicial days from 8:00 a.m. to 11:00 a.m. and 1:00 p.m. to 5:00 p.m.

(b) Clerk's Office. The Renton Municipal Court Clerk's Office shall be open on all judicial days 8:00 a.m. to 5:00 p.m.

(c) Temporary Orders for Protection. Motions for a Temporary Order For Protection may be filed on judicial days from 8:30 a.m. until 3:00 p.m.

(d) Forms: For a complete list of forms available from the court, please see www.rentonwa.gov/court.

[Adopted effective September 1, 2001. Amended effective September 1, 2002; September 1, 2007; September 1, 2011; September 2, 2013; September 2, 2014.]

FORM—ADVICE OF RIGHTS (005a) [RESCINDED]

[Amended effective September 1, 2011. Rescinded effective September 2, 2014.]

FORM—MOTION RECALLING NO CONTACT ORDER (065) [RESCINDED]

[Rescinded effective September 2, 2014.]

RMCLR 3.1. RIGHT TO A LAWYER

(a) The right to a lawyer shall extend to all criminal proceedings for offenses punishable by loss of liberty.

(b) Unless waived, a lawyer shall be provided to any person who is financially unable to obtain one without causing substantial hardship to the person or to the person's family. A lawyer shall not be denied to any person merely because his or her friends or relatives have resources adequate to retain a lawyer or because he or she has posted or is capable of posting bond.

(c) The ability to pay part of the cost of a lawyer shall not preclude assignment. The assignment of a lawyer may be conditioned upon partial payment pursuant to an established method of collection.

(d) The court, upon motion of a defendant, shall screen said defendant for the purposes of determining whether the defendant is indigent. The court may consider any factors regarding indigence it deems appropriate. The court may require proof of income at its discretion.

(e) A defendant may waive their right to be represented by an attorney. The court shall require all defendants entering a plea of guilty in the absence of an attorney to complete a Renton Municipal Court Waiver *of Right to* Attorney form. The court shall enter findings regarding whether the defendant made a knowing and voluntary waiver of an attorney before accepting a guilty plea or setting a case for trial.

[Adopted effective September 1, 2001.]

FORM—WAIVER OF ATTORNEY: ARRAIGNMENT (061) [RESCINDED]

[Rescinded effective September 2, 2014.]

FORM—WAIVER OF ATTORNEY: TRIAL (062) [RESCINDED]

[Rescinded effective September 2, 2014.]

RMCLR 3.1.1. WITHDRAWAL OF ATTORNEY

Pursuant to CrRLJ 3.1(e), no attorney may withdraw except upon consent of the court for good cause shown when a case has been set for trial. The motion shall be made in open court with notice to interested parties. Except in cases where withdrawal is mandated by the Rules of Professional Conduct, the court should not permit withdrawal unless there is simultaneous substitution of a lawyer who is prepared to proceed on the scheduled trial date. A substitution of counsel not mandated by the Rules of Professional Conduct which is accompanied by a motion to continue the trial date should only be granted upon actual payment of terms and/or costs.

[Adopted effective September 1, 2001.]

RMCLR 3.2. BAIL

When required to reasonably assure appearance in court for those persons arrested and detained in jail for new offenses, bail shall be set in accordance with a schedule approved by the Presiding Judge and available from the Court Administrator. Bail shall not be set for an accused arrested for new offenses involving domestic violence (Assault Fourth Degree, Violation of a No Contact Order, Violation of a Protection Order) or alcohol related driving offenses (Driving Under the Influence, Physical Control, Minor Operating Motor Vehicle after Alcohol Consumption). Persons held in custody accused of domestic violence or alcohol related driving offenses shall personally appear before a judge the next judicial day following booking into jail.

[Adopted effective September 1, 2001. Amended effective September 1, 2006; September 2, 2013.]

RMCLR 3.3. VIDEO CONFERENCE PROCEEDINGS

(a) Authorization. Preliminary appearances held pursuant to CrRLJ 3.2.1(d), arraignments held pursuant to CrRLJ 3.4 and 4.1, bail hearings held pursuant to CrRLJ 3.2, and trial settings held pursuant to CrRLJ 3.3(f), may be conducted by video conference in which all participants can simultaneously see, hear and speak with each other. Such proceedings shall be deemed held in open court and in the defendant's presence for the purpose of any statute, court rule or policy. All video conference hearings conducted pursuant to this rule shall be public, and the public shall be able to simultaneously see and hear all participants and speak as permitted by the Renton Municipal Court judge, judge pro-tem or court commissioner. Any party may request an in-person hearing which may be granted at the discretion of the Municipal Court judge, judge pro-tem or court commissioner.

(b) Agreement. Other trial court proceedings, including the entry of a Statement of Defendant on Plea of Guilty as provided for by CrRLJ 4.2, may be conducted by video conference only by agreement of the parties, either in writing or on the record, and upon the approval of the Renton Municipal Court judge, judge-pro tem or court commissioner.

(c) Standards for Video Conference Proceedings. The standards for video conference proceedings shall be as specified in CrRLJ 3.4(d)(3).

[Adopted effective September 1, 2011.]

RMCLR 4.1. APPEARANCE AND PLEADINGS BY ATTORNEYS

(a) Pursuant to CrRLJ 4.1, except in cases involving domestic violence or alcohol related driving crimes, an attorney may enter an appearance and/or plea of not guilty on behalf of an accused in any criminal or traffic offense if said appearance or plea is made in writing or made in open court on the record. Appearance must be accompanied by an acknowledgement by defendant that they have been advised of their rights as a person accused of a crime.

(b) A defendant must personally appear in court in cases involving domestic violence (Assault Fourth Degree, Violation of a No Contact Order, Violation of a Protection Order).

(c) A defendant must personally appear in court for arraignment in cases where the crime charged is Driving Under the Influence of Alcohol and/or Drugs or Physical Control.

(d) Unless previously commenced by an appearance made in open court, a written appearance shall commence the running of the time periods established in CrRLJ 3.3 from the date of receipt by the court. A written appearance waiving an arraignment, but without a plea, shall be considered a plea of not guilty, made in writing or in open court, and obviates the need for further arraignment and waives any defects in the complaint other than failure to state a crime.

(e) Telephonic requests or notice by defendant or defense counsel shall not constitute an arraignment, appearance or plea, and shall not commence the time periods under CrRLJ 3.3.

[Adopted effective September 1, 2001. Amended effective September 2, 2013.]

RMCLR 4.2. OFF–RECORD CONTINUANCES

The court may continue cases at the pre-trial hearing off the record at its discretion. Motions to continue cases where a prior continuation of the pre-trial hearing was approved shall be supported by a written statement.

[Adopted effective September 1, 2001. Amended effective September 2, 2013.]

RMCLR 4.5. PETITIONS FOR DEFERRED PROSECUTION

Petitions for deferred prosecution pursuant to RCW 10.05 shall be submitted no later than seven days prior to the date of any pretrial hearing. Copies shall be served on the City of Renton Prosecuting Attorney and the court. All petitions shall be in strict compliance with the requirements of RCW 10.05. Findings of Fact, Conclusions of Law, and Order shall be submitted on Renton Municipal Court form Order Granting Deferred Prosecution.

[Adopted effective September 1, 2001. Amended effective September 2, 2014.]

FORM—GRANTING DEFERRED PROSECUTION (DUI) [RESCINDED]

[Amended effective September 1, 2011. Rescinded effective September 2, 2014.]

FORM—ORDER ON PRETRIAL CONFERENCE (048) [RESCINDED]

[Rescinded effective September 2, 2014.]

RMCLR 6.13. EVIDENCE

(a) Rules of Evidence. The rules of evidence are applicable to criminal prosecutions.

(b) Rules of Evidence–Infractions. The rules of evidence and statutes that relate to evidence in infraction cases shall apply to contested hearings. The court may consider the notice of infraction and any other written report made under oath submitted by the officer who issued the notice or whose written statement was the basis for the issuance of the notice in lieu of the officer's personal appearance at the hearing, unless the defendant has caused the officer to be served with a subpoena to appear.

[Adopted effective September 1, 2001. Amended effective September 2, 2014.]

RMCLR 7.2. SENTENCING

The court shall follow the provisions of CrRLJ 7.2 on Sentencing.

[Adopted effective September 1, 2001.]

RMCLR 7.3. RECALL OF DOMESTIC VIOLENCE NO CONTACT ORDERS

The court shall follow the provisions of CrRLJ 7.3 on Recall of Domestic Violence No Contact Orders.

The calendar is conducted on a walk-in basis. The alleged victim may come to the court on any Thursday morning and petition the court for a hearing.

Upon arrival the alleged victim is provided with a form that memorializes their request to have the order recalled. Once the form is completed the alleged victim is directed into the court-room. The clerk prepares a calendar along with a standardized form/order for the judge's decision. Once the documents are prepared the judge evaluates the request in chambers and makes a decision whether to grant or deny the motion. The judge then goes into court and on the record informs the petitioner of his or her decision.

At the start of the calendar the judge informs the petitioner of the following:

There are three requirements for the judge to recall a no-contact order:

1. There must be a written motion. Since the alleged victim is not a party to the action, the motion is the mechanism to get on the calendar. The petitioner is informed that the judge does not read the motion as it may contain facts of the case before the court and since the petitioner is a potential witness it would not be appropriate for the judge to read if the case is in a pre-trial status.

2. The judge reviews the defendant's case history to determine whether there have been any allegations of a violation of the order or acts of violence since the order was entered. The judge also considers the defendant's criminal history as a whole to determine whether based on that history the judge has concerns that if the order were to be recalled there is a potential for a breach of the peace or violence against the petitioner.

3. Two weeks must have elapsed since the entry of the order was entered.

A petitioner is also informed that the judge's decision is final and that the judge will not entertain any discussion regarding the case.

Before the order is recalled the petitioner is asked by the court on the record whether they have been coerced or compelled in any way to move the court to recall the order. The petitioner is informed that they will no longer enjoy the protection of the court once the order is recalled.

Finally, the petitioner is informed that if they find they are in need of the protection of the court they may return to the court and file a petition of a civil protection order at no cost to them, or in the alternative contact the prosecutor and ask for a motion to re-enter the no-contact order.

[Adopted effective September 2, 2014.]

RENTON MUNICIPAL COURT LOCAL INFRACTION RULES

RMCLIR 1.0. MITIGATION HEARINGS

A defendant charged with an infraction who requests a hearing to explain mitigating circumstances per IRLJ 2.4(3) or RCW 46.63.070(4) shall appear before a magistrate. The magistrate's determination shall be final and is not subject to review before a judge.

[Adopted effective September 1, 2001.]

RMCLIR 1.1. SUBPOENAS

A defendant who requests a hearing to contest the determination that an infraction was committed may file upon the court a written demand that the court subpoena the officer who issued the Notice of Infraction, or whose written statement was the basis for the issuance of the notice if the demand is filed with the court at least 14 days prior to the first setting of the contested hearing. A defendant is responsible for obtaining and serving subpoenas in accordance with IRLJ 3.1 in all other circumstances.

[Adopted effective September 1, 2001.]

RMCLIR 1.2. MOTIONS

All motions, except those motions pursuant to IRLJ 2.2(d), shall be filed with the court and served on all interested parties no later than 14 days prior to the date of the Contested Hearing. Failure to comply with this rule shall constitute a waiver of the motion.

[Adopted effective September 1, 2001.]

RMCLIR 1.3. OBJECTION TO HEARING DATE

A defendant who objects to the hearing date set by the court pursuant to IRLJ 2.6 shall file with the court and serve upon the City Attorney a written motion for a speedy hearing date. Such motion shall be filed and served no later than 10 days from the date of written notice of the contested hearing date. Failure to comply with this rule shall constitute a waiver of the objection.

[Adopted effective September 1, 2001.]

RMCLIR 1.4. EXPERT WITNESS FEES [RESERVED]

[Adopted effective September 1, 2001; reserved effective September 1, 2011.]

RMCLIR 1.5. DECISIONS ON WRITTEN STATEMENTS

Mitigation and contested hearings based on written statements, given under penalty of perjury as provided for in IRLJ 2.4(b)(4) and IRLJ 2.6(c) are authorized. The procedures authorized by IRLJ 3.5 are adopted by this court. To be considered, the written statement(s) must be received by the court pursuant to written instructions provided to the defendant.

[Adopted effective September 2, 2014.]

RMCLIR 1.6. REQUEST FOR SPEED MEASURING DEVICE EXPERT

Request for Speed Measuring Device. The court shall follow the provisions of CrRLJ 6.13(d) concerning the request for a speed measuring device (SMD) expert, except that a request for a SMD expert shall be in writing and must be received by the court clerk at least seven court days prior to the original trial or hearing date.

[Adopted effective September 2, 2014.]

SAMMAMISH MUNICIPAL COURT—
[No Local Rules]

PUBLISHER'S NOTE

This municipal court follows the Local Rules of the District Court for King County.

SEATAC MUNICIPAL COURT LOCAL RULES

Including Amendments Received Through
August 15, 2015

Table of Rules

LOCAL CRIMINAL RULES

STMCLR 1.7. ADOPTION OF LOCAL RULES

These rules are adopted pursuant to CrRLJ 1.7.

[Adopted effective September 1, 2003.]

STMCLR 1.8. TITLE OF RULES

These rules may be known and cited as the SeaTac Municipal Court Local Rules and shall be referred to as STMCLR.

[Adopted effective September 1, 2003.]

STMCLR 1.9. READINESS FOR TRIAL HEARINGS

A Readiness Hearing shall be held before the Municipal Court Judge in every case in which a timely demand for jury is made. Notice shall be given in open court by the Judge to all parties indicating the date and time for this hearing. At the Readiness Hearing the Prosecuting Attorney, the Defendant, and the Defendant's counsel (if any) must be present. Furthermore, parties shall advise the court if the case can be settled in a manner other than a jury trial. The court will strike the scheduled Jury Trial and may issue a Bench Warrant for any Defendant that does not appear at the Readiness Hearing.

[Former Rule 17 adopted September 1, 1999; amended and renumbered as STMCLR 1.9 effective September 1, 2003; amended effective September 1, 2011.]

STMCLR 1.10. USE OF COLLECTION AGENCY

The court may use the services of one or more collection agencies for the purposes of collecting unpaid and delinquent penalties on infractions, criminal fines, costs, assessments and forfeitures. The terms and conditions of the contract for collection services shall be between the City of SeaTac and/or the SeaTac Municipal Court and said collection agency(ies), and may be amended as necessary. The collection agency's fee or charge, as set forth in said contract, shall be added by the collection agency as a court cost to the total judgment of the court against each defendant whose account is referred by the court to the collection agency.

[Former Rule 7 adopted March 17, 1994. Amended and renumbered as STMCLR 1.10, effective September 1, 2003. Amended effective September 2, 2013.]

STMCLR 1.11. REFUNDING OF POSTED BAIL [RESCINDED]

[Adopted effective September 1, 2003. Rescinded effective September 2, 2013.]

STMCLR 2.2. REQUIREMENTS FOR PAYMENT ON COURTESY WARRANT CALENDAR [RESCINDED]

[Former Rule 15 adopted September 15, 1997. Amended December 10, 1997; March 26, 1998; September 1, 1998; September 1, 1999; amended and renumbered as STMCLR 2.2, effective September 1, 2003. Rescinded effective September 2, 2013.]

STMCLR 3.2. BAIL IN DOMESTIC VIOLENCE CASES

A Defendant who is detained in jail after the initial arrest for a misdemeanor or gross misdemeanor shall be released upon posting bail in the amount of $500 for a misdemeanor and $1,000 for a gross misdemeanor, except for the following offenses:

1. Domestic Violence Offenses: Defendants shall be held in non-bailable status pending hearing the next court day following booking for any crime alleging domestic violence under RCW 10.99.020(5) or applicable ordinance.

2. Driving Under the Influence/Physical Control: Defendants shall be held in non-bailable status pending hearing the next court day following booking for Driving Under the Influence (RCW 46.61.502) or Physical Control of a Motor Vehicle While Under the Influence (RCW 46.61.504).

[Former Rule 3.2.1 amended and renumbered as STMCLR 3.2 effective September 1, 2011.]

STMCLR 3.4. RE: VIDEO CONFERENCE PROCEEDINGS

(1) **Authorization.** Preliminary appearances held pursuant to CrRLJ 3.2.1(d), arraignments held pursuant to CrRLJ 3.4 and CrRLJ 4.1, bail hearings held pursuant to CrRLJ 3.2, and trial settings held pursuant to CrRLJ 3.3(f), may be conducted by video conference in which all participants can simultaneously see, hear, and speak with each other. Such proceedings shall be deemed held in open court and in the defendant's presence for the purposes of any statute, court rule or policy. All video conference hearings conducted pursuant to this rule shall be public, and the public shall be able to simultaneously see and hear all participants and speak as permitted by the SeaTac Municipal Court Judge or Judge Pro–Tem. Any party may request an in-person hearing, which may be granted at the discretion of the SeaTac Municipal Court Judge or Judge Pro–Tem.

(2) **Agreement.** Other trial court proceedings including the entry of a Statement of Defendant on Plea of Guilty as provided for by CrRLJ 4.2 may be conducted by video conference only by agreement of the parties, either in writing or on the record, and upon the approval of the SeaTac Municipal Court Judge or Judge Pro–Tem.

(3) **Standards for Video Conference Proceedings.** The judge, counsel, all parties, and the public must be able to see and hear each other during proceedings, and speak as permitted by the judge. Video conference facilities must provide for confidential communications between attorney and client and security sufficient to protect the safety of all participants and observers. In interpreted proceedings, the interpreter must be located next to the defendant and the proceeding must be conducted to assure that the interpreter can hear all participants.

[Adopted effective September 1, 2007.]

STMCLR 4.1. AUTHORIZATION FOR CONTINUANCE OF ARRAIGNMENTS [RESCINDED]

[Former Rule 8 adopted March 24, 1994. Amended and renumbered as STMCLR 4.1, effective September 1, 2003. Rescinded effective September 2, 2013.]

STMCLR 4.5. PETITIONS FOR DEFERRED PROSECUTION

All petitions for deferred prosecution shall be in strict compliance with the requirements of RCW 10.05. Copies shall be served on the City of SeaTac Prosecuting Attorney. Findings of Fact, Conclusions of Law, and Order shall be submitted on SeaTac Municipal Court form *Order Granting Deferred Prosecution*.

[Adopted effective September 1, 2003.]

STMCLR 6.1. TRIAL BY JURY [RESCINDED]

[Former Rule 18 adopted September 1, 1999. Amended and renumbered as STMCLR 6.1, effective September 1, 2003. Rescinded effective September 2, 2013.]

STMCLR 10.1. ANTIHARASSMENT PROTECTION ORDERS

1. By adoption of this local rule, the SeaTac Municipal Court hereby exercises jurisdiction and cognizance of any civil actions and proceedings brought under RCW 10.14.150, as now or hereafter amended, except the SeaTac Municipal Court shall transfer such actions and proceedings to the superior court when it is shown that the respondent to the petition is under eighteen years of age.

2. The SeaTac Municipal Court's jurisdiction pursuant to this rule shall be limited to situations:

a. When the alleged acts of unlawful harassment occurred within the SeaTac city limits; or

b. When the respondent resides within the SeaTac city limits at the time the petition is filed; or

c.   When the respondent may be served within the SeaTac city limits if it is the same county or judicial district where a respondent resides.

3.   The Clerk of the Municipal Court may charge a filing fee in an amount equal to that charged by the King County District Court for the filing of a Petition for an Antiharassment Protection Order, but such filing fee shall not be less than fifty-one dollars ($51.00). The Municipal Court Judge has discretion to waive or reduce the filing fee upon a showing of indigence, financial hardship, or other good cause.

[Adopted effective September 1, 2005.]

LOCAL INFRACTION RULES

STMCLIR 1.3.   ADOPTION OF LOCAL RULES

These rules are adopted pursuant to IRLJ 1.3.

[Adopted effective September 1, 2003.]

STMCLIR 1.4.   TITLE OF RULES

These rules may be known and cited as the SeaTac Municipal Court Local Infraction Rules and shall be referred to as STMCLIR.

[Adopted effective September 1, 2003.]

STMCLIR 1.5.   REQUIREMENTS FOR PAYMENT FOLLOWING INFRACTION HEARINGS [RESCINDED]

[Former Rule 11 adopted September 15, 1994. Amended and renumbered as STMCLR 1.5, effective September 1, 2003. Rescinded effective September 2, 2013.]

STMCLIR 2.4.   HANDLING OF REQUESTS FOR CONTESTED HEARINGS AFTER FAILURE TO RESPOND [RESCINDED]

[Former Rule 9 adopted May 3, 1994. Amended and renumbered as STMCLIR 2.4, effective September 1, 2003. Rescinded effective September 2, 2013.]

STMCLIR 3.5.   AUTHORIZING DECISIONS ON WRITTEN STATEMENTS

The defendant may elect to contest or mitigate an infraction or petition for a deferred finding by submitting a written statement by mail or e-mail made under penalty of perjury pursuant to and in accordance with IRLJ 2.4, IRLJ 2.6, and IRLJ 3.5.   A defendant who elects to proceed by requesting a decision on written statement shall be deemed to have waived an in-court hearing to contest or mitigate the infraction in person. A petition for deferred finding which is denied by the Court will be treated as a request for a mitigation hearing on written statement.

[Former Rule 13, adopted April 6, 1995. Amended and renumbered as STMCLIR 3.5, effective September 1, 2003. Amended effective September 2, 2013.]

STMCLIR 6.2.   MANDATORY LIABILITY INSURANCE VIOLATIONS—PROOF OF INSURANCE [RESCINDED]

[Former Rule 5 adopted June 22, 1993. Amended and renumbered as Rule 10, effective June 6, 1994; former Rule 10 amended and renumbered as STMCLIR 6.2, effective September 1, 2003. Rescinded effective September 2, 2013.]

STMCLIR 6.6(d).   SPEED MEASURING DEVICE: DESIGN AND CONSTRUCTION CERTIFICATION [RESCINDED]

[Former LIRLJ 6.6(d) adopted effective May 21, 1996. Amended and renumbered as STMCLIR 6.6(d), effective September 1, 2003. Rescinded effective September 2, 2013.]

SEATTLE MUNICIPAL COURT LOCAL RULES

Including Amendments Received Through
August 15, 2015

Table of Rules

GENERAL RULES

SMCLR 1.7. ADOPTION OF LOCAL RULES

These rules are adopted pursuant to CrRLJ 1.7.
[Effective May 2, 1988.]

SMCLR 1.8. TITLE OF RULES

These rules may be known and cited as Seattle Municipal Court Local Rules, and shall be referred to as SMCLR.
[Effective May 2, 1988.]

SMCLR 2.4. COMPLAINT

Whenever the plaintiff refiles a case that has previously been dismissed without prejudice, the charging document must reflect the word "REFILED" and must set forth the Municipal Court of Seattle case number.

[Effective August 21, 1991.]

LOCAL ADMINISTRATIVE RULES

SMCLR 9.3. DOCUMENT AND RECORDING FEES

Fees for the duplication and preparation of documents and recordings shall be set at cost by the Court Administrator, from whom a schedule shall be available.

[Adopted effective September 1, 1997; amended effective September 1, 2004.]

SMCLR 10.1. CALL OF CALENDARS

At the start of each session the magistrate or commissioner shall order the names scheduled for hearing to be read. This procedure shall be followed for a defendant in an infraction case. The court may issue a finding that the infraction was committed, and may enter a default judgment in the amount of the bail, plus a default penalty as provided by law.

[Effective May 2, 1988; amended effective September 1, 2004.]

SMCLR 10.2. PRESIDING JUDGE

1. Election and Term of Presiding Judge.

(a) The judges shall elect by a majority of all the judges a Presiding Judge for a term of no1 t less than two years. The term of office shall commence on January 1 following election. The election should occur a minimum of two months prior to the beginning of the new term.

(b) Candidates for the position of Presiding Judge shall demonstrate their interest in the position by expressing their views to other judges about the strategic direction of the court.

(c) In the same manner, the judges will elect an Assistant Presiding Judge for a term of not less than two years. The term of office for Assistant Presiding Judge shall commence on January 1 following election. The election should occur a minimum of two months prior to the beginning of the new term.

(d) *Vacancies.* Vacancies in the office of Presiding Judge, Assistant Presiding Judge or in the event the immediate Past Presiding Judge is unavailable, the position shall be filled by a majority vote of all the judges, at a regular or special meeting of the judges, within 30 days after the vacancy occurs. In the case of a vacancy in the office of Presiding Judge, the Assistant Presiding Judge shall serve as the acting Presiding Judge until said election. In the case of vacancy in the office of Assistant Presiding Judge, the third member of the Executive Committee shall act as interim Assistant Presiding Judge. The judge elected to fill the vacancy shall serve the remainder of the term of the Presiding Judge or Assistant Presiding Judge. In the absence of both the Presiding Judge and Assistant Presiding Judge, the third member of the Executive Committee shall act as interim Presiding Judge until said election.

(e) *Failure or Refusal to Elect.* If the judges fail or refuse to elect a Presiding Judge or Assistant Presiding Judge, the Presiding Judge then in office shall notify the Supreme Court of said failure or refusal no later than 45 days after the vacancy occurs, and the Chief Justice of the Supreme Court shall appoint a Presiding Judge or Assistant Presiding Judge pursuant to GR 29.

(f) *Removal.* The Presiding Judge or Assistant Presiding Judge may be removed by majority vote of the judges at a regular or special meeting of the judges called by any judge upon at least ten days notice in writing or by court electronic mail sent to all judges stating that removal or the Presiding Judge or Assistant Presiding Judge is at issue.

(g) *Ballots.* Casting of ballots pursuant to this rule may be made in person, by court electronic mail, telephonically, by letter or other written notice or by proxy given to another judge.

2. Responsibilities of Presiding Judge.

(a) The Presiding Judge shall be responsible for leading the management and administration of the court's business, recommending policies and procedures that improve the court's effectiveness, and allocating resources in a way that maximizes the court's ability to resolve disputes fairly and expeditiously. Judicial caseload of the court shall be adjusted to provide the Presiding Judge with sufficient time and resources to properly perform the duties of office as required by GR 29.

(b) The Presiding Judge shall direct the work of the Court Administrator in managing all administrative, non-judicial functions and all other court personnel.

(c) When the Presiding Judge is unavailable, the Assistant Presiding Judge shall undertake the duties of the Presiding Judge. If both the Presiding Judge and the Assistant Presiding Judge are unavailable, the third member of the Executive Committee shall undertake the duties of the Presiding Judge.

(d) The Presiding Judge shall directly supervise non-elected judicial officers.

(e) The Presiding Judge may delegate specific supervisory responsibilities to other judges. The Presiding Judge shall make specific judicial assignments for supervisory duties to other judges for each calendar year.

(f) *Executive Committee.* The executive committee will consist of the Presiding Judge, Assistant Presiding Judge, the immediate Past Presiding Judge and the Court Administrator. The Executive Committee will act in an advisory capacity to the Presiding Judge in the management of the Court, review administrative proposals, judicial projects and proposed court policies. The Executive Committee shall make no binding policy decisions absent prior approval by the majority of judges.

(g) A Standing Advisory Committee, referred to as the Bench–Bar Committee, appointed and chaired by the Presiding Judge or his/her designee judge, may meet monthly to discuss policies, procedures and other matters that may be of mutual interest. The Bench–Bar Committee shall be comprised of the Court Administrator, Chief Clerk, Chief Bailiff, Probation Director, the City Attorney or designee and the Directors or designee of the Public Defense agencies. A member of the Washington Association of Criminal

Defense Lawyers and the chair or his/her designee of the Criminal Law Section of the King County Bar Association may also be asked to participate.

[Effective June 13, 1989; amended effective September 1, 1997; September 1, 1998; September 1, 2003; September 1, 2006; September 1, 2011; September 1, 2012; September 1, 2015.]

SMCLR 10.3. MEETING OF THE JUDGES

The judges shall meet at least once each month, except for July and August, at such hour and place as the presiding judge shall designate. The presiding judge shall preside at all such meetings and the judges shall consider such matters pertaining to the administration of justice in the court as may be brought before them. The presiding judge shall prepare an agenda for the meeting and provide a copy for the other judges in advance thereof. The judges shall at such meetings, by majority vote of those present, plus proxies, adopt rules for the proper administration of justice in the court.

[Effective May 2, 1988; amended effective September 1, 1997.]

SMCLR 10.4. MAGISTRATES

The court may employ judicial officers as Magistrates to assist in the administration of justice and accomplishment of the work of the court. The Presiding Judge shall have the authority to assign work to the Magistrates. The duties and responsibilities that have been assigned to Magistrates include the adjudication of contested civil traffic infractions, parking infractions, and various ordinance violations, presiding over mitigation and contested settlement conferences, ruling on search warrant requests, and such other duties as may be assigned by the Presiding Judge.

Magistrates are expected to perform their assigned duties and responsibilities in a timely and efficient manner, consistent with law, and with appropriate judicial demeanor and respect for the rights of court participants and court personnel. Magistrates are further expected to adhere to the Code of Judicial Conduct and to the Code of Conduct for Employees of Municipal Court. Failure of magistrate to fulfill any of his or her duties or responsibilities, as determined in the judgment and discretion of the presiding judge, may result in disciplinary action including termination of employment.

[Effective June 13, 1989; amended effective September 1, 2003; September 1, 2011; amended on an emergency basis effective September 1, 2014; amended on a permanent basis effective September 1, 2015.]

LOCAL CIVIL RULES

SMCLR 10.7. CIVIL CASE PROCEDURES

(a) **Scope of Rule.** This rule applies to civil actions filed with the Seattle Municipal Court that do not fall within the scope of infractions under the IRLJ and SMCLR.

(b) **Commencement of Action.** A civil action is commenced by filing with the court a complaint signed as required under CRLJ 11. Upon the filing of a complaint, the civil clerk will assign a case number to the matter. Plaintiff must affix the case number to the summons and complaint and serve the summons and complaint on the defendant pursuant to CRLJ 4, and file copies of the summons and proof of service with the court. Unless a statute or rule provides for a different time requirement, defendant(s) must file a written answer with the court and serve a copy on the other party no later than 20 days after being served.

(c) **Pre–Settlement Conferences.** Pre-settlement conferences are informal proceedings, presided over by a magistrate, to discuss the status of cases and possible settlement options. Either party may request a pre-settlement conference by filing a written request with the civil clerk. The civil clerk shall notify all parties of any pre-settlement conference dates.

(d) **Trial Settings.** Either party may request a case be set for trial by filing a note for trial for an available trial date with the civil clerk. Available trial dates may be obtained from the civil clerk. The proposed trial date must be scheduled at least 45 days after the note for trial is filed. The party filing the note for trial must serve a copy on all other parties on the same day the note is filed with the clerk. The note for trial may be served by first class mail.

(e) **Disclosure of Witnesses.** All parties shall disclose all persons with relevant factual or expert knowledge whom the party reserves the option to call as witnesses at trial no later than 30 days prior to the trial date. The disclosure deadline is not extended if a trial date is continued. Disclosure shall include the following:

1. The name, address, and phone number of each witness.

2. *Lay Witnesses.* A brief description of the witness' relevant knowledge.

3. *Experts.* A brief description of the subject matter of the expert's testimony and a statement of qualifications.

Any person not disclosed in compliance with this rule may not be called to testify at trial, unless the Court orders otherwise for good cause and subject to such conditions as justice requires.

(f) **Discovery.** All discovery must be completed 7 days prior to the first assigned trial date. The discovery cutoff date shall not be extended if a trial date is continued, unless approved by the Court or by agreement of the parties.

(g) Demand for Jury Trials. A demand for a jury trial shall be made by filing a jury demand with the civil clerk and paying a jury fee as authorized by RCW 3.62.060 no later than 7 days after the notice of trial date is mailed or otherwise delivered to the parties. The party requesting the jury trial must serve the demand for jury to all other parties on the same date the jury demand is filed with the civil clerk. The demand for jury may be served by first class mail. Failure to comply with this rule shall be deemed a waiver of the right to a jury trial. The deadline for demanding a jury trial shall not be extended if a trial date is continued.

(h) Motions.

1. *Dates of Filing, Hearing and Consideration.* The moving party shall file and serve all motion documents no later than 6 court days before the date the party wishes the motion to be considered. If the case is set for trial, all motions and supporting documents must be filed and served by the moving party no less than 14 days prior to the trial date. Either party may request oral argument by requesting it in the party's written documents.

2. *Note for Motion.* A Note for Motion designating an available hearing date shall be filed and served with the motion. Available hearing dates and Note for Motion forms are available from the civil clerk's office.

3. *Opposing Documents.* Any party opposing a motion shall file the original responsive papers in opposition to a motion and serve copies on all parties no later than 12:00 noon two court days before the date the motion is scheduled to be heard.

4. *Reply.* Any documents in strict reply shall be filed and copies served on parties no later than 12:00 noon on the court day before the motion is scheduled to be heard.

5. *Noncompliance.* Any material offered at a time later than required by this rule, and any reply material which is not in strict reply, will not be considered by the Court.

6. *Form of Motions and Opposition Documents.*

(a) The motion and any memorandum in opposition shall conform to the following:

    a. Relief Requested

    b. Statement of Facts

    c. Statement of Issues

    d. Evidence relied upon

    e. Authority

    f. Proposed Order for Relief clearly marked as "Proposed"

(b) The initial motion and opposing memorandum shall not exceed 12 pages and the reply memoranda shall not exceed five pages without permission of the Court.

(i) Pleadings and Other Documents. The Seattle Municipal Court case number shall be noted in the caption of all pleadings and documents filed with the Court. Pleadings and documents with incorrect or missing case numbers may be deemed null and void. Court clerks have no responsibility for obtaining or correcting case numbers, dates, times or courts.

1. Documents requiring clerk's action shall include, in the caption, above the cause number, the words "CLERK'S ACTION REQUIRED."

2. All documents filed with the court shall comply with GR 14 and GR 30. Those which do not conform with these rules may be rejected by court clerks.

(j) Motions to Reconsider. Motions for reconsideration of an order or judgment must be filed no later than 10 days after the date of entry of the order or judgment. The form of motion shall conform to section (h). The motion shall set forth specific grounds for the reconsideration, and will be considered without oral argument unless called for by the Court. No response to a motion to reconsider shall be filed unless requested by the Court. No motion for reconsideration will be granted without such a request. If a response is called for, a reply may be filed within two days of service of the response.

(k) Trial Briefs. Trial briefs and bench memorandums may be submitted at the Court's discretion.

(*l*) Case Removal to Superior Court. A party seeking case removal to Superior Court shall comply with RCW 4.14.010, RCW 4.14.020 and CRLJ 14A.

[Adopted effective September 1, 2012. Amended effective September 1, 2015.]

SMCLR 73. TRIAL DE NOVO

(a) Scope of Rule. This rule applies only to proceedings pursuant to Ch. 11.30, Seattle Municipal Code, relating to redemption of impounded vehicles and post-impoundment hearing procedures. The proceedings to which this rule applies is defined by and limited to those expressly set forth in the Seattle Municipal Code permitting de novo appeals from an administrative hearings officer to the Municipal Court of Seattle.

(b) Filing Notice of Appeal Jurisdictional—Service. When an appeal is permitted by law from a Magistrate or Commissioner to the Municipal Court, such appeal shall be taken by filing in the Municipal Court clerk's office a notice of appeal within fifteen days after the decision of the Magistrate or Commissioner and payment of a filing fee to the Municipal Court in the sum set by law, pursuant to RCW 3.62.060 and RCW 7.75.035, unless said fee is waived. The Magistrate or Commissioner shall provide, upon request, a notice of appeal form approved by the Municipal Court. A copy of the notice of appeal shall be served upon the chief of police and upon the City Attorney. Filing and serving the notice of appeal and payment of the filing fee are the only jurisdictional requirements for an appeal. The notice of appeal shall contain the mailing address of appellant.

(c) Waiver of Filing Fee for Indigents. A party seeking to appeal partially or wholly at public expense must seek a waiver of the filing fee from the Presiding Judge or his or her designee by filing and presenting to the Presiding Judge, or designee, within the fifteen day period, a proposed notice of appeal and an affidavit setting forth the moving party's total assets, expenses and liabilities. The Presiding Judge, or designee, shall notify the party of his or her decision in writing within three court days of filing the affidavit. If the Presiding Judge, or designee, determines that the filing fee shall be waived, the Presiding Judge, or designee, shall direct the clerk to file the notice of appeal.

(d) Discovery. Upon written demand, a party shall provide the other party, within seven days of receipt of the demand, with a list of witnesses, together with their addresses and telephone numbers and copies of all documents the party will offer at the de novo hearing; the city shall mail discovery demanded pursuant to this rule to appellant's address contained in the Notice of Appeal. No other discovery shall be required. If, after compliance with this rule or orders pursuant to it, a party discovers additional witnesses or information that is subject to disclosure, the party shall promptly notify the other party of the existence of such additional material. Failure to provide discovery in accordance with this rule is grounds for exclusion of evidence or such lesser sanction as the court deems just and equitable.

(e) Scheduling of De Novo Hearing. The hearing shall be scheduled not sooner than twelve but not later than 21 days from the filing of the notice of appeal, and shall be set on a Municipal Court bench trial calendar. The clerk shall notify the parties in writing of the hearing date, and shall mail notice to the parties within three days of filing of the notice of appeal. The Presiding Judge or designee has the discretion to schedule a contested hearing for a parking infraction that was alleged to occur at the time of the impoundment at the same time as the de novo hearing.

(f) Procedures at Hearing. At the hearing, the city shall be represented by a lawyer. Appellant may be represented by a lawyer. The Rules of Evidence applicable to civil cases shall apply. If an infraction is consolidated with the hearing, IRLJ 3.3(c) shall apply to the infraction. If the court finds the impoundment to have been proper, the court shall enter an order so stating. If the court finds the impoundment to have been improper, the court shall enter an order so stating, and shall order the immediate release of the

vehicle to the registered owner of the vehicle. If the costs of impoundment, towing, removal, storage and administrative fees and filing fee have been paid, the court shall enter a judgment in favor of appellant in that sum. If the court finds the impoundment to have been proper but that the fees charged for impoundment, removal, towing, storage or administration were improper, the court shall determine the correct fees to be charged and, if the costs and fees have been paid, the court shall enter a judgment against the city and in favor of the appellant for the amount of the overpayment.

(g) Time Payments. The court may grant time payments in cases of extreme financial need and where there is an effective guarantee of payment. If the court grants time payments, the court shall order the release of the vehicle immediately if authorized by law or at the end of the authorized impound period.

[Emergency rule, adopted December 4, 1998, effective January 1, 1999; amended effective September 1, 2002; September 1, 2004; September 1, 2015.]

SMCLR 74. RULES ON APPEAL OF CODE OF ETHICS VIOLATIONS

(a) Scope of Rule. This rule applies only to appeals of fines imposed by the Seattle Ethics and Elections Commission (Commission) upon city employees imposed pursuant to Ch. 4.16, Seattle Municipal Code.

(b) Filing Notice of Appeal. When an appeal is permitted by law to the Municipal Court from a fine imposed by the Commission, such appeal shall be taken by filing a notice of appeal in the Municipal Court clerk's office, and paying a filing fee to the Municipal Court in the amount set by law, pursuant to RCW 3.62.060 and RCW 7.75.035, for filing a civil action in district court, within twenty days after the date of the Commission's decision. The notice of appeal shall contain, in separate numbered paragraphs, statements of the specific findings of fact, conclusions of law, or aspects of the fine on which appellant seeks review, the basis for the appeal, and a brief statement of the relief requested. The appellant shall attach a copy of the written decision of the Commission being appealed. A copy of the notice of appeal shall be served upon the Executive Director of the Commission. Timely filing and serving the notice of appeal and payment of the filing fee are the only jurisdictional requirements for an appeal. The notice of appeal shall contain the mailing address of appellant.

(c) Stay of Proceedings. Upon timely filing and service of a notice of appeal, the fine imposed by the Commission shall be stayed.

(d) Scope of Review. An appeal pursuant to this rule is on the Commission's record and is not de novo. The court shall uphold the Commission's decision if it determines that the decision is not arbitrary, capricious or otherwise illegal and that the decision is supported by substantial evidence in the Commission's record. No new evidence shall be taken by or submitted to the court. If the court affirms the Commission, then the fine is immediately due. Otherwise, the court shall modify, reverse or remand the matter to the Commission.

(e) Procedures.

(1) *Record on Appeal.* Within thirty days after the notice of appeal is filed and served, appellant shall, at appellant's expense, provide the Executive Director of the Commission with a report of proceedings to the extent deemed necessary for review by appellant. The report of proceedings may take the form of a "verbatim report of proceedings" as provided in Rules of Appellate Procedure (RAP) 9.2 or an "agreed report of proceedings" as provided in RAP 9.4. If appellant prepares less than all of the verbatim report of proceedings, the Executive Director may prepare a transcript of additional portions of the hearing, at the Commission's expense. The Executive Director shall review the transcript. Appellant may serve and file objections to, and propose amendments to, the verbatim report of proceedings as approved by the Executive Director. If objections or amendments are served and filed, any objections or proposed amendments must be determined by the members of the Commission before whom the proceedings were held. The Executive Director shall provide appellant with a copy of the relevant papers and exhibits which were considered by the Commission, which shall be included in the record to the court. The Executive Director shall file the report of proceedings and record with the court.

(2) *Sanctions for Failure to Perfect Appeal.* The court, upon motion, may dismiss an appeal that is not diligently pursued by appellant. The court, upon motion, may reverse a fine imposed by the Commission where the court finds that the Executive Director has not, in good faith, pursued the preparation of the record.

(f) Hearing. Within thirty days of the filing of the notice of appeal, the presiding judge shall assign the appeal to a judge or judge pro tempore. Appellant shall file with the court and serve upon the Executive Director a brief, not to exceed fifteen pages, within thirty days of receipt by the court of the agreed or approved record. Respondent shall file and serve a brief, not to exceed fifteen pages, within thirty days of service of appellant's brief. Appellant may file and serve a reply brief, not to exceed five pages, within ten days of service of respondent's brief. Briefs shall conform with RAP 10.4(a). The court shall schedule oral argument, unless waived, within thirty days of filing of respondent's brief. Each party shall be allowed ten minutes for oral argument. Appellant may reserve part of his or her ten minutes for rebuttal argument.

(g) Decision. The court shall state its decision at the conclusion of oral argument or shall prepare a written decision with thirty days of oral argument.

(h) Costs. The filing fee and the costs of preparing the record may be taxed against the non-prevailing party. Where the court determines that the fine was properly imposed, then the Commission is the prevailing party. Where the court reverses the fine, then appellant is the prevailing party. Where the court modifies the fine or remands the matter to the Commission, then the court will determine which party has substantially prevailed. A prevailing party shall file a cost bill with the court and serve a copy of the bill on the non-prevailing party within ten days after the court has announced or filed its decision. The non-prevailing party may object to items in the cost bill by filing with the court objections to the cost bill within ten days after service of the cost bill. The court will determine costs within ten days after the time has expired for filing objections to the cost bill. No oral argument will be taken on costs.

[Emergency rule, adopted December 4, 1998, effective January 1, 1999; amended effective September 1, 2002; September 1, 2004.]

LOCAL CRIMINAL RULES

SMCLR 2.3. SEARCH AND SEIZURE

(c) Issuance and Contents. A search warrant may be issued only if the court determines there is probable cause for the issuance of a warrant. There must be an affidavit, a document as provided in RCW 9A.72.085 or any law amendatory thereto, or sworn testimony establishing the grounds for issuing the warrant. The sworn testimony may be an electronically recorded telephonic statement, facsimile machine document or electronically mailed document. The recording or a duplication of the recording facsimile, or electronic mail shall be a part of the court record and shall be transcribed if requested by a party if

there is a challenge to the validity of the warrant or if ordered by the court. The evidence in support of the finding of probable cause shall be preserved and shall be subject to constitutional limitations for such determinations and may be hearsay in whole or in part. If the court finds that probable cause for the issuance of a warrant exists, it shall issue a warrant or direct an individual whom it authorizes for such purpose to affix the court's signature to a warrant identifying the property or person and naming or describing the person, place or thing to be searched. The court's authorization may be done by electronic signature process. A record shall be made of any additional submitted evidence on which the court relies.

(h) Search Warrants. After execution and return, the search warrant shall be filed by number and description of the person or property to be searched. An index will be maintained and available to the public by the Clerk's Office.

[Adopted effective September 1, 2015.]

SMCLR 3.1.1. INDIGENT SERVICES OTHER THAN LAWYER

A lawyer for a defendant who is financially unable to obtain expert services necessary to an adequate defense may request them by a motion to the court. The motion must be in writing, and shall be accompanied by (1) an affidavit or sworn declaration, signed by the defendant, setting forth the defendant's assets, income, liabilities, monthly expenses, dependents and employment; (2) an affidavit or declaration setting forth the name, address of the expert, cost, qualifications of the expert and a summary of the expert's proposed testimony as it relates to the case in question; (3) a copy of all of the discovery material provided by the plaintiff; and (4) any other materials to assist the court in determining whether the services are necessary. The pleadings may be presented ex-parte to the court which heard the last pre-trial hearing. Unless otherwise directed by the court, the motion will be decided exclusively on the pleadings without oral argument. If the defendant requests that the affidavits or declarations be sealed because they contain privileged information not discoverable by the plaintiff, the court may order the clerk to place the affidavit or declaration in a sealed envelope for filing. Requests for investigative services likely to exceed $600 and requests for expert services likely to exceed $1000 should be submitted to the Presiding Judge.

[Effective May 2, 1988; amended effective September 1, 1997; September 1, 2011; September 1, 2015.]

SMCLR 3.2(o). RELEASE OF ACCUSED

Bail shall be set in accordance with CrRLJ 3.2(o)1. Bail shall not be set for accused persons arrested for new domestic violence charges, stalking, cyberstalking, violation of an anti-harassment order, no contact/protection order violation, willful violation of a no contact order and firearms offenses as set out in 12A.14.071 (discharge of a firearm), 12A.14.075 (unlawful use of weapons to intimidate another, 12A.14.130 (failure to register as a firearms offender), 12A.14.140 (unlawful carrying of pistol), 12A.14.150 (unlawful possession of loaded rifle in motor vehicle), 12A.14.180 (unlawful delivery of a pistol), 12A.14.195 (unlawful sale or transfer of firearm) 12A.14.200, (altering identifying marks of firearm), 12A.14.080(c) (possess firearm—public property) and 12A.14.080(e) (firearm—noise suppression device) except at the preliminary appearance or arraignment.

[Adopted effective July 8, 1993; amended effective September 1, 1994; September 1, 1997; September 1, 2002;

September 1, 2004; September 1, 2006; amended on an emergency basis effective June 24, 2014; amended on a permanent basis effective September 2, 2014; amended on an emergency basis effective April 6, 2015; amended on a permanent basis effective September 1, 2015.]

SMCLR 3.2.1. ELECTRONIC FILING OF PROBABLE CAUSE DOCUMENTS

For purposes of determining probable cause to detain under CrRLJ 3.2.1 (a), the court may rely on documents filed electronically by a law enforcement officer following the procedure established by GR 30. The documents must be authenticated by a law enforcement officer using a digital signature that complies with the requirements of RCW 19.34 or GR 30, or by the arresting or citing officer explicitly signing the statement and transmitting the eSuperform within the King County Booking and Referral System, as permitted by GR 30.

[Adopted on an emergency basis, effective November 28, 2012; adopted on a permanent basis, effective September 2, 2013.]

SMCLR 3.4. PRESENCE OF THE DEFENDANT

(a) Video Conference Proceedings.

(1) Pursuant to GR 19 and CrRLJ 3.4(d), proceedings in Seattle Municipal Court may be conducted via video conference or other similar technology.

[Adopted on an emergency basis, effective July 1, 2013; adopted on a permanent basis, effective September 2, 2013. Amended effective September 1, 2015.]

SMCLR 4.1(a)(2). ARRAIGNMENT

(i) Arraignments. Arraignments shall be in accordance with CrRLJ 4.1 and 4.2. A lawyer may, pursuant to CrRLJ 4.1(e) and SMCLR 8.4.1, enter an appearance on behalf of a client except in cases in which the docket or charging document states that one or more of the charges involves domestic violence, harassment, violation of an anti-harassment order, driving under the influence, physical control, assault, stalking, or firearms offenses as set out in 12A.14.071 (discharge of a firearm), 12A.14.075 (unlawful use of weapons to intimidate another) and 12A.14.080 (unlawful use of weapon) whereupon defendant's presence is mandatory. The clerk may continue an arraignment at the request of the defendant or counsel for no more than two weeks, except in cases in which the docket or charging document states that one or more of the charges involves domestic violence, violation of an anti-harassment order, harassment, driving under the influence, physical control, assault, stalking or firearms offenses as set out in 12A.14.071 (discharge of a firearm), 12A.14.075 (unlawful use of weapons to intimidate another) and 12A.14.080 (unlawful use of weapon). Where legislation mandates the defendant's appearance on the next judicial day following arrest if the defendant is served with a citation or complaint at the time of the arrest, the term "next judicial day" as applied in Seattle Municipal Court shall mean within 72 hours of arrest excluding Sundays and holidays. Appearances may be entered only after a complaint or citation and notice has been filed.

(ii) Intake Hearings. Defendants who wish to plead not guilty who are out of custody and who are not charged with an offense involving domestic violence, violation of an anti-harassment order, harassment, driving under the influence, physical control, assault, stalking or firearms offenses as set out in 12A.14.071 (discharge of a firearm), 12A.14.075 (unlawful use of weapons to intimidate another) and 12A.14.080 (unlawful use of weapon) may, at the time summoned for arraignment, appear before a clerk; the clerk shall assign a pre-trial hearing date without judicial involvement. Any defendant who so desires may appear before a judge at this initial intake appearance for formal arraignment. The clerk may continue an arraignment at the request of the defendant or counsel for no more than two weeks, except in cases in which the docket or charging document states that one or more of the charges involves domestic violence, violation of an anti-harassment order, harassment, driving under the influence, physical control, assault, stalking or firearms offenses as set out in 12A.14.071 (discharge of a firearm), 12A.14.075 (unlawful use of weapons to intimidate another) and 12A.14.080 (unlawful use of weapon).

(iii) Delays. Defendants who are released from custody prior to arraignment may delay arraignment once a complaint has been filed. The clerk may continue an arraignment or Intake Hearing at the request of the defendant or counsel for no more than two weeks, except in cases in which the docket or charging document states that one or more of the charges involves domestic violence, violation of an anti-harassment order, harassment, driving under the influence, physical control, assault, stalking, or firearms offenses as set out in 12A.14.071 (discharge of a firearm), 12A.14.075 (unlawful use of weapons to intimidate another) and 12A.14.080 (unlawful use of weapon). If a complaint has not been filed a judge must approve the delay request.

[Formerly SMCLR 4.1, adopted effective May 2, 1988; amended effective June 13, 1989; September 1, 1994; September 1, 1997, September 1, 1998, changes effective January 1, 1999; amended effective September 1, 1999; September 1, 2002; September 1, 2004; September 1, 2006; September 1, 2007; September 1, 2011; renumbered SMCLR 4.1(a)(2) and amended, effective September 1, 2012; amended on an emergency basis effective June 24, 2014; amended on a permanent basis effective September 2, 2014.]

SMCLR 5.4.   PRE–TRIAL HEARINGS

Unless a disposition of the case is entered into at the intake hearing or an arraignment, a pre-trial hearing may be held. Notice shall be issued by the clerk to the parties of the date, time and courtroom for this hearing. Defendant and all counsel must be present at the pre-trial hearing; failure of the defendant to appear may result in the issuance of a bench warrant.

[Effective June 13, 1989; amended effective September 1, 1997; September 1, 2002; September 1, 2004; September 1, 2006.]

SMCLR 6.1.   ASSIGNMENT OF TRIALS

(a) Generally, at arraignment or the pre-trial hearing, the court shall provide the parties with the jury trial date. The parties shall appear at the readiness calendar, or file a certificate of readiness. At the readiness calendar the parties will inform the court that the case is ready for trial on the assigned trial date, or will indicate witness and party scheduling conflicts that may require rescheduling of the trial date. The court may require the defendant to appear at the readiness calendar if warrants were issued previously; failure to do so appear may result in the issuance of a bench warrant and striking of the trial date.

(b) The parties may waive appearance at the readiness calendar by filing an agreed certificate of readiness on a form provided by the clerk of the court. A certificate may be filed if there is no outstanding discovery, witness or scheduling issues.

(c) Following the readiness calendar, the court will determine trial priority, taking into consideration the expiration dates, the parties' and witness' scheduling conflicts and other matters deemed appropriate by the court.

(d) All parties and counsel shall appear on the trial date, as directed by the court.

(e) Other cases may be assigned to a specific court at arraignment or pretrial. Otherwise all subsequent trials may be set on the Master Calendar from pre-trial courtrooms.

[Effective June 13, 1989; amended effective September 1, 1993; September 1, 1994; September 1, 1997; September 1, 2002; September 1, 2004; September 1, 2005; September 1, 2006; September 1, 2007; September 1, 2011; September 1, 2012; September 1, 2015.]

SMCLR 7.3(k)(1).   JUDGMENT (RESTITUTION)

Where the court orders that a defendant pay restitution but does not set an amount at the time of disposition, the City Attorney shall, within ninety days, file with the court a motion for restitution with documentation in support thereof.

[Formerly SMCLR 7.6, adopted effective September 1, 1997; amended effective September 1, 2002; September 1, 2004; September 1, 2006; renumbered SMCLR 7.3(k)(1) and amended, effective September 1, 2012.]

SMCLR 8.2.1.   MOTIONS

(a) Motions.

(1) All motions shall be noted on Trial Setting Order and shall be filed no later than the pretrial

hearing at which the matter is scheduled for trial. A party noting a motion must file a supporting affidavit pursuant to CrRLJ 3.6 at the same time, except that, upon good cause shown, a trial court may extend the time for the filing of a supporting affidavit for up to five (5) business days. Counsel shall indicate whether the motion will require live testimony. The pre-trial court shall hear testimonial motions prior to the date the case is set for trial unless the trial court finds good cause to reserve the motions to the trial date.

(2) *Copies of Motions and Supporting Material.* Not later than fourteen (14) business days prior to the hearing date, the moving Party shall serve the motion on all parties and the clerk, a supporting brief, copies of all affidavits, photographic, video, audio, documentary and all other evidence presented in support of the motion and a proposed order. Not later than five (5) days prior to the hearing date, each party opposing the motion shall file with all opposing parties and the clerk, and serve on each party that has appeared in the action, a brief in opposition to the motion, together with any supporting material.

The original motion and shall be filed in accordance with SMCLR 8.4.1.

(3) *Noncompliance.* If a party fails to file the papers required by this rule, or if a party or a necessary witness fails to appear on the day appointed for argument or hearing, the motion may be granted, or the hearing stricken by the court and the motion deemed waived. The court may, upon a showing of good cause, continue the motion.

(b) Emergency Motions. Any party may request an immediate hearing before the pretrial judge if circumstances so require. The party requesting the emergency hearing must provide appropriate notice to the opposing party, allowing both parties an opportunity to be heard on the issue presented. If immediate action is necessary and the judge assigned to the case for pretrial hearing is unavailable, any other judge may hear and dispose of the matter requiring immediate attention, but such action shall not constitute reassignment of the case or proceeding.

(c) Reconsideration of Motions. A motion for reconsideration shall be clearly labeled. The motion for reconsideration shall be noted for consideration on the court's calendar and may be summarily denied without a hearing. No response to a motion for reconsideration shall be filed unless requested by the court. The request will set a time when the response is due, and may limit the response to particular issues or points raised by the motion.

[Effective September 1, 2002; amended effective September 1, 2004; September 1, 2007; September 1, 2011; amended on an emergency basis, effective March 16, 2012; amended on a permanent basis, effective September 1, 2012; amended on an emergency basis effective June 24, 2014; amended on a permanent basis effective September 2, 2014.]

SMCLR 8.2.2. CONTINUANCES

(a) Motions for continuances of hearings and trials shall be presented to the court before which the hearing is scheduled. Once a case is assigned to a trial court for jury trial, a motion for continuance is presumed untimely and will be denied unless based upon facts unknown and not reasonably foreseeable to the moving party prior to assignment to the trial court.

(b) No case shall be continued for hearing or trial unless good cause has been shown.

(1) All motions to continue a pre-trial or trial date shall be made in writing, setting forth specific facts showing good cause and justification for the specific length of the continuance.

Motions for continuance of trials and any supporting documentation on such motions shall be served on the parties no later than two days prior to the readiness hearing, unless excused by the court for cause.

Appropriate sanctions may be imposed.

(2) In ruling on a motion to continue, the following factors will be considered by the court:

(a) The diligence of counsel in noting the motion.

(b) The proximity of the motion to the trial date, the age of the case, previous continuances;

(c) Any injury, inconvenience caused to the naming party.

(d) The earliest date all parties will be ready to proceed to trial.

(3) The following factors do not necessarily establish good cause for continuance:

(a) Convenience to or stipulation between the parties;

(b) Failure to expeditiously prepare for trial;

(c) Failure of client to adhere to financial agreement with an attorney;

(d) Settlement negotiations not yet completed, including the need to communicate an offer to a client appearing through counsel;

(e) Recent substitution of trial counsel, except where required by the Rules of Professional Conduct; and

(f) To secure a driver's license for a defendant except at intake/arraignment.

[Effective June 13, 1989; amended effective September 1, 1994; September 1, 1997; September 1, 2002; September 1, 2004; September 1, 2011.]

SMCLR 8.2.3. MOTION TO RESCIND OR MODIFY DOMESTIC VIOLENCE NO–CONTACT ORDER

Any party to the case or the protected person may request a motion to rescind or modify a no-contact order. The request must be filed using a form approved by the court. The request shall be filed with the court, together with an address form. Unless otherwise required by the Court, appearance of the defendant and attorneys is not required and absence of appearance shall be deemed a waiver of appearance. Notice of the court date shall contain language that the presence of the defendant is not required.

[Adopted on an emergency basis effective April 6, 2015; adopted on a permanent basis effective September 1, 2015.]

SMCLR 8.4.1. SERVICE, FILING AND SIGNING OF PAPERS

(a) All motions, briefs and other documents in support of motions, and arraignment waivers shall be filed and served as follows:

(1) The original shall include the date, time and court of the next hearing set forth above the caption on the first page if a hearing on the motion is already scheduled. If a hearing is not scheduled, the words "NOT SCHEDULED" shall appear above the caption;

(2) The original shall contain a certificate of mailing or a certificate or affidavit of service upon or acknowledgment of receipt by opposing counsel and judicial chambers;

(3) The original shall be filed with the clerk of the court in the Seattle Justice Center

(b) The clerk is authorized to refuse to accept for filing any documents that do not, on their face, comply with these rules.

(c) The Seattle Municipal Court cause number shall be noted in the caption. Documents with incorrect or no cause number may be deemed null and void. Court clerks have no responsibility for obtaining or correcting cause numbers, dates, times or courts. The clerk shall make available to parties the printout of all pending cases.

(d) Documents requiring clerk's action, including but not limited to arraignment waivers, shall include, in the caption, above the cause number, the words "CLERK'S ACTION REQUIRED." Arraignment waivers which do not include said words and which do not conform to SMCLR 8.4.1(a)(1) may not be processed and, upon failure to appear at arraignment, a warrant may be issued for the defendant's arrest.

(e) All papers filed with the court shall comply with GR 14. All papers filed with the court shall be submitted on letter-size paper (8–1/2 by 11 inches). Papers which do not conform with this rule may be rejected by court clerks.

[Formerly SMCLR 8.4, adopted effective June 13, 1989; amended effective September 1, 1997; September 1, 2002; September 1, 2011; renumbered SMCLR 8.4.1 and amended, effective September 1, 2012; amended on an emergency basis effective June 24, 2014; amended on a permanent basis effective September 2, 2014; September 1, 2015.]

LOCAL INFRACTION RULES

SMCLIR 2.6. SCHEDULING OF HEARINGS

(a) A defendant charged with an infraction who requests a hearing to explain mitigating circumstances, IRLJ 2.4, RCW 46.63.070, shall appear before a Magistrate. The Magistrate's determination of the disposition shall be final, and is not subject to review before a Judge.

(b) A defendant charged with an infraction who requests a hearing to contest the determination that an infraction occurred shall first appear before a Magistrate for a prehearing conference. The prehearing conference shall be held in the Magistrate's department and should be scheduled in accordance with IRLJ 2.6(a). The Presiding Judge or designee, defendant, or defendant's lawyer, may waive the prehearing conference on his/her own motion. If the prehearing conference is waived the case will be set for a contested hearing. A defendant who waives the prehearing conference is deemed to have waived any IRLJ 2.6(d) objection to the prehearing conference date. If the defendant fails to waive or appear at the settlement conference, a default judgment shall be entered.

(c) If the defendant who requests a hearing to contest the determination that an infraction was committed has a criminal charge pending in Seattle Municipal Court, and said criminal charge arises out of the same occurrence as the infraction, the hearing on the infraction may be heard at the same time as the criminal charge. The defendant, the City Attorney or the court may make this request as authorized by the Infraction Rules for Courts of Limited Jurisdiction.

(d) A defendant who objects to the hearing date set by the court pursuant to IRLJ 2.6, shall file with the court and serve upon the plaintiff a written motion for a speedy hearing date. Said motion shall be filed and served no later than ten (10) days from the date of written notice of the hearing date. Failure to comply with this rule shall be a waiver of the objection.

(e) Either party may request the court to consider setting the contested hearing on a special calendar or on Master calendar when the case involves multiple witnesses, complex motions, or other factors that require a lengthy hearing. The court, on its own motion, may set a case on a special calendar or on Master calendar when judicial economy requires or the court deems it appropriate.

[Effective September 1, 1992. Amended effective September 1, 2011; September 1, 2012; amended on an emergency basis, effective November 28, 2012; amended on a permanent basis, effective September 2, 2013.]

SMCLIR 2.6.1. CONTINUANCES— CONTESTED HEARINGS

(a) Each party is entitled to have the contested hearing continued one (1) time without judicial approval or prior notice to the opposing party if it is the first continuance for that party and the party contacts the clerk at least fifteen (15) days prior to the scheduled contested hearing.

(b) For continuance requests not covered by (a), the party who wishes to continue the contested hearing must file a written motion with the court and serve a copy of the motion on the opposing party at least fifteen (15) days prior to the scheduled contested hearing. For motions filed less than fifteen (15) days prior to the scheduled contested hearing good cause must be shown.

(c) One (1) continuance on the day of the scheduled contested hearing may be granted if there is no prejudice to the opposing party.

[Adopted on an emergency basis, effective November 28, 2012; adopted on a permanent basis, effective September 2, 2013.]

SMCLIR 3.1. CONTESTED HEARINGS— PRELIMINARY PROCEEDINGS

(a) Subpoena. A defendant who requests a hearing to contest the determination that an infraction was committed may file upon the court a written demand that the court subpoena the parking enforcement, police or other law enforcement officer who issued the citation. The demand must be filed with the court at least fifteen (15) days prior to the contested hearing. Upon receipt of such demand, the court will issue and serve the subpoena. The court may continue the hearing upon receipt of such a demand to assure the officer's presence, upon written notice to the defendant. A defendant is responsible for obtaining and serving subpoenas in accordance with IRLJ 3.1 in all other circumstances.

[Adopted on an emergency basis, effective November 28, 2012; adopted on a permanent basis, effective September 2, 2013.]

SMCLIR 3.2. FAILURE TO APPEAR

(a) If a defendant who was personally served with a notice of infraction fails to respond to within fifteen days (15), or fails to appear for a contested hearing, a prehearing conference or a mitigation hearing, the court shall enter a default judgment. If notice of the infraction was mailed to the defendant, defendant has eighteen (18) days to respond. If the defendant fails to satisfy the judgment, the court may refer the delinquent judgment to a collection agency pursuant to RCW 3.02.045. Remuneration for collection services will be assessed as costs, at the rate agreed to

between the Court and the collection agency, and added to the judgment.

(b) Motions to Set Aside a Default Judgment Under IRLJ 3.2(b). The court may consider a request to set aside a default judgment entered upon a defendant's failure to appear as provided in IRLJ 3.2(b) and CRLJ 60(b). If the request is made within 45 days of the entry of default judgment, the court may administratively schedule a hearing to determine whether there is "good cause" to set aside a default judgment entered upon a failure to appear. Requests received after 45 days must be made in writing and submitted to the Presiding Judge or designee.

(c) If the defendant fails to pay a fine and/or a default penalty, the court may refer the delinquent judgment to a collection agency pursuant to RCW 3.02.045. Remuneration for collection services will be assessed as costs, at the rate agreed to between the Court and the collection agency, and added to the judgment.

[Adopted on an emergency basis, effective November 28, 2012; adopted on a permanent basis, effective September 2, 2013. Amended effective September 1, 2015.]

SMCLIR 3.3. PROCEDURE AT CONTESTED HEARINGS

(a) The plaintiff need not be represented by a lawyer at a contested hearing unless directed to do so by the court.

(b) Only printed copies of photos or electronic copies of photos or videos saved to CD/DVD will be considered by the court.

[Adopted effective September 1, 2007; amended on an emergency basis, effective November 28, 2012; amended on a permanent basis, effective September 2, 2013; September 1, 2015.]

SMCLIR 3.5. DECISION ON WRITTEN STATEMENTS

(a) Mitigation hearings of infractions based on sworn written statements are authorized pursuant to IRLJ 2.4(b)(4), 2.6, and 3.5. The defendant shall be informed of the option to mitigate by written statement at the time defendant receives written notice of their date to appear in court for the mitigation conference. If the defendant elects to mitigate the infraction by written statement, the defendant's sworn statement must be received by the Court no later than three (3) calendar days before the scheduled mitigation conference or it will not be considered by the Court. There shall be no appeal from a decision based on written statements.

(b) Contested hearings of infractions based on sworn written statements are authorized pursuant to IRLJ 2.4(b)(4), 2.6, 3.4 and 3.5. The defendant shall be informed of the option to contest by written statement at the time defendant receives written notice of their date to appear in court for the pre hearing conference. If the defendant elects to contest the infraction by written statement, the defendant's sworn statement must be received by the Court no later than three (3) calendar days before the scheduled pre hearing conference or it will not be considered by the Court. There shall be no appeal from a decision based on written statements.

(c) The court, on its own motion, may decline to adjudicate a case by written statement and may schedule the matter for a formal court hearing.

[Adopted on an emergency basis, effective November 28, 2012; adopted on a permanent basis, effective September 2, 2013.]

SMCLIR 6.2. MONETARY PENALTY SCHEDULE FOR INFRACTIONS

(a) Schedule for Selected Infractions. (All statutory references are to Seattle Municipal Code (SMC), except as otherwise designated.)

Description	Code	Amount (including assessments)
Permit Animal to Damage Property	9.25.084(0D1)	$109
Permit Animal to Bark/Whine/Howl	9.25.084(0D2)	$109
Permit Animal to Spread or Spill Garbage	9.25.084(0D3)	$109
Tobacco License Required (3rd Offense)	6.240.020(3)	$269
Tobacco License-Change	6.240.050(3)	$269
Tobacco Vending Location (3rd Offense)	6.240.070(3)	$269
Sell Sealed Tobacco (3rd Offense)	6.240.080(3)	$269
Tobacco Samples – Give Away (3rd Offense)	6.240.120(3)	$269
Tobacco License Required (2nd Offense)	6.240.020(2)	$136
Tobacco License-Change (2nd Offense)	6.240.050(2)	$136
Tobacco Vending Location (2nd Offense)	6.240.070(2)	$136
Sell Sealed Tobacco (2nd Offense)	6.240.080(2)	$136
Tobacco Samples – Give Away (2nd Offense)	6.240.120(2)	$136
Tobacco License Required (1st Offense)	6.240.020(1)	$54
Tobacco License Change (1st Offense)	6.240.050(1)	$54
Tobacco Vending Location (1st Offense)	6.240.070(1)	$54
Sell Sealed Tobacco (1st Offense)	6.240.080(1)	$54
Tobacco Samples – Give Away (1st Offense)	6.240.120(1)	$54
Failure to Vaccinate Cats or Dogs Agains	9.25.049(I)	$54
Failure to Vaccinate Cats or Dogs Agains	9.25.049(II)	$109
Failure to Have Valid Cat or Dog License	9.25.051	$54
Fail to Obtain Lic Required by Animal Control	9.25.080(A)	$125
Fail to Display License ID Tag on Animal	9.25.080(B)	$54
Failure to Show License to Officer	9.25.080(C)	$54

Description	Code	Amount (including assessments)
Using Permit Belonging to Another	9.25.080(D)	$109
Remove Lic ID Without Owners Consent	9.25.080(E)	$109
Alter a License or License ID Tag	9.25.080(F)	$54
Making False Statements Regarding Animal	9.25.080(G)	$109
Remove Animal from City Vehicle/Shelter with	9.25.080(H)	$109
Allow Accum of Animal Feces in Cage/Yard	9.25.082(A)	$109
Failure to Remove Animal Feces from Public	9.25.082(B)	$54
Failure to have Feces Removal Equipment on Person	9.25.082(C)	$54
Have Possession of or Allow Diseased Animal	9.25.082(D)	$109
Dog Off Premises to be On Leash	9.25.084(A)	$54
Maintain Alarm w/o No of Person to Turn	10.08.150	$54
Alarm Sounding Over Ten Minutes	10.08.155	$54
Notify SPD of Alarm/ Failure to Report Alarm	10.08.160(A)	$54
Urinating in Public	12A.10.100	$27
Open/Consume Marijuana in Public	12A.20.100	$27
Consume/Possess Open Container of Liquor	12A.24.025	$27
Sitting or Lying on Sidewalk	15.48.040	$23
Failure to Obey Rules of Road	16.20.020	$87
Failure to Carry Safety Equipment	16.20.030	$87
Swimming in Prohibited Area	16.28.010	$87
Boat Speed Violations	16.20.130	$87
Anchorages Designated	16.40.030	$87
Animal at Large in Large Lake, Pond, Fountain	18.12.080(II)	$109
Animal at Large in Large Lake, Pond, Fountain	18.12.080(A)	$54
Failure to Display Valid License	18.12.080(B)	$54
Failure to Remove Animal Feces from Park	18.12.080(C)	$54
Animal at Large in Large Lake, Pond, Fountain	18.12.080(III)	$136
Animal at Large in Large Lake, Pond, Fountain	18.12.080 (IV)	$162
Skateboards at Westlake	18.16.150	$31
Littering – Less than One Cubic Foot	21.36.410	$103
Accumulation of Solid Waste	21.36.425	$54
Unlawful Use of Litter Receptacles	21.36.430	$54
Deposit Garbage in Improper Container	21.36.440	$54
Permit Dog or Cat to Be in Public Fountain	9.25.084(B)	$54
Dog or Cat Loose While in Heat	9.25.084(C)	$54
Have Possession of Anothers Animal	9.25.084(E)	$109
Tether an Animal Improperly	9.25.084(F)	$54
Miniature Goat Leave Premises	9.25.084(H)	54
Mobile Peddling in Restricted Area (Infraction)	15.17.010	$250
Vending and Display in Public Places (Infraction)	15.17.005	$250
Dangerous Animals	9.25.084G(1) or (2)	$269
Residential Disturbance	25.08.505	$269
Regulations for Posting	15.48.105	$269

(b) Schedule for Selected Parking Infractions.

Parking Infraction Description	Municipal Code	Amount (including assessments)
UNAUTHORIZED USE - DISABLED	11.23.400	$250
CARPOOL, FREE & PREFERENTIAL	11.23.410	$47
CARPOOL PERMIT	11.23.415	$47
SERVICE CONTROLLED PARKING AREA	11.26.060	$47
HOOD, CONTROLLED PARKING AREA	11.26.080	$47
HOOD, FREE PARKING AREA	11.26.100	$47
HOOD, WORK LOCATION	11.26.120	$47
HOOD ON OCCUPIED METER	11.26.140	$47
HOODED METER, UNOCCUPIED	11.26.160	$47
HOOD ON METER OVER 2 DAYS	11.26.180	$47
HOOD, PROH. HOURS	11.26.200	$47
HOOD, PASSENGER VEH.	11.26.220	$47
HOOD, REVOKED	11.26.240	$47
HOOD, VIOLATION	11.26.280	$47
ANGLE, GEN.	11.70.020	$47
PARALLEL R. SIDE	11.70.040	$47
PARALLEL 1 WAY ST.	11.70.060	$47
SHOULDER	11.70.080	$47
STALLS/SPACES	11.70.100	$47
PARK, R/W	11.70.120	$47
SECURE VEH.	11.70.140	$44
KEYS IGNITION	11.70.160	$47
REMOVE KEY, LOCK DOOR	11.70.180	$47
ILLEGAL ON STREET/ALLEY	11.70.200	$47
ADVERTISING	11.72.010	$47
ALLEY	11.72.020	$47
ALLEY/DRIVEWAY	11.72.025	$47
ANGLE/ARTERIAL OR BUS ROUTE	11.72.030	$47
BLOCK TRAF OR WALK UNOCCUPIED	11.72.035	$47
BUS SHELTER	11.72.045	$47
BUS ZONE	11.72.050	$47
CURB BULBS	11.72.051	$47
UNAUTHOR. VEH/CARPOOL	11.72.053	$47
CAR SHARING VEH ZONE	11.72.054	$47
CLASS OF VEH.	11.72.055	$47
CLEAR ROADWAY	11.72.060	$47
IN MARKED DISABLED, INVALID PLACARD	11.72.065	$250
COMMERCIAL VEH.	11.72.070	$47
RESTRICTIONS - COMM LOAD ZONE	11.72.075	$53
CROSSWALK	11.72.080	$47

XWALK APPROACH	11.72.090	$47
DOUBLE PARKED	11.72.100	$47
DRIVEWAY OR ALLEY ENTRANCE	11.72.110	$47
ELEVATED STRUCTURE	11.72.130	$47
EXCAVATION OR OBSTRUCTION	11.72.140	$47
EXPIRED/IMPROPER PLATES	11.72.145	$47
FIRE APPARATUS	11.72.150	$47
FIRE EXIT DOOR	11.72.155	$47
FIRE HYDRANT	11.72.160	$47
FIRE STATION DRIVEWAY	11.72.170	$47
FIRE AREA	11.72.180	$47
FIRE LANE	11.72.185	$47
FLASHING SIGNAL	11.72.190	$47
FUEL LOSS	11.72.200	$47
DROPPING OIL OR GREASE	11.72.205	$47
INTERSECTION	11.72.210	$47
LOAD/UNLOAD ZONE	11.72.215	$47
HOODED METERS, SIGNS	11.72.220	$47
FOOD VEHICLE ZONE	11.72.225	$42
MOVING VEHICLE OF ANOTHER	11.72.230	$47
MOVE VEH. AVOID TIME LIMIT	11.72.240	$47
PARK, MUNICIPAL PROPERTY	11.72.250	$44
OVERTIME	11.72.260	$44
REPEATED OVERTIME	11.72.270	$47
IN PARK	11.72.280	$47
PASS. LOAD ZONE	11.72.285	$47
PAVEMENT MARKINGS	11.72.290	$47
PEAK HOUR	11.72.300	$47
PLANTED AREA	11.72.310	$44
PLANTING STRIP	11.72.320	$44
SIGN POSTED LOCATIONS	11.72.330	$47
TOO CLOSE TO R.R.	11.72.350	$47
RESTRICTED PARKING ZONE	11.72.351A	$53
RPZ PERMIT ON DISPLAY IN IMPROPER LOCATION ON VEHICLE	11.72.351B	$29
ILLEGAL SALE, PURCHASE OR POSSESSION OF RPZ PERMIT	11.72.351C	$250
HUSKY STADIUM EVENT RESTRICTED PARKING	11.72.352	$53
SCHOOL LOAD ZONE	11.72.353	$47
SERVICE VEH. IN ST.	11.72.355	$47
SHUTTLE BUS LOAD ZONE	11.72.357	$47
SIDEWALK	11.72.360	$47
STOP SIGN APPROACH (30')	11.72.370	$47
LIMITED ACCESS, STREET	11.72.390	$47
TAXI CAB ZONE	11.72.400	$47
TOW AWAY ZONE	11.72.410	$47

TRAIL OR PATH (VEH/BIKE)	11.72.415	$47
TRF. CONTROL SIGNAL APPROACH	11.72.420	$47
TRL./CAMPER DETACHED	11.72.430	$47
PASS. VEH. IN TRUCK ZONE	11.72.435	$47
OVER 72 HOURS	11.72.440	$44
TYPE OF VEH.	11.72.450	$47
WALL OR FENCE	11.72.460	$47
CURB RAMP	11.72.465	$47
WRONG SIDE	11.72.470	$47
W/IN 30 FT. OF YIELD SIGN	11.72.480	$47
PARKING JUNK VEHICLE ON STREET (IMPOUND)	11.72.500	$250
STAND/ALLEY/COMM. VEH.	11.74.010	$47
TRUCK LOAD ZONE - CMCRL VEH.	11.74.020	$47
LOAD ZONE - TIME RESTRICTIONS	11.74.030	$53
LOAD/UNLOAD PROH.	11.74.060	$47
RESTRICTED AREA	11.74.120	$47
IMPROPER PARKING RECEIPT DISPLAY	11.76.005	$29
METER/COINS	11.76.010	$44
PARKING PAYMENT DEVICE VIOLATIONS	11.76.015	$44
PARKING TIME LIMIT	11.76.020	$47
METER RESTRICTION	11.76.030	$44
ILLEGAL USE, PARKING PAYMENT, TAMPERING	11.76.040	$47
LIGHTS, PARKED VEHICLE	11.82.300	$47
LIGHTS, PARKED, HIGHBEAM	11.82.320	$47
FALSE ALARM - PARKED AUTO	11.84.345	$47
RESTRICTIONS IN CERTAIN PARKS (REQ)	18.12.235	$47

[Renumbered from SMCLR 10.5(a) and SMCLR 10.5(b) and amended on an emergency basis, effective November 28, 2012; amended on a permanent basis, effective September 2, 2013; amended on an emergency basis, effective January 23, 2014; amended on a permanent basis, effective September 2, 2014; amended on an emergency basis, effective September 1, 2014; September 1, 2015.]

SMCLIR 6.6.1. CERTIFICATION OF SCALES USED IN THE MEASUREMENT OF WEIGHT FOR COMMERCIAL MOTOR VEHICLES

(a) In General. This rule applies only to contested hearings in traffic infraction cases.

(b) Scale Test Report and Certification of Inspection. In the absence of proof of a request on a separate pleading to produce a scale inspection expert served on the prosecuting authority and filed with the clerk of the court at least 30 days prior to trial or such lesser time as the court deems proper, a sworn statement setting forth the results of any inspection, test, and/or certification of any scale used primarily for the purpose of measuring the weights of commercial motor vehicles is admissible in lieu of an expert witness in any court proceeding in which the scale accuracy is an issue. Such scale test report and certification of inspection is admissible in evidence without additional foundation, and shall not be subject to objection on grounds of hearsay, provided that such document is maintained in a manner consistent with subsection (d) of this rule. Any party may present evidence supporting or attacking the result of any such measurement of weight or the inspection, test and/or certification of any such scale.

(c) Continuance. The court at the time of the formal hearing shall hear testimony concerning the infraction and, if necessary, may continue the proceeding for the purpose of obtaining evidence concerning the scale accuracy and the certification or inspection thereof. If, at the time it is supplied, the evidence is insufficient, a motion to suppress the readings of such test shall be granted.

(d) Maintaining Certificates as Public Records. Any document of inspection, test and/or certification of any State scale as set forth in subsection (b) of this rule may be filed with the court and maintained by the court as a public record. The documents will be available for inspection by the public. Copies will be provided on request. The court may charge any allowable copying fees. The documents are available without a formal request for discovery. In the alternative, or in addition, such documents may be maintained on a web site established for that purpose by the Washington State Patrol. The court is entitled to take judicial notice of the fact that the document has been filed with the court or maintained on the web site. Evidence will not be suppressed merely because there is not a representative of the prosecuting authority present who actually offers the document.

[Adopted on an emergency basis, effective April 11, 2013; adopted on a permanent basis, effective September 2, 2013.]

SHORELINE MUNICIPAL COURT—
[No Local Rules]

PUBLISHER'S NOTE

This municipal court follows the Local Rules of the District Court for King County.

SKYKOMISH MUNICIPAL COURT—
[No Local Rules]

PUBLISHER'S NOTE

This municipal court follows the Local Rules of the District Court for King County.

SNOQUALMIE MUNICIPAL COURT—
[No Local Rules]

PUBLISHER'S NOTE

This municipal court follows the Local Rules of the District Court for King County.

TUKWILA MUNICIPAL COURT LOCAL RULES

Including Amendments Received Through
August 15, 2015

Table of Rules

TMCLR 1.7. ADOPTION OF LOCAL RULES

These rules are adopted pursuant to GR7, CrRLJ 1.7 and IRLJ 1.3.

[Adopted effective January 1, 1999.]

TMCLR 1.8. TITLE OF RULES

These rules may be known and cited as the Tukwila Municipal Court Local Rules and Tukwila Municipal Court Local Infraction Rules and shall be referred to as TMCLR and TMCLIR.

[Adopted effective January 1, 1999; amended effective September 1, 2000.]

TMCLR 2.4. COMMISSIONERS

The court may employ judicial officers as commissioners, who shall serve at the pleasure of the Presiding Judge. He/she must be appointed in accordance with RCW 3.50.075 and TMC 2.68.040(B). Commissioners shall hear infraction cases as provided by the infraction rules for courts of limited jurisdiction and RCW 46.63, or any law amendatory thereof. Commissioners shall also perform such other duties and hear other matters as may be assigned to them by the Presiding Judge of the Court.

[Adopted effective January 1, 1999; amended effective September 1, 2000.]

TMCLR 3.1. PRE–TRIAL HEARINGS

A. General: Unless otherwise ordered by the court in a specific case for good cause, all cases in which a defendant enters a plea of not guilty shall be set for a pre-trial hearing. The pre-trial hearing shall provide an opportunity for negotiation between the parties. The parties shall confer in good faith regarding any agreed disposition prior to trial. The defendant shall be required to attend the pre-trial hearing unless excused by the court. Failure to attend may result in the issuance of a bench warrant and/or forfeiture of any bond. In the event of a disposition, the parties shall execute the appropriate documents for the judge to consider the matter on the record. Pre–trial hearings should be held no later than 30 days after arraignment unless otherwise approved by the court.

B. Scheduling: The court shall assign dates and give written notice to the parties for future motion hearings and trial at the time of the pre-trial conference and shall, in so far as is reasonably possible, schedule those hearings in consultation with both parties. Other factors, such as witness availability, shall also be considered.

C. Motions: In cases which proceed to trial, the parties shall identify with specificity all motions and counsel may be required to articulate on the record the basis for any motion. All rulings made at the pre-trial hearing or subsequent motions hearing(s) shall be binding on the parties and shall not be relitigated at trial. Any motion not identified at pre-trial shall be deemed waived unless otherwise allowed by the court. Counsel shall identify only those motions for which there is a good faith belief that the motion is well grounded in fact and is warranted by existing law or a good faith argument for the extension, modification or reversal of existing law. Counsel shall comply with CrRLJ 3.6.

D. Readiness: A jury call/readiness hearing will be scheduled in all cases proceeding to jury unless specifically waived by the court in a particular case for good cause shown. This calendar will be held during the week approximately one week prior to the scheduled jury trial or as otherwise set by the court. The defendant shall be required to attend this hearing unless excused by the court. Failure to attend the jury call/readiness hearing may result in the issuance of a bench warrant and/or forfeiture of bond. Both parties must have their witnesses present at the readiness hearing. This requirement does not apply to the reporting police officers, expert witnesses, or those specifically excused by the court. Absent a showing of good cause for their absence, witnesses who do not appear at the readiness calendar may be stricken from the witness list. A confirmation of readiness constitutes an assurance that the parties will be ready to begin jury selection immediately on the morning of trial and submit jury instructions at the call of the jury calendar.

[Adopted effective January 1, 1999; amended effective September 1, 2000.]

TMCLR 3.2. RELEASE OF THE ACCUSED

A. Bail: Tukwila Municipal Court will follow the bail schedule set forth in Washington Court Rule CrRLJ 3.2(*o*) with the following exceptions:

9A.88.030	Prostitution	$1,000.00
9A.88.090	Permitting Prostitution	$1,000.00
9A.88.110	Patronizing a Prostitute	$1,000.00
TMC 8.50.040	Prostitution Loitering	$1,000.00

TMC 8.30.040	Failure to Abide by Court Order	$1,000.00

Bail for unscheduled misdemeanors shall be $250.00 unless otherwise set by statute or ordinance. Bail for unscheduled gross misdemeanors shall be $500.00 unless otherwise set by statute or ordinance.

Bail shall not be set for accused persons arrested for new offenses involving domestic violence, violation of an anti-harassment order or stalking except at the preliminary appearance or arraignment.

B. Conditions of Release: The court may impose conditions of release pending trial to include, but not limited to, a No Contact Order, Ignition Interlock or any other conditions that are appropriate and are set forth in CrRLJ 3.2(a), (b) and (c).

[Adopted effective January 1, 1999; amended effective September 1, 2000; September 1, 2006.]

TMCLR 3.3. AUTHORIZATION FOR CONTINUANCE OF ARRAIGNMENTS

If a defendant requests a continuance of his or her arraignment date without having to first appear in court, the Clerk of the Court is authorized to continue and reset the arraignment date to a date not later than fourteen (14) days after the date on which the arraignment was initially set. This procedure is available on one occasion. Second and subsequent requests must be made in writing, addressed to the court with a detailed explanation for the request. The court will determine if good cause exists for an additional continuance.

This authorization for a continuance of arraignment is not permitted in cases involving alleged DUI, charges with a DV designation, Harassment or Violation of Court Order.

Any other requests for continuance of arraignment shall be presented to the court. A written motion for continuance, with notice to the opposing party or counsel for the opposing party, shall be required.

[Adopted effective January 1, 1999. Amended effective September 1, 2000; September 1, 2003; September 1, 2015.]

TMCLR 3.4. RECALL OF WARRANTS AND RESETTING OF CASES

A defendant who is charged with a criminal violation and has an outstanding warrant in the Tukwila Municipal Court may address the warrant in the following manner:

Option 1. Turn him/herself into the SCORE jail.

Option 2. Post full cash bail amount or bond with the Clerk of the Court.

Option 3. Contact his/her attorney to file a motion to quash the warrant. If the defendant is not represented by counsel, he or she may file a written request to recall the warrant with the court. Either way, the request or motion should include an explanation for his/her failure to appear.

Option 4. Personally appear at the Clerk of the Court's office and provide an explanation for his/her failure to appear for court and provide proper documentary support if appropriate and pay an administrative bench warrant fee of $100.00. The Clerk of the Court shall recall or not process the warrant, and is authorized to issue a new notice of hearing to the defendant. This option is limited to one occasion per case number. This option does not apply to charges of DUI, Domestic Violence, or Violation of Court Order.

Option 5. Sign up in person for the weekly warrant walk-in calendar no later than prescribed deadlines. Contact the court for current deadlines and calendar dates. No fee is required to sign-up for and attend this hearing. The court will address the warrant on the record and a courtesy attorney shall be provided at no cost to the defendant. The court will either recall the warrant or serve it. Additionally the court may impose a warrant fee if the court determines lack of good cause for the failure to appear and the defendant's ability to pay.

[Adopted effective January 1, 1999. Amended effective September 1, 2000; September 1, 2015.]

TMCLR 3.6. SUPPRESSION PROCEDURE

A. Pleadings; Determination regarding Hearing: Motions to suppress physical, oral or identification evidence other than motions pursuant to Rule 3.5 shall be in writing supported by an affidavit or document as provided in RCW 9A.72.085 or any law amendatory thereto, setting forth the facts the moving party anticipates will be elicited at a hearing. If there are no disputed facts, the court shall determine whether an evidentiary hearing is required. If the court determines that no evidentiary hearing is required, the court shall set forth its reasons on the record for not conducting an evidentiary hearing.

B. Time Limits: Pleadings required for compliance with this rule shall be submitted in writing to the court and the non-moving party at least 14 days in advance of the request for a 3.6 hearing. Responsive pleadings may be submitted within 7 days from date of receipt of the motion for a 3.6 hearing to the moving party and the court. Failure to provide responsive pleadings shall be considered a waiver of the right to file responsive pleadings.

C. Decision: The court, on the record, shall state findings of fact and conclusions of law based upon the pleadings submitted pursuant to TMCLR 3.6B.

[Adopted effective January 1, 1999; amended effective September 1, 2000; September 1, 2003.]

TMCLR 4.1. ARRAIGNMENTS AND CONTINUANCES OF ALL MATTERS OTHER THAN ARRAIGNMENT

A. Arraignment: Arraignments shall be in accordance with CrRLJ 4.1 and 4.2. A lawyer may, pursuant to CrRLJ 4.1(d), enter an appearance on behalf of a client except in cases in which the docket or charging document states that one or more of the charges involves DUI, Assault 4° (DV), Harassment, Violation of an Antiharassment/No Contact Order, Malicious Mischief (DV), Stalking or Harassment, whereupon defendant's presence is mandatory and cannot be waived.

B. Unless otherwise noted for motion, all requests to continue pretrial hearings, motions, trial dates and/or other final dispositions will require the agreement of both parties before such request will be submitted to the court for review except as provided for in TMCLR 3.3.

[Adopted effective January 1, 1999; amended effective September 1, 2000.]

TMCLR 4.2. FORFEITURE OF BAIL

Upon the non-appearance of a defendant at the time and place scheduled by the court and a warrant of arrest issued, the defendant's bail or bond may be ordered forfeited with or without further proceedings.

[Adopted effective January 1, 1999. Amended effective September 1, 2000; September 1, 2015.]

TMCLR 6.1. EVIDENCE—COURT'S CUSTODY OF EXHIBITS

In a criminal case every exhibit in the court's custody, which is not contraband and for which ownership is not in dispute, shall be returned to the party who produced that exhibit upon motion of that party and expiration of the appeal period. In the event of finding of guilty, for purpose of this rule, the appeal period shall begin on the day of sentencing or deferral of sentencing by the court. Exhibits not withdrawn shall be delivered by the court to the Tukwila Police Department for disposition as abandoned property; or if contraband, for destruction. The court shall not release an exhibit without it being receipted for by the receiving person.

[Adopted effective January 1, 1999.]

TMCLR 7.1. SENTENCING

The court shall follow the provisions of CrRLJ 7.2.

[Adopted effective January 1, 1999; amended effective September 1, 2000.]

TMCLR 7.2. RESTITUTION

Where the court orders that a defendant pay restitution, but does not set an amount at the time of disposition, the city attorney shall, within 60 days, file with the court a proposed amount, with documentation in support thereof. The city attorney shall mail to the defendant's last known address or to the defendant's attorney the proposed amount, with copies of the supporting documents. If the defendant wishes to contest the proposed amount, the defendant shall file with the court an objection within 30 days of the date the proposed amount was mailed to the defendant's last known address or to the defendant's attorney. Upon receipt of an objection by the court, the court shall schedule a restitution hearing, and shall send notice to the city attorney and the defendant. If the city attorney does not file a proposed amount within 60 days of disposition, the matter of restitution shall be deemed waived unless otherwise authorized by the court. If the defendant does not object, the proposed amount shall be entered as a judgment. Payment of restitution shall be made through the Clerk of the Court unless otherwise ordered by the court.

[Adopted effective January 1, 1999; amended effective September 1, 2000.]

TMCLR 8.1. USE OF A COLLECTION AGENCY AND ASSESSMENT AS COURT COST OF AMOUNTS PAID FOR COLLECTION SERVICES

A. The court may use the services of a collection agency for the purposes of collecting unpaid and delinquent penalties on infractions, criminal fines, costs, assessments and forfeitures. The terms and conditions of the contract for collection services shall be between the City of Tukwila and said collection agency, and may be amended as necessary.

B. The collection agency's fee or charge, as set forth in said contract, shall be added by the collection agency as a court cost to the total judgment of the court against each defendant whose account is referred by the court to the collection agency.

C. Nothing in this section shall prevent the court from notifying the Department of Licensing of the defendant's failure to pay a fine and/or costs as ordered by the court.

[Adopted effective January 1, 1999; amended effective September 1, 2000.]

TMCLR 8.2. MOTIONS FOR DEFERRED PROSECUTION

Petitions for deferred prosecution must be submitted pursuant to RCW 10.05. Defendants must use the deferred prosecution forms provided by the court. The petition must include the appropriate assessment and treatment plan.

[Adopted effective September 1, 2000; amended effective September 1, 2003.]

TMCLR 9.1. REQUIREMENT FOR PAYMENT OF ADMINISTRATIVE PROBATION FEES, PUBLIC DEFENDER FEES, AND JAIL BOOKING FEES

A. If a defendant is found guilty of a criminal violation the court may impose an administrative pro-

bation fee up to the maximum fee permitted under the current state statute.

B. If a defendant is provided a public defender during any phase of a criminal proceeding, the court may order recoupment of costs for public defender services.

C. If a defendant has been confined during any phase of a criminal proceeding by order of the Tukwila Municipal Court, the defendant may be ordered to pay the costs of confinement, not to exceed the cost of each booking fee associated with a case, plus the daily housing cost of the defendant at whatever jail he/she is confined, and not to exceed statutory limits.

D. The court shall, on the record, inquire of the defendant as to his/her present and future ability to pay non-mandatory costs and fees prior to imposition.

[Adopted effective January 1, 1999; amended effective September 1, 2000; September 1, 2015.]

TMCLR 10.1. REQUIREMENTS FOR PAYMENT OF JURY FEES UPON CANCELLATION OF JURY TRIAL

A. If a defendant who has been charged with a criminal violation in the Tukwila Municipal Court has requested a jury trial, and if that jury trial is summoned and the court has incurred the expense or will incur the expense because the jury has been or will be brought in, and the defendant does not waive his or her right to a jury trial within 48 hours prior to the date for which the jury trial has been scheduled, or otherwise excuses or releases the jury from hearing the case within 48 hours of the date of the scheduled jury trial, the defendant may be responsible for payment to the court in the amount of the costs incurred by the court for jury fee payments and mileage reimbursements, unless the court specifically determines that those fees and costs or the full amount of those fees and costs shall not be paid under the circumstances of the defendant's case.

B. Any such jury fee costs imposed by the court for payment and reimbursement of jury fees and mileage reimbursement shall be paid by the defendant as a condition of suspended sentence, if any, or as otherwise directed by the court.

[Adopted effective January 1, 1999; amended effective September 1, 2000.]

TMCLR 10.2. PRESIDING JUDGE

A. The Judge duly appointed as Judge of the Tukwila Municipal Court will be known as the Presiding Judge.

B. The Presiding Judge shall be responsible for the efficient administration of the court. The Presiding Judge shall supervise the preparation and filing of all reports required by statute or rule and shall perform such other duties as may be prescribed by statute, ordinance or rule.

C. The Presiding Judge shall direct the work of the Court Administrator who will have direct supervision over all administrative, non-judicial functions and all other court personnel except that the Presiding Judge shall directly supervise the Commissioner(s), Judge Pro–Tempore(s) and magistrate(s).

[Adopted effective September 1, 2000.]

TMCLR 10.3. ANTIHARASSMENT PROTECTION ORDERS

A. Pursuant to RCW 10.14.150, as amended by HB 1296 (2005), the Tukwila Municipal Court may hear and adjudicate petitions for anti-harassment protection orders filed under RCW 10.14.

B. The Tukwila Municipal Court's jurisdiction shall be limited to situations:

(1) When the alleged acts of unlawful harassment occurred within the Tukwila city limits; or

(2) When the respondent resides within the Tukwila city limits; or

(3) When the respondent may be served within the Tukwila city limits if it is the same county or judicial district a respondent resides.

C. The Clerk of the Municipal Court may charge a filing fee in an amount equal to the applicable fee charged by the King County District Court. The Municipal Court Judge has discretion to waive or reduce the filing fee upon a showing of indigence, financial hardship, or other good cause.

[Adopted effective September 1, 2006.]

TMCLR 10.6. JURY TRIAL IN CIVIL CASES [RESCINDED]

[Rescinded effective September 1, 2006.]

TMCLR 12.1. USE OF UNSWORN STATEMENT IN LIEU OF AFFIDAVIT

A. Unsworn Statement Permitted: Except as provided in section B., whenever a matter is required or permitted to be supported or proved by affidavit, the matter may be supported or proved by an unsworn written statement, declaration, verification, or certificate executed in accordance with RCW 9A.72.085. The certification or declaration may be in substantially the following form:

I certify (or declare) under penalty of perjury under the laws of the State of Washington that the foregoing is true and correct:

_____ _____
(Date and Place)   *(Signature)*

B. Exceptions: This rules does not apply to writings requiring an acknowledgment, oaths of office, or oaths required to be taken before a special official other than a notary public.

[Adopted effective January 1, 1999.]

TMCLR 13.1. VIDEO CONFERENCE PROCEEDINGS

A. Criminal: Preliminary appearances as defined by CrRLJ 3.2.1(d), arraignments as defined by CrR 3.4 and 4.1 and CrRLJ 3.4 and 4.1, bail hearings as defined by CrR3.2 and CrRLJ 3.2, and trial settings as defined by CrR 3.3 and CrRLJ 3.3(f), and pre-trial hearings as determined by the court, conducted via video conference in which all participants can simultaneously see, hear, and speak with each other shall be deemed held in open court and in the defendant's presence for the purposes of any statute, court rule or policy. All video conference hearings conducted pursuant to this rule shall be public, and the public shall be able to simultaneously see and hear all participants and speak as permitted by the court. Any party may request an in-person hearing which may, in the court's discretion, be granted.

B. Agreement: Other trial court proceedings including the entry of a Statement of Defendant on Plea of Guilty as defined by CrR 4.2 and CrRLJ 4.2 may be conducted by video conference only by agreement of the parties. The defendant will be deemed to have agreed to voluntarily participate in court proceedings in Tukwila Municipal Court by video conference unless the defendant or counsel for the defendant notifies the court at the time of the proceeding that he/she objects to the proceeding being conducted via video conference. The right to object to video conference proceedings will be deemed waived if not exercised prior to the start of the video conference hearing.

C. Standards for Video Conference Proceedings: The Judge, counsel, all parties, and the public must be able to see and hear each other during proceedings, and speak as permitted by the court. Video conference facilities must provide for confidential communications between attorney and client and security sufficient to protect the safety of all participants and observers. In interpreted proceedings, the interpreter must be located next to the defendant and the proceeding must be conducted to assure that the interpreter can hear all participants.

D. For purposes of video conference proceedings, the facsimile signature(s) of the defendant, counsel, interested parties and the court will be treated as if they were an original signature. This includes all Orders on Judgments & Sentence, No Contact Orders, S.O.A.P. and S.O.D.A. Orders, Time Pay Agreements, and other documents as the court shall determine are appropriate or necessary.

[Adopted effective January 1, 1999; amended effective September 1, 2000.]

TMCLR 14.1. ZONING, FIRE, BUILDING CODE VIOLATIONS; INFORMAL AND PRE–TRIAL SETTLEMENT CONFERENCES [RESCINDED]

[Rescinded effective September 1, 2015.]

TUKWILA ELECTRONIC HOME MONITORING [RESCINDED]

[Rescinded effective September 1, 2015.]

LOCAL INFRACTION RULES

TMCLIR 1.0. SPEED MEASURING DEVICE: DESIGN AND CONSTRUCTION CERTIFICATION

Any person who requests production of an electronic speed measuring device expert, and who is thereafter found by the court to have committed the infraction, shall be required to pay the fee charged by the expert as a cost incurred by that party, as provided in RCW 46.63.151.

[Adopted effective January 1, 1999.]

TMCLIR 2.0. REQUIREMENTS FOR PAYMENT FOLLOWING INFRACTION HEARINGS

A. If a defendant who has been charged with a traffic or other infraction filed with the Tukwila Municipal Court is found to have committed that infraction, absent extenuating circumstances, the defendant shall make payment in full of the amount of the penalty at the time of the hearing in which the defendant was found to have committed the infraction.

B. Time payments on infractions will be permitted upon a showing of exceptional and exigent circumstances in court, at the time of the hearing on the contested infraction. Time payments will be at a minimum payment of $50.00 each month, unless specifically authorized by the Judge or Commissioner. The court's decision to authorize time payments in infraction cases shall be subject to the conditions set at the time of the order authorizing time payments. The court may impose an additional administrative fee for the costs of establishing, monitoring and processing a time pay agreement.

C. Failure to make payment on the penalties on the committed infractions shall be enforceable pursuant to otherwise applicable court rules, state law or relevant administrative regulations.

[Adopted effective January 1, 1999; amended effective September 1, 2000.]

TMCLIR 3.0. TIME FOR HEARING—OBJECTIONS TO DATE

A defendant who objects to the hearing date set by the court pursuant to IRLJ 2.6, shall file with the court and serve upon the city attorney a written motion for a new speedy hearing date. Such motion shall be filed and served no later than 10 days from the date of written notice of the hearing date. Failure to comply with this rule shall become a waiver of the objection.

[Adopted effective January 1, 1999.]

TMCLIR 3.1. HANDLING OF REQUESTS FOR CONTESTED HEARINGS AFTER FAILURE TO RESPOND

A. If a defendant who has failed to appear or respond to a notice of infraction, on not more than one occasion, as required by RCW 46.63.070 and Rule 2.4 of the Infraction Rules for Courts of Limited Jurisdiction (IRLJ), requests that the court set his/her case for a contested hearing, and upon payment of a $50.00 processing fee, the Clerk of the Court shall be authorized to set a date for a contested hearing, and retrieve/recall FTA's, pleadings and/or correspondence from the Department of Licensing reflecting the failure to respond or appear, if any was sent, on the following conditions:

(1) The defendant, within one week of the date by which a request for a contested hearing should have been received by the court, delivers to the court an envelope containing his/her request for a contested hearing, with a postmark clearly indicating that the envelope was addressed and mailed to the Municipal Court within the time frame for requesting contested hearings pursuant to statute and court rule, and with the envelope indicating that it was returned to the defendant, for whatever reason; or,

(2) The court, within one week of the date by which a request for a contested hearing should have been received by the court, receives in the mail an envelope containing the defendant's request for a contested hearing, with the envelope showing a postmark clearly indicating that the envelope was mailed to the court within the time frame for requesting contested hearings pursuant to statute and court rule.

B. In all other cases, the defendant shall not be entitled to a contested hearing, and the disposition of his/her infraction shall be dealt with as provided for in the statute and/or court rule for failures to respond or appear, or as otherwise determined by the court.

C. If a defendant fails to respond to a notice of infraction within the time frames set forth in 3.0 and 3.1 above, in addition to any amount imposed by the court as a fine, the court may impose a $50.00 infraction processing fee in addition to the scheduled bail amount or fine set by the court at the time the infraction is adjudicated.

[Adopted effective January 1, 1999; amended effective September 1, 2000.]

TMCLIR 3.5.   DECISION ON WRITTEN STATEMENTS

A.   Traffic infractions may be heard by the court on the basis of written submissions from the City and the defendant.   Written submissions must be provided to the court in advance of the date set for contested hearing or mitigation as outlined on the forms provided by the court.   Defendant's must use court's mitigation/contested by mail forms.

B.   Generally.   The court shall examine the citing officer's report and any statement submitted by the defendant.   The examination shall take place within 120 days after the defendant filed the response to the notice of infraction.   The examination may be held in chambers and shall not be governed by the Rules of Evidence.

C.   Factual Determination.   The court shall determine whether the plaintiff has proved by a preponderance of all evidence submitted that the defendant has committed the infraction.

D.   Disposition.   If the court determines that the infraction has been committed, it may assess a penalty and any appropriate and permitted costs.

E.   Notice to Parties.   The court shall notify the parties in writing whether an infraction was found to have been committed and what penalty, if any, was imposed.

F.   No Appeal Permitted.   There shall be no appeal from a decision on written statements.

[Adopted effective September 1, 2000.]

TMCLIR 4.0.   PROOF OF INSURANCE [RESCINDED]

[Adopted effective September 1, 2000; rescinded effective September 1, 2008.]

WOODINVILLE MUNICIPAL COURT—
[No Local Rules]

PUBLISHER'S NOTE

This municipal court follows the Local Rules of the District Court for King County.

KITSAP COUNTY

Table of Courts

Superior Court

Local Rules of the Superior Court of Washington for Kitsap County.

District Court

Local Rules for the District Court of Kitsap County, Washington.

Municipal Courts

Bainbridge Island Municipal Court Local Rules.
Bremerton Municipal Court Local Rules.
Local Court Rules of the Port Orchard Municipal Court.
Poulsbo Municipal Court Local Rules.

SUPERIOR COURT

LOCAL RULES OF THE SUPERIOR COURT OF WASHINGTON FOR KITSAP COUNTY

**Including Amendments Received Through
August 15, 2015**

Table of Rules

Rule			Rule	
Exhibit C.	Note for Settlement Conference or Support Modification Hearing and Trial Setting.		Exhibit G.	Domestic Relations Information Form.
			Exhibit H.	Note for Arbitration Setting Initial Statement of Arbitrability (STA).
Exhibit D.	Order Setting Trial Date and Civil Case Event Schedule.		Exhibit I.	Response to Statement of Arbitrability (RSSA).
Exhibit D–2.	Order Setting Civil Case Event Schedule.		Exhibit J.	Arbitration Award (ARBA).
Exhibit E.	Note for Motion Docket (NTMTDK).		Exhibit K.	Pre–Arraignment Domestic Violence No Contact Order.
Exhibit F.	Request for Continuance (RQC).		Exhibit L.	Order Re Ad Litem Fees.

KITSAP COUNTY LOCAL GENERAL RULES [KCLGR]

KCLGR 31. ACCESS TO COURT RECORDS

(e) Personal Identifiers–Children.

(1) *Complete names of children, sealed case types.* The complete names of children shall be used in cases that are deemed confidential pursuant to state or federal statutes, including cases filed pursuant to RCW 13 (excluding offender cases); RCW 4.24; RCW 26.33 (Adoption); and, RCW 71.34 (Mental Health Services for Minors).

(2) *Confidential Information Form.* The complete names of children and other identifiers shall be included in the Confidential Information Form or similar document for cases filed under Title 26.

(3) *Domestic Relations Orders.* Court orders concerning the financial support or the custody or residential schedule of a child (including temporary or permanent parenting plans and similar documents) and orders establishing or disestablishing paternity shall include the full name of the child. The date of the birth of a child shall be included in court records only as authorized by General Rule 22.

(4) *Child who is alleged to be a victim of a crime.* The complete name of a child who is alleged to be a victim of a crime may be included in subpoenas and in jury instructions. Nothing in this rule requires that subpoenas be routinely filed in the court file.

(5) *Child who is charged with a crime.* The complete name of a child charged with a crime shall be included in any indictment or information filed with the court pursuant to CrR 2.1 or JuCR 7.2, as part of an affidavit or declaration of probable cause or for any other purpose deemed necessary for the prosecution or defense of the criminal or juvenile offender matter.

(6) *Child who is the subject of a minor settlement.* The complete name and date of birth of a child who is the subject of a minor settlement shall be included in the petition and any dispositive orders, pursuant to Rule 98.16W of the Superior Court Rules on Special Proceedings.

(7) *Orders issued for the protection of a child.* If a child is a person protected by a criminal no contact order issued pursuant to RCW 10.99, an anti-harassment order issued pursuant to RCW 10.14, an order of protection issued pursuant to RCW 26.50 or a restraining order or order of protection issued pursuant to RCW 26.09, RCW 26.10, RCW 26.26, RCW 26.52.020, or any other court order entered for the protection of the child, the child's full name and other identifiers shall be included on petitions and orders as necessary for entry of the order in the Judicial Information System (JIS) and/or the Washington Crime Information Center (WACIC).

(8) *Orders on release of criminal defendant.* If access to a child is restricted pursuant to CrR 3.2(d)(1), the court may include the full name of the child on the order if deemed necessary for effective enforcement of the order.

(9) *Orders restraining child from contacting or harassing others.* Whenever a child is named as a respondent in an order listed in (3) above, the child's full name and other personal identifiers shall be included on the petition and order as necessary for entry of the order in the Judicial Information System (JIS) and/or the Washington Crime Information Center (WACIC).

(10) *Petitions and Notices filed pursuant to RCW 11.28 (children as heirs to estate).* The full names and ages of children and other information required by RCW 11.28.110 and RCW 11.28.330 shall be included. However, the date of birth may be included only as authorized by General Rule 22.

(11) *General Authority.* Nothing in this rule shall prohibit a court from authorizing the use of a child's full name or date of birth when necessary for the orderly administration of justice, consistent with the requirements of General Rule 22.

[Adopted as an Emergency Rule effective June 20, 2005; adopted on a permanent basis effective September 1, 2005; amended effective September 1, 2011.]

KITSAP COUNTY LOCAL ADMINISTRATIVE RULES [KCLAR]

KCLAR 1. LOCAL ADMINISTRATIVE RULES

(a) **Presiding Judge and Assistant Presiding Judge.** The judges shall elect a Presiding Judge and an Assistant Presiding Judge by majority vote at a judges' meeting. The term of a Presiding Judge shall be two years and begin on January 1. The Presiding Judge and Assistant Presiding Judge shall perform all duties of the position required by General Rule 29. Vacancies in the office of Presiding Judge or Assistant Presiding Judge shall be filled by majority vote of the judges at the first judges' meeting held after the vacancy is known to exist.

(b) **Executive Committee.** The judges of the Superior Court, sitting as a whole as an executive committee, shall advise and assist the Presiding Judge in the administration of the court.

(c) **Assignments.** Judges shall be appointed to manage administrative and policy matters relating to specific areas. Any Superior Court judge may be designated to manage any of the duties set forth below.

(1) *Domestic Relations Presiding Judge.* The Presiding Domestic Relations judge shall be appointed to manage administrative and policy matters relating to domestic relations cases.

(2) *Criminal Motions Judges.* The Criminal Motions Judges shall manage administrative and policy matters relating to criminal cases in both adult and juvenile court.

(3) *Juvenile Court Judges.* The Juvenile Court Judges shall manage administrative and policy matters relating to Juvenile Court.

(4) *Truancy Judge.* The Truancy Judge shall manage administrative and policy matters relating to truancy cases.

(5) *Guardianship Delinquency Judge.* The Guardianship Delinquency Judge shall manage administrative and policy issues relating to guardianship delinquency matters.

(6) *Guardian ad Litem Committee.* The Guardian ad Litem Committee shall manage administrative and policy issues relating to guardians ad litem.

(7) *Parenting Education Committee.* The Parenting Education Committee shall consist of at least one judge, one court commissioner, one or more representatives of local dispute resolution agencies, one or more marriage and family therapists, one or more private attorneys, and others as appropriate.

[Amended effective September 1, 2002; September 1, 2005; September 1, 2011.]

KITSAP COUNTY LOCAL CIVIL RULES [KCLCR]

II. COMMENCEMENT OF ACTION; SERVICE OF PROCESS, PLEADINGS, MOTIONS AND ORDERS [No Local Rules]

III. PLEADINGS AND MOTIONS

KCLCR 7. PLEADINGS ALLOWED; FORM OF MOTIONS

(b) **Motions and Other Papers.**

(1) *How Made.*

(A) Time for filing. Parties desiring to submit an application to the Court, legal brief, memorandum of authorities, and any supporting affidavits or other documents on a motion, hearing or trial to be heard shall, unless otherwise particularized under a specific State or local rule, serve and file the same with the Clerk of Court no later than five court days before the date the party wishes the motion to be considered. Any responsive materials shall be served and filed with the Clerk of Court by 12:00 noon two days prior to the time set for the hearing or trial. Any documents in strict reply shall be similarly filed and served no later than 12:00 noon on the court day before the hearing. No documents shall be submitted to the Court unless opposing counsel or the self-represented litigants have been timely provided with copies.

(B) Bench Copies. At the time a party files any document with the office of the Clerk of Court pursuant to section (A) above the party shall be responsible for filing bench copies simultaneously with the Superior Court office along with a notation of trial or hearing date. Bench copies are mandatory for all hearings for which pleadings have been filed. If a hearing is confirmed but not held, the bench copy will be available at the Superior Court office until the end of the calendar and then discarded.

If a hearing is not confirmed and a bench copy has been filed, a party may retrieve it from the Superior Court office on, or before, the date originally set for hearing, redate it, and refile it. If bench copies have not been retrieved and refiled for a new hearing date, another set of bench copies must be filed for the new hearing unless the submitting party contacts the Court Administration office prior to the hearing and makes arrangements to move the bench copies to the next hearing date.

(C) Reapplication for Order. When an order has been applied for and refused in whole or in part (unless without prejudice), or has been granted conditionally and the condition has not been performed, the same application for an order shall not be presented to another judge.

If a subsequent application is made upon an alleged different statement of facts or law, it shall be shown by affidavit what application was made, when, and to what judge; what order or decision was made thereon; and what new facts or law are claimed to be shown.

For failure to comply with this requirement, any order made upon such subsequent application shall be set aside upon request of an opposing party.

(D) Motions in Limine. Motions to limit the introduction of evidence should be presented for resolution on the day of trial, or at other such time as arranged with the Court Scheduler.

Failure to comply with this rule may result in the Court's refusal to hear such motion on the day of trial or in the imposition of terms in favor of both the adversely affected party or parties and to Kitsap County for the expense caused by resulting delays.

(2) *Form; Necessary Provisions in Orders Requiring Personal Attendance.* In all civil proceedings wherein an order is to be issued requiring the personal attendance of a person to be examined in open court, the order shall include the following words in capital letters:

YOUR FAILURE TO APPEAR AS ABOVE SET FORTH AT THE TIME, DATE AND PLACE STATED MAY CAUSE THE COURT TO ISSUE A BENCH WARRANT FOR YOUR APPREHENSION AND CONFINEMENT IN JAIL UNTIL SUCH TIME AS THE MATTER CAN BE HEARD OR UNTIL BAIL IS POSTED.

No bench warrant shall be issued in such cases for the apprehension of the cited person if such language has been omitted.

[Amended effective September 1, 2008; September 1, 2011; September 1, 2012; September 2, 2013; September 1, 2015.]

KCLCR 16. PRETRIAL PROCEDURE AND FORMULATING ISSUES

(a) Settlement Conferences (Civil–Non–Domestic).

(1) *Attendance and Preparation Required.* Settlement conferences are mandatory, unless the parties file proof of each party's participation in a formal mediation. The mediator may not have an interest in the case's outcome and may not be related to a party, and the mediator must be: (a) an attorney licensed to practice before the courts of this state having at least five years of experience in the primary subject matter of the action; (b) an individual, who may be an attorney, with special skill or training in the subject matter of this action (e.g. administration of trusts and estates); or (c) an individual, who may be an attorney, with special skill or training as a mediator. No later than noon of the court day prior, all parties and counsel shall serve a complete memorandum for settlement upon the other parties and provide the original for the settlement conference judge. The original memorandum shall not be filed, but shall be returned to its author at the conclusion of the settlement conference. The attorney personally in charge of each party's case and trial counsel shall personally attend all settlement conferences and shall come prepared to discuss in detail and in good faith the following, which shall also be addressed in the memorandum for settlement:

- All liability issues;
- All items of special damages or property damage;
- The degree, nature, and duration of any claimed disability;
- General damages;
- Explanation of position on settlement; and
- Pretrial conference matters if the case is not settled.

(2) *Parties to be Available.*

(a) Presence in Person. The parties shall, in all cases, be present.

(b) Representative of Insurer. A party whose defense is provided by a liability insurance company shall personally attend said settlement conference and a representative of the insurer of said party shall attend or be available by telephone with sufficient authority to bind the insurer to a settlement.

(c) Court May Excuse Attendance. Attendance of a party may be excused upon notice to other parties no later than 24 hours prior to the settlement conference at the discretion of the settlement conference judge, preassigned judge, or Presiding Judge for good cause shown.

(3) *Mandatory Confirmations.* All settlement conferences must be confirmed in person, by telephoning the Superior Court office at **(360) 337–7140 (Option #2)**, or by email at **supcourtconfirm@co.kitsap.wa. us** no later than 12:00 noon on the day before the conference, but not earlier than 48 hours in advance. Failure to confirm may result in the imposition of terms and/or sanctions as the Court may deem appropriate.

(4) *Failure to Attend.* Failure to attend the settlement conference in accordance with these rules may

result in the imposition of terms and/or sanctions as the Court may deem appropriate.

(5) *Changes or Continuances.* Changes or continuances of settlement conferences may be authorized only by the Presiding Judge or preassigned judge on timely written motion and for good cause shown.

(6) *Proceedings Confidential.* Proceedings of settlement conferences shall, in all respects, be confidential and not reported or recorded. No party shall be bound unless a settlement is reached. When a settlement has been reached, the Court may, at its discretion, and with the consent of the parties, order any agreement to be placed on the record.

(7) *Pretrial Power of the Court.* If the case is not settled at the settlement conference, the Court may nevertheless make such orders as are appropriate pursuant to pretrial conference rules.

(8) *Judge Disqualified for Trial.* A judge presiding over a settlement conference shall be disqualified from acting as the trial judge or exercising discretion in regard to subsequent motions in that matter.

(b) Trial Preparation (Civil–Non–Domestic).

(1) *Exchange of Exhibit and Witness Lists.* Pursuant to the case event schedule, the parties shall exchange: (A) lists of the witnesses whom each party expects to call at trial; (B) lists of the exhibits that each party expects to offer at trial, except for exhibits to be used only for impeachment; and (C) copies of all documentary exhibits except those to be used only for illustrative purposes, and except for those items agreed to by counsel and self-represented parties, such as identical copies of items already produced to avoid unnecessary duplication. Counsel and self-represented parties are encouraged to ascertain that each has full and complete copies of any document to be presented at trial to avoid unnecessary duplication expenses. In addition, non-documentary exhibits, except for those to be used only for illustrative purposes, shall be made available for inspection by all other parties prior to the start of trial. Any witness or exhibit not listed shall not be used at trial, unless the court orders otherwise for good cause and subject to such conditions as justice requires. Copies of the actual exhibits should not be filed and should be presented at the time of the trial before the Court.

(2) *Joint Statement of Evidence.* Pursuant to the case event schedule, the parties shall file a Joint Statement of Evidence consisting of (A) a list of the witnesses whom each party expects to call at trial and (B) a list of the exhibits that each party expects to offer at trial. The Joint Statement of Evidence shall include a notation for each exhibit as to whether all parties agrees as to the exhibit's authenticity and admissibility.

[Amended effective September 1, 2011; September 1, 2012; September 2, 2014.]

Official Comment

For rules governing settlement conferences in domestic relations matters see KCLFLR 8.

IV.   PARTIES (Rules 17–25)
No Local Rules

V.   DEPOSITION AND DISCOVERY

KCLCR 26.   GENERAL PROVISIONS REGARDING DISCOVERY

(g) Objections to Discovery Responses. Any party objecting to an answer or a response to an interrogatory, requests for production or inspection, or requests for admission shall set forth each request or response objected to, the interrogatory or requests to which it relates, and the reasons for the objections.

[Adopted effective September 1, 2007; amended effective September 1, 2011.]

VI.   TRIALS

KCLCR 40.   ASSIGNMENT OF CASES

(b) Methods.

(1) *Trial Setting.*

(A) Note for Trial Setting. Any party desiring to obtain a trial date may note the matter on the trial setting calendar using the Note for Trial Setting (Exhibit A) after all named parties have been served.

The moving party must identify all counsel and/or parties and their mailing addresses. Personal appearance by counsel is not necessary. Settings will be done administratively and the Court shall mail a default case event schedule that contains all case events and deadlines listed herein and the trial date to all parties listed on the Note for Trial Setting. If a dispute arises over a setting, the matter shall be heard on the civil motion calendar.

Alternatively, a party may note a motion to set a trial date on the civil motions docket at any time. At said hearing, the Court will set a trial date and (absent good cause) a settlement conference date and the Court may set deadlines for effecting service upon unserved parties and may compel the filing of answers by parties against whom relief is sought. The Court may order the striking of pleadings of parties who/which do not comply with such orders.

After a trial date has been set, if all parties can agree upon a case schedule which includes all case events listed herein, the parties may file the agreed case schedule in place of the Court's default case event schedule. If the parties do not file a case event schedule within 60 days of the announcement of the trial date, the Court's default schedule shall prevail.

A party must file and serve a jury demand on or before the time of trial setting or the right to a jury trial will be waived. A party who/which has not appeared at the time of trial setting must file and serve a jury demand within sixty (60) days of service of the initial pleadings or the right to a jury trial will be waived.

All telephone communications regarding trial settings, special motion settings, and scheduling should initially be with the Court Scheduler at (360) 337-7008.

(B) Visiting Judge Required. The Court shall be notified at the time of trial setting if an attorney practicing in Kitsap County is a party or a witness in any matter before the Court or of any other matter needing a visiting judge.

(3) *Mental Illness Hearings.* Mental illness hearings will be set through the Court Scheduler.

(4) *Standby Calendar.* In the event that a case cannot be heard on the date set for trial it will be held on a standby calendar and counsel will be given a minimum of two hours' notice for trial.

(A) Notification. The Court Scheduler shall contact the parties to advise them of the standby status of their case.

(B) Standby Calendar at Counsel Request. A standby calendar at the parties' request may be created with the following conditions and addressed to the Court Scheduler.

(i) Trial—Kitsap County Superior Court. If an attorney is in another trial in Kitsap County Superior Court.

(ii) Trial—Other Courts. If an attorney has a conflict with another Superior Court, Appellate Court, or Federal Court, with the approval of the Presiding Judge.

(iii) Emergency. If an illness or other emergency situation arises involving the litigants, witnesses, or lawyers, with the approval of the Presiding Judge.

(iv) Other Requests. Any other request must be made to the Presiding Judge.

(v) Pending Settlement. Cases pending settlement will not be placed on standby at counsel request, but may be reset.

(5) *Notice to Court of Calendar and Jury Trial Changes.* Whenever a cause has been set for trial and thereafter is settled or will not be tried for any reason, or if a jury is thereafter waived, notice shall immediately be given to the Court Scheduler.

(6) *Case Management.* A Note For Trial Setting filed pursuant to section (1)(A) above, shall designate that the case falls within one of the following categories:

Track I Standard/General Civil Litigation
Track II Complex Litigation
Track III Domestic Relations

Once designated, counsel shall comply with the tracking procedures set forth below.

(A) Track I—Standard/General Civil Litigation.

(i) Scope. Except as otherwise provided in these rules or as otherwise ordered by the Court, this rule shall apply to all civil cases except:

- Adoptions;
- Domestic violence;
- Civil harassment;
- URESA cases;
- Juvenile proceedings;
- Paternities;
- Minor Settlements;
- Probates;
- Guardianships;
- Unlawful Detainers;
- Reviews of administrative agency actions;
- Appeals from courts of limited jurisdiction;
- Foreign judgments;
- Petitions for writs of mandamus, restitution, etc.;
- Civil commitments; and
- Proceedings under RCW 70.96A.

(ii) Preassignment and Case Schedule. At the time a matter is noted for trial setting, the Court shall randomly preassign a department of the Superior Court to hear the case. The Court shall enter an Order Setting Trial Date and a Civil Case Event Schedule in the form set forth in Exhibit D of these rules.

(iii) Amendment of Order Setting Case Event Schedule. Upon motion of any party or the Court, and upon good cause shown, the preassigned judge may modify any date in the original Order Setting Trial Date and Civil Case Event

Schedule. Copies of said amended order shall be filed and served upon all parties.

(iv) Additional Parties. A party who joins an additional party in an action shall be responsible for serving the additional party with the current Order Setting Trial Date and Civil Case Event Schedule together with the first pleading served on the additional party.

(v) Time Intervals for Case Event Schedule. Except as otherwise provided in the rules, or as otherwise ordered by the Court pursuant to section (A)(iii) above, the parties and counsel shall comply with the case event schedule, which shall include at minimum

EVENT:	DEADLINE:
Disclosure of Possible Primary Witnesses	240 days before trial date
Disclosure of Possible Additional Witnesses	150 days before trial date
Discovery Cutoff	120 days before trial date
Mandatory Settlement Conference	90 days before trial date
Last day to hear Dispositive Pretrial Motions	60 days before trial date
Exchange of Witness and Exhibit Lists	20 days before trial date
Joint Statement of the Evidence	7 days before trial date
Filing of Trial Briefs	5 days before trial date
Trial Date	

Comment: These dates will be set forth in the Civil Case Event Schedule.

(vi) Enforcement. The Court on its own initiative, or on motion of a party, may order an attorney or party to show cause as to why sanctions or terms should not be imposed for failure to comply with the case schedule established by these rules. If the Court finds that an attorney or party has failed to comply with the case schedule and has no reasonable excuse or other good cause, the Court may order the attorney or party to pay monetary sanctions to the Court, or terms to any attorney or party who has incurred expense as a result of the failure to comply, or both. In addition, the Court may impose such other sanctions or terms as justice requires. As used in this rule, "terms" mean costs, reasonable attorney fees and other expenses incurred or to be incurred as a result of the failure to comply; "monetary sanctions" mean a financial penalty payable to the Court, and "other sanctions" includes, but is not limited to, the exclusion of evidence and other sanctions available pursuant to the Civil Rules and Local Court Rules.

(vii) Discovery Cutoff. Unless otherwise ordered by the Court for good cause and subject to such terms and conditions as are just, all discovery allowed under Civil Rules 26–37, including responses and supplements thereto, must be completed no later than the date specified in the Civil Case Event Schedule. Discovery requests must be served early enough that responses will be due and depositions will have been taken prior to the cutoff date. Nothing in this rule shall modify a party's responsibility to seasonably supplement responses to discovery requests or otherwise to comply with discovery prior to the cutoff, nor shall a party be prevented from seeking relief under CR 37 after the cutoff date for discovery properly sought in accordance with this rule.

(viii) Dispositive Pretrial Motions. No hearings on dispositive pretrial motions shall be heard by the Court after the cutoff date specified in the Civil Case Event Schedule, except upon good cause shown and upon such terms and conditions as the Court may deem just, including assessment of terms and sanctions.

(ix) Settlement Conference. Reserved [See KCLCR 16(a).]

(B) Track II—Complex Litigation.

(i) Leave of Court Required. Assignment to Track II requires court approval. A request for assignment to Civil Track II may be made by filing a Note for Trial Setting (Exhibit A) in conjunction with a Request for Assignment to Civil Track II (Exhibit B).

Alternatively, a plaintiff or defendant may move for placement on Track II at filing or when an answer is filed by bringing the motion on the Presiding Judge's departmental calendar. The Court may place a case on Track II on its own motion at any time.

(ii) Scope. The following factors shall be weighed in determining whether a case will be placed on Track II:

- Nature of subject matter;
- Degree of complexity;
- Amount in controversy;
- Number of attorneys/parties involved; and
- Length of trial.

(iii) Preassignment and Case Schedule. The Presiding Judge will accept or deny a request submitted pursuant to section (B)(i) above and notify parties. A department of the Superior Court shall be preassigned to hear the case.

(iv) Management conference. A case must be at issue at the time of the initial management conference. The initial management conference shall be held within 60 days of acceptance into Track II, at which conference the following shall occur:

- Assignment of a trial date;

- Parties submit case management schedule approved by the Court; and

- Assignment of a date for the mandatory settlement conference.

(v) Amendment of Order Setting Case Schedule. Upon written motion of any party or the Court, and upon good cause shown, the preassigned judge may modify any date in an order entered pursuant to section (B)(iii) above. Copies of said amended order shall be filed and served upon all parties.

(vii)[1] Cases under the Land Use Petition Act, RCW 36.70C. When a land use petition (pursuant to RCW 36.70C) is filed with the Kitsap County Superior Court, all such cases shall be treated as Track II complex litigation and in accordance with the following procedures:

Pre–Assignment to a Superior Court Judge. Land Use Petition Act cases shall be assigned to a superior court judge, who shall hear and decide all matters in the case.

Notice of Land Use Petition. Within 7 days of the filing of a petition under the Land Use Petition Act, RCW 36.70C, the petitioner shall provide written notice of the filed petition to the Kitsap County Court Scheduler, identify it as a Land Use Petition Act case, and ask that the case be assigned to a judge. The Court Scheduler will note an initial hearing before the assigned judge.

Initial Hearing. A scheduling order setting the dates for filing the record, submitting briefs, and hearings will be issued at or shortly after the initial hearing. The parties should attempt to determine a mutually agreed upon scheduling order prior to the initial hearing. The parties may waive the initial hearing by filing a stipulated order resolving jurisdictional and procedural issued raised by the petition and setting a schedule for briefing, filing the record and transcripts and a hearing on the merits. Prior to filing a stipulated scheduling order, the petitioner shall contact the Court Scheduler to obtain a tentative date for the merits hearing.

Preparation of Administrative Record. Copies of the administrative record shall be provided to all parties. A bench copy of the record with an index and document identification tabs shall be provided to the assigned judge. A copy of the administrative record without side tabs shall be filed with the Superior Court Clerk for the court file.

Preparation of Transcripts. Verbatim transcripts shall be prepared by a certified court reporter and submitted to all parties for a period of seven days for correction of errors prior to filing.

Briefs. The petitioner shall have at least 30 days after the record and verbatim transcripts are filed to file and serve its brief. Respondent's brief shall be filed and served 30 days following filing and service of the petitioner's brief. Petitioner shall have an additional 14 days for filing a service of a reply brief. Reply briefs are in strict reply only. If a reply brief raises new issues, respondent may respond to those issues. In all statements of fact, briefs shall contain citations to the administrative record and the transcripts. Citations to the administrative record and the transcripts shall be denoted "AR" and "HR [date]," respectively, plus a page number.

Hearing on the Merits. Unless otherwise granted at the initial hearing, the Land Use Petition Act hearing on the merits shall be scheduled for one (1) day. The assigned judge shall take the first half of the day for reviewing the record, transcripts and briefs. The assigned judge will determine the amount of time granted for argument on the merits.

Related Matters. If a LUPA petition is consolidated with another claim, such as a damage action, the case may be bifurcated on stipulation of the parties or pursuant to motion. If the related matter is not bifurcated and entails a trial, a note for trial setting shall not be filed until after the record and transcripts are filed and served.

(C) TRACK III—Domestic Relations. [See KCFLR 8]

[Amended effective September 1, 1997; September 1, 2001; September 1, 2002; September 1, 2003; September 1, 2010; September 1, 2011; September 1, 2012; September 2, 2014; September 1, 2015.]

[1] As numbered in original.

Official Comment:

Parties are advised to consult the Land Use Petition Act statute for further procedural rules that apply in these proceedings. *See* RCW 36.70C.

KCLCR 47. JURORS

(a) Examination of Jurors.

(1) At the commencement of trial the clerk will assign numbers randomly, beginning with the number one, to all jurors called for trial. If a criminal defendant objects to this procedure, the numbers will be drawn by the clerk in open court at the beginning of the trial.

(A) Prior to the questioning of prospective jurors by counsel, the Court will allow time for counsel to review juror profiles and questionnaires.

(B) These jurors will be given large badges with their assigned numbers on them. These will be large enough to be easily read by the Court, counsel, and the court reporter. The jurors will arrange themselves in order as directed by the Court.

(C) If alternate jurors are to be selected, the parties are encouraged to stipulate that all peremptory challenges will be exercised against the entire panel. Otherwise, each side will only be allowed the number of peremptory challenge(s) against the alternate juror or jurors as allowed by CR 47(b).

(2) The Court will then ask general questions of the prospective jurors.

(A) "General questions" means those questions that are designed to discover those jurors who should be excused for cause (e.g., those prospective jurors who are related to a party or who cannot be available for the full time the trial is estimated to take).

(B) Counsel may request general questions to be asked by the Court as long as they meet the definition in section (2)(A) above.

(3) After prospective jurors have been excused for cause, the Court may excuse those jurors who are in excess of the number needed for the trial. The number needed for trial will be equal to 12, plus the number of alternates, plus the total number of peremptory challenges to which all parties are entitled, plus two to five additional as a cushion for possible additional challenges for cause.

(4) Counsel will then question the remaining prospective jurors.

(A) Each side will have 90 minutes for questioning. Each side may reserve that amount of the allotted time as allowed by the Court for additional questions following the questioning by the other side.

(i) Any time expended in arguing a challenge for cause will not be charged to either side.

(B) The times set forth in section (4)(A) above may be expanded by the Court for good cause shown, such as an extremely complicated case or multiple parties.

(C) Counsel may use their allotted time in any manner and may question prospective jurors in any order. Counsel may ask group questions or ask jurors to respond to remarks made by other members of the jury panel. (e.g., the first question may be addressed to juror #3 in the box, then a question to juror #21 on the benches, then to juror #9 in the box, then back to juror #3 in the box, then a question addressed to the entire panel, or just to jurors #3 and #9, etc.)

(D) Challenges for cause must be made when they are discovered.

(E) Objections to questions are made in the usual manner.

(F) If counsel is pursuing an important issue that relates to the qualifications of the prospective jurors to serve, and time has run out, counsel may request that the Court grant additional time.

(G) The entire panel of prospective jurors is passed for cause when counsel so announces or when the time allotted has been consumed.

(H) The procedure set forth in this rule shall not apply to cases involving charges of aggravated first degree murder as defined by RCW 10.95.020 if a notice of special sentencing proceeding has been filed.

(5) The parties then exercise their peremptory challenges.

(A) All peremptory challenges shall be exercised in open court.

(B) Challenges may be made to jurors who are not seated in the box.

(C) When a peremptory challenge is exercised, the next juror on the bench with the lowest number shall replace the juror who was excused from the jury box.

(D) The parties are encouraged to stipulate regarding peremptory challenges per Rule 47(a)(2)(A).

(E) Upon request of counsel, time will be allowed between voir dire and the exercise of peremptory challenges.

(6) Additional provisions.

(A) Counsel may submit, and the Court may allow, special questionnaires focused to the specific case (or type of case) to be submitted to the jurors to answer on the morning of trial before the voir dire process begins. Copies will be made and available to counsel during the questioning of the jurors. Counsel must submit proposed questionnaires to the Court and serve copies on opposing counsel at least five days prior to trial. If this is not done, the Court, in its discretion, may not allow special questionnaires. (If a standard questionnaire has been adopted by the Court for particular types of cases, counsel may refer to the standard questionnaire rather than serving copies.)

(k) Jury—Jurors. Jurors shall be called on a one trial/one day basis. Those persons selected to serve on a jury will be obligated for the duration of that one trial. Those not seated on a jury by the end of the selection will have fulfilled their jury obligation.

[Amended effective September 1, 1996; September 1, 2006; September 1, 2011.]

KCLCR 51.   INSTRUCTIONS TO JURY AND DELIBERATION

(b) Submission.

(1) *Filing.* Instructions shall be served and filed by 9:00 a.m. of the first day of trial.

(2) *Assembling and Distribution.* Jury instructions shall be assembled and distributed as follows:

(A) One set to trial judge to be unnumbered without citations.

(B) One set numbered and with supporting citations to each of the following:

- Clerk of Court for file;
- Judge for work copy; and
- Counsel for each opposing party

(C) One set containing unnumbered instructions without citations submitted electronically on CD or by email attachment (to the address provided by the trial judge). The jury instructions should be in Microsoft Word format.

(D) Jury instructions shall comply with the following formatting requirements:

- Formatted for 8–1/2″ × 11″ paper;
- One inch margins on all sides, except for verdict form which should have a three-inch top margin on the first page;
- Set for double-spacing; and
- Arial Font, 14 point font size.

(d) **Published Instructions.** Washington Pattern Jury Instructions are to be cited. On the copy of proposed jury instructions delivered to the trial court, the Clerk of Court, and opposing counsel, those Washington Pattern Jury Instructions proposed shall be so identified by WPI number. If the WPI is changed or modified in any way (except for the selection of alternate WPI wording), the citation shall include the word "modified." Modifications shall be identified on the numbered sets.

[Amended effective September 1, 2003; September 1, 2011.]

VII. JUDGMENT

KCLCR 54. JUDGMENT AND COSTS

(g) Attorney Fees.

(1) *Itemization.* Counsel requesting that the Court fix or determine the reasonableness of fees, or order payment of fees in any case, shall itemize the time expended, services rendered, or other detailed bases for the fees requested and attach a copy thereof to the request.

(2) *Temporary Attorney Fees.* The following temporary attorney fees are guidelines in domestic relations cases: $1,500.00 to the Petitioner, and $1,250.00 to the Respondent if a parenting plan is required; $1,000.00 to the Petitioner and $500.00 to the Respondent if no parenting plan is required. The Court also has the discretion to award taxable costs.

[Amended effective September 1, 2007; September 1, 2011.]

KCLCR 56. SUMMARY JUDGMENT

(c) A bench copy of the summary judgment and all supporting documents and responses shall be delivered, on the date of filing, to the Superior Court office.

[Adopted effective September 1, 2009; September 1, 2011. Amended on an emergency basis (as to comment only) effective April 1, 2013; amended on a permanent basis, effective September 2, 2013.]

Official Comment

For further guidance on the submission of bench copies see KCLCR 7. For further guidance on calendaring a motion for summary judgment, see KCLCR 77(k)(2).

KCLCR 59. NEW TRIAL, RECONSIDERATION, AND AMENDMENT OF JUDGMENTS

(b) Motion for Reconsideration; Time for Motion; Contents of Motion. A motion for reconsideration shall be filed and noted-not later than 10 days after entry of the judgment, decree, or order. The motion shall be noted on the trial judge's departmental motion docket to be heard not sooner than 30 but not later than 40 days after entry of the judgment, decree, or order, unless the Court directs otherwise. The trial judge shall be served by hand delivery of a copy of the motion and all supporting pleadings to the Law Clerk of the trial judge at the Superior Court office. [See KCLCR 7(b)(1)(B).] The documents shall be clearly identified as a motion for reconsideration, and shall clearly state the date the judgment, decree, or order was entered, and the names and addresses of opposing counsel.

(e) Hearing on Motion for Reconsideration. A motion for reconsideration shall be submitted on briefs and affidavits of the moving party only. No response shall be submitted by the opposing party, nor shall oral argument be heard, unless the Court so directs. The Court shall notify the parties, not later than 10 days before the hearing, whether: (1) the motion has been denied and the hearing stricken; or (2) oral argument and/or responsive pleadings will be allowed.

[Amended effective September 1, 1997; September 1, 1998; September 1, 2000; September 1, 2009; September 1, 2010; September 1, 2011; September 1, 2012.]

VIII.   PROVISIONAL AND FINAL REMEDIES (Rules 64–71)
[No Local Rules]

IX.   APPEALS (Rules 72–76) [Reserved]

X.   SUPERIOR COURTS AND CLERKS

KCLCR 77.   SUPERIOR COURTS AND JUDICIAL OFFICERS

(d) Superior Court Always Open. Court will be in session, unless otherwise ordered, on all judicial days, except Saturday. Court hours will be from 9:00 a.m. to 12:00 noon and from 1:30 p.m. to 4:30 p.m., except for those ex parte departments commencing at 8:30 a.m.

(f) Sessions. There shall be one continuous session of Court from January 1 through December 31 of each year.

(k) Motion Day—Local Rules.

(1) *Departmental Matters.* Departmental matters will be heard on Fridays at 1:30 p.m.

(2) *Civil Matters.* Probate, guardianship and civil motions (except Civil Rule 56 motions) in cases which are not preassigned to a specific judge will be heard on Friday at 9:00 a.m. Civil matters in cases which have been preassigned shall be heard on that judge's departmental calendar on Fridays at 1:30 p.m.

(A) In cases related to debt collections, Civil Rule 56 motions will be heard on Friday at 9:00 a.m.

(B) Motions pursuant to Civil Rule 56 in cases not solely related to debt collection should be noted for Friday at 1:30 p.m. on the "Summary Judgment" calendar. No specific judge should be named in the Note for Motion Docket.

(C) In cases other than those related to debt collections, upon filing of a Civil Rule 56 motion, the Superior Court will issue an order of preassignment to a specific judge. The Civil Rule 56 motions will be heard on the assigned judge's Friday departmental calendar at 1:30 p.m. If the matter is noted for the Trial Setting Docket, a case event schedule will issue.

(D) For purposes of KCLCR 77(k)(2), "debt collections" refer to cases where:

(i) The Complaint requests relief only in the form of a sum certain monetary judgment, with attorney fees, costs and interest, where applicable; and,

(ii) The relief requested in the Complaint is alleged to have been incurred pursuant to a contract between the parties; and,

(iii) The defendant(s) has not raised any Counterclaims.

(iv) Examples of debt collections cases under this rule include, but are not limited to: actions seeking monetary judgment based on debt alleged to have been incurred pursuant to a credit card, line of credit, or Promissory Note.

(E) The purposes of KCLCR 77(k)(2) are to keep lengthy, substantive summary judgment motions off the civil motions calendar; to ensure such motions receive sufficient review and oral argument before a decision is made; and, to ensure that once a judge has become sufficiently familiar with a case to decide a summary judgment motion, the case will stay with that judge until its final resolution to conserve judicial resources. Counsel should consider these purposes in determining where to note motions for summary judgment.

3. *Criminal Matters.* The Criminal Motion Schedule shall be as follows:

DAILY	9:00	Criminal In Custody Calendars
	10:30	Criminal Out of Custody Calendars
FRIDAY	9:00	Criminal In Custody Calendars
	11:00	Criminal After Sentencing/Restitution Calendar

(4) *Ex Parte Matters.* Noncriminal ex parte matters shall be heard Monday through Friday at 8:30 a.m. and 3:30 p.m. [See KCLCR 77(k)(10)(C)]

(5) *Domestic Relations Matters.*

(A) Settlement Conferences. Settlement conferences are heard Monday through Wednesday at 1:30 p.m. and Thursdays at 9:00 a.m., or such other times as set by the Court. [See KCLCR 16(a)(1).]

(B) Continuances. Matters for continuances in domestic relations cases shall be made in writing to be heard by the Domestic Relations Presiding Judge.

(B)[1] Pro Se Dissolutions. Pro se dissolutions without children will be heard at 1:30 p.m. on Tuesday. Pro se dissolutions with children will be heard at 2:00 p.m. on Tuesday.

(D) Domestic Violence. Domestic violence matters will be heard at 1:30 p.m. on Thursday.

(E) Temporary Relief. Show cause hearings and motions for temporary relief will be heard on Friday at 9:00 a.m. [See KCFLR 2.]

(F) Child Support Modification. All child support modifications, including applications for post

830

secondary support, shall be heard by affidavit on Tuesday at 3:00 p.m. as set by the Court Scheduler. Each side shall be limited to 10 minutes. Arguments requiring greater than 10 minutes per side shall be specially set by the Court Scheduler upon application of a party. [See KCLCR 77(k)(10).]

(G) Adoptions. Any adoptions requiring notice, including pro se adoptions, will be heard on Tuesday at 11:00 a.m. All other adoptions may be heard on any Ex Parte Calendar except Friday. [See KCLSPR 93.04.]

(H) Parentage and State Initiated Child Support Cases. The Parentage Calendar shall be heard on Tuesday at 9:00 a.m.

(i) All matters noted on the Parentage calendar must be confirmed in person, by telephoning the Superior Court office at (360) 337–7140 (Option 2), or by email at supcourtconfirm@co.kitsap.wa.us no later than 12:00 noon two business days before hearings, but no earlier than three business days before hearings.

(ii) Motions which are administratively continued must be confirmed by the moving party in order to be heard.

(iii) Matters not confirmed may be heard only at the discretion of the Court. [See KCLCR 16(a)(3) (confirmation of settlement conferences).]

Official Comment: For further guidance on the submission of bench copies see KCLCR 7.

(I) State Initiated Child Support Cases. State of Washington initiated child support cases including support modifications and parentages shall be heard on Tuesday at 9:00 a.m.

(6) *Guardianship Delinquency Matters.* Guardianship delinquency matters shall be heard at 10:00 a.m. the first Friday of each month.

(7) *Trial Settings.* Trial setting dockets shall be Friday at 9:00 a.m. [See KCLCR 40(b)(1)(A).]

(8) *Minor Settlements.* Petitions for settlement of the claims of minors shall be heard on Friday at 9:00 a.m. on the Probate Motions Calendar, except cases which are preassigned shall be heard on that judge's departmental calendar on Friday at 1:30 p.m. [See KCLSPR 98.16.]

(9) *Special Settings.* Any hearing requiring special setting shall be arranged through the Court Scheduler. A hearing may be specially set for the following reasons, by way of example only: length of argument: nature of the hearing; or need for a visiting judge. Special set hearings must be confirmed as required by KCLCR 77(k)(11)(A).

(10) *Hearing of Motions.*

(A) Mandatory Confirmations.

(iv)[2] All motions pursuant to CR 12(b)(6) and CR 56 must be confirmed in person, by telephoning the Superior Court office at (360) 337–7140 (Option 2), or by email at supcourtconfirm@co.kitsap.wa.us no later than 12:00 noon two days before hearings, but no earlier than 72 hours in advance. Motions which are administratively continued must be confirmed by the moving party in order to be heard.

(v) The Court does not require confirmation of unlawful detainer actions filed under RCW Title 59.

(vi) Hearings set by order of the a[3] judicial officer, including orders to show cause and presentation of orders set by a judicial officer in open court following that judicial officer's oral ruling, do not require confirmation and are not subject to continuance except by signed order of the judicial officer.

(vii) All other civil, domestic relations, probate, adoptions and departmental motions which are not covered by or exempt from confirmation under sections (i), (ii) or (iii) must be confirmed in person, by telephoning the Superior Court office at (360) 337–7140 (Option 2), or by email at supcourtconfirm@co.kitsap.wa.us no later than 12:00 noon one day before hearings but no earlier than 48 hours in advance.

(viii) Matters not confirmed may be heard only at the discretion of the Court. [See KCLCR 16(a)(3) (confirmation of settlement conferences).]

(B) Hearing of Calendars.

(i) Calling of Calendar. The causes on the Civil Calendar and Domestic Relations Calendar for each motion day will be called in order, oldest causes first.

(ii) Noting of Calendar Matters. Notes for motion calendars shall be filed in the office of the Clerk of Court by 4:30 p.m. on the fifth judicial day preceding the calendar on which hearing is requested and should be substantially in the form found in Exhibit E.

(iii) Failure of Party to Appear. If no one appears in opposition to a duly noted motion, the Court may grant the relief requested upon proper proof of notice. If no one appears for a motion, it will be stricken.

(iv) Continuances of Motions. Counsel, by agreement, may continue any noncriminal motion by filing a notice of continuance, signed by at least one attorney. Forms are available in the courtroom. *See* Exhibit F. Criminal motions shall be continued only with the consent of the Criminal Motions Judge. Continuances shall not be granted by telephone. Summary judgment motions which have been confirmed shall not be continued without the Civil Calendar or preassigned judge's approval.

A party who has noted a matter for hearing may unilaterally strike or re-note the hearing for a new date, except that once confirmed the hearing may be stricken or re-noted only with prior notice to the other parties.

(v) Time Allowed for Argument. Each side shall be limited to 10 minutes. Argument requiring more than 20 minutes total time may be placed by the judge or court commissioner at the end of the calendar.

If the Court desires to hear further arguments after expiration of 20 minutes, the matter may be placed in order at the end of the calendar for further argument or continued to a specified date.

(C) Hearing of Ex Parte Matters.

(i) Scope. This rule applies to all temporary restraining orders, orders to show cause, and all other ex parte matters. It includes all criminal matters except dismissal at end of probation.

(ii) Notice to Opposing Counsel or Party. Unless notice is specifically excluded by statute, no ex parte order shall be presented without notice to opposing counsel or opposing party if appearing without counsel. If counsel for any party, or a party, has appeared either formally or informally, notice is required. If necessary, notice may be by telephone. This rule applies regardless of whether service is required on the attorney or a party pursuant to CR 5(b)(4).

(iii) Reapplication for Order. Reserved. [See KCLCR 7(b)(1)(C) (reapplication for order).]

(iv) Court File. Counsel or a party is responsible for obtaining the court file when presenting ex parte matters, except for agreed orders other than domestic relations decrees.

[Amended effective September 1, 1996; September 1, 1997; September 1, 1998; July 1, 1999; September 1, 2002; September 1, 2005; amended on an emergency basis, effective April 1, 2006; amended on a permanent basis, effective September 1, 2006; September 1, 2007; amended on an emergency basis, effective January 18, 2008; amended on a permanent basis, effective September 1, 2008; September 1, 2009; September 1, 2011; September 1, 2012; amended on an emergency basis, effective October 1, 2012; December 18, 2012; April 1, 2013; amended on a permanent basis, effective September 2, 2013; amended on an emergency basis, effec-

tive November 1, 2013; January 22, 2014; April 21, 2014; amended on a permanent basis, effective September 2, 2014.]

1 Lettering as provided in original.
2 Lettering as provided in original.
3 So in original.

KCLCR 78. CLERKS

(a) Powers and Duties of Clerks.

(1) *Notifications.*

(A) Juvenile Staff Appointments. The Clerk of Court shall promptly notify the Director of Juvenile Court Services of appointment of juvenile court staff for any purpose as ordered by the Court.

(B) Appointment of Counsel. The Clerk of Court shall promptly notify appointed counsel of any court appointment.

(C) Presentence Investigations. The Clerk of Court shall promptly notify the Department of Corrections or Superior Court Investigative Officer of any orders for presentence investigation.

(2) *Action Documents.* All pleadings requiring action by the Clerk of Court, other than file stamping and docketing, shall contain the language **CLERK'S ACTION REQUIRED** in the caption beneath the case number on the first page of the document.

(3) *No Personal Checks.* The Clerk of Court shall not accept personal checks except for passport applications.

[Amended effective September 1, 1996; September 1, 2010; September 1, 2011.]

KCLCR 79. BOOKS AND RECORDS KEPT BY THE CLERK

(d) Other Books and Records of the Clerk.

(1) *Files.* The Clerk of Court has authority to grant a member in good standing of the Washington State Bar Association authorization to withdraw up to five files for a period not to exceed seven days.

(2) *Verbatim Report of Proceedings.* Verbatim reports of proceedings, after having been settled and signed, shall not be withdrawn from the office of the Clerk of Court except by order of the Court.

(3) *Disposition of Exhibits.* All exhibits not withdrawn within 90 days following the final disposition of a civil cause will be destroyed without further notice to any of the attorneys or parties in the case and without further order of the Court.

[Amended effective September 1, 2002; September 1, 2011.]

XI. GENERAL PROVISIONS

KCLCR 81. APPLICABILITY IN GENERAL

(c) Suspension of Rules. The Court may modify or suspend any of these rules, in any given case, upon

good cause being shown therefore or upon the Court's own motion.

[Amended effective September 1, 2011.]

KCLCR 83. LOCAL RULES OF SUPERIOR COURT

(a) Adoption.

(1) *Initiation of Rules Changes.* All suggestions for rules changes shall be sent to the Assistant Presiding Judge, who shall transmit them to the Practice and Procedure Committee of the Kitsap County Bar Association, to the other Superior Court judges of Kitsap County, and to other interested parties as determined by the Assistant Presiding Judge.

(2) *Consideration of Proposed Rules Changes.* All suggested rules changes shall be considered by all judges of the Superior Court of Kitsap County in consultation with the Practice and Procedure Committee of the Kitsap County Bar Association. If a proposed rule or rule change is approved, it will be published for comment as follows during the month of April: by posting on the bulletin board in the office of the Clerk of the Court and the reception counter at the Superior Court office; and by transmitting such proposals to the Kitsap County Bar Association, which shall publish the same to its members.

(3) *Consideration of Comments.* All comments on proposed rules should be directed to the Presiding Judge. The Court shall consider all comments, criticisms, objections, and suggestions submitted on, or before, the last day of May.

(4) *Final Adoption, Publication, and Effective Date.* After the comment period, and on or before September 1, the Court shall publish the rule changes, and shall submit these to the Administrative Office of the Courts on or before July 1, of each year. The Court shall publish the rule changes as finally approved on or before the effective date of September 1.

(5) *Periodic Review.* Thereafter, until the next succeeding December 31, the Court shall continue its consultation with appropriate committees of the Kitsap County Bar Association concerning the need or desirability of further rule changes.

(6) *Limitation of Amendments; Exceptions.* The Court shall make rule changes only in accordance with this rule, except in cases of emergency or other circumstances justifying immediate changes.

[Amended effective September 1, 2011; September 1, 2012.]

KITSAP COUNTY LOCAL FAMILY LAW RULES [KCLFLR]

KCLFLR 1. EX PARTE RESTRAINING ORDERS

Personal appearance of a party is required if a party requests an ex parte order seeking to restrain one party from the family home or contact with the other party or children.

[Adopted effective September 1, 2011.]

KCLFLR 2. ORDERS

The following shall apply to all contested motion hearings in which relief is sought:

(a) Responsive Affidavits. Responsive affidavits shall be served and filed no later than 12:00 noon the day before the hearing.

(b) Reply Affidavits. Reply affidavit shall be provided to opposing counsel/party no later than 5:00 p.m. the day before the hearing. Reply affidavits may be filed no later than the day of the hearing. Reply affidavits shall be limited to a maximum of three double spaced pages and shall be in strict reply to the responsive affidavit.

(c) Exhibits and Worksheets. Mandatory financial declarations and support worksheets as required by RCW 26.09 shall be filed whenever financial matters are at issue. [See KCLCR 77(k)(5).]

[Adopted effective September 1, 2011. Amended effective September 2, 2013.]

KCLFLR 3. CHILD SUPPORT

The Washington State Child Support Schedule as adopted by the legislature shall be applied by the Court and counsel in all matters involving child support, temporary or permanent.

[Adopted effective September 1, 2011.]

KCLFLR 4. FINAL HEARING ON CONTESTED MATTERS

In all final hearings or trials in domestic relations matters, each party shall file and serve on the opposing party and the court by 9:00 a.m. the day of trial, a written Domestic Relations Information Form. The Domestic Relations Information Form shall be in the form set forth on Exhibit G attached to these rules. Mandatory financial declarations and support worksheets as required by RCW 26.09 shall be filed whenever financial matters are at issue.

[Adopted effective September 1, 2011.]

KCLFLR 5. NONCONTESTED MARRIAGE DISSOLUTIONS; DELIVERY OF DECREE TO OTHER PARTY

In default dissolution cases, at the time of entry of the decree, the moving party or counsel shall immediately deliver to or mail to the other party, at their address if known, or to their counsel, a conformed copy of the decree, with the date of filing indicated on each copy so delivered or mailed.

[Adopted effective September 1, 2011.]

KCLFLR 6. MANDATORY SETTLEMENT CONFERENCES

(a) Mandatory Settlement Conferences. In each dissolution, declaration of invalidity, or legal separation, counsel and the parties shall participate in a settlement conference presided over by a judge or court commissioner. Settlement conferences are mandatory.

(b) Attendance and Preparation Required. No later than noon the day prior to a settlement conference that has been scheduled pursuant to section (a), each party shall have submitted to the other party and the Court a completed settlement conference memorandum and a completed "Domestic Relations Form" in the form of Exhibit G. The attorneys shall come prepared to discuss in detail and in good faith all unresolved issues in the case and, in addition, all pretrial matters if the case is not settled.

(1) Failure to Serve Settlement Conference Memorandum and "Domestic Relations Form"/Exhibit G. Failure to serve a completed settlement conference memorandum and a "Domestic Relations Form" in the form of Exhibit G and/or an equivalent upon the other parties and provide the original for the settlement conference judge, as required, may, at the discretion of the judge, result in the settlement conference judge striking the scheduled settlement conference and setting a subsequent settlement conference on the Court's next available date.

(c) Mandatory Confirmations. All settlement conferences must be confirmed in person, by telephoning the Superior Court office at (360) 337-7140 (Option 2), or by email at supcourtconfirm@co.kitsap.wa.us no later than 12:00 noon one day before hearings, but no earlier than 48 hours in advance. Failure to confirm may result in the imposition of terms and/or sanctions as the Court may deem appropriate.

[Adopted effective September 1, 2011. Amended effective September 1, 2012; September 2, 2013.]

KCLFLR 7. APPOINTMENT OF OPTIONAL GUARDIAN AD LITEM, ATTORNEY FOR CHILD, AND CUSTODY INVESTIGATOR IN CHILD CUSTODY MATTERS

(a) Guardian Ad Litem (Title 26).

(1) *Optional Guardian Ad Litem.* In any domestic relations matter the Court may, upon its own motion, or motion of either party, appoint a guardian ad litem to represent the interests of any child, or children, of the parties. If any decree illegitimizes a child or may result in a child becoming illegitimate, the Court may require that a guardian ad litem be appointed for the child.

(2) *Appointment.* The guardian ad litem shall be appointed from the court-approved registry for Title 26. Said person shall have such powers, as granted by the Court, to ascertain what is in the best interests of the child or children, and to take whatever steps the Court deems appropriate to effectuate a result consistent with the best interests of the child or children.

(3) *Duties of Guardian Ad Litem.* The Court may direct the guardian ad litem to report to the court, either orally or in writing. The guardian ad litem has the right to attend and participate at trial or any other proceeding, and shall be given all other rights accorded a party, including notice. The guardian ad litem may be called as a witness at trial by either party, or the Court.

(b) Attorney for Child. In any domestic relations matter the Court may, upon its own motion, or motion of either party, appoint an attorney for any children of the parties. The attorney shall be an advocate for the children and shall represent the position of the children in the action. The attorney shall have the rights of any other attorney in the action. The attorney shall not be expected to submit a report to the court, nor normally be called as a witness at trial. [See RCW 26.09.110.]

(c) Custody Investigator. The Court may, upon its own motion, or motion of either party, appoint a custody investigator in matters involving a dispute over custody of a child. [See RCW 26.09.220.]

A custody investigator shall make appropriate investigation and report to the court. Upon motion of any party, or the court, the custody investigator shall appear at trial and be subject to examination by the parties and the Court.

[Adopted effective September 1, 2011.]

KCLFLR 8. DISCOVERY SCOPE AND LIMITS

In family law matters interrogatories shall be limited to 100 in number and each subpart of an interrogatory shall be counted as a separate interrogatory for purposes of this rule. Additional interrogatories may be permitted by stipulation of the parties or by order of the Court. There shall be no limit on requests for production or requests for admission.

[Adopted effective September 1, 2011.]

KCLFLR 9. CASE PROGRESSION

(a) Note for Settlement Conference and Trial Setting. Within 90 days of the case at issue, Petitioner or Respondent shall file a Note for Settlement Conference & Trial Setting—Domestic Relations (as set forth in Exhibit C).

(b) Settlement conference. A mandatory settlement conference shall be set within 45 days of the date noted for trial setting. Settlement conferences are mandatory and shall be confirmed before 12:00 noon the day before such conference is scheduled. [See KCFLR 6.]

(c) Assignment of Trial Date. If the case is not settled at settlement conference, the Court will assign a trial date, not more than 120 days from the date of the settlement conference. Exceptions shall be addressed to the settlement conference judge.

(d) Change of Trial or Hearing Date. Upon written stipulation of the parties, or upon motion of party, the Court may order a change or continuance of the trial date, special set hearing, support modification hearing, or settlement conference date.

(e) Support Modifications. All support modifications will be heard by affidavit, 10 minutes per side for argument unless the Court requests additional affidavits or an order authorizing oral testimony is granted. Petitioner's affidavit shall be submitted not later than 14 days before the hearing. Respondent's affidavit shall be submitted not later than seven days before the hearing. The reply affidavit shall be submitted not later than 12:00 noon the day before the hearing. Settlement conferences are not required for support modifications.

[Adopted effective September 1, 2011. Amended effective September 2, 2013.]

KCLFLR 10. MANDATORY PARENTING SEMINAR

(a) Scope. This rule applies to all cases filed under Ch. 26.09, or Ch. 26.26 of the RCW (except those cases brought on behalf of the State of Washington by the Prosecuting Attorney's Child Support Office) filed after January 1, 2005, which require a parenting plan for minor children, including dissolutions, legal separations, and paternity actions. This rule does not apply to petitions to modify custody. In the case of paternity actions involving the Prosecuting Attorney's Child Support Office, the seminar shall be required only in cases that the Court has made a finding that the Parenting Seminar would benefit the parents.

(b) Definitions. As used in these rules, the following terms have these meanings.

(1) *Parenting Seminar.* Parenting seminar or seminar shall mean a seminar presented by an authorized provider as set forth in section (h) below, with content that meets the requirements specified in section (i) below.

(2) *Parent Education Committee.* The Parent Education Committee or Committee shall mean the standing committee of the Kitsap County Superior Court as provided in LCR 1(c)(5).

(c) Parenting Seminars; Mandatory Attendance. In all cases referred to in Section (a) above, and in those additional cases arising under Title 26 RCW where the Court makes a discretionary finding that a parenting seminar would be in the best interest of the children, both parents, and such other parties as the Court may direct, shall participate in, and successfully complete, an approved parenting seminar within 90 days after service of a petition on the responding parent. Successful completion shall be evidenced by a certificate of attendance filed with the Court by the provider agency.

(d) Special Considerations, Waiver.

(1) *Joint Participation Not Required.* In no case shall parents be required to attend a seminar together.

(2) *Grounds for Waiver or Alternative.* Upon a showing of any of the following, the Court shall either waive the requirement of completion of the seminar or provide an alternative to the seminar:

(A) Domestic violence, abuse, or safety concerns;

(B) Allegations of any conduct set fort at RCW 26.09.191; or

(C) Any other reason why a parent's attendance at a seminar is not in the children's best interest.

(3) *Waiver.* The Court may waive the seminar requirement for one or both parents in any case for good cause shown, including but not limited to default situations.

(e) Failure to Comply. Delay, refusal or default by one parent does not excuse timely compliance by the other parent. Unless attendance at the seminar is waived, a parent who delays beyond the 90 day deadline, or who otherwise fails or refuses to complete the parenting seminar, shall be precluded from presenting any final order affecting the parenting/residential plan in this action, until the seminar has been successfully completed. The Court may also refuse to allow the non-complying parent to seek affirmative relief in this or subsequent proceedings until the seminar is successfully completed.

(f) Finalizing Parenting Plans. All parents are required to attach to their proposed final parenting plan a true and accurate signed and dated copy of the certificate of completion of the seminar. No final parenting plan shall be entered without said certificate, except in those cases that the Court has waived attendance.

(g) Fee. Each parent attending a seminar shall pay a fee charged by the provider and sanctioned by the Court. The Court may waive the fee for indigent parents.

(h) Authorized Providers.

(1) *Certified Providers.* The Kitsap County Court Administrator shall maintain a list of seminar providers who have filed a statement of compliance with the Parent Education Committee. The statement of compliance shall certify that the content of seminars offered by the provider meet the requirements set forth in section (i) below.

If a provider's qualifications are challenged, the provider shall be notified by the Committee of the process to resolve any questions regarding the provider's future approval. The provider will then have an opportunity to respond to any challenges to its qualifications.

(2) *Equivalent Providers May be Used.* Parents may use equivalent services offered by private agencies or religious organizations, upon approval of the judge or commissioner in the individual case.

When the Court authorized the use of providers or religious organizations which have not previously been accepted by the Committee as a certified provider of parenting seminars, the Court may modify or waive the qualifications for the instructors, as listed as section (j) below, upon a showing of functional equivalency.

(i) Seminar Content. The seminar content shall include, at a minimum:

- The developmental stages of childhood;

- Stress indicators in children;

- Age appropriate expectations of children;

- The impact of divorce on children;

- The grief process;

- Reducing stress for children through an amicable divorce;

- The long term impact of parental conflict on children;

- The importance of child's relationships with both parents; fostering those relationships;

- Communication skills for divorced parents;

- Minimization of conflict;

- Practical skills for working together;

- The impact on children when stepparents and blended families enter their lives;

- Parenting children with limited time; and Involvement of extended family.

(j) Qualifications of Instructors. Parenting seminars shall be taught by a team of not less than two instructors, including one male and one female. Arrangements may be made for classes limited to one or two attendees, in which case two instructors are not required. Instructors should have the following minimum credentials and experience:

- A Master's Degree in social work, psychology or other related behavioral science suggested, with a Bachelor's Degree minimum with two years social work experience;

- Supervisory experience in treatment of emotionally disturbed children, adolescents and their families;

- Experience in providing a wide range of mental health services to children and families, with specific experience in the areas of separation/divorce, loss and grief, and blended families;

- Extensive knowledge of child development, age appropriate expectations for children, and positive parenting;

- An ability to work with others (both groups and individuals) as part of a collaborative program; and

- Strong oral communication skills.

(k) Referrals for Other Services. During the seminar, referral resources will be made available to the parents and their children, including individual and family counseling, drug/alcohol counseling, anger management counseling, parenting classes, etc. These services are optional, and the parents must seek their own funding resources.

[Adopted effective September 1, 2011.]

KCLFLR 11. PRESENTATION OF FINAL PLEADINGS IN FAMILY LAW CASES

(a) Unless presented by an attorney, no final Decree, Findings of Fact and Conclusions of Law, Parenting Plan, Order of Child Support and Worksheets, Order of Modification or other final pleadings in Family Law cases shall be presented to the Court without written verification that all such pleadings have been reviewed as to form by an attorney, the Kitsap County Courthouse Facilitator or Kitsap Legal Services. This requirement may be waived by the Court for good cause shown.

(b) Formal proof by a litigant personally appearing in Court shall be required in the finalization of all dissolution and legal separation proceedings, including when a Decree of Legal Separation is converted to a Decree of Dissolution, modification of a prior Parenting Plan, and in all other matters in which a final Parenting Plan or Residential Schedule is being presented. Upon good cause, the Court may authorize formal proof to be taken by Skype or telephone.

[Adopted effective September 1, 2011. Amended effective September 1, 2015.]

KCLFLR 12. MOTIONS FOR REVISION

A motion to revise a court commissioner's decision shall be filed within 10 days of the decision and shall be noted on the Presiding Domestic Relations Judge's departmental calendar.

[Adopted effective September 1, 2011. Amended effective September 2, 2013.]

KITSAP COUNTY LOCAL MANDATORY
ARBITRATION RULES [KCLMAR]

I. SCOPE AND PURPOSE OF RULES

KCLMAR 1.1. APPLICATION OF RULES

Application and Purpose. The purpose of mandatory arbitration of civil actions under RCW 7.06 as implemented by the Mandatory Arbitration Rules is to provide a simplified and economical procedure for obtaining the prompt and equitable resolution of disputes involving claims of $50,000 or less, exclusive of attorney fees, interest, and costs. The Mandatory Arbitration Rules as supplemented by these local rules are not designed to address every question which may arise during the arbitration process and the rules give considerable discretion to the arbitrator. The arbitrator should not hesitate to be informal and expeditious, consistent with the purpose of the statute and rules.

[Amended effective September 1, 2005; September 1, 2011.]

KCLMAR 1.2. MATTERS SUBJECT TO ARBITRATION

The following matters are subject to mandatory arbitration: (a) civil actions at issue in the Superior Court where the sole relief sought is a money judgment not in excess of $50,000, exclusive of attorney fees, interest, and costs, and (b) Small Claims Judgments appealed from District Court.

[Adopted September 1, 1995; amended effective September 1, 2005; September 1, 2011.]

KCLMAR 1.3. RELATIONSHIP TO SUPERIOR COURT JURISDICTION AND OTHER RULES

(b) Which Rules Apply. All motions before the Court relating to mandatory arbitration shall be noted on the Civil Motions Calendar in accordance with KCLCR 77, except as otherwise provided in these arbitration rules.

[Amended effective September 1, 2011.]

II. TRANSFER TO ARBITRATION AND ASSIGNMENT OF ARBITRATOR

KCLMAR 2.1. TRANSFER TO ARBITRATION

(a) Statement of Arbitrability. In every civil case, when any party has determined that the case is ready for trial and that the case is subject to arbitration, either mandatory or by stipulation, such party shall file with the Clerk a Note for Arbitration Setting & Initial Statement of Arbitrability substantially in the form of Exhibit H. A duplicate copy shall be delivered to the Superior Court office

(b) Response to Statement of Arbitrability. Any party disagreeing with the Statement of Arbitrability shall serve and file a response substantially in the form of Exhibit I. A duplicate copy of the response shall be delivered to the Superior Court office. In the absence of such a response, the Statement of Arbitrability shall be deemed correct and a non-responding party shall be deemed to have stipulated to arbitration if the Statement of Arbitrability provides that the case is arbitrable. If a party asserts that its claim exceeds $50,000 or seeks relief other than a money judgment, the case is not subject to arbitration except by stipulation.

(c) Failure to File—Amendments. A party failing to serve and file an original response within the time prescribed may later do so only upon leave of the court. A party may amend the Initial Statement of Arbitrability or response at any time before assignment of an arbitrator or assignment of a trial date, or thereafter only upon leave of the court for good cause shown.

(d) By Stipulation. A case in which all parties file a stipulation to arbitrate under MAR 8.1(b) will be placed on the arbitration calendar regardless of the nature of the case or amount in controversy.

[Amended effective September 1, 2002; September 1, 2005; September 1, 2011.]

III. ARBITRATORS

KCLMAR 3.1. QUALIFICATIONS

(a) Arbitration Panel. There shall be a panel of arbitrators in such numbers as the administrative committee may determine. A person desiring to serve as an arbitrator shall complete an information sheet on the form prescribed by the Court. A list showing the names of the arbitrators available to hear cases and information sheets will be available for public inspection in the Superior Court office. The oath of office on the form prescribed by the court must be completed and filed prior to an application being placed on the panel.

(b) Refusal; Disqualification. The appointment of an arbitrator is subject to the right of that person to refuse to serve. An arbitrator must notify the Court Administrator immediately if he or she refuses to serve or if any cause exists for the arbitrator's disqualification from the case on any of the grounds of interest, relationship, bias, or prejudice set forth in CJC Canon 3(c) governing disqualification of judges. If disqualified, the arbitrator must immediately return all materials in the case to the Court Administrator.

(c) Challenge to Qualifications. Any party may challenge the qualifications of the appointed arbitrator by motion to the Superior Court Presiding Judge

provided, however, that said motion must be made within 14 days of the appointment of the arbitrator.

[Amended effective September 1, 2004; September 1, 2011.]

KCLMAR 3.2. AWARD OF ATTORNEY FEES

In addition to the authority given to arbitrators under MAR 3.2, an arbitrator has the authority to award fees, as authorized by these rules, by a contract, or by law except CR 11 sanctions.

[Adopted effective September 1, 2000; amended effective September 1, 2011.]

Official Comment

The arbitration information sheet and oath is available on the Superior Court's website. *See* http://www.kitsapgov.com/sc/arbitrator_info.htm.

IV. PROCEDURES AFTER ASSIGNMENT

KCLMAR 4.2. DISCOVERY

(a) Additional Discovery. In determining when additional discovery beyond that directly authorized by MAR 4.2 is reasonably necessary, the arbitrator shall balance the benefits of discovery against the burdens and expenses. The arbitrator shall consider the nature and complexity of the case, the amount of controversy, the values at stake, the discovery that has already occurred, the burdens on the party from whom discovery is sought, and the possibility of unfair

surprise which may result if discovery is restricted. Authorized discovery shall be conducted in accordance with the Civil Rules except that motions concerning discovery shall be determined by the arbitrator.

(b) Discovery Pending at the Time Arbitrator is Assigned. Discovery pending at the time the case is assigned to an arbitrator is stayed pending order from the arbitrator or except as the parties may stipulate or as authorized by MAR 4.2.

[Amended effective September 1, 2011.]

V. HEARING

KCLMAR 5.1. NOTICE OF HEARING

Notice of Hearing—Time—Place—Continuance. In addition to the requirements of MAR 5.1, the arbitrator shall give reasonable notice of the hearing date and any continuance to the Court Administrator.

[Amended effective September 1, 2011.]

KCLMAR 5.2. PREHEARING STATEMENT OF PROOF

Prehearing Statement of Proof—Documents Filed with Court. In addition to the requirements of

MAR 5.2, each party shall also furnish the arbitrator with copies of pleadings and other documents contained in the court file which the party deems relevant.

[Amended effective September 1, 2011.]

VI. AWARD

KCLMAR 6.1. FORM AND CONTENT OF AWARD

(a) Form. The award shall be prepared on a form substantially compliant with Exhibit J.

(b) Return of Exhibits. When an award is filed, the arbitrator shall return all exhibits to the parties who offered them during the hearing.

[Amended effective September 1, 2011.]

KCLMAR 6.2. FILING OF AWARD

A request by an arbitrator for an extension of time for the filing of an award under MAR 6.2 must be presented to the Court Administrator.

[Amended effective September 1, 2011.]

KCLMAR 6.3. JUDGMENT ON AWARD

A judgment on an award shall be presented to the Ex Parte Judge, by any party, on notice in accordance with MAR 6.3.

[Amended effective September 1, 2011.]

VII. TRIAL DE NOVO

KCLMAR 7.1. REQUEST FOR TRIAL DE NOVO

(a) **Service and Filing.** The request for trial de novo shall be accompanied by a Note for Trial on the forms provided by the Court. [*See* Exhibit A.]

[Amended effective September 1, 2011.]

KCLMAR 7.2. PROCEDURE AFTER REQUEST FOR TRIAL DE NOVO

(e) **Trial To Be Set in Accordance with KCLCR 40.** When a trial de novo is requested as provided in MAR 7.1 and LMAR 7.1(a)(1), trial shall be set in accordance with KCLCR 40(b)(1), except that the Court will assign an accelerated trial date no sooner than 180 days and no more than 270 days from the date the request for trial de novo is filed. A request for a trial de novo may include a request for assignment of a particular trial date or dates, provided the date or dates requested have been agreed upon by all parties in writing and preauthorized by the Court Scheduler.

[Amended effective September 1, 2011; September 2, 2014.]

KCLMAR 7.3. COSTS AND ATTORNEY FEES

MAR 7.3 shall apply only to costs and reasonable attorney fees incurred since the filing of the request for a trial de novo.

[Amended effective September 1, 2011.]

VIII. GENERAL PROVISIONS

KCLMAR 8.1. STIPULATIONS

(b) **To Arbitrate Other Cases—Stipulations—Effect on Relief Granted.** If a case not otherwise subject to mandatory arbitration is transferred to arbitration by stipulation, the arbitrator may grant any relief which could have been granted if the case were determined by a judge.

[Amended effective September 1, 2011.]

KCLMAR 8.4. TITLE AND CITATION

These rules are known and cited as the Kitsap County Superior Court Mandatory Arbitration Rules. LMAR is the official abbreviation.

[Amended effective September 1, 2011.]

KCLMAR 8.6. COMPENSATION OF ARBITRATOR

(a) **Generally.** Arbitrators shall be compensated in the same amount and manner as judges pro tempore of the Superior Court; provided, the compensation shall not exceed $650.00 for any case without approval of the Presiding Judge.

(b) **Form.** When the award is filed, the arbitrator shall submit to the Superior Court office a request for payment on a form prescribed by the Court. The Presiding Judge shall determine the amount of compensation to be paid.

[Amended effective September 1, 2011; September 2, 2013.]

KCLMAR 8.7. ADMINISTRATION

(a) **Supervision.** The Presiding Judge and his or her designees shall supervise arbitration under these rules.

(b) **Administrative Committee Composition and Terms.** There shall be an administrative committee composed of the Presiding Judge and four members of the Kitsap County Bar Association. The members of the committee shall serve one year terms and may be reappointed.

(c) **Administrative Committee Power and Duties.** The administrative committee shall have the power and duty to:

(1) Select a chairperson and establish procedures;

(2) Appoint the panel of arbitrators provided in LMAR 3.1(a);

(3) Remove a person from a panel of arbitrators;

(4) Establish procedures for selecting an arbitrator not inconsistent with the Mandatory Arbitration Rules or these rules; and

(5) Review the administration and operation of the arbitration program periodically and make recommendations as it deems appropriate to improve the program and submit any recommendations to the Kitsap

County Bar Association membership for comment and to the Superior Court for ratification.

[Amended effective September 1, 2011.]

KITSAP COUNTY LOCAL SPECIAL PROCEEDINGS RULES [KCLSPR]

KCLSPR 93.04. DISPOSITION OF REPORTS—ADOPTIONS [RESCINDED]

[Amended effective September 1, 2011; rescinded effective September 1, 2012.]

KCLSPR 98.10. GUARDIANSHIPS AND TRUSTS

(h) Order Approving Guardian's Report and Accounting. Every order to approve an initial or periodic Guardian's or Trustee's report shall include a Court Summary (Required) on the first page in the following format:

COURT'S SUMMARY(Required)		
Date Guardian/Trustee Appointed:		
☐ Person:	☐ Full	☐ Limited
☐ Estate:	☐ Full	☐ Limited
Next Review Period:	to	
Accounting Due (90 Days Later), **NO LATER THAN:**		
Date for Next Hearing:	or TBD	
Letters Expire (90 Days After Accounting Due):	_____	

[Adopted effective September 1, 2015.]

KCLSPR 98.16. MINOR SETTLEMENTS

(a) Hearings.

(1) *Time for Hearing.* Petitions for Settlement of the claims of minors shall be noted on the Probate Motion Calendar at 9:00 a.m. on Friday, except cases which are preassigned shall be noted on that judge's departmental calendar on Friday at 1:30 p.m. Bench copies of all pleadings and reports shall be submitted to the court no later than 12:00 noon the day before the hearing.

(2) *Mandatory Attendance.* The attorney personally in charge of the case of the minor, if any, the minor child, and at least one parent or legal custodian shall personally appear at any hearing at which application is made for approval of a settlement. Personal attendance for any proposed guardian may be required by the court. For good cause shown, the court may excuse the personal appearance of the minor child.

(b) Deposit in Court and Disbursements; Receipts. A receipt for funds deposited in a blocked account shall be filed with the courts no later than 30 days from the date the bank receives the funds.

[Adopted September 1, 1995; amended effective September 1, 1997; September 1, 1998; September 1, 2001; September 1, 2011.]

Official Comment

For further guidance on noting motions for hearing see KCLCR 77(k). For guidance on filing motions see KCLCR 7.

KCLSPR 98.24. MANDATORY TRAINING FOR NON–CERTIFIED GUARDIANS

(a) Definition of Applicable Cases. This rule applies to all guardianship cases including those originating under RCW 11.88. The Court, in its discretion, may also direct other persons to take all or part of the mandatory guardian training.

(b) Intent. The purpose of mandatory guardian training it to provide information to prospective, non-certified guardians about their legal duties and responsibilities as a guardian.

(c) Non–Certified Guardian Training. Except as provided in (d), a non-certified guardian shall not be appointed guardian by the Court until he/she has successfully completed the mandated Lay/Family (Non–Professional) Guardian Training module located at http://www.courts.wa.gov/programs_orgs/guardian/. Successful completion shall be evidenced by submit-

ting the Declaration of Completion provided by the training module to the Court for filing.

(d) Special Consideration/Waiver. Certified Professional Guardians are not required to complete the Lay/Family (Non–Professional) Guardian Training module provided that the guardian is in good standing with the Certified Professional Guardianship Board. The Court may waive the video requirement for attorneys, bank trust officers, and other professionals who have been appointed as guardians in the past.

[Adopted effective September 1, 2009; amended effective September 1, 2011; September 1, 2012.]

KITSAP COUNTY LOCAL GUARDIAN AD LITEM RULES [KCLGALR]

KCLGALR 1. SCOPE AND DEFINITIONS

(a) Scope. These rules apply to proceedings under RCW Titles 11 and 26.

For general guidelines regarding responsibilities and authority of Guardians ad Litem and roles and responsibilities of Guardians ad Litem in Title 13 juvenile court proceedings, see Superior Court Guardian Ad Litem Rules (GALR).

(b) Definitions. As used in these rules, the following terms have these meanings.

(1) *Guardian ad Litem Registry.* Guardian ad litem registry or registry shall mean the list of individuals authorized by Kitsap County Superior Court to serve as guardians ad litem. Title 11 registry and Title 26 registry shall mean the list of individuals authorized by Kitsap County Superior Court to serve as guardians ad litem under Titles 11 and 26, respectively, of the RCW.

(2) *Registry Applicant.* Registry applicant shall mean any individual applying to be listed on the registry.

(3) *Guardian ad Litem Committee.* Guardian ad Litem Committee or Committee shall mean the committee of Kitsap County Superior Court judges appointed to manage guardians ad litem as provided in LCR 1(c)(4).

(4) *Court Administrator.* Court Administrator shall mean the Kitsap County Superior Court Administrator.

[Adopted effective September 1, 2011.]

KCLGALR 2. GENERAL RESPONSIBILITIES OF GUARDIAN AD LITEM

(a) Professional conduct. All registry applicants shall abide by the Guardian ad Litem Code of Conduct, these local rules. Violations may subject a guardian ad litem to discipline as set forth in KGALR 7.

(b) Qualifications. All applicants to the guardian ad litem registry shall meet the following qualifications at the time of their application, in addition to any qualifications required by statute:

(1) *Attorneys.* Attorney applicants must be members of the Washington State Bar Association in good standing.

(2) *Non Attorneys, Title 11.* Non-attorney applicants for the Title 11 registry must have no fewer than five years' experience in the needs of impaired elderly people, physical disabilities, mental illness, developmental disabilities and/or other areas relevant to the needs of incapacitated individuals, as documented in the applicant's curriculum vitae.

(3) *Non–Attorneys, Title 26.* Non-attorney applicants for the Title 26 registry must have no fewer than five years' experience in the needs of children and families involved in disputes over parenting issues, dissolution or parentage determinations, as documented in the applicant's curriculum vitae.

(4) *Integrity.* All applicants shall be of high moral character, and shall not have any of the following:

(A) Felony convictions or any convictions involving theft, dishonesty or moral turpitude;

(B) Professional certification or license suspension or revocation; or

(C) Pending investigation or action regarding any criminal charges or license suspension or revocation.

(5) *Applications and Annual Updates.*

(A) Timing. The Title 11 and Title 26 registries shall be open for new applications one time per year, between February 1 and June 1. All required information must be received by the Court Administrator no later than June 1 of each year. The registry shall be defined by July 1 of each year.

(B) Review. Applications for placement on the registry shall be reviewed by the Guardian ad Litem Committee to determine compliance with the court rules. The Committee shall review all applications and annual updates to determine compliance with the court rules and all applicable State laws.

(C) Contents. Each applicant, including individuals already on the registry, must annually submit the following documents to the Court Administrator:

(i) A completed application for guardian ad litem registry which includes the following: a statement certifying the applicant has read and agrees to be bound by the Kitsap County Superior Court Guardian ad Litem Registry Code of Conduct; a summary of experiences as a guardian ad litem, including years of experience and number of appointments; and the number of times the guardian ad litem has been removed for failure to perform his or her duties as guardian ad litem;

(ii) A current curriculum vitae documenting educational background, qualifications, formal training, work, professional and individual experiences in or related to the field that would assist in the performance of his/her duties;

(iii) A description of the nature, status and outcome of any professional complaint, investigation or disciplinary action, lawsuit or professional liability claim, and any order for removal of the guardian ad litem prior to completion of his or her duties;

(iv) A description of any claim or litigation that has been commenced involving allegations of improper fee charges, charges of fraud, theft or other forms of dishonesty or professional malpractice or conduct;

(v) A copy of the applicant's proposed fee schedule;

(vi) A Washington State Patrol criminal history report;

(vii) A signed release of information directed to all professional regulatory bodies which have licensed or supervised the applicant within the last ten years;

(viii) For new applicants, a Certification of Qualifications/Training for Guardian ad Litem (Title 11 or 26) as approved by the Department of Social and Health Services or the Administrative Office of the Courts; or, for those applicants currently on the registry, a certification of having completed the annual training (Title 11 or 26) approved by the Kitsap Superior Court, or if no training is so approved, the annual training offered in another county; and

(ix) Any other required information and correspondence with reference to the individual's service as a guardian ad litem and any action thereon by the Court.

(D) Notification. New registry applicants and returning guardians ad litem will be notified of their placement on the registry by July 1, and shall then be eligible for appointment as a guardian ad litem. An individual, whose application for placement on the registry does not meet the Court's requirements for placement on the registry, shall be notified of the apparent deficiency and be given an opportunity to correct the same. If after 30 days the applicant has not corrected the apparent deficiency, his or her name shall not be placed on the registry.

(F)[1] Records. The Court Administrator shall maintain a separate file on each guardian ad litem, which file will be maintained in the Superior Court office. Each file shall include the items listed in section (2)(C). The information contained in the files shall be open for public review during normal business hours.

(6) *Retention on Registry.*

(A) Maintenance of Registry. The Court Administrator shall maintain the registry of those qualified to serve as a guardian ad litem.

(B) Removal From Registry. An individual shall remain on the registry unless removed by the Court Administrator for one or more of the following reasons:

(i) The individual fails to maintain the statutory certification or court requirements for the registry;

(ii) The individual him- or herself requests that he or she be removed;

(iii) The Guardian ad Litem Committee directs the Court Administrator to remove the individual pursuant to KGALR 7;

(iv) The Guardian ad Litem Committee directs the Court Administrator to remove the individual for any reason that places the suitability of the person to act as a guardian ad litem in question; or,

(v) Any other reason provided for by law.

[Adopted effective September 1, 2011. Amended effective September 2, 2013; September 2, 2014.]

1 Lettering as provided in original.

Official Comment

Applications for the guardian ad litem registry are available at the Superior Court office or online at http://www.kitsapgov.com/sc/.

KCLGALR 5. APPOINTMENTS OF GUARDIAN AD LITEM

(a) **Title 11 Appointments.** Application to the Court for appointment of a guardian ad litem in all Title 11 guardianship proceedings shall be made by submitting an Order Appointing Guardian ad Litem to the Superior Court office. The Superior Court administrator, or designee, shall provide, and the Court shall appoint, the guardian ad litem whose name next appears on the rotational list, subject to the guardian ad litem's acceptance of the appointment.

(b) Title 26 Appointments. Application to the Court for appointment of a guardian ad litem in all Title 26 family law proceedings shall be made by submitting an Order Appointing Guardian ad Litem to the Superior Court office. The Court Administrator, or designee, shall provide three names that are next on the rotational list. Each party may, within three judicial days, strike one name from the list. The Order shall then be submitted to a judge or commissioner for signature or such other action as may be appropriate, and a copy delivered to the Superior Court office. The individual appointed guardian ad litem pursuant to this section shall have his or her named placed on the end of the rotational list.

If more than one name remains on the list, the Court shall appoint a guardian ad litem from the names on that list. The parties may make a joint recommendation for appointment of a guardian ad litem from the registry.

In the event none of the three names provided according to the rotational registry are acceptable to the parties, for good cause, the Court shall appoint the next individual on the random rotation list of approved registered guardians ad litem.

(c) Deviation from List. Any judge or commissioner who does not appoint the individual next on the rotational list, as supplied by the Court Administrator, shall comply with RCW 11.88.090(3) or RCW 26.09.220, RCW 26.12.175, and RCW 26.12.177, as appropriate, for the purposes of making an appropriate record of the reasons for the deviation. The Order, once signed, shall be presented to the Superior Court office for registry data. In the event a judge or commissioner approves an individual who is not next on the rotational list, the appointed individual's name shall go to the bottom of the rotational list.

(d) Appointment by Stipulation. If the parties stipulate to recommend the appointment of a particular registered guardian ad litem, the parties must present, prior to appointment, a written stipulation and Order signed by both parties and their attorneys which specifies the amount of the retainer charged, the agreement between the parties regarding payment of the retainer and the fees, and the hourly rate charged by the recommended individual. The Order, once signed, shall be presented to the Superior Court office for registry data. The individual appointed guardian ad litem pursuant to this section shall have his or her name placed at the end of the rotational list.

(e) Declining Appointment. In the event the individual nominated as guardian ad litem chooses not to serve, regardless of the reason, his or her name shall go to the end of the rotational list just as if he or she had served.

(f) Fees.

(1) *Limitations.* Fees paid by Kitsap County shall be at the hourly rate set by the Superior Court judges upon the recommendation of the Court Administrator, and published in the Court's administrative policy.

(i) Fees shall not exceed $500 per case in Title 11 matters or $1,500 per case in Title 26 matters. If additional fees are requested, a motion must be made to the Court with proper notice to all parties.

(ii) Reimbursement of travel costs shall only be approved for GAL travel within Kitsap County boundaries.

(2) *Authorization.* A copy of the Order authorizing County-paid fees and an affidavit of fees (Exhibit L) shall be submitted to the Court Administrator before payment will be made.

[Adopted effective September 1, 2011; amended effective September 1, 2012.]

KCLGALR 7.   GRIEVANCE PROCEDURES

(a) Submitting a Grievance

(1) *Grievances in an Ongoing Case.*

(A) Scope. This rule pertains to any grievance pertaining to a conduct by a guardian ad litem in a case currently pending before the Court.

(B) Format. A grievance under this rule must be brought to the attention of the Court in the form of a motion. For the motion to be heard by the Court it must be properly noted for hearing in compliance with local rules. In a case assigned to a particular judge, the motion must be noted for hearing before that judge. In all other cases the matter should be noted as follows: for Title 11 cases, on the guardianship calendar; or, for Title 26 cases, on the domestic relations calendar (both calendars are held Fridays at 9:00 a.m.). The grievance will be entertained only if raised by or on behalf of a party named in the case.

(C) Response by Guardian ad Litem. The guardian ad litem may respond as provided by local rules governing motion practice.

(D) Sanctions. If the Court determines that the grievance has merit, the Court may remove the guardian ad litem from the case or impose other sanctions. Grievances determined to have merit may also be forwarded to the Guardian ad Litem Committee.

(2) *Grievances Not Concerning an Ongoing Case.*

(A) Scope. This rule pertains to any grievance pertaining a guardian ad litem other than grievances concerning a case currently pending before the Court.

(B) Format. Grievances shall be submitted in a written complaint, explaining in clear and concise language the grounds for the grievance. The complaint shall be directed to the Court Administrator.

Grievances will be considered only if submitted in writing.

(C) Action upon Receipt of Complaint. Upon receipt, the Court Administrator shall forward the complaint and any supplemental materials to the Guardian ad Litem Committee. The complaint and any supplemental materials shall also be forwarded to the guardian ad litem named in the complaint, and the source of the complaint identified to the guardian ad litem.

(D) Authority of Court and Court Administrator. Nothing in these rules shall limit the authority of a judge, commissioner or the Court Administrator to communicate to the Guardian ad Litem Committee any concern about a guardian ad litem. Nor shall these rules limit the discretion of a judge or commissioner to remove, retain or sanction a guardian ad litem or party in a case before the Court.

(E) Confidentiality. Any written complaint pending against a guardian ad litem under this rule, and any associated information or documentation, shall remain confidential until the Guardian ad Litem Committee has rendered a decision.

(b) Action by Guardian Ad Litem Committee.

(1) *Scope.* The following rules apply once a grievance is forwarded to the Committee pursuant to (1)(D) or (2)(C).

(2) *Review Procedure.*

(A) Response to Grievance. A guardian ad litem who has received notice that a complaint has been filed against him or her may respond in writing within 30 days of when such notice was sent by the Court Administrator. For grievances in pending cases the Committee will consider any motion materials submitted to the Court by the guardian ad litem pursuant to (a)(1)(c).

(B) Action Pending Resolution. At the discretion of the Committee, a guardian ad litem's further participation on the registry may be suspended or denied pending resolution of the grievance. The guardian ad litem shall be notified of any decision to suspend or remove their name from the registry pending resolution of the grievance.

(C) Basis of Decision. The Committee shall consider grievances on the strength of written materials only; no oral testimony or argument shall be allowed.

(D) Time for Decision.

(i) *Grievances in an Ongoing Case.* For grievances pertaining to an ongoing case under section (a)(1), the Committee shall issue a decision no later than 25 days after the Court renders a decision on the aggrieved party's motion.

(ii) *Grievances not Concerning an Ongoing Case.* For grievances under not concerning an ongoing case pursuant to section (a)(2), the Committee shall issue a decision no later than 60 days after the complaint is received by the Court Administrator.

(E) Notice of Decision. The guardian ad litem and any complaining party shall be notified of any action or decision on the complaint or grievance. A copy of the decision of the Committee shall be placed in the guardian ad litem file maintained by the Superior Court Administrator.

(3) *Sanctions.*

(A) Action by Committee. In reaching its decision the Committee shall consider whether the guardian ad litem failed to comply with the applicable statutes, court rules and/or the guardian ad litem Code of Conduct. The Committee, at its discretion, may then take any of the following actions:

(i) Take no action;

(ii) Impose additional reasonable requirements on the guardian ad litem to permit the individual to continue to serve as a guardian ad litem; or

(ii) Remove the guardian ad litem from the registry.

(B) Removal from registry. The court administrator shall immediately notify the Administrative Office of the Courts of the name of any guardian ad litem removed from the registry. Notification to the AOC may be delayed up to 15 days to permit the guardian ad litem to seek reconsideration of the decision under these rules.

(c) Reconsideration of Decision

(1) *Time for Request.* The guardian ad litem or complaining party may seek reconsideration of a decision by the Committee by doing so in writing to the Court Administrator within 15 days of the date of decision.

(2) *Review of Request.* The Court Administrator shall forward the request for reconsideration and any supporting documents to the Presiding Judge. The Presiding Judge shall present the same to the Superior Court judges at their next regular meeting.

[Adopted effective September 1, 2011.]

Official Comment

A grievance concerning a guardian ad litem's conduct in an ongoing case must be brought to the attention of the judge or commissioner hearing that case. In bringing the issue to the Court, the aggrieved party must comply with local and state rules governing court procedure. *See, e.g.,* KCLCR 7 (local rules on filing a motion), KCLCR 77(k) (local rules on noting a motion for hearing). Grievances in ongoing cases become part of the court record and are therefore not confidential.

KITSAP COUNTY LOCAL CRIMINAL RULES [KCLCrR]

1. SCOPE, PURPOSE AND CONSTRUCTION

KCLCrR 1.1. SCOPE

The local civil rules shall apply in all criminal proceedings when not inconsistent with these rules, the Superior Court Criminal Rules or applicable statutes. Local civil rules particularly applicable to criminal cases include but are not limited to the following rules:

KCLCR 7   Motions and briefs
       Motions in limine
       Reapplication for order
       Telephonic appearances.

KCLCR 16   Pretrial and Settlement Procedures

KCLCR 40   Notice to Court of Calendar and Jury Trial Changes

KCLCR 47   Jury—Jurors
       Peremptory Challenges

KCLCR 51   Jury Instructions

KCLCR 54   Counsel Fees

KCLCR 77   Court Hours
       Hearing of Motions

KCLCR 79   Withdrawal of Files and Exhibits from Clerk's Office

[Amended effective September 1, 2011.]

2. PROCEDURES PRIOR TO ARREST AND OTHER SPECIAL PROCEEDINGS

[No Local Rules]

3. RIGHTS OF DEFENDANTS

KCLCrR 3.2. RELEASE OF ACCUSED

(a) Release of Accused; Domestic Violence.

(1) Any person arrested on Probable Cause (without a warrant) for an offense classified as a Domestic Violence offense under Chapter 10.99 of the Revised Code of Washington as the same exists or shall hereafter be amended shall be held in jail pending the defendant's first appearance.

(2) Notwithstanding Section (1), a person being held for a Domestic Violence offense classified as a felony may be released from custody prior to defendant's first appearance upon (a) the posting of $50,000 bail or bond; and (b) the person's affixing his or her signature at the appropriate location on a Pre–Arraignment Domestic Violence No Contact Order (Exhibit K) prohibiting the arrested person from having contact with the protected person or from knowingly coming within, or knowingly remaining within, 500 feet of the protected person's residence, place of work, or school.

(3) Notwithstanding Section (1), a person being held for a Domestic Violence offense classified as a misdemeanor or gross misdemeanor may be released from custody prior to defendant's first appearance upon (a) the posting of $5,000 bail or bond; and (b) the person's affixing his or her signature at the appropriate location on a Pre–Arraignment Domestic Violence No Contact Order (Exhibit K) prohibiting the arrested person from having contract with the protected person or from knowingly coming within, or knowingly remaining within, 500 feet of the protected person's residence, place of work or school.

[Adopted effective July 1, 2003. Amended on an emergency basis effective March 1, 2010; September 1, 2010; September 1, 2011.]

4. PROCEDURES PRIOR TO TRIAL

KCLCrR 4.2. PLEAS

A court commissioner authorized by Article 4, Section 23 of the Constitution of the State of Washington may accept pleas of adult criminal defendants in accordance with CrR 4.2.

[Adopted effective September 1, 2000; amended effective September 1, 2011.]

5. VENUE
[No Local Rules]

6. PROCEDURES AT TRIAL
[No Local Rules]

7. PROCEDURES FOLLOWING CONVICTION

KCLCrR 7.2. SENTENCING

At sentencing, counsel should present all available and appropriate information regarding restitution. The determination of a restitution amount may be delayed pending the receipt of necessary information.

Unless otherwise ordered by the judge, the monies paid into the registry of the court shall be distributed in the following priority order:

(1) Restitution to victims.

(2) Victims of crime compensation fund.

(3) Court costs.

(4) Attorney fees.

(5) SIU fund payments and other payments to Kitsap County funds.

(6) Fines.

[Amended effective September 1, 2011.]

KITSAP COUNTY LOCAL RULES FOR APPEAL OF DECISIONS OF COURTS OF LIMITED JURISDICTION (RALJ) [KCLRALJ]

TITLE 1. SCOPE AND PURPOSE OF RULES
[No Local Rules]

TITLE 2. INITIATING AN APPEAL

KCLRALJ 2.6. CONTENT OF NOTICE OF APPEAL

(h) Designation of Claimed Errors. The notice of appeal shall include a statement of the errors the appealing party claims were made by the court of limited jurisdiction.

(1) The notice of appeal shall identify the location of claimed errors in the transcript.

[Amended effective September 1, 1998; September 1, 2011.]

TITLE 3. ASSIGNMENT OF CASES IN SUPERIOR COURT

KCLRALJ 3.1. NOTICE OF HEARING AND ASSIGNMENT

(a) Notice; Hearing; Action That May be Taken. After an appeal has been filed, the court shall note the case for status hearing and notify counsel/parties of the hearing. This hearing will be scheduled as soon as the briefing time lines as set forth in RALJ 7.2 have elapsed. At this hearing, the following action may be taken:

(1) If appellant's brief has not been timely filed, the appeal may be dismissed on either respondent's or the court's motion;

(2) If respondent's brief has not been timely filed, a hearing shall be set and the respondent will be barred from presenting oral argument; or

(3) If both the appellant's brief and the respondent's brief have been filed, the matter will be assigned to a trial department for hearing on a date certain and the parties so notified.

(4) If good cause is shown why the appellant's brief and/or the respondent's brief have not yet been filed, the court shall set a new briefing schedule and another trial/hearing date.

(b) If, two days prior to the status hearing above scheduled, all parties notify the court scheduler and certify in writing that the briefs are filed and the matter is ready for trial, the presence of the parties or counsel at the status hearing is not required, and a trial date will be assigned and the parties notified.

This procedure shall be followed in both criminal and civil matters, excluding small claims.

[Amended effective September 1, 1997; September 1, 2011.]

TITLE 4.   AUTHORITY OF COURTS OF LIMITED JURISDICTION AND OF SUPERIOR COURT PENDING APPEAL—STAYS
[No Local Rules]

TITLE 5.   RECORDING PROCEEDINGS IN COURT OF LIMITED JURISDICTION
[No Local Rules]

TITLE 6.   RECORD ON APPEAL

KCLRALJ 6.3.1.   TRANSCRIPT OF ELECTRONIC RECORD

(a) Transcript by Appellant. The appellant shall transcribe the electronic record.

[Amended effective September 1, 2011.]

TITLE 7.   BRIEFS

KCLRALJ 7.3.   FILING AND CONTENT OF BRIEFS

. Each party shall file a brief pursuant to the requirements of RALJ 7.1 and 7.2.

(a) Content of Appellant's Brief. The brief of the appellant should contain under appropriate headings and in the order here indicated:

(1) *Title Page.* A title page, which is the cover, naming the Superior Court to which the appeal is taken and identifying: the cause number on appeal; the names of the parties; the title of the brief (for example: Brief of Appellant); and the name of the party filing the brief or the attorney filing it on his/her behalf.

(2) *Tables.* A table of contents, with page references, and a table of cases (alphabetically arranged), statutes and other authorities cited, with references to the pages of the brief where cited.

(3) *Assignments of Error.* A separate concise statement of each error a party contends was made by the trial court, together with the issues pertaining to the assignments of error.

(4) *Statement of the Case.* A fair statement of the facts and procedure relevant to the issues presented for review, without argument. Reference to the record must be included for each factual statement.

(5) *Argument.* The argument in support of the issues presented for review, together with citations to legal authority and specific references to those por-

tions of the re cord/transcript relevant to the issues argued.

(6) *Conclusion.* A short conclusion stating the precise relief sought.

(7) *Appendix.* An appendix to the brief if deemed appropriate by the party submitting the brief.

(b) Content of Respondent's Brief. The brief of respondent should conform to section (a) and answer the brief of appellant. A statement of the issues and a statement of the case need not be made if respondent is satisfied with the statement in the brief of appellant. If a respondent is also seeking review, the brief of respondent must state the assignments of error and the issues pertaining to those assignments of error presented for review by respondent and include argument of those issues making specific reference to relevant portions of the record/transcript.

(c) Reply Brief. A reply brief should be limited to a response to the issues in the brief to which the reply brief is directed.

(d) Failure To Include Information. Failure to provide specific references to those portions of the transcript relevant to argument(s) on appeal may result in the dismissal of the appeal or the imposition of terms. References to the entire transcript or electronic record will not be acceptable or considered by the court.

[Amended effective September 1, 2011.]

TITLE 8.   ORAL ARGUMENT
[No Local Rules]

TITLE 9.   SUPERIOR COURT DECISION AND PROCEDURE AFTER DECISION
[No Local Rules]

TITLE 10.   VIOLATION OF RULES—SANCTIONS AND DISMISSAL
[No Local Rules]

TITLE 11.   SUPPLEMENTAL PROVISIONS
[No Local Rules]

APPENDIX I

EXHIBIT A. NOTE FOR TRIAL SETTING

Superior Court of Washington
County of Kitsap

_____,
             (Plaintiff/Petitioner),

vs.

_____,
             (Defendant/Respondent).

No. _____

NOTE FOR TRIAL SETTING

TRACK I – STANDARD CIVIL
TRACK II – COMPLEX LITIGATION
                            (NTTS)

TO THE CLERK OF THE COURT AND TO:

Please take notice that this case will be placed on the trial setting docket for assignment of trial on the _____ day of _____, 200___ .

1. Nature of Case: _____

2. A jury ☐ has ☐ has not been demanded.

3. Estimated length of trial: ☐ _____ hours . ☐ _____ days.

4. Preferred trial dates: _____ _____

5. Dates unavailable for trial: _____

CHECK APPROPRIATE SQUARES:

☐   I have contacted all counsel and they agree the trial may be set anytime after _____ _(date)._

☐   I have contacted all counsel and am unable to obtain agreement on trial dates. The Court will set the trial date.

☐   This case has been requested to be placed on Track II, Complex Litigation. Exhibit B, Request for Assignment to Civil Track II, has been filed as a separate document. If granted, the Court will assign a trial date at the Initial Management Conference.

☐   No contact has been made with other counsel/party, but all have been served with a copy of this notice in time to allow a response within 10 days.

I HEREBY REPRESENT TO THE COURT THAT THIS CASE IS AT ISSUE AND SHOULD BE SET FOR TRIAL.

    ☐   Plaintiff's claim exceeds $50,000.00

    ☐   Plaintiff seeks relief other than a money judgment.

    ☐   Defendant's counter or cross claim exceeds $50,000.00.

    ☐   Defendant's counter or cross claim seeks relief other than a money judgment.

    ☐   A trial de novo from arbitration has been requested.

Any party not in agreement with the information or estimates given in Note for Trial Setting shall file and serve at least three (3) days prior to the trial setting date a counter notice or written objection to setting. If an objection to setting is filed, counsel shall appear on the setting day before the civil motions judge, to argue the objection.

Trial will be set only if this form is filled out completely.

DATE: _____

SIGNED _____

Lawyer for: _____

Address: _____

_____

Telephone Number: _____

List the name, address and phone number of all attorneys or parties who were provided notice:

Name: _____   Name: _____

Lawyer for: _____   Lawyer for: _____

Address: _____   Address: _____

_____   _____

Telephone Number: _____   Telephone Number: _____

Name: _____   Name: _____

Lawyer for: _____   Lawyer for: _____

Address: _____   Address: _____

_____   _____

Telephone Number: _____   Telephone Number: _____

Name: _____   Name: _____

Lawyer for: _____   Lawyer for: _____

Address: _____   Address: _____

_____   _____

Telephone Number: _____   Telephone Number: _____

[Amended effective September 1, 2001; September 1, 2002; September 1, 2005; September 1, 2011.]

EXHIBIT B. REQUEST FOR ASSIGNMENT TO CIVIL TRACK II

Superior Court of Washington
County of Kitsap

_____, Plaintiff(s),	No. _____
vs.	REQUEST FOR ASSIGNMENT TO CIVIL TRACK II
_____, Defendant(s).	(RQACT)

TO: PRESIDING JUDGE

The undersigned affirms that the above-captioned case is not subject to arbitration and requests that it be assigned to Civil Track II based on the information provided below and the supporting affidavit(s) attached hereto.

☐   Nature of subject matter, please state: _____

☐   Requires five or more days of trial.

☐   Presents unusually complex issues.

☐   Has numerous parties and witnesses.

☐   Requires extensive pre-trial motions.

Estimated length of trial: _____

Note for Trial filed: ☐ Yes   ☐ No

Trial date, if set: ☐ Jury   ☐ Non-jury

I have contacted other counsel and we agree on the following three dates within the next 60 days for our initial management conference:

(1) _____ (2) _____ (3) _____

DATED: _____   _____

                                    Attorney for _____

cc: All Counsel

[Amended effective September 1, 2001; September 1, 2011.]

851

EXHIBIT C. NOTE FOR SETTLEMENT CONFERENCE OR SUPPORT MODIFICATION HEARING AND TRIAL SETTING

Superior Court of Washington
County of Kitsap

_____,
               Petitioner,
 	
 vs.
 	
 _____,
               Respondent.
	No. _____
	
	 NOTE FOR SETTLEMENT CONFERENCE
	 OR SUPPORT MODIFICATION HEARING
	 AND TRIAL SETTING
	
	 DOMESTIC RELATIONS – TRACK III
	
	                            (NTC)

TO COURT SCHEDULER AND OPPOSING COUNSEL:

Please take notice this case will be placed on the setting docket for assignment on the _____ day of _____ , 200____ at 9:00 a.m.

☐ 1   **SETTLEMENT CONFERENCE:**

     A.   <u>Nature of Issues</u>

         ☐ Property Division   ☐ Debt Division   ☐ Maintenance

         ☐ Custody   ☐ Parenting Plan   ☐ Visitation

         ☐ Other: _____

     B.   Preferred Settlement Conference dates within 45 days from this note:

     C.   Dates unavailable for settlement conference:

     D.   Settlement conferences are mandatory in all domestic relations cases except support modifications.

     E.   All parties must attend and be prepared to seriously negotiate settlement.

☐ 2.   **SUPPORT MODIFICATIONS:**

     A.   Preferred Support Modification hearing dates within 60 days from this note:

     B.   Dates unavailable for Support Modification hearing:

☐ **3. CHECK APPROPRIATE SQUARE**:

    ☐ I have contacted by telephone or mail opposing counsel/party/guardian ad litem who agrees the settlement conference/support modification may be set anytime after _____ *(date)*.

    ☐ I have contacted the opposing counsel/party/guardian ad litem by telephone or mail and have received no response. The Court is requested to set the hearing/settlement conference date.

    ☐ I have contacted the opposing counsel/party/guardian ad litem by telephone or mail and am unable to obtain agreement on hearing dates. The Court will set the hearing/settlement conference date.

I hereby represent to the Court that this case is at issue. If the case is not settled at the pre-trial conference, the Court is requested to assign a trial date.

DATED: _____

Signed: _____

Lawyer for: _____

Address: _____

_____

Telephone: _____

Names, addresses and telephone numbers of other attorneys or pro se parties and guardian ad litem in this case:

Name: _____

Lawyer for: _____

Address: _____

_____

Telephone Number: _____

Name: _____

Lawyer for: _____

Address: _____

_____

Telephone Number: _____

Name: _____

Lawyer for: _____

Address: _____

_____

Telephone Number: _____

Name: _____

Lawyer for: _____

Address: _____

_____

Telephone Number: _____

Name: _____

Lawyer for: _____

Address: _____

_____

Telephone Number: _____

Name: _____

Lawyer for: _____

Address: _____

_____

Telephone Number: _____

[Amended effective September 1, 1998; September 1, 2001; September 1, 2011.]

EXHIBIT D. ORDER SETTING TRIAL DATE AND CIVIL CASE EVENT SCHEDULE

Superior Court of Washington
County of Kitsap

_____,
                    Plaintiff(s),

vs.

_____
                    Defendant(s).

No. _____

ORDER SETTING TRIAL DATE AND
CIVIL CASE EVENT SCHEDULE
Pursuant to KCLCR 40(b)(6)(A)(ii)

(ORSTD/ORSCS/_____/ORACS)

This case shall be heard on the following date(s):

☐ **TRIAL**   ☐ **OTHER**
- Date _____   - _____
- Time _____   - Date _____
- Trial Length _____   - Time _____
- ☐ **Jury** - ☐ 12 - ☐ 6   ☐ **Nonjury**   - Length _____
- Nature of Case _____
- JUDGE ASSIGNED: _____

NOTE: IF YOUR CASE IS PUT ON STANDBY, YOU WILL BE REQUIRED TO BE IN COURT ON TWO HOURS NOTICE. COUNSEL ARE REQUIRED TO BE PRESENT IN THE TRIAL COURTROOM AT 8:45 A.M. ON THE FIRST DAY OF TRIAL.

IT IS HEREBY ORDERED that the parties and their respective counsel shall comply with the following schedule, and that Sanctions, including but not limited to those set forth in the Local Court Rules may be imposed for noncompliance.

Last Day to File Motions to Join Parties		
Last Day to Complete all Discovery, Including Responses and Supplements (KCLCR 40[b][6][A][viii])		
Last Day for Hearing Dispositive Pretrial Motions		
Mandatory Settlement Conference Date		Time:

SETTLEMENT CONFERENCE REQUIREMENTS: At least five (5) court days prior to the Settlement Conference, all parties and counsel shall serve a complete Memorandum for Settlement upon the other party and provide the original for the Settlement Conference Judge. The parties shall, in all cases, be present, unless excused by the court for good cause shown. Parties whose defense is provided by a liability insurance company, shall personally attend said settlement conference and a representative of the insurer of said parties shall attend or be available by telephone, with sufficient authority to bind the insurer to a settlement. [See KCLCR 16(c)]

SETTLEMENT CONFERENCES ARE MANDATORY AND MUST BE CONFIRMED NO LATER THAN NOON THE COURT DAY BEFORE THE CONFERENCE AT (360) 337-7140. PARTIES MUST BE PREPARED TO SERIOUSLY NEGOTIATE SETTLEMENT.

Dated: _____

                                          _____
                                          Judge/Court Commissioner

Copies Mailed:

_____   _____

_____   _____

[Amended effective September 1, 2001; September 1, 2011.]

Exhibit D–2. ORDER SETTING CIVIL CASE EVENT SCHEDULE

SUPERIOR COURT OF WASHINGTON
COUNTY OF KITSAP

Plaintiff,	NO.
v.	ORDER SETTING CIVIL CASE EVENT SCHEDULE
Defendants.	(ORSTD/ORSCS/_____/ORACS)

IT IS HEREBY ORDERED that the parties and their respective counsel shall comply with the following schedule, and that Sanctions, including but not limited to those set forth in the Local Court Rules may be imposed for noncompliance.

SCHEDULING AND CUTOFF DATES		
DAYS PRIOR TO TRIAL	**DATE**	**DESCRIPTION**
		Disclosure of possible primary witnesses
		Disclosure of possible additional witnesses
		Discovery cutoff
		Settlement Conference
		Last day to hear Dispositive Pretrial Motions
		Exchange of Witness and Exhibit Lists

ORDER SETTING CIVIL CASE EVENT SCHEDULE (09/15) .. 13

		SCHEDULING AND CUTOFF DATES	
		Joint Statement of the Evidence	
		Filing of Trial Briefs	
		TRIAL to begin at 9:00 a.m.	

DATED this _____ day of _____, _____

_____
HONORABLE

COPIES MAILED:

ORDER SETTING CIVIL CASE EVENT SCHEDULE (09/15) . . 14

[Adopted effective September 1, 2015.]

EXHIBIT E.   NOTE FOR MOTION DOCKET (NTMTDK)

Superior Court of Washington
County of Kitsap

No. _____

_____,
                    Plaintiff/Petitioner

NOTE FOR MOTION DOCKET

_____,   (NTMTDK)
         Attorney for Plaintiff/Petitioner
vs.

_____,
                 Defendant/Respondent

_____,
        Attorney for Defendant/Respondent

TO THE CLERK OF THE COURT AND

TO:

AND:

Please take notice that the undersigned will bring on for hearing:

NATURE OF MOTION:

The hearing is to be held:

    DATE: TIME:

AT: JUDGE/DEPARTMENT NO.
      Superior Court of Kitsap County
      614 Division Street
      Port Orchard, WA   98366

COURT REPORTER REQUESTED: ☐ YES   ☐ NO
ELECTRONIC RECORDER ACCEPTABLE: ☐ YES   ☐ NO
COURT COMMISSIONER MAY HEAR THIS MOTION: ☐ YES   ☐ NO

DATED:_____   Signed: _____

                        Lawyer for: _____

                        Address: _____

                        _____

                        Telephone: _____

[Amended effective September 1, 2001; September 1, 2011.]

EXHIBIT F.   REQUEST FOR CONTINUANCE (RQC)

Superior Court of Washington
County of Kitsap

_____ Plaintiff/Petitioner	No. _____
_____ Attorney for Plaintiff/Petitioner	**REQUEST FOR CONTINUANCE** (RQC)
vs.	
_____ Defendant/Respondent	
_____ Attorney for Defendant/Respondent	

Please continue the hearing Re: _____

_____

to _____, 200_____.

This hearing should be placed on the

☐ Civil   ☐ Presiding Docket

☐ Domestic   ☐ Probate

☐ Criminal   ☐ Judge _____'s Departmental Calendar

CONTINUANCE: ☐ By Court Order

☐ Agreed

☐ Orally

☐ By Written Approval

☐ Due to Absence of Opposing Counsel

☐ On Request of Opposing Party

Dated: _____   _____
                                                              Attorney

[Amended effective June 7, 2006; September 1, 2011.]

EXHIBIT G.   DOMESTIC RELATIONS INFORMATION FORM

Superior Court of Washington
County of Kitsap

DOMESTIC RELATIONS INFORMATION FORM

Date: _____ ☐ Husband   ☐ Petitioner

Cause No.: _____ ☐ Wife   ☐ Respondent

PARTIES:

HUSBAND/FATHER		WIFE/MOTHER	
Name:	Age:	Name:	Age:
Address:		Address:	
Date of Marriage:		Date of Separation:	

DEPENDENT CHILDREN:

Name	Age	This Marriage	Prior Marriage	Percent Residential Time Father %	Mother %	Since

CHILD SUPPORT:

1.

	NET INCOME	SUPPORT
Husband/Father:	$	
Wife/Mother:	$	

2. Tax Exemptions allocated as follows: _____

3. Exceptional support considerations: _____
   _____

4. Child Support presently being paid $_____ per month; since _____

5. Summary of proposed residential arrangements for the children: _____

_____

_____

> **YOU MUST ATTACH:**
>   1.   Proposed Child Support Order, Support Worksheets and current pay stubs. Form WPF DR 01-050.
>   **2. Completed Financial Declaration. Form WPF DR 01-055**
>   **3. Proposed Parenting Plan, if disputed.**

MAINTENANCE:

1. Requested: $_____ per month, duration: _____

2. Presently being paid: $_____ per month, for _____ months.

HUSBAND/FATHER INCOME:

Employer/Other Source	Length	Gross Income	Net Income
		Total Income	

WIFE/MOTHER INCOME:

Employer/Other Source	Length	Gross Income	Net Income
		Total Income	

FACTORS RELATING TO AWARD OF MAINTENANCE: _____

_____

_____

_____

IF ATTORNEY FEES ARE AT ISSUE:

1.	Incurred to Date	$	Paid To Date	$
2.	Ordered to Date	$	Paid to Date	$
3.	Requested to Date	$	Estimate to Trial	$

PROPERTY DIVISION:

ASSETS:	Fair Market Value	Debt Owed	Net to Husband	Net to Wife
Real Estate:				

Home	$	$	$	$
Other Real Property	$	$	$	$
	$	$	$	$
Vehicles (Year/Make):				
	$	$	$	$
	$	$	$	$
Household Goods	$	$	$	$
Tools/Equipment	$	$	$	$
Recreational/Hobby Equipment	$	$	$	$
Business/Profession:				
Husband	$	$	$	$
Wife	$	$	$	$
Investments	$	$	$	$
Life Insurance Cash Value	$	$	$	$
Retirement:				
Husband	$	$	$	$
Wife	$	$	$	$
IRA's, TSP's, 401-K's, etc.:				
Husband	$	$	$	$
Wife	$	$	$	$
Receivables	$	$	$	$
Other Assets:				
	$	$	$	$
	$	$	$	$
	$	$	$	$
	$	$	$	$
Debts:	($)	($)	($)	($)
TOTALS	$	$	$	$
Equalization:	$	- $	divided by two (2)	= $

Proposed Percentage Division: _____ % to Husband   _____ % to Wife

Effects of Proposed Division: $_____ to Husband $_____ to Wife

[Amended effective September 1, 2002; September 1, 2005; September 1, 2011.]

EXHIBIT H.   NOTE FOR ARBITRATION SETTING INITIAL
STATEMENT OF ARBITRABILITY (STA)

Superior Court of Washington
County of Kitsap

	No. _____
_____,	**NOTE FOR ARBITRATION SETTING**
(Plaintiff),	**INITIAL STATEMENT OF ARBITRABILITY**
vs.	
	(STA)
_____,	
(Defendant).	

TO THE CLERK OF THE COURT AND TO:

Please take notice that this case will be placed on the arbitration setting docket at 9:00 a.m., on Friday, the _____ day of _____, 200___, for assignment to mandatory arbitration.

Nature of Case: _____

INITIAL STATEMENT OF ARBITRABILITY

☐   This case is subject to arbitration because the sole relief sought is a money judgment and involves no claim in excess of $50,000.00 exclusive of attorney fees, interest and costs. (MAR 1.2)

☐   The undersigned contends that its claim exceeds $50,000.00 but hereby waives any claim in excess of $50,000.00 for purposes of arbitration. (MAR 1.2)

Any party not in agreement with the Initial Statement of Arbitrability shall file and serve a response (KCLCR-Exhibit G) at least three (3) days prior to the arbitration setting docket date. If a response is filed, counsel shall appear on the setting day before the civil motions judge to argue the objection.

DATE: _____   SIGNED _____

Lawyer for: _____

Address: _____

_____

Telephone Number: _____

List the name, address and phone number of all attorneys or parties who were provided notice:

Name: _____	Name: _____
Lawyer for: _____	Lawyer for: _____
Address: _____	Address: _____
_____	_____
Telephone Number: _____	Telephone Number: _____

[Amended effective September 1, 2001; September 1, 2011.]

EXHIBIT I. RESPONSE TO STATEMENT OF ARBITRABILITY (RSSA)

Superior Court of Washington
County of Kitsap

	No. _____
Plaintiff(s), vs.	**RESPONSE TO STATEMENT** **OF ARBITRABILITY**
_____ Defendant(s).	**(RSSA)**

TO THE CLERK AND TO ALL OTHER LAWYERS: (Per List on Reverse Side.)

The undersigned lawyer disagrees with the prior Statement of Arbitrability filed in this case and contends that this case:

☐ Should be arbitrated   ☐ Should **not** be arbitrated

for the reasons indicated in Part II.

II. RESPONDED STATEMENT OF ARBITRABILITY

☐ This case is subject to arbitration because the sole relief is a money judgment, and it involves no claim in excess of $50,000.00, exclusive of attorney fees, interests, and costs.

☐ The undersigned contends that its claim exceeds $50,000.00, but for purposes of arbitration waives any claim in excess of that amount.

☐ This case is **not** subject to mandatory arbitration because:
☐   (a) Plaintiff's claim exceeds $50,000.00;
☐   (b) Plaintiff seeks relief other than a money judgment;
☐   (c) Defendant's counterclaim or cross claim exceeds $50,000.00;
☐   (d) Defendant's counterclaim or cross claim seeks relief other
        than a money judgment; or
☐   (e) Case is not an appeal of a Small Claims Judgment from District Court.

III. INSTRUCTIONS

3.1 Important: Type the names and address of all lawyers on reverse side.
3.2 Serve a copy on the other parties and file the original with the COUNTY CLERK.
3.3 Provide a copy to the Arbitrator Department of the Superior Court.

Dated: _____   _____

                            Attorney for _____
                            Type Name: _____

[Amended effective September 1, 2001; September 1, 2007; September 1, 2011.]

EXHIBIT J.   ARBITRATION AWARD (ARBA)

Superior Court of Washington
County of Kitsap

_____,
Plaintiff(s),

vs.

_____,
Defendant(s).

No. _____

ARBITRATION AWARD

(ARBA)

The issues in arbitration having been heard on _____, 200_____.

I make the following award:

Twenty days after the award has been filed with the clerk, if no party has sought a trial de novo under MAR 7.1, any party on notice to all parties may present to the Ex Parte Department a judgment on the arbitration award for entry as final judgment in this case.

Was any part of this award based on the failure of a party to participate at the hearing? Yes ☐ No ☐ (MAR 5.4)

If yes, please identify the party and explain:

Dated: _____   _____
                                                    ARBITRATOR

ORIGINAL TO BE FILED WITH THE SUPERIOR COURT CLERK, KITSAP COUNTY COURTHOUSE, TOGETHER WITH PROOF OF SERVICE ON THE PARTIES. A COPY MUST ALSO BE SENT TO THE SUPERIOR COURT SCHEDULER/JUDICIAL ASSISTANT.

[Amended effective September 1, 2001; September 1, 2011.]

EXHIBIT K.   PRE–ARRAIGNMENT DOMESTIC VIOLENCE NO CONTACT ORDER

☐   IN THE KITSAP COUNTY SUPERIOR COURT
☐   IN THE KITSAP COUNTY DISTRICT COURT
☐   IN THE BAINBRIDGE ISLAND MUNICIPAL COURT
☐   IN THE BREMERTON MUNICIPAL COURT
☐   IN THE PORT ORCHARD MUNICIPAL COURT
☐   IN THE POULSBO MUNICIPAL COURT

☐   STATE OF WASHINGTON,
☐   CITY OF BAINBRIDGE ISLAND,
☐   CITY OF BREMERTON,
☐   CITY OF PORT ORCHARD,
☐   CITY OF POULSBO,
 	
             Plaintiff,
 	
vs.
 	
_____,
 	
DOB: _____
       Defendant.
	LAW ENFORCEMENT NO. _____
	
	PRE-ARRAIGNMENT DOMESTIC
	VIOLENCE NO CONTACT ORDER
	                   (ORNC)
	
	Date of Arrest: _____
	
	Time of Arrest: _____
	
	Arresting Officer/No.: _____
	    ☐ Bainbridge Island Police Department
	    ☐ Bremerton Police Department
	    ☐ Kitsap County Sheriff's Office
	    ☐ Port Orchard Police Department
	    ☐ Poulsbo Police Department
	    ☐ Washington State Patrol

THE COURT FINDS THAT the Defendant has been arrested for a domestic violence offense, and further finds that to prevent possible recurrence of violence, this Pre-Arraignment Domestic Violence No Contact Order shall be entered pursuant to chapter 10.99 RCW. The person(s) protected by this order are–

_____

(Protected person(s) name, or initials if a minor, and DOB)

IT IS ORDERED THAT Defendant is PROHIBITED from causing or attempting to cause physical harm, bodily injury, assault, including sexual assault, and from molesting, harassing, threatening, or stalking the protected person(s), and

IT IS ORDERED THAT Defendant is PROHIBITED from coming near and from having any contact whatsoever, in person or through others, by phone, mail or any means, directly or indirectly, except for mailing or service of process of court documents by a third party or contact by the Defendant's lawyer(s) with the protected person(s), and

IT IS ORDERED THAT Defendant is PROHIBITED from entering or knowingly coming within or knowingly remaining within 500 feet of the protected person's residence, school, or place of work, and

IT IS ORDERED THAT this Pre-Arraignment Domestic Violence No Contact Order expires seven (7) days from the date below.

WARNINGS TO THE DEFENDANT: Violation of the provisions of this order with actual notice of its terms is a criminal offense under chapter 26.50 RCW, <u>and will subject a violator to arrest.</u> If the violation of this order involves travel across a state line or the boundary of a tribal jurisdiction, or involves conduct within the special maritime and territorial jurisdiction of the United States, which includes tribal lands, the you may be subject to criminal prosecution in federal court under 18 U.S.C. sections 2261, 2261A, or 2262.

Any assault, drive-by shooting, or reckless endangerment that is a violation of this order is a felony. Any conduct in violation of this order that is reckless and creates a substantial risk of death or serious physical injury to another person is a class C felony.

Effective immediately, and continuing as long as this order is in effect, you may not possess a firearm or ammunition. 18 U.S.C. section 922(g)(8). A violation of this federal firearms law carries a maximum possible penalty of 10 years in prison and a $250,000 fine. An exception exists for law enforcement officers and military personnel when carrying department/government-issued firearms. 18 U.S.C. section 925(a)(1). If you are convicted of an offense of domestic violence, you will be forbidden for life from possessing a firearm or ammunition. 18 U.S.C. section 922(g)(9); RCW 9.41.040.

**YOU CAN BE ARRESTED EVEN IF ANY PERSON OR PERSONS
PROTECTED BY THIS ORDER INVITES OR ALLOWS YOU TO
VIOLATE THIS ORDER'S PROHIBITIONS.**

You have the sole responsibility to avoid or refrain from violating the order's provisions. Only the court can change the order.

Pursuant to 18 U.S.C. section 2265, a court in any of the 50 states, the District of Columbia, Puerto Rico, any United States territory, and any tribal land within the United States shall accord full faith and credit to the order.

Dated: _____

Time: _____ [□ AM] [□ PM]

I agree to abide by the terms of this Pre-Arraignment Domestic Violence No Contact Order. I understand that the terms of any other court orders remain in effect notwithstanding the expiration of this order.

_____
DEFENDANT

SO ORDERED.

_____
JUDGE _____

Presiding Judge of the _____ Court

Original (Prosecutor's Office)
Copy (Defendant)
Copy (Law Enforcement Agency)

[Amended effective September 1, 2002; September 1, 2005; September 1, 2011.]

EXHIBIT L. ORDER RE AD LITEM FEES

**Superior Court of Washington
County of Kitsap**

SUPERIOR COURT FOR THE STATE OF WASHINGTON
IN AND FOR KITSAP COUNTY

In re the Guardianship of :

No.

**ORDER RE GUARDIAN AD
LITEM FEES**

The Court finds that the Guardian ad Litem fees herein are reasonable and should be granted.

ORDER

IT IS HEREBY ORDERED that fees in the amount of $_____ and costs in the amount of

$_____ shall be paid to _____ by Kitsap County,

Washington, for services in the above cited case.

Dated: _____, 20____

_____
JUDGE/COURT COMMISSIONER

Presented By:

_____

Attached is Affidavit of Fees.

[Adopted effective September 1, 2003; amended effective September 1, 2011.]

DISTRICT COURT

LOCAL RULES FOR THE DISTRICT COURT OF KITSAP COUNTY, WASHINGTON

Including Amendments Received Through
August 15, 2015

Table of Rules

I. LOCAL ADMINISTRATIVE RULES

LARLJ 9(c)(5). DEFERRED PROSECUTION

(c) Quasi–Public Documents: The following are not subject to public review, but are subject to review by the defendant and the defendant's lawyer:

(5) *Deferred Prosecution*: Petition for deferred prosecution, statement of defendant for deferred prosecution, order granting deferred prosecution, evaluation and recommendation of chemical dependency agency, status reports from chemical dependency agency, status reports and/or recommendations from probation, any aspect of a court docket which reflects the contents of a report from a chemical dependency agency or probation, any aspect of a court docket which reflects the conditions set by the court as the result of an evaluation or status report submitted by a chemical dependency agency or probation.

[Effective September 1, 1999.]

LARLJ 11. OATH OF INTERPRETER

All language interpreters serving in a legal proceeding, whether certified or uncertified, shall abide by the following:

(a) GR 11.1 and 11.2

(b) Annually, each language interpreter wishing to practice in the Kitsap County District Court shall complete and sign a written Oath of Interpreter. (The Oath is available from the Kitsap County District Court Administrative Office, 614 Division Street, MS–25, Port Orchard, WA 98366). A separate Oath is required for each language an individual is certified to interpret.

(c) At the time of interpretation of any written pleading in the case, the language interpreter shall sign the Certification of Translator, which document shall be filed with the Clerk of the Court and/or be attached to the document filed with the Clerk of the Court.

So long as the Oath of Interpreter is completed and filed with the Kitsap County District Court administrative office annually, the interpreter need only be identified and need not be sworn or further qualified during the recorded court proceeding, except at the discretion of the court.

[Adopted effective September 1, 2002; amended effective September 1, 2009.]

KITSAP COUNTY DISTRICT COURT

JAMES M. RIEHL, JUDGE DEPARTMENT NO. 1	614 Division Street, MS–25 Port Orchard, WA 98366 Phone (360) 337–7109	MARILYN G. PAJA, JUDGE DEPARTMENT NO. 3
JEFFREY J. JAHNS, JUDGE DEPARTMENT NO. 2	Fax 337–4865	STEPHEN J. HOLMAN, JUDGE DEPARTMENT NO. 4

MAURICE H. BAKER
COURT ADMINISTRATOR

OATH OF INTERPRETER

State of Washington, County of Kitsap, ss.

I, _____, do solemnly declare:

1) I have read and will abide by the Code of Conduct for Court Interpreters adopted by the Supreme Court of the State of Washington (attached on reverse and as subsequently amended).

2) When appointed to serve in legal proceedings I will interpret the material thoroughly and precisely, stating as nearly as possible what has been stated by all speakers. I will never add words to, nor omit words from, a statement made by a witness, party, judge or attorney.

3) I will maintain the respect due to the courts of justice and judicial officers, and to all parties involved in legal proceedings.

4) *IF YOU ARE CERTIFIED BY the State of Washington Office of the Administrator for the Courts*: I am certified by the State of Washington Office of the Administrator for the Courts to interpret in the _____ (insert name of language) language.

5) *IF YOU ARE NOT CERTIFIED BY the State of Washington Office of the Administrator for the Courts:*

    a)   I have been sworn to interpret in the _____
         (insert name of language) language for the following courts and/or agencies in the past: _____

(cite 2–3 representative examples).

b) I have the following educational background relevant to my ability to interpret for the courts:

_____

_____

(insert educational degrees and relevant life/work experience.

c) I will interpret simultaneously/ consecutively (choose one) with the speaker.

_____
Signature

Subscribed and sworn to before me this _____ day of _____ 20_____.

_____
Judge

RULE 11.1. CODE OF CONDUCT FOR COURT INTERPRETATION[1]

Preamble. All language interpreters serving in a legal proceeding, whether certified or uncertified, shall abide by the following Code of Conduct:

A language interpreter who violates any of the provisions of this code is subject to a citation for contempt, disciplinary action or any other sanction that may be imposed by law. The purpose of this Code of Conduct is to establish and maintain high standards of conduct to preserve the integrity and independence of the adjudicative system.

(a) A language interpreter, like an officer of the court, shall maintain high standards of personal and professional conduct that promote public confidence in the administration of justice.

(b) A language interpreter shall interpret or translate the material thoroughly and precisely, adding or omitting nothing, and stating as nearly as possible what has been stated in the language of the speaker, giving consideration to variations in grammar and syntax for both languages involved. A language interpreter shall use the level of communication that best conveys the meaning of the source, and shall not interject the interpreter's personal moods or attitudes.

(c) When a language interpreter has any reservation about ability to satisfy an assignment competently, the interpreter shall immediately convey that reservation to the parties and to the court. If the communication mode or language of the non-English speaking person cannot be readily interpreted, the interpreter shall notify the appointing authority or the court.

(d) No language interpreter shall render services in any matter in which the interpreter is a potential witness, associate, friend, or relative of a contending party, unless a specific exception is allowed by the appointing authority for good cause noted on the record. Neither shall the interpreter serve in any matter in which the interpreter has an interest, financial or otherwise, in the outcome. Nor shall any language interpreter serve in a matter where the interpreter has participated in the choice of counsel.

(e) Except in the interpreter's official capacity, no language interpreter shall discuss, report, or comment upon a matter in which the person serves as interpreter. Interpreters shall not disclose any communication that is privileged by law without the written consent of the parties to the communication, or pursuant to court order.

(f) A language interpreter shall report immediately to the appointing authority in the proceeding any solicitation or effort by another to induce or encourage the interpreter to violate any law, any provision of the rules which may be approved by the courts for the practice of language interpreting, or any provisions of this Code of Conduct.

(g) Language interpreters shall not give legal advice and shall refrain from the unauthorized practice of law.

RULE 11.2. TELEPHONIC INTERPRETATION[2]

(a) Interpreters may be appointed to serve by telephone for brief, nonevidentiary proceedings, including initial appearances and arraignments, when interpreters are not readily available to the court. Telephone interpretation is not authorized for evidentiary hearings.

(b) RCW 2.43 and GR 11.1 must be followed regarding the interpreter's qualifications and other matters.

(c) Electronic equipment used during the hearing must ensure that the non-English speaking party hears all statements made by the participants. If electronic equipment is not available for simultaneous interpreting, the hearing shall be conducted to allow consecutive interpretation of each sentence.

(d) Attorney-client consultations must be interpreted confidentially.

(e) Written documents which would normally be orally translated by the interpreter must be read aloud to allow full oral translation of the material by the interpreter.

(f) An audio recording shall be made of all statements made on the record during their interpretation, and the same shall be preserved.

KITSAP COUNTY DISTRICT COURT, STATE OF WASHINGTON	Mailing Address: 614 Division Street, MS–25 Port Orchard, WA 98366 (360) 337–7109

STATE OF WASHINGTON,   NO.
               Plaintiff,
       vs.   CERTIFICATION OF TRANSLATOR

_____,
           Defendant.

---

1. My name is: _____

    My address is: _____

2. I am fluent/certified in the _____ language. Today I have translated the following document(s) for the defendant from English into that language:

☐ Commitment
☐ DUI Information Sheet
☐ Ignition Interlock Order
☐ Judgment and Sentence
☐ Motion and Order Appointing Counsel
☐ No Contact Order
☐ Notice of Ineligibility to Possess Firearm
☐ Order Allowing Community Service Work
☐ Order of Release

☐ Order Regarding Seized Property
☐ Payment Plan
☐ Pre–Trial Diversion Agreement
☐ Rights and Procedures
☐ Statement of Defendant on Plea of Guilty
☐ Statement of Defendant on Stipulation to Facts
☐ Waiver of Speedy Trial
☐ Other: _____

The defendant has acknowledged his or her understanding of both the translation and the subject matter of these document(s).

3. I certify under penalty of perjury under the laws of the State of Washington that the foregoing is true and correct.

    DATED this _____ day of _____ 20 _____.

At: _____   _____
      Location   Interpreter

---

[1] RULE 11.1 references GR 11.1.
[2] RULE 11.2 references GR 11.2.

II. LOCAL CRIMINAL RULES
LCrRLJ 3.2.2. RELEASE OF ACCUSED

(1) Any person arrested on Probable Cause (without a warrant) for an offense classified as a Domestic Violence offense under Chapter 10.99 of the Revised Code of Washington as the same exists or shall hereafter be amended shall be held in jail pending the defendant's first appearance.

(2) Notwithstanding paragraph (1), a person being held for a Domestic Violence offense classified as a felony may be released from custody prior to defendant's first appearance upon (a) the posting of $50,000 bail or bond; and (b) the person's affixing his or her signature at the appropriate location on a Pre-Arraignment domestic Violence No Contact Order describing in paragraph (4) prohibiting the arrested person from having contact with the protected person or from knowingly coming within, or knowingly remaining within, 500 feet of the protected person's residence, place of work, or school.

(3) Notwithstanding paragraph (1), a person being held for a Domestic Violence offense classified as a misdemeanor or a gross misdemeanor may be released from custody prior to defendant's first appearance upon (a) the posting of $5,000 bail or bond; and (b) the person's affixing his or her signature in the appropriate location on a Pre-Arraignment Domestic Violence No Contact Order described in paragraph (4) prohibiting the arrested person from having contact with the protected person or from knowingly coming within, or knowingly remaining within, 500 feet of the protected person' residence, place of work, or school.

(4) The following Pre-Arraignment Domestic Violence No Contact Order, or one that is substantially similar to it, is hereby approved for use under this rule.

☐ In the Kitsap County Superior Court
☐ In the Kitsap County District Court
☐ In the Bainbridge Island Municipal Court
☐ In the Bremerton Municipal Court
☐ In the Port Orchard Municipal Court
☐ In the Poulsbo Municipal Court

☐ State of Washington, ☐ City of Bainbridge Island, ☐ City of Bremerton, ☐ City of Port Orchard, ☐ City of Poulsbo,	) Law Enforcement No. _____)) Pre-Arraignment Domestic) Violence) No Contact Order)
Plaintiff,	) Date of Arrest: _____) Time of Arrest: _____
v. _____	) Arresting Officer/No.: _____) ☐ Bainbridge Island Police) Department
_____, DOB: _____	) ☐ Bremerton Police Department) ☐ Kitsap County Sheriff's Office) ☐ Port Orchard Police Department
Defendant. _____	) ☐ Poulsbo Police Department) ☐ Washington State Patrol

The Court Finds That the Defendant has been arrested for a domestic violence offense, and further finds that to prevent possible recurrence of violence, this Pre-Arraignment Domestic Violence No Contact Order shall be entered pursuant to chapter 10.99 RCW. The person(s) protected by this order are-

_____

(Protected person(s) name, or initials if a minor, and DOB)

It Is Ordered That Defendant is Prohibited from causing or attempting to cause physical harm, bodily injury, assault, including sexual assault, and from molesting, harassing, threatening, or stalking the protected person(s), and

It Is Ordered That Defendant is Prohibited from coming near and from having any contact whatsoever, in person or through others, by phone, mail or any means, directly or indirectly, except for mailing or service of process of court documents by a third party or contact by the Defendant's lawyer(s) with the protected person(s), and

It Is Ordered That Defendant is Prohibited from entering or knowingly coming within or knowingly remaining within 500 feet of the protected person's residence, school, or place of work, and

It Is Ordered That this Pre–Arraignment Domestic Violence No Contact Order expires seven days from the date below.

Warnings To The Defendant: Violation of the provisions of this order with actual notice of its terms is a criminal offense under chapter 26.50 RCW, and will subject a violator to arrest. If the violation of this order involves travel across a state line or the boundary of a tribal jurisdiction, or involves conduct within the special maritime and territorial jurisdiction of the United States, which includes tribal lands, the you may be subject to criminal prosecution in federal court under 18 U.S.C. sections 2261, 2261 A, or 2262.

Any assault, drive-by shooting, or reckless endangerment that is a violation of this order is a felony. Any conduct in violation of this order that is reckless and creates a substantial risk of death or serious physical injury to another person is a class C felony.

Effective immediately, and continuing as long as this order is in effect, you may not possess a firearm or ammunition. 18 U.S.C. section 922(g)(8). A violation of this federal firearms law carries a maximum possible penalty of 10 years in prison and a $250,000 fine. An exception exists for law enforcement officers and military personnel when carrying department/government–issued firearms. 18 U.S.C. section 925(a)(1). If you are convicted of an offense of domestic violence, you will be forbidden for life from possessing a firearm or ammunition. 18 U.S.C. section 922(g)(9); RCW 9.41.040.

You Can Be Arrested Even If Any Person Or Persons Protected By This Order Invites Or Allows You To Violate This Order's Prohibitions.

You have the sole responsibility to avoid or refrain from violating the order's provisions. Only the court can change the order.

Pursuant to 18 U.S.C. section 2265, a court in any of the 50 states, the District of Columbia, Puerto Rico, any United States territory, and any tribal land within the United States shall accord full faith and credit to the order.

Dated: _____

Time: _____ [□ AM] [□ PM]

I agree to abide by the terms of this Pre–Arraignment Domestic Violence No Contact Order. I understand that the terms of any other court orders remain in effect notwithstanding the expiration of this order.

_____
Defendant

So Ordered.

/s/ _____

JUDGE _____
Presiding Judge of the _____ Court
Original (Prosecutor's Office)   Copy (Defendant)   Copy (Law Enforcement Agency)

[Adopted effective September 1, 2003; amended effective September 1, 2012.]

LCrRLJ 3.4.1. VIDEO CONFERENCES

Pursuant to CrRLJ 3.4(d)(2) the Kitsap District Court authorizes the use of Video Conferences Proceedings for all court proceedings.

[Adopted effective September 1, 2012.]

LCrRLJ 3.6. SUPPRESSION PROCEDURE

(c) **Hearing:** Motions to suppress physical, oral or identification evidence shall be noted for hearing by the moving party to be held before the impaneling of a jury. The moving party shall contact the court scheduler at (360) 337–7013 to obtain a hearing date.

[Effective September 1, 1999; amended effective September 1, 2012.]

LCrRLJ 3.7. DISPOSITIVE MOTIONS

(a) Motions that, if granted, would be dispositive of a case or cases shall be noted at the pre-trial hearing and heard on a date prior to the date set for trial.

[Effective September 1, 1999; amended effective September 1, 2012.]

LCrRLJ 4. PROCEDURES PRIOR TO TRIAL

4.1(d)(7) *ARRAIGNMENTS IN DUI & PHYSICAL CONTROL CASES*

(i) <u>Mandatory Appearance</u>: Unless otherwise provided for in this rule, or by statute, all defendants must appear in person for arraignment.

(ii) <u>Waiver of Arraignment</u>: If the defendant has previously appeared in person before a judge, as required by RCW 46.61.50571, and conditions of release have been ordered, then a lawyer may enter an appearance or a plea of not guilty AND WAIVER OF ARRAIGNMENT on behalf of a client. An appear-

ance that waives arraignment, but fails to state a plea, shall be deemed to constitute entry of a plea of not guilty. Upon timely receipt of a notice of appearance and the filing of proof of compliance with conditions of release, the court staff shall strike the arraignment date and issue a notice to appear for pretrial hearing.

[Effective September 1, 1999.]

LCrRLJ 4.5. PRE–TRIAL HEARING

(b) **Confirmation:** Cases shall be set for either bench or jury trial at the pre-trial hearing. To ensure the presence of a jury, a party must confirm with the court scheduler at (360) 337–7013 no later than 1:30 p.m. on the Thursday prior to the date set for trial. To elect a bench trial on the date set for jury trial, a party shall notify the court of the election no later than 1:30 p.m. on the Thursday prior to the date set for trial. Confirmed jury trials will have priority on jury trial days.

[Effective September 1, 1999; amended effective September 1, 2009. Amended on an emergency basis, effective January 4, 2010; amended on a permanent basis effective September 1, 2012.]

LCrRLJ 4.7. DISCOVERY

(h) **Discovery for Court Appointed Counsel.** The prosecuting authority shall provide discovery to counsel appointed at public expense within fourteen days of the prosecuting authority's receipt of the Order Appointing Counsel. The Order Appointing Counsel shall be considered a written demand for discovery, thereby triggering the prosecuting authority's discovery obligations under CrRLJ 4.7(a).

[Effective September 1, 1999. Amended on an emergency basis, effective January 4, 2010; amended on a permanent basis effective September 1, 2012.]

III. LOCAL INFRACTION RULES

LIRLJ 3.1. CONTESTED HEARINGS— PRELIMINARY PROCEEDINGS.

(a) **Subpoena:** The defendant and the plaintiff may subpoena witnesses necessary for the presentation of their respective cases. Witnesses should be served at least seven days before the hearing. The subpoena may be issued by a Judge, Court Commissioner, or Clerk of the Court or by a party's lawyer. If a party's lawyer issues a subpoena, a copy shall be filed with the court. A subpoena may be directed for service within their jurisdiction to the sheriff of any county or any peace officer of any municipality in the state in

which the witness may be or it may be served as provided in CR 45(c), or it may be served by first class mail, postage prepaid, sent to the witness' last known address. Service by mail shall be deemed complete upon the third day following the day upon which the subpoena was placed in the mail. If the subpoena is for a witness outside the county, the judge must approve of the subpoena.

(b)(1) All parties demanding discovery shall provide an e-mail or other electronic device address, if available, to which the discovery shall be delivered.

(i) If the defendant wishes to subpoena a witness, including a law enforcement officer, the defendant shall deliver in person to the court clerk at the Kitsap County District Court office or by mail to Kitsap County District Court, 614 Division Street, MS–25, Port Orchard, Washington 98366, at least 28 days prior to the date of the hearing, a written request for the issuance of the subpoena and for instructions regarding service of the subpoena. The written request must state the case number, date and time of the hearing, the complete address of the location of the hearing and the name and address of the witness to be named in the subpoena. The defendant shall also include a self-addressed, stamped envelope along with the written request.

Upon receipt of the written request, the court clerk shall prepare a subpoena and present it to the judge or court commissioner for signature. The clerk shall then mail the subpoena to the defendant in the self-addressed, stamped envelope, together with a return of service form.

[Effective September 1, 1999; amended effective September 1, 2009; December 1, 2010.]

LIRLJ 3.5. DECISION ON WRITTEN STATEMENTS

Mitigation and contested hearings regarding infractions are authorized. The procedure set out in IRLJ 3.5 is adopted. Defendants shall be required to comply with written instructions provided by the court. The court shall render its written decision by mail.

[Adopted effective September 1, 2009; amended effective September 1, 2012.]

LIRLJ 6.6. SPEED MEASURING DEVICE

Any certificate admissible under IRLJ 6.6(b), and any other document relating to a Speed Measuring Device, can be filed with the clerk of the court and maintained by the court as a public record, and shall be available for inspection by the public. Copies shall be provided by the clerks' office on request. There shall be no charge for the copy if it relates to an infraction filed against the person making the request. These records shall be available without a formal request for discovery. The court shall be entitled to take judicial notice of the fact that any document filed pursuant to this rule has been filed with the court. Documents filed pursuant to this rule shall not be suppressed as evidence merely because there is no prosecutor present to offer the document as an exhibit at the hearing. If the certificate or document is insufficient, then a motion to suppress the reading of the Speed Measuring Device shall be granted.

[Adopted effective September 1, 2000; amended effective September 1, 2009.]

IV. LOCAL CIVIL RULES

LCRLJ 3. COMMENCEMENT OF ACTIONS

[Deleted.]

[Effective September 1, 1999; deleted effective September 1, 2009.]

LCRLJ 4. PROCESS

(a) **Summons**—Any summons used to commence an action in the Kitsap County District Court shall contain a statement that a copy of the answer and all other responsive pleadings must be filed with the court. The summons for personal service within this state shall be substantially in the following form:

KITSAP COUNTY DISTRICT COURT, STATE OF WASHINGTON	Mailing Address: 614 Division Street, MS–25 Port Orchard, WA 98366 (360) 337–7109
	NO.
_____ Plaintiff(s), vs. _____ Defendant(s).	SUMMONS (20 days)

TO THE DEFENDANT: A lawsuit has been started against you in the above-entitled court by _____, plaintiff(s). The plaintiff(s)' claim is stated in the written complaint, a copy of which is served upon you with this summons.

In order to defend against this lawsuit, you must respond to the complaint by stating your defense in writing; serve a copy upon the person signing this summons within twenty (20) days after service of this summons, excluding the day of service; and file a copy with the court named above. If you do not, a default judgment may be entered against you without prior notice. A default judgment is one where the plaintiff is entitled to what he/she asks for because you have not responded.

If you serve a notice of appearance on the undersigned person, you are entitled to notice before a default judgment may be entered. A copy of all responsive pleadings must be filed with the court.

If you wish to seek the advice of an attorney in this matter, you should do so promptly so that your written response, if any, may be served and filed with the court on time. This summons is issued pursuant to Rule 4 of the Civil Rules for Courts of Limited Jurisdiction.

DATE _____

PLAINTIFF/PLAINTIFF(S)' ATTORNEY

Print or Type Name _____

Mailing Address _____

City _____ State _____ Zip _____

Phone Number _____

[Effective September 1, 1999; amended effective September 1, 2009.]

LCRLJ 5. SERVICE AND FILING OF PLEADINGS AND OTHER PAPERS

The Kitsap County District Court adopts the Superior Court rule CR 5(i).

[Effective September 1, 1999; amended effective September 1, 2012.]

LCRLJ 7. PLEADINGS ALLOWED: FORM OF MOTIONS

(a) **Appearance and/or Answer:** Contents—An appearance and/or answer or response of a party shall, in addition to any response to the merits of the action, contain a legible statement of the name, post office address, and telephone number (if any) of the appearing or answering party.

i. Appearance and Answer—The form of a party's Appearance and Answer may be, but is not required to be, in substantially the same format as Attachment A.

ii. Motion and Declaration—The form of a party's Motion and Declaration may be, but is not required to be, in substantially the same format as Attachment B.

iii. Note for Hearing and Declaration of Mailing or Delivery—The form of a party's Note for Hearing and Declaration of Mailing or Delivery may be, but is not

required to be, in substantially the same format as Attachment C.

(b) **Motions and Other Papers**

1) *How Made.*

(A) Reapplication for Order. When an order has been applied for and refused in whole or in part (unless without prejudice), or has been granted conditionally and the condition has not been performed, the same application for an order shall not be presented to another judge unless so directed by the court. If a subsequent application is made upon an alleged different statement of facts or law, it shall be shown by affidavit what application was made, when, and to what judge; what order or decision was made thereon; and what new facts or law are claimed to be shown. For failure to comply with this requirement, any order made upon such subsequent application shall be set aside upon request of an opposing party.

2) *Form.*

(A) Necessary Provisions in Orders Requiring Personal Attendance. In all proceedings wherein an order is to be issued requiring the personal attendance of a person to be examined in open court, the order shall include in capital letters a warning in substantially the following form:

YOUR FAILURE TO APPEAR AS ABOVE SET FORTH AT THE TIME, DATE AND PLACE STATED WILL CAUSE THE COURT TO ISSUE A BENCH WARRANT FOR YOUR APPREHENSION AND CONFINEMENT IN JAIL UNTIL SUCH TIME AS THE MATTER CAN BE HEARD OR UNTIL BAIL IS POSTED.

No Bench warrant shall be issued in such cases for the apprehension of the cited person if such language has been omitted.

[Effective September 1, 1999; amended effective September 1, 2002; September 1, 2003; September 1, 2009.]

ATTACHMENT A.   APPEARANCE AND ANSWER

KITSAP COUNTY DISTRICT COURT,
STATE OF WASHINGTON

Mailing Address: 614 Division Street, MS–25
Port Orchard, WA 98366
(360) 337–7109

_____,
Plaintiff(s),

vs.

_____,
Defendant(s).

NO.

APPEARANCE AND ANSWER

I.   This appearance and answer is made for the following defendant(s):

_____   _____

_____   _____

II. The defendant(s) answer the complaint as follows (check one and use additional sheets if necessary):

☐   (a) I (we) admit the entire claim.

☐   (b) I (we) deny the entire claim for the following reason(s):

_____

_____

_____

_____

_____

_____

_____

_____

☐   (c) I (we) admit part and deny part, as follows:

(1) I (we) admit, as follows:

_____

_____

_____

_____

(2) I (we) deny, as follows:

_____

_____

_____

_____

III. All further pleadings and notifications in this matter should be sent to the
following:

_____   _____
Name   Name

_____   _____
Mailing Address   Mailing Address

_____   _____
City   State   Zip   City   State   Zip

_____   _____
Phone Number   Phone Number

ALL DEFENDANTS ANSWERING SIGN AND PRINT NAMES:

_____   _____
Signature   Print Name

_____   _____
Signature   Print Name

_____   _____
Signature   Print Name

[Amended effective September 1, 2009.]

ATTACHMENT B. MOTION AND DECLARATION

KITSAP COUNTY DISTRICT COURT,   Mailing Address: 614 Division Street, MS–25
STATE OF WASHINGTON   Port Orchard, WA 98366
                                                                                (360) 337–7109

_____,   NO.
                          Plaintiff,
            vs.   **MOTION AND DECLARATION**

_____,   ☐ CIVIL   ☐SMALL CLAIMS
                          Defendant.

COMES NOW the ☐ plaintiff ☐ defendant and moves the court for the following relief **(briefly and clearly state what you want the court to do):** _____.
_____
_____

This motion is made for the reasons stated in the declaration below.

            Signature: _____

            Printed Name: _____

            Mailing Address: _____

                                          _____

            Telephone No.:   (____)_____

The undersigned states the following reasons for the requested motion. All statements are made to the best of my personal knowledge and belief. I certify under penalty of perjury, under the laws of the State of Washington, that the following is true and correct: _____
_____
_____
_____

            Signature: _____

            Printed Name: _____

            Signed at (City/State): _____

            Date: _____

[Amended May 10, 2000; February 12, 2001; September 1, 2009.]

ATTACHMENT C.   NOTE FOR HEARING AND DECLARATION OF MAILING OR DELIVERY

KITSAP COUNTY DISTRICT COURT, STATE OF WASHINGTON	Mailing Address: 614 Division Street, MS–25 Port Orchard, WA 98366 (360) 337–7109

_____,   NO.

               Plaintiff,

     vs.   **NOTE FOR HEARING**
AND DECLARATION OF

_____,   **MAILING OR DELIVERY**

             Defendant.   ☐ CIVIL   ☐ SMALL CLAIMS

PLEASE TAKE NOTICE that the motion attached hereto and filed with the court will be heard on _____, the _____ day of _____ 20 (6) 6d, at _____ a.m./p.m.,

at: 614 Division Street, Rm 106
       Port Orchard, Washington

USER NOTE: Please call the District Court at (360) 337–7109 to obtain the date and time for the hearing. If you fail to do so, your matter will not be heard and sanctions may be imposed against you.

USER NOTE: Your motion and this Note for Hearing must be filed with the court and delivered to the opposing party(s), at least five (5) days prior to the hearing date, exclusive of holidays and weekends. Some types of motions require more than five (5) days notice. If using the mail for delivery, add three (3) days for mailing, exclusive of holidays and weekends.

(Please review CRLJ 5, CRLJ 6 and any other applicable court rules, which are found in the Washington State Court Rules and are available for review in the county's law library.) Motions not properly delivered and with proof of delivery on file with the court will not be heard and sanctions may be imposed against you.

PROOF OF DELIVERY

☐   Hand–Delivery: The undersigned personally hand-delivered to the following party(s), at the address(es) shown, the attached Note for Hearing, Motion and Declaration:

☐   Delivery by Mail: I certify that on _____, 20 _____, at (6) 6d a.m./p.m., I did deposit into the US Mail, proper postage applied, a copy of this Note for Hearing and of the attached Motion and Declaration to the following person(s) at the address(es) shown:

_____	_____
Name	Name
_____	_____
Mailing Address	Mailing Address
_____	_____
City State Zip	City State Zip

I certify under penalty of perjury, under the laws of the State of Washington, that the foregoing statements are true and correct.

Signature: _____

                   Mailing Address

Printed Name: _____   _____

                                   City   State   Zip

Signed at (City/State): _____   Telephone No.: (____)_____

Date: _____

[Amended May 10, 2000; February 12, 2001; September 1, 2009.]

LCRLJ 26. DISCOVERY

(a) Limited Discovery Permitted. Except as provided in this rule and in CRLJ 26, the procedures authorized by Rules 26 through 37 of the Superior Court Civil Rules applicable for use in the Superior Court may be available only upon prior permission of the court. Appropriate sanctions as permitted by Rule 37 of the Superior Court Civil Rules will be applicable for a party's or person's failure to comply with this rule, with CRLJ 26 and, upon the prior permission of the court, any of the discovery procedures authorized under Rules 26 through 37 of the Superior Court Civil Rules.

(b) Evidence Deemed Admissible

(1) All provisions of Evidence Rule (ER) 904 are adopted.

(2) Subject to the time lines established in ER 904, the written statement of any witness, including the written report of an expert witness, and including a statement of opinion, which the witness would be allowed to express if testifying in person, is deemed admissible if it is made by affidavit or by declaration under penalty of perjury. Any other party may subpoena the author or maker of a document admissible under this subsection, at the party's expense, and examine the author or maker as if under cross examination.

(c) Small Claims Court Actions. No discovery shall be permitted in Small Claims Court actions.

(d) Limitations on Discovery. No blanket orders for unlimited discovery will be permitted.

(f) Time for Discovery. Twenty-one days after service of a discovery request, individually or in conjunction with the service of the summons and complaint, or counterclaim, or cross complaint, the serving party may compel discovery as set forth in section[s] (a) and (b) of CRLJ 26, or request additional discovery pursuant to section[s] (c) and (d) of CRLJ 26. Unless agreed by the parties and with the permission of the court, all discovery shall be completed within 60 days of service of the Motion to Compel, or 90 days of service of the summons and complaint, counterclaim, or cross complaint, whichever is longer.

(i) Motions: Conference of Counsel Required. Compliance with Superior Court Civil Rule (CR) 26(i) is a requirement to compelling discovery under this rule.

[Effective September 1, 1999. Amended on an emergency basis, effective January 4, 2010; amended on a permanent basis effective September 1, 2012.]

LCRLJ 38. JURY TRIAL

(a) Demand. A demand for jury trial shall be made by serving a copy of a written demand for jury trial on the opposing party, by filing the original written demand with the Kitsap County District Court clerk and by paying the nonrefundable jury fee, all prior to the time the case is set for trial. Failure to strictly comply with this rule shall be deemed a waiver of the right to a jury trial.

(b) Confirmation. A party demanding a jury trial shall, before 1:30 p.m. on the Thursday prior to the scheduled trial date, contact the Kitsap County District Court scheduler at (360) 337–7013 and confirm that the jury is still required.

[Effective September 1, 1999. Amended on an emergency basis, effective January 4, 2010.]

LCRLJ 40. ASSIGNMENT OF CASES

(a) Methods

(1) *Administrative Status Review.* On or about the ninetieth day following the filing of a complaint, the court clerk shall conduct a status review of all cases not yet set for preliminary trial to determine whether proof of service is on file for all parties defendant and whether an answer or reply has been filed by all named parties required to file an answer or to file complaints, cross-complaints, counterclaims and third party complaints. If all necessary proof of service, answers and replies are on file, the clerk shall note the cause for a preliminary trial as provided for by LCRLJ 40(b)(2). If all necessary proofs of service, answers or replies are not on file, the clerk shall notify, in writing, the respective parties that all pending claims for relief shall be scheduled for dismissal on the clerk's motion on a date no sooner than twelve (12) months from the date of filing of the most recent pleading, pursuant to LCRLJ 41(b)(2). If all necessary proofs of service, answers or replies are later filed within said twelve (12) month period, the clerk shall schedule the matter for a preliminary trial, as provided for by LCRLJ 40(b)(2).

(2) *Preliminary Trial.* When matters of fact are put in issue by responsive pleadings served and filed in conformance with these rules, the clerk shall, without prior notice to the parties, set the case on for a preliminary trial. At the preliminary trial all parties must appear in person or through counsel. If a party does not appear at the preliminary trial, the non-appearing party's pleadings shall be

stricken, unless good cause is shown, and the court may grant a judgment of default or dismissal against the non-appearing party. If no parties appear, the court may dismiss all pending claims without prejudice. At the preliminary trial, the court will also perform the following functions:

1) Hear and determine motions.

2) Assign trial and/or further motion dates.

3) Acknowledge and approve settlement agreements.

4) Enter defaults or judgments on the pleadings.

5) Pre-admit exhibits for trial.

6) Enter discovery order and completion dates.

Counsel shall appear at the preliminary trial with their schedule of dates of availability for trial.

The preliminary trial procedure shall not preclude the entry of default judgments, judgments on pleadings, or any other orders not inconsistent with these rules or the Civil Rules for Courts of Limited Jurisdiction (CRLJ) prior to the date of the preliminary trial.

(3) *Preliminary Trial/Trial Assignment: Forms.* The Assignment of Preliminary Trial Date and the Assignment of Civil Trial Date pleadings will be in substantially the following formats:

ASSIGNMENT OF PRELIMINARY TRIAL DATE

KITSAP COUNTY DISTRICT COURT, STATE OF WASHINGTON	Mailing Address: 614 Division Street, MS–25 Port Orchard, WA 98366 (360) 337–7109

_____, Plaintiff(s), vs. _____, Defendant(s).	NO. **ASSIGNMENT OF PRELIMINARY TRIAL DATE**

This case shall be heard on the following court date before Judge/ Commissioner:
_____

Preliminary Trial: Date: _____, **Time:** ___ a.m./p.m., **Room:** ___.

All Parties must appear in person or through counsel. If a party does not appear at the preliminary trial, the non-appearing party's pleadings shall be stricken unless good cause is shown and the court may grant a judgment of default or dismissal against the non-appearing party. If no parties appear, the court may dismiss all pending claims without prejudice. At the above date and time, the court will:

1. Hear and determine motions.

2. Assign trial and/or further motion dates.

3. Acknowledge and approve settlement agreements.

4. Enter defaults or judgments on the pleadings.

5. Pre-admit exhibits for trial.

6. Enter discovery order and completion dates.

All parties shall be prepared with their schedules so that further motions and/or trial dates can be set at this time.

DATED this _____ day of _____ 20_____.

_____
CLERK

cc:

PLAINTIFF (WHITE)   DEFENDANT (YELLOW)   COURT (PINK)

ASSIGNMENT OF CIVIL TRIAL DATE

KITSAP COUNTY DISTRICT COURT,
STATE OF WASHINGTON

Mailing Address: 614 Division Street, MS–25
Port Orchard, WA 98366
(360) 337–7109

_____,   NO.
                Plaintiff(s),
        vs.   **ASSIGNMENT OF CIVIL TRIAL DATE**

_____,
                Defendant(s).

This case shall be heard on the following court date before:

Judge/Commissioner: _____   Room: _____

TRIAL

Length: _____ days   No. of Jurors: ☐ 20   ☐ Other_____

Date: _____   Time: _____ a.m./p.m.

If the trial will last more than two (2) days (calculated from the morning of the assigned trial date to the rendition of the jury's verdict), a special setting of this case is required. Failure to comply will likely result in a lengthy adjournment or other relief to be established by the court.

Litigants must confirm a Jury or Bench Trial by notifying the court scheduler at (360) 337–7013 before 1:30 p.m. the judicial day prior to trial. Failure to do so will result in a jury panel not being present and/or the striking of the trial.

   DATED this _____ day of _____ 20_____.

                                    _____
                                    CLERK

cc:

PLAINTIFF (WHITE)   DEFENDANT (CANARY)   COURT (PINK)

ASSIGNMENT OF CIVIL TRIAL DATE

1. Hear and determine motions.

2. Assign trial and/or further motion dates.

3. Acknowledge and approve settlement agreements.

4. Enter defaults or judgments on the pleadings.

5. Pre-admit exhibits for trial.

6. Enter discovery order and completion dates.

All parties shall be prepared with their schedules so that further motions and/or trial dates can be set at this time.

DATED this _____ day of _____ 20_____.

_____
CLERK

cc:

PLAINTIFF (WHITE)   DEFENDANT (YELLOW)   COURT (PINK)

ASSIGNMENT OF CIVIL TRIAL DATE

KITSAP COUNTY DISTRICT COURT,   Mailing Address: 614 Division Street, MS–25
STATE OF WASHINGTON   Port Orchard, WA 98366
                                                             (360) 337–7109

_____,   NO.
                        Plaintiff(s),
            vs.   **ASSIGNMENT OF CIVIL TRIAL DATE**

_____,
                        Defendant(s).

This case shall be heard on the following court date before:

Judge/Commissioner: _____   Room: _____

TRIAL

Length: _____ days   No. of Jurors: ☐ 20 ☐ Other_____

Date: _____   Time: _____ a.m./p.m.

If the trial will last more than two (2) days (calculated from the morning of the assigned trial date to the rendition of the jury's verdict), a special setting of this case is required. Failure to comply will likely result in a lengthy adjournment or other relief to be established by the court.

Litigants must confirm a Jury or Bench Trial by notifying the court scheduler at (360) 337–7013 before 1:30 p.m. the judicial day prior to trial. Failure to do so will result in a jury panel not being present and/or the striking of the trial.

DATED this _____ day of _____ 20_____.

_____
CLERK

cc:

PLAINTIFF (WHITE)   DEFENDANT (CANARY)   COURT (PINK)

[Effective September 1, 1999; amended June 22, 2000; January 30, 2002; July 29, 2002; September 1, 2009. Amended on an emergency basis, effective January 4, 2010.]

LCRLJ 41. DISMISSAL OF ACTIONS

(b) Dismissal on Clerk's Motion

(2) *Procedure*—In all civil cases where there has been no action of record during the twelve (12) months just past, the Kitsap County District Court clerk shall mail notice to the parties or the attorneys of record that such case will be dismissed by the Kitsap County District Court for want of prosecution unless within thirty (30) days following said mailing, action of record is made or an application in writing is made to the court and good cause shown why it should be continued as a pending case. If such application is not made or good cause is not shown, the court shall dismiss each such case without prejudice. The costs of filing such order of dismissal with the clerk shall not be assessed against either party.

[Effective September 1, 1999.]

LCRLJ 45. SUBPOENA

(a) Any subpoena authorized pursuant to this rule shall be in accord with Superior Court Civil Rule 45 as governed by Kitsap County LCRLJ 26.

(b) No party shall have a right to subpoena persons, documents or things in Small Claims Court actions.

[Effective September 1, 1999.]

LCRLJ 51. INSTRUCTIONS TO JURY

(a) **Submission of Proposed Instructions**—It is the responsibility of the parties to submit proposed jury instructions to the Kitsap County District Court and to opposing parties at the time the case is called for trial. If the party demanding a jury trial fails to comply with this requirement, the right to jury trial shall be deemed waived and the jury panel dismissed unless all opposing parties move to retain the jury and the court finds good cause therefore.

[Effective September 1, 1999.]

LCRLJ 56. JUDGMENT SUMMARY

(e) Pursuant to RCW 4.64.030, the first page of all judgments presented should include the required summary in substantially the following form:

KITSAP COUNTY DISTRICT COURT, STATE OF WASHINGTON	)))	Mailing Address: 614 Division Street, MS–25 Port Orchard, WA 98366 (360) 337–7109
_____, Plaintiff, vs. _____, Defendant.	))))))))	NO. **ORDER OF DEFAULT AND DEFAULT JUDGMENT** (EXAMPLE)

JUDGMENT SUMMARY

JUDGMENT CREDITOR :
ATTORNEY FOR JUDGMENT CREDITOR :
JUDGMENT DEBTOR :
ATTORNEY FOR JUDGMENT DEBTOR :
PRINCIPAL JUDGMENT AMOUNT :
INTEREST TO DATE OF JUDGMENT :
TOTAL OF TAXABLE COSTS AND ATTORNEYS' FEES :
    ATTORNEYS' FEES :
    FILING FEE :
    SERVICE OF PROCESS :
    TOTAL :
TOTAL JUDGMENT :
INTEREST RATE ON JUDGMENT :

THIS MATTER having come on before the undersigned Judge of the above-entitled court for the entry of an Order of Default and Default Judgment against _____, and the court having reviewed the records and the files herein, including the Affidavit of ___, and otherwise being fully advised in the premises, it is now, therefore,

ORDERED, ADJUDGED AND DECREED that defendants _____ are hereby ordered and adjudged to be in default in this action for want of a pleading herein; and it is further

ORDERED, ADJUDGED AND DECREED that plaintiff _____ shall have judgment against defendant _____

Monies due and owing: $
Filing Fee: $
Service of Process: $
Attorneys' Fee: $

TOTAL JUDGMENT $

This sum shall bear interest at the rate of _____% per annum from _____, until paid in full.

(*Insert the following information if the judgment pertains to RCW 46.29.270:)

This judgment provides for damages arising from the ownership, maintenance or use of a motor vehicle and this judgment is awarded pursuant to RCW 46.29.270.

DONE IN OPEN COURT this ____ day of _____ 20____.

_____
JUDGE/COMMISSIONER

Presented by:

_____
, WSBA#
Attorney for Plaintiff

[Effective September 1, 1999; amended effective September 1, 2009.]

LCRLJ 58.   ENTRY OF JUDGMENT

(a) Attorney's Fees—When feasible, upon conclusion of a trial in Kitsap County District Court, the amount of attorney's fees shall be set by the trial judge.

(b) Fee Schedule: When a party is entitled to an award of reasonable attorney's fees (in lieu of those statutory fees provided for by RCW 12.20.060), the fees provided in the following attorney's fee schedule shall be deemed reasonable in all default cases unless the party presents evidence of circumstances that convince the court that a larger or smaller fee should be awarded; provided, however, the court shall have authority to vary from this schedule on its own motion:

SCHEDULE FOR ATTORNEY FEES IN DEFAULT CASES

(Other than Statutory Attorney Fees)

Judgment Range (excluding costs)					Fees Awarded
$	50.00 to	$	2500.00	$	375.00
$	2500.01 to	$	10,000.00	$	750.00
$	10,000.01 to	$	35,000.00	$	1,000.00
$	35,000.01 to	$	50,000.00	$	1,250.00
$	50,000.01 to	$	75,000.00	$	1,500.00

Attorney's fee requests in excess of $1,500.00 must be itemized.

[Effective September 1, 1999; amended effective September 1, 2009; September 1, 2012.]

LCRLJ 59.   MOTION FOR RECONSIDERATION

(b) Motion for Reconsideration; Time for Motion; Contents of Motion—A motion for reconsideration shall be filed, noted, and served on all parties and the trial judge not later than ten (10) days after entry of the judgment, decree, or order. The motion shall be noted on the trial judge's calendar to be heard not sooner than thirty (30) but not later than forty (40) days after entry of the judgment, decree, or order, unless the court directs otherwise. The bench copy shall be delivered to the clerk of the District Court and shall contain the date the judgment, decree, or order was entered, and the names and addresses of opposing counsel.

(e) Hearing on Motion for Reconsideration. A motion for reconsideration shall be submitted on briefs and affidavits of the moving party only. No response shall be submitted by the opposing party, nor shall oral argument be heard, unless the court so directs. The court shall notify the parties, not later than ten (10) days before the hearing, whether: (1) the motion has been denied and the hearing stricken; or (2) oral argument and/or responsive pleadings will be allowed.

[Adopted effective September 1, 2009; Amended effective September 1, 2012.]

LCRLJ 64. GARNISHMENTS

(a) Exemption Claims and Hearings

(1) *Non–Responsive Exemption Claim.* An exemption claim in the form prescribed in RCW 6.27.140, submitted by a party shall be deemed non-responsive if:

(i) The form is submitted in blank and/or does not assert a claim of exemption;

(ii) Exemption(s) specific to bank accounts are claimed and the writ is not directed to a bank;

(iii) Exemption(s) specific to child support garnishments are claimed and the writ is not issued for enforcement of a child support judgment;

(iv) Exemption(s) specific to pension or retirement benefits are claimed and the writ is not directed to the garnished party's employer or other pension or retirement benefit provider; or

(v) Exemption(s) specific to other personal property are claimed and the writ is directed to a bank, employer or other holder of monetary amounts belonging to the garnished party.

(2) *Denial of Non–Responsive Exemption Claim.* A non-responsive exemption claim, as defined in this rule, shall be denied without a court hearing if the garnishing party files and serves a Notice of Non–Responsive Exemption Claim, substantially in the form prescribed in subsection (3) of this rule, within seven days of receipt of the exemption claim. If filing and/or service is had by mail, compliance with this rule shall be deemed complete if the described notice is posted in the U.S. Mail on or before the seventh day after the garnishing party receives the exemption claim.

(3) *Notice of Non–Responsive Exemption Claim Form.* The Notice of Non–Responsive Exemption Claim shall be substantially in the following form:

KITSAP COUNTY DISTRICT COURT, STATE OF WASHINGTON	Mailing Address: 614 Division Street, MS–25 Port Orchard, WA 98366 (360) 337–7109

_____, Plaintiff(s),	NO.
vs.	
_____, Defendant(s),	**NOTICE OF NON–RESPONSIVE EXEMPTION CLAIM**

_____,
Garnishee Defendant.

The Exemption Claim submitted by the opposing party (copy attached) does not, in fact, state any claim of exemption to the Writ of Garnishment issued previously herein and, thus, creates no issue of exemption to be determined by the court.

The purported Exemption Claim fails to create an issue needing judicial resolution for the following reason(s):

☐ The Exemption Claim has been submitted in blank and/or does not assert a claim of exemption;

☐ Exemption(s) specific to bank accounts are claimed and the Writ of Garnishment herein is not directed to a bank;

☐ Exemption(s) specific to child support garnishments are claimed and the Writ of Garnishment herein is not issued for enforcement of a judgment for child support;

☐ Exemption(s) specific to pension or retirement benefits are claimed and the Writ of Garnishment is not directed to the garnished party's employer or other pension or retirement benefit provider;

☐ Exemption(s) specific to other personal property are claimed and the Writ of Garnishment is directed to a bank, employer or other holder of monetary amounts owed to the garnished party.

NO COURT HEARING TO DETERMINE YOUR RIGHT TO HAVE ANY FUNDS OR PROPERTY EXEMPTED FROM GARNISHMENT IS CURRENTLY SCHEDULED.

If you believe you have valid exemption rights different from those claimed in your recently submitted Exemption Claim and you wish to have a court hearing to determine those exemption rights, you must submit another Exemption Claim, which specifies the exemption(s) to which you believe you are entitled. Another Exemption Claim form is being provided to you with this notice.

YOU MUST SUBMIT ANY ADDITIONAL EXEMPTION CLAIM ACCORDING TO THE DIRECTIONS CONTAINED IN THE EXEMPTION CLAIM AND WITHIN THE LATER OF:
(1) 28 DAYS FROM THE DATE ON THE WRIT OF GARNISHMENT; OR
(2) SEVEN DAYS FROM THE DATE THIS NOTICE IS POSTMARKED OR SERVED ON YOU.

DATE

SIGNATURE

Print or Type Name

Mailing Address

City   State   Zip

Phone Number

(b) Federal Government as Garnishee Defendant

(i) Whenever the federal government is named as a garnishee defendant, the clerk of the court shall, upon submittal of a notice in the appropriate form by the requesting party, issue a notice that directs the garnishee defendant to disburse any non-exempt earnings to the court.

(ii) Funds received by the clerk from a garnishee defendant may be deposited into the registry of the court or, in the case of negotiable instruments, may be retained in the court file. Upon presentation of an order directing the clerk to disburse the funds received, the clerk shall pay or endorse the funds over to the party entitled to same. Except for good cause shown, the funds shall not be paid or endorsed to the judgment creditor prior to the expiration of any minimum statutory period allowed to the judgment debtor for filing an exemption claim.

(iii) The party requesting the Writ of Garnishment shall supply a copy of the notice to the garnishee defendant with a pre-addressed envelope to the court, which has the cause number displayed thereon, and to the garnished party in the same manner as is permitted for service of the Writ of Garnishment.

(iv) The notice to the federal government employer shall be in substantially the following form:

| KITSAP COUNTY DISTRICT COURT, STATE OF WASHINGTON | Mailing Address: 614 Division Street, MS–25
Port Orchard, WA 98366
(360) 337-7109 |

NO.

Plaintiff(s),

vs.

NOTICE TO FEDERAL GOVERNMENT GARNISHEE DEFENDANT

Defendant(s),

Garnishee Defendant.

TO: THE GOVERNMENT OF THE UNITED STATES AND ANY DE-
      PARTMENT, AGENCY OR DIVISION THEREOF

You have been named as the garnishee defendant in the above-entitled cause. A Writ of Garnishment accompanies this Notice. The Writ of Garnishment directs you to hold the non-exempt earnings of the above-named defendant, but does not instruct you to disburse the funds you hold.

BY THIS NOTICE THE COURT DIRECTS YOU TO WITHHOLD ALL NON–EXEMPT EARNINGS AND DISBURSE THEM, IN ACCORDANCE WITH YOUR NORMAL PAY AND DISBURSE-MENT CYCLE, TO THE FOLLOWING:

Kitsap County District Court—Civil
614 Division Street, MS–25
Port Orchard, WA 98366

PLEASE REFERENCE THE DEFENDANT EMPLOYEE'S NAME AND THE ABOVE CASE NUMBER ON ALL DISBURSE-MENTS.

The following Writ also directs you to respond to the Writ within twenty (20) days, but you are allowed thirty (30) days to respond under federal law.

DATED this _____ day of _____ 20_____.

CLERK

[Effective September 1, 1999; amended effective September 1, 2009.]

LCRLJ 68.   OFFER OF JUDGMENT

(a) **Offers of Judgment**—Offers of Judgment shall be made in accordance with CRLJ 68.

(b) **Offers of Settlement: Form**—Offers of Settlement shall clearly state it is an Offer of Settlement and specifically refer to Chapter 4.84 of the Revised Code of Washington.

(1) *Method of Service*—Service shall be made as permitted in CRLJ 5;

(2) *Time of Service*—Service shall be made in accordance with RCW 4.84. 280.

(3) *Offer of Settlement*—An Offer of Settlement served on a party shall include a statement that failure or refusal to accept the offer may result in a reasonable attorney's fee being assessed at the time of judgment. Failure to include such wording may be grounds for the court to deny reasonable attorney's

fees. The notice shall be in substantially the following form:

This Offer of Settlement is being served upon you as permitted by RCW 4.84.250–290 not sooner than thirty (30) days after completion of the service and filing of the summons and complaint and at least ten (10) days prior to trial. If you wish to accept this offer, you must do so by written notice to the undersigned attorney or party and file a copy of your response with the court named above. The response must be served within ten (10) days and not later than five (5) days before trial. If you do not accept this settlement offer within the time specified herein and if the party making the offer obtains a result, exclusive of costs, that is (i) as much as or less than the amount offered to pay to you; or (ii) as much as or more than the amount offered to accept from you, then that person will be deemed the "prevailing party." In that event, you will be responsible for payment of the prevailing party's reasonable attorney's fees to be fixed by the court as part of the costs of this action, pursuant to RCW 4.84.250.

[Effective September 1, 1999.]

LCRLJ 69. EXECUTION

(c) Warrant Quashing Procedure/Supplemental Proceedings

(1) *Procedure*—In all cases where a bench warrant has been ordered to compel the attendance of a party who has failed to appear (hereinafter "the non-appearing party"), pursuant to court order for proceedings supplemental to and in aid of a judgment, and in proceedings on or in aid of execution, the non-appearing party shall be brought before the court at the regularly scheduled in custody time. Verbal or oral notice of the bench warrant hearing will be given to the opposing party or counsel one hour or more prior to the scheduled hearing. In the event the opposing party is unavailable for said hearing, the non-appearing party may be released by order of the District Court conditioned upon the party's appearance at a rescheduled hearing.

(2) *Bail*—Nothing in this rule will prevent a person arrested from posting bail for release on condition that they appear at court on a date certain.

[Effective September 1, 1999.]

V. LOCAL SPECIAL PROCEEDINGS

LSPLJ 1.1. NAME CHANGES

(a) Requirements—An applicant who applies to the court for a change of name, pursuant to RCW 4.24.130, must meet the following requirements:

(1) *Birth Certificate*—A certified copy of any minor applicant's birth certificate or suitable identification must be presented to the clerk for verification and copying.

(2) *Minors: Parental Consent*—All applicants under eighteen (18) years of age must be represented by a parent or legal guardian and <u>both</u> biological or legal parents or guardians must approve the change of name either by personal appearance or by verified affidavit, unless good cause is shown.

(3) *Separate Applications*—Each applicant requesting a change of name must present a separate Change of Name Order and pay a separate filing fee and recording fee.

(4) *Petitions*—Change of name petitions must be in substantially the same format as Attachments A and B.

(5) *Length of Order*—Change of name orders must be no longer than one page in length and in substantially the same format as Attachments C and D.

[Amended effective September 1, 2002.]

ATTACHMENT A. PETITION FOR CHANGE OF NAME (ADULT)

KITSAP COUNTY DISTRICT COURT,   Mailing Address: 614 Division Street, MS–25
STATE OF WASHINGTON   Port Orchard, WA 98366
                                                          (360) 337–7109

In the Matter of the Change of Name of: NO.

_____,   **PETITION FOR CHANGE OF NAME**
          Petitioner.   **(ADULT)**

_____

    COMES NOW _____ and petitions the above-entitled court for an order changing his/her name to _____ and shows the court as follows:

1.   Petitioner was born on the _____ day of _____ 20____, in _____ County, State of _____; is a resident of Kitsap County, Washington; and is a citizen/legal resident of the United States of America.

2.   Petitioner has been known as _____ for a period of _____ and requests this court to change his/her name to _____ for the reason that:

3. A.   This petition is not made to avoid creditors or for an illegal or fraudulent purpose, but for the bona fide purpose of changing the petitioner's name to the name by which he/she has been and prefers his/her name to be referred.

    B.   I am not under the jurisdiction of the department of corrections.

    C.   I am not required under RCW 9A.44.130 to register as a sex offender.

    WHEREFORE, petitioner prays that his/her name be changed by order of this court from:

_____to _____
and that the latter be in place of the former.

                                          _____
                                                    Petitioner

STATE OF WASHINGTON   )
) ss.
COUNTY OF KITSAP   )

_____, being first duly sworn, upon oath, deposes and says that: I am the petitioner above-named and I have read the foregoing Petition for change of Name, know the contents thereof and believe the same to be true.

                                          _____
                                                    Petitioner

Subscribed and sworn to before me this _____ day of _____ 20____.

                                          _____
                                          Notary Public in and for the State of _____
                                          Residing in _____ (city)
                                          My appointment expires: _____

[Amended effective May 31, 2000; September 1, 2009.]

ATTACHMENT B.   PETITION FOR CHANGE OF NAME (MINOR)

| KITSAP COUNTY DISTRICT COURT, STATE OF WASHINGTON | Mailing Address: 614 Division Street, MS–25 Port Orchard, WA 98366 (360) 337–7109 |

In the Matter of the Change of Name of: NO.

_____,   **PETITION FOR CHANGE OF NAME**
          Minor Child,   **(MINOR)**

_____,
          By Guardian (Petitioner).

_____

    COMES   NOW   _____   as   guardian   of   minor   child _____ and petitions the above-entitled court for an order changing minor child's name to _____ and shows the court as follows:

1.   Minor child was born on the ____ day of _____ 20____, in _____ County, State of _____; is a resident of Kitsap County, Washington; and is a citizen/legal resident of the United States of America.

2.   Minor child has been known as _____ for a period of _____ and requests this court to change his/her name to _____ for the reason that:

3.   This petition is in the best interest of the minor child and not made for any illegal or fraudulent purpose, but for the bona fide purpose of changing the minor child's name to the name by which he/she has been and prefers his/her name to be referred.

    WHEREFORE, petitioner prays that minor child's name be changed by order of this court from:

_____to _____
and that the latter be in place of the former.

_____
    Petitioner

STATE OF WASHINGTON	)
COUNTY OF KITSAP	) ss.
	)

_____, being first duly sworn, upon oath, deposes and says that: I am the petitioner above-named and I have read the foregoing Petition for change of Name, know the contents thereof and believe the same to be true.

_____
    Petitioner

Subscribed and sworn to before me this ____ day of _____ 20____.

_____
Notary Public in and for the State of _____
Residing in _____ (city)
My appointment expires: _____

[Amended effective May 31, 2000; September 1, 2009.]

ATTACHMENT C. ORDER CHANGING NAME (ADULT)

KITSAP COUNTY DISTRICT COURT, STATE OF WASHINGTON	Mailing Address: 614 Division Street, MS–25 Port Orchard, WA 98366 (360) 337–7109

In the Matter of the Change of Name of: NO.

_____,   **ORDER CHANGING NAME (ADULT)**
               Petitioner.

THIS MATTER coming on regularly for hearing before the undersigned Judge upon the petitioner's request for an order changing the petitioner's name from: _____to _____; it appearing to the court that the petitioner is a resident of Kitsap County, Washington; and the court finding that the statements made in the petition are true, that the change of name is not for any illegal or fraudulent purpose; now, therefore, it is hereby
ORDERED, ADJUDGED AND DECREED that the petition is approved and the petitioner's name is changed to: _____ for all intents and purposes.
DONE IN OPEN COURT this ____ day of _____ 20____.

Presented by:

_____   _____
PETITIONER   JUDGE

_____
Mailing Address

_____
City   State   Zip

Date of Birth: _____

[Amended effective September 1, 2009.]

ATTACHMENT D. ORDER CHANGING NAME (MINOR)

KITSAP COUNTY DISTRICT COURT,   Mailing Address: 614 Division Street, MS–25
STATE OF WASHINGTON   Port Orchard, WA 98366
                                                   (360) 337–7109

In the Matter of the Change of Name of: NO.

_____, **ORDER CHANGING NAME (MINOR)**
               Minor Child,

By: _____,
             Guardian/Petitioner.

     THIS MATTER coming on regularly for hearing before the undersigned Judge upon the petitioner's request for an order changing the minor's name from: _____to _____; it appearing to the court that the petitioner is guardian of the minor for purposes of this change of name, that the petitioner and minor child are residents of Kitsap County, Washington; and the court finding that the statements made in the petition are true, that the change of name is not for any illegal or fraudulent purpose and that it is in the best interest of the child, now, therefore, it is hereby

     ORDERED, ADJUDGED AND DECREED that the petition is approved and the minor child's name is changed to: _____ for all intents and purposes.

     DONE IN OPEN COURT this ____ day of _____ 20____.

Presented by:

_____   _____
PETITIONER/GUARDIAN   JUDGE

_____
Mailing Address

_____
City   State   Zip

Minor's Date of Birth: _____

[Effective September 1, 1999; amended effective January 7, 2000; September 1, 2009.]

LSPLJ 2.1. UNLAWFUL HARASS-MENT/DOMESTIC VIOLENCE PROCEEDINGS

(a) Jurisdiction—Applicants for protection orders for either domestic violence or unlawful harassment shall be screened by the Kitsap County Superior Court clerk by first filing a declaration. If the circumstances alleged in the declaration meet the criteria for domestic violence or involve unlawful harassment when the respondent is a juvenile, the Kitsap County Superior Court shall hear the case. If the circumstances alleged in the declaration meet the criteria of unlawful harassment only and the parties are not already involved in a pending dissolution, dependency or paternity proceeding (in which case the Kitsap County Superior Court will hear the case), then the Kitsap County District Court shall hear the case.

(b) (Deleted)

(b) Indigent Filing—Upon request of the applicant, the court shall assess the applicant's financial resources to determine if that individual may proceed in forma pauperis. For the purpose of determining whether grounds for waiver of the filing fee exist, the applicant must complete under oath and submit an Application for Waiver of Fees. No order authorizing waiver of the filing fee shall be issued unless the mandatory financial information is submitted to the court, except in circumstances as set forth in RCW 10.14.

[Effective September 1, 1999; amended effective September 1, 2002; September 1, 2009.]

MUNICIPAL COURTS
BAINBRIDGE ISLAND MUNICIPAL COURT LOCAL RULES

Including Amendments Received Through
August 15, 2015

Table of Rules

ADMINISTRATIVE RULES

LARLJ 7. STALKING PROTECTION ORDERS

Pursuant to RCW 7.92.050 the Bainbridge Island Municipal Court shall hear and adjudicate petitions for stalking protection orders filed under Chapter 7.92 RCW.

[Adopted on an emergency basis effective June 20, 2014; adopted on a permanent basis effective September 2, 2014.]

LARLJ 9(c)(5). DEFERRED PROSECUTION

(c) Quasi-Public Documents. The following are not subject to public review, but are subject to review by the defendant and the defendant's lawyer:

(5) *Deferred Prosecution.* Petition for deferred prosecution, statement of defendant for deferred prosecution, order granting deferred prosecution, evaluation and recommendation of chemical dependency agency, status reports from chemical dependency agency, status reports and/or recommendations from probation, any aspect of a court docket which reflects the contents of a report from a chemical dependency agency or probation, any aspect of a court docket which reflects the conditions set by the court as a result of an evaluation or status report submitted by a chemical dependency agency or probation.

[Adopted effective September 1, 2000.]

LARLJ 10. ANTI-HARASSMENT PROTECTION ORDER PROCEDURE

Pursuant to RCW 10.14.150, as amended by HB 1296 (2005), the Bainbridge Island Municipal Court shall hear and adjudicate petitions for anti-harassment protection orders filed under Chapter 10.14 RCW.

[Adopted effective September 1, 2005.]

INFRACTION RULES

LIRLJ 3.1. CONTESTED HEARINGS–PRELIMINARY PROCEEDINGS

(a) Subpoena. The defendant and the plaintiff may subpoena witnesses necessary for the presentation of their respective cases. Witnesses should be served at least 7 days before the hearing. The subpoena may be issued by a judge, a court commissioner, or by a party's lawyer. If the party's lawyer issues a subpoena, a copy shall be filed with the court. A subpoena may be directed for service within their jurisdiction to the sheriff of any county or any peace officer of any municipality in the state in which the witness may be or it may be served as provided in CR 45(c), or it may be served by first class mail, postage prepaid, sent to the witness' last known address.

Service by mail shall be deemed complete upon the third day following the day upon which the subpoena was placed in the mail. If the subpoena is for a witness outside the county, the judge must approve of the subpoena.

(i) If the defendant wishes to subpoena a witness, including a law enforcement officer, the defendant shall deliver in person to the court clerk at the Bainbridge Island Municipal Court office located at 10255 NE Valley Road, Bainbridge Island, Washington, or by mail to Bainbridge Island Municipal Court, P O Box 151, Rolling Bay, Washington, 98061, at least 28 days prior to the date of the hearing, a written request for the issuance of the subpoena and for instructions regarding service of the subpoena. The written request must state the case number, date and time of the hearing, the complete address of the location of the hearing and the name and address of the witness to be named in the subpoena. The defendant shall include a self-addressed, stamped envelope along with the written request.

Upon receipt of the written request, the court clerk shall prepare a subpoena and present it to the judge for signature. The clerk shall then mail the subpoena to the defendant in the self-addressed, stamped envelope, together with a return of service form, and instructions regarding service of the subpoena.

[Adopted effective September 1, 2000.]

LIRLJ 3.5. DECISIONS ON WRITTEN STATEMENTS

Mitigation hearings on alleged traffic and parking infractions may be held upon written statements pursuant to IRLJ 2.4(b)(4), IRLJ 2.6(c) and IRLJ 3.5.

[Adopted on an emergency basis effective June 20, 2014; adopted on a permanent basis effective September 2, 2014.]

LIRLJ 6.6. SPEED MEASURING DEVICE

Any certificate admissible under LIRLJ 6.6(b), and any other document relating to a Speed Measuring Device, can be filed with the clerk of the court and maintained by the court as a public record, and shall be available for inspection by the public. Copies shall be provided by the clerk's office on request. There shall be no charge for the copy if it relates to an infraction filed against the person making the request. Otherwise, there shall be a charge of 15 cents for each page copied. These records shall be available without a formal request for discovery. The court shall be entitled to take judicial notice of the fact that any document filed pursuant to this rule has been filed with the court. Documents filed pursuant to this rule shall not be suppressed as evidence merely because there is not prosecutor present to offer the document as an exhibit at the hearing. If the certificate or document is insufficient, then a motion to suppress the reading of the Speed Measuring Device shall be granted.

[Adopted effective September 1, 2000.]

CRIMINAL RULES

LCrRLJ 3.2.2. RELEASE OF ACCUSED

(a) Release of Accused; Domestic Violence.

(1) Any person arrested on Probable Cause (without a warrant) for an offense classified as a Domestic Violence offense under Chapter 10.99 of the Revised Code of Washington as the same exists or shall hereafter be amended shall be held in jail pending the defendant's first appearance.

(2) Notwithstanding paragraph (1), a person being held for a Domestic Violence offense classified as a felony may be released from custody prior to defendant's first appearance upon (a) the posting of $50,000 bail or bond; and (b) the person's affixing his or her signature at the appropriate location on a Pre–Arraignment Domestic Violence No Contact Order described in paragraph (4) prohibiting the arrested person from having contact with the protected person or from knowingly coming within, or knowingly remaining within, 500 feet of the protected person's residence, place of work, or school.

(3) Notwithstanding paragraph (1), a person being held for a Domestic Violence offense classified as a misdemeanor or gross misdemeanor may be released from custody prior to defendant's first appearance

upon (a) the posting of $5,000 bail or bond; and (b) the person's affixing his or her signature at the appropriate location on a Pre–Arraignment Domestic Violence No Contact Order described in paragraph (4) prohibiting the arrested person from having contact with the protected person or from knowingly coming within, or knowingly remaining within, 500 feet of the protected person's residence, place of work, or school.

(4) The following Pre–Arraignment Domestic Violence No Contact Order, or one that is substantially similar to it, is hereby approved for use under this rule.

PRE–ARRAIGNMENT DOMESTIC VIOLENCE NO CONTACT ORDER The contents of this item are only available on-line.

[Adopted effective September 1, 2003. Amended on an emergency basis effective June 20, 2014; amended on a permanent basis effective September 2, 2014.]

LCrRLJ 3.4. VIDEO CONFERENCES

Pursuant to CrRLJ 3.4 (d) (2) the Bainbridge Island Municipal Court authorizes the use of Video Conference Proceedings for all court proceedings.

[Adopted on an emergency basis effective June 20, 2014; adopted on a permanent basis effective September 2, 2014.]

BREMERTON MUNICIPAL COURT LOCAL RULES

Including Amendments Received Through
August 15, 2015

Table of Rules

CRIMINAL RULES FOR COURTS OF LIMITED JURISDICTION (LCrRLJ)

LCrRLJ 3.2.2.   RELEASE OF ACCUSED

(1) Any person arrested on Probable Cause (without a warrant) for an offense classified as a Domestic Violence offense under Chapter 10.99 of the Revised Code of Washington as the same exists or shall hereafter be amended shall be held in jail pending the defendant's first appearance.

(2) Notwithstanding paragraph (1), a person being held for a Domestic Violence offense classified as a felony may be released from custody prior to defendant's first appearance upon (a) the posting of $50,000 bail or bond; and (b) the person's affixing his or her signature at the appropriate location on a Pre-Arraignment Domestic Violence No Contact Order described in paragraph (4) prohibiting the arrested person from having contact with the protected person or from knowingly coming within, or knowingly remaining within, 500 feet of the protected person's residence, place of work, or school.

(3) Notwithstanding paragraph (1), a person being held for a Domestic Violence offense classified as a misdemeanor or gross misdemeanor may be released from custody prior to defendant's first appearance upon (a) the posting of $5,000 bail or bond; and (b) the person's affixing his or her signature at the appropriate location on a Pre-Arraignment Domestic Violence No Contact Order described in paragraph (4)

prohibiting the arrested person from having contact with the protected person or from knowingly coming within, or knowingly remaining within, 500 feet of the protected person's residence, place of work, or school.

(4) The following Pre-Arraignment Domestic Violence No Contact Order, or one that is substantially similar to it, is hereby approved for use under this rule.

[Adopted effective September 1, 2003.]

LCrRLJ 3.4(d)(2).   AGREEMENT

(2) **Agreement.**   Other trial court proceedings including the entry of a Statement of Defendant on Plea of Guilty as provided for by CrRLJ 4.2 may be conducted by video conference only by agreement of the parties, either in writing or on the record, and upon the approval of the trial court judge.

[Adopted effective September 1, 2005.]

LCrRLJ 4.   JURY COST

Jury costs in the amount of $125.00 may be imposed in addition to any other courts costs on all cases that have a jury confirmed and result in a conviction or plea of guilty. These costs shall be waived if the court is notified in sufficient time to cancel the services of the jury prior to the City incurring any costs.

[Adopted effective September 2, 2013.]

ADMINISTRATIVE RULES FOR COURTS OF LIMITED JURISDICTION (LARLJ)

LARLJ 10. ANTI-HARASSMENT PROTECTION ORDER PROCEDURE

Pursuant to RCW 10.14.150, as amended by HB 1296 (2005), the Bremerton Municipal Court may hear and adjudicate petitions for anti-harassment protection orders filed under Chapter 10.14 RCW.

[Adopted effective September 1, 2005.]

INFRACTION RULES FOR COURTS OF LIMITED JURISDICTION (LIRLJ)

LIRLJ 6.6(a)(1). SPEED MEASURING DEVICE EXPERT

(a)(1) All subpoenaed appearances for an electronic or laser speed measuring device (SMD) expert will be conducted telephonically.

[Adopted effective September 1, 2005.]

FORMS

PRE-ARRAIGNMENT DOMESTIC VIOLENCE NO CONTACT ORDER

☐ IN THE KITSAP COUNTY SUPERIOR COURT
☐ IN THE KITSAP COUNTY DISTRICT COURT
☐ IN THE BAINBRIDGE ISLAND MUNICIPAL COURT
☐ IN THE BREMERTON MUNICIPAL COURT
☐ IN THE PORT ORCHARD MUNICIPAL COURT
☐ IN THE POULSBO MUNICIPAL COURT

☐ STATE OF WASHINGTON,   )
☐ CITY OF BAINBRIDGE ISLAND,   )   LAW ENFORCEMENT NO. _____
☐ CITY OF BREMERTON,   )
☐ CITY OF PORT ORCHARD,   )   PRE-ARRAIGNMENT DOMESTIC VIOLENCE
☐ CITY OF POULSBO,   )   NO CONTACT ORDER
)
                    Plaintiff,   )   Date of Arrest: _____
)   Time of Arrest: _____
            v.   )   Arresting Officer/No.: _____
)   ☐ Bainbridge Island Police Department
_____ ,)   ☐ Bremerton Police Department
DOB: _____   )   ☐ Kitsap County Sheriff's Office
)   ☐ Port Orchard Police Department
                    Defendant.   )   ☐ Poulsbo Police Department
_____)   ☐ Washington State Patrol

THE COURT FINDS THAT the Defendant has been arrested for a domestic violence offense, and further finds that to prevent possible recurrence of violence, this Pre-Arraignment Domestic Violence No Contact Order shall be entered pursuant to chapter 10.99 RCW. The person(s) protected by this order are-

_____

(Protected person(s) name, or initials if a minor, and DOB)

IT IS ORDERED THAT Defendant is PROHIBITED from causing or attempting to cause physical harm, bodily injury, assault, including sexual assault, and from molesting, harassing, threatening, or stalking the protected person(s), and

IT IS ORDERED THAT Defendant is PROHIBITED from coming near and from having any contact whatsoever, in person or through others, by phone, mail or any means, directly or indirectly, except for mailing or service of process of court documents by a third party or contact by the Defendant's lawyer(s) with the protected person(s), and

IT IS ORDERED THAT Defendant is PROHIBITED from entering or knowingly coming within or knowingly remaining within 500 feet of the protected person's residence, school, or place of work, and

IT IS ORDERED THAT this Pre-Arraignment Domestic Violence No Contact Order expires seven days from the date below.

_____

WARNINGS TO THE DEFENDANT: Violation of the provisions of this order with actual notice of its terms is a criminal offense under chapter 26. 50 RCW, <u>and will subject a violator to arrest.</u> If the violation of this order involves travel across a state line or the boundary of a tribal jurisdiction, or involves conduct within the special maritime and territorial jurisdiction of the United States, which includes tribal lands, the you may be subject to criminal prosecution in federal court under 18 U.S.C. sections 2261, 2261A, or 2262.

Any assault, drive-by shooting, or reckless endangerment that is a violation of this order is a felony. Any conduct in violation of this order that is reckless and creates a substantial risk of death or serious physical injury to another person is a class C felony.

Effective immediately, and continuing as long as this order is in effect, you may not possess a firearm or ammunition. 18 U.S.C. section 922(g)(8). A violation of this federal firearms law carries a maximum possible penalty of 10 years in prison and a $250,000 fine. An exception exists for law enforcement officers and military personnel when carrying department/government–issued firearms. 18 U.S.C. section 925(a)(1). If you are convicted of an offense of domestic violence, you will be forbidden for life from possessing a firearm or ammunition. 18 U.S.C. section 922(g)(9); RCW 9.41.040.

YOU CAN BE ARRESTED EVEN IF ANY PERSON OR PERSONS PROTECTED BY THIS ORDER INVITES OR ALLOWS YOU TO VIOLATE THIS ORDER'S PROHIBITIONS.

You have the sole responsibility to avoid or refrain from violating the order's provisions. Only the court can change the order.

Pursuant to 18 U.S.C. section 2265, a court in any of the 50 states, the District of Columbia, Puerto Rico, any United States territory, and any tribal land within the United States shall accord full faith and credit to the order.

Dated: _____
Time: _____ [☐ AM] [☐ PM]

I agree to abide by the terms of this Pre–Arraignment Domestic Violence No Contact Order. I understand that the terms of any other court orders remain in effect notwithstanding the expiration of this order.

_____
DEFENDANT

SO ORDERED.

/s/ _____
JUDGE _____
Presiding Judge of the Port Orchard Municipal Court

Original(Prosecutor's Office)   Copy(Defendant)   Copy(Law Enforcement Agency)

[Adopted Effective July 1, 2003.]

LOCAL COURT RULES OF THE PORT ORCHARD MUNICIPAL COURT

Effective September 1, 2001

Including Amendments Received Through
August 15, 2015

Table of Rules

ADMINISTRATIVE RULES

LARLJ 9(c)(5). DEFERRED PROSECUTION

(c) Quasi–Public Documents. The following are not subject to public review, but are subject to review by the defendant and the defendant's attorney:

(5) *Deferred Prosecution.* Petition for deferred prosecution, statement of defendant for deferred prosecution, order granting deferred prosecution, evaluation and recommendation of chemical dependency agency, status reports from chemical dependency agency, status reports and/or recommendations from probation, any aspect of a court docket which reflects the contents of a report from a chemical dependency agency or probation, any aspect of a court docket which reflects the conditions set by the court as the result of an evaluation or status report submitted by a chemical dependency agency or probation.

[Adopted effective September 1, 2002.]

LARLJ 11. OATH OF INTERPRETER [RESCINDED]

[Adopted effective September 1, 2002. Rescinded effective September 2, 2013.]

LARLJ 14. COURT OFFICE HOURS OF OPERATION

The Port Orchard Municipal Court office shall be open to the public for business from 8:00 am to 12:00 pm and 1:00 pm to 4:30 pm Monday through Friday of each week except for holidays scheduled by Order of the State of Washington Supreme Court and closures ordered by the Port Orchard Municipal Court Presiding Judge when necessitated by inclement weather or other emergency.

[Adopted effective September 2, 2013.]

CRIMINAL RULES
LCrRLJ 3.2.2. RELEASE OF ACCUSED

(1) Any person arrested on Probable Cause (without a warrant) for an offense classified as a Domestic Violence offense under Chapter 10.99 of the Revised Code of Washington as the same exists or shall hereafter be amended shall be held in jail pending the defendant's first appearance.

(2) Notwithstanding paragraph (1), a person being held for a Domestic Violence offense classified as a felony may be released from custody prior to defendant's first appearance upon (a) the posting of $50,000 bail or bond; and (b) the person's affixing his or her signature at the appropriate location on a Pre–Arraignment Domestic Violence No Contact Order described in paragraph (4) prohibiting the arrested person from having contact with the protected person or from knowingly coming within, or knowingly remaining within, 500 feet of the protected person's residence, place of work, or school.

(3) Notwithstanding paragraph (1), a person being held for a Domestic Violence offense classified as a misdemeanor or gross misdemeanor may be released from custody prior to defendant's first appearance upon (a) the posting of $5,000 bail or bond; and (b) the person's affixing his or her signature at the appropriate location on a Pre–Arraignment Domestic Violence No Contact Order described in paragraph (4) prohibiting the arrested person from having contact with the protected person or from knowingly coming within, or knowingly remaining within, 500 feet of the protected person's residence, place of work, or school.

(4) The following Pre–Arraignment Domestic Violence No Contact Order, or one that is substantially similar to it, is hereby approved for use under this rule.

☐ IN THE KITSAP COUNTY SUPERIOR COURT
☐ IN THE KITSAP COUNTY DISTRICT COURT
☐ IN THE BAINBRIDGE ISLAND MUNICIPAL COURT
☐ IN THE BREMERTON MUNICIPAL COURT
☐ IN THE PORT ORCHARD MUNICIPAL COURT
☐ IN THE POULSBO MUNICIPAL COURT

☐ STATE OF WASHINGTON,	)
☐ CITY OF BAINBRIDGE ISLAND,	) LAW ENFORCEMENT NO. _____
☐ CITY OF BREMERTON,	)
☐ CITY OF PORT ORCHARD,	) PRE–ARRAIGNMENT DOMESTIC VIOLENCE
☐ CITY OF POULSBO,	) NO CONTACT ORDER
	)
Plaintiff,	) Date of Arrest: _____
	) Time of Arrest: _____
v.	) Arresting Officer/No.: _____
	) ☐ Bainbridge Island Police Department
_____,)	☐ Bremerton Police Department
DOB: _____	) ☐ Kitsap County Sheriff's Office
	) ☐ Port Orchard Police Department
Defendant.	) ☐ Poulsbo Police Department
_____)	☐ Washington State Patrol

THE COURT FINDS THAT the Defendant has been arrested for a domestic violence offense, and further finds that to prevent possible recurrence of violence, this Pre–Arraignment Domestic Violence No Contact Order shall be entered pursuant to chapter 10.99 RCW. The person(s) protected by this order are-

_____

(Protected person(s) name, or initials if a minor, and DOB)

IT IS ORDERED THAT Defendant is PROHIBITED from causing or attempting to cause physical harm, bodily injury, assault, including sexual assault, and from molesting, harassing, threatening, or stalking the protected person(s), and

IT IS ORDERED THAT Defendant is PROHIBITED from coming near and from having any contact whatsoever, in person or through others, by phone, mail or any means, directly or indirectly, except for mailing or service of process of court documents by a third party or contact by the Defendant's lawyer(s) with the protected person(s), and

IT IS ORDERED THAT Defendant is PROHIBITED from entering or knowingly coming within or knowingly remaining within 500 feet of the protected person's residence, school, or place of work, and

IT IS ORDERED THAT this Pre–Arraignment Domestic Violence No Contact Order expires seven days from the date below.

WARNINGS TO THE DEFENDANT: Violation of the provisions of this order with actual notice of its terms is a criminal offense under chapter 26. 50 RCW, and will subject a violator to arrest. If the violation of this order involves travel across a state line or the boundary of a tribal jurisdiction, or involves conduct within the special maritime and territorial jurisdiction of the United States, which includes tribal lands, the you may be subject to criminal prosecution in federal court under 18 U.S. C. sections 2261, 2261A, or 2262.

Any assault, drive-by shooting, or reckless endangerment that is a violation of this order is a felony. Any conduct in violation of this order that is reckless and creates a substantial risk of death or serious physical injury to another person is a class C felony.

Effective immediately, and continuing as long as this order is in effect, you may not possess a firearm or ammunition. 18 U.S.C. section 922(g)(8). A violation of this federal firearms law carries a maximum possible penalty of 10 years in prison and a $250,000 fine. An exception exists for law enforcement officers and military personnel when carrying department/government–issued firearms. 18 U.S.C. section 925(a)(1). If you are convicted of an offense of domestic violence, you will be forbidden for life from possessing a firearm or ammunition. 18 U.S.C. section 922(g)(9); RCW 9.41.040.

YOU CAN BE ARRESTED EVEN IF ANY PERSON OR PERSONS PROTECTED BY THIS ORDER INVITES OR ALLOWS YOU TO VIOLATE THIS ORDER'S PROHIBITIONS.

You have the sole responsibility to avoid or refrain from violating the order's provisions. Only the court can change the order.

Pursuant to 18 U.S.C. section 2265, a court in any of the 50 states, the District of Columbia, Puerto Rico, any United States territory, and any tribal land within the United States shall accord full faith and credit to the order.

Dated: _____
Time: _____ [☐ AM] [☐ PM]

I agree to abide by the terms of this Pre–Arraignment Domestic Violence No Contact Order. I understand that the terms of any other court orders remain in effect notwithstanding the expiration of this order.

_____
DEFENDANT

SO ORDERED.

/s/ _____
JUDGE _____
Presiding Judge of the Port Orchard Municipal Court

Original(Prosecutor's Office)   Copy(Defendant)   Copy(Law Enforcement Agency)

[Adopted Effective July 1, 2003.]

LCrRLJ 3.4(d)(2)(a). PRESENCE OF THE DEFENDANT

(a) Agreeing to Proceed by Video Conference. Whenever parties to a criminal proceeding agree that such proceedings including entry of a Statement of Defendant on Plea of Guilty as provided for by CrRLJ 4.2 may be conducted by video conference as is provided under CrRLJ 3.4(d)(2), such agreement shall be acknowledged either on the record or in writing by execution of a form substantially following the form set forth below.

PORT ORCHARD MUNICIPAL COURT, KITSAP COUNTY, WASHINGTON	216 Prospect Street Port Orchard, WA 98366 (360) 876–1701

CITY OF PORT ORCHARD,
                              Plaintiff,

Cause Number(s): _____
_____

v.

_____,
                     Defendant.

AGREEMENT TO PROCEED BY VIDEO CONFERENCE

PURSUANT TO CrRLJ 3.4(d)(2), the undersigned parties acknowledge that today's trial court proceedings are being conducted by video conference and hereby:

☐ **AGREE** that today's proceedings may be conducted by video conference

☐ **DO NOT AGREE** that today's proceedings may be conducted by video conference

DATED this ____ day of _____ 20 ___.

_____
DEFENDANT

_____
DEFENSE ATTORNEY

_____
CITY ATTORNEY

[Adopted effective September 1, 2002.]

LCrRLJ 4.5.   PRE–TRIAL HEARING

(a) Confirmation of Trial. A case set for trial shall be set for either bench or jury trial at the pretrial hearing. To ensure the presence of a jury and/or witnesses, a party must confirm the trial with the court clerk at (360) 876–1701 no later than 1:30 p.m. the Friday prior to the date set for trial. If the Friday falls on a court holiday, the party must confirm with the court no later than 1:30 p.m. one court day prior to the Friday prior to the date set for trial. If a party wishes to change an election of a jury trial to a bench trial on the date set for jury trial, a party shall notify the court of the election change no later than at confirmation of the trial.

[Adopted effective September 1, 2001.]

INFRACTION RULES

LIRLJ 2.4(b).   RESPONSE TO NOTICE

(5) The procedure authorized in IRLJ 2.4(b)(4) for explaining mitigating circumstances is adopted by this Court.

[Adopted effective September 1, 2005; amended effective September 1, 2007.]

LIRLJ 3.1.   CONTESTED HEARINGS– PRELIMINARY PROCEEDINGS

(e) Preparing Subpoena by the Court Clerk. If the defendant wishes to subpoena a witness, including a law enforcement officer, the defendant shall deliver to the court clerk at the Port Orchard Municipal Court office located at 216 Prospect Street, Port Orchard, Washington 98366, in person or by mail at least 28 days prior to the date of the hearing, a written request for the issuance of the subpoena and for instructions regarding service of the subpoena. The written request must state the case number, date and time of the hearing, the complete address of the location of the hearing, and the name and address of the witness to be named in the subpoena. The defendant shall also include a self-addressed, stamped envelope along with the written request.

Upon receipt of the written request, the court clerk shall prepare a subpoena and present it to the judge for signature. The clerk shall then mail the subpoena along with a return of service form to the defendant in the self-addressed, stamped envelope.

[Adopted effective September 1, 2001; amended effective September 1, 2007.]

LIRLJ 3.3(b). REPRESENTATION BY LAWYER

(1) At a contested hearing, when the respondent is represented by a lawyer, the plaintiff shall be represented by a lawyer representative of the prosecuting authority.

(2) No attorney shall appear for a respondent without first filing a Notice of Appearance no less than seven (7) days prior to any scheduled hearing. Upon the filing of a Notice of Appearance, the Court shall reset the contested hearing to the appropriate calendar. Failure to timely submit a notice of appearance may result in the contested hearing being held beyond the 120 days required by IRLJ 2.6(a).

[Adopted effective September 1, 2007.]

LIRLJ 3.4. HEARING ON MITIGATING CIRCUMSTANCES

(d) **Request for Penalty Reduction on Written Statement.** If a defendant submits a timely request for a hearing to mitigate an infraction, the defendant may elect to seek a reduction of the infraction penalty by written statement pursuant to the provisions of IRLJ 2.4(b)(4), IRLJ 3.5(b), LIRLJ 2.4(b)(5), LIRLJ 3.5(c).

(1) A defendant electing to proceed for a penalty reduction by written statement must notify the court in writing within 30 days prior to the date set for the in-court mitigation hearing to request the appropriate paperwork.

(2) The completed form to request a reduction by written statement shall be filed with the court no later than fourteen (14) days prior to the date set for the in-court mitigation hearing.

(3) A defendant who elects to mitigate an infraction by written statement shall be deemed to have waived an in-court hearing to mitigate the infraction in person.

(4) A written statement submitted pursuant to this rule shall be executed in compliance with RCW 9A.72.085.

[Adopted effective September 1, 2005; amended effective September 1, 2007.]

LIRLJ 3.5. DECISION ON WRITTEN STATEMENTS (LOCAL OPTION)

(c) **Adoption of Procedure.** The procedure authorized in IRLJ 3.5(b) is adopted by this Court.

[Adopted effective September 1, 2005; amended effective September 1, 2007.]

LIRLJ 6.2(d)(5). PENALTY SCHEDULE

(d)(5) **Unscheduled Infractions.** The base penalty for any unscheduled infraction not listed in this rule, sections (1) through (4), shall be established by local ordinance adopted by the City of Port Orchard and set forth in the Port Orchard Municipal Code (POMC) or by state statute as adopted by the Washington State Legislature and set forth in the Revised Code of Washington (RCW).

[Adopted effective September 1, 2011.]

LIRLJ 6.6. SPEED MEASURING DEVICE: DESIGN AND CONSTRUCTION CERTIFICATION

(e) **Appearance of Speed Measuring Device Expert.** Any request to produce a speed measuring device expert must be filed in accordance with IRLJ 6.6(b). The court may allow the speed measuring device expert to testify from a location other than the courtroom, via speakerphone or other electronic means acceptable to the court.

[Adopted effective September 1, 2007.]

POULSBO MUNICIPAL COURT LOCAL RULES

Including Amendments Received Through
August 15, 2015

Table of Rules

RULE 1.   [NEXT JUDICIAL DAY]

The "next judicial day" as referred to in RCW 46.61.50571 means the next day upon which Court is held in the Municipal Court of the City of Poulsbo, Washington.

[Adopted effective September 1, 1999.]

INFRACTION RULES

LIRLJ 3.1.   CONTESTED HEARINGS— COSTS AND WITNESS FEES

Costs and Witness Fees. Each party is responsible for costs incurred by that party as set forth in RCW 46.63.151. In cases where a party requests a witness to be subpoenaed, the party requesting the witness shall pay the witness fees and mileage expenses due that witness.

[Adopted effective September 1, 2007.]

LIRLJ 3.5.   DECISIONS ON WRITTEN STATEMENTS

Mitigation and contested hearings on alleged traffic infractions may be held upon written statements pursuant to IRLJ 2.4(b)(4), IRLJ 2.6(c) and IRLJ 3.5.

[Adopted effective September 1, 2007.]

LIRLJ 6.6.   CONTESTED HEARINGS— SPEED MEASURING DEVICE EXPERT

1. **Speed Measuring Device Expert:** A request for a Speed Measuring Device expert may be treated by the Court as a request for a continuance to the next date on which the prosecuting attorney has scheduled the appearance of the SMD Expert.

2. When any speed measuring device expert is required to testify in a contested infraction hearing, the expert may testify by telephone, unless otherwise ordered by the Court.

[Adopted effective September 1, 2007.]

ADMINISTRATIVE RULES

LARLJ 7.   STALKING PROTECTION ORDERS

Pursuant to RCW 7.92.050 the Poulsbo Municipal Court shall hear and adjudicate petitions for stalking protection orders filed under Chapter 7.92 RCW.

[Adopted on an emergency basis, effective March 31, 2014.]

LARLJ 10.   ANTI–HARASSMENT PROTECTION ORDERS

Pursuant to RCW 10.14.150 the Poulsbo Municipal Court shall hear and adjudicate petitions for anti-harassment protection orders filed under Chapter 10.14 RCW.

[Adopted on an emergency basis, effective March 31, 2014.]

CRIMINAL RULES
LCrRLJ 3.2.2. RELEASE OF ACCUSED

(a) Release of Accused; Domestic Violence.

(1) Any person arrested on Probable Cause (without a warrant) for an offense classified as a Domestic Violence offense under Chapter 10.99 of the Revised Code of Washington as the same exists or shall hereafter be amended shall be held in jail pending the defendant's first appearance.

(2) Notwithstanding paragraph (1), a person being held for a Domestic Violence offense classified as a felony may be released from custody prior to defendant's first appearance upon (a) the posting of $50,000 bail or bond; and (b) the person's affixing his or her signature at the appropriate location on a Pre–Arraignment Domestic Violence No Contact Order described in paragraph (4) prohibiting the arrested person from having contact with the protected person or from knowingly coming within, or knowingly remaining within, 500 feet of the protected person's residence, place of work, or school.

(3) Notwithstanding paragraph (1), a person being held for a Domestic Violence offense classified as a misdemeanor or gross misdemeanor may be released from custody prior to defendant's first appearance upon (a) the posting of $5,000 bail or bond; and (b) the person's affixing his or her signature at the appropriate location on a Pre–Arraignment Domestic Violence No Contact Order described in paragraph (4) prohibiting the arrested person from having contact with the protected person or from knowingly coming within, or knowingly remaining within, 500 feet of the protected person's residence, place of work, or school.

(4) The following Pre–Arraignment Domestic Violence No Contact Order, or one that is substantially similar to it, is hereby approved for use under this rule.

Pre-Arraignment Domestic Violence No Contact Order

☐ IN THE KITSAP COUNTY SUPERIOR COURT
☐ IN THE KITSAP COUNTY DISTRICT COURT
☐ IN THE BAINBRIDGE ISLAND MUNICIPAL COURT
☐ IN THE BREMERTON MUNICIPAL COURT
☐ IN THE PORT ORCHARD MUNICIPAL COURT
☐ IN THE POULSBO MUNICIPAL COURT

☐ STATE OF WASHINGTON,)
☐ CITY OF BAINBRIDGE ISLAND,)   LAW ENFORCEMENT NO. _____
☐ CITY OF BREMERTON,)
☐ CITY OF PORT ORCHARD,)   **PRE–ARRAIGNMENT DOMESTIC VIOLENCE**
☐ CITY OF POULSBO,)   **NO CONTACT ORDER**
)   (ORNC)
       Plaintiff,)   Date of Arrest: _____
)   Time of Arrest: _____
       v.   )   Arresting Officer/No.: _____
)   ☐ Bainbridge Island Police Department
_____,)   ☐ Bremerton Police Department
)   ☐ Kitsap County Sheriff's Office
DOB: _____)   ☐ Port Orchard Police Department
)   ☐ Poulsbo Police Department
       Defendant.)   ☐ Washington State Patrol
_____)

THE COURT FINDS THAT the Defendant has been arrested for a domestic violence offense, and further finds that to prevent possible recurrence of violence, this Pre–Arraignment Domestic Violence No Contact Order shall be entered pursuant to chapter 10.99 RCW. The person(s) protected by this order are—

_____

(Protected person(s) name, or initials if a minor, and DOB)

IT IS ORDERED THAT Defendant is PROHIBITED from causing or attempting to cause physical harm, bodily injury, assault, including sexual assault, and from molesting, harassing, threatening, or stalking the protected person(s), and

IT IS ORDERED THAT Defendant is PROHIBITED from coming near and from having any contact whatsoever, in person or through others, by phone, mail or any means, directly or indirectly, except for mailing or service of process of court documents by a third party or contact by the Defendant's lawyer(s) with the protected person(s), and

IT IS ORDERED THAT Defendant is PROHIBITED from entering or knowingly coming within or knowingly remaining within 500 feet of the protected person's residence, school, or place of work, and

IT IS ORDERED THAT this Pre–Arraignment Domestic Violence No Contact Order expires seven days from the date below.

WARNINGS TO THE DEFENDANT: Violation of the provisions of this order with actual notice of its terms is a criminal offense under chapter 26. 50 RCW, and will subject a violator to arrest. If the violation of this order involves travel across a state line or the boundary of a tribal jurisdiction, or involves conduct within the special maritime and territorial jurisdiction of the United States, which includes tribal lands, the you may be subject to criminal prosecution in federal court under 18 U.S.C. sections 2261, 2261A, or 2262.

Any assault, drive-by shooting, or reckless endangerment that is a violation of this order is a felony. Any conduct in violation of this order that is reckless and creates a substantial risk of death or serious physical injury to another person is a class C felony.

Effective immediately, and continuing as long as this order is in effect, you may not possess a firearm or ammunition. 18 U.S.C. section 922(g)(8). A violation of this federal firearms law carries a maximum possible penalty of 10 years in prison and a $250,000 fine. An exception exists for law enforcement officers and military personnel when carrying department/government–issued firearms. 18 U.S.C. section 925(a)(1). If you are convicted of an offense of domestic violence, you will be forbidden for life from possessing a firearm or ammunition. 18 U.S.C. section 922(g)(9); RCW 9.41.040.

YOU CAN BE ARRESTED EVEN IF ANY PERSON OR PERSONS
PROTECTED BY THIS ORDER INVITES OR ALLOWS YOU TO
VIOLATE THIS ORDER'S PROHIBITIONS.

You have the sole responsibility to avoid or refrain from violating the order's provisions. Only the court can change the order.

Pursuant to 18 U.S.C. section 2265, a court in any of the 50 states, the District of Columbia, Puerto Rico, any United States territory, and any tribal land within the United States shall accord full faith and credit to the order.

Dated: _____
Time: _____ [☐ AM] [☐ PM]

I agree to abide by the terms of this Pre–Arraignment Domestic Violence No Contact Order. I understand that the terms of any other court orders remain in effect notwithstanding the expiration of this order.

_____
DEFENDANT

SO ORDERED.

/s/ _____
JUDGE _____

Presiding Judge of the _____ Court

Original(Prosecutor's Office)   Copy(Defendant)   Copy(Law Enforcement Agency)

[Adopted effective September 1, 2003.]

KITTITAS COUNTY

Table of Courts

Superior Court

Local Rules of the Superior Court of Washington for Kittitas County.

District Courts

Lower Kittitas County District Court Local Rules.
Local Court Rules of the Upper District Court for Kittitas County.

Municipal Courts

Cle Elum Municipal Court.
Kittitas Municipal Court—[No Local Rules].
Roslyn Municipal Court.

SUPERIOR COURT

LOCAL RULES OF THE SUPERIOR COURT OF WASHINGTON FOR KITTITAS COUNTY

Including Amendments Received Through
August 15, 2015

Table of Rules

I. GENERAL LOCAL RULES (GLR)

GLR 1. APPLICABILITY IN GENERAL

A. Authority. These rules are made pursuant to CR 83.

B. Suspension of Rules. The court may modify or suspend any of these Rules, in any given case, upon good cause being shown therefore or upon the court's own motion.

[Adopted effective September 1, 2004; amended effective September 1, 2011.]

GLR 2. SUPERIOR COURT RULE MAKING PROCEDURE

A. Initiation of Rules Changes. All suggestions for rules changes shall be sent to the members of the Kittitas County Bar Association and to other interested parties as determined by the presiding judge.

B. Consideration of Proposed Rules Changes. All suggested rules changes shall be considered by the judges of the Superior Court of Kittitas County in consultation with the Kittitas County Bar Association. If a proposed rule or rule change is approved, it will be published for comment as follows:

(1) By posting the proposed rule(s) on the bulletin board of the Office of the Clerk of the Court and of the Court Administrator's office.

(2) By transmitting the proposed rule(s) to the Kittitas County Bar Association, which shall publish the same to its members.

C. Consideration of Comments. All comments on proposed rules should be directed to the presiding judge. The court shall consider all comments, criticisms, objections and suggestions submitted within 30 days of the date for publishing for comment.

D. Final Adoption, Publication, and Effective Date. After the comment period, the court shall publish the rule changes as finally approved.

E. Limitation of Amendments; Exceptions. The court shall make rule changes only in accordance with this rule, except in cases of emergency or other circumstances justifying immediate changes.

[Adopted effective September 1, 2004; amended effective September 1, 2011.]

GLR 3. INDIGENT DEFENSE

By this rule the Kittitas County Superior court hereby adopts standards for the delivery of public defender services consistent with RCW 10.101.030 and Kittitas County Code 2.09 *et. seq.*

[Adopted effective September 1, 2004; amended effective September 1, 2011.]

II. LOCAL CIVIL RULES (LCR)

LCR 7. MOTIONS PRACTICE

(1) Filing and Noting Motion for Hearing. A note for motion substantially in the form found in Exhibit C shall be filed with the Clerk at the time the motion is filed and served on the parties in accordance with CR 6(d). To assure that timely and complete delivery of the court file to the court, notes for motion calendars should be filed with the Clerk's office by noon on the Thursday preceding the Monday calendar on which hearing is requested.

(2) Failure of Party to Appear. If no one appears in opposition to a duly noted motion, the court may grant the relief requested upon proper proof of notice. If no one appears for a motion, it will be stricken.

(3) Continuances of Motions. Counsel, by agreement, may continue any motion by executing a stipulation of continuance or by orally stipulating on the record in court to a continuance. Continuances shall not be granted by telephone. Upon agreement of counsel to continue or strike a hearing, counsel for the moving party shall advise the court of the agreement to continue or strike the hearing at the time of the agreement and no later than one day prior to the hearing.

(4) Time Allowed for Argument. Each side shall be limited to 10 minutes unless granted leave by the court. Parties anticipating argument that will require longer than 20 minutes total time shall obtain a special hearing date and time from the Court Administrator.

(5) Hearing of Ex Parte Matters.

(a) *Scope.* This rule applies to all temporary restraining orders, orders to show cause, and all other *ex parte* matters.

(b) *Notice to Opposing Counsel.* Unless notice is specifically excluded by statute, no *ex parte* order shall be presented without notice to opposing counsel. If counsel for any party has appeared either formally or informally, notice is required. If necessary, notice may be by telephone.

(c) *Court File.* Counsel is required to obtain the court file when presenting *ex parte* matters, except for agreed orders other than domestic relations decrees.

(6) Working Copies Are Required.

(a) When filing a motion or a response, provide a conformed working copy to the judge. Designate the judicial department and the date and time of your hearing on your copies. Working copies may not be emailed or faxed to the court.

(b) Any pleading filed with the Clerk of Court requiring affirmative action by the Clerk shall indicate the need for said action by placing under the caption of the pleading "(Clerk's Action Required.)"

[Adopted effective September 1, 2004; amended effective September 1, 2011; September 1, 2015.]

LCR 40.   TRIAL SETTING

A. Trial Setting. Civil cases may be noted for trial setting after the issues are joined. Criminal cases will be assigned a trial date at the time of arraignment.

1. *Note for Trial Setting.*

a. Anyone desiring to bring any issue to trial shall note the matter on the trial setting calendar. (Use Exhibit A.)

b. Counsel are <u>required</u> to ascertain from the Court Administrator the available trial date(s).

c. Counsel are also <u>required</u> to inform the Court Administrator of their available and unavailable dates.

d. Counsel must estimate the length of time needed for trial. Because the court trial calendar is preset, cases will not be permitted to continue beyond the time estimated for trial. If the non-setting parties do not agree with the estimate in the note up notice, they must file their own estimate before the trial setting date. Estimates shall include the total time for trial, not just one side.

2. *Presence of Counsel.* All trial dates will be assigned by the Court Administrator or the Court. If counsel previously have provided the Court Administrator with available and unavailable dates as required above and are otherwise agreeable to a setting on any particular date, then counsel's presence at the trial setting is not required.

3. *Visiting Judge Required.* The Court shall be notified at the time of trial setting if an attorney is a party or a witness in any matter before the Court or of any other matter needing a visiting judge. If such notification is not provided, the case will lose any priority it may otherwise have had.

4. *Continuances.* Continuances of trial may not be granted by the court except for good cause shown after hearing on the motion filed by the party seeking the continuance, or by motion of the court. In the event good cause is shown and the court grants a motion for continuance, the case will be rescheduled by the Court Administrator and given the priority of a new case (in other words, the case loses any priority it had). In the event the court strikes the trial date on its own motion due to calendar congestion, the case shall receive a priority trial setting.

B. Special Settings. Any civil motions or other matters requiring a special setting will be set by the Court Administrator.

C. Mental Illness Hearings. Mental illness hearings will be set for hearing by the Court Administrator.

D. Change of Judge; Affidavit of Prejudice. Cases will be assigned to a judicial department under the direction of the presiding judge for the county. In all cases, parties shall be notified of the assignment upon the issuance of the Scheduling Order. That assignment shall serve as a pre-assignment/assignment for purposes of change of judge pursuant to CrR 8.9, CR 40, and RALJ 3.2(c). The presiding judge shall notify the local bar when changes in judicial assignments occur.

E. Notice to Court of Calendar and Jury Trial Changes. Whenever a cause has been set for trial and thereafter is settled or will not be tried for any reason, or if a jury is thereafter waived, notice shall immediately be given to the Court Administrator so the case may be removed from the court's calendar.

F. Domestic Relations–Case Management.

1. *Settlement Conference.* At the time the Court Administrator sets the case for trial, the Administrator shall also set a date and time for a settlement conference which shall not be earlier than 10 days from the date of notification and not later than 10 days prior to trial. After the settlement conference has been set, the parties, through written agreement or the court, after a motion made by one of the parties, may strike the settlement conference.

2. *Support Modifications.* All support modifications will be noted for hearing on the regular motion day. The support modification hearing will be heard by affidavit only, 10 minutes per side for argument. If a party desires live testimony, the request shall be made by motion and allowed by the court in its discretion. After the affidavits and/or financial information have been provided in accordance with the state statutes on child support modification, either party may note the matter for hearing on the regular motion docket. Settlement conferences are not required for support modification.

[Adopted effective September 1, 2011. Amended effective September 1, 2015.]

LCR 47.   PEREMPTORY CHALLENGES

Unless good cause is show, all peremptory challenges shall be exercised in open Court at the side bar by marking the challenged juror's name on a form to be provided by the Court.

[Adopted effective September 1, 2011.]

LCR 54.   ATTORNEY FEES, TERMS AND IMPOSITION OF COSTS

If attorney fees or costs have been awarded, the prevailing party must itemize via affidavit the time expended, services rendered, or other detailed bases for the fees and costs requested and attach a copy thereof to the proposed order granting fees and costs.

[Adopted effective September 1, 2011.]

LCR 56. SUMMARY JUDGMENTS

Summary judgments require special settings and should be noted to be heard before the judge who is assigned to hear the trial. Motions and affidavits, and reply and response affidavits, must be filed in the manner and within the time limitations of CR 56. Working copies shall be provided to the judge. On any motion for summary judgment, counsel for movant is required to call the Court Administrator two business days prior to the date set for hearing to confirm that the motion will be heard.

[Adopted effective September 1, 2011. Amended effective September 1, 2015.]

LCR 59. MOTION FOR NEW TRIAL, RE-CONSIDERATION, AND AMEND-MENT OF JUDGMENTS

A motion for new trial, reconsideration, or amendment/alteration of judgment shall be submitted on briefs and affidavits of the moving party only, without response or oral argument to the trial judge by the opposing party. The trial judge shall, within 10 days, either deny the motion or advise both counsel of desired further proceedings pursuant to CR 59 and this rule. *A motion under this rule shall be filed with the Clerk and a working copy shall be served on the trial judge at the Superior Court office at the time of the filing of the motion.* A copy shall also be served on opposing counsel.

[Adopted effective September 1, 2011.]

LCR 77. SESSIONS/COURT HOURS, HEARING DAYS

(1) There shall be one continuous session of court from January 1 through December 31 of each year. Court will be in session, unless otherwise ordered, on all judicial days, except Saturday and Sunday. Court hours will be from 9:00 a.m. to 12:00 p.m. and from 1:30 p.m. to 4:30 p.m.

(2) Hearing times and days as well as Department assignments are subject to change to accommodate holidays, availability of judges and courtrooms, judicial conflicts and calendar size, but shall generally be as follows:

A. *Civil Matters.* Probate, guardianship and civil motions will be heard on Monday beginning at 9:00 a.m.

B. *Criminal Matters.* Arraignments, omnibus hearings, sentencing pursuant to guilty pleas, probation violations, bail hearings, and preliminary appearances will be heard on Mondays at 1:30 p.m. Pretrial hearings pursuant to CrR 3.5 and 3.6 will be heard on Fridays at 9:00 a.m. Status conferences will be heard on Fridays at 9:00 a.m. Criminal trials will be held Tuesday through Friday and will be set by the court at the time of arraignment.

C. *Ex Parte Matters.* *Ex parte* matters shall be heard Monday through Friday 9:00 a.m. to 12:00 p.m. and from 1:30 p.m. to 4:30 p.m. Contact Court Administrator to confirm availability of judge.

D. *Domestic Relation Matters.*

(1) Settlement Conferences. Settlement Conferences will be heard on Friday beginning at 1:30 p.m.

(2) Show Cause and Temporary Relief. Show cause hearings and motions for temporary relief, including URESA contempt hearings will be heard on Mondays at 9:00 a.m.

(3) Uncontested Dissolutions. Uncontested dissolutions in which one or both parties are represented by counsel will be heard at 9:00 a.m. on Mondays. Uncontested dissolutions in which both parties are not represented by counsel will be heard on Mondays at 10:30 a.m. Regardless of representation, jurisdictional testimony may be submitted by affidavit and is encouraged.

E. *Protection Orders.* Domestic Violence and Protection Orders not otherwise filed under a related case between the parties shall be heard on Mondays at 10:30 a.m.

F. *Adoptions.* Any adoptions requiring notice, including pro se adoptions, will be heard on Monday at 8:45 a.m.

G. *Civil Trial Settings.* Trial setting dockets shall be every Monday at 9:00 a.m. (See also LCR 6.)

H. *Juvenile Matters.*

(1) Offenders. Arraignments, pleas, dispositions and probation violations will be heard on Monday at 3:00 p.m. Offender trials will be heard on Thursdays and scheduled by the court at the time of arraignment.

(2) Dependencies. Stipulated fact-finding hearings and review hearings will be heard on the 2nd and 4th Tuesdays of each month. Contested fact-finding hearings and shelter care hearings will be scheduled by the Court Administrator.

(3) Truancy/At–Risk Youth. Adequate cause, show cause, review hearings and fact-findings will be heard on Monday afternoons at 4:00 p.m.

[Adopted effective September 1, 2011. Amended effective September 1, 2015.]

LCR 79. BOOKS AND RECORDS

A. **Files.** No file shall be taken from the clerk's custody, except to the courtroom or to a judicial officer or official reporter unless written authority has first been obtained. All files which are in the hands of a person for the purposes of any trial or hearing must be returned to the Clerk at the close thereof. The Clerk may grant written authority to an applicant to withdraw one or more files for a period not exceeding two days.

B. Verbatim Report of Proceedings. Verbatim reports of proceedings, after having been settled and signed, shall not be withdrawn from the Clerk's office except by order of the court.

C. Disposition of Exhibits. After final disposition of a civil cause, the court may order the clerk to dispose of physical evidence which cannot be retained in the case file provided that all parties of record are given 30 days written notice of any such hearing.

D. Return of Administrative Record. When a case for review of an administrative record is completed, the clerk shall return the administrative record to the officer or agency certifying the same to the court. The clerk shall treat the administrative record as an exhibit.

[Adopted effective September 1, 2011. Amended effective September 1, 2015.]

LCR 80.   COURT REPORTERS

A court reporter will not be provided for any matter heard in Kittitas County Superior Court. All matters will be digitally audio recorded. If any party wishes any matter to be reported by a court reporter, that party is responsible to provide a court reporter.

[Adopted effective September 1, 2015.]

II. SPECIAL PROCEEDINGS RULES (KCLSPR)

SPR 94.04.   FAMILY LAW ACTIONS

A. Ex Parte Restraining Orders. Personal appearance of a party may be required upon the judge's request if a party requests an *ex parte* order be entered immediately restraining the other party from the family home.

B. Temporary Orders. The initial hearing for temporary relief shall be heard on affidavits or sworn declarations only unless, after appropriate motion, the court allows live testimony. Working copies shall be provided to the Court. The following shall apply to all contested hearings in which temporary relief is sought:

(1) *Responsive Affidavits/Declarations.* Responsive affidavits or declarations shall be served and filed no later than one business day prior to hearing pursuant to CR 6(d). To ensure that pleadings are available in the court file for timely review by the court, parties are encouraged to file pleadings before noon two days prior to the hearing.

(2) *Exhibits and Worksheets.* Financial exhibits and support worksheets shall be filed in the form as provided by these rules whenever financial matters are in issue.

(3) *Temporary Parenting Plans.* Proposed parenting plans shall be filed whenever temporary parenting matters are at issue.

(4) *Temporary Child Support.* A motion concerning temporary child support must be accompanied by a child support worksheet, together with proof of income including most recent paystubs and tax returns.

C. Child Support. The Washington State Child Support Schedule as adopted and amended from time to time by the legislature shall be applied by the Court and Counsel in all matters involving child support, temporary or permanent.

D. Settlement Conferences. Settlement conferences shall be mandatory in domestic relations cases with the exception of a petition to modify child support. The Court Administrator shall set a time and date for a settlement conference at the time the matter is set for trial. The settlement conference shall be scheduled no earlier than 10 days from the notification and no later than 10 days prior to trial. The settlement conference shall be set before the judicial department of the superior court not assigned to hear the trial. The conference must be confirmed by each party before 12:00 p.m. the day prior to the scheduled conference.

E. Position Statements. In all final hearings or trials in domestic relation matters, each party shall file and serve on the opposing party and the court a written domestic relations position statement, which shall include the Washington Pattern Form financial declaration (WPF 01.1550). The petitioner is required to file his/her position statement three (3) business days prior to the scheduled final hearing. The respondent shall file his/her position statement two (2) business days prior to the scheduled final hearing, trial, or settlement conference. In preparing the position of a party to a domestic relations matter, the assumptions and alternate residential guidelines set forth on Exhibit D to these rules should be considered.

F. Noncontested Marriage Dissolutions—Delivery of Decree to Other Party. In default dissolution cases at the time of entry of the decree, the moving party or counsel shall immediately deliver to or mail to the other party, at their address if known, (or to their counsel), a conformed copy of the decree, with the date of filing indicated on each copy so delivered or mailed.

G. Date of Support Payments. If, in any marriage dissolution case, support, whether temporary or permanent, is to be paid, the order or decree shall specify the day upon which said order becomes effective and the day or days certain upon which said support shall be due.

H. Impact on Children Seminar.

(1) *Definition of Applicable Cases.* This rule applies to all domestic cases including dissolutions, legal separations, major residential modifications and paternity actions in which paternity has been established, where the parties are parents of a child or children under the age of 16, or where a party is not a parent but is seeking custody, and where a parenting plan or residential plan involving more than purely financial issues is required.

(2) *Impact on Children Seminars.* The court may require within 60 days after service of a petition or initiating motion on the respondent, both parties to participate in, and successfully complete, an approved Impact on Children Seminar. Standards for a court-approved Impact on Children Seminar are set forth in sections (7) and (8) below. Successful completion shall be evidenced by a certificate of attendance filed by the provider agency with the court. The petitioning party shall provide notice to the other party, in or with the petition, of the requirements of this rule. In the event that a party complies with this rule through the use of an alternative seminar not issuing a certificate of completion, that party shall file an Affidavit of Attendance setting forth at a minimum the date(s) and place of attendance, the sponsor or agency holding the seminar, and the title or description of the seminar.

(3) *Permissive Application.* The court may require parties with children living in the household in domestic violence actions brought under RCW 26.50, and non-parent parties in any domestic case, to attend an Impact on Children Seminar.

(4) *Special Considerations/Waiver.* In no case shall opposing parties be required to attend a seminar together, nor more than one seminar. Parties may use equivalent services offered by another courts, private agencies or religious organizations, upon approval by the judge in the individual case.

(5) *Fees.* Each party attending a seminar shall pay a fee charged by the approved provider agency directly.

(6) *Failure to Comply.* If the court requires attendance of both parties at an Impact on Children Seminar, non-participation, or default, by one party does not excuse participation by the other party. A party's refusal, delay or default shall not delay the progress of the case to a final decree. Willful refusal or delay by either party may result in sanctions imposed by the court, or may result in the imposition of monetary terms, default and/or striking of pleadings, and/or refusal to entertain postdecree motions and petitions.

(7) *Seminar Location/Content.* A court-approved Child Impact Seminar shall be available in a designated Kittitas County meeting location, on the internet, or may occur at such other sites as may be approved by the court and shall provide, at a minimum, information on:

(a) The developmental stages of childhood;

(b) Stress indicators in children;

(c) Age appropriate expectations of children;

(d) The impact of divorce on children;

(e) The grief process;

(f) Reducing stress for children through an amicable resolution of disputes;

(g) The long-term impact of parental conflict on children;

(h) Importance of child's relationships with both parents, and with extended family members, and fostering those relationships;

(i) Communication skills for divorced parents;

(j) Practical skills for working together; and

(k) The impact on children when step-parents and blended families enter their lives;

(*l*) Parenting children with limited time (alternate residential time limits) and fair parenting (impact on child when parent abstains from discipline/showers child(ren) with gifts/"sides" with child against other parent/succumbs to guilt feelings (whether self-imposed or brought on by child(ren), etc.); and

(m) Involvement of extended family.

(8) *Qualifications of Instructors.* Instructors should be familiar with the required provisions of parenting plans, and have the following minimum credentials and experience:

(a) A Master's Degree in Social Work, Psychology or other related behavioral science;

(b) Supervised experience in treatment of emotionally disturbed children, adolescents and their families;

(c) Experience in providing a wide range of mental health services to children and families, with specific experience in the areas of separation/divorce, loss and grief, and blended families;

(d) Extensive knowledge of child development, age appropriate expectations for children, and positive parenting;

(e) Substantial knowledge of the impact on children of alcohol/drug abuse by family members;

(f) An ability to work with other agencies as part of a collaborative program; and

(g) Strong oral communications skills.

When parties choose to use agencies or religious organizations which have not received prior approval by the court, the court may modify or waive the foregoing qualifications for the instructors upon a showing of functional equivalency.

(9) *Conduct of Parties.* The Court shall not consider a party's conduct, demeanor, or level of participation at the seminar in determining the provisions of a parenting plan.

I. Mandatory Settlement Conferences. In each contested action for dissolution, declaration of invalidity or legal separation, or when ordered by the court, counsel and the parties shall participate in a conference presided over by a judge, judge pro tem or court commissioner.

(1) *Excused Attendance.* A party may be excused from attendance or a settlement conference may be stricken when compelling attendance would be unduly burdensome. Request for non-attendance should be made at least 24 hours in advance to the Court and opposing counsel.

(2) *Proceedings Confidential.* Proceedings of said settlement conference shall, in all respects, be confidential. No party shall be bound unless a settlement is reached. When a settlement has been reached, the judge may in his discretion, order any agreement to be placed on the record.

(3) *Disqualification of Judge.* A judge presiding over a settlement conference is presumed to be disqualified from hearing any other matter regarding the action, but this presumption may be overcome by stipulation of the parties.

(4) *Preparation Required.* Prior to said conference, each party shall have submitted to the other party and to the court a completed position statement in accordance with SPR 94.04€11(e [1]) above.

[Adopted effective September 1, 2011. Amended effective September 1, 2015.]

[1] So in original.

III. LOCAL GUARDIAN AD LITEM RULE FOR SUPERIOR COURT (LGALR)

LGALR 1. GUARDIAN AD LITEM

The Court Administrator maintains and administers the Title 11 and 26 Guardian Ad Litem Registry. Contact the Superior Court Administrator for appointments.

[Adopted effective September 1, 2004; amended effective September 1, 2011; September 1, 2015.]

IV. LOCAL CRIMINAL RULES FOR SUPERIOR COURT (LCrR)

LCrR 1. MANDATORY APPEARANCES

Each criminal defendant shall be required to attend all scheduled pretrial hearings, including the omnibus hearing, the 3.5/3/6 hearing and the status conference, unless excused by the court.

[Adopted effective September 1, 2004; amended effective September 1, 2011.]

LCrR 2. STATUS CONFERENCE

Every criminal case shall be set for a status conference prior to trial to determine whether a scheduled case is still on track for trial.

[Adopted effective September 1, 2004; amended effective September 1, 2011.]

LCrR 3. MOTIONS IN LIMINE

Motions in limine shall be filed and served at or before the date set for status conference. Motions in limine requiring extensive argument or testimony shall be heard on the date set for the pretrial hearing or by leave of the court through the Court Administrator.

[Adopted effective September 1, 2004; amended effective September 1, 2011.]

APPENDIX

EXHIBIT A. NOTE FOR TRIAL SETTING CIVIL CASES (NOT DOMESTIC RELATIONS)

EXHIBIT A

SUPERIOR COURT OF WASHINGTON FOR KITTITAS COUNTY

Plaintiff(s),	No.
vs.	NOTE FOR TRIAL SETTING CIVIL CASES (NOT DOMESTIC RELATIONS)
Defendant(s).	

TO THE CLERK OF COURT
AND TO:

PLEASE TAKE NOTE that this case will be brought on the trial setting docket for assignment for a trial date on the ____ day of _____, 201____, at 9:00 a.m. A list of your available trial dates must be filed with the court before the setting date. **FAILURE TO PROVIDE THE COURT WITH A LIST OF AVAILABLE DATES COULD RESULT IN THE DENIAL OF ANY MOTION FOR CONTINUANCE BECAUSE OF CONFLICTS IN SCHEDULE.**

1. Nature of this Case: _____

2. Date Answer Filed: _____

3. Is a jury demanded? _____   6 member ( ) 12 member ( )
   Jury demand filed? _____
   Jury demand fee paid? _____

4. Estimated trial time: _____.
   THE COURT TRIAL CALENDAR IS PRESET. CASES WILL NOT BE PERMITTED TO CONTINUE BEYOND THE TIME ESTIMATED FOR TRIAL. IF THE NON-SETTING PARTIES DO NOT AGREE WITH THE ESTIMATE IN THIS NOTICE THEY MUST FILE THEIR OWN ESTIMATE BEFORE THE TRIAL SETTING DATE.

5. Interpreter Needed: _____
   [   ] Spanish
   [   ] Other language:
   [   ] ASL

A settlement conference is   [   ] requested in this case.
                                    [   ] not requested

DATED: _____   Signed: _____
                                 Attorney for: _____
                                 Address: _____
                                 Telephone: _____

FILE A COPY WITH THE COURT ADMINISTRATOR, ROOM 207, KITTITAS COUNTY COURTHOUSE.

[Adopted effective September 1, 2004; amended effective September 1, 2011; September 1, 2015.]

EXHIBIT B. NOTE FOR SETTLEMENT CONFERENCE AND TRIAL SETTING (DOMESTIC RELATIONS ONLY)

EXHIBIT B

SUPERIOR COURT OF WASHINGTON FOR KITTITAS COUNTY

IN RE THE MARRIAGE OF:

Petitioner,	No.
and	NOTE FOR SETTLEMENT CONFERENCE AND TRIAL SETTING (DOMESTIC RELATIONS ONLY)
Respondent.	

TO: **Court Administrator** AND OPPOSING COUNSEL:

PLEASE TAKE NOTICE that this case will be placed on the setting docket for assignment of settlement conference and trial setting on the ___ day of _____, 201____.

1. Date Response to Dissolution was filed. _____ (required).

2. Nature of Issues:
   ( ) Property Division ( ) Maintenance
   ( ) Custody ( ) Support Modification
   ( ) Other _____

Settlement conferences are mandatory in all domestic relations cases [except support modification] except through agreement of the parties or by order of the court after appropriate motion.

3. Preferred settlement conference dates: _____

4. Preferred trial date: _____

5. Dates unavailable for settlement conference, support modification hearing, and trial: _____

_____

_____

6. Estimated trial time: _____

7. **THE COURT TRIAL CALENDAR IS PRESET. CASES WILL NOT BE PERMITTED TO CONTINUE BEYOND THE TIME ESTIMATED FOR TRIAL. IF THE NON-SETTING PARTIES DO NOT AGREE WITH THE ESTIMATE IN THIS NOTICE THEY MUST FILE THEIR OWN ESTIMATE BEFORE THE TRIAL SETTING DATE.**

8. Interpretor Needed: _____
   [ ] Spanish
   [ ] Other language:
   [ ] ASL

Date: _____   Signed: _____

                                 Attorney for: _____
                                 Address: _____
                                 Telephone: _____

FILE A COPY WITH THE COURT ADMINISTRATOR, ROOM 207, KITTITAS COUNTY COURTHOUSE.

[Adopted effective September 1, 2004; amended effective September 1, 2011; September 1, 2015.]

EXHIBIT C. NOTE FOR MOTION DOCKET

EXHIBIT C

SUPERIOR COURT OF WASHINGTON FOR KITTITAS COUNTY

	)	
	)	
Plaintiff/Petitioner,	)	No.
	)	
vs.	)	NOTE FOR MOTION DOCKET
	)	
	)	
Defendant/Respondent.	)	

NATURE OF PROCEEDINGS: _____

TO:_____

AND TO THE CLERK OF THE ABOVE ENTITLED COURT:

  PLEASE TAKE NOTICE that the above matter will be brought on for hearing/to be set on the __ day of _____, 201___, at _____ a.m./p.m. in Department ____ (1 or 2) at 205 West 5th Avenue, Ellensburg, WA 98926, and the Clerk is requested to note this cause on the motion/trial docket for that date.

DATED: _____   _____
               Signature

               _____
               Print Name

[Adopted effective September 1, 2004; amended effective September 1, 2011; September 1, 2015.]

EXHIBIT D. GUIDELINES FOR DOMESTIC RELATIONS CASES

Unless otherwise stated, the court assumes the following:

(1) That each party shall be responsible for one-half of the non-insured major medical, dental, ophthalmic and orthodontic expense incurred on behalf of the child(ren).

(2) Tax Exemptions: If neither party's proportional share of income (worksheets line 6) is greater than 60%, then the tax exemption is alternated every year. If either party's proportional share of income is between 61% and 80%, the party with the higher percentage would receive the exemption two years and the other party one year. If either party's proportional share of income is over 80%, the party with the higher percentage would receive the exemption every year. These assumptions are guidelines only, and the Court reserves the authority to do equity based on individual circumstances, as well as consideration of changing federal tax regulations.

(3) That the court shall retain jurisdiction to review the issue of post-high school support for any child desiring, and having the ability to pursue vocational/technical training or a college education.

(4) That child support is due on a date certain each month.

(5) That the non-custodial spouse secure his/her support obligation by naming the child(ren) as primary beneficiaries in an amount sufficient to fund said child support obligation.

(6) Alternate residential guideline for Kittitas County.

(A) Alternate Residential Time: The court shall from time to time adopt a schedule to be used only as a guideline in setting alternate residential times.

1. **Ages 0–6 MONTHS:** One time per week for a period of 3 hours. Extended residential time not recommended.

2. **Ages 6 MOS. TO 1 YEAR:** Once per week for 4 hours. Extended residential time not recommended.

3. **Ages 1 YR TO 3 YEARS:** Once per week for 8 hours, together with alternating child's birthday, Easter, July 4th, Thanksgiving, Christmas Eve, and Christmas Day. Residential time on holidays should be for a period of 8 hours. Extended resident time not recommended.

4. **Ages 3 YRS TO 5 YEARS:** Every other weekend from Saturday morning at 9:00 a.m. until Sunday evening at 6:00 p.m.; one weekday evening from 5:30 p.m. until 7:30 p.m. every other week; alternating Easter and July 4th; alternating Thanksgiving for 2 days; Christmas Eve and 2 days before in alternating years and Christmas Day and 2 days thereafter in alternating years; one week at age 3 and two weeks at age 4 during the summer.

5. **Ages 5 YRS & OLDER:** Every other weekend from Friday at 6:00 p.m. until Sunday at 6:00 p.m., together with contiguous holidays with residential time to begin on Thursday at 6:00 p.m. if the holiday is on a Friday and terminate on Monday if the holiday is on Monday; one weekday evening from 5:30 p.m. until 7:30 p.m. every other week; alternating Thanksgivings for a period of 4 days; one-half of the Christmas school vacation with Christmas Eve and Christmas Day in alternating years alternate spring vacations and summer residential time for a period of 30 days unless the parties agree to a shorter or longer period of time or the court finds that there are extraordinary circumstances which would extend or shorten summer residential time.

(B) Father's/Mother's Day: Regardless of the above routine for residential time, the mother shall have residential time of not less than 4 hours on Mother's Day; and the father shall have residential time of not less than 4 hours on Father's day.

(C) Each parent shall be allowed to spend at least 4 hours with the child to celebrate the child's birthday and each parent's birthday, within a week of that birthday.

(D) For weekend visitation, the residential parent shall be obligated to have the child available for one (1) hour after the scheduled starting time for visitation; if the non-residential parent does not pick up the child within one (1) hour of the scheduled visitation time, the weekend visitation shall be deemed cancelled.

(E) The above provisions are designed to encourage each parent to maintain a loving, stable, and nurturing relationship with the child; and each parent shall encourage the parent/child relationship of the other party and make decisions regarding residential arrangements which are in the best interests of the child. Reasonable telephonic contact with the child is usually appropriate, and should be not less than once per week by the non-primary residential parent.

(F) The foregoing may be varied upon sufficient proof to the court.

[Adopted effective September 1, 2004; amended effective September 1, 2011; September 1, 2015.]

DISTRICT COURTS

LOWER KITTITAS COUNTY DISTRICT COURT LOCAL RULES

Including Amendments Received Through
August 15, 2015

Table of Rules

LOCAL CRIMINAL RULES

LCrR 4.5.   PRE–TRIAL PROCEDURE

(A) Pre-Trial Hearings. All cases scheduled for jury trial shall be set by the clerk for a pre-trial hearing. The state or city prosecutor, defense counsel and the defendant shall attend the pre-trial hearing to consider such matters as will promote a fair and expeditious trial. Upon agreement that the discovery process has been completed to the satisfaction of the parties and that there are no other issues to be heard by the court at the scheduled pre-trial hearing, a stipulated pre-trial statement of readiness, substantially in the form set forth as "Form 1" below, may be filed by the parties. The filing of a stipulated pre-trial statement of readiness will serve to excuse counsel and the defendant from appearing at the scheduled pre-trial hearing.

(B) Motions. All amendments to the charges, pleas or pre-trial motions shall be made prior to or at the time of the pre-trial hearing. Motions which should have been heard at a pretrial hearing shall not be considered at the time of trial unless the judge at the time of the pre-trial hearing expressly continues such motions to the time of trial. Absent good cause, motions for dismissal or suppression of evidence in criminal cases shall be in writing and shall be provided to the prosecutor or city attorney at least 24 hours before the pre-trial hearing. Motions which are lengthy, complex, or which require the presence of witnesses will be heard by the court at a subsequent 35/3.6 hearing calendar.

(C) CrRLJ 3.5 Hearings. Pursuant to CrRLJ 3.5(a) all demands for hearing on the admissibility of confessions must be made no later than the pre-trial hearing. All motions filed pursuant to this rule shall be heard by the court at a subsequent 3.5/3.6 hearing calendar.

(D) Deferred Prosecution—Time for Petition—Forms for Petition and Order. A petition for deferred prosecution shall be filed with the court at least seven days before the date set for trial but, upon written motion and affidavit establishing good cause for the delay and failure to comply with this rule, the court may waive this requirement subject to the defendant's reimbursement to the court of the witness fees and expenses due for subpoenaed witnesses who have appeared on the date set for trial. The petition for deferred prosecution shall substantially comply with CrRLJ 4.2(I). The proposed findings and order shall substantially comply with the form set forth as "Form 2" below.

(E) Stays of Proceedings—Form of Order. In the event the parties enter into a stay of proceedings, the agreement between the parties shall be reduced to writing in a form which substantially complies with the form set forth as "Form 3" below.

[Adopted effective September 1, 2000; amended effective September 1, 2005.]

Comments

The purpose of these rules is to eliminate surprise and unnecessary delay and expense. While the purpose of these rules is not to create traps for the unwary, when a party's failure to follow these rules causes unnecessary extra expense to the opposing party, the inconvenienced party may apply to the court for the imposition of sanctions. The purpose of these sanctions is not to punish but rather to insure that the appropriate party is responsible for the predictable costs of unnecessary delay.

Comment to section (A): The stipulated pre-trial statement of readiness was adopted by the court at the request of counsel who wanted to avoid the necessity of clients appearing at unproductive pre-trial hearings. Attorneys are encouraged to use the pre-trial statement of readiness to avoid the necessity of clients appearing when there are no pre-trial issues requiring his or her presence.

Comment to section (B): The purpose of this section is to provide a predictable structure to the pre-trial motions process and to insure that the non-moving party has adequate time to prepare for the hearing. However, if counsel desire to avoid multiple hearings, the parties may agree to present evidence and argue pre-trial motions at the scheduled pre-trial hearing rather than following the procedure described by this rule.

Comment to section (C): See the comments to section (B).

Comment to section (D): See RCW 10.05.010.

Comment to section (E): The stay of proceedings form set forth below is generally consistent with the forms currently in use in the Lower Kittitas County District Court. In creating a uniform stay of proceedings form, it is not the court's intention to suggest what conditions should be part of an agreement between the parties. For example, if an agreement between the parties in a specific case does not include the defendant stipulating to the admissibility of the police reports, or a stipulation that the reports are sufficient to convict, the court expects the parties to line out that portion of the stay of proceedings form.

FORM 1. STIPULATED PRE–TRIAL STATEMENT OF READINESS

A stipulation filed in substantially the following form will comply with LCrR 4.5(A):

LOWER KITTITAS COUNTY DISTRICT
COURT STATE OF WASHINGTON

[ ] State of Washington	)
[ ] City of Ellensburg,	) NO. _____
Plaintiff,	) STIPULATED PRE–TRIAL
	) STATEMENT OF READINESS
vs.	)
_____,	)
Defendant,	)
_____	)

Pre–trial hearing is currently set for _____, 20 ____.

Jury trial is currently set for _____, 20 ____.

    COMES NOW the parties in the above captioned action and, by signature of counsel, do hereby stipulate and agree that **this case has not been resolved by agreement,** and should remain on the trial calendar or be reset by the clerk as indicated below:

1. Motions:
    [ ] There will be no pretrial motions and the above noted pre-trial hearing should be stricken.

    [ ] Pre-trial motions have been filed and served. The clerk is requested to reset the pre-trial hearing for ___/___/___.

    [ ] A CrRLJ 3.5 Hearing is required. The clerk is requested to set the hearing for ___/___/___.

2. Bench/Jury Trial:

    [ ] Remain set for a jury trial at above noted date and time.

    [ ] Clerk is requested to re-set jury trial as follows: _____.

    [ ] Jury trial waiver filed; set for bench trial.

3. Discovery:
    Discovery is complete.

4. Witnesses:

    Plaintiff:
    [ ] Witness list filed
    [ ] Witnesses as follows:

Name	Address/telephone	Subject of testimony
_____	_____	_____
_____	_____	_____
_____	_____	_____

928

Defense:
[ ] Witness list filed
[ ] Witnesses as follows:

Name	Address/telephone	Subject of testimony
_____	_____	_____
_____	_____	_____
_____	_____	_____

_____   _____
Attorney for Plaintiff   W.S.B.A.   #Attorney for Defendant   W.S.B.A. #

[Amended effective September 1, 2000.]

FORM 2. DEFERRED PROSECUTION FINDINGS
OF FACT, CONCLUSIONS OF LAW & ORDER

Lower Kittitas County District Court
State of Washington

[ ] State of Washington,	)	
[ ] City of Ellensburg,	)	
Plaintiff,	)	No.
	)	Deferred Prosecution
vs.	)	Findings of Fact, Conclusions of
	)	Law & Order
_____,	)	
Defendant.	)	
_____	)	

This matter coming before the court on the defendant's Petition for Deferred
Prosecution, and the court having considered the Petition, evaluation and treatment
plan filed by the defendant, and the arguments of counsel, now makes the following
findings of fact:

I. Findings of Fact

1. The defendant was evaluated by an approved alcoholism treatment facility or an
    approved drug treatment center; said agency's evaluation meets the require-
    ments of RCW 10.05.040 and is attached to this Order. A certified alcoholism
    treatment facility or drug treatment center has prepared a treatment plan
    meeting the requirements of RCW 10.05.150 and has committed to provide
    treatment. Said treatment plan and commitment to treatment is attached to
    this Order, and incorporated by reference herein.

2. The defendant has agreed to pay, or arranged for the payment of, the costs of
    treatment.

3. The defendant has agreed to complete the two-year treatment program set forth
    in the treatment plan attached to this Order and to follow the other conditions of
    the court's Order.

4. The defendant has been advised of the following rights and has knowingly and
    voluntarily waived each of them:

    (a) The right to a jury trial;
    (b) The right to a speedy trial;
    (c) The right to present evidence in his or her defense;
    (d) The right to hear and question all witnesses who testify against the
        defendant;
    (e) The right to compel witnesses to appear and testify on behalf of the
        defendant at no cost to the defendant;
    (f) The right to testify.

5. The defendant has stipulated to the admissibility and sufficiency of the facts
    contained in the written police reports and understands these facts will be
    considered by the court in any criminal hearing on the underlying offense or
    offenses held subsequent to revocation of the order granting deferred prosecu-
    tion. The defendant has agreed that the facts contained in the stipulated police
    reports are sufficient to allow the court to find the petitioner guilty, beyond a
    reasonable doubt, of the charged offenses.

6. The defendant has agreed, and the court finds, that any statements made by the defendant contained in the stipulated police reports were made knowingly and voluntarily.

7. If the charge is a violation of RCW Title 46 or similar municipal ordinance, the defendant has affirmed, and the court finds, that the defendant has not previously participated in a prior deferred prosecution program for a violation of RCW Title 46 or any similar municipal ordinance.

From the forgoing Findings of Fact, the court makes the following conclusions of law:

II. Conclusions of Law

1. The court has jurisdiction over the subject matter and petitioner in this case.
2. The petition meets the requirements of RCW 10.05.020
3. The diagnostic evaluation and treatment plan met the requirements of RCW 10.05.040, RCW 10.05.050 and RCW 10.05.150.
4. The Petition was made freely, voluntarily and knowingly.

III. Order

Based on the foregoing Findings of Fact and Conclusions of Law, the court hereby grants the Petition for Deferred Prosecution and allows the defendant to enter into a deferred prosecution program. The defendant shall remain under the jurisdiction of the court and the supervision of Kittitas County Probation Services during the two year treatment plan, and for three years after the court receives proof of successful completion of the two-year treatment program, but not less than five years from the date of this Order. The defendant shall, while under the court's jurisdiction, comply with the following conditions:

1. The defendant shall fully comply with and complete the two-year treatment program attached to this Order and incorporated by reference in Paragraph 2 of the court's Findings. In the event there are any inconsistencies between this order and the attached treatment plan, the terms and conditions set forth in this order shall be controlling.

2. The defendant shall pay, or arrange for payment of, the costs of the treatment program.

3. The defendant shall maintain total abstinence from alcohol and all other non-prescribed mind altering drugs.

4. The defendant shall not commit any crimes. The definition of "commit" includes, but is not limited to, any criminal charge resolved by a stay of proceedings, a stipulated order of continuance, or any other agreement which consists of a continuance with conditions, even if the ultimate disposition of the criminal charge is a dismissal, amendment of charge, or a finding of not guilty.

5. The defendant shall not refuse to submit to a breath or blood test if a police officer has reasonable grounds to believe that the defendant is driving or is in physical control of a motor vehicle while under the influence of intoxicating liquor or drugs.

6. The defendant shall not operate a motor vehicle upon the public highways without a valid operator's license and proof of liability insurance in an amount not less than that established by RCW 46.29.490.

7. The defendant shall immediately report to Probation Services, and continue to report in the future as directed by Probation Services.

8. The defendant shall pay $35 per month for probation supervision. The court may, after the successful completion of the two year treatment program, reduce the level of supervision (and associated probation fees) required for the remainder of the period of supervision.

8. [1]The defendant shall not change treatment agencies without written permission of the court.

9. The treatment facility shall file with Kittitas County Probation Services **monthly** treatment status/compliance reports. Those reports shall be sent to:

> Kittitas County Probation Services
> 507 Nanum Street
> Ellensburg, Washington 98926

10. The defendant shall provide **in writing** to the court and Probation Services any change in mailing address.

11. The defendant shall not drive any motor vehicle unless the motor vehicle is equipped with a functioning ignition interlock calibrated to prevent the motor vehicle from being started when the breath sample provided has an alcohol concentration of 0.025 or more. This restriction is effective [ ] immediately; [ ] as of ___/___/___; [ ] after the completion of any suspension, revocation, or denial of driving privileges. The period of time of this restriction shall be for [ ] one year [ ] five years [ ] ten years.

12. The defendant [ ] shall [ ] shall not be required to pay a $150 administrative fee.

13. The defendant [ ] shall [ ] shall not be required to pay a $125 breath test fee.

14. [ ] The defendant [ ] shall [ ] shall not be required to reimburse Kittitas County for the cost of his/her court appointed attorney in the amount of $ _____.

15. [ ] The defendant shall pay restitution in the amount of $ _____. [ ] A restitution hearing shall be held on ___/___ /20 ___ to determine what amount of restitution should be paid by the defendant

16. The defendant shall start the two year deferred prosecution treatment program on or before:
___/___ /20 ___. ' [ ] **Prior to entry into the two year intensive treatment program, the defendant shall attend a minimum of three (3) self-help recovery support group meetings per week, and provide proof of attendance to Probation Services. The defendant shall also attend and fully participate in any pre-treatment program available from his or her treatment agency. The defendant shall report to Probation Services as directed.**

17. [ ] The defendant shall attend a DUI victim's panel in Kittitas County on: ___/___ /20 ___. [ ] The defendant shall attend a DUI victim's panel within 90 days. [ ] The defendant shall attend a Spanish language DUI victim's panel as directed by Probation Services.

18. This matter shall be set for review at any time as may be deemed appropriate by the court. In the event the defendant fails or neglects to undertake, complete or comply with any term or condition of this Order, the court, upon receiving notice of such failure, neglect, or violation, shall hold a hearing to determine whether the sufficient cause exists to remove the defendant from the deferred prosecution program. In the event the defendant is convicted of a

similar offense, the court shall remove the defendant from the deferred prosecution program.

19. In the event the court finds cause to revoke the deferred prosecution, the court (sitting without a jury) will consider the stipulated police reports, including any statements made by the defendant, and determine whether the stipulated evidence supports the charge(s) beyond a reasonable doubt

20. In the event the defendant complies with the conditions of this Order the court shall, three years after receiving proof of successful completion of the two-year treatment program, but not before five years following entry of this Order, dismiss the charges pending against the defendant.

21. Other: _____

_____

Dated _____/_____/20___   _____
                                        Judge/Court Commissioner
Presented by: Copy received; approved as to form:

_____   _____
Attorney for Defendant   WSBA   #Prosecuting Authority   WSBA #

Copy received; terms and conditions of Order accepted by:

_____
            Defendant

Attached to this Order are:
  A. **Alcohol/drug evaluation, treatment plan and commitment to provide treatment.**
  B. **Police reports.**

[Adopted effective September 1, 2000.]

1 Numbering as provided in original.

FORM 3. STIPULATION FOR AND ORDER FOR STAY OF PROCEEDINGS

LOWER KITTITAS COUNTY DISTRICT COURT
STATE OF WASHINGTON

[ ] State of Washington,   )
[ ] City of Ellensburg,   )   No. _____
                   Plaintiff,   )   Stipulation for and Order for
)   Stay of Proceedings
vs.   )
)   Charge(s) _____
_____,   )
                 Defendant.   )   _____
_____   )

_____ [ ] Deputy Prosecuting Attorney [ ] Attorney for the City of Ellensburg and _____, defendant, represented by _____, stipulate and agree to a stay of proceedings in this matter for a period of ___ months, on the following terms and conditions:

1. The defendant shall maintain good and lawful behavior during the term of the stay: the defendant shall have no criminal convictions for offenses committed after the date of this order, no charges during the term of the stay which lead to criminal convictions, no criminal charges which lead to a stay of proceedings, stipulated order of continuance or similar disposition, and no criminal charges which lead to a deferred prosecution. In addition:

    [ ] The defendant shall complete ___ hours of approved community service within ___ days and provide proof of completion to Kittitas County Probation Services.

    [ ] The defendant shall complete ___ days of Department of Corrections work crew within ___ days and provide proof of completion to Probation Services.

    [ ] The defendant shall attend a DUI victim's panel within ___ days and provide proof to Probation Services.

    [ ] The defendant shall obtain the following evaluation(s) and provide proof of such evaluation(s) to Probation Services within 30 days:
       [ ] Alcohol/Drug   [ ] Domestic Violence   [ ] Anger Management
       [ ] Other: _____

    In the event the evaluating agency recommends that the defendant obtain treatment or other Services, the defendant shall fully comply with the agency's recommendations and start any recommended classes or treatment within 45 days. In the event that extended treatment is recommended, the defendant shall direct the treating agency to provide compliance reports to Probation Services on a monthly basis.

    [ ] Other: _____

2. Probation Services shall monitor the defendant's compliance with the conditions of this order. Probation Services shall: [ ] Actively monitor the defendant.   [ ] Complete _____ record checks.
    [ ] The defendant shall immediately report to Probation Services and continue to report as directed.

3. The defendant shall pay the following assessments:
    [ ] Probation record check fees of   [ ] Probation monitoring fees of
       $_____ $_____ per month

[ ] Court appointed attorney fees of   [ ] Court costs: $_____
    $_____
[ ] Restitution in the amount of   [ ] A Time payment agreement is
    $_____   authorized

4. The defendant hereby waives his/her right to a trial within 90 days of arraignment, and agrees to a trial date of no later than 90 days from the end of the stay of proceedings. In the event that the defendant is charged with a crime during the term of the stay of proceedings, but which is not resolved until after the end of the term of the stay, the defendant agrees to a trial date no later than 90 days after final resolution of the subsequently charged criminal offense.

5. If the defendant complies with all of the above listed conditions, the prosecuting authority agrees to:

   [ ] Move the court for a dismissal of the charge(s) of: _____ filed under the above cause number.
   [ ] Move the court to amend the charge of _____ to the charge of _____ to which the defendant shall: [ ] Plead guilty [ ] Bail forfeit $ ___. [ ] Other: _____
   [ ] In the event the defendant pleads guilty the parties agree to the following sentencing recommendation:
     [ ] Prosecutor's recommendation: _____

     [ ] Defense recommendation: _____

6. In the event the court finds, after a hearing, that the defendant has failed to comply with any of the above listed conditions, the court shall, upon the request of the prosecuting authority, revoke the stay of proceedings and set a trial date.

7. As a condition of entering this stay of proceedings, the defendant agrees to waive the following rights:

   A. The right to a jury trial
   B. The right to a trial within 90 days of arraignment.
   C. The right at trial to hear and question witnesses called by the prosecuting authority.
   D. The right to testify at trial and call defense witnesses.

8. In the event the court finds cause to revoke the stay of proceedings, the defendant stipulates and agrees to the admissibility of the attached police reports (including any statements made by the defendant contained in the reports) and stipulates and agrees that the facts contained in the attached reports are sufficient to convict the defendant of the charged crime(s).

9. The parties agree that in the event the defendant fails to make payments as listed above and is delinquent by fifteen (15) days or more, the plaintiff and/or court have the authority to send such delinquent amounts to a collection agency for collection of said sums. Both parties agree that this authority exists whether or not the plaintiff chooses to have the matter set for review and bench trial. The defendant specifically waives any objection to such collection action by the plaintiff or the court, regardless of whether or not the defendant is found guilty after a trial. The defendant agrees that this document, along with any time payment agreement signed by the defendant, constitute a judgment for the amounts stated in paragraph 3 above.

10. The defendant understands and agrees that this document constitutes an agreement between the plaintiff and the defendant pertaining to the resolution

of a criminal charge(s). The defendant further understands that he/she is obligated to fully and strictly comply with all conditions set forth in this agreement. The defendant further understands that in the event the defendant fails to fully comply with the conditions of this agreement, the prosecuting authority may request a hearing in order seek revocation this stay of proceedings.

11. The parties jointly request that the court allow the above described stay of proceedings and further request that the court enter the attached order

Dated this ___ day of _____, ___   _____

                                                  Defendant

_____   _____

Prosecuting Authority   WSBA   #Attorney for Defendant   WSBA #

ORDER

Based on the parties' request for a stay of proceedings, and the above stipulation between the parties, the court hereby orders that this cause is stayed for a period of _____, under the terms and conditions contained in the attached stipulation.

Dated this ___ day of _____, ___   _____

                                      Judge/ Court Commissioner

INTERPRETER'S DECLARATION

I am a certified interpreter or have been found otherwise qualified by the court to interpret in the _____ language, which the defendant understands, and I have translated this Stipulation for and Order for Stay of Proceedings for the defendant from English into that language. The defendant has acknowledged his or her understanding of both the translation and the subject matter of this document. I certify under penalty of perjury under the laws of the state of Washington that the foregoing is true and correct.

Signed at Ellensburg, Washington on: ___/___/___   _____

                                               Interpreter

[Adopted effective September 1, 2000; amended effective September 1, 2005.]

LCrR 7.2(f). REQUIREMENTS FOR CHEMICAL DEPENDENCY ASSESSMENTS

When, as a part of a sentence or other disposition, a chemical dependency assessment is required, the alcohol/drug evaluator must be a certified Chemical Dependency Professional (CDP) or a CDP trainee (CDPT) under supervision of a CDP. The evaluator shall prepare a written report of the assessment that shall include a description of the steps taken to insure compliance with the requirements of WAC 388–805–310. The written report shall also include the following information:

1. **A description of the sources used to establish the defendant's legal history.** At a minimum, these sources must include a Defendant's Case History (DCH), a Washington Department of Licensing driver's record abstract, and police reports describing the current offense. The police reports shall contain, at a minimum, a description of the offense and the defen-dant's blood or breath alcohol level and any other drug levels at the time of arrest.

2. **A description of sources used to document the defendant's history of alcohol and other drug treatment or education.** At a minimum, these sources shall include any available drug/alcohol evaluations prepared by a CDP or CDPT concerning the defendant. The defendant shall notify the evaluator of any prior alcohol/drug evaluation and sign any releases necessary to make such alcohol/drug evaluations available to his or her current evaluating agency.

3. **A description of the method used to notify the defendant of the assessment results.** The defendant shall be supplied with a copy of his alcohol/drug evaluation along with any treatment/education recommendations made by the CDP or CDPT. If the assessment results are mailed to the defendant, the report shall state the address to which the assessment was mailed and the date of mailing.

[Adopted effective September 1, 2003.]

LOCAL RULES OF GENERAL APPLICATION

LGR 17(a)(7). FACSIMILE TRANSMISSION

The Lower Kittitas County District Court will not accept for filing a facsimile transmission of any pleading or other document for which any other court rule or statute sets a filing time-limit or filing deadline. The court will accept facsimile transmissions of other documents, including judge's working copies of trial briefs or position statements.

[Adopted effective September 1, 2003.]

LGR 30. ELECTRONIC FILING

LGR 30(b)(6). The clerk may accept any electronic document created by a Kittitas County Lower District Court judicial officer, clerk, or administrator for filing. Non-electronic documents filed with the court may be converted to electronic documents and all such electronic documents shall be deemed the equivalent of original documents.

LGR 30(b)(7). The clerk may accept for filing via email or any other reliable electronic means any certificates filed for use by the court pursuant to IRLJ 6.6(d) and LIR 6.6(f).

LGR 30(d)(2)(G). Any electronic document created by Kittitas County Lower District court requiring a signature by a judicial officer, clerk or court administrator may be signed with an electronic signature. Each person authorized to sign court generated documents with an electronic signatures will be assigned a user ID and password by the presiding judge. Documents created pursuant to this rule may be electronically filed. An electronic document shall be deemed the equivalent of an original signed document if the electronic signature thereon complies with this rule.

[Adopted effective September 1, 2015.]

Comments

LGR 30(b)(6), LGR 30(b)(7), and LGR 30(d)(2)(G) go into effect immediately and apply retroactively to any document created or filed in accordance with the provision of those rules.

LOCAL INFRACTION RULES

LIR 3.3(b). CONTESTED INFRACTION HEARING—REPRESENTATION BY LAWYER

At a contested hearing the plaintiff shall be represented by a lawyer representative of the prosecuting authority when i) a witness has been subpoenaed to appear, or ii) where a timely request for a speed measuring device (SMD) expert has been filed with the court and served on the prosecuting authority. The court in its discretion may waive the presence of plaintiff's lawyer representative if it deems it appropriate.

[Adopted effective September 1, 2015.]

Comments

The purpose of the rule regarding requiring the presence of a lawyer for the plaintiff is to minimize questioning of witnesses by the court and for the plaintiff's lawyer to be present to address various legal challenges and issues. The presence of the plaintiff's lawyer is not a "right" of the defendant and the court may waive the presence of the plaintiff's lawyer under any circumstances which it may deem appropriate.

LIR 3.5(f).   INFRACTION HEARINGS BASED ON WRITTEN STATEMENTS

The court adopts IRLJ 3.5 and will, at the request of a defendant, decide infraction cases based on written statements. A defendant requesting the court to decide the case on written statements shall do so by completing a statement in substantially the following form:

Lower Kittitas County District Court State of Washington

[ ] State of Washington,   )
[ ] City of Ellensburg,   )
        Plaintiff,   )
) No. _____
vs.   ) Defendant's Request for
) Decision on Written Statements
_____) [ ] **Mitigation Hearing**
        Defendant.   ) [ ] **Contested Hearing**
_____)

To: The Clerk of the Lower Kittitas County District Court, Room 180, Kittitas County Courthouse, Ellensburg, Washington 98926
From: _____, Defendant.
I hereby request that the court decide my case based on my following sworn statement:

_____

_____

_____

_____

_____

_____

_____

_____

_____

_____

_____

_____

_____

_____

_____

_____

_____

_____

_____

_____

_____

_____ (Attach additional pages if necessary)

I certify [or declare] under the penalty of perjury under the laws of the State of Washington that the above statement is true. I promise that if it is determined that I committed the infraction for which I was cited, I will pay the monetary penalty

authorized by law and assessed by the court. I understand that I may not appeal
the decision of the court.

_____   _____
         (Print your name)   (Sign your name)

_____
    (Street or Post Office address)

_____
      (City, state and zip code)

[Adopted effective September 1, 2000; amended effective September 1, 2005.]

LIR 6.6(e).   REQUEST FOR SPEED MEASURING DEVICE EXPERT

Request for Speed Measuring Device ("SMD") Expert. Defense requests to produce an electronic or laser SMD expert pursuant to IRLJ 6.6(b) shall be contained in a separate document clearly designated as a request for an SMD expert, served on the prosecuting authority with a conformed copy filed with the clerk of the court. If the charging law enforcement agency's SMD expert maintains a schedule for monthly appearances in the Lower Kittitas County District Court, a request for an SMD expert shall be deemed by the court to be a request to set (or re–set) the hearing to a day scheduled for the agency's SMD expert. An SMD expert called as a witness by either party may testify by telephone; however, any party intending to elicit telephonic testimony from an SMD expert shall notify the court and the opposing party at least 5 days prior to the date set for the contested hearing.

[Adopted effective September 1, 2003.]

Comments to Local Infraction Rule 6.6(e). *LIR 6.6(e) is designed to address the problem of requests for SMD experts being "buried" within discovery requests or other documents filed in contested infraction cases. A request for an SMD expert which stands alone and is clearly identified as a request for an SMD expert will eliminate continuances for defendants who desire the presence of an SMD expert but who have not made their wish sufficiently clear to the prosecuting authority. Allowing SMD expert testimony by telephone serves to reduce costs incurred by law enforcement agencies as well as assisting defendants in presenting the testimony of their own SMD experts.*

LIR 6.6(f).   PUBLIC ACCESS TO SPEED MEASURING DEVICE CERTIFICATES

Pursuant to IRLJ 6.6(d), the court maintains as public records any design and construction certifications for electronic speed measuring devices and laser speed measuring devices filed with the court. In addition to the methods of public access described in IRLJ 6.6(d), certifications filed by the Washington State Patrol are available for review and downloading at the court's web cite located at http://www.co. kittitas.wa.us/courts/lower.asp.

[Adopted effective September 1, 2005.]

LOCAL COURT RULES OF THE UPPER DISTRICT COURT FOR KITTITAS COUNTY

Including Amendments Received Through
August 15, 2015

Table of Rules

INTRODUCTION

LARLJ 2.   SCOPE OF RULES AND ADOPTION

(a) Effect of Local Rules. The provisions of the Local Rules are supplemental to the Rules for courts of Limited Jurisdiction, as adopted or hereafter amended by the Supreme Court of the State of Washington, and shall not be construed in conflict with them.

(b) Scope. The Local Rules apply to all Courts in which a Upper Kittitas County District Court Judge is appointed or elected to sit, including but not limited to the Upper Kittitas County District Court, Cle Elum Municipal Court, and the Roslyn Municipal Court.

(c) Adoption and Amendments. These Rules may be amended from time to time by the Upper Kittitas County District Court Judge.

(d) Prior Rules Repealed. All prior rules of the Upper Kittitas County District Court are repealed upon the adoption of these Rules.

[Adopted effective September 1, 2011.]

LOCAL CRIMINAL RULES

LCrRLJ 4.5.   PRE–TRIAL PROCEDURE

(A) Pre–Trial Hearings. All cases scheduled for jury trial shall be set by the clerk for a pre-trial hearing. The state or city prosecutor, defense counsel and the defendant shall attend the pre-trial hearing to consider such matters as will promote a fair and expeditious trial. Upon agreement that the discovery process has been completed to the satisfaction of the parties and that there are no other issues to be heard by the court at the scheduled pre-trial hearing, a stipulated pre-trial statement of readiness, substantially in the form set forth as "Form 1" below, may be filed by the parties. The filing of a stipulated pre-trial statement of readiness will serve to excuse counsel and the defendant from appearing at the scheduled pre-trial hearing.

(B) Motions. All amendments to the charges, pleas or pre-trial motions shall be made prior to or at

942

the time of the pre-trial hearing. Motions which should have been heard at a pretrial hearing shall not be considered at the time of trial unless the judge at the time of the pre-trial hearing expressly continues such motions to the time of trial. Absent good cause, motions for dismissal or suppression of evidence in criminal cases shall be in writing and shall be provided to the prosecutor or city attorney at least 24 hours before the pre-trial hearing. Motions which are lengthy, complex, or which require the presence of witnesses will be heard by the court at a subsequent 3.5/3.6 hearing calendar.

(C) CrRLJ 3.5 Hearings. Pursuant to CrRLJ 3.5(a) all demands for hearing on the admissibility of confessions must be made no later than the pre-trial hearing. All motions filed pursuant to this rule shall be heard by the court at a subsequent 3.5/3.6 hearing calendar.

(D) Deferred Prosecution—Time for Petition— Forms for Petition and Order. A petition for deferred prosecution shall be filed with the court at least seven days before the date set for trial but, upon written motion and affidavit establishing good cause for the delay and failure to comply with this rule, the court may waive this requirement subject to the defendant's reimbursement to the court of the witness fees and expenses due for subpoenaed witnesses who have appeared on the date set for trial. The petition for deferred prosecution shall substantially comply with CrRLJ 4.2(I). The proposed findings and order shall substantially comply with the form set forth as "Form 2" below.

(E) Stays of Proceedings—Form of Order. In the event the parties enter into a stay of proceedings, the agreement between the parties shall be reduced to writing in a form which substantially complies with the form set forth as "Form 3" below.

[Adopted effective September 1, 2011.]

Comments

The purpose of these rules is to eliminate surprise and unnecessary delay and expense. While the purpose of these rules is not to create traps for the unwary, when a party's failure to follow these rules causes unnecessary extra expense to the opposing party, the inconvenienced party may apply to the court for the imposition of sanctions. The purpose of these sanctions is not to punish but rather to insure that the appropriate party is responsible for the predictable costs of unnecessary delay.

Comment to section (A): The stipulated pre-trial statement of readiness was adopted by the court at the request of counsel who wanted to avoid the necessity of clients appearing at unproductive pre-trial hearings. Attorneys are encouraged to use the pre-trial statement of readiness to avoid the necessity of clients appearing when there are no pre-trial issues requiring his or her presence.

Comment to section (B): The purpose of this section is to provide a predictable structure to the pre-trial motions process and to insure that the non-moving party has adequate time to prepare for the hearing. However, if counsel desire to avoid multiple hearings, the parties may agree to present evidence and argue pre-trial motions at the scheduled pre-trial hearing rather than following the procedure described by this rule.

Comment to section (C): See the comments to section (B).

Comment to section (D): See RCW 10.05.010.

Comment to section (E): The stay of proceedings form set forth below is generally consistent with the forms currently in use in the Upper Kittitas County District Court. In creating a uniform stay of proceedings form, it is not the court's intention to suggest what conditions should be part of an agreement between the parties. For example, if an agreement between the parties in a specific case does not include the defendant stipulating to the admissibility of the police reports, or a stipulation that the reports are sufficient to convict, the court expects the parties to line out that portion of the stay of proceedings form.

LCrRLJ 7.2(f). REQUIREMENTS FOR CHEMICAL DEPENDENCY ASSESSMENTS

When, as a part of a sentence or other disposition, a chemical dependency assessment is required, the alcohol/drug evaluator must be a certified Chemical Dependency Professional (CDP) or a CDP trainee (CDPT) under supervision of a CDP. The evaluator shall prepare a written report of the assessment that shall include a description of the steps taken to insure compliance with the requirements of WAC 388–805–310. The written report shall also include the following information:

1. A description of the sources used to establish the defendant's legal history. At a minimum, these sources must include a Defendant's Case History (DCH), a Washington Department of Licensing driver's record abstract, and police reports describing the current offense. The police reports shall contain, at a minimum, a description of the offense and the defendant's blood or breath alcohol level and any other drug levels at the time of arrest.

2. A description of sources used to document the defendant's history of alcohol and other drug treatment or education. At a minimum, these sources shall include any available drug/alcohol evaluations prepared by a CDP or CDPT concerning the defendant. The defendant shall notify the evaluator of any prior alcohol/drug evaluation and sign any releases necessary to make such alcohol/drug evaluations available to his or her current evaluating agency.

3. A description of the method used to notify the defendant of the assessment results. The defendant shall be supplied with a copy of his alcohol/drug evaluation along with any treatment/education recommendations made by the CDP or CDPT. If the assessment results are mailed to the defendant, the

report shall state the address to which the assessment was mailed and the date of mailing.

[Adopted effective September 1, 2011.]

LOCAL RULE OF GENERAL APPLICATION

LGR 17(a)(7). FACSIMILE TRANSMISSION

The Upper Kittitas County District Court will not accept for filing a facsimile transmission of any pleading or other document for which any other court rule

or statute sets a filing time-limit or filing deadline. The court will accept facsimile transmissions of other documents, including judge's working copies of trial briefs or position statements.

[Adopted effective September 1, 2011.]

LOCAL INFRACTION RULES

LIRLJ 3.5. INFRACTION HEARINGS BASED ON WRITTEN STATEMENTS

The court adopts IRLJ 3.5 and will, at the request of a defendant, decide infraction cases based on written statements. A defendant requesting the court to decide the case on written statements shall do so by completing a statement in substantially the following form:

{see form LIRLJ 3.5 Form}

[Adopted effective September 1, 2011.]

LIRLJ 6.6.1. CERTIFICATION OF SCALES USED IN THE MEASUREMENT OF WEIGHT FOR COMMERCIAL MOTOR VEHICLES

(a) **In General.** This rule applies only to contested hearings in traffic infraction cases.

(b) **Scale Certification.** Evidence given under oath (including testimony given in person or the written report of an officer as provided in IRLJ 3.3) of the results of a measurement of the weight of any commercial motor vehicle or portion thereof shall be admissible without additional foundation. A sworn statement setting forth the results of any inspection, test and/or certification of any scale used primarily for the purpose of measuring the weights of commercial motor vehicles shall likewise be admissible in evidence without foundation, and shall not be subject to objection on grounds of hearsay, provided that such document is maintained in a manner consistent with subsection (3) of this rule. Any party may present evidence supporting or attacking the result of any such measurement of weight or the inspection, test and/or certification of any such scale.

(c) [Reserved]

(d) **Maintaining Certificates as Public Records.** Any document of inspection, test and/or certification of any State scales as set forth in subsection (b) of this rule may be filed with the court and maintained by the

court as a public record. The documents will be available for inspection by the public. Copies will be provided on request. The court may charge any allowable copying fees. The documents are available without a formal request for discovery. In the alternative, or in addition, such documents may be maintained on a web site established for that purpose by the Washington State Patrol. The court is entitled to take judicial notice of the fact that the document has been filed with the court or maintained on the web site. Evidence will not be suppressed merely because there is not a representative of the prosecuting authority present who actually offers the document.

[Adopted effective September 2, 2013.]

LIRLJ 6.6(e). REQUEST FOR SPEED MEASURING DEVICE EXPERT

Request for Speed Measuring Device ("SMD") Expert. Defense requests to produce an electronic or laser SMD expert pursuant to IRLJ 6.6(b) shall be contained in a separate document clearly designated as a request for an SMD expert, served on the prosecuting authority with a conformed copy filed with the clerk of the court. If the charging law enforcement agency's SMD expert maintains a schedule for monthly appearances in the Upper Kittitas County District Court, a request for an SMD expert shall be deemed by the court to be a request to set (or re-set) the hearing to a day scheduled for the agency's SMD expert. An SMD expert called as a witness by either party may testify by telephone; however, any party intending to elicit telephonic testimony from an SMD expert shall notify the court and the opposing party at least 5 days prior to the date set for the contested hearing.

[Adopted effective September 1, 2011.]

Comments

Comments to Local Infraction Rule 6.6(e). LIR 6.6(e) is designed to address the problem of requests for SMD experts being "buried" within discovery requests or other documents filed in contested infraction cases. A request for an SMD expert which stands alone and is clearly identified as a request for an SMD expert will eliminate continuances for defendants who desire the presence of an SMD expert but who have not made their wish sufficiently clear to the prosecuting authority. Allowing SMD expert testimony by telephone serves to reduce costs incurred by law enforcement agencies as well as assisting defendants in presenting the testimony of their own SMD experts.

LIRLJ 6.6(f). PUBLIC ACCESS TO SPEED MEASURING DEVICE CERTIFICATES

Pursuant to IRLJ 6.6(d), the court maintains as public records any design and construction certifica-

tions for electronic speed measuring devices and laser speed measuring devices filed with the court. In addition to the methods of public access described in IRLJ 6.6(d), certifications filed by the Washington State Patrol are available for review and downloading at the WSP website:

http://www.wsp.wa.gov/traveler/traveler.htm

[Adopted effective September 1, 2011.]

FORMS
DECLARATION

INTERPRETER'S DECLARATION

I am a certified interpreter or have been found otherwise qualified by the court to interpret in the _____ language, which the defendant understands, and I have translated this Stipulation for and Order for Stay of Proceedings for the defendant from English into that language. The defendant has acknowledged his or her understanding of both the translation and the subject matter of this document. I certify under penalty of perjury under the laws of the state of Washington that the foregoing is true and correct.

Signed at Cle Elum, Washington on: ___ / ___ / _____

[Adopted effective September 1, 2011.]

LCrRLJ 4.5 FORM 1.   STIPULATED PRE–TRIAL STATEMENT OF READINESS

A stipulation filed in substantially the following form will comply with LCrRLJ 4.5(A):

UPPER KITTITAS COUNTY DISTRICT COURT

STATE OF WASHINGTON

[ ] State of Washington	)	
[ ] City of Cle Elum,	)	
[ ] City of Roslyn	)	NO. _____
Plaintiff,	)	STIPULATED PRE–TRIAL
	)	STATEMENT OF READINESS
vs.	)	
_____,	)	
Defendant,	)	
_____	)	

Pre-trial hearing is currently set for _____, 20 ___.
Jury trial is currently set for _____, 20 ___.
    COMES NOW the parties in the above captioned action and, by signature of counsel, do hereby stipulate and agree that **this case has not been resolved by agreement,** and should remain on the trial calendar or be reset by the clerk as indicated below:

1. Motions:

    [ ]   There will be no pretrial motions and the above noted pre-trial hearing should be stricken.

    [ ]   Pre-trial motions have been filed and served. The clerk is requested to reset the pre-trial hearing for ___ / ___ / ___.

    [ ]   A CrRLJ 3.5 Hearing is required. The clerk is requested to set the hearing for ___ / ___ / ___.

2. Bench/Jury Trial:

    [ ]   Remain set for a jury trial at above noted date and time.

    [ ]   Clerk is requested to re-set jury trial as follows: _____.

    [ ]   Jury trial waiver filed; set for bench trial.

3. Discovery:
    Discovery is complete.

4. Witnesses:

    Plaintiff:
    [ ]   Witness list filed
    [ ]   Witnesses as follows:

Name	Address/telephone	Subject of testimony
_____	_____	_____
_____	_____	_____
_____	_____	_____

Defense:
    [ ] Witness list filed
    [ ] Witnesses as follows:

	Name	Address/telephone	Subject of testimony
	_____	_____	_____
	_____	_____	_____
	_____	_____	_____

Attorney for Plaintiff   W.S.B.A. #   Attorney for Defendant W.S.B.A. #

_____

Interpreter

[Adopted effective September 1, 2011.]

LCrRLJ 4.5 FORM 2.   DEFERRED PROSECUTION FINDINGS OF FACT, CONCLUSIONS OF LAW & ORDER

Upper Kittitas County District Court

    State of Washington

[ ] State of Washington,	)	
	)	
Plaintiff,	)	No.
	)	Deferred Prosecution
vs.	)	Findings of Fact, Conclusions of
	)	Law & Order
_____,	)	
Defendant.	)	
_____	)	

This matter coming before the court on the defendant's Petition for Deferred Prosecution, and the court having considered the Petition, evaluation and treatment plan filed by the defendant, and the arguments of counsel, now makes the following findings of fact:

I.   Findings of Fact

1. The defendant was evaluated by an approved alcoholism treatment facility or an approved drug treatment center; said agency's evaluation meets the requirements of RCW 10.05.040 and is attached to this Order. A certified alcoholism treatment facility or drug treatment center has prepared a treatment plan meeting the requirements of RCW 10.05.150 and has committed to provide treatment. Said treatment plan and commitment to treatment is attached to this Order, and incorporated by reference herein.

2. The defendant has agreed to pay, or arranged for the payment of, the costs of treatment.

3. The defendant has agreed to complete the two-year treatment program set forth in the treatment plan attached to this Order and to follow the other conditions of the court's Order.

4. The defendant has been advised of the following rights and has knowingly and voluntarily waived each of them:

(a) The right to a jury trial;

(b) The right to a speedy trial;

(c) The right to present evidence in his or her defense;

(d) The right to hear and question all witnesses who testify against the defendant;

(e) The right to compel witnesses to appear and testify on behalf of the defendant at no cost to the defendant;

(f) The right to testify.

5. The defendant has stipulated to the admissibility and sufficiency of the facts contained in the written police reports and understands these facts will be considered by the court in any criminal hearing on the underlying offense or offenses held subsequent to revocation of the order granting deferred prosecution. The defendant has agreed that the facts contained in the stipulated police reports are sufficient to allow the court to find the petitioner guilty, beyond a reasonable doubt, of the charged offenses.

6. The defendant has agreed, and the court finds, that any statements made by the defendant contained in the stipulated police reports were made knowingly and voluntarily.

7. If the charge is a violation of RCW Title 46 or similar municipal ordinance, the defendant has affirmed, and the court finds, that the defendant has not previously participated in a prior deferred prosecution program for a violation of RCW Title 46 or any similar municipal ordinance.

From the forgoing Findings of Fact, the court makes the following conclusions of law:

II. Conclusions of Law

1. The court has jurisdiction over the subject matter and petitioner in this case.

2. The petition meets the requirements of RCW 10.05.020

3. The diagnostic evaluation and treatment plan met the requirements of RCW 10.05.040, RCW 10.05.050 and RCW 10.05.150.

4. The Petition was made freely, voluntarily and knowingly.

III. Order

Based on the foregoing Findings of Fact and Conclusions of Law, the court hereby grants the Petition for Deferred Prosecution and allows the defendant to enter into a deferred prosecution program. The defendant shall remain under the jurisdiction of the court and the supervision of Kittitas County Probation Services during the two year treatment plan, and for three years after the court receives proof of successful completion of the two-year treatment program, but not less than five years from the date of this Order. The defendant shall, while under the court's jurisdiction, comply with the following conditions:

1. The defendant shall fully comply with and complete the two-year treatment program attached to this Order and incorporated by reference in Paragraph 2 of the court's Findings. In the event there are any inconsistencies between this order and the attached treatment plan, the terms and conditions set forth in this order shall be controlling.

2. The defendant shall pay, or arrange for payment of, the costs of the treatment program.

3. The defendant shall maintain total abstinence from alcohol and all other non-prescribed mind altering drugs.

4. The defendant shall not commit any crimes. The definition of "commit" includes, but is not limited to, any criminal charge resolved by a stay of proceedings, a stipulated order of continuance, or any other agreement which consists of a continuance with conditions, even if the ultimate disposition of the criminal charge is a dismissal, amendment of charge, or a finding of not guilty.

5. The defendant shall not refuse to submit to a breath or blood test if a police officer has reasonable grounds to believe that the defendant is driving or is in physical control of a motor vehicle while under the influence of intoxicating liquor or drugs.

6. The defendant shall not operate a motor vehicle upon the public highways without a valid operator's license and proof of liability insurance in an amount not less than that established by RCW 46.29.490.

7. The defendant shall immediately report to Probation Services, and continue to report in the future as directed by Probation Services.

8. The defendant shall pay $40 per month for probation supervision. The court may, after the successful completion of the two year treatment program,

reduce the level of supervision (and associated probation fees) required for the remainder of the period of supervision.

8.[1] The defendant shall not change treatment agencies without written permission of the court.

9. The treatment facility shall file with Kittitas County Probation Services **monthly** treatment status/compliance reports. Those reports shall be sent to:

Kittitas County Probation Services

507 Nanum Street

Ellensburg, Washington 98926

10. The defendant shall provide **in writing** to the court and Probation Services any change in mailing address.

11. The defendant shall not drive any motor vehicle unless the motor vehicle is equipped with a functioning ignition interlock calibrated to prevent the motor vehicle from being started when the breath sample provided has an alcohol concentration of 0.025 or more. This restriction is effective [ ] immediately; [ ] as of ___ / ___ / ___; [ ] after the completion of any suspension, revocation, or denial of driving privileges. The period of time of this restriction shall be for [ ] one year [ ] five years [ ] ten years.

12. The defendant [ ] shall [ ] shall not be required to pay a $250 administrative fee.

13. The defendant [ ] shall [ ] shall not be required to pay a $125 breath test fee.

14. [ ] The defendant [ ] shall [ ] shall not be required to reimburse Kittitas County for the cost of his/her court appointed attorney in the amount of $ ___.

15. [ ] The defendant shall pay restitution in the amount of $ ___. [ ] A restitution hearing shall be held on ___ / ___ /20___ to determine what amount of restitution should be paid by the defendant

16. The defendant shall start the two year deferred prosecution treatment program on or before: ___ / ___ /20___. [ ] **Prior to entry into the two year intensive treatment program, the defendant shall attend a minimum of three (3) self-help recovery support group meetings per week, and provide proof of attendance to Probation Services. The defendant shall also attend and fully participate in any pre-treatment program available from his or her treatment agency. The defendant shall report to Probation Services as directed.**

17. [ ] The defendant shall attend a DUI victim's panel in Kittitas County on: ___ / ___ /20___. [ ] The defendant shall attend a DUI victim's panel within 90 days. [ ] The defendant shall attend a Spanish language DUI victim's panel as directed by Probation Services.

18. This matter shall be set for review at any time as may be deemed appropriate by the court. In the event the defendant fails or neglects to undertake, complete or comply with any term or condition of this Order, the court, upon receiving notice of such failure, neglect, or violation, shall hold a hearing to determine whether the sufficient cause exists to remove the defendant from the deferred prosecution program. In the event the defendant is convicted of a similar offense, the court shall remove the defendant from the deferred prosecution program.

19. In the event the court finds cause to revoke the deferred prosecution, the court (sitting without a jury) will consider the stipulated police reports, including any statements made by the defendant, and determine whether the stipulated evidence supports the charge(s) beyond a reasonable doubt

20. In the event the defendant complies with the conditions of this Order the court shall, three years after receiving proof of successful completion of the

two-year treatment program, but not before five years following entry of this Order, dismiss the charges pending against the defendant.

21. Other: _____

_____

Dated ____/____/20____   _____
Judge/Court Commissioner

Presented by: Copy received; approved as to form:

_____   _____
Attorney for Defendant WSBA #   Prosecuting Authority   WSBA #

Copy received; terms and conditions of Order accepted by:

_____
                Defendant

Attached to this Order are:

   A. Alcohol/drug evaluation, treatment plan and commitment to provide treatment.

   B. Police reports.

[Adopted effective September 1, 2011.]

_____
1 Numbering in original.

LCrRLJ 4.5 FORM 3.   STIPULATION FOR AND ORDER FOR STAY OF PROCEEDINGS

UPPER KITTITAS COUNTY DISTRICT COURT
STATE OF WASHINGTON

[ ] State of Washington,
[ ] City of Cle Elum, [ ] City of Roslyn

Plaintiff,

vs.

_____ ,
Defendant.
_____

)
)
)
)
)
)
)
)
)
)
)

No. _____
Stipulation for and Order for
Stay of Proceedings

Charge(s) _____

_____

_____ [ ] Deputy Prosecuting Attorney and _____, defendant, represented by _____, stipulate and agree to a stay of proceedings in this matter for a period of ___ months, on the following terms and conditions:

1. The defendant shall maintain good and lawful behavior during the term of the stay: the defendant shall have no criminal convictions for offenses committed after the date of this order, no charges during the term of the stay which lead to criminal convictions, no criminal charges which lead to a stay of proceedings, stipulated order of continuance or similar disposition, and no criminal charges which lead to a deferred prosecution.   In addition:

[ ]   The defendant shall complete ___ hours of approved community service within ___ days and provide proof of completion to Kittitas County Probation Services.

[ ]   The defendant shall complete ___ days of Department of Corrections work crew within ___ days and provide proof of completion to Probation Services.

[ ]   The defendant shall attend a DUI victim's panel within ___ days and provide proof to Probation Services.

[ ]   The defendant shall obtain the following evaluation(s) and provide proof of such evaluation(s) to Probation Services within 30 days:
    [ ] Alcohol/Drug   [ ] Domestic Violence   [ ] Anger Management
    [ ] Other: _____

    In the event the evaluating agency recommends that the defendant obtain treatment or other Services, the defendant shall fully comply with the agency's recommendations and start any recommended classes or treatment within 45 days.   In the event that extended treatment is recommended, the defendant shall direct the treating agency to provide compliance reports to Probation Services on a monthly basis.

[ ]   Other: _____

2. Probation Services shall monitor the defendant's compliance with the conditions of this order. Probation Services shall:
    [ ]   Actively monitor the defendant.   [ ] Complete ___ record checks.
    [ ]   The defendant shall immediately report to Probation Services and continue to report as directed.

3. The defendant shall pay the following assessments:
    [ ] Probation record check fees of $ ___   [ ] Probation monitoring fees of $ ___ per month
    [ ] Court appointed attorney fees of $ ___   [ ] Court costs: $ ___
    [ ] Restitution in the amount of $ ___   [ ] A Time payment agreement is authorized

4. The defendant hereby waives his/her right to a trial within 90 days of arraignment, and agrees to a trial date of no later than 90 days from the end of the stay of proceedings.   In the event that the defendant is charged with a crime during the term of the stay of proceedings, but which is not resolved until after the end of the term of the stay, the defendant agrees to a trial date no later than 90 days after final resolution of the subsequently charged criminal offense.

5. If the defendant complies with all of the above listed conditions, the prosecuting authority agrees to:

    [ ]   Move the court for a dismissal of the charge(s) of: _____ filed under the above cause number.
    [ ]   Move the court to amend the charge of _____ to the charge of _____ to which the defendant shall: [ ] Plead guilty [ ] Bail forfeit $ ___ [ ] Other: _____
    [ ]   In the event the defendant pleads guilty the parties agree to the following sentencing recommendation:

[ ] Prosecutor's recommendation: _____

[ ] Defense recommendation: _____

6. In the event the court finds, after a hearing, that the defendant has failed to comply with any of the above listed conditions, the court shall, upon the request of the prosecuting authority, revoke the stay of proceedings and set a trial date.

7. As a condition of entering this stay of proceedings, the defendant agrees to waive the following rights:

   A. The right to a jury trial
   B. The right to a trial within 90 days of arraignment.
   C. The right at trial to hear and question witnesses called by the prosecuting authority.
   D. The right to testify at trial and call defense witnesses.

8. In the event the court finds cause to revoke the stay of proceedings, the defendant stipulates and agrees to the admissibility of the attached police reports (including any statements made by the defendant contained in the reports) and stipulates and agrees that the facts contained in the attached reports are sufficient to convict the defendant of the charged crime(s).

9. The parties agree that in the event the defendant fails to make payments as listed above and is delinquent by fifteen (15) days or more, the plaintiff and/or court have the authority to send such delinquent amounts to a collection agency for collection of said sums. Both parties agree that this authority exists whether or not the plaintiff chooses to have the matter set for review and bench trial. The defendant specifically waives any objection to such collection action by the plaintiff or the court, regardless of whether or not the defendant is found guilty after a trial. The defendant agrees that this document, along with any time payment agreement signed by the defendant, constitute a judgment for the amounts stated in paragraph 3 above.

10. The defendant understands and agrees that this document constitutes an agreement between the plaintiff and the defendant pertaining to the resolution of a criminal charge(s). The defendant further understands that he/she is obligated to fully and strictly comply with all conditions set forth in this agreement. The defendant further understands that in the event the defendant fails to fully comply with the conditions of this agreement, the prosecuting authority may request a hearing in order seek revocation this stay of proceedings.

11. The parties jointly request that the court allow the above described stay of proceedings and further request that the court enter the attached order

Dated this ___ day of _____, _____   _____
                                                                Defendant

_____ _____   _____ _____
Prosecuting Authority   WSBA #   Attorney for Defendant   WSBA #

ORDER

Based on the parties' request for a stay of proceedings, and the above stipulation between the parties, the court hereby orders that this cause is stayed for a period of _____, under the terms and conditions contained in the attached stipulation.

Dated this ___ day of _____, _____   _____
                                                        Judge/ Court Commissioner

[Adopted effective September 1, 2011.]

LIRLJ 3.5. FORM

UPPER KITTITAS COUNTY DISTRICT COURT

STATE OF WASHINGTON

State of Washington,
     Plaintiff

Infraction Number: _____

Defendant's Request For Decision
On Written Statements

VS.

[ ] Contested Hearing
[ ] Mitigation Hearing

_____
       Defendant

TO: Upper Kittitas County District Court
Infraction Number: _____
I hereby request that the Court decide my case based upon the following statement:

_____

_____

_____

_____

_____

_____

(Attach Additional Page(s) if necessary).

I certify (or declare) under penalty of perjury under the laws of the State of Washington that the foregoing statement is true.

I understand that Infraction Rules for Courts of Limited Jurisdiction 3. 5(e) provides "There shall be no appeal from a decision on written statements".

I promise that if it is determined that I committed the infraction for which I was cited, I will pay the monetary penalty authorized by law and assessed by the Court.

_____
(Date and Place)

Defendant's Signature
_____

Current Mailing Address
_____

[Adopted effective September 1, 2011.]

MUNICIPAL COURTS

CLE ELUM MUNICIPAL COURT LOCAL RULES

Including Amendments Received Through
August 15, 2015

Table of Rules

INTRODUCTION

LARLJ 2. SCOPE OF RULES AND ADOPTION

(a) **Effect of Local Rules.** The provisions of the Local Rules are supplemental to the Rules for courts of Limited Jurisdiction, as adopted or hereafter amended by the Supreme Court of the State of Washington, and shall not be construed in conflict with them.

(b) **Scope.** The Local Rules apply to all Courts in which a Upper Kittitas County District Court Judge is appointed or elected to sit, including but not limited to the Upper Kittitas County District Court, Cle Elum Municipal Court, and the Roslyn Municipal Court.

(c) **Adoption and Amendments.** These Rules may be amended from time to time by the Cle Elum Municipal Court Judge.

(d) **Prior Rules Repealed.** All prior rules of the Cle Elum Municipal Court are repealed upon the adoption of these Rules.

[Adopted effective September 1, 2011.]

LOCAL CRIMINAL RULES

LCrRLJ 4.5. PRE–TRIAL PROCEDURE

(A) **Pre–Trial Hearings.** All cases scheduled for jury trial shall be set by the clerk for a pre-trial hearing. The state or city prosecutor, defense counsel and the defendant shall attend the pre-trial hearing to consider such matters as will promote a fair and expeditious trial. Upon agreement that the discovery process has been completed to the satisfaction of the parties and that there are no other issues to be heard by the court at the scheduled pre-trial hearing, a stipulated pre-trial statement of readiness, substantially in the form set forth as "Form 1" below, may be filed by the parties. The filing of a stipulated pre-trial statement of readiness will serve to excuse counsel and the defendant from appearing at the scheduled pre-trial hearing.

(B) **Motions.** All amendments to the charges, pleas or pre-trial motions shall be made prior to or at the time of the pre-trial hearing. Motions which should have been heard at a pretrial hearing shall not be considered at the time of trial unless the judge at the time of the pre-trial hearing expressly continues such motions to the time of trial. Absent good cause, motions for dismissal or suppression of evidence in criminal cases shall be in writing and shall be provided to the prosecutor or city attorney at least 24 hours before the pre-trial hearing. Motions which are lengthy, complex, or which require the presence of witnesses will be heard by the court at a subsequent 3.5/3.6 hearing calendar.

(C) CrRLJ 3.5 Hearings. Pursuant to CrRLJ 3.5(a) all demands for hearing on the admissibility of confessions must be made no later than the pre-trial hearing. All motions filed pursuant to this rule shall be heard by the court at a subsequent 3.5/3.6 hearing calendar.

(D) Deferred Prosecution—Time for Petition— Forms for Petition and Order. A petition for deferred prosecution shall be filed with the court at least seven days before the date set for trial but, upon written motion and affidavit establishing good cause for the delay and failure to comply with this rule, the court may waive this requirement subject to the defendant's reimbursement to the court of the witness fees and expenses due for subpoenaed witnesses who have appeared on the date set for trial. The petition for deferred prosecution shall substantially comply with CrRLJ 4.2(I). The proposed findings and order shall substantially comply with the form set forth as "Form 2" below.

(E) Stays of Proceedings—Form of Order. In the event the parties enter into a stay of proceedings, the agreement between the parties shall be reduced to writing in a form which substantially complies with the form set forth as "Form 3" below.

[Adopted effective September 1, 2011.]

Comments

The purpose of these rules is to eliminate surprise and unnecessary delay and expense. While the purpose of these rules is not to create traps for the unwary, when a party's failure to follow these rules causes unnecessary extra expense to the opposing party, the inconvenienced party may apply to the court for the imposition of sanctions. The purpose of these sanctions is not to punish but rather to insure that the appropriate party is responsible for the predictable costs of unnecessary delay.

Comment to section (A): The stipulated pre-trial statement of readiness was adopted by the court at the request of counsel who wanted to avoid the necessity of clients appearing at unproductive pre-trial hearings. Attorneys are encouraged to use the pre-trial statement of readiness to avoid the necessity of clients appearing when there are no pre-trial issues requiring his or her presence.

Comment to section (B): The purpose of this section is to provide a predictable structure to the

pre-trial motions process and to insure that the non-moving party has adequate time to prepare for the hearing. However, if counsel desire to avoid multiple hearings, the parties may agree to present evidence and argue pre-trial motions at the scheduled pre-trial hearing rather than following the procedure described by this rule.

Comment to section (C): See the comments to section (B).

Comment to section (D): See RCW 10.05.010.

Comment to section (E): The stay of proceedings form set forth below is generally consistent with the forms currently in use in the Cle Elum Municipal Court. In creating a uniform stay of proceedings form, it is not the court's intention to suggest what conditions should be part of an agreement between the parties. For example, if an agreement between the parties in a specific case does not include the defendant stipulating to the admissibility of the police reports, or a stipulation that the reports are sufficient to convict, the court expects the parties to line out that portion of the stay of proceedings form.

LCrRLJ 7.2(f). REQUIREMENTS FOR CHEMICAL DEPENDENCY ASSESSMENTS

When, as a part of a sentence or other disposition, a chemical dependency assessment is required, the alcohol/drug evaluator must be a certified Chemical Dependency Professional (CDP) or a CDP trainee (CDPT) under supervision of a CDP. The evaluator shall prepare a written report of the assessment that shall include a description of the steps taken to insure compliance with the requirements of WAC 388–805–310. The written report shall also include the following information:

1. A description of the sources used to establish the defendant's legal history. At a minimum, these sources must include a Defendant's Case History (DCH), a Washington Department of Licensing driver's record abstract, and police reports describing the current offense. The police reports shall contain, at a minimum, a description of the offense and the defendant's blood or breath alcohol level and any other drug levels at the time of arrest.

2. A description of sources used to document the defendant's history of alcohol and other drug treatment or education. At a minimum, these sources shall include any available drug/alcohol evaluations prepared by a CDP or CDPT concerning the defendant. The defendant shall notify the evaluator of any prior alcohol/drug evaluation and sign any releases necessary to make such alcohol/drug evaluations available to his or her current evaluating agency.

3. A description of the method used to notify the defendant of the assessment results. The defendant shall be supplied with a copy of his alcohol/drug evaluation along with any treatment/education recommendations made by the CDP or CDPT. If the assessment results are mailed to the defendant, the report shall state the address to which the assessment was mailed and the date of mailing.

[Adopted effective September 1, 2011.]

LOCAL RULE OF GENERAL APPLICATION

LGR 17(a)(7).   FACSIMILE TRANSMISSION

The Cle Elum Municipal Court will not accept for filing a facsimile transmission of any pleading or other document for which any other court rule or statute sets a filing time-limit or filing deadline. The court will accept facsimile transmissions of other documents, including judge's working copies of trial briefs or position statements.

[Adopted effective September 1, 2011.]

LOCAL INFRACTION RULES

LIRLJ 3.5.   INFRACTION HEARINGS BASED ON WRITTEN STATEMENTS

The court adopts IRLJ 3.5 and will, at the request of a defendant, decide infraction cases based on written statements. A defendant requesting the court to decide the case on written statements shall do so by completing a statement in substantially the following form:

{see form LIRLJ 3.5 Form}

[Adopted effective September 1, 2011.]

LIRLJ 6.6(e).   REQUEST FOR SPEED MEASURING DEVICE EXPERT

Request for Speed Measuring Device ("SMD") Expert. Defense requests to produce an electronic or laser SMD expert pursuant to IRLJ 6.6(b) shall be contained in a separate document clearly designated as a request for an SMD expert, served on the prosecuting authority with a conformed copy filed with the clerk of the court. If the charging law enforcement agency's SMD expert maintains a schedule for monthly appearances in the Cle Elum Municipal Court, a request for an SMD expert shall be deemed by the court to be a request to set (or re–set) the hearing to a day scheduled for the agency's SMD expert. An SMD expert called as a witness by either party may testify by telephone; however, any party intending to elicit telephonic testimony from an SMD expert shall notify the court and the opposing party at least 5 days prior to the date set for the contested hearing.

[Adopted effective September 1, 2011.]

Comments

Comments to Local Infraction Rule 6.6(e). LIR 6.6(e) is designed to address the problem of requests for SMD experts being "buried" within discovery requests or other documents filed in contested infraction cases. A request for an SMD expert which stands alone and is clearly identified as a request for an SMD expert will eliminate continuances for defendants who desire the presence of an SMD expert but who have not made their wish sufficiently clear to the prosecuting authority. Allowing SMD expert testimony by telephone serves to reduce costs incurred by law enforcement agencies as well as assisting defendants in presenting the testimony of their own SMD experts.

LIR 6.6(f).   PUBLIC ACCESS TO SPEED MEASURING DEVICE CERTIFICATES

Pursuant to IRLJ 6.6(d), the court maintains as public records any design and construction certifications for electronic speed measuring devices and laser speed measuring devices filed with the court.

[Adopted effective September 1, 2011.]

FORMS
INTERPRETER'S DECLARATION

I am a certified interpreter or have been found otherwise qualified by the court to interpret in the _____ language, which the defendant understands, and I have translated this Stipulation for and Order for Stay of Proceedings for the defendant from English into that language. The defendant has acknowledged his or her understanding of both the translation and the subject matter of this document. I certify under penalty of perjury under the laws of the state of Washington that the foregoing is true and correct.

Signed at Cle Elum, Washington on: ___ / ___ / ___

[Adopted effective September 1, 2011.]

LCrRLJ 4.5 FORM 1.   STIPULATED PRE–TRIAL STATEMENT OF READINESS

A stipulation filed in substantially the following form will comply with LCrRLJ 4.5(A):

CLE ELUM MUNICIPAL COURT
STATE OF WASHINGTON

[ ] State of Washington	)
[ ] City of Cle Elum,	)
[ ] City of Roslyn	) NO. _____
Plaintiff,	) STIPULATED PRE–TRIAL
	) STATEMENT OF READINESS
vs.	)
_____,	)
Defendant,	)
_____	)

Pre-trial hearing is currently set for _____, 20___.
Jury trial is currently set for _____, 20 ___.

    COMES NOW the parties in the above captioned action and, by signature of counsel, do hereby stipulate and agree that **this case has not been resolved by agreement,** and should remain on the trial calendar or be reset by the clerk as indicated below:

1. Motions:

      [ ] There will be no pretrial motions and the above noted pre- trial hearing should be stricken.

      [ ] Pre-trial motions have been filed and served. The clerk is requested to reset the pre-trial hearing for __/__/__.
      [ ] A CrRLJ 3.5 Hearing is required. The clerk is requested to set the hearing for __/__/__.

2. Bench/Jury Trial:

      [ ] Remain set for a jury trial at above noted date and time.
      [ ] Clerk is requested to re-set jury trial as follows: _____.
      [ ] Jury trial waiver filed; set for bench trial.

3. Discovery:

      Discovery is complete.

4. Witnesses:

      Plaintiff:
      [ ] Witness list filed
      [ ] Witnesses as follows:

Name	Address/telephone	Subject of testimony

Defense:
    [ ] Witness list filed
    [ ] Witnesses as follows:

Name	Address/telephone	Subject of testimony

Attorney for Plaintiff   W.S.B.A. #   Attorney for Defendant W.S.B.A. #

Interpreter

[Adopted effective September 1, 2011.]

LCrRLJ 4.5 FORM 2.   DEFERRED PROSECUTION FINDINGS OF FACT, CONCLUSIONS OF LAW & ORDER

Cle Elum Municipal Court
State of Washington

[ ] State of Washington,	)
	)
Plaintiff,	) No.
	) Deferred Prosecution
vs.	) Findings of Fact, Conclusions of
	) Law & Order
_____,	)
Defendant.	)
_____	)

This matter coming before the court on the defendant's Petition for Deferred Prosecution, and the court having considered the Petition, evaluation and treatment plan filed by the defendant, and the arguments of counsel, now makes the following findings of fact:

I.   Findings of Fact

1. The defendant was evaluated by an approved alcoholism treatment facility or an approved drug treatment center; said agency's evaluation meets the requirements of RCW 10.05.040 and is attached to this Order. A certified alcoholism treatment facility or drug treatment center has prepared a treatment plan meeting the requirements of RCW 10.05.150 and has committed to provide treatment. Said treatment plan and commitment to treatment is attached to this Order, and incorporated by reference herein.

2. The defendant has agreed to pay, or arranged for the payment of, the costs of treatment.

3. The defendant has agreed to complete the two-year treatment program set forth in the treatment plan attached to this Order and to follow the other conditions of the court's Order.

4. The defendant has been advised of the following rights and has knowingly and voluntarily waived each of them:

(a) The right to a jury trial;

(b) The right to a speedy trial;

(c) The right to present evidence in his or her defense;

(d) The right to hear and question all witnesses who testify against the defendant;

(e) The right to compel witnesses to appear and testify on behalf of the defendant at no cost to the defendant;

(f) The right to testify.

5. The defendant has stipulated to the admissibility and sufficiency of the facts contained in the written police reports and understands these facts will be considered by the court in any criminal hearing on the underlying offense or offenses held subsequent to revocation of the order granting deferred prosecution. The defendant has agreed that the facts contained in the stipulated police reports are sufficient to allow the court to find the petitioner guilty, beyond a reasonable doubt, of the charged offenses.

6. The defendant has agreed, and the court finds, that any statements made by the defendant contained in the stipulated police reports were made knowingly and voluntarily.

962

7. If the charge is a violation of RCW Title 46 or similar municipal ordinance, the defendant has affirmed, and the court finds, that the defendant has not previously participated in a prior deferred prosecution program for a violation of RCW Title 46 or any similar municipal ordinance.

From the forgoing Findings of Fact, the court makes the following conclusions of law:

II. Conclusions of Law

1. The court has jurisdiction over the subject matter and petitioner in this case.
2. The petition meets the requirements of RCW 10.05.020
3. The diagnostic evaluation and treatment plan met the requirements of RCW 10.05.040, RCW 10.05.050 and RCW 10.05.150.
4. The Petition was made freely, voluntarily and knowingly.

III. Order

Based on the foregoing Findings of Fact and Conclusions of Law, the court hereby grants the Petition for Deferred Prosecution and allows the defendant to enter into a deferred prosecution program. The defendant shall remain under the jurisdiction of the court and the supervision of Kittitas County Probation Services during the two year treatment plan, and for three years after the court receives proof of successful completion of the two-year treatment program, but not less than five years from the date of this Order. The defendant shall, while under the court's jurisdiction, comply with the following conditions:

1. The defendant shall fully comply with and complete the two-year treatment program attached to this Order and incorporated by reference in Paragraph 2 of the court's Findings. In the event there are any inconsistencies between this order and the attached treatment plan, the terms and conditions set forth in this order shall be controlling.

2. The defendant shall pay, or arrange for payment of, the costs of the treatment program.

3. The defendant shall maintain total abstinence from alcohol and all other non-prescribed mind altering drugs.

4. The defendant shall not commit any crimes. The definition of "commit" includes, but is not limited to, any criminal charge resolved by a stay of proceedings, a stipulated order of continuance, or any other agreement which consists of a continuance with conditions, even if the ultimate disposition of the criminal charge is a dismissal, amendment of charge, or a finding of not guilty.

5. The defendant shall not refuse to submit to a breath or blood test if a police officer has reasonable grounds to believe that the defendant is driving or is in physical control of a motor vehicle while under the influence of intoxicating liquor or drugs.

6. The defendant shall not operate a motor vehicle upon the public highways without a valid operator's license and proof of liability insurance in an amount not less than that established by RCW 46.29.490.

7. The defendant shall immediately report to Probation Services, and continue to report in the future as directed by Probation Services.

8. The defendant shall pay $40 per month for probation supervision. The court may, after the successful completion of the two year treatment program, reduce the level of supervision (and associated probation fees) required for the remainder of the period of supervision.

8.[1] The defendant shall not change treatment agencies without written permission of the court.

9. The treatment facility shall file with Kittitas County Probation Services **monthly** treatment status/compliance reports. Those reports shall be sent to:

Kittitas County Probation Services

507 Nanum Street

Ellensburg, Washington 98926

10. The defendant shall provide **in writing** to the court and Probation Services any change in mailing address.

11. The defendant shall not drive any motor vehicle unless the motor vehicle is equipped with a functioning ignition interlock calibrated to prevent the motor vehicle from being started when the breath sample provided has an alcohol concentration of 0.025 or more. This restriction is effective [ ] immediately; [ ] as of ___ / ___ / ___; [ ] after the completion of any suspension, revocation, or denial of driving privileges. The period of time of this restriction shall be for [ ] one year [ ] five years [ ] ten years.

12. The defendant [ ] shall [ ] shall not be required to pay a $250 administrative fee.

13. The defendant [ ] shall [ ] shall not be required to pay a $125 breath test fee.

14. [ ] The defendant [ ] shall [ ] shall not be required to reimburse Kittitas County for the cost of his/her court appointed attorney in the amount of $ _____.

15. [ ] The defendant shall pay restitution in the amount of $ _____. [ ] A restitution hearing shall be held on ___ / ___ /20____ to determine what amount of restitution should be paid by the defendant.

16. The defendant shall start the two year deferred prosecution treatment program on or before: ___ / ___ /20____ . [ ] **Prior to entry into the two year intensive treatment program, the defendant shall attend a minimum of three (3) self-help recovery support group meetings per week, and provide proof of attendance to Probation Services. The defendant shall also attend and fully participate in any pre-treatment program available from his or her treatment agency. The defendant shall report to Probation Services as directed.**

17. [ ] The defendant shall attend a DUI victim's panel in Kittitas County on: ___ / ___ /20____ . [ ] The defendant shall attend a DUI victim's panel within 90 days. [ ] The defendant shall attend a Spanish language DUI victim's panel as directed by Probation Services.

18. This matter shall be set for review at any time as may be deemed appropriate by the court. In the event the defendant fails or neglects to undertake, complete or comply with any term or condition of this Order, the court, upon receiving notice of such failure, neglect, or violation, shall hold a hearing to determine whether the sufficient cause exists to remove the defendant from the deferred prosecution program. In the event the defendant is convicted of a similar offense, the court shall remove the defendant from the deferred prosecution program.

19. In the event the court finds cause to revoke the deferred prosecution, the court (sitting without a jury) will consider the stipulated police reports, including any statements made by the defendant, and determine whether the stipulated evidence supports the charge(s) beyond a reasonable doubt

20. In the event the defendant complies with the conditions of this Order the court shall, three years after receiving proof of successful completion of the two-year treatment program, but not before five years following entry of this Order, dismiss the charges pending against the defendant.

21. Other: _____

Dated___/___/20___
Judge/Court Commissioner

Presented by: Copy received; approved as to form:

_____   _____
Attorney for Defendant   WSBA #   Prosecuting Authority   WSBA #

Copy received; terms and conditions of Order accepted by:

_____
                    Defendant

Attached to this Order are:

    A. Alcohol/drug evaluation, treatment plan and commitment to provide treatment.

    B. Police reports.

[Adopted effective September 1, 2011.]

---

1 Numbering in original.

LCrRLJ 4.5 FORM 3.   STIPULATION FOR AND ORDER FOR STAY OF PROCEEDINGS

CLE ELUM MUNICIPAL COURT
STATE OF WASHINGTON

[ ] State of Washington,	)
[ ] State of Washington,	)
[ ] City of Cle Elum, [ ] City of Roslyn	) No. _____
Plaintiff,	) Stipulation for and Order for
	) Stay of Proceedings
vs.	)
	) Charge(s) _____
_____,	)
Defendant.	) _____
	)

_____ [ ] Deputy Prosecuting Attorney and _____, defendant, represented by _____, stipulate and agree to a stay of proceedings in this matter for a period of ___ months, on the following terms and conditions:

1. The defendant shall maintain good and lawful behavior during the term of the stay: the defendant shall have no criminal convictions for offenses committed after the date of this order, no charges during the term of the stay which lead to criminal convictions, no criminal charges which lead to a stay of proceedings, stipulated order of continuance or similar disposition, and no criminal charges which lead to a deferred prosecution. In addition:

[ ] The defendant shall complete ___ hours of approved community service within _ days and provide proof of completion to Kittitas County Probation Services.

[ ] The defendant shall complete ___ days of Department of Corrections work crew within ___ days and provide proof of completion to Probation Services.

[ ] The defendant shall attend a DUI victim's panel within ___ days and provide proof to Probation Services.

[ ] The defendant shall obtain the following evaluation(s) and provide proof of such evaluation(s) to Probation Services within 30 days:

    [ ] Alcohol/Drug   [ ] Domestic Violence   [ ] Anger Management
    [ ] Other: _____

In the event the evaluating agency recommends that the defendant obtain treatment or other Services, the defendant shall fully comply with the agency's recommendations and start any recommended classes or treatment within 45 days. In the event that extended treatment is recommended, the defendant shall direct the treating agency to provide compliance reports to Probation Services on a monthly basis.

[ ] Other: _____

2. Probation Services shall monitor the defendant's compliance with the conditions of this order. Probation Services shall:

[ ] Actively monitor the defendant. [ ] Complete ___ record checks.

[ ] The defendant shall immediately report to Probation Services and continue to report as directed.

3. The defendant shall pay the following assessments:

    [ ] Probation record check fees of $ _____   [ ] Probation monitoring fees of $ _____ per month
    [ ] Court appointed attorney fees of $ _____   [ ] Court costs: $_____
    [ ] Restitution in the amount of $_____   [ ] A Time payment agreement is authorized

4. The defendant hereby waives his/her right to a trial within 90 days of arraignment, and agrees to a trial date of no later than 90 days from the end of the stay of proceedings. In the event that the defendant is charged with a

crime during the term of the stay of proceedings, but which is not resolved until after the end of the term of the stay, the defendant agrees to a trial date no later than 90 days after final resolution of the subsequently charged criminal offense.

5. If the defendant complies with all of the above listed conditions, the prosecuting authority agrees to:

[ ] Move the court for a dismissal of the charge(s) of: _____ filed under the above cause number.

[ ] Move the court to amend the charge of _____ to the charge of _____ to which the defendant shall: [ ] Plead guilty [ ] Bail forfeit $ _____. [ ] Other: _____

[ ] In the event the defendant pleads guilty the parties agree to the following sentencing recommendation:

[ ] Prosecutor's reccomendantion [1]: _____

[ ] Defense recommendation: _____

6. In the event the court finds, after a hearing, that the defendant has failed to comply with any of the above listed conditions, the court shall, upon the request of the prosecuting authority, revoke the stay of proceedings and set a trial date.

7. As a condition of entering this stay of proceedings, the defendant agrees to waive the following rights:

A. The right to a jury trial

B. The right to a trial within 90 days of arraignment.

C. The right at trial to hear and question witnesses called by the prosecuting authority.

D. The right to testify at trial and call defense witnesses.

8. In the event the court finds cause to revoke the stay of proceedings, the defendant stipulates and agrees to the admissibility of the attached police reports (including any statements made by the defendant contained in the reports) and stipulates and agrees that the facts contained in the attached reports are sufficient to convict the defendant of the charged crime(s).

9. The parties agree that in the event the defendant fails to make payments as listed above and is delinquent by fifteen (15) days or more, the plaintiff and/or court have the authority to send such delinquent amounts to a collection agency for collection of said sums. Both parties agree that this authority exists whether or not the plaintiff chooses to have the matter set for review and bench trial. The defendant specifically waives any objection to such collection action by the plaintiff or the court, regardless of whether or not the defendant is found guilty after a trial. The defendant agrees that this document, along with any time payment agreement signed by the defendant, constitute a judgment for the amounts stated in paragraph 3 above.

10. The defendant understands and agrees that this document constitutes an agreement between the plaintiff and the defendant pertaining to the resolution of a criminal charge(s). The defendant further understands that he/she is obligated to fully and strictly comply with all conditions set forth in this agreement. The defendant further understands that in the event the defendant fails to fully comply with the conditions of this agreement, the prosecuting authority may request a hearing in order seek revocation this stay of proceedings.

11. The parties jointly request that the court allow the above described stay of proceedings and further request that the court enter the attached order.

Dated this ___ day of _____, _____   _____

                                                  Defendant

_____   _____

Prosecuting Authority   WSBA #   Attorney for Defendant   WSBA #

ORDER

Based on the parties' request for a stay of proceedings, and the above stipulation between the parties, the court hereby orders that this cause is stayed for a period of _____, under the terms and conditions contained in the attached stipulation.

Dated this ___ day of _____, _____   _____

                                                  Judge/Court Commissioner

[Adopted effective September 1, 2011.]

1 So in original.

LIRLJ 3.5 FORM. DEFENDANT'S REQUEST FOR DECISION ON WRITTEN STATEMENTS

CLE ELUM MUNICIPAL COURT
STATE OF WASHINGTON

State of Washington,   Infraction Number: _____
            Plaintiff

                                     Defendant's Request For Decision
                                     On Written Statements

VS.

                                     [ ] Contested Hearing
                                     [ ] Mitigation Hearing

_____
            Defendant

TO: Cle Elum Municipal Court
Infraction Number: _____
I hereby request that the Court decide my case based upon the following statement:

_____
_____
_____
_____
_____
_____
_____
_____

(Attach Additional Page(s) if necessary).
I certify (or declare) under penalty of perjury under the laws of the State of Washington that the foregoing statement is true.
I understand that Infraction Rules for Courts of Limited Jurisdiction 3.5(e) provides "There shall be no appeal from a decision on written statements".
I promise that if it is determined that I committed the infraction for which I was cited, I will pay the monetary penalty authorized by law and assessed by the Court.

_____   _____
(Date and Place)   Defendant's Signature

                                  _____
                                  Current Mailing Address

[Adopted effective September 1, 2011.]

KITTITAS MUNICIPAL COURT—
[No Local Rules]

ROSLYN MUNICIPAL COURT LOCAL RULES

Including Amendments Received Through
August 15, 2015

Table of Rules

INTRODUCTION

LARLJ 2. SCOPE OF RULES AND ADOPTION

(a) Effect of Local Rules. The provisions of the Local Rules are supplemental to the Rules for courts of Limited Jurisdiction, as adopted or hereafter amended by the Supreme Court of the State of Washington, and shall not be construed in conflict with them.

(b) Scope. The Local Rules apply to all Courts in which a Upper Kittitas County District Court Judge is appointed or elected to sit, including but not limited to the Upper Kittitas County District Court, Cle Elum Municipal Court, and the Roslyn Municipal Court.

(c) Adoption and Amendments. These Rules may be amended from time to time by the Roslyn Municipal Court Judge.

(d) Prior Rules Repealed. All prior rules of the Roslyn Municipal Court are repealed upon the adoption of these Rules.

[Adopted effective September 1, 2011.]

LOCAL CRIMINAL RULES

LCrRLJ 4.5. PRE–TRIAL PROCEDURE

(A) Pre–Trial Hearings. All cases scheduled for jury trial shall be set by the clerk for a pre-trial hearing. The state or city prosecutor, defense counsel and the defendant shall attend the pre-trial hearing to consider such matters as will promote a fair and expeditious trial. Upon agreement that the discovery process has been completed to the satisfaction of the parties and that there are no other issues to be heard by the court at the scheduled pre-trial hearing, a stipulated pre-trial statement of readiness, substantially in the form set forth as "Form 1" below, may be filed by the parties. The filing of a stipulated pre-trial statement of readiness will serve to excuse counsel and the defendant from appearing at the scheduled pre-trial hearing.

(B) Motions. All amendments to the charges, pleas or pre-trial motions shall be made prior to or at the time of the pre-trial hearing. Motions which should have been heard at a pretrial hearing shall not be considered at the time of trial unless the judge at the time of the pre-trial hearing expressly continues such motions to the time of trial. Absent good cause, motions for dismissal or suppression of evidence in criminal cases shall be in writing and shall be provided to the prosecutor or city attorney at least 24 hours before the pre-trial hearing. Motions which are lengthy, complex, or which require the presence of witnesses will be heard by the court at a subsequent 3.5/3.6 hearing calendar.

(C) CrRLJ 3.5 Hearings. Pursuant to CrRLJ 3.5(a) all demands for hearing on the admissibility of confessions must be made no later than the pre-trial hearing. All motions filed pursuant to this rule shall be heard by the court at a subsequent 3.5/3.6 hearing calendar.

(D) Deferred Prosecution—Time for Petition— Forms for Petition and Order. A petition for deferred prosecution shall be filed with the court at least seven days before the date set for trial but, upon written motion and affidavit establishing good cause for the delay and failure to comply with this rule, the court may waive this requirement subject to the defendant's reimbursement to the court of the witness fees and expenses due for subpoenaed witnesses who have appeared on the date set for trial. The petition for deferred prosecution shall substantially comply with CrRLJ 4.2(I). The proposed findings and order shall substantially comply with the form set forth as "Form 2" below.

(E) Stays of Proceedings—Form of Order. In the event the parties enter into a stay of proceedings, the agreement between the parties shall be reduced to writing in a form which substantially complies with the form set forth as "Form 3" below.

[Adopted effective September 1, 2011.]

Comments

The purpose of these rules is to eliminate surprise and unnecessary delay and expense. While the purpose of these rules is not to create traps for the unwary, when a party's failure to follow these rules causes unnecessary extra expense to the opposing party, the inconvenienced party may apply to the court for the imposition of sanctions. The purpose of these sanctions is not to punish but rather to insure that the appropriate party is responsible for the predictable costs of unnecessary delay.

Comment to section (A): The stipulated pre-trial statement of readiness was adopted by the court at the request of counsel who wanted to avoid the necessity of clients appearing at unproductive pre-trial hearings. Attorneys are encouraged to use the pre-trial statement of readiness to avoid the necessity of clients appearing when there are no pre-trial issues requiring his or her presence.

Comment to section (B): The purpose of this section is to provide a predictable structure to the pre-trial motions process and to insure that the non-moving party has adequate time to prepare for the hearing. However, if counsel desire to avoid multiple hearings, the parties may agree to present evidence and argue pre-trial motions at the scheduled pre-trial hearing rather than following the procedure described by this rule.

Comment to section (C): See the comments to section (B).

Comment to section (D): See RCW 10.05.010.

Comment to section (E): The stay of proceedings form set forth below is generally consistent with the forms currently in use in the Roslyn Municipal Court. In creating a uniform stay of proceedings form, it is not the court's intention to suggest what conditions should be part of an agreement between the parties. For example, if an agreement between the parties in a specific case does not include the defendant stipulating to the admissibility of the police reports, or a stipulation that the reports are sufficient to convict, the court expects the parties to line out that portion of the stay of proceedings form.

LCrRLJ 7.2(f). REQUIREMENTS FOR CHEMICAL DEPENDENCY ASSESSMENTS

When, as a part of a sentence or other disposition, a chemical dependency assessment is required, the alcohol/drug evaluator must be a certified Chemical Dependency Professional (CDP) or a CDP trainee (CDPT) under supervision of a CDP. The evaluator shall prepare a written report of the assessment that shall include a description of the steps taken to insure compliance with the requirements of WAC 388–805–310. The written report shall also include the following information:

1. A description of the sources used to establish the defendant's legal history. At a minimum, these sources must include a Defendant's Case History (DCH), a Washington Department of Licensing driver's record abstract, and police reports describing the current offense. The police reports shall contain, at a minimum, a description of the offense and the defendant's blood or breath alcohol level and any other drug levels at the time of arrest.

2. A description of sources used to document the defendant's history of alcohol and other drug treatment or education. At a minimum, these sources shall include any available drug/alcohol evaluations prepared by a CDP or CDPT concerning the defendant. The defendant shall notify the evaluator of any prior alcohol/drug evaluation and sign any releases necessary to make such alcohol/drug evaluations available to his or her current evaluating agency.

3. A description of the method used to notify the defendant of the assessment results. The defendant shall be supplied with a copy of his alcohol/drug evaluation along with any treatment/education recommendations made by the CDP or CDPT. If the assessment results are mailed to the defendant, the report shall state the address to which the assessment was mailed and the date of mailing.

[Adopted effective September 1, 2011.]

LOCAL RULE OF GENERAL APPLICATION

LGR 17(a)(7). FACSIMILE TRANSMISSION

The Roslyn Municipal Court will not accept for filing a facsimile transmission of any pleading or other document for which any other court rule or statute sets a filing time-limit or filing deadline. The court will accept facsimile transmissions of other documents, including judge's working copies of trial briefs or position statements.

[Adopted effective September 1, 2011.]

LOCAL INFRACTION RULES

LIRLJ 3.5. INFRACTION HEARINGS BASED ON WRITTEN STATEMENTS

The court adopts IRLJ 3.5 and will, at the request of a defendant, decide infraction cases based on written statements. A defendant requesting the court to decide the case on written statements shall do so by completing a statement in substantially the following form:

{see form LIRLJ 3.5 Form}

[Adopted effective September 1, 2011.]

LIRLJ 6.6(e). REQUEST FOR SPEED MEASURING DEVICE EXPERT

Request for Speed Measuring Device ("SMD") Expert. Defense requests to produce an electronic or laser SMD expert pursuant to IRLJ 6.6(b) shall be contained in a separate document clearly designated as a request for an SMD expert, served on the prosecuting authority with a conformed copy filed with the clerk of the court. If the charging law enforcement agency's SMD expert maintains a schedule for monthly appearances in the Roslyn Municipal Court, a request for an SMD expert shall be deemed by the court to be a request to set (or re-set) the hearing to a day scheduled for the agency's SMD expert. An SMD expert called as a witness by either party may testify by telephone; however, any party intending to elicit telephonic testimony from an SMD expert shall notify the court and the opposing party at least 5 days prior to the date set for the contested hearing.

[Adopted effective September 1, 2011.]

Comments

Comments to Local Infraction Rule 6.6(e). LIR 6.6(e) is designed to address the problem of requests for SMD experts being "buried" within discovery requests or other documents filed in contested infraction cases. A request for an SMD expert which stands alone and is clearly identified as a request for an SMD expert will eliminate continuances for defendants who desire the presence of an SMD expert but who have not made their wish sufficiently clear to the prosecuting authority. Allowing SMD expert testimony by telephone serves to reduce costs incurred by law enforcement agencies as well as assisting defendants in presenting the testimony of their own SMD experts.

LIR 6.6(f). PUBLIC ACCESS TO SPEED MEASURING DEVICE CERTIFICATES

Pursuant to IRLJ 6.6(d), the court maintains as public records any design and construction certifications for electronic speed measuring devices and laser speed measuring devices filed with the court.

[Adopted effective September 1, 2011.]

FORMS

DECLARATION

INTERPRETER'S DECLARATION

I am a certified interpreter or have been found otherwise qualified by the court to interpret in the _____ language, which the defendant understands, and I have translated this Stipulation for and Order for Stay of Proceedings for the defendant from English into that language. The defendant has acknowledged his or her understanding of both the translation and the subject matter of this document. I certify under penalty of perjury under the laws of the state of Washington that the foregoing is true and correct.

Signed at Cle Elum, Washington on: ___ / ___ / _____

[Adopted effective September 1, 2011.]

LCrRLJ 4.5 FORM 1.   STIPULATED PRE–TRIAL STATEMENT OF READINESS

A stipulation filed in substantially the following form will comply with LCrRLJ 4.5(A):

ROSLYN MUNICIPAL COURT

STATE OF WASHINGTON

[ ] State of Washington	)
[ ] City of Cle Elum,	)
[ ] City of Roslyn	) NO. _____
Plaintiff,	) STIPULATED PRE–TRIAL
	) STATEMENT OF READINESS
vs.	)
_____,	)
Defendant,	)
_____	)

Pre-trial hearing is currently set for _____, 20 ___.

Jury trial is currently set for _____, 20 ___.

    COMES NOW the parties in the above captioned action and, by signature of counsel, do hereby stipulate and agree that **this case has not been resolved by agreement,** and should remain on the trial calendar or be reset by the clerk as indicated below:

1.   Motions:
   > [ ] There will be no pretrial motions and the above noted pre-trial hearing should be stricken.
   >
   > [ ] Pre-trial motions have been filed and served. The clerk is requested to reset the pre-trial hearing for ___ / ___ / ___.
   >
   > [ ] A CrRLJ 3.5 Hearing is required. The clerk is requested to set the hearing for ___ / ___ / ___.

2.   Bench/Jury Trial:

   > [ ] Remain set for a jury trial at above noted date and time.
   >
   > [ ] Clerk is requested to re-set jury trial as follows: _____.
   >
   > [ ] Jury trial waiver filed; set for bench trial.

3.   Discovery:
   Discovery is complete.

4.   Witnesses:

   > **Plaintiff:**
   > [ ] Witness list filed
   > [ ] Witnesses as follows:

Name   Address/telephone   Subject of testimony

_____   _____   _____

_____   _____   _____

Defense:
    [ ] Witness list filed
    [ ] Witnesses as follows:

Name   Address/telephone   Subject of testimony

_____   _____   _____

_____   _____   _____

_____   _____   _____

Attorney for Plaintiff   W.S.B.A. #   Attorney for Defendant   W.S.B.A. #

_____

Interpreter

[Adopted effective September 1, 2011.]

LCrRLJ 4.5 FORM 2. DEFERRED PROSECUTION FINDINGS OF FACT, CONCLUSIONS OF LAW & ORDER

Roslyn Municipal Court

State of Washington

City of Roslyn,	)	
	)	
Plaintiff,	)	No.
	)	Deferred Prosecution
vs.	)	Findings of Fact, Conclusions of
	)	Law & Order
_____,	)	
Defendant.	)	
_____	)	

This matter coming before the court on the defendant's Petition for Deferred Prosecution, and the court having considered the Petition, evaluation and treatment plan filed by the defendant, and the arguments of counsel, now makes the following findings of fact:

I. Findings of Fact

1. The defendant was evaluated by an approved alcoholism treatment facility or an approved drug treatment center; said agency's evaluation meets the requirements of RCW 10.05.040 and is attached to this Order. A certified alcoholism treatment facility or drug treatment center has prepared a treatment plan meeting the requirements of RCW 10.05.150 and has committed to provide treatment. Said treatment plan and commitment to treatment is attached to this Order, and incorporated by reference herein.

2. The defendant has agreed to pay, or arranged for the payment of, the costs of treatment.

3. The defendant has agreed to complete the two-year treatment program set forth in the treatment plan attached to this Order and to follow the other conditions of the court's Order.

4. The defendant has been advised of the following rights and has knowingly and voluntarily waived each of them:

(a) The right to a jury trial;

(b) The right to a speedy trial;

(c) The right to present evidence in his or her defense;

(d) The right to hear and question all witnesses who testify against the defendant;

(e) The right to compel witnesses to appear and testify on behalf of the defendant at no cost to the defendant;

(f) The right to testify.

5. The defendant has stipulated to the admissibility and sufficiency of the facts contained in the written police reports and understands these facts will be considered by the court in any criminal hearing on the underlying offense or offenses held subsequent to revocation of the order granting deferred prosecution. The defendant has agreed that the facts contained in the stipulated police reports are sufficient to allow the court to find the petitioner guilty, beyond a reasonable doubt, of the charged offenses.

977

6. The defendant has agreed, and the court finds, that any statements made by the defendant contained in the stipulated police reports were made knowingly and voluntarily.

7. If the charge is a violation of RCW Title 46 or similar municipal ordinance, the defendant has affirmed, and the court finds, that the defendant has not previously participated in a prior deferred prosecution program for a violation of RCW Title 46 or any similar municipal ordinance.

From the forgoing Findings of Fact, the court makes the following conclusions of law:

II. Conclusions of Law

1. The court has jurisdiction over the subject matter and petitioner in this case.

2. The petition meets the requirements of RCW 10.05.020

3. The diagnostic evaluation and treatment plan met the requirements of RCW 10.05.040, RCW 10.05.050 and RCW 10.05.150.

4. The Petition was made freely, voluntarily and knowingly.

III. Order

Based on the foregoing Findings of Fact and Conclusions of Law, the court hereby grants the Petition for Deferred Prosecution and allows the defendant to enter into a deferred prosecution program. The defendant shall remain under the jurisdiction of the court and the supervision of Kittitas County Probation Services during the two year treatment plan, and for three years after the court receives proof of successful completion of the two-year treatment program, but not less than five years from the date of this Order. The defendant shall, while under the court's jurisdiction, comply with the following conditions:

1. The defendant shall fully comply with and complete the two-year treatment program attached to this Order and incorporated by reference in Paragraph 2 of the court's Findings. In the event there are any inconsistencies between this order and the attached treatment plan, the terms and conditions set forth in this order shall be controlling.

2. The defendant shall pay, or arrange for payment of, the costs of the treatment program.

3. The defendant shall maintain total abstinence from alcohol and all other non-prescribed mind altering drugs.

4. The defendant shall not commit any crimes. The definition of "commit" includes, but is not limited to, any criminal charge resolved by a stay of proceedings, a stipulated order of continuance, or any other agreement which consists of a continuance with conditions, even if the ultimate disposition of the criminal charge is a dismissal, amendment of charge, or a finding of not guilty.

5. The defendant shall not refuse to submit to a breath or blood test if a police officer has reasonable grounds to believe that the defendant is driving or is in physical control of a motor vehicle while under the influence of intoxicating liquor or drugs.

6. The defendant shall not operate a motor vehicle upon the public highways without a valid operator's license and proof of liability insurance in an amount not less than that established by RCW 46.29.490.

7. The defendant shall immediately report to Probation Services, and continue to report in the future as directed by Probation Services.

8. The defendant shall pay $40 per month for probation supervision. The court may, after the successful completion of the two year treatment program,

reduce the level of supervision (and associated probation fees) required for the remainder of the period of supervision.

8.[1] The defendant shall not change treatment agencies without written permission of the court.

9. The treatment facility shall file with Kittitas County Probation Services **monthly** treatment status/compliance reports. Those reports shall be sent to:

Kittitas County Probation Services

507 Nanum Street

Ellensburg, Washington 98926

10. The defendant shall provide **in writing** to the court and Probation Services any change in mailing address.

11. The defendant shall not drive any motor vehicle unless the motor vehicle is equipped with a functioning ignition interlock calibrated to prevent the motor vehicle from being started when the breath sample provided has an alcohol concentration of 0.025 or more. This restriction is effective [ ] immediately; [ ] as of ___ / ___ / ___; [ ] after the completion of any suspension, revocation, or denial of driving privileges. The period of time of this restriction shall be for [ ] one year [ ] five years [ ] ten years.

12. The defendant [ ] shall [ ] shall not be required to pay a $250 administrative fee.

13. The defendant [ ] shall [ ] shall not be required to pay a $125 breath test fee.

14. [ ] The defendant [ ] shall [ ] shall not be required to reimburse Kittitas County for the cost of his/her court appointed attorney in the amount of $ ___.

15. [ ] The defendant shall pay restitution in the amount of $ ___. [ ] A restitution hearing shall be held on ___ / ___ /20__ to determine what amount of restitution should be paid by the defendant

16. The defendant shall start the two year deferred prosecution treatment program on or before: ___ / ___ /20__ . [ ] **Prior to entry into the two year intensive treatment program, the defendant shall attend a minimum of three (3) self-help recovery support group meetings per week, and provide proof of attendance to Probation Services. The defendant shall also attend and fully participate in any pre-treatment program available from his or her treatment agency. The defendant shall report to Probation Services as directed.**

17. [ ] The defendant shall attend a DUI victim's panel in Kittitas County on: ___ / ___ /20__ . [ ] The defendant shall attend a DUI victim's panel within 90 days. [ ] The defendant shall attend a Spanish language DUI victim's panel as directed by Probation Services.

18. This matter shall be set for review at any time as may be deemed appropriate by the court. In the event the defendant fails or neglects to undertake, complete or comply with any term or condition of this Order, the court, upon receiving notice of such failure, neglect, or violation, shall hold a hearing to determine whether the sufficient cause exists to remove the defendant from the deferred prosecution program. In the event the defendant is convicted of a similar offense, the court shall remove the defendant from the deferred prosecution program.

19. In the event the court finds cause to revoke the deferred prosecution, the court (sitting without a jury) will consider the stipulated police reports, including any statements made by the defendant, and determine whether the stipulated evidence supports the charge(s) beyond a reasonable doubt

20. In the event the defendant complies with the conditions of this Order the court shall, three years after receiving proof of successful completion of the

two-year treatment program, but not before five years following entry of this Order, dismiss the charges pending against the defendant.

21. Other: _____

_____

Dated ___ / ___ /20_____   _____
Judge/Court Commissioner

Presented by: Copy received; approved as to form:

_____   _____
Attorney for Defendant   WSBA #   Prosecuting Authority   WSBA #

Copy received; terms and conditions of Order accepted by:

_____
          Defendant

Attached to this Order are:

A. Alcohol/drug evaluation, treatment plan and commitment to provide treatment.

B. Police reports.

[Adopted effective September 1, 2011.]

---

1 Numbering as provided in original.

LCrRLJ 4.5 FORM 3. STIPULATION FOR AND ORDER FOR STAY OF PROCEEDINGS

ROSLYN MUNICIPAL COURT
STATE OF WASHINGTON

[ ] State of Washington,	)	
[ ] City of Cle Elum,	)	No. _____
[ ] City of Roslyn	)	
Plaintiff,	)	Stipulation for and Order for
	)	Stay of Proceedings
vs.	)	
	)	Charge(s) _____
_____ ,	)	
Defendant.	)	_____
_____	)	

_____ [ ] Deputy Prosecuting Attorney and _____, defendant, represented by _____, stipulate and agree to a stay of proceedings in this matter for a
period of __ months, on the following terms and conditions:

1. The defendant shall maintain good and lawful behavior during the term of the
    stay: the defendant shall have no criminal convictions for offenses committed
    after the date of this order, no charges during the term of the stay which lead to
    criminal convictions, no criminal charges which lead to a stay of proceedings,
    stipulated order of continuance or similar disposition, and no criminal charges
    which lead to a deferred prosecution.   In addition:

    [ ] The defendant shall complete ___ hours of approved community service
         within ___ days and provide proof of completion to Kittitas County Proba-
         tion Services.
    [ ] The defendant shall complete ___ days of Department of Corrections work
         crew within ___ days and provide proof of completion to Probation Services.
    [ ] The defendant shall attend a DUI victim's panel within ___ days and
         provide proof to Probation Services.

    [ ] The defendant shall obtain the following evaluation(s) and provide proof of
         such evaluation(s) to Probation Services within 30 days:
         [ ] Alcohol/Drug   [ ] Domestic Violence   [ ] Anger Management
         [ ] Other: _____

    In the event the evaluating agency recommends that the defendant obtain
    treatment or other Services, the defendant shall fully comply with the
    agency's recommendations and start any recommended classes or treat-
    ment within 45 days.   In the event that extended treatment is recom-
    mended, the defendant shall direct the treating agency to provide compli-
    ance reports to Probation Services on a monthly basis.

    [ ] Other: _____

2. Probation Services shall monitor the defendant's compliance with the conditions
    of this order. Probation Services shall:
    [ ] Actively monitor the defendant.   [ ] Complete ___ record checks.
    [ ] The defendant shall immediately report to Probation Services and continue
         to report as directed.

3. The defendant shall pay the following assessments:

[ ] Probation record check fees of $ ___　[ ] Probation monitoring fees of $ ___ per month
[ ] Court appointed attorney fees of $ ___　[ ] Court costs: $ _____
[ ] Restitution in the amount of $ ___　[ ] A Time payment agreement is authorized

4. The defendant hereby waives his/her right to a trial within 90 days of arraignment, and agrees to a trial date of no later than 90 days from the end of the stay of proceedings. In the event that the defendant is charged with a crime during the term of the stay of proceedings, but which is not resolved until after the end of the term of the stay, the defendant agrees to a trial date no later than 90 days after final resolution of the subsequently charged criminal offense.

5. If the defendant complies with all of the above listed conditions, the prosecuting authority agrees to:

[ ] Move the court for a dismissal of the charge(s) of: _____ filed under the above cause number.
[ ] Move the court to amend the charge of _____ to the charge of _____ to which the defendant shall: [ ] Plead guilty
[ ] Bail forfeit $ ___.　[ ] Other: _____
[ ] In the event the defendant pleads guilty the parties agree to the following sentencing recommendation:
[ ] Prosecutor's recommendation: _____
_____

[ ] Defense recommendation: _____
_____

6. In the event the court finds, after a hearing, that the defendant has failed to comply with any of the above listed conditions, the court shall, upon the request of the prosecuting authority, revoke the stay of proceedings and set a trial date.

7. As a condition of entering this stay of proceedings, the defendant agrees to waive the following rights:

A. The right to a jury trial
B. The right to a trial within 90 days of arraignment.
C. The right at trial to hear and question witnesses called by the prosecuting authority.
D. The right to testify at trial and call defense witnesses.

8. In the event the court finds cause to revoke the stay of proceedings, the defendant stipulates and agrees to the admissibility of the attached police reports (including any statements made by the defendant contained in the reports) and stipulates and agrees that the facts contained in the attached reports are sufficient to convict the defendant of the charged crime(s).

9. The parties agree that in the event the defendant fails to make payments as listed above and is delinquent by fifteen (15) days or more, the plaintiff and/or court have the authority to send such delinquent amounts to a collection agency for collection of said sums. Both parties agree that this authority exists whether or not the plaintiff chooses to have the matter set for review and bench trial. The defendant specifically waives any objection to such collection action by the plaintiff or the court, regardless of whether or not the defendant is found guilty after a trial. The defendant agrees that this document, along with any time payment agreement signed by the defendant, constitute a judgment for the amounts stated in paragraph 3 above.

10. The defendant understands and agrees that this document constitutes an agreement between the plaintiff and the defendant pertaining to the resolution

of a criminal charge(s). The defendant further understands that he/she is obligated to fully and strictly comply with all conditions set forth in this agreement. The defendant further understands that in the event the defendant fails to fully comply with the conditions of this agreement, the prosecuting authority may request a hearing in order seek revocation this stay of proceedings.

11. The parties jointly request that the court allow the above described stay of proceedings and further request that the court enter the attached order

Dated this ___ day of _____, ___   _____

                                                                 Defendant

_____   _____   _____   _____
Prosecuting Authority   WSBA #   Attorney for Defendant   WSBA #

ORDER

Based on the parties' request for a stay of proceedings, and the above stipulation between the parties, the court hereby orders that this cause is stayed for a period of _____, under the terms and conditions contained in the attached stipulation.

Dated this ___ day of _____, ___   _____

                                                                 Judge/ Court Commissioner

[Adopted effective September 1, 2011.]

LIRLJ 3.5. FORM

ROSLYN MUNICIPAL COURT

STATE OF WASHINGTON

City of Roslyn,   Infraction Number: _____
                Plaintiff

                                         Defendant's Request For Decision
                                         On Written Statements

VS.

                                         [   ] Contested Hearing
                                         [   ] Mitigation Hearing

_____
                Defendant

TO: Roslyn Municipal Court
Infraction Number: _____
I hereby request that the Court decide my case based upon the following statement:

_____

_____

_____

_____

_____

_____

(Attach Additional Page(s) if necessary).

I certify (or declare) under penalty of perjury under the laws of the State of
Washington that the foregoing statement is true.

I understand that Infraction Rules for Courts of Limited Jurisdiction 3. 5(e) provides
"There shall be no appeal from a decision on written statements".

I promise that if it is determined that I committed the infraction for which I was
cited, I will pay the monetary penalty authorized by law and assessed by the Court.

_____   _____

(Date and Place)   Defendant's Signature

                                        _____

                                        _____

                                        Current Mailing Address

[Adopted effective September 1, 2011.]

KLICKITAT COUNTY

Table of Courts

Superior Court

Local Court Rules of the Superior Court for Klickitat/Skamania Counties.

District Courts

East Klickitat County District Court—[No Local Rules].
West Klickitat County District Court.

SUPERIOR COURT

LOCAL COURT RULES OF THE SUPERIOR COURT FOR KLICKITAT/SKAMANIA COUNTIES

Including Amendments Received Through
August 15, 2015

Table of Rules

RULE 1. [COURT SCHEDULE]

I. Court Schedule

A. The Court schedule in Klickitat/Skamania Judicial District shall be as follows:

1. Klickitat County

a. Criminal Motion Days: 1st, 3rd and 5th Mondays of each month. Juvenile offenders will be scheduled on the 2nd Monday and 1st, 3rd and 5th Thursday of each month. Time certain motions to be set by the Court Administrator. Where holidays conflict, motions will be heard on the next judicial day or as otherwise ordered.

b. Civil Motion Days: 1st, 3rd and 5th Tuesdays of each month. Time certain matters will be heard in the afternoon and set by the Court Administrator. Court Commissioner will hear civil motions on the Thursday of the second full week of each month.

c. Juvenile Dependencies: Tuesday of the second full week of each month and such other days as ordered by the Court.

2. Skamania County:

a. Motion Days: Thursday on weeks beginning with 2nd, 4th and 5th Mondays of each month; where holidays conflict, motions will be heard on the next judicial day or as otherwise ordered. Time certain motions to be set by the Court Administrator.

b. Juvenile Days: The Court will sit in Juvenile Court session regularly on the 1st Wednesday after the 2nd Monday of each month and such other days as set by the Court.

[Adopted effective September 1, 1996.]

RULE 2. [SESSIONS, HOURS AND RECESSES]

I. Sessions, Hours and Recesses

A. There shall be one continuous session of Court from January 1st to December 31st of each year.

B. Court will be in session on all judicial days as designated by the State Supreme Court except during recesses herein prescribed, unless otherwise ordered.

C. Except as set forth in Rule No. 5, Court hours will be as follows:

Skamania County—9:00 AM—12:00 noon, 1:30 PM—5:00 PM; recesses of 15 minutes each will be called at approximately 10:30 AM and 3:00 PM.

Klickitat County—9:30 AM—12:00 noon, 1:30 PM—5:00 PM; recesses of 15 minutes each will be called at approximately 10:45 AM and 3:00 PM.

D. December 24th to January 2 shall be Winter Holiday recess and no contested cases or matters will be set for trial or tried during said period except by consent of the parties and the Court, or by order of the Court. During Winter Holiday recess, law and motion days shall be scheduled at the direction of the Court, and motions duly noted shall be regularly heard.

[Adopted effective September 1, 1996; amended effective September 1, 2009.]

RULE 3. [COURT FILES; RETURN MAIL]

I. Court Files; Return Mail

A. No files may be removed from the Clerk's office without the express permission of the Clerk or the Clerk's designee.

B. A file or files taken from the Clerk's office by an attorney or title company with permission shall be returned within 24 hours, or before, if so requested by the Judge, Court Commissioner or Clerk of the Court.

C. The Clerk will not permit files to be taken from the Clerk's office by attorneys or title companies not complying with this rule.

D. If an attorney or any other person requests, from the Clerk, an answer to correspondence and/or confirmation of any pleading or other documents, the attorney or person so requesting shall furnish a self-addressed stamped envelope for the Clerk's convenience.

[Adopted effective September 1, 1996.]

RULE 4. [LAW AND MOTION DOCKETING; TELEPHONE ARGUMENT]

I. Law and Motion Docketing

A. *Skamania County:*

A citation or request for placement of any matter on the regularly scheduled motion calendar shall be in writing and filed with the Clerk before 5:00 PM on the Monday preceding any regularly scheduled motion calendar or on the third day preceding any specially scheduled motion calendar.

B. *Klickitat County:*

A citation or request for placement of any matter on the regularly scheduled motion calendar shall be in writing and filed with the Clerk before noon on the Friday preceding a Tuesday calendar or by noon on the second day preceding any specially scheduled motion calendar. Criminal motions shall be filed with the Clerk before noon on the Thursday preceding a Monday criminal calendar.

C. Matters not regularly noted on the motion calendar will not be heard except by consent of all parties and the Court and then heard only after all matters regularly noted shall be called and disposed of. Nothing in this rule should be interpreted as affecting the notice of Civil Rules for Superior Courts or Criminal Rules for Superior Courts.

II. Telephonic Argument

A. Telephonic arguments are discretionary with the Court and may be authorized upon the following conditions:

   1. Express approval is obtained by the Judge who is hearing the motion

   2. One or more of the attorneys' offices are outside the County where the motion is filed.

   3. All counsel agree to the telephonic argument or the telephonic argument is ordered by the Court

   4. The party requesting telephonic argument shall be responsible for initiating and paying for the conference call

B. Telephonic arguments will not be reported or recorded unless request is made twenty-four hours in advance to the Court Administrator, or as otherwise ordered by the Court.

[Adopted effective September 1, 1996.]

RULE 5. [LAW AND MOTION CALENDAR]

I. Law and Motion Calendar

A. In Skamania County the criminal motion calendar shall be heard commencing at 9:00 AM and the civil motion calendar shall be heard at 1:30 PM. Ex parte matters and adoptions will be heard at 8:30 AM in chambers. Pro se non-contested dissolutions and protection order petitions will be heard at 9:00 AM on the Friday after the criminal/civil motion day.

B. In Klickitat County the criminal and civil motion calendars shall be heard commencing at 9:30 AM. Ex parte matters and adoptions will be heard at 9:00 AM on the civil motion day in chambers. Pro se non-contested dissolutions and protection order petitions will be heard at 3:00 PM on the civil motion day.

C. Presentation of Law and Motion matters shall be limited to a hearing time of ten (10) minutes for each side. Matters requiring argument longer than above prescribed shall be scheduled on a special hearing date to be set by the Court Administrator.

D. Ex parte matters may be heard in chambers on any judicial day (preferably on Motion Days) before Court is convened or after Court is recessed. These matters need not be noted for placement on the Clerk's docket.

E. Probate matters may be submitted to the Court in chambers and shall not require testimony except as ordered by the Court upon application or as required by statute. Probate matters in which the Court is requested to find that procedural steps have been taken shall be accompanied by the Court file when presented.

F. All hearings that are to be held in courts outside of the county where the case has been filed shall be coordinated through the Klickitat/Skamania County Court Administrator. The Court Administrator shall then notify the clerk in which the case has been filed of the out-of-county hearing date and time.

[Adopted effective September 1, 1996; amended effective September 15, 2000.]

RULE 6. PRE–TRIAL STATUS AND SETTLEMENT CONFERENCES

I. Civil Pre–Trial Conferences

A. In all civil cases the Court may order a pre-trial conference on its own motion or that of any party. Pre–trial conferences in domestic relations cases are governed by Rule No. 7. The purpose of the pre-trial conference is to consider:

   1. The simplification of the issues;

   2. The necessity or the desirability of amendments to pleadings;

   3. The possibility of obtaining admissions of fact and of documents which will void unnecessary proof;

   4. The list of witnesses (including experts) which each party intends to call; and

   5. Such other matters as may aid in the disposition of the action

B. Unless otherwise ordered by the Court all pre-trial conferences shall be conducted at least two weeks before trial.

C. Attorneys for all parties shall personally attend the pre-trial conference unless the Court orders the conference to be heard by telephone.

D. The pre-trial conference shall be conducted by the Judge informally and shall not be recorded unless so ordered.

E. Any joint proposed or final pre-trial order shall be substantially in the form of exemplar No. 1.

II. Criminal Pre–Trial Status Conferences [Repealed September 1, 2009.]

III. Civil Settlement Conferences

A. Settlement conferences are encouraged but are voluntary and may be requested by any party.

B. A party requesting a settlement conference shall do so when requesting a trial date.

C. The Court Administrator shall designate the settlement conference Judge and shall set the date for the settlement conference at least two weeks prior to the trial date.

   1. Settlement conferences may be held before a Court Commissioner, Judge or Pro–Tem Judge as determined by the Court.

D. All attorneys, parties including representatives from any insurer shall be personally present or immediately available to the attorneys representing them by telephone.

E.   Proceedings of the settlement conference shall be privileged and not reported or recorded. No party shall be bound unless a settlement is reached. When a settlement has been reached, the Judge may, in his or her discretion, order the settlement agreement to be recorded or reported. The Judge or Commissioner, presiding over a settlement conference, shall be disqualified from acting as a Trial Judge in the matter unless all parties otherwise agree in writing or in open Court on the record.

[Adopted effective September 1, 1996; amended effective September 1, 1998; September 1, 2009.]

RULE 7.   DOMESTIC RELATIONS

I.   Motions for Order Pending Trial

A.   Local Rules 4 and 5 shall be followed for all motions and hearings on orders to show cause, except when an opposing party has not appeared in person or by an attorney, and except when temporary restraining orders are sought under CR 65.

B.   Hearings in respect to temporary orders in domestic relations cases other than involving child custody shall be heard only upon affidavits. Testimony shall be allowed only by special permission of the Court, granted prior to the hearing.

   1.   The affidavits of the moving party shall be filed and served in the manner provided in LR 8 and other Rules of the Court. Responding affidavits and work sheets shall be served and filed no later than one day prior to the hearing unless the Court permits a later service and filing.

C.   Residential Placement

   1.   Any motion concerning the temporary residential placement of children must be accompanied by a proposed parenting plan, unless one has been previously filed and served. Hearings involving questions of residential placement of a child requiring testimony shall be set on a date and time certain upon the request made to the Court Administrator.

D.   Temporary Child Support

   1.   Any motion for temporary child support must be accompanied by a completed and signed child support work sheet in the form approved by the State Office of the Administrator for the Courts.

E.   Temporary Maintenance or Attorney's Fees

   1.   Any motion for temporary maintenance or attorney's fees must be accompanied by an affidavit or sworn statement with information including a list of monthly living expenses, debts, employment information for the parties and net income of the parties. If a party is unemployed, the information shall indicate the length of unemployment and reasons why the party is unemployed and when and how much unemployment compensation, if any, will be received.

II.   Child Support

A.   The Washington State Child Support Schedule now in effect or as hereafter revised shall be used by the Court and counsel in all matters involving child support whether temporary or permanent unless good cause to deviate from it is established.

III.   Non–Contested Dissolutions

A.   Any non-contested dissolutions, separations, or invalidity action decrees, which have been approved for entry by both parties, or their counsel, may be presented for final hearing by setting the same on the regular civil motion calendar. Oral testimony will not be required at such hearings. Presentation of such agreed decrees may be by mail to the Clerk of the Court, however, the Judge or Court Commissioner hearing such ex parte matters may require that oral testimony or affidavits be provided prior to the entry of the final decree.

IV.   Contested Dissolution Actions

A.   In any action for dissolution of marriage, separation, or declaration of invalidity in which property division, parenting plan, spousal maintenance, or child support is an issue, each party shall serve on the other party and file with the Court a written summary setting forth:

   1.   Statement of the issues

   2.   A statement of the parties' proposed resolution issues

   3.   A description and value of the assets and liabilities of the parties together with a proposed division thereof

   4.   The parties' proposed parenting plan

   5.   Child support worksheet

   6.   Financial affidavit showing the income and expenses per month of the parties

Petitioner's summary must be served and filed no later than ten days before the pre-trial conference, settlement conference, or trial date whichever occurs first. Respondent's summary shall be filed and served no later than five days before the pre-trial conference, settlement conference, or trial date whichever occurs first. Failure to timely file and serve the summary as required may result in appropriate sanctions which may include striking the trial settings and/or imposition of terms for any delay or inconvenience caused by the Court, counsel or other party.

V.   Modification of Decree of Dissolution, Separation or Invalidity

A.   Every action to modify a decree of dissolution, separation or invalidity shall be initiated by the filing of a properly verified petition to be entitled the same as the original decree sought to be modified.

B. If the petition to modify relates only to support, maintenance or minor adjustments to the parenting plan, then it shall be heard upon the pleadings only unless the petitioner has obtained leave of the Court to hear the matter upon oral testimony; however, if the petition to modify pertains to major adjustments to the parenting plan then it shall be heard upon oral testimony unless both parties stipulate that it may be heard on affidavits.

In any case involving the modification of a parenting plan where the original plan provides for alternate dispute resolution, a petition to modify said plan shall state whether alternate dispute resolution has been exhausted. The Court shall not modify a decree unless the alternate dispute resolution process has first been exercised in good faith. Failure to participate in the alternate dispute process in good faith may result in the imposition of terms. The Court shall determine on affidavits whether alternate dispute resolution has been exercised in good faith.

C. Where modification of a decree concerning child support or spousal maintenance is sought, a financial statement and, if applicable, a child support worksheet shall be filed and served with the petition to modify. A responding financial affidavit and, if applicable, child support worksheet shall be filed and served no later than one day prior to the hearing on the petition. Failure to timely serve and file the statements and worksheets as required will result in appropriate sanctions. Only those portions of the financial statements and worksheets applicable to the issues in the petition to modify need be completed.

D. Proceedings for modification of a dissolution decree or other custody decree shall be done strictly in accordance with RCW 26.09.270.

VI. Receipt of Public Assistance

A. In any action to establish or modify child support where any child affected is subject to receiving public assistance or if either party owes any past debt for child support to the State of Washington, then the Office of Support Enforcement shall be served with a copy of the petition to establish or modify child support at least twenty days prior to the hearing on any final order and at least five days prior to the hearing on any temporary order (RCW 26.23.130). Proof of service of said petition shall be filed with the Court prior to the hearing. In Skamania County, the petition shall be served on the Prosecuting Attorney's Office of Support Enforcement.

[Adopted effective September 1, 1996.]

RULE 8. MOTIONS FOR SUMMARY JUDGMENT

I. Notification to Judge

A. A party moving for summary judgment or any other relief requiring consideration of affidavits, pleadings, depositions, interrogatories and/or legal briefings shall file with the Clerk or ascertain that the file already contains all matters and documents intended to be relied upon and the moving party shall notify the Judge directly on or before the date that request is made to place the matter on the calendar to be heard.

B. A statement of points and authorities and supporting affidavits shall be filed and served concurrently with the motion for summary judgment and complimentary copies provided to the Judge.

C. Responses to affidavits etc., cross-motions with supporting documents and statement of points and authorities in support of response and/or cross-motion intended to be relied on at the hearing shall be filed pursuant to Civil Rules for Superior Court (CR 56) and at the time of filing, complimentary copies shall be provided to the Judge.

II. Nothing [1] Summary Judgment Motions

A. Prior to noting a motion for summary judgment, a specific date and time shall be obtained from the Court Administrator. Once noted for hearing, the motion shall not be stricken or continued by the parties without approval of the Judge who is assigned to hear the motion.

B. Argument on summary judgment motions may not exceed twenty minutes per party unless otherwise extended by the Judge hearing the motion.

III. Sanctions

A. Failure to strictly adhere to this rule may result in the hearing being stricken. Late responses stricken, or not considered in ruling on the motion, terms and/or such other sanctions as the Court in its discretion may deem appropriate.

[Adopted effective September 1, 1996.]

[1] So in original.

RULE 9. TRIALS (CIVIL)

Sections IV, V, VI, VII, VIII and IX of this Rule also apply to Criminal Trials.

I. Note for Trial Setting

A. Any party desiring to bring any issue of fact to trial shall file with the County Clerk with copy to the Court Administrator and serve upon the other parties a "Note for Trial Setting" in the form prescribed in Exemplar 5.

B. If no response to the Note for Trial Setting is received by the Court Administrator within ten days from the receipt of the moving party's request the Court Administrator will schedule the trial and notify all parties of the trial date.

1. The "Note for Trial Setting" will contain a list of the names, addresses and telephone numbers of all persons entitled to notice. All parties have the obligation to inform the Court Administrator promptly of any errors in the list.

C. Each party is allowed one request for a change of date after set without hearing, if the request is made within ten judicial days after trial date has been set by the Court Administrator. Within ten days after such objection, the Court Administrator will set another date and send notice of the new date. Additional changes may be allowed for good cause shown upon motion to the Court.

II. Certificate of Readiness

A. If the case is a contested civil action, the party filing a Note for Trial Setting/Certificate of Readiness must, at that time, submit a statement by counsel with due proof of service showing:

1. That the issue has actually been joined, no affirmative pleading remains unanswered and all pleadings are on file; and,

2. That the parties have completed all necessary oral and physical examinations and discovery proceedings or have had or will have opportunity to do so prior to trial.

III. Trial Briefs

A. Trial briefs shall be filed and served three days or more before trial; the original to be filed, one copy to the Judge and one copy served on opposing counsel.

IV. Jury Instructions

A. As provided by CR 51, counsel are requested by the Court to prepare and deliver to the Court and opposing counsel on the day on which the case is set for trial, the required number of copies of proposed instructions. "Washington Pattern Jury Instructions" are recommended for use whenever possible. Counsel are requested to prepare instructions as follows:

1. One copy which shall be assembled into a set and numbered shall be filed with the Clerk;

2. One copy which shall be assembled and numbered shall be served on opposing counsel;

3. One copy which shall be assembled and numbered shall be retained by the counsel preparing them;

4. One copy which shall be assembled and numbered shall be delivered to the Judge; this copy may contain citations listed on each instruction but if citations are contained thereon said citation shall be furnished to the opposing counsel; and,

5. The original without citations and numbers shall be delivered to the Judge.

V. Voir Dire

A. The Trial Judge may examine the jury touching their qualifications to act as fair and impartial jurors in the case before the Court, provided that, thereafter, the Trial Judge shall give leave to respective counsel to ask the jurors such supplementary questions as may be deemed by the Trial Judge proper and necessary. The voir dire examination of prospective jurors shall, as nearly as possible, be limited to those matters having a reasonably direct bearing on prejudice or qualifications and shall not be used by opposing counsel as a means of arguing or trying their case on voir dire.

VI. Peremptory Challenges

A. In trial by jury cases, peremptory challenges shall be exercised secretly without disclosing the juror being challenged. The plaintiff first and then defendant alternately shall mark and initial such challenge upon a sheet furnished for that purpose by the bailiff who shall then exhibit such challenge to the opposite party, the Clerk and the Court with no disclosure to the jury as to the challenging party. A questionnaire prepared by each juror will have been submitted to counsel. It is improper for counsel to go over the details furnished in this questionnaire consuming unnecessary time of the Court.

VII. Excusing Witnesses

A. A witness subpoenaed to attend in any case criminal or civil is dismissed and excused from further attendance as soon as he/she has given his/her testimony in chief for the party in whose instance he/she was called and has been cross-examined thereon, unless either party makes request in open Court that the witness may remain in attendance. Witness fees will not be allowed any witness after the day on which his/her testimony is given except when the witness has, in open Court, been required to remain in further attendance and, when so required, the Clerk shall note that fact in the record. If the adverse party requests a witness to remain in attendance he/she shall thereafter be responsible for the cost and expense occasioned thereby.

VIII. Notice of Settlement

A. It shall be the obligation of counsel in all civil and criminal jury and non-jury cases to notify the Court Administrator when a case is settled or otherwise will not come on for trial as scheduled. Such notice shall be made by telephone to the Court Administrator's office during regular business hours.

IX. Verdicts

A. A party or attorney desiring to be present at the return of a jury verdict must remain in attendance at the courthouse or be available by telephone. If a party or attorney fails to appear within twenty minutes of telephone notice to the attorney's office, home or other number left by the attorney, the Court may proceed to take the verdict in the absence of such party or attorney. In such case, the jury shall be individually polled and the identity of any dissenting jurors recorded.

X. Civil Jury—Cost

A. If the trial of the case has been canceled because of a settlement or will not be tried for any reason or will be tried without a jury and notification to the Clerk of the Court and Court Administrator occurs after a jury has been notified to report and less than one full judicial day prior to the time set for trial, each party may, in the Court's discretion be discharged with an equal share of the per diem cost of one day's service by the number of jurors actually reporting for the trial of said case. The forgoing costs will not be waived except upon a showing of exceptional circumstances which excuse the delay notification, but may, in the discretion of the Court, be charged against either or both parties together with any additional costs reasonably incurred in anticipation of trial including but not limited to travel expenses and loss of earnings of witnesses and the like.

[Adopted effective September 1, 1996.]

RULE 10.   CRIMINAL RULES

I. Arraignments and Preliminary Appearances

A. Arraignments and preliminary appearances shall be handled at any time by arrangement with the Court and otherwise as part of the criminal motion calendar.

B. At arraignment in any criminal action, the Administrator shall set the matter for omnibus hearing, status conference and trial. The defendant shall be given a copy of the setting notice at the time of arraignment and sign the receipt therefor.

II. Change of Plea

A. In all cases where the Court is advised to cancel a trial setting for the reason that the defendant intends to enter a plea of guilty such change of plea must be entered no later than the next succeeding criminal motion day following cancellation of the trial setting or the criminal motion day preceding the trial date, whichever is sooner, and in no event later than the time limitation of the applicable speedy trial rule unless by leave of Court by good cause shown.

III. Indigent Criminal Defendants, Financial Statement

A. The first duty of counsel appointed to represent indigent accused shall be to assist such accused in completing and immediately filing with the Court a financial statement form as provided by the Court. The defendant shall make a request for Court appointed counsel on the form prescribed in Exemplar 6.

IV. Probation Violation Procedure

A. Whenever a probationer is detained as a result of alleged violation of conditions of probation an order of probation suspension, arrest and detention shall be issued by the community supervision officer. The order shall contain authorization for the appropriate law enforcement agency to hold the alleged violator and in addition shall contain the specific violations for which the probationer is being detained. A copy of such order shall be served on the probationer no later than his/her placement in detention and at the time of detention he/she shall also be served with a written notice advising him/her of his/her right to both a

preliminary hearing and a revocation hearing. He/she shall also be given an opportunity to waive preliminary hearing in writing. He/she may so waive at any time prior to such hearing.

Copies of the notice together with waiver of preliminary hearing if such is signed, as required by this rule, shall be given to the prosecuting attorney and the sentencing Court. Within one judicial day thereafter a preliminary hearing or revocation hearing, if preliminary hearing is waived, shall be scheduled by the prosecuting attorney and the probationer advised of the date thereof.

Nothing in this rule shall be construed as abrogation of a probationer's right to counsel. He/she shall be advised that he/she may consult counsel before signing the waiver of preliminary hearing. Upon exercising his/her right to consult an attorney before signing the waiver, the form for such waiver shall be left with him/her.

V. Continuances

A. Request for continuances either agreed or uncontested will not be granted by the Court unless the following procedure has been followed:

1. Defendant and his/her attorney has signed and submitted a waiver of speedy trial in the form prescribed in Exemplar 7, with the motion and order for continuance of trial date; and,

2. Motion and order for continuance of trial date has been submitted for Court approval after endorsement of a new trial date by the Court Administrator; and

3. The motion and order for continuance of trial date is submitted to the Judge not less than seven days prior to the previously established trial date.

VI. 3.5 and 3.6 Hearings

A. If the moving party in a 3.5 (Confession) or 3.6 (Suppression) hearing files a Memorandum of Authorities in support of the motion, such memorandum shall be filed and served on the opposing party at least ten days prior to the hearing on the motion. A response to the Memorandum shall be filed and served at least five days before the hearing and a reply to the response shall be filed and served at least two days prior to the hearing. Courtesy copies of all Memoranda shall be provided to the Judge hearing the matter at the time of filing.

B. Within 7 days after the Omnibus hearing where a 3.5 hearing is requested by the State, the Prosecutor must serve on the defendant (or if represented, the defendant's attorney) and file with the Court a brief description of the defendant's statement(s) the Prosecutor intends to offer in evidence.

C. Within 7 days after the Omnibus hearing where a 3.6 hearing is requested by the defendant, the defendant (or, if represented, the defendant's attorney) shall serve on the Prosecutor and file with the

Court a written motion for suppression identifying the item(s) to be suppressed and briefly stating the grounds for suppression.

(Adopted effective September 1, 1998)

VII. Pre–Trial Settlement Conferences and Status Hearings in adult criminal cases

A. On the date set for arraignment in Superior Court, or upon which the defendant is arraigned, the prosecuting attorney, defense attorneys, and the defendant(s) will subscribe to a Notice Form (a copy of which is made as Exemplar 2 and 3 to this rule). Each attorney and the defendant shall be given a copy of the completed form; the original shall be filed in the case file.

B. At least two weeks prior to the Trial Status conference date, the prosecuting attorney shall mail or deliver to the defendant's attorney or to the defendant if he/she is pro se, a written offer to settle the case.

C. In Klickitat County, on the third Friday preceding a scheduled criminal trial, the defendant shall meet with his/her attorney in his/her attorney's office or at such other place as may be designated by the defense attorney for a settlement conference to discuss any plea bargain offers made by the prosecuting attorney. If the settlement conference falls on a legal holiday, it shall be held on the day before the holiday.

Defendants' attendance is mandatory at the Settlement Conference and Status Hearing and his/her failure to attend without Court approval will result in a warrant for his/her arrest.

On the next criminal motion day following the settlement conference, or in Skamania County, the date of the settlement conference, the defendant, his/her attorney and the prosecuting attorney shall appear in the Superior Court at a time set on the Notice Form for a status hearing to determine if the matter will proceed to trial as scheduled.

At the status hearing, the attorneys shall fill out and sign and the defendant shall sign a Status Conference Report (Exemplar 4). The original of the Status Conference Report shall be filed with the Court.

If the defendant agrees to plead guilty, the plea shall be set on for entry prior to the scheduled trial date. If the matter is to proceed to trial the defense attorney and the prosecuting attorney shall verify to the Court that each has provided the other with his/her trial witness list and that any pre-trial motions have been scheduled for hearing.

VIII. Authority of Court Commissioners

A. Superior Court Commissioners shall have the power, authority and jurisdiction in adult criminal cases to accept pleas in accordance with RCW 2.24.040.

[Adopted effective September 1, 1996; amended effective October 15, 1997; September 1, 1998; September 1, 1999; January 15, 2001; September 1, 2009.]

RULE 11. GENERAL RULES

I. Filing and Endorsement of Papers

A. Every paper presented to a Judge for signature and every paper presented for filing shall bear a designation of what it purports to be, the number and title of the case and the name of counsel presenting or filing the same. Every order presented to a Judge for signature shall bear the signature of the individual attorney presenting it on the lower left hand corner of the page to be signed by the Judge.

II. Accounting Procedures

A. Before a trial is set in any matter involving an accounting, the party required to account shall submit to opposing parties and the Court a formal statement in detail of cash and other property transactions in a form which will furnish information to enable a party to make a reasonable test of the accuracy and honesty thereof.

The opposing party, by pre-trial discovery procedures, shall test the validity of the accounting statements submitted.

Issues shall be made up for trial only by specific exception to separate and specific transactions shown or not shown in the accounting statement.

Items that are set forth in the accounting statement to which no exception is taken shall be deemed correct.

III. Attorney Fees

A. Appointed Counsel submitting motions for fixing or payment of attorney fees and counsel requesting the Court fix fees in any other case, shall itemize their time, services rendered or other detailed basis for the fee requested and attach a copy thereof to the motion. Orders for payment of Court appointed attorneys' fees shall be presented in duplicate.

No fees will be paid or approved, except interim fees and fees on juvenile dependencies made on special request, until the case is concluded of record with all papers and documents required therefor signed by the Court.

IV. Suspension of Rules

A. The Court may modify or suspend any of these rules in any given case upon good cause being shown therefor or upon the Court's own motion.

V. Restitution

A. The Clerk shall pay to the person authorized by Court order to receive the same all restitution monies paid through his/her office at such times as he/she shall find convenient but not less frequently than quarterly.

[Adopted effective September 1, 1996; amended effective September 1, 2002; September 1, 2003.]

RULE 12. FINANCIAL RESPONSIBILITY FOR COST OF JUVENILE DETENTION

I. Persons Responsible

A. Pursuant to the intent and standard set forth in RCW 13.16.085 in any Juvenile Court proceeding regarding the detention of a juvenile offender, the Court may order the parent or parents, guardian or other person or persons having custody of the juvenile offender to pay or contribute to the payment of the cost of such detention.

II. Time of Payment

A. The maximum payment of per diem costs charged to the county and/or ordered by the Court shall be paid in a reasonable time unless a sworn financial statement is presented to the Court at said proceeding which could reduce or eliminate any such assessment or due to other circumstances recognized by the Court. Transportation and medical costs may also be assessed under this rule.

III. Duty of Juvenile Court Administrator

A. It shall be the duty of the Administrator of Juvenile Court to notify the parent or parents, guardian or other person or other persons having custody of the juvenile offender, of this rule prior to said proceeding and provide all necessary documents to the parent or parents, guardian or other person or persons having custody of the offender in order for such parent or person or persons to adequately prepare for said proceeding.

IV. Clerk to Receive Payments

A. The Clerk of the Court shall receive payments in a manner appropriate to local and State auditing regulations for any such assessments and shall monitor the same, reporting to the Administrator of Juvenile Court any assessments that are substantially delinquent. A show cause hearing with timely notice by the Administrator of Juvenile Court to the delinquent parent or parents, guardian or other person or persons having custody of the offender may be held to inquire into the delinquency of the assessments and the sanctions available pursuant to RCW 13.16.085.

[Adopted effective September 1, 1996.]

RULE 13. WAIVER OF AGE TO MARRY

I. Application

A. Application for waiver of minimum age to marry shall be through the Juvenile Department of the Superior Court in the County where one of the parties resides. Applications shall contain such information and supporting documentation as may be prescribed by the Juvenile Court Administrator. Before presentation to the Court, applicants must give evidence of completion of a program approved by the Juvenile Court Administrator, pre-marital counseling by a licensed counseling agency or their rabbi, priest or minister together with a counselor's written recommendation and be interviewed by the Juvenile Court Administrator or his/her designee who shall offer recommendations to the Court.

[Adopted effective September 1, 1996.]

RULE 14. FEE FOR PETITION FOR EMANCIPATION

I. There shall be charged a fee for the filing of a Petition for Emancipation as provided under RCW 13.64.020 as now in effect or hereafter amended.

[Adopted effective September 1, 1996.]

RULE 15. RECORD OF PROCEEDINGS

I. The record of proceedings in Klickitat and Skamania County Superior Courts is on videotape. Refer to "Publisher's Appendix" to Washington Court Rules, Rules on Appeal, for procedures for the use of videotape equipment in the trial court and on appeal.

[Adopted effective September 1, 1996.]

RULE 16. MANDATORY ARBITRATION

I. Scope and Purpose of Rules

A. *Application of Rules—Purpose and Definition*

1. Purpose. The purpose of mandatory arbitration of civil actions under RCW 7.06 as implemented by the Mandatory Arbitration Rules is to provide a simplified and economical procedure for obtaining the prompt and equitable resolution of disputes involving claims of fifty thousand dollars ($50,000.00) or less. The Mandatory Arbitration Rules as supplemented by these local rules are not designed to address every question which may arise during the arbitration process, and the rules give considerable discretion to the arbitrator. The arbitrator should not hesitate to exercise that discretion. Arbitration hearings should be informal and expeditious, consistent with the purpose of the statutes and rules.

2. Administration. The arbitration department shall consist of the Court Administrator under the direction of the Superior Court Judge. The arbitration department shall supervise arbitration under these rules and perform any additional duties which may be delegated.

B. *Relationship to Superior Court Jurisdiction and Other Rules—Motions*

1. All motions relating to civil cases transferred to mandatory arbitration shall be presented to the arbitrator, except (a) cases where arbitrability is at issue, (b) where assignment of an arbitrator is disputed and not resolved by the Administrator, (c) motions for involuntary dismissal, (d) motions for summary judgment, and (e) motions to dismiss for failure to state a cause of action.

II. Transfer to Arbitration and Assignment of Arbitrator

A. *Transfer to Arbitration*

1. Statement of Arbitrability. In every civil case the party filing the Note for Trial Docket shall, upon the form prescribed by the court, complete a Statement of Arbitrability (Exemplar #5). Prior to the trial-setting date any party disagreeing with the Statement of Arbitrability or willing to stipulate to arbitration shall serve and file a Response to the Statement of Arbitrability on the form prescribed by the court (Exemplar #8). In the absence of such Response, the Statement of Arbitrability shall be deemed correct, and the case shall be deemed set for arbitration. Cases transferred to the arbitration calendar shall be stricken from their position on the trial calendars. Unless otherwise ordered by the court, no trial date shall be assigned in cases which are subject to arbitration. If a party asserts that its claim exceeds $50,000.00 or seeks relief other that a money judgment, the case is not subject to arbitration except by stipulation.

2. Failure to File Amendments. A party failing to serve and file an original Response within the time prescribed may later do so only upon leave of court. A party may amend the Statement of Arbitrability or Response at any time before assignment of an arbitrator or assignment of a trial date and then only upon leave of court for good cause shown.

B. *Assignment of Arbitrator*

1. Generally; Stipulations. When a case is set for arbitration, a list of five proposed arbitrators shall be furnished to the parties. A list of other approved arbitrators shall be furnished upon request. The parties are encouraged to stipulate to an arbitrator. In the absence of the stipulation within 14 days after a case is transferred to arbitration, the arbitrators shall be chosen from among the five proposed arbitrators in the manner defined by this rule.

a. Response by Parties. Within 14 days after a list of proposed arbitrators is furnished to the parties, each party shall nominate one or two arbitrators and strike two arbitrators from the list. If both parties respond, an arbitrator nominated by both parties shall be appointed. If no arbitrator has been nominated by both parties, an arbitrator shall be appointed from among those not stricken by either party. The parties need not serve their responses on the other side, and the responses shall not be disclosed to a party by the Administrator (except for disclosure of an arbitrator selected by both parties).

b. Response by Only One Party. If only one party responds within 14 days, an arbitrator shall be appointed from that party's response.

c. No Response. If neither party responds within 14 days, the arbitrator shall be randomly appointed from the five proposed arbitrators.

d. Additional Arbitrators for Additional Parties. If there are more than two adverse parties, all represented by different counsel, two additional proposed arbitrators shall be added to the list for each additional party so represented with the above principles of selection to be applied. The number of adverse parties shall be determined by the arbitration department, subject to review by the Superior Court Judge.

III. A. *Qualifications*

1. Arbitration Panel. There shall be a panel of arbitrators in such numbers as the Superior Court Judge may from time to time determine. A person desiring to serve as an arbitrator shall complete an information sheet on the form prescribed by the court. A list showing the names of arbitrators available to hear cases and the information sheets shall be available for public inspection in the Court Administrator's office. The oath of office on the form prescribed by the court must be completed and filed prior to an applicant being placed on the panel.

2. Refusal—Disqualification. The appointment of an arbitrator is subject to the right of that person to refuse to serve. An arbitrator must notify the arbitration department immediately if refusing to serve or if any cause exists for the arbitrator's disqualification from the case upon any of the grounds of interest, relationship, bias or prejudice set forth in CJC Canon 3 (C) governing the disqualification of judges. If disqualified, the arbitrator must immediately return all materials in a case to the arbitration department.

B. *Authority of Arbitrators*

1. An arbitrator has the authority to:

a. Determine the time, place and procedure to present a motion before the arbitrator.

b. Require a party or attorney advising such party or both to pay the reasonable expenses, including attorney's fees, caused by the failure of such party or attorney or both to obey an order of the arbitrator unless the arbitrator finds that the failure was substantially justified or that other circumstances make an award of expenses unjust. The arbitrator shall make a special award for such expenses and shall file such award with the Clerk of the Court, with proof of service on each party. The aggrieved party shall have 10 days thereafter to appeal the award of such expense in accordance with the procedures described in RCW 2.24.050. If within 10 days after the award is filed no party appeals, a judgment shall be entered in a manner described generally under MAR 6.3.

c. Award attorney's fees as authorized by these rules, by contract or by law.

IV. **Procedures After Assignment**

A. *Discovery*

In determining when additional discovery beyond that directly authorized by MAR 4.2 is reasonably necessary, the arbitrator shall balance the benefits of discovery against the burdens and expenses. The arbitrator shall consider the nature and complexity of the case, the amount in controversy, values at stake, the discovery that has already occurred, the burdens on the party from whom discovery is sought, and the possibility of unfair surprise which may result if discovery is restricted. Authorized discovery shall be conducted in accordance with the Civil Rules except that motions concerning discovery shall be determined by the arbitrator.

V. Hearing

A. *Notice of Hearing*

1. Notice of Hearing—Time and Place—Continuance. An arbitration hearing may be scheduled at any reasonable time and place chosen by the arbitrator. The arbitrator may grant a continuance without court order. The parties may stipulate to a continuance only with permission of the arbitrator. The arbitrator shall give reasonable notice of the hearing date and any continuance to the arbitration department.

B. *Prehearing Statement of Proof—Documents Filed with Court*

In addition to the requirements of MAR 5.2, each party shall also furnish the arbitrator with copies of pleadings and other documents contained in the court file which that party deems relevant. The court file shall remain with the Clerk of the Court.

C. *Conduct of Hearing*

1. Recording. The hearing may be recorded electronically or otherwise by any party at that party's expense.

VI. Award

A. *Form and Content of Award*

1. Form. The award shall be prepared on the form prescribed by the court (Exemplar #9).

2. Return of Exhibits. When an award is filed, the arbitrator shall return all exhibits to the parties who offered them during the hearing.

B. *Filing of Award*

A request by an arbitrator for an extension of time for the filing of an award under MAR 6.2 may be presented to the Superior Court Judge, ex parte. The arbitrator shall give the parties notice of any extension granted.

C. *Judgment on Award*

1. Presentation. A Judgment on an award shall be presented to the Presiding Judge, by any party, on notice in accordance with MAR 6.3.

VII. General Provisions

A. *Stipulations; Effect on Relief Granted*

If a case not otherwise subject to mandatory arbitration is transferred to arbitration by stipulation and order of the court, the arbitrator may grant any relief which could have been granted if the case were determined by a judge.

B. *Title and Citation*

These rules are known and cited as the Klickitat/Skamania Court Mandatory Arbitration Rules. LMAR is the official abbreviation.

C. *Compensation of Arbitrator*

1. Generally. Arbitrators shall be compensated in the same amount and manner as Judges Pro Tempore of the Superior Court; provided, however, that said compensation shall not exceed $500.00 for any case unless prior approval is granted by the Superior Court Judge. The Superior Court Judge shall determine the amount of compensation to be paid. No county payment shall be made unless and until funding is provided by the County Commissioners of the county having jurisdiction over the action.

[Adopted effective September 1, 1996; Amended effective September 1, 2007.]

RULE 17. MANDATORY PARENTING SEMINARS

I. Applicable Cases

A. This rule shall apply to all cases filed after April 1, 1997 under Ch.26.09, Ch.26.10, or Ch.26.26 RCW which require a parenting plan or residential plan for minor children, including dissolution's, legal separations, major modifications, paternity actions in which paternity has been established, and non-parental custody actions.

II. Mandatory Attendance

A. In all cases governed by this rule, all parties shall complete a parenting seminar approved by the Court. Standards for parenting seminars shall be established by the Court and providers shall be approved by the Court.

III. Timing

A. Parties required by this rule to participate in parenting seminars shall complete an approved parenting seminar within 90 days after service of the petition or motion initiating the action which is subject to this rule. In the case of paternity actions initiated by the prosecuting attorney's office, the parenting seminar shall be required only when paternity has been established or acknowledged and a parenting plan is requested. The seminar will be completed prior to the entry of a permanent parenting or residential plan.

B. Upon completion of the parenting seminar, the seminar provider shall file a certificate of completion with the Clerk of the Court.

IV. Fees

A. Each party attending a seminar shall pay a fee charged by the approved provider and sanctioned by the Court. The Court may waive the fee for indigent parties.

V. Special Consideration/Waivers

A. In no case shall opposing parties be required to attend a seminar together.

B. If the Court determines that attendance at a seminar is not in the children's best interest, pursuant to Ch.26.12 RCW, the Court shall either:

1. Waive the requirement of completion of the seminar; or

2. Allow participation in an alternative parenting seminar, if available.

C. The Court may waive the seminar requirement or extend the time for attendance of the seminar for good cause shown.

VI. Service on Parties

A. The Clerk of the Court shall provide a copy of this rule to the initiating party for service upon all parties against whom relief is sought, together with a statement describing the program including contact telephone numbers, addresses, statement of costs, and an explanation of how to request a waiver or referral of the program registration fee.

VII. Failure to Comply

A. Willful refusal to participate in a parenting seminar or willful delay in completion of a parenting seminar by any party will constitute contempt of court and may result in sanctions, including but not limited to, imposition of monetary terms, striking of pleadings, or denial of affirmative relief to a party not in compliance with this rule.

[Adopted effective September 1, 1997.]

RULE 18. JUVENILE OFFENDER STATUS CONFERENCES

I. Status Conference Schedule/Notification

A. At the time of a juvenile's arraignment on criminal charges, the Court will set a status conference/hearing date and time. Notification will be provided on a notice form. The status conference/hearing shall be at 4:00 PM on the second regular juvenile arraignment docket following arraignment, if the case is a 60 day fact-finding set (Klickitat County), or at 4:00 PM on the second regular criminal/civil motion day following arraignment (Skamania County).

In Klickitat County, if the case is a 30 day fact-finding set, the status conference/hearing shall be held on the next regular juvenile arraignment docket following arraignment. The juvenile and the juvenile's attorney shall be present at the status conference/hearing unless the juvenile and his/her attorney have signed off on a status conference report prior to the status conference/hearing.

B. The Prosecuting Attorney and the Juvenile Court Administrator shall make available to the juvenile's attorney, or if unrepresented, to the juvenile, an offer to settle the case prior to the status conference/hearing date. No further plea bargain offers will be accepted by the Court after the status conference/hearing date unless good cause be shown.

[Adopted effective January 1, 1998; amended effective September 1, 2003; September 1, 2006.]

RULE 19. BOOKS AND RECORDS KEPT BY THE CLERK

I. Clerk of the Court Schedule of Charges

A. The Clerk of the Court will maintain a schedule of charges authorized by law for clerk's services. The schedule will be maintained in the clerk's office and available for public inspection.

II. Files

A. Filings by Clerk of Court; All original pleading or other papers with proper caption and cause number will be file stamped, docketed and secured in the legal file by the clerk in the order received.

B. Action Documents; All pleadings that require action by the clerk, other than file stamping and docketing, shall contain the language "Clerk's Action Required" in the caption beneath the case number on the first page of the document.

C. Conformed Copies; All requests to the clerk for a response to an inquiry about a court file or for return of conformed copies of pleadings must be accompanied by a self-addressed, stamped return envelope.

D. Sealed Papers; The clerk of the court shall seal and not permit examination of the following; psychological evaluations, sociological evaluations, mental evaluations, reports of the guardians ad litem and sealed financial source documents in family law matters, except by court order in conformity with GR 15 and GR 22. If sealed, papers may be unsealed only by court order, by motion and, by motion and with notice, in conformity with GR 15 and GR 22.

III. Exhibits

A. Exhibit Files; The exhibits in all cases shall be kept by the clerk separate from the files of the case.

B. Exhibit Inspection; Exhibits may be inspected in the clerk's office only in the presence of the clerk of the court or a deputy clerk.

C. Court Records as Exhibits; No original court record shall be admitted as an exhibit, but a copy may be admitted.

D. Substituted Copies of Exhibits; For cause shown, the court may permit a copy of any document admitted in evidence to be substituted for the original.

E. Exhibit Packaging and Labeling; Exhibits containing blood borne pathogens, drugs, firearms or dangerous weapons shall be properly packaged and labeled before acceptance by the court. To meet packaging and labeling requirements, exhibits shall conform to the following criteria when presented:

(1) Blood borne pathogens shall be packaged in sturdy plastic containers. If contained in a vial or hypodermic, each shall be placed in an individual sturdy plastic container. All items shall be labeled to identify the contents as potentially biologically hazardous material.

(2) Drugs shall be placed in sealed containers to prevent or reduce emissions from the container. Plainly visible labels shall identify the contents.

(3) Firearms shall be unloaded, any breach mechanism or cylinder shall be open, and a secured trigger lock shall be in place.

(4) Dangerous weapons shall have any sharp or pointed portions sheathed in a manner to prevent injury or contact with the sharp or pointed portions.

(5) Paper bags alone will not constitute proper packaging.

F. Videotaped Depositions; Videotaped depositions published in open court shall be treated as court exhibits, with the same retention standards. A party who wishes to make a published videotaped deposition part of the court file must submit a certified transcript of the deposition.

G. Unsuitable Materials as Exhibits; Whenever there is presented to the clerk of the court for filing any paper or material that the clerk of the court determines to be improper or inappropriate for filing, the clerk of the court shall affix a file mark thereto and apply to the court for a determination of the propriety of filing the material presented. If the court determines that the paper or material should not be made part of the file, an order shall be entered converting the material to an exhibit, and the clerk of the court shall retain the material as an exhibit to the cause. If the court determines that the material warrants being sealed, the court shall direct the clerk of the court to give notice to all parties to the cause and shall conduct a hearing on the court's motion to seal the material pursuant to GR 15.

IV. Withdrawal of Files and Exhibits

A. Files; Except for delivery to a courtroom, judge, court commissioner, referee, court personnel or official court reporter, files may be withdrawn from the clerk's office only pursuant to court order or written authorization by the clerk. Applications to withdraw a file must be in writing. The clerk or a deputy may authorize withdrawal of a file for a period not exceeding 24 hours. A person who withdraws a file shall return the file and all of its papers in good order, and shall not remove, even temporarily, any staples from any papers.

B. Exhibits; Temporary Withdrawal; Exhibits may be withdrawn temporarily from the clerk's office only by:

(1) The judge having the case under consideration.

(2) Official court reporters for use in connection with their duties, without court order.

(3) An attorney of record, upon court order.

The clerk shall take an itemized receipt for all exhibits withdrawn, and upon return of the exhibits they shall be checked by the clerk against the original receipts. The clerk shall keep all receipts for such exhibits for the period of three years from date of withdrawal or return.

C. Failure to Return Files or Exhibits; Sanctions; In the event that an attorney or other person fails to return within the time required a file or exhibit which was temporarily withdrawn, and fails to comply with the clerk's request for its return, the clerk may, without notice to the attorney or other person concerned, apply to the court for an order for the immediate return of such file or exhibit. A certified copy of such order, if entered shall then be served upon the attorney or other person involved.

D. Permanent Withdrawal of Exhibits; After final judgment and expiration of the time for appeal, the court may order the permanent withdrawal of an exhibit and delivery thereof to any party or other person entitled to possession.

E. Return of Contraband Exhibits; When contraband, alcoholic beverages, tobacco products or controlled substances are being held by the clerk as part of the records and files in any criminal case, and all proceedings in the case have been completed, the court may order the clerk to deliver such contraband or substances to an authorized representative of the law enforcement agency initiating the prosecution for disposition according to law. The clerk shall then deliver the contraband or substances and take from the law enforcement agency a receipt which shall be filed in the case. The clerk shall also file any certificate issued by an authorized federal or state agency and received by the clerk showing the nature of such contraband or substances.

F. Return of Exhibits and Unopened Depositions; When a civil case if finally concluded, and upon stipulation of the parties or court order, the clerk may return all exhibits and unopened depositions, or destroy the same.

G. Return of Administrative Records; When a case for review of an administrative record is finally completed, the clerk shall return the administrative record to the officer or agency certifying the same to the court. The clerk shall treat the administrative record as an exhibit, conforming with III. above.

H. Verbatim Report of Proceedings; A verbatim report of proceedings shall not be withdrawn from the clerk's office except by court order.

I. Transcripts; A request for a verbatim report of proceedings or a copy of a videotaped record of proceedings shall be referred to the Superior Court Judicial Assistant.

[Adopted effective September 1, 2002; amended effective September 1, 2003.]

RULE 20. NAMES OF MINOR CHILDREN ON COURT DOCUMENTS

The complete names of minor children is necessary for the orderly administration of justice and such complete names shall be used on all court documents except where prohibited by statute or court order. This rule does not prohibit the use of initials to identify child victims or witnesses in criminal or juvenile offender proceedings.

[Adopted effective September 1, 2005.]

RULE 21. GUARDIANSHIPS

I. Loss of Voting Rights

A. In accordance with RCW 11.88.010(5), if an incapacitated person loses the right to vote, the Order Appointing Guardian or Approving Report shall include a specific finding on the loss of the right to vote.

B. The Guardian ad Litem and/or Guardian shall also submit a Notice of Loss of Voting Rights to the Court that shall include the name, address, and date of birth of the incapacitated person and that shall direct the clerk to forward the Notice of Loss of Voting Rights to the County Auditor. (see Exemplar #11)

C. If the guardianship is terminated by a determination of competency of the individual, the court shall direct the clerk to send to the County Auditor a certified copy of the Order Restoring Voting Rights including the same personal identifiers as the Notice of Loss of Voting Rights.

D. Clerk will determine whether Notice of Loss of Voting Rights has been filed. If notice has not been filed, clerk shall complete a notice using information from guardianship petition and/or guardian ad litem report.

E. Clerk will forward Notice of Loss of Voting Rights to the County Auditor.

F. Copy of the notice will be placed in the file.

G. If the guardianship is terminated based on the Court's finding that the ward is now competent to handle affairs, the clerk will send a certified copy of the Order Restoring Voting Rights (see Exemplar #12) to the County Auditor.

II. Guardian Ad Litem Grievance Procedure

A. When the Court receives a written complaint alleging one of the following:

1) There has been a violation of the Guardian ad Litem Code of Conduct,

2) There has been a misrepresentation of his or her qualification to be a Guardian ad Litem, or

3) The Guardian ad Litem has not met the annual update requirements, or

B. When the Court becomes aware of any reason that would place the suitability of the person to act as Guardian ad Litem in question, including, but not limited to the following:

1) Breach of confidentiality.

2) Falsifying information on the application.

3) Falsifying information in a Court report.

4) Failure to report abuse of a child.

5) Ex-parte communication.

6) Representing the Court in a public forum, without prior approval of the Court.

7) Violation of state, or local laws, rules of this policy, while a Guardian ad Litem.

8) Dissemination of law enforcement records.

C. The Court Administrator/or designee shall seek a written response from the Guardian ad Litem only upon findings by the Court Administrator/or designee that a response is necessary. Should a response from the Guardian ad Litem be requested and upon receipt of the response, the Court Administrator/or designee will forward the complaint, and the response to the Presiding Judge, or his or her designee(s). The Guardian ad Litem shall be notified of any decision to suspend or remove the Guardian ad Litem from a registry. A Guardian ad Litem seeking reconsideration of the decision shall do so in writing to the Superior Court Administrator/or designee, who shall forward the request, and other documents to the Presiding Judge, or his or her designee(s). At the discretion of the Presiding Judge, or his or her designee(s), the Guardian ad Litem's participation in the registry may be suspended pending resolution of the complaint. The Guardian ad Litem shall be notified in writing of the final decision of the Court.

D. The Court's decision may deny a person listing on, or may temporarily suspend from, or permanently removed from, the registry for any reason that places the suitability of the person to act as a Guardian ad Litem in question.

E. A Guardian ad Litem who ceases to be on the registry, and who still has active or incomplete cases shall immediately report this circumstance to the Superior Court Administrator/or designee who will reassign such cases.

[Adopted effective September 1, 2006; amended effective September 1, 2009.]

EXEMPLARS

EXEMPLAR #1/LCR 6 I.E.   PRE–TRIAL ORDER

IN THE SUPERIOR COURT OF THE STATE OF WASHINGTON
IN AND FOR THE COUNTY OF SKAMANIA/KLICKITAT

Plaintiff(s),	)))) No.)) **PRE–TRIAL ORDER**))))
vs.	
Defendant(s).	

A pre-trial conference was held in the above entitled cause at Stevenson, Washington on _____, 20__ with Judge _____ presiding. Plaintiff was represented by _____ and defendant by _____, respective attorneys of record. The following pre-trial order has been formulated and settled as follows:

The following facts are agreed upon by the parties and require no proof:

1. _____
2. _____

PLAINTIFF'S CONTENTIONS

Plaintiff's contentions as to disputed issues are:

1. _____
2. _____

etc.

DEFENDANT'S CONTENTIONS

Defendant's contentions as to disputed issues are:

1. _____
2. _____

etc.

ISSUES OF FACT

The following are the issues of fact to be determined by trial:

1. _____
2. _____

etc.

ISSUES OF LAW

The following are the issues of law to be determined by the Court:

1. _____
2. _____

etc.

EXHIBITS

The following exhibits may be received in evidence, if otherwise admissible, without further authentication, it being admitted that each is what it purports to be:

Plaintiff's Exhibits:

1. _____

2. _____

etc.

Defendant's Exhibits:

1. _____

2. _____

etc.

The following plaintiff's exhibits are objected to by defendant:

1. _____

2. _____

etc.

The following defendant's exhibits are objected to by plaintiff:

1. _____

2. _____

etc.

Other than for impeachment purposes, the only exhibits admitted at trial will be exhibits identified herein or on a supplemental list filed at least 3 (three) days before trial, or at such other date as may have been set by the Court, which supplemental list shall bear counsel's certification that opposing counsel has had an opportunity to examine the exhibits.

ANTICIPATED MOTIONS

Including Motions in Limine

_____
_____
_____
_____
_____
_____

EVIDENTIARY ISSUES

Other than Foundation Issues for Exhibits

_____
_____
_____
_____
_____
_____

WITNESSES

The following witnesses may be called by plaintiff (if expert, give field of expertise):

1. _____

2. _____

etc.

The following witnesses may be called by defendant (if expert give field of expertise):

1. _____

2. _____

etc.

Other than for rebuttal purposes, no witnesses may be called unless listed above.

RELIEF SOUGHT

_____

_____

_____

_____

_____

_____

TRIAL

The parties estimate _____ days trial time, including jury selection, evidence and argument. The parties stipulate and agree that (check appropriate box):

_____ An alternate juror is recommended

_____ If a juror is excused during trial for good cause the parties stipulate to a verdict by the jurors.

_____ No stipulation reached as to above

It is hereby ORDERED that the foregoing constitutes the pre-trial order in the case and that upon the filing hereof all pleadings pass out of the case and are superseded by this order. This order may be amended by consent of the parties and approval by the Court or by the Court to prevent manifest injustice.

Dated this ___ day of _____, 20___.

_____

E. Thompson Reynolds
Superior Court Judge

EXEMPLAR #2/LCR 6 II.A. NOTICE RE; ARRAIGNMENT DATE; OMNIBUS HEARING DATE; TRIAL DATE; TIME ELAPSED FROM ARRAIGNMENT TO TRIAL; AND TIME LIMITS

IN THE SUPERIOR COURT OF THE STATE OF WASHINGTON
IN AND FOR THE COUNTY OF SKAMANIA/KLICKITAT

STATE OF WASHINGTON)	
)	No.
Plaintiff,)	
)	NOTICE RE; ARRAIGNMENT DATE;
vs.)	OMNIBUS HEARING DATE; TRIAL DATE;
)	TIME ELAPSED FROM ARRAIGNMENT
)	TO TRIAL; AND TIME LIMITS
)	
Defendant.)	

The above defendant having been arraigned before the Superior Court now, therefore, all parties and their counsel are hereby NOTIFIED AS FOLLOWS:

(1) The defendant was arraigned on the ___ day of _____, 20___.

(2) The omnibus hearing will be held on the ___ day of _____, 20___, at ___ o'clock AM/PM.

(3) The Trial Status Conference REQUIRING DEFENDANT'S PERSONAL PRESENCE* will be held on the ___ day of _____, 20___ at ___ o'clock AM/PM.

(4) The trial will be held on the ___ day of _____, 20___, at ___ o'clock AM/PM.

(5) The number of days which will elapse from the arraignment date to the trial date is ___ days.

(6) The number of days which will elapse before the trial date from the commencement of the running of time pursuant to CrR 3.3 (c)(I) is ___ days.

A PARTY WHO OBJECTS TO THE TRIAL DATE SET ON THE GROUND THAT IT IS NOT WITHIN THE TIME LIMITS PRESCRIBED BY THIS RULE MUST, WITHIN TEN (10) DAYS OF RECEIVING THIS NOTICE FROM THE COURT, MOVE THAT THE COURT SET A TRIAL DATE WITHIN THOSE TIME LIMITS. FAILURE OF A PARTY, FOR ANY REASON, TO MAKE SUCH A MOTION SHALL BE A WAIVER OF THE OBJECTION THAT A TRIAL COMMENCED ON SUCH A DATE IS NOT WITHIN THE TIME LIMITS PRESCRIBED BY CrR 3.3(c).

Dated this ___ day of _____, 20___.

_____
Judge

The original of this notice has been read:

_____ _____ _____
Defendant   Defense Counsel   Prosecutor

* NOTE: FAILURE OF DEFENDANT TO APPEAR (unless excused by the Court) WILL RESULT IN A WARRANT FOR HIS/HER ARREST.

EXEMPLAR #3/LCR 6 II.A. ORDER SETTING STATUS CONFERENCE AND TRIAL DATES

IN THE SUPERIOR COURT OF THE STATE OF WASHINGTON
IN AND FOR THE COUNTY OF SKAMANIA

JUVENILE DIVISION

STATE OF WASHINGTON vs.	)	
	)	
	)	NO.
	)	
	)	ORDER SETTING STATUS
	)	CONFERENCE & TRIAL DATES
DOB: _____ Defendant.	)	
_____	)	

The above defendant having been arraigned before the Superior Court, now, therefore, all parties and their counsel are hereby NOTIFIED AS FOLLOWS:

(1) The juvenile was arraigned on _____

(2) The status conference will be held on _____

(3) The Fact Finding Hearing will be held on _____ at ___ in the Superior Court Room.

(4) The number of days which will elapse from the arraignment date to the hearing date of fact-finding is ___ days.

A PARTY WHO OBJECTS TO THE HEARING DATE SET ON THE GROUNDS THAT IT IS NOT WITHIN THE TIME LIMITS PRESCRIBED BY THIS RULE MUST, WITHIN TEN (10) DAYS OF RECEIVING THIS NOTICE FROM THE COURT, MOVE THAT THE COURT SET A HEARING DATE WITHIN THOSE TIME LIMITS. FAILURE OF A PARTY, FOR ANY REASON, TO MAKE SUCH A MOTION SHALL BE A WAIVER OF THE OBJECTION THAT A HEARING COMMENCED ON SUCH A DATE IS NOT WITHIN THE TIME LIMITS PRESCRIBED BY JuCR 7.8(b).

DATED this ___ day of _____, 20___.

_____
JUDGE/COURT COMMISSIONER

This notice has been received and read:

_____   _____   _____
Juvenile/Defendant   Defense Counsel   Prosecutor

FAILURE TO APPEAR AT THE SCHEDULED PLACE AND TIME (without excuse by the Court) WILL RESULT IN A WARRANT FOR DEFENDANT'S ARREST.

EXEMPLAR #4/LCR 6 II.C.   STATUS CONFERENCE REPORT

IN THE SUPERIOR COURT OF THE STATE OF WASHINGTON
IN AND FOR THE COUNTY OF SKAMANIA/KLICKITAT

STATE OF WASHINGTON	)	
	)	
Plaintiff,	)	No.
	)	
vs.	)	STATUS CONFERENCE REPORT
	)	
	)	
Defendant.	)	
_____	)	

We the undersigned report as follows:

( ) The Prosecutor has <u>not</u> made an offer for plea and does not intend to do so, and

( ) The defendant will be changing his/her plea nonetheless on the next available motion/hearing date of the ___ day of _____, 20___.

. ( ) The case will proceed to trial on the previously established trial date.

( ) A continuance will be requested by Prosecutor/defense to be heard on the ___ day of _____, 20___, the next available motion/hearing date. **NOTICE OF HEARING ON THE REQUEST FOR CONTINUANCE IS HEREBY ACKNOWLEDGE BY ALL PARTIES.**

( ) The Prosecutor has made an offer to resolve this case and the undersigned defendant has responded as follows:

( ) Accepting the offer and is prepared to change his/her plea on the ___ day of _____, 20___, the next available motion/hearing date;

( ) Refusing the offer and the case will go to trial on the previously assigned trial date;

( ) Refusing the offer and a new trial date is requested by Prosecutor/defense to be heard on the _____ day of _____, 20___, the next available motion/hearing date. **NOTICE OF HEARING ON THE REQUEST FOR CONTINUANCE IS HEREBY ACKNOWLEDGED BY ALL PARTIES.**

Dated this ___ day of _____, 20___.

_____   _____   _____
Defendant   Defense Counsel   Prosecutor

EXEMPLAR #5/LCR 9, 16.　NOTE FOR TRIAL SETTING/CERTIFICATE OF READINESS/STATEMENT OF ARBITRABILITY (CIVIL)

IN THE SUPERIOR COURT OF THE STATE OF WASHINGTON
IN AND FOR THE COUNTY OF SKAMANIA/KLICKITAT

Plaintiff,	) No.
	)
and	) NOTE FOR TRIAL SETTING/
	) CERTIFICATE OF READINESS/
	) STATEMENT OF ARBITRABILITY
	) (Civil)
Defendant(s).	)

To opposing counsel or party, Clerk of Court and Court Administrator:

(Plaintiff) (Defendant) requests a trial date and certifies as follows:

1.　This case is at issue, no affirmative pleading remains unanswered and all pleadings are on file

2.　Nature of case _____

3.　Jury ( ) Non–Jury ( )

4.　Estimated trial time:　　　5.　Jury demand filed ( )
　　My case ( ) days　　　　　Jury fee paid ( )
　　Total ( ) days　　　　　　12 ( ) or 6 ( ) jury

6.　Number of witnesses I will call: _____ Doctor ( ) Other expert ( ) Non-expert ( )

7.　Dates unavailable to me: _____

8.　Discovery proceedings complete or time to complete available.　Yes ( ) No ( )

9.　In the event of an opening, trial date could ( ) could not ( ) be advanced ( ) days on a minimum notice of ( ) days.

10.　Pre–trial conference requested.　Yes ( ) No ( )

11.　Trial brief on file ( ) will be filed ( ) will not be filed ( )

12.　The names, addresses and telephone number of the attorneys or parties appearing in person are: _____

INITIAL STATEMENT OF ARBITRABILITY

( ) This case is subject to mandatory arbitration because the sole relief sought is a money judgment and involves no claim in excess of thirty-five thousand dollars ($35,000.00) exclusive of attorney's fees, interest, and costs (MAR 1.2).

( ) This case is not subject to mandatory arbitration under RCW 7.06

Any party not in agreement with the information or estimates given in the Note for Trial Setting/Certificate of Readiness/Statement of Arbitrability shall file and serve within seven days of the date of this notice, a counter notice on written objection to setting or to the Statement of Arbitrability, and note the matter on for hearing to argue the objection.

Date _____ Attorney for _____ (Plaintiff) (Defendant)

EXEMPLAR #6/LCR 10 III.A. REQUEST FOR AND ORDER APPOINTING LEGAL COUNSEL

IN THE SUPERIOR COURT OF THE STATE OF WASHINGTON IN AND FOR THE COUNTY OF SKAMANIA/KLICKITAT

STATE OF WASHINGTON,	)	
	)	
Plaintiff,	)	No
	)	
vs.	)	REQUEST FOR AND ORDER
	)	APPOINTING LEGAL COUNSEL
	)	
Defendant.	)	

I, the undersigned defendant in the above entitled case, state under oath that I am without funds with which to employ counsel and cannot acquire such funds without substantial hardship to me, and therefore request the Court to appoint legal counsel to represent me at public expense.

I, the undersigned do realize that upon a plea of guilty or a finding of guilty, the Court may assess costs for the appointment of counsel to be paid to the Court.

I also understand that it is my responsibility to keep in touch with my Court appointed attorney.

I fully understand that the representation made in this request, if false, can subject me to the penalty prescribed by law for perjury.

Dated this ____ day of _____, 20____.

_____
Defendant

It is hereby ordered that:

Robert A. Lewis, Attorney at Law   Todd Pascoe, Attorney at Law
430 NE Everett Street   11015 NE Fourth Plain Rd., Ste. D
Camas, WA 98607   Vancouver, WA 98662
(360)834–4611   (360)254–0022

is appointed to represent the above named defendant in this action throughout these proceedings.

Dated this ____ day of _____, 20____.

_____
JUDGE/COURT COMMISSIONER

EXEMPLAR #7/LCR 10 V.A.I.   WAIVER OF SPEEDY TRIAL

IN THE SUPERIOR COURT OF THE STATE OF WASHINGTON
IN AND FOR THE COUNTY OF SKAMANIA/KLICKITAT

STATE OF WASHINGTON   )
)
           Plaintiff,   )   No.
)
   vs.   )   WAIVER OF SPEEDY TRIAL
)
)
)
           Defendant(s).   )
)
_____)

     I, _____, a defendant in this case, acknowledge that I have been fully advised by my attorney of the trial time limits of Criminal Rule 3.3, as amended.

     I understand that I have a right to trial within the time noted in Criminal Rule 3.3, as amended, and I give up that right and consent to a trial date of _____.

DATED: _____   _____
                                             Defendant

Approved:

_____   _____
Judge   Defendant's Lawyer

EXEMPLAR #8/LCR 16.   RESPONSE TO STATEMENT OF ARBITRABILITY

IN THE SUPERIOR COURT OF THE STATE OF WASHINGTON
IN AND FOR THE COUNTY OF SKAMANIA/KLICKITAT

Plaintiff,)	No.
)	
v.)	RESPONSE TO STATEMENT OF
)	ARBITRABILITY
)	
Defendant(s))	

I.

To the Clerk, Court Administrator and Opposing Counsel (Per list on reverse side)

The undersigned attorney disagrees with the Statement of Arbitrability filed in this case and contends that this case:

   ( ) Should be arbitrated   ( ) Should <u>not</u> be arbitrated

for the reasons indicated in Part II.

II.   RESPONDED STATEMENT OF ARBITRABILITY

( )   2.1 This case is subject to arbitration because the sole relief is a money judgment, and it involves no claim in excess of $35,000.00, exclusive of attorney fees, interests, and costs.

( )   2.2 The undersigned contends that its claim exceeds $35,000.00, but for purposes of arbitration waives any claim in excess of that amount.

( )   2.3 This case is not subject to mandatory arbitration because:

    ( ) a.   Plaintiff's claim exceeds $35,000.00;
    ( ) b.   Plaintiff seeks relief other than a money judgment;
    ( ) c.   Defendant's counterclaim or cross claim exceeds $35,000.00;
    ( ) d.   Defendant's counterclaim or cross claim seeks relief other than a money judgment; or
    ( ) e.   Case is an appeal from a lower court

III.   INSTRUCTIONS

3.1 Important: Type names and address of all counsel on reverse side.

3.2 Serve other parties and file with Clerk.

3.3 Copy to Superior Court Administrator.

Dated _____ Attorney: _____ for _____

EXEMPLAR #9/LCR 16.   ARBITRATION AWARD

IN THE SUPERIOR COURT OF THE STATE OF WASHINGTON
IN AND FOR THE COUNTY OF SKAMANIA

Plaintiff,	)	No.
	)	
v.	)	ARBITRATION AWARD
	)	
	)	
Defendant(s).	)	
	)	

The issues in arbitration having been heard on _____, ___. I make the following award:

Twenty days after the award has been filed with the Clerk, if no party has sought a trial de novo under MAR 7.1, any party on notice to all parties may present to the Superior Court a judgment on the arbitration award for entry as final judgment in this case.

Was any part of this award based on the failure of a party to participate at the hearing?

(　) Yes　　　(　) No (MAR 5.4)

If yes, please identify the party and explain:

Dated: _____　　_____
　　　　　　　　　　　　　　　　　　　　　Arbitrator

ORIGINAL TO BE FILED WITH THE SUPERIOR COURT CLERK, TOGETHER WITH PROOF OF SERVICE ON THE PARTIES. A COPY MUST ALSO BE SENT TO THE SUPERIOR COURT ADMINISTRATOR.

EXEMPLAR #10/LCR 7IV.   PRE–TRIAL STATEMENT

IN THE SUPERIOR COURT OF THE STATE OF WASHINGTON
IN AND FOR KLICKITAT/SKAMANIA COUNTIES

In re the Marriage of   )
)   No.
)
             Petitioner,   )   PRE–TRIAL STATEMENT OF
   and   )
)   _____
)
             Respondent.   )

I.   PARTIES

HUSBAND: _____ Age: _____ DOB: _____
                  (Name)

_____
                  (Address)

WIFE: _____ Age: _____ DOB: _____

_____
                  (Address)

Date of Marriage: _____ Date of Separation: _____

II.   DEPENDENT CHILDREN

A.   Of this Marriage: Residing with:

       Name(s): _____ DOB: _____ Age: ____ _____
                  _____ DOB: _____ Age: ____ _____
                  _____ DOB: _____ Age: ____ _____

B.   Of Former Relationships:
                  Name(s)   DOB: Age: Residing with:
       Husband:

       Wife:

III.   INCOME AND EMPLOYMENT

Husband:

a.   Employer: _____
b.   Average monthly gross: _____

c.   Deductions: _____
      withholding: _____
      social security: _____
      other: _____
d.   Net income: _____
e.   Other income: _____

Total Disposable Income: _____

Wife:

a. Employer: _____
b. Average monthly gross: _____
c. Deductions: _____
    withholding: _____
    social security: _____
    other: _____
d. Net income: _____
e. Other income: _____

Total Disposable Income: _____

IV. LIVING EXPENSES (Per Month)

                Husband: Wife:

General:

food (persons) _____ _____
house/rent _____ _____
property taxes _____ _____
heat/oil/gas _____ _____
electricity _____ _____
water/garbage _____ _____
telephone _____ _____
home maintenance _____ _____
home insurance _____ _____

Auto/Transportation:

car payment _____ _____
gas _____ _____
maintenance _____ _____
license _____ _____
bridge/ferry _____ _____
parking _____ _____
public transportation _____ _____

Children:

daycare/sitter _____ _____
school lunches _____ _____
school supplies _____ _____
allowances _____ _____
activities _____ _____
music lessons _____ _____
school tuition _____ _____
other _____ _____

Health Care:

med/dental insurance _____ _____
uninsured/med _____ _____
life insurance _____ _____
eye care _____ _____
chiropractic _____ _____
RX drugs _____ _____

Non–RX
other   _____   _____

Miscellaneous:

tobacco   _____   _____
pet supplies   _____   _____
vet bills   _____   _____
cable tv   _____   _____
stamps/stationary   _____   _____
clubs/donations   _____   _____
haircuts   _____   _____
books/newspapers   _____   _____
clothing   _____   _____
laundry/dry clean   _____   _____
gifts   _____   _____
recreation   _____   _____
support/maintenance   _____   _____
other   _____   _____
Monthly payments to creditors
(from V. below)

TOTAL $_____ $_____

V. CREDITORS

Creditor	Balance due	Monthly payment	Paid by

TOTAL: $_____ $_____

VI. PARENTING PLAN

(Attach Proposed Parenting Plan)

VII. CHILD SUPPORT PROPOSAL

A.   Present: $_____   Proposed: $_____

B.   Medical & Dental Expenses:

C.   Tax Exemption:

D.   Child Support During Visitation:

E.   Due Date for Child Support Payment:

F.   Termination of Child Support Obligation:

G.   Child Support Obligation Secured by:

H.   Post High School Educational Support:

VIII. MAINTENANCE AND ATTORNEY'S FEES

A.   Maintenance:

     Present: $_____   Proposed: $_____

B.   Attorney's Fees:

X. RETIREMENT BENEFITS

Present

Husband
    Source: Term of Benefits: % accrued during marriage: Net per month:

Wife
    Source: Term of Benefits: % accrued during marriage: Net per month:

Future

Husband   Estimated Present Value:

Wife   Estimated Present Value:

XI. ASSETS

A. Community:

Description: FMV: Encumbrance: Net:

TOTAL NET VALUE: _____

B. Separate:

Husband:

Description: FMV: Encumbrance: Net:

TOTAL NET VALUE: _____

Separate:

Wife:

Description: FMV: Encumbrance: Net:

TOTAL NET VALUE: _____

XII. PROPOSED PROPERTY DISTRIBUTION

To be awarded to Wife:
Item   Fair Market Value

Value of property awarded to Wife: _____

LESS:

Debts to be assumed by Wife:

Total debts assumed by Wife: (_____)

Net value of property awarded to Wife: _____

To be Awarded to Husband:
Item   Fair market Value

Value of property awarded to Husband   _____

LESS:

Debts to be assumed by Husband:

Total debts assumed by Husband: (_____)

Net value of property awarded to Hus-_____
band

DATED _____

_____
Attorney for Petitioner/Respondent
or
Petitioner/Respondent

EXEMPLAR #11. NOTICE OF LOSS OF VOTING RIGHTS

IN THE SUPERIOR COURT OF THE STATE OF WASHINGTON
IN AND FOR THE COUNTY OF

IN RE THE GUARDIANSHIP OF   )
)   NO.
)   NOTICE OF LOSS OF
)   VOTING RIGHTS
)
          Incapacitated Person)   (CLERK'S ACTION REQUIRED —
)   send notice to County Auditor)
_____)

On _____, this matter came before the court. Pursuant to Laws of Washington RCW 11.88.010, it has been determined that the individual named in this notice lacks the capacity to understand the nature and effect of voting. The Court has appointed a guardian and has revoked the right to vote.

Name: _____ Date of Birth: _____

Address: _____

Date: _____   _____
                                 Signature of Filing Party

                                 _____
                                 Printed Name/WSBA#

                                 _____
                                 Address

I hereby certify that I personally mailed the above notice to the Auditor of the county in which the incapacitated person resides on _____.

_____
Deputy Clerk, _____ County Superior Court

[Adopted effective September 1, 2006.]

EXEMPLAR #12. ORDER RESTRAINING VOTING RIGHTS

IN THE SUPERIOR COURT OF THE STATE OF WASHINGTON
IN AND FOR THE COUNTY OF

IN THE GUARDIANSHIP OF:	)
	) NO.
	)
	) ORDER RESTORING
	) VOTING RIGHTS
	)
Incapacitated Person	) CLERK'S ACTION REQUIRED
	)

This matter having come before the Court on this day upon the Petition of the Guardian for an Order Terminating Guardianship; the Court having reviewed the Petition and the records and files herein, and being fully informed, now therefore;

IT IS HEREBY ORDERED that the Court has determined that the incapacity has terminated and that there is now the capacity to manage the personal care and administration of assets and to exercise the right to vote.

IT IS FURTHERE [1] ORDERED that the Superior Court Clerk shall send a certified copy of this order to the County Auditor.

DATED AND SIGNED IN OPEN COURT this _____ day of _____, 20 ___.

_____
Judge/Court Commissioner

Presented by:

_____
Signature of Guardian/Attorney

_____
Printed Name WSBA/CPG#

_____
Address

_____
Telephone/FAX Number

_____
City, State, Zip Code

_____
E-mail Address

[Adopted effective September 1, 2006.]

_____
[1] So in original.

DISTRICT COURTS

EAST KLICKITAT COUNTY DISTRICT COURT—
[No Local Rules]

WEST KLICKITAT COUNTY DISTRICT COURT

Including Amendments Received Through
August 15, 2015

Table of Rules

LCrRLJ 3.4.   VIDEO CONFERENCE PROCEEDINGS

Preliminary appearances, arraignments, bail hearings, and trial settings, conducted via video conference in which all participants can simultaneously see, hear, and speak as authorized by the Judge, shall be deemed held in open court and in the defendant's presence for the purposes of any statute, court rule, or policy. All video conference hearings conducted pursuant to this rule shall be public, and the public shall be able to simultaneously see and hear all participants and speak as permitted by the Judge. Any party may request an in-person hearing which may, in the Judge's discretion, be granted. Other trial court proceedings may be conducted by video conference only by agreement of the parties either in writing or on the record and upon the approval of the Judge.

[Adopted effective September 1, 2015.]

LCrRLJ 3.7.   MOTIONS

Rules CrRLJ 3.5 and 3.6 shall govern suppression motions in criminal cases. Unless a motion is made during a hearing or trial, it shall be made in writing, shall state with particularity the grounds therefore, shall state the statute, case decision, or court rule that supports the motion, and set forth the relief or order requested. Timing and briefing requirements are governed by Klickitat County Local Superior Court local rule 10 (V) (a).

[Adopted effective September 1, 2015.]

LIRLJ 3.5.   DECISIONS ON WRITTEN STATEMENTS

Mitigation and contested hearings based on written statements, given under penalty of perjury as provided for in IRLJ 2.4(b)(4) and IRLJ 2.6(c), are hereby authorized. The procedures authorized by IRLJ 3.5 are adopted by this court. A defendant requesting the court to decide the case on written statements shall do so by completing and submitting a statement in substantially the form provided by the Court staff for these matters.

[Adopted effective September 1, 2015.]

WRITTEN STATEMENTS FORM

Klickitat County West District Court
State of Washington

[ ] State of Washington,
[ ] City of Bingen
[ ] City of White Salmon,
       Plaintiff,

vs.

_____
      Defendant.

)
)
)
)
)
)
)
)
)
)
)

No. _____
Defendant's Request for
Decision on Written Statements
[   ] **Mitigation Hearing**
[   ] **Contested Hearing**

To: The Clerk of the Klickitat County West District Court, P.O. Box 435, White Salmon, WA 98672.
From: _____, Defendant.
(Print Name)

I hereby request that the court decide my case based on my following sworn statement:

_____

_____

_____

_____

_____

_____

_____

_____

_____

_____

_____

_____

_____

_____

_____

_____

_____

_____

_____

_____

_____

_____

_____

(Attach additional pages if necessary)

I certify [or declare] under the penalty of perjury under the laws of the State of Washington that the above statement is true. I promise that if it is determined that I committed the infraction for which I was cited, I will pay the monetary penalty authorized by law and assessed by the court. I understand that I may not appeal the decision of the court.

_____   _____
(Print your name)   (Sign your name)

_____
(Street or Post Office address)

_____
(City, state and zip code)

[Adopted effective September 1, 2015.]

LEWIS COUNTY

Table of Courts

Superior Court

Lewis County Superior Court Rules.

District Court

Lewis County District Court Local Rules.

Municipal Courts

Centralia Municipal Court Local Rules.
Chehalis Municipal Court Local Rules.
Morton Municipal Court—[No Local Rules].
Mossyrock Municipal Court—[No Local Rules].
Napavine Municipal Court Local Rules.
Pe Ell Municipal Court—[No Local Rules].
Toledo Municipal Court—[No Local Rules].
Winlock Municipal Court Local Rules.

SUPERIOR COURT

LEWIS COUNTY SUPERIOR COURT RULES

Including Amendments Received Through
August 15, 2015

LOCAL ADMINISTRATIVE RULES (LAR)

LAR 1. PRESIDING JUDGE

1.1 Election. Pursuant to General Rule 29(a)(1), Rules of Court (GR 29(a)(1)), the elected Superior Court Judges shall elect a Presiding Judge and an Assistant Presiding Judge by majority vote at a meeting of the Judges to be held in October of odd numbered years.

1.2 Terms. The terms of the Presiding Judge and Assistant Presiding Judge shall be for two years beginning January 1 of the even numbered year after their election.

1.3 Vacancy. A vacancy in the office of the Presiding Judge shall be filled by the then Assistant Presiding Judge. A vacancy in the office of Assistant Presiding Judge shall be filled by majority vote of the elected Superior Court Judges at the first meeting of

Judges to be held after the vacancy is known to exist. Judges filling vacancies shall serve until January 1 of the next even numbered year.

1.4 Duties and Responsibilities. The duties of the Presiding Judge and Assistant Presiding Judge shall be as provided in GR29, unless otherwise provided by written Court policy approved by a majority of the elected Judges of the Lewis County Superior Court.

1.5 Interim Term. Since the effective date of GR 29 was April 30, 2002, this rule shall be effective on the date of its adoption and the Presiding Judge and the Assistant Presiding Judge shall be elected by majority vote of the Judges of the Lewis County Superior Court upon adoption of this Rule and shall serve in the interim until January 1, 2004.

[Adopted effective June 19, 2002.]

LOCAL CIVIL RULES OF COURT

LCR 1. COURT COMMISSIONER HEARING ADULT FELONY MATTERS

Court Commissioners appointed and qualified under Article 4, Section 23 of the Washington State Constitution are authorized to preside over, and consider all matter in adult felony proceedings as specified under RCW 2.24.040(15) including accepting pleas in all cases.

[Adopted effective September 1, 2001.]

LCR 2. MOTIONS FOR REVISION OF COMMISSIONER RULINGS

A party filing a motion for revision of a ruling of a Court Commissioner shall note the motion for argument before the presiding judge such that, within 30 days of filing, the matter shall be considered and determined. Absent extraordinary circumstances, any motion for revision not heard within 30 days of filing shall be considered abandoned, stricken by the court and the commissioner's ruling affirmed.

(a) Revision by Motion and Notice. Revision shall be initiated by filing a motion with the Clerk of the Court within 10 days after entry of the order or judgment as provided in RCW 2.24.050. The motion must specify each portion of the Order for which revision is sought. The revision form shall designate a hearing date no later than 30 days after the filing of the motion. The Motion for Revision shall also be noted in accordance with Civil Rules 6 and 7. A copy of the motion for revision shall be served upon the other parties, or their counsel, if represented, within 10 days after the entry of the order or judgment and at least five court days before the hearing date. An additional three days notice shall be required if service is by mail.

(b) Transcript Required. At least two days prior to the hearing on the motion, the moving party shall file a transcript of the oral ruling of the Commissioner. The moving party shall obtain the transcript at their expense. A copy of the transcript shall, at least two days before the hearing, also be served upon the other parties and furnished to the Judge who will hear the motion. A transcript will not be required if the matter was decided by letter decision, or if no oral decision was rendered. The transcript shall be double spaced in at least eleven point type. The person preparing the transcript shall certify, under penalty of perjury, that it is an accurate transcription of the record. Failure to comply with these requirements may result in denial of the motion.

[Adopted effective September 1, 2001. Amended effective September 1, 2015.]

LCR 3. DOCKETING AND CONFIRMING CIVIL MOTIONS

A. Motion Dockets. Motions to be argued shall be heard on the respective dockets as set forth in this rule. In the event any day scheduled for a motion docket is a legal holiday or a date when the court is unavailable for any reason, the date for **such docket shall be as scheduled by the Court Administrator.** Any motions pertaining to cases assigned to a specific judge shall be heard by that judge and such motion hearings shall be scheduled through the Court Administrator, unless such judge is the Motion Judge, in which event the motions shall be heard on the civil motion docket.

1. The civil motion docket and guardianship docket shall be held on Friday. All civil motions (other than family and guardianships) and motions for revision shall be heard on the civil docket.

2. The family law docket, other than paternity, modification of final child support orders and contempt of final child support order cases, shall be heard on Friday.

3. The paternity and child support modification docket shall be heard on Wednesday.

4. The schedule for motion dockets and trial assignments shall be as Follows:

Wednesday	Court Commissioner
9:00 A.M.	Final Dissolutions
10:00 A.M.	Modification of Final Child Support Orders, Contempt of Final Child Support Orders, Paternity Motions
Friday	Motion Department
9:00 A.M.	Ex Parte, adoptions and other confidential matters
9:30 A.M.	Civil Motion Docket
11:00 A.M.	Guardianship Docket
Friday	Court Commissioner
9:00 A.M.	Family Law Motion Docket
Friday	Court Administrator
8:30 A.M.	Trial Assignments

5. All motions shall be confirmed for argument through the Clerk's Office by 12:00 noon two court days prior to the scheduled argument. Confirmations shall be made by calling the County Clerk at (360) 740–2704. Motions not confirmed will stricken unless the parties and the Court agree otherwise.

[Adopted effective September 1, 2001; amended effective September 1, 2003; September 1, 2005; September 1, 2010; amended on an emergency basis, effective April 1, 2011; July 1, 2011; amended on a permanent basis effective September 1, 2011.]

LCR 5.   SERVICE AND FILING OF MOTIONS AND RESPONSES

A.   Filing and Scheduling of Motions.

Notwithstanding any provision of CR 6(d) to the contrary, a party filing any motion shall serve and file such motion no later than seven (7) court days prior to the date noted for argument on the motion; e.g., by Wednesday 5:00 p.m. of the preceding week for a Friday docket; by Monday 5:00 p.m. of the preceding week for a Wednesday docket. Motions requiring a longer period of notice pursuant to court rule or statute shall be filed as required by the applicable court rule or statute.

All documents supporting the motion shall be filed and served with the motion.

Unless other arrangements are made with the Court Administrator, all motions shall be scheduled for the appropriate Wednesday or Friday Motion Docket and heard by the Motion Judge or by the Court Commissioner. Unless other arrangements are made with the Court Administrator, hearings on any motion shall not include live testimony and argument may be limited in time.

A notice of issue or note for the motion docket identifying the nature of the motion, names of the parties, the names of the attorneys if any, and the date and time for argument on the motion shall be filed and served with the motion. The provisions of GR 14 notwithstanding, a notice of issue or note for a motion docket should be printed on pink paper.

B.   Response Documents

Any party opposing a motion, or any part thereof shall file all original responsive documents and serve copies upon all parties no later than 12:00 noon two court days prior to the scheduled date for argument on the motion; e.g., by noon Wednesday for a Friday docket; by noon Monday for a Wednesday docket.

C.   Reply to Response Documents

All reply documents to the response documents as provided for in part B of this rule shall be filed and served on all parties no later than 12:00 noon one court day prior to the date set for argument on the motion, e.g., by noon Thursday for a Friday docket; by noon Tuesday for a Wednesday docket. No additional documents shall be filed or served after that date and time.

D.   Bench Copies

Bench copies of all motions, memoranda, responses and or replies, and all documents supporting such motions, responses or replies shall be delivered to the Judge or Court Commissioner who is to consider the motion, on the day they are filed. The name of the Judge or Court Commissioner and the date of the hearing for the matter shall be designated on the bench copies.

E.   Affidavits and Declarations.

Affidavits and declarations in support of or in opposition to any motion or part thereof shall be made only on personal knowledge, shall set forth only such facts as would be admissible in evidence, and shall show affirmatively that the affiant or declarant is competent to testify to the specific matters set forth therein. Argument, comment, and nonexpert opinion shall be excluded from affidavits and declarations.

F.   Hearing on Short Notice.

All orders shortening time shall include a provision for a service deadline upon the other party or parties.

G.   Terms

Terms and sanctions may be imposed for failure to comply with this rule, including the striking of any documents filed in violation this rule.

[Adopted effective September 1, 2001. Amended effective September 1, 2003.]

LCR 7.   PLEADINGS ALLOWED; FORM OF MOTIONS

A.   Motions and Other Papers

1. *How Made.* Reapplication for order. When an order has been applied for and refused in whole or in part (unless without prejudice), or has been granted conditionally and the condition has not been performed, the same application for an order shall not be presented to another Judge or Commissioner. If a subsequent application is made upon a different statement of facts or law, it shall be shown by affidavit or certified statement what application was made, when and to what Judge or Commissioner, what order or decision was made thereon; and what new facts or law are claimed to be shown.

Failure to comply with this requirement shall, at the request of an opposing party or counsel, result in any order thus obtained being set aside and terms assessed against the counsel or party obtaining the order.

2. *Form.* All motions and responses or replies thereto shall be in writing, shall be typewritten, or hand printed and shall be presented on paper 8-1/2 by 11 inches in size, on paper containing a vertical line of numbers at the left margin, and shall be double spaced. No pleadings shall be filed or presented which are hand written in cursive form, unless a typed or hand printed version of such pleading is attached to such pleading. The court shall not consider any hand written or cursive pleading without such a typed or hand printed version attached, for any purpose.

3. *Required Provisions in Orders Mandating Personal Appearance.* In all proceedings wherein an order is to be issued requiring or mandating the personal attendance of a person or a party in open court, the order shall include the following words in capital letters:

YOUR FAILURE TO APPEAR AS ABOVE SET FORTH AT THE TIME, DATE AND PLACE STATED MAY CAUSE THE COURT TO ISSUE A BENCH WARRANT FOR YOUR APPREHENSION AND CONFINEMENT IN JAIL UNTIL SUCH TIME AS THE MATTER CAN BE HEARD OR UNTIL BAIL IS POSTED.

No bench warrant shall be issued in such cases for the apprehension of the cited person if such language has been omitted.

4. *Failure to Appear.* If the party noting a motion fails to appear for the scheduled hearing, and the opposing party appears, the motion shall be denied or stricken. If the moving party appears and the opposing party does not appear the requested relief shall be granted, if warranted. If neither the moving nor the responding party appears, the motion shall be stricken.

5. *Motions For Reconsideration*

A. Motions for reconsideration of rulings and all pleadings and documents in support thereof, must be filed and served on opposing counsel, or the opposing party, if unrepresented, and a copy delivered to the Judge or Commissioner making the ruling, within ten (10) days after entry of the judgment or order. Such pleadings shall set forth specific grounds for the reconsideration, and the arguments and authorities in support thereof.

B. The opposing party may, within ten (10) days after receipt of the motion, file and serve on the moving party, and the Judge or Commissioner making the ruling, pleadings and documents in opposition.

C. Each party shall prepare and include in the materials submitted, a proposed order sustaining their respective position on such motion.

D. Oral argument on a motion for reconsideration shall be scheduled only if so ordered by the Judge or Commissioner to whom the motion is submitted. In no case shall a motion for reconsideration be noted for hearing on the motion calendar unless ordered by the Judge or Commissioner to whom the matter has been submitted. Twenty days after a motion for reconsideration has been submitted and served upon the parties or their counsel as provided for in this rule, and no ruling has been made, either party may submit to the Judge or Commissioner a certification that the matter is ready for a ruling on the motion for reconsideration.

B. **Filing of Documents**

1. *Filing: Case Numbers.* Except in consolidated cases, no documents shall be filed with more than one case number, unless sufficient copies are simultaneously provided for each case. Where there are multiple case numbers and no copies provided, the clerk shall place the documents only in the first case number designated.

[Adopted effective September 1, 2001.]

LCR 10. FAMILY LAW MOTIONS PAGE LIMITATION

(A) Generally. Absent prior approval from the court as set forth in (G), all declarations and affidavits from a party, and any non-expert witnesses, in support of a motion, including any reply, shall be limited to a sum total of twenty (20) pages. All declarations and affidavits submitted in response to a motion shall be limited to a sum total of twenty (20) pages.

(B) Application. This rule shall apply to all family law, paternity, and non-parental custody motions. No portion of this rule shall be construed to permit multiple motions noted for the same day and docket to avoid the page limit.

(C) Exhibits. Exhibits that consist of declaration or affidavits shall count toward the above page limits. If parties and attorneys quote only the relevant parts of the emails, journals or depositions in a declaration, and attach the full version of the email, journal or deposition as an exhibit for context, the full version of the email, journal or deposition will not count against the page limit, if labeled as such for that limited purpose. All other exhibits attached to a declaration or affidavit shall be counted toward the page limit.

(D) Financial Declarations. Financial declarations and financial documents shall not count toward the page limit.

(E) Expert Report and Evaluations. Declarations, affidavits, or reports from Guardian *Ad Litems* and expert witnesses shall not count toward the page limit.

(F) Miscellaneous Exceptions. Copies of declarations or affidavits previously filed in a motion previously ruled upon and supplied solely as a convenience to the court in lieu of the court file shall not count toward the page limit.

(G) Authorization. Upon motion of a party and for good cause shown, a party may seek authorization to exceed the page limit may do so on the ex parte calendar without notice to opposing counsel or a self-represented party.

[Adopted effective September 1, 2010.]

LCR 14. USE OF COLORED PAPER

Notwithstanding the provisions of GR14 to the contrary, Lewis County Superior Court authorizes and encourages the use of colored paper for the filing of the following notices in court files.

A. Notice of issue or note for motion docket: Pink paper

B. Notice of case setting of a trial, hearing or other court proceeding: Blue paper.

[Adopted effective September 1, 2001.]

LCR 79. BOOKS AND RECORDS KEPT BY CLERK

(1) Rejection of Unsuitable Materials.

(A) *Original Court Record.* Whenever there is presented to the clerk for filing in a cause, any paper or other material that is deemed by the clerk to be improper or inappropriate for filing, the clerk shall affix his/her file mark thereto and may forthwith orally apply to the court for a determination of the propriety of filing the material presented. If the

court determines the paper or materials should not be made a part of the original court file, an order shall be entered to that effect and the material shall be retained by the clerk as an exhibit in the cause. The court may order that the unsuitable material be sealed, in which event it shall be available for inspection only by order of the court, except to the parties or their attorneys of record.

(B) *Materials Filed Not Evidence Unless Ordered.* Exhibits filed pursuant to subsection (A) hereof shall not be evidence in the cause unless by order of the trial judge entered on notice and hearing.

[Adopted effective September 1, 2015.]

LOCAL GUARDIAN AD LITEM GRIEVANCE RULES
(Cite as LRGAL)

LRGAL 1.1. GUARDIAN AD LITEM COMPLAINT REVIEW COMMITTEE

There shall be a complaint review committee (hereinafter referred to as the "Committee"), consisting of a Superior Court Judge, as designated by the Presiding Judge, the Superior Court Administrator, and a representative of the Lewis County Bar Association designated by it's President, to administer complaints about guardians ad litems involved in Title 11, 13 and 26 RCW.

[Adopted effective September 1, 2002.]

LRGAL 1.2. SUBMISSION OF COMPLAINTS

All complaints shall be in writing, signed by at least one individual with their address and phone number, and shall be submitted to the Superior Court Administrator.

[Adopted effective September 1, 2002.]

LRGAL 1.3. REVIEW OF COMPLAINT

Upon receipt of a written complaint, the Superior Court Administrator shall convene the Complaint Review Committee with ten (10) business days to review the complaint. Upon review of the complaint, the Committee shall either:

A. Make a finding that the complaint is with regard to a case then pending in the court and decline to review the complaint and so inform the complainant. In such instances the Committee shall advise the complainant that the complaint may only be addressed in the context of the case at bar, either by seeking the removal of the guardian ad litem or by contesting the information or recommendation contained in the guardian ad litem's report or testimony. In such cases the Committee and its members shall perform its role in such a manner as to assure that the trial

judge or court commissioner remains uninformed as to the complaint; or

B. Make a finding that the complaint has no merit on it's face, and decline to review it and so inform the complaining party; or

C. Make a finding that the complaint does appear to have merit and request a written response from the guardian ad litem within ten (10) business day, detailing the specific issues in the complaint to which the committee desires a response. The Committee shall provide the guardian ad litem with a copy of the original complaint. A guardian ad litem's failure to respond within the required ten (10) business days shall result in the immediate suspension of the guardian ad litem from all registries. In considering whether the complaint has merit, the Committee shall consider whether the complaint alleges the guardian ad litem has:

1. Violated the Rules of Professional Conduct;

2. Misrepresented his or her qualifications to serve as a guardian ad litem;

3. Not met the annual training requirements set forth in the Registry requirements;

4. Breached the confidentiality of the parties;

5. Falsified information in a report to the Court or in testimony before the Court;

6. Failed to report abuse of a child;

7. Communicated with the a judge/commissioner ex-parte, except as allowed by (such as an emergency restraining order);

8. Purported to represent the Court in a public form without prior approval of the Presiding Judge;

9. Violated state or local laws, rules, or this policy in the person's capacity as guardian ad litem;

10. Taken or failed to take any other action which would reasonably place the suitability of the person to serve as guardian ad litem in question;

11. Failed to keep information confidential from non-parties or disclosed protected information to a party;

12. Intentionally lied or presented information in a false light to the Court, another party or a third party;

13. Failed to report abuse of a child as required by RCW 26.44;

14. Talked about a case for which the guardian ad litem was appointed to the media or public without the permission of all parties and/or the Court

[Adopted effective September 1, 2002.]

LRGAL 1.4. RESPONSE AND FINDINGS

Upon receipt of a written response to a complaint from the guardian ad litem, the Complaint Review Committee shall, within ten (10) business days, make a finding s to each of the issues delineated in the Committee's written request to the guardian ad litem that based on the response, there is either no merit to the issue, or that there is merit to the issue. In any case where the Committee finds that there is merit to an issue, the Committee may conduct further investigation, including the examination of witnesses, documents, and such other evidence as the Committee may, in the exercise of their discretion chose to examine. The Committee may extend the time for entering findings of fact during such examination, provided however, that no such extension shall exceed thirty (30) days, beyond the date the Committee determines that there is merit to any issue.

[Adopted effective September 1, 2002.]

LRGAL 1.5. CONFIDENTIALITY

A. A complaint shall be deemed confidential for all purposes unless the Committee has determined that it has merit under LCRGAL 1.3 C.

B. Any record of complaints filed which are not deemed by the committee to have merit shall be confidential and shall not be disclosed except by court order.

[Adopted effective September 1, 2002.]

LRGAL 1.6. COMPLAINT PROCESSING TIME STANDARDS

A. Complaint shall be resolved within twenty five (25) days of the date of receipt of the written complaint if a case is pending.

B. Complaints shall be resolved within sixty (60) days of the date or receipt of the written complaint if the complaint is filed subsequent to the conclusion of the case.

C. The complaint and the guardian ad litem shall be notified in writing of the Committee's decision within ten (10) business days of the entry of the Committee's findings and decision being signed.

D. Complaints filed under this rule must be filed within three (3) years from the date of the occurrence of the matters complained of. The Committee shall find complaints filed after this time not to have cause to proceed. This limitation applies to all complaints, whether filed during the pendency or after the conclusion of a case.

[Adopted effective September 1, 2002.]

LRGAL 1.7. SANCTIONS

The Committee shall have the authority to issue a written admonishment, a written reprimand, refer the guardian ad litem to additional testing, recommend to the Presiding Judge that the Court, on it's own motion, remove the guardian ad litem from the instant case, or suspend or remove the guardian ad litem from the registry. In considering a response, the Committee shall take into consideration any prior complaints which resulted in an admonishment, reprimand, referral to training, removal of the guardian ad litem from a particular case, or suspension or removal from a registry. If a guardian ad litem is listed on more than one registry, at the discretion of the Committee, the suspension or removal may apply to each registry on which the guardian ad litem is listed. When a guardian ad litem is removed from a registry pursuant to the disposition of a grievance, the Court shall send notice of such removal to the Administrator of the Courts.

[Adopted effective September 1, 2002.]

LRGAL 1.8. REQUEST FOR RECONSIDERATION BY GUARDIAN AD LITEM

A guardian ad litem may, within five (5) business days of receipt of notification that he or she have been suspended or removed from a registry, request a hearing to review the Committee's decision. The Presiding Judge shall designate a hearing officer, to preside over and conduct such review. The sole purpose of the review shall be to review the appropriateness of the suspension or removal from the registry. The hearing officer shall review the written record of the instant case and any prior complaints upon which the Committee relied and hear oral argument from the guardian ad litem and a representative of the Committee. Said hearing shall be conducted within twenty (20) days of receipt of a request for the hearing.

[Adopted effective September 1, 2002.]

LRGAL 1.9. MAINTAINING RECORDS OF GRIEVANCES

The Superior Court Administrator shall maintain a record of grievances filed and of any sanctions issued pursuant to the grievance procedure.

[Adopted effective September 1, 2002.]

LOCAL RULE ON GUARDIAN AD LITEM REGISTRY POLICY

LRGAL 2.1. GENERAL POLICY

Any individual desiring to serve as a Guardian ad Litem (GAL) in any matter pertaining to Adoptions, Family Law matters, Probates and Trusts, must be listed on the Guardian ad Litem (GAL) Registry maintained by the Lewis County Superior Court Administrator. A separate registry shall maintained by the Lewis County Juvenile Court Administrator for Title 13 GALS and Volunteer GALS, the program administered by the Juvenile Court.

The Court Administrator shall maintain and administer the GAL registries as provided herein and shall maintain application forms and background information records pertaining to each person applying to be listed on Title 11 and 26 registries. Persons listed on any registries shall reapply and provide additional background information annually by January 31. All application and background information, with the exception of personal identifying information in family law cases and pending complaints shall be available for public inspection.

Persons shall be selected to serve on each registry at the discretion of the Court, giving due consideration to: (1) having a sufficient number of GALS available to fulfill the requests of litigants for appointments: (2) achieving and maintaining diversity; and (3) retaining panels of persons with substantial experience and special knowledge with each given field. In the event that more qualified applicants apply than may be needed or would benefit any of the separate programs, all applicants may not be selected for the registry.

The Court shall periodically sponsor or approve training programs which registry applicants shall be required to attend to maintain and improve their level of proficiency. Training programs may be co sponsored or offered by the State or County Bar Associations under the oversight of the Court or offered or sponsored by other counties under the oversight of their courts.

Each registry may be constituted periodically after an open application period has been publicly announced. The Court may allow additional applicants to be added to any registry periodically.

The Court Administrator may impose an application processing fee and may charge a fee for any and all training programs.

[Adopted effective September 1, 2002.]

LRGAL 2.2. SPECIFIC REGISTRY REQUIREMENTS

A. Adoption Registry. Education and Experience Requirements:

a. *Attorneys*

1) Member of the Washington State Bar Association in good standing; and

2) Two years of experience in the practice of law including at least three (3) completed adoptions.

b. *Non Attorneys*

1) Bachelor level degree in any of the following fields: social work, psychology, counseling, nursing, medicine, or equivalent field or equivalent work or personal experience in the areas of child, adolescent or family counseling or casework; or

2) Certified by the State of Washington as a social worker, mental health therapist or marriage and family counselor, or licensed as a psychologist, nurse, or physician in good standing;

B. Guardianship Registry. Education and Experience Requirements

a. *Attorneys*

1) Member of the Washington State Bar Association in good standing; and

2) Minimum two years of practice of law.

b. *Non Attorneys*

1) Five years experience in the following: Needs of the impaired, elderly people, physical disabilities, mental illness, developmental disabilities, and/or other areas relevant to the needs of incapacitated persons; and

2) For initial placement on the registry, completion of any training required by RCW 11.88.090 as amended.

C. Family Law Registry. Education and Experience Requirements

a. *Attorneys*

1) Member of the Washington State Bar Association in good standing; and

2) Two years of experience in the practice of law including a minimum of 10 completed dependency and/or dissolution cases with children to include post-resolution custody modifications; or

3) Meet the requirements C (b) 1) or 2) below.

b. *Non Attorneys*

1) Bachelor level degree in any of the following fields: social work, psychology, counseling, nursing, medicine or equivalent field or equivalent work or personal experience in the areas of child, adolescent, or family counseling or casework; or

2) Certified by the State of Washington as a social worker, mental health therapist, or marriage and family counselor, or licensed as a psychologist, nurse, physician in good standing; or

3) Such other educational or employment experience that is acceptable to the court.

c. *Parentage Cases/Out of State Guardian ad Litem.* In RCW 26.26 actions, a relative of the minor mother or father may be appointed who has complied with the requirements of RCW 26.12.175 and who is otherwise suitable.

In RCW 26.33 actions involving the need for an out-of-state GAL, a non-registry GAL may be appointed so long as the appointed GAL complies with the requirements of RCW 26.12.

D. Training

1. For initial placement on the registries, all guardians shall Complete all training and continued training that is required by statute, State or County court rules.

E. Appointments

1. *Guardianships:* Any person listed on the registry may be agreed to by the parties or a party may serve a written request upon the Superior Court Administrator's office, who shall appoint a GAL whose name next appears on the registry on a rotational basis in accordance with RCW 11.88.090(3)(a) subject to that person's acceptance of the appointment.

2. *Family Law:* Absent a joint recommendation from the parties of a person listed on the family law registry who has been approved by the Court, the

3. GAL shall be appointed pursuant to RCW 26.12.177(2)(b).

4. *Adoptions:* Any person listed on the adoption registry may be appointed upon stipulation of the parties and the agreement of the GAL to accept the case. Absent an agreement, the Court Administrator shall select the name of a GAL from the registry on a rotational basis, which GAL shall be appointed by the Court, subject to the GAL's agreement to accept the case.

F. Application.
Each person requesting to be listed on any Guardian ad Litem registry shall annually submit an application on the current form provided by the Court and maintained by the Court Administrator.

[Adopted effective September 1, 2002. Amended effective September 1, 2010.]

LRGAL 2.4.   RETENTION ON REGISTRIES

1. Persons on the registries shall promptly inform the Court of any temporary unavailability to serve, or their intent to resign from the registry.

2. A person shall remain on the registry unless the person fails to maintain a current application with attachments or the person is removed or suspended because of the grievance procedure.

3. A person may be denied listing on, or may be temporarily suspended from the registry for any reason that places the suitability of the person to act as a GAL in question.

4. A GAL who ceases to be on the registry and who still has active or incomplete cases shall immediately report this circumstance to the Superior Court Administrator, who shall reassign such cases.

5. A person's retention on the registry shall be review upon the Court's receipt of a complaint regarding performance in office or the Court's receipt of adverse information regarding the suitability of a person serve as a GAL. Complaints shall be reviewed in accordance with the grievance procedure.

[Adopted effective September 1, 2002.]

LOCAL MANDATORY PARENTING SEMINAR RULES

LMPSR 1.1.   PARENTING SEMINARS

A. The parents, petitioners, and respondents shall complete a parenting seminar approved by the Court in all cases filed under RCW Chapters 26.09, 26.10, and 26.26, which require a parenting or residential plan or custody order for minor children, including marital dissolutions, legal separations, paternity residential plans, non-parent custody actions, any action where one or both of the parties is under the age of eighteen (18) years, and any action in which the Court makes a discretionary finding that a parenting seminar would be in the best interest of the children. The Court may also order additional persons involved in the parenting of the minor children to attend the parenting seminar.

B. **Major Modifications of Parenting/Residential Plans or Custody Orders**: All parents, petitioners, and respondents involved in a major modification of a parenting or residential plan or custody order need to have attended the parenting seminar at least once since the original case was filed before the court will enter modified parenting or residential plans or custody orders. A copy of the attendance certificate shall be filed with the Clerk of the Court.

[Adopted effective September 1, 1995; Amended effective September 1, 2007.]

LMPSR 2.1.   TIME OF ATTENDANCE

All parties required by this rule to participate in a parenting seminar shall complete a Court approved seminar within sixty (60) days of filing of the action if the party is the Petitioner, or sixty (60) days of filing an appearance or a response, whichever is first, if the party is the Respondent. In paternity actions wherein the State of Washington is the Petitioner, attendance shall be required within sixty (60) days after paternity has been established and a parenting plan has been requested. In all cases in which attendance is ordered by the Court and not mandated by this rule, the parenting seminar shall be completed within sixty (60) days of the date of the Court order being entered.

[Adopted effective September 1, 1995.]

LMPSR 2.2. CERTIFICATION OF COMPLETION

Successful completion of the seminar shall be evidenced by a certificate of attendance provided by the person or agency providing the seminar and filed with the Court.

[Adopted effective September 1, 1995.]

LMPSR 3.1. FEES

Every party attending a parenting seminar shall pay the fee charged by the Court approved provider. The provided may waive the fee for an indigent party.

[Adopted effective September 1, 1995.]

LMPSR 4.1. SPECIAL CONSIDERATION/WAIVER

A. In no case shall opposing parties be required to attend a parenting seminar together.

B. Upon a showing of domestic violence or abuse which would not require mutual decision making pursuant to RCW 26.09.191(1), or upon a showing that a parent's attendance at a seminar is not in the children's best interest pursuant to RCW Chapter 26.12, the Court shall either (1) waive the requirement of completion of the seminar, or (2) allow participation in an alternative voluntary parenting seminar for battered spouses.

C. The Court may waive the seminar requirement for good cause shown.

[Adopted effective September 1, 1995.]

LMPSR 5.1. FAILURE TO COMPLY/SANCTIONS

Willful failure to participate or willful delay in completion of a parenting seminar by any party may constitute contempt of Court and result in sanctions, including, but not limited to, imposition of monetary terms, striking of pleadings, or denial of affirmative relief to a party not in compliance with these rules. Nonparticipation or default by one party does not excuse participation by any other party. Refusal, delay or default by a Respondent will not delay the action. Petitioner's refusal or delay shall prevent the case from being set for trial or the entry of any final order concerning a parenting/residential plan or custody order, except in cases where there is a co-petitioner or counter petitioner who is in full compliance. Other than one motion made by either party for temporary orders that is filed within sixty (60) days of the filing of a petition requesting a parenting plan, residential plan or custody order, neither Petitioner nor Respondent shall be allowed to continue to seek affirmative relief in the pending action or any subsequent action between the same parties until the seminar has been successfully completed and a copy of the attendance certificate is filed with the Clerk of the Court. Agreement by the parties as to a final order on a parenting plan, residential plan, or custody order shall not excuse participation in the seminars by both parties. The Court may waive the seminar requirement for good cause shown.

[Adopted effective September 1, 1995; Amended effective September 1, 2007.]

LMPSR 6.1. STANDARDS

Standards for parenting seminars shall be established by the Court and all providers shall be approved by the Court.

[Adopted effective September 1, 1995.]

LOCAL MANDATORY MEDIATION RULES FOR CHILD CUSTODY AND VISITATION ISSUES (LMMR)

LMMR 1. CHILD CUSTODY PROCEEDING DEFINED

For purposes of this rule, a child custody proceeding shall be defined as any proceeding before the court in which custody or visitation is contested, except Juvenile Court dependency proceedings.

[Adopted effective April 1, 1995; amended effective September 1, 2003.]

LMMR 2. FAMILY COURT SERVICES DEFINED

Family Court Services is defined as the agency under contract with the Board of County Commissioners to provide family court services.

[Adopted effective April 1, 1995.]

LMMR 3. MEDIATION REQUIRED

Unless prohibited by law, all custody or visitation disputes shall be submitted to mandatory mediation before proceeding to trial. The mediation requirement may be waived by the Court for good cause shown. A motion for waiver shall be noted before the Court Commissioner. An Order Waiving Mediation shall be filed with the Court prior to the case being set for trial.

[Adopted effective April 1, 1995; amended effective September 1, 2003.]

LMMR 4.   CONTINUING SUPERIOR COURT JURISDICTION

The requirement of mediation shall not prevent the Court or Court Commissioner from entering temporary orders.

[Adopted effective April 1, 1995.]

LMMR 5.   NOTING FOR MEDIATION AND TRIAL SETTING

Upon the filing of a Response to the Petition which contests child custody or visitation, making the proceeding subject to these rules, the Petitioner shall immediately note the proceeding for mandatory mediation and trial setting on forms prescribed by the Court. The form for mandatory mediation shall be entitled "Order to Transfer to Mandatory Mediation", shall be substantially in the form in Appendix A to these rules, and shall be signed by the attorney for each party and each party appearing *pro se* prior to presentation to the Court for approval. The form for trial setting shall be the standard Notice of Issue available in the Lewis County Clerk's Office.

The refusal by an attorney or pro se party to sign the Order to Transfer to Mediation shall not delay a transfer to Family Court Services or trial setting. Such refusal to sign shall be noted on the Order to Transfer to Mandatory Mediation.

[Adopted effective April 1, 1995; amended effective September 1, 2003.]

LMMR 6.   APPOINTMENT OF MEDIATOR

(1) A list of Family Court Services mediators shall be available upon request. If the parties reach an agreement as to the mediator, the stipulation shall be noted on the Order to Transfer to Family Court Services for Mediation. In the absence of a stipulation the court will appoint the mediator.

(2) The appointment of a mediator is subject to the right of that person to refuse to serve. A mediator shall provide prompt notification if refusing to serve. Refusal to serve shall be based upon any grounds of interest, relationship, bias or prejudice set forth in CJC Canon 3(C) governing disqualification of judges.

(3) Notice of Appointment shall be mailed to the mediator selected with copies being mailed to each counsel or party. Mediation shall commence within three (3) weeks from the date of appointment unless otherwise agreed to by the parties and the mediator,

and shall be completed within forty-five (45) days of the appointment of the mediator.

[Adopted effective April 1, 1995.]

LMMR 7.   AUTHORITY OF MEDIATOR

Family Court Services shall determine the time and place of mediation. In appropriate cases, the mediator shall determine the duration of mediation and have the authority to terminate the mediation prior to completion.

[Adopted effective April 1, 1995.]

LMMR 8.   ATTENDANCE

Mediation sessions shall normally include the parties only, but may, by agreement of the parties, include other persons. Attendance at mediation sessions is mandatory.

[Adopted effective April 1, 1995.]

LMMR 9.   DECLARATION OF COMPLETION

Within seven (7) days of completion, a Certificate of Mediation Completion shall be filed by the mediator. Counsel and the parties shall be advised by the mediator, on a separate document attached to the Certificate of Mediation Completion, of the results and recommendations of the mediator.

[Adopted effective April 1, 1995.]

LMMR 10.   PAYMENT

Family Court Services shall be paid equally by the parties, unless either or both parties are declared to be indigent or partially indigent. Financial declarations shall be executed by each party and a Court determination of the financial status shall be made prior to the commencement of mediation for consideration of indigency. Judgment for reimbursement of mediation fees to Lewis County may be entered in the discretion of the Court.

[Adopted effective April 1, 1995; amended effective September 1, 2003.]

LMMR 11.   MEDIATION UNSUCCESSFUL

If the parties fail to reach an agreement in mediation, an investigation may be ordered. The investigator shall not be the same person who mediated the case. Upon completion of the investigation, written recommendations shall be filed with the Court.

[Adopted effective April 1, 1995.]

LMMR 12.   CONFIDENTIALITY

The work product of the mediator and all communications during mediation shall be privileged and not subject to compulsory disclosure. The mediator shall not appear or testify in any court proceedings.

[Adopted effective April 1, 1995.]

LOCAL MANDATORY ARBITRATION RULES OF THE SUPERIOR COURT FOR LEWIS COUNTY, STATE OF WASHINGTON

I. SCOPE AND PURPOSE OF RULES

LMAR 1.1. APPLICATION OF RULES— PURPOSE AND DEFINITIONS

(a) **Purpose.** The purpose of mandatory arbitration of civil actions under RCW 7.06 as implemented by the Mandatory Arbitration rules is to provide a simplified and economical procedure for obtaining the prompt and equitable resolution of disputes involving claims of $50,000.00 or less. Claims in which the sole relief sought is the establishment, modification or termination of maintenance or child support payments shall not be subject to mandatory arbitration unless stipulated to in writing by the parties or otherwise ordered by the court. The Mandatory Arbitration rules as supplemented by these local rules are not designed to address every question, which may arise during the arbitration process, and the rules give considerable discretion to the arbitrator. The arbitrator should not hesitate to exercise that discretion. Arbitration hearings should be informal and expedi-tious, consistent with the purpose of the statutes and rules.

(b) **Administration.** The arbitration department shall consist of the County Clerk, the Court Administrator or Assistant Court Administrator, or such other person designated by the Superior Court Judges. The arbitration department shall supervise arbitration under these rules and perform any additional duties, which may be delegated.

[Adopted effective November 6, 1992; amended effective October 1, 1994; September 1, 2007.]

LMAR 1.3. RELATIONSHIP TO SUPERIOR COURT JURISDICTION AND OTHER RULES—MOTIONS

All motions before the court relating to mandatory arbitration shall be noted on the civil motions calendar except as otherwise provided in these arbitration rules.

[Adopted effective November 6, 1992.]

II. TRANSFER TO ARBITRATION AND ASSIGNMENT OF ARBITRATION

LMAR 2.1. TRANSFER TO ARBITRATION

(a) **Statement of Arbitrability.** In every civil case the party filing the note for trial assignment shall upon the form provided by the court, complete a statement of arbitrability, and serve it upon opposing counsel or party, if not represented by counsel. Prior to the trial-setting date, any party disagreeing with the statement of arbitrability or willing to stipulate to arbitration shall serve and file a response to the statement or arbitrability as filed, upon the form prescribed by the court. In the absence of such a response, the statement of arbitrability shall be deemed correct, and the case shall be set for arbitration. Cases transferred to the arbitration calendar shall be stricken from the trial calendar. Unless otherwise ordered by the court, no trial date shall be assigned in cases, which are subject to arbitration.

If a party asserts that it's claim exceeds $50,000.00, or seeks relief other than a money judgment, the case is not subject to arbitration, except by stipulation.

(b) **Failure to file–amendments.** A party failing to serve and file an original response within the time prescribed may do so later only upon leave of court. A party may amend the statement of arbitrability or response thereto at any time prior to assignment of an arbitrator or assignment of a trial date and thereafter only by leave of court for good cause shown.

[Adopted effective November 6, 1992; amended effective September 1, 2007.]

LMAR 2.3. ASSIGNMENT TO ARBITRATOR

(a) **Generally; Stipulations.** When a case is set for arbitration, a list of five proposed arbitrators shall be furnished to the parties. A list of other approved arbitrators shall be furnished upon request. The parties are encouraged to stipulate to an arbitrator. In the absence of the stipulation within 14 days after a case is transferred to arbitration, the arbitrator shall be chosen from among the five proposed arbitrators in the manner defined by this rule.

1. *Response by Parties.* Within 14 days after a list of proposed arbitrators is furnished to the parties, each party shall nominate one or two arbitrators and strike two arbitrators from the list. If both parties respond, an arbitrator nominated by both parties shall be appointed. If no arbitrator has been nominated by both parties, an arbitrator shall be appointed from among those not stricken by either party.

2. *Response by Only One Party.* If only one party responds within 14 days, an arbitrator shall be appointed from that party's response.

3. *No Response.* If neither party responds within 14 days, the arbitrator shall be randomly appointed from the five proposed arbitrators.

4. *Additional Arbitrators for Additional Parties.* If there are more than two adverse parties, all represented by different counsel, two additional proposed arbitrators shall be added to the list for each additional party so represented with the above principles of selection to be applied. The number of adverse parties shall be determined by the arbitration department, subject to review by the Presiding Judge.

[Adopted effective November 6, 1992.]

III. ARBITRATORS

LMAR 3.1. QUALIFICATIONS

(a) Arbitration Panel. There shall be a panel of arbitrators in such numbers as the Superior Court Judges may from time to time determine. A person desiring to serve as an arbitrator shall complete an information sheet on the form prescribed by the court. A list showing the names of arbitrators available to hear cases and the information sheets shall be available for public inspection in the Court Administrator's office. The oath of office on the form prescribed by the court must be completed and filed prior to an applicant being placed on the panel.

(b) Refusal; Disqualification. The appointment of an arbitrator is subject to the right of that person to refuse to serve. An arbitrator must notify the arbitration department immediately if refusing to serve or if any cause exists for the arbitrator's disqualification from the case upon any of the grounds of interest, relationship, bias or prejudice set forth in CJC Canon 3(C) governing the disqualification of judges. If disqualified, the arbitrator must immediately return all materials in a case to the arbitration department.

[Adopted effective November 6, 1992.]

LMAR 3.2. AUTHORITY OF ARBITRATORS

An arbitrator has the authority to:

(a) Determine the time, place and procedure to present a motion before the arbitrator.

(b) Require a party or attorney advising such party or both to pay the reasonable expenses, including attorney's fees, caused by the failure of such party or attorney or both to obey an order of the arbitrator unless the arbitrator finds that the failure was substantially justified or that other circumstances make an award of expenses unjust. The arbitrator shall make a special award for such expenses and shall file such award with the Clerk of the Court, with proof of service on each party. The aggrieved party shall have 10 days thereafter to appeal the award of such expense in accordance with the procedures described in RCW 2.24.050. If within 10 days after the award is filed no party appeals, a judgment shall be entered in a manner described generally under MAR 6.3.

(c) Award attorney's fees as authorized by these rules, by contract or by law.

[Adopted effective November 6, 1992.]

IV. PROCEDURES AFTER ASSIGNMENT

LMAR 4.2. DISCOVERY

In determining when additional discovery beyond that directly authorized by MAR 4.2 is reasonably necessary, the arbitrator shall balance the benefits of discovery against the burdens and expenses. The arbitrator shall consider the nature and complexity of the case, the amount in controversy, values at stake, the discovery that has already occurred, the burdens on the party from whom discovery is sought, and the possibility of unfair surprise which may result if discovery is restricted. Authorized discovery shall be conducted in accordance with the Civil Rules except that motions concerning discovery shall be determined by the arbitrator.

[Adopted effective November 6, 1992.]

V. HEARING

LMAR 5.1. NOTICE OF HEARING—TIME AND PLACE—CONTINUANCE

An arbitration hearing may be scheduled at any reasonable time and place chosen by the arbitrator. The arbitrator may grant a continuance without court order. The parties may stipulate to a continuance only with the permission of the arbitrator. The arbitrator shall give reasonable notice of the hearing date and any continuance to the arbitration department.

[Adopted effective November 6, 1992.]

LMAR 5.2. PREHEARING STATEMENT OF PROOF—DOCUMENTS FILED WITH COURT

In addition to the requirements of MAR 5.2, each party shall also furnish the arbitrator with copies of pleadings and other documents contained in the court file which that party deems relevant. The court file shall remain with the Clerk of the Court.

[Adopted effective November 6, 1992.]

LMAR 5.3. CONDUCT OF HEARING— WITNESSES—RULES OF EVIDENCE

(a) **Recording.** The hearing may be recorded electronically or otherwise by any party at that party's expense.

[Adopted effective November 6, 1992.]

VI. AWARD

LMAR 6.1. FORM AND CONTENT OF AWARD

(a) **Form.** The award shall be prepared on the form prescribed by the court.

(b) **Return of Exhibits.** When an award is filed, the arbitrator shall return all exhibits to the parties who offered them during the hearing.

[Adopted effective November 6, 1992.]

LMAR 6.2. FILING OF AWARD

A request by an arbitrator for an extension of time for the filing of an award under MAR 6.2 may be presented to the Presiding Judge, ex parte. The arbitrator shall give the parties notice of any extension granted.

[Adopted effective November 6, 1992.]

LMAR 6.3. JUDGMENT ON AWARD

(a) **Presentation.** A judgment on an award shall be presented to the Presiding Judge, by any party, on notice in accordance with MAR 6.3.

[Adopted effective November 6, 1992.]

VII. GENERAL PROVISIONS

LMAR 8.1. STIPULATIONS—EFFECT ON RELIEF GRANTED

If a case not otherwise subject to mandatory arbitration is transferred to arbitration by stipulation and order of the court, the arbitrator may grant any relief which could have been granted if the case were determined by a judge.

[Adopted effective November 6, 1992.]

LMAR 8.4. TITLE AND CITATION

These rules are known and cited as the Lewis County Superior Court Mandatory Arbitration Rules. LMAR is the official abbreviation.

[Adopted effective November 6, 1992.]

LMAR 8.6. COMPENSATION OF ARBITRATOR

(a) **Generally.** Arbitrators shall be compensated in the same amount and manner as judges pro tempore of the Superior Court; provided, however, that said compensation shall not exceed $500.00 for any case unless prior approval is granted by the Presiding Judge. The Presiding Judge shall determine the amount of compensation to be paid. No county payment shall be made unless and until funding is provided by the Lewis County Commissioners.

[Adopted effective November 6, 1992.]

APPENDIX

APPENDIX A. ORDER TO TRANSFER TO MANDATORY MEDIATION

LOCAL MANDATORY MEDIATION RULES FOR CHILD CUSTODY
AND VISITATION ISSUES IN THE SUPERIOR COURT OF
THE STATE OF WASHINGTON FOR LEWIS COUNTY

In Re the	)	
	)	
Petitioner,	)	No.
	)	
and	)	ORDER TO TRANSFER TO
	)	MANDATORY MEDIATION
	)	(ORTF)
	)	
Respondent,	)	

THIS MATTER having come on regularly for hearing and it appearing that there are custody or visitation issues requiring mandatory mediation pursuant to LMMR 3, Local Rules for Superior Court, now, therefore,

IT IS HEREBY ORDERED as follows:

1.1   This matter shall be transferred to [ ] Family Court Services [ ] _____ for mandatory mediation.

1.2   The cost of mediation services shall be paid as follows:

By the Petitioner   _____ %

By the Respondent   _____ %

At County expense   _____ %

1.3   The parties shall cooperate and make themselves available in any reasonable manner deemed necessary by the Mediation Provider for the purposes of this Order.

DATED this ___ of _____, 20___.

_____
Judge

Presented by: Approved as to form/
                                  Presentation Waived

_____   _____
Attorney for: [ ] Petitioner   Attorney for: [ ] Respondent

THE FOLLOWING INFORMATION SHALL BE EITHER PRINTED OR TYPED:

Petitioner's Address: Respondent's Address:

_____   _____

_____   _____

Home Telephone: Home Telephone:

Work Telephone: _____   Work Telephone: _____

_____   _____

Order to Transfer to Mediation
[Adopted effective September 1, 2003.]

LOCAL MANDATORY SETTLEMENT CONFERENCE RULES (LMSCR)

LMSCR 1. SETTLEMENT CONFERENCES IN FAMILY LAW CASES

(A) Requirement. Unless otherwise ordered by the Court, all family law cases, including those brought pursuant to RCW 26.09, 26.10, 26.26 or 26.60, in which the parties are not in agreement as to the terms of any parenting plan, order for placement of or visitation with a child, the determination of child support as part of a parenting plan or order for placement of or visitation with a child, the division of property, division of debts and liabilities, or a claim by any party for post decree maintenance or spousal support, shall, prior to being assigned a trial date, be set for a settlement conference. Prior to setting for a settlement conference, the case shall be "at issue," with all interested parties having filed answers or responses. Upon filing a notice for a settlement conference, the Court Administrator shall assign the soonest available date.

(B) Scheduling.

(1) To obtain a date for a settlement conference, the moving party must file a notice of issue for a settlement conference and certify that the respondent and all other interested parties have filed responses to the petition or complaint, that mediation as required has been attended or waived by the court, and note the matter on the Court Administrator's assignment calendar. The notice of issue must be filed and served at least seven (7) court days prior to the date scheduled for the assignment to be made.

(2) All interested parties or their counsel shall attend the assignment meeting with the Court Administrator, and shall provide a list of unavailable dates. Once a date for settlement conference has been assigned, the date may be changed or continued only by the court for good cause shown.

(C) Attendance and Preparation Required. All parties and their counsel shall personally attend the settlement conference unless other arrangements have been made with the court in advance of the settlement conference date. At the settlement conference, all parties shall make a good faith effort to fully discuss and settle all unresolved issues in dispute and negotiate in good faith. Failure to do so shall be grounds for imposition of terms.

(D) Settlement Conference Statement. The parties or their counsel shall deliver to the court and any opposing parties a settlement conference statement no later than fourteen (14) days prior to the settlement conference date. The settlement conference statement shall be in such form as required by the court and shall be available from the Court Administrator in electronic format or hard copy. Every party shall attach to the settlement conference statement or include with it the following information in hard copy:

(1) Complete individual (or joint) tax returns for the past two calendar years with all schedules, IRS form 1099's, W–2's, and similar statements of income.

(2) Complete partnership and/or corporate tax returns for the past two years, including all schedules and attachments for any entity by whom any of the parties may be employed as an officer or director, be a member of or in which any party has an interest of 5% or more of the capital stock.

(3) All pay stubs for the past six months or since January 1 or the current calendar year, whichever period is longer

(4) Copies of the most recent statement and copies of the statements current as of the date of separation of balances due upon any mortgages, real estate purchase or sale contracts, deeds of trust and the underlying obligation secured by them, installment purchases contracts, time payment agreements or accounts, credit card accounts and all other debt owed by or to the parties.

(5) The most recent employers' ERISA or other retirement statement, together with a statement of contributions since the date of that statement of any pension or retirement plan of any party, the most recent statement together with a list of contributions since the date of that statement for any IRA, SEP, deferred compensation account or other defined contribution "retirement" account.

(6) A written appraisal or its equivalent for any and all real property and all personal property of special, unusual or extraordinary value, or a detailed summary of the evidence to be relied upon as to the value of such items. The parties may stipulate to a comparative market analysis for any real estate, provided there is no disagreement as to the value of the real property.

(7) The most recent NADA Official Used Car Guide or other similar vehicle appraisal guide showing both average loan or wholesale and retail values for any automobiles.

(8) A summary of the source and tracing of any property asserted or claimed to be the separate property of any party.

(9) A statement from each life insurance company issuing a policy of the insurance on the life of any party showing the case surrender value of the policy and any outstanding loans against its cash value.

(10) A written appraisal or business evaluation of any proprietorship, partnership or closely held corporation of any party, or a summary of the evidence to be relied upon as to value of the same.

(11) A list of expert witnesses to be called at trial, a summary of their qualifications or C.V. as well as a summary of their anticipated testimony.

(12) Any other documents which any party believes to be relevant or material to the issues remaining in dispute between the parties, together with a written explanation of the relevance and materiality of the documents.

(13) If the issues in dispute concern a parenting plan or order of placement of or for visitation with any child, a copy of a proposed parenting plan or order for such placement or visitation.

(E) Sanctions for Noncompliance. Failure of any party to comply with the settlement conference rules described above may result in the imposition of sanctions in the sum of not more than $500.00 upon the non-complying party.

(F) Other Issues and Documents. If child support is an issue of a dispute pertaining to a parenting plan, order of placement or visitation for a child, proposed child support worksheets in the form required, together with any required forms for determination of a deviation from the scheduled amount of child support.

(G) Negotiations Prior to Settlement Conference. After settlement conference statements are served, the parties are encouraged to negotiate and exchange additional documents. Any party may file and serve supplemental settlement conference statements prior to the scheduled settlement conference if the party's analysis or proposal to resolve the issues has changed after reviewing another party's settlement conference statement. If the parties resolve all issues prior to the settlement conference, they should appear at the settlement conference prepared to place the settlement on the record and/or enter final orders completing the action. If the parties resolve some of the issues in dispute, they should be prepared to discuss the issues remaining at the settlement conference.

(H) Completion. At the conclusion of the settlement conference, if the parties reach a settlement, the court shall schedule a hearing for presentment of final orders. If the parties desire to continue discussing the issues, the court may schedule a continuance of the settlement conference if warranted and time is available.

(I) Proceedings After Settlement Conference. If the parties do not reach a complete settlement of all issues in dispute, the matter shall proceed to trial as to the issues remaining in dispute. Any party may submit to any other party proposals for resolution of the remaining issues in dispute up the date of trial.

[Adopted effective September 1, 2010.]

LOCAL SPECIAL PROCEEDINGS RULES (LSPR)

LSPR 98.05. GUARDIANSHIP ORDERS AND REPORTS

(a) Appointment of Guardian. The initial Order of Appointment of a Guardian shall clearly specify the due date for filing the Inventory, Budget, Personal Care Plan and the first Annual Report, and shall schedule the hearing for approval of the Inventory, Budget, and Personal Care Plan in conformity with subsection (d) at the top of the Order in substantially the following form:

Due Date for Inventory, Budget & Personal Care Plan: _____

Court Hearing for Review for Inventory, Budget & Care Plan

_____, 20 _____ at 11:00 a.m.

Reporting Period for Annual Report:

_____, 20 _____ to _____, 20 _____

Due Date for First Annual Report: _____, 20 _____

Court Hearing for Annual Review: _____, 20 _____ at 11:00 a.m.

The Order of Appointment shall contain the language "CLERK'S ACTION REQUIRED" in the caption beneath the case number on the first page of the order.

(b) Voting Rights. Pursuant to RCW 11.88.010(5), all orders of appointment of guardian shall address whether the alleged incapacitated person retains capacity to meaningfully excise the right to vote. If the incapacitated person's capacity deteriorates after appointment of a guardian, such that the capacity to exercise the right to vote is in question, this issue may be raised by motion at any time.

(c) Proof of Security. Within five (5) days of securing a required bond or of blocking withdrawals from an account, proof of the same shall be filed with the court.

(d) Inventory, Budget and Personal Care Plan

(1) *Due Dates.* The Inventory, Budget and Personal Care Plan for an incapacitated person shall be filed within 90 days from the date of appointment of a Guardian.

(2) *Court Hearing.* A hearing for the Court to review the Inventory, Budget and Personal Care Plan shall be scheduled to occur within 14 days after the due date of the reports. At this hearing, the Court shall determine whether any required bond has been posted or accounts blocked, and review whether a bond or blocked account is required. If, after review, the Court finds the reports acceptable, the Court shall enter an order approving the inventory and care plan,

and authorizing expenditures in accordance with the budget.

(e) Annual Reports

(1) *Reporting Period and Due Date.* The Guardian shall file an Annual Report on behalf of the incapacitated person annually, unless other intervals are approved in advance by the Court. Unless modified by court order, the reporting period for each annual report shall be determined from the date of appointment of the Guardian. Each annual report shall be filed within 90 days after the ending date of the reporting period.

(2) *Report Summary.* Each annual report shall begin with a Summary of Annual Report substantially in the form included in the Appendix to these Rules. The Summary shall clearly identify the reporting period covered by the report and the due date for filing the next annual report.

(3) *Court Hearing.* A hearing for the Court to review the first annual report shall be scheduled to occur within 14 days after the due date of the report. At this hearing the Court shall review whether required bonds are in place, accounts are blocked, or whether such security should be required. If, after review, the court is satisfied the actions of the guardian have been proper, the court shall enter an order approving the report. This same procedure shall be followed for annual reports following the first annual report unless waived by the court.

(4) *Order Approving Report.* The guardian shall prepare and present any order approving report. The order approving an annual report shall identify the due date for the next report and the reporting period to be covered by that report in substantially the following form:

Reporting Period for Annual Report:

_____, 20 ___ to _____, 20 ___

Due Date for First Annual Report: _____, 20 ___

Court Hearing for Annual Review: _____, 20 ___ at 11:00 a.m.

The Order Approving Report shall contain the language "CLERK'S ACTION REQUIRED" in the caption beneath the case number on the first page of the order.

(f) Review Hearings

(1) *Delinquency.* In the event an initial, annual, or tri-annual report has not been timely filed or scheduled for Court review as required by this rule, the Court may issue to the Guardian an Order to Show Cause to compel the filing of the report or appearance at a hearing to review the report.

(2) *Hearing Schedule.* Review hearings shall be scheduled on the Friday guardianship calendar.

(3) *Sanctions.* At the review hearing, the court may approve filed reports, compel reports to be filed, impose sanctions, and take other action as necessary to protect the interests of the incapacitated person, including initiating the process for appointing a new guardian.

SUPERIOR COURT OF THE STATE OF WASHINGTON IN AND FOR THE COUNTY OF LEWIS

In the Matter of the Guardianship of: No.

GUARDIANSHIP SUMMARY FOR ANNUAL REPORT

An Incapacitated Person.

Reporting Period for This Report:

_____, 20 ___ to _____, 20 ___

Incapacitated Person   **Attorney for Guardianship**

Name: _____   Name: _____

Address: _____   Address: _____

Daytime Phone: _____   Day Phone: _____

   Email: _____

Guardian   **Co–Guardian**

Name: _____   Name: _____

Address: _____   Address: _____

Daytime Phone: _____   Daytime Phone: _____

Email: _____   Email: _____

Date of Appointment: _____   Frequency of Report: ☐ 1 year ☐ 3 year

Type of Guardianship: (check all that apply)
☐ Full Guardianship of Person   ☐ Limited Guardianship of Person
☐ Full Guardianship of Estate   ☐ Limited Guardianship of Estate

Personal Care Plan filed: ☐ Yes ☐ No ☐ Not Required
Inventory of Estate filed: ☐ Yes ☐ No ☐ Not Required
   Amount of Bond in place: $ _____
   Blocked Account receipts filed: ☐ Yes ☐ No ☐ Not Required
VA or DSHS served with report: ☐ Yes ☐ No ☐ Not Required

Standby Guardian   **Other Person Requiring Notice**

Name: _____   Name: _____

Address: _____   Address: _____

Daytime Phone: _____   Daytime Phone: _____

Email: _____

Alternate Standby Guardian

Name: _____

Address: _____

_____

Daytime Phone: _____

Email: _____

Other Person Requiring Notice

Name: _____

Address: _____

Email: _____

Other Person Requiring Notice

Name: _____

Address: _____

_____

Daytime Phone: _____

Email: _____

Other Person Requiring Notice

Name: _____

Address: _____

_____

Daytime Phone: _____

Email: _____

I declare under penalty of perjury under the laws of the State of Washington that the foregoing statement is true and correct.

Dated this ___ day of _____, 20 ___.

Signed at: City: _____, State: _____

_____
Signature of Guardian or Attorney

[Adopted effective September 1, 2010.]

DISTRICT COURT
LEWIS COUNTY DISTRICT COURT LOCAL RULES

Including Amendments Received Through
August 15, 2015

Table of Rules

LEWIS COUNTY LOCAL ADMINISTRATIVE RULES
FOR COURTS OF LIMITED JURISDICTION

PREFACE

1. Promulgation. These rules shall be known as the Local Rules for the District Court of the State of Washington for Lewis County. Copies of these rules will be filed with the Office of the Administrator of the Courts, and the Clerk of the District Court for Lewis County. Copies of these rules will be distributed to all law offices in Lewis County and to the county Law Library for public reference. To the extent possible, these rules will be placed on the Internet at the Lewis County District Court webpage. Copies will be available from the District Court Clerk for Lewis County. These rules as originally adopted were effective on September 1, 1998, and as amended or supplemented are effective on September 1, 2006, and supersede all prior rules of this court.

2. Numbering. Consistent with GR 7(b) Washington Court Rules, these rules, to the extent possible, conform in numbering system and in format to those rules adopted by the Supreme Court of the State of Washington for courts of limited jurisdiction and facilitate the use of the same. The number of each rule is preceded by the abbreviation *"LL"*, designating the rule as a *Lewis County Local Court Rule* and as being supplemental to the corresponding Washington Court Rule for Courts of Limited Jurisdiction.

[Adopted effective September 1, 1998. Amended effective September 1, 2006.]

LLARLJ 1. SCOPE OF LOCAL RULES

These rules govern the procedure in the District Court of the State of Washington for Lewis County. These rules are supplemental to the rules enacted by the Washington State Supreme Court for courts of limited jurisdiction as specifically authorized by GR 7, CRLJ 83, CrRLJ 1.7, and IRLJ 1.3 of the *Washington Court Rules*. The court may modify or suspend any of these local rules in any given case upon good cause being shown or upon the court's own motion.

[Adopted effective September 1, 1998.]

LLARLJ 2. COURT LOCATIONS

The primary office of the District Court of the State of Washington for Lewis County shall be located in Chehalis, Washington, and the Court shall hold periodic sessions in Morton, Washington, and such other locations in Lewis County as the Court may decide best serves the interest of the people of Lewis County. All criminal and civil trials will be heard at Chehalis. Arraignments, small claim trials, infraction mitigation hearings, and contested infraction hearings not involving attorneys or subpoenaed witnesses may be scheduled for Morton if it is more convenient to all parties involved.

[Adopted effective September 1, 1998. Amended effective September 1, 2006.]

LLARLJ 3. SCHEDULING

(a) Calendar. The Court Administrator shall develop and maintain a calendar for all hearings and trials.

(b) Priority. Whenever the case load of the court requires, trials and other matters will be subject to multiple settings on the same date. The order in which said matters proceed will be determined by the judge based on speedy trial rule in criminal cases, the age of the civil cases, and the availability of jurors.

(c) Transfer of Cases. If the caseload or other circumstances require, the court may appoint a Court Commissioner or *Judge Pro Tempore* to hear that trial or calendar of cases and may arrange for it to be heard in a location other than the usual courtroom.

[Adopted effective September 1, 1998.]

LLARLJ 5. COURTROOM DECORUM

All attorneys, litigants, witnesses, and other individuals in the courtroom shall abide by the following rules of conduct:

(a) Always be prompt. Be in the courtroom ready to proceed at the appointed time.

(b) Stand when the judge or the jury enters or leaves the courtroom.

(c) Do not make personal attacks on opposing counsel or parties.

(d) Do not interrupt. Wait your turn. Address all remarks to the Court. Argument between litigants or their attorneys is not permitted.

(e) After the court has ruled, ask the court's permission before arguing further.

(f) Rise when addressing the Court and when making objections as this calls the Court's attention to you.

(g) Do not approach a witness or the jury without asking permission of the Court.

(h) Dress appropriately to the serious nature of the matters before the court. Shorts and other kinds of beach apparel are not appropriate. Clothing advertising alcoholic beverages or illegal drugs are not appropriate. Hats are not to be worn in the courtroom unless required by religious custom and practice.

[Adopted effective September 1, 1998. Amended effective September 1, 2006.]

LLARLJ 6. RETURN OF EXHIBITS

Every exhibit admitted into evidence or marked for identification in any type of trial or other court proceeding, shall be returned to the party or attorney who produced that exhibit for identification. The return shall be made upon written application, not later than two weeks following the termination of the time allowed to take an appeal. Bulky exhibits not requested to be returned during that period may be delivered by the court clerk to the local police authority for disposition as abandoned property. If the exhibit is contraband or weapons, it shall be disposed of by destruction. No exhibit or identification shall be withdrawn or delivered without receipt being acknowledged by the receiving party.

[Adopted effective September 1, 1998.]

LLARLJ 7. CONTACT WITH JURORS

No litigant or attorney shall have any contact with any venire person or juror pending discharge of the jury. Any requests by a litigant or an attorney for post-trial communication shall be conveyed to the juror through the bailiff. Contact shall only occur if the juror affirmatively indicates a willingness to meet with the litigant or the attorney. The bailiff shall advise the juror that there is no obligation to discuss any matter with the requesting party.

If the juror agrees to meet with the requesting party, the conversation shall occur in the courtroom. The bailiff shall be present to insure that the juror is not challenged, threatened, or harangued, and that such conversation will not improperly influence the juror in any future trial. Questions shall be limited to the basis of the jury's decision, critiques of counsel's performance, and any alleged juror impropriety.

No litigant or any attorney shall enter the jury room corridor or any jury room without explicit authorization from the bailiff.

[Adopted effective September 1, 2006.]

LLARLJ 9(g). DISCLOSURE OF PUBLIC RECORDS

The following records and files are deemed confidential and are not available to the public for inspection or copying absent a court order after notice and hearing:

1. Affidavits, transcriptions or electronic records for search warrants prior to the return of service of such warrant;

2. Affidavits, transcriptions or electronic records for arrest warrants prior to the returns of service of such warrant;

3. Pre–sentence or post–sentence investigation reports;

4. Mental health, psychiatric, and/or medical reports and records, unless admitted into evidence and not ordered sealed;

5. Alcohol, drug, and/or controlled substance evaluations unless admitted into evidence and not ordered sealed;

6. Certified and non-certified paper copies and/or electronic representations of driving and criminal records unless admitted into evidence;

7. Judge's notes and working documents, whether written or electronic.

Access to these confidential records and files is strictly limited to persons or entities authorized by statute or court order to obtain such records. Request for access to other court files shall be made in writing on the form provided by the Court and shall be granted or denied only by a judge, or their designee, who shall state the reasons for any denial in writing. No documents or electronic data may be removed from the court offices without the prior written order of the court. The requesting party will be required to pay in advance for time expended and costs involved in researching, copying, and/or transcribing the requested court files. Such research, transcription, and copying will be done on a time available basis.

[Adopted effective September 1, 1998. Amended effective September 1, 2006.]

LLARLJ 10. ELECTION OF PRESIDING JUDGE

10.1 Election

In conformity with GR 29, on the first Monday, after January 15th, of every odd numbered year commencing in 2003, the Judges of the Lewis County District Court shall elect one of their number as Presiding Judge, and another of their number as Assistant Presiding Judge.

10.2 Conduct of Election

The election shall be conducted and witnessed by the Court Administrator and shall be by simple oral majority vote.

10.3 Term

The term of office will be for a period of two years in conformity with GR 29 (a)(2) and will be retroactive to January 1st of the year of the election.

10.4 Selection Criteria

The selection of said Presiding Judge shall be based on and in conformity with GR 29(a)(5).

10.5 Transition

Between the date of the original adoption of this rule and the election of 2003, the Judges elected in conformity with ARLJ 6 on January 22nd, 2002, continued to serve as the Presiding Judges of the Lewis County District Court.

[Adopted effective September 1, 2006.]

LEWIS COUNTY LOCAL CIVIL RULES FOR COURTS OF LIMITED JURISDICTION

LLCRLJ 26

(a) Certain Documents Presumed Admissible. The documents listed below, if relevant, are presumed admissible at the trial, but only if:

(1) the party offering the document serves on all parties at least fourteen (14) days prior to the trial date in accordance with CRLJ 5(a) notice, accompanied by a copy of the document and the name, address, and telephone number of its author or maker; and

(2) the party offering the document similarly furnishes all other parties with copies of all other related documents from the same author or maker. This rule does not restrict argument or proof related to the weight of the evidence admitted, nor does it restrict the court's authority to determine the weight of the evidence after hearing all of the evidence and the arguments of opposing parties.

(b) The documents presumed admissible under this rule are:

(i) A bill, report, chart, or record of a hospital, doctor, dentist, registered nurse, licensed practical nurse, physical therapist, psychologist or other health care provider, on a letterhead or billhead;

(ii) A bill for drugs, medical appliances or other related expenses on a letterhead or billhead;

(iii) A bill, or an estimate of, property damage on a letterhead or billhead. In the case of an estimate, the party intending to offer the estimate shall forward with the notice to the adverse party a statement indicating whether or not the property was repaired, and if it was, whether the estimated repairs were made in full or in part, attaching a copy to the receipted bill showing the items or repair and the amount paid;

(iv) A police, weather, wage loss, or traffic signal report, or standard United State government life expectancy table to the extent it is admissible under the Rules of Evidence, but without the need for formal proof of authentication or identification;

(v) A photograph, x-ray, drawing, map, blueprint or similar documentary evidence, to the extent it is admissible under the Rules of Evidence, but without the need for formal proof of authentication or identification;

(vi) The written statement of any other witness, including the written report of an expert witness, and including a statement of opinion which the witness would be allowed to express if testifying in person, if it is made by affidavit or by declaration under penalty of perjury;

(c) Any other party may subpoena the author or maker of a document admissible under this rule, at that party's expense, and examine the author or maker as if under cross examination.

[Adopted effective September 1, 2011.]

LLCRLJ 38(h). CIVIL TRIAL CONFIRMATION

(a) A date and time for a trial confirmation hearing shall be assigned to each case at the time it is set for trial. Trial confirmation hearings shall be held each Tuesday at 2:00 p.m. for the trials set for the following Thursday or Friday. Trial confirmation hearings shall be held each Thursday at 2:00 p.m. for those trials set for the following Monday, Tuesday, or Wednesday.

(b) It shall be the affirmative duty of all parties, and of their counsel, to advise the court at such hearing of their readiness to proceed to trial. Failure of a party to advise of the inability to proceed for any reason known on that date shall constitute a waiver of the right to request a continuance for that reason at a later date.

(c) The appearance of the litigants and of their counsel at trial confirmation hearings shall be mandatory unless a written confirmation of readiness on the form provided is filed with the court. Said confirmation form must be signed by a party or counsel not more than seven days prior to the hearing under penalty of perjury.

(d) Failure of any party to confirm in person or in writing will cause the trial date to be stricken. Civil litigants who fail to appear or confirm will be subject to such terms and costs as the Court determines to be reasonable.

(e) After confirmation, the failure of a party to appear at trial, or upon appearance, to be unable proceed with the trial, shall be treated as a motion for continuance, resulting in the dismissal of the jury panel, where applicable, and of the trial date. It may also constitute grounds for the dismissal of the charges and/or for the imposition of sanctions and terms against litigants and counsel.

[Adopted effective September 1, 1998. Amended effective September 1, 2006.]

LLCRLJ 87. MISCELLANEOUS PROCEEDINGS RULES

LLCRLJ 87.1. Name Change Petitions

Those persons seeking to petition the Court for a change of name for themselves or those minors in their legal custody shall comply with the procedures and requirements set forth in the Lewis County District Court Name Change Brochure, herein adopted by reference as a rule of this court. The brochure, as it currently exists or is hereafter amended, is available through the Clerk of the District Court and delineates the requirements that must be met in order for the petition to be granted.

LLCRLJ 87.2. Anti–Harassment Petitions

Those persons seeking to petition the Court for the entry of an Anti-harassment Order against another person shall comply with the procedures and requirements set forth in the Lewis County District Court Anti-harassment Brochure, herein adopted by reference as a rule of this court. The brochure, as it currently exists or is hereafter amended, is available through the Clerk of the District Court and delineates the requirements that must be met in order for either an emergency temporary order or an order to show cause may be granted and lead to the entry of a permanent order after notice and a hearing.

[Adopted effective September 1, 1998. Amended effective September 1, 2006.]

LEWIS COUNTY LOCAL CRIMINAL RULES FOR COURTS OF LIMITED JURISDICTION

LLCrRLJ 3.1(g). WAIVER OF RIGHT TO COUNSEL

Unless a written waiver of the defendant's right to counsel is signed by the defendant and filed with the Court, an attorney shall be appointed to represent the defendant at all stages of the proceedings. No criminal charge shall be set for trial involving a self represented defendant, unless such a signed waiver of counsel is filed with the Court.

[Adopted effective September 1, 1998. Amended effective September 1, 2006.]

LLCrRLJ 3.2(v). OFFENSES FOR WHICH BAIL IS NOT ALLOWED

Any person subjected to custodial arrest for the following offenses shall be held in jail without bail pending their first appearance in Court:

1. Any offense classified as Domestic Violence under Chapter 10.99 of the Revised Code of Washington or an equivalent ordinance:

2. Any offense classified as Harassment and/or Stalking under Chapters 10.14 and/or 9A.46 of the Revised Code of Washington or an equivalent ordinance;

3. The offense of Driving Under the Influence (DUI) under Revised Code of Washington 46.61.502;

4. The offense of Physical Control of Motor Vehicle Under the Influence (PC) under Revised Code of Washington 46.61.504.

[Adopted on an emergency basis effective December 23, 2005; adopted on a permanent basis effective September 1, 2006; amended on an emergency basis effective February 10, 2014; amended on a permanent basis effective September 2, 2014.]

LLCrRLJ 3.2(w). BAIL SCHEDULE

The Lewis County District Court shall periodically publish a bail schedule which will include the bail schedule and penalty schedule promulgated by the Supreme Court of the State of Washington. The schedule will also include appearance dates and times. The schedule will also be provided to all law enforcement agencies within Lewis County. The bail schedule shall be intended as a guideline but shall not be construed as limiting the authority of the Court in individual cases to set bail in a different amount.

[Adopted on an emergency basis effective December 23, 2005; adopted on a permanent basis effective September 1, 2006.]

LLCrRLJ 3.3(h). CONTINUANCES TIME FOR TRIAL

All motions for continuances shall be heard by notice and citation on the appropriate motion docket. Only in cases of extreme emergency and unforeseeable circumstances shall the presiding judge or the trial judge consider a motion for continuance without the proper notice and citation.

[Adopted effective September 1, 1998. Amended effective September 1, 2006.]

LLCrRLJ 3.6(c). SUPPRESSION HEARING PROCEDURE

A party moving to suppress evidence must file a written motion that sets forth in detail the specific factual and legal grounds for the motion. The motion should be filed with the court at least seven (7) days prior to the pretrial hearing. Said motion shall be supported by an affidavit or declaration under penalty of perjury of a person with testimonial knowledge, setting forth the facts to be elicited at an evidentiary hearing. The matter will be set for evidentiary hearing only if the judge at a pretrial hearing finds that there are facts in dispute. A copy of the motion and supporting documents must be served on the opposing party at least five court days prior to the date set for hearing.

As a matter of professional courtesy, the parties shall file bench copies of all motions, affidavits, and memoranda at the time of filing of the original documents.

[Adopted effective September 1, 1998. Amended effective September 1, 2006.]

LLCrRLJ 4.1(g). MANDATORY APPEARANCE FOR ARRAIGNMENT ON ALL GROSS MISDEMEANORS

A person who is accused of committing a criminal offense denominated as a gross misdemeanor by the enacting statute, and who is served with a criminal citation and notice or complaint shall physically appear before the Court for arraignment on the designated date to allow for determination of probable cause and the setting of conditions of release in conformity with CrRLJ 3.4(a). In conformity with CrRLJ 4.1(g), this Court is exercising its right to eliminate the option of a defendant to waive arraignment on gross misdemeanor charges under CrRLJ 4.1(g)(1).

[Adopted on an emergency basis effective December 1, 2010; adopted on a permanent basis effective September 1, 2011.]

LLCrRLJ 4.3.1(d). NO JOINDER OF CIVIL AND CRIMINAL MATTERS

A person who is served with a criminal citation and notice or complaint, and who also receives one or more notices of infraction arising out of the same incident shall not have the dates for hearings thereon set together. No civil matter will be set for hearing on a criminal calendar. Each type of case will be set on the specific calendar established for that type of case.

[Adopted effective September 1, 1998. Amended effective September 1, 2006.]

LLCrRLJ 4.5.1. PRETRIAL PROCEDURES

(a) Duty of Parties.

It is the duty of the parties and their counsel to move expeditiously to seek resolution of these matters prior to trial. It is the strong policy of this court that the Rules of Professional Conduct require the completion of investigation, discovery, and plea negotiations prior to trial setting.

(b) Pre–trial Hearings. The Court shall set all cases where a plea of not guilty has been entered for a pretrial hearing approximately 45 days after the date of first appearance. Said hearing shall provide an opportunity for execution of plea negotiations, resolution of discovery issues and trial setting. All defendants must be present, with counsel, where applicable. Failure to appear for the pretrial hearing may result in the issuance of a warrant of arrest and/or forfeiture of any bail or bond.

It is strongly suggested that all negotiations be completed prior to this hearing since no time for additional negotiations will be available on the pretrial hearing calendar. All amendments to the charges and any pretrial motions except a *motion in limine* shall be made in writing and filed with the court at, or prior to, the pretrial hearing.

Following this hearing, if a pretrial disposition of any charge does not occur, an order shall be entered setting forth the following: trial date; trial confirmation date; discovery schedule; date of hearing on pretrial motions; and the date by which witness lists must be exchanged and filed.

(c) 3.5 Hearings. All demands for a CrRLJ 3.5 hearing on admissibility of statements or confessions must be made in writing and filed no later than the pretrial hearing. The Court will set hearing dates for motions filed as part of that proceeding. See LLCrRLJ 3.6 for suppression motions.

(d) Imposition of Jury Costs. In order to efficiently schedule the calling of jurors, to avoid unnecessary disruptions of the jurors lives, and to further avoid the waste of public funds, the court will not, unless good cause is shown, permit the waiver of a jury trial nor the entry of a plea of guilty in a matter scheduled for jury trial after the date of the trial confirmation hearing unless the jury costs are imposed against the moving party.

(e) Trial Confirmation Hearing. See LLCrRLJ 6.1.1 (d)

[Adopted effective September 1, 1998. Amended effective September 1, 2006.]

LLCrRLJ 4.12. DUTY TO NOTIFY COURT AND WITNESSES

When a case docketed for trial or other hearing is settled, or for any reason will not proceed to hearing at the set time, the parties shall give notice of that fact immediately to the Court. It shall be the duty of each party to notify it's own witnesses, not only of the date and time of the trial, but also of continuances, pre-trial hearings, motions, and other proceedings. The Court will not pay witness fees to witnesses who appear for a trial or hearing which has been continued or settled. Such costs shall be borne by the party or attorney who called or subpoenaed the witness.

[Adopted effective September 1, 1998. Amended effective September 1, 2006.]

LLCrRLJ 6.1.1.(d). CRIMINAL TRIAL CONFIRMATION

(a) A date and time for a trial confirmation hearing shall be assigned to each case at the time it is set for trial. Trial confirmation hearings shall be held each Tuesday at 2:00 p.m. for the trials set for the following Thursday or Friday. Trial confirmation hearings shall be held each Thursday at 2:00 p.m. for those trials set for the following Monday, Tuesday, or Wednesday.

(b) It shall be the affirmative duty of all parties, and of their counsel, to advise the court at such hearing of their readiness to proceed to trial. Failure of a party to advise the Court of their inability to proceed for any reason known on that date shall constitute a waiver of the right to request a continuance for that reason at a later date.

(c) The appearance of criminal defendants at trial confirmation hearings shall be mandatory unless a written confirmation of readiness on the form provided is filed with the court. Said confirmation form must be signed by the defendant not more than seven days prior to the hearing, and by the defendant's attorney, under penalty of perjury. The plaintiff may confirm in person or in writing on the form provided, by signature under penalty of perjury.

(d) Failure of any party to confirm in person or in writing will cause the trial date to be stricken. Criminal defendants who fail to appear or confirm in writing shall be subject to the issuance of a warrant of arrest, upon a showing of probable cause.

(e) After confirmation, the failure of a criminal plaintiff or defendant to appear at trial, or upon appearance, to be unable proceed with the trial, shall be treated as a motion for continuance, resulting in the dismissal of the jury panel, where applicable, and of the trial date. It may also constitute grounds for the issuance of a warrant of arrest, for the dismissal of the charges or for the imposition of sanctions and terms, including jury fees, against litigants and counsel.

[Adopted effective September 1, 1998. Amended effective September 1, 2006.]

LLCrRLJ 7.2(f). PRE-SENTENCE REPORTS

In every case where the defendant has been found guilty by the trier of fact after trial or by virtue of a guilty plea, of the crimes of DUI, Physical Control, DWLS 1st, or Assault in the Fourth Degree, a pre-sentence report shall be automatically be ordered by the Court. There shall be included in this report the results of any alcohol, drug, or domestic violence evaluations which has been ordered. The costs of the preparation of the report shall be assessed against the convicted person as part of the judgment and sentence. Failure of the defendant to cooperate in the preparation of the report including ordered evaluations shall result in the issuance of a bench warrant requiring the defendant to be held in custody until sentencing is completed.

[Adopted effective September 1, 1998. Amended effective September 1, 2006.]

LLCrRLJ 7.2(g). DEFERRED PROSECUTION FORM

A petition for deferred prosecution pursuant to RCW 10.05 must be filed with the Court no later than seven (7) days prior to the Trial Confirmation Hearing unless good cause exists for delay. Said petition and the accompanying declarations shall be in a form acceptable to the Court and in conformity with Chapter 10.05 RCW. The order deferring prosecution shall require as a minimum: supervision by the LCDC Probation Department for 24 months, including monthly face-to-face meetings; payment of the costs of supervision, no conviction for any criminal offense; and compliance with all of the terms of any proposed treatment plan.

In cases involving a finding of addiction to alcohol or drugs, the order shall additionally prohibit the consumption of alcohol or drugs for a period of five years unless prescribed by a physician, and attendance at a victim impact panel within a specified period of time, and completion of the outlined treatment program.

In cases involving offenses involving the operation of motor vehicles, the order shall also include requirements that the defendant, during the period of deferral, not operate a motor vehicle unless properly licensed and insured, be convicted of no criminal traffic offenses, and comply with all DOL requirements regarding that the defendant only operate a motor vehicle equipped with an ignition interlock device.

[Adopted effective September 1, 1998. Amended effective September 1, 2006.]

LLCrRLJ 7.2(h). DEFERRED PROSECUTIONS AND ORDERS OF CONTINUANCE

Required demonstration of amenability to treatment.

(1) Prerequisites to Entry of Order

An order deferring prosecution of a criminal charge will not be entered absent sufficient evidence that the Petitioner has demonstrated her/his amenability to treatment by successfully completing two months of treatment in the proposed program. Successful completion means that the Petitioner is fully compliant with every requirement of the treatment program, and has remained so at all times during that two month period. The Order granting such a petition will not be signed unless the petitioner is physically present in the courtroom. The requirement of the presence of the Defendant is to allow inquiry of the petitioner by the Court to determine whether the petitioner is amenable to treatment and whether the Court, in conformity with the statute, will grant such a petition. The order deferring prosecution of a criminal charge will not be granted until after the completion of a standardized risk evaluation to determine the level of supervision appropriate to that petitioner.

(2) Alcohol Related Driving Offenses

No alcohol related driving offense, including DUI, Actual Physical Control, Negligent Driving in the First Degree, or Minor Driving after Consuming, Will be resolved except by plea of guilty to the original charge, plea of guilty to an amended charge, dismissal, trial, or under the terms of an RCW 10.05 "Order of Deferred Prosecution".

(3) AOC's/SOC's

The Court will no longer be a party to any form of agreement between the Plaintiff and the Defense, whether designated **"Agreed Orders of Continuance"**, **"Stipulated Orders of Continuance"** or by any other name. Neither the District Court nor its probation department shall have a duty to supervise, monitor, or oversee performance of any agreement entered into by the parties relating to such continuances. Those agreements may be filed with the Court as grounds for continuance of the time for trial only.

[Previous LLCrRLJ 8.4(f) was adopted effective September 1, 1998; amended on an emergency basis effective December 23, 2005. Renumbered and amended effective September 1, 2006. Amended on an emergency basis effective November 1, 2006.]

LLCrRLJ 8.2. MOTIONS

Rules CrRLJ 3.5 and 3.6, and CRLJ 7(b) shall govern motions in criminal cases. Unless a motion is made during a hearing or trial, it shall be made in writing, shall state with particularity the grounds therefore, shall state the statute, case decision, or court rule that supports the motion, and set forth the relief or order requested. Timing and notice requirements are governed by CrRLJ 8.1(c) and local rule LLCrRLJ 4.5.

As a matter of professional courtesy, the parties will file with the Court bench copies of motions and memoranda along with the originals documents.

[Adopted effective September 1, 1998. Amended effective September 1, 2006.]

LLCrRLJ 8.4(f). DEFERRED PROSECUTIONS AND ORDERS OF CONTINUANCE [RESCINDED]

Rescinded effective 9/01/06; See LLCrRLJ 7.2 (h)

LLCrRLJ 8.5. RETURN OF EXHIBITS

See LLARLJ 6.

[Adopted effective September 1, 1998.]

LEWIS COUNTY LOCAL INFRACTION RULES FOR COURTS OF LIMITED JURISDICTION

LLIRLJ 3.2(b). MOTION FOR VACATION OF DEFAULT JUDGMENT FOR FTA

A defendant, against whom a judgment for a traffic infraction has been entered by default for failure to appear, may file a motion in writing, on forms provided by the court, requesting that said default judgment be set aside. The motion will then be set for hearing. Defendant must be present. The motion will be evaluated in conformity with CRLJ 60(b). If the Court grants said motion, the matter will be set for a hearing of the kind requested by the defendant. Mitigation hearings may be heard at the time of the motion if the calendar allows.

[Adopted effective September 1, 1998. Amended effective September 1, 2006.]

LLIRLJ 3.5. DECISIONS AND DEFERRED FINDINGS ON WRITTEN STATEMENTS

(a) Decisions on Written Statements Authorized. Deferred findings, mitigation hearings, and contested hearings based on written statements, given under penalty of perjury as provided for in IRLJ 2.4(b) and IRLJ 2.6(c), are authorized. Forms for providing such written statements shall be available from the Lewis County District Court or its website and shall be submitted within the timeline provided by the Court. Thereupon, the Court will make its decision according to the procedures of IRLJ 3.5, considering the materials submitted both by the defendant and the State. Except as provided in subsection (c) of this rule, the Court need not consider any written statement submitted later than seven (7) calendar days before the scheduled hearing.

(b) Deferred Findings. The Court will consider written requests to defer infractions. A defendant who wants to defer a traffic infraction by mail must complete either the *Petition for Mitigation Hearing on Infraction(s) via Written Statement* form or the *Petition for Contested Hearing on Infraction(s) via Written Statement* form. Each of the two forms

contains a section in which the defendant may request a deferred finding. A defendant requesting a deferred finding shall also complete the remainder of the chosen form, either contesting or mitigating the infraction. In the event the defendant is ineligible to defer the infraction(s) or the Court finds that a deferral is not an appropriate remedy for the infraction, the Court will proceed with either a mitigation hearing on written statements or a contested hearing on written statements in accordance with the defendant's choice.

(c) Agreed Dispositions. The Court will consider written statements requesting agreed dispositions of infractions filed on or before the date of the hearing. When requested to do so as part of such a disposition, the Court may set a different penalty for an unscheduled infraction than the default, as permitted by IRLJ 6.2(b).

(d) There shall be no appeal from a decision on written statements.

[Adopted on an emergency basis effective June 29, 2015; adopted on a permanent basis effective September 1, 2015.]

LLIRLJ 3.5(f). MITIGATION HEARINGS BY MAIL

In conformity with IRLJ 3.5, this court exercises its local option to allow mitigation hearings by written document.

If a person who is cited for a civil or traffic infraction lives more than thirty (30) miles from any location where mitigation hearings are regularly heard by this Court, said person may request to mitigate the infraction by mail. Upon receipt of the request for mitigation hearing, forms for a written statement mitigation hearing will be sent to the defendant. Upon receipt of the completed forms by return mail, accompanied by the payment of the original amount of the infraction, the Court will hold a hearing based on the written documents, and render a decision. The balance of funds, in excess of the penalty, will be mailed to the defendant.

A hearing by mail with written statements shall not be available where a contested infraction hearing has been requested.

[Adopted effective September 1, 1998. Amended effective September 1, 2006.]

MUNICIPAL COURTS
CENTRALIA MUNICIPAL COURT LOCAL RULES

Including Amendments Received Through
August 15, 2015

Table of Rules

SCOPE OF LOCAL RULES

These rules govern the procedure in the Municipal Court of Centralia, County of Lewis, State of Washington. These rules are supplemental to the rules enacted by limited jurisdiction as specifically authorized by GR 7, CRLJ 83, CrRLJ 1.7, and IRLJ 1.3 of the Washington Court Rules. The court may modify or suspend any of these local rules in any given case upon good cause begin shown or upon the court's own motion.

1. Appearance following arrest.

(a) Defendant having been arrested for Driving Under the Influence, RCW 46.61.502 or Physical Control, RCW 46.61.504, or Assault 4th Domestic Violence, RCW 9A.36.041.DV, must appear in court on the earliest practicable day as defined herein.

(b) Earliest practicable day is defined as the next regularly scheduled court session.

[Adopted effective September 1, 2005.]

[RULE 1]. DECORUM

1. **Courtroom Decorum.** All attorneys and other individuals in the courtroom shall abide by the following rules of conduct.

(a) *Always be Prompt.* Be in the courtroom ready to proceed at the appointed time.

(b) *Dress Appropriately to the Serious Nature of the Matters Before the Court.* Shorts and other kinds of beach apparel are not appropriate. Clothing advertising alcoholic beverages or illegal drugs are not appropriate. Hats are not to be worn in the courtroom.

[Adopted effective September 1, 2005.]

[RULE 2]. USE OF A COLLECTION AGENCY

1. **Contract for Collections.** The court may use the services of a collection agency for the purpose of collecting unpaid and delinquent penalties on infractions, criminal fines, costs, assessments, and forfeitures, on the terms and conditions of the contract for collection services between the City of Centralia and said collection agency, and as may be subsequently amended.

[Adopted effective September 1, 2005.]

[RULE 3]. RELEASE OF ACCUSED

1. Any person arrested on probable cause (without a warrant) for an offense classified as a domestic violence offense under chapter 10.99 of the Revised Code of Washington as the same exists or shall hereafter be amended shall be held in jail pending the defendant's first appearance in court in the absence of a judicial order.

[Adopted effective September 2, 2013.]

CHEHALIS MUNICIPAL COURT LOCAL RULES

Including Amendments Received Through
August 15, 2015

Table of Rules

PREFACE

1. Promulgation. These rules shall be known as the Local Rules for Municipal Court of Chehalis, County of Lewis, State of Washington. Copies of these rules will be filed with the Office of the Administer of the Courts, and the Clerk of the Municipal Court of Chehalis. Copies of these rules will be distributed to all law offices in Lewis County and to the county Law Library for public reference. To the extent possible, these rules will be placed on the Internet at the Chehalis Municipal Court web page. Copies will be available from the Municipal Court Clerk for Chehalis. These rules will be effective on September 1, 2000, and supersede all prior rules of this court.

2. Numbering. Consistent with GR 7(b) Washington Court Rules, these rules to the extent possible, conform in numbering system and in format to those rules adopted by the Supreme Court of the State of Washington for courts of limited jurisdiction and facilitate the use of the same. The number of each rule is preceded by abbreviation "CML", designating the rule as a Chehalis Municipal Local Rule and as being supplemental to the corresponding Washington Court Rule for Courts of Limited Jurisdiction.

3. Revisions and Additions (Reserved).

[Adopted effective September 1, 2000.]

CMLARLJ 1. SCOPE OF LOCAL RULES

These rules govern the procedure in the Municipal Court of Chehalis, County of Lewis, State of Washington. These rules are supplemental to the rules enacted by limited jurisdiction as specifically authorized by GR 7, CRLJ 83, CrRLJ 1.7, and IRLJ 1.3 of the Washington Court Rules. The court may modify or suspend any of these local rules in any given case upon good cause being shown or upon the court's own motion.

1. Appearance Following Arrest.

(a) Defendant having been arrested for Driving Under the Influence, RCW 46.61.50571, must appear in court on the earliest practicable day as defined herein.

(b) Earliest practicable day is defined as the next regularly scheduled court session.

[Adopted effective September 1, 2000.]

CMLARLJ 2. DECORUM

1. Courtroom Decorum. All attorneys and other individuals in the courtroom shall abide by the following rules of conduct.

(a) *Always be Prompt.* Be in the courtroom ready to proceed at the appointed time.

(b) *Dress Appropriately to the Serious Nature of the Matters Before the Court.* Shorts and other kinds of beach apparel are not appropriate. Clothing advertising alcoholic beverages or illegal drugs are not appropriate. Hats are not to be worn in the courtroom.

[Adopted effective September 1, 2000.]

CMLARLJ 3. DECISION ON WRITTEN STATEMENTS

(a) **Written Submissions:** Traffic infractions may be heard by the Court on the basis of written documents submitted by the city and a defendant, as provided in IRLJ 2.4(b)(4) and IRLJ 2.6. A written submission must be received by the court no later than seven (7) days prior to the scheduled date of the contested or mitigation hearing, or the submission will not be considered.

(b) **Generally:** The court shall examine the citing officer's report and any written documents submitted by the defendant. The examination shall take place within 120 days after the defendant files the response to the notice of infraction. The examination may be held in chambers and shall not be governed by the Rules of Evidence.

(c) **Factual Determination**: For purposes of a contested infraction hearing, the court shall determine whether the city has established, by a preponderance of all submitted evidence, that the defendant committed the infraction.

(d) **Disposition**: If the court determines that the infraction has been committed, it may assess a penalty amount, and any appropriate and permitted costs to be paid by the defendant.

(e) **Notice to Parties**: The court shall notify the parties in writing, whether an infraction was found to have been committed and what penalty, if any, was imposed.

(f) **No Appeal Permitted**: There shall be no appeal from a court determination based upon written statements.

[Adopted effective September 1, 2006.]

CMLARLJ 4. VIDEO CONFERENCE PROCEEDINGS

1. **Authorization**: Preliminary appearances as defined by CrR 3.2(B) and CrRLJ 3.2.1(d), arraignments as defined by CrR 3.4 and 4.1 and CrRLJ 3.4 and 4.1, bail hearings as defined by CrR 3.2 and CrRLJ 3.2, and trial settings as defined by CrR 3.3 and CrRLJ 3.3(f), conducted via video conference in which all participants can simultaneously see, hear, and speak with each other shall be deemed held in open court and in the defendant's presence for the purposes of any statute, court rule or policy. All video conference hearings conducted pursuant to the rule shall be public, and the public shall be able to simultaneously see and hear all participants and speak as permitted by the Court. Any party may request an in-person hearing under this section, which may be in the Court's discretion, be granted.

2. **Agreement**: Other trial court proceedings including the entry of a Statement of Defendant on Plea of Guilty as defined by CrR 4.2 and CrRLJ 4.2 may be conducted by video conference only by agreement of the parties, either in writing or on the record, and upon the approval of the Court pursuant to this local court rule. For purposes of video conference proceedings, the facsimile signatures of the defendant, counsel, interested parties and the Court shall be treated as if they were an original signature. This includes all orders on Judgment and Sentence, No Contact Orders, Statements of Defendant on Plea of Guilty, and

other documents or pleadings as the Court shall determine are appropriate or necessary.

3. **Standards**: The judge, counsel, all parties, and the public must be able to see and hear each other during video proceedings, and may speak as permitted by the Court. Video conference facilities must provide for confidential communications between attorney and client and security sufficient to protect the safety of all participants and observers. In interpreted proceedings, the interpreter must be located next to the defendant and the proceedings must be conducted to assure that the interpreter can hear all participants.

[Adopted effective September 1, 2011.]

CMLARLJ 5. INFRACTIONS/FINES/NO PROOF OF LIABILITY INSURANCE

1. If a person who has been cited with a violation of RCW 46.30.020 (failure to provide proof of liability insurance) presents to the Court Clerk evidence that the person had in effect, at the time of the citation, liability insurance as required by RCW 46.30.020, then, upon payment of twenty-five dollars ($25.00), administrative costs, the case shall be dismissed and the Court Clerk shall be authorized to make appropriate notation of the dismissal in the Court file. This section is applicable only if the person charged has otherwise complied with all rules and procedures that govern responding to notices of infraction.

[Amended effective September 1, 2011.]

CMLARLJ 6. SENTENCE MONITORING [RESCINDED]

[Rescinded effective September 1, 2015.]

CMLARLJ 7. PARK IN SPACE FOR INDIVIDUAL W/DISABILITY WITHOUT PLACARD/PLATE

If a person is charged with violation of city ordinance 10.08.090 or with RCW 46.19.050.4, for parking in a space for individuals with disabilities without placard or plate, as now enacted or hereafter amended, presents to the Court Clerk evidence that the person had in effect at the time of citation, the required parking placard, and an identification card bearing picture, name and date of birth of the permit holder, as well as the placard's serial number, then the infraction shall be dismissed and the Court Clerk will be authorized to make the appropriate notation of the dismissal in court records.

[Adopted effective September 1, 2011.]

MORTON MUNICIPAL COURT—
[No Local Rules]

PUBLISHER'S NOTE

This municipal court follows the Lewis County District Court Local Rules.

MOSSYROCK MUNICIPAL COURT—
[No Local Rules]

PUBLISHER'S NOTE

This municipal court follows the Lewis County District Court Local Rules.

NAPAVINE MUNICIPAL COURT LOCAL RULES

Including Amendments Received Through
August 15, 2015

Table of Rules

PREFACE

1. Promulgation. These rules shall been known as the Local Rules for Municipal Court of Napavine, County of Lewis, State of Washington. Copies of these rules will be filed with the Office of the Administrator of the Courts, and the Clerk of the Municipal Court of Napavine. Copies of these rules will be distributed to the county Law Library for public reference. These rules will be effective on September 1, 2006.

2. Numbering. Consistent with GR 7 Washington Court Rules, these rules to the extent possible, conform in numbering system and in format to those rules adopted by the Supreme Court of the State of Washington for courts of limited jurisdiction and facilitate the use of the same. The number of each rule is preceded by abbreviation "NML" designation the rule as Napavine Municipal Local Rule and being supplemental to the corresponding Washington Court Rule for the Courts of Limited Jurisdiction.

3. Revisions and Additions (Reserved).

[Adopted effective September 1, 2006.]

NMLARLJ 1. SCOPE OF LOCAL COURT RULES

These rules govern the procedures in the Municipal Court of Napavine, County of Lewis, State of Washington. These rules are supplemental to the rules enacted by limited jurisdiction as specifically authorized by GR 7, CRLJ 83, CrRLJ 1.7, and IRLJ 1.3 of the Washington Court Rules. The court may modify or suspend any of these local rules in any given case upon good cause being shown or upon the court's own motion.

1. *Appearance following arrest.*

(a) Defendant having been arrested for Driving Under the Influence, RCW 46.61.50571, must appear in court on the earliest practicable day as defined herein.

(b) Earliest practicable day is defined as the next regularly scheduled court session.

[Adopted effective September 1, 2006.]

NMLARLJ 2. DECORUM

1. Courtroom Decorum. All attorneys and other individuals in the courtroom shall abide by the following rules of conduct.

(a) *Always be Prompt.* Be in the courtroom ready to proceed at the appointed time.

(b) Dress appropriately to the serious Nature of the Matter before the Court. Shorts and other kinds of beach apparel are not appropriate. Clothing advertising alcoholic beverages or illegal drugs are not appropriate. Hats are not to be worn in the courtroom.

[Effective September 1, 2006.]

NMLARLJ 3.1. HEARINGS ON WRITTEN STATEMENTS

1. The court authorizes mitigation hearings and contested hearings on written statements in lieu of a defendant's personal appearance.

(a) A defendant may submit a written statement as a response to a notice of infraction within 15 days of the date the notice is personally served or, if the notice is served by mail, within 18 days of the date the notice is mailed. Additionally, a defendant who has requested a mitigation hearing or contested hearing may submit a written statement later in lieu of personally appearing at the hearing. The written statement must be received by the time of the hearing.

(b) A written statement that does not clearly request to contest a notice of infraction will be treated as a request to explain mitigating circumstances.

(c) A written statement may be delivered to the court in person, by United States mail or any other delivery service, and by facsimile. The court's contact information is as follows:

Address: Napavine Municipal Court
            PO Box 810
            Napavine, WA 98565

Facsimile: (360) 262–9885

(d) A written statement shall contain the person's promise to pay the monetary penalty authorized by law if the infraction is found to be committed. The statement shall be executed in compliance with RCW 9A.72.085, in substantially the following form:

Name of Defendant:
Address:
Infraction Number: (***Located in the upper right hand corner of citation***)

I wish to mitigate infraction   [ ]
I wish to contest infraction   [ ]

Statement: _____
_____

I certify (or declare) under penalty of perjury under the laws of the State of Washington that the foregoing is true. I promise that if it is determined that I committed the infraction for which I was cited, I will pay the monetary penalty authorized by law and assessed by the court.

Executed this _____ day of _____, 20 ___ at _____,
_____. (City/State)

_____   _____
(Print Name)   (Signature)

[Adopted effective September 1, 2006.]

NMLARLJ 3.2. DECISION ON WRITTEN STATEMENTS

1. The court is authorized to enter decisions based upon written statements on infraction cased involving contested and mitigation hearings and request for deferred findings.

(a) In infraction cases where the respondent has requested, the court will conduct a mitigation hearing as authorized under RCW 46.63.100 as now enacted or hereafter amended, or consider a petition to defer the finding, or conduct a contested hearing based upon the written statements of the City's witness(es), if provided, and the Respondent, pursuant to IRLJ 3.5.

The examination shall take place within 120 days after the respondent filed the response to the notice of infraction. The examination may be held in chambers and shall not be governed by the Rules of Evidence.

(b) *Factual Determination.* In contested cases, the court shall determine whether the plaintiff has provided preponderance of all evidence submitted that defendant has committed the infraction.

(c) A petition for a deferred finding which is denied by the court will be treated as a request for a mitigation hearing on written statements.

(d) *Disposition.* If the court determines that the infraction has been committed, or the review was based upon a request for mitigation or a deferred finding, the court may assess a penalty and any appropriate and permitted costs.

(e) *Notice to Parties.* The court shall notify the parties in writing whether an infraction was found to have been committed and the amount of the penalty imposed, if any.

(f) *No Appeal Permitted.* There shall be no appeal from a decision on written statements.

[Adopted effective September 1, 2006.]

NMLARLJ 4. SCHEDULE OF FEES

The following shall be the schedule of fees charged for certain official services provided by the Municipal Court. These amounts are consistent with RCW 3.62.060.

Duplication of Electronic Records	$ 10.00	per Tape
Paper Copy Expense	$ .25	per page
Certified Copy	$ 5.00	document
Postage		Actual Cost
Appeals (Preparation & Tape)	$ 40.00	

[Adopted effective September 2006.]

PE ELL MUNICIPAL COURT—
[No Local Rules]

PUBLISHER'S NOTE

This municipal court follows the Lewis County District Court Local Rules.

TOLEDO MUNICIPAL COURT—
[No Local Rules]

PUBLISHER'S NOTE

This municipal court follows the Lewis County District Court Local Rules.

WINLOCK MUNICIPAL COURT LOCAL RULES

Including Amendments Received Through
August 15, 2011

Table of Rules

PREFACE

1. Promulgation. These rules shall be known as the Local Rules for Municipal Court of Winlock, County of Lewis, State of Washington. Copies of these rules will be filed with the Office of the Administer of the Courts, and the Clerk of the Municipal Court of Winlock. Copies of these rules will be distributed to all law offices in Lewis County and to the county Law Library for public reference. To the extent possible, these rules will be placed on the Internet at the Winlock Municipal Court webpage. Copies will be available from the Municipal Court Clerk for Winlock. These rules will be effective on September 1, 1999, and supersede all prior rules of this court.

2. Numbering. Consistent with GR 7(b) Washington Court Rules, these rules to the extent possible, conform in numbering system and in format to those rules adopted by the Supreme Court of the State of Washington for courts of limited jurisdiction and facilitate the use of the same. The number of each rule is preceded by abbreviation "WML", designating the rule as a Winlock Municipal Local Rule and as being supplemental to the corresponding Washington Court Rule for Courts of Limited Jurisdiction.

3. Revisions and Additions (Reserved).

[Adopted effective September 1, 2000.]

WMLARLJ 1. SCOPE OF LOCAL RULES

These rules govern the procedure in the Municipal Court of Winlock, County of Lewis, State of Washington. These rules are supplemental to the rules enacted by limited jurisdiction as specifically authorized by GR 7, CRLJ 83, CrRLJ 1.7, and IRLJ 1.3 of the Washington Court Rules. The court may modify or suspend any of these local rules in any given case upon good cause being shown or upon the court's own motion.

1. Appearance Following Arrest.

(a) Defendant having been arrested for Driving Under the Influence, RCW 46.61.50571, must appear in court on the earliest practicable day as defined herein.

(b) Earliest practicable day is defined as the next regularly scheduled court session.

[Adopted effective September 1, 2000.]

WMLARLJ 2. DECORUM

1. Courtroom Decorum. All attorneys and other individuals in the courtroom shall abide by the following rules of conduct.

(a) _Always be Prompt._ Be in the courtroom ready to proceed at the appointed time.

(b) _Dress Appropriately to the Serious Nature of the Matters Before the Court._ Shorts and other kinds of beach apparel are not appropriate. Clothing advertising alcoholic beverages or illegal drugs are not appropriate. Hats are not to be worn in the courtroom.

[Adopted effective September 1, 2000.]

WMLARLJ 3. DECISION ON WRITTEN STATEMENTS

(a) _Written Submissions:_ Traffic infractions may be heard by the Court on the basis of written documents submitted by the city and a defendant, as provided in IRLJ 2.4(b)(4) and IRLJ 2.6. A written submission must be received by the court no later than seven (7) days prior to the scheduled date of the contested or mitigation hearing, or the submission will not be considered.

(b) _Generally:_ The court shall examine the citing officer's report and any written documents submitted by the defendant. The examination shall take place within 120 days after the defendant files the response to the notice of infraction. The examination may be held in chambers and shall not be governed by the Rules of Evidence.

(c) *Factual Determination:* For purposes of a contested hearing, the court shall determine whether the city has established, by a preponderance of all submitted evidence, that the defendant committed the infraction.

(d) *Disposition:* If the court determines that the infraction has been committed, it may assess a penalty amount and any appropriate and permitted costs to be paid by the defendant. [1]

(e) *Notice to Parties:* The court shall notify the parties in writing, whether an infraction was found to have been committed and what penalty, if any, was imposed.

(f) *No Appeal Permitted:* There shall be no appeal from a court determination based upon written statements.

[Adopted effective September 1, 2007.]

[1] Subsection designations have been corrected by Publisher.

LINCOLN COUNTY

SUPERIOR COURT

LOCAL RULES OF THE SUPERIOR COURT FOR LINCOLN COUNTY

Including Amendments Received Through
August 15, 2015

Table of Rules

PREFACE

1. Promulgation. These rules shall be known as the Local Rules for the Superior Court of the State of Washington for the County of Lincoln. Copies of these rules will be filed with the Clerk for Lincoln County and will be distributed to all law offices in Lincoln County. Additional copies will be available at the office of the Clerk for Lincoln County. These rules shall be effective September 1, 2014 and supersede all prior rules of the court.

2. Numbering. Consistent with CR 83(a), Washington Court Rules, these rules conform in numbering system and format to those rules and facilitate the use of both. The number of each rule is preceded by the abbreviation "LCR" or "LCrR" designating the rules as local to this court and supplemental to the corresponding Washington Court.

[Adopted effective September 2, 2014.]

COURTROOM SAFETY

No person, (except for duly and regularly commissioned law enforcement officers of the State of Washington, of other state and the federal government of the United States of America not appearing on their own family law matter) shall be on the 2nd floor of the Lincoln County courthouse (exclusive of the north side staircase) while armed with ANY firearm or taser or explosive device or any knife having a blade length of more than three inches or any Billy club, blackjack, truncheon or bat, nor shall any such person be in any of the aforementioned areas while possessing any gas gun or other device used for the spraying of tear gas, mace or other noxious chemical substance, or any incendiary device.

Any person found having any of the articles or devices heretofore mentioned which are banned from the 2nd floor of the Lincoln County Courthouse is subject to having such articles or devices seized by law enforcement officers, bailiffs on court order, or as otherwise directed by the court.

Any person violating this rule may be subject to punishment for contempt of court and prosecuted under RCW 9.41.300.

[Adopted effective September 2, 2014.]

LCR 7. PLEADINGS AND MOTIONS

(a) Pleadings.

(1) *Working Copies to Judge.*

(A) Delivery. Bench copies of briefs, memorandum of law, affidavits, declarations, exhibits, and other legal documents requiring thorough consideration by the court shall be delivered to the judge's chambers at least two (2) days prior to the trial or hearing thereon. Any response or reply documents should be delivered twenty-four (24) hours prior to hearing.

(B) Manner of Delivery. Bench copies may be delivered to chambers personally, by mail, or by electronic transmission via email attachment.

(i) Electronic transmission via email attachment is the court's preferred method of receiving bench copies of documents. Such attachments shall be in Microsoft Word or Adobe Portable Documents (PDF) format or some other compatible format.

[Adopted effective September 2, 2014.]

LCR 16. PRETRIAL PROCEDURE AND FORMULATING ISSUES

(c) Pre–Trial Conference. In the event a pretrial conference is required by this court or requested by any party, the conference shall be held in chambers. Any order for a pre-trial conference shall be in the form of and include the provisions as set forth in Exhibit "A" attached to this rule. The pre-trial conference shall be held not less than two weeks prior to the trial date.

(d) Pre–Trial Order. If so directed by the court, a pre-trial order in the form of Exhibit "B" attached to this rule shall be prepared by counsel within ten (10) days after the conclusion of the pre-trial conference.

(e) Exhibits. Parties shall notify the trial judge and the opposing party by letter if that party anticipates offering twenty-five (25) exhibits or more at the time of the trial. Said notice shall be given no less than two (2) weeks prior to the trial date.

[Adopted effective September 2, 2014.]

LCR 39. TRIAL BY JURY OR BY THE COURT

(d) Trial Briefs and Required Documents.

(2) *Other Required Documents, Domestic Relations Matters.* In addition to the above, in all contested trials in domestic relations matters, each party shall provide the opposing party and the court with the following:

(i) A written pretrial information form indicating a proposed division of assets and liabilities, using the form set forth in Exhibit "C" attached to the rules.

(ii) If children are involved, a proposed parenting plan and child support worksheets and supporting documents including Financial Declarations and the last two (2) years of tax returns, W–2's, and current paystubs, if applicable.

[Adopted effective September 2, 2014.]

LCR 40. ASSIGNMENT OF CASES

(a) Notice of Trial–Note of Issue.

(6) Requests for trial settings in civil cases will be heard on Law and Motion Day at the time they are regularly noted for setting, upon proper written notice filed with the clerk of the court. If both parties are pro se, the Court Administrator may tentatively set the date subject to review if an objection is received within 20 (twenty) days of mailing of the trial date.

(d) Trials.

(1) *Contested Dissolutions.*

(A) Pretrial Forms. In all final hearings or trials in domestic relations matters, each party is strongly encouraged to provide to the judge and the opposing party, a written statement as to the issues in controversy at least three (3) days prior to trial. The written statement may be in any form chosen by the party or his or her attorney to convey the following:

A brief factual summary;

Issues in dispute [e.g. property, debts, custody or support];

Case law, if it will be argued, supporting the party's position;

Proposed distribution of assets and debts, proposed parenting plan and child support amount, if in dispute, see LCR 39(d)(2)(i) and (ii) above; Areas of agreement;

(i) If one of the parties is seeking maintenance or child support, both parties shall complete a financial declaration.

(ii) If the parties are in dispute as to the distribution of assets and debts, both parties shall complete Exhibit "C" as attached to these local rules. The pretrial forms shall not be filed with the clerk, but shall be given to the opposing party and judge as bench copies.

(iii) Unless explained otherwise by the parties, the values shown on the pretrial form should include fair market value and assessed value of any real property, bank accounts, proposed pension, retirement, profit sharing or other deferred benefit or financial security plan, the present value of all life insurance policies and the cash surrender value, the amount of accounts receivable, inheritance due, and any trust accounts in which the party has an interest; the fair market value of all other property including collections, antiques; and in the case of motor vehicles, the average between wholesale and retail values from Kelly Blue Book or NADA or other comparable companies.

(B) Enforcement. If either party fails to comply with the rules set above, the judge may order such party or his attorney to pay appropriate attorney's fees to the opponent for any additional work or delay caused by the failure to comply. If either party fails to comply, the trial date may be stricken.

(C) Continuances. Stipulations or motion to continue a case already on the trial calendar must be in writing, supported by a declaration showing sufficient grounds for the requested continuance. The moving party shall present a written order for entry.

(D) Dating and Mailing of Decrees and Orders. When any decree or order is filed in a dissolution matter, the attorney for the party presenting the order, or the party if the matter is presented pro se, shall promptly personally deliver to the opposing party or mail to the opposing party's last known address or to opposing counsel, if so represented, a conformed copy of the decree or order with the date of entry indicated on each copy.

[Adopted effective September 2, 2014.]

LCR 41. DISMISSAL OF ACTIONS

(e) Notice of Settlements, Jury Trials. Whenever a cause has been set for trial as a jury case and a date for trial has been assigned and the matter is settled, or will not be tried by a jury, for any reason whatsoever, notice of the fact shall immediately be given to the court so that the jury panel can be dismissed. The violation of this rule may result in unnecessary jury expense, therefore the court in its discretion, may

assess such additional costs for the jury called for the trial against the violating party or his or her attorney.

[Adopted effective September 2, 2014.]

LCR 43. TAKING OF TESTIMONY

(a) Testimony.

(3) *Electronic Testimony or Evidence.* When testimony or evidence is to be given via electronic means, it is the responsibility of the parties to obtain the proper equipment for viewing such testimony or evidence.

[Adopted effective September 2, 2014.]

LCR 49. VERDICTS

(k) Receiving Verdict and Discharging Jury.

(1) *Receiving Verdict During Absence of Counsel.* A party or attorney desiring to be present at the return of the verdict must remain in attendance at the courthouse or be available by telephone call. If a party or attorney fails to appear within twenty (20) minutes of the telephone notice to the attorney's office, home or other phone number, the court may proceed to take the verdict in the absence of such party or attorney. In such case, the jury shall be individually polled and the identity of any dissenting jurors recorded.

[Adopted effective September 2, 2014.]

LCR 52. DECISIONS, FINDINGS, AND CONCLUSIONS

(a) Requirements.

(1) *Specifically Required.*

(D) In all non-contested matters, all orders, findings, decrees, and judgments shall have the name of the presenting counselor, pro se litigants, if not represented, and signed thereon by all parties unless a proper Joinder or waiver had previously been signed. Personal appearance for presentment shall not be necessary provided one party verifies the findings to the court.

(E) In contested matters, all orders, findings, decrees, and judgments shall be approved by the attorney of record or pro se parties, if not represented, unless the same are presented for signing in open court in the presence of all counsel or pro se parties, or are signed after proper notice of presentment.

[Adopted effective September 2, 2014.]

LCR 59. NEW TRIAL, RECONSIDERATION, AND AMENDMENT OF JUDGMENTS

(e) Hearing on Motion.

(3) *Nature of Hearing.*

(i) A motion for reconsideration or for a new trial shall be submitted on briefs and declarations or affidavits only, without oral arguments, unless the judge, on application from counsel or on the judge's own motion, allows oral argument. The judge will notify counsel if oral argument is to be allowed. Copies of such motion for reconsideration, note for motion calendar and responses thereto shall be delivered to the judge at the time of filing with the clerk.

[Adopted effective September 2, 2014.]

LCR 77. SUPERIOR COURT AND JUDICIAL OFFICERS

(k) Motion Day.

(1) Law and Motion day shall be held each Tuesday commencing at 9:30 am (when necessary and at the direction of the judge, some matters may be heard at 9:00 am) except when Tuesday is a legal holiday, or when cancelled by prior order of the court. All matters requiring more than 15 minutes will need to be special set with the Court Administrator.

(2) All matters to be heard on the regular Tuesday Law and Motion docket shall be scheduled with the Clerk of the Court not later than 12 noon on the preceding Tuesday.

(3) The Clerk of the Court shall prepare a docket of all matters regularly scheduled and shall distribute the same to the judge, attorneys (on request), Juvenile Office and five copies to the Bailiff, who is responsible for posting the docket.

(o) Court Calendar.

(1) Law and Motion matters will be heard in the following order:

9:00 am	Adoptions and other matters to be heard in chambers, at the discretion of the judge, and other matters that have been approved by the court for telephonic hearings.
9:30 am	Civil/Family Law matters including: probate and guardianship matters; ex–parte matters; default judgments; default dissolutions of marriage; trial settings; change of venues; and all contested motions requiring not more than 15 minutes.
10:30 am	Criminal Matters including: preliminary appearances; arraignments; status/reviews; omnibus; pleas.
1:15 pm	Juvenile Matters including: truancies; at risk youths; dependencies; juvenile offense proceedings.
2:30 pm	The following hearings must first be special set with the Court Ad-

ministrator: show cause matters; marriage dissolutions; all motions requiring argument; and other contested matters requiring more than 20 minutes but less than one hour. Matters requiring more than such time shall be scheduled in the same manner as trials.

(2) Special setting on the motion docket may be made with prior approval of the court administrator.

(3) Matters requiring more than 30 minutes shall be scheduled in the same manner as trials.

(p) Telephonic Hearings.

Telephonic hearings are authorized for most matters other than trials either upon stipulation by the parties or with approval of the court or upon the court's own motion or authorization following a request from the requesting party upon good cause shown. The record of such hearings will be electronically recorded. The requesting party shall contact the court Administrator at least three (3) days before the hearing for permission to appear telephonically under such conditions as ordered by the court. Any party retains the right to argue motions in person, even if the other party appears by telephone.

[Adopted effective September 2, 2014.]

LCR 78. CLERKS

(g) Requirements of Clerk's office.

(1) Only on prior court order, unless authorized by the clerk, will facsimile or electronic copies be accepted as temporary file documents. The facsimile copy shall be destroyed upon receipt of the original signed document.

(2) Files may be withdrawn from the clerk's office by a judge, or the Court Administrator, or by the official Court Reporter, practicing attorney in Lincoln County, or a title company situated in Lincoln County upon signing a receipt therefore. Files may be withdrawn by attorneys outside of Lincoln County upon written order of the court. All files shall be returned within one week or sooner if requested by the judge or the Clerk of the Court.

(3) An attorney or other person requesting a written answer to correspondence or confirmation on any pleadings or other documents shall furnish to the clerk a copy to conform if requested and a stamped, self-addressed envelope for the convenience of the clerk in making a necessary reply.

(4) The clerk shall not be required to disburse any funds paid into the registry of the court unless ordered to do so by the court.

(5) Unless the order specifically provides otherwise, all payments made in civil matters shall be by money

order, cashier's check, or attorney's business or trust account check.

[Adopted effective September 2, 2014.]

LCR 80.   COURT REPORTERS

(d) Court Reporting.

(1) Pre–trial and post-trial civil motions and other proceedings will be electronically recorded unless otherwise required by the court.

(2) Civil trials will be reported only on request of a party to the action, for which said party shall arrange for a court reporter to be in attendance. The cost of such reporter shall be an expense of the requesting party or parties, unless otherwise ordered by the court for good cause shown.

(3) In criminal matters, all pre-trial motions and appearances will generally be recorded electronically, and the court may arrange for a court reporter to be in attendance for criminal trials at the expense of the county.

(4) If partial transcriptions are made of the record during proceedings in Superior Court, a copy of such transcription shall be furnished to the judge and to opposing counsel or the pro se litigant if such matters are being argued before the court.

[Adopted effective September 2, 2014.]

LCR 83.   LOCAL RULES OF COURT

(c) Suspension or Modification of Rules. The court may suspend or modify any of the foregoing rules, in any given case, upon good cause being shown thereof or upon the court's own motion.

[Adopted effective September 2, 2014.]

LCrR 3.1.   RIGHT TO AND ASSIGNMENT OF LAWYER

(d) Assignment of Lawyer.

(5) Defendants who request assignment of counsel will be required to execute and file a financial disclosure under oath, which shall substantially comply with the form set forth in Exhibit "D" attached hereto, (or any successor from[1] approved by the State or Supreme Court) or the defendant may be required to provide the information orally to the court.

(6) All appointments of counsel by reason of indigency are expressly contingent upon proven indigency and full disclosure of assets. Where income or assets are discovered or indigency status changes subsequent to appointment which enable the defendant to afford counsel, or if the defendant can afford partial payment, fees may be ordered to be reimbursed to the court.

(7) Upon appointment of counsel for indigent criminal defendants or other litigants, the clerk shall promptly provide counsel with notice of the appointment.

[Adopted effective September 2, 2014.]

1 So in original.

LCrR 3.2.   RELEASE OF ACCUSED

(p) Bail Schedule. The following schedule shall in superior court cases pertain as the specified amount of bail required in criminal cases where no bail has been otherwise set, pending first court appearance:

Class A Felonies	No Bail
Class B Felony (against a person)	No Bail
Class B Felony (not against a person)	$5,000
Class C Felony (against a person)	No Bail
Probation Violation where bench warrant issued	$2,500
Gross Misdemeanor	See District Court Schedule
Misdemeanor	See District Court Schedule

(q) Appearances. Defendants on bail or recognizance are expected to be available to appear upon 72 hours' notice to their attorney. They are expected to be present on time at all scheduled appearances when they have received either oral or written notice. Failure to appear in accordance with this rule may result in forfeiture of bail, revocation of the personal recognizance order or issuance of a bench warrant for arrest.

(r) Approving Bail. Bail bondsmen, who have justified their qualifications to the Superior Court in the manner set forth hereafter, shall be deemed approved to provide bail bonds to defendants in criminal cases in an amount not exceeding the limits prescribed in the order of justification. All petitions shall be accompanied by a proposed order of justification. An initial petition shall be accompanied by a full filing fee. Renewal petitions shall be accompanied by an ex parte fee. Petition for renewal must be filed on or before April 30 of each year otherwise a full filing fee is due. The petition for renewal will include a verified statement that either there have been no changes since the last petition or will set forth the changes.

Upon failure of a bondsman to pay into the court, within ten (10) days, the amount of any bond forfeited by order of the court, the justification of said bail bondsman shall be immediately revoked. The sum so deposited shall be held in the registry of the court for sixty (60) days and should the person for whose appearance the bond was given be produced within said period, the judge may vacate the order and judgment forfeiting the bond on such terms as may be just and equitable. In any case where the bondsman has not previously justified qualification, the bond must be submitted to and approved by the presiding judge or the judge's designee. In order to obtain prior justification and approval of the court to provide bonds as an individual surety, the following requirements shall be met:

(1) Provide the court verifiable documentary evidence of qualification, including but not limited to a current financial statement.

(2) Provide a current list of all bonds on which the bondsman is obligated in any court of this state, including on the list the name of the court and defendant and the amount of the bond.

In the case of individuals seeking prior justification to write bail bonds on behalf of a corporate surety, the applicant must provide the court with the following:

(1) A certified copy of a power of attorney showing authorization of the applicant to act for the corporate surety.

(2) A letter from the Insurance Commissioner of Washington State indicating that the corporate surety is authorized to do business in this state.

The judge of the court may approve and justify any bail bondsman upon receipt of the above information. The court shall provide notice from time to time to the Sheriff of Lincoln County of the bail bondsmen previously qualified and the extent of their authority to write bonds. In the event of disqualification, the bail bondsman shall be promptly notified and may seek a hearing before the judge on the issues of qualification.

(s) Posting of Justified Bondsmen in Jail. The Sheriff of Lincoln County is required to post in a conspicuous location in the jail booking area, the names and telephone numbers of all justified bondsmen.

[Adopted effective September 2, 2014.]

LCrR 4.5.   OMNIBUS HEARINGS

(d) Motions.

(i) If there is no dispute regarding omnibus requests, the motion may be signed by both parties and presented to the court ex parte for signature before or at the date of omnibus hearing.

(ii) Unless otherwise requested by the prosecutor and required by the court, a defendant need not appear at the omnibus hearing if there are no disputed omnibus requests.

[Adopted effective September 2, 2014.]

EXHIBIT A. ORDER FOR PRETRIAL CONFERENCE

EXHIBIT "A"

SUPERIOR COURT OF WASHINGTON **COUNTY OF LINCOLN**	

_____,
    Plaintiff(s)/Petitioner(s),
 	
vs
 	
_____,
    Defendant(s)/Respondent(s).
	Case No._____
	
	ORDER FOR PRETRIAL
	CONFERENCE

THIS CAUSE appearing to be at issue and ready for trial, it is

1.   ORDERED AND ADJUDGED that a pretrial conference will be held in
Chambers at _____ at the Lincoln County Courthouse on the _____ day
of _____. Total times allocated from the conference will be
_____. The attorneys who will conduct the trial must attend this
conference unless the court pre-authorizes other means such as telephone or an
acceptable electronic communication.

All discovery procedures shall be completed by the time of this conference.

2.   ORDERED AND ADJUDGED that at least five (5) working days prior to this
conference, the attorneys shall submit to the judge and to opposing counsel a
Pretrial Statement containing the following:

(a)   A list designating those pleadings upon which the case goes to trial;

(b)   A succinct statement of the cause of action in regard to each claim or
defense;

(c)   A clear statement of the issues to be tried;

(d)   An itemized list of the claimed special damages;

(e)   Any statement of the principles of law involved in the case, supported by
citations of authority;

(f)   A statement of facts, which the client will admit;

(g)   A list of the names and addresses of all persons who have knowledge of relevant facts and the general nature of their testimony;

(h)   A list of all exhibits and documentary evidence, which may be used at the trial;

(i)   A complete set of written jury instructions, standard and special, which will be proposed for use at a jury trial, including verdict forms;

(j)   Any request for preliminary rulings on questions of law with citations in regard thereto;

(k)   Any trial brief that either party wishes the court to consider.

3.   ORDERED AND AJUDGED that at the time of the conference, the first thirty minutes of the conference will be set aside for a meeting between counsel to:

(a)   Inspect all documentary evidence and transportable exhibits listed in the Pretrial Statements. Exhibits not easily transportable will be made available for inspection at a time and place fixed at the conference;

(b)   Mark each document and exhibit using consecutive numerals for the plaintiff and defendant; generally, defendant's numbers would start at "100."

(c)   Object to the admissibility of the evidence, reserving the appropriate objections;

(d)   Object to the jury instructions filed with the Pretrial Statements, reserving the appropriate objections;

(e)   Stipulate on all matters of fact and law upon which the parties are in agreement.

DONE AND ORDERED in Chambers in Lincoln County, Washington

this _____ day of _____, 20_____.

_____
JUDGE

[Adopted effective September 2, 2014.]

EXHIBIT B. PRETRIAL ORDER
EXHIBIT "B"

SUPERIOR COURT OF WASHINGTON **COUNTY OF LINCOLN**	
_____, Plaintiff(s)/Petitioner(s), vs. _____, Defendant(s)/Respondent(s).	Case No._____ PRETRIAL ORDER

I. BASIS

1.1   The above matter has been noted for trial setting.

1.2   A pretrial conference was held and the following persons were present:

For Plaintiff: For Defendant:

II. ORDER

2.1   Names and addresses of attendant lawyers who will try the case and are authorized to enter into binding stipulations:

For Plaintiff   For Defendant:

2.2   Summary of Plaintiff's case:

2.3   Summary of defense and counterclaim:

2.4   The following amendments are allowed to the pleadings:

2.5   Names and addresses of plaintiff's witnesses and summary of testimony expected from each:

2.6   Names and addresses of defendant's witnesses and summary of testimony expected from each:

Additional Witnesses: If additional witnesses are discovered, who by the use of reasonable diligence could not have been discovered before Pretrial Conference, the party intending to use such witnesses shall immediately report the names, addresses and summary of the testimony of such witnesses to opposing counsel and the court.

2.7   Facts admitted by stipulation and agreement:

2.8   Exhibits produced for admission:

       a.   The following exhibits were marked, identified and admitted without objection, no further identification or offers of admission shall be required at trial:

       b.   The following exhibits were produced and offered but were objected to for competency, relevancy, or materiality; they may be introduced at the trial without formal identification, their authenticity being agreed to:

       c.   The admission of the following exhibits will be contested:

       d.   The following exhibits will be sent to opposing counsel within _____ days and within five (5) days of receipt forwarded to the court with any objections thereto; in the event no objections are raised the exhibits will be admitted in accordance with the provisions of (a) above:

Additional Exhibits: If additional exhibits or documents are discovered which could not
have been discovered by reasonable diligence before the Pretrial Conference, the
party intending to use them shall immediately exhibit them to opposing counsel
and submit them to the court to be marked for identification. Opposing counsel
shall immediately indicate to the court his or her position with respect to such
exhibit, i.e., whether his or her position falls under (a), (b), or (c) above.

2.9   Unresolved issues:

2.10   Points of law passed upon by the court:

2.11   Estimated length of trial: Jury Demanded: _____

2.12   Other matters that may aid the trial:

Set for trial:

Approved, stipulated and agreed:

_____   _____
Attorney for Plaintiff   Attorney for Defendant

IT IS ORDERED that the stipulations be carried out as outlined above.

DATED: _____   _____
                                 JUDGE

[Adopted effective September 2, 2014.]

Exhibit C   LINCOLN COUNTY

EXHIBIT C.   ASSET AND LIABILITY LIST

EXHIBIT "C"

SUPERIOR COURT OF WASHINGTON **COUNTY OF LINCOLN**	

In re: the Marriage of:
 	
Petitioner: _____
 	
and
 	
Respondent: _____
	Case No._____
	
	ASSET AND LIABLITY LIST OF
	  ▪ Petitioner
	  ▪ Respondent

The attached is the Asset and Liability List of ☐ Petitioner   ☐ Respondent.

I certify under penalty of perjury under the law of the State of Washington that the attached Asset & Liability List is true and correct.

DATED:_____   _____
                              Signature

                              _____
                              Print or Type Name

ASSET & LIABILITY LIST: ASSETS

	Wife Recommends				Husband Recommends				For Court Use Only			
	Value	To Wife	To Husband	Comm. or Sep.	Value	To Wife	To Husband	Comm. or Sep.	Court's Value	To Wife	To Husband	Comm. or Sep.
1. REAL ESTATE:												
a. Home												
b. Other												
2. HOUSE-HOLD GOODS (attach goods distribution worksheet)												
3. PERSONAL EFFECTS & JEWELRY												
4. PROF EQUIP & TOOLS												
5. REC. & HOBBY EQUIP												
6. VEHICLES												
Year & Make												

Exhibit C   **LINCOLN COUNTY**

ASSET AND LIABILITY LIST: ASSETS

	Wife Recommends				Husband Recommends				For Court Use Only			
	Value	To Wife	To Husband	Comm. or Sep.	Value	To Wife	To Husband	Comm. or Sep.	Court's Value	To Wife	To Husband	Comm. or Sep.
7. BANK ACCOUNTS: Bank, Branch & Type of Act.												
8. BUSINESS												
9. STOCKS & BONDS												
10. RETIREMENT Husband:												
Wife:												
11. LIFE INSURANCE												
12. OTHER ASSETS												
Total Assets												

ASSET AND LIABILITY LIST: LIABILITIES

	Wife Recommends				Husband Recommends				For Court-Use Only			
	Value	To Wife	To Husband	Comm. or Sep.	Value	To Wife	To Husband	Comm. or Sep.	Court's Value	To Wife	To Husband	Comm. or Sep.
13. REAL ESTATE Home:												
Other:												
14. INSTALLMENT PURCHASE CONTRACTS Attach list												
15. OTHER ACTS & BILLS PAYABLE Attach List												
TOTAL LIABILITIES												

NET WORTH AND PROPOSED DIVISION

	Wife Recommends				Husband Recommends				For Court Use Only			
	Value	To Wife	To Husband	Comm. or Sep.	Value	To Wife	To Husband	Comm. or Sep.	Value	To Wife	To Husband	Comm. or Sep.
TOTAL ASSETS												
TOTAL LIABILITIES												
NET WORTH												

[Adopted effective September 2, 2014.]

EXHIBIT D. INDIGENCY SCREENING FORM

EXHIBIT "D"

INDIGENCY SCREENING FORM   **CONFIDENTIAL**
[Per RCW 10.010.020(3)]

Name_____

Address_____

City_____ State_____ Zip_____

1. Place and "x" next to any of the following types of assistance you receive:

_____ Welfare   _____ Poverty Related Veteran's Benefits
_____ Food Stamps   _____ Temporary Assistance for Needy Families
_____ SSI   _____ Refugee Settlement Benefits
_____ Medicaid   _____ Disability Lifeline Benefits
_____ Other- Please Describe _____

{If you marked an "x" by any of the above, please stop here and sign at #15 below.}

2. Do you work or have a job? _____ yes _____ no. If yes, take-home pay: $_____

Occupation: _____ Employer's name & phone #:_____

3. Do you have spouse or state registered domestic partner who lives with you? ___yes ___no

Does she/he work? ___yes _____no If yes, take-home pay: $_____

Employer's name: _____

4. Do you and/or your spouse or state registered domestic partner receive unemployment, Social Security, a pension, or workers' compensation? ____yes ____no

   If yes, which one? _____ Amount: $_____

5. Do you receive any money from any other source? _____yes _____no
   If yes, how much$_____

6. Do you have any children residing with you? ___ yes____no
   If yes, how many? _____

7. Including yourself, how many people in your household do you support? _____

8. Do you own a home? ____yes _____no.
   If yes, value: $_____ Amount owed: $_____

9. Do you own a vehicle? ____yes _____no

If yes, year(s) and model (s) of your vehicle(s):_____
Amount owed: $_____

10. How much money do you have in checking/savings account(s)? $_____

11. How much money do you have in stocks, bonds, or other investments? $_____

12. How much money are your routine living expenses (rent, food, utilities) $_____

13. Other than routine living expenses such as rent, utilities, food, etc., do you have any other expenses such as child support payments, court-ordered fines or medical bills, etc? If so, describe:_____

14. Do you have money available to hire a private attorney? ____yes ____no

15. **Please read and sign the following:**

I understand the court may ask for verification of the information provided above. I agreed to immediately report any change in my financial status to the court.

"I certify under penalty of perjury under Washington State law that the above is true and correct." (Perjury is a criminal offense-see Chapter 9A.72 RCW)

_____
Signature   Date

_____
City   State

FOR COURT USE ONLY- DETERMINATION OF INDIGENCY

_____ Eligible for a public defender at no expense

_____ Eligible for a public defender but must contribute $_____

_____ Re-screen in future regarding change of income

_____ Not eligible for a public defender

_____
JUDGE

[Adopted effective September 2, 2014.]

DISTRICT COURT

LINCOLN COUNTY DISTRICT COURT LOCAL RULES

Including Amendments Received Through
August 15, 2015

Table of Rules

INTRODUCTION

FOREWORD: These local rules have been adopted under the provisions of General Rule 7 promulgated by the Washington State Supreme Court and conform in numbering and format to GR 7. These rules supplement ARLJ, CRLJ, RALJ, and IRLJ in accordance with RCW 3.30.080 and GR 7. Insofar as practicable the Washington Court Rules are not repeated and the user of these Local Rules should refer to the pertinent rule as adopted by the Supreme Court.

[Adopted effective September 1, 2000.]

I. ADMINISTRATIVE RULES (LARLJ)

LARLJ 1. JURY ADMINISTRATIVE REIMBURSEMENT FEE

A party demanding or entitled to a jury trial shall, before 1:30 p.m. five working days prior to the scheduled trial date, contact the Lincoln County District Court Clerk and confirm that the jury is still required. When a cause assigned a date for trial as a jury case is settled, or will not be tried by a jury for any reason, notice of that fact shall be given immediately to the Court Clerk. In the event the notice is given to the Court Clerk less than five working days prior to the scheduled trial date, the party electing not to have their case heard by a jury (Criminal Cases: Defendant who waives jury, elects to enter a plea of guilty; or State if jury waiver follows Jury Demand by State; Civil Cases: jury waiver by party after demand) shall pay a jury administrative reimbursement fee equal to the actual costs incurred by the Court for jury fee payments and mileage reimbursements and all postage costs to summons the jury, unless the Judge determines that those costs and fees shall not be paid.

[Adopted effective September 1, 2000. Amended effective September 1, 2006; September 1, 2011.]

LARLJ 2. [RESERVED]

[Reserved effective September 1, 2011.]

LARLJ 3. NEXT JUDICIAL DAY

The state law requires that defendants arrested for driving while under the influence, driving under age twenty-one after consuming alcohol, or being in physical control of a vehicle while under the influence appear in court within one judicial day. Such judicial day is defined as the first date following arrest when court is in session.

[Adopted effective September 1, 2000; amended effective September 1, 2011.]

LARLJ 4. MISCELLANEOUS FEES

The following shall be the schedule of fees charged for certain official services provided by the Lincoln District Court Clerk. These amounts are consistent with RCW 3.62.060.

```
Duplication of Electronic Records....$10.00
Photocopy Expenses ..............$  .50/page
Certified Copy ....................$  6.00
Appeals (Preparation of Tapes) ......$40.00
Return of Check Fee (NSF or Ac-
    count closed checks).............$35.00
Non-traffic civil infraction—violation
    of City or Town Ordinance Filing
    Fee ...........................$12.00
Additional fee if court hearing held...$13.00
Misdemeanor—violation of City or
    Town Ordinance Filing Fee .......$25.00
```

These fees may be changed by general court order without amending these rules.

[Adopted effective September 1, 2000; amended effective September 1, 2011.]

LARLJ 5. PROBATION FEES [RESERVED]

[Adopted effective September, 1, 2000; reserved effective September 1, 2011.]

LARLJ 6. DISCLOSURE OF PUBLIC RECORDS

1. The following records and files of this Court are declared confidential:

(A) Affidavits for probable cause for arrest warrants before the warrant has been served and returned.

(B) Mental health, psychiatric, and medical reports.

(C) Alcohol and drug evaluations and follow up reports.

(D) Unless admitted into evidence, certified copies of driving records, abstracts of driving records, and compiled reports of arrests and convictions;

(E) Judges notes and work sheets.

2. Access to confidential records is limited to persons authorized by statute or who obtain a Court order.

3. **File Research Fee.** The Court Administrator shall provide procedures and staff for requests made for research in the files of the Court. In the event a request is made to research the contents of files, which have been archived, an Archive Research Fee of $25 per hour shall be charged to the requesting party with a minimum of one hour paid prior to the research commencing.

[Adopted effective September 1, 2000; amended effective June 15, 2001; September 1, 2011.]

II. CIVIL RULES (LCRLJ)

LCRLJ 1. FILING OF PLEADINGS AND OTHER PAPERS

1. Interrogatories and depositions without written permission of Lincoln County District Court unless necessary for the disposition of a motion or objection.

2. Unanswered request for admissions unless necessary for the disposition of the motion or objection.

3. Total copies of reported cases, statutes or texts appended to a brief, or otherwise, may only be filed with a copy marked "bench copy" furnished directly to the judge hearing the matter; and

4. An offer of settlement made pursuant to RCW chapter 4.84 shall not be filed or communicated to the trier of fact in violation of RCW 4.84.280 of the revised

code Washington prior to the completion of trial. A violation of this order may result in denial of the reasonable attorney fee.

[Adopted effective September 1, 2000; amended effective September 1, 2011.]

LCRLJ 2. PRE-TRIAL HEARING

When matters of fact are put in issue by responsive pleadings served and filed with the court and if one of the parties has noted the case for pretrial hearing, a pre trial will be set. If both parties stipulate the pretrial hearing may be set on the docket for a telephone conference hearing. At the pre-trial hearing all parties must appear (in person or telephonically) or through counsel. If a party does not appear at the pre-trial hearing, the non-appearing party's pleadings shall be stricken, unless good cause shown, and the court may grant a judgment of default or dismissal against the non-appearing party. If no parties appear, the court may dismiss all pending claims without prejudice. At the pre-trial hearing, the court will also perform the following functions:

1. Determine any pre-trial motions.

2. Assign trial and/or further motion dates.

3. Acknowledge and approve settlement agreements.

4. Enter default or judgments on pleadings.

5. Pre admit exhibits for trial.

6. Enter discovery order and completion dates.

Counsel shall appear at the pre-trial hearing with a schedule of dates of availability for trial or any other necessary proceeding.

The pre-trial hearing procedure shall not preclude the entry of default judgments, judgments on pleadings, or any other orders not inconsistent with these rules or the Civil Rules for Courts of Limited Jurisdiction (CRLJ) prior to the date of the pre-trial hearing.

[Adopted effective September 1, 2000; amended effective September 1, 2011.]

LCRLJ 3. INSTRUCTIONS TO JURY [RESERVED]

[Adopted effective September 1, 2000; reserved effective September 1, 2011.]

LCRLJ 4. DISMISSAL ON CLERK'S MOTION

In all cases where there has been no action of record during the 12 months just past, the Lincoln County District Court clerk shall mail notice to the parties or the attorneys of record that such case will be dismissed by the court for want of prosecution unless within thirty days following said mailing, written application of action of record is made to the court and good cause shown why the case should be continued as a pending case. If such application is not made or the cause is not shown, the court shall dismiss each such case without prejudice. The cost of filing such order of dismissal with a clerk shall not be assessed against either party.

[Adopted effective September 1, 2000; amended effective September 1, 2011.]

LCRLJ 5. ENTRY OF JUDGMENT

A. Attorney fees. When a party is entitled to an award of reasonable attorney fees (in lieu of those statutory fees provided for by R. C. W. 12.20.060), the fees provided in the following attorney fees schedule are deemed reasonable in all default cases unless the party presents evidence of circumstances which convince the court a larger or smaller fee should be

awarded; provided, however, the court shall have authority to vary from the schedule on its own motion:

Schedule for attorney fees in default cases

$0.00	to $2,500	$250.00
$2,501	to $5,000	$350.00
$5,001	to $10,000	$450.00
$10,001	to $15,000	$600.00

Attorneys' fee requests in excess of $600 must be itemized.

[Adopted effective September 1, 2000; amended effective September 1, 2011.]

LCRLJ 6. DEFAULT JUDGMENTS (NO APPEARANCE BY DEFENDANT)

(a) All necessary papers required for entry of a default judgment shall be filed at the same time as the motion for default judgment, unless extended by court order to correct a clerical error or omission or for furnishing of any proof required by the court.

(b) Default judgments shall be subject to the following:

(1) No default judgment shall be granted except upon motion by plaintiff's counsel of record, or if none, by motion of plaintiff.

(2) No default shall be granted except upon proof satisfactory to the court. The court shall require at least the following to be on file with the motion for default judgment, unless otherwise excused by the court for good cause:

(i) on assigned causes of action, the assignment instrument

(ii) on causes of action based on open account where the complaint is not specific, a written statement of account setting forth all charges and credits and the dates thereof, the nature of merchandise or services furnished, and a statement of any interest or surcharges which are included;

(iii) on causes of action on retail sales contract, chattel mortgage, or conditional sales contract, the original contract (or a copy if the original has been filed with a government agency). Where applicable, an automobile title or bill of sale must be filed;

(iv) on causes of action for rent based on an oral lease, a statement of account similar to that required in actions on open account. If any claim is made for damages or repairs to premises, such claim must be itemized separately;

(v) on causes of action based on a negotiable instrument, the original negotiable instrument.

(vi) on causes of action for rent based on a written lease, a copy of the lease and a statement of account as in subsection (b)(2)(ii) of this Rule;

(vii) on causes of action based on all other contracts, oral testimony to prove performance may be required, together with filing of a copy of the contract if written, and filing or proving the items of account and any credits;

(viii) on causes of action for tort, the proof required shall be the same as required above for proving contract balances except that the following additional proof of the amount of damage shall be required:

Property damage may be proved by repair bills or estimates;

Loss of use claims, loss of wages, and pain and suffering shall be proved by oral testimony;

Hospital, and doctor bills may be proved by written bills, whether paid or not.

(3) No judgment for interest shall be allowed unless there is on file proof of the factors necessary for computation of interest including applicable dates, rate of interest, amounts subject to interest, and a computation of the total interest claimed due.

(4) Plaintiff shall file a stamped addressed envelope with the last known address of the defendant at the time the motion for default judgment is made. No more than fifteen (15) days following the entry of the default judgment, the clerk of court shall mail a copy of the judgment to the defendant.

[Adopted effective September 1, 2000; amended effective September 1, 2011.]

LCRLJ 7. PAYMENT OF MONIES ON JUDGMENTS

All payments of monies on judgments (including awards of costs) shall be made to through the Clerk of the Court. After said funds are paid to the receiving party, or the receiving party's attorney, a satisfaction of judgment shall be filed within the following thirty (30) days of receipt of the funds and a satisfaction of judgment shall be filed within said thirty days in the amount received.

[Adopted effective September 1, 2000; amended effective September 1, 2011.]

LCRLJ 8. CIVIL JURY

(a) Pre-trial Procedure. All cases, set for jury trial shall be set for a pre-trial conference which shall be held at least two weeks prior to trial. The attorneys who are to conduct the trial and all parties shall be present (parties may be excused by the court for good cause) to consider such matters as will promote a fair and expeditious trial. All discovery shall be completed within ten (10) days following the pre-trial hearing. Opposing counsel or party must be given ten (10) days notice prior to the pre-trial conference. Opposing counsel or party must be given ten (10) days prior written notice of any pre-trial motions to be heard at the pre-trial conference. Any motions not made at the pre-trial conference shall be deemed waived.

[Adopted effective September 1, 2000; amended effective September 1, 2011.]

III. INFRACTION RULES (LIRLJ)

LIRLJ 1. DECISIONS ON WRITTEN OR EMAIL STATEMENTS

In place of the defendant's personal appearance at a contested or mitigation infraction hearing, defendants may submit their statement in writing (including email submissions). The statement may be on Form LIRLJ #1, or it may be submitted on the court's electronic hearing Form LIRLJ #2. The court shall examine the citing officers report and any statement(s) submitted by the defendant. The examination shall take place within 120 days after the defendant filed a response to the notice of infraction. The examination may be held in Chambers and shall not been governed by the rules of evidence. Any Defendant electing to request that the court hold a contested hearing under this rule waives the right to appeal the court's decision to the Superior Court under IRLJ 3.5.

[Adopted effective September 1, 2000; amended effective September 1, 2004; September 1, 2011.]

LIRLJ 2. MANDATORY LIABILITY INSURANCE VIOLATIONS– PROOF OF INSURANCE

(A) If a person who has been cited with a violation of RCW 46.30.020 presents to the Court Clerk evidence that the person had in effect at the time of the citation liability insurance as required by RCW 46.30.020, then, upon payment of twenty five dollars ($25.00) the case shall be dismissed and the court clerk shall be authorized to make appropriate notation of the dismissal in the court file.

(B) Court clerks are authorized to mitigate the penalty for Mandatory Liability Insurance Violations (RCW 46.30.020) in cases where the person cited presents, either in person at the Clerk's Counter, or by mail or email or facsimile, evidence of after citation procurement of insurance in amounts as the Court, from time to time, directs by general court order.

[Adopted effective September 1, 2000; amended effective September 1, 2007; September 1, 2011.]

LIRLJ 3. STUDENT COURT

The court from time to time may defer a Traffic Infraction of a defendant who is a high school student. The deferral shall be pursuant to RCW 46.63.070.

[Adopted effective September 1, 2000; amended effective September 1, 2011.]

LIRLJ 4. REQUEST FOR SPEED MEASURING DEVICE EXPERT; REMOTE TESTIMONY

Any request to produce a speed measuring device expert must be filed in accordance with IRLJ 6.6(b).

If the parties stipulate the court may allow the speed measuring device expert to testify from a location other than the courtroom, via speakerphone or other electronic means acceptable to the court.

Allowing SMD expert testimony by telephone serves to reduce costs incurred by law enforcement agencies as well as assisting defendants in presenting the testimony of their own SMD experts.

[Adopted effective September 1, 2006; amended effective September 1, 2007; September 1, 2011.]

IV. CRIMINAL RULES (LCrRLJ)

LCrRLJ 1. NON–APPEARANCE

Upon the non-appearance of a defendant at the time and place scheduled by the court and a Bench Warrant issued, the defendant's bail or bond may be ordered forfeited with or without further proceedings upon motion of the prosecuting attorney or upon the court's own motion. If the necessary witnesses do not appear at the time scheduled by the court, the court may dismiss such action unless a good cause for such non-appearance is shown. No such action shall be taken until thirty (30) minutes after the scheduled appearance time.

[Adopted effective September 1, 2000; amended effective September 1, 2011.]

LCrRLJ 2. EXHIBITS

In a criminal case every exhibit in the court's custody, which is not contraband and for which ownership is not in dispute, shall be returned to the party who produced that exhibit upon motion of the party, or upon the court's motion and expiration of the appeal period. Exhibits not withdrawn shall be delivered by the court to the applicable law enforcement agency for disposition as abandoned property; or if contraband, for destruction. No exhibit shall be released by the court without its being receipted for by the receiving person.

[Adopted effective September 1, 2000; amended effective September 1, 2011.]

LCrRLJ 3.1. OBLIGATION OF DEFENDANTS TO APPEAR IN COURT, AND CONSEQUENCES OF FAILURES TO APPEAR IN CASES WHERE A PUBLIC DEFENDER HAS BEEN APPOINTED

(A) The appointment of a public defender attorney, for any defendant deemed to be indigent shall be conditioned upon the defendant appearing in court for all hearings where his/her appearance has been required by the court.

(B) If any defendant for which a public defender has been appointed fails to appear in court when so required on two occasions without being excused in advance by the court, the order/appointment whereby the public defender was appointed for said defendant may be vacated immediately upon such second failure to appear.

(C) Upon such appointment being vacated the public defender shall be relieved from any requirements to appear in court with such defendant.

(D) The provisions of this rule, however, do not preclude the defendant from reapplying to the court for the appointment of a public defender to represent him/her.

[Adopted effective September 1, 2000; amended effective September 1, 2011.]

LCrRLJ 3.2. RELEASE OF ACCUSED

DUI/Physical Control Cases. In addition to posting bail as set out in CrRLJ 3.2(m)(or by local schedule) in all cases where an individual is arrested for Driving a Motor Vehicle While Under the Influence of Intoxicants and/or Drugs or for Physical Control of a Motor Vehicle While Under the Influence of Intoxicants and/or Drugs or Minor Operating a Motor Vehicle After Consuming Alcohol, the individual so arrested shall be held for eight hours from time of booking before being entitled to release by posting bail.

[Adopted effective June 15, 2001; amended effective September 1, 2011.]

LCrRLJ 4. CONDITIONS FOR RELEASE FROM JAIL [REPEALED]

[Adopted effective September 1, 2000; repealed effective June 15, 2001.]

LCrRLJ 5. PRE–JURY TRIAL HEARING

In every criminal case in which the defendant has not waived a jury trial, the clerk shall set a pre-trial hearing. The purpose of the hearing is for the presentation and setting of motions, an opportunity for plea negotiations between the parties, and the setting of dates for a readiness hearing and the jury trial. Discovery should be completed by the pre-trial hearing. See CrRLJ 3.5, and CrRLJ 3.6 for motions practice and procedure.

The defendant and counsel are required to attend pre-trial hearing unless excused by the court. Failure to attend any pre-trial hearing may result in the issuance of a bench warrant and forfeiture of any bail/bond.

[Adopted effective September 1, 2004; amended effective September 1, 2011.]

LCrRLJ 5.2. READINESS HEARING

In order to efficiently schedule the calling of jurors, to avoid unnecessary disruptions of jurors' lives, and to avoid the waste of public funds the following readiness hearing procedures have been adopted:

Not less than 14 days prior to an assigned jury trial date, there shall be held a readiness hearing. At the readiness hearing it shall be mandatory that the prosecuting attorney, the defense counsel, and the defendant be present. The requirements of this rule can be waived only by the Judge appointed to the case. In the event the defendant fails to appear, the jury trial setting shall be canceled, a bench warrant may be issued, bail or bond may be forfeited, and costs may be imposed at the discretion of the court. In the event the defendant waives the jury trial subsequent to the readiness hearing, costs may be imposed pursuant to LARLJ 1.

At the readiness hearing, the following matters will be concluded:

1. All plea negotiations.

2. Exchange of witness lists.

3. Providing of any discovery not previously completed by the pretrial hearing held prior to the readiness hearing.

4. Motions on legal issues arising subsequent to the pretrial hearing or on issues arising due to new evidence.

5. Filing with the court proposed non–WPI (Washington Pattern Instructions) jury instructions and voire dire questions for the prospective jurors which either party requests be used. NOTE WPI proposed jury instructions shall be filed no later than 7 days prior to a jury trial, including. Each set of proposed jury instructions shall be identified as that parties' proposed instructions and each shall be numbered.

At the conclusion of the readiness hearing, the court will no longer grant any further motions to amend or motions to dismiss the charge(s) unless good cause is shown (involving unique and unexpected events/factors). Therefore, the case will be tried by jury, unless waived by the defendant, or concluded by a guilty plea to the original charge(s). See LARLJ 1 regarding administrative reimbursement of jury fees for those who do not give at least 14 days notice of settlement to the clerk of the court.

[Adopted effective September 1, 2004. Amended effective September 1, 2011; September 2, 2013.]

V. RULES FOR APPEAL (LRALJ)

LRALJ 1. FAILURE TO DESIGNATE THE RECORD [DELETED]

[Adopted effective September 1, 2000; deleted effective September 1, 2007.]

LRALJ 3. COPY OF RECORDING FOR PARTIES [DELETED]

[Adopted effective September 1, 2000; deleted effective September 1, 2007.]

DEFENDANT'S REQUEST FOR DECISION ON WRITTEN STATEMENTS

DISTRICT COURT OF WASHINGTON FOR LINCOLN COUNTY

STATE OF WASHINGTON   )

_____)

            Plaintiff   ) No._____

)

vs.   ) DEFENDANT'S REQUEST FOR

) DECISION ON WRITTEN

_____) STATEMENTS

           Defendant.   )

To: CLERK of Court, PO Box 329, Davenport, WA 99122

From: _____, Defendant

I understand that by requesting that the Court hear my case by written statement that I am, by signature hereof, waiving any appeal of the Court's Decision to Superior Court. With that in mind I hereby request that the Court decide my case based on the following sworn statements:

_____

_____

_____

_____

_____

[attach additional pages if necessary]

I certify, under penalty of perjury under the laws of the State of Washington, that the foregoing and any attached statements is true.

I promise that if it is determined that I committed the infraction for which I was cited, I will pay the monetary penalty authorized by law and assessed by the court.

_____   _____

       [Date and Place]   [Defendant's Signature]

[Adopted effective September 1, 2000.]

MASON COUNTY

Table of Courts

Superior Court

Local Rules of Practice and Procedure in the Superior Court of the State of Washington in and for the County of Mason.

District Court

Mason County District Court Local Court Rules.

Municipal Court

Shelton Municipal Court Local Rules.

SUPERIOR COURT

LOCAL RULES OF PRACTICE AND PROCEDURE IN THE SUPERIOR COURT OF THE STATE OF WASHINGTON IN AND FOR THE COUNTY OF MASON

Including Amendments Received Through August 15, 2015

Table of Rules

Rule
LCrR 4.2.   Superior   Court   Commissioners—Authority—
Criminal Cases.

LOCAL RULES OF APPELLATE PROCEDURE

LRAP 9.2(a).   Verbatim Report of Proceedings/designation
of Court–Approved Transcribers.

LOCAL JUVENILE COURT RULES

LJuCR 7.1.   Dismissal for Delay in Filing Information [Re-
scinded].
LJuCR 9.2.   Additional Right to Representation by Lawyer.

Rule
LOCAL RULES FOR APPEAL OF DECISIONS OF COURTS OF LIMITED JURISDICTION
LRALJ 6.3A(c).   Content of Transcript of Electronic Rec-
ord.
LOCAL GUARDIAN AD LITEM RULES
LGAL 5.   Specific Guardian Ad Litem Registry Require-
ments.
LGAL 7.   Guardian Ad Litem Grievance and Complaint
Procedure.
LOCAL SPECIAL PROCEEDINGS RULES
LSPR 94.04.   Family Law, Probate, Guardianship and
Adoption Cases.

LOCAL SUPERIOR COURT GENERAL RULES (LGR)

LGR 29.   PRESIDING JUDGE IN SUPERIOR COURT

(a) Election, Term, Vacancies, Removal and Selection Criteria—Multiple Judge Courts.

(1) *Election.* The judges of the superior court shall elect a Presiding Judge and an Assistant Presiding Judge who shall serve for a period of two years. The election will take place in December of odd-numbered years, and the term shall commence on January 1.

The Presiding Judge and the Assistant Presiding Judge shall perform all duties of the position required by General Rule 29.

[Adopted effective September 1, 2012.]

LGR 31.   ACCESS TO COURT RECORDS [RESCINDED]

[Adopted effective September 1, 2005; rescinded effective September 1, 2012.]

LOCAL SUPERIOR COURT CIVIL RULES (LCR)

LCR 6.   CONFIRMATION PROCEDURES AND CUT–OFF DATES FOR FILING CIVIL MOTIONS AND RESPONSIVE DOCUMENTS [RESCINDED]

[Adopted effective September 1, 2005. Amended effective September 1, 2006. Rescinded effective September 1, 2010.]

LCR 7.   MOTIONS

(b) Motions and Other Papers.

(1) *How Made.*

(A) Motion Docket. There shall be a civil motion docket held according to the published schedule available at the courthouse or through the Mason County Superior Court Administrator's Office at http://www.co.mason.wa.us/superior_court. All civil motions and motions for revision shall be heard on the civil motion docket.

The schedule may change. Parties and counsel are advised to review the current schedule before noting matters for hearing. Incorrectly scheduled matters may be stricken.

(B) Confirmation Procedures. For a contested matter to be heard by the court, the hearing must be confirmed as set forth below. This includes hearings scheduled by notice of issue or court order,

including hearings which are administratively continued.

(i) Confirmations must be made by calling the Clerk of the Court at (360) 427–9670, Ext. 346, or by e-mail at superiorcourt–confirm@co.mason.wa.us, no later than 10:00 a.m. two (2) court days prior to the civil motion docket (example: for a motion on Monday, confirmation must be made by 10:00 a.m. on Thursday of the preceding week).

(ii) If the deadline for confirmation falls on a court holiday, confirmations shall be made before 10:00 a.m. on the last court day before the holiday.

(iii) Motions filed by those persons physically confined under a court order shall be deemed confirmed at filing.

(iv) Matters not confirmed may be heard at the end of the docket only at the discretion of the Court and upon agreement of all parties.

(C) Continuance of Confirmed Matters. Matters confirmed in accordance with paragraph (B) (i) and (ii) are not subject to continuance, except with permission of the Court. If not heard, these matters shall be *stricken* and may be re-noted by the moving party.

(D) Time Limits. Arguments on motions other than summary judgment shall be limited to ten (10) minutes per side. Arguments which will exceed the time limit of this rule, if allowed by the Court, will ordinarily be placed at the end of the docket.

[Adopted effective September 1, 2010. Amended effective September 1, 2012; September 2, 2013; September 1, 2015.]

LCR 16. PRETRIAL PROCEDURE AND FORMULATING ISSUES

(c) Public Records Act Cases—*In Camera* Review.

(1) *When commenced.* In a Public Records Act case, *in camera* review will occur only if the court enters an order requiring such review. Agreement between parties or submission of records to the court, without an appropriate order, will not trigger *in camera* review.

(2) *Electronic records.* Records for *in camera* review shall be submitted in an electronic form unless the court orders otherwise on a showing of good cause.

(3) *Identification of records.* Records for *in camera* review must have a unique identifying number, such as a Bates number. The system for numbering and the placement of page numbers must be uniform for all records.

(4) *Entirely exempt record.* If a record is claimed entirely exempt, it must be clearly designated as exempt or withheld on the first page of the document for *in camera* review.

(5) *Identification of redactions.* Records redacted in part must be submitted to the judge in a manner that will permit the judge to read the entire record and immediately understand which parts were withheld by redaction and which parts were produced. For example, the redactions may be outlined or indicated with a lightly shaded or colored overlay.

(6) *Submission of spreadsheet.* In cases with numerous records at issue, or if ordered by the judge, a spreadsheet shall be submitted as part of the *in camera* procedure. The spreadsheet must clearly identify which records are claimed entirely exempt and have been withheld and which records have been redacted in part. The spreadsheet(s) shall list the following information in separate fields or columns: (A) the unique identifier for the record or page being reviewed, such as a Bates number; (B) descriptive information that accurately identifies the record, including author(s), recipients(s), and date(s) (or if descriptive information is protected, other means of sufficiently identifying particular records without disclosing protected content); (C) identification of a specific exemption claimed and an explanation of how it applies to the record; and (D) an expandable cell for the court's notes. The spreadsheet shall be filed and served on all parties and also shall be submitted to the court in electronic form.

(7) *Basis for exemption.* The basis for the claim of exemption may appear on the document if doing so would not obliterate text or other information necessary for the court's review.

[Adopted effective September 2, 2013.]

LCR 40. STATUS CONFERENCES, PRETRIAL HEARINGS, MEDIATION, SETTLEMENT CONFERENCES AND TRIALS—CIVIL CASES ONLY

(b) Status Conferences, Mediation, Trial Setting Conferences

1. *Status Conferences.*

1.1 A status conference may be assigned at the time a case is filed, by notice from the court administrator's office, or upon motion of any party.

1.2 At the status conference, the court may direct the case to arbitration or mediation, and/or may set an additional status conference date. The court may determine and set a discovery deadline, a mediation deadline, a trial setting conference date, and other dates and deadlines as necessary.

2. *Mediation.*

2.1 **Presumption of Mediation.** It is presumed that all contested civil and family law matters, with the following exceptions, will have completed mediation prior to trial:

- Dependencies and termination of parental rights;
- Uniform Parentage actions, up until establishment of paternity;
- Matters in which a domestic violence or sexual assault protection order is in place;
- Petitions for Civil Commitment (Sexual Predators);
- Actions regarding seizure of property by the State;
- Matters subject to Mandatory Arbitration Rules, or that are to be arbitrated by agreement, up until a request for a trial de novo;
- Matters that have been previously mediated consistent with the standards set forth in this rule; and
- By court order upon motion of any party, upon the court's determination that there is good cause not to require mediation.

Any party may move the court for an order that there is good cause to require mediation in any matter, including those cases designated as exceptions above.

2.2 **Mediators.** Parties may agree to a mediator from among the three categories of mediators below. If the parties cannot agree, the court shall upon motion by any party appoint a mediator. Appointment of a mediator is subject to the mediator's right to decline to serve.

2.2.1 Mediation Panel. There shall be a panel of mediators established by the court. The list of court-approved mediators and their information sheets will be available to the public in the court administrator's office.

Parties may stipulate to using a mediator from the Mediation Panel. If the parties stipulate to using a mediator from the Mediation Panel, but are not able to agree on a specific mediator, a mediator will be assigned from the Mediation Panel.

2.2.2 Volunteer Mediation Panel. There shall be a panel of volunteer mediators established by the court. Parties may qualify for appointment of a mediator from the Volunteer Mediation Panel if income and asset tests as determined by the court are met. The list of court-approved volunteer mediators and their information sheets will be available to the public in the court administrator's office.

Parties who qualify may stipulate to using a mediator from the Volunteer Mediation Panel. If the parties stipulate to using a mediator from the Volunteer Mediation Panel, but are not able to agree on a specific mediator, a mediator will be assigned from the Volunteer Mediation Panel.

2.2.3 Other Mediators. Upon approval by the court, parties may stipulate to a mediator not on the Mediation Panel or the Volunteer Mediation Panel. The court may approve appointment of a proposed mediator upon satisfactory showing of qualifications and knowledge of subject matter. Any mediator certified as such by a Washington State dispute resolution center is qualified to serve as a mediator under this paragraph.

2.2.4 Application and Trainings. A person who wishes to be placed on the Mediation Panel and/or Volunteer Mediation Panel shall complete an information sheet on the form prescribed by the court, which shall demonstrate the person's qualifications as mediator, and as to specific subject matters. Mediators and any person who wishes to be considered as a mediator may participate in court-sponsored mediation trainings.

2.3 Cost of Mediation. Parties may stipulate to the allocation of mediation costs. If the parties are unable to agree, the court will order the same upon motion of any party. Parties using mediators from the Volunteer Mediation Panel may be charged an administrative fee as set by the court.

2.4 Mediation Orders and Process.

2.4.1 Mediation Status and Terms. An order shall be entered setting forth the following:

- Mediation status (whether the case is to be mediated); and

- Mediation terms (including but not limited to the mediator or category the mediator is to be chosen from, allocation of costs of mediation, mediation deadline, and identity of parties with authority required to attend mediation).

If the parties agree as to mediation status and/or terms, they may so stipulate and submit an agreed order for the court's approval prior to the status conference, or at any time thereafter prior to the discovery deadline.

If the parties are unable to agree to the status and/or all terms of mediation, a party may file and note a motion for entry of an order setting the status and terms of mediation.

2.4.2 Litigation Process During Period of Mediation. Pending mediation, all litigation processes such as discovery, motions for temporary orders, and motions for dispositive orders shall continue.

2.4.3 RCW ch. 7.07. All mediations undertaken pursuant to this Rule are subject to the provisions of RCW ch. 7.07, the Uniform Mediation Act, including its requirements regarding privilege and confidentiality.

2.4.4. Civil Mediation Statements. In civil actions, all parties shall prepare and deliver a Civil Mediation Statement to the mediator and opposing parties, no later than five working days prior to the mediation. The statement shall address the matters set forth in Appendix A. The statement shall not be filed with the court.

2.4.5. Family Law Mediation Statements. In family law actions, all parties shall prepare and deliver a Family Law Mediation Statement to the mediator, opposing parties, and the State of Washington, if the State is a party, no later than five working days prior to the mediation. The statement shall address the matters set forth in Appendix B. The statement shall not be filed with the court.

2.4.6. Appearance at Mediation. The parties shall appear in person at mediation unless the court orders in advance that they may be present by telephone or electronic means sufficient to allow full participation. Each party shall ensure the presence at mediation of persons who have sufficient authority to approve a settlement.

2.4.7 Mediation Report. Within five days after completion of mediation, the mediator shall file a Mediation Report indicating whether the case has been resolved. A copy of the Mediation Report shall be provided to the court administrator's office.

3. *Discovery.* Discovery shall be completed in accordance with the discovery schedule set at the status conference. Exceptions will be made only upon prior approval of the court, and for good cause.

4. *Trial Setting Conference.*

4.1 A date for a trial setting conference may be set at the status conference, by notice from the court administrator's office, or upon motion of any party. A party may also request an accelerated trial date by motion at any time prior to the trial setting conference date.

4.2 Trial setting conferences shall not be continued absent a showing of good cause and upon prior approval of the court.

4.3 At the trial setting conference, the court shall consider compliance with dates and deadlines, the status of mediation, and readiness for trial.

4.4 Cases shall be assigned a secondary and/or primary trial setting to be determined by the court. Where out-of-state witnesses or substantial expert testimony is anticipated, the parties may request that the court dispense with the secondary trial setting.

4.5 The court may set schedules, deadlines and other pretrial dates as appropriate.

5. *Compliance.*

5.1 Counsel for the parties and pro se parties shall appear in person or by telephone at each of the conferences set by the court. Counsel appearing for a party shall preferably be lead counsel for that party. Any counsel appearing for a party shall be prepared with an understanding of the case and authority to enter into agreements as contemplated herein.

5.2 Failure to comply with deadlines, dates, or other requirements set out in these rules, or failure to appear at a conference set by the court, may result in sanctions being imposed, including terms. The court may also strike a trial date if mediation has not been completed by the applicable deadline.

[Adopted June 2, 1989; amended September 1, 1995; amended effective September 1, 1996; September 1, 1997; September 1, 2000; September 1, 2009; September 1, 2010; September 1, 2011.]

APPENDIX A. MASON COUNTY LCR 40 (b) 2.4.4

MASON COUNTY LCR 40 (b) 2.4.4 - APPENDIX A

DO NOT FILE WITH THE COURT

SUPERIOR COURT OF THE STATE OF WASHINGTON
IN AND FOR THE COUNTY OF MASON

_____,	)
	)
Plaintiff(s),	) No. _____
	)
vs.	) CIVIL MEDIATION STATEMENT
	)
_____,	) *[ATTENTION CLERKS*: *This document*
	) *is **not** to be made a part of the*
Defendant(s).	) *court file.]*
	)

Pursuant to LCR 40(b)2.4.4, in all civil actions, all parties shall prepare and deliver a mediation statement to the mediator and opposing parties no later than five working days prior to the mediation. The statement shall address the following matters:

(a) Introduction, summary of case:

(b) Status of discovery:

(c) Undisputed facts:

(d) Disputed facts:

(e)   Legal Issues, including liability, damages or other issues:

(f)   Summary of settlement negotiations, if applicable:

(g)   Conclusion, including assessment of primary factual and legal issues:

(h)   Other:

DATED this _____ day of _____, _____.

_____
Attorney for _____ / Pro Se
Address: _____
         _____
         _____

Copies Provided To:

NAME _____	NAME _____
Attorney for _____ / Pro Se	Attorney for _____ / Pro Se
Address _____	Address _____
_____	_____
_____	_____
NAME _____	NAME _____
Attorney for _____ / Pro Se	Attorney for _____ / Pro Se
Address _____	Address _____
_____	_____
_____	_____

[Amended effective September 1, 1997; September 1, 2009; September 1, 2010; September 1, 2011.]

APPENDIX B. MASON COUNTY LCR 40 (b) 2.4.5

MASON COUNTY LCR 40 (b) 2.4.5 - APPENDIX B

DO NOT FILE WITH THE COURT

SUPERIOR COURT OF THE STATE OF WASHINGTON
IN AND FOR THE COUNTY OF MASON

IN RE   )
)
_____ ,   )
)
                         Petitioner,   ) NO. _____
)
        and   ) FAMILY LAW MEDIATION STATEMENT
)
_____ ,   ) [ATTENTION CLERKS: This document is **not**
) to be made a part of the court file.]
                         Respondent.   )
_____   )

    Pursuant to LCR 40 (b) 2.4.5, in family law actions, all parties shall prepare and deliver a mediation statement to the mediator, opposing party, and to the State of Washington, if the State is a party, no later than five working days prior to the mediation. The statement shall address the following matters if they apply to the case:

1. <u>General Information</u>:

    1.1 Personal Data:

        Name: _____ Date of Birth: _____
        Employer, occupation or former occupation: _____

    1.2 Marriage and Separation Data:

        Date of Marriage _____ Date of Separation _____

    1.3 Children:

        _____ Age _____ DOB _____
        _____ Age _____ DOB _____
        _____ Age _____ DOB _____
        _____ Age _____ DOB _____

2. <u>Issues Remaining in Dispute</u>:
   [Check only those boxes which apply.]

   [ ] Parenting Plan*   [ ] Child Support**
   [ ] Spousal Maintenance   [ ] Attorney Fees

[ ] Division of Property   [ ] Division of Debts
[ ] Division of Retirement/Pension
[ ] Other: _____
             _____
             _____
             _____

  * Provide a copy of any agreed Parenting Plan.
** A copy of any agreed Order of Child Support, worksheets and income
    information shall be provided as forth below in paragraph 14, even
    if the parties have agreed to a child support amount.

3. <u>Community Assets</u>:

4. <u>Separate Assets</u>:

5. <u>Community Debts</u>:

6. <u>Separate Debts</u>:

7. <u>Attorney Fees</u>:

8.   Proposed Parenting Plan:

   8.1 Primary Residential Parent:

   8.2 Alternate Residential Schedule:

   8.3 Basis for Restrictions, if any:

   8.4 Decision-making:

   8.5 Alternative Dispute Resolution:

   8.6 Miscellaneous Requests:

9. Income and Proposed Child Support (including any reasons for deviation from schedule amount):

NOTE: UNLESS OTHERWISE AGREED, THE FOLLOWING WILL BE ASSUMED:
  (1) Each parent shall name the child(ren) as insured on health care insurance available through the parent's employment or union, provided that the cost of the insurance does not exceed 25% of the parent's basic support set out on the support schedule worksheet; and
  (2) Each party shall be responsible for his or her proportionate share (set out on the support schedule worksheet) of the child(ren)'s uninsured health care expenses and verified work-related child care expenses; and
  (3) Child support shall be terminated at age 18 or upon graduation from high school, whichever is later; and
  (4) The Court shall retain jurisdiction to review the issue of post-secondary school support; and
  (5) The support obligation will be paid through the Washington State Support Registry; and
  (6) Child support is due by the last day of each month.

10. Proposed Property and Debt Division:

	Fair Market Value	Debt Owed	Net to Husband	Net to Wife
REAL ESTATE	$	$	$	$
	$	$	$	$
VEHICLES (Year/Make)	$	$	$	$
	$	$	$	$
	$	$	$	$
	$	$	$	$
HOUSEHOLD GOODS	$	$	$	$
TOOLS/EQUIPMENT	$	$	$	$
RECREATIONAL/HOBBY EQUIP.	$	$	$	$
BUSINESS/PROFESSION	$	$	$	$
STOCKS/BONDS	$	$	$	$
LIFE INS. CASH VALUE	$	$	$	$
RETIREMENT/IRAs	$	$	$	$
OTHER ASSETS/RECEIVABLES	$	$	$	$
TOTAL OTHER DEBT	$	$	$	$
TOTALS	$	$	$	$

11. <u>Proposed Spousal Maintenance</u>:

11.1 Reason for Request:

11.2 Proposed Amount and Length of Time Spousal Maintenance should Continue:

12. <u>Proposed Division of Attorney's Fees and Costs</u>:

13. <u>Other</u>:

14. <u>Documents to be attached</u>:

•   <u>Child Support Worksheets</u>. In all cases involving child support issues, completed child support worksheets and proposed child support order.
     Document(s) attached as Exhibit A: _____Yes _____No If no, please explain:

•   <u>Federal Income Tax Returns</u>. Copies of federal income tax returns, with schedules and W-2 forms, for the preceding three (3) tax years.
     Document(s) attached as Exhibit B: _____Yes _____No If no, please explain:

•   <u>Payroll Statements</u>. Copies of payroll statements from employers for the last six months.
     Document(s) attached as Exhibit C: _____Yes _____No If no, please explain:

•   <u>Real Estate</u>. A copy of an appraisal or market analysis for each parcel, and a copy of the most recent statement of balances due on mortgages, real estate purchase contracts, deeds of trust, or other debt secured by the real property.
     Document(s) attached as Exhibit D: _____Yes _____No If no, please explain:

•   <u>Pension Plans and Retirement Accounts</u>. The most recent employer's pension statement, and documentation of contributions since the date of that statement, of any pension plan of either party if pension division by a QDRO is proposed; otherwise, provide a statement of present value of the retirement benefits. The most recent statement of all 401K, deferred compensation or other similar account(s).
     Document(s) attached as Exhibit E: _____Yes _____No If no, please explain:

- <u>Personal Property Appraisals</u>. A written appraisal of any antiques, jewelry, or other items of special, unusual or extraordinary value or a summary of the evidence that will be relied upon.
Document(s) attached as Exhibit F: _____ Yes _____ No If no, please explain:

- <u>Automobile Values</u>. A copy of the most recent N.A.D.A. Official Used Car Guide or other appraisal guide showing both average loan or wholesale and retail values for any automobiles.
Document(s) attached as Exhibit G: _____ Yes _____ No If no, please explain:

- <u>Life Insurance</u>. A statement from each life insurance company issuing a policy of insurance on the life of either party as to its cash value and any loans against the cash value.
Document(s) attached as Exhibit I: _____ Yes _____ No If no, please explain:

- <u>Business Valuation</u>. A written appraisal of any sole proprietorship, partnership, or closely held corporation of either or both the parties, or a summary of the evidence that will be relied upon.
Document(s) attached as Exhibit J: _____ Yes _____ No If no, please explain:

- <u>Separate Property and Debt Tracing</u>. A summary of the source and tracing of any property asserted to be the separate property or obligation asserted to be the separate obligation of either party, and any community interests in separate property, or a summary of the evidence that will be relied upon.
Document(s) attached as Exhibit H: _____ Yes _____ No If no, please explain:

- <u>Debts</u>. A list of debts as of the date of separation, including minimum monthly payments.
Document(s) attached as Exhibit I: _____ Yes _____ No If no, please explain:

DATED this _____ day of _____, _____.

Attorney for _____ / Pro Se
Address: _____
_____
_____

<u>Copies Provided To</u>:

NAME _____
Attorney for _____ / Pro Se
Address _____
_____
_____

NAME _____
Attorney for _____ / Pro Se
Address _____
_____
_____

NAME _____
Attorney for _____ / Pro Se
Address _____
_____

NAME _____
Attorney for _____ / Pro Se
Address _____
_____

[Adopted effective September 1, 2010. Amended effective September 1, 2011.]

LCR 53.2. COURT COMMISSIONERS

(e) Revision by Court.

1. *Time for Motion.* A motion for revision must be filed and served within ten (10) days after the commissioner's written order is entered. The motion for revision shall be noted at the time it is filed, to be heard within thirty (30) days after entry of the commissioner's written order.

2. *Abandonment.* Unless reset by the court, a motion for revision shall be considered abandoned if not heard within thirty (30) days after the entry of the commissioner's written order.

3. *Findings of Fact and Conclusions of Law.*

3.1 Findings of fact and conclusions of law shall be entered before the hearing on the motion for revision.

3.2 A minimum of five (5) days prior to the time of presentation, the party moving for revision shall present to the court commissioner and opposing counsel proposed findings of fact and conclusions of law to support the order or judgment.

4. *Form of Motion.* A motion for revision shall:

4.1 Specify each alleged error; and

4.2 Identify each document in the court file related to the issues raised by the motion for revision.

5. *Hearing on Motion.* At the time a motion for revision is filed, the moving party shall schedule a hearing on a civil calendar by filing a notice of issue. Unless otherwise directed by the Court, the hearing on the motion for revision shall be scheduled to occur within thirty (30) days after the motion for revision is filed.

6. *The Record.*

6.1 The motion for revision shall be heard upon the record that was before the court commissioner.

6.2 In all proceedings for which a audio recording of *live* testimony is made, the party moving for revision shall, within five (5) calendar days after filing the motion, make arrangements through Superior Court Administration for a transcript of the proceedings to be provided to the court. Where a transcript is required, *the party moving for revision shall be responsible for arranging for and payment*

for the transcript and ensuring that the transcript of proceedings is filed with the court not later than five (5) calendar days before the scheduled hearing.

7. *Scope of Motion.* The court may revise any order or judgment that is related to the issues raised by the motion for revision; for example, all issues related to child support or all issues related to the parenting plan. The court will not consider issues that are not related to the motion for revision without a separate motion, except:

7.1 The court may consider requests for attorney's fees by either party for the revision proceedings; and

7.2 The court may consider issues in the original order when the motion for revision is filed as to a motion denying a motion for reconsideration.

8. *Effect of Motion.* When a motion for revision is timely filed the following shall occur:

8.1 With the exception of findings of fact and conclusions of law, until the revision proceeding is completed the court commissioner loses jurisdiction to conduct further proceedings and/or enter orders on issues that are the subject of revision proceeding.

8.2 The Court Commissioner may continue to hear proceedings and/or enter orders on issues that do not involve the subject of the revision proceeding.

8.3 A court commissioner's order shall be effective upon entry of a written order, unless stayed by a judge's order, pending a motion for revision.

[Adopted effective September 1, 2012.]

LCR 59. MOTIONS FOR REVISION OF COURT COMMISSIONER ORDERS [RESCINDED]

[Adopted effective September 1, 2001; amended effective September 1, 2003; September 1, 2004; September 1, 2008; September 1, 2009; rescinded effective September 1, 2012.]

LCR 93.04. [RESCINDED]

[Rescinded effective September 1, 2006.]

LCR 94.04. [REVOKED]

[Revoked effective September 1, 2000.]

LOCAL SUPERIOR COURT MANDATORY ARBITRATION RULES (LMAR)

LMAR 1. SCOPE AND PURPOSE OF RULES

1.1 **Application of Rules.** The purpose of mandatory arbitration of civil actions under RCW 7.06, as implemented by the Mandatory Arbitration Rules, is to provide a simplified and economical procedure for obtaining the prompt and equitable resolution of disputes. The Mandatory Arbitration Rules, as supplemented by these local rules, are not designed to address every question which may arise during the arbitration process, and the rules give considerable discretion to the arbitrator. The arbitrator should not hesitate to be informal and expeditious, consistent with the purpose of the statute and rules.

1.2 Matters Subject to Arbitration. The following matters are subject to mandatory arbitration: (a) civil actions at issue in the Superior Court where the sole relief sought is a money judgment not in excess of $50,000, exclusive of attorney fees, interest, and costs; and (b) claims in which the sole relief sought is the establishment, modification, or termination of maintenance or child support payments which are not capable of resolution on the motion docket or by agreement, regardless of the number or amount of payments.

1.3 Relationship to Superior Court Jurisdiction and Other Rules.

(c) *Motions.* All motions before the court relating to mandatory arbitration shall be noted on the civil motion calendar except as may be otherwise provided in these rules.

[Adopted February 1, 1991; amended effective April 1, 1991; September 1, 2004; September 1, 2012.]

LMAR 2. TRANSFER TO ARBITRATION AND ASSIGNMENT OF ARBITRATOR

2.1 Transfer to Arbitration

(a) *Court Order Required.* Cases shall be transferred to arbitration only by court order.

(b) *Status Conference to Address.* At the status conference provided for by LCR 40, the question of mandatory arbitration shall be addressed.

(c) *Statement of Arbitrability.* If not transferred to arbitration at the status conference, when any party determines that the case is subject to mandatory arbitration, such party shall file and serve a Statement of Arbitrability on the form prescribed by the Court. A duplicate copy shall be provided to the Superior Court Administration Office.

(d) *Response to Statement of Arbitrability.* Any party disagreeing with the Statement of Arbitrability shall, within ten (10) days after the Statement of Arbitrability has been served, file and serve a Response to the Statement of Arbitrability on the form prescribed by the Court. A duplicate copy of the response shall be provided to the Superior Court Administration Office. In the absence of such a response, the Statement of Arbitrability shall be deemed correct and a non-responding party shall be deemed to have stipulated to arbitration if the Statement of Arbitrability provides that the case is subject to mandatory arbitration.

(e) *Failure to File—Amendments.* A party failing to file and serve an original response within the time prescribed may later do so only upon leave of the court. A party may amend the Initial Statement of Arbitrability or response at any time before assignment of an arbitrator or assignment of a trial date, or thereafter only upon leave of the Court for good cause shown.

(f) *By Stipulation.* A case in which all parties file a stipulation to arbitrate under MAR 8.1(b) regardless of the nature of the case or amount in controversy may be transferred to arbitration by court order presented to the Court with the stipulation.

(g) *Interpreter.* In a case transferred to arbitration, if a party: (1) is hearing impaired or has a limited ability to speak or understand the English language, or (2) knows, or after reasonable inquiry has reason to believe, that any other party or any witness is hearing impaired or has limited ability to speak or understand the English language, the party shall advise the Arbitration Supervisor in writing that an interpreter is needed.

2.2 Assignment of Arbitrator [Rescinded]

2.3 Assignment to Arbitrator

(a) *Generally.* When a case is set for arbitration, a list of five proposed arbitrators shall be furnished to the parties. A list of other approved arbitrators shall be furnished upon request. The parties are encouraged to stipulate to an arbitrator. In the absence of the stipulation, the arbitrator shall be chosen from among the five proposed arbitrators in the manner defined by this rule.

(1) Response by Parties. Within fourteen (14) days after the list of the proposed arbitrators is furnished to the parties, each party shall nominate two arbitrators and strike two arbitrators from the list. If both parties respond, an arbitrator nominated by both parties shall be appointed. If no arbitrator has been nominated by both parties, an arbitrator shall be appointed from among those not stricken by either party.

(2) Response by Only One Party. If only one party responds within fourteen (14) days, an arbitrator shall be appointed from that party's response.

(3) No Response. If neither party responds within fourteen (14) days, the arbitrator shall be randomly appointed from the five proposed arbitrators.

(4) Additional Arbitrators for Additional Parties. If there are more than two adverse parties all represented by different counsel, one additional proposed arbitrator shall be added to the list for each additional party so represented with the above principles of selection to be applied. The number of adverse parties shall be determined by the arbitration department, subject to review by the Presiding Judge.

[Adopted February 1, 1991; amended effective April 1, 1991; September 1, 2004; September 1, 2007; September 1, 2012.]

LMAR 3. ARBITRATORS

3.1 Qualifications

(a) *Arbitration Panel.* There shall be a panel of arbitrators in such numbers as the Superior Court Judge may determine. A person desiring to serve as an arbitrator shall complete an information sheet on the form prescribed by the court. A list showing the names of the arbitrators available to hear cases and information sheets will be available for public inspection in the Superior Court Administration Office. The oath of office on the form prescribed by the court must be completed and filed prior to an applicant being placed on the panel.

(b) *Refusal—Disqualification.* The appointment of an arbitrator is subject to the right of that person to refuse to serve. An arbitrator must notify the Arbitration Supervisor immediately if refusing to serve, or if any cause exists for the arbitrator's disqualification from the case on any of the grounds of interest, relationship, bias, or prejudice set forth in the Code of Judicial Conduct governing disqualification of judges. If disqualified, the arbitrator must immediately return all materials in a case to the Arbitration Supervisor.

3.2 Authority of Arbitrator.
In addition to the authority given to arbitrators under MAR 3.2, an arbitrator has authority to require a party or attorney advising such party, or both, to pay the reasonable expenses, including attorney's fees, caused by the failure of such party or attorney, or both, to obey an order of the arbitrator unless the arbitrator finds that the failure was substantially justified, or that other circumstances make an award of expenses unjust. The arbitrator shall make a special award for such expenses and shall file such award with the Clerk of the Court, with proof of service on each party. The aggrieved party shall have ten (10) days thereafter to appeal the award of such expense in accordance with the procedures described in RCW 2.24.050. If within ten (10) days after the award is filed no party appeals, a judgment shall be entered in a manner described under MAR 6.3.

[Amended effective September 1, 2004; September 1, 2012.]

LMAR 4. PROCEDURES AFTER ASSIGNMENT

4.1 Discovery [Rescinded]

4.2 Discovery

(a) *Discovery Pending at the Time Arbitrator is Assigned.* Discovery pending at the time the case is assigned to an arbitrator is stayed pending order from the arbitrator or except as the parties may stipulate or as authorized by MAR 4.2 and LMAR 4.2 below.

(b) *Additional Discovery.* In determining when additional discovery beyond that directly authorized by MAR 4.2 is reasonably necessary, the arbitrator shall balance the benefits of discovery against the burdens and expenses. The arbitrator shall consider the nature and complexity of the case, the amount in controversy, values at stake, the discovery that has already occurred, the burdens on the party from whom discovery is sought, and the possibility of unfair surprise which may result if discovery is restricted. Authorized discovery shall be conducted in accordance with the civil rules except that motions concerning discovery shall be determined by the arbitrator.

(c) *Interrogatories.* Notwithstanding the foregoing, the following interrogatories may be submitted to any party:

(1) State the amount of general damages being claimed;

(2) State each item of special damages being claimed and the amount thereof;

(3) List the name, address and phone number of each person having knowledge of any facts regarding liability, and a short summary of their intended testimony at the arbitration hearing;

(4) List the name, address and phone number of each person having knowledge of any facts regarding the damages claimed, and a short summary of their intended testimony at the arbitration hearing;

(5) List the name, address and phone number of each expert witness you intend to call at the arbitration. For each such expert, state the subject matter on which the expert is expected to testify; state the substance of the facts and opinions to which the expert is expected to testify, and a summary of the grounds for each opinion.

Only these interrogatories, with the exact language as set out above, are permitted, except as permitted by section (a).

[Amended effective September 1, 2004; September 1, 2012.]

LMAR 5. HEARING

5.1 Notice of Hearing.
In addition to the requirements of MAR 5.1, the arbitrator shall give reasonable notice of the hearing date and any continuance to the Arbitration Supervisor.

5.2 Prehearing Statement of Proof.
In addition to the requirements of MAR 5.2, each party shall also furnish the arbitrator with copies of pleadings and other documents contained in the court file which the party deems relevant. The court file shall remain with the Clerk of the Court.

5.3 Conduct of Hearing—Witnesses—Rules of Evidence [Rescinded.]

[Amended effective September 1, 2004; September 1, 2012.]

LMAR 6. AWARD

6.1 Form and Content of Award

(a) *Form.* The award shall be prepared on the form prescribed by the Court.

(b) *Return of Exhibits.* When an award is filed, the arbitrator shall return all exhibits to the parties who offered them during the hearing.

6.2   Return of Exhibits [Rescinded]

6.3   Filing of an Award [Rescinded]

6.4   Judgment of Award [Rescinded]

[Amended effective September 1, 2004; September 1, 2012.]

LMAR 7.   TRIAL DE NOVO

7.1   Request for Trial De Novo

(a) *Service and Filing.* In addition to the provision for service and filing in MAR 7.1, a copy of the Request for Trial de Novo shall be provided to the Arbitration Supervisor.

(b) *Form.* [Reserved.]

(c) *Proof of Service.* [Reserved.]

(d) *Calendar.* When a trial de novo is requested as provided in MAR 7. 1, a status conference shall be set by the court administrator in accordance with LCR 40.

[Amended effective September 1, 2004; September 1, 2012.]

LMAR 8.   GENERAL PROVISIONS

8.1   Stipulations

(c) *To Arbitrate Other Cases—Effect on Relief Granted.* If a case not otherwise subject to mandatory arbitration is transferred to arbitration by stipulation, the arbitrator may grant any relief which could have been granted if the case were determined by a judge.

8.2   Title and Citation [Rescinded]

8.3   Compensation of Arbitrator [Rescinded]

8.4   Title and Citation. These rules are known and cited as the Mason County Superior Court Mandatory Arbitration Rules. LMAR is the official abbreviation.

8.6   Compensation of Arbitrator

(a) *Generally.* Arbitrators shall be compensated in the same amount and manner as judges pro tempore of the Superior Court; provided, however, the portion of the compensation from the Superior Court shall not exceed $1,000.00 for any case without approval of the presiding judge.

(b) *Form.* When the award is filed, the arbitrator shall submit to the Court Administrator a request for payment on a form prescribed by the Washington State Administrative Office of the Courts. The presiding judge shall determine the amount of compensation to be paid.

[Amended effective September 1, 2004; September 1, 2012.]

[EXHIBITS]
EXHIBIT A. ARBITRATION AWARD [RESCINDED]

[Amended effective September 1, 2004; rescinded effective September 1, 2012.]

EXHIBIT B. REQUEST FOR TRIAL DE NOVO AND FOR CLERK TO SEAL THE AWARD [RESCINDED]

[Amended effective September 1, 2004; rescinded effective September 1, 2012.]

LOCAL SUPERIOR COURT CRIMINAL RULES

LCrR 3.1. RIGHT TO AND ASSIGNMENT OF COUNSEL

(d) Assignment of Lawyer.

(4) Certificates of Compliance with the Standards for Indigent Defense required by CrR 3.1 shall be filed quarterly with the Mason County Clerk. All Notice of Appearance forms filed by counsel for indigent defendants shall indicate in a separate paragraph whether or not a current CrR 3.1 Certificate of Compliance with the Standards for Indigent Defense is on file with the Mason County Clerk.

[Adopted effective September 2, 2013.]

LCrR 3.4. PRESENCE OF THE DEFENDANT

(d) Video Conference Proceedings.

(2) *Agreement.* In criminal matters, proceedings may be conducted by video conference as authorized by CrR 3.4(d)(1). Other criminal proceedings may be conducted by video conference by agreement of the parties in writing or on the record, and upon approval of the judge.

[Adopted effective September 2, 2014.]

LCrR 4.2. SUPERIOR COURT COMMISSIONERS—AUTHORITY—CRIMINAL CASES

The Judges of Mason County Superior Court hereby adopt the provisions of RCW 2.24.040, as amended, and specifically authorize Mason County Superior Court Commissioners, appointed under Article 4, Section 23 of the constitution of the State of Washington, to accept and enter pleas of guilty by adult criminal defendants in accordance with CrR 4.2.

[Adopted effective September 1, 2000.]

LOCAL RULES OF APPELLATE PROCEDURE

LRAP 9.2(a). VERBATIM REPORT OF PROCEEDINGS/DESIGNATION OF COURT–APPROVED TRANSCRIBERS

Audio systems are used by Mason County Superior Court to record all proceedings. The Judges of Mason County Superior Court hereby adopt RAP 9.2(a), as amended, as a local court rule to require that only a court-approved transcriber is authorized to prepare transcripts from audio-recorded proceedings.

1. Primary Court–Approved Transcribers: Primary court-approved transcribers are employees of Mason County Superior Court. The following has been adopted concerning designation of primary court-approved transcribers:

(a) Primary court-approved transcribers are subject to qualifications set out in job descriptions adopted by Mason County.

(b) Transcripts prepared by employees of Mason County Superior Court during regular business hours will be billed either to the party or the appellate court (if the transcript is being prepared under an Order of Indigency) and the county retains the income.

(c) Primary court-approved transcribers must charge rates that are no more than the prevailing rates charged in the county. For a criminal indigent appeal, primary court-approved transcribers will receive the same rate as other transcribers and court reporters and that rate is set by the Supreme Court.

(d) Superior Court is responsible for assigning backup court-approved transcribers to assist with preparation of transcripts when required.

2. Backup Court–Approved Transcribers: Backup court-approved transcribers are required from time-to-time to assist the primary court-approved transcribers with preparation of transcripts. The following procedures have been adopted for selecting backup court-approved transcribers:

(a) Application forms will be available for all applicants interested in being designated as backup court-approved transcribers. The purpose of the application is to screen interested persons to ensure that only those with appropriate experience receive the court-approved designation. Applications will be evaluated to determine which applicants can be designated. At a minimum, all applicants must have experience in typing legal documents and in transcribing material.

(b) Applications should ask applicants what their fees are for ordinary and expedited transcription. The court is responsible for determining if these rates are within the standard range charged in the county for similar work. A backup court-approved transcriber must charge rates that are no more than the prevailing rates charged in the county. For a criminal indigent appeal, the backup court-approved transcriber will receive the same rate as other transcribers and court reporters and that rate is set by the Supreme Court.

(c) Transcripts prepared by backup court-approved transcribers will be billed either to the party or the appellate court (if the transcript is being prepared under an Order of Indigency) and that individual will retain the income.

(d) On a yearly basis, backup court-approved transcribers will be required to submit a completed transcript for verification by a primary court-approved transcriber.

3. Compliance with Rules of Appellate Procedure: All primary and backup court-approved transcribers must agree to comply with all Rules of Appellate Procedure which include, but are not limited to, the following: RAP 9.2, RAP 9.5(a), RAP 9.5(b), and RAP 15.4.

[Adopted effective September 1, 1995. Amended effective September 1, 2004.]

LOCAL JUVENILE COURT RULES

LJuCR 7.1. DISMISSAL FOR DELAY IN FILING INFORMATION [RESCINDED]

[Adopted effective March 3, 1989. Rescinded effective September 2, 2013.]

LJuCR 9.2. ADDITIONAL RIGHT TO REPRESENTATION BY LAWYER

(d) **Juvenile Offense Proceedings.**

(1) Certificates of Compliance with the Standards for Indigent Defense required by JuCR 9.2 shall be filed quarterly with the Mason County Clerk. All Notice of Appearance forms filed by counsel for indigent defendants shall indicate in a separate paragraph whether or not a current JuCR 9.2 Certificate of Compliance with the Standards for Indigent Defense is on file with the Mason County Clerk.

[Adopted effective September 2, 2013.]

LOCAL RULES FOR APPEAL OF DECISIONS OF COURTS OF LIMITED JURISDICTION

LRALJ 6.3A(c). CONTENT OF TRANSCRIPT OF ELECTRONIC RECORD

(c) **Content of Transcript.** The transcript shall contain only those portions of the electronic recording necessary to present the issues raised on appeal. In a transcript provided at public expense, approval by the Court shall be obtained prior to requesting transcription of jury voir dire, opening and/or closing state-ments, and reading of the jury instructions. If the appellant intends to urge that a verdict or finding of fact is not supported by the evidence, the appellant shall include in the transcript all testimony relevant to the disputed verdict or finding. If the appellant intends to urge that the court erred in giving or failing to give an instruction, the appellant shall include all objections to the instructions given and refused and the court's ruling.

[Adopted effective September 1, 1999.]

LOCAL GUARDIAN AD LITEM RULES

LGAL 5. SPECIFIC GUARDIAN AD LITEM REGISTRY REQUIREMENTS

1. Title 11—Guardianship Registry

1.1 All registry applicants must meet the qualifications set forth by statute and all requirements for training and certification established by statute and/or court rule to be considered for placement and retention on the Title 11 registry.

1.2 In addition to any qualifications required by statute, the following are specific education and experience requirements for inclusion on the Title 11 registry:

(a) *Attorneys.* Members of the Washington State Bar Association in good standing with a minimum of one year of practice of law with some experience in the needs of impaired elderly people, physical disabilities, mental illness, developmental disabilities and/or other areas relevant to the needs of incapacitated persons.

(b) *Non-Attorneys.* Four years experience in the needs of impaired elderly people, physical disabilities, mental illness, developmental disabilities and/or other areas relevant to the needs of incapacitated persons documented in the applicant's Statement of Qualifications.

2. Title 26—Family Law Registry

2.1 All registry applicants must meet the qualifications set forth by statute and all requirements for training and certification established by statute and/or court rule to be considered for placement and retention on the Title 26 registry.

2.2 In addition to any qualifications required by statute, the following are specific education and experience requirements for inclusion on the Title 26 registry:

(a) *Attorneys.* Members of the Washington State Bar Association in good standing with a minimum of one year of practice of law, including family law cases, and at least eight hours of family law CLE in the preceding twenty-four months.

(c)[1] *Non-Attorneys.*

(1) A minimum of a B.A. degree with four years field experience working with children and families;

(2) A Masters degree with two years of field experience working with children and families; or

(3) Licensed psychologist or psychiatrist with preference given to those who specialize, or have developed expertise, in working with children and families.

3. Retention On Registry

3.1 Each person requesting to remain on any Guardian ad Litem registry shall annually submit an updated background information report to the Court Administrator's Office. The background information report shall include, but not be limited to, the following:

(a) Level of formal education;

(b) Training related to the guardian's duties;

(c) Number of years' experience as a guardian ad litem;

(d) Number of appointments as a guardian ad litem and county or counties of appointment;

(e) The names of any counties in which the person was removed from a guardian ad litem registry pursuant to a grievance action, and the name of the court and the cause number of any case in which the court has removed the person for cause; and

(f) Criminal history, as defined in RCW 9.94A.030.

[Adopted effective September 1, 2004.]

1 Lettering as provided in original.

LGAL 7. GUARDIAN AD LITEM GRIEVANCE AND COMPLAINT PROCEDURE

(a) Guardian ad Litem Committee. A Mason County Guardian ad Litem Committee (the Committee) is created to address grievances concerning conduct by guardians ad litem involved in Title 11 and 26 RCW cases. The Committee shall consist of three members: a representative of the Mason County Superior Court, selected by the Court Administrator and approved by the Presiding Judge; an active guardian ad litem, selected by the Court Administrator and approved by the Presiding Judge; and a member of the Mason County Bar Association, selected and approved by the Association. The guardian ad litem member shall be a member of the Mason County Guardian Ad Litem Registry who has not received any sanctions in the past three years. Service on the Committee is a voluntary service for the good of the community.

(b) Submitting a Grievance.

(1) *Grievance in Ongoing Case.*

(A) Format. In an ongoing case, a grievance concerning conduct by a guardian ad litem is hereinafter referred to as a "Complaint." It shall be brought before the Court as a written motion filed by a party to the case or his or her attorney and must be properly served and noted for hearing in compliance with court rules.

(B) Response by Guardian ad Litem. The guardian ad litem may respond as provided by court rules governing motion practice.

(C) Court's Decision. If the Court determines that the Complaint has merit, the Court may remove the guardian ad litem or require other action in the case. The Court may also refer the Complaint to the Court Administrator to be forwarded to the Committee in the form of a "Grievance."

(2) *Grievance After Conclusion of Case.* After the conclusion of a case, a grievance concerning conduct by a guardian ad litem is hereinafter referred to as a "Grievance." It shall be submitted in writing within 12 months after the conclusion of the case and signed by at least one individual with their address and telephone number. It shall be based upon personal knowledge and shall explain in clear and concise language the grounds for the grievance. Supplemental materials may be attached. It shall be submitted to

the Superior Court Administrator at 419 N 4th Street, P.O. Box X, Shelton, WA 98584.

(3) *Action Upon Receipt of Grievance.* Upon receipt, the Court Administrator shall forward the Grievance and any supplemental materials to the Committee and to the guardian ad litem named in the Grievance.

(c) Action by Guardian Ad Litem Committee.

(1) *Review Procedure.* The following rules apply once a Grievance is forwarded to the Committee.

(A) Response to Grievance in Ongoing Case. For a Grievance in an ongoing case pursuant to (b)(1)(C), the Committee will consider any motion materials submitted to the Court by the guardian ad litem pursuant to (b)(1)(B). The guardian ad litem may submit additional responsive materials in writing within 10 days from the date the Grievance is forwarded by the Court Administrator.

(B) Response to Grievance After Conclusion of Case. For a Grievance after the conclusion of a case pursuant to (b)(2), the guardian ad litem shall respond in writing within 30 days from the date the Grievance is forwarded by the Court Administrator. Supplemental materials may be attached.

(C) Action Pending Resolution. The Committee may recommend to the Presiding Judge that a guardian ad litem's further participation on the registry be suspended pending resolution of the Grievance. The guardian ad litem shall be notified of any such recommendation and may respond in writing within 72 hours.

(D) Materials to Consider. The Committee shall consider written materials only, including the court file. No oral testimony or argument shall be allowed. If the Committee finds the Grievance has merit, the Committee may then consider prior Grievances which resulted in sanction.

(E) Time for Decision on Grievance in Ongoing Case. For Grievances pertaining to an ongoing case under section (b)(1)(C), the Committee shall issue a decision no later than 25 days from the date the Grievance is forwarded by the Court Administrator.

(F) Time for Decision on Grievance After Conclusion of Case. For Grievances after the conclusion of the case under section (b)(2), the Committee shall issue a decision no later than 60 days from the date the Grievance is forwarded by the Court Administrator.

(2) *Decision.*

(A) Basis. In determining whether the Grievance has merit, the Committee shall consider whether the guardian ad litem:

(i) Violated the guardian ad litem Code of Conduct;

(ii) Misrepresented his or her qualifications to serve as a guardian ad litem;

(iii) Failed to meet the annual training requirements set forth in the Registry requirements;

(iv) Breached the confidentiality of the parties;

(v) Falsified information in a report to the Court or in testimony before the Court;

(vi) Failed, when required, to report abuse of a child;

(vii) Communicated with a judicial officer ex parte concerning the case for which he or she is serving as a guardian ad litem, except as allowed (such as an emergency restraining order);

(viii) Violated state or local laws or rules in the person's capacity as a guardian ad litem;

(ix) Took or failed to take any other action which would reasonably place the suitability of the person to serve as guardian ad litem in question.

(B) Resolution by Committee. If the Committee determines the Grievance has merit, the Committee shall have the authority to issue a written admonishment or reprimand, impose additional reasonable requirements for continued service as a guardian ad litem, and/or require the guardian ad litem to take corrective action to remedy or mitigate matters. The Committee may also recommend to the Presiding Judge that the guardian ad litem be suspended or removed from the Court Registry.

(C) Notice of Decision. The guardian ad litem and any complaining party shall be notified of the decision on the Grievance. A copy of the decision of the Committee shall be placed in the guardian ad litem file maintained by the Superior Court Administrator.

(d) Review and Reconsideration of Decision.

(1) *Time for Request.* The guardian ad litem may seek review or reconsideration of a sanction by making a written request to the Court Administrator within 15 days of the date of decision.

(2) *Review of Request.* The Court Administrator shall forward the request and any supporting documents to the Presiding Judge. The Presiding Judge shall present the matter to the Superior Court judges to review and issue a final decision within 10 days. Prior Grievances which resulted in an admonishment, reprimand, referral to training, removal of the guardian ad litem from a particular case, or suspension or removal from a registry shall be taken into consideration.

(e) Removal from Registry. If the guardian ad litem is listed on more than one registry, at the discretion of the Presiding Judge, the suspension or removal may apply to each registry on which the guardian ad litem is listed. The Court Administrator shall notify the Administrative Office of the Courts of

the name of any guardian ad litem removed from the registry after such removal becomes final.

(f) Confidentiality. A Grievance shall be confidential for all purposes unless the Committee has determined that it has merit. Any record of Griev-

ances which are not found by the Committee to have merit shall be confidential and shall not be disclosed except by court order.

[Adopted effective September 1, 2001; amended effective September 1, 2003; September 2, 2014.]

LOCAL SPECIAL PROCEEDINGS RULES

LSPR 94.04. FAMILY LAW, PROBATE, GUARDIANSHIP AND ADOPTION CASES

1. Family Law, Probate, Guardianship and Adoption Motion Calendars, Confirmation Procedures and Time Limits.

1.1 *Motion Calendars.* There shall be the following motion calendars held according to the published schedule available at the courthouse or through the Mason County Superior Court Administrator's Office at http://www.co.mason.wa.us/superior_court:

- Adoption

- Probate and Guardianship

- Family Law (where at least one party is represented by an attorney at the time a matter is noted for hearing)

- Pro Se Family Law (where no party is represented by an attorney at the time a matter is noted for hearing)

- Ex Parte

The schedule for the above calendars may change. Parties and counsel are advised to review the current calendar schedules before noting matters for hearings. Incorrectly scheduled matters may be stricken.

1.2 *Confirmation Procedures.* For a contested matter to be heard by the court, the hearing must be confirmed as set forth below. This includes hearings scheduled by notice of issue, court order and hearings which are administratively continued.

    (a) Confirmation must be made by calling the Clerk of the Court at (360) 427–9670, Ext. 346, or by e-mail at superiorcourt-confirm@co.mason.wa.us, no later than 10:00 a.m. two (2) court days prior to the motion (examples: for a motion on Wednesday, confirmation must be by 10:00 a.m. on Monday; or for a motion on Friday, confirmation must be by 10:00 a.m. on Wednesday).

    (b) If the deadline for confirmation falls on a court holiday, confirmation shall be made before 10:00 a.m. on the last court day before the holiday.

    (c) Motions filed by those persons physically confined under a court order shall be deemed confirmed at filing.

    (d) Matters not confirmed may be heard at the end of the calendar only at the discretion of the Court and upon agreement of all parties.

1.3 *Continuance of Confirmed Matters.* Matters confirmed in accordance with paragraph 1.2 are not subject to continuance, except with permission of the Court. If not heard, these matters shall be *stricken* and may be re-noted by the moving party.

1.4 *Time Limits.* Arguments on motions shall be limited to ten (10) minutes per side. Arguments which will exceed the time limit of this rule, if allowed by the Court, will ordinarily be placed at the end of the docket.

2. Pleadings, Motions and Other Papers.

2.1 *Format.* All pleadings, motions and supporting documents shall use mandatory forms where applicable, follow the format required by GR 14 and meet the requirements of GR 31(e). If typed or computer printed, documents shall be in 12 point or larger type, single-sided and double-spaced. If handwritten, documents shall be single-sided, double-spaced and written legibly using black or dark blue ink. Illegible documents will not be considered.

3. Children's Statements.

3.1 *Children's Statements.* Declarations by minors in family law matters are disfavored and the Court may, in its discretion, refuse to consider such declarations.

4. Page Limitations on Declarations.

4.1 *Generally.* Absent prior authorization from the Court as set forth in paragraph 4.7 below:

    (a) The entirety of all declarations and affidavits in support of motions, including any reply, shall be limited to a total of twenty-five (25) pages for all motions scheduled on the same date in a single case.

    (b) The entirety of all declarations and affidavits submitted in response to motions shall be limited to a total of twenty-five (25) pages for all motions scheduled on the same date in a single case.

4.2 *Applicable Cases.* This rule shall apply to all family law motions.

4.3 *Exhibits.* Exhibits that consist of declarations or affidavits shall count toward the above page limits. All other exhibits attached to a declaration or affidavit, including deposition excerpts, shall not be counted towards the page limit.

4.4 *Financial Declarations.* Financial declarations and financial documents do not count toward the page limit.

4.5 *Expert Reports and Evaluations.* Declarations, affidavits or reports from guardians ad litem and expert witnesses do not count toward the page limit.

4.6 *Miscellaneous Exceptions.* Copies of declarations or affidavits previously filed for a motion already ruled upon and supplied only as a convenience to the Court in lieu of the court file do not count toward the page limit.

4.7 *Authorization.* A party seeking authorization to exceed the page limit may do so by noting a motion to exceed the page limit on the family law calendar. Parties may appear in person or by telephone; provided, however, that authorization to appear by telephone must be made in advance by calling the Court Administrator's Office at (360) 427–9670, Ext. 348. Notice of this hearing shall be given in the same manner as provided in CR 5.

4.8 *Consequences of Non–Compliance.* If the Court finds that one or more parties have violated this rule, the Court may, in its discretion, assess terms, strike or continue the matter, or refuse to consider materials that violate this rule.

5. Parenting Seminars.

5.1 *Applicable Cases.* This rule shall apply to all cases which require a custody decree, parenting plan or residential schedule for minor children.

5.2 *Mandatory Attendance.* All parties involved in cases governed by this rule shall complete an approved parenting seminar, except parties who have previously attended such a parenting seminar within the last two years. In the case of paternity actions initiated by the prosecuting attorney's office, the parenting seminar shall be required only when paternity is established or acknowledged and a parenting plan is requested.

5.3 *Seminar Providers.* A list of approved parenting seminars shall be available from the Superior Court Administrator, Family Law Facilitator and Clerk of the Court. If a parenting seminar is not included on the list, then the Court, upon proper motion, may allow other seminars to fulfill this requirement on a case-by-case basis.

5.4 *Timing.* Parties required by this rule to participate in a parenting seminar shall complete an approved parenting seminar within ninety (90) days after service of a petition.

5.5 *Proof of Completion.* Parties shall file a certificate of completion or other documentation showing proof of completion of the parenting seminar as soon as possible after completion.

5.6 *Fees.* Each party attending a seminar shall pay a fee charged by the approved provider.

5.7 *Special Consideration/Waivers.* Pursuant to RCW 26.12.172:

(a) Opposing parties shall not be required to attend seminars together.

(b) Upon a showing of domestic violence or abuse which would not require mutual decision making pursuant to RCW 26.09.191, or that a parent's attendance at the seminar is not in the children's best interests, the court shall either:

(i) Waive the requirement of completion of the seminar; or

(ii) Accept an alternative, voluntary parenting seminar.

(c) The Court may otherwise waive the seminar requirement or extend the time for attendance of the seminar for good cause shown.

5.8 *Failure to Attend/Sanctions.* Willful refusal to participate in a parenting seminar or willful delay in completing the parenting seminar by any party may constitute contempt of court and may result in sanctions including, but not limited to, imposition of monetary terms, striking of pleadings, or denial of affirmative relief to a party not in compliance with this rule.

[Adopted effective September 1, 2006. Amended effective September 1, 2010; September 1, 2012; September 2, 2013; September 2, 2014; September 1, 2015.]

DISTRICT COURT

MASON COUNTY DISTRICT
LOCAL COURT RULES

Including Amendments Received Through
August 15, 2015

Table of Rules

LOCAL DISTRICT COURT GENERAL RULES

LGRLJ 14(4).   AUDIO/VISUAL EXHIBITS

Audio/Visual Exhibits. When testimony or evidence is to be given via video tape or motion pictures, it is the responsibility of the party introducing the testimony or evidence to provide the proper equipment for viewing such testimony or evidence, or to provide the court the testimony or evidence in CD or DVD format.

[Adopted effective September 1, 2015.]

LGRLJ 14(5).   SMALL CLAIMS AND NAME CHANGE FORMAT REQUIREMENTS

All Small Claims and Name Change pleadings must conform to the Mason County District Court forms.

Prescribed forms are available at the Mason County District Court office located at—419 N. 4th St, Shelton, WA. 98584 or on the courts website: www.co.mason.wa.us/district_court. Any pleadings not meeting such requirements may be rejected for filing and returned, then resubmitted after compliance with this rule.

[Adopted effective September 1, 2015.]

LOCAL DISTRICT COURT ADMINISTRATIVE RULES

LARLJ 0.4.   RE: E–MAIL COMMUNICATION

Purpose: The purpose of this rule is to provide guidelines for the use of e-mail in communicating with Mason County District Court staff. This rule does not apply to the other forms of communication, and does not establish a preference for e-mail communication over any other form of communication.

Use of Judge's Individual Address Prohibited: The only address to be used by attorneys, pro se self-represented litigants or others who need to communicate with court staff about a case is the District Courts general e-mail address—DistrictCourt@co. mason.wa.us, unless otherwise directed by the judge and/or court clerk to e-mail to a specific e-mail address. Absent express invitation by the judge, the judge's individual e-mail address is not to be used.

Guidelines for Use of E–mail: E-mail communication with the District Court is appropriate in the following typical situations:

To obtain a date for an in-court hearing;

To submit proposed orders;

To determine the judge's availability for a settlement conference;

To determine the availability of equipment needed for trial (such as a video player or speaker phone);

To determine the judge's preference as to number of copies of jury instructions required for trial;

To advise the court of a settlement (to be immediately followed by formal written notice pursuant to CR 41(e);

To determine whether the judge will accept pleadings, jury instructions, legal memoranda, and other matters of a similar nature that would be appropriate to handle by way of a phone call to court staff.

Ex Parte Communication Prohibited: The prohibitions regarding ex parte contact with the court are fully applicable to e-mail communication. If an attorney/party is communicating substantive information to court staff, the e-mail must also be sent to opposing counsel/party and so indicate on its face. Substantive information includes information regarding the likelihood of settlement, the timing of witnesses, anticipat-

ed problems with scheduling, concerns regarding security and other case-specific issues.

Service of Working Copies and Pleadings: Absent prior permission of the court, e-mail may not be used to provide working copies of legal pleadings, including jury instructions. Absent agreement of counsel/opposing party or express permission of the court, e-mail may not be used for service of pleadings on opposing parties, even in those situations where the court has agreed to accept working copies by e-mail.

Retention of E–mail: The court is not obligated to retain any electronic communications. Original documentation shall be filed with the Mason County District Court.

[Adopted effective September 1, 2015.]

LARLJ 5.   COURTROOM DECORUM[1]

All attorneys, litigants, witnesses, and other individuals in the courtroom shall abide by the following rules of conduct:

(a) Always Be Prompt. Be in the courtroom ready to proceed at the appointed time.

(b) Stand when the judge or the jury enters or leaves the courtroom.

(c) Do not make personal attacks on opposing counsel or parties.

(d) Do Not Interrupt. Wait your turn. Address all remarks to the Court. Argument between litigants or their attorneys is not permitted.

(e) After the court has ruled, ask the court's permission before arguing further.

(f) Rise when addressing the Court and when making objections as this calls the Court's attention to you.

(g) Do not approach a witness or the jury without asking permission of the Court.

(h) Dress appropriately to the serious nature of the matters before the court. Shorts and other kinds of beach apparel are not appropriate. Clothing advertising alcoholic beverages or illegal drugs are not appropriate. Hats are not to be worn in the courtroom unless required by religious custom and practice.

[Adopted effective September 1, 2015.]

[1] Publisher's Note: This rule has been designated as "Proposed".

LOCAL DISTRICT COURT INFRACTION RULES

LIRLJ 2.4.   RESPONSE TO NOTICE OF INFRACTION

(a) Generally. A person who has been served with a notice of infraction must respond to the notice within

15 days of the date the notice is personally served or, if the notice is served by mail, within 18 days of the date the notice is mailed.

(b) Alternatives. A person may respond to a notice of infraction by:

(1) Paying the amount of the monetary penalty in accordance with applicable law, in which case the court shall enter a judgment that the defendant has committed the infraction;

(2) Contesting the determination that an infraction occurred by requesting a hearing in accordance with applicable law;

(3) Requesting a hearing to explain mitigating circumstances surrounding the commission of the infraction in accordance with applicable law; or

(4) Submitting a written statement either contesting the infraction or explaining mitigating circumstances. The statement shall contain the person's promise to pay the monetary penalty authorized by law if the infraction is found to be committed.

For contested hearing, the statement shall be executed in substantially the following form:

I hereby state as follows:

I promise that if it is determined that I committed the infraction for which

I was cited, I will pay the monetary penalty authorized by law and assessed by the court. I certify (or declare) under penalty of perjury under the laws of the State of Washington that the foregoing is true and correct.

_____ _____
(Date and Place)   (Signature)

I understand that if this form is submitted by e-mail, my typed name on the signature line will qualify as my signature for purposes of the above certification.

For mitigation hearings, the statement shall be executed in substantially the following form:

I hereby state as follows:

I promise to pay the monetary penalty authorized by law or, at the discretion of the court, any reduced penalty that may be set.

I certify (or declare) under penalty of perjury under the laws of the State of Washington that the foregoing is true and correct.

_____ _____
(Date and Place)   (Signature)

I understand that if this form is submitted by e-mail, my typed name on the signature line will qualify as my signature for purposes of the above certification.

(c) Method of Response. A person may respond to a notice of infraction either personally, by mail or by e-mail DistrictCourt@co.mason.wa.us. If the response is mailed or emailed it must be postmarked or e-mailed not later than midnight of the day the response is due.

{see form LIRLJ 2.4, LIRLJ 3.5}

[Adopted effective September 1, 2015.]

LIRLJ 2.6.   INFRACTION HEARINGS[1]

(c) Decisions on Written Statements. Mitigation hearings shall generally be held in open court. The procedure set forth in IRLJ 3.5, allowing decisions on written statements is authorized.

[Adopted effective September 1, 2015.]

1 Publisher's Note: This rule has been designated as "Proposed".

LIRLJ 3.1.   CONTESTED HEARINGS— COSTS AND WITNESS FEES

Costs and Witness Fees. Each party is responsible for costs incurred by that party as set forth in RCW 46.63.151. In cases where a party requests a witness to be subpoenaed, the party requesting the witness shall pay the witness fees and mileage expenses due that witness.

[Adopted effective September 1, 2015.]

LIRLJ 3.2.   PERSONAL APPEARANCE REQUIRED

The defendant must appear in person for contested hearings scheduled unless the contested hearing is held upon written statements per LIRLJ 3.5. The court recognizes that IRLJ 3.4 allows the defendant to be represented by a lawyer, however, this will not waive the requirement that the defendant must appear in person.

[Adopted effective September 1, 2015.]

LIRLJ 3.2(b).   MOTION FOR VACATION OF DEFAULT JUDGMENT FOR FTA[1]

A defendant, against whom a judgment for a traffic infraction has been entered by default for failure to appear, may file a motion in writing, requesting that said default judgment be set aside. The motion will then be set for hearing. Defendant must be present unless the judge authorizes otherwise. The motion will be evaluated in conformity with CRLJ 60(b). If the Court grants said motion, the matter will be set for a hearing of the kind requested by the defendant (Refer to LIRLJ 2.6). Mitigation hearings may be heard at the time of the motion if the calendar allows.

A defendant requesting the court to vacate a Default Judgment for FTA shall do so by filing a motion in substantially the following form:

{see form LIRJ 3.2 (b)}

[Adopted effective September 1, 2015.]

1 Publisher's Note: This rule has been designated as "Proposed".

LIRLJ 3.2(b) FORM. MOTION/ORDER TO VACATE DEFAULT JUDGMENT ON FINDING OF COMMISSION OF INFRACTION

MASON COUNTY DISTRICT COURT

STATE OF WASHINGTON,

                Plaintiff

Vs.

_____,
                Defendant

Cause No. _____

**Motion/Order to Vacate Default Judgment
On Finding of Commission of Infraction**

I move the Court to vacate the default judgment entered on _____

Pursuant to IRLJ 6.7 and CRLJ 60(b) for the following reason(s):

_____

_____

_____

If the Judge grants my motion to vacate, I would request the following hearing:

[   ] Mitigation hearing   [   ] Contested hearing.
Note: The hearing will be in-person unless you choose to submit in writing per LIRLJ 3.5.

I certify (or declare) under penalty of perjury under the Laws of the State of Washington that the foregoing is true and correct.

Date: _____   _____
                                        Defendant's Signature

Your current mailing address: _____

                            City   State   Zip

**If mailing form, return to: Mason County District Court, PO Box "O", Shelton, WA. 98584

Upon receipt of this completed form, a Judge will review the Motion to Vacate and you will be notified of the decision by mail per LIRLJ 3.5. If you requested a hearing and it is granted, you will be notified in writing of the date and time of the hearing at the address you provide on this form.

(Do not write in this section – Judge/Commission will complete this section at the time of your hearing)

RULING

☐   Motion Denied

☐   Motion Granted/Judgement Vacated
      ☐ Set for Mitigation Hearing
      ☐ Set for Contested Hearing
      ☐ Other:

                                   _____

DATED: _____   _____
                                        Judge/Court Commissioner/Pro-tem

LIRLJ 3.2 (b) – Motion/Order to vacate Default Judgment 9/2015

[Adopted effective September 1, 2015.]

LIRLJ 3.5. DECISION ON WRITTEN STATEMENTS

Mitigation and contested hearings on alleged traffic infractions may be held upon written statements and email statements pursuant to IRLJ 2.4 (4) IRLJ 2.6 (c) and IRLJ 3.5.

(a) Contested Hearings. The court shall examine the citing officer's report and any statement submitted by the defendant. The examination shall take place within 120 days after the defendant filed the response to the notice of infraction. The examination may be held in chambers and shall not be governed by the Rules of Evidence.

(1) *Factual Determination.* The court shall determine whether the plaintiff has proved by a preponderance of all evidence submitted that the defendant has committed the infraction.

(2) *Disposition.* If the court determines that the infraction has been committed, it may assess a penalty in accordance with rule 3.3.

(3) *Notice to Parties.* The court shall notify the parties in writing whether an Infraction was found to have been committed and what penalty, if any, was imposed.

(4) *No Appeal Permitted.* There shall be no appeal from a decision on written statements.

(b) Mitigation Hearings. Mitigation hearings based upon written statements may be held in chambers.

(c) The procedure set forth in IRLJ 3.5, allowing decisions on written statements or e-mail sent to MasonDistrict@co.mason.wa.us is authorized.

A defendant requesting the court to decide the case on written statements shall do so by completing a statement in substantially the following form:

{See form LIRLJ 2.4, LIRLJ 3.5 Form}

[Adopted effective September 1, 2015.]

LIRLJ 3.5 FORM. DEFENDANT'S REQUEST FOR DECISION ON WRITTEN STATEMENTS

MASON COUNTY DISTRICT COURT
STATE OF WASHINGTON

State of Washington,
        Plaintiff

Infraction Number: _____

Defendant's Request for Decision
On Written Statements

VS.

[ ]   Contested Hearing
[ ]   Mitigation Hearing

_____
     Defendant

TO: Mason County District Court
Infraction Number: _____

I hereby request that the Court decide my case based upon the following statement:

_____
_____
_____
_____
_____
_____
_____
_____
_____

(Attach Additional Page(s) if necessary).

- I have read and agree to abide by the rules and procedures governing hearings by mail.
- I understand that Infraction Rules for Courts of Limited Jurisdiction 3.5(e) provides "There shall be no appeal from a decision on written statements".
- I promise that if it is determined that I committed the infraction for which I was cited, I will pay the monetary penalty authorized by law and assessed by the Court.
- I understand that if this form is submitted by e-mail, my typed name on the signature line will qualify as my signature for purposed of the above certification.

I certify (or declare) under penalty of perjury under the laws of the State of Washington that the foregoing statement is true and correct.

Date and Place (City) _____

Defendant's Signature: _____

_____
Current Mailing Address

Phone #: _____

Defendant's request for Decision on Written Statement LIRLJ 2.4, LIRLJ 3.5 Form

[Adopted effective September 1, 2015.]

LOCAL DISTRICT COURT CIVIL RULES

LCRLJ 7(b). MOTIONS

(a) A party who notes a motion, but decides to strike the motion, shall immediately notify the court and the opposing party that the motion is stricken.

(b) If a moving party does not appear within thirty (30) minutes of the time set for a motion, and no request, for extension of time is received by telephone or otherwise, the motion shall be stricken and the non-moving party(ies) may be awarded costs, and if otherwise authorized, a reasonable attorney's fee.

(c) If a non-moving party does not appear within thirty (30) minutes of the time set for a motion, and no request for extension of time is received by telephone or otherwise, the Court may grant the motion.

(d) The Court may, in its discretion, assess terms against any party failing to comply with this rule.

[Adopted effective September 1, 2002.]

LCRLJ 40(a)(5) and (d). NON–APPEARANCE OF A PARTY OR PARTIES ON TRIAL DATE

(a) If the plaintiff does not appear within thirty (30) minutes of the time set for trial, and no request for extension of time is received by telephone or otherwise, defendant, upon motion, may be granted a judgment of dismissal without prejudice, be awarded costs, and if otherwise authorized, a reasonable attorney's fee, and if a counterclaim, upon satisfactory proof, may be awarded judgment thereon.

(b) If the defendant does not appear within thirty (30) minutes of the time set for trial, and no request

for extension of time is received by telephone or otherwise, the plaintiff, upon motion, may be granted judgment as prayed for, upon satisfactory proof to the court, including costs and if otherwise authorized a reasonable attorney's fee.

(c) In the event neither party appears at the time set for trial, or thirty (30) minutes thereafter, the matter shall be dismissed without prejudice, (including counterclaims) unless the court has received prior notification of agreed or confessed judgment, settlement, dismissal, or continuance. Notification may initially be oral and/or by telephone, but will not be deemed completed until it has been followed up with a clear written statement by the person making such notification, such written statement shall be caused to be on file with the court by 4:30 p.m. on the fifth day following the oral telephonic notification.

[Adopted effective September 1, 2002.]

LCRLJ 43. TAKING OF TESTIMONY[1]

(e) Evidence on Motions.

(1) Motions shall be heard on the pleadings, affidavits, published depositions and other papers filed unless otherwise directed by the Court. Any counter-affidavit shall be served upon the opposing party not later than (3) three days prior to the date of the hearing, or movant shall have the option of a postponement of the hearing. Affidavits strictly in reply to a counter-affidavit may be served and considered at the hearing.

[Adopted effective September 1, 2015.]

[1] Publisher's Note: This rule has been designated as "Proposed".

LOCAL DISTRICT COURT CRIMINAL RULES

LCrRLJ 2.2(h). WARRANTS EXPIRATION DATE[1]

All warrants for arrest issued by the Mason County District Court for misdemeanor and gross misdemeanor offenses shall carry on their face a seven (7) year expiration date.

The court will automatically reissue the warrant one time only for a total of fourteen (14) years on violent offenses and serious traffic offenses.

Violent offenses include Assault, Violation of No Contact or Protection Order, Malicious Mischief, Unlawful Imprisonment, Reckless Endangerment or as designated by the court.

Serious traffic offenses include Driving Under the Influence, Physical Control, Reckless Driving, Hit and Run, or as designated by the court.

If the warrant is not served during this time the prosecutor may file a motion to reissue for the judge's consideration prior to the expiration date. If the case is pre-disposition the motion must state that the prosecutor has a good faith belief they will be able to proceed to trial.

If not served and/or reissued during this time, the warrant expires and the case file shall be closed if no fines, fees, costs and/or restitution is owing. All fines, fees, costs, and/or restitution previously imposed remain owing unless otherwise ordered by the court.

[Adopted effective September 1, 2015.]

[1] Publisher's Note: This rule has been designated as "Proposed".

LCrRLJ 3.1(e). AUTOMATIC WITHDRAWL[1] OF ATTORNEY APPOINTED AT PUBLIC EXPENSE[2]

(1) Unless a Notice of Appeal has been filed, an attorney appointed at public expense shall be deemed automatically withdrawn from representation thirty (30) days following a final decision of the court as defined in RALJ, without further notice to the court.

(2) An attorney appointed at public expense shall be deemed automatically withdrawn from representation thirty (30) days upon the issuance of a warrant without further notice to the court.

[Adopted effective September 1, 2015.]

1 So in original.

2 Publisher's Note: This rule has been designated as "Proposed".

LCrRLJ 3.4(d). PRESENCE OF THE DEFENDANT

(d) Video Conference Proceedings.

(2) *Agreement.* In criminal matters, proceedings may be conducted by video conference as authorized by CrRLJ 3.4.(d). Other criminal proceedings may be conducted by video conference by agreement of the parties in writing or on the record and upon approval of the judge.

[Adopted effective September 2, 2014.]

LCrRLJ 3.6(c). SUPPRESSION HEARING PROCEDURES[1]

A party moving to suppress evidence must file a written motion that sets forth in detail the specific factual and legal grounds for the motion. The motion should be filed with the court at least seven (7) days prior to the pretrial hearing. Said motion shall be supported by an affidavit or declaration under penalty of perjury of a person with testimonial knowledge, setting forth the facts to be elicited at an evidentiary hearing. The matter will be set for evidentiary hearing only if the judge at a pretrial hearing finds that there are facts in dispute. A copy of the motion and supporting documents must be served on the opposing party at least five court days prior to the date set for hearing.

As a matter of professional courtesy, the parties shall file bench copies of all motions, affidavits, and memoranda at the time of filing of the original documents.

[Adopted effective September 1, 2015.]

1 Publisher's Note: This rule has been designated as "Proposed".

LCrRLJ 4.5.1. PRETRIAL PROCEDURES[1]

(a) Duty of Parties. It is the duty of the parties and their counsel to move expeditiously to seek resolution of these matters prior to trial. It is the strong policy of this court that the Rules of Professional Conduct require the completion of investigation, discovery, and plea negotiations prior to trial setting.

(b) Pre–trial Hearings. The Court shall set all out of custody cases where a plea of not guilty has been entered for a pretrial hearing approximately 45 days after the date of first appearance, all in-custody cases will be set within approximately 14 days after

arraignment. Said hearing shall provide an opportunity for execution of plea negotiations, resolution of discovery issues and trial setting. All defendants must be present, with counsel, where applicable. Failure to appear for the pretrial hearing may result in the issuance of a warrant of arrest and/or forfeiture of any bail or bond.

It is strongly suggested that all negotiations be completed prior to this hearing since no time for additional negotiations will be available on the pretrial hearing calendar. All amendments to the charges and any pretrial motions except a motion in limine shall be made in writing and filed with the court at, or prior to, the pretrial hearing.

Following this hearing, if a pretrial disposition of any charge does not occur, an order shall be entered setting forth the following: trial date; trial confirmation date; date of hearing on pretrial motions; and the date by which witness lists must be exchanged and filed. The court may set a discovery schedule.

(c) 3.5 Notice of 3.5 and 3.6 Motions. All demands for a CrRLJ 3.5 hearing on admissibility of statements or confessions must be made in writing and filed no later than the pretrial hearing. The Court will set hearing dates for motions filed as part of that proceeding. See LCrRLJ 3.6 for suppression motions.

(d) Imposition of Jury Costs. In order to efficiently schedule the calling of jurors, to avoid unnecessary disruptions of the jurors lives, and to further avoid the waste of public funds, the court will not, unless good cause is shown, permit the waiver of a jury trial nor the entry of a plea of guilty in a matter scheduled for jury trial after the date of the trial confirmation hearing unless the jury costs are imposed against the moving party.

(e) Trial Confirmation Hearing. See LCrRLJ 4.11.

[Adopted effective September 1, 2015.]

1 Publisher's Note: This rule has been designated as "Proposed".

LCrRLJ 4.11. JURY TRIAL CONFIRMATION—NOTIFICATION OF COURT[1]

(a) All cases set for a jury trial will also be set for a Confirmation Hearing prior to the jury trial date. The prosecutor, defense counsel and the defendant shall attend the confirmation hearing. If the defendant fails to appear for the confirmation hearing, a warrant for the arrest of the defendant may issue, and the court may continue or strike any scheduled hearing or trial date. If the prosecutor or defense counsel fails to appear at the pre-trial hearing, the court my impose terms and any other sanctions authorized by law, and the court may continue or strike any scheduled hearing or trial date. At the Confirmation Hearing all parties are expected to verify readiness to proceed to trial, or to propose an alternate disposition. When a case assigned for jury trial is settled or will not be tried by the jury for any reason, notice of that fact shall be given immediately to the court. The court may impose terms including requiring payment of the actual costs of the jury in the event a case settles after the Confirmation Hearing.

[Adopted effective September 1, 2015.]

1 Publisher's Note: This rule has been designated as "Proposed".

SPECIAL PROCEEDINGS

LRSP 1. NAME CHANGES

(a) **Requirements.** An applicant who applies to the court for a change of name, pursuant to RCW 4.24.130, must meet the following requirement:

(1) *Birth Certificate.* A certified copy of any applicant and/or minor's birth certificate or suitable identification must be presented to the clerk for verification and copying.

(2) *Photo Identification.* The applicant shall be prepared to show photo identification at the time of the hearing.

LCrRLJ 8.2(B). QUASHING WARRANTS [RESCINDED]

[Adopted effective September 1, 2002; rescinded effective September 1, 2009.]

(3) *Minors: Parental Consent.* All applicants under eighteen (18) years of age must be represented by a parent or legal guardian and *both* biological or legal parents or guardians must approve the change of name either by personal appearance or by verified affidavit, unless good cause is shown. Both parents must have notice of the petition.

(4) *Separate Applications.* Each applicant requesting a change of name must present a separate Change of Name Order and pay a separate filing fee and recording fee.

[Adopted effective September 1, 2002.]

MUNICIPAL COURT

SHELTON MUNICIPAL COURT LOCAL RULES

Including Amendments Received Through
August 15, 2015

Table of Rules

CRIMINAL RULES

CrRSMC 3.4. VIDEO CONFERENCE PROCEEDINGS

A. Criminal: Preliminary appearances as defined by CrRLJ 3.2.1(d), arraignments as defined by CrR 3.4 and 4.1 and CrRLJ 3.4 and 4.1, bail hearings as defined by CrR3.2 and CrRLJ 3.2, and trial settings as defined by CrR 3.3 and CrRLJ 3.3(f), and pre-trial hearings as determined by the court, conducted via video conference in which all participants can simultaneously see, hear, and speak with each other shall be deemed held in open court and in the defendant's presence for the purposes of any statute, court rule or policy. All video conference hearings conducted pursuant to this rule shall be public, and the public shall be able to simultaneously see and hear all participants and speak as permitted by the court. Any party may request an in-person hearing which may, in the court's discretion, be granted.

B. Agreement: Other trial court proceedings including the entry of a Statement of Defendant on Plea of Guilty as defined by CrR 4.2 and CrRLJ 4.2 may be conducted by video conference only by agreement of the parties. The defendant will be deemed to have agreed to voluntarily participate in court proceedings

in Shelton Municipal Court by video conference unless the defendant or counsel for the defendant notifies the court at the time of the proceeding that he/she objects to the proceeding being conducted via video conference. The right to object to video conference proceedings will be deemed waived if not exercised prior to the start of the video conference hearing.

C. Standards for Video Conference Proceedings: The Judge, counsel, all parties, and the public must be able to see and hear each other during proceedings, and speak as permitted by the court. Video conference facilities must provide for confidential communications between attorney and client and security sufficient to protect the safety of all participants and observers. In interpreted proceedings, the interpreter must be located next to the defendant and the proceeding must be conducted to assure that the interpreter can hear all participants.

D. For purposes of video conference proceedings, the facsimile or scanned and printed signature(s) of the defendant, counsel, interested parties and the court will be treated as if they were an original signature. This includes all Orders on Judgments & Sentence, No Contact Orders, any Orders purporting to be a final resolution of the case, Time Pay Agreements, and other documents as the court shall determine are appropriate or necessary.

[Adopted on an emergency basis, effective November 1, 2012; January 31, 2013; adopted on a permanent basis, effective September 2, 2013.]

CrRSMC 3.6.1.   3.6 HEARINGS

The court shall not set any 3.6 Hearings without the 3.6 Motion being submitted to the court prior and the Judge or the Judge Pro tern reviewing the motion and authorizing the hearing.

[Adopted effective September 1, 2009.]

CrRSMC 6.1.1.   CONFIRMATION OF JURY TRIAL

1) When a case is set for jury trial, there will be a Jury Status Conference at 8:45 a.m., the Wednesday before the trial is scheduled to begin. That conference shall initially be off the record. The parties shall discuss the case and prepare a stipulation, signed by the Prosecuting Authority, Defense Counsel, and Defendant that supplies the following:

a) The projected length of the trial and scheduling if the case is going to proceed to trial;

b) The defense to be offered which will be listed as,

   i) General denial;

   ii) Lawful Use of Force;

   iii) Duress;

   iv) Insanity

   v) Diminished Capacity;

   vi) Alibi;

   vii) Other, _____ ;

c) Any legal issues, discovery issues or evidentiary issues that need to be resolved prior to trial;

d) Whether the case has been settled or if there are any plea negotiations still being conducted and, without divulging any offers, the likelihood of the case resolving without trial.

2) If the parties have reached a settlement, the court, may in its discretion, allow the settlement to be placed on the record, that day, after nine o'clock. If not, the disposition will be heard on the scheduled jury trial date, with the court setting a backup jury trial date, the following jury trial day. The stipulation form shall contain a waiver of speedy trial, if the case is being placed on for disposition, with a follow up jury trial date.

3) If the parties are unable to agree on the trial issues or whether the case is ready to go to trial, the matter will be placed on the 9 o'clock calendar and be heard as soon as feasible.

4) Failure of the defendant to appear at the Jury Status Conference will result in a bench warrant and the striking of the jury trial date.

5) If a case is confirmed for jury trial and does not proceed to jury trial, such that jurors and witnesses are needlessly brought into court on the date assigned, the Court may impose sanctions including, but not limited to, jury costs, witness fees, and such other terms as the Court may find appropriate and just.

[Adopted effective September 1, 2003; amended effective September 1, 2009.]

CrRSMC 6.13.1.   EVIDENTIARY HEARINGS

Any party wishing to produce witnesses in any court proceeding other than a Jury or Bench Trial shall provide a minimum of one weeks notice to the court and the opposing party through counsel if the party is represented along with estimation as to the length the hearing will be. Any party failing to comply with this rule may be subject to sanctions and the court rescheduling the hearing to another time to accommodate the length of the hearing.

[Adopted effective September 1, 2009.]

CrRSMC 7.2(c).   SENTENCING

The court shall consider a person's ability to pay, in imposing legal financial obligations. The court will consider both a person's present ability to pay and a person's future ability to pay. The court expects the parties, through their attorneys if they have one, otherwise themselves, to notify the court, if there is not an ability to pay the legal financial obligation. Absent that issue being raised, the court will presume that the defendant either currently has or can in the future, the ability to pay the legal financial obligations outlined in an agreed plea or other disposition.

[Adopted effective September 1, 2015.]

CrRSMC 7.3.1.   COMMUNITY RESTITUTION (COMMUNITY SERVICE)

Community Service for the Shelton Municipal Court shall be performed through the Court's Community Service Work Crew Program unless, for good cause, the Court Orders otherwise.

[Adopted effective September 2, 2013.]

CrRSMC 7.3.2.   COURT ORDERED PROGRAMS

No credit will be allowed for "Online" Court Ordered Programs unless specifically authorized by the court, prior to entering into the program.

[Adopted effective September 2, 2013.]

CrRSMC 8.   MOTIONS

The judge of this court or judge pro-tem shall have the authority to review any motion, except motions brought under rule CrRLJ 3.5, to determine whether they have merit on their face. If it is decided that the motion has merit on its face, the court shall grant a hearing. If it does not, the judge or judge pro-tem shall deny scheduling a hearing.

In determining whether the motion has, on its face, merit, the court shall accept the factual allegations made in the motion and determine, whether those facts arguably support a legal basis in which to grant the motion. In determining whether an argument exists in legally supporting the motion, the presump-

tion shall be that it does have merit. Only when it is clear that there is no factual and/or legal basis on its face to grant the requested relief shall the court decline to hold a hearing.

Nothing in this rule shall be construed as authorizing the court to grant a motion on its merits without the opposing parties having a chance to respond.

[Adopted effective September 1, 2015.]

INFRACTION RULES

IRSMC 2.4.1.   TIME PAYMENTS ON INFRACTIONS

Any person who has been served with a notice of infraction and who desires to use option (1) as provided in IRLJ 2.4(b)(1), may either pay the penalty in full or arrange time payments of the monetary penalty with the clerk. The clerk is authorized to enter a finding that the infraction was committed, and make appropriate notations in the court record, relieving the person of any further obligation to appear in court in connection with the infraction, provided the person has responded to the infraction as required and pays the penalty as directed.

[Adopted effective January 1, 2003.]

IRSMC 2.4.2.   LIABILITY INSURANCE INFRACTIONS

(A) If a person who has been cited with a violation of RCW 46.30.020, as now enacted or hereafter amended, presents to the court clerk evidence that the person had in effect at the time of the citation liability insurance as required by RCW 46.30.020, and that person has had no previous violations of RCW 46.30.020, then the case shall be dismissed and the court clerk shall be authorized to make appropriate notation of the dismissal in the court file provided the person has responded timely to the notice of infraction.

(B) If a person who has been cited with a violation of RCW 46.30.020, as now enacted or hereafter amended, presents to the court clerk evidence that the person had in effect at the time of the citation liability insurance as required by RCW 46.30.020, and that person has had prior violations of RCW 46.30.020, then, upon payment of twenty-five dollars ($25.00) administrative costs, the case shall be dismissed and the court clerk shall be authorized to make appropriate notation of the dismissal in the court file provided the person has responded timely to the notice of infraction.

(C) If a person charged with violation of RCW 46.30.020, as now enacted or hereafter amended, is able to show evidence that the person has subsequently obtained liability insurance in conformity with the requirements of RCW 46.30.020, and has had no previ-

ous violation of the same statute, then the penalty shall be reduced to one hundred and twenty five dollars ($125.00) and upon payment of the one hundred and twenty five ($125.00) penalty, or arranging a payment agreement with the clerk, the clerk shall be authorized to enter a finding that the infraction was committed, and make appropriate notations in the court record, and the person will be relieved of any further need to appear in court in connection with the infraction, provided the person has responded to the notice of infraction as required and pays the penalty in full or as set forth by the payment agreement.

(D) If a person has had a previous violation of RCW 46.30.020, then the person must pay the penalty in full or in the alternative request a hearing either to contest or mitigate the notice of infraction within fifteen days of the date the infraction was issued.

(E) The court may, without amendment to this rule, adjust the penalties, fees, or costs to be imposed under this rule, to be proportionate with changes in the statewide bail schedule, fees or costs as changes are made by the Supreme Court or the Washington State Legislature, provided the Presiding Judge so orders and the Order is on file in the office of the Shelton Municipal Court.

[Adopted effective September 1, 2003.]

IRSMC 2.4.3.   NO VALID OPERATOR'S LICENSE

(A) If a person charged with violation of RCW 46.20.005, No Valid Operators License With Valid Identification. as now enacted or hereafter amended, is able to show proof of subsequently acquiring a valid operators license, then upon payment of One Hundred and One dollars ($101.00) or arrangement of a payment agreement with the clerk, the citation will be amended to the infraction RCW 46.20.015, No Driver's License on Person with a finding of committed and the court clerk shall be authorized to make appropriate notation in the court file, provided the defendant has responded to the citation as required and pays the penalty in full or as set forth by the payment agreement.

(B) If a person charged with violation of RCW 46.20.015, No Valid Operators License On Person, as now enacted or hereafter amended, is able to subsequently show proof of having a Valid Operators License and has had no previous violations regarding Operator Licenses, then the case shall be dismissed and the court clerk shall be authorized to make appropriate notation of the dismissal in the court file provided the person has responded timely to the notice of infraction.

(C) If a person charged with violation of RCW 46.20.015, No Valid Operators License On Person, as now enacted or hereafter amended, is able to subsequently show proof of having a Valid Operators License and has had previous violations regarding Operator Licenses, then upon payment of twenty-five dollars ($25.00) administrative costs, the case shall be dismissed and the court clerk shall be authorized to make appropriate notation of the dismissal in the court file provided the person has responded timely to the notice of infraction.

(D) The court may, without amendment to this rule, adjust the penalties, fees, or costs to be imposed under this rule, to be proportionate with changes in the statewide bail schedule, fees or costs as changes are made by the Supreme Court or the Washington State Legislature, provided the Presiding Judge so orders and the Order is on file in the office of the Shelton Municipal Court.

[Adopted effective September 1, 2003.]

IRSMC 2.4.4. EXPIRED VEHICLE LICENSE INFRACTIONS

(A) If a person who has been cited with a violation of RCW 46.16.010 as now enacted or hereafter amended, presents to the court clerk evidence that the person had in effect at the time of the infraction a valid vehicle license as required by RCW 46.16.010 but had failed to display it on the vehicle license plate and that person has had no previous violations of RCW 46.16.010, then the case shall be dismissed and the court clerk shall be authorized to make appropriate notation of the dismissal in the court file provided the person has responded timely to the notice of infraction.

(B) If a person who has been cited with a violation of RCW 46.16.010, as now enacted or hereafter amended, presents to the court clerk evidence that the person had in effect at the time of the infraction a valid vehicle license as required by RCW 46.16.010 but had failed to display it on the vehicle license plate, and the person has had prior violations of RCW 46.16.010, then, upon payment of twenty-five dollars ($25.00) administrative costs, the case shall be dismissed and the court clerk shall be authorized to make appropriate notation of the dismissal in the court file provided the person has responded timely to the notice of infraction.

(C) If a person charged with violation of RCW 46.16.010, for failure to renew an expired vehicle license, as now enacted or hereafter amended as now

enacted or hereafter amended, is able to show evidence that the person has subsequently obtained the vehicle license in conformity with the requirements of RCW 46.16.010, and has had no previous violation of the same statute, then the penalty shall be reduced to one hundred and forty five dollars ($145.00) if the vehicle license has been expired for over two months and fifty-five dollars ($55.00) if the vehicle license has been expired for less than two months and upon payment of the penalty, or arrangement of a payment agreement with the clerk, the clerk shall be authorized to enter a finding that the infraction was committed, and make appropriate notations in the court record, and the person will be relieved of any further need to appear in court in connection with the infraction, provided the person has responded to the notice of infraction as required and pays the penalty in full or as set forth in the payment agreement.

(D) If a person has had a previous violation of RCW 46.16.010, as now enacted or hereafter amended, then the person must pay the penalty in full or in the alternative request a hearing either to contest or mitigate the notice of infraction within fifteen days of the date the infraction was issued.

(E) The court may, without amendment to this rule, adjust the penalties, fees, or costs to be imposed under this rule, to be proportionate with changes in the statewide bail schedule, fees or costs as changes are made by the Supreme Court or the Washington State Legislature, provided the Presiding Judge so orders and the Order is on file in the office of the Shelton Municipal Court.

[Adopted effective January 1, 2003.]

IRSMC 2.4.5. EXPIRED VEHICLE LICENSE INFRACTIONS CITY ORDINANCE VIOLATION

(A) If a person who has been cited with a violation of Ordinance 11.24.070, as now enacted or hereafter amended, presents to the court clerk evidence that the person had in effect at the time of the infraction a valid vehicle license as required by RCW 46.16.010 but had failed to display it on the vehicle license plate and that person has had no previous violations of RCW 46.16.010 or Ordinance 11.24.070, then the case shall be dismissed and the court clerk shall be authorized to make appropriate notation of the dismissal in the court file provided the person has responded timely to the notice of infraction.

(B) If a person who has been cited with a violation of Ordinance 11.24.070, as now enacted or hereafter amended, presents to the court clerk evidence that the person had in effect at the time of the infraction a valid vehicle license as required by RCW 46.16.010 but had failed to display it on the vehicle license plate, and the person has had prior violations of RCW 46. 16.010 or Ordinance 11.24.070, then, upon payment of ten dollars ($10.00) administrative costs, the case shall be dismissed and the court clerk shall be authorized to make appropriate notation of the dismissal in the court file provided the person has responded timely to the notice of infraction.

(C) If a person charged with violation of Ordinance 11.24.070, as now enacted or hereafter amended, is able to show evidence that the person has subsequently obtained the vehicle license in conformity with the requirements of RCW 46.16.010, and has had no previous violation of the same statute or Ordinance 11.24.070, then the penalty shall be reduced to fifteen dollars ($15.00) and upon payment of the penalty, or arrangement of a payment agreement with the clerk, the clerk shall be authorized to enter a finding that the infraction was committed, and make appropriate notations in the court record, and the person will be relieved of any further need to appear in court in connection with the infraction, provided the person has responded to the notice of infraction as required and pays the penalty in full or as set forth in the payment agreement.

(D) If a person has had a previous violation of RCW 46.16.010 or Ordinance 11.24.070, then the person must pay the penalty in full or in the alternative request a hearing either to contest or mitigate the notice of infraction within fifteen days of the date the infraction was issued.

[Adopted effective January 1, 2003.]

IRSMC 2.4.6. PARKING IN A DISABLED SPACE WITHOUT PROPER PARKING PLACARD

If a person charged with violation of city ordinance 11.24.120 or RCW 46.16.381, for parking in disabled space without proper parking placard, license plate or picture identification, as now enacted or hereafter amended, presents to the court clerk evidence that the person had in effect at the time of citation the required parking placard, and an identification card bearing picture, name and date of birth of the permit holder, as well as the placard's serial number, then the infraction shall be dismissed and the court clerk shall be authorized to make appropriate notation of the dismissal in court records.

[Adopted effective September 1, 2003.]

IRSMC 2.4.7. FAILURE TO LICENSE DOG

(A) If a person who has been cited with a violation of Ordinance 7.04.030, as now enacted or hereafter amended, presents to the court clerk evidence that the person had in effect at the time of the infraction a valid license for the person's dog as required by Ordinance 7.04.030 but had failed to display it on the dog and that person has had no previous violations of Ordinance 7.04.030, then the case shall be dismissed and the court clerk shall be authorized to make appropriate notation of the dismissal in the court file provid-ed the person has responded timely to the notice of infraction.

(B) If a person who has been cited with a violation of Ordinance 7.04.030, as now enacted or hereafter amended, presents to the court clerk evidence that the person had in effect at the time of the infraction a valid license for the dog as required by Ordinance 7.04.030 but had failed to display it on the dog, and the person has had prior violations of Ordinance 7.04.030, then, upon payment of twenty-five dollars ($25.00) administrative costs, the case shall be dismissed and the court clerk shall be authorized to make appropriate notation of the dismissal in the court file provided the person has responded timely to the notice of infraction and pays the penalty in full or as set forth in the payment agreement.

(C) If a person charged with violation of Ordinance 7.04.030, as now enacted or hereafter amended, is able to show evidence that the person has subsequently obtained a valid license for the dog in conformity with the requirements of Ordinance 7.04.030, and has had no previous violation of Ordinance 7.04.030, then the penalty shall be reduced to fifty-five dollars ($55.00) and upon payment of the penalty, or arrangement of a payment agreement with the clerk, the clerk shall be authorized to enter a finding that the infraction was committed, and make appropriate notations in the court record, and the person will be relieved of any further need to appear in court in connection with the infraction, provided the person has responded to the notice of infraction as required and pays the penalty in full or as set forth in the payment agreement.

(D) If a person has had a previous violation of Ordinance 7.04.030, as now enacted or hereafter amended, then the person must pay the penalty in full or in the alternative request a hearing either to contest or mitigate the notice of infraction within fifteen days of the date the infraction was issued.

(E) The court may, without amendment to this rule, adjust the penalties, fees, or costs to be imposed under this rule, to be proportionate with changes in the fees or costs as changes are made by the Washington State Legislature, provided the Presiding Judge so orders and the Order is on file in the office of the Shelton Municipal Court.

[Adopted effective September 1, 2003.]

IRSMC 2.6(A)(2). INFRACTION WITNESS FEES

In an infraction or other non-criminal proceeding, the party requesting the witness shall pay the witness fees and mileage expenses due that witness. Any person who requests production of an electronic speed measuring device expert, and who is thereafter found by the court to have committed the infraction, shall be required to pay the fee charged by the expert as a cost incurred by the party.

[Adopted effective September 1, 2009. Former IRSMC 2.6(a)(2) was deleted effective September 1, 2004.]

IRSMC 3.5. DECISION ON WRITTEN STATEMENTS

Pursuant to IRLJ 3.5, the court is authorized to enter decisions based upon written statements on infraction cases involving contested and mitigation hearings and requests for deferred findings. Such written statements may be submitted to the court for consideration either by mail or email by the respondent but must certify or declare under penalty of perjury that the statement is true and must contain a statement that if it is determined that the respondent committed the cited infraction, the respondent promises to pay the monetary penalty authorized by law and assessed by the court.

(A) Generally. In infraction cases where the respondent has requested, the court will conduct a mitigation hearing as authorized by RCW 46.63.100 as now enacted or hereafter amended, or consider a petition to defer the finding, or conduct a contested hearing based upon the upon the written statements

of the City's witness(es) if provided, and the Respondent, pursuant to IRLJ 3.5.

The examination shall take place within 90 days after the respondent filed the response to the notice of infraction. The examination may be held in chambers and shall not be governed by the Rules of Evidence.

(B) Factual Determination. In contested cases, the court shall determine whether the plaintiff has proved by a preponderance of all evidence submitted that the defendant has committed the infraction.

(C) A petition for a deferred finding which is denied by the Court will be treated as a request for a mitigation hearing on written statements.

(D) Disposition. If the court determines that the infraction has been committed, or the review was based upon a request for mitigation or a deferred finding, the court may assess a penalty in accordance with rule 3.3.

(E) Notice to Parties. The court shall notify the parties in writing whether an infraction was found to have been committed and/or what penalty, if any, was imposed.

(F) No Appeal Permitted. There shall be no appeal from a decision on written statements.

[Adopted effective September 1, 2003.]

ADMINISTRATIVE RULES

ARSMC 1.1. COURT PROCEEDINGS

Court Proceedings will be conducted with appropriate decorum. The consuming of any food or beverage other than pure water is prohibited. Additionally, appropriate dress will be required. Shorts, tank tops, or exposure of the midriff will not be considered to be acceptable attire.

Additionally, all recording devices, cell phones, text messaging devices and items attached to the internet, other than the court computers, are to be turned off.

No head coverings are allowed unless required by a recognized religious faith.

[Adopted effective September 1, 2009.]

ARSMC 1.2. COMMUNITY SERVICE FEE

Anybody who is granted the option of performing community service for substitution of jail time or fines and or penalties shall be required to pay a fee to the clerk's office, which may be adjusted from time to time by the court, as reimbursement of the administrative cost of overseeing the community service. The fee shall be paid in full prior to receiving credit for the community service performed unless otherwise ordered by the court.

[Adopted effective September 1, 2009. Amended effective September 2, 2013.]

OKANOGAN COUNTY

Table of Courts

Superior Court

Local Rules of the Superior Court for Okanogan County.

District Court

Okanogan County District Court—[No Local Rules].

Municipal Courts

Brewster Municipal Court—[No Local Rules].
Elmer City Municipal Court—[No Local Rules].
Omak Municipal Court—[No Local Rules].
Tonasket Municipal Court—[No Local Rules].
Twisp Municipal Court—[No Local Rules].
Winthrop Municipal Court—[No Local Rules].

SUPERIOR COURT

LOCAL RULES OF THE SUPERIOR COURT FOR OKANOGAN COUNTY

Including Amendments Received Through
August 15, 2015

Table of Rules

LOCAL RULES (LR)

INTRODUCTORY

LR 1. TITLE AND SCOPE

(a) Preface. These rules shall take effect on September 1, 2013, and supersede all prior rules of this court. The previous rules which were adopted effective January 2, 1995, September 1, 2000 and September 1, 2010 are hereby replaced. Forms listed in Appendix A shall be effective September 1, 2013. These rules shall be known as the Local Rules of the Superior Court of the State of Washington for Okanogan County. These rules may be cited in the following form: "LR", "LGALR", "LMAR" and "LSPR".

(b) Scope. These rules apply to all matters now pending and hereafter filed in the Okanogan County Superior Court. To the extent these rules conflict with statewide rules, the statewide rules apply. Okanogan County Superior Court will follow Washington State Court Rules and only promulgate local rules as deemed necessary.

(c) Waiver and Construction. Any provision of these rules may be waived or modified by order of the court for good cause shown, or as required in the interest of justice. These rules should be construed to promote the fair, just and expeditious resolution of disputes.

[Adopted effective September 2, 2013. Amended effective September 2, 2014.]

LR 1A. JUDICIAL POSITIONS

(a) Judicial Positions. RCW 2.08.065 provides that there shall be two superior court judges for Okanogan County.

(b) Commissioners. The court may appoint up to three Court Commissioners and such pro tem Commissioners and pro tem Judges as are necessary, in the judgment of the court, to complete the business of the court.

(c) Authority of Commissioners. Court Commissioners shall perform duties as assigned by the court and shall have all powers conferred by law, including the authority to accept pleas in criminal matters. Commissioners may perform other duties as stipulated by the parties if authorized by the court.

[Adopted effective September 2, 2013.]

COMMENCEMENT OF ACTION; SERVICE OF PROCESS; PLEADINGS, MOTIONS AND ORDERS

LR 4.3. PRO SE APPEARANCE

Pro Se. All *Pro Se* litigants *(being those individuals representing themselves)* shall be required to file a *Pro Se* Notice of Appearance (Form *WPF DRPSCU 01.0320*).

The form must include that party's full name, signature, mailing address, email addresses (if available) and telephone number. A new form must be filed in the event of a change in address or phone number. Parties who fail to comply with this order may have sanctions imposed by the court, including their pleadings stricken, or other court action without notice. A copy of the *Pro Se* Notice of Appearance should be attached to any request for trial setting submitted to the court's Judicial Assistant. A form for this purpose may be obtained from the court's website, Judicial Assistant or family law facilitator. Petitioners in domestic violence or civil harassment cases may provide alternate address and contact information where their physical address is confidential.

[Adopted effective September 2, 2013. Amended effective September 2, 2014.]

PLEADINGS, MOTIONS AND SPECIAL SETTINGS

LR 7.   CIVIL MOTIONS

(a) Scope of Rules.   Except when specifically provided in another rule, this rule governs all motions in civil cases.

(b) Dates of Filing, Hearing and Consideration.

(1) *Filing.*   The moving party shall serve and file the motion and supporting documents no later than five court days before the date the party wishes the motion to be considered.

(2) *Opposing Documents.*   Any party opposing a motion shall file and serve the original responsive papers in opposition to a motion with the clerk, serve copies on parties, and deliver working copies to the hearing judge no later than twenty-four hours or one (1) judicial day before the date the motion is to be heard by the court.

(3) *Scheduling Oral Argument.*   Contested motions shall be scheduled on the Superior Court's regularly scheduled Law & Motion Calendar unless otherwise specified in (b)(4).

(4) *Limitation of Arguments.*   Oral arguments on the Law & Motion Calendar shall be limited to ten (10) minutes per side.   If it is anticipated by either party that oral arguments will be more than ten (10) minutes per side, that party shall contact the Judicial Assistant to request a special setting.

(5) *Working Copies.*   Any Working copies of the motion and all documents in support or opposition, as herein required, shall be delivered to the Judicial Assistant as set forth in section (d).

(c) Motions for Revision of a Commissioner's Order.   For all cases except juvenile and involuntary treatment proceedings:

(1) *Motion for Revision.*   A motion for revision of a commissioner's order or judgment shall be served and filed within ten (10) calendar days of entry of the written order, as provided in RCW 2.24.050, along with a written notice of hearing that gives the other party at least five (5) Judicial days' notice of the time, date and place of the hearing on the motion for revision.   The motion shall identify the error(s) claimed.

(2) *Hearing.*   A hearing on a motion for revision of a commissioner's order shall be scheduled within a reasonable time of entry of the commissioner's order.

(3) *Materials Submitted.*   All motions for revision of a commissioner's order shall be based on the written materials and evidence submitted to the commissioner, including documents and pleadings in the court file.   The moving party shall provide the assigned judge a working copy of all materials submitted to the commissioner in support of and in opposition to the motion, as well as a copy of the electronic recording, if the party wishes the electronic recording to be considered.   Oral arguments on motions to revise shall be limited to ten (10) minutes per side.

(4) *Pending Order Effective.*   The Commissioner's written order shall remain in effect pending the hearing on revision unless ordered otherwise by a Judge.

(d) Judge's Working Copies.   Working copies for the judge's use shall be provided as follows: all summary judgment materials including briefs and supporting materials; all briefs and supporting materials for any specially set matter; trial briefs, motions in limine, witness lists and similar material.   Working copies of exhibits should be provided to the court during all civil trials.   WORKING COPIES SHALL BE DELIVERED TO THE JUDICIAL ASSISTANT AT OKANOGAN SUPERIOR COURT OR MAILED TO OKANOGAN SUPERIOR COURT AT P.O. BOX 112 OKANOGAN, WA 98840 NO LATER THAN FIVE DAYS PRIOR TO THE COURT HEARING DATE.   ALL WORKING COPIES MUST HAVE THE HEARING DATE AND TIME ON THEM.

(e) Telephonic hearings.   Telephonic hearings are authorized for most matters other than trial upon stipulation by the parties and upon court approval or upon the court's own action.   The record of such hearings will be electronically recorded.   (No cellphones or in-office conferencing equipment shall be used by either party.) If authorized for regular motion calendars, arrangements shall be made through the County Clerk's Office.   For all other hearings, arrangements shall be made through the Judicial Assistants.

(f) Cancellation or Continuance.   When the parties wish to cancel or continue special set matters or law and motion matters, the party who originally set the hearing must notify the Superior Court Clerk (509) 422–7275 at least twenty-four (24) hours before the scheduled hearing.   **Notice must also be provided to** the Judicial Assistant at (509) 422–7093 and/or an email addressed to the **superiorcourt@co. okanogan.wa.us**

(g) Interpreter Services.   When there is an individual before the court who is limited English proficient (LEP) involved in litigation, it is the attorney's or individual's (if Pro Se), responsibility to make timely prior arrangements for an Interpreter thru the Office of the Interpreter Coordinator at (509) 422–7198 or by email at **superiorcourt@co. okanogan.wa.us**

[Adopted effective September 2, 2013.   Amended effective September 2, 2014.]

LR 10.   FORM OF PLEADINGS AND OTHER PAPERS

Captions.   Use of Mandatory Forms.   Where the Administrative Office of the Court has prepared mandatory forms, the parties shall comply with the format and style rules for mandatory forms as published by the Administrative Office of Courts, including use of SCOMIS codes. *See:* **http://www.courts.wa.gov/forms/?fa=forms.static&staticID=4**

[Adopted effective September 1, 2015.]

LR 16. PRETRIAL PROCEDURE AND FORMULATING ISSUES

(a) Pre–Trial Conferences. Pre-trial Conferences are required in all cases except family law cases. Any order for a pre-trial conference shall be in the form of and include the provisions as set forth in Appendix A Form A–6. The pre-trial conference shall be held not less than twenty-one (21) calendar days prior to the trial date.

(b) Pre–Trial Order. A pre-trial order as set forth in Appendix A Form A–7 shall be prepared by counsel within fourteen (14) calendar days after the conclusion of the pre-trial conference.

(c) Exhibits. Parties shall notify the trial judge and the opposing party by letter if that party anticipates offering twenty-five (25) exhibits or more at the time of trial. Said notice shall be given no less than fourteen (14) calendar days prior to the trial date.

(d) Settlement Conferences.

(1) *On Motion by Party.* Any party in any pending case may serve and file a motion for a settlement conference.

(2) *On Court's Motion.* The court to which a case is assigned for trial may, upon its own motion after a trial date has been set, order a settlement conference in any pending case, and a settlement conference shall be held unless all parties file objections thereto.

(3) *Subsequent Motion by Party.* Where a motion for a settlement conference has been defeated by the filing of an objection, any future motion must be made upon a showing of a significant change in circumstances.

(4) *Order for Settlement Conference.* Upon the entry of an order for a settlement conference, the judge shall fix a specific date and hour for the conference. If either party has a limited ability to speak or understand the English Language then the order shall provide for an interpreter and identify the language needing interpreting. The party presenting such order for entry shall at the time of entry provide a copy to the Judicial Assistant.

(5) *Preparation and Attendance.* The attorney in charge of each party's case shall personally attend all settlement conferences and shall, not less than five (5) days prior to the date set for the settlement conference, serve on the settlement judge and the attorney for the opposing party a letter succinctly addressing the following:

a. A brief factual summary;

b. Issues regarding liability;

c. Issues regarding damages, both special and general

d. History of any settlement negotiations; and

e. Current position on settlement.

In family law cases, counsel shall also serve on the settlement judge and attorney for the opposing party the completed Asset & Debt Matrix *(Appendix A form A–1)* and financial declaration *(WPF DRPSCU 01.1550)*

Each attorney shall be prepared to discuss the foregoing in detail at the settlement conference.

(6) *Attendance of Parties.* The parties shall in all cases attend the settlement conference. Only parties and attorneys shall be present during the settlement conference unless unwise [1] allowed by the court.

In subrogation cases, brought in the name of the insured party, an insurance company representative need not personally appear, provided that counsel appears and has settlement authority. Alternatively, the insurance company representative must be available by telephone or other means to authorize settlement.

Parties whose defense is provided by a liability insurance company need not personally attend said settlement conference, but a representative of the insurer of such party, if such a representative is available, shall attend with sufficient authority to bind the insurer to a settlement. In the event such a representative is not available, counsel representing the party whose defense is provided by the insurer shall make a good faith effort to obtain settlement authority to bind the insurer to a settlement prior to the settlement conference.

Upon timely request, attendance of any party may be excused by the court where by reason of health, or other good and sufficient reason, compelling their personal attendance would be unduly burdensome.

(7) *Proceedings Privileged.* Proceedings of said settlement conference shall, in all respects, be privileged and shall not be reported or recorded. When a settlement has been reached, the judge may, at the request of any party, order the settlement to be reported or recorded.

(8) *Sanctions.* Where a party has failed to comply with any of the provisions of this rule the court shall make such orders as are just, which shall include the award of reasonable expenses, including attorney's fees, caused by the failure, unless the court finds that the failure was substantially justified or that other circumstances make an award of expenses unjust. These sanctions may also include a court services assessment up to a sum of one thousand dollars ($1,000.000) to cover judicial and court staff.

(e) Agreed Statement of the Case. In all civil jury trials the parties shall jointly prepare a neutral and agreed summary description of the case. The court will read that statement during the orientation phase of selection.

[Adopted effective September 2, 2013. Amended effective September 2, 2014; September 1, 2015.]

1 So in original.

TRIALS

LR 38. JURY DEMAND

Civil Jury Demand. Any demand for a jury in a civil proceeding shall be submitted in writing to the Superior Court Clerk and the Judicial Assistant.

[Adopted effective September 2, 2013.]

LR 40. TRIAL SETTING AND PRE-TRIAL PROCEDURES

(a) Trial Setting. Any party may request a trial setting by use of the Request for Trial Setting form (Appendix A forms A–8 and A–9) which can be obtained from the Court's website or Judicial Assistant. The form must be served on all opposing counsel or Pro Se parties and delivered to: Office of the Judicial Assistant, PO Box 112, Okanogan, WA 98840 **superiorcourt@co.okanogan.wa.us** Opposing counsel and any Pro Se party shall prepare, serve and file any response to the request within fourteen (14) days. All counsel and Pro Se parties must provide unavailable dates on the form or by separate attachment. The listing of a date as unavailable is a request not to have trial set on that date. Such requests must be reasonable and should not result in unnecessary inconvenience or undue delay.

(b) Multiple Settings and Priorities. The Judicial Assistant sets trial dates based upon the information provided in the Request for Trial Setting and Response. Because of scheduling difficulties, the Judicial Assistant may give cases multiple settings with some of those being second or third place settings. Counsel and parties should be prepared for trial regardless of the priority of a specific setting. Second and third set cases are often called for trial. Counsel and parties with second and third settings are required to maintain awareness of the status of their trial setting by contacting the Judicial Assistant who will endeavor to provide current information on the status of cases set with higher priority.

(c) Settlement Confirmation. In the event parties and or their counsel reach a resolution and/ or settlement of their action, then the counsel and/or pro se party shall immediately, but not more than two (2) judicial days after executing a settlement document (ie decree, order or stipulation), shall notify and provide a copy to the Judicial Assistant by either email or in hand. Failure to provide this notification to the Judicial Assistants may result in sanctions against the parties and/ or counsel.

(d) Trial Confirmation. All counsel and Pro Se parties shall confirm by contacting the Judicial Assistant that the scheduled trial is ready to proceed. Confirmation should be made no later than noon (12:00pm) two (2) judicial days prior to the scheduled trial date. Failure to confirm may result in trial being stricken.

(e) Scheduling. Scheduling letters may be issued by the Judicial Assistant. However, they may not address issues such as discovery cutoff, disclosure of experts and any other scheduling issues except trial dates and pre-trial conference dates. The court may issue scheduling orders as appropriate for a case.

(f) Sanctions. Where a party has failed to comply with any of the provisions of this rule the court shall make such orders as are just, which shall include the award of reasonable expenses, including attorney's fees, caused by the failure, unless the court finds that the failure was substantially justified or that other circumstances make an award of expenses unjust. These sanctions may also include a court services assessment up to a sum of one thousand dollars ($1,000.000) to cover judicial and court staff.

[Adopted effective September 2, 2013. Amended effective September 2, 2014; September 1, 2015.]

LR 47. JURORS

(a) Jury Selection. Juries will be selected by the method commonly known as the "struck juror system." Before the process begins the clerk will randomly assign sequential numbers to all prospective jurors, who have appeared, and will seat them in the courtroom in that order. The judge and counsel will be provided with a seating chart or a roster of the panel as seated.

(b) Alternate Juror. In lieu of the procedure designated by statute, the parties may stipulate that the alternate juror be designated by random drawing to be announced after closing argument.

[Adopted effective September 2, 2013.]

LR 51. INSTRUCTIONS TO JURY

(a) Jury Instructions and Note–Taking. The court allows jurors to take notes and provides written copies of instructions to each juror. Juror notes are destroyed at the end of trial. The copies of instructions provided to jurors are not preserved.

(b) Jury Instructions. Each party shall file one cited and numbered copy of proposed instructions with the clerk in order to preserve the record. Each party shall also provide one cited and numbered copy and one un-cited, un-numbered and un-stapled copy of instructions to the court's Judicial Assistant for the judge's use. The parties shall provide a copy of their instructions on disk to the court's Judicial Assistant at the beginning of the trial.

(1) *Civil.* Written instructions in civil cases shall be provided by the time of the pre-trial conference or five (5) judicial days prior to commencement of trial.

(2) *Criminal.* Written instructions in criminal cases shall be provided two (2) judicial days prior to commencement of trial.

[Adopted effective September 2, 2013.]

LR 56.　SUMMARY JUDGMENT AND OTHER SPECIAL SETTINGS

(a) **Summary Judgment/Special Settings.** Summary Judgments as per CR 56 or hearings requiring more than ten minutes per side to argue must be specially set and arranged by contacting the Court Judicial Assistant (509) 422–7093. No hearing will be set without the motion and notice of hearing filed with the Superior Court Clerk. Matters requiring less than ten minutes per side may generally be placed on the appropriate Law and Motion calendar. Upon filing with the clerk a copy of the notice shall be emailed to Superior Court email address **superiorcourt@co.okanogan.wa.us**. Failure to do so shall result in the hearing being stricken.

(b) **Summary Judgment Confirmation.** Summary judgment hearings must be confirmed by call-ing/emailing **superiorcourt@co.okanogan.wa.us** to the Judicial Assistant forty-eight (48) hours before the scheduled hearing (509) 422–7093. Failure to comply may result in cancellation.

[Adopted effective September 2, 2013. Amended effective September 2, 2014.]

LR 59.　NEW TRIAL, RECONSIDER-ATION, AND AMENDMENT OF JUDGMENTS

(a) **Motion and Notice of Hearing.** The form of motion and notice of hearing shall conform to LCR 7(b). The motion will be considered without oral argument unless called for by the court.

(b) **Response and Reply.** No response to a motion for reconsideration shall be filed unless requested by the court. No motion for reconsideration will be granted without such a request. If a response is called for, a reply may be filed within two days of service of the response.

(c) **Form of Proposed Order; Mailing Envelopes.** The moving party and any party given leave to file a memorandum in opposition shall attach an original proposed order to the working copies submitted to the hearing judge. If the working copies are submitted in paper form, pre-addressed stamped envelopes for each party/counsel shall also be submitted to the hearing judge. Working copies shall be submitted pursuant to the requirements of LCR 7(d) to the extent not inconsistent with this rule.

[Adopted effective September 2, 2014.]

DOMESTIC PROCEEDINGS

LSPR 94.04.01.　FILINGS IN FAMILY LAW AND NON–MARITAL RELATIONSHIPS

(a) **Application of Rule.** This rule shall apply to all of the following types of cases that were filed after September 1, 2013:

(1) *Family Law.* Petitions seeking dissolution of marriage, legal separation, or declaration of invalidity; and

(2) *Non–Marital.* Actions brought by parties to non-marital relationships involving parenting or distribution of assets/liabilities.

(b) **Court's Automatic Temporary Restraining Order.** Upon the filing of a Summons and Petition in any of the actions specified above, the court shall issue an Automatic Temporary Restraining Order, for which no fees will be imposed, using the form set forth in Appendix A FORM A–3. The Petitioner is subject to this order from the time of filing the Petition. The Petitioner shall serve a copy of this order on the Respondent and file a declaration of service in the court file. The Respondent is subject to this order from the time that the order is served.

(c) **Limitations on Declarations.**

(1) *Application.* This rule shall apply to all family law motions, motions in paternity actions and actions to establish residential schedule, and domestic violence and anti-harassment hearings.

(2) *Formats.*

(a) All motions and pleadings in support thereof, shall use mandatory forms where applicable, follow the format required by GR 14, and meet the requirements of GR 31.

(b) All declarations shall contain information that provides the court with foundational information such as the name of the declarant, relationship to one or both of the parties, age, education, city and state of residence, and occupation. This information shall be provided in summary fashion at the beginning of each declaration.

(c) All filed documents shall be legible. If typed or computer printed, documents shall be in 11 point or larger type and double-spaced.

(3) *Page Limitations.* Absent prior authorization from the court, the entirety of all declarations and affidavits from the parties and any non-expert witnesses in support of motions, including any reply, shall be limited to a total of 15 pages. The entirety of all declarations and affidavits submitted in response to motions shall be limited to a sum total of 10 pages. This rule shall be qualified as follows:

(a) Exhibits. Exhibits that consist of declarations, statements, affidavits or any narrative document of parties or witnesses shall count toward the above page limit. All other exhibits attached to a declaration or affidavit shall not be counted toward the page limit.

(b) Expert Reports and Evaluations. Declarations, affidavits, and reports from Guardians ad litem and similar expert witnesses shall not count toward the above page limit.

(c) Previously considered declarations. Copies of declarations or affidavits previously filed for a motion already ruled upon and supplied only as a convenience to the court in lieu of the court file shall not count toward the above page limit. Such declarations or affidavits shall be counted, however, if the court is expected or is being requested to read such prior declarations and affidavits as a part of a present motion.

(d) Basic pleadings and financial declarations. The above page limits shall not apply to basic pleadings and financial declarations.

(4) *Children's Statements.* Declarations by minors are disfavored and the court may in its discretion refuse to consider such declarations.

(5) *Rules of Evidence Apply.* All submissions, including written materials in affidavits and declarations by the parties and witnesses, must comply with the rules of evidence. All declarations shall be based upon personal knowledge. Violations of this subsection may result in sanctions as set forth hereinafter.

(6) *Inappropriate Submissions.* Unless prior permission of the court is obtained, the parties shall not submit inappropriate or pornographic materials. If permission to submit or file such material is granted, it should be filed in the confidential section of the file.

(7) *Consequences of Non–Compliance.* The court, if it finds that one or both of the parties have violated this rule, may in its discretion assess terms, may require that the matter be stricken or continued, or may refuse to consider those materials that violate this rule.

(8) *Procedure for Court Authorization to Exceed or Excuse Limitations.* The court will not entertain any motion or objection with respect to a request to exceed or excuse the limitations of this rule unless counsel or the parties have first conferred with respect to the motion or objection. Counsel or the parties shall arrange for a mutually convenient conference in person or by telephone. If, after conferring, one or both of the parties believe that the limitations of this rule should be excused, then they shall arrange a telephone conference or appearance before the assigned Commissioner if they are reasonably available, or if the assigned Commissioner is not available then they shall arrange a telephone conference or appearance before the Ex Parte department to have the court determine if the rule should be excused.

(d) Service of Financial Declarations and Assets & Debt Matrix. Within thirty (30) calendar days after the filing of an answer or other responsive pleading in any of the actions specified above, each party shall be required to serve the following documents on the opposing party:

(1) *Petitioner's Obligation.* Upon receipt of the answer or response, the Petitioner shall, within fifteen (15) calendar days serve their Verified Financial Declaration and Verified Statement of Assets & Debt Matrix upon the Respondent.

(2) *Respondent's Obligation.* Upon receipt of declaration and financial statements as per (c) (1) above from Petitioner, the Respondent shall, within fifteen (15) calendar days, serve Petitioner a Verified Financial Declaration and Verified Statement of Assets & Debt Matrix.

(3) *Parties' Obligations.* Each party shall then file with the court a Declaration of Mailing, attesting that the Financial Declaration and Verified Statement of Assets & Debt Matrix has been provided to the other party within the thirty (30) calendar day time limit. All parties have a duty to supplement the financial information when additional information becomes available.

(4) *Final Statement.* The parties final Verified Statement of Assets & Debt Matrix shall be filed with the court within fourteen (14) calendar days of any scheduled trial. The Verified Financial Declarations must be filed with the court in cases involving a request for child support, maintenance or attorney's fees.

(e) Pro Se Review. Any party representing themselves (Pro Se) shall have their pleadings (except petitions for domestic violence protection orders, antiharassment protection orders or sexual assault protection orders) reviewed by the Court's Facilitator. This does not prevent anyone from filing or scheduling a hearing; however to avoid delays and in consideration of court efficiency their pleadings must be reviewed as follows:

(1) *Temporary Motion/Orders.* For temporary orders or motions at least two (2) judicial days prior to scheduled hearing.

(2) *Final Orders/Decrees.* For trials parties shall see the facilitator at least forty-five (45) calendar days prior to scheduled trial.

The Court's Facilitator may review further pleadings as necessary however; any pleadings required for completion (finalization) of the action shall be reviewed. Any pleadings required to be reviewed may be reviewed by an attorney acting as a third-party neutral in accordance with RPC 2.4, or a Limited License Legal Technician as per APR 28 who shall certify the pleadings as reviewed using the form in Appendix A form A–2.

[Adopted effective September 2, 2013. Amended effective September 2, 2014.]

LSPR 94.04.02.   PARENTING SEMINARS

(a) **Applicable Cases.** This rule shall apply to all cases under Chapter 26.09, 26.10, or 26.26 RCW which require a parenting plan or residential schedule for minor children, including major modifications and paternity actions in which paternity has been established.

(b) **Mandatory Attendance.** Except as provided in Section (e) below, within ninety (90) calendar days of filing an appearance, answer or other responsive pleading in this action, both parties shall attend, a court-approved parent education seminar on the effects of family transitions on children, unless the parties have previously attended such a course. The court may also accept any comparable class that has been approved by any other superior court. (Contact Superior Court at (509) 422–7130 for a list of approved seminars/courses) **superiorcourt@co.okanogan.wa. us**

(c) **Certificate of Completion.** Upon completion of the seminar or prior to presentment of final documents, each party shall file with the Superior Court Clerk the seminar completion certificate provided by the sponsoring agency or provider.

(d) **Fees.** Each party shall be responsible for paying any fees charged by the approved provider.

(e) **Waiver/Special Consideration.** Any waiver of attendance or special consideration may be made in accordance to RCW 26.12.172 or for good cause.

(f) **Exchange of Parenting Plans.** Within twenty-one (21) calendar days of completing the parenting seminar, each parent shall provide the other parent with a Proposed Parenting Plan, or may submit a mutually agreed proposed parenting, or a joinder.

(g) **Failure to Comply.** Willful refusal to participate in a parenting seminar or willful delay in completing or failure to exchange/provide a proposed parenting plan may result in a finding of contempt and imposition of sanctions. The Court may decline to

enter finalization documents until both parents have completed the seminar.

[Adopted effective September 2, 2013. Amended effective September 2, 2014; September 1, 2015.]

LSPR 94.04.03.   MANDATORY MEDIATION

(a) **Mediation in Contested Cases.** Except as provided in Section (b) below, in all Family law petitions seeking dissolution of marriage, legal separation, or declaration of invalidity; and actions brought by parties to non-marital relationships involving parenting or distribution of assets/liabilities having unresolved issues, both parties shall in good faith engage in mediation with Okanogan County Dispute Resolution Center, licensed attorney, mediation service or individual trained (certificated) in this specialized area in an effort to resolve the case. In cases where parenting issues exist, the mediation shall not occur until both parties have completed the parenting seminar. Mediation shall be completed prior to any settlement conference except as per subsection (b).

(b) **When Mediation may not be required.** Mediation shall not be required, but is encouraged, as provided in Section (a) in the following cases:

(1) *Good Cause.* For good cause shown upon motion and approval by the court; or

(2) *Indigent.* Upon determination of a party's indigence through procedures under GR 34 as implemented by the court; or

(3) *Domestic Violence.* Where a Domestic Violence or Anti–Harassment order is currently in effect, involving the parties and/or their dependent children whether it exists pursuant to RCW 10.99 or RCW 26.50 or RCW 26.09.016.

(c) **Requests for Mediation.** If not required under subsection (b) above, either party may by motion seek a court order requiring mediation if that party can demonstrate that it can be accomplished in a safe and reasonable manner.

(d) **Settlement Conference.** If, after mediation in good faith or where mediation is not required, there remain unresolved issues, then a settlement conference may take place pursuant to LR 16(d).

(e) **Effect on Court Proceedings.** Mediation does not stay or otherwise affect the rights and duties of the parties established by statute, court rule, or court order. The court may enter temporary orders and the parties may conduct discovery prior to or during the mediation process.

(f) **Cost of Mediation.** Mediators shall be paid by the parties in accordance with the agreement of the parties, or in the absence of agreement, as determined in mediation.

(g) **Responsibility for Compliance.** The parties shall be responsible for arranging for and completing all mediation requirements established under this rule.

(h) Failure to Comply. Willful refusal to participate in mediation or willful delay in completing mediation or non-compliance may result in a finding of contempt and imposition of sanctions.

(i) Approval of Mediators. Mediators performing mediation services pursuant to this rule must fulfill the minimum qualifications set forth in Appendix B.

(j) Selection of Mediator. The parties shall agree on the mediator. If they cannot agree then each party shall submit a list of proposed mediators to the court. The court shall then select from the proposed mediators. A mediator has the right to decline to serve in a particular case. If a mediator declines to serve, the parties or the court shall select a different mediator, using the same selection process by which the preceding mediator was selected.

(k) Authority of Mediator. The mediator has the authority to determine the time, place, manner, and duration of mediation. In appropriate cases, the mediator shall have the authority to terminate the mediation prior to completion.

(*l*) Attendance at Mediation. The parties shall personally attend all mediation sessions, unless the mediator permits telephonic or other attendance. The mediator shall have the authority to require other persons to attend.

(m) Declaration of Completion. Within seven (7) days of completion of mediation, a declaration that mediation has been completed shall be filed with the court by the mediator. The mediator shall advise counsel and the parties of the results of mediation in writing. The mediator shall advise the court only whether an agreement has been reached on some or all of the issues.

(n) Confidentiality. The work product of the mediator and all communications during the mediation shall be privileged and confidential and not subject to compulsory disclosure. The mediator shall not appear to testify in any court proceedings. See RCW 5.60.070.

[Adopted effective September 2, 2013. Amended effective September 2, 2014; September 1, 2015.]

LSPR 94.04.04. PROCESS UNDER GR 34

Application Process. Any individual, deemed indigent as defined under GR 34(a)(3), shall make an application to the Court's Judicial Assistant prior to submission of any pleadings or filings to the Okanogan County Clerk. The Judicial Assistant shall submit the application to the Judicial Officer for consideration as per GR 34(a)(2).

[Adopted effective September 2, 2013.]

GUARDIAN AD LITEM RULES

LGALR 1. SCOPE AND DEFINITIONS

Scope and Purpose. This local rule covers the maintenance and administration of the Guardian ad Litem Registry by the Judicial Assistants.

[Adopted effective September 2, 2013.]

LGALR 2. GENERAL RESPONSIBIL-ITIES OF GUARDIAN AD LITEM

(a) Education and Experience Requirements.

(1) *Attorneys.*

(a) Member of the Washington State Bar Association in good standing; and

(b) For initial placement on registry, completion of any training as required by statute. For retention on registry, completion of any continuing training, as may be required by statute or the court from time to time.

(2) *Non–attorneys.*

(a) For initial placement on registry, completion of any training as required by statute. An individual must have a Bachelor's Degree from a fully accredited college or university in social/behavioral sciences, criminal justice, counseling or other closely related field with a minimum of two years' work experience in the field. At the sole discretion of the Presiding Judge, or their designee, a combination of relevant education, training and experience may be accepted in lieu of, or as an equivalent to, the educational and/or experience requirements. For retention on registry, completion of any continuing training, as may be required by statute or the court from time to time.

(b) New registry GAL's shall complete observation hours as determined by the court.

(b) Application and Annual Renewal. Any application shall be submitted on a form provided by the court and shall be renewed annually by date specified by the court. The application shall include the following:

(1) The name, business address, and telephone number of the applicant.

(2) The level of formal education of the applicant and, if the applicant is an attorney, the year admitted to practice in Washington State and any other States in which the attorney is licensed to practice.

(3) A listing of training relating to the GAL's duties.

(4) The number of years' experience as a GAL.

(5) The number of appointments as a GAL, Counties of appointment and types of matters.

(6) The applicant's criminal history as defined by RCW 9.94A.030.

(7) The applicant shall be fingerprinted at the Okanogan County Sheriff's Department.

(8) Any additional evidence of applicant's education, knowledge, training, and experience.

(9) A statement describing the nature, status, and outcome of any complaints, investigations, disciplinary actions, lawsuits, or liability claims lodged against the GAL related to the person's duties as a GAL or their profession along with any orders for removal of the GAL entered prior to the completion of the GAL's duties for any reason other than a conflict of interest where the GAL had no prior knowledge that the conflict existed.

(10) A description of the fees to be charged by the applicant (hourly rate and any required retainer) and a statement of the applicant's willingness to accept cases on a reduced fee basis.

(11) Agreement to advise the court immediately in the event of any complaint, investigation, or action being commenced related to the applicant's duties as a GAL in the instant or any other case which could lead to:

(a) Discipline of the applicant;

(b) The suspension or revocation of the applicant's professional license(s).

(12) Agreement to advise the court immediately upon the filing of criminal charges for a felony or a crime involving allegations of theft, dishonesty, or moral turpitude.

(c) Retention on Registry.

(1) Persons on the registry shall promptly inform the court of any temporary unavailability to serve, or of their intent to resign from the registry.

(2) A person shall remain on the registry unless the person fails to maintain a current application with attachments or the person is removed or suspended as set forth in Section (g).

(3) A person may be denied listing on, or may be temporarily suspended from, the registry for any reason that places the suitability of the person to act as GAL in question.

(4) A GAL who ceases to be on the registry and who still has active or incomplete cases shall immediately report this circumstance to the Registry Administrator, who shall reassign such cases.

(5) A person's retention on the registry shall be reviewed upon the court's receipt of a complaint regarding performance in office or the court's receipt of adverse information regarding the suitability of a person to serve as a GAL. Complaints shall be reviewed in accordance with Section (g).

[Adopted effective September 2, 2013. Amended effective September 2, 2014.]

LGALR 5. APPOINTMENTS OF GUARDIAN AD LITEM

(a) Appointment of a Guardian ad Litem from Registry.

(1) For Title 26 cases only in cases where the parties agree, any GAL from the registry may be appointed.

(2) In Title 11 cases or in Title 26 cases where the parties cannot agree, a party needing an appointment from a GAL registry shall request the same from the Registry Administrator. If the requesting party is represented by counsel, the attorney shall then contact the proposed GAL to determine if he/she is available to serve. If the requesting party is pro se, the Registry Administrator shall contact the proposed GAL to determine if he/she is available to serve. The person whose name next appears on the registry on a rotational basis shall be appointed, subject to that person's acceptance of the appointment.

(3) The person appointed by the Registry Administrator shall serve upon the parties a notice of appointment.

(4) Any order providing for the appointment will then be submitted to the Registry Administrator within three days.

(b) Registry Administration. The court shall maintain a GAL registry and appoint a registry administrator (Judicial Assistant). The registry is limited to RCW Titles 11.88, 13 and 26 GAL's. These requirements and procedures apply to persons whether listed or not listed on the registry who is appointed to serve as a Guardian ad Litem.

(1) The Court shall maintain an application form and background information records pertaining to each person. Persons shall reapply and update background information annually on a date specified by the court. All application and background information, with the exception of personal identifying information in family law cases and pending complaints, shall be available for public inspection.

(2) Persons shall be selected for appointment at the discretion of the Court giving due consideration to:

(a) Having a sufficient number of GAL's available to fulfill the requests for appointment;

(b) Achieving and maintaining diversity; and

(c) Retaining panels of persons with substantial experience and special knowledge within given fields. In some cases there may be more qualified applicants that will be needed or would benefit the program, so that not all persons applying will be selected.

(d) All Guardian Ad Litem's shall comply with RCW 26.12.177

(3) The court may periodically sponsor or approve training programs which registry applicants shall be required to attend to maintain and improve their level of proficiency. Training programs may be co-sponsored or offered by the state or local bar association under the oversight of the court.

(4) The registry may be reconstituted as necessary. The court may allow additional applicants to be added to the registry upon approval of applicant.

(5) The court may impose an application processing fee and/or charge a fee for the training programs.

[Adopted effective September 2, 2013. Amended effective September 2, 2014; September 1, 2015.]

LGALR 7. GRIEVANCE PROCEDURE

Grievance Procedure.

(1) There shall be a grievance review committee consisting of the Superior Court Presiding Judge, the Court Administrator and a representative of the Okanogan County Bar Association as appointed by the then County Bar President. This attorney shall be compensated at an hourly rate of one hundred fifty dollars an hour not to exceed six hours unless otherwise authorized by the Presiding Judge.

(2) All grievances must be in writing and must be submitted to the Superior Court Presiding Judge or Administrator.

(3) Upon receipt of a written grievance, the Presiding Judge or Administrator shall convene the Grievance Review Committee within ten (10) business days to review the grievance. Upon review of the grievance, the Grievance Review Committee shall either:

(a) Make a finding that the grievance has no merit on its face, and decline to review the grievance and so inform the complainant; or

(b) Make a finding that the grievance does appear to have merit and request a written response from the GAL within ten (10) business days, detailing the specific issues in the grievance to which the Committee desires a response. The Committee shall provide the GAL with a copy of the original grievance. A GAL's failure to respond within the required ten (10) business days will result in the immediate suspension of the GAL from all registries.

(c) In considering whether the grievance has merit, the Grievance Review Committee shall consider whether the grievance alleges the GAL has:

(1) Violated the code of conduct;

(2) Misrepresented his or her qualifications to serve as GAL;

(3) Not met the annual update requirements set forth in Section (d) of this policy;

(4) Breached the confidentiality of the parties;

(5) Falsified information in a report to the court or in testimony before the court;

(6) Failed to report abuse of a child;

(7) Communicated with a judicial officer ex-parte;

(8) Represented the court in a public forum without prior approval of the court;

(9) Violated state or local laws, rules, or this policy in the person's capacity as a GAL; or,

(10) Taken or failed to take any other action which would reasonable[1] place the suitability of the person to serve as GAL in question.

(4) Upon receipt of a written response to a complaint from the GAL, the Grievance Review Committee shall, within ten (10) business days, make a finding as to each of the issues delineated in the Committee's letter to the GAL that either there is no merit to the issues based upon the GAL's response or that there is merit to the issue. The Review Committee may, at their discretion, extend the time for entering findings to conduct additional investigation if necessary; however, in no case shall that extension be for more than twenty (20) business days and the GAL shall be notified.

(5) The Grievance Review Committee shall have the authority to issue a written admonishment, a written reprimand, refer the GAL to additional training or recommend to the court, upon its own motion, to remove the GAL from the instant case, or suspend or remove the GAL from the registry. In considering a response, the Committee shall take into consideration any prior grievance which resulted in an admonishment, reprimand, referral to training, removal of the GAL from a particular case, or suspension or removal from a registry. If a GAL is listed on more than one registry, the suspension or removal may apply to each registry the GAL is listed on at the discretion of the Committee.

(6) The complainant and the GAL shall be notified in writing of the Committee's decision within 10 business days of receipt of the GAL response.

[Adopted effective September 2, 2013. Amended effective September 2, 2014.]

[1] So in original.

LGALR 8. COMPENSATION

Payment of Guardian ad Litem

(1) There shall be no payment of a GAL by anyone, except as authorized by order of the court.

(2) Each order appointing GAL shall set forth the hourly rate of compensation and/or a monetary limit for the investigative/legal work; source of payment, if determined; and unless waived, shall require the GAL to seek prior court authorization to provide services in excess of the time and/or amount previously authorized by court order including court appearances.

(3) The order appointing a GAL may include a provision for an advance payment on fees and proportionate responsibility for payment to the GAL.

(4) All fee requests by the GAL submitted to the court shall contain time records, which distinguish investigative/legal, administrative/clerical, and travel time and shall also be served upon the parties.

(5) GAL fees shall be the responsibility of a party or parties unless the court has entered an order authorizing payment at public expense. Any limitation shall be established by the court at the time of the initial appointment.

[Adopted effective September 2, 2013. Amended effective September 2, 2014; September 1, 2015.]

CRIMINAL RULES

LCrR 3.1. RIGHT TO AND ASSIGNMENT OF LAWYER

(d) Assignment of Lawyer.

(5) Upon notification of assignment, the assigned attorney shall within five (5) judicial days file their Notice of Appearance or at the arraignment hearing whichever is earlier. Further any attorney substituting shall file their notice within five (5) judicial days of assignment and/or substitution whichever is sooner.

(6) Appointed and assigned counsel shall file quarterly, with the Okanogan County Clerk, on the form recommended by the Supreme Court, a certificate declaring that counsel is in compliance with the applicable Standards for Indigent Defense promulgated by the Supreme Court of Washington. An appointed or assigned attorney who is not in compliance with the applicable standards, or who has not filed a certificate prior to appearing or filing a notice of appearance, shall so advise the court at every hearing.

[Adopted effective September 1, 2015.]

LCrR 6.15. JURY INSTRUCTIONS

Consistent with CrR 6.15, all parties shall file with the trial judge an original and one copy of their proposed instructions. The original shall not be numbered nor include any citations of authority. The copy shall contain a proposed number and any citation of authority in support of the instruction. Authorities may include any number from any published book of instructions or case name and citation. Instructions must be provided to the trial judge not later than the day prior to commencement of trial.

[Adopted effective September 1, 2015.]

LCrR 8.9. CHANGE OF JUDGE

Affidavit of Prejudice. In addition to the procedures set out in CrR 8.9 the party or their counsel shall provide a copy of the motion and affidavit to the Judicial Assistant of Superior Court of Okanogan for proper assignment of the case.

[Adopted effective September 1, 2015.]

LOCAL RULES FOR MANDATORY ARBITRATION

LMAR 1.2. MANDATORY ARBITRATION OF CIVIL ACTIONS

Scope and Purpose. The purpose of mandatory arbitration of civil actions under RCW 7.06 as implemented by the Mandatory Arbitration Rules is to provide a simplified and economical procedure for obtaining the prompt and equitable resolution of disputes involving claims of $75,000.00 or less. The Mandatory Arbitration Rules as supplemented by these local rules are not designed to address every question which may arise during the arbitration process, and the rules give considerable discretion to the Arbitrator. The Arbitrator should not hesitate to exercise that discretion. Arbitration hearings should be informal and expeditious, consistent with the purpose of the statutes and rules.

[Adopted effective September 2, 2013.]

LMAR 1.2.01. GENERAL RESPONSIBILITIES OF ARBITRATORS

Education, Application and Renewal Requirements

(1) Must be in good standing with the Washington Bar Association.

(2) Must provide the required documentation including but not limited to the Oath of an Arbitrator, W–9 tax form and Arbitrator information sheet. All required documentation must be submitted to the Judicial Assistant upon request. Once on the registry the Judicial Assistant will review annually as for compliance.

(3) Any and all grievances regarding an arbitrator must be reported in a statement describing the nature, status, outcome of any complaints, investigations, disciplinary actions, and or lawsuits lodged against the arbitrator related to the person's duties as an arbitrator or their profession along with any orders for removal as an arbitrator.

[Adopted effective September 2, 2014.]

APPENDICES

APPENDIX A

FORM A-1.   ASSET & DEBT MATRIX

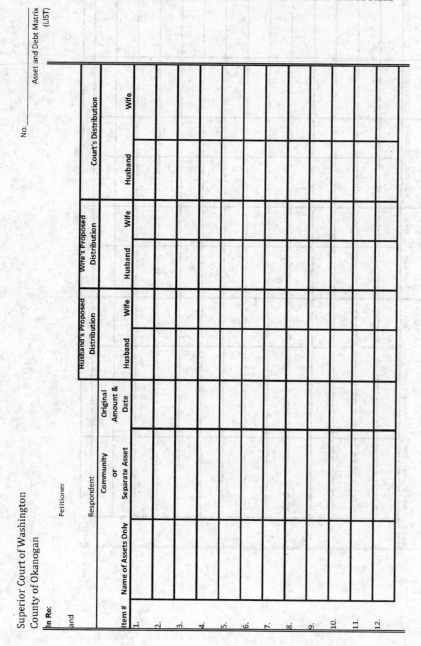

Superior Court of Washington
County of Okanogan

In Re:

        Petitioner

and

        Respondent

No. _____

Asset and Debt Matrix (LIST)

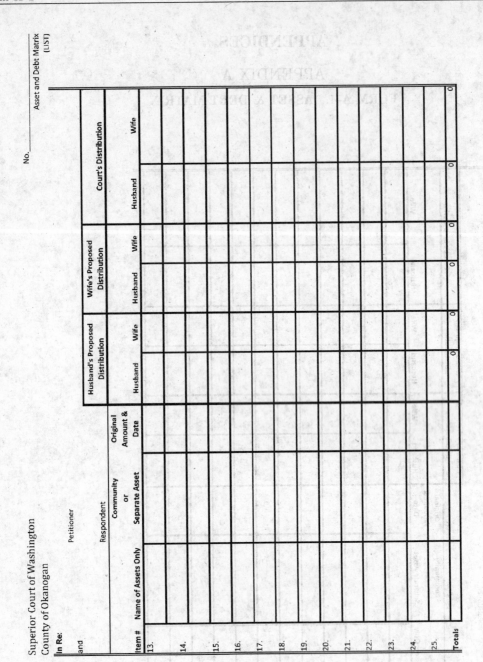

Item #	Name of Assets Only	Community or Separate Asset	Original Amount & Date	Husband's Proposed Distribution		Wife's Proposed Distribution		Court's Distribution	
				Husband	Wife	Husband	Wife	Husband	Wife
13.									
14.									
15.									
16.									
17.									
18.									
19.									
20.									
21.									
22.									
23.									
24.									
25.									
Totals				0	0	0	0	0	0

Asset Debt Matrix
Page 2

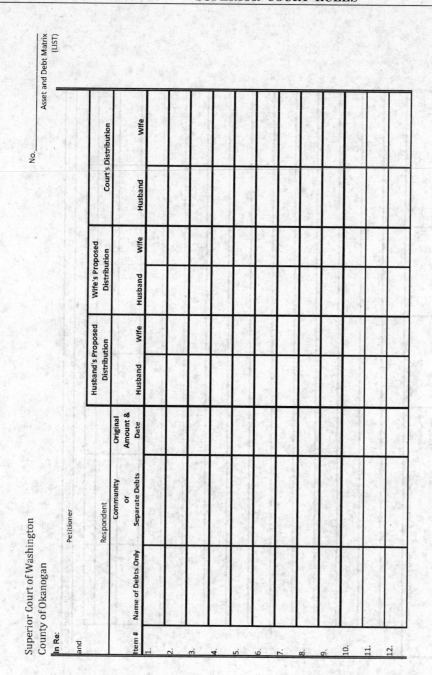

Superior Court of Washington
County of Okanogan

In Re:

Petitioner

and

Respondent

No. _____

Asset and Debt Matrix
(LIST)

Item #	Name of Debts Only	Community or Separate Debts	Original Amount & Date	Husband's Proposed Distribution		Wife's Proposed Distribution		Court's Distribution	
				Husband	Wife	Husband	Wife	Husband	Wife
1.									
2.									
3.									
4.									
5.									
6.									
7.									
8.									
9.									
10.									
11.									
12.									

Asset Debt Matrix
Page 3

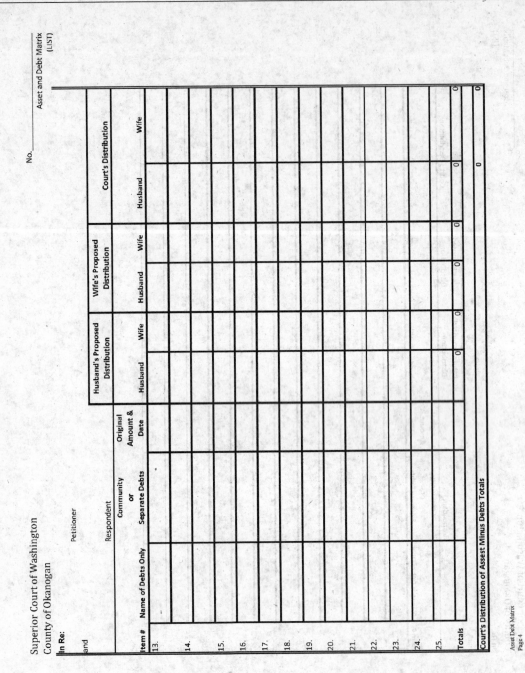

Superior Court of Washington
County of Okanogan

In Re:

    Petitioner

and

    Respondent

Asset and Debt Matrix (LIST)

No. _____

Item #	Name of Debts Only	Community or Separate Debts	Original Amount & Date	Husband's Proposed Distribution		Wife's Proposed Distribution		Court's Distribution	
				Husband	Wife	Husband	Wife	Husband	Wife
13.									
14.									
15.									
16.									
17.									
18.									
19.									
20.									
21.									
22.									
23.									
24.									
25.									
Totals				0	0	0	0	0	0

Court's Distribution of Assest Minus Debts Totals

Asset Debt Matrix
Page 4

[Adopted effective September 2, 2013. Amended effective September 2, 2014; September 1, 2015.]

FORM A-2. ATTORNEY CERTIFICATION FORM/LIMITED LICENSE CERTIFICATION FORM

Superior Court of Washington
County of Okanogan

[x] In re:

Petitioner,

And

Respondent.

Case No.

☐ Attorney Certification Form
☐ Limited License Legal Tech (APR 28)

(As reviewer of pleading)

I _____ declare as follows:

I am over the age of 18 years; I am the third-party neutral in accordance with RPC 2.4 or APR 28 in the entitled action.

On the _____ of _____ 201__, I reviewed the following documents in this action:

_____

_____

I am in compliance with Okanogan County Local Rule LSPR 94.04.01.

I declare under penalty of perjury under the laws of the state of Washington that the foregoing statement is true and correct.

Dated at _____, _____ this _____ day of _____ 201__.

_____   _____
Signature   Print

Attorney Certification Form/ Limited License Certification form
Page 1

[Adopted effective September 2, 2013. Amended effective September 2, 2014; September 1, 2015.]

FORM A-3. AUTOMATIC TEMPORARY RESTRAINING ORDER

Superior Court of Washington
County of Okanogan

[ ] In re	No.
Petitioner,	Automatic Temporary Restraining Order
And	(TMRO)
Respondent.	

I. NOTICE TO PARTIES

1.1 An action has been started in this court that affects your rights. Both parties are now required to obey the following order unless the court changes it. Either of you may ask the court to change or clarify this order. The court has the power to punish violations of this order and to require the violator to pay attorneys' fees to the party for having to bring the violation before the court.

1.2 The financial restraints in section 2.1 below and the requirement to fill out the attached "Verified Statement of Assets and Liabilities" only apply in actions for (1) dissolution of marriage, legal separation, or marriages declared to be invalid, or (2) non-marital relationships involving distribution of assets and liabilities.

II. ORDER

IT IS ORDERED:

2.1 TEMPORARY ORDERS FOR ALL PARTIES

(a.) The [x] petitioner [x] respondent are mutually restrained and enjoined from transferring, removing, encumbering, concealing or in any way disposing of any property except in the usual course of business or for the necessities of life and requiring each party to notify the other of any extraordinary expenditures made after the order is issued.

(b.) The [x] petitioner [x] respondent are mutually restrained and enjoined from assigning, transferring, borrowing, lapsing, surrendering or changing entitlement of any insurance policies of either or both parties whether medical, health, life or auto insurance.

Automatic Temporary Restraining Order
Page 1 of 2

(c.) Each party shall be immediately responsible for their own future debts whether incurred by credit card or loan, security interest or mortgage.

(d.) Both parties shall have access to all tax, financial, legal, and household records. Reasonable access to records shall not be denied without order of the court.

(e.) Within 30 days after the filing of any general appearance, answer or other responsive pleading, each party shall provide the other party with a completed Financial Declaration (WPF DR 01.1550). In all cases involving a request for child support maintenance or attorney fees, the Financial Declaration shall also be filed with the court. All parties have a duty to supplement the financial information when additional information becomes available.

2.2 TEMPORARY ORDERS FOR PARTIES WITH MINOR CHILD(REN)

(a.) The [x] petitioner [x] respondent are mutually restrained from changing the residence of the child(ren) until further order of the court or unless agreed upon in writing by the parties.

(b.) Neither parent shall make negative remarks about the other parent.

(c.) Each parent will take the parenting class as required by local court rule.

(d.) Both parents are entitled to any and all education and medical records unless otherwise ordered by the court.

2.3 EFFECTIVE DATE OF ORDER

The Petitioner is subject to this order from the time of filing the Petition. The petitioner shall serve a copy of this on the Respondent and file a Return of Service with the Okanogan County Superior Clerk's office. The Respondent is subject to this order from the time that the order is served. This shall be the order of the court until further order of the court.

This order shall not constitute a discretionary decision by the undersigned judge.

This General Order shall be effective for all Dissolution or related matters filed after the first day of September 2013.

Issued this _____ of _____ 20_.

_____
Judge

Automatic Temporary Restraining Order
Page 2 of 2

[Adopted effective September 2, 2013. Amended effective September 2, 2014.]

FORM A–4. DECLARATION OF COMPLIANCE

Superior Court of Washington
County of Okanogan

[x] In re:

_____ Petitioner,   Case No.
                                    Declaration of Compliance
                                    (DCLR)

And

_____ Respondent.

_____

I _____ the Petitioner/Respondent declare as follows:
I am over the age of 18 years. On the ___ day of _____ 201 ___, I deposited an envelope in the regular U.S. mail, postage prepaid, addressed as follows:
Name of Party (Petitioner/Respondent): _____
Mailing address (PO Box /Physical): _____
                 (City/ State/Zip): _____

The envelope contained copies of the following: **Verified Financial Declaration, Verified Asset and Debt Matrix**
I am in compliance with Okanogan County Superior Court Local Rule LSPR 94.04.01.
I declaration[1] under penalty of perjury, pursuant to the laws of the state of Washington, that the foregoing information and statement is true and correct.
Dated this ___ day of _____ 201 ___ at _____.

_____   _____
     Signature   Print

[Adopted effective September 2, 2013.]

---

1 So in original.

FORM A–5. NOTE FOR HEARING

Superior Court of Washington
County of Okanogan

Petitioner,	**No.**
And	
Respondent.	**Note for Hearing** **Clerk's Action Required** **(NTHG)**

To the Clerk of Court and to:

1. Please note that this case will be place on the hearing calendar regarding

   _____

   ☐ Civil Law and Motion Calendar for hearing on Monday, _____ at 9:00 am

(date)

   ☐ Agreed Orders Calendar on Monday, _____ at 2:00 pm

(date)

   ☐ Interpreter required _____

(language)

Place: Okanogan Superior Court (*Courtroom to be determined*)
149 3rd Ave N., Okanogan, WA 98840

Dated:_____   _____
                                    Signature of Requesting Party or Lawyer/WSBA No.

Note for Hearing
Page 1

[Adopted effective September 2, 2013. Amended effective September 2, 2014; September 1, 2015.]

FORM A–6. ORDER FOR PRETRIAL CONFERENCE

Superior Court of Washington
County of Okanogan

Plaintiff(s)

No.
ORDER FOR PRETRIAL
CONFERENCE (OR)

And

Defendant(s)

THIS CAUSE appearing to be at issue and ready for trial, it is

1. ORDERED AND ADJUDGED THAT a pretrial conference will be held in Chambers at ____.m. at the Okanogan County Courthouse on the ___ day of _____, 20 ___. Total time allocated for the conference will be _____. The attorneys who will conduct the trial must attend this conference.

All discovery procedures shall be completed by the time of this conference.

2. ORDERED AND ADJUDGED THAT at least five working days prior to this conference, the attorneys shall submit to the trial judge and to opposing counsel a Pretrial Statement containing the following:

   (a)   A list designating those pleadings upon which the case goes to trial;

   (b)   A succinct statement of the cause of action in regard to each claim or defense;

   (c)   A clear statement of the issues to be tried;

   (d)   An itemized list of the claimed special damages;

   (e)   A statement of the principles of law involved in the case, supported by citations of authority;

   (f)   A statement of facts, which his client will admit;

   (g)   A list of the names and addresses of all persons who have knowledge of relevant facts and the general nature of their testimony;

   (h)   A list of all exhibits and documentary evidence, which may be used at the trial;

   (i)   A complete set of written jury instructions, standard and special, which will be proposed for use at the trial, including verdict forms;

   (j)   Any request for preliminary rulings on questions of law with citations in regard thereto;

   (k)   Any trial brief that either party wishes the court to consider.

3. ORDERED AND ADJUDGED THAT at the time of the conference, the first thirty minutes of the conference will be set aside for a meeting between counsel to:

   (a)   Inspect all documentary evidence and transportable exhibits listed in their Pretrial Statements. Exhibits not easily transportable will be made available for inspection at a time and place fixed at the conference.

   (b)   Mark each document and exhibit using consecutive numerals for the plaintiff and the defendant.

(c)   Object to the admissibility of the evidence, reserving the appropriate objections.

(d)   Object to the jury instructions filed with the Pretrial Statements, reserving the appropriate objections.

(e)   Stipulate on all matters of fact and law upon which the parties are in agreement.

DONE AND ORDERED in Chambers in Okanogan County, Washington, this ____ day of _____ 20 ___.

_____
JUDGE

[Adopted effective September 2, 2013.]

FORM A–7.   PRETRIAL ORDER

Superior Court of Washington
County of Okanogan

                    Plaintiff(s)
                                          No.
        And   **Pretrial Order (ORPTC)**

_____
                    Defendant(s)

I. BASIS

1.1   The above matter has been noted for trial setting.
1.2   A pretrial conference was held and the following persons were present:
For Plaintiff(s):   For Defendant(s):

II. ORDER

2.1   Names and addresses of attendant lawyers who will try the case and are authorized to enter into binding stipulations:
For Plaintiff(s):   For Defendant(s):

2.2   Summary of plaintiff's case:
2.3   Summary of defense and counterclaim:
2.4   The following amendments are allowed to the pleadings:
2.5   Names and addresses of plaintiff's witnesses and summary of testimony expected from each:
2.6   Names and addresses of defendant's witnesses and summary of testimony expected from each:
Additional Witnesses: If additional witnesses are discovered, who by the use of reasonable diligence could not have been discovered before the Pretrial Conference, the party intending to use such witness shall immediately report the names, addresses and summary of the testimony of such witness to opposing counsel and the court.
2.7   Facts admitted by stipulation and agreement:
2.8   Exhibits produced for admission:
   a.   The following exhibits were marked, identified and admitted without objection, no further identification or offers of admission shall be required at trial:

   b.   The following exhibits were produced and offered but were objected to for competency, relevancy and materiality; they may be introduced at the trial without formal identification, their authenticity being agreed to:

   c.   The admission of the following exhibits will be contested:

   d.   The following exhibits will be sent to opposing counsel within ____ days and within five days of receipt forwarded to the court with any objections thereto; in the event no objections are raised the exhibits will be admitted in accordance with the provisions of (a) above.

Additional Exhibits: If additional exhibits or documents are discovered which could not have been discovered by reasonable diligence before the Pretrial Conference, the party intending to use them shall immediately exhibit them to opposing counsel and submit them to the court to be marked for identification. Opposing counsel shall immediately indicate to the court his or her position with respect to such exhibit, i.e., whether his or her position falls under (a), (b) or (c) above.

  2.9   Unresolved issues:

  2.10 Points of law passed upon by the court:

  2.11 Estimated length of trial: Jury:

  2.12 Other matters that may aid the trial:

Set for trial:

Approved, stipulated and agreed:

_____	_____
Attorney for Plaintiff	Attorney for Defendant

    IT IS ORDERED that the stipulations be carried out as outlined above.

DATED: _____   _____

                         JUDGE

[Adopted effective September 2, 2013.]

FORM A–8. REQUEST FOR TRIAL SETTING (DISSOLUTION OF MARRIAGE AND OTHER FAMILY LAW CASES) (RQTH)

Superior Court of Washington
County of Okanogan

And _____ **Petitioner,** _____ **Respondent.**	**No.** _____ **Request for Trial Setting** **(Dissolution of Marriage and** **Other Family Law Cases)** **(RQTH)**

TO: Okanogan County Superior Court   Clerk of the Court
        P.O. Box 112   P.O. Box 72
        Okanogan, WA 98840   Okanogan, WA 98840

TO: List all Attorneys or Pro Se Parties (including yourself) with addresses and telephone numbers.

TRIAL SETTING

This case should be set for Non-Jury Trial.

Estimated length of trial_____Day(s)

Dates unavailable for trial (see LR 40(a)):

_____ *Interpreter needed (make sure to specify language needed)*
              Language_____
_____ *Notice to Support Enforcement Required* (If either party is receiving state benefits)

Okanogan County Request for Trial Setting.
Page 1

CERTIFICATION

1. I have served the opposite attorney or Pro Se party with this request on the following date: _____ and in the following manner: _____

2. I have reviewed the Okanogan County Superior Court Local rules relating to dissolution myself and with any party I represent.

3. I (or the party I represent) have satisfactorily completed the required class, Your Child and Divorce sponsored by the Okanogan County Dispute Resolution Center or will attend the next session and will have the requirement completed and certificate filed prior to the court date. (Any equivalent class approved by a court may be substituted).

4. I understand the requirement for 1) the mandatory use of the Court's property and debt Itemization form and 2) providing a complete and current financial declaration at the time of trial.

5. If I am appearing Pro Se, I understand that I am required to always have a Pro Se notice of appearance with my current address and phone number on file with the Superior Clerk's Office. Failure to comply may result in cancellation of my trial.

Dated:_____

_____
Signature of Requesting Party or Lawyer/WSBA No.

_____
Print or Type Name
Notice to party: (you may list an address that is not your residential address where you agree to accept legal documents. <u>Any</u> time this address changes while this action is pending, you must notify the opposing parties in writing and file an updated Confidential Information Form (WPF DRPSCU 09.0200) with the court clerk.)

_____
Address

_____

_____
Telephone Number

Okanogan County Request for Trial Setting.
Page 2

[Adopted effective September 2, 2013. Amended effective September 2, 2014; September 1, 2015.]

FORM A–9.   REQUEST FOR TRIAL SETTING—CIVIL (CIVIL MATTERS OTHER THAN DISSOLUTION OF MARRIAGE AND OTHER FAMILY LAW CASES) (RQTH)

Superior Court of Washington
County of Okanogan

And Petitioner, Respondent.	**No.** **Request for Trial Setting-Civil** **(Civil Matters Other Than** **Dissolution of Marriage and** **Other Family Law Cases)** **(RQTH)**

TO: Okanogan County Superior Court   Clerk of the Court
        P.O. Box 112   P.O. Box 72
        Okanogan, WA 98840   Okanogan, WA 98840

TO: List all Attorneys or Pro Se Parties (including yourself) with addresses and telephone numbers.

TRIAL SETTING

This case should be set for   ☐ Non-Jury Trial.
                                ☐ Jury Trial *   ☐ Six person
                                               ☐ Twelve person

*No Jury Trial will be set until Jury Demand Fee is paid.

Estimated length of trial_____Day(s)

Dates unavailable for trial (see LR 40(a)):

Interpreter needed Yes or No *(please circle one)* Language _____

Okanogan County Request for Trial Setting
Page 1

CERTIFICATION

1. I have served the opposing attorney or Pro Se party with this request on the following date: _____ and in the following manner: _____

2. I have reviewed the Okanogan County Superior Court Local rules myself and with any party I represent.

3. If I am appearing Pro Se, I understand that I am required to always have a Pro Se notice of appearance with my current address and phone number on file with the Superior Clerk's Office. Failure to comply may result in cancellation of my trial.

Dated: _____

_____
Signature of Requesting Party or Lawyer/WSBA No.

_____
Print or Type Name

Notice to party: (you may list an address that is not your residential address where you agree to accept legal documents. Any time this address changes while this action is pending, you must notify the opposing parties in writing.)

_____
Address

_____

_____
Telephone Number

Okanogan County Request for Trial Setting
Page 2

[Adopted effective September 2, 2013. Amended effective September 2, 2014; September 1, 2015.]

APPENDIX B

MINIMUM QUALIFICATIONS FOR SUPERIOR COURT FAMILY LAW MEDIATORS

1. A Jurist Doctor Degree with extensive experience in family law related matter; or

2. A Bachelor's Degree or Master's Degree in Sociology, Psychology or other social or behavioral science plus completion of training in family law mediation upon approval of the court; or

3. A person who has completed a family law mediation training course offered by a law school in the State of Washington or the basic mediation training course and family mediation training offered by the Okanogan County Dispute Resolution Center or such other equivalent mediation training course(s) as shall be approved by the court; or

4. Such other education and experiential qualifications as shall be approved by the Superior Court judge on a case by case basis.

[Adopted effective September 2, 2013.]

DISTRICT COURT

OKANOGAN COUNTY DISTRICT COURT—
[No Local Rules]

MUNICIPAL COURTS
BREWSTER MUNICIPAL COURT—
[No Local Rules]

ELMER CITY MUNICIPAL COURT—
[No Local Rules]

OMAK MUNICIPAL COURT—
[No Local Rules]

TONASKET MUNICIPAL COURT—
[No Local Rules]

TWISP MUNICIPAL COURT—
[No Local Rules]

WINTHROP MUNICIPAL COURT—
[No Local Rules]

PACIFIC COUNTY

Table of Courts

Superior Court

Local Rules for the Superior Court of Pacific and Wahkiakum Counties.

District Courts

North Pacific District Court—[No Local Rules].
South Pacific District Court Local Court Rules.

Municipal Courts

Long Beach Municipal Court—[No Local Rules].
Raymond Municipal Court—[No Local Rules].
South Bend Municipal Court—[No Local Rules].

SUPERIOR COURT

LOCAL RULES FOR THE SUPERIOR COURT OF PACIFIC AND WAHKIAKUM COUNTIES

Including Amendments Received Through
August 15, 2015

Table of Rules

Titles in brackets added by Publisher.

[INTRODUCTION]

The following are the Local Rules for the Superior Court of Pacific County and Wahkiakum County. The Court may modify or suspend any of these Rules in any given case upon good cause being shown or upon the Court's own motion.

[Effective September 1, 2000.]

LOCAL CIVIL RULES (LCR)

RULE 1. SESSIONS, MOTION DAYS AND CALENDARS

A. Sessions. The Court shall be in session on all judicial days from 9:00 a.m. to 12:00 noon and from 1:30 p.m. to 4:30 p.m. Cases may be set by the Court for other dates and times. Court shall be in session beginning at 8:30 a.m. on Motion Day. Except for matters on the motion calendar, all trials and hearings will be set for 9:00 a.m. unless otherwise ordered by the Court (9:30 a.m. in Wahkiakum County). For jury trials counsel should be available for a chambers conference at 8:45 a.m. In the event of a conflict which prevents the second day of a trial from commencing at 9:00 a.m., the parties will be expected to be available to commence the trial at a later time in the day or week.

B. Office Hours. Office hours for the Court Administrator's Office shall be from 8:30 a.m. to 5:00 p.m., Monday through Friday, excluding holidays. Office hours for the Clerk's Office shall be from 8:30 a.m. to 4:30 a.m. Monday through Friday, excluding holidays.

C. Special Christmas Eve Hours. The Court and Superior Court Clerk's Office shall be open each year from 8:00 a.m. to 10:00 a.m. on the last day of work before Christmas Day.

D. Motion Days and Calendar Timing. In Pacific County, Motion Day shall be on Friday of each week. Motion Day may be conducted on another day of a particular week by court order. When a holiday falls on Friday, the previous Thursday may be designated as Motion Day.

In **Pacific County** the Court will hear domestic violence cases on Fridays at 8:30 a.m., adoptions (in chambers) at 8:45 a.m., civil motions at 9:00 a.m., juvenile and dependency cases at 10:00 a.m., **phone conferences between 10:30 a.m. and 11:30 a.m., (to be scheduled through the Court Administrator's Office),** and criminal motions commencing at 1:30 p.m. Domestic matters shall be heard on domestic docket days as set by the Court Administrator and shall not be scheduled on the regular civil docket except as approved by the Court Administrator's office.

In **Wahkiakum County**, Motion Day shall generally be scheduled on alternating Mondays but may be changed due to holidays and vacation schedules. A Motion Day may be conducted on another day of a particular week by court order. When a holiday falls on a normal motion day, the following Tuesday may be designated as Motion Day. The Court will hear the criminal docket at 9:30 a.m. and the civil docket at 10:30 a.m. Telephone conferences are allowed on regular Motion Days but are normally scheduled at a special time later in the morning. Telephone conferences must be scheduled through the Clerk of the Court, the Court Administrator's Office.

E. Noting Motions and Hearings. All matters for the calendar shall be noted through the Clerk's Office on a Note for Motion Docket form (Exhibit B). Notes for Motion Docket must be filed in the Clerk's Office by 1:00 p.m. two days preceding the calendar on which hearing is requested.

F. Telephone Conferences. With the consent of the Court Administrator's Office or the Judge, motions and hearings may be heard by telephone conference or set on days other than motion days. Scheduling of such motions and hearings shall be arranged through the Court Administrator's Office and then noted through the Clerk's Office with a statement on the Notice that the telephone conference was cleared through the Court Administrator's Office. The non-refundable fee for these arrangements and the cost of the call is $25.00 per party and must be paid to the Clerk's office prior to the hearing.

G. Ex Parte Matters. Ex Parte matters may be presented to the Judge in chambers between the hours of 9:00 a.m. and 4:00 p.m. Counsel should call the Court Administrator's Office **in advance** for scheduling presentations. Emergency matters may be presented any time. If the Judge is not available, they may be presented to a Court Commissioner, if available. Lawyers should not ask the Court for ex parte orders without notice to opposing counsel if counsel has appeared either formally or informally. All orders must be filed with the Clerk forthwith when signed. Orders signed away from the courthouse shall provide that they are not effective until filed.

H. Juvenile and Dependency Dockets. The Court Administrator will schedule (in advance) a specific day each month for juvenile offender cases and a specific day for dependency hearings. The Juvenile Office shall set all juvenile matters on the designated juvenile offender day at 9:00 a.m., except that the Prosecuting Attorney may set first appearance matters. Dependency actions shall be set on the designated monthly dependency day at 9:00 a.m. Dependency actions or juvenile trials that require more than one hour on the docket shall be noted for 11:00 a.m., unless otherwise set by the Court, by counsel for the respondent or the party requesting the case be tried. If a juvenile trial is scheduled for later in the day on the regular juvenile docket and the case settles, counsel for the respondent **MUST RE-NOTE** the matter for **9:00 a.m.** and advise all the parties, including witnesses, as soon as practicable.

I. Interpreters. In all cases where an interpreter is required, it shall be the responsibility of the person requesting an interpreter to make arrangements to have an interpreter present at hearings by contacting the Court Administrator's office.

The Court Administrator's Office shall be responsible for arranging for an interpreter for indigent juveniles or indigent parties in dependency proceedings, **upon the request of court appointed counsel, the Juvenile Office, or the Prosecutor's Office.** It shall be the responsibility of the requesting party's counsel to notify the Court Administrator's office of any change of hearing date(s) that require an interpreter. **Failure to do so may result in sanctions,** including, but not limited to, imposition of monetary penalties against the party not in compliance with this rule.

K.[1] Domestic Docket. Domestic Dockets will be held two days a month. The Superior Court Administrator's Office should be contacted for a list of the scheduled Domestic Docket days. All matters shall be scheduled for 9:00 a.m. If a trial is scheduled for later in the day on the regular Domestic docket and the case settles, counsel or the parties shall **must [2] re-note** the matter for 9:00 a.m. as soon as practicable.

[Effective September 1, 2000; amended effective September 1, 2004; September 1, 2008; September 1, 2012.]

1 As numbered from original.

2 So in original.

RULE 2.   ASSIGNMENT OF CASES

A.   Setting of Trial Dates. The Court Administrator shall schedule all trial dates. A Request or Trial Setting substantially in the form set forth herein (Exhibit A) shall be served by the moving party upon all parties involved in the action. The Request For Trial Setting notice shall reflect the number of days requested for trial, whether jury or non-jury, and a list of counsel's available dates for trial and settlement conference (if over one day is requested), in addition to other relevant information. The original shall be filed with the Court Clerk with **a copy to the Court Administrator**. The opposing party shall serve and file a similar form (Exhibit A) prior to the date noted for hearing indicating his or her available dates for trial and settlement conference (see Rule 3: Settlement Conferences). It is not required that counsel attend the hearing to set a trial date **but only if** they have sent a list of their available dates to the Court Administrator **prior** to the scheduled hearing date.

If available dates are not received by the Court Administrator by the date in which it appears on the motion docket for trial setting, the Court Administrator will schedule the trial using the available dates received by those counsel who have responded to the Request For Trial Setting notice. If the assigned trial date is inconvenient for any party who fails to respond to the Request For Trial Setting (i.e., forwarding available dates or appearing personally at trial setting), that party must file a motion with the Court requesting the trial date be changed.

If requesting a jury trial, the Demand For Jury must be filed and fee paid <u>prior</u> to setting a trial date.

The initial Request For Trial Setting shall be accompanied by a list of the names and addresses of all persons entitled to notice. All parties have the obligation to inform the Court Administrator promptly of any errors or changes in this list.

B.   Pacific County/Grays Harbor County Judge Trades. In the event the Pacific County Superior Court judge either voluntarily disqualifies himself from a case due to a conflict or an Affidavit of Prejudice is filed, in most instances the case will then be heard by a Grays Harbor County Superior Court judge. Motion hearings should be noted up on the Grays Harbor County Superior Court motion docket by contacting the Grays Harbor County Court Administrator's Office at (360) 249-5311 and requesting a date and time prior to preparing a Note For Motion Docket (Exhibit B). The original of the Note For Motion Docket and related pleadings should be filed with the Pacific County Superior Court Clerk with courtesy copies sent to Grays Harbor County Superior Court Administrator, 102 W. Broadway, Montesano, WA 98563 with a request that any enclosed bench copies be given to the judge hearing the matter. Upon receipt of the original Note for Motion Docket, the Pacific County Clerk will make arrangements to have the court file transferred to Grays Harbor County prior to the hearing date.

C.   Wahkiakum County/Cowlitz County Judge Trades. In the event the Wahkiakum County Superior Court Judge either voluntarily disqualifies himself from a case due to a conflict or an affidavit of Prejudice is filed, in most instances the case will then be heard by a Cowlitz County Superior Court Judge. Motion hearings should be noted upon the Cowlitz County Superior Court motion docket by contacting the Cowlitz County Court Administrator's Office and requesting a date and time prior to preparing a Note For Motion Docket (Exhibit B). The original of the Note For Motion Docket and related pleadings should be filed with the Wahkiakum County Superior Court Clerk with courtesy copies sent to Cowlitz County Superior Court with a request that any enclosed bench copies be given to the judge hearing the matter. Upon receipt of the original Note for Motion Docket, the Wahkiakum County Clerk will make arrangements to have the court file transferred to Cowlitz County prior to the hearing date.

[Effective September 1, 2000. Amended effective September 1, 2004; September 1, 2008; September 1, 2012; September 2, 2013.]

RULE 3.   SETTLEMENT CONFERENCES

Settlement conferences shall be required in all cases involving more than one day of trial time. Settlement conferences shall be scheduled at least two (2) months prior to the trial date. Settlement conferences are normally heard before a court commissioner but may be heard by the presiding judge if the case will be heard by a jury. Upon the agreement of counsel, an arbitrator or mediator of their choice may conduct the settlement conference.

Available dates for settlement conferences shall be included at the time available trial dates are submitted by counsel as set forth in Rule 2 above. Settlement conferences are informal and held off the record. All parties to the action shall be personally present or send a party with full authority to settle (telephone appearances are not allowed). Non-attorney insurance representatives need only be available by telephone. Lead counsel shall personally attend the settlement conference. Counsel should submit a pre-settlement conference brief to the settlement judge outlining their issues in the case three (3) workdays prior to the settlement conference. If the name of the settlement conference judge is not included on the Notice of Settlement Conference and Trial Date, counsel may call the Court Administrator or Asst. Court Administrator for that information. **ATTENDANCE AT SETTLEMENT CONFERENCES IS MANDATORY UNLESS WAIVED BY THE COURT. TERMS MAY BE IMPOSED FOR ANY VIOLATION OF THIS RULE.**

[Effective September 1, 2000; amended effective September 1, 2004; September 1, 2008; September 1, 2012.]

RULE 4.   PRE–TRIAL/TRIAL PROCEEDINGS

A.   Jury Trials. Counsel shall report to the Judge at least one-half hour before the scheduled beginning of a jury trial. Counsel shall be prepared to present any final pretrial matters to the Court. Pretrial matters and motions in limine requiring argument shall be noted for hearing at least two weeks prior to the morning of the trial. Jury trials should be conducted with minimal interruptions of the jury's time. To this end, matters which must be heard outside the presence of the jury should be anticipated and be considered during jury breaks or before or after the jury's day.

Unless otherwise ordered or agreed, Plaintiff shall occupy the counsel table closest to the jury.

B.   Continuances. The Court is obligated to resolve cases promptly. Continuances shall only be available for good cause shown. Motions for trial continuances shall be in writing and filed at least fourteen (14) days before the scheduled trial date. Later continuances of trials will be considered only upon the filing and noting for hearing a motion for continuance for unforeseeable emergencies with good cause shown and upon terms the Court deems just. Continuances shall be to a date certain.

C.   Notice to Court of Calendar and Trial Changes. Whenever a cause which has been set for trial is settled or will not be tried for any reason, or if jury trial is waived, the attorneys shall immediately file written notice with the Clerk and the Clerk shall provide a copy of the notice to the Court Administrator (if notice was not already provided by counsel).

If it becomes apparent that the time allocated for a trial will not be adequate to complete the trial, the parties shall promptly notify the Court Administrator's Office of that fact and of the time necessary to complete the trial. The Court may assess actual costs or other sanctions for a violation of this rule.

D.   Appeals on Written Record. All cases set for jury trial which are appeals based on a written record which is read to the jury will be heard without the presence of a judge or court reporter during the reading of the record. The rulings of the hearing official will stand unless objections are renewed prior to trial. Counsel will meet and confer before trial and negotiate on the order of the record and what portions will be read. Counsel shall notify the trial judge before the jury is empaneled of those portions of the record upon which the trial judge will be asked to rule on and of any other matters relating to the reading of the record that need to be resolved prior to trial.

E.   Motion For Reconsideration. Motions for Reconsideration shall be noted by Counsel for a civil motion docket day. Counsel shall submit their arguments on Motions For Reconsideration in writing prior to the date noted. There shall be no oral argument (unless specifically requested by the Court) and counsel need not appear. The Court will issue a written opinion based on the written argument of counsel received prior to the date the Motion for Reconsideration is noted for.

[Adopted effective September 1, 2008; amended effective September 1, 2012.]

RULE 5.   VERDICTS

A.   Proceedings When Jurors Have Agreed. A party or attorney desiring to be present at return of the verdict must remain in attendance at the courthouse or be available by telephone call. If a party or attorney fails to appear within ten (10) minutes of telephone notice to the attorney's office, home, or another number, the Court may proceed to take the verdict in the absence of such party or attorney.

[Adopted effective September 1, 2000; amended effective September 1, 2003; September 1, 2004; renumbered from

Rule 4 effective September 1, 2008; amended effective September 1, 2012.]

RULE 6. INSTRUCTIONS TO JURY AND DELIBERATION

A. Submission. Instructions shall be submitted no later than one day prior to the commencement of the trial in the following manner:

1) One copy with citations and assembled in numbered sequence shall be provided to the Clerk, Judge, and each opposing counsel.

2) The Court Administrator's office should be provided with a usable computer disk containing an uncited set of the proposed instructions in Word format.

3) The original of each Instruction, together with one copy for each party, shall be paper clipped together and provided to the trial judge. These Instructions shall be unnumbered and without citations.

Washington Pattern Instructions shall be furnished by the parties. Any modifications to the Pattern Jury Instructions shall be clearly noted on the annotated copies.

[Adopted effective September 1, 2000; amended effective September 1, 2003; September 1, 2004; renumbered from Rule 5 effective September 1, 2008; amended effective September 1, 2012.]

RULE 7. BOOKS AND RECORDS KEPT BY THE CLERK

A. Exhibits. When a proposed exhibit is marked for identification it becomes part of the court record and, except when used in the courtroom or on appeal, shall not be removed from the Clerk's custody without a court order. No one shall withdraw exhibits without a court order. After 30 days written notice to all parties of record following final disposition of a civil cause, the Court may order the Clerk to destroy or dispose of physical evidence unless good cause is shown why it should be preserved.

B. Fax Filings. Documents faxed to the Clerk's office will be delivered to the Judge but not filed.

C. E-mails. Courtesy e-mails are encouraged for notification purposes only. Parties are required to also file with the Court proper pleadings pursuant to the Local Court Rules.

[Adopted effective September 1, 2000; amended effective September 1, 2003; September 1, 2004; renumbered from Rule 6 and amended effective September 1, 2008; amended effective September 1, 2012.]

RULE 8. DOMESTIC RELATIONS/PATERNITY

A. Order Pendente Lite. The following shall apply to all contested hearings in domestic relations matters in which temporary relief is sought during the pendency of the action:

1) *Affidavits/Oral Testimony.* Such matters shall not be heard unless affidavits are served and filed as required by this rule. Oral testimony may be offered only to supplement, explain, or controvert affidavits and only upon prior approval of the Court. Such request for oral testimony shall be made no later than the day preceding hearing.

2) *Ex Parte Restraining Orders.* Ex parte orders in domestic relations matters shall not change the custody of children or possession of the family home unless the applying party appears personally before the Court and the Court finds that irreparable injury could result if the order is not entered.

[Adopted effective September 1, 2000; amended effective September 1, 2003; September 1, 2004; renumbered from Rule 7 and amended effective September 1, 2008; amended effective September 1, 2012.]

COURT RULE 8B. EMERGENCY COURT RULE FOR WAHKIAKUM COUNTY UNCONTESTED DISSOLUTIONS

Uncontested Dissolutions of Marriage, Legal Separations and Registered Domestic Partnerships:

If, at the final dissolution hearing,

a. the proposed Findings of AND CONCLUSIONS OF LAW WPF DR 04.0300) are verified by the Petitioner, and

b. there has been no Response to Petition (WPF DR 01.0300) filed by the Respondent, and

c. no formal appearance by the Respondent has been filed, **AND**

d. THE RELIEF TO BE GRANTED IN THE DECREE OF DISSOLUTION IS EXACTLY THE SAME AS THE RELIEF SOUGHT IN THE PETITION,

The personal appearance by the Petitioner shall not be required to enter the Findings of Fact AND CONCLUSIONS OF LAW (WPF DR 04.0300) and Decree of Dissolution (WPF DR 04.0400). HOWEVER, IN SUCH INSTANCES, THE PETITIONER MUST ALSO PRESENT A MOTION AND DECLARATION FOR DEFAULT (WPF DRPSCU 03.0100 AND AN ORDER ON MOTION FOR DEFAULT (WPF DRPSCU 03.0200) IF THE RESPONDENT HAS NOT SIGNED VERIFIED FINDINGS OF FACT AND CONCLUSIONS OF LAW AND THE DECREE OF DISSOLUTION, INDICATING THAT THE RESPONDENT HAS APPROVED THE DOCUMENTS AND WAIVES NOTICE OF THEIR PRESENTATION TO THE COURT.

Uncontested Dissolution of Marriage, Legal Separations and Registered Domestic Partnerships with Joinder by Respondent:

If the Respondent files a Joinder (WPF DRPSCU 01.0330) demanding service of other pleadings, or executes the Joinder in the Petition (WPF DR

01.0100) demanding notice of futher[1] proceedings, the Petitioner shall file proof of service of the Note for Dissolution Calendar (WPF DR 03.0300) fixing the date for the presentation of final orders upon the Respondent in a manner consistent with the Rules of Civil Procedure (CR 5). THE RESPONDENT MAY THEN APPEAR TO OBJECT TO ENTRY OF THE FINAL ORDERS; IF HE OR SHE DOES SO AP-PEAR, THE HEARING WILL BE CONTINUED AND THE COURT CLERK WILL INFORM THE PETITIONER OF THE DATE OF THE NEXT HEARING.

Uncontested Dissolution of Marriage. Legal Separations and Registered Domestic Partnerships When Attorney is Representing a Party:

In the event that the Petitioner and/or Respondent is represented by an attorney, the attorney(s) shall deliver a copy of the Decree of Dissolution (WPF DR 04.0400) to his or her client and shall mail a copy to the other party in a manner consistent with service as outlined by Rules of Civil Procedure (CR 5), which copy shall be properly conformed by the Clerk with the filing date indicated thereon. This Court Rule shall take effect immediately.

[Adopted on an emergency basis effective March 28, 2012.]

[1] So in original.

RULE 9. MANDATORY PARENT EDUCATION WORKSHOP

The Pacific and Wahkiakum County Superior Courts find that it is in the best interest of any child whose parents or custodians are involved in specific court proceedings to provide such parents with an educational workshop concerning the impact family restructuring has on their child(ren). The workshop offers parents tools to help ensure that their child's emotional needs will not be overlooked during the legal process, to encourage parents to agree on child related matters, and to aid in maximizing the use of court time.

A. Applicable Cases. This rule shall apply to all cases filed on or after April 1, 1997 under Ch. 26.09, Ch. 26.10, or Ch. 26.26 RCW, and as amended, which require a Parenting Plan or Residential Plan for minor children, including dissolutions, legal separations, major modifications, paternity actions in which paternity has been established, and non-parental custody actions.

B. Mandatory Attendance. In all cases governed by this rule, all parties shall complete an approved four-hour parenting seminar in-person or on-line within 90 days after service of the petition or motion initiating an action subject to this rule. In the case of paternity actions where the responding parent is not having contact with the child, the parenting seminar shall be required only when paternity is established or acknowledged and contact is requested. The class

must be completed prior to entry of a permanent Parenting or Residential Plan.

C. Fees. Each party attending a seminar shall pay a fee charged by the approved provider and sanctioned by the Court, or the provider may waive the fee for indigent parties.

D. Special Consideration/Waiver:

1) In no case shall opposing parties be required to attend a parenting seminar together. They may do so voluntarily.

2) Upon a showing of (a) domestic violence or abuse which would not require mutual decision making pursuant to RCW 26.09.191, or (b) that a parent's attendance at a seminar is not in the children's best interest pursuant to Ch. 26.12 RCW, the Court shall either:

a) Waive the requirement of completion of the parenting seminar; or

b) Allow participation in an alternative voluntary parenting seminar for battered spouses.

3) The Court may waive the parenting seminar requirement for other good cause shown.

E. Failure To Comply. Willful refusal to participate in a parenting seminar or willful delay in completion of a parenting seminar by any party may constitute contempt of court and result in sanctions, including, but not limited to, imposition of monetary penalties against the party not in compliance with this rule.

1) *Types of Proceedings Required.* Each person named as a party in the following types of proceedings must comply with Local Court Rule 9:

a) Dissolution of Marriage with child(ren) under 18 years old;

b) Legal Separation or Declaration of Invalidity of Marriage with child(ren) under 18 years old;

c) Petition to establish custody or visitation, including paternity;

d) Post-judgment petition involving custody or visitation.

2) *Service on Parties.* The Clerk of the Court shall provide a copy of this Rule to the initiating party for service upon all parties against whom relief is sought, together with a statement describing the program, including contact telephone numbers and addresses.

3) *Mandatory.* Each party who files an appearance in a proceeding of the types described above in Section A shall complete the program unless exempted by the Court. **No final order approving any residential or parenting plan shall be entered without proof of completion of such education program by the parents or legal guardians unless otherwise ordered by the Court.**

4) *Ninety (90) Day Deadline.* Each party shall attend and complete an approved parenting workshop

within ninety (90) days of filing a proceeding specified in Section A above.

5) *Exemption.* The Court may exempt one or both parties from completion of the program if, after reviewing the requesting party's motion and supporting affidavit, the Court determines that participation is unnecessary.

[Adopted effective September 1, 2000; amended effective September 1, 2003; September 1, 2004; renumbered from Rule 8 effective September 1, 2008; amended effective September 1, 2012.]

RULE 10. ENTRY OF AGREED DISSOLUTIONS BY DECLARATION (WAHKIAKUM COUNTY ONLY)

A. Wahkiakum County Superior Court Only. The Court may sign an <u>agreed</u> dissolution of marriage without a final hearing or oral testimony if (1) the parties have executed <u>all</u> approved, pattern-form documents, (2) have all their signatures notarized, including any Joinder executed by the adverse party, and (3) Execute the Request for Entry of Decree and Declaration of Jurisdictional Facts [See Exhibit D].

[Adopted effective September 1, 2008; amended effective September 1, 2012.]

RULE 11. GUARDIAN AD LITEMS

A. Registry. The Pacific County Superior Court Administrator or designee shall be responsible for maintaining a registry of those qualified to serve as a Guardian Ad Litem in guardianship proceedings as provided in RCW 11 and RCW 26.

B. Trial. Upon the filing of the Guardian Ad Litem's report, the Guardian Ad Litem is excused from attending all further court proceedings unless ordered by the court to appear.

[Adopted effective September 1, 2000; amended effective September 1, 2003; September 1, 2004; renumbered from Rule 9 effective September 1, 2008; amended effective September 1, 2012.]

RULE 12. MANDATORY MEDIATION IN DOMESTIC CASES

Prior to a trial being set in domestic cases, including dissolutions, legal separations, major modifications, paternity actions in which paternity has been established, and non-parental custody actions, the parties must pursue a resolution through mediation, unless waived by the Court. Counsel may attend mediation with their client, however they are not required to. A pamphlet containing more information on mediation can be obtained from the Court Administrator's Office or the Clerk's Office.

A. Service On Parties. The Clerk of the Court shall provide a copy of this Rule to the initiating party for service upon all parties against whom relief is sought, together with a pamphlet describing mediation, including contact telephone numbers and addresses.

B. Mandatory. Each party who files an appearance in a contested proceeding of the types described above shall attend mediation unless exempted by the Court. Attorneys are not required to attend with their clients but may do so if they wish.

C. Exemption. The Court may exempt one or both parties from attending mediation if, after reviewing the requesting party's motion and supporting affidavit, the Court determines that participation is unnecessary.

D. Fees. Each party attending the mediation shall pay one-half of the fee charged by the provider, unless otherwise ordered by the Court.

E. Failure To Comply. Willful Refusal to participate in mandatory mediation or willful delay in completion by any party contesting an action may constitute contempt of court and result in sanctions, including, but not limited to, imposition of monetary penalties against the party not in compliance with this rule.

[Adopted effective September 1, 2000; amended effective September 1, 2003; September 1, 2004; renumbered from Rule 10 and amended effective September 1, 2008; amended effective September 1, 2012.]

RULE 13. PROBATE

Initial probate matters may be submitted ex parte to the Court.

[Adopted effective September 1, 2000; amended effective September 1, 2003; September 1, 2004; renumbered from Rule 11 effective September 1, 2008; amended effective September 1, 2012.]

RULE 14. LAW LIBRARY

Volumes shelved in the courtroom or Court's chambers shall not be removed from the area of the chambers or courtroom without permission of the Judge, Court Administrator, or Clerk. If such permission is granted, a card shall be placed in the location where the volume was removed. Any volumes removed from the courtroom or chambers must be returned within ten (10) days.

[Adopted effective September 1, 2000; amended effective September 1, 2003; September 1, 2004; renumbered from Rule 12 and amended effective September 1, 2008; amended effective September 1, 2012.]

RULE 15. WITHDRAWAL OF FILES FROM CLERK'S OFFICE

The Clerk shall permit no file to be taken from her office or any other place where she has the same in charge, except by a judge, court commissioner, referee, or court administrator's staff. All files in the hands of an attorney for the purposes of any trial or hearing must be returned by him or her to the Clerk at the close thereof.   All files must be returned within ten (10) days.

[Adopted effective September 1, 2012.]

LOCAL CRIMINAL RULES (LCrR)

RULE 1.   RIGHT TO AN ASSIGNMENT OF COUNSEL

Assignment of Counsel. Appointment of counsel for indigent defendants shall be made by the Court at the preliminary appearance. A copy of the order appointing counsel shall be placed in the lawyers courthouse mailbox located in the Juvenile office. The Prosecuting Attorney shall promptly provide defendant or defense counsel with a copy of the Information or other charging document. The Court Administrator's office shall also notify appointment of counsel by electronic mail.

[Adopted effective September 1, 2000; amended effective September 1, 2003; September 1, 2004; September 1, 2008.]

RULE 2.   PROCEDURES PRIOR TO TRIAL

A. Hearings Requiring An Interpreter. The Court Administrator's Office shall be responsible for arranging for an interpreter for indigent defendants in criminal proceedings, **only upon the request of court appointed counsel or the Prosecutor's Office**. It shall be the responsibility of the indigent party's counsel to notify the Court Administrator's Office of any hearings scheduled that require an interpreter or any hearings **stricken** that require an interpreter. **Failure to do so may result in sanctions,** including, but not limited to, imposition of monetary penalties against the party not in compliance with this rule.

B. Pretrial/Omnibus Checklist Hearing. At arraignment the Court will set a time and date for an omnibus/pretrial hearing under CrR 4.5,. The State shall provide the defense attorney with copies of all officer's reports and other information within five (5) days of receipt thereof. The parties and their representatives shall confer at least once before the pretrial/omnibus checklist hearing as to any discovery problems or any possible settlements. Counsel shall submit completed omnibus hearing checklist at first pretrial hearing.

C. Motions. The moving party shall note motions in a timely manner so that all hearings and motions will be heard at least 14 days prior to the date of trial. Failure to timely note motions for hearing in accordance with this rule may be deemed a waiver of the pretrial hearing on such motions. The Local Civil Rules relating to motions and hearings also apply in criminal cases, where not inconsistent with criminal rules.

D. Omnibus Order. The parties must submit an "Omnibus Hearing Checklist" at the pretrial/omnibus checklist hearing. The parties may submit an agreed order on omnibus. If an agreed order will not be submitted, each party shall prepare and submit an omnibus application substantially in the form set forth in Exhibit C at/or before the time set for the omnibus hearing. It is not necessary to make separate written motions where such motions have been checked on the party's omnibus application. The moving party shall note such motions for hearing in accordance with these rules.   Briefs and supporting documents shall be filed with the court two (2) court days prior to the date of hearing.

E. Settlement of Criminal Cases. Counsel must notify in writing the Court Administrator and the Clerk of a settlement in a criminal case prior to 14 days of trial. Counsel for defendant shall note the matter up for entry of plea on the first Friday motion day following the resolution. See Rule 3 below.

[Adopted effective September 1, 2000; amended effective September 1, 2003; September 1, 2004; September 1, 2008.]

RULE 3.   TIME FOR WAIVER OR PLEA AGREEMENT

Any waiver of right to speedy trial or waiver of right to jury trial shall be in writing, signed in open court, at least 14 days prior to the scheduled trial date. Any plea entered based upon the State's agreement to reduce or dismiss any charges or to recommend a certain disposition must be entered at least 14 days prior to the scheduled trial date.

[Adopted effective September 1, 2000; amended effective September 1, 2003; September 1, 2004.]

RULE 4.   JURY SELECTION

Jury Selection shall be by the struck jury method. Jurors shall be randomly selected from reporting jurors and seated in the order so selected starting in the front row of the audience benches in the courtroom.

Jury Questions. The Court will ask questions and then counsel shall be allowed alternating periods of time to question the jurors.

Improper Inquiry. Questions should be directed solely to determining bias or prejudice and not to direct or implied argument of the case.

[Adopted effective September 1, 2000; amended effective September 1, 2003; September 1, 2004; September 1, 2008.]

RULE 5. ADMINISTRATIVE RULES

Constitutional Court Commissioners may take pleas in all cases except Class A felonies.

[Adopted effective September 1, 2000; amended effective September 1, 2003; September 1, 2004.]

EXHIBITS

EXHIBIT A. NOTE FOR TRIAL SETTING

IN THE SUPERIOR COURT OF THE STATE OF WASHINGTON
IN AND FOR THE COUNTY OF PACIFIC

	)
	)
	) NO. _____
Plaintiff(s)	)
	) **NOTE FOR TRIAL SETTING**
vs.	)
	)
	)
Defendant(s)	)
_____)	

TO: THE CLERK OF THE ABOVE–ENTITLED COURT; and

TO:

The above matter is at issue and will be brought on for trial setting on **FRIDAY, the ___ day of _____ at the hour of 9:00 a.m.** The Clerk is requested to note this cause on the civil docket for that date. **COUNSEL DO NOT NEED TO APPEAR FOR TRIAL SETTING IF THEY HAVE PROVIDED THE COURT ADMINISTRATOR WITH A LIST OF THEIR UNAVAILABLE DATES PRIOR TO THIS HEARING.**

LENGTH OF TRIAL: _____

JURY: (Yes) _____ (No) _____ (6–person) _____ (12–person) _____ (Demand For Jury Trial must be filed and fee paid prior to trial seting)

NATURE OF CASE: _____

NUMBER OF WITNESSES I WILL CALL: ___

NOTE TO COURT ADMINISTRATOR: The following are dates the undersigned is unavailable for trial:

DATED: _____

_____

I certify that I sent a copy of the above Note For Trial Setting to the parties listed below, the Clerk of the above-entitled Court, and the Court Administrator, postage prepaid on _____

_____

[Effective September 1, 2000; amended effective September 1, 2004.]

EXHIBIT B. NOTE FOR MOTION DOCKET

IN THE SUPERIOR COURT OF THE STATE OF WASHINGTON
IN AND FOR THE COUNTY OF PACIFIC

————————————————,)
)
      Plaintiff/Petitioner,   )   CAUSE NO. ————————————
)
           vs.   )
)
————————————————,)   NOTE FOR MOTION DOCKET
)
     Defendant/Respondent.   )
—————————————————)

TO: CLERK OF THE ABOVE–ENTITLED COURT; and

TO: —————— (Opposing counsel or party)

Please place this matter on the Motion Calendar on Monday, the —— day of —————, 2000 at 9:00 a.m.

Opposing counsel is hereby notified.

NATURE OF MOTION: ————————————————————

————————————————————————————————

————————————————————————————————

————————————————————————————————

————————————————————————————————

DATED this —— day of ————————, 2000.

                  (Signature) ————————————————————

                  (Address) ——————————————————————

                              ——————————————————————

[Effective September 1, 2000; amended effective September 1, 2004; September 1, 2008; September 1, 2012.]

Exhibit C   PACIFIC AND WAHKIAKUM COUNTIES

EXHIBIT C.   [OMNIBUS HEARING CHECKLIST]

OMNIBUS HEARING CHECKLIST

Case Name: _____   Trial Date: _____

Cause No: _____   Expiration Date: _____

PLEA NEGOTIATIONS COMPLETED

Yes ____ No ____   Plea Possible

Yes ____ No ____   Sent to Plea Calendar this date

Yes ____ No ____   Strike trial date of _____.

DISCOVERY ISSUES ADDRESSED

Provided by:

Yes ____ No ____   All documentary discovery (photos/tapes)   _____

Yes ____ No ____   Prior convictions of defendant/witness   _____

Yes ____ No ____   All medical records, expert reports, lab and
test results   _____

Yes ____ No ____   All state witnesses have been interviewed
and are ready for trial

Yes ____ No ____   All defense witnesses have been interviewed and are ready for trial

Yes ____ No ____   All remaining witnesses interviews have
been scheduled for specific dates and times
or will be completed by   _____

Yes ____ No ____   All discoverable defenses have been disclosed

Yes ____ No ____   All discovery has been completed

If no: Issues: _____

Yes ____ No ____   Motions in Limine requested. All motions in limine must be
heard not later than the Friday before the trial date. Any
Friday motions requiring more than five minutes per side
must be approved by the Court Administrator's office or in
open court.

TRIAL/READINESS ISSUED

Yes ____ No ____   The information will be amended

Yes ____ No ____   Co-defendant(s) is/are ready for trial

Yes ____ No ____   Trial length estimate, including pre-trial motions

Yes ____ No ____   Jury

Yes ____ No ____   **CrR 3.5 hearing:**
# of hours _____   # of witnesses_____

Yes ____ No ____   **CrR 3.6 hearing:**
# of hours ____ # of witnesses ____ Interview date(s)_____
Briefing schedule _____

Other: _____

_____

DATED: _____   _____

                                                 JUDGE

_____   _____
(Deputy) Prosecuting Attorney   Defendant's Attorney

[Adopted effective September 1, 2008.]

EXHIBIT D. REQUEST OF ENTRY OF DECREE AND DECLARATION OF JURISDICTIONAL FACTS

IN THE SUPERIOR COURT OF THE STATE OF WASHINGTON
IN AND FOR THE COUNTY OF WAHKIAKUM

In re the Marriage of:

_____,

Petitioner,

and

_____,

Respondent.

CAUSE NO. _____

REQUEST FOR ENTRY OF DECREE
AND DECLARATION OF
JURISDICTIONAL FACTS

The petitioner and respondent request the entry of Findings of Fact, Conclusions of Law and Decree of Dissolution of Marriage without a final hearing, and states:

Residency

Petitioner was a resident of the State of Washington when the petitioner was filed.

Notice to the Respondent

The Respondent signed all documents along with a Joinder.

Status of the Parties

The parties were married on _____, 20 ___, at (city and state only) _____ and separated on _____, 20 ___.

The marriage is irretrievably broken and at least ninety (90) days have elapsed since the date the petition was filed and since the respondent signed the joinder.

Pregnancy

The wife is not now pregnant.

Dependent Children

All dependent children of the marriage are identified in the proposed Decree. The proposed Parenting Plan is in the children's best interest; the Child Support Worksheets are accurate.

Property & Debts

All property and all debts of the parties are fairly and completely divided in the Decree.

I declare under penalty of perjury under the laws of the State of Washington that the foregoing is true and correct.

1174

STATE OF WASHINGTON))ss COUNTY OF WAHKIAKUM)	STATE OF WASHINGTON))ss COUNTY OF WAHKIAKUM)
_____, being first duly sworn upon oath, deposes and says: I am the petitioner in this case. I have read the foregoing Jurisdictional Facts, and they are true to the best of my knowledge.	_____, being first duly sworn upon oath, deposes and says: I am the respondent in this case. I have read the foregoing Jurisdictional Facts, and they are true to the best of my knowledge.
_____ Petitioner's Signature	_____ Respondent's Signature
Subscribed and Sworn to before me this _____ day of _____, 20 _____.	Subscribed and Sworn to before me this _____ day of _____, 20 _____.
_____ Notary Public for the State of Washington My appointment expires: _____.	_____ Notary Public for the State of Washington My appointment expires: _____.

[Adopted effective September 1, 2012.]

DISTRICT COURTS

NORTH PACIFIC DISTRICT COURT—
[No Local Rules]

PUBLISHER'S NOTE

See South Pacific District Court Rules.

SOUTH PACIFIC DISTRICT COURT LOCAL COURT RULES

Including Amendments Received Through
August 15, 2015

Table of Rules

RULE 1. AMENDMENT TO CITATION/COMPLAINT, WAIVER OF JURY TRIAL, AND CHANGE OF PLEA

A Defendant charged with a criminal offense punishable by a loss of freedom shall be scheduled for a jury trial unless specifically waived by filing a written waiver of jury trial.

A waiver of trial by jury must be in writing. A notice of intent to change plea and notice of intent to amend citation/complaint may be done orally to the clerk.

A notice of intent to plea to a lesser charge, and notice of intent to amend shall be effective any time prior to the Friday preceding the Trial date.

Thereafter, no amendment to the citation/complaint shall be permitted except as provided below. A waiver of jury trial shall be effective at any time prior to 2 days before the trial date.

An amendment to the citation/complaint, waiver of jury trial and a change of plea to a lesser charge may be allowed upon a showing of exigent circumstances and the payment of terms in the amount of $180.00.

A Defendant may plead guilty to the charge originally alleged at any time.

The Court deems an emergency exists and this rule shall become effective immediately.

[Adopted effective June 14, 1996.]

RULE 2. [CONTESTED INFRACTION HEARINGS; REPRESENTATION BY ATTORNEYS]

In all Contested Infraction hearings where an attorney has appeared for the Defendant, the State shall be represented by an attorney from the Prosecuting Attorney's office, or the infraction shall be dismissed with prejudice.

[Adopted effective April 1, 1998.]

RULE 3. SCHEDULING AND APPEARANCES IN TRAFFIC MATTERS

All contested traffic matters where the Defendant is represented by counsel shall be heard on Wednesday's at 11:00 A.M. or such day as the Court directs.

No Attorney shall appear for a Defendant without first filing a Notice of Appearance seven days before any scheduled hearing. If Defendant's attorney fails to so file the Court will continue the contested matter to a date available to both sides.

[Adopted effective June 5, 2001.]

RULE 4. [CIVIL INFRACTIONS; PLACE OF FILING]

All Civil Infractions, including Traffic Infractions, Criminal Citations and Criminal Complaints shall be filed in the district in which the underlying facts occurred to wit;

Offenses occurring in the following voting districts shall be filed in Pacific County South District Court:

Chinook, Ilwaco 1R, Ilwaco 2R, Ilwaco, Klipsan, Long Beach, Nahcotta, Naselle, Nemah, Ocean Park 1, Ocean Park 2, Oysterville, Pioneer, Seaview 1, Seaview 2.

Offenses occurring in the following voting districts shall be filed in Pacific County North District Court:

Baleville, Bay Center, Ekland Park, Frances, Menlo, North River, Raymond Ward 2, Raymond

Ward 3, Smith Creek, South Bend 1R, South Bend 2R, South Fork, Willapa, Raymond Ward 1P1, Raymond Ward 1P2, Raymond Ward 1P3, Raymond Ward 2, Raymond Ward 3, South Bend 1, South Bend 2, South Bend 3.

Any Citation filed in violation of this rule may be dismissed without prejudice or transferred without notice to the correct district.

[Adopted on an emergency basis effective March 17, 2009.]

Publisher's Note:

The emergency adoption of this rule has not become permanent.

MUNICIPAL COURTS

LONG BEACH MUNICIPAL COURT—
[No Local Rules]

RAYMOND MUNICIPAL COURT—
[No Local Rules]

SOUTH BEND MUNICIPAL COURT—
[No Local Rules]

PEND OREILLE COUNTY

SUPERIOR COURT

LOCAL RULES FOR THE SUPERIOR COURTS OF FERRY, PEND OREILLE AND STEVENS COUNTIES

PUBLISHER'S NOTE

The Local Rules for the Superior Courts of Ferry, Pend Oreille and Stevens Counties are set forth under Ferry County.

DISTRICT COURT

PEND OREILLE COUNTY DISTRICT COURT—
[No Local Rules]

PIERCE COUNTY

Table of Courts

Superior Court

Local Rules of the Superior Court for Pierce County.

District Courts

Local Court Rules of the Pierce County District Court.

Municipal Courts

Bonney Lake Municipal Court Local Rules.
Buckley Municipal Court—[No Local Rules].
Dupont Municipal Court—[No Local Rules].
Eatonville Municipal Court—[No Local Rules].
Fife Municipal Court Local Rules.
Local Rules, City of Fircrest Municipal Court.
Gig Harbor Municipal Court Local Rules.
Lakewood Municipal Court Local Rules.
Milton Municipal Court Rules.
Orting Municipal Court Local Rules.
Puyallup Municipal Court Local Rules.
Roy Municipal Court Local Court Rules.
Ruston Municipal Court Local Rules.
South Prairie Municipal Court—[No Local Rules].
Steilacoom Municipal Court Local Rules.
Sumner Municipal Court Local Rules.
Local Rules for the Municipal Court of the City of Tacoma.
University Place Municipal Court Local Rules.

SUPERIOR COURT

LOCAL RULES OF THE SUPERIOR COURT FOR PIERCE COUNTY

Including Amendments Received Through
August 15, 2015

Table of Rules

ADMINISTRATIVE RULES – PCLR

PCLR 0.1. CITATION—SCOPE

These rules shall be cited as PCLR (Pierce County Local Rules). They were adopted for the manage-

ment and operation of the Pierce County Superior

Court and became effective June 1, 1990, with periodic amendments thereafter.

[Amended effective September 1, 2010.]

PCLR 0.2. COURT ORGANIZATION

(a) Judicial Departments. The Superior Court of Pierce County is organized into judicial departments, numbered consecutively in the order of their creation:

Judicial Department	Created	Incumbent Judge	Date of	Qualification
No. 1	1889	Hon. James R. Orlando	Sept.	2000
No. 2	1891	Hon. Katherine M. Stolz	Jan.	2001
No. 3	1891	Hon. Thomas P. Larkin	Jan.	1997
No. 4	1925	Hon. Bryan Chushcoff	Jan.	1997
No. 5	1951	Hon. Vicki L. Hogan	Jan.	1993
No. 6	1953	Hon. Jack Nevin	Jan.	2013
No. 7	1961	Hon. Jerry Costello	Jan.	2013
No. 8	1967	Hon. Brian Tollefson	Jan.	1989
No. 9	1969	Hon. Edmund Murphy	May	2010
No. 10	1971	Hon. Garold E. Johnson	April	2011
No. 11	1978	Hon G. Helen Whitner	Jan	2015
No. 12	1981	Hon. Stephanie Arend	Sept.	1999
No. 13	1981	Hon. Kathryn J. Nelson	Jan.	2001
No. 14	1987	Hon. Susan Keers Serko	Jan.	2006
No. 15	1987	Hon. Gretchen Leanderson	Dec.	2014
No. 16	1990	Hon. Elizabeth P. Martin	May	2010
No. 17	1990	Hon. Ronald Culpepper	Feb.	2003
No. 18	1990	Hon. Stanley J. Rumbaugh	Jan.	2013
No. 19	1996	Hon. Philip K. Sorensen	April	2014
No. 20	1998	Hon. Kitty–Ann van Doorninck	Oct.	1998
No. 21	2001	Hon. Frank E. Cuthbertson	Mar.	2001
No. 22	2005	Hon. John R. Hickman	Dec.	2005

(1) *Judicial Department Location.* Each Judge has a permanently assigned courtroom, to the extent available, all located in the County–City Building, 930 Tacoma Avenue South, Tacoma, Washington 98402. Each Judge may sit for limited periods of time in other special function courts, described below. The Court Administrator's office will provide information as to the courtroom in which a Judge is currently sitting.

(2) *Judicial Department Hours.*

(A) Court Business Hours. Superior Court's regular hours are 8:30 a.m. to 4:30 p.m.

(B) Trials. Parties must appear for trial at 9:00 a.m. in the assigned judicial department on the first day of trial.

(b) Court Staff. Each Judge employs a full-time judicial assistant and court reporter. The court employs a Court Administrator, Deputy Administrator and administrative staff, who perform various support services for the Judges and Commissioners. The Court Administrator's office serves as an information and message center at those times when the Judges and staff are not available. See website: www.co.pierce.wa.us/superiorcourt.

(c) Divisions of the Superior Court.

(1) Juvenile Court is located at Remann Hall, 5501 Sixth Avenue, Tacoma, WA 98406.

(2) *Criminal Divisions.*

(A) Judicial Assignments. The specific judicial officers assigned and courtroom locations are designated by the Court Administrator's Office. See website for specific information: www.co.pierce.wa.us/superiorcourt.

(B) Subject Matter. The Superior Court has three criminal division courts: Criminal Division I (CD1), Criminal Division II (CD2) and Criminal Division Presiding Judge (CDPJ). These criminal division courts hear arraignments, omnibus hearings, pleas, sentencings, revocation hearings related to criminal offenses, and other matters but not criminal jury trials.

(C) **Drug Court.** The Superior Court has Drug Court(s).

(D) **Criminal Trial Assignment.** Judges presiding over criminal trials are determined by the Presiding Judge.

(3) *Civil Divisions.*

(A) **Judicial Assignments.** The specific judicial officers assigned and courtroom locations are designated by the Court Administrator's Office. See website for specific information: www.co.pierce.wa.us/superiorcourt.

(B) **Family Court.** The Superior Court has two Family Court Family Court 1 (FAM1) and Family Court 2 (FAM2). Cases assigned to Family Court include: Petitions to Modify Custody/ Parenting Plans/Residential Schedules, Nonparental Custody, Relocations and all Custody/Parenting Plans/Residential Schedules cases in which a Guardian ad Litem is appointed, except those cases where a Guardian ad Litem is appointed for the purpose of parentage or minority.

(C) **Civil Trial Assignment.** Judges presiding over civil trials are determined by the Presiding Judge.

[Adopted effective June 1, 1990; amended retroactively effective June 3, 1991; amended effective June 1, 1994; September 1, 1995; July 2, 1996; July 1, 1997; September 1, 1999; September 1, 2000; September 1, 2001; September 1, 2002; September 1, 2003; September 1, 2004; amended on an emergency basis effective September 24, 2004; amended effective September 1, 2005; September 1, 2006; September 1, 2007; September 1, 2008; September 1, 2009; September 1, 2010; September 1, 2011; September 2, 2013; September 2, 2014; September 1, 2015.]

PCLR 0.3. COURT MANAGEMENT

(a) **Authority.** The authority to manage and conduct the court is vested in the Superior Court Judges and shall be exercised through regular meetings of the Judges. Authority of the Superior Court located in the County–City Building is delegated to a:

Presiding Judge

Assistant Presiding Judge

Presiding Judge-elect

Executive Committee

Court Administrator

Authority of the Juvenile Court located at Remann Hall is delegated to a:

Juvenile Court Presiding Judge

Juvenile Court Deputy Presiding Judge

Juvenile Court Executive Committee

Juvenile Court Administrator

(b) **Duties—Responsibilities of the Judges of the Superior Court.**

(1) *Executive Committee.* Elect an Executive Committee.

(2) *Policies.* Establish all policies regarding judicial functions of court.

(3) *Court Organization.* Exercise final authority over any matters pertaining to court organization and operation and over any individual, employee or com-

mittee of the court, except judicial departmental staff. This includes removal for cause of the Presiding Judge and Commissioners.

(4) *Meetings.* Meet regularly once a month or at such other special meetings as may from time to time be called by the Presiding Judge or as may be voted by a majority of Judges attending a regular meeting of the Judges and participate in the management of the court.

(A) **Quorum.** A quorum shall consist of a majority of the Judges.

(B) **Governance Rules.** Meetings shall be conducted under The Modern Rules of Order, Second Edition, where not inconsistent with these rules.

(c) **Office of Presiding Judge.**

(1) *Duties.*

(A) **Court Business.** Direct the business of the court and supervise its operation as provided in **GR 29**.

(B) **Court Policy.** Initiate court policy for presentation to the Judges or to the Executive Committee.

(C) **Spokesperson.** Act as official speaker for the court. If the matter is of such a nature that the Presiding Judge requires advice and counsel, he/she shall contact the members of the Executive Committee as necessary, or as possible, under the circumstances.

(D) **Meetings.** Preside at all Judges' meetings.

(E) Executive Committee. Chair the Executive Committee.

(F) Special Meetings. Call such special meetings of the Judges and Executive Committee as may be required.

(2) *Selection of Presiding Judge.* The Presiding Judge shall be that member of the Executive Committee elected as Presiding Judge by a majority vote of the Judges as a whole. The Presiding Judge shall serve a two year term.

In January of the second year of the Presiding Judge's term, at a regularly scheduled Judges' meeting, an election shall occur for a Presiding Judge-elect. The Presiding Judge-elect shall be selected from the members of the Executive Committee.

If a vacancy occurs in the Presiding Judge position, and there is no Presiding Judge-elect, then an election shall occur at the next regularly scheduled Judges' meeting for the election of a Presiding Judge from the members of the Executive Committee. The Presiding Judge shall be elected to complete the term left in the vacant position.

(3) *Selection of Assistant Presiding Judge.* An Assistant Presiding Judge shall be elected by the Executive Committee, from the membership of the Executive Committee, at least annually in January of every year, or more frequently as needed.

(d) Executive Committee.

(1) *Policy Decisions.* The Executive Committee shall decide matters of policy affecting the court and make such decisions in writing by majority vote of the committee. Such actions shall be final unless modified or rejected by a majority of the Judges in attendance at the next regular Judges' meeting or continuation of the meeting.

(2) *Policy Recommendations.* The Executive Committee may make recommendations on policy matters to the Judges at any meeting of the Judges.

(3) *Committees.* The Executive Committee shall recommend the designation and duties of the committees of the court and nominate the members of the committees.

(4) *Advisory Capacity.* The Executive Committee shall act in an advisory capacity to the Presiding Judge.

(5) *Procedure.* The Executive Committee shall distribute promptly to the Judges written minutes of action taken by the Executive Committee. On request of any Judge, any action taken by the Executive Committee shall be subject to review for final approval or rejection at a meeting of the Judges. Any matter which should be decided by the Judges shall be presented to the next Judges' meeting before action is taken.

(6) *Meetings.* The Executive Committee shall meet at least once a month. Any Judge or Commissioner may attend any Executive Committee meeting and participate but not vote.

(7) *Selection.* The Executive Committee shall consist of five Judges. Vacancies shall be filled by election by a majority of the Judges voting at the regularly scheduled December Judges' meeting. Nominations shall be made in writing and delivered to the Presiding Judge one week prior to the December meeting. The Judge(s) receiving the majority of votes shall be elected to the Executive Committee to serve a two-year term beginning January 1.

(8) *Unexpired Term.* If any Judge serving on the Executive Committee is unable or unwilling to continue in office for any reason, the position shall be filled to serve out the balance of the term by the election process provided for in these rules. Provided further that a Presiding Judge-elect who succeeds to the office of the Presiding Judge during the term of another Presiding Judge shall serve the balance of that Judge's term as Presiding Judge and one calendar year as Presiding Judge following that term.

[Adopted effective June 1, 1990; amended effective September 1, 2000; December 2, 2002 on an emergency basis; amended effective September 1, 2007; September 1, 2009; September 1, 2010; September 1, 2015.]

PCLR 0.4. COMMISSIONERS

(a) Duties. Court Commissioners shall perform duties as assigned by the court. Full-time Court Commissioners have all powers conferred by law, including the authority to accept pleas in criminal matters. The Commissioners preside over and decide matters presented in the following divisions:

(1) *Civil Divisions A, B, C and Ex Parte.* The Commissioners hear and decide all matters brought before these divisions as set forth below. There are four civil Court Commissioners in divisions A, B, C and Ex Parte.

(A) Family Court. The Commissioners hear and decide matters arising in Family Court as set forth in **PCLSPR 94.04(c)**. All cases involving children shall be assigned to a Commissioner at the time of the first motion and all later motions will be heard by that assigned Commissioner while on Family Court rotation, unless exclusive jurisdiction is retained by a specific judicial officer.

(B) Subject Matter. The function of these civil divisions is to hear family law motions, petitions to modify child support, initial determination of adequate cause on Petitions to Modify Parenting Plans and Nonparental Custody Petitions, initial relocation hearings, probates, trust and guardianship matters (except for annual periodic reviews which are heard by the assigned judicial department on its Friday motion docket), minor settlements, transfer of structured settlement payment rights, unlawful detainer actions, applications for appointment of a receiver, injunctive relief and restraining orders, replevin actions, defaults eligible for presentation in the Ex Parte Department wherein no notice is required (including uncontested finalization of dissolution, legal separation and invalidity with attorney representation), supplemental proceedings, paternity actions, adoptions (limited to the appointment of an adoption investigator), contested show cause proceedings, domestic violence, vulnerable adult protection hearings, sexual assault protection hearings, uncontested/default dissolutions, committed intimate relationships (meretricious relationships), domestic partnerships, and uncontested/default self-represented party dissolutions, and ex parte matters.

(C) Schedule. The **Schedule of Commissioners' Calendars** for each division is contained in Appendix, **Form Q** and at the Pierce County Superior Court website: www.co.pierce.wa.us/superiorcourt and by clicking on "Civil & Family Law".

The Schedule of the Commissioners' Calendars may be changed without formal republication of these rules or appendices. Parties and counsel are advised to verify calendar schedules before noting matters for hearing and by viewing the Pierce County Superior Court website for any revisions to the Commissioners' Calendars.

(2) *Juvenile Division.* The Commissioners hear and decide matters arising under the juvenile laws and other matters at the request of the Presiding Juvenile Court Judge, including finalization of adoptions.

(3) *Civil Mental Health Division.* The Civil Mental Health Division hears matters relating to the involuntary commitment, treatment, and release of individuals alleged to be suffering from mental disorders or alcoholism. Protocols for presentation of Less Restrictive Orders are found at the Pierce County Superior Court website: www.co.pierce.wa.us/superiorcourt and by clicking on "Civil & Family Law" and "Protocols Less Restrictive Alternative Orders". When a jury trial is requested, all jury trials are assigned to one of the judicial department by the Presiding Judge.

(4) *Criminal Division.* In the event a Commissioner is assigned to this Division, this Commissioner hears and decides matters authorized pursuant to **Chapter 2.24 RCW.**

(b) **Direction.** Commissioners discharge their duties under the general direction of the Presiding Judge, except when serving in the Juvenile Court Division, during which time they are under the general direction of the Presiding Juvenile Court Judge.

(c) **Rotation of Commissioner Duties.** The above duties rotate among the Commissioners in accordance with a schedule adopted by the Executive Committee.

Information as to their current duty assignments can be obtained from the Court Administrator's Office.

[Adopted effective June 1, 1990; amended effective September 1, 1995; July 2, 1996; July 1, 1997; September 1, 2000; September 1, 2006; September 1, 2007; September 1, 2009; September 1, 2010; September 1, 2011; September 2, 2014; September 1, 2015.]

PCLR 0.5. COURT ADMINISTRATOR

(a) **Selection.** The Court Administrator shall be appointed by a majority of all of the Judges and shall serve at the pleasure of the appointing authority under the direction and supervision of the Presiding Judge.

(b) **Powers (2) and Duties.** The general powers and duties of the Court Administrator include but are not limited to:

(1) *Administrative.* Administrative control of all non-judicial activities of the court.

(2) *Policies.* Implement all policies regarding judicial functions of the court.

(3) *Supervisory.* Supervision of all court employees, except Commissioners, juvenile court employees and judicial departmental employees.

(4) *Budgetary.* Preparation and administration of the budget.

(5) *Representative.* Representation of the court in dealings with the State Court Administrator.

(6) *Assist.* Assist the Presiding Judge in meeting with representatives of governmental bodies, and other public and private groups regarding court management matters.

(7) *Agenda Preparation.* Prepare the agenda for Judges' meetings and act as recording secretary at those meetings and at committee meetings where the Administrator's presence would be reasonable and productive.

(8) *Record Preparation and Maintenance.* Prepare reports and compile statistics as required by the Judges or state court administration and maintain records of informal activities of the court.

(9) *Recommendations.* Make recommendations to the Judges for the improvement of the administration of the court.

[Adopted effective June 1, 1990. Amended effective September 1, 2010.]

PCLR 0.6. STANDING COMMITTEES

(a) **Establishment.** The following permanent standing committees of Judges and Commissioners include:

Bench Bar and Retired Judges Liaison Committee

Civil Case Management Committee

Civil Local Rules Committee

Construction Committee

County Courthouse Security Committee

Family Law Committee

Family Law Guardian ad Litem/Parenting Investigator Grievance Committee

Guardianship, Probate, Trust and Mental Illness Committee

LINX/IT/Satistics Committee

Personnel Committee

Pro Tem Commissioner and Pro Tem Judge Application and Training Committee

Strategic Planning Committee

Criminal Plus Committee, the assigned responsibilities of which include:

Criminal Justice Task Force

Criminal Local Rules

Criminal Procedures

Drug Court Committee

Any additional special committees may be appointed by the Presiding Judge with approval of the Executive Committee.

(b) Selection of Members. Committee members shall be selected by the Presiding Judge in the manner provided in **PCLR 0.3(d)(3)**.

[Adopted effective June 1, 1990; amended effective July 1, 1997; September 1, 2000; September 1, 2006; September 1, 2009; September 1, 2010; September 2, 2014; September 1, 2015.]

PCLR 0.7. LEGAL ASSISTANTS

(a) Authorized Activity. Those persons qualifying as a legal assistant pursuant to subpart (b) below are authorized to: (1) check out court files from the Clerk of the Court, subject to the Clerk's rules and regulations; (2) use the Pierce County Law Library and check out materials, subject to the rules and regulations of the Library; and (3) present Agreed Orders and Orders to Show Cause (accompanied by the clerk's file) to Judges and Commissioners respectively, based solely upon the record; provided the same have been signed as presented by the attorney of record for whom said legal assistant is acting.

(b) Qualifications of Legal Assistant. For purposes of this rule, a legal assistant is one who has been so designated by the Tacoma–Pierce County Bar Association, and who presents credentials from said association to the Pierce County Clerk, Pierce County Law Library, or Pierce County Superior Court Judge or Commissioner, provided said credentials are based upon the following criteria:

(1) *Supervising Attorney.* Is responsible directly to a supervising attorney, who has at least five (5) years experience and who will be responsible under the Rules of Professional Conduct applicable to that attorney for the performance of the legal assistant sponsored by said attorney. The sponsoring attorney shall supervise the legal assistant and shall have submitted to the Tacoma–Pierce County Bar Association certification that he or she is currently sponsoring no more than one legal assistant; and

(2) *Employment.* Has been currently employed six months or longer by a Pierce County law firm, or by a city, county, or state administrative agency or corporation under the direct supervision of an attorney; and

(3) *Nature of Work.* Seventy-five percent of the legal assistant's work time is devoted to legal assistant (non-clerical) work, consisting of the performance of tasks under the direct supervision of a lawyer, which tasks shall not include the giving of legal advice, the quoting of legal fees, or the appearance in court in contested matters; and

(4) *Education.* Has obtained a degree or certificate of completion of a legal assistant program of no less than two years duration, or has the substantially equivalent college education or work experience in the legal field which equivalency shall be determined by the Legal Assistants' Committee of the Tacoma–Pierce County Bar Association.

(c) Presentation by Out-of-County Legal Assistants. Notwithstanding the provisions of paragraph (b) above, legal assistants who are duly registered with a bar association in the state, other than the Tacoma–Pierce County Bar Association, may present Agreed Orders and Orders to Show Cause (accompanied by the Clerk's file) to Judges and Commissioners respectively, based solely upon the documents presented and the records in the file.

[Adopted effective June 1, 1990. Amended effective September 1, 2010.]

GENERAL RULES—PCLGR

PCLGR 11. COURT INTERPRETERS

The court may appoint qualified interpreters for hearing impaired or non-English speaking persons in accordance with RCW 2.42, 2.43, GR 11 and the Pierce County Superior Court Language Assistance Plan as well as with current applicable court rules and law.

[Adopted effective September 1, 2012.]

PCLGR 30. MANDATORY ELECTRONIC FILING

(a) **Definitions**—See GR 30(a)

(b) **Electronic filing authorization**—See GR 30(b)(1)–(4)

(5) *Electronic Filing Is Mandatory.* Effective January 1, 2012, unless this rule provides otherwise, attorneys are required to electronically file (e-file) all documents with the Clerk using the Clerk's e-filing system or an electronic service provider that uses the Clerk's e-filing system. Self-represented parties are not required to e-file documents but may contact the Clerk's Office to obtain a LINX account and password to enable e-filing.

(A) **Documents That Shall Not Be E–Filed.** Exceptions to mandatory e-filing include the following documents:

(i) Original Wills and codicils;

(ii) Certified records of proceedings for purposes of appeal;

(iii) Documents of foreign governments under official seal including foreign and out of state adoption documents;

(iv) Documents presented for filing during a court hearing or trial including documents submitted for in camera review pursuant to **GR 15**;

(v) Foreign (out of state) Judgments;

(vi) New cases or fee based documents filed with a request for an Order in Forma Pauperis;

(vii) Affidavits for Writs of Garnishment and Writs of Execution on Garnishment;

(viii) Voluminous Document—"voluminous document" is any document that exceeds 200 pages, including attachments.

The above-excepted documents must be filed in paper form.

(B) **Working Copies for E–Filed Documents.** Judicial working copies for e-filed documents may be electronically delivered to the Clerk using the Clerk's e-filing system. The Clerk may assess a fee for the electronic delivery of working copies. Working copies of documents 200 pages or more in length shall be submitted in paper form only and shall be delivered pursuant to **PCLR 7(a)(7)** and **PCLR 7(b)(1)(E)**.

(C) **Waiver of the Requirement to E–File.** If an attorney is unable to e-file documents, the attorney may request a waiver. The attorney must explain why he or she needs to file paper documents in that particular case. The Clerk will make waiver request forms available. The Clerk will consider each application and provide a written approval or denial to the attorney. The waiver may be for a specific case or for a specific period of time determined by the Clerk. Attorneys who receive a waiver shall file a copy of the waiver in each case in which they file documents. Attorneys who have received a waiver shall place the words "Exempt from e-filing per waiver filed on (date)" in the caption of all paper documents they file for the duration of the waiver. An attorney shall have the ability to ask for a review by the Presiding Judge if the request for waiver is denied by the Clerk.

(D) **Non–Compliance With This Rule.** If an attorney files a document in paper form and does not have an approved waiver from e-filing, the Clerk is authorized to reject the document and return it to the attorney for e-filing.

[Adopted effective September 1, 2011.]

CIVIL RULES – PCLR

PCLR 3. COMMENCEMENT OF ACTION/CASE SCHEDULE

(a) **Scope.** This rule shall apply to all civil cases including family law cases once an **Order Setting Case Schedule** as set forth in Appendix, **Form A** has been issued pursuant to **PCLR 40(d)**, except for:

(1) Cases in mandatory arbitration after they have been transferred to arbitration pursuant to **PCLMAR 2.1**. A written request for a trial de novo shall cause a new Order Setting Case Schedule to be issued by the assigned judicial department when the request for trial de novo is filed pursuant to **PCLMAR 7.1**;

(2) Change of name;

(3) Adoption;

(4) Domestic violence (**Chapter 26.50 RCW**);

(5) Harassment (**Chapter 10.14 RCW**);

(6) UIFSA actions (**Chapter 26.21A**);

(7) Review of action taken by administrative agency, except Land Use Petition Actions (LUPA) filed pursuant to **Ch. 36.70C RCW**, which shall be assigned a Case Schedule pursuant to (g) below;

(8) Appeals from courts of limited jurisdiction, except de novo appeals from courts of limited jurisdiction which shall be assigned an Order Setting Case Schedule by the assigned judicial department when filed;

(9) Foreign judgments;

(10) Abstract or transcript of judgment;

(11) Civil commitment;

(12) Proceedings under **Chapter 10.77 RCW** (Criminally Insane);

(13) Proceedings under **Chapter 70.96A RCW**;

(14) The following case types for which the Clerk shall issue, at the time of filing or when an order appointing personal representative is filed, an Order Assigning Case to Judicial Department and Setting Hearing Date as indicated:

(A) Case types to be reviewed 4 months after filing:

Absentee

Administrative Law Review

Confidential name change

Collection

Commercial

Compel/Confirm Binding Arbitration

Confidential Intermediary

Deposit of Surplus Funds

DOL Revocation—Appeal

Foreclosure

Guardianship, Limited Guardianship, Special Needs Trust and Trust, except for annual periodic reviews of guardianships and trusts which are heard by the assigned Judicial Department on its Friday motion docket, and contested guardianships which shall be assigned a Case Schedule when a trial date is requested;

Injunction

Interpleader

Lower Court Appeal—Civil

Lower Court Appeal—Infraction

Minor Settlement with or without guardianship

Miscellaneous

Petition for Writ

Proceedings for isolation and quarantine

Seizure of Property from Commission of Crime

Seizure of Property Resulting from Crime

Subpoenas

Unlawful Detainer

Writ of Habeas Corpus

Writ of Mandamus

Writ of Review

(B) Case types to be reviewed 6 months after filing:

Criminal RALJ Appeal

(C) Case types to be reviewed 12 months after filing:

Adoption

Child Support or Maintenance Modifications

Estate/probate if court supervision is required (e.g. bond required, either a guardian or guardian ad litem is appointed to represent a minor or incompetent heir, or estate insolvent) or is otherwise governed by **RCW 11.76.010**, except any will contest or litigation matter arising in a probate case shall be assigned an Order Setting Case Schedule when the Petition to Contest the Will is filed or the estate is sued.

Paternity Parent Determination

Trust and Estate Dispute Resolution Act (TEDRA)

(D) Case types to be reviewed 60 months after filing:

Estate/probate if full nonintervention powers are granted.

The purpose of the hearing in these cases shall be to assess the progress of the case and assure that the matter is being prosecuted diligently to a conclusion. If necessary, a trial date may be assigned. Failure to attend the hearing may result, when appropriate, in dismissal of the case without prejudice or closure of the matter without further notice. In paternity matters, it may result in a resolution of the case without dismissal.

(b) Case Schedule. When a new civil case is filed or as otherwise provided in these rules, the clerk shall issue and file a document entitled Order Setting Case Schedule or an Order Assigning Case to Judicial Department and Setting a Hearing date, as applicable, and shall provide one copy to the plaintiff/petitioner and one copy to the assigned judicial department. The plaintiff/petitioner shall serve a copy of the applicable Order on the defendant/respondent along with the initial pleadings; provided that if the initial pleading is served prior to filing, the plaintiff/petitioner shall within five (5) court days of filing serve the applicable Order. If the initial pleading is served by publication, the plaintiff/petitioner shall serve the applicable Order within five (5) court days of service of defendant's/respondent's first appearance. When the applicable Order is served pursuant to this section, it may be served by regular mail with proof of mailing/service to be filed promptly in the form required by these rules, see **PCLR 5**. The **Order Setting Case Schedule** shall contain the case heading and otherwise be as set forth in Appendix, **Form A**, except for estate/probate cases for which the Order Setting Case Schedule shall be in a form set forth in Appendix, **Form B (1)** or **B (2)**, depending on the time period for mandatory case review.

(c) Family Law Cases. When a new family law case is filed, the clerk shall issue and file a document entitled Order Assigning Case to Judicial Department and shall provide one copy to the petitioner and one copy to the assigned judicial department. Nonparental Custody Petitions and Petitions to Modify Parenting Plan shall be issued an Order Setting Case Schedule at filing pursuant to **PCLSPR 94.04(f)** and **(g)**. The respondent shall be served with the applicable Order as set forth in **PCLR 3(b)**. The **Order Assigning Case to Judicial Department** shall contain the case heading and otherwise be as set forth in Appendix, **Form I**.

(d) Amendment of Case Schedule. The court, either on motion of a party or on its own initiative, may modify any date in the Order Setting Case Schedule for good cause, including the track to which the case is assigned, except that the trial date may be changed only as provided in **PCLR 40(g)**. If an Order Setting Case Schedule is modified or the track assignment is changed, the court shall prepare and file the Order Amending Case Schedule and promptly mail or provide it to the attorneys and self-represented parties.

(e) Service on Additional Parties Upon Joinder. A party who joins an additional party in an action shall be responsible for serving the additional party with the current Order Setting Case Schedule together with the first pleading served on the additional party.

(f) Form of Case Schedule.

(1) Original Case Schedule. The **Order Setting Case Schedule** is set forth in Appendix, **Form A**.

(2) Amended Case Schedule. An Order Amending Case Schedule shall be in the same form as the original Order Setting Case Schedule; except that an Order Amending Case Schedule shall be entitled Order Amending Case Schedule and it need not include the Notice provisions. An Order Amending Case Schedule issued pursuant to **PCLR 40(e)(4)** shall only contain the following dates: Joint Statement of Evidence, Pretrial Conference and Trial date. Additional dates may be added to the Order Amending Case Schedule upon order of the court.

(g) Time Intervals. Except for those cases provided for in **PCLR 3(a)(1), (8), (9) and (12)** the events and time intervals included in the original Order Setting Case Schedule shall be measured in weeks from the date of filing or assignment of a Case Schedule as follows:

CASE SCHEDULE AND TRACK ASSIGNMENT–Measured in Weeks:

	EXPEDITED	STANDARD	COMPLEX	DISSOLUTION
Confirmation of Service	2	4	6	3
Confirmation of Joinder of Parties, Claims and Defenses *	8	17	26	
Jury Demand *	9	18	27	
Set Settlement Conference Date with Assigned Judicial Officer				14
Status Conference **(contact court for specific date)**	10	21	32	14
Plaintiff's/Petitioner's Disclosure of Primary Witnesses	12	25	38	18
Defendant's/Respondent's Disclosure of Primary Witnesses	15	29	42	21
Disclosure of Rebuttal Witnesses	17	36	57	23
Deadline for filing motion to Adjust Trial Date	19	40	60	25

	EXPEDITED	STANDARD	COMPLEX	DISSOLUTION
Discovery Cutoff	20	45	67	30
Exchange of Witness and Exhibit Lists and Documentary Exhibits	21	47	70	32
Deadline for Hearing Dispositive Pretrial Motions *	22	48	72	
Joint Statement of Evidence	22	48	72	32
Alternative Dispute Resolution to be held before	23	48	72	
Settlement Conference to be held before				34
Pretrial Conference (**contact Court for specific date**)	25	50	75	35
Trial	26	52	78	36

* Does not apply to dissolution cases.

LUPA CASE SCHEDULE:

CASE EVENT	DEADLINE
Petition for Review of Land Use Decision Filed and Schedule Issued (**RCW 36.70C.040**)	
DEADLINE to contact assigned Judge to confirm Initial hearing (**RCW 36.70C.080**)	7 days after Petition is filed
DEADLINE to Stipulate or File Motion for Change of Hearing Date or Adjustment of Schedule (**RCW 36.70C.080(1)**; **RCW 36.70C.090**)	28 days after Petition is filed
Initial Hearing on Jurisdictional and Preliminary Matters (FRIDAYS ONLY) (**RCW 36.70C.080**)	40 days after Petition is filed
DEADLINE to file Certified Copy of Local Jurisdiction Record (**RCW**	45 days after Initial Hearing

36.70C.110)	
DEADLINE to file Brief of Petitioner (**RCW 36.70C.080(4)**)	20 days after deadline to file Record
DEADLINE to file Brief of Respondent (**RCW 36.70C.080(4)**)	40 days after deadline to file Record
DEADLINE to file Reply Briefs (**RCW 36.70C.080(4)**)	50 days after deadline to file Record
Review Hearing/Trial Date – (**RCW 36.70C.090**)	Within 60 days of the date set for submitting the Record

(h) Track Assignment.

(1) *Track Assignment.* Each case shall be assigned to a track as set forth in this rule.

(2) *Expedited Cases.* Expedited cases shall have a discovery cutoff of 20 weeks and trial in 26 weeks. There shall be depositions of the parties only without leave of court. Interrogatories shall be limited to twenty-five (25) in number and each subpart of an interrogatory shall be counted as a separate interrogatory for purposes of this rule. There shall be no limit on requests for admissions. Any case in which it is expected there will be no more than a total of four (4) witnesses shall be presumptively an expedited track case.

(3) *Standard Cases.* Standard cases shall have a discovery cutoff of 45 weeks and trial in 52 weeks. There shall be no limitations with respect to depositions, except as otherwise ordered pursuant to the state civil rules. Interrogatories shall be limited to thirty-five (35) in number and each subpart of an interrogatory shall be counted as a separate interrogatory for purposes of this rule. There shall be no limit on requests for admissions. Actions for breach of contract, personal injury, title to land, construction claims involving questions of workmanship and discrimination claims shall presumptively be standard track cases. Any case wherein it is expected there will be no more than a total of twelve (12) witnesses shall be presumptively a standard track case.

(4) *Complex Cases.* Complex cases shall have a discovery cutoff of 67 weeks and trial in 78 weeks. There shall be no limitations with respect to depositions, except as otherwise ordered pursuant to the state civil rules. Interrogatories shall be limited to thirty-five (35) in number and each subpart of an interrogatory shall be counted as a separate interrogatory for purposes of this rule. There shall be no limit on requests for admission. Medical or professional malpractice, product liability and class action claims shall presumptively be complex track cases.

(5) *Dissolution Cases.* All dissolutions shall presumptively be a family law track at filing. If not resolved within 122 days of filing, the case will be assigned to the dissolution track by the assigned Judicial Department and an Order Setting Case Schedule will be created. There shall be no limitations with respect to depositions except as otherwise ordered pursuant to the civil rules. Interrogatories shall be limited to one hundred (100) in number and each subpart of an interrogatory shall be counted as a separate interrogatory for purposes of this rule. There shall be no limit on requests for admissions.

(6) *LUPA Cases.* All LUPA cases shall be LUPA track cases.

(7) *Collaborative Law Cases.* In the event that represented parties mutually agree to participate in Collaborative Law, they shall present to the assigned judicial department the Order and Joint Notice of Participation in Collaborative Law as set forth in the Appendix, **Form P**, and obtain a mandatory status conference date. The parties shall no longer have to comply with the Order Setting Case Schedule Requirements of **PCLR 3**. If the case does not resolve by the mandatory status conference date, the mandatory status conference shall be held to advise the Court

of the progress. Counsel and the court may agree to continue the status conference if participation in the Collaborative Law process is ongoing. Failure to comply may lead to dismissal of the case.

(i) Trial by Affidavit.

(1) *Affidavit.* Parties may agree to submit unresolved issues to the assigned judicial department by affidavit. This shall be determined at the discretion of the assigned judicial department at the status conference or as determined by agreement of the parties and approval of the assigned judicial department. If the request for trial by affidavit is granted the self-represented parties or their attorneys shall file and serve a form entitled **Trial By Affidavit Certificate**, as set forth in Appendix, **Form C**. The assigned judicial department shall issue an Order Amending Case Schedule.

(2) *Trial and Notice.* If the matter is to be submitted on affidavit, the parties shall be given a trial date approximately 20 weeks from filing. Fourteen (14) days prior to the trial date the parties shall serve and file their affidavits. Rebuttal affidavits, if any, shall be served and filed no later than seven (7) days prior to trial. Surrebuttal affidavits, if any, shall be filed and served two (2) days before the trial. Working copies of all affidavits shall be provided to the assigned judicial department. Affidavits filed beyond these deadlines shall not be considered.

(3) *Priority.* Matters set for trial by affidavit may take priority over other matters set for the same day. On the day of trial, unless otherwise ordered, each side shall have one-half hour to argue their respective positions to the court.

(4) *Case Schedule.* Once a matter is set for trial by affidavit, the self-represented parties and attorneys shall no longer be bound by the Order Setting Case Schedule, except for the new trial date in the Order Amending Case Schedule issued by the Judicial Assistant.

(j) Monitoring. Each judicial department of the Superior Court, the Superior Court Administrator's Office, and at such time as the Presiding Judge may direct, the Clerk of the Court shall monitor cases to determine compliance with these rules.

(k) Enforcement. The assigned judicial department, on its own initiative or on motion of a party, may impose sanctions or terms for failure to comply with the Order Setting Case Schedule established by these rules. If the court finds that an attorney or self-represented party has failed to comply with the Order Setting Case Schedule and has no reasonable excuse, the court may order the attorney or party to pay monetary sanctions to the court, or terms to any other party who has incurred expense as a result of the failure to comply, or both; in addition, the court may impose such other sanctions as justice requires. As used in this rule, "terms" means costs, attorney fees, and other expenses incurred or to be incurred as a result of the failure to comply; the term "monetary sanctions" means a financial penalty payable to the court; the term "other sanctions" includes but is not limited to the exclusion of evidence.

[Adopted effective July 1, 1996. Amended effective July 2, 1996; September 1, 1998; September 1, 1999; September 1, 2001; September 1, 2002; January 1, 2007; September 1, 2009; September 1, 2011; September 1, 2012; September 2, 2013; September 2, 2014; September 1, 2015.]

PCLR 5. SERVICE

(a) Scope. This rule shall apply to all cases governed by an Order Setting Case Schedule pursuant to **PCLR 3.**

(b) Confirmation of Service. No later than the date designated in the Order Setting Case Schedule, the plaintiff/petitioner shall file a Confirmation of Service. The original Confirmation of Service shall be filed with the Pierce County Clerk, with a copy delivered to the judicial department to which the case is assigned. The **Confirmation of Service** shall contain the case heading, cause number and shall otherwise be as set forth in Appendix, **Form D**.

[Amended effective September 1, 2011]

[Adopted effective July 1, 1996. Amended effective September 1, 2010; September 1, 2011.]

PCLR 6. TIME

For shortening or enlarging the time for filing of motions and briefs for the motions:

(a) Civil Motions. PCLR 7 for motions generally;

(b) Restraining Orders. PCLR 65 for applications for temporary restraining orders and injunctive relief; and

(c) Family Law. PCLSPR 94.04 for family law proceedings.

[Adopted effective June 1, 1990; amended effective July 2, 1996; September 1, 2007; September 1, 2010.]

PCLR 7. MOTIONS: JUDGES AND COMMISSIONERS

(a) Judges' Motions and Trial Assignments.

(1) *When Heard.* All motions, except motions during trial or those motions heard by the Commissioners as set forth below shall be heard on the assigned judicial department's motion calendar. All discovery motions shall be heard before the assigned judicial department. No contested summary judgment motions, motions to dismiss, or other such motions which might effectively terminate a case shall be heard, except by the assigned judicial department, unless otherwise directed by the Presiding Judge or by the assigned judicial department. Motions are heard on Friday mornings at 9:00 a.m., unless specially set by the assigned judicial department. In the event a Friday is a non-judicial day, motions shall be heard on the judicial day immediately preceding the Friday.

(2) *Recess Schedule.* Motions and assignments regularly scheduled for a time when a judicial department is at recess shall be heard in the manner and in accordance with the schedule determined by the Judges.

(3) *Scheduling Motions and Trial Assignments.*

(A) Motions. Motions shall be scheduled for hearing by filing a Note for Motion Docket, in a form approved by the court, and containing all information required by such form. The Note for Motion Docket shall be filed with the motion and supporting documents and served upon the opposing party at the same time. The Note for Motion Docket, motion and supporting documents shall be filed with the Clerk, and served on the opposing party no later than the close of business on the sixth court day before the day set for hearing. For example, if the motion is scheduled for a Friday, it shall be filed by the close of business on the Thursday of the week before the hearing date unless there is an intervening court holiday. This rule shall not relieve the moving party from any greater notice or filing requirements established by law or court rule. See **PCLR 7(c)(1)(2) & (3)** regarding Motions for Reconsideration to be heard before a judge. See also **PCLSPR 98.20** regarding periodic guardianship hearings.

(B) Trial Assignments. If the attorneys or any self-represented party fails to appear on the date set for assignment of a trial date, the case shall be dismissed without prejudice unless the assignment of a trial date has been previously obtained or the case has been fully resolved with the entry of all final documents.

(4) *Failure to File or Serve—Sanctions.* If the motion, supporting documents and Note for Motion Docket are not all filed with the clerk, the court may strike the motion. No motion shall be heard unless proof of service upon the opposing party is filed or there is an admission of such service by the opposing party. The court may also, in its discretion, impose terms upon the offending party.

(5) *Opposing Papers.* Any party opposing a motion shall file and serve responsive papers in opposition to a motion not later than noon, two court days before the date the motion is scheduled for hearing.

(6) *Reply.* Any papers in strict reply shall be served no later than noon, one court day before the date the motion is scheduled for hearing.

(7) *Working Copies.* The assigned judicial department shall be furnished with a working copy of all motion papers. The working copies shall be delivered either directly to the judicial department or to the Court Administrator's office. Anyone e-filing motion papers shall be responsible for ensuring working copies are timely provided to the assigned judicial department. All working copies are to be delivered no later than the date and time they are required to be served on opposing parties. The working copies of papers in support or opposition shall be marked on the upper right corner of the first page with the date of hearing and the name of the Judge. A fax or email transmittal of working copies shall not be acceptable delivery.

(8) *Page Limits.* The initial motion and opposing memorandum shall not exceed 12 pages without authorization of the court; reply memoranda shall not exceed five pages without the authority of the court. Provided, however, for Motions for Summary Judgment pursuant to CR 56, the parties' moving and opposing memoranda shall not exceed 24 pages without authorization of the court; reply memoranda shall not exceed 12 pages without authority of the court.

(9) *Confirmation of Motions.* All motions shall be confirmed by the moving party during the week of the hearing, but no later than 12:00 noon two court days prior to the hearing. Attorneys and any self-represented party shall confirm motions by contacting the judicial assistant of the assigned judicial department or electronically, through the internet by those with LINX accounts and PIN (Personal Identification Numbers), in accordance with the procedures adopted by the Pierce County Superior Court Clerk's Office. Motions filed by those persons physically confined under a court order shall be deemed confirmed at filing. The court may strike motions that are not timely confirmed.

(10) *Procedures for Hearing.* The cases on the motion docket for each motion day shall be called and oral argument may be presented. Motions may be continued by the court, at the court's discretion, for hearing at other specified times. The trial court may, in its discretion or for good cause shown, waive oral argument for civil motions. Motions requiring more than ten (10) minutes for argument may be placed at the end of the calendar.

(11) *Motions for Summary Judgment.*

(A) Confirmation of Motions. In the event a motion for summary judgment pursuant to **CR 56** is to be argued, the moving party shall notify the judicial department to which such motion is assigned during the week of the hearing, but no later than 12:00 noon, two (2) court days prior to the hearing; otherwise the motion shall be stricken. No hearing upon a motion for summary judgment shall be continued except upon the explicit order of the assigned Judge. Any summary judgment motion that is continued shall be reconfirmed as set forth above.

(B) Testimony. If testimony transcribed at any pretrial deposition is used in support of or in opposition to a motion for summary judgment, such testimony shall be presented by affidavit containing excerpts of the testimony relied upon by the party using such testimony, with reference to the line and the page of source.

(C) Page Limits. See **PCLR 7(a)(8)** regarding Motion for Summary Judgment page limits.

(12) *Motions for Revision of a Commissioner's Order or Judgment (this rule does not apply to CR 54(b) revision motions).* At the time a motion for revision is filed, the moving party shall provide the reviewing court copies of all documents submitted by all parties that were considered by the Court Commissioner in making the decision sought to be revised.

(A) Timing. Within 10 days of the entry of a written order or judgment by a Court Commissioner, either party may file a motion for revision. Such motion shall be scheduled for argument on the assigned judicial department's next available motion date but no sooner than six working days from the Commissioner's written order or judgment sought to be revised, unless upon an order shortening time, and no later than 30 days except for good cause shown. Failure to schedule the motion within the time prescribed shall be deemed jurisdictional.

(B) Validity of Commissioner's Orders. All orders granted by a Court Commissioner shall remain valid and in effect pending the outcome of the motion for revision, unless stayed pending the outcome of a motion for revision by the Court Commissioner granting the order, the Presiding Judge or the Judge to whom the motion for revision has been assigned.

(C) Content of Motion. All motions and cross-motions shall state with specificity any portion of the Commissioner's order or judgment sought to be revised, identifying those portions by paragraph or page and line numbers. Any portion not so specified shall be binding as if no revision motion has been made.

(D) Costs and Fees. The judicial department has the right to award reasonable costs or attorneys fees where allowed on all motions for revision without the necessity of a written motion.

(E) Transcript Required. When seeking revision of a ruling of a Court Commissioner which was based upon testimony, such testimony shall be transcribed in accordance with **RAP 9.2(e) and (f)**.

(13) *Juvenile Court Orders and Judgments.* Revision of orders and judgments made by a Court Commissioner sitting in the Juvenile Court Division shall be heard by a Judge sitting in the Juvenile Court Division.

(b) Commissioners' Motions.

(1) *Civil Divisions A, B, C and Ex Parte.* Court Commissioners hear and decide all matters brought before these divisions as set forth below. There are four civil Court Commissioners in Divisions A, B, C and Ex Parte.

(A) Family Court. Court Commissioners hear and decide matters arising in Family Court as set forth in **PCLSPR 94.04(c)**. All cases involving children shall be assigned to a Commissioner at the time of the first motion and all later motions shall be heard, if possible, by that assigned Commissioner while on Family Court rotation, unless exclusive jurisdiction is retained by a specific judicial officer.

(B) Subject Matter. The function of these Civil Divisions is to hear applications for show cause orders, motions for temporary orders, petitions to modify child support, initial determination of adequate cause on Petitions to Modify Parenting Plans and Nonparental Custody Petitions, initial relocation hearings, probates, trust and guardianship matters (except for annual periodic reviews and initial hearings under TEDRA if live testimony is to be presented or the hearing will likely last longer than twenty minutes, which are heard by the Superior Court Department assigned on its Friday motion docket), minor settlements, unlawful detainer actions, applications for appointment of a receiver, injunctive relief and restraining orders, defaults eligible for presentation in the Ex Parte Department wherein no notice is required, supplemental proceedings, paternity actions, contested show cause proceedings, domestic violence, vulnerable adult protection hearings, sexual assault protection hearings, uncontested/default dissolutions, committed intimate relationships (meretricious relationships), domestic partnerships, and uncontested/default self-represented party dissolutions, and ex parte matters. Court Commissioners do not hear discovery motions.

(C) Schedule. The **Schedule of Commissioners' Calendars** for each division is contained in Appendix, **Form Q** and at the Pierce County Superior Court website: www.co.pierce.wa.us/superiorcourt and by clicking on "Civil & Family Law". The Schedule of the Commissioners' Calendars may be changed without formal republication of these rules or appendices. Parties and counsel are advised to verify calendar schedules before noting matters for hearing and by viewing the Pierce County Superior Court website for any revisions to the Commissioners' Calendars. Incorrectly scheduled matters shall be stricken.

(D) How Motions Initiated. Attorneys shall electronically file a Note for Commissioners Calendar by using the electronic filing and scheduling process provided by LINX via the public website (https://linxonline.co.pierce.wa.us/linxweb/Main.cfm) or from a public kiosk in the Clerk's Office for all the Commissioner's dockets held at the County–City Building, 930 Tacoma Avenue South, Tacoma, WA 98402, except for the self represented dissolution docket, domestic violence, vulnerable adult protection orders and sexual assault protection orders. See also **PCLSPR 94.04** regarding family law motions, **PCLSPR 98.04** regarding Estates and Probates, **PCLSPR 98.16W** regarding Settlements of Minors and Incapacitated Persons, **PCLSPR 98.18** regarding Court Created Trusts and **PCLSPR 98.20** regarding Guardianships for specific procedures about these types of motions on the Commissioners' dockets. Self represented parties may contact the Clerk's Office for a LINX e-filing account or use the Clerk's Office kiosk to file and schedule a Note for Commissioners Calendar. **Waiver of Requirement to E-file.** See **PCLGR 30(b)(5)(C)**.

(i) Docketing for Morning Show Cause Calendars. Matters heard on the show cause calendar at 9:00 a.m. shall be docketed by electronically filing and scheduling in accordance with **PCLR 7(b)(1)(D)** a Note for Commissioner's Calendar at least fourteen (14) calendar days before the hearing, simultaneously with a motion and/or notice of hearing and any supporting pleadings, unless this is a renote of a motion or notice of hearing previously filed in which event only the Note for Commissioner's Calendar shall be e-filed. The morning show cause cases heard shall be limited in number. Case caps shall be calculated in LINX based on the number of cases rather than the Note for Commissioner's Calendar. Leave may be granted by a duly appointed Commissioner, not a Commissioner Pro Tem, to exceed the number of cases heard on any given day in that Commissioner's Division.

(ii) Counter Motions For Morning Show Cause Calendars. In the event there is an existing motion and the responding party wishes to file a counter motion to be heard the same date they may do so without leave of the court by electronically filing and scheduling in accordance with **PCLR 7(b)(1)(D)** a Note for Commissioner's Calendar, as long as the counter motion and all supporting pleadings are filed and served at least fourteen (14) calendar days before the hearing. Any necessary Order to Show Cause for the counter motion shall be signed by the Ex Parte Department.

(E) Working Copies. For matters docketed on the morning show cause calendars in Commissioner Divisions A, B, and C whether by Note for Commissioner's Calendar or by the Order Setting Case Schedule, and for probate, guardianship and minor settlement cases on the Commissioner Division A afternoon calendar, the Commissioners shall be furnished with working copies of all motions, or petitions, and supporting documents, including affidavits, declarations, certified statements, Guardian ad litem reports, responsive and reply documents. Working copies for the morning show cause calendars are subject to page limits pursuant to **PCLSPR 94.04(c)(4)**.

Working copies are encouraged but not mandatory for all other dockets conducted in Civil Divisions A, B and C and at the discretion of the court, cases may be continued to require their submission.

The working copies shall be delivered directly to Commissioner's Services Department or by using the Clerk's electronic working copy delivery process as defined in **PCLGR 30(b)(5)(C)** "Working Copies" shall be marked on the upper right corner of the first page with the date of hearing, the appropriate docket and who is delivering the copies (moving or opposing party). Anyone e-filing motion papers shall be responsible for ensuring working copies are timely provided. All working copies shall be delivered no later than 12:00 noon two (2) court days prior to the hearing, provided that this deadline shall not apply to responsive pleadings in unlawful detainer matters. A copy of the Note for Commissioner's Calendar shall be attached to the working copies. A fax or email transmittal of working copies shall not be acceptable delivery.

(F) Procedures for Hearing/Proposed Orders. Attorneys and self-represented parties shall have proposed orders prepared for presentation to the court at the time of the hearing in family law show cause matters. For probate/trust, guardianship and minor settlement cases, proposed orders shall be included with working copies.

(2) *Juvenile Division Calendars.* Court Commissioners hear and decide matters arising under the juvenile laws and other matters at the request of the Presiding Juvenile Court Judge, including finalization of adoptions.

(3) *Civil Mental Health Division.* Court Commissioners hear matters arising in this division as set forth in **PCLR 0.2(c)(4)**, except where a trial by jury is requested. Jury trials are assigned to one of the judicial departments by the Court Administrator.

(c) Motions held before Judges or Commissioners.

(1) *Motions for Reconsideration.* A Motion for Reconsideration shall be heard by the Judge or Commissioner who initially ruled on the motion or to the Presiding Judge or his/her designee upon a showing of good cause. Temporary assignment of the Judge or Commissioner to a location other than the courthouse shall not be considered good cause.

(2) *Time for and Contents of Motions for Reconsideration.* A Motion for Reconsideration shall be noted and filed not later than 10 days after entry of the judgment, decree or order. The motion shall be noted on the judge's civil motion docket that heard the original motion. The motion will be noted not sooner than 30 but not later than 40 days after the entry of the judgment, decree or order, unless the court directs otherwise. A proposed order shall be delivered to the judge along with working copies in accordance with PCLR(a)(7).

(3) *Hearings on Motions for Reconsideration before a Judge (this rule does not apply to Motions for Reconsideration to be heard before the Commissioners).* Motions for Reconsideration before a Judge shall be submitted on briefs and affidavits of the moving party only. No responses shall be required or submitted by the opposing party and there shall be no oral argument permitted unless the judge so directs. The court shall notify the parties whether: (1) the Motion for Reconsideration has been denied and the hearing stricken; or (2) oral argument and/or responsive pleadings are required.

(4) *Motion and Order to Shorten Time.*

(A) Motions to Shorten Time. All Motions to Shorten Time shall be in writing and supported by declaration or affidavit that (a) states the reasons why the matter should be heard on shortened time and (b) sets forth the manner and method by which notice, or attempted notice, was provided to all other parties regarding presentation of the Motion to Shorten Time. If the moving party has been unable to notify all parties of the Motion to Shorten Time, it is within the judicial officer's discretion to proceed with the Motion to Shorten Time. The court file shall be presented with the Motion to Shorten Time, declaration or affidavit, and the proposed Order.

(B) Judicial Department Motions. If the underlying motion is to be heard by a Judge, the Motion to Shorten Time and the underlying motion shall be presented to the assigned judicial department. If the assigned judicial department is not available to consider the Motion to Shorten Time, the matter shall be presented to the Presiding Judge for consideration. If the Presiding Judge is not available, the moving party shall contact Superior Court Administration for additional information as to which Judge can hear the Motion to Shorten Time.

(C) Commissioner Motions. If the underlying motion is to be heard by a Commissioner, the Motion to Shorten Time and the underlying motion shall be presented to the Ex Parte Division. The Motion to Shorten Time shall be heard by a duly appointed Court Commissioner and not a Commissioner Pro Tem. If granted, a copy of the Order Shortening Time and Note for Commissioner Docket shall be given to the Commissioner Services Department.

(D) Notice. The party requesting the Order to Shorten Time shall notify all opposing parties of the Motion to Shorten Time and the time and location of its presentation. Any party opposing the Motion to Shorten Time shall appear or respond by declaration or affidavit setting forth the basis of the opposition. Failure to appear or respond to the Motion to Shorten Time does not preclude a party from requesting terms.

(E) Service. If the Motion to Shorten Time is approved by the appropriate judicial officer, the party shall provide a copy of the pleadings relating to the Motion to Shorten Time as well as to the underlying motion, to all parties as soon as possible or as otherwise directed by the Court.

(5) *Reapplication.* No party shall reargue the same motion to a different judicial officer without showing by affidavit, what motion was previously made, when and to which judicial officer, what the order or decision was, and any new facts or other circumstances that would justify seeking a different ruling from another judicial officer.

(6) *Temporary Restraining Orders and Injunctive Relief.* See **PCLR 65**.

[Adopted effective June 1, 1990. Amended effective September 1, 1992; July 2, 1996; July 1, 1997; September 1, 1998; September 1, 1999; September 1, 2001; September 1, 2002; September 1, 2003; September 1, 2004; September 1, 2005; September 1, 2006; September 1, 2007; September 1, 2009; September 1, 2010; September 1, 2011; September 1, 2012; September 2, 2013; September 2, 2014.]

PCLR 10. FORM OF PLEADINGS

(d) Format Requirements.

(1) *Handwritten Documents.* To ensure access to the courts for any self-represented party, pleadings may be submitted that are legibly handwritten in black or blue ink, double spaced (unless a mandatory form authorizes the use of single spacing) using only one side of each page. Declarations shall be appropriately verified and formatted.

(2) *Font Size for Typed or Computer Generated Documents.* Except for footnotes, all typed or computer generated documents shall be prepared using a minimum of 12 point font and shall be double spaced, unless a mandatory form authorizes the use of single spacing.

(3) *Paper color.* All pleadings and working copies shall be only on white paper.

(4) *Mandatory Forms.* The Washington State Mandatory Forms shall be used except where a mandatory form is designated "optional," and local forms have been promulgated by the Court or no mandatory form exists for the particular matter.

Local forms may be obtained from the Pierce County Superior Court Clerk, the Pierce County Law Library or by accessing: www.co.pierce.wa.us/xml/abtus/supct.htm. State forms may be obtained by accessing: www.courts.wa.gov/forms.

(5) *Preparation of Transcript from Electronic/Mechanical Recorder or Videotape.* All report of proceedings produced from use of any electronic/mechanical recorder or videotaped proceedings shall be in the same form as a verbatim report as provided in **RAP 9.2(e) and (f)**. This rule applies to all transcripts prepared from hearings before any judicial officer. This rule shall not apply to appeals on small claims cases.

(e) Briefs/Memoranda. Briefs/Memoranda shall be submitted for all hearings involving disputed questions of law. A copy shall be served on opposing counsel, and a separate copy shall be delivered to the Judge/Commissioner and marked "Working Copy." The original shall be filed with the Pierce County Clerk and the working copy shall be delivered to the Court Administrator's Office or Commissioners Service Department, whichever is applicable, at the time the working copies are due. A fax or email transmittal of working copies shall not be acceptable delivery.

(f) Required Language in Pleadings Relating to Supplemental Proceedings and Show Cause Hearings for Contempt. In all supplemental proceedings wherein a show cause order is to be issued requiring the personal attendance of a party to be examined in open court, and in orders to show cause for contempt, the order shall include the following words in capital letters:

> YOUR FAILURE TO APPEAR AS SET FORTH AT THE TIME, DATE AND PLACE DESIGNATED SHALL CAUSE THE COURT TO ISSUE A BENCH WARRANT FOR YOUR APPREHENSION AND CONFINEMENT IN JAIL UNTIL SUCH TIME AS THE MATTER CAN BE HEARD.

No bench warrant shall be issued for the apprehension of the cited person if such language has been omitted. All orders directing the issuance of a warrant and all warrants in such matters shall provide that the cited person shall be brought before the presiding officer of the division or department signing the order.

[Adopted effective June 1, 1990; amended effective July 2, 1996; September 1, 2002; September 1, 2005; September 1, 2009; September 1, 2010.]

PCLR 11. SIGNING AND DRAFTING OF PLEADINGS, MOTIONS AND LEGAL MEMORANDA; SANCTIONS

(c) Address of Self Represented Party. A self represented party shall state on the pleadings, notice of appearance, and other documents filed, the person's telephone number, mailing address and street address where service of process and other papers may be served unless that information is made confidential by statute.

(d) Change of Address. Any self represented party or attorney changing their address shall immediately serve all parties and file, in each case, a Notice of Change of Address. The **Notice of Change of Address** shall contain the case heading and otherwise be as set forth in Appendix, **Form J**.

[Adopted effective June 1, 1990; amended effective July 2, 1996; September 1, 2001; September 1, 2010.]

PCLR 15. AMENDED AND SUPPLEMENTAL PLEADINGS

(e) Interlineations. No interlineations, corrections or deletions shall be made in any paper after it is signed by the judicial officer or filed with the clerk. Any such mark made prior to filing shall be initialed and dated by all persons signing the document.

[Adopted effective June 1, 1990. Amended effective September 1, 2010.]

PCLR 16. PRETRIAL AND SETTLEMENT PROCEDURES

(a) Designated Judge. Except in the case of family law matters or unless otherwise provided for herein, the judicial department to whom the case is assigned at the time of filing shall hear all pretrial matters.

(b) Pretrial Procedure.

(1) *Pretrial Conferences.* The lead trial attorney of each party represented by an attorney and each self-represented party shall attend the pretrial conference. The conference shall include those matters set forth in **CR 16** as well as any other matters that might result in a speedy, just and economical resolution of the case.

(2) *Exchange of Exhibit and Witness Lists.* In cases governed by an Order Setting Case Schedule pursuant to **PCLR 3**, the parties shall exchange: (A) lists of the witnesses whom each party expects to call at trial; (B) lists of the exhibits that each party expects to offer at trial, except for exhibits to be used

only for impeachment; and (C) copies of all documentary exhibits except for those items agreed to by counsel and self-represented parties, such as identical copies of items already produced to avoid unnecessary duplication. Counsel and self-represented parties are encouraged to ascertain that each has full and complete copies of any document to be presented at trial to avoid unnecessary duplication expenses. In addition, non-documentary exhibits shall be made available for inspection by all other parties no later than fourteen (14) days before trial. Any witness or exhibit not listed shall not be used at trial, unless the court orders otherwise for good cause and subject to such conditions as justice requires.

(3) *Pretrial Motions.* All such motions shall be served, filed and heard pursuant to **PCLR 7**; provided that no pretrial dispositive motions shall be heard after the cutoff date provided in the Order Setting Case Schedule except by order of the court and for good cause shown.

(4) *Joint Statement of Evidence.* In cases governed by an Order Setting Case Schedule pursuant to **PCLR 3** the parties shall file a Joint Statement of Evidence containing (A) a list of the witnesses whom each party expects to call at trial and (B) a list of the exhibits that each party expects to offer at trial. The Joint Statement of Evidence shall contain a notation for each exhibit as to whether all parties agrees as to the exhibit's authenticity and admissibility.

(c) **Alternative Dispute Resolution.** Some form of Alternative Dispute Resolution ("ADR") is required in all cases prior to trial except as noted otherwise below.

(1) *Non–Family Law Cases.* At least 30 days prior to trial the parties shall each submit a certification or declaration that they have participated in one or more types of Alternative Dispute Resolution, including, but not limited to: formal negotiations that included an exchange of written proposals; arbitration; or mediation.

(2) *Family Law Cases.* Judicial Officers shall make themselves available for settlement conferences in dissolutions, paternity cases involving petition/motion for establishment of residential schedule or parenting plan, post-dissolution petitions for modification of custody and related Family Law matters, except in Non–Parental Custody Petitions under RCW 26.10, which are exempt from mandatory ADR unless ordered by the Assigned Judge. The attorney or self-represented party may utilize an alternative dispute resolution process to satisfy the settlement conference requirement.

(A) Scheduling and Submission of Materials. A settlement conference Judicial Officer shall be randomly assigned by the LINX computer program at the time the family law case is filed. The parties shall conduct any settlement conference no later than the date set forth in the Case Schedule.

The assigned settlement conference Judicial Officer's judicial assistant shall schedule the exact date and time of the settlement conference. If the assigned settlement conference Judicial Officer is not available to conduct the settlement conference before the trial date the attorneys or self-represented parties shall utilize an alternative dispute resolution process to satisfy the settlement conference requirement.

The attorney or self-represented party shall prepare a **Domestic Relations Information Form** and submit the same to the settlement Judicial Officer and opposing counsel or opposing self-represented party not later than two (2) court days prior to the conference. See Appendix, **Form E.** A fax or email transmittal of working copies shall not be acceptable delivery. This form may be supplemented.

(B) Attendance. Parties shall attend the settlement conference. Attendance may be excused, in advance, by the settlement judicial officer for good cause. Failure to attend may result in the imposition of terms and sanctions as the judicial officer deems appropriate.

(C) Proceedings Privileged. Proceedings of the settlement conferences shall, in all respects, be privileged and not reported or recorded. Without disclosing any communications made at the settlement conference, the settlement conference Judicial Officer may advise the assigned judicial department in writing as to whether the use of further or alternative dispute resolution procedures, or the appointment of additional investigators or the development of additional evidence would be advisable prior to trial.

(D) Settlement of Case. When a settlement has been reached, the settlement agreement or partial agreement shall be placed on the record or reduced to writing.

(E) Disqualification. A Judicial Officer presiding over a settlement conference shall be disqualified from acting as the trial Judge in that matter, unless all parties agree in writing.

(F) Withdrawal of Attorney. If any attorney withdraws and a settlement conference has been scheduled or is required to be scheduled by the existing case schedule, the withdrawing attorney shall inform his/her client of the date, time and location of the settlement conference, as well as a brief explanation of the process, including how to schedule a settlement conference and expectations.

(G) Waivers of ADR in Family Law Matters for DV, Child Abuse or other Good Cause. Upon motion and approval of the Assigned Judge [not the settlement conference judge], ADR, including settlement conferences, may be waived in Family Law cases involving domestic violence and/or child abuse or for other good cause shown:

(i) Where a Domestic Violence Restraining Order or Protection Order (excluding Ex–Parte orders) involving the parties has been entered by a court at any time within the previous twelve (12) months; or

(ii) Where a Domestic Violence or other No Contact order involving the parties exists pursuant to RCW 10.99, or has been in effect within the past twelve (12) months; or

(iii) Where the court upon motion finds that allegations of domestic violence or other abuse between the parties are such that it would not be appropriate to mandate alternative dispute resolution; or

(iv) Where the court upon motion finds that allegations of child abuse involving at least one of the parties are such that it would not be appropriate to mandate alternative dispute resolution; or

(v) For other good cause shown.

Motions for Waivers of ADR in Family Law must be brought in accordance with the provisions of PCLR 7. The Motion to Waive Mandatory Settlement Conference shall contain the case heading and otherwise be as set forth in Appendix, Form R.

(3) *Cases Exempt from Alternative Dispute Resolution.* The following cases are exempt from participating in an alternative dispute resolution process: LUPA, RALJ, ALR, child support cases, Non–Parental Custody Petitions under RCW 26.10, trials de novo after arbitration and family law cases in which a waiver was granted pursuant to PCLR 16(c)(2)(G). Although settlement conferences are not mandatory for Non–Parental Custody Petitions brought under RCW 26.10, any party may request a settlement conference or other form of ADR by motion to the Assigned Judge.

[Adopted effective September 1, 2010. Amended effective September 1, 2011; September 2, 2013; September 2, 2014.]

PCLR 19. JOINDER

(a) Scope. This rule shall apply to all cases governed by an Order Setting Case Schedule pursuant to PCLR 3.

(b) Additional Parties, Claims, and Defenses. No additional parties may be joined, and no additional claims or defenses may be raised, after the date designated in the Order Setting Case Schedule for Confirmation of Joinder of Additional Parties, Claims and Defenses, unless the court orders otherwise for good cause and subject to such conditions as justice requires.

(c) Confirmation of Joinder; Form. No later than the designated deadline for joining additional parties and raising additional claims and defenses, as described in section (b) above, the plaintiff shall, after conferring with all other attorneys or any self-represented party pursuant to paragraph (d) of this rule,

file with the Pierce County Clerk and with the assigned judicial department, and serve by mail upon the opposing counsel or any self-represented party, a report entitled **Confirmation of Joinder of Parties, Claims, and Defenses**, which will contain the case heading and otherwise be as set forth in Appendix, **Form F**.

(d) Parties to Confer in Completing Form. The plaintiff shall confer with all other parties in completing the form. This may be in person or by telephone but requires actual contact with the attorney of record or self-represented party.

(e) Cases Subject to Mandatory Arbitration. If a statement of arbitrability pursuant to **PCLMAR 2.1** is filed on or before the deadline for filing the Confirmation of Joinder of Parties, Claims and Defenses, the Confirmation of Joinder need not be filed and no status conference will be held.

[Adopted effective September 1, 2010; amended effective September 1, 2011.]

PCLR 26. DISCOVERY: DISCLOSURE OF POSSIBLE LAY AND EXPERT WITNESSES

(a) Scope. This rule shall apply to all cases governed by an Order Setting Case Schedule pursuant to PCLR 3.

(b) Disclosure of Primary Witnesses. Each party shall, no later than the date for disclosure designated in the Order Setting Case Schedule, disclose all persons with relevant factual or expert knowledge whom the party reserves the option to call as witnesses at trial.

(c) Disclosure of Rebuttal Witnesses. Each party shall, no later than the date for disclosure designated in the Order Setting Case Schedule, disclose all persons whose knowledge did not appear relevant until the primary witnesses were disclosed and whom the party reserves the option to call as witnesses at trial.

(d) Scope of Disclosure. Disclosure of witnesses under this rule shall include the following information:

(1) *All Witnesses.* Name, address and phone number.

(2) *Lay Witnesses.* A brief description of the witness's relevant knowledge.

(3) *Experts.* A summary of the expert's anticipated opinions and the basis therefore and a brief description of the expert's qualifications or a copy of curriculum vitae if available. For the purposes of this rule, treating physicians shall be considered expert as well as fact witnesses.

(e) Discovery Not Limited/Additional Witness Identified. This rule does not modify a party's responsibility to timely supplement responses to discovery requests or otherwise to comply with discovery before the deadlines set by this rule or by other civil rules.

(f) Interrogatories. The number of interrogatories is limited depending on track assignment. See **PCLR 3(h).**

[Adopted effective September 1, 2000. Amended effective September 1, 2010; September 1, 2011; September 1, 2012; September 2, 2014.]

PCLR 38. JURY TRIALS

(a) Jury Trials. No case will be set for trial by jury unless the jury fee has been paid or waived by court order and all other requirements of statutes or court rules have been satisfied.

(b) Demand for Jury. In cases governed by an Order Setting Case Schedule pursuant to **PCLR 3,** a jury demand must be filed and served no later than the date set in the Order Setting Case Schedule, which shall be deemed the date on which the case is called to be set for trial within the meaning of **CR 38(b).**

[Adopted effective June 1, 1990; amended effective July 1, 1996; September 1, 2011.]

PCLR 40. ASSIGNMENTS OF CASES TO JUDICIAL DEPARTMENTS

(a) Presiding Judge in Charge. Assignment of cases shall be the responsibility of the Court Administrator under the supervision of the Presiding Judge.

(b) Authority of Judicial Departments. The case shall be assigned to a judicial department at the time of filing and once so assigned shall remain in such judicial department for all future proceedings unless returned to the Court Administrator by the Trial Judge for reassignment. The assigned judicial department will hear such pretrial motions as are subsequently noted. Each judicial department maintains its own hearing and trial docket.

(c) Trial Dates. Except in those cases governed by an Order Setting Case Schedule pursuant to **PCLR 3,** following the filing of a lawsuit or appeal from a court of limited jurisdiction, the matter shall be set for trial upon request of counsel. A **Note for Trial Setting** shall be filed at least six (6) court days prior to the date fixed for assignment to bring the matter before the court. In cases governed by an Order Setting Case Schedule pursuant to **PCLR 3,** the trial date shall be listed in the Order Setting Case Schedule. The trial date may be changed only as provided in section **(g)** of this rule.

(d) Trial Dates—Family Law Cases. When a new family law case is filed, except for nonparental custody petitions and petitions to modify a parenting plan or petition for parenting plan/child support, a petitioner in a family law case shall be provided with an Order Assigning Case to Judicial Department by the clerk. This order shall (1) assign the case to a trial judicial department and (2) set a date by which a trial date shall be obtained. The **Order Assigning Case to Judicial Department** shall contain the case heading and otherwise be as set forth in Appendix, **Form I.**

On the assignment for trial date, either party may appear before the assigned judicial department to obtain an Order Setting Case Schedule. Whichever party obtains the Order Setting Case Schedule shall serve a copy of the Case Schedule on all other parties. Pursuant to **PCLR 5,** the original of the **Confirmation of Service,** in Appendix, **Form D** shall be filed with the Pierce County Clerk no later than the date designated in the Order Setting Case Schedule, with a copy delivered to the judicial department to which the case is assigned. Assignment of the trial date shall conform to the dissolution track, **PCLR 3(g).**

If neither party appears on the date set for assignment for trial date, the case shall be dismissed without prejudice.

Once a response to the petition has been filed, any party may request the assignment of a trial date by filing a note for assignment at least six (6) court days prior to the date fixed for assignment to bring the matter before the court.

Nonparental Custody Petitions and Petitions to Modify Parenting Plan shall be assigned to Family Court and issued an Order Setting Case Schedule at filing pursuant to **PCLSPR 94.04(f)** and **(g).**

(e) Reassignment for Inability to Hear.

(1) *Preassigned Matter.* If the assigned judicial department is unable to hear a preassigned matter, the Court may transfer that case to the Court Administrator for reassignment.

(2) *Trial Date.* In the event the judicial department is unable to hear a case on the date set because of a conflicting schedule, the case may be transferred to the Court Administrator for reassignment.

(3) *Remain Available.* While awaiting such reassignment, litigants and their witnesses shall remain available until such time as they are excused by the Court Administrator or designee.

(4) *No Available Judicial Department.* If it is not possible for the Court Administrator to reassign a case due to the lack of an available judicial department, the case shall be returned to the previously assigned trial department. The court shall issue an Order Amending Case Schedule which shall only contain the following dates: Joint Statement of Evidence, Pretrial Conference and Trial Date. Additional dates may be added to the Order Amending Case Schedule upon order of the court.

(f) Change of Judge (Affidavits of Prejudice).

(1) *Judges.* To seek disqualification of a judge, a motion and affidavit of prejudice shall be presented to the Judge against whom the affidavit is made. It shall be in conformity with **RCW 4.12.040 and .050,**

and be presented before the Judge in question has made any ruling involving discretion and prior to the time set forth in **CR 40(f)**. Upon being presented with a motion and affidavit, the Judge shall sign a request for reassignment and direct the parties to report to the Court Administrator for assignment to a different judicial department and, if necessary, receipt of an amended case schedule from the new judicial department.

(2) *Commissioners.* Affidavits of prejudice with reference to Court Commissioners shall not be recognized, the remedy of a party being a motion for revision under **RCW 2.24.050**.

(g) Change of Trial Date.

(1) *Cases Not Governed by an Order Setting Case Schedule.* In cases not governed by an Order Setting Case Schedule pursuant to **PCLR 3**, a motion to continue a case already on the trial calendar shall be in writing, supported by an affidavit or declaration under penalty of perjury showing sufficient grounds therefore. If a motion for continuance is granted, the court may impose terms and conditions on the moving party and may set a new trial date. The moving party shall present a written order for entry.

(2) *Cases Governed by an Order Setting Case Schedule.*

(A) Limited Adjustment of Trial Date to Resolve Schedule Conflict. In cases that are governed by an Order Setting Case Schedule pursuant to **PCLR 3**, the trial date may be adjusted, prior to the Deadline for Filing Motions to Adjust Trial Date, by written agreement of counsel and the parties and the court or by court order upon motion by a party, but only to a date no more than 30 days before or 30 days after the trial date listed in the original Order Setting Case Schedule, or as otherwise ordered by the court. The new trial date shall not be selected without first consulting with the judicial department's judicial assistant in order to accommodate the court's calendar. On the court's own motion prior to the Deadline for Filing Motions to Adjust Trial Date the trial date may be adjusted to a date no more than 120 days before or 120 days after the trial date listed in the original Order Setting Case Schedule to accommodate the court's civil and criminal calendars and to attempt to insure trial on the day scheduled.

(B) Continuance of Trial Date. A request to change the trial date to a date more than 30 days before or after the original trial date shall be made by motion and will not be granted unless the motion is supported by a showing of good cause. The new trial date shall not be selected without first consulting with the judicial department's judicial assistant in order to accommodate the Court's calendar. If a motion to change the trial date is made after the Deadline to Adjust Trial Date, the motion will not be granted except under extraordinary circumstances where there is no alternative means of preventing a substantial injustice. A continuance may be granted subject to such conditions as justice requires. If an attorney moves for a continuance of the trial date under this subsection, the motion shall not be considered unless it is signed by both the attorney and the client or it contains a certification from the attorney that the client has been advised of the motion to continue the trial date as well as the basis for the motion and that the client agrees with the motion to continue.

(C) Notice of Change of Trial Date. In the event a party is not present at the time of hearing the motion to change the trial date, the party or parties requesting the change shall serve the absent party or parties with a conformed copy of the Order Amending Case Schedule within five (5) days.

[Adopted effective June 1, 1990; amended effective July 1, 1996; July 2, 1996; September 1, 1998; amended on an emergency basis effective May 15, 2000; amended effective September 1, 2001; September 1, 2002; September 1, 2007; September 1, 2008; September 1, 2009; September 1, 2010; September 1, 2011; September 2, 2014.]

PCLR 41.   DISMISSAL OF ACTIONS

(a)—(d) Reserved.

(e) Notice of Settlements.

(1) *Notice of Settlement.* After any settlement that fully resolves all claims against all parties, the plaintiff shall, within five (5) days or before the next scheduled court hearing, whichever is sooner, file and serve a written notice of settlement. Where such written notice cannot be filed before the trial date, the assigned judicial department shall be notified of the settlement by telephone, or orally in open court, to be confirmed by filing and serving the written notice of settlement within five (5) days.

(2) *Form of Notice.* The **Notice of Settlement of All Claims Against All Parties** shall contain the case heading and otherwise be as set forth in Appendix, **Form G**.

(3) *Dismissal on Court's Motion.* If an order disposing of all claims against all parties is not entered within 90 days after the written notice of settlement is filed, the court shall dismiss the matter unless good cause is shown upon motion and order.

(4) *Agreement by Stipulation.* If the parties have reached agreement and file a stipulation with the court, and the completion or execution of the agreement will take more than 90 days to complete, the requirements of paragraph (3) are waived.

[Adopted effective September 1, 2011.]

PCLR 56.   SUMMARY JUDGMENT

See PCLR 7(a)(8) regarding Summary Judgment page limits.

[Adopted effective September 2, 2014.]

PCLR 59. MOTIONS FOR RECONSIDERATION

See **PCLR 7(c)(2)** and **(3)** regarding time for filing, responsive pleadings and oral argument requirements on reconsideration heard before a Judge (not applicable to reconsiderations set before a Commissioner).

[Adopted effective September 1, 2015.]

PCLR 65. TEMPORARY RESTRAINING ORDERS AND INJUNCTIVE RELIEF

Family Law Matters. A party requesting an Ex Parte Temporary Restraining Order/Order to Show Cause or other temporary injunctive relief under **CR 65** in a family law matter shall present the proposed order to the Ex Parte Division. The party asking for an Ex Parte Restraining Order or other temporary injunctive relief (the moving party) shall give prior written or oral notice to the attorney for the opposing party or to the self-represented party. The moving party or attorney shall certify to the court in writing the efforts which have been made to give notice to the opposing party. Such notice is required in all cases unless the moving party clearly shows by sworn declaration that immediate injury, loss or damage will result if notice is given. If the injunctive relief or temporary restraining order is granted, the hearing shall be set in accordance with the timing requirements of **CR 65(b)** and shall be heard in Civil Division A, B or C as assigned by the Ex Parte Division or by the judicial department which ruled on the initial request for relief. In the interim, the adverse party may move to have the order set aside prior to the hearing in accordance with the time limits set forth in **CR 65(b)**. Such motion shall be heard in Civil Division A, B or C as assigned by the Ex Parte Division or by the judicial department which ruled on the initial request for relief.

Non-Family Law Matters. In non-family law matters, a party requesting a temporary restraining order/preliminary injunctive relief under **CR 65** shall present the proposed order to the Superior Court Presiding Judge. The party asking for an Ex Parte Restraining Order or temporary injunctive relief (the moving party) shall give prior written or oral notice to the attorney for the opposing party or to the self-represented party. The moving party or attorney shall certify to the court in writing the efforts which have been made to give notice to the opposing party. Such notice is required in all cases unless the moving party clearly shows by sworn declaration that immediate injury, loss or damage will result if notice is given. The Presiding Judge shall grant, deny, refer the matter to the assigned judicial department, or if not assigned to a department, refer the matter to court administration for assignment to a judicial department. If the injunctive relief or temporary restraining order is granted, the hearing shall be set in

accordance with the timing requirements of **CR 65(b)** and may be heard before the judicial officer who ruled on the requested order, referred to the judicial department to which the case has already been assigned, or if not assigned to a judicial department, then referred to administration for assignment to a judicial department. In the interim, the adverse party may move to have the order set aside prior to the hearing in accordance with the time limits set forth in **CR 65(b)**. Such motion shall be heard by the judicial department which ruled in the initial request for relief.

In all cases, the time period for hearing the preliminary injunction or temporary restraining order may be extended in accordance with **CR 65(b)**.

[Adopted effective June 1, 1990; amended effective July 2, 1996; July 1, 1997; September 1, 2007; September 1, 2009; September 1, 2010; September 1, 2012.]

PCLR 71.   WITHDRAWAL BY ATTORNEY

(a)—(b) Reserved.

(c) Withdrawal by Notice. Except as provided in **CR 71(b)** and **71(d)**, an attorney may withdraw by notice in the manner provided in this section.

(1) *Notice of Intent to Withdraw.* The attorney shall file and serve a Notice of Intent to Withdraw on all other parties in the proceeding. The notice shall specify a date when the attorney intends to withdraw, which date shall be at least 10 days after the service of the Notice of Intent To Withdraw. The notice shall include a statement that the withdrawal shall be effective without order of court unless an objection to the withdrawal is served upon the withdrawing attorney prior to the date set forth in the notice. If notice is given before trial, the notice shall include the date set for trial. If trial is not yet set, the notice shall include the date(s) of any mandatory future proceeding dates, including any mandatory court review, under **PCLR 3**. The notice shall include the names and last known addresses of the persons represented by the withdrawing attorney, unless disclosure of the address would violate the Rules of Professional Conduct, in which case the address may be omitted. If the address is omitted, the notice must contain a statement that after the attorney withdraws, and so long as the address of the withdrawing attorney's client remains undisclosed and no new attorney is substituted, the client may be served by leaving papers with the clerk of the court pursuant to **CR 5(b)(1)**.

(e) Reserved.

[Adopted effective September 1, 2012.]

PCLR 83. LOCAL RULES OF COURT—CIVIL

(a) Adoption/Amendment of Local Rules

(1) *Local Rules Committee.* The Local Rules Committee (see **PCLR 0.6(a)**), shall be responsible for

promulgation and/or review of all proposed local rules or amendments thereto.

(2) *Changes to Rules.* Substantive changes to local rules proposed by any other committee of the Bench or Bar shall be referred to the Local Rules Committee for review and initial approval.

(3) *Submission to County Bar Association.* Upon initial approval by the Local Rules Committee, that Committee shall forward the text of the proposed rule/amendment to the Tacoma–Pierce County Bar Association for dissemination to the members of the Tacoma–Pierce County Bar Association for comments, criticisms or objections.

(4) *Comments.* The Local Rules Committee shall consider all comments, criticisms and objections. It shall then make any changes to the proposed rules that it deems necessary. It shall then present any proposed rules/amendments to a meeting of the Judges for their consideration.

[Adopted effective June 1, 1990; amended effective July 2, 1996; September 1, 2000; September 1, 2009; September 1, 2010.]

PCLR 85. TITLE OF RULES

These rules shall be known and cited as the Pierce County Superior Court Local Court Civil Rules. PCLR is the official abbreviation.

[Adopted effective September 1, 2010.]

PCLR 86. EFFECTIVE DATES

These rules shall become effective June 1, 1990. The effective date of the amendments is September 1, 1995; July 1, 1996; July 2, 1996; July 1, 1997; September 1, 1998; September 1, 1999; May 15, 2000 on an emergency basis; September 1, 2000; September 1, 2001, September 1, 2002; December 2, 2002 on an emergency basis; September 1, 2003; September 1, 2004; September 4, 2004; September 24, 2004 on an emergency basis; September 1, 2005; September 1, 2006; September 1, 2007; July 1, 2008 and September 1, 2008; June 1, 2009 on an emergency basis; September 1, 2009; September 1, 2010 and September 1, 2011.

[Adopted effective June 1, 1990; amended effective September 1, 1995; July 1, 1996; July 2, 1996; July 1, 1997; September 1, 1998; September 1, 1999; September 1, 2000; September 1, 2001; amended on an emergency basis effective December 2, 2002; amended on a permanent basis effective September 1, 2003; September 1, 2004; amended on an emergency basis effective September 4, 2004; September 24, 2004; amended on a permanent basis effective September 1, 2005; September 1, 2006; September 1, 2007; September 1, 2008; amended on an emergency basis effective June 1, 2009; amended on a permanent basis effective September 1, 2009; amended effective September 1, 2010; September 1, 2011.]

SPECIAL PROCEEDINGS RULES—PCLSPR

PCLSPR 93.04. ADOPTIONS

(a) **Where and When Heard.** All adoption hearings and motions shall be heard every Friday morning commencing at 9:00 a.m. at Pierce County Superior Court, Juvenile Division, located at Remann Hall. Ex Parte and emergency motions can be heard at such dates and times pursuant to procedures promulgated by Juvenile Court and available at the Clerk's Office, Building A, Remann Hall.

(b) **How Initiated.** The moving party shall docket these matters by filing a Note for Juvenile Court Calendar at least six (6) court days in advance of the hearing date unless otherwise required for the hearing by law.

(c) **Appointment and Notice to Adoption Investigator.** Upon the filing of any initial pleadings for adoption of a minor child, including any preplacement reports, the Pierce County Superior Court Clerk shall generate the Order Appointing the Pierce County Adoption Investigator. Copies of all initial pleadings, including any preplacement reports, shall be immediately delivered to the Adoption Investigator. Copies of all Notes for Juvenile Court Calendar, motions for temporary custody, termination or relinquishment of parental rights or for the entry of a Decree of Adoption of a minor child shall be served upon the Adoption Investigator in conformity with paragraph (b) above.

(d) **Preplacement Reports.** No order approving voluntary relinquishment of parental rights shall be considered unless a preplacement report has been filed pursuant to statute. Said preplacement report shall be prepared by those authorized by statute.

(e) **Postplacement Reports.** The Pierce County Adoption Investigator shall provide a postplacement report to the court prior to any adoption of a minor child being finalized, unless the court authorizes an alternate person or adoption agency. No person shall provide postplacement services in a private or independent adoption until authorized by the court. Unless otherwise ordered by the court, the adoption agency having legal custody of the child may be appointed to prepare the postplacement report required by statute. In the event the court authorizes an alternate person or adoption agency to prepare the postplacement report, said report shall be immediately delivered to the Pierce County Adoption Investigator for his/her review and approval.

(f) **Disclosure of Fees and Costs.** A completed financial disclosure declaration shall be filed by the petitioner and considered by the court at any hearing that may result in the termination of parental rights, award of temporary custody or entry of an adoption decree.

[Adopted effective June 1, 1990; amended effective June 3, 1991; September 1, 2000; September 1, 2006; September 1, 2009; September 1, 2010.]

PCLSPR 94.04.   FAMILY LAW PROCEEDINGS

(a) Uncontested Applications for Marital Dissolution, Decree of Invalidity or Legal Separation, Committed Intimate Relationships (Meretricious Relationships) or Domestic Partnerships.

(1) *Presentation of Final Documents.* At the time of final hearing upon any uncontested dissolution, invalidity, legal separation, committed intimate relationship (meretricious relationship) or domestic partnership, the attorney for the applicant or the self-represented party shall present to the court for signature appropriate Findings of Fact and Conclusions of Law, Decree, Order of Child Support, Child Support Worksheets, Residential Time Summary and Parenting Plan/Residential Schedule, if applicable.

(2) *Hearings to Finalize with Attorneys.* For parties represented by counsel, all of these types of proceedings are conducted Monday through Friday in the Ex Parte Division. The location of this calendar is contained in the **Schedule of Commissioners' Calendars**, Appendix, **Form Q**, attached to these rules. The Commissioners' Calendars may be changed without formal republication of these rules or appendices.

At the time of hearing, if the Findings of Fact and Conclusions of Law are signed under penalty of perjury by the Petitioner in the form set forth below and there has been no appearance by the Respondent, no personal appearance by the Petitioner is required. In the event there has been an appearance by the Respondent, but the Respondent agrees to the entry of the final papers as proposed, neither party need personally appear except through his/her attorney, provided that both the Petitioner and Respondent have signed the Findings of Fact and Conclusions of Law under penalty of perjury in the form set forth below. If Respondent has previously signed a Joinder, only the verification of Petitioner is required.

Declaration(s) under penalty of perjury shall be as follows:

I declare under penalty of perjury under the laws of the State of Washington that the following is true and correct:

I am the Petitioner in this case and I have read the foregoing Findings of Fact and Conclusions of Law, Decree, the Order of Child Support, Child Support Worksheets, and Parenting Plan (if applicable), and they are true and accurate to the best of my knowledge. I am not seeking any relief beyond that specifically requested in the Petition. The support requested, if any, is in compliance with the Child Support

Schedule. The wife/other domestic partner is not pregnant and no other children have been born to the wife/other domestic partner since the date of marriage that have not been disclosed in the Findings of Fact and Conclusions of Law and Final Parenting Plan. The State of Washington has been notified of this case as required by the court rules if either party or the children are receiving or have ever received state cash assistance or medical public assistance.

Signed at _____, _____ on _____.
             City   State   Date

_____
Petitioner's Signature

And if agreed by Respondent, add the following declaration:

I declare under penalty of perjury under the laws of the State of Washington that the following is true and correct:

I am the Respondent in this case and I have read the foregoing Findings of Fact and Conclusions of Law, Decree, the Order of Child Support, Child Support Worksheets, and Parenting Plan (if applicable,) and they are true and accurate to the best of my knowledge. I am not seeking any relief beyond that specifically requested in the petition. The support requested, if any, is in compliance with the Child Support Schedule. The wife/other domestic partner is not pregnant and no other children have been born to the wife/other domestic partner since the date of marriage that have not been disclosed in the Findings of Fact and Conclusions of Law and Final Parenting Plan. The State of Washington has been notified of this case as required by the court rules if either party or the children are receiving or have ever received state cash assistance or medical public assistance.

Signed at _____, _____ on _____.
             City   State   Date

_____
Respondent's Signature

(3) *Hearings to Finalize without Attorney Representation.* Uncontested/default dissolutions invalidity or legal separation, committed intimate relationships (meretricious relationships) or domestic partnerships for self-represented parties are conducted every Friday morning. The moving party shall docket these matters by filing a Note for Commissioner's Calendar—Uncontested Docket six court days before the hearing date, subject to case limits. The location and exact time of this calendar is contained in the **Schedule of Commissioners' Calendars**, Appendix, **Form Q**, attached to these rules. The Commissioners' Calendars may be changed without formal republication of these rules or appendices.

(b) Reconciliation.

(1) *Notice of Reconciliation.* In the event the parties reconcile or mutually agree they wish to attempt a reconciliation, they shall jointly file in the Clerk's Office an Order and **Joint Notice of Reconciliation**

as set forth in Appendix, **Form H**, and the parties shall no longer have to comply with the Order Setting Case Schedule requirements of **PCLR 3**; provided that the matter shall automatically be dismissed by the court six months from the date of the notice unless an amended petition has been filed.

(2) *Amended Petition.* In all dissolution, invalidity, legal separation, committed intimate relationship (meretricious relationship) or domestic partnership actions where the parties have reconciled, and the reconciliation fails, an amended petition shall be filed and personally served unless otherwise authorized.

(c) Contested Matters. Before all final hearings or trials in contested dissolution, invalidity, legal separation, committed intimate relationship (meretricious relationship) or domestic partnership cases, each party shall file and serve on the opposing party a **Domestic Relations Information Form** approved by the Court. See Appendix, **Form E.** The Domestic Relations Information Form shall be filed and served two (2) court days prior to the scheduled final hearing or trial. Such information shall be verified under oath.

(d) Family Law Motions.

(1) *How Initiated.* All motions (except discovery motions which are heard on the Judges' motion docket) shall be docketed by filing a Note for Commissioner's Calendar at least fourteen (14) calendar days before the hearing, simultaneously with a Motion and Notice of Hearing and any supporting pleadings, unless this is a renote of a motion or notice for hearing previously filed, in which event only the Note for Commissioner's Calendar shall be filed. The hearing shall be heard on the basis of affidavit and/or declaration. All parties and attorneys shall electronically file a Note for Commissioners Calendar by using the electronic filing and scheduling process provided by LINX via the public website (https://linxonline.co.pierce.wa.us/linxweb/Main.cfm) or from a public kiosk in the Clerk's Office. Cases heard shall be limited in number. Case caps shall be calculated in LINX based on the number of cases rather than the Note for Commissioner's Calendar. Leave may be granted by a duly appointed Commissioner, not a Commissioner Pro Tem, to exceed the number of cases heard on any given day in that Commissioner's Division. Self represented parties may contact the Clerk's Office for a LINX e-filing account or use the Clerk's Office kiosk to file and schedule a Note for Commissioners Calendar.

(2) *Counter Motions.* In the event there is an existing motion or adequate cause hearing and the responding party wishes to file a counter motion to be heard the same date they may do so without leave of the court by e-filing a Note for Commissioner's Calendar, as long as the counter motion and all supporting pleadings are filed and served a minimum of fourteen (14) calendar days before the hearing. Any necessary Order to Show Cause shall be timely presented to the Ex Parte Department. The Note for Commissioner's Calendar shall be electronically filed and scheduled in accordance with **PCLSPR 94.04(c)(1)**.

(3) *Notice and Hearing.* Copies of the motion, counter motion, e-filed Note for Commissioner's Calendar, Notice of Adequate Cause, if applicable, together with all supporting documents including affidavits, declarations, certified statements, exhibits, and any other materials to be considered by the court, shall be served on all counsel and any self-represented party at least fourteen (14) calendar days before the hearing. Response documents, including briefs or memoranda, if any, shall be filed with the Clerk and copies served on all parties and attorneys no later than 12:00 noon four (4) court days prior to the hearing time; and documents in strict reply to the motion shall be similarly filed and served no later than 12:00 noon two (2) court days prior to the hearing.

(4) *Working Copies/Proposed Orders.* Copies of the motion, counter motion, e-filed Note for Commissioner's Calendar, together with all supporting documents including affidavits, declarations, certified statements, documents in strict reply and response documents, including briefs or memoranda and a copy of proposed orders shall be delivered to the Commissioners Service Department no later than 12:00 noon two (2) court days prior to the hearing or by using the Clerk's electronic working copy delivery process as defined in **PCLGR 30(b)(5)(B)**. A copy of the e-filed Note for Commissioner's Calendar shall be attached to each set of copies delivered to the Commissioner Services Department. All parties shall mark "Working Copies" in the upper right hand corner and indicate the name of the calendar, the date and time of the hearing and who is delivering the papers (moving party or opposing party).

Anyone e-filing documents shall be responsible for ensuring working copies are timely provided to the Commissioner Services Department. A fax or email transmittal of working copies shall not be acceptable delivery.

(5) *Page Limits.*

(A) Generally. Absent prior authorization from the court, the entirety of all declarations and affidavits from the parties and any non-expert witness in support of motions (except financial declarations), including any reply, shall be limited to a sum total of 20 pages for all motions scheduled for the same date. Prior authorization to exceed page limits under **PCLSPR 94.04(c)(5)** shall initially be presented to the Ex Parte Department and that Department shall determine whether the matter needs to be referred to the assigned Commissioner. The entirety of all declarations and affidavits submitted in response to motions shall be limited to a sum total of 20 pages for all motions scheduled for the same date. In those cases having more than one moving party, the entirety of all declarations and affidavits from each party in support of their respective motions (except financial declarations), shall be limited to a sum total of 20 pages per side.

(B) Exhibits. Exhibits that consist of declarations or affidavits of party's witnesses shall count towards the above page limits. All other exhibits attached to a declaration or affidavit shall be limited to 10 pages.

(C) Financial Declarations. Financial declarations and financial documents do not count toward the page limit.

(D) Expert Reports and Evaluations. Declarations, affidavits, and reports from Court Appointed Special Advocates (CASA), Parenting Investigators, Guardians ad Litem, Family Court Services (FCS), expert witnesses, police reports and out-of-state backgrounds checks do not count toward the page limit.

(E) Miscellaneous Exceptions. The following do not count towards the page limit:

(i) Copies of orders, declarations, or affidavits previously filed for a motion already ruled upon and supplied only as a convenience to the court in lieu of the court file;

(ii) Copies of orders, declarations, or affidavits previously filed in other cases, or from cases in other counties;

(iii) Deposition excerpts;

(iv) GR 17 affidavits/declarations regarding fax signature; and

(v) Cover sheets setting forth a caption for an attached document or declaration, however, the attached document or declaration shall count in accordance with this rule.

(6) *Confirmations.* The moving party shall confirm the motion with the Commissioner Services Department in person or by telephone by noon two (2) court days prior to the hearing; otherwise the matter shall be stricken. Motions may also be confirmed and stricken electronically, in accordance with the time deadlines set forth herein, by those with LINX accounts and PIN (Personal Identification Numbers) in accordance with the procedures adopted by the Pierce County Superior Court Clerk's Office. Motions filed by persons physically confined under a court order shall be deemed confirmed at filing.

(7) *Courtroom Assigned.* The monitors located on the first and second floor lobbies of the County City Building list which court has been assigned to hear confirmed motions. Attorneys and self-represented parties may also check the assigned courtroom by accessing the Pierce County Superior Court website: https://linxonline.co.pierce.wa.us/linxweb/Main.cfm and viewing the calendar of proceedings.

(8) *Presentation of Court Orders.* All counsel or self-represented parties are responsible for preparing and presenting court orders (using mandatory Family Law pattern forms if applicable) at the conclusion of the motion and shall remain in attendance in the court until the appropriate order(s) has been signed by counsel, all parties and the court.

(9) *Limits of Argument.* The court may direct counsel or self-represented parties to appropriate issues set forth in the motion and may place strict limits on the time for argument.

(d) Settlement Conferences. See **PCLR 16(c).** Settlement conferences are mandatory in dissolutions, paternity cases involving petition or motion for establishment of residential schedule or parenting plan and post-dissolution petitions for modification. Settlement conferences are not mandatory for cases addressing only child support and family law cases in which a waiver was granted pursuant to **PCLR 16(c)(2)(G).**

(e) Guardian ad Litem in Parenting/Custody Cases: Limitations on Appointments, Hours and Fees.

(1) *Appointment of Guardian ad Litem.* The appointment of a guardian ad litem/parenting investigator in cases involving the residential placement of minor children shall be made by court order. The guardian ad litem shall be provided a copy of the Order Setting Case Schedule, and any amendments thereto entered throughout the course of the case. If there are less than 90 days to the date of trial, any Order for Appointment of a Guardian ad Litem/Parenting Investigator shall include the trial date and shall only be signed by the assigned judicial department.

(2) *Hours and Fees.*

(A) Retainer/Additional Fees. When an order authorizing appointment of a guardian ad litem from the **RCW 26.09** Certified Registry is signed, a $1125.00 initial retainer fee shall be paid to the Clerk of the Court, unless for good cause shown a greater amount is ordered by the Court at the time of the appointment of a guardian ad litem and is reflected in the order.

The guardian ad litem's time shall be paid from this retainer at the rate of $75.00 per hour. When the retainer is exhausted, the guardian ad litem shall request payment of additional fees from the assigned Family Court. No additional fees shall be allowed without prior authorization of the assigned Family Court Judge.

(B) State Paternity Actions. Section (2) (A) does not apply to State initiated paternity contract cases.

(3) *Administrative Policy.* Pierce County Superior Court's current Administrative Policy re: **Guardian ad Litem Registry for Pierce County Family Law Proceedings** and **Code of Conduct** are set forth in Part VI, Administrative Policies, **Policies 1** and **2.** Found at: www.co.pierce.wa.us/superiorcourt and by clicking on "Local Rules."

(4) *Case Assignment.* Upon the court authorizing the appointment of a guardian ad litem/parenting investigator, the case shall be reassigned to Family Court, except for those cases where the Guardian ad Litem (GAL) is only appointed for the purpose of parentage or minority.

(f) Nonparental Custody Proceedings.

(1) *How Initiated.* An action for custody of a child brought by a nonparent is commenced by the filing of a Summons, Petition, Petitioner's Notice of Adequate Cause, and Order Directing DCFS/CPS to Release Information on the mandatory forms under a new cause number and may not be commenced under an existing dissolution, paternity or other case.

(2) *Case Schedule.* Upon filing, the Clerk's Office shall issue an **Order Setting Case Schedule**. Refer to Appendix, **Form A**.

(3) *Requirements.* The petitioner(s) shall obtain a Washington State Patrol and Child Protective Services (CPS) background checks on themselves and all adult household members. The petitioner(s) shall obtain an Order Finding Adequate Cause on the Commissioner's dockets on or before the court hearing date specified in the Order Setting Case Schedule or the petition shall be dismissed without further notice. The petitioners and respondents shall attend the mandatory Impact on Children seminar. A settlement conference, or other dispute resolution process, is required prior to trial, unless waived by the Court; see **PCLR 16(c)**.

(4) *Case Assignment.* All Nonparental Custody actions shall be assigned to Family Court.

(5) *Finalization.* Nonparental Custody actions to be finalized, by agreement or by default, shall be calendared on the Commissioners' Motion/Show Cause docket or on the motion calendar of the assigned Family Court Department. Such matters shall not be heard in the Ex Parte Division. Pro Tem Commissioners are not authorized to finalize any nonparental custody actions.

(g) Petition to Modify Parenting Plan/Residential Schedule.

(1) *How Initiated.* An action for modification of a final parenting plan/residential schedule is commenced by the filing of a Summons, Petition for Modification of Custody, Proposed Parenting Plan/Residential Schedule, and Petitioner's Notice of Adequate Cause on the mandatory forms under the existing dissolution, paternity, or other case.

(2) *Case Schedule.* Upon filing, the Clerk's Office shall issue an **Order Setting Case Schedule**. Refer to Appendix, **Form A**.

(3) *Requirements.* The petitioner(s) shall obtain an Order Finding Adequate Cause on the Commissioners' dockets on or before the court hearing date specified in the Order Setting Case Schedule or the

petition will be dismissed without further notice. The petitioner(s) and respondent(s) shall attend the mandatory Impact on Children seminar. A settlement conference, or other dispute resolution process, is required prior to trial, unless waived by the Court; see **PLCR 16(c)**.

(4) *Case Assignment.* All Petitions to Modify Parenting Plan/Residential Schedule shall be assigned to Family Court.

(h) Relocation of Children.

(1) *How Initiated.* An action for Relocation of Children is commenced by the filing of an Objection to Relocation under the existing dissolution, paternity, or other case. Prior to the trial, any hearing regarding the Objection to Relocation or temporary relocation shall be heard on the Commissioners' Show Cause/Motion docket.

(2) *Case Schedule.* The Clerk's office shall issue an Order Assigning Case to Family Court and set a date on the assigned Family Court's next available motion calendar (not less than six days from filing) for an assignment for trial date.

(3) *Case Assignment.* All Objections to Relocation shall be assigned to Family Court.

[Adopted effective June 1, 1990. Amended effective June 3, 1991; September 1, 1995; July 1, 1996; July 2, 1996; September 1, 1998; September 1, 1999; amended on an emergency basis, effective May 15, 2000; amended on a permanent basis, effective September 1, 2000; September 1, 2002; September 1, 2003; September 1, 2004; September 1, 2005; September 1, 2006; September 1, 2007; September 1, 2008; September 1, 2009; September 1, 2010; September 1, 2011; September 1, 2012; September 2, 2013; September 1, 2015.]

PCLSPR 94.05.   MANDATORY SEMINAR: IMPACT ON CHILDREN

(a) Applicable Cases. This rule shall apply to all cases filed under **Ch. 26.09, Ch. 26.10,** or **Ch. 26.26 RCW** which require a parenting plan or residential schedule for minor children. This rule does not apply to modification cases based solely upon relocation.

(b) Mandatory Attendance. In all cases governed by this rule, all parties shall complete an approved parenting seminar. Each party shall attach a copy of the Certificate of Completion to the final parenting plan. Standards for parenting seminars shall be established by the court and providers shall be approved by the court. The court may approve a seminar upon a showing of functional equivalency regarding course content and instructor qualifications. In no case shall opposing parties be required to attend a seminar together.

(c) Timing. Parties required by this rule to participate in a parenting seminar shall complete an approved parenting seminar within 60 days after service of the petition or motion initiating the action which is subject to this rule. In the case of paternity actions, the parenting seminar shall be required only when paternity is established or acknowledged and a residential schedule is requested.

(d) Fees. Each party attending a seminar shall pay a fee charged by the approved providers and sanctioned by the court. The court or an approved provider may waive the fee for indigent parties.

(e) Seminar Content/Instructor Qualifications. The Impact on Children Seminar shall provide information concerning the impact family restructuring has on children. Superior Court (or a committee designated by the Judges) shall adopt guidelines governing the content of the seminar, the number of approved providers and the minimum credentials and experience required of seminar instructors. The provider shall e-file each attendee's Certificate of Completion with the court. The provider shall give each attendee a Certificate of Completion.

(f) Waiver. The court may waive the seminar requirement for good cause shown.

(g) Failure to Comply. Willful refusal to participate in a parenting seminar or willful delay in completion of a parenting seminar by any party may constitute contempt of court and result in sanctions, including, but not limited to, imposition of monetary terms, striking of pleadings or denial of affirmative parenting plan relief, to a party not in compliance with this rule. Non-participation, or default, by one party does not excuse participation by the other.

(h) Administrative Policy. Pierce County Superior Court's current Administrative Policy re: Impact on Children Seminar is set forth in Part VI, Administrative Policies. It may also be found at: www.co.pierce.wa.us/superiorcourt and by clicking on "Local Rules."

[Adopted effective September 1, 2000; amended effective September 1, 2004; January 1, 2007; September 1, 2009; September 1, 2010; September 1, 2015.]

PCLSPR 98.04. ESTATES—PROBATE—NOTICES

(a) Presentation. The initial presentation of an order appointing a Personal Representative or Administrator in a testate or intestate estate may be presented to the Court Commissioner in the Ex Parte Division. This appointment shall be at the discretion of the court and in the event the court determines that notice shall be given, may direct the petitioner to make said presentation on the Commissioner's Probate calendar conducted in Civil Division A.

(b) Notice and Hearing. All hearings shall be scheduled with a Note for Commissioner's Calendar by using the electronic filing and scheduling process provided by LINX via the public website (https://linxonline.co.pierce.wa.us/linxweb/Main.cfm) or from a public kiosk in the Clerk's Office. The Note shall be filed at least six (6) court days prior to the scheduled hearing date. The Court Commissioner may set spe-

cial hearings at other times if complex or unusual issues are present. Self represented parties may contact the Clerk's Office for a LINX e-filing account or use the Clerk's Office kiosk to file and schedule a Note for Commissioners Calendar. Working Copies/Proposed Orders. All parties shall be responsible for ensuring working copies and proposed orders are delivered to the Commissioner Services Department no later than 12:00 noon two (2) court days prior to the hearing or by using the Clerk's electronic working copy delivery process as defined in **PCLGR 30(b)(5)(B).** A copy of the Note for Commissioner's Calendar shall be attached to each set of copies delivered to the Commissioner's Service Department. In the upper right hand corner mark "Working Copies" the name of the calendar, the date and time of the hearing and indicate who is providing the copies (moving party or opposing party). A Guardian ad Litem shall be responsible for providing a working copy of his/her report. Anyone e-filing documents shall be responsible for ensuring working copies are timely provided to the Commissioner Services Department. A fax or email transmittal of working copies shall not be acceptable delivery.

(c) Bonds. All bonds required of personal representatives/administrators shall be signed by the principal and shall contain the address of the surety.

(d) Probate Homesteads/Prior Claims. In all cases where a petition for allowance in lieu of homestead or in addition thereto is filed by the surviving spouse, receipts evidencing the payment of funeral expenses, expenses of last sickness, and of administration, including fees of appraisers, or a signed written statement by the creditor that such payment has been provided for, shall be filed at or before the time of the hearing on said petition.

(e) Oaths. The Personal Representative(s)/Administrator(s) name shall be typed or printed on the oath as it appears in the order. The oath shall conform to the requirements as set forth in **RCW 11.28.170** and **RCW 11.36.010.** When a Personal Representative/Administrator changes his or her name, he or she shall obtain an order for new letters and file an oath under the new name in order to receive new letters. The expiration date of the letters shall remain the same unless changed by the new order.

(f) Order Appointing Personal Representative/Administrator. The order shall contain the name(s) for the Personal Representative(s)/Administrator(s) as it appears in the oath.

(g) Notification of Change of Address. Any person appointed as Personal Representative or Administrator of an estate shall file a notice of change of address with the court within thirty (30) days of the change.

Waiver of Requirement to E-file. See **PCLGR 30(b)(5)(C)**.

[Adopted effective September 1, 2009; amended effective September 1, 2010; September 1, 2011; September 1, 2015.]

PCLSPR 98.16W. SETTLEMENT OF CLAIMS OF MINORS AND INCAPACITATED PERSONS

(a) Presentation. The presentation of an order to appoint an attorney to serve as the proposed Settlement Guardian ad Litem shall be presented to the Court Commissioner in the Ex Parte Division. This appointment shall be at the discretion of the court and no proposed order presented shall include a preselected name nor address the fees/cost of the court appointed Settlement Guardian ad Litem.

(b) Qualifications. The qualifications of an attorney to serve as the Settlement Guardian ad Litem shall be in compliance with **SPR 98.16W(d)**. The Settlement Guardian ad Litem report shall include the following information:

(1) the number of years the attorney has been in practice in the State of WA;

(2) a summary of the type of practice of the attorney for at least the last five (5) years;

(3) an affirmation that the attorney does not have any conflict of interest as contemplated in **SPR 98.16.W(d)**; and whether the attorney is aware of any pending Bar Association disciplinary proceedings or of any criminal charges that have been filed against his/her; and

(4) whether the attorney has any relationship with the involved parents, guardians, insurers or other attorneys in the case; and

(5) a statement as to whether or not there has been compliance with **RCW 4.24.010**, specifically, the notice requirements to a parent who is not named as a plaintiff.

(c) Attendance at Hearings. The presence of the Settlement Guardian ad Litem, custodial parent or legal custodian, and the affected person is required unless waived by the Court pursuant to an Order obtained from the Commissioner in Civil Division A, or the Ex Parte Division, in advance of the hearing for good cause shown.

(d) Report/Working Copies/Proposed Orders. The Settlement Guardian ad Litem, shall file his/her report in the Clerk's Office. The moving party shall be responsible for ensuring working copies, including proposed orders and the Settlement Guardian ad Litem report, are delivered to the Commissioner Services Department no later than 12:00 noon two (2) court days prior to the hearing or by using the Clerk's electronic working copy delivery process as defined in **PCLGR 30(b)(5)(B)**. A copy of the e-filed Note for Commissioner's Calendar shall be attached to each set of copies delivered to the Commissioner Services Department. In the upper right hand corner mark "Working Copies", the name of the calendar, the date and time of the hearing and who is providing the papers (moving party or opposing party). Anyone e-filing documents shall be responsible for ensuring working copies are timely provided to the Commissioner Services Department. A fax or email transmittal of working copies shall not be acceptable delivery.

(e) Notice and Hearing. All hearings shall be scheduled with a Note for Commissioner's Calendar by using the electronic filing and scheduling process provided by LINX via the public website (https://linxonline.co.pierce.wa.us/linxweb/Main.cfm) or from a public kiosk in the Clerk's Office. The Note shall be filed at least six (6) court days prior to the scheduled hearing date. Consistent with **RCW 4.24.010**, notice of said motion shall be given to a parent who was not originally named as a plaintiff or is no longer a custodian of the minor or incapacitated person. Self represented parties may contact the Clerk's Office for a LINX e-filing account or use the Clerk's Office kiosk to file and schedule a Note for Commissioners Calendar.

The Court Commissioner may set special hearings at other times if complex or unusual issues may be present.

(f) Multiple Minors. In the event the filed claim involves multiple minors, separate proposed court orders shall be presented to the court addressing each individual minor. Each proposed Order shall also include reference to the day, month and year of the minor's eighteenth (18th) birthday.

(g) Structured Annuity Settlements. Unless waived by the Court for good cause shown, the following language shall be inserted into any court order approving a structured annuity settlement involving a minor or incapacitated person:

"Neither the minor nor incapacitated person, nor his estate, nor any subsequent beneficiary or recipient of any payments or any part of any payments under this structured settlement shall have the right to accelerate, commute or otherwise reduce to present value or to a lump sum any of the payments or any part of the payments due under this structured annuity settlement or this order unless by later motion good cause has been shown to lift or modify these restrictions.

No payment under the structured settlement annuity contract or this order shall be transferred as defined in **RCW 19.205.010(18)**, accelerated, deferred, increased or decreased, or anticipated, sold, mortgaged, assigned or encumbered in any manner by the minor or incapacitated person or any other recipient of the payments unless by later motion good cause has been shown to lift or modify these restrictions."

(h) Receipt of Deposit of Funds. Unless waived by the Court for good cause shown, a verification of blocked account and receipt of deposit of funds into either the Registry of the Court or such institution as the court order directs shall be filed within forty-five (45) days by independent counsel for the minor or incapacitated person, counsel for the insurance carrier, or by the court appointed Settlement Guardian ad Litem should there be no independent counsel on behalf of the minor or incapacitated person. In the event a party other than the Settlement Guardian ad Litem deposits the funds, they shall provide a copy of the receipt of deposit and verification of blocked account to the Settlement Guardian ad Litem. Failure to comply with this provision may subject the parties to a noncompliance hearing and the assessment of terms.

(i) Discharge of Settlement Guardian ad Litem. No court appointed Settlement Guardian ad Litem shall be considered discharged by the court until a receipt of deposit of funds has been filed as set forth above.

(j) Disbursements. All motions relating to disbursements from the court approved settlement proceeds of a minor or incapacitated person prior to their eighteenth (18th) birthday shall be scheduled by e-filing a Note for Commissioner's Calendar, scheduling the hearing in Civil Division A and the parties shall comply with all requirements set forth in subsection **(e)** above.

(k) Fees/Costs. All fees and costs requested by the attorney for the minor and/or court appointed Settlement Guardian ad Litem are subject to court approval.

Waiver of Requirement to E–file. See **PCLGR 30(b)(5)(C)**.

[Adopted effective September 1, 2000; amended effective September 1, 2007; September 1, 2009; September 1, 2010; September 1, 2011; September 1, 2015.]

PCLSPR 98.18.   COURT CREATED TRUSTS

(a) Scope of Rule. This rule shall apply to any trust created by the court, including but not limited to trusts created pursuant to **PCLSPR 98.16W, RCW 11.88** and **RCW 11.92**, such as special needs trusts and settlement trusts.

(b) Drafting of Trust Instrument. A trust instrument shall only be drafted after a written guardian ad litem recommendation and/or a court order that specifies the relevant terms of such trust, unless the requirement of such recommendation or court order is waived by the court for good cause.

(c) Guardian ad Litem/Guardian. The court shall only order a court-created trust upon the written recommendation of a qualified guardian ad litem or guardian, unless the requirement of a guardian ad litem or guardian is specifically waived by the court for good cause. Based on the facts and circumstances, the court may authorize the petitioner, the guardian ad litem or guardian to hire trust counsel to evaluate any proposed trust instrument, to draft a trust instrument or any other duties as enumerated by the court.

The guardian ad litem's or guardian's report shall:

(1) Identify why a court-created trust is in the best interests of the beneficiary;

(2) Specifically identify any other roles expected of a trustee or trust advisory committee member in the life of the beneficiary (e.g. this requirement would include caregivers, professional advisors, family or others who might receive direct or independent economic benefit from trust expenditures); and

(3) Specifically recommend why a Trust Advisory Committee is appropriate or not appropriate if proposed by petitioner.

(d) Special Master. In its discretion, the court may appoint a Special Master to provide independent analysis to the court with regard to the proposed trust instrument or provide such assistance as ordered by the court.

(e) Declaration of Proposed Trustee. Prior to appointment, each trustee shall file with the court a **Declaration of Proposed Trustee** as set forth in Appendix, **Form K** unless waived by the court. If the proposed trustee is a bank or trust company, no Declaration shall be required, except if the court or the guardian ad litem determines that a Declaration shall be filed with the court. At the hearing for appointment, the fee schedule shall be disclosed.

(f) Notice and Hearing. All hearings shall be scheduled with a Note for Commissioner's Calendar using the electronic filing and scheduling process provided by LINX via the public website (https://linxonline.co.pierce.wa.us/linxweb/Main.cfm) or from a public kiosk in the Clerk's Office. The Note shall be e-filed at least six (6) court days prior to the scheduled hearing date. Self represented parties may contact the Clerk's Office for a LINX e-filing account or use the Clerk's Office kiosk to file and schedule a Note for Commissioners Calendar.

(g) Attendance at Hearings. The presence of the Guardian ad Litem, Guardian, Special Master and the affected person is required unless waived by the Court pursuant to an Order obtained from the Commissioner in Civil Division A in advance of the hearing for good cause shown.

(h) Report/Working Copies/Proposed Orders. The Guardian ad Litem and Special Master shall file their reports in the Clerk's Office. The moving party shall be responsible for ensuring working copies, including proposed orders, the Guardian ad Litem report and report of Special Master, are delivered to the Commissioner Services Department no later than

12:00 noon two (2) court days prior to the hearing or by using the Clerk's electronic working copy delivery process as defined in **PCLGR 30(b)(5)(B)**. A copy of the Note for Commissioner's Calendar shall be attached to each set of copies delivered to the Commissioner Services Department. In the upper right hand corner mark "Working Copies", the name of the calendar, the date and time of the hearing and who is providing the papers (moving party or opposing party). Anyone e-filing documents shall be responsible for ensuring working copies are timely provided to the Commissioner Services Department. A fax or email transmittal of working copies shall not be acceptable delivery.

(i) Order Approving/Declaring Trust. Within thirty (30) days, the Order Approving/Declaring the Trust shall be filed in a court file with a guardianship cause number to allow the court to track the matter. Likewise, the trust instrument shall be filed under the same cause number. Any guardian ad litem shall not be discharged until such filing has occurred.

(j) Fees/Costs. All fees and costs requested by the attorney for the minor and/or court appointed Settlement Guardian ad Litem are subject to court approval.

(k) Review Hearings. Upon signing the Order Approving/Declaring the Trust, the court shall specify the report interval for the first periodic report and accounting. At the time the Order Approving/Declaring the Trust is filed with the clerk's office, the clerk shall schedule the date for the initial review hearing on the assigned judicial department's Friday motion docket, not more than 120 days after the anniversary date of the Order. Trusts shall be reviewed at least annually unless the court extends the review period. The periodic reports and accountings shall be filed within 90 days after the anniversary date of the trust's creation.

Review hearings on subsequent periodic reports and accountings shall be automatically scheduled by the court and heard on the assigned judicial department's Friday motion docket not more than 120 days after the anniversary date of the trust's creation. Any change to the scheduled review date shall be noted before the assigned department. Review hearings on final reports and accountings shall be noted and heard on the assigned judicial department's Friday motion docket.

(*l*) Trust Summary. A **Trust Summary**, as set forth in Appendix, **Form L** shall be completed and placed directly below the case caption or on a separate cover page on all orders creating a trust and orders approving a trustee's periodic report or accounting.

(m) Delinquency Calendar. The assigned judicial department shall track all trust cases which require court review and shall notify the assigned judicial department of cases where periodic reports and accountings are delinquent. The department shall direct the trustee and counsel to appear at a hearing where sanctions may be imposed or the trustee removed. The department may appoint a guardian ad litem to investigate and report back to the court as to whether the trustee should be removed or other protections put in place for the benefit of the trust beneficiary.

Waiver of Requirement to E-file. See **PCLGR 30(b)(5)(C)**.

[Adopted effective September 1, 2006; amended effective September 1, 2009; September 1, 2010; September 1, 2011; September 1, 2015.]

PCLSPR 98.20. GUARDIANSHIPS

(a) Presentation of Order Appointing Guardian ad Litem. The initial Order appointing a Guardian ad Litem shall be presented to the Court Commissioner in the Ex Parte Division upon the filing of a Petition for Guardianship. The Clerk of the Court in the Ex Parte Division shall maintain the **RCW 11.88** Registry and shall select the next Guardian ad Litem on the list for insertion into the Order Appointing Guardian ad Litem, unless the alleged incapacitated person is indigent in which event the selection shall be made from those Guardians ad Litem who have contracted to serve in this capacity with Pierce County Superior Court.

(b) Notice and Hearing. The following matters shall be noted for hearing at least six (6) court days in advance and heard on the Guardianship docket in Civil Division A:

(1) All guardianship matters involving the approval of initial reports, interim accounts or the expenditure of funds prior to the appointment of a Guardian;

(2) All hearings on the appointment of a Guardian of the Person and/or Estate;

(3) Motions for confirmation of sale of real estate; or

(4) Any other matters in which the court is requested to find that certain procedural steps have been taken.

All hearings shall be scheduled with a Note for Commissioner's Calendar. Attorneys shall electronically file a Note for Commissioners Calendar by using the electronic filing and scheduling process provided by LINX via the public website (https://linxonline.co.pierce.wa.us/linxweb/Main.cfm) or from a public kiosk in the Clerk's Office. The Note shall be filed at least six (6) court days prior to the scheduled hearing date. The Court Commissioner may set special hearings at other times if complex or unusual issues are present. Self represented parties may contact the Clerk's Office for a LINX e-filing account or use the Clerk's Office kiosk to file and schedule a Note for Commissioners Calendar.

(c) Report/Working Copies/Proposed Orders. The moving party shall be responsible for ensuring working copies, including proposed orders and the Guardian ad Litem report and any medical reports are delivered to the Commissioner Services Department no later than 12:00 noon two (2) court days prior to the hearing or by using the Clerk's electronic working copy delivery process as defined in **PCLGR 30(b)(5)(B)**. A copy of the Note for Commissioner's Calendar shall be attached to each set of copies delivered to the Commissioner Services Department. In the upper right hand corner mark "Working Copies", the name of the calendar, the date and time of the hearing and who is providing the papers (moving party or opposing party). Anyone e-filing documents shall be responsible for ensuring working copies are timely provided to the Commissioner Services Department. A fax or email transmittal of working copies shall not be acceptable delivery.

(d) Declaration of Proposed Guardian. Prior to appointment, a **Declaration of Proposed Guardian** shall be filed with the Court as set forth in Appendix, **Forms M** or **N**, unless waived by the Court. If the proposed guardian is a bank or trust company, no declaration shall be required, except if the Court or the Guardian ad Litem determines that a Declaration shall be filed with the Court. At the hearing for appointment, the fee schedule for the bank or trust company shall be disclosed.

(e) Review Hearings. Upon signing the Order Appointing Guardian the court will specify: (i) the report interval for the first periodic report and accounting, and (ii) whether a review hearing will be required on the Inventory.

At the time the Order Appointing Guardian is filed, the Clerk's Office shall schedule the date for the *initial* review hearing on the assigned judicial department's Friday motion docket, not more than 120 days after the anniversary date of the guardian's appointment. Guardianships shall be reviewed at least annually unless the court extends the review period. The periodic reports and accountings shall be filed and a working copy provided to the assigned judicial department within 90 days after the anniversary date of the guardian's appointment. Anyone e-filing the periodic report and accounting shall be responsible for ensuring the working copies are timely provided to the assigned judicial department.

Review hearings on *subsequent* periodic reports and accountings shall be automatically scheduled by the court and heard on the assigned judicial department's Friday motion docket not more than 120 days after the anniversary date of the guardian's appointment. Any change to the scheduled review date shall be noted before the assigned judicial department. Review hearings on the final report and accounting must be noted and heard on the judicial assigned department's Friday motion docket. Working copies of the final report and accounting shall be provided to the assigned judicial department at the time the final report and accounting are filed. Anyone e-filing the

final report and accounting shall be responsible for ensuring the working copies are timely provided to the assigned judicial department. A fax or email transmittal of working copies shall not be acceptable delivery.

(f) Guardianship Summary. A **Guardianship Summary**, as set forth in **Form O** shall be completed and placed directly below the case caption or on a separate cover page on all Orders Appointing a Guardian and Orders Approving a Guardian's Periodic Report or Accounting.

(g) Delinquency Calendar. The assigned judicial department shall track all guardianship cases which require court review and shall notify the court of cases where periodic reports and accountings are delinquent. The department may direct the guardian, and counsel to appear at a hearing where sanctions may be imposed and/or the guardian removed. The department may appoint a guardian ad litem to investigate and report back to the court as to whether the guardian should be removed or other protections put in place for the benefit of the incapacitated person.

(h) Expiring Letters of Guardianship. The Clerk's Office shall issue Letters of Guardianship to the appointed guardian. The Letters shall expire on the 120th day after the anniversary date of the guardian's appointment, unless a different date is ordered by the court. A guardian has no authority to act on behalf of the incapacitated person without valid Letters of Guardianship.

(i) Oaths. The guardian name(s) shall be typed or printed on the oath as it appears in the order. When a guardian changes his or her name he or she shall obtain an order for new letters and file an oath under the new name in order to receive new letters of guardianship. The expiration date of the letters shall remain the same unless changed by new court order.

(j) Vulnerable Adult Protection Petitions. Any petition protecting a vulnerable adult shall be filed as a civil matter separate from any guardianship matter. If there is an existing guardianship case when the Vulnerable Adult Petition is filed, a copy of any Protection order shall be placed in that file.

(k) Loss of Voting Rights. In accordance with **RCW 11.88.010(5)**, if an incapacitated person loses the right to vote, the Order Appointing Guardian or Approving Report shall include a specific finding on the loss of the right to vote. The Guardian shall also submit a Notice of Loss of Voting Rights to the court that includes the name, address and date of birth of the incapacitated person and that directs the Clerk to forward the Notice of Loss of Voting Rights to the County Auditor. In the event the guardianship is terminated by a determination of competency of the individual, the court shall direct the Clerk to send to the County Auditor a certified copy of the Order Restoring Voting Rights including the same personal identifiers as the Notice of Loss of Voting Rights.

(*l*) **Mandatory Forms.** In the event a statewide mandatory guardianship form exists, these forms shall be utilized. If no state wide form exists, then the Pierce County Mandatory Guardianship forms shall be utilized. Both the mandatory and pattern guardianship forms can be obtained on Pierce County Superior Court's website: www.co.pierce.wa.us/superiorcourt or the Pierce County Superior Court Law Library. These forms are subject to future updates, corrections, amendments or other alterations and notice of these changes shall be placed on Superior Court's website and are available at: www.courts.wa.gov/forms/.

Waiver of Requirement to E–file. See **PCLGR 30(b)(5)(C).**

[Adopted effective June 1, 1990; amended effective July 2, 1996; September 1, 2001; September 1, 2004; September 1, 2005; September 1, 2006; September 1, 2007; September 1, 2008; September 1, 2009; September 1, 2010; September 1, 2011; September 1, 2015.]

PCLSPR 98.30. PUBLIC EXPENSE GUARDIANS AD LITEM AND ATTORNEYS FOR ALLEGED INCAPACITATED PERSONS PURSUANT TO RCW 11.88

(a) Application and Petition. All persons asserting a right to the services of an attorney or a guardian ad litem at public expense shall make application to the court at the time of the filing of the Petition for Guardianship, or as soon thereafter as the qualifying financial situation is known, setting forth:

(1) *Financial Condition.* The financial condition of the alleged incapacitated person and of persons responsible for the alleged incapacitated person's obligations, and the resulting substantial hardship, if any, if payment of fees is required.

(2) *Other.* The Petition for Guardianship shall also, whenever possible, indicate:

(A) if the assets are expected to be less than $3,000;

(B) whether there is a request that the filing fee be waived; and

(C) whether a guardian ad litem at public expense is being sought.

(b) Guardian ad Litem at Public Expense. If the court approves an application for the appointment of a guardian ad litem at public expense, the case shall be assigned in the Ex Parte Division to the appropriate guardian ad litem at public expense.

(1) *Mandatory Language in Order.* All orders appointing a guardian ad litem at public expense shall include language that:

"If the estate is found not to qualify for services at public expense, the assigned public expense guardian ad litem shall, before significant work is performed or time elapsed, return the case for reassignment to a regular **RCW 11.88** guardian ad litem from the Certified Registry If significant work by the public expense guardian ad litem has been performed or time elapsed, the public expense guardian ad litem shall perform all duties and then apply for fees at their private rate from the court."

(2) *Duty of Guardian ad Litem to Advise Court.* The Guardian ad Litem shall immediately advise the court if the guardianship case qualifies for a guardian ad litem at public expense and before significant work is performed or time elapsed and return the case for reassignment to a guardian ad litem at public expense.

(c) Attorney Assignment and Fees. When the court appoints an attorney for the alleged incapacitated person which attorney will be paid at public expense, the order shall provide that the hourly rate to be charged by the attorney is $75.00 per hour or less, and that all fees paid shall be reasonable fees as determined by the judicial officer.

[Adopted effective September 1, 2007; amended effective September 1, 2009; September 1, 2010; September 1, 2015.]

MANDATORY ARBITRATION RULES—PCLMAR

I. SCOPE AND PURPOSE OF RULES

PCLMAR 1. SCOPE AND PURPOSE OF RULES

1.1. Application of Rules—Purpose and Definitions

(a) *Purpose.* The purpose of mandatory arbitration of civil actions under **RCW 7.06**, as implemented by the Mandatory Arbitration Rules, is to provide a simplified and economical procedure for obtaining the prompt and equitable resolution of disputes involving claims of $50,000 or less. The Mandatory Arbitration Rules, as supplemented by these local rules, are not

designed to address every question which may arise during the arbitration process, and the rules give considerable discretion to the arbitrator. The arbitrator should not hesitate to exercise that discretion. Arbitration hearings should be informal and expeditious, consistent with the purpose of the statutes and rules.

(b) *"Director" Defined.* In these rules, "Director" means the Clerk of the Pierce County Superior Court.

1.2. Matters Subject to Arbitration. The limit for claims subject to mandatory arbitration is $50,000.00. For the purpose of this rule, a "claim" is defined to be the net value of the claim, after all reductions for comparative negligence or set-offs; e.g. if the plaintiff's damages are $70,000.00 and the plaintiff is 50% comparatively negligent, the plaintiff's claim is for $35,000.00.

1.3. Relationship to Superior Court Jurisdiction And Other Rules—Motions.

(a) *Motions.* All motions before the court relating to mandatory arbitration shall be noted on the civil motions calendar in accordance with **PCLR 7**, except as otherwise provided in these arbitration rules.

(b) *Assignment to Arbitrator.* A case is deemed assigned to an arbitrator upon the filing of a Statement of Arbitrability, as set forth in **PCLMAR 2.1(e)**.

[Adopted effective June 1, 1990; amended on an emergency basis effective August 4, 2008; amended on a permanent basis effective September 1, 2011.]

II. TRANSFER TO ARBITRATION AND ASSIGNMENT OF ARBITRATOR

PCLMAR 2. TRANSFER TO ARBITRATION AND ASSIGNMENT OF ARBITRATOR

2.1 Transfer to Arbitration.

(a) *Statement of Arbitrability.* In every civil case, the party filing the note for trial provided by **CR 40(a)(1)** and **PCLR 40** shall, upon the form prescribed by the court, complete a statement of arbitrability; except that a party may file a statement of arbitrability requesting arbitration at any time after filing of the complaint, but no sooner than the date the confirmation of joinder is filed and no later than the discovery cutoff date. After the deadline has passed, the statement of arbitrability may be filed only by leave of the court for good cause shown.

(b) *Response to Statement of Arbitrability.* Any person disagreeing with the statement of arbitrability shall serve and file a response to the statement of arbitrability on the forms prescribed by the court within 20 days of service of the summons and complaint, or 7 days after the receipt of the statement of arbitrability, whichever time is greater.

(c) *Failure to File—Amendments.* A person failing to serve and file an original response within the times prescribed may later do so only upon leave of the court. A party may amend a statement of arbitrability or response at any time before assignment of an arbitrator or assignment of a trial date, and thereafter only upon leave of the court for good cause shown.

(d) *By Stipulation.* A case in which all parties file a stipulation to arbitrate under **MAR 8.1** will be placed on the arbitration calendar regardless of the nature of the case or amount in controversy.

(e) *When Transfer to Arbitration Occurs for Purpose of Application of Local Rules.* The case is transferred to arbitration upon the filing of a statement of arbitrability indicating that the case is subject to arbitration, unless an objection to arbitration of the case is received within the time limits found in **PCLMAR 2.1(b)**. This transfer shall also trigger the restriction on discovery contained in **MAR 4.2** and **PCLMAR 4.2**.

2.3. Assignment to Arbitrator

(a) *Generally; Stipulations.* When a case is set for arbitration, a list of 5 proposed arbitrators will be furnished to the parties. A master list of arbitrators will be made available on request. The parties are encouraged to stipulate to an arbitrator. In the absence of a stipulation, the arbitrator will be chosen from among the five proposed arbitrators in the manner defined by this rule.

(b) *Response by Parties.* Each party may, within 14 days after a list of proposed arbitrators is furnished to the parties, nominate 1 or 2 arbitrators and strike 2 arbitrators from the list. If both parties respond, an arbitrator nominated by both parties will be appointed. If no arbitrator has been nominated by both parties, the presiding Judge or designee will randomly appoint an arbitrator from among those not stricken by either party.

(c) *Response by Only One (1) Party.* If only one party responds within 14 days, the presiding Judge or designee will appoint an arbitrator nominated by that party.

(d) *No Response.* If neither party responds within 14 days, the presiding Judge or designee will randomly appoint 1 of the 5 proposed arbitrators.

(e) *Additional Arbitrators for Additional Parties.* If there are more than 2 adverse parties, all represented by different counsel, 2 additional proposed arbitrators shall be added to the list for each additional party so represented, with the above principles of selection to be applied. The number of adverse parties shall be determined by the presiding Judge or designee.

[Adopted effective June 1, 1990. Amended effective September 1, 2015.]

III. ARBITRATORS

PCLMAR 3. ARBITRATORS

3.1. Qualifications

(a) *Arbitration Panel.* There shall be a panel of arbitrators in such numbers as the administrative committee may from time to time determine. A person desiring to serve as an arbitrator shall complete an information sheet on a form prescribed by the court. A copy of said completed sheet is available upon request by any party and will be mailed to a requesting party at the party's own expense. The oath of office on the form prescribed by the court must be completed and filed prior to an applicant being placed on the panel. An arbitrator must be a member of the Washington State Bar Association and have been admitted to the bar for a minimum of 5 years.

(b) *Refusal; Disqualification.* The appointment of an arbitrator is subject to the right of that person to refuse to serve. An arbitrator must notify the presiding Judge or designee immediately if refusing to serve or if any cause exists for the arbitrator's disqualification from the case upon any of the grounds of interest, relationship, bias or prejudice set forth in **CJC Canon 3(D)**, governing the disqualification of Judges. If disqualified, the arbitrator must immediately return all materials in a case to the presiding Judge or designee.

3.2. Authority of Arbitrators. An arbitrator has the authority to:

(a) *Payment of Expense/Attorney Fees.* Require a party or attorney, advising such party, or both, to pay the reasonable expenses, including attorney fees, caused by the failure of such party or attorney, or both, to obey an order of the arbitrator unless the arbitrator finds that the failure was substantially justified or that other circumstances make an award of expenses unjust. The arbitrator shall make a special award for such expenses and shall file such award with the clerk of the superior court, with proof of service of a party on each party. The aggrieved party shall have 10 days thereafter to appeal the award of such expense in accordance with the procedures described in **RCW 2.24.050**. If, within 10 days after the award is filed, no party appeals, a judgment shall be entered in a manner described generally under **MAR 6.3**;

(b) *Basis of Attorney Fee Award.* Award attorney fees, as authorized by these rules, by a contract or by law.

[Adopted effective September 1, 2002.]

IV. PROCEDURES AFTER ASSIGNMENT

PCLMAR 4. PROCEDURES AFTER ASSIGNMENT

4.2 Discovery.

(a) *Additional Discovery.* In determining when additional discovery beyond that directly authorized by **MAR 4.2** is reasonably necessary, the arbitrator shall balance the benefits of discovery against the burdens and expenses. The arbitrator shall consider the nature and complexity of the case, the amount in controversy, values at stake, the discovery that has already occurred, the burdens on the party from whom discovery is sought, and the possibility of unfair surprise which may result if discovery is restricted. Authorized discovery shall be conducted in accordance with the civil rules, except that motions concerning discovery shall be determined by the arbitrator.

(b) *Notwithstanding the Foregoing, the Following Interrogatories May Be Submitted to Any Party:*

(1) General Damages. State the amount of general damages being claimed;

(2) Special Damages. State each item of special damages being claimed and the amount thereof;

(3) Knowledge of Liability Witness(es). List the name, address and phone number of each person having knowledge of any facts regarding liability;

(4) Knowledge of Damages Witness(es). List the name, address and phone number of each person having knowledge of any facts regarding the damages claimed;

(5) Expert Witness(es). List the name, address and phone number of each expert witness you intend to call at the arbitration. For each such expert, state the subject matter on which the expert is expected to testify; state the substance of the facts and opinions to which the expert is expected to testify, and a summary of the grounds for each opinion.

Only these interrogatories, with the exact language as set out above, are permitted.

(c) *Restrictions Upon Discovery.* The restrictions upon discovery set out in **MAR 4.2** and **PCLMAR 4.2(a)** shall take effect upon the filing of a statement of arbitrability as set out in **PCLMAR 1.3** and **2.1(e)**.

(f) *Trial Date.* Once the statement of arbitrability has been filed, the trial date and Case Schedule shall be cancelled. A Mandatory Court Review Hearing shall be set 6 months from the filing of the statement of arbitrability.

[Adopted effective June 1, 1990. Amended effective September 1, 2015.]

V. HEARING

PCLMAR 5. HEARING

5.1. Notice of Hearing—Time and Place—Continuance. An arbitration hearing shall be scheduled to be heard in Pierce County at any reasonable time and place chosen by the arbitrator. The arbitrator may grant a continuance without court order. The parties may stipulate to a continuance only with the permission of the arbitrator. The arbitrator shall give reasonable notice of the hearing date and any continuance to the Director.

5.2. Prehearing Statement of Proof—Documents Filed with Court. In addition to the requirements of **MAR 5.2**, each party shall also furnish the arbitrator with copies of pleadings and other documents contained in the court file which that party deems relevant. The court file shall remain with the county clerk. The arbitrator shall strictly enforce the provisions of **MAR 5.2** and is encouraged to withhold permission to present evidence at time of hearing if the parties have failed to comply with this rule.

[Adopted effective June 1, 1990; amended effective February 19, 1991.]

VI. AWARD

PCLMAR 6. AWARD

6.1 Form and Content of Award.

(a) *Form.* The award shall be prepared on the form prescribed by the court.

(b) *Exhibits.* All exhibits offered during the hearing shall be returned to the offering parties.

(c) *Attorneys Fees.* Any motion for actual attorney fees, whether pursuant to contract, statute, or recognized ground in equity, must be presented to the arbitrator, as follows:

(1) Motion. Any motion for an award of attorney fees must be submitted to the arbitrator and served on opposing counsel within seven calendar days of receipt of the award. There shall be no extension of this time, unless the moving party makes a request for an extension before the seven day period has expired, in writing, served on both the arbitrator and opposing counsel;

(2) Response. Any response to the motion for fees must be submitted to the arbitrator and served on opposing counsel within seven calendar days after receipt of the motion;

(3) Decision. The arbitrator shall render a decision on the motion, in writing, within 14 days after the motion is made;

(4) Amended Award. If the arbitrator awards fees, the arbitrator shall file an amended award. If fees are denied, the decision shall be filed and served on the parties;

(5) Discretionary Hearing. It is within the arbitrator's discretion whether to hold a hearing on the issue of fees;

(6) Appeal. The time for appeal of the arbitrator's decision in any case where attorney fees have been timely requested, as set forth above, shall not start to run until the service and filing of the amended award, or the denial thereof.

6.2 Filing of Award. A request by an arbitrator for an extension of time for the filing of an award under **MAR 6.2** may be presented to the presiding Judge, ex parte. The arbitrator shall give the parties notice of an extension granted.

6.3 Judgment on Award. Failure to file a judgment within 90 days of filing the arbitration award shall result in the entry of an order of dismissal, provided no request for trial de novo has been timely filed or upon motion good cause is shown to not dismiss the case.

[Adopted effective June 1, 1990. Amended effective September 1, 2015.]

VII. TRIAL DE NOVO

PCLMAR 7. TRIAL DE NOVO

7.1 Request for Trial de Novo—Calendar.

(a) *Form.* A written request for a trial de novo shall be accompanied by a note of issue placing the matter on the assignment calendar. Failure to submit the note for assignment is not grounds for dismissal; however, the court may impose terms in its discretion.

(b) *Attorney Fees—Time for Appeal.* In any case in which a party makes a motion for attorney fees pursuant to **PCLMAR 6.1(c)**, the 20 day period for appeal shall not commence until the arbitrator has either filed and served the amended award, or the written denial thereof.

(c) *Trial Date.* When a request for a trial de novo is timely filed, an expedited case schedule shall be issued setting the trial date in 6 months.

[Adopted effective June 1, 1990; amended effective September 1, 2002; September 1, 2015.]

VIII. GENERAL PROVISIONS

PCLMAR 8. GENERAL PROVISIONS

8.1. Stipulation—Effect on Relief Granted. If a case not otherwise subject to mandatory arbitration is transferred to arbitration by stipulation, the arbitrator may grant any relief which could have been granted if the case were determined by a Judge.

8.3. Effective Date. These rules, as amended, become effective on the 1st day of January, 1989, subject to amendment thereafter, pursuant to **GR 7**.

8.4. Title and Citation. These rules are known and cited as the Pierce County Local Mandatory Arbitration Rules. PCLMAR is the official abbreviation.

8.5. Compensation of Arbitrator

(a) *Generally.* Arbitrators shall be compensated in the same amount and manner as Judges pro tempore of the superior court; provided, however, that said compensation shall not exceed $1,000.00 for any case unless prior approval is granted by the presiding Judge. Hearing time and reasonable preparation time are compensable. Arbitrators may be reimbursed a sum not to exceed $10.00 for costs incurred.

(b) *Form.* When the award is filed, the arbitrator shall submit to the presiding court ex parte a request for payment on a form prescribed by the court. The presiding Judge shall determine the amount of compensation and costs, if any to be paid.

8.6. Administration

(a) *Supervision.* The director, under the supervision of the superior court Judges shall supervise arbitration under these rules.

(b) *Committee.* There shall be a standing committee of the Tacoma–Pierce County Bar Association, appointed by the president thereof, to assist the court in the formulation and administration of these rules.

(c) *Powers.* The court, assisted by the director and standing committee of the Tacoma–Pierce County Bar Association, shall have the power and duty to:

(1) Appoint the panel of arbitrators provided in **PCLMAR 3.1(a)**;

(2) Remove a person from a panel of arbitrators;

(3) Establish procedures for selecting an arbitrator not inconsistent with the mandatory arbitration rules;

(4) Review the administration and operation of the arbitration program periodically and make recommendations as it deems appropriate to improve the program.

[Adopted effective June 1, 1990; amended effective June 19, 1990; September 1, 2000; September 1, 2008.]

CRIMINAL RULES—PCLCRR

1.1. LOCAL PROCEDURES

Procedures for handling and processing criminal cases in Pierce County Superior Court will be available in the Presiding Department, from the courtroom of the Criminal Division Presiding Judge, in Superior Court Administration and posted on the Superior Court's website at: www.co.pierce. wa.us/superiorcourt and by clicking on "Criminal Law" or "Local Rules".

[Adopted effective June 1, 1990; amended effective September 1, 2004; September 1, 2010.]

1.2. SCOPE

The following Pierce County Local Rules (PCLR) shall apply in Pierce County in criminal cases:

PCLR 10

PCLR 11

PCLR 15

PCLR 40(e)

[Amended effective September 1, 2010.]

ADMINISTRATIVE POLICIES

POLICY 1. PIERCE COUNTY SUPERIOR COURT ADMINISTRATIVE POLICY RE: GUARDIAN AD LITEM/PARENTING INVESTIGATOR REGISTRY FOR PIERCE COUNTY—FAMILY LAW PROCEEDINGS

1. Qualifications: Registry For Guardians Ad Litem/Parenting Investigators In Family Law Proceedings.

1.1 The Pierce County Superior Court Administrator or his/her designee shall be responsible for maintaining a registry of those qualified to serve as Guardians ad Litem/Parenting Investigators for parenting matters as provided in **RCW 26.09.220** and **RCW 26.12.175**.

1.2 Applicants to the Pierce County Guardian ad Litem/Parenting Investigator registry must successfully complete training requirements of the Administrative Office of the Courts (AOC).

A. Attorneys: Must be a member of the Washington State Bar Association in good standing.

B. Non–Attorneys: Must have five years experience working with children and families involved in disputes over parenting issues, dissolution or parentage determinations. A Bachelor's Degree in a related academic discipline is required and a Master's Degree in related academic discipline is preferred.

C. All Applicants: Shall be of high moral character, and shall not have any:

1. Felony convictions or any convictions involving theft, dishonesty, or moral turpitude.

2. Suspension or revocation of professional certification or license.

3. Pending investigation or action for either 1 or 2 above.

4. Agree to abide by the Guardian ad Litem/Parenting Investigator Code of Conduct, Pierce County Superior Court Administrative Policy, and all applicable statutes and Court Rules.

1.3 The Pierce County Guardian ad Litem Committee shall review applications periodically, prior to the creation of the updated Registry. Placement on the Registry does not guarantee appointment as a guardian.

1.4 The Registry shall be open for new applications at least once a year, as set by the Pierce County Superior Court. A new Registry shall be created by July 1 of each year.

1.5 Each applicant, including persons currently on the Registry, must annually complete and file the following documents with the Court Administrator:

A. Application

B. Code of Conduct

C. Washington State Patrol Request for Conviction Criminal History Record, with the results provided to the Court Administrator as part of the required application materials.

1.6 Persons applying for the Registry for the first time, or after a substantial break in service, will be notified of their provisional placement on the Registry, and shall then be eligible for appointment as a Guardian ad Litem/Parenting Investigator after meeting the requirements of the Pierce County Superior Court Guardian ad Litem Committee.

1.7 First-time registrants, or registrants returning after a substantial break in service, shall complete their required mentoring and have on file, with Superior Court Administration, the Declaration of Mentoring Completion before they may reapply for the following year's Registry. Special authorization to reapply and continue provisional placement in the second year may be granted by the Pierce County Superior Court Guardian ad Litem Committee.

1.8 Registry members shall attend continuing education as required by Pierce County Superior Court.

1.9 The Court Administrator, or designee, shall maintain a separate file for each person on the Registry. Each file shall include an Applicant's Certificate of Completion of training. In addition, the file will include all application materials and all formal complaints or grievances, related to an Applicant's service as a Guardian ad Litem/Parenting Investigator, which were retained and acted upon by Pierce County Superior Court. The information contained in the files shall be open for public review in the office of Superior Court Administration during normal business hours.

2. Appointment From Registry.

2.1 Request for appointment of a Guardian ad Litem/Parenting Investigator shall be made to a Superior Court Commissioner or Judge, who shall generate an Order for Selection of a Guardian ad Litem/Parenting Investigator. This Order contains randomly selected names from the Registry and an apportionment of responsibility for payment of the retainer. Each party shall strike one person from this randomly selected set of names within 3 days. Upon payment of the retainer in full, the Petitioner is responsible for obtaining the Order Appointing Guardian ad Litem/Parenting Investigator and the timely presentation of the Order to the Ex Parte Commissioner for approval and signature.

2.2 If the judicial officer determines from the financial affidavits that a pro bono or county pay Guardian ad Litem/Parenting Investigator is required, the parties will be directed to properly file, serve and note a motion before the assigned Family Court Judge.

2.3 Any Commissioner or Judge who deviates from the rotational order established for the Registry shall make an appropriate written record pursuant to statute.

2.4 In the event the person appointed Guardian ad Litem/Parenting Investigator chooses not to serve, regardless of the reason, the Judicial Officer shall generate a new Order for Selection of a Guardian ad Litem/Parenting Investigator.

2.5 If the parties stipulate to recommend the appointment of a particular Guardian ad Litem/Parenting Investigator, who shall be on the registry, the parties must present, prior to appointment, a written stipulation, signed by both parties and their attorneys, which specifies:

A. The amount of the retainer charged;

B. The agreement between the parties regarding payment of the retainer and all fees;

C. The hourly rate charged by the recommended Guardian ad Litem/Parenting Investigator; and

D. The statutory reasons for a non-rotational appointment.

2.6 All retainers and additional fees shall be paid into the Clerk of the Court and disbursed pursuant to Court Order. A stipulation alone is not a basis for a non-rotational appointment if the judicial officer finds the statutory factors for a non-rotational appointment are not present.

3. Placement On Registry.

3.1 Once placed on the registry, a person shall remain on the registry for one year unless:

A. The person fails to maintain current information required by law or Local Rule;

B. The person is removed by his or her own request; or

C. The person is removed pursuant to action by the Superior Court Judges under Section Four (4) below.

4. Complaint Procedures.

4.1 Complaints by a Guardian ad Litem/Parenting Investigator shall be timely addressed by the Pierce County Superior Court through its Family Law Guardian ad Litem/Parenting Investigator Grievance Committee. Such complaints shall be in writing and delivered to the Court Administrator. A written response will be provided to the Guardian ad Litem/Parenting Investigator.

4.2 Complaints against a Guardian ad Litem/Parenting Investigator during the pendency of the case.

A. Complaints shall be by written motion properly served and noted, pursuant to Pierce County Local Rules. The motion shall be made directly to the assigned trial department, its designee, or the Presiding Judge. Complaints may be made by any party to the case or his or her attorney.

B. The judicial officer may decide, in his or her discretion, to remove, retain, substitute, or stay the work or appointment of the Guardian ad Litem/Parenting Investigator in the active case. Any such decision shall be documented by a written order. The Family Law Guardian ad Litem/Parenting Investigator Grievance Committee shall be notified of any remedial action.

C. Complaints by a party to the case or his or her attorney, or the judicial officer, may be referred for remedial action after the completion of the case, and according to the processes specified in sections 4.3–4.9 below.

4.3 Complaints against Guardian ad Litem/Parenting Investigator after the case Is complete.

A. If the Court Administrator:

1. Receives a written complaint, based upon personal knowledge, alleging that a Parenting Investigator or Guardian ad Litem:

a) has violated this policy regarding the requirements for participation on the registry; or

b) has misrepresented his or her qualifications to be on the registry; or

c) is not suitable to act as a Guardian ad Litem/Parenting Investigator, or raises questions about the conduct of the Guardian ad Litem/Parenting Investigator in a particular case; or

2. In any manner becomes aware of a reason that would place the suitability of the Guardian ad Litem/Parenting Investigator in question, then under 1. or 2. above, the matter shall be referred to the Judges on the Family Law Guardian ad Litem/Parenting Investigator Grievance Committee.

B. If it is determined that the case is completed and that the complaint was submitted upon personal knowledge, the Judges on the Family Law Guardian ad Litem/Parenting Investigator Grievance Committee shall seek a written response from the Guardian ad Litem/Parenting Investigator. Such response shall be due within 30 days.

C. All matters/materials shall be submitted in writing only. There shall be no live testimony or oral testimony. A copy of the response from the Guardian ad Litem/Parenting Investigator shall be sent to the person initiating the complaint.

D. The Guardian ad Litem/Parenting Investigator may be suspended pending resolution of the complaint. The Guardian ad Litem/Parenting Investigator and complaining person shall be notified in writing of any decision to suspend the Guardian ad Litem/Parenting Investigator, pending resolution or otherwise.

4.4 Information regarding suitability to serve as a Guardian ad Litem/Parenting Investigator, which does not relate to a particular case, may be directed to the Family Law Guardian ad Litem/Parenting Investigator Grievance Committee. The source of the information and its content may be communicated to the Guardian ad Litem/Parenting Investigator for their written response.

4.5 The Committee shall forward any recommendation to remove a Guardian ad Litem/Parenting Investigator from the Registry to the Presiding Judge, who shall present the recommendation to the Superior Court Judges at their next meeting.

4.6. In the discretion of a majority of the Pierce County Superior Court Judges, a person may be denied admission to the Registry or may be removed from the Registry for any reason that places the suitability of the person to act as a Guardian ad Litem/Parenting Investigator in question, including but not limited to, failure to comply with the applicable requirements of the Administrative Policy, the Code of Conduct, State law, and Guardian ad Litem Rules (GALR).

4.7 Any person filing a grievance or complaint against the Guardian ad Litem/Parenting Investigator shall be notified in writing of the final decision of the Superior Court Judges within 60 days of the response to the complaint being received.

4.8 In addition to recommending removal, the Family Law Guardian ad Litem/Parenting Investigator Grievance Committee may order remedial measures, including but not limited to further education, additional training and mentoring, and/or suspension, as a condition to remaining on the Registry or receiving new cases. The Family Law Guardian ad Litem/Parenting Investigator Grievance Committee shall regularly make a report of all such remedial actions.

4.9 Administrative Office of the Court Reporting Requirements. As required, the Administrative Office of the Court shall be timely notified of the names on the Guardian ad Litem/Parenting Investigator Registry. The Administrative Office of the Court shall be notified immediately of the name of any Guardian ad Litem removed from the rotational Registry as a result of a grievance or decision of the Superior Court Judges.

[Adopted effective May 4, 1998; amended effective April 5, 1999; May 6, 2002; September 1, 2006; September 1, 2008; September 1, 2009; September 1, 2010.]

POLICY 2. PIERCE COUNTY SUPERIOR COURT RCW 26.09.220 AND RCW 26.12.175 GUARDIAN AD LITEM/PARENTING INVESTIGATOR CODE OF CONDUCT

All Guardian ad Litem/Parenting Investigators shall fully comply with this Code of Conduct and the requirements of Superior Court GALR.

1. The appointed Guardian ad Litem/Parenting Investigator shall decline the appointment if he/she is not qualified, competent, or able to complete the matter in a timely manner.

2. The Guardian ad Litem/Parenting Investigator shall maintain the ethical principles of his/her own profession in addition to compliance with this Code of Conduct.

3. The Guardian ad Litem/Parenting Investigator shall promptly advise the court of any grounds for disqualification or unavailability to serve.

4. The Guardian ad Litem/Parenting Investigator shall avoid self-dealing or association from which the Guardian ad Litem/Parenting Investigator might directly or indirectly benefit, other than from compensation as a Guardian ad Litem/Parenting Investigator.

5. The Guardian ad Litem/Parenting Investigator shall not guarantee or create the impression that any portion of the investigation will remain confidential, and shall inform all witnesses that the information gathered by the Guardian ad Litem/Parenting Investigator must be reported to the court.

6. All records, including contemporaneously maintained time and expense records, of the Guardian ad Litem/Parenting Investigator shall promptly be made available to the parties and their attorneys for review upon request, without formal discovery request(s) being made. Copies of the records may be made by the parties and their attorneys under circumstances that assure that the file remains complete, organized and intact.

7. The Guardian ad Litem/Parenting Investigator shall be available to testify if called by a party.

8. Once admitted to the **RCW 26.09** Certified Registry, all Guardian ad Litem/Parenting Investigator's shall fully comply with all continuing education requirements established under Pierce County Local Rules and GALR, as amended.

9. The Guardian ad Litem shall report to D.S.H.S. and the court, any child abuse as defined in **RCW 26.44.030, RCW 26.12.175** and **RCW 26.12.177**.

The undersigned acknowledges receipt of the foregoing, has read the same and GALR, and agrees to be governed by all.

_____ _____
Date   Signature

[Adopted effective May 4, 1998; amended effective May 6, 2002; September 1, 2009; September 1, 2010.]

POLICY 3. PIERCE COUNTY SUPERIOR COURT ADMINISTRATIVE POLICY RE: GUARDIAN AD LITEM REGISTRY FOR PIERCE COUNTY—GUARDIANSHIP PROCEEDINGS

1. **Qualifications: Registry for Guardians Ad Litem in Guardianship Proceedings.**

1.1 The Pierce County Superior Court Administrator or his/her designee shall be responsible for maintaining a Registry of those qualified to serve as Guardian ad Litem for guardianship matters as provided in **RCW 11.88**.

1.2 Applicants to the Pierce County **RCW 11.88** Guardian ad Litem Registry shall successfully meet all qualifications set forth in **RCW 11.88** and this Policy. Applicants shall attend and satisfactorily complete the mandatory training approved by the Pierce County Superior Court. Registry members must attend and satisfactorily complete continuing education as required by the Pierce County Superior Court as well as any statute, court rule and regulation in order to qualify for continued placement on the Registry.

1.3 A person whose application for placement or continued placement on the Registry does not, in the opinion of the majority of members of the Pierce County Superior Court Guardian ad Litem Committee, meet the Court's requirements for admission to and placement on the Registry shall not be approved.

1.4 In the sole discretion of a majority of the Pierce County Superior Court Judges, a person may be denied admission to the Registry for any reason that places the suitability of the person to act as a Guardian ad Litem in question, including but not limited to, failure to comply with the applicable requirements of this Administrative Policy, the Code of Conduct, State law, Court Rules, the Rules of Professional Conduct (RPC), and Guardian ad Litem Rules (GALR). The procedures described in Section IV below do not apply to decisions regarding the application or continued placement of an applicant for Guardian ad Litem.

A. ATTORNEYS: Must be a member of the Washington State Bar Association in good standing and demonstrate relevant experience working in the needs of impaired elderly people, an understanding of issues surrounding "abuse and neglect" of the elderly, physical disabilities, mental illness, developmental disabilities, and/or other areas relevant to the needs of incapacitated persons, legal procedure, and the Guardian ad Litem requirements of **RCW 11.88.**

B. NON–ATTORNEYS: Must have five years relevant experience working in the needs of impaired elderly people, an understanding of issues surrounding "abuse and neglect" of the elderly, physical disabilities, mental illness, developmental disabilities and/or other areas relevant to the needs of incapacitated persons, legal procedure, and the Guardian ad Litem requirements of **RCW 11.88.**

C. ALL APPLICANTS: Shall be of high moral character, and shall not have any:

1. Felony convictions or any convictions involving theft, dishonesty, or moral turpitude.

2. Suspension or revocation of professional certification or license.

3. Pending investigation or action for either 1 or 2 above.

4. Agree to abide by the current Guardian ad Litem Code of Conduct and this Pierce County Superior Court Administrative Policy, as well as all applicable statutes and Court Rules.

1.5 The Pierce County Guardian ad Litem Committee shall review applications periodically, prior to the creation of the updated Registry.

1.6 The Registry shall be open for new applications periodically, as set by the Pierce County Superior Court.

1.7 Each applicant, including persons currently on the Registry, must complete and timely file the following documents with the Court Administrator when the registry is opened:

A. Application for Pierce County Superior Court Guardian ad Litem Registry Title 11 (all new applicants) or a Renewal Application (all current registry participants);

B. Signed agreement to abide by Administrative Policy 4, Code of Conduct;

C. Current Washington State Patrol Request for Conviction Criminal History Record, with the results to be provided to the Court Administrator as part of the required application materials; and

D. Current Certificate of Attendance at applicable mandatory training.

1.8 Each applicant will be notified of the decision regarding placement on the Registry. Only those applicants approved for placement on the Registry shall be eligible for appointment as a Guardian ad Litem. Placement on the Registry does not guarantee appointment as a Guardian ad Litem.

1.9 The Court Administrator, or his/her designee, shall maintain a separate file for each person on the Registry. Each file shall include each applicant's application materials and all formal complaints related to an applicant's service as a Guardian ad Litem which were retained and acted upon by Pierce County Superior Court. The information contained in the files shall be open for public review in the office of Superior Court Administration during normal business hours.

2. Placement On Registry.

2.1 Once approved by the Superior Court and placed on the Registry, a person shall remain on the registry unless:

A. The person fails to maintain current information or qualifications required by law or court rule;

B. The person is removed by his or her own request; or

C. The person is removed pursuant to action by the Superior Court Judges under Section Four (4) below.

3. Appointment from Registry.

3.1 Request for appointment of a Guardian ad Litem in all guardianship proceedings shall be made by submitting an Order Appointing Guardian ad Litem to the Superior Court Ex Parte Department. The clerk on the Ex Parte Department shall write in the name which is next on the applicable rotational list and initial the same. The Order shall then be submitted to the Ex Parte Department for signature or such other action as may be appropriate. An Order Appointing a Guardian ad Litem for an indigent person shall only be made from the rotational list of contracted **RCW 11.88** Guardians ad Litem for Indigent Persons.

3.2   Any judicial officer who deviates from the rotational order established for the Registry shall fully comply with the provisions of **RCW 11.88** for the purposes of making an appropriate written record pursuant to statute for said deviation. In the event a person who is not next on the rotation list is approved by the Court, the appointed person's name shall go to the bottom of the rotation list.

3.3   In the event the person appointed Guardian ad Litem chooses not to serve, regardless of the reason, that person's name shall go to the bottom of the rotational list just as if they had served.

4.   **Complaint Procedures.**

4.1   Any complaint regarding a person who is on the Registry shall be timely submitted to the Court Administrator. Any such complaint shall be submitted in writing and shall be based upon personal knowledge. The Court Administrator shall refer to the Judges on the Guardian ad Litem Committee the following:

A.   A written complaint received by the Court Administrator, alleging that a Guardian ad Litem:

1.   has violated this Administrative Policy regarding requirements for participation on this Registry; or

2.   has misrepresented his or her qualifications to be on the Registry; or

3.   is not suitable to act as a Guardian ad Litem or raises questions about the conduct of the Guardian ad Litem in a particular case;

4.   exceeds the authority of the Order Appointing Guardian ad Litem;

OR

B.   Any reason, of which the Court Administrator becomes aware in any manner that would place the suitability of a person to act as a Guardian ad Litem in question.

4.2A.   If it is determined that the case is completed and that the complaint was submitted upon personal knowledge, the Judges on the Guardian ad Litem Committee shall seek a written response from the Guardian ad Litem. Such response shall be due in 30 days. If the complaint is filed by a judicial officer, the judicial officer shall not participate in the complaint procedure after submitting the written complaint. Conduct of a Guardian ad Litem in an active case shall be addressed to the assigned Judge, or to the Commissioners, pursuant to Court Rules.

4.2B.   Information regarding suitability to serve as a Guardian ad Litem, which does not relate to a particular case, may be directed to the Guardian ad Litem Committee for consideration and action. The source of the information and its content may, at the Committee's discretion, be communicated to the Guardian ad Litem for their written response.

4.3   All materials, including the complaint response and any supporting documentation, shall be submitted in writing only. There shall be no live testimony or oral testimony. A copy of the response from the Guardian ad Litem shall be sent to the person initiating the complaint.

4.4   The Guardian ad Litem may be suspended from the Registry by the Guardian ad Litem Committee pending resolution of the complaint. The Guardian ad Litem and complaining person shall be notified in writing of any decision to suspend the Guardian ad Litem, pending resolution or otherwise.

4.5   The Committee shall forward any recommendation to remove a Guardian ad Litem from the Registry to the Presiding Judge, who shall present the recommendation to the Superior Court Judges at their next meeting.

4.6   In the discretion of a majority of the Pierce County Superior Court Judges, a person may be removed from the Registry for any reason that places the suitability of the person to act as a Guardian ad Litem in question, including but not limited to, failure to comply with the applicable requirements of this Administrative Policy, the Code of Conduct, State law, court rules, the Rules of Professional Conduct (RPC), and Guardian ad Litem Rules (GALR).

4.7   In lieu of recommending removal, the Guardian ad Litem Committee may order remedial measures, including by not limited to further education, additional training and mentoring, and/or suspension or probation, as a condition to remaining on the Registry or to receiving appointments on new cases. The Guardian ad Litem Committee shall regularly make a report of all such remedial actions to the Presiding Judge.

4.8   Any person filing a complaint against a Guardian ad Litem shall be notified in writing of the final decision of the Guardian ad Litem Committee or Superior Court Judges.

4.9   Nothing herein is intended to limit the discretion of a judicial officer to remove or retain a Guardian ad Litem in an active case. Conduct of a Guardian ad Litem in an active case shall be addressed to the assigned Judge, or to the Commissioners, pursuant to Court Rules.

5.   **Administrative Office of the Court Reporting Requirements**

5.1   As required, the Administrative Office of the Court shall be timely notified of the names on the Guardian ad Litem Registry. The Administrative Office of the Court shall be notified immediately of the name of any Guardian ad Litem removed from the

Registry as a result of a complaint or decision of the Superior Court Judges.

[Adopted effective May 4, 1998; amended April 5, 1999; May 6, 2002; September 1, 2004; September 1, 2008; September 1, 2009; September 1, 2010; September 1, 2012.]

POLICY 4. PIERCE COUNTY SUPERIOR COURT RCW 11.88 GUARDIAN AD LITEM CODE OF CONDUCT

All Guardians ad Litem shall fully comply with this Code of Conduct and the requirements of Superior Court GALR:

1. The appointed Guardian ad Litem shall decline the appointment if he/she is not qualified, competent, or able to complete the matter in a timely manner.

2. The Guardian ad Litem shall maintain the ethical principles of his/her own profession in addition to compliance with this Code of Conduct.

3. The Guardian ad Litem shall promptly advise the court of any grounds for disqualification or unavailability to serve.

4. The Guardian ad Litem shall avoid self-dealing or association from which the Guardian ad Litem might directly or indirectly benefit, other than from compensation as a Guardian ad Litem.

5. The Guardian ad Litem shall not guarantee or create the impression that any portion of the investigation will remain confidential, and shall inform all witnesses that the information gathered by the Guardian ad Litem must be reported to the court.

6. All records, including contemporaneously maintained time and expense records, of the Guardian ad Litem shall promptly be made available to the parties and their attorneys for review upon request, without formal discovery request(s) being made. Copies of the records may be made by the parties and their attorneys under circumstances that assure that the file remains complete, organized and intact.

7. Once admitted to the RCW 11.88 Registry, all Guardians ad Litem shall fully comply with all continuing education requirements established under Pierce County Local Rules and GALR, as amended.

8. The Guardian ad Litem shall report to D.S.H.S. and the court, any adult abuse as defined in RCW 74.34.020(2).

9. The Guardian ad Litem shall immediately advise the court if the guardianship case qualifies for a guardian ad litem at public expense and before significant work is performed or time elapsed shall return the case for reassignment to a guardian ad litem at public expense.

The undersigned acknowledges receipt of the foregoing, has read the same and GALR, and agrees to be governed by all.

Date _____ Signature _____

[Adopted effective May 4, 1998; amended April 5, 1999; May 6, 2002; September 1, 2009; September 1, 2010.]

POLICY 5. PIERCE COUNTY SUPERIOR COURT ADMINISTRATIVE POLICY RE: IMPACT ON CHILDREN SEMINAR

Pierce County Local Rule for Special Proceedings 94.05 mandates the parties' attendance at a seminar designed to address the impact family restructuring has on children. See PCSPR 94.05.

This Administrative Policy contains the guidelines governing the content of the seminar, the minimum credentials and experience required of seminar instructors and administrative requirements of an acceptable program. The Superior Court Judges' Committee will review submitted proposals and approve those programs, which meet the outlined criteria.

1. **Seminar Content.** The seminar must contain these minimum elements:

(A) the developmental stages of childhood;

(B) stress indicators in children;

(C) age appropriate expectations of children;

(D) the impact of divorce on children;

(E) the grief process;

(F) reducing stress for children through an amicable resolution of disputes;

(G) the long term impact of parental conflict on children;

(H) importance of child's relationships with both parents, and with extended family members, and fostering those relationships;

(I) communication skills for parties caring for children;

(J) practical skills for working together;

(K) impact on children when step-parents and blended families enter their lives;

2. **Qualifications of Instructors.** A team of not less than two instructors, one male and one female shall conduct Impact on Children Seminar. Instructors should be familiar with the required statutory provisions of parenting plans and residential schedules, and have the following minimum credentials and experience:

(A) A Master's Degree in Social Work, Psychology or other related behavioral science;

(B) Supervised experience in treatment of emotionally disturbed children, adolescents and their families;

(C) Significant experience in providing a wide range of mental health services to children and families, with specific experience in the areas of separation/divorce, loss and grief, and blended families;

(D) Extensive knowledge of child development, age appropriate expectations for children, and positive parenting;

(E) Substantial knowledge of the impact on children of alcohol/drug abuse by family members;

(F) An ability to work with other agencies as part of a collaborative program; and

(G) Strong oral communications skills.

3. Administration of Program

(a) *Fees*: Each party attending a seminar shall pay a fee charged by the approved provider. The fees charged shall be approved by the Court and shall be no greater than $60.00 per seminar, unless otherwise approved by the Superior Court Judges. Collection of the fees is the responsibility of the approved provider. The seminars shall be conducted at no cost to the county's general revenue allocation to the court.

(b) *Sliding Fee Scale and Waiver*: The provider shall develop a sliding fee scale and waiver for individuals unable to pay.

(c) *Certificate of Completion*: The provider shall e-file each attendee's Certificate of Completion with the court. The provider shall give each attendee a Certificate of Completion. The certificate shall include the name of the person attending the seminar, the location and date of attendance, the Superior Court cause number, and the date of submission to the court. The certificate must be on 8.5 inch, white paper; must have a 3–inch top margin, 1–inch side margins (nothing should be in the top margin area) and the case number should be just below the top margin on the right side of the document. The provider shall also advise each attendee that he or she must file their Certificate of Completion with the court.

(d) *Attendance at Seminar*: In no case shall opposing parties be required to attend a seminar together.

(e) *Number of and Length of Seminars*: The provider shall develop a schedule of seminars that will accommodate individuals who work during the day and those who work during the evenings.

(f) *Number of Participants*: The provider shall propose a minimum and maximum number of participants for each seminar, as well as indicate the minimum number of participant required in order to present the seminar.

(g) *Location of Seminars*: The provider shall propose the location(s) of seminars to accommodate seminar attendees who will come from all areas of Pierce County.

(h) *Evaluations*: The provider shall conduct anonymous written evaluations at the end of each seminar. A report, in the format developed by the Court, summarizing the responses shall be given to the Superior Court Judges' Committee monthly.

(i) *Instructors*: Changes in instructors shall not occur without approval by the Superior Court Judges' Committee. Instructors shall not solicit business during the seminar.

[Adopted effective May 4, 1998; amended effective April 5, 1999; May 6, 2002; September 1, 2006; September 1, 2008; September 1, 2009; September 1, 2010.]

APPENDIX OF CIVIL RULE FORMS
FORM A. ORDER SETTING CASE SCHEDULE
FORM A

IN THE SUPERIOR COURT OF THE STATE OF WASHINGTON FOR PIERCE COUNTY

CASE NAME	NO.
	ORDER SETTING CASE SCHEDULE Type of Case: Track Assignment: Assigned to Judicial Department: Docket Code: ORSCS Length of Trial

Confirmation of Service
Confirmation of Joinder of Parties, Claims and Defenses
Jury Demand
Set Settlement Conf Date with Judge/Comm. _____
(See PCLR 16 & PCLSPR 94.04)
Status Conference (Contact Court for Specific Date)
Plaintiff's Disclosure of Primary Witnesses
Defendant's Disclosure of Primary Witnesses
Disclosure of Rebuttal Witnesses
Deadline for Filing Motion to Adjust Trial Date
Discovery Cutoff
Exchange of Witness and Exhibit Lists and Documentary Exhibits
Deadline for Hearing Dispositive Pretrial Motions
Joint Statement of Evidence
Settlement Conference
Pretrial Conference (Contact Court for Specific Date)
Trial

Unless otherwise instructed, ALL Attorneys/Parties shall report to the trial court at 9:00 a.m. on the date of trial.
NOTICE TO PLAINTIFF/PETITIONER
If the case has been filed, the plaintiff shall serve a copy of the Case Schedule on the defendant(s) with the summons and complaint/petition: Provided that in those cases where service is by publication the plaintiff shall serve the Case Schedule within five (5) court days of service of the defendant's first response/appearance. If the case has not been filed, but an initial pleading is served, the Case Schedule shall be served within five (5) court days of filing. See PCLR 3.
NOTICE TO ALL PARTIES
All attorneys and parties shall make themselves familiar with the Pierce County Local Rules, particularly those relating to case scheduling. Compliance with the scheduling rules is mandatory and failure to comply shall result in sanctions appropriate to the violation. If a statement of arbitrability is filed, PCLR 3 does not apply while the case is in arbitration.

DATED: _____   Judge_____

Department_____

Revised 9/1/10

[Amended effective January 1, 2007; September 1, 2010.]

FORM B(1).   ORDER ASSIGNING CASE TO JUDICIAL DEPARTMENT AND SETTING REVIEW HEARING DATE (PCLR3/PCLR40)

FORM B (1)

SUPERIOR COURT OF THE STATE OF WASHINGTON
FOR PIERCE COUNTY

NO. XX-4-XXXXX-X

ORDER ASSIGNING CASE TO JUDICIAL
DEPARTMENT AND SETTING REVIEW
HEARING DATE (PCLR3/PCLR40)

Judge: [Name]
Department: [Dept No.]
Docket Code: ORACD

Mandatory Hearing Date: September 9, 2016 9:00 AM

Failure to appear on this date may result in closure of the case by the court.

Notice to Petitioner(s):

* Petitioner(s) shall serve a copy of this Order Assigning Case to Judicial Department on all parties entitled to notice of this action.

* The timing of this mandatory review hearing assumes that Non-intervention powers will be/have been granted. The purpose of the mandatory hearing date is to review whether the matter has been completed. If a Declaration of Completion is filed prior to the mandatory review hearing date, that date will be stricken by the court.

* If non-intervention powers are not granted, a bond is required, a probate Guardian ad Litem is appointed, the personal representative is removed or resigns, or the estate is later declared insolvent, then you are required to immediately bring this issue to the attention of the judicial officer of the department to which it is assigned to obtain a different mandatory hearing date than the one listed above.

Dated: _____   _____

                                          JUDGE
                                          Department #

[Adopted effective September 1, 2012.]

FORM B(2). ORDER ASSIGNING CASE TO JUDICIAL DEPARTMENT AND SETTING REVIEW HEARING DATE (PCLR3/PCLR40)

FORM B (2)

**SUPERIOR COURT OF THE STATE OF WASHINGTON
FOR PIERCE COUNTY**

NO. **XX-4-XXXXX-X**

ORDER ASSIGNING CASE TO JUDICIAL
DEPARTMENT AND SETTING REVIEW
HEARING DATE (PCLR3/PCLR40)

Judge: **[Name]**
Department: **[Dept. No.]**
Docket Code: ORACD

Mandatory Hearing Date: September 7, 2012 9:00 AM

Failure to appear on this date may result in closure of the case by the court.

Notice to Petitioner(s):

* Petitioner(s) shall serve a copy of this Order Assigning Case to Judicial Department on all parties entitled to notice of this action.

* Under RCW 11.76.010 the petitioner shall file an annual status report with the court prior to the hearing date.

* The purpose of the mandatory hearing date is to review whether the matter has been completed. If a Decree of Distribution and/or Order Closing Estate is filed prior to the mandatory review hearing date, that date will be stricken by the court.

Dated: _____   _____
JUDGE
Department #

[Adopted effective September 1, 2012.]

FORM C. TRIAL BY AFFIDAVIT CERTIFICATE
IN THE SUPERIOR COURT OF THE STATE OF WASHINGTON FOR PIERCE COUNTY

CASE NAME	CAUSE NO.
	TRIAL BY AFFIDAVIT CERTIFICATE Docket Code: CTBA

I understand that I have the right to a trial by presenting oral testimony to the Judge or jury and that by agreeing to this alternative procedure, the trial will be limited to submission of written affidavits only and argument by counsel or a party pro se. The argument is limited to one half hour per side.

By using this alternative procedure, Trial by Affidavit, all information of a factual nature will be submitted in written affidavit form.

I am aware that by agreeing to trial by affidavit, I will receive an accelerated trial date in about twenty (20) weeks rather than the normal trial date (26 - 36 weeks). I am aware this is a voluntary procedure and I am under no obligation to agree to trial by affidavit. I understand these options and have chosen and agreed to trial by affidavit.

DATED: _____   _____
                    Client

Witness: _____   _____
                    Client

_____
Attorney of Record, WSBA #

Revised 09/09

[Amended effective September 1, 2009.]

1234

FORM D. CONFIRMATION OF SERVICE
IN THE SUPERIOR COURT OF THE STATE OF WASHINGTON FOR PIERCE COUNTY

CASE NAME

CAUSE NO.

CONFIRMATION OF SERVICE
Docket Code: CS, CSSRV

CS ☐   All the named defendants/ petitioners/respondents have been served, have joined or have accepted service in writing. (Check if appropriate; otherwise, check the box below.)

CSSRV ☐   One or more named defendants have not yet been served. (If this box is checked, an additional confirmation of service must be filed pursuant to subsection (b) when service is obtained and the following information provided.

The following defendants have been served or accepted service: _____

_____

The following defendants have not yet been served: _____

_____

Reasons why service has not been obtained: _____

_____

How service will be obtained: _____

_____

Date by which service is expected to be obtained: _____

No other named defendants remain to be served.

A status conference is requested regarding: _____

Family Law Cases only (PCLR 40(d)): The following petitioner/respondent has been served or accepted service of the Order Assigning Case to Judicial Department:_____

_____

If Service has not been made, state the reasons why and the date by which service will be accomplished:

_____

_____

Date_____   Attorney or Party_____
                        WSBA # _____

Revised 09/10

[Amended effective September 1, 2009; September 1, 2010.]

FORM E. DOMESTIC RELATIONS INFORMATION FORM

DOMESTIC RELATIONS INFORMATION FORM: Form E (PCLR 16 and PCLSPR 94.04; 9/10)

Date: _____

Cause No.: _____

☐ Husband   ☐ Petitioner
☐ Wife   ☐ Respondent

PARTIES:

PETITIONER		*RESPONDENT*	
Name:	Age:	Name	Age:
Address:		Address:	

Date of Marriage/Domestic Partnership/Cohabitation:	Date of Separation:

DEPENDENT CHILDREN:

Name	Age	This Marriage	Prior Marriage	Percent Residential Time Petitioner %	Respondent %	*Since*

CHILD SUPPORT:1.

	NET INCOME	SUPPORT
Petitioner:	$	
Respondent:	$	

2.   Tax Exemptions allocated as follows: _____

3.   Exceptional support considerations: _____

4.   Child Support presently being paid $_____ per month; since _____

5.   Summary of proposed residential arrangements for the children:
_____
_____
_____
_____

MAINTENANCE:

1. _____ per month, duration: _____

2. Presently being paid: $_____ per month, for _____ months.

PETITIONER INCOME:

Employer/Other Source	Length	Gross Income	Net Income
		Total Income	

RESPONDENT INCOME:

Employer/Other Source	Length	Gross Income	Net Income
		Total Income	

FACTORS RELATING TO AWARD OF MAINTENANCE:

_____

_____

_____

_____

IF ATTORNEY FEES ARE AT ISSUE:

1.	Incurred to Date	$	Paid To Date	$
2.	Ordered to Date	$	Paid to Date	$
3.	Requested to Date	$	Estimate to Trial	$

PROPERTY DIVISION:

ASSETS:	Fair Market Value	Debt Owed	Net to Petitioner	Net to Respondent
Real Estate:				
Home	$	$	$	$
Other Real Property	$	$	$	$
	$	$	$	$
Vehicles (Year/Make):				
	$	$	$	$
	$	$	$	$
Household Goods	$	$	$	$
Tools/Equipment	$	$	$	$
Recreational/Hobby Equipment	$	$	$	$
Business/Profession:				
Petitioner	$	$	$	$
Respondent	$	$	$	$
Investments	$	$	$	$
Life Insurance Cash Value	$	$	$	$
Retirement:				
Petitioner	$	$	$	$
Respondent	$	$	$	$
IRA's, TSP's, 401-K's, etc.:				
Petitioner	$	$	$	$
Respondent	$	$	$	$
Receivables	$	$	$	$
Other Assets:				
	$	$	$	$
	$	$	$	$
	$	$	$	$
Debts:	($)	($)	($)	($)
TOTALS	$	$	$	$
Equalization:	$	- $	divided by two (2)	= $

Proposed Percentage Division: _____ % to Petitioner _____ % to Respondent
Effects of Proposed Division: $ _____ to Petitioner $ _____ to Respondent

A copy of this form shall be served on opposing counsel/party and trial Judge not later than 2 working days prior to trial. The original shall be filed with the Clerk's Office. When this form is used for Settlement Conference purposes under PCLR 16, do not file the original with the Clerk's Office.)

YOU MUST ATTACH:
1. **Proposed Child Support Order, Support Worksheets and current pay stubs. Form WPF DR 01-050.**
2. **Completed Financial Declaration. Form WPF DR 01-055**
3. **Proposed Parenting Plan, if disputed.**

[Amended effective September 1, 2009; September 1, 2010.]

FORM F. CONFIRMATION OF JOINDER OF PARTIES, CLAIMS AND DEFENSES
IN THE SUPERIOR COURT OF THE STATE OF WASHINGTON FOR PIERCE COUNTY

CASE NAME

CAUSE NO.

**CONFIRMATION OF JOINDER OF
PARTIES, CLAIMS AND DEFENSES**
Docket Code: CJ, CJN

CJNSC   ☐ The parties make the following joint representations:
(IF THIS BOX IS CHECKED, THERE WILL NOT BE A STATUS CONFERENCE)

1. This case is not subject to mandatory arbitration. (If it is, this report should not be filed; instead, no later than the deadline for filing this report, a statement of arbitrability should be filed.)
2. No additional parties will be joined.
3. All parties have been served or have accepted service.
4. All mandatory pleadings have been filed.
5. No additional claims or defenses will be raised.
6. The parties anticipate no problems in meeting the deadlines for disclosing possible witnesses and other subsequent deadlines in the Case Schedule.
7. All parties have cooperated in completing this report.

CJ   ☐ The parties do not join in making the foregoing representation, as explained below (if appropriate, check both the box at left and every applicable box below);
*(IF THE BOX ADJACENT TO THE PRECEDING SENTENCE IS CHECKED, THERE **WILL** BE A STATUS CONFERENCE, WHICH ALL PARTIES OR THEIR ATTORNEYS MUST ATTEND.)*

☐ An additional party will be joined.
☐ A party remains to be served.
☐ A mandatory pleading remains to be filed.
☐ An additional claim or defense will be raised.
☐ One or more parties anticipate a problem in meeting the deadlines for disclosing possible witnesses or other subsequent deadlines in the Case Schedule.
☐ Other explanation:

_____

_____

_____

In order to obtain the court's direction in the matters described above, the parties will appear at an Initial Status Conference, the date of which (as stated in the Case Schedule) is:

_____

_____   _____
Date   Attorney for Plaintiff/Party Pro Se
                                    WSBA #_____
Revised 9/09

[Amended effective September 1, 2009.]

FORM G.   NOTICE OF SETTLEMENT OF ALL CLAIMS AGAINST ALL PARTIES

IN THE SUPERIOR COURT OF THE STATE OF WASHINGTON FOR PIERCE COUNTY

CASE NAME	CAUSE NO.
	NOTICE OF SETTLEMENT OF ALL CLAIMS AGAINST ALL PARTIES Docket Code: NTSSTD

Notice is hereby given that all claims against all parties in this action have been resolved. Any trials or other hearings in this matter may be stricken from the court calendar. This notice is being filed with the consent of all parties.

If an order dismissing all claims against all parties is not entered within 90 days after the written notice of settlement is filed, the case shall be dismissed by the court.

_____
Date

_____
Attorney for_____
WSBA # : _____

[Amended effective September 1, 2011.]

FORM H. JOINT NOTICE OF RECONCILIATION
IN THE SUPERIOR COURT OF THE STATE OF WASHINGTON FOR PIERCE COUNTY

CASE NAME

CAUSE NO.

JOINT NOTICE OF RECONCILIATION
PCLSPR 94.04 (a)(4)(A)
DOCKET CODE: JNR

Notice is hereby given that both parties in the above-identified matter have either reconciled or mutually agree they wish to attempt a reconciliation. All future dates reflected in the Order Setting Case Schedule shall be cancelled by the Court.

FURTHER, both parties understand that this case shall automatically be dismissed by the Court six (6) months from the date of this Notice unless an Amended Petition has been filed with the Clerk of the Court prior to that date.

_____   _____
DATE   Petitioner Pro Se/Attorney
                             WSBA #:_____

_____   _____
DATE   Respondent Pro Se/Attorney
                             WSBA #:_____

[Amended effective September 1, 2009.]

FORM I. ORDER ASSIGNING CASE TO JUDICIAL DEPARTMENT

IN THE SUPERIOR COURT OF THE STATE OF WASHINGTON FOR PIERCE COUNTY

CASE NAME

CAUSE NO.

**ORDER ASSIGNING CASE TO
JUDICIAL DEPARTMENT**
Docket Code: AST

In accordance with PCLR 40(d), this case is hereby assigned to Department _____, Judge_____

Notice to Petitioner:
Once the case has been filed, the petitioner(s) shall serve a copy of this Order Assigning Case to Judicial Department on the respondent(s) with the summons and petition. Provided, however, that in those cases where service is by publication, the petitioner shall serve a copy of this Order Assigning Case to Judicial Department to within five (5) court days of service of the respondent's first response/appearance. If the case has not been filed, but an initial pleading is served, a copy of this Order Assigning Case to Judicial Department shall be served within five (5) court days of filing. PCLR 3(b)

Trial Date:
A trial date may be obtained pursuant to PCLR 40(d) by filing a 'Note of Issue' for assignment of a trial date by noon at least six (6) court days prior to the date fixed for assignment of the trial date. PCLR 40(d)

 If a trial date is not obtained pursuant to PCLR 40(d), failure to appear on this date will result in dismissal of the case by the Court. PCLR 40(d)

Assignment to set Trial Date   _____
                                        (Date and Time)
At that time the Court will provide you with a Case Schedule which shall include the trial date. Failure to appear on this date will result in dismissal of the case by the Court. PCLR 40(d)
Certificate of Completion of Mandatory Parenting Seminar due from both parties by _____.
See PCLSPR 94.05(c)

Uncontested Dissolutions/Settlements:
If this case is agreed upon by both petitioner(s) and respondent(s) who are represented by attorneys, you are not required to wait for the trial date in order to settle your case; after appropriate time requirements have been met, final pleadings may be presented in Ex Parte. If you are self represented and settle your case and the appropriate time requirements have been met, you may file a "Note for Pro Se/Self Represented Dissolution Calendar" to appear before a Court Commissioner for entry of final papers.

Date _____

_____
(Judge Signature and Department Number)

[Amended effective September 1, 2003; September 1, 2009; September 1, 2010.]

FORM J. NOTICE OF CHANGE OF ADDRESS

IN THE SUPERIOR COURT OF THE STATE OF WASHINGTON FOR PIERCE COUNTY

CASE NAME	CAUSE NO.
	NOTICE OF CHANGE OF ADDRESS DOCKET CODE: NTACA

NOTICE IS HEREBY GIVEN that the address for the attorney and/or party identified below is changed to the following:

NAME: _____

NEW ADDRESS: _____

_____

EFFECTIVE: _____

IN THIS CASE, I AM THE: (select only one)

___ Plaintiff/Petitioner

___ Defendant/Respondent

___ Attorney for _____WSBA #_____

DATED:_____   **SIGNATURE:** _____

PRINT NAME: _____

[Amended effective January 1, 2007; September 1, 2009; September 1, 2010; September 1, 2011.]

FORM K. DECLARATION OF PROPOSED TRUSTEE

IN THE SUPERIOR COURT OF THE STATE OF WASHINGTON FOR PIERCE COUNTY

In the [NAME] of:	CAUSE NO.
	DECLARATION OF PROPOSED TRUSTEE

1) Identification of Trustee.
Name of Proposed Trustee:
WSBA/CPG#:
Mailing Address of Proposed Trustee:
Street Address (if different):
City/State/Zip:
Telephone Number: Fax Number:
Email Address:

2) Certified Status. The proposed Trustee is professionally licensed in the State of Washington as: a ☐ lawyer, ☐ guardian, ☐ trustee, or ☐ other (identify:_____).   Attached as Exhibit A to this Declaration is a summary listing the educational programs (*pertaining to fiduciary matters*) which the proposed Trustee and its employees have attended during the past twelve (12) months.

3) Business Form. The form in which the proposed Trustee does business is:
☐ sole proprietor   ☐ trust company   ☐ bank
☐ corporation   ☐ non-profit corporation   ☐ other: _____

4) Identification of Principals of Proposed Trustee. List the name of each member of the board of directors, officer, and owner of the business of the proposed Trustee and their title:

5) Relationship to Allegedly Incapacitated Person. The proposed Trustee has the following relationship with the Incapacitated Person:

6) Trustee's Organizational Structure.

(a) Date the proposed Trustee began doing business:

(b) Allocation of job responsibilities:
(*Brochures or other printed materials may be attached as an Exhibit in response to this question.*)

7) Criminal Background Checks. Does the proposed Trustee conduct criminal background checks pursuant to RCW 43.43.832 on all employees or volunteers who will or may have unsupervised access to the trust beneficiary?   ☐ Yes   ☐ No

8) Criminal and Disciplinary History. Provide the following information for the proposed Trustee and for each of its principals and employees:

(a) Circumstances leading to removal as a Trustee or as a fiduciary for breach of fiduciary duty or for any other reason:

(b) Criminal proceedings for a felony or misdemeanor involving moral turpitude, which resulted in a finding or plea of guilty (*attach an explanation as an exhibit explaining why this individual is employed by the proposed Trustee*):

(c) Civil proceedings in which there was a finding of dishonesty, misappropriation of funds, breach of fiduciary duty, or mistreatment of any person (*identify any civil proceedings where there was a settlement, even if such settlement was without specific findings by the Court*):

(d) Reported disciplinary proceedings by a disciplinary body or licensing agency that resulted in a finding of misconduct (*including proceedings by a professional organization such as a state bar association, a medical disciplinary review board, etc.*):

9) Protection of Trust Funds. The proposed Trustee has insurance coverage or security from the following forms at the following policy limits as of _____,20_

    a) **Errors and Omissions Insurance:**

        i)   Insurance Company: _____

        ii) Policy Limits: $_____

    b) **Employee Dishonesty Insurance:**

        i)   Insurance Company: _____

        ii) Policy Limits: $_____

    c) **General Surety Bond:**

        i)   Bonding Company: _____

        ii) Amount: $_____

10) Assets Under Management. As of _____,20____, the total value of all of the assets administered by the Trustee is: $_____, and the total value of all assets separately bonded or held in blocked accounts is: $_____

11) Case Load. As of _____,20____the proposed Trustee administers [*insert text-number*] trusts, and serves as a non-trustee fiduciary (e.g. Guardian, Attorney in Fact, Custodian) for _____ individuals

12) Compensation and Reimbursement. The proposed Trustee' compensation schedule is as follows (*include the different hourly rates for various services and an estimated fee in this matter if possible*):

13) Experience. The proposed Trustee's experience with similar Trusts (*for example, similar amount of assets, the family circumstances of the trust beneficiary, the proximity of the proposed Trustee to the residence of the trust beneficiary, and any relevant information*) is:

14) Asset Management. The proposed Trustee intends to manage the trust as follows:

I certify (or declare) under penalty of perjury under the laws of the State of Washington that to the best of my knowledge the statements above are true and correct.

Signed at _____, Washington

This _____ day of _____, 20____.

Signature of Proposed Trustee	Printed Name of Proposed Trustee
Address	Telephone/Fax Number
City, State, Zip Code	Email Address

[Adopted effective September 1, 2006.]

FORM L.   TRUST SUMMARY

TRUST SUMMARY

Date Trustee Appointed: _____

Date of Next Hearing: _____

Current Bond Amount: $ _____

Blocking Required: Yes ☐ No ☐

Beneficiary	Trustee
Name: Address: City, State and postal code *Phone:*	Name: Address: City, State and postal code *Phone:* *Facsimile:*

Interested Parties	Address & Phone	Relation to Beneficiary

[Adopted effective September 1, 2006.]

FORM M.   DECLARATION OF PROPOSED GUARDIAN
IN THE SUPERIOR COURT OF THE STATE OF WASHINGTON FOR PIERCE COUNTY

In Re the Guardianship of:	**CAUSE NO.**
[Name]	**DECLARATION OF PROPOSED GUARDIAN** **(Non-Certified)**
An Incapacitated Person.	

(1) Personal Information.
Name of Proposed Guardian:
Mailing Address of Proposed Guardian:
Street Address (if different):
City/State/Zip:
Telephone Number: Fax Number:
Email Address:
If the proposed Guardian does not reside in Washington, provide the name, address, phone and email for the proposed Guardian's resident agent:

(2) Non-Professional Status. I am not charging fees for carrying out the duties of court-appointed guardian of three or more incapacitated persons. I acknowledge that before I may receive fees for serving as a Guardian for three or more persons, I am required to be certified in the State of Washington. See RCW § 11.88.008.

(3) Business Form. If appointed, I will serve as a Guardian as an individual and not as an entity or representative of a business entity, such as a trust company or non-profit corporation.

(4) Background and Experience Helpful to Service as Guardian. I have the following background, education training and experience, which may be helpful in my service as Guardian:

(5) Licenses held:

(6) Relationship to Alleged Incapacitated Person. I have the following relationship to the Alleged Incapacitated Person (*such as family member, friend, etc.*):

(7) Prior History as Fiduciary or Guardian.
    (a) I have served in a fiduciary capacity (*such as an attorney-in-fact pursuant to power of attorney, a trustee, an executor, an administrator, or a Guardian*).
        ☐ Yes   ☐ No
    (b) I have been removed as a fiduciary.
        ☐ Yes   ☐ No
    If the answer above is "Yes," describe the circumstances leading to your removal as a Guardian or as a fiduciary.

(8) Criminal History. RCW 11.88.020(3) expressly provides that no person is qualified to serve as a Guardian if he or she has been "convicted of a felony or of a misdemeanor involving moral turpitude," *(a crime involving dishonesty, misappropriation of funds, breach of fiduciary duty, or mistreatment of any person).*

I have been convicted of such a crime

☐ Yes   ☐ No

If the answer to the question is "Yes," identify all such convictions dated, and whether or not your civil rights have been restored.

(9) Civil Proceedings. Describe any civil or administrative proceeding in which there was a finding that you had engaged in dishonesty, misappropriation of funds, breach of fiduciary duty, or mistreatment of any person. Also identify any proceeding(s) where there was a settlement, even if such settlement was without specific findings by the Court.

(10) Disciplinary Proceedings. Describe any disciplinary proceeding against you by any applicable disciplinary body or licensing agency that resulted in a finding of misconduct. This would include any proceedings by a professional organization such as a state bar association, a medical disciplinary review board and the like:

(11) Ability to Secure Bond. In some cases, it is necessary for the Guardian to secure a bond, which is insurance coverage providing protection to the Incapacitated Person in the event of financial loss or personal harm caused by the negligent or intentional conduct of the proposed Guardian. Is there any reason (*such as bankruptcy or poor credit record*) why you would have difficulty obtaining a Guardian's bond. If yes, please explain:

(12) Compensation and Reimbursement. State whether you intend to request hourly compensation for your services and describe the expenses (e.g. mileage, postage copies charges, etc.) for which you expect to be reimbursed.

(13) Summary of Guardian Duties: The below signed proposed Guardian understands and agrees that:

My duties as Guardian are more fully described in:
  (1) the Court Order that appoints me,
  (2) the statutes of the State of Washington – (for example see the Revised Code of Washington (RCW) at Chapters 11.88 & 11.92 and specifically 11.92.042 and 11.92.043 RCW.)
  (3) the case law.

I should consult with my attorney if I have any questions. I am presumed to understand my duties and responsibilities. I can be held personally responsible if I do not properly carry out my duties as Guardian.

As Guardian, I act in a fiduciary capacity in my dealings on behalf of the Incapacitated Person. This means that as the Guardian, I am required to put the interests of the Incapacitated Person ahead of my personal interests in all transactions, as well as any transaction in which my interests and the interests of the Incapacitated Person may be in conflict.

Additionally, if I have been appointed Guardian of the Estate, I am charged with the responsibility of acting as a reasonably prudent person in dealing with the investment and conservation of the assets of the Incapacitated Person and to avoid self dealing.

For health care decisions, "Before any person authorized to provide informed consent on behalf of a patient not competent to consent exercises that authority, the person must first determine in good faith that that patient, if competent, would consent to the proposed health care. If such a determination cannot be made, the decision to consent to the proposed health care may be made only after determining that the proposed health care is in the patient's best interests." RCW § 7.70.065(3)

If my personal beliefs could be in conflict with the interests of the Alleged Incapacitated Person, I must first do what I believe the Incapacitated Person would do if competent. If that cannot be determined, either because of lack of knowledge or because the Incapacitated Person has always been disabled, I may act in the manner that I believe is in the best interest of the Alleged Incapacitated Person. I understand that at any time I can seek direction from the court if there is any question of what is in the best interest of the Alleged Incapacitated Person.

Any attorney that I retain to assist me in this guardianship proceeding will have independent responsibilities and obligations to the Court. The attorney-client privilege may not extend to information regarding misfeasance or malfeasance of a fiduciary. The attorney-client privilege may not extend to information given by me, the Guardian, to my attorney, for any failure to follow the laws of a court-appointed Guardian.

If I am appointed the Guardian of the Person or Guardian of the Estate I must:

- file a Designation of Standby Guardian with the Court;
- keep the Court informed of any change in my name, address, or bonding status; and
- file a Change of Circumstance Report within thirty (30) days of any change of location, major or permanent changes in health or finances, or of the death of the Incapacitated Person.
- file a Final Accounting within ninety (90) days after the termination of a guardianship. 11.92.053 RCW, see also 11.88.140 RCW.

If I am appointed the Guardian of the Estate I must also:

- keep the Incapacitated Person's funds separate from my own, in a separate guardianship bank account;
- make all payments in a timely manner and with a method so there is a record of all transactions that can be verified by the Court at the time of each annual accounting (e.g. checking account);
- file, within ninety (90) days of my appointment, an Inventory of the assets in the guardianship estate, and a Budget authorizing disbursements; and
- file, within ninety (90) days of the anniversary date of my appointment (as shown on the Letters of Guardianship), an Accounting showing the receipts and disbursements made on behalf of the Incapacitated Person during the previous accounting period.

If I am appointed the Guardian of the Person I must also:

- file, within ninety (90) days of my appointment, a Personal Care Plan describing the care needs of the Incapacitated Person with the court; and
- file, within ninety (90) days of the anniversary date of my appointment, a Status Report describing the care and condition of the Incapacitated Person during the previous accounting period.

If I am appointed the Guardian of the Person or Guardian of the Estate I <u>cannot</u>:

- spend, sell, borrow, loan, invest or give away ANY of the Incapacitated Person's property (including money), without a court order;

- spend, loan, invest, or give away any of the Incapacitated Person's principal or income for any purpose without a court order;

- borrow money on behalf of the Incapacitated Person, without a court order;

- use the Incapacitated Person's money for myself or my needs, without a court order;

- pay myself a fee from the Incapacitated Person's money, without the filing of a verified petition for payment of fees with an Affidavit detailing the time spent, services provided, and compensation requested attached thereto, and a corresponding court order approving said petition; or

- force the Incapacitated Person to live ANYWHERE, including a mental institution or nursing home facility.

I certify (or declare) under penalty of perjury under the laws of the State of Washington that to the best of my knowledge the statements above are true and correct.

Signed at _____, Washington

This _____ day of _____, 20____

_____
Signature of Proposed Guardian

Printed Name of Proposed Guardian,

_____
Address

Telephone/Fax Number

_____
City, State, Zip Code

Email Address

[Adopted effective September 1, 2006.]

FORM N. DECLARATION OF PROPOSED GUARDIAN
IN THE SUPERIOR COURT OF THE STATE OF WASHINGTON FOR PIERCE COUNTY

In Re the Guardianship of:	**CAUSE NO.**
[Name]	**DECLARATION OF PROPOSED GUARDIAN (Certified)**
An Incapacitated Person.	

1) Personal Information.
Name of Proposed Guardian:
Certified Professional Guardian #:
Mailing Address of Proposed Guardian:
Street Address (if different):
City/State/Zip:
Telephone Number: Fax Number:
Email Address:

2) Certified Status. The proposed Guardian is a certified professional Guardian in the State of Washington. Attached as Exhibit A to this Declaration is a summary listing the educational programs (*pertaining to Guardianships or fiduciary matters*) which the proposed Guardian and its employees have attended during the past twelve (12) months.

3) Business Form. The form in which the proposed Guardian does business is:
☐ sole proprietor   ☐ partnership   ☐ trust company
☐ corporation   ☐ non-profit corporation

4) Identification of Principals of Proposed Guardian. List the name of each member of the board of directors, officer, and owner of the business of the proposed Guardian and their title:

5) Individual Certified Guardians. List each certified Guardian in the employ of the Guardian who may have responsibilities in this case and the individual certified Guardian who will have supervising responsibility in this case.

6) Relationship to Alleged Incapacitated Person. The proposed Guardian has the following relationship with the Incapacitated Person:

7) Guardian's Organizational Structure.

(1)   Date the proposed Guardian began doing business:

(2)   Allocation of job responsibilities:
(*Brochures or other printed materials may be attached as an Exhibit in response to this question.*)

8) Criminal Background Checks. Does the proposed Guardian conduct criminal background checks pursuant to RCW 43.43.832 on all employees or volunteers who will or may have unsupervised access to the Incapacitated Person?   ☐ Yes   ☐ No

9) Criminal and Disciplinary History. Provide the following information for the proposed Guardian <u>and</u> for each of its principals and employees who are certified professional Guardians. However, do <u>NOT</u> include employees who are neither principals nor certified Guardians:

(1) Circumstances leading to removal as a Guardian or as a fiduciary for breach of fiduciary duty or for any other reason:

(2) Criminal proceedings for a felony or misdemeanor involving moral turpitude, which resulted in a finding or plea of guilty (*attach an explanation as an exhibit explaining why this individual is employed by the proposed Guardian*):

(3) Civil proceedings in which there was a finding of dishonesty, misappropriation of funds, breach of fiduciary duty, or mistreatment of any person (*identify any civil proceedings where there was a settlement, even if such settlement was without specific findings by the Court*):

(4) Reported disciplinary proceedings by a disciplinary body or licensing agency that resulted in a finding of misconduct (*including proceedings by a professional organization such as a state bar association, a medical disciplinary review board, etc.*):

10) Bond/Insurance. The proposed Guardian has insurance coverage or security from the following forms at the following policy limits as of _____20_:

   a) **Errors and Omissions Insurance:**

      i) Insurance Company: _____

      ii) Policy Limits: $_____

   b) **Employee Dishonesty Insurance:**

      i) Insurance Company: _____

      ii) Policy Limits: $_____

   c) **General Surety Bond:**

      i) Bonding Company: _____

      ii) Amount: $_____

11) Assets Under Management. The total value of all of the assets that proposed Guardian has under management as of _____, 20___ is: $_____

12) Compensation and Reimbursement. The proposed Guardian's compensation schedule is as follows (*include the different hourly rates for various services*):

13) Experience. The proposed Guardian's experience with similar Guardianships (*for example, similar amount of assets, the family circumstances of the Incapacitated Person, the proximity of the proposed Guardian to the residence of the Alleged Incapacitated Person, and any relevant information*) is:

14) Case Load. As of _____,20____the proposed Guardian is the Court appointed Guardian for [*insert text-number*] of total individuals, and serves as a non-guardian fiduciary (e.g. Trustee, Attorney in Fact, Custodian) for _____ number of total individuals.

15) Summary of Guardian Duties: The below signed proposed Guardian understands and agrees that:
> My duties as Guardian are more fully described in:
> (1) the Court Order that appoints me,
> (2) the statutes of the State of Washington – (for example see the Revised Code of Washington (RCW) at Chapters 11.88 & 11.92 and specifically 11.92.042 and 11.92.043 RCW.)
> (3) the case law.

I should consult with my attorney if I have any questions about my duties and responsibilities. I am presumed to understand my duties and responsibilities. I can be held personally responsible if I do not properly carry out my duties as Guardian.

As Guardian, I act in a fiduciary capacity in my dealings on behalf of the Incapacitated Person. This means that as the Guardian, I am required to put the interests of the Incapacitated Person ahead of my personal interests in all transactions as well as any transaction in which my interests and the interests of the Incapacitated Party may be in conflict.

Additionally, if I have been appointed Guardian of the Estate, I am charged with the responsibility of acting as a reasonably prudent person in dealing with the investment and conservation of the assets of the Incapacitated Person; and to avoid self dealing.

Any attorney that I retain to assist me in this guardianship proceeding will have independent responsibilities and obligations to the Court. The attorney-client privilege may not extend to information regarding misfeasance or malfeasance of a fiduciary.

If I am appointed the Guardian of the Person or Guardian of the Estate I <u>must</u>:
- file a <u>Designation of Standby Guardian</u> with the Court;
- keep the Court informed of any change in my name, address, or bonding status; and
- file a <u>Change of Circumstance Report</u> within thirty (30) days of any change of location, major or permanent changes in health or finances, or of the death of the Incapacitated Person.
- file a <u>Final Accounting</u> within ninety (90) days after the termination of a guardianship. 11.92.053 RCW, see also 11.88.140 RCW

If I am appointed the Guardian of the Estate I <u>must</u> also:
- keep the Incapacitated Person's funds separate from my own, in a separate guardianship bank account;
- make all payments in a timely manner and with a method so there is a record of all transactions that can be verified by the Court at the time of each annual accounting (e.g. checking account);
- file, within ninety (90) days of my appointment, an <u>Inventory</u> of the assets in the guardianship estate, and a Budget authorizing disbursements; and

- file, within ninety (90) days of the anniversary date of my appointment (as shown on the Letters of Guardianship), an <u>Accounting</u> showing the receipts and disbursements made on behalf of the Incapacitated Person during the previous accounting period.

If I am appointed the Guardian of the Person I <u>must</u> also:

- file, within ninety (90) days of my appointment, a <u>Personal Care Plan</u> describing the care needs of the Incapacitated Person with the court; and
- file, within ninety (90) days of the anniversary date of my appointment, a <u>Status Report</u> describing the care and condition of the Incapacitated Person during the previous accounting period.

If I am appointed the Guardian of the Person or Guardian of the Estate I <u>cannot</u>:

- spend, sell, borrow, loan, invest or give away ANY of the Incapacitated Person's property (including money), without a court order;
- spend, loan, invest, or give away any of the Incapacitated Person's principal or income for any purpose without a court order;
- borrow money on behalf of the Incapacitated Person, without a court order;
- use the Incapacitated Person's money for myself or my needs, without a court order;
- pay myself a fee from the Incapacitated Person's money, without the filing of a verified petition for payment of fees with an Affidavit detailing the time spent, services provided, and compensation requested attached thereto, and a corresponding court order approving said petition; or
- force the Incapacitated Person to live ANYWHERE, including a mental institution or nursing home facility.

I certify (or declare) under penalty of perjury under the laws of the State of Washington that to the best of my knowledge the statements above are true and correct.

Signed at _____, Washington

This _____ day of _____, 20 _____.

_____	_____
Signature of Certified Professional Guardian	Printed Name of Certified Professional Guardian, WSBA/CPG#
_____	_____
Address	Telephone/Fax Number
_____	_____
City, State, Zip Code	Email Address

[Adopted effective September 1, 2006.]

FORM O. GUARDIANSHIP SUMMARY
IN THE SUPERIOR COURT OF THE STATE OF WASHINGTON FOR PIERCE COUNTY

In Re the Guardianship of:

[Name]

An Incapacitated Person.

CAUSE NO.

GUARDIANSHIP SUMMARY

Date Guardian Appointed: _____

Date of Next Hearing: _____

Current Bond Amount: $ _____

Blocking Required: Yes ☐ No ☐

Due Date for Inventory: _____

Due Date for Care Plan: _____

Loss of Voting Rights Yes ☐ No ☐

Incapacitated Person (IP)	**Guardian of:** ☐ **Estate** ☐ **Person**
Name: Address: Phone:	Name: Address: Phone: Facsimile:

Standby Guardian	**Address & Phone:**	**Relation to IP**

Interested Parties	**Address & Phone:**	**Relation to IP**

I declare under the penalty of perjury that the above information is true and correct. I agree that if any of the above information changes, I will notify the court of that change within ten days of the change.

Dated this_____ day of _____, _____ at _____

    (day)   (month)   (year)   (City & State)

_____

Signature

_____

Print

Effective 9/1/06

[Adopted effective September 1, 2006.]

FORM P. ORDER AND JOINT NOTICE OF PARTICIPATION IN COLLABORATIVE LAW

IN THE SUPERIOR COURT OF THE STATE OF WASHINGTON
FOR PIERCE COUNTY

CASE NAME	NO.
	ORDER AND JOINT NOTICE OF **PARTICIPATION** **IN COLLABORATIVE LAW**

Notice is hereby given that both parties in the above-identified matter mutually agree that they wish to participate in Collaborative Law. All future dates reflected in the Order Setting Case Schedule shall be cancelled by the Court.

FURTHER, both parties understand that should this case not resolve within six (6) months from the date of this Notice, the parties shall appear before the Court on the following date for a mandatory status conference to advise the Court of the progress in this matter.

MANDATORY HEARING DATE:_____.

Counsel and the Court may agree to continue the status conference to a later date if participation in the Collaborative Law process is ongoing as the status conference date approaches.

Done in Open Court this _____ day of _____, 20_____.

_____
JUDGE

_____   _____
DATE   Petitioner's Attorney
                           WSBA #

_____   _____
DATE   Respondent's Attorney
                           WSBA #

[Adopted effective September 1, 2010.]

FORM Q. COMMISSIONERS' CALENDARS

COMMISSIONERS' CALENDARS:

CIVIL DIVISION A (Courtroom 2A)

TIME	MONDAY	TUESDAY	WEDNESDAY	THURSDAY	FRIDAY
9:30–12:00	Show Cause	Show Cause	Show Cause	Show Cause	Prosecutor's Docket
12:00-1:00	Closed	Closed	Closed	Closed	Closed
1:30-4:30	Probate Guardianship Vulnerable Adult Minor Settlement Supp Proceedings Unlawful Detainer	Probate Guardianship Vulnerable Adult Minor Settlement Supp Proceedings Unlawful Detainer	Probate Guardianship Vulnerable Adult Minor Settlement Supp Proceedings Unlawful Detainer	Probate Guardianship Vulnerable Adult Minor Settlement Supp Proceedings Unlawful Detainer	Probate Guardianship Vulnerable Adult Minor Settlement Supp Proceedings Unlawful Detainer

CIVIL DIVISION B (Courtroom 117)

TIME	MONDAY	TUESDAY	WEDNESDAY	THURSDAY	FRIDAY
9:30–Noon	Show Cause	Show Cause	Show Cause	Show Cause	Self Represented Uncontested Dissolutions
12:00-1:00	Closed	Closed	Closed	Closed	Closed
1:00–4:30pm	Domestic Violence Sexual Assault	Domestic Violence Sexual Assault	Domestic Violence Sexual Assault	Domestic Violence Sexual Assault	Domestic Violence Sexual Assault

CIVIL DIVISION C (Courtroom 407)

TIME	MONDAY	TUESDAY	WEDNESDAY	THURSDAY	FRIDAY
9:30–Noon	Show Cause	Show Cause	Show Cause	Show Cause	Self Represented Uncontested Dissolutions
12:00-1:00	Closed	Closed	Closed	Closed	Closed
1:30–4:30	Family Support Modification	Paternity	Family Support Modification	Paternity	Family Support Modification

EXPARTE DEPARTMENT (Courtroom 105)

TIME	MONDAY	TUESDAY	WEDNESDAY	THURSDAY	FRIDAY
9:00-11:30	Exparte Presentations	Exparte Presentations	Exparte Presentations	Exparte Presentations	Exparte Presentations
12:00-1:30	Closed	Closed	Closed	Closed	Closed
1:30-3:30	Exparte Presentations	Exparte Presentations	Exparte Presentations	Exparte Presentations	Exparte Presentations

COMMISSIONERS CALENDARS/HOURS MAY BE REVISED—CHECK WEBSITE:
www.co.pierce.wa.us/superiorcourt

[Adopted effective September 1, 2007; amended effective September 1, 2008; September 1, 2009; September 1, 2010; September 1, 2011.]

FORM R. MOTION TO WAIVE MANDATORY SETTLEMENT CONFERENCE

FORM R

IN THE SUPERIOR COURT OF THE STATE OF WASHINGTON FOR PIERCE COUNTY

CASE NAME	CAUSE NO.
	MOTION TO WAIVE MANDATORY SETTLEMENT CONFERENCE

I, _____, **Petitioner/Respondent** , request the Court waive the requirement for mandatory Settlement conference for the following reason(s):

☐ A domestic violence restraining order or protection order (excluding Ex-Parte orders) involving the parties has been entered by a court within the previous twelve (12) months. A copy of the order is attached to this motion. (If an order is not attached, provide the name of the case, case number, county in which the order is issued, the date of issuance):

_____
_____

☐ A domestic violence no contact order exists pursuant to RCW 10.99, and has been in effect within the past twelve (12) months. A copy of the order is attached to this motion. (If an order is not attached, provide the name of the case, case number, county in which the order is issued, the date of issuance):

_____
_____

☐ There is a history of domestic abuse between the parties. Because of that history of abuse I believe I am in danger of physical or emotional abuse in connection with the mediation session or it would interfere with arm's-length mediation. Describe history of domestic abuse:

_____
_____
_____

☐ There is a history of child abuse that has occurred involving at least one of the parties and one or more of the children subject to the family law matter. Describe history of abuse:

_____
_____
_____

☐ I seek a waiver for other reasons (Set forth reasons:) _____

_____
_____

My Name: _____ Other Party/Attorney's Name: _____

_____ _____

Address: _____ Address: _____

_____ _____

_____ _____

_____ (check here) **I CERTIFY THAT THE STATEMENTS IN THIS MOTION ARE TRUE AND CORRECT, AND I HAVE MAILED A COPY OF THIS MOTION TO THE OTHER PARTY'S ATTORNEY OR TO THE OTHER PARTY IF UNREPRESENTED BY AN ATTORNEY .**

DATED this _____ day of _____, 20_____.

_____

Signature of Attorney or Party filing Motion if
unrepresented by an attorney

[Adopted effective September 2, 2013.]

FORM S. STATEMENT OF ARBITRABILITY

SUPERIOR COURT OF WASHINGTON
COUNTY OF PIERCE

Plaintiff(s),	No. _____
and	**STATEMENT OF ARBITRABILITY**
Defendant(s).	

CASE CATEGORY:

NAME:		NAME
ADDRESS:		ADDRESS:

CERTIFICATE OF ARBITRABILITY

___ This case is subject to arbitration because the sole relief sought is a money judgment and involves no claim in excess of Fifty Thousand Dollars ($50,000), exclusive of attorney fees, interest and costs.

___ This case is not subject to mandatory arbitration because:

   ___ Plaintiff's claim exceeds Fifty Thousand Dollars ($50,000).

   ___ Plaintiff seeks relief other than a money judgment.

   ___ Defendant's counter or cross claim exceeds Fifty Thousand Dollars ($50,000)

   ___ Defendant's counter or cross claim seeks relief other than a money judgment.

___ The undersigned contends that its claim exceeds Fifty Thousand Dollars ($50,000), but hereby waives any claim in excess of Fifty Thousand Dollars ($50,000) for the purpose of arbitration.

CERTIFICATE OF READINESS

The undersigned attorney **certifies** that:

1. All parties have been joined and served;
2. All parties have received a copy of the Case Schedule;
3. All answers and other mandatory pleadings have been filed and served; and
4. No additional claims or defenses will be raised.

ARBITRATION AWARD

NOTE: In cases where an Arbitration Award is filed and there is no timely request for trial *de novo*, either a judgment on arbitration award or an order dismissing all claims against all parties must be entered within 90 days of the filing of the Arbitration Award. Failure to do so shall result in the case being dismissed by the court.

(PAGE FOR ADDITIONAL ATTORNEYS)

[Adopted effective September 1, 2015.]

DISTRICT COURTS

LOCAL COURT RULES OF THE PIERCE COUNTY DISTRICT COURT

Including Amendments Received Through
August 15, 2015

Table of Rules

ADMINISTRATIVE RULES

LARLJ 1. LOCAL RULES SUSPENSION

Any of these rules may be suspended or modified, upon good cause shown, by written stipulation of the parties approved by the court, or by the court upon its own motion.

[Adopted effective September 1, 1993.]

LARLJ 2. FORM OF PLEADINGS—STYLE AND FORM—FACILITATING PROOF OF SERVICE AND FILING OF PAPERS

Style and Form. (See: CRLJ 5 and 10 and CrRLJs 1.5 and 8.4.)

Filing with Court. (See CrRLJ 8.4(c) and CRLJ 5.)

1. Action Documents. Pleadings or other papers requiring action on the part of the Clerk/Court (other than file stamping, docketing and placing in the court file) shall be considered action documents. Action documents shall include a special caption directly below the case number on the first page, stating: **"Clerk's Action Required: (here state the action requested)".**

2. Format Recommendations. It is recommended that all pleadings and other papers include or provide for the following:

(a) *Service and Filing.* Space should be provided at the top of the first page of a document allowing on the right half for the clerk's filing stamp, and in the left half for proof of or acknowledgment of service.

Common pleading or service forms should be two-hole punched at the page top for fastening in court files.

(b) *Numbered Paper.* All pleadings, motions, affidavits, briefs, and other supporting documents prepared by attorneys/parties should be on paper with line numbering in the left hand margin.

(c) *Handling by Clerk.* All pleadings or other papers with proper caption and cause number will be date receipted, docketed, and secured/placed in the court file by the clerk of the District Court in the order received.

[Adopted effective September 1, 1993.]

EXAMPLE LARLJ 2

SPACE FOR SERVICE PROOF   SPACE FOR COURT FILING STAMP

PIERCE COUNTY DISTRICT COURT NO. ONE,
PIERCE COUNTY WASHINGTON

Plaintiff	) Cause No.
	)
-vs-	) CLERK'S ACTION REQUIRED:
	) SET THIS MOTION FOR HEARING
	)
Defendant	) MOTION FOR _____

FOR ATTORNEY USE

Please set hearing prior to trial date.

Please set hearing day of trial.

FOR CLERK'S USE ONLY

This matter set for hearing on the _____ day of _____, 1993.

This matter to be heard on trial date, prior to start of actual trial.

SPACE FOR SERVICE PROOF   SPACE FOR COURT FILING STAMP

PIERCE COUNTY DISTRICT COURT NO. ONE,
PIERCE COUNTY WASHINGTON

Plaintiff	) Cause No.
	)
-vs-	) CLERK'S ACTION REQUIRED:
	) SET THIS MOTION FOR HEARING
	)
Defendant	) MOTION FOR _____

The clerks will not search out action items. They will not search through letters, notices of appearance, requests for discovery, or other materials, to locate possible requests for action, such as: preservation of jury trial, non-waiver of 60/90 day rule (this needs a request to set within the correct time, see CrRLJ 3.3), or concern with witnesses. Amongst CRLJs impacted by this rule are:

CRLJ 2A	Stipulations	CRLJ 38	Jury Trial
CRLJ 4	Process	CRLJ 40	Assignment of Cases
CRLJ 5	Service and Filing of	CRLJ 41	Dismissal of Actions
	Pleadings and Other	CRLJ 45	Subpoena
	Papers	CRLJ 54	Judgments/Costs
CRLJ 7	Pleadings Allowed: Form	CRLJ 55	Default
	of Motions	CRLJ 56	Summary Judgment
CRLJ 10	Form of Pleadings	CRLJ 59	New Trial, Reconsidera-
CRLJ 12	Defenses and Objections		tion, and Amendment of
CRLJ 13	Counterclaim and Cross		Judgments
	Claim	CRLJ 60	Relief from Judgment or
CRLJ 15	Amended and Supplemen-		Order
	tal Pleadings	CRLJ 71	Withdrawal by Attorney
CRLJ 26	Depositions Pending		
	Action		

[Adopted effective September 1, 1993.]

LARLJ 4. CANCELLATION NOTIFICATION OF SUMMARY JUDGMENT MOTIONS, JURY TRIALS, VISITING JUDGE CASES AND CIVIL TRIALS REQUIRING IN EXCESS OF ONE COURT DAY TO COMPLETE

Cancellation notification in writing or telephonically must be given to the Pierce County District Court No. One Civil Section at least 48 hours prior to the date and time the hearing is scheduled to take place.

If cancellation notification is not received at least 48 hours prior to the date and time of the hearing, the following sanctions may be imposed:

1. Jury Trial, Visiting Judge Case or Court Trial in Excess of One Day—Terms of up to $50.00 may be assessed against each party.

2. Summary Judgment Motion—Terms of up to $25.00 may be assessed against each party.

Trial and/or motion dates will not be rescheduled until sanction payments are received by the Court.

[Adopted effective September 1, 1993.]

LARLJ 5. RETRIEVING CASE FILES FROM STATE ARCHIVE OR DISTRICT COURT STORAGE FACILITY

Retrieval From County Archives. Case files that have been transcribed, dismissed or satisfied are processed and transmitted to the State Archive Facility in accordance with the State Retention Schedule. In order to retrieve a case file from the State's facility a request form must be completed. The cost to retrieve a case file from archives will be set by court policy per case file. This fee covers the cost charged by the State to retrieve documents.

Retrieval From District Court Facility. Due to limited storage space, some open civil case files are stored outside the County/City Building. These case files are accessed from the off-site facility on a weekly basis at no cost to the party requesting the case file.

[Adopted effective September 1, 1993.]

LARLJ 6A. SMALL CLAIMS MEDIATION

Mediation is mandatory before a trial is allowed. The court will set the date for mediation at the time of filing. Both parties must attend the mediation. If the plaintiff fails to appear, a dismissal will be entered. If the defendant fails to appear, their answer, if one was filed, will be stricken and a default judgment entered. Parties must bring their evidence to the mediation, however, no witnesses are allowed. The purpose of mediation is to settle the case if possible; if no settlement is made at mediation, the case will be set for trial. Attorneys and paralegals may not represent parties at mediation.

If the parties have already submitted the case to another type of mediation or arbitration service, the case may proceed directly to trial.

[Adopted effective September 1, 1993.]

LARLJ 6B. CONTINUANCE OF MEDIATION OR SMALL CLAIM TRIAL

The party requesting the continuance must contact the other party who must also agree to the continuance. Both parties must contact the Court in person or by telephone.

If one party will not agree to the continuance, the party seeking the continuance may make a written motion for continuance and set a hearing date prior to the scheduled mediation or trial date. The motion and notice of hearing must be served on the opposing party not less than five days prior to the date set for the motion to continue. At the hearing, the Judicial Officer will make the ruling if the matter will be continued.

If there are less than five days prior to the mediation or trial date to serve the opposing party, the party requesting the continuance may contact the Court to explain the circumstances which require the mediation or trial to be continued. The matter may be continued by the Court upon showing of good cause.

[Adopted effective September 1, 1993.]

LARLJ 7A. INFRACTION WITNESSES

The District Court will not serve or forward subpoenas issued pursuant to IRLJ 3.1. Pursuant to IRLJ 6.6, a request for a Speed Measuring Device Expert shall be made at the time of the request for a contested hearing to allow appropriate scheduling of the hearing. Failure to do so shall result in an IRLJ 6.6(c) continuance of the hearing to a subsequent hearing when an expert will be available. The defendant may in the alternative waive the presence of the expert at the hearing and accept the IRLJ 6.6 affidavit in lieu of testimony.

[Adopted effective September 1, 1993.]

LARLJ 7B. INFRACTION DISCOVERY REQUEST

Discovery requests other than a copy of the infraction, the officer's report and the speed measuring device certification must be set for hearing to determine the relevance of such requests.

[Adopted effective September 1, 1993.]

CRIMINAL TRAFFIC/CRIMINAL NON–TRAFFIC RULES

LCrRLJ 1. FORMS OF PLEADINGS–STYLE AND FORM–FACILITATING PROOF OF SERVICE AND FILING OF PAPERS/CLERKS ACTION REQUIRED

See LARLJ 2

[Adopted effective September 1, 1993.]

LCrRLJ 6.1. CRIMINAL JURY TRIAL READINESS

In all criminal jury trials a readiness hearing shall be scheduled during the week prior to the scheduled criminal jury trial. The defendant, defense attorney and prosecuting attorney must attend the readiness hearing unless prior to or at that hearing a "Declaration of Readiness for Jury Trial In Lieu of Readiness Hearing" is filed with the court.

The Readiness Hearing is scheduled to determine which matters set for trial, will in fact, go to trial. Dispositions may be presented at the readiness hearing or on the scheduled trial date. After the readiness hearing the following restrictions to the proceedings shall apply:

All Plea Negotiations shall be concluded at or before the readiness hearing. No amendments to the charges will be granted by the court, unless they have be agreed to by the parties prior to or at the readiness hearing.

Continuances on the scheduled trial date will only be granted for good cause.[1]

The Time of Trial shall be extended at or after a case is declared "ready for trial" in case of extraordinary and unforeseeable circumstances only.[2]

[Adopted effective September 1, 2001]

[1] It is the intention of the Court to not extend the time within which the case is to be tried. The Court will vigorously enforce the speedy trial rule, bringing matters to trial as soon after the alleged offense date as is practicable.

[2] These will usually involve injury, illness or death. Vacations, training or other scheduled events shall not be the basis for an extension of the speedy trial time.

LCrRLJ 6.3. CRIMINAL JURY TRIAL

1. **Voir Dire.** The court will obtain from the members of the jury panel answers to a general list of questions touching on their qualifications to serve as jurors. The form of the questionnaire will be adopted and amended by the judges and maintained in the court policy manual to allow updating without requiring a change of local rules. These questions may be supplemented at the request of the Court or the parties.

[Adopted effective September 1, 1993.]

LCrRLJ 6.15. CRIMINAL JURY TRIAL

1. **Jury Instructions.** The court will maintain, in certain types of cases, a standard set of jury instructions which will be given by the court, unless supplemented or supplanted by jury instructions provided by the parties. When the court does not maintain a standard set of jury instructions or either party wishes to supplement or supplant the standard set, the party or parties shall provide copies of said jury instructions to the court not later than the start of the defendant's case, unless the requirement for the instruction(s) was not foreseeable. The parties' proposed instructions shall consist of one original set of jury instructions without citation to Washington Pattern Jury Instructions or case law and one set with citations. A copy of the set with citations shall be served upon opposing counsel at the same time jury instructions are filed with the court.

[Adopted effective September 1, 1993.]

LCrRLJ 8.2A. PROCEDURE FOR SETTING MOTIONS

1. **Pretrial Motions and Post–Trial Motions Filed During the Appeal Period**: All motions shall be in writing and set forth the relief sought. Motions, other than those regarding warrants, should be filed at the pretrial conference whenever possible or as soon as possible thereafter. Where issues arise after the pretrial conference or after disposition, the moving party shall file and serve a written request for docketing of the motion together with the motion and supporting documents stating the general basis for the motion.

2. **Post–Trial Motions After Appeal Period Has Expired**: A request for hearing of any motion after the appeal period has expired will require the defendant or defense attorney to file and serve a written motion and declaration stating the relief requested and the basis therefore and requesting the court to set a hearing on the motion. The court will grant or deny the hearing on the motion within seven (7) days of filing the motion and notify the parties within five (5) days of the decision.

[Adopted effective September 1, 1993; amended effective September 1, 2009.]

LCrRLJ 8.2B. MOTION FOR CONTINUANCE

All motions for continuance shall be in writing and supported by an affidavit substantially in the form of attachment A hereto. The moving party will set forth in the affidavit the following information:

1. Date of arraignment;

2. Date the trial is currently set;

3. Dates of prior continuances and which party requested the same;

4. Reason for this requested continuance, including the date the information upon which this motion is made came to the attention of the moving party;

5. If the request is based on the unavailability of witnesses, include the earliest date the witnesses will be available (whether before or after the current trial date set);

6. Any other facts known to the moving party bearing on questions of due diligence in moving for the continuance or which will assist the court in setting an appropriate date if the continuance is granted.

The non-moving party if in opposition to the motion for continuance, when given five (5) working days notice of the motion, shall file an affidavit setting forth any prejudice their client will suffer if the continuance is granted. Failure to file such an affidavit shall be deemed a waiver of a claim of prejudice by the non-moving party.

[Adopted effective September 1, 1993.]

ATTACHMENT A.   AFFIDAVIT IN SUPPORT OF MOTION TO CONTINUE

In the District Court No. One, Pierce County Washington

State of Washington)
)
)   Affidavit in Support
)   of Motion to Continue
Plaintiff   )
-vs-   )   CASE NO.(s)
)
)
)
Defendant.   )
)

State of Washington   )
            ss.   )
County of Pierce   )

The undersigned, being first duly sworn on oath deposes and says:

1.   Defendant was arraigned   _____

2.   Trial date is currently set for   _____

3.   Prior continuances have been requested by   _____

4.   The reason for the prior request was   _____

5.   The basis for this motion is   _____

6.   Date information basing this motion became available is   _____

7.   If the request is based on the unavailability of witnesses, what is the earliest date the witnesses will be available, whether before or after the current trial date set

     _____

8.   Any other facts known to the moving party bearing on questions of due diligence in moving for the continuance or which will assist the court in setting an appropriate date if the continuance is granted.

     _____

     _____

     _____

     _____

                                 _____

                                 Defendant\Defense Counsel\Prosecut-
                                 ing Attorney

Subscribed and sworn to before me this ___ day of _____, 19___.

                                 _____

Notary Public in and for the State of Washington

residing at _____.

[Adopted effective September 1, 1993.]

LCrRLJ 16. MANDATORY APPEARANCE AND PLEADINGS BY ATTORNEYS

Pursuant to CrRLJ 3 & 4, an attorney may enter an appearance and/or plea of not guilty on behalf of a client in any criminal or traffic offense, if said appearance or plea is made in writing or made in open court UNLESS the defendant is charged with domestic violence, driving while under the influence or physical control.

A person charged with domestic violence, driving while under the influence or physical control shall be required to appear in person before a judicial officer on the earliest practicable day following arrest. The earliest practicable day is defined as:

For persons arrested not posting bail	The next judicial day
For persons arrested posting bail	According to schedule determined by the court
For persons not arrested	Summoned within 15 days from filing of charge

Unless previously commenced by an appearance made in open Court, when a written appearance is authorized it shall commence the running of the time periods established in CrRLJ 3.3 from the date of receipt by the Court. A written appearance, waiving an arraignment, but without plea, shall be considered a plea of not guilty, made in writing, or in open Court, and obviates the need for further arraignment and waives any defects in the complaint other than failure to state a crime. Telephonic requests or notice by defendant or defense counsel shall not constitute an arraignment, appearance or plea, and shall not commence the time periods under CrRLJ 3.3.

[Adopted effective September 1, 1993; amended effective September 1, 2004.]

CIVIL/SMALL CLAIMS RULES

LCRLJ 1. FORMS OF PLEADINGS— STYLE AND FORM—FACILITATING PROOF OF SERVICE AND FILING OF PAPERS/CLERKS ACTION REQUIRED

See LARLJ 2

[Adopted effective September 1, 1993.]

LCRLJ 5. FILING OF PLEADINGS AND OTHER PAPERS

1. Documents Not to Be Filed.

(a) Interrogatories and depositions without written permission of Pierce County District Court No. One, unless necessary for the disposition of a motion or objection;

(b) Unanswered request for admissions, unless necessary for the disposition of a motion or objection;

(c) Photocopies of reported cases, statutes, or texts appendixed to a brief or otherwise, shall not be filed, but may be furnished directly to the Judge hearing the matter; and

(d) Documents or copies thereof which should be received as exhibits rather than part of the court file.

(e) Evidence Rule 904 documents.

[Adopted effective September 1, 1993.]

LCRLJ 10. PRO SE LITIGANTS

In accordance with District Court rules, all pro se defendants must respond to the service of a Summons and Complaint by filing a Pro Se Appearance and Answer in the form of the civil rules or by utilizing the uniform form set forth in these rules. The original of the Pro Se Appearance and Answer shall be filed with the court and a copy served upon the plaintiff or plaintiff's attorney.

[Adopted effective September 1, 1993.]

PRO SE APPEARANCE AND ANSWER

PIERCE COUNTY DISTRICT COURT NO. ONE, PIERCE COUNTY WASHINGTON

	)	
	)	
Plaintiff,	)	NO.
	)	
-vs-	)	PRO SE APPEARANCE AND
	)	ANSWER
	)	
Defendant.	)	
	)	

1. My name is: _____

2. My address is: _____

3. Telephone: Home _____ Work _____

4. I am appearing:

   _____ for myself only

   _____ for myself and _____

   whose address is _____

5. I admit the following paragraph and/or subparagraph numbers of the complaint:

   _____

6. I deny the following paragraph and/or subparagraph numbers of the complaint:

   _____

7. The specific reason(s) I denied the paragraph(s) listed in number six (6) above is/are as follows: _____

   _____

   _____

I have read the above appearance and answer, the statements made are true to the best of my knowledge.

DATE: _____ SIGNATURE _____

[Adopted effective September 1, 1993.]

LCRLJ 14. REMOVAL OF SMALL CLAIM TO CIVIL STATUS

1. Cross Claim or Counter Claims. Defendant or his Counsel may file a Summons and Complaint by paying the $31.00 filing fee, and then move the Court to consolidate the Small Claim action and the Civil action under the District Court number. A date will be set hearing the motion and both parties notified.

2. Other. In a case where there will be no cross-claim or counter claim, the defense counsel shall file a motion asking that the matter be moved to the District Court. If the motion is granted, Defense Counsel must submit, within fourteen (14) days of the granting of the motion, an appearance and answer on behalf of the defendant(s) and pay the $31.00 civil filing fee. The Small Claim action will then be transferred to the Civil docket and will proceed as a Civil case from thereon. If the defendant fails to so file or pay, the order transferring the matter to the District Court Calendar shall be vacated and the matter rescheduled as a small claim.

[Adopted effective September 1, 1993.]

LCRLJ 26. DISCOVERY

1. Depositions of a Party. A party will be entitled to take one (1) deposition of another party without prior permission of the court, and in accordance with Rule 30 of the Superior court Rules.

2. Demand for Damages. A party may demand a specification of damages under RCW 4.28.360.

3. Limited Interrogatories Without Prior Approval of the Court. The following Interrogatories and Requests for Production may be submitted by either party:

A. State the amount of general damages being claimed.

B. State each item of special damages being claimed and the amount thereof.

C. List the name, address and phone number of each person having any knowledge of facts regarding liability.

D. List the name, address and phone number of each person having any knowledge of facts regarding the damages claimed.

E. List the name, address and phone number of each expert you intend to call as a witness at trial. For each expert, state the subject matter on which the expert is expected to testify. State the substance of facts and opinion to which the expert is expected to testify and a summary of the grounds for each opinion.

F. Produce a copy of any insurance agreement under which any person carrying on an insurance business may be liable to satisfy part or all of any judgment which may be entered in this action, or to indemnify or reimburse the payments and to satisfy the judgment.

G. Produce a copy of any agreement or contract or other document upon which this claim is being made.

H. Produce a copy of any bill or estimate for items for which special damages is being claimed.

4. Additional Discovery. No additional discovery shall be allowed, except as the parties may stipulate or as the court may order. The court shall have discretion to decide whether to permit any additional discovery. In exercising such discretion the court shall consider:

A. Whether all parties are represented by counsel;

B. Whether undue expense or delay in bringing the case to trial will result;

C. Whether the interests of justice will be promoted.

5. Conducting Discovery. Any discovery authorized pursuant to this rule shall be conducted in accordance with Civil Rules 26–37.

6. Limitations on Discovery. No blanket orders for unlimited discovery will be permitted.

7. Evidence Deemed Admissible.

A. All provisions of Evidence Rule (ER) 904 are adopted.

B. Subject to the time lines established in ER 904, the written statement of any witness, including the written report of an expert witness, which includes statements of opinion, which the witness would be allowed to express if testifying in person, is deemed admissible if it is made by affidavit or by declaration under penalty of perjury. Any other party may subpoena the author or maker of the written statement admissible under this subsection, at the party's expense, and examine the author or maker as if under cross examination.

[Adopted effective September 1, 1993; amended effective September 1, 2010.]

LCRLJ 38A. CONFIRMATION OF CIVIL JURY TRIAL

Whenever a civil jury trial has been demanded and scheduled, the requesting party shall notify the Civil Department at Pierce County District Court No. One during normal business hours on the Friday or the last working day of the week prior to the date the trial is set and confirm that the jury trial is to remain scheduled.

Failure to do so will be deemed as a waiver of the jury trial demand.

[Adopted effective September 1, 1993.]

LCRLJ 38B. CANCELLATION OF CIVIL JURY TRIAL

Whenever a case set for jury trial is settled or will not be tried, for any reason, the court shall be notified immediately. If notice of cancellation is not received at least 48 hours prior to the scheduled date, the court shall assess costs for the jury panel to the requesting party.

[Adopted effective September 1, 1993.]

LCRLJ 40. CIVIL TRIAL SETTINGS; CONTINUANCES; PRETRIAL SETTLEMENT CONFERENCES

Whenever a Demand for Jury Trial has been filed in a civil case, the case shall be set for mandatory mediation. All attorneys and all parties or persons representing them with authority to consent to settlement shall be present for mediation. In the event of the failure of any person identified above to appear for the mediation, terms may be assessed, at the discretion of the court, for failure to comply and the inconvenience to the opposing party.

[Adopted effective August 15, 2000.]

LCRLJ 41. NON–APPEARANCE OF A PARTY OR PARTIES ON TRIAL DATE

If the plaintiff does not appear within sixty (60) minutes of the time set for trial, and no request for extension of time is received by telephone or otherwise, defendant, upon motion, may be granted a judgment of dismissal without prejudice, be awarded costs and if otherwise authorized, a reasonable attorney's fee, and if a counterclaim, upon satisfactory proof, may be awarded judgment thereon.

If the defendant does not appear within sixty (60) minutes of the time set for trial, the plaintiff, upon motion, may be granted judgment as prayed for, upon satisfactory proof to the court, including costs and if otherwise authorized, a reasonable attorney's fee.

In the event neither party appears at the time set for trial, or within sixty (60) minutes thereafter, the matter shall be dismissed without prejudice, (including counterclaims) on or after the fourteenth (14) day following the scheduled trial date, unless the court has received prior notification of agreed or confessed judgment, settlement, dismissal, or continuance. Notification may initially be oral and/or by telephone, but will not be deemed completed until followed with a clear written statement by the person making such notification. Such written statement shall be filed with the court by 4:30 p.m. on the fifth (5) day following the oral telephonic notification.

[Adopted effective September 1, 1993.]

LCRLJ 54A. GARNISHMENT JUDGMENT ON ANSWER

Judgments on answer of garnishee defendant seeking the addition of costs to the previous judgment balance shall include a judgment balance itemization including key elements. The key elements that are required in the judgment on answer are:

1. Principal amount owed at time garnishment filed;

2. Garnishment filing fee;

3. Attorney's fee;

4. Answer fee;

5. Service fees; and

6. Postage/Certified mail costs.

Proof (in receipt form or affidavit form) must be attached regarding service fees and postage/certified mail costs.

[Adopted effective September 1, 1993.]

LCRLJ 54B. CONDITION PRECEDENT FOR ATTORNEY'S FEES ON DISHONORED CHECKS

Collection and handling charges and reasonable attorneys fees on actions brought to collect dishonored checks shall not be allowed unless proof of the following is provided:

(a) The statutory form of notice of dishonor has been sent as required by RCW Chapter 62.A–3 and a copy is filed with the court.

(b) The original check or a copy of the original check and statement as to the current disposition of the original check is filed with the court.

[Adopted effective September 1, 1993.]

LCRLJ 55. DEFAULT JUDGMENTS

1. All necessary papers required for entry of a default judgment shall be filed at the same time as the motion for default judgment, unless extended by court order to correct a clerical error or omission or for furnishing of any proof required by the court.

2. No default judgment shall be granted except upon proof satisfactory to the court. The court shall require at least the following to be on file with the motion for default judgment, unless otherwise excused by the court for good cause;

a. On assigned causes of action, the assignment instrument;

b. On causes of action based on a negotiable instrument, the original negotiable instrument;

c. On causes of action based on a retail sales contract, chattel mortgage, or conditional sales contract, the original contract (or a copy if the original has been filed with a government agency). Where applicable, an automobile title or bill of sale must be filed;

d. On causes of action based on open account where the complaint is not specific, a written statement of account setting forth all charges and credits and the dates thereof, the nature of merchandise or services furnished, and a statement of any interest or surcharges which are included;

e. On causes of action for rent based on an oral lease, a statement of account similar to that required in actions on open account. If any claim is made for damages or repairs to premises, such claim must be itemized separately;

f. On causes of action for rent based on a written lease, a copy of the lease and a statement of account as in subsection (2)(d) of this Rule;

g. On causes of action based on all other contracts, oral testimony to prove performance may be required, together with filing of a copy of the contract, if written; and filing or proving the items of account and any credits;

h. On causes of action for tort, the proof required shall be the same as required above for proving

contract balances except that the following additional proof of the amount of damage shall be required;

i. Property damage may be proved by repair bills or estimates;

j. Loss of use claims, loss of wages, and pain and suffering shall be proved by oral testimony;

k. Hospital and doctor bills may be proved by written bills, whether paid or not.

3. A sworn affidavit may be substituted in lieu of oral testimony.

4. No judgment for interest shall be allowed unless there is proof on file of the factors necessary for computation of interest including applicable dates, rate of interest, amounts subject to interest, and a computation of the total interest claimed due.

5. Plaintiff shall file a stamped, addressed envelope (with last known address of the defendant) at the time the motion for default judgment is made. The clerk of court shall mail a copy of the judgment to the defendant.

[Adopted effective September 1, 1993.]

INFRACTION RULES

LIRLJ 2.2. FILING OF NOTICE

An infraction is issued on the date the infraction is signed by the citing officer or prosecuting authority. When a Notice of Infraction has been issued, the notice shall be filed with the Court within five days of issuance of the notice, excluding the day of issuance, Saturdays, Sundays and holidays.

When the Notice of Infraction is presented to the Court, the Court clerk shall stamp the citation with the current date and the infraction shall be deemed filed on that date and not the date the infraction is entered into the case management system.

In the absence of good cause shown, a Notice of Infraction not filed within the time limits of the section shall, upon motion, be dismissed with prejudice.

[Adopted effective September 1, 2006.]

LIRLJ 3.5. DECISIONS ON WRITTEN STATEMENTS

Mitigation and contested hearings based on written statements, given under penalty of perjury as provided for in IRLJ 2.4(b)(4) and IRLJ 2.6(c) are authorized. The procedures authorized by IRLJ 3.5 are adopted by this court. To be considered, the written statement(s) must be received by the court pursuant to written instructions provided to the defendant.

[Adopted effective August 15, 2000.]

MUNICIPAL COURTS

BONNEY LAKE MUNICIPAL COURT LOCAL RULES

Including Amendments Received Through
August 15, 2015

Table of Rules

ADMINISTRATIVE RULES

BLMLcR 1.1. SCHEDULE OF FEES

The following shall be the schedule of fees charged for certain official services provided by the Municipal Court. These amounts are consistent with RCW 46.62.060

Duplication of Electronic Records	$ 10.00 per tape/CD
Paper Copy Expenses	$ .15 per page
Certified Copy	$ 5.00 Document
Postage	Actual Cost
Appeals (Preparation & Tapes)	$ 40.00

JIS Data dissemination charges will be set in accordance with the Office of the Administration of the Courts.

[Adopted October 7, 1998; amended effective June 13, 2003; June 3, 2004; September 1, 2008.]

BLMLcR 1.2. JUDGMENT

Any fine, assessment or cost that is not in an even dollar amount shall be amended to a higher amount which produces the next greatest even dollar total. Provided however, this provision shall not apply if the total monetary penalty resulting from any increase shall exceed the maximum possible fines, costs and assessments allowed by law.

[Adopted effective September 1, 2008.]

BLMLcR 1.3. PROBATION [DELETED]

[Adopted October 7, 1998; deleted effective September 1, 2008.]

BLMLcR 1.7. DELEGATING AUTHORITY TO CANCEL WARRANTS AND FTA'S AND RESCIND DELINQUENT CHARGES [DELETED]

[Adopted October 7, 1998; deleted effective September 1, 2008.]

BLMLcR 1.11. NO CONTACT ORDER CONDITIONS OF RELEASE FROM JAIL IN DOMESTIC VIOLENCE CASES [DELETED]

[Adopted October 7, 1998; deleted effective September 1, 2008.]

BLMLcR 1.14. SCHEDULING OF HEARINGS [DELETED]

[Adopted effective July 1, 2003; deleted effective September 1, 2008.]

BLMLcR 1.15. INFRACTION WITNESS FEE [DELETED]

[Adopted effective July 1, 2003; deleted effective September 1, 2008.]

INFRACTION RULES
BLMLcR 2.1. DECISIONS ON WRITTEN STATEMENTS

(a) **Request for Decision on Written Statement.** If the defendant submits a timely request for a hearing to contest or mitigate an infraction, the defendant may elect to seek a decision on written statement pursuant to the provisions of IRLJ 3.5. A defendant who elects to contest or mitigate an infraction by decision on written statement shall be deemed to have waived an in-court hearing to contest or mitigate the infraction in person.

(b) **Time for Submitting Request for Decision on Written Statement.** The request for a decision by written statements shall be submitted no later than fourteen (14) days prior to the date set for the in-court mitigation or contested hearing.

(c) **Declaration for Written Statement Required.** A defendant wishing to proceed by decision on written statement shall provide a written statement which sets forth the facts and/or defense(s) that the defendant would like the court to consider. A written statement submitted pursuant to this rule shall be submitted by declaration as follows: "I declare under penalty of perjury under the laws of the state of Washington that the foregoing is true and correct," and shall be in substantially the following form:

Name of Defendant:

Address:

Infraction Number (upper right corner of citation):

Violation Date:

I wish to mitigate the infraction   [ ]
I wish to contest the infraction   [ ]

Statement:

_____

_____

_____

_____

_____

_____

I declare under penalty of perjury under the laws of the state of Washington that the above information is true and correct.

Executed this ___ day of _____, 20___ at _____ (city/state).

_____
                          Signature

The written statement shall be submitted at the same time as the request for decision on written statement.

(d) Time for Examination, Factual Determination, Disposition and Notice to Parties. The time for examination, factual determination, disposition and notice to parties shall be pursuant to IRLJ 3.5(a)–(d).

(e) No Appeal Permitted. There shall be no appeal from a decision on written statements.

[Adopted effective September 1, 2008.]

BLMLcR 2.2. SPEED MEASURING DEVICE DESIGN AND CONSTRUCTION CERTIFICATION

(a) Any certificate admissible under IRLJ 6.6.(b), and any other document relating to a Speed Measuring Device, can be filed with the clerk of the court and maintained by the court as a public record, and shall be available for inspection by the public. The court shall be entitled to take judicial notice of any document so filed. Documents filed pursuant to this rule shall not be suppressed as evidence merely because there is not a prosecutor present to offer the document as an exhibit at the hearing. If the certificate or document is insufficient, then a motion to suppress the reading of the Speed Measuring Device shall be granted.

(b) Any person who requests production of an electronic speed measuring device expert, and who is thereafter found by the Court to have committed the infraction, shall be required to pay the fee charged by the expert as a cost incurred by that party, as provided in RCW 46.63.151.

[Adopted effective September 1, 2008. Amended effective September 2, 2013.]

BLMLcR 2.3. REQUIREMENTS FOR REQUESTS FOR CONTESTED AND MITIGATION HEARINGS AFTER FAILURE TO RESPOND

(a) If a defendant who has failed to appear or respond to a notice of infraction, as required by RCW 46.61.070 and Rule 2.4 of the Infraction Rules for Courts of Limited Jurisdiction (IRLJ) requests that the court set his/her case for a contested or mitigation hearing, the court clerk shall be authorized to set a date for a contested or mitigation hearing and retrieve pleadings and/or correspondence from the Department of Licensing reflecting the failure to respond or appear, if any was sent, on the following conditions:

(i) The defendant, within one week of the date by which a request for a contested hearing should have been received by the court, delivers to the court an envelope containing his/her request for a contested or mitigation hearing, with a postmark clearly indicating that the envelope was addressed and mailed to the Municipal Court within the time frame for requesting contested or mitigation hearings pursuant to statute and court rule, and with the envelope indicating that it

was returned to the defendant, for whatever reason; or

(ii) The court, within one week of the date by which a request for a contested or mitigation hearing should have been received by the court, receives in the mail an envelope containing the defendant's request for a contested or mitigation hearing, with the envelope showing a postmark clearly indicating that the envelope was mailed to the Municipal Court within the time frame for requesting contested or mitigation hearings pursuant to statute and court rule.

(b) In all other cases, the defendant shall not be entitled to a contested or mitigation hearing, and the disposition of his/her infraction shall be dealt with as provided for in the statute and/or court rule for failures to respond or appear.

[Adopted October 7, 1998; amended effective September 1, 1999; renumbered from BLMLcR 1.10 effective September 1, 2008.]

BLMLcR 2.4. FAILURE TO RESPOND TO NOTICE OF INFRACTION (PARKING)

Notices of Infraction involving parking offenses shall increase $25.00 in penalty after fifteen calendar days from the date of issue. At this point the registered owner of the cited vehicle shall be deemed to have "Failed to Respond" in accordance with RCW 46.63.110 (3). The infraction may be turned over to a collection agency.

[Adopted October 7, 1998; renumbered from paragraph one of BLMLcR 1.8 and amended effective September 1, 2008.]

BLMLcR 2.5. REQUIREMENTS FOR PAYMENT FOLLOWING INFRACTION HEARINGS

(a) If a defendant who has been charged with a traffic or other infraction filed with the Bonney Lake Municipal Court is found to have committed that infraction, the defendant shall make payment in full of the amount of the penalty at the time of the hearing in which the defendant was found to have committed the infraction. The court may reduce a fine penalty amount only upon a showing of exceptional circumstances.

(b) Time payments on infractions will be permitted upon court order, at the time of the hearing on the contested infraction. The court's decision to authorize time payments in infraction cases shall be subject to the conditions set at the time of the order authorizing time payments.

(c) Failure to make payment on the penalties on the committed infractions shall be enforceable pursu-ant to otherwise applicable court rules, state law or administrative code regulations.

[Adopted effective September 1, 2008.]

CRIMINAL RULES

BLMLcR 3.1. OBLIGATION OF DEFENDANTS TO APPEAR IN COURT; CONSEQUENCES OF FAILURE TO APPEAR IN CASES WHERE PUBLIC DEFENDER HAS BEEN APPOINTED

(a) The appointment by this court of a public defender attorney for any defendant deemed to be indigent shall be conditioned on the defendant appearing in court for all hearings where his/her appearance has been required by the court.

(b) If any defendant for whom a public defender has been appointed fails to appear in court when so required without being excused in advance by the court, the order/appointment whereby the public defender was appointed for said defendant may be vacated immediately upon such failure to appear.

(c) Upon such appointment being vacated, the public defender shall be relieved from any requirements to appear in court with such defendant.

(d) The provisions of this Rule, however, do not preclude the defendant from reapplying to the court for the appointment of the public defender to represent him/her.

[Adopted October 7, 1998; renumbered from BLMLcR 1.12 effective September 1, 2008.]

BLMLcR 3.2. WARRANT FOR FAILURE TO APPEAR OR PAY

At the point in time that a warrant is issued for "Failure to Appear" on a criminal citation or "Failure to Pay" on a time payment plan, the bail involved shall be increased in the amount of $100.00.

[Adopted October 7, 1998; renumbered from paragraph two of BLMLcR 1.8 and amended effective September 1, 2008.]

BLMLcR 3.3. QUASHING WARRANTS

The defendant or defendant's attorney may schedule a hearing to quash a warrant, after first non-appearance, either in person or by telephone, but the warrant will not be stayed or quashed, and the defendant will still be subject to arrest on the warrant until the defendant has appeared in open court and the Judge has quashed the warrant.

A hearing to consider the request to quash a warrant will be scheduled as soon as possible and not later than the second regularly scheduled criminal court day following the request.

No warrant will be quashed until the defendant has paid a fee of $100.00 to the clerk.

[Adopted October 7, 1998; renumbered from BLMLcR 1.6 effective September 1, 2008.]

BLMLcR 3.4. VIDEO CONFERENCE PROCEEDINGS

(1) Authorization. Preliminary appearances held pursuant to CrRLJ 3.2.1(d), arraignments held pursuant to CrRLJ 3.4 and 4.1, bail hearings held pursuant to CrRLJ 3.2, and trial settings held pursuant to CrRLJ 3.3(f), may be conducted by video conference in which all participants can simultaneously see, hear and speak with each other. Such proceedings shall be deemed held in open court and in the defendant's presence for the purpose of any statute, court rule or policy. All video conference hearings conducted pursuant to this rule shall be public, and the public shall be able to simultaneously see and hear all participants and speak as permitted by the Bonney Lake Municipal Court judge, judge pro-tem or court commissioner. Any party may request an in-person hearing which may be granted at the discretion of the Municipal Court judge, judge pro-tem or court commissioner.

(2) Agreement. Other trial court proceedings, including the entry of a Statement of Defendant on Plea of Guilty as provided for by CrRLJ 4.2, may be conducted by video conference only by agreement of the parties, either in writing or on the record, and upon the approval of the Bonney Lake Municipal Court judge, judge-pro tem or court commissioner.

(3) Standards for Video Conference Proceedings. The standards for video conference proceedings shall be as specified in CrRLJ 3.4(d)(3).

[Adopted effective September 1, 2008.]

BLMLcR 3.5. ARRAIGNMENT DATE

The arresting officer shall set the defendant's arraignment date and time when issuing a citation in all cases charging a criminal traffic and criminal non-traffic offense. The arraignment date set shall be set no later than 14 days following the next regularly scheduled court date. For citations charging Driving Under the Influence, Driver Under Twenty-one Consuming Alcohol, or Physical Control of Vehicle Under the Influence, as defined in RCW 46.61.502, 503, or 504, all such defendants shall be required to appear at the earliest practicable day following arrest, such date being defined as the first date following arrest when court is in session. Any Domestic Violence offense as defined in RCW 10.99.020 as enacted or hereinafter amended the arraignment date shall be no later than 14 days after the next day on which the court is in session.

[Effective September 1, 1999; amended effective June 28, 2005; renumbered from BLMLcR 1.13 effective September 1, 2008.]

BLMLcR 3.6. MANDATORY APPEARANCE AND PLEADINGS BY ATTORNEYS

Pursuant to CrRLJ 3 & 4, an attorney may enter an appearance and/or plea of not guilty on behalf of a client in any criminal or traffic offense, if said appearance or plea is made in writing unless the defendant is charged with domestic violence, driving while under the influence or physical control if the charge is a second or subsequent charge within a five (5) year time period (DUI and Physical Control) in which instances the defendant must appear personally before the court for arraignment.

Unless previously commenced by an appearance made in open Court, when a written appearance is authorized it shall commence the running of the time periods established in CrRLJ 3.3 from the date of receipt by the Court. A written appearance, waiving an arraignment, but without plea, shall be considered a plea of not guilty, made in writing, or in open court, and obviates the need for further arraignment and waives any defects in the complaint other than failure to state a crime. Telephonic requests or notice by defendant or defense counsel shall not constitute an arraignment, appearance, or plea, and shall not commence the time periods under CrRLJ 3.3.

[Adopted October 7, 1998; renumbered from BLMLcR 1.5 effective September 1, 2008.]

BLMLcR 3.7. SUPPRESSION HEARINGS

A party moving to suppress evidence must file a written motion that sets forth in detail the specific factual and legal grounds for the motion. The court will not conduct a hearing for any motion for which the grounds are not adequately set forth. Motions for a Rule 3.7 hearing may not be included with any other pleadings. The motion must be noted for hearing pursuant to CrRLJ 3.6.

[Adopted October 7, 1998; renumbered from BLMLcR 1.1 and amended effective September 1, 2008.]

BLMLcR 3.8. READINESS TRIAL HEARINGS

A Readiness hearing shall be held before the Municipal Court Judge/Commissioner in every case in which a timely demand for trial by jury is made. At the hearing the City Attorney, the defendant, and the defendant's counsel (if any) must be present. By the Readiness Hearing date all discovery must be completed, and all motions must have been made and completed. Furthermore, parties shall advise the Court if the case can be settled by other than a jury trial. The Readiness Hearing date shall be set no later than five (5) judicial days before the date of trial. The Court will strike the scheduled Jury Trial and may issue a Bench Warrant for any party that does not appear at the Readiness Hearing.

[Adopted October 7, 1998; renumbered from BLMLcR 1.4 and amended effective September 1, 2008.]

BUCKLEY MUNICIPAL COURT—
[No Local Rules]

DUPONT MUNICIPAL COURT—
[No Local Rules]

PUBLISHER'S NOTE

This municipal court follows the Local Court Rules of the Pierce County District Court.

EATONVILLE MUNICIPAL COURT—
[No Local Rules]

FIFE MUNICIPAL COURT LOCAL RULES

Including Amendments Received Through
August 15, 2015

Table of Rules

INTRODUCTION/ADOPTION

These Local Rules have been adopted under the provisions of General Rule 7, (GR 7), promulgated by the Washington State Supreme Court. The numbering used in these Local Rules conforms to the numbering system and format of the Administrative Rules for Courts of Limited Jurisdiction (ARLJ), Criminal Rules for Courts of Limited Jurisdiction (CrRLJ), and Infraction Rules for Courts of Limited Jurisdiction (IRLJ), which are in effect as of the adoption of these Local Rules.

COURTROOM PRACTICE AND PROFESSIONALISM

As a proud member of the legal profession, the Court endorses the following principles of civil–professional–conduct:

1. In dealing with attorneys, parties, witnesses, members of the bench, and court staff; be civil, courteous, and guided by the fundamental tenets of integrity and fairness.

2. Your word is your bond in dealing with the Court, fellow counsel, and others.

3. Endeavor to resolve differences through cooperation and negotiation, giving due consideration to alternative dispute resolution.

4. Honor appointments, commitments, and case schedules. Be timely in all communications.

5. Design the timing, manner of service, and scheduling of hearings only for proper purposes. The objective should never be to oppress or inconvenience the opponent.

6. Conduct yourself professionally during negotiations, depositions, and any other interaction with opposing counsel or a witness as if you were in the presence of a judge.

7. Be forthright and honest in dealing with the Court, opposing counsel, and others.

8. Be respectful of the Court, the legal profession, and the litigation process in attire and demeanor.

9. As an officer of the Court, as an advocate, and as an attorney; uphold the honor and dignity of the Court and of the legal profession. Strive always to instill and encourage a respectful attitude toward the Court, the litigation process, and the legal profession.

[Adopted effective September 1, 2002.]

GENERAL RULES

FMLGR 1. APPLICATION

These Rules apply only to the Fife Municipal Court.

[Adopted effective September 1, 2002.]

FMLGR 2. COURT BUSINESS HOURS/JUDICIAL DAYS

The Fife Municipal Court shall be open to the public for business Monday through Friday from 8:30 a.m. to 4:30 p.m. excluding holidays scheduled by the Washington State Supreme Court and closures ordered by the Presiding Judge when necessitated by union contract, inclement weather, or the oversight of the Court.

Judicial days shall be defined as Tuesday, Wednesday, Thursday, and Friday of each week. The Presiding Judge has the discretion to use Monday of any week as a "judicial day" when necessary in the oversight of the Court.

[Adopted effective September 1, 2002. Amended effective September 1, 2006.]

FMLGR 3. PLEADINGS

Every paper presented to the Judge for signature or delivered to the Court for filing shall be a clearly readable original and shall include: (a) number and title of case, (b) designation of what the paper purports to be, and (c) name, original signature, office address, office telephone number, and WSBA number of counsel.

[Adopted effective September 1, 2002.]

FMLGR 4. JURY INSTRUCTIONS

Where a jury is to be instructed in writing, proposed "non–WPIC" instructions shall be submitted on plain paper with no identifying mark. The original, without citations of authority and one copy with citations of authority shall be submitted to the Court at the Readiness Hearing.

[Adopted effective September 1, 2002.]

FMLGR 17. FACSIMILE TRANSMISSION

(A)(1) Except as set forth in subsection (a)(5) of GR 17, the clerks of the Court may accept for filing documents sent directly to the clerk or to another by electronic facsimile (fax) transmission. The original shall replace a fax copy within five (5) working days. Documents to be transmitted by fax shall bear the notation: "SENT ON (date) VIA FAX FOR FILING IN FIFE MUNICIPAL COURT".

[Adopted effective September 1, 2002.]

ADMINISTRATIVE RULES

FMLAR 1. COMMISSIONERS

(A) The Court may employ judicial officers as commissioners, who shall serve at the pleasure of the Presiding Judge.

(B) Each must be appointed in accordance with RCW 35.20.205 and the Fife Municipal Code as judge pro tempore.

(C) Commissioners may hear infraction cases as provided by the infraction rules for courts of limited jurisdiction and RCW 46.63, or any amendatory law thereof. Commissioners may also perform such other duties as may be assigned by the Presiding Judge.

[Adopted effective September 1, 2002.]

FMLAR 2. SCOPE OF RULES

(A) Operating and administrative policies and procedures of the Fife Municipal court shall be in accordance with these Local Rules adopted pursuant to GR 7, CrRLJ 1.7, and IRLJ 1.3.

(B) In the absence of a rule governing a particular policy or procedure, the Presiding Judge shall resolve the issue pending the establishment of a local rule.

[Adopted effective September 1, 2002.]

FMLAR 5. ADVISORY RULES COMMITTEE

(A) To facilitate regular review of established Local Rules, practices and procedures, and to insure maximum participation, an Advisory Committee shall be established and composed of the following participants: (1) Presiding Judge, (2) Court Administrator, (3) City Attorney, (4) Prosecuting Attorney, (5) Public Defender, and (6) Chief of Police.

(B) The Advisory Committee shall meet annually. The Court Administrator shall facilitate the meetings for the convenience of the Committee. Additional meetings may be called as needed by the Presiding Judge.

(C) The Committee shall evaluate written recommendations for the revision or establishment of Local Rules received by the Court during the preceding year.

(D) The Committee may also consider proposed changes in Court policy and procedure that are not governed by Court Rules.

[Adopted effective September 1, 2002.]

FMLAR 5.1. MISCELLANEOUS PROVISIONS

(A) All requests for Local Rules or rule changes must be submitted in writing on or before May 1st to be considered by the Advisory Committee at the annual meeting.

(B) Immediately following each Advisory Committee meeting, the Presiding Judge shall present the Committee recommendations to the Washington State Supreme Court for appropriate action.

(C) In evaluating any proposed Local Rule, the Presiding Judge shall take into consideration the fiscal impacts of additional services and budget constraints.

[Adopted effective September 1, 2002.]

CRIMINAL RULES

FMLCrR 3.2. RELEASE OF ACCUSED

(D) Delay of Release. (1) Bail shall not be set for a person arrested and booked into jail for violation of RCW 46.61.502, 503, 504, or RCW 46.25.110 unless set by a judge telephonically at the time of arrest or at a preliminary appearance, arraignment, or subsequent court appearance. A person arrested and released for a violation of RCW 46.61.502, 503, 504, or RCW 46.25.110 shall be required to appear before a judge pursuant to RCW 46.61.5051 the next judicial day following the arrest. Appearances are mandatory and may not be waived by the appearance of an attorney . . . (4) Bail shall not be set for a person arrested and booked into jail for a domestic violence offense unless set by a judge telephonically at the time of arrest or at a preliminary appearance, arraignment, or subsequent court appearance. In matters where a person is arrested and released for a domestic violence offense prior to appearing before a judge for arraignment, bail hearing, or any other hearing where conditions of release may be set; there shall be a *No Contact Order* imposed as a condition of release from custody prohibiting the arrested person from having any contact with the alleged victim involved in the incident and from having any contact with the alleged victim's residence, place of employment, or any other place where the alleged victim may be found or believed to be. Said *No Contact Order* shall remain effective until the next judicial day when the arrested, cited, and released person shall be required to appear before a judge OR fourteen (14) days if the arrested person is released, but not cited. Appearances are mandatory and may not be waived by the appearance of an attorney. "*Domestic Violence*" includes, but is not limited to, any misdemeanor or gross misdemeanor offenses listed in RCW 10.99.020(3) or similar municipal ordinance when committed by one family or household member against another. "*Family or household members*" are those persons listed in RCW 10.99.020(1) or similar municipal ordinance . . . (5) Bail as set forth in this Rule or any similar rule or order shall be available to those accused that have provided sufficient information to establish a positive and verifiable identity and home address. Absent such information, no bail may be accepted until established by the Court.

(K) Forfeiture. No forfeiture of bail shall be allowed except in those matters designated herein as forfeitable offenses. Provided, that in extraordinary cases the Court shall have discretion to permit forfeiture for offenses designated as nonforfeitable. In any such case, the prosecuting authority shall be permitted an opportunity to resist such forfeiture, if desired. The Court may at any time, for good cause shown, order a mandatory hearing for violations designated as forfeitable offenses.

(M) Bail. When required to reasonably assure appearance in court, the Court shall follow the bail schedule set forth in the *Fife Municipal Court Uniform Bail Schedule*, as may be amended, modified, and filed periodically by the Court for use by the Fife Police Department.

[Adopted effective September 1, 2002. Amended effective September 1, 2006.]

FMLCrR 4.2. PLEAS

(I) Deferred Prosecution. A written petition shall be filed at the time the defendant moves the Court to grant a deferred prosecution under RCW 10.05 and an order approving the deferred prosecution. A copy of the documents required by this rule will be made available upon request. Said documents may be submitted in the original form provided by the Court or may be reprinted and submitted in substantially the same form. All substantive revisions to these forms must be made known to the Court at the hearing when presented.

[Adopted effective September 1, 2002.]

FMLCrR 4.5. PRETRIAL HEARINGS

(A) Pretrial. When a plea of "not guilty" is entered, the Court shall schedule a pretrial hearing. The prosecuting authority, the defendant, and the defendant's attorney (if any) shall attend the pretrial hearing. Failure of the defendant to appear may result in the issuance of a bench warrant.

(B) Readiness Hearing. A readiness hearing shall be set prior to the trial date. All parties mentioned above shall appear unless waived in the pretrial order. Failure of the defendant to appear when required shall cause the trial date to be stricken and the issuance of a bench warrant.

(C) Telephonic Communications. Pretrial hearings may be conducted by telephonic conference call at the request of either party once approved by the Court.

[Adopted effective September 1, 2002.]

FMLCrR 6.1.1. TRIAL BY JURY

(E) Any case confirmed for jury trial at the readiness hearing shall remain set for a jury trial. On the last regular court day preceding the trial date, the prosecuting authority and defense attorney or defendant, if appearing pro se, shall confirm the jury trial telephonically to the clerk of the court before 3 p.m., or advise that some other disposition has been reached. Failure to confirm the jury trial as required shall be deemed a waiver of the right to a jury trial, cause the jury to be stricken, and the matter set before the bench. If the failure to confirm the jury trial is on behalf of the defendant and the defendant requests that the case be reset before a jury, then the defendant is deemed to have extended the time for trial to the date next scheduled for jury trial.

(F) Any case confirmed as a jury trial and not proceeding to a jury trial, whether by entry of a plea or otherwise, shall be subject to terms, including costs for the unused jury, witness fees, and other terms deemed appropriate by the Court.

[Adopted effective September 1, 2002; amended effective June 1, 2003.]

INFRACTION RULES

FMLIR 2.6. SCHEDULING OF HEARINGS

(A)(1)(i) A Respondent who requests a contested hearing may first be scheduled for a prehearing status conference, which shall be scheduled in accordance with the provisions of IRLJ 2.6(a)(1)(i).

(ii) The prehearing status conference may waived in accordance with the provisions of IRLJ 2.6(a)(1)(ii). However, if a Respondent requires certain witnesses to appear, the pretrial status conference may not be waived in order to issue the subpoenas and handle other scheduling matters. If the Respondent fails to timely waive or appear at the prehearing status conference, then a default judgment shall be entered.

[Adopted effective June 1, 2003; amended effective September 1, 2011.]

FMLIR 3.3. PROCEDURE AT CONTESTED HEARING

(B)(1) At a contested hearing, the plaintiff shall be represented by the prosecuting authority in those matters that the respondent is represented by an attorney or the plaintiff's witnesses have been subpoenaed for the hearing. The respondent may be represented by an attorney.

(2) No attorney shall appear for a respondent without first filing a Notice of Appearance no less than seven (7) days prior to any scheduled hearing. Upon the filing of a Notice of Appearance, the Court shall schedule the contested hearing on a date available to both parties.

[Adopted effective September 1, 2002.]

FMLIR 3.5. DECISION ON WRITTEN STATEMENT

(A) Generally. The Court shall examine the citing officer's report and any statement submitted by the respondent. The examination shall take place within 120 days after the respondent has filed a response to the notice of infraction. The examination may be held in chambers and shall not be governed by the Rules of Evidence.

(B) Factual Determination. The Court shall determine whether the plaintiff has proved by a preponderance of all evidence submitted that the respondent has committed the infraction if contested.

(C) Disposition. If the Court determines that the infraction has been committed, it may assess a penalty in accordance with IRLJ 3.3. If the Court defers a finding for a specified period of time on certain conditions, it may assess an administrative fee to process the infraction notice.

(D) Notice to Parties. The Court shall notify the parties in writing whether the infraction was found to be committed, deferred, or dismissed and what penalty or administrative fee, if any, was imposed.

(E) No Appeal Permitted. There shall be no appeal from a decision made upon written statements.

[Adopted effective September 1, 2002.]

LOCAL RULES, CITY OF FIRCREST MUNICIPAL COURT

Effective September 1, 2002

Including Amendments Received Through
August 15, 2015

Table of Rules

ADMINISTRATIVE RULES

LAR 1.1. JUDICIAL DAYS DEFINED

Regular judicial days shall be Mondays, Wednesday and Friday of every week, Holidays and Court Holidays excepted. In the event of holidays or other preemption, Court may be held the next weekday. Court sessions shall be at such times and places, as the Court may deem necessary for its proper administration.

[Adopted effective September 1, 2002.]

GENERAL RULES

LGR 2.1. REQUIREMENTS FOR TIME PAYMENTS [REPEALED]

[Repealed effective September 1, 2004.]

LGR 2.2. DELEGATING AUTHORITY TO QUASH WARRANTS AND FTA'S, AND RESCIND DELINQUENT CHARGES [REPEALED]

[Repealed effective September 1, 2004.]

INFRACTION RULES

LIRLJ 3.1. CONTESTED HEARINGS— PRELIMINARY

(a)(1) *Speed Measuring Device Expert*: A request for a Speed Measuring Device expert may be treated by the Court as a request for a continuance to the next date on which the prosecuting attorney has scheduled the appearance of the SMD Expert.

(2) *Costs and Witness Fees.* Each party is responsible for costs incurred by that party as set forth in RCW 46.63.151. In cases where a party requests a witness to be subpoenaed, the party requesting the witness shall pay the witness fees and mileage expenses due that witness.

[Amended effective September 1, 2003.]

LIRLJ 3.1(a). CONTESTED HEARINGS— COSTS AND WITNESS FEES

(a) Costs and Witness Fees. Each party is responsible for costs incurred by that party as set forth in RCW 46.63.151. In cases where a party requests a witness to be subpoenaed, the party requesting the witness shall pay the witness fees and mileage expenses due that witness.

[Adopted effective September 1, 2003.]

LIRLJ 3.5. DECISIONS ON WRITTEN STATEMENTS

Mitigation and contested hearings on alleged traffic infractions may be held upon written statements pursuant to IRLJ 2.4(b)(4), IRLJ 2.6(c) and IRLJ 3.5.

[Adopted effective September 1, 2003.]

LIRLJ 6.6(d). SPEED MEASURING DEVICE: DESIGN AND CONSTRUCTION CERTIFICATION

Any person who requests production of an electronic speed measuring device (SMD) expert, and who is thereafter found by the Court to have committed the infraction, may be required to pay the fee charged by the expert as a cost incurred by that party, as provided in RCW 46.63.151.

[Adopted effective September 1, 2002.]

CRIMINAL RULES

LCrRLJ 3.2.2. MANDATORY APPEARANCES

A defendant who is arrested for an offense involving driving while under the influence as defined in RCW 46.61.502, driving under twenty-one after consuming alcohol as defined in RCW 46.61.503, or being in physical control of a vehicle while under the influence as defined in RCW 46.61.504, shall be required to appear in person before a judge/commissioner on the Wednesday following arrest if the defendant is served with a citation or complaint at the time of the arrest. The following Wednesday shall be deemed the earliest practicable judicial day for the hearing. Appearances are mandatory and may not be waived. The requirements of the RCW 46.61.50571 shall be imposed at the hearing.

[Adopted effective September 1, 2002.]

LCrRLJ 4.5. READINESS TRIAL HEARINGS

A Readiness Hearing shall be held before the Municipal Court Judge in every case in which a timely demand for jury is made. Notice shall be given in open Court by the Judge to all parties indicating the date and time for this hearing. At the hearing the city attorney, defendant and the defendant's counsel (if any) must be present. By the Readiness Hearing date all discovery must be completed and all motions must have been timely filed. Furthermore, parties shall advise the Court if the case can be settled by other than a jury trial. The Readiness Hearing date shall be set no later than ten (10) judicial days before

the date of trial. The Court will strike the scheduled Jury Trial and may issue a Bench Warrant for any party that does not appear at the Readiness Hearing.

[Adopted effective September 1, 2002.]

LCrRLJ 8.2. WRITTEN MOTIONS AND BRIEFS

Written motions and briefs other than those for continuances, shall be filed with the Court and served on the opposing party not less than ten (10) judicial days before trial. Responses thereto shall be filed and served not less than five (5) judicial days before the hearing date. Motions shall be heard on Wednesdays at 9:00am in open Court, and not later than five (5) judicial days before trial.

Failure to comply with this rule may result in the Court's refusal to hear such motion or in the imposition of terms, both to the adverse party or parties and to the City of Fircrest for the expense caused by resulting delays.

[Adopted effective September 1, 2002.]

LCrRLJ 9(c)(5). DEFERRED PROSECUTION

(c) Quasi-Public Documents. The following are not subject to public review, but are subject to review by the defendant and the defendant's lawyer:

(5) *Deferred Prosecution*—the evaluation, and recommendation of chemical dependency agency, status reports from chemical dependency agency.

[Adopted effective September 1, 2002.]

GIG HARBOR MUNICIPAL COURT LOCAL RULES

Including Amendments Received Through
August 15, 2015

Table of Rules

PRE–TRIAL CONFERENCE RULE

1. Mandatory. A pre-trial conference shall be mandatory in all cases for which a jury trial is requested.

2. Permissive. A pre-trial conference may be requested by either party in any other case set for trial.

3. Purpose. At the pre-trial conference, the following issues shall be addressed:

a. List of trial witnesses shall be provided by each party to the other and the court at or before the pre-trial conference.

b. At or before the pre-trial conference, the defendant shall provide the City Prosecutor with a list of all witnesses (with address and phone numbers) requested to be subpoenaed by the court for trial.

c. At least three (3) days before the pre-trial conference, all motions to limit or exclude evidence shall be filed. If a motion is expected to take 10 minutes or less per side, it shall be heard at the pre-trial conference. If a motion will take longer or if oral testimony is required, it will be specially set by the court at the pre-trial conference. Motions not heard nor scheduled at or before the pre-trial conference may be heard at a later date, if good cause is shown, at the discretion of the judge.

d. At least three (3) days before the pre-trial conference, the defendant shall make all requests of the City Prosecutor for pre-trial discovery. The court shall set a date for compliance with all such requests. Requests for discovery not made at or before the pre-trial conference may be made at a later date, if good cause is shown, at the discretion of the judge.

e. A trial date will be set. Generally jury trials will be set to begin at 9 a.m.

4. Setting. The pre-trial conference will be set to be heard approximately one (1) month after appearance or arraignment, and generally will be heard at 1:30 p.m. on the regular court calendar.

5. Defendant's Appearance Mandatory. The defendant shall personally appear at the pre-trial conference with his/her attorney unless specifically excused by the court in advance thereof. If the defendant fails to appear for the pre-trial conference, a bench warrant may be issued for his arrest and, if set, the trial and/or jury will be stricken by the clerk.

6. Confirmation of Jury Trial Required. The defendant and prosecutor shall each contact the court clerk 72 hours prior to a scheduled jury trial to confirm, or jury panel shall be stricken automatically by the clerk.

7. Supersedes. The Pre-trial Conference Rule dated September 15, 1991, is hereby superseded.

8. Effective Date. This rule shall be effective September 1, 1993.

[Adopted effective September 1, 1993.]

LAKEWOOD MUNICIPAL COURT LOCAL RULES

Including Amendments Received Through
August 15, 2015

Table of Rules

CHAPTER I.   GENERAL RULES

LMCLR GR1.1.   SCOPE

These rules govern the procedures in the Municipal Court of the Cities of Lakewood, University Place, DuPont and the Town of Steilacoom in all proceedings, and supplemented in light of the common law and the decisional law of these jurisdictions. These rules shall not be construed to affect or derogate from the constitutional rights of any party.

[Formerly LMCLR 1.1, adopted effective June 28, 2002. Amended effective September 1, 2010. Renumbered LMCLR GR 1.1 and amended effective September 1, 2012. Amended effective September 1, 2015.]

LMCLR GR1.2.   PURPOSE AND CONSTRUCTION

These rules are intended to provide for the just determination of every proceeding. They shall be construed to secure simplicity in procedure, fairness in administration, effective justice, and the elimination of unjustifiable expense and delay.

These rules are not intended to supersede or conflict with any statutes covering procedures for criminal and infraction violations or the Criminal Rules for Courts of Limited Jurisdiction (CrRLJ), or the Infraction Rules for Courts of Limited Jurisdiction (IRLJ).

[Formerly LMCLR 1.2, adopted effective June 28, 2002; amended effective September 1, 2010; renumbered LMCLR GR 1.2 and amended effective September 1, 2012.]

LMCLR GR1.3.   EFFECT

Except as otherwise provided elsewhere in these rules, on their effective date:

1) Any acts done before the effective date in any proceedings then pending or any action taken in any

proceeding pending under rules of procedure in effect prior to the effective date of these rules are not impaired by these rules.

2) These rules also apply to any proceedings in court then pending or thereafter commenced regardless of when the proceedings were commenced, except to the extent that in the opinion of the court, the former procedures should continue to be made applicable in a particular case in the interest of justice or because of infeasibility of application of the procedures of these rules.

[Formerly LMCLR 1.3, adopted effective June 28, 2002; renumbered LMCLR GR 1.3 and amended effective September 1, 2012.]

LMCLR GR1.4.   DEFINITIONS

As used in these rules, unless the context clearly requires otherwise:

1) "Earliest practicable day" means the next regularly scheduled court calendar.

2) "Next business day" means the next day the court is open for business.

[Formerly LMCLR 1.4, adopted effective June 28, 2002; renumbered LMCLR GR 1.4 and amended effective September 1, 2012.]

LMCLR GR1.5.   SCHEDULE OF FEES

The following shall be the schedule of fees charged for certain services provided by the Municipal Court. These amounts are consistent with RCW 3.62.060.

Duplication of Electronic Records $10.00/tape or CD

Paper Copy/Fax Expenses $.50/each page

Certified Copy $5.00/document

Postage actual cost

Civil Filing Fee—as set by Pierce County District Court

Copy of DOL Abstract of Driving Record—as set by RCW 46.52.130

JIS Data Dissemination charges will be set in accordance with the Administrative Office of the Courts.

[Formerly LMCLR 8.2, adopted on an emergency basis effective March 3, 2010. Amended effective September 1, 2010. Superseded and recreated effective September 1, 2011. Renumbered LMCLR GR 1.5 and amended effective September 1, 2012. Amended effective September 2, 2013.]

LMCLR GR1.6.   WAIVER OF ACCOUNT BALANCES

1) Delinquent account balances under $10.00 on adjudicated cases where all other conditions of sentencing have been satisfied may be waived administratively and closed on a case-by-case basis.

2) Any case for which jurisdiction has expired, and the only remaining condition of sentence is to pay an account balance that has been in collections for ten years or more, and the account has been deemed uncollectible, the remaining balance may be waived administratively and closed. A docket entry will be made on each case reflecting the above for audit purposes, and the case will be closed.

[Formerly LMCLR 8.3, adopted effective June 28, 2002. Amended effective September 1, 2006; September 1, 2008; renumbered LMCLR GR 1.6 and amended effective September 1, 2012.]

CHAPTER II.   CRIMINAL RULES

LMCLR CR2.2.   WARRANT RECALL PROCEDURES

1) If a defendant has not failed to appear for a prior hearing, the defendant may appear within 2 working days by 5 pm and reset their hearing. Prior to resetting the hearing the defendant will complete a Personal Recognizance form and then be given a copy of the form with the next court appearance date noted.

2) If a defendant has failed to appear for a prior hearing, and the warrant ordered by the Judge is for a bondable amount for less than $5000, the defendant may post a $100 non-refundable warrant fee to have the warrant recalled by the clerk. The defendant shall complete a Personal Recognizance form, and be given a copy of the form with the next court appearance date noted, as well as a copy of the recalled warrant (if it has been printed).

3) A defendant may post the entire bail/bond amount with the clerk to have the warrant recalled. The defendant shall complete a Personal Recogni-

zance form, and be given a copy of the form with the next court appearance date noted, as well as a copy of the recalled warrant (if it has been printed).

4) A defendant may schedule a Motion to Recall Warrant hearing. The defendant shall complete a Motion to Recall Warrant form, and will be given a copy of the form with the next court appearance date noted. The warrant shall remain active until the motion to recall has been granted.

5) If a No Contact Order has been filed and approved by the Court, but not previously served on a defendant, the Order will be served on the defendant along with the Personal Recognizance form or notice of Motion to Recall Warrant hearing. If the defendant refuses to accept service of a No Contact Order, the warrant shall be served on the defendant.

[Formerly LMCLR 3.4, adopted effective June 28, 2002. Amended effective September 1, 2008; renumbered LMCLR CR 2.2 and amended effective September 1, 2012. Amended effective September 2, 2014; September 1, 2015.]

LMCLR CR3.2(n).　BAIL OR BOND PROCEDURES

1) Upon receipt of bail or bond for a case where charges are pending review and filing by the Prosecutor, the court shall create a case in JIS and hold the bail or bond for 30 days. If no formal charges have been filed by the Prosecutor in that time, then the bail will be returned to the payee, and/or a notice of exoneration will be mailed to the bonding agency that posted the bond.

2) When a case is dismissed or sentence imposed, any financial obligations for fines, penalties and/or costs on the case shall be deducted from bail posted by the defendant, and the remainder shall be returned to the defendant, unless the bail has already been forfeited subject to RCW 10.19.140.

3) If cash bail was posted subsequent to the issuance of a bench warrant, the court shall deduct a $100 warrant fee prior to refunding the bail. This rule shall also apply if a person other than the defendant posted the bail.

4) If bail or bond has been processed for forfeiture, and the judge has ordered the forfeited bail returned to the payee, per RCW 10.19.140 the court shall deduct a $100 warrant fee and applicable booking fee prior to the return of the bail or bond forfeiture.

[Formerly LMCLR 3.11, adopted effective September 1, 2005; amended effective September 1, 2010; renumbered LMCLR CR 3.2(n) and amended effective September 1, 2012. Amended effective September 2, 2014.]

LMCLR CR3.2(o).　BAIL FOR NEW DOMESTIC VIOLENCE OFFENSES

Subject to constitutional limitations and CrRLJ 3.2.1, a person who has been booked into jail for domestic violence as defined in RCW 10.99.020, shall be detained until they have appeared before a judge.

[Formerly LMLCLR 3.2, adopted effective June 28, 2002; renumbered LMCLR CR 3.2(o) and amended effective September 1, 2012. Amended effective September 2, 2014.]

LMCLR CR4.1.　ARRAIGNMENTS AND CONTINUANCES OF ALL MATTERS OTHER THAN ARRAIGNMENT

1) **Arraignment**: A lawyer may, pursuant to CrRLJ 4.1(d), enter an appearance on behalf of a client, except in cases in which the docket or charging document states that one or more of the charges involves DUI, Physical Control, any Domestic Violence charge, including, but not limited to Assault 4th DV, Malicious Mischief DV, Harassment, Violation of an Antiharassment/No Contact Order, Stalking or Harassment, whereupon the defendant's presence is mandatory and cannot be waived. Pursuant to RCW 46.61.50571, the Presiding Judge may waive the appearance of a defendant arrested under RCW 46.61.502, 503 and 504 from the next judicial day to the next regularly scheduled arraignment calendar.

2) Unless otherwise noted for motion, all requests to continue pretrial hearings, motions, trial dates and/or other final dispositions will require an Agreed Order signed by both parties. The signed Agreed Order for Continuance is to be filed no less than four working days before the scheduled hearing and will be either approved or denied by the Judge. If an Agreed Order of Continuance is filed less than four working days before the scheduled hearing, the prosecutor or defense is required to file the Order in open Court for the Judge's approval or denial.

[Formerly LMCLR 4.1, adopted effective June 28, 2002; amended effective September 1, 2004; renumbered LMCLR CR 4.1 and amended effective September 1, 2012.]

LMCLR CR4.2(i).　DEFERRED PROSECUTION [RESCINDED]

[Formerly LMCLR 3.6, adopted effective June 28, 2002; renumbered LMCLR CR 4.2(i) and amended effective September 1, 2012. Rescinded effective September 2, 2014.]

LMCLR CR4.5.　PRE–TRIAL HEARINGS

1) Unless otherwise ordered by the court in a specific case for good cause, all cases in which a defendant enters a plea of not guilty shall be set for a pretrial hearing.

2) The court shall assign dates and give written notice to the parties for future motion hearings and trial at the time of the pre-trial conference and shall, in so far as is reasonably possible, schedule those hearings in consultation with both parties. Other factors, such as witness availability, shall also be considered.

3)(a) A jury call/readiness hearing will be scheduled in all cases proceeding to trial unless specifically waived by the court in a particular case for good cause shown. This calendar will be held during the week approximately 1 week prior to the scheduled trial or as otherwise set by the court. The defendant shall be required to attend this hearing unless excused by the court. Failure to attend the jury call/readiness hearing may result in the issuance of a bench warrant and/or forfeiture of bond/bail.

(b) At the conclusion of the readiness hearing, the court will no longer accept any plea bargaining arrangements. Therefore, the case will be tried by jury unless waived by the defendant, or concluded by a guilty plea to the original charge(s), or a dismissal of the charge(s). When a defendant enters a plea to an offense as charged after having confirmed for jury trial at the readiness hearing, the court shall assess jury costs.

[Formerly LMCLR 4.3, adopted effective June 28, 2002; amended effective September 1, 2010; renumbered LMCLR CR 4.5 and amended effective September 1, 2012. Amended effective September 2, 2014.]

LMCLR CR4.7. DISCOVERY—ASSIGNED COUNSEL [RESCINDED]

[Rescinded effective September 1, 2015.]

LMCLR CR6.4. VOIR DIRE [RESCINDED]

[Formerly LMCLR 5.2, adopted effective June 28, 2002; renumbered LMCLR CR 6.4 and amended effective September 1, 2012. Rescinded effective September 2, 2014.]

LMCLR CR6.13. EVIDENCE—COURT'S CUSTODY OF EXHIBITS

In a criminal case every exhibit in the court's custody, which is not contraband and for which ownership is not in dispute, shall be returned to the party who produced that exhibit upon motion of that party and expiration of the appeal period. In the event of finding of guilty, for purpose of this rule, the appeal period shall begin on the day of sentencing or deferral of sentencing by the court. Exhibits not withdrawn shall be delivered by the court to the Lakewood Police Department for disposition as abandoned property, or if contraband, for destruction. The court shall release no exhibit without its being receipted for by the receiving person.

[Formerly LMCLR 5.1, adopted effective June 28, 2002; renumbered LMCLR CR 6.13 and amended effective September 1, 2012.]

LMCLR CR7.2(a). RESTITUTION

Where the court orders that a defendant pay restitution but does not set an amount at the time of disposition, a restitution hearing may be scheduled. The prosecuting attorney shall file a restitution order with supporting documentation at the time of the hearing. If the Prosecutor does not file a restitution order at the time of the hearing, the matter of restitution shall be deemed waived unless otherwise authorized by the court. If the defendant does not object, the proposed amount shall be entered as a judgment. Payment of restitution shall be made through the clerk of the court unless otherwise ordered by the court.

[Formerly LMCLR 6.1, adopted effective June 28, 2002. Amended effective September 1, 2008; renumbered LMCLR CR 7.2(a) and amended effective September 1, 2012. Amended effective September 1, 2015.]

LMCLR CR7.2(b). PAYMENT ARRANGEMENTS

For indigent defendants on Active Supervised Probation—the Court may authorize conversion of community service hours in lieu of an outstanding Probation fee. Credit will be given for up to $50. Hours are determined per LMCLR CR7.2(c).

[Formerly LMCLR 6.3, adopted effective June 28, 2002. Renumbered LMCLR CR 7.2(b) and amended effective September 1, 2012. Amended effective September 2, 2013; September 2, 2014; September 1, 2015.]

LMCLR CR7.2(c). COMMUNITY SERVICE

The court may allow a defendant to complete community service at a non-profit organization in lieu of monetary payments in appropriate cases. Unless otherwise ordered by the court, community service hours are credited at the most recent minimum wage amount used by the State of Washington, rounded off to the nearest dollar per hour worked toward any fine balances.

[Formerly LMCLR 6.4, adopted effective June 28, 2002; amended effective September 1, 2010; renumbered LMCLR CR 7.2(c) and amended effective September 1, 2012.]

LMCLR CR7.6. PROBATION DEPARTMENT SERVICES AND PROCEDURE

The role of the Municipal Court Probation Department is to assist the court in the management of criminal justice and thereby aid in the preservation of public order and safety. Pursuant to ARLJ 11, the Probation Officer shall perform the following duties and follow the following procedures:

1) Conduct pre/post-sentence investigations with face to face interviews and extensive research that may include but is not limited to: criminal history, contact with victims, personal history, social and economic needs, community resource needs, counseling/treatment needs, work history, family and employer support, and complete written pre/post-sentence reports which include sentencing recommendations to the court.

2) Probation Officer shall communicate with community agencies providing services required of offenders with input to the judicial officer regarding the following areas: alcohol/drug, domestic violence, sexual deviancy, and mental illness.

3) In addition to the duties mentioned above, the Probation Officer is also required to perform records checks on active probation clients, notify the court of violations or special circumstances through written reports and direct communication with court personnel, attend calendar proceedings as needed, and participate in accounting of fees.

6)[1] This rule is based upon the provisions of ARLJ 11.

[Formerly LMCLR 6.5, adopted effective September 1, 2006; amended effective September 1, 2010; renumbered LMCLR CR 7.6 and amended effective September 1, 2012. Amended effective September 1, 2015.]

[1] So in original.

LMCLR CR8.2. CRIMINAL MOTION PROCEDURES

1) **Purpose:** This rule governs criminal motion practice.

2) **Filings of Motions. Memoranda and Affidavits General.** The moving party shall file with the court

14 days prior to the motion hearing date the following: The motion being noted, all supporting affidavits and documentary evidence and a brief memorandum of authorities. Unless a court rule, statute or briefing schedule provides a different timeframe for a response, the responding party may file a response to the issue of law, or any counter-affidavits, briefs or memoranda of authorities no later than five (5) days before the hearing. The responding party may also file any pleading to which the motion is directed. Failure to timely comply with these filing requirements may result in a continuance or the motion being stricken from the calendar.

3) Length of Memoranda. Memoranda relating to motions shall not exceed fifteen (15) pages. Waiver of page limitations may be granted only upon motion demonstrating good cause which may be heard ex parte.

4) Copies of Motions, Memoranda and Affidavits. A copy of the motion, brief, memorandum, documents and affidavit shall be furnished to the Clerk at the time of filings for delivery to the assigned Judge for preparation. Responding briefs, memoranda and other documents shall be filed with copies provided for the preparation of the assigned Judge.

5) Motion Hearing Procedures. Oral argument on motions shall be limited to ten (10) minutes for each side unless the Judge determines otherwise.

6) The Motion hearing shall proceed upon the pleadings and any submitted police reports. If, at the time of the hearing, the City elects to provide supplementation or the court finds that additional information is necessary to adequately decide the issues presented by the moving party, a testimonial hearing shall be set. Prior to the testimonial hearing, the court should advise the parties of the issues that remain for consideration. The purpose of this rule is to efficiently and effectively resolve pre-trial issues and to focus the costs of testimonial hearings to cases that warrant it.

[Formerly LMCLR 4.4, adopted effective June 28, 2002; amended effective September 1, 2008; September 1, 2010; renumbered LMCLR CR 8.2 and amended effective September 1, 2012.]

CHAPTER III.   INFRACTION RULES

LMCLR IR2.6(a)(1). CONTINUANCES OF INFRACTION PROCEEDINGS

A motion for a continuance in a scheduled contested or mitigation hearing must be made in writing and filed 7 days prior to the date of the hearing. The motion shall show good cause for continuance. The Clerk is authorized to grant a timely request for a continuance, unless (a) the defendant has previously sought a continuance; (b) failed to appear for a hearing; or (c) the defendant has either requested that witnesses be present or witnesses have been subpoenaed. Any other requests for a continuance shall be considered by the judge, who may render a decision ex-parte.

[Formerly LMCLR 10.15, adopted effective September 1, 2010; renumbered LMCLR IR 2.6(a)(1) and amended effective September 1, 2012. Amended effective September 2, 2014.]

LMCLR IR3.1(a). PROCEDURE AT CONTESTED HEARINGS— SUBPOENAS

1) A subpoena may be obtained pursuant to IRLJ 3.1(a).

2) Subpoenas for Police Officers—Alternative Procedure. Subpoenas may be requested and served as provided by state law and court rules. In the alternative, defendants in contested infraction cases may serve subpoenas upon officers who issued the citation in the following manner:

(a) A subpoena may be requested and obtained from the court clerk;

(b) The defendant, or his/her attorney or agent, may effectuate service of the subpoena upon the officer by serving the subpoena upon an employee of the Legal Department of the City Attorney's Office in that office at least seven days before the scheduled contested hearing;

(c) The City Attorney's Office shall date-stamp the subpoena, provide a stamped copy to the person serving the subpoena, and transmit the original subpoena to the officer at the Police Department.

3) This rule is not intended to supersede or conflict with any statutes concerning procedures for infractions or the Infraction Rules for Courts of Limited Jurisdiction (IRLJ).

[Formerly LMCLR 10.1, adopted effective June 28, 2002; amended effective September 1, 2010; renumbered LMCLR IR 3.1(a) and amended effective September 1, 2012.]

LMCLR IR3.1(b). DISCOVERY REQUESTS FOR INFRACTIONS

1) Discovery requests regarding infractions that are pending hearing shall be governed by IRLJ 3.1(b).

2) All discovery requests must have the following information: Complete name of defendant, Case number and mailing address of defendant.

3) No motion to dismiss for failure to comply with IRLJ 3.1 shall be entertained absent proof of service

of such discovery request upon the opposing party on-file with the court, in conformity with CRLJ 5(b).

[Formerly LMCLR 10.5, adopted effective June 28, 2002; amended effective September 1, 2009; renumbered LMCLR IR 3.1(b) and amended effective September 1, 2012.]

LMCLR IR3.1(e). CONTESTED HEARINGS—PRELIMINARY MOTIONS

Motions challenging the authority of the Court, the constitutionality of the Court, the constitutionality of any statute, ordinance or court rule pertaining to an infraction, the authority of the prosecuting attorney prosecuting an infraction, and/or the authority of the law enforcement agency or officer filing an infraction must be made in writing. Such motions, together with citations to authority and argument, must be filed with the Court and served upon the opposing party no later than fourteen days prior to a contested infraction hearing. Such motions may be decided by the Court with or without oral argument, as the Court may determine.

[Formerly LMCLR 10.16, adopted effective September 1, 2010; renumbered LMCLR IR 3.1(e) and amended effective September 1, 2012.]

LMCLR IR3.2(b). FAILURE TO APPEAR

If a defendant appears within 48 hours of a failure to appear (FTA) on a regularly scheduled contested or mitigation hearing, has not previously failed to appear, and the plaintiff has not been prejudiced by the FTA, the FTA will be set aside and reset for the same hearing type pursuant to IRLJ 3.2 (b) and CRLJ 60 (b).

[Adopted effective September 1, 2012. Amended effective September 2, 2014.]

LMCLR IR3.3. DEFERRED FINDINGS ON INFRACTIONS

Upon entry of a deferred finding for an infraction, the court will monitor the infraction for a period of six months from the date of entry to determine compliance with the conditions set by the court. If a defendant successfully complies with the conditions after the six month period, the charge(s) will be dismissed as agreed.

If a defendant fails to pay the agreed costs within the time limit allowed by the court, fails to establish an account with Signal Management Services, or fails to complete the payment plan within the time allowed, a finding of committed will be entered for the charge(s), and collection will proceed.

If a defendant obtains a new moving violation during the first six months of jurisdiction, the court shall extend jurisdiction over the deferral to one year total. During the additional time period, the court shall monitor the new moving violation(s) and determine whether or not a committed finding has been entered.

If a committed finding is entered for the new moving violation(s), per RCW 46.63.070(5) the deferral will be revoked and the charge(s) found committed. If the new moving violation(s) is dismissed or found not committed, then the deferral will be monitored by the court until the end of the jurisdiction, which shall be no less than six months from the date of entry of the deferral.

The court will not consider a request for deferred findings under RCW 46.63.070(5) for the following violations:

RCW 46.61.440 Speeding in a School Zone
RCW 46.61.527 Speeding in a Construction Zone,
RCW 46.61.212 Emergency Zone Violations, or
RCW 46.61.370 Passing Stopped School Bus.

Defendants with a CDL (Commercial Driver's License) or who operated a commercial vehicle at the time of the violation are not eligible to enter into a Deferred Finding.

[Formerly LMCLR 10.11, adopted effective September 1, 2005. Renumbered LMCLR IR 3.3 and amended effective September 1, 2012. Amended effective September 2, 2013.]

LMCLR IR3.5. WRITTEN STATEMENT

This Court adopts IRLJ 3.5 regarding decision on written statements for infractions.

[Formerly LMCLR 10.7, adopted effective June 28, 2002; renumbered LMCLR IR 3.5 and amended effective September 1, 2012.]

LMCLR IR3.6(a). DISABLED PARKING

If a person charged with parking in a disabled parking space without proper parking placard or license plate has a valid disabled parking placard or disabled person's license plate at the time of citation, the defendant may present such proof to the court along with proper picture identification. Upon confirmation with Department of Licensing that the placard is valid, the charge will be dismissed.

[Formerly LMCLR 10.8, adopted effective June 28, 2002; renumbered LMCLR IR 3.6(a) and amended effective September 1, 2012.]

LMCLR IR3.6(b). MANDATORY LIABILITY INSURANCE

1) If a person charged with a violation of RCW 46.30.020, driving a motor vehicle without having proof of valid insurance, presents to the court clerk within 15 days of the violation, or prior to a scheduled mitigation or contested hearing evidence that they had in effect at the time of the infraction liability insurance as required by RCW 46.30.020, then, upon payment of twenty-five dollars ($25), the case shall be dismissed and the court clerk shall be authorized to make appropriate notation of the dismissal in the court file.

2) If a person charged with a violation of RCW 46.30.020, driving a motor vehicle without having proof of valid insurance, provides proof to the court clerk

within 15 days of the violation, or prior to a scheduled mitigation or contested hearing that they subsequently obtained liability insurance in conformity with the requirements of RCW 46.30.020, then the penalty shall be reduced to one hundred and fifty dollars ($150), and the clerk shall be authorized to enter a finding that the infraction was committed and make appropriate notations in the court record. The person will be relieved of any further need to appear in court in connection with this charge on the infraction.

3) If a person charged with a violation of RCW 46.30.020, driving a motor vehicle without having proof of valid insurance, provides proof during a scheduled mitigation or contested hearing that they subsequently obtained liability insurance in conformity with the requirements of RCW 46.30.020, then the penalty shall be reduced to two hundred dollars ($200). Alternately, the Judge may authorize the defendant a definite period of time to file proof of insurance with the court to reduce the fine to two hundred dollars ($200).

[Formerly LMCLR 10.10, adopted effective September 1, 2003; amended effective September 1, 2005; September 1, 2007; renumbered LMCLR IR 3.6(b) and amended effective September 1, 2012. Amended effective September 2, 2014.]

LMCLR IR3.6(c). EXPIRED VEHICLE REGISTRATION

If a person who has been cited with a violation of RCW 46.16A.030.5 provides proof to the court clerk within 14 days from the date of violation, or prior to any scheduled mitigation or contested hearing that the vehicle registration was valid at the time of the violation, and that person has had no previous violations of RCW 46.16.010, then the case shall be dismissed with no costs.

If a person charged with the violation of RCW 46.16A.030.5.L (Expired Vehicle Registration Less than Two Months) is able to acquire valid registration and provide proof to the court within 14 days from the date of violation, or prior to any scheduled mitigation or contested hearing, then the penalty shall be reduced to one hundred dollars ($100) and a finding of committed entered.

If a person is charged with the violation of RCW 46.16A.030.5.O (Expired Vehicle Registration Over Two Months) is able to acquire valid registration and provide proof to the court within 14 days from the date of violation, or prior to any scheduled mitigation or contested hearing, then the penalty shall be reduced to one hundred fifty dollars ($150) and a finding of committed entered.

[Formerly LMCLR 10.13, adopted effective September 1, 2009; renumbered LMCLR IR 3.6(c) and amended effective September 1, 2012.]

LMCLR IR3.6(d). NVOL WITH ID

If a person charged with violation of RCW 46.20.015 for No Valid Operator's License with Valid Identification (NVOL with ID) is able to acquire a valid operator's license and provide proof to the court within 14 days from the date of violation, or prior to a scheduled mitigation or contested hearing, then the penalty shall be reduced to one hundred fifty dollars ($150).

[Formerly LMCLR 3.9, adopted effective June 28, 2002. Amended effective September 1, 2004; September 1, 2006; September 1, 2007. Renumbered LMCLR IR 3.6(d) and amended effective September 1, 2012. Amended effective September 1, 2015.]

LMCLR IR3.6(e). MOTOR VEHICLE EQUIPMENT VIOLATIONS

If a person charged with a defective motor vehicle equipment violation presents to the court clerk, prior to any hearing, proof of repairs to the vehicle to correct the defect, the clerk may reduce the fine to one hundred dollars ($100).

[Adopted effective September 1, 2012.]

LMCLR IR6.2(b). MONETARY PENALTY FOR UNSCHEDULED INFRACTIONS

Infractions resulting from automated traffic safety cameras will not exceed $450 pursuant to Chapter 167, Laws of 2005.

[Formerly LMCLR 10.12, adopted effective September 1, 2005. Amended effective September 1, 2007; September 1, 2008; September 1, 2010. Renumbered LMCLR IR 6.2(b) and amended effective September 1, 2012. Amended effective September 1, 2015.]

CHAPTER IV.   APPEALS TO MUNICIPAL COURT

LMCLR AR1.1.   APPEALS

Purpose: Certain statutes and ordinances vest the Municipal Court with the authority to hear appeals. This Rule sets forth the procedure for hearing and decision regarding such appeals. This Rule is intended to provide for the expeditious consideration of timely filed notices of appeal.

1) **Timeliness.** The appeal must be filed with the Court and a copy filed with the City Attorney within the timeframe set forth by statute or municipal code

and accompanied by any applicable filing fee. An untimely appeal shall be dismissed summarily.

2) In addition to any other requirements imposed by applicable statutes or municipal code, the notice of appeal should (1) be titled "Notice of Appeal" (2) identify the party or parties appealing (3) designate each decision which the party wants reviewed (4) provide the name, address and telephone number of the appealing party or their lawyer. If the decision for which review is sought is in writing, that decision should be attached to the notice of appeal.

3) Upon receipt of a properly filed notice of appeal, the Court will set the matter for hearing on an available.[1] Documents, photographs, affidavits, and other offers of proof may be submitted if they are filed with the Court and served on the opposing party no less than five days before the appeal hearing. The provisions of ER 904 shall also apply. Upon a showing of good cause, the Court may set over the hearing.

4) The Court may make an oral ruling at the close of oral argument, or may take the matter under advisement. If the matter is taken under advisement, the Court will issue a written decision or set the matter for further hearing within 30 days.

5) **Applicability of State Rules.** To the extent not inconsistent with law, the Civil Rules for Courts of Limited Jurisdiction (CRLJ) shall apply to hearings under these rules. In addition, the provisions of Superior Court Civil Rule (CR) 16 shall apply.

6) **Monetary Judgment.** Where authorized by law, the Court will award monetary recoveries and costs upon timely application of a prevailing party. The parties shall note at the hearing whether they intend to seek a monetary recovery, and as part of its decision, the Court will make a determination whether such recoveries are allowed. In the event that such recoveries are awarded, and the prevailing party certifies that such recoveries have not been paid, the Court will certify the monetary award for enforcement as a civil judgment in accordance with RCW 3.66.020(10).

[Formerly LMCLR 10.14, adopted effective September 1, 2008; amended effective September 1, 2010; renumbered LMCLR AR 1.1 and amended effective September 1, 2012. Amended effective September 2, 2014.]

1 So in original.

MILTON MUNICIPAL COURT RULES

Including Amendments Received Through
August 15, 2015

Table of Rules

ADOPTION OF CITY OF MILTON COURT RULES

Pursuant to CrRLJ 1.7, GR 7, and {House Bill 2205, as enacted by the Washington State Legislature} the undersigned Judge of the above-mentioned court hereby adopts and requests official publication of the following Milton Municipal Court Local Rules.

Done this 20th day of June, 2003; amended effective September 1, 2008.

Sandra L. Allen

Presiding Judge

ADMINISTRATIVE RULES

LAR 1.1. JUDICIAL DAYS DEFINED

Regular judicial days shall be Tuesday of every week, Holidays and Court Holidays excepted.

In the event of holidays or other preemption, Court may be held the next scheduled Court day. Court sessions shall be at such times and places, as the Court may deem necessary for its proper administration.

[Adopted effective September 1, 2003; amended effective September 1, 2008.]

GENERAL RULES

LGR 2.2. DELEGATING AUTHORITY TO ADJUDICATE FTA'S, AND RESCHEDULE TIME PAY AGREEMENTS

In addition to the Judge the following Court personnel are hereby granted authority to allow the rescheduling of time payments and to adjudicate FTA's reported to the department of Licensing:

- Deputy Court Administrator
- Court Clerk
- Part-time Court Clerk

[Adopted effective September 1, 2003; amended effective September 1, 2008.]

INFRACTION RULES

LIRLJ 2.4(b)(4). MITIGATION AND CONTESTED HEARINGS BASED ON WRITTEN STATEMENTS

Submitting a written statement either contesting the infraction or explaining mitigating circumstances is authorized by local court rule. The statement shall contain the person's promise to pay the monetary penalty authorized by law if the infraction is found to be committed. The statement shall be sworn under penalty of perjury in compliance with RCW 9A.72.085.

[Adopted effective September 1, 2003.]

LIRLJ 2.6(c). SCHEDULING HEARINGS ON DECISIONS OF WRITTEN STATEMENTS

Decisions on Written Statements. The court has adopted a local rule authorizing decisions on written statements, and it shall, upon receipt of a statement pursuant to IRLJ 2.4(b)(4) and IRLJ 2.6(c), consider the case in accordance with IRLJ 3.5. The court is not required to notify the parties of a date for the examination of the statements.

[Adopted effective September 1, 2003.]

LIRLJ 3.5. DECISION ON WRITTEN STATEMENTS

Mitigation and Contested hearings based on written statements, given under penalty of perjury as provided for in IRLJ 2.4(b)(4) and IRLJ 2.6(c) are authorized. The procedures authorized by IRLJ 3.5 are adopted by this court. To be considered, the written statement(s) must be received by the court pursuant to written instructions provided to the Defendant.

[Adopted effective September 1, 2003.]

LIRLJ 6.6(d). SPEED MEASURING DEVICE: DESIGN AND CONSTRUCTION CERTIFICATION

Any person who requests production of an electronic speed measuring device (SMD) expert, and who is thereafter found by the Court to have committed the infraction, shall be required to pay the fee charged by the expert as a cost incurred by that party, as provided in RCW 46.63.151.

[Adopted effective September 1, 2003.]

CRIMINAL RULES

LCrRLJ 3.1. RIGHT TO AND ASSIGNMENT OF COUNSEL

1) **Types of Proceedings.** The right to a lawyer shall extend to all criminal proceedings for offenses punishable by loss of liberty.

2) **Explaining the Availability of a Lawyer.** When a person has been arrested he or she shall as soon as practical be advised of the right to a lawyer. The Milton Police Department shall allow a person in custody access to a telephone and the current contracted public defender's number if they choose to consult with an attorney.

3) **Assignment of Lawyer.** Unless waived, a lawyer shall be provided to any person who is financially unable to obtain one without causing substantial hardship to the person or to the person's family. The court will consult the current poverty guidelines as provided by RCW 10.101 to determine eligibility.

4) **Withdrawal of Lawyer.** When a case has been set for trial, no lawyer shall be allowed to withdraw, except upon consent of the court for good cause shown and upon substitution of another lawyer or upon the defendant's knowing and voluntary decision to proceed without a lawyer.

Upon completion of a case, a signed order deferring prosecution, or a Stipulated Order of Continuance, the lawyer shall be allowed to withdraw without consent of the court.

[Adopted effective September 1, 2003; amended effective September 1, 2008.]

LCrRLJ 3.2.2. MANDATORY APPEARANCES

A defendant who is arrested for an offense involving driving while under the influence as defined in RCW 46.61.502, driving under twenty-one after consuming alcohol as defined in RCW 46.61.503, or being in physical control of a vehicle while under the influence as defined in RCW 46.61.504, shall be required to appear in person before a judge on the Tuesday following arrest if the defendant is served with a citation or complaint at the time of the arrest. The following Tuesday shall be deemed the earliest practicable judicial day for the hearing.

Appearances are mandatory and may not be waived. The requirements of the RCW 46.61.50571 shall be imposed at the hearing.

A defendant who is arrested for an offense involving domestic violence as defined under RCW 10.99.020 shall be required to appear in person before a judge on the date indicated on the citation or complaint. Appearances are mandatory and may not be waived.

[Adopted effective September 1, 2003; amended effective September 1, 2008.]

LCrRLJ 3.3. MOTION FOR CONTINUANCE

All motions for continuance shall be in writing and supported by an affidavit containing the following information:

1. Date of Arraignment;

2. Dates that current hearings are scheduled;

3. Dates of prior continuances and which party requested the same; and

4. Reason for this requested continuance, including the date, which the information, which this motion is came to the attention of the moving party.

[Adopted effective September 1, 2008.]

LCrRLJ 4.2. COMMITMENT OF DEFENDANTS TO JAIL

Commitment procedures enumerated herein are consistent with statutory provisions contained in RCW Title 10. This Court Order further defines the intent of the Municipal Court Judge wherein case law or judicial discretion might determine an appropriate case disposition.

DEFENDANTS COMMITTED TO SERVE JAIL TIME ONLY:

Jail time imposed may be ordered consecutive to other jail time imposed within the discretion of the Judge. Costs of commitment may be imposed as authorized by statute.

[Adopted effective September 1, 2003.]

LCrRLJ 4.3. WARRANT RECALL PROCEDURES

1. If a defendant has not failed to appear for any prior hearing the defendant may appear within two (2) working days of their prior hearing date and reset their hearing.

2. After the warrant has been issued:

First Warrant:

Upon written Motion of the Defendant a Warrant Hearing will be scheduled. The Warrant will remain outstanding pending the hearing.

Second Warrant:

Upon payment of a $100.00 Warrant Fee and upon the written Motion of the Defendant a Warrant Hearing will be scheduled. The Warrant will remain outstanding pending the hearing.

Third/Subsequent Warrants:

Defendant will be taken into custody and held on the warrant pending hearing or posting of bail.

[Adopted effective September 1, 2008.]

LCrRLJ 4.5. READINESS TRIAL HEARINGS

A Readiness Hearing shall be held before the Municipal Court Judge in every case in which a timely demand for jury is made. Notice shall be given in open Court by the Judge to all parties indicating the date and time for this hearing. At the hearing the city prosecutor, defendant and the defendant's counsel (if any) must be present. By the Readiness Hearing date all discovery must be completed and all motions must have been timely filed. Furthermore, parties shall advise the Court if the case can be settled by other than a jury trial. The Readiness Hearing date shall be set no later than ten (10) judicial days before the date of trial. The Court will strike the scheduled Jury Trial and may issue a Bench Warrant for any defendant that does not appear at the Readiness Hearing.

After the readiness hearing the following restrictions to the proceedings shall apply:

All Plea Negotiations shall be concluded at or before the readiness hearing. The court will grant no amendments to the charges or plea bargains after the readiness hearing. Therefore, after readiness the case will be tried by a jury, unless waived by the defendant, or concluded by a guilty plea to the original charge, or dismissal of the charge(s).

Continuances on the scheduled trial date will only be granted for good cause.

[Adopted effective September 1, 2003; amended effective September 1, 2008.]

LCrRLJ 8.2. WRITTEN MOTIONS AND BRIEFS

Written motions and briefs other than those for continuances shall be filed with the Court and served on the opposing party not less than fourteen (14) days before the motion date. Responses thereto shall be filed and served not less than seven (7) days before the hearing date. Motions shall be heard on Tuesdays at the time prescribed in open Court, and not later than seven (7) days before trial.

Failure to comply with this rule may result in the Court's refusal to hear such motion or in the imposition of terms, both to the adverse party or parties and to the City of Milton for the expense caused by resulting delays.

[Adopted effective September 1, 2003; amended effective September 1, 2008.]

LCrRLJ 9.0. DEFERRED PROSECUTION

Quasi–Public Documents. The following are not subject to public review, but are subject to review by the defendant and the defendant's lawyer:

Petition for deferred prosecution, statement of defendant for deferred prosecution, order granting deferred prosecution, evaluation, and recommendation of chemical dependency agency, status reports from chemical dependency agency.

[Adopted effective September 1, 2003; amended effective September 1, 2008.]

ORTING MUNICIPAL COURT LOCAL RULES

Including Amendments Received Through
August 15, 2015

Table of Rules

PURPOSE, SCOPE, AND CONSTRUCTION

OMCLR 1.1. ADOPTION OF LOCAL RULES

THESE RULES ARE ADOPTED PURSUANT TO GR 7, CrLJ 1.7, AND IRLJ 1.3. The effective date of these rules shall be September 1st, 2011.

[Adopted effective September 1, 2011.]

OMCLR 1.2. TITLE OF RULES

These rules may be known and cited as Orting Municipal Court Local Rules and shall be referred to as OMCLR.

[Adopted effective September 1, 2011.]

OMCLR 1.3. EFFECT OF LOCAL RULES

The provisions of the Local Rules are supplemental to the Rules for Courts of Limited Jurisdiction as adopted or hereafter amended by the Supreme Court of the State of Washington and shall not be construed in conflict with them.

[Adopted effective September 1, 2011.]

OMCLR 1.4. RESERVATION OF DISCRETION

The Orting Municipal Court reserves the authority to interpret and/or suspend or modify these rules in individual cases on motion of a party for good cause or on a motion of the Court in the interest of justice and/or the efficient operation of the Court.

[Adopted effective September 1, 2011.]

OMCLR 1.5. JUDICIAL DAY

As used in these rules, unless the context clearly requires otherwise, "Judicial Day" when not otherwise defined by statute or court rule, means every first and third Tuesday of the calendar month, or another date determined by the Judge upon which the regular sessions of the Court are set.

[Adopted effective September 1, 2011.]

OMCLR 1.6. NEXT JUDICIAL DAY

The requirement of RCW 46.61.50571 that defendants arrested for driving while under the influence, driving under age twenty-one after consuming alcohol, or being in physical control of a vehicle while under the influence appear in court within one judicial day is waived. All such defendants shall be required to appear at the earliest practicable day following arrest, such date being defined as the first date following arrest when court is in session.

[Adopted effective September 1, 2011.]

OMCLR 1.7. SCHEDULE OF FEES

The following shall be the schedule for fees charged for certain official services provided by the Municipal Court. These fees are consistent with RCW 3.62.060:

Duplication of Electronic Records	$10.00 per CD
Paper Copy Expenses	$0.50 per page
Certified Copy	$5.00 per document
Postage	Actual Cost
Appeal (preparation)	$40.00
Appeals (CD)	$10.00 per CD

[Adopted effective September 1, 2011.]

LOCAL CRIMINAL RULES

OMCLR 2.1. QUASHING WARRANTS

(A) The defendant or defendant's attorney may schedule a hearing to quash a warrant, either in person or by telephone, but the warrant will not be stayed or quashed and the defendant will still be subject to arrest on the warrant until the defendant has appeared in open court and the Judge has quashed the warrant.

(B) A hearing to consider the request to quash a warrant will be scheduled not later than the next regularly scheduled Judicial Day following the request. However, a defendant or defendant's attorney may stay or quash a warrant, or request a hearing later than the next regularly scheduled Judicial Day, by paying an administrative fee of $100.00 to the Court

(C) In any case wherein Bond or Bail has been posted to ensure the defendant's appearance and the said Bond or Bail has been ordered forfeited by the Court, no warrant shall be stayed or quashed except by the appearance of the defendant before the Court or surrender of the defendant to jail.

[Adopted effective September 1, 2011.]

OMCLR 2.2. DELEGATING AUTHORITY TO CANCEL WARRANTS AND FTA'S

In addition to the Judge, the Court Administrator and Court Clerk are hereby granted authority to allow the rescheduling of time payments and to cancel arrest warrants.

[Adopted effective September 1, 2011.]

OMCLR 2.3. EXONERATION OR FORFEITURE OF POSTED BAIL OR BOND

(A) When a bench warrant has been issued, if there has been any Bail or Bond posted by or for the benefit of the defendant, then that Bail or Bond shall be forfeited without any further order of the Court. If cash Bail was posted subsequent to the issuance of a bench warrant, the court clerk is authorized to deduct a warrant fee prior to refunding Bail.

(B) When a case has been dismissed or sentence has been imposed, then any Bail or Bond posted for the defendant shall be returned to the individual who posted the Bail or Bond unless the Bail or Bond has already been forfeited subject to RCW 10.19.140.

[Adopted effective September 1, 2011.]

OMCLR 2.4. BAIL FORFEITURES FOR SPECIFIC CRIMES [REPEALED]

[Repealed effective September 1, 2011.]

OMCLR 2.5. WRITTEN MOTIONS AND BRIEFS

Written motions and briefs other than those for continuances shall be filed with the Court and served on the opposing party not less than fourteen (14) days before the motion date. Responses thereto shall be filed and served not less than seven (7) days before the hearing date. Motions shall be heard on Tuesdays at the time prescribed in open Court.

Failure to comply with this rule may result in the Court's refusal to hear such motion or in the imposition of terms, both to the adverse party or parties and to the City of Orting for the expense caused by resulting delays.

[Adopted effective September 1, 2011.]

OMCLR 2.6. QUASI–PUBLIC DOCUMENTS

The following are not subject to public review, but are subject to review by the defendant and the defendant's lawyer:

Petitions for deferred prosecution; statements of defendant for deferred prosecution; orders granting deferred prosecution; evaluations; recommendations from chemical dependency agencies; and status reports from chemical dependency agency.

[Adopted effective September 1, 2011.]

INFRACTION LOCAL RULES

OMCLR 3.1. MANDATORY INSURANCE

(A)[1] If a person who has been cited with the violation of RCW 46.30.20 presents to the court administrator/court clerk evidence that the person had in effect at the time of violation liability insurance as required by statute, then, upon payment of $25.00 for administrative costs, the case shall be dismissed and the court clerk shall be authorized to make appropriate notations of dismissal in the court file.

[Adopted effective September 1, 2011.]

  1 The rule contained no subsec. (B).

OMCLR 3.2. EXPIRED VEHICLE LICENSE [REPEALED]

[Repealed effective September 1, 2011.]

OMCLR 3.3. REQUIREMENTS FOR REQUESTING A HEARING AFTER FAILURE TO RESPOND OR APPEAR

(A) If a defendant who has failed to appear or respond to a notice of infraction on not more than one occasion requests that the Court set/reset his/her case for a hearing, the court clerk shall be authorized to set a date for such requested hearing and retrieve/recall FTA's from the Department of Licensing reflecting the failure to respond or appear, if any were sent, on the following conditions:

(1) The defendant within 30 days of the date by which a request for hearing should have been received by the Court, delivers to the Court an envelope containing his/her request for a hearing, with a postmark indicating that the envelope was addressed and mailed to the court within the time frame for requesting a hearing, and with the envelope indicating that it was returned to the defendant, for whatever reason; or,

(2) The court within 30 days of the date by which a request for hearing should have been received by the defendant's request for a hearing, with the envelope showing a postmark indicating that the envelope was mailed to the Court within the time frame for requesting a hearing.

(B) In those cases where a defendant has failed to appear or respond through his/her own neglect, and less than 60 days has elapsed since the court should have received the request for a hearing or the date of the hearing, the defendant may request a hearing and such hearing shall be scheduled upon payment of an administrative fee of $25.00. If the failure to appear/respond was reported to the Department of Licensing, the Defendant shall pay the appropriate failure to appear/respond fee in addition to the administrative fee to remove the FTA from Department of Licensing records.

(C) In all other cases, the defendant may file a motion in writing requesting that said judgment be set aside with a payment of the applicable failure to respond or appear fee and a $25.00 administrative fee. Upon receipt of the written request for hearing and payment of the applicable fees, the clerk of the court shall set or reset a hearing for the defendant and shall recall/retrieve FTA's from the Department of Licensing reflecting the failure to respond/appear, if any was sent.

[Adopted effective September 1, 2011.]

OMCLR 3.4. DECISION ON WRITTEN OR ELECTRONICALLY FILED STATEMENTS

(A) Request for Decision on Written or Electronically Filed Statement. If the defendant submits a timely request for a hearing to contest or mitigate an infraction, the defendant may elect to seek a decision on written or electronically filed statement pursuant to IRLJ 3.5. A person who elects to contest or mitigate an infraction by decision on written or electronically filed statement shall be deemed to have waived an in-court hearing to contest or mitigate the infraction in person.

(B) Time for Submitting Request for Decision on Written or Electronically Filed Statement. The request for a decision by written or electronically filed statements shall be submitted not less than five days prior to the date set for the in-court hearing.

(C) Declaration for Written or Electronically Filed Statement Required. A defendant wishing to proceed by decision on written or electronically filed statement shall provide a written statement which sets forth the facts and/or defense(s) that the defendant would like the Court to consider. A written or electronically filed statement submitted pursuant to this rule shall be submitted by declaration in substantially the following form:

NAME OF DEFENDANT:

ADDRESS:

PHONE NUMBER:

INFRACTION NUMBER:

VIOLATION DATE:

I wish to mitigate/contest the infraction.

STATEMENT:

"I declare under the penalty of perjury under the laws of the State of Washington that the foregoing is true and correct,"

I promise that if it is determined that I committed the infraction for which I was cited or costs are assessed, I will pay the monetary penalty and/or costs authorized by law and assessed by the court.

Executed this (day) of (month), (year), at (place)

Signature or electronic ID number (as provided by the Court)

(D) Factual Determination. The Court shall determine whether the plaintiff has proved by a preponderance of all evidence submitted that the respondent has committed the infraction if contested.

(E) Disposition. If the Court determines that the infraction has been committed, it may assess a penalty in accordance with IRLJ 3.3. If the court defers a finding for a specified period of time on certain conditions, it may assess an administrative fee to process the infraction notice.

(F) Notice to Parties. The Court shall notify the parties in writing whether the infraction was found to be committed, deferred, or dismissed and what penalty or administrative fee, if any, was imposed.

(G) No Appeal Permitted. There shall be no appeal from a decision made upon written or electronically filed statements.

[Adopted effective September 1, 2011.]

OMCLR 3.5. SPEED MEASURING DEVICE

(A) Speed Measuring Device. Any certificate admissible under IRLJ 6.6(b), and any other document relating to a Speed Measuring Device, can be filed with the court and maintained by the court as a public record, an shall be available for inspection by the public. Copies shall be provided by the clerk's office on request. There shall be no charge for the copy if it relates to an infraction filed against the person making the request. Otherwise, there shall be a charge for each page copied. These records shall be available without a formal request for discovery. The court shall be entitled to take judicial notice of the fact that any document filed pursuant to this rule has been filed with the court. Documents filed pursuant to this rule shall not be suppressed as evidence merely because there is not a prosecutor present to offer the document as an exhibit at the hearing. If the certificate or document is insufficient, then a motion to suppress the reading of the Speed Measuring Device can be granted [1]

(B) Request for Speed Measuring Device Expert. In the absence of proof of a request to produce an electronic speed measuring device (SMD) expert, a certificate in substantially the form provided under CrRLJ 6.13, IRLJ 6.6 is admissible in lieu of an expert witness in any court proceeding in which the design and construction of an electronic speed measuring device (SMD) is in issue.

(C) The request for an SMD expert under IRLJ 6.6 must be served on the prosecuting authority and filed with the clerk of the court at least 30 days prior to the hearing.

(D) The request to provide a speed measuring device expert cannot be combined with a Notice of Appearance or any other Pleading. Each party is responsible for costs incurred by that party as set forth in RCW 46.63.151. In cases where a party requests a witness to be subpoenaed, the party requesting the witness shall pay the witness fees and mileage expenses due to that witness.

(E) Any person who requests production of an electronic speed measuring device (SMD) expert, and who is thereafter found by the Court to have committed the infraction, may be required to pay the fee charged by the expert as a cost incurred by that party, as provided in RCW 46.63.151.

(F) The Court may allow the speed measuring device expert to testify from a location other than the courtroom via speaker phone or other electronic means acceptable to the court.

[Adopted effective September 1, 2011.]

1 Punctuation so in original.

PUYALLUP MUNICIPAL COURT LOCAL RULES

Including Amendments Received Through
August 15, 2015

Table of Rules

---

1. PURPOSE, SCOPE AND CONSTRUCTION

PUMCLR 1.1. ADOPTION

These rules are adopted pursuant to CrRlJ 1.7 and GR 7 and supersede any and all Local Court Rules heretofore adopted by the Puyallup Municipal Court.
[Adopted effective September 1, 2002.]

PUMCLR 1.2. TITLE OF RULES

These rules may be known and cited as Puyallup Municipal Court Local Rules, and shall be referred to as PUMCLR.
[Adopted effective September 1, 2002.]

PUMCLR 1.3. EFFECT OF LOCAL RULES

The provisions of the Local Rules are supplemental to the Rules for the Courts of Limited Jurisdiction, as adopted or hereafter amended by the Supreme Court of the State of Washington, and shall not be construed in conflict with them.

[Adopted effective September 1, 2002.]

PUMCLR 1.4. RESERVATION OF DISCRETION

The Puyallup Municipal Court reserves the authority to interpret and/or suspend or modify these rules in individual cases on motion of a party for good cause or on a motion of the Court in the interest of justice and/or the efficient operation of the Court.

[Adopted effective September 1, 2002.]

3. RIGHTS OF DEFENDANT

PUMCLR 3.1. ARRAIGNMENT DATE

The arresting officer shall set the defendant's arraignment date and time when issuing a citation in all cases charging a criminal traffic and criminal non-traffic offense. The arraignment date set shall be the next regularly scheduled arraignment date, except as provided below. For citations charging Driving Under the Influence, Driver Under Twenty-one Consuming Alcohol, or Physical Control of Vehicle under the Influence, as defined in R.C.W. 46.61.502, 503 or 504, or any Domestic Violence offense as defined in R.C.W. 10.99.020 as enacted or hereinafter amended, the arraignment date shall be the next regularly scheduled Court session.
[Adopted effective September 1, 2002.]

PUMCLR 3.2. RELEASE OF ACCUSED

(*o*) **Bail in Criminal Offense Cases—Mandatory Appearance.**

(1) **Bail Schedule**: When required to reasonably assure appearance in court for those persons arrested and detained in jail for new offenses, bail shall be set in accordance with the bail schedule approved by the presiding judge.

(2) **Hold Pending Appearance Before A Judge— Domestic Violence Offenses:** The bail schedule approved by the presiding judge shall require that a person subjected to custodial arrest for a Domestic Violence offense as defined in RCW 10.99.020 shall be held in custody in a non-bail status pending appearance before a judge at the next regularly scheduled in-custody. Court session following booking and shall be issued a Pre–Arraignment No Contact Order prohibit- ing the arrested person from having contact with the protected person or persons.

[Adopted effective September 1, 2009.]

PUMCLR 3.3. VIDEO CONFERENCE HEARINGS

For in custody defendants, hearings will be held by video conference as provided for in CrRLJ 3.4(d). For purposes of CrRLJ 3.4(d)(2), the defendant will be deemed to have agreed to voluntarily participate in proceedings in Puyallup Municipal Court by video conference unless the defendant or counsel notifies the Court on the record at the time of the proceeding that the defendant objects to the proceeding being conducted via video conference. Any objection will be deemed waived if not exercised at the time the case is called and prior to the start of the video conference hearing.

[Adopted effective September 1, 2015.]

4. PROCEDURES PRIOR TO TRIAL

PUMCLR 4.1. APPEARANCE OF DEFENDANT

Pursuant to CrRLJ 3 and 4, an attorney may enter an appearance and/or plea of not guilty on behalf of a defendant in any criminal non-traffic or criminal traffic offense, if said appearance or plea is made in writing or made in open court. However, if the defendant is charged with Driving Under the Influence, Driver Under Twenty-one Consuming Alcohol, or Physical Control of Vehicle Under the Influence, as defined in R.C.W. 46.61.502, 503 and 504, or any Domestic Violence offense as defined in R.C.W. 10.99.020 as enacted or hereinafter amended, the defendant must appear personally before the Court for arraignment.

[Adopted effective September 1, 2002.]

PUMCLR 4.2. CONTINUANCES

(a) All motions for continuance shall be in writing and must set forth the reason for the requested continuance and the dates of prior continuances indicating which party requested each.

(b) Requests for Continuance of Jury Trial must be received by the Court no less than 48 hours prior to jury trial.

Failure to comply with this rule may result in the imposition of terms relating to the expense incurred by the Court including, but not limited to, the costs of jury fee payments and mileage reimbursements.

[Adopted effective September 1, 2002.]

PUMCLR 4.3. PRETRIAL CONFERENCE

(a) **Hearing to be set.** In all cases in which a defendant has entered a plea of not guilty, a pretrial conference shall be set. The hearing shall provide an opportunity for plea negotiations, resolutions of discovery issues, and trial setting. If the case is to be set for trial, an order shall be entered setting forth the following, if applicable: (i) discovery schedule; (ii) date and nature of pretrial motions; (iii) date of readiness hearing; (iv) date of trial; and (v) time for filing witness lists.

(b) **Presence Required.** The prosecuting attorney, defense attorney and defendant shall be required to attend the pretrial conference. Personal appearance of any of these parties shall not be waived without prior Court approval.

[Adopted effective September 1, 2002.]

PUMCLR 4.4. TRIAL READINESS HEARING

(a) **Readiness Hearing Set.** The Court shall, in its discretion, set trial readiness hearings in criminal cases set for trial.

(b) **Appearance.** Appearance by the prosecuting attorney, defense attorney and the defendant is required. Appearance by the attorneys who will be trying the case is preferred. For good cause, substitute counsel may attend on behalf of trial counsel so long as counsel is prepared to answer the inquiries of the Court.

(c) **Procedure at Hearing.** At the trial readiness hearing, the Judge may inquire as to whether the case is expected to go to trial, whether the defendant expects to waive his/her right to jury, the number of witnesses expected to be called, the anticipated length of the trial, the number and nature of any motions and any other matter necessary to administer the trial efficiently. Any anticipated problems should be brought to the Court's attention.

(d) Failure to Appear at Hearing. The Court will strike the jury trial and may issue a bench warrant for a defendant who fails to appear at the Readiness Hearing.

[Adopted effective September 1, 2002.]

6. PROCEDURES AT TRIAL

PUMCLR 6.1. JURY INSTRUCTIONS

Jury instructions shall be filed with the Court and provided to the opposing party on the day of trial, unless otherwise ordered by the Court. Two sets of instructions shall be filed with the Court, one with citations, and one without citations. The set with citations shall be assembled in numbered sequence and stapled together. The set without citations shall be submitted to the Court in the same order as the cited set, and shall be paper clipped together. One copy of the set with citations shall be provided to the opposing counsel or party.

[Adopted effective September 1, 2002.]

8. INFRACTIONS

PUMCLR 8.1. DECISIONS ON WRITTEN STATEMENTS

Upon timely request for a hearing to contest or mitigate a traffic infraction, the Court shall send the defendant written notice of the hearing date and time. If a defendant is unable to appear for the scheduled hearing, mitigation and contested infraction hearings based on written statements, as provided for in this rule, IRLJ 2.4(b)(4), and IRLJ 2.6(c), are authorized.

A written request for a hearing by mail, and a written statement under penalty of perjury in compliance with IRLJ 2.4(b)(4), must be filed with the Court a minimum of five (5) business days in advance of the date set for hearing. A decision will be issued pursuant to IRLJ 2.6(c) and 3.5. If a written submission is not timely provided and defendant fails to appear for the in-person hearing, a committed finding may be entered and a penalty in the amount shown on the face of the citation assessed.

There shall be no appeal from a decision on written statements.

[Adopted effective September 1, 2002. Amended effective September 1, 2015.]

PUMCLR 8.2. NOTICE OF APPEARANCE— INFRACTIONS

Attorneys appearing on behalf of clients on traffic infractions shall file a Notice of Appearance with the court and with the prosecutor no later than seven (7) court days prior to the hearing. Upon filing of the Notice, the Court shall schedule the case to the next available calendar when the prosecutor will be present. Failure to timely submit a Notice of Appearance may result in the contested hearing being held beyond the 120 days required by IRLJ 2.6(a).

[Adopted effective September 2, 2013.]

PUMCLR 8.3. CONTESTED HEARINGS— SUBPOENAS AND WITNESSES

a) A request by a defendant for the Court to subpoena an officer must be made at the court in person at least 14 days prior to the date of the contested hearing. Failure to comply with the time limits set forth in this rule will be grounds for the Court to deny a request to subpoena the officer.

All officer subpoena cases shall be heard on a calendar where the prosecuting attorney is scheduled to be present and a request to subpoena the officer will result in the case being rescheduled to the next date and time of that special-set calendar.

For requests made pursuant to this rule, the Court will cause the subpoena to be served upon the officer.

b) For a non-officer witness, a subpoena may be issued in accordance with IRLJ 3.1(a). It is the responsibility of the party issuing or requesting the subpoena to arrange for proper service. Each party is responsible for the costs incurred by that party as provided in RCW 46.63.151.

c) A request for a Speed Measuring Device expert must be filed in accordance with IRLJ 6.6(b). The request must be on a separate pleading. The Court may allow the speed measuring device expert to testify telephonically from a location other than the courtroom.

All cases requiring the testimony of a Speed Measuring Device expert shall be heard on a calendar where the prosecuting attorney is scheduled to be present and a request filed pursuant to IRLJ 6.6 will result in the case being rescheduled to the next date and time of that special-set calendar.

A defendant who causes the Speed Measuring Device expert to be subpoenaed shall be responsible for all costs related to the appearance of that witness in court, including any appearance made by the expert telephonically, as provided in RCW 46.63.151 if thereafter found by the court to have committed the infraction.

[Adopted effective September 2, 2013.]

PUMCLR 8.4. INITIATION OF PHOTO ENFORCEMENT INFRACTION CASES

a) Generally. For purposes of IRJL 2.2, a photo enforcement infraction is initiated by the issuance of an infraction under the procedures set forth in PMC 10.33 and RCW 46.63.170.

b) Who May Issue. A notice of infraction for photo enforcement may be issued by an officer upon certification the officer has probable cause to believe, and does believe, that the operator of the vehicle committed an infraction contrary to law. The notice

of infraction is presumed to have been signed by the citing officer when the officer uses his or her user ID and password to access the computer system of the third party vendor authorized by the City of Puyallup to facilitate use of automated traffic safety cameras and uses that system to affix his or her name and serial number to the notice of infraction. The appearance of the officer's name and serial number on the infraction is prima facie evidence of compliance with the signature requirement listed above.

c) Service of Notice. A notice of infraction under the photo enforcement program is served when mailed according to the requirements of PMC 10.33 and RCW 46.63.170. There is a rebuttable presumption the issue date is the date the notice was mailed.

[Adopted effective September 1, 2015.]

9. MISCELLANEOUS

PUMCLR 9.1. SCHEDULE OF FEES

The following shall be the schedule of fees charged for certain official services provided by the Puyallup Municipal Court. These amounts are consistent with R.C.W. 3.62.060.

Duplication of Electronic Records	$10.00 Per Tape
Paper Copy Expense	$1.00 1st page
Each Additional Page	.15 cents
Certified Copy	$5.00 document
Postage	Actual Cost
Appeals (Preparation & Tapes)	$40.00

JIS Data dissemination charges will be set in accordance with the Administrative Office of the Courts.

This rule does not apply to law enforcement agencies, governmental agencies, or other departments within the City of Puyallup, or criminal cases involving indigent counsel.

[Adopted effective September 1, 2002.]

ROY MUNICIPAL COURT LOCAL COURT RULES

Including Amendments Received Through
August 15, 2015

Table of Rules

1. PURPOSE, SCOPE AND CONSTRUCTION

RULE 1.1. ADOPTION

These rules are adopted pursuant to CrRLJ 1.7 and GR 7 and supersede any and all Local Court Rules heretofore adopted by the Roy Municipal Court.

[Adopted effective September 1, 1999.]

RULE 1.2. TITLE OF RULES

These rules may be known and cited as Roy Municipal Court Local Rules, and shall be referred to as RMCLR.

[Adopted effective September 1, 1999.]

RULE 1.3. EFFECT OF LOCAL RULES

The provisions of the Local Rules are supplemental to the Rules for Courts of Limited Jurisdiction, as adopted or hereafter amended by the Supreme Court of the State of Washington, and shall not be construed in conflict with them.

[Adopted effective September 1, 1999.]

RULE 1.4. RESERVATION OF DISCRETION

The Roy Municipal Court reserves the authority to interpret and/or suspend or modify these rules in individual cases on motion of a party for good cause or on motion of the Court in the interest of justice and/or the efficient operation of the Court.

[Adopted effective September 1, 1999.]

3. RIGHTS OF DEFENDANTS

RULE 3.1. ARRAIGNMENT DATE

The arresting officer shall set the defendant's arraignment date and time when issuing a citation in all cases charging a criminal offense. The date set shall be the next regularly scheduled Court session if the citation is issued three or more days prior to that court session. For citations not charging Driving Under the Influence, Driver Under Twenty-one Consuming Alcohol, Physical Control of Vehicle under the Influence or Minor Under the Influence, as defined in R.C.W. 46.61.502, 503 or 504 or any Domestic Violence offense as defined in R.C.W. 10.99.020 as enacted or hereinafter amended, which are issued less than three days prior to the next regularly scheduled court session, the date set shall be the following regularly scheduled Court session.

[Adopted effective September 1, 1999.]

4. PROCEDURES PRIOR TO TRIAL

RULE 4.1. APPEARANCES OF DEFENDANT

Pursuant to CrRLJ 3 and 4, an attorney may enter an appearance and/or plea of not guilty on behalf of a client in any criminal or traffic offense, if said appearance or plea is made in writing or made in open court *unless* the defendant is charged with Driving Under the Influence, Driver Under Twenty-one Consuming Alcohol, Physical Control of Vehicle under the Influence or Minor Under the Influence, as defined in R.C.W. 46.61.502, 503 or 504 or any Domestic Violence offense as defined in R.C.W. 10.99.020 as enacted or hereinafter amended, in which instances the defendant must appear personally before the court for arraignment.

[Adopted effective September 1, 1999.]

RULE 4.2. CONTINUANCES

All motions for continuance shall be in writing and must set forth the reason for the requested continuance and the dates of prior continuances indicating which party requested each.

[Adopted effective September 1, 1999.]

RULE 4.3. PRETRIAL CONFERENCE

(a) **Hearing to Be Set.** In all cases in which a defendant has entered a plea of not guilty, a pretrial hearing shall be set. Said hearing shall provide an opportunity for plea negotiations, resolution of discovery issues, and trial setting. If a plea is not negotiated, an order shall be entered setting forth the following:

(i) discovery schedule, (ii) date and nature of pre-trial motions, (iii) date of readiness hearing, if set, (iv) date of trial and (v) time for filing witness lists.

(b) **Presence Required.** The prosecuting attorney, defense attorney and defendant shall be required to attend the pretrial hearing. Personal appearance of any of these parties shall not be waived without prior court approval.

[Adopted effective September 1, 1999.]

RULE 4.4. TRIAL READINESS HEARING

(a) **Readiness Hearing Set.** The Court shall, in its discretion, set trial readiness hearings in criminal cases set for trial.

(b) **Appearance.** Appearance by the attorneys and the defendant is required. Appearance by the attorneys who will be trying the case is preferred. For good cause, substitute counsel may attend on behalf of trial counsel so long as counsel is prepared to answer the inquiries of the court.

(c) **Procedure at Hearing.** At the trial readiness hearing, the Judge may inquire as to whether the case is expected to go to trial, whether the defendant expects to waive his/her right to jury, the number of witnesses expected to be called, the anticipated length of the trial, the number and nature of any motions and any other matter necessary to administer the trial efficiently. Any anticipated problems should be brought to the court's attention.

[Adopted effective September 1, 1999.]

6. PROCEDURES AT TRIAL

RULE 6.1. JURY INSTRUCTIONS

Jury instructions shall be filed with the Court and provided to the opposing party on the day of trial, unless otherwise ordered by the Court. Two sets of instructions shall be filed with the court, one with citations, and one without citations. The set with cita-

tions shall be assembled in numbered sequence and stapled together. The set without citations shall be submitted to the court in the same order as the cited set, and shall be paper clipped together. One copy of the set with citations shall be provided to the opposing counsel or party.

[Adopted effective September 1, 1999.]

8. INFRACTIONS

RULE 8.1. DECISION ON WRITTEN STATEMENTS

(a) **Generally.** Mitigation and contested hearings may be submitted to the Court on a written statement. The court shall examine the citing officer's report and any statement submitted by the defendant. All statements submitted by the defendant must be received by the court within 90 days after the defendant filed the response to the notice of infraction. The examination shall take place within 120 days after the

defendant filed the response to the notice of infraction. The examination may be held in chambers and shall not be governed by the Rules of Evidence.

(b) **Factual Determination.** The court shall determine whether the plaintiff has proved by a preponderance of all evidence submitted that the defendant has committed the infraction.

(c) **Disposition.** If the court determines that the infraction has been committed, it may assess a penalty in accordance with INRLJ 3.3.

(d) Notice to Parties. The court shall notify the parties in writing whether an infraction was found to have been committed and what penalty, if any, was imposed.

(e) No Appeal Permitted. There shall be no appeal from a decision on written statements.

[Adopted effective September 1, 1999.]

RUSTON MUNICIPAL COURT LOCAL RULES

Including Amendments Received Through
August 15, 2015

Table of Rules

1. PURPOSE, SCOPE AND CONSTRUCTION

RULE 1.1. ADOPTION

These rules are adopted pursuant to CrRlJ 1.7 and GR 7 and supersede any and all Local Court Rules heretofore adopted by the Ruston Municipal Court.

[Adopted effective September 1, 2002.]

RULE 1.2. TITLE OF RULES

These rules may be known and cited as Ruston Municipal Court Local Rules, and shall be referred to as RUMCLR.

[Adopted effective September 1, 2002.]

RULE 1.3. EFFECT OF LOCAL RULES

The provisions of the Local Rules are supplemental to the Rules for the Courts of Limited Jurisdiction, as adopted or hereafter amended by the Supreme Court of the State of Washington, and shall not be construed in conflict with them.

[Adopted effective September 1, 2002.]

RULE 1.4. RESERVATION OF DISCRETION

The Ruston Municipal Court reserves the authority to interpret and/or suspend or modify these rules in individual cases on motion of a party for good cause or on a motion of the Court in the interest of justice and/or the efficient operation of the Court.

[Adopted effective September 1, 2002.]

3. RIGHTS OF DEFENDANT

RULE 3.1. ARRAIGNMENT DATE

The arresting officer shall set the defendant's arraignment date and time when issuing a citation in all cases charging a criminal offense. The date set shall be the next regularly scheduled arraignment date, except as provided below. For citations charging Driving Under the Influence, Driver Under Twenty-one Consuming Alcohol, Physical Control of Vehicle under the Influence or Minor Under the Influence, as defined in R.C.W. 46.61.502, 503 or 504 or any Domestic Violence offense as defined in R.C.W. 10.99.020 as enacted or hereinafter amended, the court date shall be the next regularly scheduled court session.

[Adopted effective September 1, 2002.]

4. PROCEDURES PRIOR TO TRIAL

RULE 4.1. APPEARANCE OF DEFENDANT

Pursuant to CrRLJ 3 and 4, an attorney may enter an appearance and/or plea of not guilty on behalf of a client in any criminal or traffic offense, if said appearance or plea is made in writing or made in open court unless the defendant is charged with Driving Under the Influence, Driver Under Twenty-one Consuming Alcohol, Physical Control of Vehicle under the Influence or Minor Under the Influence, as defined in R.C.W. 46.61.502, 503 and 504 or any Domestic Violence offense as defined in R.C.W. 10.99.020 as enacted or hereinafter amended, in which instances the defendant must appear personally before the court for arraignment.

[Adopted effective September 1, 2002.]

RULE 4.2. CONTINUANCES

(a) All motions for continuance shall be in writing and must set forth the reason for the requested continuance and the dates of prior continuances indicating which party requested each.

(b) Requests for Continuance of Jury Trial must be received by the Court no less than 48 hours prior to jury trial.

Failure to comply with this rule may result in the imposition of terms relating to the expense incurred by the Court including, but not limited to, the costs of jury fee payments and mileage reimbursements.

[Adopted effective September 1, 2002.]

RULE 4.3. PRETRIAL CONFERENCE

(a) Hearing to be set. In all cases in which a defendant has entered a plea of not guilty, a pretrial hearing shall be set. The hearing shall provide an opportunity for plea negotiations, resolutions of discovery issues, and trial setting. If a plea is not negotiated, an order shall be entered setting forth the following: (i) discovery schedule, (ii) date and nature of pretrial motions, (iii) date of readiness hearing, if set, (iv) date of trial and (v) time for filing witness lists.

(b) Presence Required. The prosecuting attorney, defense attorney and defendant shall be required to attend the pretrial hearing. Personal appearance of any of these parties shall not be waived without prior court approval.

[Adopted effective September 1, 2002.]

RULE 4.4. TRIAL READINESS HEARING

(a) Readiness Hearing Set. The Court shall, in its discretion, set trial readiness hearings in criminal cases set for trial.

(b) Appearance. Appearance by the attorneys and the defendant is required. Appearance by the attorneys who will be trying the case is preferred. For good cause, substitute counsel may attend on behalf of trial counsel so long as counsel is prepared to answer the inquiries of the court.

(c) Procedure at Hearing. At the trial readiness hearing, the Judge may inquire as to whether the case is expected to go to trial, whether the defendant expects to waive his/her right to jury, the number of witnesses expected to be called, the anticipated length of the trial, the number and nature of any motions and any other matter necessary to administer the trial efficiently. Any anticipated problems should be brought to the court's attention.

(d) Failure to Appear at Hearing. The Court will strike the jury trial and may issue a bench warrant for a party who fails to appear at the Readiness Hearing.

[Adopted effective September 1, 2002.]

6. PROCEDURES AT TRIAL

RULE 6.1. JURY INSTRUCTIONS

Jury instructions shall be filed with the Court and provided to the opposing party on the day of trial, unless otherwise ordered by the Court. Two sets of instructions shall be filed with the court, one with citations, and one without citations. The set with citations shall be assembled in numbered sequence and stapled together. The set without citations shall be submitted to the court in the same order as the cited set, and shall be paper clipped together. One copy of the set with citations shall be provided to the opposing counsel or party.

[Adopted effective September 1, 2002.]

8. INFRACTIONS

RULE 8.1. DECISION ON WRITTEN STATEMENTS

Mitigation and Contested hearings based on written statements, given under penalty of perjury as provided for in IRLJ 2.4 (b)(4) and IRLJ 2.6 (c) are authorized.

The procedures authorized by IRLJ 3.5 are adopted by this court. To be considered, the written statement(s) must be received by the court pursuant to written instructions provided to the Defendant.

[Adopted effective February 8, 2002.]

9. MISCELLANEOUS

RULE 9.1. SCHEDULE OF FEES

The following shall be the schedule of fees charged for certain official services provided by the Municipal Court. These amounts are consistent with R.C.W. 3.62.060.

Duplication of Electronic Records	$10.00 Per Tape
Paper Copy Expense	$1.00 1st page
Each Additional Page	.15 cents
Certified Copy	$5.00 document
Postage	Actual Cost
Appeals (Preparation & Tapes)	$40.00

JIS Data dissemination charges will be set in accordance with the Administrative Office of the Courts.

This rules does not apply to law enforcement agencies, governmental agencies, or other departments within the Town of Ruston, or criminal cases involving indigence.

[Adopted effective September 1, 2002.]

SOUTH PRAIRIE MUNICIPAL COURT—
[No Local Rules]

STEILACOOM MUNICIPAL COURT LOCAL RULES

Including Amendments Received Through
August 15, 2015

Table of Rules

SMCLR 1.0

The Steilacoom Municipal Court hereby adopts all of the Local Rules of the Lakewood Municipal Court (LMCLR) as if set forth fully herein. All future amendments of the LMCLR will be likewise adopted.

The Lakewood Municipal Court Rules are available at http://www.courts.wa.gov/court_rules/?fa=court_rules.list&group=municipal&set=munlkd.

[Adopted effective September 1, 2015.]

LOCAL COURT GENERAL RULES [RESCINDED]

LR .01. COURTROOM SAFETY [RESCINDED]

[Rescinded effective September 1, 2015.]

LR .02. CELL PHONES, PAGERS, AND OTHER DEVICES [RESCINDED]

[Rescinded effective September 1, 2015.]

PURPOSE, SCOPE, AND CONSTRUCTION [RESCINDED]

SCMLR 1.1. ADOPTION OF LOCAL RULES [RESCINDED]

[Rescinded effective September 1, 2015.]

SCMLR 1.2. TITLE OF RULES [RESCINDED]

[Rescinded effective September 1, 2015.]

SCMLR 1.3. EFFECT OF LOCAL RULES [RESCINDED]

[Rescinded effective September 1, 2015.]

SCMLR 1.4. RESERVATION OF DISCRETION [RESCINDED]

[Rescinded effective September 1, 2015.]

CONTINUANCE REQUESTS [RESCINDED]

SCMLR 2.1. INFRACTION AND ARRAIGNMENT CONTINU- ANCES [RESCINDED]

[Rescinded effective September 1, 2015.]

SCMLR 2.2. PRETRIAL CONTINUANCES [RESCINDED]

[Rescinded effective September 1, 2015.]

WARRANTS [RESCINDED]

SCMLR 3.1. WARRANT COSTS [RESCINDED]

[Rescinded effective September 1, 2015.]

SCMLR 3.2. PROCEDURE TO QUASH WARRANT [RESCINDED]

[Rescinded effective September 1, 2015.]

BAIL FORFEITURES [RESCINDED]

SCMLR 4.1. BAIL FORFEITURES FOR SPECIFIC CRIMES [RESCINDED]

[Adopted effective September 1, 2011; rescinded effective September 1, 2012.]

INFRACTIONS [RESCINDED]

SCMLR 5.1. NVOL WITH ID [RESCINDED]

[Rescinded effective September 1, 2015.]

SCMLR 5.2. MANDATORY LIABILITY INSURANCE [RESCINDED]

[Rescinded effective September 1, 2015.]

SCMLR 5.3. EXPIRED VEHICLE REGISTRATION [RESCINDED]

[Rescinded effective September 1, 2015.]

SCMLR 5.4. DECISIONS ON WRITTEN STATEMENTS [RESCINDED]

[Rescinded effective September 1, 2015.]

SCMLR 5.6. DEFERRAL OF TRAFFIC INFRACTION [RESCINDED]

[Rescinded effective September 1, 2015.]

SUMNER MUNICIPAL COURT LOCAL RULES

Including Amendments Received Through
August 15, 2015

Table of Rules

GENERAL RULES

SUMCLR 1. LOCAL GENERAL RULE 1

Any party or attorney to a proceeding or subpoenaed witness who fails to appear within thirty minutes of the time scheduled for hearing or trial shall be deemed having failed to appear unless previously excused by the Court or timely notice having been provided to the Court for determination of an acceptable reason for such absence. The Court retains complete authority to reschedule the matter, issue warrant(s), or dismiss the case or proceeding.

[Adopted effective September 1, 2009.]

SUMCLR 2. LOCAL GENERAL RULE 2

Sixty days after sentencing and/or final disposition of a criminal case or civil infraction, the attorney of record except for the matters appointed the public defender at City of Sumner expense, unless a notice of appeal has been filed, shall file a written notification with the court indicating the attorneys desire to remain as the attorney of record on the case.

[Adopted effective September 1, 2009.]

1. PURPOSE, SCOPE AND CONSTRUCTION

SUMCLR 1.1. ADOPTION

These rules are adopted pursuant to CrRLJ 1.7 and GR 7 and supersede any and all Local Court Rules heretofore adopted by the Sumner Municipal Court.

[Adopted effective September 1, 2002.]

SUMCLR 1.2. TITLE OF RULES

These rules shall be known and cited as Sumner Municipal Court Local Rules, and shall be referred to as SUMCLR.

[Adopted effective September 1, 2002; amended effective September 1, 2009.]

SUMCLR 1.3. EFFECT OF LOCAL RULES

The provisions of the Local Rules are supplemental to the Rules for the Courts of Limited Jurisdiction, as adopted or hereafter amended by the Supreme Court of the State of Washington, and shall not be construed to be in conflict with State court rules as hereby exist or are hereafter amended or modified.

[Adopted effective September 1, 2002; amended effective September 1, 2009.]

SUMCLR 1.4. RESERVATION OF DISCRETION

The Sumner Municipal Court reserves the authority to interpret and/or suspend or modify these rules in individual cases on motion of a party for good cause or on a motion of the Court in the interest of justice and/or the efficient operation of the Court.

[Adopted effective September 1, 2002.]

3. RIGHTS OF DEFENDANT

SUMCLR 3.1. ARRAIGNMENT DATE

The arresting officer shall set the defendant's arraignment date and time when issuing a citation in all cases charging a criminal traffic and criminal non-traffic offense. The arraignment date set shall be the next regularly scheduled arraignment date, except as provided below. For citations charging Driving Under the Influence, Driver Under Twenty-one Consuming Alcohol, or Physical Control of Vehicle under the Influence, as defined in R.C.W. 46.61.502, 503 or 504, or any Domestic Violence offense as defined in R.C.W. 10.99.020 as enacted or hereinafter amended, the arraignment date shall be the next regularly scheduled Court session.

[Adopted effective September 1, 2002.]

4. PROCEDURES PRIOR TO TRIAL

SUMCLR 4.1. APPEARANCE OF DEFENDANT

Pursuant to CrRLJ 3 and 4, an attorney may enter an appearance and/or plea of not guilty on behalf of a defendant in any criminal non-traffic or criminal traffic offense, if said appearance or plea is made in writing or made in open court. However, the defendant must personally appear before the court for arraignment in cases where the appearance is mandated by statute, e.g., Driving under the influence, Driver under twenty-one consuming alcohol, or Physical control of vehicle under the influence, as defined in R.C.W. 46.61.502, 503 and 504, any Domestic violence offense as defined in R.C.W. 10.99.020 as enacted or hereinafter amended, or the following crimes required by this local rule:

- Sexual misconduct with a minor in the second degree as defined in RCW 9A.44.096 as enacted or hereinafter amended;

- Communicate with a minor for immoral purpose as defined in RCW 9.68.090 as enacted or hereinafter amended;

- Indecent exposure as defined in RCW 9A.88.010 as enacted or hereinafter amended;

- Crimes with sexual motivation, other than sex offenses as defined in RCW 9.94A.030;

- Crimes involving assault or sexual motivation that were forwarded to the County prosecutor for charging as a felony but were not charged by the County and returned to the municipality for charging as misdemeanor;

- Leaving a child unattended in a parked automobile as defined in RCW 9.91.060 as enacted or hereinafter amended;

- Abandonment of a dependent person in the third degree as defined in RCW 9A.42.080 as enacted or hereinafter amended;

- Aiming or discharging firearms, dangerous weapons as defined in RCW 9.41.230 as enacted or hereinafter amended; and

- Neglect of a child or dependent person as defined in Sumner Municipal Code (SMC) 9.04.100 as enacted or hereinafter amended.

[Adopted effective September 1, 2002; amended effective September 1, 2012.]

SUMCLR 4.2. CONTINUANCES

(a) All motions for continuance shall be in writing and shall set forth the reason for the requested continuance, and if available, the dates of prior continuances indicating which party requested each.

(b) Requests for Continuance of Jury Trial after readiness hearing shall not be granted except in extraordinary circumstances as permitted by the court.

Failure to comply with this rule may result in the imposition of terms relating to the expense incurred by the Court including, but not limited to, the costs of jury fee payments and mileage reimbursements.

[Adopted effective September 1, 2002; amended effective September 1, 2009.]

SUMCLR 4.3. PRETRIAL CONFERENCE

(a) Hearing to be set. In all cases in which a defendant has entered a plea of not guilty, a pretrial conference shall be set. The hearing shall provide an opportunity for plea negotiations, resolution of all discovery issues, and trial setting. If the case is to be set for trial, an order shall be entered setting forth the following, if applicable: (i) discovery schedule; (ii) date and nature of pretrial motions; (iii) date of readiness hearing; (iv) date of trial; and (v) time for filing witness lists.

(b) Presence Required. The prosecuting attorney, defense attorney and defendant shall be required to attend the pretrial conference. Personal appearance of any of these parties shall not be waived without prior Court approval.

[Adopted effective September 1, 2002; amended effective September 1, 2009.]

SUMCLR 4.4. TRIAL READINESS HEARING

(a) Readiness Hearing Set. The Court shall set jury trial readiness hearings in criminal cases set for trial. No readiness hearings will be set for bench trials.

(b) Appearance. Appearance by the prosecuting attorney, defense attorney and the defendant is required. Appearance by the attorneys who will be trying the case is preferred. For good cause, substitute counsel may attend on behalf of trial counsel so long as counsel is prepared to answer the inquiries of the Court.

(c) Procedure at Hearing. At the trial readiness hearing, the Judge may inquire as to whether the case is expected to go to trial, whether the defendant expects to waive his/her right to jury, the number of witnesses expected to be called, the anticipated length of the trial, the number and nature of any motions and any other matter necessary to administer the trial efficiently. Any motions other than motions in limine that can be handled in a short time prior to jury selection shall be set on a separate motion date prior to jury trial date. Any anticipated problems should be brought to the Court's attention.

(d) Failure to Appear at Hearing. The Court will strike the jury trial and may issue a bench warrant for a defendant who fails to appear at the Readiness Hearing.

[Adopted effective September 1, 2002; amended effective September 1, 2009.]

6. PROCEDURES AT TRIAL

SUMCLR 6.1. JURY INSTRUCTIONS

Standard WPIC jury instructions shall be filed with the Court and provided to the opposing party on the day of trial, unless otherwise ordered by the Court. Any specialized instructions (crafted by the individual attorneys based upon case law or other statutory authority) shall be submitted for the opposing parties and courts review no later than readiness hearing without specific authority granted by the court. Two sets of instructions shall be filed with the Court, one with citations, and one without citations. The set with citations shall be assembled in numbered sequence and stapled together. The set without citations shall be submitted to the Court in the same order as the cited set, and shall be paper clipped together. One copy of the set with citations shall be provided to the opposing counsel or party.

[Adopted effective September 1, 2002; amended effective September 1, 2009.]

8. INFRACTIONS

SUMCLR 8.1. DECISIONS ON WRITTEN STATEMENTS

Mitigation and Contested infraction hearings based on written statements, given under penalty of perjury as provided for in IRLJ 2.4 (b) (4) and IRLJ 2.6 (c), are authorized.

The procedures authorized by IRLJ 3.5 are adopted by this Court. To be considered, the written statement (s) must be received by the Court pursuant to written instructions provided to the defendant.

[Adopted effective September 1, 2002.]

SUMCLR 8.2. CITATIONS FOR NO INSURANCE

If a defendant who was cited with a violation of RCW 46.30.020 presents to a court clerk or administrator evidence that the person had in effect at the time of the citation liability insurance as required by that statute, then upon the payment of twenty-five ($25) administrative costs, the case shall be dismissed and the court clerk/administrator shall be authorized to make appropriate notation of the dismissal in the Court file.

If a defendant who was cited with a violation of RCW 46.30.020, for failure to have liability insurance is able to show evidence that the person did not have insurance at the time of the citation but has subsequently obtained liability insurance in conformity with the requirements of the statutes, then the penalty upon a first violation of such statute shall be reduced to two hundred seventy-five dollars ($275); upon a second violation shall be reduced to three hundred seventy-five dollars ($375); in either event the court clerk/administrator shall be authorized to enter a finding that the infraction was committed, and make appropriate notations in the Court record, and the person shall be relieved of any further need to appear in court in connection with that particular infraction.

[Adopted effective September 1, 2009.]

SUMCLR 8.3. CITATIONS FOR NO HAND-ICAPPED PLACARD/IDENTIFICA-TION

If a person is cited more than one time in a two year period with a violation for improper parking in a disabled space without proper parking placard, license plate or picture identification, presents to the court clerk/administrator evidence that the person had in effect at the time of the citation the required parking placard, and an identification card bearing picture, name and date of birth of the permit holder, as well as the placard's serial number, then upon payment of a twenty-five dollar ($25) administrative cost, the infraction shall be dismissed and the court clerk/administra-

tor shall be authorized to make appropriate notation of the dismissal in the Court record.

[Adopted effective September 1, 2009. Amended effective September 1, 2010.]

SUMCLR 8.4. CITATIONS FOR DOG/CAT LICENSE REQUIREMENTS

If a defendant who was cited with a violation of SMC 6.04.030 for failure to have a dog and/or cat license presents to a court clerk or administrator evidence that although the person did not have a license for their dog/cat at the time of the citation but has obtained a license in conformity with the requirements of the ordinance within 21 days from date of issuance then the penalty upon a first violation within a 5 year period shall be reduced to two hundred seventy five dollars ($275); upon a second violation shall be reduced to three hundred seventy-five dollars ($375); in either event the court clerk/administrator shall be authorized to enter a finding that the infraction was committed, and make appropriate notations in the Court record, and the person shall be relieved of any further need to appear in court in connection with that particular violation.

[Adopted effective September 1, 2011; amended effective September 1, 2012.]

9. MISCELLANEOUS

SUMCLR 9.1. SCHEDULE OF FEES

The Sumner Municipal Court shall charge fees consistent with R.C.W. 3.62.060. Any other expenses including but not limited to postage shall be imposed per the current expense to the City of Sumner.

JIS Data dissemination charges will be set in accordance with the Administrative Office of the Courts.

This rule does not apply to law enforcement agencies, governmental agencies, or other departments within the City of Sumner, or criminal cases involving indigent defense counsel.

[Adopted effective September 1, 2002; amended effective September 1, 2009.]

10. [PUBLIC RECORDS]

SUMCLR 10.1. PUBLIC RECORDS REQUEST

Public Records Requests must be submitted in writing on the Sumner Municipal Court Public Records

Request Form noting fees may apply and must be paid prior to dissemination of information.

[Adopted effective September 1, 2010.]

LOCAL RULES FOR THE MUNICIPAL COURT OF THE CITY OF TACOMA

Including Amendments Received Through August 15, 2015

Table of Rules

LGR 29. PRESIDING JUDGE [RESCINDED]

[Adopted effective June 25, 2002. Amended effective September 1, 2003. Rescinded effective September 1, 2010.]

LARLJ 5. APPOINTMENT OF PRESIDING JUDGE [RESCINDED]

[Adopted effective June 25, 2002. Amended effective September 1, 2003. Rescinded effective September 1, 2010.]

LIRLJ 3.5. DECISIONS ON WRITTEN STATEMENTS

Mitigation and contested hearings based on written statements, given under penalty of perjury as provided for in IRLJ 2.4(b)(4) and IRLJ 2.6(c) are authorized. The procedures authorized by IRLJ 3.5 are adopted by this court. To be considered, the written statement(s) must be received by the court pursuant to written instructions provided to the defendant.

[Adopted effective September 1, 2002. Amended effective September 1, 2003.]

UNIVERSITY PLACE MUNICIPAL COURT LOCAL RULES

Including Amendments Received Through
August 15, 2015

Table of Rules

Rule
UPMCLR 1.0.

UPMCLR 1.0

The University Place Municipal Court hereby adopts all of the Local Rules of the Lakewood Municipal Court (LMCLR) as if set forth fully herein. All future amendments of the LMCLR will be likewise adopted.

[Adopted effective September 1, 2011.]

WILKESON MUNICIPAL COURT—
[No Local Rules]

SAN JUAN COUNTY

Table of Courts

Superior Court

Local Rules of the Superior Court for San Juan County.

District Court

Local Rules of the District Court for San Juan County.

SUPERIOR COURT

LOCAL COURT RULES OF THE SUPERIOR COURT FOR SAN JUAN COUNTY

Including Amendments Received Through August 15, 2015

Table of Rules

PART I.   LOCAL CIVIL RULES (LCR)

1.   INTRODUCTORY
(Rules 1–2A)

LCR 1.   SCOPE OF RULES

Unless specifically designated otherwise, these rules shall supplement the Washington Court Rules for superior and juvenile court and shall govern the local procedure in San Juan County Superior Court and San Juan County Juvenile Court. These rules are subject to amendment at the direction of the judge.

Counsel and litigants should check with the court administrator or county clerk to assure that the rules applicable to their matters are currently in effect. [Adopted effective September 1, 2009; amended effective September 1, 2012.]

LCR 2–2A.   *[No Local Rules]*

2.   COMMENCEMENT OF ACTION; SERVICE OF PROCESS, PLEADINGS, MOTIONS AND ORDERS
(Rules 3–6)

LCR 3–4.2.   *[No Local Rules]*

LCR 5.   SERVICE AND FILING OF PLEADINGS AND OTHER PAPERS

(a) Service—When Required.

(1) *Emergency Orders.* A party applying for an emergency order which will require or forbid the doing of some act shall notify the opponent or his or her counsel, if known, and shall request his or her presence at presentation of the order, unless good cause to the contrary is shown. If the opponent or opponent's counsel does not appear, the judge shall require a full showing with respect to the notice given. See also, LCR 9(m).

(b)—(d) (No Local Rules)

(e) Filing With the Court. All notices for the Law and Motion calendar shall be filed with the Clerk of the court no later than 4:30 p.m. seven (7) days preceding the date of the hearing.

(f)—(i) (No Local Rules)

(j) Filing by Facsimile With Clerk. See LCR 78(i).

(k) Service of Papers by Facsimile on Attorney or Party. Service of all papers other than the summons and other process may be made by facsimile transmission as follows:

(1) *Fax Machine Availability.* Pleadings and such other papers may only be served by facsimile transmission upon a self-represented party or attorney if the intended recipient makes available a facsimile machine at the recipient's residence or place of business.

(2) *Length.* Pleadings and such other papers regarding any hearing which total more than twenty-five (25) pages in length may not be served by facsimile without prior approval of the intended recipient.

(3) *Transmittal Sheet.* Any pleadings or such other papers transmitted by facsimile must be accompanied by a facsimile transmittal sheet containing, at a minimum, the following information: identification of pleading or other paper being transmitted, number of pages of pleading or paper, sender's name and sender's telephone and facsimile numbers.

(4) *Receipt of Documents.* A pleading or such other paper transmitted by facsimile shall be deemed received at the time the recipient's facsimile machine registers the transmission of the last page. If that time is after 5 p.m., the pleading or other paper shall be deemed received the following day. If a pleading or other paper is received after any time set forth as a deadline herein, and prior to the next day, the pleading or other paper shall be deemed received the following day. If a pleading or other paper is not completely transmitted, it shall not be considered received.

(5) *Delivery of Original to Recipient.* The transmitting party shall mail or deliver a copy of the transmitted pleading or other paper to the recipient of the facsimile transmission by the next day.

(6) *Time.* Time shall be computed as set forth in Civil Rule 6 and LCR 6 herein.

(7) *Facsimile Machine Not Required.* Nothing in this rule or other rule allowing service by facsimile transmission shall require an attorney or party to have a facsimile machine.

(*l*) Service of Papers by Email on Attorney or Party. Service of all papers other than the summons and other process may be made by electronic mail (email) as follows:

(1) *Email Availability.* Pleadings and such papers may be served by email only upon an attorney or a self-represented party who makes available, as provided in this subsection, an email address to which such pleadings and papers may be served. An attorney or a self-represented party makes an email address available by giving notice, which must include:

(i) The email address to which service may be made.

(ii) Whether service on this email address will return an automatic confirmation via return email to the sender.

(iii) The phone number, if any, that the sender must call to announce service to the email address.

(iv) Whether service by email must be followed by service of hard copies. Notice of the availability of an email address for service of pleadings and papers for a specific case may be given in the Notice of Appearance or any other notice filed with the Court. Notice of the availability of an email address for service of pleadings and papers for all cases may be made in correspondence directly to attorneys and parties. Any notice of availability of an email address for service may be modified or revoked in the same manner as originally given.

(2) *Paper Format.* Pleadings and papers served by email must be formatted in the Adobe Acrobat format. Papers without color should be in black-and-white format to save space. Pleadings and papers shall be attached to an email served at the appropriate email address. No email may exceed one (1) megabyte in size. Each pleading and paper must be formatted into a single attachment unless it exceeds the size limitation, in which case the pleading or paper may be split across attachments to multiple emails.

(3) *Email Information.* Each email shall contain at a minimum the following information: identification of each pleading and paper being served in the email, the sender's name and company name, and a phone number to which transmission problems shall be reported.

(4) *Service Confirmation.* If the recipient's notice of the availability of a service email address indicates that the email address will return an automatic confir-

mation by email, then service shall be complete when the sender receives such automatic confirmation. If the recipient's notice specifies a phone number that the sender must call to announce service, then service is complete once the sender calls the phone number and announces service. Announcement by phone may be made in voicemail and shall indicate the number of emails sent. Service completed after 5:00 PM shall be considered completed the next business day.

(5) *Delivery of Hard Copy to Recipient.* If the recipient's notice of the availability of a service email address indicates that service of hard copies is required, the sender shall mail or deliver a copy of the emailed pleadings and papers to the recipient of the email by the next day.

(6) *Time.* Time shall be computed as set forth in Civil Rule 6 and LCR 6 herein.

[Adopted effective September 1, 2009; amended effective September 1, 2012; September 1, 2015.]

LCR 6. TIME

(a)—(c) (No Local Rules)

(d) For Motions—Affidavits. A written motion, other than one which may be heard ex parte, and notice of the hearing thereof shall be served no later than nine (9) court days before the time specified for the hearing, unless a different period is fixed by statute, these local rules, or by order of the court. When a motion is supported by affidavit or other documents, the affidavit or other documents shall be served with the motion; and, except as otherwise provided in Civil Rule 59(c), opposing affidavits and any other documents responsive to the motion shall be served no later than 4 p.m. four (4) court days prior to the hearing. Affidavits and any other documents in strict reply to the opposing affidavits shall be served not later than 4 p.m. two (2) court days prior to the hearing. No additional responses or replies shall be permitted from either party without permission of the court.

(e) (No Local Rules)

[Adopted effective September 1, 2009; amended effective September 1, 2012; September 1, 2015.]

3. PLEADINGS AND MOTIONS
(Rules 7–16)

LCR 7. PLEADINGS ALLOWED; FORM OF MOTIONS

(a) Pleadings. (No Local Rules)

(b) Motions and Other Papers.

(1) Motions and other papers must contain the following:

(i) Relief Requested. The specific relief the court is requested to grant;

(ii) Statement of Grounds. A concise statement of the grounds upon which the motion is based;

(iii) Statement of Issues. A concise statement of the issues of law upon which the court is requested to rule;

(iv) Evidence Relied Upon. The evidence on which the motion or reply is based shall be identified with particularity. Deposition testimony, discovery pleadings, and documentary evidence relied upon must be quoted verbatim, or a photocopy of relevant pages thereof must be attached to the motion. Deposition testimony in connection with a motion shall not require publication thereof unless a challenge is made thereto and an opposing party shows good cause for such publication. Depositions used in this fashion shall remain unopened and not a part of the court file unless otherwise ordered by the court.

(v) Legal Authority. Any legal authority relied upon must be cited.

(vi) Memorandum of Authority. Provided, however, that items (i)—(v) above may be contained in a memorandum of authority in support of the motion.

(vii) Mandatory Forms. This rule is not intended to modify or replace any mandatory forms required by law.

(b) (2)–(5) No Local Rules)

(c)–(d) (No Local Rules)

(e) Dispositive Motions. All dispositive motions shall be noted to be heard by the judge assigned to preside over the case, except (1) upon agreement of the assigned judge, (2) upon agreement of the parties or attorneys, and (3) only upon good cause shown.

(f) Limits to Replies. Replies shall be limited to the issues or facts raised by the responding party in the response to the motion.

(g) Schedule to Provide Courtesy Copies for Judge. See LCR 8(h).

(h) Motions and Orders to be Separate. Motions and orders shall not be combined into one document. Rather, an order shall always be set forth in a separate document from the motion itself. The original of any proposed order shall be lodged with the Clerk.

[Adopted effective September 1, 2009; amended effective September 1, 2012; September 1, 2015.]

LCR 8. GENERAL RULES OF PLEADINGS AND MOTIONS

(a)—(f) (No Local Rules)

(g) Special Set Hearings. In the event motions in a case are expected to take longer than a total of 15 minutes to be heard, the parties shall obtain a specially set hearing date and time from the Court Administrator. The moving party shall arrange the hearing after conferring with opposing counsel or a self-represented party with regard to conflicts.

(h) Courtesy Copies for Judge. A copy of all motions, briefs, affidavits and declarations, and other documentary evidence to be considered by the court shall be provided to the judge assigned to preside over the trial or hearing at the same time as such documents or documentary evidence are required to be served on the opposing party or a self-represented party as provided in the court rules or local rules herein.

(1) *Caption.* The upper right hand corner of the first page of each courtesy copy shall contain the words "Judge's Courtesy Copy," the judge's name, and the date and time of the hearing.

(2) *Delivery.* It is the court's preference that all courtesy copies for the judge be mailed or personally delivered to the Court Administrator. If time does not permit mailing or personal delivery, the filing party shall contact the Court Administrator at (360) 370–7480. The court reserves the right to charge a reasonable fee for fax or email copies. Do not fax or email without prior permission from the Court Administrator.

(3) *Courtesy Copies Are Discarded.* Courtesy copies are discarded after ten (10) days from the assigned hearing date, unless counsel or a self-represented party notify the Court Administrator of a new hearing date and request that the courtesy copies be retained. If either party fails to do so, it will be the responsibility of counsel or a self-represented party to provide new courtesy copies to the court as provided herein.

(i) Default Orders, Decrees or Judgments. If an order, decree or judgment has been entered by default, the prevailing party or the attorney representing the prevailing party shall immediately mail a conformed copy of the original order, decree or judgment, including the date the original was entered by the court, to the opponent or opponent's attorney at his or her last known address. An affidavit or declaration showing proof of service by mailing shall be filed with the Clerk. If an attorney does not represent the prevailing party, it shall be the prevailing party's duty to ensure compliance with this rule.

(j) Jurisdictional Declaration in Dissolution Cases. If a decree is entered under RCW 26.09 by joinder, agreement, or default, an attorney representing the petitioner or the respondent may present jurisdictional testimony pursuant to a "Request for Entry of Decree and Declaration of Jurisdictional Facts," using the form set forth in Appendix G. If both parties are self-represented, one party's presence in court is required.

[Adopted effective September 1, 2009; amended effective September 1, 2012; September 1, 2015.]

LCR 9. SPECIAL MATTERS: MOTIONS AND PLEADINGS

(a)—(l) No Local Rules

(m) Motions to Shorten Time. Motions to shorten time for a hearing shall be granted only upon good cause shown. The party requesting an order to shorten time shall give verbal and written notice as soon as possible to opposing parties regardless of when pleadings are prepared and provided. Such motions shall contain a written certification that self-represented parties or attorneys were notified of the time and place of requesting the order to shorten time, or the reasons why such notice was not given. The court may impose terms, including an award of attorney fees, where the court later finds there was insufficient need for shortening time. See also, LCR 5(a)(1).

(n) Motions in Dissolution Actions.

(1) *Standard Forms and Supporting Affidavit or Declaration.* Motions for temporary support, maintenance, restraining orders, parenting plans, costs, attorney fees and show cause orders in connection therewith shall be in compliance with any standard forms required by law and local rules herein and shall be supported by the affidavit or declaration of the moving party.

(2) *Blank Affidavit or Declaration Provided to a Self–Represented Party.* When one of the parties is self-represented, a blank affidavit or declaration shall be attached to the motion for temporary orders and show cause order and served on the other party. In addition, the motion for temporary orders and show cause order shall contain the following language: *"At the hearing, the court will consider written sworn affidavits or declarations under penalty of perjury. Oral testimony may not be allowed. If you wish to respond, prior to the hearing you must: (1) file your documents with the court; (2) provide a copy of those documents to the judge; (3) serve the other party's attorney with copies of your documents (or have the other party served if that party does not have an attorney); and (4) complete your filing and service of documents within the time period required by the local court rules in effect in your county. If you need more information, you are advised to consult an attorney or a courthouse facilitator.*

FAILURE TO APPEAR MAY RESULT IN A TEMPORARY ORDER BEING ENTERED BY THE COURT THAT GRANTS THE RELIEF REQUESTED IN THE MOTION WITHOUT FURTHER NOTICE."

(3) *Courtesy Copies.* Courtesy copies shall be delivered to the assigned judge, pursuant to LCR 8.

(4) *Evidence on Motions.* Hearings with respect to all temporary orders shall be held and determined only upon the pleadings, affidavits or declarations, and other papers filed, unless the court directs otherwise.

[Adopted effective September 1, 2009; amended effective September 1, 2012; September 1, 2015.]

LCR 10. FORM OF PLEADINGS AND OTHER PAPERS

(a)—(c) (No Local Rules)

(d) Format Requirements.

(1) All papers filed with the Court shall comply with GR 14, including the requirement that the writing or printing shall appear on only one side of the page.

(2) *Tabs.* Except on courtesy copies, any tabs or separators used within documents shall be placed at the bottom of the page. If any tabs or separators are used on the sides of documents, the tabs or separators shall be removed by the Clerk and shall not be imaged for archiving purposes. It is the Court's preference that tabs on courtesy copies be placed on the sides of documents.

(3) *Typing/Color Photographs.* All court documents submitted for filing must be typed or printed legibly using black or dark blue ink. Since color photographs do not produce usable scanned or microfilmed images, black and white reproductions are preferable to obtain a better copy for imagining [1] and microfilming reproduction.

(4) *Conformed Copies.* Court documents served on opposing counsel or a self-represented party shall be fully conformed as to signatures, dates signed, date filed if known, and all other information as it appears on the filed original. If a party serves court documents that are otherwise fully conformed, but without the date of filing on the documents, the serving party shall notify the receiving party, as soon as practical after filing, of the date the served documents were filed.

(5) *Guardianship Hearing Dates.* In all reports required by RCW 11.92 et seq., the title shall contain, in addition to the name of the report, a notation to the Clerk to set the next report date, i.e., **"Clerk's Action Required: Next Hearing Date and Time: (date) at 10:30 a.m."**

(6) *Length of Briefs and Legal Memoranda.* Briefs and legal memoranda on non-dispositive pretrial matters may not exceed ten (10) pages double-spaced. In trial matters the limit for a party's main filing is twenty (20) pages double-spaced; supplemental briefs or legal memoranda on subsidiary matters may not exceed five (5) pages double-spaced. Declarations and affidavits in such matters may not exceed five (5) pages double-spaced. There is no page limit on dispositive motions.

[Adopted effective September 1, 2009; amended effective September 1, 2012; September 1, 2015.]

1 So in original.

LCR 11. SIGNING OF PLEADINGS, MOTIONS, AND LEGAL MEMORANDA

(a)—(b) No Local Rules

(c) Sanctions. Violation of any of these local rules may result in sanctions, including but not limited to, imposition of monetary terms, striking of pleadings or denial of affirmative relief to a party not in compliance with these rules.

[Adopted effective September 1, 2009; amended effective September 1, 2012.]

LCR 12-15. *[No Local Rules]*

LCR 16. PRETRIAL PROCEDURE AND FORMULATING ISSUES

(a)—(b) (No Local Rules)

(c) Pretrial Readiness.

(1) *Time.* The Court Administrator shall set pretrial readiness hearings in all civil and domestic cases approximately a month prior to the assigned trial date.

(2) *Matters Considered.* Matters to be considered at the readiness hearing may include, but are not limited to, the following: completion of mandatory mediation, completion of mandatory parenting seminar, witness availability, confirmation of length of trial, continuance of trial date pursuant to LCR 40(e), and pretrial motions.

(3) *Completion of Discovery.* Unless otherwise stipulated by the parties, or ordered by the court upon good cause shown and on such terms and conditions as are just, all discovery allowed under CR 26–27, including responses and supplementation thereto, must be completed no later than the scheduled date of the pretrial readiness hearing. Nothing herein stated shall modify a party's responsibility to promptly supplement responses to discovery rules or otherwise comply with discovery no later than the scheduled date of the pretrial readiness hearing.

(4) *Statement of Readiness for Trial.* If there are no matters to be resolved by the court, a party's personal appearance at the readiness hearing may be waived, provided the party has certified his or her readiness for trial with a written statement of readiness for trial filed with the court using the form set forth in Appendix E, and has received confirmation from the Court Administrator that the party's personal court appearance is waived or that the party may appear via CourtCall.

(d) Settlement Conference. Except as provided in SPR 94.08.3, any party in a civil action may schedule a pretrial settlement conference through the Court Administrator.

(1) *Conference Judge.* The settlement conference shall be before a judge who has not been assigned to preside at any subsequent trial, or an attorney mediator agreed to by the parties.

(2) *Mandatory Attendance.* Attendance at the settlement conference by all parties and counsel shall be mandatory, unless the court determines that circumstances exist precluding said attendance. Any nonparty wanting to be present or participate in the settlement conference must obtain written permission of the Settlement Conference Judge. Any request to attend must be submitted in writing, and a copy provided to the other party, at least 48 hours in advance of the scheduled settlement conference.

(3) *Setting.* Settlement conferences shall be set and heard no later than 21 days prior to trial.

(4) *Issues.* The parties shall provide documentation clearly stating the issues involved to the conference judge at least two (2) days prior to the conference.

[Adopted effective September 1, 2009; amended effective September 1, 2012; September 1, 2015.]

4. PARTIES
(Rules 17–25) *[No Local Rules]*

5. DEPOSITIONS AND DISCOVERY
(Rules 26–37) *[No Local Rules]*

6. TRIALS
(Rules 38–53.4)

LCR 38. *[No Local Rules]*

LCR 39. TRIAL BY JURY OR BY THE COURT

(a)—(c) (No Local Rules)

(d) Trial Briefs and Required Documents.

(1) *Trial Brief or Memorandum.* In all contested civil trials, each party shall prepare a trial brief or memorandum of authorities containing the legal issues involved and the authorities supporting same.

(2) *Other Required Documents.* In addition to the above, in all contested trials in domestic relations matters, each party shall provide the court with the following:

(i) A written pretrial information form indicating a proposed division of assets and liabilities, using the form set forth in Appendix H.

(ii) If children are involved, a proposed parenting plan and child support worksheets.

(3) *Time.* By noon two (2) calendar days prior to the date set for commencement of trial, all required documents shall be filed with the Clerk copies served on opposing counsel or a self-represented party, and courtesy copies provided to the assigned judge.

[Adopted effective September 1, 2009; amended effective September 1, 2012; September 1, 2015.]

LCR 40. ASSIGNMENT OF CASES

(a) (No Local Rules)

(b) Methods.

(1) *Note for Trial Assignment.* All notes for trial assignment on contested cases shall, in addition to counsel's or a self-represented party's estimate of time needed for trial, indicate the issues which counsel or the self-represented party believe will be in dispute, and shall contain the names and addresses of all attorneys, guardians ad litem, or self-represented parties. Counsel and self-represented parties shall certify that the issues are joined. If opposing counsel or self-represented parties dispute that the issues are joined or disagree with the statement of issues, do not believe the case is yet ready for trial, or have any other objection to the information contained in the Notice of Trial Assignment, opposing counsel or the self-represented parties shall, prior to the trial assignment date, file and serve an Objection to the Notice of Trial Assignment and note the matter for hearing on the appropriate motion calendar. This will remove the matter from the Court Administrator's trial assignment docket. Counsel and self-represented parties are urged to request sufficient time for these matters. Overestimation is preferred to underestimation of time needed. The form of the Note for Trial Assignment is set forth in Appendix C. Time shall be computed as set forth in Civil Rule 6 and LCR 6 herein.

(2) *Mandatory Mediation.* In any proceeding where mediation is required by SPR 94.08.3, no party may note the case for trial assignment until the parties have participated in good faith in mediation and a certificate of attendance at mediation has been filed with the court, or the court has found that a party refused to participate, in good faith, in mediation.

(3) *Conflict Dates.* Counsel shall file a Notice of Conflict Dates with the Clerk of the court and provide a copy to the Court Administrator on or before 9 a.m. of the date set for trial assignment. Conflict dates shall be limited to previously scheduled vacations and trial dates. The form of the Notice of Conflict Dates is set forth in Appendix D.

(4) *Trial Date Assignment.* The Court Administrator will assign cases a specific trial date and notify the parties by mail of such date. Counsel and self-represented parties shall not appear for the trial assignment calendar. If more than one matter is set for trial for the same day, counsel and self-represented parties shall be prepared for trial on the date set regardless of the order in which the cases are set.

(c) Priority Settings. All matters are subject to the established rule that criminal cases, juvenile proceedings, and civil proceedings entitled to priority settings take precedence over all other matters and may at times cause postponement of lesser prioritized cases.

(d) (No Local Rules)

(e) Continuances. A trial date may be stricken or continued by agreement of the parties upon presentation of an order to the court.

(f) Settlement of Cases Set for Trial. Notice shall be given immediately to the Court Administrator if any case which has been assigned a trial date is settled or will not be tried for any reason whatsoever. If this rule is violated and the court incurs unnecessary expenses, such as jury expenses, the court may, in its discretion, assess such costs to the parties.

(g) Confirmation of Trials. It shall be the responsibility of the parties to confirm that their trial will proceed on the scheduled trial date. Confirmation shall be made by telephone to the Court Administrator's office (360) 370–7480 no earlier than seven (7) or later than two (2) court days prior to the scheduled trial date.

[Adopted effective September 1, 2009; amended effective September 1, 2012; September 1, 2015.]

LCR 41-42. *[No Local Rules]*

LCR 43. TAKING OF TESTIMONY; EXHIBITS

(a)—(k) (No Local Rules)

(*l*) Matters Not Reported. Unless requested by a party and expressly directed by the judge, the following matters may not be reported or recorded:

(1) Opening statements and closing arguments in non-jury civil trials;

(2) Ex parte matters on the law and motion calendar;

(3) Verbal statements in a tape recording;

(4) Video tape recording used at trial or in a hearing; and

(5) Deposition transcripts read at trial in lieu of live testimony.

(m) Trial Exhibits.

(1) *Marked in Advance of Trial Date.* In all contested matters, the parties shall cause all exhibits, except such exhibits as are intended for impeachment purposes, to be marked for identification by the Clerk in advance of the trial date; provided that a party

may present exhibits for marking on the day of trial if the number of exhibits to be marked is ten (10) or less and the exhibits are provided for marking at least one (1) hour before the start of the trial. An exhibit list, without exhibit numbers filled in, shall be given to the Clerk when the exhibits are presented for marking.

(2) *Copies.* Copies of all documents offered as exhibits, except large maps or drawings, shall be prepared and presented to opposing counsel, any self-represented parties and to the judge at such time as the exhibits are offered into evidence; provided that, with the permission of the other party, the judge's courtesy copies may be provided before or at the commencement of the trial.

(3) *Withdrawal of Exhibits.* After final judgment, if the time for appeal has elapsed and no appeal has been taken, the court, upon application of any party or other person entitled to the possession of one or more exhibits, may in its discretion order the withdrawal of such exhibit or exhibits and delivery thereof to such party or other person.

(4) *Return or Destruction of Exhibits.* When judgment in a civil case shall become final after an appeal or upon judgment of dismissal, or upon filing a satisfaction of judgment, the Clerk, on stipulation of the parties, shall return all exhibits and unopened depositions or destroy them. The court shall enter an order accordingly.

(5) *Records in Administrative Appeals.* Records of proceedings and exhibits filed as the record in an appeal of any administrative hearing shall be presumed to be exhibits to the file in the superior court. Any video conference tapes or audio tapes shall have a transcript filed in addition to the video or audio tape.

[Adopted effective September 1, 2009; amended effective September 1, 2012; September 1, 2015.]

LCR 44–50. *[No Local Rules]*

LCR 51. INSTRUCTIONS TO JURY AND DELIBERATION

(a) **Proposed.** Proposed jury instructions shall be submitted prior to commencement of trial but in no event later than 9:00 a.m. the day on which the case is called for trial.

(b) **Submission.**

(1) *Cited Instructions for Court.* The parties shall file the original proposed jury instructions with the clerk and shall provide one (1) copy to the trial judge and one (1) copy to the opposing party. The proposed instructions shall be numbered and identified as to proposing party and shall contain supporting annotation and the number of the Washington Pattern Instruction (WPI) thereon.

(2) *Uncited Instructions for Jury.* The parties shall further provide the trial judge with one (1) set of such proposed jury instructions to be given to the jury, which set shall not be numbered but shall contain a space to enter a number, no citations of authority, no reference to the WPI number, and no identification as to the proposing party. The parties shall also include a title page entitled "Court's Instructions to the Jury" pursuant to WPI 1.01.01.

(c)—(j) (No Local Rules)

[Adopted effective September 1, 2009; amended effective September 1, 2012.]

LCR 52. DECISIONS, FINDINGS AND CONCLUSIONS

(a)—(e) No Local Rules

(f) **Time Limit for Presentation.** Written findings of fact, conclusions of law, decrees, judgments or orders shall be presented to the judge hearing the matter within thirty (30) days of the judge's oral or written pronouncement. Failure to comply with this rule may be grounds for a new trial or hearing and sanctions.

(g) **Responsibility for Preparation.** If a movant's motion is granted in whole or in part, the moving party shall be responsible to prepare and present any written findings, conclusions, and orders necessary as a result of the decision, unless the court orders otherwise.

[Adopted effective September 1, 2009; amended effective September 1, 2012.]

LCR 53–53.4. *[No Local Rules]*

7. JUDGMENT
(Rules 54–63)

LCR 54–55. *[No Local Rules]*

LCR 56. SUMMARY JUDGMENT

(a)—(h) (No Local Rules)

(i) **Confirmation of Summary Judgment Motions.** It shall be the responsibility of the moving party to confirm all summary judgment motions. Confirmation shall be made by telephone to the court administrator's office at (360) 378–2399 no earlier than seven (7) or later than two (2) court days prior to the hearing.

[Adopted effective September 1, 2009; amended effective September 1, 2012.]

LCR 57–63. *[No Local Rules]*

8. PROVISIONAL AND FINAL REMEDIES
(Rules 64–71) *[No Local Rules]*

9.   APPEALS
(Rules 72–76) *[No Local Rules]*

10. SUPERIOR COURTS AND CLERKS
(Rules 77–80)

LCR 77. SUPERIOR COURTS AND JUDICIAL OFFICERS

(a)—(n) (No Local Rules)

(*o*) Visiting Judge.

(1) When the elected judge is not sitting on a case, whether from a recusal, an affidavit of prejudice or otherwise, and a visiting judge has been assigned to hear the case, all hearings and trial dates shall be scheduled with the San Juan County Superior Court Administrator.

(2) For motions to be heard on the Friday law and motion calendar and for special set motions, counsel or self-represented parties shall notify the Court Administrator before the motion is filed in order to determine if the visiting judge can be scheduled to either be present in San Juan County or be available for a telephonic hearing on the requested date.

(3) For motions that are not dispositive and are of the type that would normally be set for the Friday morning calendar, the visiting judge shall have the option of appearing by telephone to hear the motion. In that event, counsel or self-represented parties shall appear personally in the San Juan County Superior Court Courtroom or, where allowed by these rules, may appear telephonically.

(4) For special set motions, other than dispositive motions, the Court Administrator shall attempt to arrange for the visiting judge to appear personally in the San Juan County Superior Court Courtroom to hear the motion. In the event the judge is not able to appear personally, counsel or self-represented parties may appear in the San Juan County Superior Court Courtroom; appear telephonically, where allowed by these rules; or appear personally before the judge in that judge's courtroom.

(5) Trials and dispositive motions shall be held in San Juan County, absent court approval and agreement of the parties.

(6) Telephonic appearances by the visiting judge shall be arranged by the Court Administrator. Tele-phonic appearances by counsel or self-represented parties must be arranged by counsel or the parties.

(7) Counsel or self-represented parties are responsible to provide courtesy copies of their pleadings to the visiting judge.

(p) Court Administrator. The Court Administrator is subject to the general supervision of the judge. The specific powers and duties of the Court Administrator include, but are not limited to, the following, as directed by the judge:

(i) Calendaring and jury management;

(ii) Supervision and direction of the work of the court employees;

(iii) Preparation and administration of the budget of the court;

(iv) Assistance in representing the court regarding court management matters.

(q) Office Hours.. Office hours for the Court Administrator are 8:00 a.m. to 12:00 noon and from 1:00 p.m. to 5:00 p.m., Monday through Friday, except on legal holidays.

(r) Court Schedule.

(1) *Law and Motion Day.* Friday of each week shall be law and motion day. If Friday falls on a legal holiday, then the motion calendar will be heard on the preceding Thursday, except during the week of the Thanksgiving holiday, when the motion calendar shall be heard on the preceding Wednesday. Scheduling on law and motion day will be as follows:

(i) 9:00 a.m. Adult criminal matters, except sentencings;

(ii) 10:30 a.m. Open civil hearings, which shall proceed in the following order: ex parte matters; supplemental proceedings; readiness hearings; uncontested matters in probates and guardianships; uncontested dissolutions; parentage motions where paternity has previously been determined; all orders to show cause and/or motions in domestic actions; other orders to show cause, except show cause hearings in unlawful detainer actions; motions in civil cases; motions and orders subsequent to judgment; and motions for summary judgment where a special set is not required by LCR 8(g).

(iii) 10:30 a.m. Closed civil hearings, which shall follow the Open civil hearings;

(iv) 1:30 p.m. Criminal sentencing hearings special set per LCrR 8.2(c)

(v) 1:30 p.m. Show cause hearings in unlawful detainer matters and special set matters [per LCR 8(g)] scheduled in advance through the Court Administrator's office.

(2) *Protection Order Matters.* Domestic violence matters under Chapter 26.50, RCW; sexual assault matters under Chapter 7.90, RCW; stalking matters under Chapter 7.92, RCW; abuse of vulnerable adult matters under Chapter 74.34, RCW; and those anti-harassment matters transferred to Superior Court pursuant to RCW 10.14.150, shall be heard on Thursday of each week, beginning at 8:30 a.m. If Thursday falls on a legal holiday, these matters will be heard on the preceding Wednesday, except during the week of the Thanksgiving holiday, when they shall be heard on the preceding Tuesday.

(3) *Juvenile Matters.* All juvenile matters other than fact finding hearings and truancy hearings shall be heard on Thursdays, beginning at 12:30 p.m. The juvenile calendar shall proceed in the following order: offender matters; dependency matters; and matters proceeding under Chapter 13.32A, RCW; Truancy hearings shall be heard on Thursdays, beginning at 3:10 p.m.

(4) *Ex Parte Matters.* Ex Parte matters may be presented to the judge in chambers between the hours of 9:00 a.m. and 4:00 p.m. on all judicial days. Counsel or a self-represented party shall call the Court Administrator's office in advance to schedule a presentation. Parties wishing to present an ex parte matter on the record shall do so at 1:30 p.m. on any day, after

first giving notice to the County Clerk and the Court Administrator.

(5) *Jury Trials.* Jury trials will normally start on a Monday. Court will begin at 8:30 a.m. and recess for lunch from 12:00 noon to 1:30 p.m., continuing until 4:30 p.m. each day, with a minimum 15–minute recess mid-morning and again mid-afternoon.

[Adopted effective September 1, 2009; amended on an emergency basis effective Feb. 23, 2012; May 23, 2012; amended on a permanent basis effective September 1, 2012; September 1, 2015.]

LCR 78. CLERKS

(a)—(f) No Local Rules

(g) **Signing Out Court Files.** Any file signed out from the County Clerk's Office by a local attorney or title company shall be returned and signed in within five (5) days, or immediately if so requested by a judge, court commissioner or clerk. Nonresident attorneys or title companies may withdraw files only upon an order based upon such application signed by the court. The court file shall not be taken apart for any purpose, except with the express consent of the County Clerk.

(h) **Self–Addressed, Stamped Envelope.** If an attorney or any other person requests from the clerk the mailing of an answer to correspondence or conformed copies of any pleadings or other documents, the attorney or person requesting the same shall furnish a self-addressed, stamped envelope for the convenience of the clerk.

(i) **Facsimile Filing of Pleadings With Clerk.** Documents, including pleadings, may be filed with the clerk by facsimile transmission, in accordance with GR 17.

[Adopted effective September 1, 2009; amended effective September 1, 2012.]

LCR 79–80. *[No Local Rules]*

11. GENERAL PROVISIONS
(Rules 81–87)

LCR 81-83. *[No Local Rules]*

LCR 84. INVOLUNTARY COMMITMENT HEARING

Involuntary commitment hearings shall be held as occasion demands in deference to expediting the hearing, availability of medical testimony, and the convenience of the court. The office of the prosecuting attorney shall notify the court administrator immediately upon the filing of an application, and the time and place of the hearing shall be set by the court

administrator at the earliest date compatible with the foregoing factors.

[Adopted effective September 1, 2009; amended effective September 1, 2012.]

LCR 85-86. *[No Local Rules]*

LCR 87. PROFESSIONAL CONDUCT

(a) **Conduct and Dress Code.** All persons entering the courtroom shall comply with the Conduct and Dress Code posted outside the courtrooms. A copy of the Conduct and Dress Code is set forth in Appendix J.

(b) Professional Conduct. All attorneys and self-represented parties shall adhere to the "Courtroom Decorum and Practice Guidelines," a copy of which is set forth in Appendix K.

(c) Time Standards. All attorneys and self-represented parties shall make a good faith effort to meet the Advisory Case Processing Time Standards set forth in the Washington Court Rules.

[Formerly LCR 81, adopted effective September 1, 2009. Renumbered LCR 87 and amended effective September 1, 2012; September 1, 2015.]

PART II.   LOCAL RULES FOR SPECIAL PROCEEDINGS (SPR)

SPR 94.08.1.   FILINGS IN FAMILY LAW CASES

(a) Application of Rule. This rule shall apply to all of the following types of cases:

(1) Family law petitions seeking dissolution of marriage, legal separation, or declaration of invalidity; and

(2) Actions brought by parties to nonmarital relationships involving parenting or distribution of assets/liabilities.

(b) Court's Automatic Temporary Order. Upon the filing of a Summons and Petition in any of the actions specified above, the court shall automatically issue a Temporary Order using the form set forth in Appendix A. The Petitioner is subject to this order from the time of filing the Petition. The Petitioner shall serve a copy of this order on the Respondent and file a declaration of service in the court file. The Respondent is subject to this order from the time that the order is served.

(c) Filing of Parties' Financial Declarations and Verified Statement of Assets and Liabilities. Within thirty (30) days after the filing of an answer or other responsive pleading in any of the actions specified above, each party shall serve on the opposing party:

(1) A Financial Declaration, using (WPF DR 01.1550). In all cases involving a request for child support, maintenance or attorney's fees, the Declaration shall also be filed with the court; and

(2) A Verified Statement of Assets and Liabilities, including both marital and separate assets and liabilities of any kind, in the form set forth in Appendix B. The Verified Statement of Assets and Liabilities shall not be filed with the court.

(3) Each party shall then file with the court a Declaration of Mailing, attesting that the Financial Declaration and Verified Statement of Assets and Liabilities has been provided to the other party within the 30–day time limit. All parties have a duty to supplement the financial information when additional information becomes available.

(d) Self–Represented Parties—Review of Parenting Plans and Child Support Orders. In any action, including modification proceedings, in which the residential care or child support of a minor child or children is at issue and in which none of the parties are represented by counsel, any proposed parenting plan or residential schedule and any proposed child support documents, including the child support schedule worksheet, shall first be reviewed, approved as to form and initialed by the court facilitator or by an attorney acting as a third-party neutral in accordance with RPC 2.4. Provided, however, this requirement shall not apply to a proposed temporary parenting plan or residential schedule in cases where there has been a recent and substantial change in circumstances that has resulted in a serious and imminent threat to the health, safety or welfare of the child(ren).

(e) Judicial Information System Background Checks. Prior to presenting a permanent parenting plan or residential schedule to the court for approval, the party or parties shall comply with RCW 26.09.182 by submitting a completed Judicial Information System (JIS) Background Check form to the San Juan County Clerk. Such request shall include the names and dates of birth of all persons residing in each residence and must be submitted no fewer than 5 days prior to the date of presentation of the final parenting plan. Upon receipt of a completed JIS Background Check form, the Clerk shall complete a search of the Judicial Information System for the existence of any information and proceedings relevant to the placement of the child. This search shall be performed no more than 10 days prior to the proposed date of presentation of the permanent parenting plan. The results of such search shall be available to the judicial officer presiding over the entry of the permanent parenting plan at least 2 court days prior to the proposed presentation date. Per Chapter 2.28 RCW (as amended by SHB 1617, Laws of 2015), if the Court relies upon information in the results of the search in rendering a decision, a copy of the results and the JIS Background Check form must be filed as a confidential document, within the court file, with any confidential contact information such as addresses, phone numbers, or other information that might disclose the location or whereabouts of any person redacted from the document or documents. In the event the Court does not rely upon information in the results of the search, the JIS Background Check form and the results of the search shall be destroyed. JIS Background Check form is attached as Appendix I.

(f) Background Information. Before entering any order regarding custody of a child in a non parental action for child custody the Petitioner(s) shall comply with the requirements of RCW 26.10.135(2).

[Adopted effective September 1, 2009; amended effective September 1, 2012; September 1, 2015.]

SPR 94.08.2. PARENTING SEMINARS

(a) **Applicable Cases.** This rule shall apply to all cases under Chapter 26.09, 26.10, or 26.26 RCW which require a parenting plan or residential schedule for minor children, including major modifications and paternity actions in which paternity has been established.

(b) **Mandatory Attendance.** Except as provided in Section (f) below, within thirty (30) days of filing an appearance, answer or other responsive pleading in this action, both parties shall register for a court-approved parent education seminar on the effects of family transitions on children, unless the parties have previously attended such a course. Each party shall attend the seminar within sixty (60) days of registering.

(c) **Certificate of Completion.** Upon completion of the seminar, each party shall file with the court the seminar completion certificate provided by the sponsoring agency or provider. Additionally, a copy of the certificate of completion shall be provided to the judge at presentation of final documents.

(d) **Fees.** Each party attending a seminar shall pay a fee charged by the approved provider and authorized by the court.

(e) **Seminar Providers.** The court shall establish standards for parenting seminars and shall approve seminar providers. A list of approved parenting seminars shall be available from the superior court administrator, court facilitator, and county clerk. If a parenting seminar is not included on the list, then the court, upon proper motion, may allow other seminars to fulfill this requirement on a case-by-case basis.

(f) **Waiver/Special Consideration.** Pursuant to RCW 26.12.172:

(1) In no case shall opposing parties be required to attend a parenting seminar together; and

(2) Upon a showing of domestic violence or abuse which would not require mutual decision-making, pursuant to RCW 26.09.191, or if the court determines that attendance at a seminar is not in the children's best interest, the court shall either waive the requirement of completion of the seminar or allow participation in an alternative parenting seminar if available; and

(3) The Court may otherwise waive the requirement upon a showing of good cause.

(g) **Exchange of Parenting Plans.** Within fourteen (14) days of completing the parenting seminar, each parent shall provide the other parent with a Proposed Parenting Plan, if they have not already done so.

(h) **Failure to Comply.** Willful refusal to participate in a parenting seminar or willful delay in completing the parenting seminar may result in a finding of contempt and imposition of sanctions. The Court may decline to enter finalization documents until both parents have completed the seminar. [See Order to Show Cause Re: Parenting Class in Appendix F.]

[Adopted effective September 1, 2009; amended effective September 1, 2012.]

SPR 94.08.3. MANDATORY MEDIATION

(a) **Mediation in Contested Cases.** Except as provided in Section (b) below, in all cases specified in Section (a) of SPR 94.08.1 having unresolved issues, both parties shall in good faith engage in mediation with a court-approved mediator in an effort to resolve the case. In cases where parenting issues exist, the mediation shall not occur until both parties have completed the parenting seminar described in SPR 94.08.2. Mediation shall be completed at least sixty (60) days prior to the scheduled trial date.

(b) **When Mediation is Not Required.** Mediation shall not be required as provided in Section (a) in the following cases:

(1) For good cause shown upon motion and approval by the court; or

(2) Where a domestic violence restraining order or protection order (excluding ex parte orders) involving the parties has been entered by a court at any time within the previous twelve (12) months;

(3) Where a domestic violence no contact order exists pursuant to RCW 10.99;

(4) Where the court upon motion finds that domestic abuse has occurred between the parties and that such abuse would interfere with arm's-length mediation. Notwithstanding the foregoing, either party may by motion seek a court order requiring mandatory mediation in a case where it would not be required as set forth in (b)(2), (b)(3) or (b)(4) above if the moving party believes that the parties would be able to mediate their dispute at arm's-length under the particular circumstances of the case.

(c) **Settlement Conference.** If, after mediation in good faith or where mediation is not required, there remain unresolved issues in any case specified by Section (a) of SPR 94.08.1, the parties may participate in a settlement conference, pursuant to LCR 16(b).

(d) **Effect on Court Proceedings.** Mediation does not stay or otherwise affect the rights and duties of the parties established by statute, court rule, or court order. The court may enter temporary orders and the parties may conduct discovery prior to or during the mediation process.

(e) Cost of Mediation. Mediators shall be paid by the parties in accordance with the agreement of the parties, or in the absence of agreement, as determined by the Court.

(f) Responsibility for Compliance. The parties shall be responsible for arranging for and completing all mediation requirements established under this rule.

(g) Failure to Comply. Willful refusal to participate in mediation or willful delay in completing mediation may result in a finding of contempt and imposition of sanctions.

(h) Approval of Mediators. Mediators performing mediation services pursuant to this rule must fulfill the minimum qualifications set forth in Appendix L. In order to fulfill the mediation requirements of this rule, the parties must use the services of a court-approved mediator. The Court Administrator shall maintain a list of approved mediators, either persons or agencies, for distribution to the public. The list shall contain the following information: each mediator's name, organization, if any, address and telephone number, and fee schedule.

(i) Selection of Mediator; Right of Mediator to Decline. The parties may either agree to a mediator from the court-approved list or the mediator will be determined by use of a strike list. A mediator has the right to decline to serve in a particular case. If a mediator declines to serve, the parties shall select a different mediator, using the same selection process by which the preceding mediator was selected.

(j) Authority of Mediator. The mediator has the authority to determine the time, place, manner, and duration of mediation. In appropriate cases, the mediator shall have the authority to terminate the mediation prior to completion.

(k) Attendance at Mediation. The parties shall personally attend all mediation sessions, unless the mediator permits telephonic or other attendance. The mediator shall have the authority to require other persons to attend.

(l) Declaration of Completion. Within seven (7) days of completion of mediation, a declaration that mediation has been completed shall be filed with the court by the mediator. The mediator shall advise counsel and the parties of the results of mediation in writing. The mediator shall advise the court only whether an agreement has been reached on some or all of the issues.

(m) Confidentiality. The work product of the mediator and all communications during the mediation shall be privileged and confidential and not subject to compulsory disclosure. The mediator shall not appear to testify in any court proceedings. See RCW 5.60.070.

[Adopted effective September 1, 2009; amended effective September 1, 2012; September 1, 2015.]

SPR 94.08.4.   COURTCALL TELEPHONIC APPEARANCE RULE

(a) Program Overview.

(1) The CourtCall Telephonic Appearance Program ("CourtCall"), 1–888–882–6878, organizes a procedure for telephonic appearance by attorneys or self-represented parties as a reasonable alternative to personal appearances in appropriate cases and situations. CourtCall is fully voluntary and no person is required to utilize CourtCall. CourtCall is available at a fixed fee to use when circumstances are appropriate.

(2) Hearings will be held on a specific calendar in the usual manner, unless the court exercises its discretion to call cases in a different order.

(3) Hearings are conducted in open court or in private as the court may designate. All attorneys or self-represented parties making CourtCall Appearances call a designated toll free teleconference number a few minutes before the calendar is scheduled, to check in with the Clerk. Attorneys or self-represented parties remain on the court's speakerphone-telephone line and hear the same business that those present in the court may be hearing. Attorneys or self-represented parties not participating telephonically appear in person. The court calls cases for hearing. All attorneys or self-represented parties on a case participate in the hearing. All present in the courtroom hear the discourse of those making CourtCall Appearances.

(4) CourtCall Appearances are scheduled, in writing, in advance, by counsel or self-represented parties serving on all other counsel and self-represented parties and delivering (via fax, mail, or personal delivery) to CourtCall, LLC, not less than seven (7) court days prior to the hearing date, a Request for CourtCall Appearance form and by paying the stated fee for each CourtCall Appearance. The court may shorten the time for serving the request for good cause shown.

(b) Participation in CourtCall Appearances.

(1) *Court.*

(a) The court shall hear CourtCall Appearances in the order in which they are noted on the calendar, unless the court exercises its discretion to call cases in a different manner.

(b) The following matters are currently deemed unsuitable for CourtCall Appearances and shall require the personal appearance of counsel or self-represented parties, unless otherwise approved in advance by the court.

(i) Judgment Debtor Examinations;

(ii) Settlement Conferences;

(iii) Hearings and trials at which oral testimony may be presented;

(iv) Show cause hearings regarding contempt by a party.

(c) The court reserves the right, at any time, to reject any Request for CourtCall Appearance. When the court rejects a request, it shall order a refund of deposited telephonic appearance fees and notify CourtCall, LLC.

(d) The court reserves the right to halt the telephonic hearing on any matter and order the attorneys or self-represented parties to personally appear at a later date and time, in which case no refund is permitted.

(e) If a matter is continued prior to the actual hearing date, the prior filing of a Request for CourtCall Appearance form shall remain valid for the continued date of the hearing.

(f) Existing rules and procedures regarding making of the record by a court reporter or electronic device or obtaining a transcript after the hearing shall apply to hearings at which CourtCall Appearances are made. No private recordings may be made of telephonic appearances.

(g) Upon proper motion, the court in its discretion may waive the CourtCall fee for a party who is found by the court to be indigent or for his or her counsel.

(2) *Attorneys and Self–Represented Parties.*

(a) Attorneys and self-represented parties electing to make a CourtCall Appearance shall serve, on all other parties in the case, the Request for Court-Call Appearance form, fax or otherwise deliver a copy of the form to CourtCall, LLC, and pay the CourtCall Appearance Fee in the method prescribed, not less than seven (7) court days before the hearing date. The court may shorten the time for serving the request for good cause shown.

(b) When the Request for CourtCall Appearance is made at the same time as the filing of the hearing documents or response, in addition to the Request for CourtCall Appearance form, the words "Court-Call Appearance Requested" shall be printed below the department, date, and time of the hearings on the first page of the papers filed with the court and courtesy copies for the judge.

(c) **Appearance Procedure.**

(1) An attorney or a self-represented party making a Court Call Appearance shall:

(a) Eliminate to the greatest extent possible all ambient noise from the calling location;

(b) Be required, during the speaker's appearance, to speak directly into a telephone handset;

(c) Not call in with cellular or cordless telephone devices or through a personal computer.

(2) An attorney or a self-represented party making a CourtCall Appearance shall call the court's designated toll free teleconference line approximately five (5) minutes prior to the scheduled hearing time and check-in with the Clerk. All persons calling after the check-in period shall be considered to be late for the hearing and shall be treated by the court in the same manner as if the person had personally appeared late for the hearing.

(3) An attorney or a self-represented party appearing telephonically shall state his or her name for the record each time the person speaks and shall participate in the appearance with the same degree of courtesy and courtroom etiquette as is required for a personal appearance. An attorney or a self-represented party shall not utilize the "hold" button, as it is not within the policy of the court to wait for any person to rejoin the line.

[Adopted effective September 1, 2009; amended effective September 1, 2012; September 1, 2015.]

SPR 98.04.5. GUARDIANS AD LITEM

[See Superior Court Guardian ad Litem Rules (GALR) for general responsibilities of guardians ad litem.]

(a) **Appointments of Guardian Ad Litem.** All guardians ad litem shall be appointed as set forth in the policies and procedures for guardians ad litem, approved by the judges and maintained by the Superior Court Administrator's Office.

(b) **Grievance Procedures.**

(1) *Submission of Complaints.* All complaints made by or against guardians ad litem shall be in writing and shall be submitted to the court administrator. All complaints must bear the signature, name and address of the person filing the complaint.

(2) *Review of Complaint.* Upon receipt of a written complaint, the court administrator shall refer the complaint to the judge for review

(3) *Findings and Action of Complaint.* Upon review of the complaint, the judge shall either:

(A) Make a finding that the complaint is with regard to a case then pending in the court and decline to review the complaint and so inform the complainant. In such instances, the judge shall advise the complainant that the complaint may only be addressed in the context of the case at bar, either by seeking the removal of the guardian ad litem or by contesting the information or recommendation contained in the guardian ad litem's report or testimony; or

(B) Make a finding that the complaint has no merit on its face, and decline to review the complaint and so inform the complainant; or

(C) Make a finding that the complaint appears to have merit and request a written response from the guardian ad litem or other person against whom the complaint is brought within ten (10) business days, detailing the specific issues in the complaint to which the judge desires a response. The judge shall provide the guardian ad litem or other person against whom the complaint is brought with a copy of the original complaint. In considering whether any complaint against a guardian ad litem has merit, the judge shall consider whether the complaint alleges the guardian ad litem has (i) violated a code of conduct, (ii) misrepresented his or her qualifications to serve as a guardian ad litem, (iii) breached the confidentiality of the parties, (iv) falsified information in a report to the court or in testimony before the court, (v) failed, when required, to report abuse of a child, (vi) communicated with a judicial officer ex parte concerning a case for which he or she is serving as guardian ad litem, (vii) violated state or local laws or court rules, or (viii) taken or failed to take any other action which would reasonably place the suitability of the person to serve as a guardian ad litem in question.

(4) *Response and Findings on Complaint.* Upon receipt of a written response to a complaint, the judge shall make a finding as to each of the specific issues in the complaint to which the judge desires a response, as delineated in the judge's letter to the person against whom the complaint is brought. Such findings shall state that either there is no merit to the issue based upon the response or that there is merit to the issue.

(5) *Forms of Discipline.* The judge shall have the authority to issue a written admonition or a written reprimand, refer the guardian ad litem (if the complaint is against a guardian ad litem) to additional training, or suspend or remove the guardian ad litem from the registry. In considering an appropriate form of discipline, the judge shall take into consideration any prior complaints that resulted in an admonition, reprimand, referral to training, or suspension or removal from the registry. If the guardian ad litem against whom the discipline is directed is listed on more than one registry, the suspension or removal

may apply to each registry the guardian ad litem is listed on, at the discretion of the judge.

(6) *Notice to Complainant and Person Against Whom Complaint is Brought.* The complainant and the person against whom the complaint is brought shall be notified in writing of the judge's decision following receipt of the response to the complaint.

(7) *Confidentiality.* A complaint shall be deemed confidential for all purposes unless the judge reviewing the complaint has determined that the complaint has merit. Any record of complaints filed which are not deemed by the judge to have merit shall be confidential, and shall not be disclosed except by court order, upon good cause shown, after the person against whom the complaint was brought has been given notice and an opportunity to be heard.

(8) *Complaint Processing Standards.* Complaints shall be resolved within twenty-five (25) days of the date of receipt of the written complaint if a case is pending. Complaints shall be resolved within sixty (60) days of the date of receipt of the written complaint if the complaint is filed after the conclusion of a case.

(9) *Removal from Registry.* When a guardian ad litem is removed from the court's registry pursuant to the disposition of a grievance hereunder, the court administrator shall send a notice of such removal to the Administrative Office of the Courts. When the court administrator receives notice from the Administrative Office of the Courts that a guardian ad litem on the court's registry has been removed from the registry of any other Washington superior court, the court administrator shall advise the judge of such removal.

[Adopted effective September 1, 2009; amended effective September 1, 2012.]

PART III.   LOCAL CRIMINAL RULES (LCrR)

1.   SCOPE, PURPOSE AND CONSTRUCTION
(Rules 1.1–1.5) *[No Local Rules]*

2.   PROCEDURES PRIOR TO ARREST AND OTHER SPECIAL PROCEEDINGS
(Rules 2.1–2.3) *[No Local Rules]*

3.   RIGHTS OF DEFENDANTS
(Rules 3.1–3.6) *[No Local Rules]*

4.   PROCEDURES PRIOR TO TRIAL
(Rules 4.1–4.10)

LCrR 4.2(i).   AUTHORITY OF COURT COMMISSIONERS

Court Commissioners qualified under Article 4, Section 23 of the Washington Constitution are authorized to preside over arraignments, preliminary appearances, initial extradition hearings, and noncompliance proceedings pursuant to RCW 9.94A.200; accept guilty pleas as authorized in this local rule pursuant to RCW 2.24.040(15); appoint counsel; make determinations of probable cause; set, amend, and review conditions of pretrial release; set bail; set trial and hearing dates; authorize continuances and accept waivers of the right to speedy trial.

[Adopted effective September 1, 2009; amended effective September 1, 2012.]

LCrR 4.9.   PRETRIAL MOTIONS

The attorneys or self-represented parties shall specially set pretrial motions in criminal matters with the Court Administrator at least ten (10) days prior to trial.

[Adopted effective September 1, 2009; amended effective September 1, 2012; September 1, 2015.]

5.   VENUE
(Rules 5.1–5.2) *[No Local Rules]*

6.   PROCEDURES AT TRIAL
(Rules 6.1–6.16)

LCrR 6.1.   TRIAL BY JURY OR BY THE COURT

(a) **Trial Brief or Memorandum.** In criminal trials with contested legal or evidentiary issues, each party shall prepare a trial brief or memorandum of authorities containing the issues involved and the authorities supporting same and provide the same to the clerk, opposing counsel and judge by noon two (2) days prior to the date set for commencement of trial.

[Adopted effective September 1, 2009; amended effective September 1, 2012.]

7.   PROCEDURES FOLLOWING CONVICTION
(Rules 7.1–7.8) *[No Local Rules]*

8.   MISCELLANEOUS
(Rules 8.1–8.9)

LCrR 8.1.   TIME

Time shall be computed and enlarged in accordance with CR 6, and not by the civil local court rules.

[Adopted effective September 1, 2009; amended effective September 1, 2012.]

LCrR 8.2.   MOTIONS

(a) **Motion Calendar.** Criminal motion calendar shall be set at 9:00 a.m. on Fridays.

(b) Motions. Unless changed by the Local Criminal Court Rules, Criminal Rules 3.5 and 3.6, Civil Rule 7(b), and LCR 7 shall govern motions in criminal cases. CourtCall may only be utilized in limited circumstances and then only after court approval.

(c) Sentencing Hearings. For all criminal sentencing hearings the parties shall obtain a special set hearing date and time (usually 1:30 p.m. on Friday) from the Court Administrator after conferring with each other regarding conflicts.

(d) Drug/Alcohol and/or Mental Evaluations. Unless otherwise approved by the court, any evaluation required or presented to the court for consideration must meet the standards set forth in Appendix M.

(e) Presentation of Final Documents. If a movant's motion is granted in whole or in part, the moving party shall be responsible to prepare and present any written findings, conclusions, and orders necessary as a result of the decision, unless the court orders otherwise.

[Adopted effective September 1, 2009; amended effective September 1, 2012; September 1, 2015.]

LCrR 8.3-8.9. *[No Local Rules]*

PART IV. LOCAL JUVENILE COURT RULES (LJuCR)

TITLE I. SCOPE AND APPLICATION OF RULES

LJuCR 1.1-1.3. *[No Local Rules]*

LJuCR 1.5. *[No Local Rules]*

LJuCR 1.4. APPLICABILITY OF OTHER RULES

(a) Criminal Rules. The Superior Court Criminal Rules and Local Criminal Rules shall apply in juvenile offense proceedings when not inconsistent with these rules and applicable statutes.

[Adopted effective September 1, 2009; amended effective September 1, 2012.]

LJuCR 1.6. COURT APPOINTED SPECIAL ADVOCATE PROGRAM

This judicial district has a Court Appointed Special Advocate program. Rules and details may be obtained from Juvenile Court Services and from the clerk's office.

[Adopted effective September 1, 2009; amended effective September 1, 2012.]

TITLE II. SHELTER CARE PROCEEDINGS

LJuCR 2.1-2.4. *[No Local Rules]*

LJuCR 2.5. AMENDMENT OF SHELTER CARE ORDER

(a) 30–Day Shelter Care Review. If a parent, guardian ad litem, or court-appointed special advocate wishes to contest placement of a child or any service ordered at the shelter care hearing, he or she must file and serve on all parties and counsel a notice of contested issues no later than three (3) court days before the 30–day shelter care review hearing. The notice of contested hearing shall be accompanied by written evidence in support of the issue. Unless good cause is shown, failure to provide timely notice of contested issues shall constitute a waiver of the right to raise such issues at the 30–day shelter care review hearing.

[Adopted effective September 1, 2009; amended effective September 1, 2012.]

TITLE III. DEPENDENCY PROCEEDINGS

LJuCR 3.1-3.8. *[No Local Rules]*

LJuCR 3.9. REVIEW HEARING

(a) Department's Written Review Report. A written review report shall be prepared by the department and shall be filed and served on all counsel and parties not less than ten (10) days prior to the review hearing.

(b) Notice of Contested Issues. After receipt of the department's report, if a parent, guardian ad litem, or court-appointed special advocate wishes to contest any issue, he or she must file serve a notice of contested issues no later than three (3) court days before the hearing. The notice of contested hearing shall be accompanied by written evidence in support of the issue. Unless good cause is shown, failure to provide timely notice of contested issues shall constitute a waiver of the right to contest any issue, except the department's permanency plan.

[Adopted effective September 1, 2009; amended effective September 1, 2012.]

TITLE IV. PROCEEDINGS TO TERMINATE PARENT–CHILD RELATION-SHIP
(LJuCR 4.1–4.3) *[No Local Rules]*

TITLE V. PROCEEDINGS FOR CHILDREN IN NEED OF SERVICES
(LJuCR 5.1–5.7) *[No Local Rules]*

TITLE 5A. PROCEEDINGS FOR AT–RISK YOUTH
(LJuCR 5A.1–5A.6) *[No Local Rules]*

TITLE VI. JUVENILE OFFENSE PROCEEDINGS–DIVERSION AGREE-MENTS
(LJuCR 6.1–6.6) *[No Local Rules]*

TITLE VII. JUVENILE OFFENSE PROCEEDINGS IN JUVENILE COURT

LJuCR 7.1-7.2. *[No Local Rules]*

LJuCR 7.3. DETENTION FACILITIES

(g) **Facilities In San Juan County.** The San Juan County Juvenile Court shall designate appropriate juvenile detention facilities for use; provided, that the detention area within the San Juan Sheriff's Depart-ment building may be used for detention of juveniles prior to an initial court appearance if no adult prisoners are housed in the same detention area.

[Adopted effective September 1, 2009; amended effective September 1, 2012.]

LJuCR 7.4-7.15. *[No Local Rules]*

TITLE VIII. DECLINING JUVENILE COURT JURISDICTION OVER AN ALLEGED JUVENILE OFFENDER
(LJuCR 8.1–8.2) *[No Local Rules]*

TITLE IX. RIGHT TO LAWYER AND EXPERTS IN ALL JUVENILE COURT PROCEEDINGS
(LJuCR 9.1–9.3) *[No Local Rules]*

TITLE X. JUVENILE COURT RECORDS
(LJuCR 10.1–10.9) *[No Local Rules]*

TITLE XI. SUPPLEMENTAL PROVISIONS

LJuCR 11.1-11.2. *[No Local Rules]*

LJuCR 11.3. COURT SCHEDULES FOR JUVENILE MATTERS

See LCR 77(r)(3).

[Adopted effective September 1, 2009.]

LJuCR 11.4. DUTIES OF CLERKS

(1)(a) *Distribution of Funds.* [See RCW 9.94A.760(1)]

[Adopted effective September 1, 2009.]

LJuCR 11.5. FINANCIAL RESPONSIBILITY

(a) **Financial Obligation.** Pursuant to the intent and standards set forth in RCW 13.16.085 and RCW 13.40.145, in any juvenile court proceeding regarding the detention, disposition or modification regarding a juvenile offender, or in any at risk youth, CHINS, truancy or dependency proceeding, the court may order the parent or parents, guardian, or other person legally obligated to support the juvenile, to pay a reasonable sum for the cost of detention and/or legal services provided by publicly funded counsel.

(b) **Assessment of Costs.** The assessment for the cost of detention and publicly funded counsel should not exceed actual costs to the county. The costs shall be assessed and ordered paid in a reasonable time unless a sworn financial statement is presented to the court at said proceeding justifying reduction or elimination of any such assessment, or there are other circumstances recognized by the court for reducing or not imposing the assessment.

(c) **Notice.** It shall be the duty of the Juvenile Court Services and/or the prosecuting attorney, to notify the parent or parents, guardian, or other person legally obligated to support the juvenile of this rule prior to said proceeding and to provide all necessary documents in order for such person to adequately prepare for said proceeding. Notice shall be provided to the parties five days in advance of any proceeding to assess costs.

(d) **Time.** Proceedings to assess costs shall not be held prior to sentencing or contempt hearing.

(e) **Payments Forwarded.** Juvenile Court Services, the public defense department, or the county clerk's office shall receive payments in a manner appropriate to local and state auditing regulations and shall forward such payments to the county treasurer.

(f) **Sanctions.** A show cause hearing with timely notice by Juvenile Court Services or the prosecuting attorney to the delinquent person or agency may be held to inquire into the delinquency of the assessment and the sanctions available under RCW 13.16.085 and RCW 13.40.145.

[Adopted effective September 1, 2009; amended effective September 1, 2012.]

LJuCR 11.6-11.22. *[No Local Rules]*

[APPENDICES]

[Appendices were adopted effective September 1, 2009.]

APPENDIX A.   TEMPORARY RESTRAINING ORDER (TMRO)

SUPERIOR COURT OF WASHINGTON
COUNTY OF SAN JUAN

[ ] In Re the Marriage of: [ ] In Re the Parentage of: _____, Petitioner and _____, Respondent	NO. TEMPORARY RESTRAINING ORDER (TMRO)

I. NOTICE TO PARTIES

1.1 An action has been started in this court that affects your marriage. Both parties are now required to obey the following order unless the court changes it. Either of you may ask the court to change or clarify this order. The court has the authority to punish violations of this order and to require the violator to pay attorney fees to the other party for having to bring the violation before the court.

II. ORDER

IT IS ORDERED:

2.1 TEMPORARY ORDERS FOR ALL PARTIES

(a) Both parties are restrained from transferring, removing, encumbering, concealing, damaging or in any way disposing of any property except in the usual course of business or for the necessities of life or as agreed in writing by the parties. Each party shall notify the other of any extraordinary expenditure made after this order is issued.

(b) Both parties are restrained from assigning, transferring, borrowing, lapsing, surrendering or changing entitlement of any insurance policies of either or both parties or of any dependent children, whether medical, health, life or auto insurance, except as agreed in writing by the parties.

(c) Unless the court orders otherwise, both parties are responsible for their own future debts whether incurred by credit card, loan, security interest or mortgage, except as agreed in writing by the parties.

(d) Both parties shall have access to all tax, financial, legal, and household records. Reasonable access to records shall not be denied without order of the court.

(e) Within 30 days after the filing of any general appearance, answer or other responsive pleading, each party shall provide the other party with a completed Financial Declaration (WPF DR 01.1550) and a Verified Statement of Assets and Liabilities (form is Appendix B to Local Court Rules of the Superior Court for San Juan County, available at www.sanjuanco.com/suprcourt/forms.aspx. Each party shall then file a Declaration of Mailing showing that these documents have been provided to the other party within the time limit. In all cases involving a request for child support, maintenance or attorney fees, the Financial Declaration shall also be filed with the court. All parties have a duty to supplement the financial information when additional information becomes available.

RESTRAINING ORDER
SPR 94.08.01
Page 1 of 2

         FORMS APPENDIX -- A

Eff September 1, 2015

2.2 TEMPORARY ORDERS FOR PARTIES WITH MINOR CHILD(REN).

(a) Both parents are restrained from changing the residence of the child(ren) until further court order, except as agreed in writing by the parties.

(b) Each parent shall have full access to the child(ren)'s educational and medical records, unless otherwise ordered by the court.

(c) Each parent shall insure that the child(ren) are not exposed to negative comments about the other parent. Neither parent shall make negative comments about the other parent in the presence of the child(ren).

(d) Unless waived pursuant to SPR 94.08.2(f), within 30 days of filing an appearance, answer or other responsive pleading in this action, both parties shall register for a court-approved parent education seminar. Each party shall attend the seminar within 60 days of registering. Upon completion of the seminar, each party shall file with the court the seminar completion certificate provided by the sponsoring agency or provider.

(e) Within 14 days of completing the above-ordered parent education seminar, each parent shall provide the other parent with a Proposed Parenting Plan, if they have not already done so.

2.3 MEDIATION AND SETTLEMENT CONFERENCE

If the parties are not able to agree on the final terms of their Decree, they shall be required to participate in mediation in accordance with SPR 94.08.3. If, after mediation, there remain unresolved issues, the parties may participate in a settlement conference, pursuant to LCR 16(b).

2.4 EFFECTIVE DATE OF ORDER

The Petitioner is subject to this order from the time of filing the Petition. **The Petitioner shall serve a copy of this on the Respondent and file a declaration of service in the court file.** The Respondent is subject to this order from the time that the order is served. This order shall remain in effect until further court order.

Dated: _____   _____
                                         JUDGE/ Commissioner

RESTRAINING ORDER   **FORMS APPENDIX -- A**
SPR 94.08.01
Page 2 of 2

Eff September 1, 2015

[Amended effective September 1, 2012; September 1, 2015.]

APPENDIX B.   VERIFIED STATEMENT OF ASSETS AND LIABILITIES

DO NOT FILE THIS DOCUMENT WITH THE COURT

VERIFIED STATEMENT OF ASSETS AND LIABILITIES

(Attach additional sheets in the same form if necessary.)

Petitioner: _____ Respondent: _____ Case #:_____

Date of separation from Spouse: _____ Date Petition for Dissolution filed: _____

1.   I am the [ ] Petitioner [ ] Respondent in this action.

2.   To my knowledge, as of the date of separation, the following community and separate assets and liabilities existed. *(Note: Generally **"Community assets"** means those assets that were acquired during marriage, except by inheritance or gift. **"Community liabilities"** means all debts incurred during the marriage, regardless of whose name the debt is in. **"Separate assets"** means those assets owned before marriage, or acquired after separation, or acquired during the marriage by inheritance or gift. **"Separate liabilities"** means those debts incurred before the marriage or after separation.*

<table>
<tr><td>COMMUNITY ASSETS</td><td>SEPARATE ASSETS</td></tr>
</table>

Real Property:

COMMUNITY	SEPARATE
1. _____	1. _____
2. _____	2. _____

Vehicles (autos, trailers, boats, etc.):

COMMUNITY	SEPARATE
1. _____	1. _____
2. _____	2. _____
3. _____	3. _____
4. _____	4. _____

Bank Accounts:

Bank Name/Branch Account No.	Bank Name/Branch Account No.
1. _____	1. _____
2. _____	2. _____
3. _____	3. _____
4. _____	4. _____

VERIFIED STATEMENT OF ASSETS AND LIABILITIES
SPR 94.08.1
Page 1 of 5

FORMS APPENDIX -- B

Eff September 1, 2015

1351

Pensions/Retirement Accounts:

1. _____   1. _____
2. _____   2. _____

Business Interests:

1. _____   1. _____
2. _____   2. _____

Stocks/Bonds/Investments:

1. _____   1. _____
2. _____   2. _____
3. _____   3. _____

Life Insurance:

1. _____   1. _____
2. _____   2. _____

**Household Goods/Furnishings/
Appliances valued over $250:**

1. _____   1. _____
2. _____   2. _____
3. _____   3. _____
4. _____   4. _____
5. _____   5. _____
6. _____   6. _____

**Sporting Goods/Tools & Equipment
valued over $250:**

1. _____   1. _____
2. _____   2. _____
3. _____   3. _____
4. _____   4. _____

VERIFIED STATEMENT OF ASSETS AND LIABILITIES
SPR 94.08.1
Page 2 of 5

FORMS APPENDIX -- B

Eff September 1, 2015

Jewelry/Artwork valued over $250:

1. _____   1. _____
2. _____   2. _____
3. _____   3. _____
4. _____   4. _____

Electronics and Accessories valued over $250:

1. _____   1. _____
2. _____   2. _____
3. _____   3. _____
4. _____   4. _____

Other

1. _____   1. _____
2. _____   2. _____
3. _____   3. _____

COMMUNITY LIABILITIES

Mortgage: **Balance at Separation**   **Current Balance**

1. _____ $_____ $_____
2. _____ $_____ $_____

Loans (vehicles/student/personal):

1. _____ $_____ $_____
2. _____ $_____ $_____
3. _____ $_____ $_____
4. _____ $_____ $_____

Credit Cards:

1. _____ $_____ $_____
2. _____ $_____ $_____
3. _____ $_____ $_____
4. _____ $_____ $_____
5. _____ $_____ $_____

Other (overdue utility/phone bills, IRS,   **Balance at Separation**   **Current Balance**
    hospital/doctor bills, collection):

1. _____ $_____ $_____
2. _____ $_____ $_____
3. _____ $_____ $_____
4. _____ $_____ $_____
5. _____ $_____ $_____
6. _____ $_____ $_____

Business Debts:

1. _____ $_____ $_____
2. _____ $_____ $_____
3. _____ $_____ $_____
4. _____ $_____ $_____

SEPARATE LIABILITIES

Described type:

1. _____ $_____ $_____
2. _____ $_____ $_____
3. _____ $_____ $_____
4. _____ $_____ $_____
5. _____ $_____ $_____

Since the time of separation, there has been the following substantial change in the assets listed above: (NOTE: Describe how, when and why any of the above assets were sold, traded, consumed or otherwise disposed.)

_____

_____

_____

_____

_____

_____

_____

_____

_____

VERIFIED STATEMENT OF ASSETS AND LIABILITIES
SPR 94.08.1   **FORMS APPENDIX -- B**
Page 4 of 5

Eff September 1, 2015

I anticipate receiving the following in the future:

(a) Inheritance [ ] Yes [ ] No
(b) Settlement proceeds from a lawsuit [ ] Yes [ ] No
(c) Settlement proceeds from a work-related injury [ ] Yes [ ] No
(d) Money owed to me by another [ ] Yes [ ] No

I declare under penalty of perjury of the laws of the State of Washington that the above is true and correct to the best of my knowledge.

DATED this _____ day of _____, 20_____, at _____, Washington.

_____
Declarant

VERIFIED STATEMENT OF ASSETS AND LIABILITIES
SPR 94.08.1
Page 5 of 5

FORMS APPENDIX -- B

Eff September 1, 2015

[Amended effective September 1, 2012; September 1, 2015.]

APPENDIX C. NOTE FOR TRIAL ASSIGNMENT (CLERK'S ACTION REQUIRED)

SUPERIOR COURT OF WASHINGTON
COUNTY OF SAN JUAN

_____, Petitioner/Plaintiff | NO.

vs

_____, Respondent/Defendant | NOTE FOR TRIAL ASSIGNMENT
                                                    | (Clerk's Action Required)

TO: Clerk of the Court
AND TO: Court Administrator
AND TO: _____

Please take notice that the above captioned action is now at issue. The Clerk is requested to note this case on the regular <u>Trial Assignment Calendar (Every Friday of the month)</u>

Date requested for trial assignment: Friday _____
(This is an administrative calendar only; no personal appearance required)

Nature of this case: _____

Issues in Dispute: _____

Estimated Length of Trial (days): _____

A jury   ☐ of 6   ☐ of 12   ☐ has   ☐ has not been demanded.

Is the Parent Education Seminar requirement under Local Rule SPR 94.08.2 applicable? ☐ Yes   ☐ No
     If yes, have the parties attended a court-approved Parent Education Seminar and are the certificates
     filed with the court? ☐ Yes   ☐ No

Is the mandatory mediation requirement under Local Rule SPR 94.08.3 applicable? ☐ Yes   ☐ No
     If yes, have the parties completed mandatory mediation and is the declaration of completion filed
     with the court? ☐ Yes   ☐ No

Has a Title 26 Guardian ad Litem been appointed? ☐ Yes   ☐ No
     If yes, has the GAL Report been filed with the court? ☐ Yes   ☐ No

Dated: _____   _____
                                           Signature / Printed Name
                                           Attorney for _____
                                           WSBA No. _____
                                           Address: _____

NOTE FOR TRIAL ASSIGNMENT
LCR 40   **FORMS APPENDIX -- C**

Eff September 1, 2015

[Renumbered from Appendix D and amended, effective September 1, 2012; September 1, 2015.]

APPENDIX D. NOTICE OF CONFLICT DATES

SUPERIOR COURT OF WASHINGTON
COUNTY OF SAN JUAN

_____, Petitioner/Plaintiff | NO.

VS

_____, Respondent/Defendant | NOTICE OF CONFLICT DATES

TO: Clerk of the Court
AND TO: Court Administrator
AND TO: _____

Please take notice that the above captioned case has been noted for trial assignment on the following date:

The following are the undersigned's conflict dates, which are limited to previously scheduled vacations and trial dates:

Dates of Counsel's Unavailability	Reason for Unavailability	Reference (Court and Cause No.)

Dated: _____

Signature / Printed Name
Attorney for _____
WSBA No. _____
Address: _____

NOTICE OF CONFLICT DATES
LCR 40   **FORMS APPENDIX -- D**

Eff September 1, 2015

[Renumbered from Appendix E and amended effective September 1, 2012; September 1, 2015.]

APPENDIX E.   STATEMENT OF READINESS FOR TRIAL

SUPERIOR COURT OF WASHINGTON
COUNTY OF SAN JUAN

_____ , Petitioner/Plaintiff	NO.
VS	
_____ , Respondent/Defendant	STATEMENT OF READINESS FOR TRIAL

TO: Clerk of the Court
AND: _____

COMES NOW _____ by and through his/her attorney of record and pursuant to LCR 16 certifies as follows:

1. This case is subject to mandatory mediation: ☐yes ☐no
   If so, mandatory mediation has been completed: ☐yes ☐no ☐N/A

2. This case is subject to mandatory parent education seminar: ☐yes ☐no
   If so, the parent education seminar has been completed: ☐yes ☐no ☐N/A

3. Declarant's witnesses are available for trial: ☐yes ☐no ☐N/A

4. All discovery has been completed: ☐yes ☐no

5. All necessary pleadings have been filed: ☐yes ☐no

6. The parties are ready for trial: ☐yes ☐no

7. The estimated length of trial _____ is days.

Declarant   ☐   will appear personally
                      ☐   requests permission to appear via CourtCall
                      ☐   requests that his/her personal presence be waived

at the court scheduled Readiness Hearing.

Dated: _____   _____
                                                                                   Signature / Printed Name
                                                                                   Attorney for _____
                                                                                   WSBA No. _____

           Address: _____

STATEMENT OF READINESS FOR TRIAL
LCR16   **FORMS APPENDIX -- E**

Eff September 1, 2015

[Renumbered from Appendix F and amended effective September 1, 2012; September 1, 2015.]

APPENDIX F.   ORDER TO SHOW CAUSE RE: PARENT EDUCATION SEMINAR

SUPERIOR COURT OF WASHINGTON
COUNTY OF SAN JUAN

[ ] In Re the Marriage of:
[ ] In Re the Parentage of:

_____, Petitioner

and

_____, Respondent

NO.

ORDER TO SHOW CAUSE RE: PARENT EDUCATION SEMINAR

Clerk's Action Required: Para./Sect. _____

IT IS HEREBY ORDERED, ADJUDGED AND DECREED

By sua sponte order of the Court:

The Respondent herein, _____, shall complete a court-approved parent education seminar, per SPR 94.08.2, no later than _____.
Proof of completion shall be filed with the Court no later than _____.

IT IS FURTHER ORDERED:

In the event proof of completion of the class is not filed with the Court by said date, _____ shall appear in person before this court at the place and time set forth below and show cause why he / she should not be held in contempt of court for failure to abide by this order and why sanctions should not be entered for such failure to-wit:

Date: _____/ Time: _____
Place: San Juan County Courthouse
         350 Court Street
         Friday Harbor, WA 98250
Room: Superior Courtroom, Second Floor
Judge: Honorable Donald E. Eaton

IF YOU FAIL TO APPEAR IN PERSON AND SHOW CAUSE AT THESE PROCEEDINGS THE COURT MAY ORDER SANCTIONS, INCLUDING CONTEMPT, AND/OR ISSUE A BENCH WARRANT FOR YOUR ARREST WITHOUT FURTHER NOTICE TO YOU.

This order may be served by mail.

Dated: _____   _____
                                                    Donald E. Eaton, Judge

ORDER TO SHOW CAUSE RE: PARENTING CLASS
SPR 94.08.2   **FORMS APPENDIX -- F**

Eff September 1, 2015

[Renumbered from Appendix G and amended, effective September 1, 2012; September 1, 2015.]

APPENDIX G. REQUEST FOR ENTRY OF DECREE AND DECLARATION OF JURISDICTIONAL FACTS

SUPERIOR COURT OF WASHINGTON
COUNTY OF SAN JUAN

In Re the Marriage of:	NO.
_____, Petitioner	
and	REQUEST FOR ENTRY OF DEGREE AND DECLARATION OF JURISDICTIONAL FACTS
_____, Respondent	**(For Use by Attorney Only)**

REQUEST: The petitioner requests immediate entry of Findings of Fact, Conclusions of Law and • Decree of Dissolution of Marriage, • Decree of Legal Separation, or • Declaration of Invalidity without a final hearing, and states:

RESIDENCE: I was a resident of the state of Washington when the petition was filed.

TIME LIMITS: More than 90 days have elapsed since the later of _____, 20___, the date on which the Petition was filed, and _____, 20___, the date on which

1. The Respondent signed an acceptance of service of the Summons and Petition **and**
    - the Respondent has signed the original final documents; **or**
    - the Respondent waived notice **and** the final documents provide for only that relief requested in the petition; **or**
    - an order of default has been entered against Respondent;

    or

2. The Summons and Petition:
    - were personally served upon the Respondent, **or**
    - the summons was first published pursuant to a court order, **or**
    - the summons and petition were mailed pursuant to a court order;
    and
    - an order of default has been entered against Respondent.

MARRIAGE & SEPARATION: The parties were married on _____, _____, (date) at _____, (city and state) and separated on _____, _____ (date).
- The marriage is irretrievably broken, **or**
- The parties wish to be legally separated, **or**
- The marriage of the parties is invalid.

PREGNANCY: • Neither party is pregnant.
• (Name) _____ is pregnant. [Note: Under RCW 26.26.116, the other party is the presumed parent. If either party believes the other party is not the parent, this presumption may be challenged up to four years after the birth of the child or as otherwise provided in RCW 26.26.500 through 26.26.625.]

REQUEST FOR ENTRY OF DECREE AND
DECLARATION OF JURISDICTIONAL FACTS
(For use by Attorney Only)
LCR 8   **FORMS APPENDIX -- G**
Page 1 of 2

Eff September 1, 2015

DEPENDENT
CHILDREN: All dependent children of the marriage are identified and the Child Support worksheets are accurate.

PARENTING
CLASS: • Petitioner ☐ has ☐ has not / Respondent ☐ has ☐ has not completed the mandatory court-approved parent education seminar and the certificate(s) of completion is/are attached.
• The parent education seminar has been waived by the court.

PROPERTY &
DEBTS: All property and all debts of the parties are fairly and completely divided in the Decree.

IF DEFAULT: If entry of the Decree is sought after default of the Respondent, the final documents provide for only that relief requested in the petition.

PERJURY
DECLARATION: I declare under penalty of perjury under the laws of the State of Washington that the foregoing is true and correct.

Dated this _____ day of _____, 20____, at _____,
Washington.

_____
Signature of Petitioner

Presented by:

_____
Signature & Printed Name of Petitioner's Attorney

Approved, Notice of Presentation Waived:

_____   _____
Signature & Printed Name of Respondent's Attorney   Signature & Printed Name of Respondent

REQUEST FOR ENTRY OF DECREE AND
DECLARATION OF JURISDICTIONAL FACTS
(For use by Attorney Only)
LCR 8   **FORMS APPENDIX -- G**
Page 2 of 2

SUPERIOR COURT OF WASHINGTON

Eff September 1, 2015

[Renumbered from Appendix H and amended, effective September 1, 2012; September 1, 2015.]

APPENDIX H.   DOMESTIC RELATIONS PRE–TRIAL INFORMATION

COUNTY OF SAN JUAN

In Re the Marriage of:

_____, Petitioner | NO.

and

_____, Respondent | DOMESTIC RELATIONS PRE-TRIAL INFORMATION
SUBMITTED BY: _____

NOTE: This form shall be filed and served by noon two judicial days before trial.

I.   INFORMATION

    A. Ages: Petitioner _____ Respondent _____
    B. Date of Marriage: _____
    C. Dependent children living with either party:
        1. Of this marriage:

Name	Age	With Whom Residing
_____	_____	_____
_____	_____	_____

        2. Children of former marriages:

Name	Age	With Whom Residing
_____	_____	_____
_____	_____	_____

II. INCOME & EMPLOYMENT

    A. Petitioner:
        1. Employer's name and address: _____
        2. Net take-home pay per month: $_____
        3. Other income: <u>Source</u>   <u>Monthly Amount</u>
                _____ $_____
                _____ $_____

    B. Respondent:
        1. Employer's name and address: _____
        2. Net take-home pay per month: $_____
        3. Other income: <u>Source</u>   <u>Monthly Amount</u>
                _____ $_____
                _____ $_____

III. ASSETS & LIABILITIES

Instructions: Indicate your proposed division of assets and liabilities on a sheet of paper divided in the middle, vertically, by listing the property to be awarded to the petitioner on the left side of the page and listing the property to be awarded to the respondent on the right side of the page. (See **Sample** on following page.) Such lists should begin with items of community property having the greatest value and should be described in such detail as may be reasonable in

DOMESTIC RELATIONS PRE-TRIAL INFORMATION
LCR 39
Page 1 of 2   **FORMS APPENDIX --H**

Eff September 1, 2015

view of the total assets of the marital community.

Generally, assets having an individual value of more than $500 should be listed separately. Any property subject to an encumbrance or security interest should disclose the nature of such security interest, the unpaid balance owing at the time of trial and the net fair market value of such asset after the deduction of such encumbrance.

The proposed property division should conclude with a list of liabilities to be assumed by each party, including, except as may be disclosed above, the name of the creditor, amount of the monthly payment, the unpaid balance on each such debt and the total amount of all such liabilities to be assumed by each party.

Deduction of the total amount of liabilities to be assumed by each party from the net total fair market value of the community property awarded to such party will constitute the net fair market values for your proposed property division. This should be followed by a list of separate property to be awarded to each spouse.

SAMPLE

III. ASSETS & LIABILITIES

PROPERTY DIVISION PROPOSED BY PETITIONER

Property to be Awarded to Petitioner:	**Property to be Awarded to Respondent:**

Property to be Awarded to Petitioner:

Real Estate:
Family Home (FMV) $60,000
Less: Mortgage to
Hometown Bank (30,000)
Net Equity: $30,000

Motor Vehicles:
1985 Chev. Caprice
(FMV) $ 8,500
Less: Loan to
Credit Union (5,000)
Net Equity: $3,500

Household Goods:
Living room furniture $750
Console TV $600
Bedroom Furniture $500
Kitchen Appliances $300
Misc. Dishes/utensils $200
Total Household Goods $2,350

Cash: (from savings acct) $1,500

Clothing & Personal Effects: $1,000

Total Value Community Property
Awarded to Petitioner: $ 38,350

Less Debts Assumed by Petitioner:
Sears $450
VISA $600
Total Debts: ($1,050)

Net Value of Award to Petitioner: $ 37,300

Less: Lien on Family Home   ($6,375)

Total Community Property
Awarded to Petitioner: **$ 30,925**

Separate Property:
100 Shares Puget Power (from father) $ 2,000

Total Award to Petitioner: **$ 32,925**

Property to be Awarded to Respondent:

Pension (Present Cash Value
at dissolution) $20,000

Motor Vehicles:
1983 Ford pickup (FMV) $ 5,000
Less: Loan to Second
National Bank   ($2,000)
Net Equity: $ 3,000

Household Goods:
Living Room Furniture $500
Bedroom Furniture $350
Misc. Dishes/utensils $150
Total Household Goods $1,000

Cash (from checking & savings) 1,000

Power Tools $350

Clothing & Personal Effects $750

Total Value of Community Property
Awarded to Respondent: $26,100

Less Debts Assumed by Respondent:
Bon Marche $350
Mastercard $500
Ace Finance Company $700
Total Debts: ($1,550)

Net Value of Award to Respondent: $24,530

Plus: Lien on family home $ 6,375

Total Community Property
Awarded to Respondent: **$ 30,925**

I SWEAR UNDER PENALTY OF PERJURY THAT THE ABOVE IS TRUE AND CORRECT.
Dated: _____   _____
                                   Signature

DOMESTIC RELATIONS PRE-TRIAL INFORMATION
LCR 39
Page 2 of 2   **FORMS APPENDIX -- H**

Eff September 1, 2015

[Renumbered from Appendix I and amended, effective September 1, 2012; September 1, 2015.]

APPENDIX I. JIS INFORMATION COVER SHEET, PERMANENT PARENTING PLANS

SUPERIOR COURT OF WASHINGTON
COUNTY OF SAN JUAN

☐ In re the Marriage of: ☐ In re the Parentage of: Petitioner(s), and Respondent(s).	No. Sealed Cover Sheet for JIS Background Check (Permanent Parenting Plan) **CLERK'S ACTION REQUIRED:**

(JIS Background Check cannot be completed unless the information below is provided.)

The following information is provided for completion of the JIS Background Check required by SPR 94.08.1(e) of the Local Rules for San Juan County.

Permanent Parenting Plan or Residential Schedule to be noted for presentation on:
_____ [date].

Attached is JIS Background Check for **the Petitioner, the Respondent, all minor children over the age of 11 years who reside in the residence of either party, and all other adults who reside in the residence of either party based on the following information provided by the Petitioner, the Respondent, or legal counsel.** Use additional forms, if necessary, for additional children or adults.

I declare under penalty of perjury of the laws of the state of Washington that the information contained herein is true and accurate.

Dated this _____ day of _____, 20____, at _____.
         (day)   (month)   (year)   (city and state)

Petitioner: _____   Respondent: _____

County Clerk Received by: _____ Date: _____

JIS Information Cover Sheet,
Permanent Parenting Plans   **FORMS APPENDIX --I**
SPR 94.08.1(e)
Page 1 of 3

CHILD(REN) INFORMATION

Eff September 1, 2015

Child's FULL Name (Last, First, MI):	Child's FULL Name (Last, First, MI):
Child's Date of Birth (MO/DAY/YEAR):	Child's Date of Birth (MO/DAY/YEAR):
Child's CURRENT Address:	Child's CURRENT Address:
Child's FULL Name (Last, First MI):	Child's FULL Name (Last, First MI):
Child's Date of Birth (MO/DAY/YEAR):	Child's Date of Birth (MO/DAY/YEAR):
Child's CURRENT Address:	Child's CURRENT Address:

PETITIONER'S INFORMATION	
1st Petitioner's FULL Name (Last, First MI):	2nd Petitioner's FULL Name (Last, First MI):
Has the 1st Petitioner ever been known by another name? Including hyphenated or maiden names. If so, list name(s):	Has the 2nd Petitioner ever been known by another name? Including hyphenated or maiden names. If so, list name(s):
1st Petitioner's Date of Birth (MO/DAY/YEAR) :	2nd Petitioner's Date of Birth (MO/DAY/YEAR):

COURT USE ONLY		COURT USE ONLY	
JIS/JABS Checked ☐	Checks attached ☐	JIS/JABS Checked ☐	Checks attached ☐
SCOMIS Checked ☐	No information ☐	SCOMIS Checked ☐	No information ☐

RESPONDENT'S INFORMATION	
1st Respondent's FULL Name (Last, First MI):	2nd Respondent's FULL Name (Last, First MI):
Has the 1st Respondent ever been known by another name? Including hyphenated or maiden names. If so, list name(s):	Has the 2nd Respondent ever been known by another name? Including hyphenated or maiden names. If so, list name(s):
1st Respondent's Date of Birth (MO/DAY/YEAR):	2nd Respondent's Date of Birth (MO/DAY/YEAR):

COURT USE ONLY		COURT USE ONLY	
JIS/JABS Checked ☐	Checks attached ☐	JIS/JABS Checked ☐	Checks attached ☐
SCOMIS Checked ☐	No information ☐	SCOMIS Checked ☐	No information ☐

JIS Information Cover Sheet,

Permanent Parenting Plans **FORMS APPENDIX --I**
SPR 94.08.1(e)
Page 2 of 3

OTHER MINORS OR ADULTS RESIDING IN	OTHER MINORS OR ADULTS RESIDING IN

Eff September 1, 2015

PETITIONER'S HOUSEHOLD	RESPONDENT'S HOUSEHOLD
Other's FULL Name (Last, First MI):	Other's FULL Name (Last, First MI)
Has the Other ever been known by another name? Including hyphenated or maiden names. If so, list name(s):	Has the Other ever been known by another name? Including hyphenated or maiden names. If so, list name(s):
Other's Date of Birth (MO/DAY/YEAR):	Other's Date of Birth (MO/DAY/YEAR):
Other's FULL Name (Last, First, MI):	Other's FULL Name (Last, First, MI):
Has the Other ever been known by another name? Including hyphenated or maiden names. If so, list name(s):	Has the Other ever been known by another name? Including hyphenated or maiden names. If so, list name(s):
Other's Date of Birth (MO/DAY/YEAR):	Other's Date of Birth (MO/DAY/YEAR):
Other's FULL Name (Last, First MI):	Other's FULL Name (Last, First MI):
Has the Other ever been known by another name? Including hyphenated or maiden names. If so, list name(s):	Has the Other ever been known by another name? Including hyphenated or maiden names. If so, list name(s):
Other's Date of Birth (MO/DAY/YEAR):	Other's Date of Birth (MO/DAY/YEAR):

COURT USE ONLY		COURT USE ONLY	
JIS/JABS Checked ☐	Checks attached ☐	JIS/JABS Checked ☐	Checks attached ☐
SCOMIS Checked ☐	No information ☐	SCOMIS Checked ☐	No information ☐

JIS Information Cover Sheet,
Permanent Parenting Plans
SPR 94.08.1(e)
Page 3 of 3

FORMS APPENDIX --I

Eff September 1, 2015

[Adopted effective September 1, 2015.]

APPENDIX J. SAN JUAN COUNTY SUPERIOR COURT CONDUCT AND DRESS CODE

SAN JUAN COUNTY SUPERIOR COURT CONDUCT AND DRESS CODE

THE FOLLOWING CONDUCT AND DRESS CODE SHALL
APPLY WHEN COURT IS IN SESSION:

1. No firearms or other weapons, including knives, shall be allowed in the courtroom.

2. No food or drinks, except water, shall be allowed in the courtroom.

3. No cell phones or pagers with audible signals activated shall be allowed in the courtroom.

4. All persons in the courtroom, except those required to be there because of arrest or court order, shall be attired in a manner appropriate to the dignity and decorum of the courtroom setting. As minimum standards, the following rules apply:

   ♦ Men shall wear shirts, trousers and shoes.
   ♦ Women shall wear shoes and either dresses, skirts and tops, or pants and tops
   ♦ Pants shall be firmly and snuggly fastened about the waist.
   ♦ Shorts, halter-tops, tank tops, hats, caps, torn clothing, shirts or other clothing with obscene or profane pictures or messages, and flip flop type sandals shall not be worn.
   ♦ Male attorneys shall wear coats, slacks and ties. Women attorneys shall wear professionally appropriate attire.

5. All persons in the courtroom shall, in their speech and actions, conduct themselves in a manner appropriate to the dignity and decorum of the courtroom setting. As minimum standards, the following rules shall apply:

   ♦ Spectators and persons not then actively engaged in court proceedings shall be quiet; any speech which does occur shall be as an unobtrusive as possible.
   ♦ All persons shall refrain from any gestures and from conduct or behavior, which manifest disrespect for the court, counsel, litigants, witnesses, court staff, law enforcement personnel, or other persons.
   ♦ Children shall be closely controlled by adults inside and outside the courtroom.

6. No cameras or video or audio recording equipment, except members of the press with prior approval of the Court.

SAN JUAN COUNTY SUPERIOR COURT
CONDUCT AND DRESS CODE
LCR 87

FORMS APPENDIX --J

Eff September 1, 2015

[Renumbered from Appendix I and amended, effective September 1, 2012; September 1, 2015.]

APPENDIX K.   COURTROOM DECORUM AND PRACTICE GUIDELINES

COURTROOM DECORUM AND PRACTICE GUIDELINES

PREFACE

The pursuit of justice is a serious undertaking and conduct during the litigation process, both within and outside the courtroom, must at all times satisfy the appearance as well as the reality of fairness and equal treatment. Dignity, order and decorum are indispensable to the proper administration of justice.

A trial is an adversary proceeding, and lawyers must advocate for their clients' positions. However, conduct that may be characterized as discriminatory, abusive, or obstructive impedes the fundamental goal of resolving disputes rationally, peacefully and efficiently. Such conduct tends to delay and often to deny justice.

Attorneys are privileged to participate in the administration of justice in a unique way, and are responsible to their own consciences, to their clients, to one another, and to the public to conduct themselves in a manner which will facilitate, and never detract from, the administration of justice.

A trial is a truth-seeking process designed to resolve human and societal problems in a rational and efficient manner. A lawyer's conduct should be characterized at all times by personal courtesy and professional integrity in the fullest sense of those terms. A judge's conduct should be characterized at all times by courtesy, patience, and fairness toward all participants. The courts belong to the people of this state. The guidelines are intended to facilitate access to the courts for the fair resolution of disputes and should never be applied to deny access.

Application

The purpose of these guidelines is to provide lawyers, judges, and parties with a reasonable standard of conduct in judicial proceedings. However, these guidelines are not intended to homogenize conduct or remove individuality from the courtroom. To facilitate professional growth and foster voluntary compliance with these guidelines, the WSBA Court Congestion and Improvement Committee periodically review these guidelines. Comments are considered by the committee and changes are incorporated as needed.

All participants in judicial proceedings should voluntarily adhere to these guidelines. These guidelines shall not be used as a basis for litigation or for sanctions or penalties. Nothing in these guidelines supersedes or detracts from existing codes or rules of conduct or discipline or alters existing standards by which lawyer negligence may be determined.

COURTROOM DECORUM

I. General Courtroom Decorum

A. Always be prompt.
B. Stand when the judge enters or leaves the courtroom.
C. Do not make personal attacks on opposing counsel.
D. Do not interrupt. Wait your turn.
E. Enhancing courtroom decorum is a cooperative venture among bench and bar. It is appropriate to call to the attention of opposing counsel any perceived violations of these guidelines out of the presence of the jury.
F. After the court has ruled, ask the court's permission before arguing further.
G. Advise clients and witnesses of the formalities of the court, the appropriate guidelines, and any rulings on motions in limine. Encourage their cooperation. This applies both to attorneys and to

COURTROOM DECORUM AND PRACTICE GUIDELINES
LCR 87   **FORMS APPENDIX – K**
Page 1 of 3

Eff September 1, 2015

self-represented parties.

H. If there is a live microphone at counsel table, remember not to confer with others or rustle papers near the microphone. With the importance of making an accurate court record, be mindful of speaking into the microphone in an audible and clear fashion.

I. Courtrooms equipped for videotaped reporting may require special precautions, such as remaining near a microphone.

J. Treat everyone in the courtroom with fairness, consideration, and respect. Refrain from conduct that discriminates on the basis of race, color, national origin, religion, creed, sex, age, disability, sexual orientation, or marital status.

II. General Trial Conduct

A. Offers of and requests for stipulations are appropriate to facilitate the presentation of a case, but should not be employed to communicate to the jury a party's willingness or unwillingness to stipulate.

B. During trial, maintain appropriate respect for witnesses, jurors, and opposing counsel, avoiding informality. Address adults by their titles or surnames unless permission has been given to use first names. Avoid referring to adults by biased and demeaning expressions or labels such as "girl," "gal," or "boy." Address jurors individually or by name only during voir dire.

C. Treat jurors with respect and dignity, avoiding fawning, flattery, or pretended solicitude. Suggestions regarding the comfort or convenience of jurors should generally be made to the court out of the jury's hearing.

D. During the opening statement and argument of opposing counsel, never inappropriately divert the attention of the court or the jury.

E. Avoid expressing an opinion to the jury about the testimony of a witness, a ruling of the court, or argument of counsel through exaggerated facial expressions or other contrived conduct.

F. When practical, give the court advance notice of any legal issue that is likely to be complex, difficult, and which you expect to require argument.

G. Do not argue the case in the opening statement.

H. Counsel should not express to the jury personal knowledge or personal opinions about the evidence.

I. Address your remarks to the court, not to opposing counsel except when extending necessary courtesies, e.g., thank you.

J. Only attorney, parties, court personnel, and witnesses, when called to the stand, are permitted within the bar of the courtroom, unless otherwise allowed by the court.

III. Examination of Witnesses

A. When examining a witness, avoid undue repetition of the witness' answer.

B. Make objections for evidentiary reasons without delivering a speech or guiding a witness. Recapitulate testimony only as needed to put an objection in context.

C. If a witness was on the stand at a recess or adjournment, have the witness ready to proceed when the court is resumed.

D. Attempt to anticipate witness scheduling problems and discuss them with opposing counsel and the court. Try to schedule witnesses in advance of trial.

IV. Exhibits and Documents

A. Premark exhibits with the clerk for identification prior to trial where appropriate. Hand all unmarked exhibits to the clerk for marking before using them in trial.

B. If practical, have photocopies of an exhibit for the court, opposing counsel, and the witness. Avoid illegible copies if possible.

C. Return all exhibits to the clerk at each adjournment.

D. Whenever referring to an exhibit, identify the exhibit by its exhibit number.

COURTROOM DECORUM AND PRACTICE GUIDELINES
LCR 87
Page 2 of 3

FORMS APPENDIX – K

Eff September 1, 2015

E. Give to the clerk all papers intended for the court.

F. Show the proposed exhibit to opposing counsel prior to offering the exhibit in evidence.

V. Scheduling

A. When practical, consult opposing counsel before scheduling hearings and discovery appearances in an effort to avoid scheduling conflicts. Assert a scheduling conflict only if the requested time is not available, not to obtain any unfair advantage.

B. If opposing counsel fails promptly to accept or reject a time offered for hearing or discovery appearance, raises an unreasonable number of conflicts, or consistently fails to comply with this standard, agreement is not required.

C. Where time associated with scheduling agreements could cause damage or harm to a client's case, then a lawyer is justified in setting a hearing or discovery appearance without first consulting with opposing counsel.

D. Give notice of cancellation of appearances and hearings to all involved at the earliest possible time.

VI. Preferences of Individual Judges

Counsel are advised to determine the preferences of individual judges with respect to movement within the courtroom. Following are some examples of individual preferences.

A. Stand when addressing the court and when making objections.

B. Stand during opening statement and closing argument.

C. Approach the bench only with permission.

D. Maintain an appropriate distance from the witness and the jury.

E. In the presence of the jury, address the judge as "Your Honor."

VII. Discovery

A. Make reasonable efforts to conduct all discovery by agreement. Consider agreeing to an early voluntary exchange of information.

1. Comply with all reasonable discovery requests in a timely manner.

2. Stipulate to facts unless there is a genuine dispute.

B. Conduct yourself in a professional manner and treat other lawyers, the opposing party, and all involved with courtesy and civility at all times. Clients should be counseled that civility and courtesy are required.

C. Be punctual in fulfilling all professional commitments and in communicating with the court and other lawyers.

D. Concentrate discovery responses on matters of substances and content, avoiding quarrels over form or style.

E. Clearly identify for other counsel or parties all changes made in documents submitted for review.

F. Fully respond to discovery, unless making a specific and clear objection warranted by existing law or a reasonable extension thereof. Do not produce documents in a manner designed to hide or obscure the existence of particular documents.

VIII. Depositions

A. Advise clients regarding appropriate behavior, attire and other matters involved with depositions and other proceedings.

B. Take depositions only when actually needed to ascertain facts or information or to perpetuate testimony.

C. Make only good-faith objections to discovery, and avoid objections solely for the purpose of withholding or delaying the disclosure of relevant information.

COURTROOM DECORUM AND PRACTICE GUIDELINES
LCR 87
Page 3 of 3   **FORMS APPENDIX – K**

Eff September 1, 2015

[Renumbered from Appendix K and amended, effective September 1, 2012. Renumbered from Appendix J and amended effective September 1, 2015.]

APPENDIX L.   MINIMUM QUALIFICATIONS FOR FAMILY LAW MEDIATORS

> MINIMUM QUALIFICATIONS FOR
> SUPERIOR COURT FAMILY LAW MEDIATORS
> FOR SAN JUAN COUNTY

1.   A Bachelor's Degree plus a Master's Degree in sociology, psychology, or other social or behavioral science, plus completion of a family law mediation training course offered by the University of Washington School of Law, Seattle University School of Law, Gonzaga University School of Law, American Arbitration Association, or Washington Arbitration and Mediation Services, or the basic mediation training course and family mediation training course offered by the Island County Dispute Resolution Center, or such other equivalent mediation training course(s) as shall be approved by the court; or

2.   A Juris Doctor Degree plus completion of a family law mediation training course offered by the University of Washington School of Law, Seattle University School of Law, Gonzaga University School of Law, American Arbitration Association, or Washington Arbitration and Mediation Services, or the basic mediation training course and family mediation training course offered by the Island County Dispute Resolution Center, or such other equivalent mediation training course(s) as shall be approved by the court; or

3.   A Bachelor's Degree and two year's experience in a law-related or mediation related field plus completion of a family law mediation training course offered by the University of Washington School of Law, Seattle University School of Law, Gonzaga University School of Law, American Arbitration Association, or Washington Arbitration and Mediation Services, or the basic mediation training course and family mediation training course offered by the Island County Dispute Resolution Center, or such other equivalent mediation training course(s) as shall be approved by the court;

4.   A Bachelor's Degree plus completion of a family law mediation training course offered by the University of Washington School of Law, Seattle University School of Law, Gonzaga University School of Law, American Arbitration Association, or Washington Arbitration and Mediation Services, or the basic mediation training course and family mediation training course offered by the Island County Dispute Resolution Center, or such other equivalent mediation training course(s) as shall be approved by the court, 15 hours of family mediation experience through the American Arbitration Association, Washington Arbitration and Mediation Services, the Island County Dispute Resolution Center or other county-approved dispute resolution center; or

5.   Such other educational and experiential qualifications as shall be approved by the Superior Court judges on a case by case basis.

Minimum Qualifications for Family Law Mediators   **FORMS APPENDIX – L**
SPR 94.08.3(h)

Eff September 1, 2015

[Adopted effective September 1, 2012. Renumbered from Appendix K and amended, effective September 1, 2015.]

APPENDIX M.   EVALUATION STANDARDS

COUNTY OF SAN JUAN
SUPERIOR and DISTRICT COURTS
350 Court Street, Friday Harbor, WA 98250

EVALUATION STANDARDS

A defendant, who is required by the court to obtain an evaluation of any kind, must ensure that the evaluator complies with the minimum requirements set forth below. The defendant must also sign a waiver of confidentiality so that the court, probation officer and prosecutor may provide the evaluator with pertinent information, and the evaluator can provide evaluations and progress reports to the court, probation officer and prosecutor.

THE EVALUATOR must meet all certification and registration requirements for the State of Washington. The evaluation must be conducted in person. As part of the evaluation process, the evaluator must comply with all procedures required by the State of Washington and **MUST ALSO OBTAIN AND CONSIDER THE FOLLOWING:**

1.   The arrest and criminal history of the defendant;
2.   The driving record of the defendant (if charge is driving related);
3.   The police reports relating to the incident underlying the charges;
4.   Any prior relevant evaluations;
5.   Information from at least one collateral contact who has significant knowledge of the defendant;
6.   Any additional information provided by the District Court probation officer;
7.   The defendant must submit a urinalysis for alcohol and drug testing (if charge is alcohol/ drug related).

AUTHORIZATION TO RELEASE INFORMATION

I understand that federal and state laws and regulations provide that information obtained by drug, alcohol, mental health counselors and treatment agencies are confidential and may not be disclosed without my specific written consent, unless otherwise permitted by such regulations. A general authorization for the release of medical or other information is not sufficient to allow disclosure. I also understand that I may revoke this consent at any time EXCEPT to the extent that action has been taken in reliance on it for purposes of sentencing, probation or parole. I have read the above evaluation standards, and understand that the evaluator must comply with those standards.

I HAVE READ AND UNDERSTAND the evaluation standards set forth above and **AGREE TO COMPLY** with these standards and to **PROVIDE A COPY** of these standards to the person or agency that will be conducting my evaluation.

I AUTHORIZE the court, prosecutor, sheriff and probation department to release any arrest, criminal, and driving records, incident reports, and any prior evaluations relating to me, to the person(s) or agencies named below who will perform a court-ordered evaluation in this case.

I AUTHORIZE _____
(name, address & tel. of agency) to release tests results, evaluations and progress reports to the court clerk, prosecuting attorney, and District Court probation department in San Juan County.

DATE: _____
                                                              Defendant

Superior Court: 360-370-7480   Address: _____
County Clerk: 360-378-2163   _____
District Court: 360-378-4017   _____
Prosecutor: 360-378-4101   Telephone Number: _____
D.C.Probation: 360-378-8208
Juvenile Court: 360-370-7442

Evaluation Standards LCrR8.2(d)   **FORMS APPENDIX M**

Eff September 1, 2015

[Adopted effective September 1, 2015.]

DISTRICT COURT

LOCAL RULES OF THE DISTRICT COURT FOR SAN JUAN COUNTY

Including Amendments Received Through
August 15, 2015

Table of Rules

PREFACE—PROMULGATION AND ADOPTION

These rules shall be known as the Local Rules for the San Juan County District Court. Copies will be filed with the Office of the Administrator of the Courts, the San Juan County Public Law Library, and the Clerk of the San Juan County District Court. Additional copies will be available from the San Juan County District Court Clerk.

Consistent with GR 7(b) Washington Court Rules, to the extent possible, these rules conform in numbering system and in format to those rules adopted by the Supreme Court of the State of Washington for Courts of Limited Jurisdiction. The number of each rule is preceded by the abbreviation "L" designating the rule as a San Juan County Local Court Rule and as being supplemental to the corresponding Washington Court Rule for Courts of Limited Jurisdiction, and shall not be construed in conflict with them.

These rules have been adopted, or are adopted, or are amended, to be effective as noted within the body of each rule. The court may modify or suspend any of these local rules in any given case upon good cause shown or upon the court's own motion.

[Amended effective September 1, 2003.]

LOCAL ADMINISTRATIVE RULES

LARLJ 2. LOCATION OF PRIMARY OFFICE

The primary office of the San Juan County District Court shall be located in Friday Harbor, Washington. Violations of State Law and Municipal Ordinances occurring in the Town of Friday Harbor are filed and prosecuted in San Juan County District Court. These rules are binding in such cases.

[Effective September 1, 2002]

LARLJ 9. DISCLOSURE OF PUBLIC RECORDS

The following records and files of this Court are declared confidential:

A. Affidavits for probable cause for arrest warrants before the warrant has been served and returned;

B. Mental health, psychiatric, and medical reports;

C. Alcohol and drug evaluations and follow up reports;

D. Unless admitted into evidence, certified copies of driving records, abstracts of driving records, and compiled reports of arrests and convictions;

E. Judges notes and work sheets;

F. Witness statements and police reports;

G. Determinations of Indigency; and,

H. Any other item ordered to be sealed by a judge or classified as confidential by statute, rule or regulation.

Access to confidential records is limited to persons authorized by statute or who obtain a Court order.

[Effective September 1, 2002]

LOCAL CIVIL RULES

LCRLJ 38. TRIAL READINESS REPORT—REIMBURSEMENT FEE

(i) A party demanding a jury trial shall, three days prior to the scheduled trial date, contact the District Court Clerk and confirm that the jury is still required. When a cause assigned a date for trial as a jury case is settled, or will not be tried by a jury for any reason, notice of that fact shall be given immediately to the Court Clerk.

In the event the notice is given to the Court Clerk less than three days prior to the scheduled trial date, the party electing not to have it's case heard by a jury shall pay a jury administrative reimbursement fee equal to the actual costs incurred by the Court associated with the jury request, unless the Judge determines that the reimbursement shall not be paid.

[Effective September 1, 2002; amended effective September 1, 2003.]

LCRLJ 54. ATTORNEY FEES

Reasonable Fees. In civil default cases where reasonable attorney fees are authorized, the following schedule shall be deemed reasonable unless the parties present evidence of circumstances that convinces the court that a larger or smaller fee should be awarded, provided, however, the court shall have authority to vary from this schedule on its own motion:

$1.00 to $999	$300
$1,000.00 to $1,500	$325
$1,500.01 to $2,000	$350
$2,000.01 to $2,500	$375
$2,500.01 to $3,000	$400
$3,000.01 to $4,000	$425
$4,000.01 to $5,000	$450.

For judgments exceeding $5,000, additional reasonable attorney fees may be allowed of 5% of any balance over $5,000 without formal justification or documentation.

[Effective September 1, 2002]

LCRLJ 56. SUMMARY JUDGMENT MOTIONS AGAINST PRO SE LITIGANTS

(h) In all cases where a motion for summary judgment is brought against a litigant who is not represented by an attorney, the moving party must attach a copy of CRLJ 56 to the motion for summary judgment. The copy shall be attached to the motion filed with the court and the copy of the motion served on the non-moving party. In the event a copy of the rule is not attached, the motion shall be stricken subject to being re-noted without terms.

[Adopted effective September 1, 2003.]

LOCAL CRIMINAL RULES

LCrRLJ 1.1. SCOPE

Procedures in San Juan County District Court shall be in accordance with pertinent Washington statutes and Criminal Rules, and these Local Rules are only in supplement thereto.

[Former Rule No. 1, renumbered and amended effective September 1, 1997.]

LCrRLJ 1.6. CONDUCT OF COURT

(a) The court may modify or suspend any of the Court Rules in any given case upon the showing of good cause or upon the Court's motion in order to prevent the failure of justice.

[Former Rule 22, renumbered and amended effective September 1, 1997.]

LCrRLJ 3.1. AUTOMATIC WITHDRAWAL OF ATTORNEY APPOINTED AT PUBLIC EXPENSE

(e) Unless a Notice of Appeal has been filed, an attorney appointed at public expense shall be deemed automatically withdrawn from representation thirty days following a final decision of the court as defined in RALJ without need to file any document with the court.

[Adopted effective September 1, 2003.]

LCrRLJ 3.2. BAIL IN CRIMINAL AND TRAFFIC CASES

(v) Bail Schedule. Except as otherwise set forth herein, the court has adopted the uniform bail schedule of the Administrative Office of the Courts. No deviation from the bail schedule shall be permitted unless specifically authorized by the court.

(w) Domestic Violence Offenses. Any person arrested for a domestic violence offense shall be held in custody without bail pending a first appearance before a judge.

(x) Receipt of bail. Clerks are authorized to receive bail posted with the court in the form of cash, cashier's check, money order or credit card.

[Former Rule No.6 renumbered and amended September 1, 1997; amended effective September 1, 2010.]

LCrRLJ 3.3. VERIFICATION OF TRIAL DATE—CONTINUANCES

(f)(3) Counsel and parties shall be responsible for keeping themselves informed of the date and time of trials, and must contact the clerk of the court one business day prior to the trial date to verify the starting time of the trial.

(h) Continuances or other delays may be granted as follows:

(1) *By stipulation:* Upon written agreement of the parties, which must be signed by the defendant or all defendants, and with the express approval of the court. The agreement shall be effective when approved by the court on the record or in writing.

(2) *By motion:* On motion of the prosecuting authority, the court, or a party, the court may continue the case when required in the administration of justice and defendant will not be substantially prejudiced in the presentation of his or her defense. The motion must be filed on or before the date set for trial or the last day of any continuance or extension granted pursuant to this rule. The court must state on the record or in writing the reasons for the continuance. If the court grants the continuance, it may also impose such terms as would be equitable.

(3) The court will not continue a trial date or other final disposition beyond the applicable time for trial under CrRLJ 3.3 without a signed speedy trial waiver.

[Former Rules No. 2 and 11 renumbered and amended effective September 1, 1997.]

LCrRLJ 3.4. PRESENCE OF THE DEFENDANT

(c) Defendant Not Present. If in any case the defendant is not present when his or her personal attendance is necessary, the court may order the clerk to issue a bench warrant for the defendant's arrest, which may be served as a warrant of arrest in other cases. The court may also forfeit any bail, bond or other security posted by or on behalf of the defendant. If the defendant fails to appear for any pre-trial hearing, the court may also strike the trial date. If the defendant fails to appear for *any pre-trial hearing* for any reason not authorized or approved by the court, the defendant shall be deemed to have waived his or her right to a speedy trial under CrRLJ 3.3(c).

[Former Rules No. 5 and 16(C) renumbered and amended effective September 1, 1997.]

LCrRLJ 3.7. PRESENCE OF THE PROSECUTOR

In all criminal cases, a representative of the San Juan County Prosecuting Attorney's Office shall be present to conduct the case for the plaintiff, unless otherwise authorized by the court.

[Former Rule No. 3, renumbered and amended effective September 1, 1997.]

LCrRLJ 4.1. ARRAIGNMENT

Arraignments shall be in accordance with CrRLJ 4.1 and 4.2. Except as noted below, a lawyer may, pursuant to CrRLJ 4.1(d), enter an appearance on behalf of a client by filing a written notice of appearance with the clerk and serving a copy upon the prosecuting attorney. Except in the following cases, the clerk may continue an arraignment at the request of the defendant or counsel for one week, on condition that a Waiver of Speedy Arraignment is filed with the court.

A lawyer may not enter a written plea of not guilty on behalf of a client, if the charging document states that one or more of the charges involves domestic violence, harassment, violation of an anti-harassment or protection order, stalking, or driving while under the influence of intoxicants, driving while under the age of 21 after having consumed alcohol, or physical control of a vehicle while under the influence of intoxicants.

If the defendant has previously appeared in person before a judge, as required by RCW 46.61.50571, and conditions of release have been ordered, then a lawyer may enter an appearance or a plea of not guilty and waiver of arraignment on behalf of a client.

An appearance that waives arraignment, but fails to state a plea, shall be deemed to constitute entry of a plea of not guilty. Upon timely receipt of a notice of appearance and the filing of proof of compliance with conditions of release, the court staff shall strike the arraignment date and issue a notice to appear for pretrial hearing.

[Former Rule No. 4, renumbered and amended effective September 1, 1997; amended effective September 1, 2002.]

LCrRLJ 4.2. STATEMENT OF DEFENDANT ON PLEA OF GUILTY

(g) A written statement of the defendant shall be filed in accordance with CrRLJ 4.1(g). Where a defendant is represented by counsel, it shall be the duty of the defense attorney to have a properly completed written statement of defendant on plea of guilty, at the time the case is called.

[Effective September 1, 1997, amended effective September 1, 2002.]

LCrRLJ 4.5. PRE–TRIAL CONFERENCE

(a) **Date set at Arraignment.** When a plea of not guilty is entered, the court shall set a time for a pre-trial conference, approximately 30 days after the arraignment.

(b) **Mandatory Appearance.** All parties and their attorneys shall be present at the pre-trial hearing. Failure of a defendant to attend the pre-trial conference may result in the issuance of a bench warrant, the forfeiture of any bond, bail or other security posted by or on behalf of the defendant, and the striking of the trial date from the trial calendar.

(c) **Discovery Complete.** By the time of the pre-trial hearing, the parties should have completed discovery and concluded plea negotiations.

(d) **Pre–trial motions.** All pre-trial motions (including Petitions for Deferred Prosecution), other than motions in limine, must be noted at the pre-trial hearing. The court will set a time for a hearing on the motions and set a briefing schedule. The motions must be made in writing in accordance with the briefing schedule, with a memorandum of authorities and, where appropriate, an affidavit setting forth the specific facts the party expects to elicit at the hearing. Failure to note a motion at the pre-trial hearing, or comply with the briefing schedule, absent a showing of good cause, will be deemed a waiver of the issues presented in the motions.

(e) **Jury Trial.** The Trial Readiness Hearing and the Jury Trial will be scheduled at this time.

[Former Rule 16(C), renumbered and amended effective September 1, 1997, amended effective September 1, 2002; September 1, 2003.]

LCrRLJ 4.7. CHALLENGE TO BAC DATAMASTER—SANCTIONS

(b)(4) If the defendant seeks to challenge the condition or operation of the BAC Verifier DataMaster or the admissibility of any test conducted with the instrument, he or she must serve written notice of the challenge and the grounds therefore on the prosecuting attorney at least 7 days prior to the trial date. Failure to provide timely notice will constitute a waiver of such challenge.

(g)(7)(iv) Motions for sanctions may be heard on any regularly scheduled court day, provided that notice has been provided to opposing party at least 48 hours (excluding weekends and holidays) prior to the hearing, and that such motions are in writing and filed and served on the opposing party at least 6 business days before the scheduled trial date.

[Former Rules No. 10 and 15, renumbered and amended effective September 1, 1997.]

LCrRLJ 6.1. JURY TRIAL READINESS HEARING

A Jury Trial Readiness Hearing will be scheduled during the week prior to the Jury Term Week. The Defendant must be present with his or her attorney, who may appear telephonically when called. The failure of the Defendant to appear at this hearing, unless excused by the Court, may result in the issuance of a bench warrant and the jury trial being stricken, and shall be deemed a Waiver of the Defendant's Right to Speedy Trial. At the hearing the following matters will be concluded:

1. All plea negotiations;

2. Exchange of witness lists;

3. Providing any discovery not previously completed by the Pre–Trial Conference; and,

4. Motions on legal issues arising subsequent to the Jury Pre–Trial Conference or on issues arising due to new evidence.

When a cause assigned for jury trial is settled, or will not be tried by a jury for any reason, notice of that fact shall be given immediately to the Court Clerk. In the event the notice is given after the readiness hearing, the party electing not to have it's case heard by a jury shall pay a jury administrative reimbursement fee equal to the actual costs incurred by the Court for the jury trial, unless the Judge determines that those costs and fees shall not be paid.

[Effective September 1, 2002, amended effective September 1, 2003.]

LCrRLJ 6.1.1. JURY TRIAL TERM

(e) Cases required to be tried by a jury shall be so tried unless the defendant files a written waiver of jury trial and has the consent of the court. A defendant who has waived his or her right to a jury trial and who subsequently wishes to request a jury trial, must file the request with the court no later than the pre-trial hearing, or the right to jury trial will be deemed irrevocably waived.

(f) The court will set two jury trial terms each month during the weeks of the first and third Thursdays of that month.

[Former Rule 16(A), renumbered and amended September 1, 1997; amended effective September 1, 2002; September 1, 2010.]

LCrRLJ 6.1.2. BENCH TRIAL TERM

(c) Bench trials will be scheduled on Thursday afternoons, other than during the jury trial week, except where otherwise ordered by the court.

[Former Rule 16(A), renumbered and amended effective September 1, 1997. Amended effective September 1, 2002.]

LCrRLJ 6.13. EVIDENCE—COURT'S CUSTODY OF EXHIBITS

(f) In a criminal case every exhibit in the court's custody that is not contraband, and for which ownership is not in dispute, shall be returned to the party that produced that exhibit upon motion of that party and the expiration of the appeal period. Exhibits not withdrawn shall be delivered by the court to the applicable law enforcement agency for disposition as abandoned property, or if contraband, for destruction. No exhibit shall be released by the court without obtaining a receipt from the person or agency receiving it.

[Effective September 1, 1997.]

LCrRLJ 6.15. JURY INSTRUCTIONS

(a) Unless otherwise ordered by the court, proposed jury instructions shall be filed with the court and served upon opposing counsel at least 2 business days before the trial date. Each party shall file two original sets of instructions: one with citations and one without citations, and shall serve a copy with citations on each party. Additional instructions, which could not be reasonably anticipated, shall be served and filed at any time before the court has instructed the jury. Each proposed instruction shall be on a separate sheet of paper. The original without citations shall neither be numbered nor include citations of authority.

[Former Rule No. 16, renumbered and amended effective September 1, 1997.]

LCrRLJ 7.2. SENTENCING— EVALUATIONS

(e) Whenever the court orders a defendant to obtain an evaluation as a condition of sentence, the defendant shall first obtain and execute a waiver of confidentiality on a form provided by the court, and a copy of the form containing the court's evaluation standards as set forth in LCrRLJ 8.13(b). The defendant shall file signed copies of the waiver of confidentiality form and the form containing the evaluation standards, and shall provide copies of the two signed forms to the evaluator. The evaluation must be performed by a state-certified agency, counselor, or therapist and the evaluation just meet the evaluation standards set forth in LCrRLJ 8.13(b).

[Effective September 1, 1997.]

LCrRLJ 8.2. MOTIONS

(a) Motion practice shall be in accordance with CrRLJ 8.2.

(b) Deferred Prosecutions:

(1) A petition for deferred prosecution under 10.05 RCW shall be filed and served on the prosecuting attorney no later than five days before the date set for the pre-trial hearing, and in no event less than 14 days before the date set for trial. The petition must be accompanied by an evaluation that meets the court standards as set forth in LCrRLJ 8.13(b). No petition shall be heard without a recommendation from the probation department.

(2) All pleadings shall be consistent with forms approved by the court.

(3) Prior to obtaining an evaluation, the petitioner must (a) execute a waiver of confidentiality on a form approved by the court and file a copy with the court, (b) obtain a copy of the court's evaluation standards as set forth in LCrRLJ 8.13(b) and (c) provide copies of the evaluation standards and completed waiver form to the evaluator.

(4) The evaluation accompanying the petition for deferred prosecution must be performed by a state-approved treatment facility and must meet the evaluation standards set forth in LCrRLJ 8.13(b).

[Amended September 1, 1997, amended effective September 1, 2010.]

LCrRLJ 8.13. EVALUATIONS— GENERAL STANDARDS

(a) Except as otherwise approved by the court, any evaluation presented to the court for consideration must meet the evaluation standards set forth in this rule.

(b) The defendant must sign and file with the court a waiver of confidentiality on a form provided by the court, so that the court, probation officer and prosecutor may provide the evaluator with pertinent information, and the evaluator can provide evaluations and progress reports to the court, probation officer and prosecutor. The defendant must obtain a form from the court setting forth the court's evaluation standards and sign the form and file it with the court. The defendant must provide the evaluator with copies of the signed forms containing the waiver and evaluation standards.

(c) The evaluator must meet all certification and registration requirements of the state in which (s)he practices. As part of the evaluation process, the evaluator must comply with all procedures required by the State of Washington and, in addition, must obtain and consider the following:

1) The arrest and criminal history of the defendant;

2) The driving record of the defendant;

3) The police reports relating to the incident underlying the charges;

4) Any prior relevant evaluations;

5) Information from at least one collateral contact who has significant knowledge of the defendant;

6) Any additional information provided by the probation officer.

(d) Upon receipt of a request from an evaluator for information set forth in LCrRLJ 8.13(b), the prosecutor, probation officer or law enforcement agency may provide such information, provided that a proper waiver of confidentiality has been filed with the court.

[Effective September 1, 1997.]

LOCAL INFRACTIONS RULES

LIRLJ 3.1(b). CONTESTED HEARINGS— PRELIMINARY PROCEEDINGS— DISCOVERY

(1) In any case where the State intends to call or to rely upon the sworn statement of a local law enforcement officer, the duty to provide a list of witnesses to the Respondent may be met by providing a copy of the citing officer's sworn statement on which the officer is identified.

(2) No motion to dismiss or to suppress evidence will be granted for failure to provide discovery not required by IRLJ 3.1(b) unless the moving party has previously obtained an order from the Court compelling production of the additional discovery.

[Effective September 1, 2002.]

LIRLJ 3.2(b). MOTION FOR VACATION OF DEFAULT JUDGMENT FOR FTA.

(b) A defendant against whom a judgment for a traffic infraction has been entered by default for failure to appear, may file a motion in writing, on forms provided by the court, requesting that the judgment be set aside. The motion will then be presented to the court ex parte for determination. If, upon review, the court feels that a hearing upon the motion is necessary, the matter shall be set for hearing. Defendant must be present in the event the matter is set for hearing. The motion will be evaluated in conformity with CRLJ 60(b). If the Court grants said motion, the matter will be set for a hearing of the kind requested by the defendant. Miti-gation hearings may be heard at the time of the motion if the calendar allows.

[Effective September 1, 2002.]

LIRLJ 3.5. DECISION ON WRITTEN STATEMENTS

Mitigation and contested hearings based on sworn written statements, as provided in IRLJ 2.4(b)(4) and IRLJ 2.6 and IRLJ 3.5 are authorized. The written statements must be received by the Court no later than seven (7) calendar days before the scheduled hearing or it will not be considered.

[Effective September 1, 2002.]

LIRLJ 3.6. DEFERRED FINDINGS

A. Deferred Findings. The court may defer findings regarding traffic infractions either before or following a contested hearing or defer entry of an order following a mitigation hearing for up to one year and impose conditions on the person.

B. Limit. A person may not receive more than one deferral within a seven-year period for moving violations and one deferral within a seven year period for nonmoving violations.

C. Conditions. For moving violations the conditions may include attendance at traffic safety school, payment of some or all of the presumptive fine and an administrative fee. For nonmoving violations the conditions may include payment of some or all of the presumptive fine and an administrative fee.

D. Administrative Fee. An administrative fee shall be charged.

E. Dismissal. After the end of the deferral period, the court will dismiss the infraction if the person has met all the conditions of deferral and has not committed another traffic infraction during the period.

F. Subsequent Violation during the deferral period. The Court will notify a person during the pending deferment of a violation by first class mail to the address provided by the deferred person. The Court will note the deferred violation as committed and transmit the Notice of Infraction to the Department of Licensing. The Court shall have no other obligation to the deferred person in this regard.

[Effective September 1, 2002.]

LIRLJ 6.6. SPEED MEASURING DEVICE CERTIFICATION

Any certificate admissible under LIRLJ 6.6(b), and any other document related to a Speed Measuring Device, can be filed with the clerk of the court and maintained by the court as a public record, and shall be available for inspection by the public. Copies shall be provided by the clerk's office on request. There shall be no charge for the copy if it relates to an infraction filed against the person making the request. These records shall be available without a formal request for discovery. The court shall be entitled to take judicial notice of the fact that any document filed pursuant to this rule has been filed with the court. Documents filed pursuant to this rule shall not be suppressed as evidence merely because there is no prosecutor present to offer the document as an exhibit at the hearing. If the certificate or document is insufficient, then a motion to suppress the reading of the Speed Measuring Device shall be granted.

Requests to produce the electronic measuring device expert shall be contained in a separate document and served on the prosecuting attorney with a conformed copy filed with the Clerk of the Court. Unless otherwise requested, and ordered by the Court, appearance by the electronic measuring device expert shall be by telephone.

[Amended September 1, 2002, amended effective September 1, 2010.]

LOCAL SPECIAL PROCEEDINGS RULES

LRSP 1. NAME CHANGES

A. Requirements. An applicant who applies to the court for a change of name pursuant to RCW 4.24.130 must meet the following requirements:

B. Birth Certificate. A certified copy of any minor applicant's birth certificate or suitable identification must be presented to the clerk for verification and copying.

C. Minors—Parental Consent. All applicants under eighteen (18) years of age must be represented by a parent or legal guardian, and both biological or legal parents or guardian must approve the change of name either by personal appearance or by verified affidavit, unless good cause is shown.

D. Parental Notification. A parent or guardian who has not consented in writing to a minor's change of name and whose parental rights have not been previously terminated must be given actual notice or notice by publication as provided in CRLJ 4.

E. Notice by Publication. Publication of a single notice in a newspaper of general circulation in the county of the parent or guardian's last known residence shall be sufficient so long as the notice contains a hearing date, the name of the minor, the name the petitioner desires the child to assume, and sets for the reasons for requesting the change of name.

F. Separate Applications. Each applicant requesting a change of name must present a separate Petition, Change of Name Order and pay a separate filing fee and recording fee.

[Amended September 1, 2002; amended effective September 1, 2010.]

SKAGIT COUNTY

Table of Courts

Superior Court

Local Rules for Skagit County Superior Court.

District Court

Skagit County District Court Local Rules.

Municipal Courts

Anacortes Municipal Court—[No Local Rules].
Burlington Municipal Court—[No Local Rules].
Mount Vernon Municipal Court—[No Local Rules].
Sedro–Woolley Municipal Court Local Rules.

SUPERIOR COURT

LOCAL RULES FOR SKAGIT COUNTY SUPERIOR COURT

Including Amendments Received Through
August 15, 2015

Table of Rules

PART I. LOCAL ADMINISTRATIVE RULES (Cite as SCLAR)

SCLAR 0.1. SCOPE OF RULES

(a) These rules shall become effective, September 1, 2011.

(b) All proceedings in Skagit County Superior Court shall be conducted in accordance with applicable statutes and Washington State Court Rules, except as modified by these Local Court Rules.

(c) Compliance with Skagit County Local Court Rules shall be mandatory, unless waived by the Court for good cause.

[Effective September 1, 1997; amended effective September 1, 1999; September 1, 2000; September 1, 2001; September 1, 2002; September 1, 2003; September 1, 2004; amended on an emergency basis effective April 1, 2006; amended on a permanent basis effective September 1, 2006; amended on an emergency basis effective January 30, 2007; amended on a permanent basis effective September 1, 2007; amended effective September 1, 2008; renumbered and amended effective September 1, 2009; amended effective September 1, 2011.]

SCLAR 0.2. COURT ORGANIZATION

(a) **Departments.**

Dept	Created	Incumbent Judge	Date of Qualification
No. 1	1891	Hon. John M. Meyer	January 1997
No. 2	1955	Hon. Michael E. Rickert	January 1993
No. 3	1992	Hon. Susan K. Cook	January 1997
No. 4	2006	Hon. Dave Needy	January 2006

(b) **Selection of Presiding Judge.** The Presiding Judge shall be the Superior Court Judge selected by a majority vote of the Skagit County Superior Court Judges. An election shall be held during the second December of the term of the current Presiding Judge. The Presiding Judge shall serve for two calendar years.

(c) **Commissioners.** Except where otherwise required by law or court rules, the terms "judge" and "court" include commissioners. Court Commissioners authorized by Article 4, Section 23 of the Constitution of the State of Washington have the power, authority and jurisdiction established by RCW 2.24.040, including the specific authorization to accept pleas in adult criminal cases in accordance with CrR 4.2.

[Effective September 1, 1997; amended effective September 1, 1999; September 1, 2000; September 1, 2001; September 1, 2002; September 1, 2003; September 1, 2004; amended on an emergency basis effective April 1, 2006; amended on a permanent basis effective September 1, 2006; amended on an emergency basis effective January 30, 2007; amended on a permanent basis effective September 1, 2007; amended effective September 1, 2008; renumbered and amended effective September 1, 2009.]

SCLAR 0.3. SPECIAL SET HEARINGS AND COURT SCHEDULE

(a) **Special Set Hearings.** All special set hearings shall be set through the Court Administrator's Office at (360)336–9320 and, unless agreed upon by all parties and the Court, follow the nine (9) court day rule. No special set hearings should be scheduled before the criminal motions judge on Fridays.

(b) **Court Schedule [Rescinded]**

See Superior Court website www.skagitcounty.net and follow links to Superior Court.

[Effective September 1, 1997. Amended effective September 1, 1999; September 1, 2000; September 1, 2001; September 1, 2002; September 1, 2003; September 1, 2004; amended on an emergency basis effective April 1, 2006; amended on a permanent basis effective September 1, 2006; amended on an emergency basis effective January 30, 2007; amended on a permanent basis effective September 1, 2007; amended effective September 1, 2008; renumbered and amended effective September 1, 2009; amended effective September 1, 2011; amended on an emergency basis effective March 1, 2012; amended on a permanent basis effective September 1, 2012; September 2, 2013; amended on an emergency basis effective November 1, 2013; amended on a permanent basis effective September 2, 2014.]

SCLAR 0.4. RECORDS SUBMITTED FOR IN CAMERA REVIEW

Upon completion of in camera review of documents in a case, the documents shall be sealed by the clerk and maintained as an exhibit. The order sealing shall indicate the documents were presented to the court for in camera review.

[Adopted effective September 1, 2009.]

PART II. LOCAL GENERAL RULES (Cite as SCLGR)

SCLGR 1–5.   (No Local Rules)

SCLGR 6.   SPECIAL TRIAL RULES [DELETED]

[Effective September 1, 1997; amended effective September 1, 1999; September 1, 2004; September 1, 2008; deleted effective September 1, 2009.]

SCLGR 7–14.   (No Local Rules)

SCLGR 15.   PRELIMINARY CONFIDENTIAL FILING OF REPORT [RESCINDED]

[Adopted on an emergency basis effective March 1, 2008; adopted on a permanent basis effective September 1, 2008; amended on an emergency basis effective November 1, 2008; amended on a permanent basis effective September 1, 2009. Rescinded on an emergency basis, effective November 1, 2013; rescinded on a permanent basis, effective September 2, 2014.]

SCLGR 16.   COURTROOM PHOTOGRAPHY AND RECORDING BY THE NEWS MEDIA

(d) All media personnel requesting to use still or video cameras shall check in first with the bailiff of the particular court room who will direct them to an area in the courtroom conducive to the needs of the court personnel, parties to the action and the media.

(e) **Media and proof of liability insurance.** [Rescinded September 2, 2014]

[Adopted effective September 1, 2009. Amended effective September 2, 2014.]

SCLGR 17–30.   (No Local Rules)

SCLGR 31.   PERSONAL IDENTIFIERS–CHILDREN

(a) **Complete names of children, sealed case types:** The complete names of children shall be used in cases that are deemed confidential pursuant to state or federal statutes, including cases filed pursuant to Title 13 RCW (excluding offender cases); Chapter 4.24 RCW, Chapter 26.33 (Adoption) and Chapter 71.34 (Mental Health Services for Minors).

(b) **Confidential Information Form:** The complete names of children and other identifiers shall be included in the Confidential Information Form or similar document for cases filed under Title 26.

(c) **Domestic Relations Orders:** Court orders concerning the financial support or the custody or residential schedule of a child (including temporary and permanent parenting plans and similar documents) and orders establishing or disestablishing paternity shall include the full name of the child. The date of birth of a child shall be included in court records only as authorized by GR 22.

(d) **Child who is alleged to be a victim of a crime:** The complete name of a child who is alleged to be a victim of a crime may be included on subpoenas and in jury instructions. Nothing in this rule requires that subpoenas be routinely filed in the court file.

(e) **Child who is charged with a crime:** The complete name of a child charged with a crime shall be included in any indictment or information filed with the court pursuant to CrR 2.1 or JuCR 7.2, as part of an affidavit or declaration of probable cause or for any other purpose deemed necessary for the prosecution or defense of the criminal or juvenile offender matter.

(f) **Orders issued for the protection of a child:** If a child is a person protected by a criminal no contact order issued pursuant to 10.99 RCW, an anti-harassment order issued pursuant to 10.14 RCW, an order of protection issued pursuant to 26.50 RCW or a restraining order or order of protection issued pursuant to 26.09 RCW, 26.10 RCW, 26.26 RCW, RCW 26.52.020, or any other court order entered for the protection of the child, the child's full name and other identifiers shall be included on petitions and orders as necessary for entry of the order into the Judicial Information System (JIS) and/or the Washington Crime Information Center (WACIC).

(g) If access to a child is restricted pursuant to CrR 3.2(d) (1), the court may include the full name of the child on the order, if deemed necessary for effective enforcement of the order.

(h) Orders restraining child from contacting or harassing others: Whenever a child is named as a respondent in an order listed in (3) above, the child's full name and other personal identifiers shall be included on the petition and order as necessary for entry of the order in the Judicial Information System (JIS) and/or the Washington Crime Information Center (WACIC).

(i) **General authority:** Nothing in this rule shall prohibit a court from authorizing the use of a child's full name or date of birth when necessary for the orderly administration of justice, consistent with the requirements of GR 22.

[Adopted effective September 1, 2005; amended effective September 1, 2009.]

SCLGR 32. FORMS [DELETED]

[Adopted effective September 1, 2005; deleted effective September 1, 2009.]

PART III. LOCAL CIVIL RULES (Cite as SCLCR)

1. INTRODUCTORY
(Rules 1–2A) [Reserved]

2. COMMENCEMENT OF ACTION; SERVICE OF PROCESS; PLEADINGS, MOTIONS AND ORDERS
(Rules 3–6)

SCLCR 3. PLEADINGS ALLOWED; FORM OF MOTIONS; MOTIONS FOR RECONSIDERATION [DELETED]

[Effective September 1, 1997; amended effective September 1, 1999; September 1, 2001; September 1, 2004; September 1, 2006; September 1, 2007; September 1, 2008; deleted effective September 1, 2009.]

SCLCR 3–5. [RESERVED.]

SCLCR 6. TIME

(d) For Motions

(1) *Notes for Motion Calendar.* Notes for the Motion Calendar shall be filed with the clerk of the court and served on all parties at least nine (9) court days before the hearing. All Notes for the Motion Calendar must comply with SCLCR 84.

(2) *Timing for Service of Motions, Responses, Replies and Proposed Orders.*

(i) *Motions.* Motions, other than Summary Judgment motions, shall be filed and served upon all parties at least nine (9) court days before hearing. When a motion is supported by affidavit or other documents, the affidavit and other documents shall be served with the motion.

(ii) *Responses.* Responses shall be filed and served on all parties at least four (4) court days before hearing. Affidavits and other supporting documents shall be served with the Response.

(iii) *Replies.* Replies shall be filed and served on all parties at least two (2) court days before hearing. Affidavits and other supporting documents shall be served with the Reply.

(iv) *Proposed Orders.* A proposed form of order, which the Court may adopt, modify or reject consistent with the decision of the Court, shall be served with the motion or response to motion. Proposed orders should not be filed with the clerk.

[Adopted effective September 1, 2009. Amended on an emergency basis, effective March 1, 2013; June 1, 2013; amended on a permanent basis, effective September 2, 2013.]

3. PLEADINGS AND MOTIONS
(Rules 7–16)

SCLCR 7. PLEADINGS ALLOWED; FORM OF MOTIONS; MOTIONS PRACTICE

(b) Motions and Other Papers

(1)–(4) [Reserved]

(5) *Telephonic Argument.* Oral argument on civil motions, including family law motions, may be heard by conference telephone call at the discretion of the court.

(i) The CourtCall Telephonic Appearance Program ("CourtCall"), organizes a procedure for telephonic appearance by attorneys or pro se parties.

CourtCall is available for motions. Each party wanting to appear telephonically shall contact CourtCall directly at 1–888–882–6878. All DV matters require prior approval by Court Administration. All requested telephonics will be heard later in the calendar and be given a specific time. The party scheduling the telephonic must also notify the other side. Counsel shall provide the court with an original proposed order with their judge's copies prior to appearing telephonically. Any request for a telephonic appearance for a trial must be brought before the court by a motion.

(c)–(d) [Reserved]

(e) Motions Practice.

(1) *Setting of Motion.* Motions under CR56 and CR57, and other motions that may be dispositive to the outcome of the matter, including, but not limited to, motions made under CR 12(b)(1–7) at least in part, and 12 (c) shall be placed on the Thursday, 9:30 calendar and confirmed pursuant to the provisions set forth in SCLCR 56/57. All other civil motions shall be placed on the Friday 9:30 a.m. Civil Motions Calendar.

(f) Ex Parte Practice. Ex Parte matters shall be delivered to the Clerk's Office, with the appropriate ex parte fee, for transmission to court with the court file. Ex Parte matters requiring personal presentation may be presented at the beginning of any Motion Calendar or at 1:15 p.m. each day, provided the appropriate court file is available or made available to the court by the attorney presenting the motion. This is NOT an argument calendar. A paralegal working in an attorney's office, or employee working in an attorney's office may present orders on the ex parte calendar, if signed by the supervising attorney. See SCLSPR 94.04.2(j) and SCLSPR 98.16.2 for dissolution and probate matters that may be presented ex parte.

(g) Motions in Limine. All motions in limine shall be heard by the trial judge prior to trial. If a lengthy hearing is anticipated, a special set shall be requested from court administration pursuant to SCLAR 0.3(a).

[Adopted effective September 1, 2009. Amended effective September 1, 2011; amended on an emergency basis, effective March 1, 2012. Adopted on a permanent basis, effective September 1, 2012. Amended on an emergency basis, effective March 1, 2013; June 1, 2013; amended on a permanent basis, effective September 2, 2013; amended on an emergency basis effective February 19, 2014; amended on a permanent basis effective September 2, 2014; September 1, 2015.]

SCLCR 8-9. [RESERVED]

SCLCR 10. FORM OF PLEADINGS AND OTHER PAPERS

(a)–(c) [Reserved]

(d) Format Requirements

(1) *GR 14 Compliance.* All pleadings and other papers presented for filing with the Clerk shall conform to GR 14.

(2) *Length of Briefs and Legal Memoranda.* Briefs and legal memoranda on non-dispositive pretrial matters may not exceed five (5) pages double-spaced. In trial matters the limit for a party's main filing is ten (10) pages double-spaced; supplemental briefs or legal memoranda on subsidiary matters may not exceed three (3) pages double-spaced. Declarations and affidavits in such matters may not exceed five (5) pages double-spaced. There is no page limit on summary judgment motions, motions for declaratory judgment and any potentially dispositive motions as described in SCLCR 7(e)(1). The Court may strike pleadings that are longer than the page limit described in this rule upon its own motion.

(3) *Filing: Case Numbers.* No documents shall be submitted for filing with more than one case number. Where documents require filing under multiple case numbers, attorneys shall submit duplicate originals for each case number cited. Case numbers for each file shall be highlighted by circling the appropriate cause number. Where there are multiple case numbers and no duplicate originals provided, the Clerk shall place the document only in the first case number designated.

(4) *Filing: Physical Issues.* Single documents with multiple pages shall be stapled together. Multiple documents shall not be stapled together; e.g., do not staple your calendar note to the motion.

(5) *Translation of Documents.* Any documents filed in the court file in Spanish, or any other foreign language, must be accompanied by a translated version in English.

[Effective September 1, 1997; amended effective September 1, 2000; September 1, 2001; September 1, 2004; amended on an emergency basis effective March 1, 2008; amended on a permanent basis effective September 1, 2008; amended effective September 1, 2009.]

SCLCR 11–16. [RESERVED]

4. PARTIES
(Rules 17–25) [Reserved]

5. DEPOSITIONS AND DISCOVERY
(Rules 26–37) [Reserved]

6. TRIALS
(Rules 38–53.4)

SCLCR 38-39. [RESERVED]

SCLCR 40. ASSIGNMENT OF CASES

(a) [Reserved]

(b) Methods

(1) *Form of Request.* The trial assignment calendar shall be held on each Monday at 9:30 a.m. Counsel should not be present for this calendar, but should proceed according to the remainder of this rule. Trial dates shall be assigned by the Court Administrator pursuant to requests made in accordance with CR 40, using the form in Appendix H (for pro se litigants) or J to these Local Rules.

(2) *Joinder and Default.* Before filing a request for trial assignment, counsel must determine that all joinder issues under CRs 18–20 are resolved. Motions for default under CR 55 must have been heard and resolved before requesting a trial date.

(3) *Conflict Dates.* Counsel shall file with the clerk of the court, and a copy to Court Administration, a notice of conflict dates on or before the date set for the trial assignment. A trial date will be assigned even if all parties have not submitted conflicts. Conflict dates shall be limited to previously scheduled vacations, trial dates, arbitrations and mediations. Counsel is to include the name of the trial, arbitration or mediation in conflict and the location of the conflict. The form Notice of Conflict Dates may be found in the Forms Appendix.

(4) *Objections to Trial Assignment.* The Court Administrator shall set the trial date from the trial assignment calendar. Objections to having a trial date assigned shall be made by motion and noted for hearing within 14 calendar days of filing of the Note for Trial Assignment. If the Court finds the objection has merit, the trial date will be stricken.

(5) *Pre–assignment of Judge.* Parties may move the court for pre-assignment of a judge. The original should be filed and a copy should be delivered to the Court Administrator. The presiding Judge will then select a Judge for pre-assignment. A letter will then notify counsel that all pretrial motions should be heard by the assigned judge and should be scheduled through Court Administration. This is to assure that the assigned judge is on the appropriate calendar, or if a special set is necessary. If both sides do not agree to a pre-assignment, the matter can be brought on the regular Civil Motions calendar.

(c) [Reserved]

(d) Confirmation of Civil Trials.

(1) All civil jury trials shall be confirmed by noon Thursday the week before the scheduled trial date. All other bench trials, **EXCEPT unlawful detainers,** shall be confirmed by noon two court days before the scheduled trial date. Counsel shall confirm trials by calling the Superior Court Administrator's Office, (360) 336–9320. If a trial is not confirmed in accordance with this rule, the trial will be stricken.

(e) Continuances and Settlement. Attorneys shall immediately notify the Court Administrator if a trial has settled or has been continued.

(f) [Reserved]

[Effective September 1, 1997. Amended effective September 1, 1999; September 1, 2002; September 1, 2003; September 1, 2004; September 1, 2006; September 1, 2008; September 1, 2009; amended on an emergency basis, effective March 1, 2013; June 1, 2013; amended on a permanent basis, effective September 2, 2013; September 2, 2014; September 1, 2015.]

SCLCR 41–42. [RESERVED]

SCLCR 43. TAKING OF TESTIMONY

(a) Testimony

(1)–(2) [Reserved]

(3) *Exhibits.* When a documentary exhibit is used at trial during witness examination counsel shall provide extra copies of the exhibit to opposing counsel and the court.

[Adopted effective September 1, 2009.]

SCLCR 44–50. [RESERVED]

SCLCR 51. INSTRUCTIONS TO JURY AND DELIBERATION

(a) Proposed. Provide to judge when trial begins, two copies of proposed jury instructions. One copy shall be cited and the other uncited with plaintiff's proposed instructions numbered in pencil on the lower left corner and the defendant's proposed instructions numbered in pencil on the lower right corner to correlate with jury instructions.

[Adopted effective September 1, 2009.]

SCLCR 52–53. [RESERVED]

SCLCR 53.2. COURT COMMISSIONERS [DELETED]

[Effective September 1, 2000; deleted effective September 1, 2009.]

7. JUDGMENT
(Rules 54–63)

SCLCR 54–55. [RESERVED]

SCLCR 56. SUMMARY JUDGMENT

(c) Motion, Proceedings and Confirmation of Motion.

(1) All parties must conform to the motion and proceeding requirements of CR 56(c).

(2) It shall be the responsibility of the moving party to confirm all motions for Summary Judgment on the Thursday 9:30 a.m. calendar by 4:00 p.m. Friday the week before the scheduled hearing.

(3) Confirmation shall be made by telephone to the Court Administrator's Office at (360) 336–9320 between 8:30 a.m. Monday and 4:00 p.m. Friday the week before said motion is scheduled for hearing.

(4) Motions not confirmed in accordance with this rule will be stricken.

(5) SCLCR (10)(d)(2) does not apply to SCLCR 56.

[Adopted effective September 1, 2009; amended on an emergency basis, effective March 1, 2012; amended on a permanent basis effective September 1, 2012; amended on an emergency basis effective February 19, 2014; amended on a permanent basis effective September 2, 2014.]

SCLCR 57. DECLARATORY JUDGMENTS

(a) Confirmation of Motion

(1) All parties must conform to the motion and proceeding requirements of CR 57.

(2) It shall be the responsibility of the moving party to confirm all motions for Declaratory Judgment on the Thursday 9:30 a.m. calendar by 4:00 p.m. Friday the week before the scheduled hearing.

(3) Confirmation shall be made by telephone to the Court Administrator's Office at (360) 336–9320 between 8:30 a.m. Monday and 4:00 p.m. Friday the week before said motion is scheduled for hearing.

(4) Motions not confirmed in accordance with this rule will be stricken.

(5) SCLCR (10)(d)(2) does not apply to SCLCR 57.

[Adopted effective September 1, 2009; amended on an emergency basis, effective March 1, 2012; amended on a permanent basis effective September 1, 2012; amended on an

emergency basis effective February 19, 2014; amended on a permanent basis effective September 2, 2014.]

SCLCR 59. NEW TRIAL, RECONSIDERATION, AND AMENDMENT OF JUDGMENTS

(b) Time for Motion; Contents of Motion

(1) This subsection applies to Motions for Reconsideration only.

(2) Motions for reconsideration of Judge's rulings and for reconsideration or revision of Commissioner's rulings, and all pleadings and documents in support thereof, must be filed and served on opposing counsel, or on the opposing party if unrepresented, and on the Court Administrator, within ten (10) days after entry of the judgment or order. The motion must set forth specific grounds for the reconsideration, and the arguments and authorities in support thereof, and designation of the Judge making the ruling.

(3) The opposing party may, within ten (10) days after receipt of the motion, file, and serve on the moving party and the Court Administrator, pleadings and documents in opposition.

(4) Each party shall prepare and include in the materials submitted, a proposed order sustaining their position on the motion.

(5) Oral arguments will be scheduled only if the Judge involved requests the same.

(6) Motions for reconsideration and revision shall be by brief only and shall not be noted for hearing on any motion calendar, unless oral argument has been requested by the Judge. Either party, after expiration of ten (10) days following filing and service of the motion, *may* file and serve on opposing counsel and the Court Administrator, a notice containing the case heading, a designation of the Judge making the original ruling, and certifying that the matter is ready for a ruling on the motion for reconsideration. The matter will not be brought before a judge until a Notice of Readiness is filed by any party.

[Adopted effective September 1, 2009. Amended on an emergency basis, effective March 1, 2013; June 1, 2013; amended on a permanent basis, effective September 2, 2013.]

SCLCR 60–63. [RESERVED]

8. PROVISIONAL AND FINAL REMEDIES
(Rules 64–71) [Reserved]

9. APPEALS
(Rules 72–76) [Reserved]

10. SUPERIOR COURTS AND CLERKS
(Rules 77–80) [Reserved]

11. GENERAL PROVISIONS
(Rules 81–86)

SCLCR 81–83. (No Local Rules)

SCLCR 84. FORMS

(a) **Action documents.** Pleadings or other documents requiring action on the part of the Clerk/Court (other than file stamping, docketing and entry in the court file) shall be considered action documents. Action documents must contain special caption and specify the action required on the first page.

[Adopted effective September 1, 2009.]

SCLCR 85–86. (No Local Rules)

PART IV. LOCAL MANDATORY ARBITRATION RULES (Cite as SCLMAR)

SCLMAR 1. SCOPE AND PURPOSE OF RULES

1.1 PURPOSE AND APPLICATION

These local rules, to be cited as Local Mandatory Arbitration Rules (LMAR) are for the purpose of implementing RCW 7.06 and supplementing Superior Court Mandatory Arbitration Rules adopted by the Supreme Court. Mandatory Arbitration Rules (MAR) as supplemented by these local rules are not designed to address every question which may arise during the arbitration process, and the rules give considerable discretion to the arbitrator. The arbitrator should not hesitate to exercise that discretion. Arbitration proceedings should be informal and expeditious, consistent with the purpose of relevant statutes and rules.

1.2 MATTERS SUBJECT TO ARBITRATION

Any civil action filed in the Skagit County Superior Court, other than an appeal from a Court of Limited Jurisdiction, is subject to mandatory arbitration if the sole relief sought is a money judgment in which no party asserts a claim in excess of $50,000.00, exclusive of attorney fees, interest and costs, or in which all parties for purposes of arbitration waive claims in excess of $50,000.00, exclusive of attorneys fees, interests and costs. Additionally, parties may stipulate to the arbitration of any matter in controversy not subject to mandatory arbitration.

[Adopted December 12, 1990]

SCLMAR 2. TRANSFER TO ARBITRATION AND ASSIGNMENT OF ARBITRATOR

2.1 TRANSFER TO ARBITRATION

(a) *Time of Transfer*

In every civil case, when any party has determined that the case is ready for trial and that the case is subject to arbitration, either mandatory or by stipulation, such party shall file with the Clerk a Note for Motion Docket, pay associated filing fee, and file a Demand for Arbitration setting the matter on the Motion Calendar not earlier than nine days from the date such demand is filed.

(b) *Order Transferring Cause to Arbitration*

Cases shall be transferred to arbitration only by Court Order. Such order may be secured:

(1) At the hearing scheduled pursuant to 2.1(a) above.

(2) By stipulation and order agreed to by all parties.

(c) *Response to Demand for Arbitration*

Any party disagreeing with a Demand for Arbitration shall serve and file a response to demand for arbitration not less than two (2) working days prior to the date the demand is noted for hearing. In the absence of such response, the Demand for Arbitration shall be granted, and an order presented transferring the cause to arbitration. Responses asserting that the cause is not subject to arbitration shall be heard on the date noted for hearing of the Demand for Arbitration.

2.3 ASSIGNMENT OF ARBITRATOR

(a) Generally; Stipulations

Parties may stipulate to appointment of any person, including non-attorneys, as arbitrator. Such stipulation shall be filed at or before the hearing on the demand for arbitration, or, in case of a stipulated order for arbitration, with said stipulated order. In the absence of a stipulated choice of arbitrator, a list of five arbitrators shall be submitted to the parties by the Director of Arbitration in cases involving two parties. In cases involving more than two parties, two additional names shall be submitted for each additional party involved in the cause.

Within seven (7) days thereafter each party shall nominate one or two arbitrators, and shall strike one or two arbitrators on the list. The Director of Arbitration shall appoint an arbitrator from among those nominated by all parties, or, if no one has been nominated by all parties, from among those not stricken by any party. Any party unwilling to submit their cause to the arbitrator so designated must file, within five (5) days of the appointment by the Director, a request for an appointment by the Court. Said request shall be filed with the Director and acted upon by the Court without further hearing.

[Adopted December 12, 1990; amended effective September 1, 2007.]

SCLMAR 3.   ARBITRATORS [RESCINDED]

[Adopted July 1, 1996.   Rescinded effective September 1, 2010.]

SCLMAR 4.   PROCEDURES AFTER ASSIGNMENT [RESERVED]

[Amended effective September 1, 2009. Former SCLMAR 4 adopted effective December 12, 1990; amended effective September 1, 2004; September 1, 2008; renumbered as SCLMAR 5 and amended effective September 1, 2009.]

SCLMAR 5.   HEARING

5.1 NOTICE OF HEARING

An arbitration hearing may be scheduled at any reasonable time and place chosen by the Arbitrator, after giving due consideration to the time preferences and conflicts indicated by the parties. Reasonable notice of the hearing and of any continuances shall be given to all parties and to the Director. Hearings should be scheduled not sooner than 21 days nor later than 63 days from the time of appointment and assignment of the cause to the Arbitrator. The arbitrator may grant a continuance without court order and for good cause shown.

[Adopted effective December 12, 1990; amended effective September 1, 2004; September 1, 2008; renumbered from SCLMAR 4 and amended effective September 1, 2009.]

SCLMAR 6.   AWARD [RESERVED]

SCLMAR 7.   TRIAL DE NOVO [RESERVED]

SCLMAR 8.   GENERAL PROVISIONS

(a) **Director of Arbitration**

The Arbitration Department of this Court shall be administered by the Director of Arbitration. The Director of Arbitration shall be the presently designated Court Administrator. The Director of Arbitration shall develop and make available to parties and arbitrators appropriate forms for the implementation of arbitration proceedings.

(b) **Administrative Committee.** [Rescinded September 2, 2014]

(c) **Compensation.** Arbitrators shall be compensated in the same amount and manner as judges pro tempore of the Superior Court; provided, the compensation shall not exceed $1,000.00 for any case without approval of a Superior Court Judge.

(d) These rules shall take effect on January 1, 1991 with respect to transfer of causes to arbitration. They shall take effect forthwith with respect to duties of the Director of Arbitration and the Administrative Committee.

[Amended effective September 1, 2005; September 1, 2008; September 1, 2009; September 2, 2014.]

PART V. LOCAL SPECIAL PROCEEDINGS RULES (Cite as SCLSPR)

SCLSPR 94.04.1.   PARENTING SEMINARS

(a) **Applicable Cases.** This rule shall apply to all cases filed after September 1, 2001 under Chapter 26.09, Ch. 26.10, or Ch. 26.26 RCW which require a parenting plan for minor children; including dissolutions, legal separations, major modifications, paternity actions in which paternity has been established, and non-parental custody actions.

(b) **Mandatory Attendance.** In all cases governed by this rule, all parties shall complete an approved parenting seminar. Standards for parenting seminars shall be established by the Court and providers shall be approved by the Court. An approved list of providers will be available through Court Administration.

(c) **Timing.** Parties required by this rule to participate in a parenting seminar shall complete an approved parenting seminar within 90 days after service of the petition or motion initiating the action which is subject to this rule. In the case of paternity actions initiated by the prosecuting attorney's office, the parenting seminar shall be required only when paternity is established or acknowledged and a parenting plan is requested.

(d) Fees. Each party attending a seminar shall pay a fee charged by the approved provider and sanctioned by the court. The court may waive the fee for indigent parties.

(e) Special Consideration/Waiver.

(1) In no case shall opposing parties be required to attend a seminar together.

(2) Upon a showing of domestic violence or abuse which would not require mutual decision-making, pursuant to RCW 26.09.191, or that a parent's attendance at a seminar is not in the children's best interest, pursuant to Ch. 26.12 RCW, the Court shall either:

(A) waive the requirement of completion of the seminar; or

(B) allow participation in an alternative voluntary parenting seminar for battered spouses.

(3) The Court may waive the seminar requirement for good cause shown.

(f) Failure to Comply. Willful refusal to participate in a parenting seminar or willful delay in completion of a parenting seminar by any party may constitute contempt of court and result in sanctions, including, but not limited to, imposition of monetary terms, striking of pleadings, or denial of affirmative relief to a party not in compliance with this rule.

[Adopted effective September 1, 2003; renumbered from SCLSPR 94.08.1 and amended effective September 1, 2009; amended effective September 1, 2011.]

SCLSPR 94.04.2. FILINGS IN FAMILY LAW CASES

(a) Application of Rule. This rule shall apply to all cases filed after September 1, 2003:

(1) All family law petitions seeking dissolution of marriage, legal separation, or declaration of invalidity;

(2) Actions brought by parties to non-marital personal relationships involving parenting or distribution of assets/liabilities; and

(3) Actions to modify previously-entered parenting plan or child support final orders.

(b) Court's Automatic Temporary Order. Upon the filing of a Summons and Petition in any of the actions specified in Sections (a)(1) and (2) above, the court on its own motion shall automatically issue a Temporary Order that includes the following provisions:

(1) The parties shall be restrained from transferring, removing, encumbering, concealing or in any way disposing of any property except in the usual course of business or for the necessities of life or as agreed in writing by the parties. Each party shall notify the other party of any extraordinary expenditure made after the order is issued.

(2) The parties shall be restrained from assigning, transferring, borrowing, lapsing, surrendering or changing entitlement of any insurance policies of either or both parties whether medical, health, life or auto insurance, except as agreed in writing by the parties.

(3) Each party shall be immediately responsible for his or her own future debts whether incurred by credit card or loan, security interest or mortgage, except as agreed in writing by the parties.

(4) Both parties shall have access to all tax, financial, legal and household records. Reasonable access to records shall not be denied.

(5) For those actions in which children are involved:

(i) Each parent shall be restrained from changing the residence of the child(ren) until further court order, except as agreed in writing by the parties. Subsequent orders regarding parenting issues supercede previously issued orders to the extent the orders may be inconsistent.

(ii) Each parent shall insure that the child(ren) not be exposed to negative comments about the other parent in the presence of the child(ren).

(c) Mediation in Contested Cases. Mediation shall apply to all cases filed after January 1, 2004. Except as provided in Section (d) below, in all cases specified in Section (a) having unresolved issues (except child support issues), both parties shall in good faith engage in mediation with a court-approved mediator in an effort to resolve the case. The parties may either agree to a mediator from the court-approved list or the mediator will be determined by use of a strike list. Either party may seek a court apportionment of the cost of mediation. In cases where parenting issues exist, the mediation shall not occur until both parties have completed the parenting seminar described in SCLSPR 94.04.1. A certificate of completion signed by the mediator shall be filed with the clerk of the court prior to trial.

(d) When Mediation is Not Required. Mediation shall be required as provided in Section (c) except in the following cases:

(1) For good cause shown upon motion and approval by the court;

(2) Where a domestic violence restraining order or protection order (excluding ex-parte orders) involving the parties has been entered by a court at any any[1] time within the previous 12 months;

(3) Where a domestic violence no contact order exists pursuant to RCW 10.99;

(4) Where the court upon motion finds that domestic abuse has occurred between the parties and that such abuse would interfere with arm's-length mediation.

Notwithstanding the foregoing, either party may by motion seek a court order requiring mandatory mediation in a case where it would not be required as set forth in (d)(2), (d)(3) or (d)(4) above if the moving party believes that the parties would be able to mediate their dispute at arm's-length under the particular circumstances of the case.

(e) Failure to Comply. A party's compliance with the provisions of this rule may be enforced upon Motion and Order to Show Cause. Unless compliance is waived by the court for good cause shown, the court may order appropriate sanctions including costs, attorney's fees, and adoption of the complying party's proposal.

(f) Registry Administration. The Court Administrator shall maintain and administer the family law mediator registry. The application form and requirements may be obtained from the Court Administrator's office.

(g) Certificate of Completion. Prior to a final dissolution hearing or the trial date, mediation must be completed. Failure to complete mediation, prior to the trial date, will result in the trial being stricken. A certification of completion signed by the mediator shall be filed with the clerk.

(h) Page Limitation. Absent prior authorization from the court, the entirety of all declarations and affidavits from the parties and any non-expert witness in support of motions shall be limited to a sum total of twenty (20) pages. The entirety of all declarations and affidavits submitted in response to motions shall be limited to a sum of twenty (20) pages. The entirety of all declarations and affidavits submitted in reply shall be limited to a sum total of five (5) pages. All declarations and affidavits must be legibly hand printed or typed in at least twelve (12) point type, and 1½ space format. All pages, including attached declarations and affidavits shall be sequentially numbered. Working copies of previously filed documents or orders are excluded from page limitation.

(1) *Exhibits.* Exhibits that consist of declarations or affidavits of parties or witnesses shall count towards the above page limit. All other exhibits attached to a declaration or affidavits shall not be counted toward the page limit.

(2) *Financial Declarations.* Financial declarations and financial documents do not count toward the page limit.

(3) *Expert Reports and Evaluations.* Declarations, affidavits, and reports from Family Court Investigation, guardians ad litem, police reports, substance abuse evaluations, psychological evaluations and other expert witnesses do not count toward the page limitation.

(4) *Sanctions.* Failure to comply with this rule may result in sanctions that may include, but are not limited to, striking over limit pleadings.

(i) Final Dissolutions Hearings or Trials. Prior to scheduling the final dissolution hearing or trial, pro se litigants shall meet with the Courthouse Facilitator.

(j) Pretrial Affidavits in Dissolution Proceedings. A case summary affidavit in the form provided in Appendix I to these rules shall be filed and served on opposing counsel by noon of the day preceding trial. Judge's copies shall be delivered to the Court Administrator's Office at that time.

(k) Final Papers in Uncontested Dissolution Matters. Final papers in uncontested dissolution matters may be presented ex parte if accompanied by an affidavit of one of the parties setting forth jurisdictional facts and signed by at least one attorney. Final papers in pro se dissolution matters must be set on a Monday calendar after being reviewed the Courthouse Facilitator.

(l)[1] Review of All Final Pleadings. Pro se litigants, married or unmarried, are required to meet with the Courthouse Facilitator on all final decrees, final orders and accompanying findings of fact and conclusions of law, parenting plans, orders of child support, and child support worksheets for family law cases involving children. The Courthouse Facilitator must review the documents for form and completeness prior to presentation to a judicial officer at a hearing or trial.

[Adopted effective September 1, 2003. Amended effective September 1, 2004; amended on an emergency basis effective April 1, 2006; amended on a permanent basis effective September 1, 2006; renumbered from 94.08.2 and amended effective September 1, 2009; amended effective September 1, 2011; September 1, 2012; amended on an emergency basis effective November 1, 2013; amended on a permanent basis effective September 2, 2014; September 1, 2015.]

1 So in original.

SCLSPR 94.04.3. JUDICIAL INFORMATION SYSTEM BACKGROUND CHECKS

Prior to presenting a ***permanent or final*** parenting plan to the court, the party or parties presenting the final parenting plan shall submit a completed judicial information service (JIS) background check form to Skagit County Superior Court Administration. Such request must be submitted no less than three days prior to the date of presentation of the final parenting plan.

[Adopted on an emergency basis effective March 1, 2008; adopted on a permanent basis effective September 1, 2008; renumbered from SCLSPR 94.08.3 and amended effective September 1, 2009.]

SCLSPR 94.04.4. FAMILY LAW TRIAL REQUEST AND CONFIRMATION

(d) FAMILY LAW TRIAL REQUEST. The trial assignment calendar shall be held on each Monday at 9:30 a.m. Parties need not be present for this calendar, but should proceed according to the remainder of this rule. Trial dates shall be assigned by the Court Administrator pursuant to requests made in accordance with CR 40, using the form in Appendix H (for pro se litigants) or J to these Local Rules.

(1) *Parenting Seminar Required.* A parenting seminar under SCLSPR 94.04.1 must be completed, if applicable, before requesting a trial date.

(2) *Mandatory Mediation on Domestic Matters.* Certification of completed mediation must be filed prior to trial or the matter is subject to being stricken by the Court. See SCLSPR 94.04.2(c)–(g).

(3) *Conflict Dates.* The parties shall file with the clerk of the court a notice of conflict dates on or before the date set for the trial assignment. A trial date will be assigned even if all parties have not submitted conflicts. Conflict dates shall be limited to previously scheduled vacations, trial dates, arbitrations and mediations. If counsel is involved, counsel is to include the name of the trial, arbitration or mediation in conflict and the location of the conflict. The form Notice of Conflict Dates may be found in the Forms Appendix.

(4) *Objections to Trial Assignment.* The Court Administrator shall set the trial date from the trial assignment calendar. Objections to having a trial date assigned shall be made by motion and noted for hearing within 14 calendar days of filing of the Note for Trial Assignment. If the Court finds the objection has merit, the trial date will be stricken.

(5) *Continuances and Settlement.* Parties shall immediately notify the Court Administrator if a trial has settled or has been continued.

(e) CONFIRMATION OF FAMILY LAW TRIALS. All family law trials shall be confirmed by noon two court days before the scheduled trial date. Parties shall confirm trials by calling the Superior Court Administrator's Office (360) 336–9320. If a trial is not confirmed in accordance with this rule, the trial will be stricken.

[Adopted effective September 1, 2009.]

SCLSPR 94.04.5. EVIDENCE AND EXHIBITS IN FAMILY LAW: SPECIAL PROVISIONS

(a) APPRAISALS OF AUTOMOBILES AND BOATS. In addition to individual appraisals of automobiles, trucks, and boats, the Court will give judicial recognition to Kelly Blue Book, NADA, or other recognized internet appraisal services on all automobiles, trucks, and boats. The appraisal should be for fair market retail value in the local area and be consistent with the description of the item being appraised.

(b) EXHIBITS. When a documentary exhibit is used at trial during witness examination and reference to the contents of the exhibit is necessary to understand the issues, the party shall provide extra copies of the exhibit to opposing counsel and the court.

[Adopted effective September 1, 2009.]

SCLSPR 98.16.1. GUARDIANSHIP MONITORING [RESCINDED]

[Adopted on an emergency basis effective March 1, 2008; adopted on a permanent basis effective September 1, 2008; renumbered from SCLSPR 98.1 and amended effective September 1, 2009; rescinded effective September 1, 2011.]

SCLSPR 98.16.2. PROBATE MATTERS NOT REQUIRING NOTICE

(a) EX PARTE PRESENTATION. Probate matters not requiring notice may be presented ex parte.

[Adopted effective September 1, 2009.]

PART VI. LOCAL RULES FOR GUARDIAN AD LITEM REGISTRY (Titles 11 and 26) (Cite as SCLGALR)

SCLGALR 1. SCOPE AND PURPOSE

1.1 This local rule covers the administration of the Guardian ad Litem Registry maintained by the Skagit County Superior Court under RCW Chapters 11 and 26.

[Adopted July 1, 2002. Amended effective September 1, 2004; September 1, 2009.]

SCLGALR 2. REGISTRY ADMINISTRATION

2.1 The Court Administrator shall maintain and administer the Guardian ad Litem registries. These registries are limited to Titles 11 and 26 guardians ad litem. These requirements and procedures also apply to persons not listed on a registry who are appointed to serve as a guardian ad litem in a field for which there is a registry.

2.2 The Court Administrator shall maintain an application form and background information records pertaining to each person on a registry. Persons listed on the registry shall reapply annually and provide a WSP criminal background check for the September 1st review date. All application and background information, with the exception of personal identifying information in family law cases and pending complaints, shall be available for public inspection.

2.3 Persons shall be selected to serve on the registry at the discretion of the court giving due consideration to having a sufficient number of guardians ad litem available to fulfill the requests for appointment and to retain panels of persons with substantial experience and special knowledge within given fields.

In some cases there may be more qualified applicants than will be needed or would benefit the program, so that not all persons applying will be selected.

2.4 The court shall periodically sponsor or approve training programs which registry applicants shall be required to attend to maintain and improve their level of proficiency. Training programs may be co-sponsored or offered by the state or local bar association under the oversight of the court.

2.5 The registry may be reconstituted periodically after an open application period has been announced. The court may allow additional applicants to be added to the registry in March of each year. All new applications are due by March 1st for consideration.

2.6 The court may impose an application processing fee and/or charge a fee for the training programs.

[Amended effective September 1, 2010.]

SCLGALR 3.   EDUCATION AND EX-PERIENCE REQUIREMENTS

3.1 Attorneys must be a member of the Washington State Bar Association in good standing, and provide proof of successful completion of guardian ad litem training as required by Title 11 and/or 26.

3.2 Non–Attorneys

(a) *Family Law Registry (Title 26)*

(1) Bachelor level degree in any of the following fields: social work, psychology, counseling, nursing, medicine or equivalent field; or

(2) Certified by the State of Washington as a social worker, mental health therapist or marriage and family counselor, or licensed as a psychologist, nurse or physician, in good standing; or

(3) Proof of successful completion of guardian ad litem training as required by Title 26 and proof of four completed guardian ad litem assignments for any Washington State superior court within the past five years

and

Proof of successful completion of guardian ad litem training as required by Title 26 and proof of successful completion of two supervised guardian ad litem assignments as follows:

(i) One guardian ad litem assignment done in conjunction with a mentor guardian ad litem which shall include accompanying the mentor on all visits, attendance at all interviews, participation in preparation of a report, and attendance at all court hearings. The mentor is the guardian ad litem of record and this assignment is without compensation to the applicant.

(ii) One guardian ad litem assignment done under the supervision of the same mentor guardian ad litem which shall include more active participation on the part of the applicant, i.e., requesting documents, conducting interviews, preparing reports under the supervision of the mentor. The mentor is the guardian ad litem of record and this assignment is without compensation to the applicant.

(b) *Guardianship, Probate and Minor Settlement Registry (Title 11)*

(1) Two (2) years of experience in the needs of impaired elderly people, physical disabilities, mental illness, developmental disabilities/ and/or other areas relevant to the needs of incapacitated persons, and

(2) Successful completion of mandatory Title 11 training.

[Amended on an emergency basis effective November 1, 2008; amended on a permanent basis effective September 1, 2009.]

SCLGALR 4.   APPLICATION

4.1 Each person requesting to be listed on the Guardian ad Litem Registry (or registries) shall submit an application by September 1st of each year. The application form and requirements may be obtained from the Court Administrator's office.

SCLGALR 5.   APPOINTMENT OF GUARDIAN AD LITEM

5.1 When the need arises for the appointment of a guardian ad litem in a case involving a subject area for which there is a registry, the court shall appoint a person from the registry, unless good cause is found and findings are entered supporting appointment of a person not listed on the registry.

5.2 Appointments from the registries shall be made in the exercise of the court's sound discretion. The court may, but is not obligated to, appoint a person whom all parties have stipulated to serve as guardian ad litem. Agreement of all parties will not suffice when one or more parties are alleged to be under a legal disability.

5.3 In making appointments from a registry, among other factors, the court will consider the facts of the case, and the skills, experience and knowledge of persons on the registry.

5.4 Generally a guardian ad litem will be required to accept a minimum of two (2) appointments per year at public expense. These two appointments from the previous year should be listed on the application.

5.5 Generally, appointments will be made on a rotational basis from the registry.

5.6 Appointment of a guardian ad litem in all cases shall be on the form required by the court.

5.7.1 The court shall make provisions for fees and expenses pursuant to statute in the Order Appointing Guardian ad Litem or in any subsequent order. For all cases filed in Skagit County, Order Appointing Guardian ad Litem form shall be used. (See Appendix S.) All expenses must be approved in advance.

5.8 The Guardian ad Litem Review Committee will address any complaints made by any guardian ad litem regarding registry or appointment matters upon the Court Administrator's receipt of said complaint. The guardian ad litem shall be notified in writing of the Guardian ad Litem Review Committee's decision.

[Amended effective September 1, 2005; September 1, 2015.]

SCLGALR 6. RETENTION ON REGISTRY

6.1 Persons on the registry shall promptly inform the court of any temporary unavailability to serve, or of their intent to resign from the registry.

6.2 A person shall remain on the registry unless the person fails to maintain a current application with attachments or the person is removed or suspended as set forth in Section VI.

6.3 A person may be denied listing on, or may be temporarily suspended from, the registry for any reason that places the suitability of the person to act as guardian ad litem in question.

6.4 A guardian ad litem who ceases to be on the registry and who still has active or incomplete cases shall immediately report his circumstance to the Court Administrator, and the court shall reassign such cases.

6.5 A person's retention on the registry shall be reviewed upon the court's receipt of a complaint regarding performance in office or the court's receipt of adverse information regarding the suitability of a person to serve as a guardian ad litem. Complaints shall be reviewed in accordance with Section VI.

SCLGALR 7. COMPLAINT PROCEDURE

7.1 There shall be a Guardian ad Litem Review Committee consisting of the Superior Court Presiding Judge, the Superior Court Administrator, a representative of the Skagit County Bar Association, and a guardian ad litem from the registry, appointed by the Presiding Judge.

7.2 The Guardian ad Litem Review Committee, hereinafter referred to as the "Committee," will administer complaints about guardians ad litem.

7.3 All complaints must be in writing and must be submitted to the Superior Court Administrator, 205 W. Kincaid, Room 202, Mount Vernon, WA 98273. All complaints must bear the signature, name and address of the person filing the complaint.

7.4 Upon receipt of a written complaint, the Court Administrator shall convene the Committee to review the complaint. Upon review of the complaint, the Committee shall either:

(a) Making a finding that the complaint is with regard to a case then pending in the court and decline to review the complaint and so inform the complain-

ant. In such instances the Committee shall advise the complainant that the complaint may only be addressed in the context of the case at bar, either by seeking the removal of the guardian ad litem or by contesting the information or recommendation contained in the guardian ad litem's report or testimony. In such cases the Committee and its members shall perform its role in such a manner as to assure that the trial judge remains uninformed as to the complaint; or

(b) Make a finding that the complaint has no merit on its face and decline to review the complaint and so inform the complainant; or

(c) Make a finding that the complaint appears to have merit and request a written response from the guardian ad litem within 10 business days, detailing the specific issues in the complaint to which the Committee desires a response. The Committee shall provide the guardian ad litem with a copy of the original complaint. In considering whether the complaint has merit, the Committee shall consider whether the complaint alleges the guardian ad litem has:

(1) Violated a code of conduct including all Superior Court Guardian ad Litem Rules (GALR) and applicable professional codes of conduct.

(2) Misrepresented his or her qualifications to serve as a guardian ad litem;

(3) Breached the confidentiality of the parties;

(4) Falsified information in a report to the court or in testimony before the court;

(5) Failed, when required, to report abuse of a child;

(6) Communicated with a judicial officer ex-parte concerning a case for which he or she is serving as a guardian ad litem;

(7) Violated state or local laws or court rules; or

(8) Taken or failed to take any other action which would reasonably place the suitability of the person to serve as a guardian ad litem in question.

7.5 Upon receipt of a written response to a complaint from the guardian ad litem, the Committee shall make a finding as to each of the issues delineated in the Committee's letter to the guardian ad litem. Such findings shall state that either there is no merit to the issue based upon the guardian ad litem's response or that there is merit to the issue.

7.6 The Committee shall have the authority to issue a written admonishment, a written reprimand, refer the guardian ad litem to additional training, or recommend to the Presiding Judge that the court suspend or remove the guardian ad litem from the registry. In considering a response, the Committee shall take into consideration any prior complaints that resulted in an admonishment, reprimand, referral to training, or suspension or removal from a registry. If a guardian ad litem is listed on more than one registry, the suspension or removal may apply to each registry the guardian ad litem is listed on, at the discretion of the Committee.

7.7 The complainant and the guardian ad litem shall be notified in writing of the Committee's decision following receipt of the guardian ad litem's response.

7.8 Complaints shall be resolved within twenty-five (25) days of the date of receipt of the written complaint if a case is pending. Complaints shall be resolved within sixty (60) days of the date of receipt of the written complaint if the complaint is filed subsequent to the conclusion of a case.

7.9 A complaint shall be deemed confidential for all purposes unless the committee has determined that it has merit. [correction of numbering September 1, 2008]

7.10 Any record of complaints filed which are not deemed by the committee to have merit shall be confidential and shall not be disclosed except by court order.

[Amended on an emergency basis, effective April 1, 2006; amended on a permanent basis, effective September 1, 2006; amended on an emergency basis, effective March 1, 2008; amended on a permanent basis, effective September 1, 2008; amended on an emergency basis, effective March 1, 2013; June 1, 2013; amended on a permanent basis, effective September 2, 2013.]

SCLGALR 8. PAYMENT OF GUARDIAN AD LITEM

8.1. There shall be no payment of a guardian ad litem by anyone, except as authorized by order of the court.

8.2. Each order appointing guardian ad litem shall set forth the hourly rate of compensation for the investigative/guardian ad litem work; source of payment, if determined.

8.3. The order appointing a guardian ad litem may include a provision for a retainer fee, as evidenced by itemized accounting, to be returned to the parties according to their proportionate responsibility for payment of the guardian ad litem.

8.4. All fee requests by the guardian ad litem submitted to the court shall contain time records, which distinguish investigative/guardian ad litem, administrative/clerical, and travel time and shall also be served upon the parties. This should be presented to Court Administration along with an Order Authorizing Payment.

8.5. Guardian ad litem fees shall be the responsibility of a party or parties unless the court has entered an order authorizing payment at public expense.

[Adopted effective July 1, 2002. Amended effective September 1, 2003; September 1, 2004; September 1, 2006; amended on an emergency basis, effective March 1, 2008; amended on a permanent basis, effective September 1, 2008; amended effective September 1, 2009; September 1, 2011; September 2, 2013.]

SCLGALR 9. TITLE 26 GAL REPORTING

9.1 The guardian ad litem must report to the court within six months of order appointing GAL regarding the progress if not specifically stated in the order appointing.

[Adopted effective July 1, 2002; amended effective September 1, 2003; September 1, 2004; September 1, 2006; amended on an emergency basis effective March 1, 2008; amended on a permanent basis effective September 1, 2008; amended effective September 1, 2009.]

PART VII. LOCAL CRIMINAL RULES (Cite as SCLCrR)

1.   SCOPE, PURPOSE AND CONSTRUCTION
(Rules 1.1–1.5) [No Local Rules]

2.   PROCEDURES PRIOR TO ARREST AND OTHER PROCEDURES
(Rules 2.1–2.3) [No Local Rules]

3.   RIGHTS OF DEFENDANTS
(Rules 3.1–3.6)

SCLCrR 3.1. ATTORNEY CERTIFICATION

(d)(4) Attorney certification. Attorneys who anticipate being appointed to represent adult indigents in criminal cases must comply with CrR 3.1(f) by filing a certification of compliance with the Clerk of the Superior Court. The certification should be filed at least fourteen (14) days prior to each calendar quarter.

The Clerk will maintain an administrative file for such certifications. The administrative files will be open for public inspection.

[Adopted on an emergency basis, effective March 1, 2013; June 1, 2013; adopted on a permanent basis, effective September 2, 2013.]

4. PROCEDURES PRIOR TO TRIAL
(Rules 4.1–4.10) [No Local Rules]

5. VENUE
(Rules 5.1–5.2) [No Local Rules]

6. PROCEDURES AT TRIAL
(Rules 6.1–6.16)

SCLCrR 6.12. WITNESSES

(e) Exhibits. When a documentary exhibit is used at trial during witness examination and reference to the contents of the exhibit is necessary to understand the issues, counsel shall provide extra copies of the exhibit to opposing counsel and the court.

[Adopted effective September 1, 2009.]

SCLCrR 6.15. INSTRUCTIONS AND ARGUMENT

(a) Proposed Instructions.

(1) Provide to judge when trial begins, two copies of proposed jury instructions. One copy shall be cited and the other uncited with plaintiff's proposed instructions numbered in pencil on the lower left corner and the defendant's proposed instructions numbered in pencil on the lower right corner to correlate with jury instructions.

(b) Juror questionnaires for trials. Juror questionnaires must be agreed to by both sides or approved by the Court on motion of either party. Copies should be provided to Court Administration by Noon Friday.

[Adopted effective September 1, 2009; amended effective September 1, 2011.]

7. PROCEDURES FOLLOWING CONVICTION
(Rules 7.1–7.8) [No Local Rules]

8. MISCELLANEOUS
(Rules 8.1–8.9)

SCLCrR 8.2. MOTIONS

(a) Motions in Limine. All motions in limine shall be heard by the trial judge prior to trial. If a lengthy hearing is anticipated, a special set hearing may be requested under SCLAR 0.3(a).

(b) Child Hearsay Motion Hearings. Child hearsay hearings are to be special set in front of the trial judge (if possible) pursuant to special set rules under SCLAR 0.3(a). Child Hearsay Hearings shall not be scheduled on any criminal calendar.

[Adopted effective September 1, 2009.]

SCLCrR 8.4. SERVICE, FILING, AND SIGNING OF PAPERS

(a) Action documents. Pleadings or other documents requiring action on the part of the Clerk/Court (other than file stamping, docketing and entry in the court file) shall be considered action documents. Action documents must contain special caption and specify the action required on the first page.

(b) Judge's Copies. Judge's copies of legal memoranda are to be provided to the Court Administrator's Office at the time of filing for all motions. Furthermore, Judge's copies of Pre–Sentence Investigation Reports and Sentencing Briefs shall be provided to the Court Administrator's Office at the time of filing.

(c) Case Numbers. Documents may be filed with more than one case number for adult felony pleadings as provided in CrR 4.3(b) only.

[Adopted effective September 1, 2009.]

PART VIII. LOCAL RULES FOR APPEAL OF DECISIONS OF COURTS OF LIMITED JURISDICTION (Cite as SCLRALJ)

SCLRALJ 7.2. TIME FOR FILING BRIEFS

(d) Briefing Schedule

(1) *Case Schedule.* The moving party shall prepare a case scheduling order upon filing a notice of appeal.

[Adopted effective September 1, 2005; renumbered from SCLRALJ 1 and amended effective September 1, 2009.]

SCLRALJ 8.5. CONFIRMATION OF ORAL ARGUMENT

(a) It shall be the responsibility of the petitioner to confirm oral argument on the Thursday 9:30 a.m. calendar by 4:00 p.m. Friday the week before the scheduled hearing.

(b) Confirmation shall be made by telephone to the Court Administrator's Office at (360) 336–9320 be-tween 8:30 a.m. Monday and 4:00 p.m. Friday the week prior to when the oral argument is scheduled for hearing.

(c) Motions not confirmed in accordance with this rule will be stricken.

[Adopted effective September 1, 2009; amended on an emergency basis, effective March 1, 2012; amended on a permanent basis effective September 1, 2012; September 2, 2014.]

PART IX. MENTAL PROCEEDINGS RULES (Cite as SCMPR)

MPR 2.4.

(c) To assure compliance with the 72–hour hold limitation in RCW 71.05, in the event of a late detention resulting in the need for a continuance or special set probable cause hearing, the parties must either agree to the less than 24–hour continuance or obtain a special set hearing through Court Administration. The agreed order of continuance shall be presented in Superior Court no later than the first ex parte calendar following the detention.

[Adopted on an emergency basis effective March 1, 2012; adopted on a permanent basis effective September 1, 2012.]

PART X. LOCAL JUVENILE COURT RULES (Cite as SCLJuCR)

SCLJuCR 9.2. ATTORNEY CERTIFICATION

(d) **Attorney Certification.** Attorneys who anticipate being appointed to represent juvenile indigents in criminal offender cases in the Skagit County Superior Court, Juvenile Division must comply with JuCR 9.2 by filing a certification of compliance with the Clerk of the Superior Court. The certification should be filed at least fourteen (14) days prior to each calendar quarter.

The Clerk will maintain an administrative file for such certifications. The administrative files will be open for public inspection.

[Adopted on an emergency basis, effective March 1, 2013; June 1, 2013; adopted on a permanent basis, effective September 2, 2013.]

SCLJuCR 10.7.1. ADMINISTRATIVE SEALING AFTER DISPOSITION

(a) In all dispositions of offender matters in juvenile court, at the time of disposition, the Court shall determine if the charges are subject to administrative sealing pursuant to HB 1651, and if so, set a date for an administrative review in the disposition order.

(b) All juvenile offenses are subject to administrative sealing, pursuant to HB 1651, other than:

1) Most serious offenses as defined in RCW 9.94A.030.

2) Sex Offenses as defined in RCW 9A.44

3) Felony Drug Offenses as defined by RCW 9.94A.030, except possession of a controlled substance or forged prescription for a controlled substance.

(c) At disposition, the Court shall set the administrative review:

a. After the respondent turns 18; and

b. After anticipated completion of community supervision or parole if any; and

c. After anticipated release from detention or JRA.

(d) Administrative reviews shall be held monthly on or after a date as set by the court administrator. Administrative reviews may be conducted in chambers. The date set in the disposition order will indicate a month and year. Any interested party may contact the Skagit County Superior Court Clerk's Office or refer to the Skagit County Superior Court website to determine the date that the administrative hearings will occur on or after for any given month.

(e) The County Prosecutor, Public Defender, and a representative of the Office of Juvenile Court may provide input on whether a case qualifies for administrative sealing before the review. A list of cases set for administrative review shall be available to the Prosecutor, Public Defender, and representative of the Office of Juvenile Court at least one week prior to the reviews. Included with this list shall be information from the County Clerk, indicating whether the respondents have paid their legal financial obligations for the cases set for review.

(f) The respondent may, but need not, be present at the administrative review. The respondent may, but need not, retain counsel who may be present. If the respondent or counsel chose to appear, they shall notify the court clerk 5 days prior to the review date, and the court clerk shall move the review onto a regularly scheduled Juvenile Offender Calendar.

(g) If any person not a party to the case wishes to make an objection to sealing, that objection must be in writing and filed with the court 9 court days before the administrative review. If an objection is filed, the review shall be moved to a regularly scheduled Juvenile Offender Calendar.

(h) At the administrative review, unless there is an objection or the Court believes there is a compelling reason not to seal, the Court shall seal the records if:

a. The respondent has completed the terms of disposition. Completion is presumed unless a probation violation is pending or a warrant is active in the cause; and

b. The respondent has paid legal financial obligations.

(i) The Court shall seal the records, or deny sealing, using court form "Order Re: Sealing Records of Juvenile Offender (ORSF, ORSFD)."

(j) After the administrative review, the Court shall mail a copy of the order sealing or denying sealing, to the respondent at the last known address per the Judicial Information System.

(k) If the matter qualifies for administrative sealing, but there is an objection or the Court believes there is a compelling reason not to seal, the matter shall be set for a hearing on the regularly scheduled juvenile offender calendar, with at least 18 days notice provided to all parties.

(l) If the respondent has not completed his/her terms of disposition, including paying legal financial obligations, by the date of the first administrative review, the Court may continue the administrative review to another date as set by the judge.

(m) Nothing in this local court rule prevents a respondent from petitioning at another time, or in another manner, for sealing of records as authorized by law.

[Adopted effective September 2, 2014.]

SCLJuCR 10.7.2. ADMINISTRATIVE SEALING AFTER A DISMISSAL OR ACQUITTAL

Any time a charge is dismissed or acquitted, the prosecutor shall immediately file with the Court, court form "Order Re: Sealing Records of Juvenile Offender (ORSF, ORSFD)," sealing the records.

[Adopted effective September 2, 2014.]

APPENDICES

[Appendices were adopted effective September 1, 1997; amended effective September 1, 1998; amended effective September 1, 1999; renumbered and amended effective September 1, 2000; amended effective September 1, 2001; amended effective September 1, 2002; renumbered and amended effective September 1, 2004; renumbered and amended effective September 1, 2005; renumbered and amended effective September 1, 2009; renumbered and amended effective September 1, 2012; amended effective September 2, 2013.]

APPENDIX A.   DEMAND FOR ARBITRATION/NOTE FOR MOTION CALENDAR

IN THE SUPERIOR COURT OF WASHINGTON FOR SKAGIT COUNTY

Plaintiff(s),	NO.
vs.	**DEMAND FOR ARBITRATION/NOTE FOR MOTION CALENDAR**
	☐Clerk's Action Required
Defendant(s).	

TO: The Clerk of the Skagit County Superior Court and the Attorneys and Parties listed below:

DEMAND FOR ARBITRATION

☐   This case is subject to arbitration because the sole relief sought is a money judgment and involves a claim not in excess of thirty-five thousand dollars exclusive of attorney fees; interests and costs. (MAR 1.2)

☐   The undersigned contends that the claim exceeds the maximum amount authorized under RCW 7.06.020, but for purposes of arbitration waives any claim in excess of such amount.

☐   **NOTE FOR MOTION DOCKET (ARBITRATION)**

Please take note that the issue of arbitrability will be heard on the date set out below and the Clerk is requested to note the same for the Motion Docket for that date.

DATE OF HEARING: _____ at 9:30 A.M.

Any response to this Demand for Arbitration must be filed with the Clerk and served upon counsel within two (2) working days of the date Demand is scheduled for hearing.

SUBMITTED BY: Dated: _____

Signed: _____
WSBA #_____

Address/Phone _____

_____

Attorney for: _____

CERTIFICATE OF MAILING: I certify that I mailed a copy of this document to the parties listed, postage prepaid on the _____ day of _____, 200 _____.

Signature: _____

OTHER ATTORNEY/PARTY (use additional page if required)

Name: _____ WSBA #_____

NOTE:

Address/Phone: _____

File the original of this document

_____

with the County Clerk.

Attorney for: _____

APPENDIX B.   ORDER ON DEMAND FOR ARBITRATION

IN THE SUPERIOR COURT OF WASHINGTON FOR SKAGIT COUNTY

NO.

Plaintiff(s),

vs.

**ORDER ON DEMAND
FOR ARBITRATION**

Defendant(s).

THIS MATTER having come on for an Order concerning arbitrability and it appearing that the matter before the Court upon due notice to all parties, and the Court being fully advised in the premises,

NOW, THEREFORE, IT IS ORDERED that this case:

☐ IS SUBJECT TO MANDATORY ARBITRATION and is hereby transferred to arbitration.

☐ IS NOT SUBJECT TO MANDATORY ARBITRATION, because:
    ☐ Opposing party's claim exceeds $50,000;
    ☐ Opposing party seeks relief other than a money judgment;
    ☐ A party's counter or cross claim exceeds $50,000;
    ☐ A party's counter or cross claim seeks relief other than a money judgment; or
    ☐ This case is an appeal from a lower court not subject to Mandatory Arbitration.
    ☐ Other: _____

DONE IN OPEN COURT this ___ day of _____, 200 ___.

_____
JUDGE/COURT COMMISSIONER

Presented by:

_____   _____
Attorney for Plaintiff, WSBA   #Attorney for Defendant, WSBA #

Address _____   Address_____

_____   _____

Phone _____   Phone_____

APPENDIX C.　RESPONSE TO DEMAND FOR ARBITRATION

IN THE SUPERIOR COURT OF WASHINGTON FOR SKAGIT COUNTY

NO.

Plaintiff(s),

vs.

**RESPONSE TO DEMAND
FOR ARBITRATION**

Defendant(s).

TO:　The Clerk of the Skagit County Superior Court and the Attorneys and Parties listed below:

The undersigned responds to the prior Demand for Arbitration filed in this case and:

☐　AGREES TO MANDATORY ARBITRATION.

☐　OBJECTS TO MANDATORY ARBITRATION, because:

　　　☐　Opposing party's claim exceeds $35, 000;
　　　☐　Opposing party seeks relief other than a money judgment;
　　　☐　A party's counter or cross claim exceeds $35,000;
　　　☐　A party's counter or cross claim seeks relief other than a money judgment;
　　or
　　　☐　This case is an appeal from a lower court and not subject to Mandatory Arbitration.
　　　☐　Other: _____

Any response to a Demand for Arbitration must be filed with the Clerk and a copy served upon opposing counsel not less than two (2) working days prior to the date the Demand is noted for hearing [LMAR 2.1 (c)].

SUBMITTED BY:　　Dated: _____

Signed _____

WSBA # _____

Address/Phone: _____

_____

Attorney for: _____

CERTIFICATE OF MAILING: I certify that I mailed a copy of this document to the parties listed, postage prepaid on the ___ day of _____, 200 ___.

Signature: _____

Note: File the original of this document with the Clerk.

OTHER ATTORNEY/PARTY (Use additional page if required)

Name: _____

WSBA #

Address/Phone: _____

_____

Attorney for: _____

APPENDIX D. STIPULATION AND ORDER TRANSFERRING TO ARBITRATION

IN THE SUPERIOR COURT OF WASHINGTON FOR SKAGIT COUNTY

_____

NO.

Plaintiff(s),

vs.

STIPULATION AND ORDER
TRANSFERRING TO
ARBITRATION

(EX PARTE)

Defendant(s).
_____

BASED ON THE FOLLOWING STIPULATIONS:

That the case may be transferred to arbitration;

That this case is at issue; that no affirmative pleading remains unanswered; that no other parties will be served with summons; and that the case is in all respects ready for arbitration;

That the following persons has been selected and has agreed to serve as arbitrator; (leave blank if the parties are not stipulating to an arbitrator):

NAME _____

ADDRESS _____

_____

PHONE _____

ORDER

IT IS ORDERED that this case is transferred to arbitration under the provisions of LMAR.

DONE IN OPEN COURT this ___ day of _____, 200 ___.

_____

JUDGE/COURT COMMISSIONER

PRESENTED BY:

_____   _____
Attorney for Plaintiff, WSBA   #Attorney for Defendant, WSBA #

Address _____   Address_____

_____   _____

Phone _____   _____

APPENDIX E. CERTIFICATE OF COMPLETION (MEDIATION)

IN THE SUPERIOR COURT OF WASHINGTON FOR SKAGIT COUNTY

Petitioner,	NO._____
vs.	**CERTIFICATE OF COMPLETION (MEDIATION)**
Respondent.	

Per SCLSPR 94.08.2 (c) A certificate of completion provided by the mediator must be filed with the clerk of the court prior to trial.

NAME OF SKAGIT COUNTY APPROVED MEDIATOR:
_____

DATE ABOVE PARTIES COMPLETED MEDIATION: _____

I certify under penalty of perjury under the laws of the State of Washington that the foregoing is true and correct. Signed this ___ day of _____, at _____, Washington.

_____

(Signature of Mediator)

APPENDIX F. NOTE FOR CALENDAR (DOMESTIC—NON-CONTESTED) [RESCINDED]

APPENDIX G. NOTE FOR CALENDAR (DOMESTIC CASE—PRO SE MOTIONS) [RESCINDED]

APPENDIX H. NOTE FOR TRIAL ASSIGNMENT

IN THE SUPERIOR COURT OF WASHINGTON FOR SKAGIT COUNTY

_____,
                    Petitioner,   Case No.:

vs.   **NOTE FOR TRIAL ASSIGNMENT**
_____,   (Self–Represented Parties)
                    Respondent.

☐Clerk's Action Required
*File original of this document with the
County Clerk*

FILL OUT FORM COMPLETELY

TO: **The Clerk of the Skagit County Superior Court and the Parties listed below:**

This case is ready for trial. The Clerk is requested to send this case to the Court Administrator for Trial Assignment.

Have you completed the mandatory mediation? ☐Yes ☐No

Have you completed the parenting seminar, if applicable? ☐Yes ☐No

Trial Assignment Date (any Monday, no personal appearance required): _____

Issues to be Resolved: ☐ property/debt distribution; ☐ spousal maintenance; ☐ parenting plan; ☐ child support; ☐ other: _____

SUBMITTED THIS ___ DAY OF _____.

Signature: _____

Address (required): _____

Other Party(use additional page, if required)

Name: _____

Address (required): _____

CERTIFICATE OF MAILING: I certify that I mailed a copy of this document to the parties listed, postage prepaid on the ___ day of _____, 200 ___.

Signature: _____

APPENDIX I. PRETRIAL AFFIDAVIT

SUPERIOR COURT OF WASHINGTON, COUNTY OF SKAGIT

In re

NO._____

PRETRIAL AFFIDAVIT OF: ☐ PETITIONER
☐ RESPONDENT

I. PERSONAL DATA

Name: _____, Age ____ Occupation: _____

Marriage/Relationship date: _____ Employer: _____

Separation date: _____ Gross monthly income: _____

Children's ages: _____ Net monthly income: _____

II. SUGGESTED RESIDENTIAL TIME FOR CHILDREN

With Father: _____

_____

_____

With Mother: _____

_____

_____

III. SUGGESTED CHILD SUPPORT

If child support is at issue, complete and file an updated set of Washington State Child Support Worksheets.

Based on current Worksheets, the presumptive amount of child support for ____ children is $ _____ per month.

Child support should be set at $ _____ per month, because _____.

_____

_____

IV. SUGGESTED MAINTENANCE

If maintenance is at issue, complete and attach the Monthly Expense schedule, and page 1 of the Washington State Child Support Worksheets (showing income and deductions).

Maintenance of $ _____ per month should be paid to the ☐husband ☐wife, until _____, because_____

_____

V. ASSETS AND DEBTS

If the other party *has not* yet filed a Pretrial Affidavit: fill in and attach four separate schedules, listing each community asset, separate asset, community debt, and separate debt. For each item, insert your figures in the appropriate columns (for "Petitioner's Pretrial Affidavit" or "Respondent's Pretrial Affidavit").

If the other party *has* filed a Pretrial Affidavit: on their four schedules, add your own figures for each item in the appropriate columns. If the other party omitted any assets or debts, add them to the appropriate schedule. Attach copies of your completed schedules.

Transfer your totals from the Community Assets and Community Debts schedules to this chart, showing your proposed divisions of community property and debt:

	To Wife	To Husband
Community Assets:		
Community Debts:		
Subtract Debts from Assets:		
Proposed judgment transfer (+/-):		
FINAL TOTALS:		

VI. OTHER FACTORS

List any other factors which you believe should be considered at the settlement conference, such as special income situations, physical disabilities, dependent children of other relationships, etc.

_____

_____

_____

_____

_____

_____

_____

_____

_____

I certify under penalty of perjury under the laws of the State of Washington that the foregoing is true and correct. Signed this ___ day of _____, at _____, Washington.

Petitioner/Respondent_____

DATED _____, by: _____

Attorney for _____ WSBA No.____

MONTHLY EXPENSES OF _____ AND ___ DEPENDENTS:

Housing:
    Rent or house payment ...._____
    Taxes and insurance ...._____
    ...._____

Utilities:
    Heat (gas & oil)......................................._____
    Electricity ...._____
    Water, sewer, garbage ...._____
    Telephone ...._____
    Cable ...._____
    ...._____

Food and Supplies:

Food for _____ persons ....
Supplies (paper, tobacco, pets) .... _____
Meals eaten out .... _____

Children:
Day care / babysitting .... _____
Clothing .... _____
Tuition (if any) .... _____

Transportation:
Vehicle payments or leases .... _____
Vehicle insurance & license .... _____
Vehicle gas, oil, ordinary maintenance .... _____
Parking... _____

Health Care:
Insurance.. _____
Uninsured dental, orthodontic, medical, eye care .... _____

Personal Expenses (not including children):
Clothing .... _____
Hair care / personal care .... _____
Clubs & recreation .... _____
Education.. _____
Books, newspapers, magazines, photos .... _____
Gifts .... _____

Miscellaneous:
Life insurance (if *not* deducted from income) .... _____

TOTAL MONTHLY EXPENSES: .... _____

Article I.   COMMUNITY ASSETS

Asset #	Description of Community Asset	Related Debt #	Wife's Position			Husband's Position		
			Fair Mkt Value	To Wife	To Husband	Fair Mkt Value	To Wife	To Husband
CA–1								
CA–2								
CA–3								
CA–4								
CA–5								
CA–6								
CA–7								

Asset #	Description of Community Asset	Related Debt #	Wife's Position			Husband's Position		
			Fair Mkt Value	To Wife	To Husband	Fair Mkt Value	To Wife	To Husband
CA–8								
CA–9								
CA–10								
CA–11								
CA–12								
CA–13								
CA–14								

COMMUNITY ASSET TOTALS:

Article II. SEPARATE ASSETS

Asset #	Description of Separate Asset	Related Debt #	Wife's Position			Husband's Position		
			Fair Mkt Value	To Wife	To Husband	Fair Mkt Value	To Wife	To Husband
SA–1								
SA–2								
SA–3								
SA–4								
SA–5								
SA–6								
SA–7								
SA–8								
SA–9								
SA–10								
SA–11								
SA–12								
SA–13								
SA–14								

Asset #	Description of Separate Asset	Related Debt #	Wife's Position			Husband's Position		
			Fair Mkt Value	To Wife	To Husband	Fair Mkt Value	To Wife	To Husband
	SEPARATE ASSET TOTALS:							

Article III.   COMMUNITY DEBTS

Debt #	Description of Community Debt	Related Asset #	Wife's Position			Husband's Position		
			Balance at Separation	To Wife	To Husband	Balance at Separation	To Wife	To Husband
CD–1								
CD–2								
CD–3								
CD–4								
CD–5								
CD–6								
CD–7								
CD–8								
CD–9								
CD–10								
CD–11								
CD–12								
CD–13								
CD–14								
	COMMUNITY DEBT TOTALS:							

Article IV.   SEPARATE DEBTS

Debt #	Description of Separate Debt	Related Asset #	Wife's Position			Husband's Position		
			Balance at Separation	To Wife	To Husband	Balance at Separation	To Wife	To Husband
SD–1								
SD–2								
SD–3								
SD–4								
SD–5								
SD–6								
SD–7								
SD–8								
SD–9								
SD–10								
SD–11								
SD–12								
SD–13								
SD–14								

SEPARATE DEBT TOTALS:

APPENDIX J.   NOTE FOR CALENDAR MOTION DOCKET OR TRIAL ASSIGNMENT [RESCINDED EFFECTIVE MARCH 1, 2012]

APPENDIX K.   NOTICE OF CONFLICT DATES

IN THE SUPERIOR COURT OF WASHINGTON FOR SKAGIT COUNTY

NO.

Plaintiff(s),

vs.

NOTICE OF CONFLICT DATES

Defendant(s).

<u>LCR 40(b) Conflict Dates.</u> Counsel shall file with the clerk of the court a notice of conflict dates on or before the date set for the trial assignment. Conflict dates shall be limited to previously scheduled vacations and trial dates.

DATE	SCHEDULED VACATIONS, TRIALS, MEDIATION OR ARBITRATIONS

Presented by:

SUBMITTED BY: Dated: _____

Signed _____

WSBA #

Address/Phone: _____

_____

Attorney for: _____

CERTIFICATE OF MAILING: I certify that I mailed a copy of this document to the parties listed, postage prepaid on the ___ day of _____, 200 ___.

Signature: _____

Note: File the original of this document with the Clerk AND a copy to Court Administration

OTHER ATTORNEY/PARTY (Use additional page if required)

Name: _____

WSBA #

Address/Phone: _____

_____

Attorney for: _____

APPENDIX L.   JIS SEARCH FOR ALL CASES INVOLVING CHILDREN

Case Number: _____

Hearing Date: _____

SKAGIT COUNTY SUPERIOR COURT

JIS SEARCH FOR ALL CASES INVOLVING CHILDREN

PARTY	NAME	BIRTHDATE
Petitioner		
Respondent		
Other Adult in Prospective Custodial Home		
Other Adult in Prospective Custodial Home		

Date: _____

Presented By: _____

• **This form must be filed by both parties at the Court Administrator's Office at least two days before final orders are scheduled to be entered.**

• **If orders are to be presented at ex parte, Court Administration must be notified.**

APPENDIX M.   NOTE FOR CALENDAR CIVIL/PROBATE

IN THE SUPERIOR COURT OF THE STATE
OF WASHINGTON FOR SKAGIT COUNTY

Petitioner/Plaintiff, vs. Respondent/Defendant,	NO. **NOTE FOR CALENDAR** **CIVIL/PROBATE**

TO: THE CLERK OF THE COURT and to OPPOSING ATTORNEY(S) OR PARTIES
Please note that the issue of law in this case will be heard on the date indicated and the
Clerk is requested to note the same on the motion calendar for that day.

[ ]   NOTE FOR TRIAL ASSIGNMENT: MONDAY @ 9:30 _____
                                                                           DATE

The undersigned certifies that this case is at issue; that no affirmative pleading   Jury Requested: o Yes   o No
remains unanswered; that to my knowledge no other parties will be served with
summons; and that the case is in all respects ready for trial .
This case is <u>not</u> subject to mandatory to mandatory arbitration   _____
                                                                                                                        Estimated length of time for trial
Reason exempt from Mandatory Arbitration _____   Nature of Cause/Issues to be determined

---

[ ]   PROBATE   FRIDAY @ 9:00 am _____
     [ ] Minor Settlements   DATE
     [ ] Guardianships   ISSUE: _____

[ ]   CIVIL MOTIONS   FRIDAY @ 9:30 am _____
     [ ] LUPA Initial Petition/Motions   DATE
     [ ] Emancipation   ISSUE: _____

[ ]   DOMESTIC VIOLENCE   WEDNESDAY @ 1:30 pm _____
     SEXUAL/ASSAULT   DATE

[ ]   SUMMARY JUDGMENT   MONDAY @ 9:30am _____
     [ ] RALJ   DATE
     [ ] Any Dispositive Motions   ISSUE: _____

[ ]   SPECIAL SETTING   * **MUST BE PREAPPROVED**   _____ TIME: _____
                                BY COURT ADMINISTRATION   DATE
                                                                          ISSUE: _____

Dated: _____   Names/Addresses of Other Attorneys or parties

_____
Signature of Attorney or Party

_____
Print or Type Name; WSBA # if Attorney
Address:_____

APPENDIX M - Note for Calendar Civil/Probate

Telephone:_____

_____

If Attorney, Party Represented

CERTIFICATE OF MAILING: I certify that I mailed a copy of this document

to the attorneys/parties listed above, postage prepaid on ___/___/_____

SIGNED: _____

APPENDIX M - Note for Calendar Civil/Probate

[Adopted on an emergency basis effective March 1, 2012; adopted on a permanent basis effective September 1, 2012.]

APPENDIX N. GUARDIAN AD LITEM APPLICATION

SKAGIT COUNTY SUPERIOR COURT
GUARDIAN AD LITEM APPLICATION

TITLE 11.88 _____

TITLE 26 _____ *Please refer to RCW 26.12.175 for all requirements.*

(Please check which Title applying for)

CONTACT INFORMATION

LAST NAME	FIRST NAME	MIDDLE	DATE
BUSINESS NAME OR FIRM			SSN OR TAX ID (CONFIDENTIAL)
STREET AND MAILING ADDRESS			CITY STATE ZIP
BUSINESS PHONE			
RETAINER AMOUNT		COMMENTS	
HOURLY RATE		COMMENTS	

EDUCATION

LEVEL AND LOCATION OF FORMAL EDUCATION   (ATTACH DETAILED RESUME - **MANDATORY**)

CERTIFIED GUARDIAN AD LITEM TRAINING

DATE AND TYPE OF INITIAL TRAINING

DATE AND TYPE OF ANNUAL REFRESHER TRAINING (ATTACH COPY)

OTHER FORMAL TRAINING/CERTIFICATIONS/LICENSES (INCLUDE DATE AND TYPE)

RELEVANT EXPERIENCE

PUBLIC PAY APPOINTMENTS THIS YEAR (LIST NAME & CASE NUMBER)

LIST OTHER EQUIVALENT EXPERIENCE

NUMBER OF YEARS AS A GUARDIAN AD LITEM	NUMBER OF APPOINTMENTS AS A GUARDIAN AD LITEM

LIST ALL COUNTIES OF APPOINTMENTS

LIST ANY AND ALL CIRCUMSTANCES OF REMOVAL FROM ANY G.A.L. REGISTRY PURSUANT TO A GRIEVANCE ACTION. PROVIDE NAME OF COURT AND THE CASE NUMBER FROM WHICH YOU WERE REMOVED.

APPENDIX N – GUARDIAN AD LITEM APPLICATION FORM

CERTIFICATION

I certify under penalty of perjury under the laws of the State of Washington that the foregoing is true and correct. Signed this _____ day of _____, at _____, Washington.

(Signature of Applicant): _____

APPENDIX N – GUARDIAN AD LITEM APPLICATION FORM

APPENDIX O. FAMILY LAW MEDIATOR APPLICATION

SKAGIT COUNTY SUPERIOR COURT
205 W. Kincaid Street, Room 202
Mount Vernon, WA 98273
360-336-9320

FAMILY LAW MEDIATOR APPLICATION

CONTACT INFORMATION

LAST NAME	FIRST NAME	MIDDLE	DATE

BUSINESS NAME OR FIRM	SSN OR TAX ID (CONFIDENTIAL)
STREET AND MAILING ADDRESS	CITY STATE ZIP
BUSINESS PHONE	

EDUCATION

LEVEL AND LOCATION OF FORMAL EDUCATION   (ATTACH DETAILED RESUME - MANDATORY)

FAMILY LAW MEDIATOR TRAINING

DATE, SPONSOR AND HOURS ACCOMPLISHED OF BASIC MEDIATION TRAINING (MINIMUM OF 32 HRS REQUIRED)

DATE, SPONSOR AND HOURS COMPLETED OF COURT APPROVED DIVORCE MEDIATION TRAINING (MINIMUM OF 24 HRS RQUIRED)

PRACTICUM:
Observation of at least six two-hour family law mediation sessions divided among at least three different mediators. (You must engage in a discussion of the mediations at the conclusion of each session.)

DATES: MEDIATORS:

Co-mediate three family law cases from beginning to end, each with a different court-approved mediator.

CASE NAMES: MEDIATORS:

APPENDIX O – MEDIATOR APPLICATION FORM

If approved by co-mediators, mediate a family law case solo, with a court-approved mediator observing throughout the case.

CASE NAME: MEDIATOR:

CERTIFICATION

I certify under penalty of perjury under the laws of the State of Washington that the foregoing is true and correct. Signed this _____ day of _____, at _____, Washington.

(Signature of Applicant): _____

APPENDIX O - MEDIATOR APPLICATION FORM

APPENDIX P. GENERAL ORDER FORM

IN THE SUPERIOR COURT OF THE STATE OF WASHINGTON
FOR SKAGIT COUNTY

Case No.: _____

ORDER ON:

☐ Civil   ☐ Criminal
☐ Domestic   ☐ Other

☐ CLERK'S ACTION REQUIRED

THIS COURT FINDS _____
_____
_____
_____
_____
_____
_____
_____
_____

IT IS HEREBY ORDERED, ADJUDGED AND DECREED that _____
_____
_____
_____
_____

Dated:

_____   _____
                                           JUDGE/COMMISSIONER

Presented by: Approved:

_____   _____
Attorney for   Attorney for

APPENDIX P – ORDER FORM (BLANK)

APPENDIX P.   NOTE FOR SPECIAL SET HEARING*

SUPERIOR COURT OF THE STATE OF WASHINGTON FOR SKAGIT COUNTY

Plaintiff/Petitioner,	NO.
	NOTE FOR SPECIAL SET HEARING
vs.	Before: _____
	Judge
	MUST BE PREVIOUSLY APPROVED
	BY COURT ADMINISTRATION
Defendant/Respondent.	

Note for Special Set Hearing.

Please take note that the issue in this case will be heard on the date
and time indicated, and that the Clerk is requested to note the same

on the case docket for that day.

Dated: _____

Date and Time of Hearing

Nature of Hearing

Names/Addresses of Other Attorneys or Parties

Pro Se

_____
Signature of Attorney or Party

_____
Print or Type Name; WSBA # if Attorney

Address:_____
_____
Telephone:_____

If Attorney, Party Represented:

CERTIFICATE OF MAILING: I certify that I mailed a copy of this document to the attorneys/parties listed hereon,
postage prepaid on the _____ day of _____ 20_____.

Signed: _____

APPENDIX P – ORDER FORM (BLANK)

* Designation as provided in original.

APPENDIX R. NOTE FOR CALENDAR—SELF-REPRESENTED PARTIES

IN THE SUPERIOR COURT OF WASHINGTON FOR SKAGIT COUNTY

Petitioner vs. Respondent.	NO. _____ **NOTE FOR CALENDAR** (self-represented parties)

TO: THE CLERK OF COURT and to OPPOSING ATTORNEY(S) or PARTY

☐ NOTE FOR CALENDAR

Please note that the issue of law in this case will be heard on the date set out in the margin and the Clerk is requested to note the same on the motion calendar for that day.

☐DOMESTIC

Date & time of hearing:_____

_____(hour)

Nature of hearing:_____

_____

(A motion and declaration must also be filed)

☐ NOTE FOR DISSOLUTION CALENDAR
(For Non-Contested Final Decree)

Please note this case on the non-contested dissolution calendar for hearing on the date set forth.

Date of hearing:_____

Time of hearing:_____

NOTICE TO OTHER PARTIES (REQUIRED):

Name _____

Address _____

_____

(Use additional page for additional parties)

PERSON NOTING THIS MATTER:

Name _____

Address _____

_____

Phone number: _____

CERTIFICATE OF MAILING: I certify, upon penalty of perjury in the State of Washington, that I mailed a copy of this document to the parties listed, postage prepaid on the _____ day of _____, 20_____.

Signature: _____   Print Name: _____

APPENDIX R – NOTE FOR CALENDAR – SELF-REPRESENTED PARTIES

[Adopted effective September 2, 2013.]

DISTRICT COURT

SKAGIT COUNTY DISTRICT COURT LOCAL RULES

Including Amendments Received Through
August 15, 2015

Table of Rules

SKAGIT COUNTY ADMINISTRATIVE RULES FOR COURTS OF LIMITED JURISDICTION

PREFACE

1. PROMULGATION. These rules shall be known as the Local Rules for the District Court of the State of Washington for Skagit County. Copies of these rules will be filed with the Office of the Administrator of the Courts, and the Clerk of the District Court for Skagit County. Copies of these rules will be distributed to all law offices in Skagit County and to the County Law Library for public reference. Copies will be available from the District Court Clerk for Skagit County. These rules will be effective on September 1, 1999.

2. NUMBERING. Consistent with GR 7(b) Washington Court Rules, these rules, to the extent possible, conform in numbering system and in format to those rules adopted by the Supreme Court of the State of Washington for courts of limited jurisdiction and facilitate the use of the same. The number of each rule is preceded by the abbreviation "SL" designating the rule as a Skagit County Local Court Rule and as being supplemental to the corresponding Washington Court Rule for Courts of Limited Jurisdiction.

3. Revisions and Additions (Reserved).

[Adopted effective September 1, 1999; amended effective September 1, 2001; September 1, 2008; September 1, 2012.]

SLARLJ 2. SCOPE OF LOCAL RULES

These rules govern the procedure in the District Court of the State of Washington for Skagit County.

These rules are supplemental to the rules enacted by the Washington State Supreme Court for courts of limited jurisdiction as specifically authorized by GR 7, CRLJ 83, CrRLJ 1.7, and IRLJ 1.3 of the *Washington Court Rules.* The court may modify or suspend any of these local rules in any given case upon good cause being shown or upon the court's own motion.

[Formerly SLARLJ 1 adopted effective September 1, 1999; renumbered SLARLJ 2 and amended, effective September 1, 2012.]

SLARLJ 5. LOCATION OF PRIMARY OFFICE AND MUNICIPAL DEPARTMENTS

The primary office of the District Court of the State of Washington for Skagit County shall be located in Mount Vernon, Washington. The municipal courts of the Cities of Anacortes, Burlington and Mount Vernon are duly organized Municipal Departments of the Skagit County District Court sitting in its respective municipality. These rules are binding upon the Municipal Departments of the Skagit County District Court.

[Formerly SLARLJ 2 adopted effective September 1, 1999; amended effective September 1, 2008; renumbered SLARLJ 5 and amended, effective September 1, 2012.]

SLARLJ 7. SCHEDULING

(a) Calendar. The Court Administrator shall develop and maintain a calendar for all hearings and trials.

(b) Priority. Whenever the caseload of the court requires, trials and other matters will be subject to multiple settings on the same date. The order in which said matters proceed will be determined by the judge based on speedy trial rule in criminal cases, the age of the civil cases, and the availability of jurors.

(c) Transfer of Cases. If the caseload or other circumstances require, the court may appoint a Court Commissioner or Judge Pro Tempore to hear that trial or calendar of cases and may arrange for it to be heard in a location other than the usual courtroom.

[Formerly SLARLJ 3 adopted effective September 1, 1999; renumbered SLARLJ 7 and amended, effective September 1, 2012.]

SLARLJ 9(b). DISCLOSURE OF CONFIDENTIAL RECORDS

The following records and files are deemed confidential and are not available to the public for inspection or copying absent a court order:

1. Affidavits for Search Warrants before a return of service and inventory has been filed with the court:

2. Mental health, psychiatric and medical reports;

3. Alcohol and drug evaluations and compliance reports;

4. Deferred prosecution evaluations and police reports;

5. Certified copies of driving records, abstracts of driving records and compiled reports of arrests and convictions;

6. Judge's notes and worksheets;

7. Witness statements and police reports;

8. Address of Jurors

Dissemination of data by the court shall be done according to the Skagit County District Court's Data Dissemination Policy Adopted by the court on January 15, 1998 subject to revisions or amendments duly enacted by the court. A copy of said policy is available upon demand made to the Skagit District Court Clerk's Office.

[Formerly SLARLJ 9(g) adopted effective September 1, 1999; renumbered SLARLJ 9(b) and amended, effective September 1, 2012.]

SLARLJ 30. EMERGENCY ORDER ADOPTING LOCAL RULE SLARLJ 30

Pursuant to GR 7, Skagit County District Court hereby finds that an emergency exists that justifies adoption of the attached SLARLJ 30. Specifically, law enforcement seeks a method to seek search warrants electronically in non-court hours. A system has been put in place whereby said warrants may be sought via email but law enforcement is unable to proffer an affidavit directly to the on call judge via SECTOR or JINDEX and Skagit County lacks a local secured system envisioned by GR 30. SSB 6279 authorizes a method for subscription to an unsworn document in Section 4 of said legislation. This emergency rule adopts said methodology. The Court finds that it is in the best interest of the public's safety and welfare to adopt this rule on an emergency basis pending the effective date of said legislation.

This order shall be effective on March 19, 2014 and the rule adopted hereby shall be enforced after that date for a period of 90 days unless readopted pursuant to GR 7. [1]

[Adopted on an emergency basis effective March 19, 2014.]

[1] Publisher's Note: This order has not been readopted on a permanent basis.

SKAGIT COUNTY LOCAL CIVIL RULES FOR
COURTS OF LIMITED JURISDICTION

SLCLRJ 7(b)(5). MOTIONS FOR ORDERS SHORTENING TIME

No party shall seek a motion for order shortening time for hearing a motion unless said party has first notified opposing counsel or the opposing party(s) that such a motion will be sought. The moving party's motion shall be supported by an affidavit or declaration under penalty of perjury detailing the nature of the emergency necessitating the shortening of time and further stating that opposing counsel/party has been provided with a copy of the motion together and the time and place of the hearing wherein the moving party is seeking an order shortening time. Such affidavit or declaration shall state when and where opposing counsel was served with the motion and notice of hearing. The Court shall not grant an order shortening time unless it is satisfied that an emergency justifying the shortening of time truly exists and that the moving party has exercised due diligence in timely advising the opposing counsel/party of the hearing on said motion.

[Formerly SLRCLRJ 7(b)(5) adopted effective September 1, 2007; renumbered SLCLRJ 7(b)(5) and amended, effective September 1, 2012.]

SLCRLJ 40(b). NOTE FOR TRIAL ASSIGNMENT

Any party may file a notice asking that the case be set for trial. Said notice shall set a hearing date for trial setting. In lieu of appearance at said hearing, the parties may submit their trial conflicts in wiriting[1] in advance of the date for trial setting. By noting the matter for trial, the moving party certifies that discovery is complete and the case is ready for trial. By not objecting to trial setting, the non-moving party joins in the moving party's certification. A note for trial assignment must be served on the non-moving party at least ten days in advance of the date set for hearing.

[Formerly SLRCRLJ 40(b) adopted effective September 1, 2001; renumbered SLCRLJ 40(b) and amended, effective September 1, 2012.]

1 So in original.

SLCRLJ 40(g). MANDATORY MEDIATION FOR SMALL CLAIMS COURT

Mediation is mandatory before a trial is allowed in Small Claims Court. Mediation is held at the first scheduled appearance date unless continued by the court for good cause. Both parties must attend the mediation. If the plaintiff fails to appear, a dismissal may be entered. If the defendant fails to appear, their answer, if one was filed, may be stricken and default judgment entered. Parties may bring their evidence to the mediation, however, no witnesses are allowed. The purpose of mediation is to settle the case if possible; if no settlement is made at mediation, the case will be set for trial. Attorneys and paralegals may not represent parties at mediation.

[Formerly SLRCRLJ 40(g) adopted effective September 1, 1999; renumbered SLCRLJ 40(g) and amended, effective September 1, 2012.]

SLCRLJ 54. REASONABLE ATTORNEY FEES

(a) The court shall grant reasonable attorney's fees when permitted by statute or on the basis of a written instrument. A party seeking reasonable attorney's fees shall file with the court the written instrument or, in the event of a dishonored check, proof of the service of the statutory form of Notice of Dishonor in accordance with RCW 62A.3–104. If reasonable attorney fees are requested based on a contract provision, the contract provision must be conspicuously highlighted or underlined to be readily ascertainable. Specific citation of authority must accompany requests for reasonable attorney fees on any basis other than contract provision. Reasonable attorney's fees following the granting of a judgment at trial or motion shall be set by the court, in its discretion, and the court may require the filing of an affidavit in support of the request.

(b) **Offer of Judgment.** When a party is seeking reasonable attorney's fees following the entry of a judgment under the provisions of RCW 4.84.250 through RCW 4.84.300, proof of compliance with the service procedures must be shown to the court following the entry of the judgment.

(c) **Default Judgments.** Reasonable attorney's fees awarded on a default judgment, where authorized by law or contract, shall be presumed to be no more than $500 subject to modification in the court's discretion based upon the circumstances of a particular case and where supported by an affidavit or declaration in support of the request.

[Formerly SLRCRLJ 54 adopted effective September 1, 2007; renumbered SLCRLJ 54 and amended, effective September 1, 2012.]

SLCRLJ 56(h). SUMMARY JUDGMENT MOTIONS AGAINST PRO SE LITIGANTS

In all cases where a motion for summary judgment is brought against a litigant who is not represented by an attorney, the moving party must attach a copy of CRLJ 56 to the motion for summary judgment. Said copy shall be attached to the motion filed with the court and the copy of the motion served on the non-moving party. In the event a copy of said rule is not so attached, the motion shall be stricken subject to being re-noted without terms.

[Formerly SLRCRLJ 56(h) adopted effective September 1, 2001; renumbered SLCRLJ 56(h) and amended, effective September 1, 2012.]

SLCRLJ 64.1. CIVIL ARREST WARRANTS—NECESSARY INFORMATION

The Court will not issue a civil arrest warrant until the party applying for the issuance of said warrant has provided the Court with necessary information identifying the person for whom the warrant is sought. Said information includes the following minimum facts: (1) full name; (2) date of birth; (3) height or weight, and; (4) hair or eye color.

[Formerly SLRCRLJ 64.1 adopted effective September 1, 2001; renumbered SLCRLJ 64.1 and amended, effective September 1, 2012.]

SKAGIT COUNTY LOCAL CRIMINAL RULES FOR COURTS OF LIMITED JURISDICTION

SLCrRLJ 2.5. ISSUANCE OF BENCH WARRANTS

The Court Administrator or Lead Clerk is authorized to sign and issue warrants in the following cases:

(a) Failure to Appear After Signed Promise to Appear: When a defendant has failed to appear either in person or by a lawyer in answer to a citation and notice, or an order of the court, upon which the defendant has signed a notice to appear. In the event defendant's appearance is mandated by statute, defendant must appear personally.

(b) Failure to Appear in Response to a Summons: When a summons has been issued after authorization of a Judge, and determination by a Judge has been made that probable cause exists that the defendant has committed the crime alleged, and the defendant fails to appear in person or by a lawyer. In the event defendant's appearance is mandated by statute, defendant must appear personally.

(c) Failure to Appear in Response to a Notice: In any case where a defendant fails to appear in person or by a lawyer after notice directing the defendant to appear has been sent to the defendant at the defendant's last address which appears in the court file.

(d) Failure to Appear After Release on Recognizance or on Bail: When a defendant fails to appear after posting bail, or release on recognizance in any case designated as a "MANDATORY APPEARANCE" case by local rule.

(e) Failure to Appear After Probation Violation Hearing: When, after a probation violation hearing, an order has been signed by a Judge directing the defendant to perform certain terms or meet specified conditions or appear, and when there is no evidence in the file that the directed terms and conditions have

been satisfied, and the defendant, after signing the order, fails to appear at the time directed in the order.

[Adopted effective September 1, 2001.]

SLCrRLJ 3.1(e). WITHDRAWAL OF LAWYER [RESCINDED]

[Adopted effective September 1, 1999; rescinded effective September 1, 2012.]

SLCrRLJ 3.1(g). WAIVER OF RIGHT TO COUNSEL [RESCINDED]

[Adopted effective September 1, 1999; rescinded effective September 1, 2012.]

SLCrRLJ 3.3. TIME FOR TRIAL [RESCINDED]

[Original SLCrRLJ 3.3(h) was adopted effective September 1, 1999. Renumbered as SLCrRLJ 3.3 effective September 1, 2005; rescinded effective September 1, 2012.]

SLCrRLJ 3.4(a). PRESENCE OF THE DEFENDANT

Defendant must be present at all stages of the proceedings from arraignment through imposition of sentence. Defendant may waive his/her right to be present unless such waiver conflicts with statute or court rule. Such waiver of presence must be in written form and approved by the Court in advance of each hearing for which waiver of presence is sought. In the event a Defendant does not appear for a hearing and has not obtained prior court approval of a waiver of presence, such non-appearance shall constitute a failure to appear for purposes of CrRLJ 3.3(c)(2)(ii). Both Defendant and Defendant's attorney shall be present at trial confirmation unless the court has accepted Defendant's written waiver of his or her right to be present. If Defendant does not appear for trial confirmation, all of Defendant's pending trial dates shall be stricken and a warrant issued for Defendant's arrest.

[Original SLCrRLJ 3.4(d) was adopted effective September 1, 2001. Renumbered as SLCrRLJ 3.4(a) effective September 1, 2005; amended effective September 1, 2012.]

SLCrRLJ 3.6. SUPPRESSION HEARINGS [RESCINDED]

[Adopted effective September 1, 1999; rescinded effective September 1, 2012.]

SLCrRLJ 4.1(d). CRIMES REQUIRING DEFENDANT'S APPEARANCE AT ARRAIGNMENT [RESCINDED]

[Adopted effective September 1, 1999; amended effective September 1, 2001; rescinded effective September 1, 2012.]

SLCrRLJ 4.12. DUTY TO NOTIFY COURT AND WITNESSES

When a case docketed for trial or other hearing is settled, or for any reason will not proceed to hearing at the set time, the parties shall give notice of that fact immediately to the Court. Notice to the court should be in written form, however, telephonic notice is acceptable where appropriate due to time constraints provided that said notice is confirmed in writing. It shall be the duty of each party to notify their own witnesses, not only of the date and time of the trial, but also of continuances, pre-trial hearings, motions, and other proceedings. The Court will not pay witness fees to witnesses who appear for a case which has been continued or settled without trial or hearing. Such costs shall be borne by the party or attorney who called or subpoenaed the witness.

[Adopted effective September 1, 1999; amended effective September 1, 2012.]

SLCrRLJ 6.13(b). EVIDENCE—BLOOD DRAW CERTIFICATION [RESCINDED]

[Adopted effective September 1, 1999; rescinded effective September 1, 2012.]

SLCrRLJ 6.13(g). EVIDENCE—COURT'S CUSTODY OF EXHIBITS

In a criminal case, every exhibit in the court's custody which is not contraband, and for which ownership is not in dispute, shall be returned to the party who produced at exhibit upon motion of the party and the expiration of the appeal period. Exhibits not withdrawn shall be delivered by the court to the applicable law enforcement agency for disposition as abandoned property, or if contraband, for destruction. No exhibit shall be released by the court without obtaining a receipt from the person or agency receiving it.

[Formerly SLCrRLJ 6.13(f) adopted effective September 1, 2001; renumbered SLCrRLJ 6.13(g) and amended, effective September 1, 2012.]

SLCrRLJ 7.2(g). ALTERNATIVE TO SENTENCING—DEFERRED PROSECUTION

Prior to entry of an order deferring prosecution pursuant to RCW 10.05, the Defendant shall schedule an appointment and meet with a representative of the Skagit County District Court Probation. During this meeting Defendant shall be advised of the requirements for supervision of a deferred prosecution.

[Adopted effective September 1, 1999; amended effective September 1, 2001; September 1, 2007; September 1, 2008; September 1, 2012.]

SLCrRLJ 8.2. MOTIONS [RESCINDED]

[Adopted effective September 1, 1999; amended effective September 1, 2001; rescinded effective September 1, 2012.]

SKAGIT COUNTY LOCAL INFRACTION RULES FOR COURTS OF LIMITED JURISDICTION

SLIRLJ 3.2(b). MOTION FOR VACATION OF DEFAULT JUDGMENT FOR FTA

A defendant against whom a judgment for a traffic infraction has been entered by default for failure to appear, may file a motion in writing, on forms provided by the court, requesting that said judgment be set aside. The motion will then be presented to the court ex parte for determination. If, upon review, the court finds that a hearing upon the motion is necessary, the matter shall be set for hearing. Defendant must be present in the event the matter is set for hearing. The motion will be evaluated in conformity with CRLJ 60(b). If the Court grants said motion, the matter

will be set for a hearing of the kind requested by the defendant. Mitigation hearings may be heard at the time of the motion if the calendar allows.

[Adopted effective September 1, 1999; amended effective September 1, 2001.]

SLIRLJ 3.5. DECISIONS ON WRITTEN STATEMENTS

Hearings on alleged traffic infractions may be held upon written statements pursuant to IRLJ 2.4(b)(4), 2.6(c), and 3.5 for alleged infractions which are contested or where the Defendant requests a mitigation hearing.

[Adopted effective September 1, 2001.]

SLIRLJ 6.6.1. CERTIFICATION OF SCALES USED IN THE MEASUREMENT OF WEIGHT FOR COMMERCIAL MOTOR VEHICLES

(a) In General. This rule applies only to contested hearings in traffic infraction cases.

(b) Scale Certification. Evidence given under oath (including testimony given in person or the written report of an officer as provided in IRLJ 3.3) of the results of a measurement of the weight of any commercial motor vehicle or portion thereof shall be admissible without additional foundation. A sworn statement setting forth the results of any inspection, test and/or certification of any scale used primarily for the purpose of measuring the weights of commercial motor vehicles shall likewise be admissible in evidence without additional foundation, and shall not be subject to objection on grounds of hearsay, provided that such document is maintained in a manner consistent with subsection (d) of this rule. Any party may present evidence supporting or attacking the result of any such measurement of weight or the inspection, test and/or certification of any such scale.

(c) [Reserved]

(d) Maintaining Certificates as Public Records. Any document of inspection, test and/or certification of any State scale as set forth in subsection (b) of this rule may be filed with the court and maintained by the court as a public record. The documents will be available for inspection by the public. Copies will be provided on request. The court may charge any allowable copying fees. The documents are available without a formal request for discovery. In the alternative, or in addition, such documents may be maintained on a web site established for that purpose by the Washington State Patrol. The court is entitled to take judicial notice of the fact that the document has been filed with the court or maintained on the web site. Evidence will not be suppressed merely because there is not a representative of the prosecuting authority present who actually offers the document.

[Adopted effective September 1, 2007.]

MUNICIPAL COURTS

ANACORTES MUNICIPAL COURT—
[No Local Rules]

PUBLISHER'S NOTE

The Skagit County District Court Local Rules are binding upon the Anocortes Municipal Court. (See SLARLJ 2, Skagit County District Court Local Rules, Supra.)

BURLINGTON MUNICIPAL COURT—
[No Local Rules]

PUBLISHER'S NOTE

This municipal court follows the Skagit County District Court Local Rules.

MOUNT VERNON MUNICIPAL COURT—
[No Local Rules]

PUBLISHER'S NOTE

This municipal court follows the Skagit County District Court Local Rules.

SEDRO–WOOLLEY MUNICIPAL COURT LOCAL RULES

Including Amendments Received
Through August 15, 2015

Table of Rules

ADMINISTRATIVE RULES

PREFACE

1. PROMULGATION. These rules shall be known as the Local Rules for the Municipal Court of the City of Sedro–Woolley. Copies of these rules will be filed with the Office of the Administrator of the Courts, and the Clerk of the District Court for Skagit County and the Clerk of the Municipal Court of Sedro–Woolley. Copies of these rules will be distributed to all law offices in Skagit County, the County Law Library and Sedro–Woolley Public Library for public reference. Copies will be available from the Municipal Court Clerk for Sedro–Woolley. These rules will be effective on September 1, 2003.

2. NUMBERING. Consistent with GR 7(b) Washington Court Rules, these rules, to the extent possible, conform in numbering system and in format to those rules adopted by the Supreme Court of the State of Washington for Courts of Limited Jurisdiction and facilitate the use of the same. The number of each rule is preceded by the abbreviation of "SWM" designating the rule as a Sedro–Woolley Municipal Local Court Rule and as being supplemental to the corresponding Washington Court Rule for Courts of Limited Jurisdiction.

3. Revisions and Additions (Reserved).

[Adopted effective September 1, 2000; amended effective September 1, 2003.]

SWMARLJ 1. SCOPE OF LOCAL RULES

These rules govern the procedure in the Sedro–Woolley Municipal Court. These rules are supplemental to the rules enacted by the Washington State Supreme Court for Courts of Limited Jurisdiction as specifically authorized by GR 7, CrRLJ 1.7, and IRLJ 1.3 of the Washington Court Rules. The Sedro–Woolley Municipal Court may modify or suspend any of these local rules in any given case upon good cause being shown or upon the Court's own motion.

[Adopted effective September 1, 2000; amended effective September 1, 2003.]

SWMARLJ 2. SCHEDULING

(a) Calendar. The Court Administrator shall develop and maintain a calendar for all hearings and trials.

(b) Priority. Whenever the caseload of the Court requires, trials and other matters will be subject to multiple settings on the same date. The order in which said matters proceed will be determined by the Judge, based on the speedy trial rule in criminal cases and the availability of jurors.

(c) Transfer of Cases. If the caseload or other circumstances require, the Court may appoint a Court Commissioner or Judge Pro Tempore to hear that trial or calendar of cases and may arrange for it to be heard in a location other than the usual courtroom.

[Adopted effective September 1, 2000.]

SWMARLJ 9(g). DISCLOSURE OF PUBLIC RECORDS

The following records and files are deemed confidential and are not available to the public for inspection or copying absent a court order.

1. Affidavits for Search warrants before a return of service and inventory has been filed with the court;

2. Mental Health, psychiatric and medical reports;

3. Alcohol and drug evaluations and compliance reports;

4. Deferred prosecution evaluations and police reports;

5. Certified copies of driving records, abstracts of driving records and compiled reports of arrests and convictions;

6. Judge's notes and worksheets;

7. Witness statements and police reports;

8. Address of Jurors

9. Juror notes taken during trial.

Dissemination of data by the Court shall be done according to the JIS/DISCIS Policy and Sedro–Woolley Municipal Court's Data Dissemination Policy Adopted by the Court and subject to revisions or amendments duly enacted by the court. A copy of said policy is available upon demand made to the Sedro–Woolley Municipal Court Clerk's Office.

[Adopted effective September 1, 2000; amended effective September 1, 2003.]

LOCAL CRIMINAL RULES

SWMCrRLJ 3.1(e). WITHDRAWAL OF LAWYER

No withdrawal after a case has been set for trial will be recognized by the Court, except for cause deemed sufficient by the Court. Approval of withdrawal may, if necessary to prevent a continuance, be denied, and such attorney be required to proceed with the trial.

[Adopted effective September 1, 2000.]

SWMCrRLJ 3.1(e)(1). WITHDRAWAL OF PUBLIC DEFENDER

Unless a Notice of Appeal has been filed, an attorney appointed at public expense shall be deemed automatically withdrawn from representation five days following a final decision of the Court as defined in RALJ without need to file any document with the Court with the exception of domestic violence and driving under the influence cases.

[Adopted effective September 1, 2003)

SWMCrRLJ 3.1(g). WAIVER OF RIGHT TO COUNSEL

Unless a written waiver of the defendant's right to counsel is signed by the defendant and filed with the Court, an attorney shall be appointed to represent the defendant at all stages of the proceedings. No matter may be set for trial for a self-represented defendant, unless a signed Waiver of Right to Attorney is filed with the Court.

[Adopted effective September 1, 2000.]

SWMCrRLJ 3.2. RELEASE OF ACCUSED

Return of Cash Bail. The Court may apply cash bail posted in the defendant's name to pay the defendant's fines, penalties and costs on the present case or on any past due obligations to the court.

[Adopted effective September 1, 2003.]

SWMCrRLJ 3.3(h). TIME FOR TRIAL

Continuances. All contested motions for continuances shall be heard on the appropriate motion docket. Only in cases of extreme emergency and unforeseeable circumstances shall the trial judge consider motion for continuance without the proper notice and citation.

[Adopted effective September 1, 2000; amended effective September 1, 2003.]

SWMCrRLJ 3.6. SUPPRESSION HEARINGS

A party moving to suppress evidence must file a written motion that sets forth in detail the specific factual and legal grounds for the motion. The motion should be filed with the Court at least seven (7) days prior to the pre-trial hearing. Said motion shall be supported by an affidavit or declaration under penalty of perjury of a person with testimonial knowledge that sets forth the facts to be elicited at an evidentiary hearing. The matter will be set for evidentiary hearing only if the Judge at a pre-trial hearing finds that there are facts in dispute. If the parties agree to the facts, a written stipulation shall be signed by the parties setting forth the facts on which the Court will render its decision. A copy of the motion and supporting documents must be served on the opposing party at least five court days prior to the date set for hearing.

[Adopted effective September 1, 2000.]

SWMCrRLJ 4.1(d). CRIMES REQUIRING DEFENDANT'S APPEARANCE AT ARRAIGNMENT

A lawyer may not enter a written plea or not guilty plea on behalf of a client if the charging document states that one or more of the charges involves domestic violence, harassment, violation of an anti-harassment order, order of protection, or no contact order, driving while under the influence of intoxicants, driving while under the age of 21 after having consumed alcohol or physical control of a vehicle while under the influence of intoxicants. For such charges, the defendant must appear in person for arraignment; and the Court shall determine the necessity of imposing conditions of pre-trial release. Where legislation mandates the defendant's appearance on the next judicial day following arrest, the term "next judicial day" as applied to the Municipal Court shall mean the next scheduled court day for the Sedro–Woolley Municipal Court.

[Adopted effective September 1, 2000; amended effective September 1, 2003.]

SWMCrRLJ 4.11. DUTY TO NOTIFY COURT AND WITNESSES

When a case docketed for trial or other hearing is settled, or for any reason will not proceed to hearing at the set time, the parties shall give notice of that fact immediately to the Court. Notice to the Court should be in written form. Telephonic notice is acceptable where appropriate due to time constraints, provided that said notice is confirmed in writing. It shall be the duty of each party to notify it's own witnesses, not only of the date and time of the trial, but also of continuances, pre-trial hearings, motions and other proceedings. The Court will not pay witness fees to witnesses who appear for a case which has been continued or settled without trial or hearing. Such costs shall be borne by the party or attorney who called or subpoenaed the witness.

[Adopted effective September 1, 2000.]

SWMCrRLJ 6.13(b). EVIDENCE BLOOD DRAW CERTIFICATION

(1) **Certification of Qualification to Draw Blood and of Blood Draw Procedure**

(a) **Admission of Blood Draw Certificate.** In the absence of a request to produce the person who drew blood from the defendant made at least seven (7) days prior to trial, certificates substantially in the following form are admissible in lieu of a witness in any court proceeding held pursuant to RCW 46.61.502 through RCW 46.61.506 for the purpose of determining whether a person was operating or in actual physical control of a vehicle while under the influence of intoxicating liquors and/or drugs.

BLOOD DRAW CERTIFICATION

I do certify under penalty of perjury of the laws of the State of Washington, the following: I am a (physician) (registered nurse) (qualified technician) and I am qualified by medical training and experience to draw blood from the human body.

On (date) at (time) I drew (number of samples) blood samples from (name of person) at the direction and in the presence of _____ (name of officer).

I further certify that with each sample, the blood draw site was sterilized with a non-alcoholic preparation (betadine) (other _____), and that each blood sample was drawn into a chemically clean dry container (hereinafter referred to as blood draw containers) consistent with the size of the sample and sealed with an inert leak-proof stopper. The blood draw containers are known by me to contain a suitable anti-coagulant and enzyme poison sufficient in amount to prevent clotting and stabilize the alcohol concentration. The anti-coagulant and enzyme poison utilized in this blood draw were (sodium fluoride and potassium oxalate) (other:). To the best of my knowledge, no foreign substances or chemicals, including alcohol, were involved in the blood draw process other than those listed above.

Date and Place of signature.

Signature of person making certification.

[Adopted effective September 1, 2000.]

SWMCrRLJ 7.2(g). ALTERNATIVE TO SENTENCING DEFERRED PROSECUTION

A petition for deferred prosecution pursuant to RCW 10.05 must be filed with the Court no later than seven (7) days prior to the Pre-trial/Trial Confirmation Hearing unless good cause exists for delay. Said petition and the accompanying declarations shall be in a form acceptable to the Court and in conformity with the statute. A complete copy of the police report of the defendant's conduct giving rise to the charge shall be attached to the petition. Said order shall provide for supervision for 60 months, completion of a treatment plan, payment of costs, abstinence from consumption of alcohol and non-prescription mood altering drugs, attendance at a victims impact panel, no major traffic offenses, a requirement that all vehicles driven by the defendant be equipped with an ignition interlock device for at least the first two (2) years of the deferred prosecution and no driving without being properly licensed and insured.

[Adopted effective September 1, 2000.]

SWMCrRLJ 8.2. MOTIONS

(a) All motions, unless made during a hearing or trial, shall be made in writing and shall state with particularity the grounds therefore, and set forth the relief or order sought.

(b) Motions for continuance shall be made in writing, in person, via fax or e-mail by the defendant or the defense attorney. No telephone motions for continuances will be accepted.

(c) The Court, on it's own motion or motion of the defendant or the prosecuting attorney, may continue a scheduled court appearance in the interest of justice or as authorized in CrRLJ 3.3.

(d) Upon agreement by both parties, the Clerk is authorized to continue a hearing without leave of Court upon request of either party within five days of the date the case is set for hearing/trial by issuance of notice.

(e) A request to extinguish or modify a No Contact Order in a Domestic Violence case may only be made by a party to the case. The party must file a request on a form prescribed by the Court. All parties and the alleged victim must be served with written notice at least five court days before any hearing to consider such a request.

(f) A request to re-impose a No Contact Order in a Domestic Violence Case may only be made a victim/party to the case and the party must file a written motion on a form prescribed by the Court. All parties must be served with written notice at least five court days before any hearing to consider such a request.

[Adopted effective September 1, 2000; amended effective September 1, 2003.]

LOCAL INFRACTION RULES

SWMIRLJ 2.4. RESPONSE TO NOTICE

(1) Persons alleged to have committed infractions may submit a written statement, in lieu of appearing at a scheduled hearing, either contesting the infraction or explaining mitigating circumstances.

(a) Persons alleged to have committed infractions may submit a written statement via e-mail mitigation through the forms on the Sedro–Woolley Municipal Court Web Site.

(b) The e-mail mitigation hearing will be reviewed by the Judge who will make an appropriate decision and the judicial decision will be sent via e-mail and in writing.

(2) Upon receipt of a request for either a contested or mitigation hearing, the Clerk shall provide to the defendant a Hearing by Mail.

(3) The written statement must be received by the Clerk at least one court day prior to the scheduled hearing in order to be considered.

[Adopted effective September 1, 2003.]

SWMIRLJ 3.2(b). MOTION FOR VACATION OF DEFAULT JUDGMENT FOR FAILURE TO APPEAR/RESPOND

A defendant against whom a judgment for a traffic infraction has been entered by default for failure to appear/respond may file a motion in writing, on forms provided by the Court, requesting that said judgment be set aside. The motion will then be presented to the Court ex parte for determination. If, upon review, the Court feels that a hearing upon the motion is necessary, the matter shall be set for hearing. The defendant must be present in the event the matter is set for hearing. The motion will be evaluated in conformity with CRLJ 60(b). If the Court grants the motion, the matter will be set for a hearing. Mitigation hearings may be heard at the time of the motion if the calendar allows.

[Adopted effective September 1, 2000; amended effective September 1, 2003.]

SWMIRLJ 3.5(f). DECISION ON WRITTEN STATEMENTS

(1) A defendant may request the Court to make a decision on the infraction in the defendant's absence on the basis of the defendant's written affidavit, on a form provided by the court and the affidavit of the complaining officer and witnesses. The Court's decision shall be in writing whether an infraction was found to have been committed and what penalty, if any, was imposed and will be mailed to the defendant.

(2) A defendant may request the Court to make a decision on a mitigation hearing for an infraction held via e-mail on the basis of the defendant's written e-mail affidavit. The Court's decision may be an e-mailed response and in writing whether an infraction was found to have been committed and what penalty, if any, was imposed and will be e-mailed or mailed via post card to the defendant.

[Adopted effective September 1, 2000; amended effective September 1, 2003.]

SKAMANIA COUNTY

Table of Courts

Superior Court

Local Court Rules of the Superior Court for Klickitat/Skamania Counties.

District Court

Local Rules of the District Court of Skamania County, State of Washington.

Municipal Courts

North Bonneville Municipal Court.
Stevenson Municipal Court—[No Local Rules].

SUPERIOR COURT

LOCAL COURT RULES OF THE SUPERIOR COURT FOR KLICKITAT/SKAMANIA COUNTIES

PUBLISHER'S NOTE

The Local Rules for the Superior Courts of Klickitat/Skamania Counties are set forth under Klickitat County.

DISTRICT COURT

LOCAL RULES OF THE DISTRICT COURT OF SKAMANIA COUNTY, STATE OF WASHINGTON

Including Amendments Received Through
August 15, 2015

Table of Rules

PREAMBLE

These local rules pertain to the operation of the Skamania County District Court. These rules are complementary and supplemental to the Rules for Courts of Limited Jurisdiction promulgated by the Washington Supreme Court. The rules are designed to economize the time of counsel and to make efficient use of the Court's time. To be effective, the cooperation of the litigants and their counsel is required.

The rules that follow are ones that have been in effect for some time. Anyone having comments on these rules should address them in writing to the presiding Judge in care of the Court Administrator.

[Adopted March 21, 1996.]

STRUCTURE OF THE COURT

The District Court for Skamania County is located at 240 Vancouver Avenue, P.O. Box 790, Stevenson, Washington 98648–0790.

The Court is staffed by one part-time District Court Judge, two Court Commissioners, one Clerk and the Court Administrator.

Office hours are Monday through Friday, 8:30 a.m. to 5:00 p.m. This District Court does not receipt monies after 4:30 p.m. for accounting purposes.

[Adopted March 21, 1996.]

RULE 1. COURT ORGANIZATION AND MANAGEMENT

General Management. The general management of the Court shall be vested in the presiding Judge and his duties and powers are as set forth below.

Duties of the Presiding Judge. The presiding Judge will act as chief administrative Judge and will set policy to be implemented by the court personnel.

A. The presiding Judge will call meetings of the Court and preside over said meetings.

B. The presiding Judge will be responsible for scheduling of court time.

C. The presiding Judge will speak for the Court on all matters.

D. The presiding Judge will be responsible for space management and facilities planning.

E. The presiding Judge will have the responsibility for monitoring the budget with the assistance of the Court Administrator.

F. The presiding Judge will be responsible for relations with all other elected officials.

Court Commissioner. The Skamania County District Court Judge may select a Court Commissioner and/or Magistrate to provide services for the Court. The Court Commissioner shall have the following duties:

A. Conduct probable cause determinations.

B. Conduct preliminary hearings and arraignments.

C. Set bail, appoint counsel and perform other duties common to the preliminary hearing and arraignment process.

D. Signing warrants of arrest.

E. Signing normal civil ex parte matters and immediate temporary relief orders.

F. Other matters that may be, from time to time assigned by the presiding Judge.

G. Court Commissioners who have been admitted to the bar shall sign search warrants in the absence of the presiding Judge.

H. A Court Commissioner shall serve at the pleasure of the Judge.

Court Administrator.

A. Assists the District Court Judge in directing caseflow management and case assignments.

B. Assists in preparation and presentation of the department budget and directs fiscal management inventory control and purchasing.

C. Directs the activities of District Court personnel by managing work flow and overall work assignments and providing employee training and review.

D. Briefs Judge on District Court operations and status.

E. Prepares reports and complies statistics as required.

F. The District Court Administrator serves at the pleasure of the District Court Judge.

[Adopted March 21, 1996.]

RULE 2. SECURITY OF COURTROOMS AND RELATED AREAS

A. Weapons. No weapon designed for offensive or defensive purpose shall be allowed in any space assigned to District Court. A violation of this order shall constitute contempt of court.

a. *Exceptions.* Paragraph (A) shall not apply to Judges, commissioned police officers, prison or jail wardens, or federal law enforcement officers.

[Adopted March 21, 1996.]

RULE 3. APPEARANCE BONDS

A. Only those people who have been approved by the Judge of the District Court are authorized to post appearance bonds.

[Adopted March 21, 1996.]

RULE 4. JUSTICE COURT CIVIL RULES (CRLJ)

A. Format; Typed Names and Bar Numbers.

a. The names of all persons signing a pleading should have their name typed under their signatures. If signed by an attorney, the attorney's Washington State bar association number must be set forth.

B. Verification and Signing of Pleadings.

a. As collection agencies are prohibited from practicing law, all actions by collection agencies shall be by and through their attorney.

b. The civil clerk shall upon request from employees of the collection agencies over the telephone or in person, furnish them with information requested about pending cases in which they are a party; provided that such request shall not burden the time of the clerk or the Court.

c. Before judgment is entered, employees of the collection agencies shall be allowed to file cases and legal papers in those cases in which their company is a party except garnishments, executions, attachments, or other extraordinary process shall be filed by the attorney for the collection agency.

d. Checks of collection agencies for payment of fees and other Court charges shall be accepted by the Court from employees of collection agencies.

C. Assignment for Trial.

a. A trial setting must be requested in writing by either party, provided the case is at issue and all necessary answers and replies have been filed with the Court.

b. Continuances will be granted upon filing of an agreed motion and affidavit signed by all parties involved. If the request for continuance is contested, the Court will set the next available court date for a hearing on the motion for continuance.

D. Demand for Judgment; Method—Ex Parte Judgments and Orders.

a. Counsel presenting a judgment or entry of an order shall be responsible to see all applicable papers are filed and that the Court file is provided to the Judge or Court Commissioner. Out-of-county counsel may present routine ex parte or stipulated matters based on the record in the file by mail. Self addressed, stamped envelopes shall be provided for return of any conformed materials and/or rejected orders.

E. Entry of Judgments on a Promissory Note.

a. No judgment on a promissory note will be signed until the original note has been filed with the Court, absent of proof of loss or destruction.

F. Execution, Supplemental Proceedings and Garnishments.

a. Shall be governed by statute.

[Adopted March 21, 1996.]

RULE 5. JUSTICE COURT CRIMINAL RULES

A. Bail Schedule.

a. The Court may periodically publish a bail schedule which will include any bail schedule and penalty schedule promulgated by the Supreme Court of the State of Washington. Said schedule shall be provided to all law enforcement officers within the county. Said schedule shall have the force and effect of local court rule for all the courts under the authority of the District Court of Skamania County.

B. Bail.

a. Misdemeanor bail shall not be combined with felony bail. If cash is received, it shall be kept separate. If a bondsman posts bail, they shall post separate bonds.

b. If someone other than the defendant posts cash bail, it will be necessary to obtain the correct name and address of the person or persons posting the bail. That information should then be given to the District Court along with the bail.

C. Forfeiture.

a. If the defendant fails to appear as directed by the Court, a bail forfeiture shall be immediately issued. The bondsman shall have 60 days to locate the defendant. If the bondsman presents the defendant to the Court before the 60 days has elapsed, the bail forfeiture can be rescinded for cost. The cost shall be $100.00 for failure to appear at arraignment, pretrial or sentencing; $200.00 for failure to appear for trial, or $300.00 for failure to appear at a jury trial.

b. Should the 60 days elapse and the defendant has not been brought before the Court, the bond becomes due and payable immediately.

D. Pre-trial Release.

a. Court Commissioners are authorized to release persons who are charged with misdemeanor and gross misdemeanor offenses on their own recognizance.

b. The arresting officer should list an arraignment date on the citation for any defendant detained at the jail for a misdemeanor or gross misdemeanor.

c. When the District Court Judge or Court Commissioner are not available, supervisory personnel of the jail division may grant recognizance to certain defendants charged only with misdemeanor or gross misdemeanor offenses. This authority is to be used for defendants who have been residents of Washington for more than one year and who have no failures to appear or warrants outstanding.

d. The recognizance authority granted to jail division staff is to be used only in emergency situations when overcrowding becomes a problem.

E. Arraignment.
The arraignment date and time shall be written on the face of the citation by the officer. Should the officer fail to put an arraignment date and time the court will set the arraignment date and notify the defendant through the mail. The arraignment shall consist of:

a. Ascertaining the defendant's true name and address, ties to the community, employment status and past criminal history.

b. Advise the defendant of the nature of the charges and the maximum penalties pertaining to the charges.

c. Advisement of rights.

d. Appointment of counsel, determination indigency.

e. Setting of bail, personal recognizance release.

F. Right to Assignment of Counsel.

a. Unless waived, counsel shall be provided to any person who is financially unable to obtain one without causing substantial hardship to himself or his family and pursuant to standards published by the State of Washington.

b. If at any time it appears that a person has retained private counsel, has funds sufficient to do so, or is otherwise not eligible for defense services, the appointed attorney may notify the Court and ask its guidance. Conversely, if it appears that counsel previously retained by a person has withdrawn, or that a person thought to have funds sufficient to obtain private counsel is not in fact able to do so, then the Court shall make a redetermination of eligibility.

G. Reimbursement of Attorney Fees.

a. *Partial Ability to Pay.*

1. A person found to be partially eligible for defense services shall be required to make reimbursement to the Court as agreed at the time of appointment.

b. *Reimbursement as a Provision of an Order of Probation.*

1. Any defendant who is placed on probation may be required to reimburse the county for all or part of the costs of appointed counsel. Further said reimbursement may be part of a recommendation from the probation department or any agreement between prosecution and appointed counsel.

c. *Reimbursement Not Required by Appointed Counsel.*

1. In no case shall appointed counsel set or attempt to obtain reimbursement for the costs of defense services.

d. *Failure to Reimburse After Ordered to Do so.*

1. If reimbursement is part of an order of probation, failure of payment could be sufficient to be a violation of probation. The Court shall determine whether or not defendant has the present financial ability to pay without causing undue hardship to self or dependents and shall also determine that the defendant has willfully failed to make payments or willfully failed to make a good faith, reasonable effort to acquire the means to make the payment.

e. *Legal Representation Regarding Reimbursement.*

1. The appointed counsel's representation of a client shall include the ability to oppose an order of the Court requiring reimbursement for defense ser-

vices, provided there are arguable legal grounds for such opposition.

H. Arraignment—Appearance by Counsel Only.

a. Attorneys at law, admitted to practice in the State of Washington, may enter a plea of not guilty in writing on all cases filed in the District Court.

I. Pretrial Conference. The pretrial conference shall be set by the Court and used for the following purposes:

a. To file any petition for deferred prosecution.

b. To file any pretrial motion.

c. To negotiate for plea-bargaining purposes.

d. To examine the police/officer's reports and other prosecution information.

e. To dispose of the case in any other manner.

f. Pretrial does not require the attendance of the defendant and shall be set at approximately 21 days from the first appearance.

g. All pretrial motions shall be in writing and state an estimate of time for said motion.

J. Witness—Process—Subpoena.

a. If a witness in a criminal matter is to be subpoenaed, the person making the request should prepare the subpoena and present it to the Court for signature. All subpoenas must be prepared in triplicate prior to the presentation for signature.

K. Status Conference. The pretrial status conference shall be set by the Court and used for the following:

a. Status conferences shall be set approximately 14 days before trial.

b. The defendant must appear or a warrant will be issued for the arrest of defendant.

c. A status conference report shall be filed with the Court by the prosecuting authority.

d. The purpose of the status conference is to present witness lists to the Court, to resolve all issues and advise the Court of such resolution, whether it be a jury trial, bench trial, plea, dismissal or need for rescheduling a pretrial motion.

L. Jury and Trial Tracking Procedure.

a. Jury trials shall be initially set on the Court's Thursday criminal docket and are subject to being reset to a time and date certain on the Court's own

motion or that of either party upon a showing that need for a jury is confirmed.

b. If any pretrial motions are filed within 14 days of trial, the Court will, consistent with it's schedule, attempt to set the motion prior to the day of trial. Any motions set on the morning of trial shall begin at 8:15 a.m. Jury trials begin at 8:30 a.m. Should the Court rule in a manner that requires a continuance of the trial on the morning of trial, the Court shall assess the costs of the jury against the attorney who the Court finds, in it's discretion, has failed to properly recognize, note or resolve the issues at the pretrial and according to the schedule set forth in these rules.

M. Continuances.

a. All motions for continuances shall be heard by notice and citation on the appropriate motion docket. Only in extreme emergencies shall the presiding Judge or the trial Judge consider a motion for continuance without the proper notice and citation.

N. Probation.

a. Should supervised probation be ordered at arraignment, sentencing, deferred prosecution hearing or any other type of hearing, the Court will require the defendant to pay monthly probation fees at the District Court.

O. Work Crew.

a. All defendants who participate in the work crew program will be required to pay the insurance fee for that privilege or work one extra day on the work crew.

[Adopted March 21, 1996.]

RULE 6. INITIATION OF TRAFFIC CASE

A. Filing of Notice.

a. Whenever a notice of infraction has been issued and not filed with the Court within 48 hours, the clerk shall bring the untimely filing to the attention of the Judge except:

b. If the citation is filed more than 72 hours after issuance of the notice, excluding Saturdays, Sundays, and holidays. The clerk may mark the citation "dismissed without prejudice", (IRLJR 2.2) and take no further action.

[Adopted March 21, 1996.]

RULE 7. RECORD RETENTION

District Court records shall be retained pursuant to the District and Municipal Court Records Retention Schedule provided by the State of Washington.

[Adopted March 21, 1996.]

MUNICIPAL COURTS

NORTH BONNEVILLE MUNICIPAL COURT

Including Amendments Received Through
August 15, 2015

Table of Rules

PREAMBLE

These local rules pertain to the operation of the North Bonneville Municipal Court, these rules are complementary and supplemental to the Rules for Courts of Limited Jurisdiction promulgated by the Washington Supreme Court. The rules are designed to economize the time of counsel and to make efficient use of the Court's time. To be effective, the cooperation of the litigants and their counsel is required.

The rules that follow are ones that have been in effect for some time. Anyone having comments on these rules should address them in writing to the residing Judge of the Court.

[Adopted September 1, 2010.]

STRUCTURE OF THE COURT

The Municipal Court for the City of North Bonneville is located at City Hall, 214 CBD Mall, PO Box 7, North Bonneville, WA., 98639–0007.

The Court is staffed by one part-time Municipal Court Judge and one Court Clerk. Office Hours are Monday through Friday 8:00 am to 5:00 pm. Court days for trials and hearings are on the 1ST, 3RD, and the 5th Monday every month. In the event a national holiday is observed on the Monday Court day, the following Tuesday shall be a Court day.

[Adopted September 1, 2010.]

RULE 1. COURT ORGANIZATION AND MANAGEMENT

General Management: The general management of the Court shall be vested in the presiding Judge and the duties and powers are as set for below.

Duties of the Presiding Judge: The presiding Judge will act as chief administrative Judge and will set policy to be implemented by the Court personnel.

1) The presiding Judge will call meetings of the Court and preside over said meetings.

2) The presiding Judge will be responsible for scheduling of Court time.

3) The presiding Judge will speak for the Court on all matters.

4) The presiding Judge will be responsible for space management and facilities planning.

5) The presiding Judge will have the responsibility for monitoring the Court budget.

6) The presiding Judge will be responsible for communications with all other elected officials.

7) The presiding Judge will conduct probable cause determinations

8) The presiding Judge will conduct preliminary hearings and criminal arraignments.

9) The presiding Judge will set bail, appoint counsel and perform other duties common to the preliminary hearing and arraignment process.

10) The presiding Judge will shall sign warrants for arrest.

Duties of the Court Clerk: The North Bonneville Court Judge shall select a Court Clerk to provide services for the Court and shall have the following duties.

1) Assist the Municipal Court Judge in directing case-flow management.

2) Assist in the preparation and presentation of the department budget and direct fiscal management inventory control and purchasing.

3) Brief the Judge on Municipal Court operations and status.

4) Prepares reports and complies[1] statistics as required.

[Adopted September 1, 2010.]

[1] So in original. Probably should be "compiles".

RULE 2.   SECURITY OF COURTROOMS AND RELATED AREAS

Weapons: No weapon designed for offensive or defensive purposes shall be allowed in any space assigned to the Municipal Court and a violation of this order shall constitute Contempt of Court.

Exceptions: This Rule shall not apply to Judges, commissioned police officers while in duty status, and corrections officers in duty status.

[Adopted September 1, 2010.]

RULE 3.   APPEARANCE BONDS

Posting Appearance Bonds: Only those people approved by the Judge of the Municipal Court are authorized to seek and submit the post of appearance bonds.

[Adopted September 1, 2010.]

RULE 4.   MUNICIPAL COURT CRIMINAL JUSTICE RULES

Purpose and Construction: These rules are intended to provide for the just determination of every criminal proceeding. They shall be construed to secure simplicity in procedure, fairness in administration, effective justice, and the elimination of unjustifiable expense and delay. These rules are constructed to supplement and not to supplant the Criminal Rules for Courts of Limited Jurisdiction (CrRLJ).

1) Bail Schedule. The Court may periodically publish a bail schedule which will include any bail schedule and penalty schedule promulgated by the Supreme Court of the State of Washington. Said bail schedule shall be provided to law enforcement agencies within the jurisdiction of the Municipal Court.

2) Bail. Misdemeanor bail shall not be combined with felony bail. If cash funds are received, it shall be kept separate. If a bail bondsman posts bail it shall be with separate bonds for the charged offenses. If someone other than the defendant posts cash funds as bail, it will be necessary to obtain the correct name and address of the posting party to be provided to the Municipal Court with the bail.

3) Bail Forfeiture.

a) Should the defendant fail to appear as directed by the Court, bail forfeiture shall be immediately issued. The bail bondsman shall have 60 days to locate the defendant and if the bondsman presents the defendant to the Court before 60 days have elapsed, the bail forfeiture can be rescinded for cost. The cost shall be $100.00 for failure to appear at arraignment, pre-trial or sentencing proceeding; $200.00 for failure to appear for trial; or $300.00 for failure to appear for jury trial.

b) Should the permitted 60 days elapse and the defendant has not been brought before the Court, the bond becomes due and payable immediately.

c) Should the defendant fail to appear as directed by the Court, bail forfeiture shall be immediately issued for any cash funds bail posted by the defendant or any party posting same on behalf of the defendant.

4) Pre–Trial Release.

a) The arresting officer shall list on the criminal citation for any defendant, whether or not that person is detained at the jail for a misdemeanor or gross misdemeanor.

b) The arresting officer shall prepare a sworn statement for the Court describing probable cause for criminal charge for which the defendant has been arrested.

5) Arraignment.

a) The arraignment date and time shall be written on the criminal citation by the arresting officer. The date of arraignment shall be no later than 14 days post-arrest date. Should the officer fail to put an arraignment date and time, the Court will set the arraignment date and notify the defendant through the mail. The arraignment shall consist of:

i) The defendant's true full name, residential address and mailing address, ties to the community, employment status and past criminal history

ii) Advise the defendant of the nature of the charges and the maximum penalties that may be imposed upon a finding of guilt

iii) Advisement of all rights

iv) Advisement of right to legal counsel and determination of indigence

v) The setting of bail and release conditions

vi) Attorneys at law, admitted to practice in the State of Washington, may enter a notice of appearance and plea of not guilty in writing on all cases filed in the Municipal Court

6) The Right to Assignment of Counsel.

a) Unless waived by the defendant, legal counsel shall be provided to any person who is financially unable to obtain one without causing substantial financial hardship to themselves for family and pursuant to standards published by the State of Washington

b) If at any time it appears that a person has retained private counsel, has funds sufficient to do so, or is otherwise not eligible for defense services, the

appointed attorney may notify the Court and ask it
guidance

c) Conversely, it appears that counsel previously
retained by a person has withdrawn, or that a person
thought to have funds sufficient to obtain private
counsel is not in fact able to do so, than the Court
shall make a redetermination of eligibility for appointed counsel

d) Unless a written notice to withdraw is approved
by the Court, defendant's attorney must appear at all
subsequent Court dates, including post conviction reviews. If the defendant's attorney fails to appear at
any hearing, the Court may impose terms and any
other conditions authorized by law.

7) Pre-trial Conference.

a) The pre-trial conference shall be set by the
Court and used for the following purposes:

i) Pre-trial hearings shall be within 30 days of
defendant's first appearance

ii) File any pre-trial motion

iii) Negotiation for plea-bargaining purposes

iv) File petition for deferred prosecution

v) Submit a change in plea

vi) All pre-trial motions shall be in writing

vii) To dispose of the case in any other manner

8) Witness—Process—Subpoena.
If a witness in
criminal matters is to be subpoenaed, shall be requested by either party and presented to the Court for
signature

9) Status conference.

a) Status conferences shall be set by the Court for
the following purposes:

i) Defendant and counsel shall appear and failure
to appear without just cause shall result in the issue
of warrant

ii) The purpose of the status conference is to
present witness lists to the Court, resolve all issued,
determination of jury trial, bench trial, plea offering, or other resolution matters

iii) The Court shall set trial date

10) Reimbursement of Attorney Fees.

a) The Court shall determine, on information presented by accused of defendant's ability to partial to
pay appointed attorney fees

b) A person found to be partially eligible for defense services shall be required to make reimbursement to the Court as agreed at the time of adjudication

c) Any defendant who is placed on probation may
be required to reimburse the city for all or part of the
costs of appointed counsel

d) In no case shall appointed counsel set or attempt
to obtain personal reimbursement for the costs of
defense services

e) If reimbursement is part of an order of probation, failure to make payment by the defendant could
be sufficient to be a violation of probation

f) The appointed counsel's representation of a client
shall include the ability to oppose an order of the
Court requiring reimbursement for defense services,
provided there are arguable legal grounds for such
opposition

11) Jury instructions.

a) Time of submission shall be by 8:00 am the
morning prior to trial and an additional set shall be
served upon the opposing party

12) Trials.

a) Trial briefs shall be filed no later than two days
before trial

b) Any motions filed on the date of trial shall begin
at 8:15 am and jury trial shall begin at 8:30 am

c) Should the Court rule in a manner that requires
a continuance of the trial on the morning of the trial,
the Court shall assess the costs of the jury against the
attorney who the Court finds, in it's discretion, has
failed to properly recognize, note or resolve the issues
at the pre-trial hearing

d) Return of exhibits in a criminal case will be
returned to the party who produced that exhibit for
identification. The return shall be made upon written
application, following termination of the time for appeal. Exhibits not requested to be returned during
that period by the producing party may be delivered
by the Court to the local police authority for disposition by law as abandoned property; or if contraband,
for destruction. No exhibit shall be delivered without
being receipted for by the receiving party.

[Adopted September 1, 2010.]

RULE 5.   TRAFFIC CASES

1) Whenever a Notice of Infraction has been issued
and not filed with the Court within 48 hours, the Clerk
shall bring the untimely filing to the attention of the
Judge

a) If the citation is filed more than 72 hours after
issuance of the Notice of Infraction, excluding weekends and national holidays, the clerk may mark the
citation "dismissed without prejudice" and take no
further action (IRLJ 2.2)

b) Infraction witness fees incurred by a party as set
forth in RCW 46.63.151 shall pay the witness fees and
mileage expenses due that witness. Any person who
requests production of an electronic speed measuring
device expert, and is thereafter found by the Court to
have committed the infraction, shall be required to

pay the fee charged by the expert as a cost incurred by the party.

[Adopted September 1, 2010.]

RULE 6.   RECORD RETENTION

Municipal Court records shall be retained pursuant to the District and Municipal Court Records Retention Schedule provided by the State of Washington

[Adopted September 1, 2010.]

RULE 7.   RESERVATION OF DISCRETION

The Court reserves the authority to interpret and / or suspend or modify these rules in individual cases on motion or a party for good cause shown or its own motion in the interest of justice and /or the efficient operation of the Court

[Adopted September 1, 2010.]

STEVENSON MUNICIPAL COURT—
[No Local Rules]

SNOHOMISH COUNTY

Table of Courts

Superior Court

Local Rules for the Superior Court of Snohomish County.

District Courts

Snohomish County District Court Local Rules.

Municipal Courts

Brier Municipal Court—[No Local Rules].
Darrington Municipal Court—[No Local Rules].
Edmonds Municipal Court Local Court Rules.
Everett Municipal Court Rules.
Gold Bar Municipal Court—[No Local Rules].
Granite Falls Municipal Court—[No Local Rules].
Index Municipal Court—[No Local Rules].
Lynnwood Municipal Court Local Court Rules.
Marysville Municipal Court Local Rules.
Mill Creek Municipal Court—[No Local Rules].
Monroe Municipal Court.
Mountlake Terrace Municipal Court—[No Local Rules].
Mukilteo Municipal Court—[No Local Rules].
Snohomish Municipal Court—[No Local Rules].
Stanwood Municipal Court—[No Local Rules].
Sultan Municipal Court—[No Local Rules].
Woodway Municipal Court—[No Local Rules].

SUPERIOR COURT

LOCAL RULES FOR THE SUPERIOR COURT OF SNOHOMISH COUNTY

**Including Amendments Received Through
August 15, 2015**

Table of Rules

PART I.   ADMINISTRATIVE RULES
(SCLAR)

RULE 0.01.   CITATION—SCOPE

These rules shall be cited as SCLR (Snohomish County Local Rules). When a rule creates a requirement or duty of an "attorney," "counsel," or "lawyer," the rule shall equally apply to a party pro se.

RULE 0.02.   ORGANIZATION
OF THE COURT

(a) **Departments.** The Superior Court for Snohomish County is organized into the following departments: A Presiding Judge's Department; Trial Departments; Court Commissioner Departments; and Juvenile Departments. Trial departments may be given special calendar assignments.

(b) Commissioners and Clerks. Except where otherwise required by law or court rules, the terms "judge" and "court" include commissioners. The term "clerk" includes deputies and other employees authorized to act on behalf of the clerk. Court commissioners have the power, authority and jurisdiction established by RCW 2.24.040, including the specific authorization to accept pleas in adult criminal cases.

(c) Disqualification of Judge. No Judge shall be challenged or disqualified from hearing a matter except: (1) on written motion and affidavit filed in accordance with R.C.W. 4.12.040, et seq., prior to, or at the time of such challenge being made, or (2) when the judge disqualifies himself or herself.

(d) Judges Pro Tem. Judges pro tem shall be appointed by the Presiding Judge or designee, when required, in accordance with R.C.W. 2.08.180. Judges pro tem will be appointed from a list approved by the judges.

(e) Order in the Court–Arms–Recording Devices.

(1) *Sheriff and Bailiff Preserve Order.* The Sheriff or law enforcement officers, county security officers, and bailiff shall preserve order in the courtroom without special direction from the court, and may be armed.

(2) *Courtroom Security.* Commissioned peace or law enforcement officers, county security officers or bailiffs present in court shall be chargeable with maintaining courtroom security, under the direction of the judge, and pursuant thereto shall be permitted to possess firearms.

(3) *Arms and Weapons Prohibited.* No person, other than a county security officer, bailiff or commissioned peace or law enforcement officer, shall possess in court, or any area within the court's authority to prohibit or designate, any firearm or weapon, as defined by statutes relating to courtroom security, except as provided in this rule, unless such firearm or other weapon is or will be offered as an exhibit.

(4) *Recording and Photography.* The broadcasting, televising, recording or photographing of proceedings shall be allowed only with the approval of the court.

(f) Appearances–Business by Mail or Messenger.

(1) *Appearances.* All appearances before the court shall be by a party pro se, by an attorney admitted to practice in the State of Washington, by a legal intern authorized under A.P.R. 9, or by an attorney entitled to appear in a matter under A.P.R. 8(b).

(2) *Presentation by Mail.* Any order, finding, judgment or other document requiring the signature of a judge or commissioner may be presented by mail under the following conditions:

    (A) Signature on Pleadings. All such documents shall bear the personal original signature of counsel or party pro se presenting the same, and the endorsement of approval or waiver of notice of presentation signed by all non-presenting parties not previously adjudged in default, or their attorneys.

    (B) Covering Letter–Request for File. All such documents shall be accompanied by a covering letter of explanation personally signed by the presenting party pro se or an attorney and shall request the clerk to deliver the file to the judge or commissioner, if deemed appropriate.

    (C) Return Envelope. A self-addressed envelope bearing sufficient pre-paid postage for the return of any requested conformed copies shall be enclosed; and if not, all such copies may be discarded. If no such envelope is enclosed, and for any reason the presented order(s) are not signed, the same may be discarded without further notice.

    (D) Fees. A check or money order for all fees, including the clerk's processing fee, shall be included with the above documents.

(3) *Presentation by Messenger.* No order or judgment may be presented in open court or in chambers to any judge by any person not authorized to appear before the court as specified in these rules; provided, however, that an attorney or party may obtain from a judge or commissioner prior telephone or oral consent to the delivery of an order by a secretary, clerk, or messenger for signature in chambers, provided further, that such matters would not require testimony.

(g) Preassignments. Cases involving complex issues of fact or law, or in which substantial pretrial proceedings are anticipated, may be preassigned by the Presiding Judge or designee to a trial department at any time for pretrial proceedings and/or for trial. A preassignment may be made on motion of one or more parties to be decided without oral argument (unless requested by the court) or on motion of the court.

[Amended effective September, 1992; September 1, 1993; September 1, 1997; September 1, 2000.]

RULE 0.03. COURT ADMINISTRATION

Administration of the court shall be by such rules, policies and administrative orders, as defined in GR 7(a), as are established by a majority of the judges with notice to the Snohomish County Bar Association. Such rules, policies and administrative orders shall be on file with the Court Administrator and Snohomish County Law Library. They shall be made available to the Snohomish County Bar.

[Amended effective September 1, 1993; September 1, 2002.]

RULE 0.04. PILOT PROJECTS

Pilot Projects in Snohomish County Superior Court shall operate through published procedures approved by the Court.

[Adopted effective September 1, 2000.]

RULE 0.05. PRESIDING JUDGE

(a) **Election and Term.** The Judges shall meet to elect a Presiding Judge by majority vote. The election shall occur during the month of January following the first year of the term of the current Presiding Judge. Selection criteria will be in accord with those delineated in GR 29. The term of the Presiding Judge shall be three years and begin on January 1.

(b) **Assistant Presiding Judge.** The Assistant Presiding Judge shall serve as Acting Presiding Judge during the absence or upon request of the Presiding Judge. The immediate past Presiding Judge shall serve as Assistant Presiding Judge during year one of the current Presiding Judge's term. The incoming Presiding Judge shall serve as Assistant Presiding Judge during years two and three of the current Presiding Judge's term.

(c) **Duties.** The Presiding Judge and Assistant Presiding Judge shall perform all duties of the position required by General Rule 29.

(d) **Vacancies.** Vacancies in the office of Presiding Judge, or Assistant Presiding Judge shall be filled by majority vote of the judges at the first judges meeting held after the vacancy is known to exist.

(e) **Committees.** The Presiding Judge may create standing or ad-hoc committees to address policy matters relating to specific areas, and appoint Judges to chair and serve on those committees.

[Adopted effective July 1, 2002. Amended effective September 1, 2005; September 1, 2015.]

RULE 0.06. COURT RECORDS

Records Submitted for in Camera Review. Upon completion of in camera review of documents in a case, the documents shall be sealed by the clerk and maintained as an exhibit. The order sealing shall indicate the documents were presented to the court for in camera review and shall contain the notation: The court records sealed herein shall be maintained as an exhibit.

[Adopted effective March 10, 2005; amended effective September 1, 2005; rescinded effective September 1, 2006; reenacted on an emergency basis effective January 18, 2007; reenacted on a permanent basis effective September 1, 2007.]

PART II.   GENERAL RULES
(SCLGR)

RULE 15. SEALING AND REDACTION OF COURT RECORDS

(c)(1) Motions to seal or redact court records pursuant to GR 15 shall be noted before a judge or regularly appointed Court Commissioner. Motions to seal or redact may not be heard by a Judge Pro Tem or Court Commissioner Pro Tem unless the motion is brought to seal/redact Juvenile Court records pursuant to RCW 13.50.050 and is unopposed by the State.

(2) Any party or interested person who moves to seal or redact a court record shall propose written Findings of Fact and Conclusions of Law which identify the compelling privacy or safety concerns which are alleged to outweigh the public interest in access to the court record. Copies of the written Motion to Seal or Redact and proposed Findings of Fact and Conclusions of Law shall be served on all other parties and to the court at least six (6) court days before the date fixed for such hearing.

(3) Any party or interested person who moves to redact a court record shall provide the court, the clerk and each opposing party a redacted copy of the court record which is the subject of the motion to redact.

[Adopted effective September 1, 2006; amended on an emergency basis effective December 9, 2009; amended on a permanent basis effective September 1, 2010.]

PART III. CIVIL RULES
(SCLCR)

I. INTRODUCTORY (RULES 1–2A)
[RESERVED]

II. COMMENCEMENT OF ACTION: SERVICE OF PROCESS, PLEADINGS, MOTIONS AND ORDERS (RULES 3–6)

RULE 3. PETITION TO RESTORE FIREARMS

(a) Petitions to restore firearm rights shall be brought under a civil cause number pursuant to the civil rules.

(b) A party filing a petition to restore firearms rights must serve the Snohomish County Prosecutor, or his or her designee, at least 15 days before the scheduled hearing date. A petition that is not filed within the requirements of this rule will not be heard on the date noted for hearing.

(c) Service on the county prosecutor or his or her designee shall be made by (i) hand delivering a copy to the office of the prosecuting attorney and leaving it with the prosecutor, a deputy prosecutor, or clerk employed by the prosecutor's office or (ii) by mail. If service is by mail the provisions of CR5 (b)(2)(A)&(B) shall apply.

(d) The prosecutor may file a response to the petition to restore firearms rights. A response to the petition shall be filed and served at least two days before the scheduled hearing date.

[Adopted effective September 1, 2011. Amended effective September 2, 2014.]

RULE 6. TIME

(d) For Motions—Affidavits.

(1) *Notes for Civil Motions Calendar.* Responding documents and briefs must be filed with the clerk and copies served on all parties and the court no later than 12 noon two (2) court days prior to the hearing. Copies of any documents replying to the response must be filed with the clerk and served on all parties and the court not later than 12 noon of the court day prior to the hearing. This section does not apply to CR 56 summary judgment motions. Absent prior approval of the court, responsive or reply materials will not include either audio or video tape recordings.

(2) *Notes for Family Law Motion Calendar.* Any party desiring to bring any family law motion, other than a motion to reconsider (governed by SCLCR 59), on the family law motion calendar must file such motion documents with the Clerk and serve all parties and the court at least twelve (12) days before the date fixed for such hearing. Responding documents and briefs must be filed with the clerk and copies served on all parties and the court no later than 12:00 noon five (5) court days before the hearing. Copies of any additional responding or reply documents must be filed with the clerk and served on all parties and the Court not later than 12:00 noon three (3) court days before the hearing. Absent prior approval of the court, responsive or reply materials will not include either audio or video tape recordings.

[Adopted effective September 1, 2012.]

III. PLEADINGS AND MOTIONS (RULES 7–16)

RULE 7. PLEADINGS ALLOWED; FORM OF MOTIONS

(b) Motions and Other Papers.

(2) *Form.*

(A) Notes for Motion. The motion documents must include an order to show cause or a note for motion calendar, the motion, and supporting documents. The note for motion calendar must be on the form approved by the court. The note for motion calendar must be signed by the attorney or party pro se filing the same, with the designation of the party represented. The note for motion calendar must identify the type or nature of relief being sought. The note or other document shall provide a certification of mailing of all documents related to the motion. The certificate shall state the person and address to who such mailing was made, and who performed the mailing. Such mailing may not be made by a party to the action. Absent prior approval of the court, materials will not include audio or video tape recordings.

(B) Working Copies. Working copies of the motion and all documents in support or opposition shall be delivered by the party filing such documents to the judicial officer who is to consider the motion no later than the day they are to be served on all other parties. All working copies shall state, in the upper right corner, the following: the date and time of such hearing, the jurist assigned, if any, and the Department or room number of the department where the motion is to be heard.

(C) Late Filing; Terms. Any material offered at a time later than required by this rule may be stricken by the court and not considered. If the court decides to allow the late filing and consider the materials, the court may continue the matter or impose other appropriate remedies including terms, or both.

(D) Motion; Contents Of. A motion must contain the following (motions shall comply with any applicable mandatory form requirements):

1. Relief Requested. The specific relief the court is requested to grant;

2. Statement of Grounds. A concise statement of the grounds upon which the motion is based;

3. Statement of Issues. A concise statement of the issue(s) of law upon which the court is requested to rule;

4. Evidence Relied Upon. The evidence, on which the motion or reply is based, shall be identified with particularity. Absent prior court approval, this evidence shall not include audio or video tape recordings. Deposition testimony, discovery pleadings, and documentary evidence relied upon must be quoted verbatim, or a photocopy of relevant pages thereof must be attached to the motion. Deposition testimony in connection with a motion shall not require publication thereof unless a challenge is made thereto and good cause is shown for such publication by an opposing party. Depositions used in this fashion shall remain unopened and not a part of the court file unless otherwise ordered by the court. Any document in a language other than English shall be filed with a coversheet identifying the document.

5. Legal Authority. Any legal authority relied upon must be cited. Provided that items 2. through 5. above may be contained in a memorandum of authority in support of the motion.

6. Reapplication on Same Facts. Except as stated below, when a motion has been ruled upon in whole or in part, the same motion may not be later presented to another judge. If the prior ruling was made without prejudice or when the prior motion has been granted conditionally, and the condition has not been met, any subsequent motion may be presented as set forth below. Reapplication shall be made in the same manner as a motion to reconsider.

NOTE: SEE SCLCR 59 FOR MOTIONS FOR RECONSIDERATION.

7. Subsequent Motion; Different Facts. If a subsequent motion is made upon alleged different facts, the moving party must show by affidavit what motion was previously made, when and to which judge, what order or decision was made on it, and what new facts are claimed to be shown. For failure to comply with this requirement, the subsequent motion may be stricken, any order made upon such subsequent motion may be set aside, or provide such other relief as the court deems appropriate.

8. Land Use Petition Appeals.

(A) Filing. A party filing a Land Use Petition Appeal (LUPA) shall note a motion and an initial hearing, pursuant to RCW 36.70C.080, within seven days after serving the LUPA petition on the parties identified in RCW 36.70C.040(2). The motion and initial hearing will be set no sooner than 35 days and no later than 50 days after service of the parties. At the same time, the party filing the petition shall deliver working copies for the Superior Court Presiding Judge to Court Administration for pre-assignment of a Judge for the initial hearing.

(B) Motion. The Motion shall include the following:

1. Request for pre-assignment for initial LUPA Hearing

2. Specific relief and/or action sought at this time

3. List of the names, e-mail addresses (if known), telephone numbers and mailing addresses of all other attorneys in the case and/or all other parties requiring notification regarding this case

4. Proposed outline of hearing/filing deadlines based on the filing date as directed by statute.

5. Any other matters required by RCW 36.70C.080

(C) Pre-assignment. The presiding judge will assign the case to a judge who will handle the initial hearing and all other hearings in the case. The assigned judge may reschedule the initial hearing, if necessary, based on the assigned judge's availability.

(D) Other parties. The other parties shall note all matters required by RCW 36.70C.080 to be heard at the initial hearing.

9. Confirmation Process.

(A) Manner of Confirming. In order that a motion, or an order to show cause, or matter be argued or ruled upon, a party pro se or attorney for the moving party must confirm before 12 noon two (2) court days prior to the hearing;

otherwise the matter will be stricken. Only by stipulation of the parties and agreement of the court may an unconfirmed matter be heard. Confirmations shall be made electronically, in a format approved by the court, or by telephone. The case name, cause number, date and time of the motion, title or type of motion, calendar on which the motion appears, the name and telephone number of the person confirming, and E-mail address of the person confirming when confirmation is accomplished electronically, is information which must be provided to the person or recording taking the confirmation.

(B) Strikes or Continuances. The court must be notified immediately if any confirmed matter will be stricken or continued. No confirmed matter may be continued after 5:00 p.m. two court days before the hearing, except by leave of the court. Failure to notify of such continuance or strike of a confirmed motion may result in sanctions and/or terms.

10.   Time and Place of Hearing.

(A) Times, days, and locations of various motions shall be as set forth in an administrative order 11–11.

COMMISSIONER DEPARTMENTS 1st Floor of Courthouse

Type of Motions Noted for Type of Calendar

Family Law Domestic Motions Commissioner Family Law Domestic Motions calendar

Child Support Modification Motions/Final Orders Commissioner Child Support Modifications calendar

Pro Se Dissolutions Commissioner Pro Se Dissolutions calendar Domestic Violence Commissioner Domestic

Violence calendar

Motions for Summary Judgment to Establish Parentage Commissioner Family Law Domestic Motions calendar

Motions to Establish Parentage/State Initiated Commissioner State Paternity calendar

Defaults Commissioner Civil Motions calendar

Discovery Motions & enforcement thereof Commissioner Civil Motions calendar

Supplemental Proceedings Commissioner Civil Motions calendar

Unlawful Detainer/Eviction Commissioner Civil Motions calendar

Receiver Actions Commissioner Civil Motions calendar

Motions to Amend Pleadings Commissioner Civil Motions calendar

Motions for Inactive Status Commissioner Civil Motions calendar

Petitions for Restoration of Right to Possess Firearms Commissioner Civil Motions calendar

Probate Commissioner Guardianship/Probate calendar

Guardianship Commissioner Guardianship/Probate calendar

JUDICIAL CALENDARS—ASSIGNED TO DEPARTMENTS

Type of Motions Noted for Type of Calendar

All Civil Motions not Otherwise Described in this rule Judge's Civil Motions calendar

All Summary Judgment Motions not Otherwise Described in Judge's Civil Motions calendar

Initial TEDRA (Trust and Estate Dispute Resolution Act) Judge's Civil Motion calendar hearing pursuant to RCW 11.96A.100(8)

Motion to Revise Court Commissioner Rulings Judge's Civil Motions calendar

Motion to revise Juvenile Court Commissioner Rulings Juvenile Judge's calendar

Motions for pre assignment Presiding Judge

Motions regarding trial setting Presiding Judge

Motions regarding the timeliness for the demand for jury Presiding Judge

Motions for trial continuance Presiding Judge

Motions to Waive the Requirement for ADR before Trial Presiding Judge

(B) Unopposed Matters. If no one appears in opposition to a motion at the time set for hearing, the court may enter the order sought, unless the court deems it inappropriate to do so. If no one appears in support of a motion, the court may strike the matter or deny the motion unless the court deems it inappropriate to do so.

(C) Time for Argument Special Setting. No more than five (5) minutes per side will be allowed for argument unless specially permitted by the court. If more than one half (1/2) hour of judicial time, including preparation and in-court time, is required, the moving party shall at the earliest possible opportunity advise the confirmation clerk or law clerk/bailiff of the judge who will be hearing that calendar. The matter may then be preassigned, specially set, or placed on the trial calendar, at the discretion of the Presiding Judge or designee. If placed on the trial calendar, unless otherwise authorized by the court, the parties or their attorneys shall be present for the trial calendar call on the day of the setting. Upon stipulation of all parties or upon court order, a motion may be presented without oral argument.

(D) Shortening time. Before taking any action on less notice than that required by this or any other rule, a party must present a motion and affidavit, and must obtain an order to shorten time. The documents may be presented ex parte if the motion contains a written certification that the other parties prose or attorneys were notified of the time and place of the hearing requesting the order shortening time.

11. Presentation of Order. Each party shall have a proposed order prepared at the time the motion is called for hearing. Unless specifically authorized by the court, the prevailing party shall present a proposed order before the conclusion of the calendar on which the matter was heard.

12. Motions for Revision of Commissioner's Order. A party seeking revision of a commissioner's order shall, within the time specified by statute, file and serve on all other parties a motion and completed calendar note. The filing of the written order of the commissioner shall commence the running of the time. Review of rulings shall be de novo on the pleadings submitted to the commissioner. A transcript or recording of proceedings held before the commissioner shall not be filed or considered by the Court, unless specifically authorized by the judge hearing a motion to revise. Any motion for revision shall state each particular finding of fact, conclusion of law, order or ruling for which revision is sought. Any such motion shall additionally contain a brief statement, for each such claimed error, which states the movant's claim of the correct finding, conclusion, order, or ruling. The Motion for Revision shall be filed timely and shall be scheduled by the movant to be heard not more than 14 days after the motion is filed. Working Copies of the motion and all papers which were before the commissioner in support or opposition shall be delivered as provided in SCLCR 7(2)(B) by the party moving for revision.

[Amended effective October 1, 1990; July 1, 1991; September 1, 1992; September 1, 1993; September 1, 1994; September 1, 1996; September 1, 1997; September 1, 1998; September 1, 1999; September 1, 2000; September 1, 2001; September 1, 2002; September 1, 2003; September 1, 2005; September 1, 2006; September 1, 2007; amended on an emergency basis, effective December 12, 2007; amended on a permanent basis, effective September 1, 2008; amended effective September 1, 2009; amended on an emergency basis, effective January 13, 2010; amended on a permanent basis, effective September 1, 2010; September 1, 2012; amended on an emergency basis, effective December 7, 2012; amended on a permanent basis, effective September 2, 2013.]

RULE 10. FORM OF PLEADINGS AND OTHER PAPERS

(h) **Action Documents.** Pleadings or other papers requiring action on the part of the clerk, other than file stamping, docketing and placing in the file, shall be considered action documents. Action documents shall include a special caption directly below the case number on the first page, such as "Clerk's Action Required.

[Amended effective September 1, 1993; September 1, 1994; September 1, 1997; deleted effective September 1, 2001; amended effective September 1, 2012.]

RULE 11. SIGNING OF PLEADINGS

(a) **Address of Party Appearing Pro Se.** A party appearing pro se shall state on a notice of appearance, pleadings, and other documents filed by such party, his/her mailing address, street address where service of process and other papers may be made, telephone number and email address. A party pro se shall advise the court and other parties by written notice of any changes of address and/or telephone and email address. Upon request, the clerk shall provide a form, approved by the court, for this purpose.

(b) **Notice of Rule Requirements.** When a party physically appears in court, pursuant to process served upon him/her, but without an attorney and without filing a written pleading or other paper, the clerk shall deliver a printed Notice of Appearance form containing the substance of subsection (a) of this rule and approved by the court. This notice shall be completed by the party pro se and filed.

[Amended effective September 1, 1993; September 1, 2010; September 1, 2012.]

RULE 15. AMENDED AND SUPPLEMENTAL PLEADINGS

(e) **Interlineations.**

(1) *Pleadings and Other Papers.* Interlineations, corrections and deletions on pleadings and all other papers to be filed with the clerk shall be initialed by the party or counsel filing them.

[Amended effective September 1, 2009; September 1, 2012.]

RULE 16. STATUS CONFERENCES [REPEALED]

[Adopted effective September 1, 1994; amended effective September 1, 1997; September 1, 1999; repealed effective September 1, 2009.]

IV. PARTIES (RULES 17–25) [RESERVED]

V. DEPOSITIONS AND DISCOVERY (RULES 26–37)

RULE 26. GENERAL PROVISIONS GOVERNING DISCOVERY

(k) Completion of Discovery. Unless otherwise stipulated to by the parties, or ordered by the court upon good cause shown and such terms and conditions as are just, all discovery allowed under CR 26—37, including responses and supplementation thereto, must be completed no later than 35 calendar days prior to the date assigned for trial. Nothing herein stated shall modify a party's responsibility to promptly supplement responses to discovery rules or otherwise comply with discovery prior to the 35–day cutoff. In any case brought under Title 26 R.C.W. discovery will be completed no later than the date of confirmation required by Rule 40(d)(1).

[Adopted effective September 1, 2012.]

RULE 37. FAILURE TO MAKE DISCOVERY: SANCTIONS [DELETED]

[Amended effective September 1, 1992; September 1, 1996; September 1, 2009; deleted effective September 1, 2012.]

VI. TRIALS (RULES 38–53.2)

RULE 38. JURY TRIAL OF RIGHT

(b) Demand for Jury.

(1) *Must Be on Separate Document.* A Demand for Jury Trial shall be contained in a separate document.

RULE 39. TRIAL BY JURY OR BY THE COURT [DELETED]

[Adopted effective September 1, 2009; deleted effective September 1, 2012.]

RULE 40. ASSIGNMENT OF CASES; SETTING OF TRIALS—FILING OF PLEADINGS—TIME OF TRIALS—CONTINUANCES—SETTLEMENT

(b) Methods; Noting of Non-criminal Cases.

(1) The original Note for Trial and Initial Statement of Arbitrability, in the form approved by the court, is to be filed and served in the manner provided in CR 40 and a copy shall be served upon the Director of Arbitration. Such note SHALL be in the form of, and contain ALL requested information in such form as is required by the court. Presence of counsel or parties pro se is not required. In the event of non-appearance, the matter shall be set regularly and counsel of record and parties pro se indicated on the Note for Trial and Initial Statement of Arbitrability form will be notified by mail of the trial date and, where appropriate, of assignment to arbitration.

(2) If after two years, a case, other than a family law case, has not been resolved or noted for trial under this rule, the court may require the parties to appear to show cause why the matter should not be set for trial or the court should not take other appropriate action. Any trial set pursuant to this subsection shall be deemed confirmed by the court. Such hearings shall be set on the clerk's dismissal calendar

of the court commissioner, unless otherwise ordered. For family law cases, refer to SCLSPR 94.04(c) (1).

(c) Trials.

(1) *Confirmation.* It shall be the duty of each attorney of record or party pro se in a case set for trial to jointly or separately confirm, no sooner than 12 noon of the first court day of the week and no later than 12 noon of the last court day of the week two weeks prior to the trial date, in such written or electronic form as approved by the court. The court may strike the trial date and may impose sanctions and/or terms against the parties or counsel for failure to so confirm, including dismissal of the case.

(2) *Alternative Dispute Resolution.* At time of confirmation the parties shall provide proof of compliance with SCLSPR 94.04(g).

(g) Reduction or Waiver of Jury. If a jury is to be waived or reduced from a twelve (12) to a six (6) member panel, the Court Administrator MUST be so notified no later than 12 noon on the last court day of the week prior to the trial date, except as approved by the court.

(h) Reporting for Trial. All parties shall report to the Presiding Department at 9:00 a.m. on the date set for trial for assignment to a trial department unless otherwise notified by the Court Administrator. If no trial department is available for trial at such time, the Presiding Judge shall hold or excuse the parties for such time as circumstances dictate.

(i) Civil Trials; Reporting Voir Dire and Closing Arguments. Counsel must advise the court prior to trial if they wish to have voir dire, opening statements and closing arguments reported. Approval of such request shall be within the discretion of the court.

[Amended effective July 1, 1991; September 1, 1992; September 1, 1993; September 1, 1995; September 1, 1996; September 1, 1997; September 1,1999; September 1, 2000. Amended on an emergency basis effective October 3, 2005; amended on a permanent basis effective September 1, 2006; amended effective September 1, 2009; amended on an emergency basis effective January 13, 2010; amended on a permanent basis effective September 1, 2010; September 1, 2012.]

RULE 41. DISMISSAL OF ACTIONS

(g.) Request for Inactive Case Status.

(1) *How Made.* In civil cases where a point of stability has been reached such that there will be no need for further litigation, but where it may not be in the interests of the parties or of justice to dismiss the case; any party may file a motion requesting that the case be removed from the active pending caseload of the court to an inactive status.

(2) *Placement in Inactive Case Status.* Placement in an inactive case status under this rule shall be by order of the court. A case in an inactive case status shall not be subject to notice of clerk's dismissal. Every five years following placement in inactive case status, the clerk will notify all parties that unless requested otherwise by the parties, the court will order the case to be removed from inactive status. A motion for extension of the inactive status shall be made in the same manner as the initial motion for inactive status pursuant to SCLCR 7.

(3) *Removal from Inactive Case Status.* A case placed in inactive case status under this rule may not be removed from this status except upon order of the court or upon notice by the parties that the case has been disposed. Any party may file a motion requesting that a case be removed from inactive status. Such motion shall be set on the civil motions calendar of the Court Commissioner.

[Adopted effective September 1, 1993; amended effective September 1, 1999. Amended on an emergency basis effective October 3, 2005; amended on a permanent basis effective September 1, 2006; amended effective September 1, 2009; September 1, 2010.]

RULE 43. TELEPHONIC TESTIMONY [DELETED]

[Adopted on an emergency basis effective June 11, 2008; adopted on an permanent basis effective September 1, 2008; deleted effective September 1, 2012.]

RULE 47. JURORS [REPEALED]

[Adopted on an emergency basis effective June 11, 2008; adopted on an permanent basis effective September 1, 2008; repealed effective September 1, 2009.]

RULE 50. MOTION FOR A DIRECTED VERDICT AND FOR JUDGMENT NOTWITHSTANDING VERDICT OR FOR A NEW TRIAL [REPEALED]

[Adopted on an emergency basis effective June 11, 2008; adopted on an permanent basis effective September 1, 2008; repealed effective September 1, 2009.]

RULE 51. INSTRUCTIONS TO JURY AND DELIBERATIONS

(a) Proposed [Reserved]

(b) **Submission.** Proposed instructions, including supplemental instructions and copies shall be submitted as follows:

(1) An original, numbered and with citations, and stamped "original" on the first page shall be provided to the courtroom clerk.

(2) One copy, numbered and with citations, and one copy without citations or numbers shall be provided to the trial judge.

(3) One copy without citations or numbers in Word compatible electronic format shall be provided to the trial judge, unless this requirement is waived by the court.

(4) One copy, numbered and with citations, shall be served on each opposing counsel or party pro se.

[Amended effective September 1, 1993; September 1, 2003; September 1, 2007; September 1, 2009; September 1, 2012.]

RULE 52. DECISIONS, FINDINGS AND CONCLUSIONS

(1) **Findings and Conclusions;** the substantially prevailing party shall prepare proposed findings and conclusions. Any party objecting to proposed Findings of Fact and/or Conclusions of Law shall comply with:

(A) Proposed Changes in Opposition. Provide the court and opposing counsel with a copy of such proposed documents, which indicate all changes the objecting party proposes. Deletions shall be shown by a strike out and additions shown by underlining; or

(B) Alternate Proposed Documents. Provide the court and opposing counsel with a complete set of alternate proposed documents which easily identifies proposed deletions and additions.

(C) Oral objections at the time of presentation, without documentation as provided in (A) or (B) above, will not be permitted.

[Amended effective September 1, 2009.]

VII. JUDGMENT (RULES 54–63)

RULE 54. JUDGMENTS AND COSTS

(g) Interlineations.

Any interlineations, corrections, and deletions in orders and judgments signed by the judge/commissioner must be initialed by the judge/commissioner.

[Amended effective September 1, 2009; September 1, 2012.]

RULE 55. DEFAULT JUDGMENTS AND DECREES; EXCEPT FOR DISSOLUTIONS [REPEALED]

[Repealed effective September 1, 2009.]

RULE 56. SUMMARY JUDGMENT

(c) Motion and Proceedings.

(1) *Procedure.*

(A) Motions for summary judgment or other relief under CR 56 shall comply in all respects with SCLCR 7 except as modified by this rule.

(B) Time of Hearing.

(i) Motions for summary judgment are heard at a time and place as set forth in as in SCLCR 7.

(ii) Time for Argument. No more than ten (10) minutes per side will be allowed for argument unless additional time is allowed by the court. If more than one (1) hour of judicial time, including preparation and in court time, is required, the moving party shall so advise the law clerk/bailiff of the judge who will be hearing that calendar. The matter may then be preassigned, specially set, or placed on the trial calendar, at the discretion of the court.

[Amended effective October 1, 1990; September 1, 1993; September 1, 2005; September 1, 2009; September 1, 2012.]

RULE 58. ENTRY OF JUDGMENT

(a) When.

(1) *Judgments and Orders to Be Filed Forthwith.* Unless otherwise authorized by the court, any order, judgment, or decree that has been signed by the court shall not be taken from the courthouse, but must be filed forthwith in the clerk's office or with the clerk in the courtroom, by the attorney or party pro se obtaining said order.

(d) *Judgments on Notes.* An attorney or party pro se filing a judgment on a negotiable instrument must attach to the judgment the original instrument unless the original has been previously filed.

[Amended effective September 1, 2009.]

RULE 59. NEW TRIAL, RECONSIDERATION AND AMENDMENT OF JUDGMENTS; POST TRIAL MOTIONS

(e) Hearing on Motion.

(3) *Nature of Hearing.*

(A) Proposed Order. Each party must include in the materials delivered to the judge a proposed order sustaining his/her side of the argument. Should any party desire a copy of the order signed and filed by the judge, a pre-addressed, stamped envelope shall accompany the proposed order.

(B) Oral Argument. At the time of filing a motion under this rule, the moving party shall comply with CR 59(b) by filing a calendar note, setting the motion before the court which heard the motion. Absent order of the court, the motion will be taken under advisement. Oral arguments will be scheduled only if the court requests the same.

[Amended effective October 1, 1990; September 1, 1992; September 1, 1993; September 1, 1998; September 1, 2009.]

VIII. PROVISIONAL AND FINAL REMEDIES (RULES 64–71)

RULE 65. INJUNCTIONS [DELETED]

[Deleted effective September 1, 2012.]

RULE 69. EXECUTION

(b) Supplemental Proceedings.

(1) *Time.* Supplemental proceedings shall be noted as set forth in SCLCR 7, or at such other time as designated by the court.

(2) *Failure to Appear.*

(A) Debtor. Failure of the person to be examined to appear may result in issuance of a bench warrant by the court, provided that specific warning of that consequence was contained in the order directing supplemental proceedings. Service of such order must be made personally upon the debtor.

(B) Examining Attorney. Failure of the examining attorney to appear may result in release of the debtor from examination and may result in imposition of terms against the attorney if subsequent supplemental proceedings are scheduled for the same debtor.

[Amended effective September 1, 2007; September 1, 2012.]

IX. APPEALS (RULES 72–76) [RESERVED]

RULE 72. FILING OF LAND USE PETITIONS (LUPA) [REPEALED]

[Adopted effective September 1, 2004; Repealed effective September 1, 2007.]

X. SUPERIOR COURTS AND CLERKS (RULES 77–80)

RULE 77. SUPERIOR COURTS AND JUDICIAL OFFICERS

(f) Sessions. The court shall be in session generally from 9:00 a.m.—12:00 p.m. and 1:00 p.m.—4:30 p.m., Monday—Friday (excluding legal holidays) at the discretion of the judge hearing the matter.

[Amended September 1, 1993; September 1, 1997; September 1, 1999; September 1, 2009.]

RULE 79. BOOKS AND RECORDS KEPT BY THE CLERK

(d) Other Books and Records of Clerk.

(1) *Exhibits; Filing and Substitution.* All exhibits and other papers received in evidence during trial must be filed at the time, but the court may, either then or by leave granted thereafter, upon notice, permit a copy of any such exhibit or other paper to be filed or substituted in the files, in lieu of the original.

(A) Exhibits Kept Separate. Exhibits shall be kept by the clerk separate from the file(s) in the case.

(B) Exhibits; Inspection. Unless otherwise ordered by the court, exhibits shall not be inspected in the clerk's office except in the presence of a clerk.

(C) Original Court Record; Copies. An original court record shall not be admitted as an exhibit, but a copy thereof may be so admitted.

(D) Exhibits; Packaged and Labeled. Exhibits containing bloodborn pathogens, drugs, firearms or dangerous weapons shall be properly packaged and labeled before acceptance by the court. To meet packaging and labeling requirements, exhibits shall conform to the following criteria when presented:

(i) Bloodborn pathogens shall be packaged in sturdy plastic containers. If contained in a vial or hypodermic, each shall be placed in an individual sturdy plastic container or styrofoam container. All items shall be labeled to identify the contents as potentially biologically hazardous materials.

(ii) Drugs shall be placed in sealed containers to prevent or reduce emissions from the container. They shall be labeled identifying the contents.

(iii) Firearms shall be unloaded, any breech mechanism or cylinder shall be open, and a secured trigger lock shall be in place.

(iv) Dangerous weapons shall have any sharp or pointed portions sheathed in a manner to prevent injury or contact with the sharp or pointed portions.

(v) Paper bags alone shall not constitute proper packaging.

(2) *Unsuitable Materials.* Whenever any paper or other material is presented to the clerk for filing but is deemed by the clerk to be improper or inappropriate for filing, the clerk shall affix the file mark thereto and may forthwith orally apply to the court for a determination of the propriety of filing the material presented. If the court determines that the document or material should not be made a part of the file, an order shall be entered to that effect that the unsuitable document or material shall be retained by the clerk as an exhibit in the cause. The court may order that the unsuitable document or material be sealed, in which event the requirements of GR 15 shall apply.

(3) *Same; Not Evidence Unless Ordered.* Exhibits filed pursuant to subsection two (2) hereof shall not be evidence in the cause unless by order of the trial judge entered on notice and hearing.

(4) *Withdrawal of Files and Exhibits.*

(A) Files. The clerk shall permit no file to be taken from the clerk's office or the clerk's custody, except to the courtroom, or to a judge, commissioner, referee, law clerk/bailiff, official court reporter, or the Court Administrator or deputy unless written authority has first been obtained. Files that are in the custody of an attorney for the purpose of a trial or hearing must be returned to the clerk at the conclusion thereof. The court or the clerk, may with discretion and on application in writing, grant written authority to the applicant to withdraw one or more files from the clerk's custody for a period not exceeding ten (10) days. Only the court may authorize the withdrawal of specified clerk's files for a period in excess of ten (10) days. Such applicant shall return the file, and all of its papers, in good order, and shall not remove, even temporarily, any staples from any papers.

(B) Same; Verbatim Report of Proceedings. The Report of Proceedings after having been settled and signed, shall not be withdrawn from the clerk's office.

(C) Exhibits; Temporary Withdrawl[1]. Exhibits may be withdrawn temporarily from the custody of the clerk only by:

    (i) The judge having the cause under consideration.

    (ii) Official court reporters and law clerks/bailiffs, without court order, for use in connection with duties.

    (iii) Attorneys of record, upon court order, after notice to or with the consent of opposing counsel. The clerk shall require an itemized receipt for all exhibits withdrawn, and upon their return, they shall be checked against the original receipt.

(D) Failure to Return Files or Exhibits; Sanctions. If any person fails to return any file or exhibit within the time required, and fails to comply with the clerk's request for return thereof, the clerk may, without notice to the attorney or other person concerned, apply to the Presiding Judge for an order for the immediate return of such files or exhibits. A certified copy of such order, if entered, shall then be served upon the attorney or other person involved.

(E) Exhibits; Permanent Withdrawal. After final judgment and after the time for appeal, and no appeal having been taken, the court, on application of any party or other person entitled to the possession of one or more exhibits, and for good cause shown, may with discretion order the withdrawal of such exhibit(s) and delivery to such party or other person.

    (i) Same; Narcotics. When narcotics or dangerous drugs have been admitted in evidence or have been identified, and are being held by the clerk as a part of the records and files in a criminal case, and all proceedings in the cause having been completed, the prosecuting attorney may apply to the court for an order directing the clerk to deliver such drugs to an authorized representative of the law enforcement agency initiating the prosecution, for disposition according to law. If the court finds these facts and is of the opinion that there will be no further need for such drugs, it shall enter an order accordingly. The clerk shall then deliver the drugs and take from the law enforcement agent a receipt which shall be filed in the cause. The clerk shall also file any certificate issued by an authorized federal or state agency and received by a representative thereof showing the nature of such drugs.

(F) Return of Exhibits and Unopened Depositions. In any non-criminal cause, on a stipulation of the parties that when judgment in the cause shall become final, after an appeal, or upon judgment of dismissal, or upon filing of a satisfaction of judgment, the clerk may return all exhibits and unopened depositions or may destroy them. Absent such stipulation of the parties, the clerk is authorized to seek an order, under SCLCR 79(d)(E), upon notice to parties, for withdrawal and destruction of all offered and entered exhibits, opened and unopened depositions.

(G) Original Court Audio Recordings. Audio recordings produced in any court, such as a court of limited jurisdiction, and submitted to the Court Clerk, are original records of the submitting court's proceedings. These recordings will not be withdrawn from the Clerk. The Clerk shall make a copy of such recordings, or, at the Clerk's discretion, the portion of the recordings which relates only to the proceeding at issue.

(5) *Videotaped Depositions.* Videotaped depositions published in open court shall be treated as court exhibits, with the same retention standards. Except as ordered by the court, if a party wishes such published deposition to be a part of the court file, then the party shall submit a true and accurate transcript of such deposition.

(e) Destruction of Records.

(1) *Electronically Scanned Records.* Records, or portions thereof, and records that have been destroyed pursuant to R.C.W. 36.23.065, may be reproduced and used in accordance with R.C.W. 36.23.067 for a trial or hearing. The party or attorney needing a reproduction of a scanned or microfilmed record or records shall request the clerk at least six (6) court days before the scheduled court date to reproduce the necessary materials.

[Amended effective September 1, 1992; September 1, 1993; September 1, 2008; September 1, 2012.]

_____
1 So in original.

XI. GENERAL PROVISIONS (RULES 81–86)

RULE 84. FORMS [DELETED]

[Deleted effective September 1, 2012.]

PART IV. MANDATORY ARBITRATION RULES (SCLMAR)

1. SCOPE AND PURPOSE OF RULES

RULE 1.1. APPLICATION OF RULES— PURPOSE AND DEFINITION

(a) **Purpose.** The purpose of mandatory arbitration of civil actions under RCW 7.06, as implemented by the Mandatory Arbitration Rules (MAR), is to provide a simplified and economical procedure for obtaining the prompt and equitable resolution of disputes involving claims of fifty thousand dollars ($50,000.00) or less, exclusive of attorney fees, interest and costs, and claims in which the sole relief sought is the establishment, modification, or termination of maintenance or child support payments regardless of the number or amount of such payments. Mandatory Arbitration Rules (MAR) as supplemented by these Local Mandatory Arbitration Rules (SCLMAR) are not designed to address every question that may arise during the arbitration process, and the rules give considerable discretion to the arbitrator. The arbitrator should not hesitate to exercise that discretion. Arbitration hearings should be informal and expeditious, consistent with the purpose of relevant statutes and rules.

(b) **"Director" Defined.** In these rules, "Director" means the Director of Arbitration for the Snohomish County Superior Court. The appointment of the Di-

rector and other administrative matters are addressed in SCLMAR 8.6.

[Amended effective September 1, 2007.]

RULE 1.2. MATTERS SUBJECT TO ARBITRATION

Pursuant to the authority granted by statute, a claim is subject to mandatory arbitration only if it does not exceed fifty thousand dollars ($50,000), exclusive of attorney fees, interest and costs; or if it involves solely the establishment, modification, or termination of child support or maintenance payments or arrearages, regardless of the number or amount of such payments; or if it is a small claims matter appealed from District Court.

[Amended on an emergency basis effective November 9, 2005; amended on a permanent basis effective September 1, 2006.]

RULE 1.3. RELATIONSHIP TO SUPERIOR COURT JURISDICTION AND OTHER RULES—MOTIONS [DELETED]

[Amended effective September 1, 1992; September 1, 1993; deleted effective September 1, 2012.]

2. TRANSFER TO ARBITRATION AND ASSIGNMENT OF ARBITRATOR

RULE 2.1. TRANSFER TO ARBITRATION

(a) **Time of Transfer.** A matter is deemed transferred to Arbitration upon filing of the Note for Trial and Initial Statement of Arbitrability.

(b) **Note for Trial Setting and Initial Statement of Arbitrability.** In every civil case the party filing a notice for trial provided by CR 40(a)(1) and SCLCR 40(b) shall serve the Director and all parties and file with the clerk a Note for Trial and Initial Statement of Arbitrability on the form prescribed by the court.

(c) **Response to an Initial Statement of Arbitrability.** Within fourteen (14) days after the Note for Trial and Initial Statement of Arbitrability has been served and filed, any party disagreeing with the Note for Trial and Initial Statement of Arbitrability shall

serve the Director and all parties and file with the clerk a Response to the Note for Trial and Initial Statement of Arbitrability on a form prescribed by the court. In the absence of such response, the Note for Trial and Initial Statement of Arbitrability shall be deemed correct and a non-responding party shall be deemed to have stipulated to arbitration if the Note for Trial and Initial Statement of Arbitrability provides that the case is arbitrable. If a party asserts that a claim exceeds fifty thousand dollars ($50,000.00) or seeks relief other than a money judgment (except for the establishment, modification or termination of child support or maintenance payments regardless of the number or amount of such payments), the case is not subject to arbitration except by stipulation. If a party incorrectly asserts in the Note for Trial and Initial Statement of Arbitrability that a case is not arbitrable, the court may at any time prior to trial on its own motion transfer such case to mandatory arbitration and strike any scheduled trial date.

(d) Failure to File Amendments. A party failing to serve and file an original Response within the time prescribed may later do so only upon leave of court. A party may amend the Note for Trial and Initial Statement of Arbitrability or Response at any time before assignment of an arbitrator or assignment of a trial date, and thereafter only upon leave of court for good cause shown. The parties may amend a Note for Trial and Initial Statement of Arbitrability or Response from non-arbitrable to arbitrable at any time prior to trial by written stipulation served on the Director and filed with the clerk.

(e) By Stipulation. A case in which all parties file a stipulation to arbitrate under MAR 8.1(b) will be placed on the arbitration calendar regardless of the nature of the case or amount in controversy.

(f) Jury Demand. Where any party indicates, pursuant to this rule, that the case is arbitrable or stipulates to arbitration, that party may simultaneously demand a jury trial in the form and manner set forth in these local rules. The case shall then be assigned a position on the jury trial calendar as provided in section (g) of this rule. The jury demand must be made and the jury fee paid not later than the time at which the initial statement of arbitrability is filed which indicates the matter is arbitrable or by a party responding to the initial statement when the response to the statement is filed, otherwise the right to trial by jury is waived unless, after the arbitration decision, a jury demand is filed at the time in the manner set forth in SCLMAR 7.1(b)(2)(ii).

(g) Trial Calendar. A non-jury case that is assigned to arbitration shall not be assigned a position on the trial calendar except as provided in SCLMAR 7.1. A jury case that is assigned to arbitration shall simultaneously be assigned a position on the jury trial calendar.

[Amended effective October 1, 1990; July 1, 1991; September 1, 1992; September 1, 1993; September 1, 2007.]

RULE 2.2. COURT MAY DETERMINE ARBITRABILITY

(a) Motions; How Made. Motions to establish whether a case is actually subject to arbitration shall be governed by the state and local rules pertaining to civil motions practice. Such motions shall be noted for hearing on a date not more than twenty-one (21) days from the date the response is filed and served if the Note for Trial and Initial Statement of Arbitrability provides that the case is arbitrable. A party failing to timely note such cases for motion shall be deemed to have stipulated to arbitration unless otherwise ordered by the court for good cause shown. Such stipulations to arbitration under this rule shall be

established by ex parte court order and shall be filed with the clerk and shall be served upon all parties and the Director.

(b) Determination of Non-Arbitrability. If upon motion the court determines that a case is not arbitrable, all parties shall report to the trial calendar coordinator in court administration to obtain a trial date.

(c) Determination of Arbitrability. If upon motion the court determines that a case is arbitrable, the prevailing party shall serve upon the Director an order transferring the case to arbitration and if a non-jury trial date has been set, it shall be stricken by the Director subject to being renoted pursuant to SCLMAR 7.1.

[Amended October 1, 1990; September 1, 1997; September 1, 2012.]

RULE 2.3. ASSIGNMENT OF ARBITRATOR

(a) Generally; Stipulations. When a case is set for arbitration, a list of five (5) proposed arbitrators will be furnished to the parties. Except to determine the proposed arbitrator's availability, the parties shall not contact the arbitrator regarding the matter being arbitrated. A master list of arbitrators will be made available on request. The parties are encouraged to stipulate to an arbitrator. In the absence of a stipulation, the arbitrator will be chosen from among the five (5) proposed arbitrators in the manner defined by this rule.

(b) Response by Parties. Each party may, within fourteen (14) days after a list of proposed arbitrators is furnished to the parties, nominate one (1) or two (2) arbitrators and strike two (2) arbitrators from the list. If both parties respond, an arbitrator nominated by both parties will be appointed. If no arbitrator has been nominated by both parties, the Director will appoint an arbitrator from among those not stricken by either party.

(c) Response by Only One (1) Party. If only one (1) party responds within fourteen (14) days, the Director will appoint an arbitrator nominated by that party.

(d) No Response. If neither party responds within fourteen (14) days, the Director will appoint one (1) of the five (5) proposed arbitrators.

(e) Additional Arbitrators for Additional Parties. If there are more than two (2) adverse parties, such parties may request the Director to include additional proposed arbitrators on the list, with the above principles of selection to be applied. The number of adverse parties and additional proposed arbitrators shall be determined by the Director, subject to review by the Presiding Judge.

[Amended effective October 1, 1990; September 1, 1993.]

3. ARBITRATORS

RULE 3.1. QUALIFICATIONS

(a) Minimum Qualifications. An arbitrator must be a member of the Washington State Bar Association who has been admitted to the Bar for a minimum of five (5) years, or who is a retired Superior Court Judge or Commissioner. By stipulation the parties to a case may agree to an arbitrator not on the Snohomish County Arbitration Panel if the arbitrator so chosen is a duly qualified member of an arbitration panel established under Local Mandatory Arbitration Rules of another county in the State of Washington. The parties may stipulate to a non-lawyer arbitrator upon approval of the Director.

(b) Arbitration Panel. There shall be a panel of arbitrators in such numbers as the Director may from time to time determine. A person desiring to serve as an arbitrator shall complete an information sheet on the form prescribed by the court. A list showing the names of arbitrators available to hear cases and the information sheets will be available for public inspection in the Director's office. The oath of office on the form prescribed by the court must be completed and filed prior to an applicant being placed on the panel.

(c) Refusal–Disqualification. The appointment of an arbitrator is subject to the right of that person to refuse to serve. An arbitrator must notify the Director immediately if refusing to serve or if any cause exists for the arbitrator's disqualification from the case upon any of the grounds of interest, relationship, bias or prejudice set forth in CJC Canon 3(c) governing the disqualification of judges. If disqualified, the arbitrator must immediately return all materials of a case to the Director.

[Amended effective September 1, 1993; amended on an emergency basis, effective December 8, 2010; June 6, 2010; amended on a permanent basis, effective September 1, 2011.]

RULE 3.2. AUTHORITY OF ARBITRATORS

In addition to the authority conferred on arbitrators under MAR 3.2, an arbitrator has the authority to:

1. Determine the time, place and procedure to present a motion before the arbitrator;

2. Require a party or attorney representing such party, or both, to pay the reasonable expenses, including attorney's fees, caused by the failure of such party or attorney, or both, to obey an order of the arbitrator, unless the arbitrator finds that the failure was substantially justified or that other circumstances make an award of expenses unjust. The arbitrator shall make a special award for such expenses and shall file such award with the clerk, with proof of service of party(s). The aggrieved party shall have ten (10) days thereafter to appeal the award of such expenses in accordance with the procedures described in RCW 2.24.050. If within ten (10) days after the award is filed no party appeals, a judgment shall be entered in a manner described generally under MAR 6.3; and

3. Award attorney's fees as authorized by these rules, by contract or by law.

Motions for involuntary dismissal and motions for summary judgment shall be decided by the court and not by the arbitrator. Agreed orders which are dispositive shall be presented to the court.

[Amended effective July 1, 1991; September 1, 1992; September 1, 1993.]

4. PROCEDURE AFTER ASSIGNMENT

RULE 4.2. DISCOVERY

(a) Discovery Pending at the Time Case Is Transferred to Arbitration. Except upon stipulation of the parties or as may be otherwise authorized by MAR 4.2 or by SCLMAR 4.2(c) below discovery pending at the time a case is transferred to arbitration is stayed. However, interrogatories with the exact language as set out below are permitted:

1. State the amount of general damages being claimed or the amount and basis of support and arrearages being sought.

2. State each item of special damages being claimed, and the amount thereof.

3. List the name, address, and phone number of each person having knowledge of any facts regarding liability.

4. List the name, address, and phone number of each person having knowledge of any facts regarding damages claimed or the amount and basis of support and arrearages being sought.

5. List the name, address, and phone number of each expert witness you intend to call at the arbitration. For each such expert, state the subject matter on which the expert is expected to testify; state the substance of the facts and opinions to which the expert is expected to testify, and a summary of the grounds for each opinion.

(b) Additional Discovery. In determining when additional discovery beyond that directly authorized by MAR 4.2 is reasonably necessary, the arbitrator shall balance the benefits of discovery against the burdens and expenses. The arbitrator shall consider the nature and complexity of the case, the amount in controversy, values at stake, the discovery that has already occurred, the burdens on the party from whom discovery is sought, and the possibility of unfair surprise which may result if discovery is restricted. Authorized discovery shall be conducted in accordance with the Civil Rules except that motions concerning discovery shall be determined by the arbitrator.

(c) Admissibility of Discovery. All discovery admissible under the Civil Rules or Rules of Evidence will be admissible at the arbitration hearing whether or not such discovery was produced before or after the appointment of an arbitrator.

[Amended effective September 1, 1993.]

5. HEARING

RULE 5.1. NOTICE OF HEARING

(a) Notice of Hearing—Time and Place—Continuance. An arbitration hearing shall be scheduled to be heard in Snohomish County, unless otherwise agreed by the parties, at any reasonable time and place chosen by the arbitrator. The arbitrator may grant a continuance without court order for good cause shown. The parties may stipulate to a continuance only with the permission of the arbitrator. The arbitrator shall give reasonable notice of the hearing date and any continuances to the Director and all parties.

(b) Confirmation–Settlement or Other Disposition. The parties shall confirm scheduled arbitration hearing dates with the arbitrator at least one (1) week prior to the hearing. Failure to timely confirm a scheduled arbitration hearing may result in cancellation of the hearing by the arbitrator. The parties shall also promptly notify an arbitrator of any prehearing case settlement or other disposition.

(c) Waiver of Hearing–Child Support Modification Matters. In cases of child support modification, the parties may stipulate to waive oral argument and testimony. Such waiver shall be in writing, on a form approved by the court, if any. Such writing shall specify the documents and written materials to be considered by the arbitrator. It shall be submitted prior to the confirmation date as set forth in subsection (b).

[Amended effective September 1, 1994; amended on an emergency basis effective June 11, 2008; amended on a permanent basis effective September 1, 2008; amended on an emergency basis effective December 8, 2010; effective June 6, 2010; amended on a permanent basis effective September 1, 2011.]

RULE 5.2. PREHEARING STATEMENT OF PROOF—DOCUMENTS FILED WITH COURT

In addition to the requirements of MAR 5.2, each party shall also furnish the arbitrator with copies of pleadings and other documents contained in the court file which that party deems relevant. The court file shall remain with the clerk.

RULE 5.3. CONDUCT OF HEARING— WITNESSES—RULES OF EVIDENCE

(f) Offers of Settlement. The parties shall, prior to conclusion of the arbitration hearing, advise the arbitrator in general terms that an offer of settlement has been made pursuant to RCW 4.84.250. Such advisement shall disclose neither the amount nor the party making such offer of settlement. The corresponding request for attorney fees shall be made to the arbitrator by affidavit only, not later than 5 calendar days after the date of the arbitration hearing and shall be addressed by the arbitrator in the arbitration award.

(g) Length of Hearing. The arbitrator may set a reasonable time limit on the length of the arbitration hearing.

[Amended effective September 1, 1993; September 1, 2011 ; September 1, 2012.]

6. AWARD

RULE 6.1. FORM AND CONTENT OF AWARD

(a) Form. The award shall be prepared on the form prescribed by the court.

(b) Content. The award shall dispose of all issues raised in the pleadings or submitted by the parties and shall do so in specific monetary terms whenever possible.

(c) Return of Exhibits. When an award is filed, the arbitrator shall return all exhibits to the parties who offered them during the hearing.

[Amended effective September 1, 1993.]

RULE 6.2. FILING OF AWARD

A request by an arbitrator for an extension of time for the filing of an award under MAR 6.2 may be presented to the Director, ex parte. The Director may grant or deny the request, subject to review by the Presiding Judge. The arbitrator shall give the parties notice of any extension granted.

RULE 6.3. JUDGMENT ON AWARD

(a) **Presentation.** A judgment on an award shall be presented to the Civil Motions Judge or court commis-

sioner, by any party, on five (5) days notice in accordance with MAR 6.3.

[Amended effective September 1, 1997.]

7. TRIAL DE NOVO

RULE 7.1. REQUEST FOR TRIAL DE NOVO

(b) **Calendar.**

(1) *Trial De Novo—Non–jury.* When a trial de novo is requested in a non-jury case as provided in MAR 7.1, the party making the request shall simultaneously file a Note for Trial on the form prescribed by the court. If no note for trial is timely filed the party requesting a trial de novo may be subject to sanctions.

(2) *Trial De Novo—Jury.*

(i) When a trial de novo is requested as provided in MAR 7.1, and the case has been set for jury trial at the time of the initial statement of arbitrability, the trial shall be on the date originally assigned pursuant to SCLMAR 2.1(e) unless within thirty (30) days after the request for trial de novo is filed the party originally demanding the jury trial serves, files, and notes a motion to withdraw the jury demand. If such motion is granted the court may advance the trial date. If after twenty (20) days from the filing of an arbitration award, no party has requested a trial de novo under MAR 7.1, the case shall be stricken from the trial calendar.

(ii) When a trial de novo is requested as provided in MAR 7.1 and no jury trial date has been previously set, any jury demand shall be made in the following manner. Such demand shall be served and filed by the appealing party simultaneously with a Note for Trial on the form prescribed by the court, and by a non-appealing party within 14 calendar days after the request for trial de novo is

served on that party. If no jury demand is timely filed, it is deemed waived.

(3) *Trial De Novo–Service and Filing.* When a trial de novo is requested as provided in MAR 7.1 (a), the party making the request shall complete the Request for Trial De Novo form, including the trial setting information, and file the original with the clerk and serve a copy on the Director of Arbitration and all other parties.

[Amended effective October 1, 1990; September 1, 1993; September 1, 1999; September 1, 2001; September 1, 2002.]

RULE 7.2. PROCEDURE AT TRIAL

(a) The clerk shall automatically seal any award and any memorandum decision/award if a trial de novo is requested.

(b) If the trial de novo is not confirmed, the opposing party may move for entry of judgment on the arbitrator's award upon proper notice. If the trial de novo is confirmed and the party who requested the trial de novo fails to appear at trial, then the opposing party may move to strike the trial and obtain a judgment on the arbitrator's award without further notice. If the trial de novo is confirmed and the party opposing the request for trial de novo fails to appear at trial, then the trial shall proceed in the normal course.

[Amended effective September 1, 1993; September 1, 2012.]

RULE 7.3. COSTS AND ATTORNEY FEES

MAR 7.3 shall apply only to costs and reasonable attorney's fees incurred after the filing of the request for a trial de novo.

8. GENERAL PROVISIONS

RULE 8.1. STIPULATIONS; EFFECT ON RELIEF GRANTED

If a case not otherwise subject to mandatory arbitration is transferred to arbitration by stipulation, the arbitrator may grant any relief which could have been granted if the case were determined by a judge.

RULE 8.4. TITLE AND CITATION

These rules are known and cited as the Snohomish County Superior Court Local Mandatory Arbitration Rules. SCLMAR is the official abbreviation.

RULE 8.6. COMPENSATION OF ARBITRATOR

(a) **Generally.** Arbitrators shall be compensated in the same amount and manner as judges pro tem of the Superior Court. Hearing time and reasonable preparation time are compensable, and reasonable costs incurred by the arbitrator are reimbursable.

(b) **Form.** When the award is filed, the arbitrator shall submit to the Director a request for payment on a form prescribed by the court. The Director shall determine the amount of compensation and costs, if any, to be paid. The decision of the Director will be reviewed by the Presiding Judge at the request of the arbitrator. Compensation to the arbitrator shall not exceed one thousand two hundred fifty dollars ($1,250), and costs reimbursement shall not exceed fifty dollars ($50.00), without special approval by the Presiding Judge.

[Amended effective September 1, 1993; September 1, 2007.]

RULE 8.7. ADMINISTRATION

(a) Director. The Presiding Judge shall designate a person to serve as Director of Arbitration. The Director, under the supervision of the Presiding Judge or designee, shall supervise arbitration under these rules, and perform any additional duties which may be delegated by the Presiding Judge or designee.

[Amended effective September 1, 1993; September 1, 1997; September 1, 1999.]

PART V. SPECIAL PROCEEDINGS RULES (SCLSPR)

RULE 93.04. DISPOSITION OF REPORTS—ADOPTIONS

(a) Proceedings to Dispense With Consent. Applications for dispensing with the consent of a parent or terminating a parent's rights shall be noted on a commissioner's calendar. If such application is contested, the matter shall be referred to the Court Administrator's office to be assigned a trial date.

(b) Ex Parte; Other Than Final Decrees. All non-contested adoption proceedings, other than the entry of final decrees, may be heard ex parte. Application shall be made to the Civil Motions law clerk, or such other place as set forth in an administrative order, for a hearing on a final decree of adoption.

(c) Testimony Required. Testimony shall be required in the following adoption proceedings:

1. Upon entry of the findings and decree;

2. Contested matters; and

3. Hearings on relinquishments and terminations.

The court may on its own motion require testimony at any stage of an adoption.

(d) Preplacement and Post Placement Reports. It shall be the responsibility of the petitioner or counsel to insure delivery to the court of the preplacement, post placement and guardian ad litem reports required for relinquishments, approvals of consent, terminations, or for adoptions. Reports must be delivered to the appropriate department no later than one day prior to the date for hearing in which the report is required, in order for the judge or commissioner to have an opportunity to read and consider the same.

(e) Stepparent Adoptions. When the object of an adoption proceeding is to adopt the child of petitioner's spouse, i.e., a stepparent adoption, the Order for Post Placement Report may contain the following provision: "It is further ordered that a formal written report is dispensed with and in lieu thereof the petitioner and spouse shall fill out and sign, and the post placement reporter will complete and file herein a 'Post Placement Report' in the form prescribed by the Snohomish County Superior Court."

(f) Release of Adoption Information. Any release of adoption file material must be only by court order. If the applicant is an intermediary previously approved by the court, or an attorney for an adopting parent seeking only a certified copy of the Decree of Adoption, the order may be approved by a judge or court commissioner. All other orders for release must be approved by a judge or full-time commissioner.

[Amended effective October 1, 1990; September 1, 1992; September 1, 1993; September 1, 1997.]

RULE 94.04. FAMILY LAW PROCEEDINGS

(a) Applicability of the Rule. Unless otherwise specified, this rule applies to all family law proceedings, including paternity actions and non-parental custody and/or visitation actions, defined as follows: Any proceeding in which the court is requested to adjudicate or enforce the rights of the parties or their children regarding the determination or modification of child custody, visitation, parenting plan, child support or spousal maintenance, or the temporary distribution of property or obligations.

(b) Court's Automatic Temporary Order Upon Filing of Certain Family Law Cases.

(1) *Application.* This rule shall apply to the following types of cases filed after May 1, 2010:

A. All family law petitions seeking dissolution of marriage, legal separation, parentage, or declaration of invalidity; and

B. Actions brought by parties to committed intimate relationships or state registered domestic partnerships, involving parenting or distribution of assets/liabilities.

(2) *Court's Automatic Temporary Order in Dissolution, Legal Separation, Invalidity, Committed Intimate Relationship, or State Registered Domestic Partnership Actions.* Upon the filing of a Summons and Petition in any dissolution, legal separation, invalidity, committed intimate relationship, or state registered domestic partnership action, the court on its own motion shall automatically issue a Temporary Order that includes the following provisions:

A. The parties shall be restrained from transferring, removing, encumbering, concealing, damaging, or in any way disposing of any property except in the usual course of business or for the necessities of life or as agreed in writing by the parties. Each party shall notify the other party of any extraordinary expenditure made after the order is issued.

B. The parties shall be restrained from assigning, transferring, borrowing, lapsing, surrendering, or changing entitlement of any insurance policies of either or both parties, or of any dependent children whether medical, health, life, or auto insurance, except as agreed in writing by the parties.

C. Each party shall be immediately responsible for his or her own future debts whether incurred by credit card, loan, security interest, or mortgage, except as ageed[1] in writing by the parties.

D. Both parties shall have access to all tax, financial, legal, and household records. Reasonable access to records shall not be denied. This provision does not apply to documents protected by the attorney-client or attorney work product privilege.

(3) *Court's Automatic Temporary Order in Actions Involving Minor Child(ren).* Upon the filing of a Summons and Petition in any action specified in Sections (b)(1)(a) or (b)(1)(b) that involves minor children, the court on its own motion shall automatically issue a Temporary Order that includes the following provisions:

A. Under the automatic temporary order, the term "parent" is limited only to those persons listed on a valid birth certificate or a presumed father under RCW 26.26.116.

B. Each parent shall be restrained from changing the residence of the child(ren) until further court order, except as agreed in writing by the parties. Subsequent orders regarding parenting issues supersede previously issued orders to the extent that the orders may be inconsistent.

C. Each parent shall have full access to the child(ren)'s educational and medical records, unless otherwise limited by court order.

D. Each parent shall ensure that the child(ren) not be exposed to negative comments about the other parent. Neither parent shall make negative comments about the other parent in the presence of the child(ren).

(4) *Service of Automatic Temporary Order.* It is the responsibility of the Petitioner to serve a copy of the Automatic Temporary Order on the Respondent.

(c) Family Law Proceedings–Courtroom Calendars and Procedures.

(1) *Trial Date; Status Conference.* If a family law case has been active longer than 180 days and a trial is not scheduled, the Court may review the case and schedule it for a status conference. If a family law trial is not confirmed and final pleadings are not entered within thirty (30) days after the unconfirmed trial date, the Court will schedule a status conference. The status conference will be heard on a status conference calendar held at least monthly and heard by a Judge designated by the Presiding Judge. If final documents are entered before the status conference is held, the status conference will be stricken. At the status conference, the Court will set a court confirmed trial date on its own motion, unless good cause is shown to do otherwise. If the parties fail to appear at the status conference, the court may dismiss the case on its own motion without further notice to the parties.

A. Trial Continuances in Family Law Cases. In all family law cases, a motion or stipulation for trial continuance shall list the date(s) upon which trial was previously set.

B. Dismissal for Unattended Trials in Family Law Cases. In all family law cases, the Court on its own motion may dismiss any case which was properly confirmed by the parties or court confirmed, but the parties failed to appear on the date of trial, unless a motion for continuance has been previously granted. This provision applies to all cases filed on or after January 1, 2010.

(2) *Family Law Proceedings Motions.*

A. Except as otherwise provided in this rule, all motions and returns on orders to show cause shall be as set forth in SCLCR 7 or SCLCR 56.

B. Generally. Absent prior authorization from the court, the entirety of all declarations and affidavits from the parties and any non-expert witness in support of motions shall be limited to a sum total of twenty-five (25) pages. The entirety of all declarations and affidavits submitted in response to motions shall be limited to a sum of twenty-five (25) pages. The entirety of all declarations and affidavits submitted in reply shall be limited to a sum total of five (5) pages. All declarations and affidavits must be legibly hand printed or typed in at least twelve (12) point type, double-spaced, and comply with GR14. All pages, including attached declarations and affidavits shall be sequentially numbered. Working copies of previously filed documents/orders are excluded from page limitation.

C. Exhibits. Exhibits that consist of declarations or affidavits of parties or witnesses shall count towards the above page limit. All other exhibits attached to a declaration or affidavits shall not be counted toward the page limit.

D. Financial Declarations. Financial declarations and financial documents do not count toward the page limit.

E. Expert Reports and Evaluations. Declarations, affidavits, and reports from Family Court Investigation, guardians ad litem, police reports, substance abuse evaluations, psychological evaluations and other expert witnesses do not count toward the page limitation.

F. Sanctions. Failure to comply with this rule may result in sanctions that may include, but are not limited to, striking over limit pleadings.

(3) Paternity actions brought by the prosecutor shall be heard as set forth in an administrative order of the court.

(4) Return on Show Cause actions in Domestic Violence cases shall be heard as set forth in an administrative order of the court.

(5) *Formal Proof Required.* A party shall provide oral testimony in support of final pleadings in a legal separation or marriage dissolution matter unless waived by the court on written motion and upon good cause shown. Good cause may include burdensome cost if both parties are geographically distant or involuntarily unavailable. If oral testimony is waived, written declaration testimony shall be submitted.

(d) Child Custody or Parenting Plan Proceedings.

(1) *Information Required.* In child custody, visitation or parenting plan cases, each party shall timely submit all information, forms, and worksheets required by statute. Any such forms or worksheets that are not complete may be stricken or other sanctions imposed.

(2) *Evaluations.* The court may order a custody or parenting or residential evaluation, mental health evaluation, alcohol or drug evaluation, mediation, treatment, counseling investigation and/or physical examination. The issue of costs shall be addressed in the order requiring such evaluation, and shall contain an hourly rate and maximum payment if the cost is to be at public expense. Any order failing to comply will be void.

(3) *Reference to Family Court; Counseling.*

(A) Duties of Parties. It shall be the responsibility of the parties or their counsel to utilize and complete such form as required by the court for reference to Family Court for investigation or other services. The completed and signed order shall be immediately submitted to the Family Court. Such services will not be required or undertaken until such form has been properly and timely submitted.

(B) The completed Family Court report shall be filed with the Court clerk. The attorneys for the parties, or party pro se shall receive one copy of such report.

(4) *Child Advocate.*

(A) Appointment. Upon motion the court may appoint a guardian ad litem or special advocate. The order shall be on a form as approved by the court and shall designate the appointee, the duties, and make provisions for payment of fees.

(B) Notice. The guardian ad litem or child advocate shall receive notice and copies of all discovery and hearings.

(C) Discharge. The guardian ad litem or child advocate shall be discharged only by order of the court.

(5) *Parenting Seminars.*

(A) Definition of Applicable Cases. This rule applies to all cases filed under Ch. 26.09, 26.10 or Ch. 26.26 of the RCW filed after September 1, 1994, including dissolutions, legal separations, major modifications and paternity actions (in which paternity has been established) where the parties are parents of children under the age of 18, and where a parenting plan or residential plan is required which involves more than purely financial issues.

(B) Parenting Seminars; Mandatory Attendance. In all cases referred to in Section (A) above, and in those additional cases arising under Title 26 RCW where a court makes a discretionary finding that a parenting seminar would be in the best interest of the children, both parents, and such non-parent parties as the court may direct, shall participate in, and successfully complete, an approved parenting seminar within 60 days after service of a petition, or an initiating motion, on the responding party. Standards for an approved parenting seminar shall be established by Administrative Order of this court. Successful completion shall be evidenced by a certificate of attendance filed by the provider agency with the court.

(C) Special Considerations/Waiver.

(1) In no case shall opposing parties be required to attend a seminar together.

(2) Upon a showing of domestic violence or abuse which would not require mutual decision-making pursuant to RCW 26.09.191, or that a parent's attendance at a seminar is not in the children's best interest, the court shall either:

[a] waive the requirement of completion of the seminar; or

[b] provide an alternative voluntary parenting seminar for battered spouses.

(3) The court may waive the seminar requirement for one or both parents in any case for good cause shown.

(D) Failure to Comply. Delay, refusal or default by one parent does not excuse timely compliance by the other parent. However, a parent who fails to complete the parenting seminar, shall be precluded from confirming the case for trial or presenting any final order affecting the parenting/residential plan, and may be precluded from seeking affirmative relief in this or subsequent proceedings in this file, until the parenting seminar has been successfully completed. Refusal or delay by either parent may constitute contempt of court and result in sanctions imposed by the court, or may result in the imposition of monetary terms, default and/or striking of pleadings.

(6) *Judicial Information System Background Checks.* Prior to presenting a permanent parenting plan to the court for entry, the party or parties presenting the final parenting plan shall submit a completed judicial information service (JIS) background check form to Snohomish County Superior Court Family Court Services. Such request must be submitted no less than five court days prior to the date of presentation of the final parenting plan. Upon receipt of a completed JIS background check form, Superior Court staff shall complete a search of the Judicial Information System for the existence of any information and proceedings relevant to the placement of the child. This search shall be performed no more than 14 days prior to the proposed date of presentation of the permanent parenting plan.

(e) Petitioner and Respondent–Affidavits of Income. Any application or response regarding child support shall be by motion and shall include a completed child support worksheet and other information which might be required by statute. Any application or response regarding spousal maintenance, attorney's fees, or any other financial relief, except child support, shall be by motion and shall include a Financial Affidavit in the form approved by the court. Each party shall attach to this Financial Affidavit copies of sufficient W–2 forms, 1040 forms and copies of wage stubs for prior periods to adequately prove income.

All orders establishing, setting or modifying any temporary or permanent child support obligation must be in the form of a separate order, on mandatory forms where appropriate, with the adopted child support worksheet attached.

(f) Restraining Orders.

(1) *Where Presented.* Applications for Temporary Restraining Orders may be presented ex parte. Motions for relief to be effective during the pendency of litigation shall be noted for hearing on a commissioner's calendar. Agreed restraining orders may be presented ex parte.

(2) *Notice to Opponent.* If an appearance has been made by a party, notice to the party pro se or counsel must be given prior to application for any immediate temporary restraining order which will be heard by a commissioner ex parte.

(3) *Mutual Orders.* All immediate temporary restraining orders shall be made mutual where appropriate.

(4) *Motions to Quash or Terminate Temporary Restraining Orders.* A motion to quash a temporary restraining order or to terminate a restraining order shall be noted for hearing on a commissioner's calendar.

(5) *Temporary Restraining Orders; Testimony.* No temporary order removing a person from or restraining a person from entering premises in which that person then resides, or has resided within fourteen (14) days of the application; or which affects the custody of a minor child in which another person has parental rights; or which grants to a person possession of property in the name or possession of another; shall be issued except: (a) after a hearing of which the adverse party has been given prior notice deemed adequate by the court hearing the same; or (b) at which sworn testimony or statement is received from a person or persons having personal knowledge of the facts, and the court waives the notice requirement. In general, an ex parte order establishing, vacating or changing child custody or residence may only be entered under one or more of the following circumstances:

A. There is already an existing order entered in a different cause or proceeding, and this order is merely to confirm the status quo in this proceeding;

B. The parties have been separated more than fourteen (14) days, and the moving party has had the actual uninterrupted custody of the children for the last fourteen (14) days, or the other party has voluntarily vacated the family residence more than fourteen (14) days hence;

C. Less than fourteen (14) days have elapsed since separation of the parties, but during this time, the responding party has voluntarily acceded to the present arrangement by removing himself/herself from the family residence, or by leaving the children behind in the physical custody of the moving party; or

D. The parties have not as yet separated or have only recently done so, and there are substantial, documented allegations of physical, emotional, or sexual abuse of the other party or of the children which present a substantial danger of immediate irreparable harm such that an emergency order without notice ought to be entered. The applicant for such an order is expected to appear personally before a commissioner and give testimony in support of the request.

(6) *Show Cause Hearings; Testimony.* All show cause hearings, except for contempt, domestic violence, and anti-harassment hearings, shall be by affidavit and declaration only. In anti-harassment and domestic violence actions only the parties may testify without cross examination, or make statements as allowed by the court. The court may take testimony if it appears to the court necessary for an adequate determination of the matter.

(7) *Agreed or Non-contested Orders and Decrees.* In any case in which the respondent has appeared, pro se or through counsel, prior to the entry of an order of default, all orders, findings, or decrees shall be endorsed by the non-presenting party or his/her attor-

ney and shall indicate approval or waiver of notice of presentation.

(g) Modification Proceedings.

(1) *Modification of Temporary Orders.* Temporary orders may be modified by motion based upon a change of circumstances.

(2) *Entry of Modified Decree by Default.* No permanent decree of modification of support, maintenance, visitation, parenting plan, or custody shall be entered by default unless the adverse party was served with at least twenty (20) days notice of such proceedings (sixty (60) days if out of state), together with copies of pleadings.

(3) *Custody, Parenting, or Visitation Modifications.*

(A) Commencement. A proceeding to modify custody, a parenting plan, visitation or support is commenced by the filing of such documents as is required by various statutes.

(B) Threshold Hearings–Temporary Relief. Any party may, by motion or show cause order, request temporary relief or a threshold hearing based on affidavits. Responsive documents shall be served on the moving party as required by SCLCR 7.

(C) Disposition. Contested matters involving modification of support or maintenance only will be set for arbitration, unless a trial by affidavit is approved by the court upon motion.

(h) Alternative Dispute Resolution Required in Family Law.

(1) *Alternative Dispute Resolution Required in Family Law.* All contested issues in the following cases shall be submitted to settlement conference, mediation, or other ADR process with a neutral third party who offers ADR services: petitions filed under RCW 26.09; 26.10; 26.26 and committed intimate relationship cases and petitions for modifications of final orders exclusive of Child Support/Maintenance Modification actions which are in mandatory arbitration. If a guardian ad litem (GAL) has been appointed, the parties shall provide the GAL with the date of ADR at least ten (10) days prior to its scheduled occurrence.

(2) *When Alternative Dispute Resolution Is Not Required.* ADR shall NOT be required in the following cases:

A. For good cause shown upon motion and approval by the court.

B. Where a domestic violence restraining order or protection order (excluding Ex–Parte orders) involving the parties has been entered by a court at any time within the previous twelve (12) months.

C. Where a domestic violence no contact order exists pursuant to RCW 10.99;

D. Where the court upon motion finds that domestic abuse has occurred between the parties and that such abuse would interfere with arm's-length mediation.

(3) *Alternative Dispute Resolution Timing.* In all matters filed after May 1, 2010, in which ADR is required, the parties must complete ADR prior to trial confirmation, provided however that either party may by motion request an order requiring mediation sooner upon good cause shown.

(4) *Failure to Comply.* Failure to comply with Alternative Dispute Resolution when required shall result in the case not being confirmed for trial. Refusal or delay by either party may constitute contempt of court and result in sanctions imposed by the court, including the imposition of monetary terms.

(5) *Division of Costs.* The parties shall be equally responsible for the cost of ADR unless a different division of the cost is ordered by the court or agreed upon by the parties.

(6) *Where to Bring Motions.* Motions to waive ADR shall be noted before the Presiding Judge at 9:00 a.m. Motions to alter the ADR time period or change the division of the cost shall be noted on the Commissioner's Family Law Calendar. Notwithstanding the foregoing, either party may by motion seek a court order requiring mandatory mediation in a case where it would not be required as set forth in (2)(B), (2)(C) or (2)(D) above if the moving party believes that the parties would be able to mediate their dispute fairly under the particular circumstances of the case.

(i) Notice of Settlement.

When all issues in a Title 26 matter have been settled, the mediator, if any, or the attorneys or parties if there is no mediator, shall file within seven (7) days of settlement, a Notice of Settlement of All Issues in the form prescribed by the court. Facsimile or scanned image signatures are allowed. If final documents are not filed and entered within sixty (60) days after the filing of the Notice of Settlement, the Court may on its own motion dismiss the matter(s) without further notice to the parties.

[Amended effective October 1, 1990; September 1, 1992; September 1, 1993; September 1, 1994; September 1, 1995; September 1, 1996; September 1, 1997; September 1, 1999; September 1, 2002; September 1, 2005; September 1, 2007; amended on an emergency basis effective November 14, 2007; amended on a permanent basis effective September 1, 2008; September 1, 2009; amended on an emergency basis effective October 14, 2009; May 1, 2010; amended on a permanent basis effective September 1, 2010; September 1, 2011; September 1, 2012; September 1, 2015.]

1 So in original.

RULE 94.05. PARENTAGE ACTIONS—TEMPORARY PARENTING PLANS AND CHILD SUPPORT ORDERS CONVERTED TO PERMANENT ORDERS [REPEALED]

[Repealed effective September 1, 2015.]

RULE 96.01. CIVIL CONTEMPT PROCEEDINGS; REQUIREMENTS

The following shall apply to indirect, remedial or civil contempt proceedings brought under RCW 7.21.030 or similar statutes.

(a) Warnings; Failure to Appear. The Order to Show Cause shall contain language warning the responding party that failure to appear could result in a warrant for arrest.

(b) Personal Service. Unless otherwise authorized by the court, the Order to Show Cause, motion, and affidavits must be personally served upon the responding party.

(c) Arrest or Other Remedies Upon Failure to Appear. At the hearing, if the responding party fails to appear and upon showing of proof of service, and if the warning required above is in the order, the court may order an arrest. Other requested remedies may also be ordered upon default, even if a warrant is not authorized.

[Amended effective September 1, 1992.]

RULE 96.02. CHANGE OF NAME PROCEDURE [RESCINDED]

[Adopted effective October 1, 1990; rescinded September 1, 1993.]

RULE 98.04. ESTATES–PROBATE

(a) Ex Parte; Files Required. All probate matters that are not contested, and in which notice is not required by statute, rule, or a duly filed request for notice under R.C.W. 11.28.240, or where such notice has been waived, may be heard ex parte. It shall be the responsibility of the presenting party to submit to the court, the court file if the file contains any pleadings or other documents or proof on which the requested action is based. Applications by mail should be in conformance with SCLAR 0.02(f)(2). A death certificate or comparable documentation of the death of the decedent shall be filed with any petition to open a probate matter.

(b) Notice Required. All matters in probate proceedings not involving testimony in which notice is required shall be placed on the court commissioners civil calendar.

(c) Testimony for Certain Proceedings Required. Sworn testimony of any person or persons having personal knowledge of the facts may be required in certain probate proceedings as determined by the court.

[Amended effective September 1, 1993; September 1, 1997; September 1, 2015.]

RULE 98.16. ESTATES—GUARDIANSHIPS—SETTLEMENT OF CLAIMS OF MINORS

(a) Appointment of Representation. Appointment of representation of a minor for purposes of a minor settlement shall be by order of the Court.

(b) [Reserved]

(c) [Reserved]

(d) [Reserved]

(e) [Reserved]

(f) Guardianships.

(1) *Non–Certified Professional Guardian Appointments and Waiver of Training Requirements.* Upon filing of a Petition To Extend Time or Waive Guardian Training pursuant to RCW 11.88.020(3) by a non Certified Professional Guardian the court may extend the time period for completion of the lay guardian training for a period of ninety (90) days or waive the training requirement for guardians appointed prior to the effective date of July 22, 2011 for good cause. In establishing good cause, the court may consider: the length of time the lay guardian has successfully fulfilled their duties; the timeliness of filing of all required reports; whether the duties of the guardian have been monitored by a state or local agency; and any founded allegations against the guardian for abuse, neglect, or breach of fiduciary duty.

(2) *Ex Parte; Files Required.* All guardianship matters that are not contested, and in which notice is not required by statute, rule, or a duly filed request for notice under applicable statutes, or where such notice has been waived, may be heard ex parte. It shall be the responsibility of the presenting party to submit to the judge the court file if the file contains any pleadings or other documents or proof on which the requested action is based.

(3) *Notice Required.*

(A) Notes for Motion Calendar. All matters in guardianship proceedings not involving testimony in which notice is required shall be noted on the court commissioners civil calendar. The court may, in its discretion, require a guardianship matter be noted for motion.

(4) *When Guardian Ad Litem Required.*

(A) Certain Proceedings. The appointment of a guardian ad litem shall be made when required by statute and may be required in the guardianship proceedings at other times within the discretion of the court.

(5) *Order Appointing Guardian and Execution and Form of Letters of Guardianship.* All Orders Appointing Guardians shall contain the following information to ensure the timely and accurate issuance of Letters of Guardianship by the Clerk's Office. The

following information shall be completed and placed directly below the case caption or on a separate cover page in all Orders Appointing Guardians:

CLERK'S ACTION REQUIRED
Due Date for Report and Accounting: _____
New Letters Expire On:** _____
   Due Date for Initial Personal Care Plan: _____
   Due Date for Inventory: _____

** All Letters of Guardianship, unless otherwise ordered by the Court, will expire 120 days following the end of the next accounting period.

(g) Minor Settlements.

(1) *Compliance with SPR 98.16.* The requirements of SPR 98.16 will be strictly enforced in all matters in which the court is requested to approve a settlement involving a beneficial interest or claim of a person under the age of eighteen (18).

(2) *Petition.*

(A) Contents. A petition for approval of a settlement of each minor's claim shall contain:

   1. The full name and birth date of each minor;

   2. The relation of the guardian ad litem to each minor;

   3. A brief statement of the basis for the claim unless a summons and complaint have been previously filed;

   4. An itemization of special damages;

   5. A statement of the collateral sources for payment of special damages, whether reimbursement is sought and the terms thereof, including the allocation of fractional shares of the costs of recovery;

   6. A description of the injuries, length of disability and prognosis of future disability. Medical reports may be attached and incorporated in the petition;

   7. The amount of proposed settlement;

   8. The amount of attorney's fees requested or agreed upon and an itemization of the court costs and expenses incurred in preparation and prosecution of the claim; and,

   9. The proposed distribution of settlement funds.

(3) *Hearing on Approval of Settlement.*

(A) Report of Counsel or Guardian Ad Litem. At the time the petition for approval of the settlement is heard, independent counsel or the guardian ad litem should be prepared to advise the court of his/her opinion of the probable chances of recovery, including issues of primary negligence, contributory negligence, reasonableness of attorney's fees, etc., and the basis for such opinion. Reasonably current medical reports shall be available. The minor and custodial parent or the parent designated primary residential parent under the Parenting Act shall be present at the hearing, unless their presence is waived by the court. All hearings shall be reported.

(B) Time of Hearing. Application shall be made to the Civil Motion Judge's law clerk/bailiff for a time to hear the matter or for assignment to a department to hear the matter.

(4) *Filing of Receipt.* Within 30 days of the approval of the settlement, the petitioner shall file a receipt, signed by a representative of the financial institution, acknowledging receipt of the funds and acknowledging that the financial institution will hold the funds in compliance with the court order and SPR 98.16W. A copy of the receipt shall be provided to the judge approving the settlement. The copy shall bear the stamp of the clerk showing that it has been filed and shall be provided to the judge within two working days of being filed.

(i) [Reserved]

(j) Control and Orders for Remaining Funds.

(1) $25,000 or less. [Reserved]

(2) More than $25,000. [Reserved]

(3) Conditions for use of Trust. A trust established pursuant to SPR 98.16W must meet the following additional requirements:

(A) The selection of the trustee(s) and the terms of the trust shall be approved by the same judge as approved the settlement. If that judge is not available, the presiding judge may assign the matter to a different judge. A working copy of the proposed trust document, note for hearing and trustee's fee schedule shall be furnished to the judge no less than 6 court days in advance of the hearing.

[Amended effective September 1, 1992; September 1, 1993; September 1, 1997; September 1, 1999; September 1, 2001; September 1, 2003; amended on an emergency basis, effective November 9, 2011; amended on a permanent basis effective September 1, 2012.]

PART VI. CRIMINAL RULES
(SCLCrR)

1. SCOPE, PURPOSE AND CONSTRUCTION

RULE 1.1. SCOPE; APPLICATION OF CIVIL RULES

All local civil rules and Supreme Court Civil Rules shall apply in criminal cases, unless contrary provision is made in these or other rules governing criminal cases.

RULE 1.2. PURPOSE AND CONSTRUCTION

Where the term "probation" is used herein it will also apply to "community supervision".

2. PROCEDURES PRIOR TO ARREST AND OTHER SPECIAL PROCEEDINGS

RULE 2.2. WARRANT OF ARREST AND SUMMONS

(b) Issuance of Summons. Upon the Prosecuting Attorney's filing with the clerk an information without directing or requesting the issuance of a warrant for the arrest of the defendant, the clerk shall issue, or re-issue, a summons commanding the defendant to appear before the Court at a specified time and place. Summons shall also issue upon the filing of a motion for modification or revocation of probation, provided that the motion be supported with a properly executed affidavit setting forth the basis for the requested modification or revocation of probation.

3. RIGHTS OF DEFENDANTS

RULE 3.1. RESTORATION OF FIREARMS RIGHTS

An action for restoration of firearms rights pursuant to RCW 9.41 may only be commenced by filing a petition with the court in the manner provided by CR3.

[Adopted effective September 1, 2010.]

RULE 3.1B. CERTIFICATES OF COMPLIANCE FOR INDIGENT DEFENDANTS

(c) Certificates of Compliance with the Standards for Indigent Defendants required by CrR 3.1 and JuCr 9.2 shall be filed quarterly with the Snohomish County Clerk.

(d) All Notice of Appearance forms filed by counsel for indigent defendants shall indicate in a separate paragraph whether or not a current CrR 3.1/JuCr 9.2 Certificate of Compliance with the Standards for Indigent Defendants is on file with the Snohomish County Clerk.

[Adopted on an emergency basis, effective October 1, 2012; adopted on a permanent basis, effective September 2, 2013.]

RULE 3.2A. PRELIMINARY APPEARANCE OF DEFENDANT

(a) Generally. Unless a defendant has appeared or will appear before a court of limited jurisdiction for a preliminary appearance pursuant to JCrR 2.03(a), any defendant, whether detained in jail or subjected to court authorized conditions of release, and any person in whose case the Juvenile Court has entered a written order declining jurisdiction, must be taken or required to appear before the Superior Court in person or by electronic audio-visual device as soon as practicable after the detention is commenced, the conditions of release are imposed, or the order is entered, but in any event before the close of business on the next judicial day. A person is not subject to conditions of release if the person has been served with a summons and the only obligation is to appear in court on a future date.

RULE 3.3. TIME FOR TRIAL

(c) Time for Arraignment and Trial. The in-custody arraignment calendar shall be heard at the time as indicated for such in an administrative order of the court. The out-of-custody arraignment calendar shall be heard at the time as indicated for such in an administrative order of the court. All first appearances, arraignments, setting of bail, and similar matters in criminal cases shall be placed on such calendars. Guilty pleas will be taken at either omnibus hearings or plea calendars.

(1) *Setting of Omnibus Hearings.* At the time of the arraignment the court shall set the omnibus hearing.

(2) *Sentencing.* Upon the entry of a plea of guilty, sentencing shall be assigned to a judge by the judge taking the plea.

(f) Trial Settings/Confirmation Hearings. Criminal cases shall be set for trial at the time of arraignment, or entry of plea, by the judge hearing such matters.

[Amended effective July 1, 1991; September 1, 1993; September 1, 1997.]

RULE 3.4.   PRESENCE OF DEFENDANT

(a) Required—Exception. Unless otherwise ordered by the court the presence of the defendant shall be required at all proceedings, including omnibus hearing.

(d) Record. In any hearing where the defendant is in custody in the Snohomish County Jail and no sworn testimony is to be taken, including but not limited to preliminary appearance, arraignment, re-arraignment, bail review, trial setting or continuance, and/or extradition waiver, the court may in its discretion conduct such hearing with the defendant present in person or by electronic audio-visual device, and may make an electronic, mechanical, or shorthand record thereof in accordance with CR 80.

[Amended effective October 1, 1990.]

4.   PROCEDURES PRIOR TO TRIAL

RULE 4.5.   OMNIBUS HEARING

(a) Omnibus Calendar. The Omnibus Calendar shall be heard at the time indicated for such as set forth in an administrative order of the court, and in such courtroom as may be posted.

(d) Criminal Motion Calendar. Motions to suppress, Rule 3.5 hearings, and similar matters, shall be heard at the time indicated for such as set forth in an administrative order of the court and may be assigned to Trial Departments as may appear appropriate to the judge. Matters in criminal cases requiring disposition other than on the regular Arraignment, Omnibus or Criminal Motion Calendars, shall be presented to the Criminal Motions Judge, except for motions for preassignment which shall be presented to the Presiding Judge. Criminal motions requiring more than five minutes to be heard shall be confirmed by 12:30 p.m. one day prior to the hearing with the law clerk for the assigned criminal hearings judge. The moving party must notify the court as soon as possible when a confirmed matter is stricken or continued. Failure to do so may result in the imposition of sanctions or terms. The moving party's motion and brief, if any, must be filed with the court clerk and a copy served on the judge hearing the matter and opposing counsel at least six court days before the hearing. Responding documents and briefs, if any, must be filed with the court clerk, and a copy served on the judge hearing the matter and the moving party at least two court days before the hearing. Reply documents must be filed and served no later than 12 noon of the court day prior to the hearing.

[Amended effective September 1, 1992; September 1, 1993; September 1, 1997; September 1, 1998; amended on an emergency basis, effective April 4, 2011; amended on a permanent basis effective September 1, 2011.]

RULE 4.11.   COMPENTENCY DETERMINATION [1]

(a) Initial Competency Assessment Screening.

1.   Upon receiving a representation that there may be reason to doubt the competency of an in custody criminal defendant, the court shall order an initial competency assessment screening by the Snohomish County Competency Assessment Management Program at Snohomish County Corrections.

2.   The initial Competency Assessment Screening Report shall be provided in writing to the court, the Prosecuting Attorney and defense counsel within three (3) court days of the entry of the Initial Competency Assessment Screening Order.

3.   The assessment and report required by this rule shall be conducted and prepared by qualified professionals in the mental health field at Snohomish County Corrections.

(b) Court Action. At the hearing following receipt of the initial Assessment Screening Report, the court shall consider along with the report, the arguments and any factual information from the Prosecuting Attorney and the defendant's attorney and may either:

1.   Find that there is not a reason to doubt the competency of the in custody defendant and deny the motion for a further evaluation of the defendant's competency pursuant to RCW 10.77.060, or

2.   Find that there is reason to doubt the competency of the in custody defendant, and provided that the defendant has not indicated his or her intention to rely on the defense of insanity pursuant to RCW 10.77.030, stay further criminal proceedings, and order an evaluation of the mental health condition (competency) of the in custody defendant at state expense (subject to available funding) pursuant to RCW 10.77.060, by a qualified community expert, who has been preapproved by the court. Such competency evaluation shall be in writing and returned to the court not later than 15 days from the entry of such order, or

3.   Find that there is reason to doubt the competency of the in custody defendant, stay further crimi-

nal proceedings, and order that a qualified expert from Western State Hospital evaluate and report on the mental health condition (competency) of the defendant pursuant to RCW 10.77.060.

4. Find that there is reason to doubt the competency of the in-custody defendant, stay further criminal proceedings, and, finding that circumstances involving the health of the defendant require, order that the defendant be transported to Western State Hospital for an evaluation and preparation of a report on the mental health condition (competency) of the defendant, pursuant to RCW 10.77.060.

(c) Waiver of Initial Competency Screening/Rescreening.

1. The Initial Competency Assessment Screening required by this local rule may be waived by the court upon the agreement of both the Prosecuting Attorney and the defendant's attorney that such screening is unnecessary in a particular case.

2. An in custody defendant may be ordered by the court to be rescreened at any time, upon finding that it is likely that the mental condition of the defendant has changed since the last screening.

(d) Defendant Rights.

1. Any time the defendant is being assessed by court appointed experts or professional persons pursuant to the provisions of this local rule, the defendant shall be entitled to have his or her attorney present.

2. In an initial competency assessment conducted under this chapter, the defendant may refuse to answer any question if he or she believes his or her answers may tend to incriminate him or her or form links leading to evidence of an incriminating nature.

3. No provision of this local rule shall abrogate any right guaranteed or provided by the Constitution of the United States or of the State of Washington, Washington statutes or Washington State Court Rules.

[Adopted effective September 1, 2015.]

1 So in original.

5.   VENUE [RESERVED]

6.   PROCEDURES AT TRIAL

RULE 6.12.   WITNESSES

(f) Not Offered Exhibits. All exhibits marked but not offered at trial shall be subject to the same retention requirements as those admitted or rejected.

7.   PROCEDURES FOLLOWING CONVICTION

RULE 7.1.   PROCEDURES BEFORE SENTENCING

(e) Sealing of Records. No sentencing records or reports will be sealed except by order of the court pursuant to the procedures set forth in GR 15.
[Amended effective September 1, 2000.]

RULE 7.2.   SENTENCING; CONDITIONS OF PAYMENT OF COSTS, FEES, RESTITUTION AND FINES [REPEALED]

[Repealed effective September 1, 2004.]

8. MISCELLANEOUS [RESERVED]

PART VII. MENTAL PROCEEDINGS RULES (SCLMPR) [RESERVED]

PART VIII. JUVENILE COURT RULES (SCLJuCR)

TITLE 1. SCOPE AND APPLICATION OF RULES

RULE 1.4. APPLICABILITY OF OTHER RULES

(a) **Civil Rules.** The computation of any period of time prescribed or allowed by these rules shall be as set forth in CR 6.

[Adopted effective September 1, 1992.]

TITLE 2. SHELTER CARE PROCEEDINGS [RESERVED]

TITLE 3. DEPENDENCY PROCEEDINGS

RULE 3.4. NOTICE AND SUMMONS— SCHEDULING OF FACTFINDING HEARING [RESCINDED]

[Adopted effective September 1, 1992; rescinded effective September 1, 1993.]

RULE 3.6. ANSWER TO PETITION

(a) A written answer to a petition shall be made by each party and shall be filed and served on counsel and parties without counsel no later than 7 days before the preliminary hearing.

[Adopted effective September 1, 1992.]

RULE 3.6A. PRELIMINARY HEARINGS

(a) In every matter set for a dependency, guardianship, or termination fact-finding hearing, a preliminary hearing shall first be had to resolve all undisputed facts and to consider matters of law. An estimate of the length of fact-finding hearing shall be made to determine whether the hearing should be rescheduled.

(b) Preliminary hearings shall be set at least 14 days prior to the date of the fact-finding hearing.

(c) Any party not appearing at the preliminary hearing in person or by counsel, after proper notice, may be adjudged in default.

(d) Written court reports setting forth the dispositional plan shall be prepared by the agency having or requesting custody and shall be filed and served on all counsel and parties without counsel 7 days prior to the preliminary hearing.

[Adopted effective September 1, 1992.]

RULE 3.6B. ALTERNATIVE DISPUTE RESOLUTION (ADR) PROCEDURE

(a) **ADR Procedure.** Any time after filing of an answer/response to a petition for dependency or to a petition for termination of parental rights, the dispute resolution process may be initiated by agreement of the parties or by court order. The alternative dispute resolution process "ADR" includes judicial assisted settlement conferences, non-judicial settlement conferences, mediation or formal family conferencing through the DSHS family group conferencing program.

(b) **Statement of Issues.** The parties to ADR shall provide to the court, mediator or facilitator and to each other a statement of the relief each party seeks and a statement of the issues each party want addressed and/or resolved. In a dependency "non-termination matter" this statement may take the form of a proposed order of individual service plan. All parties shall provide the statement of relief and issues at least five days prior to the ADR schedule or by agreement.

(c) **Confidentiality.** Alternative dispute resolution proceedings held pursuant to this rule shall be held in private and shall be confidential. Any person serving as a mediator shall sign a statement of familiarity with applicable statutory confidentiality provisions regarding dependency and termination matters and agreeing to be bound by such provisions.

[Adopted effective September 1, 1998.]

RULE 3.9. DEPENDENCY REVIEW HEARINGS

(a) Dependency Review Reports. A written review report shall be prepared by the supervising agency which shall be filed and served on all counsel and unrepresented parties not less than 14 calendar days prior to any 6–month review or permanency planning hearings. Responsive documents shall be filed and served on said parties and counsel not less than 7 calendar days prior to any 6–month review or permanency planning hearing. Reply documents, if any, shall be filed and served on said parties and counsel not later than noon 2 court days prior to any 6–month or permanency planning hearing. Courtesy copies of all dependency review reports, responsive and reply documents shall be provided to the assigned judge at the time of filing with the court. The supervising agency shall mail a copy of the written review report to any represented party at the time it is filed with the court.

(b) Non-contested Calendar. All dependency reviews shall be set for hearing on the non-contested calendar to be heard between 5 and 6 months after the beginning of the placement episode or entry of the order of dependency, whichever occurs first; and thereafter between 5 and 6 months after entry of the previous review order. The initial review hearing shall be an in-court review and shall be set within 6 months from the beginning date of the placement episode or no more than 90 days from the entry of the disposition order, whichever comes first. A dependency review hearing order consistent with the agency court report may enter at the hearing, subject to court review.

(c) Contested Calendar.

i. If a party wishes a contested review hearing, he or she shall obtain a date from the clerk's office and serve a Notice of Contested Hearing on counsel and unrepresented parties at least 1 court day prior to the non-contested calendar date.

ii. The contested hearing date shall be at least 7 days later than the non-contested hearing date, but less than 6 months from the date of the prior review hearing.

iii. If the contested hearing is set for a time beyond the normal review period an order maintaining the status quo will be entered pending the contested hearing.

iv. The Notice of Contested Hearing shall contain the hearing date obtained from the clerk's office, the issues that are contested, and the estimated length of time needed for the hearing. The notice of contested hearing shall be accompanied by documents in support of the issue.

v. The court may set a case on the contested calendar with notice to all parties accompanied by a statement of the reasons for such action.

vi. Failure to timely note a contested review may result in entry of a dependency review hearing order on the non-contested calendar consistent with the agency's court report.

vii. Inability to contact one's client will not be deemed a basis to transfer a matter to a contested calendar. If desired, counsel can file a written statement as to non-contact as a basis for non-agreement, but the matter will be deemed non-contested.

(d) Permanency Planning Hearing. In all cases where a child has been placed in substitute care for at least 9 months and an adoption decree, guardianship order, or permanent custody order has not previously been entered, a permanency planning hearing shall be set on the "Permanency Planning Review" calendar no later than 12 months following commencement of the placement episode. Additional permanency planning hearings shall be held at 11 month intervals thereafter for so long as the child remains in substitute care. After receipt of the agency's court report, if a party or GAL contest any issue, they must file and serve on all counsel and unrepresented parties a Notice of Contested Issues no later than 7 calendar days before the hearing. The Notice of Contested Issues shall be accompanied by documents in support of the issue. Any reply documents must be filed and served on all counsel and unrepresented parties not later that noon 2 court days before the contested hearing. Courtesy copies of the Notice of Contested Issues and all reply documents shall be provided to the assigned judge at the time of filing with the court.

(e) Motions. Any party may note a motion for hearing on a regularly scheduled contested review calendar. A party wishing to note a motion for hearing shall obtain a date from the clerk's office and shall file and serve the motion, a calendar note, and all supporting documents to all counsel and unrepresented parties at least 6 court days prior to the date set for the hearing. Any reply documents must be filed and served on all counsel and unrepresented parties not later than noon 2 court days before the contested hearing. Courtesy copies of the motion, supporting documents and all reply documents shall be provided to the assigned judge at the time of filing with the court. Special settings shall be made only with the permission of the assigned judge. The form of motions, procedures, and filing and service requirements shall be as set forth in SCLCR 7 for civil motions.

[Adopted effective September 1, 1992; amended effective September 1, 2000; amended on an emergency basis effective December 12, 2007; amended on a permanent basis effective September 1, 2008; amended effective September 1, 2010.]

RULE 3.12. UNIFIED FAMILY COURT

(a) Purpose of the UFC: The purpose of the Unified Family Court is to promote effective judicial management over cases involving dependent children and their applicable family law case. UFC provides facilitation and case management promoting prompt and informed resolution of the family law matter.

(b) UFC Case Manager. The role of the case manager is to provide coordination for the cases. The case manager summarizes the current family law case for the judge, makes recommendations as to the family law actions needed for the dismissal of the dependency, circulates proposed orders, and tracks cases for timeliness. All information summaries provided to the court shall also be provided to all parties.

(c) Referrals to UFC. (1) Referrals for UFC case management may be made by any judicial officer, the parties or attorneys, Court Appointed Special Advocates, and the Department of Social and Health Services (DSHS). A party referring a matter to UFC shall set it on a UFC Preliminary Hearing calendar and provide notice to all parties to the dependency. (2) A referral shall be made to UFC when a dependent child is returned to a parent. The party filing the order to return a child to a parent shall at the same time, file and circulate to all parties an Order Setting Unified Family Court Preliminary Hearing setting the case onto the UFC Preliminary Calendar. (3) The court, upon its own motion, may set any case on the UFC Preliminary Calendar or for a UFC initial hearing.

(d) UFC Preliminary Calendar. The case manager will circulate a proposed Preliminary Hearing Order indicating the family law status and proposed action electronically. The order will enter exparte on the morning of the hearing and will be presumed agreed unless formal objection is noted. Parties can contest this order by noting their objection and serving all parties the Friday prior to the hearing. If the proposed Preliminary Hearing Order is contested, the parties shall attend the preliminary hearing for argument. If a case is accepted for UFC case management, the dependency case and all related family law cases concerning the family and the children, will be transferred to UFC and managed together as a case group by the judge assigned to hear the underlying dependency matter. When a case is transferred to UFC, the court shall enter an order transferring

limited jurisdiction and linking the family law and dependency cases.

(e) Planning Conference. A planning conference is set in the UFC preliminary order when appropriate. At the planning conference the family may meet with a family law facilitator for assistance. Families that do not appear for this assistance will be expected to obtain their own assistance and complete necessary family law filings prior to the date set by the court. Social workers and guardians ad litem should attend the planning conference to give input into the parenting plan.

(f) Motions. Motions in a UFC case shall be scheduled and heard on the assigned judge's UFC calendar. Motions in the family law action shall comply with local rule SCLR 6(d)(2).

(g) Concurrent Hearings. If available, the UFC Case Manager shall electronically circulate courtesy copies of relevant family law documents to the dependency parties for their input as to the safety of the child. Parties to the dependency objecting to dismissal of the dependency because the family law orders will not adequately protect the child shall note their objection 6 court days prior to the hearing.

(h) Nonparental custody actions. If the court has adopted a permanent plan of nonparental custody as an option and has entered a transfer of limited jurisdiction, the parties may contact the case manager for further assistance on the case or may proceed without such assistance. All hearings in such cases shall be scheduled on the unified family court calendar for the judge assigned to the related dependency action.

(i) Trials. UFC Cases that need to be set for trial at the main courthouse will be set through the case manager to ensure expedited setting. Trials to be set at juvenile court will be set by the assigned dependency judge. All family law rules pertaining to trial apply to the parties.

[Adopted effective September 1, 2012.]

TITLE 4. PROCEEDINGS TO TERMINATE PARENT–CHILD RELATIONSHIP

RULE 4.2. PLEADINGS [REPEALED]

[Repealed effective September 1, 2015.]

TITLE 5. PROCEEDINGS FOR ALTERNATIVE RESIDENTIAL PLACEMENT
[RESERVED]

TITLE 6. JUVENILE OFFENSE PROCEEDINGS—DIVERSION AGREEMENTS
[RESERVED]

TITLE 7. JUVENILE OFFENSE PROCEEDINGS IN JUVENILE COURT

RULE 7.12. DISPOSITION HEARING

(g) Disposition Order. At or after a disposition hearing, a written Disposition Order shall be signed by the judge. Unless otherwise specifically provided for in said Order, the probation counselor is authorized to thereafter fix and establish the amount of restitution and a schedule for the payment of any fines, restitution, court costs or attorney's fees, or the performance of any community service. Once such schedule is proposed in writing by the probation counselor and a copy given to the defendant, such shall be deemed to be incorporated into and a part of the Disposition Order, unless a written request for judicial review is filed within ten (10) days. Thereafter, any failure to comply with said schedule shall be deemed a violation of the Disposition Order.

(h) Fingerprints; When Required. Unless otherwise ordered by the court, the fingerprints of a juvenile adjudged to have committed an offense which would be a felony if committed by an adult, shall be affixed to such Disposition Order in the form and manner authorized by R.C.W. 10.64.110.

TITLE 8. DECLINING JUVENILE COURT JURISDICTION OVER AN ALLEGED JUVENILE OFFENDER
[RESERVED]

TITLE 9. RIGHT TO LAWYER AND EXPERTS IN ALL JUVENILE COURT PROCEEDINGS [RESERVED]

TITLE 10. JUVENILE COURT RECORDS

RULE 10.7. SEALING JUVENILE COURT RECORDS

The right to request and obtain an order sealing and/or destroying records in the manner set forth in ch. 13.50 RCW, GR 15 and SCLGR 15 shall be extended to those youth who have signed Diversion Agreements to the extent practicable in light of the Juvenile Court's limited involvement with the diversion process.

[Amended effective September 1, 2015.]

TITLE 11. SUPPLEMENTAL PROVISIONS

RULE 11.3. PRE–TRIAL CONFERENCE

(a) How Initiated. If it appears that in any hearing scheduled pursuant to the provisions of R.C.W. 13.04 through 13.40, inclusive, there are disputed issues of law or fact, the court may upon the ex parte motion of any party, or upon its own motion, order that a pre-trial conference be held as hereinafter provided.

(b) How Conducted. The attorney personally in charge of each party's case, or the party pro se, and guardian ad litem, if any, shall personally attend all pre-trial conferences, and shall come prepared to discuss in detail and in good faith, and to settle such matters as may aid in the disposition of the action, including, but not limited to the following:

1. An exchange of the names and addresses of prospective witnesses and the substance of their testimony;

2. Admit undisputed facts or legal principles and identify all disputed facts and legal principles;

3. Waive requirements for formal proof of documents and exhibits and submit intended exhibits so that they may be marked and listed in advance by the clerk; and

4. Determine if a written report of any witness shall be admitted in evidence by agreement of the parties or in the manner provided in CrR 6.13.

(c) Presence of Parties. All parties represented by counsel, parties pro se, and guardians ad litem, shall be present and readily available during the conference. If counsel cannot agree, the judge shall decide whether the parties are to be present in the conference room.

(d) Presence of Judge. The judge shall not be present during the conference, though the judge may attend if requested by any or all parties.

(e) Pre-Trial Order. At the conclusion of the conference, counsel shall prepare a pre-trial order setting forth the disputed and undisputed facts and legal principles. At their option they may make such order on the record using Juvenile Court recording equipment if such is available.

RULE 11.4. GRIEVANCE PROCEDURES FOR GUARDIANS AD LITEM

(a) Scope. This rule governs grievance procedures for Volunteer Guardians Ad Litem (VGAL/CASA) appointed pursuant to RCW 13.34.100, which are beyond the scope of RCW 13.34.100 (8) or RCW 13.34.102 (2) (c).

(b) Filing a Grievance. A person with a grievance or complaint beyond the scope of RCW 13.34.100 (8) or RCW 13.34.102 (2) (c) shall file a written complaint or grievance with the Juvenile Court Community Services Supervisor.

(c) Investigating Grievances or Complaints.

(1) The Juvenile Court Community Services Supervisor shall investigate the complaint or grievance and make an initial determination as to whether the complaint or grievance has potential merit.

(2) If the grievance or complaint is determined not to have potential merit, the grievance or complaint shall not be further reviewed and the complainant shall be so notified.

(d) Determination as to Potential Merit. In determining potential merit of the grievance or complaint, the Community Services Supervisor shall determine whether a complaint or grievance against a VGAL alleges:

1) Violation of a code of conduct;

2) Misrepresentation of qualifications to serve as a VGAL;

3) A breach of confidentiality of the parties;

4) Falsified information in a report or testimony to the court;

5) Gross negligence or recklessness in the preparation of a report to the court;

6) Failure to report child abuse, when required;

7) Violation of state or local laws or court rules;

8) Ex-parte communication with a judicial officer;

9) An actual or apparent conflict of interest or impropriety in the performance of VGAL responsibilities;

10) A lack of independence, objectivity, and the appearance of fairness in dealings with parties and professionals; and/or

11) Any other actions or failure to take action, which would reasonably place the suitability of the person to serve as a Volunteer Guardian Ad Litem in question.

(e) Notification. If the grievance or complaint is found to have potential merit, the GAL or appropriate party shall be notified in writing of the grievance or complaint. A copy of the grievance or complaint shall be provided to the VGAL or appropriate party. A written response shall be requested, to be received by the court within 10 business days of the date of the written notice.

(f) Review of Complaint or Grievance. Any complaints or grievances found to have potential merit shall be reviewed by the Assistant Administrator for Juvenile Court. The VGAL, complainant, and any relevant party named in the complaint shall be entitled to respond to the assistant administrator for the Juvenile Court to present their position regarding the issues raised in the complaint. Upon receipt of a written response to a grievance or complaint, the Assistant Administrator shall issue a written determination, making findings on the issues in the complaint or grievance.

(g) Time to Resolution.

(1) If the grievance or complaint relates to a pending case, then it shall be resolved within 25 days of the receipt of the complaint.

(2) If the grievance or complaint is made subsequent to the conclusion of a case, it shall be resolved within 60 days of the receipt of the complaint.

(h) Remedies/Sanctions. The Assistant Administrator for Juvenile Court may refer the VGAL for additional training, issue a written admonition, issue a written reprimand, suspend or remove the VGAL from the program, or impose other appropriate sanctions based on the findings. During the pendency of this process, the VGAL may continue on other appointed cases or continue to receive appointments unless otherwise specifically provided by the Assistant Administrator for Juvenile Court. The Assistant Administrator may impose an interim suspension during this process. In determining sanctions, any prior complaints or grievances which resulted in sanctions under this rule, RCW 13.34.100 (8), or RCW 13.34.102 (2)(c) or the lack of the same and any mitigating or aggravating factors found shall be considered.

(i) Confidentiality. The complaint, investigation, and any initial report shall be confidential until a finding of potential merit.

(j) Finality of Disposition. All resolutions to complaints or grievances by the assistant administrator for Juvenile Court shall be final and not subject to further appeal, except the removal of a VGAL from the program.

(k) Appeal.

(1) A VGAL who has been removed from the program may appeal to the Administrator for Superior and Juvenile Court.

(2) A VGAL shall notify the administrator in writing of such appeal within ten (10) days or receipt of a written notice of removal from the program. A notice of appeal shall clearly state the basis for appeal. The

administrator for Superior and Juvenile Court, the Presiding Judge and the Chair of the Judges Juvenile Court Committee shall jointly make a determination on appeals under this rule.

(*l*) Notification. The complainant, the VGAL, and any person named in the complaint over which the court has authority shall be notified in writing of the determination on appeal and any sanctions imposed.

(m) Record. The court shall maintain a record of complaints or grievances filed under this rule or under RCW 13.34.100 (8) or RCW 13.34.102 (2) (c) and the disposition of those complaints or grievances.

[Formerly SCLJuCR 9.4, adopted effective September 1, 2005. Renumbered SCLJuCR 11.4 and amended, effective September 1, 2015.]

PART IX.   RULES OF APPEAL OF DECISIONS OF COURTS OF LIMITED JURISDICTION (SCLRALJ)

TITLE 1.   SCOPE AND PURPOSE OF RULES
[RESERVED]

TITLE 2.   INITIATING AN APPEAL

RULE 2.6.   CONTENT OF NOTICE OF APPEAL

(a) Content of Notice of Appeal Generally. The Notice of Appeal shall include a statement of the errors the appellant claims were made by the court of limited jurisdiction and must identify the locations and

ending numerical count from the recording log. Respondent's brief must identify, in like manner, the portions of the record requested to be considered by the court. Identification of the entire record or tape of proceedings will not be acceptable or considered unless a motion to prepare and file transcript is timely granted as hereinafter provided.

TITLE 3.   ASSIGNMENT OF CASES IN SUPERIOR COURT

RULE 3.1.   NOTICE OF HEARING AND ASSIGNMENT

(a) Notice; Hearing; Action That May Be Taken. After an appeal has been filed, the clerk shall note the case on the Wednesday 10:30 Criminal Hearings Calendar which follows a date eighty-five (85) days thereafter, and if a court holiday, the next judicial day. There shall be no continuances without court order. Notice of hearing shall be mailed to each party or counsel of record and shall notify them that at such hearing the following action may be taken:

1. If appellant's brief has not been timely filed, the appeal may be dismissed on either respondent's or the court's motion;

2. If respondent's brief has not been timely filed, the relief sought by the appeal may be granted on appellant's or the court's motion; or

3. The matter will be assigned to a trial department for hearing on a date certain and the parties so notified.

This procedure shall be followed in both civil and criminal matters.

(b) If, two days prior to the hearing above scheduled, all parties notify the Law Clerk and certify in writing that the briefs are filed and the matter is ready for hearing, then the presence of the parties or counsel at the hearing is not required.

[Amended effective September 1, 1993; September 1, 1997; September 1, 2011.]

TITLE 4. AUTHORITY OF COURT OF LIMITED JURISDICTION AND OF SUPERIOR COURT PENDING APPEAL—STAYS

RULE 4.1. AUTHORITY OF COURTS PENDING APPEAL

(a) Motions Made in Superior Court Prior to Assignment for Trial. All motions made prior to assignment to a trial department shall be brought on the Civil Motion Calendar.

[Amended effective September 1, 1997.]

TITLE 5. RECORDING PROCEEDINGS IN COURT OF LIMITED JURISDICTION
[RESERVED]

TITLE 6. RECORD ON APPEAL

RULE 6.3A. TRANSCRIPT OF ELECTRONIC RECORD

(h) Transcript Required.

(1) *Exceptions.* By order of the Superior Court no transcript of the electronic proceeding shall be required unless:

1. The appellant shall serve and file, together with the notice of appeal, a motion to prepare and file transcript;

2. Another party serves and files such motion within ten (10) days of the service upon such party of the notice of appeal; or

3. The party filing and serving such motion notes the same for argument within ten (10) days thereafter.

(2) *Contents of Order.*

The order granting any such motion will:

1. State what the transcript shall contain;

2. State the time when it shall be served and filed; and

3. State who shall provide the transcript.

TITLE 7. BRIEFS
[RESERVED]

TITLE 8. ORAL ARGUMENT
[RESERVED]

TITLE 9. SUPERIOR COURT DECISION AND PROCEDURE AFTER DECISION

RULE 9.1. BASIS FOR DECISION ON APPEAL

(f) Form of Decision. At the time of oral argument both parties must submit proposed written decisions containing the reasons therefor, supporting their respective positions, and allowing adequate space for interlineations or additions, for immediate entry.

TITLE 10. VIOLATION OF RULES—SANCTIONS AND DISMISSAL
[RESERVED]

TITLE 11. SUPPLEMENTAL PROVISIONS
[RESERVED]

PART X. GUARDIAN AD LITEM RULES
(SCLGALR)

RULE 1. APPLICABILITY

These rules for guardians ad litem shall be referred to as SCLGALR. These rules apply to guardians ad litem appointed by the court pursuant to Title 11, attorney guardians ad litem appointed by the court pursuant to Title 13 and guardians ad litem appointed by the court pursuant to Title 26 RCW, and to guardians ad litem appointed pursuant to Special Proceeding Rule (SPR) 98.16W, RCW 4.08.050 and RCW 4.08.060.

These rules do not apply to guardians ad litem or Special Representatives appointed pursuant Chapter 11.96A RCW; Volunteer Guardians ad Litem (VGAL) (CASA) in RCW Title 13 cases, with respect to whom other grievance procedures apply; persons appointed to serve as Custodians for Minors pursuant to Chapter 11.114 RCW, or guardians ad litem to hold funds for incapacitated persons under Title 11 RCW.

Complaints by guardians ad litem or by other persons against guardians ad litem (also referred to as "grievances") covered by this local court rule shall be administered under this local court rule.

[Adopted effective September 1, 2002; amended effective April 13, 2005; amended on an emergency basis effective February 13, 2008; amended on a permanent basis effective September 1, 2008.]

RULE 2. DUTIES OF THE GUARDIAN AD LITEM

In addition to compliance with GALR 2 (General Responsibilities of Guardian ad Litem, a guardian ad litem (GAL) shall comply with the court's instructions as set out in the order appointing a guardian ad litem, and shall not provide or require services beyond the scope of the court's instructions unless by motion and on adequate notice to the parties, a guardian ad litem obtains additional instruction, clarification or expansion of the scope of such appointment. An attorney guardian ad litem may assist unrepresented parties with the preparation of final documents in a case for which they were appointed. Non-attorney guardians ad litem may submit a proposed Parenting Plan for the convenience of the court.

[Adopted effective April 13, 2005.]

RULE 3. ROLES AND RESPONSIBILITIES OF ATTORNEY GUARDIAN AD LITEM IN TITLE 13 RCW JUVENILE COURT PROCEEDINGS

Attorneys appointed as attorney guardians ad litem (AGALS) pursuant to Title 13 RCW in Juvenile Court proceedings shall comply with the terms and conditions for appointment to the AGAL registry as established by the Juvenile Court Committee of the Superior/Juvenile Court. The qualifications and processes for application, selection, education, compensation and retention of AGALs shall be as set forth in policies adopted by the court. These policies may be obtained by contacting the Programs Manager at Juvenile Court.

[Adopted effective April 13, 2005; amended on an emergency basis effective February 13, 2008; amended on a permanent basis effective September 1, 2008.]

RULE 4. AUTHORITY OF GUARDIAN AD LITEM

(a) **Proposed.** [Reserved.]

[Adopted effective April 13, 2005.]

RULE 5. REGISTRIES

The court shall establish registries for the appointment of guardians ad litem for whom this Rule applies. Absent a finding of good cause the court shall appoint from the registry. The qualifications and processes for application, selection, education, compensation, and retention for guardians ad litem on each of the registries shall be as set forth in administrative policies adopted by the court. These administrative policies may be obtained by contacting the Superior Court Program Administrator.

[Adopted effective April 13, 2005; amended on an emergency basis effective February 13, 2008; amended on a permanent basis effective September 1, 2008.]

RULE 6. LIMITED APPOINTMENTS

(a) **Proposed.** [Reserved.]

[Adopted effective April 13, 2005.]

RULE 7.1. GRIEVANCE PROCEDURES

(a) **Filing a Grievance.** A person with a grievance or complaint against a Guardian Ad Litem (GAL) under RCW Title 26 or RCW Title 4 or an Attorney

Guardian Ad Litem (AGAL) appointed pursuant to RCW Title 13 or a GAL or AGAL with a grievance or complaint shall file the complaint with the Superior Court Program Administrator. (See Rule 7.2 for complaint against a Non Professional Guardian or Certified Professional Guardian under RCW 11.88).

(b) Processing Grievances or Complaints.

(1) All complaints must be in writing directed to the attention of the Programs Administrator. Upon receipt of such a complaint, the Programs Administrator shall immediately deliver the complaint to the Chair of the Superior Court GAL Committee or the Presiding Judge in the absence of GAL Committee Chair.

(2) The GAL Committee Chair or Presiding Judge shall cause the complaint or grievance to be investigated and make an initial determination as to whether the complaint or grievance has potential merit. If the grievance or complaint is determined not to have potential merit, the grievance or complaint shall not be further reviewed and the complainant shall be so notified.

(3) If the grievance or complaint is found to have potential merit, the grievance or complaint shall be referred to the Superior Court GAL Committee for resolution.

(4) Any conduct of a GAL or AGAL pertaining to his/her performance of duties in a specific case, during the pendency of that case, which does not implicate the suitability of the person to continue to serve as a GAL/AGAL or involve a violation of the GAL or AGAL Rules or Code of Conduct, shall be addressed by a judicial officer in hearings in that specific case.

(c) Determination as to Potential Merit. In determining potential merit of the grievance or complaint, the GAL Committee Chair or Presiding Judge shall determine whether a complaint or grievance against a GAL or AGAL alleges:

1) Violation of a code of conduct;

2) Misrepresentation of qualifications to serve as a GAL or AGAL;

3) A breach of confidentiality of the parties;

4) Falsified information in a report or testimony to the court;

5) Gross negligence or recklessness in the preparation of a report to the court;

6) Failure to report child abuse, when required;

7) Violation of state or local laws or court rules;

8) Ex-parte communication with a judicial officer;

9) An actual or apparent conflict of interest or impropriety in the performance of GAL or AGAL responsibilities;

10) A lack of independence, objectivity, and the appearance of fairness in dealings with parties and professionals; and/or

11) Any other actions or failure to take action, which would reasonably question the suitability of the person to serve as a GAL or AGAL.

If the complaint does not allege any of these factors, the matter shall be closed.

(d) Notification. If the grievance or complaint is found to have potential merit, the GAL/AGAL or appropriate party shall be notified in writing of the grievance or complaint. A copy of the grievance or complaint shall be provided to the GAL/AGAL or appropriate party. A written response shall be requested, to be received by the court within 10 business days of the date of the written notice.

(e) GAL Committee Review. The GAL/AGAL, Complainant, and any relevant party named in the complaint shall be entitled to respond to the GAL Committee to present their position regarding the issues raised in the complaint. All such responses must be filed within ten (10) days of the responding individual's notification of the complaint. The Committee shall issue a written determination making a finding on the issues in the complaint or grievance within the timeframes listed in section (f). If a case in which a complaint or grievance is made is pending before a judicial officer serving on the GAL Committee, that judicial officer shall be deemed recused. The judicial officer shall not be informed as to the content of the complaint. In such cases, the Presiding Judge shall appoint another judicial officer to serve on the GAL Committee for the resolution of that specific case.

(f) Time to Resolution.

(1) If the grievance or complaint relates to a pending case then it shall be resolved within 25 days of the receipt of the complaint.

(2) If the grievance or complaint is made subsequent to the conclusion of a case, it shall be resolved within 60 days of receipt.

(g) Remedies/Sanctions. If the complaint is sustained, the GAL Committee may issue a written admonition, a written reprimand, refer the GAL/AGAL to additional training, suspend or remove the GAL/AGAL from the registry, or impose other appropriate sanctions based on the committee's findings. A suspension or removal may apply to each registry on which the GAL/AGAL is listed, at the discretion of the GAL Committee. During the pendency of the complaint process, a GAL/AGAL may continue to receive appointments and shall continue to serve in appointed cases, unless otherwise specifically prohibited by the GAL Committee. The GAL Committee may impose an interim suspension during this process. In its determination of sanctions, the GAL Committee shall take into consideration any prior complaints or grievances which resulted in sanctions authorized by this rule or the lack of same and any mitigating or aggravating factors found by the Committee.

(h) Confidentiality. The complaint, investigation, and any initial report shall be confidential until a finding of potential merit.

(i) Finality of disposition. All resolutions of complaints or grievances by the GAL Committee shall be final and not subject to further appeal. An action to remove a GAL/AGAL from a registry may follow the entry of a final disposition.

(j) Appeal.

(1) A GAL/AGAL who has been removed from a registry may appeal to the Superior Court bench.

(2) A GAL/AGAL shall notify the Presiding Judge in writing of such appeal within ten (10) days of receipt of a written notice of removal from a registry. The notice of appeal shall clearly state the basis for the appeal.

(3) The Superior Court bench shall consider the written material considered by the GAL Committee and any written communication from the GAL/AGAL relevant to the issues considered by the GAL Committee. Neither the GAL/AGAL nor any complainant may personally appear to argue issues to be considered by the Superior Court bench on such appeal. The Presiding Judge shall respond to the appeal in writing, on behalf of the Superior Court Bench.

(k) Notification. The complainant, the GAL/AGAL, and any person named in the complaint over which the Committee has authority shall be notified in writing of the GAL Committee determination and any sanctions imposed. Upon the removal of a GAL from the GAL registry pursuant to the disposition of a grievance, the court shall promptly send notice of the removal to the AOC. Upon removal of an AGAL from the AGAL registry, the court shall promptly send notice of the removal to the Juvenile Court Program Manager.

(*l*) Record. The court shall maintain a record of complaints or grievances filed and of the disposition of those complaints or grievances.

[Formerly SCLGALR 7, adopted effective April 13, 2005; amended on an emergency basis effective February 13, 2008; amended on a permanent basis effective September 1, 2008; renumbered SCLGALR 7.1 and amended, effective September 1, 2012.]

RULE 7.2. GRIEVANCE PROCEDURES FOR RCW 11.88

(a) Filing a grievance. These procedures shall be followed for complaints against all guardians, professional or otherwise, pursuant to RCW 11.88.

(b) Processing the grievance or complaint. All complaints must be in writing on the approved court form directed to the attention of the Programs Administrator who will then forward it to the GAL Committee Chair or Presiding Judge in the Chair's absence.

(1) The GAL Chair may assign another Judicial Officer to investigate the complaint.

(2) Within ten (10) working days of the Programs Administrator's receipt of the complaint, the GAL Chair shall direct the Programs Administrator to acknowledge receipt of the complaint by letter to the complainant.

(3) The GAL Chair/Judicial Officer designee shall review the guardianship file in its entirety within fifteen (15) working days of the judicial officer's receipt of the complaint and direct the Programs Administrator to:

- Send a letter to the complainant dismissing the complaint as insubstantial/inconclusive/ or having an insufficient basis; or

- Send a copy of the complaint to the guardian and/or attorney for the guardian to review and direct that a response be filed with the Programs Administrator within fifteen (15) working days of the guardian's/attorney's receipt of the complaint. If the guardian does not respond within fifteen (15) working days, a show cause hearing will be set and the guardian must appear.

(4) Upon receipt of the guardian's response, the GAL Chair/Judicial Officer shall review the response and forward a copy of the response to the Programs Administrator to send the following to the complainant within 10 working days:

- A letter to all interested persons that resolves or dismisses the complaint, or

- Notice of a show cause hearing, or

- Appointment of an 11.88 GAL to investigate the issues identified in writing by the GAL Chair/Judicial Officer. Notice of this appointment shall be mailed to the complainant, guardian, guardian's attorney and any other interested persons of record. The 11.88 GAL report is due within fourteen (14) days of the appointment unless the time is extended by the Judicial Officer for good cause.

(5) For cases involving a Certified Professional Guardian (CPG), the Programs Administrator shall notify the CPG Board that there is a complaint pending and the final disposition of the complaint.

(c) Hearing to review the 11.88 GAL report. The GAL Chair/ Judicial Officer shall conduct a hearing to review the GAL's report and recommendations. Following the hearing, the court shall enter Findings of Fact and an Order:

(1) Dismissing the complaint; or

(2) Directing remedial or other relief actions to be taken by the guardian; and

(3) Directing additional review dates for hearings as appropriate; and/or

(4) Determining allocation or payment of GAL fees; and/or

(5) Sanctions, which may include: Reimbursement to the incapacitated person, suspension from taking new cases (for CPGs only), removal from the case, referral for prosecution, and other appropriate sanctions.

(6) For Certified Professional Guardians (CPGs): The GAL Chair/Judicial Officer may refer the case to the CPG Board for further action regarding GR 23 Standards of Practice (ethical) violations. Such referral is mandatory in the event that the CPG is removed from a case for cause. This referral to the Board may occur at any stage of the complaint process. The CPG Board will not act upon the complaint until the Superior Court has concluded its investigation. While the Board will act on any judicial referral, it generally will not act on a pending complaint by a Superior Court until receipt of Findings of Fact, Conclusions of Law and Order.

(c) Final resolution. The complaint is closed upon entry of Findings of Fact and an Order directing same, and the discharge and compensation of the GAL. All pleadings and orders regarding the complaint will be filed in the appropriate guardianship court file. In cases involving a CPG, the Programs Administrator shall forward the final pleadings to the CPG Board.

[Adopted effective September 1, 2012.]

DISTRICT COURT

SNOHOMISH COUNTY DISTRICT COURT LOCAL RULES

Including Amendments Received Through
August 15, 2015

Table of Rules

ADMINISTRATIVE RULES—SCLARLJ

SCLARLJ 3. DEFINITIONS

(a) Name of Court. The Snohomish County District Court consists of four divisions and operates in facilities in four electoral districts. Reference to a particular physical location shall specify the electoral district that shall be known as a division of the Snohomish County District Court. The current divisions are as follows:

(1) Cascade Division

415 E. Burke Avenue, Arlington, WA 98223–1099

(2) Evergreen Division

14414 179th Avenue SE, Monroe, WA 98272–0625

(3) Everett Division

3000 Rockefeller Avenue, Everett, WA 98201–4060

(4) South Division

20520 68th Avenue W., Lynnwood, WA 98036–7406

(b) Judge. A "Judge" is defined to mean a current validly appointed or elected Snohomish County District Court Judge.

[Amended effective September 1, 2000; September 1, 2003.]

SCLARLJ 5. PRESIDING JUDGE

(a) Appointment. The Court shall be managed by the Presiding Judge, who shall be elected by a majority of the judges prior to December 1st in the year immediately occurring before the term of office. An Assistant Presiding Judge shall be elected in the same manner.

(b) Appeals.

(1) A decision of the Presiding Judge may be appealed to the judges by any judge.

(2) An affirmative majority vote of those judges voting is required to reverse a decision of the Presiding Judge.

(c) Meetings.

(1) *Regular Meetings.* Regular meetings of the judges shall be held not less than every quarter.

These meetings shall be on such a day as may be designated by the Presiding Judge.

(2) *Special Meetings.* Special meetings of the judges may be called at any time by the Presiding Judge or by any four judges acting jointly. Notice of any such meeting shall be provided each judge at least 48 hours in advance by personal contact or in writing left at the judge's assigned division.

(3) *Meeting Agendas.* The Presiding Judge shall prepare the agenda for judges' meetings. Any judge may place any item of business on the agenda.

(4) *Voting.* At a judge's meeting, each judge shall have the right to cast one vote on any issue before the judges.

(5) *Quorum.* A quorum for the conduct of business by the judges shall be five judges.

(d) **General Responsibilities.** In addition to GR 29 responsibilities, and in order to assure the expeditious and efficient handling of all cases and an equitable distribution of workload among the several divisions, the Presiding Judge may by written order, direct that certain types of cases be filed in different division(s) than otherwise provided in these rules for a designated period of time, or until further ordered. It is recommended, but not required, that the Presiding Judge consult with the affected division judges, affected law enforcement agencies, and other affected parties prior to making such decisions.

[Amended effective September 1, 2000; September 1, 2003; September 1, 2004.]

SCLARLJ 5.2. COMMISSIONERS AND JUDGES PRO TEMPORE

(a) There shall be one full time Court Commissioner who shall serve at the pleasure of the judges and under the direction of the Presiding Judge.

(b) The Commissioner shall be compensated at a rate of pay established in the Court's annual budget.

(c) Judges Pro Tempore shall be compensated in an amount that does not exceed the daily rate of compensation earned by the Commissioner.

(d) From time to time, the Presiding Judge may appoint Pro Tempore Commissioners as authorized by County ordinance. Pro Tempore Commissioners shall be compensated at the same rate as Judges Pro Tempore

[Formerly SCLARLJ 5.3, amended effective September 1, 2000. Renumbered as SCLARLJ 5.2 and amended effective September 1, 2003.]

SCLARLJ 5.3. [RENUMBERED]

[Former SCLARLJ 5.3 amended effective September 1, 2000; amended and renumbered as SCLARLJ 5.2 effective September 1, 2003.]

CIVIL RULES—SCLCRLJ

SCLCRLJ 3. FILING OF CIVIL AND SMALL CLAIMS CASES

(a) **General Provision.** Any Civil or Small Claim action brought in the Court shall be filed in the division in which the defendant, or, if there be more than one defendant, where one of the defendants resides at the time the complaint is filed or in which the defendant, or, if there be more than one defendant, where one of the defendants may be served with the notice and complaint. If the residence of the defendant is not ascertained by reasonable efforts, the action may be filed in the division in which the defendant's place of actual physical employment is located.

(b) **Recovery of Personal Property.** Any action for the recovery of possession of personal property shall be filed in the division in which the subject matter of the action or some part thereof is situated.

(c) **Actions for a Penalty.** An action for a penalty shall be filed in the division where the cause of action, or some part thereof, arose.

(d) **Personal Injuries and Property Damage.** An action for the recovery of damages for injuries to the person or for injury to personal property may be filed either in the division in which the cause of action arose, or in the division in which the defendant, or, if there be more than one defendant, where some one of the defendants resides at the time the complaint is filed.

(e) **Non-Resident Defendants.** An action brought against a non-resident of this state may be filed in any division where service of process may be had, or in which the cause of action or some part thereof arose, or in which the plaintiff or one of them resides.

(f) **Corporate Defendants.** For the purposes of this rule, the residence of a corporation defendant shall be deemed to be in any division where the corporation transacts business, or has an office for the transaction of business at the time the cause of action arose, or where any person resides upon whom process may be served upon the corporation.

(g) **Impound Hearings.** Impound Hearings shall be filed in the division in which the impound of the vehicle occurred.

(h) **Transfer of Non-Jury Civil or Small Claim Cases.** If a civil or small claim action is filed in the wrong division, the action shall remain there unless the defendant requests a transfer of the action to the proper division. Upon such demand the court may enter an order transferring the action to the proper division and may award the defendant the reasonable costs associated with the transfer of the action, including a reasonable attorneys fee, to be paid by the plaintiff.

(i) Transfer of Civil Jury Cases. Upon the court's own motion or the motion of any party the Presiding Judge may enter a written order transferring the case to a different division.

(j) The filing of a case in the improper division does not create a jurisdictional defect and does not, of itself, grant or deprive the Court of jurisdiction otherwise conferred by law.

[Amended effective September 1, 2000; September 1, 2003.]

SCLCRLJ 38. JURY TRIAL

(a) Jury Trial

(1) *Confirmation Required.* On the last court day preceding the jury trial date the party demanding a jury trial shall contact the confirmation clerk at the respective division of the Snohomish County District Court, at the telephone numbers listed below, between 9:00 AM and 3:00 PM, and confirm that the case is going to proceed to jury trial or that some other settlement has been reached.

Confirmation Clerk's telephone numbers for each division are as follows:

Cascade Division:	(360) 435–7747
Everett Division:	(425) 388–3926
Evergreen Division:	(360) 805–6787
South Division:	(425) 744–6808

Failure of a party to confirm the jury trial or to advise the confirmation clerk that settlement has been reached shall constitute a waiver of the jury trial demand and cause the case to be stricken from the jury trial calendar. Terms may be assessed if the case has to be continued to a different trial date. Stipulated settlements not yet reduced to writing may be put on the record in conformance with CRLJ 2A.

Any case confirmed for jury under this subsection and not proceeding to jury trial shall be subject to such sanctions, including but not limited to jury costs, witness fees and terms, as deemed appropriate by the trial judge.

(2) This procedure may be modified by written order entered in a particular case.

[Adopted effective September 1, 2001; amended effective September 1, 2003.]

CRIMINAL RULES—SCLCrRLJ

SCLCrRLJ 3.1. CERTIFICATES OF COMPLIANCE FOR INDIGENT DEFENDANTS

(a) Certificates of Compliance with the Standards for Indigent Defendants required by CrRLJ 3.1 shall be filed quarterly with the Snohomish County District Court Clerk's Office.

(b) All Notice of Appearance forms filed by counsel for indigent defendants shall indicate in a separate paragraph whether or not a current CrRLJ 3.1 Certificate of Compliance with the Standards for Indigent Defendants is on file with the Snohomish County District Court Clerk's Office.

[Adopted on an emergency basis effective December 7, 2012.]

SCLCrRLJ 3.2. BAIL IN FELONY OFFENSE CASES

A person subject to custodial arrest for a felony offense shall be held until they have posted bail according to the following schedule or appeared before a judge. Nothing in this rule shall limit the authority of the Court to set bail in a different amount in an individual case.

1. Class A felonies and attempts, conspiracies, and solicitations to commit Class A felonies.	Bail shall be set by a judicial officer.
2. The following Domestic Violence related felony crimes and attempts, conspiracies and solicitations to commit such crimes: -- Assault 2, DV -- Assault 3, DV -- Assault of a Child 2, DV -- Assault of a Child 3, DV -- Burglary 2, DV -- Child Molestation 2, DV -- Child Molestation 3, DV -- Criminal Mistreatment 1, DV -- Criminal Mistreatment 2, DV	Bail shall be set by a judicial officer.

-- Cyberstalking, DV
-- Drive by Shooting, DV
-- Kidnapping 2, DV
-- Malicious Mischief 1, DV
-- Malicious Mischief 2, DV
-- Rape 3, DV
-- Rape of a Child 3, DV
-- Residential Burglary, DV
-- Stalking, DV
-- Telephone Harassment, DV
-- Unlawful Imprisonment, DV
-- Violation of a temporary, permanent, or final Domestic
Violence Court Order that is punishable as a felony

3. The following, when committed as a felony offense: -- Driving under the Influence -- Physical Control	Bail shall be set by a judicial officer.
4. Class B felonies involving crimes against persons (as defined in RCW 9.94A.422(2)) and attempts, conspiracies, and solicitations to commit such crimes.	$25,000
5. The following Class B felony crimes and attempts, conspiracies, and solicitations to commit such crimes: -- Assault by Watercraft -- Bribe Received by a Witness -- Criminal Mistreatment 1 -- Drive by Shooting -- Escape 1 -- Hit & Run, Death -- Holding Hostages or Interference with Officer's Duty -- Intimidating a Judge -- Malicious Placement of an Explosive 2 -- Malicious Placement of an Imitation Device 1 -- Manslaughter 2 -- Promoting Commercial Sexual Abuse of a Minor -- Threats to Bomb -- Unlawful Possession of a Firearm 1	$25,000
6. All other Class B felonies (including attempts, conspiracies, and solicitations to commit such Class B felonies).	$10,000
7. Class C felonies involving crimes against persons (as defined in RCW 9.94A.422(2)) and attempts, conspiracies, and solicitations to commit such crimes.	$10,000
8. The following Class C felonies and attempts, conspiracies, and solicitations to commit such crimes: -- Bail Jumping with a Class B or C Offense -- Child Molestation 3 -- Criminal Mistreatment 2 -- Criminal Trespass Against Children -- Custodial Interference 1 -- Custodial Interference 2 -- Custodial Sexual Misconduct 1 -- Escape 2 -- Harassment -- Hit & Run, Injury -- Hit & Run with a Vessel, Injury -- Indecent Exposure to a Person Under Age 14 -- Luring -- Machine Gun or Short–Barreled Shotgun or Rifle Possession Prohibited	$10,000

-- Malicious Harassment
-- Sexual Exploitation of a Minor
-- Sexual Misconduct with a Minor 1
-- Tampering with a Witness
-- Telephone Harassment
-- Threats Against the Governor
-- Voyeurism

9. Class C felonies, all other cases	$5,000

[Adopted on an emergency basis effective October 16, 2007; amended on an emergency basis effective October 26, 2007; adopted on a permanent basis effective September 1, 2008.]

SCLCrRLJ 5.1. COMMENCEMENT OF ACTIONS

(a) Under Municipal Ordinances. Complaints for the violation of a municipal ordinance should be heard in the division in which the municipality exists.

(b) Under Other Laws. All criminal and criminal traffic actions should be filed in the division where the violation is alleged to have occurred.

[Amended effective September 1, 2000; September 1, 2003.]

SCLCrRLJ 5.2. TRANSFER OF CASES

Any judge may by written order direct the transfer of a criminal case to another division upon the court's own motion or motion of any party.

[Adopted effective September 1, 2003.]

SCLCrRLJ 6.1.1. TRIAL BY JURY

(a) Jury Trial

(1) *Readiness Hearings.* All cases set for jury trial shall be assigned both a readiness hearing date and a trial date. The defendant, and the defendant's attorney if the defendant is represented, shall appear at the readiness hearing. The court will inquire as to whether the case is expected to go to trial, the number of witnesses to be called by each side and the anticipated length of trial; and if all motions, discovery and plea negotiations have been concluded. Any case confirmed for jury trial at the readiness hearing shall remain set on the jury trial date. Failure to appear at the readiness hearing, as required herein, shall constitute a waiver of the defendant's speedy trial rights, and may result in a bench warrant for the defendant's arrest and forfeiture of any bail or bond.

(2) *Confirmation Required.* On the last court day preceding the jury trial date the defendant, if appearing pro se, or the defendant's attorney if represented by counsel, and the prosecutor shall contact the confirmation clerk at the respective division of the Snohomish County District Court, at the telephone numbers listed below, between 9:00 AM and 3:00 PM, and confirm that the case is going to proceed to jury trial or that some other disposition has been reached.

Confirmation Clerk's telephone numbers for each division are as follows:

Cascade Division:	(360) 435–7747
Everett Division:	(425) 388–3926
Evergreen Division:	(360) 805–6787
South Division:	(425) 744–6808

Failure of a party to confirm the jury trial or to advise the confirmation clerk that another disposition has been reached may cause the case to be stricken from the jury trial calendar. Failure of the defendant, if appearing pro se, or the defendant's attorney if represented by counsel, to confirm the jury trial or to advise the confirmation clerk that another disposition has been reached shall constitute a waiver of the defendant's speedy trial rights. Failure of the defendant to appear on the jury trial date may result in a bench warrant for the defendant's arrest and forfeiture of any bail or bond, unless it is confirmed by both parties that a disposition is to be proposed to the court.

Any case confirmed for jury under this subsection and not proceeding to jury trial shall be subject to such sanctions, including but not limited to jury costs, witness fees and terms, as deemed appropriate by the trial judge.

[Adopted effective September 1, 2001; amended effective September 1, 2003.]

SCLCrRLJ 7.1. DEFERRED PROSECUTION PETITION AND ORDER

A petition for deferred prosecution pursuant to RCW 10.05 must be filed with the court and the prosecuting authority no later than seven (7) days prior to proposed entry unless good cause exists for delay.

An order deferring prosecution will not be granted absent proof that the defendant has actually begun treatment in the program contained in the petition and order for deferred prosecution.

An order deferring prosecution will not be granted unless the petition, order and treatment plan have been reviewed and approved by the court's probation department to insure compliance with RCW 10.05 and appropriateness for said defendant.

[Adopted effective September 1, 2007.]

TRAFFIC INFRACTIONS RULES—SCLIRLJ

SCLIRLJ 2.3.   FILING

Notices of Infraction should be filed in the division where the violation is alleged to have occurred.
[Amended effective September 1, 2000; September 1, 2003.]

SCLIRLJ 2.6. HEARINGS BASED ON WRITTEN STATEMENTS

Contested and mitigation hearings based on written statements are authorized, as provided in IRLJ 2.6.
[Amended effective September 1, 2000; September 1, 2003.]

SCLIRLJ 3.1. PRELIMINARY PROCEDURES FOR CONTESTED HEARINGS

Subpoenas in Municipal Cases. In municipal cases where a party has requested that a witness be subpoenaed, the clerk may reschedule the hearing to the municipality's next available bench trial calendar.

[Amended effective September 1, 2000; September 1, 2003.]

SCLIRLJ 3.5. DECISION ON WRITTEN STATEMENTS

Decisions on written statements are authorized, as permitted in IRLJ 3.5.

[Amended effective September 1, 2000; September 1, 2003.]

SPECIAL PROCEEDINGS RULE—SCLSPRLJ

SCLSPRLJ 1. NAME CHANGES

Requirements. An applicant who applies to the court for a change of name pursuant to statute must meet the following requirements:

(a) *Birth Certificate.* A certified copy of any minor applicant's birth certificate or suitable identification shall be presented to the clerk for verification and copying.

(b) *Minors: Parental Consent.* All applicants under eighteen (18) years of age shall be represented by a parent or legal guardian, and both biological or legal parents or guardian must approve the change of name either by personal appearance or by verified affidavit. In the absence of consent from one of the biological or legal parents, the court may grant the petition if such action would be in the best interests of the child and the non-consenting parent has received notice of the hearing on the petition.

[Amended effective September 1, 2000; September 1, 2003.]

MUNICIPAL COURTS

BRIER MUNICIPAL COURT—
[No Local Rules.]

PUBLISHER'S NOTE

This municipal court follows the Snohomish County District Court Local Rules.

DARRINGTON MUNICIPAL COURT—
[No Local Rules]

PUBLISHER'S NOTE

This municipal court follows the Snohomish County District Court Local Rules.

EDMONDS MUNICIPAL COURT LOCAL COURT RULES

Including Amendments Received Through
August 15, 2015

Table of Rules

EDMGR 30. ELECTRONIC SIGNATURES AND FILING

(A) Judicial Electronic Signatures.

a. Judicial officers may sign orders and search warrants with a digital or electronic signature as defined in GR 30 in one of the following formats:

i. The judicial officer affixes the electronic signature, saves the signed document in .pdf format, and emails the document to the intended recipients using the judge's secure email account; or,

ii. The judicial officer affixes the electronic signature in the body of an email using the judge's secure email account; or,

iii. The judicial officer uses any other reliable means approved by the court by general order.

b. Documents may be signed by judicial officers using a facsimile of the judicial officer's signature so long as the original facsimile of the signature used in the document is only accessible by the judicial officer. The document or email may also be signed in the following format if the document or email is sent from the judge's secure email account:

Judge X
Edmonds Municipal Court
250 Fifth Avenue North
Edmonds, WA 98020

Telephone: 425–771–0210
Fax: 425–771–0269
Email: first.last@edmondswa.gov

c. The printed version of the document signed by the judge pursuant to this rule shall constitute an original document that shall be made part of the court file or search warrant return file.

d. Nothing herein alters the ability of the judge to sign documents in person or delegate the affixing of signatures by others if allowed by law or court rule.

(B) Supplemental rules regarding electronic filing of documents are as follows:

a. *Speed Measuring Device Certifications.*

i. Speed Measuring Device Certifications will be deemed filed with the court pursuant to IRLJ 6.6(b) at the time the document is added by the prosecutor's office to a secure website that allows the documents to be viewed by the public through a hyperlink on the court's website.

ii. Nothing herein alters the ability of the prosecutor's office to file hard copies of the certifications with the court, which also would be deemed filed with the court pursuant to IRLJ 6.6(b).

b. *Pleadings.*

i. Pleadings signed by attorneys or pro se defendants, may be filed electronically by attaching the signed document in .pdf format to an email addressed to edmcourt@edmondswa.gov. The pleadings will not be considered filed until a clerk acknowledges receipt of the document by return email.

ii. Nothing herein requires the electronic filing of documents by counsel.

c. *Infraction Hearings.*

i. Any request for a written contested or mitigation hearing may be submitted electronically through the court's website, if available, as long as the document has the defendant's digital signature as defined by RCW 19.34.020; or by scanning in the court-approved "Request for Written Hearing" form, completed with signature, and emailing it to the court at edmcourt@edmondswa.gov as an attached PDF.

[Adopted effective September 1, 2015.]

EDMLCR 1.1. RE: MANDATORY APPEARANCE AT ARRAIGNMENT—WAIVER OF ARRAIGNMENT BY ATTORNEYS—DEFINITION OF NEXT COURT DAY FOR DOMESTIC VIOLENCE, DUI AND PHYSICAL CONTROL CHARGES [TERMINATED]

[Adopted effective September 1, 2001; terminated effective September 1, 2008.]

EDMLCR 1.2. RE: READINESS HEARING [TERMINATED]

[Adopted effective September 1, 2001; terminated effective September 1, 2008.]

EDMLCR 1.3. JURY CONFIRMATION [TERMINATED]

[Adopted effective September 1, 2006; terminated effective September 1, 2008.]

EDMCrRLJ 2.5(A). QUASHING WARRANTS

a. The defendant or defendant's attorney may file a motion and order to quash a warrant or pay an administrative fee to quash a warrant subject to subsection (b). The filing of a motion to quash a warrant will not stay the warrant and the defendant remains subject to arrest on the warrant. The motion to quash the warrant will be reviewed by the Judge and the court will either grant or deny the motion, or set a show-cause hearing for the parties to appear. If a show-cause hearing is set by the Judge the warrant will remain outstanding until the proper bond is posted, the defendant is arrested, or the defendant appears in open court and the Judge quashes the warrant and the defendant signs for a new court date.

b. Warrants issued in an amount less than $5,000 are subject to an administrative warrant quash procedure whereby defendants shall pay a nonrefundable administrative fee of $50.00 to the Court. Warrants will not be quashed until defendants appear in person at the Court clerk's window with a valid photo identification and sign for their next court date to appear. Defendants may also quash warrants issued in an amount less than $5,000 by paying a nonrefundable administrative fee of $50 at another court previously approved by Edmonds Municipal Court. Warrants issued in an amount of $5,000 or more are not subject to be quashed administratively by posting the administrative fee.

[Adopted effective September 1, 2015.]

EDMCrRLJ 3.2(a). PROCEDURE FOLLOWING WARRANTLESS ARREST

The court shall determine probable cause on evidence presented by a peace officer or prosecuting authority in the same manner as provided for a warrant of arrest in rule CrRLJ 2.2(a)(2). The evidence shall be preserved and may consist of an electronically recorded telephonic statement, facsimile machine document, or by electronic mail. If the court finds that release without bail should be denied or that conditions should attach to the release on personal recognizance, other than the promise to appear for trial, the court shall proceed to determine whether probable cause exists to believe that the accused committed the offense charged, unless this determination has previously been made by a court. Before making the determination, the court may consider an affidavit, a document as provided in RCW 9A.72.085 or any law amendatory thereto, or sworn testimony, and further may examine under oath the affiant and any witnesses the affiant may produce. Said documentation may be provided to the court by facsimile machine document or electronic mail. Sworn testimony shall be electronically or stenographically recorded. The evidence shall be preserved and shall be subject to constitutional limitations for probable cause determinations, and may be hearsay in whole or in part. Court authorization may be done by electronic mail using an electronic signature process.

[Adopted effective September 1, 2015.]

EDMCrRLJ 3.2(b)(7). LOCAL BAIL SCHEDULE

Edmonds Municipal Court adopts the uniform bail schedule as set forth in CrRLJ 3.2(*o*) with the following exceptions:

(1) Any case designated as a domestic violence offense as defined in RCW 10.99. In these cases bail shall be set at $100,000 subject to judicial review under CrRLJ 3.2.1.

(2) Any driving under the influence or physical control cases cited under RCW 46.61.502 or .504. In

these cases bail shall be set at $2500 subject to judicial review under CrRLJ 3.2.1.

[Adopted effective September 1, 2009; amended effective September 1, 2010.]

EDMCrRLJ 3.2(o)(2). RESCINDED DOMESTIC VIOLENCE CASES HELD WITHOUT BAIL

Pursuant to CrRLJ 3.2(o)(2) the following classes of offenses shall be held without bail until their cases can be reviewed by a judge: Any case designated and cited as a domestic violence offense as defined in RCW 10.99.020.

[Adopted effective September 1, 2009; amended effective September 1, 2010.]

EDMCrRLJ 3.4(d). VIDEO CONFERENCE PROCEEDINGS

(1) **Authorization.** Preliminary appearances held pursuant to CrRLJ 3.2.1(d), arraignments held pursuant to CrRLJ 3.4 and 4.1, bail hearings held pursuant to CrRLJ 3.2, and trial settings held pursuant to CrRLJ 3.3(f), may be conducted by video conference in which all participants can simultaneously see, hear and speak with each other. Such proceedings shall be deemed held in open court and in the defendant's presence for the purpose of any statute, court rule or policy. All video conference hearings conducted pursuant to this rule shall be public, and the public shall be able to simultaneously see and hear all participants and speak as permitted by the judge, judge pro tem or court commissioner. Any party may request an in-person hearing which may be granted at the discretion of the judge, judge pro tem or court commissioner.

(2) **Agreement.** Other trial court proceedings, including entry of a Statement of Defendant on Plea of Guilty as provided for by CrRLJ 4.2, may be conducted by video conference only by agreement of the parties, either in writing or on the record, and upon the approval of the judge, judge pro tem or court commissioner.

(3) **Standards.** The standards for video conference proceedings shall be as specified in CrRLJ 3.4(d)(3).

[Adopted effective September 1, 2008.]

EDMCrRLJ 4.1(a). MANDATORY APPEARANCE AT ARRAIGNMENT

A defendant charged with a domestic violence offense (as defined in RCW 10.99), driving under the influence (RCW 46.61.502), physical control (RCW 46.61.504) or minor driving after consuming alcohol (RCW 46.61.503) must appear personally for arraignment on the next arraignment calendar following arrest.

[Adopted effective September 1, 2008.]

EDMCrRLJ 4.1(c). WAIVER OF ARRAIGNMENT

An attorney may enter an appearance and/or plea of not guilty on behalf of a client in any criminal or criminal traffic offense. Said appearance or plea shall be made in writing or in open court. In all cases not listed in EDM–CrRLJ 4.1(a) an attorney may waive arraignment. A written appearance and waiver of arraignment shall commence the running of the time periods established in CrRLJ 3.3 from the date of receipt by the Court. A written appearance and waiver of arraignment without a plea shall be considered a plea of not guilty and waives any defect in the complaint other than failure to state a crime. The Court does not accept telephonic notices or requests.

[Adopted effective September 1, 2008.]

EDMCrRLJ 4.5(a). CONFIRMATION READINESS HEARING

Eight (8) days prior to an assigned jury trial date there shall be held a readiness hearing. All parties must be present and the following matters will have been concluded: plea bargaining, exchange of witness lists, exchange of discovery, and motions on any newly discovered evidence creating legal issues.

Following conclusion of the confirmation readiness hearing the court may set conditions for the confirmation of the jury trial pursuant to EDM–CrRLJ 4.5(b). Conditions may include the defendant calling and/or meeting with their attorney prior to the scheduled trial date. Failure to comply with the conditions may result in the jury trial being stricken and sanctions imposed pursuant to EDM–CrRLJ 4.5(b).

[Adopted effective September 1, 2008. Amended effective September 1, 2015.]

EDMCrRLJ 4.5(b). JURY CONFIRMATION

(i) **Confirmation Required.** The defendant, if appearing pro se, or the defendant's attorney, if represented by legal counsel, and the City Prosecutor shall contact the Court Clerk between 9:00 a.m. and 4:00 p.m. two days before the first day of trial and confirm that the case will proceed to jury trial or that some other settlement has been reached.

(ii) **Failure to Confirm.** Failure of a party to confirm the jury trial or to advise the Court Clerk that another disposition has been reached may cause the case to be stricken from the jury trial calendar. Failure of the defendant, if appearing pro se, or the defendant's attorney, if represented by legal counsel, to confirm the jury trial or to advise the Court Clerk that another disposition has been reached shall constitute an excluded period of the defendant's speedy trial right pursuant to CrRLJ 3.3(e)(3). Likewise, failure to comply with any conditions set at the readiness hearing pursuant to EDM–CrRLJ 4.5(a) may result in the jury trial being stricken and the finding of an excluded period pursuant to CrRLJ 3.3(e)(3).

(iii) Failure to Appear. Failure of the defendant to appear on the jury trial date may result in the issuance of a bench warrant and the forfeiture of any posted bail unless a disposition has been confirmed by all parties. Any disposition will be heard on the next regularly scheduled court day unless an alternative date is set by the parties and is approved by the judge or judge pro tern.

(iv) Sanctions. Failure to comply with this rule or EDM–CrRLJ 4.5(a) may result in the imposition of sanctions. If a failure of a party to comply with this rule results in a jury pool actually appearing at the court unnecessarily, sanctions of not less than $250 plus jury costs will be assessed against the offending party.

[Adopted effective September 1, 2008. Amended effective September 1, 2015.]

EDMCrRLJ 7.1. DEFERRED PROSECUTION PETITION AND ORDER

A Petition for Deferred Prosecution pursuant to RCW 10.05 must be filed with the Court's Probation Department and the prosecuting authority no later than seven (7) days prior to proposed entry unless good cause exists for delay.

An Order deferring prosecution will not be granted unless proof of compliance with the following is shown:

(A) Petition for Deferred Prosecution is submitted on the form identified in CrRLJ 4.2.

(B) Petitioner uses the court's approved Order for Deferred Prosecution.

(C) Petitioner has completed at least 36 hours of Phase I Treatment.

(D) An ignition interlock device has been installed on every vehicle operated by Petitioner and has proof of insurance.

(E) If the defendant is not driving, then the defendant must complete the court's declaration of non-driving form.

[Adopted effective September 1, 2015.]

EDMCrRLJ 8.2. MOTION CONFIRMATION

When a motion has been noted for the long motions calendar, parties must confirm by 11:00 a.m. the Monday prior if the motion is going forward. Dispositions will not be heard on the long motions calendar. Parties who know that the hearing will not be going forward and fail to notify the court by this deadline may be assessed court costs.

[Adopted effective September 1, 2015.]

EDMIRLJ 2.6(a). SCHEDULING OF HEARINGS

(1) Contested hearings will be scheduled upon the respondent's request within the time limits provided by IRLJ 2.6(a). If, at the same time the respondent requests a contested hearing, the respondent also requests that an electronic speed measuring device (SMD) expert be present at the contested hearing, the court will set such hearing on the third Wednesday of a calendar month. If such a request is made subsequent to the scheduling of the hearing on a day other than the third Wednesday of a calendar month, the court will continue the hearing from the date first set to a hearing on the third Wednesday in a calendar month and the period between the date of the hearing originally set and the new hearing will be excluded from the computation of the time-for-hearing requirements of IRLJ 2.6(a). If the third Wednesday of a calendar month falls on a non-judicial day, the court may direct that such hearings be set on another day in the same calendar month.

(2) There shall be no pre-hearing conferences unless properly noted and approved by the Court.

(3) If the respondent is also charged with a criminal offense arising out of the same incident as that which gives rise to an alleged civil infraction, the hearing on the infraction may be scheduled at the same time as any hearing set for the criminal matter.

[Adopted effective September 1, 2006; amended effective September 1, 2008.]

EDMIRLJ 3.1(a). SERVICE AND FILING OF SUBPOENAS

The respondent, the plaintiff and respondent's attorney will subpoena witnesses in accordance with IRLJ 3.1(a). Service of subpoenas will be in accordance with IRLJ 3.1(a). Edmonds Municipal Court will not serve a subpoena on an officer or witness for the respondent, plaintiff or respondent's attorney. Each party must serve their own subpoenas.

[Adopted effective September 1, 2006; amended effective September 1, 2008.]

EDMIRLJ 3.1(b). DISCOVERY

(1) In any case where the City intends to call or to rely upon the sworn statement of a local law enforcement officer, the duty to provide a list of witnesses to the respondent may be met by providing a copy of the citing officer's sworn statement on which the officer is identified.

(2) No motion to dismiss or to suppress evidence will be granted for failure to provide discovery not required by IRLJ 3.1(b) unless the moving party has previously obtained an order from the Court compelling production of the additional discovery.

[Adopted effective September 1, 2006; amended effective September 1, 2008.]

EDMIRLJ 3.1(f).   CONTESTED HEARINGS PRELIMINARY MOTIONS

Motions challenging the authority of the Court, the constitutionality of the Court, the constitutionality of any statute, ordinance or court rule pertaining to an infraction, the authority of the prosecuting attorney prosecuting an infraction, and/or the authority of the law enforcement agency or officer filing an infraction must be made in writing. Such motions, together with citations to authority and argument, must be filed with the Court and served upon the opposing party no later than fourteen days prior to a contested infraction hearing. Such motions may be decided by the Court with or without oral argument, as the Court may determine.

[Adopted effective September 1, 2006; amended effective September 1, 2008.]

EDMIRLJ 3.3(b).   REPRESENTATION BY LAWYER

Attorneys appearing on behalf of clients shall file a Notice of Appearance with the Court and Prosecutor no later than seven (7) days prior to the hearing. Failure to provide such notice shall be grounds for a continuance to the next available calendar when the Prosecutor will be present, even if the date is beyond speedy trial requirements.

[Adopted effective September 1, 2006; amended effective September 1, 2008.]

EDMIRLJ 3.5.   DECISION ON WRITTEN STATEMENTS

At the request of the respondent, the Court will conduct a mitigation hearing authorized by RCW 46.63.100 or consider a petition to defer a finding under RCW 46.63.070(5), or conduct a contested hearing authorized by RCW 46.63.090, upon the written statements of the City's witness(es) and the respondent, pursuant to IRLJ 3.5. A petition for a deferred finding which is denied by the Court will be treated as a request for a mitigation hearing on written statements.

[Adopted effective September 1, 2006; amended effective September 1, 2008.]

EVERETT MUNICIPAL COURT RULES

Including Amendments Received Through
August 15, 2015

Table of Rules

Rule
1. Hours.
2. Calendars [Rescinded].
3. Mandatory Appearance.
4. Continuances.
5. Hearing on Motions.
6. Setting Jury Trials.
7. Voir Dire.
8. Miscellaneous [Rescinded].

Rule
9. Conditions of Suspended and Deferred Sentences on Criminal and Traffic Matters.
10. Deferred Prosecution.
11. Rules of Evidence.
12. Infraction Witness Fees.
13. [Facsimile (Fax) Transmissions].
14. [Suspension or Modification of Rules].
15. Video Conference Proceedings.
16. Local Bail Schedule.

Titles in brackets added by Publisher.

RULE 1. HOURS

1. Except as provided in Section 2, below, the Municipal Court of Everett is open to the public Monday—Friday 8:00 a.m. to 4:30 p.m.

The Clerk's office is closed between 12:00 p.m. and 1:00 p.m. for lunch.

2. One Wednesday each month the Court will remain open to accommodate a Bench Trial calendar beginning at 5:00 p.m. and continuing until the last case is completed.

If court is in session before 8:00 a.m. or after 4:30 p.m., or between 12:00 and 1:00 p.m., the courtroom(s) in which court is in session are open to spectators to enter, remain, and leave the proceedings in accordance with defendants' public trial rights under state and federal law.

[Adopted effective September 1, 1996. Amended effective September 1, 2000; September 1, 2002; September 1, 2005; September 2, 2013; September 1, 2015.]

RULE 2. CALENDARS [RESCINDED]

[Adopted effective September 1, 1996; amended effective September 1, 2000; September 1, 2002; September 1, 2006; September 1, 2008; September 1, 2009; September 1, 2010; September 1, 2011; September 1, 2012. Rescinded effective September 2, 2013.]

RULE 3. MANDATORY APPEARANCE

Arraignment: A defendant who is charged with DUI as defined in RCW 46.61.502, Driving under age 21 after consuming alcohol or marijuana as defined in RCW 46.61.503, or being in physical control of a vehicle while under the influence as defined in RCW 46.61.504 shall appear in person before a judge on the next available Arraignment date. Arraignments are held at the Court every Wednesday and Friday at 8:30 a.m. unless it is a holiday.

Confirmation Hearings: Appearance of the defendant and defense counsel is mandatory at the confirmation hearing. In custody defendants appearance is waived, defense counsel need to appear. The Judge may waive the appearance of defense counsel or defendant on showing good cause and it must be done prior to hearing.

[Adopted effective September 1, 1996. Amended effective September 1, 2006; September 1, 2008; September 1, 2012; September 2, 2013.]

RULE 4. CONTINUANCES

Continuances may be granted upon written stipulation. Per Rule CrRLJ 3.3 (f)(1), a written stipulation between the parties for a continuance must be signed by the defendant. In the absence of a Stipulation, a continuance may be granted on a showing of good cause; and in the absence of a showing of good cause, said motions must be in writing and noted for hearing on or before the last motion calendar prior to the confirmation or trial date. Please see CrRLJ 3.3.

[Adopted effective September 1, 1996; amended effective September 1, 2004; September 1, 2008; September 1, 2012.]

RULE 5. HEARING ON MOTIONS

All non-trial motions shall be filed, served and noted for hearing at least six days prior to the date specified for the hearing. No pre-trial motions shall be heard or noted for hearing on the trial date without prior approval by the Judge. The defendant must be present at the 3.5 hearings. 3.5 hearings or 3.6 hearings shall be heard only upon 6 (six) court days notice with a designation of the officer(s) who may be required to testify, unless the Court authorizes otherwise.

Motions shall be set forth in writing with a memorandum of points and authorities and an affidavit or declaration as permitted under RCW 9A.72.085 setting forth specifically the facts which counsel expects to elicit at a hearing. Failure to comply with this rule will result in the Motion being stricken from the calendar. Pre-trial hearings for admission of non-testimonial motions (Crawford/Davis Hearings) and motions for admission of evidence under 404B are heard the Wednesday before Jury Trial and noted on the confirmation calendar unless earlier set with Court approval. The defendant must be present for this hearing.

A request to extinguish or modify a No Contact Order in a Domestic Violence case may only be made by a party to the case. The party must file a request on a form prescribed by the Court. All parties and alleged victim must be served by written notice at least five court days before any hearing to consider such a request.

A request to re-impose a No Contact Order in a Domestic Violence case may only be made by the victim/party to the case and the party must file a written motion on a form prescribed by the Court. All parties must be served with the written notice at least five court days before any hearing to consider such a request.

[Adopted effective September 1, 1996. Amended effective September 1, 2000; September 1, 2009; September 1, 2010; September 2, 2013.]

RULE 6. SETTING JURY TRIALS

A jury trial will be set at the arraignment hearing and confirmed at the confirmation hearing if all necessary participants are present and indicate that the case is ready for jury trial. A case is ready for jury trial when discovery is completed and both parties indicate to the Court that there are no further pre-trial motions, other than those heard or scheduled. A jury trial will normally be set eighteen days after the confirmation hearing.

[Adopted effective September 1, 1996; amended effective September 1, 2002; September 1, 2006; September 1, 2011.]

RULE 7. VOIR DIRE

The voir dire examination of jurors shall be conducted under the direction and control of the Court with the following guidelines:

It is expected that voir dire, in most cases, will consume less than thirty minutes.

The Court shall ask all general questions and thereafter shall give leave to the respective parties to ask such supplementary questions as may be deemed proper and necessary by the Court. The parties shall submit all proposed general questions in writing prior to voir dire.

The Court may intervene without objection in instances of inappropriate questioning and may limit the amount of time each party has to examine a juror or jury panel.

[Adopted effective September 1, 1996; amended effective September 1, 2010; September 1, 2011; September 1, 2012.]

RULE 8. MISCELLANEOUS
[RESCINDED]

[Rescinded effective September 1, 2015.]

RULE 9. CONDITIONS OF SUSPENDED AND DEFERRED SENTENCES ON CRIMINAL AND TRAFFIC MATTERS

(1) The following provisions are applicable to all suspended and deferred sentences and to deferments of a finding of guilty given in traffic and criminal cases.

a. *General Conditions.* During the period of probation or suspension the defendant shall not be convicted, be awaiting sentencing or be under a deferred sentence or finding of guilty, with respect to any offense or claimed offense occurring after the date on which probation in this Court was granted. Further, any conduct reflecting moral turpitude or recklessness with respect to the operation of a motor vehicle will be considered a violation whether or not any charges are filed or carried to judgment.

b. *Specific Conditions.* The defendant must comply with the conditions specifically imposed by the Court and any conditions imposed by the Probation Department. Defendants generally must report to Probation within 7 days of sentencing, but must report directly after Court or release from jail if ordered to do so. If the defendant is placed on supervised Probation he/she must make an appointment to meet with a Probation Officer and attend that appointment.

(2) Probation–Related Hearings in Everett Municipal Court include, but are not limited to, the following:

a. *DUI Review.* DUI review hearings are initially set for approximately 4 months post sentence. All DUI and Physical Control charges, whether or not there was an amendment to the charge during the course of the proceedings, are set for a DUI Review hearing unless otherwise ordered by a judge.

b. *DV Review.* DV review hearings are initially set for approximately 4 months post sentence. All DV charges, whether or not there was an amendment to the charge during the course of the proceedings, are set for a DV review hearing unless otherwise ordered by a judge.

c. *Probation Revocation Hearing.* Probation Revocation hearings are scheduled when there is an alleged violation of a probation or suspension condition and the defendant does not admit the violation(s).

Those hearings are out of custody only. The City Prosecutor's office presents the evidence for proving the violation(s).

d. *Failure to Comply/Bench Warrant Hearings.* When a defendant has been ordered to appear for a probation-related hearing and fails to appear, resulting in a bench warrant, he/she may request that his/her matter be noted onto a Failure to Comply–Bench Warrant calendar at any time prior to the service of the warrant.

e. *Motions to Revoke Suspended Jail and/or Fine.* The Everett City Prosecutor's Office may file a motion to revoke suspended sentence.

i. If the motion is based on an active, pending case, the motion is generally noted onto the next calendar for the pending case, for which City witnesses should already be in attendance. The court will not summons the defendant for the motion hearing under these circumstances. If the defendant fails to appear for the hearing, a warrant may be issued in the active, pending case and the motion to revoke stricken. If the defendant does appear, the judge will preside over the hearing on the motion to revoke unless a continuance or resetting is necessitated by court congestion.

ii. If the motion to revoke is based on a case that is not an active, pending case, e.g., an allegation that has not resulted in a criminal charge, the motion is noted onto a motion calendar. The court will summon the defendant for the motion hearing under these circumstances. If the defendant fails to appear, a warrant may issue. If the defendant does appear, any required evidentiary hearing will be scheduled for a later date and time unless agreed to by the parties and approved by the judge.

f. *Show Cause Hearings.* Judges may order show cause hearings for any alleged violation of a condition of probation or suspension. The hearings may be set on a regular show cause calendar or may be set on any other court calendar, or may be specially set. The court will summons the defendant for show cause hearing unless the defendant has previously been given written notice of the hearing.

g. *Pretrial Reviews.*

i. Court Monitored Deferrals (CMD) are set for at least one review hearing following entry, generally within 4 months.

ii. Prosecutor Offer of Diversion (POD) cases are set for at least one review hearing following entry, generally at the conclusion of the agreed-upon diversion period.

iii. Any other pretrial review hearing may be scheduled as necessary and as approved by a judge.

(3) **Further Information.** The defendant should contact the probation office as often as may be necessary to understand the conditions of the deferral suspension or probation, particularly the condition[1] that are specific to the defendant's case. The defendant must at all times advise the Court of his/her current address and stay current wil[2]l all fines and costs owing.

[Adopted effective September 1, 1996. Amended September 1, 2006; September 1, 2008; September 1, 2010; September 2, 2013; September 1, 2015.]

1 So in original.
2 So in original.

RULE 10.   DEFERRED PROSECUTION

In addition to the statutory conditions and requirements of deferred prosecution, each defendant shall pay the monitoring assessment to the Municipal Court in the amount of $250.00 plus the BAC fee and any other costs related to the case. All defendants placed on a deferred prosecution will also be placed on five-year probation: Supervised Probation for two years and Monitored Probation for three years. They will be required to pay the fees for Probation. Restitution is required as a condition of a deferred prosecution if applicable. Deferred Prosecution defendants will have ignition interlock installed on all personal vehicles, which they drive, during their period of Supervised Probation. An Order will not enter without the written signed contract for treatment being presented to the Court.

[Adopted effective September 1, 1996; amended effective September 1, 2000; September 1, 2008; September 1, 2010.]

RULE 11.   RULES OF EVIDENCE

The Rules of Evidence are applicable to Criminal prosecutions.

[Adopted effective September 1, 1996.]

RULE 12.   INFRACTION WITNESS FEES

Each party is responsible for costs incurred by that party as set forth in RCW 46.63.151. The party requesting the witness shall pay the witness fees and mileage expenses due that witness. Any person who requests production of an electronic speed measuring device expert, and who is thereafter found by the court to have committed the infraction, may be required to pay the fee charged by the expert as a cost incurred by the party.

[Adopted effective September 1, 2000. Amended effective September 1, 2008.]

RULE 13.   [FACSIMILE (FAX) TRANSMISSIONS]

(1) The clerks of the court may accept for filing documents sent directly to the clerk by electronic facsimile (fax) transmission. A fax copy shall constitute an original for all court purposes. The attorney or party sending the document via fax to the clerk shall retain the original signed document until 60 days after completion of the case. Documents to be trans-

mitted by fax shall bear the notation: "SENT on DATE) VIA FAX FOR FILING IN COURT.

(2) If a document is transmitted by facsimile for filing with the court, the person responsible for the filing must attach an original affidavit as the last page of the document. The affidavit must bear the name of the court, case caption, case number, the name of the document to be filed, and a statement that the individual signing the affidavit has examined the document, determined that it consists of a stated number of pages, including the affidavit page, and that it is complete and legible. The affidavit shall bear the original signature, the printed name, address, phone number and facsimile number of the individual who received the document for filing.

(3) The clerk of the court may use fax transmission to send any document requiring personal service to one charged with personally serving the document. Notices and other documents may be transmitted by the clerk to counsel of record by fax.

(4) The Court reserves the right to charge reasonable fees for receiving, collating, and verifying lengthy fax transmissions.

(5) A document transmitted directly to the clerk of the court shall be deemed received at the time the clerk's fax machine electronically registers the transmission of the first page, regardless of when final printing of the document occurs, except that a document received after the close of normal business hours shall be considered received the next judicial day. If a document is not completely transmitted, it will not be considered received. A document transmitted to another for filing with the clerk of the court will be deemed filed when presented to the clerk in the same manner as an original document.

[Adopted effective September 1, 2004.]

RULE 14. [SUSPENSION OR MODIFICATION OF RULES]

Any of these Rules may be suspended or modified by the Court upon its own motion.

[Adopted effective September 1, 2000.]

RULE 15. VIDEO CONFERENCE PROCEEDINGS

Authorization: Preliminary appearances as defined by CrRLJ 3.2.1 (d), arraignment as defined by CrR 3.4 and 4.1 and CrRLJ 3.4 and 4.1, bail hearings as defined by CrR 3.2 and CrRLJ 3.2, and trial settings as defined by CrR 3.3 and CrRLJ 3.3 (f), and pre-trial hearings as determined by the court, conducted via video conferencing in which all participants can simultaneously see, hear, and speak with each other shall be deemed in open court and in the defendant's presence for the purposes of any statute,

court rule or policy. All video conference hearing conducted pursuant to this rule shall be public, and the public shall be able to simultaneously see and hear all participants and speak as permitted by the court. Any party may request an in-person hearing which may, in the court's discretion, be granted.

Agreement: Other trial court proceedings including the entry of a Statement of Defendant on Plea of Guilty as defined by CrR 4.2 and CrRLJ 4.2 may be conducted by video conference only by agreement of the parties. The defendant will be deemed to have agreed to voluntarily participate in court proceedings in the Everett Municipal Court by video conference unless the defendant or counsel for the defendant notifies the court at the time of the proceeding that he/she objects to the proceedings being conducted via conference. The right to object to video conference proceedings will be deemed waived if not exercised prior to the start of the video conference hearing.

Standards for Video Conference Proceedings: The standards for video conference proceedings shall be as specified in CrRLJ 3.4(d)(3).

[Adopted effective September 2, 2013.]

RULE 16. LOCAL BAIL SCHEDULE

Everett Municipal Court adopts the following bail schedule pursuant to CrRLJ 3.2(b)(7) and CrRLJ 3.2(o):

(1) **Domestic Violence Offenses.** Bail shall be set at $100,000, subject to judicial review under CrRLJ 3.2.1, for any person booked and detained in jail after the initial arrest for an offense classified as Domestic Violence under Chapter 10.99 of the Revised Code of Washington or under Title 10 of the Everett Municipal Code.

(2) **DUI, Physical Control.** Bail shall be set at $100,000, subject to judicial review under CrRLJ 3.2.1, for any person:

(a) Who is booked and detained in jail after the initial arrest for an offense involving driving under the influence as defined in RCW 46.61.502 or being in physical control of a vehicle while under the influence as defined in RCW 46.61.504, and;

(b) Who is not required, pursuant to RCW 10.31.100, to be kept in custody until appearance before a judge because the police officer has knowledge that the person has a prior offense as defined in RCW 46.61.5055 within ten years.

(3) **Other Offenses.** Bail for all other offenses shall be set according to the Uniform Bail Schedule in CrRLJ 3.2(o). A copy of the bail schedule is available for viewing upon request at the clerk's office.

[Adopted on an emergency basis effective March 1, 2015; adopted on a permanent basis effective September 1, 2015.]

GOLD BAR MUNICIPAL COURT—
[No Local Rules]

PUBLISHER'S NOTE

This municipal court follows the Snohomish County District Court Local Rules.

GRANITE FALLS MUNICIPAL COURT—
[No Local Rules]

PUBLISHER'S NOTE

This municipal court follows the Snohomish County District Court Local Rules.

INDEX MUNICIPAL COURT—
[No Local Rules]

PUBLISHER'S NOTE

This municipal court follows the Snohomish County District Court Local Rules.

LYNNWOOD MUNICIPAL COURT LOCAL COURT RULES

Including Amendments Received Through
August 15, 2015

Table of Rules

CRIMINAL RULES

LCrRLJ 2.2. WARRANT OF ARREST

(a) Warrants issued by the Court will specify whether a bond or bail may be posted to secure the release of the defendant. A warrant for $5,000 or less may be quashed administratively by the Clerk of the Court upon the payment of a $100.00 dollar warrant fee. No–bail warrants are not subject to this procedure.

(b) A written motion to quash any warrant may be made at any time and will be considered without a hearing.

[Adopted effective September 1, 2002; amended on an emergency basis effective August 17, 2007; amended on a permanent basis effective September 1, 2008.]

LCrRLJ 3.1(e). WITHDRAWAL OF COUNSEL

Once an attorney has been assigned and/or has filed notice of appearance in a criminal case and a trial date has been set, that attorney may withdraw from the case only with the consent of the court for good cause shown. If the withdrawal is mandated by the Rules of Professional Conduct, it will be granted upon the filing of a written motion and affidavit setting forth the reason. If a represented defendant fails to appear for any hearing and the Court issues a warrant for the Defendant's arrest, an oral motion to withdraw may then be granted by the Court. All other motions to withdraw will be granted only upon the simultaneous substitution of counsel who is prepared to proceed on the scheduled trial date or upon the defendant's know-

ing, voluntary and intelligent decision to proceed without counsel.

[Adopted effective September 1, 2002.]

LCrRLJ 3.2. RELEASE OF ACCUSED— BONDING REQUIREMENTS

Surety under CrRLJ 3.2(a)(5) or for any other purpose may be posted by any company and any agent authorized, licensed and/or justified to post bonds by the Washington State Department of Licensing under RCW 18.185 and by the Superior Court of Snohomish County.

[Adopted effective September 1, 2002.]

LCrRLJ 4.2(i). DEFERRED PROSECUTION

An order deferring prosecution under RCW 10.05 will be granted only to a petitioner who is participating in the proposed treatment plan at the time the order is entered.

[Adopted effective September 1, 2001.]

LCrRLJ 6.15(a). JURY INSTRUCTIONS

Proposed jury instructions which conform exactly to the latest edition of Washington Pattern Jury Instructions may be served and filed on the day of trial. Proposed jury instructions which deviate in any respect from Washington Pattern Jury Instructions shall be served upon the lawyer for each party and filed with the clerk no later than ten (10) days prior to the trial date.

[Adopted effective September 1, 2002.]

INFRACTION RULES

LIRLJ 2.6(a). SCHEDULING OF HEARINGS

(1) Contested hearings will be scheduled upon the Respondent's request within the time limits provided by IRLJ 2.6(a). If, at the same time the Respondent requests a contested hearing, the Respondent also requests that an electronic speed measuring device (SMD) expert be present at the contested hearing, the court will set such hearing on the fourth Tuesday of a calendar month. If such a request is made subsequent to the scheduling of the hearing on a day other than the fourth Tuesday of a calendar month, the court will continue the hearing from the date first set to a hearing on the fourth Tuesday in a calendar month and the period between the date of the hearing originally set and the new hearing will be excluded from the computation of the time-for-hearing requirements of IRLJ 2.6(a). If the fourth Tuesday of a calendar month falls on a non-judicial day, the court may direct that such hearings be set on another day in the same calendar month.

(2) There shall be no prehearing conferences.

(3) If the Respondent is also charged with a criminal offense arising out of the same incident as that which gives rise to an alleged civil infraction, the hearing on the infraction may be scheduled at the same time as any hearing set for the criminal matter.

[Adopted effective September 1, 2002.]

LIRLJ 3.1(b). DISCOVERY

(1) In any case where the City intends to call or to rely upon the sworn statement of a local law enforcement officer, the duty to provide a list of witnesses to the Respondent may be met by providing a copy of the citing officer's sworn statement on which the officer is identified.

(2) No motion to dismiss or to suppress evidence will be granted for failure to provide discovery not required by IRLJ 3.1(b) unless the moving party has previously obtained an order from the Court compelling production of the additional discovery.

[Adopted effective September 1, 2001.]

LIRLJ 3.1(f). CONTESTED HEARINGS— PRELIMINARY MOTIONS

Motions challenging the authority of the Court, the constitutionality of the Court, the constitutionality of any statute, ordinance or court rule pertaining to an infraction, the authority of the prosecuting attorney prosecuting an infraction, and/or the authority of the law enforcement agency or officer filing an infraction must be made in writing. Such motions, together with citations to authority and argument, must be filed with the Court and served upon the opposing party no later than fourteen days prior to a contested infraction hearing. Such motions may be decided by the Court with or without oral argument, as the Court may determine.

[Adopted effective September 1, 2002.]

LIRLJ 3.3(b). PROCEDURE AT CONTESTED HEARING

At a contested hearing, the plaintiff shall be represented by an attorney.

[Adopted effective September 1, 2002.]

LIRLJ 3.5. DECISION ON WRITTEN STATEMENTS

At the request of the Respondent, the Court will conduct a mitigation hearing authorized by RCW 46.63.100 or consider a petition to defer a finding under RCW 46.63.070(5), or conduct a contested hearing authorized by RCW 46.63.090, upon the written statements of the City's witness(es) and the Respondent, pursuant to IRLJ 3.5. A petition for a deferred finding which is denied by the Court will be treated as a request for a mitigation hearing on written statements.

[Adopted effective September 1, 2001; amended effective September 1, 2002.]

LIRLJ 6.6(b). SMD EXPERT

A request for the production of an SMD expert at the contested hearing shall be made in a document separate from any and all other requests, demands and/or notices.

[Adopted effective September 1, 2001.]

MARYSVILLE MUNICIPAL COURT LOCAL RULES

Including Amendments Received Through
August 15, 2015

Table of Rules

LOCAL GENERAL RULES

MMCLGR 1.1. INDIGENT DEFENSE CERTIFICATION

1.2 Certificates of Compliance with the Standards for Indigent Defendants required by CrRLJ 3.1 shall be filed and kept at the Marysville Municipal Court clerk's office. Certification of Compliance shall be submitted electronically in the form provided by the court or in a substantially similar format. Certifications shall be filed quarterly with the court and are due: January 1, April 1, July 1, and October 1, or the next court day, if the filing day falls on a weekend or holiday.

[Adopted on an emergency basis effective October 1, 2012.]

MMCLGR 1.2. ANTI–HARASSMENT PROTECTION ORDER

1. By adoption of this local rule, the Marysville Municipal Court hereby exercises jurisdiction and cognizance of any civil actions and proceedings brought under RCW 10.14.150, as now or hereafter amended, except the Marysville Municipal Court shall transfer such actions and proceedings to the superior court when it is shown that the respondent to the petition is under eighteen years of age.

2. The Marysville Municipal Court's jurisdiction pursuant to this rule shall be limited to situations:

a. When the alleged acts of unlawful harassment occurred within the city limits of Arlington, Lake Stevens or Marysville; or

b. When the respondent resides within the city limits of Arlington, Lake Stevens or Marysville at the time the petition is filed; or

c. When the respondent may be served within the city limits of Arlington, Lake Stevens or Marysville if it is the same county or judicial district where a respondent resides.

3. The Clerk of the Municipal Court may charge a filing fee in the amount equal to the applicable fee charged by the Snohomish County District Court. The Municipal Court Judge has discretion to waive or reduce the filing fee upon showing of indigence, financial hardship, or other good cause.

[Adopted effective September 1, 2015.]

LOCAL CRIMINAL RULES

MMCLCR 1.1. ADOPTION AND TITLE

These local court rules are adopted pursuant to GR 7, and CrRLJ 1.7. These rules shall be known as the Marysville Municipal Court Local Criminal Rules, and may be cited as "MMCLCR."

[Adopted effective September 1, 2002.]

MMCLCR 1.2. ARRAIGNMENT—DEFENDANT'S PRESENCE REQUIRED

1.2 (A) A lawyer may enter a written notice and plea of not guilty on behalf of any defendant, including a waiver of formal arraignment, except for those criminal charges listed in MMCLCR 1.2(B).

1.2 (B) Arraignment—Defendant's Presence Required: A lawyer may not enter a written plea of not guilty on behalf of a defendant if the charging document states that one or more of the charges involve domestic violence, harassment, violation of an anti-harassment or protection order, stalking, driving while under the influence, being in physical control of a vehicle while under the influence, or driving while under the age of 21 after having consumed alcohol. For such charges, the defendant must appear in person for arraignment, and the court shall determine the necessity of imposing conditions of pre-trial release. Where legislation mandates the defendant's appearance on the next judicial day following arrest, the term "next judicial day" shall be the next regularly scheduled court session.

1.2 (C) Defendants booked into custody on charges of Assault–Domestic Violence, Driving Under Influence, or Physical Control shall personally appear before a judge the next judicial day following booking into jail.

[Adopted effective September 1, 2002; amended effective September 1, 2008.]

MMCLCR 1.3. PRE–TRIAL HEARINGS AND CONFIRMATION OF JURY TRIALS

(a) Pre–Trial, Confirmation and Jury Trial Dates: All cases set for jury trial shall be assigned a pre-trial, confirmation hearing and a jury trial date. The defendant, and the defendant's attorney, if the defendant is represented, shall appear at the pre-trial and confirmation hearings. At the confirmation hearing the court will inquire whether the case is expected to go to jury trial, the number of witnesses to be called by each side and the anticipated length of trial, and if all motions, discovery and plea negotiations have been concluded. Any case confirmed for jury trial at the confirmation hearing shall remain set for the assigned jury trial date. A defendant's failure to personally appear at the pre-trial and confirmation

hearing, as required herein, shall constitute a waiver of the defendant's speedy trial rights, and may result in a bench warrant for the defendant's arrest and forfeiture of any bail or bond.

(b) Telephonic confirmation of Jury Trial Required: Two (2) days prior to the date of the assigned jury trial, the defendant, if not represented by an attorney, or the defendant's attorney and the City Prosecutor shall contact the jury confirmation line at 360–363–8071 between 9:00 AM and 3:00 PM, and confirm that the case is going to proceed to jury trial.

(c) Telephonic Confirmation of Jury Trial Using Interpreter Services: Three (3) days prior to the date of the assigned jury trial, the defendant, if not represented by an attorney or the defendant's attorney and the City Prosecutor shall contact the jury confirmation line at 360–363–8071 by 3:00 pm and confirm the case and the use of an interpreter.

(d) Failure to Confirm: Failure of a party to confirm the jury trial shall cause the case to be stricken from the jury trial calendar. Failure of the defendant, if appearing pro se, or the defendant's attorney to confirm the jury trial shall constitute a waiver of the defendant's speedy trial rights. Failure of the defendant to appear on the jury trial date may result in the issuance of a bench warrant for the defendant's arrest and forfeiture of any bail or bond.

(e) Costs and Sanctions: Any case confirmed for jury trial under this rule, and not proceeding to jury trial may be subject to sanctions, including but not limited to: jury costs, witness fees, interpreter costs and terms or other costs, as deemed appropriate by the court.

[Adopted effective September 1, 2002. Amended effective September 1, 2008; September 1, 2015.]

MMCLCR 1.4. DEFERRED PROSECUTION

(a) Petition for Deferred Prosecution: A petition for deferred prosecution pursuant to RCW 10.05 must be filed with the Court and the prosecuting authority no later than seven (7) days prior to proposed entry, unless good cause exists for the delay.

(b) An order deferring prosecution will not be granted without written verification that the defendant has actually begun treatment in the program contained in the petition and order for deferred prosecution.

(c) An order deferring prosecution will not be granted unless the petition, order and treatment plan have been reviewed and approved by the Court's probation officer, no later than seven (7) days prior to the proposed entry, to insure compliance with RCW 10.05.

(d) An order deferring prosecution must identify the assessment utilized in support of deferred prosecution, and must state the name of the agency providing treatment.

(e) No changes in treatment, nor changes in treatment provider, shall be permitted without prior written authorization from the Court.

[Adopted effective September 1, 2002; amended effective September 1, 2008.]

LOCAL INFRACTION RULES

MMCLIR 1.1. ADOPTION

These Local Traffic Rules are adopted pursuant to IRLJ 1.3. These rules shall be known as the Marysville Municipal Court Local Infraction Rules "MMCLIR".

[Adopted effective September 1, 2002.]

MMCLIR 1.2. REPRESENTATION BY LAWYER

At a contested hearing where an attorney has appeared for the defendant or witnesses have been subpoenaed, a lawyer representative of the City Prosecutor's office shall personally appear at the time of hearing. A defendant issued a Notice of Infraction and represented by an attorney must provide a written Notice of Appearance to the City Prosecutor for the municipality issuing the Notice, together with filing a copy of the Notice of Appearance with the Court Clerk. The Notice of Appearance shall be filed not later than 10 days following the date defendant's request for a contested hearing has been filed with the Court Clerk. Upon receipt of a Notice of Appearance, the Court Clerk shall set, or reset the contested hearing to an appropriate calendar. The failure to timely file a notice of appearance may result in the contested hearing being continued beyond the 120 days from the date the Notice of Infraction was issued.

[Adopted effective September 1, 2002.]

MMCLIR 1.3. CONTESTED HEARINGS— PRELIMINARY PROCEEDINGS

(a) Speed Measuring Device Expert: As provided in RCW 46.63.151, any person who requests production of an electronic speed measuring device expert, and who is thereafter found by the Court to have committed the infraction, shall be required to pay the fee charged by the expert as a cost incurred by that party. A request for the presence of a SMD Expert must be submitted, in writing, to the City Prosecutor of the municipality issuing the Notice of Infraction not less than 30–days prior to the scheduled date of the contested hearing. A untimely request for the presence of a SMD Device Expert may be treated by the Court as a request for a continuance to the next date on which the City Prosecutor has scheduled the appearance of the SMD Expert.

(b) Costs and Fees For Other Witnesses: Each party is responsible for cost incurred by that party,

including witness fees as set forth in RCW 46.63.151. In cases where a party requests a witness to be subpoenaed, the party requesting the witness shall pay the witness fees and mileage expenses due the witness.

[Adopted effective September 1, 2002.]

MMCLIR 1.4. LIABILITY INSURANCE

If a defendant is cited, with driving a motor vehicle without having proof of valid insurance pursuant to RCW 46.30.020, and the defendant presents satisfactory evidence that they have subsequently obtained valid liability insurance to the Court Clerk, within 15 days of the date of the Notice of Infraction, for the vehicle the defendant was operating on the day he or she was cited, then the bail for the offense shall be reduced to $255.00. If the defendant presents satisfactory evidence that they were in compliance with the requirements of RCW 46.30.020(1) at the time the Notice of Infraction was issued, which evidence must be presented within 15 days from the date of the notice, the infraction shall be dismissed, and a administrative cost of $25.00 shall be assessed and paid by the defendant.

[Adopted effective September 1, 2002.]

MMCLIR 1.5. DECISIONS ON WRITTEN STATEMENTS

(a) Written Submissions: Traffic infractions may be heard by the Court on the basis of written documents submitted by the City and a defendant, as provided in IRLJ 2.4(b)(4) and IRLJ 2.6. A written submission must be received by the Court no later than 7 days prior to the scheduled date of the contested or mitigation hearing, or the submission will not be considered.

(b) Generally: The Court shall examine the citing officer's report and any written documents submitted by the defendant. The examination shall take place within 120 days after the defendant filed the response to the notice of infraction. The examination may be held in chambers and shall not be governed by the Rules of Evidence.

(c) Factual Determination: For purposes of a contested infraction hearing, the Court shall determine whether the City has established, by a preponderance of all submitted evidence, that the defendant committed the infraction.

(d) Disposition: If the Court determines that the infraction has been committed, it may assess a penalty amount, and any appropriate and permitted costs to be paid by the defendant.

(e) Notice to Parties: The Court shall notify the parties in writing, whether an infraction was found to have been committed and what penalty, if any, was imposed.

(f) No Appeal Permitted: There shall be no appeal from a Court determination based upon written statements.

[Adopted effective September 1, 2002.]

MMCLIR 1.6. MONETARY PENALTY FOR UNSCHEDULED INFRACTIONS

The Administrative Office of the Courts (AOC) has interpreted School Zone Speeding pursuant to RCW 46.61.440 to be an "unscheduled" infraction under IRLJ 6.2 (b). On the assumption that this is a correct interpretation, the Marysville Municipal Court has by this rule established a local rule as permitted by IRLJ 6.2 (b) to make the School Zone Speeding penalties consistent with IRLJ 6.2 (d) and the obvious intent of the legislature in adopting RCW 46.61.440 (3).

Pursuant to IRLJ 6.2 (b) this rule adopts as the penalty for speeding in a school zone the monetary base penalty set for in IRLJ 6.2 (d) for the relevant speed, but then doubled pursuant to RCW 46.61.440 (3). The base penalty, together with the statutory assessments may not be waived, reduced or suspended. The court will not consider a request for deferred findings under RCW 46.63.070 (5) in a school zone speeding case.

Penalty schedule

1–5	mph over limit	$157.00
6–10	mph over limit	$177.00
11–15	mph over limit	$239.00
16–20	mph over limit	$321.00
21–25	mph over limit	$423.00
26–30	mph over limit	$526.00
31–35	mph over limit	$628.00
Over 35	mph over limit	$751.00

[Adopted effective September 1, 2006.]

MILL CREEK MUNICIPAL COURT—
[No Local Rules]

PUBLISHER'S NOTE

This municipal court follows the Snohomish County District Court Local Rules.

MONROE MUNICIPAL COURT

**Including Amendments Received Through
August 15, 2015**

Table of Rules

LOCAL CRIMINAL RULES

MMCLR 1. RELEASE OF ACCUSED

(a) Bail: Monroe Municipal Court will follow the bail schedule set forth in Washington Court Rule CrRLJ 3.2(*o*) except where the charges involve domestic violence offenses or charges of DUI(RCW 46.61.502) or Physical Control (RCW 46.61.504).

(b) Domestic Violence Offenses: Bail shall not be set for a person arrested for a new domestic violence offense unless set by a judge electronically at the time of arrest, or at a preliminary appearance, arraignment or subsequent court appearance. "Domestic violence" includes, but is not limited to any of the misdemeanor or gross misdemeanor offenses listed in RCW 10.99.020(5), or similar municipal ordinance, when committed by one family or household member against another. "Family or household members" are those persons listed in RCW 10.99.020(3) or similar municipal ordinance.

(c) DUI or Physical Control: Bail shall not be set for a person arrested for a new DUI or Physical Control offense unless set by a judge electronically at the time of arrest, or at a preliminary appearance, arraignment or subsequent court appearance or by written court order.

[Adopted effective September 1, 2015.]

MMCLR 2. WARRANT OF ARREST

(a) Warrants issued by the Court will specify whether a bond or bail may be posted to secure the release of the defendant. A warrant for $5,000 or less may be quashed administratively by the Clerk of the Court upon the payment of a fifty dollar ($50.00)

warrant fee. No–bail warrants are not subject to this procedure.

(b) A written motion to quash any warrant may be made at any time and will be considered without a hearing.

[Adopted effective September 1, 2015.]

MMCLR 3. ELECTRONIC MOTION FOR BAIL REVIEW

Either party may file a motion for bail review with the court in writing. The motion must also be served on the opposing party. If the party wishes to have the matter reviewed electronically, the party may electronically file the motion with the court and simultaneously file the motion with the opposing party at the email address of the opposing party. The opposing party will have 24 hours to respond electronically to the court and the moving party. Upon receipt of the response, the moving party may reply electronically by service to the court and the opposing party within 12 hours. Upon receipt of the reply, the court will render a decision in writing. Nothing herein requires the electronic filing of motions for bail review.

[Adopted effective September 1, 2015.]

MMCLR 4. MOTIONS AND OTHER PAPERS

a) **How Made.** An application to the court for an order shall be by motion which, unless made during a hearing or trial, shall be made in writing, shall state with particularity the grounds therefor, and shall set forth the relief or order sought. The requirement of writing is fulfilled if the motion is stated in a written notice of the hearing of the motion.

b) Form. The civil rules (CR) applicable to captions and other matters of form of pleadings apply to all motions and other papers provided for by these rules.

c) Signing. All motions shall be signed in accordance with CR 11 or GR 30.

d) Identification of Evidence. When a motion is supported by affidavits or other papers, it shall specify the papers to be used by the moving party.

e) Electronic Filing. Any pleading signed by attorneys, electronically or otherwise, may be filed electronically by attaching the document in .pdf format to an email addressed to court@monroewa.gov. Nothing herein requires the electronic filing of documents by counsel.

[Adopted effective September 1, 2015.]

LOCAL INFRACTION RULES

MMCLR 5. SCHEDULING OF HEARINGS

(a) Contested hearings will be scheduled upon the Respondent's request within the time limits provided by IRLJ 2.6(a). If, at the same time the Respondent requests a contested hearing, the Respondent also requests that an electronic speed measuring device (SMD) expert be present at the contested hearing, the court will set such hearing on the third Wednesday of a calendar month. If such a request is made subsequent to the scheduling of the hearing on a day other than the third Wednesday of a calendar month, the court will continue the hearing from the date first set to a hearing on the third Wednesday in a calendar month and the period between the date of the hearing originally set and the new hearing will be excluded from the computation of the time-for-hearing requirements of IRLJ 2.6(a). If the third Wednesday of a calendar month falls on a non-judicial day, the court may direct that such hearings be set on another day in the same calendar month.

(b) There shall be no prehearing conferences.

(c) If the Respondent is also charged with a criminal offense arising out of the same incident as that which gives rise to an alleged civil infraction, the hearing on the infraction may be scheduled at the same time as any hearing set for the criminal matter.

[Adopted effective September 1, 2015.]

MMCLR 6. DISCOVERY

(a) In any case where the City intends to call or to rely upon the sworn statement of a local law enforcement officer, the duty to provide a list of witnesses to the Respondent may be met by providing a copy of the citing officer's sworn statement on which the officer is identified.

(b) No motion to dismiss or to suppress evidence will be granted for failure to provide discovery not required by IRLJ 3.1(b) unless the moving party has previously obtained an order from the Court compelling production of the additional discovery.

[Adopted effective September 1, 2015.]

MMCLR 7. CONTESTED HEARINGS— PRELIMINARY MOTIONS

Motions challenging the authority of the Court, the constitutionality of the Court, the constitutionality of any statute, ordinance or court rule pertaining to an infraction, the authority of the prosecuting attorney prosecuting an infraction, and/or the authority of the law enforcement agency or officer filing an infraction must be made in writing. Such motions, together with citations to authority and argument, must be filed with the Court and served upon the opposing party no later than fourteen days prior to a contested infraction hearing. Such motions may be decided by the Court with or without oral argument, as the Court may determine.

[Adopted effective September 1, 2015.]

MMCLR 8. DECISION ON WRITTEN STATEMENTS

At the request of the Respondent, the Court will conduct a mitigation hearing authorized by RCW 46.63.100 or consider a petition to defer a finding under RCW 46.63.070(5), or conduct a contested hearing authorized by RCW 46.63.090, upon the written statements of the City's witness(es) and the Respondent, pursuant to IRLJ 3.5. A petition for a deferred finding which is denied by the Court will be treated as a request for a mitigation hearing on written statements.

[Adopted effective September 1, 2015.]

MMCLR 9. SMD EXPERT

A request for the production of an SMD expert at the contested hearing shall be made in a document separate from any and all other requests, demands and/or notices.

[Adopted effective September 1, 2015.]

MMCLR 10. Representation by Lawyer

Attorneys appearing on behalf of clients shall file a Notice of Appearance with the Court and Prosecutor no later than seven (7) days prior to the hearing. Failure to provide such notice shall be grounds for a continuance to the next available calendar when the

Prosecutor will be present, even if the date is beyond
speedy trial requirements.

[Adopted effective September 1, 2015.]

MOUNTLAKE TERRACE MUNICIPAL COURT—
[No Local Rules]

PUBLISHER'S NOTE

This municipal court follows the Snohomish County District Court Local Rules.

MUKILTEO MUNICIPAL COURT—
[No Local Rules]

PUBLISHER'S NOTE

This municipal court follows the Snohomish County District Court Local Rules.

SNOHOMISH MUNICIPAL COURT—
[No Local Rules]

PUBLISHER'S NOTE

This municipal court follows the Snohomish County District Court Local Rules.

STANWOOD MUNICIPAL COURT—
[No Local Rules]

PUBLISHER'S NOTE

This municipal court follows the Snohomish County District Court Local Rules.

SULTAN MUNICIPAL COURT—
[No Local Rules]

PUBLISHER'S NOTE

This municipal court follows the Snohomish County District Court Local Rules.

WOODWAY MUNICIPAL COURT—
[No Local Rules]

PUBLISHER'S NOTE

This municipal court follows the Snohomish County District Court Local Rules.

SPOKANE COUNTY

Table of Courts

Superior Court

Local Rules for the Superior Court of Spokane County.

District Court

Local Rules for the District Court of Spokane County, Washington.

Municipal Courts

Airway Heights Municipal Court—[No Local Rules].
Cheney Municipal Court Local Rules.
Deer Park Municipal Court Local Rules.
Medical Lake Municipal Court Local Rules.
Spokane Municipal Court Local Rules.

SUPERIOR COURT

LOCAL RULES FOR THE SUPERIOR COURT OF SPOKANE COUNTY

Originally Effective January 1, 1979

Including Amendments Received Through August 15, 2015

Table of Rules

Titles in brackets added by Publisher.

LOCAL GENERAL RULES

LGR 0.15. DESTRUCTION, SEALING, AND REDACTION OF COURT RECORDS

(a) See GR 15

(b) See GR 15

(c) Sealing or Redacting Court Records.

(1) *Motions to Destroy, Redact or Seal.* Motions to destroy, redact or seal all or part a court record shall be presented, in accordance with GR 15 to the assigned judge or Presiding Judge if there is no assigned judge.

(A) Guardianship, Trusts and Probate: (Title 11) Motions may be presented to the Ex Parte Commissioner.

(B) Vulnerable Adult Protection Order: (RCW 74.04) Motions may be presented to the Ex Parte Commissioner.

(C) Minor/Incapacitated Settlement: The motion shall be presented to the assigned judge.

(D) Name Changes Based on Domestic Violence: If no assigned judge, motion may be presented by the requesting party to the Ex Parte Commissioner.

(2) *Financial Source Documents, Personal Health Care Records and Confidential Reports in Title 26 or Title 11 Cases*: In a proceeding brought pursuant to RCW 26 or RCW 11, "financial source document", "personal health care record" and "confidential report" as defined under and submitted in accordance with GR 22 will be automatically sealed by the clerk without court order, if accompanied by the proper cover sheet.

(3) *Orders to Destroy, Redact or Seal.* Any order containing a directive to redact or seal all or part of a court record must be clearly captioned as such and may not be combined with any other order; the

clerk's office is directed to return any order that is not so captioned to the judicial officer signing it for further clarification. The clerk is directed to not accept for filing and to return to the signing judicial officer any order that is in violation of this rule.

(4) Motions to Seal/Redact Filed Contemporaneously with Confidential Document(s).

(A) Contemporaneously with filing the motion to seal, the moving party shall provide the following as working copies:

(i) the original unredacted copy of the document(s) the party seeks to file under seal to the hearing judge in an envelope for *in camera* view. The words "SEALED PER COURT ORDER DATED [insert date]" shall be written on the unredacted document(s). The following information shall be written on the envelope: The case caption and cause number; a list of the document(s) under review; and the words "SEALED PER COURT ORDER DATED [insert date]."

(ii) a proposed redacted copy of the subject documents(s).

(iii) a proposed order granting the motion to seal, with specific proposed findings setting forth the basis for sealing the document(s).

(B) If the judicial officer denies the motion to seal, the judicial officer will file the original unredacted document(s) unsealed with an order denying the motion. The words "SEALED PER COURT ORDER FILED [insert date]" will be crossed out on the unredacted document(s).

(C) If the judicial officer grants the motion to seal, in whole or in part, the judicial officer will cause to be filed the sealed document(s) contemporaneously with a separate order granting the motion. If the judicial officer grants the motion by allowing redaction, the judicial officer shall write the words "SEALED PER COURT ORDER DATED [inserted date]" in the caption of the unredacted document before filing.

(d) See GR 15

(e) Motions to Unseal or Examine, See GR 15 with respect to motions to unseal or examine a sealed court record.

(f) See GR 15.

(g) See GR 15.

(h) See GR 15.

(i) See GR 15.

(j) See GR 15.

[Adopted on an emergency basis, effective January 1, 2013; March 13, 2013; June 4, 2013; adopted on a permanent basis, effective September 2, 2013.]

LGR 0.31. ACCESS TO COURT RECORDS

a) Filing by Clerk. It is the policy of the Spokane County Superior Court to make, as a part of the public record, all documents considered by judicial officers in the course of their official duties. This includes pleadings, reports, letters, and other written materials. The Court directs the Clerk of Court to place in the public file all documents considered by the Court, unless otherwise sealed or redacted.

(1) The Court orders the following documents to be placed in the public court file after consideration by the court:

(A) Mental condition evaluations (RCW 10.77);

(B) SSOSA evaluations and reports (RCW 9.94A.670);

(C) Presentence reports (RCW 9.94A.500(1)); and

(D) Victim Impact Statements (Washington State Constitution, Article I, Section 35).

(2) *Criminal Cases.* After first appearance, pretrial first appearance evaluations and risk assessment tools used in pretrial hearings shall be placed in the public court file.

[Adopted on an emergency basis, effective January 1, 2013; March 13, 2013; June 4, 2013; adopted on a permanent basis, effective September 2, 2013.]

I. ADMINISTRATIVE AND CIVIL RULES (LAR and LCR)

1. INTRODUCTORY

LAR 0.1. DEPARTMENTS OF COURT

The Superior Court of Spokane County shall be divided into as many departments as there are judges authorized by law. The departments shall be numbered consecutively in the order of their creation, as follows:

Department	Created	Incumbent Judge
No. 1	1889	Hon. Annette S. Plese

Department	Created	Incumbent Judge
No. 2	1891	Hon. James M. Triplet
No. 3	1901	Hon. Raymond F. Clary
No. 4	1907	Hon. Kathleen M. O'Connor
No. 5	1909	Hon. Michael P. Price
No. 6	1949	Hon. Salvatore F. Cozza
No. 7	1963	Hon. Maryann C. Moreno
No. 8	1973	Hon. Harold D. Clarke III
No. 9	1977	Hon. John O. Cooney
No. 10	1979	Hon. Linda G. Tompkins
No. 11	1996	Hon. Greg D. Sypolt
No. 12	1999	Hon. Ellen Kalama Clark

[Amended effective October 1, 1989; October 19, 1990; May 31, 1994; September 1, 1996; September 1, 1997; March 5, 1998; September 1, 2003; February 1, 2004; September 1, 2005; September 1, 2009; September 1, 2011; September 2, 2013; September 1, 2015.]

LAR 0.2. COURT ORGANIZATION AND MANAGEMENT

(a) General Management. The general management of the courts shall be vested in the presiding judge under policy established by the judges at regular and special meetings.

(b) Meetings. The judges shall meet regularly on Thursday of each week during the noon hour. Special meetings may be called by the presiding judge as deemed necessary on timely notice. A written agenda shall be provided in advance of all meetings. A majority of the judges shall constitute a quorum.

(c) Presiding Court. The presiding judge and Assistant Presiding Judge shall serve a two year term and shall be selected by election by a majority of the judges in accordance with GR 29. In the absence of the presiding judge, presiding duties shall be performed by the Assistant Presiding Judge.

(d) Duties of the Presiding Judge.

(1) Supervise all business of the court and implement all policies established by the judges;

(2) Supervise the court commissioners, the court administrator, court employees not assigned to a particular department, and employees assigned to a particular department in the absence of the departmental judge;

(3) Oversee the assignment of cases and caseflow management, with the assistance of the court administrator;

(4) Select and utilize jurors, with the assistance of the court administrator;

(5) Preside at all judges' meetings and call special meetings as required;

(6) Act as spokesperson for the court, seeking advice and counsel from the judges where appropriate;

(7) Assign cases and other duties to the judges and court commissioners;

(8) Hear such ex parte civil and probate matters as are not assigned to other departments or court commissioners;

(9) Appoint standing and special committees, with the approval of the judges.

(e) Criminal Department. The criminal department shall consist of one Chief Criminal Judge, the Presiding Judge and three Criminal Trial Judges. The Chief Criminal Judge shall be responsible to manage the entire criminal docket from arraignment through plea setting or trial assignment. He or she shall preside at arraignments, decide continuance issues, hold scheduling hearings and pretrial (omnibus) hearings, and shall hear or assign all criminal motions, all probation violations, violations of conditions of sentence, and shall assign all criminal trials. The Presiding Judge will hear criminal pleas and sentencings. Additional hearings, pleas and sentencings will be assigned to the other judges by the Chief Criminal Judge as needed to keep the docket current. Judges will serve on assignment as Criminal Trial Judges for a month at a time, pursuant to a schedule established by the Court Administrator. The Chief Criminal Judge shall be selected from among the judges, other than the Presiding Judge and the Juvenile Judge, to serve for a one year term.

(1) *Drug Court.* The Presiding Judge or designee will be responsible to manage the Drug Court program, including primary responsibility to determine eligibility of defendants and revocation for violation of program rules.

(2) Court Commissioners qualified under Article 4, Section 23 of the Washington Constitution are authorized to preside over, and consider all matters in adult felony proceedings specified under RCW 2.24.040, with the limitation that they may not accept guilty pleas in matters involving felony charges under RCW 9A.44 (Sexual Offenses) or 9.68A (Sexual Exploitation of Children).

(f) Duties of the Court Administrator. The court administrator shall assist the presiding judge in administrative responsibilities. Subject to the general supervision of the presiding judge, the court administrator's duties shall include:

(1) Administrative control of all nonjudicial activities of the court;

(2) Supervision of all court employees other than court commissioners, juvenile court employees, and departmental employees;

(3) Case setting and trial calendar management;

(4) Juror selection and utilization;

(5) Preparation and administration of the budget;

(6) Coordination with the state court administrator and with the visiting judge program;

(7) Assisting the presiding judge in dealing with county government, bar association, news media, and other public and private groups having a reasonable interest in the administration of justice;

(8) Attendance of judges' meetings and preparation of the agenda for and minutes of those meetings;

(9) Preparation of such reports and compilation of such statistics as may be required by the judges or state court administrator;

(10) Making recommendations to the judges for the improvement of the administration of the court.

[Amended effective July 1, 1988; July 1, 1994; September 1, 1997; January 1, 1998; January 18, 2000; March 23, 2000; June 8, 2000; September 1, 2002; September 2, 2014.]

LAR 0.3. COMMITTEES

(a) Standing Committees. The following standing committees shall be established:

(1) Juvenile Court, composed of the juvenile court judge as chairman and the last and next succeeding juvenile court judge;

(2) Mental Illness;

(3) Jury Management;

(4) Mandatory Arbitration;

(5) Superior Court Criminal Liaison;

(6) Budget and Planning;

(7) Superior Court Civil Liaison; and

(8) Court Commissioner Liaison;

(9) Criminal Liaison Committee consisting of the Chief Criminal Judge, past Chief Criminal Judge, future Chief Criminal Judge, a judge designated by the Presiding Judge, representatives from the offices of the Prosecuting Attorney and Public Defender, a representative of private defense counsel, a representative from the Court Administrator's staff, and others designated by the chairperson to assist in the work of the committee. The Committee shall be chaired by the Chief Criminal Judge; together with such special committees as may be appointed by the Presiding Judge with approval of the judges; together with such special committees as may be appointed by the presiding judge with approval of the judges.

(b) Duties of Committees. Committees have a duty to study and make recommendations concerning the subject matters assigned to them with authority to act when specifically authorized by the judges, provided, however, that the Juvenile Court Committee is authorized to act in any matter concerning which there is unanimity among the three juvenile court committee judges.

[Amended effective July 1, 1994; January 1, 1998; September 1, 2003.]

LAR 0.4. STANDARDS FOR TIMELY DISPOSITION OF CIVIL CASES

(a) Time Standards. The court, in order to increase the rate of civil and domestic dispositions and insure trial preparation, adopts the following time standards.

(1) *General Civil.* 90% of all civil cases should be settled, tried or otherwise concluded within 12 months of the date of case filing; 98% within 18 months; and the remainder within 24 months, except for individual cases in which the court determines exceptional circumstances exist and for which a continuing review will occur.

(2) *Domestic Relations.* 90% of all domestic relations matters should be settled, tried or otherwise concluded within ten months of the date of case filing; 100% within 18 months, except for individual cases in which the court determines exceptional circumstances exist and for which a continuing review will occur.

(b) Scope. Except as otherwise provided by LAR 0.4(a), or as otherwise ordered by the court, this rule shall apply to all civil cases, except for:

(1) Modification of a decree of support or maintenance under RCW Title 26;

(2) Collection cases under $35,000;

(3) Changes of name;

(4) Adoptions;

(5) Domestic violence (RCW Chapter 26.50);

(6) Civil harassment (RCW Chapter 10.14);

(7) Uniform Interstate Family Support Act (UIFSA);

(8) Juvenile and Dependency cases (RCW 13.32A & 13.34);

(9) Paternity cases;

(10) Minor settlements;

(11) Probate cases;

(12) Guardianships;

(13) Unlawful detainers;

(14) Reviews of action taken by an administrative agency;

(15) Appeals from courts of limited jurisdiction;

(16) Foreign judgments;

(17) Abstracts or transcripts of judgments;

(18) Petitions for writs of habeas corpus, mandamus, restitution, or review, or any other writs;

(19) Civil commitment cases;

(20) Proceedings under RCW chapter 70.96A.

[Adopted effective July 1, 1988; amended effective January 1, 1991; October 1, 1992; October 1, 1993; July 1, 1994; October 1, 1994; September 1, 1996; June 18, 1998; July 1, 2001.]

LAR 0.4.1. CASE SCHEDULE ORDER AND ASSIGNMENT OF CIVIL CASES

(a) **Scope.** Except as otherwise ordered by the court, this rule shall apply to all civil cases, except for:

(1) Cases which have been transferred to mandatory arbitration, pursuant to LMAR 2.1, whether or not a Case Schedule Order has been previously signed. For cases appealed from mandatory arbitration see LAR 0.4.1(c);

(2) Modifications of child support or maintenance, except that these matters may be assigned a Case Schedule Order upon order of the court;

(3) Paternity;

(4) Change of name;

(5) Adoption;

(6) Domestic violence (RCW Chapter 26.50);

(7) Harassment (RCW Chapter 10.14);

(8) UIFSA actions;

(9) Juvenile dependency;

(10) Minor settlement;

(11) Probate, except any will contest or litigation matter arising in a probate case shall be assigned a Case Schedule Order when the petition to contest the will is filed or the estate is sued;

(12) Guardianship;

(13) Unlawful detainer;

(14) Review of action taken by administrative agency;

(15) Appeals from courts of limited jurisdiction which are governed by rules for Appeal of Decisions of Courts of Limited Jurisdictions (RALJ);

(16) Foreign judgments;

(17) Abstract of transcript of judgment;

(18) Petition for Writ;

(19) Civil commitment;

(20) Proceedings under RCW Chapter 10.77 (Criminally Insane);

(21) Proceedings under RCW Chapter 70.96A;

(22) Proceedings for isolation and quarantine;

(23) Collection cases.

(b) **Clerk Index Sheet, Case Assignment Notice and Order.** When an initial pleading is filed and a new case file is opened, the plaintiff/petitioner shall file a Spokane County Clerk Indexing Sheet in the form specified in Appendix A.

Excluding cases listed in LAR 0.4.1(a), the clerk will issue and file a Case Assignment Notice and Order with a status conference date and will provide one copy to the party filing the initial pleading and one copy to the assigned court department. The plaintiff/petitioner may serve a copy of the Case Assignment Notice and Order on the defendants/respondents along with the initial pleadings. Otherwise, the plaintiff/petitioner shall serve the Case Assignment Notice and Order on the defendants/respondents within ten days after the later of: (1) the filing of the initial pleadings, or (2) service of the defendant's/respondent's first response to the initial pleadings whether that first response is a notice of appearance, an answer, or a CR 12 motion. The Case Assignment Notice may be served by regular mail, with proof of mailing to be filed promptly in the form required by CR 5.

(c) **Assignment of Cases.** All civil cases not falling under LAR 0.4.1(a)(1) through (23), will be assigned to an individual judge when an initial pleading is filed and a new case file is opened. Cases that fall within LAR 0.4.1(a)(1) through (23) may move for assignment which the court may grant if the circumstances of the case so warrant. Termination of Parental Rights cases will be assigned to a judge 60 days after filing of the petition. Cases appealed from mandatory arbitration will be assigned to a judge when the notice of appeal is filed.

(d) **Status Conference and Case Schedule Order.** All attorneys of record and/or pro se parties must attend a status conference with the assigned judge on the date and time designated by the Case Assignment Notice. A Case Schedule Order will be issued at the status conference in the format found in Appendix A. The order will set the time period between filing and trial and the scheduled events and deadlines for that type of case, as determined to be appropriate by the assigned court department, after consultation with counsel. The court will set cases consistent with the time standards set forth in LAR 0.4(a).

(1) [Deleted]

(2) [Deleted]

(e) Joint Case Status Report. All parties shall confer and jointly prepare a Joint Case Status Report in the form found in Appendix A. The form must be brought to the status conference by the parties, or provided to the court department in advance. This form is not to be filed in the court file.

(f) Monitoring. The assigned judge and/or court administrator's office will monitor cases to determine compliance with these rules.

(g) Enforcement.

(1) Failure to comply with the Civil or Domestic Case Schedule Orders may be grounds for imposition of sanctions, including dismissal, or terms.

(2) The Court, on its own initiative or on motion of a party, may order an attorney or party to show cause why sanctions or terms should not be imposed for failure to comply with the Civil or Domestic Case Schedule Orders established by these rules.

(3) If the Court finds that an attorney or party has failed to comply with the Civil or Domestic Case Schedule Orders and has no reasonable excuse, the Court may order the attorney or party to pay monetary sanctions to the Court, or terms to any other party who has incurred expenses as a result of the failure to comply, or both; in addition, the Court may impose such other sanctions as justice requires.

(4) As used with respect to the Civil or Domestic Case Schedule Orders, "terms" means costs, attorney fees, and other expenses incurred or to be incurred as a result of the failure to comply; the term "monetary sanctions" means a financial penalty payable to the Court; the term "other sanctions" includes but is not limited to the exclusion of evidence.

(h) Relationship to Civil Rules. The issuance of a Case Schedule Order or Domestic Schedule Order does not affect the right of a party to seek a summary judgment under CR 56 or the right of a party to seek enforcement of discovery rights or obligations under CR 26–37.

[Adopted effective June 18, 1998; amended effective January 1, 1999; January 18, 2000; July 1, 2001.]

LAR 0.5. CIVIL MEDIATION

The judicial officers of the Superior Court are empowered to issue an order requiring the parties to participate, in good faith, in mediation at any time during the pendency of litigation.

[Previous LAR 0.5 was deleted effective September 1, 1996. This rule was adopted effective September 1, 2006.]

LAR 0.6. JUVENILE COURT AND FAMILY LAW DEPARTMENT

(a) Generally. There shall be a juvenile court and family law department of the court, in which shall be heard all matters arising under the juvenile and family laws. Every judge is designated a judge of the family and juvenile court. The juvenile court judge shall be determined according to a yearly rotation list provided by the court administrator, with 12 month terms beginning on January 1 of each year. The term of the juvenile court judge may be extended by agreement of the juvenile court judge and the next judge in line on the rotation list, in which case the judge surrendering their place in the rotation shall drop to the end of the rotation schedule.

(b) Assignment. The presiding judge shall assign judges or commissioners as needed to hear matters in the family law department and in the juvenile court department subject to the approval of the juvenile court judge.

(c) Sessions of Juvenile Court. Regular sessions of the juvenile court department shall be held as provided by local juvenile court rules.

(d) Sessions of Family Law. Regular sessions of the family law department shall be as provided by local court rules.

(e) Rules. The juvenile court shall make rules for the conduct of business of the department subject to the approval of a majority of the judges.

(f) Revision. Revision of orders and judgments by a commissioner in the juvenile court shall be heard by the juvenile court judge.

[Amended July 1, 1981; amended effective October 1, 1988; September 1, 1996; January 1, 1999.]

LAR 0.7. REVISION OF COURT COMMISSIONER'S ORDER OR JUDGMENT

(a) Revision by Motion and Notice. Revision shall be initiated by filing a motion on a form approved by the Court, with the Clerk of the Court within 10 days after entry of the order or judgment as provided in RCW 2.24.050. The motion must specify each portion of the Order for which revision is sought. The revision form shall designate a hearing date no later than 30 days after the filing of the motion. The Motion for Revision shall also be noted in accordance with Civil Rules 6 and 7. A copy of the motion for revision shall be served upon the other parties, or their counsel, if represented, within 10 days after the entry of the order or judgment and at least five court days before the hearing date. An additional three days notice shall be required if service is by mail.

(b) Transcript Required. At least two days prior to the hearing on the motion, the moving party shall file a transcript of the oral ruling of the Commissioner. The moving party shall obtain the transcript at their expense. A copy of the transcript shall, at least two days before the hearing, also be served upon the other parties and furnished to the Judge who will hear the motion. A transcript will not be required if the matter was decided by letter decision, or if no oral decision was rendered. The transcript shall be double spaced in at least eleven point type. The person preparing the transcript shall certify, under penalty of perjury, that it is an accurate transcription of the record. Failure to comply with these requirements may result in denial of the motion.

(c) Assignment and Procedure. Revision motions in cases that have been assigned, will be heard by the assigned judge. Family Law revision hearings involving non-assigned cases will be heard by the Chief Family Law Judge. Non–Family law revision hearings will be heard by the Presiding Judge. The Juvenile Judge will hear all Juvenile Court revision hearings. A Judge required by this rule to conduct the revision hearing, may, in the efficient administration of justice, assign the matter to another Judge.

(d) Hearing Procedure. Hearings before the Family Law Judges shall be scheduled at 1:30 p.m. on Thursdays. Hearings before other judges shall be set pursuant to motion procedures for each department. The hearing will be on the factual record made before the Commissioner. Argument will be up to 10 minutes per side. The moving party shall confirm with the other parties whether they are ready for hearing, or whether a continuance may be requested. The moving party shall notify the Judicial Assistant to the Presiding Family Law Judge by noon, two days before the hearing date, as to the ready status of the motion. Failure to comply with this rule will result in the motion being stricken. The non-moving parties may be granted sanctions if they appear at the time set for hearing and the matter is stricken due to non-compliance with the rule by the moving party. The Judge scheduled to conduct the hearing shall approve any order of continuance. If the moving party fails to appear at the time set for hearing, the Court may enter an order denying the motion. The Juvenile Judge shall determine the setting of motions in that Court. Absent good cause, a party seeking revision shall be deemed to have abandoned the motion if they fail to calendar the case and obtain a hearing within 60 days of the filing of the motion. Multiple orders of continuance shall not be freely granted. The agreement of the parties, standing alone, may not be deemed sufficient basis for a continuance.

(e) Emergency Motions. If a party can demonstrate exigent circumstances, an emergency motion may be presented to the Presiding Judge, upon reasonable notice to the opposing parties, without the necessity of meeting the requirements set forth in the above sections of this rule. The Presiding Judge may determine that exigent circumstances do not justify an emergency hearing. In that event, the moving party shall follow the procedures set forth above.

(f) Stay. The filing of a Motion for Revision does not stay the Commissioner's order. The moving party may seek a stay of the order from the Judge expected to conduct the revision hearing as set forth in this rule. A request for stay may also be addressed to the Commissioner who issued the judgment or order.

[Adopted June 18, 1981, effective August 1, 1981; amended January 1, 1983; July 1, 1994; amended effective September 1, 1996; September 1, 1997; March 1, 1998; amended on an emergency basis effective March 1, 2006; amended on a permanent basis effective September 1, 2006; amended effective September 1, 2012; September 2, 2014.]

LAR 0.8. LOCAL RULE TO IMPLEMENT GR 31 AND GR 22

(a) Personal Identifiers–Children

(1) Complete names of children, sealed case types: The complete names of children shall be used in cases that are deemed confidential pursuant to state or federal statutes, including cases filed pursuant to Title 13 RCW (excluding offender cases); Chapter 4.24 RCW, Chapter 26.33 (Adoption) and Chapter 71.34 (Mental Health Services for Minors).

(2) Confidential Information Form: The complete names of children and other identifiers shall be included in the Confidential Information Form or similar document for cases filed under Title 26.

(3) Domestic Relations Orders: Court orders concerning the financial support or the custody or residential schedule of a child (including temporary and permanent parenting plans and similar documents) and orders establishing or disestablishing paternity shall include the full name of the child. The date of birth of a child shall be included in court records only as authorized by GR 22.

(4) Child who is alleged to be a victim of a crime: The complete name of a child who is alleged to be a victim of a crime may be included on subpoenas and in jury instructions. Nothing in this rule requires that subpoenas be routinely filed in the court file.

(5) Child who is charged with a crime: The complete name of a child charged with a crime shall be included in any indictment or information filed with the court pursuant to CrR 2.1 or JuCR 7.2, as part of an affidavit or declaration of probable cause or for any

other purpose deemed necessary for the prosecution or defense of the criminal or juvenile offender matter.

(6) Orders issued for the protection of a child: If a child is a person protected by a criminal no contact order issued pursuant to 10.99 RCW, an anti-harassment order issued pursuant to 10.14 RCW, an order of protection issued pursuant to 26.50 RCW or a restraining order or order of protection issued pursuant to 26.09 RCW, 26.10 RCW, 26.26 RCW, RCW 26.52.020, or any other court order entered for the protection of the child, the child's full name and other identifiers shall be included on petitions and orders as necessary for entry of the order into the Judicial Information System (JIS) and/or the Washington Crime Information Center (WACIC).

(7) Orders on release of criminal defendant: If access to a child is restricted pursuant to CrR 3.2(d)(1), the court may include the full name of the child on the order, if deemed necessary for effective enforcement of the order.

(8) Orders restraining child from contacting or harassing others: Whenever a child is named as a respondent in an order listed herein, the child's full name and other personal identifiers shall be included on the petition and order as necessary for entry of the order in the Judicial Information System (JIS) and/or the Washington Crime Information Center (WACIC).

(9) Petitions and Notices filed pursuant to Chapter 11.28, RCW (children as heirs to estate): The full names and ages of children and other information required by RCW 11.28.110 and RCW 11.28.330 shall be included, however, the date of birth may be included only as authorized by GR 22.

(10) General authority. Nothing in this rule shall prohibit a court from authorizing the use of a child's full name or date of birth when necessary for the orderly administration of justice, consistent with the requirements of GR 22.

(b) Access

(1) Electronic access to the Superior Court Clerk's electronic records system outside of the clerk's office and outside of Spokane County's wide area network may be provided for all electronically-stored case files except those restricted by federal law, state law, court rule, case law, or court order, and

(2) Electronic access to court records shall be provided to those who have been approved to enter into a Document Viewer Subscription Agreement with Spokane County and have fulfilled all requirements of said agreement and are in current compliance with the agreement.

[Adopted effective September 1, 2005; amended on an emergency basis effective March 1, 2011; May 11, 2011; amended on a permanent basis effective September 1, 2011.]

LAR 30. ELECTRONIC FILING

(d)(2)(D)(ii) Any document initiated by a law enforcement officer is presumed to have been signed when the officer uses his or her user ID and password to electronically submit the document to a court or prosecutor through the Statewide Electronic Collision and Traffic Online Records (SECTOR) application, the Justice Information Network Data Exchange (INDEX), or the local secured system "Xpediter" used by the County of Spokane and City of Spokane. Unless otherwise specified, the signature shall be presumed to have been made under penalty of perjury under the laws of the State of Washington and on the date and at the place set forth in the document.

[Adopted on an emergency basis effective January 1, 2012; March 9, 2012; June 7, 2012; adopted on a permanent basis effective September 1, 2012.]

2. COMMENCEMENT OF ACTION

LCR 5. SERVICE AND FILING OF PLEADINGS AND OTHER PAPERS

(d) Filing.

(5) Motions. No motion for any order shall be heard unless the papers pertaining to it have been filed with the clerk.

(6) Documents Not to Be Filed. Unanswered interrogatories to parties and requests for admissions where an answer or other response is expected on the same document shall not be filed unless necessary for the disposition of a motion or objection. Photocopies of reported cases, statutes or texts shall not be filed as an appendix to a brief or otherwise but may be furnished directly to the judge hearing the matter. Documents or copies thereof produced during discovery and other items which should properly be received as exhibits rather than as a part of the court file shall not be included in the court file.

(7) Indexing Cover Sheet. An indexing cover sheet (Clerk Form 1) shall be completed and filed with all initial pleadings at the time the pleadings are assigned a cause number.

[Amended effective June 1, 1990.]

3. PLEADINGS AND MOTIONS

LCR 7. PLEADINGS

(a) Notice of Appearance. In each and every cause, after the filing of a complaint or petition, the attorney of record shall file a clearly designated "Notice of Appearance" with the court before filing any answer, motion, memorandum, or responsive pleading and shall serve a copy on the assigned trial judge.

(b) Pro Se Pleadings. Pro se pleadings shall be typewritten or neatly printed in black or dark blue ink, shall conform to the format requirements of GR 14, and shall contain the party's mailing address and street address where service of process and other papers may be made upon him/her.

[Adopted effective September 1, 1999; amended effective September 1, 2001.]

LCR 10. FORM OF PLEADINGS AND OTHER PAPERS

(e) Format Requirements.

(1) *Compliance with GR 14.* All pleadings, motions and other papers presented for filing with the Clerk shall comply with GR 14.

(2) *Paper Requirements.* All original documents filed shall be clear, legible and permanent, and printed or typewritten in black or dark blue ink on nontranslucent bond paper or other paper suitable for scanning. On documents not readable by the scanner, the original will be stamped by the clerk showing it was of poor quality for scanning. The following standards are required to assist the clerk for scanning purposes: use of binder clips on large documents; one staple per document (do not staple sub-documents within the pleading); use of bottom tabs only; no colored divider pages; and use of tape within documents (to affix small notes and receipts) instead of staples.

(3) *Consolidated Cases.* For all causes wherein an order for consolidation (for any purpose) has been entered, the caption shall include the separated titles of the consolidated actions, along with the specific cause numbers, and indication to the clerk of which cause number the pleadings shall be filed under. The party filing the pleadings shall provide copies for each cause listed. If no indication is made and/or a copy is not provided for each cause, the clerk shall place the pleadings into the lowest (or earliest filed) cause.

(4) *Bottom Notation.* Every proposed order, judgment and decree presented to a judge for signature shall be signed, on the lower left-hand corner of the page to be signed by the judge, by the individual attorney or pro se party presenting it. Attorneys signing shall include their Washington State Bar Association identification numbers.

(5) *Change of Name or Address of Attorney.* An attorney whose office address or whose name changes shall, within ten days after the change, notify in writing the Superior Court Administrator's Office and shall file a notice in each Superior Court case file in which he or she is the attorney of record. An attorney may use the same format referred to in APR 13 or the form in use by the Washington State Bar Association.

(A) Change of Address. The attorney shall furnish his or her Washington State Bar Association membership number, the previous address and telephone number, clearly identified as such, the new address and telephone number, clearly identified as such, and the effective date of the change.

(B) Change of Name. The attorney shall furnish his or her Washington State Bar Association membership number, the previous name, clearly identified as such, the full new name, clearly identified as such, and the effective date of the change.

[Amended effective July 1, 1988; amended October 1, 1990; amended effective October 1, 1990; September 1, 2001.]

LCR 12. DEFENSES

(a) Answer or Motion for Default. In all civil cases every plaintiff shall promptly move for entry of default if the answers or responsive pleadings are more than 20 days past due.

(b) How Presented.

(1) *Bankruptcy.* Any party that wishes to assert the protection of the Federal Bankruptcy laws shall, by the next judicial business day after the bankruptcy filing, file a copy of the Bankruptcy Court Notice of Commencement of Case Under Bankruptcy Code, or Voluntary Petition. The copies shall be accompanied by a certificate reflecting that the copies are true and accurate, filed under the Superior Court caption for each case to which the matter pertains. A copy shall be served on all other parties, and a copy provided to the assigned judge, if any. A claim of bankruptcy protection asserted in an answer or other pleading is not sufficient to advise the clerk or court of the pendency of bankruptcy. The parties will seasonably update the court as to the status of a bankruptcy case.

[Adopted effective October 1, 1993; amended effective September 1, 1999; January 18, 2000.]

LCR 15. AMENDED PLEADINGS

(a) Amendments. No additional parties may be joined, no additional claims or defenses may be raised after the date designated in the Case Schedule Order as the Last Date for Joinder of Additional Parties, Amendment of Claims or Defenses, unless, for good cause, the court orders otherwise subject to such conditions as justice requires.

[Adopted effective September 1, 2002.]

LCR 16. PRETRIAL PROCEDURE

(a) **Trial Management Joint Report.** In cases governed by a Civil Case Schedule Order pursuant to LAR 0.4.1, the parties must jointly prepare a Trial Management Joint Report (form CI–06.0150). The Report shall be filed with the Court, with a copy served on the assigned trial department. The Report shall contain:

(1) Nature and brief, non-argumentative summary of the case;

(2) List of issues which are not in dispute;

(3) List of issues that are disputed;

(4) Index of exhibits (excluding rebuttal or impeachment exhibits);

(5) List of plaintiff's requests for Washington Pattern Jury Instructions;

(6) List of defendant's requests for Washington Pattern Jury Instructions;

(7) List of names of all lay and expert witnesses, excluding rebuttal witnesses;

(8) Suggestions by either party for shortening the trial.

(b) **Parties to Confer in Completing Report.** The attorneys for all parties in the case shall confer in completing the Trial Management Joint Report (form CI–06.0150). If any party fails to cooperate in completing the report, any other party may file and serve the report and note the refusal to cooperate.

(c) **Pretrial Conference.** All parties must attend a pretrial management conference if scheduled by the assigned trial judge.

(d) [Deleted]

(e) [Deleted]

(f) [Deleted]

(g) [Deleted]

(h) [Deleted]

(i) [Deleted]

[Amended effective July 1, 1988; October 1, 1989; January 1, 1991; July 1, 1993; October 1, 1994; June 18, 1998; September 1, 1999.]

5. DEPOSITIONS AND DISCOVERY

LCR 37. FAILURE TO MAKE DISCOVERY: SANCTIONS

(a) **Motion for Order Compelling Discovery.** Motions to compel discovery shall be noted for hearing on Motion for Hearing Ex Parte Issue of Law before the ex parte commissioner (if the case is not pre-assigned to a judicial department) on any court day during regular business hours. If the case is pre-assigned to a judicial department, the motion shall be noted for hearing on the motion calendar for that department. The ex parte commissioner, in his or her discretion, may refer the motion to the presiding judge, if the case is not pre-assigned. The presiding judge may assign the case to a judge if it has not already been preassigned, or may return the motion to the ex parte commissioner. In the absence of emergency, no motion or objection with respect to CR 30, 31, 33, 34, or 35 will be heard unless it affirmatively appears that before the hearing counsel have conferred and attempted to resolve the issue(s). If any party has refused to confer, terms will be assessed against that party. The notice requirements of LCR 40(b)(10) apply to motions governed by this rule.

[Adopted effective August 15, 1987; amended effective July 1, 1988; October 1, 1994; June 4, 1998; September 1, 2002; September 1, 2004.]

6. TRIALS

LCR 38. JURY TRIAL OF RIGHT

(a) **Demand for Jury.**

(1) *Must Be on Separate Document.* The demand for a jury trial shall be contained on a separate document.

(2) *Deadline for Filing Jury Demand.*

(A) In cases not governed by a Civil Case Schedule Order pursuant to LAR 0.4, a jury demand shall be filed and served no later than the trial setting date.

(B) In cases governed by a Civil Case Schedule Order pursuant to LAR 0.4, a jury demand shall be filed and served no later than the date set forth in the Civil Case Schedule Order.

[Adopted effective January 1, 1991; July 1, 1993; June 18, 1998.]

LCR 40. ASSIGNMENT OF CASES

(a) **Note of Issue.**

(1) [Deleted]

(A) [Deleted]

(B) [Deleted]

(1) *Of Law.* In cases where a Case Schedule Order has been entered issues of law shall be noted for hearing on a form approved by the court and shall be

heard on Friday each week by the assigned judge. If Friday is a holiday, they will be heard on Thursday. For the issues of default, see LCR 55. For issues under CR 30, 31, 33, 34 and 35, see LCR 37.

In cases where a Domestic Case Schedule Order has been entered issues of law shall be noted for hearing on a form approved by the court on any Family Law or Paternity Calendar as appropriate. However, in the case of summary judgment motions, they shall be noted for hearing before the assigned judge.

(2) *Family Law Cases.* (Pursuant to RCW 26.09, 26.10 not otherwise specified).

The Judges shall appoint periodically judges to act as Family Law Judges who shall manage all matters of family law administration. All cases involving matters of marriage dissolution, legal separation, child custody and paternity will be under the general supervision of the Family Law Judges and one or more Family Law Commissioners.

A Financial Declaration, Asset and Liability List, and Proposed Parenting Plan and Child Support Worksheets, if applicable, shall be filed by each party, per the Domestic Case Schedule Order.

If the opposing party fails to timely file a parenting plan, the moving party shall note a motion in the ex parte court on 10 days notice to adopt their parenting plan. If the motion is granted the judge or court commissioner shall take appropriate action to include an order precluding the introduction of evidence on parenting issues, the adoption of the parenting plan and/or such other sanctions as may be required.

Trials involving petitions for marriage dissolution, legal separation, or child custody will be assigned to a Family Law Judge for trial. Paternity cases will be assigned for trial pursuant to LSPR 94.04(a)(6). A Family Law Judge may reassign any family law matter in the due administration of justice.

(b) Motion Practice.

(1) [Deleted]

(2) [Deleted]

(3) [Deleted]

  (B) [Deleted]

(4) [Deleted]

(5) [Deleted]

(6) [Deleted]

(7) [Deleted]

(8) [Deleted]

(9) [Deleted]

(10) *Motion Setting-General.* The Note for Hearing/Issue of Law (form CI.06.0300) must be served and filed no later than twelve days prior to the hearing (CR 6 and CR 40). Any responding docu-

ments must be served and filed at least seven days before the hearing. Reply documents must be served and filed at least two days before the hearing. If a judge has not been preassigned, the court administrator will notify counsel of the assigned judge. In the event a motion or one continued from a prior date is to be argued, counsel for the moving party shall confirm with all opposing counsel that they are available to argue the motion and then notify the bailiff for the assigned judge by 12:00 noon two days before the hearing. In the event an agreed or uncontested order of continuance is to be entered, or an affidavit of prejudice filed, counsel are further required to notify the assigned judge's bailiff by 12:00 noon two days before the scheduled hearing. Failure to comply with the provisions of this rule will result in the motion being stricken from the motion calendar and terms considered.

(11) *Motion Setting-Summary Judgment.* (See LCR 56).

(12) *Motion Setting-Criminal Matters.* (See LCrR 4.5)

(13) *Filing Motions, Memoranda and Affidavits-General.* The moving party shall file with the Note for Hearing/Issue of Law form the following: The motion being noted, all supporting affidavits and documentary evidence, and a brief or memorandum of authorities, unless the legal position is fully and adequately covered by the "authorities" section of the issue of law form. If the responding party files a response to the issue of law or any counter-affidavits, briefs or memoranda of authorities, such responding documents must be served and filed no later than seven days before the hearing. The responding party must also file any pleading to which the motion is directed. Any replying documents must be served and filed at least two days before the hearing. Failure to timely comply with these filing requirements will result in a continuance or strike the motion from the calendar and the imposition of terms.

(14) *Copies of Motions, Memoranda and Affidavits.* For cases where a Case Schedule Order has been entered and a judge assigned, a copy of the motion, brief, memorandum, documents and affidavit shall be furnished to the bailiff at the time of filing. For a case which does not have a Case Schedule Order pursuant to LAR 0.4.1(a), these materials shall be furnished to the Court Administrator's Office. For issues of law heard on the Family Law Calendar, these materials shall be furnished to the Family Law Coordinator for delivery to the assigned Court Commissioners.

(15) *Motion Calendar Hearing Procedures.* In cases where a Case Schedule Order has been entered and a judge assigned, the bailiff of the assigned judge will set the time for hearing the motion. In cases where a Case Schedule Order has not been entered pursuant to LAR 0.4.1(a), the Presiding Court will

assign the motion and the bailiff for the assigned judge will set the time for hearing. Motions for Default and Motions to Compel Discovery must be brought in accordance with LCR 37 and LCR 55.

(16) *Oral Argument of Motions.* All motions shall be limited to ten minutes per side unless additional time is granted by the judge or court commissioner, in which case the matter may be placed at the end of the calendar. Requests for additional time shall be made in writing at the time the motion or response is filed.

(17) [Deleted]

(c) Preferences (Reserved).

(d) Trials. When a case is set and called for trial, it shall be tried or dismissed unless good cause is shown for a continuance. The court may in a proper case, and upon terms, reset the same.

(1) [Deleted]

(e) Continuances. All continuances will be considered only upon written motion, for unforeseeable emergencies, for good cause shown, and upon terms the court deems just. No motion for continuance will be considered unless signed by attorneys of record and clients. Motions to change the trial date on a case where a Case Schedule Order has been entered pursuant to LAR 0.4.1 shall be heard by the assigned judge on or before the date designated in the Case Schedule Order.

(f) [Deleted]

[Amended effective July 1, 1981; January 1, 1983; November, 1985; August 15, 1987; July 1, 1988; October 1, 1988; October 1, 1989; January 1, 1991; March 1, 1992; October 1, 1993; October 1, 1994; September 1, 1996; March 1, 1998; June 18, 1998; January 1, 1999; September 1, 1999; January 18, 2000; July 1, 2001.]

LCR 43.   TAKING OF TESTIMONY

(a) Testimony.

(3) *Excusing Witness.* A witness under subpoena is excused from further attendance as soon as testimony has been given unless either party makes request in open court that the witness remain in attendance or be subject to recall. Witness fees will not be allowed on subsequent days unless the court has required the witness to remain in attendance which fact shall be noted by the clerk in the court journal.

(e) Evidence on Motions.

(1) *Generally.* Motions for temporary support, suit money, restraining orders, injunctions, to dissolve injunctions and to quash or dissolve attachments shall be heard only on the pleadings, affidavits, published depositions and other papers filed unless the court otherwise directs. Except as otherwise provided in LSPR 94.04(a) or (b), any counter-affidavits shall be served upon the opposing party before the expiration of one-half the time intervening between the service of the movant's affidavits and the hearing or the movant shall have the option of a postponement of the hearing. Affidavits strictly in reply to counter-affidavits may be served and considered at the hearing.

LCR 47.   JURORS

(a) Examination of Jurors

(1) *Juror Questionnaires.* The trial judge shall direct that individual questionnaires of jurors dealing with matters of a personal or sensitive nature shall be filed under seal. Juror questionnaires may not be removed from the courtroom without the express permission of the trial judge. At the conclusion of voir dire, juror questionnaires shall be returned to the court.

(2) *Juror Information Form.* Juror Information Forms will not be filed with the court file. The Juror Information Form may not be removed from the courtroom without the express permission of the trial judge. At the conclusion of voir dire, the Juror Information Forms will be returned to the court.

(d) Empaneling Jury. The Spokane County Superior Court shall employ a properly programmed electronic data processing system to make random selection of jurors as authorized by RCW 2.36.063 and RCW 2.36.093. The presiding judge is empowered to take any necessary action on behalf of the court. The master jury list shall be selected during July of each year from an unrestricted random sample from the names of all registered voters filed with the county auditor without regard to location of precinct, the judges having determined that a fair and random selection may be achieved without division of the county into jury districts. A general jury venire as now provided by law shall be issued for jurors for service for such term and at such frequency as may be required consistent with applicable law.

(e) Challenge.

(9) *Peremptory Challenges.* The exercise or waiver of peremptory challenges shall be noted secretly on the jury list.

[Amended effective June 18, 1998.]

LCR 49.   VERDICTS

(k) Receiving Verdict and Discharging Jury.

(1) *Receiving Verdict During Absence of Counsel.* A party or attorney desiring to be present at the return of the verdict must remain in attendance at the courthouse or be available by telephone call. If a party or attorney fails to appear within 20 minutes of telephone notice to the attorney's office, home or other number, the court may proceed to take the verdict in the absence of such party or attorney. In such case, the jury shall be individually polled and the identity of any dissenting jurors recorded.

LCR 51. INSTRUCTIONS TO JURY AND DELIBERATION

(a) Proposed. In addition to the proposed instructions required by CR 51, each party shall submit a brief statement of the case suitable to be read to the jury before the voir dire examination.

(c) Form. Copies of proposed instructions shall contain supporting citations or reference to a pattern jury instruction.

(d) Published Instructions.

(1) *Request.* WPI or WPIC instructions without alternate or optional language may be requested by reference to the published number. If the published instruction allows or provides for a choice of wording, the written request which designates the number of the instruction shall also designate the choice of wording which is being requested by attaching a facsimile of the proposed instruction suitable for photocopying.

LCR 52. DECISIONS, FINDINGS AND CONCLUSIONS

(a) Requirements.

(6) *Time.* Unless the judge has included formal findings of fact and conclusions of law in a written opinion or memorandum of decision pursuant to CR 52(a)(4) or they are otherwise unnecessary by reason of CR 52(a)(5), the attorney of record for the prevailing party shall prepare and note for presentation within 15 days of the decision proposed findings of fact and conclusions of law along with the proposed form of order and judgment as required by CR 54(e).

7. JUDGMENT

LCR 54. JUDGMENTS AND COSTS

(c) [Deleted]

(e) [Deleted]

(f) Presentation.

(1) *Local Counsel.* Counsel and legal interns presenting a judgment or seeking entry of an order shall be responsible to see that all pertinent papers are filed and that the court file is provided to the judge or court commissioner. Legal interns presenting ex parte or agreed orders as authorized by APR 9(c)(4) shall be sufficiently familiar with the matter so as to satisfy the court on any question reasonably to be anticipated.

(2) *Out-of-County Counsel.* Counsel outside of Spokane County may present routine ex parte or stipulated matters based on the record in the file by mail addressed to the county clerk. The presentation fee must accompany the original pleadings. Self-addressed, stamped envelopes shall be provided for return of any conformed materials and/or rejected orders.

(3) *Paralegal.* Paralegals, who are currently registered with the Spokane County Bar Association for the purpose of presentation of such orders, may personally present agreed, ex parte and uncontested orders signed by counsel, based solely upon the documents presented and the record in the file.

[Amended January 1, 1991; amended effective September 1, 1997; June 1, 2000; September 1, 2009.]

LCR 55. DEFAULT AND JUDGMENT

(a) [Deleted]

(3) [Deleted]

(1) *Required Pleadings.* All documentation required for entry of an order of default pursuant to CR 55(a) shall be filed at the same time as the motion for a default, unless extended by court order to correct a clerical error or omission or for furnishing of any proof required by the court.

(2) *Before Whom Taken.* Motions for default shall be noted for hearing on such form(s) as required by the court, before the judge to whom the matter is assigned, on such date as is approved by the judicial assistant for said judge or before the ex parte department on any court day during regular hours.

(b) Entry of Default Judgment. No default judgment shall be granted except upon proof satisfactory to the court. The court shall require at least the following to be on file with the motion for default judgment, unless otherwise excused by the court for good cause:

(1) On assigned causes of action, a copy of the assignment instrument;

(2) On causes of action based on a negotiable instrument, the original negotiable instrument or satisfactory explanation as to why the original cannot be produced;

(3) On causes of action based on a retail sales contract, chattel mortgage, or conditional sales contract, the original contract (or a copy if the original has been filed with a government agency). Where applicable, a copy of a motor vehicle title or bill of sale must be filed;

(4) On causes of action based on open account where the complaint is not specific, the last written statement of account sent to the debtor setting forth current charges and credits and the dates thereof and a statement of any interest or surcharges which are included;

(5) On causes of action for rent based on an oral agreement, a statement of account similar to that required in actions on open account. If any claim is

made for damages or repairs to premises, such claim must be itemized separately;

(6) On causes of action based on a written lease, a copy of the lease and a statement of account as stated in section (4) above;

(7) On causes of action based on all other contracts, oral testimony or affidavits may be required to prove terms, together with filing of a copy of the contract, if written; and filing or proving the items of account and any credits;

(8) On causes of action for tort, proof shall be required by way of testimony or affidavit, supplemented by repair bills or estimates, medical bills, loss of use claims, and proof of loss of wages, when relevant to the claim. The court may require that claims for non-economic damages be proved by oral testimony.

(9) No judgment for accrued interest shall be allowed unless there is on file proof of the factors necessary for computation of interest, including applicable dates, rate of interest, amounts subject to interest and a computation of the total interest claimed due.

(10) Any request for attorney fees shall be supported by an affidavit or certificate supporting any contractual basis for attorney fees, and the basis upon which attorney fees are calculated. If attorney fees are based on statute, the request for attorney fees must cite the specific statutory authority.

[Adopted effective August 15, 1987; amended effective September 1, 2001.]

LCR 56. SUMMARY JUDGMENT

(a) **Motion and Proceedings.** Motions for summary judgment, partial summary judgment or dismissal must be served and filed at least 28 days prior to the hearing and heard at least 14 calendar days prior to the date the case is set for trial. Any responding documents must be served and filed at least 11 calendar days before the hearing. Any rebuttal documents must be served and filed at least five days before the hearing. If the date for filing either the response or rebuttal falls on a Saturday, Sunday, or legal holiday, then it shall be filed and served not later than the next day nearer the hearing, which is neither a Saturday, Sunday or legal holiday. In the event a motion for summary judgment, partial summary judgment or dismissal is to be argued, counsel for the moving party is required to comply with the requirements of notice in LCR 40(b)(10).

[Adopted effective August 15, 1987; amended effective October 1, 1993; June 18, 1998.]

LCR 58. ENTRY OF JUDGMENTS

(d) **Judgment on a Promissory Note.** No judgment on a promissory note will be signed until the original note has been filed with the clerk, absent proof of loss or destruction. If the original note has been lost, destroyed or is not available, the court may enter judgment upon satisfaction of RCW 62A.3–309 and sufficient proof of existence of debt, such as written agreement, billing statement, invoice or credit application, together with an affidavit or testimony supporting the claim. If attorney fees or interest in excess of the statutory rate are claimed, the claim must be supported by evidence of written agreement or other evidence supporting the claim.

[Amended effective September 1, 2001.]

LCR 59. NEW TRIAL AND AMENDMENT OF JUDGMENTS

(e) **Hearing on Motion.** The moving party shall promptly note a motion for reconsideration or new trial for hearing, coordinating the setting with the bailiff for the trial judge and sending notice to the trial judge. The trial judge may dispose of the motion without oral argument if the hearing is not scheduled within 30 days of the filing of the motion unless the time has been extended for good cause or the judge is unavailable.

LCR 69. EXECUTION

(a) **Procedure—Delinquent Support.** No writ of execution or attachment shall be issued for the collection of delinquent child support or spousal maintenance until a judgment determining the amount due has been entered.

(b) **Supplemental Proceedings.** In all supplemental proceedings wherein a show cause order is issued pursuant thereto requiring the personal attendance of a party to be examined in open court and in orders to show cause in re contempt, the order to show cause must include the following words in capital letters:

YOUR FAILURE TO APPEAR AS SET FORTH AT THE TIME, DATE AND PLACE THEREOF MAY CAUSE THE COURT TO ISSUE A BENCH WARRANT FOR YOUR APPREHENSION AND CONFINEMENT IN JAIL UNTIL SUCH TIME AS THE MATTER CAN BE HEARD, UNLESS BAIL IS FURNISHED AS PROVIDED IN SUCH BENCH WARRANT.

The failure to include such wording will be grounds for the court to refuse to issue a bench warrant for the apprehension of such person.

[Amended effective August 15, 1987.]

10. SUPERIOR COURTS AND CLERKS

LCR 77. SUPERIOR COURTS AND JUDICIAL OFFICERS

(c) Powers of Judicial Officers.

(9) *Judges Pro Tempore.* The court administrator, with the aid of the Spokane County Bar Association, shall maintain a list of attorneys willing and capable of assuming occasional assignment as judges pro tempore. Judges pro tempore shall be utilized as available and needed, with the consent of the parties involved. Arrangements for judges pro tempore, trial scheduling, courtroom and courtroom personnel shall be made through the court administrator.

(f) Sessions—Hours of Court. Court shall be in continuous session except for non-judicial days and Saturdays. Cases will be set, however, according to the priority established by law and court rule and the availability of trial departments. The hours of court shall be as follows:

(1) *Presiding Department and Ex Parte Department.* The hours of the presiding department shall be from 9:00 a.m. until 12:00 noon and from 1:30 p.m. until 4:30 p.m. Monday through Friday, subject to change by the court for good cause. The hours of the ex parte department shall be from 9:00 a.m. until 12:00 noon and from 1:30 p.m. until 4:30 p.m. Monday through Friday, subject to change by the court for good cause.

(2) *Trial Departments.* Jury trials will normally be conducted Mondays through Thursdays from 9:00 a.m. until 12:00 noon and from 1:30 p.m. until 4:30 p.m. subject to adjustment by the trial judge. Non-jury trials shall be during the same hours subject to adjustment by the trial judge. Friday calendars shall be individually controlled by the respective trial judges and may be utilized for pretrial conferences, motions, sentencings, opinion drafting and other chambers work.

(i) Sessions Where More Than One Judge Sits.

(10) *Orders to Show Cause.* Show cause orders relating to supplemental proceedings shall be issued and made returnable on the supplemental show cause calendar on Thursday of each week at 2:00 p.m. In all other show cause matters the order shall be made returnable to presiding court for assignment at 9:00 a.m. A copy of the order shall be provided upon its issue to the court administrator's office.

(11) *Sealed Files.* [See LCR 79(i)]

(k) Motion Day. [See LCR 40(b)(11) and LSPR 94.04(a)(5)]

(*l*) Submission on Briefs. [See LCR 40(b)]

[Amended effective September 1, 1997; amended effective January 18, 2000.]

LCR 79. BOOKS AND RECORDS KEPT BY CLERK

(g) Other Books and Records of Clerk.

(1) *Exhibits.* Exhibits shall be kept separately from the court file. Any inspection of an exhibit must be in the presence of the clerk or a deputy clerk unless authorized by a court order.

(A) Hazardous or Potentially Hazardous Materials. Exhibits containing hazardous or potentially hazardous materials shall be properly packaged and labeled before acceptance by the court. To meet packaging and labeling requirements, exhibits shall conform to the following criteria when presented:

(i) Materials containing or apparently containing blood, blood residue, bloodborne pathogens, infectious material, drugs, controlled substances, or other potentially hazardous material, shall be packaged and labeled as directed in a Hazardous Exhibit Protocol adopted by the court and filed with the Clerk or as directed by the court.

(ii) Firearms shall be unloaded, any breech mechanism or cylinder shall be open, and a secured trigger lock shall be in place.

(iii) Dangerous weapons shall have any sharp or pointed portions sheathed in a manner to prevent injury or contact with the sharp or pointed portions.

(iv) Paper bags alone shall not constitute proper packaging.

(2) *Rejection of Unsuitable Materials.*

(A) Original court record. Whenever there is presented to the clerk for filing in a cause, any paper or other material that is deemed by the clerk to be improper or inappropriate for filing, the clerk shall affix his file mark thereto and may forthwith orally apply to the court for a determination of the propriety of filing the material presented. If the court determines the paper or materials should not be made a part of the original court file, an order shall be entered to that effect and the material shall be retained by the clerk as an exhibit in the cause. The court may order that the unsuitable material be sealed, in which event it shall be available for inspection only by order of the court, except to the parties or their attorneys of record.

(B) Materials filed not evidence unless ordered. Exhibits filed pursuant to subsection (2)(A) hereof shall not be evidence in the cause unless by order of the trial judge entered on notice and hearing.

(h) Withdrawal of Files and Exhibits.

(1) *Files.* Files may be withdrawn to be taken to a courtroom by the following persons on giving a written receipt: judges, court commissioners, deputy

clerks, bailiffs, official court reporters, judicial assistants, court administrator's office, court facilitator staff, representatives from bail and/or bonding companies, attorneys, paralegals registered under LCR 54(e)(3), APR 9 legal interns, guardians ad litem and representatives of adoption agencies. Violation of this rule may result in sanctions including a suspension of privilege to remove any file from the Clerk's office. Files are available for electronic reproduction by the County Clerk under the fee schedule as provided in RCW 36.18.016 (4).

(2) *Exhibits—Temporary Withdrawal.* Exhibits may be withdrawn temporarily from the custody of the clerk only by:

(A) The judge having the cause under consideration.

(B) Official court reporters and law clerks/judicial assistants, without court order, for use in connection with their duties.

(C) Attorneys of record, or paralegals employed by attorneys of record and registered under LCR 54(e)(3) upon court order, after notice to or with the consent of opposing counsel.

(3) *Exhibits—Illustrative Exhibits Return.* In any non-criminal cause, the court on its own motion, may at the conclusion of trial/hearing return all exhibits that were admitted for illustrative purposes only, to the parties, absent any objection by counsel.

(4) *Exhibits—Return of Exhibits.* In any non-criminal cause on a stipulation of the parties, that when judgment in the cause shall become final, or shall become final after an appeal, or upon judgment of dismissal or upon filing a satisfaction of judgment, each party shall withdraw all exhibits offered by such party and give the clerk a receipt therefore. In the event a party shall fail to withdraw the exhibits within ninety (90) days after the final disposition, the clerk is authorized to destroy the same exhibits after thirty (30) days from mailing to a party a notice of intent to destroy exhibits.

(5) *Exhibits—Return of Controlled Exhibits (Drugs or Dangerous Items).* When any controlled substance or dangerous items have been admitted in evidence or have been identified, and are being held by the clerk as part of the records and files in any criminal cause, and all proceedings in the cause have been completed, the prosecuting attorney may apply to the court for an order directing the clerk to deliver such drugs and/or dangerous items, to an authorized representative of the law enforcement agency initiating the prosecution for disposition according to law. If the court finds these facts, and is of the opinion that there will be no further need for such drugs and/or dangerous items, it shall enter an order accordingly. The clerk shall then deliver the drugs and/or dangerous items and take from the law enforcement agency a receipt which he shall file in the cause. He shall also file any certifi-

cate issued by an authorized federal or state agency and received by him showing the nature of such drugs.

(6) *Videotaped Deposition(s).* Videotaped deposition(s) played and reviewed in open court shall be treated as court exhibits, with the same retention standards. Except as ordered by the court, if a party wishes same reviewed deposition(s) to become part of the court file, then the party shall submit a true and accurate transcript of such deposition(s) to the clerk.

(7) *Certified Appeal Board Records and Exhibits.* Certified appeal board records and exhibits shall be kept separate from the original court file. Upon conclusion of the trial and stipulation of the parties, absent any objection or further appeal by the parties, the certified appeal board record and exhibits shall be withdrawn upon receipt to the clerk. In the event of an appeal to a higher court, when the final disposition of the appeal is filed, the parties shall withdraw the certified appeal board record and exhibits within thirty (30) days or upon notice from the clerk, authorize the clerk to destroy the above said records and exhibits. The clerk shall file any stipulation or authorization into the case file.

(8) *Destruction of Records—Reproduction of Records.*

(A) Microfilmed Or Scanned Records. Files, or portions thereof, and records that have been destroyed pursuant to RCW 36.23.065, may be reproduced and used in accordance with RCW 36.23.067 for trial or hearing. The party or attorney needing a reproduction of a microfilmed or scanned file or record shall request the clerk, at least six (6) days prior to the scheduled court date, to reproduce the necessary materials.

(B) Confidential or sealed files and materials. The clerk shall not permit the examination of any confidential or sealed file or other sealed materials except by order of the court. Such order shall include findings to meet the requirements of GR–15 and any applicable statutes.

(i) Sealed Files. The clerk shall not permit the examination of any sealed file except upon the written order of a judicial officer.

(1) *Confidential Use by Judicial Conduct Commission.* Upon request, the clerk of the court shall provide copies of, or otherwise describe the contents of sealed files to a representative of the State Commission on Judicial Conduct, who is conducting a confidential investigation pursuant to WA. Const. Art. IV, sec. 31.

(2) *Public Use.* No materials in a sealed file may be made public, unless the Judicial Conduct Commission has first obtained an order pursuant to GR 15. Motions to obtain such an order shall be made to the Presiding Judge.

(j) Filing of Court Documents.

(1) *Filed Documents Available.* Documents turned in for filing by 4:00 p.m. on any given day will be imaged in the Application Extender (AX) system and placed in the court file by 5:00 p.m. on the next work day, unless the document is a "Clerks Action Required" document or a Financial document requiring a judgment number and execution docket entry. Filed documents must be coded, entered into the computer, scanned into the clerk's imaging system and placed in the court file. These documents will not be released until they are processed and placed in the court file. The court document will be available for use by 5:00 p.m. on the first work day subsequent to filing. "Clerks Action Required" and Financial documents require additional time for review, copying, execution docket coding, JIS data entry and verification. These documents will not be released until they are processed and placed in the court file. The court documents will be available for use by 5:00 p.m. on the third to fifth work day subsequent to filing.

(2) *Action Documents—Requirements.* Pleadings or other papers requiring action on the part of the clerk, other than file stamping, docketing and placing in the case file, shall be considered action documents. Action documents shall include a special caption directly below the case number on the first page, indicating "Clerks Action Required".

[Amended effective October 1, 1990; September 1, 1997; March 5, 1998; June 1, 2000; November 1, 2004; September 1, 2005; September 1, 2007; September 1, 2009; January 1, 2010; September 1, 2010; amended on an emergency basis, effective August 5, 2011; November 3, 2011; April 24, 2012; October 11, 2012; January 8, 2013; April 2, 2013; June 11, 2013; amended on a permanent basis, effective September 2, 2013.]

LCR 80. COURT REPORTERS

(c) General Reporting Requirements.

(1) *Separate Civil and Criminal Notes.* Court reporters shall keep notes for civil and criminal cases separately.

(2) *Filing of Notes.* Reporters shall file their notes with the clerk within 120 days of the trial or proceeding, provided, however, that the notes may be stored in the courtroom under the proper supervision of the deputy clerk assigned to that courtroom. The court reporter shall provide the deputy clerk with the index number and place of storage of the notes and a minute record made of such action in the court journal. Civil and criminal notes shall be filed separately. The notes of the presiding court reporter shall be filed as a criminal matter even though containing some civil matters. An index, with number and title of all cases reported, shall be attached to and filed with said notes. Reporters may withdraw notes for the time necessary to prepare transcripts by giving a receipt therefor to the county clerk.

(3) *Argument and Informal Discussions.* Unless otherwise directed by the trial judge, the following matters will not be reported:

–Closing argument in non-jury cases;

–Closing argument in civil jury cases where counsel have so agreed in advance;

–Informal discussions relating to proposed instructions.

(d) Confession Procedure Record. Unless the trial judge directs otherwise or the defendant is found not guilty, the court reporter shall promptly transcribe at the conclusion of the trial judge's bench decision concerning the admissibility of a confession, which shall be signed by the judge and filed to comply with CrR 3.5(c).

(e) Oral Decision. Oral decisions or rulings by a judge which are transcribed for any purpose shall first be submitted to the judge for correction prior to delivery and a final copy furnished to the judge for his or her file.

12. SPECIAL PROCEEDINGS RULES (LSPR)

LSPR 91.04. GARNISHMENTS

(d) Judgment Against Garnishee. No judgment against a garnishee defendant or order to pay into court and no order to the clerk to pay out any sum received pursuant to a writ of garnishment will be signed except after judgment is entered against the defendant and until the party who caused the writ to issue shall have filed proof of service in the manner provided by statute and 20 days shall have elapsed from the filing of the answer of the garnishee defendant.

(e) Federal Employees. When a garnishee defendant is a federal employer who fails to file a written answer but submits the amount to be withheld in the garnishment to the clerk of court or the judgment creditor, the judgment creditor shall provide the judg-

ment debtor with written notice that the judgment debtor has 20 days from the mailing of the notice to file an objection with the court and that in the event they fail to file an objection and or claim an exemption within that time, the court will authorize disbursement of the funds in partial satisfaction of the judgment without further notice to the judgment debtor. Any documentation received from the garnishee containing calculations of the amount withheld by the garnishee shall be attached to the notice. The judgment creditor shall file a declaration that they have mailed such a notice and attachments and that more than 20 days have elapsed without the filing of an objection by the judgment debtor before the court shall authorize the disbursement of said funds.

[Amended effective September 2, 2013.]

LSPR 92.0. COLLABORATIVE LAW PROCESS

(a) Commencement. In the event that represented parties enter into a Collaborative Law Participation Agreement that meets all requirements for such an agreement as specified in RCW 7.77.030, then upon the filing by both legal representatives of a joint Notice of Participation in Collaborative Law there shall be an automatic stay that suspends the case scheduling requirements of LAR 0.4.1.

(b) Effect. Upon the removal of a family or civil law action from case management processes, the court shall set a status conference to occur not later than nine (9) months from the date of the matter's initial filing. The parties to the action shall then be excused from settlement conferences, discovery deadlines, GAL requirements, mediation, and any other deadlines. If the case does not resolve within this nine (9) month period, then a mandatory Collaborative Law Status Report shall be filed with the Court on the date set for the status conference. If participation in the Collaborative Law process remains ongoing, then additional periodic case status conferences shall be scheduled as the court orders. Failure to comply may lead to dismissal of the case.

(c) Termination. Upon termination of the Collaborative Law process, prior to entry of the final decree, a Notice of Withdrawal from participation in Collaborative Law shall be filed with the Court.

(d) Bench Copies. The notices contemplated by this local rule shall be filed with the Superior Court Clerk and a bench copy provided to the assigned trial judge.

[Adopted effective September 2, 2014.]

LSPR 93.04. ADOPTIONS

(a) Relinquishments.

(1) *Personal Acknowledgment.* The written consent of the birth mother shall be personally acknowledged before the court at a hearing on the Petition for Relinquishment. The hearing shall be recorded. It is recommended that the written consent of any birth father-whether admitted, presumed or alleged-be personally acknowledged before the court, but appearance at the hearing on the Petition for Relinquishment shall not be required of any birth father, *provided* the father has signed a waiver of his right to notice of and appearance at the hearing and provided he requests, in writing, that he not be required to appear at the hearing, unless otherwise required by the court per RCW 26.33.090.

(2) *Guardian Ad Litem for Minor Parent.* The guardian ad litem for any minor parent, including an alleged birth father, shall be appointed from the list of family law guardians ad litem approved by the court, unless otherwise ordered by the court for good cause. Unless otherwise ordered by the court the guardian ad litem shall be present at the hearing on the Petition for Relinquishment. The guardian ad litem shall file a written report addressing the factors set forth in RCW 26.33.070.

(3) *Form of Consent.* The written consent of any parent, alleged father or presumed father shall be in the form prescribed by RCW 26.33.160, and shall contain the address of the Spokane County Superior Court Clerk.

(4) *Statement Regarding Social/Medical/Family History.* Each parent, presumed father and alleged father who consents to the adoption and to the termination of the parent-child relationship shall also submit a written statement certifying that he or she has provided or will provide all social, medical and family history of the child and of the parent that is needed by the prospective adoptive parents to properly care for the child and to help the prospective adoptive parents maximize the developmental potential of the child. RCW 26.33.350.

(b) Involuntary Termination of Parent-Child Relationship.

(1) *Appointment of Guardian Ad Litem.* If a parent contests a petition for termination of the parent-child relationship, by appearing in the action, either personally or through an attorney, a Guardian Ad Litem shall be appointed to represent the best interests of the child.

(c) Non-agency Adoptions.

(1) *Placement Requirements.* The preplacement report must be dated not more than one year preceding the filing of a Petition for Relinquishment or for adoption or must be supplemented within that period of time. The preplacement report shall be obtained by the prospective adoptive parents at their expense from a licensed child-placing agency, the State Department of Social and Health Services, or by a court-approved individual who has a masters degree in social work or a related field and one year of experience in social work or a related field and one year of experience in social work or who is demonstrated to have reasonably equivalent experience.

(2) *Checklist of Required Pleadings.* The following documents should be filed in a non-agency relinquishment/termination/adoption proceeding:

(A) Relinquishment:

(i) Petition for Relinquishment (mother and/or father)

(ii) Prospective Adoptive Parents' Consent to Assume Custody

(iii) Consent to Adoption (mother and/or father)

(iv) Waiver of Right to Notice if applicable

(v) Petition for Adoption

(vi) Preplacement Report

(vii) Financial Affidavit

(viii) Findings of Fact, Conclusions of Law and Order Terminating Parent-Child Relationship

(B) Termination:

(i) Petition for Termination

(ii) Order Setting Time for Hearing

(iii) Summons and Notice of Hearing

(iv) Affidavit of Service/Publication

(v) Motion/Affidavit/Order of Default (if applicable)

(vi) Findings of Fact, Conclusions of Law and Order Terminating Parent-Child Relationship

(C) Finalization:

(i) Order Appointing Agency for postplacement report

(ii) Postplacement report

(iii) Acknowledgment of Receipt of All Information about child and birthparents

(iv) Financial Affidavit

(v) Findings of Fact, Conclusions of Law and Decree of Adoption

(vi) Adoption Data Card and Birth Certificate Registration Form

(d) Finalizations.

(1) *Financial Declaration.* The adoptive parents in every adoption shall set forth in a declaration or affidavit a statement of all expenses paid and expected to be paid in connection with the adoption. Said affidavit shall be upon a form approved by the court.

(e) Stepparent Adoptions.

(1) *Preplacement Reports.* A preplacement report, prepared pursuant to RCW 26.33.190, shall be required before the adoption of a child by his or her stepparent:

(A) If the petitioning stepparent and the custodial parent of the child have been married less than one year at the time the adoption is finalized; or

(B) If required by the court.

(2) *Postplacement Report.* If a preplacement report is required in a stepparent adoption, the person or agency doing that report shall be appointed to complete the postplacement investigation and report, otherwise any suitable person may be appointed to do the postplacement report. No person related by blood or marriage to the custodial parent, the child or the petitioning stepparent shall be appointed. The report must contain the information required by RCW 26.33.200, and also must verify the following:

(A) Birth certificate data of the child;

(B) Information concerning the dissolution of the marriage of the natural parents, where applicable;

(C) Marriage certificate data of the petitioning stepparent and the parent of the child/spouse of petitioner;

(D) The criminal history, if any, of the petitioning stepparent;

(E) A history of support and parental contact by the parent whose legal relationship with the child will end as a result of the adoption;

(F) Employment history of the petitioning stepparent;

(G) Whether the child or his or her parents are Native Americans.

(f) General Requirements.

(1) *Interstate Adoptions:* According to RCW 26.34 the Interstate Compact on Placement of Children shall apply to all cases in which the adoptee is born or residing in a state other than Washington, or is born and residing in Washington and is to be placed or adopted outside of Washington. Prior to any order allowing placement in cases subject to ICPC the Petitioners shall file proof of compliance with the ICPC process by filing a copy of the form 100A with signatures from both states offices indicating approval of the placement.

(2) *Attorney appointments:* Any non-consenting parent who requests an attorney to be appointed at county expense due to indigency will complete and file a Financial Declaration WPF DR 01.0550.

(3) *Court's courtesy copies:* Courtesy copies of all pleadings, notices and reports shall be provided to the Family Law Coordinator 7 days prior to any hearing for review. In the event of an emergency, the pleadings shall be provided no less than 24 hours prior to the hearing. The pleadings may be submitted in draft form in advance of the birth of the adoptee, and may be submitted prior to filing of the Petition.

(4) *Presentment of Orders:* While a Petition for Termination/Relinquishment and Adoption may be filed prior to the birth of the baby, no orders regarding default or custody shall be signed prior to the birth.

[Revised June 19, 1980; amended January 1, 1983; amended effective August 15, 1987; February 1, 1991; September 1, 2005.]

LSPR 94.03. MANDATORY PARENTING SEMINARS

(a) Definition of Applicable Cases. This rule applies to all domestic cases including dissolutions, legal separations, and paternity actions (in which paternity has been established) where the parties are parents of children under the age of 18, and where a parenting plan or residential plan is required. The rule also applies to parties in an action seeking a major modification, as defined by RCW 26.09.260, of a previous parenting or residential plan or Decree or Order regarding custody.

(b) Parenting Seminars; Mandatory Attendance. Within 60 days after service of a petition or initiating motion on the respondent, or, in the case of a paternity action, after the entry by the Court of a finding of paternity, both parties shall participate in, and successfully complete, an approved Parenting Seminar. Standards for approved parenting seminars are set forth in sections (g), (h) and (i) below. Successful completion shall be evidenced by a certificate of attendance filed by the provider agency with the court.

The provider may also provide a separate class for petitioners involved in cases where the respondent has or is expected to default. The seminar shall also meet the standards in (g), (h), and (i) below as applicable, and shall also provide any additional information which may be relevant to this type of case.

(c) Permissive Application. In additional cases arising under Title 26 RCW where a court makes a discretionary finding that a parenting seminar would be in the best interest of the children, both parents, and such non-parent parties as the court may direct, shall also participate in a parenting seminar.

(d) Special Considerations/Waiver.

(1) In no case shall opposing parties be required to attend a seminar together.

(2) Upon a showing of domestic violence or abuse which would not require mutual decision-making pursuant to RCW 26.09.191, or that a parent's attendance at a seminar is not in the children's best interest, the court shall either:

   (a) waive the requirement of completion of the seminar; or

   (b) allow the parent to attend an alternative voluntary parenting seminar for battered spouses.

(3) The court may waive the seminar requirement for one or both parents in any case for good cause shown. Factors to consider include, but are not limited to, whether the action will be resolved by default, one or more parties reside out of the geographical area and availability of parent education programs where the parties reside, the ages of the child(ren), and whether the parents have arrived at an agreed parenting plan which is approved by the court.

(e) Fees. Each parent attending a seminar shall pay a fee charged by the approved provider. The seminars shall be conducted at no cost to the county.

(f) Failure to Comply. Non-participation or default by one parent does not excuse participation by the other parent. Respondent's refusal, delay or default will not delay the progress of the case to a final decree. Petitioner's refusal or delay will prevent the case from being set for trial or any final order affecting the parenting/residential plan being entered, except in cases where there is a co-petitioner or counter petitioner who is in full compliance. Willful refusal or delay by either parent may constitute contempt of court and result in sanctions imposed by the court, or may result in the imposition of monetary terms, default and/or striking of pleadings.

The Court shall also have the discretion to continue or strike motions brought by a party during the pendency of an action until the class has been completed.

(g) Provider Agencies. Approved Parenting Seminars shall be those offered by providers who comply with seminar content requirements as specified in this rule. Parties may use equivalent services offered by private agencies or religious organizations, upon approval by the Committee. The Committee will maintain a list of providers who have filed a statement of compliance with the Committee. If the providers' qualifications are challenged, they shall be notified by the Committee of the process to resolve any questions regarding their future approval. The provider will then have an opportunity to respond to any challenges to their qualifications.

(h) Seminar Content. The seminar content will be approved by the Committee, and shall include, at a minimum:

(1) the developmental stages of childhood;

(2) stress indicators in children;

(3) age appropriate expectations of children;

(4) the impact of divorce on children;

(5) the grief process;

(6) reducing stress for children through an amicable divorce;

(7) the long term impact of parental conflict on children;

(8) visitation recommendations to enhance the child's relationship with both parents;

(9) financial obligations of child rearing;

(10) conflict management and dispute resolution;

(11) communication skills for divorced parents;

(12) practical skills for working together; and

(13) the impact on children when stepparents and blended families enter their lives.

(i) Qualifications of Instructors. Parenting seminars shall be taught by a team of not less than two instructors, including one male and one female. Arrangements may be made for classes limited to one or two attendees, in which case two instructors are not required. Instructors should have the following minimum credentials and experience:

(1) a master's degree in social work, psychology or other related behavioral science;

(2) supervised experience in treatment of emotionally disturbed children, adolescents and their families;

(3) experience in providing a wide range of mental health services to children and families, with specific experience in the areas of separation/divorce, loss and grief, and blended families;

(4) extensive knowledge of child development, age appropriate expectations for children, and positive parenting;

(5) an ability to work with others (both groups and individuals) as part of a collaborative program; and

(6) strong oral communication skills.

When parties choose to use providers or religious organizations which have not previously been accepted by the Committee as a provider of parenting seminars, the court may modify or waive the foregoing qualifications for the instructors upon a showing of functional equivalency.

(j) Referrals for Other Services. During the seminar, referral resources will be made available to the parents and their children, including individual and family counseling, drug/alcohol counseling, anger management counseling, parenting classes, etc. These services are optional, and the parties must seek their own funding resources.

(k) Parent Education Committee. The Parent Education Committee shall be a standing sub-committee of the Spokane County Superior Court and shall consist of at least one judge, one court commissioner, one or more representatives of local dispute resolution agencies, one or more marriage and family therapists, one or more private attorneys, and others as appropriate.

[Adopted effective March 1, 1995.]

LSPR 94.04. FAMILY LAW ACTIONS

(a) Preliminary and Temporary Orders.

(1) *Temporary Restraining Orders.* When the court finds that irreparable injury could result and issues a temporary restraining order without requiring notice to the other party pursuant to CR 65(b), a show cause order shall be made returnable to the assigned Commissioner's family law motion calendar. If the case is not assigned a show cause order shall be made returnable to any family law motion calendar or paternity calendar as appropriate to determine whether the restraining order shall continue pending trial. A show cause order may also include notice of hearing of a motion for temporary order pursuant to LSPR 94.04(a)(3).

(2) *Modification of Parenting Plans and Custody Orders.* Motions for temporary custody under RCW 26.10 or a temporary parenting plan under RCW 26.09 will not be heard until adequate cause has been established pursuant to LSPR 94.04(f)(1). Once adequate cause is established the court may proceed immediately to the hearing of the motion for a temporary parenting plan or temporary custody or continue the same as justice requires.

(3) *Other Temporary Orders.* Any application for temporary support, attorney's fees, preliminary injunction pending trial or other similar relief in pending actions shall be by Motion and Declaration for Temporary Order and Notice of Hearing unless the application is included in an order to show cause issued under LSPR 94.04(a)(1).

(4) *Financial Declaration.* A party applying for temporary support, attorney's fees or other financial relief pending trial must serve and file with his or her motion or show cause order the mandatory financial declaration form. A party responding to a motion for temporary support, fees or other financial relief must file and serve a completed financial declaration with their response.

(5) *Family Law Calendar.* All family law motions under this rule and LCR 40(a)(1), all show cause orders seeking similar relief and adequate cause hearings shall be heard on the family law calendar on Tuesdays, Thursdays and Fridays of each week at 8:30 a.m.

(6) *Paternity Matters.*

(A) Motions. All motions shall be set for hearing on the paternity motion calendars on Monday or Wednesday. The dockets will be called at 8:30 a.m. The notice for hearing shall be on a form approved by the court.

(B) Trials. Trials will generally be set on the Wednesday Paternity Calendar. Lengthy trials may be assigned to a Family Law Judge for calendaring. The docket shall be called at 8:30 a.m. in conjunction with the motion calendar, for all trials set on the paternity calendar.

A trial date shall be requested by filing a Certificate of Readiness and Note for Paternity Trial Setting (Certificate) form together with proof of service. A copy of the Certificate shall be provided to the Family Law Coordinator.

The opposing party may file an objection to setting within ten days from the filing of the Certificate. The objection shall be accompanied by a note for hearing to be returned to the paternity motion calendar within 20 days. If the objection is denied, an order will be entered referring the matter to the Family Law Coordinator for setting. If the objection is granted, an order will be entered setting forth the terms and conditions under which the case may be set at a future date.

If no objection has been filed within ten days of the filing of the Certificate, the Family Law Coordinator will schedule the trial date.

The setting party shall contact the Family Law Department to obtain the trial date after the time for objection has run.

The setting party shall prepare a notice of the trial date and file a copy of the notice together with proof of service on all parties. Notice shall be served by the 10th day of the month preceding trial.

(7) *Notice Requirements.*

(A) **Monday hearings.** The notice of hearing shall be filed and served no later than the second Thursday preceding the hearing date. Any responding declarations shall be served no later than 4:00 p.m. on the Tuesday prior to the hearing date. Any reply or supplemental declarations must be served by 4:00 p.m. on the Thursday immediately preceding the hearing date.

(B) **Tuesday hearings.** The notice of hearing shall be filed and served no later than the second Friday preceding the hearing date. Any responding declarations shall be served no later than 4:00 p.m. on the Wednesday prior to the hearing date. Any reply or supplemental declarations must be served by 4:00 p.m. on the Friday immediately preceding the hearing date.

(C) **Wednesday hearings.** The notice of hearing shall be filed and served no later than the second Friday preceding the hearing date. Any responding declarations shall be served no later than 4:00 p.m. on the Thursday prior to the hearing date. Any reply or supplemental declarations must be served by 4:00 p.m. on the Monday immediately preceding the hearing date.

(D) **Thursday hearings.** The notice of hearing shall be filed and served no later than the second Monday preceding the hearing date. Any responding declarations shall be served no later than 4:00 p.m. on the Friday prior to the hearing date. Any reply or supplemental declarations must be served by 4:00 p.m. on the Tuesday immediately preceding the hearing date.

(E) **Friday hearings.** The notice of hearing shall be filed and served no later than the second Tuesday preceding the hearing date. Any responding declarations shall be served no later than 4:00 p.m. on the Monday prior to the hearing date. Any reply or supplemental declarations must be served by 4:00 p.m. on the Wednesday immediately preceding the hearing date.

(F) In the event of a Court holiday occurring during these notice periods, all deadlines will be 24 hours earlier than indicated above.

(G) The Notice of Hearing Family Law Calendar will be on a form approved by the court; the Note for Hearing Paternity Motion Calendar will be on a form approved by the court and the Notice of Hearing for Adequate Cause Determination will be on the mandatory state form.

(8) *Hearing.* All matters which will take more than ten minutes on either side shall be carried to the end of the calendar or rescheduled to another date. If the ten-minute limit is exceeded in a matter that has been estimated to be within the rule, the Court may termi-

nate the presentation or continue the hearing to the end of the calendar or reschedule to another date. Matters shall be heard on declarations and arguments only, except that the Court may permit oral testimony.

(9) *Special Notice—Extensive Declarations (Family Law and Paternity Motion Calendars).* If the total narrative declarations on a motion, including response and reply declarations, equal or exceed twenty (20) pages, and/or a written Guardian ad Litem report must be reviewed by the court; the moving party shall notify the Family Law Coordinator via voice-mail system by noon of the court day preceding the motion calendar. Failure to provide notice may cause the motion to be stricken or continued. Mandatory forms such as the financial declaration or other statewide forms will not be counted toward the twenty (20) page limit.

A party filing documents pertaining to a motion described above, on or after the last day allowed under local rule, shall furnish a bench copy to the Family Law Coordinator by noon of the court day preceding the motion calendar.

(10) *Limitations on Declarations*

(A) Application. This rule shall apply to all family law motions, motions in paternity actions and actions to establish residential schedule, and domestic violence and anti-harassment hearings.

(B) Formats.

1. All motions and pleadings in support thereof, shall use mandatory forms where applicable, follow the format required by GR 14, and meet the requirements of GR 31.

2. All declarations shall contain information that provides the court with foundational information such as the name of the declarant, relationship to one or both of the parties, age, education, city and state of residence, and occupation. This information shall be provided in summary fashion at the beginning of each declaration.

3. All filed documents shall be legible. If typed or computer printed, documents shall be in 11 point or larger type and double-spaced.

(C) Page limitations. Absent prior authorization from the court, the entirety of all declarations and affidavits from the parties and any non-expert witnesses in support of motions, including any reply, shall be limited to a total of 15 pages. The entirety of all declarations and affidavits submitted in response to motions shall be limited to a sum total of 10 pages. This rule shall be qualified as follows:

1. Exhibits. Exhibits that consist of declarations, statements, affidavits or any narrative document of parties or witnesses shall count toward the above page limit. All other exhibits attached to a declaration or affidavit shall not be counted toward the page limit.

2. Expert Reports and Evaluations. Declarations, affidavits, and reports from Guardians ad litem and similar expert witnesses shall not count toward the above page limit.

3. Previously considered declarations. Copies of declarations or affidavits previously filed for a motion already ruled upon and supplied only as a convenience to the court in lieu of the court file shall not count toward the above page limit. Such declarations or affidavits shall be counted, however, if the court is expected or is being requested to read such prior declarations and affidavits as a part of a present motion.

4. Basic pleadings and financial declarations. The above page limits shall not apply to basic pleadings and financial declarations.

(D) Children's Statements. Declarations by minors are disfavored and the court may in its discretion refuse to consider such declarations.

(E) Rules of Evidence apply. All submissions, including written materials in affidavits and declarations by the parties and witnesses, must comply with the rules of evidence. All declarations shall be based upon personal knowledge. Violations of this subsection may result in sanctions as set forth hereinafter.

(F) Inappropriate submissions. Unless prior permission of the court is obtained, the parties shall not submit inappropriate or pornographic materials. If permission to submit or file such material is granted, it should be filed in the confidential section of the file.

(G) Consequences of Non–Compliance. The court, if it finds that one or both of the parties have violated this rule, may in its discretion assess terms, may require that the matter be stricken or continued, or may refuse to consider those materials that violate this rule.

(H) Procedure for Court Authorization to Exceed or Excuse Limitations. The court will not entertain any motion or objection with respect to a request to exceed or excuse the limitations of this rule unless counsel or the parties have first conferred with respect to the motion or objection. Counsel or the parties shall arrange for a mutually convenient conference in person or by telephone. If, after conferring, one or both of the parties believe that the limitations of this rule should be excused, then they shall arrange a telephone conference or appearance before the assigned Commissioner if they are reasonably available, or if the assigned Commissioner is not available then they shall arrange a telephone conference or appearance before the Ex Parte department to have the court determine if the rule should be excused.

(11) *Court's Automatic Temporary Order.* Upon the filing of a Summons and Petition for dissolution, legal separation or declaration of invalidity, the court on its own motion shall automatically issue a Temporary Order that includes the following provisions:

(A) The parties be restrained from harassing or disturbing the peace of the other party;

(B) The parties be restrained from transferring, removing, encumbering, concealing, damaging or in any way disposing of any property except in the usual course of business or for the necessities of life or as agreed in writing by the parties. Each party shall notify the other party of any extraordinary expenditure made after the order is issued. This order shall not preclude a party from accessing funds in a reasonable amount to retain counsel;

(C) The parties be restrained from assigning, transferring, borrowing, lapsing, surrendering or changing entitlement of any insurance policies of either or both parties or of any dependent child(ren), whether medical, health, life or auto insurance, except as agreed in writing by the parties;

(D) Unless the court orders otherwise, each party shall be immediately responsible for their own future debts whether incurred by credit card, loan, security interest or mortgage, except as agreed in writing by the parties;

(E) Both parties must have access to all tax, financial, legal, and household records. Reasonable access to records shall not be denied without order of the court;

(F) For those actions in which children are involved:

i) each parent be restrained from changing the residence of the child(ren) until further court order, except as agreed in writing by the parties. Subsequent orders regarding parenting issues supersede previously issued orders to the extent the orders may be inconsistent;

(ii) each parent shall have full access to the child(ren)'s educational and medical records, unless otherwise ordered by the court;

(iii) each parent shall insure that the child(ren) is(are) not exposed to negative comments about the other parent. Neither parent shall make negative comments about the other parent in the presence of the child(ren).

(G) Each parent shall attend a SHARING THE CHILDREN seminar pursuant to LSPR 94.03 within 60 days of receipt of the court's temporary order.

After completion of the appropriate seminar, each party shall file with the court the seminar completion certificate provided by the sponsoring agency or provider;

(H) Upon motion of the court or any party, the parties may be required to participate in the mediation of unresolved disputes. Mediation is not required for child support disputes nor in cases involving domestic violence. If a case is to be tried before a judge, the parties may also be required to participate in a settlement conference and exchange settlement offers;

(I) A party's compliance with the provisions of this rule may be enforced upon Motion and Order to Show Cause. Unless compliance is waived by the court for good cause shown, the court may order appropriate sanctions including costs, attorney's fees, and adoption of the complying party's proposal;

(J) If a party believes that a Guardian ad Litem (GAL) needs to be appointed for the minor child(ren), the party must make a motion for the appointment of a GAL within 30 days of the filing or service of the petition;

(K) The Petitioner is subject to this order from the time of the filing of the Petition. **The Petitioner shall serve a copy of this order on Respondent and file proof of service.** The Respondent is subject to this order from the time that it is served. This order shall remain in effect until further court order or entry of final documents.

(L) The court's Automatic Temporary Order will not be entered in any law enforcement database. This rule does not preclude any party from seeking any other restraining order(s) as may be authorized by law.

(12) *Mediation in Contested Cases.* Except as provided in section (B) below, in all cases specified in LSPR 94.04(a)(11), the Court shall on motion of either party or, on its own motion, require the parties to engage in good faith mediation with an independent, neutral, trained, mediator. Unless otherwise ordered by the Court, the cost of mediation shall be shared by the parties in proportion to their respective incomes.

(A) Procedure for Mediation. Any party may cause the matter to be subject to mediation by filing the Notice of Mediation and service to all parties. The Notice of Mediation is available at the Spokane County Superior Court website www.spokanecounty.org. The Notice shall provide that the matter shall proceed to mediation unless an objection to mediation is filed with the Court and served on the other party within ten (10) days of service of the Notice. Said Objection may be served in accordance with CR 5(b). Any party filing an Objection to mediation shall, at the time of filing, schedule a hearing on the objection that must be heard no later than ten (10) days after the filing of the objection. Notice of that hearing shall be timely if service is accomplished at least five (5) business/court days prior to the hearing. The hearing shall be before the ex parte department. The Objection to mediation shall state under oath the reasons for the objection. The only valid bases for objecting to mediation are listed in section (B) below. At the hearing, the court shall order media-

tion to proceed unless it finds one or more of those circumstances set forth in section (B) below.

(B) *When Mediation is not Required.* Mediation shall be required as provided above, except in the following cases:

1. Lack of financial resources based upon the financial declarations required by LSPR 94.04(a)(4), and/or lack of mediation resources in the community; or

2. Where a domestic violence restraining order or protection order (excluding ex parte orders) involving the parties has been entered by a court at any time within the previous 12 months; or

3. Where a domestic violence no contact order exists pursuant to RCW 10.99; or

4. Where the court finds that domestic abuse has occurred between the parties and that such abuse would interfere with arms length mediation; or

5. For good cause otherwise shown.

(b) Trial of Family Law Actions—General.

(1) *Effect of Juvenile Court Orders and Proceedings.* No residential placement/time provision or custody order in any decree shall supersede an order of Juvenile Court or affect the power of the Juvenile Court in any proceeding. All parties to a proceeding pending before the Juvenile Court are obligated to disclose to the Superior Court the pendency of any such proceeding. The Juvenile Court must be timely served with copies of all motions, petitions and orders which purport to affect the custody of juveniles under its jurisdiction.

(c) Contested Family Law Actions—Settlement/Mandatory Parenting Issues Conferences.

(1) *Settlement Conferences.* In any contested family law action (except support modifications), a voluntary settlement conference may be held. A conference may be requested in writing by the parties on a form approved by the court. Both parties or their counsel, if represented must join in the request. The court may also order the parties to attend a settlement conference. A Commissioner or Judge may preside over the conference. The Family Law Coordinator shall provide written notice to the parties of the date, place and time of the conference. The attorneys and the parties shall be present unless excused by the presiding judicial officer for good cause. The assigned judicial officer may authorize appearance by telephone when attendance might otherwise be logistically impractical or unduly burdensome.

The parties shall file and exchange the following documents per the Domestic Case Scheduling Order unless otherwise ordered by the court:

1. Financial Declaration.

2. Asset and Liability List.

3. Child Support Worksheet (if applicable).

4. Parenting Plan (if applicable).

The parties shall also exchange the following documents one week in advance of the settlement conference and provide bench copies for the settlement conference:

1. Tax returns

2. Appraisals

3. Pension statements.

(A) **[Deleted]**

(B) **[Deleted]**

(C) **[Deleted]**

(D) **[Deleted]**

(E) **[Deleted]**

(F) **[Deleted]**

(G) **[Deleted]**

(H) **[Deleted]**

(I) **[Deleted]**

(J) **[Deleted]**

(2) *Mandatory Parenting Conference.* In any contested family law action involving parenting issues, the parties are required to attend a mandatory parenting conference as follows:

(A) In cases where a Guardian Ad Litem has not been appointed, the parties are required to attend a parenting issue conference with a neutral third party. The parties shall file a certificate of completion in compliance with the Domestic Case Schedule Order. Said conference shall not be required when the court finds (1) There is a domestic violence restraining order or protection order (excluding ex parte orders) involving the parties has been entered by a court at any time within the previous 12 months; or (2) Where a domestic violence no contact order exists pursuant to RCW 10.99; or (3) Where the court finds that domestic abuse has occurred between the parties and that such abuse would interfere with arms length mediation; or (4) Good cause otherwise shown.

(B) In cases in which a Guardian Ad Litem has been appointed, the parties are required to attend a parenting issue conference that is scheduled by the Guardian Ad Litem in compliance with the Domestic Case Schedule Order.

(d) Noncontested Family Law Actions.

(1) *Ex Parte Department.* Uncontested proceedings under RCW Title 26 may be presented for entry of final decree before the assigned Commissioner or the Ex Parte Department during normal court hours. Unless requested by the court, oral testimony will not be required in marriage dissolution cases, provided the findings of fact are verified by a party.

(2) *Pro Se Matters.* A pro se party may present uncontested matters for final hearing at the Non–Contested Dissolution Calendar. They may obtain a date for presentment from the Family Law Department. The calendar will be heard each Wednesday at times set by the Family Law Department. Unless requested by the court, oral testimony will not be required in marriage dissolution cases, provided the findings of fact are verified by a party.

(3) **[Deleted]**

(4) **[Deleted]**

(e) Clarification of Visitation and/or Residential Time. Motions to clarify parenting plans as to minor children or to establish specificity in such orders shall be noted for the assigned Commissioner's family law calendar. This shall also apply to clarification of visitation in proceedings under RCW 26.10.

Motions to clarify a residential schedule or parenting plan in a parentage case (RCW 26.26) shall be noted on the paternity calendar.

(f) Modification of Orders or Decrees.

(1) *Modification of Custody and/or Residential Placement.* A proceeding for modification of the parenting plan of a decree of dissolution or other custody decree shall be commenced by filing or serving a Summons and Petition for Modification/Adjustment of Custody Decree/Parenting Plan/Residential Schedule which may be supported by additional declarations. The court shall determine whether adequate cause for a modification exists in the following manner:

(A) Ex Parte. If the non-moving party fails to respond to the Summons within the applicable period after service thereof, that party may be held in default. The court shall then determine adequate cause based upon the pleadings of the moving party.

(B) Adequate Cause Hearing. A party may serve a Notice of Hearing for Adequate Cause Determination concurrently with the Summons and Petition or at any time subsequent thereto. The hearing date shall be after the time to respond, as per the Summons, has expired.

—If adequate cause for hearing is not established by the declarations, the petition will be denied;

—If adequate cause for hearing is established the matter will be assigned to a Family Law Judge for further management.

(2) *Notice Requirements.* A party setting or responding to an adequate cause hearing shall also comply with the filing and notice requirements for motion calendars set forth in LSPR 94.04(a)(7).

(3) *Adjustment of Residential Schedule/Parenting Plan.* An action to adjust a residential schedule/parenting plan pursuant to RCW 26.09.260(5) or (10) shall be commenced by filing and serving a Summons and Petition for Modification/Adjustment of Custody Decree/Parenting Plan/Residential Schedule. If the mat-

ter is contested by the filing of a response, the matter shall be placed on the assigned Commissioner's family law motion calendar or if the case is not assigned on any family law or paternity motion calendar as appropriate using standard notice procedure. A party seeking to present oral testimony shall file a written request and a declaration as to the basis with their notice of hearing or response.

At the time of the hearing the court shall:

(A) Determine whether adequate cause exists to proceed, and

(B) Rule on the merits, or

(C) Grant the request for oral testimony and refer the matter to the Family Law Coordinator for setting or assignment to a Family Law Judge.

(4) *Relocation of Children; Adjustment of Parenting Plan or Residential Schedule.* A party filing a Notice of Intended Relocation of Children, or an Objection to Relocation based upon the failure of the party intending to move children to provide such Notice, shall provide a copy of the Notice or Objection to the Family Law Coordinator upon filing the same. In the event that the relocation issue has not been resolved by default or agreement within 30 days of filing, the matter shall be assigned to a Family Law Judge for final hearing.

(A) Ex Parte Application. The following matters shall be presented to the assigned Commissioner or to the Ex Parte Department:

i) those cases in which there has been no objection filed by the party entitled to notice within the 30–day period for objection;

ii) cases in which the parties are in agreement regarding the intended relocation and

iii) cases in which the party with whom the child resides the majority of the time is seeking to waive the requirement of the Notice of Intended Relocation pursuant to RCW 26.09.460.

(B) Motions for Temporary Orders. In those cases where a party is seeking to either restrain or permit an intended relocation of children pending a final hearing, once the matter is at issue, it shall be noted for hearing on the assigned Commissioner's family law motion calendar or if the case is not assigned on any family law or paternity calendar as appropriate, using standard notice and procedure. A party seeking oral testimony shall file a written request as to the basis with their notice of hearing or their response. At the time of the hearing the court in its discretion may:

i) rule on the merits based upon the notice or objection and declarations;

ii) grant a request for oral testimony and refer the matter to an available judicial officer to be set at a later date.

Following the courts decision on the matter of relocation the Family Law Judge who has been assigned the case will set the matter for a final hearing.

(5) *Child Support Modifications.*

(A) Commencement. A proceeding for the modification for child support will be commenced by filing the state mandatory summons and petition forms. In addition, both the petitioning party and the responding party are required to prepare and file with their petition/response Child Support Worksheets.

(B) By Default. An order of modification by default shall be submitted, on motion, to the Ex Parte Department no sooner than 20 days after service (60 days if the respondent was served outside the State of Washington).

(C) Contested Hearings. Either party, after the filing of the response and completed worksheets, may file a request to schedule a hearing on the mandatory state form. It shall be filed with the Clerk of the Court with proof of service thereof and the party requesting the hearing shall furnish a copy to the Family Law Coordinator.

If no objection has been filed within ten days of the issuance of the request to schedule hearing, the Family Law Coordinator will schedule a hearing with notice to the parties of not less than 20 days.

The party not requesting the hearing may file an objection to setting within the ten-day period referred to in the paragraph above. The objection shall be accompanied by a note for hearing to be returned to the Ex Parte Department with at least five days notice. If the objection is denied, an order will be entered referring the matter to the Family Law Coordinator for setting. If the objection is granted, an order will be entered setting forth the terms and conditions under which the case may be set at a future date.

The case shall be set for a hearing on declarations only. By filing a request for hearing a party indicates that they have served and filed their child support worksheets and initial declarations to be considered by the court. They also must have provided the other party with tax returns as required by the state guidelines. The other party shall have 14 days from service of the request for hearing to file and serve their responsive declarations and provide required tax returns. The party requesting the hearing shall then have an additional seven days to file declarations in strict reply.

If either party wishes to present oral testimony, they shall file a motion and affidavit for oral testimony and serve it on the opposing party together with a note for hearing with five days notice returnable to the Ex Parte Department. The motion must be filed within ten days of the issuance of the initial notice setting the matter for hearing on declarations only. If the motion is denied, the case will go to hearing as originally scheduled on declarations only. If the motion is granted, an Order on Motion to Present Oral Testimony will be entered. The matter may be heard on the same docket or may have to be rescheduled but arrangements should be made with the Family Law Coordinator, in advance, to secure additional time if it is reasonably anticipated that the hearing will exceed 45 minutes in length. Matters reasonably expected to exceed three hours will be specially set.

The moving party shall confirm the ready status of the hearing by telephone to the Family Law Department:

For Monday hearings by noon on Wednesday of the week preceding the scheduled hearing date.

For Wednesday hearings by noon on Friday of the week preceding the scheduled hearing date.

Hearing dates not confirmed shall be stricken. Notice of any foreseeable request for a continuance shall be provided to the Court and opposing party at least seven days prior to the hearing.

(D) Supporting Financial Documents. The parties are not required to file tax returns, pay stubs, or bank statements with the Clerk of the Court prior to hearing. However, this information must be made available to the court at the time of the hearing and to the opposing party and/or counsel at least seven days prior to the hearing. If appropriate, these documents may be filed at the time of hearing at the discretion of the judicial officer conducting the hearing.

Nothing in these rules or applicable statutes precludes a petitioning or responding party from requesting additional information and/or documentation pursuant to CR 26–37 Depositions and Discovery.

(6) *Spousal Maintenance.* An action to modify a decree as to spousal maintenance shall be commenced by filing and serving a Summons and Petition, together with the Financial Declaration and Asset and Liability List. The form shall be completed by each party. However, they need not complete that portion of the form showing a proposed distribution of assets and liabilities between husband and wife. The responding parties' form shall be due at the time required for the response. If the matter is placed at issue by the filing of a response, a party may request a hearing by filing a Notice to Request Hearing (Maintenance Modification) on a form approved by the court. The Court will set a hearing according to procedures used for child support modifications. The matter will be heard on declarations only unless a party obtains an order permitting oral testimony. A party may object to the setting of a hearing in the same manner as a child support case. If the responding party files a response, but fails to file the Financial Declaration and Asset–Liability List when due as

set forth above, the petitioner may file a motion to compel before the Ex Parte Department and seek sanctions.

(g) Interstate Support Proceedings. Show cause orders relating to matters under RCW 26.21, the Uniform Interstate Family Support Act, (UIFSA), shall be heard on the paternity motion calendar.

(h) Residential Schedule. The Court shall make available suggested child centered residential schedules for minor children whose families are not intact. The Guidelines shall be distributed through the Spokane County Bar Association Office. These may assist the parties in formulating the residential provisions of a parenting plan, domestic violence protection order or decree of custody, visitation or parentage in accord with the applicable statutory criteria. A reasonable fee, approved by the court, may be charged for the printing and distribution of the guideline. This rule will be effective starting January 1, 1997.

(i) Third Party Custody Actions. In any action brought under RCW 26.10, the petitioning party, upon filing, shall be required to complete a declaration on a form approved by the court providing information about their criminal and social history and that of all persons in their household. The failure to submit such declaration and release shall result in denial of the relief requested by the petitioning party.

[Amended January 1, 1983; November, 1985; amended effective January 1, 1986; July 1, 1988; October 1, 1988; January 1, 1991; September 1, 1991; March 1, 1992; October 1, 1993; October 1, 1994; July 1, 1995; September 1, 1996; September 1, 1997; September 1, 1999; September 1, 2000; July 1, 2001; March 1, 2003; September 1, 2005; September 1, 2006; September 1, 2007; September 1, 2009.]

LSPR 94.05. FAMILY LAW, GUARDIAN AD LITEM, AND DISCOVERY PROCEDURES

(a) Applicability. This rule applies to the following original actions and/or modifications of decrees: marriage dissolution, legal separation, declaration of invalidity, custody or parentage actions filed pursuant to RCW 26.09, RCW 26.10, or RCW 26.26.

(b) Motion. When any of the above actions is filed and where an allegation of abuse or neglect of a minor child pursuant to RCW 26.44.020 (12) has been made and no dependency or alternative residential placement petition has been filed pursuant to RCW 13.34 or RCW 13.32A; upon motion of either party or upon the court's own motion, a hearing shall be held:

(1) To appoint a guardian ad litem for the child/children pursuant to RCW 26.44.053 and

(2) To determine whether the case should be referred to the Regional Center for Child Abuse and Neglect or other appropriate professional or agency.

(3) In all other cases where the welfare of the minor child/children is at issue, the provisions of

LSPR 94.05 may be utilized upon the request of either party or upon the court's own motion.

(c) Notice to Appear. Upon the filing of the motion, a hearing shall be set on the family law calendar. That hearing may be set by notice using local form DR–01.0430. A copy of the motion, notice of hearing and all supporting documents, which shall identify the proposed guardian ad litem, shall be served upon the nonpetitioning party indicating the time and place of the hearing on the motion. The responding party shall serve and file their response and supporting documents no later than 24 hours prior to the hearing date. Hearings shall be on affidavits only unless otherwise directed by the court.

(d) Guardian Ad Litem. In those cases where a guardian ad litem is appointed, the court shall appoint a person who, through their professional qualifications or specialized training provided by the court, has the expertise to represent children. The Spokane County Superior Court judges shall appoint a committee of judges and/or court commissioners and interested members of the Spokane County Bar Association to oversee this specialized guardian ad litem program and provide training to those persons who wish to participate in the program.

(e) Discovery Stay. Upon the filing of the motion pursuant to (b), no discovery directly involving the child/children, including any interview of the child/children by investigators, psychologists, psychiatrists or other professionals, shall proceed without an order of the court. If the motion is not heard within 30 days, the discovery stay order expires unless extended, for good cause, by further order of the court.

(f) Notice to Guardian Ad Litem. If a guardian ad litem is appointed, the guardian ad litem is entitled to notice of all proceedings. The guardian ad litem shall be given ten days notice by any party seeking discovery which directly involves the child/children. The guardian ad litem has a right to be present at all interviews of the child/children unless the guardian ad litem believes it is in the best interest of the child/children not to be present. In the event the guardian ad litem objects to the proposed discovery procedure, the guardian ad litem shall schedule a hearing on the family law calendar in order to resolve the discovery issues.

(g) Report Confidential. The report of the Guardian Ad Litem in a proceeding under RCW Title 26 shall be treated as a confidential document by the Clerk of the Court, the parties and their counsel unless otherwise ordered by the court. However, attorneys of record may use and disclose such information from the report that is reasonably necessary for their investigation of the case and for trial preparation. Attorneys are prohibited from reproducing or distributing any portion of the written report to any person other than the attorney's client without further order of the court. Parties representing themselves shall be subject to the same use and disclosure limitations as attorneys. The cover sheet of the report shall be marked "Clerks Action Required" and indicate that it is confidential pursuant to LSPR 94.05(g). This rule shall not apply to Guardian Ad Litem reports provided under RCW Title 11, minor settlements or other similar matters.

[Adopted effective July 1, 1990; amended effective March 1, 1992; July 1, 1994; September 1, 1996; November 1, 2004.]

LSPR 94.06. GUARDIANS AD LITEM— RCW TITLE 26 FAMILY LAW—APPOINTMENT, GUARDIAN AD LITEM REPORT, CASE AND ANNUAL EVALUATIONS AND COMPLAINT PROCEDURES

(a) Guardians Ad Litem. When the appointment of a guardian ad litem is required, the appointee shall come from the Title 26 Family Law Guardian Ad Litem Registry maintained by the Superior Court. In order to be placed on the registry a person must present a written statement of their qualifications and complete a training program approved by the court. The Spokane County Superior Court Judges shall appoint a committee, to be known as the Family Law Guardian Ad Litem Committee, of judges and/or court commissioners and interested members of the Spokane County Bar Association to maintain the registry and provide training to those persons who wish to participate in the program. Orders to Appoint Guardian Ad Litem may be presented to the Ex Parte Department.

(b) Administration. The administration of such Guardian Ad Litem registry, including qualification, appointment, retention, evaluation, complaints and discipline of guardians ad litem under this rule, shall be in accordance with the written Policies and Procedure promulgated and approved by the Spokane County Superior Court. Copies of such written policies and procedures may be obtained from the Family Law Coordinator.

(c) Case Evaluations. At the time a guardian ad litem is discharged from a case, every attorney and the judicial officer involved in the case, will submit an evaluation of the guardian ad litem on a form to be supplied by the court. The completed evaluations will be returned to the Family Law Coordinator's Office and placed in the guardian ad litem's file. A copy of the evaluation(s) will be provided to the guardian ad litem. The guardian ad litem may respond, in writing, and the response will be placed in the guardian ad litem's file. These evaluation forms will assist the court in maintaining a registry of qualified guardians ad litem.

(d) Annual Evaluations. A judicial officer will review the complete file of every guardian ad litem at the time the Annual Updated Statement of Qualifications is reviewed. The judicial officer may refer a guardian ad litem file to the Family Law Guardian Ad Litem Committee if the judicial officer concludes, in a written report, there are specific concerns that should be addressed with the guardian ad litem. The guardian ad litem will be given a reasonable time to respond to the report. The Family Law Guardian Ad Litem Committee, or its designee, will meet with the guardian ad litem to discuss the report and appropriate remedial action(s), if any, to be taken by the guardian ad litem. The Family Law Guardian Ad Litem Committee may (1) allow the guardian ad litem to remain on the registry with no further action; (2) suspend the guardian ad litem from the registry, subject to the guardian ad litem completing other requirements as set forth by the Committee; or (3) remove the guardian ad litem from the registry. The guardian ad litem will be notified by written decision within seven days. In the event of removal from the registry, the guardian ad litem may request a meeting with the full Committee to review the decision.

(e) Complaint Procedures.

(1) *Duties of the Judicial Officer.* The court shall designate a judicial officer to review any written complaint regarding a guardian ad litem. If the complaint pertains to a pending case, the judicial officer shall immediately refer the complaint to the judge or court commissioner assigned to the pending case for disposition. If a complaint is received after a case has been completed then the judicial officer will commence an investigation.

(2) *Investigation Procedures.* The judicial officer will advise the complainant that an investigation has commenced. A copy of the complaint will be sent to the guardian ad litem. The guardian ad litem shall submit a written response within fourteen days of receipt of the complaint unless the court for good cause extends the time. The judicial officer may make any other contacts or inquiries he or she feels necessary. The judicial officer will submit a written report, within 45 days of the receipt of the written complaint, to the Family Law Guardian Ad Litem Committee. The guardian ad litem may respond to the report within 15 days of receipt of the report.

(3) *Discipline:* The judicial officer may recommend to the Family Law Guardian Ad Litem Committee to (1) allow the guardian ad litem to remain on the registry with no further action; (2) suspend the guardian ad litem from the registry, subject to the guardian ad litem completing other requirements as set forth by the Committee; or (3) remove the guardian ad litem from the registry. The Committee, or its designee, will meet and review the judicial officer's recommendation. The guardian ad litem will be notified by written decision within seven days. The guardian ad litem may request a meeting with the full Committee to review its decision.

(f) Confidentiality. A record of all complaints and grievances will be maintained by the court and treated as confidential until merit has been found. A record of any sanctions issued pursuant to the Annual Review and/or Complaint Procedures will be placed in the guardian ad litem's file.

(g) Appointments.

(1) Guardians Ad Litem in Title 26 cases (family law) will be appointed pursuant to statute (RCW 26.12) and the policies and procedures established by the Family Law GAL Committee. The policies and procedures are available from the Family Law Coordinator.

(2) Each GAL on the Family Law Registry shall be required to accept two county-pay cases each calendar year. These cases shall be paid pursuant to the Spokane County Superior Court GAL payment policies.

(3) A combination of County payment/private payment may be allowed pursuant to Spokane County Superior Court GAL payment policies.

(4) No GAL shall be appointed without his or her written approval or telephonic consent to the Family Law Coordinator.

(h) Procedure to Address Complaints. GALs may address complaints regarding registry or appointment matters as follows:

(1) Complaints should be directed in writing to the chair of the Family Law GAL Committee.

(2) The chair will review the matter, investigate as necessary and present the issue to the full committee at its next regularly scheduled meeting. The committee will decide whether any action is necessary to address the complaint, and establish a plan to enforce that action.

(3) The complainant shall be notified of the committee's decision in writing within one week of the committee meeting.

[Adopted effective July 1, 2000; amended effective November 1, 2002; September 1, 2004.]

LSPR 96.04. CHANGE OF NAME OF STEPCHILD

When a change of name of a child to that of the stepfather is sought for a child under 18 years of age, notice must be given to the natural father in the manner of giving notice to a nonconsenting parent in an adoption and, in addition, written consent will be required of any child over 14 years of age.

[Amended effective September 1, 1999.]

LSPR 98.04. ESTATES—PROBATE

(a) Estates—Probate Accounts.

(1) Receipts or cancelled checks in support of final and intermediate accounts in probate matters shall not ordinarily be filed with the clerk. Supporting documentation to accounts shall be supplied to the court as

needed to resolve any objection of an interested party or issue raised by the court.

(2) Final accounts are to be prepared in charge and discharge form, accounting for all assets received by the personal representative, all credits claimed, and reconciled to the balance of the assets on hand to be distributed.

(3) *Order for Production of Wills.* Upon filing any petition showing jurisdictional facts as to the estate of a deceased person and alleging that it is believed that a will exists and is in a safe deposit box to which the deceased had access, any person having control of such safe deposit box may be directed by court order to open such box in the presence of the petitioner, and if a document purporting to be a will of the deceased is found, the custodian of such safe deposit box shall deliver the same to counsel for the petitioner for immediate filing or to the clerk of the court. The clerk, on demand, and on payment of fees, shall issue a receipt for the same, attaching a photostatic or a like reproduction of said will to the receipt. The fees and mileage to the custodian for such delivery shall be the same as those for any witness and payable by the petitioner, together with expenses incurred.

[Amended effective April 1, 1990; September 1, 1997; September 1, 2002.]

LSPR 98.16. ATTORNEY'S FEES FIXED BY COURT IN MINOR OR INCOMPETENTS SETTLEMENTS

(f) Attorneys Fees. In those instances in which the court is called upon to set the reasonable amount of the fee for the lawyer acting on behalf of a minor or other incapacitated person, the court at the hearing shall consider the criteria set forth in RPC 1.5 and RCW 4.24.005.

(g) Court Approval of Investments. The court shall make available a set of investment guidelines for funds held in trust for a minor or other incapacitated person. The guidelines shall be distributed through the Spokane County Bar Association Office. A reasonable fee, approved by the Court, may be charged for the printing and distribution of the guidelines. These may assist a petitioning party in formulating and presenting to the Court for its approval a proposal to invest such funds. Court approval shall not be required for funds to be placed in a blocked account in a bank, trust company or other insured financial institution such as a credit union. The court need not approve the acquisition of unconditional interest bearing obligations of the state or federal government.

[Amended effective August 15, 1987; September 1, 1996.]

LSPR 98.18. COURT–CREATED TRUSTS

(a) Special Needs Trusts and Trusts governed by SPR 98.16W shall be approved in accord with the following requirements:

(1) A copy of the proposed trust document, note for hearing and trustee's fee schedule shall be furnished to the Court Administrator's designee for guardianship matters one week in advance of the hearing. The matter may be set in the Ex Parte Department, unless previously assigned to another department.

(2) An independent Guardian Ad Litem, specifically qualified in the area of court-created trusts, must be appointed to evaluate the proposed trust unless:

(a) The Court has ordered that the trust be drafted by independent trust counsel or

(b) The basis for eligibility for a special needs trust is a physical disability only and the adult beneficiary is competent. However, the Court may, in its discretion, appoint a Guardian Ad Litem for an otherwise competent beneficiary if it determines that he or she may not fully appreciate all the issues involved in creating the trust.

(3) The proponent of a trust must identify any other roles expected for trustees or members of a trust advisory committee in the life of the beneficiary. This would include caregivers, professional advisors, family or others who might receive direct or indirect economic benefit from trust expenditures.

(4) The order approving the trust may only be entered in a file with a probate/guardianship type "4" case assignment number to facilitate tracking. The order must have space designated on the face page to highlight due dates for accountings and other required filings. The trust document must be filed in the Superior Court file.

(5) The trustee is required to furnish annual accountings to the Court for approval on notice to any interested parties.

(6) The trust may not provide for removal to another venue or jurisdiction without order of this Court.

(7) A parent of a minor beneficiary is not the sole trustee or, if co-trustee, is not able to authorize a trust disbursement without Court approval.

(8) The appointment of any successor trustee is subject to approval of the Court.

(9) A trustee, other than a bank or trust company, is required to post a bond in the full amount of trust funds not placed in blocked accounts.

(10) Amendment of the trust shall only be by order of this Court.

(11) The trustee must file an inventory with the Court within 30 days of the funding of the trust. An amended inventory must be filed within 30 days if additional funding, in excess of $3,000, takes place after the filing of the initial inventory.

(12) The trustee must file with the Court an outline of the beneficiary's projected needs and significant trust expenditures within 30 days of their appointment

and annually at the time of each accounting to the Court.

[Adopted effective September 1, 2002.]

LSPR 98.19. CONFLICTS OF INTEREST OF PROPOSED GUARDIAN

(1) It shall be deemed a conflict of interest for a Certified Professional Guardian (CPG) to petition to have him or herself appointed as guardian for an alleged incapacitated person. Likewise, it shall be deemed a conflict of interest for an Attorney/CPG representing a petitioner to seek to have him or herself appointed. The conflict shall be disclosed to the Court and the procedure set forth below followed.

(2) If a CPG petitioner or an Attorney/CPG representing a petitioner seeks to have the Court appoint himself or herself as a guardian for an alleged incapacitated person he or she shall determine that:

(a) a guardianship is in the best interests of the alleged incapacitated person;

(b) there are no less restrictive alternatives; and

(c) there is no other suitable person willing to act as guardian.

(3) The conflicted party, referred to above, shall conduct an investigation and file a declaration (Declaration Pursuant to LSPR 98.19) describing the following pre-filing actions:

(a) identify any alternative nominees and provide information as to why alternate nominees who are available are not suitable or able to serve;

(b) provide a written request from the party requesting the guardianship which identifies the basis for the request and the basis for the decision by that party not to petition;

(c) provide documentation from third parties of the facts set out in the petition. Such documentation can include statements from care providers, family members, friends, or others with knowledge of the circumstances of the incapacitated person;

(d) provide documentation that the conflicted party has met with the alleged incapacitated person, the results of that meeting, and an opinion of the capacity issues faced by the alleged incapacitated person.

(e) disclose any relationship the conflicted party may have with a care facility and describe any practice the facility may have involving the referral of residents.

[Adopted on an emergency basis, effective May 14, 2014. Adopted on a permanent basis, effective September 2, 2014.]

LSPR 98.20. ESTATES–GUARDIANSHIPS– TRUSTS

(a) **Hearings**

1. If a guardianship/trust case is assigned to a trial judge, all hearings will be set before the assigned judge pursuant to LCR 40.

2. If a guardianship/trust case is not assigned to a trial judge, hearings must be scheduled through the Guardianship Monitoring Program.

3. There will be a weekly guardianship/trust calendar.

4. The first thirty minutes of the guardianship/trust calendar will be reserved for ex-parte matters.

5. The Note for Hearing or Order to Show Cause and documents pertaining to the hearing must be served and filed no later than twelve days prior to the hearing. Any responding documents must be served and filed at least seven days before the hearing. Reply documents must be served and filed at least two days before the hearing. In the event an agreed or uncontested order of continuance is to be entered, parties are required to present the order to the judicial assistant of the assigned judge or the Guardianship Monitoring Program if not assigned.

6. Copies of all documents pertaining to the hearing shall be furnished to the judicial assistant of the assigned judge or to the Guardianship Monitoring Program if not assigned.

7. *Hearing time limits.* Each party shall be given ten minutes unless additional time is granted by the judge or court commissioner. Requests for additional time shall be made in writing and provided with copies of all documents pertaining to the hearing.

8. *Confirming hearings.* A party to the proceeding must confirm the matter is ready no later than 12:00 noon, 2 days before the hearing by contacting the assigned judicial assistant of the assigned judge or to the Guardianship Monitoring Program if not assigned.

(b) **Pleadings.** Parties are required to use those guardianship forms approved by the Spokane County Superior Court for guardianship proceedings.

(c) **Presentation of Reports and Care Plans.**

(1) The original of any report, accounting or care plan shall be filed in the Clerk's Office.

(2) A date-stamped copy of the report, accounting or care plan shall be provided to the Guardianship Monitoring Program together with an original and one copy of a proposed order approving the report, accounting and/or care plan and a stamped, self-addressed envelope. Out–of–county guardians doing business by mail shall send the originals, copies and proposed order to the Guardianship Monitoring Program.

(3) Supporting documentation for accountings shall be provided to the Guardianship Monitoring Program. This shall include original monthly bank statements,

canceled checks or substitute images thereof provided by the financial institution, and receipts as appropriate. If the guardian of the estate is a bank or trust/agency company, it may file a computer printed statement of account in lieu of receipts or canceled checks. However, it must still complete the Report and Accounting form.

(d) Final Accounting. When a guardianship of the estate terminates and a guardian files a final account, an order shall be presented to the court setting a hearing on notice pursuant to RCW 11.92.053. The Guardianship Monitoring Program shall audit the final accounting. The order shall be on a form approved by the court. However, if the sole basis for the guardianship is the minority of the incapacitated person, the guardian may settle the account by filing a declaration of completion and serving notice thereof, on forms approved by the court, in accord with RCW 11.88.140. If the guardian of the estate resigns or is removed, but the guardianship continues, the court may in its discretion settle the account as an ex parte intermediate account or require a hearing on notice.

(e) Withdrawal by Attorney. Should the attorney representing the estate choose to withdraw, the attorney must advise the court of the name and address of the party to be notified, should that be necessary, of a delinquent report, accounting or Periodic Personal Care Plan. The notice to the court shall be filed prior to the effective date of the withdrawal of the attorney.

(f) Show Cause Noncompliance Calendar.

(1) *Calendar.* The clerk's office shall record all due dates for guardian's reports, and filings as set by the court. This shall include, but not be limited to an inventory, care plan, designation of standby-guardian, report and accounting or receipt for blocked account. The Guardianship Monitoring Program shall set a monthly Show Cause Noncompliance Calendar for those cases in which guardians have not met the required due dates.

(2) *Order to Appear.* If reports and filings are not presented timely, an order to appear on the guardianship show cause noncompliance calendar shall be sent to the attorney of record and/or the guardian citing the parties into court. Appearance on the calendar is mandatory. The attorney and/or the guardian shall have at least five days notice, in accordance with CR 6, to appear.

(3) *Attendance at Show Cause Noncompliance Calendar Excused.* If the guardian files the required document(s) referenced in the show cause noncompliance notice at least five days in advance of the calendar date, they shall be excused from attendance at the calendar.

(4) *Sanctions on the Show Cause Noncompliance Calendar.* The judicial officer assigned to hear the guardianship show cause noncompliance calendar may impose monetary sanctions, increase the bond, suspend the duties of the guardian, appoint a guardian ad litem, and/or remove the guardian.

(g) Review Hearing/Conference. If after initial review of a guardian's report or other filing, it is found unacceptable by the Court, the guardian shall be notified of the additional information or corrective action required. Additionally, the Court may cite the guardian in to appear at an informal review conference or in-court review hearing. The Court may then take appropriate action to resolve any concerns regarding the guardian's performance of their fiduciary duties.

(h) Deleted.

[Amended February 1, 1984; amended effective October 1, 1989; February 1, 1991; October 3, 1991; June 1, 1995; September 1, 1997; July 1, 2000; September 1, 2002; amended on an emergency basis effective January 1, 2007; amended on a permanent basis effective September 1, 2007; amended on an emergency basis effective May 14, 2014; amended on a permanent basis effective September 2, 2014.]

LSPR 98.22. GUARDIANS AD LITEM— RCW 11.88 GUARDIANSHIPS—APPOINTMENT, GUARDIAN AD LITEM REPORT, CASE AND ANNUAL EVALUATIONS AND COMPLAINT PROCEDURES

(a) Guardians Ad Litem. When the appointment of a guardian ad litem is required, the appointee shall come from the Guardian Ad Litem Registry maintained by the Superior Court. In order to be placed on the registry a person must present a written statement of their qualifications and complete a training program approved by the court. The Spokane County Superior Court Judges shall appoint a committee of judges and/or court commissioners and interested members of the Spokane County Bar Association to maintain the registry and provide training to those persons who wish to participate in the program. Orders to Appoint Guardian Ad Litem may be presented to the Ex Parte Department.

(b) Administration. The administration of such Guardian Ad Litem registry, including qualification, appointment, retention, evaluation, complaints and discipline of guardians ad litem under this rule, shall be in accordance with the written Policies and Procedures promulgated and approved by the Spokane County Superior Court. Copies of such written policies and procedures may be obtained from the Family Law Coordinator.

(c) Report of Guardian Ad Litem. When a guardian ad litem is appointed pursuant to RCW 11.88.090, the guardian ad litem shall secure a Report of Physician or Psychologist on Form GU 01.0110 and file it with the Guardian Ad Litem Report on Form GU 01.0120. The use of these forms is mandatory.

(d) Case Evaluations. At the time a guardian ad litem is discharged from a case, every attorney and the judicial officer involved in the case, will submit an evaluation of the guardian ad litem on a form to be supplied by the court. The completed evaluations will be returned to the Court Administrator's Office and placed in the guardian ad litem's file. A copy of the evaluation(s) will be provided to the guardian ad litem. The guardian ad litem may respond, in writing, and the response will be placed in the guardian ad litem's file. These evaluation forms will assist the court in maintaining a registry of qualified guardians ad litem.

(e) Annual Evaluations. A judicial officer will review the complete file of every guardian ad litem at the time the Annual Statement is reviewed. The judicial officer may refer a guardian ad litem file to the Guardianship Registry Committee if the judicial officer concludes, in a written report, there are specific concerns that should be addressed with the guardian ad litem. The guardian ad litem will be given a reasonable time to respond to the report. The Guardianship Registry Committee, or its designee, will meet with the guardian ad litem to discuss the report and appropriate remedial action(s), if any, to be taken by the guardian ad litem. The Guardianship Registry Committee may (1) allow the guardian ad litem to remain on the registry with no further action; (2) suspend the guardian ad litem from the registry, subject to the guardian ad litem completing other requirements as set forth by the Committee; or (3) remove the guardian ad litem from the registry. The guardian ad litem will be notified by written decision within seven days. In the event of removal from the registry, the guardian ad litem may request a meeting with the full Committee to review the decision.

(f) Complaint Procedures.

(1) *Duties of the Judicial Officer.* The court shall designate a judicial officer to review any written complaint regarding a guardian ad litem. If the complaint pertains to a pending case, the judicial officer shall immediately refer the complaint to the judge or court commissioner assigned to the pending case for disposition. If a complaint is received after a case has been completed then the judicial officer will commence an investigation.

(2) *Investigation Procedures.* The judicial officer will advise the complainant that an investigation has commenced. A copy of the complaint will be sent to the guardian ad litem. The guardian ad litem shall submit a written response within fourteen days of receipt of the complaint unless the court for good cause extends the time. The judicial officer may make any other contacts or inquiries he or she feels necessary. The judicial officer will submit a written report, within 45 days of the receipt of the written complaint, to the Guardianship Registry. The guardian ad litem may respond to the report within 15 days of the receipt of the report.

(3) *Discipline.* The judicial officer may recommend to the Guardianship Registry Committee to (1) allow the guardian ad litem to remain on the registry with no further action; (2) suspend the guardian ad litem from the registry, subject to the guardian ad litem completing other requirements as set for by the Committee; or (3) remove the guardian ad litem from the registry. The Committee, or its designee, will meet and review the judicial officer's recommendation. The guardian ad litem will be notified by written decision within seven days. The guardian ad litem may request a meeting with the full Committee to review its decision.

(g) Confidentiality. A record of all complaints and grievances will be maintained by the court and treated as confidential until merit has been found. A record of any sanctions issued pursuant to the Annual Review and/or Complaint Procedures will be placed in the guardian ad litem's file.

(h) Removal from the Guardianship Registry. When a guardian ad litem is removed from the Guardianship Registry, the court shall send a notice to the Office of the Administrator for the Courts.

(i) Appointments.

(1) Guardians Ad Litem in Title 11 cases (guardianship) will be appointed pursuant to statute (RCW 11.88) and the policies and procedures established by the Guardianship Registry Committee. The policies and procedures are available from the Family Law Coordinator.

(2) Each GAL on the Guardianship Registry shall be required to accept two county-pay cases each calendar year. These cases shall be paid pursuant to the Spokane County Superior Court GAL payment policies.

(3) No GAL shall be appointed without his or her written approval or telephonic consent to the Family Law Coordinator.

(j) Procedure to Address Complaints. GALs may address complaints regarding registry or appointment matters as follows:

(1) Complaints should be directed to the chair of the Guardianship Registry Committee.

(2) The chair will review the matter, investigate as necessary and present the issue to the full committee at its next regularly scheduled meeting. The committee will decide whether any action is necessary to address the complaint, and establish a plan to enforce that action.

(3) The complainant shall be notified of the committee's decision within one week of the committee meeting.

[Amended effective July 1, 2000; November 1, 2002; September 1, 2004.]

LSPR 98.24. MANDATORY GUARDIAN TRAINING

(a) Definition of Applicable Cases. This rule applies to all guardianship cases including those originating under RCW 11.88 and SPR 98.16W. The court, in its discretion, may also direct other persons to take all or part of the mandatory guardian training.

(b) Intent. The purpose of mandatory guardian training is to provide information to prospective guardians about their legal responsibilities as a guardian.

(c) Guardian Training. Except as provided in (d) no person shall be appointed guardian by the court until he/she has successfully completed the Mandatory Guardian Training sponsored by the Spokane County Superior Court. Successful completion shall be evidenced by a certificate issued by the court.

(d) Special Consideration/Waiver. Certified Professional Guardians are not required to attend guardian training as long as the guardian is in good standing with the Certified Professional Guardian Board. The court may waive the training for attorneys, bank trust officers and other professionals who have been appointed as guardians in the past.

(e) Fees. Each participant shall pay a fee to Spokane County to cover the cost of the training and guardian manual. The court may waive the fee in cases where the proposed guardian and/or the alleged incapacitated person is indigent.

[Adopted on an emergency basis effective January 1, 2007; adopted on a permanent basis effective September 1, 2007.]

LSPR 99. LOCAL RULES OF SUPERIOR COURT

(a) Adoption. These local rules were originally adopted on September 21, 1978, to be effective on January 1, 1979. They were revised August 1, 1981. They may be amended from time to time by a majority of the judges, but shall first be submitted for comment to representatives of the Spokane County Bar Association in the absence of emergency or other circumstances justifying immediate change. The provisions of these rules are supplemental to the Rules of the Supreme Court of the State of Washington and shall not be construed in conflict with them.

(b) Format. These rules shall be contained in the Spokane County electronic data processing system. Updated copies shall be available to counsel and other interested parties upon payment of a reasonable fee to cover the cost of reproduction.

(c) Filing With Administrator for the Courts. Copies of these rules and subsequent amendments shall be provided to the state court administrator without fee pursuant to GR 7.

[Amended effective July 1, 1988.]

II. LOCAL MANDATORY ARBITRATION RULES (Cite as LMAR)

1. SCOPE AND PURPOSE OF RULES

LMAR 1.1. APPLICATION OF RULES— PURPOSE AND DEFINITIONS

The purpose of mandatory arbitration of civil actions under RCW 7.06 as implemented by the Mandatory Arbitration Rules is to provide a simplified and economical procedure for obtaining the prompt and equitable resolution of disputes involving claims of $ 50,000 or less. The Mandatory Arbitration Rules as supplemented by these local rules are not designed to address every question which may arise during the arbitration process, and the rules give considerable discretion to the arbitrator. The arbitrator should not hesitate to be informal and expeditious, consistent with the purpose of the statute and rules.

[Amended effective July 1, 1987; October 1, 1989; September 1, 2005.]

LMAR 1.2. MATTERS SUBJECT TO ARBITRATION

By implementation of these rules the Superior Court of Washington for Spokane County authorizes mandatory arbitration under RCW 7.06.010, and approves such arbitrations in civil actions in which no party asserts a claim in excess of $ 50,000 exclusive of interest and costs under RCW 7.06.020 as amended.

[Amended effective July 1, 1987; October 1, 1989; September 1, 2005.]

LMAR 1.3. [DELETED]

[Deleted effective January 1, 1990.]

2. TRANSFER TO ARBITRATION AND ASSIGNMENT OF ARBITRATOR

LMAR 2.1. TRANSFER TO ARBITRATION

(a) Statement of Arbitrability. The party filing a statement of arbitrability shall do so no later than the date set forth in the Case Schedule Order using such form(s) as approved by the Court. A conformed copy shall be provided to the arbitration director. If any party objects to the matter being submitted for mandatory arbitration, said objection shall be filed within 5 days of receipt of the Statement of Arbitrability and shall be noted for hearing pursuant to LCR 40(b)(10) before the assigned judge, or if unassigned, to the presiding judge. The party objecting to the statement of arbitrability shall provide a copy to the arbitration director.

(b) By Stipulation. After the answer has been filed, the parties may stipulate to mandatory arbitration using a Stipulation for Arbitration form approved by the court. Stipulated cases will be placed on the arbitration calendar regardless of the nature of the case or amount in controversy.

(c) Limitations. For cases where a Case Schedule Order has been entered pursuant to LAR 0.4.1, no case may be assigned to mandatory arbitration after the deadline for filing for arbitration, unless consent is obtained from the assigned judge.

[Amended effective September 4, 1986; July 1, 1987; October 1, 1989; January 1, 1991; October 1, 1994; September 1, 1999; September 1, 2001; September 1, 2002.]

LMAR 2.3. ASSIGNMENT TO ARBITRATOR

(a) Generally, Stipulations. When a case is set for arbitration, a list of five proposed arbitrators will be furnished to the parties. A master list of arbitrators will be made available on request. The parties are encouraged to stipulate to an arbitrator using

Stipulation to Arbitrator (form LMAR–02.0300). In the absence of a stipulation, the arbitrator will be chosen from among the five proposed arbitrators in the manner defined by this rule.

(b) Response by Parties. Each party may, within ten days after a list of proposed arbitrators has been furnished to the parties, nominate one or two arbitrators and strike two arbitrators from the list. If both parties respond, an arbitrator nominated by both parties will be appointed. If no arbitrator has been nominated by both parties, the arbitration director will appoint an arbitrator from among those not stricken by either party.

(c) Response by Only One Party. If only one party responds within ten days, the arbitration director will appoint an arbitrator nominated by that party.

(d) No Response. If neither party responds within ten days, the arbitration director will appoint one of the five proposed arbitrators.

(e) Additional Arbitrators for Additional Parties. If there are more than two adverse parties, all represented by different counsel, two additional proposed arbitrators shall be added to the list for each additional party so represented with the above principles of selection to be applied.

[Amended effective September 1, 2001.]

3. ARBITRATORS

LMAR 3.1. QUALIFICATIONS

(a) Arbitration Panel. There shall be a panel of arbitrators in such numbers as the administrative committee may from time to time determine. A person desiring to serve as an arbitrator shall complete an application on a form prescribed by the court. A copy of said application of a person appointed as an arbitrator will be available upon request by any party and will be mailed to a requesting party at the party's own expense. The oath of office on the form prescribed by the court must be completed and filed prior to an appointed applicant being placed on the panel.

(b) Refusal, Disqualification. The appointment of an arbitrator is subject to the right of that person to refuse to serve. An arbitrator must notify the arbitration director immediately if refusing to serve or if any cause exists for the arbitrator's disqualification from the case upon any of the grounds of interest, relationship, bias or prejudice set forth in CJC Canon (3) governing the disqualification of judges.

[Amended effective September 1, 2001.]

LMAR 3.2. AUTHORITY OF ARBITRATORS

An arbitrator has the authority to:

(a) Motions. Determine the time, place and procedure to present a motion before the arbitrator, excluding motions for summary award and involuntary dismissal.

(b) Expenses. Require a party or attorney advising such party or both to pay the reasonable expenses, including attorney's fees, caused by the failure of such party or attorney or both to obey an order of the arbitrator unless the arbitrator finds that the failure was substantially justified or that other circumstances make an award of expenses unjust. The arbitrator shall make a special award for such expenses and shall file such award with the clerk of the superior court, with proof of service on each party. The aggrieved party shall have ten days thereafter to appeal the award of such expense in accordance with the procedures described in RCW 2.24.050. If within ten days after the award is filed no party appeals, a judgment shall be entered in a manner described generally under MAR 6.3.

(c) Attorney's Fees. Award attorney's fees as authorized by these rules, by contract or by law.

[Amended January 1, 1990.]

4. PROCEDURES AFTER ASSIGNMENT

LMAR 4.2. DISCOVERY

(a) **Additional Discovery.** In determining when additional discovery beyond that directly authorized by MAR 4.2 is reasonably necessary, the arbitrator shall balance the benefits of discovery against the burdens and expenses. The arbitrator shall consider the nature and complexity of the case, the amount in controversy, values at stake, the discovery that has already occurred, the burdens on the party from whom discovery is sought, and the possibility of unfair surprise which may result if discovery is restricted. Authorized discovery shall be conducted in accordance with the civil rules except that motions concerning discovery shall be determined by the arbitrator.

(b) **Discovery Pending.** Discovery pending at the time the case is assigned to an arbitrator is stayed pending order from the arbitrator or except as the parties may stipulate or except as authorized by MAR 4.2.

5. HEARING

LMAR 5.1. NOTICE OF HEARING—TIME AND PLACE—CONTINUANCE

An arbitration hearing may be scheduled at any reasonable time and place chosen by the arbitrator. The arbitrator may grant a continuance without court order as long as the new hearing date will allow the arbitration hearing and arbitrator decision to be completed 30 days before the scheduled trial date. The parties may stipulate to a continuance only with the permission of the arbitrator. A continuance of the arbitration hearing to a date less than 30 days prior to the scheduled trial date must be approved by the assigned judge. The arbitrator shall give reasonable notice of the hearing date on a Notice of Arbitration Hearing Date form approved by the court, and any continuance on an Order of Continuance of Arbitration Hearing Date form approved by the court to the arbitration director.

[Amended effective September 1, 2001.]

LMAR 5.2. PREHEARING STATEMENT OF PROOF—DOCUMENTS FILED WITH COURT

(a) **Generally.** In addition to the requirements of MAR 5.2, each party shall also furnish the arbitrator with copies of pleadings and other documents contained in the court file which that party deems relevant. The court file shall remain with the county clerk. The arbitrator shall strictly enforce the provisions of MAR 5.2 and is encouraged to withhold permission to present evidence at time of hearing if the parties have failed to comply with this rule.

(b) [Deleted].

[Amended effective September 4, 1986; amended January 1, 1990; April 1, 1990.]

LMAR 5.3. [DELETED]

[Deleted effective January 1, 1990.]

6. AWARD

LMAR 6.1. FORM AND CONTENT OF AWARD

(a) **Form.** The award shall be prepared on an Arbitration Award approved by the court and filed with the county clerk along with proof of service on the parties.

(b) **Return of Exhibits.** When an award is filed, the arbitrator shall return all exhibits to the parties who offered them during the hearing.

[Amended effective September 1, 2001.]

LMAR 6.2. FILING OF AWARD

A request by an arbitrator for an extension of time for the filing of an award shall be presented to the arbitration department, which will gain authorization from the administrative committee. The arbitrator shall give the parties notice of any extension granted. Recurring delays in the filing of awards will result in the removal of the arbitrator from the panel.

[Amended effective September 4, 1986.]

LMAR 6.3. JUDGMENT ON AWARD

(a) **Presentation.** A judgment on an award shall be presented to the ex parte department, by any party, on notice in accordance with MAR 6.3.

7. TRIAL DE NOVO

LMAR 7.1. REQUEST FOR TRIAL DE NOVO

(a) **Request.** The Request for Trial de Novo and Sealing of Award shall be filed with the county clerk on such form as approved by the court. A copy shall be provided to the assigned judge and arbitration director.

(b) [Deleted]

[Amended effective September 1, 2001.]

LMAR 7.2. [DELETED]

[Deleted effective January 1, 1990.]

LMAR 7.3. [DELETED]

[Deleted effective January 1, 1990.]

8. GENERAL PROVISIONS

LMAR 8.1. STIPULATIONS—EFFECT ON RELIEF GRANTED

If a case not otherwise subject to mandatory arbitration is transferred to arbitration by stipulation, the arbitrator may grant any relief which could have been granted if the case were determined by a judge.

LMAR 8.3. [DELETED]

[Deleted effective September 1, 2001.]

LMAR 8.4. TITLE AND CITATION

These rules are known and cited as the Spokane County Superior Court Mandatory Arbitration Rules. LMAR is the official abbreviation.

LMAR 8.5. COMPENSATION OF ARBITRATOR

(a) **Generally.** Arbitrators shall be compensated in the same amount and manner as judges pro tempore of the superior court. Hearing time and reasonable preparation time are compensable.

(b) **Form.** When the award is filed, the arbitrator shall submit to the arbitration director a request for payment on a form prescribed by the court within 60 days of the filing of the award. The director shall determine the amount of compensation and costs to be paid. The decision of the director will be reviewed by the presiding judge at the request of the arbitrator. Compensation to the arbitrator and cost reimbursement shall be pursuant to standards set and periodically revised by the court.

[Amended effective September 4, 1986; July 1, 1987; September 1, 1988; October 1, 1989; amended April 1, 1990; amended effective September 1, 2001.]

LMAR 8.6. ADMINISTRATION

(a) **Generally.** The court administrator, under the supervision of the superior court judges, shall supervise arbitration under these rules and perform any additional duties which may be delegated by the judges.

(b) **Administrative Committee.** There shall be an administrative committee composed of three judges chosen by the presiding judge and three members of the Washington State Bar Association, one each chosen by the Spokane County Bar Association, the Washington Association of Defense Counsel and the Washington State Trial Lawyers Association. The members of the committee shall serve for staggered three-year terms and may be re-appointed.

(c) **Powers and Duties.** The administrative committee shall have the power and duty to:

(1) Select its chairperson and provide for its procedures;

(2) Select and appoint the panel of arbitrators provided in Rule 3.1(a);

(3) Remove a person from a panel of arbitrators;

(4) Review the administration and operation of the arbitration program periodically and make recommendations as it deems appropriate to improve the program.

[Amended effective September 1, 2001.]

III. CRIMINAL RULES
(Cite as LCrR)

2. PROCEDURES PRIOR TO ARREST AND OTHER SPECIAL PROCEEDINGS

LCrR 0.2. COURT ORGANIZATION AND MANAGEMENT [REPEALED]

[Repealed effective January 1, 1998.]

LCrR 0.3. COMMITTEES [REPEALED]

[Repealed effective January 1, 1998.]

LCrR 2.1.   [INFORMATION]

(d) Amendment.

(1) A motion by the State prior to trial, to amend an Information in order to add counts, change the degree of an offense, change the means of commission of an offense, change the date of an offense or add a sentencing enhancement, shall be noted by the State on Form CR–06.300(a) and served on defendant's counsel of record, if represented, or on the defendant if unrepresented.   A copy of the proposed amended Information shall be filed and served with the motion. Said motions must be filed and served at least 5 days prior to the hearing of the motion.   A copy of the motion shall be given to the bailiff for the Chief Criminal Judge at least one working day prior to the hearing.   Motions to amend will be heard by the Chief Criminal Judge on Thursday afternoons unless specially set by the Court.   It is the duty of the moving party to notify the bailiff for the Chief Criminal Judge by noon of the Tuesday prior to the hearing to confirm the matter will be heard.   A motion to amend an Information to correct simple clerical or grammatical errors is not subject to the time limits set forth in this rule.

(2) A motion to amend an Information during, or after, the trial has commenced is governed by CrR 2.1(d).

[Adopted effective March 5, 1998.]

LCrR 2.2.   WARRANT OF ARREST AND SUMMONS

(b) Issuance of Summons in Lieu of Warrant. Upon the Prosecuting Attorney's filing with the clerk an Information without directing or requesting the issuance of a warrant for the arrest of the defendant, the clerk shall issue a summons commanding the defendant to appear before the Court at a specified time and place.

[Adopted effective September 1, 2001.]

LCrR 2.3.   SEARCH AND SEIZURE

(g) Search Warrant Custody and Control.   The Superior Court judge authorizing a search warrant will retain custody and control of the affidavit for search warrant and the search warrant until executed or returned unexecuted.

(1) After execution, the search warrant shall be filed by number and description of the person or property to be searched.   An index will be maintained and available to the public in the clerk's office.

(2) The affidavit and accompanying papers including the return of service shall be filed in accordance with the provisions of LCrR 2.3(h).

(h) Sealing or Destruction of Records.

(1) The destruction or sealing of court records is governed by GR 15.   A motion to seal or destroy a record shall be made before a record is filed with the clerk.   The motion shall be made to the judicial officer before which the matter is pending, or the Presiding Judge.

(2) [Deleted].

(3) [Deleted].

[Adopted effective July 1, 1993; amended effective September 1, 1997.]

3.   RIGHTS OF DEFENDANTS

LCrR 3.1.   RIGHT TO AND APPOINTMENT OF COUNSEL

(d) Appointment of Counsel.

(2) Defendants requesting appointment of counsel may be required to promptly execute an affidavit under oath disclosing their financial circumstances. This affidavit will be filed and will be reviewed by the judge who is determining assignment of court-appointed counsel for a defendant.   All appointments by reason of indigence are expressly contingent upon a finding of indigence, as defined in CrR 3.1(d)(1) and full disclosure of assets.   All appointments of counsel are subject to review at or before the omnibus hearing as provided in LCrR 4.5.   Where assets are discovered or acquired subsequent to appointment which would indicate that a defendant can afford to retain counsel in whole or in part a defendant may be ordered to retain counsel or reimburse the county for the cost of court-appointed counsel.   Court-appointed counsel who learn or have reason to believe that their client can afford to retain counsel shall notify the court's bailiff promptly of this fact in order that the court can inquire into the financial status of the defendant.

(e) [Deleted]

(g) Privately Retained Counsel.   A defendant who privately retains counsel is responsible for whatever fee is contracted or its agreed basis arranged between them.   In those cases involving privately retained counsel, the only public funds expended for the Superior Court trial shall be those authorized by CrR 3.1(f).

Attorneys retained by defendants in criminal cases must serve prompt written notice of their appearance upon the prosecuting attorney and file the same with the clerk.   Withdrawal of attorneys is governed by CrR 3.1(e).

[Amended March 1, 1984; March 5, 1998.]

LCrR 4.5. OMNIBUS HEARINGS AND MOTIONS

(d) Criminal Motions. Criminal Motions under CrR 3.5 shall ordinarily be heard by the assigned trial judge. However, CrR 3.5 motions may be specially set prior to trial date by the Chief Criminal Judge upon a showing of good cause. Criminal motions under CrR 3.6 shall be noted with the Chief Criminal Judge, who will either schedule the matter before the Chief Criminal Judge or assign it to another judge. Motions under CrR 3.6 shall be heard at least 14 days before trial and shall be accompanied by all supporting materials required by CrR 3.6. The moving party will file and serve all memoranda, affidavits and certificates no later than the second Tuesday preceding the hearing date. The responding party shall file and serve all responsive memoranda, affidavits and certificates no later than 5:00 p.m. the Monday prior to the hearing date. Any reply memoranda must be served no later than 12:00 p.m. the Wednesday prior to the hearing. The judge who will hear the CrR 3.6 motion will, pursuant to that rule, determine if an evidentiary hearing is required. The time limit prescribed by this rule may be waived by the Chief Criminal Judge upon a showing of newly discovered evidence or a basis for the motion that could not have been developed by an exercise of due diligence.

(i) All criminal motions must be filed by using form CR–06.300(a). Motions must be promptly served on the opposing party, and a copy shall be provided to the bailiff for the Chief Criminal Judge. A working copy of all memoranda, affidavits and certificates must be provided by the parties to the bailiff for the judge hearing the motion at least one working day prior to the hearing.

(ii) All criminal motions, other than those under CrR 3.5, will be heard on Thursday mornings unless specially set by the Court.

(iii) It is the duty of the moving party to notify the bailiff for the Chief Criminal Judge by noon of the Tuesday prior to the hearing to confirm the matter will be heard.

(iv) Any agreements to continue a hearing which had been confirmed as ready to be heard shall be presented to the Chief Criminal Judge and the judge assigned to hear the motion no later than 12:00 p.m. the Wednesday prior to the hearing.

(e) Restitution Hearings. Restitution hearings shall be scheduled before the Presiding Department on Thursdays at 3:30 p.m., unless specially set by the court. The party noting the hearing shall notify the judicial assistant for the Presiding Department by 12:00 noon of the previous day (Wednesday) to confirm that the matter will be heard. The parties will also advise the court if it is expected that multiple witnesses will be called. The assigned prosecutor will also advise if prisoner transport is required for the hearing.

[Amended effective July 1, 1995; March 1, 1998; September 1, 2003; February 1, 2004; September 1, 2006.]

LCrR 7.1. SENTENCING

The Clerk shall receive all Presentence Investigation (PSI) reports prepared by the Department of Corrections which shall be forwarded by the sentencing judge. The Clerk shall maintain said PSI in confidential status. For purposes of this rule, "confidential" means that the only persons who may have access to the PSI are parties, counsel of record, or such other persons who have received permission of the court upon a showing of good cause.

[Adopted effective September 1, 2003.]

LCrR 7.8. PAYMENT OF COSTS AND RESTITUTION THROUGH CLERK

Whenever the court orders costs and/or restitution it shall be paid through the clerk of the court by cash, certified check, cashier's check or money order payable to the clerk of the court. The name of the payor and the court case number will be entered on the face of the instrument of payment.

(a) Payment of Costs. In all criminal cases, except where the court order is to the contrary, the clerk shall disburse monies received from the criminal defendant in the following order:

(1) Restitution;

(2) Court Costs;

(3) Attorney's Fees;

(4) Drug Fund.

(b) Hearings on Legal–Financial Obligations. Contested Hearings to enforce legal-financial obligations (LFO) are to be scheduled at 2:30 p.m. Fridays in the Chief Criminal Department or as may be specially set by the Chief Criminal Judge.

[Amended January 1, 1983; July 1, 1988; September 1, 2007.]

IV. JUVENILE COURT RULES
(CITE AS LJuCR)

2. SHELTER CARE HEARINGS

LJuCR 2.3. NOTICE AND RIGHT TO HEARING

(a) Scheduling and Notice. A shelter care hearing may be set by court order or by scheduling a hearing with the Juvenile Court Coordinator. The party scheduling the hearing shall notify the Juvenile Court Coordinator, Clerk of Court, Attorney General's Office, CASA Program, Public Defender's Office, and any other parties and their attorneys.

(b) Guardian ad Litem. The court shall address the appointment of a Guardian ad Litem for the child at the initial shelter care hearing. The court shall appoint a Guardian ad Litem for the child or make a determination that good cause exists not to appoint one. This decision may be reviewed at each subsequent hearing including the dependency fact-finding hearing, each dependency review hearing, and prior to entry of a guardianship or termination order. A party may request that a Guardian ad Litem be appointed at any time during the dependency, guardianship or termination proceedings. A copy of the shelter care hearing order shall be provided to the CASA Program.

(e) Recommendation. The recommendation required by RCW 13.34.060(7) may be made orally at the time of hearing.

[Amended effective September 4, 1986; September 1, 1987; March 1, 1992; September 1, 1999.]

3. DEPENDENCY AND GUARDIANSHIP/TERMINATION

LJuCR 3.1. FILING AND SERVICE OF PROCESS OF DEPENDENCY, GUARDIANSHIP AND TERMINATION PETITIONS

The petitioner shall provide the Clerk of the Court with the original petition along with sufficient copies of the petition for service of process. The party filing a petition shall also file a Request for Service notifying the Clerk of Court what type of service is being requested. The Clerk of Court shall notify the petitioner when personal service packets are completed. The petitioner is responsible for completing personal service and filing a declaration of service. The Clerk is responsible for service by publication and mail and for filing a declaration of service.

[Amended effective March 1, 1992; September 1, 1999.]

LJuCR 3.3. CONTENT OF PETITION

(g) Other Information. A dependency, guardianship, or termination petition shall contain a statement whether either parent is under the age of 18.

[Amended effective September 1, 1987; March 1, 1992; September 1, 1999.]

LJuCR 3.4. APPOINTMENT OF COUNSEL AND SCHEDULING OF DEPENDENCY FACT–FINDING HEARING

(a) [Deleted]

(c) Scheduling of Hearing. Any request for continuance of the fact-finding hearing shall identify the 75th day from the filing of the petition. A motion to continue beyond the 75th day shall be supported by a declaration of exceptional circumstances. The order continuing the hearing beyond 75 days shall identify the exceptional circumstances found by the Court.

(e) Appointment of Attorney or Guardian Ad Litem.

(1) *Minor Parents.* Juvenile Court staff shall review all dependency, guardianship and termination petitions to determine whether an attorney and/or guardian ad litem should be appointed for a parent under the age of 18. Juvenile Court staff shall apply to the court for an Order Assigning Lawyer or Guardian Ad Litem for a minor parent. Juvenile Court staff shall forward the dependency, guardianship, or termination petition to the appointed attorney.

(2) *Attorney for Child.* A child over the age of 12 may request the appointment of an attorney by informing the Guardian ad Litem or by written request to Juvenile Court staff. Juvenile Court staff shall apply to the Court for an Order Assigning Lawyer for the child.

(3) *Request for Appointed Counsel by Parent/Guardian.* A parent or guardian may request appointment of counsel in a dependency, guardianship or termination proceeding by completing a Motion and Declaration for Assignment of Lawyer. Juvenile Court staff will help the parent or guardian complete the requisite documents and will present the motion and Order Assigning Lawyer to the court. If the order is signed, a copy of the order along with the dependency, termination, or guardianship petition shall be delivered immediately to the assigned lawyer by Juvenile Court staff. Copies of the order shall be furnished to all parties.

If the motion for counsel is denied, the parent or guardian may request the court to review its decision. The parent or guardian shall contact the Juvenile Court Coordinator to initiate the review process.

(f) Private Counsel. If private counsel is retained by any party to the proceedings, such counsel shall immediately file a notice of appearance with the Clerk of Court and provide a copy to Juvenile Court staff, the child's guardian ad litem, if any, the Attorney General's Office, other counsel, and the supervising agency. If the child's guardian ad litem is a CASA, providing a copy of the notice of appearance to the CASA Program is deemed notice to the guardian ad litem.

[Amended effective September 4, 1986; September 1, 1987; October 1, 1989; March 1, 1992; September 1, 1999.]

LJuCR 3.7. [DELETED]

[Amended effective September 4, 1986; October 1, 1989; March 1, 1992; deleted effective September 1, 1999.]

LJuCR 3.8. [DELETED]

[Amended effective March 1, 1992; deleted effective September 1, 1999.]

LJuCR 3.9. REVIEW HEARING

(a) Proposed Order and Supervising Agency Report. The supervising agency shall prepare a proposed order and a written report containing the information required by RCW 13.34.120. The report shall be provided to the court and copies shall be furnished to Juvenile Court staff, the guardian ad litem, if any, and to the parties and their counsel 14 days before the review hearing.

(b) First Review and Permanent Planning Review Hearings in Open Court. All first review and permanent planning review hearings will be presented in open court. A party may request that any review hearing be held in open court.

[Amended March 1, 1986; amended effective October 1, 1989; March 1, 1992; September 1, 1999; amended on an emergency basis effective January 1, 2009; amended on a permanent basis effective September 1, 2009.]

LJuCR 3.10. ASSIGNMENT TO COURT COMMISSIONER

Each dependency petition shall be assigned by the Juvenile Court to a Court Commissioner. The assigned commissioner shall hear every contested issue from fact-finding forward unless otherwise ordered by the court. Issues set on the motion calendar, except motions regarding placement or visitation, are not required to be heard by the assigned commissioner. However, a party may request the assigned commissioner to decide the issue and must schedule the motion accordingly.

[Adopted effective September 1, 1999.]

LJuCR 3.11. SETTING A CONTESTED HEARING

Prior to setting a contested hearing, a status conference shall be held with a judicial officer assigned to Juvenile Court. The parties shall contact the Juvenile Court Coordinator to schedule a status conference. At the status conference, the parties should be prepared to discuss witness and exhibit lists, contested issues, and estimated trial time. A Status Conference Report shall be completed at the conclusion of the status conference and filed with the Clerk of the Court.

[Adopted effective September 1, 1999.]

5. AT–RISK YOUTH (ARY) AND CHILD IN NEED OF SERVICES (CHINS) PROCEEDINGS

LJuCR 5.1. PROCEDURE FOR FILING

A party may file a petition by delivering it to the Juvenile Court facilitator designated for proceedings under RCW 13.32A. Upon verifying that a family assessment has been completed or has been requested, but not completed within two working days, the original petition shall be filed with the Clerk by the facilitator. The Court shall provide forms and instructions for the parties interested in filing a petition. The Court shall also provide an informational session to assist parties in preparing a petition. It is recommended that a parent or other unrepresented party attend prior to filing.

[Amended effective September 1, 1999.]

LJuCR 5.2. APPOINTMENT OF ATTORNEY

The Public Defender shall be deemed appointed to represent the minor child unless an order is entered or notice of appearance is filed providing for alternative counsel in a specific case. The appointed attorney shall be provided the minor child's address and telephone number, together with the name and telephone number of the assigned social worker at least one court day prior to the initial hearing.

[Adopted effective September 1, 1999.]

LJuCR 5.3. SCHEDULING OF FACT–FINDING HEARING

The facilitator shall assign a hearing date and time for each properly filed petition.

(a) [Deleted]

(b) [Deleted]

(c) [Deleted]

[Amended effective September 1, 1999.]

LJuCR 5.4. NOTICE OF FACT–FINDING HEARING

The facilitator shall provide a copy of the petition and notice of hearing to:

(a) Petitioner,

(b) Respondent,

(c) Department of Social and Health Services, Family Reconciliation Services,

(d) Public Defender or other assigned counsel, and

(e) Probation Officer assigned for RCW 13.13A proceedings.

The facilitator may notify the respondent by mail. However, in a CHINS proceeding the petitioner shall also arrange service on the respondent pursuant to RCW 13.32A.152.

[Amended effective September 1, 1987; September 1, 1999.]

LJuCR 5.5. DETENTION HEARING

A child taken into custody for violating a placement order under RCW 13.32A or pursuant to a pick-up order under this chapter shall be entitled to a detention hearing within twenty-four hours, excluding Saturdays, Sundays and holidays. Detention hearings shall be held at 9:00 a.m. or 1:30 p.m. The detention staff shall immediately inform the facilitator when a child is admitted under this chapter. The facilitator shall notify all interested parties of the detention hearing, including any assigned probation officer.

[Adopted effective September 1, 1999.]

LJuCR 5.6. DISPOSITION HEARING

(a) [Deleted]

(b) [Deleted]

(d) [Deleted]

(e) [Deleted]

The disposition hearing may be held at the conclusion of the fact-finding hearing or may be scheduled within fourteen days. A petitioning parent in an ARY case shall attach to the petition an outline of the requested disposition. In a CHINS case, the DSHS assessment shall set forth the dispositional services and out-of-home placement options that may be available. If a respondent requests that the disposition hearing be deferred to a later date, the Court will give due consideration to whether they have received notice of the dispositional alternatives as set forth herein. If the disposition hearing is not held at the time of fact-finding, the facilitator shall notify any interested party listed above of the hearing date and time unless they signed the order setting the disposition hearing.

[Amended effective September 1, 1987; September 1, 1999.]

LJuCR 5.7. REVIEW HEARING

The facilitator shall notify each interested party listed above and the assigned probation officer, if any, of the review hearing date and time set by the Court unless the party signed the order setting the hearing.

(a) [Deleted]

(b) [Deleted]

[Amended effective September 1, 1987; September 1, 1999.]

6. DIVERSION

LJuCR 6.4. [DELETED]

[Deleted effective September 1, 1987.]

LJuCR 6.6. TERMINATION OF DIVERSION AGREEMENT

(a) Petition. A Petition for Termination of a Diversion Agreement (form JU–06.0200–WPF) shall be filed with the clerk by the deputy prosecuting attorney. The petition shall be accompanied by an affidavit of a probation counselor stating the matter as required by JuCR 6.6(a) and RCW 13.40.080(6).

(b) Scheduling of Hearing. The clerk of court shall schedule a hearing on the daily offender calendar within 30 days of the filing of a petition to terminate a diversion agreement. Copies of the notice and accompanying affidavit shall be furnished to the administrative supervisor for probation services and to the public defender along with a notation of the scheduled hearing date. The probation counselor shall give notice of the hearing to the juvenile as required by RCW 13.40.080(6) in accordance with JuCR 11.2.

[Amended effective September 1, 1987; March 1, 1992; September 1, 1996.]

7. OFFENSE PROCEEDINGS

LJuCR 7.1. JURISDICTION

The deputy prosecuting attorney shall file the original information with the clerk of court. Upon filing the information a conformed copy shall be furnished to the administrative supervisor for probation services and to the public defender along with copies of the applicable police report and a computer print out showing the juvenile's criminal history.

[Amended effective September 1, 1996.]

LJuCR 7.3. [DELETED]

[Deleted effective September 1, 1996.]

LJuCR 7.4. DETENTION HEARING

(a) Scheduling of Hearing. For all juveniles taken into custody and held in detention, the court shall make every reasonable effort to conduct a hearing on the issue of detention the next judicial day. The prosecutor shall schedule all detention hearings on the daily 1:30 p.m. offender calendar.

(b) Procedure at Hearing. The detention hearing shall be held in accordance with JuCR 7.3 and 7.4.

(c) Determination that Detention Is or Is Not Necessary. The determination as to detention will be made in accordance with JuCR 7.4.

[Amended effective September 1, 1987; March 1, 1992; September 1, 1996.]

LJuCR 7.5. SUMMONS

(a) Generally. When an information is filed the Clerk of Court shall set an initial hearing on the daily offender calendar at 9:00 a.m. pursuant to LJuCR 7.6. The Clerk shall issue the summons commanding the juvenile and parent to appear at the initial court hearing. Copies of the summons and information shall be forwarded as soon as practicable to the probation supervisor for service.

(b) Service and Return of Summons.

(1) *Service.* The supervisor for probation services, upon receipt of copies of the summons and information, shall assign a probation counselor. The probation counselor shall immediately complete the sentencing computation and provide it to the deputy prosecutor and defense counsel. The Juvenile's Acknowledgment of Advice of Rights shall also be prepared and furnished to defense counsel together with a copy for the client. Counsel shall review this document with their client prior to the scheduled court day. It will then be presented to the court with the signatures of the juvenile and their attorney.

If the juvenile is not in custody, the probation counselor will arrange service of the summons and information by mail. If the juvenile is in custody, personal service will be effected.

(2) *Return.* Proof of service shall be filed with the Clerk by the probation department. If notice by mail cannot be accomplished due to an improper address, the probation counselor shall exercise due diligence to obtain a proper address. If notice by mail cannot be accomplished within a reasonable time, the probation counselor shall notify the prosecutor who may apply for an arrest warrant.

[Amended effective September 1, 1987; March 1, 1992; September 1, 1996; September 1, 1999.]

LJuCR 7.6. ARRAIGNMENT AND PLEAS

(a) Time and Procedure for Arraignment.

(1) As to a juvenile held in detention, upon the filing of an information the clerk of court, at the request of the prosecutor, will schedule an arraignment to be held within 14 days after the information is filed.

(2) As to a juvenile not held in detention, upon the filing of an information the clerk of court, at the request of the prosecutor, will schedule an initial hearing pursuant to LJuCR 7.5(a) within 30 days of the filing of the information. The juvenile will be arraigned at this initial hearing.

(3) An in-court appearance by the juvenile and counsel is required at the initial hearing unless a Waiver of Arraignment signed by the juvenile, the defense attorney and approved by the prosecutor has been filed with the court; or a continuance order signed by the prosecutor, the defense attorney and approved by the court has been filed.

(b) Plea.

(1) For a juvenile in detention, a pro-forma not guilty plea will be entered at the arraignment hearing. At that hearing the clerk of court will schedule a change of plea/trial setting hearing not later than five court days thereafter on the daily 9:00 a.m. offender calendar.

(2) For a juvenile who is not in detention, if a plea of not guilty is made at the time of arraignment, the court will schedule an adjudicatory hearing within the time limit prescribed by LJuCR 7.8. If a plea of guilty is made the court will proceed to a finding of guilty and disposition or continue the matter for disposition in accordance with LJuCR 7.12.

(3) If further time is requested by the juvenile to consider a plea the matter may be continued five court days if the juvenile is in detention, 15 court days if the juvenile is not in detention, to the daily offender calendar at 9:00 a.m. This time may be enlarged or reduced upon a showing of good cause.

[Amended effective September 4, 1986; September 1, 1987; March 1, 1992; September 1, 1996.]

LJuCR 7.7. STATEMENT OF JUVENILE ON PLEA OF GUILTY

The form of a statement of a juvenile on plea of guilty shall be as prescribed by JuCR 7.7 using Statement of Juvenile on Plea of Guilty and Judge's Findings and Predisposition Order (form JU–07.0600–WPF). The lawyer for the juvenile, or if the right to a lawyer has been waived, the probation counselor, shall assist the juvenile in completing the form, supplies of which will be available in the office of the clerk of court.

LJuCR 7.12. DISPOSITION HEARING

(a) Time.

(1) A disposition hearing will in most cases be held immediately following a plea or verdict of guilty upon

presentation of an oral or written predisposition report or a written risk assessment. By stipulation of counsel and approval of court the matter may proceed to disposition without the probation officer present.

(2) If disposition is continued following a plea or verdict of guilty the court will enter an order setting a time for hearing and directing the juvenile, if not in detention, to report to a probation counselor within 24 hours to schedule an interview. A copy of the order shall be given by the deputy prosecuting attorney to defense counsel at the time of entry of the finding of guilty and an additional copy furnished promptly to the supervisor.

(3) If disposition is continued a disposition hearing will be set by the court not more than 14 days following a plea or verdict of guilty if the juvenile is in detention. If the juvenile is not in detention the hearing shall be set not more than 21 days following the plea or verdict. In either case if the standard range sentence would provide for a commitment to the Juvenile Rehabilitation Administration, or if the offense is a sex offense then a written predisposition report is required unless specifically waived by the court upon a showing of good cause.

[Amended effective September 4, 1986; September 1, 1987; March 1, 1992; September 1, 1996.]

LJuCR 7.14. MODIFICATION OF DISPOSITION ORDER

(d) Preliminary Hearing if Juvenile in Detention. If the motion is contested, and whether the allegation is a juvenile offense or not, and the juvenile is held in detention, the hearing on the motion shall be held on the daily disposition calendar within three days of the date of the preliminary hearing.

(e) Scheduling and Notice of Hearing. The clerk of court shall schedule a hearing on the allegations in the motion on the weekly motion calendar [LJuCR 11.3(f)] within 14 days except that when the juvenile is held in detention the hearing shall be scheduled in accordance with section (d) of this rule. Notice of the hearing may be given by the supervisor pursuant to JuCR 11.2 or the court may issue a summons or warrant pursuant to JuCR 7.5 and LJuCR 7.5.

[Amended effective September 1, 1987; March 1, 1992.]

8. DECLINE OF JURISDICTION

LJuCR 8.1. TIME FOR DECLINE HEARING

(b) Scheduling of Hearing. Upon the filing of a Motion and Affidavit for Declining Jurisdiction [form JU–08.0100–WPF] the court shall set a decline hearing within 14 days of the detention hearing using form JU–08.0105.

(c) Notice. Notice of the decline hearing may be given by the supervisor in accordance with JuCR 11.2 by telephone.

[Amended effective September 4, 1986; March 1, 1992.]

LJuCR 8.2. PROCEDURE AT DECLINE HEARING

A decline investigation report must be prepared by a probation counselor and presented to the court with copies furnished to the juvenile or his lawyer and to the deputy prosecuting attorney on the second court day preceding the day on which the decline hearing is set.

[Amended effective March 1, 1992.]

9. RIGHT TO LAWYER AND EXPERTS

LJuCR 9.1. MANDATORY APPOINTMENT OF LAWYER

The court shall appoint a lawyer for a juvenile when required by RCW 13.32a.160(1)(c) or RCW 13.32a.190(1). This shall be accomplished by a general order to be implemented by the Probation Department in conjunction with the Department of Corrections.

[Amended effective March 1, 1992.]

LJuCR 9.2. [DELETED]

[Deleted effective September 1, 1987.]

LJuCR 9.3. RIGHT TO APPOINTMENT OF EXPERTS

(a) Appointment. An order authorizing counsel to obtain the services of an expert will not authorize payment for those services but shall define the services to be provided. If services are authorized, counsel shall advise the service provider of the provisions of this rule and the approved rates as set by the court.

(b) Compensation. Compensation in excess of an hourly rate or total amount as determined reasonable from time to time by the superior court will not be approved without a prior report and special authorization by the court. Claims submitted within the approved hourly rates and total amounts may be approved by the supervisor in accordance with the budget.

11. SUPPLEMENTAL PROVISIONS

LJuCR 11.2. JUVENILE COURT SOCIAL FILE

Every person filing a document in Juvenile Court, including an agency plan and supplemental reports, shall provide a copy to Juvenile Court staff for filing in the Juvenile Court social file.

[Adopted effective March 1, 1992; amended effective September 1, 1999.]

LJuCR 11.3. CALENDARING OF MATTERS

The Clerk of Court shall set matters on the court calendar upon receipt of an appropriate order of the court, upon an oral instruction from the bench or pursuant to these local rules. All matters shall be calendared for hearing within the following schedule unless otherwise ordered by the court:

(a) Arraignment/Change of Plea/Disposition Calendar. Offender matters involving arraignment, change of plea, modification of disposition, termination of diversion agreements, declination of jurisdiction, deferred disposition or disposition shall be set on this calendar which shall be held on days designated by the court at 9:00 a.m. The calendar shall begin with the calling of the offender docket for that day.

(b) The Daily Detention Calendar. Offender detention hearings shall be held at 1:30 p.m. each court day.

(c) Offender Adjudicatory Hearings. Hearings shall be set by written order after consultation with the Juvenile Court Coordinator.

(d) [Deleted]

(e) [Deleted]

(f) [Deleted]

(d) Calendaring Contested Dependency, Guardianship, and Termination Hearings. All contested matters shall be scheduled through the Juvenile Court Coordinator unless scheduled on the motion calendar pursuant to (e) below.

(e) Weekly Motion Calendar for Dependency, Termination and Guardianship Proceedings. Motions shall be scheduled on Fridays at 2:00 p.m. or other time approved by the Juvenile Court Coordinator. Argument is limited to 10 minutes per party unless otherwise authorized by the court. Motions requiring testimony or argument in excess of 10 minutes per party shall be scheduled through the Juvenile Court Coordinator.

(f) Weekly Review Calendar. All non-contested dependency and permanent planning review hearings will be heard on Thursday afternoons unless otherwise scheduled by the court. All post termination review hearings assigned to the Juvenile Court docket shall be heard on Tuesdays as scheduled by the Clerk of Court. Post-termination review hearings in cases assigned to a trial department shall be scheduled by contacting that department.

(j) [Deleted]

[Amended effective September 4, 1986; September 1, 1987; March 1, 1992; September 1, 1999; November 1, 2002.]

LJuCR 11.4. CONTINUANCES

A request for continuance of an uncontested hearing shall be made or presented at or before the hearing. A request for continuance of a contested hearing may be made by motion or at the weekly calendar call on Fridays at 1:30 p.m. provided prior notice is given as required by court rules to all parties.

[Amended effective September 4, 1986; March 1, 1992; September 1, 1999.]

LJuCR 11.5. CALENDAR INQUIRIES

Inquiries regarding the calendaring of cases shall be directed to the Juvenile Court Coordinator. All calendaring of matters will be done by the Clerk of Court or Juvenile Court Coordinator only upon order of the court or pursuant to these local rules.

[Amended effective March 1, 1992; September 1, 1999.]

LJuCR 11.6. WEEKLY CALENDAR CALL

All lawyers (or a representative approved by the court) with cases set on the Juvenile Court calendar for the following, week shall appear at a calendar call held every Friday at 1:30 p.m. in the Juvenile Court Judge's courtroom. Each lawyer or a representative of the lawyer shall identify the status and anticipated length of each hearing at the calendar call.

[Amended effective September 1, 1999.]

LJuCR 11.7. MEDICAL CONSENT AUTHORIZATIONS

(a) Request for Medical Treatment. Requests for authorization of medical treatment should be submitted in writing to the court stating the treatment required, the reason for the treatment and the necessity for the authorization. Such requests may be heard on the motion calendar or at such other time approved by the Juvenile Court Coordinator or ordered by the court.

(b) [Deleted]

[Amended effective March 1, 1992; September 1, 1999.]

LJuCR 11.8. JUVENILE COURT COMMITTEE

The juvenile court committee as constituted in LAR 0.3 shall meet in regular session once monthly on the second Tuesday at 7:30 a.m. at the time and location designated by the chairperson. Additional/special meetings may be called at times and locations designated by the chairperson.

(a) The committee shall meet with the juvenile court commissioner, the juvenile court administrator, the administrative supervisor for juvenile probation services and the juvenile court Detention superintendent. The juvenile court coordinator shall also attend and record the proceedings.

Also invited shall be representatives of the Department of Social and Health Services, the Office of the Attorney General, the Office of Public Defender, the Office of the Prosecuting Attorney and the Juvenile Court Citizen's Advisory Committee. Other persons may be invited by the chairperson at his or her discretion.

[Amended effective March 1, 1992.]

LJuCR 11.9. PAYMENT OF RESTITUTION THROUGH CLERK

Whenever the court orders restitution it shall be paid through the clerk of the court by cash, certified check, cashier's check or money order payable to the clerk of the court. The name of the payor and the court case number will be entered on the face of the instrument of payment.

Payment of Monetary Obligation: In all juvenile cases, except where the court order is to the contrary, the clerk of the court shall disburse monies received in the following order:

(a) Restitution.

(b) Penalty Assessment.

[Adopted January 1, 1983; amended effective July 1, 1988.]

12. TRUANCY PROCEEDINGS

LJuCR 12.1. LEGAL REPRESENTATION

(a) A child may appear in a truancy proceeding without the appointment of a guardian ad litem. The Court may appoint a guardian ad litem if the facts of a specific case indicate that justice would be served thereby.

(b) An attorney shall be appointed by the Court to represent a child when a school district requests a hearing alleging that the child is in contempt of a truancy order.

[Adopted effective September 1, 1999.]

LJuCR 12.2. NOTICE

(a) **Fact-Finding Hearings.** The Court shall, upon the filing of a truancy petition, set the date for a fact-finding hearing unless it enters a stay of proceedings. The Petitioner may serve a copy of the notice of hearing, petition for truancy and supporting declaration separately to the child and parent(s) or legal guardian(s) at their last known address by certified mail return receipt requested. If certified mail is unsuccessful or receipt is not signed by addressee, personal service shall be required. The notice shall advise the parties of their rights and options under

RCW 13.32 and the right to present evidence at the hearing. The Clerk shall also notify the school district of the date and time of hearing. If the school district obtains an order continuing the hearing, the district shall provide notice, by mail to any party that has not approved the order. It shall file proof of mailing with the Court.

(b) **Contempt Proceedings.** The school district shall personally serve a party alleged to be in contempt of a truancy order at least five court days, not including the day of service, before the hearing. The documents to be served will include the motion, declaration, and order to show cause. The child shall also be served with the notice of appointment of counsel. If the party alleged to be in contempt of an order compelling attendance was not present at the fact-finding hearing, the district shall provide evidence that the party had notice of the terms of the order. This evidence may be in the form of a declaration, under oath, that the party has been served with the order, either personally or by a form of mail requiring a return receipt.

[Adopted effective September 1, 1999.]

V. LOCAL RULES FOR APPEALS OF DECISIONS OF COURTS OF LIMITED JURISDICTION (CITE AS LRALJ)

2. INITIATING AN APPEAL

LRALJ 2.4. [DELETED]

[Amended March 1, 1988; deleted effective September 1, 1996.]

3. ASSIGNMENT OF CASES IN SUPERIOR COURT

LRALJ 3.1. ASSIGNMENT

Appeals from a court of limited jurisdiction will be assigned to an individual judge when a Notice of Appeal is received by the Clerk of Court. The Court Administrator will prepare and mail a notice of case assignment to the lawyer for each party or party appearing pro se. The assigned court will meet with counsel and set briefing deadlines consistent with RALJ 7.2, and a date for oral argument. Extensions and continuances are governed by RALJ 10.3. Parties are encouraged to prepare an agreed narrative report of the proceedings in the court of limited jurisdiction in lieu of a transcript.

[Amended March 1, 1988; October 1, 1994; January 1, 1999; January 1, 2001.]

4. AUTHORITY OF COURT PENDING APPEAL—STAYS

LRALJ 4.1. AUTHORITY OF COURT PENDING APPEAL

(a) Superior Court. After a notice of appeal has been filed the clerk of the superior court will schedule the following dates from the date of filing:

(1) *45 Days.* For the receipt of appellant's brief and a transcript of the record [See RALJ 6.3 and 7.2(a)]. If the appellant has not filed a brief and transcript the clerk will move to dismiss the appeal for lack of prosecution in accordance with LRALJ 10.2(a).

(2) *75 Days.* For the receipt of the respondent's brief [See RALJ 7.2(b)]. On the 76th day from the date of filing a Notice of Appeal the clerk will prepare and transmit a notice to the Court Administrator. The Court Administrator will mail a Note for Appeal Assignment (form JRA–08.0100–1/81) to the lawyer for each party or any party appearing pro se assigning said case to an individual judge.

[Amended March 1, 1988; amended effective September 1, 1996; September 1, 1999.]

LRALJ 4.3. STAY OF ENFORCEMENT OF JUDGMENT

(a) Civil Case. If the appellant seeks to stay enforcement of the district or municipal court judgment from which an appeal has been taken it shall be upon motion noted for hearing as an issue of law (form CI–06.0300–6/98) pursuant to LCR 40(b)(10). If an order staying enforcement is made a conformed, certified copy of the order must be filed by the appellant with the district or municipal court from which the appeal has been taken.

(b) Criminal Case. If the appellant has been granted an order staying enforcement of a sentence in a criminal case by the court of limited jurisdiction in accordance with RALJ 4.3(b) a conformed, certified copy shall be filed with the clerk of the superior court.

[Amended effective January 1, 1999.]

9. SUPERIOR COURT DECISION

LRALJ 9.1. BASIS FOR DECISION ON APPEAL

(a) Form of Decision. The decision of the superior court may be rendered orally, with a court reporter present, or recorded by electronic means. In either case the verbatim record or the electronic recording shall be transcribed and filed with the clerk of the superior court.

[Amended effective August 1, 1994.]

LRALJ 9.2. ENTRY OF DECISION

(a) The clerk of the superior court shall transmit within 30 days one copy of the transcribed decision to the clerk of the court of limited jurisdiction from which the appeal was taken, one copy to the district court or municipal court judge whose decision was appealed and one copy to each party or the attorney for each party in accordance with RALJ 9.2(b).

[Adopted effective August 1, 1994.]

10. VIOLATION OF RULES—SANCTIONS AND DISMISSAL

LRALJ 10.2. DISMISSAL OF APPEAL

(a) Involuntary Dismissal/Continuances. In the event that the provisions of RALJ 7.2(a) have not been met and if a motion to dismiss has not been filed by a party, the clerk of the superior court, pursuant to LRAJ 4.1(a)(1), will prepare and mail a Notice of Dismissal For Want of Prosecution (form JRA 10.0100–6/81) to the parties or their lawyers that the appeal will be dismissed for want of prosecution unless within 14 days good cause is shown why the case should be continued as a pending appeal. If a motion for continuance supported by good cause is not filed and noted for hearing within that time, the clerk will present a Motion and Order Dismissing Appeal to District/Municipal Court (form JRA 10.0200–4/81) to the judge to whom the appeal has been assigned or, if unassigned, to the presiding judge for signature. Hearings on motions for continuance will be noted on the motion docket for the assigned judge per LCR 40(b)(10), or if the appeal is unassigned, before the presiding judge. In the event that there has been no action of record for 90 days, the clerk may present a motion and order dismissing the appeal forthwith.

(b) In event that the appellant has not filed a designation of record per RALJ 6.2(a) the superior court clerk shall send out a notice of closure to the parties or their attorneys that the appeal has been deemed abandoned and the superior court file is closed. Such closing of the file shall only be vacated upon an order of the superior court showing good cause.

[Amended effective March 1, 1988; September 1, 1996; September 1, 1999.]

11.   SUPPLEMENTAL PROVISIONS

LRALJ 11.5.   [DELETED]

[Deleted effective September 1, 1997.]

LRALJ 11.8.   [DELETED]

[Deleted effective September 1, 1997.]

VI.   LOCAL WRIT PRACTICE RULES (LWP)

LWP 1.1.   APPLICATION FOR WRIT

(a) Filing. Any party seeking an extraordinary writ pursuant to Chapter 7.16 RCW concerning the action of a district or municipal court shall file an application or petition and schedule a show cause hearing before the presiding judge no later than 14 days after the filing to determine whether the requested writ shall be granted. The order setting a show cause hearing may stay further proceedings in the lower court if proceedings are scheduled there prior to the show cause hearing.

(b) Scheduling. If the presiding judge, or other superior court judge to whom the matter may be assigned, grants an order issuing an extraordinary writ to review a decision of a district or municipal court, the court will also enter a hearing schedule which shall state the due dates for the briefs of the parties, the filing of the written transcript, and the date on which the parties will return to court for assignment and argument. No continuance or extension shall be entered which does not also reset the hearing schedule. The time frame for scheduling shall be consistent with that of LRALJ 4.1(a) unless circumstances dictate that less time be allowed.

(c) [Deleted]

[Adopted effective August 1, 1994; amended effective June 18, 1998; January 1, 2001.]

LWP 1.2.   DISMISSAL

The clerk of the superior court may, pursuant to the procedures established by LRALJ 10.2(a), seek dismissal of any writ action involving a district or municipal court wherein more than 90 days have passed since the last action of record.

[Adopted effective August 1, 1994.]

APPENDIX A
SPOKANE COUNTY CLERK INDEXING SHEET

Please place an "X" in the box which best describes the nature of the action filed. This form will be used to statistically classify your case upon data entry. This classification in no way affects the legal action of the case.

CASE NO.

CIVIL

Tort

(MED)	_____	*Medical Malpractice
(PIN)	_____	*Personal Injury
(PRP)	_____	*Property Damage
(MAL)	_____	*Other Malpractice
(TMV)	_____	*Tort Motor Vehicle
(WDE)	_____	*Wrongful Death
(TTO)	_____	*Tort—Other

Commercial/Collection

(COL)	_____	Collection—under $35,000
(COL)	_____	Collection—over $35,000
(COM)	_____	*Commercial

Property Rights

(CON)	_____	*Condemnation
(FOR)	_____	*Foreclosure
(QTI)	_____	*Quiet Title
(LUP)	_____	Land Use Petition
(UND)	_____	Unlawful Detainer
(PFA)	_____	Property Fairness Act

Civil Harassment

(HAR)	_____	Civil Harassment

Other Petitions And Other Complaints

(CHN)	_____	Change of Name (Non–Conf.)
(INJ)	_____	Injunction
(MER)	_____	*Meretricious Relationship
(MHA)	_____	Malicious Harassment
(MST)	_____	Minor Settlements
(PCC)	_____	Petition for Civil Comm (Sexual Predator)
(SPC)	_____	Seizure of Prop from Commission of a Crime
(SPR)	_____	Seizure of Prop from a Crime
(WHC)	_____	Writ of Habeas Corpus
(WMW)	_____	Miscellaneous Writs
(WRM)	_____	Writ of Mandamus
(WRR)	_____	Writ of Restitution
(WRV)	_____	Writ of Review
(EOM)	_____	Emancipation of Minor

DOMESTIC

Domestic Relations

(CUS)	_____	*Child Custody
(DIC)	_____	*Dissolution With Children of the Marriage
(DIN)	_____	*Dissolution With No Children of the Marriage
(FJU)	_____	Foreign Judgment
(INV)	_____	Annulment–Invalidity
(MOD)	_____	Modification
(MDS)	_____	Modification: Support Only
(OSC)	_____	Out of State Custody
(SEP)	_____	**Legal Separation**
(MWA)	_____	Mandatory Wage Assignment
(MSC)	_____	Miscellaneous

Uniform Interstate Family Support Act (UIFSA)

(RIC)	_____	Interstate, Respondent–In–County
(ROC)	_____	Interstate, Respondent–Out–of–County

PROTECTED CASES

Paternity

(PAT)	_____	Paternity
(PUR)	_____	Paternity/Interstate
(MOD)	_____	Modification

Adoption

(ADP)	_____	Adoption
(MSC)	_____	Misc (Confidential Intermediary)
(REL)	_____	Relinquishment
(TER)	_____	Termination of Parent/Child Relationship
(PPR)	_____	Initial Pre–Placement Report

Change of Name

(CHN)	_____	Change of Name (Confidential)

(MSC) _____ Miscellaneous

PROBATE

Domestic Violence

(DVP) _____ Domestic Violence Protection

(FPO) _____ Foreign Protection Order

(VAP) _____ Vulnerable Adult Protection

(ABS) _____ Absentee

(DSC) _____ Disclaimer

(EST) _____ Estate

(FNW) _____ Foreign Will

(NNC) _____ Non–Probate Notice to Creditors

Appeal/Review

(ALR) _____ Administrative Law Review

(LCA) _____ Lower Court Appeal–Civil

(LCI) _____ Lower Court Appeal–Infractions

(DOL) _____ Dept. of Licensing Revocation

(WLL) _____ Will Only

(MSC) _____ Miscellaneous

Matters Filed With Clerk

(TAX) _____ Tax Warrants

(ABJ) _____ Abstract of Judgment

(TRJ) _____ Transcript of Judgment

(FJU) _____ Foreign Judgment

GUARDIANSHIP

(GDN) _____ Guardianship

(LGD) _____ Limited Guardianship

(MST) _____ Minor Settlements

---

*ATTN CASHIERS: ONLY cases in **bold face** receive a case assignment notice.

CASE ASSIGNMENT NOTICE

_____(Copy Receipt)_____   _____(Clerk's Date Stamp)_____

SUPERIOR COURT OF WASHINGTON
COUNTY OF SPOKANE

_____

_____

_____   **JUDGE** _____

Plaintiff(s)/Petitioner(s),   **CASE NO.** _____

vs.   **CASE ASSIGNMENT NOTICE AND**
                                                       ORDER
                                                       (NTAS)

_____   **CASE STATUS CONFERENCE DATE:** _____
Defendant(s)/Respondent(s).

ORDER

YOU ARE HEREBY NOTIFIED that this case is preassigned for all further proceedings to the judge noted above. **You are required to attend a Case Status Conference on the date also noted above. The Joint Case Status Report must be completed and brought to the Status Conference. A case schedule Order, with the trial date, will be issued at the Status Conference.**

Under the individual calendar system, the court will operate on a four-day trial week. Trials will commence on Monday, Tuesday, Wednesday or Thursday. Motion Calendars are held on Friday. All motions, other than ex parte motions, must be scheduled with the assigned judge. Counsel must contact the assigned court to schedule motions and working copies of all motion pleadings must be provided to the assigned court at the time of filing with the Clerk of Court. Pursuant to LCR 40(b)(10), motions must be confirmed no later than 12:00 noon two days before the hearing by notifying the judicial assistant for the assigned judge.

Please contact the assigned court to schedule matters regarding this case. You may contact the assigned court by phone, court department email or through the Spokane County Superior Court web page at www.spokanecounty.org/superior court.

DATED: _____   _____
                                                       PRESIDING JUDGE

NOTICE TO PLAINTIFF: Plaintiff shall serve a copy of the Case Assignment Notice on the defendant(s).

DOMESTIC CASE ASSIGNMENT NOTICE

SUPERIOR COURT OF		(Clerk's Date Stamp)
WASHINGTON		
COUNTY OF SPOKANE		

	JUDGE
	CASE NO. XXXX–XX–XXXXX–X
vs. Petitioner	DOMESTIC CASE ASSIGNMENT
	NOTICE AND ORDER (NTAS)
	CASE STATUS CONFERENCE DATE
Respondent	XXXXXXXXXX AT XXXX A.M.

ORDER

YOU ARE HEREBY NOTIFIED that this case is preassigned to the judge noted above. **You are required to attend a Case Status Conference on the date also noted above. If the matter is resolved by entry of a decree the Status Conference is canceled, you need not appear at the Status Conference. The Joint Case Status Report must be completed and brought to the Status Conference. A Case Schedule Order, with trial date, will be issued at the Status Conference.**

Under the individual calendar system, the court will operate on a four-day trial week. Trials will commence on Monday, Tuesday, Wednesday and Friday. Any motions regarding trial or case scheduling will be heard by the assigned judge. Counsel and/or parties (if self represented) must contact the assigned court to schedule motions. Working copies of all motion pleadings must be provided to the assigned court at the time of filing with the Clerk of the Court. You may contact the assigned court by phone, court department e-mail or through the Spokane County Superior Court web page at www.spokanecounty.org/superiorcourt.

ALL OTHER MOTIONS will be heard on the Family Law Calendar, pursuant to LCR 94.04. You may contact the Family Law Center by phone, Family Law Department e-mail or through the Spokane County Superior Court web page at www.spokanecounty.org/superiorcourt.

PRESIDING JUDGE

NOTICE TO PETITIONER: Petitioner shall serve a copy of the Case Assignment Notice on the respondent(s). Parties representing themselves may contact the Family Law Center for clarification of this notice.

CIVIL JOINT CASE STATUS REPORT

SUPERIOR COURT OF WASHINGTON
COUNTY OF SPOKANE

Petitioner: _____

vs.

Respondent: _____

CASE NO. _____

CIVIL JOINT CASE STATUS REPORT

DO NOT FILE   (JSR)

1. Case Information:

    a. Case type (e.g. personal injury-auto, malpractice-medical): _____
    b. List the parties and who represent them.

Party _____	Party _____
Attorney _____	Attorney _____
Address _____	Address _____
_____	_____
Phone No. _____	Phone No. _____
Email Address _____	Email Address _____
Contact Person _____	Contact Person _____
Participated in Preparation of Joint Case Status Report: Yes No	Participated in Preparation of Joint Case Status Report: Yes No
Party _____	Party _____
Attorney _____	Attorney _____
Address _____	Address _____
_____	_____
Phone No. _____	Phone No. _____
Email Address _____	Email Address _____
Contact Person _____	Contact Person _____
Participated in Preparation of Joint Case Status Report: Yes No	Participated in Preparation of Joint Case Status Report: Yes No

If there are additional parties, list above information on separate page.

    c. Amount in controversy and range of damages requested, including cross-claims and Counter claims: _____

    d. Specify equitable relief requested.

e. Subject to Mandatory Arbitration?   Yes [ ] No [ ]

f. Have answers been filed?   Yes [ ] No [ ]

g. Have all parties been joined?   Yes [ ] No [ ]

h. Have all parties been served?   Yes [ ] No [ ]

2. Case Management Information:

a. Pursuant to LAR 0.4(a), the court expects this case to be resolved within 12 months. If there is a reason why this is impractical, please explain:

b. The parties agree to go through medi-   Yes [ ] No [ ]
    ation/alternative dispute resolution?

c. The parties agree to stipulate to the   Yes [ ] No [ ]
    appointment of a judge pro tempore?

d. Are there any unique issues requiring   Yes [ ] No [ ]
    special preparation by the court?
    If yes, explain

e. Estimated length of trial days or hours required: _____

f. Will a jury be demanded?   Six person [ ] Twelve person [ ]
    Yes [ ] No [ ]

FOR JUDICIAL USE ONLY

Next Anticipated Event and Date of Event _____

Second Status Conference Date _____

Judge's Notes

DOMESTIC JOINT CASE STATUS REPORT

(Copy Receipt)   (Clerk's Date Stamp)

**SUPERIOR COURT OF WASHINGTON
COUNTY OF SPOKANE**

Petitioner: _____

vs.

Respondent: _____

CASE NO. _____

DOMESTIC JOINT CASE STATUS
REPORT

DO NOT FILE   (JSR)

1. Case Information: ☐ Dissolution with Children   ☐ Legal Separation   ☐ Paternity
   a. Case Type   ☐ Dissolution without Children   ☐ Third Party Custody ☐ Mod.

   b. List the parties and who represent them.

   Party _____   Party _____

   Attorney _____   Attorney _____

   Address _____   Address _____

   _____   _____

   Phone No _____   Phone No _____

   Email Address _____   Email Address _____

   Contact Person _____ Contact Person _____

   Participated in Preparation of Joint Case Status   Participated in Preparation of Joint Case Status
   Report: ☐ Yes   ☐ No   Report   ☐ Yes   ☐ No

   If there are additional parties, list above information on separate page.

   c. ☐ The parties agree to be scheduled as a Fast Track case.

   d. ☐ The parties are trying to reconcile and request another status conference be set.

DOMESTIC JOINT CASE STATUS REPORT   PAGE 1 OF 3
LAR 0.4.1(e)   (Rev: 01/2011)

e. ☐ The parties agree to a Voluntary Settlement Conference.

f. Have responses been filed?   ☐ Yes   ☐ No

g. Have all parties been served?   ☐ Yes   ☐ No

2. Case Management Information:

a. Pursuant to LAR 0.4(a), the court expects this case to be resolved within 10 months. If there is a reason why this is impractical, please explain:

b. The parties agree to go through mediation/alternative dispute resolution? ☐ Yes   ☐ No

c. Should a Guardian Ad Litem be appointed?   ☐ Yes   ☐ No

d. The parties agree to stipulate to the appointment of a judge pro tempore? ☐ Yes ☐ No

     If yes ,who? _____

e. Are there any unique issues requiring special preparation by the court? Yes ☐   No ☐
     If yes, explain.

f. Estimated length of trial days or hours required _____

FOR JUDICIAL USE ONLY

Next Anticipated Event and Date of Event _____

Second Status Conference Date _____

Judge's Notes

_____   _____
Petitioner   Respondent

Guardian Ad Litem: _____   **Other:** _____

Party _____	Party _____
Attorney _____	Attorney _____
Address _____	Address _____
_____	_____
Phone No _____	Phone No _____
Email Address _____	Email Address _____
Contact Person _____	Contact Person _____

Other: _____   **Other:** _____

Party _____	Party _____
Attorney _____	Attorney _____
Address _____	Address _____
_____	_____
Phone No _____	Phone No _____
Email Address _____	Email Address _____
Contact Person _____	Contact Person _____

Other: _____

_____

_____

_____

_____

_____

_____

[Amended effective September 1, 2011.]

CIVIL CASE SCHEDULE ORDER

(Copy Receipt)　　　　　　　　(Clerk's Date Stamp)

SUPERIOR COURT OF WASHINGTON
COUNTY OF SPOKANE

_____

Plaintiff(s),

vs.

CASE NO. _____

CIVIL CASE SCHEDULE ORDER
(ORSCS)

Defendant(s).

I. BASIS

Pursuant to LAR 0.4.1 IT IS ORDERED that all parties shall comply with the following schedule:

II. SCHEDULE

DUE DATE

1.　Last Date for: Joinder of Additional Parties, Amendment of Claims or Defenses

2.　Plaintiff's Disclosure of Lay and Expert Witnesses

3.　Defendant's Disclosure of Lay and Expert Witnesses

4.　Disclosure of Plaintiff Rebuttal Witnesses

5.　Disclosure of Defendant Rebuttal Witnesses

6.　Last Date for Filing: Motions to Change Trial Date, Note for Arbitration, Jury Demand

7.　Discovery Cutoff

8.　Last Date for Hearing Dispositive Pretrial Motions

9.　Exchange Witness List, Exhibit List and Documentary Exhibits

10.　Last Date for Filing and Serving Trial Management Joint Report, including Jury Instructions

11.　Trial Memoranda, Motions In Limine

12.　Pretrial Conference

13.　Trial Date

III. ORDER

IT IS ORDERED that all parties comply with the foregoing schedule pursuant to Local Court Rules 0.4.1 and 16.

DATED: _____　　　_____

　　　　　　　　　　　　　　　　　　　　　Judge

DOMESTIC CASE SCHEDULE ORDER

<u>(Copy Receipt)</u>   <u>(Clerk's Date Stamp)</u>

SUPERIOR COURT OF
WASHINGTON
COUNTY OF SPOKANE

_____   CASE NO. _____

           Petitioner,

vs.   **DOMESTIC CASE SCHEDULE ORDER**

_____   **(ORSCS)**
           Respondent.

I. BASIS

Pursuant to LAR 0.4.1 IT IS ORDERED that all parties shall comply with the following schedule:

II. SCHEDULE

DUE DATE

1. Petitioner's/Respondent's Disclosure of Witnesses

2. Discovery Cutoff and filing of the Parenting Plan

3. File Financial Declaration, Asset Liability List and Child Support Worksheet.

4. Mandatory Conference-Parenting Issues.

5. Last Day for filing motion to change Trial Date.

6. Last Day for filing GAL Report or Affidavit.

7. Last Date for Filing and Serving Trial Management Joint Report and Exchanging of Witness and Exhibit Lists.

8. Pretrial Conference

9. Trial Date

III. ORDER

IT IS ORDERED that all parties comply with the foregoing schedule pursuant to Local Court Rules 0.4.1 and 16.

DATED: _____   _____
                                             Judge

PATERNITY CASE SCHEDULE ORDER

_____   _____
        (Copy Receipt)   (Clerk's Date Stamp)

**SUPERIOR COURT OF
WASHINGTON
COUNTY OF SPOKANE**
_____

_____   CASE NO. _____
                    Petitioner,
vs.   **PATERNITY CASE SCHEDULE ORDER**

_____   (ORSCS)
                    Respondent.   _____

I. BASIS

Pursuant to LAR 0.4.1 IT IS ORDERED that all parties shall comply with the
following schedule:

II. SCHEDULE

                                                              DUE DATE

1. Petitioner's/Respondent's Disclosure of Witnesses

2. Discovery Cutoff and filing of the Parenting Plan

3. File Financial Declaration and Child Support Worksheet.

4. Mandatory Conference-Parenting Issues.

5. Last Day for filing motion to change Trial Date.

6. Last Day for filing GAL Report of Affidavit.

7. Last Date for Filing and Serving Trial Management Joint Report and Exchanging of Witness and Exhibit Lists.

8. Pretrial Conference

9. Trial Date

III. ORDER

   IT IS ORDERED that all parties comply with the foregoing schedule pursuant to
Local Court Rules 0.4.1 and 16.

DATED: _____   _____
                                                              Judge

DISTRICT COURT

LOCAL RULES FOR THE DISTRICT COURT OF SPOKANE COUNTY, WASHINGTON

Including Amendments Received Through
August 15, 2015

Table of Rules

Titles in brackets added by Publisher.

I. INTRODUCTION

LARLJ 2. SCOPE OF RULES AND ADOPTION

(a) Effect of Local Rules. The provisions of the Local Rules are supplemental to the Rules for Courts of Limited Jurisdiction, as adopted or hereafter amended by the Supreme Court of the State of Washington, and shall not be construed in conflict with them.

(b) Scope. The Local Rules apply to all Courts in which a Spokane County District Court Judge is appointed or elected to sit, including but not limited to the Spokane County District Court and Cheney Municipal Court

(c) Adoption and Amendments. These Rules may be amended from time to time by a majority of the Judges.

(d) Prior Rules Repealed. All prior rules of the Spokane County District Court are repealed upon the adoption of these Rules.

[Adopted effective September 1, 1988; amended effective September 1, 1995; September 1, 2009; September 1, 2012.]

LARLJ 3. DEFINITION OF TERMS AND SENIORITY

(8) Departmental Numbers and Seniority.

(a) *Departmental Numbers.* The District Court of Spokane County shall be divided into as many Departments as there are Judges authorized by law. Department numbers are assigned as follows:

Department	Incumbent Judge
No. 1	Hon. Vance W. Peterson
No. 2	Hon. Sara B. Derr
No. 3	Hon. Donna Wilson
No. 4	Hon. Patti Connolly Walker
No. 5	Hon. Gregory J. Tripp
No. 6	Hon. Debra R. Hayes
No. 7	Hon. Randy A. Brandt
No. 8	Hon. Richard M. Leland

Whenever a Judge vacates his or her office, the Department number shall be assigned to the successor.

(b) *Seniority.* Seniority of District Court Judges is as follows:

1. Hon. Donna Wilson
2. Hon. Sara B. Derr
3. Hon. Gregory J. Tripp
4. Hon. Vance W. Peterson
5. Hon. Patti Connolly Walker
6. Hon. Debra R. Hayes
7. Hon. Randy A. Brandt
8. Hon. Richard M. Leland

Hereafter, seniority will be determined by the length of service as a Spokane County District Court Judge. If two (2) or more Judges have equal length of service, their seniority shall be determined by lot. Each Judge shall select an unassigned chamber in order of their seniority.

(c) *Seniority—Court Commissioners.* Seniority for Court Commissioners shall be determined by date of hire with continuous service. Court Commissioner chamber assignments shall be determined by seniority, provided that there is no over-arching need to locate a commissioner in a certain chamber which supersedes seniority assignment. Docket assignments for the Court Commissioners is at the discretion of the Presiding Judge with consideration given to advice provided by the Bench.

[Adopted effective September 1, 1988. Amended August 5, 1991; amended effective September 1, 1995; September 1, 1997; September 1, 1998; September 1, 1999; September 1, 2001; September 1, 2003; September 1, 2005; September 1, 2007; September 1, 2009; September 1, 2012; September 2, 2013.]

LARLJ 5. PRESIDING JUDGE

(c) Court Organization and Management.

(1) *General Management.* The general management of the Courts shall be vested in the Presiding Judge under policy established by the Judges at regular and special meetings.

(A) Executive Committee

(1) The Executive Committee shall consist of the immediate past Presiding Judge, Presiding Judge, and acting Presiding Judge. The Court may elect one (1) additional Judge to serve on the Executive Committee.

(2) The Executive Committee will act in an advisory capacity to the Presiding Judge in the daily management of the Court, in accordance with the general policy established by the majority vote of the Judges at the regular or special meetings; and have such other duties assigned by the Presiding judge or conferred by the court.

(2) *Meetings.*

(A) The Judges shall meet regularly once each week during the noon hour unless cancelled by the Presiding Judge. The meeting day shall be determined by the judges annually for the following calendar year no later than December 15 of the preceding year. The Presiding Judge may schedule one meeting each calendar quarter as a one-half day meeting in lieu of a noon hour meeting.

(B) A Judge may request an item be placed on a meeting agenda. The request and any materials for reproduction and distribution are to be submitted to the Presiding Judge no later than noon of two business days preceding the weekly meeting day. All meeting materials shall be distributed to the judges no later than noon one business day preceding the meeting day.

(C) A quorum consists of a simple majority of Judges and shall be required at all meetings.

(D) Special meetings shall be called by the Presiding judge as deemed necessary by Presiding, with timely notice to all Judges.

(3) *Election of Presiding Judge.*

(A) The Presiding Judge shall be elected for a term of two (2) years pursuant to the provisions of General Rule 29.

(B) The Presiding Judge and Assistant Presiding Judge shall be elected by a majority vote of the Judges.

(C) In the event the Presiding Judge or Assistant Presiding Judge is unwilling or unable to fulfill the duties of such office, the vacancy or position will be filled by majority vote of the Judges.

(4) *Duties of Presiding Judge.* The Presiding Judge shall:

(A) Perform all the duties required by General Rule 29;

(B) Implement all policies established by the Judges and pursuant to said policies, exercise general management of the Court including but not limited to personnel matters, judicial assignments, fiscal matters and supervision of Court Commissioners;

(C) Assign duties to the Court Administrator as deemed necessary;

(D) Act as spokesperson for the Court after seeking advice and counsel from the Judges where appropriate;

(E) Preside at all Judges' meetings and shall call special meetings as necessary;

(F) Make docket and case assignments, including ex parte and conflict cases, which are not assigned to existing departments, and assign dockets as necessary, provided that the preference of the judges by seniority shall be given priority in any docket assignments; and

(G) Appoint committees to study and make recommendations concerning the subject matter assigned and allow the committee to take necessary action when authorized by the Judges.

(5) *Court Commissioner.*

(A) Selection. Upon a vacancy for Court Commissioner, the Court may advertise the vacancy and accept applications. A Personnel Committee of not less than three (3) Judges shall screen the written applications.

The Personnel Committee shall decide which candidates to interview, conduct interviews and make recommendations to the Judges. Any Judge of this Court may attend, participate and vote as a member of the Personnel Committee for the selection process. The selection shall be by majority vote of the Judges present at a regularly scheduled Judges' meeting or a meeting called by the Presiding Judge for this purpose.

(B) Termination. A Court Commissioner shall serve at the pleasure of the Judges and shall be terminated by a majority vote of Judges at a Judges' meeting.

(C) Attorney–Commissioner—Authority and Jurisdiction. A lawyer appointed Commissioner of this Court shall have such power, authority and jurisdiction in criminal and civil matters as the appointing Judges possess unless otherwise restricted by court rule, statute or case law.

(D) Non–Attorney Commissioner. Court employees qualified to act as a judicial officer under Supreme Court General Rule 8 (GR 8) may be appointed Court Commissioner by a majority of the Judges. The appointee shall perform such duties as authorized by the Judges, in addition to the duties of his or her regular position. The appointment and designation of Court Commissioner shall be for a period prescribed by the Judges.

(E) A Pro–Tempore Judicial Officer shall receive the necessary orientation and training before assignment. The Pro–Tempore Judicial Officer will be assigned only to a calendar on which they have received training and orientation.

(1) The regularly appointed Court Commissioner shall be first utilized for judicial calendars and only in their absence or unavailability shall Pro–Tempore Judicial Officers be used on a judicial calendar.

(2) The Judicial Operations Manager shall notify and schedule the Pro–Tempore Judicial Officers.

(F) The Pro–Tempore Judicial Officers shall be administered the Oath of Office as required in section 3.34.080 of the Revised Code of Washington only by the Judicial Operations Manager, the Presiding Judge or the Acting Presiding judge in the absence or unavailability of Presiding judge. No other person shall be authorized to administer the Oath of Office on behalf of the Court.

(6) *Court Administrator.*

(A) Selection. Upon a vacancy, the Presiding Judge and not less than two (2) additional Judges selected in a Judges' meeting shall act as a Personnel Committee. The Personnel Committee shall take the necessary step to obtain qualified applicants. The Committee shall screen the written applications, conduct interviews, and make recommendations to the Judges. Any Judge may attend, participate, and vote as a member of the Personnel Committee. Selection of the Court Administrator shall be by majority vote of Judges present at a regularly scheduled Judges' meeting.

(B) Termination. The Court Administrator shall serve at the pleasure of the Judges and shall be terminated by a majority vote of judges at a regularly scheduled Judges' meeting.

(7) *Duties of Court Administrator.* The Court Administrator shall assist the Presiding Judge in his or her administrative responsibilities. Subject to the general supervision of the Presiding Judge, the Administrator's duties shall include but not be limited to those duties set forth in the job description for the Court Administrator.

(8) *Departmental Employees.* Departmental employees are those employees assigned to a Judge, or Judges, and shall include, but are not limited to Judicial Assistants and Judicial Secretaries. The Judicial Operations Manager shall be the immediate supervisor of the Judicial Assistants and Judicial Secretaries with such duties and responsibilities as assigned by the Judges. Departmental Employees shall be selected and serve at the pleasure of the Judges in accordance with policies approved by the Court and procedures contained in the District Court Employee Handbook.

(9) *Employer–Employee Relations.* The Court shall issue an employee handbook which will set forth the general employment policies and practices of the Court, and a code of conduct for all employees. Except as otherwise provided in the Local Rules of the Spokane County District Court, and the Policies adopted by the District Court, all employees of the Spokane County District Court shall comply with the provisions of the handbook.

(10) *Courtrooms.* The Court shall have its main facility at the Spokane County Courthouse site located at the Public Safety Building and the Broadway Center Building. The Court shall sit from time to time at the branch sites including the City of Spokane Valley, Cheney, and such other location designated by the County Legislative authority. Only those types of cases specifically approved by the Court shall be heard at branch sites.

[Adopted effective September 1, 1988. Amended effective August 5, 1991; April 22, 1992; September 1, 1992; September 1, 1995; September 1, 1997; September 1, 1998; September 1, 1999; September 1, 2001; September 1, 2002; September 1, 2008; September 1, 2009; September 1, 2012; September 2, 2013; amended on an emergency basis effective February 23, 2015.]

LARLJ 10.   PARALEGALS

Paralegals who are currently registered with the Spokane County Bar Association for the purpose of presentation of such orders may personally present agreed, ex-parte and uncontested orders signed by counsel, based solely upon the documents presented and the record in the file. Said privilege may be revoked or limited by the Court for noncompliance with this rule, or other misconduct, regardless of whether the Paralegal is permitted to present orders before other Courts.

[Amended Sept. 1, 1995; amended effective September 1, 2000.]

LARLJ 11.   RECEIVING SERVICE OF PROCESS

Service of Process of legal suits, writs, or other actions on or against Spokane District Court shall be served upon the Court Administrator or Presiding Judge in his or her official capacity.

[Adopted effective September 1, 2004; amended effective September 1, 2009.]

LARLJ 12.   INVESTIGATIONS BY THE JUDICIAL CONDUCT COMMISSION: ACCESS TO SEALED FILES AND DOCUMENTS

(a) **Confidential Use:** Upon request, the clerk of the court shall provide copies of or otherwise describe the contents of sealed files to a representative of the State Commission on Judicial Conduct, who is conducting a confidential investigation pursuant to WA Const. Art. IV sec. 31.

(b) **Public Use:** No materials in a sealed file may be made public, unless the Commission has first obtained an order pursuant to GR 15 and LR 79(d)(5). Motions to obtain such an order shall be made to the Presiding Judge.

[Adopted effective September 1, 2007.]

LARLJ 30.   ELECTRONIC FILING

(d)(2)(D)(ii) Any document initiated by a law enforcement officer is presumed to have been signed when the officer uses his or her user ID and password to electronically submit the document to a court or prosecutor through the Statewide Electronic Collision & Traffic Online Records (SECTOR) application, the Justice Information Network Data Exchange (JINDEX), or the local secured system "Xpediter" used by the County of Spokane and City of Spokane. Unless otherwise specified, the signature shall be presumed to have been made under penalty of perjury under the laws of the State of Washington and on the date and at the place set forth in the citation.

[Adopted effective September 1, 2011.]

II. CIVIL PROCEEDINGS

LCRLJ 1. LOCAL CIVIL RULES AND SCOPE

[See LARLJ 2]

[Adopted effective September 1, 1988.]

LCRLJ 5. SERVICE AND FILING OF PLEADINGS AND OTHER PAPERS

(d) Filing

(5) *Motions.* No motion for any order shall be heard unless the papers pertaining to it have been filed with the Clerk.

(6) *Documents Not to be Filed:*

(A) Interrogatories and depositions without written permission of Court, unless necessary for the disposition of a motion or objection;

(B) Unanswered request for admissions unless necessary for the disposition of a motion or objection;

(C) Photocopies of reported cases, statutes or texts appendixed to a brief or otherwise, shall not be filed, but may be furnished directly to the Judge hearing the matter;

(D) Documents or copies thereof which should be received as exhibit rather than part of the Court file.

(E) Request for discovery and/or answer shall not be filed unless necessary for the disposition of a motion or objection.

(7) *Offers of Settlement.* An offer of settlement made pursuant to Chapter 4.84 of the Revised Code of Washington shall not be filed or communicated to the trier of fact in violation of Section 4.84.280 of the Revised Code of Washington prior to the completion of trial. A violation of this order shall result in the denial of the reasonable attorney fee. [See LCRLJ 68]

[Adopted effective September 1, 1988; amended August 5, 1991; September 1, 1992; September 1, 1998.]

LCRLJ 10. FORM OF PLEADINGS

(d) Bottom Notation. At the left side of the bottom of each page of all pleadings and other papers prepared by an attorney, an abbreviated name of the pleading or other paper should be repeated, followed by the page number. At the right side of the bottom of the first page of each pleading or other paper, the name, mailing address and telephone number of the attorney or firm preparing the paper should be printed or typed.

(1) Every proposed order or judgment and decree presented to a Judge for signature shall be signed by the individual attorney or prose party. Attorneys signing shall include their Washington State Bar Association identification number.

(2) *Change of Name or Address of Attorney.* An attorney whose office address or whose name changes shall, within 10 days after the change, notify in writing the District Court Administrator's Office. An attorney may use the same format referred to in APR 13 or the form in use by the Washington State Bar Association.

(A) **Change of Address.** The Attorney shall furnish his or her Washington State Bar Association membership number, the previous address and telephone number, clearly identified as such, the new address and telephone number, clearly identified as such, and the effective date of the change.

(B) **Change of Name.** The attorney shall furnish his or her Washington State Bar Association membership number, the previous name, clearly identified as such, the full new name, clearly identified as such, and the effective date of the change.

(e) Paper Weight and Type Style. Unless otherwise authorized, pleadings, motions, and other papers filed with the Court shall be on standard 20 weight paper. Forms and pleadings shall be printed in standard text fonts (e.g. Arial or Times New Roman) and in standard point sizes (e.g. 12 point or 10 point). Other point sizes may be used for captions and footers so long as the captions and footers are legible when faxed, photocopied or scanned. Bold, underlined and italicized type is acceptable where appropriate.

(f) Format Recommendation

(1) Documents to be filed with the County Auditor, such as Name Change Orders, etc., shall conform to the format requirements set forth in R.C.W. 65.04.045.

[Adopted effective September 1, 1988; amended August 5, 1991; September 1, 1999; September 1, 2001; September 1, 2007.]

LCRLJ 11. SIGNING OF PLEADINGS

(a) Failure of a party to comply with the Local Rules of this Court may be grounds for imposition of appropriate sanctions.

(1) The term party shall include the attorney for such party unless the context of the rule excludes such meaning.

[Adopted effective September 1, 1988; amended August 5, 1991.]

LCRLJ 33. INTERROGATORIES TO PARTIES [DELETED]

[Adopted effective September 1, 1988; amended September 1, 1992; September 1, 1995; deleted effective September 1, 2001.]

LCRLJ 38. JURY TRIALS

(d) Impaneling the Jury

(1) *Voir Dire*

(A) **Completion of Voir Dire—Juror Questionnaires and Information Form**. At the conclusion of voir dire, Juror Questionnaires, if any, and Information Forms shall be immediately returned to the Court. Juror Questionnaires and Information Forms may not be removed from the courtroom without the express permission of the trial Judge. Juror Information Forms and Questionnaires will not be filed with the Court file. The trial Judge shall direct that individual Questionnaires of jurors dealing with matters of a personal or sensitive nature, if required to be filed by rule or statute, shall be separately filed under seal.

(3) *Peremptory Challenges*

(A) The exercise or waiver of peremptory challenges shall be noted secretly on the jury list.

[Adopted effective September 1, 1988; September 1, 1998; amended effective September 1, 2005.]

LCRLJ 40. ASSIGNMENT OF CASES

(a) Notice of Trial—Note of Issue—Civil

(1) Of Fact. Any party desiring to bring an issue of fact to trial shall serve and file, not later than seven (7) Court days preceding the setting day, a properly completed Note for Trial Setting. The Civil Clerk shall place on the setting calendar only those cases which are properly and timely noted. A party noting a case for trial thereby certifies that the case is at issue and that necessary witnesses will be available. Any party contending a case is not ready for trial shall do by serving and filing a counter Notice of Trial or objection to the setting at least three (3) days prior to setting day. The objection will be heard by the Civil Department Judge. (Amended Sept. 1, 2005).

Failure to comply with this rule by any party may result in the imposition of terms; and/or the striking of the case from the calendar; and/or the refusal to grant a requested continuance.

(2) Of Law. Issue of Law may be noted for hearing on the Note For Hearing–Issue of Law form, and shall be heard on Friday of each week at 10:00 a.m. For issue of default, see LCRLJ 55.

(b) Method

(1) Civil Trial Setting Day. Note for trial shall be set for 9:00 A.M. on Fridays. The Civil Department Judge shall hear all objections to setting at that time. (Amended Sept. 1, 2005, Amended Sept. 1, 2009).

(2) Civil Trial Date and Uncontested Setting. The Civil Clerk shall determine the trial date on all uncontested trial settings and place such case on the assigned trial calendar with proper notification to all parties by the Court. (Amended Sept. 1, 2005).

(3) Pro–Se Party—Civil Case. In every action in which there is a pro-se party, a Civil Clerk shall set the trial date when the pleadings are completed. The Clerk's Office shall notify the parties of the trial setting by regular first class mail and complete a certificate of mailing. (Amended Sept. 1, 2005).

(4) Civil Case—Notification of Out-of-County Counsel. Spokane County Counsel shall notify in writing, within five (5) days of the notice of case setting, all out-of-county counsel of the trial date of the case in which they are concerned and file a copy of such notice with a certificate of mailing.

(5) Motion Setting—Civil

(A) Filing Note for Hearing. The Note for Hearing–Issue of Law must be served and filed no later than twelve (12) days prior to the hearing (CRLJ 6 and CRLJ 40). Any responding documents must be served and filed at least seven (7) days before the hearing. Reply documents must be served and filed at least two (2) days before the hearing. In the event a motion or one continued from a prior date is to be argued, counsel for the moving party shall notify the District Court Civil Clerk by 12:00 Noon two (2) days before the hearing. At the time reporting counsel will be informed which Judge will be hearing the motion calendar. In the event an agreed or uncontested Order of Continuance is to be entered, or an Order to change Judge filed, counsel are further required to so file and notify the District Court Civil Clerk by 4:30 p.m. two (2) days before the scheduled hearing. Failure to comply with the provisions of this rule will result in the motion being stricken from the motion calendar. (Amended Sept. 1, 2005, Amended Sept. 1, 2009)

(6) Motion Setting—Summary Judgment. Motion for summary judgment and dismissal must be served and filed at least twelve (12) days prior to the hearing (CRLJ 56) and heard at least two (2) weeks prior to the date the case is set for trial. The motion shall be set in accordance with the provisions of paragraph (5) above; and a continuance may be granted only in accordance with the provisions of paragraph (e) below.

(7) Filing of Motions, Memoranda and Affidavits—General. The moving party shall file with the Note for Hearing–Issue of Law form, the following: The motion being noted, all supporting affidavits and documentary evidence, and a brief memorandum of authorities, unless the legal position is fully and adequately covered by the "authorities" section of the Issue of Law form. If the responding party files a response to the issue of Law or any counter-affidavits, briefs, or memoranda of authorities, such document must be served and filed no later than seven (7) days before the hearing. The responding party must also file any pleading to which the motion is directed. Failure to timely comply with these filing requirements may

result in a continuance or the motion being stricken from the calendar and imposition of terms.

(A) Length of Memoranda. Memoranda relating to motions shall not exceed ten (10) pages. Attached copies of foreign and federal decisions are not included in the ten (10) page limitation. Waiver of page limitations may be granted only upon motion demonstrating good cause which may be heard ex-parte.

(8) Copies of Motions, Memoranda and Affidavits. A copy of the motion, brief, memorandum, documents and affidavit shall be furnished to the clerk at the time of filing for delivery to the assigned Judge for preparation. Responding briefs, memoranda and other documents shall be filed with copies provided for the preparation of the assigned Judge. Failure to comply with this requirement may result in a continuance and imposition of terms.

(9) Motion Hearing Procedures. Oral argument on motions shall be limited to ten (10) minutes for each side unless the assigned Judge determines otherwise, in which case the motion may be placed at the end of the calendar. (Amended Sept. 1, 2005).

(10) Pre–Assignment of Cases. All cases shall be pre-assigned to a Judicial Department except Ex-Parte matters. (Amended Sept. 1, 2005).

(11) Civil Ex–Parte Matters. Any Agreed Orders may be granted or denied by the judicial officer presiding in the Ex Parte department, or by any judge or court commissioner provided that the assigned judge is unavailable.

In the event a non-assigned judicial officer elects to deny to sign an agreed order, a denial of an order shall be noted on the order and filed in the legal file. (Amended effective Sept. 1, 1995, Sept. 1, 1999, Sept. 1, 2008.)

(d) Trials

(1) Daily Calendar Procedure. The daily trial calendar shall be called at 9:00 a.m. and 1:30 p.m. by the assigned Judicial Departments.

(2) Case Assignment Procedure. Cases which are ready for trial but are not brought to trial because of non-availability of the trial Court, shall be carried forward on the calendar to a day certain.

(3) Notice of Change in Status. Trial counsel are to report changes in the status of cases on the trial calendar to the Clerk. Special problems which affect readiness, such as unavailability of a witness, a party, or counsel, must be reported immediately. Neglect of this duty resulting in expense or inconvenience to the Court or other litigants may result in the imposition of terms, the refusal to grant a requested continuance, or the case being stricken from the calendar.

(e) Continuances

(1) Contested Continuances. If an attorney needs to have a case continued and the continuance is opposed, a motion for continuance shall be served on the opposing party and submitted to the assigned Judge not less than three (3) Court days in advance of the trial date. The motion shall be accompanied by an affidavit stating the reasons of necessity of the continuance. The three-day requirement may be waived if an emergency exists in fact. Terms may be imposed in the discretion of the Court. If a continuance is granted, it shall be reflected on the appropriate Court form or a comparable order. (Amended effective Sept. 1, 2005, Amended effective Sept. 1, 2009.)

(A) Pro–Se Parties. A pro-se party may request a continuance at the time of the hearing without compliance with the provisions of paragraph (1) above. Upon a showing of good cause, in the interest of justice, and/or the imposition of terms, the Court may grant a continuance. The continuance shall be noted on the case file.

(2) Agreed Continuances. In cases where all parties agree, an Order of Continuance will be presented for the assigned Judge's consideration not later than one (1) day prior to the date set for trial, unless otherwise authorized by the Court.

(A) Jury Trials. No jury trial will be continued, absent exigent circumstances, unless the agreed Order of Continuance is submitted to the assigned Judge for his or her consideration, not less than three (3) working days prior to the scheduled jury trial date.

(g) Pre–Trial Conference

(1) The Judicial Department assigned to the case will determine whether a case would benefit from a Pre–Trial Conference. The proceedings of the settlement conference are privileged and shall not be recorded. The attorneys for both parties shall attend with their respective clients. The parties shall confer in good faith prior to the date of the Pre–Trial Conference and attempt to reach an agreed disposition.

[Adopted effective September 1, 1988; amended August 5, 1991; September 1, 1993; amended effective September 1, 1995; September 1, 1999; September 1, 2005; September 1, 2008; September 1, 2009.]

LCRLJ 43. TAKING OF TESTIMONY

(e) Evidence on Motions

(1) Motions shall be heard only on the pleadings, affidavits published deposition and other papers filed unless otherwise directed by the Court. Any counter-affidavit shall be served on the opposing party within seven (7) days pursuant to LCRLJ 40(b)(9), or the movant shall have the option of a postponement of the

hearing. Affidavits strictly in reply to a counter-affidavit may be served and considered at the hearing.

[Adopted effective September 1, 1988; amended August 5, 1991.]

LCRLJ 43.1. COURTROOM PRACTICE AND DECORUM

(a) Examination of Witnesses and Arguments

(1) During opening statement, examination of witnesses and arguments, counsel should remain at counsel table unless otherwise authorized by Court.

(2) Do not approach a witness without asking permission of the Court. When permission is granted for the purpose of working with an exhibit, resume the examination from counsel table when finished with the exhibit.

(3) Rise when addressing the Court and when making objections as this calls the Court's attention to you.

(b) Objections to Questions and Evidence

(1) When objecting, state only that you are objecting and specify the ground or grounds of objection. Do not use objections for the purpose of making a speech, recapitulating testimony or attempting to guide the witness.

(2) Argument upon the objection will not be heard until permission is given or argument is requested by the Court.

(c) Decorum

(1) Address all remarks to the Court. Colloquy or argument between attorneys is not permitted.

(2) In a jury case, if there is an offer of stipulation, first confer with opposing counsel and obtain the Court's permission before submitting it to the jury.

(3) Counsel during trial shall not exhibit familiarity with witnesses, jurors, or opposing counsel. The use of first names or nicknames is to be avoided. During jury argument, no juror shall be addressed individually or by name.

(4) During the argument of opposing counsel, remain seated at the counsel table and be respectful. Never divert the attention of the Court or the jury.

(d) Witnesses and Ruling of the Court

(1) Witnesses shall at all times be treated with fairness, consideration and respect.

(2) No person shall ever by facial expression or other conduct exhibit any opinion concerning any testimony which is being given by a witness, or as to a ruling by the Court. Counsel will admonish their clients and witnesses about this very common occurrence.

(e) Court Hours and Promptness

(1) The Court will make every effort to commence proceeding at the time set. Promptness is expected from counsel and witnesses.

(2) Counsel should make every effort to schedule witnesses in order to ensure full utilization of the trial day.

(f) Exhibits

(1) All exhibits should be pre-marked for identification prior to trial. The Judicial Assistant assigned to each Judge will cooperate with counsel in facilitating the marking and management of the exhibits. (Amended effective Sept. 1, 2009)

(2) Documents and other exhibits should be shown to opposing counsel before their use in Court.

(3) Ordinarily, exhibits should be offered in evidence when they become admissible rather than at the end of counsel's case.

(4) Marking on exhibits should only be made after receiving the Court's permission to do so.

(g) Opening Statements. Confine your opening statement to what you expect the evidence to show. It is not proper to use the opening statement to argue your case or instruct as to the law.

[Adopted effective September 1, 1988; amended August 5, 1991; September 1, 2009.]

LCRLJ 47. JURORS

(a) Examination of Jurors (See Local Rule 38)

[Adopted effective September 1, 1998.]

LCRLJ 49. VERDICTS

(f) Manner of Giving Verdict

(1) *Receiving Verdict During Absence of Counsel.* A party or attorney desiring to be present at the return of the verdict must remain in attendance at the courthouse or be available by telephone call. If a party or attorney fails to appear within twenty (20) minutes of telephone notice to the attorney's office, home or other number, the Court may proceed to take the verdict in the absence of such party or attorney. In such case, the jury shall be individually polled and the identity of any dissenting jurors recorded.

[Adopted effective September 1, 1988.]

LCRLJ 51. INSTRUCTIONS TO JURY AND DELIBERATIONS

(a) Proposed. In addition to the proposed instructions required by CRLJ 51, each party shall submit a brief statement of the case suitable to be read to the jury before the voir dire examination.

(c) Form. Copies of proposed instructions shall contain supporting citations or reference to a pattern jury instruction.

(d) Published Instructions.

(3) Request of WPI or WPIC by reference. (Reserved.)

[Adopted effective September 1, 1988.]

LCRLJ 54. JUDGMENTS AND COSTS

(c) Demand for Judgment

(1) ***Method—Ex–Parte Judgments and Orders.*** Counsel, legal interns and paralegals registered with the Spokane County Bar Association presenting a judgment or seeking entry of an order shall be responsible to see that all papers pertaining thereto are filed and that the Court file is provided to the Judge. Legal Interns presenting ex-parte or other agreed orders as authorized by APR 9(c)(4) shall be sufficiently familiar with the matter so as to satisfy the Court on any question reasonably to be anticipated. Counsel may present routine ex-parte or stipulated matters based on the record in the file by mail addressed to the Civil Clerk. Self–addressed, stamped envelopes shall be provided for return of any conformed materials and/or rejected orders.

(d) Cost–Attorney Fees

(1) Reasonable attorney fees when allowed by statute or contract will be determined on a case by case basis and awarded in the sound discretion of the Court upon satisfactory justification, which may include documentation of time and charges.

In appropriate cases, when a Default Judgment is entered, reasonable attorney fees may be allowed on the basis of a maximum of 50% of the first $500 of the principal amount of the judgment, plus 10% of any balance over $500, without formal justification or documentation.

(2) If reasonable attorneys fees are requested based on a contract provision, the contract provision must be conspicuously highlighted or underlined to be readily ascertainable.

(3) Specific citation of authority must accompany requests for reasonable attorney fees on any basis other than contract provision.

(4) Statutory attorney fees may be granted when reasonable attorney fees are not authorized. (See RCW 12.20.060)

(5) ***Assigned Claims.*** Before costs and attorney fees will be allowed by the Court on assigned claims, proof shall be furnished the Court that Notice and Demand for Payment of disputed amount has been sent to the defendant by the assignee, and he or she has had reasonable opportunity of not less than thirty (30) days to pay the disputed amount prior to the suit. Reasonable attorney fees, when allowed, shall not exceed either ten percent (10%) of the disputed amount or the statutory attorney fee, whichever is greater unless there is documentation of time and charges.

(A) **Payment Prior to Trial.** A statutory attorney fee shall be allowed when the amount in dispute is paid any time prior to trial on assigned claims. A reasonable attorney fee shall not be allowed absent satisfactory justification including documentation of time and charges.

(6) ***Offers of Settlement.*** Improper communication of an offer of settlement shall result in the denial of reasonable attorney fees. [See LCRLJ 5(d)(7) and LCRLJ 68.]

[Adopted effective September 1, 1988; amended August 5, 1991; amended effective September 1, 1995; amended effective September 1, 2000; September 1, 2007.]

LCRLJ 55. DEFAULT

(b) Entry of Default

(5) *Form and Documentation*

(A) Orders for Default and Default Judgments must be accompanied by the original and two copies of the following:

(1) Supporting documentation of debt or Affidavit of Indebtedness.

(2) Declaration or Affidavit of Service if not previously filed.

(3) Affidavit Regarding Military Service on the form provided by the court for each defendant against whom the plaintiff is requesting an order of default or default judgment.

(4) Affidavit of Venue and other requirements under CRLJ 55 (a) and (b).

(5) On NSF checks, a separate pleading itemizing all charges and penalties claimed pursuant to RCW 62A.3–515.

(6) If the default motion is mailed or left with the court, a stamped, self addressed envelope for the clerk to return a conformed copy to the plaintiff.

(B) Prejudgment Interest will be governed in accordance with RCW 19.52 and RCW 62A.3–515. Specific citation of authority must accompany requests for Pre–Judgment Interest on any other basis.

(6) Presentation and entry of defaults may be noted for hearing before the Civil Department Judge on Friday morning at 10:00 A.M.

(7) Post–Judgment Interest will accrue in accordance with RCW 4.56.110. Specific citation of authority must accompany requests for Post–Judgment Interest on any other basis.

(8) (i) Any plaintiff who obtains an average of five (5) or less default judgments per month from this Court may do so on any form or forms that comply with State statutes and the Rule for Courts of Limited Jurisdiction.

(ii) Any plaintiff averaging more than five (5) default judgments per month, unless leave of Court is granted, shall use the Motion and Affidavit for Default and the Order for Default and Default Judgment form provided by the Court. The Motion and Affidavit for Order of Default and Default judgment shall be available in the Clerk's Office and on the court's official website.

[Adopted effective September 1, 1988; amended August 5, 1991; amended effective September 1, 1995; September 1, 2005; September 1, 2007.]

LCRLJ 56. SUMMARY JUDGMENT

(See LCRLJ 40)

[Adopted effective September 1, 1988.]

LCRLJ 58. ENTRY OF JUDGMENT

(a) Judgment on a Promissory Note. No Judgment on a promissory note will be signed until the original note has been filed with the Court, absent proof of loss or destruction.

[Adopted effective September 1, 1988; amended effective September 1, 2005; September 1, 2009.]

LCRLJ 60(c). RELIEF FROM JUDGMENT OR ORDER [REPEALED]

[Adopted effective September 1, 2004; repealed effective September 1, 2009.]

LCRLJ 68. OFFER OF JUDGMENT

(a) Form. Offers of Settlement shall clearly state it is an Offer of Settlement and specifically refer to Chapter 4.84 of the Revised Code of Washington.

(1) *Method of Service.* Service shall be made as permitted in CRLJ 5;

(2) *Time of Service.* Service shall be made in accordance with RCW 4.84.280.

(3) *Pro-Se Parties.* Offers of Settlement served on pro-se parties shall include a statement that failure or refusal to accept this offer may result in a reasonable attorney fee being assessed at the time of judgment. Failure to include such wording will be grounds for the Court to deny reasonable attorney fees.

[Adopted effective September 1, 1988.]

LCRLJ 69. EXECUTION, SUPPLE-MENTAL PROCEEDINGS AND GARNISHMENTS

(a) Scope. Execution, supplemental proceedings and garnishments are governed by Statute (see Title 6 and 7 of the Revised Code of Washington).

(1) *Supplemental Proceedings.* In all supplemental proceedings wherein a show cause order is issued pursuant thereto requiring the personal attendance of a party to be examined in open Court and in orders to show cause in re contempt, the order to show cause must include the following words in capital letters:

YOUR FAILURE TO APPEAR AS SET FORTH AT THE TIME, DATE AND PLACE THEREOF MAY CAUSE THE COURT TO ISSUE A BENCH WARRANT FOR YOUR APPREHENSION AND CONFINEMENT IN JAIL UNTIL SUCH TIME AS THE MATTER CAN BE HEARD, UNLESS BAIL IS FURNISHED AS PROVIDED IN SUCH BENCH WARRANT.

The failure to include such wording will be grounds for the Court to refuse to issue a bench warrant.

(2) *Bench Warrant.* In the event the judgment debtor fails to appear for examination in supplemental proceedings, the Court may issue a Bench Warrant for the defendant's arrest upon plaintiff's motion, provided that proof of service on the judgment debtor of the order to appear for examination has been filed. Such Bench Warrant shall provide for bail in the amount of $500.00 unless the total judgment, including costs and fees, is less than $500.00, in which case bail shall be set at such lesser amount. Upon arrest on a Civil Bench Warrant, the defendant shall be released by the jail upon posting the bail amount in cash or surety bond. The jail shall require the defendant to sign a jail release form to appear at. the. the Civil counter within 24 hours of release to make a court date. The Clerk shall set a new date and time for the Supplemental Proceeding and notify both parties.

If the judgment debtor is not released on bail or bond, he or she shall be brought before a Judge, not later than the next judicial day, who shall set a new date and time for the examination on Supplemental Proceedings, and notify both parties.

Upon completion of the examination of the judgment debtor, and the bail shall be exonerated unless the Court orders otherwise.

(3) (Deleted)

(b) Judgment Against Garnishee Defendant.

(1) In the event a garnishee defendant answers a writ of garnishment, judgment against the garnishee may be entered only after:

(A) Twenty days have elapsed from the date of filing of the answer or the second answer in the event of a continuing lien;

(B) Proof of service of the writ, and other documents required by the statute to be served is filed with the Court.

(2) A judgment upon an answer of a garnishee defendant may be entered on an *ex parte basis*.

(3) In the event a garnishee defendant fails to answer the writ of garnishment, a default judgment against the garnishee defendant may be entered only after:

(A) Twenty days have elapsed from the filing and service of the writ;

(B) Notice of intent to present the default judgment shall be personally served or sent by certified mail giving at least 10 calendar days notice before the default judgment is taken. Proof of mailing must be filed before the default judgment is taken.

(c) Exemption Claims to Writ of Garnishment

(1) *Exemption Claims and Hearings*

Non-Responsive Exemption Claim. An Exemption Claim in the form prescribed in RCW 6.27.140, submitted by a party shall be deemed Non-Responsive if:

(A) The form is submitted in blank and/or does not assert a claim of exemption;

(B) Exemption(s) specific to bank accounts are claimed and the Writ is not directed to a bank;

(C) Exemption(s) specific to Child Support Garnishments are claimed and the Writ is not issued for enforcement of a child support judgment;

(D) Exemption(s) specific to pension or retirement benefits are claimed and the Writ is not directed to the garnished party's employer or other pension or retirement benefit provider; or

(E) Exemption(s) specific to other personal property are claimed and the Writ is directed to a bank, employer or other holder of monetary amounts belonging to the garnished party.

(2) *Denial of Non-Responsive Exemption Claim:*

(A) Claim as defined in this rule shall be denied without a Court hearing if the garnishing party files and serves a Notice of Non-Responsive Exemption Claim, substantially in the form prescribed in subsection (3) of this rule, within seven (7) days of receipt of the Exemption Claim. If filing and/or service is had by mail, compliance with this rule shall be deemed complete if the described Notice is posted in the U.S. Mail on or before the seventh day after the garnishing party receives the Exemption Claim.

(B) **Notice of Non-Responsive Exemption Claim Form.** The Notice of Non–Responsive Exemption Claim shall be substantially in the form approved by the Court.

(d) Federal Government as Garnishee Defendant

(1) Whenever the federal government is named as a garnishee defendant, the Clerk of Court shall, upon submittal of a notice in the appropriate form by the requesting party, issue a notice which directs the garnishee defendant to disburse any non-exempt earnings to the Court.

(2) Funds received by the Clerk from a garnishee defendant may be deposited into the registry of the Court, or in case of negotiable instruments, may be retained in the Court file. Upon presentation of an order directing the Clerk to disburse the funds received, the Clerk shall pay or endorse the fund over to the party entitled to the same. Except for good cause shown, the funds shall not be paid or endorsed to the judgment creditor prior to the expiration of any minimum statutory period allowed to the judgment debtor for filing an exemption claim.

(3) The party requesting the Writ of Garnishment shall supply a copy of the notice to the garnishee defendant with a pre-addressed envelope to the Court which has the cause number displayed thereon and to the garnished party in the same manner as is permitted for the service of the Writ of Garnishment.

(4) The notice to the federal government employer shall be in substantially the form approved by the Court.

[Adopted effective September 1, 1988; amended August 5, 1991; amended effective September 1, 1995; September 1, 1998; September 1, 1999; September 1, 2004; September 1, 2005.]

LCRLJ 79. BOOKS AND RECORDS KEPT BY THE CLERK

(a) Records. Records are governed by Title 3 of the Revised Code of Washington.

(b) Other Books and Records Kept by Clerk

(1) *Exhibits.* Exhibits shall be kept with the Court file unless they are oversize. Any inspection of an exhibit must be in the presence of the Clerk or a Deputy Clerk unless authorized by an order of the Court.

(2) *Rejection of Unsuitable Material.* The Clerk shall not accept for filing in the Court file matters which should be filed as an exhibit or other material not to be included by reason of LCRLJ 5(d)(6). When the Clerk is uncertain as to whether a matter is suitable for filing, he or she shall seek the advice of the Civil Judge before filing the same.

(3) *Withdrawal of Files.* No file may be removed from the Clerk's Office without an order of the Court, except as herein provided: an attorney, legal intern, paralegal registered with the Spokane County Bar Association, District Court Probation Officer, or Pre–Trial Release Evaluator may withdraw a file without a specific order of the Court. A person withdrawing a file and failing to return same file by the close of business of the same day the file was withdrawn, shall lose the privilege of withdrawing files until the previously withdrawn file is returned. Failure to return the file after notice from the Clerk's Office of a violation of this rule may result in the imposition of terms or other appropriate sanctions. Any person withdrawing a file and leaving it with a Judge or Judicial Secretary shall have the duty to immediately correct the check out record in the Clerk's Office, showing the file was, in fact, left with a Judge or Judicial Secretary.

(4) *Items Required to be Sealed by the Clerk's Office are as follows:*

(A) Probation Department Investigation reports for sentencing procedures;

(B) Alcohol evaluations and reports;

(C) Mental Health evaluations and reports;

(D) Drug Evaluations and reports;

(E) Pre-trial release evaluations and recommendations; and

(F) Any other item ordered to be sealed by a Judge or classified as confidential by statute, rule or regulation. [See LARLJ 9.]

[Adopted effective September 1, 1988; amended August 5, 1991; amended effective September 1, 1995; amended effective September 1, 2000; September 1, 2005.]

III. CRIMINAL MATTERS

LCrRLJ 1.6. CONDUCT OF COURT

(a) The Local Civil Rules (LCRLJ) will supplement the Criminal Rules (CrRLJ) in the absence of an appropriate Local Criminal Rule (LCrRLJ).

[Adopted effective September 1, 1988; amended August 5, 1991.]

LCrRLJ 1.7. LOCAL CRIMINAL RULES

(a) **Adoption and Amendments.** [See LARLJ 2.]

[Adopted effective September 1, 1988.]

LCrRLJ 2.3. SEARCH AND SEIZURE

(c) **Issuance and Contents.** A search warrant may be issued only if the court determines there is probable cause for the issuance of a warrant. There must be an affidavit, a document as provided in RCW 9A.72.085 or any law amendatory thereto, or sworn testimony establishing the grounds for issuing the warrant. The sworn testimony may be an electronically recorded telephonic statement, facsimile machine document or electronically mailed document. The recording or a duplication of the recording facsimile, or electronic mail shall be a part of the court record and shall be transcribed if requested by a party if there is a challenge to the validity of the warrant or if ordered by the court. The evidence in support of the finding of probable cause shall be preserved and shall be subject to constitutional limitations for such determinations and may be hearsay in whole or in part. If the court finds that probable cause for the issuance of a warrant exists, it shall issue a warrant or direct an individual whom it authorizes for such purpose to affix the court's signature to a warrant identifying the property or person and naming or describing the person, place or thing to be searched. The court's authorization may be done by electronic signature process. A record shall be made of any additional submitted evidence on which the court relies.

(h) **Search Warrants.**

(1) After execution, the search warrant shall be filed by number and description of the person or property to be searched. An index will be maintained and available to the public by the Clerk's Office.

LCRLJ 83. LOCAL RULES OF THE DISTRICT COURT

(a) **Adoption and Amendments.** [See LARLJ.]

[Adopted effective September 1, 1988.]

(2) The affidavit and accompanying papers including the return of service shall be filed in accordance with the provisions of CrRLJ 8.10 and ARLJ 9.

[Adopted effective September 1, 1988; amended effective September 1, 1995; September 1, 2003; September 1, 2012.]

LCrRLJ 2.5. PROCEDURE ON FAILURE TO OBEY CITATION AND NOTICE TO APPEAR

(a) **Recall of Failure to Respond Arrest Warrants.** The Court Administrator or delegate shall have authority to recall Failure To Respond Arrest Warrants under the following provisions:

(1) The Failure To Respond Arrest Warrant was issued because the defendant failed to respond to the citation or a Summons and Complaint.

(2) The defendant personally appears at the counter to sign for a court date, or appears through counsel.

[Adopted effective September 1, 1988. Amended effective September 1, 1995.]

LCrRLJ 3.1(e). WITHDRAWAL OF LAWYER

(e)

(1) Unless a Notice of Appeal has been filed, an attorney appointed at public expense shall be deemed automatically withdrawn from representation thirty days following a final decision of the court as defined in RALJ without need to file any document with the court.

[Adopted effective September 1, 2010.]

LCrRLJ 3.2. RELEASE OF ACCUSED

(k) [Deleted]

(m) **Bail Schedule.** [Deleted]

(n) **Personal Recognizance Release.** Reserved

(o) **Bail in Criminal Offense Cases—Mandatory Appearance.**

(2) Any person arrested by a Law Enforcement Officer on Probable Cause (without an arrest warrant) for the below listed offenses shall be held in jail

pending the Defendant's First Appearance in the absence of a judicial order:

(A) An offense classified as a Domestic Violence under Chapter 10.99 of the Revised Code of Washington or an equivalent local ordinance.

(B) An offense classified as Harassment and/or Stalking under Chapters 10.14 and/or 9A.46 of the Revised Code of Washington or an equivalent local ordinance.

(C) An offense classified as a Felony.

(3) Any person arrested and booked into jail for Driving Under the Influence, (RCW 46.61.502), or Physical Control of Vehicle Under the Influence (RCW 46.61.504), shall be held in jail without bail pending the Defendant's First Appearance before a judge, in the absence of a judicial order.

[Adopted effective September 1, 1988. Amended August 5, 1991; September 1, 1993; amended effective September 1, 1995; September 1, 1999; September 1, 2007. Reserved September 1, 2010. Amended effective September 2, 2013.]

LCrRLJ 3.2.1. PROCEDURE FOLLOWING WARRANTLESS ARREST—PRELIMINARY APPEARANCE

(b) How Determined. The court shall determine probable cause on evidence presented by a peace officer or prosecuting authority in the same manner as provided for a warrant of arrest in rule 2.2(a). The evidence shall be preserved and may consist of an electronically recorded telephonic statement, facsimile machine document, or by electronic mail. If the court finds that release without bail should be denied or that conditions should attach to the release on personal recognizance, other than the promise to appear for trial, the court shall proceed to determine whether probable cause exists to believe that the accused committed the offense charged, unless this determination has previously been made by a court. Before making the determination, the court may consider an affidavit, a document as provided in RCW 9A.72.085 or any law amendatory thereto, or sworn testimony, and further may examine under oath the affiant and any witnesses the affiant may produce. Said documentation may be provided to the court by facsimile machine document or electronic mail. Sworn testimony shall be electronically or stenographically recorded. The evidence shall be preserved and shall be subject to constitutional limitations for probable cause determinations, and may be hearsay in whole or in part. Court authorization may be done by electronic mail using an electronic signature process.

[Adopted effective September 1, 2012.]

LCrRLJ 3.3. TIME FOR TRIAL

(f) Continuances

(3) Form and Procedure. A continuance in a criminal matter shall be requested on a Case Scheduling Order, and submitted to the assigned Judge for approval in accordance with the provisions of LCRLJ 40(e).

(k) Deferred Prosecution

(1) (A) Petition for Deferred Prosecution under Section 10.05 of the Revised Code of Washington, shall be filed fourteen (14) days before the date set for trial on forms approved by the Court.

(B) The written assessment prepared by an approved treatment facility shall be accompanied by a recommendation from the Probation Office, or such other Court Appointee authorized under Chapter 10.05 of the Revised Code of Washington.

(2) When the Court denies the Petition for a Deferred Prosecution, timely filed under this rule, the case shall proceed to trial as previously set.

(3) In the event the Petition for Deferred Prosecution is approved by the Court, the defendant may be under the supervision of the Probation Department, or Court Appointee pursuant to Section 10.05.170 of the Revised code of Washington. A defendant who refuses, fails or neglects to comply with an order, or request of the Probation Office or Court Appointee, or the terms of supervision, or conditions of supervision, or conditions of deferred prosecution may have the deferred prosecution revoked.

[Adopted effective September 1, 1988; amended effective September 1, 1993; September 1, 1995; September 1, 2007.]

LCrRLJ 3.4. PRESENCE OF THE DEFENDANT

(a) When Necessary

(1) *Pre–trial Hearings.* The assigned Judge will determine if a Pre-trial hearing shall be scheduled after the arraignment. The parties shall confer in good faith prior to the Pre-trial or readiness hearing in an attempt to reach an agreed disposition. The defendant shall be required to attend the Pre-trial hearing unless excused by the Court. Failure to attend may result in issuance of a bench warrant and/or forfeiture of any bond.

(d) Video Conference Proceedings

(2) Approval of the assigned Judge must be obtained in advance to conduct by video conference such proceedings as provided for by CrRLJ 3.4 (d)(2).

[Adopted September 1, 1999; amended effective September 1, 2007.]

LCrRLJ 4.1. PROCEEDINGS BEFORE THE JUDGE—APPEARANCE— BAIL

(d) Appearance by Defendant's Lawyer

(7) Attorneys retained by defendants, or public defenders who have assumed representation of defendants must promptly serve written notice of their appearance upon the prosecuting attorney, and file the

same with the Clerk. The notice of appearance shall be contained in a separate document.

(e) Counter–Appearance. A defendant, in response to a Summons and Complaint, Citation and Notice to Appear, or a Jail Release Appearance form, may first appear at the Court Appearance Counter to obtain an Arraignment or Pre–Trial Conference date. A defendant wishing to be represented by the Public Defender shall be referred to the Probation Department for a determination of eligibility.

(g) For the Municipal Court of the City of Cheney the requirement for appearance by the Defendant in person within one judicial day after arrest as set forth in RCW 46.61.50571 is waived; however, such defendants are required to appear in person at the Municipal Court of the City of Cheney at the next regularly-scheduled Court day of such Court. The Judge assigned to the Municipal Court shall file in advance a schedule of Court dates with the Clerk of the Municipal Court of the City of Cheney.

[Adopted effective September 1, 1988; amended August 5, 1991; amended effective September 1, 1995; September 1, 1999; September 1, 2007; September 1, 2012.]

LCrRLJ 4.2. PROCEDURE UPON A PLEA OF GUILTY

(i) Guilty Plea Statement. It shall be the duty of the defense attorney to have a properly completed written statement of the defendant on a guilty plea.

[Adopted effective September 1, 1995; amended effective September 1, 2009.]

LCrRLJ 4.7. DISCOVERY

(e) Discretionary Disclosure

(3) Any motion for items and information not covered by Section (a) and (d) of CrRLJ 4.7 shall be accompanied by an affidavit setting forth in detail the reasons the requested items and information are material and significant enough to amount to a denial of the right to a fair trial, if not ordered discoverable, so that the Court may have a basis for its ruling.

[Adopted effective September 1, 1988; amended August 5, 1991; September 1, 1998.]

LCrRLJ 6.1.1. TRIAL BY JURY OR BY THE COURT [DELETED]

[Adopted effective September 1, 1988; amended August 5, 1991; deleted effective September 1, 2007.]

LCrRLJ 6.13. EVIDENCE [REPEALED]

[Adopted effective September 1, 1988; amended August 5, 1991; repealed effective September 1, 2009.]

LCrRLJ 7.2. SENTENCING [DELETED]

[Adopted effective September 1, 1988; amended August 5, 1991; September 1, 1998; deleted effective September 1, 2001.]

LCrRLJ 8.2. MOTIONS

(a) Calendar Settings. All motions for dismissal, suppression and post-sentence relief, except motions pursuant to rule 3.5, shall comply with the provisions of CrRLJ 3.6.

(b) Motions to Dismiss and Motions to Suppress Evidence. Said Motions shall be filed and served at least three (3) weeks prior to the hearing and heard not later than one (1) week before the case is set for trial. The responding party shall file and serve any responding brief or memoranda one (1) week prior to Motion Hearing. Provided, however, that the Court may waive this requirement if due diligence has been shown or justice otherwise requires. It is the duty of the moving party to notify the assigned Judge by noon of the day prior to the motion day if oral testimony is required and estimated length of time required for the Motion. This rule does not authorize oral testimony when the facts can be adequately presented by affidavit and other documentary evidence.

(c) Agreed Orders–Criminal Cases. The following Agreed Orders may be approved or denied by any Judge or Commissioner PROVIDED the assigned Judge is absent or unavailable unless otherwise noted on and after review of the case file:

(1) Agreed Order of Dismissal

(2) Agreed Order of Misdemeanor Compromise

(3) Agreed Order of Bond Forfeiture

(4) Agreed Order of Pre–Trial Jail Release

(5) Agreed Order of Pre–Trial Bond Release

(6) Agreed Order of Pre–Trial Bond Reduction

(7) Agreed Order of Continuance of Pre–Trial Conference

It is understood that the non-assigned judicial officer being asked to sign any of the above Orders may refuse to sign. An Order not listed above shall be presented only to the Judge assigned to the case for his/her approval or denial. Orders denied must be noted on the Court file.

(d) Agreed Orders—Criminal Cases. Any Agreed Orders may be approved or denied by the judicial officer presiding in the ex parte department, or by any judge or commissioner provided the assigned judge is unavailable.

In the event a non-assigned judicial officer elects to deny to sign an agreed order, a denial of an order shall be noted on the order and filed in the legal file.

(e) Copies of Motions, Memoranda and Affidavits. A copy of the motion, brief, memorandum, documents and affidavits shall be furnished to the Judge after the originals have been filed. Responding briefs, memoranda, and other documents shall also be filed with the Clerk, and copies furnished to the assigned Judge. The copy provided to the assigned judge should indicate the date and time of the hearing on the motion. Failure to comply with these requirements may result in a continuance and imposition of terms.

(f) Motion Hearing Procedure. Oral argument on motions shall be limited to ten (10) minutes for each side unless the Judge determines otherwise, in which case the motion may be placed at the end of the calendar.

[Adopted effective September 1, 1988. Amended August 5, 1991; amended effective September 1, 1995; September 1, 1998; September 1, 1999; September 1, 2002; September 1, 2007; September 1, 2008; September 1, 2009; September 2, 2013.]

LCrRLJ 8.10. CLOSURE OF PROCEEDINGS AND CLOSURE OF RECORDS [RESERVED].

IV. INFRACTIONS

LIRLJ 1.1. SCOPE AND ADOPTION [SEE LARLJ 2.]

[Adopted effective September 1, 1988; amended September 1, 1992.]

LIRLJ 2.2. INITIATION OF TRAFFIC CASES [REPEALED AND RESERVED]

[Repealed and Reserved effective September 1, 2006.]

LIRLJ 2.4. RESPONSE TO NOTICE

The procedure authorized in IRLJ 2.4(b)(4) is adopted by this Court.

[Adopted effective September 1, 1988; amended September 1, 1992; October 10, 2003; March 29, 2004; September 1, 2005.]

LIRLJ 2.5. FAILURE TO RESPOND

(a) Out-of-State Residents—Penalty Assessment. An out-of-state resident failing to timely respond to an Infraction notice shall be mailed a thirty day letter authorizing a penalty forfeiture in the original penalty amount if the defendant remits the required amount within 30 days of the date of the letter.

(b) In-State Resident—Penalty Assessment. An in-state resident failing to timely respond to an Infraction shall have the privilege to remit and forfeit the original penalty not later than 30 days after the response period expired.

[Adopted effective September 1, 1988; amended September 1, 1992; September 1, 1993.]

LIRLJ 3.2. FAILURE TO APPEAR

(b) Setting Aside Judgment Upon Failure to Appear—Good Cause Petition

(1) A defendant may file a Good Cause Petition to set aside a default judgment for Failure to Appear at a requested hearing. Only one (1) Petition shall be allowed on a Failure to Appear judgment. A Mitigation hearing may be granted upon setting aside the judgment. A Contested Hearing shall not be allowed unless by special written Order of the assigned Judge or Court Commissioner.

[Adopted effective September 1, 1988; amended September 1, 1992.]

LIRLJ 3.4. HEARING ON MITIGATING CIRCUMSTANCES

(c) Disposition

(1) *Written Request for Penalty Reduction.* A defendant requesting a reduction of the Infraction penalty may have such determination based on his or her prior driving record without an explanation of the event cited. The amount of the reduction shall be set by the Court in a written Order maintained in the Clerk's Office and available upon request.

(2) Infractions disposable by a reduced bond forfeiture, with conditions precedent, shall be established by a majority vote of the Judges. A public list of Infractions, bond amount, and conditions shall be maintained in the Clerk's Office and available upon request.

[Adopted effective September 1, 1988; amended September 1, 1992.]

LIRLJ 3.5. DECISION ON WRITTEN STATEMENTS

The procedure authorized by IRLJ 3.5 is adopted by this Court.

[Adopted effective September 1, 1988; amended September 1, 1992.]

LIRLJ 6.2. MONETARY PENALTY SCHEDULE [DELETED]

[Adopted effective September 1, 1988. Amended September 1, 1992. Deleted effective September 2, 2013.]

LIRLJ 6.6. SPEED MEASURING DEVICE: DESIGN AND CONSTRUCTION CERTIFICATION

(b) Any certificate, affidavit, or foundation evidentiary document allowed or required by IRLJ 6.6 can be filed with the Clerk of the Court and maintained by the court as a public record. The records will be available for inspection by the public. Copies will be provided on request, subject to a charge for any allowable copying fees.

(d) Requests to produce the electronic measuring device expert shall be contained in a separate document and served on the prosecutor with a conformed copy filed with the Clerk of the Court. The Motion and Order–Issue of Law, Form 1503, may be used to demand the expert.

(1) The party filing the above demand shall specifically call it to the Court Clerk's attention so the case will be set on the appropriate radar expert trial date so as to avoid a continuance under IRLJ 6.6(c).

[Adopted effective September 1, 1988; amended August 5, 1991; September 1, 1992; September 1, 1999; amended effective September 1, 2000.]

LIRLJ 6.8. MOTION PRACTICE

All motion settings shall be served on the Prosecuting Attorney for the County five (5) days prior to the date set on the Motion and Order Form 1503. The District Court Clerk's Office shall furnish dates each week for the hearing of motions on contested infractions. It will be at the discretion of the Judge or Commissioner, after ruling on the motion, whether the infraction can then proceed to contested hearing immediately, or be reset on a contested docket. Motions in infraction cases shall comply with the above procedure or may be stricken by the Court.

[Adopted effective September 1, 1997; amended September 1, 1998; September 1, 2009.]

Committee Comments

LIRLJ 6.8 has been adopted for the purpose of assisting attorneys and defendants contesting infractions that require the determination of a motion to: dismiss, suppress evidence, objection to jurisdiction, objection to written statements or other issues, and will be considered by the Court only if the above Rule is followed.

V. SMALL CLAIM PROCEDURES

LJSC 0.1. SCOPE AND ADOPTION
[SEE LARLJ 2]

Local Rules on Small Claims actions supplement Chapter 12.40 of the Revised Code of Washington.

[Adopted effective September 1, 1988.]

LJSC 0.2. HEARING

(a) Defendant. When a party against who a judgment is sought fails to appear at the time and place specified in the Notice issued pursuant to RCW 12.40.060, a default judgment shall be entered upon proof of valid service, presentation of supporting evidence of indebtedness, and proof of venue.

(b) Plaintiff. When a plaintiff fails to appear at the time and place specified in the Notice issued pursuant to RCW 12.40.060, the plaintiff's claim shall be dismissed without prejudice.

[Adopted effective September 1, 1988.]

LJSC 0.3. MOTION TO VACATE
DEFAULT JUDGMENTS

(a) A Motion to Vacate a Small Claims Court Judgment shall be governed by CRLJ 55(c).

[Adopted effective September 1, 1988.]

LJSC 0.4. NEW TRIAL, RECONSIDERATION AND AMENDED JUDGMENTS

(a) Time. A Motion for a new trial, reconsideration, or amended judgment shall be filed within the statutory appeal period.

(b) Procedure. The Motion shall be set for hearing only with the permission of the Court and shall require notice to the opposing party.

[Adopted effective September 1. 1988.]

LJSC 0.5. PAYMENT OF MONETARY JUDGMENT

(a) Payment Plan. A Judgment debtor may petition the Court for a payment plan prior to a transcript of such judgment being entered on the District Court Judgment Docket.

(b) Form of Petition. The petition shall be on a Court approved form available in the Clerk's Office. The pertinent financial information shall be under oath. Upon the filing of Petition for Installment Payment, the Clerk's Office shall set a hearing date and notify both parties.

[Adopted effective September 1, 1988.]

LJSC 0.6. REASONABLE ATTORNEY FEE ON CERTIFICATION
[RESCINDED]

[Rescinded effective September 1, 2011.]

VI. RULES FOR APPEAL OF DECISIONS FOR COURTS OF LIMITED JURISDICTION

LRALJ 2.4. FILING NOTICE OF APPEAL

(a) **Where to File Notice of Appeal.** A Notice of Appeal from a final decision of the Spokane County District Court must be filed with the Clerk of Court on forms approved by the Court. Upon payment of the filing fee, if applicable, or determination that no fee is due, the Clerk shall transmit a copy of the Notice of Appeal, and all other necessary materials to the Superior Court Clerk.

(b) **Filing Fee.** Appellant(s) shall pay the Superior Court filing fee as defined by law, unless specifically excused by law, or upon obtaining an Order to Proceed in Forma Pauperis. Appellant shall file any Motion and Affidavit for Order to Proceed in Forma Pauperis with the Judge or Commissioner who heard the case, or in his or her absence, by the Presiding Judge. In Forma Pauperis Petitions shall be filed on forms approved by the Court.

[Adopted effective September 1, 1995; amended effective September 1, 2009.]

LRALJ 4.3. [STAY OF ENFORCEMENT OF JUDGMENT]

(b) **Criminal Case.** In order to stay a sentence, the party appealing the judgment must file with the Clerk of the Court a Stay Order signed by the assigned Judge, or in his or her absence, the Presiding Judge, setting forth the conditions of release.

[Adopted effective September 1, 2001.]

LRALJ 5.1. RECORDING GENERALLY

(a) **Generally**

(1) *Preservation of Court Recording Tapes.* Court proceedings recorded by tape recording machines shall be preserved for a period of two (2) years after entry of the final judgment.

[Adopted effective September 1, 1995.]

MUNICIPAL COURTS

AIRWAY HEIGHTS MUNICIPAL COURT—
[No Local Rules]

CHENEY MUNICIPAL COURT LOCAL RULES

PUBLISHER'S NOTE

The Local Rules for the District Court of Spokane County, Washington apply to the Cheney Municipal Court. (See LARLJ 2, Local Rules for the District Court of Spokane County, Washington, supra.)

DEER PARK MUNICIPAL COURT LOCAL RULES

PUBLISHER'S NOTE

The Local Rules for the District Court of Spokane County, Washington apply to the Deer Park Municipal Court. (See LARLJ 2, Local Rules for the District Court of Spokane County, Washington, supra.)

MEDICAL LAKE MUNICIPAL COURT LOCAL RULES

Including Amendments Received Through
August 15, 2015

Table of Rules

Titles in brackets added by Publisher.

RULE 1. [NEXT JUDICIAL DAY]

The "next judicial day" as referred to in RCW 46.61.50571 means the next day upon which Court is held in the Municipal Court of the City of Medical Lake, Washington.

[Adopted effective September 1, 1999.]

RULE 2. [ADOPTION]

The Local Rules of the Spokane County District Court are hereby adopted by this Court. Said rules shall apply unless superceded by specific rules adopted by this Court.

[Adopted effective September 1, 1999.]

RULE 3. [ANTIHARASSMENT PROTECT ORDER]

Pursuant to House Bill 1296 2205 Regular Session, the Medical Lake Municipal Court hereby adopts this rule whereby it shall hereafter exercise jurisdiction and cognizance of any civil action or proceedings brought under RCW 10.14 for antiharassment protect order, *provided that,* (1) the alleged act(s) of unlawful harassment occurred within the City of Medical Lake, Washington; or (2) when, at the time the petition is filed, any respondent resides within the City of Medical Lake, Washington. In the event that the respondent does not reside within the City of Medical Lake, the defendant must be amenable to service within Spokane County; *provided further that* all actions and proceedings under RCW 10.14 in which the respondent is under the age of eighteen (18) years shall be transferred to Spokane Superior Court.

[Adopted effective September 1, 2006.]

[BAIL SCHEDULE [GENERAL ORDER NO. 01–96]]

TO: THE POLICE DEPARTMENT OF MEDICAL LAKE WASHINGTON.

Except as otherwise provided by the Supreme Court of the State of Washington in Criminal Rule CrRLJ 3.2, copy attached, the following Bail Schedule is hereby adopted by the Medical Lake Municipal Court:

1.) PROBABLE CAUSE ARREST FOR DOMESTIC VIOLENCE, HARASSMENT AND/OR STALKING. (MCA RULE)

(a) Any person arrested by a Law Enforcement Officer on Probable Cause (without an arrest warrant for the below listed offenses shall be held in jail pending the Defendant's First Appearance in the absence of a judicial order:

(1) A probable cause arrest for an offense classified as Domestic Violence under RCW 10.99.

(2) A probable cause arrest for an offense classified as Harassment and/or Stalking under RCW 10.14 and/or RCW 9A.46.

2.) INTERFERENCE WITH HEALTH CARE FACILITIES OR HEALTH CARE PROVIDERS — PROBABLE CAUSE ARREST. (1st offense $1,000 Bail and Condition of Release Form; 2nd offense MCA)

(a) First (1st) Offense Bail Rule:

Any person arrested by a Law Enforcement Officer on probable cause for a violation of RCW 9A.50 shall be released from jail pending First Appearance upon posting a cash or surety bond of $1,000 and signing for receipt of the "Additional Conditions for Release Pending Trial" (copy attached to this order.)

(b) Second (2nd) Offense Bail Rule:

Any person arrested for violation of RCW 9A.50 after having been previously released from jail within the immediate past 72 hours for a prior violation of RCW 9A.50 and having previously signed the Additional Conditions for Release Pending Trial shall upon the second (2nd) arrest be held in jail pending his/her First Appearance before a Judicial Officer.

3.) GROSS MISDEMEANOR OR MISDEMEANOR PROBABLE CAUSE ARREST.

(a) EXCEPT AN OFFENSE LISTED IN SECTION ONE (1) OR SECTION TWO (2) ABOVE, THE GENERAL RULE FOR A PERSON ARRESTED ON PROBABLE CAUSE FOR A MISDEMEANOR OR A GROSS MISDEMEANOR SHALL BE A RELEASE PRIOR TO FIRST APPEARANCE UPON THE POSTING OF A SURETY BOND OF $250.00 FOR MISDEMEANORS AND $500.00 FOR GROSS MISDEMEANORS, UNLESS THE ARRESTEE QUALIFIES FOR AN UNSECURED RECOGNIZANCE BOND AS FOLLOWS:

(1) The Defendant is a resident of the State of Washington and lives within 50 miles of the City of Medical Lake, and

(2) The Defendant has been properly identified by fingerprints or other appropriate means; and

(3) The Defendant's physical or mental condition will not jeopardize his/her safety or the safety of other persons, and there is no articulable reason to believe that he/he will seek to intimidate witnesses, or otherwise unlawfully interfere with the administration of justice or the Court, and

(4) The Defendant signs an Unsecured Recognizance Bond and Promise to Appear in Court.

    A. The Unsecured Recognizance Bond on MISDEMEANORS is $250.00.

    B. The Unsecured Recognizance Bond on GROSS MISDEMEANORS is $500.00.

(5) The Defendant has not otherwise demonstrated a failure to respond to any Court process.

4.) WARRANT ARREST

(a) Any person arrested pursuant to a Warrant for the below listed fourteen (14) offenses or the five (5) special warrant categories shall be released only after meeting the conditions set forth on the Warrant:

OFFENSES:

(1) DOMESTIC VIOLENCE OFFENSES charged under RCW 10.99.

(2) HARASSMENT OFFENSES and/or STALKING charged under RCW 10.14 and/or RCW 9A.46.

(3) DRIVING a motor vehicle UNDER THE INFLUENCE of Alcohol and/or Drugs.

(4) PHYSICAL CONTROL of a Motor Vehicle Under the Influence of Alcohol and/or Drugs.

(5) HIT AND RUN ATTENDED vehicle.

(6) DRIVING WHILE SUSPENDED/REVOKED—FIRST or SECOND DEGREE.

(7) RECKLESS DRIVING or RACING of vehicles.

(8) ASSAULT in the 4th degree.

(9) Violation of the PROSTITUTION LAWS.

(10) INTERFERENCE WITH HEALTH CARE FACILITIES OR HEALTH CARE PROVIDERS under RCW 9A.50.

(11) VIOLATION OF RCW 69.50, Uniform Controlled Substances Act, including POSSESSION OF MARIJUANA and DRUG PARAPHERNALIA.

(12) INTIMIDATION WITH A WEAPON.

(13) RECKLESS ENDANGERMENT.

(14) PEDESTRIAN INTERFERENCE.

WARRANT CATEGORIES:

(1) PROBATION VIOLATION and/or MANDATORY COURT APPEARANCE WARRANT.

(2) FELONY WARRANT.

(3) SUPERIOR COURT WARRANT.

(4) A SPOKANE COUNTY DISTRICT COURT OR SPOKANE MUNICIPAL COURT WARRANT issued after June 26, 1995, requiring a cash bond.

(5) A MEDICAL LAKE MUNICIPAL COURT WARRANT issued after March 1, 1996 requiring a cash bond.

EXCEPT AS PROVIDED IN THE FOURTEEN (14) OFFENSES AND FIVE (5) SPECIFIC WARRANT CATEGORIES LISTED ABOVE, a person arrested on a Spokane County District, any other Municipal Court within Spokane County, or Medical Lake Municipal Court Warrant for a Misdemeanor or Gross Misdemeanor may be released on an unsecured recognizance bond under the same terms and conditions itemized in Section Three (3). This Bail Provision shall supersede any contrary bail amount or provision noted on the Misdemeanor or Gross Misdemeanor Warrant, except for the fourteen (14) offenses and five (5) specific warrant categories listed above.

5.) FAILURE TO PAY FINES AND COST WARRANT ARREST—CASH BOND EQUALING OUTSTANDING FINES AND COSTS—MAXIMUM $250.

Any person arrested on a warrant for failing to pay fines and/or cost shall be released pending First Appearance upon the posting of a cash bond equal to the amount of the outstanding fines and costs, provided that the amount of such bond shall in no event exceed $250.00. The provisions of Section Four (4) above shall apply to Warrants issued for failure to comply with probation due to failure to pay restitution.

THIS ORDER SHALL BE IN FULL FORCE AND EFFECT MARCH 1, 1996.

[Adopted effective March 1, 1996.]

SPOKANE MUNICIPAL COURT LOCAL RULES

Including Amendments Received Through
August 15, 2015

Table of Rules

I. INTRODUCTION

SPMGR 7. LOCAL RULES—FILING AND EFFECTIVE DATE

(g) Reference. The provisions of the Local Rules are supplemental to the Rules for Courts of Limited Jurisdiction, as adopted or hereafter amended by the Supreme Court of the State of Washington, and shall not be construed in conflict with them and are submitted pursuant to GR 7(e) with an intent to adopt as changed. These rules may be known and cited as Spokane Municipal Court Local Rules, and shall be referred to as "SPM" along with the corresponding rule abbreviation.

(h) Prior Rules Repealed. These rules supersede and replace any prior rules.

[Adopted effective January 2, 2009; amended effective September 1, 2011.]

SPMGR 14. FORMAT FOR PLEADINGS AND OTHER PAPERS

(a)(i) All pleadings, motions and other papers filed with the court, except original citations, should be legibly written or printed on 8–1/2 by 11 inch paper. The top margin should be at least one inch except as otherwise approved by the court on certain forms.

(ii) Colored pages are allowed for certain court-approved forms.

(iii) All papers filed with the court should be two-hole punched with holes 2 ¾ inches apart centered approximately ½ inch from the top edge of the paper.

[Adopted effective September 1, 2011.]

SPMGR 29. PRESIDING JUDGE

(c) (Reserved)

(f) Duties and Authority of Presiding Judge.

(f)(5)(a) Personnel Assigned to Perform Court Functions

(i) Court Commissioners—Selection. Upon a vacancy for Court Commissioner, the Court may advertise the vacancy and accept applications.

The majority of the Judges shall decide which candidates to interview, and conduct interviews. Any Judge of this Court may attend, participate and vote during the selection process. The selection shall be by majority vote of the Judges present at a regularly scheduled Judges' meeting or a meeting called by the Presiding Judge for this purpose.

(ii) Court Commissioners—Termination. A Court Commissioner shall serve at the pleasure of the Judges and any decision to terminate shall be by a majority vote of Judges at a Judges' meeting.

(f)(5)(c) Court Administrator

(i) Selection. Upon a vacancy, the Judges shall take the necessary step to obtain qualified applicants. The Judges shall screen the written applications, and conduct interviews. Any Judge may attend, participate, and vote. Selection of the Court Administrator shall be by majority vote of Judges present at a regularly scheduled Judges' meeting.

(ii) Termination. The Court Administrator shall serve at the pleasure of the Judges and shall be terminated by a majority vote of judges at a regularly scheduled Judges' meeting.

(iii) Duties of Court Administrator. The Court Administrator shall assist the Presiding Judge in his or her administrative responsibilities. Subject to the general supervision of the Presiding Judge, the Administrator's duties shall include but not be limited to those duties set forth in the job description for the Court Administrator.

(f)(14) Paralegals who are currently registered with the Spokane County Bar Association for the purpose of presentation of such orders may personally present agreed, ex-parte and uncontested orders signed by counsel, based solely upon the documents presented and the record in the file. Said privilege may be revoked or limited by the Court for noncompliance with this rule, or other misconduct, regardless of whether the Paralegal is permitted to present orders before other Courts.

(h) Oversight of Judicial Officers.

(1) The Presiding Judge shall maintain a record of absences by each judicial officer. All Judicial Officers must advise the Presiding Judge if they will not be on campus for the day and whether the reason is work-related or not. This information will be made available to the public by request at the end of each calendar year, provided that information about an ongoing leave will not be made available until after the leave has ended.

[Adopted effective January 2, 2009; amended effective September 1, 2011.]

SPMGR 30. ELECTRONIC FILING

(A)(1)(a) Judicial Signatures: Judicial officers may sign orders with a digital signature, as defined in GR 30. In addition, documents may be signed by judicial officers using an electronic form that contains an electronic copy of the judicial officer's signature so long as the form is saved only on a directory that is accessible only by the judicial officers and so long as the electronic signature is protected so that it cannot be electronically copied. The printed version of these documents shall constitute an original order and shall be placed in the court file. This rule may be amended or supplemented during the year by general order.

(B)(5) Notices of Appearance may be filed electronically by attaching a Notice in Word or .pdf format to an email addressed to eramcnoa@spokanecity.org.

(D)(2)(D)(iii) Any document initiated by a law enforcement officer is presumed to have been signed when the officer uses his or her user ID and password to electronically submit the document to a court or prosecutor through the Statewide Electronic Collision & Traffic Online Records application, the Justice Information Network Data Exchange, or the local secured system "Xpediter" used by the County of Spokane and City of Spokane. Unless otherwise specified, the signature shall be presumed to have been made under penalty of perjury under the laws of the State of Washington and on the date and at the place set forth in the citation.

[Adopted effective September 1, 2011; amended on an emergency basis retroactively effective June 23, 2011; amended on a permanent basis effective September 1, 2012.]

II. CIVIL PROCEEDINGS

SPMCR 1. SCOPE OF RULES

The Spokane Municipal Court has adopted this Local Rule to allow it to exercise jurisdiction granted in ch. 84, § 4 Laws of Wash. 2013 (ESHB 1383.SL, eff. 7/28/13) to hear civil petitions for stalking anti-harassment protection orders and stalking anti-harassment no contact orders as set forth in that law. Upon exercising such jurisdiction, it will transfer to Superior Court any petition when it is shown that (a) the petitioner, victim, or respondent to the petition is under eighteen years of age; (b) the action involves title or possession of real property; (c) a superior court has exercised or is exercising jurisdiction over a proceeding involving the parties; or (d) the action would have the effect of interfering with a respondent's care, control, or custody of the respondent's minor child.

[Adopted effective September 2, 2013.]

III. CRIMINAL MATTERS

SPMCrRLJ 3.1. ASSIGNMENT OF COUNSEL

(d) Assignment of Lawyer.

(1)(a) A determination of financial eligibility is valid for 180 days so long as the Defendant's financial circumstances are not materially changed.

(e) Withdrawal of Public Defender. Unless a Notice of Appeal has been filed, an attorney appointed at public expense shall be deemed automatically withdrawn from representation immediately upon the filing of an order dismissing the case, or sixty days following a final decision of the court as defined in the RALJ without having to file any document with the court. A "final decision" includes an order of dismissal, a judgment and sentence, a deferred prosecution, a Stipulated Order of Continuance, or any other similar disposition.

[Adopted effective January 2, 2009; amended effective September 1, 2011.]

SPMCrRLJ 3.2.   RELEASE OF ACCUSED

(k) Reserved

(*o*) Bail in Criminal Offense Cases—Mandatory Appearance.

(1) A bail schedule for persons arrested on probable cause, except such schedule as is mandated by CrRLJ 3.2(*o*), may be established by a majority vote of the Judges. The Schedule may be revised from time to time in the interests of justice and available in the Clerk's office. The bail schedule shall be a General Order and not part of the Local Rules. A copy of the General Order setting forth the bail schedule shall be furnished to the jail.

(2) Any person arrested by a Law Enforcement Officer on Probable Cause (without an arrest warrant) for the below listed offenses shall be held in jail pending the Defendant's First Appearance in the absence of a judicial order:

(a) An offense classified as Domestic Violence under Chapter 10.99 of the Revised Code of Washington or an equivalent local ordinance.

(b) An offense classified as Harassment and/or Stalking under Chapters 10.14 and/or 9A.46 of the Revised Code of Washington or an equivalent local ordinance.

[Adopted effective January 2, 2009; amended effective September 1, 2011.]

SPMCrRLJ 3.3.   TIME FOR TRIAL

(f) Continuances.

Form and Procedure. A continuance in a criminal matter shall be requested on a Case Scheduling Order, stating the reason necessitating the continuance request.

[Adopted effective January 2, 2009; amended effective September 1, 2011.]

SPMCrRLJ 3.4.   PRESENCE OF THE DEFENDANT

(a) When Necessary.

(1) *Pre-trial Hearings.* The assigned Judge will determine if a Pre-trial hearing shall be scheduled after the arraignment. The defendant shall be required to attend the Pre-trial hearing unless excused

by the Court. Failure to attend may result in issuance of a bench warrant and/or forfeiture of any bond.

(2) *Counter–Appearance.* A defendant who receives a Jail Release Appearance form that does not include a hearing date must appear at the Court Appearance Counter within the time provided in the notice to obtain a hearing date. A defendant wishing to be represented by the Public Defender, and who has not been screened in the last six months, will be screened for eligibility.

(d) Video Conference Proceedings.

(2)(i) Agreement. The trial court judge may approve other trial court proceedings, including the entry of a Statement of Defendant on Plea of Guilty as provided by CrRLJ 4.2, upon agreement of the parties, either in writing or on the record.

[Adopted effective January 2, 2009; amended effective September 1, 2011.]

SPMCrRLJ 4.1.   ARRAIGNMENT

(g) Appearance by Defendant's Lawyer. Attorneys retained by defendants, or public defenders who have assumed representation of defendants must promptly serve written notice of their appearance upon the prosecuting attorney, and file the same with the Clerk. The notice of appearance shall be contained in a separate document.

[Adopted effective January 2, 2009; amended effective September 1, 2011.]

SPMCrRLJ 4.2.   PROCEDURE UPON A PLEA OF GUILTY

(g) Written Statement. Guilty plea forms are available on the Washington State Court website http://www.courts.wa.gov/forms.

(i) Deferred Prosecution

a. A Petition for Deferred Prosecution shall be filed at the time a defendant moves the court to grant a deferred prosecution under RCW Chapter 10.05. The petition shall be substantially in the form provided on the Washington State Court website (http://www.courts.wa.gov/forms).

b. The written assessment prepared by an approved treatment facility shall be accompanied by a recommendation from Municipal Probation, or such other Court Designee authorized under Chapter 10.05 of the Revised Code of Washington.

[Adopted effective January 2, 2009; amended effective September 1, 2011.]

SPMCrRLJ 4.7.   DISCOVERY

(e) Discretionary Disclosures.

(3) Any motion for items and information not covered by Section (a) and (d) of CrRLJ 4.7 shall be accompanied by an affidavit setting forth in detail the reasons the requested items and information are material and significant enough to amount to a denial of

the right to a fair trial, if not ordered discoverable, so that the Court may have a basis for its ruling.

[Adopted effective January 2, 2009; amended effective September 1, 2011.]

SPMCrRLJ 8.2. MOTIONS

(a) **Calendar Settings.** All motions shall be initiated and scheduled by filing a court-approved "Motion" form with the court clerk.

(b) **Dispositive Motions and Motions to Suppress Evidence.** Dispositive Motions and Motions to Suppress shall be filed and served at least three (3) weeks prior to the hearing and heard not later than one (1) week before the case is set for trial. The responding party shall file and serve any responding brief or memoranda one (1) week prior to Motion Hearing. Provided, however, that the Court may waive this requirement if due diligence has been shown or justice otherwise requires. It is the duty of the moving party to notify the assigned Judge by noon of the day prior to the motion day if oral testimony is required and estimated length of time required for the Motion. This rule does not authorize oral testimony when the facts can be adequately presented by affidavit and other documentary evidence.

(c) **Agreed Orders—Criminal Cases.** Agreed Orders may be presented ex parte for approval or denial by any Judge or Commissioner. Submitted orders that are denied must be noted on the Order and initialed by the judicial officer making that decision.

(d) **Copies of Motions, Memoranda and Affidavits.** A copy of the motion, brief, memorandum, documents and affidavits shall be furnished to the Judge after the originals have been filed. Responding briefs, memoranda, and other documents shall also be filed with the Clerk, and copies furnished to the assigned Judge. Working copies may be delivered to the Judicial Secretary by hard copy or email in Microsoft Word or Adobe Acrobat format. Working copies must contain a notation in the caption with the date of the motion and the notation "Working Copy." Failure to comply with this requirement may result in a continuance and imposition of terms.

(e) **Motion Hearing Procedure.** Oral argument on motions shall be limited to ten (10) minutes for each side unless the Judge determines otherwise, in which case the motion may be placed at the end of the calendar.

(f) **Reconsideration of Motions.** A motion for reconsideration shall be clearly labeled. Motions for Reconsideration may not simply re-argue the original motion, but must allege a change in law or circumstances that would materially affect the court's prior decision on the motion and may be summarily denied. A response to a motion for reconsideration may be filed, but is not required unless requested by the court. The request will set a time when the response is due, and may limit the response to particular issues or points raised by the motion.

[Adopted effective January 2, 2009; amended effective September 1, 2011.]

SPMCrRLJ 8.4. SERVICE, FILING AND SIGNING OF PAPERS

(c) **Filing with the Court.**

(1) All pleadings must contain the case number(s) noted above the document title. Pleadings that do not include the correct case number may be refused by the Clerk or returned by the Court.

[Adopted effective September 1, 2011.]

IV. INFRACTIONS

SPMIRLJ 2.2. INITIATION OF INFRACTION CASES

(d) **Filing of Notice.**

(1) Whenever a Notice of Infraction has been issued and not filed with the Court within 5 days of issuance, the Clerk or his/her designee may note the citation "Dismissed without prejudice per SPMIRLJ 2.2," and take no further action.

[Adopted effective January 2, 2009; amended effective September 1, 2011.]

SPMIRLJ 2.4. RESPONSE TO NOTICE

(b) **Alternatives.**

(4) The procedure authorized in IRLJ 2.4(b)(4) is adopted by this Court.

[Adopted effective January 2, 2009; amended effective September 1, 2011.]

SPMIRLJ 2.6. SCHEDULING OF HEARINGS

(a) **Contested Hearings.**

(1)(i) The procedure authorized in IRLJ 2.6 (a)(1)(i) for scheduling of a prehearing conference is adopted by this Court.

[Adopted on an emergency basis effective January 27, 2012; adopted on a permanent basis effective September 1, 2012.]

SPMIRLJ 3.4. HEARING ON MITIGATING CIRCUMSTANCES

(c) **Disposition.**

(1) *Written Request for Penalty Reduction.* A defendant requesting a reduction of the Infraction penalty may have such determination based on his or her prior driving record without an explanation of the event cited. The amount of the reduction shall be set

by the Court in a written Order maintained in the Clerk's Office and available upon request.

[Adopted effective January 2, 2009; amended effective September 1, 2011.]

SPMIRLJ 3.5. DECISION ON WRITTEN STATEMENTS

The Spokane Municipal Court has adopted a local option as set forth in IRLJ 3.5 for those electing to submit their case for decision on written statement in lieu of contesting or mitigating at a hearing on the record.

[Adopted effective January 2, 2009; amended effective September 1, 2011; September 1, 2012.]

SPMIRLJ 6.8. MOTION PRACTICE

All motion settings shall be served on the Prosecuting Attorney for the City five (5) days prior to the date set on the Motion and Order Form. The Municipal Court Clerk's Office shall furnish dates each week for the hearing of motions on contested infractions. It will be at the discretion of the Judge or Commissioner, after ruling on the motion, whether the infraction can then proceed to contested hearing immediately, or be reset on a contested docket. Failure to comply with the above procedure may result in the Court striking the motion.

[Adopted effective January 2, 2009; amended effective September 1, 2011.]

STEVENS COUNTY

Table of Courts

Superior Court

Local Rules for the Superior Courts of Ferry, Pend Oreille and Stevens Counties.

District Court

Stevens County District Court.

SUPERIOR COURT

LOCAL RULES FOR THE SUPERIOR COURTS OF FERRY, PEND OREILLE AND STEVENS COUNTIES

PUBLISHER'S NOTE

The Local Rules for the Superior Courts of Ferry, Pend Oreille and Stevens Counties are set forth under Ferry County.

DISTRICT COURT

LOCAL RULES FOR THE DISTRICT COURT IN AND FOR STEVENS COUNTY

Including Amendments Received Through August 15, 2015

Table of Rules

I. LOCAL ADMINISTRATIVE RULES

SCLGR 11. INTERPRETERS

All language interpreters serving in a legal proceeding, whether certified or uncertified, shall abide by General Rule 11.1 and General Rule 11.2

[Adopted effective September 1, 2009.]

SCLARLJ 2. SCOPE OF LOCAL RULES

These rules govern the procedure in the District Court of the State of Washington for Stevens County. These rules are supplemental to the rules enacted by the Washington State Supreme Court for courts of limited jurisdiction as specifically authorized by GR 7, CRLJ 83, CrRLJ 1.7, and IRLJ 1.3 of the Washington Court Rules. The court may modify or suspend any of these local rules in any given case upon good cause being shown or upon the court's own motion.

[Adopted effective September 1, 2009.]

SCLARLJ 2.1. DECORUM

Courtroom Decorum. All attorneys and other individuals in the courtroom shall abide by the following rules of conduct:

(a) **Always be prompt.** Be in the courtroom ready to proceed at the appointed time.

(b) **Stand** when the judge or the jury enters or leaves the courtroom.

(c) **Do not** make personal attacks on opposing counsel or parties.

(d) **Do not interrupt.** Wait your turn. Address all remarks to the Judge. Argument between litigants or their attorneys is not permitted.

(e) After the judge has ruled, **ask** the Judge's permission before arguing further.

(f) **Rise** when addressing the judge and when making objections as this calls the Judge's attention to you.

(g) **Do not** approach a witness, the jury or the Judge without asking permission of the Judge.

(h) **Dress Appropriately to the Serious Nature of the Matters Before the Court.** Shorts and other kinds of beach apparel are not appropriate. Clothing advertising alcoholic beverages or illegal drugs are not appropriate. Hats are not to be worn in the courtroom.

(i) **No food or beverages** of any kind are to be brought into the courtroom.

(j) **Cell phones, pagers, electronic games** are to be turned off in the courtroom.

[Adopted effective September 1, 2009.]

SCLARLJ 3. RETURN OF EXHIBITS

Every exhibit admitted into evidence or marked for identification in any type of trial or other court proceeding, shall be returned to the party or attorney who produced that exhibit for identification. The return shall be made upon written application, not later than two weeks following the termination of the time allowed to take an appeal. Bulky exhibits not requested to be returned during that period may be delivered by the court clerk to the local law enforcement authority for disposition as abandoned property. If the exhibit is contraband or weapons, it shall be disposed of by destruction. No exhibit or identification shall be withdrawn or delivered without receipt being acknowledged by the receiving party.

[Adopted effective September 1, 2009.]

SCLARLJ 6. APPEARANCE BY TELEPHONE

Hearings of any type will not be conducted by telephone without prior approval of the judge on a showing of good cause.

[Adopted effective September 1, 2009.]

SCLARLJ 9. DISCLOSURE OF PUBLIC RECORDS

The following records and files are deemed confidential and are not available to the public for inspection or copying absent a court order:

1. Affidavits, transcriptions or electronic records for search warrants prior to the return of service of such warrants;

2. Affidavits, transcriptions or electronic records for arrest warrants prior to the return of service of such warrants;

3. Pre-sentence or post-sentence investigation reports;

4. Mental health, psychiatric, and/or medical reports and records, unless admitted into evidence and not ordered sealed;

5. Alcohol, drug, and/or controlled substance evaluations unless admitted into evidence and not ordered sealed;

6. Certified and non-certified paper copies and electronic representation of driving and criminal records unless admitted into evidence;

7. Judge's notes and working documents, whether written or electronic.

Access to confidential records is strictly limited to persons or entities authorized by statute or court order to obtain such records. Persons requesting access to court records must have proper identification.

[Adopted effective September 1, 2009.]

II. LOCAL CIVIL RULES
SCLCRLJ 54. JUDGMENTS AND COSTS

(c) **Demand for Judgment.**

(1) *Ex Parte Judgments and Orders.* Counsel, legal interns and legal assistants presenting a judgment or seeking entry of an order shall be responsible to see that all papers pertaining thereto are filed and that the court file is provided to the judge. Counsel may present routine ex parte or stipulated matters based on the record in the file by mail addressed to the Court. Self-addressed, stamped envelopes shall be provided for return of any conformed materials and/or rejected orders. Only one conformed copy will be returned to the presenting counsel.

(d) **Attorney Fees**

(1) Statutory attorney fees may be granted when reasonable attorney fees are not authorized. Statutory attorney fees will be as specified in RCW 12.20.060: if plaintiff obtains judgment, exclusive of costs, of at least $200.00, attorney fees of $200.00 shall be included; if plaintiff obtains judgment, exclusive of costs, of less than $200.00, then attorney fees of $125.00 shall be included.

(2) If reasonable attorney fees are requested based on a contract provision, the contract provision must be conspicuously highlighted to be readily ascertainable.

(3) Reasonable attorney fees when allowed by statute or contract will be authorized pursuant to the following attorney fee schedule in all default cases unless the parties present evidence of circumstances which convince the court that a greater or

lesser amount should be awarded. The Court shall have the authority to vary from the following schedule on its own motion.

Amount of principal and interest	Attorney fee
$0 --- $500.00	$250.00
$500 --- $1000.00	$300.00
$1000.01 --- $1500.00	$350.00
$1500.01 --- $2000.00	$400.00
$2000.01 --- $2500.00	$450.00
$2500.01 --- $3000.00	$500.00
$3000.01 --- $4000.00	$550.00
$4000.01 --- $5000.00	$600.00
$5000.01 --- $6000.00	$650.00
$6000.01 --- $7500.00	$700.00
$7500.01 --- $10,000.00	$850.00
Over $10,000.00	10%

(4) Specific citation of authority must accompany requests for reasonable attorney fees on any basis other than contract provision.

[Adopted effective September 1, 2009.]

SCLCRLJ 55. DEFAULT

(a) Entry of Default Judgment.

(5) All necessary papers required for entry of a default judgment shall be filed at the same time as the motion for default judgment, unless extended by court order to correct a clerical error or omission or for furnishing of any proof required by the court. Default judgments shall be subject to the following:

(6) No default judgment shall be granted except upon motion by plaintiff's attorney of record, or if none, by motion of plaintiff.

(7) No default judgment shall be granted except upon proof satisfactory to the court. The court shall require at least the following to be on file with the motion for default judgment, unless otherwise excused by the court for good cause:

(i) on assigned causes of action, the assignment instrument;

(ii) on causes of action based on a negotiable instrument, the original negotiable instrument;

(iii) on causes of action based on a retail sales contract, chattel mortgage, or conditional sales contract, the original contract (or a copy if the original has been filed with a government agency). Where applicable, an automobile title or bill of sale must be filed;

(iv) on causes of action based on open account where the complaint is not specific, a written statement of account setting forth all charges and credits and the dates thereof, the nature of merchandise or services furnished, and a statement of any interest or surcharges which are included;

(v) on causes of action for rent based on an oral lease, a statement of account setting forth the dates of accrued rent, dates of delinquency, late charges and any other costs. If any claim is made for damages or repairs to premises, such claim must be itemized separately;

(vi) on causes of action for rent based on a written lease, a copy of the lease and a statement of account setting forth the dates of accrued rent, dates of delinquency, late charges and any other costs. If any claim is made for damages or repairs to premises, such claim must be itemized separately;

(vii) on causes of action based on all other contracts, oral testimony to prove performance may be required, together with filing of a copy of the contract, if written; and filing or proving the items of account and any credits;

(viii) on causes of action for tort, the proof required shall be the same as required above for proving contract balances except that the following additional proof of the amount of damage shall be required:

* Property damage may be proved by repair bills or estimates;

* Loss of use claims, loss of wages, and pain and suffering shall be proved by oral testimony;

* Hospital and doctor bills may be proved by written bills, whether paid or not.

(8) No judgment for interest shall be allowed unless citation to applicable authority is presented and there is on file proof of the factors necessary for computation of interest including applicable dates, rate of

interest, amounts subject to interest, and a computation of the total interest claimed due.

(9) Default Judgments must be accompanied by:

(i) Affidavit of Service if not previously filed.

(ii) Affidavit of Soldiers' and Sailors' Relief Act.

(g) Collection and handling charges and attorney fees on actions brought to collect dishonored checks shall not be allowed unless proof of the following is provided:

(1) The statutory form of notice of dishonor has been sent as required by RCW chapter 62.A–3 and a copy is filed with the court.

(2) An accounting statement, or some reasonable alternate means of determining the plaintiffs collection costs, is filed with the court.

[Adopted effective September 1, 2009.]

SCLCRLJ 65.   NAME CHANGES

(a) Separate Petitions Required. A separate petition shall be filed for each name a party wishes changed.

(b) Petitioner must produce some form of identification, preferably picture ID, to the clerk for verification and copying.

(c) Hearing. All hearings on petitions for name changes shall be in open court and on the record.

(d) Minors.

(1) *Birth Certificate.* A certified copy of any minor applicant's birth certificate or suitable identification must be presented to the clerk for verification and copying.

(2) *Parental Consent.* All applicants under eighteen (18) years of age must be represented by a parent or legal guardian and both biological or legal parents or guardians must approve the change of name either by personal appearance or by verified affidavit, unless good cause is shown.

(3) *Parental Notification.* A parent or guardian who has not consented in writing to a minor's change of name and whose parental rights have not been previously terminated must be given actual notice or notice by publication as provided in CRLJ 4.

(4) *Notice by Publication.* Publication of a single notice in a newspaper of general circulation in the county of the parent or guardian's last known residence shall be sufficient so long as the notice contains a hearing date, the name of the minor, the name the petitioner desires the child to assume, and sets forth the reasons for requesting the change of name.

(e) Contents of Petition. A petition for change of name must be sworn under oath and state the following:

(1) The Petitioner's full present name and the full name the petitioner wishes to assume;

(2) The Petitioner's date of birth;

(3) That the Petitioner resides in Stevens County;

(4) The reason for the request;

(5) The application is not made for any illegal or fraudulent purposes;

(6) The name change will not be detrimental to the interests of any other person or agency;

(7) The name of the minor's father and mother, if brought on behalf of a minor;

(8) Whether the Petitioner is subject to the jurisdiction of the Washington State Department of Corrections and, if so, that Petitioner has provided a copy of the Petition to the Department at least five (5) days before any hearing on the name change request;

(9) Whether the Petitioner is subject to the sex offender registration laws of the state of Washington and, if so, that Petitioner has provided copies of the Petition to the county sheriff and the Washington State Patrol at least five (5) days before any hearing on the name change request.

[Adopted effective September 1, 2009.]

III.   LOCAL CRIMINAL RULES

SCLCrRLJ 2.1(c).   CITIZEN COMPLAINTS

Any person filing a criminal citizen complaint pursuant to CrRLJ 2.1(c) must provide a sworn written statement of the probable cause supporting the crimes alleged. The judge will review the alleged crimes and the probable cause statement to determine whether the request should be granted or denied. At the discretion of the judge, a hearing may be set to hear additional evidence or to allow the named defendant or the prosecuting attorney an opportunity to present evidence in opposition to the filing of the complaint. If the judge grants or denies the filing of the complaint on the basis of the sworn affidavit without

hearing, the judge shall state in writing the reasons for granting or denying the filing of the complaint.

[Adopted effective September 1, 2009.]

SCLCrRLJ 4.1(f).   CRIMES REQUIRING DEFENDANT'S APPEARANCE AT ARRAIGNMENT

A written plea of not guilty may not be entered by defendant's lawyer if the charging document accuses the defendant of any of the following crimes:

1. any crime charged as involving domestic violence;

2. harassment;

3. violation of a D.V. protection order;

4. violation of an anti-harassment order;

5. stalking;

6. driving or being in physical control while under the influence of intoxicants;

7. driving while under the age of 21 after having consumed alcohol.

For such charges, the defendant must appear in person for arraignment in order that the court may determine the necessity of imposing conditions of pre-trial release, or modifying any pre-trial release conditions entered at a preliminary hearing and to schedule further hearings.

[Adopted effective September 1, 2009.]

SCLCrRLJ 4.2(i). DEFERRED PROSECUTION

Petitions for deferred prosecutions may be filed at any time prior to or at the trial readiness hearing unless good cause is shown. The petition should be in the form as specified in CrRLJ 4.2(i). The evaluation and the stipulated police reports should be attached to the petition. Upon filing of the petition, the defendant and defense attorney should, but are not required, meet with probation to verify that the evaluation and the defendant's history meet the requirements of RCW Chapter 10.05.

[Adopted effective September 1, 2009.]

SCLCrRLJ 4.5. PRE-TRIAL HEARING

(a) All cases shall be set for a pre-trial hearing no later than 45 days after arraignment. Defendant, defense attorney, and the prosecuting attorney are required to attend the pre-trial hearing unless excused prior to the hearing by the court upon a showing of good cause. If the defendant fails to appear for the pre-trial hearing, a failure to appear may be entered and the scheduled jury trial be struck, or a warrant for the arrest of the defendant may issue. If the prosecuting attorney or the defense attorney fails to appear at the pre-trial hearing without a prior showing of good cause, the court may impose terms and any other sanctions authorized by law.

(b) Any amendments to the charge(s), pre-trial motions, including motions for continuances and discovery motions shall be made at the pre-trial hearing. At the pre-trial hearing, the court will schedule dates and times for any pre-trial motions.

[Adopted effective September 1, 2009.]

SCLCrRLJ 4.5.1. TRIAL READINESS HEARING

(a) All cases shall be set for a trial readiness hearing at least 2 weeks prior to the scheduled trial week. Defendant, defense attorney, and the prosecuting attorney are required to attend the trial readiness hearing. If the defendant fails to appear, a warrant for the arrest of the defendant may be issued. If the prosecuting attorney or the defense attorney fails to appear for the trial readiness hearing without a prior showing of good cause, the court may impose terms.

(b) Any additional amendments to the charge(s), negotiated pleas, alternate dispositions, continuances, etc. shall be made at the trial readiness hearing.

(c) At the trial readiness hearing, the court shall set the actual trial date.

(d) After the trial readiness hearing and setting of the trial date, no negotiated pleas or alternative dispositions will be entered without a showing of good cause. Without a showing of good cause the matter will proceed to trial as charged, or the defendant may enter a plea to the crime as charged, or the case dismissed by the prosecuting attorney.

[Adopted effective September 1, 2009.]

SCLCrRLJ 8.2. MOTIONS

Rules CrRLJ 3.5 and 3.6 and CRLJ 7(b) shall govern motions in criminal cases. Unless a motion is made during a hearing (other than the pre-trial hearing) or trial, it shall be made in writing, shall state with particularity the grounds therefore, and set forth the relief or order sought. The motion shall be filed prior to or at the pre-trial hearing, except for good cause shown. A hearing date and time for the motion will be set by the court at the pre-trial hearing.

(a) Any brief, memorandum, documents and affidavits in support of the motion must be filed and served on opposing counsel two weeks prior to the actual hearing date on the motion, except for good cause. Any response brief, memorandum, documents and affidavits must be filed and served on opposing counsel one week prior to the actual hearing date, except for good cause.

(b) A courtesy copy of any brief, memorandum, documents and affidavits filed in support of and in response to the motion must be provided for the Judge at the time of filing.

[Adopted effective September 1, 2009.]

SCLCrRLJ 8.13. NOTE FOR HEARING

Adding Case To Docket. In order to add a case to the court's docket, a written note for hearing must be filed with the District Court Clerk's office and served on the opposing party at least two hours prior to the time of the hearing.

[Adopted effective September 1, 2009.]

IV. LOCAL INFRACTION RULES

SCLIRLJ 2.6(b). MITIGATION HEARINGS BY MAIL

In conformity with IRLJ 2.6, this court exercises its local option to allow mitigation by written document.

A person who has been cited for a civil or traffic infraction may request to mitigate the infraction by mail. Upon receipt of the request for a mitigation hearing, forms for a written statement in mitigation will be sent to the cited person. The person should complete the form and return it to the court. Upon receipt of the completed forms by return mail, the Judge will review the citation and the written statement in mitigation. Upon reaching a decision, the court will then notify the person of the Judge's determination. The person then must remit any amount set by the Judge. If the amount set by the Judge is not paid by the specified date the failure to respond fee will be added and the matter will be turned over to a collection agency. If the citation is a traffic infraction, the Department of Licensing will be notified if the person fails to respond or to pay.

This court does not accept written statements for contested infractions.

This court does not accept written statements submitted by e-mail for mitigation or contested civil or traffic infractions.

[Adopted effective September 1, 2009.]

SCLIRLJ 3.6. PRESENCE OF PROSECUTING ATTORNEY

The prosecuting attorney's office shall appear in any contested hearing in which a request has been made to subpoena an officer or a witness. The prosecuting attorney's office shall also appear in any contested hearing in which the alleged infraction was not conducted in the presence of the officer or when the appearance of witnesses is necessary to establish the commission of the infraction.

[Adopted effective September 1, 2009.]

THURSTON COUNTY

Table of Courts

Superior Court

Thurston County Superior Court Local Court Rules.

District Court

Thurston County District Court Local Rules.

Municipal Courts

Olympia Municipal Court Local Court Rules.
Rainier Municipal Court—[No Local Rules].
Tenino Municipal Court—[No Local Rules].
Tumwater Municipal Court Local Court Rules.
Yelm Municipal Court [No Local Rules].

SUPERIOR COURT

THURSTON COUNTY SUPERIOR COURT LOCAL COURT RULES

Including Amendments Received Through August 15, 2015

Table of Rules

LOCAL GENERAL RULES

LGR 7.   LOCAL RULES—FILING AND EFFECTIVE DATE

(d) Availability of Local Rules. The appendix of forms and appendix of calendar information, referenced throughout these local rules, are available to the public on the Thurston County Superior Court web site, as well as in the Thurston County Superior Court libraries, court administration, and courtrooms at the main campus and Family and Juvenile Court.

[Adopted effective September 1, 2011.]

LGR 28.   JURY SERVICE POSTPONE-MENT, EXCUSAL, AND DISQUAL-IFICATION

(b) Delegation of authority to postpone, excuse, or disqualify.

(1) The Thurston County Superior Court judges delegate to court administration staff the authority to disqualify, postpone, or excuse a potential juror from jury duty for the reasons stated in this local court rule.

(c) Grounds for postponement of service. Court administration staff may postpone jury service as provided in GR 28(c).

(d) Grounds for excusal from service.

(1) The following are reasons jurors may be granted an excuse from jury duty:

(A) Verified medical condition if documented by a physician's statement, and elderly persons who have a medical or physical condition that prevents service as a juror.

(B) Jury service within the last year as described in RCW 2.36.100(3) ("at least two weeks of jury service within the preceding twelve months.").

(C) Sole care provider for dependent family members.

(D) Undue financial hardship, outlined in writing, when a person is not compensated for jury service by an employer, or self-employed persons who would incur financial hardship.

(E) Employee who is indispensable, as documented by employer with employee's knowledge and agreement, but only if they are unable to be assigned to serve on a short jury trial. College students may have their jury service postponed to a time when courses are not being conducted; and

(F) A showing that excusal from jury service is a public necessity.

(2) The court may require written documentation to support a request for excusal from jury service. Requests to be excused that are not made before the day of jury service must be referred directly to the judge hearing the case.

[Adopted effective September 2, 2014.]

LGR 29.   PRESIDING JUDGE IN SUPERI-OR COURT DISTRICT AND LIMITED JURISDICTION COURT DISTRICT

(a) Election, Term, Vacancies, Removal and Selection Criteria—Multiple Judge Courts.

(1) *Election.* The Board of Judges shall elect a Presiding Judge and an Assistant Presiding Judge by majority vote at a Board of Judges meeting held during October or November of odd numbered years. Vacancies in the office of Presiding Judge or Assistant Presiding Judge shall be filled by majority vote of the Board of Judges at the first Board of Judges meeting held after the vacancy is known to exist.

(g) Executive Committee.

(1) *Membership.* The judges of the superior court, sitting as a whole as an executive committee, shall advise and assist the Presiding Judge in the administration of the court.

(2) *Liaison Judges.* Each judge shall be assigned responsibility for certain management areas and court functions. The responsibility of the assigned judge is to act as a liaison between the court and others concerned about court management or function. The superior court administrator shall keep a list of the liaison assignments that is available to the public.

[Adopted effective September 1, 2010.]

LGR 30. ELECTRONIC FILING

(b) Electronic Filing Authorization, Exception, Service, and Technology Equipment.

(1) The clerk may accept for filing an electronic document that complies with the court rules and the Electronic Filing Technical Standards. Electronic filing of documents with the clerk using the Thurston County Clerk's eFile Service or an electronic service provider that uses the Clerk's eFile Service is permitted if the transmission of documents is done in a manner approved by the clerk. All electronically filed pleadings shall be formatted in accordance with the applicable rules governing formatting of paper pleadings, including GR 14.

(2) A document that is required by law to be filed in non-electronic media may not be electronically filed. The following documents must be filed in paper form, not electronically filed:

(i) Original wills and codicils, including new probate cases that include original wills or codicils;

(ii) Certified records of proceedings for purposes of appeal;

(iii) Documents presented for filing during a court hearing or trial;

(iv) Documents for filing in an aggravated murder case;

(v) Administrative law review (ALR) petitions;

(vi) Interpleader or surplus funds petitions;

(vii) Documents submitted for in camera review under GR 15,

(viii) Affidavits for writs of garnishment and writs of execution; and

(ix) New cases or fee based documents filed with a motion and order to waive filing fees.

(5) Documents that are electronically filed do not need to be submitted to the clerk's office for filing on paper, unless paper is required under LCR 30(b)(2). However, parties are required to follow the local court rules regarding judge's copies, LCR 5(k).

(c) Time for Filing, Confirmation, and Rejection.

(1) An electronic document is considered filed with the clerk when it is received by the clerk's designated computer during the clerk's business hours. Any document electronically filed with the clerk by 5:00 p.m. Pacific Time on a business day shall be deemed filed with the clerk on that date. A document filed after 5:00 p.m. or on a non-business day shall be considered filed on the next business day.

(3) The clerk may reject a document that fails to comply with applicable electronic filing requirements. The clerk must notify the filing party of the rejection and the reason therefore. The clerk may also reject a document under its faulty documents policy, which can be found on the clerk's web site.

(d) Authentication of Electronic Documents.

(3) *Court Facilitated Electronically Captured Signatures*—Use of electronic filing by a party or attorney shall constitute compliance with CR 11's signature requirement. Documents containing signatures of third-parties (for example, affidavits and stipulations) may also be filed electronically as set forth in GR 30(d)(2). A copy of the electronically filed document with signatures shall be maintained in paper or electronic form by the filing party and made available for inspection by other parties or the court upon request.

(e) Filing Fees, Electronic Filing Fees.

(1) All statutory filing fees shall be collected and paid for electronically filed documents according to the methods approved by the Thurston County Clerk.

[Adopted effective September 2, 2013.]

LGR 31. ACCESS TO COURT RECORDS [RESCINDED]

[Rescinded effective September 1, 2006.]

LGR 33. REQUESTS FOR ACCOMMODATION UNDER THE ADA

(b) Process for Requesting Accommodation.

(1) Requests for accommodation under GR 33 shall be presented to either the Superior Court Administrator or the Assistant Superior Court Administrator, provided, that a need for accommodation that arises less than 48 hours before a scheduled hearing, may be presented to the judicial officer scheduled to hear the proceeding.

[Adopted effective September 1, 2007.]

LOCAL CIVIL RULES FOR SUPERIOR COURT

I. INTRODUCTORY

LCR 0.1 DEPARTMENT NUMBERS [REPEALED]

[Effective October 1, 1982; amended effective September 1, 1997; January 10, 2005; amended effective November 29, 2006. Repealed effective September 1, 2010.]

LCR 0.2. COURT MANAGEMENT AND ORGANIZATION [REPEALED]

[Amended effective September 1, 1994; September 1, 2000; May 2, 2002; September 1, 2003; September 1, 2006. Repealed effective September 1, 2010.]

LCR 0.3. STANDING AND SPECIAL COMMITTEES [REPEALED]

[Repealed effective September 1, 2010.]

LCR 0.4. SPECIAL DEPARTMENTS OR DIVISIONS [REPEALED]

[Amended effective September 1, 1994; September 1, 1997; September 1, 2003. Repealed effective September 1, 2010.]

LCR 0.5. DEPARTMENTS AND DIVISIONS OF THE COURT, ASSIGNMENTS AND SCHEDULES [REPEALED]

[Amended effective September 1, 1997; September 1, 2000; January 1, 2007. Repealed effective September 1, 2010.]

LCR 0.6. SPECIAL PROCEEDINGS [REPEALED]

[Amended effective September 1, 1997; January 1, 2007. Repealed effective September 1, 2010.]

LCR 1. SCOPE OF RULES

These local civil rules do not apply to proceedings heard at Family and Juvenile Court pursuant to LSPR 94.00.

[Adopted effective September 1, 2010.]

II. COMMENCEMENT OF ACTION: SERVICE OF PROCESS PLEADINGS, MOTIONS AND ORDERS (Rules 3–6)

LCR 3. COMMENCEMENT OF ACTIONS

(e) Procedures at Time of Filing. The following procedures shall be followed when a civil case is filed, unless a special procedure applies or otherwise directed by the court.

(1) *Assignment and Reassignment of Judge.*

(A) Cases that are assigned to a judge. All civil cases shall be assigned to a trial judge, unless these rules provide otherwise. The court clerk will assign the case by random selection to a judge in the trial department, who will hear and decide all issues in the case unless the assigned judge or the court's presiding judge directs otherwise. The case will be reassigned if the assigned judge recuses, is disqualified from hearing the case, or is no longer assigned to the trial department. The court will not individually notify parties when a case is reassigned because a judge is no longer assigned to the trial department. The court will instead make public notices about such reassignments.

(B) Cases that are not assigned to a judge. The court clerk will not assign a judge for the following types of cases:

(i) Unlawful detainer cases;

(ii) Appeals from a department of licensing revocation;

(iii) Civil, non-traffic infraction appeal cases;

(iv) Civil, traffic infraction appeal cases;

(v) Tax warrants;

(vi) Petitions for relief from registration as a sex or kidnapping offender;

(vii) Petitions to restore firearm rights; and

(viii) Foreign subpoenas.

A party may file a motion to ask for a judge assignment for these cases. The court may also direct the clerk to issue a judge assignment on its own motion.

(2) *Assignment of Trial Scheduling Date.* The court clerk shall assign a trial scheduling date to all civil cases subject to this rule, unless it is the following type of case:

(A) Unlawful detainer cases

(B) Tax warrants;

(C) Petitions for relief from registration as a sex or kidnapping offender;

(D) Petitions to restore firearm rights;

(E) Transcripts of judgments;

(F) Subpoenas;

(G) Abstracts of judgments or filing of a judgment from another jurisdiction;

(H) Minor settlements; or

(I) Public Records Act Cases. Public Records Act cases have expedited scheduling under LCR 16, "Pretrial Procedure and Motions."

Further, a party requesting a trial de novo shall obtain a trial scheduling date under the procedure outlined in the Local Mandatory Arbitration Rules (LMAR 7.1).

(3) *Notice of Assignment and Notice of Trial Scheduling.* The court clerk will prepare and file a "notice of assignment and notice of trial scheduling" in accordance with these rules and court policy, on a form that the court approved. The clerk will provide one copy to the plaintiff or petitioner. The notice of assignment and notice of trial scheduling will designate the case title and cause number, the date of filing, the judge to whom the case is assigned, and the date for the trial scheduling.

[Adopted effective September 1, 2010. Amended effective September 1, 2011; September 2, 2013; September 2, 2014.]

LCR 4. SERVICE ADDRESS REQUIRED [REPEALED]

[Adopted effective September 1, 2006. Repealed effective September 1, 2010.]

LCR 5. SERVICE AND FILING OF PLEADINGS AND OTHER PAPERS

(d) Filing.

(1) *Time.* Briefs shall be submitted on the following schedules, unless the court orders otherwise or a state-wide law or rule provides otherwise:

(A) Trial briefs. Trial briefs shall be filed and served at least two days before trial.

(B) Appeals from administrative agency action. The petitioner's brief shall be filed and served not later than 45 calendar days before oral argument. The respondent's brief shall be filed and served 25 calendar days before oral argument. The petitioner's reply brief shall be filed and served not later than 15 calendar days before argument.

(C) Civil motions. Unless otherwise provided in these rules, briefs and all supporting materials for motions shall be filed and served before 12:00 noon, five court days before the hearing. Opposing briefs and materials shall be filed and served before 12:00 noon, two court days before the hearing. Reply

briefs shall be filed and served before 12:00 noon, one court day before the date scheduled for hearing.

(D) Motions for Summary Judgment, CR 12(b)(6) Motions, and Motions for Judgment on the Pleadings. Motions for summary judgment (CR 56) and motions filed under CR 12(b)(6) or CR 12(c) for which matters outside the pleadings are presented to and not excluded by the court shall be filed, scheduled, and served as provided in CR 56.

(E) Motions for Reconsideration. Motions for reconsideration shall be filed and served as provided in these local rules and state rules governing such motions (CR 59 and LCR 59).

(F) Sexually Violent Predator Annual Review Hearings. Annual review hearings regarding sexually violent predators shall be briefed on a schedule provided by the court when the court approves scheduling the hearing under LCR 7(b)(6).

(k) Judge's Copy. A copy of all briefs, attachments and exhibits shall be provided to the judge's judicial assistant at or before the time of filing the originals with the court clerk.

(1) *Generally.* Each judge's copy of a brief shall be identified as the judge's copy and shall identify the date, time, and the judge before whom the matter is scheduled to be heard in substantially the following format in the top left hand corner of the first page. If the brief does not meet these guidelines, it is subject to being returned:

```
: □ EXPEDITE            :
: □ No hearing set      :
: □ Hearing is set      :
: Date: _____      :
: Time: _____      :
: Judge/Calendar: ____  :
:_____ :
```

(2) *Electronic Copy.* Parties may not submit electronic judge's copies of pleadings or attachments unless the court asks the parties to do so.

[Amended effective September 1, 1994; September 1, 1997; September 1, 2000; September 1, 2004; September 1, 2005; September 1, 2010; September 1, 2011; September 2, 2013; September 2, 2014.]

III. PLEADINGS AND MOTIONS (Rules 7–16)

LCR 7. PLEADINGS ALLOWED; FORMS OF MOTIONS

(b) Motions and Other Papers.

(1) *How Made.*

(A) Documents necessary for ex parte presentation. Ex parte orders presented for entry must be accompanied by a written motion and supporting documents.

(B) In–person ex parte presentation. Ex parte matters may be submitted as follows:

(i) By presentation on the ex parte calendar.

(ii) By presentation at the beginning of the assigned judge's Friday motion calendar.

(iii) When time sensitive materials must be presented to the assigned judge, such as a temporary restraining order, special presentation may be arranged with the assigned judge's judicial assistant.

(C) Alternative presentation by mail or commercial delivery. Agreed orders, orders when notice of presentation is waived, and ex parte orders based on the record in the file may be presented by mail or commercial delivery to the court clerk. The original order, supporting materials, and the required fee as set forth in the clerk's fee schedule must be included in the mail or delivery. The materials should identify the assigned judge. If accepted by the clerk, the proposed order will be presented to a judicial officer for consideration. If rejected by the clerk, the proposed order will be returned to the sender for resubmission or in-person presentation as permitted in subsection (B) above. Self-addressed, stamped envelopes, along with copies of the proposed order, must be provided if return of any conformed materials or rejected orders is sought.

(5) *Telephonic Argument for Motion Hearings.*

(A) Generally. This rule applies to all matters held in the "main campus" courthouse, including adult criminal matters and civil matters, but does not apply to matters held at the Family & Juvenile Court. The preferrence[1] is for personal appearances. Telephonic appearances are sometimes appropriate as a disability accommodation or under other extenuating circumstances.

(B) Motion. A party who seeks to request a telephonic appearance shall file a timely motion. Such a motion may be brought by any party to assist a person with limited communications, such as an inmate.

(i) Civil Cases and Trials. Motions for telephonic appearance in civil cases must be presented on the assigned judge's civil motion calendar. The motion to appear telephonically must be noted for hearing at least one week before the matter for which a telephonic appearance is sought. The assigned judge will rule on the motion to appear telephonically without oral argument.

(ii) Criminal Motions. Motions for telephonic appearance for criminal motion calendars must be presented to a criminal presiding judge. The motion may be made ex parte at the beginning of any criminal calendar. The moving party may also note the motion for consideration on the criminal miscellaneous calendar, and the criminal presiding judge will rule on the motion to appear telephonically without oral argument.

(C) Procedure. The party who was granted a telephonic hearing may contact the assigned judge's judicial assistant for instructions at least two business days before the telephonic hearing. A party who is granted a telephonic hearing has the same duties as parties who appear in person, including

the duties to provide judges' copies of pleadings and to provide a proposed order.

(6) *Motion Calendar.* Civil motions will be heard by the assigned judge during a Friday motion calendar. The assigned judge's judicial assistant must pre-approve scheduling of the following types of motions:

(A) motions for summary judgment (CR 56);

(B) motions to dismiss for failure to state a claim upon which relief can be granted (CR 12(b)(6));

(C) motions for judgment on the pleadings (CR 12(c));

(D) motions for class certification (CR 23); and

(E) motions regarding Sexually Violent Predator annual reviews.

The judicial assistant must also pre-approve hearing dates for continuances of such motions that were previously scheduled.

(7) *Confirmations.* The Court will eliminate all confirmation requirements when the Odyssey Case Management System is implemented. This is currently anticipated to occur around November 2015. The court will announce implementation on the court's web sites.

(A) Confirmations Required Until Odyssey Case Management System is Implemented. Until the Odyssey Case Management System is implemented, all contested motions to be considered on a judge's Friday civil motion calendar must be confirmed. Motions on the unlawful detainer calendar and civil miscellaneous calendar do not require confirmation. Confirmation that a hearing on a contested motion will occur as scheduled permits the judge to prepare for the hearing. A hearing for a contested motion that is not confirmed may be postponed by the court until adequate preparation can be had. Failure to confirm a matter, when required, does not result in the matter being stricken or continued. The moving party has a separate duty, explained below, to strike or continue a hearing date that is no longer necessary.

(B) Confirmations No Longer Required After the Odyssey Case Management System is Implemented. When Odyssey is implemented at the court, confirmations will not be required for any matters. Parties must strike or continue all matters that will not be heard at least two court days before the hearing date, as provided in this rule.

* (8) *Striking or Continuing Hearing Dates.* The moving party must timely strike or continue any hearing that will not go forward on the scheduled date. This rule applies to all Superior Court matters, including civil, criminal, juvenile, and family court cases. Strikes and continuances must be communicated to the clerk's office, which shall then promptly inform the court. This rule applies even if the matter is subject to confirmation and the matter was not

confirmed. Violation of this rule may result in sanctions imposed against the moving party or parties.

(A) Deadline. Hearings that must be scheduled on 28 days' notice to the clerk shall be stricken or continued at least five court days before the hearing. All other hearings shall be stricken or continued at least two court days before the hearing.

(B) Sanctions. If a party fails to properly strike or continue a hearing under this rule, the court may impose sanctions against that party. The court shall give five days' notice of its motion for sanctions, and the parties may present briefing and oral argument regarding whether sanctions are appropriate. Sanctions may include, but are not limited to, judgment against the moving party for costs and terms relating to the violation and hearing on sanctions, including a reasonable attorney fee and sanctions payable to the court up to $500.

(C) Factors in Imposing Sanctions. Sanctions shall not be imposed upon a showing of good cause or if justice requires foregoing sanctions. Monetary sanctions shall not be imposed upon a showing of indigency or if the sanctions would hamper the party's ability to access the court system. Further, sanctions shall not be imposed when a hearing was not necessary due to settlement or agreement by the parties to resolve the matter outside the court system, unless the settlement or agreement was known to the parties before the deadline to strike or confirm the hearing.

(9) *Time for Oral Argument.* Each side will be allowed ten minutes to argue a contested motion, including rebuttal, unless the court allows additional time.

(e) Show Cause Returns. Orders to show cause, summons containing return dates and citations shall be returnable to the assigned judge's Friday motions calendar.

[Adopted effective September 1, 2010. Amended effective September 2, 2013; September 2, 2014; September 1, 2015.]

1 So in original.

Commentary:

The purpose of this rule is to provide notice to the parties and the court when motions will not be heard, in consideration of the phase-out of the confirmation process.

LCR 10. FORM OF PLEADINGS AND OTHER PAPERS

(d) Format Requirements. In addition to the General Rules' requirements for Format for Pleadings and Other Papers (GR 14), all briefs must comply with the following requirements:

(1) *Brief Titles.* Briefs shall be titled with the submitting party's designation (e.g., plaintiff, defendant) and (A) "Opening Brief" or "Brief in Support of Motion . . ."; (B) "Responding Brief" or "Brief Opposing Motion . . ."; or (C) "Reply Brief."

(2) *Length of Brief.* Opening and responding briefs for trials, appeals from administrative agency rulings, Sexually Violent Predator annual review hearings, and motions to dismiss or for summary judgment shall not exceed 25 pages. Reply briefs for these matters shall not exceed ten pages. Opening and responding briefs for non-dispositive motions shall not exceed fifteen pages. Reply briefs for non-dispositive motions shall not exceed eight pages. For the purpose of determining compliance with this rule, the title sheet, table of contents, and table of authorities are not included. For compelling reasons, the court may grant a motion to file an over-length brief. Motions for over-length briefs must be timely filed to allow a decision before the date the brief is due.

(3) *Font.* The text of any brief must appear double spaced and in print as twelve point or larger type in the following fonts or their equivalent: Times New Roman, Courier, CG Times, or Arial. Footnotes may be single spaced in print as ten point or larger type.

(4) *Service and Filing.* Every filed document shall contain the following information in substantially the following format in the top left hand corner of the first page. If the document does not meet these guidelines, it is subject to being returned:

```
: □  EXPEDITE               :
: □  No hearing set         :
: □  Hearing is set         :
: Date: _____     :
: Time: _____     :
: Judge/Calendar: _____    :
```

[Amended effective September 1, 2002; September 1, 2004; September 1, 2005; September 1, 2010; September 1, 2011; September 2, 2014.]

LCR 11. SIGNING AND DRAFTING OF PLEADINGS, MOTIONS, AND LEGAL MEMORANDA; SANCTIONS

(a)(1) *Required Information.* Each party appearing pro se (*i.e.,* self-represented without an attorney) must state on every pleading and other documents submitted to the court or filed with the court clerk: (1) a telephone or message number, (2) a mailing address where materials may be sent to the party, and (3) a physical address where service may be made on that party. The designation of a post office box, mail stop, or the like shall not be sufficient. If the party cannot provide a physical address, then the party must provide a reasonable alternative to personal service, such as a fax number at which the party agrees to accept service.

(2) *Notice to Opposing Parties.* Each party appearing pro se (*i.e.,* self-represented without an attor-

ney) must deliver or mail to each opposing party or attorney a copy of every pleading or other document submitted to the court or filed with the court clerk in the same manner required of attorneys in the Civil Rules. All copies must contain the required information identified in subpart (a)(1) of this rule.

(3) *Sanctions.* The court on its own initiative or on motion of a party may order a party or counsel who uses these rules for purposes of delay or who fails to comply with these rules to pay terms or compensatory damages to any other party who has been harmed by the delay or the failure to comply. The court may condition a party's right to participate further in the matter on compliance with terms of an order or ruling, including payment of an award to a party. Any such order or ruling may be reduced to judgment.

[Amended effective September 1, 1994; September 1, 2006; September 1, 2010.]

LCR 16. PRETRIAL PROCEDURE AND MOTIONS

(a) **Hearing Matters Considered.** A pretrial conference shall be held in each case subject to this rule. Lead counsel for each party shall attend the pretrial conference. The assigned judge shall set the agenda and may consider any matter relating to trial administration, even if not provided in this rule. The conference shall be conducted in chambers or as a hearing in open court if matters of record are argued and decided. At the conclusion of the conference, a pretrial order, including any discretionary supplemental orders, may be entered.

(c) **Public Records Act Cases.**

(1) *Identification and Scheduling of Public Records Act Cases.*

(A) Every case filed under the Public Records Act shall be clearly identified as a Public Records Act case on the front page of the first filed pleading and noted on the Case Information Cover Sheet as a Public Records Act (PRA) cause of action.

(B) At the time the case is filed, the clerk's office will provide the plaintiff with a notice setting a status hearing within 21 days. The plaintiff shall provide this notice to all parties when the complaint or motion is served. If service of the complaint or motion is completed before the case is filed, the plaintiff shall provide the notice by delivery, mail, facsimile, or email within five days after filing the case.

(C) In the event a Public Records Act case is not identified at filing, the defendant or intervenor may make the identification and request the status hearing be reset.

(D) If a defendant or intervenor has not been served by the time of the status hearing, the status hearing may be continued up to 21 days.

(E) The status hearing will be held before the assigned judge and will be used to:

(i) Identify issues in dispute;

(ii) Set a hearing date and briefing schedule for resolution of issues;

(iii) Determine whether in camera review is likely to be needed and, if necessary, order the protocol for submission of the records to be reviewed; and

(iv) Refer to mediation if appropriate.

(F) Nothing in this rule affects the right of any party to schedule a hearing to show cause or enjoin, or any other hearing authorized by law or rule.

(2) *In Camera Review of Public Records Act Cases.*

(A) When commenced. In a Public Records Act case, in camera review will occur only if the assigned judge enters an order requiring such review. Agreement between parties or submission of records to the assigned judge, without an appropriate order, will not trigger in camera review.

(B) Electronic records. Records for in camera review shall be submitted in an electronic form unless the court orders otherwise on a showing of good cause.

(C) Identification of records. Records for in camera review must have a unique identifying number, such as a Bates number. The system for numbering and the placement of page numbers must be uniform for all records.

(D) Allegedly entirely exempt documents. If a record is claimed entirely exempt, it must be clearly designated as exempt or withheld on the first page of the record for in camera review.

(E) Identification of redactions. Records redacted in part must be presented to the judge in a manner that will permit the judge to read the entire record and immediately understand which parts were withheld by redaction and which parts were produced. For example, the redactions may be outlined or indicated with a shaded or colored overlay.

(F) Submission of table. In cases with numerous records at issue, or if ordered by the judge, a table shall be submitted as part of the in camera procedure. Any table, grid, or spreadsheet is acceptable if it complies with the terms of this rule. The table must clearly identify which records are claimed entirely exempt and have been withheld and which records have been redacted in part. The table(s) shall list the following information in separate fields or columns: (1) the unique identifier for the record or page being reviewed, such as a Bates number; (2) descriptive information that accurately identifies the record, including author(s), recipient(s), and date(s) (or if descriptive information is protected, other means of sufficiently identifying particular records without disclosing protected content); (3)

identification of a specific exemption claimed and an explanation of how it applies to the record; and (4) an expandable cell for the court's notes. The table shall be filed and served on all parties and also shall be submitted to the court in electronic form.

(G) Basis for exemption. The basis for the claim of exemption may appear on the document if doing so would not obliterate text or other information necessary for the court's review.

[Amended effective September 1, 1994; September 1, 1997; May 4, 1998; September 1, 1999; September 1, 2000; September 1, 2003; September 1, 2004; September 1, 2006; September 1, 2010; September 1, 2011; September 2, 2013.]

VI. TRIALS (Rules 38–53.4)

LCR 38. JURY TRIAL OF RIGHT

(b) Demand for Jury. The demand for jury trial shall be on a separate document.

LCR 40. ASSIGNMENT OF CASES

(b) Methods.

(1) *Trial Scheduling.* Trials are scheduled through an administrative docket that is conducted by the assigned judge's judicial assistant, or other court staff as directed by the presiding judge. The court shall regularly hold this administrative docket in order to issue case schedule orders and schedule trials. Parties do not appear on the trial scheduling date, and they may not communicate with the court regarding scheduling trials in any manner except through the scheduling questionnaire or a motion to the assigned judge. This prohibition applies to cases in which a trial continuance is sought or granted. On or shortly after the trial scheduling date, the court will review the case for readiness and will review any scheduling questionnaires that the parties submit. The court will attempt to resolve conflicts administratively, and will refer the matter for a hearing if necessary. The court will issue a case schedule order if the case is ready and all conflicts are resolved.

(2) *Scheduling Questionnaire.* A scheduling questionnaire is a form that allows parties to present information that is relevant to creating a case schedule order. The form is found in the forms appendix to these rules, the web sites for the court and court clerk, and at the clerk's office. It asks questions such as the anticipated length of trial, whether a jury demand has been filed, and dates on which the parties and counsel are unavailable for trial. All parties are strongly encouraged to complete a scheduling questionnaire. The questionnaire is the sole means to communicate with the court about information related to scheduling the trial and the deadlines in the case schedule order. Failure to timely file the questionnaire is not grounds to continue the trial scheduling date.

(A) Service of notice of assignment, notice of trial scheduling, and blank scheduling questionnaire. The plaintiff or petitioner shall serve the notice of assignment, notice of trial scheduling, and a blank scheduling questionnaire to all defendants and respondents at least 14 calendar days before the trial scheduling date for the case. A counterclaimant or cross-claimant shall also serve all responsive parties to the counterclaim or cross-claim at least 14 calendar days before the trial scheduling date for the case.

(B) Deadlines for completing scheduling questionnaires. The plaintiff or petitioner must file and serve any completed scheduling questionnaire five court days before the trial scheduling date. Respondents, defendants, and all other parties must file and serve any completed scheduling questionnaire two court days before the trial scheduling date by 12:00 p.m. Agreed scheduling questionnaires may also be submitted two court days before the trial scheduling date by 12:00 p.m. Parties are encouraged to meet and confer about the case scheduling before submitting scheduling questionnaires, and are encouraged to submit agreed scheduling questionnaires.

(3) *Readiness for Scheduling.* The court will enter a case schedule order only if the case is ready to be scheduled. If a case is not ready on its trial scheduling date, the court will strike the matter from the administrative docket and will not continue it.

(A) Readiness generally. A case is not ready to be scheduled unless there is timely proof of service of the scheduling questionnaire on all defendants or respondents. A case may be ready regardless of whether any party has timely completed and filed a questionnaire. The court will enter a case schedule order without input from parties if they have not completed and filed questionnaires.

(B) Civil litigation. Civil litigation is not ready to be scheduled until:

(i) it appears that the court has obtained personal jurisdiction over every defendant or respondent;

(ii) the time for filing answers has elapsed; and

(iii) at least one answer or responsive pleading has been filed.

(C) Appeals from administrative agencies, district court, and municipal courts. Cases in which the court is sitting in an appellate capacity are ready to be scheduled only after the appellate record has been filed with the court clerk. Additionally, the court may determine that the appeal is not ready if the administrative record was submitted in a form that does not substantially comply with these local court rules.

(D) Mandatory arbitration. Cases subject to the mandatory arbitration rule shall be transferred to mandatory arbitration before the trial scheduling date for the case, according to the procedure outlined in the local mandatory arbitration rules.

(4) *Striking Trial Scheduling Dates.* The court will strike a trial scheduling date if the case is not ready to be scheduled. The court will not notify parties that the scheduling date has been stricken. A party must consult the case file to determine whether the scheduling date was stricken or to view a case schedule order that the party has not yet received. If a matter is stricken, a party must schedule a new trial scheduling date in order to receive a case schedule order. The court will not continue trial scheduling dates on the ground that they are not ready to be scheduled.

(5) *Parties May Obtain a Trial Scheduling Date.* For most cases, the court clerk will issue a trial scheduling date when the case is filed. A party may also obtain a trial scheduling date by filing a timely notice of issue form and timely serving the other parties with notice and a blank copy of the scheduling questionnaire. Further, all parties may, by agreement, arrange an earlier date for scheduling than the date provided by the clerk by filing a notice of issue form and proof of the agreement. This procedure also applies when a judge has granted a motion for a continuance. A party may also move the court, with notice to other parties, for an order allowing an earlier trial scheduling date.

(6) *Special Scheduling Procedures and Deadlines.* These local court rules do not replace or modify scheduling procedures or deadlines that are required by law, such as the Land Use Petition Act or Trust and Estate Dispute Resolution Act.

(7) *Entry and Modification of Case Schedule Order.* On or after the trial scheduling date, the judicial assistant will present the case schedule order to the assigned judge for entry without further notice. Amendments to the schedule may be obtained only by obtaining an amended case schedule order. Agreed amendments to change any date in the case schedule order except for the deadline for dispositive motions, alternative dispute resolution, or the trial date may be presented ex parte to the assigned judge with a written explanation for the proposed change and the parties' certification that the agreement will not serve as a basis to change the trial date. Contested motions to amend and motions to amend the deadline for dispositive motions, alternative dispute resolution, or trial must be scheduled for a hearing on the assigned judge's civil motion calendar. The court may amend deadlines affecting the court, including the trial date, on its own motion. In that event, the judicial assis-

tant will prepare, file, and serve the amended case schedule order.

(8) *Additional Parties.* Any party who joins an additional party to an action shall be responsible for serving the additional party with a current case schedule order, together with all other pleadings required by law.

(e) Continuances.

(1) *Form of the Motion.* A motion to continue a trial must be timely filed and served not less than ten calendar days before the trial date. A motion for continuance must (A) contain written acknowledgment of the motion by the client, (B) be accompanied by an affidavit or declaration containing specific reasons necessitating a continuance, and (C) if agreed or uncontested, contain written acknowledgment of the motion by all parties to the case.

(2) *Presentation of Motion.* A motion to continue a deadline on the case schedule order must be presented in the manner described in this rule regarding "entry and modification of case schedule order."

(3) *Conditions of Order for Continuance.* A continuance will be ordered only for good cause. The court may impose terms upon a party or counsel who is not prepared for trial. When a continuance is sought after a jury has been summoned, and where the cause for continuance was or should have been known earlier, terms may be imposed to defray the court's costs incurred in summoning a jury for trial. If the trial is continued, a new trial date must be established in an amended case schedule order.

(4) *Obtaining a New Trial Date.* If a motion for continuance is granted, parties may obtain a new trial date by following the procedure outlined above in the section entitled "parties may obtain a trial scheduling date." The general prohibition on contacting judicial assistants on trial scheduling matters applies to continuances.

(f) Change of Judge. If a timely affidavit of prejudice under RCW 4.12.050 is filed, the superior court scheduling coordinator shall assign a new judge. Notice of the new assignment and trial scheduling date shall be provided to all parties and attorneys of record.

[Amended effective September 1, 1994; March 4, 1996; September 1, 1997; September 1, 2006; September 1, 2008; September 1, 2010; September 1, 2011; September 2, 2013; September 2, 2014.]

LCR 41.   DISMISSAL OF ACTIONS

(e) Notice of Settlements.

(1) *Procedure After Settlement.* After notice to the court of settlement as provided in CR 41(e), the parties shall cause to be entered a final judgment or order concluding the case. After 45 days, the court, on its own motion, may order that the parties show

cause why such final judgment or order should not be entered.

[Adopted effective September 1, 1997. Amended effective September 1, 2010.]

LCR 42.   CONSOLIDATION; SEPARATE TRIALS

(a) Consolidation. Consolidated actions shall be consolidated into the case that was filed first. Motions to consolidate must be presented to the judge who was assigned to the case that was filed first. The court may waive these requirements for good cause.

[Adopted effective September 2, 2014.]

LCR 43.   EVIDENCE [REPEALED]

[Amended effective September 1, 1994. Repealed effective September 1, 2010.]

LCR 47.   JURORS [REPEALED]

[Effective October, 1982; amended January 11, 1993; amended effective September 1, 1996; September 1, 2000; September 1, 2003. Repealed effective September 1, 2010.]

LCR 51.   INSTRUCTIONS TO JURY AND DELIBERATION

(b) Submissions.

(1) *Time for Submission.* Unless otherwise ordered by the court, proposed jury instructions shall be filed and served no later than when the case is called for trial.

(2) *Proposed Instructions.* Sets of proposed instructions shall be submitted as follows:

(A) To the Clerk: A set of instructions numbered and with citations shall be filed with the court clerk.

(B) To Counsel: A set of instructions numbered and with citations shall be served on every other counsel or pro se party appearing in the case.

(C) To the Judge: A set of instructions shall be provided to the judge as follows:

(i) a set of instructions numbered and with citations in electronic word processing format, not .pdf format, submitted via e-mail attachment to the assigned judge's judicial assistant, with all proposed instructions in a single computer file; and

(ii) a hard copy set of printed instructions numbered and with citations; and

(iii) a hard copy set of printed instructions without numbers or citations.

(c) Form. Proposed jury instructions shall be printed or typewritten, double spaced, and submitted each on a separate letter size sheet of paper (8.5 × 11 inches) that bears no markings identifying the submitting party or counsel. A cover sheet with a case

caption which reads "Court's Instructions To The Jury" shall be included.

[Amended effective February 1, 1994; September 1, 1997; September 1, 2004; September 1, 2010.]

LCR 53.2.   COURT COMMISSIONERS

(e) Revision by Court.

(1) *Scope of Rule.* This rule applies to all motions for revision, whether the court commissioner presided over a hearing at the Main Campus Courthouse or at Family & Juvenile Court.

(2) *Filing and Service Deadline.* A motion for revision must be filed within ten days after the commissioner's order or judgment is entered. (RCW 2.24.050.)

(3) *Findings of Fact and Conclusions of Law.*

(A) A party moving for revision shall present to the court commissioner proposed findings of fact and conclusions of law to support the order or judgment. Other parties may submit their proposals at the time for presentation.

(B) Findings of fact and conclusions of law shall be entered before the hearing on the motion for revision.

(C) The Administrative Office of the Court-approved form Order of Child Support and Child Support Worksheets may constitute findings of fact and conclusions of law for motions for revision on issues of child support.

(4) *Form of Motion.* A party moving for revision is encouraged to specify each alleged error and identify each document in the court file related to the issues raised by the motion for revision.

(5) *Hearing on Motion.* At the time a motion for revision is filed, the moving party shall schedule a hearing by filing a notice of issue. The hearing on the motion for revision shall be scheduled to occur within 30 days after the motion for revision is filed.

(A) Motions at Family & Juvenile Court. Revision motions for matters heard at the Family & Juvenile Court shall be scheduled on the Family & Juvenile Court revision calendar.

(B) All Other Motions. Revision motions for matters that were not heard at the Family & Juvenile Court shall be scheduled on the assigned judge's civil motion calendar if a judge is assigned. If the case does not have a judge assignment, the motion shall be scheduled on the civil miscellaneous calendar.

(6) *The Record.*

(A) The motion for revision shall be heard upon the record before the court commissioner.

(B) A transcript is required for all motions for revision in which there was live testimony. A party moving for revision is responsible for ensuring that the transcript of the proceedings is filed with the court at least five court days before the hearing for the motion. To order the transcript, the moving party must contact the official court reporter who is assigned to Family and Juvenile Court within five days of filing the motion for revision. The moving party is responsible for paying for the transcript or obtaining a fee waiver if he or she is indigent.

(7) *Scope of Motion.* The court may revise any order or judgment that is related to the issues raised by the motion for revision (for example, all issues related to child support or all issues related to the parenting plan). The court will not consider issues that are not related to the motion for revision without a separate motion, except:

(A) the court may consider requests for attorney fees by either party for the revision proceedings; and

(B) the court may consider issues in the original order when the motion for revision is filed for an order denying a motion for reconsideration.

(8) *Effect of Motion.*

(A) When a motion for revision is timely filed, the court commissioner loses jurisdiction to conduct further proceedings or enter orders on issues that are the subject of the revision proceeding until the revision proceeding is completed, except findings of fact and conclusions of law required by this rule.

(B) A court commissioner's order or judgment shall be effective upon entry of an order or judgment unless stayed by court order pending hearing on a motion for revision.

[Adopted effective September 1, 2015.]

VII. JUDGMENT (Rules 54–63)

LCR 54. JUDGMENTS AND COSTS— ORDERS [REPEALED]

[Amended effective September 1, 1994; September 1, 1997. Repealed effective September 1, 2010.]

LCR 56. SUMMARY JUDGMENT

(i) Appeals from Administrative and Industrial Insurance Rulings. Summary judgment motions will not be heard in administrative review cases or industrial insurance appeals if reference to the administrative record or transcript of the administrative proceedings is required.

[Amended effective September 1, 1994; September 1, 2010.]

LCR 59. NEW TRIAL, RECONSIDERATION, AND AMENDMENT OF JUDGMENTS

(b) Time for Motion; Contents of Motion.

(1) *Procedures for Orders for Reconsideration.* Briefs and affidavits or declarations in support of a motion for reconsideration shall be filed and served when the motion is filed. At the time of filing, the moving party shall provide judge's copies of the motion, brief, affidavit, proposed order, and notice of issue to the judicial officer's assistant. Each judicial officer reserves the right to strike the hearing and decide the motion without oral argument. Moving parties shall comply with the state-wide rule governing reconsideration, CR 59. Briefs and materials opposing a motion for reconsideration, and reply briefs and materials shall be filed in accordance with the local rule for "service and filing of pleadings and other papers" (LCR 5).

[Amended effective September 1, 1994; September 1, 1997; February 9, 1999; September 1, 2000; September 1, 2003; amended as emergency rule December 30, 2003; amended effective September 1, 2004; September 1, 2006; September 1, 2007; September 1, 2010; September 1, 2011; September 2, 2013; September 2, 2014.]

VIII. PROVISIONAL AND FINAL REMEDIES (Rules 64–71)

LCR 65. INJUNCTIONS
(b) Temporary Restraining Order; Notice; Hearing; Duration.
(1) *Procedure.* A party seeking a temporary restraining order shall promptly contact the assigned judge's judicial assistant to schedule a hearing at the first opportunity.

[Adopted effective September 1, 2010.]

X. SUPERIOR COURTS AND CLERKS (Rules 77–80)

LCR 77. SUPERIOR COURTS AND JUDICIAL OFFICERS

(*o*) **Divisions of the Court, Assignments and Schedules.**

(1) *Divisions.* The divisions of the court are:

(A) Criminal Presiding. The Criminal Presiding division will hear all criminal pretrial proceedings, including preliminary appearances, arraignments, omnibus hearings and pretrial conferences, pretrial motions, changes of plea, sentencings, and noncompliance. The Criminal Presiding Department will also hear unlawful detainer hearings and trials, writs of habeas corpus in criminal matters, petitions for certificates of rehabilitation, and other matters as assigned.

(B) Family and Juvenile Court. The Family and Juvenile Court division will hear all matters brought pursuant to RCW Titles 11, 13, and 26, and truancy petitions filed in Superior Court. Other cases may be heard by the Family and Juvenile Court division as set forth in the Local Rule for Family and Juvenile Court Proceedings (LSPR 94.00).

(C) Trial. The Trial division will hear all civil matters except cases designated as Family and Juvenile Court cases and those special proceedings assigned to a different division by these rules or court order. A judge in this division will hear all matters in the cases assigned to the judge.

(2) *Retaining Assignment of Case.* A judge may, at his or her discretion, retain assignment of a case after being reassigned to a different division.

[Amended effective September 1, 1997; September 1, 2010; September 1, 2011; September 2, 2013.]

LCR 79. BOOKS AND RECORDS KEPT BY THE CLERK

(a) **Clerk of Court Schedule of Charges.** The clerk of the court will maintain a schedule of charges authorized by law for clerk's services. The schedule is available for public inspection and will be maintained in the clerk's office and on the clerk's web site.

(b) **Files.**

(1) *Filing by Clerk of Court.* All original pleading or other papers with proper caption and cause number will be file stamped, docketed and secured in the legal file by the Clerk in the order received.

(2) *Action Documents.* All pleadings that require action by the clerk, other than file stamping and docketing, shall contain the language "CLERK'S ACTION REQUIRED" in the caption beneath the case number on the first page of the document.

(3) *Conformed Copies.* All requests to the clerk for a response to an inquiry about a court file or for return of conformed copies of pleadings must be accompanied by a self-addressed, stamped return envelope.

(4) *Sealed Papers.* The court clerk shall seal and not permit examination of records sealed by court order or by operation of law (GR 15, GR 22). If sealed, papers may be unsealed only by court order, by motion and with notice, in conformity with GR 15.

(c) **Exhibits.**

(1) *Exhibit Files.* The exhibits in all cases shall be kept by the clerk separate from the files of the case.

(2) *Exhibit Inspection.* Exhibits may be inspected in the clerk's office only in the presence of the clerk of the court or a deputy clerk.

(3) *Court Records as Exhibits.* No original court record shall be admitted as an exhibit, but a copy may be admitted.

(4) *Substituted Copies of Exhibits.* For cause shown, the court may permit a copy of any document admitted in evidence to be substituted for the original.

(5) *Exhibit Packaging and Labeling.* Exhibits containing blood borne pathogens, drugs, firearms or dangerous weapons shall be properly packaged and labeled before acceptance by the court. To meet packaging and labeling requirements, exhibits shall conform to the following criteria when presented:

(A) Blood borne pathogens shall be packaged in sturdy plastic containers. If contained in a vial or hypodermic, each shall be placed in an individual sturdy plastic container. All items shall be labeled to identify the contents as potentially biologically hazardous material.

(B) Drugs shall be placed in sealed containers to prevent or reduce emissions from the container. Plainly visible labels shall identify the contents.

(C) Firearms shall be unloaded, any breech mechanism or cylinder shall be open, and a secured trigger lock shall be in place.

(D) Dangerous weapons shall have any sharp or pointed portions sheathed in a manner to prevent injury or contact with the sharp or pointed portions.

(E) Paper bags alone will not constitute proper packaging.

(6) *Videotaped Depositions.* Videotaped depositions published in open court shall be treated as court exhibits, with the same retention standards. A party who wishes to make a published videotaped deposition part of the court file must submit a certified transcript of the deposition.

(7) *Unsuitable Materials as Exhibits.* Whenever there is presented to the clerk of the court for filing any paper or material that the clerk of the court

determines to be improper or inappropriate for filing, the clerk of the court shall affix a file mark thereto and apply to the court for a determination of the propriety of filing the material presented. If the court determines that the paper or material should not be made part of the file, an order shall be entered converting the material to an exhibit, and the clerk of the court shall retain the material as an exhibit to the cause. If the court determines that the material warrants being sealed, the court shall direct the clerk of the court to give notice to all parties to the cause and shall conduct a hearing on the court's motion to seal the material pursuant to GR 15.

(d) Withdrawal of Files and Exhibits.

(1) *Files.* Except for delivery to a courtroom, judge, court commissioner, referee, court personnel or official court reporter, files may be withdrawn from the clerk's office only pursuant to court order or written authorization. Applications to withdraw a file must be in writing. The clerk or a deputy may authorize withdrawal of a file for a period not exceeding three days. The official court reporter of a case may withdraw a file for up to ten days to prepare a verbatim report of proceedings. A person who withdraws a file shall return the file and all of its papers in good order, and shall not remove, even temporarily, any staples from any papers.

(2) *Exhibits; Temporary Withdrawal.* Exhibits may be withdrawn temporarily from the clerk's office only by:

(i) The judge having the case under consideration.

(ii) Official court reporters for use in connection with their duties, without court order.

(iii) An attorney of record, upon court order.

The clerk shall take an itemized receipt for all exhibits withdrawn, and upon return of the exhibits they shall be checked by the clerk against the original receipts. The clerk shall keep all receipts for such exhibits for the period of three years from date of withdrawal or return.

(3) *Failure to Return Files or Exhibits; Sanctions.* In the event that an attorney or other person fails to return within the time required a file or exhibit which was temporarily withdrawn, and fails to comply with the clerk's request for its return, the clerk may, without notice to the attorney or other person concerned, apply to the court for an order for the immediate return of such file or exhibit. A certified copy of such order, if entered, shall then be served upon the attorney or other person involved.

(4) *Permanent Withdrawal of Exhibits.* After final judgment and expiration of the time for appeal, the court may order the permanent withdrawal of an exhibit and delivery thereof to any party or other person entitled to possession.

(5) *Return of Contraband Exhibits.* When contraband, alcoholic beverages, tobacco products or controlled substances are being held by the clerk as part of the records and files in any criminal case, and all proceedings in the case have been completed, the court may order the clerk to deliver such contraband or substances to an authorized representative of the law enforcement agency initiating the prosecution for disposition according to law. The clerk shall then deliver the contraband or substances and take from the law enforcement agency a receipt which shall be filed in the case. The clerk shall also file any certificate issued by an authorized federal or state agency and received by the clerk showing the nature of such contraband or substances.

(6) *Return of Exhibits and Unopened Depositions.* When a civil case is finally concluded, and upon stipulation of the parties or court order, the clerk may return all exhibits and unopened depositions, or destroy the same.

(7) *Return of Administrative Records.* When a case for review of an administrative record is finally completed, the clerk shall return the administrative record to the officer or agency certifying the same to the court.

(8) *Verbatim Report of Proceedings.* A verbatim report of proceedings shall not be withdrawn from the clerk's office except by court order.

(10)[1] *Transcripts.* A request for a copy of a transcript prepared by a court reporter in the possession of the clerk of the court, shall be referred to the appropriate court reporter.

[Amended effective September 1, 1994; September 1, 2005; September 1, 2011; September 1, 2012.]

1 Numbering as provided in official copy.

LCR 80. COURT REPORTERS

(d) Scope of Rule. The provisions of this rule shall apply to official court reporters, visiting judge court reporters, and court reporters pro tempore.

(e) General Reporting Requirements.

(1) *Separate Civil and Criminal Notes.* Court reporters shall keep separate notes for civil and criminal cases.

(2) *Matters Reported.* Unless otherwise ordered by the court, all court proceedings will be reported by a court reporter or electronic means. Settlement conferences will not be reported or recorded except for the settlement agreement.

(3) *Electronic and Tape Recorder Reporting.* All Family and Juvenile Court proceedings heard by court commissioners may be reported by electronic or tape recording.

(4) *Oral Rulings and Decisions.* Oral decisions of the court that are transcribed for any purpose from court reporter notes or electronic recording shall be

prepared by a court reporter and submitted to the judge for review and correction prior to delivery of the transcript.

(5) *Transcripts and Statement of Facts.*

(A) Transcripts; notice to opposing counsel. Subject to making satisfactory arrangements for payment of costs, court reporters shall furnish promptly all transcripts ordered by counsel. Upon request by one party for transcripts of any portion of the record, the court reporter shall give prompt notice of the request to all other parties.

(B) Statements of fact (verbatim report of proceedings); ordered in writing. An order for verbatim report of proceedings shall be in writing and shall be timely. Subject to making satisfactory arrangement for payment of the cost, court reporters shall furnish promptly all verbatim reports that have been ordered.

(C) Substitute court reporters. Substitute court reporters, prior to being placed on the pro tempore court reporter roster, must have the approval of the judicial administrative officer. In the event there is a substitution of court reporter, a party may order the transcript or verbatim report of proceedings from the court reporter first assigned, who shall notify the substitute court reporter of the order.

(D) Electronic recordings. To constitute an official record, transcripts of court proceedings recorded electronically shall be produced by an official court reporter or other court-approved designee.

(f) Filing Notes. A court reporter shall file his or her notes with the court clerk within 30 days after the conclusion of the trial or proceedings. Notes from civil and criminal cases shall be filed separately.

(g) One Official Reporter. Only one official reporter may report the proceedings in court. Private reporters and tape or electronic recording are not permitted.

[Amended effective September 1, 1994; September 1, 2000; September 1, 2001; September 1, 2004; September 1, 2010.]

XI. GENERAL PROVISIONS (Rules 81–87)

LCR 83. LOCAL RULES OF SUPERIOR COURT [REPEALED]

[Amended effective September 1, 1994; September 1, 1997; September 1, 2007. Repealed effective September 1, 2010.]

LCR 87. ALTERNATIVE DISPUTE RESOLUTION

(a) Alternative Dispute Resolution Choices. Thurston County Superior Court encourages resolution of disputes without trial. To this end, the Court makes Alternative Dispute Resolution (ADR) available for civil cases in the form of settlement conferences and mediation through the program outlined in this rule. A panel of attorneys and mediators has agreed to facilitate ADR at economical, court approved rates for all parties. Alternatively, the parties may mutually agree to participate in private ADR of their choice.

(b) Family Law Cases. Family law cases are not covered by this rule. Settlement conferences and mediation in family law cases are addressed in LSPR 94.03(f) and 94.05.

(c) Definitions.

(1) *Civil case* includes all civil cases except those enumerated in LSPR 94.00.

(2) *Settlement conference attorney* means an attorney registered on the panel of ADR settlement conference attorneys maintained by the Court under this rule. See Section (g) for qualifications.

(3) *Mediator* means a person registered on the panel of ADR mediators maintained by the Court under this rule. See Section (g) for qualifications.

(4) *Facilitator* means a settlement conference attorney or mediator on the appropriate panel for the type of ADR selected.

(5) *Private ADR* means mediation or other ADR privately arranged and paid for by the parties.

(d) ADR and the Case Schedule Order.

(1) When ADR is a requirement of the Case Schedule Order, at the time of entry of the Case Schedule Order, the type of ADR shall be selected and identified on the Order (Court settlement conference, Court mediation, or private ADR) and a deadline for completion of ADR shall be set

(2) In the event the Court's ADR program is chosen and identified in the Case Schedule Order, at any time, but no later than 60 days before the ADR deadline, the requesting party shall request that the ADR Coordinator assign a facilitator from the panel maintained by the Court by filing and serving a Request to Participate in ADR and providing a copy to the ADR Coordinator. The parties may stipulate to a facilitator from the panel maintained by the Court.

(3) Within 14 days of being notified of the appointment of the facilitator, the requesting party or its attorney shall schedule the ADR with the facilitator.

(e) Procedures for the Court's ADR program.

(1) *Scope of this section.* The requirements of this section and the remainder of this rule apply only to the Court's ADR program, and not to private ADR. The Court's ADR program may be requested independent from, and in addition to, the Case Schedule Order.

(2) *Requests for ADR.* When the Court's ADR program has not been identified in the Case Schedule Order, any party desiring to participate in the Court's ADR program shall file a Notice of Request to Participate in ADR and provide a copy to the ADR Coordinator (see Forms Appendix). The Notice shall designate the ADR model selected (settlement conference or mediation).

(3) *Notice.* A party requesting to participate in the Court's ADR program shall serve a copy of the Notice of Request to Participate in ADR and a copy of this rule on all parties, counsel and the ADR Coordinator.

(4) *Participation Required.* All parties and counsel notified shall be required to participate in the Court's ADR program, unless an objection is made pursuant to Section 6 below and the Court grants a waiver.

(5) *Selection of Facilitator.* The ADR Coordinator shall select a facilitator from the panel maintained by the Court. The parties will be notified as soon as the facilitator has been appointed. Alternatively, the parties may stipulate to a facilitator from the panel maintained by the court.

(6) *Objection and Waiver.* Any party objecting to participation in the Court's ADR program shall immediately notify all other parties. If the objection is not resolved between the parties within 14 days from the notice of the Request to Participate in ADR, the requesting party shall request that the judicial assistant for the assigned department schedule a teleconference between the parties and the assigned judge. The judge may require ADR or waive participation.

(f) ADR Session.

(1) *Scheduling.* When the Court's ADR program is included in the Case Schedule Order, the requesting party shall schedule the ADR directly with the facilitator. When ADR results from a Request to Participate, the requesting party shall also schedule the ADR. Scheduling shall be done within 14 days from assignment of the facilitator. ADR may be conducted at the facilitator's private office, the courthouse, or any other agreed upon and available location.

(2) *Statements.* At least three days before the ADR session, each party shall deliver to the facilitator and all other parties or counsel a statement containing a concise discussion of all relevant factual and legal issues presented by the lawsuit. Written statements are not required for mediations conducted by the Thurston County Dispute Resolution Center.

(3) *Fees.* A fee of $100 per participating party will be charged for the first two hours of the ADR session. The fee is payable to the facilitator by check or money order at the start of the ADR session. Facilitators will charge for additional sessions or time at their customary rates. The initial two-hour session fee may be waived by the Court on proof of indigency.

(4) *Participation.* All parties and counsel shall attend the ADR session.

(5) *ADR Report.* Within 5 days after the completion of ADR, the facilitator shall file an ADR Report indicating whether the case has been resolved. A copy of the ADR Report shall be provided to the judicial assistant of the assigned judicial department and to the ADR Coordinator.

(g) Qualifications.

(1) *Settlement Conference Panel.* Settlement conferences shall be conducted by attorneys. To conduct a settlement conference under this rule, an attorney must be a member of the Washington State Bar Association who has been admitted to the Bar for a minimum of 10 years and who has included the type of case assigned in the attorney's areas of practice for at least 10 years.

(2) *Mediator Panel.* To mediate under this rule, a mediator must have completed a recognized program with at least 40 hours of instruction or training and be approved by the Court.

[Adopted effective September 1, 1997; amended effective December 30, 1999; June 1, 2000; September 1, 2004; September 1, 2005; September 1, 2007.]

LOCAL RULES FOR MANDATORY ARBITRATION

I. SCOPE AND PURPOSE OF RULES

LMAR 1.1 APPLICATION OF RULES

The purpose of mandatory arbitration of civil actions under chapter 7.06 RCW, as implemented by the Mandatory Arbitration Rules, is to provide a simplified and economical procedure for obtaining the prompt and equitable resolution of disputes involving claims of $50,000 or less. The Mandatory Arbitration Rules, as supplemented by these local rules, are not designed to address every question which may arise during the arbitration process, and the rules give considerable discretion to the arbitrator. The arbitrator should not hesitate to exercise that discretion. Arbitration hearings should be informal and expeditious, consistent with the purpose of the statutes and rules.

[Adopted effective April 1, 1984; amended effective May 1, 1990; September 1, 2000; September 1, 2007; September 1, 2011.]

LMAR 1.2. MATTERS SUBJECT TO ARBITRATION

Claims valued up to $50,000, exclusive of interest and costs, are subject to arbitration.

[Adopted effective September 1, 2011.]

LMAR 1.3. RELATIONSHIP TO SUPERIOR COURT JURISDICTION AND OTHER RULES—MOTIONS [RESCINDED]

[Rescinded effective September 1, 2011.]

II. TRANSFER TO ARBITRATION AND ASSIGNMENT OF ARBITRATOR

LMAR 2.1. TRANSFER TO ARBITRATION

(a) **Transfer Procedure.** A party to a civil case should file and serve a completed notice of arbitration setting at least 10 calendar days before the trial scheduling date. The notice of arbitration setting shall be in the form prescribed by the court. If all parties do not agree to the notice of arbitration setting, an objecting party shall file and serve an objection to arbitration before the trial scheduling date. Objections will be addressed on the date the case is noted for transfer to arbitration. If no party objects, the case shall be transferred to arbitration after payment of any required fee. Mandatory arbitration fees are subject to General Rule 34, and shall not be required from indigent parties. After assignment of an arbitrator, a party may object to arbitration only by motion to the court.

(b) **Effect of Transfer.** The assigned judge will retain the assignment after the case is transferred to arbitration.

[Adopted effective April 1, 1984. Amended effective May 1, 1990; September 1, 1997; September 1, 2000; September 1, 2008; September 1, 2011; September 2, 2013; September 1, 2015.]

LMAR 2.3. ASSIGNMENT TO ARBITRATOR

(a) **Generally; Stipulations.** When a case is set for arbitration, a list of five proposed arbitrators shall be furnished to the parties. A list of other approved arbitrators shall be available on the Thurston County Superior Court web site and at court administration. The parties are encouraged to stipulate to an arbitrator. In the absence of the stipulation within 14 days after a case is transferred to arbitration, the arbitrator shall be chosen from among the five proposed arbitrators in the manner defined by this rule.

(1) *Response by Parties.* Within 14 days after a list of proposed arbitrators is furnished to the parties, each party shall nominate one or two arbitrators and strike two arbitrators from the list. If both parties respond, an arbitrator nominated by both parties shall be appointed. If no arbitrator has been nominated by both parties, an arbitrator shall be appointed from among those not stricken by the either party.

(2) *Response by Only One Party.* If only one party responds within 14 days, an arbitrator shall be appointed from that party's response.

(3) *No Response.* If neither party responds within 14 days, the arbitrator shall be randomly appointed from the five proposed arbitrators.

(4) *Additional Arbitrators for Additional Parties.* If there are more than two adverse parties, all represented by different counsel, two additional proposed arbitrators shall be added to the list for each additional party so represented with the above principles of selection to be applied. The number of adverse parties shall be determined by the arbitration department, subject to review by the presiding judge.

[Adopted effective April 1, 1984; amended effective May 1, 1990; September 1, 2011.]

III. ARBITRATORS

LMAR 3.1. QUALIFICATIONS

(a) **Arbitration Panel.** There shall be a panel of arbitrators in such numbers as the superior court judges may from time to time determine. A person desiring to serve as an arbitrator shall complete an information sheet on the form prescribed by the court. A list showing the names of arbitrators available to hear cases and brief biographies shall be available for public inspection on the Thurston County Superior Court web site and at court administration. The oath of office on the form prescribed by the court must be completed and filed prior to an applicant being placed on the panel.

(b) **Refusal; Disqualification.** The appointment of an arbitrator is subject to the right of that person to refuse to serve. An arbitrator must notify the arbitration coordinator immediately if refusing to serve or if any cause exists for the arbitrator's disqualification from the case upon any of the grounds of interest, relationship, bias or prejudice set forth in CJC Canon 3(C) governing the disqualification of judges. If disqualified, the arbitrator must immediately return all materials in a case to the arbitration administrator.

[Adopted effective April 1, 1984; amended effective May 1, 1990; September 1, 2011.]

LMAR 3.2. AUTHORITY OF ARBITRATORS

An arbitrator has the authority to:

(a) Determine the time, place and procedure to present a motion before the arbitrator.

(b) Require a party or attorney advising such party or both to pay the reasonable expenses, including attorney's fees, caused by the failure of such party or attorney or both to obey an order of the arbitrator unless the arbitrator finds that the failure was substantially justified or that other circumstances make an award of expenses unjust. The arbitrator shall make a special award for such expenses and shall file such award with the clerk of the court, with proof of service on each party. The aggrieved party shall have 10 days thereafter to appeal the award of such expense in accordance with the procedures for revision of a court commissioner's ruling (see RCW 2.24.050). If within 10 days after the award is filed no party appeals, a judgment shall be entered in a manner described generally under MAR 6.3.

(c) Award attorney's fees as authorized by these rules, by contract or by law.

[Adopted effective April 1, 1984; amended effective May 1, 1990; September 1, 2007; September 1, 2011.]

IV. PROCEDURES AFTER ASSIGNMENT

LMAR 4.2. DISCOVERY

(a) Permitted by Arbitrator. In determining when additional discovery beyond that directly authorized by MAR 4.2 is reasonably necessary, the arbitrator shall balance the benefits of discovery against the burdens and expenses. The arbitrator shall consider the nature and complexity of the case, the amount in controversy, values at stake, the discovery that has already occurred, the burdens on the party from whom discovery is sought, and the possibility of unfair surprise that may result if discovery is restricted. Authorized discovery shall be conducted in accordance with the civil rules except that motions concerning discovery shall be determined by the arbitrator.

(b) Permitted Interrogatories. Notwithstanding the foregoing subsection (a), the following interrogatories may be submitted to any party:

(1) State the amount of general damages being claimed;

(2) State each item of special damages being claimed and the amount thereof;

(3) List the name, address and phone number of each person having knowledge of any facts regarding liability;

(4) List the name, address and phone number of each person having knowledge of any facts regarding the damages claimed;

(5) List the name, address and phone number of each expert witness you intend to call at the arbitration. For each such expert, state the subject matter on which the expert is expected to testify; state the substance of the facts and opinions to which the expert is expected to testify, and a summary of the grounds for each opinion.

(6) Provide the name, address and phone number of all health care providers, including physicians, chiropractors, dentists, physical therapists, osteopaths, hospitals, and all others who have treated you in the last seven years and the reason for the treatment.

Only the foregoing interrogatories, with the exact language as set out above, are permitted, except as permitted by subsection (a). Interrogatory (6) is permitted only in cases alleging personal injury.

(c) Effect of Limitation. The restrictions upon discovery set out in MAR 4.2 and LMAR 4.2 shall take effect upon the filing of a statement of arbitrability.

[Adopted effective April 1, 1984; amended effective September 1, 1997; September 1, 2011.]

LMAR 4.4. SETTLEMENT

(a) Notice of Settlements. If a case is settled after it has been assigned to an arbitrator, it shall be the duty of the attorneys or of any party appearing pro se to notify the court and arbitrator *promptly* of the settlement. Notice of settlement shall be in writing to the Arbitration Coordinator within 10 court days of the settlement, with a copy to the arbitrator and the assigned judge. If the settlement is made within five days before the trial date, the notice shall also be made by telephone or in person.

(b) Procedure After Settlement. After notice of settlement to the court as provided above, the parties shall cause to be entered a final judgment or order concluding the case. After 45 days, the court may, on its own motion, order that the parties show cause why such final judgment or order should not be entered.

[Adopted effective September 1, 1997; amended effective September 1, 2011.]

V. HEARING

LMAR 5.1. NOTICE OF HEARING—TIME AND PLACE—CONTINUANCE

An arbitration hearing may be scheduled at any reasonable time and place chosen by the arbitrator. The arbitrator may grant a continuance without court order. The parties may stipulate to a continuance only with the permission of the arbitrator. The arbitrator shall give reasonable notice of the hearing date and any continuance to the arbitration coordinator.

[Adopted effective April 1, 1984; amended effective May 1, 1990; September 1, 2011.]

LMAR 5.2. PREHEARING STATEMENT OF PROOF

In addition to the requirements of MAR 5.2, each party shall also furnish the arbitrator with copies of pleadings and other documents contained in the court file that the party deems relevant. The court file shall remain with the court clerk.

[Adopted effective April 1, 1984; amended effective September 1, 2011.]

LMAR 5.3. CONDUCT OF HEARING— WITNESSES—RULES OF EVIDENCE

(b) **Recording.** The hearing may be recorded electronically or otherwise by any party at that party's expense.

[Effective April 1, 1984, amended May 1, 1990.]

VI. AWARD

LMAR 6.1. FORM AND CONTENT OF AWARD

(a) **Form.** The award shall be prepared on the form prescribed by the court.

(b) **Return of Exhibits.** When an award is filed, the arbitrator shall return all exhibits to the parties who offered them during the hearing.

[Effective April 1, 1984.]

LMAR 6.2. FILING OF AWARD [RESCINDED]

[Rescinded effective September 1, 2011.]

LMAR 6.3. JUDGMENT ON AWARD [RESCINDED]

[Rescinded effective September 1, 2011.]

VII. TRIAL DE NOVO

LMAR 7.1. REQUEST FOR TRIAL DE NOVO

Cases transferred to the arbitration calendar shall be stricken from their positions on the trial calendars. Unless otherwise ordered by the court, no trial date will be assigned in cases that are subject to arbitration. Requests for trial de novo shall include a trial scheduling date that is within 30 days of service of the request, as provided in the LMAR forms. The judge initially assigned to the case retains the assignment when trial de novo is requested.

[Effective April 1, 1984. Amended May 1, 1990; amended effective September 1, 1997; September 1, 2011; September 2, 2013.]

VIII. GENERAL PROVISIONS

LMAR 8.1. STIPULATIONS

If a case not otherwise subject to mandatory arbitration is transferred to arbitration by stipulation and court order, the arbitrator may grant any relief that could have been granted if a judge determined the case.

[Adopted effective April 1, 1984; amended effective September 1, 2011.]

LMAR 8.4. TITLE AND CITATION [RESCINDED]

[Rescinded effective September 1, 2011.]

LMAR 8.6. COMPENSATION OF ARBITRATOR

(a) **Generally.** Arbitrators shall be compensated in the same amount and manner as judges pro tempore of the Thurston County Superior Court; provided, however, that the portion of the compensation received from Thurston County shall not exceed $500.00 for any case unless prior approval is granted by the presiding judge for good cause shown.

(b) **Compensation.** Compensation shall be allowed for time related to decision making functions, including review of the file, research, hearings and preparation of the decision. In addition, an arbitrator is permitted to bill for up to one hour of administrative time to schedule hearings in the proceeding.

[Effective April 1, 1984; amended May 1, 1990; amended March 1, 1995; September 1, 1997; September 1, 2003; September 1, 2005.]

LOCAL SPECIAL PROCEEDINGS RULES

I. ADOPTIONS

LSPR 93.04. ADOPTION REPORTS [REPEALED]

Repealed—covered by RCW 26.33.343 and standard order appointing Confidential Intermediaries.

[Effective October 1, 1982; amended effective December 5, 1988; May 1, 1990; repealed February 1, 1999.]

II. FAMILY AND JUVENILE COURT

LSPR 94.00. FAMILY AND JUVENILE COURT PROCEEDINGS

(a) Proceedings in the Family and Juvenile Court. The following categories of proceedings shall be heard at the Family and Juvenile Court:

(1) All actions under Title 26 RCW, including:

  (i) dissolution of marriages;

  (ii) dissolution of registered domestic partnerships;

  (iii) petitions concerning the validity of marriage;

  (iv) petitions concerning the validity of a registered domestic partnership;

  (v) paternity actions;

  (vi) non-parental custody actions; and

  (vii) adoptions.

(2) All actions under Title 13 RCW, including:

  (i) dependency and related proceedings;

  (ii) termination of parental rights;

  (iii) juvenile offender actions;

  (iv) Youth at Risk proceedings; and

  (v) Children in Need of Services proceedings.

(3) Other actions, including:

  (i) domestic violence petitions (chapter 26.50 RCW);

  (ii) anti-harassment petitions that are heard by the superior court, rather than district court (RCW 10.14.150);

  (iii) Sexual Assault Protection petitions (chapter 7.90 RCW);

  (iv) truancy actions (chapter 28A.225 RCW);

  (v) actions arising from meretricious relationship;

  (vi) name change petitions that are heard by the superior court, rather than district court, because the person seeking a name change is a domestic violence victim and moves to seal the name change record (RCW 4.24.130(5)); and

  (vii) actions regarding the abuse of vulnerable adults (chapter 74.34 RCW).

(4) All actions under Title 11 RCW, including probate, guardianship, and trusts, except that trials under the Trust and Estate Dispute Resolution Act (chapter 11.96A RCW) shall be conducted at the main campus courthouse.

(b) Location of Actions.

(1) *Generally.* A case may be relocated from the main campus courthouse to Family and Juvenile Court, or vice versa, upon motion by a party by filing a motion and supporting declaration, or by a judge by entry of an order. Upon entry of an order relocating the action, the court clerk shall transfer the file to the appropriate location until the action is completed.

(2) *Reasons to Relocate an Action.* The following types of cases may be relocated from the main campus to the Family and Juvenile Court if the court finds good cause for such a relocation:

  (i) actions for the division of marital property interests not previously distributed in a dissolution action;

  (ii) actions in which any party alleges a committed intimate relationship; and

  (ii)[1] any other action involving a party or child with another case in Family and Juvenile Court.

(c) Court Files, Hearings and Filing of Pleadings.

(1) *Case Files.* The files for all cases assigned to Family and Juvenile Court shall be maintained by the court clerk at the Family and Juvenile Court building.

(2) *Hearings.* Hearings in matters assigned to the Family and Juvenile Court shall be held at the Family and Juvenile Court building, unless otherwise directed by the Court.

(3) *Filing of Pleadings.* Initial pleadings commencing a case shall be filed at the courthouse to which that type of case is normally assigned. Only cases identified in sections (a)(1), (2), (3), and (4) may be commenced at the Family and Juvenile Court. All others must be commenced at the Superior Court, main campus, Building Two. All subsequent pleadings in a case may be filed at either courthouse. However, papers needing to be expedited should be filed at the courthouse where the hearing on the matter will be heard.

[Amended effective February 9, 1999; September 1, 2006; September 1, 2008; September 1, 2011.]

¹ So in original, probably should be (iii).

LSPR 94.01. CONCURRENT JURISDICTION OVER FAMILY COURT AND JUVENILE COURT ACTIONS

(a) Contemporaneous Actions. Contemporaneous actions are actions filed in Family and Juvenile Court involving the same family or child and having court action within the previous twelve (12) months.

(b) Concurrent Jurisdiction by Rule. The Family and Juvenile Court shall have concurrent jurisdiction over any contemporaneous action under chapters 13.32A or 13.34 RCW or title 26 RCW, except chapter 26.33 RCW, unless a party shows good cause why the Court should not exercise concurrent jurisdiction, or, unless on its own motion, the Court determines that concurrent jurisdiction should not be exercised.

(c) Concurrent Actions by Court Order. Actions filed under chapter 26.33 RCW, chapter 28A.225 RCW, title 13 RCW, and any other action assigned to Family and Juvenile Court may be subject to concurrent jurisdiction upon a showing of good cause. An order shall be entered identifying any case subject to concurrent jurisdiction that is not identified in subsection (b).

(d) Case Information Cover Sheet. To assist in the identification of concurrent actions, a Case Information Cover Sheet shall be completed upon filing of any action in the Family and Juvenile Court. The Case Information Cover Sheet may be found in the Forms Appendix.

[Adopted effective September 1, 1997; amended effective February 9, 1999.]

LSPR 94.02. MANAGEMENT OF CONCURRENT CASES

(a) Assignment of Cases. To the extent practical, and taking into account the use of court commissioners and schedules for judges' rotations, the same judicial officer will be assigned the concurrent actions of a family as identified in LSPR 94.01. The judicial officer first hearing the family's case will be assigned all subsequent concurrent actions, unless there is good cause for a different assignment. Generally, court commissioners will hear pre-trial matters, except motions for revision and settlement conferences.

(b) Scope of Concurrent Jurisdiction.

(1) *Access to Court Files.* The Court, after notice, hearing, and entry of an appropriate protective order, may authorize to parties and their attorneys in a concurrent case access to concurrent case court records and files and any files or records maintained by the Guardians ad Litem unless prohibited by law.

(2) *Party Status.* A finding of concurrent jurisdiction shall not automatically confer party status in one action on any party in another action.

(3) *Guardians Ad Litem.* The Guardian ad Litem in one proceeding may be appointed Guardian ad Litem in any concurrent action.

(4) *Parenting Plans.* Entry of a parenting plan in any concurrent case shall be conditioned upon the filing of a proper motion in a Title 26 RCW action.

(5) *Applicability of Other Rules.* In concurrent jurisdiction actions, the Superior Court Civil Rules, Juvenile Court Rules, and the Local Rules will be applicable to each action.

[Adopted effective September 1, 1997; amended effective February 9, 1999; September 1, 2005.]

LSPR 94.03. PRETRIAL PROCEDURE, TRIAL SCHEDULING, AND TRIAL IN TITLE 26 RCW CASES [REPEALED]

[Adopted effective September 1, 1997; amended effective February 9, 1999; September 1, 2000; September 1, 2002; September 1, 2003; September 1, 2006; September 1, 2008. Repealed effective September 1, 2010.]

LSPR 94.03A. CASE ASSIGNMENT

(a) Master Calendar. Cases under title 26 RCW (family law) are tried under a master calendar system.

(b) Early Assignment of Judge. Upon motion by any party, or upon the court's own motion, the court may direct assignment of an appropriate case to a single judge for all purposes, including trial.

(c) Affidavits of Prejudice. An affidavit of prejudice should be filed with the court clerk as soon as possible after the assignment of a judge has been made. The family court judicial assistant shall assign the case to a new department.

[Adopted effective September 1, 2010.]

LSPR 94.03B. MOTION PRACTICE

(a) Court Calendars.

(1) *Limits on Calendars.* The court may direct the clerk to limit the number of cases to be heard on a particular calendar. Once those cases have been confirmed for argument, if necessary, any further confirmations for that calendar will be continued to the next available family law calendar. The clerk will inform the moving or petitioning party of the continuance.

(2) *Scheduling Hearings.*

(A) Appendix of Calendar Information. The schedules and confirmation requirements for family law calendars and ex parte matters are contained in the Appendix of Calendar Information available on the court web site and in the courthouses. The schedule for these calendars may be changed throughout the year. Parties and counsel who are not familiar with Thurston County practice are advised to confirm calendar schedules before noting matters for hearings. Incorrectly scheduled matters will be stricken.

(B) Commissioners' Calendars. All motions in family law cases, except those identified below, shall be noted for hearing before the assigned court commissioner.

(C) Judges' Calendars. Motions for revision, motions for continuance of trial dates, objections to relocation, and motions in cases where all court commissioners are unable to hear the case shall be noted for hearing on the judges' motion calendar.

(D) Change of Venue Motions. Motions for change of venue shall be heard by a judge unless the parties to the case provide a written waiver prior to the hearing on the motion for change of venue. If a waiver is filed, a court commissioner may hear the motion for change of venue.

(E) Domestic Violence Cases. Parties petitioning for temporary protection orders in domestic violence cases shall be heard on a daily basis at a time specified at the time of filing. If the party can demonstrate a need for an earlier hearing, the matter may be heard pursuant to ex parte procedures.

(b) Filing Deadlines.

(1) Motions, briefs, and all supporting documents must be filed and served before 12:00 noon five court days before the motion calendar day (for example, by noon on Tuesday of the week preceding a Tuesday calendar). Upon objection, motions that violate this requirement may be stricken or continued. This rule does not affect the notice requirements of the Civil Rules or any statute.

(2) All responding documents must be filed and served before 12:00 noon two court days before the motion calendar day (for example, by noon Friday for a Tuesday calendar).

(3) All reply documents must be filed and served before 12:00 noon, one court day preceding the motion calendar day (for example, by noon Monday for a Tuesday calendar). Upon objection, late filing of responding and reply documents may result in striking the documents or a continuance and terms.

(4) *Judge's Copy.*

(A) A copy of all briefs, attachments and exhibits shall be provided to court administration at or before the time of filing the originals with the clerk. Each judge's copy shall be identified as the judge's copy and shall identify the date, time, and the judge or commissioner before whom the matter is scheduled to be heard in the top left hand corner of the first page.

(B) Judge's copies are not accepted by electronic means except as provided in this rule. In addition to a hard copy, a party may provide an additional, exact copy of judge's copies by e-mail. In emergency situations, and only if granted prior approval by court administration, a party may submit a judge's copy by facsimile.

(C) If the brief or other material does not meet these guidelines, it is subject to being returned.

(c) Confirmation of Hearings.

(1) *Calendars Requiring Confirmation.* Until the Odyssey Case Management System is implemented, all motions on a family law calendar, a commissioner's concurrent cases calendar, the relocation calendar, and a judge's motion calendar must be confirmed. Cases are confirmed by contacting the clerk's office. Parties should consult the appendix of calendar information or the notice of issue form to determine whether their matter must be confirmed.

(2) *Calendars with No Confirmation Requirement.* Confirmation is not required for motions on the State family law calendar, the self-represented parties' family law motion calendar, or the guardianship and probate calendar. Further, confirmation will no longer be required after the Odyssey Case Management System is implemented. Parties should refer to the appendix of calendar information for a complete list of confirmation requirements.

(3) *Strikes and Continuances.* Parties must strike or continue all matters that will not be heard at least two court days before the hearing date, as provided in LCR 7(b)(8).

(4) *Deadlines.* Confirmations on the family law calendar and commissioner's concurrent case calendar are due at 10:00 a.m. two court days before the hearing. Confirmations on the relocation calendar and the judge's motion calendar are due at 10:00 a.m. three court days before the hearing. If the deadline for confirmation falls on a court holiday, confirmations are due by noon on the last court day before the holiday.

(5) *Result of Failure to Confirm.* Motions that are not confirmed will be stricken or continued at the court's discretion.

(d) Submission Requirements.

(1) *Document Requirements.* All declarations and affidavits filed shall be legible and printed or typewritten in black or dark blue ink on paper suitable for scanning. Declarations and affidavits shall be one-sided only.

(2) *Page Limits.*

(A) Absent prior authorization from the court as set forth in (D) below, the entirety of all declarations and affidavits from the parties and any non-expert witnesses in support of motions, including any reply, shall be limited to a sum total of 20 pages. The entirety of all declarations and affidavits submitted in response to motions shall be limited to a sum total of 20 pages. The court will disregard every page after the first 20 pages if the court has not authorized the party to exceed the page limit.

(B) Exhibits Included In Page Limits. All exhibits that consist of declarations or affidavits will count toward the above page limits, unless listed in (C) below or authorized as set forth in (D).

(C) Exhibits Not Included In Page Limits. The following are not included in the 20 page limit:

(i) financial declarations and supporting financial documents;

(ii) declarations, affidavits, or reports from guardians ad litem and expert witnesses;

(iii) copies of declarations or affidavits previously filed for a motion already ruled upon and supplied only as a convenience in lieu of the court file; and

(iv) if parties and attorneys quote only the relevant parts of the e-mails, journals, or depositions in the declaration or brief and attach the full version of e-mail, journal or deposition as an exhibit for context, the full version of the materials will not count against the page limit if labeled as such for that limited purpose.

(D) Authorization. A party seeking authorization to exceed the page limit may do so on the *ex parte* calendar with notice to opposing counsel or a self-represented party. Opposing counsel or the self-represented party may appear telephonically for the authorization hearing.

(e) Hearings—Time for Argument. Each side will be allowed ten minutes to argue a contested motion, including rebuttal, unless the court allows additional time. Arguments requiring more than ten minutes per side may be specially set.

[Adopted effective September 1, 2010. Amended effective September 1, 2011; September 2, 2013; September 2, 2014; September 1, 2015.]

LSPR 94.03C.   EX PARTE REQUESTS

(a) Ex Parte Departments. Ex parte matters will be heard at the Family and Juvenile Court on a schedule set forth in the Appendix of Calendar Information. In addition, a call for ex parte matters will be made at the beginning of each morning and afternoon session in each courtroom and at such other times when the court's schedule can accommodate a matter. Ex parte matters should be presented to the most appropriate department in session.

(b) Presentation of Order. Ex parte orders presented for entry must be accompanied by a written motion, original supporting documents, and the case file from the court clerk.

(c) Presentation in Self–Represented Cases. Any ex parte motion and order to be presented by a self-represented party shall be reviewed by the Family Law Courthouse Facilitator before the motion is submitted to a judicial officer for consideration.

(d) Alternative Presentation by Mail or Drop Box.

(1) *What is allowed.*

(A) By mail. Agreed orders, orders when notice of presentation is waived, and ex parte orders based upon the record in the file may be presented by mail.

(B) By drop box. Agreed orders and orders when notice of presentation is waived, and which do not require reference to the case file, may be left at the desk of the court receptionist for presentation.

(2) *Who may present.* Except for good cause, these alternative methods of presentation are available only to counsel licensed to practice law.

(3) *Required documents.* A person presenting an order under this rule must send the original order, supporting materials, and the required fee in the clerk's fee schedule (LCR 79(a)) to the court clerk. Self addressed, stamped envelopes, along with copies of the order to be signed, shall also be provided for return of any conformed materials or rejected orders.

(4) *Judicial procedure.* Orders will be directed to the ex parte judicial officer. When accepted, the court will sign the order and cause it to be entered. When rejected, the papers will be returned by mail to the counsel sending them without prejudice to presentation by counsel in person to the same judge.

[Adopted effective September 1, 2010.]

LSPR 94.03D.   SETTLEMENT AND PRETRIAL CONFERENCES

(a) Settlement Conferences.

(1) *Requirement.* All contested family law cases shall be set for settlement conference before assignment of a trial date, unless otherwise ordered by the court. Upon filing of notice for settlement conference setting, the court shall assign the earliest available date. The case must be at issue before the settlement conference setting. In dissolution actions, paternity, and nonparental custody actions, if a settlement conference setting has not been requested within four months from the date the action was filed, the court may order a settlement conference setting with notice to the parties or counsel of record.

(2) *Scheduling.*

(A) To initiate the setting of a settlement conference, the moving party must file a Note for Settlement Conference and set the matter for hearing in accordance with the court's calendar. The scheduling shall occur within 120 days of the filing of the first responsive pleading, unless required mediation has not been completed. The Note for and Response to Settlement Conference setting may be found in the forms appendix. The note for hearing must be filed fourteen days before the date scheduled for the hearing.

(B) The responding party to a Note for Settlement Conference Setting must file a Note for and Response to Settlement Conference Setting seven days before the date scheduled for the hearing. The Note for and Response to Settlement Conference Setting may be found in the forms appendix.

(C) A party may object that a case is not ready for a settlement conference by filing and serving an objection no later than noon, three court days preceding the date noted. The matter shall then be referred to a judge to determine whether the case is ready for a settlement conference. The court may require a hearing. If the matter is determined to be ready for settlement conference setting, the case will be returned to the case scheduler for settlement conference assignment. Otherwise, the judge may order a date by which the case shall be made ready for settlement conference setting. The court may also determine, on its own motion, that the case is not ready for a settlement conference.

(3) *Attendance and Preparation Required.* The parties and their attorneys shall personally attend the settlement conference unless other arrangements are approved by the court prior to the settlement conference. At the settlement conference, each party shall be prepared to address the unresolved issues and negotiate settlement of the case in good faith.

(4) *Mandatory Discovery.* Parties shall exchange, as appropriate, the following documents no later than fourteen days before the conference. If a document is not produced, a brief explanation of why it is not produced is required:

(A) complete individual or joint tax returns for the past two calendar years, together with all schedules, 1099s and similar statements of income, and W–2s;

(B) complete partnership and/or corporate tax returns for the past two years together with all schedules and attachments for all partnerships and corporations in which a party has had an interest of five per cent or greater;

(C) all pay stubs showing income for the past six months or since January 1 of the calendar year, whichever period is longer;

(D) a copy of the most recent statements and a copy of statements current as of the date of the parties' separation, of balances due on mortgages, real estate purchase contracts, deeds of trust, installment purchase contracts, time payment accounts, credit cards, and other debt owed by or to the parties;

(E) the most recent employers' Employee Retirement Income Security Act (ERISA) statement and a statement of contributions since that statement of any pension plan of either party; the most recent statements, and statements as of the date of separation, for any Individual Retirement Account (IRA), Simplified Employee Pension plan (SEP), deferred compensation account, or other defined contribution "retirement" account;

(F) a written appraisal of any real estate and/or personal property of special, unusual, or extraordinary value, or a summary of the evidence that will be relied upon to value such items;

(G) the most recent National Automobile Dealers Association (N.A.D.A.) Official Used Car Guide, or other similar vehicle appraisal guide showing both average loan or wholesale and retail values for any automobiles;

(H) a summary of the source and tracing of any property asserted to be the separate property of either party;

(I) a statement from each life insurance company issuing a policy of insurance on the life of either party as to its cash value and any loans against its cash value;

(J) a written appraisal/business evaluation of any proprietorship, partnership, or closely held corporation of the parties, or a summary of the evidence that will be relied upon to value the same; and

(K) expert witnesses shall be disclosed no later than at the time of the discovery exchange.

(5) *Settlement Conference Statement.* Each party shall serve upon the other party and provide to the court a settlement conference statement no later than fourteen calendar days prior to the settlement conference, unless the parties agree to a shorter period of time. The shorter period for exchange shall not be less than seven calendar days before the settlement conference. The settlement conference statement should be in a form similar to that contained in the Forms Appendix—Family and Juvenile Court Forms. Parties may supplement the information provided in

the preferred form with a written statement further describing the issues.

(6) *Sanctions.* If a party fails to comply with the provisions of (3), (4), and (5) above, then the court may immediately impose sanctions not to exceed $500.

(7) *Other Documents.* If child support or a parenting plan is at issue in the action, a proposed child support worksheet and a proposed final parenting plan shall be attached to the settlement conference statement of each party.

(8) *Negotiations Before Settlement Conference.* After the settlement conference statements are served, the parties are encouraged to negotiate and exchange additional documentation. Parties may file supplemental settlement conference statements at any time prior to the settlement conference if the party's analysis or proposal to resolve all issues has changed after reviewing the other party's settlement conference statement. If the parties are able to resolve all issues prior to the settlement conference, they should appear at the conference prepared to present testimony and enter final orders completing the dissolution or to put the settlement agreement on the record.

(9) *Completion.* At the completion of a settlement conference, the court shall schedule a hearing for presentation of final papers if settlement is achieved, schedule a continuation of the settlement conference if warranted and time is available, or schedule the matter for trial.

(10) *Negotiations After Settlement Conference.* If the settlement conference does not result in complete resolution of the case, each party shall submit to the other a written settlement proposal addressing all unresolved issues. This offer shall be submitted within 30 days after the settlement conference, but not less than 21 days before trial.

(b) Pretrial Conferences.

(1) *Requirement.* All family law (RCW titles 26.09, 26.10, and 26.26), dependency, and termination of parental rights actions shall have a pretrial conference with the trial judge prior to trial. Other cases set for an evidentiary hearing at Family and Juvenile Court may have a pretrial conference if requested by the trial judge. This rule does not apply to juvenile offender proceedings.

(2) *Scheduling.* The pretrial conference shall be held within three weeks of trial. The date of the pretrial conference shall be included on the Case Schedule Order in dependency and termination cases.

(3) *Subjects for the Conference.* The pretrial conference shall address:

(A) the length of the trial, including opening and closing;

(B) confirmation of witnesses and coordination of scheduling;

(C) identification of exhibits and agreement on admission where possible; and

(D) discussion of anticipated pretrial motions or problems.

(4) *Attendance.* Attorneys for the State and the parents shall be required to attend the pretrial conference in dependency and termination cases. Attorneys for the parties and the parties shall be required to attend the pretrial conference in family law cases.

[Adopted effective September 1, 2010. Amended effective September 1, 2011; September 2, 2013.]

LSPR 94.03E.   TRIALS

(a) Trial Date Priorities. Cases involving the relocation of children, determination of dependency, or termination of parental rights where children are not in the care of a parent shall be accorded the highest priority in setting a trial date.

(b) Assignment for Trial.

(1) In cases where a settlement conference is required, a trial date shall be set at the conclusion of the conference if settlement is not reached.

(2) In cases where a settlement conference is not required, a party or counsel may schedule the matter for trial setting by filing a note for trial setting for hearing on the calendar for settlement conference settings, as shown in the Appendix of Calendar Information. The note for trial should be filed 14 days before the time for hearing on the calendar and should indicate the nature of the case, the number of expected factual witnesses, the number of expert witnesses, the expected length of trial, and available dates. The responding party may file a response to this note for trial setting not less than seven days prior to the hearing, providing similar information for that party's case. If the responding party objects to trial setting, the matter shall be referred to a judge for determination of whether the case is ready for trial setting. The objection shall be filed not later than three days before the date scheduled for trial setting. If the judge determines the matter is ready for trial, the case will be referred back to the case scheduler for trial setting. If the judge determines the matter is not ready for trial setting, the judge may enter an order determining when the case shall be ready for trial setting.

(3) Cases set for trial will be assigned to a week for trial. No specific starting date will be assigned, except early assignment of a judge may be ordered in appropriate cases under these Local Special Rules of Proceeding's rule regarding case assignments (LSPR 94.03A). During a week of trial, priorities among the cases scheduled will be determined at scheduling conference. In those cases where a date certain for trial is necessary due to out-of-state parties or other limited circumstances, a party may move for a trial starting on a date certain prior to the time of trial setting. Failure to seek a date certain trial prior to the time

the matter is set for trial shall constitute a waiver of the right to a date certain trial.

(c) Scheduling Conference. Each case which has been scheduled for trial but which has not settled will have a scheduling conference on the Thursday before the week for trial. If the day for scheduling conference is a legal holiday, the scheduling conferences will be held on the Wednesday before the week for trial. The purpose of this conference will be to assist the court in determining priorities among cases set for trial the following week, the issues for trial, and the length of trial.

(d) Trailing Trial Week. Any case that is not called for trial during its assigned week shall trail to the last week of that month for trial. The trailing week shall be the last week of a month that contains the last Wednesday of that month.

(e) Continuances. A case shall proceed to trial or shall be dismissed when it is called unless a continuance is ordered by the court.

(1) *Form of the Motion.* A motion for continuance of trial shall be filed, served and heard by a judge before the scheduling conference. A motion for continuance must (i) contain written acknowledgment of the motion by the client, and (ii) be accompanied by an affidavit giving the specific reasons necessitating a continuance.

(2) *Conditions of Order for Continuance.* A continuance will be ordered only for good cause. The court may impose terms upon a party or counsel who is not prepared for trial. Any case that is continued will be immediately referred to the case scheduler for a new trial date.

(f) Trial Briefs and Required Information. In all dissolution and legal separation trials where property or liabilities are at issue, each party shall submit a proposed division of assets and liabilities. In any family law matter where child support, maintenance, attorney fees, or costs are at issue, each party shall prepare a current Financial Declaration (Washington Pattern Form DR 01.0550), attaching, if necessary, the materials identified in the LSPR regarding motion practice (LSPR 94.03B). If child support is at issue, each party shall prepare the Washington State Child Support Worksheets. In any family law matter where a parenting plan is at issue, each party shall prepare a proposed parenting plan. The above information shall be submitted as a bench copy to the judge and served on opposing counsel or self-represented party by noon two judicial days prior to trial. Additionally, each party shall file a trial brief with the clerk and serve a copy on opposing counsel or self-represented party by noon two judicial days before trial.

(g) Exhibits. Before trial convenes, each party shall provide the other parties an opportunity to review all exhibits to be offered, and the other parties shall review such exhibits to determine which exhibits may be admitted by stipulation.

(h) Proposed Final Orders. Each party to a family law trial may provide proposed findings of fact and conclusions of law and proposed decrees to be used as trial exhibits. In proceedings involving children, each party shall provide a proposed parenting plan and a proposed order of child support and child support worksheets for use as trial exhibits.

(i) Attorney Fees and Costs. In considering a request for an award of attorney fees and costs at trial based on bad faith or intransigence, the court may consider settlement proposals that have been communicated in writing before trial. However, these settlement proposals shall not be submitted to the court or referred to in argument until a ruling on all other issues has been rendered.

[Adopted effective September 1, 2010; amended effective September 1, 2011.]

LSPR 94.04.   FINALIZING FAMILY LAW ACTIONS

(a) Uncontested Dissolutions.

(1) *Calendar.* Any uncontested dissolution action may be brought on for final hearing by noting it for the calendar for final dissolutions with attorneys or the calendar for final dissolutions without attorneys, as appropriate.

(2) *Note for Final Dissolution Calendar.* A notice of hearing for the calendar for final dissolutions must be filed with the clerk no later than five court days before the hearing on the calendar for final dissolutions.

(3) *Self Represented Parties.* Self represented parties are encouraged to note the matter for final hearing and to provide proposed final papers to the clerk more than thirty days before the hearing. Matters shall be placed on this calendar only if the file shows the following:

(A) The petitioner's opponent has joined in the petition for dissolution of marriage; or

(B) The respondent has agreed in writing to entry of the proposed final papers; or

(C) An order of default has been entered or is appropriate and available for entry at the time of hearing.

(b) Final Testimony. In cases in which neither party is represented by an attorney (LSPR 94.04(c)(5)), brief testimony shall be required before entry of a Decree of Dissolution of Marriage, a Decree of Dissolution of Registered Domestic Partnership, a Decree of Legal Separation, a Declaration Concerning Validity of Marriage, a Declaration Concerning Validity of Registered Domestic Partnership, a Judgment and Order Establishing Residential Schedule and Child Support, a Non-parental Custody Decree or a

Judgment and Order Determining Parentage. The testimony shall be scheduled on the following calendars:

(1) Dissolution of Marriage, Dissolution of domestic Partnership Legal Separation, Declaration Concerning Validity of Marriage, Declaration Concerning Validity of Registered Domestic Partnership, or Judgment and Order Establishing Residential Schedule and Child Support: Final Dissolution Calendar, with or without attorneys as appropriate.

(2) *Parentage:* State Parentage/Support Calendar or Family Law Motion Calendar, with or without attorneys as appropriate.

(3) *Non-parental Custody: Non-parental Custody Calendar.* Testimony may also be presented at a settlement conference or a trial.

(c) Entry of Decree.

(1) *Time of Presenting Documents for Signature.* At the time of hearing of an uncontested dissolution case, the necessary documents to be signed must be presented to the court for signature. If signed, they shall be filed with the clerk. For good cause, the Court may extend the time for presentation.

(2) *Review of Final Pleadings.* All final decrees, final orders and any accompanying Findings of Fact/Conclusions of Law, Parenting Plans, Orders of Child Support and Child Support Worksheets for family law cases shall be reviewed for form and completeness before presentation to a judicial officer by an attorney of record in the case, an attorney who approves the pleadings as to form and completeness, the Courthouse Facilitator, or the Thurston County Volunteer Legal Clinic. The Guardian ad Litem's approval of the parenting plan shall meet the review requirement for the parenting plan.

(3) *Notice to State of Washington.* No final decree or accompanying orders for child support and child support worksheets shall be entered in any family law case where a party to receive support for any dependent child shall be, at that time, a beneficiary of public assistance unless and until notice has been given to the Washington State Department of Social and Health Services, Office of Support Enforcement, or the Thurston County Prosecuting Attorney's Office, Family Support Division.

(4) *Documents.* In matters involving minor children, a decree of dissolution shall not be entered unless support worksheets and a proposed or agreed parenting plan have been filed by each party and the LSPR 94.06 requirements have been satisfied.

(5) *Testimony Not Required.* The court may enter agreed or default final orders without a final hearing or oral testimony when (a) at least one of the parties is represented by an attorney, (b) the findings of fact are verified by the petitioner or the respondent as provided in this rule, and (c) the matter is the following type of case:

(A) dissolution,

(B) legal separation,

(C) invalidity of marriage,

(D) parenting plan modification,

(E) child support modification,

(F) non-parental custody,

(G) paternity, or

(H) residential schedule, parenting plan, or child support for unmarried parents with a paternity acknowledgment.

Verification shall be as follows:

State of Washington)
) ss.
County of Thurston)

_____ (name) being first duly sworn on oath deposes and says:

I am the Petitioner or Respondent in this case and I have read the foregoing findings of fact and conclusions of law, parenting plan, support order, and related documents, if included herein, and they are true and accurate to the best of my knowledge. If this is a default, I am not seeking any relief beyond that specifically requested in the petition. The support requested, if any, is in compliance with the Washington State Child Support Schedule.

(s) _____
    Petitioner's or Respondent's Signature

SUBSCRIBED AND SWORN TO before me this _____ day of _____, 20_____.

(s) _____
Notary Public for the State of Washington,
residing at _____.
My commission expires _____.

(6) *Mailing of Final Documents.* Following the entry of final documents by default in a family law matter, the moving party or attorney for the moving party shall immediately deliver or mail to the other party, at his or her last known address, a conformed copy of all final pleadings.

(d) Non-Parental Custody Actions. In all actions for non-parental custody, at the time the Temporary Order is entered, the court shall set a review hearing six (6) months from the entry of the Temporary Order. If a matter is not ready to be finalized at the six (6) month review hearing, then the matter shall immediately be set for a settlement conference.

[Effective October 1, 1982; amended July 1, 1988; December 1, 1988; May 1, 1990; September 1, 1991; September 1, 1997; February 9, 1999; amended effective September 1, 2006; September 1, 2008; September 2, 2014.]

LSPR 94.05. MANDATORY MEDIATION FOR PARENTING PLANS AND RESIDENTIAL SCHEDULES

(a) Scope. This rule applies to any proceeding before the court in which a parenting plan or residential schedule is at issue, except juvenile court dependency proceedings. A copy of the form entitled "Mandatory Parenting Plan Mediation Program" shall be served with the petition and included on the affidavit of service. The form is available on the Thurston County Superior Court web site and in the courthouse.

(b) Mediation Required. All parenting plan and residential schedule issues shall be submitted to mandatory mediation within 120 days after the Respondent files a pleading. The mediation requirement may be waived by the court in cases involving domestic violence or in other cases upon a showing of good cause. A motion for waiver shall be noted before the court commissioner. An Order Waiving Mediation shall be filed with the court prior to the case being set for settlement conference or trial.

(c) Superior Court Jurisdiction and Other Rules—Show Cause Hearings. The requirement for mediation shall not prevent the judicial officer from entering temporary orders.

(d) Mediators. The court maintains a list of approved family law mediators, including the Thurston County Dispute Resolution Center. If the parties do not agree on a mediator, the court will assign a mediator upon request.

(e) Authority of Mediator. The mediator has the authority to determine the time, place and duration of mediation. In appropriate cases, the mediator shall have the authority to terminate the mediation prior to completion.

(f) Attendance. Mediation sessions shall normally include the parties only, but may, by agreement of the parties, include other persons. Further, the court may authorize the presence of an advocate during mediation, under the court's discretion or under RCW 26.09.016. Attendance at mediation sessions is mandatory.

(g) Declaration of Completion. Within seven days of completion, a declaration of completion shall be filed by the mediator. The mediator shall advise the court only whether an agreement has been reached.

(h) Noting for Settlement Conference and Trial Setting. Either party may request a settlement conference at the commencement of mediation if issues in addition to a parenting plan or residential schedule are disputed. In cases in which a parenting plan or residential schedule are the ONLY issues, the parties may request a trial date after the case has been in mediation for a period of 60 days, or sooner if a

Declaration of Completion has been filed. The period shall begin when a mediator is appointed.

(i) Confidentiality. The work product of the mediator and all communications during mediation may be admissible for limited purposes (RCW 26.09.015). The mediator shall not appear or testify in any court proceedings except by court order (RCW 26.09.015).

[Adopted effective April 1, 1987; amended effective May 1, 199; February 1, 1994; July 1, 1998; February 9, 1999; September 1, 2011; September 1, 2012; September 2, 2014.]

LSPR 94.06. PARENTING SEMINARS

(a) Applicable Cases. This rule shall apply to all cases filed after December 1, 1994 under Ch. 26.09 and Ch. 26.26 RCW which require a parenting plan for minor children; including dissolutions of marriage with children, dissolutions of registered domestic partnerships with children, legal separations, major modifications, and paternity actions in which paternity has been established. A copy of the form entitled "Information for Persons Involved in a Custody Action" shall be served with the petition and included in the affidavit of service. The form is available in the Appendix of Forms.

(b) Mandatory Attendance. All parties involved in cases governed by this rule shall complete an approved four-hour parenting seminar, except parties who have previously attended the parenting seminar within the last two years. Standards for parenting seminars shall be established by the Court and providers shall be approved by the Court.

(c) Timing. Parties required by this rule to participate in a parenting seminar shall complete an approved parenting seminar within 45 days after service of the petition or motion initiating the action which is subject to this rule. Parties should file proof of completion of the parenting seminar as soon as possible after completion. In the case of paternity actions initiated by the prosecuting attorney's office, the parenting seminar shall be required only when paternity is established or acknowledged and a parenting plan is requested.

(d) Fees. Each party attending a seminar shall pay a fee charged by the approved provider and sanctioned by the Court. The Court may waive the fee for indigent parties.

(e) Special Consideration/Waiver.

(1) In no case shall opposing parties be required to attend a seminar together.

(2) Upon a showing of domestic violence or abuse which would not require mutual decision-making, pursuant to RCW 26.09.191, or that a parents attendance at a seminar is not in the children's best interest, pursuant to Ch. 26.12 RCW, the Court shall either:

(A) waive the requirement of completion of the seminar; or

(B) allow participation in an alternative voluntary parenting seminar for battered spouses.

(3) The Court may waive the seminar requirement for good cause shown.

(f) Failure to Attend/Sanctions. Willful failure to participate in a parenting seminar or willful delay in completion of a parenting seminar by any party may constitute contempt of court and result in sanctions, including, but not limited to, imposition of monetary terms, striking of pleadings, or denial of affirmative relief to a party not in compliance with this rule.

[Amended effective July 1, 1998; September 1, 2006; September 1, 2008.]

LSPR 94.07. APPOINTMENTS OF GUARDIANS AD LITEM

(a) Supplemental Order. In all family law cases in which a Guardian ad Litem is appointed for a minor, the Court shall enter an "Order Appointing Guardian ad Litem (Supplemental)" in addition to the mandatory "Order Appointing Guardian ad Litem" form. The form of the Supplemental Order may be found in the Forms Appendix.

(b) Order Authorizing Release (Criminal History Release). In all family law cases in which a Guardian ad Litem is appointed for a minor, the Court shall enter an "Order Authorizing Release of Criminal History Records and CPS Records To Guardian ad Litem (Criminal History Release)." Each party and adult residing in a party's household shall attach a legible copy of their current drivers' license or State Identification to the Order Authorizing Release of Criminal History Records and CPS Records to Guardian ad Litem, which may be found in the Forms Appendix.

[Effective February 1, 1999. Amended effective September 1, 2006.]

LSPR 94.08. JUDICIAL OFFICER TRAINING

(a) Initial Training. All judicial officers assigned to Family and Juvenile Court for six months or more in a calendar year shall complete training including the subject areas of childhood development, domestic violence, cultural awareness, child abuse and neglect, chemical dependency, and mental illness. The training requirement may be satisfied by training programs attended within 12 months prior to the assignment or within six months after beginning the assignment.

(b) Continuing Training. Subsequent to initial training, judicial officers assigned to Family and Juvenile Court under paragraph (a) above shall annually attend a minimum of eight hours of continuing education on subjects relevant to families and children in the court.

(c) Training for Court Commissioners and Pro Tempore Judges. To serve as a court commissioner

or pro tem judge at Family and Juvenile Court on a regular or substitute assignment, an attorney shall have completed the Guardian ad Litem training curriculum or its equivalent, except for good cause, and any other training required by the court.

[Adopted effective September 1, 2000; amended effective September 1, 2011.]

LSPR 94.09. FINALIZING FAMILY LAW CASES

Recodified into LSPR 94.04.

[Adopted effective September 1, 2001. Amended effective September 1, 2005; September 1, 2006; recodified effective September 1, 2008.]

LSPR 94.10. RESPONSE TO DEPENDENCY OR TERMINATION PETITION [REPEALED]

[Adopted effective September 1, 2002. Repealed effective September 1, 2010.]

LSPR 94.11. ORIENTATION IN FAMILY LAW MATTERS

(a) Description. In an effort to promote less adversarial choices for parties with children beginning family law actions, the Thurston County Superior Court provides an Orientation Program. This Orientation may include:

(1) information from a courthouse facilitator on court processes,

(2) an introduction to the Parenting Seminar regarding how children are affected by their parents' separation, and an opportunity to schedule an appointment for the Seminar required under the local rule regarding parenting seminars (LSPR 94.06), and

(3) a video presentation on mediation and an opportunity for schedule a mediation appointment through court administration.

Following completion of the Orientation, and mediation, if applicable, any unresolved motions or show cause issues that have been properly filed and scheduled will be heard by the Court.

(b) Requirement.

(1) *Dissolutions/Legal Separations with Children.* In dissolutions of marriage with children, legal separations with children, and dissolutions of registered domestic partnerships with children, the parties to the action shall be required to complete an Orientation to the Family Court System.

(2) *Out of State Resident.* A party residing outside the State of Washington shall be excused from attending the Orientation if attendance would be a hardship.

(3) *Out of County Residents.* A party residing outside of Thurston County may be excused from attending the Orientation if attendance would be a hardship.

(4) *Represented Parties.* Attendance at the Orientation shall be excused for a party who is represented by an attorney upon filing a declaration that the party shall attend the Parenting Seminar in compliance with these local rules (LSPR 94.06(c)) and mediation shall be scheduled for disputed issues related to the parenting plan within 30 days from the date of filing or service. If an attorney withdraws from a case without substitution of new counsel, then the notice of withdrawal under Washington State Civil Court Rules (CR 71) shall provide notice of the party's responsibility to attend the Orientation. The withdrawing attorney shall file a Notice of Issue scheduling the Orientation for the party. This requirement for completion of the Orientation may be excused as otherwise permitted. A petitioner shall be required to schedule the Orientation for the respondent and serve notice as otherwise required by this rule.

(5) *Good Cause.* Participation in the Orientation Program may be excused or modified upon a showing of good cause.

(c) **Renewal.** The court may renew the requirement of attendance at the Orientation Program at any time in cases where attendance was previously excused.

(d) **Scheduling.** At the time an action requiring Orientation is filed, the petitioner shall schedule attendance at the Orientation Program for both parties to occur within 30 days of filing. The parties shall not be required to attend the same Orientation session. The summons and petition for dissolution shall not be accepted for filing by the Court Clerk unless the notice of issue scheduling the Orientation for both parties is filed at the same time, or attendance at Orientation is excused under the "requirement" section of this rule. Any party requesting a hearing, and any party responding to a request for hearing, shall attend the Orientation before the hearing. Initial hearings for temporary orders and on Orders to Show Cause shall be scheduled on the same day as the Orientation Program absent good cause. Attendance at the Orientation Program is not required prior to emergency hearings.

(e) **Service.** The petitioner shall serve the notice of issue scheduling the Orientation Program on the respondent at the time the Summons and Petition is served. In the event a joinder in the petition is filed, the petitioner shall serve the notice of issue scheduling the Orientation Program on the respondent within seven days of filing.

[Adopted as emergency rule effective December 29, 2003; April 2, 2004; amended effective September 1, 2005; September 1, 2006; September 1, 2008; September 1, 2011.]

LSPR 94.12. COLLABORATIVE LAW PROCESS

(a) **Commencement.** Parties to a family law action may enter a Collaborative Law Participation Agreement, and upon filing of a Notice of Participation in Collaborative Law by both parties, the action may be removed from case management processes by court order.

(b) **Effect.** Upon removal of a family law action from case management processes, the parties to the action may be excused by court order from orientation, settlement conferences, and mediation, for a period of nine months from the date the Petition for Dissolution was filed, or the date the Notice of Participation in Collaborative Law was filed. Entry into a Collaborative Law Participation Agreement shall not excuse completion of the Parenting Seminar required by LSPR 94.06 by parties with children. If the parties return to the case management processes, the parties' participation in Collaborative Law shall serve to satisfy mediation requirements.

(c) **Termination.** Upon completion or termination of the Collaborative Law process, a Notice of Withdrawal from Participation in Collaborative Law shall be filed with the court.

[Adopted effective September 1, 2006.]

LSPR 94.13. PARENTING COORDINATION

(a) **Purpose.** In order to better serve high conflict families who are subject to parenting plans, the court may appoint parenting coordinators to provide timely intervention in parenting disputes. The parenting coordinator will assist parents in making decisions regarding their children in accordance with the parenting plan, without involving the children or the court.

(b) **Qualifications of Parenting Coordinators.** Individuals serving on the Thurston County Title 26 Guardian ad Litem or Mediation Registries may request to serve as a parenting coordinator. An applicant shall complete an interview and court-approved parenting coordination training and is subject to court approval. Parenting coordinators shall be listed on a separate registry.

(c) **Appointment.**

(1) A parenting coordinator may be appointed at any time after entry of a temporary or final parenting plan.

(2) A parenting coordinator may be appointed upon the request of a party, an attorney, the guardian ad litem, or on the court's own determination.

(3) An initial appointment of a parenting coordinator shall be for no more than ten hours. Appointments may be extended by agreement of the parties in writing or court order.

(d) **Payment.** The costs of a parenting coordinator shall be paid by the parties in such proportions as determined by the court. A parenting coordinator shall bill for no more than three hours of background preparation done upon appointment, including initial parent interviews.

(e) Authority of the Parenting Coordinator.

(1) A parenting coordinator will assist the parties in resolving disputed issues by clarifying misunderstandings, interpreting the parenting plan, working on compromise where appropriate, and making recommendations for resolution.

(2) A parenting coordinator will not have authority to order the parents to do anything unless the parties grant this authority in writing.

(f) Responsibilities of Parents.

(1) Each parent shall sign releases of records for the parenting coordinator.

(2) Each parent shall contact the parenting coordinator within seven days of the appointment.

(3) Each parent shall attempt to resolve parenting disputes through the parenting coordinator before initiating court action, except on issues of safety.

(g) Responsibilities of the Parenting Coordinator.

(1) The parenting coordinator shall meet with each parent after appointment.

(2) The parenting coordinator shall review the current parenting plan, any restraining or protection orders, and any guardian ad litem report.

(3) The parenting coordinator shall determine whether any hearings are scheduled and may request the hearings be postponed.

(4) The parenting coordinator shall maintain a log of contacts, agreements, recommendations, and follow-through of the parties.

(5) The parenting coordinator is not required to attend hearings unless requested by the court. If there is a contested hearing related to parenting issues during the time of the appointment, the parenting coordinator shall file with the court the relevant portions of the service log or a summary report of no more than two pages.

(h) Terminating from Parent Coordination. In the event a party or attorney believes the services of a parent coordinator are not beneficial, he or she may request the court terminate the parent coordinator's appointment. The court may terminate a parent coordinator's appointment for good cause.

[Adopted effective September 1, 2009. Amended effective September 1, 2010.]

LSPR 94.14. MOTIONS FOR RECONSIDERATION AND REVISION

(a) Motions for Reconsideration. Motions for reconsideration of family law matters shall comply with the procedure in the Thurston County Local Court Rules for motions for reconsideration (LCR 59).

(b) Motions for Revision of Court Commissioner's Order or Judgment. Motions for revision are governed by Local Court Rule 53.2.

[Adopted effective September 2, 2013. Amended effective September 2, 2014; September 1, 2015.]

III.   ESTATES—PROBATE—GUARDIANSHIPS

LSPR 98.04.   HEARINGS

(a) Ex Parte Hearings. All probate matters that are not contested, and in which notice is not required by statute, rule, or a duly filed request for notice under RCW 11.28.240, or where such notice has been waived, may be heard ex parte. When a probate matter is presented ex parte, counsel shall procure the court file from the clerk and present it to the court at the time of hearing. Ex parte probate matters may be presented by mail in compliance with the requirements of LCR 16(g)(3).

(b) Testimony. Testimony required to open a proceedings may be presented orally, by affidavit or by verified petition.

(c) Bonds to be Signed by Principal. All bonds required of personal representative shall be signed by the principal and sureties.

(d) Order for Production of Wills. Upon filing a petition showing jurisdictional facts as to the estate of a deceased person and alleging that a will exists and is

in a safety deposit box to which the deceased had access, any person having control of such safety deposit box may be directed by court order to open such box in the presence of the petitioner. If a document purporting to be a will of the deceased is found, the custodian of such safety deposit box shall deliver the same to the clerk of the court. The clerk, on demand, and on payment of fees, shall issue a receipt for the same, attaching a copy of the will. The fees and mileage to the custodian for such delivery shall be the same as those for any witness and shall be paid by the petitioner, together with expenses incurred.

(e) Probate Homesteads; Prior Claims. In all cases where a petition for allowance in lieu of homestead is filed by the surviving spouse, vouchers showing payment of funeral expenses, expenses of last sickness and of administration including fees of appraisers, or that such payment has been provided for, must be filed at or before the time of the hearing.

[Effective October 1, 1982; amended May 1, 1990; March 1, 1995.]

LSPR 98.05. GUARDIANSHIP ORDERS AND REPORTS [RESCINDED]

[Amended effective September 1, 2005; September 1, 2008; September 1, 2011; rescinded effective September 1, 2012.]

LSPR 98.16W. ESTATES—GUARDIANSHIP—SETTLEMENT OF CLAIMS OF MINORS AND INCAPACITATED PERSONS

(a) Hearing.

(1) The party who is petitioning for approval of a settlement under this rule must nominate a Settlement Guardian ad Litem and present the nominee's qualifications to the court. The motion to appoint a SGAL may be presented ex parte.

(2) Petitions for approval of settlements shall be noted on the Friday Motion Calendar of the assigned judge, absent good cause for immediate action. The court may excuse the appearance of counsel at its discretion.

(3) Judge's copies of the guardian ad litem's or independent counsel's report and the petition for approval of the settlement shall be submitted to the court not later than noon seven calendar days before the scheduled hearing.

[Adopted effective September 1, 2002. Amended effective September 1, 2011; September 1, 2015.]

LOCAL GUARDIAN AD LITEM RULES

LGALR 5. GUARDIAN AD LITEM APPOINTMENT PROCEDURES

(a) Appointment of Guardians Ad Litem—Title 26.

(1) *Joint Recommendation.* The parties or their attorneys may agree to jointly recommend a GAL from the registry. The court may adopt the joint recommendation or require the parties to use the procedures set forth in (2), below.

(2) *By Rotation.* If the parties are not in agreement to a GAL from the registry, then the court will direct the parties to contact the Registry Manager for a list of the next three names from the GAL registry.

(A) If after reviewing the three names the parties agree upon a GAL from the list, then they may present an Order of Appointment to the court for approval by stipulation.

(B) If after reviewing the three names the parties cannot agree, each party may strike one name from the list of three. The court will appoint as GAL the first remaining name on the strike list. The Registry Manager will notify the parties or attorneys of the GAL appointed. If the court chooses a GAL other than from the list provided to the parties, then the court shall make findings on the record.

(3) *Failure of Guardian Ad Litem to Accept Appointment.* A GAL chosen to serve by stipulation or from the rotational list who chooses not to serve shall go to the bottom of the rotational list.

(4) *Indigent Parties.* If either of the parties are found to be indigent, then the court shall determine whether to appoint the Family Court Investigator or a GAL from the registry at whole or partial county expense. The court may require either or both parties to contribute to the cost of the GAL investigation.

(b) Appointment of Guardians Ad Litem—Title 11

Appointment of GALs in Title 11 RCW cases is a strict rotation selection. The party seeking appointment of a GAL shall contact the Registry Manager for the next name on the register. The party shall be responsible for contacting that GAL to determine if the GAL is able to take the case. If the GAL is unavailable for whatever reason, the party shall contact the Registry Manager for the next name on the register.

(c) Appointment of Guardians Ad Litem—Title 13

These GAL rules do not apply to appointment or management of Title 13 RCW GALs or CASAs. The CASA program is managed separately.

(d) Complaints from Guardians Ad Litem. Complaints from guardians ad litem regarding registry or appointment matters shall be made in writing and be addressed to the GAL Coordinator. A response to the complaint shall be provided within fifteen working days of receipt of the complaint.

[Adopted effective September 1, 2002. Amended as emergency rule December 30, 2003; April 2, 2004; amended effective September 1, 2004; September 1, 2007.]

LGALR 5.1. GAL REPORT REVIEW HEARING—TITLE 26

(a) Scheduling Review Hearings: When a Guardian ad Litem is appointed, an Order shall be entered setting a court hearing to review the Guardian ad Litem report.

(b) Continuances: In the event the GAL report is not completed on the date of the review hearing, the hearing may be continued for up to two weeks by agreement of the parties. Any request for a longer delay shall be presented on the record to the judicial officer at the scheduled hearing.

(c) Review Hearing: A GAL Report Review hearing will not be stricken without a court appearance unless a parenting plan has been agreed upon and entered. In the event there is no appearance at the hearing and no new parenting plan has been filed, the matter shall be continued for up to two weeks for follow up by Court Administration.

(d) Confirmation: No confirmation is required for GAL Report Review hearings. The hearing may only be stricken once there is confirmation of payment of the retainer.

[Adopted effective September 1, 2009.]

LGALR 7. GUARDIAN AD LITEM GRIEVANCE AND COMPLAINT PROCEDURES

(a) General Terms.

(1) *Complaint Review Board.* A Thurston County Complaint Review Board (the Board) is created. The Board shall consist of the Superior Court Administrator or designee, two Thurston County citizens, a member of the Thurston County Bar Association (selected by the County Bar), and one *guardian ad litem* who is active on the Thurston County *Guardian ad Litem* registry and who has not received any sanctions pursuant to a *guardian ad litem* complaint procedure in the past three years, selected by the Judicial Administrative Officer. The *guardian ad litem* representative shall be from the applicable Title 11, Title 13 or 26, or CASA registry. Service on the board is a voluntary service for the good of the community, and is made without receipt of any additional compensation from this service on the board.

(2) *Application of Rules.* These rules shall apply to *guardians ad litem* and Court Appointed Special Advocates (CASAs) appointed on any case heard by this court under Titles 11, 13, and 26 of the Revised Code of Washington (RCW).

(3) *Filing of Complaint.* Any person may file a complaint against a *guardian ad litem.* The complaint must be submitted in writing and filed with the Superior Court Administrator under Titles 11, 13 and 26. The complaint must state the specific *guardian ad litem* act or failure to act of concern to the complaining person and shall include the following information:

(A) The name, mailing address, telephone number, and e-mail address of the person filing the complaint;

(B) The status of any underlying case including the case number and case name;

(C) Whether the complaining person told the *guardian ad litem* about the complaint;

(D) What action, if any, the *guardian ad litem* has taken to address the complaint;

(E) Which section(s) of the Thurston County Superior Court Guardian ad Litem Code of Conduct was violated and the specific facts involved for each violation. A copy of the Code of Conduct is avail-

able from the Superior Court Administrator or the CASA Program Coordinator.

(F) Which provision(s) in the Order of Appointment the complaining person feels the *guardian ad litem* has violated and the specific facts supporting each alleged violation;

(G) What the complaining person would like done to fix the problem which is the subject of the complaint.

The complaint shall not exceed ten pages in length without prior permission for an overlength complaint having been given by the Superior Court Administrator or designee. The complaint may be accompanied by exhibits and attachments without limitation on length.

(4) *Limitation on Filing Complaints.* Complaints filed under this rule must be filed within one year from the date of occurrence of the matters complained of.

(5) *Removal.* If the *guardian ad litem* is removed from the Court registry, the Court shall enter findings of fact and an order of removal. Upon removing a *guardian ad litem* from the registry, the Court shall forward a copy of the Order to the Office for the Administrator of the Courts for circulation to other counties.

(6) *Confidentiality.* The complaint, and the Board's initial decision, shall be kept confidential from everyone but the complaining person, unless the Board finds cause to proceed with the complaint. Any requests to disclose information from complaint or guardian ad litem files are subject to redaction of case identifying information, including party names and case numbers; any information that could endanger a victim of domestic violence; and any information prohibited by law from disclosure.

(A) No cause to proceed. If the Board finds no cause to proceed with the complaint, no record of the complaint will be kept in the *guardian ad litem*'s file, although a copy may be kept in separate complaint files with safeguards for confidentiality. After three years, the complaint documents shall be destroyed, with a notation in the file including the names of the complaining person and *guardian ad litem,* the filing date of the complaint, and that the Board found no cause to proceed with the complaint. However, if a complaining person discloses to a third party that a complaint has been filed, the *guardian ad litem* may see a copy of the complaint and the Board's decision in the matter and may file a written response to be placed in the confidential file.

(B) Cause to proceed. If the Board finds cause to proceed, the complaint and all relating documents shall be kept in a *guardian ad litem* complaint file, including copies of the initial and final decisions, and any judicial decisions regarding the complaint.

(7) *Extension of Timelines.* Timelines stated herein can be extended by the Board or by a Judicial Officer for good cause.

(b) Grievance Procedure.

(1) *Motion in Court.* At any time, a party may bring a motion in court to address the issues raised by a complaint pursuant to LGAL 7(a).

(A) Such a motion shall be heard by a Judicial Officer other than the one making rulings in the underlying case(s) at issue in the complaint. A Judicial Officer who has heard a motion regarding a *guardian ad litem* complaint shall not make further rulings in the case except those necessary to resolve the issues raised in the *guardian ad litem* complaint.

(B) If such a motion is brought by the complaining party during or after a complaint has been filed with the Board, the party shall disclose to the Court the status of the Board's involvement. A decision by the Board is not binding on the Judicial Officer.

(2) *Initial Review by Board.* Within 10 working days after the Superior Court Administrator receives the written complaint, the Board shall review the complaint and make an initial determination of whether there is cause to proceed.

(A) The initial decision shall be in writing and state whether the Board finds cause to proceed with the complaint and the reasons for that decision.

(B) The Board shall mail the initial decision to the complaining person within 10 working days after receipt of the complaint by the appropriate administrative officer.

(C) At its discretion, the Board may request additional information from the complaining person. The Board may also extend the time to respond if needed. The extension shall not be for more than a total of 10 additional working days. The failure of a complaining person to provide more information requested by the Board may be a factor in whether the Board finds cause to proceed.

(D) If the Superior Court Administrator determines that the complaint concerns a case currently pending before the court, the Superior Court Administrator shall refer the complaint to the Family Court Presiding Judge in titles 13 and 26 RCW cases and to the Presiding Judge in title 11 RCW cases, and shall so inform the complaining person in writing.

(3) *Review of Determination of No Cause to Proceed.* If the Board finds no cause to proceed, the complaining person may seek review of that decision by bringing a motion before a Judicial Officer consistent with the provisions of this rule.

(4) *Procedure Following Determination of Cause to Proceed.* If the Board finds there is cause to proceed, the Board shall notify the *guardian ad litem* in writ-

ing at the same time the complaining person is notified of the Board's finding of cause to proceed. The notice to the *guardian ad litem* shall include a copy of the complaint and a copy of the Board's initial decision.

(A) The *guardian ad litem* shall respond in writing to the Board within 15 days of the mailing of the decision.

(B) The *guardian ad litem* shall mail a copy of the *guardian ad litem*'s response to the complaining person.

(5) *Board's Authority Following Determination of Cause to Proceed.* After reviewing the *guardian ad litem*'s response, and any replies, the Board shall have the authority to do the following:

(A) find that, based on the information provided, the *guardian ad litem* did not violate applicable laws, rules, or policies;

(B) issue a written reprimand;

(C) issue an advisory letter to the *guardian ad litem* summarizing concerns for the *guardian ad litem* to take notice and/or address;

(D) refer the *guardian ad litem* to additional training;

(E) require the *guardian ad litem* to take corrective action to remedy the matters complained about or mitigate the harm caused by those matters;

(F) require the *guardian ad litem* to bring or support a motion to add, seal, or remove information to/in/from the court file or to/in/from the *guardian ad litem* report;

(G) recommend to the Judicial Officer hearing an underlying case that it remove the *guardian ad litem* from the case; and/or

(H) recommend to the Court that the *guardian ad litem* be removed or suspended from the registry;

(6) *Decision.* Following consideration of all material submitted, the Board shall issue its final decision within 10 working days following receipt of the *guardian ad litem*'s response or passage of the time allowed for response.

(A) The Board shall mail the final decision to the complaining person, the *guardian ad litem*, and all parties in any underlying case.

(B) The Court shall ensure that the final decision is placed in the *guardian ad litem*'s file and the *guardian ad litem* complaint file.

(7) *Judicial Review of Board Decisions.*

(A) Two methods of Review. There shall be two methods for seeking judicial review of a Board decision.

(i) *Appeal.* The right to appeal a decision of the Board finding misconduct shall be available only to the *guardian ad* litem, and only in cases where the decision of the Board recommends removal or suspension of the *guardian ad litem* from the registry.

(ii) *Discretionary Review.* Decisions of the Board which do not recommend suspension or removal from the registry are subject to review by the Court only through discretionary review. Discretionary review will be accepted only in cases involving significant questions of law or allegations that there was no substantial evidence in the record to support a material finding of fact upon which the decision of the Board was based. Either a *guardian ad litem* or a complaining person may seek discretionary review of a Board decision.

(B) Procedure on Filing Review. Judicial review of a Board decision must be commenced by filing a petition for judicial review with the clerk of the court and serving the petition on the Judicial Administrative Officer, all parties to the underlying action, the complaining person, and the *guardian ad litem.* Filing and service must be obtained within 20 days of the mailing date of the final decision by the Board. The Superior Court Administrator shall assign the petition for judicial review to a Judicial Officer who has not heard matters in any underlying case at issue in the complaint.

(i) *Costs.* The person seeking judicial review shall be responsible for any filing fees, and costs associated with producing the record for review.

(C) Response and Argument.

(i) *Appeal.* Any response to an appeal of right shall be filed within 10 days of the filing and service of a notice of appeal of right. Oral arguments will be scheduled by the Judicial Officer.

(ii) *Discretionary review.* No response is required and no oral argument will be had unless otherwise directed by the Judicial Officer. If written response or oral argument is directed, the briefing schedule and the date for argument will be set by the Judicial Officer.

(D) Scope of Review. The Judicial Officer shall review the written record and any oral argument, if permitted, to determine whether the *guardian ad litem* violated any applicable laws, rules, and/or policies and if so, the appropriate remedy. The Judicial Officer shall issue findings and a decision on the issues in the complaint based on an independent review of the record.

(E) Consideration of Prior Complaints. If the Judicial Officer determines that a violation occurred, the Judicial Officer may, in fashioning a remedy, consider any prior complaints against the

guardian ad litem where the Board found cause to proceed.

[Emergency rule effective June 8, 2000; amended effective September 8, 2000; September 1, 2003; September 1, 2004; September 1, 2005.]

LGALR 8. GUARDIAN AD LITEM REGISTRIES

(a) Maintenance of Registry. The Family and Juvenile Court shall maintain and administer guardian ad litem (GAL) registries for actions under title 26 RCW and for actions under title 11 RCW. The Title 26 Registry shall be managed by a Registry Manager at Family and Juvenile Court.

(b) Maintenance of Guardian Ad Litem Files. The Family and Juvenile Court shall maintain a file for each GAL listed on a current registry. The GAL's application form, writing sample, resume or curriculum vitae, and other records pertaining to the GAL shall be maintained in his or her file. These documents shall be available for public inspection.

(c) Title 26 Registry Committee. The Title 26 Registry Committee shall consist of the GAL Coordinator and two other individuals designated by the Presiding Judge at Family and Juvenile Court. The Registry Committee shall be responsible for approving any applicant's request to be placed on the Title 26 GAL Registry, shall ensure that an interview with GAL applicants is conducted and shall conduct an annual review of each GAL as set forth below in LGALR 11(b).

[Adopted effective September 1, 2007. Amended effective September 1, 2010.]

LGALR 9. TITLE 26 GUARDIAN AD LITEM REQUIREMENTS

(a) Initial Application Requirements. New applicants may apply for placement on the Title 26 Guardian ad Litem (GAL) Registry between January 1–31 of each year. To be qualified for consideration for placement on the GAL Registry, in addition to statutory requirements, an applicant must:

(1) have a four year degree from an accredited institution of higher education;

(2) provide a current resume or curriculum vitae;

(3) complete the GAL application form provided by the GAL Coordinator;

(4) complete the Background Check Information/Authorization Form provided by the GAL Coordinator;

(5) provide a sample GAL report of three to five pages in length, double spaced, based on a fact scenario to be provided by the GAL Coordinator;

(6) complete an interview as directed by the Registry Committee;

(7) if an attorney, be a member in good standing of the Washington State Bar Association; and

(8) complete the required state and local GAL training courses as set forth in LGALR 10 (note: completion of the mentoring component is not required for application but is required prior to appointment to a case).

(b) Practicum. All applicants must provide proof of four completed GAL assignments for any Washington State Superior Court within the last five years or proof of successful completion of two supervised GAL assignments as follows:

(1) One GAL assignment done in conjunction with a mentor GAL that includes accompanying the mentor on all visits, attendance at all interviews, participation in preparation of a report, and attendance at all court hearings. The mentor is the GAL of record and this assignment is without compensation to the applicant; and

(2) One GAL assignment done under the supervision of the same mentor GAL that includes more active participation on the part of the applicant, such as requesting documents, conducting interviews, and preparing reports under the supervision of the mentor. The mentor is the GAL of record and this assignment is without compensation to the applicant.

(c) Selection Process. The Registry Committee shall review all information provided by the applicants, including the sample GAL report, and ensure the conduct of interviews and reference checks as deemed appropriate. The Registry Committee shall issue a letter to each applicant by March 31 of each year indicating whether the applicant's request to be placed on the GAL Registry is accepted or declined.

[Adopted effective September 1, 2007. Amended effective September 1, 2010.]

LGALR 10. CONTINUING REQUIRE- MENTS FOR TITLE 26 AND TITLE 11 RCW GUARDIANS AD LITEM

(a) Title 26 RCW Guardians Ad Litem

(1) *Continuing Training.* The court may periodically sponsor or approve training programs that title 26 RCW guardians ad litem (GALs) are required to attend to maintain and improve their level of proficiency. Local continuing training may be offered periodically and the curricula may include: instruction using examples of reports, pleadings, and fee agreements; billing procedure and format information; court procedures; information on local resources; and other topics from the state curriculum.

(2) *Annual Update.* Any person who is currently listed on the Title 26 GAL Registry and who desires to remain on the registry shall provide an annual update by February 28 of each year by completing the annual update form and the criminal background check authorization, as well as providing an updated

resume or curriculum vitae. The annual update form and updated resume or curriculum vitae shall be available for public inspection.

(b) Title 11 RCW Guardians Ad Litem

(1) *Continuing Requirements.* By February 28 in even numbered years, GALs shall provide an update to the court on a form provided by the court. The update shall include:

(A) current resume;

(B) signed criminal background check authorization;

(C) proof of attendance at eight hours of continuing education related to guardianship work during the past two calendar years; and

(D) disclosure of any complaints related to the GAL's work during the past two calendar years.

(2) *Failure to Fulfill Continuing Requirements.* A GAL may be dropped from the registry for failure to meet the continuing requirements above.

(c) Leave from the Registry. A GAL on a registry may notify the court of periods in which he or she is unavailable to accept appointments.

[Adopted effective September 1, 2007. Amended effective September 1, 2010.]

LGALR 11. EVALUATION OF TITLE 26 GUARDIAN AD LITEM WORK

(a) Case Evaluations. When a guardian ad litem (GAL) is discharged from a case, every attorney and self-represented party and judicial officer involved in the case is encouraged to submit an evaluation of the GAL on a form approved by the court. The completed evaluations will be returned to Family Court Administration. The GAL may review and respond to the evaluations in writing. Any responses shall be placed in the GAL's file. The purpose of these evaluation forms is to assist the court in maintaining a registry of qualified GALs.

(b) Annual Evaluations. The Registry Committee shall review the complete file of every GAL in February of each year.

(1) *Presenting Issues.* The Registry Committee shall determine if there are specific concerns from the evaluations that should be addressed with each GAL and shall issue a written report regarding any specific concerns. If a written report is issued, the GAL will have seven days to respond in writing to the report. The Registry Committee shall then conduct an in-person review with the GAL to discuss the report and appropriate remedial actions, if any, the GAL should take. The Registry Committee may (A) allow the GAL to remain on the registry with no further action; (B) suspend the GAL from the registry, subject to the GAL completing requirements as set forth by the committee; or (C) remove the GAL from the registry. The GAL shall be notified in writing within seven days of the in-person review. In the event the committee

recommends removal from the registry, the GAL shall have ten days to appeal the decision in writing to the Presiding Judge at Family and Juvenile Court. A written decision on the appeal from the Presiding Judge shall be issued within fourteen days of receipt of the appeal.

(2) *No Presenting Issues.* If no specific concerns are identified for a GAL, then a written report and in-person review is not required.

[Adopted effective September 1, 2010.]

LGALR 12.   TITLE 11 GUARDIAN AD LITEM REPORTS

Title 11 guardian ad litem reports addressing a petition for appointment of a Title 11 guardian shall be in the format approved by the court and shall contain the information required by RCW 11.88.090(f).

[Adopted effective September 1, 2010.]

LOCAL CRIMINAL RULES
I.   SCOPE, PURPOSE AND CONSTRUCTION

LCrR 1.6.   FORMS FOR PLEADINGS

Forms for pleadings approved or required by these Local Criminal Rules are contained in an appendix to these rules. All submissions of said approved or required pleadings should be in a form substantially similar to those illustrated in the forms appendix.

[Effective January 11, 1993; amended effective September 1, 2004.]

II.   PROCEDURES PRIOR TO ARREST

LCrR 2.2.   WARRANT UPON INDICTMENT OR INFORMATION

(g) Information to be Supplied to the Court. When a charge is filed in the Superior Court and an order for a warrant or a summons is requested, the court shall be provided with the following information about the person charged:

(1) The pretrial release interview form, if one has been completed by the Pretrial Services Unit.

(2) By the prosecuting attorney, insofar as possible:

(A) A brief summary of the alleged facts of the charge;

(B) Information concerning other known pending or potential charges;

(C) A summary of any known criminal record;

(D) Any other facts deemed material to the issue of pretrial release.

(3) Any ruling of the court at a preliminary hearing or appearance.

[Effective October 1, 1982.]

III.   RIGHTS OF DEFENDANTS

LCrR 3.1.   RIGHT TO AND ASSIGNMENT OF COUNSEL

(d) Assignment of Counsel.

(3) *Declaration of Financial Status.* Defendants who request appointment of counsel shall be required to promptly execute a declaration under penalty of perjury disclosing their financial circumstances. This declaration shall be filed and shall be reviewed by the judge who is determining assignment of court appointed counsel for a defendant. All appointments by reason of indigency are expressly contingent upon a finding of indigency, as defined in CrR 3.1(d)(1) and full disclosure of assets. All appointments of counsel are subject to review. Where assets are discovered or acquired subsequent to appointment which would indicate that a defendant can afford to retain counsel in whole or in part, a defendant may be ordered to retain counsel or reimburse the county for cost of court-appointed counsel. Court appointed counsel who learn or have reason to believe that their client can afford to retain counsel shall notify the court promptly of this fact in order that the court can inquire into the financial status of the defendant.

(4) *Payment of Costs.* In all criminal cases, except where the court order is to be contrary, the clerk shall disperse monies received from the criminal defendant in the following order:

(A) Restitution

(B) Crime Victims' Compensation

(C) Court Costs

(D) Attorney's Fees

(E) Drug Fund

(F) Fines

(G) Extradition Costs

(e) (i) *Withdrawal of Lawyer.* Whenever a criminal case has been set for trial, no lawyer shall be allowed to withdraw from such cause, except upon written consent of the court for good and sufficient reason shown. In cases where an attorney is attempting to withdraw because of ethical issues, a motion must be made and notice given to all involved parties. The Court may hold a hearing on the record in open court with all counsel present and may further hold a hearing on the record in chambers with only defense counsel present. The record of the latter may be sealed in appropriate cases until after the case has been completed.

(ii) *Substitution of Counsel.* In cases where a new lawyer wishes to substitute for a current lawyer, substituting counsel must file a motion requesting substitution. Notice must be given to all other counsel of record and the client. A hearing shall be set and all parties shall appear. A Notice of Appearance or Notice of Substitution and Withdrawal is insufficient to allow substitution once a case has been set for trial.

At the hearing requesting substitution, the Court, mindful of the right to counsel of one's own choosing, will address substituting counsel's ability to assume representation. The Court will consider (1) whether substituting counsel is prepared to proceed to trial on the current case schedule and (2) whether other parties and alleged victims are agreeable to any trial continuance or are not subject to any substantial adverse impact.

Approval from the Court will usually be granted in cases involving conflicts of interest or in cases involving a disability that prevents counsel from proceeding with the case.

In appropriate cases, the Court reserves the right to disallow withdrawal and substitution.

(f) Services Other Than Counsel.

(2) The Director of the Office of Assigned Counsel shall authorize assigned counsel to obtain services provided for under CrR 3.1(f) on behalf of a defendant upon a showing that the services are necessary and that the defendant is financially unable to obtain these services. This authorization shall be obtained prior to the procurement of the necessary services.

(g) Privately Retained Counsel. Attorneys retained by defendants in criminal cases must serve prompt written notice of their appearance upon the prosecuting attorney and file the same with the clerk.

[Effective October 1, 1982; amended effective December 19, 1988; May 1, 1990; September 1, 2007.]

LCrR 3.2. PRETRIAL RELEASE

(n) Interview. A defendant arrested on a felony charge who is not released prior to the defendant's preliminary appearance in court shall be interviewed by a representative of the Thurston County Pretrial Services Unit prior to the defendant's preliminary appearance. This interview shall be conducted as soon as possible after arrest. The purpose of the interview shall be to collect, assess, and verify information necessary to determine the financial status of the defendant for purposes of court-appointed counsel and to determine appropriate conditions of release. The information shall be reported in a Court Information Report and shall be delivered to the judge presiding at the defendant's preliminary appearance. Copies of the report shall be provided to the prosecuting attorney's office and to the Office of Assigned Counsel for the court-appointed counsel or any retained counsel. The prosecuting attorney's office shall advise a defendant who is summoned to answer charges in the Superior Court and who desires court-appointed counsel to contact the Pretrial Services Unit to complete a financial status report for the defendant prior to the defendant's first appearance in court.

(*o*) **Appearances.** Defendants on bail or recognizance are expected to be available to appear upon 72 hours notice to their attorney. They are expected to be present on time at all scheduled appearances when they have received either oral or written notice. Failure to appear in accordance with this rule may result in forfeiture of bail, revocation of the personal recognizance order or issuance of a bench warrant for arrest.

(**p**) **Approving Bail.** Bail bondsmen, who have justified their qualifications to the Superior Court in the manner set forth hereafter, shall be deemed approved to provide bail bonds to defendants in criminal cases in an amount not exceeding the limits prescribed in the order of justification. The justification of a bail bondsman shall continue to exist until revoked, provided, that the court shall no less frequently than once a year review the qualifications of any justified bail bondsman. Upon failure of a bondsman to pay into the court, within ten days, the amount of any bond forfeited by order of the court, the justification of said bail bondsman shall be immediately revoked. The sum so deposited shall be held in the registry of the court for 60 days and should the person for whose appearance the bond was given be produced within said period, the judge may vacate the order and judgment forfeiting the bond on such terms as may be just and equitable. Anyone seeking to provide bond for a defendant in any case where the bondsman has not previously justified qualification, the bond must be submitted to and approved by the presiding judge or the judge's designee. In order to obtain prior justification and approval of the court to provide bonds as an individual surety the following requirements shall be met:

(1) Provide the court verifiable documentary evidence of qualification, including but not limited to a current financial statement.

(2) Provide a current list of all bonds on which the bondsman is obligated in any court of this state, including on the list the name of the court and defendant and the amount of the bond.

In the case of individuals seeking prior justification to write bail bonds on behalf of a corporate surety, the applicant must provide the court with the following:

(1) A certified copy of a power of attorney showing authorization of the applicant to act for the corporate surety.

(2) A letter from the Insurance Commissioner of Washington State indicating that the corporate surety is authorized to do business in this state.

The presiding judge or his or her designee, may approve and justify any bail bondsman upon receipt of the above information. The court shall provide notice by January 31 of each year to the Thurston County Prosecuting Attorney, the Thurston County Office of Assigned Counsel, the Thurston County Sheriff, and the Chiefs of Police of any incorporated cities within the county of the bail bondsman previously qualified and the extent of their authority to write bonds. Further, the court shall notify these agencies promptly after there is a major change in the list of qualified bail bondsmen, such as a disqualification or newly justified bail bondsman. In the event of disqualification, the bail bondsman shall be promptly notified and may seek a hearing before the judge or judges of the court on the issues of qualification.

(q) Posting of Justified Bondsmen in Jail. The Sheriff of Thurston County is required to post in a conspicuous location in the jail booking area, the names and telephone numbers of all justified bondsmen.

[Effective April 4, 1983. Amended May 1, 1990; February 1, 1994; September 1, 2002; amended on an emergency basis, effective January 19, 2011; amended on a permanent basis, effective September 1, 2011; September 2, 2013.]

LCrR 3.2A. PRELIMINARY APPEARANCE

(a) Preliminary Appearances.

(3) The Superior Court shall conduct, as necessary, pursuant to CrR 3.2A, a preliminary appearance calendar to be presided over by the presiding judge or designated judge or court commissioner of the Superior Court. In all cases where an individual has been arrested for a felony offense but an information has not been filed this proceeding shall be reported verbatim.

[Effective October 1, 1982; amended May 1, 1990.]

LCrR 3.3. TIME FOR TRIAL

(f) Continuances.

(1) Agreed or stipulated continuances shall be presented in the form of the Stipulation and Order for Continuance, illustrated in the forms appendix to these local rules (LCrR 1.6), and shall be signed by the presiding judge or judge pre-assigned to the case.

(2) No continuance of trial shall be granted without counsel presenting on the record the reasons therefor. Written stipulation or agreement without court approval is ineffective to strike or continue trial dates.

(g) Status Hearings

(1) A hearing shall be held the Wednesday before the week of trial to determine if the case is ready to proceed to trial. Counsel for all parties shall appear and advise the court of the expected length of trial, any restrictions as to particular days of the week, and readiness for trial. Counsel shall be notified the following day of the trial department and the day of the week on which trial shall commence.

[Effective October 1, 1982; amended effective May 1, 1990; January 11, 1993; September 1, 2007.]

LCrR 3.4. PRESENCE OF THE DEFENDANT

(d) Video Conference Proceedings.

(2) *Agreement.* In criminal matters, proceedings may be conducted by video conference if specifically authorized by the state-wide criminal court rule regarding video conference proceedings. (CrR 3.4(d)(1)). Additionally, other criminal trial court proceedings may be conducted by video conference only by agreement of the parties either in writing or on the record and upon the approval of the judge.

[Adopted effective September 1, 2012.]

LCrR 3.5. CONFIRMATION

Hearings for CrR 3.5 and CrR 3.6 issues shall be scheduled for Mondays in the criminal presiding department. Any CrR 3.5 or CrR 3.6 hearing requiring argument shall be confirmed before Noon on Thursday preceding the Monday noted for hearing. Counsel shall notify the criminal scheduling coordinator at telephone number (360) 754-4544. Any hearing not confirmed for argument may be continued at the discretion of the court.

[Effective January 11, 1993; amended effective September 1, 2000.]

LCrR 3.6. CONFIRMATION

See LCrR 3.5.

IV. PROCEDURES PRIOR TO TRIAL

LCrR 4.2. PLEAS

(i) Time for entry. Change of pleas shall not be set for entry later than the last business day before commencement of trial. Witnesses shall not be released until after the court has accepted a change of plea.

[Adopted effective September 1, 2007.]

LCrR 4.5. PRETRIAL CONFERENCE

(a) When Required. In every case where a Not Guilty Plea is entered the criminal scheduling coordinator shall set a pretrial conference on a date not later than three weeks before trial.

(b) Pre-Hearing Disclosure and Discovery. Counsel for both parties shall comply with LCrR 4.7.

(c) Procedure. The pretrial conference hearing shall be a time for (1) the parties to negotiate a final disposition of the case and/or (2) the parties and the court to consider and resolve omnibus issues and schedule evidentiary matters, if necessary. The defendant must personally appear for this hearing unless the parties agree otherwise and defendant files in advance of the hearing a written waiver of his right to be present. The parties shall inform the court of the status of the case following their negotiations. If necessary, the court will consider omnibus issues, hear simple motions or set a future time for more involved issues to be heard.

(d) Order. Either a Consolidated Omnibus Order or Pretrial—Plea Order shall be entered memorializing the matters agreed upon by the parties and ordered by the court. A change of plea may be heard at that time if the court's schedule permits. Either order shall be in a form which substantially conforms to the orders illustrated in the forms appendix (LCrR 1.6). Forms will be available at the court clerk's station.

(e) Call of the Calendar. The pretrial conference calendar will commence each Tuesday at 9:00 a.m. Individual cases will be called when requested by counsel of a first come first served basis. No case shall be removed from the calendar without entry of an order identified in the preceding section.

(f) Waiver of Hearing. The pretrial conference may not be stricken unless an agreed Pretrial—Plea Order or Consolidated Omnibus Order shall be first entered or other good cause shown.

[Effective October 1, 1982; amended January 11, 1993; September 1, 2000.]

LCrR 4.7. PRE–HEARING DISCLOSURE AND DISCOVERY

At least one full week before the hearing date each party shall fully discharge the responsibilities imposed by CrR 4.7(a) Prosecutor's Obligations and CrR 4.7(b) Defendant's Obligations; provided, however:

(a) Agreement. The parties may agree to a posthearing schedule for disclosure and discovery. Said schedule shall be made part of the Consolidated Omnibus Order.

(b) Disagreement. In the event of disagreement over the rights and responsibilities of CrR 4.7, only disclosure and discovery of the items of disagreement may be delayed and the issue raised in the omnibus portion of the hearing.

(c) Protective Order. In the event a party seeks a protective order authorized by CrR 4.7, disclosure and discovery of the items for which protection is sought may be delayed until court order at the omnibus portion of the hearing. A motion for protective order shall be made and served in advance of the hearing, in the manner required by court rules.

[Effective January 11, 1993.]

VI. PROCEDURES AT TRIAL

LCrR 6.3. STRUCK–JURY METHOD OF SELECTION [REPEALED]

[Effective January 11, 1993. Repealed effective September 1, 2010.]

LCrR 6.15. JURY INSTRUCTIONS

(a) Time for Submission. Unless otherwise ordered by the court, proposed jury instructions shall be filed and served no later than when the case is called for trial.

(b) Format. Proposed jury instructions shall be printed or typewritten, double spaced, each on a separate letter size sheet of paper which bears no markings identifying the submitting party or counsel. A

cover sheet with a case caption which reads, "Court's Instructions To The Jury" shall be included.

(c) Submissions. Sets of proposed instructions shall be submitted as follows:

(1) *To the Clerk:* A set of instructions numbered and with citations shall be filed with the clerk.

(2) *To Counsel:* A set of instructions numbered and with citations shall be served on each other counsel or pro se party appearing in the case.

(3) *To the Judge:* A set of instructions shall be provided to the judge as follows:

(A) A set of instructions numbered and with citations in electronic format via e-mail, or on disk, preferably in Word for Windows format but acceptable in WordPerfect format, with all proposed instructions in a single computer file; and

(B) a hardcopy set of printed instructions numbered and with; and

(C) a hardcopy set of printed instructions without numbers or citations.

[Effective September 1, 1997; amended effective September 1, 2004.]

LCrR 7.2. SENTENCING

(b) **Procedure at Time of Sentencing.** All sentencings shall be scheduled for Tuesdays in the criminal presiding department. Sentencings with a Pre-Sentence Investigation may be noted for a 1:30 p.m. setting.

[Effective January 11, 1993; amended effective September 1, 2000.]

LOCAL JUVENILE COURT RULES

LJuCR 3.6. ANSWER TO PETITION

(a) **Response Required.** The parents or other respondents shall file a response to a petition for dependency in accordance with time requirements for other civil actions.

(b) **Nature of Responses.** The response shall specifically address and admit or deny each allegation in the petition or indicate there is not sufficient knowledge or information to form a belief as to the truth of the allegation.

(c) **Signature Required.** The response shall be signed by the parent or other respondent or their attorney. If the response is signed only by the attorney, the response shall include a certification that the specific admissions and denials have been discussed by the attorney with the represented parent or respondent.

[Adopted effective September 1, 2010.]

LJuCR 4. SETTLEMENT AND PRETRIAL CONFERENCES FOR DEPENDENCY AND TERMINATION CASES

(a) **Settlement Conferences for Termination Cases.**

(1) *Request for Conference.* Settlement conferences will be scheduled upon the request of any party to a termination action. The settlement conference should be requested when the trial date is set at the first-set appearance, or within 30 days.

(2) *Timing of Conference.* The settlement conference shall be held at least 30 days before the scheduling conference for the termination trial.

(3) *Settlement Conference Statements.* Settlement conference statements shall be required from all parties and shall contain:

(A) a brief history of the case;

(B) reasons for or against termination of parental rights; and

(C) any relevant legal authority.

(4) *Statement Length.* Settlement conference statements shall not exceed three pages in length.

The person conducting the settlement conference will also be provided the dependency and termination files.

(5) *Statement Due Date.* Settlement conference statements shall be provided to the court, other counsel, and the court appointed special advocate (CASA) and/or guardian ad litem (GAL) seven calendar days before the conference.

(6) *Confidentiality.* Settlement conference statements are confidential and will not be filed. Settlement conference negotiations are confidential and shall not be used at trial.

(7) *Required Attendance.* Any parent contesting termination, the currently assigned social worker, the social worker's supervisor, counsel for all parties, and the CASA or GAL shall be required to attend the settlement conference. Others may be present at the conference with the approval of the judicial officer.

(8) *Judicial Officer.* Any judicial officer presiding over a settlement conference shall be disqualified from subsequent hearings in the same case.

(b) **Settlement Conferences for Dependences**[1] **Cases.** Settlement conferences may be ordered by the court in dependency cases, subject to the requirements of section (a) of this rule.

(c) **Pretrial Conferences.** Termination cases are subject to pretrial conferences in accordance with these local rules' requirement for pretrial conferences in family law cases (LSPR 94.03D).

[Adopted effective September 1, 200; amended effective September 1, 2010; September 1, 2011.]

1 So in original.

LJuCR 4.2. PLEADINGS

(c) **Answer.** The parents or other respondents shall respond to a petition for termination in accordance with LJuCR 3.6.

[Adopted effective September 1, 2010.]

LJuCR 12. WAIVER OF AGE TO MARRY AND PETITIONS FOR EMANCIPATION

(a) **Waiver of Age to Marry.** Applications for waiver of the minimum age to marry shall be made through the Family and Juvenile Court. The application shall contain information and supporting documentation establishing the necessity of the waiver, and such additional information as may be prescribed by the Presiding Judge of the Family and Juvenile Court.

(i) Both parties seeking waiver of the minimum age to marry shall complete a program of pre-marital counseling by a licensed counselor, a counseling agency, or a religious professional, and provide the Court with that person's recommendation prior to any hearing on the application.

(ii) Both parties shall be interviewed by a probation counselor of the Juvenile Department of the Superior Court who may offer a recommendation to the Court.

(b) Petitions for Emancipation. Petitions for emancipation of minors shall be made through the Family and Juvenile Court. The petition and supporting documentation shall contain information sufficient for the Court to find by clear and convincing evidence that the minor is over the age of sixteen, has the ability to manage the petitioner's own financial affairs,

and has the ability to manage the petitioner's own social, educational and other non-financial personal affairs.

(i) Petitions for Emancipation in the form approved by the Office of the Administrator of the Court.

(ii) The petition should be accompanied by information showing ability to manage the petitioner's financial affairs, such as employment status and income verification and budgetary information.

(iii) The petition should be accompanied by information showing the ability to manage nonfinancial personal affairs, such as written reports from school indicating education level or GED completion, or letters of support for emancipation from school counselors, adult friends, or community professionals.

(iv) Prior to the time of the hearing on the emancipation petition, the petitioner shall be interviewed by an intake officer of the Juvenile Department of the Superior Court who may offer a recommendation to the Court.

[Effective October 1, 1982; amended February 9, 1999.]

LOCAL RULES FOR APPEAL OF DECISION OF COURTS OF LIMITED JURISDICTIONS

LRALJ 10.2. DISMISSAL OF APPEAL

(d) Dismissal on Clerk's Motion. The court may, on motion of the clerk of the superior court, after 28 days notice, dismiss an appeal of the case: 1) when the appellant fails to timely file a brief and the Transcript by Appellant of the electronic recording of proceedings; or 2) when there has been no action of record for 90 days. The clerk of the court shall note the case on the dismissal calendar and mail notices of the dismissal hearing to counsel of record or to a person who is not represented by counsel at the addresses contained in the notice of appeal. A dismissal will result in a remand of the matter to the originating court for the enforcement of judgment or imposition of sentence.

[Adopted effective September 1, 1997.]

THURSTON COUNTY CLERK'S FEE SCHEDULE
CIVIL

Title	Service Provided	Fee	RCW
Abstract of Judgment	Filing	15.00	36.18.012(2)
Abstract of Judgment	Preparation	2.00	36.18.016(5)
Arbitration Request for Trial de Novo	Filing	250.00	36.18.016(24) Ordinance #12112
Anti-harassment Petition/Unlawful Harassment Petition	Forms and Filing	41.00	10.14.040, HB2328 36.18.020(2)(d)
Bail Bondsmen Justification	Filing	110.00	LCrR 3.2(p) 36.18.020(2)(a)
Civil Filing	Filing	110.00	36.18.020(2)(a)
Common Law Lien	Petition to Invalidate Lien	35.00	60.70.060 36.18.012(8)
Deeds of Trust, Surplus Funds	Filing	110.00	61.24.080(3), 36.18.020(2)(a)
Election—Affidavit of Elector Contesting Election of Person	Filing	110.00	29.65.020 28A.305.070 36.18.020(2)(a)
Emancipation of a Minor	Filing	50.00	36.18.014 13.64.020
Frivolous Claim Statute	Filing of Application for Order	35.00	60.04.081(3) 36.18.012(8)
Foreign Judgment	Filing	110.00	36.18.020(2)(a)
Jury Demand	12 Member Jury 6 Member Jury	250.00 125.00	36.18.016(3)
Land Use Petition	Filing	110.00	36.70C.040 36.18.020(2)(a)
Legal Newspaper (effective 06–11–41)	Petition and Order	110.00	65.16.040, 36.18.020(2)(a)
Property Taxes, Certification of Delinquency, Application For Judgment	Each Contestant at Time of Filing Appeal	2.00	84.64.120 84.64.040
Protection of Vulnerable Adults	Filing	110.00	74.34.110 36.18.020(2)(a)
Registration of Land Titles (Torrens Act)	Application for Registration	5.00	65.12.780 36.18.016(14)
Restrictive Covenant	Petition to Strike Discriminatory Provision re real property	20.00	49.60.227, 36.18.012(6)
Transcript of Judgment	Filing	15.00	36.18.012(2)
Unlawful Detainer	1. Original Filing 2. Upon Filing of any Order other than Default Order and Default Judgment (or When Answer Filed) balance is due of	30.00 80.00	36.18.020(2)(a) 36.18.012(5)
Warrant for unpaid taxes or for overpayment of benefits by any agency of State of Wash.	Filing (prior to 7/1/03) Filing (on or after 7/1/03)	5.00 20.00	36.18.012(10) 82.38.235
Water Rights Statement	Filing	25.00	90.03.180 36.18.016(17)
Water System Requirements (Enforcement Of)	Filing of Certified Copy of Administrative Order	110.00	70.119A.040(6)
Writs—Attachment - Garnishment - Execution on Real Property - Restitution	Each Filing	20.00	36.18.016(6) 36.18.016(6) 36.18.050 36.18.050

[Amended effective September 1, 2000; September 1, 2001; October 1, 2002.]

DOMESTIC

Title	Service Provided	Fee	RCW
Domestic Relations (Dissolution, Legal Separation, Invalidity, Custody)	Filing	120.00	36.18.020(2)(a) 26.12.240
Family Court Facilitator	Fee for Services (User Fee)	10.00	26.12.240 36.18.016(16)
Modification of Decree - of Thurston County cases - of all other Counties/States	Filing in Existing Case New Filing	30.00 120.00	36.18.016(2) 36.18.020(2)(a), AGLO dated 9-9-87
	Agreed Mod in Existing Case	30.00	36.18.050 26.12.240
Out of State Custody Decree	Filing	120.00	36.18.020(2)(a) 26.27.150(1) 26.12.240
Relocation Notice	Filing in Existing Case	30.00	26.09.260 26.09.410-.560 36.18.050 26.12.240 LR 79(a)
Wage Assignment, Spousal Maintenance or Child Support	Filing of Original Action	120.00	26.18.070, 36.18.020(2)(a) 26.12.240

[Amended effective September 1, 2000; September 1, 2001.]

PROBATE/ADOPTION

Title	Service Provided	Fee	RCW
Adoption	Filing	120.00	36.18.020(2)(a) 26.12.240
Appointment of Special Representative	Filing	2.00	11.96.170, 36.18.050
Certificate of Qualification	Issuance (Form K)	2.00	36.18.016(8)
Certified Copy of Letters (Administration, Testamentary, Guardianship)	Certified Copy	2.00	36.18.016(8)
Disclaimer of Interest (no probate commenced)	Filing	2.00	11.86.031(4) 36.18.016(13)
Escheat—Probate Proceedings	Filing Claim Filing Revenue Dept. Affidavit	110.00 2.00	36.18.020(2)(f) 11.08.300
Estate (Probate)	Filing	110.00	36.18.020(2)(f)
Guardianship	Filing	110.00	36.18.020(2)(f)
Non–Judicial Resolution	Petition, Agreement or Memorandum	2.00	11.96.170, 36.18.012(7)
Non–Probate Notice to Creditors	Filing	110.00	11.42.010(3)(a) 36.18.020(2)(f)
Notice of Probate (when probate filed in a county other than where decedent resided)	Filing	20.00	11.40.020(2) 36.18.050
Petition Objecting to Non–Judicial Resolution	Filing	110.00	36.18.020(2)(g)
Petition Contesting Will	Filing	110.00	36.18.020(2)(g)
Petition To Admit Rejected Will	Filing	110.00	36.18.020(2)(g)
Small Estate Affidavit	Filing	20.00	11.62.010 36.18.050
Termination of Parent–Child Relationship	Filing	120.00	26.12.240 36.18.020(2)(a)
Will Only (before or after death –	Filing	20.00	36.18.012(6)

Title	Service Provided	Fee	RCW
no probate contemplated)			

[Amended effective September 1, 2000; September 1, 2001; October 1, 2002.]

APPEALS

Title	Service Provided	Fee	RCW
Appeals From Administrative Hearing Decision	Filing (also see non-fee schedule)	110.00	34.05.514, 36.18.020(2)(c)
Appeal From Court of Limited Jurisdiction—Civil case	Filing (to be paid at lower court)	110.00	36.18.020(2)(b)
Appeal From Court of Limited Jurisdiction—Criminal case	Filing (imposed when affirmed or dismissed) (to be paid at lower court)	110.00	36.18.020(2)(h)
Clerk's Papers	Designation Reproduction	per pg .50	36.18.016(19) RAP 9.7(a), 15.4(e)
Notice of Appeal to Appellate Court	Filing (payable to Thurston County Clerk–RAP 5.1(b))	250.00	36.18.018(2) 2.32.070
Petition For Review of a Court of Appeals Decision Terminating Review	Filing	200.00	2.32.070
Transmittal of Record and Exhibits		Actual Cost	RAP 9.8;15.4(e)
Upon Conviction or Plea of Guilty, Failure to Prosecute Appeal, or Upon Affirmance of a Conviction by a Court of Limited Jurisdiction	Filing	110.00	36.18.020(2)(h)

[Amended effective September 1, 2000; September 1, 2001; October 1, 2002.]

MISCELLANEOUS

Title	Service Provided	Fee	RCW
Approving Bonds, in other than civil or probate		2.00	36.18.016(7)
Authenticated or Exemplified Certificate	First Page Each Additional Page (in addition to normal copy fees for documents attached to certificate)	4.00 1.00	36.18.016(4)
Bench Warrants, Notices, Summons, Subpoenas, Certificates of Deposition for Out of State Depositions	Issuance	20.00	36.18.050
Change of Venue	Filing fee (payable to clerk of county to which case is transferred)	110.00	4.12.090, .100 36.18.020(2)(a) CR 82(d)
	Process fee payable to Thurston County Clerk	20.00	LCR 79(a) 11.18.016(10)
Copies, With or Without Seal; Copy Case/Docket Print Fee	First Page Each Additional Page	2.00 1.00	36.18.016(4) 36.23.067
Diking, Drainage and Sewerage Improvement District	Petition for Review	110.00	85.15.110 36.18.020(2)(a)
Executing Certificates, With or Without Seal	Execution	2.00	36.18.016(5)
Ex Parte	Presentation of Order	20.00/ presentation	LCR 79(a) 36.18.016(10)
Extension of Judgment	Filing	110.00	6.17.010; 9.94A 36.18.016(15)
Fees In Special Cases	Where no fee is provided for—fees similar and equal	Variable	36.18.050

Title	Service Provided	Fee	RCW
	to those allowed for services of the same kind		
Filing of Papers Not Related to Litigation and No Other Amount Specified	Filing	20.00	36.18.012(4)
Investment Service Fee—if Written Request Received for Service	Service Fee for Interest Investments	5% of Income Earned	36.48.090
Legal Financial Obligation	Collection fee	50.00	
	Statement fee	100.00	
Local Court Rules	Copy	10.00	
NSF Check Service Charge, Per Check		50.00	36.18.016(22)
Oaths and Affirmations	Filing	20.00	5.28
Passport Application (Adult renewals if made by applicant by mail $55—if applicant can use DSP–82)	Payables to Passport Services: - $55.00—adult - $40.00—under 16 - $60.00—if expedited Plus any Expedited Postage	30.00	31 U.S.C. § 9701 22 U.S.C. § 4219 36.18.016(9)
Petition to Restore Right to Possess Firearms	Filing	110.00	9.41.047 36.18.020(2)(a)
Reports & Copies Produced at the Local Level as Permitted by 2.68.020 and Supreme Court Policy	Copies and Reports	Variable	36.18.016(20)
Roadmap to Thurston County Clerk's Office	Copy	20.00	
Searching Records and Issuing a Written Report/Special Services	Per Hour	20.00	36.18.016(10)
Stop Payment Service Charge, per check		50.00	36.18.016(22)
Tape Duplication -cassette tape - video tape	Duplication	10.00/tape 25.00/tape	36.18.016(11)
Witness Fee		10.00/day .345/mile	

Fees to be charged to all cities, other counties, other states, unless specifically stated by statute.

Fees to be charged to all state agencies unless there is a specific statutory authority (98 Wn2d 606).

No statutory authority to <u>NOT</u> charge federal agencies except U.S. Immigration and V.A.

Fees to be paid in advance except for state and county (36.18.060). (Clerk's Office can voucher the State and cities).

Civil filing fees need to be paid by County

[Amended effective June 28, 2000; September 1, 2001; October 1, 2002.]

FEE EXEMPTIONS

Category	Description	RCW
ABSTRACTS	To Department of Licenses	AGO 61–62 No. 136
ADOPTION	–No filing fee if filed under another Petition already pending under Chapter 26.33 RCW	26.33.030(2)
	–Preplacement report filed prior to petition for adoption	26.33.190(5)
	–Revocation of Consent pursuant to 26.33.160	
ALIENS, COMMITMENT OF	No charge to U.S. Immigration office for copies	10.70.150
ANTI–HARASS-MENT	No charge for forms and brochures	10.14.040(4)
APPEALS TO SUPREME COURT	By state or municipality	2.32.070

Category	Description	RCW
OR COURT OF APPEALS	By indigent party	4.88.330
APPEALS, CRIMINAL RALJ	No initial filing fee—See Criminal	36.18.020(2)(b)
APPEALS, EXPLANATORY STATEMENTS	No costs to either party	29.81.230(3)
ATTORNEY GENERAL	Exempt from filing fees relating to paternity or support	74.20.300
BALLOT TITLE	No charge to either party	29.79.060
CHILD SUPPORT/ SPOUSAL MAINTENANCE PETITIONS	No filing fee if filed by State of Washington	26.18.040(2)
CONDEMNATION (Eminent Domain)	No fee for school districts, except on appeal	8.16.150
CRIMINAL	No fee for filing—costs assessed upon conviction or plea of guilty, upon failure to prosecute RALJ appeal or affirmance of lower court conviction	36.18.020(2)(h)
DISCLAIMER	Upon deposit of money/property (required)—No costs to determine conflicting claims of property (costs may be assessed by court)	4.08.170
DOMESTIC VIOLENCE	No charge for forms, brochures or obtaining Protection Orders	26.50.030(4), 36.18.020(3)
DOMESTIC VIOLENCE	No charge for filing or service of process; No charge for certified copies to petitioners	26.50.040
DSHS	See Social and Health Services, Department of	
EMINENT DOMAIN	See Condemnation	
EMPLOYMENT SECURITY	(Judicial Review on Unemployment Compensation) - No fees of any kind chargeable to individuals - No fees for department for any of Clerks services	50.32.110 50.32.190
EXPLANATORY STATEMENT APPEALS	No costs to either party	29.81.230
FORMS AND BROCHURES	No fee for forms and brochures under the Domestic Violence Act	36.18.020(3) 26.50.030(4)
FORMS AND BROCHURES	No fee for forms and brochures under the Unlawful Harassment Act	10.14.040(4)
GUARDIANSHIP or LIMITED GUARDIANSHIP	- No fee for filing when assets less than $3,000.00 - No prepayment when filed by AG—may be ordered paid by estate	11.88.030(3) 11.88.030(2)(b)
GUARDIANSHIP TO ESTATE	Cause Code migration/ no additional fee is charged to transfer the guardianship file to a probate proceeding when migration is ordered	11.88.150(2)
IMMIGRATION, US	See Aliens, Commitment of	10.70.150
IRRIGATION DISTRICT	No fee for Oath of Commissioner/Board Member of Joint Irrigation District	87.80.100
IN FORMA PAUPERIS	Waiver of filing fee due to financial hardship	36.18.022
INSURANCE COMMISSIONER	Exempt from filing fees	48.31.230
JUVENILE OFFENDER	No fee for filing or service	13.04.160
JUVENILE DEPENDENCY	- No fee for filing or service on Dependency, Guardianship, Terminations - No filing fee on Truancy	13.34.040 36.18.020(2)(a)
LABOR & INDUSTRIES	No filing fee to file complaint to prosecute for collection of wage assignments	49.48.040(2)
MENTAL ILLNESS JURY	No jury fee	MPR 3.3
PROPERTY	Filing to determine conflicting claims of, see Disclaimer	
PROSECUTOR	Exempt from filing fees related to paternity or support	74.20.300
PROSECUTOR (State of WA)	No fees for copies of criminal pleadings	9.94A.110
PUBLIC	See Social & Health Services, Department of (Judicial	

Category	Description	RCW
ASSISTANCE	Review)	
RECIPROCAL (URESA)	See UIFSA	
RELINQUISH-MENT OF A CHILD	No filing fee to a department, agency or prospective adoptive parent under RCW 26.33.080	36.18.020(3)
SERVICE PERSONNEL	No fees for copies to service personnel of US armed forces (for determining entitlements to family allowances and other benefits)	73.04.120
SOCIAL & HEALTH SERVICES	- Judicial review, no filing fees for individuals - Exempt from filing and copy fees relating to paternity or support	74.08.080(3)(a) 74.20.300
SUPPORT ENFORCEMENT	(DSHS) Exempt from filing and copy fees relating to paternity or support (also see UIFSA)	74.20.300
UIFSA	(Uniform Interstate Family Support Act) No filing fee—fees may be assessed	26.21.325
UNEMPLOYMENT COMPENSATION	See Employment Security	
URESA	See UIFSA	
VETERANS	(Marital Status) No fees for copies for family or legal representative of deceased for VA or other governmental agencies when required in connection with any claim pending before Veterans' Bureau or governmental agency administering benefits to war veterans	73.04.120
VETERANS	(Pension, Bounty, Back Pay) No fee for administering oaths, preparing official certificate or perfecting a voucher to procure a pension, bounty or back pay for Honorably Discharged, or spouse, orphan or legal representative	73.04.010
VETERANS	(VA Administration For Benefit Eligibility) No charge for copies to VA, applicant or person acting on applicant's behalf	73.36.155
WAGE CLAIM ASSIGNMENTS	Court costs by L & I for Prosecution	49.48.040(2)
WASHINGTON STATE BAR ASSN	No fee for requested copies of any order or other document evidencing the conviction of an attorney of a crime; Clerk to provide notification to Bar Assn (see Procedure 96–19)	RLD 3.1

No charge for federal agencies listed above
No charge for state agencies listed above
No charge for Thurston County Departments (36.18.140)
Limited Partnerships now filed with Secretary of State. Certificates of Osteopath, Osteopathy Surgery, Chiropractors, Chiropody, Optometry, etc., now filed with Department of Licenses.

[Adopted effective September 1, 2003.]

DISTRICT COURT

THURSTON COUNTY DISTRICT COURT LOCAL RULES

Including Amendments Received Through
August 15, 2015

Table of Rules

CIVIL RULES

LCRLJ 7. PRO SE APPEARANCE AND ANSWER [RESCINDED]

[Rescinded effective September 1, 2015.]

FORM. PRO SE APPEARANCE AND ANSWER

THURSTON COUNTY DISTRICT COURT
THURSTON COUNTY, STATE OF WASHINGTON

```
_____ )
                        ) No. _____
             Plaintiff, )
                        )
   V.                   ) PRO SE APPEARANCE
                        ) AND ANSWER
_____ )
             Defendant. )
```

1. My name and address is: _____

_____

2. Telephone: Home _____ Work _____

3. I am appearing: _____ for myself only _____ for myself and
_____ whose address is: _____

4. I admit the following paragraph and/or subparagraph numbers of the complaint:

_____

_____

5. I deny the following paragraph and/or subparagraph numbers of the complaint:

_____

_____

6. The specific reason(s) I denied the paragraph(s) listed in #5 above is/are as follows:

_____

_____

I have read the above appearance and answer. The statements made are true to the best of my knowledge.

_____   _____
          Date   Signature

LCRLJ 26. CIVIL DISCOVERY

26 (a) Civil Discovery.

(1) Discovery shall be permitted pursuant to CRLJ 26 without further order of the court. All discovery pursuant to CRLJ 26 shall be completed by the date of the settlement conference if a jury has been demanded, or, in the case of a non-jury trial, sixty (60) days prior to the non-jury trial date.

(2) Additional discovery may be conducted only by order of the court after motion and hearing. The settlement conference Judge has the authority to authorize additional discovery and set timelines in accordance with this rule. No orders for unlimited discovery pursuant to Superior Court Civil Rules 26—37 shall be permitted.

(3) Either party may request a hearing for the purpose of setting a discovery schedule.

(4) All discovery must be complete no later than sixty (60) days prior to the jury trial or non-jury trial date.

26 (b) Admissibility of Documents.

The documents listed below, if relevant, are presumed admissible at the trial, but only if the party offering the document serves on all parties at least 30 days prior to the trial date a notice, accompanied by a copy of the document and the name, address and telephone number of its author or maker. This rule does not restrict argument or proof related to the weight of the evidence admitted, nor does it restrict the court's authority to determine the weight of the evidence after hearing all of the evidence and the arguments of opposing parties.

The documents presumed admissible under this rule are:

(1) A bill, report, chart, or record of a hospital, doctor, dentist, registered nurse, licensed practical nurse, physical therapist, psychologist or other health care provider, on a letterhead or bill head;

(2) A bill for drugs, medical appliances, or other related expenses on a letterhead or billhead.

(3) A bill, or an estimate of, property damage on a letterhead or billhead. In the case of an estimate, the party intending to offer the estimate shall forward with the notice to the adverse party a statement indicating whether or not the property was repaired, and if it was, whether the estimated repairs were made in full or in part, attaching a copy to the receipted bill showing the items or repair and the amount paid;

(4) A police, weather, wage loss, or traffic signal report, or standard United States government table to the extent it is admissible under the Rules of Evidence, but without the need for formal proof of authentication or identification;

(5) A photograph, x-ray, drawing, map, blueprint or similar documentary evidence, to the extent it is admissible under the Rules of Evidence, but without the need for formal proof of authentication or identification;

(6) The written statement of any other witness, including the written report of an expert witness, and including a statement of opinion which the witness would be allowed to express if testifying in person, if it is made by affidavit or by declaration under penalty of perjury.

(7) A document not specifically covered by any of the foregoing provisions but having equivalent circumstantial guarantees of trustworthiness, the admission of which would serve the interests of justice.

Any other party may subpoena the author or maker of a document, admissible under this rule, at the party's expense, and examine the author or maker as if under cross examination.

[Adopted effective January 7,1987. Amended September 1, 1998; September 1, 2002; September 1, 2015.]

LCRLJ 40. CIVIL TRIAL SETTINGS, SETTLEMENT CONFERENCES, PRETRIAL ORDERS, CONFIRMATION HEARINGS

(a) Civil Trial Settings—Jury and Non–Jury.

(1) After the defendant's answer has been filed, any party may request the court set the matter for a trial.

(2) The party requesting a trial setting, jury or non-jury, shall file a Note for Civil Trial Setting and indicate by written affidavit the following:

- Certify that the defendant's answer has been filed,
- Certify that the request for a trial setting has been served on all parties and attorneys,
- State the nature of the action,
- State the estimated length of the trial,
- State the number of witnesses to be called for trial and provide the name, and contact information for each witness,
- State the name and contact information for all parties and attorneys,
- Propose a selection of dates for trial agreeable to all parties.

(3) Demand for a jury trial must be made no later than five (5) days after the Note for Civil Trial Setting is served. The party filing the demand shall at the time of filing pay the required jury fee and indicate by affidavit that the jury demand was served on all parties.

(4) In the case of jury demand, the plaintiff shall, within fourteen (14) days of receipt of the jury demand, initiate a telephone conference call with the District Court civil clerk and the defendant to set the

settlement conference date, the confirmation hearing date, and the jury trial date.

(5) In the case of a request for a non-jury trial, the plaintiff shall, within fourteen (14) days of receipt of the request for a non-jury trial, initiate a telephone conference call with the District Court civil clerk and the defendant to set the non-jury trial date.

(6) Thereafter, the Court will send notice to the parties of the settlement conference date, the confirmation hearing date, and the date of the jury or non-jury trial.

(7) Whenever any case set for trial is settled (other than at settlement conference), or will not be tried for any reason, notice of that fact shall be given immediately to the Court. If notification is not given 48 hours prior to the time of the trial, the Court in its discretion, may order any party to pay terms.

(b) Settlement Conferences. Whenever a demand for jury trial has been filed, the case will be set for a settlement conference approximately ninety (90) days prior to the trial date. All parties, their attorneys, and a person with authority to consent to settlement for each party shall be present at this hearing. All discovery pursuant to CRLJ 26 shall be completed prior to the settlement conference.

(c) Pretrial Orders. If settlement is not reached at the settlement conference, the settlement conference Judge will enter a pretrial order. The pretrial order will state the nature of the claims and defenses, list the names of witnesses & exhibits anticipated to be presented by each party at trial, indicate the additional discovery authorized by the Court with a timeline for completion, and will set a briefing schedule for motions.

(d) Confirmation Hearing. A confirmation hearing shall be set approximately one week prior to all civil jury trials. At confirmation hearing, all parties are expected to verify readiness to proceed to jury trial or propose an alternate disposition. All trial briefs, proposed jury instructions, motions in limine, and any remaining pre-trial motions shall be filed and served no later than seven (7) days prior to the confirmation hearing. Motions will be heard at the confirmation hearing.

[Adopted effective September 1, 1998. Amended effective September 1, 2002; September 1, 2015.]

FORM. NOTE FOR CIVIL TRIAL SETTING [RESCINDED]

[Rescinded effective September 1, 2015.]

FORM. PRE–TRIAL ORDER [RESCINDED]

[Rescinded effective September 1, 2015.]

LCRLJ 54. FEE SCHEDULE FOR ATTORNEY FEES IN DEFAULT JUDGMENTS

(Other than statutory attorney fees)

When a party is entitled to an award of reasonable attorney fees, where authorized by law or contract, the amounts provided in the following fee schedule shall be deemed reasonable in all cases where default judgment is granted unless the party presents evidence of circumstances that persuade the court to award a larger or smaller fee. The court shall retain the authority to vary from the following fee schedule on its own motion.

JUDGMENT PRINCIPLE	ATTORNEY FEE
$0—$5,000	$500
$5,000.01—$10,000	$1000
10,000.01—+	$1500

[Adopted effective January 7, 1987. Amended September 1, 1998; September 1, 2015.]

FORM. JUDGMENT FOLLOWING TRIAL [RESCINDED]

[Rescinded effective September 1, 2015.]

FORM. OFFER OF JUDGMENT [RESCINDED]

[Rescinded effective September 1, 2015.]

LCRLJ 55. DEFAULT JUDGMENTS

(a) The granting of default judgment shall be subject to the following key elements and will not be granted except on proof satisfactory to the court:

(1) Proof of service on all defendants against who judgment is sought;

(2) Proof of inquiry into military status of all defendants against who judgment is sought in compliance with the Service Members Civil Relief Act (SCRA);

(3) Proof of the debt owed;

(4) Proof of the basis for an award of reasonable attorney fees beyond a statutory allowance. This information shall be highlighted for the ease of review by the Court.

(5) No judgment for accrued interest shall be allowed unless there is on file proof of the factors necessary for computation of interest, including applicable dates, rate of interest, amounts subject to interest, and a computation of the total interest claimed due.

[Adopted effective January 7, 1987. Amended effective September 1, 1998; September 1, 2015.]

LCRLJ 65. [GARNISHMENTS; SUPPLEMENTAL PROCEEDINGS] [RESCINDED]

[Rescinded effective September 1, 2015.]

FORM. NOTICE TO FEDERAL GOVERNMENT GARNISHEE DEFENDANT [RESCINDED]

[Rescinded effective September 1, 2015.]

FORM. AFFIDAVIT AND ORDER FOR WARRANT OF CONTEMPT OF COURT AND BENCH WARRANT [RESCINDED]

[Rescinded effective September 1, 2015.]

FORM. VITAL STATISTIC INFORMATION [RESCINDED]

[Rescinded effective September 1, 2015.]

CRIMINAL RULES

LCrRLJ 3.2. BAIL & REVIEW OF INCARCERATED DEFENDANTS

(a) Any person arrested for the following offenses shall be held in jail without bail pending the first appearance:

(1) Any offense classified under Section 10.99 of the Revised Code of Washington as Domestic Violence.

(2) A violation of RCW 46.61.502 (Driving Under the Influence), RCW 46.61.503 (Driver Under 21 Consuming Alcohol), or RCW 46.61.504 (Physical Control of Vehicle Under the Influence), when the person has previously been convicted of or had a deferred prosecution granted for one or more of any of these offenses.

(b) Incarcerated defendants may be reviewed upon request of either party or at the court's discretion. The request shall be in writing, which includes electronic mail. The request shall include the defendant's name, court docket number, and purpose for the review. The request will be made to the Court by notifying the court coordinator and the in-custody clerk. The party requesting the review shall ensure that the other party is served notice of the request at the time that the request is made of the Court. The in-custody clerk will set the review no sooner than the following court day, unless prior court approval is granted.

[Adopted January 7, 1987. Amended effective September 1, 1991; August 6, 2001; May 1, 2003; September 1, 2015.]

Note:

Definition of domestic violence per RCW 10.99.020:

"(3) 'Domestic violence' includes but is not limited to any of the following crimes when committed by one family or household member against another:

"(a) Assault in the first degree (RCW 9A.36.011);

"(b) Assault in the second degree (RCW 9A.36.021);

"(c) Assault in the third degree (RCW 9A.36.031);

"(d) Assault in the fourth degree (RCW 9A.36.041);

"(e) Drive–by shooting (RCW 9A.36.045);

"(f) Reckless endangerment (RCW 9A.36.050);

"(g) Coercion (RCW 9A.36.070);

"(h) Burglary in the first degree (RCW 9A.52.020);

"(i) Burglary in the second degree (RCW 9A.52.030);

"(j) Criminal trespass in the first degree (RCW 9A.52.070);

"(k) Criminal trespass in the second degree (RCW 9A.52.080);

"(*l*) Malicious mischief in the first degree (RCW 9A.48.070);

"(m) Malicious mischief in the second degree (RCW 9A.48.080);

"(n) Malicious mischief in the third degree (RCW 9A.48.090);

"(o) Kidnapping in the first degree (RCW 9A.40.020);

"(p) Kidnapping in the second degree (RCW 9A.40.030);

"(q) Unlawful imprisonment (RCW 9A.40.040);

"(r) Violation of the provisions of a restraining order restraining the person or restraining the person from going onto the grounds of or entering a residence, workplace, school, or day care (RCW 26.09.300, 26.10.220, or 26.26.138);

"(s) Violation of the provisions of a protection order or no-contact order restraining the person or restraining the person from going onto the grounds of or entering a residence, workplace, school, or day care (RCW 26.50.060, 26.50.070, 26.50.130, 10.99.040, or 10.99.050);

"(t) Rape in the first degree (RCW 9A.44.040);

"(u) Rape in the second degree (RCW 9A.44.050);

"(v) Residential burglary (RCW 9A.52.025);

"(w) Stalking (RCW 9A.46.110); and

"(x) Interference with the reporting of domestic violence (RCW 9A.36.150)."

LCrRLJ 3.3. CONTINUANCE OF COURT DATES [RESCINDED]

[Rescinded effective September 1, 2015.]

LCrRLJ 3.4. VIDEO CONFERENCES

Pursuant to CrRLJ 3.4(d)(2), Thurston County District Court authorizes the use of video conferences for court proceedings.

[Adopted January 5, 2000 as Emergency Rule; effective as Permanent Rule September 1, 2000. Amended effective September 1, 2015.]

FORM.   AGREEMENT TO PROCEED BY VIDEO CONFERENCE

IN THE DISTRICT COURT OF
THURSTON COUNTY, WASHINGTON

STATE OF WASHINGTON	) Cause Number(s) _____
CITY OF	)
	) _____
Vs	)
	) _____
	)
_____	) AGREEMENT TO PROCEED BY
Defendant	) VIDEO CONFERENCE
_____	)

Pursuant to CrRLJ 3.4(d), the undersigned parties acknowledge that today's trial court proceedings are being conducted by video conference and hereby

[ ] AGREE that today's proceedings may be conducted by video conference; or

[ ] DO NOT AGREE that today's proceedings may be conducted by video conference

DATED _____, 20 ___.

_____	_____
Defendant	Attorney for Plaintiff
_____	
Attorney for Defendant	

LCrRLJ 3.7. PRETRIAL MOTIONS

(a) All pretrial motions pursuant to CrRLJ 3.5 and CrRLJ 3.6 shall be in writing, served upon the opposing counsel or pro se party, and filed with the court within 10 days after the hearing requesting a trial setting. Supporting briefs shall be filed and served at the time the pretrial motion is filed.

(b) Upon receipt of a pretrial motion, the calendar coordinator will schedule a hearing on the motion prior to the date set for the confirmation hearing.

(c) Responsive briefs shall be filed and served on opposing counsel or pro se party no later than 14 days after service of moving party's brief.

(d) The court may lengthen or shorten the time for filing on a showing of good cause.

[Adopted effective September 1, 1998. Amended effective September 1, 2015.]

LCrRLJ 4.5. PRETRIAL HEARINGS [RESCINDED]

[Rescinded effective September 1, 2015.]

LCrRLJ 6.1.1. CRIMINAL TRIAL

(a) Waiver of Jury Trial. A defendant may waive his or her right to a jury trial at any time prior to a jury being impaneled. Waiver of jury trial shall be in writing. If the waiver occurs after the confirmation hearing, the court may order costs to be imposed. A motion to withdraw a waiver of jury trial shall be in writing.

(b) Confirmation of Trial. The calendar coordinator shall set a confirmation hearing prior to the trial date in all cases where a trial has been requested. At the confirmation hearing, all parties are expected to verify readiness to proceed to trial, or to propose an alternate disposition. If a case settles after the confirmation hearing, the court may, in its discretion, order a party to pay any costs incurred as a result.

(c) Witness, Subpoenas, Costs. Where prospective witnesses, who will be compelled to appear by subpoena, reside outside the boundaries of Thurston County, leave of the court to issue a subpoena shall be obtained by written motion. The party requesting the subpoena, shall file the motion no later than fourteen (14) days prior to the date set for trial. If leave is not obtained or the request is not timely made, then the party requesting the subpoena, shall be responsible for all costs associated with the appearance of the person subject to the subpoena, unless good cause is shown.

[Adopted effective January 7, 1987. Amended September 1, 1991; June 27, 1994; September 1, 1998; September 1, 2015.]

LCrRLJ 7.2. VICTIM IMPACT STATEMENT [RESCINDED]

[Rescinded effective September 1, 2015.]

INFRACTION RULES

LIRLJ 3.1(e). PRE–HEARING MOTIONS IN INFRACTION CASES [REPEALED]

[Repealed effective September 1, 2006.]

LIRLJ 3.5. DECISION ON WRITTEN STATEMENTS

Mitigation hearings based on written statements, as provided for in IRLJ 2.4(b)(4) and IRLJ 2.6(c), are authorized. This court adopts the procedures authorized by IRLJ 3.5(b). In accordance with the provisions of IRLJ 3.5, such hearings are not governed by the Rules of Evidence, and there shall be no appeal from a decision on written statement(s).

[Adopted effective September 1, 2002. Amended effective September 1, 2015.]

LIRLJ 6.6. SPEED MEASURING DEVICE EXPERT

A request to produce the electronic speed measuring device expert at the contested hearing shall be contained in a separate pleading entitled, "Request to Subpoena Speed Measuring Device Expert". This pleading shall be served on the prosecutor with a conformed copy filed with the court clerk. Such request must be filed in accordance with the time limitations set forth in IRLJ 6.6 (b)

[Adopted effective September 1, 1998. Amended effective September 1, 2015.]

MUNICIPAL COURTS

OLYMPIA MUNICIPAL COURT LOCAL COURT RULES

Including Amendments Received Through
August 15, 2015

Table of Rules

OMCLR 1. ADOPTION AND SCOPE OF LOCAL RULES

These rules are adopted pursuant to GR 7, CrRLJ 1.7 and IRLJ 1.3 of the Washington Court rules. These rules govern the procedure in the City of Olympia Municipal Court and are supplemental to the rules enacted by the Washington State Supreme Court for Courts of Limited Jurisdiction. The Court may modify or suspend any of these local Court rules in any given case upon good cause being shown or upon the Court's own motion.

[Adopted effective September 1, 2000.]

OMCLR 2. TITLE OF RULES

These rules shall be known as the Olympia Municipal Court Local Rules and may be cited as OMCLR.

[Adopted effective September 1, 2000.]

OMCLR 3. VIDEO CONFERENCE PROCEEDINGS

A. Preliminary appearances as defined by CrR 3.2(B) and CrRLJ 3.2.1(d), arraignments as defined by CrR 3.4 and 4.1 and CrRLJ 3.4 and 4.1, bail hearings as defined by CrR 3.2 and CrRLJ 3.2, and trial settings as defined by CrR 3.3 and CrRLJ 3.3(f), conducted via video conference in which all participants can simultaneously see, hear, and speak with each other shall be deemed held in open court and in the defendant's presence for the purposes of any statute, court rule or policy. All video conference hearings conducted pursuant to this rule shall be public, and the public shall be able to simultaneously see and hear all participants and speak as permitted by the Court. Any party may request an in-person hearing under this section, which *may in the Court's discretion* be granted.

B. Other trial court proceedings including the entry of a statement of Defendant on Plea of Guilty as defined by CrR 4.2 and CrRLJ 4.2 may be conducted by video conference only by agreement of the parties, either in writing or on the record, and upon the approval of the Court pursuant to this local court rule.

C. The judge, counsel, all parties, and the public must be able to see and hear each other during video proceedings, and may speak as permitted by the Court. Video conference facilities must provide for confidential communications between attorney and client and security sufficient to protect the safety of all participants and observers. In interpreted proceedings, the interpreter must be located next to the defendant and the proceeding must be conducted to assure that the interpreter can hear all participants.

D. For purposes of video conference proceedings, the facsimile signatures of the defendant, counsel, interested parties and the Court will be treated as if they were an original signature. This includes all orders on Judgment and Sentence, No Contact Orders, Statements of Defendant on Plea of Guilty, and other documents or pleadings as the Court shall determine are appropriate or necessary.

[Adopted effective September 1, 2000.]

OMCLR 4.   ARRAIGNMENT

Arraignments shall be in accordance with CrRLJ 3.4 and 4.1. A lawyer may, pursuant to CrRLJ 4.1(d), enter an appearance on behalf of a client **except** in cases in which the docket or charging document states that one or more of the charges involves domestic violence, harassment, violation of a no contact order, protection order or anti-harassment order, stalking, driving under the influence, physical control, or minor under 21 operating motor vehicle after consuming alcohol—whereupon defendant's presence is mandatory. The Court Clerk may continue an arraignment at the request of the defendant or counsel for no more than two weeks, except in cases in which the docket or charging document states that one or more of the charges involves an offense listed above.

[Adopted effective September 1, 2000.]

OMCLR 5.   DISCOVERY ASSIGNED COUNSEL

The prosecuting authority shall provide discovery to counsel appointed at public expense within fourteen (14) days of the prosecuting authority's receipt of the order appointing counsel or other notification of appointment by the Court. The order appointing counsel or other notification of appointment by the Court shall be considered a written demand for discovery, thereby triggering the prosecuting authority's discovery obligations under CrRLJ 4.7(a).

[Adopted effective September 1, 2000.]

OMCLR 6.   PRETRIAL MOTIONS

A.   Motions to dismiss or suppress physical, oral or identification evidence other than motions made pursuant to CrRLJ 3.5 shall be in writing supported by legal grounds or authorities, and by an affidavit or document as provided in CrRLJ 3.6 and RCW 9A.72.085 or any law amendatory thereto, setting forth the facts the moving party anticipates will be elicited at a hearing. If there are no disputed facts, the Court shall determine whether an evidentiary hearing is required. If the Court determines no evidentiary hearing is required, the Court shall set forth its reasons for not conducting an evidentiary hearing.

B.   Pleadings required for compliance with this rule shall be submitted in writing and filed by the moving party at least 14 days prior to the pretrial motion hearing with the Court and City Prosecutor's Office. Responsive pleadings shall be filed within 10 days from the date of receipt of the motion and supporting pleadings with the moving party and the Court.

[Adopted effective September 1, 2000.]

OMCLR 7.   PRETRIAL HEARINGS

Unless otherwise ordered by the Court in a specific case for good cause, all cases in which a defendant enters a plea of Not Guilty shall be set for a pretrial hearing. The pretrial hearing shall provide an opportunity for negotiation between the parties. The defendant shall be required to attend the pretrial hearing unless specifically excused by the Court. Failure to appear at the pretrial hearing may result in the issuance of a bench warrant and /or forfeiture of any bond or bail. Any disposition reached between the parties shall be stated on the record at the pretrial hearing unless otherwise agreed.

[Adopted effective September 1, 2000.]

OMCLR 8.   CONTINUANCES

Unless otherwise duly noted for motion, all requests to continue pretrial hearings, motions, trial dates, failure to comply hearings, and/or other final dispositions will require the agreement of both parties before such request will be submitted to the Court for approval except as otherwise provided under OMCLR 4. All motions for continuances must be made in writing or on the record.

[Adopted effective September 1, 2000.]

OMCLR 9.   EVIDENCE COURT'S CUSTODY OF EXHIBITS

In a criminal case, every exhibit in the Court's custody, which is not contraband and for which ownership is not in dispute, shall be returned to the party who produced that exhibit upon motion of that party and expiration of the appeal period. For purposes of this rule, the appeal period shall begin on the day of sentencing or deferral of sentencing following a finding of Guilty by the Court. Exhibits not withdrawn shall be delivered by the Court to the Olympia Police Department for disposition as abandoned property; or, if contraband, for destruction. No exhibit shall be released by the Court without its first being receipted for by the receiving person.

[Adopted effective September 1, 2000.]

OMCLR 10.   INFRACTIONS DISCOVERY [RESCINDED]

[Adopted effective September 1, 2000; rescinded effective September 1, 2009.]

OMCLR 10.1.   DECISION ON WRITTEN STATEMENTS

Mitigation and contested hearings based on written or e-mail statements, given under penalty of perjury as provided for in IRLJ 2.4(b)(4) and IRLJ 2.6(c), are authorized. This court adopts the procedures authorized by IRLJ 3.5. To be considered by the court, the court must receive written or e-mail statement(s) no later than seven (7) calendar days before the scheduled hearing. In accordance with the provisions of IRLJ 3.5, such hearings are not governed by the Rules of Evidence, and there shall be no appeal from a decision on written or e-mail statement(s). Statements authorized by this rule shall be in substantially the following format:

For **contested** hearings:

I hereby state as follows:

I promise that if it is determined that I committed the infraction for which I was cited, I will pay the monetary penalty authorized by law and assessed by the court. I understand that the court's decision is final and there shall be no reconsideration or appeal from a decision on a written statement.

I certify (or declare) under penalty of perjury under the laws of the State of Washington that the foregoing is true and correct.

_____   _____
Date and Place   Signature

I understand that if this form is submitted by e-mail, my typed name on the signature line will qualify as my signature for purposes of the above certification.

For **mitigation** hearings:

I hereby state as follows:

I promise to pay the monetary penalty authorized by law or, at the discretion of the court, any reduced penalty that may be set. I understand that the court's decision is final and there shall be no reconsideration or appeal from a decision on a written statement.

I certify (or declare) under penalty of perjury under the laws of the State of Washington that the foregoing is true and correct.

_____   _____
Date and Place   Signature

I understand that if this form is submitted by e-mail, my typed name on the signature line will qualify as my signature for purposes of the above certification.

[Adopted on an emergency basis effective January 13, 2006; amended effective September 1, 2009.]

OMCLR 11. INFRACTIONS FINES— NO PROOF OF LIABILITY INSURANCE

1. If a person who has been cited with a violation of RCW 46.30.020 (failure to have proof of liability insurance) presents to the Court Clerk evidence that the person had in effect at the time of the citation liability insurance as required by RCW 46.30.020, then, upon payment of twenty-five dollars ($25.00) administrative costs, the case shall be dismissed and the Court Clerk shall be authorized to make appropriate notation of the dismissal in the Court file. This section is applicable only if the person charged has otherwise complied with all rules and procedures that govern responding to notices of infraction.

2. If a person charged with violation of RCW 46.30.020 (failure to have proof of liability insurance) is

able to show evidence that the person has subsequently obtained liability insurance in conformity with the requirements of RCW 46.30.020, then the penalty shall be reduced to one hundred fifty dollars ($150.00) for a first offense, two hundred dollars ($200.00) for a second offense, and two hundred fifty dollars ($250.00) for a third or more offense, unless otherwise ordered by the Court. Upon payment of the required penalty as set forth above, the Court Clerk shall be authorized to enter a finding that the infraction was committed, make appropriate notations in the Court record, and the person will be relieved of any further need to appear in Court in connection with the infraction. This section is applicable only if the person charged has otherwise complied with all rules and procedures that govern responding to notices of infraction.

[Adopted effective September 1, 2000; amended effective September 1, 2005.]

OMCLR 12. INFRACTIONS FINES—NO VALID LICENSE WITH VALID ID

If a person charged with violation of RCW 46.20.015 (No Valid Operator's License With Valid Identification) is able to show proof of subsequently acquiring a valid operator's license, then the fine shall be reduced to one hundred fifty dollars ($150.00) unless otherwise ordered by the Court. Upon payment of the required penalty as set forth above, the Court Clerk shall be authorized to enter a finding that the infraction was committed, make appropriate notations in the Court record, and the person will be relieved of any further need to appear in Court in connection with the infraction. This section is applicable only if the person charged has otherwise complied with all rules and procedures that govern responding to notices of infraction.

[Adopted effective September 1, 2000; amended effective September 1, 2005.]

OMCLR 13. SPEED MEASURING DEVICE—INFRACTION [RESCINDED]

[Adopted effective September 1, 2001; rescinded effective September 1, 2010.]

RAINIER MUNICIPAL COURT—
[No Local Rules]

TENINO MUNICIPAL COURT—
[No Local Rules]

TUMWATER MUNICIPAL COURT LOCAL COURT RULES

Including Amendments Received Through
August 15, 2015

Table of Rules

LCrRLJ 3.2. BAIL

A. The court shall by written order filed with the court administrator establish bail schedules for use by the Tumwater Police Department. The schedule shall, in addition, designate those types of criminal cases, if any, wherein the defendant may forfeit bail in lieu of arraignment.

B. Except for the criminal cases covered by paragraph A, the court adopts the uniform bail schedule of CrRLJ 3.2.

C. Bail for unscheduled misdemeanors shall be $250.00 unless otherwise set by statute or ordinance. Bail for unscheduled gross misdemeanors shall be $500.00 unless set by statute or ordinance.

[Adopted effective September 1, 2006.]

LCrRLJ 3.2.2. RELEASE OF ACCUSED; DOMESTIC VIOLENCE

(a) Any person arrested on Probable Cause (without a warrant) for an offense classified as a Domestic Violence offense under Chapter 10.99 of the Revised Code of Washington, as the same exists or shall hereafter be amended, shall be held in jail pending the defendant's first appearance.

(b) Notwithstanding paragraph (a), a person being held for a Domestic Violence offense classified as a misdemeanor or gross misdemeanor may be released from custody prior to defendant's first appearance upon (1) the posting of $1,000 bail or bond; and (2) the person's affixing his or her signature in the appropriate location on a Pre–Arraignment Domestic Violence No Contact Order (Exhibit A) prohibiting the arrested person from having contact with the protected person or from knowingly coming within, or knowingly remaining within, 500 feet of the protected person's residence, place of work, or school.

(c) The following Pre–Arraignment Domestic Violence No Contact Order, or one that is substantially similar to it, is hereby approved for use under this rule.

Pre-Arraignment Domestic Violence No Contact Order

CITY OF TUMWATER,

LAW ENFORCEMENT NO. _____

Plaintiff,

vs.

PRE–ARRAIGNMENT DOMESTIC VIOLENCE NO CONTACT ORDER

_____,

DOB: _____

Date of Arrest: _____

Time of Arrest: _____

Defendant.

THE COURT FINDS THAT the Defendant has been arrested for a domestic violence offense, and further finds that to prevent possible recurrence of violence, this Pre–Arraignment Domestic Violence No Contact Order shall be entered pursuant to chapter 10.99 RCW. The person(s) protected by this order are:

_____

(Protected person(s) name, or initials if a minor, and DOB)

IT IS ORDERED THAT Defendant is **PROHIBITED** from causing or attempting to cause physical harm, bodily injury, assault, including sexual assault, and from molesting, harassing, threatening, or stalking the protected person(s), and

IT IS ORDERED THAT Defendant is **PROHIBITED** from coming near and from having any contact whatsoever, in person or through others, by phone, mail or any means, directly or indirectly, except for mailing or service of process of court documents by a third party or contact by the Defendant's lawyer(s) with the protected person(s), and

IT IS ORDERED THAT Defendant is **PROHIBITED** from entering or knowingly coming within or knowingly remaining within 500 feet of the protected person's residence, school, or place of work, and

IT IS ORDERED THAT this Pre–Arraignment Domestic Violence No Contact Order expires seven (7) days from the date below.

WARNINGS TO THE DEFENDANT: Violation of the provisions of this order with actual notice of its terms is a criminal offense under chapter 26.50 RCW, and will subject a violator to arrest. If the violation of this order involves travel across a state line or the boundary of a tribal jurisdiction, or involves conduct within the special maritime and territorial jurisdiction of the United States, which includes tribal lands, then you may be subject to criminal prosecution in federal court under 18 U.S.C. sections 2261, 2261A, or 2262.

Any assault, drive-by shooting, or reckless endangerment that is a violation of this order is a felony. Any conduct in violation of this order that is reckless and creates a substantial risk of death or serious physical injury to another person is a class C felony.

Effective immediately, and continuing as long as this order is in effect, you may not possess a firearm or ammunition. 18 U.S.C. section 922(g)(8). A violation of this federal firearms law carries a maximum possible penalty of 10 years in prison and a $250,000 fine. An exception exists for law enforcement officers and military personnel when carrying department/government–issued firearms. 18 U.S.C. section 925(a)(1). If you are convicted of an offense of domestic violence, you will be forbidden for life from possessing a firearm or ammunition. 18 U.S.C. section 922(g)(9); RCW 9.41.040.

YOU CAN BE ARRESTED EVEN IF ANY PERSON OR PERSONS

PROTECTED BY THIS ORDER INVITES OR ALLOWS YOU TO

VIOLATE THIS ORDER'S PROHIBITIONS.

You have the sole responsibility to avoid or refrain from violating the order's provisions. Only the court can change the order.

Pursuant to 18 U.S.C. section 2265, a court in any of the 50 states, the District of Columbia, Puerto Rico, any United States territory, and any tribal land within the United States shall accord full faith and credit to the order.

Dated: ____
Time: ____ [AM] [PM]

I agree to abide by the terms of this Pre–Arraignment Domestic Violence No Contact Order. I understand that the terms of any other court orders remain in effect notwithstanding the expiration of this order.

DEFENDANT

So Ordered.

JUDGE

[Adopted effective September 1, 2004.]

YELM MUNICIPAL COURT—
[No Local Rules]

WAHKIAKUM COUNTY

Table of Courts

Superior Court

Local Court Rules of the Superior Court of Washington for Pacific and Wahkiakum Counties.

District Court

Wahkiakum County District Court Local Court Rules.

SUPERIOR COURT

LOCAL COURT RULES OF THE SUPERIOR COURT OF WASHINGTON FOR PACIFIC AND WAHKIAKUM COUNTIES

PUBLISHER'S NOTE

The Local Rules for the Superior Courts of Pacific and Wahkiakum Counties are set forth under Pacific County.

DISTRICT COURT

WAHKIAKUM COUNTY DISTRICT COURT
LOCAL COURT RULES

Including Amendments Received Through
August 15, 2015

Table of Rules

RULE 0.1.   DEFERRED PROSECUTION FEE

1.   There is hereby imposed by Local Court Rule a One Hundred Fifty Dollar ($150.00) fee for filing a Petition for Deferred Prosecution in the District Court of Wahkiakum County; and

2.   The Clerk of the Court is directed to pay said monies monthly to the Wahkiakum County Treasurer for crediting to the current expense fund to defray the costs of such program.

[Adopted July 17, 1991.]

RULE 0.2.   PROBATION FEE

1.   The following sliding fee schedule for supervision services is implemented forthwith:

Gross Monthly Income	Monthly Supervision Fee
$ 0.00 to $ 999.99	$15.00 per month (unless waived)
$1,000.00 to $1,999.99	$20.00 per month
$2,000.00 to $2,999.00	$30.00 per month
over $3,000.00	$40.00 per month

2.   The Clerk of the Court is directed to pay said monies monthly to the Wahkiakum County Treasurer for crediting to the current expense fund to defray the costs of such program; and

3.   This Order shall be effective February 1st, 1995.

When supervising individuals who earn less than $1,000.00 per month, the probation officer will closely review the client's finances, provide a payment recommendation to the Court and obtain approval from the referring Judge to assess a fee less than $15.00 per month, if appropriate.

[Adopted effective February 1, 1995.]

LOCAL CRIMINAL RULES

LCrRLJ 1.5.   COMBINING DOCUMENTS

The notice of appearance and plea of not guilty may be in one document. A waiver of a jury trial or speedy trial shall be separate and signed by the defendant or the defendant's attorney if the attorney certifies that the waiver has been expressly approved by the defendant. A demand for the appearance of a breathalyzer/verifier maintenance operator shall be by a separate document. Discovery demands shall be by a separate document.

[Adopted October 9, 1987.]

LCrRLJ 4.1.   PRE–TRIAL HEARINGS

(A) **Hearings.** All cases scheduled for a jury trial shall be set for a pre-trial hearing not less than two weeks prior to the trial. The Prosecuting Attorney, the defendant and the defense attorney, if any, shall attend the hearing. If a defendant not represented by counsel fails to appear for the hearing, a warrant for his or her arrest shall issue, and the jury trial setting stricken. If a defendant represented by counsel fails to appear, a warrant for the defendant's arrest may issue, and the jury trial setting may be stricken. In any case where a defendant fails to appear for the hearing, the period of time from that hearing to the defendant's next personal appearance in court shall not be included in any time limitation requirements.

(B) Motions. All amendments to the charges, pleas or other motions shall be heard at the pre-trial hearing. Motions may not be considered at the time of trial unless they could not have been raised at the pre-trial hearing, or the court, on its motion, continues a matter to the time of trial. The party wishing the attendance of a witness at the pre-trial hearing shall be responsible for subpoenas of such witness except that the Prosecuting Attorney shall subpoena necessary witnesses for a CrRLJ 3.5 hearing if the defendant or his attorney has requested in writing such attendance.

[Adopted October 9, 1987.]

LCrRLJ 4.7. DISCOVERY

"Blanket" discovery forms may be used provided that each item requested shall contain a box or square in the left margin and shall be checked by the demanding party if that item is to be applicable to the particular case. Demands not applicable shall not be checked. Sanctions may be imposed for violation of this rule including, but not limited to, the quashing of the entire demand. Failure to provide discovery materials, including bills of particulars, shall be deemed waived unless the court is notified in writing not less than two weeks prior to trial.

[Adopted October 9, 1987.]

LOCAL TRAFFIC INFRACTION RULES

LJTIR 3.3. SPEED MEASURING DEVICE: DESIGN AND CERTIFICATION

(a) Admission of Certificate. In the absence of a request to produce an electronic speed measuring devise (SMD) expert made at least 7 days prior to trial or such lesser time as the Court deems proper, a certificate substantially in the following form is admissible in lieu of an expert witness in any contested hearing relating to a Notice of Traffic Infraction in which the design and construction of an electronic speed measuring device (SMD) is an issue:

CERTIFICATION CONCERNING DESIGN AND CONSTRUCTION OF ELECTRONIC SPEED MEASURING DEVICE

I, _____, do certify under penalty of perjury as follows:

I am employed with _____ as a _____. I have been employed in such a capacity for ____ years and hold the rank of _____. Part of my duties include supervising the purchase, maintenance, and repair of all electronic speed measuring devices (SMD) used by my agency.

This agency currently uses the following SMD's:

(List All SMD's used and their Manufacturers)

I have the following qualifications with respect to the above SMD's:

(List all degrees held and any special schooling regarding the SMD's listed above)

Our agency maintains manuals for all of the above stated SMD's. I am personally familiar with these manuals and how each of the SMD's are designed and operated. All initial testing of the SMD's was performed under my direction. The units were evaluated to meet or exceed existing performance standards. Our agency maintains a testing and certification program. This program requires:

(State the program in detail)

Based upon my education, training, and experience and my knowledge of the SMD's listed above, it is my opinion that each of these pieces of equipment is so designed and constructed as to accurately employ the Doppler effect in such a manner that it will give accurate measurements of the speed of motor vehicles when properly calibrated and operated by a trained operator.

_____
Signature

DATED: _____

(b) Continuance. The Court at the time of trial shall hear testimony concerning the alleged offense and, if necessary, may continue the proceedings for the purpose of obtaining evidence concerning an electronic speed measuring device and the certification thereof. If, at the time it is supplied, the evidence is insufficient, the results of such test or readings shall not be admitted.

[Adopted October 9, 1987.]

WAHKIAKUM COUNTY BAIL SCHEDULE
EXPLANATION OF SYMBOLS

* <u>MANDATORY APPEARANCE.</u> Court appearance for these violations is mandatory. Forfeiture of bail shall not constitute a final disposition for those violations without a special order of the Court showing the reasons thereto.

PSEA Public Safety Education Assessment—90% of Penalty

BAIL AND PENALTY SCHEDULE
TRAFFIC INFRACTIONS

		Penalty	+ PSEA	= Total
SERIOUS INFRACTIONS:				
1.	Driving w/o Valid Driver License with Expired License on Person RCW 46.20.	130	120	250
2.	Violation of Posted Road Restriction RCW 46.44.105.4	175	157	285
3.	Negligent Driving 2nd Degree RCW 46.61.525.2	250	225	475
4.	Wrong Way on Freeway RCW 46.61.150	175	157	332
5.	Wrong Way on Freeway Access RCW 46.61.155	80	72	152
6.	Passing Stopped School Bus RCW 46.61.370 Penalty Cannot be Reduced, Suspended or Waived	80	72	152
7.	Disobeying School Patrol RCW 46.61.385	80	72	152
8.	Backing on Limited Access Highway RCW 46.61.605	80	72	152
9.	Throwing or Depositing Debris on Highway RCW 46.61.645	80	72	152
10.	Spilling of Loaded Material RCW 46.61.655	80	72	152
OPERATOR'S LICENSE INFRACTIONS (RCW 46.20):				
1.	No Valid Driver License RCW 46.20.021.1	250	225	475
2.	Violation of License Restrictions RCW 46.20.041	35	31	66
3.	Violation of Instruction Permit RCW 46.20.055	35	31	66

	Penalty +	PSEA =	Total
4. No Driver License on Person RCW 46.20.190	35	31	66
5. Display or Possess Canceled, Revoked or Suspended Drivers License or ID Card RCW 46.20.338	35	31	66
6. Allow Unauthorized Minor to Operate Vehicle RCW 46.20.343	35	31	66
7. Allow Unauthorized Driver to Operate Vehicle RCW 46.20.344	35	31	66

VEHICLE LICENSE INFRACTIONS (RCW 46.16):

1. Expired Vehicle License RCW 46.16.010	35	31	66
RCW 46.16.010.L—2 Months or Less	35	31	66
RCW 46.16.010.O—Over Two Months	80	72	152
2. No Gross Weight Signs Displayed RCW 46.16.170	35	31	66
3. Switching, Altering, Loan or Use of Another's License Plate RCW 46.16.240	80	72	152
4. Operate w/o or Illegal License Plates RCW 46.16.240.1	35	31	66
5. Obscured or Illegible License Plates RCW 46.16.240.3	35	31	66
3. Fail to Carry Certificate of Registration or Display on Demand RCW 46.16.260	35	31	66

Speeding (RCW 46.61.400):

1. Speeding if Speed Limit is Over 40 MPH:

1 – 5 mph over limit	20	18	38
6 – 10 mph over limit	30	27	57
11 – 15 mph over limit	45	40	85
16 – 20 mph over limit	60	54	114
21 – 25 mph over limit	75	67	142
26 – 30 mph over limit	95	85	180
31 – 35 mph over limit	120	108	228
36 – 40 mph over limit	145	130	275
Over 40 mph over limit	175	157	332

2. Speeding if Speed Limit is 40 MPH or Less:

1 – 5 mph over limit	30	27	57
6 – 10 mph over limit	35	31	66
11 – 15 mph over limit	50	45	95
16 – 20 mph over limit	70	63	133
21 – 25 mph over limit	95	85	180

26 – 30 mph over limit	120	108	228
31 – 35 mph over limit	145	130	275
Over 35 mph over limit	175	157	332

3. Speed Too Fast for Conditions   35   31   66
    RCW 46.61.400

4. Speeding in School or   132   0   132
    Playground Zone
    RCW 46.61.440   Penalty Cannot be Reduced, Suspended or Waived

5. Speeding in Marked   **DOUBLE LISTED PENALTY AMOUNT**
    Construction Zone
    RCW 46.61.527(3)   Penalty Cannot be Reduced, Suspended or Waived

RULES OF THE ROAD:

1. Driving without Lights   35   31   66
    RCW 46.37.020

2. Fail to Dim Lights–Passing or Following   35   31   66
    RCW 46.37.230

3. Fail to Obey Traffic Control Device   35   31   66
    RCW 46.61.050

4. Fail to Obey Flashing Red Signal   35   31   66
    RCW 46.61.065

5. Crossing Double Yellow Line Left of Center   35   31   66
    RCW 46.61.100

6. Fail to Give Clearance to Overtaken Vehicle   35   31   66
    RCW 46.61.110

7. Pass on the Right   35   31   66
    RCW 46.61.115

8. Pass with Approaching Vehicle w/200 Feet   35   31   66
    RCW 46.61.120

9. Pass With Obstructed View   35   31   66
    RCW 46.61.125

10. Pass in Marked no Passing Zone   35   31   66
    RCW 46.61.130

11. Wrong Way on One–Way Street   35   31   66
    RCW 46.61.135

12. Improper Lane Usage or Travel   35   31   66
    RCW 46.61.140

13. Following Too Close   35   31   66
    RCW 46.61.145

14. Fail to Yield Right of Way   35   31   66
    RCW 46.61.180

15. Vehicle Turning Left—Fail to Yield   35   31   66

RCW 46.61.185

16.	Fail to Stop/Yield at Intersection RCW 46.61.190	35	31	66
17.	Fail to Stop/Yield Entering Arterial Highway RCW 46.61.195	35	31	66
18.	Fail to Stop at Stop Sign RCW 46.61.200	35	31	66
19.	Obstructing Intersection or Crosswalk RCW 46.61.202	35	31	66
20.	Fail to Yield When Emerging from Driveway RCW 46.61.205	35	31	66
21.	Fail to Stop/Yield to Emergency Vehicle RCW 46.61.210	35	31	66
22.	Fail to Yield to Pedestrian RCW 46.61.235	35	31	66
23.	Improper or Prohibited Turn RCW 46.61.290	35	31	66
24.	Prohibited U–Turn RCW 46.61.295	35	31	66
25.	Unsafe Starting from Parked Position RCW 46.61.300	35	31	66
26.	Fail to Signal RCW 46.61.310	35	31	66
27.	Impeding Traffic RCW 46.61.425	35	31	66
28.	Fail of Slow Moving Vehicle to Turn Off When Five or More Vehicles Follow RCW 46.61.427	35	31	66
29.	Driving on Shoulder RCW 46.61.428	35	31	66
30.	Driving on Sidewalk RCW 46.61.606	35	31	66
31.	Operating With Obstructed Vision RCW 46.61.615	35	31	66
32.	Carry Passengers on Outside of Vehicle RCW 46.61.660	35	31	66
33.	Drive with Wheels Off Roadway RCW 46.61.670	35	31	66

ACCIDENT:

If an accident occurs in conjunction with any of the listed rules of the road infractions or speed too fast for conditions, the penalty for the infraction shall be:

Penalty: $60.00 + PSEA of $54.00 TOTAL: $114.00

1.	Failure to Report Accident RCW 46.52.030	35	31	66
2.	Furnish False Information in Accident RCW 46.52.088	35	31	66

EQUIPMENT (RCW 46.37)

1.	Any Other Equipment Infraction RCW 46.37.010	35	31	66
2.	Defective Headlights RCW 46.37.020	35	31	66
3.	Defective Tail–Lights RCW 46.37.050	35	31	66
4.	Illegal Use of Emergency Equipment RCW 46.37.190	80	72	152
5.	Defective Stop Lamps or Turn Signals RCW 46.37.200	35	31	66
6.	Defective Brakes RCW 46.37.360	35	31	66
7.	Defective Steering RCW 46.37.375	35	31	66
8.	Defective or Modified Exhaust Systems, Mufflers, Prevention of Noise and Smoke			
	a. First Offense RCW 46.37.390	40	36	76
	b. Second Offense RCW 46.37.390.2	60	54	114
	c. Third or Subsequent Offense RCW 46.37.390.3	80	72	152
9.	Defective or Improper Mirrors RCW 46.37.400	35	31	66
10.	Defective Windshields/Wipers RCW 46.37.410	35	31	66
11.	Defective Tires RCW 46.37.425	35	31	66
12.	Seatbelt or Shoulder Harness Required RCW 46.37.510	35	31	66

MOTORCYCLES:

1.	No Valid Motorcycle Endorsement RCW 46.20.500	35	31	66

2.	Fail to Wear Motorcycle Helmet RCW 46.37.530	35	31	66
3.	Motorcycle Equipment Violation RCW 46.37.537	35	31	66
4.	Improper Riding on Motorcycle RCW 46.61.610	35	31	66

PARKING INFRACTIONS:

1.	Unauthorized Use of Disabled Parking Place RCW 46.16.381.7	175	0	175
2.	Illegal Parking on Roadway RCW 46.61.560.1	30	0	30
3.	Any Other Parking Infraction Not Defined by City or County Ordinance	20	0	20
5.	Fail to Lock Ignition, Remove Keys or Stop Engine Upon Parking RCW 46.61.600	35	31	66

PEDESTRIAN INFRACTIONS (46.61):

1.	Hitch-hiking RCW 46.61.255	20	18	38
2.	Intoxicated Pedestrian on Public Roadway RCW 46.61.266	20	18	38
3.	Any Infraction Regarding Pedestrians Not Defined	20	18	38

BICYCLE INFRACTIONS (RCW 308.330):

1.	Any Infraction Regarding Bicycles RCW 308.330.5	25	22	47

LOAD AND TRUCK VIOLATIONS:

1.	Violation of Reciprocity Agreement RCW 46.16.030	35	31	66
2.	Over License Capacity			
	a. First Offense RCW 46.16.145.1	50	45	95
	b. Second Offense RCW 46.16.145.2	95	85	180
	c. Third or Subsequent Offense RCW 46.16.145.3	110	99	209
3.	Improper or No Gross Weight Signs RCW 46.16.170	35	31	66
4.	Registration or Tonnage Not Displayed RCW 46.16.260	35	31	66
5.	Illegal Vehicle Combination	60	54	114

RCW 46.44.036

6.	Failure to Obtain Special Permit RCW 46.44.105	50	45	95
7.	Violation of Special Permit—Height/Length			
	a. First Offense RCW 46.44.105.1	65	58	123
	b. Second Offense RCW 46.44.105.2	95	85	180
	c. Third or Subsequent Offense RCW 46.44.105.3	110	99	209
8.	Failure to Submit to Being Weighed RCW 46.44.105.5	60	54	114
9.	Illegally Transporting Mobile Home RCW 46.44.170	110	99	209
10.	Any Other Trucking or Load Infraction Defined in RCW 46.44	45	40	85

PRIVATE CARRIER (RCW 46.73)

1.	Private Carrier Violation RCW 46.73.010	35	31	66
2.	Fail to Display Valid Medical Exam RCW 46.73.030	62	55	117

MANDATORY LIABILITY INSURANCE (RCW 46.30)

1.	Operate Motor Vehicle Without Liability Insurance RCW 46.30.020	250	225	475

OFF ROAD VEHICLES—ATV'S (RCW 46.09):

	Any RCW 46.09 Infraction	40	36	76

SNOWMOBILES (RCW 46.10):

	Any RCW 46.10 Infraction	40	36	76

ALCOHOL CONTAINER (RCW 46.61):

1.	Open Alcoholic Beverage Container in Motor Vehicle RCW 46.61.519	35	31	66
2.	Disguising Alcoholic Beverage Container RCW 46.61.519.5	35	31	66

SAFETY BELT (RCW 46.61):

1.	Failure to Use Child Passenger Restraint in Vehicle RCW 46.61.687	35	31	66
2.	Failure to Wear Safety (Seat) Belt	35	31	66

RCW 46.61.688

NON–TRAFFIC CIVIL INFRACTIONS

1. Purchasing, Obtaining or Possessing   50   45   95
   Tobacco by Persons Under Age of 18
   RCW 70.155.080

2. Smoking in Public Place   100   90   190
   RCW 70.160.070

Other Chapter 7.80 RCW Infractions:

Class 1	250	225	475
Class 2	125	112	237
Class 3	50	45	95
Class 4	25	22	47

1. Class 1—Discarding Cigarette, Cigar or Other Tobacco Products
   Capable of Starting a Fire
   RCW 70.93.060

2. Class 3—Littering Less Than or Equal to 1 Cubic Foot
   RCW 70.93.060.2A

3. Class 1—Littering Greater Than 1 Cubic Foot—Plus
   $25 per Cubic Foot Litter Clean–Up Fee
   RCW 70.93.060.2B

CRIMINAL TRAFFIC BAIL SCHEDULE

BAIL IN TRAFFIC OFFENSES—MANDATORY APPEARANCE: " * "

	Bail	+ PSEA	= Total
1. Driving Under the Influence; Non Highway Vehicle or Snowmobile RCW 46.09.120.2; RCW 46.10.090.2	400	360	760*
2. Operate Nonhighway Vehicle or Snowmobile so as to Endanger Human Life, etc RCW 46.09.130; RCW 46.10.130	400	360	760*
3. Fail to Acquire Vehicle License RCW 46.16.010.F	200	180	380*
4. Driving Motor Vehicle without Valid Driver's License Issued to WA State Resident While In Violation of RCW 46.20.342.1 or RCW 46.20.420 And without Expired License RCW 46.20	250	225	475*
5. No Valid Driver's License RCW 46.20.021.1	250	225	475*
6. Unlawful Possession or Use of a Driver's License RCW 46.20.336.1	200	180	380*
7. Operating Motor Vehicle With Suspended and/or Revoked License			
a. First Degree RCW 46.20.342.1	500	450	950*
b. Second Degree	400	360	760*

		Bail	+ PSEA	= Total
	RCW 46.20.342.2			
c.	Third Degree	250	225	475*
	RCW 46.20.342.3			
8.	Violating Occupational License Restrictions RCW 46.20.410	200	180	380*
9.	Transporting Dangerous Articles RCW 46.48.175; See Laws of 1980, Chapter 104	250	225	475*
10.	Unattended Hit & Run RCW 46.52.010	300	270	570*
11.	Attended Hit & Run RCW 46.52.020	300	270	570*
12.	Reports of Repairs, Concealing Evidence RCW 46.52.090	250	225	475*
13.	Confidentially of Driving Records RCW 46.52.130	250	225	475*
14.	Fail to Obey Police Officer, Flagman, or Fire Fighter RCW 46.61.015	200	180	380*
15.	Failure To Cooperate With or Give Information to Police Officer RCW 46.61.020	100	90	190*
16.	Failure to Stop or Give Information RCW 46.61.022	100	90	180*
17.	Reckless Driving RCW 46.61.500	500	450	950*
18.	Driving Under the Influence of Intoxicants RCW 46.61.502	500	450	950*
19.	Minor Operating Vehicle After Consuming Alcohol RCW 46.61.503	130	120	250*
20.	Physical Control RCW 46.61.504	500	450	950*
21.	Negligent Driving 1st Degree RCW 46.61.525.1	250	225	475*
22.	Reckless Endangerment of Road workers RCW 46.61.527.4	400	360	760*
23.	Racing RCW 46.61.530	400	360	760*
24.	Leaving Children Unattended RCW 46.61.685	250	225	475*

		Bail	+	PSEA	=	Total
25.	Unfair Motor Vehicle Business Practices RCW 46.70.180	250		225		475*
26.	Unlawful Operation of For Hire Vehicles RCW 46.72.100	250		225		475*
27.	Motor Vehicle Wreckers RCW 46.80.170	250		225		475*
28.	Driving Training Schools RCW 46.82.390	250		225		475*

COMMERCIAL DRIVERS LICENSE VIOLATIONS:

		Bail		PSEA		Total
1.	Possession of More Than One Driver's License RCW 46.25.020	250		225		475*
2.	Violation of Driver's Duties RCW 46.25.030	250		225		475*
3.	Violation of Employer's Duties RCW 46.25.040	250		225		475*
4.	Failure to Obtain Commercial Driver's License RCW 46.25.050	250		225		475*
5.	Driving Commercial Vehicle While Suspended, Revoked or Canceled RCW 46.25.050.2	250		225		475*
6.	Driving with Alcohol in System RCW 46.25.110	500		450		950*
7.	Physical Control with Alcohol in System RCW 46.25.110	500		450		950*

OTHER TRAFFIC RELATED CRIMINAL VIOLATIONS:

		Bail		PSEA		Total
1.	Operate Vehicle without Certificate Of Ownership RCW 46.12.010	100		90		190
2.	Transferee Failing to Transfer Certificate of Ownership within 15 Days RCW 46.12.101.3	100		90		190
3.	Any Other RCW 46.12 Violations	100		90		190
4.	Dealer Plate Violations Chapter 46.70 RCW	100		90		190
5.	Fail to Keep and Use Litter Bag in Vehicle or Water Craft RCW 70.93.100	50		45		95
6.	Throwing Burning Material in Forest Area From April 15 to October 15	150		135		285*

		Bail	+ PSEA	= Total
	RCW 76.04.455			
7.	Violations of Specialized Forest Products Act RCW 76.48	440	396	836*
8.	Harvesting Specialized Forest Products Without Validated Harvesting Permit RCW 76.48.030	440	396	836*
9.	Unlawful Possession and/or Transportation of Specialized Forest Products RCW 76.48.030	440	396	836*
10.	Loaded Shotgun or Rifle in Motor Vehicle RCW 77.16.250	50	45	95
11.	Shooting Firearm From, Across, or Along Public Highway RCW 77.16.260	100	90	190*
12.	No Name and Permit Number Displayed RCW 81.70.330	50	45	95
13.	Operate without Permit RCW 81.80.060	50	45	95
14.	No Identification Cab Card RCW 81.80.305	50	45	95
15.	Fail to Obtain Trip Permit RCW 81.80.318	50	45	95

NON–TRAFFIC RELATED CRIMINAL BAIL SCHEDULE:

		Bail	+ PSEA	= Total
1.	Tampering with Fire Alarms or Fire Fighting Equipment RCW 9.40.100.1	250	225	475*
2.	Carry Concealed Weapon without a Permit RCW 9.41.050	150	135	285*
3.	Unlawful Aiming or Discharging Firearm RCW 9.41.230	130	120	250*
4.	Use of Firearm by a Minor RCW 9.41.240	130	120	250*
5.	Unlawful Possession of Dangerous Weapon RCW 9.41.250	250	225	475*
6.	Unlawful Display of Dangerous Weapon RCW 9.41.270	250	225	475*
7.	Student Carrying Weapon on School Grounds RCW 9.41.280	265	235	500*
8.	Commit or Maintain Public Nuisance RCW 9.66.030	130	120	250*

	Bail	+ PSEA	= Total
9. Communication with a Minor for Immoral Purposes RCW 9.68A.090	265	235	500*
10. Intercept/Record Private Communications RCW 9.73.030	265	235	500*
11. Leave Children Under Age 12 in Vehicle While Visiting Liquor Place RCW 9.91.060	250	225	475*
12. Assault 4th Degree RCW 9A.36.041	440	396	836*
13. Assault 4th Degree—Domestic Violence RCW 9A.36.041.DV		Hold Pending 1st Appearance	
14. Reckless Endangerment 2nd Degree RCW 9A.36.050	400	360	760*
15. Coercion RCW 9A.36.070	250	225	475*
16. Interfere with Reporting of Domestic Violence RCW 9A.36.150	265	235	500*
17. Custodial Interference 2nd Degree RCW 9A.40.070	440	396	836*
18. Fail to Register as Sex Offender or Submit Change of Address RCW 9A.44.130.7	530	470	1000
19. Stalking RCW 9A.46.110.M	440	396	836*
20. Reckless Burning 2nd Degree RCW 9A.48.050	440	396	836*
21. Malicious Mischief 3rd Degree RCW 9A.48.090			
a. Damage Not Exceeding $50	250	225	475*
b. Damage Exceeding $50	440	396	836*
22. Making or Having Burglar Tools RCW 9A.52.060	440	396	836*
23. Criminal Trespass 1st Degree RCW 9A.52.070	440	396	836*
24. Criminal Trespass 2nd Degree RCW 9A.52.080	250	225	475*
25. Vehicle Prowling 2nd Degree RCW 9A.52.100	440	396	836*
26. Computer Trespass 2nd Degree RCW 9A.52.120	265	235	500*

	Bail	+ PSEA	= Total
27. Theft 3rd Degree RCW 9A.56.050	440	396	836*
28. Unlawful Issuance of Bank Checks Value of $250 or Less RCW 9A.56.060	440	396	836*
29. Possessing Stolen Property 3rd Degree RCW 9A.56.170	440	396	836*
30. Obscuring Identity of a Machine RCW 9A.56.180	440	396	836*
31. Criminal Impersonation RCW 9A.60.040	440	396	836*
32. False Certification RCW 9A.60.050	440	396	836*
33. Defrauding Public Utility 3rd Degree RCW 9A.61.050	265	235	500*
34. False Swearing RCW 9A.72.040	440	396	836*
35. Jury Tampering RCW 9A.72.140	440	396	836*
36. Tampering With Physical Evidence RCW 9A.72.150	440	396	836*
37. Obstructing a Law Enforcement Officer RCW 9A.76.020	150	135	285*
38. Refusing to Summon Aid for Peace Officer RCW 9A.76.030	150	135	285*
39. Resisting Arrest RCW 9A.76.040	200	180	380*
40. Rendering Criminal Assistance 2nd Degree RCW 9A.76.080	440	396	836*
41. Rendering Criminal Assistance 3rd Degree RCW 9A.76.090	250	225	475*
42. Compounding RCW 9A.76.100	440	396	836*
43. Escape 3rd Degree RCW 9A.76.130	440	396	836*
44. Introducing Contraband 3rd Degree RCW 9A.76.160	440	396	836*
45. Bail Jumping (Charge pending was Gross Misdemeanor or Misdemeanor) RCW 9A.76.170.2D	250	225	475*

	Bail	+ PSEA	= Total
46. Failure to Disperse RCW 9A.84.020	150	135	285*
47. Disorderly Conduct RCW 9A.84.030	150	135	285*
48. False Reporting RCW 9A.84.040	440	396	836*
49. Indecent Exposure RCW 9A.88.010	440	396	836*
50. Prostitution RCW 9A.88.030	250	225	475*
51. Permitting Prostitution RCW 9A.88.090	250	225	475*
52. Willful Disobedience of Anti–Harassment Protection Order—Gross Misdemeanor RCW 10.14.170	530	470	1000*
53. Violation of No Contact Order RCW 10.99.050	530	470	1000*
54. Defrauding an Inn Keeper RCW 19.48.110	200	180	380*
55. Violation of Domestic Relations Restraining Order—Misdemeanor RCW 26.09.300.DV	530	470	1000*
56. Sell/Give Tobacco to Minor RCW 26.28.080	250	225	475*
57. Violation of Child Abuse Restraining Order RCW 26.44.063	400	360	760*
58. Violation of Temporary Order for Protection RCW 26.50.020	530	470	1000*
59. Violation of Domestic Violence Protection Order—Gross Misdemeanor RCW 26.50.110	530	470	1000*
60. Abusing or Insulting Teacher RCW 28A.635.010	53	47	100
61. Wilfully Disobeying School Administrative Personnel or Refusing to Leave School Property RCW 28A.635.020	150	135	285*
62. Disturbing School Activities or Meetings RCW 28A.635.030	27	23	50
63. Consuming Liquor in Public Place RCW 66.44.100	100	90	190*

		Bail	+ PSEA	= Total
64.	Sale of Liquor to Person Under the Influence RCW 66.44.200	250	225	475*
65.	Consuming Liquor in Public Conveyance RCW 66.44.250	130	120	250*
66.	Supplying Liquor to Minor RCW 66.44.270.1	250	225	475*
67.	Unlawful Possession/Consumption by Minor RCW 66.44.270.2.a	150	135	285*
68.	Minor in Public Exhibiting Effects of Having Consumed Liquor RCW 66.44.270.2.b	150	135	285*
69.	Minor Purchase/Attempt to Purchase Liquor RCW 66.44.290	150	135	285*
70.	Serving or Allowing Minor to Remain on Premises of Tavern RCW 66.44.310.a	250	225	475*
71.	Minor Frequenting Tavern RCW 66.44.310.b	100	90	190*
72.	Supply Minor with Unlawful Age Identification RCW 66.44.325	250	225	475*
73.	Damage to Graves, Markers or Shrubs RCW 68.56.010.1	250	225	475*
74.	Interfering with Funeral Procession, etc. RCW 68.56.010.3	250	225	475*
75.	Unlawful Possession of Marijuana Under 40 Grams RCW 69.50.401.e	300	270	570*
76.	Possession of Drug Paraphernalia RCW 69.50.412	130	120	250*

COUNTY ORDINANCE VIOLATION

1.	Violation of Stock Restricted Area RCW 16.24.070	50	45	95*

GENERAL FISHERIES VIOLATIONS

1.	Resisting or Obstructing Arrest RCW 75.10.040.3	200	180	380*
2.	Explosive in State Waters RCW 75.12.070.2	1000	900	1900*
3.	Theft of Foodfish or Shellfish RCW 75.12.090.1	400	360	760

4. Theft or Molesting of Fishing Gear   300   270   570
     RCW 75.12.090.2

5. Buy, Sell or Possess Illegal Foodfish   300   270   570
     RCW 75.12.100

6. Unlawfully Waste Foodfish   500   450   950
     RCW 75.12.120

7. Remove/Possess/Alter/Damage Signs 200   180   380
     RCW 75.12.410

8. Fail to Make Reports & Returns   125   112   237
     RCW 75.12.420

9. Give False Information   125   112   237
     RCW 75.12.430

10. Fish In or Interfere With Fishway   250   225   475
      RCW 75.12.031

11. Fail to Submit Gear for Inspection   100   90   190
      WAC 220.20.010.7

12. Fail to Submit Catch for Inspection 100   90   190
      WAC 220.20.010.8

13. Fail to Comply With Permit   100   90   190
      WAC 220.20.010.15

SPORTS FISHERIES INFRACTIONS

Infraction Subject to Chapter 7.84—Maximum Penalty is $500.00

1. Failure to Enter Punch Card Data   50   45   95
     WAC 220.56.175.1

2. Use of Barbed Hooks in a Barbless   25   22   47
     Hook Only Fishery—Salmon
     WAC 220.56.116

3. Use of Barbed Hooks in a Barbless   25   22   47
     Hook Only Fishery—Sturgeon
     WAC 220.56.282

SPORT FISHERIES VIOLATIONS

1. Take/Molest Fish at/near Racks or Dams 300   270   570
     RCW 75.12.020

2. Shoot, Gaff, Snag or Molest   300   270   570*
     Foodfish or Attempt RCW 75.12.070.1
     WAC 220.20.010.11—or Possess

3. Fail to Possess Valid Salmon License   50   45   95
     RCW 75.25.090

4. Falsify Information on License   75   67   142
     RCW 75.25.160

5.	Fail to Validate Salmon License—Dealer WAC 22.55.125	66	59	125
6.	Sport Fishing With Excess Gear WAC 220.56.115.1	50	45	95
7.	Fail to Maintain Physical Control WAC 220.56.115.3	50	45	95
8.	Possess Foodfish in Unlawful Condition WAC 220.56.145	188	169	357
9.	Unlawful to Take Another's Limit WAC 220.56.150	50	45	95
10.	Failure to Return Punch Card WAC 220.56.175.4	50	45	95
11.	Fail to Display Punch Card WAC 220.56.175.5	38	34	72
12.	Borrow, Transfer or Alter Punch Card WAC 220.56.175.6	50	45	95
13.	Sport Fishing with Unlawful Gear WAC 220.56.205.3.4	50	45	95
14.	Unlawful Possession of Salmon Eggs WAC 220.56.220	200	180	380
15.	Fish or Possess Salmon During Closed Hours WAC 220.56.225	100	90	190
16.	Possession of Undersized Sturgeon Possession of Oversized Sturgeon WAC 220.56.240.1	100 400	90 360	190 760*
17.	Exceed Possession Limit of Sturgeon WAC 220.56.240.1 per fish plus $50.00	75	67	142
18.	Exceed Possession Limit of Smelt WAC 220.56.240.2 plus $1.00 per lb. over 40 lbs.	38	34	72
19.	Fish Sturgeon During Closed Hours WAC 220.56.290	100	90	190
20.	Unlawful Possession of Sturgeon, Head or Tail Removed WAC 220.56.295.1	200	180	380
21.	Unlawful Use of Gaff for Sturgeon WAC 220.56.295.2	100	90	190
22.	Fail to Release Sturgeon Immediately WAC 220.56.295.3	100	90	190
23.	Take, Fish for or Possess	100	90	190

Salmon During Closed Season
WAC 220.57.001

24.	Exceed Bag Limit for Salmon WAC 220.57.001 plus $75.00 per fish	75	67	142

FISH TICKET VIOLATIONS

1.	Fish Ticket Violation WAC 220.69.215.1	313	281	594
2.	Misrepresent, Falsify or Omit Data WAC 220.69.215.2	188	168	356
3.	Use Improper Form WAC 220.69.215.3	50	45	95

HYDRAULICS VIOLATION

Hydraulics Violations
RCW 75.20.100

	a.	No Permit—Major Damage	1000	900	1900*
	b.	No Permit—Minor Damage	275	247	522
	c.	Violation of Provisions of Permit	275	247	522

COMMERCIAL FISHERIES VIOLATIONS

1.	Gillnet in Columbia River in Excess of 250 Fathoms RCW 75.12.040.1	250	225	475
2.	Use Net or Fixed Appliance RCW 75.12.040.2	1000	900	1900*
3.	Mix Commercial and Sport Caught Foodfish RCW 75.12.125	250	225	475
4.	Commercial Salmon With Illegal Gear RCW 75.12.650	250	225	475
5.	Fish Without Valid Commercial License License RCW 75.28.010.2	500	450	950*
6.	Fail to Display Registration Decals RCW 75.28.035	75	67	142
7.	Sport & Commercial Fishing Same Day RCW 75.28.095.4	250	225	475
8.	Take Foodfish Illegally WAC 220.20.010.1	250	225	475
9.	Possess Commercial Foodfish Illegally WAC 220.20.010.2	300	270	570
10.	Unattended Commercial Gear WAC 220.20.010.5	250	225	475
11.	Possession of Undersize Foodfish	100	90	190

WAC 220.20.010.12

12.	Possess Foodfish in Unlawful Condition WAC 220.20.010.13	200	180	380
13.	Buy or Sell Sport Caught Foodfish WAC 220.20.012	250	225	475*
14.	Operate Snag Net Without Permit WAC 220.20.015.2	94	84	178
15.	Possess or Unlawfully Sell Commercial Salmon WAC 220.20.016	400	360	760
16.	Possess Sturgeon Less than 48 Inches WAC 220.20.020.1	100	90	190
17.	Possess Sturgeon More than 72 Inches WAC 220.20.020.1	400	360	760
18.	Retain/Possess or Sell Unlawful Sturgeon WAC 220.20.021.1A	300	270	570
19.	Unlawful Sale of Sturgeon Eggs WAC 220.20.021.1C	1000	900	1900*
20.	Unlawful Purchase of Sturgeon Eggs WAC 220.20.021.2	250	225	475
21.	Unlawful Commercial Smelt Gear WAC 220.32.021	250	225	475
22.	Possess Sturgeon With Tail or Head Removed WAC 220.32.022.2	200	180	380
23.	Sturgeon Set Line Closed Season/Area WAC 220.32.040.1–4	250	225	475*

GAME VIOLATIONS

1.	Hunting and Fishing Contest Without Permit RCW 77.16.010			
	Big Game	250	225	475
	Other	100	90	190
2.	Illegal Killing or Possession of Wildlife During Closed Season RCW 77.16.020			
	Elk, Deer, Black Bear, Cougar plus $2,000.00 per Animal	475	427	902*
	Trophy Elk or Deer plus $6,000.00 per Animal	475	427	902*
3.	Hunt or Fish During Closed Season RCW 77.16.020.1			
	Fish	70	63	133
	Other	200	180	380
4.	Exceeding Bag Limit Per Animal			

RCW 77.16.020.2

Big Game	475	427	902*
Fish	28	25	53
Steelhead Per Fish	50	45	95
Other Per Bird/Animal	50	45	95

5. Fish in Closed Waters   70   63   133
RCW 77.16.020.3

6. Hunt in Closed Area
RCW 77.16.020.4

Big Game	475	427	902*
Other	100	90	190

7. Hunt or Fish Without
a License, Tag, Permit or Card
RCW 77.16.020.5

Big Game—Residential	100	90	190
Big Game—Non-residential	250	225	475
Other—Residential	70	63	133
Other—Non-residential	100	90	190
Taxidermist, Fur Dealer, Guide or Game Farmer	250	225	475

8. Trafficking Endangered Species   820   738   1558*
RCW 77.16.040

9. Hunt With Aid of Artificial Light   475   427   902*
RCW 77.16.050

10. Netting Game Fish   820   738   1558*
RCW 77.16.060

11. Hunting While Intoxicated   400   360   760*
RCW 77.16.070

12. Unlawful Use, Possession of Drugs,   820   738   1558*
Poisons, Explosives, While Hunting
RCW 77.16.080

13. Wastage RCW 77.16.090

Big Game	475	427	902
Other	100	90	190

14. Mutilation of Games Species
RCW 77.16.095

Big Game	100	90	190
Other	50	45	95

15. Use of Dogs While Hunting   100   90   190
RCW 77.16.100

16. Taking, Hunting, or Attracting   530   470   1000*
Black Bear with Bait
RCW 77.16

17. Pursuit of Black Bear, Cougar, Bobcat,   530   470   1000*
Or Lynx with the Aid of Dog or Dogs
Gross Misdemeanor
RCW 77.16.

18.	Use of Weapons, Traps, or Dogs on Game Reserve RCW 77.16.110	300	270	570
19.	Hunt Protected Wildlife RCW 77.16.120			
	Endangered Species	820	738	1558*
	Protected Species	250	225	475
	Nest & Eggs	100	90	190
20.	Resist/Obstruct a Game Officer RCW 77.16.130	250	225	475*
21.	Releasing Wildlife RCW 77.16.150	250	225	475
22.	Tampering With Fish Ladders RCW 77.16.160	100	90	190
23.	Traps, ID–Interference RCW 77.16.170			
	Less Than Ten (10)	50	45	95
	Ten (10) Plus	100	90	190
24.	Damage of Game Department Signs RCW 77.16.180	100	90	190
25.	Unlawful Posting of Land RCW 77.16.190	100	90	190
26.	Fishways RCW 77.16.210	475	427	902*
27.	Fish Screens RCW 77.16.220	475	427	902*
28.	Carry Loaded Rifle or Shotgun in Motor Vehicle RCW 77.16.250	50	45	95
29.	Discharge Firearm From Roadway RCW 77.16.260	100	90	190*
30.	Illegal License, Tag, or Stamp Card RCW 77.16.310	250	225	475*
31.	Hunt Albino Animals RCW 77.16.320	250	225	475*

-------- End of RCW --------

-------- WAC Citations --------

1.	Deleterious Exotic Wildlife WAC 232–12–017	250	225	475
2.	Non–Residential Wildlife Import WAC 232–12–021	100	90	190*

3.	Tagging Bobcat, Lynx, Otter WAC 232–12–024	100	90	190
4.	Game Farm Provisions WAC 232–12–027	250	225	475
5.	Game Farm Invoice WAC 232–12–031	100	90	190
6.	Game Farm Acquisition WAC 232–12–034	100	90	190
7.	Shooting Preserves WAC 232–12–037	250	225	475
8.	Dog Field Trials WAC 232–12–041	100	90	190
9.	Training With Game WAC 232–12–044	100	90	190
10.	Unlawful Firearms WAC 232–12–047	50	45	95
11.	Unlawful Muzzle Loaders WAC 232–12–051	50	45	95
12.	Unlawful Archery Equipment WAC 232–12–054	50	45	95
13.	Fail to Wear Hunter Orange WAC 232–12–055	50	45	95
14.	Hunt With Vehicles, Boats, Aircraft WAC 232–12–057	250	225	475
15.	Tagging Required WAC 232–12–061	100	90	190
16.	Hold Live Wildlife WAC 232–12–064	100	90	190
17.	Buy or Sell Game WAC 232–12–071	250	225	475*
18.	Retention of Game WAC 232–12–074	28	25	53
19.	Wildlife Taken By Another WAC 232–12–081	50	45	95
20.	Indian Caught Fish WAC 232–12–087	50	45	95
21.	Commercially Buy or Sell Game Fish WAC 232–12–091	250	225	475*
22.	Commercial Fish Records WAC 232–12–094	250	225	475

23.	Commercial Fish Transportation WAC 232–12–097	250	225	475
24.	Indian Net Gear ID WAC 232–12–099	100	90	190
25.	Falconry Permit, Propagation WAC 232–12–101	100	90	190
26.	Falconry Permit, Practice WAC 232–12–107	100	90	190
27.	Falconry Capture, Import–Export Transfers WAC 232–12–114	100	90	190
28.	Falconry ID WAC 232–12–117	100	90	190
29.	Falconry Reports WAC 232–12–121	100	90	190
30.	Falconry Capture Methods WAC 232–12–124	100	90	190
31.	Special Hunt Permits—Reapplying WAC 232–12–131	100	90	190
32.	Trapper Reports WAC 232–12–134	100	90	190
33.	Unlawful Trapping Baits WAC 232–12–137	70	63	133
34.	Illegal Trap Sizes WAC 232–12–137	50	45	95
35.	Use of Live Fish for Bait WAC 232–12–144	50	45	95
36.	Maximum Number of Lines, Unattended Gear WAC 232–12–147	28	25	53
	Snag/Gaff	200	180	380*
37.	Violation of Fly Fishing Rules WAC 232–12–151	28	25	53
38.	Juvenile Fishing Waters WAC 232–12–154	50	45	95
39.	Steelhead Punchcard WAC 232–12–157			
	Without Card	50	45	95
	Fail to Punch	28	25	53
40.	Fishing Guide Reports WAC 232–12–161	100	90	190
41.	Fish Within 400′ of Dams, Ladders, Traps WAC 232–12–167	70	63	133

42.	Domestic Animals on Department Lands WAC 232–12–174	250	225	475
43.	Use of Vehicles on Department Lands WAC 232–12–177	70	63	133
44.	Livestock Grazing Permits WAC 232–12–181	250	225	475
45.	Aircraft on Department Lands WAC 232–12–184	100	90	190
46.	Access Area Controls WAC 232–12–187	50	45	95
47.	Indian Possessing Game Off Reservation WAC 232–12–187	100	90	190
48.	Transmission Lines—Unlawful Hunting WAC 232–12–247	100	90	190
49.	Removal of Minerals or Wood on Department Lands WAC 232–12–251	100	90	190
50.	Litter on Department Lands WAC 232–12–254	50	45	95
51.	Unattended Decoys on Department Land WAC 232–12–257	50	45	95
52.	Unlawful Use of Decoys on Dept Land WAC 232–12–261	50	45	95
53.	Baiting Game Birds WAC 232–12–264	250	225	475*
54.	Field ID Wildlife WAC 232–12–267			
	Big Game	100	90	190
	Other	28	25	53
55.	Release of Wildlife—Conditions WAC 232–12–271	250	225	475
56.	Collection, Research, Display Permits WAC 232–12–271	250	225	475
57.	Taxidermy & Fur Dealer Records WAC 232–12–277	100	90	190
58.	Bighorn Sheep—Branding ID WAC 232–12–284	100	90	190
59.	Possession of Found Dead Wildlife WAC 232–12–287	100	90	190
60.	Violation of Early or Late Hunting Hours WAC 232–12–291	50	45	95

BOATING INFRACTIONS

1.	Operation of Vessel in Negligent Manner RCW 88.12.020	160	144	304
2.	Motor Propelled Vessels Must Have Effective Muffler in Good Working Order and Constant Use RCW 88.12.085.1	35	31	66
3.	No Personal Flotation Device (PFD) on Vessel for Each Person RCW 88.12.115.1.A	35	31	66
4.	Personal Flotation Device Not Appropriate Size RCW 88.12.115.1.B	35	31	66
5.	Personal Flotation Device Not Accessible RCW 88.12.115.1.C	35	31	66
6.	Observer Required on Water Skier Towing Vessel RCW 88.12.125.2.A	35	31	66
7.	Overloading of Vessel Beyond Safe Carrying Ability RCW 88.12.135.1.A	110	99	209
8.	Not Wearing Personal Flotation Device on Personal Watercraft RCW 88.12.145.1	60	54	114
9.	Navigation Lights/Sound Signals WAC 352–60–060	35	31	66

BOATING CRIMINAL NON–TRAFFIC VIOLATIONS

1.	Operation of Vessel in Reckless Manner RCW 88.12.025.1	250	225	475*
2.	Operation of Vessel Under the Influence RCW 88.12.025.2	250	225	475*

WALLA WALLA COUNTY

Table of Courts

Superior Court

Local Rules of the Superior Court of the State of Washington, for Walla Walla County.

District Court

Walla Walla County District Court Local Rules.

Municipal Courts

College Place Municipal Court Local Rules.
Prescott Municipal Court—[No Local Rules].
Waitsburg Municipal Court—[No Local Rules].

SUPERIOR COURT

LOCAL RULES OF THE SUPERIOR COURT OF THE STATE OF WASHINGTON, FOR WALLA WALLA COUNTY

Including Amendments Received Through
August 15, 2015

Table of Rules

WWCSCLR 1. SUPERIOR COURTS AND JUDICIAL OFFICERS

(CR 77(d) and (f))

(A) Departments: Walla Walla County Superior Court consists of two departments. At this time, Judge John W. Lohrmann is Department I and Judge Donald W. Schacht is Department II.

(B) Court Hours: Court is in session, unless otherwise ordered, on all judicial days except Saturdays. Trial hours are from 9:30 a.m. to 12:00 noon, and from 1:30 p.m. to 4:00 p.m. Counsel shall be present in court ready to proceed at 9:00 a.m. on the first day of a jury trial. In criminal cases, defense counsel shall have the defendant in court at 9:00 a.m. the first day of trial unless the defendant is in custody. If the defendant is in custody, the jail staff shall have the defendant in court by 9:15 a.m. each day of trial.

(C) Christmas recess: From December 20 to January 2 shall be Christmas recess, and no contested cases or matters will be set for trial or tried during said period except by consent of all counsel involved and the court, or by order of the court.

(D) Motion Days:

(1) *Dockets:* Monday of each week shall be Law and Motion Day for the disposition of issues of law regularly noted and docketed for hearing and for the setting of trial dates for all cases properly noted as hereinafter set forth. The Law and Motion Docket shall alternate between departments. The Court will conduct the Monday docket according to the following schedule:

(a) 9:30 a.m.—Civil and Domestic Relations: Assignments for trial; civil motions and entry of orders; domestic relations motions and entry of orders.

(b) 1:30 p.m.—Adult Criminal Docket: Assignments for trial; sentencings; motions and entry of orders; orders to show cause; non-contested probation violation hearings.

(c) 3:00 p.m.—Adult Criminal Docket: Adult arraignments; change of pleas; omnibus applications; first appearances by summons.

(2) During the months of August through December, on the Wednesday of the week in which Department I hears the Monday Law and Motion Docket, Department II shall hear the Truancy Docket beginning at 8:30 a.m. During the months of January through May, on the Wednesday of the week Department II hears the Monday Law and Motion Docket, Department I shall hear the Truancy Docket beginning at 8:30 a.m.

(3) On the Friday of the week in which one department hears the Monday Law and Motion Docket, the other department shall hear the Friday Juvenile and Domestic Relations Docket. The Court will conduct the Friday docket according to the following schedule:

(a) 9:30 a.m.—Juvenile Court Docket: First appearances; arraignments; change of pleas; dispositions; motions; trial assignments.

(b) 11:00—Paternity Docket: Every week when Department I has the Monday Law and Motion Docket, the Court Commissioner shall hear all paternity matters so noted.

(c) 1:30—Domestic Docket: Non-contested dissolutions; domestic violence protection orders.

(4) The department holding Law and Motion Day on Monday shall, at 8:45 a.m., Monday through Friday, that same week conduct all criminal first appearances on probable cause for adult and juvenile defendants in custody, pretrial release hearings and extradition hearings.

(5) From 1:00 to 1:30 p.m. daily, the department that heard the Monday Docket will that week be available to sign criminal, civil and probate ex parte orders, including, but not limited to agreed orders, orders on hearing where notice of presentment is waived.

(6) From 1:00 to 1:30 p.m. daily, the Court Commissioner shall be available to sign domestic violence temporary protection orders.

[Adopted effective January 1, 1999; amended on an emergency basis effective December 1, 2009.]

WWCSCLR 1(a). PRESIDING JUDGE RULE

One department of the court shall be designated the presiding department, and that judge the Presiding Judge. The Presiding Judge shall be designated pursuant to GR 29 and this rule.

The Presiding Judge shall be elected by vote of all of the judges of the superior court district. In the same manner, the judges shall elect an Assistant Presiding Judge, who shall act in the absence of or upon the request of the Presiding Judge.

The term of the Presiding Judge shall be 2 years, subject to reelection. The term shall commence on January 1 of the year in which the Presiding Judge's term begins.

The Presiding Judge shall be responsible for the general management and administration of the court's business, and these duties shall include those set forth in GR 29.

The Presiding judge shall preside over official ceremonial functions of the court, including memorials for bench and bar members and shall swear in attorneys and public officials.

General correspondence directed to the court shall be referred to the Presiding Judge who may respond or direct it to the appropriate judge for response.

[Adopted effective September 1, 2002.]

WWCSCLR 2. JUVENILE DEPARTMENT

Each Department of the Walla Walla County Superior Court shall sit as a Juvenile Court Division of the Superior Court and hear all matters arising under Title 13 RCW and Chapters 26.34 RCW and 26.44 RCW. Each Department will alternate weekly hearing the juvenile court docket, as set forth in WWCSCLR 1.

[Adopted effective January 1, 1999.]

WWCSCLR 3. FAMILY COURT

There shall be a Department of the Superior Court under the jurisdiction conferred by Chapter 26.12 RCW, known as the "Family Court." Both Superior Court judges shall sit as Family Court judges.

The Superior Court judges also grant to the "Family Court" the power, authority, and jurisdiction, concurrent with the Juvenile Court, to hear and decide cases under Title 13 RCW.

The Superior Court judges may also appoint an attorney to act as a Family Court commissioner, and such other staff as are necessary to carry on the work of the Family Court, the Juvenile Court, and any other commissioner position authorized by law.

The Family Court commissioner's duties and powers are as set forth in RCW 26.12.060 and such other statutes as are applicable, subject to final approval of and under the direction of the Superior Court judges.

[Adopted effective January 1, 1999.]

WWCSCLR 4. LAW, MOTION AND TRIAL SETTING DAY

(CR 40(a) and CR 77(f))

(A) All written motions, other than one which may be heard ex parte, and notices of the hearing thereof and notices of trial settings shall be served not later than five (5) days before the time specified for the hearing, unless a different period is fixed by the civil rules for Superior Court or by order of the court or by state statute. Such an order may for good cause shown be made on ex parte application. A motion shall be supported by affidavit, with the affidavit served with the motion, and, except as otherwise provided in Rule 59(c) of the Civil Rules for Superior Court, opposing affidavits shall be served not later than one (1) day before the hearing, unless the court permits them to be served at some other time. (See CR 6(d))

(B) Matters requiring a special setting for hearing shall be noted on the appropriate docket before the proper department (e.g., contested probate hearings, lengthy probation violations and criminal pretrial

hearings). A hearing time will be set in the same manner as trial assignments.

(C) The matters on the law and motion docket will be called in the order of their being noted, provided case settings and all other matters requiring less than ten minutes shall be heard first. The moving party, if no one appears in opposition, may take the order moved for unless the court shall deem it manifestly unauthorized; or the adverse party, if no one appears on the motion, may take an order denying the same; or the court may grant the same, if deemed well taken. If no attorney or party appears to argue for or against the motion, and neither party requests a continuance, the motion shall be stricken by the court. Any motion may also be continued by the Court for hearing at another specified time, and the court may alter the order of hearings as may be necessary to expedite the business of the court.

(D) Matters not ready for hearing in the order above specified will go to the bottom of the docket. Matters not ready for hearing when all other regularly noted matters have been called shall not be heard on that day except by consent of the court.

(E) Matters not regularly noted on the motion docket will not be heard except by the consent of all parties and the court, and shall then be heard only after all other matters regularly noted have been heard.

(F) The clerk shall prepare a Law and Motion calendar on Thursday of each week and shall enter on such calendar the notation of hearing, the number and title of the case, the names of the attorneys appearing for the respective parties and the nature of the application.

(G) Notices for Monday's Law and Motion dockets shall be filed in the clerk's office no later than 4:00 p.m. on the preceding Wednesday. Notices for Friday's Domestic Relations and Juvenile dockets shall be filed in the clerk's office no later than 4:00 p.m. the preceding Tuesday. Matters not noted for hearing as set forth above will not be heard without consent of the parties and the court.

(H) A copy of the calendar shall be available in the clerk's office on Friday of each week preceding the next Law and Motion Day (Monday), and copies of the calendar shall be available on the counsel tables on Law and Motion Day.

(I) The clerk shall keep a daily docket for the court of all matters for which a time of hearing had been fixed by the court.

(1) The clerk will furnish to counsel of record a notice advising counsel of the date and time a case is set for trial.

(J) If either docket falls on a legal holiday, matters noted will be heard on the preceding or succeeding judicial day, as appropriate.

[Adopted effective January 1, 1999.]

WWCSCLR 5.   NOTE FOR TRIAL SETTINGS

(CR 40(a))

(A) Any party desiring to bring any issue of fact to trial shall file with the Clerk a notice for trial setting which shall contain:

(1) The title of the court;

(2) The clerk's court file number;

(3) A brief title of the case;

(4) The names of the attorneys representing each party;

(5) The nature of the case;

(6) An estimate of the time that will be required for hearing said case;

(7) Whether the case is to be tried by the court or jury;

(8) Dates counsel are unavailable;

(9) A statement that the issue of fact has actually been joined and that no affirmative pleading remains unanswered and all pleadings are on file;

(10) That the parties have completed all necessary discovery, or that they will have an opportunity to complete all necessary discovery prior to the date the case is set for trial;

(11) That the case is in all respects at issue and ready for trial;

(B) The notice for trial setting must show that service was made on all counsel representing the other party or parties to the said action.

[Adopted effective January 1, 1999.]

WWCSCLR 6.   RESETTING OF CASES

(CR 40(a))

Cases which have been set for trial and then stricken or continued for any reason will not automatically be reset. The stricken or continued cases must be noted for resetting as provided in Rules 2 and 3 of these rules, unless at the time of striking or continuing the case, the court sets a later trial date with the approval of all parties to the case.

[Adopted effective January 1, 1999.]

WWCSCLR 7.   SIGNING OF PLEADINGS, MOTIONS AND LEGAL MEMORANDA: SANCTIONS

(CR 11)

Every pleading, motion and legal memorandum filed by an attorney or a pro se litigant shall be signed in conformity with CR 11, which is by this rule adopted in its entirety.

[Adopted effective January 1, 1999.]

WWCSCLR 8. INSTRUCTIONS/DELIBERATION

(CR 51)

Instructions to the jury and deliberation of the case shall be submitted and carried out in accordance with CR 51 of the Civil Rules for Superior Court, except as hereinafter set forth.

The original clean copy and one cited copy of each party's proposed instructions shall be submitted to the court at the time of the pretrial conference.

WPI and WPIC instructions proposed by the plaintiff(s) do not have to be resubmitted by the opposing party or parties.

[Adopted effective January 1, 1999.]

WWCSCLR 9.   JURY TERMS

Beginning July 31, 1995, jury terms shall commence on the first calendar day of each month and shall end on the last calendar day of each month unless the day of commencing or ending said term be changed by order of the Superior Court. In addition, the term of any juror called for a case during the juror's term, which case is not concluded by the end of the juror's regular term, shall automatically be extended until the conclusion of the case.

[Adopted November 17, 1995.]

WWCSCLR 10.   EXCUSING WITNESSES

(CR 45 (g))

A witness subpoenaed to attend in any case, criminal or civil, is dismissed and excused from further attendance as soon as he has given his/her testimony in chief for the party in whose instance he/she was called and has been cross-examined thereon, unless a party makes a request in open court that the witness remain in attendance. Witness fees will not be allowed any witness after the day on which their testimony is given except when the witness has in open court been required to remain in further attendance, and when so required, the clerk shall note that fact in his/her minutes.

[Adopted effective January 1, 1999.]

WWCSCLR 11.   VOIR DIRE EXAMINATION OF JURORS

(CR 47 (a))

The court may examine prospective jurors to the extent it deems appropriate to determine if they can act as fair and impartial jurors in the case called for trial. Thereafter, the court shall give leave to the respective counsel or pro se litigants to ask the jurors such supplementary questions as may be deemed by the court to be reasonable. The voir dire examination of prospective jurors shall be limited to those matters having a reasonably direct bearing on prejudice, bias or qualifications, and shall not be used as a means of arguing or trying the case during voir dire.

[Adopted effective January 1, 1999.]

WWCSCLR 12. SECURITY IN HANDLING COURT EXHIBITS

(GR 20)

Any exhibit admitted into evidence in a proceeding in Superior Court, which is a weapon, money, an item of negotiable value, a controlled or dangerous substance or deemed by the Court to be bulky, inappropriate or difficult for the Clerk to store, may be admitted and then withdrawn upon the substitution of photographs(s), videotape(s), samples or other facsimile representations as provided by order of the Court.

Disposition of the original evidence shall be by order of the Court entered in each proceeding as necessary. All other applicable portions of General Rule 20 are incorporated herein and made a part hereof.

[Adopted effective January 1, 1999.]

WWCSCLR 13. PRESENTATION OF FINDINGS/CONCLUSIONS, JUDGMENTS AND ORDERS

(CR 52 and CR 54(e) and (f))

(A) Within fifteen (15) days after a decision is rendered, any party desiring to submit Findings of Facts and Conclusions of Law, a Judgment, Order or other appropriate document (proposed document) for the Court's signature shall serve opposing counsel with the same.

(B) Any party objecting to the proposed document shall within fifteen (15) days after receipt thereof serve opposing counsel, and mail/deliver to the trial Judge, objections thereto in writing, together with any proposed substitutions if deemed appropriate. Upon receipt of the proposed document and objections/substitutions, the trial Judge will within fifteen (15) days sign and file those documents accurately reflecting the Court's decision.

(C) If no objections/substitutions have been received within the above-described fifteen (15) day period, counsel shall mail/deliver the original of the proposed documents to the trial court, together with an affidavit of service upon the opposing counsel, and upon receipt thereof, the Court shall sign such proposed documents, or if deficient, return such docu-

ments and inform all counsel as to such deficiencies and any requested changes or additions thereto.

(D) The preceding shall be the exclusive method for presenting Judgments and Findings of Facts and Conclusions of Law. Orders and other documents also may be presented pursuant to CR 54(f)(2), without oral argument. Any proposed document may be presented ex parte to the Court if opposing counsel has approved in writing entry of the proposed document or notice of presentment has been waived in writing.

(E) If deemed appropriate in some circumstances, the Court may shorten the preceding time frames for presentation and shall so notify all counsel/parties.

[Adopted effective January 1, 1999.]

WWCSCLR 14. POST TRIAL MOTIONS

A. Motions for New Trial, Reconsideration or Judgment NOV. Motions for New Trial, Reconsideration or Judgment NOV shall be submitted without oral argument unless the Court orders otherwise. The motion shall be served and filed as provided in CR 59(b). At the time of filing the motion, the moving party shall serve and file a memorandum of authorities and deliver a copy of the motion and memorandum to the trial judge. The trial judge may (1) deny the motion, (2) call for a written response from opposing counsel, or (3) call for oral argument.

[Adopted November 17, 1995.]

WWCSCLR 15. JUSTIFICATION OF SURETIES

(1) Any person or corporation desiring to post bail bonds in Walla Walla County Superior Court shall first obtain an Order of Justification.

(2) All petitions for an Order of Justification shall be in writing to the court filed with the Walla Walla County Superior Court Clerk, and shall provide the following information:

(A) *All Sureties:*

1. Types of bonds, an outline of the types of bonds posted by the surety.

2. Current suretyship obligations, a current list of all suretyship obligations to all courts within the geographical limits of Washington state, including the following:

    a. The name of the court.

    b. The name of the defendant.

    c. The amount of the bond.

    d. The date issued.

3. Current bond foreclosures, a list of the current obligations to the courts in the way of bond forfeitures or other obligations incurred by the surety which have not been paid, or a statement that there are none.

4. Presentation, identity of the names and addresses of all persons who will be delivering or presenting bonds on behalf of the bonding surety.

5. Jurisdictions where surety has previously been authorized to post bail bonds and jurisdictions denying such authorization.

(B) *Corporations.*

1. Power of Attorney.

a. Names of the agents authorized to execute bonds on behalf of the surety.

b. The maximum dollar amount of any single bond which each agent is authorized to execute.

2. A copy of the current Certificate of Authority issued by the insurance commissioner for the State of Washington.

3. Resident Corporate Agent.

a. The name of the resident agent(s) for the corporate surety in the State of Washington authorized to appear and accept service on behalf of the corporate surety.

b. A copy of the power of attorney appointing said person(s) as resident agent(s).

(C) *Individuals.*

1. Individual name(s) of applicant(s).

2. Any fictitious names used by the applicant(s).

3. Resident address of individual applicant(s).

4. Business address of all individual applicant(s).

5. Marital status of applicant(s) and, if applicable, name(s) of spouse(s).

6. Verified financial statement:

A. Assets.

(i) Real property.

a. Street address and legal description of property.

b. Current appraisal of the property by a qualified real estate appraiser who is a member of the American Institute of Appraisers, or a statement of the appraiser that there has been no change in the value of the property since the last appraisal of the property.

c. If the real estate is being purchased on contract or subject to mortgage, deed of trust, or other encumbrance, disclose:

1. How the property is being obtained.

2. Amount of purchase price.

3. Amount of unpaid balance.

4. Notarized confirmation, etc.

d. Property tax statements and verification that real property taxes have been paid in full.

e. Verification that real property and structures thereon are insured against loss or damage.

(ii) Personal property.

a. Statement that the personalty is properly insured against loss, including a statement indicating the insurance coverage limits.

(iii) Savings (bank deposits).

(iv) Stocks and bonds.

a. Lists of individual stocks and bonds.

b. Statement of current value of stocks and bonds.

(v) Cash (including checking accounts).

(vi) Other investments.

B. Liabilities, including unsatisfied judgments. If unsatisfied judgments(s) is included, list court, title of cause, cause number, judgment creditor, and amount of unsatisfied judgment.

C. Net worth.

7. Current property bond obligations in the State of Washington.

a. Name of court.

b. Name of defendant.

c. Amount of the bond.

d. Date of issuance of bond.

8. Driver's license

a. Driver's license number.

b. State of issuance.

9. Criminal history—provide any criminal history conviction information for all persons identified in paragraph (C) 1 and (C) 5.

a. Name of criminal offense convicted of committing.

b. Type of criminal offense (misdemeanor, gross misdemeanor, felony) exclude traffic infractions unless five or more in last five years.

c. Name of sentencing court.

d. Date of offense.

e. Date of sentencing.

(3) All petitioners for an Order of Justification shall be verified under oath or certified under penalty of perjury as authorized by RCW 9A.72.985.

(4) All initial Orders of Justification shall be effective until the 30th day of April, next following the entry of the Order of Justification.

(5) All Orders of Justification, other than the initial order for that surety, shall be effective from May 1 of one year until April 30 of the following year.

(6) All petitions for an Order of Justification shall be accompanied by a proposed Order of Justification in substantially the form set out in Exhibit A of these rules.

(7) All initial petitions for an Order of Justification shall also be accompanied by the civil filing fee, currently $110.

(8) As of the date this local court rule is approved, if not previously paid, the $110 filing fee shall accompany the petition for renewal.

(9) On or before April 30 of each year, a petition for renewal of Order of Justification shall be filed with the Walla Walla county Superior Court Clerk, requesting renewal of the Order of Justification.

(10) Said petition shall include a statement under oath or certified under penalty of perjury as authorized by RCW 9A.72.088 that there have been no changes in the information provided in the initial petition for Order of Justification, or setting forth those changes.

[Adopted effective January 1, 1999.]

WWCSCLR 16. ATTORNEY'S FEES IN MINOR'S OR INCOMPETENT'S SETTLEMENTS

[SPR 98.16 iv]

When the Court is called upon to fix the compensation for acting on behalf of a minor or other incompetent, the following guidelines shall be considered.

(A) Settlement Less Than $100,000. If the case is settled and the amount of settlement is in the amount of $100,000 or less, the attorney's fees should not exceed 1/3 of the amount recovered after deduction of costs of suit.

(B) Settlement Between $100,000 and $200,000. If the amount of settlement is in the amount of $100,000 to $200,000, the attorney's fees should not exceed 1/3 of the first $100,000 recovered after costs of suit have been paid and 25% of the balance after deduction of costs of suit.

(C) Settlement Over $200,000. If the amount of a settlement is in the amount of $200,000 or more, the attorney's fees should not exceed 1/3 of the first $100,000 recovered after costs of suit have been paid, 25% of the second $100,000 after costs of suit have been paid and 20% of the balance after deduction of costs of suit.

(D) Costs of Suit Defined. For these purposes, "costs of suit" shall mean the expenses of litigation.

(E) Appeal. If there is an appeal, an additional reasonable fee will be considered.

[Adopted effective January 1, 1999.]

WWCSCLR 17. DOMESTIC RELATIONS PRETRIAL CONFERENCES

(A) Pretrial Conference. A pretrial conference shall be held in all contested domestic relations cases. The purpose of the conference is to identify disputed issues. Attendance by all counsel is mandatory.

(B) Discovery; Filing Position Statements. All discovery must be completed 10 days before the conference. Each party shall file and serve his or her position statement seven days prior to the conference. If either party fails to comply, the judge may impose terms on the offending party or the party's attorney, and require that the other party's reasonable attorney's fees be paid for any additional work or delay caused by the failure to comply. If neither party has filed a position statement as required, the Court may impose terms.

(C) Position statements.

(1) Position statements must be substantially in the form of Exemplar 1. The position statement will indicate the proposed disposition of assets and liabilities, as well as proposed maintenance and residential placement of children, as applicable. The position statement shall not be used for any purpose at trial, unless otherwise agreed by the parties.

(2) *Asset/Liability List.* If distribution of assets or liabilities is an issue, each party shall file and serve a list of assets and liabilities known to the party, together with the position statement, and shall indicate the party's good faith opinion as to the fair market value of any asset as of the date of separation. The parties may also indicate the current fair market value if there is a significant difference. This list shall be signed by the party under penalty of perjury. This list may be used at trial, subject to the rules of evidence or agreement of the parties.

(3) *Needs/Abilities Statement.* If spousal maintenance or attorney's fees is at issue, each party shall file and serve a statement containing a list of all income and assets, including any retirement benefits, together with a list of current monthly living expenses. The information regarding liabilities shall indicate the total amount owed as of the date of separation, the amount the party has paid on the debts since the separation, and the monthly payment on the debt. The statement shall also include information concerning the needs and abilities of the party, including age, education, training, work experience, and mental and physical health. This statement of assets, liabilities, needs and abilities shall be signed by the party under penalty of perjury. This statement may be used at trial subject to the Rules of Evidence or agreement of the parties.

(4) At the time of the conference or before, all exhibits intended to be used at trial will be disclosed and a copy provided to the opposing party.

(5) *Pretrial Statement.* At the conclusion of the conference, to the extent issues remain unresolved, the parties shall complete a Joint Pretrial Statement, in the form of Exemplar 2. The Joint Pretrial Statement may be submitted in a handwritten form if it is legible. Both parties and attorneys shall sign it.

(D) Discovery Required. The parties are required to file and exchange as appropriate the following documents no later than ten days prior to the pretrial conference:

(1) *Support Worksheet.* If child support is an issue, Washington State Child Support Worksheets (ALL PAGES), signed by the submitting party;

(2) *Tax Returns.* Complete tax returns for the past two calendar years together with all schedules and W–2's;

(3) *Partnership and Corporate Tax Returns.* Complete partnership and/or Corporate tax returns for the past two years together with all schedules and attachments for all partnerships and corporations in which a party has had an interest of five percent or greater.

(4) *Pay Stubs.* All pay stubs showing income for the past six months or since January 1 of the calendar year, whichever period is greater.

(5) A copy of the most recent statements of balances due on mortgages, real estate purchase contracts, deeds of trust, installment purchase contracts and time payment accounts owed by or to the parties;

(6) The most recent employers' ERISA statement, and a statement of contribution since that statement, of any pension plan of either party;

(7) A written appraisal of any real estate, antiques, jewelry or other items of special, unusual or extraordinary value or a summary of the evidence which will be relied upon;

(8) A verified extract or copy of the most recent N.A.D.A. Official Used Car Guide or Appraisal Guide showing both average loan or wholesale and retail values for any automobiles.

(9) A summary of the source and tracing of any property asserted to be the separate property or obligation of either party;

(10) A statement from each life insurance company issuing a policy of insurance on the life of either party as to its cash value and any loans on the cash value;

(11) A written appraisal of any proprietorship, partnership or closely held corporation of the parties, or a summary of the evidence which will be relied upon.

(12) Expert witnesses shall be disclosed at or before the pretrial conference.

[Adopted effective January 1, 1999.]

EXEMPLAR 1. POSITION STATEMENT

IN THE SUPERIOR COURT OF THE STATE OF WASHINGTON
IN AND FOR WALLA WALLA COUNTY

In Re the Marriage of)

_____) NO. _____

 Petitioner,) POSITION STATEMENT

and) _____ HUSBAND _____ WIFE

_____)

 Respondent.)

I. PERSONAL DATA

 Name: Date of Marriage:
 Age: Ages of Dependent Children:
 Occupation: Employer:

II. INCOME (only if support or maintenance is an issue)

 A. Average gross monthly wage $_____

 Deductions:
  Withholding Tax $_____
  Social Security (FICA)   _____

  _____   _____

  _____   _____

 Total Deductions $_____

 Net Take Home Per Month $_____

 B. Other Income (Pensions, ADC, Rents, Support, Soc. Sec.)

  _____ $_____

  _____

 TOTAL INCOME $_____

III. ESTIMATED MONTHLY EXPENSES (only if support or
                                 maintenance is an issue)

Rent or house payment	$_____	Life Insurance	$_____
Heat	_____	Auto Insurance	_____
Water, Refuse	_____	Fire Insurance	_____
Telephone	_____	Transportation	_____
Food	_____	Babysitter	_____
Clothing	_____	_____	_____
Laundry & Cleaning	_____	_____	_____
Electricity	_____	_____	_____
Medical	_____	_____	_____
Prescription–Drugs	_____	_____	_____
		TOTAL	$_____

IV. SUGGESTED SUPPORT

Spousal support: _____

Child support: _____
　　　　　　　　　(attach worksheets if contested)

V.　SUGGESTED VISITATION
　　(summarize issues if contested)

VI.　<u>ASSETS</u> (Reference Exhibit A. You may attach a photocopy of Exhibit A, adding an indication of who you suggest should be awarded the particular assets. Use supplementary schedules where necessary. List <u>all</u> assets, tangible and intangible. Include present worth of pension rights, annuities, life insurance, etc.)

Description of Item	Fair Mkt. Value	Encumbrance	Net Value	Suggested Division Husband	Wife

1.　<u>Community Personal Property</u>:

2.　<u>Separate Personal Property</u>:

3.　<u>Community</u> :

4.　<u>Separate</u> :

TOTALS					

VII.　<u>LIABILITIES</u> (Reference Exhibit B. You may attach a photocopy of Exhibit B, indicating who you suggest should assume particular debts.)

Creditor	Monthly Payment	Unpaid Balance	Should be Assumed by Husband	Wife

TOTALS				

VIII.　<u>OTHER FACTORS, IF ANY, BEARING ON FINANCIAL ISSUES</u> (e.g., physical disabilities, dependent children of prior marriages, etc.)

IX.　<u>SUMMARY</u>
　　Assets to Husband　　　　　　$_____
　　Debts to Husband　　　　　　　_____
　　Less/plus judgment/lien　　　　_____

　　　　　TOTAL　　　　　　　　$_____
　　Assets to Wife　　　　　　　$_____
　　Debts to Wife　　　　　　　　_____
　　Less/plus judgment/lien　　　　_____

　　　　　TOTAL　　　　　　　　$_____

Respectfully submitted by:

_____

Attorney for _____

THIS POSITION STATEMENT IS PREPARED FOR SETTLEMENT PUR-
POSES ONLY AND SHALL NOT BE USED FOR ANY OTHER PURPOSE,
EXCEPT EXHIBITS A AND B (ASSET AND LIABILITY LISTS) WHICH DO
NOT INDICATE THE SUGGESTED DIVISION COULD BE USED AT TRIAL.

[Adopted effective January 1, 1999.]

EXHIBIT "A" TO POSITION STATEMENT

COMMUNITY ASSET AND LIABILITY LIST

DIRECTIONS: List all property owned by both husband and wife as community
property. Use additional pages if necessary. If the marital community has an
interest in a business, use a separate sheet showing the community interest or
liability in all business assets and debts, including tangibles and such intangibles as
"goodwill."

DESCRIPTION OF ITEM	FAIR MARKET VALUE AT TIME OF SEPARATION	ENCUMBRANCE AT TIME OF SEPARATION	NET VALUE

PERSONAL PROPERTY

Vehicles:

Household Goods and Furnishings
(specify):

Tools:

Other/Miscellaneous (specify):

Specific Bank Accounts:

Pensions, IRAs, etc.:

Insurance:

TOTAL NET PERSONAL COMMUNITY PROPERTY: $_____

REAL PROPERTY

Address or Description:

Other interests in real property such as contracts:

_____

TOTAL NET REAL COMMUNITY PROPERTY: $_____

_____
_____

GRAND TOTAL NET VALUE OF ALL COMMUNITY ASSETS: $_____
(This amount excludes unsecured debt.)

COMMUNITY LIABILITIES

Directions: List all community debts as they existed at the time of separation, even if they
               are already shown as an encumbrance on the asset list.

Real estate loans:

Bank/institution	Property	Principal at Sep.	Monthly Pmt.

Bank loans secured by personal property:

Bank/institution   Property   Principal at Sep.   Monthly Pmt.

Bank loans unsecured:
Bank/institution   Orig. Amt.   Date   Purpose   Principal   Mthly. Pmt.
                                                              at Sep.

Credit cards:
Specify Visa, store, etc.   Principal at Sep.   Monthly Pmt.

Personal loans from friends or relatives:
Date of loan   Source   Purpose   In writing?   Orig.   Amt.   Terms
                                              Yes/No   Amt.   at Sep.

Other debts:
Specify to whom owed   Purpose   Amt.   Terms
                                                                     at Sep.

TOTAL COMMUNITY DEBT: $_____   Monthly Pmt. $_____

SUMMARY OF COMMUNITY ASSETS AND LIABILITIES

Personal property (net value at separation) $_____
Real property (net value at separation) $_____
Unsecured debts $ (_____)

Total net value $_____

I swear under penalty of perjury under the laws of the State of Washington that the foregoing information about our community assets and liabilities is true.
DATE: _____   Signed: _____
                                                    (Husband/Wife)

[Adopted effective January 1, 1999.]

EXHIBIT "B" TO POSITION STATEMENT

SEPARATE ASSET AND LIABILITY LIST

This list reflects my own separate assets and liabilities. It also reflects the separate assets and liabilities of my spouse to the extent that I have particular knowledge of them.

MY SEPARATE PROPERTY AND ASSETS

DESCRIPTION	DATE ACQUIRED	FAIR MARKET VALUE AT TIME OF SEPARATION	ENCUMBRANCE AT TIME OF SEPARATION	NET VALUE

PERSONAL PROPERTY

Vehicles:

Household Goods and Furnishings:

Tools:

Miscellaneous: (specify)

Bank Accounts:

DESCRIPTION	DATE ACQUIRED	FAIR MARKET VALUE AT TIME OF SEPARATION	ENCUMBRANCE AT TIME OF SEPARATION	NET VALUE
Pensions, IRAs, etc.				

Insurance:

TOTAL Personal property and assets

REAL PROPERTY

TOTAL Real property

GRAND TOTAL, net value of my separate property: $_____
(This amount excludes unsecured debt.)

MY SPOUSE'S SEPARATE PROPERTY (if known)

PERSONAL PROPERTY

TOTAL spouse's separate personal property (net): $_____

REAL PROPERTY

TOTAL spouse's separate real property (net): $_____

Other debts (unsecured) of spouse's: $_____

GRAND TOTAL of my spouse's separate property: $_____

MY SEPARATE LIABILITIES

DIRECTIONS: List all of your separate debts as they existed at the time of separation, even if they are already shown as an encumbrance on the asset list.

Real estate loans:

Bank/institution	Property	Principal at Separation		Monthly Pmt.

Bank loans secured by personal property:

Bank/institution	Property	Principal at separation		Monthly Pmt.

Bank loans unsecured:

Bank/institution	Orig.Amt.	Purpose	Date	Amt. at Sep.	Mthly. Pmt.

Credit cards:

Specify Visa, store, etc.	Principal at Separation	Mthly. Pmt.

Personal loans from friends or relatives:

Date of loan	Source	Purpose	In writing? Yes/No	Orig. Amt.	Amt. at Sep.	Terms

Other debts:

Specify to whom owed	Purpose	Amount at Sep.	Terms

MY TOTAL SEPARATE DEBT $_____   Mthly. Pmt. $_____

SUMMARY OF MY SEPARATE ASSETS AND LIABILITIES

Personal property (net value at separation)	$_____
Real property (net value at separation)	$_____
Unsecured debts	$ (_____)

TOTAL NET VALUE: $_____

I swear under penalty of perjury under the laws of the State of Washington that the foregoing information about our community assets and liabilities is true.

DATE: _____   Signed: _____

                                                     (Husband/Wife)

[Adopted effective January 1, 1999.]

EXEMPLAR 2. DOMESTIC RELATIONS JOINT PRETRIAL STATEMENT

SUPERIOR COURT OF THE STATE OF WASHINGTON
FOR WALLA WALLA COUNTY

In Re the Marriage of:)
)
)
_____) NO.
                          Petitioner,   )
)   DOMESTIC RELATIONS
       vs.   )   JOINT PRETRIAL STATEMENT
)
_____)
                          Respondent)

The following pretrial statement has been stipulated and agreed to by the parties in the case:

1. The following issues have been resolved (set forth the issue and the specific manner of resolution, including agreed valuations, if applicable):

2. The following facts have been stipulated and agreed upon and require no further proof: (Include also any agreed valuations, of property)

3. The following specific issues remain in dispute to be determined at trial or hearing:

4. The following proposed exhibits are those intended by the parties to be used at the hearing or trial in this case and may be received in evidence by the court:

5. The following proposed exhibits are objected to by a party: (Indicate which party objecting)

6. The following witnesses may be called by the parties: (Identify specifically any expert witnesses.)

Petitioner   Respondent

7. The parties estimate the trial or hearing in this case will take ____ (hrs.) (days).

The parties stipulate and agree to be bound by all representations made herein and further stipulate and agree that this pretrial statement may be considered by the trial judge in its determination of this case.

_____   _____
        Petitioner   Respondent

_____   _____
   Petitioner's Attorney   Respondent's Attorney

[Adopted effective January 1, 1999.]

WWCSCLR 18. ALTERNATE RESIDENTIAL TIME GUIDELINES FOR WALLA WALLA COUNTY

(A) Alternate Residential Time. In order to facilitate reasonable resolution of visitation issues, the parties should consider the following guidelines which the Court would be inclined to accept as reasonable in most cases, based on the child's age and the geographical location of the parents:

0 to 6 months: Two hours, twice per week.

6 months to 1 year: Two hours, twice per week; and four hours, once per week.

1 year to 3 years: Two hours, twice per week; and eight hours, once per week. These holidays alternated each year, for eight hours each: Easter, July 4th, Thanksgiving, Christmas Eve, and Christmas Day. Overnight residential time is not usually recommended.

3 years to 5 years: Two hours, twice per week.

Alternating weekends from Saturday at 9:00 a.m. until Sunday at 6:00 p.m.

These holidays alternated each year: Easter, July 4th, Thanksgiving for 2 days; Christmas Eve and 2 days before and Christmas Day and 2 days thereafter.

Summer residential time: Two non-consecutive one-week periods.

5 years and older: Every other weekend from Friday at 6:00 p.m. until Sunday at 6:00 p.m. If Friday is a school holiday, the weekend begins Thursday at 6:00 p.m. If Monday is a school holiday, the weekend ends Monday at 6:00 p.m.

One weekday from 5:30 p.m. until 7:30 p.m., once per week.

These holidays alternated each year: Martin Luther King Day, President's Day, Memorial Day, July 4th, Labor Day, Veteran's Day, Thanksgiving (from 6:00 p.m. the Wednesday before Thanksgiving Day to 6:00 p.m. the Sunday immediately following the holiday) and Winter Holidays (on even years from 6:00 p.m. on the day school recesses to December 24 at 8:00 p.m., and on odd years, from 8:00 p.m. on December 24th to 6:00 p.m. the day before school commences.)

Summer and Spring Vacation residential time: Five weeks during the summer, commencing one week after school is out in even-numbered years and commencing six weeks before the start of school in odd-numbered years (during which times the residential parent shall have residential time with the child on an alternating weekend basis as set forth above, except during extended trips/vacations). Spring break shall be alternated each year, commencing at 6:00 p.m. on the day before the vacation begins and ending at 6:00 p.m. on the day before school starts.

(B) Father's/Mother's Day. Regardless of the residential time suggested above, the mother shall have residential time of at least 4 hours on Mother's Day; and the father shall have residential time of at least 4 hours on Father's Day.

(C) Birthdays. Each parent shall be allowed to spend at least 4 hours with the child to celebrate the child's birthday, and that parent's birthday, within two days of that birthday.

(D) Telephone Contact. Reasonable telephonic contact with the child is usually appropriate, and should not be less than once per week for each parent during that parent's nonresidential time.

(E) Different Age Groups. When children of different age groups are involved, the preference shall be to follow the guideline for the oldest child, so that the children remain together.

(F) Cancellation. For weekend visits, the primary parent shall have the child available for one hour after the scheduled starting time. If the other parent does not pick up the child within that hour, then the weekend visit shall be deemed cancelled.

(G) Priorities Under the Residential Schedule. Holidays have priority over other special occasions. Special occasions have priority over school vacations.

(H) Parental Cooperation. These provisions are designed to encourage each parent to maintain a loving, stable, and nurturing relationship with the child. Each parent shall encourage the parent/child relationship of the other parent, and shall make residential arrangement decisions which are in the best interest of the child.

[Adopted effective January 1, 1999.]

WWCSCLR 19. MANDATORY PARENTING SEMINAR RULES

(A) Parenting Seminars. The parents and all parties ordered by the Court shall complete a parenting seminar approved by the Court in all cases filed under RCW Chapters 26.09, 26.10, and 26.26, which require a parenting plan for minor children, including marital dissolutions, legal separations, modifications of the residential provisions of an approved parenting plan, paternity actions in which paternity has been established, non-parent custody actions, any action where one or both of the parties is under the age of eighteen (18) years, and any action in which the Court makes a discretionary finding that a parenting seminar would be in the best interest of the children.

(B) Time of Attendance. All parties required by this rule to participate in a parenting seminar shall complete a Court approved seminar within sixty (60) days of filing of the action if the party is the Petitioner, or sixty (60) days of filing an appearance or a response, whichever is first, if the party is the Respondent. In paternity actions wherein the State of Washington is the Petitioner, attendance shall be required within sixty (60) days after paternity has been established and a parenting plan has been requested. In all cases in which attendance is ordered by the Court and not mandated by this rule, the parenting seminar shall be completed within sixty (60) days of the date of the Court order being entered.

(C) Certification of Completion. Successful completion of the seminar shall be evidenced by a certificate of attendance provided by the person or agency providing the seminar and filed with the Court.

(D) Fees. Every party attending a parenting seminar shall pay the fee charged be the Court approved provider.

(E) Special Consideration/Waiver.

(1) In no case shall opposing parties be required to attend a parenting seminar together.

(2) Upon a showing of domestic violence or abuse which would not require mutual decision making pursuant to RCW 26.09.191(1), or upon a showing that a parent's attendance at a seminar is not in the children's best interest pursuant to RCW Chapter 26.12, the Court shall either (1) waive the requirement of completion of the seminar, or (2) allow participation in an alternative voluntary parenting seminar for battered spouses.

(3) The Court may waive the seminar requirement for good cause shown.

(F) Failure to Comply/Sanctions. Willful failure to participate or willful delay in completion of a parenting seminar by any party may constitute contempt of Court and result in sanctions including, but not limited to, imposition of monetary terms, striking of pleadings, or denial of affirmative relief to a party not in compliance with these rules. Nonparticipation or default by one party does not excuse participation by any other party. Refusal, delay or default by a Respondent will not delay the action, however, such Respondent shall not be allowed to seek affirmative relief in the pending action or any subsequent action between the same parties until the seminar has been successfully completed. Petitioner's refusal or delay shall prevent the case from being set for trial or the entry of any final order concerning a parenting or residential plan, except in cases where there is a co-petitioner or counter petitioner who is in full compliance. Agreement by the parties as to issues of parenting/residential plans shall not excuse participation in the seminars by both parties.

(G) Standards. Standards for parenting seminars shall be established by the Court and all providers shall be approved by the Court.

[Adopted effective January 1, 1999.]

WWCSCLR 20.   FAMILY LAW MANDATORY MEDIATION

(A) Mediation Required. All contested issues in the following cases shall be submitted to mandatory mediation before proceeding to trial: (a) all family law petitions, including marriage dissolutions, legal separation, and declaration of invalidity; (b) nonparental child custody proceedings; (c) paternity child custody proceedings; (d) actions brought by parties to nonmarital personal relationships involving parenting and/or distribution of assets/liabilities; and (e) petitions for modification of final orders (excluding child support modifications or adjustments). No contested matter described above shall be set for trial without proof of commencement of mediation proceedings. Mediation shall be completed no less than 30 days prior to the scheduled trial date. The mediation requirement or time limits may be waived or modified by the Court upon motion for good cause shown or upon the Court's own motion. The parties shall mediate in good faith.

(B) Mediation Does Not Stay Court Proceedings. Mediation does not stay or otherwise affect the rights and duties of the parties established by statute, court rule, or court order. The Court may enter temporary orders and the parties may conduct discovery prior to or during the mediation process.

(C) Approval of Mediators. Mediators performing mediation services pursuant to this rule must fulfill certain minimum qualifications established by the Court. The Court shall maintain a list of such minimum qualifications for distribution to the public. In order to fulfill the mediation requirements of this rule, the parties must use the services of a court-approved mediator or mediators. The Court shall maintain a list of approved mediators (whether persons or agencies) for distribution to the public. The list shall contain the following information: Each mediator's name, organization (if any), address and telephone number, and fee schedule.

(D) Selection of Mediator.

(1) The parties may have their case mediated by the mediator of their choice. If the parties cannot agree on the method of selection of the mediator, upon motion the Court shall select a mediator from among the court-approved mediators.

(2) A mediator has the right to decline to serve in a particular case. If the parties select a mediator who declines to serve, the parties shall select a different mediator, using the same selection process by which the preceding mediator was selected.

(E) Authority of Mediator. The mediator has the authority to determine the time, place, manner, and duration of mediation. In appropriate cases, the mediator shall have the authority to terminate the mediation prior to completion.

(F) Attendance. The parties shall personally attend all mediation sessions, unless the mediator permits telephonic or other attendance. The mediator shall have the authority to require other persons to attend.

(G) Declaration of Completion. Within seven (7) days of completion of mediation, a declaration of completion shall be filed with the Court by the mediator. Counsel and the parties shall be advised by the mediator of the results of mediation in writing. The mediator shall advise the Court only whether an agreement has been reached on some or all of the issues.

(H) Payment. Mediators shall be paid by the parties in accordance with the agreement of the parties, or, in the absence of agreement, as determined in mediation.

(I) Confidentiality. The work product of the mediator and all communications during the mediation shall be privileged and confidential and not subject to compulsory disclosure. The mediator shall not appear to testify in any court proceedings.

(J) Responsibility for Compliance With Mediation Requirements. The parties shall be responsible for arranging for and completing all mediation requirements established under this rule.

(K) Effective Date. This rule shall apply to all cases described in section (a) above filed after January 1, 1999, and shall also apply to petitions filed after January 1, 1999 modifying final orders entered before January 1, 1999.

[Adopted effective January 1, 1999.]

WWCSCLR 21. PRO SE PARENTING PLANS/CHILD SUPPORT ORDERS

In any action in which child support or residential care of a minor child or children is an issue and in which none of the parties is represented by counsel, the parenting plan and child support documents shall first be reviewed, approved, and initiated by the Courthouse Facilitator. If a proposed parenting plan is filed, it need not be initialed or approved by the Courthouse Facilitator, but any parenting plan submitted for court approval must be so initialed and approved.

If the parenting plan or child support order is the result of mediation, the mediator shall affix a declaration to the parenting plan or child support order submitted for court approval, signed under penalty of perjury, that the parenting plan/child support order is the result of mediation, the date(s) such mediation occurred and the name of the mediator and the mediation service. The proposed parenting plan, the proposed child support order and the mediator's declaration shall be provided to the Courthouse Facilitator for review and approval.

[Adopted effective January 1, 1999]

WWCSCLR 22. GUARDIAN AD LITEM GRIEVANCE PROCEDURES

Any grievances by or complaints against a Guardian ad Litem, including any CASA volunteer, shall be investigated, processed and resolved by the two Superior Court Judges on an individual case basis. The Court recognizes that separate procedures will be required for grievances or complaints filed during the pendency of a case, and those filed subsequent to the conclusion of a case. Complaints filed while a case is pending shall be resolved within 25 days and those filed after the conclusion of a case shall be resolved within 60 days. The Court also recognizes the need to provide, on a case by case basis, fair treatment of grievance issues, such as appearance of fairness and conflict issues.

All complaints shall be confidential unless merit is found. The Court shall provide procedures for a Guardian ad Litem who is the subject of a complaint to respond in a timely manner. The Court shall maintain a record of grievances and complaints filed, as well as any sanctions issued. If a Guardian ad Litem is removed from any registry of this Court pursuant to the disposition of a grievance or complaint, the Court shall send notice of such removal to the Office of the Administrator of the Courts.

[Adopted March 19, 2001.]

WWCSCLR 31. ACCESS TO COURT RECORDS

It is this Court's intent to comply with GR 31 and by this Local Court Rule adopt in its entirety the policy, purpose, scope and access requirements therein. Also, see Local Court Rule 31(a).

[Adopted effective November 22, 2004.]

WWCSCLR 31(a). REDACTION POLICY

(1) Complete names of children, sealed case types: The complete names of children shall be used in cases that are deemed confidential pursuant to state or federal statutes, including cases filed pursuant to Title 13 RCW (excluding offender cases); Chapter 4.24 RCW, Chapter 26.33 (Adoption) and Chapter 71.34 (Mental Health Services for Minors).

(2) Confidential Information Form: The complete names of children and other identifiers shall be included in the Confidential Information Form or similar document for cases filed under Title 26.

(3) Domestic Relations Orders: Court orders concerning the financial support or the custody or residential schedule of a child (including temporary and permanent parenting plans and similar documents) and orders establishing or disestablishing paternity shall include the full name of the child. The date of birth of a child shall be included in court records only as authorized by GR 22.

(4) Child who is alleged to be a victim of a crime: The complete name of a child who is alleged to be a victim of a crime may be included on subpoenas and in jury instructions. Nothing in this rule requires that subpoenas be routinely filed in the court file.

(5) Child who is charged with a crime: The complete name of a child charged with a crime shall be included in any indictment or information filed with the court pursuant to CrR 2.1 or JuCR 7.2, as part of an affidavit or declaration of probable cause or for any other purpose deemed necessary for the prosecution or defense of the criminal or juvenile offender matter.

(6) Orders issued for the protection of a child: If a child is a person protected by a criminal no contact order issued pursuant to 10.99 RCW, an anti-harassment order issued pursuant to 10.14 RCW, an order of protection under issued pursuant to 26.50 RCW or a restraining order or order of protection issued pursuant to 26.09 RCW, 26.10 RCW, 26.26 RCW, RCW 26.52.020, or any other court order entered for the protection of the child, the child's full name and other identifiers shall be included on petitions and orders as necessary for entry of the order into the Judicial Information System (JIS) and/or the Washington Crime Information Center (WACIC).

(7) If access to a child is restricted pursuant to CrR 3.2(d)(1), the court may include the full name of the child on the order, if deemed necessary for effective enforcement of the order.

(8) Orders restraining child from contacting or harassing others: Whenever a child is named as a respondent in an order listed in (3) above, the child's full name and other personal identifiers shall be included on the petition and order as necessary for entry of the order in the Judicial Information System (JIS) and/or the Washington Crime Information Center (WACIC).

(9) General authority: Nothing in this rule shall prohibit a court from authorizing the use of a child's full name or date of birth when necessary for the orderly administration of justice, consistent with the requirements of GR 22.

[Adopted effective November 22, 2004.]

DISTRICT COURT
WALLA WALLA COUNTY DISTRICT COURT LOCAL RULES

Including Amendments Received Through
August 15, 2015

Table of Rules

Rule
WWDIR 3.5. Decisions on Written Statements.

WWDIR 3.5. DECISIONS ON WRITTEN STATEMENTS

Mitigation and contested hearings based on written statements, given under penalty of perjury as provided for in IRLJ 2.4(b)(4) and IRLJ 2.6(c), are authorized. The procedures authorized by IRLJ 3.5 are adopted by this court. To be considered, the written statement(s) must be received by the court pursuant to written instructions provided to the defendant.

[Adopted effective September 1, 2006.]

MUNICIPAL COURTS

COLLEGE PLACE MUNICIPAL COURT LOCAL RULES

Including Amendments Received Through
August 15, 2015

Table of Rules

CPMCLR 1.   ADOPTION OF LOCAL RULES

These rules are adopted pursuant to GR 7, CrRLJ 1.7 and IRLJ 1.3.

[Adopted effective September 1, 2003.]

CPMCLR 2.   TITLE OF RULES

These rules shall be known and cited as College Place Municipal Court Local Rules and may be referred to as CPMCLR.

[Adopted effective September 1, 2003.]

CPMCLR 3.   BAIL

Any person arrested for a crime classified as Domestic Violence per Section 10.99 or Harassment per Section 10.14 of the Revised Code of Washington shall be held in jail without bail pending their first appearance before the Court.

[Adopted effective September 1, 2003.]

PRESCOTT MUNICIPAL COURT—
[No Local Rules]

WAITSBURG MUNICIPAL COURT—
[No Local Rules]

WHATCOM COUNTY

Table of Courts

Superior Court

Whatcom County Superior Court Local Rules.

District Court

Whatcom County District Court Local Court Rules.

Municipal Courts

Bellingham Municipal Court Local Court Rules.
Blaine Municipal Court Local Court Rules.
Everson—Nooksack Municipal Court.
Ferndale Municipal Court.
Lynden Municipal Local Court Rules.
Sumas Municipal Court Local Rules.

SUPERIOR COURT

WHATCOM COUNTY SUPERIOR COURT LOCAL RULES

Including Amendments Received Through
August 15, 2015

Table of Rules

RULE FORMAT

These rules conform in numbering and format to the Washington Rules of Court as directed by the Supreme Court of the State of Washington in CR 7(b). Each local rule is given the same number as the corresponding Supreme Court rule, or is given a new number where no corresponding Supreme Court rule exists. Gaps in numerical sequence occur because local rules do not exist for every subject.

ADMINISTRATIVE RULES
(Cite as WCAR)

WCAR 0.1. PURPOSE AND CITATION

(a) Purpose. Procedure in the Superior Court of the State of Washington for Whatcom County shall comply with Washington statutes, Rules of Court and these rules.

(b) Citation. These rules are collectively referred to as "Whatcom County Superior Court Local Rules" or "WCLR". Individual rules are known and cited as "WCAR 0.2", "WCCR 54", etc.

[Adopted effective June 1, 1991.]

WCAR 0.2. DEFINITIONS

A rule applying to an "attorney", "counsel", or "lawyer" shall equally apply to a party pro se. Except where otherwise required by law or court rule, the terms "judge" and "court" include commissioners. The term "clerk" includes deputies and other employees authorized to act on behalf of the Clerk of the Superior Court.

[Adopted effective June 1, 1991.]

WCAR 0.3. ORGANIZATION OF THE COURT

(a) The Superior Court of the State of Washington for Whatcom County is organized into three judge's departments, Departments One, Two, and Three. Business of the court is also conducted by three court commissioners, mental health commissioners, and a family court commissioner.

(b) Court Commissioners shall have authority in all matters allowed by the Constitution of the State of Washington, case law and statutes, including, but not limited to, the authority noted in RCW 2.24.040 to accept guilty pleas.

[Adopted effective June 1, 1991; amended effective September 1, 2000; September 1, 2002.]

WCAR 0.4. SUSPENSION OF RULES

The court may modify or suspend any WCLR for good cause or upon the court's own motion in order to prevent the failure of justice.

[Adopted effective June 1, 1991.]

WCAR 0.5. UNSUITABLE MATERIALS AS EXHIBITS

Whenever there is presented to the clerk for filing in a cause any paper or other material that is deemed by the clerk to be improper or inappropriate for filing, the clerk shall affix his/her file mark thereto and may forthwith orally apply to the court for a determination of the propriety of filing the material presented. If the court determines that the paper or material should not be made a part of the file, an order shall be entered to that effect and the clerk shall retain the material s as an exhibit in the cause. The court may order that the unsuitable material be sealed, in which event it shall be available for inspection only by order of the court except to the parties or their attorneys of record.

[Adopted effective September 1, 2004.]

WCAR 29. PRESIDING JUDGE

(a) Election, Term, Vacancies, Removal and Selection Criteria

(1) *Election.* The Presiding Judge shall be elected by a majority of the judges of the Whatcom County Superior Court. In the same manner, the judges shall elect an Assistant Presiding Judge of the court who shall serve as Acting Presiding Judge during the absence or upon the request of the Presiding Judge and who shall perform such further duties as the Presiding Judge, the Executive Committee, if any, or the majority of the judges shall direct.

(2) *Term.* The Presiding Judge shall be elected for a term of not fewer than two years, subject to reelection. The term of the Presiding Judge shall commence on January 1 of the year in which the Presiding Judge's term begins.

(3) *Vacancies.* Interim vacancies of the office of Presiding Judge or Acting Presiding Judge shall be filled as provided in (a)(1).

(4) *Removal.* The Presiding Judge may be removed by a majority vote of the judges of the court.

(5) *Selection Criteria.* A Presiding Judge must have at least four years of experience as a judge, unless this requirement is waived by a majority vote of the judges of the court. Selection of a Presiding Judge should be based on the judge's

1) Management and administrative ability,

2) Interest in serving in the position,

3) Experience and familiarity with a variety of trial court assignments, and

4) Ability to motivate and educate other judicial officers and court personnel.

(b) Selection and Term—Single Judge Courts. (No Local Rule)

(c) Notification of Chief Justice. The Presiding Judge so elected shall send notice of the election of the Presiding Judge and Assistant Presiding Judge to the Chief Justice of the Supreme Court within 30 days of election.

(d) Caseload Adjustment. To the extent possible, the judicial caseload should be adjusted to provide the Presiding Judge with sufficient time and resources to devote to the management and administrative duties of the office.

(e) General Responsibilities. The Presiding Judge is responsible for leading the management and administration of the court's business, recommending policies and procedures that improve the court's effectiveness, and allocating resources in a way that maximizes the court's ability to resolve disputes fairly and expeditiously.

(f) Duties and Authority. The judicial and administrative duties set forth in this rule cannot be delegated to persons in either the legislative or executive branches of government. A Presiding Judge may delegate the performance of ministerial duties to court employees; however, it is still the Presiding Judge's responsibility to ensure they are performed in accordance with this rule. In addition to exercising general administrative supervision over the court, except those duties assigned to clerks of the superior court pursuant to law, the Presiding Judge shall:

(1) Supervise the business of the court and judicial officers in such manner as to ensure the expeditious and efficient processing of all cases and equitable distribution of the workload among judicial officers;

(2) Assign judicial officers to hear cases pursuant to statute or rule. The court may establish general policies governing the assignment of judges;

(3) Coordinate judicial officers' vacations, attendance at education programs, and similar matters;

(4) Develop and coordinate statistical and management information;

(5) Supervise the daily operation of the court including:

(a) All personnel assigned to perform court functions; and

(b) All personnel employed under the judicial branch of government including but not limited to working conditions, hiring, discipline, and termination decisions except wages, or benefits directly related to wages; and

(c) The court administrator, or equivalent employee, who shall report directly to the Presiding Judge.

(6) Supervise the court's accounts and auditing the procurement and disbursement of appropriations and preparation of the court's annual budget request;

(7) Appoint standing and special committees of judicial officers necessary for the proper performance of the duties of the court;

(8) Promulgate local rules as a majority of the judges may approve or as the Supreme Court shall direct;

(9) Supervise the preparation and filing of reports required by statute and court rule;

(10) Act as the official spokesperson for the court in all matters with the executive or legislative branches of state and local government and the community unless the Presiding Judge shall designate another judge or employee to serve in this capacity;

(11) Preside at meetings of the judicial officers of the court;

(12) Determine the qualifications of and establish a training program for pro tem judges and pro tem court commissioners; and

(13) Perform other duties as may be assigned by statute or court rule.

(g) Executive Committee. (No local rule)

(h) Oversight of judicial officers. It shall be the duty of the Presiding Judge to supervise judicial officers to the extent necessary to ensure the timely and efficient processing of cases. The Presiding Judge shall have the authority to address a judicial officer's failure to perform judicial duties and to propose remedial action. If remedial action is not successful, the Presiding Judge shall notify the Commission on Judicial Conduct of a judge's substantial failure to perform judicial duties, which includes habitual neglect of duty or persistent refusal to carry out assignments or directives made by the Presiding Judge, as authorized by this rule.

(i) Multiple Court Districts. (No Local Rule)

(j) Multiple Court Level Agreement. (No Local Rule)

(k) Judicial Services Contracts. (No Local Rule)

[Adopted effective September 1, 2002.]

GENERAL RULES
(Cite as WCGR)

WCGR 31. PERSONAL IDENTIFIERS—CHILDREN

(1) **Complete names of children, sealed case types:** The complete names of children shall be used in cases that are deemed confidential pursuant to state or federal statutes, including cases filed pursuant to Title 13 RCW (excluding offender cases); Chapter 4.24 RCW, Chapter 26.33 (Adoption) and Chapter 71.34 (Mental Health Services for Minors).

(2) **Confidential Information Form:** The complete names of children and other identifiers shall be included in the Confidential Information Form or similar document for cases filed under Title 26.

(3) Domestic Relations Orders: Court orders concerning the financial support or the custody or residential schedule of a child (including temporary and permanent parenting plans and similar documents) and orders establishing or disestablishing paternity shall include the full name of the child. The date of birth of a child shall be included in court records only as authorized by GR 22.

(4) Child who is alleged to be a victim of a crime: The complete name of a child who is alleged to be a victim of a crime may be included on subpoenas and in jury instructions. Nothing in this rule requires that subpoenas be routinely filed in the court file.

(5) Child who is charged with a crime: The complete name of a child charged with a crime shall be included in any indictment or information filed with the court pursuant to CrR 2.1 or JuCR 7.2, as part of an affidavit or declaration of probable cause or for any other purpose deemed necessary for the prosecution or defense of the criminal or juvenile offender matter.

(6) Orders issued for the protection of or restricting access to a child: If a child is a person protected by a criminal no contact order issued pursuant to 10.99 RCW, an anti-harassment order issued pursuant to 10.14 RCW, an order of protection under issued pursuant to 26.50 RCW or a restraining order or order of protection issued pursuant to 26.09 RCW, 26.10 RCW, 26.26 RCW, RCW 26.52.020, or any other court order entered for the protection of the child, the child's full name and other identifiers shall be included on petitions and orders as necessary for entry of the order into the Judicial Information System (JIS) and/or the Washington Crime Information Center (WACIC). If access to a child is restricted pursuant to CrR 3.2(d) (1), the court may include the full name of the child on the order, if deemed necessary for effective enforcement of the order.

(7) Orders restraining child from contacting or harassing others: Whenever a child is named as a respondent in an order listed in (3) above, the child's full name and other personal identifiers shall be included on the petition and order as necessary for entry of the order in the Judicial Information System (JIS) and/or the Washington Crime Information Center (WACIC).

(8) General authority: Nothing in this rule shall prohibit a court from authorizing the use of a child's full name or date of birth when necessary for the orderly administration of justice, consistent with the requirements of GR 22.

[Adopted effective January 21, 2005.]

CIVIL RULES
(Cite as WCCR)

WCCR 4. ORDER FOR SERVICE OF SUMMONS BY PUBLICATION

A party must obtain an Order for Service of Summons by Publication in any case where that party serves summons by publication. The party shall file a Declaration for Service by Publication which shows that the requirements of RCW 4.28.100 have been satisfied and shows specific facts delineating the attempts that were made to locate the other party.

[Adopted effective September 1, 1993.]

WCCR 7.1. REAPPLICATION FOR AN ORDER

An order refused in whole or in part (or granted conditionally and the condition has not been performed) shall not be presented to a different judge or commissioner unless authorized by the judge or commissioner who refused or conditionally granted the order.

[Adopted effective June 1, 1991.]

WCCR 7.2. NECESSARY PROVISIONS FOR CIVIL BENCH WARRANT NON–DOMESTIC RELATIONS CASES

No civil bench warrant for failure to appear shall issue without an affidavit by the attorney for the moving party setting forth:

(a) a statement that the order requiring the attendance of a party in court contained the following caption:

```
)  NO.
)  ORDER REQUIRING
)  ATTENDANCE OF PARTY
)  IN COURT
```

and that the order contained the following notice:

YOUR FAILURE TO APPEAR AT THE TIME, DATE, AND PLACE REQUIRED MAY CAUSE THIS COURT TO ISSUE A BENCH WARRANT FOR YOUR APPREHENSION AND CONFINEMENT IN JAIL UNTIL SUCH TIME AS THIS MATTER CAN BE HEARD AND/OR UNTIL BAIL IS POSTED. THE RELIEF REQUESTED IN THE MOTION MAY ALSO BE GRANTED.

(b) confirmation of personal service;

(c) the date(s) of service;

(d) the time required by law to lapse between service and granting of relief;

(e) that such time has in fact lapsed.

[Adopted effective December 1, 1992.]

WCCR 10.1.   DOCUMENTARY EXHIBITS

(a) When a documentary exhibit is used at trial during witness examination and reference to the contents of the exhibit is necessary to understand the issues, counsel shall provide extra copies of the exhibit for opposing counsel and the court.

(b) An 8.5 by 11 inch photo-reduction of each large-scale exhibit shall be submitted for marking and filing except with permission of the court.

[Adopted effective June 1, 1991.]

WCCR 10.2.   PLEADING REQUIREMENTS

The provisions of CR 10 shall apply.   Additionally, the following are required:

(a) Letter–size paper (8.5 by 11 inches) is required, printed on one side only.

(b) All pleadings and orders shall bear the signature and bar association membership number of the attorney presenting the order or other paper, and shall identify the party or parties represented by the attorney.   In the event that an attorney represents some but not all of the petitioners/plaintiffs or the respondents/defendants, the signature block shall bear the names of only those parties represented by the attorney.

(c) Motions, and the orders granting the relief requested in the motions, shall be separate papers.

(d) Titles of pleadings, orders, and other papers shall be specific.   In cases with multiple parties, titles shall include the names of the parties affected by such papers.

(e) Orders of default against unnamed "Jane Doe" or "John Doe" spouses may be entered.   Judgments against unnamed spouses will not be entered against such unnamed spouses unless the file contains adequate affidavits stating reasonable grounds to believe that the defaulting party is married and reciting reasonable efforts made to obtain the complete name of, and service upon, the otherwise unnamed spouse.

(f) A party appearing pro se shall state on court papers filed by him or her, the telephone number, mailing address, and street address where service of process may be made upon such pro se party.

(g) No party may file separately or as an attachment or exhibit to a new document a document already filed as part of the court record.   New pleadings should refer to already-filed documents when appropriate, including in the reference the date of the referenced filing or the name and date of the referenced pleading to which it was attached.

[Adopted effective December 1, 1992.   Amended effective September 1, 2006.]

WCCR 10.3.   PAGE LIMITS

(a) **Motion.**   Absent prior authorization from the court, no individual document, whether titled as a motion, declaration, affidavit, memorandum or brief shall exceed fifteen (15) pages, not including exhibits thereto.   All such documents shall be double-spaced and typed in a font no smaller than 12 point.

(b) **Response to Motion.**   Absent prior authorization from the court, no response to any motion, declaration, affidavit, memorandum or brief shall exceed fifteen (15) pages, not including exhibits thereto.   No response may include any document attached to or a part of the initial motion or pleading already filed as part of the court record [WCCR 10.2(g)], but instead shall cite to the relevant portion of the initial document.   All such documents shall be double-spaced and typed in a font no smaller than 12 point.

(c) **Reply to Response.**   Absent prior authorization from the court, no reply to a response to motion, declaration, affidavit, memorandum or brief shall exceed five (5) pages, not including exhibits thereto.   No reply may include any document attached to or a part of the initial motion or response thereto or pleading already filed as part of the court record, but instead shall cite to the relevant portion of the initial document.   All such documents shall be double-spaced and typed in a font no smaller than 12 point.

(d) **Family Law Declarations.**   Notwithstanding the above provisions, absent prior authorization from the court, declarations or affidavits in family law cases (whether initial or responsive declarations or affidavits) are limited to a combined total of fifteen (15) pages per party and no single declaration or affidavit may exceed five (5) pages.   Replies to responsive declarations or affidavits are limited to a total of five (5) pages.

(e) **Exhibits to Motions, Declarations, etc.**   Exhibits that consist of declarations or affidavits of parties or witnesses shall count towards the above page limit.   All other exhibits attached to a declaration or affidavit shall not be counted toward the page limit.

(f) **Financial Declarations.**   Financial Declarations and financial documents in family law cases do not count toward the page limit.

(g) **Expert Reports and Evaluations.**   Declarations, affidavits, and reports from guardians ad litem and expert witnesses in family law cases do not count toward the page limit but should be properly authenticated and filed as separate documents, under seal if required.

(h) **Previously filed documents.**   Any document already filed as part of the court record is subject to the provisions of WCCR 10.2(g).

(i) **Miscellaneous Exceptions.**   Deposition excerpts shall not count toward the page limit but motions, affidavits, declarations or briefs shall include citations to the relevant page and line.

(j) **Failure to Comply with Page Limits.**   In the event a filing party exceeds the page limits set out above, the court reserves the right to strike the pleadings, continue the hearing and/or impose sanctions.

[Adopted effective September 1, 2006; amended effective September 1, 2009.]

WCCR 17. UNLAWFUL DETAINER/EVICTION

Complaints for writs of restitution, money judgments, and other orders in unlawful detainer cases will be granted only under the following conditions:

(a) Individual property owners, lessors, sublessors, or their duly appointed representatives who are not lawyers but who are also plaintiffs may represent themselves if they choose not to be represented by a lawyer. All other plaintiffs (corporations, limited liability corporations and partnerships) must be represented by a lawyer and may not be represented by a corporate officer, partner, a person holding a power of attorney, property manager or any other non-lawyer.

(b) Real property owners, lessors, sublessors, or any person designated as their representative may properly be a plaintiff in unlawful detainer actions. All complaints must include the following:

(1) A copy of the rental agreement shall be filed with the complaint.

(2) Plaintiff owners of the real property must state ownership in their complaint.

(3) Plaintiff lessors and sublessors must state their status as lessor or sublessor in their complaint.

(4) Plaintiffs, such as property managers, who are representatives of property owners must state their status as representative in their complaint and must file with their complaint a copy of their written designation as representative.

(c) The court may order a writ of restitution to a property owner, lessor, sublessor, or representative of the property owner.

(d) The court will grant a money judgment only when:

(1) The plaintiff is the owner of the real property, or

(2) The plaintiff is a lessor or sublessor and the rental agreement requires payments to be made directly to the lessor or sublessor, or

(3) The plaintiff is a representative of the owner, the rental agreement requires payments to be made directly to the representative, and the appointment of the representative filed with the complaint authorizes the representative to collect judgments in their individual capacity.

[Adopted on an emergency basis, effective September 16, 2005. Amended and adopted on a permanent basis, effective September 1, 2006.]

WCCR 26. FILING OF DISCOVERY MATERIALS

Interrogatories, requests for production or inspection, requests for admissions, and the responses thereto shall not be filed with the court or clerk until required to support an application to the court for relief. The originals of such documents, including answers, shall be maintained by the issuing attorney for production at trial.

[Adopted effective June 1, 1991.]

WCCR 38. NOTICE OF JURY WAIVER

When a jury is waived after being demanded, notice shall be immediately given to the Calendar Clerk. Upon violation of this rule, the court may in its discretion assess full costs. A jury demand fee once paid will not be refunded.

[Adopted effective June 1, 1991.]

WCCR 40.1. TRIAL SETTINGS

(a) Note for Trial Docket. An attorney who desires to bring an issue of fact to trial shall serve and file a note for trial docket, noting the matter before the Calendar Clerk at the time shown on the Court Calendar Schedule. The note for trial docket shall contain:

(1) The title of the court, clerk's file number, a brief title of the cause, the words "Note for Trial Docket,"

(2) Name or names of the attorneys, or parties pro se, for both plaintiff and defendant,

(3) The nature of the cause, whether to be tried to a jury or to the court, date of service of last pleading,

(4) The attorney's or party's certification that all issues have been joined, and that all responsive pleadings as to all named parties have been filed or that proper defaults have been taken,

(5) An estimate of the time that will be required for trial,

(6) A statement that the case is not subject to mandatory arbitration (stating the grounds for exception from mandatory arbitration required under WCMAR) or that the cause is an appeal from an arbitration award, and

(7) The bar association membership number and signature of the attorney filing the note, designating the party(ies) represented by the attorney.

(8) A statement that either (i) all discovery in the case has been completed, or (ii) that the parties have filed an Agreed Order on Discovery, which order shall specify the order of discovery and completion dates of all discovery in the case and that all discovery will be concluded at least 30 days prior to the appointed trial date. A party who seeks a trial date but who cannot satisfy either (i) or (ii) must note the case for a scheduling conference with the trial judge.

(b) Trial Assignment.

(1) Counsel shall consult with the Calendar Clerk at or before the time of the trial setting calendar to secure a mutually agreeable trial date. If counsel are unable for any reason to obtain an agreed trial date, they shall appear before the Assigned Judge at the time of the trial setting calendar for trial setting.

(2) To be entitled to a trial assignment, the noting attorney must be present at the trial setting calendar in person or must have previously notified the Calendar Clerk of conflicting dates. However, if the noted attorney appears and requests a trial date, a date will be assigned even if the noting attorney fails to appear or provide conflicting dates. All parties will be held to the date assigned.

(c) Formal Order Required. No trial setting is complete until a judge has signed a formal order. The Trial Setting Order may contain additional information for all parties to follow in pre-trial practice.

(d) Service of Order. When an attorney obtains a trial setting order at a case setting calendar when opposing counsel or pro se party has not appeared, the order may indicate on the signature line that the party was noted, but did not appear. If the party was not noted for trial setting, then the order must have opposing counsel's signature on it before it shall be presented for judicial signature. The party presenting the order shall provide a copy of the trial setting order to opposing counsel or pro se party.

(e) Stacked Domestic Relations Calendar. In a domestic relations proceeding, the clerk will ordinarily assign trial of the case to the monthly stacked domestic relations calendar. If more than one or two hours will be required for trial of the case, the case will not be placed on the stacked calendar but will be given a regular trial date.

(f) Department Settings Tentative. A trial setting to a particular department is tentative only and does not assure trial before that department.

[Adopted effective June 1, 1991. Amended effective September 1, 1998; September 1, 2009.]

WCCR 40.2. RESPONSIBILITY TO BE READY FOR TRIAL, MOTIONS IN LIMINE

(a) Responsibility to be Ready for Trial

Counsel and parties in cases given a second or third setting shall be ready for trial on the date set. It is the obligation of the attorneys to be aware of the status of the trial calendar, keeping in mind WCCR 40.1 which provides that a case may be transferred to a different department for trial. A party is not released from a trial setting until noon of the last judicial day before trial, although the release time may be extended by the Presiding Judge for good cause.

(b) Motions in Limine

Routine motions in Limine may be heard the morning of trial. Notice should be given to the Assigned Judge's Judicial Assistant as to the nature, number, and expected time required for hearing of motions in Limine. For cases requiring substantial hearing time on multiple motions in Limine, that may affect the framing of issues for trial, parties should contact the Assigned Judge's Judicial Assistant at least two weeks prior to trial to arrange a special hearing time. Parties shall adhere to the timelines contained in WCCR 77.2 for substantial, written motions in Limine.

[Adopted effective June 1, 1991; amended effective September 1, 2009.]

WCCR 40.3. TRIAL CONTINUANCES

When a cause is set for trial, it must be tried or dismissed unless good cause is shown for continuance. No trial continuance will be granted merely upon stipulation of the parties. All motions for continuance shall be in writing and supported by an affidavit. The court may impose terms if a continuance is granted.

[Adopted effective June 1, 1991.]

WCCR 41.1. NOTICE OF SETTLEMENT

When a cause has been set for trial and then is settled, notice shall be immediately given to the Calendar Clerk. Upon violation of this rule, the court may in its discretion assess full costs. A jury demand fee once paid will not be refunded.

[Adopted effective June 1, 1991.]

WCCR 47.1. JUROR QUESTIONNAIRES

(a) Proposed questionnaires must be circulated and submitted to the Court for approval by noon on Thursday the week preceding trial. Proposed questionnaires will be approved by the Court no later than noon on Friday the week preceding trial. Questionnaires received after the noon deadline will not be accepted. Proposed questionnaires may be sent to the Assigned Judge using the calendar confirmation email address on the Court's home page at www. whatcomcounty.us/superior. Once approved by the Court, the party submitting the questionnaire shall prepare sufficient copies for the prospective jurors to complete, and *immediately* deliver said copies to the Assigned Judge's Judicial Assistant/Bailiff not later than 2:30 p.m. on Friday the week preceding trial.

(b) Unless otherwise directed, the Judicial Assistant/Bailiff will distribute case-specific questionnaires (including any case description cover sheet) at the conclusion of jury orientation. Once the questionnaires are completed, the Judicial Assistant/Bailiff will direct the jurors to return at a time specific for commencement of voir dire. The juror number on the questionnaire will match the predetermined, randomly selected seating order.

(c) Unless otherwise approved by the Court at the time the proposed questionnaire is approved, and in order to conserve significant taxpayer money in the form of juror compensation, the Court will commence voir dire the same day as the jurors initially report and complete any questionnaire. If there is known media interest in a specific case, and in such other cases as the Assigned Judge in his or her discretion deems proper, a Judge or Commissioner shall administer the jury oath to the jurors and instruct them to avoid the media and otherwise as appropriate.

(d) Once the Judicial Assistant/Bailiff has finished collecting and sorting the answered questionnaires, the attorney submitting the questionnaire shall retrieve the originals from the Judicial Assistant/Bailiff and prepare and deliver copies to opposing counsel. Copies of the seating order will also be available at this time. The original questionnaires shall then *immediately* be returned to the Judicial Assistant/Bailiff for filing with the Clerk. In the alternative, the answered questionnaires may be scanned for retrieval by both parties.

[Adopted effective September 1, 2009.]

WCCR 51. JURY INSTRUCTIONS

(a) Proposed jury instructions must be submitted by the beginning of trial in the following form:

1) *Civil Cases*: Prepare no fewer than five copies of each instruction, including any Washington Pattern Instructions. If there are more than two parties, prepare an additional copy for each additional party.

   a) Prepare one set of instructions with no numbering and no citations to be used by the Judge for the preparation of the final instructions given to the jury.

   b) Assemble four or more sets of proposed instructions, cited and numbered sequentially (e.g. P–1, D–6) in the lower right-hand corner, for distribution as follows:

   (1) One set to the clerk to file in the court file (marked Original),

   (2) One set to the judge (marked Judge Working Copy),

   (3) One set for the proponent and

   (4) One set for each opposing party

2) *Criminal Cases*: the prosecuting attorney will furnish the proposed instructions for the case; defense counsel need only furnish additional instructions felt to be applicable to the case. All jury instructions must be prepared as described in 1 a) and b), above.

[Adopted effective December 1, 1992; amended effective September 1, 2002.]

WCCR 53.2. REVIEW OF COMMISSIONER RULINGS

(a) All revisions of Commissioner rulings shall be de novo on the record made by the Commissioner, based only those materials, papers and pleadings in the court file and previously submitted to the Commissioner.

(b) Any party seeking a revision of a Commissioner's decision shall, in accordance with CR 59, file a Motion for Revision to be heard on the Assigned Judge's civil motion calendar in accordance with WCCR 77.2. Such a motion must be filed within 10 days of the entry of the order, and shall include the following:

(1) A statement of the issue or issues sought to be revised

(2) A brief statement why the moving party is seeking a revision

(3) A transcript of the hearing before the Commissioner

(4) Citations to the record where applicable

(c) Oral arguments shall be limited to ten minutes per side.

(d) No additional affidavits or other materials shall be filed, other than a brief setting forth the legal issue and argument of the parties. If a brief or legal memorandum was filed by a party before the Commissioner, no new brief or memorandum shall be submitted by that party on the Motion for Revision.

[Adopted effective September 1, 1995; amended effective September 1, 2009.]

WCCR 54. ENTRY OF ORDERS AND JUDGMENTS

(a) In civil cases tried to the court, findings, conclusions, and judgments shall be presented to the assigned or ruling judge within 20 days of the court's oral order or memorandum decision. Normally, hearings for presentation of judgments and post-trial motions will all be noted for the same time.

(b) When no appeal is intended, counsel by stipulation may eliminate findings and conclusions and may present a judgment only for signature, if allowed by CR 52.

(c) No judgment shall be taken upon a negotiable instrument until the original instrument has been filed.

(d) No judgment shall be taken upon an assigned cause of action until the written assignment is filed.

(e) Every judgment providing for payment of money shall include on its first page a judgment summary conforming to RCW 4.64.030.

(f) Presentation:

(1) *Time.* Orders and judgments may be presented pursuant to CR 52 and CR 54.

(2) *Conference of Counsel Required.* The court will not entertain any objection to properly served proposed orders, findings, conclusions and judgments unless counsel has conferred with respect to the objection. Counsel for the objecting party shall arrange for a mutually convenient conference in person or by telephone. If the court finds that counsel for any party has willfully refused or failed to confer in good faith, the court may require counsel or client or both to pay the reasonable expenses, including attorney fees, caused by the failure. The court may continue the hearing.

(3) *Written Objections.* Though not mandatory, the court urges counsel to prepare written objections so the court can compare paperwork easily. The preferred form is that used in session laws, where undesired language is struck through and new language is underlined.

(**g**) The Assigned Judge may impose sanctions in the case of excessive delay in presenting orders and judgments.

[Adopted effective June 1, 1991; amended effective September 1, 1996; September 1, 2009.]

WCCR 77.1. COURTROOM DRESS AND DECORUM

Persons who appear in court should dress in a manner appropriate to the dignity of the forum. Counsel should wear business attire; men should be in coat and tie. Counsel and pro se litigants should observe the formality consistent with good courtroom practice. This includes rising to address the court, deference to other counsel while speaking, and professional behavior at all times.

[Adopted effective June 1, 1991; amended effective September 1, 2009.]

WCCR 77.2. COURT CALENDAR SCHEDULE, PRE–ARRANGED SETTINGS, MOTION CALENDAR PROCEDURES, CONFIRMATION

(**a**) **Court Calendar Schedule:** Non-trial matters are scheduled on various calendars before the Assigned Judge and commissioners. Accompanying these rules as Appendix A is a copy of the current Court Calendar Schedule that contains information about each of the regular court calendars. The Court Calendar Schedule may be modified from time to time (including one-time changes for holidays or judicial conferences) without formal republication. Current calendar information, including a copy of the latest edition of the Court Calendar Schedule, may be obtained from the Clerk of the Superior Court, 311 Grand Avenue, Bellingham, WA 98225, (360) 676–6777, or from the Court's web page at www.whatcomcounty. us/superior/calendars/by subject. The Court Calendar Schedule details which matters require pre-arrangement, confirmation, or both.

(**b**) **Pre–Arranged Settings:** Counsel must pre-arrange non-trial special set matters by contacting the judicial assistant for the assigned judge for a setting in order for the matter to be placed on the judge's appropriate calendar. Special sets do not need to be confirmed, but should be in compliance with the timelines and page limits imposed by these local rules.

(**c**) **Friday Civil Motions:** The Friday civil/probate law and motion settings may be made without pre-arrangement subject to judicial unavailability as posted on the court's web page under "calendars" and must be confirmed no sooner than five judicial days prior to the hearing and no later than noon two judicial days prior to the hearing. Confirmations must be directed to the appropriate judicial assistant and may be made by email or telephonically, as indicated on the court's web page at www.whatcomcounty. us/superior. Otherwise, the matter will be stricken from the docket.

(**d**) **Motion Calendar Procedures**:

(1) Motions to be noted on the Motion Calendar shall be filed with the court and served on all parties by noon nine (9) court days prior to the hearing. A proposed form of an order, which the Court may adopt, modify or reject consistent with the Decision of the Court, shall be filed and served with the motion. Responses shall be filed and served on all parties by noon four (4) court days before hearing. Replies shall be filed and served on all parties-no later than noon two (2) days prior to the hearing. Parties should come to the motion calendar with original orders so that they may be entered without an additional hearing or expense wherever possible.

(2) Time for filing and service of motions as prescribed by these rules shall not apply to summary judgment motions. Summary judgment motions shall be served and filed pursuant to CR 56 and should comply with the terms of WCCR 10.3.

(3) If no one appears in opposition to a motion, upon proof of proper service the moving party may take the order requested unless the court shall deem it manifestly unauthorized. If no party appears, the motion may be deemed waived or stricken. No more than ten minutes will be allowed to each side for argument unless the court otherwise directs.

(4) Counsel shall immediately notify the assigned judge's Judicial Assistant when matters are continued or stricken by the parties prior to the time set for hearing. Motions may be continued to a subsequent motion day by filing and serving a "re-note" for motion docket or set down by the court for hearing at other specified times. Continuances are only tentative until a judge signs a written order of continuance.

(5) Counsel who fail to timely file papers, serve papers on opposing counsel or submit bench copies as

required by these rules may cause matters to be stricken, sanctions imposed, or terms assessed. Judge's copies of all documents, including proposed orders, are due at the time the motion/response/reply is filed with the court.

(6) Counsel may request telephonic appearance at a hearing, at the discretion of the assigned judge, by contacting the assigned judge's Judicial Assistant.

[Amended September 1, 1995; amended effective September 1, 1996; September 1, 2003; amended on an emergency basis effective June 11, 2007; amended effective September 1, 2009.]

WCCR 78. FURNISHING ENVELOPE TO CLERK

Whenever a person requests from the clerk a conformed copy of pleadings filed, or other written confirmation of duties performed or photocopies, that person shall furnish a stamped, self-addressed envelope or an appropriate pre-paid courier service voucher, along with such copies of a document a person wishes conformed.

[Adopted effective September 1, 1995; amended effective September 1, 2009.]

SPECIAL PROCEEDING RULES
(Cite as WCSPR)

WCSPR 93.04. PRE–SUBMISSION OF ADOPTION DOCUMENTS

All necessary consents shall be filed and judge copies of the proposed findings, conclusions, and de-

cree of adoption shall be submitted by noon two judicial days prior to the hearing.

[Adopted effective June 1, 1991.]

DOMESTIC RELATIONS PROCEEDINGS

WCSPR 94.04. SUPPORT MODIFICATION

(a) **Post-decree Discovery.** Post-decree formal discovery requests seeking financial information form an opposing party shall be allowed only when a support modification action has been filed unless:

(1) a duty to provide the requested information was imposed by a previous court order; or

(2) discovery has been ordered pursuant to a show cause hearing.

(b) **Service.** When a party serves a child support modification petition or answer, the party shall also serve the following papers:

(1) Washington State Child Support Worksheets and a Financial Declaration (Washington Pattern Form DR 01.0550), completed with all information known to the party;

(2) tax returns for the preceding three years, including all schedules, attachments, and W–2 forms;

(3) the party's current pay stub; and

(4) if a deviation from the standard calculation of child support is requested, additional affidavits to establish the basis for granting or denying the deviation.

(c) **Filing, Tax Returns.** Do not file tax returns, schedules, attachments, or W–2 forms. If a support modification order is appealed, the appellant shall supplement the record on appeal with the tax records referred to at the hearing.

(d) **Bench Copies.** Each party shall provide a bench copy of the following to the commissioner by noon two judicial days prior to the hearing:

(1) pleadings, worksheets, affidavits, tax information, memoranda, wage information, and other information which were served on opposing counsel; and

(2) Washington State Child Support Worksheets for the various reasonably possible scenarios, clearly presented in a form which lends itself to comparison and discussion.

(e) **Note for Motion Docket.** Child support modification matters are heard by a court commissioner. Child support modification matters shall be noted for any domestic calendar utilizing the court's form for that purpose, in which the filing attorney or party shall certify that the case is ready for hearing, that all issues have been joined, that all responsive pleadings as to all named parties have been filed or proper defaults have been taken, that all outstanding discovery in the case has been completed or that all parties have filed an agreed order on discovery which specifies the order and timing of discovery and terminates discovery 30 days before the hearing date noted.

(f) **Testimony Limited.** Testimony at the hearing will be allowed only upon prior authorization or when deemed necessary by the court. Only brief argument should be required.

[Amended September 1, 1995; amended on an emergency basis effective December 11, 2006; June 11, 2007.]

WCSPR 94.05. DOMESTIC RELATIONS SHOW CAUSE HEARINGS AND MOTIONS

(a) **Motion Calendar Procedures:** Motions to be noted on the Motion Calendar, including Motions for

Show Cause, shall be filed with the court by noon nine (9) court days prior to the hearing. Motions shall be filed and served upon all parties nine (9) court days before hearing. A proposed form of an order, which the Court may adopt, modify or reject consistent with the Decision of the Court, shall be served with the motion. Responses shall be filed and served on all parties by noon four (4) court days before hearing. Replies shall be filed and served on all parties-no later than noon two (2) days prior to the hearing. The moving party's affidavits shall be served with the motion; the responding party's affidavits shall be served with the response. All motions shall be in compliance with WCCR 10.3.

(b) Confirmation. A matter noted on the Domestic Relations Calendar must be confirmed with the Calendar Clerk no sooner than five judicial days prior to the hearing and no later than Noon two judicial days prior to the hearing. Confirmations may be made by email or telephonically, as indicated on the court's web page at www.whatcomcounty.us/superior. Otherwise, the matter will be stricken from the docket.

(c) Financial affidavits. When temporary support, maintenance, attorney fees, or costs are at issue, both parties shall file and serve with their pleadings a Financial Declaration (Washington Pattern Form DR 01.0550).

(d) Bench copies. Parties shall provide bench copies of pleadings in all cases consistent with WCCR 77.2(d)(5).

(e) Testimony limited. Domestic issues will normally be determined by affidavits alone. Where temporary custody is in dispute the court may set a time for taking oral testimony. Oral testimony may be permitted whenever the court feels that unusual circumstances make it necessary or the other party appears in court without counsel.

(f) Counsel may request telephonic appearance at a hearing, at the discretion of the assigned judge, by contacting the assigned judge's Judicial Assistant.

[Amended September 1, 1995; amended effective September 1, 1996; September 1, 2003; amended on an emergency basis effective June 11, 2007; amended effective September 1, 2009.]

WCSPR 94.06. PRETRIAL INFORMATION FORM, FINANCIAL AFFIDAVIT, AND TRIAL BRIEF

In all contested trials in domestic relations matters, except those placed on the stacked calendar, each party shall prepare a written pretrial information form indicating a proposed division of assets and liabilities in the form set forth in Appendix B. If child support, spousal maintenance, attorney fees, or costs are at issue, each party shall prepare a Financial Declaration, (Washington Pattern Form DR 01.0550.) The original forms and trial briefs shall be filed with

the clerk and copies served on opposing counsel by noon two judicial days prior to trial.

[Amended September 1, 1993.]

WCSPR 94.07. ENTRY OF DISSOLUTION DECREE BY DECLARATION OF JURISDICTIONAL FACTS

The court will enter an agreed or default decree of dissolution of marriage without a final hearing or oral testimony when at least one of the parties is represented by an attorney, the petitioner completes a Request for Entry of Decree and Declaration of Jurisdictional Facts in the form set forth in Appendix C, and:

(a) the respondent or respondent's attorney approves all of the final papers including the Request for Entry of Decree and Declaration of Jurisdictional Facts, or

(b) if the respondent is in default, the decree provides for only that relief requested in the petition, or

(c) if the respondent or co-petitioner joined in the petition and is unavailable to sign the final papers, the decree provides for only that relief requested in the petition.

[Adopted effective December 1, 1992.]

WCSPR 94.08. FILINGS IN FAMILY LAW CASES

(a) Application of Rule. This rule shall apply to:

(1) All family law petitions seeking dissolution of marriage, legal separation, or declaration of invalidity;

(2) Actions brought by parties to non-marital personal relationships involving parenting or distribution of assets/liabilities; and

(3) Actions to modify previously entered parenting plan final orders.

(b) Court's Automatic Temporary Order. Upon the filing of a Summons and Petition in any of the actions specified in Sections (a) (1) and (2) above, the court on its own motion shall automatically issue a Temporary Order that includes the following provisions:

(1) The parties be restrained from transferring, removing, encumbering, concealing or in any way disposing of any property except in the usual course of business or for the necessities of life or as agreed in writing by the parties. Each party shall notify the other party of any extraordinary expenditure made after the order is issued.

(2) The parties be restrained from assigning, transferring, borrowing, lapsing, surrendering or changing entitlement of any insurance policies of either or both parties whether medical, health, life or auto insurance, except as agreed in writing by the parties.

(3) Each party shall be immediately responsible for his or her own future debts whether incurred by credit card or loan, security interest or mortgage, except as agreed in writing by the parties.

(4) Both parties must have access to all tax, financial, legal, and household records. Reasonable access to records shall not be denied.

(5) For those actions in which children are involved:

i. each parent be restrained from changing the residence of the child(ren) until further court order, except as agreed in writing by the parties. Subsequent orders regarding parenting issues supercede previously issued orders to the extent the orders may be inconsistent.

ii. each parent shall insure that the child(ren) not be exposed to negative comments about the other parent. Neither parent shall make negative comments about the other parent in the presence of the child(ren).

(c) Filing of Parties' Financial Declarations and Verified Statement of Assets and Liabilities. Within 30 days after the filing of an answer or other responsive pleading in any of the actions specified in section (a) (1) and (2) above, each party shall serve on the opposing party:

(1) A Financial Declaration (in all cases involving a request for child support, maintenance or attorney fee, the declaration shall also be filed with the court); and

(2) A Verified Statement of Assets and Liabilities including both marital and separate assets and liabilities of any kind in the form set out in Appendix E. The Verified Statement of Assets and Liabilities shall not be filed with the court. Each party shall then file with the court a Declaration of Service attesting that the Financial Declaration and Verified Statement of Assets and Liabilities has been provided to the other party within the 30-day time limit. All parties have a duty to supplement the financial information when additional information becomes available.

(d) Required Attendance at Parenting Seminar. Within 30 days after the filing of an appearance or answer or other responsive pleading in any of the actions specified in Section (a) above which involves minor children, the parties shall register for a court approved parenting program on the effects of family transitions on children, unless the parties have previously attended such a course. In cases filed pursuant to the Uniform Parentage Act, RCW 26.26, the parenting program is required only if a party petitions for a permanent court-ordered residential schedule when no such schedule exists. If domestic violence has occurred in the relationship as evidenced by the criteria set forth in (g) (2)-(4) below, then the parties shall individually attend a court-approved parenting program which includes the effects of family violence on children. Each party shall attend the appropriate seminar within 60 days of registering.

(e) After completion of the appropriate seminar, each party shall file with the court the seminar completion certificate provided by the sponsoring agency or provider.

(f) The court may waive attendance at the parenting program upon motion for good cause shown. Unless waived by the court, failure to attend the appropriate parenting program may result in a finding of contempt and imposition of sanctions.

(g) Exchange of Parenting Plans. Within 14 days of completing the appropriate program as described in (d) above, each parent shall provide the other parent with a Proposed Parenting Plan if they have not already done so. The requirement of a "behavioral evaluation" shall be added as a sub-category to non-emergency health care in the Major Decisions section of the Parenting Plan. Where there is joint decision-making, the following "red flag" behavior provision shall be included in the Parenting Plan:

(1) The parents shall be responsible to observe and note at-risk behavior of the children, including, but not limited to:

(i) Depressed mood or verbalizing suicidal thoughts,

(ii) Increase in aggressive behavior or acting out,

(iii) Running away from home,

(iv) Abnormal amount of physical illness,

(v) Changes in sleeping or eating habits,

(vi) Undesirable changes in school confirmed by teacher, such as significant drop in grades, missing classes, disciplinary problems, etc.,

(vii) Juvenile delinquency problems.

(2) If any of the above symptoms or problems occur and last for two weeks or more, the parents shall address the problem with each other and with the child.

(3) If the parents see no change in the symptoms or behavior within two weeks, the child's health care physician shall evaluate the child. The parents have designated Dr. _____ as the child's health care physician.

(h) Mediation in Contested Cases. Except as provided in Section (g) below, in all cases specified in Section (a) having unresolved issues (except child support issues), both parties shall in good faith engage in mediation with a court-approved mediator in an effort to resolve the case. The parties may either agree to a mediator from the court-approved list or the mediator will be determined by use of a strike list. The cost of mediation shall be paid by the parties in proportion to their incomes. Either party may seek a court apportionment of the cost of mediation.

(i) When Mediation Is Not Required. Mediation shall be required as provided in section (f), except in the following cases:

(1) For good cause shown upon motion and approval by the court; or

(2) Where a domestic violence restraining order or protection order (excluding ex-parte orders) involving the parties has been entered by a court at any time within the previous 12 months;

(3) Where a domestic violence no contact order exists pursuant to RCW 10.99;

(4) Where the court upon motion finds that domestic abuse has occurred between the parties and that such abuse would interfere with arms length mediation.

(j) Notwithstanding the foregoing, either party may by motion seek a court order requiring mandatory mediation in a case where it would not be required as set forth in (g)(2), (g)(3) or (g)(4) above if the moving party believes that the parties would be able to mediate their dispute at arms length under the particular circumstances of the case.

(k) Settlement Conferences. If, after mediation in good faith, or where mediation is not required, there remain unresolved issues in any case specified in Section (a), the parties shall personally participate in a settlement conference conducted by a judicial officer or, for good cause shown, a person approved by the court in advance. Five days prior to the settlement conference, each party shall submit their list of unresolved issues to the settlement officer. The settlement conference shall take place no later than 2 weeks prior to trial.

(l) Exchange of Settlement Offers. If the settlement conference does not result in complete resolution of the case, each party shall submit to the other a written settlement proposal addressing all unresolved issues. This offer shall be submitted within 5 days of the settlement conference.

(m) Failure to Comply. A party's compliance with the provisions of this rule may be enforced upon Motion and Order to Show Cause. Unless compliance is waived by the court for good cause shown, the court may order appropriate sanctions including costs, attorney's fees, and adoption of the complying party's proposal.

(n) Award of Attorney's Fees. Requests for fees at the conclusion of trial may be denied unless the settlement proposals required in section (i) are filed with the court. In no event shall the settlement proposals be filed or otherwise communicated to the court until after trial. In awarding fees and costs the court may, in addition to other considerations required by law, consider the settlement proposals.

(o) Judicial Information System Background Checks. Prior to presenting a permanent parenting plan to the court for approval, the party or parties shall submit a completed judicial information service (JIS) background check form to the Whatcom County Clerk. Such request shall include the names and dates of birth of all persons residing in each residence and must be submitted no fewer than fourteen days prior to the date of presentation of the final parenting plan. Upon receipt of a completed JIS background check form, the Court shall complete a search of the Judicial Information System for the existence of any information and proceedings relevant to the placement of the child. This search shall be performed no more than 30 days prior to the proposed date of presentation of the permanent parenting plan. The results of such search shall be available to the judicial officer presiding over the entry of the permanent parenting plan at least two court days prior to the proposed presentation date. Both the completed JIS background check form and the results of the search shall be filed under seal in the GR 22 file.

[Adopted effective September 1, 1998; amended effective September 1, 2000; September 1, 2002; amended on an emergency basis effective January 18, 2007; amended effective September 1, 2009.]

WCSPR 98.16.　PROBATE AND GUARDIANSHIP

(a) Probate. Wills may be admitted and personal representative appointed upon either oral testimony or appropriate affidavits. A copy of the death certificate shall be filed with the Social Security number redacted unless otherwise ordered by the court.

(b) Guardianship.

(1) All interim and final reports, together with a proposed order, shall be filed with the clerk and a judge's copy provided to the court by noon two judicial days prior to the hearing. If a hearing is not required on an interim report, it shall be so stated on the judge's copy supplied at the time the original is filed.

(2) The report shall contain a statement of compliance with the Internal Revenue Code.

(3) All accountings shall list the opening balance, receipts, disbursements, and ending balance. Vouchers and receipts shall be available for inspection but shall not be filed unless ordered by the court.

(4) Time sheets of guardians, guardians ad litem (whether county paid or privately paid) and attorneys are required to assist the court in fixing fees. Judge's copies shall be supplied no later than noon two days prior to the hearing.

(5) Failure without excuse to file reports as required by law or by this rule may result in sanctions by the court and imposition of terms, including but not limited to denial or reduction of requested fees.

[Adopted effective June 1, 1991; amended effective September 1, 2009.]

GUARDIAN AD LITEM RULES
(Cite as WCGALR)

WCGALR 4. AUTHORITY OF GUARDIAN AD LITEM

In addition to other elements required and contained in any order appointing a guardian ad litem, the following provisions shall be included:

(a) Guardianship Cases. Orders appointing guardians and guardians ad litem in guardianship matters shall include the following provisions:

IT IS FURTHER ORDERED, that within thirty (30) days of the entry of the order appointing a guardian herein the guardian shall file a receipt for the blocked funds of the guardianship and a bond, if any, as ordered by this court. The guardian or the guardian's attorney shall serve the guardian ad litem with a conformed copy of the receipt and a copy of the filed bond. If no receipt or bond has been filed within thirty days of the entry of the order appointing a guardian, the guardian ad litem shall contact the guardian and determine the reason why the receipt or bond has not been filed. The guardian ad litem shall file a status report about the reason for the delay, and if the guardian ad litem has any cause for concern about the protection of the ward's assets, the guardian ad litem should immediately advise the court that a show cause hearing is warranted.

Once the guardian ad litem receives satisfactory proof that the receipt or bond has been filed, the guardian ad litem or petitioner's attorney, if any, shall move the court for an order discharging the guardian ad litem and approving any additional fees and costs to be charged to the guardianship estate which were incurred by the guardian ad litem in monitoring the receipt and bond status.

The court may not authorize compensation to the guardian ad litem for any action by the guardian ad litem taken beyond the duties outlined in order.

(b) All Cases: Orders appointing guardians ad litem in guardianship matters shall include the following provisions:

The guardian ad litem will provide the parties with an itemized accounting of time, billing and costs for services each month. Payment is due within fifteen days after billing each month. Should a party disagree with an amount billed, he or she shall immediately contact the Guardian ad Litem to discuss the billing. If the matter is not resolved, the party shall note the matter upon the court's calendar for review and notify the guardian ad litem of the date and time of the hearing. A party shall be liable to the guardian ad litem for court costs, interest and attorney fees if collection action is required because payment was not made on time.

The parties' obligation to pay guardian ad litem fees and costs is reasonably related to their support obligation and may be enforced by contempt proceedings at any time notwithstanding the entry of a final decree or order of dismissal of this action. At a contempt hearing, the responding party has the burden of establishing a justifiable excuse for non-payment. If non-payment is not excused, the party may be subject to jail time, fines, attorney fees, and other compensatory relief.

[Adopted effective September 1, 2006.]

GUARDIAN AD LITEM GRIEVANCE PROCEDURES
(Cite as WCGAL)

WCGAL 7.1. GUARDIAN AD LITEM ADVISORY COMMITTEE

The Court's Guardian ad Litem Advisory Committee, hereinafter referred to as the "Committee," will administer complaints about guardians ad litem.

[Adopted effective September 1, 2000.]

WCGAL 7.2. SUBMISSION OF COMPLAINTS

All complaints must be in writing and must be submitted to the Superior Court Administrator. All complaints must bear the signature, name and address of the person filing the complaint.

[Adopted effective September 1, 2000.]

WCGAL 7.3. REVIEW OF COMPLAINT

1. Upon receipt of a written complaint, the Court Administrator shall convene the Committee to review the complaint. Upon review of the complaint, the Committee shall either:

A. Make a finding that the complaint is with regard to a case then pending in the court and decline to review the complaint and so inform the complainant. In such instances the Committee shall advise the complainant that the complaint may only be addressed in the context of the case at bar, either by seeking the removal of the guardian ad litem or by contesting the information or recommendation contained in the guardian ad litem's report or testimony. In such cases the Committee and its members shall perform its role in such a manner as to assure that the trial judge remains uninformed as to the complaint; or

B.   Make a finding that the complaint has no merit on its face, and decline to review the complaint and so inform the complainant; or

C.   Make a finding that the complaint appears to have merit and request a written response from the Guardian ad Litem within 10 business days, detailing the specific issues in the complaint to which the Committee desires a response. The Committee shall provide the Guardian ad Litem with a copy of the original complaint. In considering whether the complaint has merit, the Committee shall consider whether the complaint alleges the Guardian ad Litem has:

  1) Violated a code of conduct;

  2) Misrepresented his or her qualifications to serve as a Guardian ad Litem;

  3) Breached the confidentiality of the parties;

  4) Falsified information in a report to the court or in testimony before the court;

  5) Failed, when required, to report abuse of a child;

  6) Communicated with a judicial officer ex-parte concerning a case for which he or she is serving as a guardian ad litem;

  7) Violated state or local laws or court rules; or,

  8) Taken or failed to take any other action which would reasonably place the suitability of the person to serve as a Guardian ad Litem in question.

[Adopted effective September 1, 2000.]

WCGAL 7.4.   RESPONSE AND FINDINGS

1.   Upon receipt of a written response to a complaint from the Guardian ad Litem, the Committee shall make a finding as to each of the specific issues in the complaint to which the Committee desires a response, as delineated in the Committee's letter to the Guardian ad Litem. Such findings shall state that either there is no merit to the issue based upon the Guardian ad Litem's response or that there is merit to the issue.

2.   The Committee shall have the authority to issue a written admonishment, a written reprimand, refer the Guardian ad Litem to additional training, or recommend to the Presiding Judge that the Court suspend or remove the Guardian ad Litem from the

registry. In considering a response, the Committee shall take into consideration any prior complaints that resulted in an admonishment, reprimand, referral to training, or suspension or removal from a registry. If a Guardian ad Litem is listed on more than one registry, the suspension or removal may apply to each registry the Guardian ad Litem is listed on, at the discretion of the Committee.

3.   The complainant and the Guardian ad Litem shall be notified in writing of the Committee's decision following receipt of the Guardian ad Litem's response.

[Adopted effective September 1, 2000.]

WCGAL 7.5.   CONFIDENTIALITY

1.   A complaint shall be deemed confidential for all purposes unless the committee has determined that it has merit under WCMAR 7.4, above.

2.   Any record of complaints filed which are not deemed by the committee to have merit shall be confidential and shall not be disclosed except by court order.

[Adopted effective September 1, 2000.]

WCGAL 7.6.   COMPLAINT PROCESSING TIME STANDARDS

1.   Complaints shall be resolved within twenty-five (25) days of the date of receipt of the written complaint if a case is pending.

2.   Complaints shall be resolved within sixty (60) days of the date of receipt of the written complaint if the complaint is filed subsequent to the conclusion of a case.

[Adopted effective September 1, 2000.]

WCGAL 7.7.   REMOVAL FROM REGISTRY

1.   When a guardian ad litem is removed from the court's registry pursuant to the disposition of a grievance hereunder, the Court Administrator shall send a notice of such removal to the Office of the Administrator for the Courts.

2.   When the Court Administrator receives notice from the Office of the Administrator for the Courts that a guardian ad litem on the court's registry has been removed from the registry of any other Washington Superior Court the Administrator shall advise the Presiding Judge of such removal.

[Adopted effective September 1, 2000.]

CRIMINAL RULES
(Cite as WCCrR)

WCCrR 3.1. COUNSEL FEES IN CRIMINAL CASES

(a) Following a two-week period for evaluation, a commitment to represent a person in a criminal proceeding and the acceptance of fees requires the attorney to continue representing the client throughout the proceedings.

(b) A commitment to represent includes an assessment of the investigation required, the need for experts and the client's ability to pay fees and costs. Ordinarily, the court will not order payment for expert and investigation costs at public expense where private representation has been retained. In any event, the county will not pay for expenses incurred without prior court order authorizing such expense to be incurred.

[Adopted effective June 1, 1991.]

WCCrR 6.17. JUROR QUESTIONNAIRES

Juror questionnaires may be used in accordance with WCCR 47.1.

[Adopted effective September 1, 2009.]

WCCrR 6.18. RESPONSIBILITY TO BE READY FOR TRIAL, MOTIONS IN LIMINE

(a) Responsibility to be Ready for Trial

A party is not released from a trial setting until noon of the last judicial day before trial, although the release time may be extended by the Presiding Judge for good cause.

(b) Motions in Limine

Routine motions in Limine can be heard the morning of trial or by special set in accordance with WCCR 40.2(b).

[Adopted effective September 1, 2009.]

WCCrR 7.2. CRIMINAL SENTENCE FINANCIAL OBLIGATIONS

This rule applies to any criminal judgment and sentence which orders a defendant to pay a fine, assessment, restitution, court costs, or attorney fees. This rule shall be referred to and incorporated by reference in any such judgment and sentence.

(a) **Time Payments.** The ordered financial obligations shall be paid in equal monthly installments sufficient to completely pay the entire amount during the defendant's term of supervision by the Department of Corrections, unless a different rate is set by the court. The first payment shall be due 30 days after the date of judgment or defendant's release from total confinement, whichever occurs last. Subsequent payments shall be due on the same day of each following month.

(b) **Failure to Pay, Report by Defendant.** If a monthly payment is not made when due, the defendant shall, by the payment due date, submit to the Department a written report. The report may be submitted on a form available from the Department. It shall contain the following information:

(1) Gross income of defendant and spouse from all sources for the prior calendar month;

(2) All mandatory deductions from gross income (income tax, FICA, union dues, etc.);

(3) All fixed monthly obligations paid (rent, mortgage, loans, purchase contracts, etc.), setting out the name and addresses of the payees and the purpose of the payments;

(4) All other expenditures, setting out the name and addresses of the payees and the purpose of the payments. ("Miscellaneous" expenditures shall not exceed five percent of the gross monthly income.)

(5) *Employment.* If the defendant claims that the failure to make a monthly payment was due to lack of employment of the defendant or spouse, the report shall state all efforts made by the defendant or spouse to obtain employment, setting out the name and address or the prospective employers or employment resources or agencies contacted and the name of the person to whom application for employment was made.

(6) *Employment Termination.* If the defendant claims that the failure to make a monthly payment was due to employment termination of the defendant or spouse, the defendant shall attach to the report a written statement of the employer stating the reasons for the employment termination.

(7) *Disability.* If the defendant claims that the failure to make a monthly payment was due to a physical or emotional inability to obtain or hold employment, the defendant shall attach to the report a written physician's statement setting out the nature and cause of the physical or emotional disability.

(8) *Defendant's Signature.* The report shall be signed by the defendant under penalty of perjury, and shall be admissible in a hearing held pursuant to RCW 9.94A to determine whether a condition or requirement of a sentence has been violated.

(c) **Failure to Pay or Report, Effect.** If the defendant fails to make a required monthly payment and also fails to file a required report, the court may modify its order of judgment and sentence and impose further punishment in accordance with RCW 9.94A.

(d) Petition to Modify. The defendant may, at any time, petition the court to adjust the amount of installment payments or adjust the total amount due to fit the defendant's changed financial situation, or to relieve undue hardship to the defendant or the defendant's dependents.

[Adopted effective June 1, 1991.]

MANDATORY ARBITRATION RULES
(Cite as WCMAR)

SCOPE AND PURPOSE OF RULES

WCMAR 1.1. APPLICATION OF RULES— PURPOSE AND DEFINITIONS

(a) Purpose. The Whatcom County Mandatory Arbitration Rules (hereinafter referred to as WCMAR) implement RCW 7.06 and the Superior Court Mandatory Arbitration Rules (MAR) adopted by the Supreme Court. Mandatory arbitration provides a simplified and economical procedure for obtaining the prompt and equitable resolution of disputes. Mandatory Arbitration Rules (MAR) as supplemented by these local rules (WCMARs) are not designed to address every question which may arise during the arbitration process, and the rules give considerate discretion to the arbitrator. The arbitrator should not hesitate to exercise that discretion. Arbitration hearings should be informal and expeditious, consistent with the purpose of relevant statutes and rules.

(b) "Director" Defined. In these rules, "Director" means the Director of Arbitration for the Whatcom County Superior Court. The appointment of the director and other administrative matters are addressed in WCMAR 8.6, Administration.

[Adopted effective December 1, 1992.]

WCMAR 1.2. MATTERS SUBJECT TO MANDATORY ARBITRATION

Any civil action filed in Whatcom County Superior Court, other than an appeal from a court of limited jurisdiction, is subject to mandatory arbitration under these rules if the sole relief sought is as money judgment (a) in which no party asserts a claim in excess of the amount authorized by RCW 7.06.020, exclusive of attorney fees, interest, and costs, or, (b) in which all parties for purposes of arbitration waive claims in excess of the amount authorized in RCW 7.06.020, exclusive of attorney fees, interest, and costs. Parties are encouraged to stipulate to the arbitration of any matter in controversy. See WCMAR 8.1.

[Adopted effective June 1, 1991.]

WCMAR 1.3. RELATIONSHIP TO SUPERIOR COURT JURISDICTION AND OTHER RULES—MOTIONS

All motions before the court relating to arbitrability or the assignment of an arbitrator shall be noted on the civil motions calendar in accordance with WCCR 77.2, except as otherwise provided in these arbitration rules. Once cases have been transferred to arbitration, all motions shall be heard by the arbitrator. In the event that motions concerning arbitrability or the assignment of an arbitrator are filed after a case has been transferred to arbitration but before an arbitrator has been assigned, then such motions may be noted for consideration by the Superior Court or may be noted for consideration by the arbitrator once assigned. See also WCMAR 2.2 and 3.2.

[Adopted effective June 1, 1991.]

TRANSFER TO ARBITRATION AND ASSIGNMENT OF ARBITRATOR

WCMAR 2.1. TRANSFER TO ARBITRATION

(a) Demand for Arbitration. In every civil case, when any party has determined that the case is ready for trial and that the case is subject to mandatory arbitration, such party shall file with the clerk its Note for Motion Docket and Demand for Arbitration, setting the matter on the Motion Docket not earlier than the next motion calendar after the expiration of 14 days from the date such Demand is filed. At the same time the party demanding arbitration shall submit its proposed order on the form prescribed by the court. Cases shall be transferred to arbitration only by court order.

An order of transfer to arbitration may be secured:

(1) Upon stipulation and order submitted by all the parties;

(2) Upon Demand for Arbitration filed by a party, set for hearing on the court's motion docket, when no object has been filed prior to the hearing;

(3) By order of the Court after hearing on the merits.

(b) Response to a Demand for Arbitration. Within 14 days after the date the Demand for Arbitration, Note for the Motion Docket, and Order have been filed and mailed to all parties or their attorneys, or the later of such dates, any party disagreeing with the Demand for Arbitration shall serve and file a response to the Demand for Arbitration with the clerk and on all other parties. In the absence of such response, the Demand for Arbitration shall be deemed correct and the non-responding party shall be deemed to have stipulated to arbitration. Responses asserting that the case is not subject to mandatory arbitration shall be heard on the date noted for hearing on the Demand for Arbitration.

(c) Failure to File—Amendments. A party failing to serve and file an original response within the time prescribed may later do so only upon leave of court. A party may amend the Demand for Arbitration or response at any time before the hearing on the Demand for Arbitration.

(d) Stipulation. A cause in which all parties file a stipulation to arbitrate under MAR 8.1(b) may be transferred to arbitration by court order presented to the court with the stipulation.

[Adopted effective June 1, 1991.]

WCMAR 2.2. HEARING TO DETERMINE ARBITRABILITY

A motion to establish whether a case is subject to arbitration shall be governed by the state and local rules pertaining to civil motions practice. See WCMAR 2.1(c).

[Adopted effective June 1, 1991.]

WCMAR 2.3. ASSIGNMENT OF ARBITRATOR

(a) Generally; Stipulations. The parties are encouraged to stipulate to an arbitrator. A master list of arbitrators will be furnished upon request. In the absence of a stipulation, a list of five arbitrators will be provided to the parties and the arbitrator will be chosen from among the five proposed arbitrators in the manner defined by this rule.

(b) Response by Parties. Each party may, within 14 days after a list of proposed arbitrators is mailed to the parties, nominate one or two arbitrators and strike two arbitrators from the list. If both parties respond, an arbitrator nominated by both parties will be appointed. If no arbitrator has been nominated by both parties, the Director will appoint an arbitrator from among those not stricken by either party.

(c) Response by Only One Party. If only one party responds within 14 days, the Director will appoint an arbitrator nominated by that party.

(d) No Response. If neither party responds within 14 days, the Director will appoint one of the five proposed arbitrators.

(e) Additional Arbitrators for Additional Parties. If there are more than two adverse parties, such parties may request the Director to include additional proposed arbitrators on the list, with the above principles of selection to be applied. The number of adverse parties and the number of additional proposed arbitrators shall be determined by the Director, subject to review by the Presiding Judge.

[Adopted effective June 1, 1991.]

ARBITRATORS

WCMAR 3.1. QUALIFICATIONS

(a) Minimum Qualifications. An arbitrator must be a member of the Washington State Bar Association who has been admitted to the Bar for a minimum of five years and who is a current member of the Whatcom County Bar Association, or who is a retired judge. By stipulation, the parties to a case may waive this requirement.

(b) Arbitration Panel. There shall be a panel of arbitrators in such numbers as the Administrative Committee may from time to time determine. A person desiring to serve as an arbitrator shall complete an information sheet on the form prescribed by the court. A list showing the names of arbitrators available to hear cases and the information sheets will be available for public inspection in the Director's office. The oath of office on the form prescribed by the court must be completed and filed prior to an applicant being placed on the panel.

(c) Refusal; Disqualification. The appointment of an arbitrator is subject to the right of that person to refuse to serve. An arbitrator should notify the

Director if his impartiality might reasonably be questioned. Counsel knowing any facts which would raise a reasonable question of the impartiality of the assigned arbitrator shall notify the arbitrator and the Director. In the absence of such notice, the grounds there for are deemed waived. If disqualified, the arbitrator must immediately return all materials in a case to the Director.

[Adopted effective June 1, 1991.]

WCMAR 3.2. AUTHORITY AND RESPONSIBILITY OF ARBITRATORS

An arbitrator has the authority and the responsibility to:

(a) Conduct the arbitration in an equitable and impartial manner, in accordance with applicable statutes and rules, and to make awards;

(b) Determine the time, place, and procedure to present a motion before the arbitrator.

(c) Require a party or attorney representing such party, or both, to pay the reasonable expenses, including attorney's fees, caused by the failure of such party or attorney, or both, to obey an order of the arbitrator, unless the arbitrator finds that the failure was substantially justified or that other circumstances make an award of expenses unjust. The arbitrator shall make a special award for such expenses and shall file such award with the County Clerk, with proof of service on each party. The aggrieved party shall have 10 days thereafter to appeal the award of such expenses in accordance with the procedures prescribed in RCW 2.24.050. If within 10 days after the award is filed no party appeals, a judgment shall be entered in a manner described generally under MAR 6.3;

(d) Award attorney's fees as authorized by these rules, by contract or by law, as if the matter were tried in court;

(e) Issue a subpoena in accordance with MAR 4.3.

[Amended September 1, 1995.]

PROCEDURES AFTER ASSIGNMENT

WCMAR 4.1. RESTRICTION ON COMMUNICATION BETWEEN ARBITRATOR AND PARTIES

(No Local Rule)

WCMAR 4.2. DISCOVERY

(a) Generally. In determining when additional discovery beyond that directly authorized by MAR 4.2 is reasonably necessary, the arbitrator shall balance the benefits of discovery against the burdens and expenses. Authorized discovery shall be conducted in accordance with the Civil Rules except that motions concerning discovery shall be determined by the arbitrator.

(b) Discovery Pending at the Time Arbitrator Is Assigned. Discovery pending at the time the case is assigned to an arbitrator is stayed unless reinstated by the arbitrator, except as the parties may stipulate or as authorized by MAR 4.2.

(c) Admissibility of Discovery. All discovery admissible under the Civil Rules or Rules of Evidence will be admissible at the arbitration hearing, whether or not such discovery was produced before or after the appointment of an arbitrator.

[Adopted effective June 1, 1991.]

WCMAR 4.3. SUBPOENA

(No Local Rule)

HEARING

WCMAR 5.1. NOTICE OF HEARING— TIME AND PLACE— CONTINUANCE

An arbitration hearing may be scheduled at any reasonable time and place chosen by the arbitrator. The arbitrator shall give reasonable notice of the hearing date and any continuance to the Director. The parties may stipulate to a continuance without court order. However, no continuance, or combination of continuances, shall be for more than 60 days, without a court order.

[Adopted effective June 1, 1991.]

WCMAR 5.2. PRE–HEARING STATE- MENT OF PROOF—DOCUMENTS FILED WITH COURT

In addition to the requirements of MAR 5.2, at least 14 days prior to the date of the arbitration hearing, each party shall furnish the arbitrator with copies of pertinent pleadings previously filed by such party, a list of witnesses whom the party intends to call at the arbitration hearing and any other documents contained in the court file which that party deems rele- vant. The court file shall remain with the County Clerk.

[Amended September 1995.]

WCMAR 5.3. CONDUCT OF HEARING— RULES OF EVIDENCE

(a) Conduct of Hearing. The hearing shall be conducted pursuant to MAR 5.3.

(b) Recording. The hearing may be recorded electronically or otherwise by any party at the party's expense.

(c) Rules of Evidence, Generally. The Arbitrator shall determine to what extent the Rules of Evidence shall apply.

(d) Certain Documents Presumed Admissible. The documents listed below, if relevant, are presumed admissible at an arbitration hearing, subject to the discretion of the Arbitrator, but only if (1) the party offering the document serves on all parties a notice identifying the documents to be introduced, accompanied by a copy of the document and the name, address, and telephone number of its author or maker, at least 14 days prior to the hearing in accordance with MAR 5.2; and (2) the party offering the document similarly has furnished all other parties copies of all other related documents from the same author or maker. This rule does not restrict argument or proof relating to the weight of the evidence admitted, nor does it restrict the arbitrator's authority to determine the weight of the evidence after hearing all of the evidence and the arguments of opposing parties. The documents presumed admissible under this rule are:

(1) A bill, report, chart, or record of a hospital, doctor, dentist, registered nurse, licensed practical nurse, physical therapist, psychiatrist, psychologist, or other health care provider, on a letterhead or billhead;

(2) A bill for drugs, medical appliances, or other related expenses on a letterhead or billhead;

(3) A bill for, or an estimate of, property damage on a letterhead or billhead. In the case of a bill for repairs completed, a paid receipt showing that the repairs were made, stating whether the bill represents complete or partial repairs and in the case of partial repairs an estimate of the cost to complete the remaining repairs;

(4) A police, weather, wage loss, or traffic signal report, generated in the normal course of business, without the need for formal proof of authentication or identification;

(5) A standard life expectancy table provided in Appendix "B" to the Washington Pattern Instructions (WPI);

(6) A photograph, x-ray, drawing, map, blueprint, or similar documentary evidence, without the need for formal proof or authentication or identification;

(7) The written statement of any other witness, including the written report of an expert witness, and including a statement of opinion which the witness would be allowed to express if testifying in person, if it is made by affidavit or by declaration under penalty of perjury;

(8) A document not specifically covered by any of the foregoing provisions but having equivalent circumstantial guarantees of trustworthiness, the admission of which would serve the interests of justice.

(e) Opposing Party May Subpoena Author or Maker as Witness. Any other party may subpoena the author or maker of a document admissible under this rule, at that party's expense, and examine the author or maker as if under cross examination.

[Adopted effective June 1, 1991.]

WCMAR 5.4. ABSENCE OF PARTY AT HEARING

(No Local Rule)

AWARD

WCMAR 6.1. FORM AND CONTENT OF AWARD

(a) Form. The award shall be prepared on the form prescribed by the court.

(b) Return of Exhibits. When an award is filed, the arbitrator shall return all exhibits to the parties who offered them during the hearing, after allowing opportunity for opposing counsel to make copies, when requested.

[Adopted effective June 1, 1991.]

WCMAR 6.2. FILING OF AWARD

A request by an arbitrator for an extension of time for the filing of an award under MAR 6.2 may be presented to the Director, ex parte. The Director

may grant or deny the request, subject to review by the Presiding Judge. The arbitrator shall give the parties notice of any extension granted.

[Adopted effective June 1, 1991.]

WCMAR 6.3. JUDGMENT ON AWARD

(a) Presentation. Any party may note the arbitration award on any civil law and motion calendar, on five days' notice in accordance with MAR 6.3.

(b) Modification or Correction of Award. Any application for the modification or correction of any award permitted by statute shall be made in accordance with RCW 7.04.090.

[Adopted effective June 1, 1991.]

TRIAL DE NOVO

WCMAR 7.1. REQUEST FOR TRIAL DE NOVO—CALENDAR

When a trial de novo is requested as provided in MAR 7.1, the party requesting the trial de novo shall simultaneously file with the clerk its note for trial setting, its jury demand and jury fee, if appropriate.

[Adopted effective June 1, 1991.]

WCMAR 7.2. PROCEDURE AT TRIAL

The clerk shall seal any award if a trial de novo is requested.

[Adopted effective June 1, 1991.]

WCMAR 7.3.   COSTS AND ATTORNEY FEES

MAR 7.3 shall apply only to costs and reasonable attorney's fees incurred since the filing of the request for a trial de novo.

[Adopted effective June 1, 1991.]

GENERAL PROVISIONS

WCMAR 8.1.   STIPULATIONS—EFFECT ON RELIEF GRANTED

If a case not otherwise subject to mandatory arbitration is transferred to arbitration by stipulation, the arbitrator may grant any relief which could have been granted if the case were determined by a judge.

[Adopted effective June 1, 1991.]

WCMAR 8.2.   LOCAL RULES

(No Local Rule)

WCMAR 8.3.   EFFECTIVE DATE

(No Local Rule)

WCMAR 8.4.   TITLE AND CITATION

These rules are known and cited as the Whatcom County Superior Court Local Mandatory Arbitration Rules. "WCMAR" is the official abbreviation.

[Adopted effective June 1, 1991.]

WCMAR 8.5.   COMPENSATION OF ARBITRATOR

(a) **Generally.** Arbitrators shall be compensated in the same amount and manner as judges pro tempore of the Superior Court. Hearing time and reasonable preparation time are compensable, and reasonable costs incurred by the arbitrator are reimbursable.

(b) **Form.** When the award is filed, the arbitrator shall submit to the Director a request for payment on a form prescribed by the court. The Director shall determine the amount of compensation and costs, if any, to be paid. The decision of the Director will be reviewed by the Presiding Judge at the request of the arbitrator. Compensation to the arbitrator and costs

reimbursement shall not exceed amounts set by statute, in any case, without special approval by the Presiding Judge.

[Adopted effective June 1, 1991.]

WCMAR 8.6.   ADMINISTRATION

(a) The Presiding Judge shall designate a person to serve as Director of Arbitration. The Director, under the supervision of the Presiding Judge, shall supervise arbitration under these rules, and perform any additional duties which may be delegated by the Presiding Judge.

(b) There shall be an Administrative Committee composed of the Presiding Judge, the Assistant to the Superior Court, and three members of the Whatcom County Bar Association. The members of the Whatcom County Bar Association shall be appointed by said Association and shall serve for staggered three year terms during which terms they shall not be eligible to serve as an arbitrator hereunder. They may be reappointed.

(c) The Administrative Committee shall have the power and duty to:

(1) Appoint the panel of arbitrators provided in Local Mandatory Arbitration Rule 23.1(b);

(2) Remove a person from a panel of arbitrators;

(3) Establish procedures for selecting arbitrators not inconsistent with the Mandatory Arbitration Rules or these rules; and

(4) Review the administration and operation of the arbitration program at least annually and make recommendations as it deems appropriate to improve the program.

[Adopted effective June 1, 1991.]

JUVENILE COURT RULES, JUVENILE OFFENSE PROCEEDINGS
(Cite as WCJCrR)

WCJCrR 6.0.   REFERRAL OF MATTERS TO DIVERSION OR FILING IN JUVENILE COURT

Consistent with the purposes of RCW 13.40.010, the Whatcom County Juvenile Court shall encourage the prompt referral and resolution of juvenile offense

matters at all stages of the proceedings and shall discourage delays in the processing of said matters at all stages of the proceedings. To affect these purposes, the court shall require that:

(a) *Referral of matters to diversion.* The Prosecuting Attorney's Office shall refer appropriate misdemeanor, gross misdemeanor and Class C felony matters to diversion promptly after receiving the completed law enforcement reports regarding juvenile offenses.

(b) *Filing of Informations.* If, in the Prosecuting Attorney's discretion charges are to be filed, the Prosecuting Attorney's Office shall file charges against an alleged juvenile respondent promptly after receiving the completed law enforcement report of investigation of the offense. Failure to promptly file charges may be grounds for dismissal of the charges.

[Adopted effective September 1, 2006.]

WCJCrR 6.2. RIGHT TO COUNSEL

(a) **Notice of Appearance.** Attorneys, representing parties in juvenile matters, except for appointed attorneys, must serve prompt written notice of their appearance upon all other parties or their counsel of record, the legal process unit of the court and file the same with the Clerk of the Court.

(b) **Recovery of County Expense for Appointed Counsel.** Nothing in this rule shall prevent the court from ordering, as a condition of community supervision, that a juvenile offender pay court costs and fees for court-appointed counsel.

[Adopted effective September 1, 2006.]

WCJCrR 7.0. RELEASE FROM DETENTION

(a) **Generally.** All juveniles held on probable cause or charged with an offense by information in Whatcom County shall have the right to post a bond and be released from detention. The court may impose additional conditions of release pursuant to RCW 13.40.040(4).

(b) **Procedure.** The following steps shall be followed:

(1) The issue of bail shall be first addressed at the probable cause or detention hearing;

(2) The court may adjust the amount of bail originally set in the arrest warrant based on the particular facts and circumstances of each case;

(3) All bonds shall be reviewed and approved by the Prosecuting Attorney or his deputy;

(4) If approved by the Prosecuting Attorney, bail shall be posted or filed in the Office of the Clerk of the Court;

(5) The Clerk of the Court shall issue a written notice indicating the bail or bond has been posted or filed;

(c) **Release on Bail from Detention.** Pre–Disposition Detainees: In the absence of an order setting bail a youth held in detention on probable cause may be released by detention staff only with physical possession of an order from the Court or telephonic approval by the Court or Prosecuting Attorney.

(d) **Post–Disposition Detainees and Youth From Other Jurisdictions:** No juvenile offender from this Court's jurisdiction or any other Court's jurisdiction will be released from detention unless a written Order to that effect has been signed by a Court Commissioner or Superior Court Judge.

[Adopted effective September 1, 2006.]

WCJCrR 7.12. DISPOSITIONAL HEARING—OFFENDER PROCEEDINGS

(a) **Who must be present.** The prosecuting attorney, the respondent, defense counsel, respondent's parent/ guardian and juvenile court probation staff shall be present at all disposition hearings. The court may excuse a parent's presence at the disposition hearing upon good cause shown.

(b) **Time.** If the respondent pleads guilty or is found guilty of the allegations in the information, the court shall enter its findings upon the record and proceed immediately to the disposition unless:

(1) The court believes additional information is necessary, or

(2) The court believes additional time is needed to determine an appropriate custody or living situation, or

(3) Commitment is to be considered and additional time is necessary to seek alternatives, or

(4) The court deems a continuance is otherwise necessary.

(c) **Sources.** Pre–dispositional reports may be ordered by the court from one or more of the following sources:

(1) The Whatcom County Juvenile court staff;

(2) Any other source that can provide relevant and material information on the issue of an appropriate disposition.

(d) **Form.** All pre-dispositional reports shall address the various factors required by RCW 13.40.150. All pre-dispositional reports should present potential alternatives, if any, to commitment in those cases in which it may appear that public safety can be assured and the offender's behavior improved by such an alternative. All reports shall be provided to the court and counsel no later than one (1) day prior to the dispositional hearing.

(e) **Community Diagnostic Evaluation.** A diagnostic evaluation may be ordered by the court if a showing is made that such evaluation is necessary to aid the court to reach an appropriate disposition.

(f) **Restitution.** The court shall fix the amount of restitution at the dispositional hearing or shall set a hearing to determine the restitution amount.

(g) **Manifest Injustice Findings.** If the court imposes a sentence based upon a finding of manifest injustice, the court shall set forth those portions of the record material to the disposition.

[Adopted effective September 1, 2006.]

WCJCrR 7.15. VIOLATION OF COMMUNITY SUPERVISION

(a) Generally. Juvenile Probation officers shall make referrals to the court alleging violations of community supervision pursuant to RCW 13.04.040(1)(2) and (5). After review of the referral, the court may on its own motion issue a summons or warrant to compel the respondent's appearance at a hearing to review the terms of community supervision. Juvenile Probation shall provide copies of the summons and referral to all appropriate parties.

(b) If the referral includes allegation(s) on which the prosecutor elects to file an information charging a new offense per 13.40.070(3), the prosecutor may move to strike said allegation(s) from the referral at anytime before or at the hearing on the referral. Upon hearing on the motion, the Court shall strike said allegation(s).

(c) Nothing in this rule shall prohibit or limit the Prosecutor's Office from filing and noting a motion to modify the terms of community supervision pursuant to RCW 13.40.070(3) or RCW 13.40.200(1). Prosecutors shall serve copies of the summons, motions and affidavits to all appropriate parties, and juvenile court probation.

(d) Hearing.

(1) The juvenile probation department shall be present at such hearing to respond to questions and make recommendations concerning the matter.

(2) If the offender denies the allegations of the petition, the matter may be continued for a reasonable period of time for a contested hearing.

(e) Absconding From Placement. A juvenile respondent's voluntary absence from his/her placement pursuant to the terms of community supervision is sufficient grounds for a warrant of arrest to be issued.

(f) Warrants. Upon a showing of the reasons therefore, by declaration, or testimony upon the record, the court may order a warrant for the arrest of a juvenile respondent who violates conditions of community supervision and whose whereabouts are unknown or who is likely to fail to appear for a review hearing. A warrant may be served by law enforcement or a juvenile probation officer.

[Adopted effective September 1, 2006; amended effective September 1, 2009.]

WCJCrR 7.16. COURT FORMS

(a) Generally. It shall be the policy of the court to use standardized court forms whenever possible.

(b) Review. All court forms shall be reviewed and approved by the Judges and Court Commissioners

[Adopted effective September 1, 2006.]

WCJCrR 7.4. VIOLATION OF PRE–TRIAL RELEASE CONDITIONS

Juvenile Court Probation Officers shall make referrals to the court regarding a respondent's non-compliance with pre-trial release conditions ordered pursuant to RCW 13.40.040(6) and make recommendations to the court regarding the need for detention pursuant to RCW 13.04.040(2). The court on its own motion may require the youth to appear at a hearing to review modification or release conditions.

At the court's direction, juvenile probation shall notify all appropriate parties of the time set by the court for the youth to appear. Nothing in this rule shall prevent the prosecutor or respondent from noting up a motion to review release conditions upon notice to all parties, the respondent's parent/guardian, and juvenile probation.

At the hearing to review release conditions the court shall hear from the state, respondent's counsel, parent/guardian, juvenile probation and others with information pertinent to the court's review regarding the need for detention or modification of release conditions.

[Adopted effective September 1, 2006.]

WCJCrR 7.5. ISSUANCE AND SERVICE OF NOTICE/SUMMONS

(a) Generally. Juvenile offenders and their parent(s), guardian(s), or custodian(s) may be served by mail, postage prepaid. The Court or Prosecuting Attorney's Office shall be responsible for the preparation and mailing of the necessary pre-adjudication documents including an Affidavit of Service. Juvenile Court Administration shall be responsible for the preparation and mailing of the necessary post-disposition documents including an Affidavit of Service.

(b) Failure to Appear on Summons. If a respondent fails to appear in response to a Notice/Summons, or if service is not affected within a reasonable time, a warrant for arrest may be issued. A reasonable time to effect service shall be defined as service within ten (10) days of the filing of the information.

[Adopted effective September 1, 2006.]

WCJCrR 7.6. ARRAIGNMENT

(a) Procedure. The juvenile and his/her counsel shall prepare, review, and complete the following forms and present them to the court at the hearing:

(1) Juvenile's Acknowledgement of Advisement of Rights; and

(2) Juvenile's Notice/Advisement of Records.

(b) Name and Date of Birth. The juvenile respondent shall be asked his/her true name and date of birth. If the juvenile alleges that his/her true name and/or date of birth is other than indicated on the information, it shall be entered in the minutes of the court.

(c) At arraignment, the court shall:

(1) Confirm that respondent is represented by counsel or that counsel is waived;

(2) Confirm the respondent is aware of his/her rights and the record provisions of RCW 13.50;

(3) Read the information to respondent, unless the reading is waived, and confirm that a copy has been provided to the respondent and his/her counsel;

(4) Take a plea from the juvenile of guilty, not guilty or not guilty by reason of insanity;

(5) Determine if discovery has been given; and

(6) Set the next appropriate court date and conditions of release after hearing from the parties, juvenile probation and the juvenile's parent(s)/guardian(s);

(7) If the matter has been returned from diversion for failure to complete a diversion contract, the court shall set a diversion termination hearing no later than two (2) weeks after the arraignment.

(8) Group Arraignments. The court may advise juvenile respondents of their rights and explain the record provisions of RCW 13.50 in a group proceeding. All other portions of the arraignment shall be accomplished individually.

[Adopted effective September 1, 2006.]

WCJCrR 7.6.1. NOTICE AND ADVISEMENT JUVENILE OFFENDER RECORDS

(a) Generally. Any juvenile to whom the record provisions of RCW 13.50.050 may apply shall be given written notice of his or her rights under the referenced statute.

(b) Procedure. The following procedure shall be followed:

(1) In the case of a juvenile offender, a written form signed by the juvenile in which a juvenile is advised of rights pursuant to RCW 13.50.050 and acknowledges being so advised shall be filed with the Clerk of the Court at the time of his or her arraignment.

(2) In the case of a juvenile referred to a diversion unit, a similar written form as in the above paragraph shall be signed by the juvenile and filed as part of the diversion agreement.

[Adopted effective September 1, 2006.]

WCJCrR 7.7. GUILTY PLEAS

(a) Hearing. The parties, the juvenile's parent/guardian and Juvenile Court Probation shall be given timely notice of the guilty plea hearing. Juvenile Court Probation staff shall be present at all guilty pleas.

(b) Procedure. The juvenile respondent and his/her counsel shall prepare and complete a Statement of Juvenile on Plea of Guilty before appearing in court. The juvenile respondent and his/her counsel shall present the completed statement to the court. After receiving the completed statement, the court shall conduct a detailed inquiry addressing:

(1) The meaning and effect of a plea of guilty;

(2) The elements of the offense alleged;

(3) The juvenile's acknowledgement of his/her guilt to the offense

(4) The standard sentencing range and the maximum punishment for the offense alleged;

(5) Any other appropriate matters. Upon acceptance of the plea, the statement shall be filed with the Clerk of the Court.

(c) Withdrawal of Plea of Guilty. A motion to withdraw a plea of guilty may be made only before sentence is imposed and upon a showing of good cause. The court may set aside an Order of Disposition and permit a juvenile respondent to withdraw his/her plea of guilty to correct an injustice.

(d) Form. The Statement of Juvenile on Plea of Guilty will conform substantially with JuCr 7.7.

[Adopted effective September 1, 2006.]

WCJCrR 7.8. MOTIONS, JUVENILE OFFENDER PROCEEDINGS

(a) Generally. Unless otherwise provided in the Civil Rules, Criminal Rules and these rules, all motions, including motions to suppress evidence, motions regarding statements, confessions and any other motion requiring testimony, shall be heard at the time of trial unless otherwise set by the Court. All motions together with a brief which shall include a summary of the facts upon which the motions are based, shall be filed and served not later than five (5) days before the adjudicatory hearing. Reply briefs shall be served and filed with the Court no later than noon of the Court day before the hearing.

(b) Continuances. Motions for continuance may be granted only as follows:

(1) All motions for continuance by parties shall be by written motion and affidavit, noted and served on the other party and juvenile court probation at least 5 days before the motion day that precedes the adjudicatory hearing.

(2) All motions for continuance of a trial date shall be presented in open court by the moving party.

(3) On the motion of a party, the court may continue a juvenile offender matter when required in the due administration of justice and none of the parties

to the action will be substantially prejudiced in the presentation of their case.

(4) The court must state its reasons on the record for granting a motion for a continuance.

(5) All continuances shall be to a date certain and confirmed by written order.

(c) To dismiss for Delay in Referral of Offense. The Court may dismiss an information if it is established that there has been an unreasonable delay in referral of the offense to the Court and the delay results in prejudice to a party. Upon a prima facie showing of unreasonable delay, the Court shall then determine whether or not dismissal or other appropriate sanction will be imposed. Among those factors otherwise considered, the Court shall consider the following:

(1) The length of the delay;

(2) The reason for the delay;

(3) The impact of the delay on ability to defend against the charge; and

(4) The seriousness of the alleged offense.

(d) Unreasonable delay shall constitute an affirmative defense that must be raised by motion not later than one (1) week after arraignment. Such motion may be considered by affidavit.

(e) Revisions: Motions for revision of a Commissioner's ruling shall be made by pre-arranged special set through a Judicial Assistant pursuant to WCCR77.2(b) and shall be in accordance with the provisions of WCCCR 53.2.

[Adopted effective September 1, 2006; amended effective September 1, 2009.]

WCJCrR 8.2. DECLINING JUVENILE COURT JURISDICTION OVER AN ALLEGED JUVENILE OFFENDER

(a) Generally. In accordance with RCW 13.40.110, any party may file an appropriate motion and supporting affidavit to decline jurisdiction with the Clerk of the Court.

(b) Report. A declination investigation report shall be prepared by the juvenile court staff. The report shall:

(1) Address the following factors:

(i) The seriousness of the alleged offense to the community and whether the protection of the community requires waiver of juvenile court jurisdiction;

(ii) Whether the alleged offense was committed in an aggressive, violent, premeditated or willful manner;

(iii) Whether the alleged offense was against persons or against property;

(iv) The prosecutorial merit of the complaint;

(v) The desirability of trial and disposition of the entire offense in one court;

(vi) The sophistication and maturity of the juvenile as determined by consideration of his home, environmental situation, emotional attitude and pattern of living;

(vii) The record and previous history of the juvenile, including previous contacts with law enforcement agencies, juvenile courts and other jurisdictions, prior periods of probation/community supervision, or prior commitments to juvenile institutions;

(viii) The prospects for adequate protection of the public and the likelihood of reasonable rehabilitation of the juvenile (if he is found to have committed the alleged offense) by the use of procedures, services and facilities currently available to the juvenile court.

(2) Address any other factors relevant to the motion; and

(3) Make a recommendation to the court as to the motion.

(c) Hearing. The author of the declination investigation report shall be present at the declination hearing to testify, if so requested.

[Adopted effective September 1, 2006.]

WCJCrR 10.2. RECORDING JUVENILE COURT PROCEEDINGS

Generally. All proceedings in the Whatcom County Superior Court Juvenile Division shall be recorded unless waived pursuant to statute. The electronic recording device approved by the court is approved for all hearings and for all purposes.

[Adopted effective September 1, 2006.]

WCJCrR 77.1. ATTIRE AND DECORUM

Attire. Persons who appear in Court should dress in a manner appropriate to the dignity of the forum.

(a) Legal Counsel and Probation Officers shall wear business attire; men should be in sport-coat/blazer and tie; women should wear a sport-coat/blazer or sweater if wearing a blouse.

(b) Inappropriate courtroom attire for the public includes: shorts, tank tops, ripped or torn jeans, hats, thong sandals, shirts with lewd language or alcohol/drug slogans, or gang attire/colors (including bandanas worn, carried, or visible in any way.)

(c) Shirts and shoes are required. Bare midriffs are inappropriate.

(d) All electronic equipment such as personal music players, cell phones and pagers must be turned off during court, and may be forfeited to the court for at least the remainder of the court day if they are used during court or if they interfere with the operation of the court in anyway.

[Adopted effective September 1, 2006.]

APPENDICES
APPENDIX A.   COURT CALENDAR SCHEDULE

WHATCOM COUNTY SUPERIOR COURT

Current calendar information, including a copy of the latest edition of this schedule, may be obtained from the Clerk of the Superior Court, 311 Grand Avenue, Bellingham, WA 98225; (360) 676–6777.

Matter	Time and Place		Clerk Setting and Confirmation
ADOPTION—Final Hearing, uncontested only	8:30—9:30 am—Wed	Judge's Chambers	Call Calendar Clerk at 676–7687 for setting.
CIVIL LAW & MOTION CALENDARS – Summary Judgment, Injunctive Relief, Discovery, Revisions, Writs, Supplemental Examinations, Civil Lower Court Appeals, etc.	1:30 pm—Friday	Assigned Judge's Courtroom	**Must confirm by calling Calendar Clerk at 676–7687 by noon Wednesday.**
CRIMINAL – Arraignments, Omnibus, Violation Hrgs	9:30 am—Friday	Comm. Courtroom, **2nd** floor	Call Pros. Office at 676–6784 for setting.
Drug Court	3:00 pm—Thursday	Judge Moynihan's Courtroom	
First Appearances	In–custody; 3:00 pm daily	Jail Courtroom	Call Pros. Office at 676–6784 for setting.
	Out–of–custody; 9:30 am Friday	Comm. Courtroom, **2nd** floor	
Guilty Pleas/ Sentencing/LC Appeals/Motions	8:30 am—Thursday	Presiding Judge's Courtroom	
Suppression/Confession Hearings	8:30 am—9:30 am	Trial Judge's Courtroom	Call Calendar Clerk at 676–7687 for setting.
Trial Settings/Case Scheduling	8:00 am—Friday	Dept. 2 Jury Room, with Clerk	
DOMESTIC RELATIONS – Child Support Modification Calendar	10:00 am, last two Thursdays each month	Comm. Courtroom, **2nd** floor	Call Clerk at 676–6777, ext. 50007 for setting. **Trial setting order required. Must confirm by calling Clerk at 676–6777, ext. 50007 by noon two days before hearing.**
Domestic Relations Motions & Show Cause (1st hearing **only** before Commissioner – all subsequent hearings to Assigned Judge)	1:30 pm, Tues/ Wed/Fri **See local rule WCSPR 94.05(a) for Show Cause Order nine-day notice requirement.**	Comm. Courtroom, **2nd** floor	Call Clerk at 676–6777, ext. 50007 for setting. Must confirm by calling Clerk at 676–6777, ext. 50007 by noon two days before hearing.
Domestic Relations Motions/Show Cause/Revisions - Assigned Judge	9:00 am—Friday	Assigned Judge's Courtroom	**Must confirm by calling Calendar Clerk at 676–7687 by noon Wednesday.**
Domestic Violence and Transferred Anti–Harassment Petitions	9:00 am, Mon/Wed/Thurs **[weeks with Monday holiday will have a DV calendar on Tuesday]**	Comm. Courtroom, **2nd** floor	Call Domestic Violence Office at 676–6803 for setting.
Final Dissolution Hearing, uncontested only	9:00 am—Friday	Assigned Judge's Courtroom	**Must confirm by calling Calendar Clerk at 676–7687 by noon Wednesday.**
Parentage, Support Enforcement	10:00 am, first two Thursdays each month	Comm. Courtroom, **2nd** floor	Call Clerk at 676–6777, ext. 50007 for setting. **Must confirm by calling Clerk at 676–6777, ext. 5007 by noon two days before hearing.**
Settlement Conferences	as scheduled	Comm. Jury Room, **2nd** floor	Call Calendar Clerk at 676–7687 for setting
Stacked Domestic Calendar	8:30 am, last Monday of month	Presiding Judge's Courtroom	Call Calendar Clerk at 676–7687 for setting. **Trial setting order required.**
EX PARTE CALENDAR	8:30—9:00 am, Mon/Wed/ Fri	Becca Courtroom, 4th floor	No setting required
GUARDIANSHIP/PROBATE	9:00 am—Friday	Assigned Judge's Courtroom	**Must confirm by calling Calendar Clerk at 676–7687 by noon Wednesday.**

Matter	Time and Place		Clerk Setting and Confirmation
JUVENILE—Dependency, Shelter Care, Term.		Becca Courtroom, 4th floor	Call Juvenile Probation at 676–6780 for setting.
Dependency Drug Court	10:00 am—Thursday	Becca Courtroom, 4th floor	
Offender Drug Court	3:00 pm—Tues.(start date to be set)	Juvenile Courtroom, 5th floor	
Offender Hearings, Trial Settings		Juvenile Courtroom, 5th floor	Call Pros. Office at 676–6784 for setting.
Truancy, CHINS, At–Risk		Becca Courtroom, 4th floor	Call Juvenile Probation at 676–6780 for setting.
MENTAL COMMITMENT HEARINGS	1:30 pm, Mon—Fri	St. Joseph Hospital, South Campus	Call Clerk at 676–6777, ext. 50007 for setting.
TEEN COURT	6:00 pm, 2nd Wed. of month	3rd floor Courtrooms	
TRIAL SETTINGS [Civil Trials, Small Claims Court Appeals & Domestic Trials only]	1:00 pm—Friday	3rd floor Atty. Conference Room/Court	**Must confirm by calling Calendar Clerk at 676–7687 by noon Wednesday.**
	See local rule WCCR 40.1 for trial setting procedure.		

[Amended effective May 7, 2002.]

APPENDIX B. DOMESTIC RELATIONS PRE–TRIAL INFORMATION

SUPERIOR COURT OF
THE STATE OF WASHINGTON
FOR WHATCOM COUNTY

(Clerk's File Stamp)

In Re the Marriage of

_____,   No._____

Petitioner,

vs.   DOMESTIC RELATIONS
                                                PRE–TRIAL INFORMATION
_____,   SUBMITTED BY _____

Respondent.

Note: This form shall be filed and served by Noon two judicial days before trial.

I.   GENERAL INFORMATION

    A.   Ages: Wife_____ Husband_____
    B.   Date of Marriage:_____
    C.   Dependent children living with either party:

        (1) Of this marriage:

            Name   Age   With Whom Residing

        (2) Children of former marriages:

            Name   Age   With Whom Residing

II.   INCOME & EMPLOYMENT

    A.   Husband:

        (1) Employer's name and address:_____
        (2) Net take-home pay per month: $_____
        (3) Other income: Source   Monthly Amount

    B.   Wife:

        (1) Employer's name and address:_____
        (2) Net take-home pay per month: $_____
        (3) Other income: Source   Monthly Amount

III.   ASSETS & LIABILITIES

Instructions: Indicate your proposed division of assets and liabilities on a sheet of paper divided in the middle, vertically, by listing the property to be awarded to the Wife on the left side of the page and listing the property to be awarded to the

Husband on the right side of the page. (See **Sample** *on following page.) Such lists should begin with the items of community property having the greatest value and should be described in such detail as may be reasonable in view of the total assets of the marital community.*

Generally, assets having an individual value of more than $500 should be listed separately. Any property subject to an encumbrance or security interest should disclose the nature of such security interest, the unpaid balance owing at the time of trial and the net fair market value of such asset after the deduction of such encumbrance.

The proposed property division should conclude with a list of liabilities to be assumed by each party, including, except as may be disclosed above, the name of the creditor, amount of the monthly payment, the unpaid balance on each such debt and the total amount of all such liabilities to be assumed by each party.

Deduction of the total amount of liabilities to be assumed by each party from the net total fair market value of the community property awarded to such party will constitute the net fair market values for your proposed property division. This should be followed by a list of separate property to be awarded to each spouse.

SAMPLE

III. ASSETS & LIABILITIES:

PROPERTY DIVISION PROPOSED BY WIFE

Property to be Awarded to Wife:		
Real Estate:		
Family home (FMV)	$60,000	
Less: Mortgage to		
Hometown Bank	(30,000)	
Net Equity:		$30,000
Motor Vehicles:		
1985 Chev. Caprice		
(FMV)	8,500	
Less: Loan to Credit		
Union	(5,000)	
Net Equity:		3,500
Household Goods:		
Living room furniture	750	
Console TV	600	
Bedroom furniture	500	
Kitchen Appliances	300	
Misc. dishes/utensils	200	
Total Household Goods:		2,350
Cash: (from savings account)		1,500
Clothing & Personal: Effects:		1,000
Total Value Community Property Awarded to Wife:		$38,350
Less Debts Assumed by Wife:		
Sears	450	
VISA	600	
Total Debts:		−1,050
Net Value of Award to Wife:		$37,300
Less: Lien on family home		−6,375
Total Community Property Awarded to Wife:		$30,925
Separate Property: 100 Shares Puget Power stock received from father		2,000
Total Award to Wife:		$32,925

Property to be Awarded to Husband:		
Pension (Present cash value at dissolution)		$20,000
Motor Vehicles:		
1983 Ford pickup (FMV)	5,000	
Less: Loan to Second National Bank	2,000	
Net Equity:		3,000
Household Goods:		
Living room furniture	500	
Bedroom furniture	350	
Misc. dishes/ utensils	150	
Total Household Goods:		1,000
Cash (from checking and savings)		1,000
Power Tools		350
Clothing & Personal Effects		750
Total Value of Community Property Awarded to Husband:		$26,100
Less Debts Assumed by Husband:		
Bon Marche	350	
Mastercard	500	
Ace Finance Company	700	
Total Debts:		−1,550
Net Value of Award to Husband:		$24,550
Plus: Lien on family home		6,375
Total Community Property Awarded to Husband:		$30,925

APPENDIX C. REQUEST FOR ENTRY OF DECREE AND
DECLARATION OF JURISDICTIONAL FACTS

SUPERIOR COURT OF WASHINGTON
COUNTY OF WHATCOM

In Re the Marriage of:

_____ No._____
                    Petitioner,   REQUEST FOR ENTRY OF
and   DECREE AND DECLARATION OF
                                  JURISDICTIONAL FACTS

_____
                    Respondent.

REQUEST	The petitioner requests immediate entry of Findings of Fact, Conclusions of Law and Decree of Dissolution of Marriage without a final hearing, and states:
RESIDENCE	I was a resident of the state of Washington when the petition was filed.
TIME LIMITS	More than 90 days have elapsed since the later of _____ _____, 19___, the date on which the Petition was filed, and _____ _____, 19___, the date:

[ ] the respondent signed an acceptance of service.
[ ] the summons and petition were personally served upon the respondent.
[ ] the summons and petition were mailed pursuant to an order for service by mail.
[ ] the summons was first published pursuant to an order for service by publication.

MARRIAGE & SEPARATION	The parties were married on _____ _____, 19___, at [city, state] _____ and separated on _____ _____, 19___.
	The marriage is now irretrievably broken.
PREGNANCY	The wife is not now pregnant.
DEPENDENT CHILDREN	All dependent children of the marriage are identified in the proposed Decree. The proposed Parenting Plan is in the children's best interest; the Child Support Worksheets are accurate.
PROPERTY & DEBTS	All property and all debts of the parties are fairly and completely divided in the Decree.
IF DEFAULT	If entry of the Decree is sought after default of the Respondent, the Decree provides for only that relief requested in the petition.
PERJURY DECLARATION	I declare under penalty of perjury under the laws of the State of Washington that the foregoing is true and correct.

Dated: _____ _____, 19___   [Signed]_____
at _____, Washington.   Petitioner

Presented by: Approved, notice of presentation waived:

[Signed]_____   [Signed]_____
      Attorney for Petitioner   Respondent or Respondent's
                                                Attorney

REQUEST FOR ENTRY OF DECREE
AND DECLARATION OF JURISDICTIONAL FACTS
No Mandatory Form.
For use when at least one party is represented by counsel. 6/92

APPENDIX D. SAMPLE ARBITRATION FORMS

DEMAND FOR ARBITRATION/NOTE FOR MOTION DOCKET

SUPERIOR COURT OF
THE STATE OF WASHINGTON
FOR WHATCOM COUNTY

(Clerk's File Stamp)

_____, Plaintiff/Petitioner, vs. _____, Defendant/Respondent	No. _____ **DEMAND FOR ARBITRATION** & **NOTE FOR MOTION DOCKET**

TO: The Clerk of the Superior Court and the Attorneys and Parties listed below:

I hereby affirm that this case is at issue; that no affirmative pleading remains unanswered; that to my knowledge no other parties will be served with summons; and that the case is in all respects ready for trial or arbitration.

DEMAND FOR ARBITRATION: (Check appropriate choices)

[ ]   This case is subject to arbitration subject to WCMAR 1.3.

[ ]   The undersigned contends that the claim exceeds the maximum amount authorized under RCW 7.06.020, but for purposes of arbitration waives any claim in excess of such amount.

NOTE FOR MOTION DOCKET:

Please take note that the issue of arbitrability will be heard on the date set out below and the Clerk is requested to note the same on the Motion Docket for that date, which date is the next Friday after the expiration of 14 days from the date this Demand and Note is filed:

   Date of Hearing:_____   **Time of Hearing:**_____

Any response to this Demand for Arbitration must be filed with the Clerk and a copy served upon counsel within 14 days of the date this Demand and Note is filed and mailed. WCMAR 2.1(b)

CERTIFICATE OF MAILING:

I certify that I mailed a copy of this document to the attorneys listed hereon, postage prepaid on the _____ day of _____, 19___.

Signed: _____

SUBMITTED BY:

Signed: _____ Date: _____
Typed Name: _____
Address/Phone: _____
_____
Attorney for: _____

NOTE:

Name: _____

Address/Phone: _____

_____

**File the original of this document
with the County Clerk.**

Attorney for: _____

[DEMAND FOR ARBITRATION/NOTE FOR MOTION DOCKET]

RESPONSE TO DEMAND FOR ARBITRATION

SUPERIOR COURT OF
THE STATE OF WASHINGTON
FOR WHATCOM COUNTY

(Clerk's File Stamp)

_____,   No. _____

Plaintiff/Petitioner,

vs.   RESPONSE TO DEMAND
                                             FOR ARBITRATION

_____,

Defendant/Respondent

TO: The Clerk of the Superior Court and the Attorneys and Parties listed below:

The undersigned responds to the prior **Demand for Arbitration** filed in this cause and:

[ ]   **AGREES TO ARBITRATION**

[ ]   **OBJECTS TO MANDATORY ARBITRATION,** because:

    [ ]   Opposing party's claim exceeds the amount authorized by RCW 7.02.020;

    [ ]   Opposing party seeks relief other than a money judgment;

    [ ]   A party's counter or cross claim exceeds the amount authorized by RCW 7.06.020;

    [ ]   A party's counter or cross claim seeks relief other than a money judgment; or

    [ ]   This case is an appeal from a lower court not subject to mandatory arbitration.

    [ ]   Other: _____

_____

CERTIFICATE OF MAILING:

I certify that I mailed a copy of this document to the attorneys listed hereon, postage prepaid on the _____ day of _____, 19___.

Signed: _____

SUBMITTED BY:

Signed: _____ Date: _____
Typed Name: _____
Address/Phone: _____
_____
Attorney for: _____

OTHER ATTORNEY/PARTY:

Name: _____
Address/Phone: _____
_____
Attorney for: _____

NOTE:

File the original of this document with the County Clerk.

[RESPONSE TO DEMAND FOR ARBITRATION]

AMENDMENT TO DEMAND FOR ARBITRATION OR RESPONSE

SUPERIOR COURT OF
THE STATE OF WASHINGTON
FOR WHATCOM COUNTY

(Clerk's File Stamp)

_____, No._____

Plaintiff/Petitioner,

vs.   AMENDMENT TO DEMAND FOR
                                            ARBITRATION OR RESPONSE

_____
Defendant/Respondent

TO: The Clerk of the Superior Court and the Attorneys and Parties listed below:
[ ] This form amends the undersigned's **Demand for Arbitration; or**
[ ] This form amends the undersigned's **Response to Demand for Arbitration.**

THE UNDERSIGNED NOW CONTENDS THAT THIS CASE:

[ ] **SHOULD BE ARBITRATED,** because:
    [ ] The sole relief sought is a money judgment and it involves no claim in excess of the amount authorized by RCW 7.06.020, exclusive of attorney fees, interest and costs.
    [ ] The undersigned contends that its claim exceeds the amount authorized by RCW 7.06.020, but for purposes of arbitration waives any claim in excess of such amount.

[ ] **IS NOT SUBJECT TO MANDATORY ARBITRATION,** because:
    [ ] Opposing party's claim exceeds the amount authorized by RCW 7.02.020;
    [ ] Opposing party seeks relief other than a money judgment;
    [ ] A party's counter or cross claim exceeds the amount authorized by RCW 7.06.020;
    [ ] A party's counter or cross claim seeks relief other than a money judgment; or
    [ ] This case is an appeal from a lower court not subject to mandatory arbitration.
    [ ] Other: _____

An amendment to a **Demand for Arbitration** or a **Response** thereto must be filed with the Clerk and a copy served upon counsel prior to the date it is set for hearing as to arbitrability. WCMAR 2.1(c)

CERTIFICATE OF MAILING: **SUBMITTED BY:**

I certify that I mailed a copy of this   Signed: _____ Date: _____
document to the attorneys listed   Typed Name: _____
hereon, postage prepaid on the _____   Address/Phone: _____
day of _____, 19___.   _____

Signed: _____   Attorney for: _____

                                         OTHER ATTORNEY/PARTY:

NOTE: Name: _____
                                         Address/Phone: _____
File the original of this document   _____
with the County Clerk.   Attorney for: _____
[AMENDMENT TO DEMAND/RESPONSE]

ORDER ON DEMAND FOR ARBITRATION

SUPERIOR COURT OF
THE STATE OF WASHINGTON
FOR WHATCOM COUNTY

(Clerk's File Stamp)

_____,
                    Plaintiff/Petitioner,

vs.

_____,
            Defendant/Respondent

No. _____

ORDER ON DEMAND

FOR ARBITRATION

THIS MATTER having come on for an order concerning arbitrability and it appearing that the matter is properly before the Court upon due notice to all parties, the Court having heard oral argument, and the Court being fully advised in the premises,

NOW THEREFORE, IT IS ORDERED that this case

[ ] **IS SUBJECT TO MANDATORY ARBITRATION** and is hereby transferred to arbitration.

[ ] **IS NOT SUBJECT TO MANDATORY ARBITRATION,** because:

    [ ] Opposing party's claim exceeds the amount authorized by RCW 7.02.020;
    [ ] Opposing party seeks relief other than a money judgment;
    [ ] A party's counter or cross claim exceeds the amount authorized by RCW 7.06.020;
    [ ] A party's counter or cross claim seeks relief other than a money judgment; or
    [ ] This case is an appeal from a lower court not subject to mandatory arbitration.

    [ ] Other: _____

DONE IN OPEN COURT this the _____ day of _____, 19___.

_____
                    Judge

CERTIFICATE OF MAILING:

I certify that I mailed a copy of this document to the attorneys listed hereon, postage prepaid on the _____ day of _____, 19___.

Signed: _____

NOTE:

File the original of this document with the County Clerk.

SUBMITTED BY:

Signed: _____ Date: _____
Typed Name: _____
Address/Phone: _____
_____
Attorney for: _____

APPROVED FOR ENTRY:

Name: _____
Address/Phone: _____
_____
Attorney for: _____

[ORDER ON ARBITRATION DEMAND]

ORDER TRANSFERRING TO ARBITRATION (ON STIPULATION)

SUPERIOR COURT OF
THE STATE OF WASHINGTON
FOR WHATCOM COUNTY

(Clerk's File Stamp)

_____, No. _____
Plaintiff/Petitioner,

vs. ORDER TRANSFERRING TO
ARBITRATION ON STIPULATION

_____,
Defendant/Respondent

BASED ON THE FOLLOWING STIPULATIONS:

That the case may be transferred to arbitration,

That this case is at issue; that no affirmative pleading remains unanswered; that no other parties will be served with summons; and that the case is in all respects ready for arbitration,

That the following person has been selected and has agreed to serve as arbitrator: *(leave blank if the parties are not stipulating to an arbitrator)*

NAME: _____

ADDRESS/PHONE: _____

_____

IT IS THEREFORE ORDERED that this case is transferred to arbitration under the provisions of WCMAR.

DONE IN OPEN COURT this the _____ day of _____, 19____.

_____
Judge

PRESENTED BY:

_____ Signed: _____
Attorney for Plaintiff Attorney for Defendant
Typed Name: _____ Typed Name: _____
Address/Phone: _____ Address/Phone: _____
_____ _____

OTHER ATTORNEY/PARTY: **OTHER ATTORNEY/PARTY:**

Name: _____ Name: _____
Address/Phone: _____ Address/Phone: _____
_____ _____

Attorney for: _____ Attorney for: _____

[ORDER TRANSFERRING TO ARBITRATION on STIPULATION]
[File with County Clerk]

STIPULATION TO ARBITRATOR

SUPERIOR COURT OF
THE STATE OF WASHINGTON
FOR WHATCOM COUNTY

(Clerk's File Stamp)

_____,   No. _____

Plaintiff/Petitioner,

vs.   **STIPULATION TO ARBITRATOR**

_____,

Defendant/Respondent

THE UNDERSIGNED ATTORNEYS/PARTIES STIPULATE:

That the following person has been selected and has agreed to serve as an arbitrator:

NAME: _____

ADDRESS/PHONE: _____

_____

IT IS THEREFORE ORDERED that this case is transferred to arbitration under the provisions of WCMAR.

DONE IN OPEN COURT this the _____ day of _____, 19___.

_____
                        Judge

SUBMITTED BY:

Signed: _____   Signed: _____
Attorney for Plaintiff   Attorney for Defendant
Typed Name: _____   Typed Name: _____
Address/Phone: _____   Address/Phone: _____

_____   _____

OTHER ATTORNEY/PARTY: **OTHER ATTORNEY/PARTY:**

Signed: _____   Signed: _____
Typed Name: _____   Typed Name: _____
Address/Phone: _____   Address/Phone: _____

_____   _____

Attorney for: _____   Attorney for: _____

The original, signed stipulation must be returned to:

Director of Arbitration
Whatcom County Superior Court
311 Grand Avenue
Bellingham, Washington 98225

(DO NOT FILE WITH COUNTY CLERK)

[STIPULATION TO ARBITRATOR]

ARBITRATION AWARD

SUPERIOR COURT OF
THE STATE OF WASHINGTON
FOR WHATCOM COUNTY

(Clerk's File Stamp)

_____, No. _____

Plaintiff/Petitioner,

vs. **ARBITRATION AWARD**

_____,

Defendant/Respondent

The issues in arbitration having been heard on _____, 19___, I make the following award:

DATED this the _____ day of _____, 19___.

_____

Arbitrator

ADDRESS/PHONE: _____

CERTIFICATE OF MAILING:

I certify that I mailed a copy of this document to the attorneys listed hereon, postage prepaid on the _____ day of _____, 19___.

Name: _____ Name: _____
Attorney for Plaintiff Attorney for Plaintiff
Address/Phone: _____ Address/Phone: _____
_____ _____

OTHER ATTORNEY/PARTY: **OTHER ATTORNEY/PARTY:**

Name: _____ Name: _____
Address/Phone: _____ Address/Phone: _____
_____ _____

Attorney for: _____ Attorney for: _____

[File with County Clerk]

[ARBITRATION AWARD]

APPENDIX E.   VERIFIED STATEMENT OF ASSETS AND LIABILITIES

DO NOT FILE THIS DOCUMENT WITH THE COURT
VERIFIED STATEMENT OF ASSETS AND LIABILITIES

(Attach additional sheets in the same form if necessary.)

Petitioner: _____ Respondent: _____ Case #: ___

Date of separation from Spouse: _____ Date Petition for Dissolution filed: _____

1.   I am the [ ] Petitioner [ ] Respondent in this action.

2.   To my knowledge, as of the date of separation, the following community and separate assets and liabilities existed. *(Note: Generally* ***"Community assets"*** *means those assets that were acquired during marriage, except by inheritance or gift.* ***"Community liabilities"*** *means all debts incurred during the marriage, regardless of whose name the debt is in.* ***"Separate assets"*** *means those assets owned before marriage, or acquired after separation, or acquired during the marriage by inheritance or gift.* ***"Separate liabilities"*** *means those debts incurred before the marriage or after separation.*

COMMUNITY ASSETS   **SEPARATE ASSETS**

Real Property:
1. _____   1. _____
2. _____   2. _____

Vehicles (autos, trailers, boats, etc.):
1. _____   1. _____
2. _____   2. _____
3. _____   3. _____
4. _____   4. _____

Bank Accounts:

Bank Name/Branch   Account No.   **Bank Name/Branch   Account No.**
1. _____   1. _____
2. _____   2. _____
3. _____   3. _____
4. _____   4. _____

Pensions/Retirement Accounts:
1. _____   1. _____
2. _____   2. _____

Business Interests:
1. _____   1. _____
2. _____   2. _____

Stocks/Bonds/Investments:
1. _____   1. _____
2. _____   2. _____
3. _____   3. _____

Life Insurance:
1. _____   1. _____
2. _____   2. _____

Household Goods/furnishings/Appliances valued over $250:

1. _____	1. _____
2. _____	2. _____
3. _____	3. _____
4. _____	4. _____
5. _____	5. _____
6. _____	6. _____

Sporting Goods/Tools & Equipment valued over $250:

1. _____	1. _____
2. _____	2. _____
3. _____	3. _____
4. _____	4. _____

Jewelry/Artwork valued over $250:

1. _____	1. _____
2. _____	2. _____
3. _____	3. _____
4. _____	4. _____

Electronics and Accessories valued over $250:

1. _____	1. _____
2. _____	2. _____
3. _____	3. _____
4. _____	4. _____

Other:

1. _____	1. _____
2. _____	2. _____
3. _____	3. _____

COMMUNITY LIABILTIES [1]

Mortgage: Balance at   Current Balance
                                 Separation

1. _____ $ _____ $ _____
2. _____ $ _____ $ _____

Loans (vehicles/student/personal):

1. _____ $ _____ $ _____
2. _____ $ _____ $ _____
3. _____ $ _____ $ _____
4. _____ $ _____ $ _____

Credit Cards:

1. _____ $ _____ $ _____
2. _____ $ _____ $ _____
3. _____ $ _____ $ _____
4. _____ $ _____ $ _____
5. _____ $ _____ $ _____
6. _____ $ _____ $ _____

Other (overdue utility/phone bills, IRS, hospital/doctor bills, collection):

1. _____ $ _____ $ _____
2. _____ $ _____ $ _____
3. _____ $ _____ $ _____
4. _____ $ _____ $ _____
5. _____ $ _____ $ _____
6. _____ $ _____ $ _____

Business Debts:

1. _____ $ _____ $ _____
2. _____ $ _____ $ _____
3. _____ $ _____ $ _____
4. _____ $ _____ $ _____

SEPARATE LIABILITIES

Describe type:

1. _____ $ _____ $ _____
2. _____ $ _____ $ _____
3. _____ $ _____ $ _____
4. _____ $ _____ $ _____
5. _____ $ _____ $ _____

Since the time of separation, there has been the following substantial change in the assets listed above: *(NOTE: Describe how, when and why any of the above assets were sold, traded, consumed or otherwise disposed.)*

_____

I anticipate receiving the following in the future:

   a) Inheritance [ ] Yes [ ] No

   b) Settlement proceeds from a lawsuit [ ] Yes [ ] No

   c) Settlement proceeds from a work-related injury [ ] Yes [ ] No

   d) Money owed to me by another [ ] Yes [ ] No

I declare under penalty of perjury of the laws of the State of Washington that the above is true and correct to the best of my knowledge.

DATED this ___ day of _____, 20 ___.

_____
Declarant

1 So in original.

DISTRICT COURT

WHATCOM COUNTY DISTRICT COURT LOCAL COURT RULES

Including Amendments Received Through
August 15, 2015

Table of Rules

ADMINISTRATIVE RULES (Cite as WDARLJ)
Reserved [Effective September 1, 2008]

RULES FOR APPEAL (Cite as WDRALJ) Reserved
[Effective September 1, 2008]

CIVIL RULES (Cite as WDCRLJ) Reserved [Effective September 1, 2008]

CRIMINAL RULES (Cite as WDCrRLJ) [Effective September 1, 2008]

WDCrRLJ 1. ADOPTION, CITATION, AND APPLICABILITY

(a) These rules are adopted pursuant to GR 7 and CrRLJ 1.7, and are to be cited as WDCrRLJ 1 (Whatcom County District Court Criminal Rule).

(b) Any of these Rules may be suspended or modified, upon good cause shown, by written stipulation of the parties approved by the court, or by the court upon its own motion.

[Adopted effective September 1, 2003; amended effective September 1, 2008.]

WDCrRLJ 2. OMNIBUS PROCEDURE

(a) Omnibus Hearings. At or about the time of arraignment, all criminal cases scheduled for trial shall also be set by the court for an omnibus hearing, which shall be held approximately two weeks prior to the trial date. The state, defense counsel, and the defendant shall attend the omnibus hearing, the purpose of which is to consider unresolved issues, including, but not limited to, outstanding discovery, witness lists, witness availability, the estimated length of trial, and such other matters as will promote a fair and expeditious trial. All motions are to be resolved prior to the omnibus hearing. If the parties agree that the case is ready for trial, a stipulated omnibus statement of readiness, substantially in the form set forth in Appendix 1 to these rules, may be filed by the parties. The filing of a stipulated omnibus statement of readiness will serve to excuse counsel and the defendant from appearing at the scheduled omnibus hearing.

Cases not ready for trial by the scheduled omnibus hearing shall be reset or otherwise resolved at the omnibus hearing. The court will not allow unreasonable delay in bringing a case to trial, and the court shall make the determination of whether a case shall be ordered to proceed to trial or to be reset to a new omnibus hearing date.

(b) Trial Assignment. Following the omnibus hearing, the court will prioritize the cases determined to be ready for trial and publish this information. The order in which they are listed shall be the presumptive order of priority for trial. Once confirmed and prioritized for trial, a case may not be continued without order of the court. The court will update this list as appropriate and strike those cases from the list that it determines will not proceed to trial as scheduled. No later than noon on the last business day preceding the trial date, the clerk of, the court will make a final posting of the trial calendar and shall attempt to notify the parties in the cases that are expected to proceed to trial. The inability of the clerk of the court to contact a party for any reason shall not excuse such party from being prepared for trial. Any case that has been set for trial but does not proceed to trial on the assigned date shall be assigned to the omnibus calendar on that date, at which time it will be reset or otherwise resolved.

[Adopted effective September 1, 2003; amended effective September 1, 2008.]

WDCrRLJ 3. BRIEFS AND MEMORANDA

Whenever any brief, motion, memorandum, or other such document is filed with the court, a copy clearly marked "Judge's Copy" must also be filed. The Judge's Copy shall also clearly state the day and time the case is set for hearing. All documents in support of any motion shall be filed with the court and served upon opposing counsel (or the opposing party if such party is unrepresented) no later than five days before the hearing on the motion, and responsive or reply documents are to be filed at least one full business day

before the hearing. Trial briefs shall be submitted no later than two days before trial.

[Adopted effective September 1, 2003; amended effective September 1, 2008.]

WDCrRLJ 4. JURY INSTRUCTIONS

Proposed jury instructions and verdict forms shall be submitted when the case is called for trial. Two sets of instructions, one with and one with- out citations, shall be submitted to the court, with an appropriate cover sheet for each. One additional set with citations shall be served upon opposing counsel (or the opposing party is such party is unrepresented).

[Adopted effective September 1, 2003; amended effective September 1, 2008.]

WDCrRLJ 5. NOTICE, COSTS, WITNESS AND JURY COSTS, AND WITNESS FEES

When a case docketed for trial or other hearing is settled or will not otherwise proceed to hearing, the parties shall immediately give written notice of that fact to the court. The court will not pay witness fees to witnesses who appear for a case that has been continued or settled without trial or hearing. Such costs shall be borne by the party or attorney, who called, subpoenaed, or requested a subpoena for the witness.

In the event that a party fails to provide written notice to the court by 9:00 a.m. on the last business day prior to trial that a case will not be tried to a jury on the date set, the court may impose terms, including payment of the actual costs of the jury. Any party requesting a continuance or other delay of a case confirmed as ready for trial at the omnibus hearing must make proper application to the court with proper notice to all parties.

[Adopted effective September 1, 2003; amended effective September 1, 2008.]

INFRACTION RULES (Cite as WDIRLJ)

WDIRLJ 1.1. ADOPTION AND CITATION

These rules are adopted pursuant to GR 7 and IRLJ 1.3, and are to be cited as WDIRLJ (Whatcom County District Court Infraction Rule).

[Adopted effective September 1, 2008.]

WDIRLJ 2.4. RESPONSE TO NOTICE

The procedure authorized in IRLJ 2.4(b)(4) is adopted by this court.

[Adopted effective September 1, 2008.]

WDIRLJ 2.6. ADOPTION AND CITATION

The procedure authorized in IRLJ 2.6(c) is adopted by this court.

[Adopted effective September 1, 2008.]

WDIRLJ 3.5. DECISION ON WRITTEN STATEMENTS

Decisions on written and/or e-mail statements are authorized as permitted by IRLJ 3.5.

[Adopted effective September 1, 2008.]

SPECIAL PROCEEDINGS (Cite as WDSPLJ)
Reserved [Effective September 1, 2008]
APPENDIX 1. STIPULATED OMNIBUS STATEMENT OF READINESS

WHATCOM COUNTY DISTRICT COURT STATE OF WASHINGTON

State of Washington,

                    No.

            Plaintiff,

    vs.   STIPULATED OMNIBUS AND
                              STATEMENT OF READINESS

            Defendant.

Omnibus hearing currently set for ___ / ___ /20___.

Trial currently set for ___ / ___ /20___.

The parties in the above captioned action hereby stipulate and agree that:

This case has not been resolved by agreement, is ready for trial, and should remain on the trial calendar.

Discovery is complete.

Witnesses:

Plaintiff:

[ ] Witness list filed

[ ] Witnesses are as follows:

Name:	Address/telephone	Subject of testimony
_____	_____	_____
_____	_____	_____

Defendant:

[ ] Witness list filed

[ ] Witnesses are as follows:

Name:	Address/telephone	Subject of testimony
_____	_____	_____
_____	_____	_____

_____   _____
Attorney for Plaintiff   Attorney for Defendant/Defendant
W.S.B.A.   #W.S.B.A. #

[Adopted effective September 1, 2003; amended effective September 1, 2008.]

MUNICIPAL COURTS

BELLINGHAM MUNICIPAL COURT LOCAL COURT RULES

Including Amendments Received Through
August 15, 2015

Table of Rules

RULE 1. DELEGATING AUTHORITY TO CANCEL WARRANTS AND FTA'S AND RESCIND DELINQUENT CHARGES

In addition to the Judge, Court Commissioner, and Court Administrator, the following Court personnel are hereby granted authority to allow the rescheduling of time payments, to cancel arrest warrants issued for Failure to Pay fines or costs as agreed; and to rescind delinquent charges on warrants and FTA's reported to the Department of Licensing: Acting Court Administrator and Legal Process Supervisor.

[Adopted effective June 1, 1998. Amended on an emergency basis effective December 6, 2013; amended on a permanent basis effective September 1, 2015.]

RULE 2. MANDATORY APPEARANCE AND PLEADINGS BY ATTORNEYS

1) Pursuant to CrRLJ 3 & 4, an attorney may enter an appearance and/or plea of not guilty on behalf of a client in any criminal or traffic offense, if said appearance or plea is made in writing or made in open court unless the defendant is charged with any offense of domestic violence, assault in the fourth degree, harassment, indecent exposure, violation of any court order, cyber stalking, cruelty to animals, negligent driving in the first degree, driving while under the influence or physical control, in which instances the defendant must appear personally before the Court for arraignment in order to properly determine any pre-trial conditions of release, or bail, which may be appropriate.

2) Unless previously commenced by an appearance made in open Court, when a written appearance is authorized it shall commence the running of the time periods established in CrRLJ 3.3 from the date of receipt by the Court. A written appearance, waiving an arraignment, but without plea, shall be considered a plea of not guilty, made in writing, or in open Court, and obviates the need for further arraignment and waives any defects in the complaint other than failure to state a crime. Telephonic requests or notice by defendant or defense counsel shall not constitute an arraignment, appearance or plea, and shall not commence the time periods under CrRLJ 3.3.

3) Personal appearance at arraignment by a defendant charged with any offense of domestic violence, assault in the fourth degree, harassment, indecent exposure, driving while under the influence or physical control is mandated by law. The "next Court day" for this Court means the next regularly scheduled Court session at least one calendar day after the violation date of the citation.

[Adopted effective June 1, 1998; amended effective September 1, 1999; September 1, 2012; September 1, 2015.]

RULE 3. TRIAL BY JURY/PRE-TRIAL CONFERENCE/READINESS HEARING

1) In every criminal case in which the defendant pleads not guilty, the Clerk shall set a date for a pretrial conference. The purpose of said conference is for presentation of motions, completion of plea bargaining, and to set a trial date and readiness hearing. Discovery shall be provided to the party requesting same at least two (2) working days PRIOR TO said conference. Unless the pre-trial conference is continued to another date or the case is resolved at the hearing, the Clerk will set a jury trial and readiness hearing. If the right to jury trial is waived, however, the Clerk shall set a bench trial date and no readiness hearing is required.

2) If the defendant fails to appear at the pre-trial conference without good cause, forfeiture of bail will be ordered and the Court will order a bench warrant for the arrest of the defendant.

3) Within twenty-two (22) days prior to an assigned jury trial date there shall be held a readiness hearing. At such hearing, it shall be mandatory that the prosecuting authority, the defense counsel, and the defendant be present. At such hearing, the following matters will be concluded: 1) All plea bargaining, 2) Exchange of witness lists, 3) Providing of any discovery not previously exchanged at the pre-trial conference, and 4) Motions on legal issues arising subsequent to the pre-trial conference or on issues arising due to new evidence.

4) At the readiness hearing, the parties will notify the Court that they are ready or not ready for trial. If both parties state that they are ready for trial, the case will subsequently be tried by jury unless waived by the defendant, or concluded by a guilty plea, or a dismissal of the charge(s), except as provided in paragraphs (5), (6), and (7) below.

5) If, after the readiness hearing, the defendant decides to plead guilty, the plaintiff moves to dismiss, or if either party seeks a continuance of the trial date, the parties shall notify the other party and the Chief Clerk, or designee, no later than noon on the court day prior to the scheduled jury trial nor later than noon on the Friday before the scheduled jury trial if the defendant is in custody. The Chief Clerk shall then set the matter for a plea hearing or a motion hearing on the afternoon calendar on the court day prior to the scheduled jury trial date, or on the jail calendar for the same date if the Defendant is in custody.

6) A failure of the defendant to be present at the readiness hearing will result in the issuance of a bench warrant for failure to appear, forfeiture of bail, and the striking of the jury trial date.

7) **Final Confirmation Required:** After the readiness hearing, but no later than noon on the court day before the jury trial is scheduled to begin nor later than noon on the Friday before the jury trial is scheduled to begin if the defendant is in custody, both parties shall notify the Chief Clerk, or designee, that the case is ready to proceed to trial. If either party fails to confirm that the trial is ready to proceed by that time, the Chief Clerk, or designee, shall set the matter for a status conference on the afternoon calendar of the court day prior to the scheduled jury trial, or on the jail calendar for the same date if the defendant is in custody, and both parties shall appear for the status conference. If either party fails to appear for the status conference, the jury trial date shall be stricken and a bench warrant may be issued.

8) Any case confirmed for trial under paragraph (7) that does not proceed to trial may subject the culpable party/parties to such sanctions, including but not limited to, jury costs, witness fees and other terms, as deemed appropriate by the Judge/Commissioner.

9) A bench warrant issued for failure to appear at a jury trial or status conference will not be quashed absent a clear and convincing showing of extraordinary circumstances that justify such a failure to appear.

10) If any attorney fails to appear for a scheduled conference, hearing, or trial, the Court may assess costs and/or sanctions against the attorney.

11) The requirements of this rule can be waived only by the Judge/Commissioner.

[Adopted effective June 1, 1998; amended effective September 1, 2004; March 1, 2005; September 1, 2008.]

RULE 4. MOTIONS AND APPLICATIONS—NOTICE—SERVICE

1) **Note for Motion.** Except as provided by paragraph 4, either party may note a motion upon the motion calendar in writing, with proper and timely notice to opposing counsel. Motions may only be noted on other calendars with the prior permission of the Judge or Commissioner for good cause shown. Each note for motion form shall include an estimate of the amount of time the party believes the motion will take. Motions improperly noted may be stricken by the Clerk.

2) **Memoranda.** Memoranda relating to motions shall not exceed ten (10) pages, not including attachments and exhibits. Requests for waiver of page limitations may be granted for good cause shown, and may be heard ex parte. Copies of any statutes, ordinances, reported cases, or other authorities the advocate deems important to his or her argument shall be attached to the memoranda. Parties are encouraged, but not required, to electronically file a "courtesy copy" of their written memoranda by e-mailing the Judge and Commissioner with electronic copies sent to opposing counsel.

3) Motion Hearing Procedures. Oral argument on motions shall be limited to five (5) minutes for each side, exclusive of testimony, unless the assigned Judge or Commissioner determines otherwise.

4) Motion to Rescind or Modify a No Contact Order or Anti–Harassment Order. A motion to rescind or modify a no contact order or anti-harassment order shall be noted in the following manner: (1) The motion shall be noted on the domestic violence calendar if the defendant and victim are not in custody, or if the defendant and/or victim are incarcerated at the Whatcom County Jail, upon the Thursday in-custody calendar, (2) the motion may be noted by the victim advocate on behalf of the victim, the city attorney's office, the court, the defendant (if pro se), or the defendant's attorney, (3) the moving party shall provide written notice to the opposing party at least five court days prior to the hearing date, and (4) the moving party shall complete and file a written "Request to Rescind or Modify No Contact Order" to note the hearing. The Clerk shall limit the number of motions for rescission or modification heard in court on each domestic violence calendar as directed by the Presiding Judge. Motions for rescission or modification of no contact orders issued before trial shall be made in writing and may only be set for in-court hearing by the Judge or Commissioner upon a finding that an actual emergency or significant change in circumstances regarding the safety of the victim exists requiring potential relief. Any victim or alleged victim requesting a hearing to modify or rescind a no contact order shall be referred to the victim advocate in the City Attorney's Office for assistance in completing this process.

[Adopted effective June 1, 1998. Amended effective September 1, 2003; amended on an emergency basis effective April 21, 2011; December 6, 2013; amended on a permanent basis effective September 1, 2015.]

RULE 5. JURY SETTINGS

A matter set for jury may be heard by the Judge or Commissioner. A party wishing to file an affidavit of prejudice must do so before any discretionary ruling, and prior to the pre-trial date.

[Adopted effective June 1, 1998.]

RULE 6. WRITTEN JUROR INSTRUCTIONS

When a jury is to be instructed in writing, proposed instructions shall be submitted on plain paper with no mark identifying the attorney or party. The original, which shall be free of citations of authority, and one copy with the citation of authority, shall be submitted to the Court at the readiness hearing.

[Adopted effective June 1, 1998.]

RULE 7. VOIR DIRE

The voir dire examination of jurors shall be conducted under the direction and control of the Court with the following guidelines:

1) It is expected that voir dire, in most cases, will consume one hour of time or less. Generally, the Struck Jury Method of voir dire will be used.

2) The Court shall ask all general questions and thereafter shall give leave to the respective parties to ask such supplementary questions as may be deemed proper and necessary by the Court. The parties may submit all proposed general questions in writing prior to voir dire.

3) The Court may intervene without objection in instances of inappropriate questioning and may limit the amount of time each party has to examine a juror or jury panel.

[Adopted effective June 1, 1998; amended effective September 1, 2003.]

RULE 8. REQUIREMENTS FOR PAYMENT OF JURY FEES UPON CANCELLATION OF JURY TRIAL

If a defendant who has been charged with a criminal violation has requested a jury trial, and if that jury panel is summoned and the Court has incurred the expense, or will incur the expense because the jury has been brought in, and if the defendant waives his or her right to a jury trial less than 48 hours prior to the date for which the jury trial had been scheduled, or otherwise causes the excusal or release of the jury from hearing the case, the defendant shall be responsible for payment to the Court of the amount of the actual costs incurred by the Court for jury fee payments and mileage reimbursements. Provided, however, that the Judge/Commissioner presiding over the case specifically determines that payment of those fees and costs shall be waived for good cause shown.

Any such jury fee costs imposed by the Court for payment and reimbursement of jury fees and mileage reimbursement shall be paid by the defendant as a condition of suspended sentence, if any, or as otherwise directed by the Court.

[Adopted effective June 1, 1998.]

RULE 9. CIVIL INFRACTION—HEARING ON MITIGATING CIRCUMSTANCES

A defendant requesting a reduction of a civil infraction penalty may have such determination based on his or her prior record and/or on other relevant information available to the Court. A timely request may be made in writing or by email.

[Adopted effective June 1, 1998. Amended effective September 1, 2003; amended on an emergency basis effective December 6, 2013; amended on a permanent basis effective September 1, 2015.]

RULE 10. PROCEDURES FOR QUASHING BENCH WARRANTS

If any Defendant fails to appear in Court for a required hearing and a bench warrant has been issued, the Clerk may set a motion to quash. The motion to quash the bench warrant may only be set under the following circumstances.

1) If no bail bond or cash bail has been ordered forfeit in any of the Defendant's cases for which warrants have been issued and are then outstanding, the Clerk may set a motion to quash upon the warrant quash calendar. The motion may only be set upon receipt of $25 per Defendant payable in advance in cash, debit/credit card, or money order.

2) If a bail bond or cash bail has been ordered forfeit in any of the Defendant's cases for which warrants have been issued and are then outstanding, the Clerk may set a motion to quash upon the warrant quash calendar. The motion may only be set if ALL of the following conditions are met:

(a) Upon receipt of $25 per Defendant payable in advance in cash, debit/credit card, or money order, and

(b) If cash bail was ordered forfeit, the Defendant posts cash bail in an amount equal to the amount of bail ordered forfeit; and

(c) If a bond was ordered forfeit, the Defendant posts a new bond in the amount ordered forfeit or provides a written request from the bail bondsman requesting reinstatement of the bond, however, a request to reinstate a bond that has previously been exonerated shall not be sufficient to satisfy this requirement,

3) All fees collected in this manner shall be applied to the costs assessed for bench warrants.

[Adopted effective June 1, 1998. Amended effective September 1, 2003; amended on an emergency basis effective December 6, 2013; September 26, 2014; amended on a permanent basis effective September 1, 2015.]

RULE 11. PROCEDURE AT CONTESTED HEARINGS

1) Speed Measuring Device Experts. When any speed measuring device expert is required to testify in a contested infraction hearing, the expert may testify by telephone, unless otherwise ordered by the Court. The party required to produce such evidence shall be responsible for arranging the expert's telephonic testimony and advising the Court Clerk prior to the scheduled time for the contested hearing.

2) Handling of Requests for Contested Hearings After Failure to Respond. If a defendant who has failed to respond to a notice of infraction, as required by RCW 46.63.070 and Rule 2.4 of the Infraction Rules for Courts of Limited Jurisdiction (IRLJ), requests that the Court set his/her case for a contested hearing, the Court Clerk shall be authorized to set a date for a contested hearing, and retrieve pleadings and/or correspondence from the Department of Licensing reflecting the failure to respond or appear, if any was sent, only upon the following conditions:

a) The defendant, within one week of the date by which a request for a contested hearing should have been received by the Court, delivers to the Court an envelope containing his/her request for a contested hearing, with a postmark clearly indicating that the envelope was addressed and mailed to the Court within the time frame for requesting contested hearings pursuant to statute and Court rule, and with the envelope indicating that it was returned to the defendant, for whatever reason; or,

b) The Court, within one week of the date by which a request for contested hearing should have been received by the Court, receives in the mail an envelope containing the defendant's request for a contested hearing, with the envelope showing a postmark clearly indicating that the envelope was mailed to the Court within the time frame for requesting contested hearings pursuant to statute and Court rule.

In all other cases, the defendant shall not be entitled to a contested hearing, and the disposition of the infraction shall be dealt with as provided by statute or Court rules for failure to respond or appear.

3) Discovery Demands. Any party alleging a violation of the rules of discovery set forth in IRLJ 3.1(b) shall document service of the discovery demand upon the opposing party by either providing a copy of the discovery demand with a stamp from the opposing party indicating the demand was received in a timely manner or by providing a return receipt from the U.S. Postal Service or private postal carrier documenting that the opposing party was served with the discovery demand in a timely manner. Discovery demands made to the City in infraction matters shall be directed to the prosecution unit of the Office of the City Attorney, which shall date-stamp all discovery demands when received.

4) Subpoenas for Bellingham Police Officers— Alternative Procedure. Subpoenas may be requested and served as provided by state law and court rules. In the alternative, defendants in contested infraction cases may serve subpoenas upon officers of the Bellingham Police Department in the following manner:

a) A subpoena may be requested and obtained from the court clerk;

b) The defendant, or his or her attorney or agent, may effectuate service of the subpoena upon the officer by serving the subpoena upon an employee of the Criminal Division of the Bellingham City Attorney's Office in that office at least seven days before the scheduled contested hearing;

c) The Bellingham City Attorney's Office shall date-stamp the subpoena, provide a stamped copy to the person serving the subpoena, and transmit the original subpoena to the officer at the Bellingham Police Department;

d) All subpoenas served pursuant to this alternative procedure shall indicate that the subject of the subpoena shall appear to testify one hour after the commencement of the calendar upon which the case is scheduled;

e) The City of Bellingham has consented to this alternative procedure. A subpoena served pursuant to this alternative procedure shall be deemed valid unless objected to in a timely fashion for good cause shown; and

f) This alternative procedure does not apply to requests for Speed Measuring Device experts employed by or contracted with the Bellingham Police Department.

5) City Attorney. Pursuant to IRLJ 3.3, the City Attorney's Office need not appear in any contested infraction unless requested by the Judge or Commissioner.

6) This rule is not intended to supersede or conflict with any statutes concerning procedures for infractions or the Infraction Rules For Courts of Limited Jurisdiction (IRLJ).

[Adopted effective June 1, 1998; amended effective October 8, 2004; March 1, 2005; September 1, 2008; amended on an emergency basis effective June 16, 2009; amended on a permanent basis effective September 1, 2012.]

RULE 12. PAYMENT OF FINES AND PENALTIES

1) Infractions. Any person who has been served with a notice of infraction and who desires to use option (1) as provided in IRLJ 2.4(b) (1), may arrange time payments on the monetary penalty according to the policy then in force.

2) Attorney and Jury Fees—Reimbursement. The Court may require partial or full reimbursement to the City for the cost of court appointed counsel and/or jury fees from those defendants the Court finds able to pay such.

3) Jail Costs—Reimbursement. The Court may require partial or full reimbursement to the City for the cost of jail time, as set by the Whatcom County Sheriff's Department, from those defendants the Court finds are able to pay the same.

[Adopted effective June 1, 1998. Amended effective September 1, 2003; amended on an emergency basis effective December 6, 2013; amended on a permanent basis effective September 1, 2015.]

RULE 13. WEAPONS IN COURT BUILDING PROHIBITED

1) Pursuant to RCW 9.41.300(1)(b), the Court has determined that weapons shall be prohibited from all indoor areas of the Bellingham Municipal Court Building, located at 2014 "C" Street.

2) Exceptions:

a) Pursuant to RCW 9.41.300(7), paragraph (a) shall not apply to weapons carried by a person engaged in military activities sponsored by the federal or state governments while engaged in official duties, to law enforcement personnel, or to courthouse security officers engaged in official duties;

b) Paragraph (a) shall not apply to weapons carried by persons proceeding directly and promptly between the exterior doors at the public entrance of the Bellingham Municipal Court Building and any official lock box or public official expressly designated by the City Council for the storage or retention of weapons.

[Adopted effective September 1, 2003.]

RULE 14. COURT FILES AND AUDIO TAPES—INSPECTION AND COPYING PROCEDURES

1) All documents, including pleadings, filed with the Court and all CD recordings of court proceedings are presumed to be available for public inspection and/or copying during Court business hours upon request, except as otherwise provided herein.

2) If any party wishes to seal any document, that party must do so by motion to the Court with proper notice to all parties. If the Court finds sufficient cause to seal the document, the Court will direct the Clerk to seal the document and the document will be placed in a sealed envelope in the Court file.

3) No sealed documents will be accepted for filing without a written court order.

4) Sealed documents will not be available for public inspection or copying.

5) Any person may request that a sealed document be unsealed, but must do so by motion to the Court with proper notice to all parties.

6) Social security numbers, mental health evaluations, and medical evaluations pertaining to drug or alcohol dependency shall not be subject to inspection or copying except where the defendant or defendant's attorney so requests, or upon Court order after a showing of good cause.

7) Private records: Pursuant to ARLJ 9(b), the following records are deemed to be "private records" and shall not be subject to inspection or copying unless they have been admitted into evidence, incorporated into a court pleading, or are the subject of a stipulation on the record which places them into public records:

a) Witness statements and police reports;

b) Pre-sentence reports and reports related to compliance with conditions of sentence;

c) Copies of driving records or criminal history records subject to RCW 10.97;

d) Correspondence received by the Court regarding sentencing and compliance with the terms of probation.

8) Quasi-public records: Pursuant to ARLJ 9(c) and RCW 10.101.020(3), the following records are deemed to be "quasi-public records" and are not subject to inspection or copying, but are subject to inspection or copying by the defendant or the defendant's attorney:

a) Witness statements;

b) Pre-sentence reports and reports related to compliance with conditions of sentence;

c) Copies of driving records or criminal history records subject to RCW 10.97;

d) Correspondence received by the Court regarding sentencing and compliance with the terms of probation, except when the information is provided on condition it remain confidential or when a finding of good cause is made for its confidentiality.

e) Any application submitted in support of a determination of indigency.

9) Copying and other charges: Pursuant to RCW 3.50.100 and RCW 3.62.060, the following fees shall be collected:

a) The charge for copying documents without a seal is fifty cents per page;

b) The charge for preparing a certified copy of an instrument on file or of record in the clerk's office is five dollars for the first page or portion of the first page and one dollar for each additional page or portion of an additional page;

c) The charge for certifying any document on file or of record in the clerk's office is five dollars. The charge for authenticating or exemplifying an instrument is two dollars for each additional seal affixed;

d) The charge for copying a document without a seal or file that is in electronic format is twenty-five cents per page;

e) The charge for copying electronic recordings of proceedings on compact discs is ten dollars per disc. The charge for any other records copied to compact disc shall be twenty dollars per disc;

f) The charge for clerk's services for ex parte orders, performing historical searches, compiling statistical reports, and conducting exceptional records searches is twenty dollars per hour or per portion of an hour;

g) For preparing a record for appeal to superior court, a fee of forty dollars including any costs of tape duplication as governed by the RALJ;

h) There shall be no charge for inspecting any document or CD; and

i) Payment for copies of CDs and documents shall be received before copies are distributed unless the Clerk, Judge, or Commissioner determines that there is good cause to waive this requirement;

10) Pursuant to ARLJ 9(e), judicial review of disclosure may be requested by the prosecutor, defendant, defense attorney, court staff, or any other interested parties. If such a request is made, the Court may withhold dissemination of the record until a hearing may reasonably be held. Following the hearing, the Court may make such restrictive orders as are necessary.

11) To ensure the integrity of court files and property, unless otherwise authorized in writing by the Judge or Commissioner:

a) All copying of court files and CDs shall be conducted by court staff;

b) Inspection of court files shall take place in the designated court file viewing area; and

c) The Clerk shall have the discretion to determine the appropriate location and equipment to be used in reviewing CDs.

Nothing in this rule shall be construed to supersede existing statutes or subsequent amendments thereto.

[Adopted effective September 1, 2003; amended on an emergency basis, effective February 16, 2010.]

RULE 15. BAIL

Effective immediately, the following policy shall govern the calculation of bail for all criminal matters:

1) If the Court determines that the defendant is not likely to appear if released on personal recognizance, the Court may require conditions of release, including the posting of cash or bond, as provided by CrRLJ 3.2(b).

2) If the Court determines that the defendant poses a substantial danger to the public to commit a violent crime, intimidate witnesses, or otherwise unlawfully interfere with the administration of justice, the Court may require conditions of release, including posting of cash or bond to guarantee performance of release conditions, as provided by CrRLJ 3.2(d). Performance bail shall be posted in the Defendant's name, as required by CrRLJ 3.2(d)(6). Any bond posted to guarantee performance of release conditions ("performance bond") must be approved by the Judge or Commissioner in writing prior to the Defendant's release.

3) If the Court, upon issuing a bench warrant, determines that bail shall be "cash" or "cash only," the defendant may post an appearance bond in the

amount of ten times the cash bail requirement in lieu of cash, prior to the defendant's first appearance in Court. If "cash" or "cash only" is not indicated on the bench warrant, the defendant may post either cash or bond in the amount specified.

4) The Court may apply cash bail posted in the defendant's name to pay the defendant's fines, penalties and costs on the present case or on any past due obligations to the Court.

5) In any case for which bail forfeiture in lieu of criminal prosecution has been authorized, bail must be received by the Court before arraignment unless previously authorized in writing by the Judge or Commissioner.

6) This rule shall be retroactively applied to all cases in which bail has previously been set.

[Adopted effective September 1, 2003; amended on an emergency basis effective September 1, 2008; November 29, 2010.]

RULE 16. CASES OF BROAD PUBLIC IMPORT

1) The assigned Judge or Commissioner may declare, in any case where the resolution of novel legal issues or particularly significant factual disputes have ramifications beyond that of a single case, that the case is a case of broad public import subject to this rule.

2) The Court may order that related or similar motions in cases of broad public import be heard together in the interests of judicial economy, may set cases upon a special motion calendar for that purpose, and may make such orders as the Court may deem necessary to expeditiously and effectively resolve said motions

3) In the interest of an informed citizenry and bar, the Clerk shall solicit and maintain a list of interested attorneys, media representatives, and any other citizens who wish to be notified when the Court reaches a decision in cases of broad public import. When a special or joint broad public import, the Clerk shall notify all members fo the list and provide a brief summary of the nature of the motion. The Court may direct that such notice include an invitation to other attorneys to file related motions for the same time as the special or joint hearing. When a written decision is filed on a case of broad public import, the Clerk shall electronically transmit a copy of the written decision to all members of said list, but only after copies are sent to the attorneys of record in the case.

[Adopted on an emergency basis effective August 12, 2004.]

RULE 17. EMERGENCY CLOSURES

1) The Judge, Commissioner, and/or Judicial Services Director may declare an emergency closure of the Court when s/he deems that severe weather conditions, natural disaster, or other emergency so requires. The Court will publicize the closure as soon

as practical, file a written administrative order closing the Court, and notify the Office of the Administrator for the Courts as soon as practical, pursuant to GR 21.

2) While the emergency persists, no hearings will be held except that the Judge, Commissioner, or Judge Pro Tem of the Court will, if circumstances permit, determine probable cause, set release conditions, and otherwise adjudicate required first appearance hearings for Defendants who are in custody. Such hearings may be held by telephone if deemed necessary due to the emergency.

3) Following an emergency closure, the Judge, Commissioner, and/or Judicial Services Director may declare the Court to re-open when the severe weather conditions, natural disaster or other emergency allows. The Court will publicize the re-opening as soon as practical.

4) All parties other than the City shall contact the Clerk's Office within two (2) business days after the re-opening of the Court has been publicly announced to reschedule any hearings that were not held due to emergency closure. Failure to do so may be deemed a failure to appear.

5) This rule shall only apply to the business of the Court, and shall not be construed to govern activities of the other branches of City government.

[Adopted effective September 1, 2008.]

RULE 18. OATHS OF INTERPRETERS AND PROSECUTORS

Any oaths or affirmations required for certified interpreters and city prosecutors, including the oath or affirmation to testify under penalty of perjury in support of an application for probable cause and the oaths required by RCW 2.42 or RCW 2.43, may be made in writing and shall endure in perpetuity, rather than on a case-by-case basis, unless revoked in writing. Certified interpreters and city prosecutors shall execute oaths or such affirmations made pursuant to this rule in writing with the original filed with the Court.

[Adopted effective September 1, 2008.]

RULE 19. JAIL AND JAIL ALTERNATIVES

1) **Use of Jail Alternatives.** Unless otherwise ordered in writing, a sentence to jail shall permit the defendant to apply for jail alternatives and the defendant may serve the defendant's jail sentence on jail alternatives at the defendant's expense if deemed eligible by the Whatcom County Jail. The Court does not permit its sentences to be served at privately-operated jails or privately-operated jail alternative programs. The Court may consider a defendant's request to serve a jail term at another jail or jail alternative facility administered by a law enforcement agency at the defendant's expense if the defendant is deemed eligible by that law enforcement agency, and

the defendant shall prove service of such sentence to the satisfaction of the Whatcom County Jail. The Court will not order the Whatcom County Jail to accept any inmate for any jail alternatives program who is not deemed eligible by the Whatcom County Jail.

2) Temporary Release. Requests for temporary release from custody will only be considered by the Court in cases of urgent medical necessity as recommended by the Whatcom County Jail medical staff or, under circumstances and upon conditions deemed appropriate by the Court, for release to an in-patient treatment facility. The Court will not consider nor grant temporary releases for funerals, work, family care, or any other circumstances.

3) Jail Supervision. The Whatcom County Sheriff, not the Court, is responsible for the operation and supervision of the Whatcom County Jail and jail alternative programs. The Court will not enter any order contrary to the Sheriff's lawful policies regarding the operation of the Jail or jail alternative programs.
[Adopted effective September 1, 2012.]

RULE 20. ELECTRONIC FILING OF LAW ENFORCEMENT REPORTS AND NOTICES OF APPEARANCE

1) Pursuant to GR 30(d)(2)(D)(ii), the Presiding Judge designates Cardinal Tracking Inc. Parking Management (also known as "TickeTrak") software and Longarm software to be "local secured system[s]."

2) Reports electronically entered into the Statewide Electronic Collision & Traffic Online Records application, the Justice Information Network Data Exchange, the Cardinal Tracking Inc. Parking Management software and/or the Longarm software by law enforcement officers pursuant to GR 30(d)(2)(D)(ii) and/or this rule shall be deemed submitted to and filed with the Court as provided by GR 30.

3) Notices of appearance may be filed electronically with the Court and opposing counsel by email. Parties filing an electronic notice of appearance thereby consent to electronic service of opposing party's notice of appearance and demand(s) for discovery, and such materials may be filed by email to the Court. All parties utilizing such procedures shall use email addresses and electronic formats acceptable to the other party and to the Court Administrator. The effective date for filing shall be as set forth in GR 30.

4) This rule shall apply retroactively to any pending cases.

[Adopted on an emergency basis effective September 26, 2014; adopted on a permanent basis effective September 1, 2015.]

BLAINE MUNICIPAL COURT LOCAL COURT RULES

Including Amendments Received Through
August 15, 2014

PREFACE

RULE 1. PROMULGATION

These rules shall be known as the Local Rules for Municipal Court of Blaine, County of Whatcom, and State of Washington. Copies of these rules will be filed with the Office of the Administer of the Courts, and the Clerk of the Municipal Court of Blaine. Copies of these rules will be distributed to the Whatcom Law Library for public reference. To the extent possible, these rules will be placed on the Internet at the Blaine Municipal Court web page. Copies will be available from the Municipal Court Clerk for Blaine. These rules will be effective on September 1, 2015, and supersede all prior rules of this court.

[Adopted effective September 1, 2012. Amended effective September 2, 2014; September 1, 2015.]

RULE 2. NUMBERING

Consistent with GR 7(b) Washington Court Rules, these rules to the extent possible conform in numbering system and in format to those rules adopted by the Supreme Court of the State of Washington for courts of limited jurisdiction and facilitate the use of the same. Each rule should be considered supplemental to the Washington Court Rules applicable to Courts of Limited Jurisdiction.

[Adopted effective September 1, 2012. Amended effective September 2, 2014.]

RULE 3. REVISIONS AND ADDITIONS
[RESERVED]

GENERAL RULES

BNMGR 1. SCOPE & ADOPTION OF RULES

These rules are adopted pursuant to GR 7 and govern the procedure in the Blaine Municipal Court in Whatcom County in the State of Washington. These rules are supplemental to the rules enacted by the Washington State Supreme Court for Courts of Limited Jurisdiction as specifically authorized by GR 7, CrRLJ 1.7, and IRLJ 1.3 of the Washington Court Rules. The Blaine Municipal Court may modify or suspend any of these local rules in any given case upon good cause being shown or upon the court's own motion in the interests of justice and/or the efficient operation of the court.

[Adopted effective September 1, 2012.]

BNMGR 21. EMERGENCY CLOSURES

a) The Judge, and/or Court Administrator may declare an emergency closure of the Court when s/he deems that severe weather conditions, natural disaster, or other emergency so requires. The Court will publicize the closure as soon as practical, file a written administrative order closing the Court, and notify the Office of the Administrator for the Courts as soon as practical, pursuant to GR21.

b) While the emergency persists, no hearings will be held except that the Judge, or Judge Pro Tem of the Court will, if circumstances permit, determine probable cause, set release conditions, and otherwise conduct required first appearance hearings for Defendants who are in custody. Such hearings may be held by telephone of [1] through video conference if deemed necessary due to the emergency.

c) Following an emergency closure, the Judge, and/or Pro–Tem Judge may order the Court reopened when the severe weather conditions, natural disaster or other emergency allows. The court will publicize the re-opening as soon as practical.

d) All parties other than the City shall contact the Clerk's Office within two (2) business days after the re-opening of the Court has been publicly announced to reschedule any hearings that were not held due to emergency closure. Failure to do so may be deemed a failure to appear.

e) This rule shall only apply to the business of the Court, and shall not be construed to govern activities of the other branches of City government.

[Adopted effective September 2, 2014.]

[1] So in original.

BNMGR 24. COURTROOM DECORUM

All attorneys and other individuals in the courtroom shall abide by the following rules of conduct:

(a) Always be Prompt. Be in the courtroom ready to proceed at the appointed time.

(b) Dress Appropriately to the Serious Nature of the Matters Before the Court. Shorts and other kinds of beach apparel are not appropriate. Clothing advertising alcoholic beverages or illegal drugs are not appropriate. Hats are not to be worn in the courtroom.

(c) Do Not Disrupt the Court Proceedings. Disruptive behavior that interferes with the functioning of the judicial system, including preventing or blocking attorneys, defendants, court officials and staff from hearing the proceedings, will be presumptively considered to be eligible for sanction as Contempt of Court under RCW 7.21, *et al.*

[Adopted effective September 1, 2012.]

BNMGR 26. JUDGES PRO TEMPORE

Except as limited by statute, Judges Pro Tempore shall have the authority of a regular judge during regular Court sessions for which he or she is appointed.

[Adopted effective September 1, 2012.]

BNMGR 30. FILING

All pleadings and other papers shall be filed with this court by mail, messenger or hand delivery, and copies of said filings or notices will also be served on other parties to the suit by mail, messenger or hand delivery. The court does not accept facsimile transmission of original pleadings or papers. Without prior agreement, service of pleadings or notices will not be considered complete on other parties by facsimile transmission, without prior written or electronic consent.

[Adopted effective September 1, 2012. Amended effective September 2, 2014.]

BNMGR 30(d). ELECTRONIC FILING OF LAW ENFORCEMENT REPORTS

1) Pursuant to GR30(d)1(D)(ii), the Presiding Judge designates Coban software, Judicial Information System, Spillman, and Long arm software to be "local secured system[s]."

2) Reports electronically entered into the Statewide Electronic Collision & Traffic Online Records application, the Justice Information Network Data Exchange, Coban, the Judicial Information System and/or the Long arm software by law enforcement officers pursuant to GR 30(d)(1)(ii) and/or this rule shall be deemed submitted to and filed with the Court upon entry into these respective secured system(s). Unless otherwise specified, any such document submitted by an officer is deemed to be signed under penalty of perjury under the laws of the State of Washington and on the date and at the place set forth in the citation.

[Adopted effective September 2, 2014.]

BNMGR 31. DISCLOSURE OF COURT RECORDS

(a) The following records and files are deemed confidential and are not available to the public for inspection or copying absent a court order, unless clearly authorized my [1] statute or court rules.

(1) Affidavits for search warrants before a return of service and inventory have been filed with the court;

(2) Mental Health, psychiatric and medical reports;

(3) Alcohol and drug evaluations and compliance reports;

(4) Deferred prosecution evaluations and police reports and any video or audio recordings maintained by the police records;

(5) Certified copies of driving records, abstracts of driving records (except for a person who has a pending case before Blaine Municipal Court for a suspended license violation or an open infraction or criminal case that has resulted in the suspension of a person's driver's license) and compiled reports of arrests and convictions;

(6) Judge's notes and worksheets;

(7) Witness statements;

(8) Address of jurors;

(9) Juror notes taken during trial.

(b) Document Requests and Fees. All requests for release of records/information shall be governed by the Judicial Information System Committee's Data Dissemination Policy, GR 31. Fees for the duplication and preparation of documents and recordings shall be maintained and made available by the Court Clerk. Payment for copies of documents and recordings must be received before copies are made, unless otherwise ordered by the court.

[Adopted effective September 1, 2012. Amended effective September 2, 2014.]

1 So in original.

BNMGR 34. ORDER OF DOCKET

(a) Criminal matters will be heard first, starting with arraignments. At the court's discretion, priority can be given to criminal matters in which the defendant is represented by an attorney, in order to minimize the effect of attorney fees on the criminal justice system. After criminal matters are complete, then civil matters, including infractions, will be heard, regardless of whether or not either party is represented by an attorney.

(b) For good cause shown, the Court may adjust the schedule to accommodate conflicts, disabilities, or other good causes and set any matter at other times and days, or adjust the order of the docket.

[Adopted effective September 1, 2012.]

CRIMINAL RULES

BNMCrR 2.2. QUASHING WARRANTS

The defendant or defendant's attorney may schedule a hearing to quash a warrant, either in person or by telephone. The warrant will not be stayed or quashed and the defendant will still be subject to arrest on the warrant until the defendant has appeared in open court and the judge has quashed the warrant, unless otherwise authorized by the Court after a telephonic hearing. Court Personnel are hereby granted authority to allow the rescheduling of time payments, to cancel arrest warrants issued for Failure to Pay fines or costs as agreed; and to rescind delinquent charges on warrants and FTA's reported to the Department of Licensing: Acting Court Administrator, Judicial & Support Services Manager.

No warrant issued for anything but failing to appear for a fine review hearing will be quashed unless the amount of bail has been posted, plus a $100.00 bench warrant fee, unless otherwise ordered by the court at a hearing, telephonically, or electronically.

[Adopted effective September 1, 2012. Amended effective September 2, 2014.]

BNMCrR 4.1. CRIMES REQUIRING DEFENDANT'S APPEARANCE AT ARRAIGNMENT

A lawyer may not enter a written plea or not guilty plea on behalf of a client if the charging document states that one or more of the charges involves domestic violence, violation of a no contact order, driving under the influence of intoxicants, driving while under the age of 21 after having consumed alcohol, or physical control of a vehicle while under the influence of intoxicants. For such charges, the defendant must appear in person for arraignments and the court shall determine appropriate conditions of pretrial release. Where legislation mandates the defendant's appearance on the next judicial day following arrest, the term "next judicial day" as applied to the municipal court shall mean the next regularly scheduled court day for the Blaine Municipal Court.

[Adopted effective September 1, 2012.]

BNMCrR 4.5. REQUIRED PRESENCE AT PRETRIAL HEARINGS

Unless a disposition of the case is entered into at the first appearance hearing or arraignment, a pretrial hearing shall be scheduled and held. Defendant and all counsel must be present at any pretrial hearing. Failure of the defendant to appear may result in the issuance of a bench warrant.

[Adopted effective September 1, 2012.]

BNMCrR 4.8. REQUEST FOR SUBPOENA

Any request for a subpoena to be issued by the court must be filed in writing at least fourteen (14) days before the hearing, or such lesser time as the court deems proper. The request may not be combined with a Notice of Appearance or any other pleading.

[Adopted effective September 1, 2012.]

BNMCrR 6.1. TRIAL BY JURY, PRE-TRIAL HEARING, READINESS HEARING

In every criminal case in which the defendant pleads not guilty, the clerk shall set a date for a pretrial hearing. The purpose of said hearing is for presentation of motions, completion of plea bargaining, or to set a trial date and readiness hearing. Unless the pretrial hearing is continued to another date or the case is resolved at the hearing, a trial date shall be scheduled at the pre-trial hearing. If a jury trial date is set a readiness hearing date will be set. If the right to jury trial is waived it must be done so in writing.

If the defendant fails to appear at the pretrial hearing without good cause, forfeiture of bail may be ordered and the court may order a bench warrant for the arrest of the defendant if probable cause is established.

Prior to an assigned jury trial date, a readiness hearing shall be held. At such hearing, it shall be mandatory that the prosecuting authority, the defense counsel, and the defendant be present unless otherwise authorized by the court. At such hearing, the following matters will be concluded:

(a) Exchange of witness lists,

(b) Providing of any discovery not previously exchanged at the pretrial hearing, and,

(c) Motions on legal issues arising subsequent to the pretrial hearing based on new evidence or on matters related to the trial itself.

At the readiness hearing, the parties will inform the Court of any issues related to the jury trial date and raise appropriate motions related to the conduct of the trial.

Any continuance of the trial date after the readiness hearing shall be authorized by the Judge. The clerk shall then set a new hearing date in the matter.

Failure of the defendant to be present at the readiness hearing may result in the issuance of a bench warrant for failure to appear, forfeiture of bail, and the striking of the jury trial date.

[Adopted effective September 1, 2012. Amended effective September 2, 2014.]

BNMCrR 6.2. WRITTEN JURY INSTRUCTIONS

Proposed jury instructions shall be submitted on plain paper with no mark identifying the attorney or party. The original, which shall be free of citations of authority, and one copy, with the citation of authority, shall be submitted to the court at the readiness hearing by each party. Copies of the original of each parties proposed jury instructions shall be emailed to the court clerk as a document that can be modified, before the trial date to facilitate changes to instructions by the Court during the jury trial.

[Adopted effective September 1, 2012.]

BNMCrR 7.2. JAIL AND JAIL ALTERNATIVES

a.) Use of Jail Alternatives. Unless otherwise ordered in writing, a sentence to jail shall permit the defendant to apply for jail alternatives and the defendant may serve the defendant's jail sentence on jail alternatives at the defendant's expense if deemed eligible by the Whatcom County Jail. The Court does not permit its sentences to be served at privately-operated jails or privately-operated jail alternative programs. The Court may consider a defendant's request to serve a jail term at another jail or jail alternative facility administered by a law enforcement agency at the defendant's expense if the defendant is deemed eligible by that law enforcement agency. The Court will not order the Whatcom County Jail to accept any inmate for any jail alternatives program who is not deemed eligible by the Whatcom County Jail.

b.) Temporary Release. Requests for temporary release from custody will be considered by the Court in cases of urgent medical necessity as recommended by the Whatcom County Jail medical staff or, under circumstances and upon conditions deemed appropriate by the Court, for release to an in-patient treatment facility.

c.) Fit for Jail Release. Should the jail require a fit for jail prior to booking, the defendant will still be considered in custody unless otherwise ordered by the judge or pro-tem judge. A temporary release order may be granted telephonically or electronically so long as probable cause is established.

d.) Jail Supervision. The Whatcom County Sheriff, not the Court, is responsible for the operation and supervision of the Whatcom County Jail and jail alternative programs. The Court will not enter any order contrary to the Sheriff's lawful policies regarding the operation of the Jail or jail alternative programs.

[Adopted effective September 2, 2014. Amended effective September 1, 2015.]

BNMCrR 8.2. MOTIONS—JUDICIAL COPIES

Judicial physical copies of all cases cited or relied upon, will be delivered to the Clerk of the Court at the time of the filing of the motion. Such judicial copies will be clearly marked as such, with the date and time of the hearing indicated.

To facilitate judicial preparation Judge's copies maybe sent by email so long as all parties are emailed copies at the same time.

[Adopted effective September 1, 2012.]

INFRACTION RULES

BNM IR 2.6. SCHEDULING OF HEARINGS

(a) Mitigation. Mitigation hearings may be conducted based upon written statements or requests. Pursuant to IRLJ 2.6(c) the court is not required to notify the parties of a date for the examination of the mitigation request.

(b) Traffic Calendar. Infraction hearings shall be set on the traffic calendar unless a request for discovery has been made or the presence of the officer has been requested at which time the court date may be reset or set on the criminal calendar.

(c) Tracking with Criminal Offenses. If the respondent is also charged with a criminal offense arising out of the same incident as that which gives rise to an alleged civil infraction, the hearing on the infraction may be scheduled at the same time as any hearing set for a criminal matter.

(d) Infraction Continuances. A court clerk may grant one (1) request for a continuance via telephone. The continuance must be requested at least seven (7) days prior to the scheduled hearing. Thereafter, all requests must be made in writing and will be approved only by the court and will be granted only where a clear showing of necessity has been made to the satisfaction of the court.

[Adopted effective September 1, 2012. Amended effective September 2, 2014.]

BNM IR 3.1. PRE–HEARING PROCEDURES

(a) Request For Subpoena. Any request for a subpoena to be issued by the court must be filed in writing at least fourteen (14) days before the hearing, or such lesser time as the court deems proper. The request may not be combined with a Notice of Appearance or any other pleading.

(b)(1) *Infractions Discovery.* Defense discovery requests for material other than a copy of the infraction, the officer's report and the speed measuring device certification must be by written Motion and set for hearing to determine the relevance of such requests.

(b)(2) *Discovery Violations.* Any party alleging a violation of the rules of discovery set forth in IRLJ 3.1 (b), or a failure to respond to a discovery request, shall document proper and completed service of the discovery demand upon the opposing party by either providing a copy of the discovery demand with a stamp from the opposing party indicating the demand was received in a timely manner or providing a return receipt from the US Postal Service or private postal carrier documenting that the opposing party was served with the discovery demand in a timely manner

or a copy of the declaration of mailing on the retained copy which was originally stamped on the original demand. Discovery demands made to the City in infraction matters shall be directed to the City Prosecutor's Office, which shall date-stamp all discovery demands when received.

(b)(3) *Advance Notice of Evidence.* No party shall introduce evidence or witnesses not listed in the police reports, information filed pursuant to BNM GR 30, or publicly available SMD certifications filed with the court, without disclosing such evidence to the opposing party, no later than 14 days prior to the date set for the hearing. Such Evidence includes the names and addresses of lay and expert witnesses, the subject of their testimony and any reports relating to the subject of their testimony. Such evidence also includes any books, papers, documents, photographs, or tangible objects which a party intends to use in the hearing or trial.

(c) Motions. Respondent's motions shall be made in writing and served on the Prosecutor for the City, and filed with the Clerk of the Court, at least fourteen (14) days before the infraction hearing. Untimely motions will be denied. Motions challenging the authority of the Court, the constitutionality of the Court, the constitutionality of any statute, ordinance or court rule pertaining to an infraction, the suppression of evidence, the authority of the prosecuting attorney prosecuting an infraction, and/or the authority of the law enforcement agency or officer filing an infraction must be made with citations to authority and legal argument, and will be decided by the Court without oral argument, as per Washington State's IRLJ 3.5.

(d) Witnesses. In any case where the City intends to call or to rely upon the sworn statement of a witness, the duty to provide a list of witnesses to the Respondent may be met by providing a copy of a citing officer's sworn statement on which the witness is identified.

(e) Dismissal by Suppression. No defendant's motion to dismiss or to suppress evidence for failure to provide discovery not required by IRLJ 3.1(b) may be heard by the Court unless the moving party has previously obtained an order from the Court compelling production of the additional discovery.

[Adopted effective September 1, 2012. Amended effective September 2, 2014; September 1, 2015.]

BNM IR 6.6. TELEPHONIC PROCEDURE AT CONTESTED HEARINGS

When any speed measuring device expert is requested to testify in a contested infraction hearing, the expert may testify by telephone, unless otherwise ordered by the court prior to the scheduled hearing date in response to a written motion, filed, noted, and heard prior to the date set for the contested hearing.

[Adopted effective September 1, 2012.]

BNM IR 7. INFRACTION WITNESS FEE

Each party is responsible for costs incurred by that party as set forth in RCW 46.63.151. The party requesting the subpoena of a witness shall pay the witness fees and mileage expenses due that witness.

[Adopted effective September 1, 2012.]

BNM IR 8. INFRACTION FINES— NO PROOF OF LIABILITY INSURANCE

If a person who has been cited with a violation of RCW 46.30.020 (failure to have proof of liability insur-ance) presents to the court clerk, by mail, email, or fax only, evidence that the person had in effect at the time of the citation liability insurance as required by RCW 46.30.020, then, upon payment of twenty-five ($25.00) administrative costs, the case shall be dismissed and the court clerk shall be authorized to make appropri-ate notation of the dismissal in the court file. This section is applicable only if the person charged has otherwise complied with all rules and procedures that govern responding to notices of infraction.

[Adopted effective September 1, 2012.]

EVERSON—NOOKSACK MUNICIPAL COURT

Including Amendments Received Through
August 15, 2015

Table of Rules

PREFACE

RULE 1. PROMULGATION

These rules shall be known as the Local Rules for Municipal Court of Everson/Nooksack, County of Whatcom, and State of Washington. Copies of these rules will be filed with the Office of the Administer of the Courts, and the Clerk of the Municipal Court of Everson/Nooksack. Copies of these rules will be distributed to the Whatcom Law Library for public reference. To the extent possible, these rules will be placed on the Internet at the City of Everson web page. Copies will be available from the Municipal Court Clerk for Everson/Nooksack. These rules will be effective on September 1, 2015, and supersede all prior rules of this court.

[Adopted effective September 1, 2015.]

RULE 2. NUMBERING

Consistent with GR 7(b) Washington Court Rules, these rules to the extent possible conform in numbering system and in format to those rules adopted by the Supreme Court of the State of Washington for courts of limited jurisdiction and facilitate the use of the same. Each rule should be considered supplemental to the Washington Court Rules applicable to Courts of Limited Jurisdiction.

[Adopted effective September 1, 2015.]

RULE 3. REVISIONS AND ADDITIONS (RESERVED)

[Adopted effective September 1, 2015.]

ENMGR. GENERAL RULES

ENMGR 1. SCOPE & ADOPTION OF RULES

These rules are adopted pursuant to GR 7 and govern the procedure in the Everson/Nooksack Municipal Court in Whatcom County in the State of Washington. These rules are supplemental to the rules enacted by the Washington State Supreme Court for Courts of Limited Jurisdiction as specifically authorized by GR 7, CrRLJ 1.7, and IRLJ 1.3 of the

Washington Court Rules. The Everson/Nooksack Municipal Court may modify or suspend any of these local rules in any given case upon good cause being shown or upon the court's own motion in the interests of justice and/or the efficient operation of the court.

[Adopted effective September 1, 2015.]

ENMGR 21. EMERGENCY CLOSURES

a.) The Judge, and/or Court Administrator may declare an emergency closure of the Court when s/he deems that severe weather conditions, natural disaster, or other emergency so requires. The Court will publicize the closure as soon as practical, file a written administrative order closing the Court, and notify the Office of the Administrator for the Courts as soon as practical, pursuant to GR21.

b.) While the emergency persists, no hearings will be held except that the Judge, or Judge Pro Tem of the Court will, if circumstances permit, determine probable cause, set release conditions, and otherwise conduct required first appearance hearings for Defendants who are in custody. Such hearings may be held by telephone of[1] through video conference if deemed necessary due to the emergency.

c.) Following an emergency closure, the Judge, and/or Pro–Tem Judge may order the Court reopened when the severe weather conditions, natural disaster or other emergency allows. The court will publicize the re-opening as soon as practical.

d.) All parties other than the City shall contact the Clerk's Office within two (2) business days after the re-opening of the Court has been publicly announced to reschedule any hearings that were not held due to emergency closure. Failure to do so may be deemed a failure to appear.

e.) This rule shall only apply to the business of the Court, and shall not be construed to govern activities of the other branches of City government.

[Adopted effective September 1, 2015.]

[1] So in original.

ENMGR 24. COURTROOM DECORUM

All attorneys and other individuals in the courtroom shall abide by the following rules of conduct:

(a) Always Be Prompt. Be in the courtroom ready to proceed at the appointed time.

(b) Dress Appropriately to the Serious Nature of the Matters Before the Court. Clothing advertising alcoholic beverages or illegal drugs are not appropriate. Hats are not to be worn in the courtroom.

(c) Do Not Disrupt the Court Proceedings. Disruptive behavior that interferes with the functioning of the judicial system, including preventing or blocking attorneys, defendants, court officials and staff from hearing the proceedings, will be presumptively considered to be eligible for sanction as Contempt of Court under RCW 7.21, *et al.*

[Adopted effective September 1, 2015.]

ENMGR 26. JUDGES PRO TEMPORE

Except as limited by statute, Judges Pro Tempore shall have the authority of a regular judge during regular Court sessions for which he or she is appointed.

[Adopted effective September 1, 2015.]

ENMGR 30(d). ELECTRONIC FILING OF LAW ENFORCEMENT REPORTS

1) Pursuant to GR30(d)2(D)(ii), the Presiding Judge designates Coban software, Judicial Information System, Spillman, Crimestar and Long arm software to be "local secured system[s]."

2) Reports electronically entered by law enforcement officers pursuant to GR 30 shall be deemed submitted to and filed with the Court as set forth in GR 30. Unless otherwise specified, any such document submitted by an officer is deemed to be signed under penalty of perjury under the laws of the State of Washington and on the date and at the place set forth in the citation.

[Adopted effective September 1, 2015.]

ENMCrR. CRIMINAL RULES

ENMCrR 2.2. QUASHING WARRANTS

The defendant or defendant's attorney may schedule a hearing to quash a warrant, either in person or by telephone. The warrant will not be stayed or quashed and the defendant will still be subject to arrest on the warrant until the defendant has appeared in open court and the judge has quashed the warrant, unless otherwise authorized by the Court after a telephonic hearing. Court Personnel are hereby granted authority to allow the rescheduling of time payments, to cancel arrest warrants issued for Failure to Pay fines or costs as agreed; and to rescind delinquent charges on warrants and FTA's reported to the Department of Licensing: Acting Court Administrator, Judicial & Support Services Manager.

No warrant issued for anything but failing to appear for a fine review hearing will be quashed unless the amount of bail has been posted, plus a $100.00 bench warrant fee, unless otherwise ordered by the court at a hearing, telephonically, or electronically.

[Adopted effective September 1, 2015.]

ENMCrR 4.1. CRIMES REQUIRING DEFENDANT'S APPEARANCE AT ARRAIGNMENT

A lawyer may not enter a written plea or not guilty plea on behalf of a client if the charging document states that one or more of the charges involves domestic violence, violation of a no contact order, driving under the influence of intoxicants, driving while under the age of 21 after having consumed alcohol, or physical control of a vehicle while under the influence of intoxicants. For such charges, the defendant must appear in person for arraignments and the court shall determine appropriate conditions of pretrial release. Where legislation mandates the defendant's appearance on the next judicial day following arrest, the term "next judicial day" as applied to the municipal court shall mean the next regularly scheduled court day for the Everson/Nooksack Municipal Court.

[Adopted effective September 1, 2015.]

ENMCrR 4.5. REQUIRED PRESENCE AT PRETRIAL HEARINGS

Unless a disposition of the case is entered into at the first appearance hearing or arraignment, a pretrial hearing shall be scheduled and held. Defendant and all counsel must be present at any pretrial hearing. Failure of the defendant to appear may result in the issuance of a bench warrant.

[Adopted effective September 1, 2015.]

ENMCrR 4.8. REQUEST FOR SUBPOENA

Any request for a subpoena to be issued by the court must be filed in writing at least fourteen (14) days before the hearing, or such lesser time as the court deems proper. The request may not be combined with a Notice of Appearance or any other pleading.

[Adopted effective September 1, 2015.]

ENMCrR 6.1. TRIAL BY JURY, PRE-TRIAL HEARING, READINESS HEARING

In every criminal case in which the defendant pleads not guilty, the clerk shall set a date for a pretrial hearing. The purpose of said hearing is for presentation of motions, completion of plea bargaining, or to set a trial date and readiness hearing. Unless the pretrial hearing is continued to another date or the case is resolved at the hearing, a trial date shall be scheduled at the pre-trial hearing. If a jury trial date is set a readiness hearing date will be set.

If the defendant fails to appear at the pretrial hearing without good cause, forfeiture of bail may be ordered and the court may order a bench warrant for the arrest of the defendant if probable cause is established.

Prior to an assigned jury trial date, a readiness hearing shall be held. At such hearing, it shall be mandatory that the prosecuting authority, the defense counsel, and the defendant be present unless otherwise authorized by the court. At such hearing, the following matters will be concluded:

(a) Exchange of witness lists,

(b) Providing of any discovery not previously exchanged at the pretrial hearing, and,

(c) Motions on legal issues arising subsequent to the pretrial hearing based on new evidence or on matters related to the trial itself.

At the readiness hearing, the parties will inform the Court of any issues related to the jury trial date and raise appropriate motions related to the conduct of the trial.

Any continuance of the trial date after the readiness hearing shall be authorized by the Judge. The clerk shall then set a new hearing date in the matter.

Failure of the defendant to be present at the readiness hearing may result in the issuance of a bench warrant for failure to appear, forfeiture of bail, and the striking of the jury trial date.

[Adopted effective September 1, 2015.]

ENMCrR 6.2. WRITTEN JURY INSTRUCTIONS

Proposed jury instructions shall be submitted on plain paper with no mark identifying the attorney or party. The original, which shall be free of citations of authority, and one copy, with the citation of authority, shall be submitted to the court at the readiness hearing by each party. Copies of the original of each parties proposed jury instructions shall be emailed to the court clerk as a document that can be modified, before the trial date to facilitate changes to instructions by the Court during the jury trial.

[Adopted effective September 1, 2015.]

ENMCrR 7.2. JAIL AND JAIL ALTERNATIVES

a.) **Use of Jail Alternatives.** Unless otherwise ordered in writing, a sentence to jail shall permit the defendant to apply for jail alternatives and the defendant may serve the defendant's jail sentence on jail alternatives at the defendant's expense if deemed eligible by the Whatcom County Jail. The Court does not permit its sentences to be served at privately-operated jails or privately-operated jail alternative programs. The Court may consider a defendant's request to serve a jail term at another jail or jail alternative facility administered by a law enforcement agency at the defendant's expense if the defendant is deemed eligible by that law enforcement agency. The Court will not order the Whatcom County Jail to accept any inmate for any jail alternatives program who is not deemed eligible by the Whatcom County Jail.

b.) Temporary Release. Requests for temporary release from custody will be considered by the Court in cases of urgent medical necessity as recommended by the Whatcom County Jail medical staff or, under circumstances and upon conditions deemed appropriate by the Court, for release to an in-patient treatment facility.

c.) Fit for Jail Release. Should the jail require a fit for jail prior to booking, the defendant will still be considered in custody unless further order by the judge or pro-tem judge. A temporary release order may be granted telephonically or electronically so long as probable cause is established.

d.) Jail Supervision. The Whatcom County Sheriff, not the Court, is responsible for the operation and supervision of the Whatcom County Jail and jail alternative programs. The Court will not enter any order contrary to the Sheriff's lawful policies regarding the operation of the Jail or jail alternative programs.

[Adopted effective September 1, 2015.]

ENMCrR 8.2. MOTIONS—JUDICIAL COPIES

Judicial physical copies of all cases cited or relied upon, will be delivered to the Clerk of the Court at the time of the filing of the motion. Such judicial copies will be clearly marked as such, with the date and time of the hearing indicated.

To facilitate judicial preparation Judge's copies maybe sent by email so long as all parties are emailed copies at the same time.

[Adopted effective September 1, 2015.]

ENM IR. INFRACTION RULES

ENM IR 2.6. SCHEDULING OF HEARINGS

(a) Mitigation. Mitigation hearings may be conducted based upon written statements or requests. Pursuant to IRLJ 2.6(c) the court is not required to notify the parties of a date for the examination of the mitigation request.

(b) Tracking With Criminal Offenses. If the respondent is also charged with a criminal offense arising out of the same incident as that which gives rise to an alleged civil infraction, the hearing on the infraction, if requested, may be scheduled at the same time as any hearing set for a criminal matter.

[Adopted effective September 1, 2015.]

ENM IR 3.1. PRE–HEARING PROCEDURES

Request for Subpoena. Any request for a subpoena to be issued by the court must be filed in writing at least fourteen (14) days before the hearing, or such lesser time as the court deems proper. The request may not be combined with a Notice of Appearance or any other pleading.

[Adopted effective September 1, 2015.]

ENM IR 6.6. TELEPHONIC PROCEDURE AT CONTESTED HEARINGS

When any speed measuring device expert is requested to testify in a contested infraction hearing, the expert may testify by telephone, unless otherwise ordered by the court prior to the scheduled hearing date in response to a written motion, filed, noted, and heard prior to the date set for the contested hearing.

[Adopted effective September 1, 2015.]

ENM IR 7. INFRACTION WITNESS FEE

Each party is responsible for costs incurred by that party as set forth in RCW 46.63.151. The party requesting the subpoena of a witness shall pay the witness fees and mileage expenses due that witness.

[Adopted effective September 1, 2015.]

ENM IR 8. INFRACTION FINES—NO PROOF OF LIABILITY INSURANCE

If a person who has been cited with a violation of RCW 46.30.020 (failure to have proof of liability insurance) presents to the court clerk, by mail, email, or fax only, sufficient evidence that the person had in effect at the time of the citation liability insurance as required by RCW 46.30.020, then, upon payment of twenty-five ($25.00) administrative costs, the case shall be dismissed and the court clerk shall be authorized to make appropriate notation of the dismissal in the court file. This section is applicable only if the person charged has otherwise complied with all rules and procedures that govern responding to notices of infraction.

[Adopted effective September 1, 2015.]

FERNDALE MUNICIPAL COURT

Including Amendments Received Through
August 15, 2015

Table of Rules

RULE 1. ADOPTION OF RULES

These rules are adopted pursuant to CrRLJ 1.7 and govern the procedure in the Ferndale Municipal Court. These rules are supplemental to the rules enacted by the Washington State Supreme Court for Courts of Limited Jurisdiction as specifically authorized by GR 7, CrRLJ 1.7, and IRLJ 1.3 of the Washington Court Rules. The Ferndale Municipal Court may modify or suspend any of these local rules in any given case upon good cause being shown or upon the court's own motion in the interests of justice and/or the efficient operation of the court.

[Adopted effective September 1, 2009.]

RULE 2. FILING

All pleadings and other papers shall be filed with this court by mail, messenger or hand delivery. The court does not accept facsimile transmission or e-mail of original pleadings or papers.

[Adopted effective September 1, 2009.]

RULE 3. DOCUMENT REQUESTS AND FEES

All requests for release of records/information shall be governed by the Judicial Information System Committee's Data Dissemination Policy, GR 31, and ARLJ 9.

Fees for the duplication and preparation of documents and recordings shall be maintained and made available by the Court Services Manager.

Payment for copies of documents and recordings must be received before copies are made.

[Adopted effective September 1, 2009.]

RULE 4. RETURN OF EXHIBITS

Every exhibit shall be returned to the party who produced it in a case that is not appealed, upon application, not earlier than thirty (30) days following the trial or entry of judgment and sentence, whichever is later. Exhibits not so returned may be destroyed after sixty (60) days following the trial or entry of judgment, unless an appeal is filed, or, if contraband, delivered to the police department for destruction.

[Adopted effective September 1, 2009.]

RULE 5. DISCLOSURE OF PUBLIC RECORDS

The following records and files are deemed confidential and are not available to the public for inspection or copying absent a court order.

- Affidavits for search warrants before a return of service and inventory have been filed with the court;

- Mental Health, psychiatric and medical reports;

- Alcohol and drug evaluations and compliance reports;

- Deferred prosecution evaluations and police reports;

- Certified copies of driving records, abstracts of driving records (except for a person who has a pending case before Ferndale Municipal Court for a suspended license violation or an open infraction or criminal case that has resulted in the suspension of a person's driver's license) and compiled reports of arrests and convictions;

- Judge's notes and worksheets;
- Witness statements;
- Address of jurors;
- Juror notes taken during trial.

[Adopted effective September 1, 2009.]

RULE 6. CRIMES REQUIRING DEFENDANT'S APPEARANCE AT ARRAIGNMENT

A lawyer may not enter a written plea or not guilty plea on behalf of a client if the charging document states that one or more of the charges involves domestic violence, violation of a no contact order, driving under the influence of intoxicants, driving while under the age of 21 after having consumed alcohol, or physical control of a vehicle while under the influence of intoxicants. For such charges, the defendant must appear in person for arraignments and the court shall determine the necessity of imposing conditions of pretrial release. Where legislation mandates the defendant's appearance on the next judicial day following arrest, the term "next judicial day" as applied to the municipal court shall mean the next scheduled court day for the Ferndale Municipal Court.

[Adopted effective September 1, 2009.]

RULE 7. PRETRIAL HEARINGS

Unless a disposition of the case is entered into at the first appearance hearing or arraignment, a pretrial hearing shall be held. Defendant and all counsel must be present at the pretrial hearing. Failure of the defendant to appear may result in the issuance of a bench warrant.

[Adopted effective September 1, 2009.]

RULE 8. TRIAL BY JURY, PRETRIAL HEARING, READINESS HEARING

In every criminal case in which the defendant pleads not guilty, the clerk shall set a date for a pretrial hearing. The purpose of said hearing is for presentation of motions, completion of plea bargaining, or to set a trial date and readiness hearing. Unless the pretrial hearing is continued to another date or the case is resolved at the hearing, the clerk will set a jury trial and readiness hearing. If the right to jury trial is waived, the clerk shall set a bench trial date.

If the defendant fails to appear at the pretrial hearing without good cause, forfeiture of bail will be ordered and the court will order a bench warrant for the arrest of the defendant.

Within fifteen (15) days prior to an assigned jury trial date, a readiness hearing shall be held. At such hearing, it shall be mandatory that the prosecuting authority, the defense counsel, and the defendant be present. At such hearing, the following matters will be concluded:

- All plea bargaining,
- Exchange of witness lists,
- Providing of any discovery not previously exchanged at the pretrial hearing, and,
- Motions on legal issues arising subsequent to the pretrial hearing or on issues arising due to new evidence.

At the readiness hearing, the parties will notify the court that they are ready or not for trial. If both parties state that they are ready for trial, the case will subsequently be tried by jury, unless waived by the defendant, or concluded by a guilty plea or a dismissal of the charge(s).

If, after the readiness hearing the defendant decides to plead guilty, the plaintiff moves to dismiss, or if either party seeks a continuance of the trial date, the parties shall notify the other party and the clerk of the court or designee immediately. The clerk shall then set the matter for a plea hearing or a motion hearing on the next available court calendar.

Failure of the defendant to be present at the readiness hearing will result in the issuance of a bench warrant for failure to appear, forfeiture of bail, and the striking of the jury trial date.

[Adopted effective September 1, 2009.]

RULE 9. WRITTEN JURY INSTRUCTIONS

When a jury is to be instructed in writing, proposed instructions shall be submitted on plain paper with no mark identifying the attorney or party. The original, which shall be free of citations of authority, and one copy, with the citation of authority, shall be submitted to the court at the readiness hearing.

[Adopted effective September 1, 2009.]

RULE 10. QUASHING WARRANTS

The defendant or defendant's attorney may schedule a hearing to quash a warrant, either in person or by telephone, but the warrant will not be stayed or quashed and the defendant will still be subject to arrest on the warrant until the defendant has appeared in open court and the judge has quashed the warrant.

No warrant will be quashed until the defendant has paid a fee pursuant to a schedule maintained and made available by the Court Services Manager.

[Adopted effective September 1, 2009.]

RULE 11. PROCEDURE AT CONTESTED HEARINGS

When any speed measuring device expert is requested to testify in a contested infraction hearing, the expert may testify by telephone, unless otherwise ordered by the court. The party requesting production of such evidence shall be responsible for arranging the expert's testimony and advising the court clerk in writing prior to the scheduled time for the contested hearing.

[Adopted effective September 1, 2009.]

RULE 12. INFRACTION CONTINUANCES

A court clerk may grant one (1) request for a continuance. The continuance must be requested by 12:00 pm the day before the scheduled hearing. Thereafter, all requests must be in writing and approved by the court.

[Adopted effective September 1, 2009.]

RULE 13. INFRACTION WITNESS FEES

Each party is responsible for costs incurred by that party as set forth in RCW 46.63.151. The party requesting the witness shall pay the witness fees and mileage expenses due that witness. Any person who requests production of an electronic speed measuring device expert and who is thereafter found by the court to have committed the infraction shall be required to pay the fee charged by the expert as a cost incurred by the party.

[Adopted effective September 1, 2009.]

RULE 14. INFRACTION FINES— NO PROOF OF LIABILITY INSURANCE

If a person who has been cited with a violation of RCW 46.30.020 (failure to have proof of liability insur-

ance) presents to the court clerk evidence that the person had in effect at the time of the citation liability insurance as required by RCW 46.30.020, then, upon payment of twenty-five ($25.00) administrative costs, the case shall be dismissed and the court clerk shall be authorized to make appropriate notation of the dismissal in the court file. This section is applicable only if the person charged has otherwise complied with all rules and procedures that govern responding to notices of infraction.

[Adopted effective September 1, 2009.]

RULE 15. INFRACTIONS DISCOVERY

Discovery requests for material other than a copy of the infraction, the officer's report and the speed measuring device certification must be set for hearing to determine the relevance of such requests.

[Adopted effective September 1, 2009.]

RULE 16. REQUEST FOR SUBPOENA

Any request for a subpoena to be issued by the court must be filed in writing at least fourteen (14) days before the hearing, or such lesser time as the court deems proper. The request may not be combined with a Notice of Appearance or any other pleading.

[Adopted effective September 1, 2009.]

LYNDEN MUNICIPAL LOCAL COURT RULES

Effective August 3, 2000

Including Amendments Received Through
August 15, 2015

Table of Rules

RULE 1. INTRODUCTORY

(a) Scope of Rules. These rules shall become effective August 3, 2000.

All proceedings in Lynden Municipal Court, Whatcom County, Washington shall be conducted in accordance with applicable statutes and Washington State Court Rules, except as modified by these Local Court Rules.

Compliance with Lynden Municipal Court Rules shall be mandatory unless waived by the Court for good cause.

[Adopted effective August 3, 2000.]

RULE 2. ALCOHOL VIOLATORS— MANDATORY APPEARANCES

A defendant who is charged by citation, complaint, or information with an offense involving driving while under the influence as defined in RCW 46.61.502, driving under age twenty-one (21) after consuming alcohol as defined in RCW 46.61.503, or being in physical control of a vehicle while under the influence as defined in RCW 46.61.504, and who is not arrested, shall appear in court for arraignment in person on the next scheduled hearing date for Municipal Court (the 2nd and 4th Wednesdays of each month), but in no event later than fourteen (14) days after the next day on which court is in session following the issuance of the citation or the filing of the complaint or information.

Appearances required by this local court rule are mandatory and may not be waived.

[Adopted effective August 3, 2000.]

RULE 3. JURY TRIAL SCHEDULING

When a jury trial is scheduled, the case will proceed to trial except in the following circumstances:

a. A plea agreement is reached, and the Court Clerk is notified prior to 12:00 noon on the Friday before trial; or

b. The Defendant enters a plea of guilty to the charge for which the trial was scheduled; or

c. The City dismisses the charge for which the trial was scheduled.

[Adopted effective August 3, 2000.]

RULE 4. PROCEDURE AT CONTESTED HEARINGS

Speed Measuring Device Experts

When any speed measuring device expert is required to testify in a contested infraction hearing, the expert may testify by telephone, unless otherwise ordered by the Court. The party required to produce such evidence shall be responsible for arranging the expert's telephonic testimony and advising the Court Clerk prior to the scheduled time for the contested hearing.

[Adopted effective September 1, 2007.]

SUMAS MUNICIPAL COURT LOCAL RULES

Including Amendments Received Through
August 15, 2015

Table of Rules

PREFACE

RULE 1. PROMULGATION

These rules shall be known as the Local Rules for Municipal Court of Sumas, County of Whatcom, and State of Washington. Copies of these rules will be filed with the Office of the Administer of the Courts, and the Clerk of the Municipal Court of Sumas. Copies of these rules will be distributed to the Whatcom Law Library for public reference. To the extent possible, these rules will be placed on the Internet at the City of Sumas web page. Copies will be available from the Municipal Court Clerk for Sumas. These rules will be effective on September 1, 2015, and supersede all prior rules of this court.

[Adopted effective September 1, 2015.]

RULE 2. NUMBERING

Consistent with GR 7(b) Washington Court Rules, these rules to the extent possible conform in numbering system and in format to those rules adopted by the Supreme Court of the State of Washington for courts of limited jurisdiction and facilitate the use of the same. Each rule should be considered supplemental to the Washington Court Rules applicable to Courts of Limited Jurisdiction.

[Adopted effective September 1, 2015.]

RULE 3. REVISIONS AND ADDITIONS (RESERVED)

[Adopted effective September 1, 2015.]

SMMGR. GENERAL RULES

SMMGR 1. SCOPE & ADOPTION OF RULES

These rules are adopted pursuant to GR 7 and govern the procedure in the Sumas Municipal Court in Whatcom County in the State of Washington. These rules are supplemental to the rules enacted by the Washington State Supreme Court for Courts of Limited Jurisdiction as specifically authorized by GR 7, CrRLJ 1.7, and IRLJ 1.3 of the Washington Court Rules. The Sumas Municipal Court may modify or suspend any of these local rules in any given case upon good cause being shown or upon the court's own motion in the interests of justice and/or the efficient operation of the court.

[Adopted effective September 1, 2015.]

SMMGR 21.   EMERGENCY CLOSURES

a.) The Judge, and/or Court Administrator may declare an emergency closure of the Court when s/he deems that severe weather conditions, natural disaster, or other emergency so requires. The Court will publicize the closure as soon as practical, file a written administrative order closing the Court, and notify the Office of the Administrator for the Courts as soon as practical, pursuant to GR21.

b.) While the emergency persists, no hearings will be held except that the Judge, or Judge Pro Tem of the Court will, if circumstances permit, determine probable cause, set release conditions, and otherwise conduct required first appearance hearings for Defendants who are in custody. Such hearings may be held by telephone of[1] through video conference if deemed necessary due to the emergency.

c.) Following an emergency closure, the Judge, and/or Pro–Tem Judge may order the Court re-opened when the severe weather conditions, natural disaster or other emergency allows. The court will publicize the re-opening as soon as practical.

d.) All parties other than the City shall contact the Clerk's Office within two (2) business days after the re-opening of the Court has been publicly announced to reschedule any hearings that were not held due to emergency closure. Failure to do so may be deemed a failure to appear.

e.) This rule shall only apply to the business of the Court, and shall not be construed to govern activities of the other branches of City government.

[Adopted effective September 1, 2015.]

[1] So in original.

SMMGR 24.   COURTROOM DECORUM

All attorneys and other individuals in the courtroom shall abide by the following rules of conduct:

(a) Always Be Prompt. Be in the courtroom ready to proceed at the appointed time.

(b) Dress Appropriately to the Serious Nature of the Matters Before the Court. Clothing advertising alcoholic beverages or illegal drugs are not appropriate. Hats are not to be worn in the courtroom.

(c) Do Not Disrupt the Court Proceedings. Disruptive behavior that interferes with the functioning of the judicial system, including preventing or blocking attorneys, defendants, court officials and staff from hearing the proceedings, will be presumptively considered to be eligible for sanction as Contempt of Court under RCW 7.21, *et al.*

[Adopted effective September 1, 2015.]

SMMGR 26.   JUDGES PRO TEMPORE

Except as limited by statute, Judges Pro Tempore shall have the authority of a regular judge during regular Court sessions for which he or she is appointed.

[Adopted effective September 1, 2015.]

SMMGR 30(d).   ELECTRONIC FILING OF LAW ENFORCEMENT REPORTS

1) Pursuant to GR30(d)2(D)(ii), the Presiding Judge designates Coban software, Judicial Information System, Spillman, Crimestar and Long arm software to be "local secured system[s]."

2) Reports electronically entered by law enforcement officers pursuant to GR 30 shall be deemed submitted to and filed with the Court as set forth in GR 30. Unless otherwise specified, any such document submitted by an officer is deemed to be signed under penalty of perjury under the laws of the State of Washington and on the date and at the place set forth in the citation.

[Adopted effective September 1, 2015.]

SMMCrR.   CRIMINAL RULES

SMMCrR 2.2.   QUASHING WARRANTS

The defendant or defendant's attorney may schedule a hearing to quash a warrant, either in person or by telephone. The warrant will not be stayed or quashed and the defendant will still be subject to arrest on the warrant until the defendant has appeared in open court and the judge has quashed the warrant, unless otherwise authorized by the Court after a telephonic hearing. Court Personnel are hereby granted authority to allow the rescheduling of time payments, to cancel arrest warrants issued for Failure to Pay fines or costs as agreed; and to rescind delinquent charges on warrants and FTA's reported

to the Department of Licensing: Acting Court Administrator, Judicial & Support Services Manager.

No warrant issued for anything but failing to appear for a fine review hearing will be quashed unless the amount of bail has been posted, plus a $100.00 bench warrant fee, unless otherwise ordered by the court at a hearing, telephonically, or electronically.

[Adopted effective September 1, 2015.]

SMMCrR 4.1.   CRIMES REQUIRING DEFENDANT'S APPEARANCE AT ARRAIGNMENT

A lawyer may not enter a written plea or not guilty plea on behalf of a client if the charging document states that one or more of the charges involves domestic violence, violation of a no contact order, driving under the influence of intoxicants, driving while under the age of 21 after having consumed alcohol, or physical control of a vehicle while under the influence of intoxicants. For such charges, the defendant must appear in person for arraignments and the court shall determine appropriate conditions of pretrial release. Where legislation mandates the defendant's appearance on the next judicial day following arrest, the term "next judicial day" as applied to the municipal court shall mean the next regularly scheduled court day for the Sumas Municipal Court.

[Adopted effective September 1, 2015.]

SMMCrR 4.5. REQUIRED PRESENCE AT PRETRIAL HEARINGS

Unless a disposition of the case is entered into at the first appearance hearing or arraignment, a pretrial hearing shall be scheduled and held. Defendant and all counsel must be present at any pretrial hearing. Failure of the defendant to appear may result in the issuance of a bench warrant.

[Adopted effective September 1, 2015.]

SMMCrR 4.8. REQUEST FOR SUBPOENA

Any request for a subpoena to be issued by the court must be filed in writing at least fourteen (14) days before the hearing, or such lesser time as the court deems proper. The request may not be combined with a Notice of Appearance or any other pleading.

[Adopted effective September 1, 2015.]

SMMCrR 6.1. TRIAL BY JURY, PRE-TRIAL HEARING, READINESS HEARING

In every criminal case in which the defendant pleads not guilty, the clerk shall set a date for a pretrial hearing. The purpose of said hearing is for presentation of motions, completion of plea bargaining, or to set a trial date and readiness hearing. Unless the pretrial hearing is continued to another date or the case is resolved at the hearing, a trial date shall be scheduled at the pre-trial hearing. If a jury trial date is set a readiness hearing date will be set.

If the defendant fails to appear at the pretrial hearing without good cause, forfeiture of bail may be ordered and the court may order a bench warrant for the arrest of the defendant if probable cause is established.

Prior to an assigned jury trial date, a readiness hearing shall be held. At such hearing, it shall be mandatory that the prosecuting authority, the defense counsel, and the defendant be present unless otherwise authorized by the court. At such hearing, the following matters will be concluded:

(a) Exchange of witness lists,

(b) Providing of any discovery not previously exchanged at the pretrial hearing, and,

(c) Motions on legal issues arising subsequent to the pretrial hearing based on new evidence or on matters related to the trial itself.

At the readiness hearing, the parties will inform the Court of any issues related to the jury trial date and raise appropriate motions related to the conduct of the trial.

Any continuance of the trial date after the readiness hearing shall be authorized by the Judge. The clerk shall then set a new hearing date in the matter.

Failure of the defendant to be present at the readiness hearing may result in the issuance of a bench warrant for failure to appear, forfeiture of bail, and the striking of the jury trial date.

[Adopted effective September 1, 2015.]

SMMCrR 6.2. WRITTEN JURY INSTRUCTIONS

Proposed jury instructions shall be submitted on plain paper with no mark identifying the attorney or party. The original, which shall be free of citations of authority, and one copy, with the citation of authority, shall be submitted to the court at the readiness hearing by each party. Copies of the original of each parties proposed jury instructions shall be emailed to the court clerk as a document that can be modified, before the trial date to facilitate changes to instructions by the Court during the jury trial.

[Adopted effective September 1, 2015.]

SMMCrR 7.2. JAIL AND JAIL ALTERNATIVES

a.) Use of Jail Alternatives. Unless otherwise ordered in writing, a sentence to jail shall permit the defendant to apply for jail alternatives and the defendant may serve the defendant's jail sentence on jail alternatives at the defendant's expense if deemed eligible by the Whatcom County Jail. The Court does not permit its sentences to be served at privately-operated jails or privately-operated jail alternative programs. The Court may consider a defendant's request to serve a jail term at another jail or jail alternative facility administered by a law enforcement agency at the defendant's expense if the defendant is deemed eligible by that law enforcement agency. The Court will not order the Whatcom County Jail to accept any inmate for any jail alternatives program who is not deemed eligible by the Whatcom County Jail.

b.) Temporary Release. Requests for temporary release from custody will be considered by the Court in cases of urgent medical necessity as recommended by the Whatcom County Jail medical staff or, under circumstances and upon conditions deemed appropriate by the Court, for release to an in-patient treatment facility.

c.) Fit for Jail Release. Should the jail require a fit for jail prior to booking, the defendant will still be considered in custody unless further order by the judge or pro-tem judge. A temporary release order may be granted telephonically or electronically so long as probable cause is established.

d.) Jail Supervision. The Whatcom County Sheriff, not the Court, is responsible for the operation and supervision of the Whatcom County Jail and jail alternative programs. The Court will not enter any order contrary to the Sheriff's lawful policies regarding the operation of the Jail or jail alternative programs.

[Adopted effective September 1, 2015.]

SMMCrR 8.2. MOTIONS— JUDICIAL COPIES

Judicial physical copies of all cases cited or relied upon, will be delivered to the Clerk of the Court at the time of the filing of the motion. Such judicial copies will be clearly marked as such, with the date and time of the hearing indicated.

To facilitate judicial preparation Judge's copies maybe sent by email so long as all parties are emailed copies at the same time.

[Adopted effective September 1, 2015.]

SMM IR. INFRACTION RULES

SMM IR 2.6. SCHEDULING OF HEARINGS

(a) Mitigation. Mitigation hearings may be conducted based upon written statements or requests. Pursuant to IRLJ 2.6(c) the court is not required to notify the parties of a date for the examination of the mitigation request.

(b) Tracking With Criminal Offenses. If the respondent is also charged with a criminal offense arising out of the same incident as that which gives rise to an alleged civil infraction, the hearing on the infraction, if requested, may be scheduled at the same time as any hearing set for a criminal matter.

[Adopted effective September 1, 2015.]

SMM IR 3.1. PRE–HEARING PROCEDURES

Request for Subpoena. Any request for a subpoena to be issued by the court must be filed in writing at least fourteen (14) days before the hearing, or such lesser time as the court deems proper. The request may not be combined with a Notice of Appearance or any other pleading.

[Adopted effective September 1, 2015.]

SMM IR 6.6. TELEPHONIC PROCEDURE AT CONTESTED HEARINGS

When any speed measuring device expert is requested to testify in a contested infraction hearing, the expert may testify by telephone, unless otherwise ordered by the court prior to the scheduled hearing date in response to a written motion, filed, noted, and heard prior to the date set for the contested hearing.

[Adopted effective September 1, 2015.]

SMM IR 7. INFRACTION WITNESS FEE

Each party is responsible for costs incurred by that party as set forth in RCW 46.63.151. The party requesting the subpoena of a witness shall pay the witness fees and mileage expenses due that witness.

[Adopted effective September 1, 2015.]

SMM IR 8. INFRACTION FINES— NO PROOF OF LIABILITY INSURANCE

If a person who has been cited with a violation of RCW 46.30.020 (failure to have proof of liability insurance) presents to the court clerk, by mail, email, or fax only, sufficient evidence that the person had in effect at the time of the citation liability insurance as required by RCW 46.30.020, then, upon payment of twenty-five ($25.00) administrative costs, the case shall be dismissed and the court clerk shall be authorized to make appropriate notation of the dismissal in the court file. This section is applicable only if the person charged has otherwise complied with all rules and procedures that govern responding to notices of infraction.

[Adopted effective September 1, 2015.]

WHITMAN COUNTY

Table of Courts

Superior Court

Whitman County Superior Court Local Rules of Court.

District Court

Local Rules for Whitman County District Court.

Municipal Courts

Albion Municipal Court—[No Local Rules].
Colfax Municipal Court.
Colton Municipal Court—[No Local Rules].
Tekoa Municipal Court—[No Local Rules].
Uniontown Municipal Court—[No Local Rules].

SUPERIOR COURT
WHITMAN COUNTY SUPERIOR COURT LOCAL RULES OF COURT

Including Amendments Received Through
August 15, 2015

Table of Rules

Rule
6. Jury Instructions [Repealed].
7. Attorney's Fees in Minor's or Incompetent's Settlements [Repealed].
8. Dissolution Actions [Repealed].
9. Security for Costs [Repealed].
10. Sureties on Bonds [Repealed].
11. Filing Orders, Judgments and Decrees [Repealed].

Rule
12. Jury Venire [Repealed].
13. Probate of Estates [Repealed].
14. Clerk's Files [Repealed].
15. Guardian Ad Litem Training and Qualification [Repealed].
16. Statement for Determination of Probable Cause [Repealed].

WHITMAN COUNTY LOCAL ADMINISTRATIVE RULES (WCLAR)

WCLAR 1. SCOPE AND PURPOSE

(a) **Classification of Local Rules.** The Local Rules for Whitman County Superior Court are adopted for the management and operation of the court. These local rules shall be classified and organized as follows:

Rules	Citation Form	Purpose
Whitman County Local Administrative Rules	WCLAR	Governs the general operation and the internal management of Whitman County Superior Court
Whitman County Local Civil Rules	WCLCR	Governs local procedures in civil cases filed in Whitman County Superior Court
Whitman County Local Guardian ad Litem Rules	WCLGALR	Governs local procedures concerning cases where the court appoints a guardian ad litem
Whitman County Local Criminal Rules	WCLCrR	Governs local procedures in criminal cases filed in Whitman County Superior Court
Whitman County Local Juvenile Court Rules	WCLJuCR	Governs local procedures in juvenile court cases filed in Whitman County Superior Court
Whitman County Local Family Law Civil Rules	WCLFLCR	Governs local procedures in family law cases filed in Whitman County Superior Court

(b) **Effective Date.** Pursuant to GR 7(a), the Whitman County Local Administrative Rules (WCLAR) take effect on July 1, 2009, as such rules describe only the internal management and organization of Whitman County Superior Court. All remaining rules, unless otherwise noted at the end of a particular rule, shall take effect on September 1, 2009.

[Adopted effective September 1, 2009.]

WCLAR 2. SUPERIOR COURT ADMINISTRATOR

(a) Appointment. The Whitman County Superior Court Administrator shall be appointed by the Superior Court Judge, and shall serve at the pleasure of the Judge.

(b) Powers and Duties. Under the direction and supervision of the Superior Court Judge, the powers and duties of the Court Administrator shall include, but are not limited to the following:

(1) Administer all non-judicial activities of the court, including case scheduling and caseload management.

(2) Prepare and administer the budget of the court.

(3) Manage and administer the financial affairs of the court.

(4) Represent the court in dealing with the Washington State Administrative Office of the Courts.

(5) Assist the Judge in representing the court on all management matters in dealing with governmental bodies and other public and private groups having an interest in the administration of the court.

(6) Provide secretarial services for the Superior Court Judge.

(7) Serve as Bailiff for jury trials and other court proceedings.

[Adopted effective September 1, 2009.]

WCLAR 3. ADDRESSES OF COURT AND COURT PERSONNEL

(a) Physical Address. The Whitman County Superior Court is located on the second floor of the Whitman County Courthouse, 400 N. Main Street, Colfax, WA 99111.

(b) Contact Information. Contact information for Whitman County Superior Court departments and personnel is as follows:

(1) *Superior Court Clerk.*

Court Clerk	Shirley Bafus
Deputy Clerks	Brenda Cloninger Lorena Lynch
Mailing Address	P.O. Box 390, Colfax, WA 99111
Telephone	509–397–6240
Fax	509–397–3546
Web Page	www.whitmancounty.org Department: Clerk

(2) *Superior Court Administrator.*

Administrator	Sonya Goldsby
Mailing Address	P.O. Box 679, Colfax, WA 99111
Email	sonyam@co.whitman.wa.us
Telephone	509–397–6244
Fax	509–397–2728
Web Page	www.whitmancounty.org Department: Superior Court

(3) *Superior Court Judge.*

Judge	David Frazier
Mailing Address	P.O. Box 679, Colfax, WA 99111
Bench Copy Email	superiorcourt@co.whitman.wa.us

Telephone	509–397–6244	
Fax	509–397–2728	
Web Page	www.whitmancounty.org	Department: Superior Court

(4) *Juvenile Court Services.*

Administrator	Kimberly S. Kopf	
Mailing Address	P.O. Box 598, Colfax, WA 99111	
Email	kimk@co.whitman.wa.us	
Telephone	509–397–5300	
Fax	509–397–5591	
Web Page	www.whitmancounty.org	Department: Juvenile & Family Courts

[Adopted effective September 1, 2009. Amended effective September 2, 2013.]

WCLAR 4. SESSIONS OF COURT

(a) Court Hours. The court will be in session from 9:00 a.m. until 12:00 noon and from 1:30 p.m. until 5:00 p.m., except on law and motion day, when the court will be in session from 8:30 a.m. until 12:00 noon, and from 1:30 p.m. until 5:00 p.m.

(b) Modification of Court Hours. The court may modify court hours as may be deemed appropriate on a case-by-case basis.

[Adopted effective September 1, 2009.]

WCLAR 5. LAW AND MOTION DAY

(a) Day Established. Except as otherwise ordered by the court, Friday of each week shall be law and motion day.

(b) Civil Docket. Civil cases heard on the law and motion docket shall include ex parte matters, adoptions, default and uncontested dissolutions, probate and guardianship issues, discovery motions, protection order hearings, unlawful detainer, family law, and other civil motions or issues of law that involve no more than 10 minutes on each side to present.

(c) Criminal Docket. Criminal matters to be heard on the law and motion docket shall include first appearances, bail hearings, arraignments, omnibus hearings, status and/or scheduling hearings, readiness hearings, sentencings, and criminal motions or issues of law involving no more than 10 minutes on each side to present.

(d) Law and Motion Calendar. The arrangement of the law and motion calendar shall be as follows:

8:30 a.m.	Civil Docket
10:00 a.m.	Criminal Docket
1:30 p.m.	Criminal Sentencings
3:00 p.m.	RALJ and Administrative Appeals, Mental Health Hearings, Specially–Set Hearings

(e) Special Settings. Law and motion matters requiring testimony and/or argument exceeding more than 10 minutes per side shall be specially set by the parties through the court administrator.

[Adopted effective September 1, 2009.]

WCLAR 6. WORKING COPIES TO JUDGE

(a) **Delivery.** Bench copies of briefs, memoranda of law, affidavits, declarations, exhibits, and other legal documents requiring thorough consideration by the court shall be delivered to the judge's chamber an appropriate period prior to the trial or hearing thereon.

(b) **Manner of Delivery.** Bench copies may be delivered to chambers personally, by mail, by fax, or by electronic transmission via e-mail attachment.

(1) Electronic transmission via email attachment is the court's preferred method of receiving bench copies of documents. Such attachments shall be in Microsoft Word or Adobe Portable Document (PDF) format. The email address for purposes of the electronic delivery of bench copies is as follows: *superiorcourt@co. whitman.wa.us.*

(2) Delivery of bench copies by fax transmission will only be permitted for documents not exceeding 10 pages in length.

[Adopted effective September 1, 2009.]

WCLAR 7. SETTING CASES FOR TRIAL AND OTHER HEARINGS

(a) **Civil and Family Law Cases.** The Court Administrator is primarily responsible for setting civil and family cases for trial or other hearings that are not set on the law and motion calendar. The court administrator will generally be involved in trial setting hearings, and counsel and/or parties involved in scheduling civil and domestic cases are encouraged to confer with one another and with the court administrator as to available dates. In lieu of a trial setting hearing, counsel and/or the parties may schedule trial dates through a joint telephone or other conference directly with the court administrator.

(b) **Criminal Cases.** The scheduling of hearings and trials relating to criminal matters will generally be handled by the judge in open court and in the presence of the defendant and counsel. Suppression and other evidentiary hearings or special criminal hearings, however, shall be scheduled by counsel through a joint telephone or other conference directly with the court administrator.

[Adopted effective September 1, 2009.]

WCLAR 8. EXHIBITS

(a) **Pre–Marking.** Counsel shall arrange with the clerk for the marking of all exhibits prior to trial. Generally, the plaintiff or petitioner will be assigned exhibit numbers 1 through 199, and the defendant or respondent will be assigned exhibit numbers 200 through 299.

(b) **Copies.** Unless the making of copies is impractical, legible copies of exhibits shall be furnished to opposing counsel and the court, numbered the same as marked by the clerk. This rule shall not apply to rebuttal or impeachment exhibits not required to be offered in the party's case in chief.

(c) **Organization.** Where possible, counsel shall organize the original set of exhibits, and the copies for the court and opposing counsel or party in numerical order in a loose leaf notebook or similarly organized fashion.

[Adopted effective September 1, 2009.]

WCLAR 9. TELEPHONE HEARINGS

(a) **Telephone Hearings Allowed.** Hearings on issues not involving witness testimony, and most other pretrial motions, including brief summary judgment motions, may be heard by telephone conference call in lieu of a personal appearance by counsel and/or a party.

(b) **Arranging Telephone Hearings.** Telephone conference call hearings shall be arranged through the court administrator.

(c) **Conduct of Telephone Hearings.** The judge shall initiate the calls for telephone hearings and shall conduct such hearings in open court and on the record by use of the courtroom speaker telephone system.

(d) **Cost of Telephone Hearings.** Unless otherwise agreed, each attorney or party appearing by telephone shall bear the cost of the conference call. The court's charge to each attorney or party appearing by telephone shall be $20.00 for each half hour or part thereof of the duration of the call. In appropriate cases, this charge may be waived by the court.

[Adopted effective September 1, 2009. Amended effective September 2, 2013.]

WCLAR 10. WITNESS TESTIMONY BY TELEPHONE

(a) **Witness Testimony By Telephone.** If agreed by all parties involved in a case, witness testimony may be presented by telephone in lieu of a personal appearance by the witness.

(b) **Arranging Telephone Testimony.** The attorney or party intending to call a witness by telephone is responsible for arranging the timing and availability of the witnesses' testimony, and for obtaining a telephone number where the witness can be immediately reached. Calls to witnesses will be placed in court on the courtroom speaker telephone system.

(c) **Cost of Telephone Testimony.** The attorney or party calling a witness by telephone shall pay the court's charge for such service at the rate of $20.00 for each half hour or part thereof of the duration of the call. In appropriate cases, this charge may be waived by the court.

[Adopted effective September 1, 2009.]

WHITMAN COUNTY LOCAL CIVIL RULES (WCLCR)

WCLCR 40(b). METHOD OF SETTING MATTERS FOR TRIAL

WCLAR 7(a) shall govern the method and manner of setting civil case or other hearings, except matters to be heard on the Law and Motion Docket, in Whitman County Superior Court.

[Adopted effective September 1, 2009.]

WCLCR 43(a)(1). WITNESS TESTIMONY BY TELEPHONE

The presentation of witness testimony at trial or other evidentiary hearing is governed by WCLAR 9.

[Adopted effective September 1, 2009.]

WCLCR 43(e)(1). EVIDENCE IN DEFAULT AND UNCONTESTED DISSOLUTION OF MARRIAGE

In default and uncontested dissolution of marriage cases, the jurisdictional evidence and other testimony in support of the petition may be presented through Findings of Fact and Conclusions of Law verified by the petitioner, respondent, or both, or through a separate affidavit or declaration of either or both of the parties. The final paperwork in default and uncontested dissolution of marriage cases may be presented to the judge in chambers or by mail, in lieu of an appearance at a court hearing.

[Adopted effective September 1, 2009.]

WCLCR 47(a). EXAMINATION OF JURORS

(a) **Struck Jury Method.** Unless otherwise ordered in a particular case, the "struck jury" method shall be utilized for jury selection in civil trials in Whitman County Superior Court. Under this method:

(1) Jurors shall be each given a number and will be seated in numerical order in the spectator section of the courtroom;

(2) The lawyers will be given an equal amount of time to question prospective jurors;

(3) When a juror is struck or excused, the jury panel will consist of the first 12 jurors in numerical order then remaining;

(4) If a party passes on a peremptory challenge, the party accepts the first 12 jurors then existing, and that party cannot thereafter exercise a peremptory challenge against any one of these 12 jurors. Passing on a peremptory challenge does not waive the right to exercise an available peremptory challenge against any of the other prospective jurors.

[Adopted effective September 1, 2009.]

WCLCR 56. SUMMARY JUDGMENT

(a) **Motion and Proceedings.** A party filing a motion for summary judgment under CR 56 shall obtain a date for scheduling the hearing with the court administrator. Summary judgment hearings must be specially set and shall not be heard on the law and motion calendar.

[Adopted effective September 2, 2013.]

WCLCR 77. SESSIONS OF COURT

(f) **Sessions.** Whitman County Superior Court shall hold sessions in accordance with the hours set forth in WCLAR 4.

(k) **Motion Day.** The schedule for law and motion days in Whitman County Superior Court is set forth in WCLAR 5.

[Adopted effective September 1, 2009.]

WCLCR 80(b). ELECTRONIC RECORDING

Pursuant to WCLAR 11, the official record of all court proceedings in Whitman County Superior Court shall be recorded and maintained on electronic or mechanical recording devices.

[Adopted effective September 1, 2009.]

WHITMAN COUNTY LOCAL GUARDIAN AD LITEM RULES (WCLGALR)

WCLGALR 7. GRIEVANCE PROCEDURES

The following policies and procedures shall govern the filing, investigating, and adjudication of grievances made by or against guardians ad litem under Titles 11, 13, and 26 RCW:

(a) **Submission of Complaints.** All complaints must be in writing and must be submitted to the Superior Court Presiding Judge. All complaints must bear the signature, name, and address of the person filing the complaint.

(b) **Review of Complaint.** Upon receipt of a written complaint, the Presiding Judge shall review the complaint or in the case of a conflict, refer the complaint to another judge or court commissioner.

(c) **Findings and Action on Complaint.** The reviewing judge shall either:

(1) Make a finding that the complaint is with regard to a case then pending in the court and decline to

review the complaint and so inform the complainant. In such instances, the judge shall advise the complainant that the complaint may only be addressed in the context of the case at bar, either by seeking the removal of the guardian ad litem or by contesting the information or recommendation contained in the guardian ad litem's report or testimony;

(2) Make a finding that the complaint has no merit on its face, and decline to review the complaint and so inform the complainant; or,

(3) Make a finding that the complaint appears to have merit and request a written response from the guardian ad litem or other person, against whom the complaint is brought within 10 business days, detailing the specific issues in the complaint to which the reviewing judge desires a response. The reviewing judge shall provide the guardian ad litem or other person against whom the complaint is brought with a copy of the original complaint. In considering whether any complaint against a guardian ad litem has merit, the reviewing judge shall consider whether the complaint alleges the guardian ad litem has (i) violated a code of conduct, (ii) misrepresented his or her qualifications to serve as a guardian ad litem, (iii) breached the confidentiality of the parties, (iv) falsified information in a report or in testimony before the court, (v) failed, when required, to report abuse of a child, (vi) communicated with a judicial officer ex parte concerning a case for which he or she is serving as a guardian ad litem, (vii) violated state or local laws or court rules, or (viii) taken or failed to take any other action which would reasonably place the suitability of the person to serve as guardian ad litem in question.

(4) *Response and Findings on Complaint.* Upon receipt of a written response to a complaint, the reviewing judge may schedule a hearing, request additional materials, or enter a decision based upon the review of the record alone. The reviewing judge shall make a finding as to each of the specific issues in the complaint to which the reviewing judge desired a response as delineated in the judge's letter to the person against whom the complaint is brought. Such finding shall state that either there is no merit to the issue based upon the response or that there is merit to the issue.

(d) Forms of Discipline. The reviewing judge shall have authority to issue a written admonition or a written reprimand, refer the guardian ad litem to additional training, or suspend or remove the guardian ad litem from the registry. In considering an appropriate form of discipline, the judge shall take into consideration any prior complaints that resulted in an admonition, reprimand, referral to training, or suspension or removal from the registry. If the guardian ad litem against whom the discipline is directed is listed on more than one registry, the suspension or removal may apply to each registry on which the guardian ad litem is listed, at the direction of the reviewing judge.

(e) Notice of Decision. The complainant and the person against whom the complaint is brought shall be notified in writing of the reviewing judge's decision following the receipt of the response to the complaint.

(f) Confidentiality. A complaint shall be deemed confidential for all purposes unless the judge reviewing the complaint has determined that the complaint has merit. Any record of complaints filed which are not deemed by the judge to have merit shall be confidential, and shall not be disclosed except by court order, upon good cause shown, after the person against whom the complaint was brought has been given notice and an opportunity to be heard.

(g) Processing Standards. Complaints shall be resolved within 25 days of the date of receipt of the written complaint if a case is pending. Complaints shall be resolved within 60 days of the date of receipt of the written complaint if the complaint is filed after the conclusion of the case.

(h) Removal from Registry. When a guardian ad litem is removed from the court's registry pursuant to the disposition of a grievance hereunder, the court administrator shall send notice of such removal to the Administrative Office of the Courts. When the court administrator receives notice from the Administrative Office of the Courts that a guardian ad litem on the court's registry has been removed from the registry of any other Washington Superior Court, the court administrator shall advise of the judge of such removal.

[Adopted effective September 1, 2009.]

WHITMAN COUNTY LOCAL CRIMINAL RULES (WCLCrR)

WCLCrR 3.3. TIME FOR TRIAL AND READINESS HEARING

(d)(1) Initial Setting of Trial and Readiness Hearing. At the time of arraignment, unless a delay is requested by either party and granted by the court, the court shall set the date for trial within the time limits prescribed by CrR 3.3.

(i) Readiness Hearing.

(1) At the time a criminal case is set for trial, the court shall also set a readiness hearing. The readiness hearing shall be set approximately 10 days before the date trial is scheduled to commence. Prior to such hearing, the following matters shall be concluded: (i) all plea bargaining, (ii) all hearings on motions to suppress and other legal and evidentiary pretrial issues, and (iii) the full exchange of discovery.

(2) At the conclusion of the readiness hearing, the court will no longer accept any plea bargaining arrangements. Thereafter, the case will be tried by jury, unless waived by the defendant, or concluded by guilty plea(s) to the original charge(s), or by a dismissal of the charge(s).

(3) A failure of the defendant to be present at the readiness hearing shall result in the issuance of a bench warrant for failure to appear and the vacation of the scheduled trial date.

(4) The requirements of this readiness hearing rule can be waived or modified only by order of the court.

[Adopted effective September 1, 2009.]

WCLCrR 4.5.　OMNIBUS HEARING

(d) Motions. The failure of a party to appear for the Omnibus Hearing or to submit a joint Summary Memorandum in accordance with subsection (h) hereof, may constitute a waiver of the subsequent filing of motions or the raising of issues, objections and errors required to be addressed at the Omnibus Hearing under CrR 4.5.

(h) Memorandum. In lieu of a hearing in open court and on the record, the Omnibus procedure set forth in CrR 4.5 may be complied with by the completion, submission and filing of a joint Summary Memorandum substantially in the form set forth in CrR 4.5(h).

(i) Appearance of Defendant. Unless ordered by the court, the appearance of the defendant at the Omnibus Hearing is optional and not mandatory.

[Adopted effective September 1, 2009.]

WCLCrR 6.4.　VOIR DIRE AND JUROR CHALLENGES

Unless otherwise ordered by the court in a particular case, the "struck jury" method shall be utilized for jury selection in criminal trials in Whitman County Superior Court. The voir dire procedures in criminal trials shall be the same as the procedures adopted for civil trials under WCLCR 47(a).

[Adopted effective September 1, 2009.]

WHITMAN COUNTY LOCAL JUVENILE COURT RULES (WCLJuR) [Reserved]

WHITMAN COUNTY LOCAL FAMILY LAW CIVIL RULES (WCLFLCR) [Repealed]

WCLFLCR 88.　PARENTING SEMINARS [REPEALED]

[Adopted effective September 1, 2009. Repealed effective September 2, 2013.]

WHITMAN COUNTY LOCAL COURT RULES [Repealed]

RULE 1.　SESSIONS OF COURT [REPEALED]

[Adopted effective September 15, 1991; repealed effective September 1, 2009.]

RULE 2.　LAW AND MOTION DAY [REPEALED]

[Adopted effective September 15, 1991; repealed effective September 1, 2009.]

RULE 3.　WORKING COPIES TO JUDGE [REPEALED]

[Adopted effective September 15, 1991; repealed effective September 1, 2009.]

RULE 4.　SETTING CASES FOR TRIAL [REPEALED]

[Adopted effective September 15, 1991; repealed effective September 1, 2009.]

RULE 5.　EXHIBITS [REPEALED]

[Adopted effective September 15, 1991; repealed effective September 1, 2009.]

RULE 6.　JURY INSTRUCTIONS [REPEALED]

[Adopted effective September 15, 1991; repealed effective September 1, 2009.]

RULE 7.　ATTORNEY'S FEES IN MINOR'S OR INCOMPETENT'S SETTLEMENTS [REPEALED]

[Adopted effective September 15, 1991; repealed effective September 1, 2009.]

RULE 8.　DISSOLUTION ACTIONS [REPEALED]

[Adopted effective September 15, 1991; repealed effective September 1, 2009.]

RULE 9. SECURITY FOR COSTS [REPEALED]

[Adopted effective September 15, 1991; repealed effective September 1, 2009.]

RULE 10. SURETIES ON BONDS [REPEALED]

[Adopted effective September 15, 1991; repealed effective September 1, 2009.]

RULE 11. FILING ORDERS, JUDGMENTS AND DECREES [REPEALED]

[Adopted effective September 15, 1991; repealed effective September 1, 2009.]

RULE 12. JURY VENIRE [REPEALED]

[Adopted effective September 15, 1991; repealed effective September 1, 2009.]

RULE 13. PROBATE OF ESTATES [REPEALED]

[Adopted effective September 15, 1991; repealed effective September 1, 2009.]

RULE 14. CLERK'S FILES [REPEALED]

[Adopted effective September 15, 1991; repealed effective September 1, 2009.]

RULE 15. GUARDIAN AD LITEM TRAINING AND QUALIFICATION [REPEALED]

[Adopted effective September 15, 1991; repealed effective September 1, 2009.]

RULE 16. STATEMENT FOR DETERMINATION OF PROBABLE CAUSE [REPEALED]

[Adopted effective August 25, 1997; amended effective September 1, 1998; repealed effective September 1, 2009.]

DISTRICT COURT

LOCAL RULES FOR WHITMAN COUNTY DISTRICT COURT

Including Amendments Received Through
August 15, 2015

Table of Rules

CHAPTER ONE. SCOPE AND CONSTRUCTION

RULE 1.01. SCOPE

These rules govern the procedure in Whitman County District Court. The court may modify or suspend any of these local rules in any given case upon good cause being shown or upon the court's own motion.

[Adopted effective September 15, 1991.]

RULE 1.02.   COURTS

The main office of Whitman County District Court shall be in Colfax, Washington, and the court shall maintain a satellite office in Pullman, Washington. Cases arising within the jurisdiction of Whitman County District Court may be heard in either location, and cases may be transferred between offices at the discretion of the Judge or Court Administrator.

[Adopted effective September 15, 1991.]

RULE 1.03.   SCHEDULING

(a) **Calendar.** The Court Administrator shall maintain a calendar for all cases set for arraignment, trial or other hearing.

(b) **Priority of Settings.** Whenever the case load of the court requires, trials and other hearings will be given multiple settings on the calendar, and will proceed according to the order determined by the judge.

(c) **Transfer of Cases.** If the caseload or other circumstances so require, the court may appoint a Court Commissioner or Judge Pro Tempore to hear cases and/or may transfer cases to another court location for hearing.

(d) **Case Processing Time Standards.** The Case Processing Time Standards established by the Board for Judicial Administration, Court Management Council and published by the Washington State Office of the Administrator for the Courts in August 1990 are hereby adopted as case processing time standards for Whitman County District Court.

[Adopted effective September 15, 1991.]

CHAPTER TWO.   CRIMINAL RULES

RULE 3.2.   DISPOSITION BY FORFEITURE OF BAIL

The court may permit the disposition of any case or class of cases by forfeiture of bail by the entry of a written order showing the reasons. If the court allows forfeiture of bail, it may accept the bail as full payment including all statutory assessments.

[Adopted effective September 15, 1991.]

RULE 4.05. PRETRIAL APPLICATION

(a) Pretrial Screening Application. In every criminal case, the plaintiff and defendant shall file a written Pretrial Screening Application. The purpose of the application is to assist in determining whether the case will be disposed of other than by trial, and to arrange for the disposition of all preliminary motions and issues prior to trial.

(b) Pretrial Screening Application Issues. Issues and motions to be addressed in the Pretrial Screening Application shall include the following:

(1) Motions to dismiss.

(2) Motions to suppress evidence.

(3) Discovery motions.

(4) Motions in limine.

(5) Motions to amend.

(6) Notice of intent to resolve case without trial.

(7) Notice of intent to seek Deferred Prosecution.

(8) Waiver of right to trial by jury.

(9) Readiness for trial.

(10) Unavailable trial or hearing dates.

(11) Request for Bill of Particulars

(c) Deadline for Filing Application.* The court or a court clerk shall schedule a deadline for the filing of Pretrial Screening Applications. The Pretrial Screening Application deadline shall be scheduled approximately 45 days after the date of the arraignment. Written notice shall be provided to all parties at least 30 days prior to this deadline date. The Pretrial Screening Application deadline shall not be continued or stayed for any reason except under extraordinary circumstances. Failure to consult with clients, witnesses, or to have done any necessary research shall not be considered an extraordinary circumstance.

(d) Content, Filing, and Service of Application.* The Pretrial Screening Application must address all pretrial issues to be raised in the case, and must be accompanied with any necessary supporting motions, affidavits, briefs, waivers, memoranda or other documentation. The application must be filed with the court and served on the opposing counsel or party on or before the scheduled deadline. Opposing counsel shall have 14 days from this deadline to serve and file opposing motions, affidavits, briefs, memorandums or other documents. Any party wishing to present witnesses at any motion hearing shall so advise opposing counsel or party and the court by naming said witnesses and by providing a written statement detailing the general testimony anticipated. The court may provide a Pretrial Screening Application form which will be made available to parties for use in complying with this rule.

(e) Scheduling or Other Orders.* The court shall promptly determine all pretrial issues after reviewing the Pretrial Screening Application, and shall thereafter enter such scheduling or other orders as deemed necessary. If additional testimony, evidence or argument is necessary, the Court shall set the matter for a formal pretrial hearing.

(f) Failure to Raise Pretrial Issues.* The failure to raise a pretrial issue in the Pretrial Screening Application or to fully comply with Rule 4.05(d), shall be deemed a waiver of that issue, unless it is determined that it could not have been reasonably raised at the time of the Pretrial Screening Application filing deadline.

(g) Failure to Timely File Application.* Failure to timely file a Pretrial Screening Application shall constitute a determination that the party has waived all pretrial motions and is prepared to proceed to trial. To facilitate scheduling, the court may thereupon schedule a mandatory appearance pretrial hearing where the defendant, defense counsel, and the prosecuting attorney shall appear to confirm readiness for trial.

(h) Dispositions Allowed After Trial Is Scheduled.* Once a trial is scheduled and/or confirmed by the parties, no settlement offers will be accepted by the court. The only dispositions which will be allowed after that date will be a plea of guilty as charged, trial, or dismissal on prosecutor's motion.

[Adopted effective September 15, 1991.]

* Suggested title added by Publisher.

RULE 4.07. DISCOVERY

(a) Case Reports. The prosecuting attorney shall provide the defense attorney or defendant, upon payment of costs, with a copy of the police or other investigative case report concerning filed charges within five (5) business days from receipt of written demand therefor. Reports shall be provided without costs in cases where counsel has been appointed because of indigency. The prosecuting attorney shall have the discretion to excise any portions of any report for the protection of the victims, witnesses, or for the general welfare of the community, provided the defendant or his or her attorney is advised that an excision or deletion has been made.

(b) Other Discoverable Material. Except for police or other investigative reports required under the previous section, other discovery demands and requests made pursuant to CrRLJ 4.7 shall be answered within 14 days of arraignment or within 14 days of receipt of written demand or request, whichever is later.

(c) BAC Verifier DataMaster Records. To facilitate the availability of discoverable material, the prosecuting attorney shall file BAC Verifier DataMaster certificates concerning machine and simulator solution certifications with the court clerk at the Colfax office of the court. In addition, the prosecuting attorney may file database records concerning BAC Verifier

DataMaster machines operated in Whitman County with said court clerk. The clerk shall maintain such information as a public record, and shall make these records available for inspection and copying when requested. Filing with the court shall satisfy the prosecution's discovery obligations with respect to these records.

(d) Preservation of Simulator Solutions. BAC Verifier Datamaster simulator solutions are subject to defense discovery after said solutions are taken out of service. In no event, however, shall a law enforcement agency be required to retain a particular simulator solution for more than 120 days after the solution is taken out of service. Samples of simulator solutions which are still in service are not subject to discovery. Unless a determination of indigency has been made by the court, costs incurred in obtaining and retesting simulator solution samples shall be borne by the defendant.

(e) Protective Orders. Nothing in this rule shall preclude a party from seeking a protective order or other limitations or restrictions on discovery authorized by CrRLJ 4.7.

[Adopted effective September 15, 1991.]

RULE 6.01.   RESOLUTION WITHOUT TRIAL

(a) Notice to the Court. When a case scheduled for trial or other hearing is settled or will otherwise be resolved without the need for trial or other hearing, notice of that fact shall be immediately given by the parties to the court.

(b) Notice of Witnesses. It shall be the duty of each party to notify it's own witnesses, not only of the date and time of trial, but also of continuances, pretrial hearings, motions and other proceedings. The court will not pay witness fees to witnesses who appear for a case which has been continued or settled without trial or hearing. Such costs shall be borne by the party or attorney who called or subpoenaed the witness.

[Adopted effective September 15, 1991.]

CHAPTER THREE.   TRAFFIC INFRACTION CASES

RULE 3.01.   CONTESTED HEARINGS— PRELIMINARY PROCEEDINGS

(a) Subpoena. In contested cases, the defendant and the plaintiff may subpoena witnesses necessary for the presentation of their respective cases. The subpoena may be issued by a judge, court commissioner, or clerk of court or by a party's lawyer. A subpoena directed to the officer or officers that signed and issued the Notice of Infraction shall be served by the court. Such service shall be effected by the court's mailing or delivering a copy of the subpoena to the business address of the officer's law enforcement agency. The responsibility for serving subpoenas on other witnesses, including other police witnesses, is upon the party requesting the subpoena. Such subpoenas may be directed to the sheriff of any county or any peace officer of any municipality in the state in which the witness may be or it may be served as provided in CR 45(c).

(b) Discovery of Case Reports. The plaintiff shall provide the defendant or the defendant's attorney with a copy of the officer's written report or any other written statement it intends to introduce into evidence within five (5) business days from receipt of written demand therefor.

(c) Discovery of Radar Records. The plaintiff may file Speed Measuring Device Certificates authorized by JTIR 6.6 with the court clerk at the Colfax office of the court. In addition, the plaintiff may file other certificates and records with respect to radar units and other speed measuring devices used in Whitman County with said court clerk. The clerk shall maintain such information as a public record, and shall make these records available for inspection and copying when requested.

(d) Other Discovery. Except as provided herein, no additional discovery shall be authorized in traffic infraction cases without prior written order of the court. Such an order shall be entered only after a hearing brought on by proper motion and notice, or upon the stipulation of the parties.

[Adopted effective September 15, 1991.]

RULE 3.03.   TRAFFIC INFRACTION HEARINGS

Contested hearings and mitigation hearings shall be held in open court and shall be on the record. Such hearings shall not be held by telephone or mail, except upon order of the court for good cause shown.

[Adopted effective September 15, 1991.]

MUNICIPAL COURTS
ALBION MUNICIPAL COURT—
[No Local Rules]

COLFAX MUNICIPAL COURT

PUBLISHER'S NOTE

The Colfax Municipal Court does not have any separate local rules. However, the Court requires one-week notice to reschedule a hearing date, and permits a matter to be rescheduled only one time.

COLTON MUNICIPAL COURT—
[No Local Rules]

TEKOA MUNICIPAL COURT—
[No Local Rules]

UNIONTOWN MUNICIPAL COURT—
[No Local Rules]

YAKIMA COUNTY

Table of Courts

Superior Court

Yakima County Superior Court Local Rules.

District Court

Local Rules for Yakima County District Court.

Municipal Courts

Grandview Municipal Court—[No Local Rules].
Granger Municipal Court—[No Local Rules].
Moxee City Municipal Court Local Rules.
Selah Municipal Court Local Rules.
Sunnyside Municipal Court—[No Local Rules].
Toppenish Municipal Court—[No Local Rules].
Local Rules of Practice and Procedure for the Union Gap Municipal Court.
Wapato Municipal Court.
Local Rules of Practice and Procedure for the Yakima Municipal Court.
Zillah Municipal Court—[No Local Rules].

SUPERIOR COURT

YAKIMA COUNTY SUPERIOR COURT LOCAL RULES

Including Amendments Received Through
August 15, 2015

Table of Rules

GENERAL RULES (Cite as LGR)

GENERAL RULE 7. YAKIMA COUNTY SUPERIOR COURT RULEMAKING PROCEDURE

(e) Definitions. As used in this rule, the following terms have these meanings:

(1) "Judges" means the Superior Court Judges of Yakima County.

(2) "President" means the President of the Yakima County Bar Association.

(3) "Association" means the Yakima County Bar Association.

(f) Initiation of Rules Changes.

(1) Any person may recommend to the Judges the adoption of any changes in the Local Rules of the Superior Court.

(2) The text of all proposed rules shall be typed and the purpose and the necessity for the proposed rule shall be stated. If the proposed rule affects an existing rule, this should be so stated and the effects on the existing rule shall be clearly set forth.

(g) Receipt of Proposed Rules by Superior Court.

(1) Proposed rule changes may be submitted to any Judge who shall immediately transmit them to the Administrative Judge.

(2) The Administrative Judge shall present such proposed rule changes to the Judges at their next regular meeting.

(h) Action by Superior Court.

(1) All action taken with respect to any proposed rule shall be by a majority of the Judges.

If a proposed rule is amended or rejected by the Judges, the individual, association or committee submitting it will be notified in writing.

(2) If a proposed rule is approved pending adoption, a copy of said rule shall be published by transmitting to the President for dissemination to the Association and by filing with the County Clerk.

(i) Comment on Proposed Rule. Any person may comment on any proposed rule change. Such comment shall be in writing and directed to the Administrative Judge.

(j) Except as otherwise provided, the following schedule shall be used for adopting local rules:

April 1 — Deadline for submitting proposed rule changes to the Judges for adoption effective the subsequent September 1.

April 15 — Judges to publish pending rules by transmitting them to the President.

June 1 — Deadline for comment on proposed rule published by the Judges.

July 1 — Deadline for final action by Judges.

(k) Final Adoption, Distribution and Effective Dates.

(1) The Judges will adopt, amend or reject a proposed rule or take such other action as they deem appropriate.

(2) All adopted rules shall be filed with the County Clerk and shall be made available to the members of the Association and the public at cost.

(3) All proposed rules shall become effective September 1 following their adoption, unless an emergency determined by the Judges necessitates a different effective date.

(l) Miscellaneous Provisions. The Judges, in their discretion, may adopt, amend or rescind a rule without following the procedures set forth in this rule.

[Adopted effective January 14, 1991; amended effective July 16, 1992.]

GENERAL RULE 15. SEALED REPORTS; ADULT CRIMINAL AND JUVENILE OFFENDER PROCEEDINGS; PSYCHOLOGICAL, CHEMICAL DEPENDENCY, AND MENTAL EVALUATIONS AND REPORTS [SUSPENDED]

[Adopted effective September 1, 2012. Suspended on an emergency basis effective March 2, 2015; suspended on a permanent basis effective September 1, 2015.]

GENERAL RULE 29. PRESIDING JUDGE AND COURT GOVERNANCE

(f) Duties and Authority of the Presiding Judge. The primary function of the Presiding Judge is to resolve court administrative policy matters. The Presiding Judge may delegate administrative ministerial functions to the Court Administrator to implement court policy. The Court Administrator shall also implement court policy at the direction of the Executive Committee.

Once a year the Superior Court Judges shall create an Executive Committee. The Executive Committee shall serve for the calendar year, and shall be designated by December 1 of the preceding year. The Executive Committee shall consist of the Presiding Judge and two other judges, one of whom shall be elected at large and one of whom shall rotate into position numerically according to each judges' public elective position, also known as department number. Department Two is designated as the rotated position for 2002.

(g)(i) The Presiding Judge shall be elected and may serve consecutive terms. The term of office shall be one year unless expanded by state court rule. If expanded by state court rule, the currently elected Presiding Judge shall continue serving as Presiding

Judge with the expanded term relating back in time to the beginning of the present term. If a vacancy occurs during the term of a presiding Judge, the judges shall immediately elect a new presiding Judge to fill the vacancy and complete the term The remaining two judges' terms of office shall be for one year. The judge elected at large may serve consecutive terms.

(ii) The Presiding Judge shall be determined before the election of the at large member of the Executive Committee.

(iii) The Juvenile Judge shall not be one of the three members of the Executive Committee. If the usual turn for the rotated position coincides with a judge's assignment as juvenile Judge, the rotation shall skip to the next department number. When the Juvenile Judge completes his or her year's assignment, he or she shall then become the rotated member of the Executive Committee. He or she shall then be followed in numerical rotation by the next department number judge who has not yet served in a rotation position.

(iv) The Court Administrator is not a member of the Executive Committee but is expected to attend Executive Committee meetings and meetings of the bench as a whole, and participate in discussions unless unavailable or unless an executive session is called.

(v) The Executive Committee shall be the governing body of the Superior Court. The elected member of the Executive Committee shall serve as Assistant Presiding Judge during that person's term of office.

(vi) The Executive Committee shall share in all of the responsibilities of the Presiding Judge including any responsibilities and duties established by state court rule. The two Executive Committee members and the Presiding Judge shall each have one vote and shall resolve issues by majority vote. If there is a tie vote the issue being considered shall be referred to the judges as a whole for resolution by vote. A quorum of the judges as a whole shall resolve such issues by majority vote. Prior notice of the issue to be determined must be given before a quorum exists.

(vii) The Presiding Judge shall call a meeting of all of the judges on a monthly basis to advise the judges of developments concerning the court. Agenda and minutes for these meetings will be posted and distributed to all judges.

(viii) The Executive Committee shall meet a minimum of twice a month. Agenda and minutes for those meetings will be posted and distributed to all judges.

(ix) The Presiding Judge may determine that a matter should be brought to the vote of all of the judges; otherwise the opinions of the judges not on the Executive Committee are advisory only. If a matter is brought to all the judges for a vote, a quorum of the judges as a whole shall resolve such issues by majority vote. Prior notice of the issue to be determined must be given before a quorum exists. Full-time Court Commissioners are ex-officio members of the bench as a whole and shall not have the right to vote. The Presiding Judge can call the bench into executive session and exclude the Court Administrator and Court Commissioners from the session.

[Adopted effective November 1, 2002.]

NOTE: The judges have reserved for future consideration how abstentions should be counted in voting of the judges as a whole.

GENERAL RULE 31. PERSONAL IDENTIFIERS—CHILDREN [REPEALED]

[Repealed effective September 1, 2006.]

CIVIL RULES (Cite as LCR)

III. PLEADINGS AND MOTIONS

RULE 7. PLEADINGS ALLOWED; FORM OF MOTIONS

(b) Motions and Other Papers

(1) *How made.*

(A) Note for Motion Docket

(i) Any party may bring any issue of law on for hearing. The moving party shall file contemporaneously the motion, note for motion docket and any necessary supporting affidavit, and shall serve these upon the opposing party. The moving party shall abide by the following procedure:

(1) File and serve a motion with the clerk and serve on the opposing party not later than five (5) days prior to the day the moving party desires it to be heard. The motion shall briefly state the legal basis for relief requested.

(2) File and serve a Note for Motion Docket which shall conform to Exemplar No. 1.

(3) File and serve an affidavit or verified statement supporting the motion. The affidavit or verified statement shall briefly and concisely state the facts known to the affiant which form the basis of the motion.

(ii) The time for notice of summary judgments, motions for reconsideration, revisions and motions to dismiss for failure to state a claim and motions on the pleadings is designated by LCR 56, LCR 59 and LCR 87.

(iii) Motions on a judge's personal motion calendar shall be scheduled through the Court Administrator's Office. A copy of the motion shall be filed with the Court Administrator's Office.

Personal motions are those motions required to be heard by a particular judge, wither because the case has been preassigned or because it relates to a previous ruling by the same judge.

(iv) Arguments on motions should not exceed ten (10) minutes per party. [7(b)(1)(B)]

(B) Confirmation Process

All civil motions, except motions for summary judgment, motions on a judge's personal motion calendar, reconsideration, revisions, domestic relations, probate, guardianship, paternity and adoption matters, must be confirmed by noon two (2) court days prior to the hearing or they will be stricken. To confirm a motion as required by this rule the moving party shall call (509) 574–2690 and leave the following information: the caller's name, the case name, cause number, date and time the motion is scheduled to be heard, and the date and time of the call. Confirmation shall not be effective unless this telephone procedure is used.

Once confirmed, a motion can be stricken by the moving party who shall place a call to the same telephone number listed above and who shall leave the appropriate message. For a motion to be effectively stricken the call must be made no later than 4:00 p.m. on the afternoon before the motion is scheduled.

The phone number listed above shall be on a dedicated phone line in the Clerk's Office equipped to record messages.

Motions on a judge's personal motion calendar shall be confirmed with the Court Administrator's Office at 574–2705.

If the moving party fails to appear after confirming the motion, the court may strike the motion, deny the motion, impose terms, and may order any other relief the court deems appropriate. If the responding party fails to appear, the court may grant the relief requested.

[Adopted effective January 14, 1991; amended effective January 1, 1994, permanently effective September 30, 1994; amended effective April 19, 1996; September 1, 2003.]

RULE 10. FORM OF PLEADINGS OR OTHER PAPERS

(e) Format Recommendations.

(3) *Bottom Notation.*

(A) Endorsement of Orders by Attorneys. Every order presented to a judge for signature shall bear the signature of the person presenting it on the lower left-hand corner of the page to be signed by the judge.

[Adopted effective January 14, 1991.]

RULE 16. MANDATORY MEDIATION OF CIVIL CASES

(a) Applicable Cases: Mediation is required for all cases in which a Case Scheduling Order is required under LCR 40 (a).

(b) Procedure and Standard for Opt-out: Parties may not opt-out of mandatory mediation by stipulation. If *all* parties wish to opt-out, they shall note a joint motion for argument to the court. The court will grant the motion only if firmly convinced that the benefits of mediation, i.e., settlement or resolution of contested issues, are outweighed by the costs of mediation.

(c) Timing: Mediation shall be concluded at least 30 days prior to the date set for trial. If the parties fail to timely mediate, the Court Administrator shall strike the trial.

(d) Qualified Mediators: The Court Administrator shall maintain a list of qualified mediators under this rule which shall include the following information: Each mediator's name, organization, if any, address, telephone number, and fee schedule. A qualified mediator is an attorney with 10 or more years of civil practice, who has completed mediation training, and who is approved by the judges of this Court.

(e) Selection of Mediator: The parties shall use the services of a Court approved mediator. The parties are encouraged to agree upon a mediator. If the parties agree upon a mediator, they shall notify the Court Administrator in writing of the agreed upon mediator. If the parties are unable to agree upon a mediator, they shall request that the Court Administrator send out a short list of potential mediators. The process for determining the number of potential mediators on the short list and selecting the mediator shall be the same process as is used to select an arbitrator under the MAR.

(f) Appointment of Mediator: The Court Administrator shall notify the mediator of his or her appointment, with a copy of the notification to all parties.

(g) Mediation Date and Materials: The mediator shall determine the mediation date, and whether and when the parties are to exchange mediation statements. If mediation statements are to be exchanged, a party may send a separate statement directed to the mediator only.

(h) Procedure of Mediation: (1) The mediator shall determine the procedure of the mediation. (2) Unless excused by the mediator, the parties and their attorneys shall personally attend all mediation sessions. In every case there must be a person present at the mediation who has authority to negotiate for a settlement on behalf of each party. All insurance companies that may be liable for any portion of a settlement must have a representative with full settlement authority at the mediation or readily available by telephone. (3) Parties shall provide their own interpreters, as they deem necessary. Interpreters need not be court certified. (4) If a settlement is reached in mediation, the mediator shall prepare a Settlement Agreement which must be signed by the parties, their attorneys, and their insurers, if any. Promptly after execution of a Settlement Agreement, Plaintiff shall provide written notice to the Court Administrator that the case has settled.

(i) Notice of Compliance: If no settlement results from the mediation, the mediator shall promptly file with the Clerk, with copies to the Court Administrator and all parties, a certificate that there has been compliance with the mediation requirements of this rule but that no settlement has been reached.

(j) Payment of Mediator: The mediator shall be paid by the parties. Payment responsibilities and arrangements are to be determined between the mediator and the parties.

(k) Incorporation of RCW 7.07: The Uniform Mediation Act, RCW 7.07, applies to mediations conducted under this rule.

[Adopted effective September 1, 2011.]

V.   DEPOSITIONS AND DISCOVERY

RULE 26.   GENERAL PROVISIONS GOVERNING DISCOVERY

(h) Use of Discovery Materials. Only those portions of discovery materials relied upon shall be filed. The portions of the discovery filed shall include the cover sheet or first page of the material necessary to identify the document, or shall otherwise be identified in writing.

[Adopted effective January 14, 1991.]

RULE 33.   INTERROGATORIES TO PARTIES

(a) Procedure.

(1) *Form of Written Interrogatories.*

(A) The party proposing interrogatories shall include a verification form at the end.

(B) The proposing party shall serve at least two sets on the responding party, and shall serve a set on all other parties in the case. The responding party shall insert answers in the space provided.

(2) *Service of Answers.* The responding party may retain one set of answered interrogatories and shall serve a set on the proponent and on all other parties.

[Adopted effective January 14, 1991.]

VI.   TRIALS

RULE 40.   PRE–TRIAL PROCEDURES

(a) Notice of Trial and Civil Case Scheduling Order.

(1) Any party may note a case for trial by completing and filing either Exemplar 2 or Exemplar 3. Exemplar 2 is required for cases which require a Case Scheduling Order. Exemplar 3 is required for cases which do not require a Case Scheduling Order. The form shall be filed with the Clerk, with a copy to the Court Administrator and to all parties.

(2) Unless exempted by LCR 40(a)(3), a party noting a case for trial shall consult with all counsel toward filing a Civil Case Scheduling Order for Trial substantially in the form provided in Exemplar 2. Upon the order being entered, it shall be filed with the Clerk, with a copy to the Court Administrator and to all parties. If the parties cannot agree on how or if Exemplar 2 is to be completed, any party may note the issue for a hearing.

(3) A Case Scheduling Order is not required:

A.   When all counsel of record enter and file a stipulation opting out of a case scheduling order; or

B.   If so ordered by the court; or

C.   In the following cases:

(1) Proceedings under RCW 7.06 (MAR) and appeals thereof;

(2) Proceedings under RCW Title 26;

(3) Paternity;

(4) Proceedings under RCW 10.14 (Harassment);

(5) Proceedings under RCW Title 13;

(6) Unlawful detainer;

(7) Foreign judgment;

(8) Abstract or transcript of judgment;

(9) Petition for Writ of Habeas Corpus, Mandamus, Restitution, or Review, or any other Writ;

(10) Civil Commitment;

(11) Proceedings under RCW Chapter 10.77;

(12) Proceedings under RCW Chapter 70.96A;

(13) Proceedings for isolation and quarantine;

(14) Guardianship;

(15) Probate;

(16) Proceedings under RCW Chapter 36.70C;

(17) Tax Warrants;

(18) Lower Court Appeals;

(19) Administrative Law Reviews;

(20) Appeals of Department of Licensing driver's license revocations; and

(21) Emancipation of minor.

(22) Name Changes.

(b) Methods.

(1) *Notice of trial by jury.* If to be tried by a jury and no party serves or files a demand that the case be tried by a jury of twelve (12), it shall be tried by a jury of six (6) members, with concurrence of five (5) being required to reach a verdict. To comply with CR 38(b), which refers to a case being "called to be set for trial," a procedure not used in Yakima County, a case shall be deemed "called to be set for trial" ten (10) days after filing and service of the Note for Trial Docket as above provided. If the Note for Trial Docket indicates a nonjury trial, any party desiring a jury trial shall file a "Demand for Jury," with the required deposit, before the case is "called to be set for trial" or a jury shall be deemed to have been waived by all parties. A copy of such demand for jury shall also be filed with the Court Administrator.

(2) *Assignment of trial dates.* The Court Administrator shall assign trial dates under the supervision of the administrative judge who shall be in direct charge of the trial calendar. Cases shall be set chronologically according to noting dates, except for cases given statutory preference.

(3) *Objections to jury trial/Objections to trial date.* An objection to the case being determined by a jury or an objection to the trial date must be made within 15 days of assignment by the Court Administrator of the trial date. An objection is made, for purposes of this rule, by noting a motion objecting thereto.

(4) *Confirmation of Trial Date (Civil & Domestic Relations).* Even though scheduled for trial, no case will be heard unless a party confirms the trial with the Court Administrator **five (5) judicial days** before the trial. Confirmation shall be made by telephone or via E-mail. The Administrator shall have the authority to strike the trial date of any case that is not confirmed.

Telephone Confirmation: 509–574–2705

Email Address: Superior.Court@co.yakima.wa. us

(5) *Calendar Management; Conflict Notification.* The Court Administrator shall not release the attorneys from responsibility for appearing at a trial on the date it is set any earlier than noon the date before it is set, or 3:00 p.m. on the preceding Friday when set for a Monday, when it appears that the trial cannot proceed due to unavailability of judges or courtrooms

(6) *Notice of Settlement.* It shall be the obligation of counsel in all civil and criminal jury and nonjury cases to notify the Court Administrator in writing or by email when a case is settled or otherwise will not come on for trial as scheduled. Telephone calls may be made to the Court Administrator's office Monday through Friday from 8:30 a.m. to 12:00 noon and 1:00 p.m. to 4:00 p.m.

(c) Pre-trial disclosures.

(1) Rule LCR 40(c) applies only to those cases in which a court has entered a Civil Case Scheduling Order.

(2) *Enforcement; Sanctions; Dismissal; Terms.*

A. Disclosure of Possible Lay and Expert Witnesses.

(i) Disclosure of Primary Witnesses. Each party shall, no later than the date for disclosure designated in the order, disclose all persons with relevant factual or expert knowledge whom the party reserves the option to call as witnesses at trial.

(ii) Disclosure of Rebuttal Witnesses. Each party shall, no later than the date for disclosure designated in the order, disclose all persons with relevant factual or expert knowledge who did not appear relevant until the primary witnesses were disclosed and whom the party reserves the option to call as witnesses at trial.

(iii) Scope of Disclosure. Disclosure of witnesses under this rule shall include the following information:

(a) All witnesses. Name, address, and telephone number.

(b) Lay witnesses. A brief description of the anticipated subject matter of the witness' testimony.

(c) Experts. A summary of the expert's opinions and the basis thereof and a brief description of the expert's qualifications. If the expert has prepared a report, the report shall be produced with these disclosures.

(iv) Exclusion of Testimony. Any person not disclosed in compliance with this rule may not be called to testify at trial, unless the Court orders otherwise for good cause and subject to such conditions as justice requires.

(v) Discovery Not Limited. This rule does not modify a party's responsibility under court rules to reasonably supplement responses to discovery or otherwise to comply with discovery before the deadlines set by this rule.

(vi) Failure to Comply. If the Court finds that an attorney or party has failed to comply with the Case Scheduling Order and has no reasonable excuse, the Court may order the attorney or party to pay monetary sanctions to the Court, or terms to any other party who has incurred expense as a result of the failure to comply, or both; in addition, the Court may impose such other sanctions as justice requires.

(vii) Definitions. For purpose of the above rule, "terms" means costs, attorney fees, and other expenses incurred or to be incurred as a result of the failure to comply; "monetary sanctions" means a financial penalty payable to the Court; "other sanctions" includes but is not limited to the exclusion of evidence.

(d) Sanctions for Cases Not Completed in Time Allotted. The parties have an obligation to confer and cooperate in determining the length of trial and in trying the case so that all evidence is presented within the time allotted. Should a case go beyond the time allotted, the trial judge may fine the responsible attorney, attorneys, party, or parties. The fine may be as much as $500 per half day that the trial goes beyond the time allotted.

(e) Pre-trial Organization of Exhibits and Admissibility Without Authentication.

(1) The week prior to trial, counsel for all parties shall provide a copy of their likely exhibits to all counsel. Counsel shall endeavor to agree on which exhibits are admissible.

(2) The parties shall prepare original separate exhibit books, copies and an index of proposed exhibits. Sufficient copies should be made for each attorney, the court, and the testifying witness.

(3) The parties shall arrive at least 30 minutes prior to trial to assist the clerk in numbering all exhibits.

(4) The parties shall notify the court at the commencement of trial which exhibits are agreed to. Those exhibits will be admitted without need for authentication.

(f) Pre-assignment of Cases. Either party may request, or the court may itself suggest, that a particular case be pre-assigned. Without limiting the court's discretion, the following factors should be considered prior to ordering pre-assignment of a case: (1) The extent that one judge has become familiar with the facts and law of the case; (2) The extent that one judge has made rulings that disposed of one or more claims; (3) The likelihood that the case might require multiple motions which will require familiarity with the case history; (4) The number of experts, especially experts from outside Yakima County; and (5) The complexity of the case.

(g) Affidavit of Prejudice. Should any party elect to file an Affidavit of Prejudice against the judge to whom such case is preassigned, such affidavit shall be filed not later than ten (10) days after notification of the preassigned judge. Should additional parties thereafter be added, it shall be the duty of the party adding such additional party to notify additional party's attorney, as soon as known, in writing, the name of the judge to whom such case is preassigned and such additional party shall file any such affidavit within ten (10 days) thereafter.

[Adopted effective January 14, 1991. Amended effective September 1, 2010.]

RULE 47. JURORS

(a) Examination of Jurors.

(1) *Voir Dire.* The voir dire examination of prospective jurors shall, as nearly as possible, be limited to those matters having a reasonably direct bearing on prejudice, and shall not be used by counsel:

(1) as a means of arguing or trying their cases, or

(2) as an effort to indoctrinate, visit with or establish "rapport" with jurors, or

(3) for the purpose of questioning concerning anticipated instructions of the court or theories of law, or

(4) for the purpose of asking the jurors what kind of verdict they might return under any circumstances.

Questions are to be asked collectively of the entire panel whenever possible.

(e) Challenge.

(1) *Peremptory Challenges.* All peremptory challenges allowed by law shall be exercised in writing. Each party shall in turn indicate the juror challenged by name and seat number or shall indicate whether a peremptory challenge for the existing panel is waived. The purpose of this rule is to preserve the secrecy of the peremptory challenge process and all parties and their counsel shall conduct themselves to that end.

[Adopted effective January 14, 1991.]

RULE 51. INSTRUCTIONS TO JURY AND DELIBERATION

(a) Proposed.

(1) *Introductory Instruction.* Prior to jury selection, the parties shall submit in writing an agreed instruction to the court briefly outlining the essential factual issues in the case, or if unable to agree, shall submit separate instructions.

(b) Submission.

(1) *Distribution.* All instructions, including Washington Pattern Instructions, shall be submitted in writing. Numbered and assembled sets, with citations, shall be distributed as follows:

One (1) copy shall be filed with the Clerk;

One (1) copy shall be served on each other party;

One (1) copy shall be retained by the party proposing them;

One (1) copy shall be delivered to the judge.

In addition, one (1) unassembled set, without citations or numbers, shall be delivered to the judge.

(d) Published Instructions.

(1) *Request.*

(A) Request for Pattern Instructions. If a proposed Washington Pattern Instruction is modified, it must so indicate with the citation.

[Adopted effective January 14, 1991.]

VII. JUDGMENT

RULE 56. SUMMARY JUDGMENTS

(e) Statement of Points and Authorities and Supporting Affidavits. A statement of points and authorities and supporting affidavits shall be filed and served contemporaneously with the filing of any motion for summary judgment.

(i) Noting Summary Judgment Hearings. The Court Administrator will assign a specific date and time for all summary judgment motions. The specific date and time for hearing any summary judgment shall be obtained from the Court Administrator prior to noting any such motion. This may be done telephonically. The moving party shall then immediately file and serve the Note for Motion and send a copy to the Court Administrator.

The Court Administrator will schedule summary judgment hearings and designate judges to hear those motions as soon as possible based on the availability of judges. Information regarding the judge scheduled to hear summary judgments will be available and can be obtained from the Court Administrator's office within five days of the scheduled hearing.

In those cases where a judge has prepared for a summary judgment motion that is continued or stricken, or if after hearing the summary judgment motion there remain issues in the case, the Court Administrator will endeavor, but is not required, to assign that judge to hear any subsequent matters in that case, including the trial.

(j) Confirmation of Hearing. All summary judgment motions must be confirmed. Summary judgment motions will not be heard even though previously noted unless the hearing is confirmed with the Court Administrator. The confirmation is a representation that all pleadings and documents necessary for the motion have been timely filed by that party and the moving party is prepared to have the motion heard at the date and time noted.

Motions must be confirmed with the Court Administrator not later than 4:00 PM the Thursday preceding the week in which the motion is scheduled. Once the hearing is confirmed, the motion may not be stricken or continued without approval of the judge assigned to hear the matter.

(k) Summary Judgment Hearing. The judge hearing the motion will determine the amount of time allowed each party for oral argument at the summary judgment hearing. Unless otherwise indicated by the judge, oral argument may not exceed twenty (20) minutes per party.

(*l*) Affidavits of Prejudice. The rescheduling of the hearing on a motion for summary judgment because of a party filing an affidavit of prejudice against the assigned judge does not expand the time provided in CR 56(c) for filing any pleadings or documents with reference to the motion.

[Adopted effective January 14, 1991; amended as an emergency rule effective June 1, 1995; September 1, 1998; amended effective September 1, 2001; September 1, 2002; September 1, 2006.]

RULE 59. MOTION FOR RECONSIDERATION

(e) Hearing on Motion.

(3) *Nature of Hearing.* Any motion for reconsideration not heard within thirty (30) days of the written decision shall be deemed denied unless otherwise ordered by the court. The judge to whom the motion for reconsideration is made shall determine whether the motion shall be heard on oral arguments or submitted on the briefs. It will be presumed that there will be no oral argument unless requested by the judge.

[Adopted effective January 14, 1991; amended effective September 1, 2002.]

VIII. PROVISIONAL AND FINAL REMEDIES

RULE 71. WITHDRAWAL BY ATTORNEYS

(e) Notice to Court Administrator. An attorney filing any Notice of Intent to Withdraw, Order Autho-

rizing Withdrawal, Notice of Withdrawal and Substitution, or Notice of Appearance by any subsequent attorney shall give a copy of the notice or order to the Administrator.

[Adopted effective January 14, 1991.]

X. SUPERIOR COURTS AND CLERKS

RULE 77. SUPERIOR COURTS AND JUDICIAL OFFICERS

(c) Powers of Judicial Officers.

(1) *Criminal Presiding Department.* One department shall be designated the Presiding Department. The daily calendar shall indicate which judge or commissioner is sitting in this department. The criminal docket shall be heard each judicial day at such times and courtroom as designated on the daily calendar or otherwise ordered by the court.

(f) Sessions

(1) *Court Hours.* Court hours for all departments in session on all judicial days shall be designated on the daily court calendar or as ordered by the Court. The daily calendar shall indicate the time and courtroom for all criminal, civil and domestic relations matters.

(2) *Presence for Jury Trial.* Attorneys and parties shall be present at 9:00 a.m. on the first day of trial unless otherwise ordered by the court.

(j) Trials and Hearings; Orders in Chambers

(1) *Post–Trial Briefs.* Any party submitting a brief in support of a post-trial motion shall deliver a copy to the trial judge at the time the original is filed with the clerk, which shall be at least five (5) days prior to hearing on the motion. The responding party shall serve and file any brief in opposition to the motion at least two (2) days prior to the hearing and provide a copy to the trial judge on the date of filing. A reply brief may be filed prior to the hearing.

(k) Motion Practice

(1) *Law and Motion Day.* Motions in civil cases, except family law matters, are heard Fridays at 1:30 p.m. unless otherwise ordered by the Court or designated by the Court Administrator. Any motion which must be heard by a particular judge shall be set for 1:30 p.m. on Friday before that judge, unless otherwise directed by that judge. The Court may limit the number of motions to be heard on any particular day.

(2) *Call of the Calendar.* All matters on the motion and show cause docket that have been confirmed or set pursuant to court order shall be called. If no one appears when the matter is called, the court may grant or deny the motion or may strike the motion. Any matter stricken by the court must be re-noted.

(3) *Continuances.* At the call of the calendar, and upon the request of any party, any motion and/or show cause matter may be continued by the court to a particular day and time. Hearings on motions continued by order of the Court must be confirmed unless the order specifically states otherwise.

(7) *Telephonic Hearings*

(a) Telephonic arguments are allowed by approval of the judge hearing the motion which approval is obtained through the court administrator or by order of the court on its own motion.

(b) The party requesting telephonic argument shall be responsible for initiating and paying for the conference call. If the court orders telephonic argument, the judge shall designate which party is responsible for initiating and paying for the conference call.

(c) For all telephonic hearings the moving party shall provide a proposed order granting or denying the motion prior to such hearing.

[Adopted effective January 14, 1991; amended effective September 1, 2002.]

RULE 79. BOOKS AND RECORDS KEPT BY THE CLERK

(d) Other Books and Records of Clerk.

(1) *Removal of Files.* No file, or portion thereof, may be removed from the office of the clerk except upon a receipt thereof as prescribed by the clerk. No bond, estate or receivership claim, will, property settlement agreement, instrument of conveyance, or other document that the clerk may designate, may be removed from the office of the clerk except upon order of the court first entered. In any event, no documents removed from the clerk's office shall be taken outside of Yakima County without court order except by members of the Washington State Bar Association.

(2) *Removal of Files in Certain Proceedings.* Except for matters noted for hearing, counsel shall procure the original file from the clerk and present it to the court at the time of hearing any of the following matters:

All guardianship and decedent's estate matters involving the approval of periodic report, final accounts or the expenditure of funds.

Petitions for orders of solvency.

Interim accounts in estate matters.

Uncontested marriage dissolutions.

Any other matter in which the court is requested to find that certain procedural steps have been taken.

(e) Destruction of Records.

(1) *Disposition of Exhibits.* Within ninety (90) days after the final disposition of any cause, including all appellate processes, each party shall withdraw all exhibits offered by such party, giving the clerk a receipt therefor, which receipt shall constitute a sufficient discharge of the duties of the clerk. In the

event a party shall fail to withdraw the exhibits within such time, the clerk is authorized to destroy the same.

[Adopted effective January 14, 1991.]

RULE 87. MOTION FOR REVISION

(RCW 2.24.050)

(a) Deadline for Hearing Motion. A motion for revision must be filed with the Clerk within ten days of the entry of the order from which the motion arises. At the time it is filed, a motion for revision shall be noted for hearing at a time that has been scheduled with the Court Administrator. A revision motion not heard within thirty days after filing shall be deemed denied unless otherwise ordered by the Court.

(b) Form of Motion. The motion must clearly identify the order from which revision is sought, specify those portions of the order allegedly in error, identify the documents that were submitted to the court commissioner for hearing on the ruling from which revision is requested, and include a summary of the legal and factual grounds upon which the moving party relies. A copy of the order from which revision is sought shall accompany the motion.

(c) Transcript Required. At least five court days before the hearing on the revision motion, the moving party shall file a transcript of the hearing before the commissioner, serve a copy on all opposing parties, and provide a copy to the judge who will hear the motion. The person preparing the transcript shall certify, under penalty of perjury, that it is an accurate transcription of the record.

(d) Confirmation. Motions must be confirmed with the Court Administrator not later than four court days before the date and time set for the hearing. Once the hearing is confirmed, the motion may not be stricken or continued without approval of the judge assigned to hear the matter. The Court Administrator shall strike unconfirmed motions from the calendar.

(e) Stay of Commissioner's Order. The filing of a motion for revision does not stay the Commissioner's order. The moving party may seek a stay order from a Judge or the Commissioner who signed the order.

[Adopted as an emergency rule effective November 1, 2002; amended effective September 1, 2003; September 1, 2004; amended as an emergency rule effective March 21, 2005; permanently amended effective September 1, 2005; amended effective September 1, 2010; September 1, 2012.]

SPECIAL PROCEEDINGS RULES (Cite as LSPR)

RULE 94.04G. ALTERNATE RESIDENTIAL TIME GUIDELINES FOR YAKIMA COUNTY

1. Alternate Residential Time: The following schedule shall be used only as a guideline in setting alternative residential time, based on the child's age:

0 to 6 months: Two hours, twice per week.

6 months to 1 year: Two hours, twice per week; and four hours, once per week.

1 year to 3 years: Two hours, twice per week; and eight hours, once per week. These holidays alternated each year, for eight hours each: Easter, July 4th, Thanksgiving, Christmas Eve, and Christmas Day. Overnight residential time is not usually recommended.

3 years to 5 years: Two hours, twice per week.

Alternating weekends from Saturday 9:00 a.m. until Sunday at 6:00 p.m.

These holidays alternated each year: Easter, July 4th, Thanksgiving for 2 days; Christmas Eve and 2 days before Christmas Day and two days thereafter.

Summer residential time: Two non-consecutive one-week periods.

5 years and older: Every other weekend from Friday at 6:00 p.m. until Sunday at 6:00 p.m. If Friday is a school holiday, the weekend begins Thursday at 6:00 p.m. If Monday is a school holiday, the weekend ends Monday at 6:00 p.m.

One weekday from 5:30 p.m. until 7:30 p.m., once per week.

These holidays alternated each year: Thanksgiving for 4 days, the first half of Christmas school vacation the first year and the second half of Christmas school vacation the next year, and spring vacation.

Summer residential time: 30 days, unless the parents agree to a shorter or longer period of time, or the Court finds that there are circumstances which would extend or shorten summer residential time. During this summer time, the primary residential parent shall have residential time with the child during one weekend (except during extended trips, etc.).

2. Father's/Mother's Day: Regardless of the residential times suggested above, the mother shall have residential time of at least 4 hours on Mother's Day, and the father shall have residential time of at least 4 hours on Father's Day.

3. Birthdays: Each parent shall be allowed to spend at least 4 hours with the child to celebrate the child's birthday, and that parent's birthday, within two days of that birthday.

4. Telephone Contact: Reasonable telephonic contact with the child is usually appropriate, and should not be less than once per week for each parent during that parent's nonresidential time.

5. Different Age Groups: When children of different age groups are involved, the preference shall be to follow the guideline for the oldest child, so that the children remain together.

6. Cancellation: For weekend visits, the primary parent shall have the child available for one hour after the scheduled starting time. If the other parent does not pick up the child within that hour, then the weekend visit shall be deemed cancelled.

7. These provisions are designed to encourage each parent to maintain a loving, stable, and nurturing relationship with the child. Each parent shall encourage the parent/child relationship of the other parent, and shall make residential agreement decisions which are in the best interest of the child.

[Amended effective September 1, 2001.]

RULE 94.04H. LOCAL RULE REQUIRING PARENTING CLASS

1. Definition of Applicable Cases. This rule applies to all domestic cases including dissolutions, legal separations, major modifications and paternity actions (in which paternity has been established) where the parties are parents of children under the age of 18, or where a party is not a parent but is seeking custody, and where a parenting plan or residential plan involving more than purely financial issues is required.

2. Impact on Children Seminars; Mandatory Attendance. Within 60 days after service of a petition or initiating motion on the respondent, both parties shall participate in, and successfully complete, an approved Impact on Children Seminar. Standards for a court-approved Impact on Children Seminar are set forth in sections (7), (8) and (9) below. Successful completion shall be evidence by a certificate of attendance filed by the provider agency with the court.

3. Permissive Application. The court may require parties in domestic violence actions brought under RCW 26.50, and non-parent parties in any domestic case, to attend an Impact on Children Seminar.

4. Special considerations/waiver.

A. In no case shall opposing parties be required to attend a seminar together.

B. Upon a showing of domestic violence or abuse which would not require mutual decision-making pursuant to RCW 26.09.191, or that a party's attendance at a seminar is not in the children's best interest, the court shall either:

    1. waive the requirement of completion of the seminar; or

    2. provide an alternative voluntary parenting seminar for battered spouses or partners.

C. The court may waive the seminar requirement for one or both parties in any case for good cause shown, or may approve an alternative delivery system so the party affected can still receive the same or similar child impact information.

5. Fees. Each party attending a seminar shall pay a fee charged by the approved provider agency. The fees charged shall not be cost-prohibitive to the parties. The seminars shall be conducted at no cost to the county's general revenue allocation to the court.

6. Failure to Comply.

A. Non-participation, or default, by one party does not excuse participation by the other party. Respondent's refusal, delay or default will not delay the progress of the case to a final decree. Petitioner's refusal or delay will prevent the case from being set for trial or any final order affecting the parenting/residential plan being entered. Willful refusal or delay by either party may constitute contempt of court and result in sanctions imposed by the court, or may result in the imposition of monetary terms, default and/or striking of pleadings.

B. In post-decree actions in which attendance had previously been required but not completed, or considered and waived, the moving party's motion or petition affecting a parenting plan shall not be entertained until that party has first completed a child impact seminar, unless approved by the court for good cause shown.

7. Provider Agencies. Approved Child Impact Seminars shall be those offered by one or more individuals or counseling agencies approved by the court. "Approval by the court" means approval by a majority of the judges. Parties may use equivalent services offered by other courts, private agencies or religious organizations, upon approval by the judge in the individual case.

8. Seminar content. A court-approved child impact seminar shall include, at a minimum:

    (A) the developmental stages of childhood;

    (B) stress indicators in children;

    (C) age appropriate expectations of children;

    (D) the impact of divorce on children;

    (E) the grief process;

    (F) reducing stress for children through an amicable divorce; mediation as alternative to litigation;

    (G) the long-term impact of parental conflict on children;

    (H) importance of child's relationships with both parents; fostering those relationships;

    (I) communication skills for divorced parents;

    (J) practical skills for working together; and

    (K) the impact on children when step-parents and blended families enter their lives;

    (L) parenting children with limited time (alternate residential time limits);

(M) involvement of extended family.

9. Qualifications of Instructors. Child impact seminars should be conducted by a team of not less than two instructors, including one male and one female. Instructors should have the following minimum credentials and experience:

(A) a master's degree in social work, psychology or other related behavioral science;

(B) supervised experience in treatment of emotionally disturbed children, adolescents and their families;

(C) experience in providing a wide range of mental health services to children and families, with specific experience in the areas of separation/divorce, loss and grief, and blended families;

(D) extensive knowledge of child development, age appropriate expectations for children, and positive parenting;

(E) an ability to work with other agencies as part of a collaborative program; and

(F) strong oral communication skills.

When parties choose to use agencies or religious organizations which have not received prior approval by the court, the court may modify or waive the foregoing qualifications for the instructors upon a showing of functional equivalency.

10. Referrals for other services. During the seminar, referral resources may be made available to the parties, and their children, including individual and family counseling, drug/alcohol counseling, anger management counseling, parenting classes, etc. These services are optional, and the parties must seek their own funding resources.

[Adopted effective September 21, 1995; amended effective September 1, 2001.]

RULE 94.04W. FAMILY LAW PROCEEDINGS

(A) Proceedings Pending Trial.

(1) *Court's Automatic Order.* Upon the filing of a Summons and Petition for dissolution, legal separation or declaration of invalidity, the Court on its own motion shall automatically issue a Temporary Order consistent with Exemplar 11. The petitioner is subject to this order from the date of filing. The petitioner shall serve a copy of this order on respondent and file proof of service. The respondent is subject to this order from the time it is served. The order shall remain in effect until further order or entry of final documents. This order shall not be entered in any law enforcement data base, and shall not preclude any party from seeking any other restraining order as may be permitted by statute. If the order is violated, either party may seek a finding of contempt and/or request fees.

(2) *Motions for Temporary Orders.* Any party may file a motion for temporary orders pending trial.

(a) Form of pleadings, basis and limitations.

(i) Form. All documents and copies provided shall be legible. If typed, documents shall be in 12 point or larger type, 1.5 spaced between the lines and conform to GR 14. Mandatory forms shall be used.

(ii) Basis. Evidence, including written evidence in affidavits and declarations by the parties and witnesses, must comply with the rules of evidence.

(iii) Children's Statements. Declarations by minors are disfavored.

(iv) Page Limitations. Absent prior authorization of the court, the entirety of all declarations and affidavits from the parties and non-expert witnesses in support of motions (except financial declarations, financial documents and sealed source documents), shall be limited to a sum total of twenty (20) pages.

The entirety of all declarations and affidavits submitted in response to motions shall not exceed twenty (20) pages.

The entirety of all declarations and affidavits submitted in reply to the response shall not exceed ten (10) pages.

Exhibits to any declarations shall count toward the above page limits.

Declarations, affidavits and reports from the Family Court Investigator, GAL, CPS or law enforcement shall not count toward the page limit. Declarations in support of Parenting Plans shall not count toward the page limit but shall not exceed three (3) pages.

(v) Violations of this rule. If the Court finds that one or more of the parties violated this rule, the Court may, in its discretion, assess terms, strike or continue the matter, or refuse to consider the materials that violate this rule.

(b) Filing and Service. The moving party shall, no later than 14 calendar days prior to the hearing date, file with the clerk and serve on each other's party/counsel his/her motion, note for motion, and all supporting documents. Unless previously filed and still current, the moving party's supporting documents shall include these mandatory forms, fully completed and signed by the moving party:

(i) Residential Placement. A motion concerning temporary residential placement of children must be accompanied by a Proposed Parenting Plan (WPF DR 01.0400), and a Declaration in Support of Parenting Plan (WPF DR 04.0120).

(ii) Temporary Child Support. A motion concerning temporary child support must be accompanied by a Child Support Worksheet (CSW), together with proof of income including the party's most recent paystub and tax return with all attachments.

(iii) Temporary Spousal Maintenance or Attorney Fees. A motion for temporary maintenance or attorney fees must be accompanied by a Financial Declaration (WPF DR 01.0550).

(c) Response to Temporary Motions. The opposing party's response must be filed and served no later than noon three (3) court days prior to the date scheduled for hearing; provided, however, if the response requests affirmative relief, it must be filed and served no later than five (5) calendar days prior to the hearing. Documents filed in strict reply to issues raised in the response must be filed and served the day prior to the hearing by noon. Responses filed and/or served later will not be considered. If the disputed issues include residential placement, temporary child support or spousal maintenance, or attorney fees, the appropriate mandatory forms shall be completed and signed by the responding party (unless previously filed and still current). Working copies should be provided to the court.

(d) Confirmation/Strike Process. All domestic motions must be confirmed by the moving party **by 10:00 a.m., two (2) court days prior to the court hearing** or the motion will be stricken. The moving party shall confirm the motion by notifying the clerk (at the specific confirmation telephone number or e-mail address designated by the clerk) and any other party. The confirmation shall include the caller's name and telephone number, the case name and cause number, the date and time of the motion, and the date and time of the confirmation. Confirmation will not be effective unless this procedure is used. If the moving party fails to appear after confirming the motion, the court may strike the motion, deny the motion, impose terms, and order any other relief the court deems appropriate. If the responding party fails to appear, the court may grant the relief requested.

A moving party voluntarily striking a hearing shall notify the Clerk and other party no later than 4:00 PM the court day prior to the hearing.

(e) Renotes. Matters which have been previously noted in conformance with this rule may be renoted upon five (5) court days notice. The motion shall be confirmed as provided above or it will be stricken.

(f) Hearings on Temporary Motions. All motions shall be determined on sworn declarations unless the court determines that testimony is necessary. Argument on temporary motions shall be limited to five minutes per side, except that the court may in its discretion increase or reduce the time for argument. Argument shall be limited to matters contained in the record. By agreement of the parties

or order of the court, the matter may be submitted solely on the record.

(g) Orders Shortening Time. Motions may be heard on shortened time only in the event of an emergency and where an Order Shortening Time has been signed by the court.

(3) *Orders to Show Cause.* Where required by statute or court rule, a party may obtain an Order to Show Cause requiring the other party to appear and show cause why certain relief should not be granted. The return date on the show cause order shall not be sooner than fourteen (14) days after filing and service. In all other respects, the requirements of LR 94.04W (A)(1) shall apply.

(4) *Mediation by Court Order.* In addition to mandatory mediation set forth below, in all contested Title 26 matters, a party may request, or the Court may order the parties to engage in mediation. Mediation shall take place as specified in the order of mediation. Failure to mediate in good faith may result in sanctions. The assigned mediator shall advise the Court of the date of the mediation, the parties participating and the outcome. If the matter is not resolved, the substance of the mediation shall remain confidential and the mediator may not be called as a witness in any proceeding.

(5) *Status Hearings.* At any time pending trial, the Court may order that a status hearing be held. The purpose of the status hearing shall be to set deadlines for the completion of discovery, set deadlines for the completion of the guardian ad litem's report, or address other matters necessary to the timely resolution of the case. A party may set a status hearing by following the procedures set forth in 94.04(A)(1). Status hearings shall be heard on the motions calendar.

(B) Noncontested Dissolutions.

(1) No testimony or declaration will be required in cases in which the parties have stipulated to entry of the Decree or in cases in which the relief requested is the same as the relief requested in the petition and the other party is in default.

(2) In cases in which the relief requested is different or more specific than the original petition and the respondent has defaulted, the party requesting relief must appear and present testimony in support of the request.

(C) Contested Domestic Matters.

(1) *Mandatory Mediation.*

(a) Applicable Cases: This rule shall apply to all pending and newly filed contested cases under Chapter 26.09, 26.10, and 26.26 except support modifications and parentage cases initiated by the State of Washington.

(b) Note for Trial: Except as provided in (c) below, a party may not note a matter for trial until the parties have attempted mediation in good faith with a court approved mediator. The matter shall be noted for trial using Exemplar 3A, which shall include a certificate of compliance with this rule.

(c) When Mediation is not Required. Mediation shall not be required in the following cases:

(i) For good cause shown upon motion and approval by the court; or

(ii) Where a domestic violence restraining order or protection order (excluding ex parte orders) involving the parties is currently in effect;

(iii) Where a domestic violence no contact order exists pursuant to RCW 10.99;

(iv) Where the court upon motion finds that domestic violence abuse has occurred between the parties and that such abuse would interfere with arm's-length mediation.

Notwithstanding the foregoing, either party may by motion seek a court order requiring mandatory mediation in a case where it would not be required as set forth in (c)(2), (c)(3), or (c)(4) above if the moving party believes that the parties would be able to mediate their dispute at arm's-length under the particular circumstances of the case.

(d) Settlement Conference: Where mediation is not required or the parties have not mediated in good faith, the parties shall participate in a settlement conference as provided in (2). If the settlement conference does not result in an agreement, the matter shall be set for trial.

(e) Effect on Court Proceedings. Mediation does not stay or otherwise affect the rights and duties of the parties established by statute, court rule, or court order. The court may enter temporary orders and the parties may conduct discovery prior to or during the mediation process.

(f) Qualified Mediators: The Yakima Superior Court shall maintain a list of qualified mediators which shall include the following information: each mediator's name and organization, if any, address, telephone number and fee schedule. A qualified mediator shall be either an attorney with at least five years domestic relations experience and mediation training or a non attorney with at least five years of domestic relations experience and mediation training. Mediators must be approved by the Superior Court. The Dispute Resolution Center of Yakima and Kittitas Counties shall be considered a qualified mediator. The Court may approve upon motion by a party or parties the services provided by a mediator that is not on the Court's list, but is otherwise qualified.

(g) Selection of Mediators: The parties may either agree to a mediator from the court approved list or the mediator will be determined by use of a strike list. If the parties are unable to afford a private mediator, the Dispute Resolution Center of Yakima and Kittitas Counties shall be utilized. The

parties shall notify the court and the mediator of the mediator selected. A mediator may decline an appointment, in which case the parties shall select a new mediator utilizing the same procedure.

(h) Mediation date and materials: The mediator shall determine the mediation time and dates and whether or not mediation statements are required.

(i) Mediation Procedure: The mediator shall determine how the mediation is conducted. The parties and their lawyers shall personally attend the mediation unless there is a written agreement between the lawyer and the client that the lawyer will not attend. In the event of such agreement, the mediator and the other party/lawyer will be notified in advance of the mediation. The mediator may approve telephonic appearances for parties who reside out of state.

(j) Cost of Mediation: The mediator shall be paid by the parties. Payment responsibilities and arrangements shall be determined by the mediator and the parties.

(k) Failure to Comply: Willful refusal to participate in mediation or willful delay in completing mediation may result in a finding of contempt or imposition of sanctions.

(*l*) Notice of Compliance/Agreement: If no settlement is reached, the mediator shall, within 7 days, file with the Clerk with copies to the parties, a certificate showing that there has been compliance with this rule. If an agreement is reached in mediation, that agreement shall be reduced to writing and signed by the parties and their lawyers.

(m) Incorporation of RCW 7.07: The Uniform Mediation Act, RCW 7.07, is incorporated herein by reference, including but limited to the confidentiality of documents and mediator privilege protections of that Act.

(n) Effective Date: September 1, 2014.

(2) *Settlement/Status Conference and Trial.* In the event that mediation is not required a settlement/status conference shall be held in all contested domestic relations cases, including custody modifications, paternity actions, other than those initiated by the State of Washington, non parental custody cases and meretricious relationship and civil union matters. The purpose of the settlement/status conference is to set timelines for the completion of discovery and guardian ad litem reports, identify disputed issues and pursue settlement of the case. Domestic relations cases shall not be set for trial unless ordered and after a full settlement conference has been held. Parties and assigned guardians ad litem shall attend the settlement conference.

(a) Note for Settlement Conference. Once a response to a petition has been filed, and, if applicable, the Children Cope With Divorce class has been completed by the noting party, a party may request a settlement conference date by filing a Note For Settlement Conference (Exemplar 3A), together with a fully completed Position Statement (Exemplar 5). If there is a guardian ad litem or family court investigator assigned to the case, his/her name shall be listed on the Note for Settlement Conference.

(b) Filing Position Statements. The party who notes the matter for settlement conference shall file and serve his/her Position Statement contemporaneously. The other party shall file and serve a Position Statement no later than fourteen (14) days prior to the settlement conference. If either party fails to timely file a Position Statement or files an incomplete Position Statement, the judge/court commissioner may strike the settlement conference and impose terms.

(c) Settlement Conference and Trial Dates. Upon receiving the Note for Settlement Conference and completed Position Statement, the Court Administrator shall schedule a settlement conference and shall send notice to the parties and any assigned guardian ad litem or family court investigator. The settlement conference shall not be scheduled sooner than sixty days after the Note for Settlement Conference is filed. At the conclusion of the settlement conference the Judge/Court Commissioner may direct the Court Administrator to set the matter for trial or may schedule an additional settlement conference. At the conclusion of the conference, the Court shall complete and the parties shall sign a Settlement/Status Conference order. (Exemplar 6)

(d) Position Statements.

(i) Position statements must be in the form of Exemplar No. 5. The Position Statement shall be filed as a sealed source document and shall not be used for any other purpose or reviewed by the trial judge, unless specifically agreed by the parties. The Position statement shall indicate the proposed disposition of assets and liabilities, as well as proposed spousal maintenance, child support and residential placement of children, as applicable.

(ii) Asset List: If distribution of assets is at issue, each party shall complete a list of assets, both community and separate. For each asset listed, the party shall provide a good faith opinion as to the fair market value of the asset as of the date of separation. With respect to real property assets, the party shall provide a copy of any appraisal or market analysis intended to be used at trial. With respect to retirements, pensions, investment or bank accounts, the party shall provide a copy of all statements referencing the value of such accounts as of the date of separation and the most recent statement. With respect business assets, the party shall provide a copy of the most recent profit/loss statement available

and a copy of the most recent tax return with all schedules attached.

(iii) Liabilities List: If distribution of debts is at issue, each party will provide copies of statements from the creditors listed, both as of the date of separation and the most recent statement.

(iv) Spousal Maintenance and Child Support: If spousal maintenance or child support is at issue, each party shall file a copy of his/her most recent paycheck, together with the most recent tax return if not already on file. Each party shall fill out a statement regarding monthly expenses.

(D) Modification of Decree of Dissolution.

(1) *Parenting Plans.*

(a) Ex Parte Requests for Change in Primary Residential Care. An ex parte request to change custody shall be denied unless an emergency is clearly established by the sworn declaration of the party seeking the change.

(b) Petitions for Modification of Custody or Residential Placement. A petition for a major modification of a parenting plan shall be commenced by filing a Summons, Petition, Proposed Parenting Plan and supporting declarations. The matter may be noted for adequate cause and temporary orders in conformance with LR 94.04(A)(1). If adequate cause is found, the matter may be noted for settlement conference by either party. If adequate cause is not found, the matter shall be dismissed.

(c) Petitions for Minor Modification of Parenting Plans. In any case in which the parenting plan provides for alternative dispute resolution, the party seeking a minor modification shall state whether alternative dispute resolution has been exhausted prior to filing the Petition. The court shall not consider the petition unless the alternate dispute resolution shall have been exercised in good faith. Failure to participate in good faith may result in the imposition of terms.

(2) *Child Support Orders.*

(a) A petition to modify a child support order shall be commenced by filing a Summons, Petition, Child Support Worksheet and proof of income, including a copy of the party's most recent paystub and tax return with all attachments.

(b) The documents, above-described, shall be served on the opposing party as provided by statute.

(c) The matter shall be noted for hearing in conformance with the procedures described in LR 94.01(1). The matter shall not be scheduled for hearing until at least 20 days have elapsed since service on the opposing party.

(d) The petition shall be determined on declarations unless the court determines that oral testimony is required.

(3) *Modification of Spousal Maintenance.*

(a) A Petition to modify spousal maintenance shall be filed and served as provided by statute and civil rules.

(b) The Petition shall be noted for hearing and served as provided by LR 94.04(1). If the court determines that there has been a sufficient change of circumstances since entry of the Decree, the matter shall be set for an evidentiary hearing. If the court finds there has not been a sufficient change of circumstances, the petition shall be dismissed.

(E) Child Support.

(1) *Tax Exemption.* In determining how to award exemptions, the court should look to the percentage of the basic child support obligation paid by each parent, as well as each parent's obligation for day care expenses. In awarding the exemption, the court should also consider tax benefits available to either parent, for example, head of household status, child credits and day care credits.

(2) Child support affidavit requirement regarding Public Assistance and notice to Office of Support Enforcement.

No temporary or permanent order for future or past due child support shall be entered by the court unless:

(a) One or both parties shall have filed an affidavit declaring that the affiant has no children or stepchildren, who are the subject of the present order, who currently receive public assistance or live in a state funded placement out of the family home, and that neither spouse owes any past debt to the Washington State Department of Social and Health Services, (the affidavit shall be in the same form as Exemplar No. 7); or

The Office of Support Enforcement has been served with notice of the application for an order of support prior to hearing, fifteen (15) days for temporary orders and twenty-one (21) days for final orders.

(F) Temporary/Permanent Parenting Plans. When implementing temporary or permanent parenting plans, and in addition to considering the criteria set forth in applicable statute and case law, the court may consider the following guidelines for alternative residential time.

(1) *Alternate Residential Time Guidelines For Yakima County.*

(a) Alternate Residential Time: The following schedule shall be used only as a guideline in setting alternate residential time, based on the child's age:

(i) 0 to 6 months: Two hours, twice per week.

(ii) 6 months to 1 year: Two hours, twice per week; and

a. four hours, once per week.

(iii) 1 year to 3 years: Two hours, twice per week; and

a. eight hours, once per week.

b. These holidays alternated each year, for eight hours each: Easter, July 4th, Thanksgiving, Christmas Eve, and Christmas Day.

c. Overnight residential time is not usually recommended.

(iv) 3 years to 5 years: Two hours, twice per week; and

a. Alternating weekends from Saturday at 9:00 a.m. until Sunday at 6:00 p.m.

b. These holidays alternated each year: Easter, July 4th, Thanksgiving for 2 days; Christmas Eve and 2 days before and Christmas Day and 2 days thereafter.

c. Summer residential time: Two non-consecutive one-week periods.

(v) 5 years and older: Every other weekend from Friday at 6:00 p.m. until Sunday at 6:00 p.m. If Friday is a school holiday, the weekend begins Thursday at 6:00 p.m. If Monday is a school holiday, the weekend ends Monday at 6:00 p.m; and

a. One weekday from 5:30 p.m. until 7:30 p.m., once per week.

b. These holidays alternated each year: Thanksgiving for 4 days, the first half of Christmas school vacation the first year and the second half of Christmas school vacation the next year, and spring vacation.

c. Summer residential time: 30 days, unless the parents agree to a shorter or longer period of time, or the Court finds that there are circumstances which would extend or shorten summer residential time. During this summer time, the primary residential parent shall have residential time with the child during one weekend (except during extended trips, etc.).

(b) Father's/Mother's Day: Regardless of the residential times suggested above, the mother shall have residential time of at least 4 hours on Mother's Day, and the father shall have residential time of at least 4 hours on Father's Day.

(c) Birthdays: Each parent shall be allowed to spend at least 4 hours with the child to celebrate the child's birthday, and that parent's birthday, within two days of that birthday.

(d) Telephone Contact: Reasonable telephonic contact with the child is usually appropriate, and should not be less that [1] once per week for each parent during that parent's nonresidential time.

(e) Different Age Groups: When children of different age groups are involved, the preference shall be to follow the guideline for the oldest child, so that the children remain together.

(f) Cancellation: For weekend visits, the primary parent shall have the child available for one hour after the scheduled starting time. If the other parent does not pick up the child within that hour, then the weekend visit shall be deemed canceled.

(g) These provisions are designed to encourage each parent to maintain a loving, stable, and nurturing relationship with the child. Each parent shall encourage the parent/child relationship of the other parent, and shall make residential arrangement decisions which are in the best interest of the child.

(G) Parenting Seminars.

(1) *Definition of Applicable Cases.* All domestic cases including dissolutions, legal separations, major modifications and non-state initiated paternity actions where the parties are parents of children under the age of 18, and where a parenting plan or residential schedule is required, the parties shall attend an approved Impact on Children Seminar.

(2) *Impact on Children Seminars; Mandatory Attendance.* Within 60 days after service of a petition or initiating motion on the respondent, both parties shall participate in, and successfully complete, an approved Impact on Children Seminar. Standards for a court-approved Impact on Children Seminar are set forth in sections (7), (8) and (9) below. Successful completion shall be evidence by a certificate of attendance filed by the provider agency with the court.

(3) *Permissive Application.* The court may require parties in domestic violence actions brought under RCW 26.50, and non-parent parties in any domestic case, to attend an Impact on Children Seminar.

(4) *Special considerations/waiver.*

(a) In no case shall opposing parties be required to attend a seminar together.

(b) Upon a showing of domestic violence or abuse which would not require mutual decision-making pursuant to RCW 26.09.191, or that a party's attendance at a seminar is not in the children's best interest, the court shall either:

(i) waive the requirement of completion of the seminar; or

(ii) provide an alternative voluntary parenting seminar for battered spouses or partners.

(c) The court may waive the seminar requirement for one or both parties in any case for good cause shown, or may approve an alternative delivery system so the party affected can still receive the same or similar child impact information.

(5) *Fees.* Each party attending a seminar shall pay a fee charged by the approved provider agency. The fees charged shall not be cost-prohibitive to the parties. The seminars shall be conducted at no cost to the county's general revenue allocation to the court.

(6) *Failure to comply.*

(a) Non-participation, or default, by one party does not excuse participation by the other party. Respondent's refusal, delay or default will not delay the progress of the case to a final decree. Petitioner's refusal or delay will prevent the case from being set for trial or any final order affecting the parenting/residential plan being entered. Willful refusal or delay by either party may constitute contempt of court and result in sanctions imposed by the court, or may result in the imposition of monetary terms, default and/or striking of pleadings.

(b) In post-decree actions in which attendance had previously been required but not completed or considered and waived, the moving party's motion or petition affecting a parenting plan shall not be entertained until that party has first completed a child impact seminar, unless approved by the court for good cause shown.

(7) *Provider Agencies.* Approved Child Impact Seminars shall be those offered by one or more individuals or counseling agencies approved by the court. "Approval by the court" means approval by a majority of the judges. Parties may use equivalent services offered by other courts, private agencies or religious organizations, upon approval by the judge in the individual case.

(8) *Seminar content.* A court-approved child impact seminar shall include, at a minimum:

(a) the developmental stages of childhood;

(b) stress indicators in children;

(c) age appropriate expectations of children;

(d) the impact of divorce on children;

(e) the grief process;

(f) reducing stress for children through an amicable divorce; mediation as alternative to litigation

(g) the long-term impact of parental conflict on children;

(h) importance of child's relationships with both parents; fostering those relationships;

(i) communication skills for divorced parents;

(j) practical skills for working together; and

(k) the impact on children when step-parents and blended families enter their lives.

(*l*) parenting children with limited time (alternate residential time limits)

(m) involvement of extended family

(9) *Qualifications of Instructors.* Child impact seminars should be conducted by a team of not less than two instructors, including one male and one

female. Instructors should have the following minimum credentials and experience;

(a) a master's degree in social work, psychology or other related behavioral science;

(b) supervised experience in treatment of emotionally disturbed children, adolescents and their families;

(c) experience in providing a wide range of mental health services to children and families, with specific experience in the areas of separation/divorce, loss and grief, and blended families;

(d) extensive knowledge of child development, age appropriate expectations for children, and positive parenting;

(e) an ability to work with other agencies as part of a collaborative program; and

(f) strong oral communication skills.

When parties choose to use agencies or religious organizations which have not received prior approval by the court, the court may modify or waive the foregoing qualifications for the instructors upon a showing of functional equivalency.

(10) *Referrals for other services.* During the seminar, referral resources may be made available to the parties, and their children, including individual and family counseling, drug/alcohol counseling, anger management counseling, parenting classes, etc. These services are optional, and the parties must seek their own funding resources.

(H) Guardians Ad Litem.

(1) *Registry Administration.*

(a) The court shall maintain and administer Guardian ad Litem registries for Family Law and Guardianship/Probate/Trusts. These registries shall not include Juvenile Court volunteer Guardians ad Litem or CASAs, which shall continue to be administered independently by their respective programs.

(b) The court shall maintain the application form and background information records pertaining to each person listed on a registry. Persons listed on a registry or registries shall update information annually on a date specified for each registry.

(c) The application forms as described in paragraph 2, curriculum vitae, certificate of attendance at training, and guardianship certificates of qualification under Title 11 shall be available for public review.

(d) All guardians ad litem on the registry shall be required to complete mandatory training. The court shall periodically sponsor or approve training programs which registry applicants shall be required to attend to maintain and improve their level of proficiency.

(e) Each registry shall continuously open for new applications and persons applying shall be notified of their placement on the registry and the date thereof.

(f) The court may impose an application processing fee and/or charge a fee for the training programs.

(2) *Requirements for Listing on Registries.*

(a) Education and Experience Requirements.

(i) Attorneys.

(1) Guardianship, Probate Registry. Member of the Washington State Bar Association in good standing and five years of relevant experience in the practice of law.

(2) Family Law Registry. Member of the Washington State Bar Association in good standing and five years of experience in the practice of law, with at least 50 percent of that practice in family law or dependency cases.

(ii) Non-attorneys.

(1) Guardianship Registry. Bachelor's degree in relevant subject area and five years' experience in the following: needs of impaired elderly people, physical disabilities, mental illness, developmental disabilities and/or other areas relevant to the needs of incapacitated persons.

(2) Family Law Registry. A minimum of a Bachelor's degree in a relevant field and a minimum of five years' experience working with families and children.

(3) Parentage Cases. In RCW 26.26 actions, a relative of the minor mother or father may be appointed who has complied with the requirements of RCW 26.12.175 and who is otherwise suitable.

(b) Application Process. Each application shall be accompanied by the following:

(i) Copy of the certificate evidencing successful completion of the current training required for the area of Guardian ad Litem practice;

(ii) Application and fee allowing the court to obtain a current Washington State Patrol Certificate regarding criminal history;

(iii) Curriculum vitae, showing work and professional or personal experience in or related to the field that would assist in the performance and completion of Guardian ad Litem duties;

(iv) Signed release of information directed to all professional regulatory bodies which have licensed or supervised the applicant within the last ten years;

(v) Certificate of Qualification for Guardians ad Litem seeking appointment under RCW Title 11;

(vi) Description of the nature, status and outcome of any professional complaints, investigations or disciplinary actions, lawsuits or professional liability claims, and any order for removal of the Guardian ad Litem prior to completion of the Guardian ad Litem's duties;

(vii) Description of any claims, or litigation that has been commenced, involving allegations of improper fee charges, charges of fraud, theft or other forms of dishonesty or professional malpractice or misconduct.

(viii) Description of fees charged.

(c) The applicant shall be of high moral character, and shall not have any of the following:

(i) Conviction of a felony or of a crime involving theft, dishonesty or moral turpitude;

(ii) A professional certification or license suspension or revocation;

(iii) Pending investigations or actions for any of the above.

(3) *Appointment of Guardian ad Litem.*

(a) When the need arises for the appointment of a Guardian ad Litem in a case involving a subject area for which there is a registry, the court shall appoint a person from the registry unless exceptional circumstances are found and findings are entered supporting appointment of a person not listed on the registry.

(b) Appointments from the registries shall be made in the exercise of the court's sound discretion. The court may, but is not obligated to, appoint a person whom all the parties have stipulated to serve as Guardian ad Litem. Agreement of all parties will not suffice when one or more parties is alleged to be under a legal disability.

(c) In making appointments from a registry, among other factors, the court will consider the facts of the case, and the skills, experience and knowledge of persons on the registry.

(d) Guardians ad Litem shall be appointed from the registry in a manner which, to the extent possible, equalizes the workload among persons on the registry. Guardians ad Litem shall periodically notify the court of their current caseload, and shall promptly notify the court of any temporary unavailability to serve.

(4) *Retention on Registry/Grievance Procedures.*

(a) A person shall remain on the registry unless the person fails to maintain current application and training requirements, the person notifies the registry of his/her desire to be removed from the registry, or the person is removed or suspended as provided herein.

(b) Complaints regarding a Guardian ad Litem shall be directed to the Court Administrator. All complaints shall be in writing on a form prescribed by the court and shall bear the name, signature and address of the complainant. A complaint must be filed within one year from the date of the acts complained of.

(c) Complaints shall be forwarded to the presiding judge or his/her designee(s) and shall be processed as follows:

(i) If the complaint related to an on-going case, the complainant shall be advised that the complaint may be addressed only in the case at bar, either by seeking the removal of the Guardian ad Litem or by contesting the information contained in the Guardian ad Litem's report or testimony. Such complaints shall be processed in a manner which assures that the trial judge remains uninformed of the complaint. This process shall be completed in 25 days.

(ii) If the complaint relates to a case in which final orders have been entered, the presiding judge or his/her designee(s), shall review the complaint and either:

(1) make a finding that the complaint has no merit on its face and so inform the complainant in writing; or

(2) make a finding that the complaint may have merit and require the Guardian ad Litem to provide a written response within 10 business days. The Guardian ad Litem shall be provided with a copy of the complaint. The Guardian ad Litem's response to the complaint shall be reviewed and such additional investigation as deemed necessary shall be conducted. Findings shall be made as to whether and on what basis the complaint has merit, and such findings shall be forwarded to the Guardian ad Litem and complainant. If a complaint is found to have merit, the Guardian ad Litem may be admonished, reprimanded, referred for additional training, or suspended or removed from the registry. This process shall be completed within 60 days. If the Guardian ad Litem is removed or suspended, an order shall be signed.

(d) Complaints shall be confidential unless they are deemed to have merit. Findings regarding complaints determined to have merit shall be made part of the Guardian ad Litem's file and shall be made available upon request, provided, however, confidential information regarding the parties shall not be made available.

(e) If a Guardian ad Litem is removed from the registry pursuant to disposition of a grievance under this rule, the registry manager shall send notice of such removal to the Administrative Office of the Courts.

(5) *Payment of Guardians ad Litem:*

(a) In Family Law cases, the order appointing a Guardian ad Litem shall provide for payment of the

Guardian ad Litem's fees. The court may order either or both parents to pay for the Guardian ad Litem's fees based upon their ability to pay. The Guardian ad Litem shall provide a monthly accounting of his/her time and billing for services to the parties. The order appointing the Guardian ad Litem shall provide that the Guardian ad Litem may charge up to $3,000.00 without further court approval. Additional fees may be charged only with court approval.

(b) In Title 11 matters, the fee of the Guardian ad Litem shall be approved by the court. The fee shall be charged to the alleged incapacitated person unless the court finds such payment would result in financial hardship, in which case, the county shall be responsible for such costs. In matters where no guardian is appointed, the fee may be charged to the petitioner, the alleged incapacitated person or apportioned. If the petition is found to be brought in bad faith, the fee shall be charged to the petitioner.

(c) Guardians ad Litem paid at public expense shall accept compensation provided under the court's administrative order regarding such payment.

[Adopted effective January 14, 1991. Amended effective February 1, 1991; September 1, 1991; July 16, 1992; May 1, 1996; September 1, 2001; September 1, 2004; September 1, 2009; amended on an emergency basis effective September 8, 2009; amended on a permanent basis effective September 1, 2010; January 1, 2012; September 1, 2012; September 2, 2014.]

1 So in original.

RULE 94.05W. GUARDIANS AD LITEM [REPEALED]

[Adopted effective September 1, 2003; repealed effective September 1, 2009.]

RULE 98.01. LOCAL GUARDIANSHIP RULE FOR YAKIMA COUNTY

1. All orders granting powers to a guardian or renewing Letters of Guardianship shall include the information shown in Exemplar 9, using that format. It may be included in the body of the Order, or as a referenced attachment.

2. All Letters of Guardianship shall be in the form shown in Exemplar 10.

[Adopted on an emergency basis effective June 12, 2007; adopted on a permanent basis effective September 1, 2007.]

LOCAL CRIMINAL RULES FOR SUPERIOR COURT (Cite as LCrR)

1.0 SCOPE, PURPOSE AND CONSTRUCTION

RULE 1.1. SCOPE

These rules govern the procedure of all criminal matters in the Superior Courts of Yakima County, Washington.

[Adopted effective January 14, 1991.]

RULE 1.2. PURPOSE AND CONSTRUCTION

These rules are intended to supplement the Criminal Rules for Superior Court (CrR) and shall be interpreted and construed to facilitate the Criminal Rules for Superior Court in the administration of justice.

[Adopted effective January 14, 1991.]

RULE 1.3. EFFECT

These rules shall apply to any proceeding in court then pending, except to the extent that time limits provided or required by these rules may be impossible or infeasible to meet, in which case the court shall extend such time limits or make other appropriate provisions.

[Adopted effective January 14, 1991.]

3.0 RIGHTS OF DEFENDANTS

RULE 3.1. ATTORNEY CERTIFICATION

(d)(4) Attorneys who anticipate being appointed to represent adult indigents in criminal cases must comply with CrR 3.1(d)(4) by filing a certification of compliance with the Clerk of the Superior Court. The certification should be filed at least fourteen days prior to each calendar quarter.

The Clerk will maintain an administrative file for such certifications. The administrative files will be open for public inspection.

At the time of filing a certification, the attorney shall serve a copy of the certification on the Yakima County Department of Assigned Counsel and file proof of service with the original filed with the Clerk.

The Yakima County Department of Assigned Counsel will, at the beginning of each calendar quarter, compile a list of attorneys who have filed the certification required. A copy of the list will be distributed to each judge of the Superior Court. The list will be updated from time to time during each quarter to reflect changes in certification.

The certification list will be available for inspection at the office of the Yakima County Department of Assigned Counsel and may be otherwise published by that agency.

[Adopted on an emergency basis, effective December 3, 2012. Adopted on a permanent basis, effective September 2, 2013.]

RULE 3.3. TIME FOR TRIAL

(f) Setting of Trial Date. At the arraignment of any defendant in a criminal action, the Administrator shall set the case for trial. The defendant shall be given a copy of the trial setting notice at the time of arraignment.

(h) Continuances. Continuances or other delays of criminal trials shall be granted only upon written motion, and for reasons provided in CrR 3.3. Orders granting continuances or other delays of criminal trials must be in writing. These motions shall be heard by the presiding department unless the matter has been assigned to another department.

[Adopted effective January 14, 1991.]

RULE 4.1.1. HEARINGS FOLLOWING ARRAIGNMENT

(a) Omnibus Hearing. At the time of arraignment, the court shall set a time for an omnibus hearing in addition to a time for trial. This is a mandatory appearance hearing for the defendant.

(1) *Time of Omnibus Hearing.* The omnibus hearing shall be set on the Superior Court morning criminal docket approximately 11 days before the assigned trial date.

(2) *Content.* The defendant shall comply with CrR 4.5 if the defendant indicates an intention to go to trial. If the court grants a motion for continuance, a new omnibus hearing date shall be assigned.

(i) The parties must exchange witness lists pursuant to CrR 4.5 within three court days of the day of the omnibus hearing.

(ii) If a defendant indicates he or she intends to plead guilty, the court will set a date certain prior to the trial date for entry of the plea(s).

(b) Pre–Trial Hearing. (Reserved for further consideration by the court and no longer in effect until further amendment is issued.)

(c) Triage Hearing. If at the time of the omnibus hearing the parties wish to proceed to trial on the assigned trial date the matter shall be set for a triage hearing at 9:00 AM on the daily criminal motion docket on the Friday immediately preceding the trial. This is a mandatory appearance hearing for the defendant. Counsel shall submit a completed Status Order to the court at the triage hearing. If a case is resolved or continued before the triage hearing the parties need not appear.

(d) Failure to Appear. A defendant's failure to appear for a mandatory appearance hearing will result in a pending trial date being stricken. Absent an acceptable explanation and acquiescence by the prosecution, an order for a Bench Warrant will be entered. Time for trial shall recommence pursuant to CrR 3.3.

[Adopted effective October 1, 2003; amended effective September 1, 2004; amended on an emergency basis effective March 26, 2007; revised on an emergency basis effective May 22, 2007 and June 14, 2007; amended on a permanent basis effective September 1, 2007.]

RULE 4.1.2. SPECIAL SET MOTION HEARINGS

Definition: Special Set Motion Hearing:

A hearing set through the Court Administrator's Office which may require extensive time or court resources.

Process:

1. Counsel will contact the Court Administrator's Office to obtain a date and time for the hearing. Counsel will disclose to the Court Administrator's Office Information regarding the hearing; names of parties, case number, length of the hearing, and resource requirements (i.e., interpreter needs, custody status, or special accommodations).

2. The party requesting the hearing will file the original noting document with the County Clerk's Office and a copy with the Court Administrator's Office.

3. The noting party must provide the opposing party at least 7 court days written notice of the hearing unless the parties agree to a shorter setting and the Court Administrator can accommodate the request.

4. When a brief is required, the moving party shall file it with the original noting document and deliver a copy to the Court Administrator's Office and opposing counsel. The responding party shall file the original response with the Clerk and a copy to the Court Administrator's Office and opposing counsel no later than 4 court days prior to the hearing.

5. Special set hearings can only be stricken by the noting counsel and this must be done by court order. The order can be presented *ex parte*. If the noting party wishes to reset the hearing, it must be re-noted as outlined above.

[Adopted on an emergency basis effective March 19, 2007; adopted on a permanent basis effective September 1, 2007.]

RULE 4.2. PLEAS

(a) Types. A defendant may enter a plea of not guilty in writing. Such plea shall be signed by the defendant and his or her counsel, filed with the court and a copy served on the prosecuting attorney and the Administrator.

The failure to enter any plea prior to trial shall be construed as a plea of not guilty.

(h) Scheduling. The prosecuting attorneys and defense attorneys, acting through the prosecutor's office, shall advise the Administrator each day of all matters pertaining to criminal cases to come before the court the following day.

Neither party shall, except in emergent situations, set any guilty plea or sentencing hearing on any day that the presence of counsel for either party is required in another department for trial or other proceedings. Any counsel whose presence in another department is required shall notify the Presiding Department and such counsel shall be given time preference in the Presiding Department. In no event shall any attorney set a matter in the Presiding Department when his or her presence is required in another department on the first day of any jury trial.

(i) Court Commissioners qualified under Article 4, Section 23 of the Washington State Constitution may accept pleas of adult criminal defendants in accordance with CrR 4.2 unless otherwise restricted by administrative order of the Superior Court.

[Adopted effective January 14, 1991; amended effective September 1, 2000.]

RULE 4.5. OMNIBUS HEARING [REPEALED]

[Adopted effective January 14, 1991; amended effective July 9, 1992; repealed on an emergency basis effective April 17, 2007; repealed on a permanent basis effective September 1, 2007.]

RULE 4.7. DISCOVERY

(h) Regulation of Discovery.

(9) Unless otherwise ordered, in cases where no omnibus hearing is held and no discovery request is made, the material so required by court rule shall be furnished no less than fifteen (15) days before trial, if known and available.

(10) Unless otherwise ordered, a party has five (5) days from the entry of a discovery order to comply with the order.

[Adopted effective January 14, 1991.]

RULE 6.1. TRIAL BY JURY OR BY THE COURT

(e) Trial Notification Requirements. All parties shall contact the Administrator's office two (2) days prior to the date set for trial and notify the Administrator whether (a) the case will proceed to trial; (b)

the anticipated length of trial; (c) existence of a jury trial waiver, if any; and (d) if pretrial matters remain for hearing.

(f) Order on Hearings or Trial. Unless otherwise ordered, the prevailing party shall file and serve proposed findings of fact, conclusions of law and/or order and a Notice of Hearing within five (5) days of the conclusion of any trial or hearing requiring findings, conclusions, or order.

[Adopted effective January 14, 1991.]

RULE 6.15. INSTRUCTIONS TO JURY AND DELIBERATION

(a) Proposed Instructions.

(1) *Distribution.* All instructions, including Washington Pattern Instructions, shall be submitted in writing. Numbered and assembled sets, with citations, shall be distributed as follows:

The original shall be filed with the Clerk;

One copy shall be served on each other party;

One copy shall be retained by the party proposing them;

One copy shall be delivered to the judge.

In addition, one unassembled set, without citations or numbers, shall be delivered to the judge. Counsel should also be prepared to email to the judge a set of the instructions without citations or numbers.

(2) *Published Instructions.* If a proposed Washington Pattern Instruction is modified, it must so indicate with the citation.

[Adopted on an emergency basis effective August 16, 2006; adopted on a permanent basis effective September 1, 2007.]

RULE 7.4. POST–TRIAL MOTIONS

(b) Time for Motion; Memoranda. Post-trial motions pursuant to CrR 7.4 or CrR 7.6 shall be accompanied with a note for setting. A memorandum of points and authorities may accompany such motion and shall be served and filed with the motion. Such statement shall be concise and state with specificity the grounds for relief. The opposing party may serve and file a statement of points and authorities not less than two (2) days prior to the hearing on such motion.

[Adopted effective January 14, 1991.]

RULE 8.9. SANCTIONS

Any violation of these rules, in addition to the court's inherent right to enter or deny such orders as it deems proper, shall subject the offending attorney to such terms as the court may order.

[Adopted effective January 14, 1991.]

LOCAL JUVENILE COURT RULES FOR
YAKIMA COUNTY (Cite as LRJuCR)

III. DEPENDENCY PROCEEDINGS

RULE 3.4. NOTICE AND SUMMONS— SCHEDULING OF FACTFINDING HEARING

(c) Settlement Conference for Child Dependency Proceedings:

(1) At the time the case is set for fact finding, the court will also schedule a settlement conference for the parties. Notice of both the settlement conference and fact finding shall be provided in the notice and summons issued by the clerk and served by the petitioner as required by statute. All parties and their attorney, if any, must attend the settlement conference unless excused by the court. Failure of a party to attend will, at the request of any appearing party, be grounds for continuance of the scheduled fact finding. Incarcerated parties are excused from attending but may attend telephonically if feasible and requested in advance.

(2) At the settlement conference, all parties will meet to discuss in good faith their positions on the issues in the dependency petition and confer on settlement of the case. If settlement is not reached, the parties will make an effort to narrow the issues for trial and select a date and time for contested trial. Any agreement reached shall be reduced to writing, signed by all parties, and presented to the court at a date and time agreed upon by the parties. If the written agreement specifies the date and time for a contested fact finding, then the signing parties are excused from attending the originally scheduled fact finding and the written agreement shall constitute notice to them of the new date for the contested hearing.

[Adopted effective September 1, 2001.]

VII. JUVENILE OFFENSE PROCEEDINGS
RULE 7.3(c). DETENTION AND RELEASE

(1) Subject to space availability within the Detention Center's policies for capacity, the Detention Center shall accept juveniles for detention who are suspected of the misdemeanors or gross misdemeanors listed within section (c)(3) of this rule, upon referral by law enforcement. A suspect information report must be provided to detention before detention shall admit a juvenile.

(2) For suspected misdemeanants held in detention, cash bail shall presumptively be set in the amount shown in subsection (c)(3), to be posted by a parent or guardian. A juvenile detained for a misdemeanor or gross misdemeanor listed in this rule shall be released only to a parent or guardian when bail is posted, and shall be required to appear in court the next judicial day. At that appearance, the court may reconsider the amount of bail, and may impose other conditions of release. If the juvenile does not appear in court, bail may be forfeited. Forfeiture of bail shall not constitute a final disposition. The presumptive amount shall be used absent other order of the court. Nothing in this rule shall prohibit the court from setting bail for any crime not listed in subsection (c)(3). Nothing in this rule shall prohibit the court from changing the presumptive amount of bail for crimes listed in subsection (c)(3).

At the time of release from detention, both the parent or guardian and the juvenile shall be provided with a notice of hearing substantially in the form set forth below, and shall be required to sign it before the juvenile can be released from detention:

Superior Court of the State of Washington, Yakima County
Juvenile Division

State of Washington, Petitioner   )
) Notice of Hearing
vs.   )
)
                  Respondent)
DOB:)

Respondent and respondent's parent or guardian must appear in court at the Yakima County Juvenile Justice Center, 1728 Jerome Avenue, Yakima, Washington at the following date and time:

_____ at 1:30 PM.

Juvenile Detention releases the respondent to the parent or guardian undersigned, who has posted cash bail in the amount of $ _____. At the scheduled court hearing, the court may increase or decrease the amount of bail, or choose to maintain the same amount.

If the respondent fails to appear in court when scheduled, the bail may be forfeited and a warrant may issue for the respondent's arrest, and the separate felony criminal charge of bail jumping may be filed against the respondent.

Forfeiture of bail for failing to appear in court when scheduled does not constitute a final disposition of this case.

The name and address of the parent or guardian posting the bail:

Name _____

Address _____

_____

Telephone: _____

Relationship: ___ Parent ___ Guardian

Date: _____

I have read this form or have had it read to me.

_____   _____
Parent or Guardian   Juvenile

(3) The presumptive bail schedule for this rule is as follows:

Crime	Presumptive cash bail To be posted by parent or guardian
Assault Fourth Degree (non–DV)	100.00
Malicious Mischief Third Degree (includes graffiti)	50.00
Domestic violence crimes, over 16, all misdemeanors except Assault Fourth Degree	100.00
Domestic Violence Assault Fourth Degree	150.00
Communicating with a Minor for Immoral Purposes	250.00
Vehicle Prowling	$50.00
DUI	$50.00
Student carrying a firearm at school (mandatory admission regardless of space availability)	No bail until mandatory MH evaluation is completed. Then set by a judge.
All other misdemeanor or gross misdemeanor firearms crimes	$100.00
Resisting Arrest	$50.00
Escape Third Degree	No bail

[Adopted effective September 1, 2001.]

YAKIMA COUNTY LOCAL RULES FOR MANDATORY ARBITRATION (Cite as LMAR)

I. SCOPE AND PURPOSE OF RULES

RULE 1.1. APPLICATIONS OF RULES/PURPOSE AND DEFINITIONS

(a) Purpose

The purpose of mandatory arbitration of civil actions under RCW 7.06 as implemented by the Mandatory Arbitration Rules is to provide a simplified and economical procedure for obtaining the prompt and equitable resolution of monetary disputes. The Mandatory Arbitration Rules as supplemented by these local rules are not designed to address every question which may arise during the arbitration process. The rules give considerable discretion to the arbitrator, which the arbitrator should not hesitate to exercise. Arbitration hearings should be informal and expeditious, consistent with the purpose of the statutes and rules.

(b) "Director" Defined

In these rules, "Director" means the Court Administrator's Office for the Yakima County Superior Court.

[Adopted effective January 14, 1991. Amended on an emergency basis effective August 12, 2005. Amended on a permanent basis effective September 1, 2006.]

RULE 1.2. MATTERS SUBJECT TO ARBITRATION

A civil action, other than an appeal from a court of limited jurisdiction, is subject to arbitration under these rules if the action is at issue, if the sole relief sought is a money judgment, and if no party asserts a claim in excess of $50,000, exclusive of attorney's fees, interest and costs.

[Adopted effective January 14, 1991. Amended on an emergency basis effective August 12, 2005. Amended on a permanent basis effective September 1, 2006.]

II. TRANSFER TO ARBITRATION AND ASSIGNMENT OF ARBITRATOR

RULE 2.1. TRANSFER TO ARBITRATION

(a) Statement of Arbitrability

In every civil case the party filing the Note for Trial Docket provided by Local Rule 40 shall complete a Statement of Arbitrability using the form in Exemplar No. 3. With fourteen (14) days after the Note for Trial Docket and Statement of Arbitrability have been served and filed, any party disagreeing with the Statement of Arbitrability or unwilling to stipulate to arbitration, shall serve and file a response to the Statement of Arbitrability on the form prescribed by the court. In the absence of such response, the Statement of Arbitrability shall be deemed correct, and the case shall be designated an arbitration case. If a party asserts that its claim exceeds $50,000, or seeks relief other than a money judgment, the case is not subject to arbitration except by stipulation.

(b) Failure to File—Amendments

A party failing to serve and file an original response within the time prescribed may later do so only upon leave of court. A party may amend the Statement of Arbitrability or response at any time before assignment of an arbitrator or assignment of a trial date and thereafter only upon leave of court for good cause shown.

[Adopted effective January 14, 1991; amended effective April 14, 1994. Amended on an emergency basis effective August 12, 2005. Amended on a permanent basis effective September 1, 2006.]

RULE 2.3. ASSIGNMENT TO ARBITRATOR

(a) Generally; Stipulations. When a case is set for arbitration, a list of five (5) proposed arbitrators will be furnished to the parties. A master list of arbitrators will be made available on request. The parties are encouraged to stipulate to an arbitrator. In the absence of a stipulation, the arbitrator will be chosen from among the five (5) proposed arbitrators in the manner defined by this rule.

(b) Response by Parties. Each party may, within fourteen (14) days after a list of proposed arbitrators is furnished to the parties, nominate one or two arbitrators and strike two arbitrators from the list. If both parties respond, an arbitrator nominated by both parties will be appointed. If no arbitrator has been nominated by both parties, the Director will randomly appoint an arbitrator from among those not stricken by either party.

(c) Response by Only One Party. If only one party responds within fourteen (14) days, the Director will appoint an arbitrator nominated by that party.

(d) No Response. If neither party responds within fourteen (14) days, the Director will randomly appoint one of the five (5) proposed arbitrators.

(e) Additional Arbitrators for Additional Parties. If there are more than two adverse parties, all represented by different counsel, two additional proposed arbitrators shall be added to the list for each additional party so represented with the above principles of selection to be applied. The number of adverse parties shall be determined by the Director, subject to review by the Presiding Judge.

[Adopted effective January 14, 1991.]

III. ARBITRATORS

RULE 3.1. QUALIFICATIONS

(a) Arbitration Panel. There shall be a panel of arbitrators in such numbers as the Superior Court judges may from time to time determine. A person desiring to serve as an arbitrator shall complete an information sheet on the form prescribed by the court. A list showing the names of arbitrators available to hear cases and the information sheets will be available for public inspection in the Director's office. The oath of office on the form prescribed by the court must be completed and filed prior to an applicant being placed on the panel.

(b) Refusal/Disqualification. The appointment of an arbitrator is subject to the right of that person to refuse to serve. An arbitrator must notify the Director immediately if refusing to serve or if any cause exists for the arbitrator's disqualification from the case upon any of the grounds of interest, relationship, bias or prejudice set forth in CJC Canon 3(c) governing the disqualification of judges. If disqualified, the arbitrator must immediately return all materials in a case to the Director.

[Adopted effective January 14, 1991.]

RULE 3.2. AUTHORITY OF ARBITRATORS

An arbitrator has the authority to:

(a) Determine the time, place and procedure to present a motion before the arbitrator.

(b) Award attorney's fees as authorized by these rules by contract or by law.

[Adopted effective January 14, 1991.]

IV. PROCEDURES AFTER ASSIGNMENT

RULE 4.2. DISCOVERY

In determining when additional discovery beyond that directly authorized by MAR 4.2 is reasonably necessary, the arbitrator shall balance the benefits of discovery against the burdens and expenses. The arbitrator shall consider the nature and complexity of the case, the amount in controversy, values at stake, the discovery that has already occurred, the burdens on the party from whom discovery is sought, and the possibility of unfair surprise which may result if discovery is restricted. Authorized discovery shall be conducted in accordance with the civil rules except that motions concerning discovery shall be determined by the arbitrator.

[Adopted effective January 14, 1991.]

V. HEARING

RULE 5.1. NOTICE OF HEARING TIME AND PLACE—CONTINUANCE

An arbitration hearing may be scheduled at any reasonable time and place chosen by the arbitrator. The arbitrator may grant a continuance without court order. The parties may stipulate to a continuance only with the permission of the arbitrator. The arbitrator shall give reasonable notice of the hearing date and any continuance to the Director.

[Adopted effective January 14, 1991.]

RULE 5.2. PREHEARING STATEMENT OF PROOF DOCUMENTS FILED WITH COURT

In addition to the requirements of MAR 5.2, each party shall also furnish the arbitrator with copies of pleadings and other documents contained in the court file which that party deems relevant. The court file shall remain with the County Clerk.

[Adopted effective January 14, 1991.]

RULE 5.3. CONDUCT OF HEARING WITNESSES RULES OF EVIDENCE

(b) Recording. The hearing may be recorded electronically or otherwise by any party at his or her expense.

[Adopted effective January 14, 1991.]

VI. AWARD

RULE 6.1. FORM AND CONTENT OF AWARD

(a) **Form.** The award shall be prepared on the form prescribed by the court.

(b) **Exhibits.** The arbitrator shall return all exhibits to the parties.

[Adopted effective January 14, 1991.]

RULE 6.2. FILING OF AWARD

A request by an arbitrator for an extension of time for the filing of an award under MAR 6.2 may be presented to the Presiding Judge, ex parte. The arbitrator shall give the parties notice of any extension granted.

[Adopted effective January 14, 1991.]

RULE 6.3. JUDGMENT ON AWARD

(a) **Presentation.** A judgment on an award shall be presented to the Presiding Judge, by any party, on notice in accordance with MAR 6.3.

[Adopted effective January 14, 1991.]

VII. TRIAL DE NOVO

RULE 7.1. REQUEST FOR TRIAL DE NOVO—CALENDAR

(a) **Service and Filing.** A copy of the request for a trial de novo shall be served upon the Yakima County Superior Court Administrator. However, failure to do so shall not affect the validity of the request for the trial de novo.

(b) **Trial Date; Jury Demand.** Every case transferred to the arbitration calendar shall maintain its position on the trial calendar as if the case had not been transferred to arbitration. A case that has been given a trial date will not lose that date by reason of being transferred to arbitration. The case shall be stricken from the trial calendar after the twenty (20)–day period within which a party may request a trial de novo has elapsed. A jury demand can be filed and the fee paid at the time the trial de novo is requested. The non-appealing party shall have fourteen (14) days from the date of filing of the request for trial de novo to file a jury demand. If no jury demand is timely filed, it is deemed waived.

[Adopted effective January 14, 1991.]

VIII. GENERAL PROVISIONS

RULE 8.1. STIPULATIONS—EFFECT ON RELIEF GRANTED

If a case not otherwise subject to mandatory arbitration is transferred to arbitration by stipulation, the arbitrator may grant any relief which could have been granted if the case were determined by a judge.

[Adopted effective January 14, 1991. Amended effective September 1, 2010.]

RULE 8.4. TITLE AND CITATION

These rules are known and cited as the Yakima County Superior Court Mandatory Arbitration Rules. LMAR is the official abbreviation.

[Adopted effective January 14, 1991. Amended effective September 1, 2010.]

RULE 8.5. COMPENSATION OF ARBITRATOR

(a) **Generally.** Arbitrators shall be compensated in the same amount and manner as judges pro tempore of the superior court; except that said compensation shall not exceed $1,000.00 for any case unless prior approval is granted by the Presiding Judge. Hearing time and reasonable preparation time are compensable.

(b) **Form.** When the award is filed, the arbitrator shall submit to the Director a request for payment on a form prescribed by the court. The Director shall determine the amount of compensation to be paid. The decision of the Director will be reviewed by the Presiding Judge at the request of the arbitrator.

[Adopted effective January 14, 1991. Amended effective September 1, 2010.]

RULE 8.6. ADMINISTRATION

The Director, under the supervision of the Superior Court judges shall supervise arbitration under these rules and perform any additional duties which may be delegated by the judges.

[Adopted effective January 14, 1991. Amended effective September 1, 2010.]

LOCAL RULES FOR APPEAL OF DECISIONS OF COURTS OF LIMITED JURISDICTION (Cite as L–RALJ)

(Local rule numbers correspond to the RALJ rule numbers)

RULE 1.2. INTERPRETATION AND APPLICATION OF RULES

(b) Application of Rules. These rules shall apply to the appeal of cases tried in the courts of limited jurisdiction, as defined in Rule 1.1(a) after January 14, 1991.

[Adopted effective January 14, 1991.]

RULE 2.4. HOW TO INITIATE AN APPEAL

(c) Designation of Nature of Case. The party appealing to Superior Court shall designate in the notice of appeal the nature of the case appealed; namely, criminal, civil or infraction. At the time that a notice of appeal is filed, a copy of the notice of appeal shall be provided to the Administrator.

[Adopted effective January 14, 1991.]

RULE 3.1. ASSIGNMENT AND SCHEDULING OF CASE

When a notice of appeal is filed, the Administrator shall set the matter for oral argument. The case shall be set to be heard no less than ninety (90) days, and no more than one hundred twenty (120) days from the date the notice of appeal was filed. The Administrator shall designate on the notice of hearing the judge who will hear the case. The case shall be heard as scheduled unless otherwise ordered by the judge assigned to hear it. If a party does not appear at the time set for argument, the court will decide the case on the brief submitted.

[Adopted effective January 14, 1991.]

RULE 4.3. STAY OF ENFORCEMENT OF JUDGMENT

(a) Civil Case.

(1) The Superior Court, upon the application of a party, may stay the enforcement of any civil judgment upon the filing or posting by the applicant of a bond or other security approved by the court; provided, however, the stay in a case involving an infraction shall be automatic and no bond shall be required in such cases. The application for stay of judgment must be filed with the notice of appeal and noted for hearing at the next timely date for hearing motions before the Superior Court according to its existing rules. If the application for stay of judgment is not filed with the notice of appeal, the appellant's right to obtain a stay of judgment is waived.

(2) The bond must be conditioned on the satisfaction of the judgment in full together with interest and costs and the satisfaction in full of any probable modification of the judgment by the Superior Court. If the stay applied for is for only part of a decision the amount of the bond may be accordingly adjusted.

(3) If the judgment is for the recovery of money not wholly secured, the amount of the bond shall be fixed at such sum as will cover the whole amount of the judgment remaining unsatisfied and unsecured unless the Superior Court for good cause shown fixes a different amount.

[Adopted effective January 14, 1991.]

RULE 7.2. TIME FOR FILING BRIEFS

(a) Brief of Appellant. At the time the appellant's brief is filed, a copy shall be provided to the judge assigned to hear the matter.

(b) Brief of Respondent. At the time the respondent's brief is filed, a copy shall be provided to the judge assigned to hear the matter.

(c) Violation of Time Requirements. Upon the failure of either party to comply with the time requirements herein, the opposing party, or the court on its own initiative, may direct the defaulting party to show cause why the appeal should not be dismissed, the relief requested granted, or terms imposed.

(d) Computation of Time. Any computation of time mentioned herein, or the enlargement thereof, shall be made in accordance with CR 6(a) and (b).

[Adopted effective January 14, 1991.]

RULE 9.2. ENTRY OF DECISION AND JUDGMENT

Within two (2) weeks of the hearing, the prevailing party shall present a proposed order consistent with the judge's oral ruling, with at least three (3) days' notice to the opposing party.

In the event the court orders a remand or removal of the case to the Limited Jurisdiction Court, the prevailing party shall deliver a copy of the court's order to the lower court within one (1) week of its entry.

[Adopted effective January 14, 1991.]

RULE 10.2. DISMISSAL OF APPEAL

(c) Effect of Dismissal. Any dismissal of an appeal under any of these rules by the Superior Court shall result in an automatic removal of the matter to the appropriate court of limited jurisdiction for enforcement of judgment or imposition of sentence.

[Adopted effective January 14, 1991.]

LOCAL ADMINISTRATIVE RULE (Cite as LAR)

RULE 1. SERVICES OTHER THAN A LAWYER

Yakima County Superior Court designates the Yakima County Board of County Commissioners, or its appointed designee, as the agency responsible for the administration of services for indigent defendants.

[Adopted effective September 1, 2011.]

LAR 2. ADOPTION AND IMPLEMENTATION OF ODYSSEY

1. Introduction. The current state-wide Superior Court Case Management System (SCOMIS), developed in 1977, is outdated and lacks modern capabilities necessary for efficient court function, such as calendaring, document imaging, and document management. SCOMIS has become so antiquated it is in danger of complete failure. The Washington Administrative Office of the Courts (AOC), the Superior Courts of the State of Washington, and the Washington Association of County Clerks formed the Judicial Information System Committee (JISC) in a joint effort to search for software to replace SCOMIS. The JISC has overall responsibility for the scope, schedule and budget of the project. A request for proposals was issued and, after extensive negotiations, the JISC determined that the Odyssey software offered by Tyler Technologies was the best product available to meet the needs of the Washington Superior Courts and County Clerks. Odyssey is expected to enhance the ability of Superior Courts and County Clerks to efficiently direct and monitor court case progress, schedule case events, enforce court business rules, and view and communicate case schedules and orders.

In 2013 AOC entered into a contract with Tyler Technologies and developed a plan for installing the Odyssey software at the state and county level. Neither Tyler Technologies nor AOC has the capacity to install Odyssey in all Washington counties at the same time. Lewis County was selected as the pilot county for the initial implementation of Odyssey (case management, calendaring and document management) and is currently scheduled to "go live" in June, 2015. Yakima, Franklin, and Thurston Counties will follow in November, 2015 as early adopters. The remaining counties will implement Odyssey through 2018.

On December 13, 2013 Yakima County was approved as an early adopter site for the Superior Court Case Management System (SC–CMS), which replaces SCOMIS. This early adopter status is particularly crucial for Yakima County Superior Court because it uses a calendaring system called CAPS. The CAPS program uses an obsolete computer software language, will not be supported by AOC in the event of failure, and is inefficient and prone to disruptive outages. Calendaring is an essential core function of both the Yakima County Superior Court and the Yakima County Court Clerk. Accurate judicial calendaring is critical to access to justice through effective administration and to ensure the timely scheduling of trials, both civil and criminal, and supplemental hearings as needed to allow litigants' matters to be resolved. Reliance on the CAPS calendaring software is a threat to the Court's continuing ability to operate. In the event of a CAPS failure before Odyssey is fully implemented the Superior Court and Clerk of the Court would have a limited and unreliable ability to identify cases previously scheduled for hearing. Calendaring would have to be performed manually for cases previously scheduled and for all new cases entering the system. This manual calendaring system has an estimated extra cost of $50,000 or more per year. Early adopter status gives Yakima County a valuable opportunity to avoid the threat to the effective administration of justice and the extra calendaring costs.

The Yakima County Superior Court, having conducted a hearing in which the Yakima County Superior Court Clerk announced her decision to implement the Odyssey case management and Odyssey document imaging and management service as an early adopter, and with the support of the Yakima County Board of County Commissioners, the Yakima County Superior Court now resolves as follows:

2. Order for Adoption and Implementation of Odyssey. The Yakima County Superior Court hereby adopts the Odyssey case management system as recommended by AOC, which includes the document imaging and management system, and orders its full implementation with all possible speed. The Yakima County Superior Court and the Yakima County Superior Court Clerk shall immediately participate in the early adopter program with AOC for the adoption and implementation of Odyssey. Each shall allocate sufficient resources to ensure compliance with the Odyssey Early Adopter Implementation Schedule provided by AOC and ultimately the successful implementation of Odyssey scheduled for November of 2015.

3. Implementation. Superior Court Judges. Superior Court Administration, the Board of County Commissioners, the County Clerk. Office of Technology Services, all of Yakima County, the Administrative Office of the Courts, and Tyler Technologies must all work diligently, collaboratively, and harmoniously to support the successful implementation of the Odyssey case management system in Yakima County by November 2015. This includes, but is not limited to:

- Resolving issues in a timely manner, utilizing open, honest and respectful communication;
- Ensuring the availability of appropriate resources as required for project related activ-

ities, e.g. conversion data review, end user training and business process reviews.

● Acknowledging and working within the decisions of the JISC Project Steering Committee, Court User Work Group (CUWG) and AOC project team regarding the implementation, configuration, and release schedule.

● Fulfilling all expectations and deadlines described in the Odyssey Early Adopter Implementation Planning Checklist, Odyssey Early Adopter Implementation Schedule, and the Early Adopter Work Plans provided by the AOC SC–CMS Project team as currently drafted and as may be amended from time to time, including but not limited to the following:

● Ensure that Power Users are identified and registered for Tyler University Training By March 27, 2015.

● Identify and notify AOC of the Power Users who will attend Odyssey Pilot Site End User Training sessions in the AOC Computer Lab during the weeks of May 18–22, 2015 or June 1–5, 2015

● Ensure that the Power User(s) who are registered for training attend the training.

● Actively participate in project stakeholder executive meetings involving the presiding judge, county clerk, court administrator, county information technology staff, and AOC that will occur at least monthly until November 2015.

● Cooperate with the AOC project team to review local business processes.

● Complete business process documentation when requested and return in a timely manner to the SC–CMS project team.

● Encourage and enable staff to be open to changing business processes and look for opportunities to improve processes and efficiencies.

● Actively participate in reviews of the county's converted data and provide timely feedback regarding configuring Odyssey to meet specific county business needs.

● Arrange for all staff to attend one week of Odyssey End User Training in September or October 2015.

● Arrange for staff to work on the weekend before the actual "Go–Live" date so they will be prepared for turning Odyssey "on".

● Enable staff to actively participate in the "ride along" strategy to assist with training and implementation in other counties.

● Collaborating with the Office of Technology Services, Administrator of the Courts, and Tyler to ensure that document images are

successfully converted for use in Odyssey prior to November, 2015.

[Adopted on an emergency basis effective March 19, 2015; adopted on a permanent basis effective September 1, 2015.]

LAR 3. COURTROOM RESPONSIBILITIES AND PROCEDURES ASSIGNED TO CLERK

This rule describes actual current courtroom procedures and the responsibilities of the Clerk of the Court while in court. The purpose of the rule is to maintain and continue current practice without interruption. The Clerk of the Court does not have the authority to modify or regulate these procedures without the express, written permission of the Presiding Judge.

The Clerk of the Court or her/his deputy shall be responsible for the following courtroom duties: opening and closing the courtroom before or after each court session, ensuring the courtroom is provided with supplies and such other customary requirements as directed by the judicial officer, and announcing the opening and closing of each session of court. The Clerk of the Court or her/his deputy shall continue to assist in efficiently carrying out the court process and assist in court as directed by the judicial officer. Such assistance shall include, but is not limited to, providing the judicial officer any forms necessary for the administration of the docket, calling the CourtCall operator to connect attorneys and/or parties on line, calling for security, paging interpreters, etc. The Clerk of the Court or her/his deputy shall ensure the scanned files for all cases and/or hearings assigned to the individual judicial officers shall be loaded into said judicial officers' Liberty/Odyssey folders as soon as possible but no later than 4:30 PM the day before the matters are scheduled. This requirement does not apply to last minute re-assignments of judicial officers.

During those court sessions in which the proceedings are digitally recorded, the Clerk of the Court or her/his deputy shall before each session of court ensure the digital recording system is working correctly by performing a systems test. The Clerk of the Court or her/his deputy shall activate the recording for each session and ensure the integrity of the recordings by periodic checks.

Contemporaneous with the recording of each court session the Clerk of the Court or her/his deputy shall maintain a log which describes the events which occur in the courtroom and are the subject of the recording. For high volume court sessions which do not involve testimony the log may be limited to the items described in Attachment A, unless otherwise directed by the court. For hearings or trials in which evidence is presented the log shall be more specific and detailed and shall capture the events described in Attachment B and C, Attachment D is an exemplar of the log which shall be used and completed by the Clerk of the Court or her/his deputy for each session.

The Clerk of the Court or her/his deputy, as custodian, shall save, maintain and catalog each recorded session in a manner allowing ease of access.

On request of the court, a lawyer, or the public, the Clerk of the Court or her/his deputy shall make available copies of such digital recordings. The Clerk of the Court may charge a reasonable fee of the public

and lawyers for the copying of the requested recordings. The Clerk of the Court shall have the authority to certify such recordings as authentic.

During all court proceedings the Clerk of the Court or her/his deputy shall comply with all statutory requirements and otherwise conform to the order and direction of the court.

[Adopted on an emergency basis effective April 20, 2015; adopted on a permanent basis effective September 1, 2015.]

ATT. A.   MULTIPLE CASE SESSIONS

MULTIPLE CASE SESSIONS

Personal Motions Community Motions Protection Order Docket Domestic Relations Docket Unlawful Detainer Docket Summary Judgments Preliminary Injunctions Ex-Parte	Criminal Docket Supplemental Proceeding Docket Dependency Docket Juvenile Offender Docket Family, Gang, Drug, and MHT Dockets Adoption Docket Ceremonial Sessions

- Convened

- Introduction of case

- Case number – Complete 10-digit number

- Case name

- Attorneys

- Exhibits
  - Marked
  - Identified
  - Introduced
  - Admitted or Objection –not admitted

- Witness name/Witness Sworn

- Sworn Testimony

- On the record/Off the record
  - On Record - Waiting
  - Court Recessed
  - Court Reconvened
  - Adjournment

- Playback

❖ **Capture any time the Court
  "notes for the record" and
  attorney requests a situation
  being noted for the record**

[Adopted on an emergency basis effective April 20, 2015; adopted on a permanent basis effective September 1, 2015.]

ATT. B. REQUIRED LOG NOTE ENTRIES PRE–TRIAL/BENCH TRIAL

REQUIRED LOG NOTE ENTRIES
PRE-TRIAL / BENCH TRIAL

- Convened

- Introduction of case

- Case number – complete 10 digit number

- Case name

- Attorneys

- Type of hearing

- Preliminary remarks

- Opening Statement (plaintiff/ defendant/ waived opening)

- Recess

- Court reconvened

- Objections (nature of objection)
  - Response
  - Court's ruling on objection

- Motions – indicate type of motion

- Ruling on motion

- Exhibits
  - Marked
  - Identified
  - Introduced
  - Admitted or Objection –not admitted

- Witness name

- Witness called/ sworn

- Witness excused

- Witness Examination
  - Direct Examination
  - Cross Examination
  - Redirect Examination
  - Recross Examination
  - Rebuttal
  - Surrebuttal

- Return to Examination

- Stipulations

- Judge's ruling
  - Findings / Ruling

- Colloquy

- Playback

- Closing argument (plaintiff/defendant/plaintiff rebuttal)

- On the record/Off the record
  - On Record - Waiting
  - Court Recessed
  - Court Reconvened

- Plaintiff Rests

- Defendant rests

- Adjournment

- ❖ Capture any time the Court "notes for the record" and attorney requests a situation being noted for the record

[Adopted on an emergency basis effective April 20, 2015; adopted on a permanent basis effective September 1, 2015.]

ATT. C.   REQUIRED LOG NOTE ENTRIES JURY TRIAL
REQUIRED LOG NOTE ENTRIES
JURY TRIAL

- Convened

- Introduction of case
  - Case number – complete 10 digit number
  - Case name
  - Attorneys
  - Bailiff
- Type of hearing

- Preliminary remarks

- Voir dire
  - Juror excused
  - Challenges during voir dire
  - Change of juror (optional)
  - Change of attorney
  - Peremptory challenges

- Opening Statement (plaintiff/ defendant/ waived opening)

- Recess

- Court reconvened

- Objections (nature of objection)
  - Response
  - Court's ruling on objection

- Motions – indicate type of motion

- Ruling on motion

- Jury entering / jury exiting

- Exhibits
  - Marked
  - Identified
  - Introduced
  - Admitted or Objection –not admitted

- Witness name

- Witness called/ sworn

- Witness excused

- Witness Examination
  - Direct Examination
  - Cross Examination
  - Redirect Examination
  - Recross Examination
  - Rebuttal
  - Surrebuttal

- Return to Examination

- Stipulations

- Judge's ruling
  - Findings / Ruling

- Colloquy

- Playback

- Bench Conference (sidebar)

- Jury Instruction Conference

- Closing argument (plaintiff/defendant/plaintiff rebuttal)

- Jury Instructions

- Verdict

- On the record/Off the record

- Plaintiff Rests

- Defendant rests

- Adjournment

- ❖ Capture any time the Court "notes for the record" and attorney requests a situation being noted for the record

[Adopted on an emergency basis effective April 20, 2015; adopted on a permanent basis effective September 1, 2015.]

YAKIMA COUNTY

ATT. D.

Description			
Date		Location	
Time	Speaker	Note	

Produced by FTR Gold 5.1
www.fortherecord.com

[Adopted on an emergency basis effective April 20, 2015; adopted on a permanent basis effective September 1, 2015.]

RULE 6.   ELECTED JUDGES
PRO TEMPORE

1. PROCEDURE FOR DESIGNATION OF ELECTED JUDGES PRO TEMPORE.

At least thirty (30) days prior to the deadline for submitting the names of pro tem superior court judges to the Administrative Office of the Courts, the Presiding Judge or his or her designee shall inquire of all eligible judges to determine whether they would like to be considered for appointment. The designation of pro tem judges for purposes of the portability rule shall be submitted to all the judges and shall be determined by majority vote. If there is a tie vote, the Presiding Judge shall make the determination.

[Adopted effective September 1, 2002.]

EXEMPLARS
EXEMPLAR 1. NOTE FOR MOTION DOCKET

(LCR 7(b)(1)(A) and LSPR 94.04(A)(1)(a))

IN THE SUPERIOR COURT OF THE STATE OF WASHINGTON
IN AND FOR YAKIMA COUNTY

_____)	
)	
) NO.	
vs.)	
) NOTE FOR MOTION DOCKET	
_____)	
)	

TO: County Clerk

AND TO: (List all parties by using names of attorneys, or the name of any party who does not have an attorney, e.g., Pat Jones, attorney for petitioner.

TAKE NOTICE that this case will be set for a hearing in Yakima County Superior Court on the motion of _____ (party bringing the motion) as follows:

DAY AND DATE: _____

TIME: _____
(Particular judge, if applicable) _____

NATURE OF MOTION: (Briefly describe the motion, e.g., Motion for Default, Motion for Continuance, Motion to Compel Answers to Interrogatories, Motion to Adopt Parenting Plan, Motion for Temporary Child Support, etc.) _____

_____

_____

If you (or your attorney on your behalf) do not appear in court at the time shown above, the relief requested in the motion may be granted by the court in your absence.

Date: _____   _____

                                   Attorney for _____

[Adopted effective January 14, 1991.]

EXEMPLAR 2.   (CASES REQUIRING DISCOVERY ORDERS)

(LCR 40)

SUPERIOR COURT OF THE STATE OF WASHINGTON
FOR YAKIMA COUNTY

_____	)	
Plaintiff,	)	NO.
	)	
vs.	)	CIVIL CASE SCHEDULING
	)	ORDER FOR TRIAL
_____	)	
Defendant.	)	

Come now the parties, and enter into the following stipulation:

I.   Stipulation

A.   Discovery and Amendment Deadlines

1. Disclosure of Plaintiff's fact witnesses: _____.
2. Disclosure of Plaintiff's expert witnesses: _____.
3. Disclosure of Defendant's fact witnesses: _____.
4. Disclosure of Defendant's expert witnesses: _____.
5. Disclosure of Plaintiff's rebuttal witnesses: _____.
6. Disclosure of Defendant's rebuttal witnesses: _____.
7. Deadline to amend pleadings: _____.
8. All parties shall serve supplemental responses to outstanding written discovery requests by: _____.
9. Discovery Completed: _____.

B.   Amendment and Enforcement. The parties may amend any deadline by written agreement. The Court may amend any deadline upon motion and good cause shown and upon such terms as the Court deems appropriate. Absent good cause, a non-complying party shall be precluded from calling any witness or using any exhibit that this order required be identified or produced and that the non-complying party failed to properly identify or produce. The duty to disclose witnesses and the scope of disclosures are set forth in LCR 40(c)(2).

C.   Note for Trial.

1. Nature of case: _____ (See Case Information Cover Sheet).

2. Is jury demanded: _____

3. Number of jurors: _____

4. If jury is demanded, include statutory jury fee.

5. Estimated trial time needed by plaintiff(s): _____. (See LCR 40(d)).

6. Estimated trial time needed by defendant(s): _____. (See LCR 40(d)).

7. Estimated rebuttal time needed by parties: _____.

8. Total trial time: ___ days.

9. This case may ___ / ___ may not be placed on a Call Docket.

10. Names, addresses, and telephone numbers of the attorneys or parties:

DATED: _____   SIGNED: _____

Attorney for _____

SIGNED: _____

Attorney for _____

II. Order

This matter having come on regularly before the undersigned judge of the above entitled court, and this court having either received the above stipulation or considered arguments of counsel, the above scheduling of disclosures is adopted as an order of this court, and the Court Administrator is instructed to set the matter for trial.

Dated this ___ day of _____.

_____

Superior Court Judge/Commissioner

_____

Attorney for _____

_____

Attorney for _____

[Adopted effective January 14, 1991. Amended effective September 1, 2010.]

EXEMPLAR 3. NOTE FOR TRIAL DOCKET AND
INITIAL STATEMENT OF ARBITRABILITY

(LCR 40(a)(3))

SUPERIOR COURT OF THE STATE OF WASHINGTON
FOR YAKIMA COUNTY

_____	)	
Plaintiff,	)	NO.
	)	
vs.	)	NOTE FOR TRIAL DOCKET AND
	)	INITIAL STATEMENT OF
	)	ARBITRABILITY
	)	
	)	(Discovery Orders Not Required)
_____	)	
Defendant.	)	

To opposing counsel or party and Court Administrator of the above-entitled court:

The Court Administrator is requested to assign a trial date and notify counsel thereof.

Nature of case: _____

Date when last pleading served: _____

Is jury demanded? _____ 6–member _____ 12–member

After consulting with the other parties, we agree that the estimated time for the entire trial, including jury selection, evidence and argument, will be.

The names, addresses and telephone numbers of the attorneys or of parties appearing in person are:

I hereby represent to the Court that this case is at issue, that no affirmative pleadings remain unanswered, and all pleadings are on file; that to my knowledge no other parties will be served with summons and no further pleadings will be filed prior to trial; that the parties have completed all necessary oral and physical examinations and discovery proceedings or have had or will have opportunity to do so prior to trial; that the case in all respects is ready for trial.

INITIAL STATEMENT OF ARBITRABILITY

(LMAR 2.1)

____ This case is subject to arbitration because the sole relief sought is a money judgment and involves no claim in excess of $50,000, exclusive of attorney fees, interest and costs. (MAR 1.2)

____ This case is not subject to mandatory arbitration because:

    ____ Plaintiff's claim exceeds $50,000.

    ____ Plaintiff seeks relief other than a money judgment.

    ____ Defendant's counter or cross-claim exceeds $50,000.

    ____ Defendant's counter or cross-claim seeks relief other than a money judgment.

____ The undersigned contends that its claim exceeds $50,000, but hereby waives any claim in excess of $50,000 for purposes of arbitration. (MAR 1.2)

Dated: _____   Signed _____

Attorney for _____

Serve on all parties and file with the County Clerk.   Also, a copy must be filed with the Court Administrator, Room 314, Yakima County Courthouse, Yakima, WA 98901.

[Adopted effective January 14, 1991.   Amended effective September 1, 2010.]

EXEMPLAR 3A.   NOTE FOR SETTLEMENT CONFERENCE/TRIAL

SUPERIOR COURT OF WASHINGTON COUNTY OF YAKIMA

In re:	)	NO.
	)	
	)	
	)	
Petitioner,	)	NOTE FOR SETTLEMENT
and	)	CONFERENCE/TRIAL
	)	
	)	
	)	
Respondent.	)	

☐ I request that dates be set for a Settlement Conference.
☐ I request that dates be set for Trial.
The relief requested is: ☐ Dissolution of Marriage ☐ Parenting Plan Modification
   ☐ Paternity ☐ Legal Separation ☐ Child Support Modification
The Response was filed on:
The mandatory Parenting Class was taken: by Petitioner on:
                                            by Respondent on:

All discovery: ☐ has been done ☐ will be done before settlement conference.
The parties have participated in mandatory mediation pursuant to LSPR ___.   A
copy of the mediator's declaration of completion is attached hereto.
Mandatory mediation is not required pursuant to LSPR ___ (c).   A copy of the
court's order waiving mediation is attached hereto.
After consulting with the other parties, we agree that the estimated time needed will
be * hour(s) for settlement conference and * day(s) for trial.
I have conferred with opposing counsel/party and the dates, during the next six
months, when we will not be available for settlement conference are:
I have conferred with opposing counsel/party and the dates, during the next six
months, when we will not be available for trial are:
I request that this matter be preassigned for the following reasons:
Attorney for Petitioner: Attorney for Respondent:

The names, address and telephone numbers of the attorneys (or pro se parties) are:
Petitioner: Guardian
                                      Ad Litem:

Respondent: Other:

        DATED this ___ day of _____, 20 ___.

                                      _____
                                      _____, WSBA # _____

[Adopted effective July 1, 1998. Amended effective September 1, 2004; September 1, 2009;
September 1, 2011.]

EXEMPLAR 4. CIVIL PRETRIAL STATEMENT

(LCR 40(b)(5))

IN THE SUPERIOR COURT OF THE STATE OF WASHINGTON
IN AND FOR YAKIMA COUNTY

	)	
_____,	)	NO.
Plaintiff,	)	
	)	
vs.	)	CIVIL PRETRIAL
	)	STATEMENT
_____,	)	
Defendant.	)	

TO: County Clerk, Ct. Administrator, County Courthouse, Rm. 314, Yakima, WA 98901

I, the undersigned attorney for _____, do hereby certify as follows:

1. This case has been set for trial on _____ (Date)
2. The following have been added as additional parties since the filing of Note for Trial Docket:

         Name   Designation (Party)   Attorney

3. No additional parties will be added.
4. All discovery procedures have been completed, including depositions and disclosure and identification of all witnesses.
5. All pretrial motions have been made and heard.
6. I intend to call _____ witnesses. (Number)
7. Within the past 15 days all witnesses, including experts, have been contacted and their availability for trial confirmed.
8. After consulting with all other parties, I estimate the time for the entire trial, including jury selection, evidence and argument, will be _____ days.
9. No continuances will be requested except for extreme emergency. (Procedural matters, incomplete discovery and unavailability of witnesses are not extreme emergencies.)
10. I currently have no other conflicting cases pending in any other court.

This statement shall be filed with the Court Administrator by counsel for each party not less than 40 days prior to date of trial.

DATED this ___ day of _____, 19___.

PLEASE FORWARD TO:
Superior Court Administrator
Yakima County Courthouse
Room 314   _____
Yakima, WA 98901   Attorney for _____
(Note: You must send a copy to the Court Administrator).

[Adopted effective January 14, 1991.]

EXEMPLAR 5. POSITION STATEMENT

SUPERIOR COURT OF WASHINGTON,
COUNTY OF YAKIMA

In re

NO._____

POSITION STATEMENT OF: ☐HUSBAND
                                              ☐WIFE

I. PERSONAL DATA

Name: _____, age ____   Occupation: _____
Marriage date: _____   Employer: _____
Separation date: _____   Gross monthly income: _____
Children's ages: _____   Net monthly income: _____

II. SUGGESTED RESIDENTIAL TIME FOR CHILDREN

With Father: _____

_____

_____

With Mother: _____

_____

_____

III. SUGGESTED CHILD SUPPORT

If child support is at issue, complete and file an updated set of Washington State Child Support Worksheets. Based on current Worksheets, the presumptive amount of child support for ____ children is $____ per month. Child support should be set at $____ per month, because _____

_____

_____

IV. SUGGESTED SPOUSAL MAINTENANCE

If spousal maintenance is at issue, complete and attach the Monthly Expense schedule, and page 1 of the Washington State Child Support Worksheets (showing income and deductions).

Spousal maintenance of $____ per month should be paid to the ☐husband ☐wife, until _____, because _____

_____

V. ASSETS AND DEBTS

If the other party has not yet filed a Position Statement: fill in and attach four separate schedules, listing each community asset, separate asset, community debt, and separate debt. For each item, insert your figures in the appropriate columns (for "Husband's Position" or "Wife's Position").

If the other party *has* filed a Position Statement: on their four schedules, add your own figures for each item in the appropriate columns. If the other party omitted any assets or debts, add them to the appropriate schedule. Attach copies of your completed schedules.

Transfer your totals from the Community Assets and Community Debts schedules to this chart, showing your proposed divisions of community property and debt:

	To Husband	To Wife
Community Assets:		
Community Debts:		
Subtract Debts from Assets:		
Proposed judgment transfer (+/-):		
FINAL TOTALS:		

VI. OTHER FACTORS

List any other factors which you believe should be considered at the settlement conference, such as special income situations, physical disabilities, dependent children of other relationships, etc.

_____

_____

_____

_____

_____

_____

_____

_____

_____

_____

_____

_____

_____

_____

DATED _____, by: _____

Attorney for _____ WSBA No. _____

This position statement is prepared for settlement purposes only.

MONTHLY EXPENSES OF _____ AND _____ DEPENDENTS:

Housing:
    Rent or house payment .... _____
    Taxes and insurance .... _____
    _____ ...... _____

Utilities:
    Heat (gas & oil) .... _____
    Electricity .... _____
    Water, sewer, garbage .... _____
    Telephone .... _____
    Cable .... _____
    _____ ...... _____

Food and Supplies:
    Food for ____ persons .... _____
    Supplies (paper, tobacco, pets) .... _____
    Meals eaten out .... _____
    _____ ...... _____

Children:
    Day care / babysitting .... _____
    Clothing .... _____
    Tuition (if any) .... _____
    _____ ...... _____

Transportation:
    Vehicle payments or leases .... _____
    Vehicle insurance & license .... _____
    Vehicle gas, oil, ordinary maintenance .... _____
    Parking .... _____
    _____ ...... _____

Health Care:
    Insurance .... _____
    Uninsured dental, orthodontic, medical, eye care .... _____
Personal Expenses (not including children):
    Clothing .... _____
    Hair care / personal care .... _____
    Clubs & recreation .... _____
    Education .... _____
    Books, newspapers, magazines, photos .... _____
    Gifts .... _____
    _____ ...... _____

Miscellaneous:
    Life insurance (if not deducted from income) .... _____
    _____ ...... _____
    _____ ...... _____
    _____ ...... _____
    _____ ...... _____
    _____ ...... _____
    _____ ...... _____
    _____ ...... _____

TOTAL MONTHLY EXPENSES: .... _____
COMMUNITY ASSETS

Asset #	Description of Community Asset	Related Debt #	Husband's Position			Wife's Position		
			Fair Mkt Value	To Husband	To Wife	Fair Mkt Value	To Husband	To Wife
CA-1								
CA-2								
CA-3								
CA-4								

CA-5	
CA-6	
CA-7	
CA-8	
CA-9	
CA-10	
CA-11	
CA-12	
CA-13	
CA-14	

COMMUNITY ASSET TOTALS:

SEPARATE ASSETS

			Husband's Position			Wife's Position		
Asset #	Description of Separate Asset	Related Debt #	Fair Mkt Value	To Husband	To Wife	Fair Mkt Value	To Husband	To Wife
SA-1								
SA-2								
SA-3								
SA-4								
SA-5								
SA-6								
SA-7								
SA-8								
SA-9								
SA-10								
SA-11								
SA-12								
SA-13								
SA-14								

SEPARATE ASSET TOTALS:

COMMUNITY DEBTS

			Husband's Position			Wife's Position		
Asset #	Description of Community Debt	Related Asset	Balance at Separation	To Husband	To Wife	Balance at Separation	To Husband	To Wife
CD-1								
CD-2								
CD-3								
CD-4								
CD-5								
CD-6								
CD-7								
CD-8								
CD-9								
CD-10								
CD-11								
CD-12								
CD-13								
CD-14								

COMMUNITY DEBT TOTALS:

SEPARATE DEBTS

			Husband's Position			Wife's Position		
Debt #	Description of Separate Debt	Related Asset	Balance at Separation	To Husband	To Wife	Balance at Separation	To Husband	To Wife
SD-1								
SD-2								

SD-3	
SD-4	
SD-5	
SD-6	
SD-7	
SD-8	
SD-9	
SD-10	
SD-11	
SD-12	
SD-13	
SD-14	
SEPARATE DEBT TOTALS:	

[Adopted effective January 14, 1991; amended effective July 1, 1998.]

EXEMPLAR 6.   STATUS/SETTLEMENT CONFERENCE ORDER

(SPR 94.04C(2))

IN THE SUPERIOR COURT OF THE STATE OF WASHINGTON
IN AND FOR THE COUNTY OF YAKIMA

In re: NO.

                                                  STATUS/SETTLEMENT CONFERENCE
                                                              ORDER

           ( ) **Trial date of** _____ **is stricken.**
           ( ) **Trial date of** _____ **is continued to** _____

A status/settlement conference was held on this date.

(1)   Petitioner and his/her attorney did/did not attend.

(2)   Respondent and his/her attorney did/did not attend.

(3)   Position Statements were/were not timely filed.   Terms are awarded as follows: _____

_____

(4)   No settlement was reached and the matter shall proceed to trial.   The Court Administration shall set this matter for a _____ day trial.   The disputed issues for trial are:

_____

_____

The parties intend to call the following witnesses: _____

_____

(5)   A full or partial settlement was reached.   The terms of the settlement are: _____

_____

_____

_____

_____

or the settlement was placed on the record by: _____

(6)   An additional settlement conference will be helpful.   It shall be held: _____

_____

The following shall be accomplished before the next conference: _____

_____

_____

(7)   The following discovery shall be completed: _____

_____

_____by (date) _____

(8)   The following shall be completed by the guardian ad litem/ Investigator: _____

_____by (date) _____

Dated this _____ day of _____, _____.

_____
Judge/Court Commissioner

_____
Petitioner

_____
Respondent

_____
Petitioner's Lawyer

_____
Respondent's Lawyer

If pro se, Petitioner's current address:

If pro se, Respondent's current address:

_____

_____

[Adopted effective September 1, 2001; amended effective September 1, 2004; September 1, 2009.]

EXEMPLAR 7.   CHILD SUPPORT AFFIDAVIT REGARDING PUBLIC ASSISTANCE

(LSPR 94.04(F)(3))

SUPERIOR COURT OF THE STATE OF WASHINGTON
FOR YAKIMA COUNTY

In Re the Marriage of:)	
)	NO.
_____,)	
Petitioner,)	CHILD SUPPORT AFFIDAVIT
vs.)	REGARDING PUBLIC
)	ASSISTANCE
_____,)	
Respondent.)	

STATE OF WASHINGTON   )
)   ss.
County of Yakima   )

I, _____, being first duly sworn, state as follows to the best of my knowledge and belief:

I have no children or stepchildren who are currently public assistance recipients or living in a state funded placement out of the family home.

Neither I nor my spouse owes any past child support debt to the Washington State Department of Social and Health Services.

                               _____

                          (Petitioner)   (Respondent)

SUBSCRIBED AND SWORN to before me this ___ day of _____, 19___.

                               _____

                               NOTARY PUBLIC in and for the
                               State of Washington, residing at
                               _____

[Adopted effective January 14, 1991.]

EXEMPLAR 8. NOTE FOR MOTION DOCKET FOR PRETRIAL EVIDENTIARY HEARING

(LCrR 4.5(d)(A)(ii))

SUPERIOR COURT OF THE STATE OF WASHINGTON
FOR YAKIMA COUNTY

State of Washington,	)	
	)	
Plaintiff,	)	NO.
	)	
vs.	)	NOTE FOR MOTION DOCKET
	)	FOR PRETRIAL EVIDENTIARY
	)	HEARING
Defendant.	)	

TO: _____ (Opposing Counsel)

    Clerk of the Court
    Court Administrator

Please take notice that the following pretrial motion requires an evidentiary hearing:

(State the nature of the hearing, e.g., suppression, identification) _____

After consulting with opposing counsel, I estimate the length of the hearing to be

_____

Check all appropriate boxes:

1. ☐ If granted, this motion will be dispositive of the case or a portion of the case.
2. ☐ The hearing will not dispose of the case and will be less than 15 minutes.

If box 2 is the only box checked, the Administrator may set the motion the day of trial; otherwise it will be set before the first day of trial.

DATED this ___ day of _____, 19___.

_____

                         Attorney for _____

[Adopted effective January 14, 1991.]

EXEMPLAR 9. GUARDIANSHIP SUMMARY

(Relating to LSPR 98.01)

GUARDIANSHIP SUMMARY:

1. This is a guardianship of the: ☐person only ☐estate only ☐person and estate.

2. The Ward's information is:

Name:

Birth date:

Address:

Telephone number:

3. The Guardian's information is:

Name:

Birth date:

Address:

Telephone number:

The Ward and Guardian are related in this way:

4. The amount of bond which must be posted by the Guardian is:

☐ none. Upon any significant change in the Ward's assets or income, the estate Guardian shall schedule a court hearing to consider whether a bond should be required.

☐ $ _____ .

5. After the initial inventory and personal care plan, the reporting cycle for this guardianship is every ☐12 months ☐24 months ☐36 months from the date of entry of the original guardianship order, which was on _____ . The next report due is a:

☐ verification of blocked account, due 10 days from today, by _____ .

☐ verified initial inventory, due 3 months from today, by _____ .

☐ initial personal care plan, due 3 months from today, by _____ .

☐ verified account of administration, due by _____ .

☐ report on status of the incapacitated person, due by _____ .

☐ final verified account, due by _____ .

6. Expiration of Letters of Guardianship:

The Guardian's powers and Letters expire on _____ , which is 30 days after the date specified in paragraph 5.

7. Next Court hearing date:

Shortly before the expiration date specified in paragraph 6, a court hearing will be held to consider the Guardian's report, and decide whether the Guardian's powers and Letters should be extended. That court hearing is scheduled for _____ at _____ .

8. The people entitled to receive copies of future pleadings and reports and notice of court hearings are: ☐ none. ☐ the following (list names and mailing addresses):

SPECIAL INSTRUCTIONS TO GUARDIAN:

Your powers as Guardian, and your Letters of Guardianship, expire on the date stated above. If you wish to have your letters extended, you must attend the court hearing, ask the judge to review your report, and ask for a new order authorizing new Letters. If you do not attend, your powers and Letters will expire, and you will no longer be the Guardian.

You must in writing designate a Standby Guardian to serve in the event of your non-availability, incapacity or death. You must file that document with the court and give it to certain other people. See RCW 11.88.125.

You are required to file ongoing reports, by the dates specified above. You must send copies to each person who is listed above as entitled to notice of proceedings in this guardianship, and to each person who files a request for notice under RCW 11.92.150.

You must keep the court advised of any changes in your name or address, or the Ward's name or address. File that written information promptly with the court clerk. If you can not be located, your powers as Guardian could be terminated, and you would remain liable for your actions as Guardian.

GENERAL DUTIES OF A GUARDIAN:

1. If you are Guardian of an **estate**, you have these special obligations:

a. You must keep the Ward's money and property separate from your own. You should put the Ward's money in a separate checking or savings account, as appropriate, and make all payments by check.

b. You may not sell or give away any of the Ward's property without a court order.

c. You may not spend any of the Ward's money for any purpose, without a court order.

d. You may not borrow money on behalf of your Ward without a court order, nor may you or your Ward loan the Ward's money or property to anyone, nor may you use your Ward's money or property for yourself.

e. Within 3 months after your appointment and qualification, you must file an initial verified inventory. In that inventory you must list all assets of the Ward which have come into your hands or which you have knowledge of. See RCW 11.92.040.

f. Each year, within 90 days after the anniversary date of the order which originally appointed you, you must file a verified account of administration. The one year period might have been extended to up to 36 months in your court order. If the Ward is a minor and *all* funds are held in a blocked account, then the reports are not required (but those funds may not be withdrawn until authorized by a court order). See RCW 11.92.040.

g. You must file a report within 30 days after any substantial change in the Ward's income or assets.

h. If the guardianship was created only because the Ward is a minor, then when the Ward reaches age 18, you must turn over any money and property to the Ward and obtain a notarized receipt from the Ward. You must file your final report and the receipt with the court clerk (see RCW 11.88.140), or in the alternative you must file your final verified accounting within 90 days after the Ward reaches age 18 and follow the steps in the next paragraph.

i. If the guardianship ends for any other reason, you must file a final verified accounting within 90 days after the guardianship ends, with a petition asking the court for an order settling the account. You must send copies to each person entitled to notice of proceedings in this guardianship, and schedule a court hearing date.

2. If you are Guardian of a **person**, you have these special obligations:

a. Within 3 months after your appointment, you must file a Personal Care Plan for the incapacitated person. Include the information required by RCW 11.92.043.

b. Each year, within 60 days after the anniversary date of the order which appointed you, you must file a report on the personal and medical status of the

Ward, noting any major events that have occurred in the reporting period, and updating the Personal Care Plan for the next period. The one year period might have been extended to up to 36 months in your court order. See RCW 11.92.043.

c. You must file a report within 30 days after any substantial change in the incapacitated person's condition or residence.

3. If you are preparing your own papers or reports for a guardianship, you may want to start with the forms offered by King County, and modify them to fit your Yakima County case. You can find King County's forms at www.metrokc.gov/kcscc/guardianship.htm.

4. Fees may be allowed or paid to a Guardian only upon court order, after a verified request is filed with the court. In your request list the hours you have spent on the guardianship, the services you have provided, and the amount of pay which you are seeking. See RCW 11.92.180.

5. If you hire an attorney to assist you with this guardianship proceeding, the attorney will have independent responsibilities and obligations to the court. The attorney-client privilege will not extend to information regarding wrongdoing by you as a Guardian if you violate your obligations.

6. This is just a brief summary of your obligations as a Guardian. Most of your duties and responsibilities are set out in the Revised Code of Washington, at Chapters 11.88 and 11.92.

[Adopted on an emergency basis effective June 12, 2007; adopted on a permanent basis effective September 1, 2007.]

EXEMPLAR 10. LOCAL GUARDIANSHIP RULE

(Relating to LSPR 98.01)

IN THE SUPERIOR COURT OF THE STATE OF WASHINGTON
IN AND FOR YAKIMA COUNTY

In re the Guardianship of:

Cause No.

An incapacitated person.

LETTERS OF GUARDIANSHIP
(LTRGDN)

By order of the Yakima County Superior Court: _____ is authorized to act as Guardian of the above-named incapacitated person, as to the ☐person only ☐estate only ☐person and estate.

These Letters of Guardianship expire on _____. They can only be renewed by a new court order. If the court grants an extension, new letters will be issued.

Witness my hand and seal of said Court on _____:

KIM EATON, Yakima County Clerk

By: _____,

Deputy Clerk.

[Adopted on an emergency basis effective June 12, 2007; adopted on a permanent basis effective September 1, 2007.]

EXEMPLAR 11. TEMPORARY RESTRAINING ORDER (TMRO)

IN THE SUPERIOR COURT OF THE STATE OF WASHINGTON
IN AND FOR THE COUNTY OF YAKIMA

In re the Marriage of:

	NO.
Petitioner,	
and	TEMPORARY RESTRAINING ORDER (TMRO)
Respondent.	

I. NOTICE TO PARTIES

1.1 An action has been started in this court that affects your marriage. Both parties are now required to obey the following order unless the court changes it. Either of you may ask the court to change or clarify this order. The court has the authority to punish violations of this order by a finding of contempt and to require the violator to pay attorney fees to the other party for having to bring the violation before the court. This order shall not be entered into any law enforcement system.

2. ORDER

IT IS ORDERED:

2.1 TEMPORARY ORDERS FOR ALL PARTIES

(a) Both parties are restrained from transferring, removing, encumbering, concealing, damaging or in any way disposing of any property except in the usual course of business or for the necessities of life or as agreed in writing by the parties. Each party shall notify the other of any extraordinary expenditure made after this order is issued.

(b) Both parties are restrained from assigning, transferring, borrowing, lapsing, surrendering or changing entitlement of any insurance policies of either or both parties or of any dependent children, whether medical, health, life or auto insurance, except as agreed in writing by the parties.

(c) Unless the court orders otherwise, both parties are responsible for their own future debts whether incurred by credit card, loan, security interest or mortgage, except as agreed in writing by the parties.

(d) Both parties shall have access to all tax, financial, legal, and household records. Reasonable access to records shall not be denied without order of the court.

2.2 TEMPORARY ORDERS FOR PARTIES WITH MINOR CHILD(REN)

(a) Both parents are restrained from changing the residence of the child(ren) from Yakima County until further court order, except as agreed in writing by the parties.

(b) Each parent shall have full access to the child(ren)'s educational and medical records, unless otherwise ordered by the court.

(c) Each parent shall insure that the child(ren) are not exposed to negative comments about the other parent. Neither parent shall make negative comments about the other parent in the presence of the child(ren).

(d) Within 30 days of filing an appearance, answer or other responsive pleading in this action, both parties shall register for the Children Cope with Divorce seminar. Each party shall attend the seminar within 60 days of registering. Upon completion of the seminar, each party shall file with the court the seminar completion certificate provided by the sponsoring agency or provider. In no case shall opposing parties be required to attend a seminar together.

2.3 FILING AND SERVICE OF DOCUMENTS

In all cases involving issues of child support, spousal support, and/or property and debt division, and within 40 days after filing of any general appearance, answer or responsive pleading, each party shall file and serve on the other party the following documents:

(a) Complete tax returns for the last two calendar years together with all schedules, W–2 and 1099 forms;

(b) Most recent paystub with current and year-to-date information;

(c) Complete partnership and/or corporate tax returns for the past two years, together with all schedules and attachments;

(d) A copy of the most recent statement of balances due on mortgages, real estate purchase contracts, deeds of trust, installment purchase contracts, and time payment accounts owed by or to the parties;

(e) Statements showing the value, as of the date of separation, of any bank accounts, investment accounts, retirement and/or pension accounts;

(f) A copy of any appraisal of any real property owned by the parties conducted within the last two years which is intended to be used in the proceedings.

2.4 SETTLEMENT CONFERENCE

If the parties are not able to agree on the final terms of the Decree, they shall be required to participate in mediation before their case may be set for trial. If mediation is waived for good cause, a settlement conference shall be held.

2.5 EFFECTIVE DATE OF ORDER

The Petitioner is subject to this order from the time of filing the Petition. **The Petitioner shall serve a copy of this on the Respondent and file a declaration of service in the court file.** The Respondent is subject to this order from the time that the order is served. This order shall remain in effect until further court order.

Dated: _____   _____

JUDGE/Commissioner

Clerk's Initials _____

[Adopted effective September 1, 2009. Amended effective September 1, 2014.]

DISTRICT COURT

LOCAL RULES FOR YAKIMA COUNTY DISTRICT COURT

Including Amendments Received Through
August 15, 2015

Table of Rules

ADMINISTRATIVE RULES

L–ARLJ .01. FOREWORD

These Local Rules for Civil, Criminal, Infraction, and Appeals are assembled to conform in numbering system and in format to the rules adopted by the Supreme Court as required by GR 7.

These rules supplement ARLJ, CRLJ, CrRLJ, RALJ, and IRLJ in accordance with RCW 3.30.080 and GR 7. Local rules are cited as L—ARLJ, L—CRLJ, L—CrRLJ, L—RALJ, and L—IRLJ. Insofar as practicable the Washington Court Rules are not repeated and the user of these Local Rules should refer to the pertinent rule as adopted by the Supreme Court.

[Effective September 1, 1997.]

L–ARLJ 1. OFFICE HOURS

The Yakima County District Court Yakima office with a clerk in attendance shall be open to the public each judicial day, except Saturday and Sunday, from 8:00 a.m. to 4:30 pm. The Yakima County District Court Grandview office with a clerk in attendance shall be open to the public each judicial day, except Saturday and Sunday, from 8:30 a.m. to 4:30 p.m., and closed from 12:00 p.m. to 1:00 p.m. for lunch.

[Effective September 1, 1997; amended effective September 1, 2012; September 2, 2014.]

L–ARLJ 9. DISCLOSURE OF PUBLIC RECORDS [RESCINDED]

[Adopted effective September 1, 1997; rescinded effective September 1, 2012.]

L–ARLJ 10. COURT COMMISSIONERS AND JUDGES PRO TEMPORE

Part-time District Court Commissioners and Judges Pro Tempore shall have all of the powers of the Judge appointing them during court business hours while actively serving in a Commissioner or Judge Pro Tempore capacity. A full-time Court Commissioner is authorized by the appointing judges to exercise all powers of a District Court Judge at all times.

[Effective September 1, 1997; amended effective September 1, 1998.]

L–ARLJ 11. SERVICES OTHER THAN A LAWYER

The Yakima County District Court hereby designates the Yakima County Board of County Commissioners, or its appointed designee, as the agency responsible for the administration of services for indigent defendants.

[Adopted as an emergency rule on June 7, 2010, and shall be permanently adopted, effective September 1, 2010.]

RULES FOR APPEAL

L–RALJ 6.2. TRANSMITTAL OF RECORD OF PROCEEDINGS

(c) **Form of Designation.** A designation of the record to be transmitted to Superior Court on appeal must specifically identify each document or exhibit the party wishes transmitted. The electronic record will not be transmitted to Superior Court absent a specific Superior Court order. The electronic record will be provided to a party for review or transcription as provided in RALJ 6.3 and RALJ 6.3A.

(d) **Failure to Designate the Record.** The Court will advise Superior Court in writing if a party fails to designate the portions of the record necessary for review as provided in RALJ 6.2(a). Failure to designate the record may be considered a failure to diligently pursue the appeal and cause the court to revoke any stay of enforcement of the judgment under RALJ 4.2 and RALJ 4.3.

[Effective September 1, 1997. Amended effective September 1, 2003.]

L–RALJ 6.3. COPY OF RECORDING FOR PARTIES

Requests for duplicates of recordings shall be in writing on a form prescribed by the Court. Duplicates of recordings and of the log for the record shall be delivered only after payment of the actual costs as determined by statute, unless the party is excused by statute or by the Constitution.

[Effective September 1, 1997; amended effective September 1, 2002; September 1, 2003.]

CIVIL RULES

L–CRLJ 26. DISCOVERY [DELETED]

[Adopted effective September 1, 2002. Deleted on an emergency basis, effective January 1, 2010, permanently adopted effective September 1, 2010.]

L–CRLJ 38. JURY TRIAL

(a) **Demand.** The demand for a jury trial in civil cases shall be made by filing a written demand with the clerk and paying the jury fee not later than fourteen days from the first date the parties receive notice of trial setting or at such time as directed by the court. Failure to comply with this rule is a waiver of the right to a jury trial.

(j) **Trial Day Conference.** Attorneys for each party or any pro se party shall be present at least one-half hour before the time of trial and available to the Judge. A conference will be held with the trial judge to discuss matters which will expedite the trial. All exhibits should be marked by the Clerk prior to the start of the trial whenever possible.

[Effective September 1, 1997; amended effective September 1, 2012.]

L–CRLJ 40. ASSIGNMENT OF CASES

(b) **Notice of Trial—Methods.**

(1) *Note for Trial.* All trial settings will be made at the discretion of the Court after the issues have been joined.

(2) *Persons Notified.* Notice of the trial date will be given to the parties in person or by ordinary mail. Notice will also be provided to attorneys who have filed written notice of appearance.

(3) *Confirmation Hearing.* Every case set for jury trial or Wednesday bench trial shall also be scheduled for a Confirmation Hearing approximately one week before trial. At the Confirmation Hearing, the court will determine whether the case is ready for trial, the estimated length of trial, whether discovery is complete, and any other matters that will promote the just, speedy, and inexpensive determination of the case.

[Effective September 1, 1997; amended effective September 1, 1998. Amended on an emergency basis, effective January

1, 2010, permanently adopted effective September 1, 2010; amended effective September 1, 2012.]

L–CRLJ 47. JURORS [DELETED]

[Effective September 1, 1997. Deleted on an emergency basis, effective January 1, 2010, permanently adopted effective September 1, 2010.]

L–CRLJ 52. FINDINGS BY THE COURT

Written findings of fact and conclusions of law may be proposed by either party in civil actions tried without a jury except traffic infractions. Unless an emergency shall be shown to exist or the defendant failed to appear at trial, the Court shall not sign the same until the opposing party shall have signed and waived notice of presentation, or the opposing party shall have received five days notice of presentation. Any written proposed findings and conclusions must be presented to the Court within 30 days of the Court's decision. Failure to do so may cause the court to impose terms upon the prevailing party on the court's motion or that of another party.

[Effective September 1, 1997; amended effective September 1, 2002.]

L–CRLJ 54. JUDGMENTS AND COSTS

(d) Costs. The original note and any checks sued upon shall be filed as a condition for the award of reasonable attorney fees and collection costs. In all other cases where reasonable attorney fees are claimed either by virtue of a written instrument or a bona fide offer of settlement in a claim for damages, the original of the offer of settlement or copy of the written instrument shall be filed. An attorney's fee as provided for in RCW 4.84.250–.310 shall not be awarded upon a default judgment except when either a Notice of Appearance or responsive pleading (other than a consent to judgment) has been filed and an offer of settlement is served thereafter pursuant to statute or Court rule.

(f) Attorney Fee Guidelines. The following attorney fee schedule shall apply in all default cases unless the parties present evidence of circumstances which convince the court a greater or lesser amount should be awarded. The Court shall have the authority to vary from the following schedule on its own motion.

NSF checks: Statutory attorney fees as set by RCW 4.84.080.

All other cases where attorney fees are permitted by statute or contract:

Amount of principal and interest	Attorney fee
0—$1000.00	$250
$1000.01—$1500.00	$300
$1500.01—$2000.00	$350
$2000.01—$2500.00	$400
$2500.01—$3000.00	$450
$3000.01—$4000.00	$500
$4000.01—$5000.00	$550
$5000.01—$6000.00	$600
$6000.01—$7500.00	$700
$7500.01—$10,000.00	$850
Over $10,000	10 per cent

[Effective September 1, 1997; amended effective October 10, 1997; September 1, 2002.]

L–CRLJ 65. NAME CHANGES

(a) Separate Petitions Required. A separate petition shall be filed for each name a party wishes changed.

(b) Hearing. All hearings on petitions for name changes shall be in open court and on the record.

(c) Minors.

(1) *Birth Certificate.* A certified copy of any minor applicant's birth certificate or suitable identification must be presented to the clerk for verification and copying.

(2) *Parental Notification.* A parent or guardian who has not consented in writing to a minor's change of name and whose parental rights have not been previously terminated must be given actual notice or notice by publication as provided in CRLJ 4.

(3) *Notice by Publication.* Publication of a single notice in a newspaper of general circulation in the county of the parent or guardian's last known residence shall be sufficient so long as the notice contains a hearing date, the name of the minor, the name the petitioner desires the child to assume, and sets forth the reasons for requesting the change of name.

(d) Contents of Petition. A petition for change of name must be sworn under oath and state the following:

(1) The Petitioner's full present name and the full name the petitioner wishes to assume;

(2) The Petitioner's date of birth;

(3) That the Petitioner resides in Yakima County;

(4) The reason for the request;

(5) The application is not made for any illegal or fraudulent purpose;

(6) The name change will not be detrimental to the interests of any other person;

(7) The name of the Petitioner's father and mother, or, if brought on behalf of a minor, the name of the minor's father and mother;

(8) Whether the Petitioner is subject to the jurisdiction of the Washington State Department of Corrections and, if so, that Petitioner has provided a copy of the Petition to the Department at least five days before any hearing on the name change request;

(9) Whether the Petitioner is subject to the sex offender registration laws of the State of Washington and, if so, that Petitioner has provided copies of the Petition to the county sheriff and the Washington State Patrol at least five days before any hearing on the name change request.

(e) Contents of Proposed Order. A Petitioner for change of name must file a proposed Order Changing Name that includes the following:

(1) The Petitioner's full name;

(2) The full name Petitioner seeks to assume;

(3) If the Petition is brought on behalf of a minor, a finding that both parents or guardians consent to the change, or that a non-consenting parent was served with notice of the proposed change as required by these rules, or that a non-consenting parent's legal rights were previously terminated by court order;

(4) A finding whether the Petitioner is subject to the jurisdiction of the Washington State Department of Corrections and, if so, whether Petitioner provided a copy of the Petition to the Department at least five days before the Order is to be entered;

(5) A finding whether the Petitioner is subject to the sex offender registration laws of the State of Washington and, if so, whether Petitioner provided copies of the Petition to the county sheriff and Wash-

ington State Patrol at least five days before the Order is to be entered;

(6) A finding that the Petition is not made for illegal or fraudulent purposes;

(7) A finding that the change of name will not be detrimental to the interests of any other person;

(8) If the Petition is brought on behalf of a minor, a finding that the name change is in the best interests of the minor.

[Effective September 1, 1997. Amended effective September 1, 1998.]

L–CRLJ 66. SMALL CLAIMS

(a) Filing. Small Claims shall be filed by the Plaintiff in person on a form provided by the Court.

(b) Mediation. Every Small Claim, except a claim based upon default in an agreement made during a Small Claim mediation conference, shall be set for a mandatory mediation conference before trial. The Notice of Claim shall give the date, time, and place of the conference and shall advise the defendant that:

(1) Attendance is mandatory;

(2) Defendant's failure to attend may result in entry of a default judgment; and

(3) Plaintiff's failure to attend may result in dismissal of the case.

(c) Informational Brochure. A brochure with information about the mediation process provided by the court shall be served with the Notice of Claim.

(d) Proof of Service. Unless good cause is shown, Plaintiff's failure to provide proof of service at the time of the mediation conference will cause the court to dismiss the claim.

(e)(1) *Defendant.* When a party against whom a judgment is sought fails to appear at the time and location specified in the notice issued pursuant to RCW 12.40.060, a default judgment may be entered upon proof of valid service and venue.

(e)(2) *Plaintiff.* When a plaintiff fails to appear at the time and place specified in the notice issued pursuant to RCW 12.40.060, the plaintiff's claim may be dismissed.

(e)(3) *Motion to Vacate Default Judgments.* A motion to vacate a Small Claims Default Judgment shall be governed by CRLJ559(c).

(e)(4) *Reconsideration/New Trial.* There is no provision for a Motion for Reconsideration and/or New Trial following a Small Claim trial.

(f)(1) *Settlement.* All settlements of Small Claims pursuant to mandatory mediation under Yakima County Local Court Rule L–CRLJ 66(b) shall be placed on the record and may be incorporated into a Small Claim judgment. If the settlement is not incorporated into a judgment, the case may be dismissed.

Any action to enforce a settlement reached pursuant to mandatory mediation, which was not incorporated into a Small Claims judgment, shall require the filing of a new Small Claims action.

[Effective September 1, 1997; amended effective September 1, 2009; amended effective September 1, 2012.]

L–CRLJ 67.   PETITIONS FOR PROTECTION FROM UNLAWFUL HARASSMENT

(a) Form. A Petition for protection from unlawful harassment under RCW 10.14 shall be filed on a form or forms prescribed by the Court;

(b) Joint Petitions.

(1) A single Petition for protection from unlawful harassment may be filed on behalf of a marital community where both parties reside at the same address, or on behalf of minor children who reside at the Petitioner's address. In all other cases, a separate Petition must be filed by each adult requesting relief.

(2) A separate petition for protection from unlawful harassment shall be filed for each respondent.

(c) Minors. A parent or guardian of a child under age eighteen may petition to restrain a person over age eighteen from contact with the child that is detrimental to the welfare of the child. The court shall not enter an order restraining the actions of any person under the age of eighteen.

[Effective September 1, 1998.]

L–CRLJ 68.   VACATION OF RECORDS CONVICTION [DELETED]

[Adopted July 22, 2001 as Emergency Rule; effective as Permanent Rule September 1, 2001. Deleted effective September 1, 2005.]

CRIMINAL RULES

L–CrRLJ 2.5.   PROCEDURE ON FAILURE TO OBEY CITATION AND NOTICE [RESCINDED]

[Adopted effective September 1, 1997; rescinded effective September 1, 2012.]

L–CrRLJ 3.1.   RIGHT TO AND ASSIGNMENT OF LAWYER

(e) Unless a Notice of Appeal has been filed, an attorney appointed at public expense shall be deemed automatically withdrawn from representation thirty days following a final decision of the Court as defined in RALJ without need to file any document with the Court.

[Effective September 1, 1997.]

L–CrRLJ 3.2.   RELEASE OF ACCUSED

(m) Bail Schedule. A bail schedule may be established by a majority vote of the judges. The schedule may be revised from time to time in the interest of justice. A copy of the bail schedule shall be available in the Clerk's office. The bail schedule shall be intended as a guideline, but shall not be construed as limiting the authority of the Court in individual cases to set bail in a different amount.

(n) Domestic Violence Cases. A defendant arrested on a Domestic Violence offense shall be detained without bail until first appearance on the next judicial day. Standard bail for Domestic Violence cases after arraignment shall be $1,000, but the court may reduce or increase the amount of bail in an individual case giving due consideration to the factors specified in CrRLJ 3.2.

(p) Return of Cash Bail. The court may apply cash bail posted in the defendant's name to pay the defendant's fines, penalties and costs on the present case or on any past due obligations to the court.

[Effective September 1, 1997; amended effective September 1, 2012.]

L–CrRLJ 3.3.   TIME FOR TRIAL [RESCINDED]

[Effective September 1, 1997; rescinded effective September 1, 2012.]

L–CrRLJ 3.4.   MANDATORY APPEARANCE [RESCINDED]

[Effective September 1, 1997; rescinded effective September 1, 2012.]

L–CrRLJ 4.1.   ARRAIGNMENT

(d) Appearance by Defendant's Lawyer. A defendant or defendant's lawyer may not waive personal appearance at arraignment on any gross misdemeanor offense.

(e) Deferred Prosecution. A Petition for Deferred Prosecution and Order Deferring Prosecution shall only be considered when presented on forms provided by the Court.

(1) Defendant must file a separate Petition for Deferred Prosecution and proposed Order Deferring Prosecution for each cause number on which Deferred Prosecution is sought.

(2) Defendant must file reports and related materials, including, but not limited to, breath test printouts, blood test results, and abstracts of the defendant's driving record at the time the Petition for Deferred Prosecution is filed. Defendant must file a copy for

District Court Probation of the aforementioned documents for the Court file of each cause number. Defendant shall also provide copies of the Petition, proposed Order, evaluation and proposed treatment plan for review by the Prosecuting Authority.

[Effective September 1, 1997 as amended effective March 10, 1998 and September 1, 1998; September 1, 1999; September 1, 2012.]

L–CrRLJ 4.2. PLEAS

(i) Scheduling. Pleas of guilty may be scheduled by written notice filed no later than noon the day prior to the requested hearing.

(j) Forms. A written statement on plea of guilty shall be prepared by the defendant's lawyer on a form prescribed by the Court or as set forth in CrRLJ 4.2(g).

[Effective September 1, 1997.]

L–CrRLJ 4.7. DISCOVERY [RESCINDED]

[Adopted September 1, 1997; rescinded effective September 1, 2012.]

L–CrRLJ 4.11. STATUS CONFERENCES

(a) Scheduling. A Status Conference shall be held before trial on every criminal case. Status conferences and trials shall be set at approximately the following intervals from arraignment:

In Custody: Two weeks after arraignment. Trial two weeks thereafter.

Out of Custody: Six weeks after arraignment. Trial two weeks thereafter.

(b) Purpose. The Status Conference is designed to determine the readiness of the case for trial and to provide accurate information to the Court about which cases are actually going to be tried. The parties shall conduct themselves with this objective in mind.

(c) Level of Preparation. It is expected that prior to the Status Conference:

(1) The prosecutor will have made a good faith effort to contact, Interview, and confer with the principal witnesses (if other than a law enforcement officer). The prosecutor should be able to assure the court that the case will proceed to trial and that he or she reasonably believes a prima facie case can be established.

(2) The defense attorney will have made a good faith effort to interview and confer with the defendant.

(3) Both counsel will have, to the extent possible, complied with all local and Supreme Court rules pertaining to discovery.

(4) Both counsel will have, to the extent possible, identified witnesses needed for trial, any motions that should be heard before trial, and have estimated the length of trial.

(5) Both counsel will have conferred concerning the status of the case and discussed possible plea agreements.

(d) Procedures.

(1) Those defendants wishing to enter guilty pleas at the time of the Status Conference will be provided by the Court with an appropriate written statement which shall be completed by the Defense Counsel, if any. Such cases may be moved to the end of that day's Status Conference docket or to such other time as ordered by the Court and normally available for entry of guilty pleas.

[Effective September 1, 1997; amended effective September 1, 2012.]

L–CrRLJ 5.1.1. TRIAL BY JURY

(e) Confirmation of Jury Trials.

(1) Any case set for jury trial at the status conference shall be set for jury trial on a date certain. A confirmation hearing shall be set in the week prior to the jury trial date. All parties, including the defendant, shall be present. If the defendant fails to appear at the confirmation hearing, the jury trial shall be stricken and a warrant may be issued for the failure to appear. At the confirmation hearing, the parties shall advise the court either that the case shall proceed to jury trial as scheduled or that some other disposition has been reached.

(2) Any case confirmed for jury trial not proceeding to jury trial shall be subject to such sanctions as deemed appropriate by the judge including but not limited to jury costs, witness fees and terms.

[Adopted effective September 1, 1997; amended on an emergency basis, effective January 1, 2010, permanently adopted effective September 1, 2010; amended effective September 1, 2011.]

L–CrRLJ 6.4. CHALLENGES [RESCINDED]

[Effective September 1, 1997; amended effective September 1, 2003; rescinded effective September 1, 2012.]

L–CrRLJ 8.0. VACATION OF RECORDS OF CONVICTION

(1) All applications for vacation of records of conviction shall be initiated by the filing of a Motion for each record of conviction sought to be vacated.

(2) In addition to any other information required by the law, the Motion shall include the following:

(a) a current Criminal History Conviction Record issued by the Washington State Patrol;

(b) a current Criminal History Conviction Record issued by the Federal Bureau of Investigation;

(c) if the Petitioner was subject to probation supervision as to any conviction for which vacation is sought, a written statement from Probation Services including the ending date of supervision, date of suc-

cessful completion of treatment and date when financial obligations to Probation Service were satisfied in
full. Petitioner shall pay a fee to Probation Services
for such certification, unless previously authorized to
proceed in forma pauperis.

(3) The Motion shall be noted for hearing not less
than 20 days after filing.

(4) If the offense for which vacation is sought was
prosecuted in the name of the State of Washington,
the Motion and Note for Hearing shall be personally
served upon the Prosecuting Attorney's Office not less
than 14 days prior to the hearing. If the offense was
prosecuted in the name of another plaintiff, the Motion and Note for Hearing shall also be personally
served upon the Prosecuting Authority for that plaintiff.

[Adopted effective September 1, 2005.]

L–CrRLJ 8.2. MOTIONS

(a) **Notation for Hearing.** Motions may be noted
on the Court's docket by filing a written Note for
Motion Docket. Counsel shall indicate on the document whether the motion will require live testimony
and the estimated time for disposition.

(b) **Copies of Motions and Supporting Material.**
A party filing a motion other than a motion to continue shall also file at the same time a clearly identified
working copy for the judge. The party shall also
provide a clearly identified working copy for the judge
of any supporting affidavits, sworn statements, or
memorandum of authority on such motions.

[Effective September 1, 1997; amended effective September
1, 1998; September 1, 2003; September 1, 2012.]

TRAFFIC INFRACTION RULES

L–IRLJ 2.4. RESPONSE TO NOTICE

(1) Persons alleged to have committed infractions
may submit a written statement, in lieu of appearing
at a scheduled hearing, either contesting the infraction
or explaining mitigating circumstances.

(2) Upon receipt of a request for either a contested
or mitigation hearing, the Clerk shall provide to the
defendant a form substantially in conformity with
Exemplar No. 2.

(3) The written statement may be returned or filed
by mail or e-mail. It must be postmarked or e-mailed
not later than midnight of the judicial day preceding
the scheduled hearing.

[Adopted effective September 1, 2001; amended effective
September 1, 2003. Amended on an emergency basis effective October 9, 2006; amended on a permanent basis effective September 1, 2007.]

L–IRLJ 2.6. SCHEDULING OF HEARINGS

(a) (3) Hearings on a contested traffic infraction
and a crime arising out of the same occurrence shall
not be scheduled at the same time except with the
express permission of the trial Judge.

[Effective September 1, 1997; amended effective September
1, 2003.]

L–IRLJ 3.3. PROCEDURE AT
CONTESTED HEARINGS
[DELETED]

[Effective September 1, 1997. Amended effective September
1, 2001; September 1, 2003. Deleted on an emergency basis,

effective March 15, 2013; June 24, 2013; deleted on a
permanent basis, effective September 2, 2013.]

L–IRLJ 4.2. FAILURE TO PAY OR COM-
PLETE COMMUNITY SERVICE FOR
TRAFFIC INFRACTION

(d) **Failure to Make Payment Arrangements.**
Defendants who owe penalties on traffic infractions
must report to the cashier immediately after leaving
the courtroom. Failure to do so will be considered a
failure to pay and the appropriate penalty for failure
to pay or appear will be assessed.

[Effective September 1, 1997; amended effective September
1, 2003. Amended on an emergency basis effective October
9, 2006; amended on a permanent basis effective September
1, 2007.]

L–IRLJ 6.2. MONETARY PENALTY
SCHEDULE FOR INFRACTIONS

(b) **Unscheduled infractions.** The base penalty
for violations of RCW 46.61.440 (speeding in a school
or playground zone) and RCW 46.41.527 (speeding in
a construction zone) shall be determined by doubling
the base penalty for Speeding as provided in IRLJ
6.2(d)(1) now in existence or as hereafter amended by
the Supreme Court.

[Effective October 10, 1997; amended effective July 22, 2001;
September 1, 2003.]

UNIFORM EXEMPLAR NO. 1. TRIAL CONFIRMATION

IN THE DISTRICT COURT OF YAKIMA COUNTY
STATE OF WASHINGTON

STATE OF WASHINGTON,   )
☐ City of Yakima,   ) Case No. _____
☐ Town of Tieton,   )
)
_____,)
           Plaintiff,) TRIAL CONFIRMATION BY:
vs.   ) ☐ Plaintiff
) ☐ Defendant
_____,) ☐ Agreement of both Parties
        Defendant.)

The undersigned certifies under penalty of perjury under the laws of the State of Washington that the following is true and correct:

1. This statement is made by ☐ Plaintiff ☐ Defendant ☐ Agreement of the parties pursuant to L–CRLJ 40 or L–CrRLJ 5.1.1;

2. The above-referenced case is scheduled for trial on _____;

3.   ☐ I am prepared for trial and this case will proceed to trial as scheduled;
       ☐ This case will not proceed to trial as scheduled because:
           ☐ the parties have reached a resolution. Please set this case for hearing on _____ at _____.
           ☐ other: _____
               _____
               _____.

DATED: _____   Signed: _____
                              ☐ Attorney for Plaintiff WSBA # _____
                              ☐ Attorney for Defendant WSBA # _____
                              ☐ Other: _____

[Effective September 1, 1997.]

UNIFORM EXEMPLAR NO. 2. WRITTEN STATEMENT

_____ _____
Defendant's Name   Case Number

The local rules of the Yakima County District Court allow you to submit a written statement instead of appearing at the hearing, notice of which is enclosed with this form. If you wish to submit a written statement in lieu of appearing at the hearing, please use this form. It must be received by the Clerk at least **one court day before the hearing**. You also must provide the Clerk with a **stamped, self-addressed envelope** so that you can be advised of the result of the hearing. **No appeal may be taken from the result**. You may attach photocopies of any documents you believe are relevant to your statement. Do not attach original documents.

_____

_____

_____

_____

_____

_____

_____

_____

_____

_____

_____

_____

_____

_____

_____

_____

_____

I hereby certify or affirm under penalty of perjury of the laws of the State of Washington that the foregoing is true. I promise that if it is determined that I committed the infraction(s) for which I was cited, I will pay the monetary penalty assessed by the Court.

Signed this _____ day of _____, 20___, at _____, WA
                                             place where signed

                                              _____
                                                  your signature

Bring or mail this form to Yakima County District Court, Room 225 County Courthouse, 128 No. 2nd Street, Yakima WA 98901: Tel: 509–574–1800. Include a stamped, self-addressed envelope.

[Adopted effective September 1, 2001.]

MUNICIPAL COURTS

GRANDVIEW MUNICIPAL COURT—
[No Local Rules]

GRANGER MUNICIPAL COURT—
[No Local Rules]

MOXEE CITY MUNICIPAL COURT LOCAL RULES

Including Amendments Received Through
August 15, 2015

Table of Rules

RULE 2.4. RESPONSE TO NOTICE

(a) Generally. A person who has been served with a notice of infraction must respond to the notice within 14 days of the date the notice is personally served or, if the notice is served by mail, within 10 days of the date the notice is mailed.

(b) Alternatives. A person may respond to a notice of infraction by:

(1) Paying the amount of the monetary penalty in accordance with applicable law, in which case the court shall enter a judgment that the defendant has committed the infraction;

(2) Contesting the determination that an infraction occurred by requesting a hearing in accordance with applicable law;

(3) Requesting a hearing to explain mitigating circumstances surrounding the commission of the infraction in accordance with applicable law;

(4) Submitting a written statement either contesting the infraction or explaining mitigating circumstances. The statement shall contain the person's promise to pay the monetary penalty authorized by law if the infraction is found to be committed. The statement shall be executed in compliance with RCW 9A.72.085, in substantially the following form:

I certify [or declare] under penalty of perjury under the laws of the State of Washington that the following is true:

I promise that if it is determined that I committed the infraction for which I was cited, I will pay the monetary penalty authorized by law and assessed by the court.

Date and Place   Signature

(c) Method of Response. A person may respond to a notice of infraction either personally or by mail. If the response is mailed, it must be mailed not later than midnight of the day the response is due.

[Adopted August 16, 1993.]

RULE 3.5. DECISION ON WRITTEN STATEMENTS

(a) Generally. The court shall examine the citing officer's report and any statement submitted by the defendant. The examination shall take place within 90 days after the defendant filed the response to the notice of infraction. The examination may be held in chambers and shall not be governed by the Rules of Evidence.

(b) Factual Determination. The court shall determine whether the plaintiff has proved by a preponderance of all evidence submitted that the defendant has committed the infraction.

(c) Disposition. If the court determines that the infraction has been committed, it may assess a penalty in accordance with IRLJ 3.3.

(d) Notice to Parties. The court shall notify the parties in writing whether an infraction was found to have been committed and what penalty, if any, was imposed.

(e) No Appeal Permitted. There shall be no appeal from a decision on written statements.

[Adopted August 16, 1993.]

SELAH MUNICIPAL COURT LOCAL RULES

Including Amendments Received Through
August 15, 2015

Table of Rules

SEMAR 1.1. PREAMBLE

These local rules are assembled and numbered to conform to the numbering system and format adopted by the Supreme Court of the State of Washington as required under Rule GR 7. These rules supplement the Criminal Rules of Courts of Limited Jurisdiction as well as the Infraction Rules for Courts of Limited Jurisdiction.

[Adopted effective September 1, 2005.]

SEMAR 1.2. SCOPE AND EFFECTIVE DATE

The Court may modify or suspend these local rules in any given case upon good cause being shown or upon the Court's own motion when justice so requires. These rules shall be effective on January 1, 2015.

[Adopted effective September 1, 2005. Amended effective September 1, 2015.]

SEMAR 1.3. CITATION

These Rules should be cited as SEMAR (Administrative Rules), SEMCrR (Criminal Rules), or SEMIR (Infraction Rules).

[Adopted effective September 1, 2005.]

SEMAR 1.4. PLACE OF COURT

Unless otherwise ordered, the Court shall sit in the courtroom of the Selah City Hall, Selah, Washington. The Clerk's office also shall be at the Selah City Hall, Selah, Washington.

[Adopted effective September 1, 2005.]

SEMAR 1.5. SESSIONS

Tuesdays are hereby designated as Judicial Days. If a legal holiday falls on a Monday, Court shall, unless otherwise ordered by the Presiding Judge, still be held on Tuesday following the Monday Holiday.

[Adopted effective September 1, 2005.]

SEMAR 1.6. ORDER OF DOCKET

The docket of the Court shall be arranged, generally, in the following fashion:

7:45 AM	Bench Reviews.
8:00 AM	Pre-trial Conferences, Status Hearings, Reviews, Probation Violations, Change of Plea and any other matters as the Court may direct.
9:00 AM	Arraignments.
9:30 AM	Spanish Language Interpreter and Infraction Hearings.

Bench Trials shall be held On Tuesdays. Jury Trials on Thursdays.

[Adopted effective September 1, 2005. Amended effective September 1, 2015.]

SEMAR 1.7. OFFICE HOURS

The Clerk's Office shall be open Monday through Friday (legal holidays excepted) from 8:00 AM to 5:00 PM. The Court may, under extraordinary circumstances, authorize closure of the Clerk's Office for a specific period of time during its otherwise normal hours of operation.

[Adopted effective September 1, 2005.]

SEMAR 1.8. PROBATION DEPARTMENT

Yakima County Probation Services is designated to provide services in all matters requiring supervision of Defendants. The Court shall specify, by written order, the Defendant subject to such supervision and the terms of such supervision.

In connection with Probation Orders, Orders Deferring Prosecution, or Stipulated Orders for Continuance, if the Court issues an order staying the same, Probation Services is relieved of any duty to supervise the subject of the order, pending further directive of the Court.

[Adopted effective September 1, 2005. Amended effective September 1, 2015.]

SEMAR 1.9. JUDGES PRO TEMPORE

Judges Pro Tempore shall have the full powers of the regular Judge during regular Court sessions for which he or she is appointed. Judges Pro Tempore may also, in the absence or unavailability of the Presiding Judge, have such powers as may be necessary to carry out the essential functions of the Court.

[Adopted effective September 1, 2005.]

SEMAR 1.10. DISCLOSURE OF RECORDS

(1) The following records and files of the Court are declared confidential:

(a) Affidavits for search warrants before a return of service have been filed.

(b) Affidavits for probable cause for arrest warrants before the warrant has been served and returned to the court.

(c) Pre-sentence and after-sentence reports.

(d) Mental health, psychiatric, and medical reports.

(e) Alcohol and drug evaluations.

(f) Deferred Prosecution petitions and stipulations of rights.

(g) Unless admitted into evidence, certified copies of driving records, abstracts of driving records, and compliance reports of arrest and convictions.

(h) Judges' notes and work sheets.

(2) Access to confidential records is limited to person authorized by statute or Court order.

(3) Persons requesting access to court records shall file a written request, on a form provided by the Court. Any person objecting to a denial of access may file a Motion for Reconsideration, which will be set by the Clerk, for hearing and determination by the Court.

(4) A charge of 50 cents per page shall apply to photocopies of all documents.

(5) Request for duplicates of recorded CDs shall be in writing on a form prescribed by the court. Duplicates of CDs and photocopies of the record shall be delivered only after payment of the costs for the same, unless payor is excused from payment by statute or appropriate order of the Court.

[Adopted effective September 1, 2005.]

SEMCrR 2.5. PROCEDURE ON FAILURE TO OBEY CITATION OR NOTICE

(1) **Warrant Costs.** The maximum warrant preparation fee permitted under RCW 10.01.160 shall be assessed whenever the Court orders a warrant based on a Defendant's failure to appear for any mandatory court appearance on a jailable offense. The fee shall include any cost for service of the warrant.

(2) The Court, in its discretion, may quash a warrant in the interests of justice.

[Adopted effective September 1, 2005.]

SEMCrR 3.2. RELEASE OF ACCUSED

Cash deposited as bail is presumed to be the property of the accused, unless otherwise shown upon the record of the Court.

[Adopted effective September 1, 2005.]

SEMCrR 3.3. TIME FOR TRIAL

(1) The clerk shall set a Status Hearing on each case set for Jury Trial.

(2) Status Hearings shall be set not less than two weeks prior to the trial date.

(3) Failure of a Defendant to appear at the Status Hearing shall cause the trial date to be stricken.

(4) Failure of a Defendant to contact counsel prior to the Status Hearing may result in the imposition of sanctions upon the Defendant if such results in delay or inconvenience to the Plaintiff.

(5) The Court may continue a case pursuant to CrRLJ 3.3 (d)(1).

[Adopted effective September 1, 2005.]

SEMCrR 3.4. MANDATORY APPEARANCE

(1) Defendants under the age of eighteen shall upon court order, be accompanied by a Parent or Guardian at the time of Arraignment, Status, Trial,

and Sentencing Hearings, The Court may continue such proceedings until the presence of the Parent or Guardian can be secured.

(2) Defendants charged with DUI (RCW 46.61.502), Driver under 21 Years of Age Consuming Alcohol (RCW 46.61.503), Physical Control (RCW 46.61.504), Negligent Driving in the First Degree (RCW 46.61.5249) and Domestic Violence Assault must appear for Arraignment on the next judicial day following arrest or signing of a promise to appear on a citation.

[Adopted effective September 1, 2005. Amended effective September 1, 2015.]

SEMCrR 3.6. SUPPRESSION PROCEDURE

(1) The Court may hold Suppression Hearings immediately prior to jury selection or at such other time as set a hearing pursuant to CrRLJ 3.5 and/or 3.6.

(2) At the time of the Status Conference, appropriate arrangements shall be made to set a date and time for CrRLJ 3.5 and/or 3.6.

[Adopted effective September 1, 2005.]

SEMCrR 4.2. PLEAS

Pleas of Guilty may be entered on any regular court day, but may be subject to terms pursuant to SEMCrR 6.1.1 (f).

[Adopted effective September 1, 2005.]

SEMCrR 4.7. DISCOVERY

(1) Unless otherwise ordered by the Court, the Prosecutor shall provide all discoverable materials in the Prosecutor's possession to the Defense within 14 days of arraignment or as soon as is reasonably possible, and without written demand.

(2) Unless otherwise ordered by the court, the Defendant (if appearing pro se) or the Defendant's Attorney shall provide, without written demand, all discoverable materials to the Prosecutor not less than three days prior to the Status Hearing, or in cases where no Status Hearing has been set, not less than 14 days, or as soon as is reasonably possible, prior to the date set for trial.

[Adopted effective September 1, 2005.]

SEMCrR 4.11. STATUS HEARING

(1) The Status Hearing is designed to determine the readiness of the case for trial, to provide accurate information to the Court as to which cases are actually expected to proceed to Jury Trial and to address Pre-Trial issues.

(2) The Parties and/or their Attorneys should be prepared to exchange witness lists, address Pre–Trial motions and stipulations, discuss jury instructions where applicable, evidentiary issues other than those requiring a hearing pursuant to CrRLJ 3.5 and 3.6,

the amount of time required for trial, whether or not a jury will be waived, and any other relevant issues.

(3) Petitions or Notices of Intent to File Deferred Prosecution may be filed at the Status Hearing and then scheduled for subsequent hearing by the Court.

[Adopted effective September 1, 2005.]

SEMCrR 6.1.1. TRIAL BY JURY

(1) Any case confirmed for Jury Trial at the Status Hearing shall remain set for a Jury Trial, unless the Clerk of the Court is advised by the parties that the jury panel need not be summoned or that the jury panel may be called off.

(2) At the time of the Status Hearing, the Court will set a specific date and time by which the parties can advise the Clerk that the jury panel need not be summoned.

(3) Otherwise, in any case confirmed as a Jury Trial and not proceeding to a Jury Trial, whether by entry of a plea or otherwise, terms, including costs for an unused jury panel, costs incurred in summoning a jury panel and witness fees, may be imposed by the Court.

[Adopted effective September 1, 2005.]

SEMIR 2.4. RESPONSE TO NOTICE

(1) Written responses either contesting or mitigating an infraction shall be permitted, provided such statement shall be either notarized or certified in the manner provided in IRLJ 2.4 (b)(4).

(2) Upon request of the Defendant, the Clerk shall provide information so that the Defendant may comply with this requirement, in substantially the following form:

"You have requested a hearing on your written statement, asking for a ( ) Contested ( ) Mitigation Infraction Hearing. Under Court rules, your statement must contain the following language: "I hereby certify under penalty of perjury of the laws of the State of Washington that the foregoing is true and correct." Sign and date the statement and note next to your signature the place where you signed it; (i.e. Yakima, WA, Selah, WA etc ...). Your statement must also contain your written promise to pay the monetary penalty that may be imposed if the infraction is found committed. Hearings based upon written statement cannot be appealed.

YOUR RESPONSE MUST BE POSTMARKED BY; _____ TO BE CONSIDERED.

[Adopted effective September 1, 2005.]

SEMIR 2.6. SCHEDULING OF HEARINGS

(1) Hearings on infractions may be scheduled, upon request of the Defendant, at the same time as hearings or trials on criminal matters arising out of the same occurrence. Multiple infractions arising out of

the same occurrence may be heard at the same time whether denoted as Mitigation or Contested.

[Adopted effective September 1, 2005.]

SUNNYSIDE MUNICIPAL COURT—
[No Local Rules]

TOPPENISH MUNICIPAL COURT—
[No Local Rules]

LOCAL RULES OF PRACTICE AND PROCEDURE FOR THE UNION GAP MUNICIPAL COURT

Including Amendments Received Through
August 15, 2015

Table of Rules

UGAR 1.1.   PREAMBLE

These local rules are assembled and numbered to conform with the numbering system and format adopted by the Supreme Court of the State of Washington as required under GR 7. These rules supplement the Criminal Rules for Courts of Limited Jurisdiction as well as the Infraction Rules for Courts of Limited Jurisdiction.

[Adopted effective September 1, 1999.]

UGAR 1.2.   SCOPE AND EFFECTIVE DATE

The Court may modify or suspend these local rules in any given case upon good cause being shown or upon the Court's own motion when justice so requires.

These rules shall be effective on September 1, 1999.

[Adopted effective September 1, 1999.]

UGAR 1.3.   CITATION

These Rules should be cited as UGAR [Administrative Rules], UGCrR [Criminal Rules], or UGIR [Infraction Rules]

[Adopted effective September 1, 1999.]

UGAR 1.4.   PLACE OF COURT

Unless otherwise ordered, the Court shall sit in the Courtroom of the Union Gap City Hall, Union Gap, Washington. The clerk's office shall be at the Union Gap City Hall, Union Gap, Washington.

[Adopted effective September 1, 1999.]

UGAR 1.5.   SESSIONS

Mondays, Thursdays and Wednesdays are hereby designated as Judicial Days. If a Judicial Day falls on a legal holiday, the Court shall, unless otherwise ordered by the Presiding Judge, be in session on the next following day, excluding Saturdays, Sundays, and legal holidays.

[Adopted effective September 1, 1999; amended effective September 1, 2008.]

UGAR 1.6.   ORDER OF DOCKET

The docket of the Court shall be arranged, generally, in the following fashion:

Monday

8:00 a.m.   All matters concerning defendants in custody.

9:30 a.m.   Status Hearings, Probation Violation Arraignments and Hearings on such other matters as the Court may direct.

11:00 a.m.   Status Hearings, Probation Violation Arraignments and Hearings on such other matters as the Court may direct.

1:30 p.m. Status Hearings, Probation Violation Arraignments and Hearings on such other matters as the Court may direct.

Wednesday

9:00 a.m. All matters set for jury trial.

Thursday

8:00 a.m. All matters concerning defendants in custody.

9:30 a.m. Out of custody, arraignments, motions requiring the testimony, trials, and probation violation arraignments and such other matters as the Court may direct, including Jury trials

1:30 p.m. Hearings on infractions and special-set for criminal hearings or trials or such other matters as the Court may direct.

[Adopted effective September 1, 1999; amended effective April 16, 2002; amended on an emergency basis effective January 18, 2006; amended on a permanent basis effective September 1, 2006; amended effective September 1, 2008.]

UGAR 1.7. OFFICE HOURS

The Clerk's Office shall be open Monday through Friday [legal holidays excepted] from 8:00 AM to 12:00 and 1:00 PM to 5:00 PM. The Court may, under extraordinary circumstances, authorize closure of the Clerk's Office for a specific period of time during its otherwise normal hours of operation.

[Adopted effective September 1, 1999.]

UGAR 1.8. PROBATION DEPARTMENT

Yakima County Probation Services is designated to provide services in all matters requiring supervision of defendants. The court shall specify, by written order, the defendants subject to such supervision and the terms of such supervision.

In connection with Probation Orders, Orders Deferring Prosecution, or Stipulated Orders for Continuance, if the Court issues an order staying the same, Probation Services is relieved of any duty to supervise the subject of the order, pending further directive of the Court.

[Adopted effective September 1, 1999; amended effective September 1, 2008.]

UGAR 1.9. JUDGES PRO TEMPORE

Judges Pro Tempore shall have the full powers of the regular judge during regular Court sessions for which he or she is appointed. Judges Pro Tempore may also, in the absence or unavailability of the Presiding Judge, have such powers as may be necessary to carry out the essential functions of the Court.

[Adopted effective September 1, 1999.]

UGAR 1.10. DISCLOSURE OF RECORDS

(1) The following records and files of this Court are declared confidential:

(a) Affidavits for search warrants before a return of service has been filed;

(b) Affidavits for probable cause for arrest warrants before the warrant has been served and returned to the Court:

(c) Pre-sentence and after-sentence reports;

(d) Mental health, psychiatric, and medical reports;

(e) Alcohol and drug evaluations;

(f) Deferred Prosecution petitions and stipulations of rights;

(g) Unless admitted into evidence, certified copies of driving records, abstracts of driving records, and compiled reports of arrests and convictions;

(h) Judges' notes and work sheets.

(2) Access to confidential records is limited to persons authorized by statute or Court order.

(3) Persons requesting access to court records shall file a written request. on a form provided by the Court. Any person objecting to a denial of access may file a Motion for Reconsideration, which will be set, by the Clerk, for hearing and determination by the Court.

(4) A charge of 50 cents per page shall apply to photocopies of all documents.

(5) Requests for duplicates of recorded tapes shall be in writing on a form prescribed by the court. Duplicates of tapes and photocopies the log for the record shall be delivered only after payment of the costs for the same, unless payment is excused from payment by statute or appropriate order of the court.

[Adopted effective September 1, 1999.]

CRIMINAL RULES

UGCrR 2.5. PROCEDURE ON FAILURE TO OBEY CITATION OR NOTICE

(1) **Warrant Costs.** The maximum warrant preparation fee permitted under RCW 10.01.160 shall be assessed whenever the Court orders a warrant based on a defendant's failure to appear for any mandatory court appearance on a jailable offense. The fee shall include any costs for service of the warrant.

(2) **Quashing Warrants.** The Court, in its discretion, may quash a warrant under the following circumstances:

(a) The defendant may personally appear at the clerk's office and pay the amount of the warrant fee in cash. The defendant shall then personally sign a promise to appear at a hearing no later than the next judicial day. The Court will determine the appropriate conditions for the defendant's continued release at that hearing.

(b) Nothing in this rule shall be construed to limit the Court's power to quash a warrant when justice otherwise requires.

[Adopted effective September 1, 1999.]

UGCrR 3.2.   RELEASE OF ACCUSED

Cash deposited as bail is presumed to be the property of the accused, unless otherwise shown upon the record of the Court.

[Adopted effective September 1, 1999.]

UGCrR 3.3.   TIME FOR TRIAL

(1) The clerk shall set a status hearing on each case set for trial.

(2) Status hearings shall be set not less than two weeks prior to the trial date.

(3) Failure of a defendant to appear at the status hearing shall cause the trial date to be stricken.

(4) Failure of a defendant to contact counsel prior to the status hearing may result in the imposition of terms upon the defendant if such results in delay or inconvenience to the plaintiff.

(5) The Court may continue a case pursuant to CrRLJ 3.3(d)(1).

[Adopted effective September 1, 1999.]

UGCrR 3.4.   MANDATORY APPEARANCE

(1) Defendants under the age of eighteen shall be accompanied by a parent or guardian at the time of arraignment, status, trial, and sentencing hearings. The Court may continue such proceedings until the presence of the parent or guardian can be secured.

(2) Defendants charged with Domestic Violence Offenses as defined in RCW 10.99, DUI (RCW 46.61.502), Driver Under 21 Years of Age Consuming Alcohol (RCW 46.61.503), Physical Control (RCW 46.61.504) and Negligent Driving in the First Degree (RCW 46.61.5249) must appear for arraignment on the next judicial day following arrest or signing of a promise to appear on a citation.

(3) Appearance at arraignment for defendants charged with other offenses may be waived by the Court upon filing of a written appearance as provided under CrRLJ 4.1(d) by an attorney admitted to practice in the State of Washington, and upon such conditions as the Court may deem necessary.

[Adopted effective September 1, 1999.]

UGCrR 3.5.   BAIL/BOND

Upon a defendant's being released from jail on bail or bond, unless otherwise directed by court, the defendant shall appear in Union Gap Municipal Court, at 9:30 a.m. on the next Monday or Thursday thereafter, unless it is a legal holiday, in which case the defendant shall appear at 9:30 a.m. on the next immediately following Monday or Thursday.

[Adopted effective September 1, 2008.]

UGCrR 3.6.   SUPPRESSION PROCEDURE

(1) A hearing pursuant to CrRLJ 3.5 and/or 3.6 may be held immediately prior to jury selection or at such other time as set by the Court.

(2) At the time of the status conference, appropriate arrangements shall be made to set a date and time for CrRLJ 3.5 and/or 3.6 hearings.

[Adopted effective September 1, 1999.]

UGCrR 4.2.   PLEAS

Pleas of Guilty may be entered on any regular court day, but may be subject to terms pursuant to UGCrR 6.1.1(f).

[Adopted effective September 1, 1999.]

UGCrR 4.7.   DISCOVERY

(1) Unless otherwise ordered by the Court, the prosecutor shall provide all discoverable materials in the prosecutor's possession to the defense within 14 days of arraignment or as soon as is reasonably possible, and without written demand.

(2) Unless otherwise ordered by the Court, the defendant (if appearing pro se) or the defendant's attorney shall provide, without written demand, all discoverable materials to the prosecutor not less than three days prior to the status hearing, or in cases where there no status hearing has been set, not less than 14 days, or as soon as is reasonably possible, prior to the date set for trial.

[Adopted effective September 1, 1999.]

UGCrR 4.11.   STATUS HEARINGS

(1) The status-hearing is designed to determine the readiness of the case for trial, to provide accurate information to the Court as to which cases are actually expected to proceed to jury trial, or where appropriate, bench trial, and to address pre-trial issues.

(2) The parties and/or their attorneys should be prepared to exchange witness lists, address pre-trial motions and stipulations, discuss jury instructions where applicable, evidentiary issues other than those requiring a hearing pursuant to CrRLJ 3.5 and 3.6, the amount of time required for trial, whether or not a jury will be waived, and any other relevant issues.

(3) Petitions or Notices of Intent to File for Deferred Prosecution may be filed at the status hearing and then scheduled for subsequent hearing by the Court.

[Adopted effective September 1, 1999.]

UGCrR 6.1.1.   TRIAL BY JURY

(1) Any case confirmed for jury trial at the status hearing shall remain set for a jury trial, unless the

Clerk of the Court is advised by the parties that the jury panel need not be summoned or that the jury panel may be called off.

(2) At the time of the status hearing, the Court will set a specific date and time by which the parties can advise the Clerk that the jury panel need not be summoned.

(3) Otherwise, in any case confirmed as a jury trial and not proceeding to a jury trial, whether by entry of a plea or otherwise, terms, including costs for an unused jury panel, costs incurred in summoning a jury panel and witness fees, may be imposed by the Court.

[Adopted effective September 1, 1999.]

INFRACTION RULES

UGIR 2.4.   RESPONSE TO NOTICE

(1) Written responses either contesting or mitigating an infraction shall be permitted, provided such statement shall be either notarized or certified in the manner provided in IRLJ 2.4(b)(4).

(2) Upon request of the defendant, the clerk shall provide information so that the defendant may comply with this requirement, in substantially the following form:

"You have requested a hearing on your written statement ( ) contesting ( ) mitigating an infraction. Under the Court rules, your statement must bear the following language: "I hereby certify under penalty of perjury of the laws of the State of Washington that the foregoing is true and correct." Sign and date the statement and note next to your signature the place where you signed it; i.e. Yakima WA, Seattle WA etc. Your statement must also contain your written promise to pay the monetary penalty that may be imposed if the infraction is found to be committed.

YOUR RESPONSE MUST BE POSTMARKED BY: _____ TO BE CONSIDERED.

[Adopted effective September 1, 1999.]

UGIR 2.6.   SCHEDULING OF HEARINGS

(1) Hearings on infractions may be scheduled at the same time as hearings or trials on criminal matters arising out of the same occurrence. Multiple infractions arising out of the same occurrence may be heard at the same time, whether denoted as mitigation or contested.

[Adopted effective September 1, 1999.]

WAPATO MUNICIPAL COURT LOCAL RULES

Including Amendments Received Through
August 15, 2015

Table of Rules

WMLAR 1.1. PREAMBLE

These local rules for Criminal matters, Infractions and Appeals are assembled and numbered to conform with the numbering system and format adopted by the Supreme Court of the State of Washington as required under GR 7.

These rules supplement CrRLJ, ARLJ, CRLJ, and IRLJ

[Adopted effective September 1, 2011.]

WMLAR 1.2. CITATION

These Rules should be cited as WMAR, WMCrR, WMCR, or WMIR

[Adopted effective September 1, 2011.]

WMLAR 1.3. PLACE OF COURT

Unless otherwise ordered, the court shall sit in the Courtroom of the Wapato Law and Justice Center at 205 S. Simcoe Ave, Wapato, Washington. The clerk's office shall be at the Wapato Law and Justice Center, 205 S. Simcoe Ave. Wapato, Washington.

[Adopted effective September 1, 2011.]

WMLAR 1.4. SESSIONS

Regular Court sessions shall be held every Monday afternoon for In Custody matters along with out of custody, Arraignment, Mitigation, Contested and Probation Violations and the first and third Thursday of the month for pre-trial and bench trials. Holidays and Court Holidays excluded.

[Adopted effective September 1, 2011.]

WMLAR 1.5. ORDER OF DOCKET

(a) During sessions, the docket shall proceed according to the calendar posted and available from the clerk of the Court, except as modified from time to time by the court or except as provided by WMLAR 1.5 (b).

(b) Unusually complicated or lengthy trials and hearings may be specially set by the Court so as to expedite the matter and minimize the impact of the regular business of the Court. Parties in such cases may move the Court for a special setting, which motion shall be heard upon written affidavits, or may be granted upon the stipulation of the parties, The court may, sua sponte, schedule a special setting for a matter.

(c) Civil matters, other than infractions, shall be set as special settings, provided that no civil trial or hearing shall be set absent full compliance with CRLJ 40.

(d) For good cause shown, the Court may set any matter at other times and days.

[Adopted effective September 1, 2011.]

WMLAR 1.6. OFFICE HOURS

The Clerk's Office shall be open Monday through Friday {except legal holidays} from 8:00 AM to 1:00 PM and from 2:00 PM to 5:00 PM. The Court may, under extraordinary circumstances, authorize closure of the Clerk's office for a specific period of time during its otherwise normal hours of operation.

[Adopted effective September 1, 2011.]

WMLAR 1.7. PROBATION DEPARTMENT

The Court shall contract with Yakima County Probation Services to provide services in all matters requiring supervision of defendants. The department shall be staffed with a full time probation officer and assistants as may be deemed necessary.

[Adopted effective September 1, 2011.]

WMLAR 1.8. JUDGES PRO TEMPORE

Except as limited by statute, Judges Pro Tempore shall have the authority of a regular Judge during regular Court sessions for which he or she is appointed.

[Adopted effective September 1, 2011.]

WMLAR 9. DISCLOSURE OF RECORDS

(g)(1) The following records and files are deemed confidential:

    a. Affidavits, transcriptions or electronic records for search warrants prior to the return of service of such warrant;

    b. Pre-sentence or after-sentence investigation reports;

    c. Mental health, psychiatric and medical reports and records;

    d. Alcohol, drug and controlled substance evaluations;

    e. Deferred Prosecution Petitions and Stipulations

    f. Certified copies of driving and criminal records unless duly admitted into evidence; and

    g. Judge's notes and working documents, whether written or electronic.

(g)(2) Access to confidential records is strictly limited to persons or entities authorized by statute or Court order to obtain such records.

(g)(3) Requests for access to Court Records shall be made in writing on the form provided by the court, and shall be granted or denied only by the judge, who shall state reasons for denial in writing.

(g)(4) Costs of copying and transcription shall be borne by the person or entity requesting any copies. Unless otherwise ordered by the Court, copy costs shall be $.15 per page and $5.00 for certification of requested document.

(g)(5) Copies of Audio Court Proceedings shall be $20 per CD.

(g)(65)[1] No documents or electronic data may be removed from the court office, chambers, court room, or probation department, except for storage, without prior written order of the Court.

[Adopted effective September 1, 2011.]

[1] So in original, probably should be (g)(6).

WMLAR 11. FORMS

The Court may require pleadings, written motions, petitions or orders to be in a prescribed form and style or submitted on preprinted forms provided by the Court.

[Adopted effective September 1, 2011.]

RULES FOR APPEAL

WMLRA 6.3. COPIES OF RECORDING

On appeal, the appellant shall make a written request for duplicates of CD's of court recording, and shall specify the name and number of the case and the date of trial. Unless waived by statute, constitutional provision, or the court, duplicates of CD's and of any log or index thereto shall not be delivered until full payment of the actual preparation costs as determined by the Court Administrator.

[Adopted effective September 1, 2011.]

CIVIL RULES

WMLCR 1A. CRLJ ADOPTED

Except as modified by these rules from time to time, the Washington Civil Rules for Courts of Limited Jurisdiction shall apply to all civil actions filed and tried in Wapato Municipal Court.

[Adopted effective September 1, 2011.]

WMLCR 4.0(g). FORMS

All filings pursuant to CRLJ 40 shall be in substantial compliance with requirements of LCR 40 of the Superior Court of the State of Washington in and for the County of Yakima, provided that no statement of arbitrability shall be appended.

[Adopted effective September 1, 2011.]

WMLCR 8.1(c). LIMITATION OF APPLICABILITY

These rules do not apply to civil infractions unless otherwise provided by WMCR or CRLJ.

[Adopted effective September 1, 2011.]

CRIMINAL RULES

WMLCrRLJ 3.1(e). WITHDRAWAL OF LAWYER

(e) Unless a Notice of Appeal has been filed, an attorney appointed at public expense shall be deemed automatically withdrawn from representation thirty days following a final decision of the court as defined in RALJ without need to file any document with the court.

[Adopted effective September 1, 2011.]

WMLCrRLJ 3.2. RELEASE OF ACCUSED

(n) **Domestic Violence Cases.** A defendant arrested on domestic violence offences shall be detained without bail until arraignment on the next judicial day. Standard bail for domestic violence cases after arraignment shall be $1,000, but the court may reduce or increase the amount of bail in an individual case giving due consideration to the factors specified in CrRLJ 3.2.

(p) In any case where bail has been required, such bail shall not be waived or reduced without a hearing at which the defendant shall be present.

(r)(i) Cash deposited as bail is presumed to be the property of the accused regardless of who actually made such deposit. Such bail may be forfeited or applied to any fines and assessments.

(p)(i) A payor may request a hearing pursuant to these rules by filing a request in person and in writing with the clerk of the court within 30 days of the entry of the order forfeiting such bail. Such payor shall have the burden of proving by a preponderance of evidence that the bail was either unjustly forfeited or that the funds were neither the property of nor a gift to the defendant.

(p)(ii) At such hearing, the court may consider written evidence, properly presented, such as promissory notes or loan statements, but such evidence alone shall not be deemed decisive.

[Adopted effective September 1, 2011.]

WMLCrRLJ 3.3. TIME FOR TRIAL

WMCrRLJ 3.3(h)(3): Any agreed order or stipulation for continuance, or resetting shall be signed by the parties or their attorneys, prior to presentation to the judge or commissioner. Unsigned stipulations, agreed orders for continuance or resetting shall be deemed incomplete and not entertained by the court.

WMCrRLJ 3.3(h)(4): Properly prepared agreed orders or stipulations for continuance or resetting may be granted without hearing, but the clerk shall make the appropriate docket entry.

WMCrRLJ 3.3(h)(5): The Court may impose terms for continuance or resetting.

WMCrRLJ 3.3(k)(1): The Clerk shall set a status conference on each case set for trial.

WMCrRLJ 3.3(k)(2): Status conferences shall be set not less than two weeks prior to this trial date.

WMCrRLJ 3.3(k)(3): Failure of a defendant to appear at the status conference shall be grounds for striking the trial date and issuance of a warrant for defendant's arrest.

WMCrRLJ 3.3(k)(4): Failure of a defendant to contact counsel prior to the status conference may result in such terms and attorney's fees as the court may deem necessary being imposed against the defendant.

WMCrRLJ 3.3(k)(5): Failure of a defendant to appear at the time and date scheduled for any mandatory hearing or trial, or appearing after the time set for the case it shall be considered a failure to appear for speedy trial purposes, apprehension or subsequent appearance.

[Adopted effective September 1, 2011.]

WMLCrRLJ 3.4. MANDATORY APPEARANCE

(d) Defendants under the age of eighteen shall be accompanied by a parent or guardian at the time of arraignment, pre-trial, trial, and sentencing hearings. The Court may continue proceedings in the case until the presence of the parent or guardian can be secured, or the Court may waive the presence of the parent or guardian if satisfied that the minor is capable of understanding the proceedings and his or her peril.

(e) All defendants must be present at arraignment, status conference, suppression hearings, trial or other hearings, except the Court may, upon filing of a written notice of appearance as provided under CrRLJ 4.1 (d) by an attorney admitted to practice in the State of Washington, and upon such conditions as the Court may deem necessary and as provided by WMCrR 4.1, waive attendance at arraignment, or hearings on motions for continuance.

(f) Without exception, a defendant accused of Domestic Violence and DUI must be actually present at arraignment, status conferences, suppression hearings, trial or other hearings.

[Adopted effective September 1, 2011.]

WMLCrRLJ 3.6. SUPPRESSION PROCEDURE

(1) A hearing pursuant to CrRLJ 3.5 and/or 3.6 may be held immediately prior to jury selection or at such other time as set by the Court.

(2) At the time of the status conference, appropriate arrangements shall be made to set a date and time for CrRLJ 3.5 and/or 3.6 hearings.

[Adopted effective September 1, 2011.]

WMLCrRLJ 4.1. ARRAIGNMENT

(e)(i) The defendant's personal presence is mandatory when the charging document states that one or more of the charges involves DUI or domestic violence. This requirement shall not be waived.

(f) Deferred Prosecution. A petition for Deferred Prosecution and Order Deferring Prosecution may be considered by the court if it meets the statutory requirements.

(1) Defendant must include the cause/citation number for each Petition for Deferred Prosecution and proposed Order Deferring Prosecution for on which Deferred Prosecution is sought.

(2) Defendant must file copies of all offense reports and related materials, including, but not limited to, breath test printouts, blood test results, abstracts of the defendant's driving record, evaluation and treatment plan at the time the Petition and Order for Deferred Prosecution are filed. Defendant must file a sufficient number of copies of the aforementioned documents for the court file of each cause/citation number, probation and treating agency. Defendant shall also provide copies of the Petition, proposed Order, evaluation and proposed treatment agency. Defendant shall also provide copies of the Petition, proposed Order, evaluation and proposed treatment plan for review by the Prosecuting Authority.

(3) In addition to the statutory conditions and requirements of deferred prosecution, each defendant shall pay the monitoring assessment to the Municipal Curt in the amount of $150 plus any other costs related to the case, All defendants placed on a deferred prosecution will also be placed on five-year probation: Active Supervised Probation for two years and Monitored Probation for three years, They will be required to pay the fees for Probation. Restitution is required as a condition of a deferred prosecution if applicable. Deferred Prosecution defendants will have ignition interlock installed on all person vehicles, which they drive, during their period of Active Supervised Probation. An order will not enter without the written signed contract for treatment being presented to the Court.

[Adopted effective September 1, 2011.]

WMLCrRLJ 4.2. PLEAS (1)

A guilty plea may be entered at any time, provided that in cases wherein a defendant is represented by an attorney, not less than one day actual notice of such plea shall be given to the city, and provided further that a defendant may, at any hearing or trial scheduled in the case, enter a plea of guilty with or without notice.

[Adopted effective September 1, 2011.]

WMLCrRLJ 4.7. DISCOVERY

(1) Unless otherwise ordered by the Court, the prosecutor shall provide all discoverable materials in the prosecutor's possession to the defense within 14 days of arraignment or as soon as is reasonably possible, and without written demand.

(2) Unless otherwise ordered by the Court, the defendant (if appearing pro se) or the defendant's attorney shall provide, without written demand, all discoverable materials to the prosecutor not less than three days prior to the status hearing, or in cases where there no status hearing has been set, not less than 4 days, or as soon as is reasonably possible, prior to the date set for trial.

[Adopted effective September 1, 2011.]

WMLCrRLJ 4.11. STATUS CONFERENCES

(a) The Clerk of the Court shall set a pre-trial status/readiness hearing for every case set for jury trial. The conference shall be set two weeks prior to jury trial date. All parties must be in attendance at the readiness hearing in order to proceed to trial. Should the defendant fail to appear for the readiness hearing, the trial will be stricken, the F T A will be noted and a summons will be ordered for the appearance of the defendant.

[Adopted effective September 1, 2011.]

WMLCrRLJ 6.1. RESTITUTION

Where the court orders that a defendant pay restitution, but does not set an amount at the time of disposition, a restitution hearing shall be scheduled. The prosecuting attorney shall file a restitution order with supporting documentation at the time of the hearing. If the Prosecutor does not file a restitution order at the time of the hearing, the matter of restitution shall be deemed waived unless otherwise authorized by the court. If the defendant does not object, the proposed amount shall be entered as judgment.

Payment of restitution shall be made through the clerk of court unless otherwise ordered by the court.

[Adopted effective September 1, 2011.]

WMLCrRLJ 6.1.1.   TRIAL BY JURY

(1) Any Case confirmed for jury trial at the status hearing shall remain set for a jury trial, unless the Clerk of the Court is advised by the parties that the jury panel need not be summoned or that the jury panel may be called off.

(2) At the time of the status hearing, the Court will instruct counsel that should there be a settlement the clerk of court must be notified by 3:00 P.M. one day prior to trial which both parties can advise the Clerk that the jury panel need not be summoned.

(3) Otherwise, in any case confirmed as a jury trial and not proceeding to a jury trial, whether by entry of a plea or otherwise, terms, including costs for an unused jury panel, costs incurred in summoning a jury panel and witness fees, may be imposed by the Court.

[Adopted effective September 1, 2011.]

INFRACTIONS

WMLIR 2.4.   RESPONSE TO NOTICE

(b)(5) Written responses to mitigate an infraction or request a deferred finding, pursuant to RCW 46.63.070 (5), may be permitted

(b)(6) Upon request of the defendant, the clerk shall provide information so that the defendant may comply with this requirement. The defendant must respond within fifteen (15) days of the date the infraction was personally served or within eighteen (18) days of the date the notice was mailed. Responses by mail must be post marked within 15 days of personal receipt or 18 days of the date the notice was mailed.

(d) An attorney appearing on behalf of a defendant shall file and serve a written notice of appearance, which notice shall be substantially in the same form as the notice of appearance in a criminal case.

(e) A request for a speed measuring device expert (SMD) shall be made in writing and served upon all parties within fourteen (14) days prior to the contested hearing. The court shall set a hearing to include the SMD expert in accordance with the SMD expert's schedule.

[Adopted effective September 1, 2011.]

WMLIR 2.6.   SCHEDULING OF HEARINGS

(a)(3) Hearings on infractions may be scheduled at the same time as hearings or trials on criminal matters arising out of the same occurrence. Multiple infractions arising out of the same occurrence may be heard at the same time, whether denoted as mitigation or contested.

[Adopted effective September 1, 2011.]

WMLIR 2.7.   DEFERRED FINDINGS ON INFRACTIONS

The clerk of court is authorized to resolve an infraction through a deferred finding as authorized b [1] RCW 46.63.070 (5). The conditions of a deferred finding are that the defendant waives their contested/mitigation hearing, have no deferred findings within the prior seven years, pay an administrative fee of $150 within

120 days, and within one year complete defensive driving school and have no other traffic infractions, Successful compliance with the conditions shall result in a dismissal of the infraction. Failure of a defendant to comply with any of the terms of the deferred finding shall result in a finding of committed and assessment of the original infraction penalty as well as any assessment mandated by the State. Any monies previously paid shall not be credited toward the penalty imposed or the assessment. For non-moving violations for a deferred finding the conditions shall be $150 administrative fee and no violations for a period of one year. Upon successful completion of the deferred finding the violation will be dismissed.

[Adopted effective September 1, 2011.]

1 So in original.

WMLIR 2.8.   [EVIDENCE OF LIABILITY INSURANCE] [1]

(1) If a person who has been cited with a violation of RCW 46.30.020 presents to the court clerk evidence that the person had in effect at the time of the citation liability insurance as required by RCW 46.30.020, then upon payment of twenty-five dollars ($25.00) administrative costs, the case shall be dismissed and the court clerk shall be authorized to make appropriate notation of the dismissal in the court file.

(2) If a person charged with violation of RCW 46.30.020, for failure to have liability insurance is able to show evidence that the person has subsequently obtained liability insurance in conformity with the requirement of RCW 46.30.020, then the penalty shall be reduced to two hundred and fifty dollars ($250.00) and upon payment of the two hundred and fifty dollar ($250.00) penalty, the clerk shall be authorized to enter a finding that the infraction was committed, and make appropriate notations in the court record, and the person will be relived [2] of any further need to appear in court in connection with the infraction.

[Adopted effective September 2, 2013.]

1 Caption editorially supplied.
2 So in original.

LOCAL RULES OF PRACTICE AND PROCEDURE FOR THE YAKIMA MUNICIPAL COURT

Including Amendments Received Through
August 15, 2015

Table of Rules

ADMINISTRATIVE

YMLAR 1.1. PREAMBLE

These local rules for Criminal matters, Infractions and Appeals are assembled and numbered to conform with the numbering system and format adopted by the Supreme Court of the State of Washington as required under GR 7.

These rules supplement CrRLJ, ARLJ, CRLJ, and IRLJ.

[Adopted effective September 1, 1997; amended effective September 1, 2000; September 1, 2009; September 1, 2010.]

YMLAR 1.2. PLACE OF COURT

Unless otherwise ordered, the Court shall sit in the Courtrooms of the Yakima Law and Justice Center, 200 South Third Street, Yakima, Washington. The clerk's office shall be at the Yakima Law and Justice Center, 200 South Third Street, Yakima, Washington.

[Formerly YMLAR 1.3, adopted effective September 1, 1997; amended effective September 1, 2009; September 1, 2010. Renumbered YMLAR 1.2, effective September 2, 2014.]

YMLAR 1.3. SESSIONS

Regular Court sessions shall be held every weekday, Holidays and Court Holidays excluded.

[Formerly YMLAR 1.4, adopted effective September 1, 1997; amended effective September 1, 2009; September 1, 2010. Renumbered YMLAR 1.3, effective September 2, 2014.]

YMLAR 1.4. ORDER OF DOCKET

(a) During regular sessions, the docket shall be posted and available from the clerk of the Court, except as modified from time to time by the Court or except as provided by YMLAR 1.5(b).

(b) Suppression motions pursuant to CrRLJ 3.5 and/or 3.6 may be specially set by the Court so as to minimize the impact on regular court business. Such motions shall be heard on the second and third Monday afternoon of the month or any other time designated by the judge hearing the motion. Before noon on the Wednesday before the motion hearing, the prosecutor, defense attorney or the defendant, if appearing pro se, shall confirm the motion, or advise that some other type of disposition has been reached, to the clerk of the court by written mailed confirmation, attorney messenger service or faxing the court. Confirmation must be received by the noon deadline to be effective.

(c) Civil matters, other than infractions, may be set on a docket designated to accommodate the parties.

(d) For good cause shown, the Court may set any matter at other times and days.

[Former Rule 1.5 renumbered as Rule 1.5(a) adopted effective September 1, 1997; amended effective January 19, 1998; September 1, 2000; September 1, 2009; September 1, 2010. Renumbered YMLAR 1.4, effective September 2, 2014.]

YMLAR 1.5. OFFICE HOURS

The Clerk's Office shall be open to the public and a clerk or assistant in attendance at the public window on every regular judicial day from 9:00 a.m. to 11:00 a.m. and 1:30 p.m. to 3:30 p.m. Due to the ongoing and unstable nature of the budget and economy, the public window hours may be adjusted upon determination of the presiding judge. Office hours shall be 0800 until 1600 each judicial day.

[Formerly YMLAR 1.6, adopted effective September 1, 1997; amended effective September 1, 2009; September 1, 2010. Renumbered YMLAR 1.5, effective September 2, 2014.]

YMLAR 1.6. PROBATION DEPARTMENT

Probation services are provided in conjunction with Yakima County Probation Services.

[Formerly YMLAR 1.7, adopted effective September 1, 1997; amended effective September 1, 2009; September 1, 2010. Renumbered YMLAR 1.6, effective September 2, 2014.]

YMLAR 1.7. JUDGES PRO TEMPORE

Except as limited by statute, Judges Pro Tempore shall have the authority of a regular judge during regular Court sessions for which he or she is appointed.

[Formerly YMLAR 1.8, adopted effective September 1, 1997; amended effective September 1, 2009; September 1, 2010. Renumbered YMLAR 1.7, effective September 2, 2014.]

YMLAR 1.8. FILING OF ATTORNEY CERTIFICATION

To assure compliance with CrR 3.1/CrRLJ 3.1/JuCR 9.2, those attorneys who have been appointed as counsel in a criminal case shall file a signed certification of compliance with Applicable Standards with the Yakima Municipal Court Services Manager on a quarterly basis. The certification shall state what percentage of the attorney's practice is devoted to indigent defense. The certification shall also state that the attorney is familiar with the applicable Standards adopted by the Supreme Court for attorneys who are appointed to represent the indigent, including basic qualifications, office, investigators and caseload. An attorney shall immediately notify Yakima Municipal Court in the event he/she fails to maintain compliance with CrR 31. [1]/CrRLJ 3.1 or JuCR 9.2.

[Formerly YMLAR 1.9, adopted effective September 2, 2013. Renumbered YMLAR 1.8, effective September 2, 2014.]

[1] So in original. Probably should read "3.1".

YMLAR 9. DISCLOSURE OF RECORDS

(g)(1) The following records and files are deemed confidential:

a. Affidavits, transcriptions or electronic records for search warrants prior to the return of service of such warrant;

b. Affidavits, transcriptions or electronic records for arrest warrants prior to the return of service of such warrant;

c. Pre-sentence or after-sentence investigation reports;

d. Mental health, psychiatric and medical reports and records;

e. Alcohol, drug and controlled substance evaluations;

f. Deferred Prosecution Petitions and Stipulations;.

g. Certified copies of driving and criminal records unless duly admitted into evidence; and

h. Judge's notes and working documents, whether written or electronic.

(g)(2) Access to confidential records is strictly limited to persons or entities authorized by statute or Court order to obtain such records.

(g)(3) Requests for access to Court Records shall be made in writing in the form provided by the Court, and shall be granted or denied by the designated public disclosure clerk, subject to review by the judge, who shall state reasons for denial in writing. Any person objecting to such denial of access may file a motion for reconsideration along with a supporting affidavit.

(g)(4) Costs of copying and transcription shall be borne by the person or entity requesting any copies. Unless otherwise ordered by the Court, copy costs shall be as follows:

a) Preparing a certified copy of an instrument on file or of record in the clerk's office: $5.00 for the first page or a portion of the first page and $1.00 for each additional page;

b) Authenticating, exemplifying an instrument or document: $2.00 for each additional seal affixed;

c) Preparing a copy of an instrument or document on file or of record without a seal: .50 cents per page;

d) Copying a document without a seal or that is in an electronic format: .25 cents per page;

e) Copies made on a CD: $20.00 per CD;

f) Receiving faxed documents authorized by court rules: up to $3.00 for the first page and $1.00 for each additional page; and

g) Exceptionally lengthy or time-consuming requests for services: up to $20.00 per hour or portion of an hour.

(g)(5) No documents or electronic data may be removed from the court office, chambers, court room,, except for storage, without prior written order of the Court.

[Adopted effective September 1, 1997; amended effective September 1, 2009; September 1, 2010.]

YMLAR 11. FORMS [DELETED]

[Adopted effective September 1, 2000; deleted effective September 1, 2009.]

RULES FOR APPEAL

YMLRA 6.3. TRANSCRIPTION OR COPIES OF RECORDING

On appeal, the appellant shall make a written request for transcription or duplicates of CDs, and shall specify the name and number of the case and the date of trial. Unless waived by statute, constitutional provision, or the Court, duplicates of tapes and of any log or index thereto shall not be delivered until full payment of the actual preparation costs as determined by the Court Administrator.

[Adopted effective September 1, 1997; amended effective September 1, 2009; September 1, 2010.]

CIVIL RULES [RESCINDED]

YMLCR 1A. CRLJ ADOPTED [RESCINDED]

[Adopted effective September 1, 2000; amended effective September 1, 2009; September 1, 2010. Rescinded effective September 2, 2014.]

YCR 40(g). FORMS [DELETED]

[Adopted effective September 1, 2000; deleted effective September 1, 2009.]

YCR 81(c). LIMITATION OF APPLICABILITY [DELETED]

[Adopted effective September 1, 2000; deleted effective September 1, 2009.]

CRIMINAL RULES

YMLCrRLJ 2.5. PROCEDURE ON FAILURE TO OBEY CITATION AND NOTICE

The court may order an issuance of a bench warrant for the arrest of any defendant who has failed to appear before the court, either in person or by a lawyer, in answer to a citation and notice, or the order of the court, upon which the defendant has promised in writing to appear, or of which the defendant has been served with or otherwise received notice to appear, if the sentence for the offense charged may include confinement in jail.

(a) Warrant Costs. The maximum warrant preparation fee permitted under RCW 10.01.160 shall be assessed whenever the court orders a warrant based upon a defendant's failure to appear for any mandatory court appearance on a jailable offense. The fee shall include any costs for service of the warrant and may be waived only if the defendant is later acquitted.

(b) Quashing Warrants. The court, in its discretion, may quash a failure to appear warrant under the following circumstances:

(1) Unless specifically prohibited by the court at the time the warrant was ordered, the defendant may personally appear at the clerk's office and pay the amount of the warrant fee in cash. The defendant shall then personally sign a promise to appear at a hearing no later than the next available judicial day. The court will determine the appropriate conditions for the defendant's continued release at that hearing which may include a requirement that the defendant be detained in lieu of bail; or

(2) If the defendant establishes good cause for the failure to appear in a document sworn under oath or otherwise, the court may hear a motion to quash the warrant without requiring payment of the warrant fee in advance. Inadvertence or oversight by the defendant or defense counsel shall not constitute good cause for failure to appear.

[Adopted effective September 1, 2009. Amended effective September 1, 2010.]

YMLCrRLJ 3.1. WITHDRAWAL OF LAWYER [RESCINDED]

[Adopted effective September 1, 2009. Amended effective September 1, 2010. Rescinded effective September 2, 2014.]

YMLCrRLJ 3.2. RELEASE OF ACCUSED

(n) Domestic Violence Cases. A defendant arrested on domestic violence offences shall be detained without bail until arraignment on the next judicial day. Standard bail for domestic violence cases after arraignment shall be $1,000, but the court may reduce or increase the amount of bail in an individual case giving due consideration to the factors specified in CrRLJ 3.2.

(o) Yakima Municipal Court elects not to adopt the bail schedule set forth in CrRLJ 3.2 (o–u). Yakima Municipal Court's bail schedule may be located in the clerk's office and is available for viewing upon request. The bail schedule is intended as a guideline and may be revised from time to time in the interest of justice.

(r)(i) Cash deposited as bail is presumed to be the property of the accused regardless of who actually made such deposit. Such bail may be forfeited or applied to any fines and assessments.

(p)(i) A bailor may request a hearing pursuant to these rules by filing a request in person and in writing with the clerk of the court within 30 days of the entry of the order forfeiting such bail. Such bailor shall have the burden of proving by a preponderance of evidence that the bail was either unjustly forfeited or that the funds were neither the property of nor a gift to the defendant.

(p)(ii) At such hearing, the Court may consider written evidence, properly presented, such as promissory notes or loan statements, but such evidence alone shall not be deemed decisive.

[Adopted effective September 1, 1997; amended effective September 1, 2000; September 1, 2009; September 1, 2010.]

YMLCrRLJ 3.3. TIME FOR TRIAL

(k) Scheduling. Each criminal case set for trial shall be scheduled for a status conference before trial. Failure of the Defendant to appear at the status conference shall be grounds for striking any trial date and issuance of a warrant for the Defendant's arrest. Defendants who appear at the status conference but who have failed to make necessary contact with coun-

sel prior to the status conference may be detained in lieu of bail to facilitate future contact and terms may be imposed upon such a defendant as a condition for a continuance necessary to facilitate contact between attorney and client. The court may continue the case pursuant to CrRLJ 3.3(d)(1)

[Adopted effective September 1, 1997; amended effective January 19, 1998; September 1, 2000; September 1, 2009; September 1, 2010.]

YMLCrRLJ 3.4. MANDATORY APPEARANCE [RESCINDED]

[Adopted effective September 1, 1997; amended effective September 1, 2000; September 1, 2009; September 1, 2010; rescinded effective September 2, 2014.]

YMLCrRLJ 3.5(f). [UNTITLED] [DELETED]

[Adopted effective September 1, 2000; deleted effective September 1, 2009.]

YMLCrRLJ 3.6. SUPPRESSION PROCEDURE [DELETED]

[Adopted effective September 1, 1997; amended effective September 1, 2000; deleted effective September 1, 2009.]

YMLCrRLJ 4.1. ARRAIGNMENT [RESCINDED]

[Adopted effective September 1, 1997; amended effective September 1, 2000; September 1, 2009; September 1, 2010; rescinded effective September 2, 2014.]

YMLCrRLJ 4.2. PLEAS [RESCINDED]

[Adopted effective September 1, 1997; amended effective September 1, 2000; September 1, 2009; September 1, 2010; rescinded effective September 2, 2014.]

YMLCrRLJ 4.11. STATUS CONFERENCE [RESCINDED]

[Adopted effective September 1, 1997; amended effective September 1, 2000; September 1, 2009; September 1, 2010; rescinded effective September 2, 2014.]

YMLCrRLJ 4.12. STIPULATED ORDERS OF CONTINUANCE [DELETED]

[Adopted effective September 1, 2000; deleted effective September 1, 2009.]

YMLCrRLJ 6.1.1. TRIAL BY JURY

(e)(1) Any case confirmed for jury trial by both parties at the disposition hearing shall remain set for a jury trial.

(e)(2)(i) Before noon on the Tuesday before the disposition hearing, the prosecutor, the defense attorney or the defendant, if appearing pro se, shall confirm the jury trial to the clerk of the court or advise that some other disposition has been reached by written mailed confirmation attorney messenger service or by faxing the court. The confirmation must be received by the noon deadline to be effective. Cases confirmed by both parties at disposition shall be set for readiness the next Wednesday prior to the jury trial at 10:00 a.m. in Courtroom #2.

(e)(2)(ii) Failure of a party to confirm the jury trial as required shall cause the case to be stricken as a jury trial.

(f) Except for good cause shown, any case confirmed for jury trial and not proceeding to a jury trial as scheduled, unless such delay is the result of jury trial priority, shall be subject to terms, including costs for an unused jury of not less than $250.00, witness fees, and other terms deemed appropriate by the Court.

(g) Scheduled and confirmed jury trials shall proceed and be called according to the priority of speedy trial limits. In the event of more than one jury trial being scheduled and confirmed, cases having a lower priority shall be set as trailing, to be called as soon as possible that day or the next available judicial day.

(h) Upon settlement of a case scheduled for jury trial prior to the confirmation/settlement deadline provided according to these rules, the parties shall notify the Court in writing, to strike the jury.

[Adopted effective September 1, 1997; amended effective September 1, 2000; September 1, 2002; September 1, 2009; September 1, 2010; September 2, 2014.]

YMLCrRLJ 7.8(d). SENTENCE REVIEWS [DELETED]

[Adopted effective September 1, 1997; deleted effective September 1, 2009.]

YMLCrRLJ 8.2(a). MOTIONS [RESCINDED]

[Adopted effective September 1, 1997; amended effective September 1, 2000; September 1, 2009; September 1, 2010; rescinded effective September 2, 2014.]

YMLCrRLJ 8.2(b). TIME LIMITATIONS FOR MOTION HEARINGS [DELETED]

[Adopted effective September 1, 2000; deleted effective September 1, 2009.]

YMLCrRLJ 8.4(g). MULTIPLE FILINGS [DELETED]

[Adopted effective September 1, 2000; deleted effective September 1, 2009.]

INFRACTIONS

YMLIR 2.4. RESPONSE TO NOTICE

(b)(5) Written responses to mitigate an infraction or request a deferred finding, pursuant to RCW 46.63.070(5), may be permitted.

(b)(6) Upon request of the defendant, the clerk shall provide information so that the defendant may comply with this requirement. The defendant must respond within fifteen (15) days of the date the infraction was personally served or within eighteen (18) days of the date the notice was mailed. Responses by mail must be post marked within 15 days of personal receipt or 18 days of the date the notice was mailed.

(d) An attorney appearing on behalf of a defendant shall file and serve a written notice of appearance, which notice shall be substantially in the same form as the notice of appearance in a criminal case.

(e) A request for a speed measuring device expert (SMD) shall be made in writing and served upon all parties within fourteen (14) days prior to the contested hearing. The court shall set a hearing to include the SMD expert in accordance with the SMD expert's schedule.

[Adopted effective September 1, 1997; amended effective September 1, 2009; September 1, 2010.]

YMLIR 2.6. SCHEDULING OF HEARINGS

(a)(3) Hearings on infractions may be scheduled at the same time as hearings or trials on criminal matters arising out of the same occurrence. Multiple infractions arising out of the same occurrence may be heard at the same time, whether denoted as mitigation or contested.

[Adopted effective September 1, 1997; amended effective September 1, 2009; September 1, 2010.]

COURT SCHEDULE

MONDAYS

9:30 a.m. In–Custody Arraignments, Courtroom #1

10:30 a.m. Out-of-Custody Arraignments, Courtroom #1

9:30 a.m. Mitigation Hearings, Courtroom #2 (First Monday of the month)

1:30 p.m. Bench Trials and Status Conferences, Courtroom #1

1:30 p.m. Special Set Hearings (2nd and 3rd Monday of the month), Courtroom #2

TUESDAYS

9:30 a.m. In–Custody Arraignments, Courtroom #1

8:30 a.m. Plea Calendar/Mental Health, Courtroom #2

10:30 a.m. Out-of-Custody Arraignments, Courtroom #1

1:30 p.m. Bench Trials and Status Conferences, Courtroom #1

1:30 p.m. Mitigation Hearings, Courtroom #2

2:30 p.m. Mitigation Hearings, Courtroom #2

3:00 p.m. Infraction Review Hearings, Courtroom #2

WEDNESDAYS

9:30 a.m. In–Custody Arraignments, Courtroom #1

8:30 a.m. Disposition Calendar, Courtroom #2

10:00 a.m. Trial Readiness Calendar, Courtroom #2

10:30 a.m. Out-of-Custody Arraignments, Courtroom #1

1:30 p.m. Bench Trials and Status Conferences, Courtroom #1

1:30 p.m. Contested Hearings, Courtroom #2

3:00 p.m. Special Set Impound Hearings, Courtroom #2

THURSDAYS

9:30 a.m. In–Custody Arraignments, Courtroom #1

8:30 a.m. Jury Trials, Courtroom #2

10:30 a.m. Out-of-Custody Arraignments, Courtroom #1

Second jury trial after arraignments, Courtroom #1

FRIDAYS

9:30 a.m. In–Custody Arraignments, Courtroom #1

8:30 a.m. Bench Trials and Status Conferences, Courtroom #2

10:30 a.m. Out-of-Custody Arraignments, Courtroom #1

1:30 p.m. Status Conferences/Failure to Comply Hearings, Courtroom #1

[Adopted effective September 1, 2010. Amended effective September 2, 2013.]

ZILLAH MUNICIPAL COURT—
[No Local Rules]